GREENE'S BIOGRAPHICAL
ENCYCLOPEDIA OF COMPOSERS

GREENE'S BIOGRAPHICAL ENCYCLOPEDIA OF COMPOSERS

DAVID MASON GREENE

DOUBLEDAY & COMPANY, INC., GARDEN CITY, NEW YORK
1985

Library of Congress Cataloging in Publication Data

Greene, David Mason
Greene's biographical encyclopedia of composers
1. Composers—Biography. I. Title. II. Title:
Biographical encyclopedia of composers.
ML390.G85   1985   780'.92'2 [B]   79-6863
ISBN 0-385-14278-1

PREFACE

This book was conceived as part of a series of biographical dictionaries for the general public that began some years ago with *Asimov's Biographical Encyclopedia of Science and Technology*. It is hoped furthermore that the book will fill a real need: there are current dictionaries of music and musicians (e.g., *The New Grove Dictionary*) and of musicians in general (e.g., *Baker's Biographical Dictionary*), but as far as I know, there is no current dictionary of any real scope limited solely to composers.

When I first took on this project, I spent several months making a card index of worthy composers. As it mounted into the tens of thousands, I began to see that such an approach would not do. Obviously I needed some sort of control, however arbitrary. It occurred to me that the composers who seemed three-dimensional were those whose music I had heard, primarily on phonograph records, which in the LP era have provided a much broader and more easily accessible base for such familiarity than the concert hall and opera house. On the theory then that for most people heard music is sweet and that music unheard does not in effect exist, I decided to limit the dictionary to those composers whose music has been reasonably available on records in the United States. Even here I had no intention of being thoroughgoing—I did not mean, for example, to comb every recorded anthology of galliards, Victorian parlor songs, or military marches to make sure someone had not been left out. Frankly I depended on my own library of 15,000 LPs plus whatever was stored in my mind for such information.

But since I made that choice, much has changed. In the years and months and weeks and days this book has been a-writing, hundreds more obscure composers (and some not so obscure) have been added to the record catalogs. Moreover as American producers have cut back or ceased production, hitherto unavailable material from foreign publishers has made its way into our markets. And European relaxation of strictures on recordings made from broadcasts has flooded the market with all sorts of unusual material, especially in the operatic field. In one or two instances we have been able to add important composers who were completely ignored on records until very recently (e.g., Sorabji, Zemlinsky) by excluding very, very minor ones. But the format of the book makes such action well nigh impossible, and so major changes will have to await a second edition. The continued lack of recordings in some instances has also dictated the omission of a few composers of historical significance—J. A. Hiller, for example. The dictionary has, perforce, been limited to "serious" or "art" composers, which does not entirely preclude writers of what used to be called "semiclassical" music, though I have drawn the line at those whose compositions have been whistled or one-fingered to an arranger. In other words, "composer" means here someone who writes notes on paper (though whether that can be held true of troubadours and *Minnesingers* is debatable).

In the name of consistency, I have preserved the basic format of Mr. Asimov's book: the entries are arranged chronologically by birthdate. This was not a wholly mechanical solution. I know of no other such work that places composers in a historical perspective—that might in fact be read through as a sort of history of music in Western civilization. The arrangement poses, of course, some small inconvenience, since the entry number will have to be sought in the alphabetical index at the back. But in the index entry numbers will take the place of page numbers (as well as standing at the head of each entry), and the extra step will therefore cost a minimum of effort. Moreover, virtually every reference within a given article to another composer included in this volume is cross-indexed by his entry number.

A note about birthdates: where known, they have been recorded according to the latest available information. Where there are conflicts in such information, such have been noted. However, in earlier times the facts of many composer's lives and careers, including such vital statistics, remain undiscovered. In such instances, I have given a putative birthdate, using the decade that seems most likely from the other known statistics. To put it another way, "c. 1350" and the like usually denotes an educated guess.

Each entry is headed by its assigned number, the composer's name (with suggestions for its pronunciation), and the places and dates of his birth and death. A fourth (actually the second) line notes his professional activities apart from writing music. (Following this rubric through the centuries, down to a time when ninety-five out of a hundred composers are college professors, is an instructive pursuit in itself.)

Asked to write a biographical dictionary, I took "biographical" at its root value and attempted to write about my subjects as human beings rather than as music machines. Recent books of this kind have tended to follow the now outmoded view of literary "New Criticism," which, in T. S. Eliot's formula, maintains that the life of a creative artist has nothing to do with his work. Thus, in them, composers rarely love, marry, beget children, or suffer accident or illness, and are, at the end of the line, wafted off to heaven by Divine Command. I have tried not to overlook the fact that a composer is so called because of his compositions (though limitations of space have in most cases precluded comprehensive listings); but at the same time I have attempted to suggest that composers were—and are—made of flesh and blood.

Since this dictionary is aimed at the layman rather than the scholar, we decided to eschew bibliographies. Those who wish to pursue further information should consult, say, *Grove* at the public library, which offers excellent bibliographies up to 1980. The new seventh edition of *Baker's* will, no doubt, cite at least major works published since.

We did, however, decide to include lists of recordings. These are not meant to be comprehensive, but merely to suggest the degree to which the composer's work can be heard on records. Since records go out of print so rapidly and turn up as re-pressings in other catalogs, we decided not to include numbers and labels. Where no listing appears at the end of an entry, it is to be understood that recordings of small works will be found scattered in various appropriate anthologies. For example, troubadour songs are most likely to be found in collections of troubadour songs, most such composers' works not pres-

ently existing in significant numbers or bulk for other treatment. We shall be happy to be reminded of important omissions but shall not stop the presses when we learn that a juvenile minuet by Mateo Albéñiz has been privately recorded in Las Palmas.

Whereas, for better or worse, I allowed recordings to dictate my selection of composers throughout nine tenths of the book, I found that as I got into the present century it would be advisable for me to do so on an increasingly selective basis, even at the risk of angering some people. There were several reasons for this decision. First, to be exhaustive would have required another volume, which at this juncture would have been infeasible. Second, even if all other matters were equal, contemporary composers enjoy a certain advantage with regard to recordings by the mere accident of being active at the time when sound recordings came into full flower. Thus their appearance on records would not necessarily testify to their importance or even their typicality in the history of music. Third, all other matters are not equal, and the fact puts in doubt the qualifications of at least some of those who appear on records. The LP age has seen a proliferation of small record publishers committed to backing one or another sort of hobbyhorse, companies and grant sources that promote the academic establishment or help assure the tenure of aspiring young assistant professors and the phonographic equivalent of the vanity press. Hence in the main for twentieth-century composers—and particularly for those born after 1920—I have limited my selections to the apparent Big Boys, at least as their time values them. If there are future editions, the settling of the dust will, I hope, allow the correction of any injustices done here.

Since the research, writing, and typing of this work have been largely a one-man job, I can thank my wife, relatives, friends, and academic associates chiefly for bearing with my seeming unfriendliness and for leaving me alone. I am grateful to my editor Harold Kuebler for his patience and encouragement and a couple of lunches. I particularly thank copy editor Scott Kurtz for his painstaking care, for his useful suggestions, and his innumerable additions to the record listings.

DAVID M. GREENE
Lehigh University

GREENE'S BIOGRAPHICAL
ENCYCLOPEDIA OF COMPOSERS

LIST OF COMPOSERS

ABEL, Karl Friedrich [829]
ABRAHAM, Paul [1871]
ABSIL, Jean [1889]
ABT, Franz Wilhelm [1268]
ADAM, Adolphe [1172]
ADAM, Claus [2272]
ADAM de la Hale [29]
ADAM von Fulda [72]
ADASKIN, Murray [2085]
ADDINSELL, Richard [2047]
ADDISON, John [1048]
ADDISON, John [2298]
ADLER, Samuel [2372]
ADOLPHUS, Milton [2200]
ADSON, John [389]
AGRELL, Johann Joachim [745]
AGRICOLA, Alexander [76]
AGUADO, Dionisio [1113]
AGUILERA DE HEREDIA, Sebastian
   [324]
AGUIRRE, Julián [1594]
AHLE, Johann Rudolf [500]
ÅHLSTRÖM, Olof [999]
AHROLD, Frank [2398]
AICHINGER, Gregor [321]
AITKEN, Hugh [2343]
AKUTAGAWA, Yasushi [2348]
ALAIN, Jehan [2168]
ALARD, Delphin [1240]
ALBÉNIZ, Isaac [1523]
ALBÉNIZ, Mateo [991]
ALBERT, Charles d' [1201]
ALBERT, Eugen d' [1562]
ALBERT, Heinrich [469]
ALBERT, Prince Consort of England
   [1266]
ALBERTI, Domenico [785]
ALBERTI, Giuseppe Matteo [686]
ALBICASTRO, Enrico [621]
ALBINONI, Tomaso [630]
ALBRECHTSBERGER, Johann Georg
   [889]
ALBRIGHT, William [2433]

ALDROVANDINI, Giuseppe Antonio
   [636]
ALEXANDER, Josef [2152]
ALFANO, Franco [1683]
ALFONSO X of Castile, "el Sabio," [27]
ALFVÉN, Hugo [1630]
ALKAN, Charles-Henri Valentin [1233]
ALLENDE-BLIN, Juan [2371]
ALMEIDA MOTTA, João Pedro de [968]
ALMQVIST, Carl Jonas Love [1144]
ALPAERTS, Flor [1687]
ALTENBURG, Johann Ernst [881]
ALVARADO, Diego de [342]
ALWOOD, Richard [202]
ALWYN, William [2076]
ALYABIEV, Alexander [1125]
AMBROSE, St. [3]
AMBROSIUS, Hermann [1940]
AMIROV, Fikret [2325]
AMMERBACH, Elias Nikolaus [213]
AMRAM, David Werner [2392]
AMY, Gilbert [2418]
ANCHIETA, Juan de [89]
ANDERSEN, Anton Jörgen [1438]
ANERIO, Giovanni Francesco [335]
ANGLÉS, Rafael [860]
ANHALT, István [2288]
ANNA AMALIE, Duchess of Saxe-
   Weimar [905]
ANNA AMALIE, Princess of Prussia
   [828]
ANTEGNATI, Costanzo [260]
ANTES, John [913]
ANTHEIL, George [1981]
ANTILL, John Henry [2051]
ARÁMBARRI, Jesús [2012]
ARAÑÉS, Juan [430]
ARAUJO, Juan de [546]
ARBEAU, Thoinot [189]
ARCADELT, Jacques [156]
ARDITI, Luigi [1283]
AREL, Bülent [2289]
ARENSKY, Anton [1536]

ARGENTO, Dominick [2368]
ARIOSTI, Attilio [606]
ARNE, Michael [916]
ARNE, Thomas Augustine [783]
ARNELL, Richard [2270]
ARNOLD, Malcolm [2317]
ARNOLD, Samuel [915]
ARRESTI, Giulio Cesare [501]
ARRIAGA, Juan Crisostomo [1187]
ARRIETA, Pascual Juan Emilio [1288]
ARRIEU, Claude [2045]
ARUTYUNIAN, Alexander [2307]
ASHLEY, Robert [2389]
ASIOLI, Bonifazio [1057]
ASPLMAYR, Franz [850]
ASTON, Hugh [115]
ATTAINGNANT, Pierre [134]
ATTERBURY, Luffman [917]
ATTEY, John [452]
AUBER, Daniel François Esprit [1103]
AUBERT, Jacques [701]
AUBERT, Louis [1693]
AUDRAN, Edmond [1376]
AUFFMANN, Josef Anton [819]
AULETTA, Domenico [830]
AULIN, Tor [1581]
AURIC, Georges [1962]
AUSTIN, Larry [2390]
AVISON, Charles [775]
AVONDANO, Pedro Antonio [802]
AVSHALOMOV, Aaron [1901]
AVSHALOMOV, Jacob [2287]
AZZAIOLO, Filippo [214]

BABBITT, Milton [2247]
BACARISSE, Salvador [1954]
BACEWICZ, Grażyna [2133]
BACH, Carl Philipp Emanuel [801]
BACH, Heinrich [488]
BACH, Johann [470]
BACH, Johann Bernhard [646]
BACH, Johann Christian [886]
BACH, Johann Christoph [536]
BACH, Johann Christoph Friedrich [872]
BACH, Johann Ernst [822]
BACH, Johann Lorenz [722]

BACH, Johann Ludwig [648]
BACH, Johann Michael [550]
BACH, Johann Sebastian [684]
BACH, Wilhelm Friedemann [784]
BACH, Wilhelm Friedrich Ernst [1012]
BACHELET, Alfred Georges [1560]
BÄCK, Sven-Erik [2292]
BACKER-GRØNDAHL, Agathe [1440]
BACKOFEN, Johann Georg Heinrich
   [1053]
BACON, Ernst [1949]
BĄDARZEWSKA-BARANOWSKA,
   Tekla [1336]
BADINGS, Henk [2101]
BAINES, Francis [2265]
BAINES, William [1964]
BAIRD, Tadeusz [2376]
BAIRSTOW, Sir Edward [1656]
BAKFARK, Bálint [160]
BALAKIREV, Mily [1348]
BALANCHIVADZE, Andrei [2089]
BALASANYAN, Sergei [2021]
BALBASTRE, Claude-Bénigne [843]
BALFE, Michael William [1195]
BALLARD, Robert [370]
BALLIF, Claude [2340]
BANCHIERI, Adriano [337]
BANFIELD, Rafaello de [2322]
BANISTER, John, the Elder [502]
BANTOCK, Sir Granville [1600]
BAQUIERO FÓSTER, Gerónimo [1945]
BARANOVIĆ, Krešimir [1897]
BARATI, George [2203]
BARBER, Samuel [2149]
BARBIERI, Francisco Asenjo [1287]
BARBIREAU, Jacques [68]
BÁRDOS, Lajos [1972]
BARLOW, Wayne [2193]
BARNBY, Sir Joseph [1362]
BARON, Ernst Gottlieb [724]
BARRAUD, Henry [1976]
BARRIOS, Pio Augustín [1795]
BARSANTI, Francesco [709]
BARTÓK, Béla [1734]
BARTOLOZZI, Bruno [2174]
BASSANI, Giovanni Battista [577]

BASSANO, Giovanni [292]
BATAILLE, Gabriel [371]
BATESON, Thomas [343]
BATH, Hubert [1770]
BAX, Sir Arnold [1771]
BAYER, Josef [1465]
BAZIN, François [1247]
BAZZINI, Antonio [1256]
BEACH, Mrs. H. H. A. [1590]
BEALE, William [1110]
BEAUJOYEULX, Baltasar de [215]
BEAULIEU, Eustorg de [135]
BÉCAUD, Gilbert [2367]
BECK, Conrad [1997]
BECKER, John [1802]
BEDYNGHAM, John [58]
BEECKE, Franz von [875]
BEESON, Jack [2316]
BEETHOVEN, Ludwig van [1063]
BEHR, Franz [1354]
BELKNAP, Daniel [1070]
BELL'HAVER, Vincenzo [216]
BELLINI, Vincenzo [1164]
BELLMAN, Carl Michael [911]
BEMBERG, Herman [1514]
BENATZKY, Ralph [1780]
BENDA, Františék [776]
BENDA, Jiří Antonín [824]
BENDUSI, Francesco [105]
BENEDETTI, Pietro [413]
BENEDICT, Sir Julius [1180]
BENET, John [59]
BENEVOLI, Orazio [472]
BEN-HAIM, Paul [1939]
BENJAMIN, Arthur [1887]
BENNET, John [372]
BENNETT, John [861]
BENNETT, Richard Rodney [2417]
BENNETT, Robert Russell [1895]
BENNETT, Sir William Sterndale [1246]
BENTZON, Niels Viggo [2290]
BEREZOVSKY, Maxim Sozontovich [938]
BEREZOWSKY, Nicolai [1979]
BERG, Alban [1789]
BERG, Isak Albert [1173]
BERGER, Arthur [2185]

BERGER, Jean [2144]
BERGER, Ludwig [1088]
BERGER, Theodor [2069]
BERGMAN, Erik Valdemar [2181]
BERGSMA, William [2313]
BERIO, Luciano [2352]
BERKELEY, Sir Lennox [2036]
BERLINSKI, Herman [2160]
BERLIOZ, Hector [1175]
BERMUDO, Juan [162]
BERNART de Ventadorn [11]
BERNER, Friedrich Wilhelm [1095]
BERNERS, Gerald Hugh Tyrwhitt-Wilson, Lord [1769]
BERNHARD, Christoph [508]
BERNICAT, Firmin [1413]
BERNIER, Nicolas [599]
BERNSTEIN, Leonard [2282]
BERTI, Giovanni Pietro [441]
BERTIN, Louise-Angélique [1181]
BERTON, Pierre Montan [841]
BERTONI, Ferdinando Gasparo [834]
BERTOUILLE, Gérard [1950]
BERTRAND, Antoine de [233]
BERWALD, Franz Adolf [1151]
BESARD, Jean-Baptiste [336]
BESLY, Maurice [1827]
BESOZZI, Alessandro [750]
BESOZZI, Carlo [901]
BEVIN, Elway [279]
BIANCIARDI, Francesco [363]
BIBER, Heinrich Ignaz Franz von [539]
BILLINGS, William [946]
BINCHOIS, Gilles [60]
BINDER, Abraham Wolfe [1904]
BINKERD, Gordon [2248]
BIRTWISTLE, Harrison [2410]
BISCOGLI, Francesco [806]
BISHOP, Sir Henry Rowley [1123]
BITTI, Martino [602]
BITTNER, Jacques [555]
BIUMI, Giacomo Filippo [390]
BIZET, Georges [1363]
BJÖRKANDER, Nils Frank [1880]
BLACHER, Boris [2030]
BLACK, John [190]

BLACKWOOD, Easley [2406]

BLANCHARD, Esprit Joseph Antoine [725]

BLANCHET, Émile-Robert [1695]

BLANCO, José [969]

BLANGINI, Giuseppe [1101]

BLANKENBURG, Quirinus [572]

BLANTER, Matvey [2033]

BLASCO DE NEBRA, Manuel [967]

BLASIUS, Matthieu Frédéric [1006]

BLAVET, Michel [737]

BLISS, Sir Arthur [1854]

BLITHEMAN, John [203]

BLITZSTEIN, Marc [2065]

BLOCH, Ernest [1729]

BLODEK, Vilém [1335]

BLOMDAHL, Karl-Birger [2253]

BLONDEL de Nesle [15]

BLOW, John [552]

BLUMENFELD, Felix [1551]

BOCCHERINI, Luigi [927]

BOCHSA, Robert Nicolas Charles [1131]

BODINUS, Sebastian [740]

BOËLLMANN, Léon [1549]

BOERO, Felipe [1779]

BOËSSET, Anthoine [423]

BOGATIREV, Anatoli [2212]

BÖHM, Georg [590]

BOIELDIEU, François-Adrien [1084]

BOISMORTIER, Joseph Bodin de [702]

BOITO, Arrigo [1393]

BOLCOM, William [2425]

BOND, Capel [859]

BOND, Carrie Jacobs [1546]

BONDON, Jacques [2369]

BONNET, Pierre [300]

BONONCINI, Giovanni [620]

BONPORTI, Francesco Antonio [633]

BOŘKOVEC, Pavel [1894]

BORLET [44]

BORODIN, Alexander Porfirievitch [1331]

BØRRESEN, Hakon [1686]

BORTKIEVICH, Sergei [1694]

BORTNIANSKY, Dmitri [976]

BOSSI, Marco Enrico [1534]

BOTTEGARI, Cosimo [278]

BOTTESINI, Giovanni [1278]

BOUCOURECHLIEV, André [2349]

BOUGHTON, Rutland [1702]

BOULANGER, Lili [1886]

BOULEZ, Pierre [2346]

BOURGEOIS, Loys [163]

BOUTMY, Josse [731]

BOUVARD, François [676]

BOUZIGNAC, Guillaume [431]

BOWLES, Paul [2165]

BOYCE, William [787]

BOYDELL, Brian [2262]

BOZZA, Eugène [2066]

BRADE, William [299]

BRAGA, Gaetano [1308]

BRAHAM, John [1079]

BRAHMS, Johannes [1329]

BRANT, Henry [2213]

BREE, Johannes Bernardus van [1159]

BRÉHY, Pierre-Hercule [637]

BREMNER, James [820]

BRETAN, Nicolae [1819]

BRETÓN, Tomás [1458]

BRÉVAL, Jean-Baptiste Sébastien [1000]

BRÉVILLE, Pierre de [1531]

BRIAN, Havergal [1681]

BRIDGE, Frank [1713]

BRISTOW, George Frederick [1296]

BRITTEN, Benjamin [2215]

BRIXI, František Xaver [870]

BRONSART VON SCHELLENDORF, Hans August [1312]

BROSSARD, Sébastien de [573]

BROTT, Alexander [2231]

BROUWER, Leo [2430]

BROWN, Earle [2365]

BROWN, Rayner [2183]

BRUBECK, David [2310]

BRUBECK, Howard [2250]

BRUCH, Max [1358]

BRUCKNER, Anton [1293]

BRUHIER, Antoine [106]

BRUHNS, Nicolaus [600]

BRÜLL, Ignaz [1434]

BRUMEL, Antoine [85]

BRUMEL, Jacques [143]

BRÜN, Herbert [2280]
BRUNA, Pablo [483]
BRUNCKHORST, Arnold Melchior [622]
BRUNEAU, Alfred [1497]
BRUNETTI, Gaetano [934]
BRUNSWICK, Mark [2009]
BUCCHI, Valentino [2255]
BUCHNER, Hans [113]
BUCK, Dudley, Sr. [1367]
BÜHLER, Franz [1017]
BULL, John [315]
BULL, Ole [1206]
BULLOCK, Sir Ernest [1840]
BÜLOW, Hans von [1310]
BUNGERT, August [1423]
BUONAMENTE, Giovanni Battista [414]
BURGMÜLLER, Franz [1190]
BURGMÜLLER, Norbert [1207]
BURKHARD, Willy [1976]
BURLEIGH, Henry Thacker [1584]
BURNS, Robert [1009]
BUSCH, William [1999]
BUSH, Alan [1987]
BUSNOIS, Antoine [69]
BUSONI, Ferruccio [1577]
BÜSSER, Henri [1627]
BUSSOTTI, Sylvano [2396]
BUTTERWORTH, George [1797]
BUTTSTÄDT, Johann Heinrich [605]
BUXTEHUDE, Dietrich [525]
BYRD, William [248]
BYTTERING, Thomas [46]

CABANILLES, Juan Bautista José [540]
CABEZÓN, Antonio de [164]
CACCINI, Giulio [252]
CADMAN, Charles Wakefield [1741]
CAGE, John [2192]
CAIMO, Giuseppe [253]
CAIX D'HERVELOIS, Louis de [623]
CALDARA, Antonio [624]
CALESTANI, Vincenzo [429]
CALL, Leonhard von [1049]
CALLCOTT, John Wall [1047]
CAMBINI, Giuseppe Maria [940]
CAMPANA, Fabio [1261]

CAMPION, Thomas [332]
CAMPRA, André [584]
CANALE, Floriano [266]
CANNABICH, Johann Christian [868]
CANOVA, Francesco, da Milano [140]
CANTELOUBE DE MALARET, Joseph [1722]
CAPIROLA, Vincenzo [101]
CAPLET, André [1708]
CAPORALE, Andrea [763]
CAPUA, Rinaldo di [771]
CARA, Marco [98]
CARDOSO, Manuel [331]
CAREY, Henry [703]
CARISSIMI, Giacomo [471]
CARLETON, Nicholas [344]
CARLID, Göte [2311]
CARLTON, Richard [293]
CAROSO, Marco Fabrizio [217]
CARPENTER, John Alden [1682]
CARR, Benjamin [1054]
CARREIRA, António [204]
CARRILLO, Julián [1663]
CARTER, Elliott [2130]
CARULLI, Ferdinando [1060]
CARVALHO, João de Sousa [935]
CASADESUS, Robert [1965]
CASALS, Pablo [1690]
CASANOVAS, Narciso [947]
CASELLA, Alfredo [1767]
CASTELNUOVO-TEDESCO, Mario [1906]
CASTRO, Jean de [238]
CATALANI, Alfredo [1477]
CATEL, Charles-Simon [1076]
CATO, Diomedes [325]
CATURLA, Alejandro García [2083]
CAVACCIO, Giovanni [285]
CAVALIERI, Emilio de' [267]
CAVALLI, Francesco [464]
CAVAZZONI, Girolamo [205]
CAVAZZONI, Marco Antonio [122]
CAZDEN, Norman [2225]
CAZZATI, Maurizio [495]
CENNICK, John [813]
CEREROLS, Joan [491]

ČERNOHORSKÝ, Bohuslav Matěj [677]
CERTON, Pierre [165]
CESTI, Antonio [499]
CHABRIER, Alexis-Emmanuel [1382]
CHADWICK, George [1483]
CHAJES, Julius [2164]
CHAMBONNIÈRES, Jacques Champion
   de [465]
CHAMINADE, Cécile [1502]
CHAMPAGNE, Claude [1852]
CHANLER, Theodore [2013]
CHAPÍ, Ruperto [1461]
CHARPENTIER, Gustave [1524]
CHARPENTIER, Marc-Antoine [544]
CHAUMONT, Lambert [512]
CHAUSSON, Ernest [1484]
CHÁVEZ, Carlos [1968]
CHAYNES, Charles [2347]
CHÉDEVILLE, Nicolas [762]
CHERUBINI, Luigi [1019]
CHIESA, Melchiorre [836]
CHIHARA, Paul [2427]
CHILCOT, Thomas [741]
CHILDS, Barney [2356]
CHOPIN, Frédéric François [1208]
CHOU Wen-Chung [2331]
CHRISTOV, Dobri [1678]
CHUECA, Federico [1430]
CICONIA, Johannes [37]
CIFRA, Antonio [411]
CILÈA, Francesco [1580]
CIMA, Giovanni Paolo [345]
CIMAROSA, Domenico [962]
CIRRI, Giovanni Battista [832]
CITKOWITZ, Israel [2134]
CLARKE, Jeremiah [638]
CLARKE, Rebecca [1811]
CLARKE, Robert Coningsby [1715]
CLEMENS non Papa [166]
CLEMENTI, Muzio [977]
CLÉRAMBAULT, Louis Nicolas [647]
COATES, Eric [1812]
COBBOLD, William [297]
COCLICO, Adrien Petit [144]
CODAX, Martin [25]
COHN, Arthur [2163]

COLASSE, Pascal [551]
COLERIDGE-TAYLOR, Samuel [1674]
COLGRASS, Michael [2401]
COLIN de BLAMONT, François [707]
COLONNA, Giovanni Paolo [523]
COMPÈRE, Loyset [73]
CONFALONIERI, Giulio [1922]
CONON de Béthune [18]
CONSEIL, Jean [141]
CONSTANT, Marius [2345]
CONVERSE, Frederick [1618]
COOKE, Arnold [2098]
COOKE, John [47]
COOKE, Thomas [1107]
COOLIDGE, Peggy Stuart [2210]
COPLAND, Aaron [1986]
COPRARIO, John [373]
CORDERO, Roque [2268]
CORDIER, Baude [45]
CORELLI, Arcangelo [565]
CORIGLIANO, John, Jr. [2423]
CORKINE, William [391]
CORNELIUS, Peter [1294]
CORNYSHE, William [91]
CORREA DE ARAUXO, Francisco [386]
CORRETTE, Gaspard [643]
CORRETTE, Michel [779]
COSSET, François [478]
COSTA, Sir Michael [1193]
COSTE, Gabriel [167]
COSTE, Napoléon [1189]
COSTELEY, Guillaume [218]
COSYN, Benjamin [346]
COTTRAU, Teodoro [1302]
COUCY, Le Châtelain de [21]
COUPERIN, Armand-Louis [844]
COUPERIN, François, Le Grand [616]
COUPERIN, Louis [504]
COURBOIS, Philippe [660]
COWELL, Henry [1934]
COWEN, Sir Frederic [1464]
CRAMER, Johann Baptist [1067]
CRAMER, Wilhelm [942]
CRAWFORD, Ruth [2000]
CRECQUILLON, Thomas [145]
CRESTON, Paul [2095]

CROCE, Giovanni [290]
CROFT, William [652]
CROSSE, Gordon [2422]
CROUCH, Frederick [1197]
CRÜGER, Johann [447]
CRUMB, George [2386]
CRUSELL, Bernhard Henrik [1082]
CUI, César [1337]
CUSHING, Charles [2077]
CUTTING, Francis [301]
CZERNY, Carl [1137]
CZIBULKA, Alphons [1398]

DAGINCOURT, François [681]
DAHL, Ingolf [2188]
DALL'ABACO, Evaristo Felice [642]
DALLAPICCOLA, Luigi [2049]
DALVIMARE, Martin Pierre [1072]
DALZA, Joanambrosio [107]
DAMASE, Jean-Michel [2370]
DAMETT, Thomas [53]
DAMROSCH, Walter [1540]
DANDRIEU, Jean-François [671]
DANDRIEU, Pierre [586]
D'ANGLEBERT, Jean-Henri [520]
DANIEL, Arnaut [14]
DANIEL-LESUR [2127]
DANIELS, Mabel Wheeler [1709]
DANNSTRÖM, Johan Isidor [1225]
DANZI, Franz Ignaz [1035]
DAQUIN, Louis-Claude [717]
DARGOMIZHSKY, Alexander [1228]
DAUPRAT, Louis François [1098]
DAUS, Avraham [2016]
DAUVERGNE, Antoine [797]
DAVID, Félicien-César [1209]
DÁVID, Gyula [2205]
DAVID, Johann Nepomuk [1917]
DAVIDOV, Karl Yulyevich [1360]
DAVIDOVSKY, Mario [2408]
DAVIES, Sir Henry Walford [1609]
DAVIES, Peter Maxwell [2411]
DAVY, Richard [95]
DAWSON, William Levi [1971]
DAZA, Esteban [239]
DEBUSSY, Claude [1547]

DECKER, Joachim [374]
DECKER, Johann [448]
DE CROES, Henri-Jacques [760]
DEERING, Richard [392]
DEGEN, Helmut [2166]
DE KOVEN, Reginald [1515]
DELA, Maurice [2291]
DELAGE, Maurice [1723]
DELALANDE, Michel-Richard [576]
DE LARA, Isidore [1508]
DELIBES, Léo [1344]
DELIUS, Frederick [1539]
DELLA CIAIA, Azzolino Bernardino [629]
DELLINGER, Rudolf [1501]
DELLO JOIO, Norman [2198]
DEL TREDICI, David [2421]
DELVINCOURT, Claude [1826]
DEMANTIUS, Christoph [334]
DEMAR, Johann Sebastian [1037]
DENCKE, Jeremiah [835]
DENISOV, Edison [2381]
DENZA, Luigi [1426]
DESMARETS, Henri [589]
DESSAU, Paul [1902]
DESTOUCHES, André-Cardinal [632]
DETT, Nathaniel [1756]
DEVIENNE, François [1010]
DE VOIS, Pieter [402]
DIABELLI, Anton [1100]
DIACK, J. Michael [1607]
DIAMOND, David [2238]
DIAZ DE LA PEÑA, Eugène Émile [1350]
DIBDIN, Charles [936]
DIEPENBROCK, Alphons [1548]
DIEREN, Bernard van [1786]
DIETER, Christian Ludwig [1002]
DIEUPART, François [625]
DISTLER, Hugo [2120]
DITTERSDORF, Karl Ditters von [906]
DLUGORAJ, Wojciech [291]
DLUGOSZEWSKI, Lucia [2394]
DOCHE, Joseph Denis [1046]
DODGSON, Stephen [2338]
DOHNÁNYI, Ernö [1696]

DONATO, Baldassare [219]
DONAUDY, Stefano [1712]
DONIZETTI, Gaetano [1155]
DONOVAN, Richard [1858]
DOPPLER, Albert Franz [1276]
DORATI, Antal [2086]
DORET, Gustave [1582]
DORNEL, Louis-Antoine [661]
DOSTAL, Nico [1915]
DOUGHERTY, Celius [2015]
DOW, Daniel [873]
DOWLAND, John [316]
DRAESEKE, Felix [1342]
DRAGONETTI, Domenico [1033]
DRDLA, František [1603]
DREYSCHOCK, Alexander [1260]
DRIGO, Riccardo [1433]
DRUCKMAN, Jacob [2375]
DUBENSKY, Arcady [1844]
DUBOIS, Théodore [1356]
DU CAURROY, François Eustache [259]
DUFAY, Guillaume [56]
DUKAS, Paul [1574]
DUKELSKY, Vladimir (Vernon Duke)
  [2041]
DULICHIUS, Philipp [314]
DUMAGE, Pierre [641]
DUMITRESCU, Ion [2206]
DU MONT, Henry [476]
DUNHILL, Thomas [1691]
DUNSTABLE, John [54]
DUPARC, Henri [1442]
DUPONT, Gabriel [1704]
DUPONT, Pierre [1274]
DUPORT, Jean-Louis [961]
DUPORT, Pierre [970]
DUPRÉ, Marcel [1806]
DUPUY, Jean-Baptiste Edouard [1064]
DURAND, Auguste [1316]
DURANTE, Francesco [678]
DUREY, Louis [1828]
DURÓN, Diego [579]
DURUFLÉ, Maurice [2010]
DUŠEK, František Xaver [867]
DUSSEK, Jan Ladislav [1016]
DUTILLEUX, Henri [2244]

DUVERNOY, Frédéric [1043]
DUVERNOY, Victor [1400]
DVOŘÁK, Antonín [1386]
DZERZHINSKY, Ivan [2136]

EASDALE, Brian [2142]
EAST, Michael [393]
EBERLIN, Johann Ernst [747]
ECCARD, Johannes [274]
ECCLES, Henry [644]
ECCLES, John [617]
ECHEVARRÍA, Agustin de [862]
ECKERT, Karl [1273]
EDELMANN, Johann Friedrich [959]
EDER, Helmut [2256]
EDMUNDS, John [2207]
EDWARDS, Richard [198]
EFFINGER, Cecil [2222]
EGGE, Klaus [2092]
EGGEN, Arne [1739]
EGK, Werner [1993]
EGUIGUREN, Fernando [928]
EICHNER, Ernst Dietrich [912]
EIMERT, Herbert [1935]
EINEM, Gottfried von [2276]
EISLER, Hanns [1952]
ELGAR, Sir Edward [1499]
ELKUS, Jonathan [2395]
ELLINGTON, Edward Kennedy "Duke"
  [1967]
ELWELL, Herbert [1948]
EMMANUEL, Maurice [1544]
EMMETT, Daniel [1245]
ENCINA, Juan del [96]
ENESCO, Georges [1738]
ENRIQUEZ DE VALDERRABANO,
  Enrique [168]
ERBACH, Christian [347]
ERICKSON, Robert [2261]
ERKEL, Ferenc [1214]
ERLANGER, Baron Frédéric d' [1598]
ERLEBACH, Philipp Heinrich [575]
ERNST, Heinrich Wilhelm [1236]
ERNST LUDWIG, Landgraf von Hesse-
  Darmstadt [609]
ESCOBAR, Pedro de [92]

ESPERANÇA, Dom Pedro de [449]
ESPLÁ, Oscar [1809]
ETLER, Alvin [2201]
ETT, Kaspar [1127]
EULENBERG, Philipp zu [1436]
EVETT, Robert [2326]
EWALD, Viktor [1528]
EXAUDET, André-Joseph [786]
EYCK, Jacob van [432]
EYSLER, Edmund [1652]

FABRICIUS, Petrus [427]
FACOLI, Marco [302]
FALCONIERI, Andrea [424]
FALL, Leo [1636]
FALLA, Manuel de [1688]
FANTINI, Girolamo [453]
FARMER, John [348]
FARNABY, Giles [317]
FARNABY, Richard [439]
FARRANT, Daniel [415]
FARRENC, Louise [1178]
FARWELL, Arthur [1629]
FASCH, Johann Friedrich [696]
FAURÉ, Gabriel [1424]
FAURE, Jean-Baptiste [1311]
FAYRFAX, Robert [90]
FELDERHOF, Jan [2113]
FELDMAN, Morton [2355]
FERDINAND III, Holy Roman Emperor [475]
FERGUSON, Howard [2126]
FERNÁNDEZ, Hipolito [1031]
FERNANDEZ, Oscar Lorenzo [1942]
FERNÁNDEZ CABALLERO, Manuel [1338]
FERNÁNDEZ HIDALGO, Gutierre [275]
FERRABOSCO, Alfonso the younger [375]
FERRARI, Gabrielle [1463]
FESCA, Alexander [1271]
FESCH, Willem de [692]
FESTA, Costanzo [123]
FÉTIS, François-Joseph [1111]
FETLER, Paul [2297]
FÉVIN, Antoine de [100]

FÉVRIER, Henri [1676]
FIALA, Josef [953]
FIBICH, Zdeněk [1457]
FIELD, John [1104]
FILTZ, Johann Anton [874]
FINCK, Heinrich [74]
FINE, Irving [2228]
FINE, Vivian [2214]
FINNEY, Ross Lee [2099]
FINZI, Gerald [2001]
FIOCCO, Joseph-Hector [752]
FIORAVANTI, Valentino [1040]
FIORENZA, Nicola [765]
FISCHER, Johann Caspar Ferdinand [626]
FISCHER, Johann Christian [876]
FIŠER, Luboš [2415]
FLAGELLO, Nicolas [2373]
FLAGG, Josiah [893]
FLANAGAN, William [2332]
FLECHA, Mateo, the elder [112]
FLÉGIER, Ange [1427]
FLIES, Bernhard [1065]
FLOTOW, Friedrich von [1222]
FLOYD, Carlisle [2360]
FOERSTER, Josef Bohuslav [1520]
FOGLIANO, Giacomo [97]
FOLPRECHT, Zdeněk [2132]
FONGAARD, Björn [2286]
FONTAINE, Pierre [55]
FONTANA, Giovanni Battista [394]
FOOTE, Arthur [1471]
FORD, Thomas [395]
FORQUERAY, Antoine [635]
FOSS, Lukas [2324]
FOSTER, Stephen Collins [1299]
FRANÇAIX, Jean [2186]
FRANCESCHINI, Petronio [556]
FRANCHETTI, Barón Alberto [1526]
FRANCISQUE, Anthoine [376]
FRANCK, César [1284]
FRANCK, Johann Wolfgang [538]
FRANCK, Melchior [388]
FRANCO, Hernando [227]
FRANCO, Johan [2121]
FRANCOEUR, François [734]
FRANKLIN, Benjamin [766]

FRANZ, Robert [1242]
FRAUENLOB [31]
FREDERICK II, (Frederick the Great) [791]
FRENCH, Jacob [986]
FRESCOBALDI, Girolamo [407]
FREYER, August [1176]
FRICKER, Peter Racine [2305]
FRID, Géza [2048]
FRIML, Rudolf [1726]
FROBERGER, Johann Jakob [490]
FROMM, Herbert [2062]
FRUMERIE, Gunnar de [2122]
FRY, William Henry [1231]
FRYE, Walter [64]
FRYKLÖF, Harald Leonard [1754]
FUČIK, Julius [1631]
FUENLLANA, Miguel de [169]
FÜRSTENAU, Caspar [1071]
FURTWÄNGLER, Wilhelm [1803]
FUSZ, János [1089]
FUX, Johann Joseph [585]

GABRIEL the Musician [109]
GABRIELI, Andrea [180]
GABRIELI, Giovanni [286]
GABRIELLI, Domenico [562]
GABRIELSKI, Johann Wilhelm [1139]
GABURO, Kenneth [2363]
GACE BRULÉ [19]
GADE, Niels Wilhelm [1248]
GAGLIANO, Marco da [404]
GÁL, Hans [1837]
GALILEI, Vincenzo [208]
GALINDO, Blas [2148]
GALKIN, Nikolai [1494]
GALLES, José [1024]
GALLET, Luciano [1881]
GALLIARD, Johann Ernst [695]
GALLOIS-MONTBRUN, Raymond [2281]
GALLON, Noël [1856]
GALUPPI, Baldassare [768]
GAMARRA, Manuel de [863]
GANASSI, Sylvestro di [131]
GANNE, Louis [1542]

GARANT, Serge [2385]
GARAT, Pierre [1026]
GARDNER, John [2260]
GASPARINI, Francesco [615]
GASSMANN, Florian Leopold [851]
GASTALDON, Stanislas [1532]
GASTOLDI, Giovanni Giacomo [280]
GAUBERT, Philippe [1717]
GAULTIER, Denis [468]
GAUTIER, Pierre [537]
GAVEAUX, Pierre [1020]
GAZTAMBIDE, Joaquín Romualdo [1279]
GEBAUER, François René [1075]
GEBAUER, Michel Joseph [1038]
GEIJER, Erik Gustaf [1108]
GEIST, Christian [530]
GELBRUN, Artur [2209]
GEMINIANI, Francesco [693]
GENET, Elzéar [99]
GENZMER, Harald [2135]
GEORGES, Alexandre [1450]
GERHARD, Roberto [1926]
GERLE, Hans [146]
GERMAN, Sir Edward [1541]
GERNSHEIM, Friedrich [1373]
GERSCHEFSKI, Edwin [2139]
GERSHWIN, George [1955]
GERVAISE, Claude [170]
GESE, Barthel [282]
GESENSWAY, Louis [2081]
GESUALDO, Don Carlo [310]
GEVAERT, François Auguste [1303]
GHISELIN, Joannes [86]
GHYS, Joseph [1166]
GIANNINI, Vittorio [2042]
GIBBONS, Ellis [367]
GIBBONS, Orlando [408]
GIBBS, C. Armstrong [1836]
GIDEON, Miriam [2096]
GIGAULT, Nicolas [507]
GIGOUT, Eugène [1417]
GILBERT, Henry F. [1601]
GILLES, Jean [614]
GILLIS, Don [2189]
GILSON, Paul [1572]

GIMÉNEZ, Jerónimo [1481]
GINASTERA, Alberto [2246]
GINTZLER, Simon [147]
GIORDANI, Giuseppe [984]
GIORDANI, Tommaso [877]
GIORDANO, Umberto [1589]
GIOVANNI da Cascia [34]
GIROUST, François [891]
GIULIANI, Giovanni Francesco [1021]
GIULIANI, Mauro [1099]
GIULINI, Giorgio [808]
GIUSTINI, Lodovico Maria [688]
GLANVILLE-HICKS, Peggy [2197]
GLASS, Philip [2420]
GLAZUNOV, Alexander [1573]
GLIÈRE, Reinhold [1662]
GLINKA, Mikhail Ivanovich [1179]
GLUCK, Christoph Willibald von [803]
GNATTALI, Radamés [2079]
GOBBAERTS, Jean-Louis [1341]
GODARD, Benjamin [1445]
GODOWSKY, Leopold [1612]
GODRIC, St. [7]
GOEB, Roger [2227]
GOEHR, Alexander [2403]
GOETZ, Hermann [1380]
GOETZE, Walter [1765]
GOLĄBEK, Jakub [907]
GOLD, Ernest [2315]
GOLDMAN, Edwin Franko [1701]
GOLDMARK, Karl [1315]
GOLESTAN, Stan [1670]
GOLLER, Vinzenz [1650]
GOMBERT, Nicolas [148]
GOMES, Antônio Carlos [1347]
GOMÓLKA, Mikołaj [234]
GOOSSENS, Sir Eugene [1878]
GORCZYCKI, Grzegorz Gerwazy [612]
GORDIGIANI, Luigi [1188]
GORDON, Gavin [2006]
GÖRNER, Johann Valentin [746]
GORZANIS, Giacomo [192]
GOSSEC, François-Joseph [879]
GOSSWIN, Antonius [255]
GOTTSCHALK, Louis Moreau [1306]
GOUDIMEL, Claude [181]

GOULD, Morton [2216]
GOUNOD, Charles [1258]
GRAENER, Paul [1626]
GRAF, Christian Ernst [827]
GRAF, Friedrich Hartmann [846]
GRAINGER, Percy [1749]
GRAMMANN, Karl [1419]
GRANADOS, Enrique [1588]
GRANDI, Alessandro [377]
GRANDJANY, Marcel [1855]
GRAUN, Johann Gottlieb [751]
GRAUN, Karl Heinrich [757]
GRAUPNER, Johann Christoph [673]
GRAZIOLI, Giovanni Battista [944]
GREAVES, Thomas [349]
GRECHANINOV, Alexander [1567]
GREENE, Maurice [727]
GREFINGER, Wolfgang [108]
GREGH, Louis [1405]
GREGORY, St. [4]
GRÉTRY, André [919]
GRIEG, Edvard [1410]
GRIFFES, Charles Tomlinson [1783]
GRIGNY, Nicolas de [634]
GRILLO, Giovanni Battista [350]
GRIMACE [36]
GROBE, Charles [1254]
GROFÉ, Ferde [1862]
GROSS, Robert Arthur [2219]
GROVEN, Eivind [2005]
GRUBER, Franz Xaver [1126]
GRUENBERG, Louis [1782]
GRÜNENWALD, Jean-Jacques [2167]
GRÜNFELD, Alfred [1466]
GUAMI, Gioseffo [240]
GUARNIERI, Camargo [2103]
GUÉDRON, Pierre [351]
GUERAU, Francisco [511]
GUERRERO, Francisco [209]
GUGEL, Georg Anton [930]
GUILHEM of Aquitaine [8]
GUILLAUME Legrant [49]
GUILMANT, Alexandre [1351]
GUIRAUD, Ernest [1352]
GUIRAUT de Bornelh [13]
GUMPELZHAIMER, Adam [294]

GUNGL, Joseph [1215]
GURIDI, Jesús [1814]
GURILEV, Alexander [1174]
GURNEY, Ivor [1839]
GYROWETZ, Adalbert [1032]

HÁBA, Alois [1879]
HACQUART, Carolus [531]
HADLEY, Henry [1623]
HADZIDAKIS, Manos [2351]
HAGEMAN, Richard [1750]
HAHN, Reynaldo [1672]
HAIEFF, Alexei [2223]
HAINDL, Franz Sebastian [842]
HALÉVY, Fromental [1157]
HALFFTER, Ernesto [2060]
HALFFTER, Rodolfo [1985]
HALVORSEN, Johan [1561]
HAMAL, Henri [932]
HAMAL, Jean-Noël [778]
HAMERIK, Ebbe [1953]
HAMILTON, Iain [2323]
HAMMERSCHMIDT, Andreas [484]
HANDEL, George Friderick [683]
HANDL, Jakob [264]
HANFF, Nicolaus [601]
HANSON, Howard [1927]
HANUŠ, Jan [2233]
HARANT, Kryštof [322]
HARDIN, Louis T. ("Moondog") [2249]
HARDING, James [268]
HARDOUIN, Henri [845]
HARRIS, Roy [1947]
HARRISON, Lou [2266]
HARST, Coelestin [735]
HARTMANN, Johann Peder Emilius [1182]
HARTMANN, Karl Amadeus [2072]
HARTMANN, Thomas de [1798]
HARTY, Sir Hamilton [1725]
HASPRES, Jehan Simon de [43]
HASSE, Johann Adolf [736]
HASSE, Peter [416]
HASSLER, Hans Leo [320]
HÄSSLER, Johann Wilhelm [948]
HATTON, John Liptrot [1204]

HAUBENSTOCK-RAMATI, Roman [2285]
HAUBIEL, Charles [1859]
HAUER, Josef Matthias [1763]
HAUSSMANN, Valentin [326]
HAYDN, Franz Joseph [871]
HAYDN, Michael [894]
HEAD, Michael [1975]
HEIDEN, Bernhard [2161]
HEILLER, Anton [2333]
HEINICHEN, Johann David [674]
HEINRICH, Anthony Philip [1097]
HEISE, Peter Arnold [1313]
HEISS, John [2428]
HELDER, Bartholomäus [417]
HELLER, Stephen [1229]
HELMONT, Charles-Joseph van [805]
HELPS, Robert [2379]
HELY-HUTCHINSON, Victor [2008]
HENRY VIII, King of England [130]
HENSCHEL, Sir George [1449]
HENSELT, Adolf von [1237]
HENZE, Hans Werner [2361]
HERBERT, Victor [1513]
HERBST, Johannes [885]
HERMANNUS Contractus [6]
HÉROLD, Ferdinand [1136]
HERRMANN, Bernard [2175]
HERRMANN, Hugo [1920]
HERTEL, Johann Wilhelm [847]
HERVIG, Richard [2275]
HERZ, Henri [1170]
HESDIN, Nicolle des Celliers d' [149]
HESSE, Adolf Friedrich [1203]
HEUBERGER, Richard [1451]
HEWITT, James [1061]
HILDACH, Eugen [1447]
HILL, Edward Burlingame [1632]
HILLEMACHER, Paul [1470]
HILLER, Ferdinand von [1219]
HILLER, Lejaren [2337]
HILTON, John, the elder [303]
HILTON, John, the younger [450]
HINDEMITH, Paul [1914]
HINGESTON, John [474]
HIVELY, Wells [2028]

HODDINOTT, Alun [2384]
HOFER, Andreas [509]
HOFFMAN, Richard [1320]
HOFFMANN, E. T. A. [1086]
HOFFMANN, Giovanni [1066]
HOFFMEISTER, Franz Anton [985]
HOFHAIMER, Paul [83]
HOFMANN, Josef [1680]
HOFMANN, Leopold [899]
HOIBY, Lee [2357]
HOLBORNE, Anthony [304]
HOLBROOKE, Joseph [1706]
HOLDEN, Oliver [1041]
HÖLLER, Karl [2110]
HOLLMANN, Joseph [1468]
HOLMBOE, Vagn [2145]
HOLMÈS, Augusta [1441]
HOLMES, John [327]
HOLST, Gustav [1658]
HOLTZNER, Anton [451]
HOLYOKE, Samuel [1027]
HOLZBAUER, Ignaz [788]
HOMER, Sidney [1568]
HOMILIUS, Gottfried August [800]
HOMS OLLER, Joaquin [2093]
HONEGGER, Arthur [1861]
HOOK, James [943]
HOOPER, Edmund [276]
HOPKINS, Charles Jerome [1345]
HOPKINSON, Francis [895]
HORN, Charles Edward [1120]
HORNEMAN, Christian Frederick Emil
    [1381]
HOTTETERRE, Jacques-Martin [640]
HOTTETERRE, Jean [662]
HOVHANESS, Alan [2170]
HOWE, Mary [1745]
HOWELLS, Herbert [1870]
HOYER, Karl [1847]
HOYOUL, Baudouin [257]
HUBAY, Jenö [1509]
HÜE, Georges [1505]
HUGHES, Herbert [1742]
HULLAH, John [1223]
HÜLLMANDEL, Nicolas Joseph [997]
HUME, Capt. Tobias [339]

HUMFREY, Pelham [548]
HUMMEL, Johann Nepomuk [1091]
HUMPERDINCK, Engelbert [1480]
HUNT, Thomas [378]
HÜNTEN, Franz [1145]
HUSTON, Scott [2252]

IBERT, Jacques [1838]
ILYINSKY, Alexander [1512]
IMBRIE, Andrew [2314]
INDIA, Sigismondo d' [405]
INDY, Vincent d' [1462]
INFANTE, Manuel [1768]
INGALLS, Jeremiah [1039]
INGEGNERI, Marc' Antonio [256]
INGHELBRECHT, Désiré-Émile [1731]
IPPOLITOV-IVANOV, Mikhail [1517]
IRELAND, John [1719]
IRGENS JENSEN, Ludvig [1892]
ISAAC, Heinrich [78]
ISOUARD, Nicolas [1083]
IVANOV, Mikhail [1446]
IVANOVICI, Iosif [1425]
IVES, Charles [1659]

JACCHINI, Giuseppe Maria [595]
JACOB, Gordon [1911]
JACOBI, Frederick [1850]
JACOBUS de Senleches [42]
JACQUET DE LA GUERRE, Elisabeth
    [610]
JACQUET de Mantoue [114]
JADIN, Hyacinthe [1058]
JADIN, Louis Emmanuel [1055]
JAKUB POLAK [244]
JANÁČEK, Leoš [1478]
JANEQUIN, Clément [116]
JANIEWICZ, Feliks [1029]
JÄRNEFELT, Armas [1608]
JARZĘBSKI, Adam [433]
JEEP, Johann [401]
JEHANNOT de L'Escurel [32]
JELIĆ, Vinko [445]
JENKINS, John [436]
JENSEN, Adolf [1349]
JERGER, Wilhelm Franz [2022]

JIMÉNEZ, José [461]
JOACHIM, Joseph [1321]
JOHANN ERNST, Prince of Saxe-Weimar [729]
JOHANSEN, David Monrad [1830]
JOHNSON, John [241]
JOHNSON, Robert [409]
JOHNSTON, Ben [2359]
JOLAS, Betsy [2364]
JOLIVET, André [2073]
JONES, Charles [2155]
JONES, Daniel [2196]
JONES, Robert [328]
JONES, Sidney [1535]
JONGEN, Joseph [1649]
JONGEN, Léon [1776]
JOPLIN, Scott [1602]
JORDAN, Sverre [1834]
JOSEPH I, Holy Roman Emperor [651]
JOSEPHSON, Jacob Axel [1257]
JOSQUIN des Prez [71]
JOSTEN, Werner [1796]
JUDENKÜNIG, Hans [79]
JULLIEN, Gilles [568]

KABALEVSKY, Dmitri [2058]
KADOSA, Pál [2040]
KAGEL, Mauricio [2399]
KALINNIKOV, Vassily [1576]
KALKBRENNER, Friedrich [1118]
KALLIWODA, Johann Wenzel [1161]
KÁLMÁN, Imre [1757]
KALNIŅŠ, Jānis [2056]
KAMINSKI, Joseph [2043]
KANITZ, Ernest [1891]
KAPR, Jan [2218]
KARATIGHIN, Viacheslav [1675]
KARGEL, Sixt [242]
KARG-ELERT, Sigfrid [1700]
KARŁOWICZ, Mieczysław [1689]
KASTALSKY, Alexander [1493]
KAUFFMANN, Georg Friedrich [655]
KAUFFMANN, Leo Justinus [2004]
KAUFMANN, Armin [2024]
KAUFMANN, Walter [2107]
KAY, Hershy [2294]

KAY, Ulysses [2257]
KAYSER, Isfrid [792]
KAZURO, Stanisław [1736]
KEISER, Reinhard [639]
KELEMEN, Milko [2339]
KELLNER, Johann Peter [761]
KELLY, Michael [1028]
KENNAN, Kent [2204]
KERLE, Jacobus de [225]
KERLL, Johann Kaspar [506]
KERN, Jerome [1787]
KETÈLBEY, Albert [1673]
KHACHATURIAN, Aram [2038]
KHACHATURIAN, Karen [2306]
KHRENNIKOV, Tikhon [2208]
KIENZL, Wilhelm [1496]
KILPINEN, Yrjö [1860]
KIM, Earl [2296]
KINDERMANN, Johann Erasmus [489]
KIRBYE, George [329]
KIRCHNER, Leon [2284]
KIRCHNER, Theodor [1290]
KIRNBERGER, Johann Philipp [821]
KJERULF, Halfdan [1244]
KLABON, Krzystof [269]
KLEBER, Leonhard [136]
KLEMPERER, Otto [1794]
KLING, Henri [1392]
KLOSÉ, Hyacinthe [1198]
KLUGHARDT, August Friedrich Martin [1439]
KNECHT, Justin Heinrich [979]
KNELLER, Andreas [554]
KNIGHT, Joseph Philip [1224]
KNIPPER, Lev [1958]
KNORR, Ernst-Lothar von [1918]
KODÁLY, Zoltán [1760]
KOECHLIN, Charles [1592]
KOHAUT, Wenzel Joseph Thomas [898]
KOKKONEN, Joonas [2318]
KOLB, Barbara [2429]
KOMMA, Karl Michael [2217]
KOMZÁK, Karel, Jr. [1454]
KÖNIGSPERGER, Marianus [774]
KORBAY, Ferenc [1431]
KORN, Peter Jona [2320]

KORNGOLD, Erich Wolfgang [1937]
KORTE, Karl [2378]
KOTTER, Hans [117]
KOUGUELL, Arkadie [1944]
KOUSSEVITZKY, Sergei [1655]
KOUTZEN, Boris [1990]
KOWALSKI, Max [1751]
KOŽELUH, Jan Antonín [950]
KRAUS, Joseph Martin [998]
KREBS, Johann Ludwig [798]
KREISLER, Fritz [1664]
KRENEK, Ernst [1984]
KREUTZER, Conradin [1096]
KŘIČKA, Jaroslav [1752]
KRIEGER, Adam [519]
KRIEGER, Johann [563]
KRIEGER, Johann Philipp [553]
KRIUKOV, Vladimir [2019]
KROL, Bernhard [2302]
KROMMER, Franz Vinzenz [1013]
KRUMLOVSKÝ, Jan [817]
KRUMPHOLTZ, Johann Baptist [925]
KUBIK, Gail [2224]
KUCHAŘ, Jan Křtitel [974]
KÜFFNER, Joseph [1087]
KUGELMANN, Hans [137]
KUHLAU, Friedrich [1121]
KUHNAU, Johann [582]
KÜNNECKE, Eduard [1788]
KUPFERMAN, Meyer [2362]
KURKA, Robert [2319]
KURPIŃSKI, Karol [1117]

LABITZKY, August [1327]
LABUNSKI, Feliks [1872]
LACHNER, Franz [1171]
LACHNER, Ignaz [1192]
LACÔME, Paul [1359]
LADERMAN, Ezra [2342]
LA GROTTE, Nicolas [220]
LALO, Édouard [1286]
LAMBERT, Constant [2074]
LAMBERT, Michel [477]
LAMMERS, Thorvald [1390]
LA MONTAINE, John [2299]
LAMPUGNANI, Giovanni Battista [769]

LANDINI, Francesco [38]
LANDOWSKI, Marcel [2229]
LANDRÉ, Guillaume [2064]
LANG, Johann Georg [825]
LANG, Margaret Ruthven [1593]
LANGE, Gustav [1317]
LANGE-MÜLLER, Peter [1456]
LANGGAARD, Rued [1883]
LANGLAIS, Jean [2104]
LANIER, Sidney [1391]
LANNER, Josef [1162]
LANTINS, Arnold de [61]
LANTINS, Hugho de [57]
LAPARRA, Raoul [1685]
LARCHET, John F. [1781]
LARRANAGA, José [837]
LA RUE, Pierre de [87]
LASCEUX, Guillaume [910]
LASERNA, Blas de [973]
LASSEN, Eduard [1314]
LASSUS, Orlande de [228]
LA TORRE, Francisco de [80]
LAURO, Antonio [2267]
LAVIGNE, Philibert [743]
LAVRY, Marc [2046]
LAW, Andrew [957]
LAWES, Henry [444]
LAWES, William [463]
LAYOLLE, François de [132]
LAZAROF, Henri [2400]
LEBÈGUE, Nicolas Antoine [515]
LE BEL, Jacotin [124]
LE CAMUS, Sebastian [479]
LECHNER, Leonhard [277]
LECLAIR, Jean-Marie, L'ainé [732]
LECOCQ, Charles [1322]
LECUONA, Ernesto [1924]
LEDUC, Simon [924]
LEE, Dai-Keong [2240]
LEE, Noël [2344]
LEES, Benjamin [2335]
LEFÉBURE-WÉLY, Louis [1253]
LEFFLOTH, Johann Matthias [759]
LE GALLIENNE, Dorian [2232]
LEGINSKA, Ethel [1805]
LEGLEY, Victor [2237]

LEGNANI, Luigi [1135]
LEGRANT, Jean [62]
LEGRENZI, Giovanni [503]
LEHÁR, Franz [1614]
LEHMANN, Liza [1545]
LEIDING, Georg Dietrich [596]
LEIGH, Walter [2071]
LE JEUNE, Claude [211]
LEKEU, Guillaume [1610]
LELEU, Jehan [159]
LEMAIRE, Louis [716]
LEO, Leonardo [718]
LEONCAVALLO, Ruggero [1498]
LEONI, Franco [1566]
LÉONIN [12]
LEOPOLD I, Holy Roman Emperor [528]
LEOPOLITA, Marcin [221]
LEROUX, Xavier [1557]
LE ROY, Adrian [193]
LE SAGE DE RICHÉE, Philipp Franz [557]
LESSARD, John [2303]
LETOREY, Omer [1640]
LEVA, Enrico de [1586]
LEVADÉ, Charles Gaston [1604]
LEVERIDGE, Richard [627]
LEYBACH, Ignace Xavier Joseph [1250]
LHOTKA, Fran [1775]
LIADOV, Anatol [1485]
LIAPUNOV, Sergei [1518]
LIDHOLM, Ingvar [2312]
LIE, Sigurd [1620]
LIEBERMANN, Rolf [2162]
LIEBERSON, Goddard [2171]
LIGETI, György [2329]
LILBURN, Douglas [2241]
LILIUS, Franciszek [454]
LIMENIOS [1]
LINCKE, Paul [1583]
LINDBERG, Oskar Fredrik [1816]
LINDBLAD, Adolf Fredrik [1160]
LINLEY, Thomas, Jr. [995]
LINLEY, William [1068]
LIPATTI, Dinu [2263]
LISHIN, Grigori [1475]
LISINSKI, Vatroslav [1265]

LISLEY, John [379]
LISZT, Franz [1218]
LITAIZE, Gaston [2143]
LITOLFF, Henry Charles [1259]
LLOBET, Miguel [1677]
LOCATELLI, Pietro [721]
LOCKE, Matthew [497]
LOCKWOOD, Normand [2084]
LOEFFELHOLZ VON COLBERG, Christoph [364]
LOEFFLER, Charles Martin [1530]
LOEILLET, Jacques [685]
LOEILLET, Jean-Baptiste, of Ghent [697]
LOEILLET, Jean-Baptiste, of London [659]
LOEWE, Carl [1152]
LOHET, Simon [261]
LONBIDE, Juan Andres [939]
LONGAS, Federico [1913]
LONGO, Alessandro [1569]
LOPATNIKOFF, Nikolai [2034]
LÓPEZ, Miguel [618]
LÓPEZ BUCHARDO, Carlos [1740]
LORTZING, Albert [1163]
LOSY VON LOSYMTHAL, Jan Antonín [558]
LOTHAR, Mark [2014]
LOTTI, Antonio [613]
LOUCHEUR, Raymond [1959]
LOUIS XIII, King of France [460]
LOUIS FERDINAND, Prince of Prussia [1073]
LOUIS FERDINAND VON HOHENZOLLERN, Prince [2115]
LOVER, Samuel [1154]
LÜBECK, Vincent [571]
LUENING, Otto [1980]
LUKAČÍC, Marko Ivan [425]
LULLY, Jean-Baptiste [517]
LUMBYE, Hans Christian [1210]
LUNDQUIST, Torbjörn [2308]
LUPO, Thomas [352]
LURANO, Filippo de [102]
LUTOSLAWSKI, Witold [2199]
LUTYENS, Elisabeth [2091]

LUZZASCHI, Luzzasco [251]
LYON, James [884]

MCBRIDE, Robert [2169]
MCCAULEY, William [2259]
MACCUNN, Hamish [1595]
MACDOWELL, Edward [1529]
MACE, Thomas [485]
MACHAUT, Guillaume de [35]
MACMILLAN, Sir Ernest [1885]
MACONCHY, Elizabeth [2106]
MCPHEE, Colin [1989]
MADERNA, Bruno [2300]
MADETOJA, Leevi [1815]
MADLSEDER, Nonnosus [858]
MAGNARD, Albéric [1570]
MAHLER, Gustav [1525]
MAICHELBECK, Franz Anton [748]
MAILLART, Louis [1249]
MAINERIO, Giorgio [235]
MALASHKIN, Leonid [1401]
MALDERE, Pierre van [852]
MALIPIERO, Gian Francesco [1743]
MANCINI, Francesco [631]
MANÉN, Joan [1762]
MANEVICH, Alexander [2117]
MANFREDINI, Francesco Onofrio [679]
MANFREDINI, Vincenzo [896]
MARAIS, Marin [574]
MARCABRU [9]
MARCELLO, Alessandro [682]
MARCELLO, Benedetto [689]
MARCHAND, Louis [619]
MARCHETTI, Filippo [1319]
MARELLA, Giovanni Battista [864]
MARENZIO, Luca [273]
MARINI, Biagio [428]
MARLIANI, Count Marco Aurelio [1185]
MARQUÉS, Joan [397]
MARQUÉS, Pedro Miguel [1407]
MARSCHNER, Heinrich [1147]
MARSICK, Armand [1697]
MARSON, George [368]
MARTIN, Frank [1841]
MARTINI, Giovanni Battista [767]
MARTINI, Johann Paul Aegidius [922]

MARTINO, Donald [2393]
MARTINON, Jean [2146]
MARTINŮ, Bohuslav [1846]
MARTIRANO, Salvatore [2366]
MARTUCCI, Giuseppe [1487]
MARX, Joseph [1747]
MARX, Karl [1943]
MASCAGNI, Pietro [1559]
MASCHERA, Florentio [243]
MASCHERONI, Edoardo [1516]
MASCITTI, Michele [598]
MASON, Daniel Gregory [1648]
MASON, William [1305]
MASSAINI, Tiburtio [262]
MASSÉ, Victor [1281]
MASSENET, Jules [1396]
MATELART, Ioanne [222]
MATHIAS, William [2412]
MATIEGKA, Wenzel [1077]
MATIELLI, Giovanni Antonio [878]
MATSUDAIRA, Yoritsune [2109]
MATTEI, Tito [1387]
MATTHESON, Johann [668]
MAUDUIT, Jacques [288]
MAURY, Lowndes [2176]
MAW, Nicholas [2416]
MAYER, William [2353]
MAYR, Johannes Simon [1034]
MAYR, Rupert Ignaz [547]
MAYUZUMI, Toshiro [2380]
MAZAS, Jacques Féréol [1105]
MEDIŅŠ, Jānis [1842]
MEDTNER, Nikolai [1727]
MÉHUL, Étienne-Nicolas [1036]
MELARTIN, Erkki [1665]
MELLERS, Wilfrid [2220]
MENDELSSOHN-BARTHOLDY, Fanny [1186]
MENDELSSOHN-BARTHOLDY, Felix [1200]
MENNIN, Peter [2328]
MENOTTI, Gian Carlo [2177]
MERCADANTE, Saverio [1148]
MERIKANTO, Aarre [1882]
MERIKANTO, Oskar [1599]
MERKEL, Gustav Adolf [1301]

MERTEL, Elias [311]
MERULA, Tarquinio [442]
MERULO, Claudio [230]
MESOMEDES [2]
MESSAGER, André [1474]
MESSIAEN, Olivier [2129]
MEYER, Philippe-Jacques [897]
MEYERBEER, Giacomo [1142]
MEYER-HELMUND, Erik [1533]
MIASKOVSKY, Nikolai [1735]
MICHAEL, David Moritz [975]
MICHELET, Michel [1896]
MICHNA Z OTRADOVIC, Adam Václav [455]
MIELCZEWSKI, Marcin [434]
MIGNONE, Francisco [1941]
MIHALOVICI, Marcel [1957]
MIHÁLY, András [2273]
MIKOLAJ of Cracow [150]
MILÁN, Luys de [151]
MILHAUD, Darius [1868]
MILLÁN, Francisco [103]
MILLÖCKER, Karl [1395]
MILTON, John, the elder [319]
MINKUS, Léon [1298]
MIRON, Issachar [2304]
MODERNE, Jacques [152]
MOERAN, Ernest John [1903]
MOEVS, Robert [2309]
MOHAUPT, Richard [2055]
MOLINARO, Simone [330]
MOLINO, Francesco [1085]
MOLIQUE, Wilhelm Bernhard [1169]
MOLLER, John Christopher [989]
MOLLOY, James Lyman [1355]
MOMPOU, Federico [1877]
MONCAYO, José Pablo [2190]
MONCKTON, Lionel [1538]
MONDONVILLE, Jean-Joseph Cassanéa de [789]
MONIUSZKO, Stanisław [1263]
MONN, Matthias Georg [809]
MONRO, George [723]
MONTE, Philippe de [197]
MONTÉCLAIR, Michel Pignolet de [608]
MONTEMEZZI, Italo [1671]

MONTERO, José Angel [1328]
MONTEVERDI, Claudio [333]
MONTSALVATGE, Xavier [2184]
MOORE, Douglas [1884]
MOORE, Thomas [1093]
MORALES, Cristóbal de [153]
MORAWETZ, Oscar [2258]
MORENO TORROBA, Federico [1849]
MORGAN, Justin [951]
MORIN, Jean-Baptiste [649]
MORLACCHI, Francesco [1114]
MORLEY, Thomas [289]
MORNABLE, Antoine [182]
MOROSS, Jerome [2211]
MORTENSEN, Otto [2111]
MOSCHELES, Ignaz [1146]
MOSONYI, Mihály [1238]
MOSSOLOV, Alexander [1983]
MOSTO, Giovanni Battista [263]
MOSZKOWSKI, Moritz [1479]
MOULINIÉ, Étienne [456]
MOURAVIEFF, Léon [2078]
MOURET, Jean Joseph [669]
MOUTON, Charles [505]
MOUTON, Jean [84]
MOZART, Franz Xaver Wolfgang [1141]
MOZART, Leopold [816]
MOZART, Wolfgang Amadeus [992]
MUDARRA, Alonso [171]
MUDGE, Richard [814]
MUFFAT, Georg [566]
MUFFAT, Gottlieb [706]
MUGNONE, Leopoldo [1510]
MÜLLER, Johann Peter [1140]
MÜLLER, Marian [833]
MÜLLER, Paul [1951]
MUNDY, John [281]
MUNDY, William [212]
MURSCHHAUSER, Franz Xaver Anton [593]
MUSET, Colin [24]
MUSGRAVE, Thea [2374]
MUSHEL, Georgi [2141]
MUSSORGSKY, Modest [1369]
MÜTHEL, Johann Gottfried [849]
MYSLIVEČEK, Josef [890]

NADERMANN, Jean François [1102]
NAGINSKI, Charles [2137]
NANCARROW, Conlon [2195]
NÁPRAVNÍK, Eduard [1374]
NARDINI, Pietro [823]
NARVÁEZ, Luys de [154]
NAUDOT, Jacques-Christophe [710]
NAUMANN, Johann Gottlieb [920]
NEEFE, Christian Gottlob [954]
NEGRI, Cesare [236]
NEIDHART von Reuenthal [23]
NELHÝBEL, Václav [2293]
NENNA, Pomponio [284]
NEPOMUCENO, Alberto [1565]
NESSLER, Victor Ernst [1383]
NEUBAUER, Franz Christoph [1022]
NEUENDORFF, Adolf [1409]
NEUMANN, František [1654]
NEUPERT, Edmund [1394]
NEVIN, Ethelbert [1550]
NEWSIDLER, Hans [161]
NEWSIDLER, Melchior [226]
NICHELMANN, Christoph [812]
NICHOLAS of Radom [50]
NICHOLSON, Charles [1149]
NICHOLSON, Richard [353]
NICODÉ, Jean-Louis [1473]
NICOLAI, Otto [1212]
NIEDERMEYER, Louis [1167]
NIELSEN, Carl [1571]
NIETZSCHE, Friedrich [1422]
NIGG, Serge [2341]
NILES, John Jacob [1864]
NIN, Joaquín [1721]
NIN-CULMELL, Joaquín [2124]
NISLE, Johannes [883]
NIVERS, Guillaume [518]
NOLA, Gian Domenico da [183]
NONO, Luigi [2336]
NORCOMBE, Daniel [387]
NORDQVIST, Gustav [1804]
NÖRMIGER, August [305]
NOTKER of St. Gall [5]
NOUGUÈS, Jean [1669]
NOVÁK, Vítězslav [1617]
NOVELLO, Ivor [1874]

NOWAK, Lionel [2179]
NOWOWIEJSKI, Feliks [1692]
NUFFEL, Jules van [1764]
NUNES GARCIA, José Maurício [1050]
NUSSIO, Otmar [2023]
NYSTROEM, Gösta [1843]

OBRECHT, Jacob [77]
OCHSENKUN, Sebastian [196]
OCKEGHEM, Joannes de [65]
OESTEN, Theodor [1235]
OFFENBACH, Jacques [1264]
OGIŃSKI, Michel Kleofas [1042]
OHANA, Maurice [2221]
OLIVEROS, Pauline [2402]
OLSEN, Sparre [2035]
ONSLOW, George [1115]
OREJÓN, José de [770]
ORFF, Carl [1912]
ORR, Robin [2138]
ORREGO-SALAS, Juan Antonio [2283]
ORTIZ, Diego [172]
OSWALD, James [790]
OTHMAYR, Caspar [179]
OVALLE, Jayme [1898]
OVSIANKO-KULIKOVSKY, Nikolai
  [1056]
OXINAGAS, Joaquín de [815]

PACHELBEL, Carl Theodor [708]
PACHELBEL, Johann [567]
PADEREWSKI, Ignacy Jan [1527]
PADILLA, José [1835]
PADILLA, Juan Gutiérrez de [435]
PADOVANO, Annibale [207]
PAËR, Ferdinando [1069]
PAGANINI, Niccolò [1106]
PAINE, John Knowles [1366]
PAISIELLO, Giovanni [914]
PAIX, Jakob [287]
PALADILHE, Émile [1420]
PALAU-BOIX, Manuel [1873]
PALESTRINA, Giovanni Pierluigi da
  [201]
PALMA, John [865]
PALMER, Robert [2235]

PALMGREN, Selim [1703]
PALOMINO, José [990]
PALUSELLI, Stefan [952]
PANNAIN, Guido [1857]
PANSERON, Auguste [1150]
PANUFNIK, Andrzej [2226]
PAPINEAU-COUTURE, Jean [2254]
PARABOSCO, Girolamo [199]
PARADIS, Maria Theresia von [1011]
PARADISI, Pietro Domenico [772]
PARAY, Paul [1808]
PARCHAM, Andrew [587]
PARISH-ALVARS, Elias [1194]
PARKER, Horatio [1556]
PARROTT, Ian [2245]
PARRY, Sir Charles [1443]
PARSONS, Robert [223]
PARTCH, Harry [1998]
PARTOS, Ödön [2114]
PASQUINI, Bernardo [524]
PASSEREAU, Pierre [110]
PASTERWIZ, Georg Robert von [856]
PAUMANN, Conrad [66]
PEDRELL, Carlos [1707]
PEDRELL, Felipe [1384]
PEDRO DE CRISTO, Dom [254]
PEDROLLO, Arrigo [1710]
PEDROTTI, Carlo [1252]
PEEL, Graham [1697]
PEERSON, Martin [366]
PĘKIEL, Bartołomiej [457]
PELISSIER, Victor [971]
PELLEGRINI, Vincenzo [354]
PENDERECKI, Krzysztof [2407]
PEPPING, Ernst [2003]
PEPUSCH, John Christopher [611]
PERAGALLO, Mario [2151]
PERAZA, Francisco de [323]
PERCEVAL, Julio [2039]
PEREZ BOCANEGRA, Juan [355]
PERGAMENT, Moses [1888]
PERGOLESI, Giovanni Battista [782]
PERI, Jacopo [309]
PERLE, George [2234]
PEROSI, Dom Lorenzo [1634]
PÉROTIN [20]

PERSICHETTI, Vincent [2236]
PESCETTI, Giovanni Battista [758]
PESENTI, Martino [458]
PESSARD, Émile [1408]
PETER, Johann Friedrich [941]
PETER, Simon [929]
PETERSON-BERGER, Wilhelm [1587]
PETRASSI, Goffredo [2052]
PETRELLA, Errico [1234]
PETROVICS, Emil [2387]
PETRUS de Cruce [30]
PETTERSON, Allan [2178]
PEUERL, Paul [340]
PEZ, Johann Christoph [597]
PEZEL, Johann [527]
PFITZNER, Hans [1606]
PHILE, Philip [882]
PHILIDOR, André Danican, the elder [549]
PHILIDOR, Anne Danican [666]
PHILIDOR, Pierre Danican [667]
PHILIPPE de Vitry [33]
PHILIPS, Peter [312]
PHILIPS, Thomas [81]
PHILLIPS, Burrill [2116]
PIAZZA, Gaetano [838]
PICCHI, Giovanni [380]
PICCINNI, Niccolò [848]
PICHL, Václav [923]
PICKA, František [1641]
PIERNÉ, Gabriel [1555]
PIETRI, Giuseppe [1807]
PIJPER, Willem [1899]
PILKINGTON, Francis [356]
PINELLI, Ettore [1412]
PINKHAM, Daniel [2330]
PINSUTI, Ciro [1307]
PINTO, Octavio [1845]
PIPELARE, Matthaeus [82]
PIPKOV, Lyubomir [2053]
PISADOR, Diego [173]
PISENDEL, Johann Georg [694]
PISTON, Walter [1890]
PITTALUGA, Gustavo [2080]
PIXIS, Johann Peter [1128]
PIZZETTI, Ildebrando [1732]

PLANEL, Robert [2118]
PLANQUETTE, Jean Robert [1444]
PLANSON, Jean [295]
PLATTI, Giovanni Benedetto [742]
PLEYEL, Ignaz [1003]
POGLIETTI, Alessandro [513]
POITEVIN, Guillaume [545]
POKORNÝ, František Xaver [855]
POLLAROLO, Carlo Francesco [569]
PONCE, Juan [111]
PONCE, Manuel [1758]
PONCHIELLI, Amilcare [1334]
PONGRÁCZ, Zoltán [2182]
PONIRIDY, Georges [1869]
POOT, Marcel [1992]
POPOV, Gavriil [2054]
POPPER, David [1411]
PORPORA, Nicola Antonio [690]
PORRINO, Ennio [2147]
PORTER, Cole [1853]
PORTER, Quincy [1932]
POSCH, Isaac [396]
POULENC, Francis [1960]
POUND, Ezra [1800]
POUSSEUR, Henri [2383]
POWELL, John [1753]
POWELL, Mel [2327]
POWER, Leonel [51]
PRAETORIUS, Hieronymus [298]
PRAETORIUS, Jakob [420]
PRAETORIUS, Michael [360]
PREGER, Leo [2102]
PROCH, Heinrich [1202]
PROKOFIEV, Sergei [1851]
PUCCINI, Domenico [1074]
PUCCINI, Giacomo [1511]
PUGNANI, Gaetano [866]
PUGNI, Cesare [1168]
PURCELL, Daniel [603]
PURCELL, Henry [581]
PYKINI [39]

QUANTZ, Johann Joachim [730]
QUILTER, Roger [1699]

RABAUD, Henri [1647]
RACHMANINOFF, Sergei [1638]
RADECKE, Robert [1318]
RAFF, Joachim [1282]
RAIMBAUT de Vaqueiras [16]
RAINIER, Priaulx [2031]
RAMEAU, Jean-Philippe [675]
RAMIN, Günther [1956]
RANGSTRÖM, Ture [1785]
RASSE, François [1635]
RATHGEBER, Johann Valentin [670]
RAVEL, Maurice [1666]
RAVENSCROFT, Thomas [406]
RAWSTHORNE, Alan [2067]
READ, Daniel [1004]
REBEL, Jean-Féry [604]
REDFORD, John [125]
REED, H. Owen [2154]
REESEN, Emil [1820]
REFICE, Licinio [1790]
REGER, Max [1637]
REGNART, François [250]
REGNART, Jacques [247]
REICH, Steve [2419]
REICHA, Antonín [1059]
REICHA, Josef [978]
REICHARDT, Johann Friedrich [980]
REICHE, Johann Gottfried [607]
REIF, Paul [2150]
REINAGLE, Alexander [994]
REINCKEN, Johann Adam [498]
REINECKE, Carl [1292]
REINER, Jakob [296]
REIZENSTEIN, Franz [2173]
RESINARIUS, Balthasar [118]
RESPIGHI, Ottorino [1718]
REUBKE, Julius [1333]
REUSNER, Esajas, the elder [480]
REUSNER, Esajas, the younger [521]
REUTTER, Johann Adam [773]
REVUELTAS, Silvestre [1973]
REYER, Ernest [1289]
REYNOLDS, Roger [2409]
REZNIČEK, Emil Nikolaus von [1522]
RHEINBERGER, Joseph [1368]
RIBERA, Antonio de [138]

RICCI, Federico [1205]
RICCI, Luigi [1183]
RICHARD I, Coeur de Lion, King of
England [17]
RICHTER, Franz Xaver [777]
RIEGGER, Wallingford [1793]
RIES, Ferdinand [1116]
RIETI, Vittorio [1946]
RIETZ, Julius [1227]
RIISAGER, Knudåge [1933]
RILEY, Terry [2413]
RIMSKY-KORSAKOV, Nikolai [1416]
RIQUIER, Guiraut [28]
RITTER, Alexander [1330]
RIVAFRECHA, Martín de [93]
RIVIER, Jean [1923]
RIZZIO, David [206]
ROBERT, Pierre [492]
ROBERTSON, Leroy [1930]
ROBINSON, Earl [2157]
ROBINSON, Thomas [357]
ROCCA, Lodovico [1916]
ROCHBERG, George [2279]
ROCKSTRO, William Smith [1285]
RODGERS, Richard [2018]
RODRIGO, Joaquín [2025]
RODRIGUES COELHO, Manuel [283]
RODRIGUEZ, Felipe [1014]
ROGALSKI, Theodor [1991]
ROGER-DUCASSE, Jean [1639]
ROGERS, Bernard [1875]
ROGUSKI, Gustaw [1370]
ROHDE, Friedrich Wilhelm [1495]
ROLDÁN, Amadeo [1982]
ROLLA, Alessandro [1001]
RÖLLIG, Karl Leopold [887]
ROMAN, Johan Helmich [719]
ROMBERG, Bernhard Heinrich [1051]
ROMBERG, Sigmund [1821]
ROMERO, Mateo [381]
RONALD, Sir Landon [1643]
RONCALLI, Lodovico [564]
RONTANI, Rafaello [358]
ROOS, Robert de [2105]
ROOT, George Frederick [1272]
ROPARTZ, Guy [1564]

RORE, Cipriano de [184]
ROREM, Ned [2334]
ROSA, Salvatore [487]
ROSEINGRAVE, Thomas [699]
ROSENBERG, Hilding [1866]
ROSENMÜLLER, Johann [493]
ROSETTI, Francesco Antonio [972]
ROSIER, Carl [529]
ROSKOVSKY, Josef [880]
ROSSETER, Philip [338]
ROSSI, Luigi [446]
ROSSI, Michelangelo [466]
ROSSI, Salamone [341]
ROSSINI, Gioacchino [1143]
ROTOLI, Augusto [1435]
ROUGET DE L'ISLE, Claude Joseph
[1018]
ROUSSEAU, Jean-Jacques [793]
ROUSSEL, Albert [1605]
ROVIGO, Francesco [246]
ROYER, Pancrace [764]
RÓZSA, Miklós [2108]
RÓŻYCKI, Ludomir [1784]
RUBBRA, Edmund [1995]
RUBINSTEIN, Anton [1309]
RUBINUS [67]
RUDEL, Jaufré [10]
RUDHYAR, Dane [1905]
RUDNICK, Wilhelm [1459]
RUDZIŃSKI, Witold [2202]
RUGGIERI, Giovanni Maria [588]
RUGGLES, Carl [1684]
RUIZ DE RIBAYEZ, Lucas [532]
RUNG, Henrik [1191]
RUSSELL, Henry [1226]
RUST, Friedrich Wilhelm [904]
RUTINI, Giovanni Marco [826]
RYDER, Thomas Philander [1346]

SABADINI, Bernardo [559]
SACCHINI, Antonio [857]
SACIIS, Hans [133]
SACRATI, Francesco [473]
SAEVERUD, Harald [1936]
SAINT-GEORGES, Joseph Boulogne,
Chevalier de [908]

SAINT-LUBIN, Léon de [1184]
SAINT-LUC, Laurent de [592]
SAINT-SAËNS, Camille [1343]
SALIERI, Antonio [966]
SALMHOFER, Felix [1974]
SALOMON, Hector [1361]
SALZEDO, Carlos [1791]
SAMARA, Spiro [1558]
SAMMARTINI, Giovanni Battista [738]
SAMMARTINI, Giuseppe [720]
SANDERS, Robert [2090]
SANDI, Luis [2061]
SANDOVAL, Miguel [2044]
SANDRIN [126]
SANTA CRUZ, Domingo [1969]
SANTA MARÍA, Tomás de [174]
SANTÓRSOLA, Guido [2057]
SANZ, Gaspar [533]
SARACINI, Claudio [422]
SARASATE, Pablo de [1415]
SARRO, Domenico [658]
SARTI, Giuseppe [853]
SARTORIO, Antonio [510]
SATIE, Erik [1578]
SAUGUET, Henri [1994]
SAUMELL REBREDO, Manuel [1255]
SAVAGE, William [818]
SAVAGNONE, Giuseppe [2026]
SCACCHI, Marco [459]
SCANDELLO, Antonio [187]
SCARLATTI, Alessandro [583]
SCARLATTI, Domenico [687]
SCARLATTI, Pietro Filippo [654]
SCHACHT, Theodor von [956]
SCHAEFFER, Pierre [2159]
SCHAEUBLE, Hans Joachim [2088]
SCHAFFRATH, Christoph [780]
SCHARWENKA, Philipp [1437]
SCHARWENKA, Xaver [1448]
SCHEIDEMANN, Heinrich [443]
SCHEIDLER, Christian Gottlieb [794]
SCHEIDT, Samuel [426]
SCHEIN, Johann Hermann [419]
SCHENCK, Johann Baptist [982]
SCHERER, Sebastian Anton [514]
SCHICKELE, Peter [2414]

SCHICKHARDT, Johann Christian [672]
SCHIEFFERDECKER, Johann Christian
  [657]
SCHILDT, Melchior [438]
SCHILLINGS, Max von [1597]
SCHLICK, Arnolt [88]
SCHLICK, Johann Conrad [1015]
SCHMELZER, Johann Heinrich [496]
SCHMID, Bernhard [231]
SCHMIDT, Franz [1661]
SCHMITT, Florent [1615]
SCHNABEL, Artur [1746]
SCHNEIDER, Johann [749]
SCHNYDER VON WARTENSEE, Franz
  Xaver [1119]
SCHOBERT, Johann [888]
SCHOECK, Othmar [1813]
SCHOENBERG, Arnold [1657]
SCHOENFELD, Johann Philipp [926]
SCHREKER, Franz [1705]
SCHROETER, Leonhard [229]
SCHUBERT, Franz ("François") [1196]
SCHUBERT, Franz Peter [1153]
SCHULLER, Gunther [2354]
SCHULZ, Johann Abraham Peter [949]
SCHUMAN, William [2158]
SCHUMANN, Clara [1267]
SCHUMANN, Robert [1211]
SCHÜTT, Eduard [1491]
SCHÜTZ, Heinrich [412]
SCHWINDL, Friedrich [892]
SCOTT, Cyril [1720]
SCOTT, Tom [2187]
SCRIABIN, Alexander [1625]
SCULTHORPE, Peter [2382]
SEARLE, Humphrey [2239]
SECHTER, Simon [1129]
SECKENDORFF, Karl Siegmund [933]
SEGER, Josef [807]
SEGNI, Giulio [142]
SEIBER, Mátyás [2068]
SEIXAS, José Antonio Carlos de [755]
SELBY, William [902]
SELMA Y SALAVERDE, Bartolomeo
  [418]
SENFL, Ludwig [120]

SERLY, Tibor [2007]
SERMISY, Claudin de [127]
SEROV, Alexander [1269]
SERRANO, José [1646]
SESSIONS, Roger [1931]
SÉVÉRAC, Déodat de [1644]
SEYFERT, Johann Caspar [733]
SGAMBATI, Giovanni [1385]
SHAPERO, Harold [2301]
SHAPORIN, Yuri [1823]
SHAW, Geoffrey [1724]
SHAW, Martin [1667]
SHAW, Oliver [1092]
SHCHEDRIN, Rodion [2404]
SHEBALIN, Vissarion [2017]
SHEPHERD, Arthur [1728]
SHIELD, William [955]
SHIFRIN, Seymour [2358]
SHOSTAKOVICH, Dmitri [2094]
SIBELIUS, Jean [1575]
SICHER, Fridolin [121]
SIEFERT, Paul [421]
SIEGMEISTER, Elie [2131]
SILCHER, Philipp Friedrich [1130]
SILVER, Charles [1596]
SIMON, Johann Kaspar [744]
SIMPSON, Thomas [403]
SINDING, Christian [1488]
SITT, Hans [1452]
SJÖBERG, Svante Leonard [1645]
SJÖGREN, Emil [1472]
SKALKOTTAS, Nikos [2050]
SLAVENSKI, Josip [1921]
SLONIMSKY, Nicolas [1893]
SMERT, Richard [63]
SMETANA, Bedřich [1291]
SMITH, Alice Mary [1371]
SMITH, John Christopher, the younger [795]
SMITH, Sydney [1372]
SMITH, William [467]
SMYTH, Dame Ethel [1503]
SODERINI, Agostino [382]
SÖDERMAN, Johan August [1323]
SOJO, Vicente Emilio [1825]
SOLAGE [41]

SOLER, Antonio [854]
SOLLBERGER, Harvey [2424]
SOMERS, Harry [2350]
SOMERVELL, Sir Arthur [1553]
SONDHEIM, Stephen [2388]
SOR, Fernando [1090]
SORABJI, Kaikhosru [1867]
SORGE, Georg Andreas [753]
SOSTOA, Manuel [958]
SOTO, Francisco de [175]
SOUSA, John Philip [1482]
SOWA V SÓWKA, Jakób [306]
SOWANDE, Fela [2070]
SOWERBY, Leo [1908]
SPEER, Daniel [522]
SPELMAN, Timothy Mather [1848]
SPERANDIO, Bertoldo [224]
SPERGER, Johann Mathias [964]
SPOHR, Louis [1112]
SPONTINI, Gaspare [1081]
STADEN, Johann [400]
STADLER, Anton Paul [981]
STAINER, Sir John [1378]
STAMITZ, Carl [937]
STAMITZ, Johann Wenzel [810]
STANFORD, Sir Charles Villiers [1467]
STANLEY, Charles John [796]
STAROKADOMSKY, Mikhail [1996]
STATKOWSKI, Roman [1519]
STEENWICK, Gisbert [481]
STEFFANI, Agostino [570]
STEHMAN, Jacques [2191]
STEIBELT, Daniel [1044]
STEIGLEDER, Hans Ulrich [437]
STENHAMMAR, Wilhelm [1619]
ŠTĚPÁN, Josef Antonín [840]
STERN, Leo [1543]
STEVENS, Halsey [2128]
STICH, Johann Wenzel (Giovanni Punto) [945]
STILL, Robert [2153]
STILL, William Grant [1909]
STOCKHAUSEN, Karlheinz [2377]
STOKHEM, Johannes de [75]
STOLTZER, Thomas [119]
STOLZ, Robert [1730]

STÖLZEL, Gottfried Heinrich [704]
STONE, Robert [185]
STORACE, Stephen [1025]
STRADELLA, Alessandro [541]
STRAKOSCH, Maurice [1297]
STRATTNER, Georg Christoph [543]
STRAUBE, Rudolf [811]
STRAUS, Oscar [1613]
STRAUSS, Eduard [1339]
STRAUSS, Franz Josef [1280]
STRAUSS, Johann, Jr. [1295]
STRAUSS, Johann, Sr. [1177]
STRAUSS, Josef [1300]
STRAUSS, Richard [1563]
STRAVINSKY, Igor [1748]
STREICHER, Theodor [1653]
STRONG, George Templeton, Jr. [1490]
STRUNGK, Delphin [462]
STURGEON, Nicholas [52]
SUBOTNICK, Morton [2405]
SUCHOŇ, Eugen [2125]
SUDDS, William F. [1403]
SUK, Josef [1651]
SULLIVAN, Sir Arthur [1397]
SUPPÉ, Franz von [1262]
SURINACH, Carlos [2230]
SURZYŃSKI, Józef [1460]
SURZYŃSKI, Mieczysław [1585]
SUSATO, Tielman [155]
SVEDBOM, Per Jonas [1404]
SVENDSEN, Johan [1379]
SVIRIDOV, Georgi [2242]
SWAN, Timothy [1007]
SWANSON, Howard [2112]
SWEELINCK, Jan Pieterszoon [313]
SZABELSKI, Bolesław [1929]
SZABÓ, Ferenc [2027]
SZARZYŃSKI, Stanisław Sylwester [560]
SZELIGOWSKI, Tadeusz [1925]
SZULC, Józef [1668]
SZYMANOWSKA, Maria Agata [1133]
SZYMANOWSKI, Karol [1755]

TADOLINI, Giovanni [1132]
TAFFANEL, Paul [1421]
TAILLEFERRE, Germaine [1863]

TAKEMITSU, Toru [2391]
TALLIS, Thomas [157]
TALMA, Louise [2097]
TALTABULL, Cristofor [1829]
TANEYEV, Sergei [1492]
TANSMAN, Alexandre [1938]
TANS'UR, William [739]
TAPRAY, Jean-François [900]
TARDOS, Béla [2156]
TARP, Svend Erik [2123]
TÁRREGA, Francisco [1469]
TARTINI, Giuseppe [714]
TASKIN, Henri Joseph [1094]
TATE, Phyllis [2172]
TAUBER, Richard [1865]
TAUBERT, Wilhelm [1216]
TAUSIG, Carl [1389]
TAVENER, John [2432]
TAVERNER, John [128]
TAYLOR, Deems [1801]
TAYLOR, Franklin [1402]
TCHAIKOVSKY, Piotr Ilyich [1377]
TCHEREPNIN, Alexander [1961]
TCHEREPNIN, Nikolai [1642]
TCHESNOKOV, Pavel [1698]
TCHISHKO, Oles [1910]
TELEMANN, Georg Philipp [665]
TEMPLETON, Alec [2140]
TERTRE, Estienne du [191]
TERZI, Giovanni Antonio [307]
TESSARINI, Carlo [711]
TESSIER, Charles [270]
THALBERG, Sigismund [1220]
THAYER, Whitney Eugene [1364]
THIBAUT de Navarre [26]
THOMAS, Ambroise [1217]
THOMAS, Arthur Goring [1455]
THOMÉ, François [1453]
THOMPSON, Randall [1966]
THOMSON, Virgil [1928]
THUILLE, Ludwig [1537]
TIERSOT, Julien [1500]
TIESSEN, Heinz [1819]
TINCTORIS, Johannes [70]
TIPPETT, Sir Michael [2059]
TIRINDELLI, Pier Adolfo [1504]

TISHCHENKO, Boris [2431]
TITELOUZE, Jehan [318]
TOCH, Ernst [1824]
TOLDRÁ, Eduardo [1907]
TOMÁŠEK, Václav Jan Křtítel [1080]
TOMASI, Henri [2002]
TOMASINI, Luigi [921]
TOMKINS, Thomas [365]
TORELLI, Giuseppe [578]
TORREJÓN, Tomás de [542]
TOSELLI, Enrico [1761]
TOSTI, Sir Francesco Paolo [1429]
TOURNEMIRE, Charles [1611]
TOURS, Berthold [1365]
TRABACI, Giovanni Maria [383]
TRAVERS, John [754]
TREXLER, Georg [2032]
TRIGGS, Harold [1988]
TRNEČEK, Hanuš [1506]
TROFEO, Ruggiero [271]
TROMBONCINO, Bartolomeo [94]
TRUNK, Richard [1711]
TUFTS, John [700]
TULOU, Jean-Louis [1122]
TŮMA, František [756]
TUNDER, Franz [486]
TURINA, Joaquín [1759]
TÜRK, Daniel Gottlob [965]
TURNHOUT, Gérard de [194]
TURRINI, Ferdinando [963]
TUTHILL, Burnet [1831]
TYE, Christopher [158]

USSACHEVSKY, Vladimir [2180]
UTTINI, Francesco [831]

VACCAI, Nicola [1134]
VADO, Juan del [482]
VAILLANT, Jehan [40]
VAINBERG, Moisei [2295]
VALEN, Fartein [1822]
VALENTE, Antonio [195]
VALENTINE, Robert [663]
VALENTINI, Giuseppe [664]
VALLERAND, Jean [2243]
VALLET, Nicolas [410]

VALVERDE, Joaquín [1428]
VANHAL, Jan Křtitl [903]
VAN VACTOR, David [2087]
VARÈSE, Edgard [1774]
VARLAMOV, Alexander [1165]
VARNEY, Louis [1418]
VÁSQUEZ, Juan [176]
VASSILENKO, Sergei [1628]
VAUGHAN WILLIAMS, Ralph [1633]
VAUTOR, Thomas [384]
VECCHI, Orazio [265]
VÉCSEY, Franz von [1876]
VEDEL, Artemiy [1052]
VEGGIO, Claudio Maria [177]
VEJVANOVSKÝ, Pavel Josef [534]
VENEGAS DE HENESTROSA, Luys [178]
VENTO, Ivo de [249]
VENZANO, Luigi [1239]
VERACINI, Francesco Maria [705]
VERDELOT, Philippe [104]
VERDI, Giuseppe [1232]
VERNON, Joseph [909]
VERRALL, John [2119]
VERSTOVSKY, Alexei [1156]
VETTER, Daniel [580]
VIADANA, Lodovico Grossi da [308]
VICTORIA, Tomás Luis de [258]
VIDAL, Paul Antonin [1554]
VIERNE, Louis [1616]
VIEUXTEMPS, Henri [1270]
VILLA-LOBOS, Heitor [1817]
VINCI, Leonardo [712]
VIOTTI, Giovanni Battista [988]
VISÉE, Robert de [561]
VISETTI, Alberto Antonio [1432]
VITALI, Giovanni Battista [516]
VITALI, Tommaso Antonio [591]
VITTADINI, Franco [1778]
VIVALDI, Antonio [650]
VIVES, Amadeo [1622]
VIVIANI, Giovanni Buonaventura [526]
VLADIGEROV, Panchu [1963]
VLASOV, Vladimir [2029]
VOGEL, Johann Christoph [993]
VOGLER, Georg Joseph [960]

VOGLER, Johann Kaspar [726]
VOLKMANN, Robert [1241]
VOŘÍŠEK, Jan Václav [1138]
VRANICKÝ, Antonín [1023]
VULPIUS, Melchior [359]

WACŁAW of Szamotuł [200]
WAELRANT, Hubert [188]
WAGENSEIL, Georg Christoph [804]
WAGNER, Josef Franz [1489]
WAGNER, Richard [1230]
WAILLY, Louis de [1476]
WAISSEL, Matthäus [245]
WALDTEUFEL, Émile [1357]
WALLACE, William Vincent [1221]
WALMISLEY, Thomas Forbes [1109]
WALOND, William [839]
WALTER, Thomas [728]
WALTHER, Johann [139]
WALTHER, Johann Gottfried [680]
WALTHER von der Vogelweide [22]
WALTON, Sir William [2011]
WAŃSKI, Jan [1030]
WARD, John [361]
WARD, Robert [2269]
WARLOCK, Peter [1900]
WARREN, Elinor Remick [2063]
WARREN, George William [1304]
WATTS, Wintter [1777]
WAXMAN, Franz [2100]
WAYDITCH, Gabriel von [1832]
WEBBER, Amherst [1591]
WEBER, Ben [2251]
WEBER, Carl Maria von [1124]
WEBERN, Anton [1773]
WECKERLIN, Jean-Baptiste [1277]
WECKMANN, Matthias [494]
WEELKES, Thomas [385]
WEIGL, Karl [1733]
WEIGL, Vally [1970]
WEILL, Kurt [1978]
WEINBERGER, Jaromír [1919]
WEINER, Léo [1792]
WEINGARTNER, Felix [1552]
WEINZIERL, Max von [1388]
WEISGALL, Hugo [2194]

WEISS, Silvius Leopold [691]
WELDON, John [645]
WELLESZ, Egon [1799]
WENNERBERG, Gunnar [1251]
WERNER, Gregor Joseph [715]
WERNER, Heinrich [1158]
WERT, Giaches de [232]
WESLEY, Charles, Jr. [1005]
WESLEY, Samuel [1045]
WESLEY, Samuel Sebastian [1213]
WETZEL, Justus Hermann [1714]
WEYSE, Christoph Ernst Friedrich [1078]
WHITE, José [1375]
WHITE, Maude Valérie [1486]
WHITE, Robert [237]
WHITLOCK, Percy [2037]
WHYTHORNE, Thomas [210]
WIDMANN, Erasmus [362]
WIDOR, Charles-Marie [1414]
WIEDERMANN, Bedřich Antonín [1772]
WIENIAWSKI, Henryk [1340]
WIGGLESWORTH, Frank [2277]
WIGTHORP, William [398]
WIKLUND, Adolf [1716]
WIKMANSON, Johan [983]
WILBYE, John [369]
WILHELM, Karl Friedrich von [1243]
WILHELMINE, Markgräfin of Bayreuth
  [781]
WILLAERT, Adrian [129]
WILLIAMS, Aaron [869]
WILLIAMS, Grace [2082]
WILLIAMS, William [628]
WILLIAMSON, Malcolm [2397]
WILSON, H. Lane [1624]
WILSON, John [440]
WINTER, Peter von [987]
WIRÉN, Dag, [2075]
WITT, Jeremias Friedrich [1062]
WOLF, Hugo [1521]
WOLFF, Erich [1660]
WOLF-FERRARI, Ermanno [1679]
WOLKENSTEIN, Oswalt von [48]
WOLPE, Stefan [2020]
WOOD, Charles [1579]
WOOD, Haydn [1744]

WOODCOCK, Robert [713]
WOODWARD, Richard, Jr. [931]
WORK, Henry Clay [1326]
WUORINEN, Charles [2426]
WYMAN, Addison P. [1324]

XARABA, Diego [535]
XENAKIS, Iannis [2321]

YARDUMIAN, Richard [2264]
YON, Pietro [1810]
YOULL, Henry [399]
YRADIER, Sebastián [1199]
YSAYË, Eugène [1507]
YUN, Isang [2271]

ZABEL, Albert Heinrich [1332]
ZACHAU, Friedrich Wilhelm [594]
ZAJC, Ivan [1325]

ZANDONAI, Riccardo [1766]
ZAREMBA, Nicolai [1275]
ZARLINO, Gioseffo [186]
ZBINDEN, Julien-François [2274]
ZEIDLER, Josef [918]
ZELENKA, Jan Dismas [656]
ŻELEŃSKI, Władysław [1353]
ZELLER, Carl [1399]
ZELTER, Carl Friedrich [1008]
ZEMLINSKY, Alexander von [1621]
ZIEHRER, Carl Michael [1406]
ZIELEŃSKI, Mikołaj [272]
ZILCHER, Hermann [1737]
ZIMBALIST, Efrem, Sr. [1833]
ZIMMERMANN, Bernd Alois [2278]
ZIPOLI, Domenico [698]
ZUMAYA, Manuel de [653]
ZWIERZCHOWSKI, Mateusz [799]
ŻYWNY, Wojciech [996]

PRONUNCIATION GUIDE

Symbol	Examples	Symbol	Examples
a	at, cast	o	cot, otter
ā	able, rate	ō	cold, foal
ä	awful, sauce	ô	corn, normal
â	German *Herr*	ö	French *feu*, German *schön*
à	French *mal*	oi	boil, soy
b	boy, tub	ou	how, foul
ch	charm, church	oo	book, crook
d	dog, fad	o͞o	fool, moon
e	effort, pet	p	peep, spell
ē	eel, reach	r	roar, frog
f	fat, left	s	sister, less
g	good, tug	*s*	Basque *Andres*
h	ham, hug	sh	shark, ash
hw	what, when	t	tool, water
i	ill, pit	th	thin, wrath
ī	bile, style	*th*	then, there
j	jump, stage	u	butter, cut
k	cut, kick	ü	French *une*, German *kühl*
kh	German *sich, mutig*	v	velvet, knave
kw	queen, quota	w	west, win
l	lily, real	y	yarn, yell
lw	bell	z	zoo, doze
m	man, tom	zh	azure
n	nun, throne	ə	dozen, above
n	French *bon*	'	German *Knabe, Hadl*
ng	ring, tingle		

Comments

â   Represents a sound between ā and e.

à   Denotes a sound midway between a and ä.

kh   Indicates several sounds in German and other languages, ranging from the hard **kh** in *ach,* to the intermediate **kh** in *ich* to the soft **kh** at the end of *mutig.*

lw   In Polish names, represents the "dark-*l*" sound of the Polish letter *l,* a sound which can be approximated by saying English l with the tongue positioned firmly on the roof of the mouth just above the teeth than in regular l. In non-Polish names, lw simply represents l plus w.

n   The nasal sound which verges on silence in some words and occurs most frequently in French and Portuguese.

ô   Similar to ō but shorter, without the faint w sound trailing at the end as in ō.

ö   Represents several similar sounds in French, German, and other languages. Pronounced, roughly, by positioning the lips as for ō and saying ā or ē.

s   A Basque sound, midway between s and sh.

ü   Pronounced by positioning the lips as for $\overline{oo}$ while saying ē.

ə   This symbol, called the schwa, represents a sound similar to u or oo but which is *completely* unstressed.

'   An apostrophe following a phonetic symbol at the beginning of a syllable indicates that the sound is to be run in with that syllable rather than pronounced separately. An apostrophe in the middle of a syllable indicates that the syllable is to be pronounced as a single syllable but with the hint of a second syllable. An apostrophe preceding a symbol at the end of a word likewise indicates that the sound is to be run in with the syllable.

Note: This pronunciation guide and the system of phonetic symbols used throughout the book is designed to provide English-speaking readers with a basic knowledge of how to pronounce the composers' names. Effort has been made to keep this as simple as possible, while remaining accurate; therefore, certain subtleties (e.g., trilled r's in Spanish, complex diphthongs in Russian or Portuguese, secondary accents, and most variant pronunciations) have been omitted.

GREENE'S BIOGRAPHICAL
ENCYCLOPEDIA OF COMPOSERS

[1] LIMENIOS (Lē-mān'-yōs)
KITHARA (LYRE) PLAYER
BORN: Greece, second century B.C.
DIED: ?

Limenios composed the earliest extant piece of music to which we can attach a name— the so-called "Second Delphic Hymn" (to Apollo) of 128 B.C., imperfectly preserved in a stone carving. Of Limenios we know only that he was an Athenian citizen, the son of one Thoenos, that he played the kithara professionally, and that he was a member in good standing of the musicians' union (which he designates as "the great ecstatic sacred hive of Bacchus's artists"). He probably also wrote the "First Delphic Hymn"— like the second, intended for the Pythian Games. RECORDINGS: Various recorded histories of music contain interpretations of ancient Greek compositions, all known examples of which are contained on a record by the Atrium Musicae of Madrid under Gregorio Paniagua.

[2] MESOMEDES (Mā-sō'-mā-dēz)
SINGER
BORN: Crete, second century A.D.
DIED: Rome

Mesomedes, a freedman, became the musicopoetical superstar of Emperor Hadrian's court. As was customary, he made up his own tunes to his own lyrics and sang them to his own kithara (lyre) accompaniment. Such musical favorites, like opera singers of more recent times, were treasured chiefly for their technical feats, and were adulated, pampered, and panted after. Like the athletes they were, they competed at the annual Capitoline Games. Among the several poems by, or attributed to, Mesomedes, five include musical notation. One of them, once called *Hymn to the Muses,* is really three separate addresses to two Muses and Apollo; the others are hymns to the sun and to Nemesis (a big cult figure in those days). How accurately the notation represents the composer's intentions is debatable, since the versions we have are from much later Byzantine sources. And, indeed, experts do not agree that the hymns were really composed by Mesomedes.

[3] ST. AMBROSE
CLERIC
BORN: Trier (Augusta Treverorum),
   c. 340
DIED: Milan (Mediolanum), April 4, 397

Though he is accorded an important place in Western musical history, it is uncertain what, if anything, St. Ambrose composed. The son of a high Roman colonial official, he was born in Gaul, followed the paternal path, and became consular prefect of northwest Italy, with headquarters in Milan. In 374, the see of that city having been vacant for some time, owing to political infighting, the Milanese appointed him their bishop, bypassing the fact that he was not yet officially a Christian. He rectified that omission, and for his remaining twenty-three years distinguished himself both as a theologian and statesman, artfully holding off threats from both heretics and political invaders.

It is generally agreed that Ambrose had a good deal to do with the antiphonal singing and the hymns introduced into the Milanese rite in his time, and he almost certainly wrote some hymn texts—though we may discount the story that when St. Augustine of Hippo was baptizing him the two were inspired to compose the *Te Deum* improvisationally. In the early Church, hymn singing had apparently gotten out of hand (too much stomping and clapping, and had been largely suppressed. Then it caught on again in the Near East. Shortly before Ambrose became bishop, St. Hilary of Poitiers had brought the practice, and perhaps some examples, back from his Syrian exile, though without making much impact. According to St. Augustine, hymn singing was introduced into Ambrosian Milan in an effort to buck up the faithful in the face of a particularly severe threat from the Arian heretics. Intended for congregational singing, the music would appear to have been melodious and simple—in a word, folklike—and possibly borrowed from the folk or taken over from Eastern hymn tunes.

There is no doubt that Ambrosian chant (still used in Milan) is very old, preceding the Gregorian variety. But what, in its known form, it has to do with St. Ambrose, or with the chant introduced in his time, is quite uncertain, since no known source goes back before the high Middle Ages. (The notion that Ambrose devised the so-called "authentic" Church modes has long since been exploded, as has the belief that Ambrosian chant adheres to them only.)

RECORDINGS: Ambrosian chants appear fairly frequently in recorded histories of music; there are also several collections.

[4] ST. GREGORY "the Great" (Pope Gregory I)
POLITICIAN, CLERIC

BORN: Rome, c. 540
DIED: Rome, March 12, 604

Ancient tradition makes Gregory one of the most important of all composers, though, like St. Ambrose [3], he may not even have been particularly musical. He came of an old patrician family and, like Ambrose, initially undertook a governmental career. But in his thirties he heard the Call of God, resigned, and set about founding monasteries, in one of which he became an inmate. Pope Pelagius II sent him off to represent Church and Empire in Byzantium; he stayed there seven years, apparently disliking everything Greek, including cultural history. In the mid 580s he returned to his monastery as its abbot. When Pelagius succumbed to plague in 590, Gregory was unanimously chosen as his successor.

Some twenty years earlier, the Arian Langobards had swept into northern Italy, and continued to harass it. (Their name of Langobards, "longbeards," was derived, legend says, from their women's trick of tying their long hair under their chins to make it appear there were more fighting men than there really were.) By making peace with the Langobards, Gregory undermined imperial power and effectively established the Bishop of Rome (himself) as head of the Western Church, though his primacy was not uncontested until the Frankish King Pepin the Short gave his not entirely altruistic support to the papacy a century and a half later.

Though frail and ascetic, Gregory was a brilliant organizer, administrator, and politician. He insisted on the doctrine of papal supremacy, held well-nigh imperial sway in Italy, and did everything he could to impress the sees of Western Europe and North Africa that he was in charge. He had once had it in mind to go convert the inhabitants of England, and after he became pope he sent "the other" St. Augustine to do the job (in which he succeeded so well that he became first Archbishop of Canterbury). One would like to believe that the pun attributed to Gregory by the Venerable Bede was his: seeing some fair-haired boys in a slave market and told that they were Angles, he supposedly replied that they were not Angles but angels; but humor seems not to have been Gregory's long suit. He wrote many useful theological works, including manuals for recognizing angels and devils. His best-known such work, however, is the *Liber pastoralis curae (Pastoral Care)* on how to be a bishop. As a devout proponent of no-nonsense monasticism, he seems to have had little interest in the arts and virtually none in the Classical past.

He gets into a musicobiographical dictionary, of course, through whatever connection he may have had with what became known as Gregorian chant, the standard music for the Latin liturgy in most parts of the world. In fact it is only one manifestation of Christian chant, whose beginnings are obscure. The vast body of Gregorian chant that has come down to us cannot have been composed by Gregory, who was once credited with it, since it clearly accreted over many centuries. It may be that he did not even oversee the compilation of the music that bears his name, though it is possible that he set scholars to sifting, codifying, and legitimizing it. But the generic name does not seem to have been used until nearly three centuries after he died, and the story of his link with it is largely owing to a biography written by one John the Deacon about the same time, and to an ensuing iconographic tradition that shows the Pope dictating to scribes what was cooed into his ear by the Holy Spirit in the form of a dove.

RECORDINGS: Many collections exist, from before the LP era up to the present.

[5] NOTKER OF ST. GALL (Not'-ker)
MONK
BORN: Elg or Jonschwyll (Switzerland), c. 840
DIED: St. Gall, April 6, 912

Notker was called Balbulus ("the Stammerer") presumably because he stammered and probably to distinguish him from other monastic Notkers, who were fairly common in his day. He was long credited with having invented the musical form known as the *sequence.* In Gregorian *Alleluia* chants, the final syllable of that word was often extended —by way of expressing rejoicing—into long and ornate vocalises. Such length demanded their being broken up into phrases to permit the singers to breathe. Most monastic choristers, being not particularly gifted, had trouble recalling the precise outlines of such passages. Someone had the bright idea of equipping them with appropriate lyrics, which would provide a mnemonic device. Such developments were called *sequences.* There is no doubt that Notker wrote sequence texts. (He was a poet of stature.) In the preface to his hymnbook he claims that he did not invent the sequence, but merely tried to imitate the new form he was shown by a refugee French monk. If Notker contributed anything, it may have been the idea of giving a note to each syllable of the text. He was also long credited with the composition of a catchy religious song, *"Media vita,"* which supposedly had magical force, but he probably had nothing to do with it. Nor did he with some musicotheoretical pieces written by "Notker," their author having most likely been Notker Labeo, who was at St. Gall about a century later. However, the Stammerer's other writings, including a martyrology, were sufficient to win him canonization in 1513; and, apparently to honor him, a brief late school of sequence poetry sprang up at St. Gall in Switzerland after that. RECORDINGS: Some of Notker's sequences appear in anthologies of medieval music under his name.

[6] HERMANNUS CONTRACTUS (alias Heriman, Hermann von Reichenau, Hermannus Augiensis, Herman the Lame)

MONK, TEACHER, THEORETICIAN, SCIENTIST
BORN: Saulgau, Swabia, July 18, 1013
DIED: Altshausen, September 24, 1054

Hermannus was born of a noble family, though *which* noble family is uncertain. Various sources call him the son of Count Hermann of Vehringen or Count Wolferad of Alshausen *(sic)*. Moreover he is sometimes said to have been born at Sulgen in Switzerland and to have died at Alleshausen *(sic)*. As his sobriquet indicates, he was crippled, by an illness suffered in early childhood; one might guess it to have been poliomyelitis. He was educated from the age of seven, possibly at the Monastery of St. Gall or perhaps that of Reichenau, where he became a Benedictine at thirty and took up teaching. A brilliant man, he is said to have developed timepieces and musical, mathematical, and astronomical instruments. Although he did not invent the astrolabe (a predecessor of the sextant), as was once supposed, he was probably the first medieval man to write a treatise on it. He was particularly authoritative, apparently, in the *quadrivium*, which embraced arithmetic, astronomy, geometry, and music, but wrote on other matters as well—a poem on the vices, a continuation of Notker's [5] martyrology, and a world history, particularly rich in information about his own era. His tract *Musica* is a highly specialized study of acoustics and its relation to the Church modes. Hermannus solved the riddle of the elusive eighth mode, which other theorists had insisted, in the interests of logical neatness, *must* exist. He found it in the plagal hypomixolydian mode, which begins, like the Dorian, on D, a fourth below the mixolydian, but has its dominant (or *tenor)* on C instead of on A. (Everyone else had been expecting a *hyper*mixolydian because the Roman philosopher Boethius, on the authority of Ptolemy, had said that such a thing existed.) Hermannus also invented a new system of musical notation which, though it did not catch on, had the virtue of being more precise than the neumes then in use. He is known to have composed, and a number of pieces have been claimed for him —the most popular being *"Salve Regina"* and another Marian hymn, *"Alma Redemptoris Mater,"* which, it may be recalled, was the theme song of the hapless schoolboy in Chaucer's "Prioress's Tale." But only two or three items can be so ascribed with much confidence, though labelers of phonograph records are not so scrupulous.

[7] ST. GODRIC

MERCHANT, SAILOR, HERMIT
BORN: Hanapol, Norfolk, c. 1069
DIED: Finchale, May 21, 1170

Thanks to two biographies by people acquainted with him and his family, we know more about St. Godric than we usually do about obscure and remote persons, and some of it is probably accurate. Of his early life, however, we know only that he was born, about the time of the Norman Conquest, to "Saxon" parents and became a small-time peddler. A brush with drowning, while trying either to capture or rescue a stranded porpoise, seems rather inexplicably to have given him a taste for the sea—or at least of it. For sixteen years he was a seafarer, and perhaps something more, since he is identified with the Gudericus, *piratus de regno Angliae,* who ferried the defeated Baldwin I of Jerusalem from Arsuf to Jaffa during the First Crusade. Afterward he made pilgrimages to Santiago de Compostela and to Rome, and then became a hermit. However, he returned to Jerusalem on the instructions of a vision, which promised him ultimate quietude at a place called Finchale. On his return to England, he made his living ringing the bells and guarding the doors of Durham churches. One day he discovered that Finchale was only a short distance from Durham, and settled there under the protection of the Flambards, who owned it. Here he lived a life of self-denial for sixty years, and founded what would become Finchale Priory. In his later years he had his family with him and servants to tend to his needs, but spoke to them only when told by his ecclesiastical superiors to do so. During the last eight of his more than one hundred years, he became senile and bedridden.

Godric frequently saw visions, some of them prophetic, such as the one of the elevation of Thomas à Becket, whom he had never encountered, to the archbishopric of Canterbury. One of the manuscript biographies contains the words and music of three hymns—all that remain (save for another text) of several sung to him by various visionary saints and the shade of his sister—and these also appear in other manuscripts. Since Godric was illiterate, someone else must have noted them down. Some doubt has been expressed as to their authenticity, but the Middle English is of the period.

RECORDINGS: Several recorded anthologies contain one or more of these pieces.

[8] GUILHEM OF AQUITAINE (William, Guillaume), Ninth Duke of Aquitaine and Seventh Count of Poitou (Gwē-yem')

CRUSADER, TROUBADOUR
BORN: Poitiers, October 22 (?), 1071
DIED: Poitiers, February 10, 1127

The son of Guilhem ("Gui-Geoffroi") VIII of Aquitaine and the Princess Audiart of Burgundy, Guilhem succeeded his father in 1086 as ruler of most of south-central France. Eight years later he married the dowager Queen of Aragon, variously designated as Philippa and Matilda, daughter of the Count of Toulouse. The county had gone to her uncle, Raymond IV; when he marched off on a crusade in 1096, Guilhem seized Toulouse on the grounds that it was properly his wife's and then cast his lot with William Rufus of England in a struggle with France. Initially unmoved by Pope Urban II's crusade call, Guilhem found himself suddenly interested when news of the fall of Jerusalem reached him and persuaded his ally to join him in raising an army. But just as things were getting under way, William of England was struck down by an arrow while hunting, and the duke was forced to sell Toulouse to meet his expenses. He raised a force of 30,000 or 300,000 men, depending on what source one reads, set out in 1101 through the Germanies, was entertained by Emperor Alexius Comnenus in Byzantium, and in September saw his army, which had paused for a drink from a river in Asia Minor near Heraclea Pontica (now Eregli), wiped out in a Turkish ambush. Guilhem escaped to Antioch, made it to the Holy City by Easter, and was home again in October 1102. For the next eighteen years, he seems to have occupied his time chiefly in founding religious institutions and chasing women. (According to some of his clerical contemporaries, the first activity was insufficient to offset the second.) He died after another, more successful crusade and was succeeded by his son and namesake, who in 1137 left his lands to his daughter Eleanor, successively queen to Louis VII of France and Henry II of England, and perhaps the most significant secular figure of the so-called twelfth-century Renaissance.

The chronicler-clerics of the time depicted Guilhem as a buffoon, a profligate, and a bad man (he was twice excommunicated). Modern historians prefer to see him as a humorist, an astute politician, and a sophisticate—the very model of a corporation executive. But he is chiefly remembered as a poet and composer, though only part of the music to a single song is presently known, and the earliest, if not perhaps the first, of the troubadours. The troubadours (or *trobaires),* whose initial impetus may have come from Spain, are one of the important cultural phenomena of the twelfth century—and one of the most obscure, when it comes to their origins, a question too involved to explore here. They seem to have represented a new impulse in poetry and in music, and, one might say, a new attitude to human life. Their verse was composed in their own vernacular, Provençal or the *langue d'oc,* rather than in Latin; its forms, both poetic and musical, appear to have been new. The dominant view it espouses is that in love desire is more valuable than its consummation—the chief tenet of romantic love forever after. The root of the generic name is thought to be the Latin *tropus,* a figure of speech, a fresh way of saying something, which, through a late Latin verb form *tropar,* spawned Provençal *trobar* and French *trouver,* both meaning "to find" or "to discover," and thus "to invent." But even this derivation is not entirely certain.

Contrary to popular opinion, troubadours were not rather effeminate young men who put on funny clothes and caterwauled under donjon windows, but often lusty he-men like Guilhem. The basic notion behind their activities—a notion cultivated by Eleanor of Aquitaine to bring her obstreperous courtiers to heel in the "Courts of Love"—was that one selected a hopelessly unavailable ladylove and channeled his energies into the art of wooing through music and poetry. In fact, the ladies were not always so unavailable as they appeared to be and the songs covered many other aspects of life as well—politics, religion, morality, and personal misfortune, for example, often from a satirical viewpoint—but their impact on subsequent European literature and music was incalculable.

It has been speculated that the music was possibly created not by the poets but by professional *jongleurs*—at least for troubadours of the highest estate. Perhaps so, but since in early times words and music (i.e., melody, for harmony and counterpoint had not yet been invented) were twin products of the creative impulse, it is hard to imagine that the troubadours did not make up their own tunes, though *jongleurs* may have been called in to set them down.

RECORDINGS: A number of pieces attributed to Guilhem appear in various recorded histories of music, and in recent years there has been a notable increase in records devoted entirely to the troubadours.

[9] MARCABRU (Mär′-kà-brōō)
TROUBADOUR
BORN: Gascony, c. 1105
DIED: after 1150

Marcabru appears to be the first French troubadour for whose songs we have complete tunes—four in all. What we know of him depends mostly on two *vidas* (lives)—highly suspect biographical sketches of the period, such as we have of several of his confreres. His name, which means "Dark Spot," would appear to be derived from the name of his alleged mother, a poor Gascon woman named Marcabruna, or perhaps simply Bruna. Or so one version says; the other has him a foundling. He was also called Panperdut, meaning either "Lost Bread" or "Lost Pants," though we have no clue as to why. Whatever his origins, he was supposedly brought up by a nobleman named Aldric of Vilar, and learned his troubadour skills and outlook from one Cercamon, who belonged to the court of Guilhem X of Aquitaine. Presumably Marcabru also found a place there. He was regarded as unnecessarily scurrilous, but this is a misunderstanding of his troubadour point of view. His attacks are against hypocrites, particularly of the female persuasion, who pretend to be models of virtue but who secretly practice "false love"—that is, sexual promiscuity. What he himself longs for is *fin' amours*—"right love"—which confers all good things on those who keep its chaste laws and leads them to heaven. Marcabru's sallies at the greed, venality, and general piggishness he observed did not, the story says, sit well with the lords of Guyenne, who had him murdered. His satire apart, he is, in his lyrics, witty, allusive, and a master of rhetoric, well grounded in both scripture and classical mythology. He likes odd words and figures of speech: in his song *"Pax in nomine Domine"*

("Peace in the Lord's Name"), he likens the crusade he is recommending to Alfonso VII of Castile to a washtub which will purify those sinners who get into it.

[10] RUDEL, Jaufré (Rōō-del′, Zhō-frā′)
TROUBADOUR
BORN: Blaye before 1125
DIED: after 1147

Sometimes called Rudel de Blaja or Blaia, Jaufré was third Prince of Blaye, a town on the Gironde estuary north of Bordeaux. Probably when he was a child, his father, Girard, rebelled against his overlord, Guilhem IX of Aquitaine [8], who in retaliation bashed down large sections of the Blaye family castle. About Jaufré we know little that is dependable. An official document of 1125 mentions him, and his contemporary Marcabru [9] remarks his joining the so-called Second Crusade in 1147. Seven of his lyrics survive, four with music, reflecting both the Christian militance of the times and troubadour romanticism, though his attitude to love does not rule out physicality. The later German *Minnesinger* Walther von der Vogelweide [22] used both the theme and the melody of one of Rudel's extant songs for a famous crusade song of his own. Another tells of the troubadour's spring longing for a "distant beloved." Legend identifies her as the "Princess of Tripoli," of whose beauty he knew only from hearsay. Finding it irresistible, he took a trans-Mediterranean cruise, but fell ill en route and, on reaching the African shore, was taken dying to an inn. The princess, hearing of his remarkable devotion, hastened to his bedside. He thereupon revived sufficiently to thank God, then died in her arms. Brokenhearted, she became a nun. It is not a likely story, unless perhaps the princess is to be understood as Jerusalem (in the terrestrial or heavenly senses).

[11] BERNART de Ventadorn (or Ventadour) (Ber-när′ də Vàn′-ta-dôrn)
TROUBADOUR
BORN: Ventadorn, c. 1130
DIED: c. 1195

The modern age sees Bernart as perhaps the most attractive of the troubadour songsters. Certainly in his pose of almost religious subservience to an almost divine lady, he is one of the most archetypal. And, in the way of courtly love, he is given (like Alice in the old song) to weeping with delight when she gives him a smile, and trembling with fear—

or frustration—at her frown. He is both sensitive and sensual; his agony comes from the gnaw of sex, and it is body as much as soul that draws him. Among his forty-four extant lyrics are eighteen with music—more than we have from any other troubadour.

What we know of Bernart comes from two clearly untrustworthy *vidas* (lives), a satire by his contemporary Peire d'Alvernhe, hints from his own poems, and legend. His parents are said to have been lowborn, probably retainers of one of the viscounts of Ventadorn in the Limousin (the remains of the castle still exist). One of them was a baker in the kitchen, though there is disagreement as to which. He must have grown up there in the days of Eble II, "the Singer," who took a personal interest in troubadouring and did a bit of it himself. Probably around 1150, it is hinted, he became involved with the viscountess (presumably the wife of Eble III) and was banished. Then he seems to have taken service with Eleanor of Aquitaine, who soon after married Henry of Anjou in 1152. Bernart wrote admiring songs in the troubadour tradition, but it is doubtful that Eleanor became his mistress in any real sense. The evidence is fairly strong that he accompanied the royal couple to their coronation in Westminster Abbey when Henry became Henry II of England in 1154. After that he allegedly returned to France and took service first with Ermengarde of Narbonne and then with Raymond V of Toulouse. According to Uc of St. Circ, the reputed author of the longer *vida*, he ended his days as a monk in the Abbey of Dalon in the Dordogne.

[12] LÉONIN (or Magister Leoninus)
(Lā'-ō-nān*)*
CHOIRMASTER (?)
BORN: Paris (?), c. 1130 (?)
DIED: Paris (?), c. 1200 (?)

Forty years ago, Master Leo stood proudly in the history books and on record labels as the First Great Composer in Western history, a man who had revolutionized the art of music with one powerful stroke by inventing counterpoint. He was, we learned, choirmaster at the Cathedral of Notre-Dame de Paris, and it was easy to imagine the two-part *organa* he devised echoing through the dark vaults of that great building. Not only had he left a *Magnus Liber*, a Big Book, of such radical compositions; he had also taken a modern "rational" approach to rhythm and founded a school of composition that was to account for the whole early contra-

puntal approach later labeled the *Ars Antiqua*, the Old Art.

Since then confidence in Léonin's place has steadily weakened, until now his very existence seems doubtful. The bulk of our information about him—such as it is—comes from a questionable paragraph in the writings of a late-thirteenth-century English theorist known only as Anonymous IV. It says that Léonin was the greatest *organista* and that he *made* a Big Book of *organa*. In the simplest form of *organum* (the two-voice kind, taken from liturgical chant) the lower voice moves slowly while the upper voice develops a florid discant over it, consistent with certain harmonic or mathematical rules. We now know that such improvisational discanting was practiced for a long time before Léonin's era, so in principle he did not invent it. Anonymous IV's ambiguous term *organista* may indeed mean that Léonin, as a choir singer, was admired for his improvisations. The Big Book, then, may not have been so much a matter of composition, per se, as of noting down examples of what was then common usage. As for his vaunted invention of metrical rhythm, it depends on how one reads the notes, and it has been objected that those who find it in the Big Book are indulging in wishful thinking. In any case, the versions of the Big Book that we know are from a century or so later and may have been in some degree adapted to the needs of that time. Finally, if Léonin was a choirmaster, it was probably not at Notre-Dame, since it was only a-building in the years when he was supposedly most active and did not open for business until 1185.

RECORDINGS: A fair number of recordings exist.

[13] GUIRAUT de Bornelh (Gĕ-rōt' də Bôr-nā')
TROUBADOUR, TEACHER, SOLDIER
BORN: Bourneix, c. 1140
DIED: after 1212

Despite his high reputation in his own time (Dante speaks admiringly of him), we know little of Guiraut (or Giraut). He appears to have been born in the Dordogne, probably to middle-class parents, and to have received an unusually good education, perhaps under the patronage of Viscount Adémar of Limoges. At the height of his popularity he moved, accompanied by two *jongleurs,* from court to court—among them, those of Auvergne, Castile, and Aragon. At what must have been a fairly mature age for the times, he seems to have gone off on the Third Crusade, which began in 1189. He last turns up in 1212 in a battle in Poitou between the forces of John of England and Philippe Auguste of France. Known as the *maestre dels trobadors,* he apparently taught his art in the off-season. Many of his rather artificial and self-conscious verses survive, but only a few with music (one recent source says 18, another only 4). His most famous song is a sort of dawn hymn, *"Reis glorios,"* praying God to protect two adulterous lovers.

[14] DANIEL, Arnaut (Dàn-yel', Är-nō')
TROUBADOUR
BORN: Ribérac, c. 1150
DIED: c. 1210

High on Mount Purgatory, on the cornice of the lustful, just below the Earthly Paradise, Dante encounters Arnaut Daniel, whom the shade of the Italian poet Guinizelli introduces to him as *il miglior fabbro* (the better poet of the two—a phrase that T. S. Eliot later bestowed on Ezra Pound). Daniel, who addresses Dante in Provençal, is presumably atoning for his affair with the wife of one Guillaume de Bouville, though Petrarch's appellation *gran maestro d'amore* (in the *Trionfi)* may indicate that he had more than one reason for being in Purgatory. Most of what we know about Daniel is owing to a *vida* (life), which tells us that he was well-born and intended by his parents for the Church. But he became fascinated with poetry, gave up his vocation, and *"fetz se joglars"*—which may mean that he became a *jongleur* but probably indicates that he took to singing his own songs. He did not fare very well at first, owing to his fondness for backgammon and dice. According to Benvenuto da Imola, writing two hundred years later, his fortunes changed when he tendered some of his songs to the kings of both France and England, though exactly how is not clear. At any rate he *was* at the coronation of Philippe Auguste in 1180, and is said later to have joined the entourage of Richard I [17] of England. Daniel was a master of *trobar clus,* an extremely obscure and intellectual troubadour approach to poetry, and he supposedly invented the poetic form known as the sestina. He was undoubtedly a fine technician, but his poetry now seems extremely artificial and unnecessarily difficult. Only 2 of his tunes are extant.

[15] BLONDEL de Nesle (Blon-del' də Nâl)
TROUVÈRE
BORN: Nesle (France), c. 1155
DIED: after 1200

The *trouvères,* of whom Blondel is one of the best-known representatives and presumably one of the first, were the northern counterparts and imitators of the troubadours, the greatest difference being that they wrote in French instead of Provençal. But whereas writers were inclined to compose *vidas* for the troubadours, the *trouvères* seem to have inspired no such activity, with the result that our information about most of them is very sketchy. Fifty years ago, however, every educated child knew about Blondel, faithful retainer to the *trouvère*-king Richard I, Coeur de Lion [17] and who, when his master was imprisoned in Austria incommunicado, went about Europe singing "their" song until Richard one day responded from his lonely tower. Unfortunately, though the story goes back almost to Blondel's own day—and provided André Grétry [919] with an opera plot 600 years later—it is probably baseless. It is assumed that Blondel was born in or near Nesle, a village between Compiègne and St. Quentin in Picardy. Beyond that assumption, we know only that he knew and was known to other important *trouvères* and that, to judge from the high survival rate of his verses and melodies, he was quite popular.

[16] RAIMBAUT DE VAQUEIRAS (Räm-bō' də Vä-kā'-räs)
TROUBADOUR, SOLDIER
BORN: Vaqueiras, Provence (France), c. 1155
DIED: Messiople, Greece, September 4, 1207 (?)

The shaky biographical material of a *vida* is aided, in Raimbaut's case, by what his poems tell us about him and by certain historic events. The son of an impoverished knight, he is said to have been befriended by Guillaume de Baux, Prince of Orange, who admired his musical talents. Later he found his way to Montferrat, a town then in Italy, and became boon companion of Boniface, heir-apparent to the local ruler, Count William III. In 1194, while fighting in Sicily, he saved the life of Boniface, who by then had succeeded his father and who made him a knight out of gratitude. According to the *vida* and some of the poems, Raimbaut's ladylove was Boniface's sister Beatrice, but more dependable evidence is lacking. In 1201, Boniface was named leader of the Fourth Crusade and personally arranged the infamous attack on Constantinople (see also 18). Raimbaut was at his side. Frustrated in his attempt to be named Emperor of Byzantium, Boniface was given Salonika, Macedonia, and Crete in recompense. While attempting to get his territories under control in 1207, Boniface and his men were massacred in a Bulgarian ambush, and assumedly Raimbaut de Vaqueiras went with them. Someone of the same name turns up in a Provençal document of 1243, but unless our Raimbaut was terribly precocious, he would by then have been nearly ninety. He was a skillful poet and left thirty-five examples of his work, which often show an ear for foreign languages. Of the seven extant works with text, *"Kalenda Maya,"* a spring song, is well known and is said to be the earliest example we have of the dance form called *estampie* or *estampida.*

[17] RICHARD I, Coeur de Lion
COUNT OF POITOU, DUKE OF AQUI-
TAINE, KING OF ENGLAND, TROU-
VÈRE
BORN: Oxford, September, 1157
DIED: Limoges, April 11, 1199

In consideration of his minuscule role in the history of music, this is not the place to detail King Richard's checkered and violent military and political career. Despite his popular reputation, largely fostered by medieval romancers and Sir Walter Scott, he was about as romantic as a *Mafioso.* He seems to have devoted his life to alienating most of the potentates of Europe, including his father, Henry II, and his brothers, Henry, Geoffrey, and John. Doubtless he had daring and a certain panache, but he is often described as arrogant, foolhardy, and indecisive ("Richard Yea-and-Nay"). One finds a certain charm in his rescuing and marrying Berengaria of Navarre on the way to the Third Crusade (from which he emerged as its hero, perhaps because there were no other real contenders), though modern revisionists say that he was homosexual. Cecil B. DeMille to the contrary, Richard never even met the great Saracen leader Saladin, much less chummed about with him, and in fact he had a couple of thousand paynim prisoners murdered out of sheer vindictiveness. As King of England, he was a Frenchman, in point both of language and residence, and let others run his kingdom. By the time the crusade was over, he was so hated throughout Europe that there was no safe route home and, passing through Austria, he was captured by Duke Leopold's men, though he was in "a mean disguise" (which was type-casting for him) and locked up in Schloss Dürnstein. It was probably there that he wrote his only surviving song, *"Ja nun hons pris"* ("Yes, No Prisoner Can

Tell His Story"), but he did not sing his way out through his fellow *trouvère* Blondel de Nesle [15]. Instead Leopold sold him to the emperor, who turned him loose when he swore to be a good boy and pay an enormous ransom. To raise it, Richard invented the property tax. Five years later, trying to grab a treasure unearthed by the Viscount of Limoges, he was struck by an arrow and died of the resultant gangrene at forty-one. He was buried with his father and mother in the Abbey of Fontevrault, where his effigy may still be seen.

[18] CONON de Béthune (Kō-nōn' də Bā-tün')
SOLDIER, STATESMAN, TROUVÈRE
BORN: Béthune, France, c. 1160
DIED: Constantinople (?), December 7, 1219 or 1220

In 1201, Pope Innocent III, sensing a crusade in the air again, had the need for a fourth one preached. His chief preacher in France was a chap named Foulkes (no first name—just plain Foulkes), who had no particular success until some of the higher nobles got together for a tournament in northern France and had so much fun that they decided a little real battling would not be so bad after all. One of them was Conon de Béthune, a younger son of that town's overlord, who had apparently taken part in the Third Crusade, and whose brother Guillaume also signed up. He had grown up at the French court, had learned the *trouvère's* art from Huon d'Oisi, and was acquainted with such other *trouvères* as Blondel de Nesle [15] and Gace Brulé [19]. A fleet awaited the crusaders in Venice, but, finding themselves short of funds there, they went on to attack Constantinople at the request of the deposed Emperor Isaac II and his son Alexius, who promised to foot the bill if they successfully ousted the usurper Alexius III. By 1204 the city was in the crusaders' hands, the Byzantine claimants were dead or had fled, and Baldwin of Flanders was on the throne. In all this, Conon, whom the chronicler Villehardouin calls "a man of high intelligence," played a major role, negotiating with the Doge, and, in the latter days of the struggle, running the city of Constantinople itself. He may also have been involved in the Fifth Crusade. When last heard from, he was still in Constantinople, holding the office of Imperial Regent. As a poet, he has been called the most original of the *trouvères,* and indeed his lyrics give a strong sense of individual character. His melodies, 9 of which are extant, are simple and direct.

[19] GACE BRULÉ (Gás Brü-lā')
TROUVÈRE
BORN: Nanteuil-lès-Meaux (?), France,
c. 1160
DIED: after 1213

Gace Brulé (a nom de plume) seems to have been both well known to other *trouvères* and extremely popular, perhaps less for his originality than for adherence to the troubadour musicopoetic stereotype. A landowner, and probably a knight, he was connected with the courts of Geoffrey of Brittany (brother of Richard I, Coeur de Lion [17]) and his half sister, Marie de France (who promoted the Courts of Love, like her mother, Eleanor of Aquitaine). His songs were often imitated and some of his tunes were used by other composers. Dante admired one of his pieces at least, though he thought it was by Thibaut de Navarre [26]. There exists a manuscript miniature of Gace; unhappily, he is in full armor with his visor down—but it is probably not from life anyway.

[20] PÉROTIN (Magister Perotinus) (Pā-rō-tan')
CHOIRMASTER (?)
BORN: Paris (?), c. 1160
DIED: c. 1203 or c. 1225

Like his supposed master Léonin [12], Pérotin ("Little Pierre" or "Petey") has been accorded a pivotal position in the history of Western music, though on more solid grounds. But the man himself is almost as shadowy. Anonymous IV (see 12) called him "the greatest discantor," whatever that may have meant. It has so far been impossible to prove or disprove his connection with Notre-Dame de Paris or its "school." The approximate date of his birth is arguable, that of his death even more so. What is now generally accepted as credible is that he revised the Big Book of *organa* attributed to Léonin, in the interests of conciseness, and that he composed, and probably invented, *organa* for three and even four voices, thus opening the road for the polyphonic developments of the next century.

The most important revisions of "Léonin's" work involve the substitution of *clausulae* for the endless melismatic cadences. The *clausula* is similarly a cadential section, but by using a mere phrase extracted from a chant for a *cantus firmus* instead of the whole chant, it achieves both compactness and shape. Some musicologists assume that, in his development of polyphony, Pérotin began with the addition of a second upper voice to his organa, and proceeded to the addition of a third, but this view is by no means universally accepted. Some of his three-voice clausulae have separate texts for each of the upper voices, pointing toward the motet of the thirteenth century. Besides the 13 *organa* and many *clausulae* attributed to Pérotin, there are 3 *conducti*, works in which the *cantus firmus* is secular or specially composed rather than ecclesiastical.

RECORDINGS: There are various in recorded histories of music or surveys of early liturgical music.

[21] CHÂTELAIN de COUCY (Sha-te-lan' də Kōō-sē')
TROUVÈRE
BORN: c. 1165
DIED: late spring, 1203

The name of Coucy has become something of a household word since the publication of *A Distant Mirror*, Barbara Tuchman's study of the fourteenth century, which has Enguerrand VII de Coucy as a sort of protagonist. The ruins of his vast fortress-castle, begun in the century previous and destroyed in World War I, may still be seen on a hilltop not far from Soissons. Obviously it was not the castle of which the Châtelain had charge. That, Miss Tuchman tells us, bore the name of Château Renault. The Châtelain was probably Gui IV de Torote or Thourotte, who participated in the Third Crusade, served as regent for the young Enguerrand IV, died on the way to the Fourth Crusade, and was buried at sea. A hundred years later there appeared a verse romance of some eight thousand lines called *Li Roman du Chastelain de Couci et de la Dame de Fayel*. In it, the Châtelain is tricked into the Crusade by the faithless lady's husband and poisoned en route. He orders that his heart be sent her in token of his love. The Sieur de Fayel intercepts it, has it cooked, and serves it up to her. When she discovers what she has eaten, she gracefully dies. Her guilt-stricken husband spends the rest of his life atoning. But the story is widely spread in folklore and undoubtedly has no application to truth here. Though somewhat conventional, the Châtelain was one of the more skillful *trouvères*. Fifteen of his songs have survived with music, and several others are attributed to him.

[22] WALTHER von der Vogelweide (Vol'-ter fun dâr Fō'-gel-vī-də)
MINNESINGER

BORN: c. 1170
DIED: Würzburg, c. 1230

Walther, who ranks among the greatest of lyric poets, is the best-known of the *Minnesinger* (and not merely because he appears in Wagner's opera *Tannhäuser*). The *Minnesinger* were the German artistic descendants of the troubadours and *trouvères*. Their name derives from the fact that their chief subject was *Minne,* or courtly love. Though the Germans had already established a tradition of vernacular song, the influence from France (ever a style setter) was overwhelming. Some have traced its inception to the court of Friedrich Barbarossa, whose empress, Béatrix of Upper Burgundy, had included the *trouvère* Guiot de Provins among her retinue. One of the earliest *Minnesinger* was her son, "Keyser Heynrich"—i.e., Henry VI (1165–97).

Most of what we know of Walther is in his verses. Exactly which "bird meadow" *(Vogelweide)* he was from, no one knows: his birthplace has been variously guessed to be Wipptal in the Tyrol or Würzburg in Franconia. Despite his *von,* he was probably the son of a gentleman *(Dienstadel)* rather than of a noble. He tells us that he was educated in his craft in Austria. Early in his career he was in Vienna at the court of Duke Leopold V and his successor Friedrich I. There he seems to have indulged in a friendly rivalry with (and perhaps studied with) another *Minnesinger,* Reinmar von Hagenau, called *"der Alte"* (the Old Man). When Duke Friedrich died in 1198, Walther took up the life of a wandering minstrel. At various times he was at the courts of Philip of Swabia, Dietrich of Meissen, Bernhard of Carinthia, Otto of Brunswick, and the Holy Roman Emperor. We know that he was at that of Bishop Wolfger of Passau in 1203, because we have from there the only official document to name Walther—a requisition for a new fur coat. After 1205 he was for a time at the Wartburg, presided over by Landgraf Hermann of Thuringia, where he took part in the famous song contest commemorated in Wagner's opera *Die Meistersinger,* though on the whole he found the place too noisy. Politically active (his *Sprüche,* or satirical songs, were much admired and quite effective) and a proponent of a unified imperial Germany, he was rewarded by Friedrich II, around 1220, with a little place of his own, said to be near Würzburg. There he settled down (as much as he ever did anywhere), though there is a hint that he may at least have started on the Sixth Crusade in 1228.

His *"Palestinalied"* ("Palestine Song"), which he wrote around then with more than a little help from a piece by Jaufré Rudel [10], expresses his hope of finding in crusading a meaningful escape from a world grown stale.

[23] NEIDHART von Reuenthal (Nīt'-härt fun Roi'-en-tol)
MINNESINGER
BORN: c. 1180
DIED: Austria, after 1237

Neidhart is notable for bringing, with his "summer" and "winter" songs (for outdoor and indoor dancing, respectively), a new direction to *Minnesang.* The texts focus, with a good deal of realistic detail, on the world of nature and peasant life. The tunes, to catchy dance rhythms, may have been modeled on folk song. But the songs, somewhat atypically, tell us little about their composer. It is generally agreed that he was of noble birth and probably Bavarian. He often laments his penury and homelessness, but this may be no more than a reflection of the self-pity generally exhibited by artists and intellectuals. For a time he was apparently patronized by Duke Ludwig I of Bavaria. Later he moved to Austria, and may have gone on the Fifth Crusade along with the Austrian Duke Leopold I. Later Duke Friedrich bestowed an estate on him. (One source tells us that in 1230 he fell out of favor with Duke Ottoman II—whoever he may have been.) Neidhart's compositions appear to have been extremely popular and much imitated. RECORDINGS: A good many of those that appear on records under his name really belong to the later so-called "Pseudo-Neidhart" corpus.

[24] MUSET, Colin (Mü-zā', Kō-la n')
JONGLEUR
BORN: c. 1185 (?)
DIED: after 1234

Of Muset virtually nothing is known. He may have been of peasant or bourgeois origin and apparently led the career of a wandering minstrel in northeastern France, chiefly Lorraine in the first half of the thirteenth century. His songs are in the *trouvère* line, though he is more given to wit than most. His tunes are simple and folklike. But to tell the truth, there is much confusion about the authenticity of many pieces attributed to him.

[25] CODAX (or CODAZ), Martin (or Martim) (Kō-däsh, Mär-tēn')

BORN: c. 1200
DIED: after 1230

Nothing at all is known of Codax as a person, though it has been conjectured that he came from Coruña in northwest Spain and served at the court of (St.) Ferdinand III of Castile. In 1914 a sort of song cycle (seven poems, six with tunes) by him was discovered inside the binding of an ancient book. The texts are Galician and have to do with the seaside longings of a woman for her lover, but there is nothing else to connect these pieces with troubadour tradition. They are said to be the earliest Spanish songs whose notation has been deciphered. RECORDINGS: He is recorded in the Hispavox History of Spanish Music.

[26] THIBAUT de Navarre (Tē-bō')

KING, TROUVÈRE
BORN: Troyes, May 30, 1201
DIED: Pamplona, July 7, 1253

Thibaut was the grandson of Marie de France and the great-grandson of Eleanor of Aquitaine, and thus born to the courtly tradition. From his father, Thibaut III, he inherited at birth the most delectable counties in France, Brie and Champagne, the elder Thibaut having unexpectedly died six days before. To protect them against other aspirants, he had to swear fealty to the King of France, Philippe Auguste, in whose court he grew up. His early songs, in the trouvère tradition, indicate an uncommon fondness for Blanche of Castile, queen to Philippe Auguste's successor Louis VIII. Thibaut, however, fought dutifully for his liege lords. But, after helping Louis slaughter the heretical Cathari in Provence, thus effectively putting an end to Provençal culture, he defected in 1224, shortly before the king died of suspicious causes. He was soon shown his mistake and brought back into the fold until ten years later through his mother, Blanche of Navarre, he succeeded her brother Sancho the Strong on the throne of that Pyrenean kingdom. After that he apparently gave Blanche up, married three successive wives, and got religion. After personally overseeing the roasting of 183 Navarrese heretics, he took a force to the Holy Land in 1237 and, through some rather slippery maneuvering, managed to mitigate the shaky Christian position there, if only temporarily. After coming home in 1240, he ruled so effectively that his subjects referred to him as Thibaut the Good—an opinion not shared by the

Church, which excommunicated him, necessitating his going to Rome and doing a certain amount of cringing to assure the salvation of his soul. Though listed as a trouvère, Thibaut was enormously prolific in all kinds of lyric—military, religious, pastoral, and quasi-dramatic, as well as amatory. Some 60 melodies are extant, and he was much quoted and imitated in his own time and long afterward.

[27] ALFONSO X, el Sabio (the Wise or the Learned)

KING OF CASTILE AND LEÓN
BORN: Toledo, November 23, 1221
DIED: Seville, April 4, 1284

His father a future saint, his mother the granddaughter of Friedrich Barbarossa, Alfonso was reared in the homes of tutors, where he developed his inquiring mind and possibly gained his taste for the troubadour art and the Galician-Portuguese dialect in which most of his poetry is couched. He was linked by blood or marriage with many of the important royal houses of Europe. His lifetime saw an increase in Castilian power and the beginnings of the final ebb of the Moorish tide. A successful soldier and a better ruler than he is often accounted, he was conversant with astronomy, poetry, history, and the law. His astrological tables were deemed authoritative for some centuries. He laid the basis for Hispanic law with the code known as Siete Partidas. He promoted the drawing-up of both a world history and a history of Spain (the latter before Spain existed as such!). He had a number of translations made from the Arabic and himself wrote poetry in the style of the troubadours. The middle years of his reign were weakened by his misguided attempt (on the basis of his mother's ancestry) to have himself elected Holy Roman Emperor. (He overlooked the fact that his relatives were on the wrong side in the papal-imperial Guelf-Ghibelline feud.) Driven from the throne in a quarrel over the succession, Alfonso spent his last years as a refugee in Seville.

His presence here is occasioned by the great collection of more than four hundred songs to and about the Virgin, known as Las Cantigas de Santa Maria. These include hymns, songs of praise, and accounts of Marian miracles. Tradition long ascribed both texts and music to Alfonso. Now he is regarded primarily as the force that had the material brought together from all over Europe, versified, and outfitted with music. Clearly influenced by the troubadours, the collection is regarded as one of the monuments of medieval music. The interpretation of the notation has provided a source of scholarly disputation, one school insisting that there is direct Arabic inspiration there. It is most likely that the poems and the tunes—like the themes—came from many sources. However, scholars generally agree that Alfonso wrote some of the lyrics. Moreover, some are willing to grant him a tune or two, pointing out that he was himself musical, patronized musicians, and founded a music course at Salamanca.

[28] RIQUIER, Guiraut (Rē-kyä´, Gwē-rō´)
TROUBADOUR
BORN: Narbonne, c. 1233
DIED: Rodez, c. 1292

Riquier, often called "the last of the troubadours," reflects the sorry state of things in Provence following the Albigensian Crusade. The Albigenses, or Cathari (whose links with the troubadour cult are too many to be ignored), were a widespread heretical sect centered in Albi. Their creed was essentially Manichaean, assuming opposed good and evil deities. They rejected such doctrines as those of Purgatory, the Incarnation, the Resurrection, and the fleshly existence of the Virgin. Ascetic and self-denying, they were divided into two classes, the Believers and the Perfect; the latter forswore meat and women. The Albigensians practiced both pacifism and a kind of euthanasia, and they were common in the Provençal courts. It is generally believed that the notions of the troubadours developed from Catharism. Crusades being in style, the significantly named Innocent III preached one against them in 1209. Under the leadership of Simon de Montfort (who collected Béziers, Carcassonne, Narbonne, and Toulouse for his efforts), the French swooped down from the north and slaughtered the Albigensians, and whoever else got in the way, with unflagging enthusiasm (see 26). Louis VIII thereby won Languedoc, and the papacy won Avignon, which, in the light of subsequent history, was no more than it deserved. Riquier was born, probably to a poor family, after the excitement was over. After some years at the court of the Viscount of Narbonne (his poems are quite explicit about the events in his life), he, like the troubadour impulse, migrated to northern Spain and found a place at the court of Alfonso X of Castile [27]. When his patron was deposed, he returned to France and made his headquarters at the court of Count Henri II of Rodez. In his poems he laments that his kind of music no

longer interests anyone, wryly suggests that Alfonso should grant such as he the title of "Doctor" to indicate their superiority to modern-day songsters, and concludes that he has outlived his time. He thinks the praise of God infinitely more worth his time than that of women. He wrote prolifically in all the standard forms and invented the *serena* (evening song). Eighty-nine of his poems have survived, an incredible 48 of them with music.

[29] ADAM (or ADAN) de la Hale (or Halle) (A´-dän də lä Ál)
POET, DRAMATIST, MUSICIAN
BORN: Arras, c. 1245
DIED: Naples, 1287 (?)

As Guiraut Riquier [28] is called "the last of the troubadours," so his near contemporary Adam is called (with less justification) "the last of the *trouvères.*" In his day Adam was also called *le bossu d'Arras* ("the hunchback of Arras"), which leads one to suppose him so deformed; but he himself protests that he was not, so perhaps the sobriquet was used to distinguish his branch of the family from others. The facts of his life are almost as puzzling. His comedy *La Feuillée* indicates (if it can be believed) that his father, Maistre Henri, was a small-time civil servant in Arras, and possibly bigamous. Evidently the family was not rich, since Adam's career was furthered by outsiders. The more romantic stories about his early life are now discounted: he was not, as far as we can tell, a theological dropout, nor was he exiled to Douai for protesting a tax levied by the king to promote a crusade. Evidence suggests, but does not prove, that he studied in Paris. He tells us that one summer he fell in love with a girl named Maroie and quit school to marry her, but where these events fit into the sequence of his life is uncertain. After Paris, he apparently returned to Arras, where he was active in the local *puy*, or *trouvère* academy. Shortly afterward he seems to have entered the service of Robert II, Count of Artois. Legend has Adam visiting North Africa and the Holy Land in the count's retinue, but ascertainable fact suggests Navarre and, particularly, Italy. Robert's uncle, Charles I d'Anjou (brother to St. Louis, alias Louis IX) was King of Sicily when, in 1282, his throne tottered under the impact of the uprising known as the Sicilian Vespers (the signal for the massacre of the French to begin was the vesper bell). Robert went south to aid him, taking Adam with him. Adam stayed at Charles's court in Naples and died there in 1287. However, there is puzzling evidence that a Maître Adam le Bossu was at the court of Edward II of England in 1307, when the poet-composer would have been only sixtyish.

Though he was versed in the *trouvère* tradition, Adam is a pivotal figure who looks both farther back to the old quasi-epic *chansons de geste* and ahead to secular contrapuntalism. (He may have picked up counterpoint in Paris.) He also shows music changing from a patrician avocation to a bourgeois profession. He was perhaps better as poet than as composer, and his plays loom large in his output. One of them, *Li jeus de Robin et Marion (The Play of Robin and Marion—*not the Sherwood Forest lovers), is his best-known work. Probably written in Naples, it is sometimes called the first comic opera. Liturgical musical plays by then had a long tradition, but Adam's is secular, and its songs are folklike. Atypically for that era, it continued to be performed long after its author was dead, but seems to have inspired no imitations.

RECORDINGS: *Li jeus de Robin et Marion* has been recorded several times, both with and without dialogue. There are also examples of Adam's songs, both monophonic and polyphonic.

[30] PETRUS de Cruce (Pierre de la Croix) (Pā-trōōz' də Krōōs)
THEORIST
BORN: Amiens, after 1250 (?)
DIED: c. 1300 (?)

Other than his birthplace and the fact that he was active toward the end of the thirteenth century, nothing at all is known of Petrus de Cruce. His importance is in connection with the rhythms used in the motet, of which form he left us two certain examples. Around 1280, Franco of Cologne wrote a treatise codifying the time values and time relationships of the notational symbols, a system based on divisions of three. Thus three *semibreves* equaled one *breve,* and three *breves* equaled one *long.* Now, in the motet the two lower voices *(tenor* and *duplum)* customarily moved in slower note values, whereas the top voice *(triplum),* often set to a vernacular text, required more, and shorter, notes. In the so-called Franconian system, however, it remained largely under the rigid control of the formalized rhythmic modes. According to his contemporaries, it was Petrus who freed the *triplum* by permitting the *breve* to equal anywhere from two to nine *semibreves* (depending on the rhythmic requirements of the text), relationships between the voices being indicated

by points of division, so that the performers could see what notes went with what notes. RECORDINGS: Motets by or attributed to Petrus have been recorded.

[31] FRAUENLOB (Heinrich von Meissen) (Frou'-en-lōp)
MINNESINGER
BORN: Meissen, c. 1255
DIED: Mainz, November 29, 1318

Exactly why Heinrich von Meissen was called "Frauenlob" or "Vrouwenlop" (Praise of Women) is not certain. Traditionally the name is supposed to have come from a professional quarrel between Heinrich and a poet named Regenbogen (Rainbow). Heinrich didn't care for Regenbogen's term *wîp* (modern *Weib)* for womankind, preferring *Vrouwe (Frau)* as more respectful. (The difference is roughly that between our "woman" and "lady.") But *Frauenlob* may also have to do with his espousal of the Marian cult (the Virgin is *die heilige Jungfrau).* Most other information we have about Heinrich von Meissen is equally tentative. He tells us that he soldiered for Rudolf I, progenitor of the Hapsburg dynasty, and he was probably with him when he whipped Ottokar of Bohemia, the other claimant to the imperial throne, at the battle of Marchfeld in 1278. Six years later he attended the ceremonial knighting of Wenceslas II of Bohemia in Prague. After that he was at various courts throughout the Germanies until finally he settled in Mainz in 1312. According to legend, he founded a school of *Meistersang,* the ultimate bourgeois outgrowth of the troubadour-minnesinger impulse. And indeed the *Meistersinger* revered him as their spiritual ancestor, but there was no direct link between the two approaches. Nevertheless in his poetic attention to topical matters and in his often high-flown and artificial style, one can see why the *Meistersinger* admired him. His tomb may still be seen in Mainz Cathedral.

[32] JEHANNOT de l'Escurel (Zhä-nō' də Les-kōō-rel')
CLERIC
BORN: c. 1280
DIED: Paris, May 23, 1304

All we know of Jehannot ("Johnny") is, so to speak, what one might have read on the 1304 police blotter. Scion of a good family and clerk of Notre-Dame de Paris, he was hanged that May for lewd living and doing improper things to women. He left 31 songs in the increasingly popular *ballade, rondeau,* and *virelai* forms. One is polyphonic and shows some anticipations of the motet style that was to characterize the coming *Ars Nova,* or New Art (see 33).

[33] PHILIPPE de Vitry (Fē-lēp' də Vē-trē')

CLERIC, ADMINISTRATOR, THEORIST
BORN: October 31, 1291
DIED: Paris, June 9, 1361

There are several Vitrys in northern France from which Philippe might have come, and several of his contemporaries called "de Vitry" with whom he may have been connected in some way, though it is now believed that he was born in Paris, the son of a royal notary. He seems to have taken holy orders at a fairly early age, and when he was thirty-one Pope John XXII made him a canon of the church of St. Martin at Clermont-en-Beauvaisis (i.e., he was at least nominally attached to it and shared in its income). By 1332 he also held canonicates at Cambrai, St. Quentin, Soissons, Vertus, and Verdun Cathedral, the last giving him the Archdeaconate of Brie. No doubt royal favor helped elevate him to such affluence. Just when and how he first acquired it we don't know, but he served as secretary and counselor to three kings of France, beginning with Charles IV, who died in 1328. By 1340 he was master clerk of the Parlement or session of the royal court, and a few years later master of requests at the Hôtel du Roi under Philippe VI, a post he retained under Jean II. He seems to have been particularly close to Jean. They were together at the relief of Aiguillon in 1345, when Jean was still Dauphin, both living like soldiers. Before he was crowned in 1350, Jean sent him on a special mission to Pope Clement VI in Avignon. A year later Philippe was appointed Bishop of Meaux and given a mansion in Paris. Though he seems to have had some sort of falling-out with his king in 1356, Philippe kept his bishopric until his death at sixty-nine.

Philippe de Vitry was a scholar and was widely admired as a poet and composer, notably by Petrarch, who probably knew him personally and who left two letters to him. Of his compositions (all motets in the new style), only a dozen that are assigned to him with reasonable assurance have survived. These are particularly interesting as representing the theories formulated in the important theoretical work assigned to Philippe, the *Ars Nova* (New Art), which lent its name to the music of the new century. Though Philippe probably did not actually write the work—at least not in the form that it has come down to us—it clearly represents his ideas. These are, most importantly, concerned with the matter of rhythm. When regular rhythmic structures came into use in the previous century, they were in triplet divisions (i.e., a "long note" could be broken down rhythmically into three short notes of equal value). Such divisions were termed "perfect," possibly on Trinitarian grounds. Divisions into two or four were "imperfect." Philippe not only granted equal importance to perfection and imperfection, but also provided notation and time indications that make clear how they are to be read.

Other characteristics of the *Ars Nova* (but not formulated by Philippe) are a breakaway from the restrictions of modality, the adaptation of counterpoint to secular composition, isorhythms, the motet, and in sacred music an increasing tendency to set portions of the Mass, notably of the Ordinary (those parts common to all celebrations). The motet characteristically involved the superimposition of two or more separate songs (texts as well as music), contrapuntally compatible, over a *cantus firmus.* (This sort of thing, plus such fashionable devices as *hocketing* [hiccuping!], a jerky sort of syncopation, brought a speedy attempted crackdown on the use of *Ars Nova* in church music.) Since the term *motet* comes from the French term *mot* ("word"), one should not be surprised to find emphasis on expression of the texts.

A word is perhaps in order here about *isorhythms,* since they loom large over many subsequent decades. Isorhythmic techniques have to do with the relation of melody to rhythm. Since Pérotin [20] at least, it had been common to use as *cantus firmus* a short phrase repeated as many times as necessary. Such a phrase was, like any musical phrase, made up of a sequence of tones. To it the composer applied a (usually arbitrary) rhythmic pattern. In *Ars Nova* music the melodic pattern and the rhythmic pattern were commonly of unequal lengths, but both were sequentially repeated for the length of the composition. If the melodic pattern were shorter than the rhythmic, its next repetition would pick up at whatever point in the rhythmic progression the initial statement had left off, so that each repeat of the *cantus firmus* would be rhythmically different, though melodically the same.

[34] GIOVANNI da Cascia (or da Firenze)
(Jō-vän'-nē dä Käsh'-yä)
ORGANIST (?)

BORN: Cascia, Tuscany, c. 1300
DIED: after 1352

Like most of the first generation of significant Italian composers, Giovanni is little more than a name and a few pieces of music. He must have come from the village of Cascia near Florence. Tradition says he was organist at the Cathedral of Santa Maria del Fiore (begun only in 1296), but there is nothing to prove it. If he played the organ in Florence at all, it was more likely to have been at Santa Reparata (the old cathedral) or the Santa Trinità, whose rolls list a "Ser Giovanni degli organi" as late as 1360. Earlier he seems to have been in Verona, during the time of the alleged Montague-Capulet feud, at the court of Mastino della Scala, nephew of Dante's patron, Can Grande. There he supposedly engaged in a madrigal-writing contest with two other important (but nearly anonymous) Italian pioneers, Jacopo da Bologna and Maestro Piero. At other times he was in the Visconti court in Milan, and perhaps in Padua.

The music composed by Giovanni, Jacopo, and their contemporaries, representing a brief and perhaps premature flowering of Italian music, is often subsumed under the rubric of *Ars Nova* (see 33). But it was primarily a secular phenomenon and its links with France were tenuous at best. It came to a head in Florence with Francesco Landini [38], then spread southward and petered out. The characteristic forms were the *madrigal* and the *caccia,* for two and sometimes three voices. The madrigal, which has nothing but its name in common with the madrigal of the Renaissance, was based on an iambic pentameter text of two or three three-line stanzas (ABB), concluding with a couplet. Each stanza was sung to the same music, but the couplet (refrain or ritornello) called for a different setting. Its subjects were chiefly love and nature. Or so it was in Giovanni's time and later. The generic name is obscure: one cogent suggestion is that it derives from something like *cantus matricalis*—a song in the vernacular. Not so with the *caccia,* which is a chase or hunt in which one voice pursues another in canon, and in which the subject frequently is a hunt. Both forms were rather quickly eclipsed by the *ballata* (see 38).

[35] MACHAUT, Guillaume de (Ma-shō', Gē-yōm' də)
CLERIC, POET
BORN: c. 1300
DIED: Rheims, April 13, 1377

The Machauts probably derived their name from a town in Champagne. It is conjectured that Guillaume was born in Rheims, but nothing is known of his first two decades save that he took minor orders but never advanced to the priesthood. Around 1323 he entered the service of John, Count of Luxembourg and King of Bohemia (brother-in-law to Charles IV of France, father-in-law to John II, and son of Dante's hero-emperor Henry VII). Though Guillaume was awarded several benefices within the decade, his function at John's court seems to have been chiefly literary and scribal. John was an ambitious and quixotic man—a dashing soldier but a careless administrator—who apparently took his rather fragile secretary all over Europe on his sometimes desperate campaigns. In 1337, Machaut traded in his other livings for one at Rheims Cathedral and bought a house nearby in 1340, no doubt to facilitate the singing of the Masses required by his contract. Six years later John went blind at the age of fifty, but he continued to ride at the head of his troops and was killed at Crécy shortly afterward. Whether by that time Machaut had left his court for that of John's daughter Bonne is uncertain, but when she died in 1349 he took service with Charles II of Navarre (who was called "the Bad" because he stirred up a lot of trouble and seems not to have been very nice personally). These were, of course, terrible times, what with the Hundred Years War and the Black Death being added to the usual discomforts of medieval life; but, except for some depredations inflicted on Rheims by the English, Machaut seems to have got through it all rather well. However, he tells us that he suffered from gout, general debility, and a game eye. At other times (there are no details) he probably served John II and Charles V of France; John, Duke of Berry; and perhaps Peter I of Cyprus and Amadeus of Savoy. In his later years his house in Rheims was frequented by the great, including King Charles V himself (for whose coronation we now know that Machaut did not write his so-called "Notre-Dame" *Mass).*

As he tells it, when he was in his sixties, he got a letter from a noble mademoiselle from Armentières called Péronne or Péronnelle, who said she had fallen in love with his poems. According to his *voir dit,* an affair (properly courtly but nonetheless genuine) ensued, despite the forty-odd years that separated the lovers. To get together, they joined pilgrimages. After three or four years, they parted amicably and Péronne married someone else. It may all be true.

As a poet, Machaut was greatly admired

by the *cognoscenti* of his day, and the French like to pretend that he was their counterpart of his contemporaries Petrarch and Chaucer, though less chauvinistic readers usually wish for more wit with less matter. As a composer, however, he stands unchallenged as the greatest of his era, and must be regarded as one of the supreme creative musicians of all time. He is a pivotal figure who sums up the chief musical developments up to his time and who looks ahead to new ones; moreover, unlike many of his contemporaries, he sees his music not as a mere prop for his verse, but as an art important in itself.

The surviving manuscripts of Machaut's work make this last point clear, for he evidently established the sequence in which he wanted it presented: the pure poetry first—seventeen titles, mostly of long works, prefaced by a special prologue; then the musical compositions by categories—*lais*, motets, *ballades, rondeaux, virelais*, the Mass, and the "David" instrumental hocket. Altogether more than 130 musical works have survived. The general prologue speaks eloquently of music, and the *Remède de Fortune* includes a treatise on lyric, with examples of each of seven forms, including the *complainte* and the *chanson royale*, of which Machaut seems to have written no other examples.

Machaut took up and developed the old *trouvère* song forms. His *lais*, which take that genre to its highest point (typically, twelve stanzas each, save for the first and last, both musically and poetically different) are mostly monophonic, but four are at least partly polyphonic, and two experiment with canon. So too with the *virelais* (or *chansons balladées*), of which a few are for two voices and one for three. Here Machaut likes a three-stanza form but retains the old refrain device, and within this structure plays all sorts of musical and poetic variations, adhering at the same time to an almost folklike simplicity. On the other hand, with the exception of a single *ballade*, the *ballades* and *rondeaux* are all polyphonic, running to as many as four parts, some of which are clearly intended for instruments. Here Machaut sticks to poetic forms established a century earlier, but his music again shows considerable variety and often great polyphonic ingenuity. Indeed, Machaut's notion of the rondeau as music seems to have come out of his own head. In the motets (two of them liturgical) he shows himself, particularly in his handling of isorhythms, as a master of the *Ars Nova*.

Such techniques are also found in Machaut's *Mass*, apparently written for Rheims Cathedral. It is not only a monumental work but a landmark. Other *Ars Nova* musicians wrote isolated Mass movements, but Machaut's appears to have been the first Mass composed as such by one man —and there would be no other for a half century. It is not unified, like later polyphonic Masses, by being based on a single *cantus firmus*, but it is clear that Machaut meant it to be performed as one work.

RECORDINGS: Since the advent of LP records, considerable attention has been given to Machaut's work, all facets of which have been plentifully represented.

[36] GRIMACE (Grē-mäs′)
BORN: c. 1325 (?)
DIED: ?

Absolutely nothing is known of this composer except that he was strongly influenced by Machaut [35] and was thus probably a younger contemporary. He left 3 *ballades*, 3 *virelais* (two of them dubious), and a *rondeau*. There have been several recordings of the rather hysterical amatory *virelai* entitled *"Alarme! Alarme!"*

[37] CICONIA, Johannes (Sē-kōn′-yà, Yō-ản′-nez)
CLERIC, TEACHER, THEORETICIAN
BORN: Liège, c. 1330
DIED: Padua, mid-December 1411

Ciconia's surname means "stork" and is a Latin translation. It has been determined that his father was a Walloon furrier who called himself Johan Ciwagne, which seems to dispose of the notion that the composer was really a Fleming named Ooijevaar. Ciconia, together with his brother William, is first encountered at the papal court in Avignon in 1350. Between 1358 and 1367, Johannes traveled all over Italy in the employ of the warlike Cardinal Albornoz, who, in 1362, procured him benefices in Cesena and back home in the church of St. John in Liège. Though he was supposed to go to the latter city to reap the fruits of his appointment, he apparently preferred to stay with the cardinal until the latter's death in Viterbo. Even then, evidence in his songs suggests, he remained in Italy, and was variously at the Visconti court in Milan and the Carrara court in Padua. He finally went home to Liège in 1372 but seems to have traveled back and forth between there and Italy until 1401, when Francesco Zabarella (later a cardinal) offered him a living at a Paduan church and he moved there permanently. A year later he was attached to the cathedral as a canon and instructor to the choirboys. Of his life in Liège we know little, save that he wrote some of his music there and apparently acquired an unofficial wife and family.

Ciconia is sometimes numbered among the third generation of Italian *trecento* composers, but it is perhaps more accurate to see him as the first ripple of the northern cultural tide that would soon wash over the Alps. He was almost certainly trained in Flanders and France, though most of his secular pieces are in Italian forms (mostly *ballate),* but some of these show the influence of the French *Ars Nova,* and conversely one of his two French songs bears earmarks of the madrigal. His religious works, probably written during his mature years in Liège, are in the advanced *Ars Nova* style, which has been designated as *Ars Subtilior,* and occasionally seem to look forward to something like tonic-dominant relationships. Ciconia's magnum opus of musical theory is his *Nova musica,* which in its professorial thoroughness rather obscures its ostensible subject (new music) with its coverage of earlier views and abstruse speculations.

[38] LANDINI, Francesco (Làn-dē'-nē, Fràn-chà'-skō)
ORGANIST, SINGER, POET, SCHOLAR, ORGAN BUILDER
BORN: Fiesole, c. 1335
DIED: Florence, September 2, 1397

The birthplace and birth date of Francesco Landini, the first great native Italian composer of the late Middle Ages, are uncertain. His father was the painter Jacopo del Casentino, some of whose paintings remain in the Church of San Miniato. Francesco was stricken blind in childhood, probably as a result of smallpox. He is said to have studied music with Jacopo da Bologna, and became proficient on a number of instruments, including the lute, the recorder, and something of his own devising designated as the *serena serenarum,* but was most admired as a singer and organist. He played first at Santa Trinità and later served as a chaplain in San Lorenzo, where his tomb effigy shows him with the portative organ he took about with him. It and he figure prominently in Giovanni del Prato's poem *Il Paradiso degli Alberti,* which tells of the Alberti villa, appropriately called "Paradise," where the intellectual and artistic elite of Florence delighted to gather. Possessed of an inquiring mind and being a lover of learning, Landini could apparently more than hold his own

with such important Humanists as Colluccio Salutati and Filippo Villani. He was also a notable poet and a friend of poets (a correspondence with Franco Sacchetti survives). In Venice in 1364, the King of Cyprus awarded him the laureate crown when he lost an organ competition, in which one of the judges was Petrarch. As an expert on organs, he helped plan instruments for the church of the Santissima Annunziata and for the new cathedral.

Landini was not only the most important Italian composer of his time, but also one of the most prolific. Of his 154 surviving works (mostly Italian and French vocal forms) the bulk are to be found in the magnificent Squarcialupi Codex (once the property of Antonio Squarcialupi, organist to Lorenzo de' Medici), which also contains a miniature of Landini and his portative. The compositions show how, in a very short time, the popularity of madrigal and *caccia* (of which Landini left twelve and one respectively) had been superseded by that of the *ballata* (of which he left 139). In the *ballata* the eight-line stanza begins with a refrain identical in words and music; it perhaps derives from the *virelai,* and may have involved dancing in performance. Some of Landini's are for two voices, some for three, with the implication that the two lower voices are instrumental. Like no one else of his time, he was conscious of the melodic expressivity of the human voice, and his use of thirds and sixths hints at what one thinks of as "Italian melody."

RECORDINGS: Though there are recordings of individual Landini works in anthologies, no one, so far, seems to have given him serious attention phonographically.

[39] PYKINI (Pē-kē-nē')
BORN: possibly c. 1340
DIED: late 14th century (?)

Pykini left a single *virelai,* which, from internal evidence, may have been written in or for Avignon. The surname, if that is what it is, may refer to Picquigny, a town near Amiens. Pykini may have been Robert de Picquigny, a retainer of Charles the Bad of Navarre, but one source calls him Jean de Picquigny without further identification.

[40] VAILLANT, Jehan (Vä-ē-yàn', Zhàn)
BORN: c. 1340 (?)
DIED: c. 1395 (?)

The Jehan Vaillant who left 3 *rondeaux,* a *virelai,* and a *ballade* in the style of Machaut

[35] has been variously identified with a Jean Vaillant who had a music school in Paris, another who sang in the papal choir in Avignon, and various others (the name being a common one); none of them, however, really suit the circumstances. Vaillant's songs were written in or before 1369.

[41] SOLAGE (Sō-làzh')
BORN: c. 1340 (?)
DIED: end of fourteenth century (?)

A double handful of *Ars Nova* songs by Solage are included with the works of thirty-one of his shadowy contemporaries, including Jehan Vaillant [40] in the Chantilly Codex. One of them, the *rondeau "Fumeux fume"* ("Smoky Fume"), is a distinctly odd piece, described as a rare example of medieval chromaticism. It is indeed unstable of tonality and is set to a text whose wordplay is well nigh Joycean. It was probably written for a cult known as the *fumeurs*, who seem to have found it delightfully shocking to dwell on their own fussbudget reactions, in the manner of certain latter-day omphalophiliacs. Of the composer nothing is known, though it is suspected that he was connected with the House of Berry.

[42] JACOBUS de Senleches (Yà-kō'-bōōs də Sàn-lesh')
HARPIST
BORN: St. Luc, c. 1350 (?)
DIED: after 1395

This musician, who left a few quite stylistically advanced *virelais* and *rondeaux,* also turns up as Jacopinus or Jacques Selesses, and under other more or less similar names. He is thought to have come from St. Luc, a village west of Paris. He first turns up in Aragon in 1378, getting permission to attend the annual minstrels' convention or "school" in Flanders. The following year he joined the court of John I of Castile, who was married to the former Princess Eleanor of Aragon, and who assumed the throne that year. There he was known as "Jacomi Senlechos," not to be confused with another Jacomi, who was a virtuoso bagpiper. When Eleanor died in 1382, Jacomi wrote a lament for her, left the court, and wound up playing harp for Cardinal Pedro de Luna, who, as Benedict XIII, was to become in 1394 the last diehard Avignonese pope. But Jacomi did not accompany him, having returned, in 1391, to the court of Aragon, now presided over by Eleanor's brother, who also held the title of John I. After John's death in 1395,

Jacomi drops out of sight. One of his *virelais* is a famous "shape piece," a sort of canon noted down in the form of a harp.

[43] HASPRES, Jehan Simon de (Às'-prə, Zhàn Sē-môn' də)
CLERIC, SINGER, NOTARY
BORN: Arras, c. 1355
DIED: Avignon, 1428

Also called "Hasprois" and various similar names, this composer of a handful of polyphonic songs was in the service of Ferdinand of Portugal in 1378. Shortly afterward he was at the French court until the death of Charles V in 1380. After a period as a member of the choir of Notre-Dame de Cambrai, he joined the papal choir during the last years of the Avignonese Papacy, rising to the post of apostolic notary, and surviving the last pope, Benedict XIII, by four years. Of his *ballades,* one, with an odd text, was apparently written for the *Fumeurs* (see 41).

[44] BORLET (Bôr-là')
BORN: c. 1360 (?)
DIED: after 1409 (?)

Borlet is known solely for a so-called birdsong *virelai, "Hé, tres doulz roussignol,"* ("Hey, Sweetest Nightingale") preserved in a manuscript at Modena, Italy, and rather frequently recorded. It is not known whether he was French or Spanish. Some people think that "Borlet" is a reversal of the name of Trebol, a musician in the employ of Martin I, King of Aragon, in 1409. However, it is suspected that Trebol may have been identical with the Trebor who wrote ballades for John I, Martin's predecessor. And since Trebor's name is clearly "Robert" spelled backward, *he* has been identified with several musicians of that name. One is a Robert Nyot, who was in the papal choir at Avignon in 1394. No one had commented that "Nyot" is an anagram of Tony, but one source insists that, on the evidence of letters, Trebor was really Jacques de Jean.

[45] CORDIER, Baude (Kôrd-yā', Bōd)
BORN: Rheims, c. 1360 (?)
DIED: c. 1398 (?)

All we know for sure about Baude Cordier, the man, is that he was a native of Rheims and was "known as far away as Rome." Of his compositions, we have a *Gloria* and 10 secular pieces. Two of the latter are unusual in that they are notated in the shapes of a heart (a love song) and a circle (a perpetual canon). The music occurs in mss. deriving from places as far flung as northern France and northern Italy.

Writing in the *Musical Quarterly* in 1973, Craig Wright suggests, on the basis of certain analogies, that "Cordier" may be a nickname reflecting Baude's profession (i.e., he was a string fellow or a cord plunker), and that he may really have been the harper Baude Fresnol of Rheims, whom Philip the Bold, Duke of Burgundy, hired as his personal musician on January 10, 1384, for a daily salary of eight sous, plus two horses, board and lodging in the ducal establishment, and a body servant. To judge from the account books, this Baude used up seven harps in the next decade! He was also an organist and a near relative of the man who officiated at the console in Notre-Dame de Paris. In time his master elevated him to the prestigious post of valet of the bedchamber, and entrusted him with important embassages. Together they visited the papal palace in Avignon (often figuratively called "Rome") in 1391 and 1395. In the latter year, Baude Fresnol took unto himself a wife but died before the century was out. A pretty story, but some experts find the evidence too flimsy to accept it. At any rate, Baude Cordier is an interesting transitional figure. His melodic lines eschew mannerism for a more natural flow, and the canon cited above is perhaps influenced by the Italian *caccia*.

[46] BYTTERING, Thomas (?)
CLERIC (?)
BORN: c. 1370 (?)
DIED: after 1414 (?)

The Old Hall Manuscript (formerly at the College of St. Edmund at Old Hall in Hertfordshire) is the most important single collection of the early English polyphonists— among them one Byttering (some have read the name as "Gyttering"), represented by 3 Mass movements, an antiphon, and a motet. It was once thought, because the motet seemed to relate to the marriage of Catherine of Valois in 1420 to Henry V of England, that Byttering might have been a member of the Chapel Royal, but the work is now seen to be much earlier. Present thinking is that he was probably a clergyman named Thomas Byttering or Bytering, active in the first fifteen years of the new century in and around London.

[47] COOKE, John
SINGER
BORN: c. 1375 (?)
DIED: 1419 or c. 1455

"J. Cooke" is represented in the Old Hall Manuscript (see 46) by 7 Mass movements, 2 antiphons, and a motet. Evidence suggests that he was a member of the Chapel Royal which, however, boasted two John Cookes in the first half of the fifteenth century. John Cooke No. 1, who was a member as early as 1402, seems the better bet, since the works ascribed to Cooke seem to have been written down in or before 1419, the probable year of his death. John Cooke No. 2 survived until at least 1455. The motet has been thought by some to reflect English post-Agincourt euphoria.

[48] WOLKENSTEIN, Oswalt von (Võl'-ken-shtīn, Ōz'-vàlt fun)
KNIGHT, SINGER, ADVENTURER
BORN: Schöneck, Pustertal, Austrian Tyrol (now Italy), c. 1377
DIED: Burg Hauenstein near Bozen (now Bolzano), August 2, 1445

Oswalt has been called the "last *Minnesinger*" and the "first *Meistersinger*." Though there are some bases for both sobriquets, he seems, as artist, to have been rather a law unto himself. He was the second son of a noble family. Most of what we know of him comes from his songs. At the age of ten, with a piece of bread and a single copper in his purse, he took to the road (he tells us), supporting himself by "fiddling, drumming, playing the kettledrums, and whistling." Later he became a sort of professional ambassador, traveled to Prussia, Lithuania, Russia ("Tartary"), Turkey, Persia, North Africa, Spain, and France, picking up no fewer than ten languages in the process. In 1401, under the banner of Rupert, Elector of the Palatinate and newly crowned King of Germany, he marched into Italy in an ineffectual attack on Gian Galeazzo Visconti, Duke of Milan. Six years later a client, the Bishop of Brixen, left him a part interest in the castle of Hauenstein. Feeling that he deserved a whole interest, he took the other heirs to court. The case dragged on forever, but he managed to fall in love with one of the defendants, Anna Haumann, the object of many of his songs; twice his legal (or illegal) ploys got him thrown into prison, and at least once his life was threatened. After Rupert died in 1410, Oswalt cast his lot with Sigismund, his successor as king (and later Holy Roman Emperor). He was at the

Council of Constance (1414–18), and in 1417, though still mooning over Anna, he married Margarete von Schwangau, who bore him seven children and was the object of several more of his songs. (He must have had more charm than meets the eye: a famous portrait from the Innsbruck ms. of his work shows what looks to be a jut-jawed, blue-jowled thug, his ruined right eye squinted shut.) Finally, in 1427, the Tyrolean Duke Friedrich settled the dispute in his favor, and he seems to have spent his golden years in relative calm, though he continued to run errands for Sigismund (e.g., to the Council of Basle and the Diet of Nuremberg in 1431).

Oswalt was certainly more ingenious as a poet than as a composer. In fact he borrowed a number of his tunes from other sources, both German and French, and he sometimes used the same music for more than one text. There are extant nearly 100 monophonic songs and around 40 for two, three, or four voices. Apart from the love songs, he also wrote religious and instructive pieces. Those melodies that appear to be his own are often folklike.

RECORDINGS: At least two LPs have been devoted to Wolkenstein's music.

[49] GUILLAUME LEGRANT (Gē-yōm′ Lə-grän′)
SINGER, CLERIC
BORN: c. 1380 (?)
DIED: after 1449

"Guillaume Legrant" was apparently a nickname (meaning something like "Big Bill"); the man's real surname was Lemacherier. He sang in the papal choir in Rome (under Martin V, the first Roman pope elected after the healing of the Great Schism) from 1419 to 1421. He held a canonry in Rouen in 1449, and perhaps sang in the chapel of the Duke of Orléans in 1455. He left 3 *virelais* and 3 Mass movements; in the latter he specifies the use of soloists as well as the full choir.

[50] NICHOLAS of Radom (Mikołaj z Radomia, or Mikołaj Radomski)
BORN: Radom (?), c. 1380 (?)
DIED: after 1430

If the Eastern Slavs remained unaffected by the cultural currents flowing from the West, those of what are now Poland and Czechoslovakia soon felt the early stirrings of the Renaissance. Nicholas of Radom was the first important Polish composer of record and the earliest known Slav polyphonist. The few pieces—6 Mass movements, a

psalm, a motet, and what is probably an instrumental work—now extant are all for three voices. He seems to have been well informed on contemporary Franco-Flemish music. His motet suggests that he was at the Cracow court of Wladisłaus II, who was formerly a pagan Lithuanian warlord named Jagiełło, and who thus became the progenitor of the Jagiełłonian line of Polish monarchs. But nothing positive is known about Nicholas, save that he was still composing in about 1430.

[51] POWER, Leonel
CHOIRMASTER, TEACHER
BORN: c. 1380
DIED: Canterbury, June 5, 1445

Evidence (at least 40 surviving works, including 2 complete Masses) suggests that Leonel Power was regarded as an important composer in his day. Twenty-one of his pieces are included in the Old Hall Manuscript (see 46), but the appearance of most of his work in Italian sources seems to suggest that he traveled and perhaps even resided in Italy for a time. But the little we know of him has him squarely in England. The allegation that he was Irish-born has never been substantiated. Some of the Old Hall pieces are from the first years of the fifteenth century, but the first mention of him has him teaching the choirboys in the Duke of Clarence's chapel as late as 1421. Two years later he was associated with the chapter of Canterbury Cathedral, but we are not certain that he was a resident of Canterbury until 1438. A year after that we find him directing one of the chapel choirs in the cathedral, and he seems to have remained in his post until six months before his death.

It used to be said that the Old Hall composers represented a native insular tradition, as contrasted with the international tradition exemplified by John Dunstable [54], but Power clearly demonstrates a knowledge of what was musically up to date in both France and Italy, though he often sweetens it with English sequences of thirds and sixths and with full triads. Though he was apparently not a cleric, his music is all for the Church. He was a pioneer in linking sung portions of the Mass by using a common *cantus firmus*, and may have beaten Dunstable to the draw in this respect. But one of the Masses ascribed to Power has also been claimed for Dunstable, and there are those who will not grant him the other as well, so that one can make no rash claims for him as the composer of the first cyclic Mass.

[52] STURGEON, Nicholas
CLERIC, SINGER
BORN: Devonshire, c. 1385
DIED: London, c. June 1, 1454

The composer designated as "Sturgeon" in the Old Hall Manuscript (see 46) was almost certainly the Nicholas Sturgeon who became a scholar of Winchester College in 1399. He must have entered the Chapel Royal shortly after the accession of Henry V (1413), accompanied the king to France in 1415, and was granted a royal pension in 1419. He remained a member of the chapel until 1452, well into the reign of Henry VI. He held various benefices, including one at Windsor (from 1441), where he apparently lived and held administrative offices. In 1442 he became music director of St. Paul's Cathedral in London (where he was also a canon) and was asked to select six English singers for the chapel of the Emperor Frederick III. He made his will on his deathbed on May 31, 1454. The 6 Mass movements (one fragmentary) and the motet that survive in the Old Hall Manuscript may be in Sturgeon's own hand, and it was once thought that the whole manuscript was his.

[53] DAMETT, Thomas
CLERIC, SINGER
BORN: c. 1390
DIED: 1436 or 1437

Damett was the bastard son of a man of wealth and status from the south of England, about whom nothing else is known. "Damett" may actually have been his name; at any rate, there is no truth in the report that it derives from what he said on learning from the future composer's mother that she was pregnant. Like Nicholas Sturgeon [52], the boy studied at Winchester College, leaving in 1407, and after a short stay in a rectory in Wilshire was admitted to the Chapel Royal in 1413 following the accession of Henry V. Together with Sturgeon, he went to France with his king on the expedition that culminated in Agincourt. Henry granted him the Rugmere prebend in St. Paul's in 1418, and under Henry VI he became a canon at Windsor, where he resided at least until mid-July of 1436, dying at some time between then and April 14, 1437, when a will was filed in his name leaving his mother a chased silver cup and his motet, one of his 9 extant compositions, all in the Old Hall Manuscript (see 46). Most of the others are Mass movements, two of which share a common *cantus*.

[54] DUNSTABLE, John
MATHEMATICIAN, ASTRONOMER, CLERIC
BORN: Bedfordshire (?), c. 1390
DIED: December 24, 1453

Dunstable was in his time the most famous, probably the greatest, and certainly, as a historical figure, one of the most obscure of the fifteenth-century English school of composers. He wrote works on astronomy and on latitude and longitude. He died on the date noted above and was buried in the London church of St. Stephen's Walbrook, which burned down in 1666. These are the known facts about the man who may fairly be said to have been the first important Renaissance composer. Persistent legend has him born in the town of Dunstable, about thirty miles northwest of London, in Bedfordshire, but no records substantiate it. One of his treatises contains a notation saying that he was in the service of the Duke of Bedford (Henry V's younger brother, who appears as Prince John in Shakespeare's historical plays). Bedford became regent for the infant Henry VI, and was for a long time in France shoring up the crumbling English claims there. Presumably Dunstable was a member of the duke's chapel, which traveled with him. Since Bedford entered into an alliance with Philip the Good of Burgundy and married his sister Anne, Dunstable very likely came to know the musicians of the Burgundian court. The majority of his extant works are in Continental mss.; and in a long poem, *Le Champion des dames (The Ladies' Champion),* Martin le Franc makes no bones about calling Dunstable the source of the "English countenance" exhibited by subsequent composers of the Burgundian School. Johannes Tinctoris [70], an important theoretician of the next generation, considered Dunstable the equal of, and perhaps superior to, such important Burgundian composers as Guillaume Dufay [56] and Gilles Binchois [60], and it was common for early Renaissance writers to hail him as the fountainhead of the new music.

It used to be said that Dunstable represents an international or expatriate school of English composers, in contradistinction to the stay-at-homes of the Old Hall group, but this view is no longer tenable. Dunstable was also once supposed to be the inventor of *fauxbourdon,* a Burgundian polyphonic technique basically involving consonances of the sixth and the octave between the top and bottom voices, but he was not, though he used—and perhaps introduced to the Continent—the related English *faburden* as well as other characteristically English practices whose common denominator might be described, in a later sense, as sweetness and harmoniousness. To sum them up, they tended to focus the chief melodic interest in the top voice, emphasize consonances and avoid dissonances, and move in something like what we think of as harmonic progressions. Like some other composers of his day (and earlier), Dunstable tends to link Mass segments with a common *cantus,* to use on occasion a *cantus* made up by himself, and once in a while to indulge in cryptic notation. In his mature works he also specifies the use of soloists *and* choir. More than 50 compositions remain that are surely his, and many others are attributed to him. Virtually all of them are religious, and include 2 cyclic Masses, but one or both of the latter may be by Leonel Power [51], and the "invention" of the form, ascribed by their partisans to both the composers, remains up for grabs. Apparently Dunstable's best-known work, both then and now, is a lovely three-part song *"O rosa bella,"* set to a text by the Italian humanist Leonardo Giustiniani, but in recent years its authorship too has been cast in doubt (see 58). Considering its importance, Dunstable's music has had relatively few recordings.

[55] FONTAINE, Pierre (Fôn-tăn', Pĕ-yâr')
SINGER, PRIEST
BORN: Rouen (?), c. 1395
DIED: Dijon (?), after 1447

Fontaine first turns up as a child, "Perrinet de Fontaines," in the chapel of Philippe le Hardi, Duke of Burgundy, in 1403, a year before Philippe's death. He appears to have stayed on through the reign of Philippe's successor Jean Sans Peur. After the latter's death in 1419, Philippe served in the papal choir in Rome under Pope Martin V, where he would have known Guillaume Legrant [49]. After about a decade, he found his way back to Burgundy, where he was ordained in 1433 and where he remained a member of the ducal chapel until at least 1447, presumably dying before 1451, when the records indicate that he was replaced. His compositions, so far as we know, are limited to a handful of secular songs, though it was once suggested, on no basis other than a similarity of sobriquets, that a religious piece in the Old Hall Manuscript (see 46) by "Fonteyns" was his.

[56] DUFAY, Guillaume (Dü-fă', Gĕ-yŏm')
SINGER, LAWYER

BORN: c. 1398
DIED: Cambrai, November 27, 1474

Dufay was a native of northern France, though just where he was born is still unknown. In 1409 he was recruited as one of the six choirboys of Cambrai Cathedral (he was also an altar boy). There he studied under the composer Richard de Loqueville, a married man who moonlighted as harpist to a local court and who was appointed master to the choirboys in 1413. In the summer of 1420, Dufay seems to have been in Paris, and, for the six years immediately following, at the court of Carlo Malatesta, Lord of Rimini and Pesaro, as is evidenced by ceremonial motets written for Malatesta weddings and the like. It has been conjectured that Dufay attended the Council of Constance with the Bishop of Cambrai and encountered Malatesta there. In a chanson of 1426, he bids farewell to the wine, ladies, and friends of the town of Laon, though the circumstances are not clear. A year later he was in Bologna, perhaps at the university. In Rome in December 1428 he joined the papal choir of Martin V (and later of Eugene IV), where he sang and wrote liturgical music until August 1433. He seems to have made a stopover that year at the Ferrara court of Nicholas III and Parisina d'Este (the latter the subject of operas by Donizetti [1155] and Mascagni [1559]; she was executed on a charge of adultery with her stepson). In 1434, Dufay joined the chapel of Amadeus VIII of Savoy (who shortly afterward became a hermit and five years later, Pope Felix V); under Amadeus' successor, Louis, Dufay became director of the chapel, with which he seems to have been connected off and on into the 1450s. He went home to visit his mother in 1434–35, and in the latter year rejoined the papal choir for a two-year stint in Florence. (Eugene IV was then leading a parlous existence on the run, having been deposed by the Council of Basel in favor of Felix V, who was not even a cleric!) During the period of his connection with the choir, Dufay was given a number of livings in Laon, Cambrai, Tournai, Bruges, and Lausanne. (In 1434 he turned up as curate of Versoye in Savoy.) Tournai Cathedral, where he was a canon, gradually became his headquarters. Oddly, in 1438, he was its delegate to the rebellious Council of Basel. Repeated contemporary evidence connects him with the famous Burgundian court of Philippe le Bon, where he would have known Gilles Binchois [60], though dates are lacking. (Some say they met at a clerical get-together in Mons in 1449. There is a famous miniature in Martin le Franc's *Champion des dames* that shows the two chatting while resting from their organ and harp performances.) After 1440, Dufay seems to have been rather regularly in Cambrai (when he was not in Savoy); in that year he ordered thirty-six lots of wine for celebration of the Feast of St. John the Baptist, and eight years later he held the post of cellarer. In 1446 he is described as a bachelor of canon law, and in 1458 he was sent to Besançon to adjudicate a quarrel over a problem of the liturgy. He kept up a correspondence with the Medici court, where Piero and Lorenzo regarded him as the greatest living composer (they were not alone); he must have established the link in 1435–37, when he was in Florence and when he celebrated, in the motet *Nuper rosarum flores,* the consecration of the Cathedral of Santa Maria del Fiore. He also attended the dedication of Cambrai Cathedral in 1472. In August two years later he made his will, listing among his valuables a knife given him by the King of Sicily (presumably René I) and a portrait of Louis XI, which he received from the hands of that monarch. He died quietly at the chapter house a few months later. The motet *Ave Regina coelorum,* which he had written for singing him to his last sleep, was sung instead at his funeral. His tombstone is preserved in the Lille Museum.

It was no fluke or fad that Dufay was repeatedly hailed in his time as the greatest of the great; the study of his music in modern times has indicated that he was quite simply the most titanic musical figure between Machaut [35] and Josquin des Prez [71]. In the way of most great artists, he both sums up and prophesies. He knows and uses all the musical resources current in his day. He is at home in both the sacred and secular realms. He is thoroughly familiar not only with French music, but also with the new currents flowing in from Italy and England. He surely knew and may have studied with Dunstable, and had possibly known the music of the Liègeois Johannes Ciconia [37] from an early age. He wrote in all the current forms. But most significantly, perhaps, he stamped indelibly on his compositions the imprint of his own imagination and personality, thus identifying himself as a man of the Renaissance.

A pleasant introduction to Dufay might be his Petrarch setting *Vergine bella,* a three-part work that is, in essence, an art song in the modern sense, and of the surpassing sweetness that is Dufay's hallmark. His other secular works, mostly *rondeaux* (fifty-nine extant), love songs, and celebrations of spring and the new year, are culminations of the French tradition. The notion of Dufay's representing a special "Burgundian" or "Netherlands" school has been largely abandoned.

Dufay's religious music consists of motets, Mass movements (mostly in motet form), and complete Masses (8, with another attributed). Some of the motets and Mass movements are for everyday use and are conceived simply. Others, for such state occasions as noted above, or in celebration of the election of Eugene IV or lamenting the fall of Constantinople, are more complex and demanding. Not all the motets are religious, but with Dufay the term at last begins to take on the religious application it was to have for the next several centuries. What marks the best of his motets is his concern for bringing out the verbal meaning and emotion, and his refusal to be hamstrung by purely mechanical musical recipes. The later Masses are cyclical—bound together by the use of a common *cantus firmus* throughout; it is less likely that he invented this device, as some argue, than that he borrowed it from his English forerunners. (Someone has noted that the French insist on giving credit here to the English, and the English to the French!) To achieve great freedom and flexibility, Dufay often uses the *cantus* literally as a tenor, inventing his own bass line. Sometimes he invents his own *cantus,* but even more significantly, in the light of later practice, he borrows from secular music rather than from the liturgy—from popular songs, the famous *"L'Homme armé,"* or on *chansons* of his own, such as *"Se la face ay pale."* (Imagine a Mass on "Minnie the Moocher" or "Eleanor Rigby"!) Melody—in the English and the modern sense—is a Dufayan characteristic from the beginning, but more and more he inclines to true polyphony, in which each voice has its own melodic interest and independence, and more and more tonic-dominant harmony and chordal progression become increasingly obvious.

RECORDINGS: There are many.

[57] LANTINS, Hugho de (Làn-tan′, OO-gō′ də)
SINGER
BORN: Lantin, c. 1398
DIED: after 1430

"Lantins" probably is derived from this composer's origin in a village near Liège rather than a family name, though one automatically thinks of Hugho and Arnold [61] as the "Lantins brothers" because of the overlapping and similarity of the little we know of their lives. In the previous generation the cantor of the church of St. Jean in Liège was one Berthold de Lantins, so we are possibly dealing with a heredity or an environment favorable to musicality. Perhaps the two younger Lantins were inspired by Johannes Ciconia [37], for both made the long trek to Italy to seek their fortunes. Hugho seems to have arrived first, leading some to think he was slightly the elder of the two. He was in Venice for a time; and there, in 1421, he wrote a motet celebrating the wedding of a Malatesta princess to the Prince of Sparta—as did Dufay [56]—and another marking an official seizure of territory by Francesco Foscari, the Doge who was later to be brought low both in historical fact and in Verdi's [1232] opera *I due Foscari*. Whether a motet having to do with St. Nicholas of Bari was actually written in Bari or merely for the saint's church in Venice is not clear, but it does indicate familiarity with Dufay's music and probably with the composer himself. Hugho de Lantins left Mass movements, motets, and *chansons,* particularly characterized by their use of the new imitative polyphonic techniques.

[58] BEDYNGHAM, John
CLERIC
BORN: c. 1400 (?)
DIED: Westminster, 1459 or 1460

Bedyngham (a name spelled in innumerable ways) is known to have been a member of the Guild of Parish Clerks in London in 1449, and the verger of the chapel of St. Stephen, Westminster, early in 1458, when, for whatever reason, he deeded all his property to several people. He was apparently known as "Longstrides." These are the only ascertainable facts about the man. Some have identified him with like-named persons, such as a John Boddenham, who was born in 1422 and studied law at Oxford twenty-five or so years later. Whatever the truth, Bedyngham seems to have been a composer of stature, at times confusable with such as Dunstable [54] and Dufay [56]. He is now thought to be the author of the song "O rosa bella," long attributed to Dunstable. He left 2 Masses, as many Mass movements, and a number of songs to English, French, and Italian texts.

[59] BENET, John
TEACHER (?)
BORN: c. 1400 (?)
DIED: in or around 1449

The earliest of several composing John Benets or Bennetts, this one has left little trace besides his music. He may have been born as early as 1380. He was probably the John Benet who was master to the choirboys at St. Anthony's Hospital, London, in 1443, and a member of the Guild of Parish Clerks six years later. A contemporary and apparent admirer of Dunstable [54], Benet left (probably) 3 incomplete Masses, several movements, and 3 motets.

[60] BINCHOIS (or DE BINCHE), Gilles
(Ba*n*sh-wà', Zhēl)
SINGER
BORN: Mons, c. 1400
DIED: Soignies, September 20, 1460

Binchois stands, with Dufay [56] and Dunstable [54], as one of the three greatest composers of his time and as the founder of the Burgundian School (if one agrees that such a school exists independent of the general Franco-Flemish current). His father, Jean de Binche, who must have come from a village called Binche near Mons, had married Jeanne Paulouche of the latter city, where he apparently throve as an important citizen, serving as councilor to Guillaume IV of Hainault and his daughter, Jacqueline of Bavaria. We know nothing certain of Gilles's childhood and youth, until we encounter him in 1419 playing the organ at the church of Ste. Waudru, of whose board his father was a member. Four years later he moved to Lille. Shortly afterward he may have seen military service with William de la Pole, Earl (later Duke) of Suffolk, and spent some time thus in Paris. The earl, an amateur poet and musician who was Geoffrey Chaucer's grandson-in-law, was a friend of the regent, Prince John, then master of John Dunstable, who was then in France with his retinue, so it seems likely that the two composers must have met. Sometime before 1430, Binchois joined the chapel of Prince John's ally, Philippe le Bon of Burgundy. There he seems to have remained for thirty years, gradually working his way up to the post of second chaplain. Though he never took orders, he held several benefices, including one at his hometown church of Ste. Waudru, where he was in company with Dufay in 1449 at a get-together of canons, though they probably already knew each other. A famous manuscript miniature purports to show both of them conversing during a break in performance. (Two pictures by—or after—Jan van Eyck, are said to be portraits of Binchois, but both ascriptions are extremely iffy.) In 1452, Binchois was awarded a canonry in

Soignies, where he ultimately retired and died, leaving property to a brother, two nieces, and a cousin.

Like Dunstable's and Dufay's, Binchois's importance was recognized in his day and frequently remarked on by contemporary writers. Joannes de Ockeghem [65] marked his demise with a famous musical *Déploration*. Nearly 60 of his *chansons* survive, and almost as many religious works ranging from psalms and Mass movements (but no complete Masses) to hymns. Musically speaking, Binchois seems to have been happier in his secular vein, and indeed many of his religious pieces show a strong secular impulse. Like Dufay, he obviously took heed of the English "innovations," and he often exhibits pronounced harmonic and melodic tendencies. But he lacks Dufay's range and imagination, and his output is uneven. His songs are mostly *rondeaux,* generally for a voice and two instruments. He sometimes let his concern for word meanings get in the way of his music (he had good poetic taste and set poems by a number of important poets), and occasionally he is seduced by form for form's sake. Nevertheless, particularly as a writer of *chansons,* he is one of the most significant figures and influences of his time.

RECORDINGS: The Pro Cantione Antiqua has recorded a selection of Binchois motets.

[61] LANTINS, Arnold de (Làn-tan', Àr-nôld' də)
SINGER
BORN: Lantin, c. 1400
DIED: 1432 or later

For Arnold's possible origins and background see Hugho de Lantins [57]. Like his presumed brother and/or fellow-townsman, Arnold migrated to Venice, where two dated *chansons* place him in 1428. From November 1431 he spent a few months in the papal choir in Rome, after which he was not heard of again. Like Hugho, Arnold left some music of high quality—so high in fact that it was, in its time, equated with that of Dufay [56] and Binchois [60]. His three-voice *Mass,* though not cyclic, appears to be one of the earliest complete settings, though two movements are by Ciconia [37]. There is also a cyclic Mass, some separate Mass movements, 3 motets, and 15 secular songs.

[62] LEGRANT, Jean (Lə-gràn', Zhàn)
BORN: c. 1400 (?)
DIED: ?

Nothing is known of Jean or Johannes Legrant except that he probably wrote between 1420 and 1440. Some have called him a native of Hainault, and one source says that he died before 1474, which seems a safe conjecture. He left a few pieces, both sacred and secular, which exhibit the early "imitative" polyphonic style.

[63] SMERT, Richard
PRIEST, SINGER
BORN: c. 1405 (?)
DIED: in or after 1477

Smert was a vicar choral in the choir of Exeter Cathedral from 1428, and in 1435 became rector of Plymtree, a Devon village, where he was last listed in 1477. His musical composition is represented by 13 carols, five of them written in collaboration with a colleague named John Truelove. Carols supposedly originated in pagan times as dance songs for the solstice festivals. In the fifteenth century, when they enjoyed great popularity in England, they abandoned their terpsichorean aspect and were directed to the great religious festivals, especially Christmas. All of those in question here were for that feast. They are for two voices, with a three-part (presumably choral) refrain.

[64] FRYE, Walter
CLERIC
BORN: c. 1410 (?)
DIED: London, 1475

Walter Frye seems to have been one of the few significant English composers in the troubled times between the fifth and eighth Henrys. Because his music exists largely in Continental manuscripts, and was evidently both popular and influential in Europe, it has been suggested that he was an expatriate, but there is no other supporting evidence. The musicologist Gustave Reese suggested that because the root of his name meant "free," he was identical with a Gualterius Libertas who was in the papal choir in 1429, but we now know that singer to have been a Frenchman, Gaultier Libert. Frye may have been connected with Ely Cathedral in the middle of the century, joined the Guild of Parish Clerks in London in 1456, and probably was the man who drew up a will on June 5, 1475. He left 3 complete Masses and a fragment of another, a few motets, and some *chansons,* several of which have been assigned variously to Binchois [60] and Bedyngham [58]. His shorter works are found all over Europe and provided *cantus* for such later composers as Agricola [76], Josquin des Prez [71], Obrecht [77], and Tinctoris [70].

[65] OCKEGHEM, Joannes de (Ō'-kä-gem, Yo-àn'-nes də)

SINGER

BORN: c. 1410

DIED: Tours, February 6, 1497

For so important a figure, much of Ockeghem's life is maddeningly obscure. The erratic spellings of his name—Ockenheim, Okenghem, Okchem, Ogkeguam, Hoquegan, HoqQueham, etc.—are to be expected. It has been argued that he was born at least two decades later, though he appears to have lived to be very old. There is a village called Ockeghem (or however one spells it) in East Flanders, and around 1400 there were people of that name in Termonde, which seems since to have become Dendermonde. It has been said, without any real evidence, that Joannes (or Johannes or Jehan or Jean) was a pupil of Dufay [56], or Binchois [60], or maybe Barbireau [68]. The first clear fact that we have, however, is that in June 1443 he was a left-hand choir singer in Antwerp Cathedral. ("Left-handers" sang composed music; "right-handers" sang chant. Ockeghem is said to have sung a fine baritone.) He departed a year later, presumably for Moulins, where he became one of the twelve chaplains (i.e., choir singers) of Charles I, Duke of Bourbon, as records of 1446–48 indicate. Legend says that in 1449 he took a sabbatical to study with Dufay, but in fact he dropped out of sight until 1452, when he was a member of the Chapel Royal of Charles VII (Jeanne d'Arc's Dauphin); apparently he joined it a year previously. In 1459 the king, one of whose titles was Abbot of St. Martin-de-Tours, the wealthiest monastery in France, named Ockeghem its treasurer. Under Louis XI he was placed in charge of the chapel, granted a benefice at Notre-Dame de Paris, and sent on a diplomatic mission to Spain in 1470. Charles VIII may have sent him on another to Flanders in 1484, and there is a hint that he was in Italy at some time. Since the records for the period are missing, we do not know when he left the chapel, though someone else had taken his place by 1496. He made out his will in 1487 but was still active in connection with the abbey seven years later, which perhaps argues for his recovered health. His death inspired several *déplorations* from poets and musicians (e.g., Erasmus and Josquin des Prez [71]), lamenting the passing of not only a great artist but also of an admirable and lovable human being. His fame lasted, and a quarter century later we find him being likened to the Creator Himself. Tradition and wishful thinking have called him the teacher of Josquin and just about every other Franco-Flemish composer of consequence in the ensuing generation, though substantive support remains elusive.

Ockeghem is the most significant composer between Dufay and Josquin. Once regarded as the founder and chief apostle of the "Second Netherlands School," he is now seen rather as one of the peaks of the French Renaissance tradition. He left twenty or so *chansons* that are pretty certainly his, but the bulk (and the best) of his music is religious. But even there the legacy is surprisingly small—10 motets (most of them to the Virgin) and 15 cyclic Masses, plus the first polyphonic Mass for the dead, or Requiem, to have come down to us.

Space does not permit any detailed discussion of the characteristics of Ockeghem's music. Indeed, its scope and variety are among the best. Like all great creators, he looks behind him as well as ahead, some of his music calling to mind Dufay and even Machaut [35]. But elsewhere he is clearly a Renaissance polyphonist, weaving a seamless fabric of lines that in themselves have equal importance and equal interest. He knew all the tricks and invented some of his own. Indeed, he was especially admired for his near-miraculous technical aplomb, which unfortunately blinded later times to his musicality and expressiveness. His *Missa Cuiusvis Toni (Whatever Mode Mass)* is so written that it can be sung in any of the four "authentic" Church modes, depending on what clef one imposes on the staves. One puzzle canon has remained precisely that for a number of modern musicologists, and another canon involves thirty-six separate vocal lines. Present-day scholars, perhaps more at ease with the idiom than their forebears, find in the music such qualities as "passion," "profundity," and "religious mysticism."

Ockeghem is greatest in his Masses, where he has room to breathe. Some are freely composed; others make use of both liturgical and secular *cantus*, some of the latter from the composer's own *chansons*. There are clear predictions of the soon-to-be-common "parody" technique, wherein other compositions supply not merely the tenor but the entire raw material of the Mass.

RECORDINGS: There are recordings of the *Requiem*, several of the other Masses, and a generous helping of the smaller works.

[66] PAUMANN, Conrad (Pou'-mån, Kon'-rad)

ORGANIST, TEACHER, LUTENIST, HARP-
IST, RECORDER PLAYER, FIDDLER
BORN: Nuremberg, c. 1410
DIED: Munich, January 24, 1473

The first internationally great and widely influential German organist, Paumann (the
name is a variant of Baumann) left us—alas!
—only a few little pieces. He was born blind
but seems to have been musically precocious
and was backed by a philanthropic family in
his hometown. Otherwise we know little or
nothing of his life until 1446, when he got
married, became organist of St. Sebald's,
and signed an agreement never to leave Nuremberg without the permission of the kind
and generous city fathers. But four years
later he sneaked out to take the post of court
organist to Albrecht III of Bavaria in Munich, the duke salting the offer with a home
of his own, title clear. This action understandably caused some hard feelings in Nuremberg, but Paumann's contract was eventually bought up and he held his post, under
two subsequent dukes, for the rest of his life.
Munich evidently placed no restrictions on
his freedom to travel, and he seems to have
become one of the first touring performers,
having special success in Italy in 1470, winning a knighthood in Mantua, and playing
for the Emperor Frederick III at Regensburg a year later. He by no means limited
himself to the keyboard in these appearances. He was also a consultant in the matter of the installation of new organs in various places. He turned down an offer from
Galeazzo Maria Sforza to become court organist in Milan because, he said, he feared
the wrath of his Italian counterparts and he
didn't like Italian cooking. On his death, he
was succeeded by his son Paul and was buried in the Frauenkirche, where a memorial
plaque may still be seen. In his day
Paumann was rivaled, as an organist, only
by the Florentine Antonio Squarcialupi. His
chief musical monument is his treatise
*Fundamentum organisandi (Basics of Play-
ing the Organ)*, which contains, along with
verbal instructions, some simple two-part
pieces, mostly based on popular songs. He
also left a single three-part *Lied*. He also
supposedly invented lute tablature, an alphabetical system for annotating lute and keyboard music, which drew guffaws from some
of his less sensitive contemporaries, who
couldn't imagine what a blind man needed
with notes. (He needed them, presumably, to
dictate music of his that got written down.)

[67] RUBINUS (Roo-bē'-nus)

PRIEST, SINGER
BORN: Fouseran, March 30, 1415 (?)
DIED: Watten Abbey, September 17,
1478 (?)

"Rubinus" was the composer of a popular
piece, found in the Glogauer Liederbuch,
called *Der Bauern Schwantz*, usually translated "The Peasant's Dance" though
Schwantz usually means "tail," "train," or
"penis." He is also credited with a *chanson*
entitled *"Entre Peronne et Saint Quentin."*
He has been variously identified with the
Rubino who sang in the papal choir in Rome
in 1446, the Rubinet who left 6 *chansons* in a
Florentine manuscript, and Guillaume
Ruby, who was a chorister of Rouen Cathedral and in 1415 became a member of the
Burgundian ducal choir. Ruby has been also
identified with G. Le Rouge and W. Le
Rouge, both of whom composed and were
probably one and the same (Guillaume or
Willem). Rubinus, Rubino, and Rubinet are
now said to be Robert LePelé, alias Robinet
de la Magdalaine, born near Rouen, trained
at Beauvais, ordained, for a short time a
member of the papal choir, and from 1448
chaplain to Philippe le Bon, who appointed
him provost of the Monastery of Watten,
near St. Omer, in 1462, where he probably
died, and was certainly buried.

[68] BARBIREAU, Jacques (Bär-bē-rō', Zhåk)

CHOIRMASTER
BORN: c. 1420
DIED: Antwerp, August 8, 1491

Some accounts say that Barbireau was born
in Mons, the son of a citizen named Jean
Barbireau, and that he served as a chorister
in the church of Ste. Waudru. But the first
sure information that we have is that he took
over the choir of Antwerp Cathedral in 1448,
where he nearly doubled the number of singers and improved its quality. In 1490 the future Emperor Maximilian I sent him to Budapest, perhaps to recruit members of the
just-disbanded royal chapel, and he was received with considerable fuss. But in 1491 he
was removed from his post, either because of
illness or senility, and was replaced by Jacob
Obrecht [77], who was, however, not his pupil as he was once thought to be. Though his
name suffered various spellings, present
thinking is that he is not to be identified with
a contemporary called Barbingant, who left
a Mass and 3 small pieces, but who is otherwise a cipher. Barbireau himself is credited
with 3 Masses, a motet, and 3 (probably) in-

strumental *chansons.* One of the last, *"Een vroylic wesen,"* seems to have been a smash hit in its day, to judge from the number of copies preserved.

[69] BUSNOIS, Antoine (Bün-wả', Ản-twản')

CLERIC, SINGER, TEACHER, CHOIRMAS-TER, POET, PRIEST
BORN: c. 1430
DIED: Bruges, November 6, 1492

We have no positive knowledge of Busnois's origins, birth, or youth. His name (also spelled "de Busnes") suggests that he or his family came from a crossroads hamlet in what is now the northern tip of France. Somewhere along the way he became a churchman. He (and others) says he was a disciple of Joannes de Ockeghem [65]. History first records him in late 1467 in the chapel of the last duke of independent Burgundy, Charles the Bold. But in a musical work (apparently directed to Ockeghem), Busnois calls himself an "humble musician of the Count of Charlerois"—Charles's title before he became duke in 1467. Recent evidence has shown that Busnois was one of Charles's teachers. (Charles was addicted to music, played the harp, and composed in a small way.) One would think that with all this evidence someone could suggest a reasonable birth date, but no one seems to have.

Charles's musicians traveled with him in peace and war. Thus it has been guessed that Busnois met the poet Jean Molinet during the duke's futile siege of Neuss in 1474, and the theorist Tinctoris [70] on a state visit to Naples in 1475; both certainly seem to have known and admired him, though perhaps they were only acquaintances of Busnois. Among the composer's *chansons* are some love lyrics (he wrote many of his own) to one Jacqueline d'Hacqueville, her name thinly disguised by some horribly strained puns; she has been called his mistress, though it is likely she was so only in a Petrarchan or *amour courtois* sense, since she was married to one court bigwig and was the sister of another. When Charles, quarreling with René of Lorraine over the ownership of that hapless territory, was slain before Nancy in 1477, the chapel was transferred to his daughter Mary, who presumably took it to Ghent with her when she married the future Emperor Maximilian I later that year. (Busnois had been her teacher, too.) When, five years later, she tumbled from her horse while hunting and died, the chapel went over to Maximilian. Despite statements that Busnois stayed on until 1487—or entered the

service of Louis XI—he probably left at that time. By then he had been granted benefices all over northern France, Flanders, and Holland, and he seems to have retired to Bruges to live on his revenues and keep the choirboys in line at St. Sauveur.

In his own time Busnois was ranked with Ockeghem, and there is little doubt that he was the best of that great man's contemporaries. But there is a sort of Dufay [56]-Binchois [60] difference here, for Busnois' reputation rested (and rests) primarily on his *chansons,* of which more than 75 are presently attributed to him, some scattered all over Western and Central Europe. Perhaps the most famous, *"Fortuna desperata,"* is one of a handful set to Italian texts. Busnois looks both backward (he often uses earlier techniques and such old forms as virelai, motet, rondeau, and ballade) and forward (polyphonic imitation, expanded vocal ranges, careful attention to textual meanings, and occasionally musical illustration of verbal ideas). As a lyricist, he is an incorrigible punster. If there is a single general characteristic of his songs, they may be said to incline toward the melancholic. He did not, by the way, invent the *bergerette,* a one-stanza *virelai* popular in his time, though he wrote some. As for his sacred music, he left a Mass (on the tune *"L'Homme armé)* and at least 2 others are possibly his; there is also a *Magnificat* and a handful of motets.

RECORDINGS: Joshua Rifkin has devoted an LP to eight *chansons.* The Pro Cantione Antiqua has recorded the *Missa "L'Homme armé."*

[70] TINCTORIS, Johannes (Tink'-tôr-is, Yō-ản'-nes)

THEORIST, TEACHER, LAWYER
BORN: Braine-l'Alleud, c. 1435
DIED: October 1511

It is assumed that "Tinctoris" is a Latinized form of the name Dyer, in whatever language (Vaerwere? Teinturier?). He was born in a village about twenty miles south of Brussels, but we know nothing more of his origins than that. At the time he entered the University of Orléans in 1463, he was obviously already a man of learning and experience. He was a canon of a church in Nivelles near his home, had served in some capacity in the choir at Cambrai in Dufay's [56] time, had been master of the choristers at Chartres Cathedral, and assumed a similar function at Orléans Cathedral while in that city. A contemporaneous biographical sketch tells us that he held doctorates in both canon and civil law, of which subjects he terms himself a professor. He was also a mathematician and probably the most respected musical authority of his time. Rumor had it that he was a magician. In the early 1470s he was employed as first chaplain and cantor in the Neapolitan court of Ferdinand I, and tutor to the king's daughter Beatrice. It is said, without proof, that when she married Matthias Corvinus, King of Hungary, in 1476, Tinctoris went to Budapest with her, but since records show him in Naples in 1480, this is probably untenable. The court of Naples was at that time one of the intellectual centers of Europe, and it seems to have been there that Tinctoris wrote his treatises on counterpoint, mensural notation, modes, and other subjects. In his tract on the invention and use of music, he lists Jesus Christ as the greatest singer of all time—unfortunately phonographic support is lacking. The *Terminorum musicae diffinitorium*, printed in Treviso in 1495, is the first published music dictionary. In 1487 the chancellor, Giovanni Pontano, authorized him to travel to round up singers for the chapels of Charles VIII of France and the future Emperor Maximilian I. What Tinctoris did in his last two decades is obscure. He was in Rome in 1492, but whether he died there, in Naples, or in Nivelles is uncertain. As a composer, he wrote eclectically, intellectually, and (expectedly) learnedly, but his music is not uninteresting. He left some *chansons*, some shorter religious pieces, a *Lamentations*, and 5 Masses. RECORDINGS: At least one of the Masses has been recorded.

[71] JOSQUIN des Prez (Zhōs-kan′ dā Prä)

SINGER, CLERIC, TEACHER
BORN: c. 1440
DIED: Condé-sur-l'Escaut, August 27, 1521

Nothing is known of Josquin's birthplace or parentage. Educated conjecture puts the former in Flanders or, more likely, Picardy. Some argue for Condé, a small town now near the Belgian border south of Ghent, and others for St. Quentin. "Josquin" would seem to be a Gallicized version of the Flemish name Jossekin (Joey); "des Prez" or "Desprez," synonymous with the Flemish "van der Weyden" (from the fields), may indicate that he was a country boy. Supposedly he was a child chorister in St. Quentin, but there are no records that prove it. His setting of Jean Molinet's *Déploration* for Ockeghem [65] has led to a belief that he was Ockeghem's pupil, for it orders Josquin,

Brumel [85], Compère [73], and Pierre de La Rue [87] to mourn their "dear father," but the phrase is probably figurative.

The ascertainable facts about the rest of Josquin's life offer only glimpses. He went to Italy and appears in 1459 as a singer in the choir of Milan Cathedral. The fact that he was grossly underpaid probably attests to his youth. He retained his post, however, until the end of 1472. The following year Duke Galeazzo Maria Sforza bestowed a lucrative benefice on him, and he was by then presumably a member of the duke's chapel, though he does not appear in the records until 1474 (as "Juschino"). Among his colleagues was Loyset Compère. The duke commissioned Josquin to make him "a book of music" and provided his musicians with thirty-three gowns of "peach-flower color, turquoise blue, and greenish." We do not know the color of Josquin's. On the day after Christmas, 1476, the tyrannical Galeazzo Maria was assassinated in the cathedral square by three high-minded youths, leaving his son under the regency of his widow, much to the disgruntlement of his three brothers. Josquin apparently held his job until 1479, when the heir's uncle, Lodovico "il Moro," seized power, at which time Josquin joined the chapel of Lodovico's brother Ascanio, who was named a cardinal five years later. In Ascanio's court Josquin came to know the poet Serafino dall'Aquila, who mentioned him in his verses, and, presumably, the painter Pinturicchio. Some have found rather dubious evidence in some of the texts set by Josquin that Ascanio was a tightwad with his employees, though he thought nothing of shelling out a hundred ducats for a parakeet that could whistle a *Gloria* or do something equally devout. In any case, Ascanio's favorite sounds seem to have been horn-winding and dog-baying. In and out of favor with his brother, he was in and out of Milan, and presumably took his retinue into his exiles with him. Josquin certainly was in Rome with him when he went to procure his hat, and by late 1486 was also singing in the papal choir. He was there, off and on for some years, but may also have remained in the cardinal's employ. However, the period between 1486 and 1501 is obscure, but there are hints that at some time or other Josquin was back in Milan and perhaps in Florence and Modena. In 1493 the accounts of Duke René II of Lorraine record a payment to a singer named Josquin, but he may have been someone else.

Just when Josquin severed his connections with St. Peter's and the cardinal is uncertain. We know that he was not at the former place in or after 1501 (earlier records are missing), and later that year an envoy of the Duke of Ferrara encountered him at the court of Louis XII of France at Blois, ostensibly on a mission to Flanders to find singers for the duke's chapel. Whether or not he was there on any sort of permanent basis is questionable. We do know that he was at Lyons in the spring of 1503, as the king was, but this was a matter of only a few days. If Josquin was in any court on a regular basis before that date, it was most likely that of Duke Ercole of Ferrara, a friend of Cardinal Sforza. It is possible that the *Missa Hercules Dux Ferrariae* betokens an early association, though its date is uncertain. There is evidence that he, or his music at least, was known at the Ferrarese court, and that as early as 1502 there was talk of making him *maestro di cappella* there, but that did not become a reality until the following spring, when Johannes Ghiselin (alias Jean Verbonnet), a former member of the chapel, was rehired and instructed to escort Josquin from Paris. (Josquin was chosen over Heinrich Isaac [78], who had been highly recommended for the post.) The two arrived in state and were colleagues until Josquin left the following year, apparently to escape an outbreak of plague—to which his successor Jacob Obrecht [77] succumbed. Josquin seems to have gone straight to Condé, where he held a canonry, and where he became provost. He died there seventeen years later, leaving his property to the church, which was destroyed in 1793. Several of his musical contemporaries composed laments.

There was no doubt in the Renaissance that Josquin was its greatest composer, though after the sixteenth century his star was temporarily eclipsed by the myth of Palestrina [201]. Nor does modern musicology find any reason to quarrel with that view. Martin Luther, whose life overlapped Josquin's, called him "the supreme master of the notes," adding that they "must express whatever he wants them to, whereas other musicians can only do what the notes demand." A present-day writer unreservedly calls him the first composer to exhibit individuality in his music. Both views are perhaps extreme, but the fact remains that Josquin is one of the great watersheds in the history of Western music, dividing the Middle Ages from the Renaissance, and his impact on those who came after was enormous. (Many younger musicians were said to be, or claimed to be, his pupils, but in no case has the allegation been proved. One of them, Adrien Petit Coclico [144], however, paints an attractive picture of a man who despised hyperbole, advocated a solid grounding, and refused to flatter his ego by trying to make silk purses out of sows' ears; but whether it is taken from the life is uncertain.

What does all this praise mean? Josquin's enormous range and skill are best understood from analyses of his work, available in any good history of Renaissance music. But here only a few generalities are in order. For one thing, Josquin left a much larger output than any other considerable composer of his time, covering the full spread of forms and genres. There are 18 Masses for certain (and others attributed), some Mass movements, more than 100 motets, and as many songs (a few of them in Italian or German). The majority of these works were printed—and reprinted—in Josquin's own time. His most conservative works are the Masses, perhaps owing to their very nature, but they exhibit every contrapuntal technique developed up to that time, as well as Josquin's own trick of creating an intricate fabric by working with short phrases, with canonic and other imitations moving from voice to voice, the voices being treated as all equal in importance. The mature Masses look ahead to the devices of "parody" (the fabrication of a piece from the musical materials of another) and "paraphrase" (the elaboration of borrowed material), which were to characterize the church music of the new century.

Josquin is at his best and most individual in his *chansons* and motets. Here he can work with texts of his own choosing, and he is greatly concerned to bring out verbal meanings and feelings by musical means. To do so, he resorts to all kinds of vividly imaginative devices, achieving enormous variety without ever resorting to unmusical trickery. Particularly in the later motets, he achieves a kind of luminous simplicity that has been seen as deriving from the mystical pietism that swept over the Netherlands in his time. Some have seen his "chordal" effects in such works as a harbinger of diatonic harmony, but this notion is moot. Half a century after Josquin's death, a certain Cosimo Bartoli wrote that if Ockeghem was the Donatello of music, Josquin was its Michelangelo. It is an apt figure.

RECORDINGS: Josquin's work has been much recorded in all categories, sacred and secular, though no complete edition has been forthcoming so far, either intentionally or fortuitously.

[72] **ADAM von Fulda** (À′-dàm fun Fool′-dà)

MONK, THEORIST, HISTORIAN, TEACHER
BORN: Fulda, c. 1445
DIED: Wittenberg, 1505

Born in a Benedictine center, Adam joined that order, and lived in the monastery of Vormbach, near Passau, in Bavaria. Evidently he found his life growing drearier and drearier, for in his forties he defected, got married, took a post with the Saxon Elector Friedrich III, and became his *Kapellmeister.* In 1500 he conducted Mass at Torgau on the occasion of the wedding of his employer's brother (and eventual successor), Johann. When the University of Wittenberg was opened in 1502, Adam was appointed its first professor of music. At the time of his death, in the plague epidemic of 1505, he was writing a history of Saxony, but his most famous work is his treatise *De musica,* important for its view of the new polyphony, and the first known writing to differentiate between instrumental and vocal music. He left a Mass, a Magnificat, a handful of shorter religious works, and 3 songs, two of them to his own texts. The third of them, *Ach, hülf mir Leid,"* ("Ah, Sorrow, Help Me") seems to have been something of a hit.

[73] COMPÈRE, Loyset (Kom-pâr', Loi-sä')
CLERIC, SINGER, LAWYER
BORN: c. 1445
DIED: St. Quentin, August 1518

It is clear that Compère was from the north, but conflicting documents trace his origins to Hainaut or Artois. Nothing, however, is known of his origins or training. (His first name is a diminutive, meaning "Little Louis.") In the mid-1470s he was a colleague of Josquin des Prez [71] and Agricola [76] at the Milanese court (registered as "Aluyseto"), though it has been suggested that he came there from the chapel of Louis XI of France. When Duke Galeazzo Maria was assassinated in 1476, Compère was one of the singers laid off as an unnecessary expense. Presumably he went back to France, where he turns up in 1486 as a singer in the chapel of sixteen-year-old Charles VIII. In 1494 the king granted him French citizenship to give him certain legal rights to church livings. A few months later Compère returned to Italy with the king and his troops, by way of invasion, and got as far south as Rome. After the war was over, he was attached to churches in Cambrai, though he retained his place as court composer; at one point his church and home were vandalized by angry civic leaders for reasons that are obscure. About 1509 he moved to St. Quentin, of whose collegiate church he was a canon. He represents the musical establishment of his time and was spoken of admiringly by various of his confreres. Some of his music was published in his lifetime, by Ottaviano dei Petrucci and others. He left several Masses, some Mass movements, motets, *chansons,* and *frottole.* A couple of the Masses are "substitution" Masses, in which motets take the place of the usual sections. Compère is an oddly conservative composer who seems drawn to older forms, especially in his *chansons,* several of which have comic and even bawdy texts. He was a close friend of the poet Jean Molinet. It has been argued that his apparent pedantry is a humorous stance. RECORDINGS: The Pro Cantione Antiqua has recorded the motet *Crux Triumphans.*

[74] FINCK, Heinrich (Fĕnk, Hĭn'-rikh)
CHOIRMASTER, PRIEST
BORN: Bamberg, c. 1445
DIED: Vienna, June 9, 1527

Much of the biographical information about Heinrich Finck that has come down to us we owe to a sketch by his grandnephew, Hermann Finck, in the latter's textbook *Practica musica.* But since Hermann was not yet three months old when his aged relative died, it is unlikely that he got his purported facts direct. In any case, the elder Finck's beginnings are obscure. The city of Bamberg has long claimed him as a native, and nothing points to another birthplace. He was apparently taken into the chapel of Casimir IV of Poland at about the age of ten and remained there for over thirty-five years. In 1482, His Majesty's "royal liberality" gave him time off, presumably to attend the University of Leipzig, where a "Henricus Finck de Bamberga" first signed the rolls that summer. He seems to have been back in Cracow around the end of the decade, but on the death in 1492 of King Casimir, he, perhaps dismissed, went to Budapest and other centers vainly seeking employment. At some point he was showered with gifts by Matthias Corvinus, King of Hungary, a constant thorn in the side of the Polish monarchy, but this must have been earlier, since Matthias died in 1490. If, as Hermann tells us, he was truly the pet finch *(Finck)* of four successive Jagiełłonian kings, he must have returned to Cracow before the death of Casimir's eldest son, John Albert, in 1501. However, in 1498 he belonged to the chapel of Alexander of Lithuania, John Albert's brother and successor, and returned to Cracow with him. He was still there in 1505. His fourth Polish employer would have been Sigismund, still another son of Casimir, who came to the throne a year later. By the end of 1510, however, Finck was *Kapellmeister* to Duke Ulrich I of Württemberg in Stuttgart, where he wrote a *Missa in summis* for his employer's wedding to Sabine of Bavaria the following spring. By the time Ulrich gave up his chapel in 1514, Finck may have been in that of Maximilian I in Vienna. If he was, he did not remain there long, for by 1516 he seems to have joined the establishment of Cardinal Matthäus Lang, with whom he moved to Salzburg when Lang became its prince-archbishop in 1519. It is assumed that much of Finck's music was destroyed when the cathedral burned—as it frequently did—less than a century later. Finck was not happy in Salzburg, and in 1525 he retired to the Schottenkloster (Scottish Cloister—so called because it was founded by Irish monks) in Vienna. Still active at eighty, he founded and directed a choir there. Two years later the Emperor Ferdinand I named him his *Kapellmeister,* but Finck died before he could take over his duties. The emperor had a medal "to the most excellent of musicians" struck in his memory; it shows him in profile, apparently suffering from the same sort of nasal enlargement that afflicted Federigo da Montefeltro, Duke of Urbino.

Finck represents the sudden burst of artistic fervor that hit the Germanies in the late fifteenth century, producing painters and writers as well as composers. He was a friend of sculptor Veit Stoss, a lifelong correspondent of the humanist Conrad Celtis, and the teacher of composer Thomas Stoltzer [119]. Finck left 4 Masses, 2 Magnificats, about 50 other religious works, and around 40 *Lieder.* The sacred music is quite skillful, though its chief interest is perhaps technical. (Hermann called it "hard.") The songs are another matter. Dispensing with ready-made *cantus,* except in two instances where he uses popular songs, Finck here lets the music flow from the heart. The results are lively, sometimes rowdy, and show a considerable advance over the anonymous *Lieder* that had appeared in earlier collections.

RECORDINGS: Finck has at least one LP (by the Bamberg Musica Canterey) all to himself and is often anthologized with composers of the Maximilianian era.

---

[75] **STOKHEM, Joannes de** (Stok´-hem, Yō-àn´-nes də)
CHOIRMASTER, SINGER
BORN: c. 1445
DIED: after 1501

Stokhem (alias Johannes de Prato) was probably born in and around Liège, for he was a choirboy in the church of St. Lambert in 1455, and, as far as we can tell from incomplete records, was connected with various choirs in that city until 1481, when he went to Budapest to head the chapel of Matthias Corvinus, King of Hungary. It is likely that he was recommended by his friend Joannes Tinctoris [70]. Stokhem remained in Budapest until at least 1484, but toward the end of the decade he was a member of the papal choir in Rome. All certain traces of him vanish after 1501, though he may have been in Maximilian I's chapel (as Johannes de Prato) for a few years after that. Some of his attractive and skillful *chansons* were published by the Italian printer Ottaviano dei Petrucci around this time. He also left two sacred works.

---

[76] **AGRICOLA, Alexander** (A-grē´-kō-là, Al-eks-àn´-der)
SINGER
BORN: c. 1446
DIED: Valladolid [Spain], August 1506

Agricola's origins are uncertain. He is designated in various documents as both a Fleming *(Belgam)* and a German *(de Alamannia),* though the latter term is ambiguous. His real family name seems to have been *Ackermann* or *Akkerman.* He was a singer in the chapel of Duke Galeazzo Maria Sforza in Milan from 1471 to 1474, and probably was a colleague of Josquin des Prez [71]. In the summer of the latter year, he was in Florence and two years later in Cambrai, though his reasons for being in either place are obscure. Then he dropped out of sight until 1491–92, when he spent a few months in the choir of Florence Cathedral. In the spring of 1492 he left for Naples, hotly pursued by orders from Charles VIII of France that he return immediately to the royal chapel, from which he had apparently defected. King Ferdinand I of Naples packed him up and sent him home. After another gap (seven years) we find him being hired for what turns out to be his last post as a member of the chapel of Philip the Handsome, the Hapsburg Duke of Burgundy. Four years earlier Philip had married Juana, the daughter of Ferdinand and Isabella of Spain, in a union whose issue, the later Emperor Charles V, would link the Spanish, Burgundian, and Austrian thrones. Philip liked to travel and took his chapel with him. In 1506 he visited Spain, where both he and Agricola succumbed to the plague epidemic. (Juana went mad with grief and was afterwards known as "Juana la loca" or "Crazy Jane.") In his time Agricola was regarded as one of the great masters of the polyphonic style, though his music adheres, apparently uninfluenced by Italian currents, to the older northern style. He left Masses, shorter religious pieces, *chansons,* and a number of instrumental arrangements of popular tunes. RECORDINGS: None of his larger works appear to have been recorded.

[77] OBRECHT, Jacob (Ōb'-rekht, Yä'-kōb)
PRIEST, CHOIRMASTER
BORN: Bergen op Zoom, November 22, 1450 (?)
DIED: Ferrara, 1505

According to his own statement, Obrecht was propitiously born on the Feast of St. Cecilia, patron saint of music, though he neglected to say in what year. The son of one Willem Obrecht, he may have attended the University of Louvain (Leuven) from 1470; to be sure, the student's father's name is also given as Jacob, but university registrars have never been noted for infallibility. Presumably he studied theology there. Six or so years after his matriculation, he was in charge of the Utrecht Cathedral choirboys, one of whom was the future humanist Desiderius Erasmus, who developed, under his tutelage, a lifelong hatred of music. After about a five-year stint as choirmaster at St. Gertrude's in his hometown, where he officiated at his first Mass (1480), he went to Cambrai as master to the cathedral choirboys. Erasmus apparently had good cause for his reactions, for in 1485 Obrecht was fired for neglecting and mistreating his charges, and had to fork over a number of his manuscripts to the authorities to cover mishandled funds. Almost immediately, however, he was appointed assistant choirmaster at St. Donatien, Bruges—an appointment sweetened with a large consignment of wine. Meanwhile his fame had penetrated Italy, and in midsummer of 1487 he got six months' leave to visit Ferrara on the invitation of Duke Ercole, but did not get back for nearly a year. Two years later he was promoted to the choirmastership anyhow, but left early in 1491 to relieve the apparently ailing Jacques Barbireau [68] in Antwerp, a post that became Obrecht's when Barbireau died later that year. Five years later Obrecht himself became ill and resigned. After that he worked sporadically in Bergen op Zoom, Bruges, and Antwerp before returning to Ferrara in 1504 in time for the plague epidemic, which carried off so many of his colleagues throughout Europe in 1505–6. Of the Franco-Flemish composers born

around the middle of the fifteenth century, Obrecht was, and still is, regarded as second only to Josquin des Prez [71]. He seems to have been happiest in writing Masses, of which around twenty-five are extant. Ottaviano dei Petrucci published a collection of them in 1503. Obrecht is conservative to the degree that he adheres to *cantus firmus* technique, but he uses it with great ingenuity and considerable dramatic instinct. In his frequent quotation of music by other composers, he moves toward the later "parody" Mass. He is sometimes hampered by a sort of glibness and, when stuck for an idea, is given to using mechanical filler. He is even more conservative in his motets, where he sometimes self-consciously strains to emphasize verbal meanings. Most of his *chansons* appear to be instrumentally intended. It is now doubted that he wrote the earliest known *St. Matthew Passion,* once credited to him.

RECORDINGS: A number of Masses and shorter works have been recorded.

[78] ISAAC, Heinrich (Ē'-zàk, Hīn'-rikh)
SINGER, TEACHER, DIPLOMAT
BORN: c. 1450
DIED: Florence, March 26, 1517

Isaac's will tells us that he was a Fleming, but not his precise birthplace. Some German patriots have gone to considerable lengths to prove him a fellow-countryman (or a Bohemian at worst) on the basis of his being sometimes called "Arrigo il Tedesco," but that sobriquet means little more than its English counterpart "Harry the Dutchman" does. Nor does there seem to be any authority for the notion that he was originally named Huygens.

The first dependable fact that we have about Isaac is that in 1484 he stopped in Innsbruck on his way over the Brenner Pass to take an appointment offered him by Lorenzo de' Medici (Il Magnifico, or Lorenzo the Magnificent) in Florence. There he sang in the Duomo, in the Baptistery, and in the new Santissima Annunziata, and taught music to the Medici children, who probably included Il Magnifico's successor Piero (later thrown out of the city), Giovanni (who became Pope Leo X), and Giuliano (who figures in Baldassare Castiglione's book of "civil conversation" *Il Cortegiano [The Courtier]).* Another of Isaac's responsibilities was composing music, not only for worship, but for festivities. Some of his carnival songs were to texts by his employer, but, because of the employer's too worldly nature, they probably went up in the smoke of

Savonarola's purifying fire. Isaac was apparently quite content in Florence. Lorenzo arranged for him to marry a butcher's daughter, Bartolomea, and they were given a small farm where they made their home. But Il Magnifico's death in 1492 (on which occasion Isaac and the poet Angelo Poliziano collaborated in a moving tribute), and the religiopolitical upheaval that followed it apparently made it difficult for them to remain. The arrival of Emperor Maximilian I at Pisa in 1496, to try to counter the French invasion, offered an escape, especially since the composer had dedicated some of his work to Maximilian. The Isaacs were dispatched forthwith to Vienna, and a year later Heinrich was named composer to the imperial court in Innsbruck, the emperor's favorite town. His salary was 150 florins, and there was a clause in his contract that his wife would be provided for if she outlived him. The post was perhaps more honorific than demanding, for over the next eighteen years he seems to have moved rather freely between south Germany and northern Italy. At some point Niccolò Machiavelli ran into him in Konstanz; Machiavelli had a rather low opinion of the intelligence of musicians, but one gathers that Isaac was there in some diplomatic capacity. In 1502 he was in Ferrara, probably being looked over for the directorship of the duke's chapel, which, however, went to Josquin des Prez [71] the following year. In 1510 Maximilian gave him a farm at Valpolicella (one hopes with a vineyard). Four years later he settled for good in Florence as a sort of ambassador-without-portfolio for the emperor, and made comfortable by a pension procured for him by the recently elected Pope Leo X, his sometime pupil. Another pupil, Ludwig Senfl [120], took over his duties at the imperial court.

Isaac's enormous output includes some of the most immediately attractive music written in his time. Most music lovers know his plaintive (second) setting of *"Innsbruck, ich muss dich lassen"* ("Innsbruck, I Have to Leave You") whose foursquare form prefigures the German chorale—and, in fact, the song became one as *"O Welt, ich muss dich lassen"* ("O World . . .") It is not, however, connected with the rude ejection of Maximilian by the Innsbruckers. One of the contributing factors to the argument over Isaac's origins is his remarkable ability to adapt his secular works to national styles—German *Lieder,* Italian *frottole,* and French *chansons.* Moreover, his songs range from the knottily polyphonic to what amount to simple tunes with chordal accompaniment. There are extant more than 100 secular pieces, including a number of instrumental ones. Many were printed in Isaac's lifetime and many were later used by other composers as bases for works of their own.

Some of Isaac's 35 known Masses were published too, by Ottaviano dei Petrucci and others. In the Masses his "Flemishness" comes through most clearly, and his handling of polyphony has been likened to that of Jacob Obrecht [77]. He shows a love and respect for Gregorian melodies, but he also used secular *cantus,* notably in the *Missa carminum (Song Mass),* a veritable tapestry of hits, which may have been intended for private rather than public use. Isaac's greatest religious monument is probably his three-volume *Choralis Constantinus,* the first attempt (as far as we know) to provide music for the Proper of the Mass (those sections pertinent to specific days and services) for the whole ecclesiastical year. It takes its name from the second volume, commissioned by the churches in Konstanz. It was left to Ludwig Senfl [120] to complete and was not published until more than thirty years after Isaac's death, 1550–55.

RECORDINGS: Isaac is represented on records by Masses, smaller religious works, songs, and instrumental pieces—albeit still rather sparsely.

[79] JUDENKÜNIG, Hans (Yōō'-den-kü'-nikh, Hans)
LUTENIST
BORN: Schwäbisch Gmünd, c. 1450
DIED: Vienna, March 4, 1526

There is no indication that the man named "King of the Jews" was Jewish. In fact we know very little about him. He was born near Stuttgart, and for the six years before his death was living in Vienna. He taught the lute and perhaps made such instruments. At the time of his demise he was said to have reached an advanced age, which probably means seventy or more. During his known Vienna years he published two lute books, written in German lute tablature (a cumbersome system of notation that indicates, among other things, finger placement). Both books are of the do-it-yourself instructional type, and the second in particular (translated as *A Pretty Artistic Method for Learning the Lute and the Fiddle)* contains many pieces written or arranged for the instrument.

[80] LA TORRE, Francisco de (Là Tôr'-rā, Frán-thēs-kō dā)
SINGER, CHOIRMASTER, PRIEST

BORN: c. 1450
DIED: after 1504

Probably a native of Seville, La Torre sang
in the royal choir of King Ferdinand the
Catholic from 1483 to 1494. Later (1503) he
was briefly master of the choirboys in the
Cathedral of Seville. He left a funeral service, some *villancicos* (Christmas songs), and
other songs, but his most famous work,
found in the great manuscript collection
Cancionero Musical de Palacio, is a three-
voice instrumental piece, *"Danza alta"*
("High Dance"), based on a traditional tune
called *"La España."* This is the first known
music for "high" dancing. The high dances
were vigorous, involving leaps and such that
kept the feet off the floor (at least some of
the time), in contrast to the *baxa danza* (low
dance), which called for a gliding motion
that kept the feet on the floor. The high
dance came to Burgundy with Isabella of
Portugal, third wife of Philippe le Bon, and
swept over Europe in the first great dance
craze. It was traditionally accompanied by
wind instruments, in contrast to the string-
accompanied low dance. The two were later
paired, as in the English pavan and galliard.
The older folk took part in the low dance
but stepped aside in the high dance for the
youngsters. Curiously, Francisco's theme
provides that for the earliest known low
dance, composed by one Domenichino of
Piacenza.

[81] PHILIPS, Thomas
SINGER
BORN: c. 1450
DIED: after 1490

The composer of a three-voice carol "This
Day Daws" is probably the Thomas Philips
who was a chorister at Salisbury Cathedral
in 1465 and boy-bishop in the Feast of Fools
celebration. He remained there until at least
1473, then sang in the choir of St. George's
at Windsor Castle from 1477 to 1490.

[82] PIPELARE, Matthaeus (Pē-pe-lä′-rə, Mà-tà′-us)
TEACHER
BORN: c. 1450
DIED: c. 1515

Undoubtedly a Fleming, Pipelare was master of the boys to the Illustrious Confraternity of Our Lady at 's Hertogenbosch, Holland, at the very end of the century. Though
he was widely admired and composed a
good deal of music, including at least 11

Masses, nothing more is known of him than
that he lived and worked in Antwerp at a
slightly earlier date. He liked to sign his
works with the open fifth A–D or "la–re,"
the last two syllables of his surname. He was
flexible as to style, being equally at home in
polyphony and homophony, seriousness and
gaiety.

[83] HOFHAIMER, Paul (Hōf′-hī-mer, Poul)
ORGANIST
BORN: Radstadt, Austria, January 25,
1459
DIED: Salzburg, 1537

Hofhaimer must have been one of the
brightest ornaments of the splendid court
chapel built up by Emperor Maximilian I. In
Hans Burgkmair's series of processional engravings *The Triumph of Maximilian,*
Hofhaimer, beardless, wearing a Thomas
More costume and a Mona Lisa smile, has a
float all to himself, save for the flunkey who
pumps the bellows of the splendid positive
organ he is playing. Born near Salzburg, he
was the son of a salt-mine supervisor, who
played the organ. In his teens he was supposedly at the Graz court of Emperor Frederick III, and he was certainly, from the age
of nineteen, at that of Sigismund, the Hapsburg Archduke of the Tyrol, in Innsbruck.
Married and widowed young, he married
again in 1486, the year he was sent to Maximilian's coronation in Frankfurt am Main.
Since the emperor loved Innsbruck and
spent much time there, it is not surprising to
find Hofhaimer also in his service by 1489.
Demands on his time, however, seem not to
have been stringent, as he visited other
courts, including those of Saxony and Bavaria, and lived for a time in Passau and
later in Augsburg. He also went on various
imperial progresses, though probably not in
the manner illustrated by Burgkmair. At
fifty-six he was awarded the Order of the
Golden Spur and a patent of nobility. After
Maximilian's death in 1519, Hofhaimer went
back to Salzburg and ended his days as organist to the prince-archbishop. Not only
was he the finest organist of his time, he was
also regarded as an expert on organs and
was frequently called as a consultant. Of his
compositions there remain only a cycle of
songs to odes of Horace, 2 original organ
works, and a number of charming if simple
organ arrangements of popular songs.

[84] MOUTON, Jean (Mōō-tôn′, Zhàn)
SINGER, TEACHER, PRIEST

BORN: Haut-Wignes, c. 1459
DIED: St. Quentin, October 30, 1522

A misreading of his now vanished epitaph caused some to think Mouton a native of Hollingue, or Holling, near Metz; but it is now clear that he came from what was then Holluigue, about twenty miles south of Calais. In the years 1478–85 he joined the choir of the church of Notre-Dame in Nesle, near St. Quentin, was ordained and made choirmaster. By 1500, however, he was calling the tune for the choirboys in Amiens Cathedral, and a year later he was doing the same thing at St. André's in Grenoble, a job that he left in 1502. He had written, three years earlier, a motet celebrating the nuptials of Louis XII to Anne of Brittany, and in 1509 he followed it with another on the birth of their daughter Renée, in which year the queen obtained a canonry for him at St. André's, so despite the lack of records it is assumed that he went into the royal service. Other quasi-official or occasional compositions clearly indicate that he was regarded as a sort of composer laureate; these include motets on the election of Giovanni de' Medici to the papacy, the death of Queen Anne in 1514, and the welcome of the new queen, Mary Tudor, the same year, the accession of Francis I in 1515, his victory at Marignano, and the birth of an heir apparent. At the end of 1515 he went with the royal party to Bologna for François's meeting with the Pope, with the result that the latter made him an apostolic notary. In 1520 he participated in what seems to have been a royal-chapel "superbowl" at that flashy but empty summit conference between Francis and Henry VIII of England, known as the Field of the Cloth of Gold. In his last years Mouton held a benefice at St. Quentin, where he died.

Like so many others, Mouton was called, by later writers, a pupil of Josquin des Prez [71], which seems to mean little more than that he wrote in the post-Josquinian contrapuntal style. He was in fact a total master of that art, though his later works move toward a more homophonic and chordal style. He was particularly admired for the smoothness of both his melody and his technique, and indeed smoothness is the hallmark of his music, which is marked by calm and serenity, by a moderate pace, and by vocal lines that avoid excitement and leaping about. In a modern university he would have got tenure in short order. He left well over a hundred motets, 15 Masses (some admired by Leo X and some printed by Ottaviano dei Petrucci), and some *chansons,* including some of the newfangled *chansons rurales*

(yokel songs) that dispensed with *cantus* and sounded like folk music.

[85] BRUMEL, Antoine (Brü-mel', Ản-twản')
SINGER, TEACHER, PRIEST, CHOIRMASTER
BORN: Brunelles (?), c. 1460
DIED: after 1510

Brumel was apparently born near Chartres, at whose cathedral he was a choir singer in 1483. There is probably no foundation to the story that he was a pupil of Ockeghem [65]. He seems to have led a somewhat stormy life where his employment was concerned. From 1486 to 1492 he was nominally master of the boys at St. Peter's in Geneva, but he spent part of that time at the court of the Duke of Savoy in Chambéry, and eventually marched off into obscurity after a set-to with his fellows. He turned up at Laon Cathedral in 1497, was named master of the boys of Notre-Dame de Paris early in the New Year but quit in a huff when the chapter disapproved his choice of a chorister, and, ignoring pleas that he return, trekked back to Chambéry, where he sang in the ducal chapel until 1502. In Lyons in 1505 he was appointed *maestro di cappella* to Sigismondo Cantelmi, the apparently itinerant Duke of Sora (in the Abruzzi) and brother-in-law to Alfonso d'Este of Ferrara. The contract provided a house in Ferrara, expenses for getting there, and an annual salary of 100 ducats. But all this ended in 1510 when the chapel was disbanded. There is evidence of further composition after that, and a late and unreliable report places him in Rome in 1513, but otherwise we know nothing of the end of his life. He left 15 Masses (including the first known Requiem to use the *Dies Irae* section), a number of other sacred pieces, and a few *chansons,* both vocal and instrumental. He supposedly wrote his *Missa de Beata Virgine* in competition with Josquin des Prez [71], but no one says who won. His contemporary, the Swiss theorist Heinrich Loris ("Glareanus"), thought his music a triumph of will over small talent, but others of the time praise him extravagantly. As a composer of sacred music, he is now generally regarded as one of the best of the second rank.

[86] GHISELIN, Joannes (alias "Verbonnet") (Gĕs-lan', Yō-ản'-nes; Vâr-bun-nã')
SINGER

BORN: c. 1460
DIED: after 1507

Some minor skirmishing among musicologists as to whether Ghiselin was Verbonnet, and if so, why, was resolved by the discovery in Florence of a signature that admitted the alias. We know he was a Fleming from Picardy, but not his exact place of origin. He was in Ferrara at the court of Ercole I d'Este, after whom he had apparently named his infant son Hercules, as early as 1491, but he moved to Florence a year later and sang at the Baptistery till at least the late winter or early spring of 1493. At some point after that, he was in the French Chapel Royal at Blois, where he was already ensconced in 1501. Two years later he returned to Ferrara, bringing with him the new *maestro de cappella* Josquin des Prez [71] on the old duke's orders. He may have been sent to fetch Obrecht [77] in 1504 but fled back to the Netherlands ahead of the plague in 1505. When last heard from, he was with the Marian Brothers in Bergen op Zoom in 1507. Ottaviano dei Petrucci published 5 of his 9 extant Masses in 1502, and he also left motets and *chansons*. He was especially admired for his contrapuntal skill.

[87] **LA RUE, Pierre de** (Là Rü, Pē-âr′ də)
SINGER
BORN: Tournai (?), c. 1460
DIED: Courtrai, November 20, 1518

Because he had more aliases than one can shake a stick at (e.g., Pieter van Der Straeten, Pierazon de La Ruellien, Petrus Platensis, Pierson, Petrus LaVic), it has proved hard to keep tabs on La Rue. We know that his father was named Jehan and his mother (from The Hague) Gertrud, but we are not entirely sure of his birthplace and know nothing of his first two decades. In the early 1480s he was a singer at Siena Cathedral, but at the end of the decade he was back in the Lowlands singing in the cathedral at 's Hertogenbosch. In 1492 he became a member of the Marian Brotherhood and a member of the chapel that the future Maximilian I maintained in the Netherlands. Maximilian claimed the area through his first wife, Mary of Burgundy, and their son, Philip the Handsome, though he was anything but popular there. A year later, when he ascended to the imperial throne, the choir went over to Philip, who had married the Infanta Juana of Spain. Philip took his musicians with him to Spain in 1501 and again on his fatal journey in 1506, in the course of

which the ship carrying them encountered a storm that swept two overboard and forced the survivors to put in at Falmouth until it was over. La Rue remained in Valladolid for about two years, then came home to Malines (Mechelen) to sing for Maximilian's sister, Margaret of Austria, Protectress of the Netherlands and regent for Philip's son Charles (later Charles V). After the latter came of age, La Rue sang for a short time in his personal chapel, then retired in 1516 to Courtrai, where he held a benifice. Margaret had a magnificent two-volume collection of his Masses (of which more than 30 are extant) published in his memory. He also left Mass movements, motets, Magnificats, and *chansons*. His technique leans strongly in the direction of imitative polyphony, though he does not approach the technical marvels in that style that mark the high Renaissance. Music obviously interested him more than words, whose meanings he is content to suggest only very generally. He preferred dark colors, even in his *chansons*, which are notably lacking in sweetness and light. It is therefore not surprising that his masterpiece is his *Requiem*, which makes rather unusual use of the lower vocal ranges. RECORDINGS: The *Requiem*, some motets, and various short pieces have been recorded.

[88] **SCHLICK, Arnolt** (Shlik, Är′-nōlt)
ORGANIST, ORGAN BUILDER
BORN: in or near Heidelberg, c. 1460
DIED: Heidelberg, after 1521

Though Schlick has been claimed for Bavaria, Bohemia, and other lands, present evidence suggests that he remained close to home for most of his life. Whether he was born blind or became so later is not clear. As so often with early composers, we know nothing of his parentage or youth. He owned property in Heidelberg, and in 1482 he married Barbara Strupperlin, a court lady there, by whom he had at least one child, a son. In 1486 he went to Frankfurt to play at Maximilian's coronation as emperor-elect, and in 1490 he fled the plague westward, visiting the Lowlands and Strasbourg. Five years later he attended the Imperial Diet at Worms, where the emperor announced, rather optimistically, a perpetual peace. Perhaps it was at such an encounter with Maximilian that he obtained the title of imperial organist, for he seems not to have been directly connected with the Hapsburg court; but he did receive a lifetime appointment in 1509 to the Palatine court, which was his base of operations. After the turn of the century he traveled widely as a performer and was in great demand as an authority on organs and organ building. In 1516 he met Paul Hofhaimer [83] at Torgau and apparently competed with him. In 1520 he probably attended the coronation of Emperor Charles V, for which he wrote an ambitious set of variations, the last two in ten parts, four to be played on the pedals. After 1521, Schlick drops out of sight.

In 1511 he published his *Spiegel der Orgelmacher und Organisten (Mirror for Organ Builders and Organists)*, a very important manual and the first of its kind in German. He followed it with a collection of pieces, *Tablaturen etlicher Lobgesang und Lidlein uff die Orgeln un Lauten (Tablatures of a Few Hymns and Ditties for the Organ and Lute)*. It was the first printed collection of organ pieces and the first known German lute book. The former works are based on plainsong, but are clearly conceived for the instrument and take some cognizance of imitative polyphony. Some of the lute pieces are for "plucking and singing," others merely for "plucking."

RECORDINGS: Pierre Froidebise has committed to disc a selection of organ pieces.

[89] ANCHIETA, Juan de (Án-kyā'-tà, Hwàn dä)
PRIEST, SINGER
BORN: Urrestilla, 1462
DIED: Azpeitia, July 30, 1523

Born in the Spanish Basque country, Anchieta came of a noble family and was a first cousin of St. Ignatius of Loyola on his mother's side. In 1489 he was appointed to the chapel of Queen Isabella, with which he got to see perhaps more of Spain than he wanted to, the queen being notoriously restless. He probably taught the crown prince, Don Juan, and served him as his *maestro de capilla* during the last two years (1495–97) of that young man's brief life. He then returned to Her Majesty's service, where he was several times rewarded with salary raises and benefices, and on her death was transferred to the chapel of the Infanta Juana, wife of Philip the Handsome of Burgundy, with whom she made her headquarters in Flanders. Anchieta returned to Spain on the pair's storm-tossed voyage in 1506, during which he lost a couple of colleagues to the sea, and at the end of which the duke died. The musician remained in the mad Juana's service until 1516. In the year previous he had been beaten up by the future saint, his cousin Ignatius, and Ignatius' brother as the consequence of a family quarrel. In 1518 he was named abbot of Arbos (he already held several livings and other ecclesiastical

posts), and a year later was retired from court by Charles V as "too old," though he was only fifty-seven. Perhaps his beating incapacitated him, for in 1520 he was reported to be sick in bed at home, and a few months later his church income was transferred to his home territory. He made his will in February of 1522 and died a year and a half later. He wrote Masses and other sacred works, and a handful of very popular and hardy songs. Measured against what his northern contemporaries were doing at the time, Anchieta's work seems rather old-fashioned and simplistic, though it is not without charm. Columbus' nephew owned the manuscript of one of the songs, and Cervantes cites another.

[90] FAYRFAX, Robert
ORGANIST, SINGER
BORN: Deeping Gate, Lincolnshire, April 23, 1464
DIED: St. Albans, Hertfordshire, October 24, 1521

Fayrfax is thought to have been the younger son of a knight. Aside from the record of his baptism, the first notice we have of him indicates his membership in the Chapel Royal in 1496. A year or so later he was made organist at St. Albans Abbey, which fact suggests that he was a particularly fine organist or that he knew someone, for the organ at St. Alban's was considered the finest in all England. Over the next decade or so he acquired a B.A. and a D.Mus, from Cambridge and, in 1511, the first musical doctorate ever granted by Oxford. One of the earliest acts of Henry VIII was to assign to Fayrfax, who is always listed as First Gentleman of his chapel, an annuity from a farm in Hampshire. There are also records of his having been granted two ecclesiastical livings, both of which he was forced to surrender at one time or another for reasons that are not clear. There are also records of grants for dress for various state occasions and for boarding and tutoring various choirboys. In 1514 he was made a "Poor Knight of Windsor," which title brought with it a lifetime income of twelve pennies a day. On four successive Christmases, beginning in 1516, he presented Henry with books of anthems and part-songs of his own composition, for which he was given sums ranging between thirteen and twenty pounds. (Since there was no publication of music in the modern sense, such exchanges between a composer and a patron represented the chief way of realizing a return on one's creations.) Fayrfax fronted the Chapel Royal when it accompanied the king to the Field of the Cloth of Gold, that early ostentatious "summit" meeting of Henry and Francis I of France (about as productive as most later "summits"). The next year Fayrfax died and was buried at St. Albans, thereby missing by more than a decade its dissolution and ruination by his royal master.

In the English Renaissance, Robert Fayrfax was regarded as the first great English composer since the age of Dunstable [54], and, though he was largely forgotten in the intervening centuries, there seems no reason to argue otherwise today. He left (entire or incomplete) 6 Masses, 2 Magnificats, 13 motets, 9 part-songs, and 2 instrumental pieces. His works are primarily polyphonic, showing considerable awareness of the techniques and discoveries of the Franco-Flemish composers, and occasional archaisms, such as the use of melismata. The Mass *O bone Jesu*, based on a motet by Fayrfax, is thought to be the first English parody Mass.

[91] CORNYSHE, William
POET, ACTOR, DRAMATIST, CHOIRMASTER, TEACHER
BORN: East Greenwich, c. 1465 (?)
DIED: Hylden, Kent, 1523

There is some confusion about how many musical William (and other) Cornyshes (or Cornishes) are involved in the accounts given. It is thought by some that the William Cornyshe who was master (probably the first) of the Singing Boys of Westminster Abbey between 1490 and 1491 is the one who died around 1500. The Cornyshe described above was presumably the son of a John Cornyshe (although he signed himself "William Jr.," probably to distinguish himself from his musical predecessor). It is guessed that he became a member of Henry VII's Chapel Royal in the 1490s. (Records show that in 1493 he was paid 13s. 4d. for a "prophecy," which was probably the going rate, though the word seems to have indicated merely a poem.) In 1504 he managed to get himself thrown into the Fleet Prison for libel, having written a satirical poem about a prominent lawyer named Empson. In 1509, following the death of the king and the illness of the incumbent, he supposedly took over as master of the royal Singing Boys, though the records do not show him in that post before December 1513. At any rate, he seems to have ingratiated himself with Henry VIII, though it is doubtful they ever became the cronies some have imagined. It was Cornyshe's function to provide music for all state and ceremonial occasions.

He also wrote and presented plays and interludes, apparently of a quasi–moral–allegorical ilk. (He was a friend of the poet John Skelton. He sometimes signed himself "Nyshewhete," a punning inversion of his surname.) Together with the avian Messrs Crane and Kite, he was also one of the chief performers in such presentations. His duties as what seems to have amounted to the Mastership of the Revels extended to more homely matters as well. In 1516, for example, he was paid for "paving, gutters of lead for urinals, and other necessaries" for the Whitsuntide festivities at Greenwich. (That was the year he appeared in his own *Troilus and Pandar*.) In 1513 the chapel, under Cornyshe's direction, wowed the French when Henry went abroad, and again, at the Field of the Cloth of Gold, in 1520. A good deal of Cornyshe's time must have been taken up—as the records suggest—with procuring and teaching choristers. (In 1518 Henry apparently raided Cardinal Wolsey's chapel, of which he was envious.) Cornyshe's health began to decline in 1521, and two years later he was pensioned off to a manor in Kent where he died.

Not much of Cornyshe's output is left. The 6 religious works (some of them fragmentary) include a *Stabat Mater* and a *Magnificat*. Of more interest are the part-songs, frankly popular, often lusty, sometimes comical. One and perhaps two involve Skelton texts, and another supposedly sets a poem by Sir Thomas Wyatt.

[92] ESCOBAR, Pedro de (Es-kō-bär', Pā'-drō dā)
SINGER, CHOIRMASTER
BORN: Oporto, c. 1465 (?)
DIED: Évora, after 1535 (?)

Pedro de Escobar is the victim of an identity crisis. In the first place, there is a good bit of Spanish Renaissance music that is indicated to be merely by "Escobar." Pedro had a contemporary named Cristóbal, who wrote a treatise on plainchant, and there was a slightly later musician named André. Pedro sang from 1489 to 1499 in the chapel of Queen Isabella, where he collaborated on a Mass with Juan de Anchieta [89]. He then went to Portugal but returned in 1507 as master of the choirboys at Seville Cathedral. Finding himself unable to carry out his duties and subsist on his income, he resigned in 1514 (some say he died) and was succeeded by Pedro Fernández de Castilleja. It is argued that Pedro de Escobar and the Portuguese Pedro de Oporto (or de Porto—anyhow he came from wine country) were one and the same. If so, he was serving Cardinal Dom Affonso, son of King Manuel I, in 1521. Later, however, the port got to him and he is last heard of as the town drunk in Évora, about fifty miles east of Lisbon. The compositions accorded this oddly composite figure show much more polyphonic boldness than those of Juan de Anchieta. He left a *Mass*, a *Requiem*, 25 smaller religious works, and 18 *villancicos* in a popular vein.

[93] RIVAFRECHA, Martín de (Rē-vàfrä'-shà, Mär-tēn' dā)
CHOIRMASTER, TEACHER, PRIEST
BORN: c. 1465 (?)
DIED: Palencia, June 24, 1528

Rivafrecha (or Rivaflecha), a priest, became choirmaster at the cathedral of Palencia, in Castile, left in 1521, sang in the cathedral choir at Calahorra for two years, returned to Palencia as a singer, and once again became choirmaster, as well as master of the boys in 1525. He was relieved of the latter post for utter incompetence within a few weeks. However, he was greatly admired as a musician and composer and was buried with honor in the cathedral's Chapel of the Holy Cross. He left only 5 short religious pieces that we know of, and one of these is of dubious authorship.

[94] TROMBONCINO, Bartolomeo (Trŏm-bōn-chē'-nō, Bär-tō-lō-mä'-ō)
TROMBONIST
BORN: c. 1465
DIED: after 1535

"Little Trombone" was said to have been a Veronese and possibly was. His father was a musician (a recorder player, as his name Bernardino Piffaro indicates) and was part of the musical establishment at the Mantuan court, from sometime in the 1470s, for more than fifty years. Tromboncino seems to have been a rather unsettled fellow. He was at the Mantuan court in his capacity of sackbut player in the late 1480s, then apparently went into the service of Lorenzo de' Medici in Florence. Meanwhile, in 1490 the Marchese Gian Francesco III of Mantua, married the sixteen-year-old Isabella d'Este, who set about turning the court into a vital artistic center. Tromboncino returned there shortly after the death of Lorenzo (1492), but in 1495 he ran away to Venice. His father convinced him of the error of his ways, and he was back within the month. Four years later, however, he caught his wife Antonia *in flagrante delicto* with another man, slew

her, and headed for the hills again. Told that his action was justified, he came back, but two years later he took off again, this time for good. (His employer noted that his action was deplorable, especially considering the money they were paying him, and later tried to sue him for back taxes.) Tromboncino wound up in Ferrara, in the employ of Lucrezia Borgia, supplying the music for her wedding to Isabella's brother, Duke Alfonso. He almost certainly had a link with the court of Urbino, for Duke Guidobaldo and Duchess Elisabetta (Isabella's sister) had frequent dealings with Ferrara. In 1506 he furnished music for an Urbinate performance of Baldassare Castiglione's pastoral *Tirsi*, and he may have known the painters Raphael, Mantegna, and Giulio Romano. Tromboncino remained in Ferrara until at least 1513. After a gap, he turns up in Venice requesting citizenship, which he probably obtained, for he seems to have remained in Venetian territory until 1535, after which the trail goes cold, so that we may assume that he did too.

Though he composed a few religious works, Tromboncino is remarkable for the 175 or so *frottole* he left. The *frottola* was the Italian counterpart of the French *chanson*, but simpler, more metrically regular, and tending toward the chordal. It is regarded as a forerunner of the sixteenth-century madrigal. Tromboncino's *frottole* turn up in manuscripts scattered from Cracow to Seville, many were published, and some were transcribed by other musicians for instrumental or solo vocal performance.

[95] DAVY, Richard
SINGER, TEACHER, ORGANIST
BORN: c. 1467
DIED: c. 1507

There is some confusion about the identity of the composer Richard Davy, but it is now generally ruled out that he was the man who from 1501 to c. 1516 was chaplain at the Norfolk estate of Sir Richard Bullen and his son Sir Thomas. (Sir Richard Bullen—or Boleyn—was a parvenu, a former London mercer; Sir Thomas, described as a "grasping nonentity," was father to two mistresses of Henry VIII, one of them later briefly the queen.) Assuming the two were not one and the same, the "other" Richard Davy entered Magdalen College at Oxford in 1483, was there in the early years of the next decade as master of the boys and organist, and a member of the Exeter Cathedral choir from 1497 to 1506. He seems to have been a brilliant composer, but only a few works—religious pieces, carols, and songs—are left, and many of these are fragmentary. RECORDINGS: His most important work, a *St. Matthew Passion,* is unhappily among this last group, though it has been "reconstructed" and recorded.

[96] ENCINA, Juan del (En-thē'-nà, Hwàn del)
PLAYWRIGHT, LAWYER, SINGER, PRIEST
BORN: Salamanca, July 12, 1468
DIED: León, 1529/30

The name "del Encina" possibly indicates the place of family origin (near Salamanca) or the maternal maiden name. In either case, Juan was properly "de Fermoselle," son of a Salamanca shoemaker of that name, and brother to Diego del Fermoselle, professor of music at the local university. He served as page to the university chancellor, took a law degree there, and sang in the cathedral choir from 1484. In 1492 he entered the service of the Duke of Alva (brother to the chancellor) and remained in his employ until 1498. It was in this period that he began writing and producing plays, the first known dramas written for the stage in Spain. He also directed and acted in his creations. Since they required songs, Juan wrote *villancicos* to go with them. Earlier he had taken minor orders but had no luck in getting even one benefice, and so in 1498 he went to Rome and attached himself to the court of Pope Alexander VI, a Spaniard, *né* Rodrigo de Borja (in Italian, Borgia), who kindly obliged him. Among the livings he conferred on him was the one at Salamanca that Juan coveted, but in the end all he got out of it was a losing legal battle with the incumbent. He remained headquartered at the Vatican through the pontificates of Julius II and Leo X. Julius appointed him, despite his never having been ordained, archdeacon of Málaga Cathedral, after which date, 1506, he divided his time between Rome and Spain. He seems to have given up his writing and composition after about 1513. In 1519 he got himself ordained, was rewarded with the priorship of León Cathedral, and in gratitude betook himself to the Holy Land to celebrate his first Mass on location, as it were. On his return, he wrote his travels, then settled down in León. Four years after his death, his body was at his wish reinterred beneath the choir in Salamanca Cathedral.

According to Juan himself, all his compositions—*villancicos,* romances, *coplas,* etc.—were written before he was twenty-five. None of them are strictly religious, though his earlier plays celebrate Christmas and other Church festivals. (Later *villancicos* became synonymous with Christmas carols.) Many of them are to be found with other quasi-popular songs in the great *Cancionero Musical de Palacio* in Madrid. There may be some Italian and Flemish influence here and there, but these are basically popular music written by a highly skilled craftsman.

RECORDINGS: Several *villancicos* appear on records in an anthology by Gregorio Paniagua and the Atrium Musicae de Madrid.

[97] FOGLIANO, Giacomo (Fōl-yà'-nō, Jà'-kō-mō)
ORGANIST, HARPSICHORDIST, TEACHER, SINGER
BORN: Modena, 1468
DIED: Modena, April 10, 1548

Fogliano was sometimes called "Fogliano da Modena," possibly to distinguish him from his brother Lodovico, a theorist who published *Musica theorica* in 1529. The sons of Alessandro Fogliano of Modena, they both sang in the choir of the cathedral. Giacomo was also organist from 1479 until his death, save for an apparent seven-year gap at the turn of the century, and at times master of the boys. One of his pupils was the organist-composer Giulio Segni [142], sent him by Cardinal Ippolito d'Este. He left motets, *laude,* madrigals, and *frottole,* and 4 *ricercari* for organ, among the earliest examples of that important instrumental subgenre, a forerunner of the fugue.

[98] CARA, Marco (Kà'-rà, Mär'-kō)
LUTENIST, CHOIRMASTER, SINGER
BORN: c. 1470
DIED: Mantua, c. 1525

Like his colleague Tromboncino [94] at the Gonzaga court in Mantua, Cara (called "Marchetto") seems to have come from the neighborhood of Verona. He came to the court in or before 1494 and apparently remained there until his death. He was a great favorite of the Marchese Francesco and his wife, Isabella d'Este, who rewarded him with money and real estate in and around Mantua. He seems also to have been admired by the Este connections in the courts of Ferrara and Urbino. He set a poem by Baldassare Castiglione, a habitué of the latter, who cites him in *Il Cortegiano* for the serenity and sweetness of his lute playing. He was music director to the Gonzagas in the latter half of his career, and went to Venice in 1510 to cheer up the marchese, then a

Venetian prisoner. Cara was twice married—first to Giovanna de Marasechi, and then in 1512 to a lady named Leali, who survived him and remarried within a year of his death. Though he wrote a *Salve regina* and a handful of *laude* (religious songs), he was, like Tromboncino, a fine composer of *frottole*, some of which were transcribed for lute or for voice and lute.

[99] GENET, Elzéar (Zhe-nä', El-zä'-är)
CHOIR DIRECTOR, SINGER
BORN: Carpentras, c. 1470
DIED: Avignon, June 14, 1548

Born in the Vaucluse, Genet was called "Carpentras" or "Il Carpentrasso," after his birthplace. He took holy orders and from 1505 to 1508 sang in the choir at Avignon. In the latter year he was summoned to Rome by Pope Julius II, ex-Bishop of Avignon, but shortly afterward took service in the royal chapel of Louis XII. Pope Leo X called him back to Rome around 1513 and made him his *maestro di cappella*. When Leo was succeeded by the unmusical Adrian VI, Genet absented himself from felicity awhile back in Avignon, but returned to take up his duties under Clement VII in 1524. Two years later his health gave way (apparently from overwork), and he seems to have abandoned his musical career. He returned to Avignon for good, as Dean of St. Agricole. He set great store by his compositions, for between 1532 and 1537 he had them published in four splendid volumes, in an edition of 500 copies, by one Jean de Channey, who apparently learned the music-printing trade on the job. These were devoted to his major religious works (a few songs and motets are scattered through various manuscripts) and include 5 Masses, Magnificats, psalms, hymns, and a set of *Lamentations for Holy Week*. These last he had had published earlier for Pope Clement when he heard the Vatican Choir sing a version that was so corrupt as to be hardly recognizable. They remained the standard for the papal services until they were replaced in 1587 by Palestrina's setting. The collected works (of which only two copies remain) were the first known printed music to contain notes with round heads. RECORDINGS: There is a recording of the *Lamentations*.

[100] FÉVIN, Antoine de (Fä-van', Àn-twàn' də)
PRIEST, SINGER
BORN: Arras, c. 1470
DIED: Blois, c. January 1512

Antoine de Févin was of noble birth, a cadet son of Pierre de Févin, Sieur de Graincour et Garinet, and a town official of Arras. (The suppositions that he was a Spaniard or an Orléanais have no foundation.) Antoine was also probably a brother of the composer Robert de Févin, a musician of Cambrai. He was ordained and became a member of Louis XII's chapel at Blois, perhaps as early as 1501. Louis evidently thought a good deal of him, for in 1507, during one of his Italian excursions, he sent for some of Févin's music to astound the Italian ladies. Févin probably composed the motet sung at Louis's meeting with Ferdinand of Castile in Savona that year. He was highly regarded by other musicians. His colleagues Jean Mouton [84] and Claudin de Sermisy [127] borrowed themes from him, and Mouton wrote a *déploration* on the too early death of *"gentil Févin."* He left at least 12 Masses (some published by Ottaviano dei Petrucci), some other religious works, and a few *chansons*. Like so many musicians of his day, he was strongly influenced by Josquin des Prez [71], though he was no mere epigone. His music has a profile of its own, and a smooth handling of melodic line is especially characteristic.

[101] CAPIROLA, Vincenzo (Kà-pē'-rō-là, Vēn-chent'-zō)
LUTENIST
BORN: Brescia, 1474
DIED: Brescia, c. 1548

All that is known of Capirola is that he was a nobleman and lute virtuoso who spent his early and later years in Brescia, and who was in Venice (and perhaps briefly in England) in the second decade of the sixteenth century. From those same years comes the *Capirola Lute-Book*, a gorgeous manuscript written by one Vitale, who says that his purpose for so doing is to save the music for posterity, since musicians lack the foresight to do it for themselves. It contains song transcriptions, dances, and some enterprising *ricercari*.

[102] LURANO, Filippo de (Lōō'-rà-nō, Fē-lēp'-pō dä)
CHOIRMASTER
BORN: Cremona (?), c. 1475
DIED: in or after 1520

Lurano, one of the important early writers of *frottole* and other secular songs, apparently came from Cremona. Not much is known about him. (He also appears as "Luprano.") He seems to have been in

Rome in the first decade of the sixteenth century, where we learn that he was the composer of Cesare Borgia's favorite °song. From at least 1512 to 1515, however, he was cathedral choirmaster in Cividale, in the foothills of the eastern Alps, and from 1519 to 1520 he occupied the same post in the cathedral at Aquileia, near the north end of the Gulf of Venice. Besides songs, he wrote a few small religious pieces.

[103] MILLÁN, Francisco (Mē-yàn', Fràn-thēs'-kō)
SINGER
BORN: c. 1475 (?)
DIED: ?

Francisco Millán should not be confused with the somewhat later (and not quite as obscure) Luys de Milán **[151].** We know only that Francisco sang in Queen Isabella's chapel around the turn of the century and was a popular composer of *villancicos,* of which *Durandarte* was a particular favorite. Oddly enough Milán wrote a song of the same name.

[104] VERDELOT, Philippe (Vâr-də-lō', Fē-lēp')
SINGER, CHOIRMASTER
BORN: c. 1475
DIED: c. 1530 (?)

It is now generally agreed by scholars that Verdelot, a northerner, invented the Italian madrigal of the High Renaissance (which has little or nothing to do with the earlier madrigal form). Though his connection with various historical events can be deduced from some of his compositions, little factual material about the composer is at hand. It is assumed that he was born at a crossroads called Verdelot, a little east of Paris. He probably went to Italy in the first years of the new century and spent perhaps a decade or more before migrating to Florence, where he served as *maestro di cappella* at the cathedral from 1523 to 1527 and concurrently at the Baptistery until 1525. The end of his term coincides with the second expulsion of the Medici from Florence and the establishment of a short-lived republic (1527–30), of which he was apparently in favor. He disappears entirely after that period. His extant works include 2 Masses (one dubious), a *Magnificat,* nearly 60 motets, a few *chansons* (undoubtedly early), and more than 100 madrigals for four, five, and six voices. The chief characteristics of the madrigal at this juncture were its use of poetry in the Pe-

trarchan tradition (chiefly amatory and in various forms, some rather free) and of music tailored to the requirement of the text and usually giving no voice primacy over the others. Among the poets set by Verdelot were Petrarch himself, Aretino, and Machiavelli. Verdelot's first published madrigals appeared in Rome in 1530 in a collection *Madrigali di diversi musici,* but it is now known that he was writing such works at least four years earlier.

[105] BENDUSI, Francesco (Ben-dōō'-zē, Fràn-ches'-kō)
BORN: Siena, c. 1480 (?)
DIED: after 1553 (?)

Bendusi assembled a collection of instrumental four-part dance pieces published in 1553 as *Opera nova di ballo.* There is no evidence that Bendusi was still alive at that time. The appearance of a few of the tunes in the lute book of Joanambrosio Dalza **[107],** published in 1507–8, may argue for a birth date somewhere around that suggested above.

[106] BRUHIER, Antoine (Brü-hyā', Àn-twàn')
SINGER
BORN: c. 1480 (?)
DIED: after 1521

Though his name looks French, we know from contemporary documents that Bruhier did not speak that language. He was probably a Fleming. From 1513 he was a member of Pope Leo X's private choir and probably of the papal chapel, and seems to have attended the Bolognese meeting between the pope and François I in 1515. He drops out of sight after Leo's death in 1521. He left a *Mass* and a few short pieces, but the French *chansons* ascribed to him are not likely to be his.

[107] DALZA, Joanambrosio (Dàlt'-sà, Yō-àn-àm-brōz'-yō)
LUTENIST
BORN: c. 1480
DIED: after 1508

In 1507–8 the publisher and printer Ottaviano dei Petrucci brought out the first four printed lute books. The first two consisted largely of transcriptions; the third has vanished; the fourth, by Dalza, made up mostly of dances, is the first known collection of music specifically for the lute. Dalza also includes a few transcriptions and some warm-up exercises that he calls *ricercari*. The dances, we are told, should be played in sequences of three—*pavana, saltarella, piva*. All the Petrucci books are printed in a tablature quite different from the German kind. Of Dalza himself, nothing is known.

[108] GREFINGER, Wolfgang (Grā'-finger, Vôlf'-gàng)
PRIEST, ORGANIST
BORN: c. 1480
DIED: after 1515

No one knows for sure where Grefinger came from. He studied with Paul Hofhaimer [83], settled in Vienna, became a priest and organist at St. Stephen's Cathedral, and attended the university for a time. He apparently either left Vienna or died around 1515. Some think that he is to be identified with a Master Wolfgang who was court organist to King Lajos II of Hungary in 1525. He was editor of a collection of psalms. Most of his original sacred works have disappeared, but his songs were much admired and anthologized.

[109] GABRIEL the Musician
SINGER, POET
BORN: c. 1480 (?)
DIED: after 1530

If the *villancico* writer known as Gabriel the Musician was Gabriel (de) Mena, as seems likely, he sang in the chapel of King Ferdinand "the Catholic" (of Castile) in 1511. If, as seems likely, Gabriel Mena was also called "Gabriel de Texerana," he had sung there for more than a decade, and went on in 1516 to the chapel of Admiral Fadrique Enríquez. Later we discover that he is married and living near Valladolid.

[110] PASSEREAU, Pierre (Pàs-se-rō', Pē-âr')
SINGER
BORN: c. 1480 (?)
DIED: after 1547 (?)

The facts that we have about Passereau are very few. His name really was Passereau (Sparrow), he sang in the chapel of Francis I in 1509 when that future monarch was still the Duke of d'Angoulême, and Pierre Attaingnant [134] published some of his *chansons* in a volume that included others by Clément Janequin [116]. Before 1509, Passereau may have been in Paris; later he may have been at Cambrai. He is said to have

been a priest. If he was, he was a merry one. Apart from one motet, he left only Paris-style chansons (in a simple quasi-popular vein), most of them lighthearted and some frankly bawdy. The best known of them is *"Il est bel et bon"* ("He Is Fair and Good"), in which, over the onomatopoeic sounds of a henyard, two women discuss the unsuspecting cuckold husband of one of them.

[111] PONCE, Juan (Pôn'-sā, Hwàn)
SINGER
BORN: c. 1480
DIED: after 1521

Ponce was probably a relative of his namesake from León who discovered the fountain of rejuvenescence that attracted so many to Florida. He attended the University of Salamanca, sang in the choir of King Ferdinand "the Catholic" (of Castile) and perhaps in that of Ferdinand's successor, Charles V. His legacy consists of a *Salve regina* and 12 well-crafted songs.

[112] FLECHA, Mateo, the elder (Flā'-chà, Mà-tā'-ō)
SINGER, CHOIRMASTER
BORN: Prades, 1481
DIED: Poblet, 1553

Flecha's birthplace is usually given as being a village near Tarragona, south of Barcelona, but the sixth edition of *Grove* offers no qualifier, leaving the possibility that the more familiar Prades (now in southern France) is intended. Flecha is said to have studied in Barcelona. He served as singer and choirmaster at Lérida Cathedral from 1523 to 1525. He then took charge of the chapel of the Duke of Infantado; then, from 1534 to 1543, he occupied the analogous post in Valencia in the household of the Duke of Calabria. One of his choirboy-pupils there was his own nephew and namesake. Next he was named *maestro de capilla* to the Infantas María and Juana, the young daughters of Emperor Charles V. In 1548 Flecha retired to the Carmelite monastery at Poblet, where he died. His remaining works consist entirely of festal *villancicos* and *ensaladas*. (The latter—"salads" of the tossed, rather than the jellied, variety—are clever pastiches, of dramatic intent, made up of quotations from all sorts of music, sometimes with texts in several languages. The elder Flecha is said to have invented the form, and the younger published several of his uncle's, together with a few of his own. Cristóbal de

Morales [153] based a Mass on an *ensalada* by the former.)

[113] BUCHNER, Hans (Bōōkh'-ner, Hånts)
ORGANIST
BORN: Ravensburg, October 26, 1483
DIED: 1538

The son and namesake of a Ravensburg organist, Johann Buchner, better known as Hans, was a pupil of Paul Hofhaimer [83] and apparently deputized for him at the imperial court when Hofhaimer was absent. In 1506, on the recommendation of Emperor Maximilian I, he was appointed organist of Konstanz Cathedral and given tenure in that post six years later. Tenure, however, did not foresee the Lutheran upheaval, and the Catholic clergy was run out of town in 1526, closely followed by Buchner. He went to Meersburg, and then to Überlingen, and then, it is said, to Zürich to live with his daughter, one of six children. His wife died in 1534, and his last years were spent in poverty. His magnum opus is his *Fundamentum,* a theoretical textbook, a work on the theory and practice of organ music, including a considerable number of liturgical pieces for the instrument intended to illustrate the text. He also left a few other organ pieces and songs.

[114] JACQUET de Mantoue (Zhà-kā' də Mån-tōō')
SINGER, CHOIRMASTER
BORN: Vitré, 1483
DIED: Mantua, October 2, 1559

Many of this composer's works are credited in manuscripts simply to "Jachet" or "Giacchetto," creating both musical and biographical confusion with Jachet de (or van) Berchem, a Flemish musician active in Venice and Verona. But it is now clear that the Mantuan Jacquet was Jacques Collebaud or Colebault, born in Brittany near Rennes. Nothing is known of Jacquet's youth, training, or emigration to Italy. By 1520 he was a singer in the employ of a noble family in Modena. Five years later he was at the Ferrara court. A year or two afterward he went to Mantua, where his first wife died in 1527. He sang in the cathedral choir, became a citizen in 1534, and that same year, under the patronage of the bishop, Cardinal Ercole Gonzaga, took charge of the choir and the bishop's private chapel. He remarried at some time shortly afterward and had a daughter. His employer came to their rescue

when Jacquet died penniless. He was an immensely successful composer of sacred music, including a number of parody Masses, and was regarded as a master of polyphonic imitative style.

[115] ASTON, Hugh
TEACHER
BORN: c. 1485
DIED: November 1558

There is considerable historical confusion about the several Hugh Astons scattered about England at the turn of the sixteenth century. The most likely of them to have composed the music ascribed to "Hugh Aston" took a bachelor's degree in music from Oxford in 1510. He may have been somehow attached to the court of Henry VIII for the next decade and a half, after which he became master of the boys at St. Mary Newarke Hospital in the city of Leicester, having been beaten for the post at Cardinal College (now Christ Church), Oxford, by John Taverner [128]. When the institution was dissolved after Henry's espousal of Protestantism, Aston was pensioned off. He left two Masses and other liturgical pieces, but deserves particular note for a *Hornpipe,* perhaps the earliest piece of English music specifically for keyboard. A couple of other keyboard pieces have been ascribed to him.

[116] JANEQUIN, Clément (Zhàn-ka*n'*, Klā-mà*n'*)
CLERIC, CHOIRMASTER
BORN: Châtellerault, c. 1485
DIED: Paris, 1558

Janequin (or Jannequin) one of the most imaginative composers of *chansons* in his time, has been over the years accorded about as much speculative and fictional biography as one could ask for. He is said to have been born as early as 1470, to have studied with Josquin des Prez [71], to have been a retainer of Loys de Ronsard (butler of Francis I and father of the poet Pierre de Ronsard), a witness at (and perhaps participant in) the battles of Marignano and Pavia, and a servant to the Cardinal of Lorraine, Jean de Guise. Nothing is known of his training. From around the turn of the century until 1529 he was in Bordeaux, at first in the household of Lancelot de Fau, a prominent scholar, politician, and churchman. When Fau died as bishop of the diocese in 1523, Janequin worked for his successor, Jean de Foix. He was apparently ordained about that time and soon held several local canonries and curacies. These were, however, all vacated on the bishop's death in 1529. After a short term as master of the boys at Auch Cathedral, Janequin settled in Angers early in the 1530s, where he already held some livings. He obtained at least one curacy in an Angers church and was for three years (1534–37) choirmaster of the cathedral. He is said to have been a member of a sort of club in Angers centered on the poet Clément Marot, creator of the popular poetic device known as the *blazon* (which catalogues the beloved's physical points of interest), and later translator of the Psalms into French verse. In 1545 Janequin became curate of Unverre near Chartres, but had to use the entire income to help clear up a large debt to his nephew. In 1548 we find him (now in his sixties) listed as a student at the University of Angers; a year later he has apparently transferred to the University of Paris. He remained in Paris, becoming a member of the Chapel Royal, and was the first to be given the official title of Composer to the King. There seems to be no foundation for the story that he died in want and neglect (his will is extant) or that he turned Protestant in his last years.

The latter notion derived from the publication in 1549 and 1559 of two volumes of Janequin psalms to French texts, based on tunes from the Huguenot psalter. But these probably betoken nothing more than an interest in the trends of the times, which argument seems to be supported by the acceptance of their dedication to her by Queen Catherine de' Medici, the bane of French Protestantism. Besides these religious works, Janequin also produced a book of motets, a setting in the vernacular of Proverbs, some *chansons spirituelles,* and 2 parody Masses based on *chansons* of his own. But his chief fame resides—and justly—in his more than 250 *chansons.* He is regarded as joint father with Claudin de Sermisy [127] of the popular-style "Paris" *chanson.* With Janequin, the keynote is wit rather than feeling. His texts cover a considerable range of subject matter and are often by ranking poets (Marot, Ronsard, King Francis himself), but mostly they are in some degree amatory and often ribald. Though he was thoroughly conversant with the musical techniques of his time, he is particularly attentive to words and verbal rhythms. His most famous *chansons* are a series of rather large-scale pieces devoted to scene painting, sometimes by means more onomatopoeic than strictly musical. One of the best-known, *"La Guerre"* ("The War"), has been assumed to depict the French victory at Marignano—battle cries, drum rolls, charging cavalry, and the curses of the defeated Swiss. There were many instrumental transcriptions (the last wish of one of the court ladies was to hear one such), and Philippe Verdelot [104] wrote an extra voice part for the original, which is said to have pleased Janequin very much. Another famous *chanson, "La chant des oyseaux"* ("The Song of the Birds") must delight French composer Olivier Messiaen [2129].

Janequin is intimately connected with the birth of music publishing in France. One of Pierre Attaingnant's [134] pioneer efforts was a 1529 volume of Janequin *chansons,* which he followed with 1½ others (part of the second volume was given over to someone else), and Janequin was later taken up by other early publishers such as Jacques Moderne of Lyon, known in the trade as Grand Jacques, "Fat Jim."

RECORDINGS: There have been numerous recordings of works by Janequin over the years, but relatively few of these remain readily available domestically.

[117] **KOTTER, Hans** (Kot'-ter, Hånts)
ORGANIST, TEACHER
BORN: Strassburg, c. 1485
DIED: Berne, 1541

From his early teens Kotter studied with Paul Hofhaimer [83], then served as his assistant and deputy in the Saxon court at Torgau. His career from 1508 to 1514, when he became organist of the church of St. Nikolaus in Fribourg, Switzerland, is obscure. In Fribourg he was taken with the teachings of the Swiss religious reformer Huldreich Zwingli, with the result that in 1530 he was denounced as a heretic, jailed, tortured, and kicked out. He went home to Strassburg, then to Basel (where he had friends), and finally settled in Berne as a schoolteacher in the middle 1530s. He went to Konstanz in 1538 to take a better teaching post, but it fell through, and he returned to Berne. Whether his students welcomed Kotter back is not recorded. He left an autograph manuscript of sixty-seven organ pieces, most of them arrangements, written in an unusual six-line tablature. It once belonged to the Basel humanist Bonifacius Amerbach and was probably compiled for him. Other such pieces are also extant.

[118] **RESINARIUS, Balthasar** (Re-zē-nä'-rē-ōōs, Bàl'-tà-zär)
SINGER, PRIEST, CLERGYMAN
BORN: Tetschen, c. 1485
DIED: Böhmisch-Leipa, April 12, 1544

This composer's real name was Harzer, *Harz* being the German term for resin. (The publisher Georg Rhaw, oddly, brought out his music variously under both names.) Some sources hesitantly give his birthplace as Jessen, a town about halfway between Leipzig and Berlin, but it was undoubtedly Tetschen in Bohemia (now Děčín, on the northwest Czech border). Resinarius served for a time in the imperial chapel of Maximilian I, where he probably studied under Heinrich Isaac [78]. In 1515, under the name of Balthazar Harczer, he enrolled at the University of Leipzig, presumably to study theology. At any rate, he went back home as a priest, where, in 1523, he got into a dispute with a wandering Lutheran minister that the combatants eventually had to call in King Louis of Bohemia (and Hungary) and Martin Luther himself. Whether the encounter sowed doubt in Harzer's heart we don't know, but eleven years later he was functioning himself as a Lutheran pastor in Böhmisch-Leipa (now Česka Lípa), where he is said to have been made bishop a year before he died. His music (religious works on both sides of the fence) was praised by musical pundits in his time, but in retrospect appears devout, solid, and a bit old-fashioned for its time.

[119] **STOLTZER, Thomas** (Shtōlt'-zer, Tō'-màs)
PRIEST, CHOIRMASTER
BORN: Schweidnitz, c. 1485
DIED: Moravia, March 1526

Stoltzer's Silesian birthplace is now the Polish town of Świdnica. Nothing is known of his youth, though he may have studied with Heinrich Finck [74], whose music he was given to quoting. As a composer, he seems to have been a late bloomer, though as early as 1518 a writer named Joachim Vadian was commenting on his extraordinary ability to transcribe or perform almost any piece of music after only one or two hearings. A year later he held a living at a church in Breslau (now Wroclaw) and was listed at that city's cathedral as a *vicarius discontinuus,* an office less insubstantial than it sounds (i.e., he was a nonresident). In 1522, Louis II of Hungary (and Bohemia)—six months after he took the throne, five after he married Mary of Austria—appointed Stoltzer master of the Royal Chapel in Ofen. Queen Mary commissioned him to set four psalms in Martin Luther's German translation, the first such works known. In 1524 he sent one to Albert of Prussia by way of apology for having been unable to take the *Kapellmeisterschaft* in his

court, conditions at Ofen having been made irresistible. (Stoltzer had Protestant leanings but was apparently afraid to follow them up.) Unhappily, two years later he came, quite literally, to the end of the road: on a journey to Prague, he lost his footing and drowned in a Carpathian torrent. (For centuries the legend persisted that he died five months later at his king's side at Mohacs Field, where the Hungarians were routed by the Turks, leaving the door open for the Hapsburg takeover.)

Stoltzer was one of the most important German composers of his day—a man fully conversant with both the German and Flemish schools. His later pieces show a humanist's concern for textual meanings, and he was obviously enchanted with discovering the expressive possibilities of the vernacular, though the bulk of his religious music is in Latin. He also wrote Masses, Magnificats, a cycle of introits for the church year, hymns, and *Lieder*—both secular and sacred. An interesting set of interlinked *Melodies in the Eight Church Modes* seems to look ahead to variation technique. Much of Stoltzer's output was published after his death by such as Georg Rhaw and Johannes Ott.

RECORDINGS: At least two LP records have been devoted to his music.

[120] **SENFL, Ludwig** (Zen'-fəl, Lōōd'-vikh)
CLERIC, SINGER, POET, EDITOR
BORN: c. 1486
DIED: Munich, c. 1543

Despite German claims to Senfl (known as *Der Schweizer),* he was the son of Bernhart Senfli of Fribourg (not Freiburg im Breisgau), was probably born in Basel, and almost certainly grew up in Zürich. He was taken into the chapel of Emperor Maximilian I in 1496 as a treble, where the *Kapellmeister* from 1498 was Georg Slatkonia, later first Bishop of Vienna. However, his chief teacher was Heinrich Isaac [78]; between the two there seems to have been great mutual admiration. Except for a couple of interruptions, Senfl remained a member of the emperor's musical establishment until Maximilian's death in 1519, having succeeded Isaac as court composer in 1513. (Hans Burgkmair's *Triumph of Maximilian* depicts him—a dumpy man with a Dutch boy haircut and a laurel wreath—side by side with Slatkonia.) In 1508–9, after the 1507 Reichstag, Senfl remained in Konstanz with Isaac as his copyist for the *Choralis constantinus* (a work that Senfl completed later, after Isaac's death). After that the two apparently went to Italy together. In 1510, the year the emperor bestowed a Veronese farm on Isaac, he granted Senfl a benefice in the same area. (Senfl had apparently taken orders in some degree earlier.) The year before Maximilian's death, according to a letter of Paul Hofhaimer [83], Senfl dropped a loaded gun that went off and blew a toe off, incapacitating him for some time. From 1520, when the chapel was disbanded by Charles V, who had his own musicians (mostly Spanish), until 1523, Senfl was unemployed, and his imperial pension was cut from 150 gulden annually to only 50. He lived in Augsburg for some months, hoping to be called to the imperial court or the Austrian, and whiled away the time putting together a book of motets, *Liber selectarum cantionum,* the first such work published in Germany. Then he traveled for a time, producing music for royal weddings and such on what might be called a freelance basis. One such offering or commission eventually led to an appointment at the Bavarian court of William IV. Though Senfl was not given the title of *Kapellmeister,* his chief initial function seems to have been to bring the chapel up to international standards, which he did. He remained in this post, which seems to have been analogous to the one he had held in Vienna, until the end of his life, devoting himself to composition and a great deal of editing. Whether he converted to Protestantism is questionable, but he was a friend of Martin Luther and one of his patrons was the Lutheran prince, Albert of Prussia, and he married an affluent bourgeoise from Passau in 1529. Old age or bad health seems to have stilled his pen by 1540. The precise date of his death is uncertain.

Isaac's faith in his pupil was not misplaced. Senfl was greatly admired in his day, according to a deal of written testimony, and modern investigation has proved him one of the most fertile and prolific composers of his time. At least five collections of his music were printed in the era, and there are now extant 7 Masses, about 250 other religious works, and another 250 or so *Lieder,* odes, and other secular songs. It is in this last field that Senfl is most himself, and indeed he may be said to represent the high-water mark of the German Renaissance *Lied.* Here his output runs from settings of Horace and Virgil to folksy ditties, many to naughty or downright bawdy texts.

RECORDINGS: Several LP's have been given over to Senfl's music, and he is well represented in recorded anthologies.

[121] SICHER, Fridolin (Zēkh'-er, Frē'-dō-lin)
ORGANIST, SCRIBE
BORN: Bischofszell, March 6, 1490
DIED: Bischofszell, June 13, 1546

Early in the 1500s young Fridolin Sicher was a pupil of the Konstanz organist Martin Vogelmaier. After studying theology he returned to Bischofszell, where in 1510 he became organist at, and canon of, St. Agnes Church. He left after two years and went back to Konstanz, where he had further lessons with Hans Buchner [113] before becoming organist of the collegiate church in St. Gall in 1516. He remained there for fifteen years, then was run out by the Zwinglian uprising and found refuge as organist at Ensisheim in Alsace. In 1537 he was restored to his old position in Bischofszell, where he died after an operation. He left a large organ tablature of some 176 pieces, mostly arrangements of liturgical works.

[122] CAVAZZONI, Marco Antonio (Kà-vàd-zō'-nē, Mär'-kō Àn-tōn'-yō)
ORGANIST, HARPSICHORDIST, SINGER
BORN: Bologna, c. 1490
DIED: Venice, c. 1560

The prevalence of musicians named Marco Antonio in northeast Italy in the first half of the sixteenth century makes keeping track of Cavazzoni difficult, and the difficulty is compounded by his own proclivity to move about a great deal. Though he was often called Marc'Antonio da Urbino, he came from an upper-class Bolognese family. He seems to have spent the early years of his maturity at the Urbinate court of Francescomaria della Rovere and Eleanora Gonzaga. After 1517 he lived in Venice for a time, but was in Rome in 1520–21 as keyboardist to Pope Leo X. About four years later he was in Padua in the household of Cardinal Pietro Bembo, a longtime habitué of the Urbino court. He was soon back in Venice, however, teaching, and perhaps singing at St. Mark's. (He identifies himself in his will, drawn up thirty years later, as a member of the choir there, but there were two Marc'Antonios so employed for many years, and it is impossible to tell which is meant in the relevant documents.) Cavazzoni spent a year as organist in Chioggia Cathedral, a short way down the coast. Perhaps the environment of mudflats and fisherfolk did not suit him, or perhaps he was invited back to Rome by Paul III. If he was, it didn't work out, and he returned to Venice. He certainly spent his last fifteen years at St. Mark's under the direction of Adrian Willaert [129].

In 1523, Cavazzoni published a book of organ pieces, *Recercari, motetti, canzoni.* (It was called "Vol. I," but no sequel is known.) The motets and songs may be transcriptions, but it is interesting that no originals are known. The *ricercari*, however, are conceived in purely instrumental terms and are the first known keyboard examples.

[123] FESTA, Costanzo (Fä'-stà, Kō-stánt'-zō)
SINGER, TEACHER
BORN: c. 1490
DIED: Rome, April 10, 1545

Festa's first quarter century must be pieced together from hints and circumstantial evidence. Tradition has it that he was born into a propertied Turinese family of a place called Villafranca Sabaudo, but the appellation *Florentinus Italus* probably comes nearer to the truth. In and after 1510 he was a member of the household of the Duchess of Francavilla (see Villafranca above) on the Neapolitan isle of Ischia, as music tutor to her nephews. At some time within the next five years, he was probably a member of the Chapel Royal in France. In 1517, however, he joined the papal choir, where he, as a native Italian, must have felt lonely among all those foreigners. Nevertheless he served there under four popes: Leo X, Adrian VI, Clement VII, and Paul III. He may have been in bad health during his last years, since he was not among those who accompanied the papal party on its junket to Nice in 1538 and to Bologna five years later. On his death, his confreres gave him what amounted to a state funeral.

Expectably, Festa was a composer of religious music, and his output—4 Masses, some Mass movements, Magnificats, lamentations, hymns, and more than 60 motets— is of extremely high quality. In it he skillfully combines Italian traits with those of the Franco-Flemish school and is sometimes regarded as a forerunner of Palestrina [201], who was a Roman choirboy in Festa's later years. Festa is perhaps best known as an early composer of the new madrigal. He was once credited with having invented the form, but that honor has since been given to Philippe Verdelot [104], though the first published collection of madrigals (of 1530) contains works by both. Festa left nearly a hundred for three, four, and five voices. A recording of his funeral motet for the French queen, Anne of Brittany, *Quis dabit oculos nostros (Would That Our Eyes Were Founts*

of Tears), is improperly ascribed (as a version of it has long been) to Ludwig Senfl [120].

[124] LE BEL, Jacotin (Lə Bel, Zhà-kō-tan')
SINGER
BORN: Picardy, c. 1490
DIED: after 1556 (?)

The otherwise unidentified "Jacotin" (Jimmy) was a composer of *chansons* and shorter religious works in the first half of the sixteenth century. There were several composers so familiarly called, but this one seems to have been the man named above, who sang in the papal choir under Leo X and (probably) in the Royal chapel of France under Francis I and Henry II from 1532 to 1555. He was a brilliant writer of popular-style *chansons*, many of which were published by Pierre Attaingnant [134].

[125] REDFORD, John
SINGER, TEACHER, ORGANIST, WRITER
BORN: c. 1490 (?)
DIED: London, October 1547

John Redford was a member of the choir of old St. Paul's Cathedral in London in 1534, and was later appointed almoner and master of the boys. He wrote a morality, *Wyt and Science,* apparently for them to perform, as was the custom there at the time, and also left some poetry. Circumstantial evidence suggests that he served as organist. At any rate, 42 organ pieces for church use by Redford survive, mostly in the *Mulliner Book.* They may be the first extant works specifically for organ by an Englishman. RECORDINGS: A number of titles have been recorded by Hans Kann and Gian Lyman.

[126] SANDRIN (Pierre Regnault) (Sàn-dran')
SINGER, ACTOR, CHOIRMASTER
BORN: c. 1490
DIED: after 1561

"Sandrin" apparently took his professional name from that of a farcical shoemaker in a play in which he once acted. He allegedly came from a town near Paris called St. Marcel, but by the time he first appears on the stage of history he is nearly forty and a cleric in rural Picardy. After that he seems to have divided his time between France, where he sang in the Chapel Royal, and Italy, where he was choir director for Ippolito,

Cardinal d'Este. Curiously he left no sacred music, his reputation resting solely on his *chansons* and a single madrigal. His most famous song is *"Douce mémoire,"* on which Lassus [228] based a Mass and which is found in manuscripts as far afield as Poland.

[127] SERMISY, Claudin de (Sâr-mē-sē', Klō-dan' də)
CLERIC, SINGER, CHOIRMASTER
BORN: c. 1490
DIED: Paris, 1562

No one knows where Sermisy came from. His first name *(né* Claude) as yet undiminished, he first appears at the Ste. Chapelle in Paris as a churchman in 1508. Seven years later he was listed as having been one of the chapel singers of the late Louis XII. Except for a time in the 1520s, when he was apparently a canon in Rouen and afterward a parish priest in Cambron, he was a member of the Chapel Royal throughout the reign of Francis I and into that of Henry II. He must therefore have been at the meetings with Leo X in Bologna and with Henry VIII at the Field of the Cloth of Gold and at Boulogne, where the French singers and their music mightily impressed the foreign dignitaries. In or before 1532, Francis appointed Sermisy assistant *maître de chapelle.* Since the titular director was the king's friend, Cardinal François de Tournon, this meant that Sermisy, in effect, was in charge. He was paid 400 livres a year (a livre would buy a man meat for one month or wine for three) and had an annual expense account of 1300 livres. A year later, the king presented him with a nonresident canonry at the Ste. Chapelle, which included a residence and a considerable income. (Twenty-nine years later he was buried there.) When Henry II came to the throne, he dismissed Cardinal de Tournon from the choir, but Sermisy continued to run it in tandem with Louis Hérault. There is a suggestion that he retired to live on his benefices about 1554, but he may have stayed on until his death.

Sermisy enjoyed both great esteem and unusual popularity in his lifetime. His music was printed not only in France but also in Italy and the Netherlands. His songs were known as far afield as Poland and were frequently transcribed for the lute and for keyboard instruments. Some of them, such as *"D'où vient cela"* ("Whence Comes It"), were obviously major hits. Together with Janequin [116], Sermisy is regarded as one of the originators of the Paris *chanson.* His are perhaps more typical of the genre than Janequin's. He liked to work with contemporary verses (his favorite lyricist was Clément Marot), in rhymed stanzas of octosyllabic or decasyllabic lines. The settings, usually for four voices, are simple, chordal, and tuneful, following the texts closely, and pointing toward later song forms. They exhibit none of the rhetoric of the Franco-Flemish school or the "madrigalism" of the Italians, though Sermisy sometimes allows himself a bit of discreet contrapuntal decoration.

There is more Franco-Flemish influence in the church music, which includes 12 "parody" Masses (one a requiem), several Magnificats, lamentations, a *St. Matthew Passion,* and many motets. In some of these there is a tension between the old approach that ignores word meanings and the new expressive one. The Masses in particular tend toward the simplification that increasingly came to characterize the French Mass settings. The *St. Matthew Passion* exemplified Claudin's apparent taste for the darkly emotional.

[128] TAVERNER, John
CLERK, TEACHER, POLITICIAN
BORN: Lincolnshire, c. 1490
DIED: Boston, Lincolnshire, October 18, 1545

Until very recently the biography of John Taverner was the stuff of which historical romances are made. Torn from his ladylove to teach in Cardinal College (now Christ Church), Oxford, he was charged by Cardinal Wolsey, its patron, with Protestant heresy and (according to the martyrologist John Foxe) immured in a "deep cave under ground." Eventually the cardinal let him go on the grounds that musicians were too stupid to be dangerous. After Henry VIII broke with Rome, Taverner supposedly gave up writing "songes to popish ditties," embraced the new faith with passion, and went back to Lincolnshire to become a merciless agent for Thomas Cromwell in rooting out and getting rid of Catholics.

As such things usually turn out, fiction is here stranger than truth. The first date we have for Taverner is 1524, when he was a lay clerk in the choir of Tattershall Church in Lincolnshire. A year later he was invited to become master of the boys in Wolsey's newly founded college, but declined. There was a woman behind his decision, but his motive was dowry rather than affection. Apparently the union did not pan out, and he was installed at the college in time for the grand opening in 1526. Two years later two members of the choir were ousted for their change of faith, but Taverner seems at the time to have been sufficiently devout, in all apparent sincerity, to have shared no blame. But Wolsey's own downfall came in 1529, and in 1530 Taverner returned to his home territory to instruct the youth in the fine choir of St. Botolph's in Boston. He married a widow, apparently of some substance, named Rose Parrow, took over the rearing of her two daughters, and began to acquire property. When government funds to the choir were cut off in 1535, he left it and seemingly gave up church music altogether. He became a member of the board of the Boston parish church and at Cromwell's instigation had the rood screen destroyed as an idolatrous object. But that seems to have been the extent of his alleged depredations. In the year of his death he was named a town alderman.

Taverner was the first of the "Three T's" of pre-Elizabethan Tudor music, the others being Christopher Tye [158] and Thomas Tallis [157]. His music—most of it apparently from the Oxford years—is chiefly religious (Catholic and Protestant), though there are a handful of songs and a couple of instrumental pieces. It includes 8 Masses, some isolated movements, 3 Magnificats, and about 25 motets. (The Anglican works are adaptations.) Taverner does not merely summarize the tendencies of previous English church music; he also synthesizes them with some from across the Channel. Possessed of drive and imagination and near-limitless technical expertise, he brilliantly combines such things as imitation, canon, melismatic writing, and metrical clashes. Some of the later Masses show a turn away from the old methods toward something more transparent. The most famous of these is really a set of variations on the lovely anonymous song "Westron Wynd, When Wilt Thou Blow?," which tune was also used in Masses by Tye and John Sheppard, and the first popular song to become the basis of an English Mass. The *Missa Gloria tibi Trinitas* is also of historical interest: the section *"In nomine Domini"* became detached in an instrumental arrangement for four instruments and spawned a whole line of instrumental *"In nomines"* based on its *cantus*. Indeed it has been suggested that the tradition of English consort music (music for ensembles of instruments—particularly viols) stems from this and Taverner's six-part *Quemadmodum*.

Peter Maxwell Davies [2411] has written an opera *Taverner*, premiered in 1972, based on Taverner's life and music. Another contemporary English composer, John Tavener [2432], believes he is a descendant.

RECORDINGS: Sadly, the only major Taverner work recorded at this writing is the *Westron Wynd Mass.*

[129] WILLAERT, Adrian (Vil-lârt', Ã'-drē-àn)
CHOIRMASTER, TEACHER
BORN: c. 1490
DIED: Venice, December 17, 1562

It has been argued that Willaert was a native of the (Belgian) town of Roeselare/Roulers, but he is more likely to have been from Bruges, where his father, Denys, and his brother, Anton, were connected with the church of St. Donatien. After having acquired a solid humanistic education somewhere, he is said to have been packed off to Paris to study law. He had acquired at least a nodding acquaintance with it but was seduced by music to give it up and study with Jean Mouton [84], though inevitably there were those who called him a pupil of Josquin des Prez [71]. By 1515 he was in Rome, though why he was there is uncertain. His pupil Gioseffo Zarlino [186] says that Willaert went one day to hear the papal choir sing a motet by Josquin, and was stunned to hear his own *Verbum bonum et soave (Word Good and Sweet).* When he pointed out the error, the choir hurriedly dropped the piece from its repertory. At any rate, while in Rome Willaert was taken into the chapel of Cardinal Ippolito I d'Este, brother of Alfonso, Duke of Ferrara. He went to Ferrara with his master but after two years left with him for Hungary, where Ippolito had been appointed Bishop of Esztergom (about thirty miles northwest of Budapest). Willaert may have received an honorary title of official composer to the Hungarian king, but he was apparently not resident at the Ofen (Buda) court. He went back to Ferrara in 1519, and when Ippolito died the following year, Willaert went into Alfonso's service. In 1525 he transferred to the chapel of the duke's son, Cardinal Ippolito II, Archbishop of Milan, though it is questionable whether Willaert ever lived in Milan himself.

In 1527 he entered the competition for the post of *maestro di cappella* of St. Mark's in Venice, a position that had been vacated in 1525, when illness and senility forced the retirement of the intendant, one Pietro de Fossis. Doge Andrea Gritti, who had traveled in France and had heard Franco-Flemish music, ruled in favor of Willaert over Pietro Lupato, a local boy who had been filling in meanwhile. Thus it was that on December 12, 1527, the most glorious century of Venetian music began. For thirty-five years, apart from trips back to the Netherlands in 1542 and 1556, "Messer Adriano," as he was known, guided the fortunes of what became, largely through his own efforts, one of the most magnificent musical establishments in Europe. He founded a music school attached to the church and taught many important musicians including Zarlino, Cipriano de Rore [184], and Girolamo Parabosco [199]. He regarded uniform training of his charges as indispensable, and those who took it lightly did not long survive as members of the chapel. Willaert was honored by musicians and patrons alike, and when he died he was able to leave his widow a fortune of 10,000 ducats, invested with the banking firm of Fugger in Augsburg.

Willaert is a watershed figure who sums up the Franco-Flemish era and heralds a new one, and this fact was widely recognized in his own day. He produced music in most of the then current forms—Masses, motets, psalms, hymns, *chansons,* madrigals, and *ricercari* (in this instance instrumental motets). His earlier music is clearly in the Franco-Flemish tradition—if not readily mistakable for that of Josquin des Prez [71], some of it might be taken for that of some of his followers. The Masses are "parodies," replete with canons, imitative devices, and the whole bag of polyphonic tricks. But in the motets (3½ volumes of which were published in Willaert's lifetime) there are some important novelties. First, undoubtedly inspired by St. Mark's two choir lofts and two organs, Willaert experimented with polychoral music. He did not invent the kind of early stereophony that this implies, but he points the way toward the Gabrielis—Andrea [180] and his nephew Giovanni [286]—and the Baroque. Secondly, his motets exhibit a growing concern with text (he could not ignore his humanist upbringing), manifested in a scrupulous attention to articulation, meaning, and aesthetic impact. This also applies to his madrigals, in which he goes some way toward "madrigalism," that manneristic concern for finding the right musical formula for every image that ultimately turned trite and wore out its welcome. Some have argued that Willaert foreshadows the expressiveness of Claudio Monteverdi [333]. Finally one might note the voice-and-lute transcriptions that Willaert made of madrigals by Philippe Verdelot [104] and that seem to look ahead to the French *air de cour* and the English ayre.

[130] **HENRY VIII, King of England**
POLYMATH
BORN: Greenwich, June 28, 1491
DIED: London, January 28, 1547

It would not be pertinent to discuss here the lineage of this great-grandson of a bibulous Welsh flunky who lived sinfully with Henry V's French widow and begat five children on her before being chased away by the authorities. No reader now (thanks to the magic of television) needs to be told that Prince Henry was a handsome, lusty, magnetic, arrogant, and gifted young man who died a bloated syphilitic at fifty-five. News about his six wives is hardly germane to our purpose, though we might note that the lament "O Death, Rock Me Asleep" has been rather timidly assigned to the second queen, six-fingered Anne Boleyn, supposedly written in the Tower as she waited for the ax to fall. Any discussion of Henry's posturings and blusterings to prove himself the royal equal of Francis I of France, or his little half-island kingdom as important as the holdings of the Holy Roman Emperor, Charles V, might appear digressive. Nor can one argue as relevant the account that he went from being Catholicism's Defender of the Faith to a breakaway Anglican pope, bathed his country in blood and turmoil, and, in the sack of the English abbeys and their libraries, destroyed important parts of its cultural heritage.

No, our concern here is with Henry as composer—carrying on the tradition, as it were, of his step-ancestor Henry V, assuming him to have been the "Roy Henry" of the Old Hall Manuscript (see 46). Because Henry's brother, the ill-fated Arthur, stood to inherit the throne, Henry himself was slated for the Church and was given a suitable education, which included music, though no teacher of that subject is remembered in the records. He evidently had a modest talent, as well as a vast enthusiasm for the subject. To his credit, unlike most of his successors he actively fostered music and had an impressive court establishment of his own. As for his own compositions, they make one think of Dr. Johnson's biped dog: the wonder is not that they were done well, but that they were done at all (though if Henry had written popular songs in the latter twentieth century, he would have been hailed, no doubt, as a genius). Two Masses, probably from his student days, are lost. There remain a motet, 13 instrumental pieces, and 20 songs. Two of the last, *"Pastyme with Good Companye"* and *"Green Growth the Holly",* are expectably bluff and quite hardy, if not of certain authorship. Henry's contributions to some of the others range from small to imperceptible.

RECORDINGS: Most of the secular music has been recorded on an LP by the St. George Singers.

[131] GANASSI, Sylvestro di (Gä-näs'-sē, Sil-väs'-trō dē)
INSTRUMENTALIST
BORN: Fontego, 1492
DIED: Venice, after 1543

All we know of Ganassi himself is that he was born on Venetian soil and worked, at least in his later years, as an official musician to the Most Serene Republic itself. In 1535 he brought out a book called *Fontegara*, which set forth just about anything one could wish to know about the recorder and how to play it, and which provided copious examples of what one could make it do. During 1542–43 he produced an even more comprehensive method for the viola da gamba, in two volumes, *Regola rubertina* and *Lettione seconda*. All three appear to be firsts, and all three are in Venetian dialect; the viol books are also in lute tablature. The *ricercari* for viola da gamba include some double-stopping and may be the first works written for a solo stringed instrument. Ganassi's works are gold mines of information on Renaissance musical practice.

[132] LAYOLLE, François de (Lä-yōl', Frän-swä' də)
ORGANIST, EDITOR, TEACHER
BORN: Florence, March 4, 1492
DIED: Lyons, c. 1540

Born Francesco dell'Aiole, Layolle was a chorister and organ student at the Church of the Santissima Annunziata, where Andrea del Sarto depicted him in one of his frescoes. He became well known as an organist, married the sister of his teacher's wife, and himself taught others, including Benvenuto Cellini, who mentions him in his autobiography. He had friends among the anti-Medici faction, but had moved to Lyons before the abortive Florentine revolt of 1521, where he provided a haven for some of its perpetrators. His son Alamanno, later to return to Florence, where he played the organ, taught, and composed, was born soon after Francesco's arrival in Lyons. The elder Layolle became organist of the church of Notre-Dame de Confort and, as he had in Florence, became an important figure in artistic and intellectual circles. After doing some freelance editing and anthologizing, he went into partnership with the publisher Jacques Moderne [152]. Layolle was a highly skillful composer of both sacred and secular works. Of the first he wrote Masses, psalms, and motets (many of the last now lost) that combine Flemish and Italian techniques. His ex-tant secular works are chiefly contained in two books of madrigals.

[133] SACHS, Hans (Zåkhs, Hånts)
SHOEMAKER, POET
BORN: Nuremberg, November 5, 1494
DIED: Nuremberg, January 19, 1576

Sachs was, it is generally agreed, the greatest of the *Meistersinger*. The mastersingers represent the last gasp of the troubadour tradition as filtered through the (long-dead) *Minnesinger* into the keeping of solid, earnest, successful urban tradesmen anxious to justify their rising social position with commensurate intellectual and artistic endeavor. The movement, allegedly begun in Mainz by Frauenlob [31], was brought to Nuremberg by Hans Folz, the sometime barber of Worms, who has a bit part in Wagner's opera *Die Meistersinger von Nürnberg*. The practice and ritual of the *Meistersinger* were almost as rulebound and bureaucratized as Wagner [1230] depicts them.

Hans Sachs was a tailor's son who eschewed the family profession and went over to the cobblers. He got a better-than-usual education in the Nuremberg Latin School, and no doubt a practical one in his peregrinations about Germany as a journeyman. He was a master shoemaker back home at twenty-three, and married for the first time two years later. Wagner's portrait of him in middle age as a kindly and humorous widower may not be far off the mark. He later married again, but his bride was not Eva Pogner, whom, if she existed, he probably never even dated. As poet and composer, he was nothing if not industrious. Nine years before he died, he reckoned that he had written 4,275 songs (some, as was customary, to readymade tunes), some 1,700 verse narratives (including the legend of Siegfried), and 208 plays—and the end was not then in sight. He made, we are told, some modifications in the stringent requirements of the *Meistersinger*, for whom rules transcended inspiration and even logic. And he helped make vernacular song a tool of the German Reformation. But he does not really escape the fact that *Meistergesang* was a hermetic art (if that noun really describes it), wherein lyrics and tunes were turned out by mechanical methods and the admonition to "make it new" overlooked this fact and the general irrelevance of what was being produced to the larger musical currents of the times.

RECORDINGS: There is, of course, a historical fascination here, and Deutsche Grammophon once devoted a whole LP side to Sachs's music, sung unaccompanied.

[134] ATTAINGNANT, Pierre (At-tīn'-yản, Pĕ-âr')
PRINTER, BOOKSELLER
BORN: c. 1494
DIED: Paris, 1552

Attaingnant's is a familiar sort of success story: he married the boss's daughter and inherited the firm. Born near Douai, he may have come to Paris as a music student. By the time he was twenty, however, he was working for the printer Philippe Pigouchet. By 1525 he was turning out religious and educational texts. He probably went into music publishing about two years later. This was facilitated by a new kind of movable type of his own invention. Previously music had been printed either from wood blocks on which a whole page was engraved, or by a clumsy double process in which first the staves and then the notes were printed. Attaingnant's breakthrough involved type heads that included the note(s) on a segment of staff. For a quarter of a century printed music—religious compositions, lute pieces, and especially *chansons* and dances—poured from his presses in a manner unprecedented. He evidently died around the time noted above, since his widow was running the operation by 1553.

It is highly questionable that Attaingnant himself ever composed or arranged a note (though he may have had at least choirboy training). What, then, is he doing in a dictionary of composers? Because, *faute de mieux,* he is usually listed as the author of the many anonymous dance pieces that he published (and it is not impossible that he was).

RECORDINGS: There are innumerable recordings of such works.

[135] BEAULIEU, Eustorg de (Bō-lyü', Ü'-stôrg də)
POET, PRIEST, PROTESTANT MINISTER, TEACHER, ORGANIST
BORN: Beaulieu-sur-Ménoire, c. 1495
DIED: Basel, January 8, 1552

This odd person used to be identified as "Hector Eustorg of Beaulieu" (a village about seventy miles southeast of Limoges), but it appears that "Hector" was merely his poetical persona. In his late twenties he played organ at Lectoure Cathedral, near Auch, then taught at Tulle, back in the Limousin, and was ordained. In 1534 he was in Lyons as a retainer of the governor, Pomponio Trivulzio (or Pompone Trivulce). There he became known as a poet, influenced by Clément Marot, and as a friend of some other important poets of the day. He converted to Protestantism, went to Switzerland in 1537, studied theology in Lausanne, and in 1540 became pastor of Thierrens and Moudon, two little towns north of Lausanne. There he tried marriage, but his wife did not like his sexual preferences and left him. A second attempt six months later also ended scandalously, and he left his pastorate. In 1548 he entered the University of Basel as a student and died in that city four years later. Beaulieu several times intimated that he had written or was going to write music, but only 3 songs have survived.

[136] KLEBER, Leonhard (Klā'-ber, Lā'-ōn-hart)
ORGANIST, TEACHER, SINGER
BORN: Göppingen, c. 1495
DIED: Pforzheim, March 4, 1556

A native of Württemberg (Wiesenstein also claims him), Kleber studied theology at Heidelberg from 1512 but left without a degree. After holding musical posts in southwest Germany (Horb and Esslingen), he settled down as organist and canon at Pforzheim. Though he never was associated with any major urban centers, he became widely known as an organ teacher. Shortly after coming to Pforzheim, he compiled a collection of 119 organ pieces, mostly transcriptions of music by his contemporaries, in the usual German tablature. The first part is for manuals only, the second for manuals and pedals, showing that he thought specifically in terms of the instrument.

[137] KUGELMANN, Hans (Koo'-gel-mản, Hȧnts)
TRUMPETER, CHOIRMASTER
BORN: Augsburg, 1495
DIED: Königsberg, Prussia, summer 1542

After five years as imperial court trumpeter in Innsbruck (1518–23), Kugelmann turned Protestant and went to the Königsberg court of Albert V and worked his way up to being first trumpeter and general music director of the chapel. At various times his brothers, Christoph, Melchior, and Paul, and his nephew, Barthel, also played trumpet in Königsberg. His compositional fame rests chiefly on his 1540 songbook, *Concentus novi,* described as "three-part songs for church and school" (one is actually in eight parts), of which most are of Kugelmann's own composition. One of these is the chorale *"Allein Gott in der Höh' sei Ehr"* ("To God Alone on High Be Honor"), based on a Gregorian tune. Next to that of Johann Walther

[139], this is the earliest printed Protestant hymnbook.

[138] RIBERA, Antonio de (Rē-ver'-à, Àn-tōn'-yō dä)
SINGER
BORN: c. 1495 (?)
DIED: after 1527

All that is known of Ribera, other than that he was Spanish, is that he sang in the papal choir from at least 1520 to 1527, the year Rome was invaded and sacked by the starving soldiers of Charles de Bourbon. He left 2 Masses, other religious works, a few Spanish songs (some of which exist in keyboard arrangements), and some of the music for *El Misterio de Elche*. This is a mystery play, performed annually in Elche, the manuscript of which, together with a statue of the Virgin, supposedly came there in an "ark" in either 1226 or 1370. The music now used is of more recent vintage. RECORDINGS: There is a complete recording in the Hispavox History of Spanish Music series.

[139] WALTHER, Johann (Vàl'-ter, Yō'-hàn)
SINGER, CHOIRMASTER, TEACHER, POET
BORN: Kahla, 1496
DIED: Torgau, March 25, 1570

According to Walther himself, his real name was Blankenmüller, and he was adopted as an orphan by a taverner of Kahla (near Jena, Thuringia) named Hans Walther. He entered the University of Leipzig in 1521 and the same year was signed on as a basso in the chapel of Frederick III "der Weise," Elector of Saxony, protector of Martin Luther, and in 1502 founder of the University of Wittenberg. In 1524 Walther published in Wittenberg his *Geystliches gesangk Buchleyn,* with a preface by Luther himself. It contained mostly four-part arrangements of Lutheran hymn tunes (some by Luther), including such familiar examples as *"In dulci Jubilo"* and *"Joseph, lieber Joseph mein."* The arrangements are in the style of the *Tenorlieder* of the day (with the melody in the tenor), and there is little in the way of decoration, they being intended for the edification and delectation of the young. The work is the first Protestant hymnbook, and the foursquare phrasing and what amounts to chordal harmonies foreshadow a whole era of German chorales. When the elector died in 1525, Luther urged the continuance of the electoral chapel, then at Torgau. Later that year Walther spent some time with him helping to work out the form of the new Mass for Lutheran worship. Walther then settled down in Torgau, where the following summer he married Anna Hesse. Their son and only child, Johann Jr. (1527–78), became a musician of sorts and left a few compositions. Walther Sr. continued to direct a choir, though it is not clear under whose auspices, served as teacher to the town choirboys, and in 1532 became a citizen. The grant of a house by the municipality in that year enabled him and his family to move out of the schoolhouse.

In 1547 Maurice (Moritz), of the Albertine branch of the Saxon line, won the electorate, with the connivance of Emperor Charles V, from the incumbent John Frederick ("the Magnanimous") and settled the government in Dresden. On the recommendation of Philipp Melanchthon, Luther's right-hand man, Walther became his *Kapellmeister* the next year and remained in the post until 1554, when he returned to Torgau on his pension. After the hymnbook, which went through many editions, Walther published a few other things, including a cycle of Magnificats and a book of hymns for miners, though by then Lutheranism was no longer an underground matter. In manuscript he left 2 Passions, some motets, and a set of instrumental "fugues" (really canons). His chief importance, however, was in his impact on the chorale tradition.

[140] CANOVA, da Milano, Francesco (Kà-nō'-và dà Mē-là'-nō, Fràn-chäs'-kō)
LUTENIST, GAMBIST, ORGANIST (?)
BORN: Monza, August 18, 1497
DIED: Monza, April 15, 1543

Canova was apparently called "da Milano" because he was a native of Monza (close enough, one supposes) and spent most of his life in Rome. He was also called *"Il Divino"* because of his lute playing (which he learned from Giovanni Testagrossa), and *"da Parigi"* because he went to Nice with Pope Paul III in 1538. In the late 1520s, probably fleeing the marauding French soldiers in Rome, he lived for a time in Piacenza and afterward may have been organist at Milan Cathedral for a short time. Otherwise he was in the service of three consecutive popes (Leo X, Clement VII, and Paul III) off and on, as well as in that of Cardinals Ippolito de'Medici (illegitimate son of Clement) and Alessandro Farnese (nephew of Pope Paul). The greatest lutenist of his time, and a teacher of other lutenists, he left a very large body of work. Besides the usual transcriptions of vocal pieces, he wrote many polyphonic compositions of real complexity, demanding virtuoso performance. He was the first to compose imitative *ricercari* for the lute (though he called them *fantasie)* and the first, apparently, to designate a piece as a *toccata.* He also wrote 2 lute duets. His works were published both in collections devoted to them and in anthologies.

[141] CONSEIL, Jean (Kôn-sä', Zhàn)
SINGER, CLERIC
BORN: Paris, 1498
DIED: Rome, 1535

Also known by his Latin name Consilium, Conseil was a boy singer in 1509. Four years later he went to Rome to join the papal choir of Leo X. Save for occasional visits to France and Florence, he apparently remained in the Vatican for the rest of his life. He was given charge of the chapel in 1526. He held several benefices in France. Conseil was much admired as a composer in his time. His surviving works consist entirely of *chansons* and motets in the new simplified Parisian style.

[142] SEGNI, Giulio (Sän'-yē, Jōōl'-yō)
ORGANIST, HARPSICHORDIST
BORN: Modena, 1498
DIED: Rome, July 23, 1561

Segni was also known as Julius (or Julio) de Modena and Il Biondino (The Little Blond). He studied in Modena with his uncle, Gaspare da Signa, with Vincenzo Lusignano, Antonio Collebaudo (alias Bidon d'Asti), and the organist Jacopo Fogliano. In 1513 he was a chorister of Modena Cathedral. Afterward he seems to have spent some time in Rome. His harpsichord playing at a papal political conference, probably held in 1530, is said to have stilled the confabulation, which seems to bespeak his considerable skill, not to say magic. Later that year, however, he was organist at the "old" organ of St. Mark's, Venice, under the leadership of Adrian Willaert **[129]**. During his two years in Venice, he became a friend of Titian and other prominent figures in the arts. After 1532 we lose sight of him until 1541, when he is back in Rome, now in the service of Cardinal Sforza, where he remained until he died. He was regarded as perhaps the outstanding Italian keyboard player of his time. He left a number of *ricercari*—one for keyboard, several for ensembles of unspecified instruments, and several more for lute (probably transcriptions of other ensemble works). All

are notable for the composer's mastery of imitative technique.

[143] BRUMEL, Jacques (Brü-mel', Zhàk)
ORGANIST
BORN: c. 1500 (?)
DIED: Ferrara, 1564

Brumel, or Brunel, had more than his share of aliases—e.g., Giaches Brumel, Jacomo Brunello or Brumello, Jaches Gallico, Jaches de Ferrara—so it is difficult to say whether he was the organist Jacques Brunel who was at Rouen Cathedral in 1524, or a relative of Antoine Brumel **[85]** (whose name may have been Jean Brunelle), court organist at Ferrara from 1505 to 1510. However, Jacques did hold the same post there from 1532 until his death. Account books show that for several years during that period he also had charge of the ducal chapels in Reggio Emilia and Modena, for visiting which he was provided a horse and its upkeep. He seems to have been greatly admired as a performer. He left a Mass, 3 *ricercari* for organ, and a son named Virginio, who carried on the family trade. RECORDINGS: The *Mass* has been recorded.

[144] COCLICO, Adrien Petit (Kō'-klē-kō, Á'-drē-àn Pə-tē')
THEORIST
BORN: Flanders, 1500
DIED: Copenhagen, 1562

Coclico is an odd figure in every sense. An engraved portrait shows him as a dwarfish little fellow (hence "Petit"?) with a great beard hanging about his knees. He said he was Flemish, though his surname sounds like a cockcrow in one of the lesser Romance tongues. In his theoretical work *Compendium musices* he paints a lovely picture of his teacher, Josquin des Prez **[71]**, at work, but there is nothing to support his claim of apprenticeship. (Did Josquin teach anyone?) Indeed, Coclico takes a Münchausenesque approach to autobiography: he says, for example, that he was the pope's *maestro di cappella* (though no records show him as even a member of the papal choir) and that he was once "Bishop of Ducatum" (wherever that may be). Reared a Catholic, he converted to Protestantism in middle life, may have been imprisoned for a while as a heretic, and either jumped or was pushed into Germany, where in 1545 he enrolled at the University of Wittenberg, giving us the first irrefutable datum in his career. He gave music lessons but was turned down for the professorship of music. In 1546 he married, but his bride soon walked out on him. The following year, after stopovers at Frankfurt an der Oder and Stettin, he entered the University of Königsberg. Albert of Prussia, a compulsive collector of Protestant musicians, hired him for his chapel. But he soon quarreled with the Lutheran authorities, and when his housekeeper bore him a child, he had to leave town, even though his princely employer backed him in both matters. He went to Nuremberg and moved in with a Fleming called Johann vom Berg, who owned half of the publishing house of Montanus and Neuber. Coclico persuaded the city fathers to set him up in a school and to finance the publication by Montanus and Neuber of the *Compendium* and a collection of his motets. Apparently the school, which specialized in music and modern foreign languages, was not a success, for the subsidy was soon withdrawn. It is not clear when Coclico left Nuremberg, but in 1555 he became master of the boys in the *Kapelle* of Duke John Albert I of Mecklenburg at Wismar, a Baltic port city. There he found a new ladylove, whom the death of his wife at last enabled him to marry. He is said to have gone to London at some point during this period, but evidence is against it. In 1556 he joined the Royal Chapel in Copenhagen and succumbed to the plague there six years later. His motets bear the subtitle *musica reservata,* a rare and little understood Renaissance term. He claims that it refers to an earlier musical practice that he is there reviving, but one suspects it represents more humbug, since the works evidence nothing of the sort and display no great talent.

[145] CRECQUILLON, Thomas (Krā-kē-yôn', Tō-màs')
CLERIC
BORN: c. 1500 (?)
DIED: 1557

On no very good evidence, it has been guessed that Crecquillon was born in Ghent, perhaps a few years earlier than the date given above. Of the few facts we possess about his life, the most important is that he was a member of the chapel of Emperor Charles V from at least 1540. He seems to have been in charge of it at that time; however, he may have stepped down around 1550. Other than that, we know that at various times he held benefices, canonries, etc., in such northern towns as Béthune, Louvain, Namur, and Termonde. He is said to have died of the plague, a lot of which was

going around at the time, probably at Béthune, where he went after Charles's abdication. He left a dozen Masses, more than a hundred motets, and almost two hundred *chansons.* One of the more admired and talented composers of his time, he is representative of the Franco-Flemish school near its final flowering. His *chansons* were immensely popular and were frequently arranged for lute, vihuela, and keyboard, and as solo songs, but his religious music reflects his best work. Some modern writers see in him a tendency to try to underline verbal meanings, but others—perhaps a majority— find him almost as abstract and "pure" as Palestrina [**201**]. It is perhaps significant that Claudio Monteverdi [**333**] lists him as representative of the "first practice"—that sort of composition in which music takes precedence over text. RECORDINGS: An LP performed by the Ensemble Per Cantar e Sonar and the Stéphane Caillat Chorale has been devoted to his shorter works.

[146] GERLE, Hans (Gâr'-lə, Hànts)
LUTENIST, LUTEMAKER
BORN: Nuremberg, c. 1500
DIED: Nuremberg, 1570

There were in the sixteenth century a number of lutemaking Gerles (all boys) in Germany and Austria. Though their interrelationships have not been determined, it is probable that Hans was the son of Conrad Gerle, a Nuremberg *luthier* who died in 1521, and that he sired another Hans who carried on the tradition. He published three collections of lute music, of which the first, *Musica teusch (German Music)* is the most interesting in that it includes music for string ensembles and some helpful hints on playing the violin, viola da gamba, and lute. It sticks mostly to arrangements of pieces by German composers; the two other books, also made up of arrangements, wander farther afield.

[147] GINTZLER, Simon (Gints'-ler, Sē'-mon)
LUTENIST
BORN: c. 1500
DIED: 1547 or later

All that is known of Gintzler's life is that he was lutenist to Cardinal Madruzzo, Bishop of Trent and host to the famous council—as those who know the 1917 opera *Palestrina,* by Hans Pfitzner [**1606**], will recall. As a member of the cardinal's retinue, he would have traveled widely in Europe. In 1547 he brought out a lute book in Italian tablature containing song transcriptions and 6 *ricercari* of his own composition.

[148] GOMBERT, Nicolas (Gôm-bâr′, Nē-kō-làs′)
CLERIC, SINGER
BORN: c. 1500
DIED: c. 1560

Although he was regarded in his time as the equal of Adrian Willaert **[129]** and Clemens non Papa **[166]**, Gombert left few traces, except for his music. It has been suggested that he was born in southern Flanders, since Gomberts were common there; his birthdate may have been earlier or later than that given above. Supposedly he was (as who was not?) a pupil of Josquin des Prez **[71]**, for whom he wrote a memorial piece. From 1526 he sang and traveled with the chapel of Emperor Charles V, who awarded him various livings in Flanders and northern France (Béthune, Courtrai, Lens, Metz, Tournai). In 1529 he was appointed master of the boys. The story has it that around 1540 he overmastered one of them, was sent to the galleys for crimes against nature, and eventually wrote his way back into the emperor's good graces. He apparently retired to Tournai, where he was a cathedral canon, perhaps as early as 1547.

Gombert's genius, individuality, and inventiveness are admired by modern musicologists, as they were by his contemporaries. He is one of the great masters of the imitative polyphonic style, which is reflected alike in his 10 extant Masses, his Magnificat cycle, his more than 160 motets, and his 70-odd *chansons* and other songs. It is said that by 1575 at least 90 collections of his works had been printed, though this figure perhaps includes the volumes of *chansons* that Pierre Attaingnant **[134]** ascribed to "Nicolas" and that are now known not to be Gombert's. His style is marked by a free sort of polyphony involving the imitation of themes and motifs from voice to voice, with constant transmutation and variation. The resulting texture has been described by such adjectives as "smooth" and "thick." He goes farther than his purported teacher in making technical considerations subservient to beauty of sound and sonic beauty to textual meanings. He tends to set verse as it reads rather than as it scans, giving the music a characteristic asymmetry. For his song texts he seems to have preferred pastoral scenes and other images of natural serenity (although there is a rabbit-hunting piece). Such choices are consistent with his rather tran-

quil musical profile, which has caused some to see him as a forerunner of Palestrina **[201]**. It should be noted that his *chansons* were particularly popular for instrumental transcription.

RECORDINGS: At least two of the Masses, *Da pacem* and *Je suis desheritée*, have been recorded. *Musae Jovis: Déplorations sur la Mort de Josquin* has also been committed to disc.

[149] D'HESDIN, Nicolle des Celliers (Dez-dan′, Nē-kōl′ dä Sel-yä′)
TEACHER
BORN: c. 1500 (?)
DIED: Beauvais, August 21, 1538

D'Hesdin was master of the boys at Beauvais Cathedral (where he is buried) for at least the last two years of his short life. Nothing else is known of him, though evidence suggests that he may have spent some time in Italy, where his music was highly regarded. There is still much confusion over what he wrote and what he did not, though he can pretty certainly claim 3 extant Masses, some isolated Mass movements, 2 Magnificats, and about a dozen each of motets and *chansons*.

[150] MIKOLAJ of Cracow (Mē′-kô-lwī)
BORN: c. 1500 (?)
DIED: after 1540

Mikołaj was a composer represented in the tablature of Jan of Lublin and in a tablature from Cracow. There are nearly 40 compositions in all, including religious works, secular songs, and dances, all reduced to keyboard tablature, plus a couple of improvisatory preludes. The vocally derived pieces are initialed N.C. (Nicolas Cracoviensis). There has been some confusion with pieces initialed N.Ch., which supposedly stands for Nicolas Chrzanowita or Mikołaj of Chrzanow. A few of the N.C. pieces are dated 1540. RECORDINGS: Examples are recorded as part of the Muza series of Polish historical music and in recordings of the Jan of Lublin tablature.

[151] MILÁN, Luys de (Mē-làn′, Lōō-ēs′ dä)
VIHUELIST, WRITER
BORN: Valencia, c. 1500
DIED: c. 1562 (?)

Most of what we know of Milán he tells us himself—or permits us to deduce. He was the third son of a pair of noble Valencian Miláns, Don Luys and Violanta *(née* Eixarch). Faced with the traditional younger-son dilemma, he decided to become a gentleman. This was, in Western Europe, an increasingly popular solution that owed a great deal to the book *Il Cortegiano (The Courtier),* by Baldassare Castiglione, who had spent his twilight years in Spain as Bishop of Ávila. Accordingly, Milán attached himself to the model Renaissance court of Ferdinand, Duke of Calabria. When Ferdinand V (El Católico) and Louis XII carved up the Kingdom of Naples, to which the duke was heir, Charles brought the lad to Spain and locked him up for ten years for his own good. Later the duke married his longtime sweetheart, Germaine de Foix, whom the Spaniards regarded as "somewhat lewd" and hopelessly addicted to gourmet dining. Milán tells us that he had, in the proper Castiglionean fashion, taught himself to play the *vihuela de mano,* a forerunner of the guitar, which filled the place of the lute in Spain. This turned out to be a Good Thing, for the noble pair—particularly the duchess—adored music. But Milán had more than one string to his vihuela in the matter of making himself popular. In 1535 he published his *Libro de motes,* a manual of party pastimes for polite people. And twenty-six years later, he paid homage to Castiglione with his own Iberian guide to courtiership, *El Cortesano.* In between (1536) he turned out his contribution to music, *El Maestro.* Perhaps it was this, or the game book, that inspired John III of Portugal to give him a pension of 7,000 cruzados.

El Maestro was the first known published collection of vihuela pieces; there were only six more. Designed as method rather than mere anthology, it is progressive, much of the music being rather easy. Part One contains forty improvisatory fantasias, six pavanes ("low" dances), and the first four known *tientos* ("essays," somewhat like the Italian *ricercari).* Part Two consists of twenty vihuela-accompanied songs in Spanish, Portuguese, and Italian—among the earliest solo songs to appear in print. The book is a monument among those for plucked strings.

RECORDINGS: With the upsurge of interest recently in such instruments, Milán has been well represented on records, particularly in the Hispavox History of Spanish Music.

[152] MODERNE, Jacques (Mō-dârn', Zhàk)
PRINTER

BORN: Pinguente, c. 1500
DIED: Lyons, 1562 or later

Born (Giacomo Moderno?) in what is now the Yugoslavian town of Buzet, a few miles south of Trieste, Moderne migrated to Lyons in the early 1520s and opened a bookshop there. Using the new music type invented by Pierre Attaingnant [134], he went into the music-publishing business in 1532 and became Attaingnant's chief rival. His editor was his compatriot François de Layolle [132]. Moderne was evidently quite successful, since he acquired property, was familiar with the *lyonnais* upper class, and held municipal offices. He seems to have been popularly known as "Grand Jacques," which indicates that he was fat or tall—or perhaps just a good fellow. His output declined significantly after Layolle's death. Some modern accounts say that he was *maître de chapelle* at Notre-Dame de Confort (where Layolle was organist) and that his own compositions have not survived, but there appears to be no shred of evidence that he was musical at all. He appears here because, as with Attaingnant, he often is given credit for writing the dance pieces and such that he published.

[153] MORALES, Cristóbal de (Mō-rà'-làs, Krĕ-stō'-bàl dā)
SINGER, CHOIRMASTER
BORN: Seville, c. 1500
DIED: autumn 1553

Morales was justly proud of having been born in Seville—a fact that he insisted be made plain on the title pages and elsewhere in some of his published music. Seville was, after all, one of the few Spanish cities with much claim to musical culture at the time. Morales assumedly got his training as a cathedral choirboy—according to tradition, from Pedro Fernández de Castilleja, choirmaster there from 1514. Or perhaps he (also) studied with Fernández's predecessor, Pedro de Escobar, or the canon Francisco de Peñalosa. He also managed to acquire somewhere an excellent, if traditional, academic education and went into minor orders. By 1526 he had won an appointment as *maestro de capilla* at the cathedral of Ávila. Apparently, however, the salary did not suit him (salaries rarely did), and after two years he moved on to Plasencia in western Spain, where he almost doubled his take. But he was soon at loggerheads with the chapter there and quit in 1531. There he vanishes for four years, to turn up in 1535 as a baritone in Pope Paul III's chapel. The papal choir under Paul was not a bad place to be, after one had paid the ten-ducat initiation fee ensuring the tyro's benefiting from the fringes—purses and gifts from heads of state and church in various degrees offered in gratitude for ceremonial performances and the like. Morales at the outset got eight ducats a month, room, board, a valet, a horse for road trips, Wednesdays off, and a sabbatical of ten months every five years (with pay). Increasingly, at the summit meetings and ritual handshakings where their services were required, the choir sang works by Morales—at the treaty signing between Charles V and Francis I in Nice in 1538, at the celebration of Ippolito II d'Este's elevation to cardinal in Ferrara a year later, at the Sacred House at Loreto later that same year, and so on. Back in Rome the choir increasingly sang in the Sistine Chapel, in spite of all Michelangelo's scaffolding and drop cloths.

When his first sabbatical came due in 1540, Morales was off like a shot for Seville. But he returned for a second hitch and, to borrow an academic term, was even more productive than before. But something seems to have been amiss, for he suffered several long spells of illness (nature unspecified). He not very secretly sounded out various secular princes for positions in their households, with no luck. He waxed testy and at one point got into a sort of locker-room brawl with a colleague and was fined 200 baiocchi. Instead of claiming his second sabbatical in 1545, he resigned and shook the dust of Rome from his sandals forever. But back in Spain he could find nothing better than the directorship of the cathedral choir in Toledo (analogous to Leonard Bernstein's having to take the helm of the Wichita Symphony). The salary was low, the prices were high, and, having written all his life for *a cappella* choir, he found he had to adjust his sights to two choirs with organ. Accordingly, he fell behind in his composition. On top of all this, he sank what money he had in some investment scheme and lost it. Shortly (and not unexpectedly) he became ill again, and early in August 1547 he resigned. After some three years as music director to the Duke of Arcos at Marchena, back in his home territory, he took over the choir of Málaga Cathedral. This proved to be another mistake. He was unable to keep discipline among his charges, who took pains to embarrass him in public. In June 1548 he begged permission to go home; clearly there must have been extenuating circumstances, for not only was it given him, but he was also excused for his part in the most recent hostilities. Hearing that his old job at Toledo

was again open, Morales swallowed his pride and asked if he might have it back. He was told that all applicants had to compete. He sent a protest, and while it was being pulverized by a committee he died—probably around the first of October, for his house in Málaga was declared available for occupancy a week after that. An ignominious end for the first Spanish composer of international fame and stature!

Morales' first publications came from the press of Jacques Moderne [152]; later publishers all over Western Europe contended for his works. Much of it is still extant, some in multiple editions, very little in manuscript. The most famous and magnificent examples were the two volumes of Masses that he brought out in Rome in 1544; the most popular were the 2 Magnificat cycles. He left 23 Masses in all (including 2 requiems), about 90 motets, lamentations, and a mere handful of secular songs. The music shows a sure knowledge of all the current fashions and techniques. Some historians have wondered whether, in his occasional dealings with the Imperial Chapel, Morales may have learned a thing or two from Nicolas Gombert [148]. But he has a style of his own —grave, dark, austere: in a word, Spanish (though some of his compatriots regarded him as foreign). The popularity of his work carried it to the New World and ensured vihuela transcriptions for home consumption.

RECORDINGS: The Masses *Mille regrets* and *Quaerimus cum pastoribus* have been recorded, as well as various shorter works and transcriptions.

[154] NARVÁEZ, Luys de (När-vä'-eth, Lōō-ēs' dä)
VIHUELIST, TEACHER
BORN: Granada, c. 1500 (?)
DIED: after 1550

In his vihuela book, *Los seys libros del Delphin,* published in 1538, Narváez says that music has been his lifelong obsession, and implies that he had excellent training. At that time he was in the employ of Don Francisco de los Cobos, governor of León. Later he was master of the boys in the *capilla* of the Infante Felipe (later Philip II), with which group he made journeys to Flanders and Italy. His performing ability was greatly admired; one contemporary said that it seemed wonderful to the layman and miraculous to the professional. His son Andrés was also reputedly a fine player. Narváez called his vihuela book "the Dolphin" because, he says, the dolphin adores and is very sensitive to music. The work contains the usual heterogeny of materials. Though Narváez shows greater knowledge of the vihuela's potential than does Luys de Milán [151], the collection's chief interest lies in the several sets of *diferencias,* which show the composer an early master of variation form, which he may have introduced to Spain. He also left a couple of motets.

[155] SUSATO, Tielman (Sōō-sá'-tō, Tēl'-màn)
TRUMPETER, PRINTER
BORN: c. 1500
DIED: Antwerp, c. 1561 or later

The name Susato indicates origin in Soest, a town northeast of Cologne, but it is uncertain whether it was Tielman Susato or an ancestor who emigrated to Antwerp. At any rate, he does not appear in the records until 1529, when he was employed as a copyist by the cathedral. From at least 1532 he was also a municipal musician, playing flute, *velt-trompet,* and *teneur-pipe* (according to an inventory). In 1541 he went into the music publishing business with two printers, Henry ter Bruggen and Willem van Vissenaecken. A year later he regrouped with Vissenaecken alone and by mid-1543 was on his own. In 1549 he gave up, or was dropped from, his performing job. Two years later he moved his home and business to new quarters, "at the Sign of the Krummhorn." After his death about a decade afterward, his son, Jakob, took over the printery, but he died in 1563 and the Widow Susato sold the equipment to the great printer Christoph Plantin.

Unlike such publishers as Attaingnant [134] and Moderne [152], Susato was certifiably a musician and published many of his own compositions, as well as early works by Lassus [228] and the vernacular psalm settings *(Souterliedekens)* by Clemens non Papa [166], to which latter Susato himself contributed a few. His other works include a Mass, some motets, and many *chansons,* both French and Flemish. His series of *Musyck boexken,* dedicated to the promotion of Flemish music, contains his best-known work, a volume of dances, today beloved of amateur old-instrument groups and much recorded. (One example, called *Hoboken Dance,* after the Dutch town of that name, was once erroneously cited by a German musicologist as possibly the earliest example of a dance tune from North America.)

[156] ARCADELT, Jacques (Jacob?) (Är'-kà-delt, Zhàk)
BORN: c. 1505 (?)
DIED: Paris, October 14 (?), 1568

Now that historians have decided that Arcadelt and a certain Jacobus Flandrus were two different people, we can reconstruct his career chiefly by inference. Present thinking is that he was French rather than Flemish, and perhaps a companion of Philippe Verdelot [104] on a journey from Florence to Lyons. After apparently spending some time in Venice on his own in the late 1530s, he was (1540–51) in the employ and good graces of Pope Paul III in Rome, where he madrigalized a couple of Michelangelo's sonnets. He then went to France and joined the retinue of Charles de Guise, Cardinal of Lorraine, brother of Francis of Lorraine, the Duke of Guise, and one of the architects of the Treaty of Cateau-Cambrésis between England, France, and Spain. Arcadelt remained with the cardinal until 1562, though he may also have been affiliated with the Royal Chapel during that period. He spent his last years in Paris, living on his benefices in that city, Rheims, and Liège. It is by no means clear whether he was a performer or solely a composer in his various ecclesiastical positions. At any rate, he was primarily a secular composer—and an important one. Together with Verdelot and Costanzo Festa [123], he helped put the Renaissance madrigal on the map. The first of his five published collections, from 1539, went through more than forty editions, the last of them published nearly a century and a quarter later. He was particularly adept at the four-voice madrigal, which, at his hands, was tuneful, lucid, harmonious, clearly recalling the *frottola* origins of the form. His *Il bianco e dolce cigno (The White and Gentle Swan)* is perhaps the best-known Italian madrigal of the century. (Orlando Gibbons [408] imitated it in *The Silver Swan.)* In Paris Arcadelt switched to *chansons,* with which he was almost as successful, though he did not often stoop to the then popular Paris style. (But one of his more frivolous examples was adapted in the nineteenth century to become the famous "Arcadelt *Ave Maria.")* His sacred works include 4 Masses, a Magnificat, 3 sets of lamentations, and about 25 motets. RECORDINGS: The Christmas parody Mass *"Noël! Noël!"* (after Jean Mouton [84]) is included in an LP devoted to various Arcadelt works, performed by the Capella Cordina under Alejandro Planchart.

[157] TALLIS, Thomas
ORGANIST, SINGER, PUBLISHER
BORN: c. 1505
DIED: Greenwich, November 23, 1585

The name of Thomas Tallis is more likely to be known to the average musical layman than any other listed so far in this book because of Ralph Vaughan Williams' [1633] popular orchestral variations on a Tallis tune to one of a set of metrical psalms from the pen of his contemporary William Parker, Archbishop of Canterbury. Both Kent and Leicestershire have claimed Tallis as a native, and tradition has him trebling in the choir of St. Paul's or the Royal Chapel (or perhaps both). But there is no solid information on the first third of his life up to 1532, when he became organist at Dover Priory. Five years later he was in London, playing at St. Mary-at-Hill in Billingsgate, a district famous for its fishwives, from which in 1538 he moved on to Waltham Abbey, just north of the capital and beloved of Henry VIII until amatory considerations forced him to change his views. Thus Tallis was turned out, along with the other inmates, in 1540, taking with him forty shillings of back salary and forty in severance pay. After a couple of years at Canterbury Cathedral, he was taken into the Chapel Royal, where he served four English monarchs (or five, if one includes the luckless Lady Jane Grey). He seems to have had no problem weathering the switches from Anglicanism to Catholicism and back again that marked his tenure. He is several times mentioned in the chapel records. In 1545, for example, he was paid a pound a day, like the thirty-one other Gentlemen, and like them he was issued appropriate garb for the funeral of King Henry and for the coronation of King Edward. In 1552 he married a woman known to history only as "Joan," with whom according to his epitaph (now lost) he "lived in love full three and thirty years," despite—or perhaps owing to—the fact that the union was not blessed with issue. The couple seems to have lived comfortably, and in 1557 Queen Mary granted Tallis and his friend Richard Bowyer, master of the chapel children, a twenty-one-year lease for a manor on the Isle of Thanet, where Tallis had a relative named John Sayer. In 1572, Tallis's pupil, William Byrd [248] joined him as co-organist of the chapel. (Byrd was a lifelong Roman Catholic, and on such flimsy grounds it has been argued that his old teacher had also kept the faith.) Despite the difference in their ages, the two men seem to have been very close. In 1575, inflation having made chapel salaries insufficient, the pair was granted a license by Queen Elizabeth to print music and music paper as a monopoly. They responded by publishing a volume of motets, *Cantiones sacrae,* to which each contributed seventeen, ostensibly to honor Elizabeth's seventeenth anniversary on the throne. But evidently the business did not prosper, and they had to seek royal relief (granted)—Tallis on the grounds that he was "verie aged" and had served the chapel these forty years. Shortly afterward, he seems to have withdrawn from both his occupations and retired to Greenwich, where he died, even more aged, leaving his property to Joan and his share in the business to his godson, Thomas Byrd.

Tallis's long career reflects the changes in English music in one of its most important periods. He wrote both Catholic polyphony and the more austere music of the Anglican rite. Was it as easy as shifting gears? Was he unmoved by the destruction by politicians and fanatics of ecclesiastical buildings, libraries, statuary, paintings, and stained glass? Was survival more important to him than belief? There is no way of knowing. He left 2 Masses (both incomplete), 2 Magnificats, 2 sets of lamentations, around 50 motets and Latin hymns, 3 Anglican services, parts of others, English psalms, and a number of anthems (some arranged from earlier motets). There are also a very few secular part-songs and some keyboard pieces and consort works. The Latin polyphonic works range from a very early Mass to the *Cantiones,* and show a rather leisurely progress from old-fashioned and clumsy notions of polyphony to the absolute mastery shown in the forty-voice motet *Spem in alium.* At his most inspired, Tallis is one of the greatest of the Tudor composers, but he seems not always to have been in the vein.

RECORDINGS: National pride has treated Tallis well on records. There are recordings of both Masses (restored), *Spem in alium* (in a two-record survey of Tallis's music from Sir David Willcocks), the magnificent *Lamentations* for the first lection of Maundy Thursday Matins, the *Cantiones* (from the *Cantores in Ecclesia),* and several programs of miscellaneous shorter works.

[158] TYE, Christopher
TEACHER, CLERIC, POET
BORN: c. 1505
DIED: Doddington-cum-Marche, c. 1572

The third "T" of Tudor music (with Thomas Tallis [157] and John Taverner [128]), Tye is variously said to have been born in the west country, Cambridge, and Westminster. He was, in fact, the recipient of a B.Mus. at

King's College, Cambridge, 1536, and a clerk there, which facts have caused him to be confused with a Richard Tye, who was connected with King's College earlier, concurrently, and later. All we know of Christopher Tye before that time is that he had been studying, composing, and teaching for ten years at the time he submitted the Mass that won him his degree. A fellow alumnus of King's, Richard Cox, by then Archdeacon of Ely Cathedral, got him a post there as master of the boys in 1543. Cox later became Chancellor of Oxford University and, with such dedicated educators as Roger Ascham and Sir John Cheke, taught the future Edward VI. The legends that Tye also was one of the prince's tutors may therefore have some basis in fact; evidence suggests that at least he was at court during Edward's brief reign. Having got a doctorate in music from Cambridge in 1545, he was himself at Oxford in some capacity within a year of Cox's installation. In 1553 he published (with a friendly dedication to King Edward) a collection of his easy four-part settings (particularly recommended to students "to synge and also to play vpon the Lute) of his own doggerel translations of *The Actes of the Apostles,* promising a sequel if it was well received. Evidently it was not. At some point in the years when he was nominally at Ely, Tye married a woman named Katherine, on whom he sired several children. Shortly after England settled down to being Anglican under Queen Elizabeth in 1558 and Richard Cox became Bishop of Ely in 1559, Tye decided to enter the ministry, becoming a deacon in 1559 and receiving ordination the next year. Also in 1560, his daughter, Mary, married Robert Rowley; one of their children was the playwright Samuel Rowley, who forty-five years later depicted his grandfather in a small part in his play *When you see me, you know me.* In 1561 Tye left Ely Cathedral to become rector at nearby Doddington-cum-Marche. The post paid handsomely, though he seems to have been considered a better composer than preacher. In his later years, he is said to have become rather cranky. There is a story that when the queen sent someone to tell him that the organ he was playing was off pitch, he told the messenger to tell her to get her ears tuned. He was succeeded at Doddington by another son-in-law, Robert Whyte. His own son, Peter, became rector of Trinity Church in Ely by misrepresenting his qualifications to the bishop, who was not happy about the affair.

Tye left 3 Latin Masses *(Euge bone, The Westron Wynd,* and one unnamed). The two "named" Masses are among the chief monuments of Tudor contrapuntal music. There are also some motets and a number of English anthems. Tye has been called "the father of the anthem," but those he left are musically scarcely distinguishable from motets, save that they affect a certain simplicity. There are also more than 30 pieces for instrumental consort, including 22 *in nomine*s.

RECORDINGS: Both of the named Masses have been recorded by the choir of Tye's old college.

[159] **LELEU, Jehan** (Lə-lü′, Zhà*n)*
SINGER, TEACHER
BORN: c. 1506
DIED: Cambrai, December 20, 1539

Despite his considerable talent, Leleu (alias Joannes Lupi) seems to have been a feckless sort. His entire brief career was centered in Cambrai Cathedral, where he sang for seven years as a choirboy before trekking off to Louvain to study philosophy in 1522. Four years later he returned to the choir, where, in 1527, he was put in charge of the boys, succeeding Jean Rémy. His mother kept house for him and several of the choristers. As an officer of one of the most notable ecclesiastical musical establishments in Europe, he evidently left something to be desired, for he was constantly being cited for laxity and inefficiency, and was finally ordered to get his mother out of the house. Just over two years after that crisis, in 1535, he had to withdraw for reasons of health. In 1537 he gave it one more try, but was not up to it and succumbed in his early thirties. His not inconsiderable output includes 2 Masses, a number of motets, and about as many *chansons.* He was a master hand at imitative polyphony and had an inventive turn of mind.

[160] **BAKFARK, Bálint** (Bàk′-färk, Bä′-lint)
LUTENIST, SPY
BORN: Braşov, 1507
DIED: Padua, mid-August 1576

Not the least interesting thing about Bálint (alias Valentin) Bakfark is the instability of his surname, which appears in such versions as Bacfarc, Backfarckh, Bacfart, Bekwark, and so on. Because he was reared from infancy by his sister-in-law's family, he was also known as Greff, Graew, Graevius, Gereb, Greff-Bakfark, and Bakfark-Greff. Even his Transylvanian (Romanian) birthplace, founded by the Teutonic Knights, did not escape the vagaries of nomenclature, being also Austrian Kronstadt and presently Romanian Braşov. While still quite young, Bakfark entered the service of Janos Szápolyai (John Zapolya), governor of Transylvania. Janos, noted for frying the revolutionary nobleman György Dózsa on a red-hot throne, and for (in effect) turning Hungary over to the Ottoman Turks, became king when Lajos (Louis) II was killed at the Battle of Mohács. By that time Bakfark had become a crackerjack lutenist, for which attainment the king rewarded him with a title. With the death of the latter in 1540, Bakfark began the restless peregrinations that characterized the rest of his career. He may have gone to Italy for a time; then he moved on to France, where he joined the court of François de Tournon, Archbishop of Béthune. In 1540 the archbishop moved to Rome and a new king, Sigismund II, brother-in-law of the late Lajos, took the Polish throne. Laden with imposing recommendations, Bakfark hurried to Cracow, where he was apparently received right royally and put on the payroll. In his years at the Polish court he struck up a correspondence with Albert, Duke of Prussia, and in 1552 he got permission to visit him and to take another swing through Europe. Sigismund, preoccupied with trying to produce an heir on a succession of three queens (and his mistresses), let him go. Bakfark and Albert quickly cemented their relationship, as will appear shortly. Hearing that his old employer in France had just been made Cardinal Archbishop of Lyons, the lutenist hurried thither to offer congratulations. Though there proved to be no vacancy in the court, he managed to get Jacques Moderne [152] to publish a book of his lute pieces. In 1554 he undertook the homeward journey with stop-offs in Italy and Germany and another check-in in Königsberg with Albert. Protestant Albert, last Grand Master of the Teutonic Knights, was not in good odor in Poland, having got hold of Prussia, a Polish dependency, by posing as a defender of the Faith. In 1566, King Sigismund came to the conclusion that Bakfark's dealings with him had to do with more than mere frets and catgut. The militia trashed his home and he made it to the border a few steps ahead of the bloodhounds. After two years at the imperial court in Vienna, and another three with the Prince of Transylvania, the son of his first patron, he settled at the University of Padua in 1571, then fell victim to the plague five years later, ordering his manuscripts to be burned. He was evidently one of the most remarkable lutenists of all time. Besides his 2 lute books (the second published in Cracow in 1565), a few scattered manuscripts still exist. RECORDINGS: The Hungarian state recording company has brought out the complete works.

[161] NEWSIDLER, Hans (Noi'-sēd-ler, Hänts)
LUTENIST, LUTEMAKER, TEACHER
BORN: Pressburg (Bratislava), c. 1509
DIED: Nuremberg, February 2, 1563

The philoprogenitive Newsidler (or Neusidler), arrived in Nuremberg in the dawn of 1530, got married, took out citizenship, bought a house, and set up as a lute teacher and maker of lutes, all within a few months. He also wrote and published eight collections of lute music. Despite all this industry, Newsidler's fortunes steadily declined as his family grew, until he was forced to go on welfare, as it were, and sell his home. After twenty-six years and half as many children (among them the lutenist-composers Melchior Newsidler [226] and Conrad Newsidler), Frau N. died in 1556 and was superseded by a second wife four months later. She bore Hans four more children in the six years remaining to her, dying in August 1562. Her husband followed her to the grave six months later.

Newsidler was one of the most important German lute composers. His collections include improvisatory fantasias or preludes, as well as arrangements of polyphonic works and of many popular songs and dances. Some of the dances, such as "The Jews' Dance," "The Gypsy Dance," and several *welsch* (foreign—i.e., Italian) dances have a piquant flavor. The collections are variously classified according to the skills of the intended users, and the first of them includes a self-teaching method that shows the recommended fingerings for the exercises—an innovation.

[162] BERMUDO, Juan (Bâr-moō'-thō, Hwàn)
MONK, ORGANIST, THEORIST
BORN: Écija, c. 1510
DIED: after 1560

Born near Seville into a good family, Bermudo studied music as a youngster, joined the Observant Minorities (a Franciscan order), and after basic religious training enrolled at the University of Alcalá to study mathematics. Incapacitated by illness for some time, he turned to music (then taught as a branch of mathematics). He may have served the Archbishop of Seville as organist around 1550. Active as a preacher, he became a high official in his order in Andalucía in 1560. Bermudo was a friend and admirer of Cristóbal de Morales **[153]**. His 1555 *Declaración de instrumentos musicales,* which incorporates two earlier theoretical treatises of his, provides not only material on musical instruments and how to play them, but also a comprehensive survey of music as practiced in the mid-sixteenth century. It includes a few organ pieces by its author—the first such works printed in Spain.

[163] BOURGEOIS, Loys (Boor-zhwä', Loi)
TEACHER, SINGER
BORN: Paris, c. 1510
DIED: Paris (?), 1560 or later

John Calvin, on (he supposed) the authority of St. Paul, was all for singing in church, so long as the texts were biblical and the tunes were not corrupted by harmonizations and accompaniments. On the grounds that worshipers should also know what was being sung, he was also in favor of vernacular texts. When in 1539 he put together in Strasbourg his first psalter, he tried his hand at nine himself, and borrowed the remaining thirteen from Clément Marot (1496–1544). A witty and sophisticated court poet and royal *valet de chambre,* Marot had been run out of France in 1534, and had wound up in Ferrara, where he met John Calvin in 1536. Allowed to come home by the general amnesty declared by Francis I that year, Marot spent the rest of his life enlarging and revising his collection of metrical Psalm translations, which had begun with the first fifteen in sequence, and eventually included thirty-five others. He was encouraged by Emperor Charles V, but not by the French, who made it necessary for him to flee to Geneva in 1542. The year before, Calvin had brought out his first Geneva Psalter, an enlargement of the Strasbourg prototype. In 1543, Marot brought out his revised and augmented volume of fifty translations, and Calvin responded in kind with a similarly enlarged psalter.

Though this psalter was apparently reprinted several times, no copy has survived; hence we cannot guess what, if anything, Loys Bourgeois had to do with it. Bourgeois was probably no more respectable than any other Genevan, though the council cited his eminent respectability when it granted his citizenship in 1547. He had come there no later than 1545 (we know nothing of him before), when he was appointed psalm singer and master of the boys at the churches of St.

Pierre and St. Gervais, the previous intendant, Guillaume Le Franc, having just walked out, calling the authorities tightwads. However, the hundred florins a year seems to have struck Bourgeois as sufficient, since he married two years later— though one should note that he was also provided with a house and exempted from guard duty. In 1546 he hit on the novel scheme of posting the numbers of the psalms for the service on a bulletin board. In 1550 he reached the climax of his Genevan career when Calvin allowed him to publish his singing manual *Le droict chemin de musique (The Right Road to Music),* the council chipping in with a small emolument by way of reward. It was the first French text on singing and sightreading and the first to introduce a modern notion of solmization (the do-re-mi's). Given a two-months leave at the end of the year, Bourgeois returned to a less enthusiastic reception.

In 1551 Bourgeois published *Pseaumes octantetrois de David,* using the Marot texts, and another 34 by Théodore de Bèze, alias "Beza," scholar, theologian, and poetical hack. In its preface, Bourgeois says that he has provided new tunes to all the Beza psalms and has made more or less radical changes in 36 of the others. The authorities were scandalized and in December threw him in jail for what amounted to sacrilege. It took Calvin himself to spring him, but afterward the Swiss Protestant establishment made things uncomfortable for him. When his salary was cut, he protested, and the council magnanimously voted him a one-shot bonus of two measures of grain because Madame Bourgeois was *enceinte.* A year later the musician got leave to travel to Lyons and never returned; the council sent his wife along the following spring. They apparently lived in Lyons for some years, but are last heard of in Paris, where the birth of a daughter was recorded in May 1560. Apart from his psalms, Bourgeois left only 4 *chansons.* Many of the psalm tunes (among them "Old Hundredth") have found their way into other Protestant hymnals and have provided thematic material for other compositions.

[164] CABEZÓN, Antonio de (Kä-bä-thōn', Än-tōn'-yō dä)
ORGANIST
BORN: near Burgos, 1510
DIED: Madrid, March 26, 1566

Born into a noble family, probably on its estate at Castrillo de Matajudíos, or possibly the one at Castrojeriz, Cabezón was somehow blinded in childhood. As what seems, in musical circles, a logical consequence, he was put to studying the organ—some say with Gonzalo Martínez de Biscargui at Burgos Cathedral, where he would have encountered the choirmaster Martín de Rivafrecha [93]. (But Cabezón's younger brother and future colleague in the royal chapel, Juan, was also an organist.) Apparently already a notable tickler of the *tecla* (keyboard) at eleven, Antonio went to Palencia, where he lived with his paternal relative Estéban Martínez de Cabezón, head of the diocese, and studied with the cathedral organist García de Baeza, a kinsman of King (Emperor) Charles's treasurer. With such connections and such talent, it is not surprising that when Charles V married Isabella of Portugal in 1525, the sixteen-year-old organist was not only a member of the wedding, but remained as musician to their imperial majesties. A year later Isabella gave her husband the son he richly deserved, the future Philip II, to whom Charles turned Cabezón over when the queen-empress died in 1539. Meanwhile, at Valladolid, the organist had made friends with some of his musical contemporaries, notably Tomás de Santa María [174] and Luys de Narváez [154]. He had also acquired a home in Ávila, where in 1538 he married a local girl, Luisa Núñez. They lived near the families of St. Teresa and the composer Tomás Luis de Victoria [258], and perhaps discussed theology and polyphony with them. As part of Philip's entourage, Cabezón traveled through much of Western Europe and came to meet many other important musicians. A rather endearing jacket note for a Cabezón record says that in 1554 he went to England "for the wedding of a daughter of Henry VIII." The daughter was Mary I, the happy bridegroom Philip himself, though the union was blessed only with a false pregnancy. Philip stayed around until that was over, perhaps allowing his organist to have some impact on English musicians. In 1560 the whole royal establishment moved to the Escorial near Madrid, and Cabezón lived out his days there. Of his five children, two sons, Agustín and Hernando, were musicians, the latter succeeding his father. In 1578 Hernando published a collection of his father's works, which included also a few pieces by his uncle Juan, his brother, and himself. (About 40 pieces by the elder Cabezón had been published in 1557 in a similar tablature by Luys Venegas de Henestrosa [178]).

Antonio de Cabezón seems not only to have been universally admired as a musician, but also much loved as a man. King Philip had a portrait of him painted (it was lost in a fire) and issued a memorial to him four years after he died. Cabezón wrote for vihuela and harp as well as for keyboards, and left a single choral piece, though once there were perhaps more. His music is mature, demanding, serious, and thoroughly Spanish, reflecting a native tradition of long standing rather than the Italian and Flemish schools. It includes *tientos*, *versillos* (preludes for establishing the mode of the piece to follow), organ hymns, *diferencias* (variations), and *glosas* (ornamented transcriptions). Modern musicology is discovering that he may have had a large impact on keyboard music in the Low Countries, Germany, and England, as well as in Spain.

RECORDINGS: By now there have been at least three or four recorded anthologies of Cabezón pieces.

[165] CERTON, Pierre (Sâr-tôn' Pē-âr')
CLERIC, TEACHER
BORN: c. 1510
DIED: Paris, February 23, 1572

There were Certons in Melun, near Paris, and Pierre held a canonry at the church of Notre-Dame there, but otherwise his origins are uncertain. A fledgling clerk at Notre-Dame de Paris in 1529, he was convicted of Sunday ball playing a few months later but was let off because of his tender years. He must have shaped up after that, for in 1532 he was taken into the Ste. Chapelle, where he became master of the boys in four years and with which he was associated for the rest of his life. Apparently things were not uniformly easy there, for at least once we catch a glimpse of him going out to work in the now paved-over fields. But later he seems to have done well enough, for he obviously hobnobbed with some of the best musicians in Paris, was somehow associated with the royal court, and financed the celebration of an annual Annunciation Mass at Melun. Of his music there are extant 8 Masses, about 50 motets and other religious pieces, some vernacular psalms, and more than 250 *chansons*. Certon seems to have been a merry man and a rather glib composer. A collection of psalms has come down to us transcribed for voice and lute, and the pieces seem little different musically from the *chansons*, many of which are light and strophic and point toward the *air de cour* that characterizes the end of the century.

[166] CLEMENS NON PAPA (Kle'-menz
Nôn Pä'-pà)
SINGER, CLERIC
BORN: c. 1510
DIED: c. 1556

It used to be asserted that Jacob Clemens (or
perhaps Jacques Clément) was called
"Clemens non Papa" to distinguish him
from Pope Clement VII (died 1534). But
since the pope did not compose and the
composer was never more than a priest at
best, the whole idea seems rather silly, even
as a jest. More recently it has been argued
that the tag was given to prevent confusing
the musician with an Ypres poetaster named
Jacobus Papa. There has also been the suggestion that the sobriquet somehow evolved
from his being known as "Father Clemens."
(No one has suggested that it derived from
his winning a paternity suit.) Little else is
known for certain about him. He has been
said to have come from the Ypres (Ieper)
area, but also from the former Dutch island
of Walcheren (now a peninsula). Pierre Attaingnant [134] published one of his *chansons* in Paris as early as 1536, but the first
certain appearance of the man himself is as a
fledgling priest at St. Donatien in Bruges in
1544. Immediately thereafter (until the summer of 1545) he was assistant choirmaster at
the cathedral. His association with Tielman
Susato [155] from 1545 to 1547 may or may
not argue for a sojourn in Antwerp. In late
1550 he was somehow connected with the
Marian Brothers at 's Hertogenbosch. There
are hints that he was from time to time in
the service of Charles V, at Dordrecht, Leyden, and Ypres. German composer Hermann Finck (1527– noted that he was still
living in 1556, but two years later Flemish
composer Jacob Vaet wrote a memorial motet to him. He was buried at Dixmude
(Dixmuiden) near Ypres.

Together with Nicolas Gombert [148],
Clemens represents the high-water mark of
Franco-Flemish music in the generation af-
ter Josquin des Prez [71]. Clemens, however,
has more latitude and more verve than
Gombert and was much more prolific: fif-
teen Masses (one a requiem), two cycles of
Magnificats, more than 230 motets, 140
Dutch psalms *[Souterliedekens]*, 97 *chansons*
and other songs, and a few instrumental and
miscellaneous pieces. Except in his songs,
Clemens is determinedly polyphonic. The
Souterliedekens (a collaboration with
Susato, who printed them) are in four-part
polyphony, using as a basis the folk tunes
adapted to the vernacular psalms in Simon
Cock's pioneering Dutch psalter of 1540.
Like the *chansons,* these show Clemens at

his most lucid. In the curious chromaticism
of some of the motets some have professed
to find a code declaring the composer's Protestant sympathies. Pursued farther, this sort
of thing may ultimately reveal them to have
been written by Clement VII.

RECORDINGS: Record companies have
paid only minor attention to Clemens.

[167] COSTE, Gabriel (Kôst, Gàb-rē-el')
BORN: c. 1510 (?)
DIED: after 1542

Now that the confusion of Gabriel Coste
and the Italian organist Gasparo Costa has
been cleared up, we know nothing of the former save that he was apparently active in
Lyons, where Jacques Moderne [152] published his 2 motets, 16 *chansons,* and a single
pioneering French *ricercare* between 1538
and 1542.

**[168] ENRIQUEZ DE VALDER-
RÁBANO, Enrique** (En-rē'-kāz dä
Väl-der-rä'-bvà-nō, En-rē'-kā)
VIHUELIST
BORN: c. 1510 (?)
DIED: after 1547

Said to be a musician in the employ of the
Count of Miranda, Enriquez published a
vihuela book, *Silva de sirenas (The Sirens'
Woods)* at Valladolid in 1547. He says in his
preface that he lives at Peñaranda de Duero
and that it took him twelve years to complete the work. One of the largest of the sixteenth-century vihuela tablatures, it contains
fantasias, dances, transcriptions, lute songs,
and the only known music for two vihuelas
(which is printed to indicate that the performers must read it sitting *vis-à-vis.* RE-
CORDINGS: A good sampling on various
discs in the recorded Hispavox History of
Spanish Music.

[169] FUENLLANA, Miguel de (Fwen-
lyä'-nà, Mē-hwel' dä)
VIHUELIST
BORN: Navalcarnero, c. 1510
DIED: after 1568

Blind Miguel de Fuenllana was born near
Madrid and passed from the service of the
Marquesa de Tarifa to that of the Infante
Felipe (the future Philip II). For the six
years before her death in 1568, he was part of
the musical establishment of Philip's third
wife, Elizabeth of Valois (the heroine of
Schiller's play and Verdi's opera *Don Car-*

los). He may have died at Valladolid in 1579. In 1554 he published the next to last of the Spanish vihuela tablatures, *Orphenica lyra (The Orphic Lyre).* It is the largest of the lot, containing not only transcriptions but also many original pieces (chiefly fantasias) that show the composer as an excellent polyphonist. It also bodes ill for the vihuela, because it includes pieces for the upstart guitar which would soon supersede it. RECORDINGS: Both songs and vihuela pieces are included in the recorded Hispavox History of Spanish Music.

[170] GERVAISE, Claude (Zhâr-vāz′, Klōd)
EDITOR, VIOL PLAYER
BORN: c. 1510 (?)
DIED: after 1558

All that is known for certain of Gervaise is that he was an editor for the publishing house of Pierre Attaingnant [134] from about 1541 to after 1558. In 1550 he published a viol book (now lost) and is said to have been attached to the French court as a performer on that instrument. Attaingnant brought out a book each of his *chansons* and dances, and more *chansons* are scattered through other collections. On the assertion of the title pages, Gervaise arranged and edited at least 3 other Attaingnant collections of dances.

[171] MUDARRA, Alonso (Mōō-där′-rà, Á-lôn′-zō)
VIHUELIST, CLERIC
BORN: Palencia (or nearby), c. 1510
DIED: Seville, April 1, 1580

Mudarra's *Tres libros de música in cifras* (Seville, 1546) is chronologically the third of the seven vihuela collections published in sixteenth-century Spain. As an embryo musician and student of theology, Mudarra was a protégé of the third and fourth dukes of Infantado in the city of Guadalajara. In the same year that he published his book, the records of Seville Cathedral show him as a canon there, where he remained for the rest of his life, playing an increasingly important role in the musical life of the cathedral. At various times he directed the Corpus Christi ceremonies, was in charge of the ciborium, acted as bursar, and helped select the new organ. He died on Good Friday, leaving his goods to the Church to be sold for relief of the poor. His collection of pieces contains songs, fantasias, *tientos,* dances, and the usual transcriptions—seventy-seven works

in all, including a few designated for the guitar. One of the fantasias makes fun of King Ferdinand's harpist Ludovico, who was evidently given to curious harmonies and rhetorical flourishes. RECORDINGS: Mudarra is included in the Hispavox History of Spanish Music and other collections.

[172] ORTIZ, Diego (Ôr-tēth, Dē-ā′-gō)
CHOIRMASTER, VIOL PLAYER
BORN: Toledo, c. 1510
DIED: c. 1570

In his Italian edition of his viol book, *Tratado de glosas* (Rome, 1553), Ortiz calls himself a Toledan. His birth date has been traditionally given as c. 1525, but the portrait in the Spanish edition (published simultaneously) shows a man considerably older. At the time the book came out, Ortiz was living in Naples, where not long afterward he was directing the chapel of the Spanish viceroy, the infamous Duke of Alva (the butcher of the Netherlands). He remained with Alva's successor, the Duke of Alcalá. In a treatise by Scipione Cerreto published in 1602, we are told that Ortiz has died, but there is no indication of how long since. The *Tratado* is a gold mine for those interested in Renaissance performance practice, for besides being one of the earliest published viol books (and the only one by a Spaniard), it contains innumerable ornamentation formulas (all written out) with directions as to how and why to choose the most appropriate. The *recercadas* (not only on popular *chansons* and madrigals, but also on native themes) are useful in understanding the growing art of variation. In 1565, Ortiz also published, from Venice, *Musices liber primus,* a collection of 69 religious works for voices, in a rather conservative vein and dedicated to the Duke of Alcalá. Other contemporary works ascribed to "Ortiz" are either manifestly or apparently not by Diego. RECORDINGS: Both Deutsche Grammophon and Hispavox have given over LPs to the viol music.

[173] PISADOR, Diego (Pē-sá′-dôr, Dē-ā′-gō)
CLERIC, VIHUELIST
BORN: Salamanca, c. 1510
DIED: after 1557

Diego Pisador, author of the imaginatively titled *Libro de música de vihuela (Book of Music for Vihuela),* which he himself printed in 1552, seems to have spent all his life in Salamanca, where he was cathedral majordomo from 1532. His father, Alonso, who worked for the archbishop, was of good family (or, as a record annotator puts it, Diego was born "in the heart of a family of certain nobility"). Neither his nobility nor his heart, however, prevented Alonso from skipping town in pursuit of a better job in 1532, leaving the tyro majordomo (who had taken minor orders in 1526) to care for his mother and brother. When Isabel Pisador died twelve years later, leaving her money to Diego, the brother cried foul and sued. The father turned up at that point to back the elder, then switched sides, but after three years Diego won. He dedicated his book to Philip II, which some take to mean that he was by then a royal courtier. The *Libro*, the fifth of the seven Spanish vihuela collections in point of publication, includes 39 vernacular songs (some original), *fantasías, diferencias,* a single dance piece, transcriptions of motets and of 8 Masses by Josquin des Prez [71]. Pisador has no hesitation in saying that this is the best book of its kind in print. RECORDINGS: There are recordings in the Hispavox History of Spanish Music series.

[174] SANTA MARÍA, Tomás de (Sản'-tả Mả-rē'-ả, Tō-mảs' dả)
MONK, ORGANIST
BORN: Madrid, c. 1510 (?)
DIED: Ribadavia, 1570

Admitted to the Dominican order in 1536, Fray Tomás served as organist at the royal city of Valladolid and elsewhere in Castile. His musical fame rests on his *Arte de tañer fantasía* (roughly, *Art of Improvising)*, which he published after several delays in 1565. It goes far beyond the implications of its title, including long sections on theory, harmony, performance practice, and the earliest serious keyboard method, and was much imitated. By way of illustration, Fray Tomás included a number of *ricercare*-like *fantasías.*

[175] SOTO, Francisco de (Sō'-tō, Frản-thēs'-ko dả)
SINGER
BORN: c. 1510 (?)
DIED: Portugal after 1552

In the *Libro de cifra nueva* by Luys Venegas de Henestrosa [178], two *tientos* are credited to "Soto." It was long assumed that this was Pedro de Soto, royal organist at Granada. But recently a Portuguese manuscript was found of one of the pieces bearing the name of Francisco de Soto. He was a member of the chapel of the Empress Isabella (of Portu-

gal). After her death he was transferred to that of Charles V, who passed him on to Philip II. He was a friend of Antonio de Cabezón [164] and court records show him to have been better paid than most of the musicians. When Philip's sister Juana married Prince Juan of Portugal, Soto was a member of her entourage. He is not to be confused with the slightly later Padre Francisco de Soto de Langa, who was in the papal choir and wrote some *laude.*

[176] VÁSQUEZ, Juan (Vảs'-kảz, Hwản)
SINGER, CHOIRMASTER, PRIEST
BORN: Badajoz, c. 1510
DIED: c. 1560

A plethora of shadowy musical Juan Vásquezes has muddied the biographical waters. This one was a singer and later master of the boys at Badajoz Cathedral from at least 1530 to at least 1535. By 1539 he had transferred to Palencia, from which he was hired away by the Archbishop of Toledo to grace his court in Madrid. In 1545 he returned to Badajoz to direct the choir, remaining there until at least 1550, but by 1551 he was in Seville in the employ of a certain Don Antonio de Zuñiga. When last heard from (1560) he was still living in that city. His most famous work was his *Villancicos y canciones,* published in 1551 and republished in 1560, in a much enlarged edition, as *Recopilacion de sonetos y villancicos.* Here Vásquez reveals himself as a charming and ingenious musician and a lyricist of talent. His only other work is a setting of the Office for the Dead *(Agenda defunctorum),* published in Seville in 1556 with a dedication to "Juan Bravo." RECORDINGS: Several *villancicos* have been recorded by Gregorio Paniagua and the Atrium Musicae de Madrid.

[177] VEGGIO, Claudio Maria (Vả'-jyo, Kloud'-yō Mả-rē'-ả)
HARPSICHORDIST
BORN: Piacenza, c. 1510
DIED: after 1544

From contemporary letters, dedications, etc., we know that Veggio was a harpsichordist, that he was active in Piacenza, and that he was a friend of the writer Antonfrancesco Doni (1513–74), who makes him one of his three confabulators in his *Dialogo della musica* (1544). And that is all. He brought out a book of madrigals in Venice in 1540 and left a manuscript of keyboard pieces *(ricercari* and transcriptions) in his own hand, with his own corrections and emendations.

[178] VENEGAS DE HENESTROSA, Luys (Vä-nä'-gàs dä Hä-nä-strö'-sä, Lōō-ēs')
PRIEST
BORN: c. 1510
DIED: after 1557

We know very little about Venegas. From about 1535 to 1545 he was a member of the Toledan chapter of Cardinal Don Juan Tavera, governor of Castile, and during part of that period functioned as a priest at Hontova. In 1557 he published his *Libro de cifra nueva (Book of New Tablature*—so called because his notation was new; it was later taken up by Antonio de Cabezón [164] and others). Venegas tells us that he had it ready to go by 1540, but it was held up by a ground swell against keyboard transcriptions, the difficulty of obtaining a printer, the cardinal's death, and other vicissitudes. Though he says it may be used by vihuelists and harpists, it is really for *tecla* (keyboard). It contains nearly 150 selections, including keyboard and lute or vihuela pieces by Venegas' contemporaries and the usual transcriptions of sacred and secular vocal pieces, many with *glosas*. RECORDINGS: A disc in the Hispavox History of Spanish Music anthologizes some of this material.

[179] OTHMAYR, Caspar (Ōt'-mīr, Kàs'-pàr)
CLERIC, ADMINISTRATOR
BORN: Amberg, March 12, 1515
DIED: Nuremberg, February 4, 1553

Save for the years of his schooling at Heidelberg (1533–36), all of Othmayr's short life was spent within a thirty-five-mile radius of Nuremberg. Born in the Upper Palatinate, he was probably a chorister in the elector's chapel and certainly sang there in his university days. At thirty he was rector of the Latin School at Klosterheilsbronn, a former Cistercian monastery west of Nuremberg, which had turned Protestant. Two years later he married Anna Hartung, the daughter of one of the officials, and became a canon at the Lutheran monastery of St. Gumbertus in Ansbach. The following year he was named to the provostship, but there was a problem over the moneys supposed to go with the post, and it seems never to have been settled. He spent his final years in ill health in Nuremberg. His surviving religious compositions, all Protestant, include some motets, two memorials to Martin Luther, a set of bicinia on psalm tunes and hymn tunes, and another of tricinia set to the apothegms of St. John of Damascus. He also wrote a number of secular motets on the impresas or heraldic mottoes, of famous people, but his most widely popular works were his *Lieder,* many of which appeared in anthologies, and fifty of which he published as *Reutterische und jägerische Liedlein (Knightly and Hunterly Ditties).*

[180] GABRIELI, Andrea (Gàb-rē-ā'-lē, An-drä'-à)
ORGANIST
BORN: Venice, c. 1515
DIED: Venice, 1586

Andrea Gabrieli da Canareggio emerges, historically speaking, full grown from the dank canals of Venice (as the poet Richard Aldington, apparently familiar with un-dank canals, once called them). No evidence has been discovered to prove him a previous choirboy at St. Mark's, a pupil of Adrian Willaert [129], or an inhabitant of Verona. In 1557 he surfaces briefly as organist of the church of San Geremia in the Canareggio district, in which he was probably born. There is talk of subsequent travel in Germany, and in 1562 he did indeed accompany Albert V of Bavaria (presumably as one of his musicians) to the imperial coronation of the duke's father-in-law, Emperor Maximilian II, at Frankfurt am Main. Andrea later dedicated a volume of his works to Albert, probably with good reason, for Albert was given to squeezing his subjects to support the arts, and Andrea was apparently well acquainted with Albert's chief musician, Orlande de Lassus [228]. One source says that he was still in Albert's service in 1564 at a salary of ten ducats a month.

In 1557 Andrea had entered the competition for the post of first organist at St. Mark's, left vacant by the death of Girolamo Parabosco [199], but was beaten out by Claudio Merulo [230]. In 1566, however, Annibale Padovano [207], the number-two organist, defected to Graz to become Archduke Karl's *Kapellmeister.* Gabrieli competed again for his job, and this time he lost. When Merulo left in 1583, Giovanni Gabrieli [286], Andrea's twenty-six-year-old nephew and protégé, won the competition but (so it is said) stepped aside in favor of his uncle, who, however, died three years later. Andrea's secondary position in the musical hierarchy at St. Mark's seems not to have hurt his reputation, and it can be fairly said that he was the first native Venetian composer to attain international stature. His works were published all over Europe, and he attracted many pupils, among them not only his famous nephew, but also such as Hans Leo Hassler [320], Gregor Aichinger [321], and Vincenzo Bell'haver [216], who took over the second organ at Andrea's death. Among Andrea's patrons were the Fuggers of Augsburg, then among the wealthiest private citizens in Europe, who employed Aichinger and the Hassler brothers, and who were represented in the choir of St. Mark's by a family member designated as Gian Giacomo (Johann Jakob?) Fugger.

Andrea Gabrieli was an exact contemporary of the Venetian painters Tintoretto and Veronese and, as in their pictures, one sees in Gabrieli's music the Renaissance turning Baroque. All the new impulses are there, however embryonically—instrumentalism, pastoralism, drama, grandiosity, and spectacularity—though his roots are clearly in the Renaissance tradition. The greatest influence on his musical thinking came from his association with Lassus. In his final thirty years, Gabrieli was particularly productive. His output includes 7 Masses, about 130 motets, nearly 200 madrigals and other secular vocal works, and many instrumental pieces for organ or ensembles. (A volume of *sonate à 5* has never turned up, though it undoubtedly contained "sounding pieces" rather than sonatas in any modern sense.) Among his more unusual works are settings of the choruses from a translation of Sophocles' *Oedipus tyrannos* for a production given in Palladio's Teatro Olimpico in Vicenza.

In both the motet and the madrigal, Gabrieli moves from rather conservative beginnings down the path of word coloration, mood painting, and dramatic effect. In the dialogue madrigals, requiring a give-and-take between two groups of voices, and in the polychoral motets (especially those for such state occasions as the welcome accorded Henry III of France, late of Poland), we are, as in the *Oedipus* music, moving toward opera. (Tintoretto, incidentally, recorded the fete noted above in a fresco in one of the *palazzi* Contarini in Venice, in which he depicted his musical colleague.) Three *mascherate* clearly foreshadow the madrigal comedy, as do such comic madrigalesque subforms as *greghesche,* which use a polyglot Levantine dialect, and *giustiniane,* supposedly stuttered and spluttered by tottery Venetian aristocrats.

Significantly, Gabrieli describes one of his collections of polychoral motets as suitable for voices or instruments, and in at least one collection he clearly intends a choir of instruments as opposed to a vocal choir. In his purely instrumental music Gabrieli brought the organ *ricercare* into its own, making of it a music freed at last of verbal considerations and uncircumscribed by the range of the human voice. Some examples are monothematic, with nonthematic interludes. The *canzoni* include fairly straightforward transcriptions of *chansons*—but also independent pieces in the style of the *chanson.* We might also note a set of organ *intonationi,* once thought to be by Giovanni Gabrieli; although these toccatalike quasi-improvisations are intended to give the pitch to a choir, they can also stand alone.

RECORDINGS: Andrea Gabrieli is represented in various recorded collections, especially in a number devoted to music of the Gabrielis, but there has apparently been no disc given over entirely to his music, and indeed his work has so far not been given serious attention on records.

[181] GOUDIMEL, Claude (Gōō-dē-mel', Klōd)

EDITOR, PUBLISHER
BORN: Besançon, c. 1515 or later
DIED: Lyons, August 1572

Goudimel has nothing to do with the probably mythical "Gaudio Mell" with whom Palestrina [201] is alleged to have studied in Rome, having apparently never gotten out of France. Nothing is known of his youth. He studied at the University of Paris and was an excellent Latinist. In 1549, while he was still there, the Parisian publisher Nicolas du Chemin brought out his collection of *chansons.* Not long after, Chemin took him on as an editor and then (1552–55) as his partner. In his Paris years Goudimel seems to have been staunchly Catholic, writing Masses and other liturgical music and making life miserable for a Huguenot colleague. After the partnership ended, Goudimel moved to Metz, a Protestant stronghold, where he appears to have worked for more than a decade on his setting of the psalter *(en forme de motetz)* in the Calvin-approved vernacular settings by Clément Marot and Théodore de Bèze. When things began to get too warm for Huguenots in Metz, Goudimel went back to Besançon but soon moved on to Lyons, which turned out to have been the wrong thing to do. On August 24, 1572, St. Bartholemew's Day, as a result of a power struggle between the Dowager Queen Catherine de' Medici and the Huguenot Admiral Coligny, Parisian Catholics slaughtered their Protestant neighbors in droves. Massacring quickly established itself as the fad of the day and was taken up in city after city, including Lyons during the last three days of August. Goudimel was one of the victims. Catherine, incidentally, won a medal from Pope Gregory XIII, who ordained that the faithful celebrate her victory wherever two or three were gathered together.

Goudimel left 5 Masses, 3 Magnificats, and a few motets from his unreformed days, all reflecting the new, simpler, chordal "French" style. His *chansons spirituelles* and his Horatian odes have vanished. His many *chansons* include settings of poems by his friend Pierre de Ronsard. But he is most famous for his psalms, which are based on the tunes from the Geneva Psalter and were still being used two hundred years later.

[182] MORNABLE, Antoine (Môr-nàb'l', Ăn-twän')
SINGER, CHOIRMASTER
BORN: c. 1515
DIED: after 1553

Mornable was a chorister at the Ste. Chapelle in Paris, and in 1530 was given a scholarship to the University of Paris. Sixteen years later he is briefly glimpsed as *maître de chapelle* to Guy XVII, Count of Laval, a brother-in-law of the Huguenot leader Gaspard de Coligny. In 1538 and for the next fifteen years, Pierre Attaingnant [134] published more than twoscore attractive Paris-style *chansons* by Mornable. In 1546 he brought out a volume of motets and one of psalms (designated as *"Livre second")*, the latter said to be the first published polyphonic settings of the Clément Marot translations.

[183] NOLA, Gian Domenico da (Nō'-là, Jän Dō-mä'-nē-kō dà)
CHOIRMASTER, TEACHER
BORN: Nola, c. 1515
DIED: Naples, May 1592

Gian Domenico del Giovane, called "Don Joan," acquired the name "Nola" from his birthplace just east of Naples. Apart from his publications, we know nothing of him until 1563, when he became *maestro di cappella* at La Nontiata (the Santissima Annunziata) in Naples, a post he retained until at least 1588. He also taught singing to the young wards of that institution. He wrote some motets, but his chief fame rests in his madrigals, and especially in his dialect pieces. His first published works were a collection of *mascherate* of quasi-dramatic intent and *villanesche*, the latter the first such works to which a composer's name can be

linked. The *villanesca* or *villanella* (short for *canzon villanesca alla napolitana*—"country music in the Neapolitan style") was a southern phenomenon. If we let X stand for refrain lines, a typical lyric would be ABXX ABXX ABXX CCXX, the music being strophic throughout. *Villanesche* were satiric and not infrequently bawdy, and implied "staging" by three costumed singers. They were probably intended as a spoof of the more ambitious madrigals from the north, southerners traditionally having had a contempt for the *Svizzeri* (Swiss) up there. Generally simple and chordal, the music deliberately courted "crudeness" with parallel fifths, false accents, and general mistreatment of stress and verbal meanings. It is pleasant to be able to report that the north went along with the gag. Adrian Willaert [129] published in 1546 a volume of his own *villanesche*, thematically indebted to Nola's, and in 1567 Claudio Merulo [230] republished Nola's. The *villanesche* also inspired such Venetian subgenres as the *greghescha* and the *giustiniana*.

[184] RORE, Cipriano de (Rō'-rā, Chē-prē-à'-nō dà)
CHOIRMASTER
BORN: 1516
DIED: Parma, autumn 1565

Known by his Italianized name, Cyprien de Rore was a Fleming, claimed, on the basis of a minimum of evidence and a maximum of scholarly ingenuity, by Antwerp, Mechelen (Malines), and Machelen (a suburb of Brussels). He was almost certainly trained in his homeland. By 1542 he was already established in Venice, where he knew, and perhaps served at St. Mark's under, Adrian Willaert [129]. At some time in the middle of that same decade he took over direction of the chapel of Ercole d'Este II, Duke of Ferrara. The Duchess Renée, daughter of Louis XII, was a Huguenot, so Rore would have accompanied some of those of her faith, such as Calvin and Clément Marot, who passed through the court. In 1558 he got leave to visit his parents in Antwerp. En route he appears to have stopped off in Munich, where Duke Albert had one of the resident painters do Rore's portrait. When he reached Antwerp, he found his parents undergoing what today is described as a financial crisis. Despite his assurances to Ferrara that he would be back by All Souls' Day, he was still in Antwerp a year later, Duke Ercole was dead, and Duke Alfonso was ignoring his letters. Though it meant that he would have to miss such literary giants as the poets Torquato Tasso and Giovanni Guarini, Rore sadly gave up Ferrara. Instead he went into the service of Margaret of Austria, bastard daughter of Charles V and Protectress of the Netherlands. Soon afterward her husband, Ottavio Farnese, Duke of Parma, dropped in and took Rore back to Italy with him. Though conditions in Parma were pleasant enough, the musician was too flattered by the offer, in 1563, of the late Willaert's old job at St. Mark's in Venice to turn it down. After some resistance from Duke Ottavio, who wanted to keep his chapel in shape just in case Margaret ever came home, he was let go. He soon wished Ottavio had said no. He began writing letters back to Parma complaining of hard work, low pay, insubordinate choristers, and smelly canals. All he wanted, he said, was to be allowed to come back to Parma and die. His wishes were granted seriatim in the two ensuing years.

As a madrigalist, Rore represents the second generation, more sophisticated than that of Jacques Arcadelt [156]. He published 5 books, most of them in five parts. He is sometimes called the "inventor" of the Monteverdian "second practice," wherein verbal considerations are paramount to musical ones. Certainly Rore took great pains to underline emotional content (he was less interested in scene painting and onomatopoeia), and "passionate" is a common term used in descriptions of his music. He took no interest in the lighter and more frivolous forms. Petrarch is his guide. Among his Petrarch settings are two of the first madrigal cycles; his are actually treatments of long stanzaic poems, each stanza in effect becoming the basis of a madrigal of its own. A recent assertion that Rore set the entire *Canzoniere*, however, seems to be based on a misunderstanding. As a madrigalist, he is the keystone in the development of the form. He also wrote a few *chansons* and a considerable amount of sacred music. Of his 5 Masses, two are not only dedicated to Duke Ercole, but also make thematic usage of his name. A third was sent as a gift to Duke Albert, who included 25 Rore motets and the aforementioned portrait in a magnificent manuscript he had made up. Rore's motets (some 80 in all) move from fairly pure Franco-Flemish polyphony toward madrigalism and chromaticism. He also left 16 secular examples, 2 Magnificats, and a *St. John Passion*.

RECORDINGS: His music has received minimal attention on records.

[185] STONE, Robert
SINGER
BORN: Alphington, Devon, 1516
DIED: London, July 2, 1613

A Devonshire man, he sang first at Exeter Cathedral, and then, in 1543, became a Gentleman of the Chapel Royal. If the date of his birth is correct, he was eighty-seven when he sang at the funeral of Queen Elizabeth, and he was still active in the year of his death, a decade later. Stone immortalized himself with a single work—a setting of the Lord's Prayer that has become part of the Anglican service.

[186] ZARLINO, Gioseffo (Tsär-lē'-nō, Jō-zef'-fō)
PRIEST, CHOIR DIRECTOR, SCHOLAR, THEORIST
BORN: Chioggia, January 31 (?), 1517
DIED: Venice, February 14, 1590

Son to Zanni (Giovanni) Zarlino, Gioseffo was slated for the Church from childhood. He studied liberal arts in Chioggia with the Franciscans and joined their order at fifteen. He progressed up the theological ladder with all deliberate speed, sang in the cathedral choir, played the organ, and, after being ordained at around twenty-two, then served as priest and chaplain at the Franciscan school. However, when he went to Venice in 1541 and encountered Adrian Willaert [129], he realized what he wanted to do with his life, and took up study with him. Exactly what he did for the next fourteen years is not clear, though he spent some of that time working on his *Istitutioni harmoniche,* which he published in 1558. He was admired as a theologian, had mastered Latin, Greek, and Hebrew, and was a friend of such as Titian and Tintoretto. After the brief intendancy of Willaert's successor, Cipriano de Rore [184], at St. Mark's, Zarlino became *maestro* there in 1565 and remained until he died. In 1583 there was an attempt to make him Bishop of Chioggia, but the Venetian authorities protested, and it fell through. Zarlino ran the choir during one of its most glorious periods, and left many important pupils, including Giovanni Croce [290], Vincenzo Galilei [208], and Claudio Merulo [230].

Zarlino not only wrote and made music but thought deeply about it, and his theoretical works, which created a storm in their time, remain landmarks. The *Istitutioni* is an odd admixture of ancient folksay and almost prophetic reasoning. What caused a protracted paper war between Zarlino and his sometime disciple Galilei was the former's espousal of the acoustical theories of Ptolemy over those of Pythagoras, long regarded as the ultimate authority. These theories had to do with the divisions of the tetrachord, Ptolemy's notions permitting more perfect consonances of the intervals of the third and the sixth, which was what Zarlino was seeking. Esoteric as this may seem, it pointed toward later concepts of harmony. Zarlino recognized that European music operated in terms of what we know as "major" and "minor," and argued, heretically as it seemed to some, that the Ionian or major mode, not the Dorian, was the important one. He also set forth the first detailed discussion of the possibilities of double counterpoint and twelve fascinating rules for setting words that reflect the Renaissance concern with the semantic function of music. The later (1571) *Dimostrationi harmoniche* is a series of Socratic dialogues between gouty old Willaert and his pupils, supposed to have taken place a decade earlier.

In his day Zarlino had both force and importance as a composer. He was called on to provide music for every splendid event that took place in Venice—such as the celebration of the victory at Lepanto in 1571 and the visit of Henry III of France en route from his Cracovian throne to a more promising one in Paris. It would no doubt be instructive to see and hear Zarlino's *Orfeo* of 1574 for its bearing on the pioneering Florentine operas of a quarter century later. But alas! Unless they are still moldering in some Venetian archive, we are likely to encounter none of them. What remains are some rather pedantic motets and a few madrigals that belie their composer's reputation as an avant-garde thinker.

[187] SCANDELLO, Antonio (Skän-del'-lō, Àn-tōn'-yō)

CHOIRMASTER, CORNETIST, SACKBUTIST
BORN: Bergamo, January 17, 1517
DIED: Dresden, January 18, 1580

Scandello was a cornetist at the church of Santa Maria Maggiore in Bergamo in 1541 and probably got his training there. After two years as an instrumentalist in the establishment of Cardinal Madruzzo, Archbishop of Trent, he was hired away in 1549 by the Elector Maurice (Moritz) of Saxony, a militant Protestant, for his Dresden chapel. Maurice died in 1553 as a result of his victory over Albert Alcibiades of Bayreuth, but Scandello stayed on under his brother and successor August I. The chapel throve and by 1555 it numbered six Italians among its

membership, including Scandello's brother, Angelo. At that time Antonio was being paid more than 250 florins a year; in fact, the imports were generally paid more than the homegrown products, which fact was a source of dissension in the ranks. Scandello diplomatically turned Protestant and in 1562 became a citizen. By 1566 the Dutch *Kapellmeister* Matthaeus Le Maistre, successor to Johann Walther [139], was ailing, and Scandello took over most of his duties, but the next year an outbreak of plague caused him to take his family back to Italy for some months. In 1568 he was back and officially appointed Le Maistre's replacement. (Le Maistre dragged out another nine years.) Scandello's wife having died, he married Agnese Tola, daughter of the court painter that summer. Their son, August (1570–1609), followed in his father's footsteps and for a time was one of his charges in the chapel.

A late starter, Scandello left a considerable body of music both sacred and secular. Notable are the great *Mass* he wrote as a memorial to Maurice, a *St. John Passion,* and a *Resurrection Story* (the latter two works among the earliest vernacular-homophonic treatments of such material), and a book of *Napolitane* (the first collection of Italian songs written and published in Germany). His German *Lieder* were quite popular, and in some of his later songs he incorporated both German and Italian elements.

[188] WAELRANT, Hubert (Wäl'-rànt, Hōō'-bert)

SINGER, TEACHER, PUBLISHER
BORN: Tongerloo, 1517
DIED: Antwerp, November 19, 1595

Owing to a confusion with two lawyers of the same name, Hubert Waelrant was long thought to be a native Antwerper, but he seems to have been born in what is now the south central Netherlands. However, by 1544 he was in Antwerp singing tenor in one of the chapel choirs in the cathedral. Ten years later he was still there teaching bocedization in a music school. Bocedization is one of several bobizations, like bebezation and damenization (but not fasola, invented in an attempt to supplant solmization, the system of syllabic names given by Guido d'Arezzo to the notes of the scale and used in sight-singing. Waelrant's notes (he allegedly invented bocedization, for what it was worth) were *bo, ce, di, ga, lo, ma,* and *ni,* which caused his singing lessons to sound a little like Chinese opera. He is also supposed to have junked the old hexachord system in favor of a more modern one involving the octave. In 1551 romance entered his life in the person of a painter named Marie Corecoopers (who preferred being called Loockenberg) and led to marriage. In 1554 Waelrant branched out into publishing with Jean de Laet, who was sometimes known as Jan van Stabroeck, and brought out sixteen collections of sacred music before the venture folded in 1556. That year also terminated the marriage, Mrs. Waelrant having apparently succumbed to a surfeit of childbearing. The bereaved promptly married Anne Ablyn, a woman of property, whose house he turned into a school of his own. After that he becomes quite shadowy, and we know little more about him than his death date.

Waelrant left a slender legacy of motets, psalms, *chansons*, madrigals, and *napolitane*. The collection of motets which he and Laet published all have to do with the life of Christ, and the psalms are to Clément Marot's vernacular texts, suggesting that he at least toyed with Protestantism. The presence in his music of rather cleverly handled chromaticism has caused talk of his using the "secret chromatic language" of the Anabaptist underground. At any rate, the Inquisition saw fit to ban his motets. His music also often tends toward harmonic, rather than contrapuntal, considerations. His writing of Italian songs may support the argument (for which there is no other evidence) that he was Italian-trained.

[189] ARBEAU, Thoinot (Är-bō', Twȧ-nō')
LAWYER, PRIEST
BORN: Dijon, November 17, 1520
DIED: Langres, July 23, 1595

"Thoinot Arbeau" is a fiction, anagrammed from the name of Jehan Tabourot, the son of the Dijon lawyer Étienne Tabourot and uncle to the like-named poet. "Arbeau" studied law at Dijon and Poitiers, but, after recovering from a near-fatal illness, dedicated his life to God and entered the Church. In 1542 he was attached to the diocesan chapter at Langres, between Dijon and Nancy, holding various offices until in 1574 he became vicar-general. In his later years he found the leisure to write the work he had evidently had in mind since his student days. What we should call "ballroom dancing" had gotten its start in the previous century, and Tabouret, by his own admission, had developed a mania for it. *Orchésographie*, 1588–89, is an exhaustive illustrated treatise on the fashionable dances of the day, complete with choreography and musical examples, and with se-

rious arguments as to why the art is both manly and socially useful. It is cast in the form of a dialogue between "Arbeau" and a lawyer named "Capriol," who thinks that proficiency in dancing is necessary to his profession. (Peter Warlock **[1900]** calls his modern transcription of some of the dances *Capriol Suite.*) RECORDINGS: There have been a number of recordings of material from *Orchésographie*, including one by the Telemann Society.

[190] BLACK, John
TEACHER
BORN: c. 1520
DIED: before 1587

Around mid-century John Black was connected with the Aberdeen song school, of which he became master in 1556. For some reason, he apparently left the country in the 1560s but later returned to his job and probably died in Aberdeen. His settings of the Geneva Psalter tunes show a decided French influence. He also wrote consort pieces, some with odd names like *Report Upon "When Shall My Sorrowful Sighing Slack"* and *Lytill Blak.*

[191] TERTRE, Estienne du (Târ'tr, Est-yen' dü)
ORGANIST, EDITOR
BORN: c. 1520 (?)
DIED: after 1568

An organist, perhaps connected with the French court, Tertre married a daughter of Loys Bourgeois **[163]** and was known around Paris as a *savant musicien.* He succeeded Claude Gervaise **[170]** as Pierre Attaingnant's **[134]** dance arranger and was responsible for the posthumous collection brought out by the latter's widow in 1557. Later he was published by, and perhaps worked for, Nicolas du Chemin (c. 1515–76). His 70-odd *chansons* show dance influence and move, over a twenty-five-year period, toward increasing simplification. He was apparently the first to use the term *suite* for a group of related dances.

[192] GORZANIS, Giacomo (Gôrt-zȧ'-nis, Jȧ'-kō-mō)
LUTENIST
BORN: c. 1520
DIED: Trieste, after 1575

Gorzanis was born in southern Italy and was probably blind from birth. Shortly after mid-century he made his way to Austria and eventually settled in Trieste, where he was granted citizenship. His several volumes of lute pieces and *napolitane* were published in his northern years. The first of them, *Intabolatura di liuto* (1561), groups the dances in short variation suites. One such grouping, a *pass'e mezzo e padoana,* is the first known piece of music to be termed *sonata* (i.e., a work for "sounding" rather than singing). He also left a manuscript of such dance pairings in what we would now call all the major and minor keys—quite adventurous then.

[193] LE ROY, Adrian (Lə Rwȧ, Á-drē-àn')
PUBLISHER, LUTENIST
BORN: Montreuil-sur-Mer, c. 1520
DIED: Paris, 1598

Born to affluence near Calais, Le Roy early became connected with the French court in Paris. He married Denise de Brouilly, daughter of a publisher, acquired property, and eventually took over his father-in-law's establishment. In 1551, with a license from Henry II, he and his cousin Robert Ballard began publishing music at the sign of Montparnasse, and two years later were granted the royal monopoly formerly held by the late Pierre Attaingnant [134]. The venture was enormously successful and enormously influential. Le Roy became musical adviser to Charles IX and was *au courant* with the latest fads and cultural turns. He was at home with such artistic cliques as the Pléiad and Jean-Antoine de Baïf's Académie de Poésie et de Musique, and was a fixture at the salons of the Comtesse de Retz. Friend and publisher to Orlande de Lassus [228], he brought him to Paris in 1571 and almost persuaded him to become the royal *maître de chapelle.* Appropriate to his name (Vive Le Roy!), he enjoyed the friendship and patronage of four French monarchs. Ballard died in 1588, but Le Roy went it alone until his own death ten years later. He left no heirs, his wife having died childless many years before.

Le Roy himself wrote songs and dances that show the growing trend toward homophony. Though he did not invent the lute song, he may have coined the term *air de cour* (court air) for the lute-accompanied solo arrangements he made of polyphonic *chansons.* He may also have invented the *double,* the repetition of a dance tune in variation form. Capitalizing on the growing craze for plectrum instruments, he wrote successful methods for the lute, the guitar,

and the cittern. He also wrote and published a basic theory text.

[194] TURNHOUT, Gérard de (Tirn'-hōōt, Jā-rärd' də)
PRIEST, CHOIRMASTER
BORN: Turnhout, c. 1520
DIED: Madrid, September 15, 1580

Turnhout (originally Jacob Gheert or Gheert Jacques, depending on what account one reads) is called after his birthplace, a town near Antwerp that is noted for leech breeding. He had a musical relative, Jean-Jacques or Jan-Jakob, who was either his much younger brother or his son. Gérard was at Antwerp Cathedral from around 1540 and became choirmaster at St. Gommaire's in nearby Lier (or Lierre) in 1559. At some time during this period, he entered the priesthood. He returned to Antwerp four years later, was appointed master of the boys in 1563, and helped welcome the protectress, Margaret of Austria, Duchess of Parma, in 1564. The severity of Spanish rule and the Inquisition soon began to produce sporadic uprisings of the more fanatic Calvinists, and in 1565 they smashed the "idols" in the cathedral, including the organ, and destroyed much of the music. Turnhout devoted intense personal effort, including long hours spent in copying, to their restoration. In 1571, Philip II, through his viceroy, the infamous Duke of Alva, offered him the directorship of the Royal Chapel in Madrid. Turnhout accepted and arrived in 1572 with a contingent of homegrown musicians. Though the king rewarded him with the expectable benefices, he seems to have done nothing special after he reached Madrid. He left us a Mass, a few motets, and *chansons* in French and Flemish.

[195] VALENTE, Antonio (Vȧ-lān'-tā, Ȧn-tōn'-yō)
ORGANIST
BORN: c. 1520
DIED: Naples, c. 1580

Known as "Il Cieco" (possibly "Blinky") because he was blind, probably from birth, Valente seems not to have been a native Neapolitan, as he was once said to be. He spent the last fifteen or so years of his life in Naples as organist of Sant'Angelo a Nido. He published two keyboard collections in 1576 and 1580, the first, *Intavolatura de cimbalo,* one of the earliest representations of the Neapolitan keyboard school, mostly secular; the second, *Versi spirituali,* intended for church use. The *Intavolatura,* notated in something like Spanish tablature, contains the first known example of an improvised piece, a *fantasia* that is essentially a *ricercare* —the sort of thing expected of organists in job competitions.

[196] OCHSENKUN, Sebastian (Ōkh'-zen-kōōn, Se-bàs'-tyán)

LUTENIST
BORN: Nuremberg, February 6, 1521
DIED: Heidelberg, August 20, 1574

The son of a barber-surgeon who made trumpets on the side, Ochsenkun studied music with a Nuremberg lutenist named Hans Vogel. From the early 1540s he was musician to the Count Palatine Otto Heinrich, at Neuburg and Heidelberg, and through Otto's brief reign (1556–59) as Elector of the Palatinate Otto Heinrich "the Magnanimous." His magnanimity extended to building the Otto Heinrich wing of Heidelberg Castle and financing publication of Ochsenkun's lute book in 1558. It consists entirely of transcriptions of works both by local composers and some international ones.

[197] MONTE, Philippe de (Mōn'-tä, Fē-lēp' dä)

SINGER, TEACHER, CHOIRMASTER
BORN: Mechelen (Malines), 1521
DIED: Prague, July 4, 1603

The surname de Monte, by which this composer is known, is an Italianization of the name he was born with—probably van den Berghe. He was one of the last of the horde of Flemish musicians who had poured into Italy. Around 1542, when there were still wealthy people in Naples, he went there to teach Cosimo Pinelli's children. Either there were lots of children or they were singularly intractable, for he stayed for nearly a decade. During that period, he seems to have struck up a friendship with Orlande de Lassus [228], who was passing through in the train of the Sicilian viceroy, Ferdinand Gonzaga. Sometime in or after 1551, Monte himself headed north, stopping in Rome long enough to create some interest among music lovers there and to publish a first book of madrigals in 1554 shortly before arriving in Antwerp. There Philip of Spain, in town to seek instructions from his father, Charles V, on whom to marry, hired him for his chapel. The bride turned out to be Queen Mary of England, elder daughter of Henry VIII, and so the entourage went to London. Monte stayed long enough to meet Master William Byrd [248], age about eleven, but, as the only non-Iberian in the chapel and used to warmer climes, he went back to Antwerp the following autumn.

After that, though his credentials were excellent, Monte seems to have had difficulty finding a good post. In 1555, Albert of Bavaria looked them over and turned him down. Monte returned to Italy and entertained proposals from Ferdinando de' Medici and from St. Mark's in Venice, where Adrian Willaert [129] was feeling his years, but they came to nothing. In 1568, when he was back in Rome, he finally got a solid offer to become *Kapellmeister* to Emperor Maximilian II in Vienna, which he accepted. (The job had first been tendered Giovanni Palestrina [201], who, despite his reputation for unworldliness, wanted so much that the emperor was shocked.) Monte remained imperial *Kapellmeister* until his death, continuing to serve after the accession of Rudolf II in 1576. He was given a lucrative canonry and honorary office at Cambrai Cathedral and in 1570 was sent back to the Lowlands to recruit musicians. He returned with a young woman composer and virginalist, who seems to have been as virginal as her calling, and is also the first female composer to appear chronologically in this volume, however fleetingly. In Prague, the alternative locale of the Hapsburg court, he also taught another precocious young woman, the English poetess Elizabeth Weston. He died there in 1603, leaving Rudolf saddened. But that was Rudolf's natural state, to the degree that he was deposed as incompetent three years later.

Just what Monte did with his time between London and Vienna is not clear, but he certainly published very little. Once he took the imperial post, however, he seems to have made up for lost time. In the way of church music, he turned out more than 40 Masses (mostly of the "parody" variety) and around 250 motets. Here he shows great mastery of polyphonic techniques, but he also experiments with polychoral effects and with chromaticism. Some of the Masses seem to reflect the "purification" demanded by the Council of Trent. But Monte was particularly prolific in secular music, notably the madrigal. Like the late Merrill Moore with the sonnet, Monte's motto seems to have been "no day without a madrigal," and he left well over 1,000, including 5 books of *madrigali spirituali.* He also did about 50 *chansons,* mostly to poems by Pierre de Ronsard. His music is essentially serious but is lightened by rhythmic verve. He paid close attention to verbal meanings and often wrote in chordal (and sometimes in tonal) style.

RECORDINGS: So far he has been shockingly neglected by record producers.

[198] EDWARDS, Richard
PLAYWRIGHT, POET, TEACHER, EDITOR
BORN: Somerset, c. 1524
DIED: London, October 31, 1566

Edwards is more prominent in the annals of literature than in those of music. He took his B.A. from Corpus Christi College, Oxford, of which he was a Fellow, in 1544, and his M.A. in 1547 from the newly named Christ Church College (previously Cardinal College, founded by Cardinal Wolsey). His musical training supposedly came from George Etheridge, who, besides being a musician, was a physician and Regius Professor of Greek. Edwards was taken into the Chapel Royal at about the time of Queen Mary's coronation and rose to be master of the children in 1561. Presumably he was a Catholic and in orders, for Mary gave him some church posts, but if so, it was not held against him when Elizabeth came to the throne. In the last years of his life, he became a pioneering playwright and lyricist. Of his dramas, written for performance by his charges, only *Damon and Pithias* is extant. He also compiled, in imitation of Richard Tottel's so-called miscellany (really *Songs and Sonnets),* that rather tiresome grab bag of lyrics *The Paradise of Dainty Devices,* but did not live to see it published (ten years after his demise). Apart from a motet and a setting of the Lord's Prayer, Edwards's only extant compositions are a few songs. One of the servants in Shakespeare's *Romeo and Juliet* quotes the one that begins "When griping grief . . ." Another, "On Going to My Naked Bed" (the text of which appears in *The Paradise* as *"Amantium irae amoris redintegratio est"),* has attracted considerable notice because of its likenesses to French *airs de cour* and Italian madrigals of the Verdelot-Arcadelt type.

[199] PARABOSCO, Girolamo (Pà-ràbōs'-kō, Jē-rō'-là-mō)
ORGANIST, POET, NOVELIST, PLAYWRIGHT
BORN: Piacenza, c. 1524
DIED: Venice, April 21, 1557

After lessons with his father, the organist Vincenzo Parabosco of Brescia, Girolamo came to Venice in his teens to study with Adrian Willaert [129]. Between 1546, when he wrote his comedy *La Notte* and published his only collection of madrigals, and 1551, he traveled widely in Italy. In the latter year he was appointed first organist at St. Mark's, Venice, and there are tales of organ duels between him and the second organist, Annibale Padovano [207]. Professional considerations aside, Parabosco led a brief and apparently highly charged life. Author of plays, lyrics, and novellas *(I Diporti),* he was at home in the literary and artistic, as well as the musical, circles of Venice. If it was he that his friend Titian painted in *Venus and the Organist* (now in the Prado in Madrid), the portrait is in keeping with his reputation, for his eye is not on the organ he is playing. His madrigals, all erotic, appear to take a dim view of women, perhaps understandably. When he came a-calling after hours one night, one of his *innamorate* is said to have dumped a brazier of coals on his head, charitably following it with a pitcher of water. But the story is as apocryphal as the one that he starved to death when his house was quarantined during a plague epidemic. Apart from his madrigals, only 3 early instrumental pieces have survived.

[200] WACŁAW of Szamotuł (Vàsh'-lwàv ov Sàm-ō-tōōlw')
POET
BORN: Szamotuł, c. 1524
DIED: c. 1560

Wacław was born near Poznań, though guesses as to the date of his birth vary widely. He studied in Poznań and from 1538 at the University of Cracow. After two years as secretary to the governor of a Lithuanian province, during which he made a name for himself as a poet, he was made composer to the chapel of King Sigismund I in 1547. One of his works was played at the wedding of Sigismund II to Catherine of Austria (his third wife). About this time he seems to have turned Protestant, and by 1554 was at the Protestant court of the Duke of Lithuania, Mikołaj Radziwiłł (called "The Black"), father of Sigismund's second wife, who died under mysterious circumstances shortly before the nuptials noted above. Though Wacław's music was widely known in Europe, little of it has survived—a set of lamentations, 2 motets (all in sophisticated Flemish polyphonic style), and some psalms, hymns, and songs, mostly in the vernacular and in a simple chordal style.

[201] PALESTRINA, Giovanni Pierluigi da (Pä-les-trē'-nä)

ORGANIST, CHOIRMASTER, SINGER,
WINE MERCHANT, FURRIER, TEACHER
BORN: Palestrina, 1525
DIED: Rome, February 2, 1594

In the first act of his 1917 opera *Palestrina,* Hans Pfitzner [1606] shows the composer Palestrina weighted down with personal problems, "modern" musical trends, and most of all the threat to polyphony from the Council of Trent. Alone, in a kind of trance, in his darkened room, he writes the *Pope Marcellus Mass,* inspired by the voice of his dead wife, the shades of sixteen Old Masters, and several flights of angels. Following a second act that shows the pettiness of the Council, all Rome acclaims Palestrina as the savior of music. Act One is extraordinarily compelling, and the whole opera stands as a kind of apotheosis of the Palestrina legend. The reality, however, is somewhat different.

Emperor Charles V convened the Council in 1544, and it met a year later in Trento in the mountains of northeastern Italy. Though it may be quite properly viewed as an engine of the Counter-Reformation, its underlying motives were as much how to reform the Church itself as how to come to grips with the new heresy. It sat fitfully over an eighteen-year period, finally adjourning in December 1563. Music was one of the least and last of its concerns. Pope Marcellus, Julius III's successor, who died in April 1555 after only three weeks in office, had expressed the opinion that what was sung in church should be intelligible—*primo le parole e poi la musica.* This was, no doubt, one concern of the committee assigned to study the need for musical reforms, though its chief business was separating the sacred from the profane. A move away from worldliness would appear chiefly to mean an abandonment of frivolousness, melodrama, and particularly the thematic use of popular songs and the like in religious compositions. There was a small reactionary faction that demanded a return to plainsong, but it was opposed by powerful princes who savored the incense of polyphony in their private chapels. If there was a composer who had any significant impact on the Council, it would probably have been Jacobus de Kerle [225], whose austere prayers opened the 1562 sessions. As far as we know, Palestrina made no appearances in Trento, though he knew, and was known to, many of the participants there. Modern thinking is that it is not beyond the realm of possibility that the *Missa Papae Marcelli (Pope Marcellus Mass)*—the name appears to have been an afterthought—was written,

like several such Masses, to aid the committee's thinking with regard to verbal clarity in music, or in line with its conclusions. But it was no landmark in musical history or even in its composer's career. (Even if the Church had banned polyphonic music, the effect on the art as a whole would probably have been slight, for Rome had lost its grip on much of Western Europe, secular music was beginning its rise, and polyphony, at least for the nonce, was gradually becoming unfashionable.

Palestrina, it must be said, helped contribute to his own legend. In his dedications he was careful to point out that he was on the side of right, and took pains to dedicate his music to people who counted. On the other hand, he went on using popular material as a basis for his music. Early on, he made no secret of it (e.g., *Missa "L'homme armé"),* though later such works were given neutral titles *(Missa sine nomine).* The only early master to maintain magisterial status before the advent of modern musicology, he was venerated for three centuries as a sort of saint, though in real life he was a rather paradoxical fellow. He did not hesitate to grovel before potential patrons, but he knew his own worth and, when the chips were down, refused to undersell himself. Moreover, he was not beyond treading on the toes of others when it was to his advantage, or turning a few quick *scudi* when the opportunity arose. But such human failings take nothing away from his extraordinary industry and his ability to overcome disappointment and personal tragedy.

Born Giovanni Pierluigi, Palestrina took his name from that little foothill city east of Rome, though some have lately tried to prove him a native Roman. His people were petit bourgeois of no great means. His father, Sante, owned a home near the Cathedral of Sant'Agapito, another house, and some land. He had married a woman named Palma Veccia and had sired at least four sons on her before she died in 1536. (Two of them, Bernardino and Silla, played important roles in Giovanni's later career.) By the time he was twelve, Palestrina was a chorister at the basilica of Santa Maria Maggiore in Rome, possibly taken there by Cardinal Andrea della Valle when he was transferred from Palestrina to Rome (though the myth has it that the child was taken aboard when he was heard singing in the street). Palestrina probably studied with the various *maestri* of Santa Maria (notably Robin Mallapert and Firmin Le Bel, but not Claude Goudimel [181]) between 1537 and 1544, in which latter year he went home to play the organ, help the choirmaster, and teach the choirboys at Sant'Agapito. Three years later he married a local girl, Lucrezia Gori, whose dowry included title to a house, fields, and vineyards, and a chestnut donkey, and who bore her husband, in 1549 and 1551 respectively, sons named Rodolfo and Angelo. In 1550 the Bishop of Palestrina was elected, as Julius III, successor to Pope Paul III. The next year Julius appointed his former organist *maestro* of the Cappella Giulia, the choir of St. Peter's founded by Julius II. The recipient of this favor was so pleased that he wrote the Missa *"Ecce sacerdos magnus" (Behold the High Priest),* had it magnificently printed and bound, and presented it to his patron. Said patron was in his turn so delighted that he promoted Palestrina to the Sistine Chapel, even though he had a terrible voice, was married, and had not been submitted to the scrutiny of his peers; moreover there had been no vacancy. On top of that, Palestrina managed to get his brother Bernardino transferred there from the Cappella Giulia. None of this sat very well with his colleagues. In 1555 Julius and his successor, Marcellus, both died, and Paul IV took over. When it came to reform, Paul believed in action. He called in Daniele da Volterra to trouser all those naked people on the Sistine walls and ceiling, and he fired Palestrina and two other singers from the choir, ostensibly because they were married, but probably because they had published madrigal books flaunting their connections with the chapel. To the pope's credit, he cut them off with lifetime monthly pensions of six *scudi,* but what with inflation and all that was hard for men who had been drawing ten. A few months later Palestrina doubled the take by succeeding Orlande de Lassus [228] as *maestro* at the basilica of San Giovanni in Laterano. His son Rodolfo became a choirboy there, and shortly (1558) another son, Iginio, was born. Times were bad, and the authorities kept lowering wages and reducing personnel until in 1560 Palestrina simply walked off the job. (If there were hard feelings, they were temporary, for seven years later he was awarded two goats for helping out at San Giovanni Laterano at Easter.) Early in 1561 Palestrina was back at Santa Maria Maggiore again, this time as *maestro.* When he heard that the Vatican might cut off his pension, he presented the Sistine Chapel with a number of his unpublished pieces, of which he had a plethora by then. In 1564 he found a patron in Cardinal Ippolito II d'Este, for whom he worked in the summers at his newly built Villa d'Este at Tivoli. About a year later he was put in charge of the musical wing of the new Seminario Romano, where his two older

sons were educated and where he probably taught Tomás Luis de Victoria [258]. His fame and publications having now spread all over Europe, he was approached by emissaries from Emperor Maximilian II asking if he would like to be imperial *Kapellmeister,* but when he named his price, the offer was quickly withdrawn. In 1567 he resigned from Santa Maria Maggiore and in 1570 bought a house. The next year he was again appointed director of the Cappella Giulia and had to rent a larger dwelling to accommodate the choirboys he was obligated to put up. Later he bought it too.

Then things suddenly went bad. As a result of a series of epidemics Rodolfo died in 1572, Silla in 1573. In the latter year, Angelo married the girl next door, Doralice Uberti, but in 1575 he too succumbed, leaving his wife with two infants and forcing his father into debt to repay the dowry. Palestrina squeezed a fifty-percent salary raise from St. Peter's by threatening to return to Santa Maria Maggiore, and Iginio's marriage and the sale of some property the next year improved the family finances. In 1577 the Church entrusted Palestrina with revision of the Gradual (the collection of chants for the Proper of the Mass). He never completed the task, and Iginio's later attempt to substitute some hackwork fooled no one. One thing that interrupted him was a serious illness in 1578. When yet another epidemic carried off Lucrezia in 1580, Palestrina was so downcast that he determined to enter the priesthood and had gotten as far as the tonsure when a widowed heiress to a fur shop hove into sight. Palestrina backed up and married her, taking on the fur business as a sideline. With the profits he bought two more houses as rental properties. Meanwhile in 1581 he lost three grandchildren—the two left by Angelo and one of Iginio's children. (A century later his last male descendant was dead.)

Years before Palestrina and Duke Guglielmo Gonzaga of Mantua had struck up a correspondence. In 1583 the composer hinted that he might be available, but his demand of 200 ducats a year plus free room and board for his household quickly ended the negotiations—but not the friendship. Two years later there was a small Sistine scandal, wherein Palestrina was said to be trying to subvert some of the members to achieve a choirmasterly coup. The Pope (now Sixtus V) eventually alleviated the problem by making the directorship a one-year rotating office. That same year Palestrina wrote a motet to accompany the setting up of the Egyptian obelisk in St. Peter's Square. In 1592, Clement VIII—Palestrina's

Roman years saw the passage of twelve Popes—raised his salary to sixteen *scudi* a month, and a galaxy of important composers issued a *Festschrift* of psalm settings in his honor. By 1593, however, Palestrina, feeling a bit seedy, had decided to spend his sunset years back at Sant'Agapito, but before he could put his affairs in order, he died. He was buried in old St. Peter's, but during the rebuilding that shortly followed his remains were mislaid and have not been found to this day.

The revisionists, in their attempt to discredit Palestrina as "the savior of music," have tended to throw out the baby with the bath water. There is no denying that he was a musician of great genius and immense fertility. He is neither a pathbreaker nor an atavist. He brought together the two great musical currents of his day, one "Netherlandish," the other Italian, combining contrapuntal considerations with the demands of melody and harmony, thereby summing up and synthesizing the religious music of the Renaissance. What would follow pointed to a different age and a new synthesis.

Palestrina's output was simply enormous. It includes, first of all, more than 100 Masses, which embody every genre and technique known to his predecessors—*cantus firmus*, canon, paraphrase, parody, and free-composed technique. Then there are some 260 motets written for four to twelve voices, many of them polychoral, as are some of the Masses. Beyond these there are dozens of hymns, offertories, lamentations, Magnificats, litanies, psalms, spiritual madrigals, and other lesser religious works. Finally there are nearly 100 secular madrigals, plus a few *ricercari* and "exercises," though these are of dubious authorship. It was the composer's hope to publish all of his music in his lifetime, but even with copious assistance from patrons he failed. The standard modern edition runs to 33 volumes; a new edition is still in progress.

The two words one regularly encounters in discussions of the Palestrinan style are *smooth* and *balanced*. A century ago the favorite term was *angelic*. So perfect was his music deemed that Fux [585] and others derived from it systems for "correct" composition. But these systems are arbitrary, and the "Palestrinan counterpoint" to which generations of students have been subjected is largely a fiction. Like most great composers, Palestrina was flexible in his approach and cannot be reduced to formula. Generally, however, it can be said that he prefers successive arches or waves of melody that move as nearly stepwise as possible without slipping into chromaticism, and that every as-

cent is somewhere, somehow counterbalanced by a descent. One might also say that the wider the leap, the more it is to be avoided; fifths and sixths are not very common and the octave provides the outside limit. Great care is to be taken in approaching and resolving dissonances where they are unavoidable. If we tend to see dissonances in early music as exciting harbingers of the twentieth century, Palestrina seems to regard them as crudities perpetrated by the ignorant. He is very much a man of his time and very little a prophet. He is, for example, thoroughly aware of harmonic demands, but he works within the confines of the mode he is using, not within those of "major" and "minor." Some call him unemotional and say that his music pays little heed to the words it accompanies. And in truth it is sometimes easy to dismiss him as bland. But when emotion is appropriate, as in the lamentations, he expresses, in his own way, deep feeling—which is to say not theatrically. And he does occasionally indulge in word painting, though in madrigalian terms he is not a particularly effective madrigalist.

RECORDINGS: Consistent with his reputation, recordings of Palestrina, including the *Missa Papae Marcelli,* go back before the LP era, and in recent years he has been well treated on records. Perhaps a fourth of his Masses have been made available, as well as the motets on the Song of Songs, the set of spiritual madrigals called *Le Vergini,* the *Stabat Mater,* and numerous shorter individual works—though the surface of that vast catalogue has as yet barely been scratched.

[202] ALWOOD, Richard
PRIEST
BORN: c. 1525 (?)
DIED: ?

All we know of Richard Alwood was that he was a priest (denomination unknown) who was active around the middle of the sixteenth century. He left a *Mass* and 7 keyboard compositions, 3 of them *"in nomines."*

[203] BLITHEMAN, John
ORGANIST
BORN: c. 1525
DIED: London, May 23, 1591

Older accounts say that Blitheman was master of the boys at Christ Church, Oxford, but they also call him "William." He had a living from Christ Church, but there is no indication that he lived in Oxford at any time. He was admitted to the Chapel Royal in 1555, where he taught John Bull [315] in his choirboy phase. He was still a Gentleman of the Chapel when he died. He was buried in the Church of St. Nicholas Olave, and his epitaph says that he was a fine man who loved God and his fellows and played a mean organ. He left 2 religious choral pieces and a handful of keyboard works (mostly organ hymns).

[204] CARREIRA, António (Kä-rä′-rà, Än-tōn′-yō)
ORGANIST, CHOIRMASTER
BORN: c. 1525
DIED: c. 1589

Probably a native of Lisbon, Carreira was trained as a choirboy in the chapel of King John III by Bartolomeo Trozelho. He spent his entire life in the Portuguese Royal Chapel, under four kings, the others being Sebastian, the Cardinal-King Henry, and Philip II of Spain, who succeeded on Henry's death as Philip I. Carreira became chapel organist in 1571 and *mestre de capela* a few years later. He was known as a brilliant organist. Called "the Portuguese Cabezón," he probably knew Hernando Cabezón, son of the great Antonio [164], and Francisco de Soto [175]. Although he was a pioneer of Portuguese music, Carreira brought cosmopolitan understanding to it, for he was obviously well informed of musical trends not only in Spain but throughout Europe in general. A namesake nephew was also an organist and composer. The elder Carreira left a small collection of keyboard pieces.

[205] CAVAZZONI, Girolamo (Kä-väd-zō′-nē, Jē-rō′-là-mō)
ORGANIST
BORN: c. 1525
DIED: Mantua, 1577 or later

In his first musical publication, Vol. I of his *Intavolatura* (Venice, 1543), Cavazzoni, son of Marco Antonio Cavazzoni [122], calls himself "still a youth" *(quasi fanciullo)*. He also let it be known that he was born when his father was in the service of Cardinal Bembo, and he was commonly known as "Hieronimo d'Urbino." Since Bembo was at Urbino in the first decade of the century, it has been assumed that Cavazzoni was born around 1510 and was merely being modest about his inexperience when he claimed extreme immaturity. However, he was probably born about the year noted above, when his father and the cardinal were associated

at Padua. He seems to have stayed around the general area of Venice for a time, but by the middle 1560s he was at the court of the music-loving Duke Guglielmo Gonzaga in Mantua, where he served as organist at the church of Santa Barbara. Among his pupils there was Costanzo Antegnati [260], whose father installed the organ. His 2 organ volumes (the second of uncertain date) include organ hymns, organ Masses, Magnificats, *ricercari*, and *canzone*. Cavazzoni treats his organ hymns (a genre intended to replace the sung chant) like Franco-Flemish motets conceived in organ terms. The Magnificats alternate, verse for verse, sung plainchant and what amounts to organ variations—standard practice. The Masses follow a similar pattern but use freely composed material for the instrumental sections. The *ricercari* and *canzone* are something new. Girolamo's *ricercari* are as pathbreaking as his father's but quite different: reminiscent of imitative motets, they use fewer and more highly developed themes and fall into clear-cut sections that terminate in elaborate cadences. In short, they provide a model for the future "organ *ricercare.*" Similarly, Cavazzoni "invents" the keyboard *canzona,* a contrapuntal form regarded as an ancestor of the fugue.

[206] RIZZIO, David
SINGER, COURTIER
BORN: Turin (?), c. 1525
DIED: Edinburgh, March 9, 1566

Though his name figures in Scottish history as given above, he was probably Davidde Riccio, supposedly the son of a dancing master. Whatever his origins, he was apparently trained in the Castigleonian concept of courtiership. In 1561 he and his brother Giuseppe arrived at Holyrood Palace, Edinburgh, with the Marchese Moreta, on embassy from the court of Savoy to Mary of Scotland. Rizzio was small, slightly twisted, dark, and ugly, but he sang bass. Mary loved music and needed a good basso, so he stayed on at eighty pounds a year as *valet de chambre.* But "Davie," as he came to be known, had several strings to his bow, and he was, much to the disgust of the Scots contingent, soon handling the queen's French correspondence. When a young Scots noble, Lord Darnley, came a-wooing Mary, his distant cousin, in 1565, he and Davie became fast friends, tennis partners, and even bedfellows. Possibly anxious to see his employer wed to a Catholic, Rizzio pressed his friend's suit (or at least his doublet), and the pair went to the altar that summer. But

Mary had many enemies among the nobility, and it was easy to imagine Rizzio a Machiavelli and a tool of the Counter-Reformation. It was also easy to persuade Darnley, who, like most of the principals in the drama, was none too bright, that there was an Italian cuckoo in his nest—especially as Mary had quickly lost interest in the young ninny and had not given him the power he had hoped for. On the evening of March 9, 1566, Darnley and his men surprised Mary and Rizzio having an intimate dinner, dragged the screaming Davie into the next room, where they perforated him thoroughly and tossed his body out of the window. Sentimental or opportunistic later tradition attributed to the hapless Davie a number of such favorite Scots songs as "Auld Rob Morris," "Bessie Bell," and "Doun the Burn," but there is not a shred of evidence to prove it. If Rizzio composed anything that has come down to us, it may have been *Las! En mon doux printemps,"* lyric by Mary as a widow (of Francis II) of eighteen springs.

[207] PADOVANO, Annibale (Pà-dō-và'-nō, Ăn-nē-bà'-lä)

ORGANIST

BORN: Padua, 1527
DIED: Graz, March 15, 1575

It is not clear whether Padovano was his true surname or he was "Paduan Hannibal." In 1552 he successfully competed for the post of second organist at St. Mark's in Venice, previously held by Fra Armonio (Brother Harmony) dei Crocicchieri. After serving thirteen years, during which he would have played antiphonally with Girolamo Parabosco [199] and later with Claudio Merulo [230], he got leave to take a month's vacation in France. When he did not return, he was succeeded by Andrea Gabrieli [180]. Padovano soon found his way to the archducal court of Karl of Styria in Graz, where he had probably been headed in the first place, and where he became *Kapellmeister.* He wrote Masses, motets, and madrigals (one volume in collaboration with Cipriano de Rore [184], typical of their time but not strikingly individual. He also left a set of four-part *ricercari* from 1556, apparently meant for consort performance but probably originally organ works. A posthumous collection of *ricercari* and *toccate* is specifically for organ.

[208] GALILEI, Vincenzo (Gà-lē-lä'-ē, Vin-chănt'-zō)

MATHEMATICIAN, LUTENIST, VIOL
PLAYER, THEORIST, SINGER

BORN: Santa Maria in Monte, Tuscany, c. 1528
DIED: Florence, c. July 1, 1591

The father of Galileo Galilei, the great astronomer, was born into a poor family of noble blood in a Florentine hill town. Educated in the humanistic way, he also became a fine lutenist and had a good bass singing voice. He may have worked in Florence for a time for Count Giovanni de'Bardi, a notable soldier and courtier who dabbled in the arts. Probably in the late 1550s or early 1560s, Galilei moved to Pisa, where he married in 1562, the most famous of his several children and his firstborn arriving there two years later. At some point in between, Galilei, at Bardi's urging and expense, had taken a course of study with Gioseffo Zarlino [186] in Venice. Afterward he became increasingly involved in musical theory, which led him eventually to a violent disagreement with his old teacher on the matter of proper tuning and the nature of dissonance, among other matters. In 1572 he returned to Florence, where the Bardi *palazzo* was now a meeting place for the group of avant-garde humanists and esthetes who called themselves the Camerata, which was particularly interested in Greek music and the nature of its use in drama. Galilei's dealings on these points with Girolamo Mei, a Florentine living in Rome, convinced him that the Greek tragedies were sung. To demonstrate what that might have been like, he set Dante's passage on the cannibalistic Count Ugolino *(Inferno XXXIII)* for solo voice and viols and performed it to considerable applause and a few titters. Encouraged, he subjected part of the Lamentations of Jeremiah to similar treatment. Whether Galilei "invented" the monodic style used in the first operas is uncertain, since both works are lost, but there is no doubt that his notions played a role in the creation of the first operas. Later his fame as a musical thinker won him a number of other patrons. His *Fronimo* of 1568, a dialogue on how to transcribe for the lute, with musical illustrations, is a valuable source book on that subject and contains some important ideas on music as an emotive language. His *Dialogo della musica antica e della moderna* begins as a history but develops into a diatribe against Zarlino. When Zarlino tried to defend his viewpoint, Galilei launched another in his *Discorso* (1589). Some unpublished pieces show him using his mathematics in some pertinent deductions about acoustics. He came down heavily on the side of tonality as against modality, a taste reflected in many of his compositions. He claimed to have written or transcribed more than 4,000 lute pieces, but most of them, like the first of his 2 books of madrigals, have vanished.

[209] GUERRERO, Francisco (Gwâr-rā'-rō, Frán-thēs'-kō)
CHOIRMASTER, WRITER
BORN: Seville, October 4, 1528
DIED: Seville, November 8, 1599

For a long time neglected, Guerrero is now generally regarded as one of the most important figures of early Spanish music. He was the son of Gonzalo Sanchez Guerrero, a painter of no great importance, and the younger brother of Pedro Guerrero, who provided his musical grounding and later went to Italy, where he sang in the choir of Santa Maria Maggiore and wrote some motets and songs. Francisco Guerrero also claimed to be a pupil of Cristóbal de Morales [153], but one can't imagine when, unless on the fly after the latter's return from Italy. At fourteen he was a choirboy at Seville Cathedral, where he would probably have studied with the *maestro de capilla*, Pedro Fernández de Castilleja. Three years later he himself became choirmaster of the cathedral of Jaén in the mountains of south-central Spain. Not unexpectably, his immaturity got in his way, he was chastened for being remiss in his duties, and finally, after three years, having gotten leave to visit Seville, he failed to return. Instead he joined his old choir again, taking a considerable cut in income. In 1551 he dickered for the directorship at Málaga, which, however, went to Morales. When Morales died in 1553, Guerrero was named his successor, but he never got there, presumably because Seville promised him that he could be Fernandez's successor, the old man by that time being in his late sixties. Guerrero assumed *de facto* charge, though he did not acquire title until Fernandez's death a decade later. Meanwhile, Guerrero did a lot of politicking on his own behalf. Some music presented to the retired Emperor Charles V was badly received by its dedicatee, who called Guerrero, among other unpleasant things, a thief and a cheat. He had better luck with the volume of Masses he took to King Sebastian of Portugal in Lisbon—but then Sebastian was only twelve. Guerrero and his choir were part of the official greeting committee for Anne of Austria, Philip II's fourth and final bride, in 1570–71. In 1579 he got a year's leave to go to Rome, but it took so long to put all the manuscripts he wanted to publish there in order that he did not embark for two years. In 1588 he traveled to Venice with the Archbishop of Seville, and there, deciding to fulfill a lifetime ambition, proceeded to the Holy Land. On his return trip he crossed the Italian peninsula and sailed from Genoa. Between there and Marseilles he was twice robbed by pirates and left very low on funds. Back home he tried boarding choristers and writing up his travels, but by 1591 he was in debtor's prison and had to be bailed out by the cathedral chapter. At seventy he decided to return to Palestine, but the plague got him before he could take off. His travel book, published twelve years after he died, became a bestseller and continued to sell for two centuries.

Guerrero's music had a comparable record. Tonal, tuneful, wearing its heart on its sleeve, it was enormously popular in Spanish and Latin-American churches. This is not to say that it was trivial or simple-minded: underneath the pleasant surface was the work of a master who knew his counterpoint. A great deal of it has obviously disappeared, but there remain 18 Masses, dozens of motets, and 4 Passions (according to each of the four Evangelists). Guerrero was a notable writer of secular songs, but though only a relative handful remains, he published 61 as *Spiritual Songs and Villancicos* with substituted religious texts. At one time he was remembered largely for his Marian pieces and came to be called *"El Cantor de María."* He was thus misrepresented as an adherent of the so-called Cult of the Virgin, a sort of musical Murillo who wrote sweetly sentimental and characterless pieces. But he is now viewed as being on the same plane as Morales and Victoria [258].

[210] WHYTHORNE, Thomas
CHOIRMASTER, TEACHER
BORN: Ilminster, Somerset, 1528
DIED: London, July 31, 1596

Today Whythorne lives as few other Renaissance musicians do. He does so in part because in the 1920s Philip Heseltine—"Peter Warlock" [1900]—took the trouble to edit and publish some of his songs, demonstrating that Whythorne was a pioneer in the rise of the English madrigal. He lives even more because in 1955 his manuscript autobiography turned up at Sotheby's in a box of oddments submitted for appraisal. And a fascinating work it is: with its combination of verse and prose it is as important to the history of English literature as it is to English music, even without the exaggerated claims made for it.

Briefly the story goes like this: Whythorne was born to middle-class parents of small means and at ten was farmed out to an uncle-priest near Oxford. That worthy, after inculcating his charge in the advantages of various professions and callings, to his eternal credit allowed the boy to do what he wanted, which was to study music. In 1545, having attended Magdalen College on scholarship, and determined to support himself by his chosen calling, young Thomas was taken on as secretary by none other than the poet and dramatist John Heywood. After three years, in which he learned a great deal about music and poetry that they didn't teach one in college, he decided to go up to London and teach music. Whythorne's life was one of good and bad luck. His good luck was repeatedly to be employed by important and powerful people. Though he is reticent to name them, we can identify, besides John Heywood, Lord Ambrose Dudley (son of the late Earl of Northumberland), William Bromfield (Lieutenant-General of the Ordnance under both Mary and Elizabeth), and Matthew Parker, Archbishop of Canterbury (whose earlier choirmaster had been Thomas Tallis). Not only did he work for the great and near-great (there was also a privy councillor and a court lady, unidentified), but he pleased them so well that twice he was promised lifelong annuities. Alas! death or financial ruin regularly burst the bubble.

At one point in his career, feeling particularly flush, Whythorne made the mandatory grand tour of the Continent, sampling music and musical practice in the Lowlands, Germany, Italy, and France. No doubt the experience made its impact—notably on his decision to peddle his songs—but he tells us little about it, on the grounds that he means to devote a separate book to his travels. It has not yet turned up.

Whythorne is neither a great writer nor a great composer, but he is fascinating in both metiers. The song volume, published in 1571, contains music that is likable and competent if not first rate. If the pieces are not quite madrigals, they are interesting forerunners of the accompanied consort song. Later Whythorne published a book of duos *(bicinia)*, designed for singing or playing or both, which has, hyperbolically been called the first English book of instrumental music.

RECORDINGS: Some of the songs have been recorded by Alfred Deller, Edgar Fleet, and Jennifer Partridge, *inter alia.*

[211] LE JEUNE, Claude (Lə Zhön, Klōd)
TEACHER
BORN: Valenciennes, c. 1528
DIED: Paris, c. September 25, 1600

If the *chansons* ascribed to Le Jeune in publications of 1552 were really by someone else (and why should they have been ascribed to him?), his birth date may have been somewhat later than indicated above. A Protestant, he went to Paris and in 1564 published some four-part psalms to the vernacular texts by Théodore de Bèze. After that we catch no clear view of him for nearly twenty years. Very obviously, as his later work shows, he was connected with the Académie de Poésie et de Musique, founded by the poet Jean-Antoine de Baïf and the musician Joachim Thibault de Courville in 1570, which, in one form and another, met from 1571 to 1584. The body's chief concern was *vers mesurés* and how to set them to music. *Vers mesurés* were a product of the humanistic notion that, entropy being what it is, antiquity was better than modernity and that therefore modern poetry should be made to subscribe to the metrical rules of the Greeks and Romans. The notion ignored the fact that classical stresses were based on vowel-lengths and modern stresses on accent, but poets like Baïf in France and Richard Stanyhurst and Thomas Campion **[332]** in England strove mightily to overcome the difficulty.

Le Jeune had a number of powerful Protestant patrons, which may explain how he escaped the St. Bartholomew's Day Massacre in 1572. It is said that in 1578 he was in the service of William the Silent, Prince of Orange, in the Netherlands. Shortly thereafter he was hired as master of the children of the chapel of Henry III's brother, François, Duke of Anjou (whom Elizabeth of England called her "Little Frog" when he came a-courting). In 1581 Le Jeune was asked to provide the music for one of the splashiest weddings of the century—that of Anne, Duc de Joyeuse, the king's *mignon,* to the queen's half-sister, Marie. (Joyeuse was afterward promoted to the rank of admiral and made governor of Normandy, but the union was without issue.) Le Jeune's chief contribution was, we are told, a battle piece that stirred one old soldier to such a berserk display of militarism that the musicians were asked to switch to something more soothing and less dangerous to the onlookers.

In 1588 the religious struggle broke out afresh, with fighting between Henry's adherents and those of his Catholic rivals. Le Jeune, legend has it, was apprehended trying to flee Paris with his manuscripts. Both were saved by the fortuitous appearance of his friend and fellow-academician, the Catholic composer Jacques Mauduit [288]. For a time Le Jeune holed up in the Huguenot stronghold of La Rochelle, but when Henry was dispatched by the dagger of a vengeful monk, he returned to welcome the new (Protestant) king, Henry IV, who made him his official chamber composer. (Henry's twenty-two *Violons du Roi* may be regarded as the first modern orchestra.)

Most of Le Jeune's music that has come down to us was published late in his career or posthumously. It shows a remarkable eclecticism, blending techniques of the polyphonists, the Paris school, and the new impulses from Italy (as in his madrigals and instrumental fantasias). Le Jeune was the first to publish *vers mesurée* settings (in 1583), thitherto accessible only to members of the Académie de Poésie, and continued to do so. Syllabic in treatment (i.e., one note to each syllable), they recognize the primacy of verbal meanings and strive to bring them out. Le Jeune also made experiments in trying to approximate the Greek modes and had clearly read Gioseffo Zarlino [186] on the subject, since he arranged the contents of several of his publications according to the Zarlinesque modes. In his *Le Printemps,* a collection of airs and *chansons,* he allowed poetic stress to determine musical accent, a procedure that worked quite well. Another interesting work is the *Octonaires de la vanité et inconstance du monde,* setting of a cycle of allegorical eight-line verses by the Calvinist divine Antoine de La Roche-Chandieu (published 1606). The largest portion of Le Jeune's output is his nearly 350 psalms. The 2 volumes published in his lifetime are conceived in large quasi-polyphonic terms, in the manner of grand motets. Others, including some simple three-part treatments and some to *vers mesurée* translations, were published after his death. Many of them enjoyed two hundred years of church use.

RECORDINGS: Besides individual pieces in anthologies, there is a complete recording of the *Octonaires* and a selection of fifteen *chansons* from *Le Printemps.*

[212] MUNDY, William
SINGER
BORN: c. 1529
DIED: London, 1591

Nothing is known of Mundy's origins or his childhood. He was first chorister at Westminster Abbey in 1543 under Henry VIII. In 1547, the first year of Edward VI's reign, Mundy was usher at the London church of St. Martin Vintry, and for a decade thereafter he was parish clerk at St. Mary's-at-Hill (i.e., to the end of the reign of Mary I). In 1564 he became a Gentleman of the Chapel Royal (some sources give the year as 1563). The record tells us that he had at that time been a member of the choir at St. Paul's Cathedral, and that he was brought in to replace a Master Walker, who "was slaine the 27th of November" previous (how or why, we are not informed). On October 12, 1591, one Anthony Anderson took Mundy's place, so we may assume that he had died shortly before. Mundy produced an Anglican service, some English anthems, some Latin motets, and a son named John, who became a composer mainly of madrigals. Thomas Morley [289] implies that he remained Catholic, but none of the scant evidence gives us much basis for agreement. One wonders if there were those who blew as the wind blew, religiously speaking. He left both Catholic and Anglican works. Some of the pieces ascribed to him, however, may be by his son. His most famous is the anthem *O Lord, the Maker of All Things,* the composition of which, however, by long tradition is usually accorded to Henry VIII.

[213] AMMERBACH, Elias Nikolaus
(Ám'-mer-bákh, Ā-le'-ás Nē'-kō-lous)
ORGANIST
BORN: Naumburg, c. 1530
DIED: Leipzig, c. January 28, 1597

Ammerbach's Naumburg is the one on the River Saale, now in East Germany. He said he yearned to be a musician from birth, and studied with many foreign masters at great cost to himself, though the only record we have of his education is that of a semester at the University of Leipzig. In 1561 he was appointed organist of St. Thomas Church there, where he played the services for thirty-four years. He was thrice married, had a hard time making ends meet, and left five children. Because of the florid ornamentation of some of his organ pieces and his statement that he had "colored" them as well as he could, he is regarded as the founder of the so-called "Colorist School" of organ writing. He also apparently invented the form of tablature known as "new German tablature," and his 1571 collection (intended, he tells us, for keyboards of all kinds) is the first known organ book to be published in Germany. It is largely made up of songs and dances, graduated as to difficulty (i.e., amount of ornamentation). Ammerbach published a second collection four years later, and a revised and enlarged edition of the first in 1583.

[214] AZZAIOLO, Filippo (Ăd-ză-yō'-lō, Fē-lēp'-pō)
SINGER (?)
BORN: Bologna, c. 1530 (?)
DIED: after 1569

Nothing concrete is known about Azzaiolo, who is supposed to have been a choir singer around Bologna. His fame rests on three books of *villotte* (which he calls *Villotte del fiore alla Paduana*, or *Flower Villottas in Paduan Style)* published between 1557 and 1569. The *villotta* was basically a four-part arrangement of a popular or folk song. Some that appear in Azzaiolo's collections were used by other composers; Lassus himself **[228]** sang *Chi passar per 'sta strada (Who Passes Through This Street)* at the wedding of William V of Bavaria and Renée of Lorraine. RECORDINGS: At least half an LP has been devoted to a selection of *villotte.*

[215] BEAUJOYEULX, Baltasar de *(né Baldassare da Belgioso, called "Baltazarini")* (Bō-zhwă-ö', Băl-tă-zär də)
VIOLINIST, CHOREOGRAPHER (?), PRODUCER
BORN: Italy, c. 1530
DIED: Paris, c. 1587

Nothing is known of Beaujoyeulx's early life. Reportedly the Maréchal de Brissac found him in the Piedmont heading an orchestra of the newfangled violins and was so taken with what he heard that he dispatched the whole group in 1555 to Catherine de Médici. Beaujoyeulx served as *valet de chambre* to her, to Mary of Scotland (when she was briefly Queen of France), to Charles IX, to the Duc d'Alençon, and to Henry III before returning to the queen mother in 1584 as equerry. At that time he was given the title of Seigneur des Landes. He was succeeded as *valet de chambre* by his son. The Abbé de Brantôme thought him "the finest violinist in Christendom."

Beaujoyeulx's role as a composer is obscure, but his place in the history of the musical theater is an important one. Like most good things French, the *ballet de cour* saw its beginnings with the importation of a Milanese dancing master, Pompeo Diobono (Pompey Goodgod) the year before Beaujoyeulx arrived. Over the next two and a half decades the court ballet—related to

the English court masque, which it probably helped spawn, and the Italian pastoral plays, which probably contributed to it—developed. It came to include songs, allegory, and "special effects" (machines) along with the dancing. In October 1581 the king's favorite, the Duc de Joyeuse, married the queen's half-sister, Marie, and Beaujoyeulx got permission to celebrate with a project he had in mind. The result, which occupied five and a half hours on the night of October 15, was *Circe, ou le Balet comique de la Royne.* The work had a plot—the king's triumph over the witch Circe and his restoration of sanity and reason to his realm, and the term *comique* indicated that it was essentially a drama, not an entertainment or revue, like its predecessors. The work was carefully planned so that it would be what has come to be called "total theater," with all parts integrated—songs, dances, choreography, effects, scenery, costumes, etc., and it reflected the latest in humanistic thinking. Not only did it set the standard for the court ballet (which flickered out in the ensuing troubled times, but it returned under Louis XIII and forecast the Lullyan opera; the French also maintain that it set the standard for that Gallic shibboleth *le bon goût* (good taste). It also set the exchequer back 200,000 livres. The piece was a collaborative effort, but the idea and the plot outline came from Beaujoyeulx, who oversaw the production, and it is believed by many that he contributed the music for the dances.

[216] BELL'HAVER, Vincenzo (Bel-ă'-ver, Vēn-chänt'-zō)
ORGANIST
BORN: c. 1530
DIED: Venice, late summer 1587

A pupil of Andrea Gabrieli **[180]**, Bell'haver was an organist in Padua until 1568, when he moved to Venice to play at the Scuola di San Rocco. In 1579 he was one of several Venetian composers who contributed music for the wedding of Francesco de' Medici, Grand Duke of Tuscany, to Bianca Capello. The festivities took place in both Florence and Venice, but a year after the event itself. Bianca, the lovely and gifted daughter of a Venetian noble, had eloped in 1560 with an impecunious Florentine. In 1563 she became the duke's mistress, but he had to wait for his wife to die to make it official. Titian painted her, and she became the subject of legends, both romantic and gruesome. In June 1584, Bell'haver became organist of Padua Cathedral (he had failed in the 1567 competition). But he had not been in place long when he decided, without permission, to indulge a wish to travel and was sacked. In 1586 he briefly succeeded Giovanni Gabrieli as second organist of St. Mark's but died after a few months. Save for some fugitive pieces (2 Magnificats, a few motets, an organ piece, madrigals), his only surviving work is his second book of madrigals.

[217] CAROSO, Marco Fabrizio (Kȧ-rō′-zō, Mär′-kō Fȧ-britz′-yō)
DANCING MASTER
BORN: Sermoneta, c. 1530
DIED: Rome, after 1605

According to tradition, Caroso came from a little duchy south of Rome, where he was very likely in the employ of the Caetani, the ruling family. Later in Rome he seems to have made himself known to most of the important nobles of Italy, but we know nothing of the details of his life. In 1581, with a dedication to Bianca Capello, new Grand Duchess of Tuscany (see 216), he published *Il Ballerino (The Little Dancer),* a dance manual with choreography that shows him very *au courant,* and with illustrative dance pieces in lute tablature. In 1600, with a new dedication to Ranuccio I, the gloomy Duke of Parma, he brought out a considerably updated and expanded version as *Nobiltà di dame,* which went through several editions.

[218] COSTELEY, Guillaume (Kō-tə-lā′, Gĕ-yōm′)
ORGANIST
BORN: Fontanges, 1530 or 1531
DIED: Evreux, January 28, 1606

Music historians used to be obsessed with the notion that Costeley was a transplanted Irishman named Costello (or at least the descendant of one), but it is now known that he came from an Auvergnat village. He probably settled in Paris in his early twenties, for he was publishing there by 1554. He evidently found friends at court (he seems to have been an intimate of the poet Pierre de Ronsard and the Pléiade), and in 1560 became *valet de chambre,* organist in ordinary, and music teacher to the preadolescent Charles IX, who had just taken the throne on the death of his brother, Francis II. Costeley seems to have married for the first time in 1567, but his big year was 1570, when he became a charter member of Jean-Antoine de Baïf's Académie de Poésie et de Musique (see 211). He bought a house in Evreux, west of Paris, and was excused from his court duties, save in the first quarter of each year. At

Evreux he inaugurated what seem to have been the first musical celebrations honoring St. Cecilia, patroness of the art, sponsored by the Confraternity of St. Cecilia, which he founded that year. (In 1575 he added a competition in which Orlande de Lassus won the first prize, a silver medal engraved with an organ.) And in 1570 he seems to have given up writing music, at least for publication. He eventually retired from court entirely and served for a time as a municipal tax assessor in Evreux. Widowed, he remarried at some time in his penultimate decade.

Besides 3 motets and one of the first French keyboard pieces to have come down to us, Costeley wrote mostly *chansons,* among them a justly famous and exquisitely sensitive setting of Ronsard's *"Mignonne, allons voir si la rose."* Influenced by Italian theorists, he created one *chanson* in microtones, a pioneering effort that found few followers before the present century. He also may have originated the term *air* to describe his simpler strophic *chansons.*

[219] DONATO, Baldassare (Dō-nȧ′-tō, Bȧl-dȧ-sȧ′-rȧ)
SINGER, CHOIRMASTER, TEACHER
BORN: Venice, c. 1530
DIED: Venice, 1603

A singer at St. Mark's in Venice from 1550 at the latest, Donato became master of the choirboys in 1562. Two years later he was made director of the Small Choir (Piccola Cappella), a sort of training school for apprentice members. This arrangement was supposed to take the pressure off of the *maestro di cappella,* Cipriano de Rore **[184]**, but it didn't. When Gioseffo Zarlino **[186]** succeeded Rore the following year, he decided the whole thing was a needless expense, ended the bipartite division, and reduced Donato to a mere singer again. Perhaps Donato felt humiliated. At any rate, when in 1569 Zarlino asked the choir for a special effort on a feast day, Donato led a protest. When it went unheeded, the dissidents proceeded to caterwaul their way through the performance, winning the leader a heavy fine. However, he stayed on and in 1577 became director of the best elite musical confraternity, the Scuola di San Rocco. Again he had trouble with the authorities and soon resigned. Evidently, however, he was considered a valuable property, for when in 1580 Padua Cathedral tried to lure him away as choir director, his salary was boosted and he was given the post of teacher of singing in the Gregorian seminary attached to the basilica. He became *de facto* director at St.

Mark's during Zarlino's last illness, and when the latter died in 1590, Donato succeeded him. He continued to hold down his teaching duties until the seminary was moved across town some years later. Then he was permitted to focus what remained of his energies on the choir, which, not unexpectably, declined under his leadership. Donato is best known as a composer of secular music. His initial publication, a collection of polished and sophisticated *villanelle* and some four-part madrigals, went through six editions in as many years. Two other madrigal books followed. Donato shows the drift toward diatonicism, and some of the later madrigals are in quasi-dramatic dialogue form or tend toward monody, the other voices providing harmonic backup for what is in essence a soloist. A late collection of motets published in 1599 is less interesting.

[220] LA GROTTE, Nicolas (Là Grôt, Nē-kō-làs')
KEYBOARD PLAYER
BORN: 1530
DIED: c. 1600

When first heard from, La Grotte was royal organist at the court of the little rump kingdom of Navarre in 1557. But the next year he married and moved to Paris (or vice versa) and four years later was in the train of the Duke of Anjou, the future Henry III. When that prince became king in 1574, La Grotte probably took the place of Guillaume Costeley [218] as *valet de chambre* and organist-in-ordinary. In 1581 he helped Claude Le Jeune [211] and Baltasar de Beaujoyeulx [215] with the music for the wedding of the Duc de Joyeuse. He evidently throve at court, for by 1590 he had become a man of property. His output consists almost entirely of *chansons,* many of which are, in everything but name, *airs de cour* (solo songs with accompaniment).

[221] LEOPOLITA, Marcin (Là-ō-pol'-i-tà, Mär-tsēn)
BORN: Lvov, c. 1530 (?)
DIED: Lvov, 1589

Also known as Marcin Lvovczyk and Martinus Leopolitanus, Leopolita was hired in 1560 as court composer to King Sigismund Augustus of Poland and dismissed four years later (rationale not provided). He presumably came from Lvov and is said to have been an alumnus of the Cracow Academy.

Three of his Masses were extant a century ago, but only one seems to have survived. There are also a few motets in organ score and some miscellaneous organ pieces. Leopolita was obviously an old-school polyphonist. RECORDINGS: The surviving *Mass* and some of the organ music have been recorded.

[222] MATELART, Ioanne (Må'-tel-ärt, Yō-àn'-nä)
CHOIRMASTER, LUTENIST
BORN: Flanders, c. 1530
DIED: Rome, June 7, 1607

Though he also appears under such names as Giovanni Martellato, Matelart was surely a Fleming who emigrated to Italy in the 1550s. In 1565 he became choirmaster at the church of San Lorenzo in Damaso, in Rome, and remained at that post until he died. He is chiefly known for his 1559 lute book, which went through several editions and which contains both original pieces and transcriptions. Late in his life, in 1596, he also published a collection of processional hymns, antiphons, and responsories, including a number of his own.

[223] PARSONS, Robert
SINGER
BORN: c. 1530
DIED: Newark-upon-Trent, England, January 25, 1570

Parsons (apparently unrelated to a later Robert Parsons from Devon) was certifiably a Gentleman of the Chapel Royal from 1563, but there is some small evidence that he was in London considerably earlier. Four years later he obtained a lease on some rectories in Lincolnshire. When he was drowned in the River Trent two and a half years afterward, he may have been on his way to do whatever he planned to do with them. He was evidently highly regarded by his peers. He was succeeded in the Chapel Royal by William Byrd [248]. Parsons left a number of religious compositions, including at least one Anglican service, a few consort songs, and a number of pieces of viol consort, including 5 *In nomines.*

[224] SPERANDIO, Bertoldo (Spâr-ànd'-yō, Bâr-tōl'-dō)
ORGANIST
BORN: Modena, c. 1530
DIED: Padua, August 13, 1570

Sperandio became organist of Padua Cathedral in 1552. In the summer of 1567 he was fired for insubordination and had to get his job back by competing for it. When he died, it was offered to Baldassare Donato [219], who found it inexpedient to accept it. Sperandio was obviously of the Venetian school of composition. He left 2 books of madrigals (some for two groups of singers), and a number of organ *canzone, toccate,* and *ricercari.*

[225] KERLE, Jacobus de (Kârl, Yä´-kō-bus də)
CHOIRMASTER, ORGANIST, CARILLON-
NEUR, PRIEST, SINGER
BORN: Ieper (Ypres), 1531 or 1532
DIED: Prague, January 7, 1571

Not to be confused with the later Johann Kaspar Kerll [506], Jacobus (or Jacques) de Kerle was a Fleming, the son of Robert and Marie de Kerle. He went to Italy, probably when in his early twenties, became a singer, *carillonneur,* and master of the choristers at Orvieto Cathedral (by 1555), and was ordained. In 1561 he there encountered the Archbishop of Augsburg, Cardinal Otto. (The cardinal is sometimes called "Otto Truchsess" or "von Truchsess," but this was his title as Lord High Steward of Waldburg.) Otto, a delegate to the Council of Trent entrusted with musical considerations, commissioned from Kerle a set of prayers to open the 1562 sessions and to illustrate the principle that the words should be intelligible. The cardinal rewarded him by putting him in charge of his chapel, then in Rome, and before settling down in Dillingen, Bavaria, where he had his headquarters, took him and it on junkets that reached as far as Spain. There, having apparently overjunketed, he disbanded the choir in 1565 for economic reasons. Kerle went home to become choir director in his hometown cathedral. However, a set-to with the cathedral chapter culminated in a lawsuit and Kerle's excommunication. Crying "unfair," he set out to Rome, where he ran into his old employer, who, having apparently fixed the ticket, installed him in Augsburg Cathedral. Here Kerle became vicar choral and then organist and was given a lucrative benefice. However, when a new *Kapellmeister* was needed in 1574, he was passed over. Apparently piqued, he traded his benefice for one at Cambrai, dickered for a post at Kempten, and quit Augsburg a year later. What happened next is uncertain, but by 1579 hostilities in the area caused him to flee from Cambrai to Mons. Soon after he took service with Gebhard, Archbishop-Elector of Co-

logne, nephew to Cardinal Otto. Shortly afterward, in 1582, he was back in Augsburg in the chapel of Emperor Rudolf. From there, still in the imperial service, he moved to Vienna. In 1583 he went to Prague, where, his post being really a sinecure, he seems to have spent his last years quietly. Except for some madrigals, Kerle's work (Masses, motets, hymns, psalms, etc.) was all religious, much of it representing a union of conservative Renaissance polyphony with Italian influences. But the Tridentine *Prayers* had an important impact on post-Council music, which is reflected in some of his later music.

[226] NEWSIDLER, Melchior (Noi´-sēd-ler, Mel´-khē-ôr)
LUTENIST
BORN: Nuremberg, 1531
DIED: Augsburg, 1590

It has been established that Melchior Newsidler was the son, not the younger brother, of Hans [161]. He moved to Augsburg in his early twenties, took out citizenship in 1552, and worked there as a municipal musician. Ten years later, his father having fallen on hard times, Melchior took over the rearing of his younger brothers. In 1566 he went to Venice to publish his two-volume collection of lute pieces in Italian tablature. Eight years later, he published another collection (in German tablature) in Strasbourg, which, according to his message, contained artistic motet transcriptions, favorite German, French, and Italian tunes, merry passamezzos, saltarellos, and German dances, and three undescribed fantasias. After several unsuccessful attempts to win patronage he spent several months in 1580–81 at the court of Ferdinand, Archduke of the Tyrol, in Innsbruck. He was also patronized by various members of the banking family of Fugger (worth 60,000,000 florins in 1560). Toward the end of his life, Newsidler was incapacitated by gout and had to live on charity.

[227] FRANCO, Hernando (Fräng´-kō, Er-nán´-dō)
CHOIRMASTER
BORN: Galizuela, Spain, 1532
DIED: Mexico City, November 28, 1585

Franco is the first "American" composer whose works are known to have survived. Born in extreme west-central Spain, he spent his adolescence in the cathedral choir at Segovia, and while there fell in with a magnate named Mather de Arévalo Sedeño, who had connections with the Central American colonies. By 1573, thanks apparently to Sedeño, Franco was in charge of the cathedral choir in the city of Guatemala, which numbered in its ranks a former colleague and a cousin. When the chapter proved impecunious or stingy, Arévalo took the choir to Mexico City in 1574. When, a year later, the *maestro de capilla* somehow ran afoul of the viceroy, Franco was named to replace him at a starting salary of 600 gold pesos. Six years later, he and his cousin were named to what appeared to be handsome benefices. However, the whole thing turned out to be pie in the sky, for construction costs for the new cathedral ran far beyond the original estimates, and the authorities tried to make up the deficit by stringent cuts in salaries and other expenditures. The result was that Franco resigned, and the chapel, which he had so carefully built up, went on strike. After several years of negotiations, he was victorious, winning supreme authority in his bailiwick. Unfortunately he died shortly afterward. They did what they could to make it up to him by burying him in the cathedral and, in 1611, by bringing out a handsome and expensive volume of his double Magnificat cycle. Franco also left a number of motets, and a Lamentations setting. He was a skillful if sober polyphonist who shows the influence of Cristóbal de Morales [153]. RECORDINGS: At least two of his Magnificats have been recorded.

[228] LASSUS, Orlande de (Làs'-sōōs, Ôr-lánd' də)

SINGER, CHOIRMASTER
BORN: Mons, 1532
DIED: Munich, June 14, 1594

Orlande (or Roland) de Lassus was also called Orlandus Lassus (or Lassusius), but at the height of his career seems to have preferred "Orlando di Lasso." There is no shred of evidence that he was ever Roland de Lattre. Whatever his name, he represents the culmination of the Renaissance vocal tradition. If he could carry polyphony no farther than Josquin des Prez [71] had, he at least equaled him in knowledge and his scope was broader, for he was a master not only of both sacred and secular forms, but also of national styles, and he had an unerring sense of what was musically appropriate to the text at hand. Moreover, his output was enormous, running to nearly 1,500 works.

Considering Lassus's fame and prestige in his own time, the facts of his life that have come down to us are surprisingly sketchy. The much-repeated story that he was thrice kidnapped in boyhood by agents of princes who wanted him for their chapels is unsubstantiated. However, in about 1544 he was, as a chorister, taken into the service of Ferdinando Gonzaga, Viceroy of Sicily, who happened to be on a military campaign in the neighborhood of Mons. In Gonzaga's retinue he passed through Paris, stopped briefly in the Gonzaga town of Mantua, reached Palermo in 1545, and moved on to Milan two years later. Then, his chirping days past, he found some sort of post with a Marchese della Terza in Naples. Around 1552 he made his way to Rome, where he was taken in by the Archbishop of Florence and shortly afterward was appointed *maestro di cappella* in the basilica of San Giovanni Laterano (where, fortuitously, he was Palestrina's [201] immediate predecessor). There he served until late in 1554, when word reached him that his parents lay gravely ill back home. He immediately set out for Mons, but when he got there they were both dead and buried. A subsequent alleged visit to France and England is unsubstantiated. By 1555 he had established himself in Antwerp, where he fell in with the publisher Tielman Susato [155], who forthwith brought out a collection of his *chansons*, madrigals, and motets. A volume of madrigals had been published in Venice earlier that year. A motet collection issued in 1556 was dedicated to the Bishop of Arras, Antoine Perrenot (later Cardinal Granvelle), who soon afterward may have been influential in placing him, as a tenor singer, in the chapel of Albert V, Duke of Bavaria. His salary was good, and its steady improvement enabled him, in 1558, to marry Regina Weckinger, the daughter of locally important parents, by whom he had four sons and two daughters.

Much of what we know of Lassus beyond this point is the history of his publications, his advancements at the court, and his occasional journeys. A second book of madrigals appeared in 1559, the *Sacrae cantiones* for five voices in 1562, and in between Adrian Le Roy and Robert Ballard in Paris published a number of *chansons*. Around 1563 the Munich *Kapellmeister* Ludwig Daser was pensioned off to make room for Lassus. (Daser was only around thirty-five, but it is not certain whether health, religion, or expediency caused his downfall.) At about the same time, Duke Albert was so taken with Lassus's settings of the penitential psalms that he ordered for his library a magnificent manuscript copy, decorated with paintings and a portrait of the composer by the painter Hans Mülich; it took seven years to complete. Between then and 1567 Lassus published a third book of madrigals, two more books of *chansons,* and three more of motets, as well as the *Sacrae lectiones* from the Book of Job, dedicated to the duke. In the same year Lassus was sent to Italy to hunt for musicians, and among those he brought back were the Guami brothers (see 240) and Ivo de Vento [249]. While in Italy he stopped by Ferrara to present Duke Alfonso II d'Este with the fourth book of madrigals, having made his acquaintance in Munich, but the duke seems to have been in an unfriendly mood. The same year Lassus also published a collection of Magnificats in all the church tones, and his first book of German *Lieder,* which he dedicated to Albert's heir, William, through whose friendship he had bought his own home. The next year he furnished the music for Duke William's wedding. More collections of motets and chansons followed in the next few years.

At the Diet of Speyer in 1570, Emperor Maximilian II conferred on Lassus a hereditary title and a coat of arms (with a sharp, a flat, and a natural sign). Following this event, Lassus visited Paris, where he stayed with Le Roy and made a great hit with Charles IX. It is said that Charles offered him a post at court but that he died before it was possible for Lassus to wind up his affairs in Munich. In the early years of the decade there sprang up a rather close friendship between Lassus and Duke William, evidenced by a series of macaronic letters from Lassus in French, German, Italian, and Latin, in which he switches from one language to another in mid-phrase. In 1573 he wrote, on commission, an allegorical dialogue to serve as a ballet to celebrate the election of Prince Henry of France to the Polish throne. The next year he went again to Italy, where Pope Gregory XIII, in token of thanks for the dedication of the Masses in the *Patrocinium musices* made him a knight of the Golden Spur.

On the death of Duke Albert in 1579, William was forced to cut back on expenditures, and the chapel suffered, though Lassus did not, at least financially. William, partly, it is suggested, at the urging of his Jesuit advisers, became stringently orthodox, and soon after Lassus's church music took on a simpler, soberer, and less polyphonic overtone. Though he also continued to write and publish merrier things—e.g., a new book of *Lieder* in 1583—there followed a new setting of the Job material, a publication (at long last) of the *Psalmi Davidis poenitentiales (Penitential Psalms),* a set of lamentations, and a Stabat Mater. Even the new madrigals took on a spiritual coloration. In 1585, Lassus went for a last journey to Italy—significantly on a pilgrimage to Loreto. A year later his health and mental alertness began to decline, and his productivity to fall off. The duke gave him another house, out in the country, in which to recuperate and made every provision for his welfare, and as a result there was some improvement. (Three of his sons were by now members of the ducal chapel, and one and another sometimes filled in for him.) But in 1590 he lapsed into amnesia and speechlessness, and it took the court physician, Dr. Mermann, three years to bring him back to anything like normal, the intervening years being marked by deep depression and paranoia. By 1593 Lassus was able to go with the duke to the Diet of Ratisbon, and to begin work on his spiritual madrigal cycle, *Le Lagrime di San Pietro,* which he completed in the spring. It was his last work, for he died less than a month later. His sons Ferdinand and Rudolf became composers of some note and busied themselves to publish their father's manuscript works. Ferdinand became *Kapellmeister* at the Bavarian court from 1602 until his death in 1609.

RECORDINGS: The recording companies have barely scratched the surface of Lassus's works. There are selections from the songs and motets, but relatively few, and only a handful of the Masses. There have been recordings of the *Penitential Psalms,* the *Sacrae lectiones,* the *Prophetae Sybillarum,* the *St. Matthew Passion,* and the *Lagrime,* but much more needs to be done.

[229] SCHROETER, Leonhard (Shrö'-ter, Lā'-ōn-härt)
CANTOR, LIBRARIAN
BORN: Torgau, c. 1532
DIED: Magdeburg, c. 1601

The son of a Lutheran minister, Schroeter studied at the local Latin school, where he was undoubtedly a pupil of Johann Walther [139]. Later he studied at Annaberg (near the present Czech border) and from 1545 to 1547 at the princely school at Meissen. Around 1560 he became municipal cantor (choir director and headmaster) at Saalfeld. He was dismissed in a doctrinal dispute in 1571 and was tided over by the Duke of Wolfenbüttel, who made him his librarian until Saalfeld forgave him in 1573. In 1576 he took a cantorial post in Magdeburg at the Latin school. Save for a period in 1586–87, when he spent in the Brunswick city of Helmstedt, Schroeter spent the rest of his life there. It was in the Helmstedt period that he published what are perhaps his best-known works, the *Hymni sacri* and the

Weihnachtsliedlein (Christmas carols). Based largely on Lutheran chorale melodies, these are lovely works, though hardly, as one enthusiastic proponent claims, comparable with the music of Palestrina [201] and Tomás Luis de Victoria [258]. Schroeter leans toward homophony and, like so many Germans of his time, shows the influence of the Venetians.

[230] MERULO, Claudio (Mã-rōō′-lō, Kloud′-yō)

ORGANIST, TEACHER, PUBLISHER
BORN: Correggio, April 8, 1533
DIED: Parma, May 5, 1604

Not to be confused with the later Tarquinio Merula [442], Claudio Merulo was really Merlotti (Blackbirds), Merulo being the Latin form. He was born eleven months before the death of the painter Antonio Allegri, who, as "Correggio," had put his birthplace on the map. Merulo studied there with a transplanted Frenchman known as Tuttovale Menon and with a certain Girolamo Donati or Donato. At twenty-three he succeeded Girolamo Parabosco's father (see 199) as organist of Brescia Cathedral. Despite his five-year contract, a year later he competed for, and won, the post of first organist of St. Mark's in Venice, left vacant by the death of the younger Parabosco, beating out Andrea Gabrieli [180]. He quickly won a reputation as a brilliant performer, and for years was a feature of the Sunday afternoon concerts in the basilica. In 1566 he took on music printing and publishing as a sideline, bringing out madrigal books by Philippe Verdelot [104], Costanzo Festa [123], and himself, among others. Just why, despite several salary increases, he elected to leave Venice in 1584 is not known. Perhaps he thought he could do better elsewhere. And indeed, as things turned out, he could. After a brief stopover in Mantua, he was appointed court organist to Ranuccio Farnese, Duke of Parma, at double his St. Mark's salary and with a knighthood thrown in as a fringe benefit. In 1587 he also became cathedral organist, and a year later married (his first wife had died, leaving a daughter) a lady called Amabile (Lovable) Banzola. By 1591 the duke's paranoia may have got to him, for he became organist in the church of the Steccate, a wealthy Parmese family. On the night of April 25, 1604, Merulo was awakened by what were apparently the classic symptoms of appendicitis, suffered terribly for more than a week, and died, probably from the radical measures resorted to by

his doctors. He was given a state funeral and buried in the cathedral.

Merulo composed and published in all the current forms and genres. His madrigals (4 books) are less daring than those of some of his Venetian colleagues, but they look ahead in their occasional use of dramatic declamation. His 6 Masses, his Magnificats, litanies, and motets (some of them polychoral) also are excellent but break no new ground. His dramatic music—choruses for Lodovico Dolce's *Le Troiane (The Trojans)* of 1566 and intermezzi for a collaborative effort imaginatively called *Tragedia* presented before the visiting Henry III in 1574—anticipates opera. But Merulo shines brightest in his organ pieces, particularly his toccatas. The toccata was originally meant to give the pitch to the singers, but under his hands it became a brilliant virtuoso display, alternating quasi-improvisatory passages with contrapuntal sections that smack of fugue.

[231] SCHMID, Bernhard (Shmit, Bârn′-härt)

ORGANIST, POET
BORN: Strasbourg, 1535
DIED: Strasbourg, 1592

The son of Bernhard Schmid, school administrator, and the former Prisca Wolfenkinder, Bernhard Schmid, Jr., married Catharina Klein when he was seventeen. Ten years later he became organist at Strasbourg Cathedral and the local St. Thomas Church, and spent most of the rest of his life in those posts. The year 1567 saw the marriage blessed with Bernhard Schmid III, who also became an organist and succeeded his father at St. Thomas Church in 1589. In 1592 he also took over at the cathedral when the elder Schmid moved to the less demanding Jung Petruskirche. As composers, both are classified with the organ colorists (see 213). The elder published two collections in the "new German tablature" invented by Elias Ammerbach [213], which contain, *inter alia*, motets by Orlande de Lassus [228] and dances, including the first known *courante*.

[232] WERT, Giaches (or Jachet) de (Vârt, Zhàk de)

SINGER, CHOIR DIRECTOR
BORN: Weert, Netherlands, summer 1535
DIED: Mantua, May 6, 1596

There seems to be no speculation that Wert's name was originally Jacob van Weert (Weert is in southeast Holland, near Neer). One reads variously that as a child he was brought or sent to the court of Maria di Cardona, Marchesa della Padulla, or that he "followed her" to her headquarters in Avellino in the mountains east of Naples. (Does one scent one of the choirboy kidnappings so prevalent then?) It is suggested that later he studied under Cipriano de Rore [184] at Ferrara. In any event, he was somehow swept into the orbit of the Gonzagas, and in the early 1550s set to work as *maestro di cappella* to a junior branch of the family at Novellara, a town south of Mantua. There he served under three counts, Francesco II, Camillo I, and Alfonso I, and in the course of things married a woman who owned a house and lands, and probably had money. After a while the senior branch of the Gonzagas began to sense that Wert was a treasure, and in 1565 Duke Guglielmo put him in charge of the choir in the church of Santa Barbara in Mantua, though he continued for some years to help out when needed at Novellara. In 1566 he went with his master to the summit meeting at Augsburg, convened to deal with the Turkish threat, and impressed Emperor Maximilian II, who tried to hire him away, without success. As an outlander—one of the last of the great flood of such artists who had swept into Italy for two centuries—Wert was eyed with resentment by some of his Italian colleagues, and his reputation was not helped when his wife was found to be carrying on an affair in 1570 with one of them. The man was fired, and Signora Wert was shipped back to Novellara, where she proceeded to get herself in further trouble by becoming involved (or so it was said) in some sort of anti-Gonzaga conspiracy. Her property was seized and she was imprisoned or placed under restraint for the rest of her days. She died in 1580. That was the year that Wert's assiduity and fidelity and talent paid off, for he and his children were given the freedom of Mantua in perpetuity, and the duke added a small fortune to boot. In 1581, Guglielmo transferred him to his private chapel, and in 1584 restored to him his wife's property in Novellara. At about this time Wert seems to have spent considerable time off and on at the court of Alfonso II d'Este at Ferrara, where he met the poet Torquato Tasso and pioneered in setting his verses. At Ferrara, the musicians included three talented women, Laura Peperara, Lucrezia Bendidio, and Tarquinia Molza. The last, who played, sang, conducted, and composed, was the woman of Wert's dreams and he proposed to her. But she was of noble birth, her family objected, she was fired and sent to Modena, and Wert was dispatched posthaste back to Mantua, where the duke also chewed him

out. In 1587 Guglielmo died and was succeeded by Vicenzo I. In 1590 the court acquired a new lead singer called Claudio Monteverdi [333], who became something of a favorite of the duke's. Meanwhile, Wert's health had been failing. In 1592 Giovanni Gastoldi [280] took his place as *maestro di cappella,* and while the duke and Monteverdi were off at the Turkish Wars, Wert died in 1596. Much to Monteverdi's surprise and chagrin, he was not appointed to succeed Wert.

Wert's fame rests primarily on his madrigals, of which he published twelve books between 1558 and 1595 (plus a volume of *Villanelle).* Though his early work shows his Franco-Flemish background, he rapidly adopted the Italian style and was one of those who brought it to its height. He is a master of word painting and understands chromaticism and its impact, never using it merely for its own sake. The settings from Tasso's epic *Gerusalemme liberata* are highly dramatic; an auditor reports hearing one such work performed with three soloists and what was, for that time, a large orchestra (actually a "broken" consort made up of instruments of more than one family). This sort of thing and the monodic tendencies of Wert's later pieces show him clearly a link between Rore and the new world of Monteverdi and the opera. He also published four books of motets. If Wert was the victim of xenophobia at home, he was widely admired and appreciated by the Italian musicians who mattered, Palestrina [201] among them—as well as by their counterparts abroad, such as Thomas Morley [289]. His music was widely printed and circulated in innumerable collections and continued to be popular for a century after his death. In recent years a Mass by Wert has been discovered, as well as four instrumental fantasias.

RECORDINGS: A record giving a sampling of all of his output except the motets (and including the only known madrigal in classical Greek) has been made by Denis Stevens.

[233] BERTRAND, Antoine de (Bâr-
tránd', Àn-twán' də)
BORN: Fontanges, c. 1535
DIED: Toulouse, c. 1581

Despite the considerable claims made in recent years for Bertrand's greatness, he used to be regularly omitted from most musical reference works. All that is known of his youth is that he came from the same Auvergnat village as his contemporary Guillaume Costeley [218]. He first appears in

Toulouse around 1560 as a member of the humanist circle fostered there by Cardinal Georges d'Armagnac. One of his friends, a law student named Robert Garnier who dedicated two sonnets to him, later became a notable playwright (and the butt of the satire of his own pupil, Cyrano de Bergerac). Among Bertrand's *chansons* are a number of settings of verses by others of the group. Probably around 1560 he married Anne Carrière, a lady of sufficient real estate to allow them to live comfortably off the income. It is possible that around 1570 the Bertrands lived in Paris, where Antoine was associated with Pierre de Ronsard and the Pléiade, and where he found a patron in Charles de Bourbon. Toward the end of his life, he seems to have undergone a born-again religious experience, which caused him to put away foolish things and turn to religious composition as a doctrinaire Catholic. It won him a martyr's crown, for, while on his way to look over one of his estates, he was murdered, allegedly by equally doctrinaire Huguenots. The *Airs spirituels* (1582) thus became his memorial. He also published three volumes of *chansons,* the first two, called *Les Amours de Ronsard,* containing sixty settings of that poet (1576–78). Shortly afterward a Huguenot preacher named Simon Goulart brought out two volumes (in 1576 and 1578) of this music adapted to religious texts as *Sonets chrestiens.* Whether this event had any bearing on Bertrand's conversion is not clear. His special hallmarks are most clearly seen in *Les Amours.* To a degree, he looks back to the old polyphony and has a fondness for canon. But his melody sounds spontaneous and he is concerned to fit music to textual meaning. In fact he inveighs against art for art's sake. He appears fully conscious of harmonic demands, though his pieces often straddle a line between modality and diatonicism. He appears to have taken Gioseffo Zarlino's [186] modernistic ideas to heart: he likes to fool around with chromaticism and even uses quarter tones in a couple of works.

[234] **GOMÓLKA, Mikołaj** (Gō-molw′-kà, Mě-kō′-lwī)
SINGER, TRUMPETER, FLUTIST, POLITICIAN
BORN: Sandomierz, Poland, c. 1535
DIED: after 1591

Gomółka's early life is fairly well documented, but his last decades proceed from dimness to obscurity. His parents were a bourgeois couple named Tomasz and Agnieszka Gomółka. At about the age of ten he was taken as a boy soprano into the royal chapel of King Sigismund I at Cracow. He was taught there by the flutist Jan Claus. In the brilliant court of Sigismund Augustus, who succeeded his father, he served first as *tubinator* and later as *fistulator* (trumpeter and flute player). Eventually he left the court, married Jadwiga Kusmierzowicz, sired a son, Michal (1564–1609), who became a famous musician and *Kapellmeister,* and in 1566 went back to Sandomierz to settle the estate of his deceased parents. Respected for his learning there, he was elected alderman in 1567 and vice-advocate in 1572. In 1573 he resigned, and his tracks begin to grow dimmer. By 1580 he seems to have been back in Cracow, perhaps in the employ of Bishop Myszkowski, to whom the collection of Psalms he published in that year are dedicated. By the end of the decade he was working for Jan Zamoyski, the Chancellor. After 1591 nothing more is heard of him. Not even his gravesite is known.

Whatever else Gomółka may have written and/or published, his only musical remains are the 152 psalms of *Melodiae na psalterz polski.* This collection is analogous to psalters that were for home use, such as the *Souterliedekens* of Clemens Non Papa [166], and that in the wake of the Reformation were appearing all over Europe. In the present instance the translations were by the important Polish poet Jan Kochanowski. Both textually and musically the work is so ideologically neutral that it is impossible to tell if Gomółka identified with Protestants or Catholics. The Psalms are set for four voices (two of them twice, accounting for the odd numbering). The melodies on which they are based are drawn from various sources, including Gregorian chant, Lutheran chorales, and Hussite hymns. Some appear to be based on dances. The general style is contrapuntal rather than chordal, with no special emphasis on any melodic line. There is considerable chromaticism for no discernible reason, and many parallel fifths and octaves. The conclusion drawn by modern scholars is that Gomółka knew no better. Nevertheless he clearly has a natural musical instinct and the collection stands as an important document.

RECORDINGS: A record of twenty-odd Psalms has been made by a choir under Stefan Stuligrosz.

[235] **MAINERIO, Giorgio** (Mī-när′-yō, Jôr′-jō)
PRIEST, CHOIRMASTER, SINGER
BORN: Parma, c. 1535
DIED: Aquileia, c. May 3, 1582

In the decade of the 1560s Mainerio was a member of the choir and later a canon at Udine Cathedral. In 1570 he moved to the cathedral of Aquileia, where he served as master of the boys and from 1576 as *maestro di cappella.* Though he left some sacred music, he is chiefly remembered for his dance book, *Il Primo libro di balli,* for instrumental consort, which includes the first known dance suites for concerted instruments, and the first consort variations.

[236] NEGRI, Cesare (Nä′-grē, Chä′-sä-rä)
DANCING MASTER
BORN: Milan, c. 1535
DIED: after 1604

Negri was called "Il Trombone," which means either "The Trombone" or "The Big Horn"—in which latter case Tromboncino **[94]** would have been "Little Big Horn." Dancing masters usually supplied their own music, but Negri's instrument appears to have been the lute, which he learned from Pompeo Diobono, rather than the trombone. By the time he got to the Milanese court, where he seems to have been in demand, all the Viscontis and Sforzas were gone and the place was overrun with Spaniards. In 1602 he published a dance treatise, *Le Gratie d'amore (Love's Graces),* in which he tells what it was like to be a successful dancing master, with a catalog of his students and an annotated one of his rivals, descriptions of the more spectacular productions in which he had a hand, general rules for dancing, specific choreographies of ballroom dances, ballets, and processional events, and music for 42 dances in lute tablature. He republished the book in 1604 as *Nuove inventioni di balli.*

[237] WHITE, Robert
CHOIR DIRECTOR, ORGANIST
BORN: c. 1538
DIED: London, November 10, 1574

Robert White, though less well known than the three T's of early Tudor music (Tallis, Taverner, Tye), seems to have been almost as highly regarded as they. Nothing is known of his place of birth or of his early years, but there is fairly strong circumstantial evidence that his father was also Robert White, an organ builder of repute. Young Robert took his B.Mus. at Cambridge in December 1560, after working at it for ten years, producing a service setting as his graduation project. By 1562 he was master of the choristers and organist at Ely Cathedral,

succeeding the great Christopher Tye **[158]**, with a salary of ten pounds a year. He also married his predecessor's daughter, Ellen, who between 1565 and 1573 bore him five daughters. In 1566 he was succeeded at Ely by John Farrant. From Ely, White apparently went to Chester, where in 1567 he is listed as master of the choristers (but no first name is given in the records). While there, he appeared in the mystery plays presented traditionally on Whitsunday. By 1570 he had moved to London to be master of the choristers at Westminster Abbey, his father becoming part of the White household. In 1574 a particularly virulent wave of the plague struck the city and when it was over, only his father and two daughters were left.

White was, expectably, primarily a composer of church music. There are extant a few pieces—*In nomine*s and such—for lute, organ, and consort. The considerable body of vocal music to Latin texts includes a *Magnificat,* 2 Lamentations, and about 20 motets (some of the last also appearing in lute transcriptions). The *Lamentations for Five Voices* is said to be fit to stand with the best works of the period. There are also 10 English anthems that are White's for certain, and several others that may be his.

RECORDINGS: The *Lamentations* and four motets have been recorded by the Clerkes of Oxenford.

[238] CASTRO, Jean de (Kås′-trō, Zhàn də)
BORN: Liège, c. 1540
DIED: c. 1600

For long something of a mystery man, Castro, most probably of Spanish descent, was almost certainly born in Liège. From about the time he was thirty, he seems to have led a peripatetic career that is now possible to trace in outline. From around 1570 until at least 1575 he lived in Antwerp. Then, perhaps as a result of the religious upheaval in the Netherlands, he left the country, ultimately settled in Lyons until the mid-1580s, when he returned to Antwerp. Shortly afterward he became a court musician to Duke Johann Wilhelm of Jülich, Berg, and Cleves. In the last decade during which we have any record of him, he seems to have been firmly established at the electoral court of Cologne. He left 3 parody Masses, 7 volumes of motets (many of them secular and occasional), and innumerable *chansons* and madrigals. His music shows an awareness of current trends and styles and was quite popular in its day, though it has no very personal characteristics.

[239] DAZA, Esteban (Dá'-thȧ, Ās-tā'-bȧn)
VIHUELIST
BORN: c. 1540 (?)
DIED: after 1576

All we know of Daza is that he was a gentleman of Valladolid who in 1576 dedicated to Hernando de Habalos de Soto-Mayor, adviser to Philip II, his vihuela book, *El Parnasso*. It contains three sections devoted respectively to fantasias, motet intabulations, and popular songs (which Daza indicates that he would prefer to have played than sung). *El Parnasso* was the last and least of published vihuela books and seems to mark the end of the vogue for the instrument, which soon gave place to the guitar.

[240] GUAMI, Gioseffo (Gwȧ'-mē, Jō-zef'-fō)
ORGANIST, CHOIRMASTER, SINGER
BORN: Lucca, c. 1540
DIED: Lucca, 1611

Like the Puccinis, the Guamis represent a Lucchese musical dynasty. Gioseffo's younger brother Francesco (c. 1544–1602), a composer and trombonist, worked variously in Münich, Baden-Baden, Venice, Udine, and Lucca. From his early twenties Gioseffo studied in Venice with Adrian Willaert [129] and Annibale Padovano [207], and sang at St. Mark's. He spent more than a decade as organist in the Bavarian electoral *Kapelle,* under Orlande de Lassus [228], with whom he went talent-hunting in Italy in the early 1570s. In 1579 he returned to Lucca as organist at San Michele, but after a few years accepted the directorship of the *cappella* of Gian-Andrea Doria, great-nephew and successor of the great admiral. In 1588 he was named organist at St. Mark's, to succeed the late Vincenzo Bell'haver [216]. Despite the high esteem in which his playing was held there, he left in an unexplained huff three years later and spent the rest of his life as organist of Lucca Cathedral. His son, Domenico, spelled him at the organ there, and he was succeeded by two other sons, (in order) Vincenzo (d. 1615) and Valerio (1587–1649). Gioseffo Guami produced both church and secular music of fine, if not highly individual, quality. He was clearly influenced both by the Venetian modernists and by Lassus. Some of his madrigals show a quasi-instrumental approach, and some of his motets call specifically for instruments. He left a number of instrumental *canzone* but, curiously, considering his enormous

reputation as a performer, only a single piece (a toccata) specifically for organ.

[241] JOHNSON, John
LUTENIST
BORN: c. 1540 (?)
DIED: c. 1594

John Johnson, probably the father of the English lutenist-composer Robert Johnson [409], was himself the first of the significant English lutenists. Records show that he held a court appointment from 1579 to 1594. A year later, Queen Elizabeth conferred on his widow, Alice, a lease on a Dorset estate in gratitude for his services. He left a number of lute pieces (mostly dances) and at least 10 lute duets.

[242] KARGEL, Sixt (Kâr'-gel, Zikst)
LUTENIST, EDITOR
BORN: c. 1540
DIED: after 1594

In his twenties Kargel lived in Mainz. In the mid-1570s he moved to Alsace, where he was musician to Charles de Guise, Cardinal of Lorraine, and to Johann von Manderscheid-Blankenheim, Prince-Bishop of Alsace, and music editor for the Strasbourg printer Bernhard Jobin. In his last years he was in Bishop Johann's establishment at Zabern (now Saverne). As a lute composer, he was influenced by the Italian school. He published 2 lute books in 1574 and 1586, and 2 collections for the wire-strung cittern in 1575 and 1578.

[243] MASCHERA, Florentio (Mȧs-kā'-rȧ, Flō-rȧnt'-yō)
ORGANIST
BORN: c. 1540
DIED: Brescia, c. 1584

Son of the Brescia Cathedral Latin teacher, Maschera studied organ with Claudio Merulo [230]. His first job was at the church of Santo Spirito in Venice, but when Merulo defected to St. Mark's in 1557, Maschera succeeded him at his hometown basilica. He was also a famous violinist. He was succeeded in 1584, when he presumably died, by Costanzo Antegnati [260]. He left more than a score of *canzone,* among the earliest composed specifically for instruments, though the composer does not say what kind. RECORDINGS: Samples have been recorded both by organists and consorts.

[244] JAKUB POLAK or JACQUES LE POLONOIS (Yä'-kōōb Pō'-låk)
LUTENIST
BORN: Poland, c. 1540
DIED: Paris, c. 1605

"Polish Jim" turns out to be Jakub Reys (many spellings), a brilliant lutenist. When Henry III abandoned the Polish throne to take over the French one, Reys came along as his *valet de chambre*, married a French merchant's daughter in 1585, and spent the rest of his life in France, where his playing was much admired. He is said to have invented a new way of playing the lute, but specifics are lacking. He left a scattering of *ricercare*-like fantasias and almost wholly diatonic dance pieces.

[245] WAISSEL, Matthäus (Vī'-sel, Mä-tä'-us)
LUTENIST, PRIEST
BORN: Bartenstein [Poland], c. 1540
DIED: 1602

A native of East Prussia (the town is now Bartoszyce, Poland), Waissel (or Waisselius, as he preferred to be called) studied at the University of Königsberg, then went abroad for his musical instruction. In 1574 he was rector of a school in Schippenbeil, back in home country, and a year later began a hitch of at least thirteen years as a country parson. His last years were spent in Königsberg (now Kaliningrad, U.S.S.R.). He published 4 lute books, containing mostly arrangements, and was the last to use German tablature.

[246] ROVIGO, Francesco (Rō-vē'-gō, Fràn-chäs'-kō)
ORGANIST
BORN: c. 1541
DIED: Mantua, October 7, 1597

A student of Claudio Merulo [230] in Venice (when Rovigo was nearly thirty), Rovigo began working for the Gonzaga court in Mantua about three years later. In 1582 he was lured away to Graz by the promise of a healthy rise in salary chiefly to teach the children of Charles II, Archduke of Styria. On the latter's death eight years later, he returned to Mantua, where the welcome mat had been out all along, and became organist of the ducal chapel, Santa Barbara. When Giaches de Wert [232], the much-honored court *maestro di cappella,* died in 1596, Rovigo assumed his duties but died soon thereafter. *(His* successor was Benedetto

Pallavicino, much to the chagrin of Claudio Monteverdi [333].) He left some Masses, a *St. Luke Passion,* other liturgical music, some rather popular madrigals, and a few instrumental pieces.

[247] REGNART, Jacques (Rän-yärt', Zhàk)
CHOIRMASTER, TEACHER
BORN: Douai, c. 1542
DIED: Prague, October 16, 1599

At just about the time that the Guamis of Lucca were producing two musical sons [240], the Regnarts of Douai were producing five—Augustin, Jacques, François, Paschaise, and Charles (who may be encountered *ensemble* in a motet collection edited by Augustin in 1590). Jacques was probably the second oldest, the best-known, and the most-remembered. He had his musical education as a choirboy in the Prague chapel of Maximilian, the so-called King of Bohemia, and remained in his employ when, as Holy Roman Emperor, Maximilian II moved to Vienna in 1564. By that time Regnart was a tenor. In 1568 he took a two-year leave to survey the Italian musical scene. Whatever he may have learned there, it impressed Maximilian, who put him in charge of the choirboys' education on his return, and the next year elevated him to the status of a gentleman. He continued in the imperial chapel under Rudolf II, who became emperor in 1576. Rudolf moved him back to Prague and three years later named him second-in-command. Regnart turned down an offer from the Saxon elector, Augustus, in 1580, but apparently was unable to resist one a year or so later from Archduke Ferdinand of the Tyrol. He settled in Innsbruck in 1582, became *Kapellmeister* in 1585, and by the time he left had become very rich, owned his own home (still standing), and had been ennobled. When Ferdinand died, Regnart stayed on for a few months but in 1596 decided to return to his old post in Prague, where he died three and a half years afterward.

Regnart wrote a number of Masses and motets, but his enormous popularity and his latter-day fame are owing chiefly to his Italian and German songs, especially the three-part *Lieder* modeled on the *villanelle,* which, with their hummable tunes and simple harmonies, helped establish the direction of German popular song.

[248] BYRD, William
ORGANIST, SINGER, PUBLISHER
BORN: 1543

DIED: Stondon Massey, Essex, July 4, 1623

The brief but glorious upsurge of English music in the last years of Queen Elizabeth's reign and at the beginning of the first James's was initiated by its greatest figure, William Byrd. Indeed, in terms of depth, breadth, and productivity, Byrd is comparable to the greatest composers of the century, wherever they were. As with most of them, his early life can only be guessed at. His will, made in his eightieth year, tells us about when he was born but not where. Because Lincolnshire, where the first facts of his life are to be found, was a Byrd rookery, it is reasonable to think him a native. At twenty he was organist and master of the choristers at Lincoln Cathedral, supposedly trained by Thomas Tallis [157]. Five years later he married Juliana Birley there. When Robert Parsons [223] was drowned, Byrd was appointed to his place in the Chapel Royal but continued to hold his job at the cathedral. It was only after the births of their first two children that the Byrds left Lincoln. About 1573 they took out a lease on Battylshall Manor in Essex from the poetical Edward de Vere, Seventeenth Earl of Oxford, contingent upon the death of the latter's Uncle Aubrey. That melancholy event came to pass six years later. But the estate had been given over to Aubrey when his elder brother had been politically disgraced, and, the title being in some doubt, a certain Lewyn now came forward with a claim that Byrd had enfeoffed (transferred) his rights to one Anthony Luther, a relative of Lewyn's. In the subsequent trial, Lewyn succeeded in packing the jury with his adherents, and Byrd lost the case.

By 1575 Byrd and his old teacher, Tallis, were jointly serving the Chapel Royal as organists. That was the year they decided to go into business together and won a royal monopoly in the printing and sales of part music and musical manuscript paper. Their first effort was the jointly composed collection of motets *Cantiones sacrae,* dedicated to the queen by way of thanks. (That the texts were Latin proves nothing, since the queen liked her church music in Latin, but Byrd was a lifelong Catholic, a fact that caused him trouble from time to time.) The business did not prosper, however, and by 1577 the owners had to petition the queen for what is now known as "government aid," which was granted in the form of another manorial lease to Byrd.

Around this time the Byrd family, which now included Thomas, Rachel, and Mary, moved to Harlington in West Middlesex, perhaps on the notion that their religious sympathies would attract less notice there. Nevertheless the senior Byrds and their servants were constantly being cited for nonattendance at Anglican services, though apparently William's pull at court managed to get most of the fines fixed or mitigated. The Byrd home was also clearly under observation as a potential nest of popish treachery.

Old Tallis died in 1585, followed by Juliana Byrd about a year later. Byrd remarried (his second wife is known to the rolls only as "Byrd, Ellen"), and carried on the publishing business alone, using Thomas East (see under 393) as his printer, until the license expired in 1596 and it went over to Thomas Morley [289]. In 1589 he was once again the loser to a sharper named Boxe in a suit over his rights as the lessee of another property. In 1593 he moved his family, for the last time, to the Essex village of Stondon Massey, into a house previously owned by a Catholic named Shelley, who had been convicted of trying to place Mary Stuart on the English throne. Part of it, however, was occupied by a Mr. Lolly, who had a lease on "the parlour, the bed-room, half the hopground, and the right of using the pond" (for what the document does not specify). This occasioned another suit over who could claim what. It was settled amicably, but in 1603, when ownership was returned by the Crown to private hands, the Widow Shelley tried to evict the Byrds, who had made many improvements, including the installation of running water in the house. Once again Byrd went to court, and once again he lost, this time after seven years of litigation. But the widow died soon after, and he was able to buy the place outright. At the same time, he was involved in yet another suit having to do with the lease on the Gloucestershire manor granted him long before by the queen, though the details are now murky. Ellen Byrd had died around 1605, and by 1618 William had retired from the Chapel Royal. His successors were Edmund Hooper [276] and Orlando Gibbons [408]. He died at eighty and was presumably buried in the village churchyard, though no gravesite is known.

Byrd was immensely productive, particularly in his later years, and was equally at home in the Mass, the Anglican service, the motet, and the anthem; he also wrote much secular and instrumental music. His three Masses are among the monuments of English Renaissance music, and he was perhaps the first significant composer of the verse anthem, with its alternation of solo and choral passages. His consort songs, although often set to verse of the so-called "Leaden Age," are the first great secular songs of the English Renaissance, and point the way for such composers as John Dowland [316] and Thomas Campion [332]. He was also notable as a composer of songs for the stage. His consort pieces continue an older tradition but in some ways seem also to look ahead to the chamber music of the next century. Perhaps most important, Byrd was the first great composer of music for the harpsichord (or virginal). The 1611 collection *Parthenia,* in which he appears jointly with Gibbons and John Bull [315], was the first engraved book of such pieces and sold like hotcakes (which were evidently even more popular then than now). Notice should also be taken of the so-called *My Ladye Nevilles Booke,* a collection of keyboard works by Byrd, copied out by John Baldwin. (No one knows for sure who Lady Neville was.) In more than one sense, the title "Father of English Music" bestowed on Byrd after his death is applicable.

RECORDINGS: Among important works by Byrd on records are the 3 Masses, the "Great" Service, the *Cantiones sacrae,* and the Lady Neville collection. A number of LPs are given over to collections of shorter works.

[249] VENTO, Ivo de (Ven'-tō, Ē'-vō de)
ORGANIST, CHOIRMASTER
BORN: c. 1543
DIED: Munich, autumn 1575

Though Ivo de Vento hardly sounds like a Flemish name, none other has been found for him, and all roads seem to lead to his origin in Antwerp. He was a choirboy in the Bavarian ducal chapel from 1556 to 1559. A year later his employer, Albrecht V, shipped him off to study with Claudio Merulo [230] in Venice. He returned after four or five years to become number-three organist at the Munich court, a post that he held until his death, except for the year (1568–69) that he served as *Kapellmeister* to Prince Wilhelm at Landshut. He left 3 Masses, 4 collections of motets, a handful of madrigals, and 6 collections of German *Lieder* (a few of them dialogue numbers). The *Lieder* enjoyed considerable popularity.

[250] REGNART, François (Rän-yärt', Frä*n*-swä')
SINGER, CHOIRMASTER
BORN: Douai, c. 1544
DIED: c. 1600

Next to Jacques Regnart [247], François was the most famous and productive of the five musical *frères* Regnart. The birth dates of both are often given as c. 1540, which would have made it a busy year for Madame Regnart. François was a student at Douai University. After serving as choirmaster at Tournai Cathedral and the church of St. Lenaerd, he headed the chapel of the Austrian Archduke Mathias, son of Emperor Maximilian II. François published a book of Masses (now lost), some motets (in company with some by his brothers), and a volume of *chansons,* heavy on Pierre de Ronsard settings.

[251] LUZZASCHI, Luzzasco (Lo͞od-zås'-kē, Lo͞od-zås'-kō)
ORGANIST, CHOIRMASTER, TEACHER
BORN: Ferrara, 1545
DIED: Ferrara, September 10, 1607

Apparently precocious, Luzzaschi studied, when he was little more than a child, with Cipriano de Rore [184]. Shortly afterward, he was made organist and (probably) *maestro di cappella* to Duke Alfonso II d'Este. He became widely known throughout Italy and attracted numerous pupils, among them the madrigalist Girolamo Belli and, most important, Girolamo Frescobaldi [407]. He seems to have attracted Carlo Gesualdo [310] to Florence at least as strongly as the prospect of a bride, and the two seem to have worked together, (Italian) hand in (velvet) glove, plotting "whither the madrigal?" during Gesualdo's stay there. After Alfonso died in 1597 and Ferrara reverted to the Papacy, Luzzaschi seems to have gone on living and working there, though in what capacity is not clear.

Luzzaschi was an experimenter with the new chromaticism. He published seven books of five-part madrigals and at least one volume of motets. The penultimate madrigal book includes a preface containing Luzzaschi's thoughts on the future of the genre. He also left a few organ pieces—a toccata and a couple of *ricercari* of the imitative type. His most important work, historically, however, is the *Madrigali per cantare e sonare (Madrigals to Sing and Play),* published in 1601 but written far earlier. It was intended for the famous three singing ladies of the Ferrara court, and its publication was delayed by the duke, who wanted the music to be heard nowhere else but in Ferrara. It consists of madrigals for one, two, and three voices with written-out accompaniment. Though this last amounts to little more than a reduction of the vocal harmonies, it is probably the earliest work of the sort. Moreover, the embellishments of the vocal lines are written in, giving another important clue to performance practice in that time.

[252] CACCINI, Giulio (Kȧ-chē′-nē, Jōōl′-yō)

SINGER, VIOLIST, LUTENIST, HARPIST, TEACHER, MUSIC DIRECTOR
BORN: in or near Rome, c. 1545
DIED: Florence, c. December 9, 1618

Caccini was not only a singer, he was a *virtuoso* singer and the teacher of vocal *virtuosi*, including most members of his own family. He is thus a sort of ancestor of the whole Cacchination of Italian opera singers, besides being one of the fathers of opera itself. Indeed his own singing must have been, as they say, something else, for by the time he had reached his majority he was, as "Giulio Romano" or "Julie the Roman," famous all over northern Italy. He studied in Rome with Giovanni Animuccia, Palestrina's successor when he was dismissed from the Cappella Giulia (see 201). The first Grand Duke of Tuscany, Cosimo I de' Medici, heard him sing and brought him back to Florence when Caccini was around nineteen or twenty, where he undertook further study with Scipione de' Vecchi, known as Scipione delle Palle. Except for a couple of short journeys, he remained in Florence the rest of his life. Around 1573 he became one of the charter members of an informal group which he referred to as the Camerata (i.e., "club") and which met in the *palazzo* of ex-soldier Giovanni de' Bardi, Count del Vernio (a local hill town). Bardi was also a humanist, mathematician, amateur musician, and scholar who was particularly interested in finding out how Greek drama was actually produced. Influenced by Vincenzo Galilei [208], he had some special notions about the role played therein by music. Caccini, who was given to hyperbole where the avant-garde and his own talents were concerned, claimed to have learned more about music from Bardi than he had from thirty years' study of formal counterpoint. (Since he left no contrapuntal compositions, he may have been right.)

In 1575, Caccini particularly endeared himself to his employer, Grand Duke Francesco, who had succeeded his father the year before. Given a letter by Eleonora di Toledo, wife of the duke's brother Pietro, to deliver to her lover, Caccini gave it instead to Francesco, who immediately had the lover, Bernardino Antinori, already in prison for killing a man in an argument, beheaded. Pietro,

who seems to have been a loathsome character, ordered the twenty-year-old Eleonora to meet him at one of his suburban villas and there murdered her. Or so the story, to which a good many doubts adhere, has come down.

In 1579, Caccini, in the person of Night, was a featured soloist at the delayed celebration of the long-delayed marriage of Francesco to his fair Venetian, Bianca Capello. Ten years later he wrote and directed an interlude for the wedding of the new grand duke, Francesco's brother Ferdinand I, to Christine of Lorraine. Since the ms. has disappeared, we cannot know whether it was written in the new monodic style that Caccini claimed to have invented at least four years earlier. At any rate it impressed the Ferrarese ambassador, who recommended to his master that he hire Caccini as *maestro di cappella* and gardener-in-chief, the musician also being noted for his green thumb. In 1592, when Bardi was called to an official post in the Vatican, Caccini went along, apparently for a visit, because he was back in Florence by 1594. By then he was already noted for the composition of his "monodies" —solo songs accompanied by a single stringed instrument designed to bring out the emotive impact of the words to which they were set. His career and his musical efforts climaxed in 1600, in connection with the wedding of the late Francesco's daughter, Maria, to Henry of Navarre (Henry IV of France). Here his chief function was to contribute the arias to the pastoral *Il Rapimento di Cefalo (The Abduction of Cephalus)*. To his chagrin, this was to be preceded by Jacopo Peri's [309] opera *Euridice*. But it turned out that Caccini had the upper hand there: several of his singers were in the cast, and he threatened to pull them out if they sang Peri's music. In the end they sang Caccini's setting of their lines. Caccini then hastened to recompose the rest of the libretto and managed to get his version to the printer before Peri could submit his. The bridal couple were evidently impressed, for in 1604 they invited Caccini, his second wife, Margherita, and his daughters, Francesca and Settimia, to Paris for the winter. Perhaps as a consequence, French court ballet soon replaced poetic recitation with solo song. Caccini seems to have been content to rest on his laurels thereafter. Francesca, called *"La Cecchina"* or "the Little Magpie," was a composer of consequence and the first woman to write operas.

Musically considered, *Euridice,* the only one of Caccini's stage works to have survived, lacks any real variety or theatricality. Nevertheless, Caccini has a firm place in the history of opera, not least for his written explanations of how vocal ornamentation should be carried out. More important, however, are his two published books of monodies, *Le nuove musiche* (1602), which is a real landmark, and *Nuove musiche* (1614), in which these principles are spelled out and illustrated. His claim to have invented a new approach to song is probably substantiated here. He was also a pioneer in the use of continuo, or figured bass.

RECORDINGS: Rodrigo de Zayas has recorded *Euridice.*

[253] CAIMO, Giuseppe (Kā-ē'-mō, Jōō-sep'-pā)
ORGANIST
BORN: Milan, c. 1545
DIED: Milan, 1584

The younger son of an aristocratic family, Caimo was a known composer by 1563, and organist at the church of Sant' Ambrogio Maggiore in Milan no later than the next year. In 1580 he became organist of the cathedral there, but his career was suddenly ended by his death in the autumn of 1584. He left several books of madrigals and *canzonette,* dating from 1564 to the end of his life; several others seem to have vanished. In some of his later works he exhibits an interesting and forward-looking use of dissonance, though on the whole he tends to conservatism.

[254] PEDRO DE CRISTO, Dom (Pā'-thrōō de Krēs'-tō, Don)
PRIEST, TEACHER
BORN: Coimbra, c. 1545
DIED: Coimbra, December 10, 1618

Dom Pedro is one of the earliest of native Portuguese composers whose name has come down to us. Nothing solid is known of him before he became a novice in the monastery of Santa Cruz (Holy Cross) in Coimbra in 1571, where he worked for the rest of his life. He won fame as a composer, a teacher, and organist, and a performer on the *baixao,* a variety of kortholt, or primitive bassoon. His music is said to show international influence rather than merely that of the Iberian school. He died as the result of a fall in the cloisters of his monastery. He left some motets and other religious music.

[255] GOSSWIN, Antonius (Gos'-swin, Ån-tōn'-yus)
SINGER, CHOIRMASTER

BORN: c. 1546
DIED: 1597 or 1598 (?)

Gosswin, who may have come from around Liège, was in the chapel of Albrecht V of Bavaria, probably as a choirboy, by 1558 and is said to have been the first pupil of Orlande de Lassus [228]. As a composer he imitated Lassus and built compositions on music by him to such a degree that he was termed a "female Lassus." Around 1566 he married Maria Praum in Münich and became a citizen within the next year or so. Like his colleague Ivo de Vento [249], Gosswin was siphoned off to Landshut in 1569 to grace the chapel of the heir apparent, Prince Wilhelm, but when the prince ran out of money for such amenities a year later, Gosswin returned to his old post. He was, by report, a perfectly splendid singer, and Emperor Maximilian II knighted him in 1574, whereupon Gosswin went to Vienna to present him personally with a couple of Masses of his composition in token of his gratitude. Despite the generally high esteem in which he was held, he was dismissed as an economic measure in 1579 after Albrecht's death. Almost immediately, however, he won lifetime tenure at the court of Albrecht's son, Ernst, Bishop of Freising, and moved to that city. But shortly afterward Ernst was named Bishop of Liège, whither he took his court. Whether Gosswin followed him immediately or later is not clear, but he left Mrs. Gosswin in Bavaria. In 1584, Bishop Ernst settled in Bonn, but Gosswin seems to have remained in Liège, where he probably died, some say in 1594, but, more likely, in the second half of 1597 or the first of 1598. He left some parody Masses, a few motets, a book of *Lieder,* and several madrigals.

[256] INGEGNERI, Marc' Antonio (In-gān-yā'-rē, Märk Ån-tōn'-yō)
SINGER, CHOIRMASTER
BORN: Verona, c. 1547
DIED: Cremona, July 1, 1592

Remembered particularly as the teacher of Claudio Monteverdi [333], Ingegneri was himself trained by Vincenzo Ruffo, choirmaster at his hometown cathedral, and by Cipriano de Rore [184] in Mantua. He came to Cremona around or shortly before 1570, a city noted more for its fiddle makers than for its composers. He joined the choir of the mighty-towered cathedral and by the end of the decade had become its *maestro.* He was a great friend of the local bishop, Nicolo Sfondrato, who reigned briefly as Pope Gregory

XIV in 1590–91. Ingegneri married in 1581. Something of a throwback polyphonist, he wrote Masses, motets, and other sacred works, but also published 9 books of madrigals. His responsories for Holy Week were long claimed for Palestrina.

[257] **HOYOUL, Baudouin** (Ō-yōōl', Bōd-wä*n'*)

SINGER, TEACHER, CHOIRMASTER
BORN: Liège, c. 1548
DIED: Stuttgart, November 26, 1594

From the same area as Antonius Gosswin [255] and, like him, a pupil of Lassus [228], Hoyoul got his start as a chorister in the ducal chapel of Württemberg in Stuttgart. When he was sixteen, his employer paid his way and expenses that he might study with Lassus in Munich. He returned two years later to sing as a countertenor in the chapel and to write music for it. He was later entrusted with the musical upbringing of the choristers. In 1574 he married the daughter of Ludwig Daser, who had become *Kapellmeister* two years earlier, after having been booted out of the ducal chapel in Munich in favor of Lassus. When Daser died in 1589, it was Hoyoul who succeeded him in Stuttgart. Perhaps grown ambitious, he angled in 1593 for a more prestigious post in Dresden but failed to get it, and was struck down by the plague a year later. His surviving output, all religious, includes both Catholic and Protestant music. Expectably, Hoyoul was strongly influenced by Lassus.

[258] **VICTORIA, Tomás Luis de** (Vik-tôr'-yà, Tō-màs' Lōō-ēs' dä)

CLERIC, ORGANIST, CHOIRMASTER,
SINGER, TEACHER
BORN: Ávila, 1548
DIED: Madrid, August 20, 1611

If Palestrina [201] sang with the dispassionate voice of the angels, his young friend and protégé Victoria worshipped his God with profoundly human (not to say Spanish) emotions. Together they stand as the cornerstones of Church music in the sixteenth century and the summation of the great polyphonic tradition. Victoria (called by the Italians Tommaso Lodovico da Vittoria) was born either in the city of Ávila or in the nearby village of Sanchidrián. As with so many of that era, his early life is obscure. It is fairly certain that from around the age of ten until his voice broke he sang in the cathedral choir, and may have had his earliest training from one or more of the successive choirmasters, Espinar, Ribera, and Navarro, though there are conjectures that his teacher was Bartolomeo Escobedo or even Antonio de Cabezón [164]. His mystical strain may owe something to contact with St. Teresa, who is known to have been acquainted with his brother.

At any rate, it is certain that in 1565 he went to Rome to study at the Collegium Germanicum, founded thirteen years earlier by St. Ignatius Loyola to train anti-Protestant missionaries for the Germanies. Owing to the tastes of certain of its benefactors, there seems to have been considerable emphasis on music there, and Victoria became one of the choral singers. The previous year, Pius V had founded the Seminario Romano, which was then an adjunct to the Collegium, and a year after Victoria entered the latter, Palestrina became choirmaster at the former, to which his two sons were admitted as students. The three young men were of an age, and Palestrina took an interest in the Spaniard and may well have taught him. After four years Victoria left the college and became organist-choirmaster at Santa Maria di Monserrato, a Spanish church in Rome. In 1571 he also took on teaching duties back at the Collegium Germanicum. The same year Palestrina returned to his original stamping grounds as *maestro* of the Cappella Giulia in St. Peter's, and Victoria succeeded him at the seminary. Two years later the new pope, Gregory XIII, put the two schools on separate footings, and Victoria was made choirmaster of the German College. About this time he also began occasionally singing in the choir of the church of San Giacomo di Spagnoli. In 1574 he left Santa Maria to complete his priestly training, taking orders the following year. It was about this period that his first publications—a book of motets, 1572; and one of miscellaneous religious pieces, 1576—appeared. Thanks to his having attracted wealthy admirers, such as the German Cardinal Otto Truchsess, these and all of Victoria's subsequent works were magnificently printed and bound.

In 1578 Victoria resigned his post for the lowly one of almoner at the church of San Girolamo della Carità. Though he left no explanation for this move, two reasons seem likely. First, the duty of distributing alms to the needy would give him much more time to compose. Second, as the focal center for the new spirituality represented by the future Oratorians and their leader (the future San) Filippo Neri, the atmosphere of "personal" religion appears to have attracted him. It is certain that he was close to two of the congregation, the monks Fra Juvenal

Ancina and Fra Francisco Soto de Longa, who wrote lyrics for the *laude,* and he may well have been close to Neri himself. Certainly the period produced a great deal of music from Victoria—two more books of motets, all of the Magnificats, the hymns, the offices for Holy Week, and a collection of Masses. But in the dedication which he addressed to Philip II in this last work (1583), he confesses that he is tired of music-making, and would like to go home and be a simple parish priest. He did the former at some time between that date and 1587; as for the latter, he was appointed chaplain to Philip's sister María, widow of Emperor Maximilian II. María lived at the Convent of Las Descalzas de Santa Clara in Madrid, where her daughter, Margaret, was a nun, and Victoria served as choirmaster there and later as organist. On the occasion of the empress's death in 1603 he wrote a *Requiem,* perhaps his most admired work, and almost certainly his last. He was left a comfortable pension by terms of the empress's will, and followed her eight years later.

Victoria left 52 motets, 22 Masses, 18 Magnificats, 2 sets of offices, a *Litany of the Blessed Virgin,* 2 Passions, and many hymns, psalms, antiphons, and sequences. Formally, his approach was up to date but not pathbreaking. What makes him a great composer is the passion of his feeling, which has been called manneristic and reminds one perhaps of his contemporary El Greco in painting; be that as it may, it presages the Baroque.

RECORDINGS: offices for Holy Week; an office for the Dead (including the *Requiem);* several of the Masses but by no means all; and a scattering of the briefer works, with much duplication of certain pieces.

---

[259] **DU CAURROY, François Eustache du, Sieur de St. Frémin** (Dü Kôr-wà', Fràn-swà' Ös-tàsh')
SINGER, CHOIRMASTER, ADMINISTRATOR, CLERIC
BORN: Gerberoy, February 1549
DIED: Paris, August 7, 1609

Born near the cathedral town of Beauvais, Eustache du Caurroy was the son of a nobleman who served as royal attorney and registrar of the census there. Becoming, in or about 1569, a singer at the Ste. Chapelle in Paris, Eustache made steady progress. In 1573 he was appointed (nonresident) prior of the abbey of St. Aïoul near Provins. Later he was given benefices in Dijon, Orléans, and elsewhere. He worked his way up to deputy choirmaster and later to the post of *maître de chapelle,* apparently delighting no less

than three kings en route. When Henry IV came to the throne in 1589, it was Caurroy's *Te Deum* that was sung at the coronation—at Chartres, because Rheims, the traditional site, was under occupation by dissidents who opposed a Protestant-tainted monarch. (Caurroy also wrote a requiem sung at royal funerals for a century afterward.) In 1599, Henry created for him the overseer post of superintendent of the King's music. The superintendent was buried in l'Église des Grands-Augustins in the French capital.

In his lifetime, Caurroy won extravagant praise from his musical countrymen, being placed on the same level as Palestrina [201] and Lassus [228]. He twice carried off the prize at Guillaume Costeley's [218] St. Cecilia festivities in Evreux, and it was once taken as gospel that he more or less sired all French music that came after him. There is little in the music that has come down to us to support such claims. In the main it consists of a collection of devotional music for court use *(Meslanges),* another collection of sacred music *(Preces ecclesiasticae),* the *Mass for the Dead,* a book of instrumental motetlike fantasies, and *chansons* scattered through various collections. Caurroy is essentially conservative and sometimes stuffy. Turned off by the quantitative musicopoetical experiments of Jean-Antoine de Baïf's (see 211) followers, he later decided to try his hand at the technique, and the results were hailed as the greatest yet; but the impetus to praise was probably more political than musical.

RECORDINGS: The fantasies have attracted most attention from recording artists; there are examples by the Concentus Musicus and the Wenzinger Viol Consort. Stéphane Caillat has recorded the *Te Deum.*

---

[260] **ANTEGNATI, Costanzo** (Àn-tān-yà'-tē, Kô-stànt'-zō)
ORGAN BUILDER, ORGANIST, THEORIST
BORN: Brescia, c. December 9, 1549
DIED: Brescia, November 14, 1624

The most famous member of a family that dominated Italian organ building for nearly two centuries, Costanzo was the great-grandson of Bartolomeo, who installed the chief organ in Milan Cathedral in 1490, and the son of Graziadio (i.e., "Thankgod"). Costanzo himself designed and oversaw the erection of nearly 150 instruments. In 1584 he became organist of Brescia Cathedral and served in that capacity until his death forty years later. He was also a productive composer, turning out published collections of Masses, motets, psalms, and madrigals. His most famous work, however, was *L'Arte organica* of 1608, which contains, besides some interesting *ricercari*, an organ method with some notions on tuning and registration.

[261] LOHET (or LOXHAY), Simon (Lō-khā', Sē-môn')
ORGANIST, TEACHER
BORN: probably in or near Liège before 1550
DIED: Stuttgart, July 1611

Lohet was presumably a compatriot of Baudouin Hoyoul [257], and certainly his colleague in the Württemberg *Kapelle* of Duke Ludwig, where he was appointed organist in 1571 as assistant to Utz Steigleder, who was getting shaky. Later he became chief organist and was assisted by his son Louis, one of his many pupils. He retired ten years before his death. He left a few organ pieces, notably a number of brief so-called fugues (really imitative fantasias).

[262] MASSAINI (or MASSAINO), Tiburtio (Màs-sà-ē'-nē, Tē-bōōrt'-zē-ō)
CHOIRMASTER, SINGER
BORN: Cremona, before 1550
DIED: after 1609

An Augustinian monk, Massaini seems to have been one of the men who gave the cloistered life a bad name. Certainly his peripatetic existence was not always the result of his own restlessness. Obviously a capable musician, he is first heard of as *maestro di cappella* in Salò, on Lake Garda, in 1587. Then he crossed the Alps and worked in the same capacity for Archduke Ferdinand of the Tyrol in Innsbruck in 1589–90. Next he assumed the directorship of the chapel of Wolfdietrich, Prince-Archbishop of Salzburg in 1591. After a thwarted attempt to steal musicians from his former employer at Innsbruck, he was run out of town in 1591 on suspicion of "flagrant crimes against nature," which in those days did not refer to throwing garbage in the Salzach. In 1592 he was in the chapel of Emperor Rudolf II in Prague. After a gap in the record he surfaces again in 1598, back in Italy, at Lodi. In 1600–8 he was in Piacenza for an unusually long stopover, but in 1609, the last year in which his name turns up, he was back in Lodi.

As a composer, Massaini published the expectable Masses, motets, and other religious works, and some secular vocal music, including a madrigal for *Il Trionfo di Dori,* the model for the English *Triumphes of Ori-*

ana. The music for which he is chiefly remembered, however, is the three instrumental *canzone* included in the collection published in Venice by Allesandro Raverii in 1608. These—for eight trombones, for sixteen trombones, and for four each of violins and lutes—are among the earliest consort pieces whose instrumentation is specified.

[263] MOSTO, Giovanni Battista (Mōs'-tō, Jō-vàn'-nē Bàt-tēs'-tà)
WIND PLAYER, CHOIR DIRECTOR
BORN: Udine, before 1550
DIED: Gyulafehérvár, 1597

Mosto came from a family of municipal wind players, or *pifferari*, in northeastern Italy: his father and three brothers, Bernardo, Francesco, and Nicolò, were all thus employed at various times and places. Giovanni Battista studied in Venice with Claudio Merulo [230], and in 1568 he and his three brothers were all part of the instrumental complement of the Bavarian ducal chapel in Munich. In 1569, Francesco, Giovanni Battista, and Nicolò quit, and a year later the last two had replaced their late father in the Udine town band. In the middle 1570s Giovanni went back to Münich for a time, but in 1580 he was director of the cathedral choir in Padua. Nine years later, the chapter dropped him for reasons unknown. After a brief time in the Cracow court of Sigismund III, he went into the service of Zsigmond Báthory, Prince of Transylvania and nephew to Stephen Báthory, the recently deceased King of Poland. In 1595, the Paduan chapter, consistent with its inconsistency, called him back to the cathedral. Some months later he returned to Transylvania to pick up his family and personal belongings, but on the way home he died at Gyulafehérvár (also known as Karlsburg; now called Alba Iulia in west-central Romania). Mosto produced at least 4 madrigal books and apparently nothing else.

[264] HANDL, Jakob (alias Jacobus Gallus) (Hàn'-dǝl, Yā'-kōp)
SINGER, CHOIRMASTER
BORN: Reifnitz, Austria, 1550
DIED: Prague, July 18, 1591

Handl is not to be confused with the later George Friderick Handel [683] nor with the sixteenth-century Joannes Gallus, whose real name was probably Jean LeCocq. What *Handl's* real name was has long been a point of argument. Its German and Latin forms both mean "cockerel," but because he came from Slovenia (his birthplace is now Ribnica, just south of Ljubljana, Yugoslavia), there are those who maintain that he was probably originally Petelin. No doubt that would make of him a Slovene musical pioneer, but one wonders why he would adopt a German dialectal form and then Latinize it. Like other composers from his area, he shows Venetian influence but nothing especially Slavic, and since Slovenia is just over the hill from the German-language province of Carinthia, one assumes that German families must have lived there when there was no international border to cross. Nor does the fact that he spent some years in what is now Czechoslovakia really strengthen the argument for his Slavic origins.

Despite speculations about where he may have stayed and visited in his youth along the Adriatic coast, we know of his whereabouts only after he moved to Austria proper and became a Cistercian at the great monastery at Melk. In 1574 he sang in the imperial chapel in Vienna, then spent some months in Prague and Breslau, eventually settling down for a while (1578) as *Kapellmeister* to Jan Pavlovský, Bishop of Olmütz (now Olomouc in central Czechoslovakia). From 1585 he was choirmaster of the church of St. Jan in Vado in Prague.

Handl was a devout Catholic in the spirit of the Counter-Reformation, and even his secular works are highly and determinedly moral. He wrote eighteen Masses (mostly of the parody ilk), and a quantity of motets and madrigals. The latter are not only untainted by frivolity, they are also in Latin! Of the motets, his largest and most important collection is the *Opus musicum,* a cycle for all sorts of vocal combinations to cover the entire liturgical year. Most of his music was printed in his lifetime in Prague, under a special dispensation from Emperor Joseph II. It combines features of both the contrapuntal and the Venetian schools, but is highly individual—so much so that some of his contemporaries thought him a wild man.

[265] VECCHI, Orazio Tiberio (Vek'-kē, Ō-rāts'-yō Tē-bâr'-yō)

CLERIC, CHOIRMASTER, MASTER OF CEREMONIES

BORN: Modena, December 5 (?), 1550
DIED: Modena, February 19, 1605

Vecchi is one of those rare Renaissance composers of whom one catches enough fascinating glimpses to make one want to know him better—or not at all! He is described variously as "merry" and "belligerent," and

there is evidence to support both evaluations. He seems to have come from the lower social strata, and for most of his life he seems to have had money problems; these in part stemmed from family difficulties, what with his father going broke and blind. Not that he was unpopular, both for his personality and his music; now and again cardinals (Alessandro d'Este), kings (Sigismund III of Poland), and emperors (Rudolf II) sought his services, and he was obviously *persona grata* at the Este court back home, where he planned the parties and taught the princelings.

Vecchi was a pupil of Salvatore Essenga, Modenese monk and madrigalist, and at sixteen saw one of his compositions included in his teacher's book of madrigals. In his younger years, he seems to have traveled the cities of northern Italy and to have taught music in the interim in his native town, which remained the focus of his whole life. Just when he entered holy orders we don't know, but they seem to have weighed lightly on him. His first publication was a volume of *canzonette,* lighthearted, dancelike secular works of which he is regarded as the past master. Even the sacred pieces that he wrote in the line of duty are decidedly madrigalesque.

In 1584, Vecchi became choirmaster at the cathedral of Salò on the western shore of Lake Garda, but quit because, he claimed, someone was out to get him. He tried for a similar and very lucrative post in Reggio Emilia, but instead had to be content with Correggio, where he went in 1586. Though he was a canon and later archdeacon there, he said it was all he could do to make ends meet. The next year he published, along with the music he wrote for the wedding of Clelia Farnese, unofficial daughter of Cardinal Alessandro, builder of the Palazzo Farnese in Rome, a sort of an account of his existence, including such fascinating minutiae as what he liked to eat. Having gotten in good with both the Church and the Venetian musical establishment (of which he is sometimes accounted a member), he was asked in 1591 (the year of his archdeaconate) to help Giovanni Gabrieli and others edit the Gregorian Gradual.

But Vecchi seems not to have been able to resist the bright lights of the Este court in Modena, where in 1594 they produced his *L'Amfiparnaso* (Both Sides of Mount Parnassus? Parnassus of Two Kinds?). This is described as a madrigal comedy, and historians of opera like to claim it as an ancestor of that form, but it hardly qualifies—as Vecchi was the first to admit. He said specifically that the story was for the ears and mind, not for the stage. It consists mostly of witty five-part madrigals, plus one of four parts and one monologue. The comical libretto, derived from *commedia dell'arte,* was by the composer, no mean poetic talent.

L'Amfiparnaso may have made Vecchi's musical reputation, but it—and his neglect of duty—lost him his cathedral job; yet Modena took care of its own and by 1596 was installed as *maestro* in the local cathedral and two years later as general musical and celebratory factotum to the court. It was largely this decade of his life that gave rise to the charges of uncontrollable irascibility. True, he had a brother, Annibale, whom he managed to get out of a conviction for a triple murder—but that was his brother. In 1595, Vecchi intervened in a fight between his brother (the same one?) and his sister-in-law's boyfriend and ended it by whopping the latter over the head twice with a short sword—but this argues for "cool" rather than heat of passion. We can hardly put the blame on Vecchi for being, that same year, nearly murdered in the dark with a stiletto by an unknown assailant (perhaps the jealous student who is said eventually to have wrought his downfall). The only cited instance in which he seems directly culpable was the one in 1596 when, during Mass in the church of St. Augustine, his running battle with the organist got out of control, culminating in the two trying to drown out each other during Vecchi's pre-Communion solo. In 1600 he went to Rome with Cardinal d'Este on what seems to have been a lovely trip, including a hearing of Jacopo Peri's [309] music drama *Euridice* on the way back through Florence. But four years later they got him at last. Supposedly at the instigation of a pupil who wanted the directorship in the cathedral, the bishop canned him for insisting on giving lessons or concerts or something in a local convent. Poor Vecchi went home and died, apparently of chagrin.

Besides the 6 books of *canzonette,* 2 of madrigals, *L'Amfiparnaso,* some Masses, motets, and Lamentations, as well as some miscellaneous works (both vocal and instru-mental), Vecchi published 2 volumes of satirical madrigals, *Il Convito (The Feast)* and *Le Veglie di Siena (The Sienese Soirees).*

RECORDINGS: Selections from *Il Convito* have been recorded, and there are several recordings of *L'Amfiparnaso.*

[266] CANALE, Floriano (Kä-nä'-lä, Flôr-yä'-nō)
ORGANIST, MEDICAL WRITER (?)
BORN: Brescia, c. 1550
DIED: Brescia, after 1612

Nothing more is known of Canale than that he was a monk and the organist at San Giovanni Evangelista in Brescia from 1581 to 1603 and that he published several volumes of his music (religious choral works, *canzonette,* and instrumental pieces) between 1575 and 1603. A medical treatise, *Dei secreti universali,* signed "Florian Canale" from Brescia in 1612 (but not published, apparently, until 1640) would appear to be his. It has been argued, not very convincingly, that he was really a Hollander named Florian Pijpe. His instrumental music, some of it for two "orchestras," shows the influence of Andrea and Giovanni Gabrieli [180, 286].

[267] CAVALIERI, Emilio de' (Kä-väl-yä'-rē, Ā-mēl'-yō dä)
ORGANIST, PRODUCER, ADMINISTRATOR, DIPLOMAT
BORN: Rome, c. 1550
DIED: Rome, March 11, 1602

Long hailed mistakenly as the inventor of the oratorio (but certainly to be regarded as a pioneer of opera), Emilio de' Cavalieri probably studied music as any gentleman of his time would have. He was the son of Tommaso de' Cavalieri, architect, friend of Michelangelo, and scion of an old Roman noble family. Little seems to be known about his first quarter century or so. In 1578 he became organist in the Oratorio del Crocifisso* at the church of San Marcello

---

* Presumably this was an offshoot of the Oratorians founded by the priest Filippo Neri, sainted soon after his death. Neri, a Florentine, came to Rome as a monk and devoted himself to such charitable work as caring for the sick and for pilgrims down on their luck. Around 1550, in the spirit of the Counter-Reformation, he began meeting with friends in his quarters at San Girolamo della Carità to pray, meditate, sing simple hymns called *laude,* and discuss things spiritual. In the revivalistic fervor of the reformed Church, the meetings overflowed, and a prayer hall, or *oratorio,* was built in the church to accommodate them. Gregory XIII gave the "Congregation of the Oratorians" official status as an order in 1575, and it soon had its headquarters at the church of Santa Maria in Valicella, where a whole new structure was erected for it. It is said that Neri and Cavalieri knew each other, and one supposes that the Oratorio del Crocifisso in the "church of the Florentines" took its cue from that in the Florentine Neri's San Girolamo. Music played an important role with the Oratorians. Some accounts have the premiere of the *Rappresentazione* occurring at the new church of Santa Maria in Valicella, but this appears to derive from a misunderstanding.

("the church of the Florentines") and a year later superseded his brother, Mario, as the person in charge of the musical arrangements for Lent. There he met Cardinal Ferdinando de' Medici, who, when in 1587 he was called back to Florence to succeed his brother, Francesco as Grand Duke of Tuscany, took Cavalieri along and made him his superintendent of arts and artists. This, in effect, meant that he was Master of the Revels, in general charge of fetes and ceremonies. His first real chance to prove himself came in 1589 with the wedding of his master to Christine of Lorraine. He evidently succeeded, for he called in everyone who was anyone in the relevant arts and crafts, and produced what must have been the sixteenth-century equivalent of a Hollywood spectacular, featuring mock battles (by land and artificial sea), banquets, tournaments, and a plethora of mythological and allegorical interludes. Over the next several years he supplied music for a number of pastorals, though Ferdinando seems to have had more use for him in helping to engineer the successive papal elections of Urban VII, Gregory XIV, Innocent IX, and Clement VIII. The frequent trips to Rome that such activity necessitated apparently allowed him to keep his hand in at San Marcello.

Most of Cavalieri's music has vanished, but we know that he was interested in the new musical ideas then brewing. He was a friend of Giovanni de' Bardi (see 252), even claimed to have invented the new recitative style, wrote for figured bass, and had an organ built that could handle quarter tones. In 1599 he wrote for Lent a set of lamentations and responsories that used these various devices. The following winter he twice produced at San Marcello his so-called "oratorio" *Rappresentazione di anima e di corpo (Play of the Soul and the Body)*. It was, in fact, an allegorical opera on the model of the old moralities and cut out of the same musical cloth as the secular examples by Peri [309] and Caccini [252]. Later that year there was another grandiose state wedding in Florence—that of Ferdinando's niece Maria to Henry IV of France. Too many other producers got into the act, Cavalieri's original conception was not fulfilled, and, considering the whole thing a disgrace, he decamped to Rome, where he died eighteen months later. The opera (which has been recorded), the lamentations, and a few madrigals have survived. The *Rappresentazione* was the first known work to have been published with continuo.

[268] HARDING, James
FLUTIST
BORN: c. 1550
DIED: London, January 28, 1626

Harding was employed as a royal musician from as early as 1575 to at least 1625. Listed as a flutist, he probably played the recorder. He may have been the father of a John Harding who was a Gentleman of the Chapel Royal under the two Charleses (though the older man also appears as Harden, Hardyn, and Hardynge). A few dances appear in English manuscripts and German anthologies.

[269] KLABON, Krzystof (Klä'-bōn, K'zhis'-tōf)
SINGER, LUTENIST, CHOIRMASTER
BORN: c. 1550
DIED: 1616 or later

Klabon, also known as Christophorus Clabonius, was a choirboy in the Cracow chapel of Sigismund August of Poland and then became a court instrumentalist. It is clear that he got himself into the good graces of the scholarly Polish kingmaker Jan Zamoyski. He wrote and sang songs in his honor on the occasion of his wedding, his defeat of Ivan the Terrible at Smolensk, and his capture of the Archduke Maximilian of Austria in Silesia. When Zamoyski brought the Transylvanian Prince Stephen Báthory to the throne in 1576 as successor to the absconded Henry III, Klabon became his chapelmaster. He continued under the Swedish-born Sigismund III, serving at both his Warsaw and Stockholm courts. In 1596 he was replaced by Luca Marenzio [273] but later was reestablished in his post, which he held until 1601. He was still living in 1616. Of his music there survive whole only a single *Kyrie* and *The Polish Calliope,* a set of six songs in honor of Zamoyski. RECORDINGS: *The Polish Calliope* songs have been recorded.

[270] TESSIER, Charles (Tes-yā', Shärl)
LUTENIST
BORN: c. 1550 (?)
DIED: after 1610

There were several late-Renaissance Tessier musicians, notably Charles and Richard, both of whom seem to have known their way around English court circles. Charles evidently had some connections with the Earl of Essex in the latter's heyday, and in 1597 dedicated a collection of airs and *chansons* to his sister, Lady Rich, supposedly the model for the female protagonist of Sir Philip Sidney's sonnet cycle *Astrophel and Stella,* from which Richard Tessier set a text. At the time he published his book, Charles Tessier was a chamber musician to Henry IV of France but was angling for a job in England. A second collection, published in 1604, was dedicated to Moritz, Landgraf von Hesse-Kassel, and a second printing of it, in 1610, to Matthias, King of Hungary. Both hinted that Tessier would welcome a move to Germany, but there seem to have been no takers.

[271] **TROFEO, Ruggiero** (Trō-fā'-ō, Rōō-jyâr'-ō)
ORGANIST, CHOIRMASTER
BORN: Mantua, c. 1550
DIED: Turin, September 19, 1614

Trofeo seems to have spent most of his first four decades in Mantua, where he was briefly cathedral organist in the mid-1570s and later organist of the ducal chapel of Santa Barbara. In 1587, Duke Guglielmo found him in a back street chatting with a woman whose company he deemed unfitting for a church organist, and when Trofeo told him to mind his business, the duke punctured him to a considerable depth with his sword. What the duke was doing in a back street, history does not say, and he died three months later anyhow. Trofeo recovered and at some time in the 1590s became organist of the church of San Marco in Milan. Lastly he settled in Turin early in the new century where he played at the cathedral and functioned as *maestro* to the Savoyard royal chamber chapel. He had a son named Giovanni Cristoforo who was also an organist. Ruggiero Trofeo published a book of *canzonette* and wrote some organ pieces.

[272] **ZIELEŃSKI, Mikołaj** (Zē-el-en'-skē, Mē-kō'-lwī)
ORGANIST, CHOIRMASTER
BORN: c. 1550 (?)
DIED: after 1615

Since the relevant records were all destroyed in the Thirty Years War, we are unlikely to ever know more about Zieleński than the little we now know. That boils down to his having served Wojciech Baranowski, Archbishop of Gniezno and chief of the Polish Catholic hierarchy, at his palace at Lowicz (between Warsaw and Łódź) as organist and choirmaster from at least 1608 until the archbishop's death in 1615. In 1611, Baranowski underwrote the publication, in Venice, of

Zieleński's two-volume collection of "offertories and communions for the whole year." Actually they contain 44 offertory motets, 61 Communion motets, 12 miscellaneous motets, a *Magnificat,* and 3 instrumental fantasias. It is clear that Zieleński knew his contemporary Venetian music. The motets in the offertory volume are antiphonal; the *Magnificat* is for three choirs, and there are instrumental parts and an organ bass (so-called *basso seguente,* indicating the lowest notes of the bass line). RECORDINGS: The Polish state recording company, Muza, has produced a disc containing the *Magnificat* and some motets.

[273] **MARENZIO, Luca** (Mà-rents'-yō, Lōō'-kà)
SINGER, CHOIRMASTER
BORN: Coccaglio, 1553
DIED: Rome, August 22, 1599

The son of a notary, Giovanni Francesco Marenzio, Luca Marenzio was born in a village near Brescia. Early accounts say that he grew up in poverty, that the local priest financed his education, and that his music teacher was Giovanni Contino, then *maestro di cappella* of the cathedral. There is some small evidence that Contino took his pupil with him when he became employed at the court of Mantua. It was almost certainly Contino who recommended Marenzio to his former employer Cardinal Madruzzo, erstwhile Archbishop of Trento, with whom he took service in Rome as a singer around 1574. When Madruzzo died four years later, Marenzio became chief musician to Cardinal Luigi d'Este, younger brother to Alfonso II, Duke of Ferrara, at a monthly emolument of five scudi, plus, no doubt, room and board. He dedicated his first book of madrigals (for five voices) to his new employer in 1580, and published fifteen more volumes of madrigals, *madrigali spirituali, villanelle,* and *canzonette* in his remaining years in his service. He spent some time in Ferrara in the cardinal's train in the early 1580s, and went to Venice to see one of his books through the press. Marenzio seems not to have been entirely happy in Luigi's service. Luigi at one time considered packing him off to Paris as a present to Henry III; more than once Marenzio had to complain that his salary was not arriving on time or even after it; and a dedication to Bianca Capello, the hapless Grand Duchess of Tuscany, indicates that he felt he would have been happier in Florence. After the deaths of Bianca, her husband Francesco, and Cardinal d'Este, all in 1587, Marenzio got his wish, being called to

Florentine duty by ex-Cardinal, now Grand Duke, Ferdinando de' Medici, primarily to help celebrate his marriage to Christine of Lorraine—which, owing to circumstances beyond their control, had to be postponed until 1589 (see 267). Marenzio's contribution, if any, to the festivities remains obscure. Suffice it to say he was back in Rome by the end of 1589, in the household of the Duke of Bracciano, Virginio Orsini. In 1593 he left him for service in the Vatican with Clement VIII's nephew, Cardinal Cinzio Aldobrandini. In 1595, on Aldobrandini's recommendation, he set out for the court of King Stephen Báthory in Poland, where in 1596 he replaced Krzysztof Klabon as choirmaster. But things did not work out there, and he returned to Rome early in 1598. On an August day a year later, while in the gardens of the Villa Medici, he dropped dead.

Although Marenzio's secular output dropped off sharply after 1587, the size of its totality (23 books in nineteen years) is significant—i.e., it sold, betokening a decided upsurge in amateur musicmaking. Moreover, it sold abroad, indicating the ascendancy of Italian music. The first books of Italian madrigals published in England—Nicholas Yonge's *Musica Transalpina* (1588) and *Italian Madrigals* translated into English by Thomas Watson (author of the first published English "sonnet" sequence)—were heavy on Marenzio and clearly helped inspire the subsequent burgeoning of the English madrigal.

As a madrigalist, Marenzio forms a bridge from the earlier Cipriano de Rore [184] and Andrea Gabrieli [180] to such advanced writers as Monteverdi [333] and Gesualdo [310]. His technical range is inexhaustible: there is no device of homophony or polyphony that he does not use. With him the word is of crucial importance, and he obviously chose his poets—Petrarch, Guarini, Sannazaro, Tasso, Dante, and others—with care and taste. He is perhaps the supreme practitioner of "madrigalism," seeking and finding a musical equivalent for every image and idea in the text. Moreover, his work displays a broad spectrum, moving over the years from pastoral lightness to the somber and apparently heartfelt—in a word, toward the melancholy that became the hallmark of the waning century. He also wrote about 75 motets and perhaps a couple of Masses.

RECORDINGS: There have been a few recorded collections of Marenzio madrigals, but his relatively scant treatment on records is inconsistent with his worth and reputation.

[274] ECCARD, Johannes (Ek'-kärt, Yō-hän'-nes)
SINGER, CHOIRMASTER
BORN: Mühlhausen, 1553
DIED: Berlin, 1611

Born in Thuringia (now western East Germany), Johannes Eccard was the son of Magdalene and Blasius Eccard, a sexton who had previously worked as a butcher. He attended the local Latin school, which opened in 1563 and whose music master was the seventeen-year-old Joachim a Burck. In 1567 he joined the chapel of the Duke of Saxe-Weimar and four years later that of the Bavarian court in Munich, where he studied with Orlande de Lassus [228] for two years. In 1573 he returned to Mühlhausen. From 1577 to 1578 he worked in Augsburg for the banker Jakob Fugger. The next year he went to Königsberg in Prussia to join the chapel of Margrave Georg Friedrich of Brandenburg-Ansbach, Governor of Prussia. He became second in command in the chapel and remained there when Georg Friedrich returned to Ansbach in 1586, maintaining his rank but actually in charge of the resident musical establishment. There a new governor, the Brandenburg Elector Joachim Friedrich, found him and promptly promoted him to *Kapellmeister*. Soon thereafter he took him back to his palace in Berlin and put him in charge there. There Eccard remained until he died in the reign of Joachim Friedrich's son Johann Sigismund.

Though he also wrote some *Lieder*, most of Eccard's work consists of polyphonic chorale settings and chorale-motets. (He and his friend Burck—his erstwhile teacher—also brought out a number of joint publications that consisted chiefly of settings by their poet-friend Ludwig Helmbold.) As a pioneer in the Germanic chorale tradition, Eccard had lasting influence.

[275] FERNÁNDEZ HIDALGO, Gutierre (Fâr-nán'-dā*th* Hē-dàl'-gō, Gōō-tyâr'-rā)
CHOIRMASTER, TEACHER, ADMINISTRATOR
BORN: Andalusia, 1553
DIED: La Plata, Bolivia, 1620 or later

Fernández Hidalgo was brought to Bogotá, Colombia, to replace the ineffectual Gonzalo García Zorro (who had not made his mark) as *maestro de capilla* at the cathedral, and to teach in the seminary. He was installed, after a fight, in 1585 and was shortly afterward made rector of the seminary. But when he established a rule that the seminarians had to sing at the cathedral services, they went on strike and ran him out of town. In 1588 he found an exactly analogous post in Quito, Ecuador, but left in 1591 for what seemed a better one in Cuzco, Peru. Two years later the cathedral chapter demanded that the musicians of the managerial class (e.g., Fernández Hidalgo) get out in the parish and do some real work for the high pay they were drawing. The shoe now being on the other foot, the *maestro* resigned and was persuaded to stay on only with an extra emolument from the chapter treasury. That kept him quiet for four years, but in 1597 he trekked off to La Plata (now Sucre), Bolivia, where they were offering a hundred pesos more per annum for identical duties. And there he seems to have stayed, building up an impressive musical establishment. In 1607 he put all his manuscripts in order and sent them back to Spain with a friend for publication, but the galleon appears to have vanished en route—as so many did. After he retired in 1620, he said he would like to end his days in Cuzco, but, we are told, he ended them in La Plata. Most of what is left of his output is in the cathedral archives in Bogotá and is said to compare favorably with that of the best of the sixteenth-century Spanish religious composers. RECORDINGS: There is a recording of one of his 9 Magnificats.

[276] HOOPER, Edmund
ORGANIST, TEACHER
BORN: North Halberton, c. 1553
DIED: Westminster, July 14, 1621

All we know of Devon-born Edmund Hooper's early life is that he may have been a choirboy at Exeter, but he first steps into the spotlight in 1582 as a singer at Westminster Abbey. By 1588 he was training the trebles there. On March 1, 1604, he succeeded a Mr. Randoll as a Gentleman of the Chapel Royal. Before that he had been a Gentleman Extraordinary—a title that, though it may also reflect his breeding, was something like the modern "steady extra musician" in orchestra personnel listings. He continued his connection with the abbey and in 1606 became its first steady organist. He was clearly a fine player, for he also shared a similar appointment in the Chapel Royal with Orlando Gibbons [408]. The abbey post carried with it such additional duties as making copies of the choirbooks and keeping the organ in playing order. He was twice married; on his death he left a widow, Margaret, and several children, of whom the eldest, James, sang in the abbey choir. A grandson, William, a friend of Samuel Pepys, carried on

the tradition. Edmund Hooper was succeeded at the abbey by Thomas Tomkins [365]. The bulk of his extant music consists of services, anthems, and other works for the Anglican ritual; there are also a few keyboard pieces. Some of the later pieces reflect the trend toward diatonicism and the contemporary concern with chromatic effects.

[277] LECHNER, Leonhard (Lekh'-ner, Lä'-on-härt)
SINGER, TEACHER, CHOIR DIRECTOR, EDITOR
BORN: Etschtal (i.e., the Adige Valley), South Tyrol, c. 1553
DIED: Stuttgart, September 9, 1606

Lechner makes an awkward entrance onto the historical stage as a dischargee (c. 1569) of the hapless chapel that Prince Wilhelm of Bavaria found himself unable to support in Landshut. Since Lechner noted his admiration for, and thanks to, Orlande de Lassus [228] for whatever musical abilities he had, he had probably spent his formative years at the ducal court in Munich. After the Landshut disaster, he says, he wandered (perhaps to Italy) before settling down in Nuremberg in the early 1570s as a lowly assistant teacher at the Lorenzschule. He stayed there for the better part of a decade, during which he married a town piper's widow, Dorothea Kast, and sired a son named Gabriel. A scholar of parts and an industrious composer whose fame steadily grew both at home and abroad, he failed to advance in the academic ranks, and the receipt of a rather empty title, *Archimusicus,* from the city fathers did little to temper his impatience. In 1584, therefore, he accepted an appointment as *Kapellmeister* to the Count of Hohenzollern-Hechingen, Eitelfriedrich IV (one of the *eitel Reich),* and then moved to Hechingen. The pay was nearly double what he had been making, but the count, it turned out, was a doctrinaire Catholic and Lechner was a fervent Lutheran (a convert); thus the two were unable to see eye to eye on the conduct of chapel services, and a year later Lechner fled to Württemberg, having failed to tie down a job in Dresden. Eitelfriedrich blacklisted him and sent out an all-points bulletin demanding his apprehension and return at whatever cost. Duke Ludwig of Württemberg, who was of Lechner's religious persuasion, paid no attention, however, to his fellow prince. He took the musician into his chapel (as a singer, with the expectable reduction in income), managed to get Nuremberg to let his wife and son emigrate, and made frequent payments to him for his compositions. Lechner became assistant to Ludwig Daser, the *Kapellmeister,* and to his successor, Baudouin Hoyoul [257], and was himself elevated to the post in 1595, after the latter's death. Faced at first with severe disciplinary problems, he got the backing of the duke, who threatened dire consequences for insubordination, and by 1603 had whipped the chapel into such shape that it won a musical contest with a visiting delegation of musicians from the English court. In his last few years, Lechner was frequently incapacitated by illness, for which he sought cures at various spas, but he managed to keep in harness until he died. He was buried with the dukes of Württemberg in the Spitalkirche.

Long largely forgotten, Lechner has emerged in recent years as one of the great German vocal composers of his time. He wrote both Latin and German liturgical music, including an important St. John Passion, a number of occasional pieces, and many *Lieder.* His music shows not only the impact of his acquaintance with Lassus, but also strong Italian influence, especially from the Venetian choralists and the madrigalists.

RECORDINGS: There are recordings of the *St. John Passion,* the *Deutsche Sprüche von Leben und Tod (German Proverbs About Life and Death),* and a number of the *Lieder.*

[278] BOTTEGARI, Cosimo (Bot-tä-gä'-rē, Kô'-zē-mō)
SINGER, LUTENIST
BORN: Florence, 1554
DIED: 1620

In the decade of the 1570s Bottegari was a member of Duke Albrecht of Bavaria's star-studded *Kapelle* in Munich. Albrecht evidently thought highly of him, for he conferred on him a patent of nobility. Afterward he returned to Florence, where he was known as a performer at the Medici court, apparently on an amateur basis. He put together a collection of lute songs, which includes a number of his own making.

[279] BEVIN, Elway
SINGER, ORGANIST, THEORIST, TEACHER
BORN: c. 1554
DIED: Bristol, October 1638

Bevin's name indicates that he was Welsh, or at least of Welsh descent. Unconfirmed rumor calls Thomas Tallis [157] his teacher, but the first ascertainable fact about him is that he joined the choir at Wells Cathedral in 1579. Early the following year he was suspended for a four-year failure to communi-

cate. (He was not stubbornly silent; he had merely neglected to partake in the Eucharist.) Evidently he mended his ways, as he was adjured to do, for he was shortly reinstated. By 1585, however, he had moved to Bristol Cathedral, where he became master of the boys and later organist. Prior to 1590 he took unto himself a wife named Alice, who by 1603 had borne him at least six children. In 1605 he was made a Gentleman Extraordinary of the Chapel Royal, but seems to have lived out his long life in Bristol. In 1631 he published *A Briefe and Short Instruction in the Art of Musicke,* which tells one mostly how difficult writing music is and offers some examples of canonic composition. He was almost certainly the "verie old" organist whom Archbishop Laud met at the Cathedral in 1634. (Eighty was an extraordinary age in those days.) On St. Valentine's Day, 1638, the chapter officially dismissed him from the cathedral. Unconfirmed rumor says that he had been found to be a Catholic. He was buried at St. Augustine-the-Less, the church of the parish in which he lived, on October 19, 1638. Bevin left a few anthems, a service (and fragments of others), a handful of songs, keyboard pieces, consort works, and innumerable canons.

[280] GASTOLDI, Giovanni Giacomo (Gás-tōl'-dē, Jō-vàn'-nē Jä'-kō-mō)
TEACHER, CHOIRMASTER
BORN: Caravaggio, 1554
DIED: 1622 (?)

Gastoldi was born in the little city between Brescia and Milan that, fifteen to twenty years after he arrived there, produced the future painter Michelangelo Amerighi, who would be remembered as "Caravaggio." Gastoldi may have sung as a lad at Santa Barbara, the Mantuan ducal chapel; he was certainly there as a subdeacon and deacon in the early 1570s. In 1581 he was one of the singers and also taught counterpoint to the novices. He probably stood in for the choirmaster, Giaches de Wert [232], during his illnesses, and was named to succeed him in 1592. In that same year he contributed settings of the choruses for a production of Giovanni Guarini's *Il Pastor fido,* some vesper motets for a collection dedicated to Duke Guglielmo's friend Palestrina [201], and a madrigal for the nuptial cycle *Il Trionfo di Dori* (on which the English *The Triumphes of Oriana* of a decade later was modeled). It is uncertain when Gastoldi left his post; it was declared vacant in 1605, but he was still in Mantua in 1608, when he wrote music for a production of Guarini's

L'Idropica (The Man with Dropsy). Supposedly after that he went to Milan. There he is said to have been *maestro di cappella* at the cathedral, but the records do not name him. He is also said to have entered secular life, but little is really known of his last years—even the place and date of his death.

Gastoldi not only wrote the expectable Masses, motets, psalms, etc., but produced at least eleven published collections of madrigals and other secular songs and some instrumental *bicinia* (pieces for two melody-instruments). His fame, however, has always rested on his *balletti.* The first of the two collections was popular for seventy years and went through many editions. The *balletti* are light and lively dance songs, many with the "fa-la-la" refrains that so many people suppose essential to the madrigal. The earlier collection, which appeared in 1591, is a real cycle, with big opening and closing numbers between which are "portraits" of various kinds of lovers. It has been seen as a forebear or close relative of the madrigal comedies popular around the end of the century, and was a chief influence on the balletts of Thomas Morley [289].

RECORDINGS: There are several more or less complete recordings of the 1591 cycle.

[281] MUNDY, John
KEYBOARDIST
BORN: London, c. 1554
DIED: Windsor, June 29, 1630

John Mundy was the son and pupil of the singer-composer William Mundy [212]. Early on, he is said to have been organist at Eton. He took a B.A. in music from Oxford University in 1586, about the same time that he was appointed organist of St. George's Chapel at Windsor—a post he apparently held the rest of his life. Six years before he died he attained the D.Mus. degree. He was especially admired for his playing, both on the organ and the harpsichord.

Mundy's output as a composer was not large. In his lifetime he published a madrigal in *The Triumphes of Oriana* and a 1594 collection of *Songes and Psalmes.* Other odds and ends exist in manuscript, notably 4 pieces—"Robin," "Goe from My Window," and 2 *fantasias*—in the *Fitzwilliam Virginal Book.* One of the *fantasias* is an early piece of program music, depicting a nice day several times interrupted by storms replete with thunder and lightning.

[282] GESE, Barthel (Gä'-zə, Bär'-tel)
CANTOR, TEACHER

BORN: Müncheberg, c. 1555
DIED: Frankfurt an der Öder, 1613

Barthel Gese (or Göse) wrote under the Latinized name of Bartholomaeus Gesius, and properly so, for he had studied theology at the University of Frankfurt. Around 1582 he returned to Müncheberg (thirty miles east of Berlin) to direct the church choir and run the attached school, but he did not stay long. Within the next few years he took service as a tutor in the household of the poetical Baron Hans Georg von Schönaich in Muskau (now in East Germany). He probably stayed there until late 1592, when he was asked to return to Frankfurt as cantor of the Marienkirche, where he spent his last twenty years. All of Gese's music is religious, most of it based on chorale tunes and quite influential among composers of the next generation in Germany. Of his 2 Passions *(St. John,* 1588, and *St. Matthew,* 1613), the earlier is the more interesting in that it combines the dramatic approach (in the person of the Evangelist who sings solo, in plainsong) and the motet-passion (the other characters sing in from three to five parts). RECORDINGS: A few of his popular Christmas songs have been recorded.

[283] RODRIGUES COELHO, Manuel
(Rō-drē'-gwez Kwāl'-yō, Mán'-ōō-wel)
ORGANIST
BORN: Elvas, c. 1555
DIED: Lisbon, c. 1635

Rodrigues Coelho presumably had his first music lessons in his birthplace near the Spanish border. In his late teens and early twenties he was an organist at Badajoz Cathedral, then became organist at the cathedral of Elvas until 1602, when he went to Lisbon to serve as royal organist to Philip III, King of Spain and Portugal. He was pensioned off in 1633 by Philip IV and died shortly afterward. Influenced as a composer by the Spanish, English, and Dutch keyboardists, he left a single collection of keyboard (or harp) pieces, *Flores de musica,* 1620, the first known to have been printed in Portugal.

[284] NENNA, Pomponio (Nen'-nà, Pôm-pōn'-yō)
BORN: Bari, c. 1555
DIED: 1613

For reasons that are obscure, one of Nenna's immediate forebears had been raised to the hereditary nobility by Emperor Charles V, and Nenna himself reminded people of his title in his publications. He came at some point into the orbit of Don Fabrizio Carafa, Duke of Andria, who appointed him governor of Andria, near Bari, Carafa being apparently otherwise occupied in Naples. When Don Carlo Gesualdo [310] slew the duke *in flagrante delicto* with his wife, Nenna seems to have passed into Gesualdo's service. It is possible that Gesualdo learned music from Nenna, but it is now thought more likely that Nenna was influenced by Gesualdo. In 1608 Nenna left Naples for Rome, the probable site of his death, apparently within a few weeks of Gesualdo's. Nenna wrote eight books of madrigals and a few sacred pieces (mostly, as with Gesualdo, responsories), which show him remarkably adaptable to the progressive tastes of his times. RECORDINGS: At least one LP has been devoted to Nenna.

[285] CAVACCIO, Giovanni (Kȧ-vȧch'-yō, Jō-vȧn'-nē)
ORGANIST, SINGER, CHOIRMASTER, POET
BORN: Bergamo, c. 1556
DIED: Bergamo, August 11, 1626

Though he was possibly a juvenile member of the ducal chapel in Munich, Cavaccio spent most of his life in his native city—twenty-three years as *maestro di cappella* at the cathedral and twenty-two more at Santa Maria Maggiore. As a publishing poet of considerable reputation, he was elected to the Accademia degli Elevati in Florence. His music seems to have had even wider circulation. His church compositions—Masses, a requiem, Magnificats, motets, psalms—are in the grandiose Venetian vein. He also published several books of madrigals and other secular songs, and some instrumental music, including an organ book with the title of *Sudori musicali (Musical Sweat)*. He was succeeded at Santa Maria Maggiore by Alessandro Grandi [377].

[286] GABRIELI, Giovanni (Gȧb-rē-ā'-lē, Jō-vȧn'-nē)
ORGANIST, TEACHER
BORN: Venice, 1556
DIED: Venice, August 12, 1612

Giovanni was the son of Andrea Gabrieli's [180] brother, but the childless Andrea seems to have brought him up as though he were his own, and there is everywhere evidence of deep love and admiration between the two. Andrea was, of course, Giovanni's teacher and probably provided the strongest

musical impulse in his career. At eighteen Giovanni went to the ducal court at Munich. (One reads that Andrea's old friend Lassus [228] took him along, that he perhaps went in company with musical theorist Lodovico Zacconi, that his uncle sent him on some pretext to protect him from the plague, or that he may not have gone at all!) For some four years he seems to have remained there in the capacity of an aide to Lassus. In 1584, Claudio Merulo [230], first organist of St. Mark's in Venice, quit his post. Giovanni entered the competition for the post and won but apparently turned it over to second organist Andrea, he himself becoming Number Two. On Andrea's death in 1586, Giovanni moved up to the first organ, remaining there until a spell of ill health forced his retirement in 1607. Along with Andrea's job, he also inherited his pupils, notably Gregor Aichinger [321] and Hans Leo Hassler [320], the latter of whom became his lifelong friend and correspondent and died two months before he did. Among his own pupils, he numbered Hassler's younger brother Jakob, Alessandro Grandi [377], and, above all, Heinrich Schütz [412], who became his favorite and his assistant, and to whom he left his ring. Gabrieli lived five years beyond his retirement, succumbing to an attack of kidney stones.

If this author may be allowed a moment of subjectivity, the personal experience of entering St. Mark's Square for the first time and being overcome by the impact of the basilica, with its oriental arches, domes, and finials counterbalanced by the pink-and-white facade of the Renaissance Doge's Palace and the red brick upthrust of the Campanile, was to *see* Giovanni Gabrieli's music. (The resemblance to the titanic Venetian painters of his period, Tintoretto, Titian, and Veronese, has been too often noted to require repetition.) In Gabrieli one finds the culmination of the Venetian Renaissance —and the beginning of the Baroque. His advent was inevitable for the material—Adrian Willaert's [129] development of polychoralism, Gioseffo Zarlino's [186] revolutionary theories, the tone painting and chromaticism of the later madrigalists, the tendencies toward soloistic performance and *basso continuo*, the evolution of instrumental forms, the increased popularity of the violins, the use of ceremonial brasses—and one is tempted to say that if no Giovanni Gabrieli had appeared, someone else would have had to do what he did.

Considered superficially from a generic standpoint, Gabrieli's compositions appear to be merely what one has come to expect of the Venetian Renaissance—madrigals, motets, a Mass (of sorts), *ricercari, canzone,* and sonatas. Most of the collections (published in the last twenty-five years of his life and posthumously in 1615) include Andrea's music as well as his own—his greatest testimonial to his beloved uncle. But there are terms in the titles that give one pause: *concerti* and *symphoniae*—these are designations that were at least exotic previously, if not unknown. One should not, of course, expect here Liszt or Beethoven. *Concerto* seems to have its basic meaning of a contest; if later the struggle was between soloist and orchestra, with Gabrieli it is between groups —but groups carefully designed to offset each other. Polychoralism is now no longer merely a chat between equals, but a counterposing of one kind of sound against another. It also indicates choral music with specifically instrumental accompaniment. *Symphoniae sacrae* is a less easily definable title, but suffice it to say that it involves instruments as well as voices, and more importantly instruments that, *ensemble,* have their own prescribed interludes. In his choral and choral-instrumental works, it pleases Gabrieli to work with all kinds of combinations, using anywhere from three to twenty-two parts and up to four separate groups. It is clear that acoustical considerations were of great significance to his musical thinking and that he obviously studied how to make St. Mark's itself a part of his music-producing apparatus. It has been noted that in his polyvocal works Gabrieli writes a real part for each voice. But his effects are harmonic and coloristic rather than polyphonic in the old sense. Not only does he expand music numerically, but he also expands it in terms of range. Even where the instruments are not specified, it is clear that he often has them in mind, for he indicates high and low notes beyond the capabilities of most trained voices. But, importantly, he *does* specify at times what he wants used—pointing in a new direction. In the much-cited *In ecclesiis,* for instance, he demands vocal soloists, two choirs, an organ, and an orchestra of three cornets, a violin (viola?), and two trombones.

The *canzone* and sonatas carry the polychoral practice into the instrumental domain. The *canzone* in particular represent a new manifestation of that genre in that they tend to be made up of a succession of short movements of contrasting natures with no common thematic material and little or no repetition of segments. The *Sonata pian e forte* (soft-and-loud sounding piece) not only has the instrumentation of its two groups indicated but is apparently the first piece of music in which dynamics are indicated.

In Gabrieli one also sees change and dissolution. His so-called "Mass" is a mere series of Mass segments with no common musical bond, each movement treated according to its proper sense. The Mass as a unified composition, which ruled since the early fifteenth century, was fading out. Indeed, with Gabrieli the word becomes paramount. Musical rhythms are dictated by those of the text, the dramatic or affective approach of the contemporary madrigal is applied without reservation to religious material, and one can descry Monteverdi [333] just over the hill. More than ever the old modes are giving way to the major-minor concept, and Gabrieli seems positively to rejoice in tonic-dominant sequences. Deliberate breaking of the "rules" is common, and dissonances that would have stood an earlier generation's hair on end (but not ours!) are used for emphasis and color. There is forward movement in the use of figured bass and of a repeated, or *ostinato,* bass-line, as in the later passacaglia.

RECORDINGS: Giovanni Gabrieli has been well represented on records since the days of short-play discs. (G. Wallace Woodworth did a pioneering album forty years ago and the *Sonata pian e forte* goes back to the *Anthologie Sonore.*) Of particular note are four records made by E. Power Biggs, Gregg Smith, and Vittorio Negri in St. Mark's itself. A warning to purists: These performances, as well as most other representations of the instrumental music, are inclined to use modern brasses rather than the originally intended instruments.

[287] PAIX, Jakob (Pā, Yä′-kōp)
ORGANIST, TEACHER
BORN: Augsburg, 1556
DIED: after 1623

If Paix seems an odd name for Augsburg, it was brought there by a Netherlands organist Peter (Pierre?) Paix, father and teacher to Jakob. Jakob took up the paternal calling, and at twenty the newlywed husband of Anna Neunhofer was installed as organist of the Martinskirche in Lauingen on the Danube, where, in a time-honored tradition of Central Europe, he also taught school. What with a large family to rear, his income barely sufficed, but in 1609 he was put in charge of instrumental music in the ducal court of nearby Neuburg. Eight years later, however, he, as a Protestant, had to leave when Neuburg reverted to Catholicism. His last known address was a village called Hiltpolstein. Though he wrote sacred choral music, he is chiefly remembered for his organ book.

[288] MAUDUIT, Jacques (Mōd-wē', Zhàk)

BUREAUCRAT, THEORIST, CONDUCTOR
BORN: Paris, September 16, 1557
DIED: Paris, August 21, 1627

Mauduit was a true Renaissance man, if slightly after the fact. The son and successor of a royal secretary and law court official, he was solidly grounded in the liberal arts, multilingual, passionately interested in science and technology, and self-taught in music. At twenty-four he went off to the annual St. Cecilia's Day festivities at Evreux and came home with a first prize for the motet he had submitted. At about the same time he was taken into the Academy of Music and Poetry as Antoine de Baïf's right-hand man. Though the ostensible purpose of the academy was the imposition of classical metrics on French poetry, Mauduit tells us that by this time it had embraced a larger view and was in fact a sort of educational institution that dealt in the most advanced notions in that area, including a sort of ROTC branch. On Sundays it sponsored concerts which were attended by the elite and which also had some of the other ritual aspects of the modern concert, discouraging, for example, latecoming and chattering. As for the metrical concerns, Mauduit agreed with Baïf that the music should always take a rhythmic back seat to the verse, and in 1586 produced his *Chansonnettes mesurées,* which did precisely that, syllable for syllable. He also set some of Baïf's psalms, but these, like most of his other music, have vanished. In 1586 he also wrote a famous requiem for the funeral of Pierre de Ronsard, which was later sung at his own, but only the first section is extant. During the religious uprisings in 1589, Mauduit is supposed to have rescued his friend and colleague Claude Le Jeune [211] and his manuscripts from soldierly harm. After Baïf's death in 1589, Mauduit took over the academy concerts, for which he was a nonpareil time beater, and, as we might say, conductor. At one of them, in 1599, Henry IV's mistress, slated to be his bride, suddenly complained of feeling unwell, went home, and died. Medical history does not say whether the cause of her illness was the warmth of the hall (which she mentioned), anticipation of regality, or the concert itself. Henry was forced to marry Marie de Médicis instead.

A few years later, the French mathematician-philosopher-musician-cleric Marin Mersenne (1588–1648) set down the results of his conversations with Mauduit in *Quaestiones celeberrimae in Genesim,* in which he notes his plan to publish all of Mauduit's music. He apparently did not. Only the *chansonnettes* and a few fugitive pieces survive intact.

[289] MORLEY, Thomas

ORGANIST, PUBLISHER, EDITOR, SPY, TEACHER
BORN: Norwich, 1557
DIED: London, October 1602

From his links with Norwich Cathedral, it has been determined that Thomas Morley, who almost single-handedly was responsible for the madrigal craze in England, was the son of Francis Morley, a Norwich brewer. At some point young Thomas studied with William Byrd [248] for a year or two, probably in the early 1570s. By 1574 he was back in Norwich at the cathedral, where in 1583 he succeeded William Inglott as organist and master of the choirboys. But by 1587 he had pulled up stakes, probably for London. A year later he acquired a B.Mus. from Oxford. Probably around the same time he married, for a son and namesake (probably an infant) was buried at St. Giles, Cripplegate, London (later John Milton's church) a year later. At that time Morley was organist at St. Paul's Cathedral. He seems to have been employed, like Christopher Marlowe, as an anti-Catholic spy by the Crown. There was strong suspicion that he was really a Catholic and was playing both ends against the middle, and at least once his life was threatened. In 1592 he was taken into the Chapel Royal, to fill the slot previously occupied by a Mr. Greene, and soon after, by way of promotion, moved from the Epistle to the Gospel side.

There is no indication as to when Morley's first wife died, but in the early 1590s he took a second, named Susan. In 1596 the Morleys settled in "little" St. Helen's parish, Bishopsgate, where a daughter, Frances (d. 1599), was born. In 1598, Morley, for tax purposes, was listed as being worth two pounds—the same as William Shakespeare, whom he may have known and for whose song "It Was a Lover and His Lass" (from *As You Like It)* he provided the most famous of its many settings. In that same year Morley managed to acquire the music-printing monopoly long ago granted his old teacher. It is thought that he was aided by one of his co-parishioners, a judge named Sir Julius Caesar. Almost immediately there was an uproar over rights to a psalter that Morley published, which resulted in Parliament's abolishing any further such monopoly. Shortly afterward Morley, who had been feeling poorly for some years, withdrew from the business. Since he was replaced in the Chapel Royal by one George Woodson and his estate turned over to Susan Morley early in October 1602, he must have died early that fall. He was survived also by two young children, Christopher and Anne. Thomas Weelkes [385] wrote a lament for his "dearest friend," and later Thomas Ravenscroft [406] hailed him as "the sun in the firmament of our art."

Usually thought of as a madrigalist, Morley wrote in other forms as well. His religious music—services, anthems, funeral music, some Latin motets—expectably shows the imprint of Byrd most clearly. Highly regarded by some, it is generally considered not to rank with the greatest of its kind. There are a number of keyboard pieces, the bulk of them in the *Fitzwilliam Virginal Book* (compiled by a Catholic prisoner, Francis Tregian the Younger). Some two-part fantasias follow up Thomas Why-thorne's [210] pioneering *bicinia,* and there are a few for more ambitious instrumental combinations. Of particular interest and importance is the 1599 *First Booke of Consort Lessons.* This contains mostly arrangements of dances by Morley's contemporaries, but the "orchestration" is precisely specified—so far as is known for the first time in musical history. The prescribed combination, a so-called "broken" consort because it calls for instruments of more than one family, consists of three plucked instruments (say, lute, cittern, and pandora), viols (one high, one low), and a flute or recorder.

As for the madrigals, Morley published only one collection of his own, subsumed under that generic title, in 1594. But it was preceded and followed by collections of modestly called "canzonets," which actually *are* madrigals. Morley is happiest when his subjects are happy ones, as in the *Canzonets or Little Short Songs of Three Voices* published in 1593. Here he establishes the standard for the English madrigal by combining the Italian impulse with Byrdian counterpoint, but never forgetting the demands of the English words. The madrigals of the next year are cast mostly in the same lighthearted vein. In 1595 he brought out a book of two-part canzonets (it included the instrumental *bicinia),* based mostly on madrigals by Felice Anerio, and a book of "balletts" for five voices that owed not a little to Gastoldi's [280] *balletti* (but are infinitely more thought-out compositions, the infamous "falas" serving as developed interludes here);

indeed both works were published in dual editions with English and Italian texts. 1597 brought another collection of canzonets, this time in five and six parts, and 1600 brought Morley's only book of ayres (for solo voice with lute and viola da gamba accompaniment), which includes the Shakespeare song. It was also Morley who drew together the famous *Triumphes of Oriana,* ostensibly dedicated to Queen Elizabeth (1601), modeled on the Italian *Trionfo di Dori.* It included madrigals, bound together with references to the fair Oriana, written by most of the best madrigalists in England (including two by Morley), as well as a few by composers who weren't quite sure what a madrigal was. Finally there should be mentioned Morley's invaluable textbook of 1597, *A Plaine and Easie Introduction to Practicall Musicke,* the first English treatise of its kind, and a fascinating source book for information on musical practice.

RECORDINGS: Collections of Morley's madrigalesque pieces have been recorded by the Deller Consort, the Golden Age Singers, the New York Pro Musica, and groups under Denis Stevens. Both René Soames and Nigel Rogers have recorded the ayres and David Munrow a selection from the *First Booke of Consort Lessons.* Three versions of *Triumphes of Oriana* have appeared.

[290] CROCE, Giovanni (Krō'-chä, Jō-vän'-nē)
PRIEST, CHOIRMASTER, TEACHER
BORN: Chioggia, c. 1557
DIED: Venice, May 15, 1609

Nicknamed "Il Chiozzotto" (the Chioggian), he was also known as Joanne a Cruce Clodiensis. In boyhood he was a chorister at St. Mark's, Venice, under Gioseffo Zarlino [186], with whom he presumably studied. He may also have studied theology, for he is said to have been an ordained priest when he sang at the church of Santa Maria Formosa in Venice. In 1592 he became assistant *maestro di cappella* at St. Mark's, though his chief duties seem to have been riding herd on the choirboys over at the "seminary." When the incumbent *maestro,* Giuseppe Donato, died eleven years later, Croce was voted into his post, with a single dissent from a man who thought they should set up a search committee, and with a good deal of pressure from his friend, Doge Marino Grimani (for whom Croce later wrote a requiem). Toward the end of his career, he suffered from gout and needed an assistant. He succumbed to an attack of fever and spots, and was succeeded by one Giulio Cesare

Martinengo, whose successor four years later was Claudio Monteverdi [333]. Whereas some historians make rather exaggerated claims for Croce's importance, others overlook him entirely. If he used, in his religious music, episodes featuring solo voices, or organ basses, or instrumental choirs, one would guess that such things were less innovative than imitative of his colleague Giovanni Gabrieli [286]. His tendencies, however, were less flamboyant and he was inclined to a simple chordal style. He published numerous motets, 2 sets of lamentations, a *Magnificat,* psalms, and 3 books of Masses. The last have some interest in that Croce espoused the *Missa brevis*—not only formally abbreviated, but in his hands very compact indeed. (But then, the life-style no longer tolerated endless big productions.)

Croce also published 9 books of madrigals and related genres. His 2 comic cycles, *Mascharate piacevole et ridicolose (Pleasant and Laughable Masquerades),* and *Triaca musicale (Musical Prescription),* with their satirical and *commedia dell'arte* references, their characterizations, and use of quasi-recitative, obviously have some place in the history of madrigal comedy and perhaps of opera. As a madrigalist, Croce is best in the *canzonette* and other lighthearted works. Some of his madrigals came to England in *Musica Transalpina,* causing both his name and influence to be magnified—especially with Thomas Morley, who not only reworked one of his pieces for *The Triumphes of Oriana* but also included the original (which came from *Il Trionfo di Dori).*

[291] DLUGORAJ, Wojciech (Dlwōō-gō'-rī, Voi'-chekh)
LUTENIST
BORN: c. 1557
DIED: c. 1619

According to the musicologist Gustave Reese, Dlugoraj "marred his good name by betraying one of his patrons" (though it might have been easy enough to mar it just by trying to say it—which may explain why he was sometimes called Adalbert or simply Albert). He was reputedly a pupil of Bálint Bakfark [160], who also marred his name. Dlugoraj seems to have had some justice on his side in his alleged treachery. He originally worked for a political magnate named Samuel Zborowski, who treated him so badly that in 1579 the lutenist fled to a Cracow monastery. However, he was tossed out two years later for not living a properly monastic life and was promptly hauled back to the Zborowski establishment. In 1583 he

managed to tip off King Stephen Báthory that the Zborowskis were up to no good. Samuel was summarily executed, his brother exiled, and Dlugoraj made court lutenist. But threats, real or imagined, from the remaining Zborowskis finally got to him, and in 1586 he fled to Germany, where he apparently spent the rest of his life. He left a number of Polish and Italian dances and other lute pieces, and may have compiled an anonymous tablature in Leipzig in 1619.

[292] BASSANO, Giovanni (Bàs-sà'-nō, Jō-vàn'-nē)
SINGER, INSTRUMENTALIST, DIRECTOR, TEACHER
BORN: Venice, c. 1558
DIED: Venice, summer 1617

Bassano (often called Bassani) is not to be confused with the later Giovanni Battista Bassani. He was possibly related to the Bassanos who emigrated to England and produced a number of instrumentalists there in the seventeenth century. As early as 1576, Giovanni was one of four instrumentalists attached to the choir of St. Mark's in Venice, though we are not sure what he played. We are told that he invented a sort of soft-toned oboe, but no example or description has come down to us. He doubled as a singer in the choir. In the early 1590s he succeeded Giuseppe Donato as singing master at the seminary, and around the turn of the century he was put in charge of the instrumentalists at St. Mark's as successor to his old *maestro* Girolamo della Casa da Udine, with the impressive title of *Capo de' concerti dei stromenti di fiato dell Illustrissimo Signoria di Venetia* (Head of the Most Illustrious Venetian Signoria's Wind Consort). He enlarged and added strings to the group and is said to have acted as first violin.

Bassano published instrumental fantasias, madrigals, *canzonette,* and religious works (the last with early examples of organ basses). His most important work for us, however, is his 1591 *Motetti, madrigali, e canzoni francese,* an anthology with "diminutions for playing on all sorts of instruments or for solo singing." Diminutions were the ornate embellishments that every performer was expected to improvise on a given tune, and Bassano's book, which spells them out, is a gold mine of knowledge on how it was done.

RECORDINGS: Michel Corboz has made a recording of *chansons* and madrigals with Bassano's instrumental versions played by Michel Piguet and Anthony Bailes.

[293] CARLTON, Richard
ANGLICAN MINISTER, CHOIRMASTER
BORN: Norfolk (?), c. 1558
DIED: Norfolk (?), 1638

There is only the name to suggest that Richard Carlton was the son of the nearly anonymous composer Nicholas Carlton. Awarded a B.A. degree from Clare College, where he completed theological studies in 1577, he was ordained, became vicar of St. Stephen's, Norwich, at the same time that he served as choirmaster at Norwich Cathedral. He is said also to have taken a B.Mus. degree. In 1612 he took over the church at Bawsey-cum-Glosthorpe in Norfolk. Fifteen years later a substitute rector was brought in, and the post was declared vacant in 1638. On this evidence, it is guessed that Carlton was ill or otherwise incapacitated during his final years. Oddly, his chief compositions are madrigals, of which he published a five-voice collection in 1601. They are said to be curiously individual in their treatment of harmony and discord. He also contributed a single madrigal to *The Triumphes of Oriana*.
RECORDINGS: The madrigal appears in recordings of that collection.

[294] GUMPELZHAIMER, Adam
(Goōm'-pelts-hī-mer, Ăd'-ăm)
CANTOR, WRITER
BORN: Trostberg, 1559
DIED: Augsburg, November 3, 1625

Gumpelzhaimer was born about twenty miles north of Salzburg in the lower part of Bavaria, which is known as Upper Bavaria because of the mountains. However, he learned his music in Augsburg from a certain Jodocus Entzenmüller at the monastery school attached to the twin churches of Sts. Ulrich and Afra, and remained in that city for the rest of his life. At twenty-two he was entrusted with the choir of the Lutheran church of St. Anna and with the operation of its Latin school. There he carried out his duties in a way that apparently delighted everyone who knew about him. He was invited, after twenty-five years, to come be *Kapellmeister* at the Württemberg ducal court in Stuttgart, but declined. In his declining years Gumpelzhaimer was plagued by chronic illness. In 1591 he brought out a musical textbook, *Compendium musicae,* which, though heavily indebted to a work brought out forty years earlier by Heinrich Faber, remained a standard in Germany for the better part of a hundred years. He otherwise seems to have written mostly sacred music, including German "spiritual songs" (including Christmas hymns) and Latin motets, many of which show Venetian polychoral influence.

[295] PLANSON, Jean (Plăn-sôn', Zhăn)
ORGANIST
BORN: c. 1559
DIED: after 1612

Primarily a writer of *chansons,* both bawdy-secular and pietist-religious, and similar *airs de cour,* Planson carried off two prizes from the 1578 St. Cecilia competition at Evreux. Before that he had served as organist at St. Germain-l'Auxerrois in Paris. Eight years later he held the same post at St. Sauveur. When last heard of, in 1612, he was apparently functioning as a "bourgeois merchant." He was among the first to set the popular religious verses of Guy du Faur, Sieur de Pibrac, which were later to enjoy epidemic popularity. In his 1587 *Airs,* published by Adrian Le Roy [193] and Robert Ballard, bar lines appear for the first time in printed French music, but to indicate the ends of the poetic verses rather than the meter of the music.

[296] REINER, Jakob (Rī'-ner, Yä'-kōp)
SINGER, CHOIRMASTER
BORN: Altdorf-Weingarten, c. 1559
DIED: Weingarten, August 12, 1606

Reiner, from a musical family, had his first training in the Benedictine monastery in Weingarten, just north of Lake Constance. After that he studied with Lassus [228] in Munich. At some point in the 1580s he went back to Weingarten, where he was the monastery's choirmaster (but not a monk) until his death. That he was a favorite pupil of Lassus may be attested to by that master's dedication of a collection of his Masses to the abbot of the monastery. Reiner wrote a good deal of religious music, including three Passions and a couple of volumes of German songs. His son Ambrosius (1604–72) served as archducal and then as imperial *Kapellmeister* in Innsbruck from 1648 until his death.

[297] COBBOLD, William
ORGANIST, SINGER
BORN: Norwich, January 5, 1560
DIED: Beccles, Suffolk, November 7, 1639

Born in the parish of St. Andrew's in Norwich, Cobbold was cathedral organist of that city by 1599 and remained in that post until 1608, when he gave it up to a Mr. Inglott and became a member of the choir instead. In 1630 his wife died and Cobbold let it be known that it was his wish to be buried beside her. Unfortunately he happened to be in Beccles, several miles away, when his hour struck, and, refrigeration being what it was, they buried him there.

As a composer, Cobbold could lay claim to renown for having been one of the ten contributors to Thomas East's *The Whole Booke of Psalmes.* He also supplied a madrigal to *The Triumphes of Oriana.* His consort songs all, like supermarket fowl, have parts missing.

[298] PRAETORIUS, Hieronymus (Prī-tô'-rē-oos, Hēr-on'-ē-moos)

ORGANIST, CANTOR
BORN: Hamburg, August 10, 1560
DIED: Hamburg, January 27, 1629

Hieronymus Praetorius is not to be confused with the more famous Michael Praetorius [360], much less with Godescalcus or Bartholomaeus. In fact his father, organist at the Jacobikirche in Hamburg, was just plain Jakob Schulze. Hieronymus, as a matter of course, studied with him, and in 1580 went off to Erfurt to be cantor there. But when his father decided he needed help two years later, the son came back and served as his assistant, taking over when he died in 1586. That same year, Hieronymus' second son, Jakob [420], later a successful organist and composer, was born. Hieronymus and Jakob collaborated with two other local church musicians, Joachim Decker [374] and David Scheidemann, on the important collection of chorales *Melodeyen Gesangbuch.* Two of Hieronymus' three other sons, Michael and Johannes, also wrote a few compositions. During the years 1522–25, Hieronymus published, at his own expense, his collected works, in five big volumes (the first of which also contains three motets by young Jakob). These include 98 Latin motets, 5 German hymns, 6 "parody" Masses, and 9 Magnificats with Christmas-chorale insertions. Praetorius was strongly influenced by currents from Venice and liked to write for a multiplicity of voices and for up to four choirs. He uses ad lib continuos but no specific instrumental parts.

[299] BRADE, William

VIOLIST, CONDUCTOR
BORN: England, 1560
DIED: Hamburg, February 26, 1630

Most of the known facts of William Brade's life derive from title pages, dedications, and the like in his publications. They suggest a man who was either inordinately popular in northern Germany and Denmark or who couldn't settle down. We know nothing of him until he pops up in Berlin in 1594 in the service of the Elector of Brandenburg. Whether, like so many Englishmen of the period, he was expatriated for religious or political reasons, or whether he sensed where the money was, there is no hint. Between then and 1606 he shuttled back and forth between Berlin and the court of King Christian IV in Denmark. He was already married, for his eldest son was born in Copenhagen; two others followed. For the next three years he worked for the Danish Duke of Holstein-Gottorp, at Gottorp, working with the Hamburg town band in his spare time. In 1610 he quit both jobs and went south to the court of Count Ernst of Schaumburg-Lippe at Bückeburg. But apparently they liked him in Hamburg, for three years later he was back there, this time as band director. A year later it was off to Gottorp again. In 1618–19, Brade moved successively down to Halle (near Leipzig), up to Güstrow (near Rostock), and back to Berlin, where he became the Elector's *Kapellmeister* at 500 thalers a year, with room and board, all the wine he could drink, and two suits for ceremonial occasions. Clearly, with Brade, affluence was no object, for he returned to Copenhagen a year later, Gottorp two years after that (becoming *Kapellmeister* in 1625, and finally settling down at last in Hamburg, being, no doubt, a Hamburger at heart).

As a composer, Brade specialized in the dances of the day (particularly pavanes and galliards), of which he published several collections. His suites of dances are said to have had considerable impact on the German composer who came after him. His music is not wholly utilitarian, for there are some curious and interesting experiments with rhythm and meter (analogous to writing part of a waltz in 4/4 time, say).

[300] BONNET, Pierre (Bô-nä', Pē-âr')

BORN: c. 1560 (?)
DIED: after 1600

All that is known of Bonnet comes from the dedications of his two books of *airs.* In 1585 he was in the service of the governor and lieutenant general of the Haute et Basse Marche, Georges de Villequier, in Poitou. By 1600 he was probably in that of the Marquis de Montemart, Gaspard de Rochechouart. At some time he is believed to have been in the court of Catherine de Médicis, Queen of France.

[301] CUTTING, Francis
LUTENIST
BORN: c. 1560 (?)
DIED: after 1600

Few composers of stature in so late a period remain so stubbornly obscure as Francis Cutting. Apart from the fact that he wrote a number of lute pieces and works for consort, we know for sure only that between 1583 and 1589 he was assessed fourpence per year for the poor rate. Various of his lute pieces were published in collections of the time. It has been conjectured that he was a gentleman of independent means, and perhaps a brother of Thomas Cutting, who worked at the royal courts of England and Denmark in the early years of the new century.

[302] FACOLI, Marco (Fä'-kō-lē, Mär'-kō)
BORN: c. 1560 (?)
DIED: ?

Facoli is even more of a cipher than Francis Cutting [301]. In 1586 and 1588 he published two books of harpsichord pieces in Venice. Only the second, which includes a dozen "airs" *(aeri)* for the instrument, is extant.

[303] HILTON, John (the elder)
SINGER, ORGANIST
BORN: c. 1560 (?)
DIED: Cambridge, winter 1608

Hilton served for at least a decade as countertenor, organist, and poor clerk at Lincoln Cathedral, where in 1593 he directed two choirboy plays. The next year, when he left to become organist at Trinity College, Cambridge, he was cited for his good and faithful service. He would appear to have acquired his B.Mus. at Cambridge, where he lived in the parish of St. Sepulchre and where his son and namesake [450] was born in 1599. (It used to be said that he was born at Oxford, which clearly does not make for biographical neatness.) The elder Hilton died intestate, leaving, according to the assessors, an estate of nearly fourteen pounds. He contributed a madrigal to *The Triumphes of Oriana* and left at least one anthem. Other pieces by "John Hilton" remain ambiguous as to authorship.

[304] HOLBORNE, Anthony
COURTIER, LUTENIST (?)
BORN: c. 1560 (?)
DIED: late November 1602

The first apparent date we have for Holborne is that of his wedding—his wife was named Elizabeth—in June 1584. From his contributions to their publications and his dedications in his own, it is clear that he was a friend of Thomas Morley [289], Giles Farnaby [317], and John and Robert Dowland. John Dowland [316], in a dedication of his own, hails him as "most famous," which seems to have been not far off the mark. Holborne termed himself "gentleman and servant to her most excellent majesty," and Robert Dowland (John's son) in 1610 specified the service as having been that of a gentleman usher. (Holborne would have made way for the queen.) Around the turn of the century he seems to have served as a diplomatic courier to Sir Robert Cecil, Lord Burghley's hunchbacked son and successor. According to a letter from Holborne's wife to his employer, he got his death on one of his missions, though she fails to be specific. He had a (presumably younger) brother named William, who briefly tried his hand at composition. The results are included in Anthony's *The Cittharn Schoole* (1597), which, he says, he brought out to counter piratical issuance of William's "six short Aers Neapolitan like to three voices," which, considering their triviality, is a likely story. The cittharn (or cittern) family was wire-strung and included such members as the bandora, the orpharion, the penorcon, and the polyphant. (Queen Elizabeth was deemed a more than competent polyphantist.) Holborne wrote for such instruments, both solo and with viol accompaniment, reflecting the special fad for them in England. Two years later he brought out his other collection, *Pauans, Galliards, Almains, and Other Short Aeirs, Both Graue, and Light.* It was designated for a consort either of viols or winds and is an important document in the history of English instrumental music, being mostly made up of early examples of pavane-galliard combinations.

[305] NÖRMIGER, August (Nör'-mi-ger, Ou'-gŏŏst)
ORGANIST, ORGAN BUILDER, TEACHER
BORN: Dresden, c. 1560
DIED: Dresden, July 22, 1613

August Nörmiger succeeded his late father, Friedrich, as organist to Augustus I, Elector of Saxony. He also taught various princelings and princesses and played at the Schlosskirche, for which, shortly before he died, he installed an organ of his own design. He left a manuscript containing intabulations of chorales, *Lieder,* and dances for organ.

[306] SOWA V SÓWKA, Jakób (So'-vä v'Sōv'-kä, Yä-kōb')
ORGANIST
BORN: Cracow, c. 1560 (?)
DIED: Cracow, February 15, 1593

Sowa was appointed royal organist to King Sigismund III of Poland in 1590. He was a virtuoso performer whose concerts attracted large crowds. We are told that he was murdered, but not why or how. He wrote some organ pieces.

[307] TERZI, Giovanni Antonio (Tärt'-zē, Jō-vän'-nē Än-tōn'-yō)
LUTENIST, SINGER
BORN: c. 1560 (?)
DIED: after 1620

Terzi spent his career in Bergamo, Italy, where he was equally admired for his celestial singing and his angelic lute playing. He published a lute book in 1593 and a sequel six years later. Besides the usual arrangements, they contain duets (whose parts may be played solo) and works for lute ensembles. Terzi was particularly adept at the "variation" suite of dances.

[308] VIADANA, Lodovico Grossi da (Vē-ä-dä'-nä, Lō-dō-vē'-kō Grôs'-sē dä)
CHOIR DIRECTOR, FRIAR
BORN: Viadana, c. 1560
DIED: Gualtieri, May 2, 1645

Like Palestrina [201], Lodovico Grossi is remembered by the name of his birthplace, a small town near Parma, in which city he is supposed to have studied with the learned Costanzo Porta, a Minorite friar and pupil of Adrian Willaert [129]. In the mid-1590s he was choir director of Mantua Cathedral at a time when he would have rubbed elbows with Gastoldi [280], Monteverdi [333], and Giaches de Wert [232]. In 1596 he became a Franciscan monk. From that time on he seems to have led a peripatetic and restless life. We catch glimpses of him in Padua, Rome, and Venice before he comes to rest as *maestro di cappella* at the convent of San Luca in Cremona in 1602. After another hiatus, he turns up in the analogous post at the cathedral of Concordia, between Mantua and Modena. A year later he is at Fano Cathedral, south of Pesaro on the Adriatic. In 1614 he was back in the Po Valley as an official of his order. Differences with his brethren plagued him for nearly ten years. After a brief time in Busseto, he retired to the monastery of San Andrea in Gualtieri near the Po River.

Though in his later works Viadana used a *basso seguente* ("organ bass," indicating the bass line only, with the harmonies to be filled in), he did not, as is sometimes claimed, invent *basso continuo.* He wrote the expectable Masses and motets, as well as 2 volumes of *canzonette,* and a collection of *sinfonie* for double choirs of instruments. His reputation chiefly rests, however, on his "ecclesiastical concerti" for one or more voices (4 books). These include the first published religious music with a continuo part (which Viadana tells us is indispensable) and also show monody put to sacred use. (There is a Mass for a single voice!) In his 1612 *Psalms* for four "choirs" (including obligatory instruments) Viadana pits the groups against each other in true *concerto* style.

RECORDINGS: Viadana's music appears to have been grossly neglected on records.

[309] PERI, Jacopo (Pä'-rē, Yä-kō-pō)
SINGER, ORGANIST
BORN: Rome, August 20, 1561
DIED: Florence, August 12, 1633

Peri, composer of the first known opera, was, like his rival Giulio Caccini [252] one of the first of the virtuoso singers. Many accounts make nearly as much of the fact that he was known as "Il Zazzerino" (the little longhair or the little shock-head), going into raptures about his "plenitude of carroty locks" or his "long, golden curls" or his "thick, abundant hair." The only portrait of him (if it is a portrait) is a costume sketch for his role as Arion in an intermezzo played at the wedding of Grand Duke Ferdinando to Christine of Lorraine. It shows nothing extraordinary beneath a laurel wreath, but perhaps in an age when close cropping was in fashion it took nothing spectacular in the way of hair length to win notice.

At twelve, Peri was a choirboy at the Santissima Annunziata in Florence. He studied with Cristofano Malvezzi, sometime choirmaster at the cathedral and the baptistry and organist of San Lorenzo, and was himself appointed organist at the Badia (the Baptistery near the Duomo) in 1579, remaining there, into his glory days, for more than a quarter century. He was also for a time a singer in the Baptistery choir. By 1583 he was participating, as both performer and composer, in court presentations and, as noted, was a featured performer in the wedding festivities of 1589, by which time he was on the Medici payroll. There is strong evidence that he frequented the Camerata meetings at the *palazzo* of Count Giovanni de' Bardi (see 208, 252), and it is certain that after Bardi moved to Rome, Peri joined the circle of Jacopo Corsi, which focused its interests largely on the practicalities of "recreating" Greek tragedy. For the play *Dafne*, written by Ottavio Rinuccini, Peri, with a little help from his friend Corsi, wrote a score, which he is said to have completed by 1594. The first public performance, however, seems not to have taken place until 1598. The first opera was sufficiently successful to produce several revivals before it vanished, save for a few fragments, forever. (Later composers used the libretto.) It also encouraged composer and librettist to write another opera, *Euridice*, for the wedding of Maria de' Medici and Henry of Navarre, which was premiered in the Pitti Palace on October 6, 1600. Peri probably sang the role of Orpheus, the protagonist. The producer-director was Emilio de' Cavalieri [267]. Some of Caccini's pupils were cast in the title role and in some smaller parts, and in a pet he insisted that they sing *his* music rather than Peri's. (Later he rewrote and published the entire opera.)

Peri remained at the Medici court for the rest of his life. After Cavalieri's defection, he took over the post of chief director of art and artists with the title of *camerlengo generale* (lord chamberlain). He continued to perform at least until 1611 but never produced another operatic score. He collaborated in some degree with Marco da Gagliano [404] on *Lo Sposalizio di Medoro e Angelica (The Wedding of Medoro and Angelica)* in 1619 and *La Flora* in 1628, and with Gagliano's younger brother, Giovanni Battista, on three Cavalierian "oratorios" in 1622–24. He also provided music for a variety of musical spectacles including an equestrian ballet, *Guerra di bellezza (The War of Beauty)*, and tinkered with various operatic commissions from both Florence and Mantua, which he either did not complete or which went unperformed. Unhappily, with the signal exceptions of the published *Euridice* and *Le Varie musiche*, a 1609 book of monodies, most of Peri's output has disappeared. The *Euridice* score contains no hint of orchestration, the instruments being represented only by a continuo line, and the only recording is, as it must be, a realization. The results are pleasant in a pastel way, and

Peri's recitative is often ingenious, but the work lacks real dramatic peaks and valleys and inhabits a different world from that of Monteverdi's [333] treatment of the same story *(L'Orfeo)* four years after Peri's.

[310] GESUALDO, Don Carlo, Prince of Venosa (Jā-zoo-ál'-dō, Don Kär'-lō)
PRINCE
BORN: probably 1561
DIED: Gesualdo, September 8, 1613

Even without the romantic and lurid encrustations that have attached themselves to it, Don Carlo Gesualdo's story is the stuff of Italian opera. The lords of Gesualdo had operated in their rocky domains from a hilltop castle sixty miles east of Naples since Norman times. When Don Carlo's father, Don Fabrizio, married Girolama, sister of the sainted Carlo Borromeo, and not incidentally niece of Pope Pius IV, King Philip II of Spain rewarded him for his good taste by making him Prince of Venosa, while the pope named his brother Alfonso a cardinal. Carlo was brought up in a house where there was a complement of musicians, and it is possible that he may have learned his music from either Pomponio Nenna [284] or the Netherlander Jean de Macque, though he would have done so late rather than early. He also came to know the poet Torquato Tasso in Naples. In 1586 he was married to his first cousin, Donna Maria d'Avalos, already twice widowed. (Rumor had it that at least her first husband died trying to satisfy her sexual appetite.) She bore him a son, Emmanuele, but by 1590 had entered into an affair with a young-man-about-Naples, Don Fabrizio Carafa, Duke of Andria. Supposedly Don Carlo's uncle blew the whistle on them when he was not permitted to join in the fun. One night when the lovers were abed in the Palazzo di San Severo in Naples, Don Carlo and some retainers tiptoed up the steps and burst in on them. The servants, or whoever they were, dispatched the duke and Don Carlo himself took care of Donna Maria—all very savagely, the coroner's report indicating that the victims were severely punctured in innumerable places. Don Carlo disappeared until things cooled off. The duke's widow said she had foreseen it all in a dream, and eighteen years later entered a convent, where she kept the other inmates awake with sounds of anguish. Novella writers painted the slain couple as more romantic than Bonnie and Clyde, and even Tasso wrote several thinly veiled sonnet-laments. Meanwhile, up in Ferrara, Duke Alfonso II, alarmed that his Last Duchess had, like her predecessors, not given him a male heir, was facing the threat, led by Cardinal Gesualdo, that his dukedom would revert to the Church on his death. A wedding between his young cousin Eleonora d'Este and the newly widowed new Prince of Venosa (Carlo's older brother and his father both died in 1591) offered some hope. In 1593 the marriage contract was signed, and the prince set off north with 150 retainers (including 2 musicians), 24 mules, and 300 pieces of baggage. The duke's emissary, who met him a day or so out of Ferrara, reported back that he wasn't much to look at, but that he grew on you, that he was extremely loquacious, especially about hunting and music, and that he played some rather strange music of his own composition after dinner. The marriage was duly celebrated and the happy couple installed in the famous Palazzo dei Diamanti (Diamond Palace). We know little of Gesualdo's activities in Ferrara, but he must have found the musical atmosphere stimulating, particularly since one of his musical heroes, Luzzaschi [251], was there. During his stay he published his first two books of madrigals (one of which had actually appeared before, pseudonymously). Business called him back to Naples in May, and he went without his bride, stopping over in Venice for a few weeks to meet the musical celebrities there. Back home, he had the castle redone, did some composing, and set out for Ferrara again in December. Bad weather caused him to stop over in Florence, where he met and talked with Count Corsi, Bardi's successor in the Camerata. By year's end he was once more in Ferrara, where he lived for two years.

There are stories that he was eventually asked to leave for misbehaving and for treating Eleonora badly. (By this time she had presented him with a second son, called Alfonsino. There is, by the way, no evidence of Donna Maria's ever having had the second child she is supposed to have murdered.) After a year in Gesualdo and Naples, he was demanding that his family be shipped to him, adding that bad health prevented his coming for them. Alfonso of Ferrara died soon thereafter, and Eleonora arrived in her new home in September of 1597. She soon wished she hadn't. The many letters the prince left say nothing of his personal (or musical!) life, and hers are very circumspect, but clearly she was put through hell. Legend whispers of mistresses and beatings and other cruelties, physical and psychological. Her brother, Cesare, and her bastard half brother, Cardinal Alessandro, talked of getting the pope to intervene. Her child died in 1600 and Alessandro paid her a visit, trying

to persuade her to come back to Modena with him. (The rumors mutter of incest!) After Emmanuele's wedding in 1608, Carlo finally let her go. When she returned, on his insistence, she became so ill that he finally sent her back in desperation. (We catch a picture by now of a man who is beaten on demand by a servant or servants regularly, though whether to pleasure him or to act as a laxative, the rumormakers aren't sure.) Eventually Eleonora returned for good—or ill. In the summer of 1613 Emmanuele died, and his father followed close behind him. Eleonora gave the rest of her life to prayer and good works, and the female heirs let Gesualdo go down the drain.

Despite Don Carlo's fascination—even obsession—with music, we have almost no information about his own beyond the printed pages. He left us 6 books of madrigals, 2 of *Sacrae cantiones*, one of responses for Holy Week, and some odds and ends in other collections and in manuscript. The first two books of madrigals were written relatively early—before the Ferrara-Venice experience—and show a thorough knowledge of counterpoint and of the state of the "modern" madrigal. But the later works are something else. All of the expressive tendencies that had been developing in the genre come to a head here. Making calculated use of chromaticism, vocal color, and harmonic progressions that, one is tempted to say, were not met with again for three centuries, he wrings the withers of his usually anguished and suffering texts. It has long been fashionable to see Gesualdo as a man tortured and driven half mad by the memory of his "crime," but in fact such slayings in the name of honor besmirched were pretty much par for the course, and however queer a duck the prince may have been, what his music seems to exemplify is not insanity but pure calculation. In his time he was seen by musical thinkers as something miraculous. But at the same time, he pushed the possibilities of the madrigal as far as they would go. As he did not biologically, so musically he left no heirs. After him, the madrigal was a dead issue. There is evidence that there was some awakening of interest in his work in the eighteenth century, but the fulminations of Dr. Burney have tended to drown it out. In our own day Igor Stravinsky [1748] took it on himself in his old age to "reconstruct" the missing voice parts in some of the religious music, and one of his last major works was his *Monumentum pro Gesualdo* of 1960.

RECORDINGS: With the reawakening of interest in Gesualdo there have been many recordings. Notable are some discs by Robert

Craft, the Montserrat Monastery Schola, a complete version of the madrigals by the Quintetto Vocale Italiano, and the Deller Consort's traversal of the religious music.

[311] MERTEL, Elias (Mâr'-tel, Ā'-lē-ås)
LUTENIST
BORN: Wangen, Alsace, c. 1561
DIED: Strasbourg, July 21, 1626

Mertel's father was a Lutheran pastor. Elias worked in Heidelberg for Elector Frederick IV of the Pfalz (a fancier of lutenists) until 1595. At the beginning of the next year he married Susanna Kirn, a Strasbourg goldsmith's daughter—a step that gave him the right to declare himself a citizen of that city, which he did a few months later. He seems to have held some interesting posts there— *Kanzlei-Verwandter* (Chancellery-Relative?) in 1596, and from 1608 quaestor of the university. But the elector seemed unable to get along without him; every time there was a big do in Heidelberg, he fetched him back. This happened in 1600, 1601, 1605, and 1606. In 1620 Mertel was in Basel for a while.

Mertel's chief contribution to music was his lute book, printed in French tablature, and called *Hortus musicalis novus*. It contains 225 preludes and 120 fantasies and fugues, all anonymous. Whether Mertel actually composed any of them is questionable, though a few fugitive dances are known to be his.

[312] PHILIPS, Peter
ORGANIST, CLERIC
BORN: England, c. 1561
DIED: Brussels, 1628

Peter Philips, alias Pierre Philippe, alias Pietro Filippo, is regarded by the Lowlanders as one of their important composers, though the British, with the fierceness born of a musical inferiority complex, insist that he is one of the great English virginalists. The Lowlanders have more going for them. Philips's English years are wrapped in darkness. All we know is that he was a ward of a Sebastian Westcote, the Catholic almoner of St. Paul's Cathedral, where he served as a choirboy around 1574. Westcote died early in 1582, and Philips, a devout Catholic, saw the handwriting on the wall and left for the Continent the following summer. From Douai he made his way to Rome, where he became part of the household of old Cardinal Alessandro Farnese, the art-loving nephew and namesake of Pope Paul III. At the same time Philips served as organist at

the English College, where he undoubtedly came under the influence of its *maestro,* the composer Felice Anerio. In 1595 he attached himself to another English Catholic expatriate, Lord Thomas Paget, and traveled about the Continent with him, first to Spain, then to France, and finally to the Netherlands, where Lord Thomas took sick and died in 1590.

Philips then moved to Antwerp, where he taught keyboard (he was a virtuoso) and took unto himself a wife (anonymous) and a patron (a Lucchese import named Giulio Balbani). In 1593 he went up to Amsterdam to meet his fellow keyboardist, the great Dutchman Jan Pieterszoon Sweelinck [313], with whom he remained friends. Becoming ill on his way home, he was met with an accusation of high treason against Queen Elizabeth of England (implication in conspiracy to murder, burning Her Majesty in effigy, etc.), and spent the fall in The Hague seeing the charges dismissed for lack of evidence. In 1597 he took what turned out to be a lifetime job as organist of the Chapel Royal in Brussels to the newly appointed Spanish governor-general of the "loyal" Belgian provinces, Archduke Albert, nephew of Philip II. He continued to serve in this post under the Archduchess Isabella, daughter of Philip II.

At some date unknown, the wraithlike Mrs. Philips must have died, subsequent to which event Peter took holy orders. It is suspected that he did so to be eligible for the canonry at Soignies that the archduke dealt him in 1610, though such thinking may be grossly unfair. By now he was an important figure, called upon to play on state occasions and approve new organs in important churches. In the next decade he was being paid almost a thousand florins a year. The Archduke passed away in 1621, and the next year Philips led the memorial procession and his portrait was included in the illustrated commemorative booklet that enabled one to identify the participants. Also in 1621 Philips traded his living at Soignies for a chaplainship at Tirlemont, and picked up another living at Béthune at about the same time.

Between 1590 and 1603, Peter Philips published an anthology of madrigals that included a few of his own making, and three collections of "originals" of from six to eight voices. A number of others appeared in various collections, including Thomas Morley's [289] of 1598. If these are not English in style, neither are they Netherlandish, but purely Italian. As much has been said about his instrumental pieces, which include dances, some trios, and so on, scattered through many collections and manuscripts, including a fantasia on a madrigal by Alessandro Striggio written for a water-powered barrel organ! (In the "hearing" panel of the Five Senses series of paintings by Jan Brueghel—now in the Prado, Madrid—a madrigal score by Philips is clearly and prominently displayed.) But the nineteen pieces by Philips in the *Fitzwilliam Virginal Book* are more properly "English," one or two having apparently been written before he left his homeland, and the lot representative of the best of the English virginal school (which, particularly through such expatriates as Philips and John Bull [315], influenced the keyboard music of the Netherlands and Germany). After taking orders Philips seems to have limited himself to religious music. His Masses and psalms have not survived, but his motets—particularly the earlier ones—show that there is considerable basis for calling him a "Netherlands" composer.

RECORDINGS: Samplings of the keyboard pieces appear in various recorded anthologies.

[313] SWEELINCK, Jan Pieterszoon
(Svä'-lingk, Yän Pē'-ter-sun)
ORGANIST
BORN: Deventer (Netherlands), May 1562
DIED: Amsterdam, October 16, 1621

Deventer, Sweelinck's birthplace, is noted for being at the junction of the Yser and the Schipbeek, and for having once been the seat of the Brothers of Common Life. His mother was the local surgeon's daughter, Elsken Sweling that was, and his father, an organist, was known only as Pieter Swybertszoon (i.e., son of Swybert). Since Jan could not very comfortably call himself Pieterszoon Swybertszoon or Pieterszoonszoon, he signed himself Sweelinck, which was as close as he could get to his mother's maiden name. When Jan was still a baby (c. 1564) the family moved to Amsterdam, where Pieter became organist at the church of St. Niklaus. (It is known now as the Oude Kerk, or Old Church, though it wasn't then, probably for good reason.) In time Jan succeeded him—in or before 1580—and held onto the job for more than forty years.

Indeed, on the face of it, Sweelinck seems not to have led a very exciting life, although he did have six children, one of whom, Dirck Janszoon, carried on the paternal trade. (Jan's wife was Claesgen Puyner, a merchant's daughter, whom he wed in 1590.) He never went to Venice to study with Gioseffo Zarlino [186] as was once fairly popu-

larly believed. He may not even have gone to Haarlem to study with a certain Jan Lossy. Except when they asked him to have a look at new organ installations in nearby towns or recommend harpsichords, he stuck pretty much to Amsterdam. Curiously, he was on the city payroll, not that of the church. His duties seem to have been to preludize and postludize the sermons (the church was by now Protestant) and to play concerts. He did not have to play the carillon or tune the organ, for the records show that others were paid for those duties. Moreover, his fame spread outside Holland, and especially into Germany, and pupils flocked to him—notably Samuel Scheidt [426], Jakob Praetorius [420], and Heinrich Scheidemann [443]. He also became friends with two famous English expatriates, Peter Philips [312] and John Bull [315].

Before the three B's arrived and established themselves as the *ne plus ultra* of Germanic music, that role was played by the four S's, of whom Sweelinck was one (the others, in alphabetical order, were Scheidt, Schein [419], and Schütz [412]. As a teacher Sweelinck can be said to have initiated the so-called North German organ school, of which Johann Sebastian Bach [684] was the ultimate product. Despite his fame as an organist, Sweelinck's largest compositional output was in the area of vocal music, he having left over 250 examples, both sacred and secular (besides others that have been lost). These include 153 psalm settings (to the Huguenot Psalter texts), the rest divided more or less evenly among *cantiones sacrae, chansons,* and what he termed "rimes" to French and Italian texts. Sweelinck was thoroughly acquainted with the work of the recent Italians (he did his own version of Zarlino's rules of composition) and shows in his vocal music their scrupulosity about words. But rather than being the dawn breaking over fresh fields and pastures new, it is really the last sunset blaze of the old Franco-Flemish polyphony—even down to the use of *cantus firmus* in most of the religious pieces.

Though comprising only a little more than a third of the total works, the instrumental efforts (all for keyboard) are another matter. Starting from virtually nothing in terms of a Netherlandish keyboard tradition, Sweelinck welds together the English and Italian school, with results that foreshadow the future of German keyboard music. Basically, the music breaks down into fantasias and variations—the latter on hymn tunes, popular songs, and dances. The fantasias clearly are moving in the direction of fugue. (They are sometimes so designated.) And the variations are only a generation or so removed from the chorale prelude and its relatives, the chorale partita and chorale variations.

RECORDINGS: Programs of the keyboard music have been recorded by E. Power Biggs, Helma Elsner, Gustav Leonhardt, Pamela Cook, et al., and samplings appear in innumerable anthologies of Renaissance keyboard music. Felix DeNobel has made a record of some of the psalms and *cantiones sacrae.*

[314] DULICHIUS, Philipp (Dō-likh'-yōōs, Fē'-lip)
PROTESTANT CANTOR
BORN: Chemnitz, December 18, 1562
DIED: Stettin, March 24, 1631

Dulichius' parents, mayor and mayoress of what is now East Germany's Karl-Marx-Stadt, were named Deulich, but their son fancied it up after he graduated from the University of Leipzig with a Ph.D. (The letters probably did not signify what they do today, which may be just as well.) In 1587, Dulichius settled in Stettin, where he was in charge of music at the Marienkirche, the Gymnasium, and the court of Pomerania. Except for the year 1604-5, when he substituted for a colleague in Danzig, he remained in Stettin for the rest of his life, retiring in 1630. Known as "the Pomeranian Lassus" (a sobriquet that may confuse dog lovers), he turned out 14 volumes with resounding Latin titles that contain religious music of a rather conservative cast.

[315] BULL, John
ORGANIST, TEACHER
BORN: c. 1562
DIED: Antwerp, c. March 13, 1628

The composer John Bull has nothing to do with Dr. John Arbuthnot's tubby eighteenth-century personification of England. In fact a portrait from his late twenties shows him to have been thin and long-faced with a slightly rodentlike look. Nothing is known for certain about his origins. After a year as a chorister at Hereford Cathedral, he was taken into the Chapel Royal in 1574. There he came under the tutelage of John Blitheman [203], who evidently knew a good thing when he met it and, according to report, took great pains with his young charge. In 1582 he became organist at Hereford and, a year later, master of the boys. Dividing his time between London and Hereford, he did not always keep his commitments at the ca-

thedral and at least once was fired temporarily for his absences. In 1586 he became a full-fledged Gentleman of the Chapel Royal, which evidently impressed the Hereforders, who treated him with more respect thereafter. That same year he also received from Oxford University the B.Mus. on which he was said to have been working for fourteen years, but was thwarted in his efforts toward the D.Mus. by a faction of what he termed "Clownes and rigid Puritans" and had to come in by the back door—that is, the degree was awarded by Cambridge in 1589 and in 1592 was "incorporated" at Oxford. From the earlier date he was known as "Dr. Bull" (or sometimes "Mr. Dr. Bull").

Bull's cadaverous look may have had something to do with his financial state, for there is ample evidence that he was usually hard up, a state not improved by an encounter with a highwayman in 1592, the year that Queen Elizabeth finally came across with the assistance for which the musician had been petitioning for some years, though it seems, by then, to have been too little and too late. However, five years later Elizabeth made Bull the first Public Reader in music at Gresham College, London. That institution was built in accordance with the will of Sir Thomas Gresham, founder of the Royal Exchange and supposedly the originator of Gresham's Law—"Bad money drives out good"—which was actually formulated in principle by Copernicus and others. In this post Bull was committed to living on campus but found his rooms occupied by Gresham's stepson, who refused to let him in. In a panic Bull had a mason break through the wall, resulting in a court case. He excused himself from reading his inaugural address in Latin, on the reasonable argument that he did not know that language. The fact that it was in English may in part account for the large audience present. However, he did not get on at the college and took a leave, ostensibly on grounds of poor health, in 1601, entrusting his duties to William Byrd's [248] son, Thomas. Supposedly he crossed the Channel, and a hoary yarn has him in St. Omer adding, on a bet, forty new parts to a forty-part composition. When he delivered the goods, the composer of the piece (unnamed) exclaimed that he must be either the devil or Dr. Bull. When he revealed himself as the latter, the composer knelt to do him reverence. He was back in 1603 for the queen's funeral and later that year returned to Gresham. James, the new king, boosted his salary at the Chapel Royal, and Bull played for that monarch at a dinner tendered the latter by the Merchant Taylors' Company in 1607. The company was so impressed—particularly because Bull waived his fee—that they elected him a full member, with all the rights and privileges appertaining thereto, which were considerable. Later that year, however, a shotgun marriage to Elizabeth Walter, described as a maiden of twenty-four, forced Bull's resignation from Gresham, the readership being reserved to bachelors-in-fact. To make ends meet, Bull went into organ-building, an art he had practiced on the side for some time. He accepted in 1609 a retainer of 1,000 pounds from Archduke Albert, in charge of the Spanish Netherlands, for an instrument. Unable to find the proper materials for it, he went to Spain to get them and, with his usual luck, was cleaned out by pirates on the way home. Meanwhile Bull had been entrusted with the musical education of at least two of the royal children.

It all came crashing down in 1613. Bull's marriage seems not to have been a success, its sole known issue having been the daughter whose imminence precipitated it. Moreover, Bull seems to have lived up to his name. Charged with adultery, he fled to the Continent (where the incontinent were looked on more tolerantly) and into the service of Archduke Albert, who had evidently forgiven him. When King James demanded his extradition, Bull claimed to be a religious refugee, but the claim did not stick. In the interests of international harmony, the archduke publicly fired him but privately continued to support him. For all that, he seems to have remained poor much of the time, and had (in modern terms) to go on welfare. From 1615 he was employed at Antwerp Cathedral, first as assistant organist and then as organist, and soon after also as organist and consultant to various guilds. Incapacitated by illness in 1626, he died two years later.

There seems to be little to challenge the claims of Bull's era that he was its greatest keyboard virtuoso and understood the potentialities of his instruments as no one else did. A century later professional virtuosi wondered how much of his output could have been played without months of rehearsal. Though he left a few pieces for voices, most of his music is instrumental, and the bulk of that for keyboard. His impact on continental composers, especially Sweelinck [313], is inescapable, even though he published little. His keyboard pieces, like those of many a later virtuoso, are uneven in quality, some being of interest chiefly as explorations, but others qualifying as, of their kind, great. The manuscript known as the *Fitzwilliam Virginal Book* contains nearly 50 examples—truly a lot of Bull by contrast with the other composers represented. But many others are to be found in *Parthenia,* a publication shared with Byrd and Orlando Gibbons [408]; in the *Cosyns Virginal Book;* and in a number of other manuscripts.

RECORDINGS: One or two LPs have been devoted to Bull's *solus,* and his music is found in many recorded anthologies of early keyboard music.

[316] DOWLAND, John
LUTENIST, SINGER
BORN: 1563
DIED: London, c. February 19, 1626

It was long said in some quarters that if you spelled Dowland's name as it was produced —"Doolan" or "Dolan"—it would be clear that his origins were Irish. Did not his impresa *"Semper Dowland, semper dolens"* (Always Dowland, always grieving) bear witness? And so a birthplace was found for him in County Dublin, and the rolls of Trinity College showed that he had studied at that institution in Dublin itself. But his younger contemporary, the writer Thomas Fuller, remarked casually that the composer was a Westminster man. And if the name scrawled in the Trinity register is indeed "Dowland," it almost certainly belonged to someone else. As a matter of fact, we know nothing of John Dowland before he was a teenage retainer of the English ambassador, Sir Henry Cobham, in Paris, where, according to his own word, he took up with a bad crowd—Catholic priests, English recusants, and others of a papist stripe. Then again, over the next decade, there is only sporadic information. He came back to London in the middle 1580s, took a B.Mus. at Christ Church, Oxford on July 8, 1588, about the same time that Thomas Morley [289] took his, married a stubbornly anonymous wife, who seems, Solveig-like, patiently to have sat out his later wanderings, and in 1590 or so sired a son Robert, who himself became a well-known lutenist.

In 1594 he applied to Queen Elizabeth as a candidate for the court vacancy left by the death of lutenist John Johnson [241], but was turned down—for being of the wrong faith, Dowland insisted. *Semper dolens,* he packed his bags, kissed his wife and son goodbye, and crossed the Channel to broaden his mind and seek his fortune. He shortly found that his talent was so much appreciated that he could, if he wished, write his own ticket. At Wolfenbüttel, the Duke of Brunswick bestowed on him a gold chain, some rich cloth for suiting, twenty-three pounds in coin of the realm, and an invitation to stay. But Dowland moved on to

Cassel, where Moritz "the Learned," Landgraf of Hesse-Kassel (1572–1632), musician and connoisseur, gave him a ring worth twenty pounds to forward to Mrs. Dowland, and for himself "a great standing cup with cover gilt, full of dollars." This gift, perhaps understandably, seems to have bolstered Dowland's wish to see the world, especially beyond the Alps, where he entertained notions of studying with Luca Marenzio [273]. So he visited Genoa; Venice where he met Giovanni Croce [290]; and Florence. In the last-named he paused to breathe the heady artistic atmosphere and to play for Grand Duke Ferdinando I, who, like his German counterparts, showered him with largesse. There too he fell in with an English Catholic priest named Skidmore or Scudamore, newly arrived for a conclave at Santa Maria Novella, who unintentionally convinced him that the papist conspiracy against the English throne was more than rumor. He understood that if he went to Rome to study with Marenzio, he, as a loyal adherent of His Holiness, would find the way made smooth. In patriotic horror, Dowland (he says) ran with the news to the English authorities in Florence, and agreed to work in Rome on their behalf as a spy. In the end, he seems to have thought better of the whole scheme and fled north, via Bologna and Venice, to Nuremberg, which he reached in November 1595. From there he wrote Sir Robert Cecil, Secretary of State, a long and abject letter, spelling out the whole story of his temptation and flight, recanting his faith, and insisting that his only wishes now were to see his family and serve his country.

Informed by his friend Sir Henry Noel that there was a new vacancy at court and that the queen herself had been heard wondering what had become of him, Dowland returned to England—just in time to write music for Noel's funeral in early 1597. He was again turned down, but set about to publish his first book of ayres, which turned out to be extremely popular. A year after Dowland's failure Landgraf Moritz cordially invited him back to Hesse on a full-time basis, but by November 1598 Dowland had somehow found employment at the court of Christian IV of Denmark. Perhaps he was drawn there by the really princely salary of 500 rixdalers annually, which Christian regularly sweetened with gifts, including the royal portrait. But he—ignoring Polonius' advice and becoming a chronic borrower—did not find popularity with the rest of the court. In 1603 he went home for a visit and to publish the third collection of ayres (he had mailed the second back in 1600) and, the return voyage hampered by

stormy seas, remained for a year or more, taking a London house in Fetter Lane and publishing, in 1604, his *Lachrimae* for viols. The next year he returned to Elsinore, from which, the king being out of town, he was ejected for good in 1606, and returned to Fetter Lane to stay, in a deplorably insolvent condition. For a time he was in the service of Theophilus Howard, Lord Walden, but for some of the ensuing years he was unemployed and, true to his motto, quite unhappy. Finally, in 1612, King James, perhaps tired of his whining, appointed Dowland a court lutenist—by which time he appears virtually to have burned himself out as a composer. Nevertheless he lived out his last fourteen years honored and admired, and was succeeded in his post by his son. (There is said to be evidence that John Dowland was briefly at the ducal court of Pomerania-Wolgast in 1622–23, though this is hard to account for, since English court records show him listed as first lutenist from the former year on.)

Dowland's funeral psalms constitute his most important sacred music, which otherwise consists of psalm-tune arrangements for the popular collections of the music printer Thomas East and Thomas Ravenscroft [406]. Similarly, the *Lachrimae*—7 remarkable variations on his own song "Flow, my tears" *(semper dolens!)* and some dances—contains the bulk of his consort music. The greatest part of his instrumental output is, expectably, for his own instrument. Little of that, however, was published in his lifetime, and what was, as he frequently complained, was "stolen" by his contemporaries. It is now recognized as the finest English music ever written for the lute, and among the finest from anywhere.

But it is as a writer of songs that Dowland stands among the greatest of composers. Besides the 3 *Bookes of Songes or Ayres,* he left *A Pilgrimes Solace* and three examples in Robert Dowland's collection *A Musicall Banquet.* John Dowland was hardly the inventor of the solo song (even in England), but we may grant him the *ayre,* wherein the chief interest lies in the top voice. The underlying voices may be sung but are preferably left to the lute. In his treatment of words (his texts seem to have been mostly his own), Dowland comes close to the ideal of the later *Lied,* wherein music and lyric are intimately bound up with and expressive of each other.

RECORDINGS: Dowland has been copiously recorded, and at this writing the Oiseau-Lyre label has just completed an integral recording of his entire output.

[317] FARNABY, Giles
VIRGINALIST
BORN: c. 1563
DIED: London, November 24 (?), 1640

It has been said that the Farnabys were Cornishmen, but it is likely that Giles was born in London to Jane and Thomas Farnaby. Thomas was a joiner (woodworker, cabinet maker), as was a cousin Nicholas who specialized in making virginals. Giles apparently also began in the family trade. In 1587 he married Katherine Roane at the church of St. Helen's, Bishopsgate, and settled in the parish, where he would have been a neighbor of Thomas Morley [289]. Over the next seventeen years the couple produced at least five children: a daughter named Philadelphia, who died; Richard (later a composer, see 439); Joyous; a second Philadelphia; and Edward. (There is no record of young Farnabys named Schenectady or Barnaby.)

From about 1580, Giles Farnaby worked toward a B.Mus. at Christ Church, Oxford, finally graduating in July 1592, the year in which he contributed nine settings to Thomas East's *Whole Booke of Psalms.* His only other publications seem to have been the 1598 collection of twenty *Canzonets to Four Voices* and *The Psalmes of David* for voices and viols (date unknown), of which only a single voice part is extant. Shortly after the turn of the century the Giles Farnabys moved to a hamlet called Aisthorpe in Lincolnshire, where they traded off the musical instruction of Sir Nicholas Saunderson's children for a lease on an estate. But by 1611 they were back in London. (Farnaby's absence may explain his omission from *The Triumphes of Oriana.)* Two decades later they were domiciled in Grub Street, in John Milton's parish of St. Giles, Cripplegate, where Giles was buried on November 25, 1640.

Farnaby's Morley-influenced canzonets (modestly so called), though generally light, have the complexion of fully developed madrigals, characterized by interesting harmonic and chromatic experiments that do not always quite come off. His keyboard pieces, of which the *Fitzwilliam Virginal Book* contains more than 50, also show an awareness of advanced idioms. Here he is at his best in the variation form, wherein he treats mostly popular songs with titles like "The New Sa-Hoo" and "Up Tails All!" An *Alman for Two Virginals* may be the earliest piece so designated.

RECORDINGS: Farnaby is well represented in anthologies, and an EMS label LP is devoted to a selection of the canzonets and keyboard pieces.

[318] TITELOUZE, Jehan (Tēt-lōōz', Zhàn)
PRIEST, ORGANIST, POET
BORN: St. Omer, 1562/3
DIED: Rouen, October 24, 1633

Jehan Titelouze's grandfather, father, and uncle were all employed as town musicians in St. Omer, where the family had settled around the turn of the century. (St. Omer, then in the Spanish Netherlands, seems to have been a sort of staging area for Catholics come over from England, who included John Bull [315], and probably Peter Philips [312] and John Dowland [316].) Jehan was already an organist and priest when he moved to Rouen in 1585 to play at the church of St. Jean. Three years later he won the post of chief organist at the cathedral, where he played for forty-five years. It was Titelouze who personally brought in his friend Crespin Carlier to redo the tired old instrument to his specifications. He himself won fame abroad both as a performer and an expert on organs. He became a French citizen in 1604 and a canon of the cathedral in 1610. He obviously liked to write and turned out both prose and poetry of an old-fashioned, rhetorical, and dense style, not unlike that of his music. In his later years he was often ill, and was forced to cut back on his duties after 1623. He proposed to train a successor in what he felt was an endangered tradition, but death overtook him before he could do so.

Considering the fact that the organ has been for so long the French instrument *par excellence,* it seems odd that so late a musician as Titelouze was the first French keyboardist of any note. Indeed his was the first French music specifically for organ—and virtually the only for nearly forty years. He published 2 organ books—a 1623 collection of hymns "with fugues and researches on their plainchants" and an organ Magnificat in the eight church modes. (Three Masses have vanished.) Though he occasionally used dissonant and chromatic touches, his music looks back to the polyphonic past that he loved. But it has a life of its own and a visionary quality.

[319] MILTON, John, the elder
SCRIVENER
BORN: Stanton St. John, Oxfordshire, c. 1563
DIED: London, mid-March 1647

The elder John Milton's father, Richard, a staunch Catholic, was a man of property. John Aubrey, in his *Brief Lives,* says that John was "brought up" at Christ Church in nearby Oxford, which could mean that he was educated at the college of that name or sang in the choir of the church itself. The records of the era, which neither confirm nor deny, are at least as unreliable as Aubrey. If Milton did hang out at the university (not unlikely in any case), he no doubt would have picked up some of the radical ideas going around. In 1585 (Aubrey again), Richard Milton found an English Bible in his son's room and kicked him out of the house. John hiked down to London and, after ten years that remain unaccounted for, joined the Worshipful Company of Scriveners on an apprentice footing. By then scriveners were something more than mere public scribes: they also functioned as legal advisers, investment counselors, financial agents, and moneylenders (at rather stiff rates). In 1600 Milton became a master scrivener, bought a house in Bread Street (wherein the Great Fire began sixty-six years on), and married a weak-eyed lady (probably a widow) named Sarah Jeffrey, who bore him five children. Three survived infancy—Anne (later Mrs. Phillips), John (the poet), and Christopher (later a knight and a judge). Old rumor to the contrary, it is unlikely that the senior Milton's musical efforts contributed to the family's welfare, though they gave his namesake a passionate love of the art. But in financial terms, he was a decided success. He was able not only to educate his sons in the manner in which they wished to be accustomed, even though young John disappointed paternal expectations by not taking the cloth; he even indulgently sent his youngest off to Italy for the mandatory broadening, equipped with a manservant to keep him in clean linen and such. In his sixties, the old scrivener, honored and wealthy, retired to his country estate at Horton in Buckinghamshire. After the death of Sarah Milton, he moved in with his son the judge, who transferred to Reading in the later years of the Puritan Revolution. When it was over, old John came back to London, at first to live with his younger son, and then in a house of his own in the Barbican. He was buried in St. Giles', Cripplegate, on March 15, 1647.

Music was an avocation with Milton, but his compositions were well regarded and he was one of the contributors to *The Triumphes of Oriana,* that all-star Elizabethan *Festschrift.* According to his grandson, Edward Phillips, John Aubrey, and other contemporaries, in his Christ Church years he wrote an *In nomine* or some such thing in forty, or perhaps eighty, parts, for which he won a gold medal or other prize from a Polish prince or Count Moritz of Hesse. In any case, the piece is lost. His other music includes anthems, psalms, madrigals, a motet, and instrumental works.

[320] HASSLER, Hans Leo (Hås-ler, Hånts Lä'-ō)
ORGANIST, BAND DIRECTOR, ENTREPRENEUR
BORN: Nuremberg, October 25 or 26, 1564
DIED: Frankfurt am Main, June 8, 1612

Hassler was the second of the three musical sons of Isaak Hassler, Nuremberg organist. Kaspar, the oldest, was an organist and editor. Jakob, the youngest, was an organist and composer who, like Hans Leo, studied in Venice and worked for the Fuggers in Augsburg (until he was run out of town). All three youths were taught by their father. In 1584, Hans became one of the first of the new wave of northern musicians to go to Italy for training (probably at municipal expense, like his brother after him). He studied with Andrea Gabrieli [180] and possibly with Giovanni [286], whose lifelong friend and correspondent he became. A year later he was hired by Oktavian II Fugger as organist, playing for him until his death in 1600. Hassler thought he would like to stay on in Augsburg, and got himself appointed director of the municipal band. Perhaps the location was beneficial to his business interests. Thanks, no doubt, to the Fuggers, who were experienced in such matters, he became a mineowner and metals dealer, raking in some 12,000 gulden a year. As a fairly natural consequence he also became a moneylender. On the side, he manufactured musical clocks. He thus would appear to be the first capitalist composer. Apparently there were those who doubted his honesty in his business dealings, so that he was constantly being dragged into court by dissatisfied customers and the like. Anyhow, after a year he decided he didn't like Augsburg all that much, and by buttering up the town council back home, managed to get the band directorship in Nuremberg, plus the job of organist at the Frauenkirche. In 1602 he was ennobled by Emperor Rudolf II and appointed chamber-organist to the imperial court—largely an honorary post. Two years later he gave up his Nuremberg tasks, retired to Ulm, got married, and apparently settled down to composing full-time. But in 1608 he went back to work as chapel organist to

Christian I, Elector of Saxony, in Dresden, remaining when that ruler died and was succeeded by his brother John George I. But like his friend Giovanni Gabrieli, Hassler's health had been in decline for some time (he suffered from tuberculosis) and the trip to Frankfurt to attend the coronation of Emperor Ferdinand II proved too much for him.

Hassler is generally reckoned by those who know as the greatest German composer of the late Renaissance. A musical public that knows very little of his work almost certainly knows his so-called "Passion chorale," used by J. S. Bach in his *St. Matthew Passion* to the text *O Haupt voll Blut und Wunden* (O bloody head sore wounded). That was not, however, the passion Hassler had in mind, for the work started out as a song *"Mein G'müt ist mir verwirret"* ("My Head Is All in a Whirl"—over a girl, of course). Whatever he may have been in his life, Hassler was a merry man in his songs. It is not surprising that his earliest separate publication was a volume of twenty-four *canzonette*. Like Thomas Morley [289] in England, Hassler seems to have been particularly fetched by the *balletti* of Giovanni Gastoldi [280] and such like, and imported their "fa-la's" and other characteristics into his native land. He also did a book of madrigals for various combinations of voices, but his chief contributions to secular music were in the *Lied*, wherein, as Morley did in England, he hybridized the local product with the imported stock (especially in the latter's dancy aspects), sending German song spinning off in a new direction. Hassler's chief efforts here are obtained in the *Neue teutsche Gesäng (New German Songs)*—specifically after Italian models—of 1596 and the *Lustgarten (Pleasure Garden)* of 1601. The latter work is of special interest, for its several purely instrumental intradas may be said to contain the seeds of German orchestral music.

As a composer of religious music, which makes up most of the rest of his output, Hassler, like certain of the early post-Reformation composers, seems to have had no qualms about writing music for both Catholic and Protestant worship, though he himself was of the latter persuasion. As with so many of the German composers of this period, his 8 Masses and his Latin motets are on the conservative side, reflecting a mastery of contrapuntal technique more than they do the innovations of the Venetians. On the other hand, Hassler leaves his personal imprint on them with the dance impulse of the secular songs. Of the "Lutheran" music, the *Psalmen* of 1607 are the most important ex-

amples, building up complex structures on chorale tunes and opening up, together with Michael Praetorius [360], from whom he took his cue, the development of the German "chorale motet." The *Kirchengesänge (Church Songs)* of 1608, however, are simple chorale harmonizations, probably for congregational (or village choir) use. Nowhere does Hassler use the newfangled *basso continuo*. He apparently wrote nothing in the last four years of his life.

RECORDINGS: The only systematic representations of Hassler on records seem to be the fairly extensive samplings from *Neue teutsche Gesäng* directed by Günther Arndt and from *Lustgarten* by Dietrich Knothe, both in the Deutsche Grammophon Archiv series. A few samples of the sacred music occur in anthologies.

[321] AICHINGER, Gregor (Ĭkh'-ing-er, Grä'-gôr)
ORGANIST, PRIEST
BORN: Regensburg, 1564/5
DIED: Augsburg, c. January 20, 1628

Aichinger was already composing when he matriculated at the University of Ingolstadt at the age of fifteen or so. There he met and became fast friends with young Jakob Fugger, a scion of the great Augsburg banking house. In 1584 he took, under Fugger patronage, what turned out to be a lifetime job as organist of the church of St. Ulrich in Augsburg. Shortly afterward young Fugger's Uncle Jakob sent Aichinger off to Venice to study with the Gabrielis [180, 286]. While in Italy he visited Rome and indulged his apparent love of academic life by enrolling in the University of Padua. Back in Augsburg in 1588, he again attended Ingolstadt, and on a second journey to Italy eleven years later he studied for a time at the University of Perugia, perhaps in connection with his entering the priesthood, which he probably did in Rome in 1600. His vocation was apparently quite serious, for he abjured secular music and in due course published a volume of meditations. No doubt thanks to his close association with the Fuggers, he was awarded several benefices, and for the rest of his life continued to compose and make music in Augsburg.

All of Aichinger's surviving works (of which there is a plenitude) are vocal, and most of them are devotional. In his musical development he shows variously the influences of Orlande de Lassus [228], Palestrina [201], and, expectably, Giovanni Gabrieli. Aichinger's *Cantiones ecclesiasticae* of 1607 may be the first German publication to include a continuo part, and is certainly the first to explain how the continuo works. Many of his later compositions are in the vocal concerto style. He was one of the contributors to the *Rosetum Marianum*, a collection of Marian hymns all composed on the same theme at the behest of Bernhard Klingenstein, *Kapellmeister* of Augsburg Cathedral.

[322] HARANT, Kryštof, a Polžic a Bedružic, (Ha'-ránt, Krě'-shtŏf)
COURTIER, SOLDIER, SCHOLAR
BORN: near Klatovy (Bohemia), 1564
DIED: Prague, June 21, 1621

Harant was a Bohemian noble, whose estate, Klenové Castle, was in the vicinity of Pilsen (Plzeň). From his early teens he served as a page in the Innsbruck court of the doctrinaire and militant Catholic Archduke of Styria, Ferdinand. Here he received a brilliant humanistic education, including musical training from the Dutchmen Gerard van Roo and Alexander Utendal. After a decade managing the family properties, he distinguished himself from 1593 to 1597 fighting the invading Turks for Emperor Rudolf II, whose court he joined in 1603, when he returned from a pilgrimage to Jerusalem (which he described in an account he published in 1608). That same year he acquired, through his second marriage, Pecka Castle, where he kept an impressive chapel. By the time his old master, Ferdinand, had wangled his way onto the throne in 1618, Harant had joined the Hussite patriots in Bohemia, was responsible for the shelling of the imperial palace in the ensuing rebellion, and was made a counselor to the "Winter King," Frederick V, promoted by the Bohemians to their throne from the electorship of the Palatinate. But, in what turned out to be the opening blast of the Thirty Years War, Frederick was run out a few months later and the Bohemians defeated at the White Mountain. Harant was arrested as a traitor. Unmoved by memories of old times, Ferdinand had him beheaded along with twenty-six other rebels.

Harant was apparently a talented but conservative composer of the old polyphonic persuasion. Only a single parody Mass and a handful of shorter religious works are known to exist. One of the latter is his contribution to Bernhard Klingenstein's collection *Rosetum Marianum* (see under Gregor Aichinger, 321).

[323] PERAZA, Francisco de (Pā-rá'-thà, Frán-thēs'-kō dā)
ORGANIST
BORN: Salamanca, 1564
DIED: Seville, June 23, 1598

Peraza came from a musical family. His father played the shawm for the Duke of Calabria in Valencia and later for the cathedrals of Salamanca and Madrid. His elder brother, Jerónimo (1550–1617), his namesake son, and a nephew were all noted organists. In his tryout for the post of cathedral organist in Seville when he was only twenty, he performed such prodigal feats of virtuosity and improvisation that the archbishop hired him forthwith at a wage of 200 ducats a year. He fulfilled expectations to the degree that his salary was quintupled inside of two years. Local merchants who hired a room in the cathedral for their exchange demanded that the door be left open so that they might hear him practice. Francisco Guerrero [209], the choirmaster, said that he had angels in his fingers. He was often called to court and elsewhere to perform. He allegedly composed a large number of works, but today only a single organ work survives (and its authorship has been challenged).

[324] AGUILERA DE HEREDIA, Sebastian (Ȧ-gwē-lā'-rà dā Ā-rā'-*thē*-à)
ORGANIST, PRIEST
BORN: c. 1565
DIED: Zaragoza, December 16, 1627

Without any concrete evidence, both Huesca (in the Pyrenean foothills) and Zaragoza have claimed Aguilera as a native son. In 1585 he became cathedral organist in the former city and remained in that post for eighteen years before moving on to the analogous one in the former cathedral, La Seo, in Zaragoza. There he was highly regarded and he founded a school that produced several notable musicians. He left perhaps a score of organ pieces notable for their use of dissonance and other "affective" devices reminiscent of the mannerism exhibited at about the same time in the Italian madrigal. Aguilera may have invented the term *falsas* to describe compositions particularly rich in this sort of thing. The only extant choral work that is certainly his is a cycle of 36 Magnificat settings, *Canticum Beatissimae Virginis deiparae Mariae* of 1618, which also shows a keen awareness of changing styles.

[325] CATO, Diomedes (Kä'-tō, Dē'-ō-mä-dēz)
LUTENIST
BORN: Venice, c. 1565 (?)
DIED: after 1607

One source gives this composer's name as "Catone Diomede," which, considering his origins, is more likely than the Latinized form, in whatever order. Lutenists were popular in Poland, which fact may explain his migration thither, though some think he went there to study. In any case, it was as a lutenist that he entered the service of Stanisław Kostka, grand treasurer of Pomerania, who liked his playing so well that he eventually willed him 1,000 (or perhaps 10,000) złoty—a lot of złoty, whatever the figure. From 1588 to 1600 he was employed by Sigismund III, King of Poland and Sweden, who was by no means so generous, owing to his realm's financial problems and his own tightwad instincts. After Sigismund lost Sweden, Cato returned to the Kostka household until his patron's death, after which he could afford the royal court again. He left 2 part-songs in Polish, a motet, a madrigal, some fantasias and other pieces for consort, and a few organ works, but is best known for his 50-odd lute compositions, many of which appeared in published anthologies of the time throughout Europe.

[326] HAUSSMANN, Valentin (Hous'-män, Fä'-len-tēn)
ORGANIST, TEACHER, EDITOR, POET,
  POLITICIAN
BORN: Gerbstedt, c. 1565
DIED: c. 1614

Haussmann was the second in a lineal succession of five musicians all named Valentin. His father, a Nuremberger, wrote chorales and was a friend of Martin Luther and Johann Walther [139]. His son built and played organs at Löbejün, near Halle, and his grandson was a predecessor of J. S. Bach [684] at the Cöthen court. His great-grandson, Bach's contemporary, after serving as organist in Merseburg and Halle, wound up as Mayor of Lauchstädt. Our man, Valentin II, was trained by Andreas Raselius, cantor at the Regensburg Gymnasium. In the early part of his mature life, his base of operations seems to have been Nuremberg, but he was obviously on the move much of the time, turning up as he does in Steyr, Ulm, Hanover, Wolfenbüttel, Halberstadt, Poland, Königsberg, Magdeburg, and Hamburg. Around the turn of the century he seems to have settled in Gerbstedt (also in the vicinity of Halle), where he served as organist and town councilor. Haussmann was an indefatigable composer of Lieder, dance songs, and dances. He also edited, translated, and published collections of Italian madrigals for the German market. His best-known work is the Venusgarten of 1601, a collection of 100 harmonized dance tunes, many of which he says he himself collected in Poland and Prussia and about half of which he fitted out with "fine courtly-amoristical texts" of his own composition. There are also extant a few sacred pieces and a number of occasional works that reflect Haussmann's peripatetic life.

[327] HOLMES, John
ORGANIST, TEACHER
BORN: c. 1565 (?)
DIED: Salisbury, January 30, 1629

What we know of Holmes's career is bound up with the cathedrals of Winchester and Salisbury, in that order. He is said to have been organist at the former from 1599 (in which post his son, Thomas, served from 1631 until his death in 1638), and would seem also to have been master of the boys, since Adrian Batten (1591–1637), a choirboy there in the first decade of the new century, claimed him as his teacher. He had some connection with Salisbury from as early as 1613 and went there in 1621 as lay vicar and master of the boys. He left anthems and other church music, a handful of instrumental pieces, and the madrigal "Thus Bonny-Boots the Birthday Celebrated" in The Triumphes of Oriana.

[328] JONES, Robert
LUTENIST (?), IMPRESARIO
BORN: c. 1565 (?)
DIED: 1616 or later

This Robert Jones, a Jacobean-ayres man, is not to be confused with his namesake of nearly a century earlier, who was a Gentleman of the Chapel Royal in the time of Henry VIII. After some sixteen years, the later Jones acquired a B.Mus. from Oxford in 1597. Between 1600 and 1610 he published five books of ayres and one of madrigals, as well as the madrigal "Oriana Seeming to Wink" in The Triumphes of Oriana. Apparently they did not sell very well, and in 1610, having decided that theatricals were more promising, he got together with Philip Rosseter [338], Ralph Reeve, and Philip Kingham to train and promote a company of child actors, duly licensed as the Children of the Revels to the Queene in Whitefriars. Though by then the novelty of such companies must have been somewhat dulled (Hamlet was complaining about the "little eyases" c. 1600), the venture evidently throve, for by 1615 the partners had gotten a permit to erect a theater in Blackfriars near Puddle Wharf, where Jones was then living. The building was just about up when the lord mayor and the City Council got into a still-unexplained snit about it, managed to obtain a royal condemnation, and pulled it down. At that point Jones vanishes from the pages of history—perhaps a suicide from Puddle Wharf?

Only 10 of Jones's 24 known madrigals have survived intact, and they inspire no confidence that the loss of the others qualifies as cataclysmic. His ayres seem to be throwbacks, and though some of them are melodically and rhythmically attractive, it is clear that Jones was rather a jackleg composer. The third book is tantalizingly called *Ultimum Vale (Last Farewell*—positively no more performances). In the fourth, Jones attacks the critics for pointing out his shortcomings. Perhaps his dedication of the fifth to a Lady Wroth is to ward off further unfavorable reviews.

[329] KIRBYE, George
MUSIC TEACHER (?)
BORN: c. 1565
DIED: Bury St. Edmunds, October 5 (?), 1634

Like John Farmer's [348], Kirbye's name first turns up in 1592 in Thomas East's *Whole Booke of Psalms* (to which only Farmer contributed more numbers). Probably at some time in the same decade he was employed by Sir Robert Jermyn of Bury St. Edmunds, Suffolk, possibly as teacher to his daughters, to whom Kirbye dedicated his one published book of 24 madrigals in 1597. In February 1598 he married Anne Saxye, and apparently settled down in Bury St. Edmunds for the rest of his life, acquiring a house in Whiting Street. In 1601 he contributed a madrigal "With Angel's face" to *The Triumphes of Oriana* collection—later changed to "Bright Phoebus" because Daniel Norcombe [387] had already contributed a setting of the same poem. Anne Kirbye died in 1626. It appears that there were no children, since George left what he possessed to his housekeeper, Agnes Seamon, a relative of Anne, and to his brother and sister, Walter and Alice.

Kirbye's madrigals, like those of Giles Farnaby [317], indulge in "expressive" experiments. Save for his published works only scraps exist (in manuscript) of the rest of his output.

[330] MOLINARO, Simone (Mô-lē-nà'-rō, Sē'-mō-nā)
CHOIRMASTER, LUTENIST, EDITOR
BORN: c. 1565
DIED: Genoa, after 1613

Molinaro learned music from his maternal uncle, Giovanni Battista della Gostena, a pupil of Philippe de Monte [197] and *maestro di cappella* at Genoa Cathedral. He also succeeded his uncle as choirmaster, though exactly when seems a point of argument, Gostena's death being pegged variously at 1598, 1602, and 1605. In 1599, Molinaro brought out his most famous work, a lute tablature containing dance suites (extended *passamezzo* and *gagliarda* (galliard) combinations, the *passamezzo* being the Italian substitute for the pavane; there are also some *saltarelle* in place of the galliards), *canzone,* and fantasias (including some by Gostena). These works tend to be more chordal-melodic than polyphonic, but exhibit some rather far-out modulations. Molinaro also wrote a good deal of vocal music, both secular and sacred, some of the latter with *basso seguente,* implying the use of organ ad lib. Some of the religious music was rather widely known, Hans Leo Hassler's [320] older brother, Kaspar, for instance, including some pieces in one of his anthologies. Molinaro is also notable for having edited a score edition of Don Carlo Gesualdo's [310] madrigals in 1613.

[331] CARDOSO, Manuel (Kär-dō'-zō, Mán-ōō-el')
ORGANIST, CHOIRMASTER, ADMINISTRATOR
BORN: Fronteira, December 11, 1566
DIED: Lisbon, November 24, 1650

In accordance with an old Portuguese custom that should appeal to modern feminists, this composer adopted (with proper adjustment for gender) the surname of his mother, Isobel Cardosa. (His father was Francisco Vaz.) Born near the Spanish border, due east of Lisbon, he was schooled in music and theology at Évora (east of Lisbon) and served for a short time as *mestre de capela* at the cathedral there. He became a Carmelite in 1588 and a year later began his sixty-year career as organist and choirmaster of the order's Lisbon monastery, where he also from time to time held various offices. He was a close friend and adviser to the young Duke of Braganza, a composer of talent who underwrote publication of several of Cardoso's collections and who, when Portugal broke away from Spain in 1640, was named John IV, later called "the Fortunate." Cardoso was one of the greatest, and certainly in his time one of the most widely known of Portuguese composers, though the hand of Palestrina [201] lies rather heavily on his music. He left 3 volumes of Masses, one of Magnificats, and one of motets. Most of his manuscripts were destroyed in the great Lisbon earthquake and fire of 1755. RECORDINGS: There is a recording of the *Missa miserere mihi Domine.*

[332] CAMPION, Thomas (Kam-pyun, Tom'-us)
POET, THEORIST, PHYSICIAN
BORN: London, February 12 (?), 1567
DIED: London, c. February 29, 1620

In earlier times poets were deemed prophets and musicians servants, which may explain why we know more about Thomas Campion than we do about, say, Giles Farnaby [317]. He was born in the parish of St. Andrew's, Holborn, to John Campion, a law clerk in the chancery courts, and his wife, a widow named Lucy Searle. At nine he lost his father. His mother then married Augustine Steward and died shortly afterward. Steward proved to be one of the better stepfathers, sending both young Campion and another stepson from a later marriage off to Cambridge. Campion spent five years (1581–86) at Peterhouse College, where he seems to have picked up a taste for Latin, Greek, and music, but no degree. A go at the law at Gray's Inn appears also to have led nowhere. In 1591 he tried soldiering with the Earl of Essex in a pointless attempt to assist Henry of Navarre against the Catholic League. Meanwhile he had been writing poetry, some of which appeared that same year in an appendix to the pirated edition of Sir Philip Sidney's *Astrophel and Stella* that launched the sonnet epidemic in England. In 1595 he brought out a collection of his own Latin verse, *Thomae Campiani poemata,* but it was yet another half decade before he made his first real impact as a composer, sharing a fat book of ayres with his friend Philip Rosseter [338]. Campion, as he did thereafter, supplied his own lyrics. The songs are to be sung to "the Lute, Orpharian [a species of cittern], and Base Violl," says Rosseter, who notes also that Campion's contributions are

"but the superfluous blossoms of his deeper studies." Those deeper studies appear to have borne fruit the following year, 1602, when Campion published *Observations on the Art of English Poesie,* raising something of a teapot tempest by declaring the current rhymed verse "vulgar and unartificial" and (like an English Jean Baïf) plumping for a return to classical meters. Though such meters, owing to different notions of stresses, are impossible in English, Campion offered some examples that he thought did the trick. Though they don't, they show a master lyricist, with an extraordinary ear for rhythms, at work.

Apparently Campion was also undertaking deeper studies in other areas, for in 1605 he received the degree of Doctor of Medicine from the University of Caën and was thereafter called "Dr. Campion." His new occupation seems not, however, to have interfered with his artistic interests. He was active for a time at the court of James I, supplying music and lyrics for several masques, that balletic form of compliment so much the rage there, and writing a set of elegies on the death of Henry, Prince of Wales, which were set by John Coprario [373]. He also published 4 subsequent books of his own ayres (dates uncertain), a revised edition of his Latin poems, and a little manual, several times reprinted, *A New Way of Making Fowre Parts in Counter-point,* which was basically an explanation of how to write songs without breaking harmonic rules. In the middle of the second decade of the new century, he was under suspicion of being an accessory to the notorious murder of Sir Thomas Overbury (Campion had unwittingly delivered a bribe to one of the suspects), but after some unpleasantness, was cleared. When he died, he left his estate to Rosseter. Evidently the medical profession was not then what it is now, for he was at that time worth only around twenty pounds.

Of Campion it might be said that he is a great poet to musicians and a great musician to poets. Though he himself seems to have made light of his creative efforts, he was capable of greater profundity than he is sometimes given credit for, and has perhaps been undervalued, though his output is uneven. It is fair to say that his music is usually subservient to his lyrics, but it is rarely less than graceful and, blessed with a lack of pretension, it often exhibits a lovely simplicity and occasionally a grave beauty. He appears to have written nothing musical beyond his ayres and masking songs.

[333] **MONTEVERDI, Claudio Giovanni Antonio** (Môn-te-vâr'-dē, Klou'-dyō Jō-vàn'-ne Àn-tōn'-yō)
SINGER, VIOLIST, CHOIRMASTER
BORN: Cremona, May 15, 1567
DIED: Venice, November 29, 1643

Claudio Monteverdi was born three years after William Shakespeare and five after Lope de Vega. The fact may not be wholly trivial. The first two ushered in what became—in England, Spain, and France—the greatest age of the theater since Athenian times. The third, supreme musician that he was, was at his greatest in the new genre of opera. Now, as we sometimes forget, opera appeared in Italy as a result of the same impulse that inspired spoken drama elsewhere, and is in fact the peculiarly Italian form of the dramatic art. Hence it is possible to see Monteverdi as not only a contemporary but a counterpart of Shakespeare.

Monteverdi was born in a city of 10,000 inhabitants, then under Spanish rule and already declining in size and importance. But Andrea Amati, the first of its great violin makers, was already at work there. Baldassare Monteverdi, the composer's father, was a druggist who practiced medicine after a fashion. The mother, the former Maddalena Zigani, died in 1573, shortly after giving birth to her third child, Claudio's only brother, Giulio Cesare, who would also become a musician. By 1584 she had been succeeded by two stepmothers. We have Claudio's own word that he was trained by Marc' Antonio Ingegneri [256], *maestro di cappella* in the town's mighty-towered cathedral. His nonmusical learning suggests that he may have also studied at the local university. Whatever the details, he spent his first twenty years in this cultural backwater, but already precociously composing and publishing—23 *cantiunculae* (little motets) at fifteen, 21 *madrigali spirituali* a year later, and 21 three-part *canzonette* in 1584. Then, when he was twenty, came the first of that incredible series of madrigal books that was to map the crossover from the old polyphony to the new monophony, harmony, and instrumentalism—i.e., to music as most of us conceived it up to c. 1945.

Apparently by the time the madrigal book appeared, Monteverdi was chafing to escape Cremona. He went to Milan in 1589, where he failed, as a violist, to attract a patron or an employer. But his opportunity came the next year, after he published his second book of madrigals, and was honored with election to the Congregation and Academy of St. Cecilia in Rome, when he was hired as singer and instrumentalist by Vincenzo

Gonzaga, Duke of Mantua. The duke may have been as frivolous as his projection in Giuseppe Verdi's [1232] *Rigoletto,* but he knew a musician when he met one. At various times during his term in Mantua, Monteverdi found himself colleagues with such composers as Giaches de Wert [232], from whom he learned much, Giovanni Gastoldi [280], Francesco Rovigo [246], Benedetto Pallavicino, Lodovico Viadana [308], and the "Mantuan Hebrew" Salamone Rossi [341], as well as the poets Guarini, Rinuccini, and probably Tasso, and the painters Pieter Pourbus and Peter Paul Rubens. Monteverdi played a viol of some sort and wrote more madrigals—the third book came out in 1592. None of this made much difference in his skimpy paycheck, but in 1595, when Duke Vincenzo marched off to war against the Turks in Hungary, he considered Monteverdi indispensable enough to the inspiration of his martial ardors to include him among the musicians he took with him. However, he did not consider him good enough to replace the dead Wert the next year, the job going to Monteverdi's fellow townsman Benedetto Pallavicino, probably on a basis of seniority. In 1599 Monteverdi improved his financial position to a degree by marrying Claudia Cattaneo, who was on the court payroll as a singer. Their honeymoon was, however, brief, for a few weeks after the wedding the duke decided he needed to take the waters at Spa. Monteverdi parked Claudia with his father in Cremona and dutifully went along, passing through Austria, Switzerland, and Lorraine, visiting Liège, Antwerp, and Brussels, and returning in October along with young Rubens and a haul of French music. In 1600 the duke attended the wedding of Henry of Navarre and Maria de' Medici, and was perhaps intrigued by the performance of Jacopo Peri's [309] *Euridice,* especially as he had recently had an up-to-date theater of his own built.

In 1601, Monteverdi succeeded Pallavicino as the duke's *maestro,* and Claudia bore him his first son, Baldassare, later one of his singers at St. Mark's in Venice. Having remained, in point of published compositions, silent for a decade (no one knows why), he brought out the fourth book of madrigals in 1603, the year his daughter Leonora was born and died. She was followed by another son, Massimiliano, in 1604, who was to follow in his grandfather's footsteps as a Cremona physician—a real one. The next year saw the publication of the fifth book of madrigals. The fourth had already shown signs of moving away from earlier traditions, especially in terms of recitative-like utterance and daring, though not revolutionary, harmonic experiments. Now Monteverdi also added a continuo, indispensable in several of the examples. The ensuing *Scherzi musicali* of 1607 contained a preface by Giulio Cesare Monteverdi on behalf of his brother, implying that these pieces had been influenced by the French *air* (perhaps the mensural experiments of the Jean Baïf circle) and differentiating between the old polyphonic style *(prima prattica)* and the new monophonic-harmonic concept *(seconda prattica)*. Early that same year Monteverdi completed his first opera, *L'Orfeo,* which was forthwith performed (under circumstances which remain obscure) before the Accademia degli Invaghiti. Here the genre stands before us already full-blown and still viable.

But Orpheus' loss was soon to be Monteverdi's own. Claudia had sickened the previous year, and so that she might have better care, he sent her to his family in Cremona. But she worsened and he joined her there in the summer of 1607, during which his townsfolk honored him with election to the Accademia degli Animosi. But on September 10, Claudia died and her grief-stricken husband buried her there. At first he refused to return to work, but his commitment to another opera, *Arianna,* took him back to Mantua in October. It being by then too late to count on it for the 1608 Carnival, it was postponed to the hometown celebration of the wedding of the Marquis Francesco of Mantua and Margaret of Savoy, slated for Turin later that spring. For the same occasion, Monteverdi was also entrusted with the music for Guarini's comedy *Idropica* and an opera-ballet, *Il Ballo delle ingrate.* Rehearsals for the opera went on for some months, marred by the death (from smallpox) of the lovely eighteen-year-old Caterina Martinelli, for whom the composer had tailored the title role. The work was presented on May 28, the great *lamento* (all that remains of it), establishing itself as a hit. Monteverdi's labors won him orders for more work. He reacted with a sort of nervous breakdown, went back to Cremona, and vainly tried to quit. Having had charge of the cathedral music since 1601, he put together a collection of his sacred pieces and presented them to Paul V in Rome, in an effort to win a seminary fellowship for Baldassare, and no doubt a place for himself.

In 1612, Fate took matters into her own hands. The duchess died, followed closely by the duke, and Francesco dismissed the musicians. Monteverdi notes with understandable bitterness that after twenty-one years of faithful and underpaid service, he left Mantua with a capital of 25 scudi. By 1613, however, his fame had won him the choirmastership of St. Mark's in Venice at 300 ducats a year. While on his way thither, he was robbed by bravos and then had to suffer the ignominy, during a fluvial segment of the journey, of being marooned on a sandbar all night. The next year he published the sixth madrigal book, which contained, *inter alia,* the madrigalian version of the *Arianna* lament and the great funerary cycle *Lagrime d'amante (A Lover's Tears).* Francesco Gonzaga had been succeeded in Mantua by Ferdinando, for whom Monteverdi wrote a ballet, *Tirsi e Clori.* But two commissioned operas never reached fruition, and when, in 1620, Ferdinando indicated that the composer would be welcome in his old post, Monteverdi rebuffed him in no uncertain terms. For one thing, he was trying to rebuild a musical establishment that had slipped to a sad state of decline; for another, he was doing far better financially in Venice than he could ever hope to do in Mantua. In 1626 he was once again invited to Mantua by the sickly new duke, Vincenzo II. The composer again declined but wrote an opera for him, *La Finta pazza Licori (Licoris Feigning Madness);* it was never produced and is now lost. The duke died without issue two years later, and with him Mantua, as a state, went too. War erupted, the city was sacked, and the invading soldiers brought with them a plague epidemic that scoured northern Italy —events depicted in Alessandro Manzoni's nineteenth-century novel *I Promessi sposi (The Betrothed).* In 1631 Monteverdi wrote a memorial Mass, and a year later he took holy orders.

The seventh book of madrigals had appeared in 1619. It was the watershed volume in his nondramatic secular output. The contents are at a far remove from the conventional madrigals of his youth, consisting mostly of solos and duets with instrumental accompaniment that owe perhaps more to the Venetian *concerto* (the collection's primary title) than to the Florentine monody. In 1632, Monteverdi produced a second book of lighthearted *scherzi,* all for one or two voices with continuo. The eighth and final book of madrigals that he published in his lifetime (there is a posthumous ninth book), which treats the twin themes of love and war, is drawn from various periods in his mature career, but in such a late work as the "dramatic madrigal" *Il Combattimento di Tancredi e Clorinda (The Battle Between Tancredi and Clorinda)* he shows how far and how radically his dramatic art has developed. The book was published in 1638, a year after the first public opera house in the world had opened in Venice. Although the composer was chiefly occupied with sacred music (for example, the *Selva morale e spirituale* of 1640), the notion of an available stage obviously stirred his blood, and he returned to operatic composition in his fecund old age. *Le Nozze d'Enea con Lavinia (The Wedding of Aeneas and Lavinia,* 1641), has, like all the earlier operas except *L'Orfeo,* vanished, but *Il Ritorno d'Ulisse in patria (Ulysses' Homecoming,* 1641) and *L'Incoronazione di Poppea (Poppea's Crowning,* 1642) remain two of the towering masterpieces of early operatic literature.

Having completed *Poppea,* Monteverdi, now seventy-five, was given leave to see Cremona and Mantua for one last time. The trip was a triumphal progress, but it sapped his strength. Returning to Venice in November of 1643, he fell ill and died. The republic gave him a magnificent funeral and buried him in the Church of the Frari.

Once viewed as a revolutionary who overturned the whole Western concept of music, Monteverdi is now seen, in the light of musicological research, as representative of changing times. But as much can be said of Beethoven or Wagner, and it takes away nothing of his greatness.

RECORDINGS: By now all the extant operas have been several times recorded, in ever more "authentic" editions. Michel Corboz has done a complete survey of the religious music, and there are a number of individual versions of the big works (the Masses and the 1610 *Vespers).* Various of the madrigal books have had integral representation, but the complete edition embarked on by Raymond Leppard some years ago has yet to be completed and, at this writing, there are still gaps, albeit minor, in representation of the secular nondramatic works.

[334] DEMANTIUS, Christoph (Dā-
   mȧnt'-yōōs, Krēs'-tȯf)
CANTOR (Lutheran)
BORN: Reichenberg, December 15, 1567
DIED: Freiberg, April 20, 1643

Demantius' birthplace, now in northern Czechoslovakia, today is called Liberec. In 1592 he published a musical textbook in Bautzen, where he was probably teaching. A year later, he entered the University of Wittenberg, but by 1594 he was living in Leipzig, where he probably married. Three years later he took the post of municipal cantor in Zittau, a few miles north of Reichenberg. In 1603 his wife, Anna, succumbed to the plague, and the next year he moved on to Freiberg, near Dresden, where he served for the rest of his life as cantor at the cathedral

and the attached school. In 1613 he married Sabina Wecker, daughter of a rich Saxon furrier. He must have fancied her name, for after she died he married another Sabina (c. 1624). She did not last long, and Demantius took a fourth wife (name unknown) in 1627. The sparsity of his publications after that time perhaps reflects the depredations of the Thirty Years War.

Demantius wrote a great deal of church music, most of it in a conservative *a cappella* style that finds its chief inspiration in Lassus [228]. Some such compositions are so-called "gospel" motets, based on the evangelistic text for the day. He also wrote a large amount of occasional music. His German *Lieder* show the influence of Hassler [320], many of them intended for the increasingly popular choral festivals. His dances show Italian influence, but also specifically include Polish dances, which seem to have been in vogue at the time. A curious work is the *Tympanum Militare,* a collection of "Hungarian war-drums and battle-cries, together with Hungarian songs of combat and victory," which reflected recent gains against the Turkish threat. Besides his textbook, Demantius published, in 1632, the first alphabetized German musical dictionary.

RECORDINGS: Among recordings are versions of the admirable *Johannespassion (St. John Passion),* 1631, and the *Weissagung des unschuldigen Leidens und Sterbens Jesu Christi (Prophecy of the Guiltless Suffering and Death of Jesus Christ).*

[335] ANERIO, Giovanni Francesco (Ä-
   när'-yō, Jō-vän'-nē Frän-chäs'-kō)
CHOIR DIRECTOR, PRIEST, ORGANIST
BORN: Rome, c. 1567
DIED: Graz, June 10 (?), 1630

The younger brother of the singer-priest-composer Felice Anerio (c. 1560–1614) and son of the chapel singer Maurizio Anerio, Giovanni Francesco declared his religious vocation in 1583. Records of his early career are decidedly spotty. In 1595 he played the organ for the Lenten observances of the Oratorian societies. It is thought that around 1600 he became *maestro di cappella* at San Giovanni Laterano, and that some five years later he took over the identical post at San Spirito in Sassia. In 1609 he went to Verona to head the cathedral choir there, but shortly resigned, though he lived in Verona until 1611, when he went back to Rome to serve for about a year. From 1613 to 1620 he was choirmaster at Santa Trinità dei Monti. It was during this period that he was at last ordained, in 1616. After another period of obscurity he went to Warsaw as director of the chapel of Sigismund III, probably around 1624. In 1628 he was succeeded by his pupil, the musical polemicist Marco Scacchi, whom he had brought with him. On what must have been a rather slow journey home, Anerio died and was buried in Graz in June 1630.

It is possible that, like his elder brother, Giovanni Francesco Anerio was a choirboy under Palestrina [201], whom he certainly knew as a member of the Compagnia di Musici, a supportive and beneficial association from which sprang the Accademia di Santa Cecilia. At any rate, in his sacred music he is generally content to walk in that great man's footsteps. (His transcription for four voices of Palestrina's *Missa Papae Marcelli* was extremely popular.) However, he is credited with pioneer work in the oratorio, his collection *Teatro armonico spirituale* (1619) containing the first known examples in Italian, and the first Roman specification of instrumental parts. Elsewhere, particularly in his madrigals, he adopts some of the new musical devices.

RECORDINGS: There are recordings of two oratorios, *Vivean felice* and *La Conversione di San Paolo*, and of the *Requiem*.

[336] BESARD, Jean-Baptiste (Bā-zàr', Zhàn Bà-tēst')
LUTENIST, LAWYER, PHYSICIAN, EDITOR, WRITER
BORN: Besançon, c. 1567
DIED: after 1617

Besard liked to call himself "Besardus Vesontinus" because it made him sound as learned as he was. The son of a wealthy merchant elevated to the nobility, he was sent up the river (the Doubs) to Dôle to get an education at the university. In 1587 he graduated with a Ph.D. and LL.D. Still distressed by his ignorance, he took off for ten further years of study in Rome, where he added an M.D. to his alphabetical trophies and (he says) studied with Lorenzino il Liuto (Larry the Lute). In 1602 he was back in Besançon marrying Péronne Jacquot, a lady of substance—in good time, too, for he was (understandably) running out of money. No doubt her dowry helped him publish his monster lute manual, the *Thesaurus harmonicus*, which he personally brought out in Cologne in 1603 and which contains over four hundred lute pieces by composers from all over (including the editor himself). About the same time, he edited a nonmusical volume, *Mercurii gallobelgici (The Franco-Belgian Mercury)*, devoted to treaties

and such. When last heard of, Besard was living in Augsburg, where in 1617 he published an addendum *(Novus partus)* containing 59 pieces, 24 of them for two and three lutes, a second edition of his lute manual, and a dictionary of diseases with suggested remedies. Ottorino Respighi [1718] claims Besard as the source of two of his *Antiche arie e danze (Ancient Airs and Dances)*.

[337] BANCHIERI, Adriano (Bàn-kyā'-rē, A-drē-à'-nō)
ORGANIST, THEORIST, MONK, PLAYWRIGHT
BORN: Bologna, September 3, 1568
DIED: Bologna, 1634

Banchieri's first teacher was one Lucio Barbieri; later he studied with Gioseffo Guami [240], but whether in Venice or in Lucca we are not told. Five days after his twenty-first birthday, he cast his lot with the Olivetans. (The Olivetans are a monastic offshoot of the Benedictines, founded in 1324 by Bernardo Tolomei, now in a last-ditch decline. They still maintain headquarters at the lovely monastery of Monte Oliveto Maggiore, located among the cypresses and olive trees south of Siena.) His first years as a monk were spent at the monastery of San Michele in Bosco (also known as Monte Oliveto) outside Bologna. Then he went to Lucca in 1592, to Siena in 1593, and was back at San Michele as organist in 1596, doubtless having profited from his work with Guami. From 1600 to 1607 he was in Imola, organist at the church of Santa Maria in Regola. Invited back to San Michele to give the new organ its maiden voyage, he obviously found it to his liking, for in 1608 he came home to stay. In 1616 he founded in Bologna one of those quasi-Platonic, quasi–secret-society organizations so popular in Renaissance Italy, the *Accademia de' Floridi* (Academy of the Flowery People), in which his code name was *Il Dissonante* (The Discordant One). It later became the *Accademia Filharmonica* (Philharmonic Academy). (Banchieri was the most important Bolognese musician of his time and is still regarded there as the founder of what became an important facet of Bolognese life in the next century or so.) For all his outside activity, Banchieri was also highly regarded by his brethren, who elected him abbot in 1620. He held that post until his death of a stroke. On the side he wrote plays under the pen name of Camillo Scaliggeri della Fratta.

Adriano da Bologna, as he was known, was obviously brilliant and energetic. He was also a merry man with an earthy streak.

Strongly affected by the new currents, and a great admirer of Claudio Monteverdi [333], he wrote and published music of all kinds, sacred and secular, vocal and instrumental, as well as a number of theoretical books and treatises. He was one of the first composers to publish music with an "organ bass" (the *Concerti ecclesiastici* of 1595, which, in the Venetian manner, are for double chorus) and apparently the first to use the *p* and *f* signs indicating soft *(piano)* and loud *(forte)*. In his *L'Organo suonarino* of 1605, he spells out how to improvise an accompaniment on a figured bass line. His writings are also useful for information on instrumental practice, harmonic concepts, and ornamentation as they existed in his day. (He claimed to have invented a stringed instrument called an *arpichitarrone,* apparently a cross between a harp and a large lute.)

For all his Masses, motets, psalms, canzonets, madrigals, *canzone,* etc., Banchieri is best remembered today for his madrigal comedies. No doubt he was here strongly influenced by Orazio Vecchi [265], who lived in nearby Modena, and whom he knew, but Banchieri's works are more inventive, more imaginative, and funnier. His first success was *La Pazzia senile (The Dotty Old Muddlehead),* its hero the Pantalone of the *commedia dell'arte.* As with Vecchi, there is no intent (or possibility) that these works be staged, though Banchieri does sometimes supply a narrator to let the audience know what is going on. The (translated) titles of some of the others give the wild flavor: "The Nobility of the Ass of Atahualpa of Peru," "The Boat from Venice to Padua," "The Musical Custard," and "Youthful Wisdom." By all odds the most famous is *Il Festino nella sera del Giovedì Grasso avanti cena (The Pre-Dinner Entertainment on Mardi Gras Eve),* which features among other things a dance of the old folks of Chioggia (who sing in their native dialect), a commercial for matches, another for spindles, a madrigal for a nightingale (text by Guarini), and a piece for four animals, who bark, moo, etc., over a *cantus firmus.* The work closes with a preview of coming attractions!

RECORDINGS: *Il Festino* has attracted several recordings, and there is at least one of *La Pazzia senile,* as well as a number of instrumental pieces in anthologies.

[338] ROSSETER, Philip
IMPRESARIO, LUTENIST
BORN: 1568
DIED: London, May 5, 1623

Not a great deal is known of Philip Rosseter. He was a friend or associate of Thomas Campion [332], with whom he shared a book of ayres, John Dowland [316], and Robert Jones [328]. He lived on Fleet Street and later on Fetter Lane, was married to a woman named Elizabeth, and had sons named Thomas and Dudley. (A namesake who became a *luthier* in The Hague was perhaps another.) Shortly after James I came to the throne, he appointed Rosseter as a court lutenist, a post he held until his death. In 1609, Rosseter went into dramatic production with a troupe of child actors known as the Children of Whitefriars. Later he joined forces with Jones and others in a disastrous theatrical venture (see 328). Besides the ayres, Rosseter published a book of consort "lessons" (extant only in fragmentary form) and some lute pieces. His songs, like Campion's, are unpretentious and in terms of harmony rather advanced.

[339] HUME, Captain Tobias
SOLDIER, VIOLA DA GAMBA PLAYER
BORN: c. 1569
DIED: London, April 16, 1645

Hume insisted that his one true calling was soldiering and that music was his "onely effeminate part." He also insisted on his amateur status as a musician, though he is said to have been a virtuoso gambist. He seems to have acquired his captaincy in England, though he served the Swedes as a mercenary. There was apparently always a streak of oddity in him (the musicologist and keyboard player Thurston Dart terms him "lovable and eccentric"), and tradition has it that he was the model for Sir Andrew Aguecheek in Shakespeare's *Twelfth Night.* By 1642 he had fallen, one way or another, on hard times and became a pensioner at the Charterhouse, a charitable institution founded thirty years before by Thomas Sutton, a mineowner, in the ancient London Carthusian monastery. There his mental condition degenerated. In 1642 he promoted himself to colonel and issued a pamphlet offering to defeat the rebel Irish if the government would have him. There were no takers.

The captain published 2 books of viol music, in 1605 and 1607, which included some consort songs. The first one, called *The First Part of Ayres* claimed sources for its tunes as far afield as Poland; it contains songs and dances for solo "Viole de Gambo," for two viols, and "an Invention for two to play upon one Viole." The second work, *Captain Humes Poeticall Musicke* is dedicated to Queen Anne, with the plaintive hint that he is at the end of his economic rope. It contains music for two and three gambas, again including some songs. For all Hume's eccentricity, it is clear that he was a splendid musician, and his compositions have an important place in gamba music. Had there been anything analogous to radio in his day, his song "Tobacco" might well have become an early commercial.

[340] PEUERL, Paul (Poi'-erl, Poul)
ORGANIST, ORGAN BUILDER
BORN: c. June 13, 1570
DIED: after 1625

Peuerl is thought to have come from Stuttgart. Having (understandably) never heard of Grimm's Law, he often thought of himself as "Bäwerl" or "Bäuerl" or even "Beurlin." Wherever he originated, by 1602 he was playing organ at Horn, northwest of Vienna, where in the course of time he built a new instrument. Later in the decade he became organist of the Protestant school in Steyr, Styria, in which district he built several more organs. None of his instruments have survived. In 1625 the Catholics ran him out of town, and all trace of him is lost thereafter. In his Styrian period he published a book of Lieder (Weltspiegel, 1613) and three of dances. He was one of the first, if not the first, to arrange his dances in four-movement variation suites (dance-paduana-intrada-galliard), the last three dances being variants of the first. In the last of the dance volumes, of 1625, he scores for two melody instruments and continuo, thus foreshadowing the German trio sonata. Both his songs and his dances are intended for social use.

[341] ROSSI, Salamone (Rôs'-sē, Sà-là-mō'-nā)
STRING PLAYER
BORN: Mantua, August 19, 1570
DIED: c. 1630

One of the first Jewish musicians to make a name for himself in the history of Western music, the "Ebreo di Mantova" sometimes called himself by his Hebrew name, Shlomo Me-ha-Adumim. Though he seems to have been only what the Musicians' Union calls a "steady extra performer" at the Mantuan court, he obviously won the admiration of its rulers, and Duke Vincenzo specifically excused him from wearing the yellow badge mandatory for persons of his faith. It is uncertain just what instrument or instruments he played; some think him to have been a violinist. He had a sister who was a virtuoso

singer and was popularly known as "Madama Europa," after her role in Guarini's comedy L'Idropica, on the music for which Rossi collaborated (with Claudio Monteverdi [333] among others). Attempts to connect the composer with other Mantuan Rossis, whether Jewish or Christian, have drawn a blank. Rossi may have been connected with a local Jewish theatrical company. In 1617 he again collaborated with Monteverdi on a sacra rappresentazione entitled La Maddalena. He is last heard of in 1628, when he published a collection of "madrigaletti"—vocal duets with accompaniment, in the new style. In 1630 the city was sacked by Austrian troops, who brought a plague epidemic with them. Rossi presumably died of, or during, these horrors, though it is possible that he escaped to Venice.

After bringing out a book of three-part canzonette in 1589, Rossi published five books of madrigals between 1600 and 1622. Much has been made of the fact that the last four have "organ bass," or continuo, parts, but it has been suggested that this probably merely reflects current practice and is not a true innovation. Otherwise, the works themselves are pleasant but rather conservative. (Book five is, however, represented now only by the continuo part.) Much also has been made of his collection Hashirim asher lish'lomo (The Songs of Solomon—or Salamone!). But despite the language of the texts (Psalms and such), there is nothing particularly "Jewish" about them. The four books of instrumental music (1607–23), which contain variously "sonate, sinfonie, gagliarde, brandi, e corrente," are, like the madrigaletti, more in the modern style, and with their use of two melody instruments with continuo, they seem to look ahead to the so-called trio sonata. Rossi also holds some interest as a developer of variation form, often using for his basis both popular Italian tunes and songs from the ghetto. It is interesting that Vincent d'Indy [1462], self-proclaimed anti-Semite, was one of Rossi's first modern editors.

RECORDINGS: The New York Pro Musica Antiqua has recorded a Rossi anthology.

[342] ALVARADO, Diego de (Ȧl-vȧ-rȧ'-thō, Dē-ā'-gō dā)
ORGANIST
BORN: c. 1570
DIED: Lisbon, February 12, 1643

Appointed a court musician to Philip III of Spain c. 1600, Alvarado was installed in 1602 in the Portuguese court in Lisbon (the Spaniards being temporarily rulers of Portugal at the time). He was still in place when John V, "the Fortunate," seized the throne for Portugal in 1640. Of his music, only a couple of organ pieces have survived.

[343] BATESON, Thomas
ORGANIST, SINGER
BORN: c. 1570
DIED: Dublin, March 1630

Presumably a Cheshireman, Bateson married in the early 1590s, sired a son named John (b. 1592), and became organist of Chester Cathedral in 1599. His duties also included maintenance of his instrument. Between 1603 and 1608 the Batesons produced at least three more children—Tom Jr., Jane, and Sarah. Between Tom and Jane, publisher Thomas East brought out Bateson's first book of madrigals, including "When Oriana Walked," which, he noted, had arrived too late for inclusion in *The Triumphes of Oriana*. In 1609, Bateson moved his tribe to Dublin, where he had secured a position as singer and organist at Christ Church Cathedral. Perhaps he was drawn by the educational advantages, for in 1612 he took a B.Mus. (said to be the first) from Trinity College. He published his second and last madrigal book in 1618, and was awarded an M.A. in 1622, by which time he is said to have been promoted to choirmaster at Christ Church. And that is all we know of Thomas Bateson, save that he died two weeks before his rent came due.

For a time ranked among the best of the English madrigalists, Bateson is now seen rather as a competent and often appealing craftsman who shows flashes of originality but lacks real daring and individuality. He seems to have had a preference for poetry of the pastoral-mythological-Anacreontic variety, though occasionally he sets more demanding stuff.

RECORDINGS: The Randolph Singers have devoted an LP side to his madrigals.

[344] CARLETON, Nicholas
BORN: c. 1570
DIED: Beoley, Worcestershire, 1630

Carleton (or Carlton) is in no wise to be identified with the slightly earlier Richard Carlton [293]. A sometime chorister associated with St. Paul's Cathedral, London, and a friend of Thomas Tomkins [365], he left few traces, musical or otherwise. A handful of keyboard pieces survive in a British Mu-

seum ms. (once the property of Tomkins), including *A Verse for Two to Play upon one Virginall,* one of the earliest known four-hand pieces.

[345] CIMA, Giovanni Paolo (Chē'-mà, Jō-vàn'-nē Pà'-ō-lō)
ORGANIST, CHOIR DIRECTOR
BORN: c. 1570
DIED: after 1622

Cima was one of two musical brothers, both active in Milanese church music. Andrea (dates unknown) was organist at Santa Maria della Rosa and then at Santa Maria delle Grazie (in whose refectory the remains of Leonardo da Vinci's *Last Supper* are to be found). Giovanni Paolo was *maestro di cappella* and organist at San Celso (some accounts say the cathedral) in Milan. He published some motets and a *Mass,* but his most interesting works are instrumental. In 1602 he brought out a volume of organ *ricercari* and followed it four years later with another of *ricercari* and *canzone,* with an appendix on how to tune a clavichord. His 1610 miscellany is particularly notable in that it contains one of the earliest trio sonatas and the first sonata for violin and continuo to be so specified. Andrea wrote motets, a *Mass,* and a few instrumental pieces.

[346] COSYN, Benjamin
ORGANIST
BORN: c. 1570
DIED: after 1652

Benjamin Cosyn may have been a son or nephew of the musician John Cosyn who died in London in 1609, but otherwise nothing is known of him before 1622, when he was organist at the school known as Dulwich College in the purlieus of south London. In 1626 he became the first organist at the Charterhouse, the charity-school established in the former Carthusian monastery in London. When, in 1623, the Puritans banned organs as "heathenish" (save for those saved for the delectation of Oliver Cromwell, an organ fancier), they kicked him out, but later granted him a small pension of concern for his age and infirmity. He is best remembered as the compiler of the Cosyn *Virginal Book* (British Museum). He also added a number of works to a ms. begun by John Bull (Bibliothèque Nationale). In both volumes several pieces are of his own composition. He also left a couple of sacred vocal works.

[347] ERBACH, Christian (Âr'-bàkh, Krēst'-yàn)
ORGANIST, POLITICIAN
BORN: Gau-Algesheim, c. 1570
DIED: Augsburg, summer 1635

A second-generation representative of the South German organ school, which took its cues from the Venetians, Erbach walked in the footsteps of first-generation Hans Leo Hassler [320]. Born near Mainz, he entered the service of the Fugger family in Augsburg in the 1590s. In 1602 he succeeded Hassler as town organist and head of the Stadtpfeifer Guild. In 1614 he was made, concurrently, assistant organist at the cathedral and moved up to the head organist's job in 1625. His numerous pupils included two *Kapellmeisters* of the cathedral. In 1631 he was appointed to the city council but was ousted the next year when the invading Swedes put in their own men. He was dismissed from his municipal post in June 1635 and died sometime that summer. Erbach left a considerable number of both sacred and instrumental compositions. The first in particular show Venetian influence.

[348] FARMER, John
ORGANIST, SINGER
BORN: c. 1570
DIED: after 1601

Farmer enters the pages of history "in youth" with the 1591 publication of his *Divers and Sundry Waies of two parts in one . . . vpon one playn Song,* in which he shows off his ability at canon-writing. The following year he was a major contributor to the psalms of Thomas East. In 1595 he makes an appearance *in propria persona* as newly appointed organist and master of the boys at Christ Church Cathedral in Dublin. By the following year he had been shifted to the choir. Apparently there was something uncongenial about the place, for by July 1597 he had gone AWOL and was being notified that if he did not return immediately his job would be forfeit. Perhaps things were no better in the outside world, for he obeyed. However, two years later he got leave to go to London (perhaps in connection with the publication of his only book of madrigals). This time he did not return, but settled on Broad Street. The cathedral gave up on him and replaced him. Both his publications are dedicated to Edward de Vere, the hotheaded and free-spending Earl of Oxford, who, according to some, wrote Shakespeare's plays, but it is not known whether Farmer was actually in his employ or merely optimistic.

The last we hear of the composer is by way of the madrigal "Fair nymphs, I Heard One Telling" contributed to *The Triumphes of Oriana,* 1601. His religious pieces (in Thomas East's collection) have been admired for their clarity and simplicity. His madrigals are skillful but minor, though "Fair Phyllis I Saw Sitting" is very well known.

[349] GREAVES, Thomas
LUTENIST
BORN: c. 1570 (?)
DIED: after 1604

In the dedication to his only known publication, Greaves tells us in 1604 that he was lutenist to Sir Henry Pierpont (or Pierrepoint, as he spells it). The latter lived on an estate in Nottinghamshire, and his wife was a cousin of the composer Michael Cavendish. The publication *Songes of Sundrie Kindes* is just that; it contains 21 works including ayres, consort songs, and madrigals.

[350] GRILLO, Giovanni Battista (Gril'-lō, Jō-vàn'-nē Bàt-tēs'-tà)
ORGANIST
BORN: c. 1570 (?)
DIED: Venice, 1622

After a period at the Styrian court at Graz, Austria, Grillo was elected in 1612 to the post of organist of the Scuola Grande di San Rocco in Venice. He also served in the same capacity (apparently concurrently) at Santa Madonna dell'Orto and from 1619 at St. Mark's (as number-one organist). It is evident from his collection of sacred *concerti* and *symphoniae* that he was strongly influenced by Giovanni Gabrieli [286], with whom he is thought to have studied.

[351] GUÉDRON, Pierre (Gwā-drôn', Pē-âr')
SINGER, TEACHER, ADMINISTRATOR
BORN: Normandy, c. 1570
DIED: c. 1620

In his teens Guédron was a chorister in the chapel of Louis II de Lorraine, Cardinal de Guise, murdered in prison in 1588 by order of Henry III. Evidently His Majesty did not hold prior associations against the musician, since he took him into his own service. After Henry was himself done in by the monk Jacques Clément a year later, his successor, Henry IV, elevated Guédron to the post of singing teacher to the vocalists of the royal chamber. After that he went right on up the ladder. In 1601 he succeeded Claude Le Jeune [211] as composer to the secular arm of the King's Music *(La Chambre du Roi),* and by 1617 he was in full charge of the court music. His chief duty was to provide music for, and oversee, the court ballets, those specially French amalgams of dance and song that were to lead to the Lullian opera (see 517). King Henry tried his hand at one himself. Guédron's forte was the *air du cour,* France's contribution to the then current fashion for accompanied solo song, and her answer to the Italian monody and the English ayre. Its components were, not unsurprisingly, wit, good taste, and the quality of a dry wine. Guédron helped put it on the map as a genre of its own (rather than, as so often previously, an arrangement of the polyphonic *chanson).* The *récits* (recitatives) he wrote for the ballets are more dramatic and less tuneful but avoid the display of their Italian counterparts. He published 5 books of airs, and his son-in-law, Anthoine Boësset [423], brought out a sixth after his death. Generally Guédron's accompaniments are written out, but he makes a few pussyfooting stabs at continuo.

[352] LUPO, Thomas
    BORN: c. 1570
    DIED: London, January 1628

The Lupos, six viol players, migrated en masse from Milan to England around 1540 and found work at the court of Henry VIII. Thomas was the son of Joseph, né Gioseffo or Giuseppe, and the nephew of Ambrose, né Ambrogio. He became a court musician to Queen Elizabeth on the death of his uncle in 1591 and served until his own demise thirty-seven years later. He carried on the family performing tradition, probably as a violinist, since he was at one point Composer to the Violins. He left some anthems and motets, a small handful of secular vocal works, and a large number of consort pieces. It has been concluded that some of this output was not written by one or another musician of the same name, as it was once said to have been.

[353] NICHOLSON, Richard
    TEACHER, ORGANIST
    BORN: c. 1570 (?)
    DIED: Oxford, 1639

Nicholson was appointed organist and put in charge of the choirboys at Magdalen College, Oxford, in 1595, a year before the university awarded him a B.Mus. Thirty years

after the latter event, still in harness at Magdalen, he became the first Lecturer in Music at the university, thanks to the generosity of William Heather, who endowed the chair. He resigned his Magdalen posts shortly before he died. Academic publication apparently not having attained the importance it is presently said to have, all of Nicholson's extant works were left in manuscript. They include anthems, madrigals, consort songs, and a few instrumental pieces. A sort of three-voice madrigal cycle is a genre piece representing the wooing, marriage, and subsequent history of a country couple, Johan and Joan. Nicholson also contributed a madrigal to *The Triumphes of Oriana.*

[354] PELLEGRINI, Vincenzo (Pel-lä-grē'-nē, Vēn-chänt'-zō)
    CHOIRMASTER, ORGANIST, PRIEST
    BORN: Pesaro, c. 1570 (?)
    DIED: Milan, 1631

Organist of the cathedral in his hometown, Pellegrini became choirmaster of that of Milan at the end of 1611. He served there for twenty years, reportedly succumbing to the plague—none too soon for some of his detractors, who felt he had done a miserable job. Apart from a considerable body of Masses and other sacred works, he left a volume (indicated as "Book I") of organ *canzone.*

[355] PEREZ BOCANEGRA, Juan (Pereth' Bō-kà-nä'-grà, Hwàn)
    BORN: c. 1570 (?)
    DIED: Andahuaylas, Peru, after 1631

It is known that Perez Bocanegra worked for a time in Cuzco, Peru, and afterward in Andahuaylas, about sixty miles to the westward. His piece *Hanacpachap cussicuinin,* to a text in the Quechua tongue, published at Lima in 1631 is thought to be the first piece of polyphonic choral music published in the western hemisphere.

[356] PILKINGTON, Francis
    SINGER, CLERGYMAN
    BORN: c. 1570
    DIED: Chester, 1638

Pilkington took a B.Mus. from Lincoln College, Oxford, in 1595, for which he said he had studied the (usual) sixteen years. Shortly after the turn of the century he had found a place in the cathedral choir at Chester, no doubt with the aid of William

Stanley, Earl of Derby (brother of the poetic earl Ferdinando Stanley), whose family had patronized his own. In 1604 his first book of ayres was dedicated to that worthy. Pilkington obviously knew that other Chester composer Thomas Bateson [343], for they set some of the same texts. Around 1612 Pilkington seems to have heard the call and entered holy orders, and by 1614 had been ordained and was serving as curate at Holy Trinity Church in Chester. He seems to have celebrated by publishing a second work, a collection of madrigals. One of these, *When Oriana walkt,* is a posthumous Oriana madrigal, not included in the collection (Bateson's variant is), but to be found in the Randolph Singers' recording of *The Triumphes of Oriana.* He also contributed to that year to Sir William Leighton's anthem collection *Teares or Lamentacions.* He went on to become curate of St. Bridget's, then of St. Martin's (both in Chester), and finally rector of the village church in nearby Aldford in 1631. He was also precentor at the cathedral from 1623. In 1624 he published his second book of madrigals. Details of his death and burial are unknown. He had a large family, and two of his sons, Zacharias and Thomas, had some small claim to musical fame. Pilkington's songs and madrigals range from pleasant to superb. (The texts lean rather heavily to mythological and pastoral subjects.) He also left a few instrumental pieces. RECORDINGS: The favorite song among recording artists appears to be "Come, Sweet Nymphs," but a few others grace various anthologies.

[357] ROBINSON, Thomas
LUTENIST
BORN: c. 1570 (?)
DIED: after 1609

His two extant publications tell us all we know of Thomas Robinson. His father was a retainer of the first Lord Burghley, and he himself had been in the household of Burghley's elder son and successor, Thomas Cecil, later Earl of Exeter. At some point before 1603 Robinson was, like Dowland [316], a musician of the Danish court at Elsinore. In the year noted he brought out his *Schoole of Musicke* in the form of a dialogue between an anxious parent and a reassuring teacher —useful for learning the lute, orpharion, and bass viol, and for teaching oneself to read prick song (i.e., musical notation). It was a splendidly practical treatise and included a number of pieces for the lute. Another Robinson work licensed for publication in 1603 as *Medulla Musicke,* has van-

ished. Six years later Robinson made his last appearance on the stage of history with his *New Citharen Lessons* (for the wire-strung citterns), also in dialogue form. In both books the style is informal and amusing. Robinson notes, for example, that "Painefull playing causeth many odde anticke faces."

[358] RONTANI, Rafaello (Rōn-tä'-nē, Räf-fä-yäl'-lō)
CHOIRMASTER
BORN: c. 1570 (?)
DIED: Rome, 1622

Between 1610 and 1615, Rontani was employed in Florence in some capacity as a musician by Antonio Medici, a bastard son of Francesco I and Bianca Capello. For the remainder of his life he was in Rome as choir director at San Giovanni de' Fiorentini and as chief musician to a Duke Sforza. (Question: Which Sforza? The male line ended in 1535.) In the latter period he published six books of songs for one, two, and three voices and continuo, called *Varie musiche.* Though his music obviously had some popularity, to judge from reprints and anthologies, he was a minor figure generally outside the tradition of his day. He has some importance in the development of the cantata by way of "strophic variation" songs.

[359] VULPIUS, Melchior (Vo͞olp'-yo͞os, Mel'-khē-ôr)
TEACHER, LUTHERAN CANTOR
BORN: Wasungen, c. 1570
DIED: Weimar, early August 1615

The Vulpius family was, before Melchior's generation, called Fuchs. (A later Weimar representative, Christiane Vulpius, became mistress and later wife to the poet Goethe.) Born in straitened circumstances in a small town near Meiningen, Melchior Vulpius was educated in the local Latin school and then at Speyer. In 1589 he became a sort of teaching assistant in the Latin school at Schleusingen (south of Erfurt). By 1592 he had risen to the lowest grade of teacher and was the institution's *de facto* cantor. After scrubbing along on the pittance they paid him for four years, he found his talents better rewarded in Weimar, where he fulfilled the same functions. It was there that he published his highly successful updated version of Heinrich Faber's 1548 musical treatise *Compendium musicae latino germanicum* (1608). Enormously prolific, Vulpius left several collections of Latin motets and some occasional works. Of more interest, however, are his

German religious works, which include a *St. Matthew Passion*, featuring a tenor evangelist and choral outbursts from the *turba* (crowd). His *Sprüche* (Sunday Gospel proverbs) is a pioneering collection, but even better musically are his many hymns, some of which contain some of the finest and most familiar chorale tunes.

[360] **PRAETORIUS, Michael** (Prī-tô'-rē-ōōs, Mēkh'-à-el)
CHOIRMASTER, ORGANIST, SECRETARY, THEORIST
BORN: Kreuzberg an der Werra, Thuringia, February 15, 1571
DIED: Wolfenbüttel, February 15, 1621

Apparently unrelated to the various other Praetoriuses of musical history (see 298, 420), Michael's family was, like theirs, originally Schulze or Schultheiss. (A *Schultheiss*, with its various contractions, was a village mayor—something less than a burgomaster; the Latinization represents something a bit grander.) His father, Michael, was a Lutheran parson, who had taught under Johann Walther [139] in the Latin school at Torgau, where he married. He was later run out of town for belonging to the wrong wing of the church. Young Michael's birth date (in a small town near Eisenach) is traditionally given as above, much being made of his dying on his (fiftieth?) birthday, but it may have been a year or two earlier or later. When he was still an infant, the Schultheisses ran into further Christian tolerance and went back to Torgau, where the boy attended the Latin school, in whose choir he chirped. He left in 1582 to study theology at the University of Frankfurt an der Oder, which he did, with interruptions, for a time. In 1587 he was appointed organist at the Marienkirche in that city and held the post for the better part of three years. Despite assertions that he then entered the service of Heinrich Julius, Duke of Braunschweig-Wolfenbüttel and Prince-Bishop of Halberstadt, the records show the connection dating from 1595 at the earliest, leaving six years a blank. He was featured the following year at a sort of all-German organ festival held in connection with the dedication of a new organ his master had had built at Gröningen. Early in the new century he took time off to travel to Regensburg, and perhaps elsewhere, but he had settled down at Wolfenbüttel by 1603, when he married Anna Lakemacher there. A year later, the duke, who thought highly of him, added the duties and wages of *Kapellmeister* to those of organist. Praetorius quickly won himself a

reputation as an excellent rebuilder of run-down musical organizations, and Heinrich Julius apparently loaned him out to others in such need—e.g., Landgrave Moritz of Hesse-Kassel.

In 1613 the duke died, and his successor, Friedrich Ulrich, who seems to have had no special interest in music, sent Praetorius off for a year at the Dresden court, at the request of the Elector Johann Georg I (who, a year later, using his feudal clout, managed to pry Heinrich Schütz [412] away from Landgraf Moritz). In 1614 Friedrich Ulrich made Praetorius prior of the monastery of Ringelheim (splendid income, no duties or residence requirement), but the appointment apparently did not bring him home. Instead, he continued to work for the elector and also took on the post of episcopal *Kapellmeister* at Magdeburg. He was also, from time to time, at Halle, Sondershausen, Kassel, Leipzig, Nuremberg, Bayreuth, and heaven knows where else, doctoring sick chapels and helping out with musical ceremonies and festivities. As a result, both the Wolfenbüttel chapel and his health suffered, and when he finally tottered into town in 1620, his shocked friends said, *"Der alter grauer Schultheiss scheint nicht wie er war!"* (The old gray mayor's not what he used to be!) He was, in fact, too ill to resume his job, and died a few months later, leaving two sons and a fortune, most of which last he willed to charity.

Apparently largely self-taught, Praetorius was extraordinarily productive and one of the giants of the early German Baroque. Most people probably know him only as the composer of the Christmas hymn *"Es ist ein Ros entsprungen"* (usually sung here as "Lo! How a Rose E'er Blooming"). It comes from a 9-volume work called *Musae Sionae (The Muses of Sion)*, a sort of encyclopedia of the chorale in all its then possible manifestations, from simple harmonizations to vast frescoes. There Praetorius notes that the chorale may be used in three major ways: (1) motet style, with the tune passing from voice to voice; (2) madrigal style, with segments of the melody used thematically; (3) as *cantus firmus*. It is perhaps no exaggeration to say that with Praetorius the genre came of age. The *Musae Sionae* was published piecemeal between 1605 and 1610. Almost all of his published composition dates from the busy decade 1605–15. It was by no means his last word on sacred music, being followed by several further volumes of motets, hymns, litanies, epithalamia, sacred songs for children, etc.

As a man who thought big, Praetorius also projected a secular counterpart of the

Musae Sionae, designated as *Musa Aonia (The Aonian Muse).* Whether he composed more of it, only the (published) 2-volume *Terpsichore* has survived. It contains more than 300 dances, mostly French ones garnered from the Wolfenbüttel dancing master Antoine Emeraud, though some are drawn from other sources, and about 80 settings are collaborations of Praetorius and his violinist-colleague Pierre Francisque Caroubel. Set for instruments specified only by the clefs used, this collection gives an invaluable picture of the popular dance music of the day.

Praetorius' most important and ambitious work is his *Syntagma musicum,* intended to be a survey of all music, past, present, and possibly future. The first volume, largely of antiquarian interest, is a historical survey from a 1614 viewpoint. Volume two, *Organographia,* is an exhaustive study of available musical instruments—how they are played, how used in combination, and so on. (There is a detailed segment on the organ.) It provides us with one of our most important sources of knowledge about early performance practice. Volume three deals with forms and techniques, with some attention to national characteristics. Volume four, on counterpoint, either was never written or is lost.

RECORDINGS: Apart from the expectable representation in recorded anthologies, there are a few LPs dedicated in whole or in part to excerpts from *Terpsichore,* and even fewer to *Musae Sionae.* The organist Wolfgang Dallmann has recorded an *intégrale* of the few scattered organ pieces. But the surface has not even been scratched, phonographically speaking.

[361] WARD, John
CIVIL SERVANT
BORN: Canterbury, c. September 8, 1571
DIED: summer 1638

After growing up in Canterbury, where he probably sang at the cathedral, Ward moved to London, found a job in the Exchequer, and married Thomasina Clee, who bore him three children called John, Thomas, and Susan. He evidently came into the good graces of his boss, Sir Henry Fanshawe, Remembrancer of the Exchequer (who presided over the Court of Exchequer). Sir Henry also employed Ward as a household musician, saw to it that he profited from his office, and on his death in 1616 left him all his musical instruments "except the great Wind Instrument in my howse in Warwyck Lane." (Whatever that may have been, it was not Lady Fanshawe.) By the time of his own

death, Ward had acquired an estate at Ilford Magna in Essex, held the rank of attorney in the Exchequer, was reckoned a gentleman, and was obviously a success. In 1613 he published a book of generally superior madrigals, with an understandably fulsome dedication to Sir Henry. He also left some anthems and a few other sacred pieces, and a large quantity of consort pieces, all indicating him to have been one of the more talented composers of his time.

[362] WIDMANN, Erasmus (Vēd′-màn, E-ràz′-mōōs)
ORGANIST, TEACHER, CHOIRMASTER, POET
BORN: Schwäbisch Hall, c. September 15, 1572
DIED: Rothenburg ob der Tauber, October 31, 1634

Educated in the town of his birth on the *Romantische Strasse* and proficient in voice, winds, strings, and keyboards, Widmann later (in 1590) graduated from the University of Tübingen. Then, for reasons that remain obscure, he migrated to Styria and worked there as an organist, at first at Eisenerz, then at Graz. All his life Widmann had the reputation of being something of a swinger, and in 1598 he found himself in trouble with at least three young Graz ladies, one of whom, Margarethe Ehetreiber, he married that June. Later that year Archduke Ferdinand cracked down on Protestants and Widmann headed back for his birthplace, where he became town cantor. In 1602 he moved into the great Hohenlohe Castle at nearby Weikersheim as teacher (academic) to the *Jünglinge* of Count Wolfgang and general musical factotum. Later Wolfgang relieved him of his teaching duties, but after the count died in 1610, demands on his time and energies became even more severe, and in 1613 he became town cantor in Rothenburg, where his duties were scarcely less exacting. In 1614 he also took on that of playing the organ at the Jakobikirche. A poet and lyricist of no mean ability, he was crowned laureate by his fellow townsmen. He survived the siege of the city in the Thirty Years War and no doubt saw it saved from pillage by Tilly's troops in 1631 when the burgomaster downed the heroic draught of beer commemorated annually in the local play *Der Meistertrunk.* But plague came on the heels of war and took first Margarethe and daughter and then Widmann himself. A son, Georg Friedrich, survived as an organist.

Widmann's music is designed for general use, a fact reflected in his numerous hymns, songs, and dances, though some of his early work is contrapuntally fairly demanding. The dances are particularly interesting, and show movement in the direction of the suite. Those in his miscellany *Musikalischer Tugendtspiegel (A Musical Mirror for Virtue)* are rather charmingly given the names of girls (e.g., "Anna," "Agathe," "Clara," etc.). Like his contemporary Melchior Vulpius [359], he also published a *Musicae praecepta latino-germanica* in 1616.

[363] BIANCIARDI, Francesco (Byán-chârʹ-dē, Frȧn-châʹ-skō)
ORGANIST, CHOIRMASTER, THEORIST
BORN: Casole d'Elsa, c. 1572
DIED: Siena, spring or summer 1607

Tradition says that Bianciardi was born in the *rocca,* or citadel, at Siena. If so, the place must have been the fortress (since replaced by the public gardens) erected in 1557 by Cosimo I de' Medici, the new ruler thanks to Philip II of Spain, for no earlier bastion was still in running order. Recent sources, however, suggest (rather gingerly) the Tuscan village noted above, which seems to suit Bianciardi's own statement that his origins were humble. He may have studied in Rome with Palestrina [201], whom he rather sedulously imitated. He served as organist and then as *maestro di cappella* at Siena Cathedral. A leading member of the Accademia degl' Intronati, he is said also to have founded the Accademia Senese. Adriano Banchieri [337] thought highly of him. Besides his motets, Masses, and vesper psalms, he wrote some sacred *canzonette* and some madrigals. He was a pioneer in the use of continuo and wrote a brochure explaining its principles.

[364] LOEFFELHOLZ VON COLBERG, Christoph (Löfʹ-fel-hōlts fun Kōlʹ-berg, Krēsʹ-tōf)
POLITICIAN
BORN: Nuremberg, December 4, 1572
DIED: Nuremberg, January 20, 1619

Of noble family, Loeffelholz grew up in Prague, studied in Altdorf, and spent most of the rest of his life in local government in his birthplace. In 1585 he compiled or completed, in the colorist manner, a manuscript organ tablature of vocal works and dances, both German and foreign.

[365] TOMKINS, Thomas
ORGANIST, TEACHER
BORN: St. David's, Wales, 1572
DIED: Martin Hussingtree, c. June 8, 1656

Tomkins was the son of the former Margaret Pore and Thomas Tomkins, a Cornishman, singer, organist, and master of the boys in the local cathedral. His elder brother was also named Thomas, a fact that must have occasioned considerable confusion at the family dining table. Thomas I was for a time a chorister at the cathedral, but he was evidently what is now known as a "discipline problem," was kicked out, ran away to sea, and died aboard the *Revenge* when that little ship took on the Spanish navy. The brothers also had a sister named Bridget. When Margaret Tomkins died, the father remarried and sired seven other children, of whom John, Giles, and Robert undertook musical careers. Thomas II seems to have studied with William Byrd [248] and may have been a chorister in the Chapel Royal. At twenty-four he became organist of Worcester Cathedral, acquiring into the bargain his predecessor's widow, Alice (or maybe Eleanor) Patrick. By the turn of the century he must have been fairly well known, for he contributed a madrigal, "The Nymphs and Satyrs Tripping," to *The Triumphes of Oriana.* Six years later Magdalen College, Oxford, conferred on him a B.Mus. He seems to have known more about building organs than how to play them, for he was involved in some organ building at Worcester in 1613–14, and again in 1639–40. At some point before the end of June 1620 he became a Gentleman of the Chapel Royal, and soon succeeded Edmund Hooper as junior organist with Orlando Gibbons [408], to whose place he was elevated when Gibbons died in 1625. Exactly what happened next in terms of his progress is confused. He either did or did not succeed Alfonso Ferrabosco the Younger [375] as composer-in-ordinary on the latter's death in 1628. Subsequent evidence finds him mostly in Worcester. In 1646 Cromwell's men destroyed the organ and banned further use of the choir. Tomkins apparently continued to live in the town until his eighty-second year, when he moved in with his son Nathaniel (1599–1681), a divine and musician who lived not far from Worcester.

As one might expect of a Byrd pupil, Tomkins, especially in his large body of church music and his consort pieces, looks back to the polyphonic past and is in a sense a "last Renaissance musician." Many of the sacred works—five services (three in forward-looking verse-style with solo parts and organ accompaniment) and nearly a hundred anthems (the best are of the "full" variety)—were published, under the probable editorship of Nathaniel Tomkins, as *Musica Deo sacra* in 1668. The *Songs* of 1622 is a mixed bag, containing Morleyesque balletts, pastoral and erotic madrigals, and scriptural pieces. An earlier tendency to dismiss the collection as a sort of last gasp of the English madrigal seems to have been supplanted by the view that many of the pieces are deeply felt and highly expressive (e.g., "When David Heard That Absalom Was Dead"—a lament for black sheep brother Tom?).

Tomkins was also a fine keyboard composer, though an "old-fashioned one"—the last of the virginal school. Though few of his pieces found their way into the great virginal manuscripts, a number of them have survived in Tomkins' own hand.

RECORDINGS: He has been rather well treated on records—for example a two-LP collection of vocal and consort works under the direction of Denis Stevens, an anthology of sacred music (Bernard Rose), a disc of the songs (Margaret Field-Hyde), and a side of keyboard pieces (Thurston Dart).

[366] PEERSON, Martin
KEYBOARDIST, TEACHER
BORN: March, Cambridgeshire, c. 1572
DIED: London, mid-January 1651

Peerson's parents, hight Thomas and Margaret, were wed and settled down in the fen country in 1570. But their idyll was brief, for three years later Thomas was (presumably) dead and Margaret remarried. Nothing else is known of Martin's first thirty years, though he may have been for a time in the household of Sir Fulke Greville, first Baron Brooke, sonneteer, and close friend to Sir Philip Sidney. Peerson's first known composition was a song for the Mayday masque presented at the new Stuart court in 1604. On at least one occasion he was in trouble with the authorities for failure to attend the prescribed form of worship, and his several Latin motets also hint that he was a Catholic. In 1609 he married a widow named Amy Wiles, with whom he made his home in the London suburb of Stoke Newington. Four years later he received a B.Mus. from Lincoln College, Oxford. A dozen years later he was master of the boys at St. Paul's, London, in whose precincts he took up his lodgings. He was dislodged by what might be described as urban renewal in 1633, the year Amy died. However, he continued to serve at the cathedral until the Puritan upheaval ended musical activities there—though he continued on as almoner until the end of his

life. However he acquired it, he left his second wife a good deal of money and could even ask that a hundred pounds be invested to buy bread for the poor. He was buried in the cathedral (which was, of course, the old one).

Peerson is probably best known today for two of his 4 extant keyboard pieces, *The Primerose* and *The Falle of the Leafe*. He published 2 volumes of songs, *Private Musicke* (in 1620) and *Mottects or Grave Chamber Musique* (in 1630). Both call for accompaniments by a viol consort, but in the first Peerson includes the advice that these instruments may be replaced by virginals. The second contains a number of settings of Greville. There are also extant some fantasias for consort, 11 Latin motets, and 21 English anthems (several defective).

[367] GIBBONS, Ellis
BORN: Cambridge, November 1573
DIED: May 1603

Ellis Gibbons was the third son of William Gibbons, previously a wait (municipal musician) at Oxford, but at the time of Ellis' birth holding a similar post at Cambridge. Three other sons, Edward (1568–c. 1650), Ferdinando, and Orlando [408], also took up music. Of Ellis we know only that his wife was named Joan, that he acquired property, that he contributed 2 madrigals ("Long Live Fair Oriana!" and "Round About Her Charret") to *The Triumphes of Oriana*, and that he died at twenty-nine (place unknown).

[368] MARSON, George
ORGANIST, TEACHER, PRIEST
BORN: Worcester, c. 1573
DIED: Canterbury, February 3, 1632

In the past sixty years research has given a human shape to the name of the composer of "The Nymphs and Shepherds Danced Lavoltas," contributed by George Marson to *The Triumphes of Oriana*. A 1598 B.Mus. from Trinity College, Cambridge, he married the following year and accepted an appointment as organist and master of the boys at Canterbury Cathedral. Five years later he was ordained and became rector of the church of St. Mary Magdalene in Canterbury and of the village church in nearby Nackington, the while he continued to serve at the cathedral. He was obviously in ill health in his last years and gave over his rectorate to his son, John, four months before he died. Besides his one published madrigal, he left some Anglican church music in manuscript.

[369] WILBYE, John
LUTENIST, VIOL PLAYER, FARMER
BORN: Diss, Norfolk, March 1574
DIED: Colchester, autumn 1638

That Wilbye was really an Italian import called Gualtiero "Che" Sarà, who anglicized himself to "Wat Wilbye," is a vile canard, perhaps promoted by the Muscovy Company. His father Matthew was a successful tanner of Diss, in Norfolk near the Suffolk border, where earlier in the century the poet John Skelton had been parson. Matt Wilbye may have been musical, for he left his son a lute. Whatever his musical background, at nineteen John was taken into the household of Sir Thomas Kytson, some twenty miles away at Bury St. Edmunds, and put in charge of matters musical. He was given his own quarters and apparently the family's affection. When Sir Thomas went up to London, where he maintained a city home in the parish of Austin Friars, Wilbye often accompanied him. On one such visit in 1598 he saw the first of his two madrigal books through the press. No doubt its appearance accounts for his contribution of "The Lady Oriana" to the *Triumphes* of some three years later. Sir Thomas died in 1602, but Wilbye (whose father died in 1605) stayed on with Lady Elizabeth, who had herself come from near Diss. He brought out his second and last book of madrigals in 1609 and contributed, in or around 1614, 2 anthems to *The Teares and Lamentacions of a Sorrowfull Soule,* a compilation made by Sir William Leighton to alleviate the tedium of debtor's prison, where he was spending some time. The pieces seem to have been his swan song. A year earlier Lady Elizabeth had given him a lease on Sexten's Farm, the best grazing land on the Kytson estates, where he took up sheep farming—not unsuccessfully, to judge from his will. When she died in 1628, Wilbye transferred to the household of her younger daughter, Lady Rivers, at Colchester, where he spent his final decade. He never married. His estate included considerable land and 500 pounds in cash to be divided among some nieces and nephews. He also left his best viol (why, no one knows) to the eight-year-old princeling who would be Charles II.

Wilbye's reputation depends entirely on his 65 madrigals, but it is an impressive reputation, for, rivaled only by Thomas Weelkes [385], he is generally regarded as the finest English practitioner of the genre. His treat-

ment of it has little to do with the Monteverdian avant-garde, despite his liking for solo passages. If his sources are William Byrd's [248] contrapuntalism and Thomas Morley's "Englishness," he is by no means unaware of the madrigalism of such as Luca Marenzio [273], several of whose Englished texts he set. Though he shows great verbal sensitivity, word meanings do not override his music: illustrative touches appear only where it logically allows them. A master of counterpoint and form, he allows neither, on the other hand, to distort the lyrics. The second collection shows a considerable advance over the first.

RECORDINGS: Though no integral recording has yet appeared, several discs have been devoted to Wilbye (e.g., by the Deller Consort, the Wilbye Consort, and the Randolph Singers).

[370] BALLARD, Robert (Bàl-lärd', Rō-bâr')
LUTENIST, TEACHER
BORN: Paris, c. 1575
DIED: 1650 or later

Ballard was the son of Lucrèce and Robert Ballard, the latter Adrian Le Roy's [193] cousin and partner in the most successful music-printing business in France in the late sixteenth century. Young Robert was probably a pupil of Le Roy. At any rate he was an established lutenist by 1600 and published a collection of preludes and dances for the instrument in 1611, which he dedicated to the dowager Queen Marie de Médicis. Evidently the ploy paid off, for a year later the pupil of Le Roy became teacher to *le Roi,* the eleven-year-old Louis XIII. He remained attached to the court in one capacity or another until 1650, when his name drops out of sight.

[371] BATAILLE, Gabriel (Bà-tī', Gà-brē-el')
CLERK, LUTENIST, POET, ADMINISTRATOR
BORN: c. 1575
DIED: Paris, December 17, 1630

At the time of his marriage in 1600, Bataille gave his occupation as *clerc* (to a politician) but was known at court as a lutenist and composer before the reign of Henry IV ended. His rise to eminence was no doubt fostered by the publisher Pierre Ballard, successor to the elder Robert and brother to the younger one [370], who between 1608 and 1615 brought out six of Bataille's *Airs de différents autheurs.* These contained arrangements for voice and lute of polyphonic *airs du cour* (many of them by Pierre Guédron [351]. To these, Bataille's colleague Anthoine Boësset added nine more collections. From 1619 the two of them shared the superintendency of the music of the young queen, Anne of Austria, daughter of Philip III of Spain. Bataille himself was a writer of airs—some of them for court ballets—many of them to be found in his and Boësset's collections. When he died, his post went to his son, Gabriel, who was then only in his midteens. Another son, Pierre, was also a court musician.

[372] BENNET, John
BORN: c. 1575
DIED: after 1614

John Bennet is not to be confused with earlier [59] or later [861] musical John Bennets, however spelled. In the preface to his 1599 collection of madrigals, he routinely protests his youth and dedicates the collection to a Lancashire justice of the peace. This latter fact and his use of West Country dialect in a song "A Borgen's a Borgen" probably indicate him to have come from thereabouts. He was evidently a musician of some repute, for he contributed to *The Triumphes of Oriana*, William Barley's psalter, and Thomas Ravenscroft's treatise *A Brief Discourse of the True (but Neglected) Use of Charact'ring the Degrees*. In this last, Ravenscroft [406] waxes fulsome about Bennet, calling him "a Gentleman admirable for all kindes of *Composures*" and implying that he is nothing less than a genius. Bennet's other known works are a couple of consort songs and an anthem.

[373] COPRARIO, John (Kō-prä′-rē-ō, Jon)
VIOL PLAYER, TEACHER
BORN: c. 1575
DIED: early summer 1626

Not long ago we thought of this composer as Giovanni Coperario, alias John Cooper, but nowadays he is generally listed as above (certainly his own version) and is somewhat gingerly said to have started life as John Cowper. Despite assertions that he changed his name as a result of going to Italy to study, there is no other evidence of such a journey, though he *did* go to the Lowlands in 1603, for purposes that remain obscure. His first known composition was his *Funeral Teares* of 1606, memorializing the death of Charles Blount, Earl of Devonshire. (The

first seven, he notes, are to be sung as accompanied solos.) A year later some of his music was featured at that royal banquet given James I by the Merchant Taylors' Company, at which John Bull [315] won approval by playing the organ for free. Up to at least 1613, Coprario seems pretty clearly to have been in the employ of Sir Robert Cecil, Earl of Salisbury, and of Edward Seymour, Earl of Hertford. As the latter's music master, he taught young William Lawes [463].

Coprario's earliest connection with the royal court seems to date from 1613, when he published his *Songs of Mourning* on the death of Henry, Prince of Wales, and composed music for a masque by Thomas Campion [332] celebrating the marriage of the Princess Elizabeth to Friedrich, Elector of the Palatinate. He went with the wedding party to Heidelberg and made two other trips to Europe in the next four years. Whether or not Coprario taught Charles I, he was, from at least 1622, one of his favorite musicians, with all the rights and privileges, including an excuse from paying certain taxes, appertaining thereto. In 1625 the newly crowned king made him composer-in-ordinary, but he did not survive to enjoy the post for long. In July a year later he was succeeded by the younger Alfonso Ferrabosco [375].

Besides the works noted, Coprario left a number of songs from masques, some *villanelle* and madrigals, and a couple of anthems. But the bulk of his music and the best of it lies in his large output for consort, mostly consisting of fantasias. King Charles thought some of these "incomparable" and loved to play the bass viol part in court chamber-music sessions. In these works, Coprario lightened the English tradition with Italianisms. He seems to have been a pioneer in writing for the lyra viol, and his fantasias for two viole da gamba were apparently something new. He also wrote a little manual of composition, *Rules How to Compose*, probably for Henry Lawes's [444] patron, the Earl of Bridgewater (for whom the poet John Milton and Lawes wrote the masque now known as *Comus*).

RECORDINGS: There are recorded examples of the fantasias, some of consort songs by the Copenhagen Concentus Musicus, and a reading of the *Songs of Mourning* by Martyn Hill.

[374] DECKER, Joachim (Deck′-er, Yō-à′-khēm)
ORGANIST
BORN: Hamburg, c. 1575
DIED: Hamburg, March 15, 1611

Decker was the middle man of three generations of musical Hamburgers. His father, Eberhard, was town cantor, his son Johann organist of the local cathedral. Joachim himself was organist of the Nikolaikirche for the last third of his life. He collaborated with Heinrich Scheidemann [443], Hieronymus Praetorius [298], and the latter's son, Jakob [420], on a popular collection of four-part chorales, the *Melodeyen Gesangbuch* of 1604, which contains 30 pieces by Decker.

[375] FERRABOSCO, Alfonso the Younger (Fer-rȧ-bos'-kō, Al-fon'-sō)
SINGER, VIOL PLAYER
BORN: Greenwich, c. 1575
DIED: Greenwich, March 10, 1628

Unlike his contemporary Coprario, Ferrabosco did not change his name. (Had he done so, it would probably have been "Wildwood.") He was the first English-born member of a Bolognese family that had distinguished itself musically for over a century. His grandfather Domenico (1513–74) was, with Palestrina [201] and a man named Leonardo Barré, one of the three singers kicked out of the Sistine Choir by Pope Paul IV in 1555 for being married. That was a status that seems not to have hampered the activities of Domenico's son Alfonso the Elder (1543–88). He emigrated to England as a youth, bringing with him some of the music of the Italian Renaissance that inspired the likes of Morley, and eventually wangled a lifetime contract as royal musician from Queen Elizabeth, to whose terms that he remain in England he paid not the slightest heed. Indeed, in his wheeling and dealing, his work as spy and counterspy, and his alleged murder of another musician there was sufficient material to fire the English notion of the Italian-as-Machiavel for the next fifty years. When last heard of, he was in Turin serving as musician and food taster to Carlo Emanuele I, Duke of Savoy.

While on the Continent in the early 1570s, Alfonso married a French lady, Suzanne Simon, but she seems to have had nothing to do with the two small children he left with his colleague Gomer van Austerwyke when he skedaddled for good, one of them being the namesake with whom we are concerned here. So far as is known, Austerwyke never was able to reclaim a cent for their keep. When, in 1584, Ferrabosco demanded that his children be shipped to him, the queen refused to give permission. Small matter, for by then he had replaced them with two legitimate ones, discreetly named for the Duke

and Duchess of Savoy. (The duchess was a daughter of Philip II of Spain.)

Evidently the queen took pity on the Ferrabosco waifs, for she settled an annuity on young Alfonso amounting to more than 25 pounds a year, and apparently she also footed the bill for his education. Under James I he served as a member of the King's Violins (ancestral to the modern orchestra) for the rest of his life. In 1604 he was named music master to Henry, Prince of Wales, and, after the latter's premature death in 1612, to his successor, Prince Charles (later Charles I). Coprario also held some such post, but we are not told whether the two men worked in tandem or just how they shared their duties, if that is what they did.

Between 1605 and 1611, Ferrabosco worked closely with Ben Jonson, writing music for many of his most famous masques, on which another collaborator was the great architect and stage designer Inigo Jones. He also wrote the incidental music for Jonson's comedy *Volpone*, which includes the well-known song "Come, My Celia." (It is thought that Ferrabosco may have provided the music for an even more famous Jonson song, "Have You Seene but a Whyte Lilly Grow?") The friendship, though, seems to have ended on a sour note.

Evidently, however, he pleased King James, who granted him and two associates, in 1619, the right to sell sand and gravel dredged from the Thames, plus a handsome rake-off from import and export duties. Under Charles I he succeeded Coprario as composer-in-ordinary and was also given the title of composer to the king. (His combined annual salary and pension, exclusive of the fringe benefits noted above, came to nearly 200 pounds, an enormous wage in those days.) He was succeeded in at least some of his royal posts by Thomas Tomkins. He left three sons, Alfonso III, Henry, and John, all of them royal musicians.

Ferrabosco's book of ayres, from 1609, is to some degree a rehash of masque songs. His other publication of that year, a collection of dances and the like for one or more viols, is of interest in the development of string music. The instrument that Ferrabosco had in mind was the lyra viol, which, to facilitate the playing of chords in double and triple stops, he tuned like the larger viola da gamba; the music is written in lute tablature. The fantasias that he left in manuscript are of even more interest, representing a step further in consort music than had been reached by Coprario. Like him, Ferrabosco also contributed to Sir William Leighton's jail-bred anthology of religious

pieces, *Teares and Lamentacions of a Sorrowfull Soule,* 1614.
RECORDINGS: The songs noted appear in recorded anthologies. Some of the viol pieces have been committed to record by the English Consort of Viols, and the Wenzinger Viol Consort.

[376] FRANCISQUE, Anthoine (Frànsēsk', Àn-twàn')
LUTENIST
BORN: St. Quentin, c. 1575
DIED: Paris, c. October 4, 1605

There is a hint of pathos here. Francisque seems to have conducted his brief career in obscurity. In 1596, in Cambrai, he married an innkeeper's daughter, Marguerite Behour or Bonhour or Bouhour (as she appears in various legal documents); at the time he may have been even younger than his conjectured birth date indicates, since he was described as a "youth" *(jeune fils).* The young couple, after some months, went to Paris to seek their fortune, and in 1600 Anthoine published his lute book, *Le Trésor d'Orphée (Orpheus' Treasure),* dedicating it (apparently tongue-in-cheek) to Henri, Prince de Condé, a gentleman who seems to have spent a good deal of time in hot water not always of his own drawing. In 1605 the composer, described by now as a "master lutenist," died in his house on the Rue Ste. Geneviève in the parish of St. Étienne-du-Mont. There were no children, and the lute book seems to have rested quietly waiting for modern researchers to discover it.

Together with Besard's *Thesaurus harmonicus,* Francisque's *Trésor* is one of the most significant monuments of early French lute music. Written for a nine-course lute (a course is a pair of octave-tuned strings), it consists for the most part of original dances in all the popular forms of the day. These, together with the preludes, point ahead to the dance suites to come. A second point of interest is that whereas transcriptions of songs and the like were the chief material of early lute collections, this one contains only two.

[377] GRANDI, Alessandro (Grän'-dē, Àl-es-sàn'-drō)
CHOIR DIRECTOR, SINGER, TEACHER
BORN: c. 1575
DIED: Bergamo, summer 1630

This Alessandro Grandi is not to be confused (though he has been) with the Alessandro Grandi of Rimini (1638–97), nor with the twentieth-century operatic tenor Alessandro Granda. He operated for twenty years (1597–1617) in Ferrara as music director of the Accademia della Morte, then of the Accademia dello Spirito Santo, and finally of the cathedral. In 1617 he was taken into Claudio Monteverdi's [333] choir at St. Mark's in Venice as a singer. A year later he was appointed singing teacher at the Seminario, and in 1620 he became Monteverdi's assistant at a fairly handsome salary. But his inferior position cramped his opportunity to compose, and in 1627 he moved on to Bergamo, where he took charge of music at Santa Maria Maggiore. The change may have been a mistake, however, for three years later Grandi and his entire family were wiped out by plague.

Said to have studied with Giovanni Gabrieli [286], Grandi was certainly an admirer and practitioner of the new music. He himself was highly respected as a composer, both at home and in the Germanies. He seems to have reveled in the new *concertato* approach to church music, and shows particular ingenuity in his innumerable motets, especially in those for two and three voices. His 2 books of *madrigali concertati* (from 1615 and 1622) testify to his admiration for Monteverdi. He also left Masses and psalms, mostly dating from the Bergamo period, in which he was able to spread his wings. But perhaps his most interesting works are to be found in his *cantade ed arie* (only one volume of four has survived intact). These are monodic songs, of considerable effectiveness and charm, constructed on the principle of strophic variation, each stanza of the lyric being set to a variant of the initial melody. The briefer ones are *arie,* but the more ambitious examples Grandi terms *cantade* (cantatas), the first known use of the term in such a context. These pieces show considerable melodic invention and a sort of synthesis of the Venetian and Florentine traditions.
RECORDINGS: Denis Stevens has devoted an LP to Grandi.

[378] HUNT, Thomas
ORGANIST (?)
BORN: c. 1575 (?)
DIED: ?

The man who contributed *"Hark! Did You Ever Hear?"* to *The Triumphes of Oriana* in 1601 is one of the most obscure figures in the history of music. He is thought to have taken a B.Mus. at Cambridge around the same time and may have served as organist at Wells Cathedral. His only other known surviving work is an Anglican service.

[379] LISLEY, John
BORN: c. 1575 (?)
DIED: ?

The single fact, supposition, or conjecture that we have about Lisley is that he contributed the madrigal "Faire Citharea" to *The Triumphes of Oriana* in 1601.

[380] PICCHI, Giovanni (Pēk'-kē, Jō-vån'-nē)
ORGANIST, LUTENIST
BORN: c. 1575 (?)
DIED: after 1625

In the last decade of his known career Picchi was organist in Venice at the Ca'Grande and later at the Scuola di San Rocco, but failed to obtain the subsidiary organist's post at St. Mark's in 1624. In 1621 he published a collection of dance pieces for harpsichord, *Intavolatura di balli*—purported the first of four. It was followed four years later by his *Canzoni di sonar* for various (specified) instrumental combinations. An early keyboard toccata made its way to England and was included in the *Fitzwilliam Virginal Book* (No. 94, as by "Giouanni Pichi").

[381] ROMERO, Mateo (Rō-mâ'-rō, Mà-tā'-ō)
CHOIRMASTER, PRIEST
BORN: Liège, c. 1575
DIED: Madrid, May 10, 1647

After a good deal of scholarly wrangling over whether Romero was a Flemish-born Spaniard or a Spanish-born Fleming, it has been finally agreed that he was a Flemish-born Fleming (probably of German ancestry) baptized Mathieu Rosmarin. When his father died, he was recruited for the choir of Philip II and went to Spain, where he sang as a choirboy, studied music with his fellow-countryman Philippe Rogier, and hispanicized his name. In 1594 he was an adult singer in the Capilla Flamenca (Flemish Chapel: has nothing to do with heeltaps) at Madrid, and four years later succeeded Rogier as its director. He got himself known as a formidable musician and was referred to all over Spain as "El Maestro Capitán." (The sobriquet means merely that he was considered Number One among musicians, and not, as some have conjectured, that he had a military career.) In 1609 he entered the priesthood and in 1624 the young King Philip IV gave him a chaplaincy at Toledo Cathedral. He retired on a royal pension in 1633, but five years later he was taken out of

mothballs and shipped off to the Duke of Braganza, a passionate lover of music who was even then plotting to retrieve the Portuguese throne from Spanish hands and backsides. This he did by popular acclaim in 1640, and in 1644 he conferred on Romero the resounding title of Chaplain-Cantor to the Portuguese Crown, whose chief weight consisted of a large monetary emolument. The king, known as John the Fortunate, meant to publish Romero's entire output, but he was evidently not that lucky, for nothing apparently came of his plan. A few Masses, motets, *villancicos*, and songs remain, showing Romero to have been a progressive, but much of his work has vanished.

[382] SODERINI, Agostino (Sō-der-ē'-nē, À-gōs-te'-nō)
ORGANIST
BORN: c. 1575 (?)
DIED: after 1608

In 1599 Soderini published his *Sacrarum cantionum* for voices and instruments in Milan. Nine years later, when he was organist at the Milanese church of Santa Maria della Rosa, he brought out an instrumental collection, *Canzoni a 4 e 8 voci.* And that is all that is known of him, save that he was much admired by the *cognoscenti* in Milan.

[383] TRABACI, Giovanni Maria (Trà-bà'-chē, Jō-vån'-nē Mà-rē'-à)
SINGER, ORGANIST, CHOIR DIRECTOR
BORN: Montepelusio, c. 1575
DIED: Naples, December 31, 1647

Trabaci's birthplace, in the Basilicatan hills of southern Italy, is now called Irsina. He studied in Naples with Jean (alias Giovanni) de Macque, a pupil of Philippe de Monte [197]. Macque was the sometime retainer of Don Carlo Gesualdo's [310] father, sometime organist at the Santa Casa dell' Annunziata, and from 1594 was organist and later *maestro di cappella* to the Spanish viceroy. Trabaci entered the choir of the Annunziata as a tenor at about the time Macque left there, and in 1597 became organist of the Oratorio dei Filippini. In 1601 he succeeded his old teacher as viceregal organist, and replaced him as *maestro* when he died in 1614.

Trabaci's connection with the court was not altogether lucky, for Spanish rule was unpopular in Naples. In July 1647 the Spanish levied a tax on fresh fruit, said to be the dietary staple of the Neapolitan poor. This action produced riots that soon flared into revolt. The leader was a fisherman named Tommaso Aniello, called "Masaniello" (the hero of the 1828 opera *Masianello, ou la Muette de Portici* by Auber [1103]), who insisted that he had the interests of both sides at heart. Nevertheless the viceroy fled to the island of Castello Nuovo out in the bay, and Trabaci received sanctuary in the monastery of the Trinità degli Spagnuoli. The inconvenience was over in a few days, Masaniello having been taken care of in mid-oration by a hit man, but Trabaci took sick in his shelter and died a few hours before the year was out.

Trabaci left nearly 400 works, including Masses, motets, and other sacred works, madrigals and *villanelle*, and a considerable number of pieces for keyboard (also usable for consorts). Of his religious music one might note four Passions of 1635 and some *Sacrae cantiones* from 1603 that have a Gesualdo-like flavor. Most interesting, however, are some of his keyboard pieces, full of daring chromaticisms and unexpected harmonic changes, which show a transition from the Venetian style to that of Girolamo Frescobaldi [407], whom he is said to have influenced.

[384] VAUTOR, Thomas
BORN: c. 1575 (?)
DIED: after 1620

Vautor is said to have been a native of Leicestershire. According to him, he was a retainer of George Villiers, father of the Duke of Buckingham, and, prior to that, of the Beaumonts, the duke's maternal relatives. In the summer of 1616 he took a B.Mus. from Lincoln College, Oxford. And that is all that is presently known about one of the more interesting English madrigalists, whose 1620 collection, optimistically designated *The First Set* ("apt for vyols and voyces"), seems to have been his only one. His "Sweet Suffolk Owl" is particularly well known. His "Shepherds and Nymphs" was intended for *The Triumphes of Oriana* but failed to be included.

[385] WEELKES, Thomas (Wēks, Tō'-mus)
ORGANIST, TEACHER, SINGER
BORN: October 25 (?), 1576
DIED: London, November 30, 1623

The name Weelkes (which would probably nowadays be Wilks or Wilkes) took an uncommonly rough orthographic beating in earlier times, making it difficult to be sure of

certain facts of Thomas Weelkes's life. He may have been the son of a clergyman, John Weeke or Wyke, rector of Elsted in the diocese of Chichester and later a vicar in the Winchester diocese. If so, there is a remote possibility that he was the Thomas Wikes who was a choirboy at Winchester Cathedral from 1582 to 1584, though the dates would argue a remarkable precocity. According to his own testimony, he spent some of his youth in the service of Edward Darcy, groom to Her Majesty's Privy Chamber. He published his first madrigal book in 1597 and a volume of *Balletts and Madrigals* in 1598; in both he protests his youth and inexperience. At about the same time he became organist of Winchester College at a salary of 53s. 4d. a year plus room and board. During his stay there he published his third and best madrigal book, and contributed the outstanding "As Vesta Was from Latmos Hill Descending" to *The Triumphes of Oriana*. He left the college around the end of 1601, and late the next year was appointed organist, Sherborne clerk (subsidized singer), and master of the children at Chichester Cathedral for 15 pounds a year, with lodging and other fringe benefits. Earlier that year New College, Oxford, had awarded him the B.Mus. toward which he said he had been progressing for sixteen years. On February 20, 1603, he entered into what was obviously a shotgun marriage with a local girl named Elizabeth Sandham, who bore him a son, named after his father, in June. Two daughters, Alice and Katherine, followed in due course.

Chichester seems to have been a chaotic place in Weelkes's day. Absenteeism was rife in the choir, and there were occasional graver lapses, such as fistfights among the members, and the churchyard suffered from incursions of "hogs and dogs and lewd persons that do play or do worse therein." The morale seems to have gotten to the composer. His last book, *Ayeres or Phantasticke Spirites*, 1608, is by far his weakest. A year later he was reprimanded for missing the bishop's visit. Ensuing evidence of his laxity was crowned in 1613 with a charge of being drunk in public. Weelkes pleaded not guilty and produced a witness to support his innocence. The next year he contributed two consort songs—his last publications, it turned out—to Sir William Leighton's *Teares and Lamentacions of a Sorrowfull Soule*. In 1616 Elizabeth Weelkes sued one John Eagle for defamation: in a drunken rage in her mother's home, he had called her a whore before witnesses. But when the court got her to admit that her son was conceived out of wedlock, it dismissed the case.

Doubtless the publicity did not help the cause of her husband, who by now was known not only as a lush, but also as a "notorious swearer and blasphemer." Early in 1617 the bishop, perhaps still smarting from being neglected, stripped him of his playing and teaching posts, replacing him with one John Fidge, though Weelkes continued to stagger into the choir and bawl away in disgraceful fashion. A new administration, apparently charitably but unwisely, renamed him organist. Elizabeth Weelkes died in 1622, and her husband followed her a little over a year later, dying (ironically) at the home of a London acquaintance named Drinkwater, to whom his will paid a debt of 50 shillings for room and board. Otherwise he left Thomas and Katherine five shillings each, and the rest of his assets to Alice. He was buried in the St. Bride's churchyard, London.

At his best Weelkes was one of the greatest of the English madrigalists after the pioneering William Byrd [248] and Thomas Morley [289], challenged for supremacy only by John Wilbye [369]. He was influenced strongly by the first two and particularly admired Morley. Weelkes can be disarmingly simple or startlingly "modern." Neither an outstanding melodist nor a passionate writer, he shines as a formalist and as one who knows how to make an impact. He is perhaps the most Baroque of his breed, a tendency that shows particularly in his choice of such texts as *Thule, the Period of Cosmography.* His balletts, however, lean heavily on Morley; and, limited in contrapuntal opportunities, he is obviously uncomfortable in his ayres, though they show his cynical and satirical side. The unpublished *Cries of London* is a fascinating and witty vocal fantasia on street cries and other urban noises. He also wrote several services, a considerable number of anthems (both verse and full), and a few instrumental pieces.

RECORDINGS: Fairly generous recorded samples of the madrigals have been provided by the Wilbye Consort and the Randolph Singers, and there are various scattered recordings of some of the church music. Alfred Deller and Grayston Burgess have both directed versions of *The Cries of London.*

[386] CORREA DE ARAUXO, Francisco
(Kôr-rä'-à dä À-rou'-hō, Frän-thēs'-kō)
ORGANIST, PRIEST, THEORIST
BORN: c. 1576
DIED: Segovia, end of October 1654

Probably Portuguese-born, Correa became organist of the Collegiate Church of San Salvador in Seville in 1599, where he commanded an unusually high salary and played for nearly forty years. In 1626 he published his *Facultad organica,* an important theoretical work that also contains all his surviving organ compositions (mostly *tientos),* and later that year he became a priest. In 1630 he organized a tax revolt among his fellow musicians and as a result was jailed, but later returned to his post. In 1636, however, he took a similar job at Jaén Cathedral, where he sold some of his music to the choir. (His last years were marred by recurrent illness and by poverty.) Four years later he made a final move to Segovia Cathedral, where for reasons of health he was put out to pasture at the end of 1653. He left some vocal works (sacred and secular) in manuscript, but these are outstripped in importance by his organ music, which is, in its harmonic daring and extravagance of expression, decidedly Baroque. (Correa is sometimes called the Spanish Frescobaldi [407]). RECORDINGS: A disc in the Hispavox History of Spanish Music is given over to seven of his organ pieces.

[387] NORCOMBE, Daniel
LUTENIST (OR VIOL PLAYER)
BORN: 1576 (?)
DIED: see below

Because it appears on records, we are here concerned with the composer of the madrigal "With Angel's Face" included in *The Triumphes of Oriana.* The problem is that there were at least two musical Daniel Norcombes active around 1601. The favorite candidate is the lutenist son of John Norcombe, a lay clerk of St. George's Chapel, Windsor. From 1599 to 1601 he was a colleague of John Dowland [316] at the Danish court of Christian IV. In the latter year he and one John Maynard ran away, and, with Danish agents in hot pursuit, made it to Venice, from whence Norcombe managed to get back to England by 1602. He returned to Windsor and took minor orders, predeceasing his wife, who died in 1626. Another Daniel Norcombe, of uncertain origins, fled England as an undesirable Catholic in 1602 and found a haven as a viol player at the court of Archduke Albert in Brussels, disappearing from the records in 1647. He is credited with the composition of several viol pieces. But one must ask: If he was in England in 1600–1 and his namesake was absent therefrom at the same time, does it not seem reasonable to assume the man who wrote other music to have composed the madrigal, rather than the one who produced no other known compositions?

[388] FRANCK, Melchior (Fränk, Mel'-khē-ôr)
TEACHER, CHOIRMASTER
BORN: Zittau, c. 1579
DIED: Coburg, June 1, 1639

A son of a painter named Hans Franck, Melchior Franck is said to have studied in Zittau with Christoph Demantius [334] and later with Adam Gumpelzhaimer [294], under whom he was singing around 1600 at St. Anna's in Augsburg. From 1601 to early 1603, Franck taught at the choir school of St. Egidien in Nuremberg, where he came strongly under the influence of Hans Leo Hassler [320]. He then became court *Kapellmeister* to the music-loving Duke Johann Casimir of Coburg, where his duties were to provide music for worship and "merry songs and dances . . . whether we have guests or not." Franck's mother died in 1603, and he married four years later, subsequently producing at least two children. For the next quarter of a century, he produced a flood of motets, psalms, hymns, occasional pieces, songs, and instrumental dance pieces. Toward the end of this period, however, things began to fall apart. He lost his entire family. The Thirty Years War ruined the Coburg economy (or brought on hard times, as one used to say). The duke died in 1633, and Johann Ernst, his successor, made his expenditures, notably in his *Kapelle,* demoting Franck to municipal music inspector and reducing his salary. The composer's last years were obviously not happy ones, and he is said to have succumbed to his deprivations.

The bulk of Franck's work consists of more than 600 motets. In the earlier ones he deliberately returns to contrapuntalism, arguing that through such an approach a Protestant may testify to God's glory just as well as a Catholic. His later antiphonal experiments may be described as cautious, but in some pieces he used continuo. For all his conservatism, his music, carefully designed not to pose needless problems for his singers, is sturdy and effective.

RECORDINGS: The New York Pro Musica Antiqua has recorded a miscellany of Franck pieces, and the Camerata Vocale of Bremen has devoted a disc to the *Deutsche Evangeliensprüche (German Gospel Proverbs).*

[389] ADSON, John
WIND PLAYER, TEACHER
BORN: c. 1580 (?)
DIED: London, 1640

Adson, who specialized in "loud" instruments (recorder, flute, and cornett), was sufficiently adept by 1604 to be taken into the service of Leopold, Duke of Lorraine. (Leopold, having been forced to give up his forts and military forces, had had to turn to the ways of peace, which, to his surprise, turned out to pay off.) Adson remained with him for at least four years. In 1614 he became a "wait" (municipal musician) in London, and shortly after the death of King James I joined the court band. In 1634, King Charles, not foreseeing the irony, appointed him royal music teacher for life. One assumes the title to have been largely ceremonial, though it ultimately assured him of a salary of 46 pounds a year. As it turned out, Adson died before his employer's execution, probably in the summer of 1640, since he was replaced (because deceased) that July. Adson's sole publication was his *Courtly Masking Ayres* of 1611—31 instrumental pieces of which some are designated for "sagbuts and cornetts." They have proved favorites of brass ensembles looking for early music to record.

[390] BIUMI, Giacomo Filippo (Byōō'-mē, Jä'-kō-mō Fē-lēp'-pō)
ORGANIST
BORN: c. 1580
DIED: Milan, November 24, 1653

After stints as organist at various Milanese churches, including San Ambrogio, Biumi was, in 1623, appointed second organist of the cathedral, and died in harness, albeit somewhat decrepit, thirty and a half years later. He left some sacred music and some more forward-looking organ pieces.

[391] CORKINE, William
BORN: c. 1580 (?)
DIED: in or after 1612

All we know about William Corkine was that he considered himself economically underprivileged (i.e., poor) and published, in 1610 and 1612 respectively, two volumes of ayres and dances. One hopes that they helped alleviate his difficulties. He otherwise left only a fragmentary anthem in manuscript.

[392] DEERING, Richard
ORGANIST, LUTENIST, SINGER

BORN: c. 1580
DIED: London, March 21, 1630

According to an old manuscript, Richard Deering was the bastard son of one Henry Deering of Liss, a town near the West Sussex border of Hampshire. The Deerings or Derings or FitzDerings were an old family traceable back to the time of Henry III. Richard's mother was the Lady Elizabeth Grey, sister of the Earl of Kent. (The objection that there are no official records to substantiate this strikes me as fatuous, since the earl's family would hardly want this blot on their scutcheon available to pokers and pryers.) Legend has it that young Deering was sent to Italy for his musical education, but again evidence lacks. If his birth date was around the conjectured time, such a Continental period would not have been impossible. In applying for a B.Mus. at Oxford in 1610, Deering notes that he has been studying (presumably in England) for ten years, so that he would have returned when he was around twenty, c. 1600. No doubt the Italian experience would have also fostered the Roman Catholic faith he professed. Apparently —whether his degree was granted or not— he returned to Italy in 1612, as secretary or cicerone to a Sir John Harrington (apparently not the Harrington who translated Ariosto, invented the flush toilet, and died in England in 1612). According to that old chatterbox Anthony à Wood, the English nuns in Brussels insisted on hiring Deering as their convent organist in or about 1617, though the likelihood is far greater that he found England too uncomfortable and, like so many others, fled to Belgium. Apparently he stayed there until Charles I took the throne with his Catholic queen, Henrietta Maria, and things cooled down. On his return in 1625 he was appointed Her Majesty's organist and the following year was given, in addition, the post of lute singer to the king. On his death in 1630 he was succeeded by Giles Tomkins, brother of Thomas Tomkins, the composer. Deering's will shows that he was unmarried; he left most of his money to the king and queen, but he endowed a Mr. Fonthill with five pounds to buy "a lute or what ells."

Though a century later Dr. Charles Burney harrumphed that Deering's music was "sober, innocent, dry, psalmodic, and uninteresting," his knowledgeable contemporaries thought it among the best of its kind. We even have a strange glimpse of Oliver Cromwell listening rapt to his Latin motets! In his lifetime he printed, between 1617 and 1620, 3 volumes of *Cantiones sacrae* for five and six voices, and two sets of *Canzonette* for three and four. A volume of two- and three-part *Cantica sacra* appeared posthumously in 1662, and John Playford published others in a collection of 1674. All of these works contain continuo parts—another argument for Deering's Italian training. If the reported 1597 edition of his first book existed in any form other than as a typo, it would have been the first English work to contain such a part.

Deering also left a number of works in manuscript, including a number of interesting fantasias and dances for viol consort. He is perhaps best known today for his *London Cries* and *Country Crie,* clever farragos of the urban and rural sounds of the day (cf. Thomas Weelkes [385] and Orlando Gibbons [408]). *Country Crie* contains a good deal of Kentish dialect.

RECORDINGS: The Deller Consort has recorded both works and a few motets.

[393] EAST, Michael
SINGER, TEACHER
BORN: c. 1580
DIED: Lichfield, 1648

Michael East was surely related to the music printer Thomas East (d. 1608)—perhaps even a son, though there is no solid evidence —for the latter published the first two of his seven collections of music, and gave to his *Hence, stars, too dim of light* pride of place in *The Triumphes of Oriana,* but on the grounds that he had received it late and had to squeeze it in thus. In 1606, the year Michael received his B.Mus. from Cambridge and published his second book (madrigals), he was apparently singing at Ely Cathedral, where he remained until at least 1614. He probably married during this period—a lady named Dorothy—and later we hear of a daughter, a son, and a grandson, the two latter his namesakes. He left Ely to become master of the boys of Lichfield Cathedral. One presumes that his function there ended with the Puritan triumph, but he remained in his home on the cathedral precincts until his death. His later collections, 1610–38, abandon madrigals as, no doubt, outmoded, including instead consort songs, anthems, and instrumental pieces. East was a capable (if glib) composer but not a particularly inspired one.

[394] FONTANA, Giovanni Battista (Fōn-tà'-nà, Jō-vàn'-nē Bàt-tēs'-tà)
VIOLINIST
BORN: Brescia, c. 1580 (?)
DIED: Padua, 1630 or 1631

One of the first musicians to win notice as a violinist, Fontana, already famous, left Brescia in or after 1608. After he had worked in Rome and Venice, a wave of plague caught him in Padua and killed him. Eleven years later, Giovanni Battista Reghius, choirmaster of the Brescian church of Santa Maria delle Grazie, where Fontana used to play, brought out a memorial collection of sonatas for one and two violins and continuo (adaptable to *cornetti*), the bass part playable on the bassoon, cello, chitarrone, etc. Though not sonatas in the modern formal sense, these represent very early examples of the accompanied sonata. The work is also the first known to us to indicate the use of the cello *(violoncino)*.

[395] FORD, Thomas
LUTENIST, VIOL PLAYER, SINGER
BORN: c. 1580 (?)
DIED: London, c. November 15 or 16, 1648

Nothing is known of Ford's parentage, birth, possible relationship to the dramatist John Ford, upbringing, or education. He published a lone book of ayres and dances, *Musicke of Sundrie Kindes,* in 1607. He joined the musical establishment of the ill-fated Henry, Prince of Wales, four years later. In 1614 he contributed two anthems to Sir William Leighton's *Teares or Lamentacions.* He served Charles I throughout his reign. At the time of his death (when, to judge from his will, he was doing rather well for himself), he was designated both a viol player and a royal composer. In his published collection the dances are scored for two lyra viols, the songs (more attractive) for solo voice (or quartet) to be accompanied by "Lute, Orphorion, or Basse-viol." A number of anthems, canons, secular part-songs, and consort pieces have survived in manuscript.

[396] POSCH, Isaac (Pōsh, Ē′-zȧk)
ORGANIST
BORN: c. 1580 (?)
DIED: c. 1622

The musically named Posch (a *Posch,* from Fr. *poche* [pocket], is a kit violin), first appears dimly as an organist in the vicinity of Klagenfurt in southeast Austria around 1614. Three or four years later he had established himself in what is now northwest Yugoslavia, in or around Ljubljana (then Laibach).

In 1618 he published an interesting collection of three-movement variation suites, *Musikalische Ehrenfreudt,* and followed it up in 1621 with another book of dances, *Musikalische Tafelfreudt.* A third publication, *Harmonia concertans,* consisting of rather forward-looking vocal *concerti,* appeared shortly after his death, in 1623.

[397] MARQUÉS, Joan (Mär-kȧs′, Hō-ȧn)
ORGANIST, CHOIRMASTER
BORN: c. 1580 (?)
DIED: Montserrat, 1636

A Catalan, Marqués was master of the choristers at the Benedictine monastery of Montserrat from 1625 until his death. Among his pupils was Joan Cererols [491]. He was also famous as an organist. RECORDINGS: The Montserrat Choir has recorded his responsorium *O vos omnes.*

[398] WIGTHORP, William
ORGANIST
BORN: c. 1580
DIED: in or after 1610

After singing as a choirboy at Winchester Cathedral, Wigthorp entered New College, Oxford, in 1598, from which he took a B.Mus. in 1605. He stayed on as organist and seems to have been active in Oxford musical circles, until 1610, after which no more is heard of him. Of his compositions there are extant only 4 original consort songs, 2 arranged from ayres by Dowland [316] and Daniel Bacheler, and a handful of fragmentary church pieces.

[399] YOULL, Henry (Yōol, Hen′-rē)
TEACHER
BORN: Newark, Nottinghamshire
c. 1580 (?)
DIED: after 1608

Youll served a seven-year apprenticeship to a Newark singing master named Peter Newcombe (from 1590). Later, he tells us in his sole publication, *Canzonets to Three Voyces* (1608), that he taught the four sons of Edward Bacon, though he does not say who Edward Bacon was. He is also said to have contributed some pieces to Ben Jonson's 1600 masque *Cynthia's Revels.* His so-called canzonets are mostly imitation Morley [289].

[400] STADEN, Johann (Shtá'-den, Yō'-hàn)
ORGANIST, TEACHER
BORN: Nuremberg, July 2, 1581
DIED: Nuremberg, c. November 14, 1634

The son of Nuremberg citizen Hans Staden and his second wife, Elisabeth (Löbele), Johann Staden had already won a reputation as a fine organist before he was out of his teens. He went to Bayreuth as organist to the Markgraf, Christian Ernst at some time before 1604, the year he was married. When a fire in 1605 made the princely establishment uninhabitable, the Markgraf moved his court to Kulmbach, where Staden's sons, Johann and Sigmund Theophil, and another child were born. By 1610 the court had returned to the capital city of Bayreuth, but within the year Staden left it to return to Nuremberg, and the births of at least three more progeny. In 1616 he became organist of the Spitalkirche and two years later of the Sebalduskirche. He was a notable teacher, his pupils including his four sons and Johann Erasmus Kindermann [489], and was frequently called in by the city fathers as consultant on musical matters. His son Sigmund Theophil composed, in the early 1640s, the first known German *Singspiel* (comic opera), *Seelewig*. Johann Staden, like so many early composers, died of plague.

Unfortunately, much of Johann Staden's music is extant only in fragmentary form. Most of his publications in his years with the Markgraf consisted of secular songs ("also playable on instruments"). In Nuremberg he, expectably, concentrated on church music, wherein he makes a synthesis of the new Italian *concertato* style and the Protestant German chorale. He also left nearly 200 instrumental pieces of high quality.

[401] JEEP, Johann (Yāp, Yō'-hàn)
ORGANIST, CHOIRMASTER, COURT OFFICIAL
BORN: Dransfeld, c. 1581
DIED: Hanau, November 19, 1644

It is improbable that the late cartoonist Elzie Segar, creator of Popeye, borrowed Jeep's name for the fictitious little animal that lent *its* name to an army vehicle. Born near Göttingen, Johann Jeep studied there and in Celle, in which latter town he was a chorister. From about 1600 to 1610 he was in Nuremberg and Altdorf, and then journeyed to Italy. In 1613 he went to Weikersheim to fill the organist's post in the Hohenlohe castle vacated by Erasmus Widmann [362]. He won the confidence and respect of his employer, Count Friedrich, and when wartime conditions made it impossible to maintain a *Kapelle* in 1625, he kept Jeep on as his chief steward. In 1635, Jeep deputized for the organist of the cathedral of Frankfurt am Main, and, in 1637, Weikersheim having been occupied by the masters of the Teutonic Order, he accepted a job in Frankfurt as town *Kapellmeister*. But his health broke down, and after three frustrating years he was fired. However, he found a school post in nearby Hanau and in 1642 was named organist of the Marienkirche and *Kapellmeister* to the local count—the latter little more than a sinecure, since the *Kapelle* had been decimated by wartime conditions. Jeep's chief musical legacy consists of *Lieder* and hymns. In the latter area his 1629 *Geistliche Psalmen und Kirchengesänge*—known as the "Weikersheim Hymnbook" and begun as an update of Widmann's *Geistliche Psalmen und Lieder*—was immensely popular.

[402] DE VOIS, Pieter Alewynszoon (Dā Vwà, Pē'-ter A-le'-wĭn-sun)
ORGANIST
BORN: c. 1581
DIED: The Hague, 1654

Born blind, De Vois became organist of the church of St. James in The Hague, and remained there until his death fifty years later. He attained considerable fame both as organist and violinist, and in 1621 was asked to succeed Sweelinck at the Oude Kerk in Amsterdam, but he turned the job down. RECORDINGS: A set of variations of his have been recorded by Henk Herzog on the carillon of De Vois's own church.

[403] SIMPSON, Thomas
VIOL PLAYER, EDITOR
BORN: Milton-next-Sittingbourne, Kent, April 1 (?), 1582
DIED: after 1625

Once thought to come from Yorkshire and to be a relative of Christopher Simpson, a contemporary viol player, Thomas Simpson is now known to have been a native of what is now Milton Regis, a suburb of Sittingbourne. He made his career chiefly in Germany and Denmark, though whether for religious or economic reasons we do not know. From 1608 or before to 1610 or later, he served the Elector Palatine, Friedrich IV, in Heidelberg. A few years later he was at the Bückeburg court of the Count of Holstein-Schaumburg, Ernst III, and in 1622 became one of the boys in Christian IV's band in Copenhagen. A manuscript of songs by one Thomas Simpson seems to indicate that he had returned to England by the end of the decade, but the evidence is shaky and there is no other. All his published works (3 volumes of pieces that he wrote or arranged) are instrumental dances, which show considerable inventiveness. His first volume in particular seems to have had some impact on the next generation of German composers.

[404] GAGLIANO, Marco da (Gàl-yà'-nō, Mär'-kō dà)
PRIEST, LUTENIST, KEYBOARDIST, CHOIRMASTER, TEACHER
BORN: Florence, May 1, 1582
DIED: Florence, February 25, 1643

The Gagliano brothers, Marco and Giovanni Battista, both notable musicians in Florence, were the sons of Zanobi and Camilla da Gagliano, whose surname came from a hill town in the vicinity. In 1587 Marco began his education and musical career (as a choirboy) in a lay confraternity, the Compagnia dell' Arcangelo Raffaello. Later he studied with Luca Bati, choirmaster of the Medici church, San Lorenzo, and at twenty took over some of his master's teaching duties. Later he entered the priesthood. The year 1607 seems to have been when he "arrived," musically speaking. Early that summer he founded an elite musical society, the Accademia degli Elevati, whose membership seems to have included just about everyone who was anyone in the arts in Florence, and which had rather demanding rules and, in the current mode for Italian academies, code names for its members. (Gagliano's was "L'Affannato," meaning generally "the Excited.") Befriended by Ferdinando Gonzaga, who stood patron to the venture, Gagliano was called to Mantua in December—a fact that may help explain why his election at that time to the musical directorship of the Compagnia of which he was an alumnus was voided in favor of someone else.

Earlier in 1607 Claudio Monteverdi [333] had created a sensation with his opera L'Orfeo and was now working on Arianna for the upcoming wedding of Francesco Gonzaga to Margarita di Savoia. It was decided by someone that the event would be a sort of opera festival and that the clever young Florentine priest might contribute. As a result Gagliano worked up a setting of Ottavio Rinuccini's revision of the first opera libretto (his), Dafne (see 309) which was produced in January 1608 (and has since proved one of the most viable of the early

operas). Gagliano also provided a ballet on the Iphigenia theme and contributed one of the interludes for Giovanni Battista Guarini's play L'Idropico. Later that year, back home, he succeeded his dead master Bati as maestro di cappella at the cathedral. In 1609 his post at the Compagnia was also restored to him, and he was given the musical directorship of the ducal court. Early in 1615 he was appointed apostolic prothonotary by Pope Paul V. He also frequently played and sang at court. Between 1602 and 1617 he published 6 books of madrigals, one of other secular pieces, and a setting of the Office for the Dead. Afterward he published only sacred works—Masses, motets, and responsories—but continued to compose for the stage, both alone and in collaboration with Peri [309], Caccini [252], and others, but only La Flora, an opera to which Peri contributed, has survived. After 1630 Gagliano is said to have suffered from ill health, and was perhaps incapacitated for his final decade. There is a portrait bust at San Lorenzo.

Gagliano is said to have been ruthlessly self-critical and to have withheld or destroyed much that he wrote. What he published, however, he evidently approved of. When a cocky young upstart named Muzio Effrem publicly attacked his madrigals in print in 1623 as "incorrect," Gagliano did not deign to reply. (They have "modern" touches, but are for the most part tastefully restrained.) Most of his published sacred works are lost or fragmentary.

RECORDINGS: There are now at least three recordings of Dafne. (The orchestration, of course, has had to be "reconstructed.")

[405] INDIA, Sigismondo d' (Dēnd'-yà, Sē-gēz-môn'-dō)
MUSIC DIRECTOR
BORN: Palermo, c. 1582
DIED: c. 1629

Very little is known of d'India's first three decades. He came of a noble and apparently wealthy Sicilian family, and may have grown up in Naples. Between 1600 and 1610 he was in Florence, then in Mantua, Florence again, Rome, and finally Parma. In 1611 he began a twelve-year stay at the court of Savoia in Turin as director of the private music of Duke Carlo Emanuele I, a great patron of the arts and himself a poet and painter. In 1623 a campaign of gossip drove him away. Whether it had to do with the poet Count Lodovico San Martino d'Aglie, the source that describes him as d'India's "constant friend and companion" does not say. At any rate, after a stopover of some months in Modena, the composer found a Roman patron in Carlo Emanuele's son, Cardinal Maurizio, who produced his sacred opera *Sant' Eustachio* (text by Count Lodovico), and may have persuaded Pope Urban VIII to commission d'India's only known Mass (now lost). In 1626, he was given a post at the Este court in Modena. Three years later he won an appointment at the Munich court of Maximilian I of Bavaria, but since he apparently died soon afterward, he probably never went there.

Sigismondo d'India is known chiefly as a composer of monodies and duets in the new style, obviously influenced to some degree by Claudio Monteverdi **[333]**, of which he published 5 volumes called *Le Musiche* (1609–23). But he also wrote 8 books of madrigals (some of which offer more than chance echoes of Don Carlo Gesualdo **[310]** and the latter volumes of which are with continuo), one of *villanelle,* 2 of sacred *concerti,* and one of motets. The *Sant' Eustachio* is lost and a stage pastoral *Zalizura* is extant only in incomplete form.

RECORDINGS: At least one LP has been devoted to the monodies.

[406] RAVENSCROFT, Thomas
EDITOR, THEORIST
BORN: c. 1582
DIED: c. 1635

For a man who occupies such an important (albeit not very respectable) place in the history of English music, Thomas Ravenscroft remains surprisingly elusive. Was he a child prodigy? Or are the vital dates wrong? In 1614 he was hailed as a youth of twenty-two, which would put his birth date at around 1592. That he took a B.Mus. from Cambridge is clear; that he took it in 1607, at fourteen (according to a contemporary statement) after ten years of study (according to the university) is supported neither by hard evidence nor by logic. What *is* clear about his early life is that he was a St. Paul's choirboy in London as early as 1598 and as late as 1600 (which facts seem to argue for a birth date later than 1582). But apparently he was involved with the cathedral's company of boy actors (for whom he wrote some music), which probability may explain his tardiness in leaving. The other clear fact about Ravenscroft's life, apart from composition and publication, is that he was in charge of music at Christ's Hospital from 1618 to 1622. Christ's was not a medical institution but a shelter and school for orphans. Established

about seventy years earlier by Edward VI, it was popularly known as the Blue-Coat School because of the boys' uniform—blue gown, knee pants, yellow petticoat and stockings, neckband, and blue caps. In Ravenscroft's day it occupied the old Greyfriars Abbey in Newgate Street.

Behind Ravenscroft, one hears the distant din of Tin Pan Alley. Though he may have been both prodigy and pedant, he clearly saw music as a salable commodity and had a keen eye for the swift shilling. His first three publications—*Pammelia* and *Deuteromelia* in 1609, and *Melismata* in 1611—were explicitly aimed at a mass public. To the title of the first, Ravenscroft added the rubric "None so ordinary as musicall, none so musicall, as not to all very pleasing and acceptable," and the second bears the motto "Qui canere potest canat. Catch that Catch Can." (Like all good ad men, Ravenscroft liked the catchy phrase. *Melismata,* he says, is "To all delightful except the spiteful; to none offensive except to the Pensive.") The bulk of the contents of the three volumes consists of rounds and catches, just then becoming a popular indoor musical sport, and *Deuteromelia* is the source of "Three Blind Mice." Some of the pieces in *Melismata* depict "Court, Citie, and Country Humours" by using street cries as their basis.

In 1614 Ravenscroft published a theoretical work, *A Briefe Discourse of the True (but Neglected) Use of Charact'ring the Degrees,* in which he rather redundantly went over the argument for "classical" meters, learnedly citing the opinions of many musty musical mentors. This, unlike his earlier publications, contained 12 songs of his own making, including the cycle *Hodge Trillindle to his Zweet hort Malkyn* in Kentish dialect. But his most influential work was his 1621 *The Whole Booke of Psalmes* (alias *Ravenscroft's Psalter),* containing four-part settings of tunes for the Elizabethan metrical translations by Thomas Sternhold and John Hopkins. Though some of the arrangements are by musicians of stature—Tallis **[157]**, Morley **[289]**, Kirbye **[329]**, the senior Milton **[319]**, the Tomkins brothers **[365]**—most are by Ravenscroft himself, who introduces a good many new tunes. This book was one of the chief sources of early American church music, approved even by the Puritans.

[407] FRESCOBALDI, Girolamo (Fres-kō-bàl'-dē, Ji-rō'-là-mō)
ORGANIST, HARPSICHORDIST, SINGER
BORN: Ferrara, September 13, 1583
DIED: Rome, March 1, 1643

His hair abundant but neatly trimmed and framing his forehead in spit curls, the eyes thick-lidded under heavy, arching brows, a long, appropriately Roman nose, high cheekbones, thick mustache, small full lips, a tiny goatee, a fringe of chin beard, Girolamo Frescobaldi looks proudly out of his portrait at the age of thirty-six. And well he might, for he was probably the first of the great virtuoso keyboardists. He was educated in Ferrara largely by Luzzasco Luzzaschi, the cathedral organist and one of the pioneers of the New Music. To his other talents, he also added a beautiful singing voice.

In the very early years of the new century he migrated to Rome and, apparently, quickly established himself as a performer. By 1604 he had been inaugurated into the prestigious musical organization that was to become the Accademia di Santa Cecilia, and had acquired a patron in Guido Bentivoglio, the papal nuncio. Duty called the nuncio to the Lowlands for a year in the summer of 1607 and Frescobaldi went with him. No doubt he observed and learned from Flemish music. Before his return to Rome, he also made use of the excellent Flemish presses, issuing his first book of madrigals in Antwerp. On the way home in the fall, he seems to have stopped in Milan, where his keyboard fantasias were published. In November, when he was barely twenty-five, his performing career peaked: he was appointed organist at St. Peter's in Rome. (That huge exhalation was still far from completed: Bramante's plans had long since been abandoned, the dome was finished, the obelisk had been erected in the piazza, Bernini was still hacking away at the baldacchino, and the great colonnades were more than thirty years in the future.) Legend has it that 30,000 auditors turned up to hear Frescobaldi's first performance; perhaps the unfinished state of the building made so large a crowd possible.

For twenty years Frescobaldi sat at the console (though not uninterruptedly). In 1613 he married a lady named Orsola del Pino, who figures in a work of his called La Frescobalda. She facilitated his production to the tune of five little Frescobalde, the first born a year before the wedding. But he appears to have been not entirely happy in his post—it is said that he felt he was not paid what he was worth. In 1615, for example, the year in which his volume of ricercari and canzone and his first books of toccatas appeared, he dickered unsuccessfully for a job at the Mantuan court. The second book of toccatas came out the next year; the capriccios waited until 1624. Finally in 1628 he secured a leave of absence, supplied a substi-

tute organist to the basilica, and trudged off to Florence to sample the air of Ferdinando II's court. The eighteen-year-old duke, who had been in Rome some months before, had just assumed power, and there must be a connection of events. It was in Florence that Frescobaldi published his Arie musicale for several voices. But Florence did not work out, and in 1534 Frescobaldi went back to the Julian Chapel, where he remained for what was left of his life. In 1635, he crowned his publishing career with the three Baroque organ Masses of the Fiori musicali (Musical Flowers), published in Venice. Among his pupils in this period was the great German organist Johann Jakob Froberger [490], who worked with him from 1637 to 1641.

Frescobaldi's fame as a virtuoso did not obscure the fact that he was one of the pivotal figures of the early Baroque. To be sure, the bulk of his work is limited to the keyboard (and improvisation being his chief stock in trade, we are necessarily deprived of an important side of that limited field), but one must remember that this was a time when instrumental music was beginning to assert itself as an independent phenomenon. If his "sound" and his generic titles at first strike one as less adventurous than what the contemporary Florentines and Venetians were doing, the effect is deceptive. If he sometimes anchors himself to a cantus firmus, it is in a way far removed from the old practice. His chromaticism and his shifting, uncertain tonalities make one think of the late music of a more modern virtuoso, Franz Liszt [1218]. The keynotes of Frescobaldi's music are—as they are with the paintings of El Greco and the poems of John Donne—drama and mysticism. From the performer he insists on interpretation of the feeling of a piece, through the use of dynamic contrasts and fudging of the rhythm (tempo rubato). Many of his organ pieces are structured (if that is the word) on a succession of contrasting and unrelated musical cells; but at the same time he was one of the early masters of the use of an ostinato (unchanging) bass pattern, as exemplified in his variations on the passacaglia (which is closer to chaconne than to passacaglia in conception). Nowhere, however, is there note wasting for virtuosity's sake. The Fiori strike one as being as devout as Palestrina [201]. Johann Sebastian Bach [684] admiringly copied them out, and an early hearer speaks of them as "the audible ecstasy of souls in prayer."

RECORDINGS: A complete recording of the Fiori musicali has been made by Lucienne Antonini (abetted by the Ensemble Vocale d'Avignon). Copious excerpts are owing to Eduard Müller, and generous samplings of the toccatas to Blandine Verlet and Edward Brewer. There are innumerable records of miscellaneous keyboard pieces by Gustav Leonhardt, E. Power Biggs, Paul Wolfe, Sylvia Marlowe, Giuseppe di Dona, and many others. The *canzone* and *arie* for instrumental ensembles may be heard in versions by Gerard Schwarz, Noah Greenberg, Richard Burgin, and others. Four pieces orchestrated by Giorgio Ghedini (1892–1965) are directed by Fernando Previtali.

[408] GIBBONS, Orlando
KEYBOARDIST
BORN: Oxford, December, 1583
DIED: Canterbury, June 5, 1625

Orlando came from a family of apparently solid Oxford citizens. His grandfather, Richard, was a chamberlain of the city, and his father, William, was both a councilor ("hanaster") and a civic musician ("wait"). At some time in the early 1560s, William went to rival Cambridge in the latter capacity, where the first three of his four sons were born. Evidently the family later moved back to Oxford at some point, for Orlando was baptized there on Christmas Day 1583. But by 1589, the Gibbonses were back in Cambridge, where, as a boy of twelve, Orlando joined the choir of King's College, under the direction and tutelage of his eldest brother, Edward, who was fifteen years older than he. Two years later Orlando was admitted to the college as a scholarship student, or "sizar." He evidently showed precocious talent, for by the time King James took the throne in 1603 he was already a member of the Chapel Royal and early in 1605 he succeeded Arthur Cock (dead two months) as organist. Shortly afterward he married Jane Patten, a Westminster girl and daughter to the future Keeper of the King's Closet. (Considering the skeletons he kept there, King James no doubt needed him.) In due course the couple produced seven progeny, the most notable of whom was Christopher (1615–76), himself a composer and organist of stature. In 1606 Orlando Gibbons graduated with a B.Mus. from Cambridge, and the following year he was admitted to Oxford University. He evidently won the attention of his king, who showered him with gifts, included him in his private music, and named him, in 1619, his personal "Musician for the Virginals." By 1615 he was being relieved at the chapel keyboard by Edmund Hooper [276], who was succeeded by Thomas Tomkins [365] in 1620.

In 1622, when the Chair of History,

founded by his friend the antiquarian William Cambridge and, for the record, first occupied by Degory Wheare, was inaugurated at Oxford, Gibbons was awarded a D.Mus. and contributed the occasional anthem *O clap your hands* in behalf of his friend and colleague William Heyther (or Heather), who was being similarly honored. The next year, when the organist of Westminster Abbey died, the post was awarded to Gibbons (who continued to hold his others). His first important duty—alas!—was to furnish the music for King James's funeral on April 5, 1625. Two months later he went to Canterbury with King Charles I and the chapel to welcome the new queen, Henrietta Maria, from France. They reached their destination on June 1, but the bride's arrival was delayed for more than a week. In the interim Gibbons fell ill, though apparently not of the plague as was first feared, for his very Shakespearean symptoms did not correspond with those of that disease. According to medical reports, he passed from a lethargy into convulsions and then into an apoplexy, from which he died. He was buried in the cathedral, where a monumental bust remains.

The English consider Gibbons—with Byrd and Purcell—as part of a sort of Holy Trinity of English music, and tend to become dewy-eyed and reverential at the mention of his name. But his place in music is more English than international. His chief contributions were to the Anglican liturgy. Besides 2 services, prayers, and psalms, he left a number of anthems. In the "full" variety (in the minority), he takes a last long look at the old polyphonic tradition, of which he was, in his own special way, a master. The verse anthems are more experimental, but—though they may be properly viewed as a link between those of William Byrd [248] and Henry Purcell [581]—even their defenders admit their weaknesses. A fine writer of madrigals in the old style, Gibbons left only a published collection of 13— though it contains the exquisite *The Silver Swan* of 1612. Though he was reputedly one of the great keyboardists of his time, little of his keyboard music was printed in his day— mostly in the 1610 *Parthenia, or the Maydenhead of the first musicke that ever was printed for the Virginalls.* (The pun is extended in *parthenia*—Greek for "virgin.") For the most part, it consists of dances, fantasies, masking tunes, and variations on such popular songs as "Whoope! Do Me No Harm, Good Man!" Probably more important are the 40-odd fantasias and dances for consort. Gibbons also tried his hand at a *Cries of London,* for voices and strings, which he cast as an *In nomine.* If *last* means

"latest-born," Gibbons probably qualifies as "the last of the Elizabethans."
RECORDINGS: The madrigal book has been recorded entire by the Consort of Musicke. There are collections of the keyboard music played by Christopher Hogwood, Glenn Gould, and others, and choral miscellanies by the Deller Consort, the Clerkes of Oxenford, and the King's College Choir, among others.

[409] JOHNSON, Robert
LUTENIST
BORN: c. 1583
DIED: London, autumn 1633

Robert Johnson must not be confused with an earlier namesake, a Scots composer-priest who, declared a heretic, fled to England c. 1535. Our man was almost certainly son to John Johnson [241], admired as a lutenist at Elizabeth's court. In 1596 Robert undertook a seven-year indenture to the lord chamberlain, Sir George Carey, in return for a musical education and the necessaries of life. Having paid out his time, he became lutenist to King James in the first year of his reign and, save for a year or two on the staff of the short-lived Prince Henry, retained that post until his death. In 1628 he was also named "Composer for the Lute and Voices," replacing the late Thomas Lupo [352]. He commanded a salary of forty pounds a year and King Charles granted him an additional twenty pounds to replace strings, on which he must have been very hard. Because, no doubt, of his association with the lord chamberlain, who was in charge of such matters at court, Johnson wrote songs for the important playwrights of the time, including Shakespeare (notably *The Tempest),* Ben Jonson, John Webster, and Francis Beaumont/John Fletcher. These often show what appears to be the influence of the new Italian dramatic music. He also left a number of excellent lute pieces, several religious songs, and some instrumental dances. He is credited with a number of dances for court masques, but for most of them his authorship remains unproved.

[410] VALLET, Nicolas (Vàl-lā', Nē-kō-làs')
LUTENIST, TEACHER
BORN: c. 1583
DIED: after 1642

Said to have been born in the Île-de-France, Vallet moved to Amsterdam in or before 1614, where he established himself as a formi-

dable performer and, between 1615 and 1620, published several books for lute, or voice and lute (notably psalm settings). Later he became increasingly occupied with teaching, and in 1626, together with several English émigrés, set up a school. It must not have succeeded, however, for by 1633 Vallet was bankrupt and destitute. In 1642 he brought out a collection of dances for viol and continuo, and is said to have followed it with another for consort a year or so later, but no copy has ever turned up.

[411] CIFRA, Antonio (Chē'-frà, Àn-tō'-nyō)
CHOIRMASTER
BORN: 1584
DIED: Loreto, October 2, 1629

Cifra's birthplace is variously given as Rome or Terracina (a coastal city between Rome and Naples). Between the ages of ten and twelve he was a chorister in the choir of San Luigi (St. Louis) in Rome and is variously said to have studied with Giovanni Bernardino Nanini, Palestrina [201], and the *castrato* Girolamo Rosini. In 1609, after having served some four years as *maestro di cappella* of the Seminario Romano and then of the Collegio Germanico, Cifra left Rome to direct the choir of the Shrine of the Holy House in Loreto, near the Adriatic. (The Holy House was the birthplace and home of the Virgin in Nazareth; in 1295 it was deposited in an Italian laurel thicket by angels to save it from the Turks.) In 1622 he returned to Rome for four years as *maestro* at the San Giovanni Laterano, then went back to Loreto for good.

Identified with the Roman progressives, such as Girolamo Frescobaldi [407], Cifra was an enormously fertile and highly talented composer. He wrote with equal aptitude in both the polyphonic and the "modern" styles, though his works in the latter category tend toward conservatism. He published numbers of Masses, motets, and psalms, and around 200 of the new-style vocal *concerti.* There are also instrumental pieces (organ *ricercari)* and vocal *scherzi* to be sung to harpsichord accompaniment. The poet John Milton was taken with his music on his Italian junket and apparently lent Cifra's songs to his friend Henry Lawes [444] on his return, for Henry had his little joke in publishing an Italian song *"Tavola"* ("Index"), whose text was Cifra's index of first lines (or rather such parts of it as suited him).
RECORDINGS: Helen Watts has recorded *"Tavola"* together with Cifra's *"In quel ge-*

lato core" ("In That Frozen Heart"), the song whose title initiates *"Tavola."*

[412] SCHÜTZ, Heinrich (Shüts, Hīn'-rikh)
ORGANIST, CHOIRMASTER
BORN: Köstritz, October 8, 1585
DIED: Dresden, November 6, 1672

Of the three S's of German Baroque music —Scheidt [426], Schein [419], and Schütz—the last-named is now viewed as immeasurably the most important. It was he who made the final great synthesis of the German Lutheran tradition and the new impulses from Italy, and pointed German music in the direction that was to reach its next peak in J. S. Bach [684]. The first German to write opera and ballet scores, he was equally at home in Gabrielian polyphony and Monteverdian dramatic monody. None of which explains his endless fertility of invention or his ability to overcome performance problems that might well have broken any other composer.

Heinrich Schütz came of solid burgher stock. His paternal grandfather, Albrecht, was an innkeeper, first in Köstritz, then in Weissenfels. Schütz's father, Christoph, took over the Köstritz establishment in the 1570s and became town clerk there. Widowed, he married the burgomaster's daughter, Elisabeth Piegert or Bieger, in 1583; Heinrich was preceded by a sister and followed by six more siblings. In 1590 Albrecht died, and the family moved to Weissenfels to run Zum güldenen Ring (At the Sign of the Golden Ring). There the Schütz boys, as they reached the proper age, were packed off to the local Latin school for a good liberal education. Heinrich sang in the choir there, and when, in 1598, Landgraf Moritz "der Gelehrte" of Hesse-Kassel (himself a good composer) stopped over at the Golden Ring one night, he was so taken by the boy's performance that he offered to stake him to an education in "the fine arts and laudable virtues" if he would only agree to grace his *Kapelle*. The parents, who thought music an unsuitable career for young men of a respectable family, hesitated but eventually succumbed to the economic appeal and sent the lad off to Kassel in the summer of 1599. There, besides doing the required gracing, he attended the Collegium Mauritianum, the Landgraf's special pride, which he personally oversaw and in which he could have taught most of the courses. Heinrich learned music as a standard branch of mathematics, and distinguished himself both as a brilliant learner and a fashionable dresser. In 1607,

thinking his musical career behind him, he followed his brother, Georg, into the law curriculum at the University of Marburg. Again he acquitted himself with *éclat*. But Moritz, visiting the institution, was horrified to discover that Schütz was neglecting what he, the Landgraf, felt to be his real talent. Forthwith he offered him an annual stipend of 200 thalers to go to Venice for two years and to study with Giovanni Gabrieli [286], although the latter was in poor health. Schütz was not terribly interested but finally acceded when he was promised that he could return to the law if things did not work out.

With Gabrieli's music Schütz was at first puzzled and then delighted, and he was soon master of the new techniques. In 1611 he sent back to the Landgraf his first publication, a book of Italian madrigals that delighted everyone at home, even his parents, who thereupon resigned themselves to the inevitable. A year later Gabrieli died, leaving Schütz his ring as a token of his admiration. But Schütz was still, at twenty-seven, not convinced that he was a musician and returned to Germany to his legal studies. At the same time he accepted a post as Moritz's organist —not very demanding work that continued his former stipend. However, his fame filtered to nearby artistic centers, and in 1614 the Saxon elector, Johann Georg I, asked to borrow Schütz to oversee the music for the baptism of his son, August, his *Kapellmeister* Rogier Michael being too tottery and Michael Praetorius [360] off gallivanting God knew where. Schütz fulfilled his mission, and a year later the elector offered him the *Kapellmeisterschaft*, an offer that Schütz always saw as the divine omen that settled his career. Moritz reluctantly gave him a two-year leave.

Johann Georg was the antithesis of Moritz—a rather insensitive type whose chief interests were hunting, fighting, eating, and drinking—but he knew the value of preserving a cultural front and so kept a fine chapel, consisting of a precentor, two organists, fifteen singers, and nine instrumentalists. It was a situation that boded well for Schütz's reputation. The following year a rich man named Burckhardt Grossmann, miraculously recovered from a severe illness, commissioned, by way of thanksgiving, settings of Psalm 116. Schütz was one of those chosen, along with Schein, Franck, Demantius, Michael Praetorius, Altenburg, and several others. By the end of the year, however, Moritz was getting nervous about the status of his investment, and besought the elector to return Schütz on the grounds that his (Moritz's) children were not getting any younger and needed a musical education. Johann Georg was not sure what all the fuss was about and consulted his counselors, who explained that possessing a Schütz would lend glitter to his establishment. So he explained the relationship between greater princes and lesser princes to Moritz, who, graciously and out of true affection, relinquished his claim. When Schütz came back to Kassel to gather up his effects, Moritz gave him his blessing and a handsome portrait-medal to remember him by. When his own *Kapellmeister,* Georg Otto, died in 1619, Moritz made one more feeble attempt and gave it up forever.

Throughout his long Dresden career, Schütz seems to have been a sort of father to his charges. He housed, fed, and educated choirboys, saw to it that the elector dealt out educational grants to the more promising musicians, and, when hard times came, often helped support the others out of his own pocket. His duties included the regaling of visiting dignitaries—e.g., Emperor Matthias. He was also obligated to attend his master to princely conclaves, such as that in Bayreuth in 1619, where his German reputation became firmly established, and the state visit to Breslau in 1621, which included a retinue of 855 persons and 878 horses. His home became a sort of unofficial hotel for folk from back home come to Dresden on business. At one time during this period he housed for some months a delegation from Weissenfels, complete with servants. (The bill was 294 florins, breakfasts included.) Copies of his publications forwarded to various local and municipal authorities brought him in a steady stream of gifts of money and silverware.

In 1619, Schütz married Magdalena Wildeck, the daughter of a customs official; oddly, the marriage contract specified that he would never leave Dresden or the elector's service. In 1623 she bore him a daughter named Euphrosyne after his mother, and two years later another, Anna Justina, shortly after which event she died. Schütz, who had produced the Resurrection Story in 1623 and the *Cantiones sacrae* that spring, was so grief-stricken that he was at first unable to function, but later he found solace in setting the vernacular psalter of Cornelius Becker in simple "practical" versions. In 1627 the wedding of the Saxon princess Sophie Eleanore to Georg of Hesse-Darmstadt called for something special, and Schütz elected to try his hand at an opera. The poet Martin Opitz reworked Rinuccini's *Dafne* into German, and it was produced in the great hall of Hartenfels Castle in Torgau on April 13. (The music is now lost, alas!) Not

unreasonably, Schütz had been agitating to be allowed to return to Italy to catch up on the latest musical developments, and finally, in the late summer of 1628, the elector let him go, with no offer to pay his expenses. While in Venice, Schütz observed the progress made in such things as continuo, monody, the use of the violin, and the career of Claudio Monteverdi [333]. Shortly after his arrival, he had to beg Johann Georg for subsistence money and, in August 1629, for fare home.

As early as 1628 Schütz had had to protest the elector's tardy payment of salaries, which was already causing dissension in the ranks of the chapel. After 1630 the treasury was so depleted that the chapel began seriously to fall apart. Nor was Schütz exactly buoyed up by a series of personal tragedies around this time—the successive deaths of his sister Dorothea, his friend Schein, his father, and his father-in-law. He was trying to get a leave when fate, in the person of Christian, Crown Prince of Denmark, stepped in with a request that he come provide the music for his wedding to Magdalena Sybille of Saxony. In the later summer of 1633 the elector grudgingly let him go. In Copenhagen he was named *Kapellmeister* with an annual salary of 800 rixdalers and a home in the city. His chief contribution to the wedding the following autumn was a ballet, but all his music was destroyed in a later fire. He came back to Dresden in the spring of 1635 to find only the skeleton of a chapel, but he dealt with these problems in the *Kleine Geistliche Konzerte* for solo voices and continuo with occasional obbligato instruments. But the situation was so frustrating and depressing that he again sought leave to return to Copenhagen, even offering his house and daughters as security against his eventual return. When the elector finally let him go, Schütz managed to wrest from him money to permit his pupil and protégé Matthias Weckmann to study in Hamburg for three years with Jakob Praetorius [420]. He remained in the Danish court for two years, until 1638, and then secured a rather loose arrangement as *Kapellmeister* in Wolfenbüttel to the Duke of Braunschweig-Lüneburg. That year he lost his thirteen-year-old daughter Anna Justina. He seems also to have had some link with the court of Hanover in 1639–40. Though he occasionally looked in on the Dresden situation, he continued this unstable existence until the mid-1640s. Meanwhile the crown prince, later Johann Georg II, had married and established his own chapel under Weckmann's direction. The fact that it consisted largely of Italians and fared better than that of the elector made Schütz's task no easier. He was called to Halle in 1646 to arbitrate the musical dispute between Marco Scacchi [459] and Paul Siefert [421]. (Eventually he pronounced Siefert unfit to kiss Scacchi's boots.) Otherwise he seems to have moved around fitfully, turning up in Weimar, Dresden, and Weissenfels sporadically. By 1651 he was urging the elector to let him live in Weissenfels as *Kapellmeister* in name only or to dismiss him entirely, but without result. Eventually the first Johann Georg died, in 1656, and his son merged his chapel with the remnants of his father's. Schütz was co-*Kapellmeister* with two Italians, with whom he seems to have got on better than his German underlings did. But in 1657 he was at last permitted to step down, to retire to Weissenfels, leaving his post to his favorite pupil, Christian Bernhard (who was later ousted by the Italians). Despite increasing deafness and the loss of his other daughter, Schütz continued to compose, producing such things as the Christmas Story and two of the Passions. In his eighty-sixth year he became increasingly ill but continued to function until felled in his tracks by a massive stroke. He died a month after his eighty-seventh birthday.

RECORDINGS: Schütz has been well treated on records. Most of the large works —the *Seven Last Words,* the *German Magnificat,* the three Passions, and the two oratorios based on the Christmas and Resurrection stories—have been several times recorded. Of the collections of sacred music, Wilhelm Ehmann has overseen recordings of the *Kleine Geistliche Konzerte* and the *Geistliche Chormusik* of 1648, there are at least two recordings of the *Cantiones sacrae,* and one of the 1618 *Psalmen Davids,* as well as generous selections from the Becker Psalter and the *Symphoniae sacrae,* though these need more attention. Finally there are complete recordings of the madrigals, both Italian and German.

[413] BENEDETTI, Pietro (Bā-nä-det′-tē, Pē-ā′-trō)
CLERIC
BORN: Florence, c. 1585
DIED: Florence, July 1649

A musical amateur, Benedetti was one of the first to jump aboard the "new music" bandwagon set rolling by the Florentine monodists. He was a charter member of Marco da Gagliano's [404] Accademia degli Elevati, in which he was known as "L'Invaghito" or "The Enamored." Indeed, he seems to have been very close to Gagliano. He went with him to Mantua to help with the 1608 wedding festivities (for Francesco Gonzaga and Margaret of Savoy), where, apparently wishing to help preserve his amateur status, they offered him no pay. (It is therefore understandable that a couple of years later he refused, on economic grounds, to join Cardinal Gonzaga's entourage in Rome.) Between 1611 and 1617 he published at least three books of *Musiche* (monodies), apparently his entire musical output. Either some of these pieces are extremely adventurous or Benedetti didn't know what he was doing. Later he was a court chaplain, and then, as "San Amato Abate," held, as did Gagliano, a canonry at the church of San Lorenzo in Florence.

[414] BUONAMENTE, (Fra) Giovanni Battista (Bwō-nä-mān′-tä, Jō-vàn′-nē Bàt-tēs′-tà)
MONK, SINGER, VIOLINIST, CHOIRMASTER
BORN: Mantua, c. 1585
DIED: Assisi, August 29, 1642

After serving for a time at the Mantuan court, Buonamente probably went to Vienna in the retinue of Eleanora Gonzaga when she went in 1622 to marry the Emperor Ferdinand II. He seems to have served the emperor as a violinist until 1631, when he ostensibly left to join the head chapter of his order (the Franciscans) in Assisi. Instead, however, he went to Bergamo to take a lucrative job as instrumentalist and countertenor at the basilica of Santa Maria Maggiore. But when the emperor waxed wroth, Buonamente suddenly went AWOL. On his way to Assisi, however, he found employment in the ducal church in Parma. But he was soon on his way again, and by 1633 he was running the choir in the basilica in Assisi. Two years later his health gave way, and he was relieved of his duties, though not of his title. Time has not been kind to Buonamente. Although he appears to have been a key figure in the development of violin music and of the sonata, only the last four of his eight known instrumental publications are extant, and all but a handful of his considerable number of religious compositions have vanished.

[415] FARRANT, Daniel
VIOL PLAYER, VIOLINIST, TROMBONIST
BORN: c. 1585 (?)
DIED: after 1640, before 1661

There were several musical Farrants in the Elizabethan and Jacobean eras. Daniel seems to have been related to none of the others, even though some historians argue that there must have been two people with this name. Daniel Farrant became a violinist to King James I in 1607. At some point he married Katherine Lanier, the daughter of one of Elizabeth's recorder players. Later in James's reign, in 1619, he was listed as a viol player, replacing one Thomas Browne, and in the days of Charles I he officially performed on the sackbut. He was still in harness in 1640 but was dead by the time Charles II restored the Royal Music in 1661. His contemporaries admired him as a pioneer, with John Coprario [373] and the younger Alfonso Ferrabosco [375], in writing for the gamba tuned "lyra-way" (i.e., like a lute). The publisher John Playford attributed to him the invention of wire-strung bowed instruments called the polyphant and the stump. However, Queen Elizabeth was supposedly playing the polyphant when Farrant was a child. (Later politicians have preferred the stump.) Farrant's sole known legacy is a handful of pieces for lute, for viol, and for consort.

[416] HASSE, Peter (Hȧs'-sə, Pȧ'-ter)
ORGANIST, TEACHER
BORN: Franconia, c. 1585
DIED: Lübeck, c. June 15, 1640

Peter Hasse was the first significantly musical member of the dynasty that culminated in the redoubtable Johann Adolf Hasse [736]. Evidence suggests that he studied in Amsterdam with Sweelinck [313] before taking over the Marienkirche organ in Lübeck, where he officiated until his death twenty-four years later. Among his many pupils, one of the more notable was his son, Nikolaus, a composer of parts and a Rostock organist. Three other sons also studied with him. A granddaughter married the organist-composer Nicolaus Bruhns [600]. Hasse was succeeded by Franz Tunder [486]. Of his music only 2 choral pieces and 3 organ works are presently known.

[417] HELDER, Bartholomäus (Hel'-der, Bär-tō-lō-mä'-ōōs)
PASTOR, SCHOOLMASTER, POET
BORN: Gotha, 1585
DIED: Remstedt, October 28, 1635

Son of the rector of the local Gymnasium, Helder studied theology at the University of Leipzig (1603–c. 6). Beginning in 1607 he taught school in Friemar, a village near Gotha, until he was appointed pastor in Remstedt, another town in the vicinity, in 1616. He died of the plague. His compositions consist mostly of hymns and Lieder, the former including the well-known New Year's chorale Das alte Jahr vergangen ist (The Old Year Has Gone). At their best his hymns are simple and obviously deeply felt.

[418] SELMA Y SALAVERDE, Bartolomeo (Sel'-mä ē Sä-lä-vâr'-thä, Bär-tō-lō-mä'-ō)
MONK, BASSOONIST
BORN: c. 1585 (?)
DIED: 1638 or later

The son of a Spanish court musician, Selma joined the Augustinian order and developed into perhaps the first great virtuoso bassoonist. His international acclaim won him a job at the Innsbruck court of Archduke Leopold in 1628. Later he may have been employed by the Bishop of Breslau. In 1638 he published a collection of "canzoni, fantasie, & correnti" for one or more bassoons and continuo—the first bassoon music, apparently, to be printed. RECORDINGS: Arthur Grossman has recorded seven solo fantasias.

[419] SCHEIN, Johann Hermann (Shīn, Yō'-hȧn Hâr'-mȧn)
CHOIR DIRECTOR
BORN: Grünhain, January 20, 1586
DIED: Leipzig, November 19, 1630

Chronologically speaking, the second of the three S's of German Baroque music—Schütz [412], Schein, Scheidt [426]—Schein was the son of a Lutheran pastor of nearby Meissen. The latter died when his son was seven, and the family moved to Dresden, where six years later the boy was taken into the Chapel of Christian II. When his soprano days were over in 1603, the elector sent him for four years to the school founded two generations before by the Elector Moritz at Pforta. There followed a four-year study of the law at Leipzig, during which, in 1609, Schein published a collection of songs, Venus Kräntzlein (Venus's Garland). After his graduation Schein briefly became tutor to the children of an old school friend, Captain Gottfried von Wolffersdorf, in Weissenfels. This connection soon won him the post of Kapellmeister to Johann Ernst II at Weimar, in 1615. A year later he married a girl from his native village, Sidonia Hösel, and later that year was named successor to Seth Calvisius as cantor of the Thomaskirche in

Leipzig, thus becoming a predecessor of Bach (in that post). Whatever the job was worth in money and prestige, the duties were backbreaking, and the tubercular Schein's health worsened under the burden. Four of his five children died, followed by his wife in the summer of 1624. Eight months later he married Elisabeth von der Perre, but they had no better luck with their five children. Schein developed other ailments, including gout and kidney stones, which increasingly incapacitated him. Shortly before his death (at forty-three) he was visited by his friend Heinrich Schütz [412].

Despite the brevity of his life and the pressure of his duties, Schein turned out, mainly in the first Leipzig decade, a large amount of music, most of it vocal. His chief importance is in the history of the German chorale, which had assumed, in the Protestant liturgy of Mitteleuropa, a place not unlike that of Gregorian chant in the Catholic. His last publication, the *Cantional oder Gesangbuch Augspurgischer Confession* of 1627, contained over 200 chorales for church and home use; he wrote some of the texts, about a third of the tunes, and all the arrangements (which abandon the Church modes for modern diatonic harmonies). Even more important to the history of music was the use to which he put the chorale tunes. The new wine demanded new bottles, and these were imported from Italy. In the 2 volumes of the *Opella nova* (from 1618 and 1626), subtitled *Geistliche Konzerte* (spiritual concerti)—a term that Schein seems to have coined—he brings together the chorale and the vocal *concerto* (with accompaniment). Schein has been said to have taken his cue from Lodovico Viadana [308], but in rhythmic and harmonic terms his bass line is more logically planned, and his word settings reflect the "affect" or implied emotion with an almost Monteverdian passion. Schein's method is to use his chorale melody not straightforwardly but thematically, embellishing it, varying it, and fragmenting it to bring the parts together in new juxtapositions.

Italian traits appear in Schein's other vocal music as well. The songs of *Venus Kräntzlein* are in effect German *canzonette*. Those of *Musica boscareccia (Sylvan Music; 3 volumes, 1621–28)* are three-part *villanesche* which may be sung *a cappella*, accompanied, or as lute songs. The *Diletti pastorali (Pastoral Delights, 1624)* and *Fontana d'Israel (Israel's Fount, 1623)* are pastoral madrigals in the "new style," to secular and sacred texts. (Schein wrote his own lyrics.) And the 1615 *Cymbalum Sionium* is a collec-

tion of Venetian-style motets, some of them polychoral. Finally, Schein also has a place in the history of instrumental music. The *Banchetto musicale (Musical Banquet, 1617)* takes the variation suite beyond Paul Peuerl [340], extending it to four movements, which are sometimes abstract music rather than functional dances.

RECORDINGS: For a composer of his importance, Schein has received shockingly little phonographic attention, at least in this country. The Whikehart Chorale has produced a disc of Latin and German choral pieces, and suites from the *Banchetto* have been included in programs of Baroque dance music, but other representation depends on anthologies.

[420] PRAETORIUS, Jakob (Prī-tô'-rē-ōōs, Yä'-kōp)
ORGANIST, TEACHER
BORN: Hamburg, February 8, 1586
DIED: Hamburg, October 22, 1651

Jakob Praetorius was the second of the four sons of Hieronymus Praetorius [298], the Hamburg organist, and there is no need to rehearse the origin of his surname. His earliest lessons were probably with his father, but he is known chiefly as a pupil of Sweelinck [313]. He evidently studied with him when still quite young, for he became the organist of the Petrikirche in his home town when he was seventeen, held the post until his death forty-eight years later. Among his pupils was Matthias Weckmann. He contributed motets to his father's *Opus musicum* and chorale settings to the *Melodeyen Gesangbuch*. He also left some wedding pieces, chorale preludes, and other organ works.

[421] SIEFERT, Paul (Zē'-fert, Poul)
ORGANIST
BORN: Danzig (now Gdansk), June 28, 1586
DIED: Danzig, May 6, 1666

Like Jakob Praetorius [420], Siefert was a pupil of Sweelinck [313] and a representative of the North German organ school. From 1609 to 1616 he played in Danzig churches, then became organist at the Warsaw court of Sigismund III of Poland (and occasionally Sweden). Siefert did not get on well with people there, and in 1623 he returned permanently to the Marienkirche in Danzig, where he had had his first job. There he quarreled constantly with the choir director, Kaspar Förster, largely for misinterpreting his music, demanding that he be disciplined or dismissed. In 1643 Marco Scacchi [459], director of the Royal Chapel in Warsaw since c. 1628, took up the cudgels for Förster, attacking Siefert in a tract *Cribrum musicum at triticum Syferticum (Musical Sieve for Siefertian Wheat)* for compositional errors (by Italian standards). Siefert responded in kind with *Anticribratio musica,* saying that he was in effect not Italian and that Scacchi was a lousy composer himself, whereupon Scacchi unleashed a fusillade of published letters by noted musicians defending his position. Siefert was probably the loser, but to judge from his extant compositions—notably a 2-volume collection of psalms—he was a composer of considerable inventiveness and looked ahead to the chorale cantata that would culminate in J. S. Bach [684].

[422] SARACINI, Claudio (Sà-rà-chē'-nē, Kloud'-yō)
SINGER, LUTENIST
BORN: Siena, July 1, 1586
DIED: after 1649

Saracini was a musical dilettante (in the proper sense) and a gentleman of leisure who spent much time in traveling and in hobnobbing with other Italian nobles of consequence. His family home, the Palazzo Saracini, one of several modeled after the Palazzo Pubblico in Siena, still stands— "rude yet distinguished," says James Schevill in his history of the city—and the family musical tradition is still carried on by Count Guido Chigi-Saracini, a great patron of music. From his nickname, "Il Palusi," it has been guessed that Claudio Saracini was a member of one of the fashionable academies. For all that he was technically an amateur, he was one of the finest composers of monodic song of the generation after Monteverdi [333], with whom he may have studied. Of his 6 *Musiche,* 1614–24, for voice (or two voices in Vol. 1) and lute, 5 are extant.

[423] BOËSSET, Anthoine, Sieur de Villedieu (Bwô-sā', Àn'-twàn)
COURT DIRECTOR OF MUSIC
BORN: Blois, 1586
DIED: Paris, December 8, 1643

Little or nothing seems to be known of Boësset's background or of his life before February 1616, in which month he married Jeanne Guédron, daughter of Pierre Guédron [351], Claude Le Jeune's [211] successor as Master of the Music of the King's Chamber. At that time Boësset was apparently already in charge of the Queen's Music. (The king was Louis XIII, not Louis XII as one respected writer on music has it; the queen was Anne of Austria, and there were musketeers all over the place.) Boësset is said to have bought his father-in-law's title from him, and certainly after 1623 he was officially Superintendent of the King's Music and Master of the Queen's; he was also Councillor and Steward-in-Ordinary to the King. His eldest son, Jean Baptiste (later Seigneur de Dehault) (c. 1613–85), succeeded him, and was in turn succeeded by *his* son, Claude Jean Baptiste, Seigneur de Launay (1664–?) until he was ousted by Lully's [517] son.

From about 1613, Boësset was one of the chief musical collaborators on the songs and dances of the court ballets. Among his dramatic works was something called *La Mort d'Adonis (Adonis' Death),* which may have been an early stab at opera; unfortunately, it was never performed. Boësset was—and is— best known for his *airs de cour,* many of which came from his ballet pieces. He published, between 1617 and 1642, nine volumes for ensembles of four and five voices. As early as 1620 he was including occasional passages for solo lute, and toward the end of his life he was experimenting with the newfangled *basso continuo.* He also edited Vols. XI–XVI of the publisher Pierre Ballard's series *Airs de différents auteurs,* with lute tablature, in which many of his own songs were included. He was a notable melodist, and his instincts were lyric rather than dramatic; his music demonstrates no special cognizance of developments in Italy. There are, however, some unsubstantiated hints that he was a pioneer in the French solo cantata, and it is true that as he developed he worked harder to make his music reflect his texts.

[424] FALCONIERI, Andrea (Fal-kôn-yer'-ē, Àn'-drā-à)
LUTENIST
BORN: Naples, 1586
DIED: Naples, July 29, 1656

In the sketchy facts that we have about Falconieri's life, one seems to see outlined a restless and freewheeling spirit. He left Naples quite young and at eighteen wound up playing for his room and board at the court of Ranuccio I Farnese, Duke of Parma, described as "a gloomy bigot." Seven years later the duke decided that Falconieri's lute playing during breakfast and supper made him feel less gloomy (if no less bigoted) and put him on salary. Perhaps Andrea felt that his Parmesan studies with Santino Garsi had qualified him for better things, or perhaps the gloom got to him, for in 1614 he cut and ran. He probably went to Mantua, though we first hear of him in a letter written to Duke Vincenzo II from Florence in 1615. The next year he was in Rome, where he published his *villanelle* for one or more voices and Spanish guitar (an instrument he would have known, perhaps, from Spanish Naples). After another stopover in Florence in 1619, Falconieri seems to have found a place at the court of Modena. There he married and ostensibly settled down, but by 1621 he was off to Spain, together with his music but not his wife, perhaps to study the guitar, on which he seems to have been an authority, in its native habitat. From Spain he went to France, and when he finally returned to Italy in 1629, it was not to Modena but back to Parma, where he worked until 1535. He certainly did not then return to Modena because of the Gloomy Duke's death, that having occurred thirteen years earlier, the current duke being the bellicose Odoardo. But by 1637, Falconieri was off to Genoa and two years later we find him strumming his lute in the viceregal chapel back home in Naples, where he succeeded Giovanni Maria Trabaci [383] as *maestro* in 1647. In 1642 he took a leave to visit his wife and daughter in Modena! He died a victim of the plague epidemic of 1656.

Falconieri published at least 6 books of songs for one, two, and three voices with guitar (in Spanish tablature), but only three are extant. As a song composer in the "new style," he is one of the most tuneful and attractive, and some of his pieces look ahead to the recitative-and-aria form. There is also a late collection, from 1650, of pieces for strings and continuo, entitled *Canzoni, sinfonie, fantasie.*

RECORDINGS: Songs have been recorded by Hugues Cuénod and (in modern arrangements) by Igor Gorin, Gérard Souzay, Ezio Pinza, and Conchita Supervia, among others.

[425] LUKAČÍC, Marko Ivan (Lōō-kå'-chĕkh, Mär'-kō Ĩ'-vån)
CHOIR DIRECTOR, ADMINISTRATOR, MONK
BORN: Šibenik, April 17 (?), 1587
DIED: Spalato, September 20, 1648

Born about twenty-five miles upcoast from Spalato (now Split) in Dalmatia, Lukačíc joined the Franciscans in childhood or early adolescence. He took an M.Mus. in Rome in 1615, and three years later returned to Spalato, where he became director of the cathe-dral choir and soon afterward *padre guardiano* of the Franciscan monastery as well. In the latter post he seems not to have satisfied everyone. In 1634, for instance, he was ousted in favor of one Bonaventura Rinaldi from Krk, Croatia, but returned to his job when Rinaldi failed to claim it. Six years later he was replaced by another monk, whose administration turned out so badly that Lukačíc had to take over again. He finally retired in 1644. His Croatian name should lead no one to expect wild Slavic music from him, for the Dalmatian coast had been long since Italianized, and he was clearly *au courant* with recent developments across the Adriatic. His only known publication, the *Sacrae cantiones* (Venice, 1620), makes considerable use of solo voices and of continuo. RECORDINGS: Selections have been recorded by Denis Stevens.

[426] SCHEIDT, Samuel (Shīt, Zå'-mōō-el)
ORGANIST, CHOIR DIRECTOR, TEACHER
BORN: Halle, November 3 (?), 1587
DIED: Halle, March 24, 1654

Born ninety-eight years before another musical native of Halle, George Friderick Handel [683], Scheidt was the youngest of the three *S*'s of German Baroque music. (He later collaborated on occasion with Schütz [412] in providing music for special programs, and Schein [419] stood godfather to Susanna Scheidt in 1623.) His father, Konrad, was a city official; his mother, Anna Achtmann, was a baker's daughter; and his younger brothers Gottfried and Christian followed him in the organ-playing business. Samuel studied at the local *Gymnasium* and was already ensconced at the organ of the fourteenth-century Moritzkirche at the age of sixteen. After a few years he went—as did brother Gottfried a bit later—to Amsterdam to study with Sweelinck [313], whose best pupil he turned out to be. In 1609, Christian Wilhelm, Markgraf of Brandenburg, became administrator of the district, which was under the rule of the Archbishop of Magdeburg, and appointed Scheidt his court organist (who was also cathedral organist). After serving under a series of *Kapellmeisters*, including the restless Michael Praetorius [360] and the peripatetic William Brade [299], Scheidt was himself given the post in Halle, c. 1620, in addition to his other duties. He evidently throve on work, for in the next five years he built up the musical organization, published at least nine collections of his vocal and instrumental music, and helped build a new organ in the Moritzkirche. By

1625, however, the Thirty Years War was turning ugly, and the Markgraf marched off to help the Protestants, leaving his chapel in limbo. Scheidt seems to have survived by freelancing and giving lessons. In 1628, a year after his marriage, he was, for what it was worth, named municipal music director, his chief duty being to play and compose for the Marktkirche. But there he locked horns with the rector of the *Gymnasium,* one Gueinz, over who had the final say on the choirboys' musical education, and was forced out in 1630. Very hard times followed. Magdeburg was destroyed and its inhabitants massacred in 1631. In 1634 the Marktkirche organist claimed that Scheidt's freelance composing was invading his turf, and that source of income was cut off, at least locally. Two years later the plague took all his children, and in 1637 the castle, known as the Moritzburg, burned down. Scheidt, however, managed to go on writing and publishing. In 1638 the Markgraf dropped the reins and went off to live in Königsberg, and the city was taken over by Duke August of Saxony, who restored Scheidt to his former position. It is hard to tell what his last years were like. In 1642 he was seeking the patronage of the Duke of Braunschweig, and in 1650 he fulfilled, with a collection of organ chorales, a commission from the city fathers of Görlitz (now on the East German–Polish frontier). He was still teaching in that year, for his best-known pupil, Adam Krieger [519], came to him about then. Frau Scheidt died two years before her husband. It is said he was by that time reduced to penury, but that can hardly be true, since he left money for the upkeep of the Moritzkirche organ.

Though Scheidt, like Schein, is an important figure in the history of the chorale, he is most notable for his application of it to organ music, the realm wherein he shines brightest. Indeed he may not improperly be thought of as the German Frescobaldi [407]. If his own era valued him most for his vocal compositions, it was perhaps because they—notably the *Geistliche Konzerte* of the early 1620s—were, at least superficially, cast in the mold of the big Venetian polychoral motet. This is not, however, to deny their importance. In the earlier *Cantiones sacrae* of 1620, he, by applying the variation technique he had learned from Sweelinck to chorale melodies, looks toward the Bachian cantata of a century later. In the bad years, Scheidt, like Schütz, lowered his sights and wrote for small scratch ensembles.

Scheidt's monument is his tripartite *Tablatura nova* of 1624, dedicated to his employer, for it marks not only the abandonment of the antiquated organ tablature in favor of modern notation, but also the coming of age of German organ music. The first two parts contain song variations, both sacred and secular, as well as dances, fantasias, and so-called fugues. The third is (like Frescobaldi's *Fiori musicali)* devoted to music for worship—versets to be played in response to the ministerial intonations. Here chorales provide the *cantus* and the harmonies are in the new diatonic style. In his chorale variations Scheidt eschews the prescribed figurations then customarily inserted between the notes of the tune, and permits the variant to develop from the demands of the tune itself. Moreover, he writes for what we term a "Baroque" organ, with pedal board and expanded range of stops. In the third part the chorale melody is kept intact in the pedal, and Scheidt specifies the registers and stops he wants used, in the name of color and contrast, for the embellishments. A volume of "musical games" for consort, a fragmentary set of *Symphonien* for two melody instruments and continuo, and a collection of canons round out his extant output.

RECORDINGS: Scheidt has been rather sparsely treated on records, most representations appearing in anthologies, though Luther Noss and Michael Schneider have devoted a disc apiece to the *Tabulatura.*

---

[427] **FABRICIUS, Petrus** (Fà-brēs'-yo͞os, Pä'-tro͞os)

PASTOR, ASTRONOMER, MATHEMATICIAN, LUTENIST

BORN: Tondern, 1587
DIED: Warnitz, 1651

Born plain Peter Schmidt in what is now Tønder, Fabricius spent most of his life in country that now belongs to Denmark but was then part of Germany. In 1603 he entered the University of Rostock, where, after studying mathematics and astronomy, he took an M.Th. in 1608. Two years later he became assistant to the pastor at Bülderup (Bjolderup), succeeding him in 1613. After marrying Maria Jacobi, the daughter of a colleague, he became pastor of Warnitz (now part of Åbenrå in 1617) and spent the rest of his days there, devoting his nights to the stars. We have no information on his musical training or accomplishments, other than the collection of popular songs and dances for lute that he intabulated during his last years in school.

[428] MARINI, Biagio (Mȧ-rē'-nē, Byȧ'-jō)
VIOLINIST, CHOIRMASTER
BORN: Brescia, c. 1587
DIED: Venice, 1663

Like his fellow Brescian, Giovanni Battista Fontana **[394]**—who was *not* his teacher—Marini was one of the first composers known to have been a professional violinist (possibly a virtuoso). He seems to have been a restless sort. He began his known career under Monteverdi **[333]** at St. Mark's, Venice, in 1615, went home no more than five years later to direct the Accademia degli Erranti, and in 1621 became a musician to Duke Ranuccio I Farnese in Parma. A year or so later he became, at least nominally, *Kapellmeister* of the little princely court at Neuburg on the Bavarian Danube, a post he held for a quarter century, during which he turns up in Brussels, Düsseldorf, and several Italian cities. In 1649 he returned to Italy as *maestro di cappella* at Santa Maria della Scala in Milan, but three years later he was in Ferrara, then Venice, and then Vicenza. His last years he divided between Venice and his birthplace. He published at least 22 opuses (several are lost). His vocal works show the influence of Monteverdi and other moderns but are of less interest than his instrumental pieces. His Op. 1 of 1617—a miscellany of dances, *canzoni*, etc., for from one to three violins or cornetts and continuo—includes three *sonate*, one of them for solo instrument and continuo. Another piece calls for string tremolo eight years before Monteverdi's vaunted "invention" of that effect. About half of the 1626 Op. 8 is devoted to "sonatas," some of them quite ingeniously conceived, and here and there calling for such advanced violinistic techniques as double stopping and *scordatura* (special tunings). His last publication, in 1655, shows *sonata* now divided into two species, "church" and "chamber" (though these terms do not indicate what they came to later), and offers clear examples of the solo-accompanied concept.

[429] CALESTANI, Vincenzo (Kȧ-le-stȧ'-nē, Vēn-chȧnt'-zō)
TEACHER
BORN: Lucca, March 10, 1589
DIED: 1617 or later

This obscure composer of the *Madrigali ed arie* of 1617 may have been related to the even more obscure Lucchese composer Girolamo Calestani, author of the *Sacri fiori musicali* of 1603. He lived and taught in Pisa

prior to publication of his book, and may have been associated there with the religious order Cavalieri di San Stefano. His most famous song (much recorded) is *"Damigella, tutta bella."* The collection also includes an essay on problems of word setting.

[430] ARAÑÉS, Juan (Ȧ-rȧn-yȧz', Hwȧn)
CHOIRMASTER, PRIEST
BORN: Catalonia, c. 1590 (?)
DIED: after 1649

Arañés studied theology at the University of Alcalá de Henares and was ordained. From 1623 he was briefly chaplain in Rome to Don Ruy Gómez de Silva, Spanish ambassador to the Vatican, and published there in 1624 his only known volume, a second collection of *tonos y villancicos* for one or more voices and guitar (the instrument that had by then superseded the vihuela). Back in Spain by 1627, he was singing master at Urgel Cathedral for seven years. After that he drops out of sight until 1649, when he was rehired for a year at Urgel. A few other fugitive pieces by him have turned up.

[431] BOUZIGNAC, Guillaume (Boō-zēn-yȧk', Gwē-yōm')
CHOIRMASTER (?), TEACHER
BORN: Narbonne, c. 1590
DIED: after 1641

A curiously isolated and independent figure, this shadowy composer apparently spent his whole life in the provinces. After several years as a choirboy in the now defunct cathedral at Narbonne, he stayed on for a time as teacher to choirboys. In 1609 he was holding a similar post at the church of St. André in Grenoble. After that, most of what we know of him derives from hints in the texts to which he set his music. We catch tantalizing glimpses of him at Carcassonne, Angoulême, and Rodez. Toward the end of his life he is said to have been in Tours, either at the cathedral of St. Martin or the abbey of Marmoutiers; there are no surviving records to prove or disprove it, but the discovery of a large number of anonymous manuscripts in Tours that are almost certainly Bouzignac's suggests the story to be so. Apart from a few songs, all the surviving works, certain or attributed, are motets, save for a *Lamentations*. Though, like many of his contemporaries, he opposes a large choir and a small one, Bouzignac's approach is quite atypical. He uses his forces for dramatic effect, sometimes having a solo voice "argue" with the main body. He likes to use speech rhythms, staccato phrases, and word painting. He invented a whole lexicon of musical devices to represent specific emotional values. He seems at times to anticipate the oratorios of Carissimi [471], and thus of Marc-Antoine Charpentier [544], but it is highly doubtful that either composer ever heard of him or his music. RECORDINGS: Four of his motets have been recorded (appropriately) by the choir of St. Martin de Tours.

[432] VAN EYCK, Jacob (Jonkheer) (Van Ĭk, Yä-kōb)
CARILLONNEUR, RECORDER PLAYER, TEACHER, ACOUSTICIAN
BORN: c. 1590
DIED: Utrecht, March 26, 1657

Van Eyck was of noble descent and was blind. In 1625 he went from Heusden in North Brabant to Utrecht as cathedral carillonneur. Three years later his salary was boosted from 400 to 500 guilders because of his handicap. By 1632 he was general overseer of bells in Utrecht and a noted teacher. Later he was given the curious additional duty of playing the recorder before and after services in the churchyard of St. Jan's. Van Eyck worked out the mathematical relationship of bell shape to purity of tone, and his findings produced superior carillon bells. Today he is chiefly remembered for his 2-volume *Der fluyten lust-hof* (1644–46), a big collection of variations for solo recorder, which has enjoyed much popularity in the latter-day recorder renaissance.

[433] JARZĘBSKI, Adam (Yä-zheb'-skē, Ä'-dàm)
VIOLINIST, POET, ARCHITECT
BORN: Warka, Poland, c. 1590
DIED: Warsaw, c. 1649

Greatly admired as a performer, Jarzębski had more than one string to his bow. Apart from his birthplace (about thirty miles southeast of Warsaw on the River Pilica), we know nothing of his background, youth, or education. The first landmark is his appointment as violinist to the Elector Johann Siegmund of Brandenburg in Berlin in 1612. In the electoral court he was thrown in contact with excellent musicians from all over Europe. In 1615 he went to Italy to study for a year. Johann Siegmund died in 1619, and his successor, Georg Wilhelm, being interested chiefly in hunting and horseflesh, the chapel went to pot. Jarzębski thereupon returned to Poland, which happily was still there, and in

1620 was appointed violinist in Warsaw to King Sigismund (or Zygmunt) III, sometime King of Sweden. He remained there until his death. Designated as "Royal Architect," he was given the task of designing the Ujázdow Palace outside Warsaw. In 1643 he published a versified description of Warsaw, and five years later was named a patrician of that city. His son, Szymon (c. 1630–79), was also a violinist at the Warsaw court.

All of Jarzębski's known compositions date from the Berlin years, and all are, unusually for that date, instrumental chamber works for two, three, and four unspecified instruments and continuo. Some at least show the marks of his Italian experience. The four-part pieces are termed simply *canzone,* without other titles. The others *(concerti)* are designated by fanciful names *(Sentinella, Bentrovata),* some of which *(Berlinesa, Königsberga)* perhaps indicate where they were written.

RECORDINGS: The Polish state recording company, Muza, dedicates a whole record to Jarzębski in its Musica Antiqua Polonica series and also includes him in several collections.

[434] MIELCZEWSKI, Marcin (Myel-chev'-skē, Mär-tsēn')
CHOIRMASTER
BORN: c. 1590 (?)
DIED: Warsaw, September 1651

The first known fact about Mielczewski is that in 1638 he was a member of the Warsaw chapel of King Ladislas IV. We do not know in what capacity he then served, nor when he was promoted to *maestro,* but we do know that he was replaced in the latter post by the Italian Marco Scacchi [459] in 1643. Obviously Scacchi thought well of him because he included some of Mielczewski's works in his *Cribrum musicum* that same year. By 1645, however, Mielczewski was a member of the little chapel maintained by the king's brother, Karol Ferdynand, Bishop of Płock, remaining there until he died.

In his sacred music, which represents the majority of his extant work, Mielczewski is a watershed figure. Many of his Masses and motets are of the old polyphonic *cantus firmus* style, but other pieces are in the new Venetian *concertato* tradition, opposing voices (solo and choral) and instruments. A *Benedictio et claritas,* for instance, calls for six vocal parts, two violins, and four other instruments. A *Deus in nomine tuo* is a *sacro concerto*—i.e., solo cantata. His seven preserved instrumental *canzoni* specify the instrumentation.

RECORDINGS: His Sunday Vesper service has been recorded by Edmund Kajdasz, and most of the *canzoni* appear on various records of the Muza series of Polish historical music. The *Deus in nomine tuo* has been recorded by Paul Matthen and by Witold Piłewski.

[435] PADILLA, Juan Gutiérrez de (Pä-dē'-yä, Hwàn Gōōt-yâr'-*eth* dä)
SINGER, CHOIRMASTER, PRIEST
BORN: Málaga, c. 1590
DIED: Puebla, Mexico, spring 1664

Until recently accounts of the life of this early American composer were hopelessly confused with those of his Spanish contemporary Juan de Padilla (1605–73). The present Padilla was a choirboy at Málaga Cathedral and in early manhood choir director of Jerez de la Frontera. After ordination he held the same post at Cádiz Cathedral from 1616 to at least 1620. Two years later he is found, inexplicably, singing in the cathedral choir at Puebla, Mexico, a town seventy-five miles southeast of Mexico City, for some time established as a musical center and one on which the Church continued to lavish money. Seven years later he was in charge there, and remained so, growing rich and famous, for thirty-five years. During that time he saw the cathedral completed and dedicated, in 1649. Besides directing the choir, he personally trained the choristers, taught chant to the other clergy, and ran an instrument shop from his home. His music, carefully preserved by the chapter, includes 5 Masses, a *St. Matthew Passion,* motets, lamentations, litanies, and a large number of *villancicos.* His church music is conservative, looking back to the polyphonic era, though he writes diatonically rather than modally and delights in polychoral effects. The secular pieces are less ambitious, incorporating popular elements. Padilla ranks very high among early Latin American composers.

[436] JENKINS, John
VIOL PLAYER, LUTENIST, TEACHER
BORN: Maidstone, 1592
DIED: Kimberley, Norfolk, October 27, 1678

Much of what we know of John Jenkins is owing to the *Memoires of Musick,* by his adoring pupil Roger North. The first child of the 1591 marriage of Henry Jenkins, a musical carpenter, and Anne Jordaine, he inherited a pandora from his father in 1617. Virtually nothing else is known of his life prior to the Puritan takeover, save that he helped with a court masque in London in 1634. After that he seems to have survived on his skill at being a nice man and making himself welcome to his many friends in the countryside. When he showed up at a front door, people were prepared for him to stay, and many a home had a "Jenkins Room" awaiting him. During the Commonwealth he could usually be found at the Derehams' (or Derings') in Norfolk or at the home of Sir Hamon L'Estrange, whose son Roger, later a Royalist pamphleteer, translator, and pioneer newspaperman, studied the viola da gamba with him. At the Restoration, Charles II appointed him to the King's Music, but by then he was staying with the family of Dudley, fourth Baron North, at Kirtling in Cambridgeshire, where he tutored the fifth and sixth sons, Montague and Roger. Roger was later solicitor general under James II and the family biographer. According to his testimony, Jenkins was perfectly happy to accept the Norths' hospitality and the token four pounds annual salary that Lord North tendered him. Though so enfeebled in his last years that he could not carry out his court commitments, he was kept on the royal payroll to the end. He died at the home of Sir Philip Wodehouse and was buried in the Kimberley churchyard. His tombstone bears a rhymed epitaph that concludes "Aged eighty-six, October twenty-seven,/In anno seventy-eight he went to heaven." Among his many friends were the poet Thomas Shadwell, the composer William Lawes [463], for whom he wrote an elegy, and no doubt the antiquarian Anthony à Wood, who called him "the little man with the great soul."

Roger North says that Jenkins wrote "horseloads of music." Fewer than 30 vocal pieces have survived, but his instrumental pieces run to around 150. These range from early consort fantasias of a decidedly contrapuntal bent to works for violin(s) and continuo. Though he seems increasingly to have been influenced by currents blowing from Italy and by King Charles's taste for the Frenchified violins, the foreign elements never obliterate his Englishness, and there is always a leavening of personal warmth and feeling. Among the instrumental works are several "rants" *(Mitter Rant, Fleece Tavern Rant, Peterborough Rant);* these turn out not to be musical rodomontades but dance pieces, which may take their generic name from *courant.* Jenkins is said to have published the first English sonatas—a set of 12 trio sonatas—in 1660. Unhappily for that notion, a certain William Young had published some sonatas in Austria as early as

1653, and no trace of the Jenkins opus has ever showed up. However, he did leave in manuscript five pieces that he called sonatas. RECORDINGS: Most of the scattered Jenkins recordings are of the consort pieces.

[437] STEIGLEDER, Hans Ulrich (Shtīg'-lä-der, Hänts OŌl'-rēkh)
ORGANIST, ENGRAVER
BORN: Schwäbisch Hall (Württemberg), March 22, 1593
DIED: Stuttgart, October 10, 1635

Like his exact contemporary Melchior Schildt [438], the crippled Steigleder was a third-generation organist. A pupil of his father, Adam (1561–1633), he first served as organist of the Stefanskirche in Lindau, then in 1617 returned to his native territory as organist of the Stiftskirche in Stuttgart, a post held earlier by his father and his grandfather, Utz Steigleder (d. 1581). In 1624 he published (from his own copperplates) his organ book *Ricercar tablatura*, like Samuel Scheidt [426] in that same year eschewing tablature for a five-line score in musical notation. It was, incidentally, the first German music to use the copperplate process. In 1627, when he became ducal organist (a post also held by old Utz), he published a second work, *Tablatur Buch*, a set of 40 chorale variations on the Lord's Prayer. He died at forty-two of the war-bred plague epidemic. The first book shows not only the expectable Italian influence typical of the South German organ school, but also an acquaintance with the music of the English virginalists.

[438] SCHILDT, Melchior (Shēlt, Mel'-khē-ôr)
ORGANIST
BORN: Hanover, 1593
DIED: Hanover, May 18, 1667

Representing the third generation of a family of Hanover church organists, Schildt, after studying with his father, Antonius, and the local composer Andreas Crappius (c. 1542–1623), went off to Amsterdam for three years as disciple to Sweelinck [313]. What became of him during the next decade no one presently knows, but by 1623 he was court organist to Duke Friedrich Ulrich of Braunschweig-Wolfenbüttel, employer to the late Michael Praetorius [360]. He spent three years there and three more at the Danish court in a similar capacity. After the death of Antonius Schildt and the defeat of Christian IV of Denmark, Melchior came home to succeed his father at the

Marktkirche, where he held forth for the next thirty-eight years. He left a single *Geistliche Konzert* and a handful of masterly organ works, including a set of variations on the *Lachrymae* pavane of John Dowland [316].

[439] FARNABY, Richard
VIRGINALIST
BORN: London, c. 1594
DIED: before 1665

"Sonne to Giles Farnaby" [317], according to the *Fitzwilliam Virginal Book*, Richard Farnaby went as a boy with his family to Lincolnshire, where in 1608 he was indentured to Sir Nicholas Saunderson, ostensibly to teach music to the young Saundersons. Evidently the contract did not take, for he was back in London in 1614 to marry Elizabeth Sendye. Presumably she was the widowed Elizabeth Farnaby who remarried in 1665. His only musical legacy is the 4 pieces in the Fitzwilliam collection.

[440] WILSON, John
LUTENIST, SINGER, PROFESSOR
BORN: April 5, 1595
DIED: Westminster, February 22, 1674

Wilson was born within a year of his lifelong friend Henry Lawes [444], according to long tradition, in Faversham, near Canterbury. In adolescence or young manhood he moved to London and by 1614 was writing songs for Shakespeare's theatrical company, the King's Men (though the Bard had retired by then). He obviously knew Ben Jonson, who inscribed a set of his works to him, and, using the name of "Jack" Wilson, was already winning a reputation as a clown, albeit probably not a professional one. (He sang, however, in a revival of *Much Ado About Nothing.*) In 1622 he became a town musician, or "wait," to the city of London. Two years later his wife, Jone, died, leaving him presumably with the daughter remembered in his will fifty years later. In 1635 he joined Lawes as a member of King Charles's Musick. When the king fled to Oxford in 1641, as the civil war gathered momentum, Wilson cast his lot with his employer and used the opportunity to pick up a D.Mus. from the university in March 1645. He so dazzled Anthony à Wood that he pronounced Wilson "the best at the lute in all England" and "the greatest judge of music that ever was." After the collapse of the monarchy, Wilson lived for a decade at the home of Sir William Walter in the nearby countryside. In 1656, however, he moved to rooms in Balliol College when he was appointed University Coragus, a post that would now be called the Professorship of Music. At the Restoration he resigned to take up his place at court. In 1662 he was named a Gentleman of the Chapel Royal, a title he had coveted all his mature life, though doubtless not through the death of Lawes, whose place he took. (Lawes had praised Wilson's integrity, his "true and honest heart," and "his great art, which I but dully understand.") In January 1671, posing, according to the official record, as a "widower about 66," he married the widow Anne Penniall in Westminster Abbey —where he was buried three years later, having magically added twelve years to his age in the interim.

Wilson published 2 collections for three voices and continuo, the *Psalterium Carolinum* in 1657 and *Cheerfull Ayres and Ballads* in 1660, but he left many more secular songs (including Shakespeare settings) and some lute pieces, both published (in collections) and unpublished.

[441] BERTI, Giovanni Pietro (Bâr'-tē, Jō-vàn'-nē Pē-ā'-trō)
ORGANIST, SINGER
BORN: c. 1595 (?)
DIED: Venice, 1638

What we know of Berti relates to his employment at St. Mark's in Venice, where he sang tenor under the direction of Monteverdi [333], and in 1624 was appointed number-two organist. Though paid almost as well as any organist in Europe, he insisted on moonlighting, thereby drawing several reprimands from his superiors. On his sudden and unexpected death, he was succeeded by Cavalli [464]. Despite his identification with the organ, Berti, as a composer, has most bearing on the history of solo song. Most of his efforts are to be found in 2 books of *Cantade ed arie* (published in 1624 and 1627), in which the chief concentration is on arias, notably of the strophic variety and marked by a fine melodic gift. The "cantatas" are not quite that, but point to the soon to be popular solo cantata, with its alternations of recitative and aria.

[442] MERULA, Tarquinio (Mä-rōō'-là, Tär-kwĕn'-yō)
ORGANIST, CHOIRMASTER
BORN: Cremona, 1594 or 1595
DIED: Cremona, December 10, 1665

Not to be confused with his older contemporary, Claudio Merulo [230], Tarquinio Merula seems, perhaps with reason, to have been a restless and uneasy man. In 1616 he went to Lodi as organist of the church of Santa Maria Incoronata. After five years he migrated to Warsaw, where he was organist to Sigismund III for about four years. From 1626 for perhaps another five years he was back home in Cremona directing music for the Marian services in the cathedral and playing the organ at Santa Agata. After the death of Alessandro Grandi [377], he was called to Bergamo in 1631 to rebuild and direct the musical organization of Santa Maria Maggiore, but at the end of the following year he was sacked for hanky-panky with the choirboys. Merula blustered until the authorities showed him that he had no case, and he went back to his old job at Cremona Cathedral. But that lasted only for a couple of years, for he got into a quarrel with his superiors and quit. No later than 1638 he returned to Bergamo as *maestro di cappella* of the cathedral. Evidently his proclivities were the same, for the choir at Santa Maria, which was sometimes loaned to the cathedral, was warned to stay away from it. In 1646 he settled in Cremona as *maestro* of its cathedral.

Honored by the pope with the Order of the Golden Spur and by the increasingly prestigious Accademia dei Filomusici in Bologna, Merula was an avant-gardist of stature. He published at least 18 opuses that included Masses, psalms, motets, madrigals, *canzonette,* and instrumental *canzone.* He was also an early experimenter in the realm of the sonata and in 1643 collaborated with four other composers on an opera produced in Venice. Like many Baroque composers, he liked odd titles for his publications, such as *Pegasus, Curtius Leaping,* and *David's Harp.* He had obviously a sense of humor, as one sees in his "grammatical madrigal" entitled *Nominativo: hic, haec, hoc.*

RECORDINGS: To date he has been represented on records chiefly by organ pieces.

[443] SCHEIDEMANN, Heinrich (Shī'-də-màn, Hīn'-rikh)
ORGANIST, TEACHER
BORN: Wöhrden, c. 1595
DIED: Hamburg, 1663

David Scheidemann, village organist of Wöhrden in Holstein, moved to Hamburg, soon after the birth of his son, to become organist at the Katharinenkirche, and to collaborate with Hieronymus Praetorius [298], Jakob Praetorius [420], and Joachim Decker

[374] on the *Melodeyen Gesangbuch.* (Or so the most recent information indicates. Earlier accounts name David as Heinrich's uncle and Michaelskirche organist and give Heinrich's father's name as Hans.) After studies with his father, Heinrich went to Amsterdam for what by then had become the mandatory three years with Sweelinck [313]. After 1614 we hear no more of him until he turns up in 1629 as successor to David (or Hans) at the Katharinenkirche. There he remained, a modest and unassuming man, apparently unruffled by his growing fame as performer and composer and his popularity as a teacher. His most famous pupil was Johann Adam Reincken [498], who succeeded him (after Scheidemann succumbed to the plague) and held the post for sixty-eight years. With Scheidt [426], Scheidemann is one of the most important North German organists in the development of an organ (as distinguished from keyboard) style. Apart from a collection of hymn tunes, he left a considerable body of organ and harpsichord works.

[444] LAWES, Henry
SINGER, ACTOR
BORN: Dinton, Wiltshire, January 5, 1596
DIED: London, October 21, 1662

Henry Lawes was born in a village near Salisbury to Thomas Lawes and the former Lucris Shepherd. Around the turn of the century, the family moved into the city, where the father became a singing man in the cathedral choir in 1602 at 12 pounds a year. (Toward the end of his life his son persuaded the authorities to promote him to vicar choral.) Henry, the oldest of five children (William, Elizabeth, Thomas Jr., and John), probably received his early musical training as a chorister under John Bartlett. At some time before 1615 he went up to London, where he is traditionally said to have studied with John Coprario [373]; if he did, he probably came to know John Egerton, future Earl of Bridgwater, who was also a pupil of Coprario. In January 1626 he was admitted to the Chapel Royal in the probationary status of "epistoler." (Legend says he attracted King James's notice when the latter heard him sing at Salisbury Cathedral the previous autumn.) On the following October 28 he became a Gentleman of the Chapel at something over 16 pounds a year plus the usual fringe benefits (room, board, clothing, free time, bonuses, etc.). Later he was appointed a member of the King's Musick at an additional 20 pounds. Among his duties

was that of performing in the court masques, as well as providing music for them. His first music for the stage was probably that for Peter Hausted's Cambridge comedy *The Rival Friends,* played before King Charles I on March 19, 1632. The chapel accompanied His Majesty to Edinburgh on his belated Scottish coronation trip, and was spattered with mud by the mob, angry because Anglican ritual was used. In 1633, Lawes set Thomas Carew's masque *Coelum Britannicum,* and a year later played the role of a Constellation in *The Triumph of Peace,* by James Shirley, presented by the Inns of Court.

September of 1634 saw the presentation at Ludlow Castle in Shropshire of the work for which Lawes is best remembered—John Milton's nameless masque now known as *Comus.* The occasion was the raising of John Egerton, who was now Earl of Bridgwater, to the ceremonial post of President of Wales, and the performers included his children and Henry Lawes as the Attendant Spirit. The outlines of the work follow closely those of *Coelum Britannicum,* and there is little doubt that Lawes worked closely with Milton. (He probably did so with the earlier *Arcades* as well.) Of the music, however, only the 5 songs remain. The following February, Lawes collaborated with his brother William and William Davenant, the future Poet Laureate. (Lawes was also a friend of Robert Herrick and seems to have known Edmund Waller, John Suckling, Richard Lovelace, and other important poets.) At the end of July 1636, on the occasion of the king's Oxford visit, Lawes furnished music for the plays *The Floating Island* by William Strode (not the parliamentarian) and *The Royal Slave* by William Cartwright. In 1637 there appeared Lawes's first publication, a setting for voice and continuo of some of George Sandys's metrical psalms and selections from *Job.* A year later he intervened to help Milton get a passport to Rome for his Italian tour.

Little is known of Lawes during the Civil War and the Commonwealth. He was possibly with the royal party at Oxford prior to the king's escape and capture. In 1642 a Henry Lawes married an Elizabeth Dally and in 1650 a Henry Lawes married an Elizabeth Miles, but in his will composer Henry Lawes calls his wife Eleanor, so his marital history remains obscure. Letters written during the period indicate that he was for a while in tight financial straits. Milton's sonnet on Lawes was written in 1645, shortly before the death of William Lawes in battle. By 1647 Henry had returned to London, where in 1648 he published a new version of

the psalms, in three-part settings by himself
and William, and including his own elegy
for his brother. Henry set up as a music
master and apparently attracted a clientele
of wealthy and noble ladies. His household
concerts came to be a fashionable social focus. In 1656 (the theaters being closed by Puritan ban), he and poet William Davenant
wrote a musical quasi-dramatic piece, which
they presented at Rutland House. It was so
well received that they followed it up with a
pastiche musical play, *The Siege of Rhodes,*
now lost but said to be the first English opera. (The Puritans had not been foresighted
enough to ban that form of theater.) With
the Restoration, Lawes was given his old
posts back, made Clerk of the Cheque
(records keeper) in the chapel, and asked to
write the coronation anthem, *Zadok the
Priest.* (He never received any pay under
Charles II.) Lawes fell ill before the coronation and died not quite two years later. He
was buried in Westminster Abbey, but all
trace of his tomb has gone.

Henry Lawes is an interesting figure, immensely respected as a composer in his own
day. The psalms aside, most of what is extant consists of songs for voice and continuo
—the medium for which he was chiefly
noted. If his contemporaries, such as Milton
and Herrick, overrated him, there has been a
tendency since to underrate him. His taste in
poetry was excellent, and his chief concern
seems to have been to bring out the meaning
and feeling of the words. The result is something more tuneful than the Italian monodies—an early attempt at the "art song," if
you will.

RECORDINGS: There is a fine recorded anthology by Helen Watts and one of *Comus*
that includes the songs.

[445] JELIĆ, Vinko (alias Vincenz Jelich)
  (Ye'-lich, Vin'-kō)
  SINGER, LUTENIST, PRIEST
  BORN: Fiume, 1596
  DIED: Zabern (now Saverne), Alsace (?),
  1636

Vinko Jelić was originally called Jeličić, and
his birthplace on the Croatian coast is now
called Rijeka. At the age of ten he went to
Graz as a chorister to Archduke Ferdinand
of Styria (later emperor as Ferdinand III).
When Vinko's brother, Peter, also a chorister in the archduke's chapel, died, the boy
went home for a year but returned in 1610 to
study at the Ferdinandeum and later at the
university. He kept up his link with the
chapel, traveling with it, for example, to
Wiener Neustadt in 1614 as an instrumental-

ist. (His teacher was one Matteo Ferrabosco,
of the non-English branch of that innumerable musical clan.) In 1616 Jelić embarked on
his theological career, attaining ordination
two years later and the vicarate of the
church of St. Mary in Zabern, Alsace, where
he had gone to serve Archduke Leopold. He
also, however, continued to function as a
court musician. During the Thirty Years
War, Zabern was repeatedly ravaged by various armies. The archduke fled in 1625, much
of the town was destroyed, and the population suffered from plague and hunger. Jelić
was still there when the French took it in
1636, but is not heard from afterward.

All of Jelić's music seems to have been
published in Strasbourg in the war years. It
is contained in 3 volumes: *Parnassia militia*
of 1622, *Arion I,* and *Arion II* (both 1628).
All these show a strong Venetian influence—
concerti for one or more voices, continuo or
organ accompaniment, and the use of instruments (notably brasses). Jelić's entire output
is religious in application.

RECORDINGS: Denis Stevens and the Accademia Monteverdiana have recorded six
selections. He is also represented on several
Jugoton (a Yugoslav label) recordings.

[446] ROSSI, Luigi (Rôs'-sē, Loo-ē'-jē)
  ORGANIST, LUTENIST, TEACHER
  BORN: Torremaggiore, c. 1597
  DIED: Rome, February 20, 1653

Apparently unrelated to Salamone Rossi
[341] or Michelangelo Rossi [466], Luigi
was the son of Donato Rossi of Torremaggiore, northeastward across the boot from
Naples. As a youth he studied in the latter
city with Jean ("Giovanni") de Macque.
Probably in the early 1620s he took service
in Rome with Marc'Antonio Borghese, and
there married the household harpist, Costanza de Ponte, in 1627. In 1633 he was appointed organist of the church of San Luigi
dei Francesi. Two years later he and Costanza were given leave to spend six months
at the Florentine court, at the invitation of
Grand Duke Ferdinando II. This was indicative of the spread of Rossi's fame, and he
was soon being acknowledged as the foremost composer in Rome. In 1641 he was
lured away from the Borghese by Cardinal
Antonio Barberini, an ex-soldier whose
brother, Maffeo, had in 1623 been elected
pope as Urban VIII. During that autumn
Rossi fell so gravely sick that he made out
his will but fortunately recovered to write
his first opera, a seven-hour Ariostan extravaganza called *Il Palazzo incantato,* which the

cardinal produced in his own *palazzo* the following February.

In 1644 Pope Urban died, and was succeeded by a Roman rival, Giovanni Battista Pamfili, elevated to the see as Innocent X. Belying his name, the pope immediately cast his lot with the emperor and began seizing the property of the pro-French Barberini. The cardinal and his relatives fled to Paris, where they found a friend and protector in Cardinal Mazarin *(né* Giulio Mazarini), the power behind a throne nominally occupied by the seven-year-old Louis XIV. Evidently the newly arrived cardinal quickly convinced the established one of the genius of his sometime musician, for in 1646 Mazarin sent for him to write a second opera which he would produce. The result was *Orfeo,* premiered in the Palais Royal in March 1647, at a cost to the French taxpayers of 300,000 écus. The audience considered Rossi's alternation of recitatives and arias not to its taste, but it adored the special-effects "machines" designed by Giacomo Torelli, the leading theatrical engineer of the day. During preparations Costanza Rossi died, and the widower returned briefly to Rome but was back in time to see his opera. That summer he went back to his church job, but before the year was out Mazarin had invited him to come write yet another opera, to impress the high quality of Italian music on the stubborn French. But by then the stubborn French had had it with Mazarin and were threatening to do more than withhold their applause. Shortly after Rossi reached Paris, the civil upheaval known as *La Fronde* (from the slingshots used to smash Mazarin's windows) began. Cardinal Barberini discreetly holed up near Lyons, where Rossi caught up with him in September 1649. Toward the end of the year he returned to Rome for good. He was survived by three sons and his brother Giovan Carlo, a harpist.

Rossi's chief impact was in his vocal music. Besides his two operas, he left several oratorios, and around 300 cantatas for one and two voices with continuo, all reflecting a new tendency. For a long time, it was the word that had primacy, the chief function of the music being to bring out its meaning. In Rossi we see the reaction in an emphasis on musical beauty (the *bel canto* notion) for its own sake. Though general attention was paid to meaning, the stress was on sensuous melody—sometimes to the detriment of the harmony, which tended to become a stripped-down tonic-dominant affair. Earlier cantatas had been cast either as extended monodies—dramatic musical recitations— or as strophic variations. Rossi's were, at

their simplest, neatly structured songs, and, at their most ambitious, successions of recitative, arioso, and aria. Frequently these are given shape and continuity through the use of a recurrent *ritornello.* In his operas and oratorios one already sees the direction such forms would take, with the chief emphasis on aria and the recitative reduced to a means of advancing the action and linking one set piece with the next. Obviously an important composer, Rossi remains largely neglected.

RECORDINGS: The only major representation of his music on records to date is his oratorio *Giuseppe, figlio di Giacobbe* of 1624.

[447] CRÜGER, Johann (Krü′-ger, Yō′-hàn)
TEACHER, THEORIST, CANTOR
BORN: Gross Breesen, April 9, 1598
DIED: Berlin, February 23, 1662

Crüger came from near Guben, now on the East German–Polish frontier southeast of Berlin. At fifteen he set out on his travels, stopping by Regensburg for some musical tutoring from Paul Homburger, cantor of the Gymnasium Poeticum, then proceeding through Austria, Hungary, modern Czechoslovakia, and Saxony before winding up in Berlin in 1615 as tutor to the children of an army officer, Christoph von Blumenthal. In 1619 he published some wedding music there, but the next year enrolled at Wittenberg as a theology student. Probably that plan did not work out, for by 1622 he was back in Berlin as cantor to the Nikolaikirche and Greyfriars Gymnasium, where he officiated for the next forty years.

Crüger published a number of musical manuals of no great originality and some miscellaneous compositions but is remembered chiefly as one of the towering figures in the history of the chorale. His magnum opus was *Praxis pietatis melica,* a collection of 137 hymn tunes, fitted to texts by the hymnologist Paul Gerhardt and others, with continuo rather than vocal harmonizations —the first such collection issued and the most popular of its time. Eighteen of the tunes, including *Jesu, meine Freude,* are Crüger's. Nine years later, in 1649, he reissued the collection as *Geistliche Kirchen-Melodeien,* with upper instrumental parts for melody instruments added. Crüger claimed to have invented the notion, which shows how much he knew.

[448] DECKER, Johann (Dek′-ker, Yō′-hàn)
ORGANIST

BORN: Hamburg, October 6, 1598
DIED: Hamburg, September 19, 1668

Decker was in all probability a pupil of his father, Hamburg organist Joachim Decker [374]. In 1624, after stints at the Magdalenkirche and the Michaelskirche, he became organist of the cathedral and remained there for the rest of his life. A few of his organ pieces are extant.

[449] ESPERANÇA, Dom Pedro de (Ás-per-àn'-sà, Dŏn Pā'-thrōō)
ORGANIST
BORN: c. 1598
DIED: Coimbra, June 24, 1660

Dom Pedro's origins are obscure. He evidently became a monk at an early age and lived to regret it. An attempt to flee the cloister in 1617 got him a five-year sentence on bread and water, or whatever the going subsistence diet was. Ten years later he was transferred from Lisbon to Coimbra, where they obviously thought better of him. He was organist (and perhaps choir director) there until his death. Of his compositions, only a few choral works have survived. RECORDINGS: Most surviving works have been recorded by Denys Darlow and the Tilford Bach Festival choir.

[450] HILTON, John (the younger)
ORGANIST, EDITOR
BORN: Cambridge, 1599
DIED: Westminster, c. March 20, 1657

If, as seems most likely, the younger Hilton was the son of the elder [303], he would have been born at Cambridge, not at Oxford, as some earlier accounts suggest. At any rate, he was awarded a B.Mus. in 1626 by Cambridge's Trinity College. A year later he dedicated his first publication, *Ayres or Fa La's*, to "William Heather" (Heyther), member of the Chapel Royal and founder of the Oxford professorship of music, with the implication that he had been Hilton's teacher. In 1628 he became organist of St. Margaret's, Westminster. Though the job presumably ended with the Civil War, he lived in that suburb for the rest of his life. In 1652 he brought out a collection of catches with the catchy title of *Catch that Catch Can*. It caught on and was frequently reprinted—but unhappily not in its editor's lifetime. His ayres represent the last gasp of that tradition, but he left in manuscript a number of excellent songs and musical dialogues, as well as a few fantasias for viols.

There is also a body of church music—services, a *Te Deum*, and anthems—by "Johr Hilton," but no one seemed certain whicl John Hilton is intended.

[451] HOLTZNER, Anton (Hōlz'-ner, Àn'-tōn)
ORGANIST
BORN: c. 1599
DIED: Munich, 1635

A chorister at the Bavarian court in 1607, Holtzner traveled in Italy (presumably to study) after his voice broke and returned in 1619 as court organist. Between then and 1631 he published 4 collections, including one of Masses and one of Magnificats. He also wrote some organ canzonas. His music shows some Italian influence.

[452] ATTEY, John
LUTENIST
BORN: c. 1600 (?)
DIED: Ross, 1640

John Attey was the last English lutenist to put on true ayres publicly. He did so in 1622 in a book of same, optimistically called "the first." In it he says that he had been in the service of John Egerton, Earl of Bridgwater, in Hertfordshire, tutoring his daughters—and, as such, must have known Henry Lawes [444]. There appears to be no substantiation for the date and place (near Gloucester) given for Attey's death.

[453] FANTINI, Girolamo (Fàn-tē'-nē, Jē-rō'-là-mō)
TRUMPETER
BORN: Spoleto, c. 1600
DIED: after 1638

Little is known about Fantini before 1630, when he was appointed head trumpeter at the court of Grand Duke Ferdinando II in Florence. He was apparently a virtuoso performer on what was then a severely limited instrument. He once played in the Palazzo Borghese in Rome, accompanied by none other than Girolamo Frescobaldi [407]. His trumpet method of 1638 was one of the earliest (probably the second to be printed), but its musical contents—120 pieces, including 8 solo sonatas for one or two trumpets and continuo—offer the first known music specifically for accompanied trumpet. RECORDINGS: Edward Tarr, who edited the trumpet sonatas, has recorded several of them.

[454] **LILIUS, Franciszek** (Lē'-lōōs, Frán'-
tsi-shek)
CHOIRMASTER, PRIEST
BORN: c. 1600 (?)
DIED: Gromnik, Poland, late summer
1657

According to some sources, Lilius was a son
and pupil of a Roman musician, Vincenzo
Gigli, who served the Polish King Sigismund III from c. 1600. In any case, they
were certainly related, and were colleagues
at the Warsaw court. In 1630 Franziszek became choirmaster of Cracow Cathedral and
was ordained six years later. The approach
of the Swedish army in 1655, as a result of
the so-called Thirteen Years War, caused
him to flee the city. He is said to have died
two years later in the Carpathians. Only a
dozen or so of his (religious) works have survived intact. They show him working in
both the polyphonic and polychoral styles.
RECORDINGS: Edmund Kajdasz has recorded a *Missa brevissima* in the latter vein.

[455] **MICHNA Z OTRADOVIC, Adam
Václav** (Mikh'-ná zə Ō-trá-dō'-vits, Á'-
dám Vá'-tsláf)
ORGANIST, POET, MERCHANT, POLITI-
CIAN
BORN: Jindřichův Hradec, c. 1600
DIED: Jindřichův Hradec, November 7,
1676

The Michnas are said to have been a noble
family. Adam's father was town organist of
Jindřichův Hradek in southeast Bohemia
and overseer at the local castle. Adam, who
succeeded him as organist, was educated by
the local Jesuits, which order later published
much of his music. A man of wealth and
property, he dabbled in local politics and
charities, but his chief occupation was as a
wine merchant. He left a fund for establishing a foundation for needy music students.
As a composer, he was quite influential in
his own time and has his place in the history
of Czech music. His more ambitious works
(all liturgical) are solidly Baroque, calling
for soloists, multiple choirs, and instruments. His *Missa sancti Wenceslai,* for instance, calls for soloists, a six-part choir, violins, violas, trumpets, and continuo. His
best-known works (designed for use in village churches) were his collections of hymn
tunes, arranged for four or more voices and
set to his own texts. These include (titles
translated) *Czech Marian Music,* 1647; *The
Czech Lute,* 1653; and especially *Music for*

the *Holy Year,* 1661. RECORDINGS: Selections
have been recorded by Miroslav Venhoda
and (in instrumental arrangements) by the
Czech Philharmonic's Ensemble Pro Arte
Antiqua.

[456] **MOULINIÉ, Étienne** (Mōō-lan-yā',
Āt'-yen)
CONDUCTOR, TEACHER
BORN: c. 1600
DIED: after 1669

Moulinié came from somewhere near Narbonne, in whose cathedral choir he sang as a
child. In his early twenties he joined his
brother, Antoine, a court musician, in Paris.
In 1626, Louis XIII [460] named his scapegrace brother, Gaston, the Duke of Orléans.
Two years later, thanks to Antoine, Étienne
found himself in charge of the music of
"Monsieur," as the duke was popularly
known. Monsieur kept him busy grinding
out songs and dances for the ballets to which
he was addicted, as well as liturgical pieces
for the chapel. In 1634 he was entrusted with
the musical upbringing of the duke's seven-
year-old daughter, Anne-Marie, the Duchess of Montpensier—"La Grande Mademoiselle." (A dozen years later she was to acquire a musical page named Giovanni Battista Lulli.) Both Monsieur and Mademoiselle had a bad habit of choosing the wrong
political allies and, after the Fronde had
failed, the duke, who had espoused the cause
of the revolutionaries, was put under house
arrest at Blois in 1652, and took his musical
staff with him. When he died eight years
later, Moulinié went home to the south
where, according to his own statement, he
worked as "musician to the Estates of
Languedoc."

His *airs de cour*—three of his five published volumes have survived—were quite
popular. The pretty, simple tunes, which
have only a general bearing on their texts,
were, according to documentary evidence,
somewhat more ornate in performance.
Moulinié seems to have liked to subject
them to rather instrumentally conceived
"diminutions" (variations), which did not
help underline the words. The fifth book of
airs includes a few instrumental fantasias.
He also left a *Requiem* and a collection of
motets and such with continuo—unusual for
French works of the time, in which Moulinié fancied himself an *avant-gardist.*
RECORDINGS: There are recordings of fantasias, songs, and music for a court ballet
(directed by Charles Ravier).

[457] PĘKIEL, Bartolomiej (Pek'-yēl, Bär-tō'-lwō-mye)
ORGANIST, TEACHER, CONDUCTOR
BORN: c. 1600
DIED: c. 1670

Space does not permit a discussion of the orthographic vicissitudes suffered by Pękiel's name. Nothing is known of his early years. By 1637 he was organist at the Warsaw court of Władisław IV. Later he became master of the boys and eventually assistant to Kapellmeister Marco Scacchi [459]. On the accession of Jan Kazimierz in 1648 and Scacchi's subsequent retirement, Pękiel became court music director in fact, though he was not named to the post until 1653. His eminence, however, was short-lived, for in the face of the invasion by Charles X of Sweden the king fled to Silesia in 1655 and Pękiel to Cracow. There he succeeded Franciszek Lilius [454], who had left for similar reasons about the same time, as cathedral choirmaster, a post he presumably held until his death. His musical legacy includes a number of Masses and motets, plus some lute dances and two organ pieces. In his Warsaw days, Pękiel wrote brilliantly in the new Venetian style. In Cracow he came under the influence of the so-called Rorantists, an all-male choir of one of the cathedral chapels, who insisted on a more conservative and "purer" approach. RE-CORDINGS: The *Missa Pulcherrima*, in this quasi-Palestrinan style, has been recorded by Edmund Kajdasz.

[458] PESENTI, Martino (Pā-zän'-tē, Mär-tē'-nō)
HARPSICHORDIST
BORN: Venice, c. 1600
DIED: Venice, c. 1648

There were several musical Pesentis in Venice in the Renaissance, though Martino's connection with them, if any, is unknown. Born blind, he studied with G. B. Grillo, organist of the Scuola Grande di San Rocco, and became popular among the Beautiful People in Venice as a chamber musician. He published a book of motets (with a Mass) in 1643, but the bulk of his output consists of madrigals (6 books extant), arias, and dances (for harpsichord or consort).

[459] SCACCHI, Marco (Shàk'-kē, Mär'-kō)
CHOIRMASTER, THEORIST

BORN: Gallese, c. 1600
DIED: Gallese, before 1687

Long assumed to have been a Roman, Scacchi was actually born (and died) in a village near Viterbo. But he studied in Rome with Giovanni Francesco Anerio [335], who got him a job at the Warsaw court of Sigismund III when he went there c. 1625 as director of the chapel. By 1628, for reasons unknown, he himself held the post and Anerio was on his fatal trip home. He retained it until 1649, when he resigned because he was not feeling at all well. During the Polish years—specifically 1643–49—he created a teapot tempest with his attack on the supposed compositional conservatism and ineptitude of his sometime colleague Paul Siefert (for details, see 421). After resigning, Scacchi returned to Gallese where, his health obviously having improved, he taught for thirty-odd years. Much of Scacchi's music, including about a dozen operas, has vanished. There remain some Masses, motets, and madrigals. He wrote learnedly about musical styles and himself used a highly eclectic approach. RECORD-INGS: There is a recording of a cantata on the election of King Jan Kazimierz by Stefan Sutkowski.

[460] LOUIS XIII, King of France
BORN: Paris, September 27, 1601
DIED: Paris, May 14, 1643

Monarchic composers are not unknown, but Louis XIII appears to be the only serious French contender to the name. The son of Henry IV of Navarre and Marie de Médicis, he became king in name on his father's assassination in 1610, though his mother, who was not a Medici for nothing, took what amounted to total charge of both kingdom and kinglet. Among the things she saw to was his musical education. He had shown an unusual passion for both music and dancing from early childhood, and the musical establishment he inherited included that forerunner of the modern orchestra, the *24 Violons du Roy*. His chief teacher was the lutenist Robert Ballard **[370]**, and when, in 1615 he brought home a child bride, the Spanish Princess Anne of Austria, Marie detailed another lutenist, Ennemond Gaultier, to teach her. One need hardly inquire why the lute became so popular in seventeenth-century France. Even Cardinal Richelieu, under whose thumb Louis permitted himself to be placed to escape maternal suffocation, occasionally used that digit to strum the strings.

Even more popular, and much more spectacular, than the lute were the court ballets, which got started under Henry III and reached something like their apogee in Louis's reign. In such works His Majesty often kicked up his own heels. He prided himself on his choreographic ability, and to help celebrate his own governmental attainments in 1617, he chose the subject of a spectacular ballet, *La Délivrance de Renaud*, in which he danced the role of a fire demon, and to which he may have contributed some music. His *chef d'oeuvre*, however, was the 1635 *Ballet de la Merlaison*, which in sixteen *entrées* depicted one of the king's favorite sports, blackbird hunting. Here he wrote the book, choreographed the dances, designed the costumes, danced the leading role (that of a farmer), and composed the music. Alexandre Dumas *père* mentions the performance, given at Chantilly, in chapter twenty-two of *Les trois mousquetaires*.

Louis also took an interest in sacred music and occasionally directed the royal chapel, singing away lustily with the choir. He is said to have written some motets while sweating out the siege of La Rochelle, and 4 settings of psalm paraphrases by Antoine Godeau are said to be his. Of his several *airs de cour*, only one, *"Tu crois, o beau soleil"* ("You Think, Fair Sun"), is known to survive. Another, "Amaryllis" (transcribed by Fritz Kreisler as *"Chanson Louis XIII"*), said to have been a bridal present for Anne, is highly dubious. One scholar unhesitatingly calls it authentic, whereas another says it is from a ballet of Baltasar de Beaujoyeulx [215].

RECORDINGS: Roger Cotte has recorded the ballet, the psalms, and the song on one LP.

[461] JIMÉNEZ, José (Hē-mä'-ne*th,* Hō-zä')
ORGANIST
BORN: Zaragoza, c. December 25, 1601
DIED: Zaragoza, August 9, 1672

Jiménez (or Ximénez) became assistant organist to Aguilera de Heredia [324] at the cathedral of his native city in 1620 and succeeded him on his death seven years later. He must have liked the job, for in 1654 he turned down an invitation to become royal organist in Madrid, even though the king, Philip IV, was noted for his support of the fine arts (but not for much else). Jiménez left a small body of organ pieces.

[462] STRUNGK, Delphin (Shtroönk, Del'-fin)
ORGANIST
BORN: c. 1601
DIED: Braunschweig, c. October 10, 1694

Strungk is said to have come from Braunschweig. He became organist of the church of the Blessed Virgin in Wolfenbüttel c. 1630 —some accounts say as successor to Melchior Schildt [438], though Schildt appears to have left as early as 1626. A few years later (dates are variously given as 1632 and 1634), he became court organist to the Duke of Lüneberg-Celle, and then around 1637 went (or returned) to Brunswick as organist of the Marienkirche. His son, Nicolaus Adam, who became a notable composer of operas, was born there in 1640 and was his father's assistant at the Magnuskirche, where Delphin also officiated, twelve years later. Strungk remained in Braunschweig for the last fifty-six of his ninety-three years. He attained great fame as a performer and was one of the composers whom J. S. Bach took careful note of. Six choral works and as many organ pieces are all that are left of it.

[463] LAWES, William
VIOL PLAYER
BORN: Salisbury, c. May 1, 1602
DIED: Chester, September 24, 1645

Because there was a William Lawes (alias Coldbeck) who was a vicar choral (and not a very nice fellow) at Winchester Cathedral as early as 1591, it used to be thought that our William Lawes must be a half-brother of Henry Lawes [444] and at least a generation older. But he was, in fact, six years younger, having been born shortly after the family settled in Salisbury. Though there is no hard evidence, he supposedly sang at the local cathedral and at the age of ten was indentured to the Earl of Hertford, who had him taught by John Coprario [373]. He apparently was, in some capacity, a court musician before officially succeeding a John Lawrence as musician-in-ordinary for the lutes and voices in 1635. Like his brother, he was involved in the writing of masques and incidental music—e.g., James Shirley's *The Triumph of Peace*, Davenant's *The Triumphe of the Prince Damour* (a brotherly collaboration), and Jasper Mayne's comedy *The City Match*, produced for the visiting king's delectation at Oxford in 1636, as well as plays for the King's Men. His songs and catches (some of them naughty, as was the fashion) were immensely popular, and he seems to have been a favorite of King Charles. When, in the face of the Civil War, the king went to Oxford, Lawes stuck with him and went so far as to join the army. His commander, Lord Gerrard, solicitous of his safety, tried to protect him from his own self-sacrificing instincts by assigning him to the commissary department. But in 1645, in the ill-fated attempt to raise the siege of Chester, "gentle Willy" (as Henry's memorial elegy termed him) rashly got caught in a crossfire and was killed. Among the many memorials dedicated to him by the literary and musical world was Henry's *Choice Psalmes*, of 1648, which included works by both brothers and represents the first music by William to reach print.

William Lawes was a more prolific and a more talented composer than his brother. Despite the fame of his songs in their own day, they have been neglected since. He also left a number of anthems, vocal canons, dances, and miscellaneous instrumental pieces. But his best work is in his suites for various groupings of viols, for ingenious "broken" consorts, and for one or two violins and continuo. The best of these show imagination and considerable formal and harmonic ingenuity.

RECORDINGS: Thurston Dart devoted an LP to a selection of these.

[464] CAVALLI, Francesco (Kȧ-vȧl′-lē, Frȧn-ches′-kō)
SINGER, ORGANIST
BORN: Crema, February 14, 1602
DIED: Venice, February 14, 1676

Francesco Cavalli first opened his eyes as Francesco Caletti in a Venetian town between Milan and Cremona. His father and first teacher was Gian Battista Caletti, choirmaster of the local cathedral. Taken with Francesco's voice and talent, the governor, Federico Cavalli, made him his protégé and found him a place in the choir of Monteverdi [333] at St. Mark's in Venice in 1616. There, for some reason, he was called Francesco Bruni. His treble days soon over, he became a tenor (as Francesco Caletto). In 1620 he found an additional job as organist of San Zanipolo (as the Venetians call Santi Giovanni e Paolo). He also seems to have done a considerable amount of moonlighting. In the end, he was forced to neglect some of his commitments, and in 1630 San Zanipolo dropped him (shortly before a severe plague epidemic closed it). By that time, however, he probably did not care, since a few months earlier he had married a wealthy widow, Maria Sozomeno (who

brought him some stepchildren). Evidently his reduced work load and his relative affluence permitted him time to compose, and by mid-decade he was producing music that he signed "Francesco Cavalli," in honor of the man who had made it all (or most of it) possible.

By now Cavalli was known as a formidable organist, and when Giovanni Pietro Berti [441], St. Mark's second organist, died in 1638, he was elected his successor. Though he commanded a high salary and came to be regarded as a rival to Girolamo Frescobaldi [407], he retained the inferior post until Massimiliano Neri (who had pull with the emperor) abandoned the first organ for a court job in Cologne in 1664. Meanwhile, in 1637 Venetian opera had gone public, and two days after he opened at the console of St. Mark's, Cavalli's first opera, *Le nozze di Teti e di Peleo*, opened at the Teatro San Cassiano, a few months before Monteverdi inaugurated the Teatro San Mosè with a revival of *Arianna*. But Monteverdi's swan song, *L'Incoronazione di Poppea*, in 1642, left Cavalli king of the operatic hill. Over the next decade he brought out at least sixteen more works at San Cassiano and other Venetian theaters. In 1652, Maria Caletti died, leaving her estate to her husband (they were childless). By then his fame had spread, and there were prestigious commissions from Milan and Florence, and stagings of others of his works in Naples.

In 1659, Louis XIV reached his majority and, France having won her war against Spain, married Maria Theresia, daughter of the defeated Philip IV. A celebration was planned to make all Europe reel, thanks to the fine Italian hand of Cardinal Mazarin. The preparations involved a grand grand theater in the Tuileries. Though his earlier attempt with Luigi Rossi [446] had been no success, Mazarin decided that this was the ideal opportunity to peddle Italian opera to the French, and that nothing less than a new work from Italy's greatest operatic composer would do. After some rather strenuous negotiations, he was able to get the Venetian authorities to loan him Cavalli in the spring of 1660. He and his party came by way of Innsbruck and München, arriving in midsummer. He began work on the opera, but there was no hurry, the theater being nowhere near ready, much less the wondrous "machines" that the architect-engineer Gasparo Vigarini had been commissioned to furnish. In order that something be gotten on the boards, Mazarin arranged to have Cavalli's 1654 *Xerse* (also known as *Serse*) performed in the Louvre. It was decided that the choruses were either inessential or impracticable, and they were replaced by dance interludes composed by Lully [517], who, under the cardinal's eye, took care to make them sound Italian. The theater was at last ready for *Ercole amante (Hercules in Love)* in 1662. By then Mazarin was dead, but it was decided that considering the money that had gone into it, the show must go on. By prior agreement Lully again supplied the dances, but left to his own devices he tailored them to French tastes. In the end the piece, which played for over six hours, became a ballet with dramatic interludes. The audience is said to have cheered the ex-Florentine and sat on its hands for the adoptive Venetian. Swearing never to write another opera, Cavalli headed for home, bearing the solace of the enormous sum the French had paid him. In the event, he was not as good as his word, and wrote five more operas, but none was particularly successful, and the last two were dropped before they opened. Having become first organist of St. Mark's, as noted, in 1664, he was further elevated four years later, succeeding Monteverdi's pupil and protégé, Giovanni Rovetta, as *maestro di cappella*. A few months before he died, he published a Vesper service—only his second publication in that field (the first, in 1656, included a Mass and some motets). He was buried at San Lorenzo, to whose nuns he left most of his impressive estate, providing a fund to have his requiem sung at St. Mark's twice a year in his memory.

Cavalli's reputation as an operatic composer has been retrieved by modern musicology after centuries of neglect. Thanks to his entrusting his scores to a favorite pupil, twenty-eight of his operas are still extant in as full score as the practice of the time allowed. Whether Cavalli ever studied the genre with Monteverdi, he was strongly influenced by him, especially in starting out. But he was a natural melodist, and even in the earliest examples there is an inclination toward a kind of formal and rhythmic aria that had little place in Monteverdi's work. In fact, in the end it is impossible to say who influenced whom, for this sort of thing does turn up in Monteverdi's final operas, and it is thought that Cavalli may even have had a hand in writing *Poppea*. Cavalli also developed the dramatic lament with *ostinato* bass (see *Dido and Aeneas* of Henry Purcell [581]) and injected comic relief into serious works (as Monteverdi did in *Ulisse* and *Poppea*). He moved toward the duet and other ensemble numbers, and away from the quasi-Greek chorus of the Florentine school. Toward the end one finds him regularly using the short *da capo* aria (the open-

ing section repeated following a contrasting second section.) One might say that with Cavalli *bel canto* came to opera.

In recent years there have been a number of productions of Cavalli—most notoriously Raymond Leppard's at Glyndebourne. Mr. Leppard has been much criticized for playing fast and loose with both plot and music, but evidence suggests that such tampering was not uncommon in the composer's day.

RECORDINGS: Raymond Leppard has recorded his versions of the 1652 *La Calisto* and *L'Ormindo* from 1644, as well as a disc of selections from other works. *L'Erismena* of 1656 has been recorded by Alan Curtis in *his* edition. There are also recordings of the polychoral *Messa concertata* by Hans Ludwig Hirsch and Umberto Cattini, the *Ercole amante* by Michel Corboz, and the *Missa pro defunctis* by Hans Ludwig Hirsch.

[465] CHAMBONNIÈRES, Jacques Champion, Sieur de (Shàn-bun-yâr', Zhàk Shàmp-yôn', Syör də)
HARPSICHORDIST
BORN: Paris, c. 1602
DIED: Paris, spring 1672

Jacques Champion came from a line of court musicians extending at least back to Nicolas Champion, a member of Francis I's chapel. Nicolas' grandson, Thomas, and *his* son, Jacques *l'aîné*, were harpsichordists. In 1601 the last-named married Anne Chartriot, and Jacques *cadet* was the first fruit of the union. At that time the father was known as the Sieur de La Chapelle. Anne's father, Robert, however, was a fairly big cheese in Brie—a nobleman of uncertain title known as the Sieur de Chambonnières. Since virtually everything about young Jacques's early years is murky, we do not know how he came to be so called. We do know, however, that he showed early talent, for he was not yet ten when he was named legal successor to his father's post at court. Within another decade he had married a certain Marie Leclerc and sired a son. But it was not apparently until the early 1630s that, as Gentleman Ordinary to the King's Chamber, he began to make a real impression as a virtuoso—regarded with the kind of awe one attaches to the Victorian keyboard kings. He was also a demon dancer, who footed it side by side with Louis XIV and Jean-Baptiste Lully [517] in the court ballets. In 1641 he inaugurated a series of concerts, the *Assemblée des Honnestes Curieux* (Assembly of the Truly Inquisitive), involving a band of ten and guest artists performing on Wednesdays and Saturdays. His father died the next year, and Chambonnières acquired the title of Spinet Player to the King—but not for long, because Louis XIII died a few months later, and the dowager queen had her own musical establishment.

The morning of the Feast of St. James, probably in 1650, Chambonnières was back at his table in Brie, probably enjoying the breakfast of Champions, when he was unexpectedly treated to an *aubade,* performed by the Couperin brothers, Louis [504], François (Sieur de Crouilly), and Charles, who lived just down the road. He was so delighted that he invited them all to Paris to be his pupils, and later introduced Louis at one of his concerts. But then things began to take a turn for the worse. Marie died and in 1652 Chambonnières married Marguerite Ferret, daughter of an official in the law courts. The Fronde was turning the country upside down, and Chambonnières, who seems to have been something of a pompous ass, was making enemies among his associates. By 1654 he was begging his great friend and admirer Constantijn Huygens, the Dutch poet and diplomat, to find him another post, and there were some negotiations between him and Queen Christina of Sweden that came to nothing. Three years later the king, Louis XIV, without notice, replaced him as royal harpsichord teacher, he lost the estate of Chambonnières in a lawsuit, and Marguerite obtained a legal separation (though they went on living under the same roof). Only Louis Couperin's loyalty prevented a coup in which he would have replaced his old teacher altogether. With Lully's rise to power, Chambonnières was deprived of his pension. Moreover, his musical abilities began to fail. Called upon to play continuo for Lully's orchestra, he refused on the grounds that he could not read figured bass parts and had no intention of learning to. In 1662 he sold his court post to Jean-Henri D'Anglebert [520], and apparently spent his final decade teaching and occasionally concertizing. Two years before he died he brought out his only publications: 2 books containing 60 keyboard pieces. (Others survive in manuscript.)

It now seems hardly likely that Chambonnières was really the "father of French harpsichord music," as he used to be termed, but he was the first performer of international repute, the first significant composer in the "French harpsichord style," a great teacher, and a strong influence on such foreigners as Johann Jakob Froberger [490]. Much has been made of how he supposedly adapted lute technique to his own instrument (see 468), and it is true that the great days of Chambonnières followed hard on the heels of the great age of French lute music, but the alleged connection may be merely a case of *post hoc, ergo propter hoc.* Like lute music, Chambonnières' harpsichord works are characterized by broken chords and arpeggios, odd titles, and a whole battery of figurations. (Our knowledge of the interrelations is hampered, says an unfortunate typo, by the "high morality rate" of seventeenth-century harpsichords.) In his two published collections, Chambonnières arranges his pieces as dance suites, usually involving allemandes, courantes, sarabandes, and other optional forms; the links between them, however, are tonic rather than thematic.

RECORDINGS: Programs have been recorded by, among others, Lionel Party, Daniel Pinkham, and Edward Smith.

[466] ROSSI, Michelangelo (Rôs'-sē, Mē-kel-àn'-jel-ō)
KEYBOARDIST, VIOLINIST
BORN: Genoa, c. 1602
DIED: Rome, c. July 5, 1656

Unrelated, so far as we know, to other Rossis treated here [341, 446], Michelangelo Rossi, son of Carlo, was taught by his father's brother, Lelio, cathedral organist in Genoa, and later served as his assistant. He moved to Rome in the early 1620s, joined the musical establishment of Cardinal Maurizio di Savoia, and studied further with Frescobaldi [407]. Just how and where he learned to play the violin is not known, but he was obviously one of the first great virtuosi and was called "the Michelangelo of the violin." Later he was patronized by the Barberini, one of whose number reigned during this period as Pope Urban VIII, and it was for a production in the Palazzo Barberini in 1633 (sets by Gian Lorenzo Bernini) that Rossi wrote his opera *Erminia sul Giordano.* Manfred Bukofzer describes it as "biblical," but its only biblical aspect is the River Jordan, the plot being taken from Torquato Tasso. (There is a big part for Apollo as virtuoso violinist.) Five years later he went north, and we catch glimpses of him in Modena, Ferrara (another opera, *Andromeda,* now lost), and Bologna. Rossi is now chiefly remembered for his keyboard pieces—mostly toccatas and *corrente,* about three dozen in all—which show his affiliation with Frescobaldi.

[467] SMITH, William
CLERGYMAN, SINGER

BORN: Durham, c. April 3, 1603
DIED: Durham, April 19, 1645

Smith's (church) music was long assigned to an earlier Durham organist, William Smythe, who died about the time he was born. William was orphaned as a small child, reared by relatives, sang treble in the cathedral choir, attended Cambridge, married Grace Hodgeson when he was twenty-two, and for the rest of his life was connected with various local churches as well as with the cathedral. He evidently played the organ, for he once filled in at the cathedral while the intendant was serving a jail sentence. He left some anthems, preces, and responses, all very ingeniously polyphonic and High Church in sound.

[468] GAULTIER, Denis (Gōt-yā', Də-nēs')

LUTENIST
BORN: 1603
DIED: Paris, 1672

In the high noon of French lute music, Paris boasted several lutenists named Gaultier (variously spelled). Denis ("Gaultier le jeune") seems to have been related (as a cousin) only to Ennemond ("Gaultier le vieux"), lute tutor to Anne of Austria (see 460). Denis taught and worked in Paris (but not at court) from 1625 or earlier. Ennemond retired to the Dauphiné in 1631. Among his pupils, Denis probably numbered Charles Mouton [505] and the Sieur de Lenclos (the father of Ninon, the famous courtesan and social arbiter). Otherwise their contemporaries and subsequent history have hopelessly confused the careers of the two. However, two lute collections, *La Rhétorique des dieux* and *Pièces de luth* (dates uncertain) are surely Denis's.

In the first quarter of the seventeenth century in Paris, the lute was the instrument *par excellence* (owing in part to its court associations). Gaultier brought it to its apogee, and the edge of its swift decline. Previously it had been devoted to playing *chanson* transcriptions or accompanying *airs*. Taking his cue, to all appearances, from the English virginalists, Gaultier made it an instrument with a profile and a repertoire all its own. A magnificent technician, he developed the *style brisé* (broken style), whereby, largely through the use of ornament and arpeggiation, an instrument ill suited to polyphony could be made to sound polyphonic. Gaultier also advanced the dance suite, adding to the mandatory allemande, courante, and sarabande a "tuning-up" pre-

lude (undoubtedly from an improvisatory tradition) and other dances, such as the chaconne and gigue, ad lib. These last, not designed for dancing, but abstracted and stylized, were given quaint names, such as *La Belle homicide* (The Pretty Murderess), indicating that they were meant to be musical portraits. Finally, Gaultier (or the Gaultiers) probably invented the *tombeau*, a sort of slow allemande, intended as a memorial to some well-known person.

RECORDINGS: Besides considerable representation of Gaultier in anthologies, there is a recording of the *Rhétorique*.

[469] ALBERT, Heinrich (Ä1'-bârt, Hīn'-rikh)

ORGANIST, LAWYER, ENGINEER
BORN: Lobenstein, July 8, 1604
DIED: Königsberg, October 6, 1651

Saxon-born Heinrich Albert called Heinrich Schütz [412] "uncle," but they were probably cousins at one remove. At eighteen Albert went off to Dresden to study with his relative, but his family had more practical plans for him, and the next several years found him working on a law degree in Leipzig instead, though he began composing while there. In 1626 he moved to Königsberg (now Kaliningrad, Russia). But a year later he joined a Dutch peace mission bound for Warsaw, and managed to get himself taken prisoner by the Swedes. He returned to Königsberg in 1628, worked for a time as a military engineer, and studied music with the Brandenburg court *Kapellmeister*, Johann Stobaeus, a pupil of Johannes Eccard [274]. In 1631 he got what turned out to be a lifetime appointment as cathedral organist, and in 1638 married a citizeness, Elisabeth Starke. Between the latter year and 1650 he published the eight volumes of *Arien* (ranging from hymns to drinking songs) on which his fame as a composer chiefly rests. Albert looms large in the history of the *Lied*, being the most important practitioner of the continuo song in North Germany before the much later Adam Krieger [519]. His *Lieder*, consisting of melody and bass, were designed for home use. Basically strophic, they are, however, not doggedly repetitious, and recitativelike links make some of them almost small cantatas.

[470] BACH, Johann (Bàkh, Yō'-hàn)

STADTPFEIFER, ORGANIST
BORN: Wechmar, November 26, 1604
DIED: Erfurt, May 13, 1673

Though legend says the Bachs came from Hungary, Veit Bach, progenitor of the main line, probably migrated from Bohemia to Thuringia in the mid-sixteenth century. He settled in Wechmar, a village near Gotha, as a miller and baker, dying there c. 1575. His son Hans (c. 1550–1626), a carpetmaker, moonlighted as a *Spielmann* (itinerant musician), inherited the paternal business, and died of the plague. Hans's son, Johann, probably went on gigs with his father to nearby towns and was eventually apprenticed to Johann Christian Hoffmann, a *Stadtpfeifer* of Suhl. A *Stadtpfeifer* played chorales to announce reveille, dinnertime, and bedtime, sounded the alarm in case of attack, and performed at social functions. Johann finished out his required seven years, but owing to the disruptions of the Thirty Years War, he had trouble finding employment. Finally, when a drunken Swedish soldier, awakened from his coma by the Erfurt town band, wiped it out under the impression that the enemy was upon him, the town hired Bach. Faced with possible solvency, in 1635, he married Hoffmann's daughter, Barbara, and acquired several orphaned relatives to support. The next year he was made organist of the Predigerkirche at a wage of 250 pounds of grain per annum. (Thirty-three years later he complained that it had been paid him only once.) Shortly after he took the post, Barbara died in childbirth. Johann then married Hedwig Lämmerhirt, a member of a family whose history was to be closely bound up with that of the Bachs, and they produced three musical sons: Johann Christian, Johann Egidius, and Johann Nikolaus. Of Johann Bach's compositions, only an aria and two double-choir motets are known. RECORDINGS: Philippe Caillard has recorded one of the latter, *Unser Leben ist ein Schatten (Our Life Is a Shadow)*.

[471] CARISSIMI, Giacomo (Kȧ-rēs'-sē-mē, Jȧ'-kō-mō)
SINGER, ORGANIST, CHOIRMASTER,
TEACHER, PRIEST
BORN: Marino [Italy], c. April 18, 1605
DIED: Rome, January 12, 1674

The son of a cooper, Carissimi was born in a small town in the Alban Hills just southeast of Rome. His father is said to have been named Amico, who called himself "Amico di Carissimi," the latter name being that given his own father. Nothing else is known of the boy's childhood and youth. At eighteen he was singing in the cathedral choir at

Tivoli, and he became organist there a year or so later. In 1628 he went to Assisi as an employee of the apostolic vicar there, and for a brief time directed the choir of the cathedral church of San Ruffino. He must have made an impression, for at twenty-four he was placed in charge of musical training at the Jesuit Collegio Germanico in Rome, and of the musical services at the attached church of San Apollinare. Eight years later, in 1637, he was ordained. He remained there for the last thirty-seven years of his life, nor does he seem to have been tempted by offers from St. Mark's in Venice, the governor of the Netherlands, or the emperor. He lived quietly and economically, invested his money astutely, died quite well off, and was buried in his own church.

It is said that Carissimi introduced the Baroque into Roman music. This must be qualified: his few extant Masses, with a single exception, adhere to the earlier polyphonic tradition. (There are seven altogether, but four are doubtful.) However, his oratorios—his best known and most influential works—show him clearly a musician of the new age. (He was somehow connected with the Oratorians of the Santissimo Crocifisso.) Eighteen such works are attributed to him, though the three examples in Italian and one of the Latin ones are suspect. If we overlook earlier "sacred operas" and various extensions of the *laud,* and agree that an oratorio is a musicodramatic treatment of sacred material that does not call for stage action and often includes a narrator, we have to say that Carissimi invented the genre as we recognize it today. Doubtless impelled by Counter-Reformation militancy, his are clearly didactic in intent and mostly biblically derived. Making effective use of recitative, dramatic monody, and choruses (double and triple), they are highly rhetorical, in the best sense of the term. Their effectiveness lies in their rhythmic energy, for they are harmonically simplex and melodically not very interesting (excerption would be unthinkable).

The other area in which Carissimi shone was that of the cantata. He uses a cantata-like approach in his motets but is at his best in his numerous secular cantatas, for one and two voices, some of them humorous. (There is a vast number of dubious motets and cantatas as well.) Here the composer shows greater flexibility and a more adventurous approach to melody than in the oratorios. It is thus not surprising that the cantatas have contributed several numbers to those "old Italian airs" ladled out to vocal students—e.g., *Vittoria, mio core!*
RECORDINGS: There presently exist one

or more recordings of each of 9 of the oratorios: *Balthazar; Felicitas beatorum (Happiness of the Blessed); Historia Abrahae et Isaac; Ezechia; Jephte; Jonas; Judicium extremum (The Last Judgment); Judicium Salomonis (Judgment of Solomon);* and *Lamentatio damnorum (Lament of the Damned).* Philippe Corboz has recorded the *Missa septimi toni* and Alberto Zedda the *Missa a 5 et a 9,* and there are a few motets. The cantatas have been somewhat neglected, but there is a recording of eight of them by Christopher Hogwood.

[472] BENEVOLI, Orazio (Bā-nā'-vō-lē, Ō-rädz'-yō)
CHOIRMASTER
BORN: Rome, April 19, 1605
DIED: Rome, June 17, 1672

Benevoli was not Italian, nor was he, as was long rumored, a bastard son of Albert, Duke of Lorraine. His father was a French baker or candymaker who moved to Rome and renamed himself Benevolo. Between the ages of twelve and eighteen, Orazio sang in the choir of San Luigi dei Francesi, and then began his career as a choir director. He was successively at Santa Maria in Trastevere (1624–30), Santo Spirito in Sassia (1630–38), and then back at San Luigi (1638–44). After two years in Vienna in the service of Archduke Leopold Wilhelm, he returned briefly to San Luigi, then spent six months at Santa Maria Maggiore before being named director of the Cappella Giulia in St. Peter's, where he spent his last quarter century. He left 11 Masses, and a number of motets, Magnificats, psalms, and other sacred works. In his big pieces, Benevoli was a practitioner of what has been called the "Colossal Baroque," which strives to overawe by sheer grandiosity. To the polyphony of the Roman tradition he added the polychoralism of the Venetian. He loved to work with many voice parts (up to twenty-four) and with many separate "choirs," both vocal and instrumental.

Benevoli is best known for a Mass of fifty-three parts—four solo quartets, 2 eight-part choirs, 2 six-part string orchestras, 1 eight-part wind band, three brass ensembles adding up to thirteen parts, two organs, and timpani—said to have been performed at the opening of the cathedral at Salzburg in 1628. It was once recorded in that cathedral by Josef Messner (and later reissued as by the "St. Anthony Cathedral Choir directed by Otto Schneider"!). Unhappily for Benevoli, it turns out to have been written by someone else, the favorite candidates be-

ing Heinrich Biber [539] and Andreas Hofer [509].

[473] SACRATI, Francesco (Sà-krä'-tē, Frän-chäs'-kō)
CONDUCTOR, CHOIRMASTER
BORN: Parma, September 17, 1605
DIED: Modena, May 20, 1650

Sacrati produced several operas in Venice in the decade after the first public opera houses opened there, where he was regarded by some as second only to Monteverdi [333]. His *La finta pazza (The Counterfeit Madwoman)* of 1641 was one of the very first comic operas to be attempted and, under the auspices of the ever-hopeful Cardinal Mazarin (see 446, 464), was produced in Paris four years later—with the mandatory "machines" and the "unrealistic" recitative replaced with dialogue. In the latter 1640s Sacrati seems to have conducted various itinerant opera troupes in northern Italy. Though he had once rejected an offer from St. Mark's in Venice, on the grounds that people like him were unsuited to the holy surroundings, he eventually settled down (with a year to live) as choirmaster of Modena Cathedral. His operas, arias, and madrigals have all vanished. RECORDINGS: Victoria de los Angeles once recorded a selection from *Proserpina rapita* (which may not have been Sacrati's).

[474] HINGESTON, John
ORGANIST, VIOL PLAYER, TEACHER
BORN: c. 1605 (?)
DIED: Westminster, c. December 15, 1683

Hingeston was a choirboy at York Minster and probably a pupil of Orlando Gibbons [408]. Not much else is known of him before the days of the Commonwealth. Then Oliver Cromwell, as part of his campaign to rid his people of the deleterious effects of organs, had the one from Magdalen College, Oxford, installed in his quarters at Hampton Palace. There he pondered the Bad Old Days while listening to choirboys sing Latin motets, accompanied by Hingeston, who doubled as virginal teacher to the Protector's daughters. Once when Roger L'Estrange, royalist and gamba player, was sitting in on a session at Hingeston's, Cromwell dropped by and forever after termed L'Estrange "Roger the Fiddler." In 1656, Hingeston rounded up a committee to promote music, on the grounds that the new regime had left a lot of musicians unemployed, but the venture did not get very far.

Shortly after Charles II returned to the throne in 1660, he made Hingeston a Musician for the Viols to fill the place of the younger Ferrabosco [375], and two weeks later also named him royal instrumental repairman. In that capacity Hingeston enlarged the organ loft at Whitehall Palace, and got a new instrument put up in the banqueting hall. In 1673 he acquired a fourteen-year-old assistant named Henry Purcell [581], who eventually succeeded him. He is also said to have taught Purcell's teacher, John Blow [552]. In 1676 he was threatened with suit by a debtor named Smyth, which suggests that, like many English Carolingian court musicians, he had trouble collecting his wages. He gave six volumes of his music to Oxford University, but all that are left now are a number of Italian-influenced dance suites reminiscent of those of William Lawes [463].

[475] FERDINAND III
HOLY ROMAN EMPEROR
BORN: Graz, July 13, 1608
DIED: Vienna, April 2, 1657

Ferd the Third was the son of Ferdinand II and his cousin Maria Anna of Bavaria, and was, like his father before him, educated and indoctrinated by the Jesuits. Thanks to old Ferdinand's machinations, his son became King of Hungary at seventeen and King of Bohemia two years later. In the Thirty Years War, Albrecht von Wallenstein, the imperial commander-in-chief, refused to entrust him with a command. But when Wallenstein was cashiered in 1634 for high treason (and subsequently murdered), Ferdinand succeeded him. Two years later he was elected King of the Romans, and followed his father to the imperial throne in February 1637. Though he wanted to end the fighting, he feared that he might have to grant religious freedom in his realm, and so it dragged on for another decade, permitting him to win his point. He was, in his short life, thrice married—to Maria Anna of Spain, to his first cousin Maria, and to Eleonora of Mantua. For all his political, religious, and military wheeling and dealing, Ferdinand was a man of wide education and cultural interests. He studied music with the Venetian organist-composer Giovanni Valentini, and patronized such musicians as Cesti [499] and Monteverdi [333]. Ferdinand's brother, Archduke Leopold Wilhelm, sometime employer of Orazio Benevoli [472], made the great collection of paintings that is the nucleus of the Kunsthistorisches Museum in Vienna. Ferdinand

was a composer of some real ability. (The historian and theorist Athanasius Kircher said he was unrivaled among sovereigns, which was playing it fairly safe.) He left 2 Masses and other sacred works, but his most famous composition is an operatic allegory with the imaginative title of *Drama musicum*. His son and heir, Leopold I [528], was also a composer of talent.

[476] DU MONT, Henry (Dü Môn, Àn-rē′)
ORGANIST, MUSIC DIRECTOR
BORN: Villers-l'Evêque, 1610
DIED: Paris, May 8, 1684

Born near Liège, Henry de Thier (as he was properly called) soon moved with his family to Maastricht, Holland, where, from the age of eleven, he was a cathedral chorister. After serving the cathedral as organist from 1630 to 1632, he returned to Liège for advanced study. Then he returned to his Maastricht post for a time but left in 1638 to seek his fortune in Paris, where he became Du Mont, the French equivalent of his Walloon name. In 1643 he accepted a lifetime appointment as organist of the church of St. Paul. For most of the following decade, he also held a court appointment as keyboardist to Louis XIV's brother, Philippe, Duke of Anjou and future Duke of Orléans, called "Monsieur" like his predecessor, and a leading authority on female fashions, which he preferred to wear. When the king married María Teresa (or "Marie Thérèse") of Spain in 1660, Du Mont was transferred to her service. At some point he returned to Maastricht to marry. In 1663 he became one of the two (and sometimes four) rotating directors of the royal chapel, a post that gave him special clout. In 1672 his official title became "Composer of Music to the Royal Chapel." Around this time his shadowy spouse died, and in 1676 Du Mont was named abbot of the monastery of Notre-Dame de Silly in Normandy. It is said that in his study years in Liège he had been ordained, but this seems preposterous, and no doubt his abbacy was merely honorary, as was his later canonry in Maastricht.

A product of Flemish training, which was by no means so backward or chauvinistic as that available in France, Du Mont was keenly aware of what was going on out in the big musical world. He did not, as he claimed, pioneer the use of continuo in France when he published his *Cantica sacra* in 1652, but it was the first French publication to offer continuo parts on a separate staff with figures. The *Cantica*, which are clearly patterned on Italian vocal-concerto practice, often being cast as dramatic dialogues, are the forerunners of the French *petit motet.* Later, to please French taste, he wove in dance rhythms and motifs from popular songs. He also helped initiate the *grand motet,* big, long rhetorical gestures involving soloists, large choir, orchestra, and organ, which more nearly accorded with Louis's self-image. A collection of 20 appeared posthumously in 1685. His so-called "Royal Masses," based on Gregorian tunes that Du Mont straitjacketed with regular rhythms and diatonic harmonies, are also interesting. RECORDINGS: Among the relatively small number of available recordings, the *Motets pour la chapelle du roy* for chorus and orchestra and a *Pavane* for harpsichord should be mentioned.

[477] LAMBERT, Michel (Làn-bâr', Mē-shel')
SINGER, TEACHER, VIOLINIST, DANCER
BORN: Champigny-sur-Veude, 1610
DIED: Paris, June 29, 1696

Native of a small town between Poitiers and the Loire, Lambert rose from village choirboy to page in the household of Louis XIII's brother "Monsieur," the Duke of Orléans. He then became a singer to Monsieur's daughter, Mademoiselle de Montpensier, and later on director of her little orchestra. Under her roof he first became acquainted with her Italian page, Lully **[517]**, whom, some sources say, Lambert taught to play the violin. From 1650 he frequently danced in the ballets at the royal court. Evidently he recommended himself to Louis XIV, for in 1659 he was awarded a license to print and publish his own compositions, and, once the king had mounted the throne in his own right, Lambert was named Music Master to the Royal Chamber, which title he retained all of his long life. In 1662, Lully, now Lambert's superior, rewarded his old colleague by taking his daughter, Madeleine, to wife. Lambert's extant output is small—some contributions to ballets, a *Tenebrae* service, a motet, and a couple of books of *airs.* It was in the last genre that Lambert made his chief reputation, and indeed his contemporaries considered him to represent the state of the art. (He is said actually to have published some 20 collections.)

[478] COSSET, François (Kus-sā', Frän-swà')
TEACHER, CHOIRMASTER
BORN: St. Quentin, c. 1610 (?)
DIED: after 1664

The data available for Cosset (who also appears as "Cossette" and "Cozette") are so confused that one wonders if one is actually dealing with two separate men. If not native to St. Quentin, he was certainly educated there. If it was really he who helped teach the choirboys at Laon Cathedral in the mid-1620s, he must have done so at a very early age, for he took a similar job at Rheims in 1628. After that, he turns up at Rheims at various times—in later years described as music director. But from 1643 to 1646 (when, on the complaint of the queen mother, he was fired for incompetency), he apparently worked at Notre-Dame de Paris as master of the boys. Though the title pages of his Masses, published mostly in the late 1650s, call him by his Rheims title, the cathedral records seem to show that he was replaced there in 1652. In 1658 he seems to have been choir director of Amiens Cathedral, where he is listed as a priest. In 1664 he resigned both from his job and the pages of subsequent history. His 5 remaining Masses (all that is known of his extant output) are curious throwbacks, written in the polyphonic *a cappella* style of the previous century. This seems to have puzzled some of his contemporaries, and Cosset's later contemporary, Sébastien de Brossard (1655–1730), went so far as to add orchestral parts to two of them. RECORDINGS: Arsène Muzerelle has recorded the *Missa "Cantate Domino"* (original version) with the Rheims Cathedral choir.

[479] LE CAMUS, Sébastien (Lə Kà-mü', Sā-bàst-yen')
VIOL PLAYER, LUTENIST, MUSIC DIRECTOR
BORN: c. 1610
DIED: Paris, March 24, 1677

From being a supernumerary musician in the establishment of Louis XIII, Le Camus rose to be music director to "Monsieur," His Majesty's brother, and then to Queen Marie Thérèse, as well as her husband's personal viol player. Extremely popular at court, he is said to have lived the life of Riley, which is more than his neglected wife did. Like Michel Lambert **[477]**, he was considered a genius at writing *airs,* but the only samples we have are in a posthumous volume published by his son.

[480] REUSNER, Esajas, the elder
(Roiz'-ner, Ez-ī'-yás)
LUTENIST
BORN: c. 1610 (?)
DIED: after 1660

The known facts about the elder Reusner are: he sired the younger Esajas Reusner [521]; he was lutenist at one of the Silesian ducal courts; in 1645 he published a collection of 80 chorales arranged for the lute.

[481] STEENWICK, Gisbert (Stän'-wik, Gis'-bert)
ORGANIST, CARILLONNEUR
BORN: c. 1610
DIED: Kampen, Holland, 1679

In the middle 1660s Steenwick was a member of a musical society in Arnhem and organist at the church of St. Eusebius. There he compiled a book of keyboard variations on popular tunes for his pupil Anna Maria van Eyl. He spent his last four years pulling stops and ringing bells in Kampen.

[482] VADO, Juan del (Bvá'-dō, Hwàn del)
ORGANIST, VIOLINIST, TEACHER
BORN: c. 1610 (?)
DIED: after 1675

Some accounts say that Vado had a brother who, like him, was a violinist at the Spanish court. Juan was also court organist and the king's (presumably Philip IV) music master. He left, among other things, some old-style polyphonic Masses, 6 puzzle canons (!), and some songs.

[483] BRUNA, Pablo (Brōō'-nà, Páb'-lō)
ORGANIST, CHOIRMASTER
BORN: Daroca, Spain, c. June 22, 1611
DIED: Daroca, June 26, 1679

The greatest Spanish organist of his day, Bruna was blind from infancy as a result of smallpox. He spent his entire life in Daroca, about 50 miles south of Zaragoza, where he was organist of the collegiate church from 1635 and director of its choir during his last five years. Among his many pupils was his nephew Diego Xaraba [535]. He left about 35 organ pieces, including some notable *tientos*, and a single four-part vocal work.

[484] HAMMERSCHMIDT, Andreas
(Hàm'-mer-shmit, Àn'-drā-às)
ORGANIST, TEACHER
BORN: Brüx, Czechoslovakia, c. 1612
DIED: Zittau, October 29, 1675

Andreas Hammerschmidt's father, Hans, was, when his son was born, a thriving German-born Protestant saddler in a Bohemian town now called Most (on the East German border). Religious persecution drove the family back to Saxony, where they settled in the late 1620s in Freiberg, near Dresden. Nothing is known of Andreas' education (musical or otherwise, though he seems somehow to have gotten a good bit of it). By 1633 he was serving a local Count von Bünau as his castle organist. The following year he applied for and got the organist's job at the Petrikirche in Freiberg, where he married Ursula Teuffel from Prague, in 1637. Two years later he moved to Zittau, where he took over the organ of the Johanniskirche and lived out his life. Though the Thirty Years War had played havoc with the local music scene, leaving Hammerschmidt and his cantor Simon Crusius the only professionals in town, they seem to have worked wonders with what local forces they could recruit. Hammerschmidt, who to judge from his portrait looked like a worried Afghan hound, came to be immensely beloved. Known as "the Orpheus of Zittau," he was the only keyboard teacher in the city, was rewarded with political sinecures, and managed to amass considerable wealth and property. A hoary yarn speaks of his inflammability, illustrated by a beerhall fistfight with the composer Johann Rosenmüller [493], but such tales should be taken *cum grano salis*. In his last years Hammerschmidt suffered from senile dementia.

In fact, Hammerschmidt's music was popular throughout Germany, and he might well be thought of as the poor man's Schütz [412], who admired him. Often in imitation of the older musician, he espoused the Venetian approach. The bulk of his work is religious or occasional. His three-volume *Musikalischer Andachten (Musical Devotions,* of 1639–42) gives a notion of his approach; it includes sacred *concerti* (one or more voices and continuo), sacred madrigals (four to six parts), sacred *symphoniae* (one or two voices, strings, continuo), and motets (five to twelve voices with instruments ad lib). His dialogues—a form soon common in German devotional music—are of special interest. He also wrote a number of so-called Lutheran Masses *(Kyrie* and *Gloria),* as J. S. Bach [684] was to do seventy-five years later. Early in his career he also published several collections of songs and of dance suites for viols. His style is lighter, simpler, and more popular than Schütz's, and there is no denying its attractiveness.

RECORDINGS: On records Hammerschmidt is occasionally encountered in anthologies.

[485] MACE, Thomas
LUTENIST, SINGER, WRITER
BORN: Cambridge, c. 1613
DIED: 1706 (?)

Most of what we know of Mace he tells us in passing in his chatty and informative 1676 treatise *Musick's Monument.* He spent most of his life in Cambridge. If he was the Thomas Mace who was replaced in the Trinity College choir in 1706, then he was a member for seventy years. In the middle 1630s he married a Yorkshire woman. One rainy morning while she was sewing, he improvised a lute piece that she took such a liking to that he wrote it down as *Mistress Mace.* The couple also produced progeny, and John, the youngest son, taught himself lute from his father's book. Toward the end of the civil war, the family moved temporarily to York, where they underwent Cromwell's siege, and twenty years after their return managed to survive the Great Plague of 1665–66. At some point Mace managed to break both arms, which, improperly set, made lute playing difficult thereafter. Progressive deafness increased his problem, and to try to counteract it, he invented a sort of giant amplifying double lute, which he called a "dyphone." In 1698 he published a guide to longevity called *Riddles, Mervels and Rarities.* His long life is generally said to have ended in "Dire Poverty," a scene known to many of his musical contemporaries—though one account says he fell into "Great Straits" (where the currents are notoriously treacherous). At any rate, we know that he put most of his musical effects up for sale in 1690. (He also wrote a book on English highways, which, not surprisingly, seems not to have been a bestseller.)

Musick's Monument, for all its quirkiness and chauvinism, is a valuable source book, notable for information about English performance practice. Its three sections treat, rather freely, of church music, "the Noble Lute," and "the Generous Viol." He speaks of "the necessity for singing the Psalms well . . . or not to sing at all." He greatly prefers the good old viol to the newfangled vio-

lin, which makes a "high-priz'd Noise, fit to make a Man's Ear Glow, and fill his brain full of frisks." He includes pieces for the lute and for consort. A D-minor lute suite includes a movement called *Tattle-de-moy,* which, Mace says, is "a new thing, similar to the Sarabande, but it contains more witty ideas, as the sound of the words 'Tattle de Moy' indicates, and more temperament."

[486] TUNDER, Franz (Tōōn´-der, Frànts)
ORGANIST
BORN: Bannesdorf, 1614
DIED: Lübeck, November 5, 1667

Born on the Baltic island of Fehmarn, the son of Hans Tunder, Franz Tunder was named organist to the Danish ducal court of Holstein-Gottorp. (Owing to politics and Werner's Law, Gottorp is now Gottorf and German.) It was long said that he was a pupil of Frescobaldi [407], but that, in the words of Eliza Doolittle, is not bloody likely. After nine years, thanks to his knowing the right people, Tunder became organist of the Marienkirche in Lübeck—one of the few thereabouts not in the line of Sweelinck [313]. Soon after, Tunder became chief elder of the church and thus its chief policy maker. Finding that tradition allowed the use of a lutenist and a viol player for special occasions, he went on to build up his instrumental forces until he had a neat little chamber orchestra of considerable virtuosity. This enabled him to present evening concerts which, under his successor, were to become internationally famous. His successor was Dietrich Buxtehude [525], who married Tunder's youngest daughter, Anna Margarethe. Whether she represented a required fringe benefit is not known, but thereafter it became necessary to marry the daughter (if any) of the Marienkirche organist to get the appointment.

Tunder, doubtless because he had tenure, bothered to publish none of his music. Thus we now have only about 30 works, about half vocal and half instrumental (except for one *sinfonia,* all of them include an organ part). He was obviously influenced by the prevailing transmontane winds from the south. The orchestrally accompanied chorale cantatas show ingenious *concertato* effects and clearly point to those of J. S. Bach [684]. The choral works, long presumed lost, eventually turned up in composer-musician Gustav Düben's manuscript collection in Uppsala, Sweden. In his chorale fantasias for organ, Tunder moves in the direction of virtuosic rhapsody.

RECORDINGS: Hans Knall has recorded one of the cantatas, and organ pieces appear in anthologies.

[487] ROSA, Salvatore (Rô'-sà, Sàl-và-tō'-rä)
PAINTER, POET, SATIRIST
BORN: Arenella (near Naples), July 21, 1615
DIED: Rome, March 15, 1673

Rosa was a fascinating figure, a Renaissance man born out of his time. One finds him listed also as a lutenist, an actor—and a bandit! Passionate and stormy, he was run out of Naples for joining Masaniello's rebellion and out of Rome for lampooning Gian Lorenzo Bernini, the leading artistic light of the time. His paintings are full of storm and stress and recommended him to the nineteenth-century Romantics as one of their spiritual forebears. Liszt included in his second set of *Années de pèlerinage* a *"Canzona di Salvator Rosa,"* a transcription of the song *"Vado ben spesso,"* recorded by Igor Gorin. The song came from a manuscript volume that Dr. Charles Burney, the eighteenth-century English musical scholar, bought in Italy, which purported to contain a number of arias by Rosa and which passed as his for many years. But the good doctor was taken in by a slick Italian operator; whoever wrote the songs wrote them long after Rosa was dead!

[488] BACH, Heinrich (Bàkh, Hīn'-rikh)
ORGANIST
BORN: Wechmar, September 16, 1615
DIED: Arnstadt, July 10, 1692

Heinrich was the youngest of the three sons of Johannes Bach, ergo the brother of Johann [470], who taught him to play the organ and sheltered him for six years in return for his assistance. In 1641, Heinrich won the job of organist in nearby Arnstadt, the seat of the Counts of Schwarzburg, and served there for fifty-one years. Shortly thereafter he married Eva Hoffmann, the younger sister of Johann's first wife and daughter of that *Stadtpfeiffer* of Suhl who had given Johann his musical training. The marriage lasted happily until her death thirty-seven years later and produced six children, five of whom lived to maturity. The three sons were all considerable musicians, and the middle one, Johann Michael, sired Maria Barbara, who became Johann Sebastian's [684] first wife. When Heinrich came to Arnstadt, the city had been financially ruined by the war and he often had to whistle for his salary. But as with everything else, he seems to have borne hardship with equanimity and unfailing good humor. (Testing an aspiring but untalented organist at the request of another town, he wrote that the fellow's performance was up to the salary that went with the post for which he was trying. He got the job.) Something of a free spirit, he was constantly being called on the carpet for going a-journeying without official sanction. In his old age he went to live with one of his daughters and her husband, a kitchen aide to the count and an organist on the side. Son-in-law Christoph Hertum gradually took over Heinrich's duties, and one of the last actions of the old man, blind and bedridden by then, was (successfully) to petition that Christoph succeed him.

Heinrich, according to all reports, was a crackerjack organist and wrote a great deal of music for his instrument, as well as choral pieces, but very little is extant, and of that only a motet, *Ich danke dir, Gott,* is not suspect.

RECORDINGS: Franz Lehrndorfer has recorded a chorale prelude attributed to Heinrich Bach.

[489] KINDERMANN, Johann Erasmus (Kin'-der-màn, Yō'-hàn Â-ràs'-mōōs)
ORGANIST, TEACHER, SINGER, VIOLINIST
BORN: Nuremberg, March 29, 1616
DIED: Nuremberg, April 14, 1655

An apparently precocious student of Johann Staden [400], Kindermann was hired by the local Frauenkirche at fifteen to play the violin and sing (as a basso!). He evidently made an impression on the town fathers, for at the end of 1634 they voted him funds on which to study for two years in Italy. We don't know with whom he studied there (some sources guess Cavalli [464]), or even if he went, for by early 1636 he was back home as number-two organist at the Frauenkirche. By 1640 he was number-one organist in Schwäbisch Hall, with a salary that included six wagonloads of wood. Evidently, however, the water or the air there did not agree with him, for scarcely had he arrived than he was stricken with a mysterious illness that required him to return to Nuremberg just in time to claim the vacancy at the Aegidienkirche, which he held onto for the rest of his rather brief life. He was known as a splendid organ teacher. Like most of the South German organists, he was influenced (perhaps directly) by the

Venetians. This is seen especially in his vocal music, which includes sacred *concerti,* dialogue pieces, chorale cantatas, and solo songs with continuo or other accompaniment, as well as more traditional motets and part-songs. His 1645 *Harmonia organica* (specifically for organ, not "keyboard"), a minor monument in the history of German organ music, is said to have been one of the first German musical publications printed from engraved plates and one of the very last in tablature. A later collection of *Canzoni, sonatae* is specifically for violin(s), cello, and continuo. For a Nuremberger, Kindermann was remarkably advanced.

[490] FROBERGER, Johann Jakob
(Frō'-bâr-ger, Yō'-hán Yä'-kōp)
ORGANIST, HARPSICHORDIST
BORN: Stuttgart, c. May 19, 1616
DIED: Héricourt, c. May 6, 1667

Thanks to the gossipy encyclopedia of old Johann Mattheson [668], much nonsense about Froberger has long passed for gospel. He was the youngest son of Basilius Froberger of Halle, who was court *Kapellmeister* in Stuttgart at the time. Four of his brothers were also musicians there at one time or another. We know nothing certain of his upbringing or education until 1637, when he turns up as imperial organist (to Ferdinand III [475]) in Vienna, though he probably arrived there earlier. At the end of the year, with the emperor's blessing and a purse of 200 gulden, he went off to Rome to study with Frescobaldi [407], returning in 1641. Between 1645 and 1649 he seems to have been traveling in Italy again. He was in Vienna in the latter year but seems almost immediately to have taken off for Brussels, Paris (where he made an enormous impact), and other points to the north and west. At last, in 1653, he resumed his court post in Vienna. Four years later Ferdinand died and was succeeded by his equally musical son, Leopold I [528]. A year later Froberger was out—tradition says because he had somehow displeased his new master. It is not certain where he went from there. Mattheson tells a marvelous story of how, c. 1662, he set out for London, was robbed first by highwaymen and then by pirates, landed destitute in England, made his way to the capital, was hired by Christopher Gibbons to pump the organ in Westminster Abbey, was distracted from his duty by the splendor of Charles II's nuptials, causing Gibbons to flee in chagrin, replaced the organist at the console, played furiously until the wind gave out, was recognized by a

guest, and wound up as royal organist. But history offers no evidence that Froberger was in England later than the early 1650s. Eventually he found a haven with an old acquaintance from Stuttgart, the Princess Sibylla of Württemberg-Montbéliard, living in retirement, until he died, on her estate in eastern France. He died of a heart attack or a stroke during Vespers.

The vast majority of Froberger's music (none of which he published) is understandably for the keyboard, for he was one of the great performers of his century thereon. Though he was obviously Frescobaldi's pupil and though he assimilated to his own uses keyboard developments from Germany, the Netherlands, France, and England, he constitutes one of the landmarks in the development of German *Klavier* music. His music may look surprisingly simple, but his patroness told his friend and promoter, Constantijn Huygens, that what Froberger put on paper was only an outline and that one needed to have worked with him to understand what he intended. His output includes toccatas, capriccios, *ricercari, canzoni,* fantasias, and 30 dance suites, all apparently written before his final exit from Vienna. The toccatas, particularly forceful and with real fugal finales, impressed Sebastian Bach [684]. The *canzoni* combine traits of both Frescobaldi and Sweelinck [313]. But it is in the suites that Froberger looms largest. Here he was perhaps influenced by Chambonnières [465] whom he knew in Paris (though he also wrote variation suites), but he set the pattern, with his sequence of allemande-courante-sarabande linked by tonality, for the keyboard suite for a long time to come.

RECORDINGS: There are records by such performers as Gustav Leonhardt, Franz Haselböck, and Thurston Dart devoted to Froberger, and he is extremely well represented in anthologies.

[491] CEREROLS, Joan (Se'-re-rôls, Zhwän)
MONK, THEOLOGIAN, POET, MUSIC DIRECTOR, ORGANIST, HARPIST, VIOLINIST
BORN: Martorell, Spain, September 9, 1618
DIED: Montserrat, August 28, 1676

Cererols is one of several important early Catalan religious composers resurrected by the efforts of Ireneu Segarra, music director at the monastery of Montserrat. Cererols came to the monastery as a boy chorister, studied with Joan Marqués, joined the Benedictine order, and succeeded his teacher as director of both school and chapel. He left a body of religious music, including several Masses, characterized by his fondness for polychoral effects and by a use of soloists, instruments, and continuo. There are also a number of extremely attractive *villancicos.* RECORDINGS: Father Segarra has recorded several examples of Cererols' work.

[492] ROBERT, Pierre (Rō-bâr′, Pē-âr′)
CHOIRMASTER, PRIEST
BORN: Louvres, c. 1618
DIED: Paris, c. December 28, 1699

A native of a small town between Paris and Senlis, Robert sang as a child at Notre-Dame de Paris. From that time until 1648, when he became choirmaster at Senlis Cathedral, we know nothing of his activities, though he was supposedly ordained in 1637. In 1650 he became choirmaster at Chartres and then was recalled in the same capacity to Notre-Dame in 1653. Ten years later Louis XIV divided the responsibility of his own chapel, on a quarterly basis, between Robert, Henry Du Mont [476], Thomas Gobert, and Gabriel Expilly. But at the end of the decade the last two dropped out and the two others shared the duties and the title of Composer to the King (both religious and secular). Robert retired on a pension in 1683, a few months before Du Mont died. Like Du Mont, he was a titular abbot of not one but two monasteries. Robert, like Du Mont (and their chief, Lully [517]), cultivated the *grand* and *petit* forms of the motet. He is the least individual of the three but likes to explore the coloristic possibilities of various combinations of soloists. (The new chapel at Versailles, finished in 1682, could handle as many as eighty performers, the point being, as someone has said, more the glorification of the king than his Maker.) RECORDINGS: Stéphane Caillat has recorded a Robert *grand* motet.

[493] ROSENMÜLLER, Johann (Rō′-zen-mü′-ler, Yō′-hàn)
ORGANIST, TROMBONIST, TEACHER, DIRECTOR
BORN: Oelsnitz, c. 1619
DIED: Wolfenbüttel, c. September 10, 1684

Born to parents in straitened circumstances in a small Saxon city between Zwickau and Chemnitz, Rosenmüller was educated at the local Latin school and then, in 1640, went to the University of Leipzig to study theology.

Two years later he was a teaching assistant to Tobias Michael, cantor of the Thomaskirche. As age and ill health began to circumscribe Michael's strength and energy, he came increasingly to rely on Rosenmüller, who in 1651 also became organist of the Nikolaikirche. By 1653 he had convinced the city fathers that he should be Michael's successor, and in 1654 he was named honorary *Kapellmeister* to the Duke of Saxe-Altenburg. Tobias Michael died in 1657, but by then Rosenmüller had wrecked his career. Two years before, the authorities were warned that he was up to no good. He was duly jailed for what the older books described as "a grave moral breach" and for what the newer ones bluntly indicate was seduction of some of his choirboys. Finding his new surroundings decidedly unpleasant, he escaped. An old story, not to be trusted, says that he went pseudonymously to Hamburg and eventually wrote the elector a letter begging forgiveness and reinstatement, enclosing a setting of the chorale *Herr, straf mich nicht in deinem Zorn (Lord, Punish Me Not in Thy Wrath).* No sooner had he sent it off than he realized he had blown his cover and went over the hills to Venice. At any rate, he really was there by 1658, playing trombone at St. Mark's. He remained until at least 1682, supporting himself by commissions and by teaching. For a time, he was official composer to the Ospedale della Pietà, where Antonio Vivaldi [650] would hold the same post somewhat later. Rosenmüller ended his life as *Kapellmeister* to the Duke of Braunschweig-Wolfenbüttel, whom he had buttered up with some dedications.

Despite the severe disruption of his life, Rosenmüller was a fairly prolific composer, chiefly of sacred music, but also of sonatas, dance suites, and other instrumental pieces. Even before the Venetian exile he shows an Italianate sweetness. The 1682 sonatas, which follow Corelli's Op.1 [565] by only a year, are of considerable interest historically and otherwise. The *Kern-Sprüche,* two collections of sacred *concerti,* show the influence of Schütz [412]. The Latin works, written in Venice, are decidedly Italianate.

RECORDINGS: There have been sporadic Rosenmüller recordings, chiefly of the instrumental music, for fifty years.

[494] WECKMANN, Matthias (Vek′-màn, Mà-tē′-às)
ORGANIST, DIRECTOR
BORN: Niederdorla, c. 1619
DIED: Hamburg, February 24, 1674

At the time of Weckmann's birth, his father, a Lutheran pastor, was stationed in a small (now East German) town near Mühlhausen. Nine years later he was transferred to a church in Oppershausen. From there, in 1630, he went to Dresden to sing in the chapel of Elector Johann George I, where he became a favorite pupil of Heinrich Schütz [412]. By 1663, the war effort having eroded the chapel, Schütz persuaded the elector to finance Weckmann's studies in Hamburg with Jakob Praetorius [420]. He (Schütz) would see him there, since it was on his way to the Danish court, where he was in charge of music for the wedding of the elector's daughter. It is said that Weckmann also studied in Hamburg with Praetorius' friend Heinrich Scheidemann [443], and with his pupil Adam Reincken [498]. He was back in Dresden as court organist by 1637, when he was sent to the Danish court to pick up music that Schütz claimed accidentally to have left there. (He seems actually to have left it as an escape valve.) In 1640 he was *Kapellmeister* to the prince, the future Johann Georg II. But conditions remained difficult there, and when Schütz left for Denmark again in 1642, Weckmann followed him to become organist to Crown Prince Frederik at Nyköping. After five years he again returned to Dresden, where he is alleged to have "dueled" Johann Jakob Froberger [490] at the organ. Froberger supposedly labeled him a "true virtuoso" and became his friend for life. But the growing tension between the Italians and the native musicians in the chapel began to get to Weckmann, and in 1654 he applied for and won the organist's post at the Jakobikirche in Hamburg. There, aided and abetted by his friends from the old days, he formed a Collegium Musicum, or performing group. Though the original intent was to benefit the musicians themselves, its concerts became a popular feature of Hamburg cultural life, beginning a tradition of public performance there. However, Weckmann's collegium was disbanded after he died. He was twice married, the organist Franz Tunder [486] standing best man at his first wedding. His son, Thomas, was organist at the Thomaskirche in Leipzig until his death in 1680.

Though a considerable body of music was once claimed for Weckmann, much of it has been found to have been misattributed. The dozen or so sacred pieces show him building on Schütz's style. There are about as many organ pieces, and 10 sonatas, probably for the Collegium, appear to be *sui generis*, reflecting neither the Italian form nor the dance suite.

RECORDINGS: Recordings are mostly of organ pieces.

[495] CAZZATI, Maurizio (Kàd-zà'-tē, Mou-rēdz'-yō)
CHOIRMASTER, TEACHER, PRIEST
BORN: Lucera, Guastalla, c. 1620
DIED: Mantua, 1677

Of Cazzati's first twenty years nothing is known save that he was born in the Po Valley between Mantua and Parma, near Reggio Emilia, and that, toward the end of this period, he was ordained. In 1641, the year in which he published the psalms and Masses of his Op. 1, he was choirmaster at the church of San Andrea in Mantua. Between 1647 and 1657 he held directorial posts at Bozzolo in the *cappella* of the Duke of Sabbioneta, at Ferrara with the Accademia della Morte, and at Santa Maria Maggiore —apparently in that sequence, but the evidence is conflicting at some points. At any rate, in 1659 he became *maestro* at the basilica of San Petronio in Bologna, where he achieved his greatest fame and notoriety. He introduced reforms that were to make the church (and the town) one of the great musical centers of the day. He laid particular emphasis on instrumental music and built up a stable of virtuoso instrumentalists. More than half of his 66 opuses was written for Bologna, plus about 12 oratorios and 2 (of 5) operas. But change does not set well with most people, and Cazzati was soon under attack from the priest Lorenzo Perti and the organist Giulio Cesare Arresti [501]. The bone of contention was certain alleged errors (musical) in some Masses he had published. Cazzati's response (familiar in modern academic circles) was that people who hadn't published were beneath contempt. The hassle went on for nearly a decade until Arresti made an ass of himself. Cazzati, who had by that time alienated most of musical Bologna, including, apparently, the Philharmonic Society and the printers, then backed down and republished the offending works (on his own press), corrected. But the atmosphere seems never to have cleared, and in 1671 he was dismissed. He spent the rest of his life back in Mantua as *maestro* to the Duchess Anna Isabella Gonzaga.

For all his productivity, Cazzati was only an average composer. His chief interest lies in his sonatas, for he was the first composer known to have written violin sonatas (Op. 55) in Bologna and his trumpet sonatas (Op.

35) inaugurate the peculiarly Bolognese tradition of such works.

RECORDINGS: There are recordings of two of the sonatas by the Teatro Comunale Orchestra of Bologna under Tito Gotti. (The oratorios and operas have all vanished.)

[496] SCHMELZER, Johann Heinrich
(Shmelt'-zer, Yō'-hán Hīn'-rikh)
VIOLINIST, MUSIC DIRECTOR, CORNETTIST
BORN: Scheibbs, c. 1620
DIED: Prague, late winter 1680

It is unlikely that the son of Daniel Schmelzer, baker of Scheibbs (about fifty miles west of Vienna) was born in 1623, as is usually speculated. Evidence indicates that he was playing violin in the emperor's *Kapelle* as early as 1635, though he does not appear on the official roster until 1649. He was married for the first time in 1643 and was then listed as a cornettist at St. Stephen's Cathedral. Other information about his life and career is equally spotty. His first two sons, Andreas Anton (later court ballet composer) and Georg Joseph, were born in 1653 and 1655 respectively, presumably of his second marriage. In 1658 Schmelzer directed the instrumental music at the imperial coronation of Leopold I at Frankfurt am Main, and he seems to have served as musical adviser to the emperor for the rest of his days. Leopold showered him with gifts and honors, made him assistant to his moribund *Kapellmeister,* Giovanni Felice Sances, ennobled him as "Schmelzer von Ehrenrüf" in 1673, and raised him to the *Kapellmeisterschaft* on Sances's death in 1679. By then the court had moved to Prague to avoid the plague, which, however, caught up with Schmelzer a few months later. A third son, Peter Clemens, was born in 1672, and he became a court violinist twenty years later.

Schmelzer wrote a great deal of vocal music, both sacred and secular, but the little that survives suggests that it was nothing special. But as a composer of dance suites for the court ballets (some of which survive in full score, showing a talent for orchestration) and his sonatas (including the 1664 *Sonatae unarum fidium,* the first printed collection of German sonatas for violin and continuo), he must be considered as the first important Austrian composer of modern instrumental music.

RECORDINGS: Sonatas have been recorded by the Vienna Concentus Musicus and by Libor Hlaváček, and a string *serenata* by Theodor Guschlbauer.

[497] LOCKE, Matthew
ORGANIST, SINGER
BORN: Devon, c. 1622
DIED: London, August 1677

Locke was a chorister at Exeter Cathedral from at least 1638 to at least 1641, as we learn from his name and initials carved on the altar screen, probably during dull sermons. His master there was Edward Gibbons, eldest brother of the late Orlando Gibbons [408] and adoptive father of Locke's friend Christopher. Locke's copies of some religious music, mostly Italian, tell us that he was in the Netherlands in 1648 and suggest that it was then that he turned Catholic. (It has been suggested that, considering his later closeness to Charles II, he may have been with the exiled royal family.) He was back in England by 1651, and two years later, when he and Christopher Gibbons collaborated on the music for James Shirley's masque *Cupid and Death,* he entered what he came to consider his native element, the theater. Shortly after that he married a Miss Garnons from Herefordshire. (Matthew Locke's marriage in 1664 to an Alice Smith, spinster, has to do with another Locke.) In 1656 he was one of the collaborators on William Davenant's "opera" *The Siege of Rhodes;* he not only wrote the fourth-act music but sang the role of the Admiral. He was not, however, a career singer at the London Opera, as one account has it; for one thing, there was no such institution—though it was the title of a collection of his songs. From then on he was the leading stage composer of his time, writing chiefly for Davenant, but also for D'Urfey, Settle, Shadwell, Etherege, and for various Shakespeare revivals. As such he was a friend of Pepys, Henry Lawes [444], and Henry Purcell's father and uncle (see 581), and many other people of consequence.

In 1660 King Charles awarded him not one but three places in the Royal Music, two of them in succession to Coprario [373] and Alfonso Ferrabosco the Younger [375]. The following year Locke supplied the music to accompany the pre-Coronation procession from the Tower to Whitehall. This is supposedly represented by the "Musick for ye king's sagbutts and cornets," preserved in a Cambridge manuscript written by someone with an apparent speech defect —e.g., "Five partt tthings ffor the Cornetts." When Charles married Catherine of Braganza in 1662, he appointed the Catholic Locke as his organist. This did not suit her mostly foreign contingent of musicians, and Locke was able to function on a small positive until the king, in a burst of economy, sent most of the others packing. But these were not the only musicians who resented him (he seems to have been an impossible fellow): in 1666 the Chapel Royal deliberately caterwauled its way, in the king's presence, through a set of rather ingenious responses to the Commandments he had written for them. In 1672, one Thomas Salmon, whom Locke had once turned down as a student, proposed a new musical staff that would abolish "cliffs" (clefs). In a paper war that went on for some months, Locke demolished him in a succession of pamphlets whose invective does him no credit. Meanwhile he continued to compose successfully for the stage until shortly before his death. He had little patience with the court's taste for things French, being an Englishman and an English musician to the core, but his dream of being the "inventor" of a native form of opera was not to be. He was succeeded as royal composer by Henry Purcell, on whom his music had great influence.

Locke was widely and deeply admired by his English contemporaries and can properly be called a popular composer. His countrymen continue to rate him highly—perhaps too highly, for even to be the greatest English composer of the mid-seventeenth century is not to be judged against very formidable competition. To be sure, his dramatic music points to Purcell. (The Shirley masque, by the way, is the only complete masque score now extant.) And his brass music perhaps owes something to Giovanni Gabrieli [286]. But, like most of his fellows, he was a conservative—indeed, deliberately so. His consort and chamber music, however, exhibits great skill and even some inventiveness.

RECORDINGS: A record by the Golden Age Singers and the Elizabethan Consort offers a general survey, Thurston Dart has recorded some keyboard pieces, and the Academy of Ancient Music has recorded the complete (collaborative) music for Shakespeare's *The Tempest.*

[498] REINCKEN, Johann Adam (Rīn'-ken, Yō'-hàn Ä'-dàm)
ORGANIST, IMPRESARIO
BORN: April 27, 1623
DIED: Hamburg, November 24, 1722

Adam Reincken, the official records show, moved his family to Deventer in Holland in 1637 from "Wilhuisen"—but whether that place was in Holland, Alsace, or Bremen has never been resolved. Of young Reincken we know nothing until 1654, when he went to Hamburg to study with his fellow Deventerian, the Katherinenkirche organist Heinrich Scheidemann [443]. After three years he returned to Deventer to play at the Berghkercke for a few months until Scheidemann summoned him back as his assistant. When the latter died in 1663, Reincken remained an incredible fifty-nine years as chief organist of the church. In 1678, in partnership with Gerhard Schott, a city councillor and a man of considerable wealth, he opened Hamburg's first opera house in the Gänsemarkt (Goose Market), by the River Alster, with—appropriately!—*Adam und Eva* by Johann Theile (1646–1744), a pupil of Schütz [412]. Reincken continued to direct the company for some years. Meanwhile he had built up a continent-wide reputation as a virtuoso. In 1701 a student named Johann Sebastian Bach [684], aged sixteen, walked the thirty miles from Lüneburg to hear him play. Reincken was then seventy-eight, but he did not hire an assistant until 1703. In 1720, when Bach was trying to find a way out of Cöthen, he heard there was an opening at the Jakobikirche in Hamburg and journeyed thither to see what his chances were. They turned out to be inconsiderable, but he took the opportunity to play for old Reincken. He chose to improvise on the chorale *Am Wasserfluten Babylons (By the Waters of Babylon)*, which he had heard Reincken use similarly long ago. Reincken, reputedly a pompous, stiff-necked, and suspicious old fellow, was visibly shaken, and remarked, uncharacteristically, that Bach possessed an art he had supposed long dead. He lived for three more years, dying five months short of his hundredth birthday, active to the end. He left numerous pupils, including his son-in-law Andreas Kneller [554] and perhaps Georg Böhm [590].

But he did not leave much in the way of music. His few organ pieces show the virtuosity typical of the second generation of North German organists, and appear in recorded anthologies. There are also one or two vocal works, and, most important, the *Hortus musicus (Garden of Music)* for strings and continuo—6 works that combine sonata and dance suite, which Bach not only copied but borrowed from.

RECORDINGS: The Cologne Musica Antiqua has recorded two sonatas (in A minor and E minor) for two violins, viola da gamba, and continuo.

[499] **CESTI, Antonio** (Chäs'-tē, Àn-tōn'-yō)
SINGER, ORGANIST, TEACHER, CHOIR
DIRECTOR, MONK
BORN: Arezzo, August 5, 1623
DIED: Florence, October 14, 1669

Born in the little Umbrian city that also produced the poet Petrarch, Cesti received his basic training as a choirboy there. Evidence makes it clear that he was further musically educated in Rome, but it is difficult to say when. At fourteen, in Volterra, he became a Franciscan, calling himself Fra Antonio (he had been baptized Pietro). He was sent to Santa Croce in Florence, where in some capacity he played the organ, returned to Arezzo in 1640, and three years later was summoned back to Volterra. There, with increasing distractions, he served until around 1650, as organist, master to the choirboys, and *maestro di cappella*. (His brother, confusingly named Antonio, replaced him at the organ in 1645.)

Meanwhile he seems to have been making powerful friends in the secular sector. In 1649 his first opera, *Orontea*, was premiered in Venice with great success, and from then on his monastic garb rested heavy on his shoulders. This is reflected in a long correspondence with the painter-poet Salvatore Rosa [487]. Evidently Cesti was behaving in a manner that ill sorted with his vows of celibacy, but at the same time he was beginning to be hailed as the most likely composer since Cavalli [464] appeared in the scene. Indeed, it is said that Cavalli's return to operatic composing after the *insuccès d'estime* of his *Ercole amante* in Paris in 1662 was motivated in part by the fear that Cesti would eclipse him. In 1652 he left Italy for a post in the *Kapelle* of Ferdinand Karl, Archduke of the Tyrol, in Innsbruck, where, in the newly built theater, he saw productions of his *Cleopatra* (in 1654) and *Argia* (in 1655, for the visiting Queen Christina in flight from Sweden).

By the end of the decade, Cesti knew he could no longer play the role of the holy man, and in 1658 went to Rome to seek release from his vows. Pope Alexander VII, much taken with his singing voice (Cesti had appeared as an operatic tenor), agreed to oblige him if he would fill a vacancy in the Sistine Choir. In 1661 he was lent to the future Grand Duke Cosimo III of Tuscany to help celebrate the latter's wedding (he put on his 1657 *La Dori* and, the festivities over, fled back to Innsbruck, where he used his political clout to placate the pope. In

1662, Ferdinand Karl died and his successor, brother Siegmund Franz, outlived him by only three years. Cesti, with most of the other Innsbruck musicians, was then absorbed by the Vienna court of Leopold I [528], where Cesti was named intendant of the theater. At some juncture the emperor conferred the title of marquis (Italian *marchese*) on him, and references to Marc. Antonio Cesti got him into generations of history books as "Marc' Antonio." Evidently the composer's new freedom and prestige opened his creative vein, for in the next three years he wrote five operas. The crown of his career came with *Il pomo d'oro (The Golden Apple)*, produced in 1667 to celebrate the emperor's recent wedding to Margarita of Spain. A true blockbuster, it is in sheer size perhaps also the crown of Baroque opera, with its five interminable acts, twenty-four scene changes, and huge orchestral and vocal forces. *(Le disgrazie d'Amore [Love's Misfortunes]*, produced a year earlier, featured a prologue by Leopold himself; there was also a 1657 equestrian ballet, *Germania esultante [Germany Rejoicing]*, written jointly with Johann Schmelzer [496]). But by 1668 Cesti was thinking of retirement in Venice. Salvatore Rosa, however, advised him that he had too many enemies there, so he went to Florence instead. If ancient rumor is to be credited, he was no more popular there, for it says he died of poisoning.

Cesti was primarily interested in the voice, and his operas, for all his use of instruments, have little orchestral interest. Apart from opera, his chief efforts went into cantatas, mostly secular, though there is nothing in the music to differentiate them. Cesti was a practitioner of *bel canto*, and his works are notably melodic, often sensuously so, with a striving for emotional feeling that produces interesting chromatic and harmonic experiments—typically, frequent recurrence to diminished and "Neapolitan" sixths. He was not afraid to use tunes in the popular mode, and he makes further advances in the concept of the operatic aria. He also seems to have established certain musicodramatic conventions, such as the use of solemn chords to introduce supernatural elements.

RECORDINGS: Except for arias in a few anthologies, Cesti is poorly represented on records, one of the few examples of any magnitude being an orchestral (!) suite by Theodor Guschlbauer from *Il pomo d'oro*. The complete opera *Orontea* has been done by René Jacobs.

[500] **AHLE, Johann Rudolf** (Ä'-lə, Yō'-hän Rōō'-dolf)
ORGANIST, POET, WRITER, POLITICIAN
BORN: Mühlhausen, December 24, 1625
DIED: Mühlhausen, July 9, 1673

Having gotten his secondary education in his Saxon hometown and in Göttingen, Ahle studied theology at the University of Erfurt and at the same time served as cantor to the Andreaskirche and its attached school. In 1650 he went back to Mühlhausen, married, and produced a son, Johann Georg (1651–1706). In 1654 he was appointed organist at the Blasiuskirche. A popular citizen, he was active in local politics, and became burgomaster in 1673. He left a large number of sacred vocal compositions, among them some chorales that enjoyed great popularity, and a collection of dances. He also wrote a singing method for elementary schools. His son was a notable poet (given the laurel crown by Emperor Leopold I) and composer. He too took up politics and received his father's appointment at the Blasiuskirche, where he was succeeded in 1707 by J. S. Bach [684].

[501] **ARRESTI, Giulio Cesare** (Är-rās'-tē, Jōōl'-yō Chä'-zä-rä)
ORGANIST
BORN: Bologna, 1625
DIED: Bologna, c. 1708

Nothing much is known of Arresti before he became an organist of San Petronio in Bologna—at second rank from 1649 to 1659, then first from 1659 to 1699, with time out (1661–71) for his famous quarrel with Maurizio Cazzati, his superior (see 495 for details). Though he seemed to have been bested, Cazzati's ouster permitted his return. He is thought to have studied with Ottavio Vernizzi, the man he succeeded in 1649. During the years of the battle, he served as music director at San Salvatore, and helped found, in 1666, the soon to be internationally prestigious Accademia Filarmonica. From 1674 to 1704 he also served as *maestro di cappella* at San Domenico. One of his now vanished oratorios was performed in Bologna in 1708, perhaps posthumously, though Arresti noted in an undated document that he had worked for seventy years as a professional musician. His son Floriano (c. 1660–1719) became second organist at San Petronio in 1692 and was known as a composer. Only a few of Giulio Cesare's works are extant, including a collection of violin sonatas, and an organ an-

thology including a few pieces of his own, of which there are recordings.

[502] **BANISTER, John, the Elder**
VIOLINIST, FLAGEOLETIST, CONDUCTOR, CONCERT PROMOTER
BORN: London, 1625
DIED: London, October 3, 1679

There were several generations of musical Banisters, of whom the first and second John (father and son), Jeffrey and James (relationship uncertain) were court musicians. *Grove's* (fifth edition) evokes a touching picture in stating that John the elder was "the son of one of the waifs of the parish of St. Giles-in-the-Fields." He was, of course, a "wait." John Banister became not only a virtuoso flageolet player but also at least a competent violinist. He was a member of the orchestra for the 1656 *The Siege of Rhodes* by William Davenant, the collaborative "first English opera," and four years later was appointed a violinist-in-ordinary by the newly returned Charles II. Evidently the king took a shine to him, for in 1661 he dispatched him to France, where he himself had spent his exile, doubtless to observe how court music operated there under Lully [517]. In 1662 Banister was elevated a step higher and a month later was put in charge of a sort of elite chamber orchestra made up of twelve of the twenty-four King's Violins. But whereas Charles was an ardent Francophile, Banister was not, and he was more than a little miffed when in 1666 he was asked to share his directorship with the imported Louis Grabu, who turned out to be an incompetent, if not a fraud. To add injury to insult, it was alleged a year later that Banister had been pocketing part of the payroll, and thereafter Grabu had charge of it. Hard evidence shows that in fact Banister himself often went unpaid. Poverty pursued him to the end, though in 1671 he took a second wife. Beginning the following year, he undertook to improve things by becoming one of England's first promoters of public concerts, which, according to the *London Gazette*, England's first twice-weekly newspaper (founded 1666), were given in his home in Whitefriars every Monday afternoon at 4 P.M. He continued these, at various locations, up to 1678. A year later he acquired a passport to go abroad (reason unstated) but fell ill and died before he could embark. He wrote innumerable songs for plays by the popular Restoration playwrights (including Dryden's recension of Shakespeare's *The Tempest*). RECORDINGS:

Some of these incidental songs and instrumental dances have been recorded.

[503] LEGRENZI, Giovanni (Lā-grent'-zē, Jô-vän'-nē)

ORGANIST, CHOIRMASTER, PRIEST
BORN: Clusone, c. August 12, 1626
DIED: Venice, May 27, 1690

Born near Bergamo, Legrenzi was trained by his father, Giovanni Maria, the village organist, and himself was elected number-two organist of Santa Maria Maggiore, Bergamo, when he was nineteen. In the late summer of 1653, two and a half years after his ordination, he became first organist, under Maurizio Cazzati [495]. But bad luck plagued Legrenzi much of his life, and owing to some sort of political struggle in the church council, his contract was not renewed the next year. In 1655 he was reinstated, but he resigned at the end of the year. In 1656 he went to Ferrara as director of the musical Accademia dello Santo Spirito. Early in the next decade he produced there three operas and an oratorio (of these, only the opera *Zenobia e Radamisto* is extant). By 1665 he was trying to find a better post. He was turned down by Emperor Leopold I in 1665, by Milan Cathedral in 1669, by the Duke of Parma in 1670, and by San Petronio at Bologna in 1671. He himself rejected offers from Modena Cathedral and his former church in Bergamo early in the same period. In 1668 he accepted one from Louis XIV but fell ill and was unable to make the journey to Paris. He moved to Venice sometime before 1673, where he worked for the Conservatorio dei Mendicanti and was connected with the Oratorians at Santa Maria della Fava. It is clear, however, that during these years of relative obscurity Legrenzi was not starving. During the 1670s he made quite a splash with his five operas produced in Venice (he went on to write ten more) and an equal number of oratorios premiered in Ferrara. After failing by one vote to be elected to the directorship at St. Mark's in 1676, he was unanimously named *vice-maestro di cappella* there five years later, and eventually gained the top post in 1685. He was highly instrumental (if the term may be forgiven) in revamping the orchestra and augmenting the choir to a membership of thirty-six. His final decade was one of success and recognition. His home was the site of much-attended concerts, and he is said to have commanded the highest salary paid to a *maestro* at St. Mark's up to his time. Afflicted by a terminal illness late in 1687, he died less than

three years later. He was a much sought-after teacher, and, according to tradition, taught Caldara [624], Gasparini [615], and Lotti [613]. But his music had a clear impact on the likes of J. S. Bach [684], Handel [683], Torelli [578], and Vivaldi [650].

Of Legrenzi's 19 known operas, only 6 survive entire, and only 2 of his 7 oratorios. He published 10 collections of sacred music, 3 of secular (mostly cantatas), and 6 of instrumental works (5 of sonatas, 1 of dances). Here he distinguishes between four-movement sonatas and dance suites, which he was one of the first to call *sonate da camera,* and is notable for fugal experiments.

RECORDINGS: Legrenzi is so far sparsely recorded—a few sonatas (Camerata Lutetiensis, Vienna Concentus Musicus), the familiar old Italian air *"Che fiero costume"* from *Eteocle e Polinice* of 1675, and the oratorio *La Vendita del core (The Sale of the Heart)* directed by Roger Blanchard.

[504] COUPERIN, Louis (Kōō-per-àn', Lōō-ē')

KEYBOARDIST
BORN: Chaumes, c. 1626
DIED: Paris, August 29, 1661

The uncle of the "great" Couperin [616] was the third son of Charles Couperin, a successful merchant of Brie, though he did not sell it. He played the organ at a local monastery, and sired eight children on his wife, the former Marie Andry. Three of them—Louis, François (Sieur de Crouilly), and Charles—all mastered the keyboard instruments and the violin. The story has already been told of how, c. 1650, they became protégés of their neighbor Chambonnières [465]. Supposedly he took Louis back to Paris (only about twenty miles away) and the others followed in due course. By 1653, Louis was organist at the church of St. Gervais, and lived with his brothers in the house provided for that functionary, overlooking the cemetery. He is also said to have held a court appointment as a harpsichordist, and he apparently worked at some time for the diplomat Abel Servien. Offered Chambonnières' post when the latter was on the skids, he refused it out of respect for his old teacher. But he was unable to overlook the cemetery for long: at thirty-five he died, leaving his brothers his spinet and the money owed him by Servien. Charles succeeded him, but died at forty-one, leaving a widow and a ten-year-old son, François, who later became known as Le Grand. The elder François lived out his threescore and ten but was killed in a street accident.

Louis Couperin left all his compositions in manuscript. Today we have a handful of ensemble pieces (including 2 for five shawms), about 130 dances and preludes for harpsichord, and about 75 organ works. Of the last, 70 were discovered in a single manuscript in 1955. So far Couperin is best known for the harpsichord music. There the composer obviously had suites in mind, but the individual pieces, as we have them, are grouped by key, inviting the performer to make up his own sequence. They are harmonically richer and more daring than those by Chambonnières and Couperin ventures into keys uncommon in the meantone tuning of the day; the use of such keys on the harpsichord was a flirtation with sonic disaster. His music is often described as grave and serious—qualities best seen in his sarabandes and chaconnes and in his *tombeau* (memorial) for the lutenist Blancrocher. (Froberger [490], whose impact on Couperin is clear, also wrote such a piece.) The unbarred preludes appear to be no more than improvisational warm-ups, but are actually ingenious structures that might be termed controlled-rhapsodic.

RECORDINGS: There are a number of recorded anthologies of Couperin's keyboard music by such players as Marie-Claire Alain, Michel Chapuis, Alan Curtis, Ruggero Gerlin, Gustav Leonhardt, Daniel Pinkham, and Blandine Verlet.

[505] MOUTON, Charles (Moo-tôn', Shárl)
LUTENIST, TEACHER
BORN: c. 1626
DIED: Paris, after 1699

Mouton studied with Denis Gaultier [468]. He lived in Turin from at least 1670 but visited Paris several times, settling there around 1678. (The assertion that he lived there from 1700 to 1720 seems to be incorrect, but very little is known for sure about the man.) Among his pupils was Philippe François Le Sage de Richée [557]. Mouton, who was among the last representatives of the seventeenth-century French lute school, published 4 books of lute music, of which 2 have survived. *(Pièces de luth sur différens modes,* 1699.) These are made up of suites, of varying length, of dance pieces with amusing titles—*The Contented Lover, The Graces' Conversation About Iris*—but each suite has its own carefully conceived coloration and unity. RECORDINGS: Samples

have been recorded by, for example, Walter Gerwig and Michael Schaeffer.

[506] KERLL, Johann Kaspar (Kârl, Yō'-hán Kàs'-par)
ORGANIST, TEACHER, MUSIC DIRECTOR
BORN: Adorf, April 9, 1627
DIED: Munich, February 13, 1693

Son and pupil of a Saxon organist, Kaspar Kerll, Johann went, still a mere youth, to be court organist to Archduke Leopold Wilhelm in Vienna, where he undertook further study with Giovanni Valentini, *Kapellmeister* and teacher to Ferdinand III [475]. Shortly his employer sent him off to Italy to study with Carissimi [471]. (There is a legend that he also studied with Frescobaldi [407], but it is difficult to make dates and places fit.) He then returned to the archduke's establishment and served with him during the latter's stint as governor in Brussels. In 1656 the Bavarian elector, Ferdinand Maria, made him assistant *Kapellmeister,* then promoted him to chief before the year was out. In 1657 *Oronte,* the first of Kerll's II operas (all lost), opened the new Munich opera house. The year following, he accompanied his prince to the Frankfurt coronation of Emperor Leopold I [528], for which he wrote a Mass. Probably through the agency of Schmelzer [496] he performed for the emperor, who is said to have been mightily impressed. In 1659 the elector named him a councillor, and five years later Leopold ennobled him (as "von Kerll"). Despite the success of his music in Munich, Kerll found himself unable to get along with the conservative Italian court musicians. In 1673 he abruptly quit and returned to Vienna, where he taught. The next year he was made organist of St. Stephen's Cathedral and three years later became organist to Leopold's court. Having survived a monstrous plague epidemic and the siege of the city by the Turks, Kerll returned to Munich and lived out his life there.

Much of Kerll's music has vanished. What remains (aside from a school drama, *Pia et fortis mulier [The Devout and Strong Woman]),* consists entirely of religious music (18 Masses) and organ pieces. The two are combined in the *Modulatio organica,* a treatment of the Magnificat with organ versets in all eight tones. The Masses and motets generally include a full complement of instruments, in some instances trumpets and trombones.

RECORDINGS: Franz Haselböck has recorded selections from the *Modulatio organica.*

[507] GIGAULT, Nicolas (Zhē-gō', Nē-
kō-làs')
ORGANIST, TEACHER
BORN: c. 1627
DIED: Paris, August 20, 1707

The first child of poor parents, Gigault was
to become rich and famous as organist of
the Paris churches of St. Honoré, St. Nicolas des Champs, St. Martin des Champs,
and the Hôpital du Saint Esprit, though he
is perhaps best remembered as a teacher of
Lully [517]. He was twice married and had
at least five children. The year before his
death he was part of the jury that pronounced Rameau [675] a suitable organist
for La Madeleine. Gigault published 2 organ books, one in 1683, the other in 1685.
The first contains the earliest known noëls
d'orgue, or variations on Christmas carols,
later a vastly popular genre. The second
consists of liturgical pieces and fugues, notable for their unusual chromaticism (for
the times) and for their frequent use of
dance rhythms.

[508] BERNHARD, Christoph (Bârn'-
härt, Krēs'-tōf)
SINGER, MUSIC DIRECTOR, THEORIST
BORN: Kolberg, January 1, 1628
DIED: Dresden, November 14, 1692

Long supposed a native of Danzig, Bernhard probably came from what is now the
Polish town of Kołobrzeg, though he may
have studied in Danzig (now Gdansk)—
some sources name his teacher as the irascible Paul Siefert [421]. In 1649 he went to the
Dresden court as a countertenor and master
of the boys, and became a protégé of
Heinrich Schütz [412]. He was evidently
not satisfied in Dresden, however, and for a
time considered becoming a lawyer. After
the accession of Elector Johann Georg II in
1656, Bernhard was sent to Italy to fetch
some Italian musicians. (It is said that at
some point he studied with Carissimi [471]
in Rome, but there is no proof.) Inevitably
Bernhard became a victim of the international wrangling among the Dresden musicians, and in 1663—his friend Matthias
Weckmann [494] having done some p.r.
work for him—he went to Hamburg as civic
director of church music. The city fathers,
though they had elected him by a one-vote
margin, rolled out the red carpet to greet
him. He remained in Hamburg until 1674,
when, following the demises of Schütz (for
whose funeral he wrote a motet) and
Weckmann, the elector called him back to
Dresden as assistant Kapellmeister and

teacher to his grandchildren. Under the
next two Johann Georg's he served as Kapellmeister, though they provided him with
a very minimal Kapelle to run.
    Apart from a few songs and some funeral
motets (that for Schütz is lost), Bernhard's
legacy consists entirely of liturgical music
(both Latin and German. His only significant musical publication was the Geistliche
Harmonien of 1665, a collection of sacred
concerti, though he was also a master of the
old contrapuntal style. He also wrote an important treatise, Tractatis compositionis aug-
mentatus, in which he distinguishes between
musical styles in terms of the relative importance of music and text.
    RECORDINGS: Some of the concerti have
been recorded—e.g., by the Collegium
Sagittarii and the Hamburg Petrikirche
Choir.

[509] HOFER, Andreas (Hō'-fer, Àn'-drā-
às)
ORGANIST, MUSIC DIRECTOR, PRIEST
BORN: (Bad) Reichenhall, 1629
DIED: Salzburg, February 25, 1684

Unrelated to his later namesake, the
Tyrolese patriot of the Napoleonic era, Hofer was born near Salzburg. He studied at
that city's university, then from 1651 to 1653
was organist at St. Lambrecht, a Benedictine abbey in Styria. At the end of that period he was ordained, and returned to Salzburg as assistant Kapellmeister to Prince-
Bishop Guidobald Thun. From 1666 he also
served as Kapellmeister of the cathedral.
Guidobald's successor, Max Gandolf von
Kuenberg, promoted Hofer to the directorship of his musical establishment in 1679. Of
Hofer's few extant works (including 4 musical school dramas), some are cast as small-
scale sacred concerti, and others in the Colossal Baroque vein. RECORDINGS: A Te
Deum of the colossal kind has been recorded by the Collegium Musicum of the
University of Missouri. Some credit Hofer
with the Salzburg Mass once thought to be
by Orazio Benevoli [472].

[510] SARTORIO, Antonio (Sär-tō'-rē-ō,
An-tōn'-yō)
MUSIC DIRECTOR
BORN: Venice, 1630
DIED: Venice, December 30, 1680

Antonio Sartorio, one of the first notable
Venetian opera composers of the new bel
canto school, was brother to Gasparo
Sartorio, who also produced operas, and

Girolamo Sartorio, an architect. The first of Antonio's fifteen known operas, *Gl'amori infruttuosi di Pirro (Pyrrhus's Fruitless Loves)* was premiered in January 1661. Five years later he went to Hanover as *Kapellmeister* to Johann Friedrich, Duke of Braunschweig-Lüneburg, who had probably encountered him on one of the duke's Italian junkets. For the next nine years Sartorio divided his time between the German court and the Venetian theaters, though in the latter part of the period sieges of ill health sometimes prevented his traveling. In 1675 he and the duke agreed to his permanently returning to Venice. There, a year later, he was elected assistant choirmaster of St. Mark's by a narrow margin. On his death he was succeeded by Giovanni Legrenzi [503]. As an operatic composer Sartorio was notable for his use of the aria and for his musical evocation of emotions. He also left some cantatas, isolated arias, and some psalms. RECORDINGS: A few recordings of arias exist and a complete opera, *L'Orfeo.*

[511] GUERAU, Francisco (Gwä-rä'-o͞o, Frän-thēs'-kō)
GUITARIST, PRIEST
BORN: c. 1630 (?)
DIED: after 1694

In the seventeenth century the guitar superseded the vihuela in Spain. Guerau, who became a court musician to Charles II in 1659, played it and wrote for it. His tablature (one of the last) for five-string instrument, *Poema harmónico,* which he published in 1694, consists of 27 dance variations, mostly *pasacalles,* of high quality.

[512] CHAUMONT, Lambert (Shō-môn', Läm-bâr')
ORGANIST, PRIEST
BORN: in or near Liège, c. 1630
DIED: Huy, April 23, 1712

Brother (or Father) Lambert de St. Théodore, as he was known for most of his life, first is heard of as a lay brother tending the gardens at the monastery of the Reformed ("Island") Carmelites in Liège in 1649. Ten years later we learn that he has completed his novitiate and theological studies in Rheims. There is no record of his musical training or his ordination. He does not surface again—the land was racked in the interim by the struggle between Louis XIV and the emperor—until 1674, when he was appointed successor to Père Augustin de la Nativité as pastor to the tiny (only three householders!) and poverty-stricken parish of St. Martin-Across-the-Meuse in Huy. Fourteen years later he was transferred to the adjacent parish of St. Germain, where he had also to assume the role of father confessor and business manager of the local convent of White Ladies (Carmelites). The remainder of his career seems to have been marked by displays of stubborn determination in contests with one higher authority or another. In 1695 he published his organ book in Liège. It is indicated to be Op. 2, but no forerunner is known. Except for that of Nicolas de Grigny [634], it was also the penultimate French organ book of the century. In 1709 Father Lambert published a book of prayers. Three years later he died unexpectedly. He left his library to his successor, requesting that he return any borrowed volumes he found there to their rightful owners. Chaumont's 8 organ suites (in the eight "tones") include 12 to 15 pieces each. Their music is notable for a sense of melody, a fondness for contrapuntal effects (there are several fugues), and a mastery of ornament. RECORDINGS: They have been recorded in their entirety by Hubert Schoonbrodt.

[513] POGLIETTI, Alessandro (Pōl-yet'-tē, Ä-les-sàn'-drō)
KEYBOARDIST, TEACHER, CHOIRMASTER
BORN: c. 1630 (?)
DIED: Vienna, July 1683

Born and probably educated in Italy, Poglietti came to Vienna, where he was organist and choirmaster at the church of the Nine Angelic Choirs in 1661. Later the same year Leopold I [528] named him imperial court organist, and later ennobled him. By the time of his death (resulting from the Turkish bombardment of Vienna), he was also a papal noble and the possessor of lands and wealth. He was a popular teacher. Poglietti left a single opera, some Masses, and other religious compositions but is particularly celebrated for his keyboard music. He was a superb contrapuntist but is even better known for his amusing program pieces, such as toccatas on the Hungarian revolt of 1671 and on the Battle of Philippsburg, or a suite depicting the activities of a henyard. Another suite, *Rossignolo (Nightingale),* written for the Empress Eleanor, contains 23 inventive variations on a German song in various national styles.

[514] SCHERER, Sebastian Anton (Shâr'-er, Se-bắst'-yản Ản'-tōn)
ORGANIST, TEACHER
BORN: Ulm, October 3, 1631
DIED: Ulm, August 26, 1712

Save for making a journey to Strasbourg in 1684 to inspect an organ, Scherer spent his whole life in Ulm. A *Stadtpfeifer* by 1653, he married the daughter of the cathedral organist, Tobias Eberlin, whose assistant he was. In 1668 he became cantor of the local school, and three years later succeeded his father-in-law. He published some sacred music, a volume of Italian-influenced organ pieces, and a book of trio sonatas.

[515] LEBÈGUE, Nicolas Antoine (Lə-beg', Nē-kō-lås' Ản-twản')
ORGANIST, TEACHER
BORN: Laon, c. 1631
DIED: Paris, July 6, 1702

Lebègue is often said to have studied with his uncle, Nicolas Antoine, in Laon and with Chambonnières [465] in Paris, but there is nothing but probability to substantiate the first assumption and stylistic likeness to back up the second. He had made his name in Paris by 1661 (where and how, no one knows), and was named organist of St. Méderic ("St. Merry") three years later. In 1678 he also became one of the four royal organists at Versailles. Among his many pupils were François Dagincourt [681] and Nicolas de Grigny [634]. He published a collection of *petits* motets, but (more important) 3 organ books and 2 for harpsichord. The third *Livre d'orgue,* which includes some *noëls* and other quasi-religious pieces, is particularly adventurous. His harpsichord suites are identified by key, though Lebègue, instead of adhering to the tonic, is not afraid to explore related keys in the course of a suite. He avoids the usual cute titles beloved of French clavecinists and dispenses with outmoded dances (bransles, galliards, etc.) in favor of more up-to-date ones (e.g., gavottes and minuets). RECORDINGS: Generous samples of the organ music have been recorded by Marie-Claire Alain, Xavier Darasse, Raphael Tambyeff, and others.

[516] VITALI, Giovanni Battista (Vē-tả'-lē, Jō-vản'-nē Bảt-tēs'-tả)
VIOLINIST, VIOLIST, CELLIST, SINGER
BORN: Bologna, February 18, 1632
DIED: Bologna, October 12, 1692

It used to be said that Vitali's affinity for stringed instruments derived from his having been a Cremonese, but recently discovered records prove him a native of Bologna. At twenty-six he became a singer in the choir of San Petronio and a student of its recently appointed maestro, Maurizio Cazzati [495]. In 1666 his first son, the future violinist and composer Tommaso Antonio Vitali [591], was born, and not long after he himself was accepted into the Accademia Filarmonica. After Cazzati leaped (or was pushed) from authority, Vitali became, in 1673, the *maestro* at the church of the Holy Rosary, and a year later went to the ducal court at Modena as assistant music director. In 1684 he was briefly promoted to *maestro* but resumed his old post in 1686.

Vitali wrote half a dozen oratorios (some of them in collaborations and all but two lost), cantatas, psalms, and hymns, but his chief importance and influence lies in his instrumental music. Of his 12 published collections in this area, 5 are distinguished as *sonate,* a term that with Vitali signifies the four-movement *sonata da chiesa* (not necessarily intended for ecclesiastical use). Here the form has not quite jelled into the slow-fast-slow-fast pattern, but there is a definite alteration of moods, and a tendency toward symmetry. Vitali also published several collections of dances, mostly for the trio-sonata ensemble, but not arranged as suites. He was one of the first Italians to borrow the new minuet from the French. Of special interest is his penultimate publication, *Artificii musicali,* an exposition of his remarkable understanding of instrumental counterpoint illustrated in 60 canons, capriccios, and other appropriate compositions—probably the first Baroque work of its kind.

RECORDINGS: Vitali has enjoyed little recording. One notes a violin sonata and 2 capriccios played by Gabriella Armuzzi-Romei.

[517] LULLY, Jean-Baptiste (Lü-lē', Zhản Bả-tēst')
ACTOR, CONDUCTOR, DANCER, SINGER, PRODUCER, VIOLINIST
BORN: Florence, November 28, 1632
DIED: Paris, March 22, 1687

If Lully was not the greatest musician of his day in France, he was the most important. Though he could be utterly charming, he was also utterly ruthless when it came to getting ahead, and the word *moralité* (in whatever language) seems not to have been in his lexicon. Whether he possessed true musical genius is arguable, but he had endless skill and intelligence, and he was a perfectionist. In not a few ways he reminds one of Richard Wagner [1230]—or a *mafioso.*

Over the centuries his life has been romanticized, positively and negative—not the least by Lully and his rivals—and the purported facts are sometimes dubious. He listed his parents as Laurent de Lully, *gentilhomme de Florence,* and Catherine de Sera. In reality, his father, hight Lorenzo, was a poor miller, and the boy was baptized Giovanni Battista Lulli. Lully (the French spelling of his name) is said to have received a rudimentary education, including guitar lessons, from a friendly neighborhood monk. When he was thirteen, he somehow attracted the attention of Roger de Lorraine, Chevalier de Guise. The chevalier's young cousin, Anne Marie d'Orléans, Duchess of Montpensier and daughter of Louis XIII's brother, "Monsieur," herself only a few years older than Lully, had delegated him to bring her back from his Italian journey "a pretty little Italian" to teach her to speak his language. The pretty little Italian became her page and presumably received more systematic training under her patronage. We know he studied the harpsichord with Gigault [507] and François Roberday, but not when. Where he acquired his remarkable skill as a violinist is even more uncertain, but it is said that the Count de Nogent was so taken with his playing that he persuaded the duchess to make him one of her household musicians. He left her service in 1652. An old yarn has it that she fired him when she discovered a nasty ditty he had written about her. But the greater likelihood is that he saw that the lady, now locked up in her château for having sided with the Fronde against the king, was of no further use to him.

At any rate, Lully's next stop was the palace, where legend has him starting as a scullion. But that seems quite unlikely, for two months after his arrival he and the kinglet were dancing in the *Ballet de la nuit,* and a month after that he was appointed one of four composers of instrumental music to Louis XIV. As a member of the king's violins or Grande Bande (often joined by the stable winds of the Grande Écurie), he could not stand the sloppiness of the ensemble and soon managed to wangle his own chamber orchestra, a sixteen-string Petite Bande, which he soon honed to such a pitch of virtuosity that all Europe marveled.

In 1657 Lully so delighted Louis with the ballet *L'Amour malade (Cupid Ailing)* that he permitted him another, in collaboration with royal librettist Isaac de Benserade, all to himself. The result *Alcidiane,* produced

in February 1659, featured the king as Hatred, Aeolus, a Demon, and a Moor, and from that time on Lully was chief composer of *ballets du cour.* Later that year Cardinal Mazarin countered by importing his countryman Cavalli [464] to dazzle the world with an Italian opera, *Ercole amante (Hercules in Love),* especially composed for Louis's wedding to the Spanish princess Maria Teresa. But because the new theater in the Tuileries remained unfinished, Cavalli's *Xerse (Xerxes)* was substituted, and Lully managed to get six of his own ballet *entrées* included in it. Shortly afterward, Louis, now of age and out from under his mother's thumb, made Lully his musical commander-in-chief (Superintendent of Music and Composer to the Royal Chamber). In 1662, when *Ercole* was finally ready, Lully smothered it with ballets and sent its composer cursing back to Venice.

Mazarin was dead, the Italian invasion thwarted, and Lully in the driver's seat, now officially a Frenchman. In July he acquired another title, Music Master to the Royal Family. His combined posts gave him an annual income of 30,000 livres, guaranteed to him and his heirs in perpetuity. Later that month, to further cement his place and augment his fortunes, he married Madeleine Lambert (dowry 20,000 livres), daughter of Michel Lambert [477], Lully's colleague from the years with Mademoiselle de Montpensier, and presently only just below Lully himself in the court musical hierarchy. The match was hardly propitious in itself—Lully's amorous escapades included several anonymous mistresses, a page named Brunet, and the Duchess of La Ferté —but Madeleine bore him six children (three of each sex) and the king stood as godfather to Louis, the eldest son, born in 1664. The year previous, the composer had supplied the incidental music for Molière's comedy *L'Impromptu de Versailles,* beginning a seven-year association in which, so to speak, Lully played Sullivan to Molière's Gilbert. The partnership produced a hybrid form known as *comédie-ballet*—at worst, a comedy with balletic interludes or a ballet with comic scenes, at best a comedy to which the musical portion was indispensable. The culmination came with *M. de Porceaugnac* and *Le Bourgeois gentilhomme (The Middle-Class Gentleman),* produced at Chambord, where the king went to hunt, in the autumns of 1670 and 1671 respectively. The king nearly fell out of his chair at Lully's performances, and both works came perilously close to opera. He and Benserade (whose exclusive partnership ended with *Flore* in 1669) had been moving in the same direction with the court ballet—though it must be understood that save for purposes of parody, Lully was carefully avoiding any taint of Italian music.

Meanwhile, in 1659, a poet, the Abbé Pierre Perrin (1620–75), and a composer, Robert Cambert (c. 1627–77) had presented, at a patron's home in Issy, *La Pastorale*, a work they maintained was the first true French opera. (It probably wasn't.) The king had already established academies to control every other branch of art and learning, and so, after several tries, they obtained, in 1669, a patent to establish operatic academies throughout France. Naturally they began in Paris, producing another opera, *Pomone*, in 1671. It was too successful. Their backers pocketed all the take and disappeared. Perrin was thrown in debtors' prison and Cambert fled to England. Lully saw his chance and struck. Having persuaded the hapless poet to sell him his monopoly (with Louis's approval), he claimed and won the right to set his own prices, to perform the same repertoire he performed at the palace, and to exercise proprietary rights over it. Moreover he was granted a monopoly on the production of opera in France. There was a howl of protest, which Molière joined, but Lully had acquired in Philippe Quinault a librettist for bigger and better things, and he not only dumped Molière but did everything in his considerable power to deprive Molière's theater of music. In February 1673 the comedian died, and shortly afterward, with the king's help, Lully wrested the troupe's theater in the Palais Royal from them as his personal opera house.

From *comédie-ballet* Lully and Quinault turned to *trágedie-lyrique*, which, like the heroic drama about the same time in England, usually focused on the conflict between love and duty. The subjects were largely from classical literature and history and from Renaissance epic, and the king often chose them. In five acts, they eschewed spoken lines but were heavy on recitative and "machines," sneaked in the balletic by way of *divertissements* that had some bearing on the story and contained orchestral and choral segments. There were solo airs, but they were a far remove from the showpieces of the Italians. Over the next fourteen years, Lully established the bases of French opera with sixteen such works. Most of the librettos were by Quinault, but in 1678–79 the poet ran temporarily afoul of some rivals who got him disgraced, and Lully had to turn to others, such as La Fontaine (unsuccessfully) and Thomas Corneille, younger brother of the great drama-

tist. Around the same time Lully brought suit against a rival, Henri Guichard, for infringing on his privileges (and allegedly trying to poison him). Guichard was acquitted in 1677, after a three-year battle, but decided to leave the country.

In 1681, having again pleased the king with a performance of *Le Bourgeois gentilhomme,* Lully was permitted to purchase, for 63,000 livres, the office of Secretary to the King, which the publicly conferred on him a title (which he had already privately received). Despite some opposition from the Church to his operas, Lully was at his apogee for the next six years. However, on January 8, 1687, while he was conducting his *Te Deum* in celebration of the king's recovery from an illness, he drove the point of the staff, with which he was pounding out the rhythm, into one of his toes. An abscess formed, the physician botched it, and Lully developed gangrene. Seeing himself doomed, he dramatically consigned his unfinished *Achille et Polixène* to the flames—after making a fair copy. He died after nearly three months of suffering. At his death he owned five hotels in Paris (the equivalent of those on Boardwalk), two country retreats, and nearly a million livres. All three of his sons—Louis, Jean-Baptiste, and Jean-Louis—were court *surintendants de musique,* at one time or another, and his son-in-law Nicolas Francine was royal major-domo.

For one so famous in the annals of music, much of Lully's output is surprisingly weak. Much of his ceremonial music is cut by the yard—glittering and clangorous but ultimately empty and (to use a common summary term) cold. He makes only rudimentary use of counterpoint, and his harmonies are often of the simplest. There is too much cadencing, so that one has the feeling of jerkiness. His arias do not develop at all, and all seem to be cast in the same mold. Yet for all that, Lully is an important figure. He created French opera—not, of course, deifically from nothing, but by synthesis. He had a natural sense of the stage, and he knew how to blend those things that would work thereon. His operas derive from, among other things, *ballet du cour,* pastoral, *comédie-ballet,* Corneillean tragedy, court air, popular dance, masque, allegory, and even Italian opera. Their orchestral aspects were premised on the kind of orchestra—the first real one—that he had developed. Though he never learned to speak unaccented French, he tailored his vocal lines to the language until they fit like a glove. He invented the two-movement, slow-fast "French overture," which was later to assume considerable formal importance in the history of music. Above all, he was probably the first to conceive of his productions as "total theater." He was, moreover, the first great conductor. He insisted on meticulous ensemble, tolerated no nonsense or slacking from either the instrumentalists or the singers, and was observed on more than one occasion smashing an erring violinist's instrument.

RECORDINGS: On records, Lully has been best represented so far by his religious music—the *Te Deum*, the *Miserere*, and others of the *grand* motets. There are also suites from a number of the Molière collaborations, but the ballet music seems largely to have been ignored, save for a recording of the 1685 *Temple de la paix (Temple of Peace)* and two of the *Xerse* pieces. The 1674 opera *Alceste* has received a complete account, and there are two new recordings of the complete *Armide*. An older mono recording of *Bourgeois gentilhomme* also exists. In addition there are excerpts from *Isis* and *Amadis*, and an orchestral suite for *Amadis de Gaule*.

[518] NIVERS, Guillaume Gabriel (Nē-vârz', Gwē-yōm' Gà-brē-el')
ORGANIST, TEACHER, THEORETICIAN
BORN: c. 1632
DIED: Paris, November 30, 1714

Nivers was one of the many keyboardists said to have studied with Jacques Chambonnières [465], but there is no proof that he did. When he was about twenty, he became organist of St. Sulpice, in the Faubourg St. Germain and held the post for more than sixty years. He took a master's degree from the University of Paris in 1661. Seven years later, his friend Nicolas Lebègue [515] witnessed his marriage contract. He was appointed a royal organist in 1678, and in 1681, on the retirement of Henry Du Mont [476], became music master to that neglected featherbrain Queen Marie Thérèse. Five years later he was given charge of the music at the Maison Royale de St. Louis at St. Cyr (France's West Point). The school, designed to educate and acculturate the wives and daughters of the officers, was a pet project of Madame de Maintenon, Louis XIV's morganatic second wife, in whose arms the poor little queen died in 1683. Besides teaching and playing at the chapel, Nivers supplied the music for Racine's *Esther*, written for Madame de Maintenon's "girls" in 1691. He apparently did not get on with her very well. She was offended at his setting of the Song of Songs.

(Though she had been the king's mistress for years, she was, paradoxically, a prude.) When Nivers was in his seventies, she accused him of hanky-panky with his pupils. Nivers wrote several theoretical books. His composition manual was used throughout Europe and his pamphlet on thoroughbass is still useful. He also wrote on Gregorian chant, as the seventeenth century understood it, and edited a number of plainsong collections. He composed a Mass and some motets but is now remembered almost entirely for his organ music. He was an authority on the instrument, and his awareness of its possibilities shows in his 3 *Livres d'orgue*. The first, of 1665, seems to have been the first such work published in France since that of Jehan Titelouze [318] nearly forty years earlier. It set the pattern for those to follow. The second includes an organ Mass, and the third, like the first, is made up of suites in the eight tones. Some of these have been recorded—e.g., by Marie-Claire Alain and Xavier Darasse.

[519] KRIEGER, Adam (Krē'-ger, À'-dàm)
ORGANIST, TEACHER, CONDUCTOR, POET
BORN: Driesen, January 7, 1634
DIED: Dresden, June 30, 1666

An officer's son from a Prussian village now in westernmost Poland, Adam, first of the musical Kriegers, seems to have been unrelated to the others, Johann Philipp [553] and Johann [563]. Beginning somewhere in his middle teens, he studied organ with Samuel Scheidt [426] in Halle and attended the University of Leipzig, where he purportedly ran a student Collegium Musicum. When they threw the hapless Johann Rosenmüller [493] in the clink in 1655, they picked Krieger to succeed him at the Nikolaikirche organ. He was not so successful two years later in his application for the vacancy left at the Thomaskirche by the death of Tobias Michael, being passed over for Sebastian Knüpfer. Nevertheless it was a good year for him, for it saw the publication of his successful *Arien* and his hiring by Elector Johann Georg II to teach his daughter in Dresden. He had not been there long before he was also appointed court organist. His death at thirty-two ended a highly promising career. A posthumous second book of *Arien* appeared a year later. Though a few cantatas and such exist in manuscript, his reputation rests on his instrumentally accompanied songs. (The first book has been reconstructed from defective copies.)

Here he made a remarkable synthesis, using what may be described as an Italian approach to German tunes, designed for household and student use. Many of the lyrics are his own. Fritz Neumeyer has recorded an LP from the *Neue Arien.*

[520] d'ANGLEBERT, Jean-Henri
(Dàng'l-bâr', Zhàn Àn-rē')
KEYBOARDIST
BORN: Paris, 1635
DIED: Paris, April 23, 1691

Over the protests of Louis Couperin [504], d'Anglebert is often called Chambonnières' [465] best pupil, but there is no solid evidence that he was Chambonnières' pupil at all. By 1661 he was serving as harpsichordist to the king's brother, Philippe, Duke of Orléans. A year later Chambonnières, on the skids, sold him his court post. He was called Harpsichordist-in-Ordinary to the King's Chamber for the rest of his life, though in fact his son, Jean-Baptiste-Henri, seems to have taken over most of his duties in 1674. The senior d'Anglebert did not get around to publishing until 1689, when he brought out his fine *Pièces de clavessin* (orthography seems not to have been his long suit). He dedicated it to the Princesse de Conti, which was not a bad idea, since she was the king's daughter, and explained in a preface that the pieces were all in G major, D major, B minor, and E minor (arranged in suites) because he had written in the other keys earlier and meant eventually to make that material available. But he didn't. Besides the suites, which contain not only the expectable dances but transcriptions of Lullyan stage pieces and *vaudevilles,* there are also 6 fugues for organ, one of which is said to be suitable also to four harpsichords, and the only French keyboard variations on *La Folia,* an epidemically popular Spanish tune, known to have been composed in d'Anglebert's century. Some see him as a master contrapuntist, but others object to his thick textures and overuse of ornamentation. (The younger d'Anglebert [1661–1747] was a sickly, near-sighted fellow who was ousted in everything but title by François Couperin [616].) RECORDINGS: Gustav Leonhardt has recorded several harpsichord pieces by d'Anglebert. There are also recordings of organ and harpsichord pieces by a number of other artists.

[521] REUSNER, Esajas, the younger
(Roiz'-ner, Ez-ī'-yàs)
LUTENIST, TEACHER

BORN: Löwenberg, April 29, 1636
DIED: Berlin, May 1, 1679

The son, namesake, and pupil of the elder Reusner [480] was born in Silesia in the now Polish town of Lwówek Śląski. A precocious performer on the lute, he worked in Breslau from about 1648 successively in the households of Count Wittenberg (a Swede), a bureaucrat named Müller, and the Princess Radziwiłł (with whom he was exposed to French music). In 1655 he became court lutenist to the Duke of Silesia, Georg III, in Brieg (now Brzeg). When the ducal line ran out with Georg's death seventeen years later and the duchy was absorbed by Austria, Reusner went to Leipzig and taught at the university for a year. After that he served Friedrich Wilhelm, Elector of Brandenburg, in Berlin for the last five years of his life. He left two books of lute suites that show strong French influence and, like his father, a collection of chorales for lute. One of the most sophisticated of the German lutenists, he exercised considerable influence on those who came after him. He also published two collections of suites for strings and continuo. RECORDINGS: Arthur Fiedler has recorded one suite for strings and continuo.

[522] SPEER, Daniel (Shpâr, Dàn'-yel)
STADTPFEIFFER, CANTOR, WRITER
BORN: Breslau, July 2, 1636
DIED: Göppingen, October 5, 1707

Orphaned at the age of eight, Speer was educated in the local *Gymnasium* and later traveled in the Balkans and other exotic climes sufficiently to produce three volumes of recollections. In the middle 1660s (when he may also have been known as Daniel Rutge, unless Daniel Rutge was someone else), he held cantorial posts in Stuttgart and Tübingen. In 1667 he accepted such a post in Göppingen, but for reasons unknown his appointment was vetoed by the Duke of Württemberg a year later. From 1668 to 1673, when he returned to his Göppingen job, he was in the nearby towns of Gross Bottwar and Leonberg, during which period he married. In 1689 he was imprisoned for sedition (he had called the government cowardly), but his fellow citizens rallied to his support, and he was released and exiled to Waiblingen for four years. After the turn of the century, his health deteriorated and he died in the aftermath of a stroke. He published some practical books of church music and 3 quaintly titled collections of quodlibets (polyphonic potpourris of familiar tunes) under such even quainter pseudonyms as "Dacianischer Simplicissimus zu Güntz," "Asne de Rilpe," and (translated) "A German Spaniard in Greece." His most influential work, however, was a 1687 textbook, *Grundrichtiger Unterricht der musikalischen Kunst (Basic Instructions in the Art of Music)*. Besides offering what the title implies, it also includes detailed instructions (with charts in the second edition) for playing currently popular instruments, together with pieces composed to illustrate their potentials. RECORDINGS: Joshua Rifkin has recorded some of these and some of the quodlibets. The Cambridge Brass Quintet has recorded two sonatas for brass quintet. There are also recordings of excerpts from the 1688 *Musickalisch Türckischer Eulen-Spiegel.*

[523] COLONNA, Giovanni Paolo (Kō-lôn'-nä, Jō-vä'-nē Pà-ō'-lō)
ORGANIST, CHOIRMASTER
BORN: Bologna, June 16, 1637
DIED: Bologna, November 29, 1695

Colonna learned how to build organs from his father, Antonio, and how to play them from Antonio Filipucci, organist of several Bolognese churches. He then went off to Rome to learn his compositional ABCs from Abbatini, Orazio Benevoli [472], and Giacomo Carissimi [471]. Having played for a time at the Roman church of San Apollinare, he returned to Bologna as number-two organist at San Petronio, moving up to number-one two years later. In 1666, together with his old teacher and forty-eight other Bolognese musicians, he became a founding father of the Accademia Filarmonica, of which he was four times president. After the departure of Maurizio Cazzati [495] in 1671, Colonna became *maestro di cappella* at San Petronio for the rest of his days. In 1685 he made a fool of himself by publicly attacking Arcangelo Corelli [565] for writing "incorrectly" and his name became mud in Roman musical circles, but Pope Innocent XII set things right in 1694 by inviting him to head the Julian Choir. Unfortunately by then Colonna was in no shape to accept.
Colonna was widely admired in his time as composer, teacher, and performer, and Emperor Leopold I [528] bought copies of all his sacred works for the imperial *Kapelle.* These show an excellent grasp of Palestrinan counterpoint, a tempered fondness for Benevoli-style polychoralism, and a clear understanding of Carissimi's dramatic *concertato* approach. To his Bolognese compositions he added the instrumental brilliance peculiarly available to him there, producing music at times as radiant as that of George Friderick Handel [683]. Colonna was in fact an important writer of pre-Handelian oratorio, though all but a few of his efforts have vanished.
RECORDINGS: A solo motet, *O lucidissima dies,* has been recorded by both Yves Tinayre and Mirella Freni, and Bolognese forces under Tito Gotti have recorded a *Mass à 5* and 2 psalms.

[524] PASQUINI, Bernardo (Pàs-kwē'-nē, Bâr-när'-dō)
KEYBOARDIST, TEACHER
BORN: Massa di Valdinievole, December 7, 1637
DIED: Rome, November 21, 1710

Pasquini, the greatest keyboard performer of his generation, was born in a village now known as Massa e Cozzili, near Lucca. There is serious disagreement about the facts of his youth and early education. He went to Rome in or before 1650 and became thoroughly acquainted with the music of Palestrina [201] and Frescobaldi [407]. After a year as organist at Santa Maria Maggiore, he took a lifetime job in 1664 as organist of Santa Maria in Aracoeli. His enormous virtuosity attracted many important patrons to him, including the exiled Queen Christina of Sweden, Cardinal Ottoboni, and Prince Giambattista Borghese, in whose palace he lived for the last thirty years of his life. He was a close friend of Alessandro Scarlatti [583] and Arcangelo Corelli [565]. He was considered to be to the keyboard what Corelli was to the violin, and the two sometimes played together. Both were officers in the Accademia di Santa Cecilia (the musicians' union of the day), and all three, in 1706, were simultaneously initiated into the prestigious Accademia Arcadiana. Pasquini was also applauded by the crowned heads in Paris and Vienna. He attracted innumerable pupils, among whom are often named Francesco Gasparini [615], J. P. Krieger [553], Georg Muffat [566], and Domenico Zipoli [698], but this is another area in which historical agreement is far from unanimous.
Pasquini wrote many operas and oratorios, but time has removed many of them from consideration, and what remains has not been studied. As the keyboard composer who links Frescobaldi with Domenico Scarlatti [687], his reputation today rests chiefly on the 4 autograph collections of cembalo pieces preserved in Berlin and London. These include dances, toccatas, varia-

tions, and miscellaneous pieces, some of which show exquisite polyphonic technique. Pasquini was also among the first to write "real" three-movement sonatas for keyboard instruments. Unfortunately, for most of them only the figured-bass parts exist. Of these, several musicians have recorded their own "reconstructions" of the set of 14 for two keyboards.

[525] BUXTEHUDE, Dietrich (Bōōks-te-hōō'-de, Dēt'-rikh)
ORGANIST, CONDUCTOR
BORN: c. 1637
DIED: Lübeck, May 9, 1707

The Buxtehudes probably came from the like-named town to the west of Hamburg, but by the time Dietrich came along, they had considered themselves Danes for several generations. The father, Hans Jensen Buxtehude, was a native of (Bad) Oldesloe in Holstein, roughly halfway between Lübeck and Hamburg. Dietrich (or probably Diderik) was his oldest child, but the only Mrs. Buxtehude we know about, *née* Helle Jespersdatter, seems to have been his stepmother. If he was born in or before 1637, he was probably also born in Oldesloe; if later, he must have been born in Hälsingborg, the coastal city in southwest Sweden (then under Danish rule) whither Hans moved in 1638 to become organist of St. Mary's. After about three years he removed across the Øresund to the island of Sjaelland or Zealand, to take the analogous post at St. Olaf's in Helsingør (Hamlet's "Elsinore").

There has been a good deal of speculation about Dietrich's early years, but the fact is that history does not again remark him until the late 1650s, when he turns up in his father's old job in Hälsingborg. Not long after, Denmark lost the town to the Swedes, and Buxtehude came back to Helsingør, where he became organist at the local St. Mary's. Being unmarried, he did not merit free lodging, and so lived under the parental roof again. That situation was remedied eight years later (1668), following the death of Franz Tunder [486], organist of St. Mary's in Lübeck. Buxtehude applied for the job and got it, along with Tunder's virgin younger daughter, Anna Margarethe (the elder was already married). And there he settled for the rest of his life. (The two organs on which he played were—alas!—destroyed in a 1942 air raid.) It must have been a cozy situation, since Samuel Franck, the choirmaster, was Anna Margarethe's brother-in-law. Besides carrying out his normal duties, Buxtehude revived the con-

certs begun by Tunder, presenting them at 4 P.M. on five Sunday afternoons (three of them in Advent) each year. This *Abendmusik* became internationally famous. He also held the office of *Werkmeister*—literally "overseer" but actually financial executive—and it is a curious coincidence that one of his correspondents and admirers was a Thuringian theorist and organist named Andreas Werckmeister.

Though Buxtehude had a number of pupils, the only one of any renown was Nicolaus Bruhns [600]. Toward the end of his career, however, such likely youngsters as Handel [683], Johann Mattheson [668], and Johann Sebastian Bach [684] visited him—ostensibly to hear him play, but no doubt with an eye to a future vacancy at the Marienkirche and for a look at the daughter, Anna Margareta, whose hand and person went with the job. Buxtehude died a year and a half after Bach took his famous hike from Arnstadt to Lübeck.

It is no doubt Buxtehude's reputation in his own time that accounts for the preservation of so much of his music, for he published only fourteen trio sonatas, and no autographs are known to exist. But admirers were at pains to make copies, notably the indefatigable Swedish collector Gustaf Düben (c. 1628–90), to whom Buxtehude dedicated his choral Passion-cycle *Membra Jesu nostri,* and J. S. Bach's cousin Johann Gottfried Walther [680], through the agency of Werckmeister. Thus we have more than a hundred cantatas and other vocal works, a large body of organ music, a score of suites and some sets of variations for harpsichord, and a few manuscript sonatas.

Buxtehude's fame in his own time, the inherent attractiveness of his musical language, and the attention given him by the recording companies have served perhaps to make his music loom larger than it should. Though he was something of a synthesist—the North German organ school, the Italians as filtered through Heinrich Schütz [412], the French clavecinists—he was no innovator. His cantatas are still loosely articulated vocal *concerti,* his organ fugues are rhapsodic rather than strict. Two qualities are particularly characteristic: (1.) his subjectivity—a sense of total involvement with his music as a means of spiritual communication, no doubt related to the pervasive Pietism of the times, which argued a personal communicatory link between the individual human being and his God; (2.) a passion, an emotional drive (obviously related to the first point), that sees the message as more important than its medium, that uses form chiefly as a springboard to the attainment of mystic vision. It was this aspect of Buxtehude that particularly appealed to Bach (on whom the impact of the organ music cannot be gainsaid), and it is amusing to see modern writers summing it up with terms like *untidy* and *turbulent* (which, they admit, are not wholly satisfactory). Buxtehude seems least happy and least himself when he is handcuffed by a structure or a stricture. RECORDINGS: The organ music has been recorded *in toto* at least four times—by Marie-Claire Alain, Michel Chapuis, Walter Kraft, and Alf Linder. Lionel Rogg has devoted a disc to the harpsichord pieces, and Heinz Markus Göttsche has done the *Jüngste Gericht (Last Judgment),* the largest choral work. Rolf Schweitzer offers *Membra Jesu nostri,* and there are increasing numbers of cantata recordings, though no systematic traversal as yet. A considerable variety of instrumental miscellani (suites, sonatas, etc.) has also been recorded.

[526] VIVIANI, Giovanni Buonaventura (Vē-vē-å'-nē, Jō-vån'-nē Bwō-nà-vān-tōō'-rà)
VIOLINIST, CONDUCTOR
BORN: Florence, July 15, 1638
DIED: 1692 or later

Once thought to have been a Lucchese, Viviani remains a nebulous figure. He was violinist and later *Kapellmeister* at the Innsbruck court for at least twenty years. In 1678 or thereabouts he went back to Italy, surfacing briefly in Venice to produce an opera and in Rome to conduct an oratorio. By then he was sporting an imperial title, which he may have brought with him from Austria. After a time in Naples, where he directed an opera company, he became choirmaster of the cathedral in Pistoia in 1687 but drops out of all records toward the end of 1692. An imitator of Cesti [499], he left a small body of operas, a smaller one of oratorios, some cantatas and other vocal works, and a few sonatas. RECORDINGS: A pair of the last for trumpet and continuo have enjoyed several recordings (e.g., Edward Tarr, Maurice André).

[527] PEZEL, Johann (Pet'-zel, Yō'-hàn)
VIOLINIST, STADTPFEIFFER
BORN: Glatz, 1639
DIED: Bautzen, October 13, 1694

A man whose name seems never to have been spelled the same way twice, Pezel is

not to be confused with Pez [597] or Pecelius, even though he has been. He came to Leipzig in 1661 or so from a region about halfway between Berlin and Dresden, and became a violinist in the municipal musicians' guild. By 1670 he had reached the top rank as *Stadtpfeiffer,* which seems to have meant that he now played the trumpet (rather than the cornett), though the point is moot. He evidently aspired higher, for he applied for the post of Thomaskirche cantor on the death of Sebastian Knüpfer in 1676 but was not even considered. He also tried to transfer to Dresden. Eventually a plague epidemic in 1681 drove him back to his home country, where he seems to have remained. Though he wrote some sacred vocal music, his reputation rests on his instrumental publications, and particularly on his *Stadtpfeiffer* pieces in *Hora decima (The Tenth Hour)* and *Fünff-stimmige blasende Musik (Five-Voice Tooting Music).* Such works were customarily played from the tower of the Leipzig Rathaus at 10 A.M. and 6 P.M. There also survive *Musica vespertina (Evening Music), Musikalische Gemüths-Ergötzung (Musical Pleasure for the Spirit),* and *Deliciae musicales (Musical Goodies),* all consisting of suites for strings and continuo, *Opus musicum* (one-movement sonatas for same), and a big volume of *bicinia* for two melody instruments and continuo. Pezel had a good sense of form, and his pieces, taken in the small increments in which they were intended to be taken, are quite attractive. RECORDINGS: Today's infatuation with brasses (especially on records) has given, through innumerable recordings, undue prominence to the tower pieces.

[528] LEOPOLD I (Lā'-ō-pōlt)
HOLY ROMAN EMPEROR
BORN: Vienna, June 9, 1640
DIED: Vienna, May 5, 1705

The second son of Ferdinand III was, like his father, reared as a hard-line Roman Catholic. His name indicated that he was a bold fellow, but he was in fact a scholarly and artistic type who began writing music in his early teens and was probably intended for the Church. But his elder brother, also named Ferdinand, died in 1654, so they made him King of Hungary and then of Bohemia and finally, in 1658, after his father's demise, Holy Roman Emperor. A peaceable man who married three times and sired two more emperors (Joseph I and Charles VI), he seems to have wanted no more than a harmonious realm and a musical court. To the latter end he collected music and musicians as if they were endangered species, and if his tastes inclined toward Italy he at least appointed the first German imperial *Kapellmeister* in Johann Schmelzer [496]. In the broader area he was constantly being hassled by Louis XIV, who liked wars (it would seem) because they ended in treaties that could be celebrated with Te Deums composed and sung to the greater glory of himself and God, approximately in that order. At other times he was bothered by Swedes and Turks and plague, but he had the satisfaction of seeing the Duke of Marlborough, in the name of the Grand Alliance, beat the peruke off of the French king at Blenheim. The wars, of course, proved costlier than keeping up what was the best musical establishment in Europe, so Leopold was forced to make concessions, not the lest of which was letting Frederick III, Elector of Brandenburg, become Frederick I, King of Prussia, the result of which, as he noted with resignation, was to start the slide of the other German states away from Austria.

Leopold was himself a talented and fairly prolific composer, if not an earthshaking one. His output was largely religious but included a number of stage works, oratorios, and *sepolcri* (a kind of Easter oratorio), and more than 100 *balletti* (dances) for orchestra.

RECORDINGS: Dietfried Bernet has recorded a suite of the *balletti,* and orchestral excerpts from the opera *La Felicità* and the *sepolcro* oratorio *Il lutto dell' universo (The Universal Struggle).* Wolfgang Gabriel conducts in a recording of the *Missa Angeli Custodis.*

[529] ROSIER, Carl (or Charles Rosiers?) (Rôs-yā', Kärl)
VIOLINIST, MUSIC DIRECTOR
BORN: Liège, December 26, 1640
DIED: Cologne, autumn 1725

There has been considerable argument over whether this composer's genes were Flemish or French, which may seem nitpicking, save that he may have been the first Frenchman to write sonatas. He was an early predecessor of another musician of Belgian descent, Ludwig van Beethoven [1063], at the electoral court in Bonn, where he played violin and rose to the eminence of vice-*Kapellmeister.* He moved to Cologne in 1675, where he eventually became the city's chief musician in both the religious and secular wings, but he also worked in Holland before the end of the century. In 1711 his daughter Maria Anna married Willem De Fesch

[692], who is said to have been his pupil. He wrote a good deal of religious music, but is most effective in his instrumental pieces. The 14 sonatas noted above are for trumpet, strings, and continuo. RECORDINGS: Several have been recorded—one by Helmut Hunger and another in The Hague Philharmonic–sponsored boxed set, *400 Years of Dutch Music,* Vol. I.

[530] GEIST, Christian (Gīst, Krēst'-yǎn)
ORGANIST, SINGER
BORN: Güstrow, c. 1640
DIED: Copenhagen, 1711

Son of the cantor of Güstrow (near Rostock in Germany), Geist went to Copenhagen to sing bass in the royal Danish *Kapelle* in 1670, and then spent a decade as organist of the Swedish court in Stockholm. In 1685 he took to wife the widow of Copenhagen organist Johann Martin Radeck and thus fell heir to several church jobs. He was thrice married, and he and his entire family were wiped out by the plague. Christian Geist was apparently sufficiently inspired by *der heilige Geist* to turn out a considerable body of *geistliche Konzerte* that are generally melodious, sensitive, and sometimes instrumentally demanding. RECORDINGS: One has been recorded by Derek McCulloch.

[531] HACQUART, Carolus (Håk'-kärt, Kär'-ō-lōōs)
LUTENIST, VIOL PLAYER, ORGANIST
BORN: Bruges, c. 1640
DIED: 1701 or later

Hacquart began his significant musical career in Amsterdam, where he settled around 1670. He provided the music in 1678 to a play by Dirck Buseyro celebrating the Treaty of Nijmegen, which concluded the war with Louis XIV. He moved to The Hague, where the music-loving diplomat Constantijn Huygens seems to have gotten him a post playing the viola da gamba in the orchestra of the *Stadtholder,* William of Orange (where he was for a time a colleague of the violinist Carl Rosier [529]). A 1686 engraving shows Hacquart conducting the court orchestra. He probably went to England with William, who became that country's king as William III, following the ouster of James II in the Glorious Revolution. The most important of his few extant compositions are the 10 sonatas of *Harmonia parnassia* of 1686, which are as advanced as any contemporary work in the form. RECORDINGS: One of the sonatas has been recorded by the Sonata Da Camera Ensemble.

[532] **RUIZ DE RIBAYEZ, Lucas** (Rōō-ĕth′ dä Rī-bī′-eth, Lōō′-kås)
GUITARIST, HARPIST, PRIEST
BORN: Santa Maria de Ribarredonda, c. 1640 (?)
DIED: after 1677

Most of the little we know of Ruiz he tells us in the preface to his 1677 *Luz y norte musical*. He studied for the priesthood at Villafranca del Bierzo in western León, was ordained, and went into the service of various noble families, at which time he took up music. He seems also to have spent some time in South or Central America. His book is a tutor for the two instruments in which he specialized, the double-strung harp and the guitar *(not* the outmoded vihuela, as one reference has it). It provides a number of dances for the aspirant to test his skills on.

[533] **SANZ, Gaspar** (Sånth, Gås′-pär)
GUITARIST, PRIEST, AUTHOR
BORN: Calanda, c. 1640 (?)
DIED: after 1681

Born in an Aragonese town about fifty miles southeast of Zaragoza, Sanz studied theology at Salamanca and then went to Italy to study music. (One of his teachers was Orazio Benevoli [472].) He is said to have proved himself a fine organist, to have served as *maestro di cappella* to the Spanish viceroy in Naples, and to have been guitar teacher to Don Juan of Austria, brilliant soldier and acknowledged but unofficial son of Philip IV. At least he dedicated to Don Juan his 1674 *Instrucción de música sobre la guitarra española*. Besides including everything one needed to know to master the instrument, it contained a series of pieces of graded difficulty. It enjoyed great popularity; Lucas Ruiz de Ribayez [532] was well acquainted with it. Sanz also wrote on letters and religion. RECORDINGS: His pieces appear in many recorded guitar recitals, and some of them form the basis for the 1955 *Fantasía para un gentilhombre* by Joaquín Rodrigo [2025].

[534] **VEJVANOVSKÝ, Pavel Josef** (Ve-vå-nōv′-skē, På′-vel Yō′-sef)
TRUMPETER, MUSIC DIRECTOR, COPYIST
BORN: c. 1640
DIED: Kroměříž, c. September 23, 1693

Thanks to the assiduity of recent musicologists, Vejvanovský is now regarded as one of the earliest important composers from what is now Czechoslovakia, though not very long ago he was not even a name in most reference works. He is claimed by both Hukvaldy in Moravia and a Silesian town called Hlučín. Matriculating in 1656, he spent four years in the Jesuit college at Opava. In 1661 he joined the music of Leopold Wilhelm, Prince-Bishop of Olmütz (now Olomouc), at Kremsier (now Kroměříž) as a trumpeter. Since he liked to style himself "tubicen campestris," we may assume that his initial duties were venatic or military or both. Three years later the bishop, a younger son of Emperor Ferdinand II, died and was succeeded by a gentleman with a sonorous name, Karl Lichtenstein-Kastelkorn. He took a shine to Vejvanovský, whom he promoted to *Hof-und-Feldtrömpeter* and in 1670, after Heinrich von Biber [539] defected, to *Kapellmeister*. The bishop paid him handsomely, but on the debit side he had to copy all the music and direct the church choir. Yet he must be rated a success, for he married the mayor's daughter, bought a mansion, collected a fine music library, and died decidedly solvent. A prolific composer, he composed at least a dozen Masses and much other religious music, almost all of it with instruments imaginatively used. But he is chiefly remembered for his brilliant sonatas, *serenate,* and dances for instruments, especially those calling for trumpets—in some instances of various sizes. RECORDINGS: There is an LP sampler directed by Libor Pišek, brass music by the Jones Brass Ensemble, and chamber orchestra pieces by the Paris Chamber Orchestra.

[535] **XARABA, Diego** (Hä-räbv′-ä, Dē-ä′-gō)
ORGANIST
BORN: c. 1640 (?)
DIED: Madrid, c. 1700

Xaraba was a nephew of the organist Pablo Bruna [483] and studied with him at Daroca. In about 1676 he was organist at El Pilar in Zaragoza, and later served in Madrid in the chapel of Charles II. RECORDINGS: A few of his organ works have been recorded.

[536] **BACH, Johann Christoph** (Båkh, Yō′-hån Krēs′-tōf)
ORGANIST, HARPSICHORDIST

BORN: Arnstadt, December 8, 1642
DIED: Eisenach, March 31, 1703

Johann Christoph Bach (the first of that name) was the eldest of the three sons of Heinrich Bach [488] and Eva Hoffmann. Thus he was a first cousin of Christoph's twin sons, Johann Christoph and Johann Ambrosius. Johann Ambrosius was father to Johann Sebastian [684] and a third Johann Christoph, who served in Heinrich's old age as his assistant. Heinrich's own Johann Christoph was appointed organist in his hometown to the Count of Schwarzburg-Arnstadt when he was not quite twenty-one. In 1665 the town organist of Eisenach died and Christoph was a no-contest winner in the competition for his job. His success there also won him a position as keyboard player to the resident duke, in whose band he was a sometime colleague of Pachelbel [567] and Telemann [665]. Two years later he married Maria Elisabeth Wedemann, the town clerk's daughter, and sister to brother Johann Michael's wife Catharina, who was the mother of Maria Barbara Bach, who married her first cousin, Johann Sebastian.

Christoph's letters to the city fathers suggest that he led a wretched life in Eisenach. His salary seems never to have been paid; the housing promised him was substandard or nonexistent; the townspeople withheld the customary tips at weddings and funerals. He was full of helpful suggestions as to how things might be put right—suggestions that the council turned down. The organ was in dreadful shape. He was not permitted to go to Schweinfurt to take a job that might have kept his family from starving. He was falsely accused of pocketing charity monies that he had been delegated to collect. Most of his family was sick abed all winter. At one point Duke Johann Georg, apparently flush enough not to need any more money, turned the mint over to the hapless Bachs as a home, but following his death two years later, in 1698, they were turned out on the street so that more coins could be stamped.

Most of this jeremiad seems to have been true, but viewed from another perspective, Johann Christoph Bach looks like a rather canny operator. For all his troubles with the city, he seems to have been well paid and highly regarded at the court. He sired seven children, and though they do seem to have been, in their early years, a rather unhealthy lot, the four boys (all musically inclined) got a somewhat better education than the state required. Johann Nikolaus, the eldest, even went to college (at Jena)—the first Bach to

do so. The family was related not only to the civic clerk but also to the burgomaster and seems, from the few accounts preserved, to have lived rather well. And Johann Christoph's success in getting a new organ for the Georgikirche shows that his nagging—and, no doubt, his pull—was sometimes effective, even though he did not live to see the instrument inaugurated.

Though no more than a local celebrity in his day, Johann Christoph Bach was the most notable composer of the tribe prior to Johann Sebastian. Johann Sebastian's son, Carl Philipp Emanuel [801], was especially taken with his music, which he thought remarkably expressive, seeing that it came from such an antediluvian old fossil. The old fossil was influenced by the Venetian tradition as filtered through Schütz [412].

The bulk of his extant output is religious, ranging from a couple of sincere four-part hymns to accompanied cantatas (or *concerti*) and polychoral motets of considerable complexity. The Michaelmas cantata *Es erhub sich ein Streit (A Fight Broke Out)*, for ten voices, four trumpets, timpani, and strings, is a particularly bold and grandiose conception. (To the wedding cantata *Mein Freundin, du bist schön [My Love, Thou Art Fair]* Christoph added, apparently for his own amusement, a hilarious prose program.) There are also some short chorale preludes and other keyboard pieces.

RECORDINGS: The two-choir motet *Ich lasse dich nicht (I Shall Not Leave Thee)*, in which Bach incorporates a melody by Hans Sachs [133] has been recorded by both Philippe Caillard and Uwe Gronostay, and there are some organ pieces played by Wilhelm Krumbach and Franz Lehrndorfer. A flute sonata recorded by Jean-Pierre Rampal is really by Johann Christoph Friedrich Bach [872].

[537] GAUTIER, Pierre, de Marseilles
(Gōt-yā' Pē-âr')
KEYBOARDIST, TEACHER, IMPRESARIO
BORN: La Ciotat, c. 1642
DIED: at sea, off Sète, December 1696

Though he was born near, rather than in, Marseilles, Gautier is "de Marseilles" to distinguish him from a passel of contemporary lute-playing Gautiers and Gaultiers (see 468)—especially Pierre Gautier d'Orléans—to none of whom he appears to have been related. Both Provençal and provincial, he was that rare French musician who seems never to have worked in Paris. He was playing and teaching in and around Marseilles when in 1684 he obtained a li-

cense from the monopolistic Lully [517] to
open an opera house (the first one permitted). Besides works by Gautier himself, the
company played the Lully repertoire,
which, under the circumstances, was not
surprising. Following three seasons in Marseilles and Avignon, Gautier (who was
scrupulous about paying his performers)
was in 1688 thrown into debtors' prison. His
incarceration lasted only a few days, at the
end of which he went to Lyons, where he
served another company as conductor until
it collapsed in 1692. Gautier then returned
to Marseilles and inaugurated another company with his brother Jacques, which successfully toured the Midi until the end of
1696. The Gautiers and some of their fellows then loaded the sets and instruments
on a ship bound from Sète to Marseilles and
set sail. They were never seen again. Gautier's operas are lost, but some songs and
pièces en trio survive. RECORDINGS: Flutist
André Pepin has recorded a suite in G minor. There is also a motet, *Ad te clamo
(Unto Thee I Cry),* conducted by Louis
Frémaux, which is attributed to Gautier.

[538] FRANCK, Johann Wolfgang (Fränk,
Yō'-hàn Vōolf'-gàng)
TEACHER, CHOIRMASTER, IMPRESARIO
BORN: Unterschwaningen, c. June 17,
1644
DIED: after 1702 (?)

Except that he was born in Franconia, nothing is known of Franck's origins or youth
before he registered, at nineteen, as a student at Wittenberg. Two years later he was
working for the *Markgraf* of Ansbach
(where he may have grown up) as assistant
recorder and tutor to his employer's daughters. In 1668 he was let go, apparently to
study in Venice. Four years later he was
back, in charge of the *Markgraf*'s theater
and its orchestra. With an obvious awareness of what was going on internationally,
he began, it is safe to say, German ballet
and German opera. Unfortunately he blew
his chances in 1679 when, in a fit of jealous
rage, he killed a colleague, Johann Ul-
brecht. He fled, with his wife of thirteen
years, the former Anna Susanna Wilbel, and
their several children, to the free city of
Hamburg. There he was welcomed by
Adam Reincken [498] who, supposing him
sent from heaven, appointed him director of
his new opera house in the Goose Market,
where he staged at least seventeen of his
own operas in less than a decade. From 1682
to 1685 he also served as choirmaster at the
cathedral. At some time during the next five

years, Franck took to the road again, leaving Anna Susanna and their now-ten offspring to fend for themselves. In 1690 he
surfaced in London as a concert manager at
the Sign of the Two Golden Balls in Covent
Garden. Shortly thereafter he took on a
partner, Robert King, and together they
provided competition for the former small-
coal man, Thomas Britton (who was later
frightened to death by a ventriloquist).
Their efforts continued until at least 1693.
After that we know only that Franck wrote
music for Colley Cibber's play *Love's Last
Shift* in 1696 and that an opera, *The Judgment of Paris,* was slated for performance in
February 1702.

Most of Franck's stage music has vanished, though the full score of the 1679 *Die
drei Töchter des Cecrops (Cecrops' Three
Daughters)* is the first such German document known to have survived, and the
anthologies of hits from *Vespasianus* and
Aneas are the first such collections to have
seen publication. He left solo cantatas and
published collections of sacred songs in
Germany. He also wrote secular songs in
England which appeared in periodicals.

RECORDINGS: A number of the *Geistliche
Lieder* appear in recorded anthologies (e.g.,
by Yves Tinayre and Kirsten Flagstad.)

[539] BIBER, Heinrich Ignaz Franz von
(Bē'-ber, Hĭn'-rikh Ĕg'-nàts fun)
VIOLINIST, CONDUCTOR
BORN: Wartenberg, August 12, 1644
DIED: Salzburg, May 3, 1704

Biber was the son of a forester (or perhaps
huntsman) on an estate near what is now
Liberec in Czechoslovakia. He probably
had his basic training from the castle organist, Wiegan Knöffel. Because of certain sim-
ilarities in their music, it is thought that he
later studied with Schmelzer [496], "the al-
most-best violinist in Europe," whom he
would one day outstrip. At some time before 1668 he joined the orchestra of the
Prince-Bishop of Olmütz (now Olomouc),
Karl Lichtenstein-Kastelkorn, at Kremsier
(see 534), as a string player. Exactly what
went wrong in 1670 is uncertain, but Biber
fled, closely followed by a warrant for his
arrest. After holing up for a time with his
fiddle maker, Jakob Stainer, in Absam (near
Innsbruck), he found a place in the *Kapelle*
of Maximilian Gandolf, Reichsgraf von
Khünberg, Prince-Bishop of Salzburg—the
lure of whose service may have caused all
the fuss in the first place. (But the rift with
Bishop Karl must have been soon healed,
for Biber made a point of sending him his

compositions.) Two years after he settled in, he married the daughter of a respectable Salzburg merchant and afterward rose steadily in rank and reputation. He became singing master in 1677, vice-*Kapellmeister* in 1679 (his rank in the pecking order was just below that of superior-court justices), and *Kapellmeister* in 1684, with the title of *Truchsess,* or "Lord High Steward." Max Gandolf died in 1687, but Biber continued to thrive under his successor, Graf Johann Ernst von Thun, and in 1690 received the ultimate accolade, a patent of nobility from Emperor Leopold I [528], enabling him to sign himself thereafter "Biber von Bibern." His son Carl Heinrich seems also to have been a musician.

As a violinist, Biber seems to have been the Niccolò Paganini [1106] of his time. Whether, as Paul Hindemith [1914] is said once to have announced, he was also the greatest composer before Johann Sebastian Bach [684] is arguable, but he is certainly an interesting one. (He was also no Charles Ives [1659], as someone rashly claimed him to be, though he did leave a handful of experimental *jeux d'esprit.*) He wrote operas (only one extant) and "school plays" (all lost). He also left a few religious pieces, ranging from *concerti* through *a cappella* old-style contrapuntal pieces to Masses in the "colossal Baroque" style. (He is a favorite candidate for the authorship of the *Salzburg Mass* in 51 parts once attributed to Benevoli [472].) But it is his instrumental works that are perhaps most interesting. The sonatas, of which nearly 60 survive, are about equally divided between those for a single instrument (with bass) and those for several (including a few trio sonatas).

The most famous are the *Rosenkrantz-Sonaten (Rosary Sonatas on the Fifteen Mysteries of the Life of the Virgin Mary).* Composed relatively early (c. 1676), they show—as Biber's violin music generally does—that however formidable his playing technique, he did not seek virtuosity for its own sake. If formal considerations are not paramount with him, he does not ignore them—albeit here "sonata" often includes pieces proper to the dance suite. Though the cycle has been termed an early example of program music, Biber is less concerned with image than with emotion. It also demonstrates the use of *scordatura,* for which the composer is famous though he did not invent the device. Borrowed from the lutenists, it involves altered tunings of the strings, permitting, on the violin, unusual double-stops and other tricks, and resulting in new and richer colors. (Since the notation is such that it permits the performer to read it as though the

tuning were normal, it baffled many a subsequent musician.) The set ends with a Guardian Angel Sonata, actually a passacaglia for solo violin on a Salzburg hymn "An Angel Sent Me by God," associated with the local cult of the Rosary. Another set of *scordatura* pieces is the *Harmonia artificiosa-ariosa,* consisting of suites for two violins and continuo. The *Sonatae tam aris quam aulis servientes (Sonatas Suitable for Both Altar and Hall)* involve trumpets in several instances, and there are a number of miscellaneous compositions for brasses and brass ensembles.

RECORDINGS: The *Rosary* sonatas have been made available by several violinists, including Suzanne Lautenbacher, Eduard Melkus, and Sonia Monosoff. Joshua Rifkin has devoted an LP to selections from the altar-and-hall series, and the Vienna Concentus Musicus has devoted two or three to the miscellaneous instrumental music (some of it played on Stainer instruments). There are versions of the *Nachtwächter (Night Watchman) Serenade* by Karl Ristenpart, Carl Baumgartner, and Günther Kehr and of the programmatic *Battalia* by Newell Jenkins. Heinz Zickler performs the Concerto in C Major for Trumpet.

[540] CABANILLES, Juan Bautista José
(Kȧb-vȧ-nē´-yes, Hwȧn Bou-tēs´-tȧ Hō-zȧ)
ORGANIST, PRIEST
BORN: Algemesí, c. September 6, 1644
DIED: Valencia, April 29, 1712

Born near Valencia, Cabanilles lived and worked in that city for most of his life. Brought to the cathedral as a choirboy, he is said to have studied with Urbano de Vargas, the choirmaster, and Jerónimo de La Torre, the second organist. When the latter died in 1665, the Cabildo unanimously voted Cabanilles into the post, waiving for the nonce the requirement that the intendant must be a priest. Cabanilles, however, quickly set about rectifying the omission, taking initial orders a month later. In 1666 he was elevated to the first organ, and in 1668 he was ordained. Except for occasional excursions to play (by request) in France and Italy, he remained at the cathedral for forty-six years, though he was ailing during much of his last decade.

Cabanilles is regarded as the culmination of Spanish organ music and the greatest Spanish organist of his day. Moreover, he was influential as a teacher. He was enormously prolific; the hundreds of manuscript pages that have survived are said to represent less than half of his output. None of his music was published in his lifetime, and a modern edition foundered with Vol. 4, issued in 1952. Save for a few vocal works (including an incomplete Mass), it is all for organ. In general it tends to be rhapsodic rather than formal, and in this regard Cabanilles has been likened to Buxtehude [525]. His variations show great fecundity of invention, but his *tientos* (his most usual genre) are also remarkable, particularly the so-called *tientos de falsas,* which exhibit some rather far-out use of dissonance.

RECORDINGS: There are recorded samplings by a number of organists, such as Franz Haselböck, Paulino Ortiz, and Helmut Rilling.

[541] STRADELLA, Alessandro (Strä-del'-lä, Ä-les-sän'-drō)
TEACHER, ADVENTURER
BORN: Rome, October 1, 1644
DIED: Genoa, February 25, 1682

The only opera by Friedrich von Flotow [1222] other than his *Martha* that has any currency today is *Alessandro Stradella* of 1844. In it the composer, smitten by a Venetian beauty, elopes with her in Carnival disguise. Later, accosted by assassins in their Roman love nest, Stradella turns them to gelatin with his singing. Free at last, he and his Leonora ride off into the sunset. It seems the kind of treatment due a man on whose murdered body were bestowed epithets like *"Orfeo assassinato!"* It's the sort of story that, thanks to a 1705 account by Pierre Bonnet-Bourdelot, further embroidered by Dr. Charles Burney and other antiquarians, everyone chose to believe until modern research put some holes in it.

Stradella's career needs no fictional coloring. His father was Marcantonio Stradella, sometime governor of Vignola (near Modena), whose abandonment of it to papal troops smacked of cowardice or treason. His mother was born Simona Garofali, to a noble Modenese family. By the time he was an eleven-year-old choirboy at San Marcello del Crocifisso in Rome, Alessandro was an orphan. He is said to have been a pupil of Ercole Bernabei, a pupil of Benevoli [472]. Stradella succeeded Kerll [506] as music director of the Münich court. At nineteen he was a retainer of the exiled Queen Christina of Sweden. Two years later—now known as "Cavaliere" Stradella—he was in the service of Lorenzo Onofrio Colonna, scion of the powerful Roman family, and his wife, *née* Maria Mancini, niece of Cardinal Mazarin, with whom he visited Venice and possibly

Florence. An intimate of the Roman "Beautiful People" of the day, Stradella also cultivated more dubious companions, such as the violinist Carlo Ambrogio Lonati, known as "the queen's hunchback," who became his henchman and copyist, and the Abbate Antonio Sforza, with whom he became involved in a charity swindle. Meanwhile his womanizing was growing notorious, and he even tried to kidnap a highborn nun.

In 1669 Pope Clement IX (himself a librettist) gave Christina's adviser, Count d'Alibert, permission to build a commercial opera house in Rome. It opened the following year as the Teatro Tordinona; Stradella was involved from the outset, offering his revisions of works by Antonio Cesti [499] and Giacomo Carissimi [471]. For the next several years he seems to have been quite busy with such things (mostly prologues and intermezzos) until Pope Innocent XI closed all the theaters for the 1675 Jubilee. Two years later he ran afoul of Cardinal Cibo, the papal foreign secretary, and was forced to leave town. He took with him a pupil, Ortensia Grimaldi or Grimani, mistress of a Venetian nobleman, Alvise Contarini. Or perhaps he acquired her en route. At any rate, Florence would not shelter them, and they had to go on to Turin, where the dowager Duchess of Savoy, Jeanne de Nemours, took them in. The pursuing posse, led by Contarini himself, was thwarted, but on October 10, 1677, Stradella was set upon and seriously wounded by a pair of Contarini's hired bravos, who were given sanctuary in the French Embassy, precipitating an international crisis. Ortensia sought refuge in the Convento della Consolata and disappeared from the tale.

Recovered, Stradella and his sidekick Lonati moved to Genoa, where they engaged in a Mafiaesque venture that offered hairstyling, gigolos, musical entertainment, and gambling. The composer also produced several operas there and wrote at least one oratorio and some other music for Modena, back in his ancestral country. Among his Genoese pupils was Francesca Lomellini, wife of a man of importance, and herself a member of a noble family. Evidently the relationship was—or was thought to be— more than professional, for her brothers hired a Sparafucile (not an Egyptian, as he is sometimes called, but a native of Alessandria in Piedmont) who stabbed Stradella to death in the Piazza di Banchi on the night of February 25, 1682. One of the Lomellini was arrested, and the trial produced a jealous actress who had betrayed the composer, but the defendant was eventually acquitted for lack of evidence.

Stradella's few extant operas seem to be musically not very interesting. His oratorios offer more variety. He considered *San Giovanni Battista* (Rome, 1675) his best large work. Here one finds brilliant use of the orchestra (divided into *concerto* and *concertino,* an introductory *sinfonia* in three movements, a reversion to polyphonic writing, constant contrasts of mood and form, and strongly emotional expression. The final scene, wherein Herod laments his murder of the holy man while Salome rejoices, represents something new and nonlinear, and, as a good deal of Stradella did, probably influenced Handel [683]. One sees this sort of thing also in the cantatas, which make the same sort of use of dramatic contrast, of instrumental interlude, and of functional accompaniment. (Oddly, the one "Stradella" vocal work that everyone knows, the aria *"Pietà, Signor,"* is a nineteenth-century forgery, probably by Louis Niedermeyer [1167].)

Stradella's chief importance lies in his instrumental writing, both in his non-operatic vocal works and in his small body of sonatas and *sinfonie.* Here one finds, in a few instances—such as that noted above and the *Sonata di viole* in D—the opposition of large and small instrumental groups that seems to look toward the coming of the *concerto grosso.*

RECORDINGS: There are scattered recordings of some of the instrumental works, as well as of several cantatas. The oratorio *San Giovanni Battista* has been recorded by Carlo Felice Cillario.

[542] TORREJÓN Y VELASCO, Tomás de (Tôr-rä-hōn′ ē Bvel-às′-kō, Tō-màs′ dä)
JUDGE, CHOIRMASTER
BORN: Spain, December 23, 1644
DIED: Lima, April 23, 1728

At the age of fourteen Torrejón entered the service of Pedro Fernández de Castro y Andrade, who took him to Lima in 1667 when he was appointed viceroy of Peru. For five years Torrejón was in charge of the armory. In 1672 he became chief magistrate of Chachapoyas Province in the northern part of the colony, returning to Lima in 1676 to spend the rest of his life as *maestro de capilla* of the cathedral. He left a few motets and many *villancicos,* the manuscripts of most of which are for some reason in Guatemala Cathedral. In 1701 the viceroy put on a performance of his opera *La Púrpura de la rosa (The Scarlet of the Rose,* libretto by Calderón), the first known opera in the New

World. RECORDINGS: Roger Wagner has recorded a chorus and dances from it.

[543] STRATTNER, Georg Christoph (Stràt′-ner, Gä-ôrg′ Krēs′-tōf)
CHOIRMASTER, SINGER, RÉGISSEUR
BORN: Gols, c. 1644
DIED: Weimar, c. April 10, 1704

Born near Pressburg (now Bratislava, Czechoslovakia), Strattner sang as a choirboy in that city under the direction of his cousin Samuel Bockshorn, alias Capricornus, with whom he resided. Capricornus took him to Stuttgart in 1657 when he was appointed court *Kapellmeister* there. In 1666, Strattner became court music director at Durlach, near Karlsruhe, and sixteen years later choirmaster of the church of the Barefoot Friars in Frankfurt am Main, where he also taught. (While he was there the French, in a meaningless rampage connected with the War of the League of Augsburg, obliterated Durlach, including the court library.) After a decade as one of the most important musical figures in Frankfurt, Strattner was banished for appropriating someone's wife. After two years, he found employment as a choir singer in Weimar, where he was soon promoted to assistant *Kapellmeister* of the court. In 1697 he was also appointed director of the newly built court opera house. Though he wrote several ballets and perhaps some operas, most of what is extant of Strattner's work consists of a few cantatas and some pietistic hymns.

[544] CHARPENTIER, Marc-Antoine (Shàr-pont-yā′, Märk Àn-twàn′)
MUSIC DIRECTOR, TEACHER, SINGER
BORN: c. 1645 (?)
DIED: Paris, February 24, 1704

Though he lacked the drive and peculiar genius of his incubus, Lully [517], Charpentier was a better composer. It is probably because Lully feared him and consequently thwarted his career that he has remained so little known until recently. The discovery of twenty-four large manuscript volumes of his music in the Bibliothèque Nationale in Paris, the dedication of modern musicologists, and the efforts of a couple of Charpentier societies have combined in the last thirty years to bring his music to the attention of the general public.

They have not, however, been able to cast much light on his origins and early career. We know that he studied in Rome with

Carissimi [471] but not how long or exactly when (three years and the middle 1660s are the usual surmises). An old story says that he was the son of a painter (a real one) from the Touraine, that he was sent to Italy to study the paternal trade, and that when he heard Carissimi's music he threw away his brushes. There is not a shred of evidence to support any of it, and most scholars suspect that he was Paris-born. At some point after his return from Rome he was employed as a countertenor by the Duchesse de Guise, but there are no precise dates until much later in their association. It is in 1672 that Charpentier first emerges clearly as composer of the overture to Molière's *La Comtesse d'Escarbagnas* and incidental music to his *Le Mariage forcé (The Shotgun Wedding)*. This partnership resulted from the playwright's break with Lully. Lully, expectably, took note and placed such strictures on the use of music and musicians in theaters other than those that had his approval that Charpentier was forced to rewrite his music for *Le Malade imaginaire (The Hypochondriac)* twice. Molière died backstage after playing the title role in the fourth performance, but Charpentier continued to work with the company at the Théâtre de Guénégaud, after Lully had kicked it out of the Palais-Royal, for a dozen years.

Around 1679 Charpentier became somehow attached to the private musical establishment of the Dauphin Louis (who did not live to be king), serving at times as its director. A year later La Guise promoted him to that status in her household, a post that he retained until she died in 1688. In 1683 Henry Du Mont [476] and Pierre Robert [492], the last of the king's four rotating *maîtres de chapelle*, retired, and there was a national competition to select four successors. Charpentier made it to the finals, but then got sick and was unable to appear. Louis, recognizing his worth, awarded him a decent pension anyhow. The next year Charpentier became music master to the Jesuit College of Louis-le-Grand, for which he wrote some *tragédies spirituelles*, notably *David et Jonathan*, produced there a year after Lully died. It was apparently shortly after this that Charpentier was appointed music tutor to Philippe d'Orléans, the young son of Louis's profligate brother "Monsieur" and future regent for the infant Louis XV. And a little later he was called on to write some music for the Jansenist nuns of the Convent of Port-Royal. In 1693 his *Médée* was produced in the Académie Royale—in a sense, a sort of ultimate triumph, though unhappily it was a failure. Finally in 1698 Charpentier reached his zenith, in terms of prestige, when he was appointed music master to La Sainte Chapelle.

Whereas the immigrant Lully strove to rid French music of even a suspicion of Italianism, Charpentier, Italian-trained, championed the Italian approach and skillfully adapted it to French use. He wrote prodigally in many genres, though the bulk of his output is sacred (nearly 400 works, including 12 Masses). Of his dramatic music the sole opera is quite effective musically but lacks Lully's feel for the theater and is hampered by the younger Corneille's libretto. One of the Masses is for instruments only (without continuo) and is admittedly modeled on the organ Mass. The vocal examples (which include 3 Requiems) are in *concertato* style and are in some instances polychoral; they show both Roman and Venetian influences. One is for eight vocal and eighteen instrumental parts, another for four and eight. The most famous, the *Messe de minuit* for Christmas Eve, is a fabric of popular *noëls*. In such works Charpentier is often extremely specific about the deployment of his forces and the effects he intends.

Undoubtedly his most interesting works are his oratorios and cantatas. These forms he imported. Save for the eccentric examples by Guillaume Bouzignac [431], Charpentier's were the first oratorios written in France, and though they fell on barren ground, they have been viewed as a sort of link between those of Carissimi [471] and Handel [683]. The cantatas aroused more interest, as subsequent events would show.

RECORDINGS: So far, these two forms, oratorios and cantatas, have been largely neglected on records, but by now virtually all of the Masses have been recorded, as has the little *Christmas Oratorio,* and the *Epithalamium* for the Bavarian Elector. Roger Blanchard has provided a disc of the Port-Royal pieces, and there have been several sets of highlights from *Médée*. Other recordings include a *Requiem* in D minor and one in G minor, conducted by Louis Devas; two short oratorios, *Caecila, Virgo et Martyr* and *Filius Prodigus,* conducted by William Christie; *Le Jugement dernier* and *Beatus vir,* conducted by Michel Corboz; *Actéon,* again conducted by William Christie; and a *Suite for Strings,* conducted by Richard Kapp. Just released is a complete recording of *Médée* conducted by William Christie.

[545] POITEVIN, Guillaume (Pwă-tə-văn′, Gwē-yōm′)

PRIEST, TEACHER, SERPENT PLAYER
BORN: Boulbon, October 20, 1646
DIED: Aix-en-Provence, January 26, 1706

An important teacher, Père Guillaume lived all of his life in Provence. While a choirboy at St. Trophime in Arles, he learned to play the serpent, that primitive predecessor of the tuba, which got him a post at the cathedral in Aix when he had just turned seventeen. Four years later he was named music master. Among his many pupils were Esprit Blanchard [725], André Campra [584], and Jean Gilles [614]. He was ordained in 1672. Twenty-one years later he retired, but the pupils who succeeded him (Gilles and Jacques Cabassol) proved unsatisfactory, and in 1698 the chapter persuaded him to come back. RECORDINGS: Stéphane Caillat has recorded the offertory from his *Requiem*. Otherwise, of his compositions only a couple of psalms and a few bits of Masses are known to exist.

[546] ARAUJO, Juan de (À-rou′-hō, Hwàn dā)

CHOIRMASTER, PRIEST
BORN: Villafranca de los Barros, Spain, 1646
DIED: La Plata, Bolivia, 1712

It was once said that Araujo was one of the first composers to have been born in the New World, but it turns out that he was actually a native of Extremadura, Spain, and was brought to Peru by his father, a government official. He attended the University of San Marcos in Lima but, because of his involvement in some sort of student protest, was expelled c. 1669 and ordered out of the country by the viceroy, Count de Lemos. He somehow made his way to Panama City, where he was ordained and became a choirmaster. On the viceroy's death in 1672, Araujo returned to Lima, where he was made cathedral choirmaster. Four years later he was appointed to the analogous post in the wealthy cathedral of La Plata (now Sucre), in Bolivia, where he remained until he died. Besides a few motets he left a large number of *villancicos,* some of them with a strain of comedy. RECORDINGS: Roger Wagner has recorded a polyphonic hymn and an Epiphany *villancico, Los Negritos,* in which the Three Kings sing in the dialect of Lima blacks.

[547] MAYR, Rupert Ignaz (Mi-er, Rōō′-pârt Ēg′-nàts)

VIOLINIST, CONDUCTOR
BORN: Schärding, 1646
DIED: Freising, February 7, 1712

Born on the River Inn in Lower Austria, Mayr found employment as a violinist in the episcopal court at Freising, Upper Austria. After functioning at various other Bavarian cities, he joined the elector's court band in Münich in 1683, and was a colleague of Evaristo Felice Dall'Abaco for a time. The elector, Maximilian Emanuel, paid his way to Paris to study composition with Lully [517]. He returned to his post in 1685. In 1704 the elector was defeated at the Battle of Höchstädt and exiled, and subsequently the country was, laid waste in the War of the Spanish Succession. In 1706 Mayr returned to Freising, where he was *Kapellmeister* for the rest of his days. Mayr's Masses, psalms, school operas, and sacred *concerti* all show a strong Italian influence, but his sonatas and instrumental dance pieces, etc., show the fingerprints of Lully. RECORDINGS: See the two *sinfoniae* recorded by Joseph Kraus. There is also a sacred *concerto* sung by Georg Jelden and the *Pythagorische Schmidsfunklein* Suite No. 2 conducted by Erich Keller.

[548] HUMFREY, Pelham

SINGER, VIOLINIST, LUTENIST, TEACHER
BORN: 1647
DIED: Windsor, July 14, 1674

Humfrey was the most likely English composer of the generation before Henry Purcell's [581], his promise nipped in the bud by his early death. Anthony à Wood says that he learned his first music from his uncle, Roundhead Sir John Humfrey, and he was one of the first contingent to be named in 1660 to the newly revived Chapel Royal. He began writing music shortly thereafter and had written several anthems by the time his voice broke in 1664. The most famous was "I Will Always Give Thanks," known as the "Club Anthem" because it was the work of a clique of boon companions: Humfrey, John Blow [552], and William Turner. King Charles was particularly solicitous of his welfare and on Humfrey's retirement came up with 450 pounds to send him to study in Italy and France, where there was real music. (The money came from the secret service fund, which shows us that government hasn't changed much.) By the time he got back,

Humfrey found he had been named to succeed Nicolas Lanier as a royal lutenist and had been made a Gentleman of the Chapel Royal. He was only twenty and it all went to his head and made him insufferable. For the next few years he seems to have done nothing spectacular, but the king rewarded him for his 1672 New Year's ode by naming him (along with Thomas Purcell) a Composer to the Violins. It turned out to be a banner year for Humfrey, for in June he was made a warden of the Corporation for Regulating the Art and Science of Music (organized in imitation of the French Academy), in July he was promoted to the office of Master of the Children in the Chapel Royal, and that autumn he married Katherine Cooke, the daughter of his predecessor in that office. He was admired as a teacher; Henry Purcell was one of his charges. Late in the winter of 1674, Humfrey's infant daughter Mary died, and he followed her in the summer. He was twenty-six. He left fewer than threescore works, all vocal, but the mature ones (not unsurprisingly) show that he knew the Renaissance was over. The orchestral parts in his anthems show the French influence, but elsewhere he is Italianate. There is also an Anglican service, 3 odes, music for a 1674 revival of *The Tempest*, and about 25 songs, both sacred and secular (some of the latter for plays). One, "I Pass All My Hours in a Shady Old Grove" (lyric by H. M. Charles II), seems to have been a runaway hit.

RECORDINGS: There are scattered recordings of anthems and songs, notably a setting of John Donne's "Hymn to God the Father" (by Alfred Deller, John Shirley-Quirk).

[549] PHILIDOR, André Danican, the elder (Fē-lē-dôr', Àn-drä' Dà'-nē-kàn)
INSTRUMENTALIST, LIBRARIAN
BORN: Versailles, c. 1647
DIED: Dreux, August 11, 1730

The Philidor tribe was originally called Danican. Supposedly Louis XIV complimented Michel (c. 1600–59), a reed player in the Grande Écurie (the "outdoor" band attached to the royal stables), by naming him after an Italian oboe virtuoso named Filidori. Jean, either his son or his younger brother (d. 1679) and his colleague, adopted the name in a Frenchified form and passed it on to the dynasty of musicians and chess players that he sired. André was probably his eldest son.

A composer of some talent, he is notable for (1) siring more progeny than J. S. Bach

[684]—sixteen on the former Marguerite Monigot, and five more on Elisabeth LeRoy (the youngest born when he was in his late seventies); (2) having, as Royal Music Librarian, copied out an invaluable archive of French court music dating back to the previous century—at least 150 volumes, of which most are still extant; (3) being a one-man band: as a member of the Écurie and later of both royal chamber and royal chapel, he played oboe, krummhorn, bassoon, timpani, and the tromba marina, a sort of one-string bass, also called a "nun's fiddle." In 1683 the king conferred on him and his musical brother Jacques (1657–1708) estates at Versailles. He was granted a pension in 1722 but continued to putter about the royal library until he died. He left at least 7 opera-ballets or divertissements, which he astutely waited to write until Lully [517] was out of the way, and a number of dances and other instrumental pieces, notably the *Pièces de trompettes et timbales*, consisting of marches and other simpleminded pieces for the Grande Écurie.

RECORDINGS: These works, which delight those who prefer high fidelity to music, have been recorded several times by Jean-François Paillard, Karl Haas, and others.

[550] BACH, Johann Michael (Bàkh, Yō'-hàn Mēkh'-à-el)
ORGANIST, TOWN CLERK, INSTRUMENT MAKER
BORN: Arnstadt, August 6, 1648
DIED: Gehren, Thuringia, May 1694

The second of Heinrich Bach's [488] three sons, and thus Johann Christoph's [536] younger brother, Johann Michael Bach was taught by his father, and when his brother left the Arnstadt court in 1665, he succeeded him at the chapel organ. In 1673, his Uncle Johann's death left a vacancy at the Predigerkirche in Erfurt that was filled by Johann Effler, erstwhile town organist at Gehren (near Arnstadt) and Johann Sebastian Bach's [684] predecessor at Weimar. The count recommended Michael Bach to take his place. The town council was so impressed that they boosted the salary by ten florins on the condition that Bach would also serve as town clerk. Fringe benefits included a house, fuel for the winter, a garden, and donations of food, which probably explains his decision to marry two years later. The bride was Catharina Wedemann, sister to brother Christoph's wife. She bore him six children—five girls and a boy named Gottfried who died a baby. Michael, described by his employers as a quiet, intro-

spective type, also made organs, clavi-
chords, and violins—which skills he presumably imparted to his youngest brother
Johann Günther and to his nephew Johann
Nikolaus (Christoph's boy). Michael died at
forty-six and his wife followed him a decade
later. Their orphaned daughter, Maria Barbara, was taken in by her aunt and her
spouse Martin Feldhaus, burgomaster of
Arnstadt. It was in their house that she met
her future husband, Johann Sebastian Bach.
    Much of Michael Bach's music has disap-
peared. Of the instrumental compositions,
only 8 chorale preludes and partitas survive,
but there are also 11 motets and 5 cantatas.
These are obviously the work of a thoroughly competent composer who shows
himself capable, on occasion, of very fine
things in the traditon of Heinrich Schütz
[412].
    RECORDINGS: Helmut Rilling has re-
corded *Wie bist du denn, o Gott, in Zorn auf
mich entbrannt.*

[551] COLASSE, Pascal (Kō-làs', Pàs-
      kȧl')
CONDUCTOR, TEACHER, IMPRESARIO
BORN: Rheims, c. January 22, 1649
DIED: Versailles, July 17, 1709

A Parisian from infancy, young Colasse
trebled in the choir at St. Paul and was later
at the Collège de Navarre. By the middle
1670s he had gotten in good with Lully
[517]. In 1677, when Lully's assistant Jean-
François Lallouette announced to the world
that he had helped compose the opera *Isis*,
he was forthwith replaced with Colasse. Colasse was required to beat time at rehearsals
and to fill out the harmonies and other minor details in Lully's scores. Colasse was evidently a good and faithful servant, for
when Lully left the running of the Opéra to
his wife and son, he stipulated that they
must always seek Colasse's advice. In 1683
the king discovered that he was fresh out of
superintendents for the royal chapel and decreed a grand competition to produce four
new ones, who would again serve on a rotating quarterly basis. When the envelopes
were opened, the winners were Colasse, two
priests named Jean Minoret and Jean
Goupillet or Coupillet, and Michel-Richard
Delalande [576]. Only the last did the office
real credit, and despite the energetic efforts
of Colasse, he was appointed Superintendent of the Royal Music after Lully died.
    That melancholy event, however, pro-
vided Colasse with an opportunity to shine.
He pieced out Lully's unfinished *Achille et
Polixène,* added a prologue depicting Louis

XIV as the New Achilles, and mounted it at
the Opéra in November 1687. *Tout le monde*
attended and *tout le monde* sat on its hands.
His own *Thétis et Pélée* two years later was
more successful, probably because it made a
case for the French rape of Germany in the
current War of the Augsburg League. The
public also applauded the prologue to the
1690 *Énée et Lavine,* which pointed out that
even though the guns were fully deployed
French tables still had plenty of butter. But
the Lully family was not impressed, and
pointing out that a good deal of Colasse's
music was really Lully's, they sued him successfully. Nor was his road made smoother
by attacks in the press and parodies in the
theaters (though his 1695 *divertissement, Le
Ballet des saisons,* inexplicably lasted for a
quarter of a century). In 1696, with the king
running interference through the Lullyan
strictures, Colasse opened his own opera
house in Lyons. Four years later it burned,
wiping him out. Bitter and depressed, he
turned to alchemy, hoping to recoup his
losses, but what was left of his money and
his mind went, and in 1708 they let him return to Versailles to die.
    Colasse is chiefly important as a symbol
of the collapse of Lully's empire minus Lully's genius. He showed that more was not
better, and his little short-winded arias (one
recorded by Ettel Sussman), however
pretty, lacked drama and pertinence. But
his feeble storm in *Thétis* kicked off a whole
era of nature imitation.

[552] BLOW, John
KEYBOARDIST, TEACHER
BORN: Newark-on-Trent, c. February 23,
      1649
DIED: Westminster, October 1, 1708

For the early part of it, Blow's career was
closely linked with that of his friend Pelham
Humfrey [548], which it in some ways resembles. John Blow was the son of Henry
and Katharine Blow, the latter a widow
who had married again three years earlier.
Henry Blow died when John was six, leaving at least two other children, named for
their parents. In 1660 John was apparently
one of the five boys "fetched" from Newark
and Lincoln by Henry Cooke, Master of the
Children in the Chapel Royal, to restaff that
organization after Charles II's return. Like
Humfrey, he was a precocious composer
(see 548). When his voice passed the estate
of angelicism, he was deemed worth keeping
on the basis of his musical promise, and
Cooke was allotted thirty pounds a year for
his upkeep. It was at this time that he prob-

ably studied organ with Christopher Gibbons, Orlando Gibbons's [408] boy. He certainly studied it with someone, for at nineteen he was appointed organist of Westminster Abbey, replacing Albertus Bryne, and at twenty he succeeded Giles Tomkins, half-brother to Thomas [365], as virginalist to the King's Private Musick. The year 1674 was climactic for him: in March he succeeded one Roger Hill as a Gentleman of the Chapel Royal. In July he succeeded the ill-fated Humfrey (whose will he witnessed) as Master of the Children. (Among those he taught were William Croft [652], Jeremiah Clarke [638], Daniel Roseingrave (see 699), and the Purcell brothers, Henry [581] and Daniel [603].) In September he married Elizabeth Braddock, daughter of the Master of the Children at the Abbey.

In 1676 Christopher Gibbons died and it was also certainly then that Blow became one of the chapel organists. The following year the Dean of Canterbury made him Dr. Blow. He resigned his post at the Abbey in 1679 in favor of his brilliant pupil Henry Purcell, who joined him as one of three chapel organists in 1682. Two years later the Temple Church reached an impasse over purchasing a new organ. As a result, the officers had two installed—one built by Renatus Harris, the other by "Father" Bernard Smith (né Bernhardt Schmidt), the royal organ builder—the choice to be made on hearing them played by experts. Giovanni Battista Draghi tested the Harris; Blow and Purcell, the Smith. Smith won.

Blow contributed 3 anthems to the coronation of James II in 1685 and was kept busy with ceremonial music for much of the decade. In 1687 he became Almoner and Master of the Choristers of St. Paul's Cathedral Choir. (The old building had been largely destroyed in the great fire of 1666; the new one was still abuilding, and Blow, in fact, inaugurated the opening of its choir a decade later with an anthem.) About this same time King James sent a church dignitary to congratulate Blow on a piece of his music. The emissary added that, in his view, the thing went on too long, and Blow replied that that was merely one fool's opinion. The clergyman demanded his ouster, but Blow survived both that attack and the Glorious Revolution. On Purcell's demise in 1695, his old teacher went back to the Abbey organ; he also inherited, in tandem with "Father" Smith, his pupil's office of Tuner of the Royal Instruments. It was at this time, of course, that Blow wrote, to Dryden's lyrics, his *Ode on the Death of Mr. Purcell.* In 1699 he was elevated to the

largely honorific post of Composer to the Chapel Royal.

Evidently from then on he suffered a decline. Elizabeth Blow had died in childbed in 1683. The couple's surviving son followed her a decade later, though three daughters lived on. In 1703 Blow turned his cathedral jobs over to the organist, his onetime pupil Jeremiah Clarke. He died, relatively well to do, five years later and was buried near Purcell in the Abbey.

Blow was unquestionably gifted, but his reputation is somewhat overblown, owing in part to his influence on the next generation, in part to his relative eminence in a musical flatland, and in part to English chauvinism. The bulk of his music—anthems and odes—was made to order for a king who wanted to emulate his French rival in self-admiration. Blow was almost certainly overworked and asked to produce too much in areas not particularly suited to his talents. His real abilities lay in intimate music so that what was intended to be magnificent too often came out merely windy. Nonetheless, he was the finest writer of orchestral ("symphony") anthems before Purcell—who learned from him and from whom he learned. Blow is even happier, however, in the continuo songs of his 1700 collection, *Amphion Anglicus,* where he often attains considerable drama, passion, and beauty. The Purcell memorial seems to express real grief, and some of the odes for St. Cecilia's day are masterly of their kind. Perhaps his most telling work is the "masque" *Venus and Adonis* (really the first true English opera), from the 1680s, which builds to a climax of exquisite poignancy.

RECORDINGS: Sir David Willcocks has recorded a few of the anthems, and there are scattered accounts of a few organ voluntaries and harpsichord pieces. Groups directed by Alfred Deller and Gustav Leonhardt have recorded songs from *Amphion Anglicus,* and the Purcell memorial has been frequently recorded. Anthony Lewis recorded the masque.

[553] KRIEGER, Johann Philipp (Krē'-ger, Yō'-hän Fē'-lip)
KEYBOARDIST, CHOIRMASTER
BORN: Nuremberg, February 25, 1649
DIED: Weissenfels, February 7, 1725

Current accounts give us a general notion of the wanderings of Johann Philipp Krieger, elder brother of Johann Krieger [563], and unrelated to Adam Krieger [519], though these accounts conflict here and there and are not always borne out by extant records.

A keyboard prodigy, he supposedly studied with Johannes Dretzel and Gabriel Schütz, both members of Nuremberg musical dynasties, before trekking off in his mid-teens to the Danish court to study with the organist Johann Schröder, whose assistant he became. He returned to Germany around 1670 and found employment as organist to Markgraf Christian Ernst in Bayreuth. When the Markgraf suspended musical activities in 1673 to go off to war, he sent Krieger, with his blessing and a continuance of his salary, to upgrade his education in Italy. There he is said to have studied with Bernardo Pasquini [524]—as who wasn't?—and was almost certainly a pupil of the self-exiled Johann Rosenmüller [493] in Venice. On the way home in 1675, he stopped by Vienna to regale Emperor Leopold I [528] with his playing. Leopold was sufficiently impressed to issue a patent of nobility to the whole Krieger family, male and female. Then Krieger returned to Bayreuth but left immediately, finally settling down at the ducal court in Halle. Three years later, in 1680, the ducal court moved to Weissenfels, where Krieger became *Kapellmeister*, a post he held for forty-five years.

Krieger was extraordinarily prolific. Apart from at least 18 operas (all lost), a Mass, sonatas, and keyboard music, his own meticulous chapel records show that he composed 2,000 or more cantatas, of which fewer than 100 have survived. These are mostly late works which show the influence of the court deacon, Erdmann Neumeister, of Hamburg, regarded as the "inventor" of the so-called reform cantata. Textually (which was where Neumeister figured) such works involved rather rhetorical interpretations of, or commentaries on, the scriptural lessons for the day. Musically, they emerged as a sequence of clearly defined sinfonias, recitatives, arias, duets, and choruses. Obviously they reflected Italian practice, and Neumeister made no bones about their being essentially operatic. Hence Krieger would seem to be a direct progenitor of Johann Sebastian Bach [684] in this area. For all his importance, he has made a small showing on records so far.

RECORDINGS: I am aware of a single cantata sung by Georg Jelden, a few songs performed by Edith Mathis and Benno Kusche, and a pair of sonatas from the pre-LP era.

[554] KNELLER, Andreas (K'nel'-ler, Àn'-drä-às)
ORGANIST

BORN: Lübeck, April 23, 1649
DIED: Hamburg, August 24, 1724

Andreas Kneller was the son of Zacharias Knüller or Kniller of Eisleben, chief accountant of the Katharinenkirche in Lübeck. His elder brother, Gottfried, took up portrait painting and in 1674 emigrated to London, where he eventually became Sir Godfrey Kneller, Bart. Andreas, at eighteen was named to succeed Melchior Schildt [438] as organist of the Marktkirche in Hanover. There seems to be a difference of opinion about his move in 1685 to the Petrikirche in Hamburg. Some accounts say that he married the daughter of Adam Reincken [498] and that Reincken subsequently recommended him for the job at the Petrikirche; others say that he met Reincken and his future bride after he got to Hamburg. He was pensioned off a few months before he died. Of 7 organ works ascribed to him, at least 3—preludes and fugues, one of them recorded by Helmut Tramnitz—are certainly his.

[555] BITTNER, Jacques (Bit'-ner, Zhàk)
LUTENIST
BORN: c. 1650 (?)
DIED: after 1682

Bittner published in 1682 a collection of *Pièces de lut,* in Nuremberg, printed in French tablature and dedicated to the internationally named banker Pedro Petroni von Treynfels. The rest of his life and career is a cipher. RECORDINGS: Suites from the collection have been recorded by Walter Gerwig and Michael Schäffer.

[556] FRANCESCHINI, Petronio (Fràn-chä-skē'-nē, Pä-trōn'-yō)
CELLIST, CONDUCTOR, TEACHER
BORN: Bologna, c. 1650
DIED: Venice, c. December 18, 1680

Originally a pupil of the priest Lorenzo Perti (whose more famous nephew Giacomo Antonio Perti he himself later taught), Franceschini went to Rome for further study with Giuseppe Corsi, a protégé of Giacomo Carissimi [471]. One of the forty founders of the Accademia Filarmonica, he was its president in 1673. Between then and 1680 he played cello at the cathedral of San Pietro and produced at least 4 operas. In 1680 he went to Venice to serve as maestro at the Ospedaletto. He was at work on an opera when he died, age thirty. His brother Marco Antonio (1648–1729) was the last considerable painter of the Bolognese School. Besides 2 earlier operas and the unfinished *Dionisio,* Petronio Franceschini left religious works and sonatas. RECORDINGS: Edward Tarr and Robert Bodenroder have recorded a sonata for two trumpets.

[557] LE SAGE DE RICHÉE, Philipp Franz (Lə Sàzh də Rē-shä′, Fē-lēp′ Frànts)
LUTENIST
BORN: c. 1650 (?)
DIED: after 1695

Though Le Sage's name appears thus in his only known publication, *Cabinet der Lauten (Lute Cabinet),* he was probably baptized Philippe François. He is said to have been of noble blood and to have studied with Charles Mouton [505]. At the time the collection was published, he was living in Breslau, as lutenist to a Freiherr von Neidhart. In its 12 suites, several movements are specified as being by various contemporary lutenists. RECORDINGS: Michael Schäffer has recorded the *ouverture* to one.

[558] LOSY VON LOSYMTHAL, (Graf) Jan Antonín (Lō′-si fun Lō′-sim-tàl, Yàn Àn′-tō-nyēn)
LUTENIST, BUREAUCRAT
BORN: near Strakonice (Bohemia), c. 1650 (?)
DIED: Prague, late summer 1721

Losy frequently appears as "Logy" in both ancient and modern accounts, and his Christian names are generally given in the German form, "Johann Anton." His family, originally from the Losintal in Switzerland, owned the castle of Štekeň in southwestern Bohemia. He took a Ph.D. from Charles University in Prague in 1668 (some think he was born as early as 1638). He then traveled in Italy and France, spent some time in Leipzig, and served the Prague court as chamberlain and councilor. He was noted for the concerts he gave in his palace and was admired by many contemporary lutenists. Philipp Franz Le Sage de Richée [557] includes music by him in his collection, and Sylvius Weiss [691] wrote a *tombeau* on the occasion of his death. Losy left suites and other lute pieces, some of which have been recorded by such as Siegfried Behrend, William Matthews, and Karl Scheit.

[559] SABADINI, Bernardo (Sà-bà-dē′-nē, Bär-när′-do)
ORGANIST, MUSIC DIRECTOR
BORN: c. 1650 (?)
DIED: Parma, November 26, 1718

Sabadini, a priest who probably came from Venice, was appointed court organist to Ranuccio II Farnese, Duke of Parma, in 1681, and was elevated to Court Composer in 1686 and to *maestro di cappella* in 1689. He and a team of theater experts were responsible for operatic productions in Ranuccio's newly built (completed in 1688) Teatro Ducale in Parma and in the duchy's other major city, Piacenza, and he is said to have put Parma on a par with the major Italian cities in that respect. He wrote operas himself but was apparently chiefly busy as a play doctor, adding arias and such to other composers' works. His greatest production was the ducal wedding of 1690, which delighted many and outraged some with its lavishness. Sabadini was also organist and choir director of the ducal chapel. Little of his output remains. RECORDINGS: An organ piece has been recorded by Clemente Terni.

[560] SZARZYŃSKI, Stanisław Sylwester (Shàr-zhin′-skē, Stä-nē′-slwäf Sil-ves′-ter)
MONK
BORN: c. 1650
DIED: after 1713

The Poles are said to regard Szarzyński as their leading composer of his era, but he is a wraithlike creature indeed. All that is known of him for certain is that he belonged to the Cistercian Order. Seven of his church works and a sonata are extant, though the manuscripts were lost in World War II. An attractive and fluent melodist, Szarzyński obviously knew his Italians. RECORDINGS: Edmund Kajdasz has recorded the motet *Ad hymnos, ad cantus,* and Zygmunt Lednicki and Igor Iwanow the sonata.

[561] VISÉE, Robert de (də Vē-zä′, Hwō-bär′)
GUITARIST, SINGER
BORN: c. 1650
DIED: c. 1733

Visée owes his fame in no small part to Louis XIV's passion for the Spanish guitar, which Visée taught him to play. In the early 1680s he became guitarist to the Royal Chamber and is said to have played the king to sleep every night. He was also detailed to entertain the dauphin and Madame de Maintenon. In 1709 he was appointed singer-in-ordinary, and in 1719 guitar master to the king (by that time a strictly honorary title). He apparently resigned his posts a year in favor of his son François. He also played lute and viola da gamba. One of the first important guitarists outside of Spain (though Jan Antonín Losy [558] may have played the instrument), he published 2 guitar books, containing 12 suites (1682 and 1686), and a book of lute pieces, some of which duplicate guitar pieces and some of which are the work of others. The suites show the form fully developed: allemande-courant-sarabande-gigue-modern   dance (minuet, gavotte, etc.). Two of them have been recorded by, respectively, Turibio Santos and Michael Schäffer.

[562] GABRIELLI, Domenico (Gà-brē-el'-lē, Dō-mā'-nē-kō)
CELLIST
BORN: Bologna, April 15, 1651
DIED: Bologna, July 10, 1690

Though his name is sometimes spelled like theirs, Gabrielli was apparently unrelated to the Venetian Gabrielis [180, 286]. He studied cello with Petronio Franceschini [556] and took his place at the cathedral of San Pietro in Bologna when Franceschini left in 1680 for death in Venice. Gabrielli is said also to have studied with Giovanni Legrenzi [503]. In 1676 he was elected to the Accademia Filarmonica and served as its president in 1683. After that time he was frequently in Venice in connection with the production of his operas, and at the court of Modena, where he played. He was probably the first cellist to establish more than a local reputation as a virtuoso, and was known popularly in Bologna as "Mingàn dal viulunzel," meaning roughly "Cello Dom." In 1687 the church fired him for failing to play the feast of its patron saint. It took him back a year later. He died at thirty-nine. His most famous pupil was Giuseppe Maria Jacchini [595]. Though he wrote at least 12 operas and 3 oratorios, as well as smaller vocal works, Gabrielli is remembered chiefly for his instrumental music and his virtuoso writing for his own instrument, which shows a thorough knowledge of what it could do. (That he should have been a close contemporary of the great French gamba virtuoso Marin Marais [574] sheds an interesting light on the state of music in their two countries.) Gabrielli was one of the first composers of cello sonatas, and his

ricercari are the earliest known music for solo cello. RECORDINGS: A cello sonata and a *ricercare* were recorded by R. Brancaleon. Davis Shuman recorded a *ricercare* on trombone, apparently under the impression that the composer was a Gabrieli. Maurice André has recorded some of the typically Bolognese trumpet sonatas.

[563] KRIEGER, Johann (Krē'-ger, Yō'-hàn)
ORGANIST, CHOIRMASTER
BORN: Nuremberg, December 28, 1651
DIED: Zittau, July 18, 1735

Johann Krieger was a choirboy at St. Sebaldus, studying with Cantor Heinrich Schwemmer, then with organist Georg Kaspar Wecker, a pupil of Johann Kindermann [489], and possibly with his own brother, Johann Philipp [553], in whose shadow he walked for some years. He succeeded him as organist at the Bayreuth court in 1672 and supposedly retained his post until 1677, though the *Kapelle* did not function from 1673. In 1678 he became *Kapellmeister* to Count Heinrich I von Reuss in Greiz, about forty miles south of Leipzig. Heinrich died two years later, and after a few months at the nearby ducal court of Eisenberg he was appointed town organist and conductor of the old Wendish city of Zittau. He died there fifty-three years later, a day after playing the usual church service. Among his pupils were Johann Philipp's son, Johann Gotthelf, and his own son, Adolf Gottlob, who succeeded him.

Much of Johann Krieger's church music and all of his several operas are lost, though some Magnificats, cantatas, and hymns are extant. There is also a published volume of *Lieder* for five to nine accompanied voices set to texts by the Zittau poet and schoolmaster Christian Weise. Krieger was especially admired in his day for his contrapuntal organ works (including multiple fugues) and his *Anmuthige Clavier-Übung (Pleasant Keyboard Exercises)* was George Friderick Handel's [683] musical bible, and some of its contents prophesy Johann Sebastian Bach [684].
RECORDINGS: There are organ recordings (e.g., by Franz Haselböck and Franz Lehrndorfer).

[564] RONCALLI, Lodovico (Run-kál'-lē, Lō-dō-vē'-kō)
GUITARIST
BORN: c. 1652 (?)
DIED: after 1692

For all that he was of the Italian nobility, Count Roncalli remains a stubborn enigma. (No basis is provided for the birthdate given in some reference works.) He published what purported to be his Op. I, 9 guitar suites called collectively *Capricci armonici,* in Bergamo in 1692, dedicating them to Cardinal Panfilio, the papal legate in Bologna. Presumably, therefore, he was somehow connected with one city or both. RECORDINGS: Charles ("Charlie") Byrd recorded four of the suites, and selections may be found in various recorded anthologies.

[565] **CORELLI, Arcangelo** (Kō-rel'-lē, Ärk-än'-jel-ō)
VIOLINIST, CONDUCTOR
BORN: Fusignano, February 17, 1653
DIED: Rome, January 8, 1713

Fusignano at the time of Corelli's birth was under the rule of nearby Ravenna. The father, also Arcangelo, was of noble blood. Having previously sired four children on his wife, *née* Santa Raffini, he died a month before his namesake was born, leaving his family comfortably off. There persist pretty tales of young Arcangelo fiddling to drooling cows and gawking *paisani* on his way to his lesson, his adoption by a musical uncle-priest, the furtherance of his career by a Cardinal Ottoboni transfixed, by the boy's playing, as he passed through Fusignano. Most of them are probably compacted of moonshine, for we know nothing certainly of Corelli's youth. He is said to have studied in Lugo and then in Faenza (home of faience pottery and the aneroid barometer, invented there by Evangelista Torricelli a decade before Corelli was born). It is fairly certain that he went to Bologna c. 1666, though who taught him there is a matter of strong disagreement. There is no doubt, however, that at the age of seventeen he was elected to the Accademia Filarmonica, the only musician other than Mozart to be admitted before the mandatory age of twenty.

Corelli is supposed to have gone to Rome early in the 1670s, but there is no record of him there until 1675, when he was listed as one of four violinists playing at San Luigi dei Francesi on the feast day of its patron; he reappeared there on the same occasion with at least fair regularity for the next thirty-three years. In 1679 he was in the orchestra when the opera *Dove è amore è pietà (Where There's Love There's Compassion)* by his friend Bernardo Pasquini [524] and the Teatro Capranica had their concurrent premieres. A few months later he was in the service of Queen Christina of Sweden, to whom in 1681 he dedicated his Op. I, a set of a dozen trio *sonate da chiesa.* The supposed German tour in the interim is no better substantiated than those to Spain and France. However, Sir John Hawkins's story of a 1685 quarrel between Corelli and the visiting N. A. Strungk suggests that he did speak German. The sonatas and the notice that Corelli attracted as performer in, and director of, Christina's *soirées* won him the patronage of Cardinal Benedetto Pamphili, nephew to the late Pope Innocent X. In 1684 Corelli and his friend Alessandro Scarlatti [583] were inducted into the Congregazione dei Virtuosi di Santa Cecilia, ancestor of the present-day Accademia. This was no big deal in itself, for in that year Innocent XI ordered all professional musicians to join what amounted to the Roman musicians' union, though Corelli later became its president. Two years later he published a second dozen trio sonatas, these of the *sonate da camera* variety. Early in 1687 at Christina's Palazzo Riario (now Palazzo Corsini), conducted a hundred singers and 150 players in a Pasquini cantata to welcome the Earl of Castelmain, dispatched by Catholic James of England to be his Man in the Vatican. A few months later the cardinal appointed him his *maestro di musica* and installed him and his inseparable companion, the violinist Matteo Fornari, whom he had taught, in an apartment in the Palazzo Pamphili. Two years later the rivalry between Corelli's patrons was terminated by circumstances beyond their respective controls. Early in 1689, Corelli directed in the Palazzo Pamphili an oratorio, *Santa Beatrice d'Este,* by his sidekick, resident cellist Giovanni Battista Lulier (with whom he liked to play sonatas); for this the cardinal hired him an orchestra of some eighty players. About this time the queen, now sixty-three, fell gravely ill. In March she rallied, and Corelli conducted two festal Masses in the churches of the Gesù and the Santa Casa di Loreto, but on April 19 she died. So did Pope Innocent in August. His successor, Alexander VIII, whom his detractors called "Papa Pantaloon," whisked Pamphili away to Bologna and installed as cardinal and vice-chancellor his own nephew, Pietro Ottoboni, who installed himself in the Palazzo della Cancelleria. There he surrounded himself with art and artists in every field. It has been argued that Corelli's dedication of his Op. 3 sonatas to the Duke of Modena, Francesco II, was a bid to escape from Rome, but there is nothing to indicate that it was, and their composer was soon ensconced in Ottoboni's palace. His employer, half his age, treated him as an intimate and put him in charge of his music, both domestic and ecclesiastical. Under his roof Corelli met the best painters and sculptors of the day, was made a member of the Accademia di Disegna, and indulged his hobby of picture collecting, for which he had eventually to rent an extra apartment in the Palazzetto Ermini.

In 1694 Corelli dedicated his fourth set of trio sonatas to his patron, and six years later, a fifth to Sophie Charlotte, Electress of Brandenburg—why, we can't be sure. Meanwhile he apparently continued to produce occasional examples of the orchestral concerti he had been turning out since the early 1680s, and to direct operas in the Roman theaters. In 1702 he went to Naples for an opera. An old story says that he was stunned to find that Neapolitans could play the violin so well, and then made a botch of his own playing during public performance. So much of the story may be true, though it is hard to believe it of the greatest violinist of his time. The sequel that he went back to Rome and died of chagrin is not. Four years later he was inducted into the Accademia Arcadiana (as "Arcomelo Erimenteo") together with his friends Scarlatti and Pasquini. Over the next two years he participated in performances of Handel's [683] oratorios *Il Trionfo del tempo* and *La Resurrezione.* There may be some truth in much later reports that his playing was deteriorating, for he played no more after 1708. Purportedly he spent his last years polishing his concerti for publication. Late in 1712 he moved into the apartment in the Palazzetto, where his older brother Giacinto lived, and died there a couple of weeks later. Though not entitled to it, being in the wrong parish, he was buried through ecclesiastical intervention in the Pantheon next to Raphael as he had wished. In his will Corelli specified that the cardinal could have any painting he wished, left his instruments and manuscripts to Fornari, and everything else to Giacinto and his other surviving brother Ippolito. Fornari saw the concerti (Op. 6) through the press the next year.

Whether Corelli "invented" the *concerto grosso* is arguable—Alessandro Stradella [541] has a claim to the principle at least— but if, as appears likely, he was producing such works in 1682, we must probably credit him with the form. Basically an application of the trio sonata (of which he was past master) to the orchestra, it also draws on the Venetian *concertato* idea, Lullyan orchestral developments, *bel canto,* and probably the five-voice Bolognese sonata. To a *ripieno*—a string orchestra with continuo—Corelli opposed a *concertino* of two violins and bass (cello). His published examples in Op. 6 (for whose primitiveness a strong case has been made, for all their late date) include 8 in the "church" mode and 4 in the "chamber" mode, though neither adheres to any rigid overall pattern. There is, as usually with Corelli, nothing ostentatious or virtuoso—only masterly music making, logical, poised, and serene.

His importance to the sonata—he wrote 48 (4 sets) of the "trio" and 12 of the "solo" varieties—is hardly less. Those of the first type are half *da chiesa* and half *da camera,* yet the former often use dance rhythms and the latter "free" movements. In other words, Corelli is on his way to synthesizing the two forms. As in all his music, the watchwords are clarity, rationality, and decorum, but they do not preclude intensity and profundity of feeling—expressed in the simplest terms. The same thing applies to the solo sonatas of Op. 5—6 *da chiesa,* 5 *da camera,* and the last a set of variations on the old Spanish theme *La Folia*—which Corelli's pupil Francesco Geminiani [693] later arranged as *concerti grossi!*

Corelli's successors found him a model for solo-sonata writing and for violin technique. Unlike his German contemporaries, he did not see his instrument as a device for making funny sounds or showing off athletic ability. He rarely asks the performer to go beyond the fourth position, and he eschews the "chest voice" of the G-string. As he worked in the summer of *bel canto,* his idea was to make the violin sing, and he had a powerful impact on those who met him. His influence on Handel, for example, is obvious. Georg Muffat [566], who claimed to have heard Corellian concerti in Rome in 1682, imitated him in his sonatas *(Armonico tributo)* of the same year. And Corelli's pupils spread his influence all over Europe —Geminiani to England, Locatelli [721] to Holland, Gasparini [615] to Venice, Dall'-Abaco [642] to Belgium and Germany, Giovanni Battista Somis (1686–1763) to France, and so on. Sebastian Bach [684] copied out many of Corelli's works, though they never met.

RECORDINGS: Many of the Op. 6 concerti (Dean Eckertsen, Argeo Quadri, Jørgen Ernst Hansen, Max Goberman, Ettore Gracis, Neville Marriner, Raymond Leppard, I Musici, among others.) The solo sonatas have also enjoyed several complete recordings (Eduard Melkus, Sonia Monosoff, Stanley Plummer), and Eckertsen has done the Geminiani transcriptions. All four sets of trio sonatas were once available in versions by Musicorum Arcadia, and Goberman has duplicated Op. 4.

[566] **MUFFAT, Georg** (Moo'-fåt, Gä-ôrg')
ORGANIST, CONDUCTOR
BORN: Mégève, c. June 1, 1653
DIED: Passau, February 23, 1704

Muffat thought of himself as a German and so did everyone else until his baptismal record turned up in his Savoyard birthplace near Mont Blanc. His people probably emigrated there from Scotland earlier in the century for religious reasons. (He may have been related to a seventeenth-century Dr. Thomas Muffet, a London amateur arachnologist, whose daughter Patience was supposedly the little Miss Muffet of the nursery rhyme.) Georg had his primary schooling in Alsace, then went to Paris at the age of ten to study with Lully [517]. From 1669 to 1671 he attended Jesuit schools in Sélestat and Molsheim, where in the latter year he became organist to the choir of Strasbourg Cathedral, the chapter having been driven out of that city. With the onslaught of the so-called Dutch War in 1672, however, Muffat left. In 1674 he undertook legal studies in Ingolstadt, then moved on to Vienna, where he came to know Fux [585]; in 1677 he moved to Prague and a year later to Salzburg, where he became a colleague of Biber [539] in the *Kapelle* of Archbishop Maximilian Gandolf. In or before 1682 he went to Italy for further study, which he is said to have gotten with Pasquini [524] in Rome. There, he reported, he marveled at concerti written by Corelli [565], by whom he was greatly influenced. Max Gandolf died in 1687. Muffat stayed on for three years under Archbishop Johann Ernst, but, denied advancement, he took the job of *Kapellmeister* to Bishop Johann Philipp of Passau. The city suffered under siege in 1703-4, during the War of the Spanish Succession. Muffat died shortly after it was relieved, leaving a thirteen-year-old son, Gottlieb, who became a composer of note himself.

Save for 5 publications, most of Muffat's music is gone. The Corelli-inspired sonatas of *Armonico tributo* have already been noted (see 565). In 1701 Muffat issued a set of *concerti grossi* of his own, 5 of the 12 being reworkings of the earlier sonatas. On the other hand, the 2 volumes of orchestral suites published in 1695 and 1698 as *Florilegia* are strongly influenced by Lully. The two currents meet in the *Apparatus musico-organisticus* of 1690 containing 12 toccatas, a passacaglia, a chaconne, and an air-and-variations for organ. These are interesting not only in terms of organ technique, but also for their use of a sort of standardized musicoemotional rhetoric.

RECORDINGS: Individual sonatas have been recorded by Theodor Guschlbauer and Nikolaus Harnoncourt, individual concerti by Gunther Kehr and Karl Ristenpart. The *Apparatus musico-organisticus* have been recorded by Leena Jacobson.

[567] **PACHELBEL, Johann** (Påkh'-el-bel, Yō'-hån)
ORGANIST
BORN: Nuremberg, September 1, 1653
DIED: Nuremberg, c. March 7, 1706

Barely known to the general public a dozen years ago, Pachelbel's has become one of the best known names of the German baroque because of the unprecedented success of Jean-François Paillard's recording of the *Canon in D* for three violins and continuo. (Oddly a recording made by Arthur Fiedler in the 1940s seems to have had little or no impact.) Perhaps Pachelbel's time has come, for renewed interest in him has cleared up many obscure spots in his life and career. Like his fellow-townsman and contemporary Johann Krieger [563], he studied with Heinrich Schwemmer and Georg Wecker (1632-95) in Nuremberg and attended lectures at the Auditorium Aegidianum, a sort of highbrow lyceum. Family finances were insufficient to maintain his studies at the University of Altdorf, which he entered at sixteen, but he won an extraordinary scholarship the next year to the Gymnasium Poeticum in Regensburg. He studied music extracurricularly with Kaspar Prentz, a pupil of Kerll [506], and in 1673 was hired as second organist of the Stefansdom in Vienna. Four years later he went to Eisenach as organist to Duke Johann Georg, in whose household he would have shared the keyboard duties with Johann Christoph Bach [536]. Perhaps he found Bach too well ensconced there, for a year later he left, bearing a letter of recommendation from Kapellmeister Eberlin, which within a month secured him a job as organist of the Predigerkirche. His contract demanded, among other things, that he give an annual organ recital as a sort of progress report to show what he had learned in the interim. Erfurt was full of Bachs, and he was well acquainted with Ambrosius and perhaps, before he left, with his young son Johann Sebastian [684]. In 1681 Pachelbel married Barbara Gabler. In due time she bore him a boy, but both died in the plague epidemic of 1683. Eleven months later Pachelbel was married again, this time to Judith Drommer. Two of their sons, Wilhelm Hieronymus (1686-1764) and Carl

Theodor [708], were known as composers; there were three others and two daughters. After a dozen years, in which he became widely known, Pachelbel thought he could do better, and in 1690, two weeks after he had severed connections, found a post as organist to Duchess Magdalene Sibylla of Württemberg in Stuttgart, but the approach of Louis XIV's armies drove him to Gotha in 1692. There he became municipal organist and stayed despite an offer from Oxford and a summons back to Stuttgart. In 1695 his old organ teacher Wecker died in Nuremberg, and Pachelbel was invited home to succeed him at St. Sebaldus. He spent the rest of his life there. He was succeeded by a local organist named Richter, who was in turn succeeded by Wilhelm Hieronymus Pachelbel. A third son, Johann Michael, established himself in Nuremberg as an instrument maker, and a daughter, Amalia, became a successful painter.

Despite a busy and peripatetic life, Pachelbel was a fairly prolific composer. The chamber-music canon is rather atypical and represents the least significant category in his output. Perhaps the most significant is his keyboard music. As an organ composer, he is one of the greatest of the era before Sebastian Bach, and attains a synthesis of the north German and south German traditions. Sixty-nine of his organ works are chorale-based and provide a sort of survey of approaches to the chorale up to that time. To these must be added the 94 fugues written to precede the singing of the Magnificat at vespers in St. Sebaldus. Besides such liturgical pieces there are 26 abstract fugues, a prelude and fugue, a toccata and fugue, 16 toccatas, 7 preludes, 6 each of ciaconas and fantasias, and 3 *ricercari*. For harpsichord there are 21 suites, the *Musicalische Sterbens-Gedancken* (7 sets of chorale variations in memory of his first wife), and the *Hexachordum Apollonis*, a set of 6 arias-with-variations, arranged in a cryptic order. As a keyboard composer, there is no doubt that Pachelbel was a direct and powerful influence on Sebastian Bach.

He is also reckoned an important composer of cantatas, through his look backward toward the Schützian *concertato* and the variation-cantata. These and his other vocal church works, however, are not often heard. (It should be noted that Pachelbel is one of the first composers to have taken note of Matthias Weckmann's attempts at mean-tone tuning, which explains his use of keys generally avoided previously.)

RECORDINGS: There are several discs of the organ music, played by, for example, Ludwig Altman, Jørgen Ernst Hansen, Diethard Hellmann, Walter Kraft, Luther Noss, Helmut Winter; Martha Scheurich has recorded the *Hexachordum Apollonis*. There are string suites by Hansen and Jean-François Paillard. One motet has been recorded by the Windsbach Boys Choir.

[568] JULLIEN, Gilles (Zhül-yàn', Zhēl)
ORGANIST
BORN: c. 1653
DIED: Chartres, September 14, 1703

If, as the official record of his death implies, Jullien was born in the year noted above, he became organist of Chartres Cathedral at fourteen and served there for thirty-six of his fifty years. He was succeeded by his son Jean-François. In 1690 he published his first organ book, containing 8 suites of miscellaneous pieces in the church modes and a choral work. The second was not forthcoming. RECORDINGS: The *Mode VII* suite has been recorded by Marie-Louise Girod; other selections appear in anthologies.

[569] POLLAROLO, Carlo Francesco
(Pul-là-rō'-lō, Kär'-lō Fràn-chäs'-kō)
ORGANIST, CHOIRMASTER
BORN: c. 1653
DIED: Venice, February 7, 1723

Pollarolo may have been born in Brescia, where his father, Orazio, was an organist from the middle 1660s. He himself was married in 1674 and succeeded Orazio (presumably dead) at the cathedral two years later. (There seems to be no evidence that he was ever a choirboy at St. Mark's or a student of Legrenzi [503] in Venice.) Beginning with Antonio in 1676, he and his wife produced seven children by 1689. Beginning with *I Deliri per amore (Love Crazy)* in 1685, he also turned out at least 8 operas, produced not only in Brescia but in Venice, Milan, Mantua, Verona, and Livorno, as well as 2 oratorios. In 1680 he became director of music at the cathedral, and a year later, of the Accademia degli Erranti as well. At the end of the decade he moved to Venice, where he became second organist at St. Mark's in 1690 and *vicemaestro* in 1692 (celebrating the arrival of another son). By 1696 he was also director of the conservatory run by the Ospedale degli Incurabili. By 1702, when he lost by one vote the chance to be *maestro di cappella* at the basilica, he had written and seen produced more than forty more operas. Perhaps understandably, he was retired, with his title and salary intact, a few months later, and went on grinding out operas and oratorios to within four months of his death. (The grand total of operas was more than 80; of oratorios, 13.)

Pollarolo as an operatic composer was immensely successful all over Europe in his day and promptly forgotten thereafter. Only about a fourth of the scores are now known to exist. There are also a few liturgical works and a number of cantatas and arias. He is regarded as a transitional figure between the old Venetian opera and the new "Neapolitan" opera with its alternation of recitative and aria.

RECORDINGS: On records he is represented only by an organ fugue—his only known instrumental composition—played by Clemente Terni.

[570] STEFFANI, Agostino (Stef-fà'-nē, Á-gus-tē'-nō)
ORGANIST, SINGER, CONDUCTOR, CLERIC, DIPLOMAT
BORN: Castelfranco Veneto, July 25, 1654
DIED: Frankfurt am Main, February 12, 1728

Of Venetian stock, Steffani, the fifth of seven children, was born in a little town north of Padua. At thirteen he joined the *Kapelle* of Ferdinand Maria, the Bavarian elector, in Munich and, after a year as protégé of Count von Tattenbach, was entrusted to Kerll [506] for training. In 1672 he was sent to Rome to study with Ercole Bernabei, Benevoli's [472] pupil and his successor as director of the Julian Chapel in St. Peter's. Two years later Kerll left München for Vienna and Bernabei came to fill his place, bringing his pupil with him. Shortly thereafter, the elector, obviously pleased with Steffani's progress, promoted him to court organist. In the last two years of the decade he traveled in Italy and France, playing for Louis XIV in Paris. While he was gone, the elector died, and in 1681 his successor, Maximilian II Emanuel, named him director of his private music, to which he responded with an opera, *Marco Aurelio,* written with his brother, a professional dramatist who was known as Ventura Terzago. Meanwhile, Steffani had been busy acquiring a thorough nonmusical education (he was obviously no slouch intellectually) and had been ordained in 1680. The elector saw him as a likely diplomat and sent him off to look into the possibility of a marriage between the houses of Bavaria and Hanover, in which peregrinations Steffani made some valuable contacts. The union did not work out, but he was rewarded with the titular abbacy of Lep-

singen, good for a nice annual income and an outright gift of 1,200 florins. At court Steffani continued to write operas, one of which, *Servio Tullio,* graced the festivities surrounding the elector's eventual wedding to Maria Antonia of Hapsburg, daughter of Leopold I [528] in 1686. When Steffani complained of feeling poorly, the elector sent him off to Italy to recuperate, and two years later he produced another opera for the electress's birthday, and got another Italian vacation, together with three years extra salary as spending money. But the serpent's tooth has nothing in acerbity on a musician scorned. The death that same year of Bernabei, and the elector's decision to elevate Giuseppe Antonio Bernabei to his father's post, provided Steffani with the chance for which he had evidently been waiting. He handed in his resignation and went to Hanover as *Kapellmeister* to Duke Ernst August. His first significant contribution to Hanoverian cultural life was the opera *Enrico il Leone,* which opened the new court opera (of which he was named director) in 1689. He was to produce seven more of his works there before the other side of his life caught up with him in 1695.

In the meantime Emperor Leopold had decided that it might be a good idea to raise the duke to electoral status, but this turned out to require more political jockeying than he had counted on, and by 1693 Ernst August's cause looked hopeless. At that point the elector-elect's librarian and private brain trust, the philosopher-mathematician Leibnitz, recalled Steffani's Machiavellian gifts and heritage, and they packed him off to Brussels to butter up his old employer, Elector Max, now in charge of the Spanish Netherlands. He succeeded in that mission, but in 1695 it was decided that he was more valuable as a diplomat than as a musician and he was sent to Brussels. But he failed to keep Max from siding with Louis XIV in the War of the Spanish Succession, and Ernst August died in 1698. Steffani went back to Hanover finally in 1702 to amuse himself with writing chamber duets. A year later he went to Düsseldorf to work for Johann Wilhelm, Elector Palatine, whom he served as privy councillor and general-president of the government. He also held other high offices, such as president of the Spiritual Council, chief rector of the University of Heidelberg, and apostolic prothonotary. In 1706, Pope Clement XI named him Bishop of Spiga, a diocese in Asia Minor; residence was not demanded because it was then in the hands of the Turks. Later, for his services to the Holy See, he was given other ecclesiastical posts, culminating in his appointment as apostolic vicar of northern Germany, with his headquarters in Hanover. He was largely responsible for the appointment of Handel [683] as court *Kapellmeister* in 1710, having met and admired him in Rome. His own last opera *Tassilone*—his only such effort in fourteen years—was produced in Hanover the year of his return. (It was long attributed to the copyist Gregorio Piva, who signed the score.) Limited now to his incomes from three benefices—two of them on foreign soil and often impossible to collect—he had a very difficult time of it. In 1722 he tried to retire to Padua, but the Vatican ordered him back to Hanover in 1725. Meanwhile, Handel had gone to London, and the elector had followed to become George I of England, and in 1727 Steffani received news that he had been elected president (with an emolument) of the Academy of Vocal Arts, which stirred him momentarily to composition again. But he was still economically troubled and in midwinter 1728, on his way to Rome, he stopped by Frankfurt to sell some valuables. There he died of a massive stroke and was buried.

Steffani was a fluent composer and wrote in several genres. Famous in his time for his operas (few of which have survived intact), he shows himself there a fine technician but no pathbreaker. Yet they do possess a remarkable blend of Italian, French, and German characteristics that must have affected Handel. Nowadays Steffani is perhaps better known (among musicologists anyhow) for his dozens of exquisite *bel canto* duets—some, it is said, written for King George's hapless Electress Sophia Dorothea. These Handel imitated but never surpassed. RECORDINGS: There is a European recording of *Tassilone* by Newell Jenkins, one of the late *Stabat Mater* by Nikolaus Harnoncourt, and a few scattered arias.

[571] LÜBECK, Vincent (Lü'-bek, Fin'-zent)
ORGANIST, TEACHER
BORN: Padingbüttel, c. September 1654
DIED: Hamburg, February 9, 1740

Born to an organist (for whom he was named) in the northern reaches of Bremen, Lübeck grew up in Flensburg in northernmost Schleswig-Holstein. (Whether the family came ultimately from Lübeck is unknown.) There seems to be no basis for the story that he was Buxtehude's pupil. When he reached his maturity, he was rewarded, for marrying the former incumbent's daughter, with the organ loft (complete with instrument) of the church of Sts. Cos-

mas and Damian in Stade (between Bremerhaven and Hamburg). He established such a fine reputation as performer and teacher that after only twenty-seven years he was invited to cross the Elbe to play at the Jakobikirche in Hamburg, leaving his Stade job to his son Peter Paul. Another son (a third Vincent) succeeded him in Hamburg, after assisting him in his old age. Lübeck published a book of harpsichord pieces. RECORDINGS: Some of the harpsichord pieces have been recorded by Edith Weiss-Mann. Michel Chapuis has recorded the 9 survivors of his organ output, which show a brilliant and virtuoso composer. There are also 3 extant cantatas.

[572] BLANKENBURG, Quirinus Gerbrandszoon van (Blånk'-en-bōōrg, Kwē'-rē-nus Ge-brånt'-sun vån)
ORGANIST, PHYSICIAN, THEORIST
BORN: Gouda, 1654
DIED: The Hague, May 12, 1739

Blankenburg's father and teacher, Gerbrant Quirijnszoon, was organist of the Janskerk in Gouda. Quirinus, sometimes called "Gideon," became organist of the Church of the Remonstrants in Rotterdam at sixteen; five years later he took a similar post in nearby Gorinchem. In 1679 he matriculated at the University of Leiden, from which he eventually emerged with both a Ph.D. and an M.D. At that time (c. 1685) he settled at The Hague, where he was organist of the court church and also (from 1702) of the Nieuwe Kerk. He was a much sought-after expert on organs and carillons. He spelled out his opposition to tuning by the newfangled equal temperament in his *Elementa musica,* published in the last year of his long life. Most of his extant music is contained in two published collections, both for keyboard. The 1732 organ book is a collection of psalm-tune paraphrases. *De verdubbelde harmonie* of 1733, written as a wedding gift to a patron, contains little trick pieces that can be played (on two instruments) right side up, inverted, forward, or backward. A few other pieces survive in manuscript, notably the cantata *L'Apologie des femmes (Women's Apologia),* written in answer to André Campra's [584] misogynistic *Les Femmes.* RECORDINGS: *L'Apologie des Femmes* has been recorded by Bernard Kruysen.

[573] BROSSARD, Sébastien de (Brussärd', Sā-båst-yån' də)
LUTENIST, CONDUCTOR, THEORIST,

PRIEST, BIBLIOPHILE, LEXICOGRA-
PHER
BORN: Dompierre, Orne, c. September
12, 1655
DIED: Meaux, August 10, 1730

Author of the first French musical dictionary, Sébastien de Brossard, descended by
way of an ancestral bend sinister from the
Valois, was born in rural eastern Normandy, not far from Caen. He taught himself to play the lute and to write for it.
When he was about sixteen, he went to
Caen to study philosophy and theology, and
there compiled a collection of lute pieces in
1672. Ordained in 1675, he went to Paris,
where, by the middle of the next decade, he
was stationed at Notre-Dame. In 1687 he
went to Strasbourg to direct the cathedral
choir. In his eleven years there he wrote and
published a number of *airs* (a few recorded
by, for example, Edith Selig). There is also
some instrumental music from this period.
He built up a remarkable music library and
used it as the basis of the concerts he conducted in Strasbourg. In 1698 he went to
Meaux to teach the cathedral choirboys and
there wrote most of his religious music—
Masses, motets, cantatas, lamentations, etc.
In 1701 he published his dictionary of musical terms (second edition, 1703). In 1725 he
gave his library to the king in exchange for
a pension; it is now in the Bibliothèque Nationale, Paris.

[574] MARAIS, Marin (Mà-rā', Mà-ra*n*')
VIOLA DA GAMBA PLAYER
BORN: Paris, March 31, 1656
DIED: Paris, August 15, 1728

Marais is said to have been a cobbler's son.
When he entered the world, the viola da
gamba, though still popular in England, was
obsolete on the Continent. However, it was
about to enjoy a brief revival in France,
thanks to the quixotic André Maugars,
sometime court musician to James I, who
became a virtuoso and trained the equally
virtuosic Nicholas Hotman, who trained the
Sieur de Saint-Colombe, who took on young
Marais as a pupil. But according to an old
yarn, Saint-Colombe told him after six
months that there was nothing more he
could teach him. (Another unsubstantiated
story has Marais a choirboy and student at
Ste. Chapelle.) He probably began his studies with Jean-Baptiste Lully [517] at about
that time and joined the king's chamber
group in 1676, at around which time he
married Catherine Damicourt. Over the
years Catherine produced nineteen little

Marais. Many of them took up the gamba,
and such a sawing as there must have been
in the home one can't imagine. Marais and
three of his offspring once played as a quartet before Louis XIV, and his son Roland
wrote a theory text and some viol pieces.
In 1679 Marais became a viol-player-in-
ordinary to the king, and by 1685 he was
sharing executive responsibility in the orchestra with Pascal Colasse [551]. A year
later he brought out the first of his five
books of viol pieces, dedicating it to Lully.
After the latter was out of the way, Marais
composed and staged four operas: *Alcide*,
1693 (with Louis Lully); *Ariane et Bacchus*,
1696; *Alcyone*, 1706; and *Sémélé*, 1709. *Alcyone*, which has not survived complete, was
the hit of the lot, mostly because of its
"storm music." His other extant works are
the *Pièces en trio* (in effect, trio sonatas),
published in 1692, and a set of "symphonies" for violin and continuo, *La Gamme*.
In 1725, the year of the last-named work,
Marais turned his duties over to his son
Vincent and retired to putter in his greenhouse. He died three years later and was
buried in the church of St. Hippolyte, which
was destroyed in the Revolution.

Marais and Antoine Forqueray [635]
were the Paganinis of the gamba. (It was
said that Marais played like an angel and
that Forqueray played like the devil.) Their
music for their chosen instrument is of immense importance in its history—though
not to all modern tastes. Marais's books
contain over 600 pieces arranged in suites
by key (but not intended to be so played).
Though, doubtless for economic reasons, he
indicated that they were playable on any
melody instrument, there is no doubt which
one he had in mind. There are many improvisatory pieces and a number of "character sketches" in the manner of François
"le Grand" Couperin [616]. Here one finds
more than a few echoes of the French
lutenists, and in the music for trio Lully
rubs elbows with unnaturalized Italians.

RECORDINGS: John Hsu has recorded several LPs of the viol pieces, including the famous sonata depicting an operation for the
removal of cystoliths. Other considerable
representations are owing to Eva Heinitz,
August Wenzinger, and Paul Doktor (the
last arranged for viola). Nikolaus
Harnoncourt offers examples from the violin and trio collections, and Jean-François
Paillard a suite from *Alcyone*. There are also
numerous recordings of *La Sonnerie de
Sainte Geneviève du Mont de Paris*, and a
variety of instrumental pieces have been
committed to disc by the Oberlin Baroque
Ensemble.

[575] ERLEBACH, Philipp Heinrich
(Âr'-le-bákh, Fē'-lip Hīn'-rikh)
CONDUCTOR
BORN: Esens, July 25, 1657
DIED: Rudolstadt, April 17, 1714

Erlebach supposedly spent some of his boyhood in the court of East Frisia, in his
hometown. When he became a man, he was
shipped off, with his master's blessing, to
serve Count Albert Anton von Schwarzburg
at Rudolstadt in Thuringia, who appointed
him his *Kapellmeister* in 1681. There he became known as a fairly large frog in his little puddle, where he remained the rest of his
life. He was immensely prolific, turning out
24 Masses, several Passions and oratorios, a
number of operas, and other stage works, at
least 6 cantata cycles, and innumerable instrumental pieces and small choral works.
Almost all of his output was destroyed in a
fire twenty years after his death. There remain some 60 cantatas, 6 violin sonatas, 6
orchestral overtures, a collection of his
arias, and a ceremonial cantata celebrating
the accession of Emperor Joseph I. The earlier pieces show Lully's [517] influence,
though Erlebach insists that he never visited
France, but later there is strong evidence of
the impact of Corelli [565] and perhaps
even of Handel [683]. His operas were
among the first to draw on German history.
RECORDINGS: Klaus Knall has recorded a
Christmas cantata.

[576] DELALANDE, Michel-Richard
(Dä-là-lånd', Mē-shel' Rē-shärd')
VIOLINIST, KEYBOARDIST, CONDUCTOR,
TEACHER, ADMINISTRATOR
BORN: Paris, December 15, 1657
DIED: Versailles, June 18, 1726

Delalande (he spelled his name thus) was
the fifteenth child of a tailor, which fact
should lay at rest the old question of that
profession's virility. At the age of ten or so
he was taken into the choir of St. Germain
l'Auxerrois, where he was trained by François Chaperon. He took up the violin and
became so good at it that he applied for a
place in the Royal Chamber but was turned
down by Lully [517]. Vowing to play no
more, he, legend has it, smashed his fiddle
and turned to the keyboards, whereon he
soon attained great proficiency. The
Maréchal de Noailles hired him to teach his
daughter and recommended him to the king
as tutor to two of his bastards by La Montespan, the Mesdemoiselles de Nantes and
de Blois. He also served as organist of four
Paris churches, notably at St. Gervais,

where he was regent between the death of
Charles Couperin and the maturity of his
son François [616] and at the Jesuit church
of St. Louis, where he was a colleague of
Marc-Antoine Charpentier [544]. In 1683,
the year the latter association began, he
competed for one of the four available appointments as Superintendent of the Royal
Chapel. After three relative incompetents
had been selected (see 551: one, Père Coupillet, was later ousted for plagiarism), the
king pulled rank and chose Delalande as the
January–March incumbent, thus making up
for an earlier refusal to hire him as royal
organist. A year later Delalande married
Anne Rebel, court *prima donna* and sister
of Jean-Féry Rebel [604]. Louis furnished
the wedding and a handsome dowry. On
Lully's fatal indisposition in 1687, Delalande
was asked to write a stage work, much to
Lully's rage. The result, *Le Ballet de la jeunesse (The Ballet of Youth)*, has been called
the first opera-ballet, a form that would climax in Rameau [675]. Later that year he
provided wedding music for the Mademoiselle de Nantes and the Duke of Bourbon.

After Lully died, Delalande became the
chief musical power at court. He was eventually not only sole superintendent of the
chapel and its official composer, but also
held similar posts in the Royal Chamber.
By 1690 he had built the chapel up to imposing size and quality—eighty-five singers
with a string orchestra augmented by five
winds and a lute, with additional forces
from the Chamber and Stable at his command. His two daughters, Marie-Anne and
Jeanne, became notable court sopranos. Unhappily the great smallpox epidemic of 1711
carried them off, as it did the Dauphin
Louis and his wife Marie. The king wrote
his musician a father-to-father note of con-
dolence, which ended *Lalande, il faut nous
soumettre* ("Lalande, we must bear it").
Four years later the king followed his son,
having outlived everyone, leaving the
throne to Delalande's pupil, his own five-
year-old great-grandson, as Louis XV. In
1720, now aged ten, he danced in Delalande's *L'Inconnu (The Stranger)* and *Les
Folies de Cardenio (The Insanities of
Cardenio*, after Cervantes), the last of the
old-style court ballets. Despite his personal
griefs, Delalande may be said to have arrived by this time. He had an apartment at
Versailles, an *hôtel* in Paris, a retreat in the
country, a salary of 6,000 livres, and his
own coach-and-four.

In 1722 he lost Anne, his wife of thirty-six
years. Depressed and suddenly feeling old,
he offered to take a 75 percent pay-cut if the
king would return to the old system of hav-

ing four superintendents, offering as candidates for the other three slots Nicolas Bernier [599], André Campra [584], and Charles-Hubert Gervais. Louis hired all three and gave Delalande a pension of 3,000 livres. The next year the composer, obviously having cheered up, married the daughter of a court surgeon named Cury. In 1725 he produced his major stage work, the opera-ballet Les Éléments, in which the king again played a role. That same year Anne Danican Philidor [666], son of André Danican Philidor [549], inaugurated, at the Salle des Suisses in the Tuileries, the Concerts Spirituels, the world's first subscription concert series, which lasted until the Revolution. The first performance included a Corelli [565] concerto and a suite and two motets by Delalande (whose music for a time was the backbone of the series). A year later Delalande died. The Requiem by Charles d'Helfer, sung at his funeral, was performed again forty-eight years later at that of Louis XV.

Delalande, Lully, and Charpentier make up the grande trinité of French baroque music, though Lully's reputation, thanks to his gift for self-aggrandizement, has outstripped that of the others until recently. Delalande's forte was the grand motet, wherein he rivaled and eventually bested the competition. After his death his pupil Colin de Blamont [707] published, with royal support, a memorial edition of 40, but at least another 20 or so exist in manuscript. Delalande's motets are an ingenious synthesis. They incorporate elements of the grandiose "Versailles" style with operatic flights and both homophonic and polyphonic choruses. In the latter, he uses as many as ten voice parts but keeps the texture open to admit air and light. What Delalande brought to the genre that Lully did not was deep feeling, sometimes approaching the mystical, together with strong melodic appeal and a feeling of simplicity. Latterly his motets took on an intriguing resemblance to the German "reform" cantata, beginning with a sinfonia and dividing up into independent and self-contained movements, which include vocal-instrumental colloquies. At times, using a Gregorian basis, he developed something akin to Bach's chorale fantasias. A master of counterpoint, he had a natural instinct for setting words, and he made dramatic use of such "advanced" chords as the diminished seventh. In the later works the orchestral parts are often independent of the voices. Delalande is said to have contemplated setting all the Psalms en motet, but he did not live to do it. Mention should also be made of the instrumental symphonies—

dance movements, free fantasias, noëls, etc., designed as background music for the king's supper and other boring functions.

RECORDINGS: Of the motets, the De profundis has been recorded by Stéphane Caillat, Michel Corboz, Marcel Couraud, and Alfred Deller; the Regina coeli by Caillat and Corboz; the Beatus vir, and the Usquequo Domine (with the cantique Sur le bonheur des justes) by Louis Frémaux; the Psallite Domino by McNeil Robinson; the Sacris solemnis by Caillat; the Te Deum by Boyd Neel and Jean-François Paillard; and the Confitemini by Neel. Leslie Heward has given us the occasional cantata Les Fontaines de Versailles and the attributed Concert d'Esculaipe by Roger Blanchard. There are many recordings of selections from the symphonies.

[577] BASSANI, Giovanni Battista (Bàs-sà'-nē, Jō-vàn'-nē Bàt-tēs'-tà)
VIOLINIST, ORGANIST, CONDUCTOR
BORN: Padua, c. 1657
DIED: Bergamo, October 1, 1716

Not to be confused with the earlier Giovanni Bassano [292] or various English Bassanos, G. B. Bassano was also not Corelli's teacher [565], as was long maintained. The facts of his early life are obscure. He is first heard of as organist to the Accademia della Morte in Ferrara. (Or so the account in the New Grove Dictionary of Music and Musicians, which places him there at the shockingly early age of ten. Older accounts locate the Accademia at Finale di Modena—the River Finale flows near that city. The Grove writer says he produced several oratorios in Ferrara before going to Modena in 1677 as music director of the Confraternità del Finale but lists his earliest oratorios—from 1675—as having been premiered in Modena.) In 1680 Bassani served at the little court of nearby Mirandola as maestro to Duke Alessandro II Pico and in 1682 was president of the Bolognese Accademia Filarmonica, to which he had been elected five years earlier. He then went (or returned) to Ferrara as maestro di cappella of the Accademia della Morte, and from 1686 as music director of the cathedral. He remained there until 1712, turning out operas (all lost), oratorios, and an enormous amount of sacred music, including 12 Masses, many motets and psalms, and 78 offices. He spent his last four years in Bergamo directing the choir at Santa Maria Maggiore and teaching. His sacred compositions are in the concertato style but markedly influenced by Bolognese practice. His chamber and church sonatas bear comparison with Corelli's. In the nineteenth century anthologists of "old Italian airs" plundered his cantatas for arias. RECORDINGS: Some of the plundered arias so arranged appear on records.

[578] TORELLI, Giuseppe (Tô-rel'-lē, Jōō-sep'-pē)
VIOLINIST, VIOLIST, CONDUCTOR
BORN: Verona, April 22, 1658
DIED: Bologna, February 8, 1709

It is easy to confuse Torelli with Corelli **[565]**, not only because they were contemporaries and had similar names, but also because both are linked with Bologna and with the early history of the concerto. One sketch of Torelli's life notes that he was called "Giuseppe Torelli Veronese" and wonders if he was related to the painter Paolo Veronese. Anything is, of course, possible, but in both instances "Veronese" merely indicates place of origin. (The painter's surname was Cagliari.) But Torelli *was* related to a lesser graphic artist—his youngest brother Felice. They were the children (Nos. 6 and 9) of a well-to-do Veronese customs official, Stefano Torelli, and his wife, the former Anna Boninsegna. Nothing else is known of Giuseppe until his not quite unanimous election to the Accademia Filarmonica in Bologna in 1684, though there is evidence that he was previously *maestro di cappella* at Imola Cathedral. He studied with Giacomo Antonio Perti (1661–1756), played at San Petronio as an extra musician, and was taken into the orchestra in 1686 to play viola and viol. Since he was by trade a superb violinist, it is no wonder that he took time off to play his own instrument elsewhere. In 1696 a financial crisis caused the chapter of the basilica to scrap the orchestra, and Torelli went to seek his fortune in the Germanies. By 1698 he was serving the Markgraf of Brandenburg as *Konzertmeister* in Ansbach, under the direction of his friend the castrato Francesco Antonio Pistocchi, but by early 1700 they were both in Vienna, striving to get some meaningful notice from Leopold I **[528]** but not succeeding. Understandably Torelli was by now (as he notes in a letter) suffering from depression. A year later, however, Perti reorganized the San Petronio orchestra and hired both men back under especially favorable terms, which no doubt cheered our man up. He was only fifty when he died. Among his numerous pupils was Francesco Manfredini **[679]**.

Torelli's output, like Corelli's, seems to have been entirely instrumental. Though he

uses the generic terms *sonata, sinfonia,* and *concerto* rather indiscriminately, his progress is from chamber to orchestral music— or from sonata to concerto. Some people used to say that he invented the *concerto grosso*—the evidence residing in his posthumous Op. 8, published by Felice Torelli in 1709—but it is now generally conceded that Corelli has the better claim. But the *Concerti musicali,* Op. 6 (from 1698; Op. 7 is unknown) contain two works that may well be regarded as the earliest violin concerti, and the chamber-size *Concerti a 4* of Op. 5 (of 1692) often give the first violinist a real workout. And all of these have some relation to the so-called sonatas for trumpet and strings, of which Torelli produced several but which were already a Bolognese tradition. It should be noted that in the Op. 8 concerti, Torelli turns from the polyphonic to the homophonic-melodic, and from the sonata forms to the fast-slow-fast sequence of the *sinfonia*—both characteristic of the later Venetian concerto as purveyed by Vivaldi **[650]**.

RECORDINGS: There are complete recordings of the set by Louis Kaufman and by Rolf Reinhardt and a one-LP selection by I Musici. There are several recorded Torelli anthologies by Antonio Janigro, Newell Jenkins, Jean-François Paillard, and Zlatko Topolski, among others.

[579] DURÓN, Diego (Dōō-rōn', Dē-ā'-gō)
CHOIRMASTER
BORN: Brihuega, c. 1658
DIED: Las Palmas, March 15, 1731

Born in a river town near Guadalajara in New Castile, Spain, Diego Durón was the product of the first marriage of the local sacristan, Sebastián Durón, and half-brother to his father's namesake, a prolific composer who eventually became director of the Royal Chapel. Diego studied in Cuenca, some sixty miles to the southeast, with Alonso Xuárez. In 1676 he went to Las Palmas in the Canary Islands and served there as *maestro de capilla* of the cathedral for fifty-five years. He left 3 Masses, other religious works, and an enormous number of *villancicos.* RECORDINGS: Ireneu Segarra has recorded 2 motets for voices and instruments.

[580] VETTER, Daniel (Fet'-ter, Dàn'-yel)
ORGANIST

BORN: Breslau, c. 1658
DIED: Leipzig, February 7, 1721

Daniel Vetter must not be confused with Andreas Nicolaus Vetter (1666–1734), a pupil of Johann Pachelbel [567] and court organist at Rudolstadt. He studied in Leipzig with the Nikolaikirche organist Werner Fabricius, himself a pupil of Heinrich Scheidemann [443] and succeeded him in 1679. He maintained his post for the rest of his life. His best-known work is *Musikalische Kirch- und Hauss-Ergötzlichkeit (Musical Delight for Church and Home)*, a series of chorales (some of his own composition) arranged very simply for the organ, with variations for the cembalo. Vetter's most famous tune is *"Liebster Gott, wann muss ich sterben"* ("Dear God, When Must I Die"), later used by J. S. Bach [684]. Gérard Souzay has recorded it.

[581] PURCELL, Henry
KEYBOARDIST, SINGER, REPAIRMAN
BORN: 1659
DIED: Westminster, November 21, 1695

In the centuries between John Dowland [316] and Edward Elgar [1499], England produced some competent composers but only one unquestioned genius: Henry Purcell. Yet, as with so many musicians of earlier times, we know only the general outline of his career and even less of the man himself. Perhaps the most vexed question about him is his parentage. There were two Purcells of the previous generation, Henry and Thomas, in Charles II's Chapel Royal, and it is supposed that they were brothers, though there is no proof. Birth records show that Henry and his wife Elizabeth had a daughter, Katherine, born in 1662. Thomas and his wife Katherine produced six known children—two girls and four boys, the latter named Charles, Edward, Francis, and Matthew. In a letter of 1679, however, Thomas mentions a son named Henry. But John Hingeston [474] left a small sum to his godson Henry, whose mother he calls Elizabeth. And Henry the composer had brothers named Edward, Joseph, and Daniel [603]. It has been generally assumed that he was Thomas's son, though F. W. Zimmermann's 1967 biography makes a tempting case for the elder Henry as father. If he is right, young Henry would have been born in a Westminster house, next door to that of Henry Lawes [444], into which the family had moved a few months earlier, and would have been left fatherless on the eve of the great plague

epidemic of 1665 and the great fire of 1666. He must have been as prodigious as Mozart [992], for the publisher John Playford issued a catch by him in 1667. At around ten he joined the Chapel Royal as a soprano under the tutelage of Henry Cooke, who, in 1670, complained to His Majesty that his charges' livery was too motheaten to be seen in public. In 1672 Cooke died and his post went over to ex-prodigy Pelham Humfrey [548], who taught not only Henry but also his brother Daniel.

The first solid historical fact that we have about Henry Purcell, however, dates from 1673. In that year, rendered *hors de combat* by a case of the goslings, he was granted by royal decree a new suit and an annuity of thirty pounds. He was also apprentice to Hingeston, who served the king as musical repairman. A year later, on Humfrey's premature demise, John Blow [552], his successor, took over Purcell's training. In 1674 Purcell was up to tuning the organ of Westminster Abbey, and a year later was earning some loose change as a copyist. He may also have been a pupil or protégé of Matthew Locke [497], for at eighteen he succeeded him as composer-in-ordinary to the King's Violins. A year later, though overage, he was granted a scholarship to St. Peter's College in Westminster, undoubtedly through its principal, Dr. Busby, who taught Locke, Dryden, and Christopher Wren, and who willed Purcell his ring. In 1679, Purcell, though still an unpaid aide to Hingeston, was named organist of the Abbey when Blow stepped aside in his favor. Within the next few months he began composing in earnest, producing the string fantasias, a welcome song for the king, and music for Nathaniel Lee's play *Theodosius*—the first of more than fifty dramatic works in which he had a hand. Around the turn of the decade he married, perhaps to make an honest woman of his wife, known to history only as Frances, who bore him a namesake son on July 9, 1681. The baby died after a week, nor did they fare better with John Baptista (b. 1682), Thomas (b. 1686), and Henry II (b. 1687); but their last three—Frances, Edward, and Mary Peters—survived, the two elder to marry and have children of their own, and Edward to become a successful organist in Westminster. In 1682, having disproved a charge that he was a Dissenter, Purcell became a Gentleman of the Chapel Royal, in which he now sang bass and served as one of the three organists. Shortly after moving his family to a new house in Great St. Ann's Lane, Westminster, he accompanied the king to Windsor and produced the expected ceremonial and occasional pieces.

For the remaining thirteen years of his brief life, our record of Purcell is largely the account of his compositions. In 1683, for example, he published his sonatas for two violins and wrote the first of the several odes he turned out for the observance of St. Cecilia's Day. In that year too he succeeded John Hingeston as Royal Repairman at sixty pounds a year. This was the period of the hassle over who would build the new Temple Church organ (see 552), settled by Purcell's and Blow's advocacy of "Father" Bernard Smith's entry (after considerable brain-racking by Judge Jeffreys, who later proved himself happier at making more fatal decisions). Renatus Harris's unsuccessful entry was, incidentally, installed in St. Andrew's, Holborn, where Purcell's son Edward played it. Late in 1684, Henry and Frances Purcell moved again, this time to Bowling Alley East, near the Abbey.

On February 2, 1685, Charles II suffered a stroke and died four days later. Purcell wrote an anthem and built an organ for the coronation of James II, who named him Royal Harpsichordist. One hopes that the new title was worth more than the older ones, for by 1687 Purcell was complaining that he had not been paid for his maintenance job and wasn't even sure if he still officially had it; even so, it took him another two years to collect. Meanwhile, perhaps because court services were now Catholic, he became increasingly involved in writing for the theater and for publication. In 1688 King James was replaced with William of Orange and his wife Mary, for whose coronation Purcell assumed the perquisite of peddling seats in the organ loft. A week later, much to his chagrin, he was ordered to turn over the proceeds or forfeit his job—all the more annoying since he had got the organ in shape out of his own pocket. It is also clear that he was not in favor with the new administration in its early days.

If work was light at court, however, the private sector gave Purcell plenty to do: 1689 saw the production, at a girl's school run by Josiah Priest (but with a cast that was not all-girl), of Dido and Aeneas, Purcell's only through-composed opera—and, if one excepts Blow's "masque" Venus and Adonis, the first by an Englishman (and one of the few English masterpieces of that genre). (The other so-called operas—King Arthur, The Fairy Queen, The Indian Queen, and The Tempest—are better described as "musicals" or extravaganzas.) But for all the increasing pressure from the theaters, Purcell went to Holland in 1691

along with King William and his singers, violinists, and "hooboys." In that same year he worked with Dryden on King Arthur (designed as a monster compliment to William), which, with the music for Thomas Betterton's Dioclesian in 1690, was praised in print for its fusion of the French and Italian styles—one of Purcell's major achievements. The year 1692 brought The Fairy Queen, loosely based on A Midsummer Night's Dream of William Shakespeare.

At some time shortly thereafter Purcell moved again, this time to Marsham St.—perhaps to provide room for students, for by 1693 he was teaching a number of them, including the composer John Weldon [645] and Lady Katherine Howard. In 1694 he marked the termination of the Irish struggle with an ode for Dublin's Trinity College, and approved "Father" Bernard Smith's bid to rebuild the Abbey organ. At the year's end Queen Mary, much beloved and the recipient of an annual birthday ode from Purcell's pen, died. He paid his last respects with music for the funeral and, later, with the songs or cantata The Queen's Epicedium. Meanwhile, he was becoming inundated with theatrical commissions and called in his brother Daniel from Oxford to help him. Among the works on which they collaborated was Dryden's The Indian Queen, for which Daniel provided the final masque, and which was produced in 1695. In mid-Autumn Henry fell ill. His sickness has been called tuberculosis, exhaustion, and the upshot of loose living. We can discount the yarn that it was the result of having been locked out all night in the rain by an irate wife. He left his estate to his widow and died late on St. Cecilia's Eve. He was buried in the Abbey (free of charge) to the singing of its choir and that of the Chapel Royal in full regalia.

Purcell represents a point of juncture and culmination of the chief musical currents of his time. If in his dramatic music he blends French and Italian influences, he is strongly English in his church music. The sonatas represent the Italian avant-garde, but the fantasias look back to English consort music. Like Monteverdi [333], Purcell had an unfailing dramatic instinct and an incredible sensitivity to words. He is the greatest English song composer between the "Elizabethan" lutenists and the twentieth century.

RECORDINGS: The instrumental music, including the not very important harpsichord pieces, has been thoroughly surveyed. There has been more than one version of each of the "operas" (including Dioclesian) and Oiseau-Lyre has been engaged in recording all the dramatic music, which for some plays is extensive and for many others consists of a song or two apiece. (In all recordings of the stage works to date, dialogue has been omitted, which is in most cases a blessing.) A number of records of anthems, odes, and the like have appeared, though this territory has not been comprehensively covered—and, considering the hack texts that Purcell often had to work with, perhaps does not need to be. The weakest area of recorded representation is that of the catches and part-songs.

[582] KUHNAU, Johann (Kōō'-nou, Yō'-hän)
ORGANIST, CONDUCTOR, THEORIST, LAWYER, NOVELIST
BORN: Geising, April 6, 1660
DIED: Leipzig, June 5, 1722

The German composer Johann Kuhnau is not to be confused with the later German-Danish composer Friedrich Kuhlau [1121]. Kuhnau's ancestors were originally Kuhns who for religious reasons had left Bohemia and settled in Geising in Saxony, just across the border. Johann, at the age of ten, went to nearby Dresden to study and wound up singing soprano in the famous Kreuzchor. He was befriended by the court *Kapellmeister*, Vincenzo Albrici, and he learned French and Italian. The plague epidemic of 1680 drove him home, but went almost immediately to Zittau to study at the *Gymnasium*. The deaths a few months later of the organist at the Johanniskirche and the cantor of the school (who had taught him in Dresden) earned him temporary jobs as replacements for both. In 1682, however, he matriculated at the University of Leipzig to study law, and two years later, being in the right place at the right time, found himself organist of the Thomaskirche. (It was during this period that he became "Kuhnau," having tried on "Cuno" for size.) In 1688 he acquired his doctorate with a dissertation on the laws of religious music and in the same year established a *collegium musicum*. The next year he married and in the course of events sired eight children. In 1700 he was put in charge of music at the university and in 1702 succeeded Johann Schelle as cantor of the Thomaskirche and Thomasschule, which gave him musical charge of the Nikolaikirche and later of the Peterskirche. In 1715, at the request of the authorities, he went to Halle as part of a three-man committee picked to judge the new organ at the Frauenkirche. His co-members were

Christian Friedrich Rolle of Quedlinburg and Johann Sebastian Bach [684] of Weimar. They spent some time in each other's company and were feted at a banquet that featured on the menu beef, pike, sausages, ham, mutton, and veal, with the appropriate trimmings.

Kuhnau was an unusual man. He was a busy lawyer. He wrote fluently in five languages other than his own—French, Italian, Greek, Latin, and Hebrew. Apart from his dissertation he published a work on the fundamentals of composition, treatises on the triad and the tetrachord, and a novel *Der Musikalische Quack-salber (The Musical Humbug)*, as well as works in other fields. He was also a mathematician, a philosopher, and a poet. But for all his skill and learning, his way in Leipzig was not always easy. Between 1701 and 1705, the brash young Telemann [665] threatened to undermine his authority at the university, as did Johann Friedrich Fasch [696], one of his students, and the choir at the church was weakened by blandishments from the local opera management. Moreover, he was hampered by illness for much of his later life. Three daughters outlived him, and he left many successful students. His successor was J. S. Bach.

Kuhnau's several stage works and much of his vocal music—mostly cantatas, ecclesiastical and occasional, in German and Latin—have disappeared, and what has survived is not well known. His name today lives chiefly through his 4 books of published keyboard music—the two parts of the *Neuer Clavier-Übung (New Keyboard Exercises:* 14 suites and a sonata), the *Frische Clavier Früchte (Fresh Keyboard Fruit:* 7 sonatas), and the famous "Biblical" sonatas (or "musical representation of a few Bible stories," as he put it). He shows generally that he has absorbed the transmontaine influences and combined them with the central German tradition; moreover, the suites exhibit an interesting use of French techniques. The sonata that accompanies these last seems to be the first for keyboard published in Germany. The "Biblical" sonatas —quite loosely structured—are forays into the then novel realm of program music, though Kuhnau is less interested in Straussian image-painting than he is in music as an art of the emotions.

RECORDINGS: Eiji Hashimoto has recorded 9 suites and sonatas from the first 3 collections. There are versions of the "Biblical" sonatas by Colin Tilney and others.

[583] SCARLATTI, Pietro Alessandro Gasparo (Skär-låt'-tē, Pē-ā'-trō Ål-es-sán'-drō Gås'-pär-ō)
ORGANIST, CONDUCTOR
BORN: Palermo, May 2, 1660
DIED: Naples, October 22, 1725

Alessandro Scarlatti was the eldest son of Pietro Scarlata, who had come to Palermo from Trapani (at the western extreme of Sicily) and married Eleonora d'Amato, a native, two years earlier. Four of the seven other children—Anna Maria, Melchiorra Brigida, Francesco, and Tommaso—also survived. The boys were all musical, the girls apparently sexually precocious. The family seems to have been poor, and the father died just before Alessandro turned eighteen. The youth and his sisters, however, had been sent to Rome to live with relatives six years earlier, and the younger boys became charity students at the conservatory in Naples. There has been much speculation about just who taught Alessandro, but the fact is we don't know. In 1678 he married Antonia Anzalone, a Roman, who presented him with his first son, Pietro Filippo [654], nine months later. Nine other children had arrived by 1700, though apparently only five lived to maturity. The sixth was the future composer and keyboard virtuoso Domenico [687].

In 1679 the Arciconfraternità della Santissimo Crocifisso, sponsor of many of Carissimi's [471] oratorios, ordered one from "little Scarlatti, alias 'The Sicilian'" for Lent, and in February his first known opera *Gli equivoci nel sembiante (Misunderstandings from Appearance)* was a decided hit at the Teatro Capranica. Queen Christina of Sweden, an exile in Rome, attended and announced herself Scarlatti's future patroness and his protector against the usually saintly, not to say ascetic, Pope Innocent XI. She disliked such things as the pope's stand against women's right to bare arms, and the pope was understandably exercised over the affair that Anna Maria Scarlatti was conducting with a high churchman. A year later Scarlatti was signing himself the queen's *maestro di cappella,* a title he also held at San Girolamo della Carità. However, by 1684 Rome had apparently gotten too hot for him, for he accepted the post of music director of the viceregal *cappella* in Naples.

The way thither had apparently been paved for him by his other sister, Melchiorra, who by showering her favors on important politicos also managed to get her younger brother Francesco the job of first violin. A scandal ensued: the *vicemaestro,*

who had reasonably expected advancement, quit in protest with several adherents; there was an investigation that ousted one of Melchiorra's lovers; and Scarlatti's podium tottered, but in the end he managed to stay. There were times when he wished he hadn't. In the Neapolitan years he may have ground out as many as 80 operas (some of them for Rome, to be sure). Moreover, he was forced to keep the Neapolitan court crowd, whose tastes were notoriously infantile, amused with reams of lightweight stuff. On top of all that, they kept forgetting to pay him—and he had all those mouths to feed. After eighteen years, he decided he had had enough and got what was supposed to be a four-month sabbatical. He and his brilliant, if timid, son Domenico (then seventeen) headed for Florence, where they were taken under the wing of Ferdinando de' Medici, the heir-apparent to the Grand Duke Cosimo. There were a number of commissions from his patron and some extremely courtly and florid correspondence, but no job—which may have been just as well, for Ferdinando died a few years later, and Scarlatti would not have liked the Florentine court as it became. Rather than return to Naples, however, he went back to Rome to serve as assistant choirmaster at Santa Maria Maggiore. But Rome proved stifling to his talents, for the pope had banned opera there. For a while he found a market in Florence for his dramatic compositions, but eventually Ferdinando tired of them.

In 1707, he gained production of two operas in Venice and went there to oversee them. He remained until the next spring, stopped at Urbino, where his son Pietro was cathedral *maestro,* but, having had no offers, went back to Rome. Meanwhile, however, Naples had become increasingly dissatisfied with his successors, and told him that he could name his price, which he happily did. He probably returned there in 1709, though there is nothing official on the books before 1713. By then several of the Scarlattis loomed large in the city's musical life. (Melchiorra, a singer, had done penance in a convent and married a double-bass player who was now running a theater.) Scarlatti remained in Naples this time for perhaps a decade, enjoying enormous success. In 1716 Pope Clement XI conferred knighthood on him. It was well that he had admirers in Rome, for Neapolitan tastes were turning to comic opera. In 1718 Scarlatti managed one example, *Il Trionfo dell'onore* but suddenly found himself outmoded. He again asked for leave and returned to Rome, where old friends enabled him to put on his last three known operas, ending with *La Griselda* in 1721. His star had set. He spent his last years in Naples. At the end of his life, he took on Johann Adolf Hasse [736] as a pupil. Hasse, overcoming the old fellow's bias against wind players, introduced him to young Johann Joachim Quantz [730], afterward flute tutor to Frederick the Great. Both Hasse and Quantz wrote highly unreliable sketches of Scarlatti. He died the following October and was buried at Santa Maria di Montesanto in Naples. His Roman friend and patron, Cardinal Ottoboni, wrote his epitaph.

People are often surprised at the fairly lofty eminence given Scarlatti in the history books—especially those who confused him with his son Domenico, who is known chiefly for his exquisite keyboard sonatas. One sees Alessandro hailed as the founder of the "Neapolitan school," the inventor of *opera buffa*, etc. And one wonders just what it was that he did, for even in this electronically enlightened age his music is little heard—perhaps not even as much as fifty years ago when certain of his arias (in garb he would not have recognized) were essential to the career of the budding singer.

Scarlatti was primarily a vocal composer who understood the voice and had an endless gift for melody. He wrote an enormous number of operas, an even larger number of cantatas, a great deal of religious music, several oratorios, and more than his share in lesser vocal genres. The secular material, at least, would seem not to time-travel well. The surviving operas, for example, have mostly to do with ancient kings and queens torn between love and duty—the *opera seria* plot as it would exist for a century, but not original with him. In context, at least, the arias (often of the *da capo* variety with a contrasting B section sandwiched between two statements of A) are too short for modern tastes, the *secco* recitatives too long. There are few duets and even fewer concerted numbers. The orchestra, perhaps, is given a more prominent role than previously, and Scarlatti standardizes the tripartite opening *sinfonia*, which would soon come to have a life of its own. Scarlatti did not invent the comic opera, nor was he, as noted, much interested in it, though his one mature example seems to look ahead to Pergolesi [782] and beyond.

Scarlatti may well have been the ultimate master of the solo cantata (he wrote more than 700!). He also used it as a testing ground for his larger vocal concepts. Here one finds him working out his notions of recitative and aria and obbligato. Here one also finds some extraordinary harmonic experiments—some so outré as to seem "modern"—and a return to a sort of "madrigalistic" symbolic tonal language. On the other hand, the religious music is conservative (though often strong and stark), influenced by Carissimi [471] and Palestrina [201]. But two of the 10 Masses (not 200 as Quantz so glibly claimed), in calling for orchestral accompaniment, look ahead to eighteenth-century practice.

Scarlatti did not turn to purely instrumental composition until his final decade. Despite his skill at the keyboard, his keyboard pieces offer nothing unusual and seem dull and old-hat beside Domenico's. The *sonate a quattro* for strings are supposed by some to herald the string quartet, but they do so at a long remove. The orchestral concerti *(12 Sinfonie di concerto grosso)* offer little that is new beyond nomenclature and instrumentation (flutes, oboe, trumpet, strings). Six incomplete concerti for keyboard and orchestra are highly suspect. In short, chiefly in his vocal music, Scarlatti is a summer-up—the culmination of the currents of the Italian Baroque.

RECORDINGS: Of the operas *Il Trionfo dell'onore* exists in a radio performance by Carlo Maria Giulini, Hans Stadlmair conducts *Il giardino di amore,* and there is a piracy of *La Griselda.* Other significant recordings include the oratorio *San Filippo Neri* (Franco Caracciolo); the *St. John Passion* (Louis Devos); the *Stabat Mater* (Angelo Ephrikian, Paul Kuentz); the 1706 *Papal Mass* and some motets (Michel Corboz); the *Vespers of St. Cecilia* (Denis Stevens); several recordings of cantatas (Uros Lajovic); and chamber cantatas (Five Centuries Ensemble). The instrumental music has, oddly, received much attention.

[584] CAMPRA, André (Kàm-prä', Àn-drä')
CHOIRMASTER, TEACHER, ADMINISTRATOR, CLERIC
BORN: Aix-en-Provence, c. December 4, 1660
DIED: Versailles, June 29, 1744

Campra's father, a surgeon, came from Turin, which may help explain the son's enthusiasm for Italian music. He sang at St. Sauveur in Aix under Guillaume Poitevin [545] but showed no particular musical talent until he suddenly blossomed in his midteens. He entered holy orders in 1678 and was probably ordained, though he seems to have been torn all his life between the church and the theater. In 1681 he went to Arles to direct the choir at St. Trophime but after nearly two years moved on to Toulon to teach the choristers at St. Etienne. In 1694 he got leave to go to Paris for further study and never returned. Instead he seems to have fallen into the analogous post at Notre-Dame de Paris, where he persuaded the chapter, which was rather behind the times in such matters, that it would be a good thing to have violins accompany the choir.

Meanwhile Campra was making some important contacts at the court, and in 1697 he produced the first of his great opera-ballets, *L'Europe galant (Europe A-courting)*. He pretended that it was by his brother Joseph (1662–1744), sometime conductor for Pierre Gautier [537] and concurrently a contrabass player in the Opéra orchestra, but no one was fooled. The work was clearly modeled on Pascal Colasse's [551] *Ballet des saisons*, but it was Campra's piece that firmly established the opera-ballet and began his reign as the most effective French stage composer between Lully [517] and Rameau [675]. It has been said that the genre substituted chaos for the sacrosanct dramatic "unities," but that is not really fair. *L'Europe*, like most opera-ballets, plays variations on a theme—here the supposed conventions of wooing in France, Spain, Italy, and Turkey, each nation treated in its own playlet, each playlet moving to a *grand divertissement*. In adopting such a subject, it makes a radical break with its Lullyan predecessors: there are no gods and no machines, and the characters, however exotic, are supposed to be real people in real places.

In 1699, Campra, still incognito, returned to the Opéra with *Le Carnaval de Venise* (which has only its title in common with Julius Benedict's [1180] variations, beloved of bandstand cornettists). Though it was a relative failure, it is important in that there is a single action, that it introduces comedy to the French operatic stage, and that it encloses a little one-act Italian opera, *Orfeo nell'inferni (Orpheus in the Underworld)*, showing that Italian music was gaining a foothold. People were soon singing a ditty to the effect that if the archbishop found out who was writing these stage pieces Campra would have to decamp. It is not certain whether he jumped or was pushed, but he left Notre-Dame in 1700 for a post with the Opéra. Once out of the closet, he produced, under his own name, his first *tragédie lyrique* that year. Aside from the fact that it wasn't Lully (though it tried), some people complained that there were too many twittering birds, murmuring streams, and other programmatic effects—though such things later became one of Campra's hallmarks. In 1702 he patched together a ballet, *Fragments*

de M. Lully, that might have been called "Lully's Greatest Hits," though Campra added some things of his own. Under the patronage of Philippe d'Orléans, future regent of France, operas and ballets flowed from his pen. Meanwhile his motets and *cantates* were increasingly marked by Italianisms, at first without comment, then later with his plea that the two "tastes" be reconciled, to mix French refinement with Italian vivacity.

All these currents flowed together in *Les Fêtes vénitiennes*, Campra's next successful opera-ballet (1710). In it comedy asserted its right to the operatic stage. So did Italian-style music, for each of the three *divertissements* involved a *cantate*, made up of a recitative, an *ariette* (really an *aria da capo*), and a dance. King Louis having been disastrously defeated at Blenheim, flattery and flag waving (for which Campra had a flair) were not in order here. Indeed, Louis, grown ascetic in his old age, had largely withdrawn from the operatic scene, and the allegory in Campra's prologue of Folly besting Reason was a sign of the times. But audiences commented favorably on the naturalness (the real Palazzo Grimani was depicted), the simplicity, and the wit of the piece.

The old king died in 1715, and three years later Campra produced *Les Ages*, the last of his opera-ballets. The new child-king, undoubtedly coached by the regent, bestowed on him a 500-livre pension. In 1723, when Campra was working as music director for the Prince de Conti, he was at last given a court post on Delalande's [576] partial retirement, as one of the four *surintendants* of the Royal Chapel (later as one of two). From 1730 he also served as Inspector General of the Opéra. His two posts drained his energies and his health went bad. In 1733 he attended the first performance of Rameau's *Hippolyte et Aricie* and saw that the old kind of opera was obsolete. It is not certain that his last opera, *Les Noces de Vénus (The Marriage of Venus*, 1740), was even produced. He lived out the last of his eighty-four years in retirement, almost forgotten.

Campra wrote about 40 operas, ballets, and lesser stage works, 3 volumes of cantatas, 2 Masses, a Requiem, and many motets, both *petits* and *grands*.

RECORDINGS: None of the operatic works have been recorded complete, though there are orchestral suites from *Les Fêtes vénitiennes* (Collegium Aureum, Andrée Colson), *L'Europe galante* (Raymond Leppard), *Les Ages* and *Le Bal interrompu* (Malgoire), as well as a few arias (e.g., Lily Pons, Ettel Sussman). Louis Frémaux has recorded the

De profundis, Omnes gentes, Te Deum, and *Requiem,* and Gérard Souzay the cantata *Les Femmes.* One should also note the Campra-based *Suite provençale* of 1937 by Darius Milhaud (1868), which catches the popular flavor of Campra's music.

[585] FUX, Johann Joseph (Fŏŏks, Yŏ'-hàn Yŏ'-zef)
ORGANIST, CONDUCTOR, THEORIST
BORN: Hirtenfeld, 1660
DIED: Vienna, February 13, 1741

An important composer, Fux has acquired something of a bad name from what have been misconstrued as negative opinions from two later composers. (I do not refer to his surname, which is merely an alternative spelling of "Fuchs.") The eighteenth-century composer and writer Johann Mattheson [668] spoke of him, in his *Ehrenpforte,* as "old-fashioned," but it is clear that Mattheson thought highly of his music. Claude Debussy [1547] called one of his *Children's Corner* pieces "Dr. Gradus ad Parnassum" (in reference to Fux's famous counterpoint text); but its picture of wearisome pedantry is intended as a child's-eye view.

Fux was born into a peasant family in a hamlet near Graz, Austria. Nothing certain is known of his first twenty years. He studied at the University of Graz in 1680, transferred to the Ferdinandeum the next year, and by 1683 was in Ingolstadt studying logic and playing the organ at the Moritzkirche. From 1688 there is another gap in the record. Supposedly he got to Vienna in the retinue of Archbishop Leopold, Count von Kollonitsch. At any rate, he became organist of the Schottenkirche there before 1696, the year of his marriage to an anonymous local girl, and two years later Emperor Leopold named him *Kammerkomponist,* court composer. From then on he went steadily up the ladder of success—vice-*Kapellmeister* at St. Stephen's in 1705 and to Emperor Charles VI in 1711, *Kapellmeister* of the cathedral in 1712 and to the emperor in 1715. Having reached that last eminence, he resigned his other posts to give his master his full attention. A kindly and considerate man who brooked no musical nonsense, he was greatly beloved by both his superiors and his students. (A quarrel over theoretical points soured Mattheson on the man and caused him to paint an unflattering portrait of him.) Some of his pupils once worked up a five-voice canon to the text "I Have Found a Man After My Own Heart" to serenade him with. When, in 1623, Fux was laid up with an attack of gout, the emperor arranged for him to be carried, oh! so gently, to Prague in a litter to attend the premiere of his opera *Costanza e fortezza (Patience and Fortitude).* Among his more successful students Fux counted Muffat [706], Zelenka [656], and Wagenseil [804]. J. S. Bach [684] admired his work, and so did Joseph Haydn [871], who perhaps recognized the peasant element that is sometimes heard in it. He was buried in St. Stephen's. He left no children.

Fux was probably the most learned composer of his time (though no one knows who taught him) and, to be sure, his learning shows. No innovator he was, in his more formal compositions, way behind the times, reflecting Lully [517] and the Venetians rather than Rameau [675] and Corelli [565]. He wrote an enormous amount of music; still extant, mostly in manuscript, are 20 operas, 14 oratorios, more than 80 Masses, about 250 other religious works, sonatas, suites, and keyboard pieces. In the suites he shows a lighter, more unbuttoned side of himself than he generally does elsewhere. His vast mastery of counterpoint is said to be best exhibited in the *Missa canonica,* a veritable encyclopedia of canonic practice.

For centuries, however, Fux has been proverbial for his counterpoint text, *Gradus ad Parnassum (The Climb to Parnassus).* Cast in the form of a Latin dialogue and first published in 1725, its chief purpose was to bring order out of the chaos into which counterpoint had fallen. To do so, Fux proposed to return to "his teacher" Palestrina [201], whom he deemed to have represented the art in its purest form. In point of fact, not all that much of Palestrina's music was available to him, and the rules that Fux set forth were much stricter than those that the Roman had gone by. Nonetheless the book established guidelines on rational principles and established the pattern by which counterpoint has been taught ever since. It went through many editions, the most recent English version dating from 1965.

As a matter of interest, Fux's music was catalogued by the same Ludwig von Koechel who catalogued Mozart's [992], and, like Mozart's is designated by "K" numbers.

RECORDINGS: Surveys are offered on record by René Clemencic and Kurt Rapf (keyboard works), and Edgar Seipenbusch has recorded two orchestral suites. The sacred cantata *Plaudite, sonat tuba* is performed by Uros Lajovic and the RIAS Sinfonietta.

[586] DANDRIEU, Pierre (Dàn-drē-ö',
Pē-âr')
ORGANIST, CLERIC
BORN: c. 1660 (?)
DIED: Paris, 1733

Pierre Dandrieu was the uncle of the better-known Jean-François Dandrieu [671]. Little is known of him. Some accounts call him an abbé, others a priest. He was organist of the former Paris church of St. Barthélemy, and in 1691 Louis Marchand [619] tried to steal his job. He put together a book of organ *noëls,* some of which have found their way into recorded anthologies (e.g., by André Marchal and Raphael Tambyeff).

[587] PARCHAM, Andrew
BORN: c. 1660 (?)
DIED: ?

A few pieces of Parcham's music date from the beginning of the eighteenth century, but otherwise nothing is known of him, though he may be presumed to have been British. RECORDINGS: Ferdinand Conrad has recorded a flute sonata published in Holland.

[588] RUGGIERI, Giovanni Maria (Rōō-jyer'-rē, Jō-vàn'-nē Mà-rē'-à)
CHOIRMASTER
BORN: c. 1660 (?)
DIED: after 1725 (?)

Ruggieri published 4 books of trio sonatas in Venice, in the first of which, in 1689, he terms himself an amateur. By 1696, however, he had become professional enough to produce the first of at least 12 operas (at the Teatro San Cassiano). Later, in 1715, he was conducting in Pesaro. The first 2 sets of trio sonatas—*Bizzarie armoniche (Harmonic Whimsies)* and *Scherzi geniali (Clever Jokes)* of 1690—involve such gimmicks as making the bass line a mirror image of the top line. RECORDINGS: Franco Gulli and C. Ferraresi have recorded one of the later nongimmick sonatas.

[589] DESMARETS, Henri (Dā-mà-rā', Àn-rē')
CONDUCTOR
BORN: Paris, February 1661
DIED: Lunéville, September 7, 1741

A child of the Sun King's chapel, Desmarets (or Demarest) has been called, for what it is worth, the most talented of Lully's [517] pupils. At twenty-two he entered the competition to pick four new *surintendants* for the Royal Chapel. His piece was deemed a winner, but the king vetoed his appointment on the basis of his youth, awarding him an annuity of 900 livres to ease the pain. However, Desmarets managed to have his cake and eat it by ghost-writing for Père Coupillet, one of the winners, for a decade, until the latter was exposed and sacked. In 1682, Desmarets embarked on what he hoped would be a successful operatic career with *Endymion;* it wasn't. Not until 1693 did he produce another opera, *Didon.* Of his half dozen others, only *Vénus et Adonis* met with approval. Its librettist, Jean-Baptiste Rousseau, was later permanently exiled for slander. Desmarets' other operas suffered chiefly from being pale imitations of Lully, having too many frills, and exhibiting Desmarets' penchant for buttering up the king. At some point early in the new century, Desmarets, recently widowed, "secretly married" or abducted the daughter of a tax-office bigwig in Senlis. Wheels were put in motion, and in 1704, before he could complete his *Iphigénie en Tauride,* he had to skip the country. (Campra [584] finished the opera, but it didn't help much.) A price was put on Desmarets' head, but he soon found steady work as music master to Philip V of Spain and made the liaison with his traveling companion legal by Spanish law. But the Spanish preferred Italian music, and in 1707 he moved on to Lunéville to take charge of the musical affairs of Leopold I, Duke of Lorraine. Following the death of Louis XIV, the regent (brother of Leopold's duchess) pardoned him and legalized his marriage, and Louis XV reinstated his pension. But, lacking a court appointment, he remained where he was. His second wife died in 1727 and he himself fourteen years later, aged eighty.

Desmarets' church music, notably his *grands motets,* has been favorably compared with Delalande's [576]. The motets show interesting use of the orchestra, a mastery of counterpoint, and a keen musical intelligence.

RECORDINGS: The only considerable work of his to reach discs so far, however, seems to be *Les Mystères de Notre-Seigneur Jésus Christ,* recorded by Guy Cornut.

[590] BÖHM, Georg (Böm, Gä-ôrg')
ORGANIST
BORN: Hohenkirchen, September 2, 1661
DIED: Lüneburg, May 18, 1733

Böhm came from the Bach-woods of Thuringia. His first teacher was his father, Johann Balthasar, who, as was then common, doubled as village schoolmaster and organist. But he died when his son was fourteen, and Georg continued his education at the Latin school in nearby Goldbach and the Gymnasium at equally nearby Gotha. In 1683 he entered the not-so-nearby-but-close University of Jena. (The statement that he went to the University of Vienna apparently stems from an English-language aural error.) Then we lose track of him until he turns up in Hamburg in 1693. No doubt he knew of and perhaps knew Reincken [498], and he could conceivably have gone to Lübeck to hear Buxtehude (or to Stade to hear Lübeck), but there is no proof that he actually studied with any of them, nor do we even know why he went to Hamburg or what he did there. In 1698 he tried out for the organist's job at the Johanniskirche in Lüneburg a few miles to the south, and won an appointment that lasted his remaining thirty-five years. In 1700 young Sebastian Bach [684] came there to sing and study at the Michaelskirche. There has been much speculation about whether Böhm was responsible for Bach's coming there and whether or not he taught him, but again the evidence is lacking. Otherwise Böhm's life seems to have been uneventful. He had five children, and was eventually succeeded by his son-in-law, Ludwig Ernst Hartmann.

Whether or not Bach studied with Böhm, he admired his organ music. Böhm was a master of the organ chorale, particularly of the large-scale *choral partita*. Eighteen of his chorale pieces are extant, plus a few other organ pieces and some latterly discovered harpsichord suites, which show a thorough knowledge of French styles and an awareness of advanced harmonic practice. His cantatas are conservative, cast in the old variation and *concertato* forms.

RECORDINGS: Böhm's organ music has been recorded by a number of organists, such as Finn Viderø, Luther Noss, Hans Heintze, Lawrence Moe, Albert DeKlerk, Franz Lehrndorfer, and Herfried Mencke. Volker Gwinner has recorded a set of chorale variations on Böhm's own Lüneburg organ (rebuilt under Böhm's direction in 1712–14). Gustav Leonhardt has recorded some of the harpsichord suites.

[591] VITALI, Tommaso Antonio (Vē-tä'-lē, Tōm-mä'-zō Än-tōn'-yō)
VIOLINIST
BORN: Bologna, March 7, 1663
DIED: Modena, May 9, 1745

Tommaso was the son of Giovanni Battista Vitali [516] and presumably his pupil. At the age of twelve he became a member of the Modenese court orchestra, of which his father was vice-*maestro* and was still playing there sixty-seven years later. In 1706 he was elected to the Accademia Filarmonica in Bologna. Evaristo Felice Dall'Abaco [642] was his pupil. His 4 volumes of sonatas (one solo, three trio) are obviously inspired by Corelli [565]. RECORDINGS: Franco Gulli and C. Ferraresi have recorded one of the two-violin examples. The famous (and much-recorded) chaconne attributed in the nineteenth century to Vitali is, according to modern musicologists, not his. They have no idea who wrote it.

[592] SAINT-LUC, Laurent de (San-Lük', Lō-rán' də)
LUTENIST
BORN: Brussels, June 8, 1663
DIED: after 1700

Laurent de Saint-Luc, a.k.a. Jacques-Alexandre, was the son of Jacques de Saint-Luc, who was a court-and-chapel lutenist in Brussels and was admired by Constantijn Huygens. Laurent at one time played in the private music ensemble of Louis XIV. In 1700, as an employee of Prince Eugène of Savoy, he performed in Vienna at the wedding festivities of Friedrich of Hesse-Kassel and Luise Dorothee Sophie of Brandenburg. He is also said to have worked for Prince Lobkowitz. He wrote dozens of little pieces for lute and dozens more for lute, melody instrument, and continuo. He liked to give them pictorial-military titles having to do with the capture or destruction of cities (e.g., Barcelona, Gaeta, Lille, Naples). RECORDINGS: One of the trio suites has been recorded by members of the Brussels Pro Musica Antiqua.

[593] MURSCHHAUSER, Franz Xaver Anton (Mōōrsh'-hou-zer, Fränts Eksä'-ver Än'-tōn)
CHOIRMASTER, THEORIST
BORN: Zabern (Saverne), c. July 1, 1663
DIED: Munich, January 6, 1738

Alsatian-born, Murschhauser went to school in Munich and studied there later (1683–93) with Kerll [506]. In 1691 he took on what turned out to be a lifetime appointment as *Kapellmeister* of the Liebfrauenkirche. Between 1696 and 1707 he published 3 organ books and a collection of vesper psalms, as well as an introduction to church music. In 1721 he brought out the first part of a stunningly old-fashioned composition manual, *Academia musico-poetica bipartita*. In it he made a mischievously uncomplimentary reference to the terrible-tempered composer and writer Johann Mattheson (1681–1764), whereupon Mattheson laid the work flat with one blast in his own *Critica musica*. Murschhauser apparently thought it unwise to go on with the project, for no Part II ever appeared. RECORDINGS: Samplings of the organ music appear in recorded anthologies (e.g., by Ernst Günthert, Franz Lehrndorfer).

[594] ZACHAU, Friedrich Wilhelm
(Tsàkh'-ou, Frēd'-rikh Vil'-helm)
KEYBOARDIST, CONDUCTOR, VIOLINIST, OBOIST, TEACHER
BORN: Leipzig, c. November 13, 1663
DIED: Halle, August 7, 1712

Zachau's father, a Leipzig municipal musician, taught his talented son a number of instruments, of which young Zachau seems to have preferred the oboe and the violin. Who taught him the *klavier* is unknown. When he was thirteen, the family moved to Eilenburg, a little city about twenty miles east of Munich. Three months before he turned twenty-one, he was named organist of the Marienkirche in Halle, where he also directed the monthly concerts. He taught a number of pupils. In 1693 a local eight-year-old, Georg Friedrich Händel (see 683), was turned over to him and remained with him for three years. Zachau had apparently an insatiable craving for new music and had acquired a library of avant-garde stuff, through which young Händel undoubtedly learned what the Italians were up to. He adored his teacher, kept in touch with him until Zachau died, and helped support his widow. A few years later Händel assisted the organist of the local Calvinist cathedral, a certain Johann Christoph Leporin, eventually succeeding him in 1702. Leporin seems to have been a poisonous fellow, and his sins, in Handel biographies, somehow got visited on poor old Zachau.

About a third of Zachau's religious music (mostly German cantatas) and a fair number of organ pieces (mostly chorale-based preludes or fugues) have survived. He was particularly adept at the cantata, some of the more advanced examples of which point down a short road to Bach.

RECORDINGS: Two cantatas have been recorded by Fritz Werner. The Trio in F Major for flute, bassoon, and cello has been recorded by Hungarian performers.

[595] JACCHINI, Giuseppe Maria (Yàk-kē'-nē, Jōō-sep'-pē Mà-rē'-à)
CELLIST, CLERIC, CHOIRMASTER
BORN: Bologna, c. 1663
DIED: Bologna, May 2, 1727

Not a great deal is known of Jacchini's life. He studied with Giacomo Antonio Perti and seems to have been Domenico Gabrielli's [562] star cello pupil. After some years as a steady extra player, he was appointed a regular cellist at San Petronio in 1689, probably in succession to his teacher, who was fatally ill. Except for the period 1696–1701, when economics permitted no orchestra, he played there the rest of his life. He was a man of the cloth, though in what degree is not certain. Named to the Accademia Filarmonica in 1688, he was elected president in 1709 but refused to serve or to be again considered on the grounds that he was unworthy. He was also choirmaster at the church of San Luigi. He published 5 books of chamber music, variously designated as sonatas, concerti, and *trattenimenti* (entertainments), all for strings, with a heavy emphasis on the cello, and some of the last (in good Bolognese style) with solo trumpet. (A few other trumpet sonatas exist in manuscript.) Like Gabrielli, Jacchini apparently saw the cello as a solo instrument rather than as a mere workhorse. RECORDINGS: Trumpet sonatas have been recorded by Helmut Hunger, Maurice André, Ludovic Vaillant, and others.

[596] LEIDING, Georg Dietrich (Lī'-ding, Gà-ôrg' Dē'-trikh)
ORGANIST
BORN: Bücken, February 23, 1664
DIED: Braunschweig, May 10, 1710

Born in the village between Bremen and Hanover where his father, a cavalry riding master, had retired, Leiding studied the organ with Jakob Bölsche in Braunschweig. When he was twenty he went to Hamburg and Lübeck, where he studied briefly with Reincken [498] and Buxtehude [525], until he had to return to Braunschweig to take over for the ailing Bölsche. The teacher died before the year was out, leaving the Ulrichkirche and Blasiuskirche organs to his pupil, who was later also appointed organist at the Magnuskirche. At a later time he had composition lessons in Wolfenbüttel with the court *Kapellmeister* Johann Theile, a pupil of Schütz [412]. Leiding died at forty-six. Only 5 of his organ compositions —3 preludes and 2 sets of chorale variations —appear to have survived him. RECORD-

INGS: His works turn up in recorded organ anthologies (by, for example, Jørgen Ernst Hansen, Franz Lehrndorfer, Herbert Leidecke).

[597] PEZ, Johann Christoph (Pets, Yō'-hán Krĕs'-tŏf)
VIOL PLAYER, LUTENIST, CONDUCTOR
BORN: Munich, September 9, 1664
DIED: Stuttgart, September 1716

Pez should not be confused with Johann Christoph Pezel [527]. Pez's first thirty years were closely linked with his native city. He studied and sang at the Petrikirche and, after further seasoning at the local Jesuit college, returned to become *Kapellmeister* there in 1687. A year later Elector Maximilian Emanuel hired him as a court musician and shipped him off to Italy for three years of study in 1689. (Presumably he studied with Johann Kerll [506] in Munich.) Owing to Max Emanuel's habitual absenteeism, Pez defected in 1694 to become *valet de chambre* and *Kapellmeister* to Josef Clemens, Archbishop of Cologne, in Bonn. In 1695 he produced a dramatic cantata in Liège, which was also under the archbishop's jurisdiction. War forced him back to vegetating in Munich in 1701. In 1705 he may have tried his luck in London briefly, but early the next year he was firmly settled for life in Stuttgart, as *Kapellmeister* to Eberhard IV, Duke of Württemberg.

Pez wrote a dozen school operas and other minor stage pieces, but not much is left of them. He published 3 volumes of Masses and other religious music (including 12 solo cantatas). There are also 2 books of sonatas and some other instrumental works in manuscript, which exhibit both Italian and French influences.

RECORDINGS: Zlatko Topolski has recorded the *Concerto pastorale* for flutes, strings, and continuo.

[598] MASCITTI, Michele (Má-shit'-tē, Mē-kä'-lä)
VIOLINIST
BORN: Santa Maria, c. 1664
DIED: Paris, April 24, 1760

Though his admirers thought him as good as Corelli [565] (whom most of them had not heard), Mascitti did not study with him, as he is often said to have done. Born near Naples, he was a pupil of his uncle, Pietro Marchitelli. Failing to find a job at the court there, he wandered north, finally arriving in Paris in 1704. As a representative of the legendary Italian violin school, he was made much of, was employed by the Duke of Orléans, and later by Pierre Crozat, the Royal Treasurer and a noted art collector. He became a citizen in 1739 and married and retired in 1740. Between 1704 and 1738, he published 12 collections of "sonatas"—100 for violin and continuo, 12 for trio, and the first 4 string concerti to be issued by a resident of France. There are also some keyboard sonatas in manuscript. Whatever his training, the Corellian influence is strong in Mascitti's music. RECORDINGS: A violin sonata subtitled "Psyche" has been recorded by Eduard Melkus and Lionel Rogg.

[599] BERNIER, Nicolas (Bârn-yā', Nē-kō-làs')
TEACHER, ADMINISTRATOR
BORN: Mantes-la-Jolie, June 5 or 6, 1665
DIED: Paris, July 6, 1734

Other than that he was born in a Seine river town, we know nothing of Bernier's early life, though it is said that somewhere in the course of it he went to Rome to study with Caldara [624], which seems unlikely, for Bernier was the older. In 1693 he flunked his audition for the job of teaching the choristers at Rouen Cathedral, but a year later his appointment to the same post at Chartres must have salved his hurt pride. In 1698 he was called to Paris to be music master at St. Germain l'Auxerrois, from which in 1704 he moved to Ste. Chapelle to fill the vacancy left by the death of Marc-Antoine Charpentier [544]. His religious duties seemingly did not prevent his writing secular music—*airs* and especially *cantates,* notably those written for Anne-Louise-Bénédicte de Bourbon, Duchess de Maine, and her "Grandes nuits de Sceaux." (These were 16 magnificent *al fresco* entertainments that she presented on summer evenings in 1714 and 1715, reportedly because she had trouble sleeping.) When, in 1723, Delalande [576] decided he was getting too old to handle the Royal Chapel administration alone, Bernier was one of the three he hand-picked to share the duties with him. When Delalande died three years later, Bernier turned over his post at Ste. Chapelle to his friend François de la Croix, but he carried on his educational function at Versailles. A much-admired teacher (Daquin [717] was one of his pupils), he wrote a no-nonsense composition manual.

Bernier wrote a good deal of church music; what survives, besides a Tenebrae Service, consists of motets, both *petits* and *grands*. But he is more important as a pioneer of the *cantate,* which, though Italian-based, becomes in his hands a French form. Jean-Baptiste Morin **[649]** may have been the first to produce a successful hybrid, but Bernier's first *cantate* publication was three years earlier than his. (Charpentier wrote some twenty years earlier, but his French ones are not Italian enough, and his Italian ones are in no wise French.) Bernier's earlier examples were chains of recitatives and airs, but in the Sceaux works he introduces a dramatic ambience and instrumental scene painting (borrowed from the operatic craze of the day).

RECORDINGS: From the Sceaux collection Janine Micheau has recorded *Le Café (On the Relative Merits of Coffee and Wine).* Jocelyne Chamonin has recorded the solo *Motet du Saint-Esprit.*

[600] BRUHNS, Nicolaus (Brōōnz, Nē'-kō-lous)
ORGANIST, STRING PLAYER
BORN: Schwabstädt, December 1665
DIED: Husum, March 29, 1697

Scion of a family of professional musicians that included his grandfather, his father, two uncles, and his brother, Nicolaus Bruhns was born in a small town on the west coast of Slesvig (now Schleswig-Holstein). He was musically precocious and no doubt learned the rudiments from his father, Paul, the town organist. When he was sixteen, he went off to Lübeck to polish his organ-playing skills under Dietrich Buxtehude **[525]**, who came to think highly of him. While there, he lived with his Uncle Peter, a municipal musician and something of a virtuoso, who taught him violin and gamba. Afterward he spent some time in Copenhagen, where his activities remain obscure. Eventually, in 1689, the town of Husum, near his birthplace, asked him to try out for the vacancy at the Stadtkirche, and when the officials heard him play they hired him on the spot. He remained in Husum for the rest of his short life, the wonder of his fellow townsmen, especially when they heard him perform trios by playing double stops on the violin while accompanying himself on the organ pedals. When he died, he was succeeded by his brother Georg, his son having opted for the ministry. Bruhns's music was much admired by J. S. Bach **[684]**. Bruhns wrote some works for strings, but all that is now left of his output consists of 12 cantatas, a chorale fantasia for organ, and 3 preludes and fugues. The organ pieces are in the North German tradition. RECORDINGS: Helmut Winter has recorded three organ pieces and Herfried Mencke the remaining prelude and fugue (authenticity in doubt). Various of them may also be found in anthologies. Some of the cantatas are strongly influenced by the Italian cantata tradition, but none seem to have been recorded.

[601] HANFF, Johann Nikolaus (Hânf, Yō'-hán Nē'-kō-lous)
ORGANIST, TEACHER
BORN: Wechmar, 1665
DIED: Schleswig, 1711/12

Hanff came from the Thuringian town to which the earliest Bachs can be traced. He must have migrated to Hamburg in early manhood, for little Johann Mattheson **[668]** studied with him there from 1688 to 1692. Shortly afterward he became organist to August Friedrich, the episcopal ruler of Lübeck, at Eutin, until the latter's death in 1705, when he returned to Hamburg to rear his family. After a considerable wait, he became organist at the cathedral in Slesvig (Schleswig) in 1711, but died that winter at forty-six. A sterling representative (on the skimpy evidence that remains) of the North German Baroque at its zenith, Hanff is said to have been particularly adept at the chorale prelude. But only the 6 that J. G. Walther **[680]** copied out, plus 3 cantatas, have survived. RECORDINGS: Various of the preludes appear in recorded anthologies.

[602] BITTI, Martino (Bit'-tē, Mâr-tē'-nō)
VIOLINIST
BORN: Genoa, c. 1665
DIED: Florence, February 2, 1743

Bitti was an obscure and workaday composer, best known in his time as a violinist. The jacket note to the record cited below has him working for the Herzogs in Florence, c. 1717. Historically aware German readers will recognize the main Herzog as Cosimo III de' Medici, Grand Duke of Tuscany. Bitti was actually at the Florentine court as first violin from 1696 to after 1720, but remained on the payroll until he died. He left a set of sonatas, a few concerti, a handful of keyboard pieces, and a cantata. RECORDINGS: One sonata has been recorded by Ferdinand Conrad.

[603] PURCELL, Daniel
ORGANIST
BORN: c. 1665 (?)
DIED: London, c. November 24, 1717

Daniel Purcell's origins are just as puzzling as those of his brother Henry [581] and for the same reasons. Like Henry, he was a chorister in the Chapel Royal. In 1688 he became organist of Magdalen College, Oxford. He returned to London in 1695, either to aid his overworked brother or to attend him in his last illness. At any rate, he contributed to *The Indian Queen* and *Pausanias.* For the next decade he was kept busy writing music for largely ephemeral plays by Colley Cibber, Aphra Behn, Thomas D'Urfey, and Nathaniel Lee— though in fairness one should note also John Vanbrugh's *The Relapse* and George Farquhar's *The Beaux's Stratagem.* He was asked to write the odes for the 1698 and 1699 St. Cecilia ceremonies (both have disappeared). In 1700 he came in third, behind John Weldon [645] and John Eccles [617], in a competition for the best setting of Congreve's *The Judgement of Paris*—which tells us something about either Purcell's musical gifts or the acumen of the judges. When the theater yielded (temporarily) to the rage for Italian opera, Purcell gave the concert-promotion business a try, then settled down as organist of St. Andrew's, Holborn. On his death, his nephew Edward, Henry's son, applied for the job but was turned down. Daniel Purcell also left some anthems, odes, cantatas, sonatas, and keyboard pieces, none of them within shouting distance of his brother's efforts. RECORDINGS: Sonatas have been recorded by Jean-Pierre Rampal and Ferdinand Conrad.

[604] REBEL, Jean-Féry (Rə-bel', Zhàn-Fā-rē')
VIOLINIST, HARPSICHORDIST, CONDUCTOR
BORN: Paris, April 18, 1666
DIED: Paris, January 2, 1747

Jean-Féry Rebel represented the third of at least four generations of Rebel musicians. He had his earliest training with his father, Jean, a court singer, and became a violin prodigy, winning the attention and favor of Lully [517]. In 1699 he became first violin at the Opéra. A year later he went to Spain for the coronation of Louis XIV's grandson Philippe, Duke of Anjou, as Philip V of Spain, and his subsequent marriage to Marie Louise of Savoy. When he got back in 1705, he was also appointed to the 24 Violins of the King. He became harpsichordist at the Opéra in 1713, and its music master in 1716. The 1684 marriage of his sister, the singer and royal favorite Anne-Renée Rebel, to Delalande [576], who became Lord-

High-Everything-Else at court, did nothing to hurt the Rebel cause. On Delalande's death in 1726, Rebel assumed his title of Chamber Composer and his general supervisory functions. When, after a period of ineffectual management, the Concert Spirituel were put under the control of the Opéra in 1634, Rebel became their conductor. In 1740, his son François (1701–75)—who would succeed him—presented a retrospective concert of his father's music.

In 1703 Rebel's only opera, *Ulysse,* failed. He also wrote songs and collaborated with Delalande on a Tenebrae service, but he was at his best as an instrumental composer. He was a pioneer in the French sonata (both solo and trio), his efforts showing solid Lullyan grounding and Corellian feeling. (His contemporaries praised him for being able to temper Italian unruliness with French good taste.) But Rebel really came into his own late in life with his dance scores, which he called *symphonies* but which, instead of being cut-and-dried chains of dances, are more like modern ballets. His final work, *Les Éléments,* is really a sort of symphonic poem that bristles with (not always successful) pictorialism, notably the huge tone cluster that stands for Chaos.

RECORDINGS: *Les Éléments* has been recorded by Christopher Hogwood and others. A *Tombeau de Monsieur de Lully* is performed by the Cologne Musica Antiqua, and Edward Melkus has recorded a "character" sonata, *Les Cloches (The Bells).*

[605] BUTTSTÄDT, Johann Heinrich (Boot'-shtāt, Yō'-hàn Hīn'-rikh)
ORGANIST, TEACHER
BORN: Bindersleben, April 25, 1666
DIED: Erfurt, December 1, 1727

The son of a parson, Buttstädt (whose composer-grandson Franz spelled it Buttstett) was sent at twelve to study with Johann Pachelbel [567], organist of the Predigerkirche in nearby Erfurt. Three years later he also entered secondary school there. At eighteen he became organist of the Reglerkirche, and at twenty-one of the Kaufmannskirche; he taught Latin in the schools attached to both churches. In 1687 he also married. The bride was Martha Lämmerhirt, a member of a family that had intermarried with the Bachs beginning with old Johann [470] and that produced Johann Sebastian Bach's [684] mother. Martha was no mean producer herself—ten children in fifteen years. Pachelbel left town in 1690, and his successor, Nikolaus Vetter, a few months later, leaving the Predigerkirche organ (once Johann Bach's) to Buttstädt. In 1693 Buttstädt was named town councillor (for music, as one might now say) and remained chief musician in Erfurt for the rest of his life. He was extraordinarily fertile and announced his plan to publish hundreds of organ works of all sorts, but never got past Book I. He also left a couple of Masses written for the Erfurt Catholic congregation. He was a fine composer but a firm believer in tradition, a point over which he got into a paper war with that feisty revolutionary Johann Mattheson [668], which, of course, he lost. His most famous pupil was J. S. Bach's cousin Johann Gottfried Walther [680]. RECORDINGS: Some of his chorale preludes appear in recorded anthologies.

[606] ARIOSTI, Attilio Malachia (Ä-rē-ô′-stē, Ät-tēl′-yō Mà-lä-kē′-à)
KEYBOARD AND STRING PLAYER, MONK, SINGER
BORN: Bologna, November 5, 1666
DIED: England, c. 1729

Ariosti was already a skilled performer when he became, as Fra Ottavio, a Servite monk in 1688. (The Order of Santa Maria de' Servi, a mendicant order, had split off from the Augustinians in fourteenth-century Florence.) Attilio's brother, Giovanni Battista, also became his brother-in-faith as "Fra Odoardo" and published a method and collection of dances for the *timpano*, a simple glockenspiel. By the mid-1690s Attilio had got as far as the rank of deacon and was organist in the local Servite church. But apparently he found his cell too confining, for in 1696 he was at the court of Mantua, writing operas for the Venetian stage. The next year, on request, the duke shipped him to Berlin to work for the Electress of Brandenburg, Sophie Charlotte, with whom he seems to have become something more than a servant if less than a *Kapellmeister*. His operatic career continued to flourish, but religio-political pressure was brought to bear on him, and in 1703 the Servites ordered him home. On the way he stopped off at the Viennese court, made a powerful impression on Joseph I [651], and decided to ignore the summons. He produced more operatic works, lived scandalously, and got himself sent to Italy in 1707 as minister plenipotentiary. But in 1711 Joseph was struck down by a fatal attack of smallpox, and his relict had the musician unfrocked and kicked out of the empire. Then we lose track of him until 1716, when he crops up in London playing the viola d'amore (on which he was a virtuoso) between the acts

of Handel's [683] *Amadigi.* After that h appears sporadically in and around Londo until 1719, when he joined forces with Han del and Bononcini [620] in organizing th Royal Academy of Music, under whose au pices he produced several successful opera between 1722 and 1727. Deciding to cash in on his popularity, he published in 1724 a collection of cantatas and sonatas ("lessons") for the viola d'amore by subscription, dedicating it to the king, George I, brother of his Berlin patroness. The subscription list contained the name of anyone who was anyone in British royal and noble circles, though it has been said that merely asking an important person to subscribe was enough to permit Ariosti to add his name. But the public, as publics will do, proved fickle. His last opera, *Teuzzone*, was a failure, and he was quickly forgotten. Presumably he died in London, but all we know is that he was noted as deceased by late summer 1729.

In the spirit of his times, Ariosti was primarily a vocal composer—about 20 operas, several oratorios, and many cantatas—but these are little known today. Many of the operas are lost, and those from the London period survive mostly in collections of hit tunes, but they are highly spoken of, especially for their use of orchestra. The viola d'amore lessons, as arranged for cello or viola, are, however, well known and much admired. Recently 57 other pieces for the instrument have been discovered in manuscript.

RECORDINGS: There is an integral recording on the viola d'amore by Nane Calabrese. There are also recordings of cantatas by Charlotte Lehmann.

[607] REICHE, Johann Gottfried (Rī′-khə, Yō′-hàn Got′-frēd)
TRUMPETER
BORN: Weissenfels, February 5, 1667
DIED: Leipzig, October 6, 1734

Reiche migrated to Leipzig when he was about to attain his majority, and apprenticed himself to the *Stadtpfeiffer* to learn the high brasses. He learned them well enough to be admitted to guild membership in 1700, to be declared a master in 1707, and named head of the guild in 1719. When Sebastian Bach [684] arrived four years later, he was impressed with Reiche's musicianship and virtuosity, and it was for him that he wrote all those high trumpet parts. Perhaps in the end he demanded too much from him, for Reiche, at sixty-seven, literally blew himself out playing Cantata No. 215 for the anniversary of August III's elevation to the throne of Poland. (It is said that the thick smoke from the torches contributed to his death.) Reiche left a collection of *24 Neue Quatricinia* for trumpet and four trombones, which suggest that trumpeters could play higher notes and longer phrases than they could in Pezel's [527] time. RECORDINGS: A few of the *24 Neue Quatricinia* have been recorded by brasses of the Boston Symphony under Richard Burgin.

[608] **MONTÉCLAIR, Michel Pignolet de** (Mon-tä-clâr', Mē-shel' Pēn-yō-lä' də)
CONTRABASSIST, TEACHER, THEORIST
BORN: Andelot, December 4, 1667
DIED: Aumont, September 22, 1737

The seventh and last child of a Lorrainese weaver, Adrien Pignolet, young Michel got his training as a chorister at the cathedral in nearby Langres. We have his word that he then took service with "le Prince de Vaudémont" (presumably Charles, Duke of Lorraine) and traveled to Italy with him as his music master, but otherwise we know very little of his career before 1700. He seems to have settled in Paris in 1687 and there became "de Montéclair," a name borrowed from a fortress in Andelot. By 1699 he was playing at the Opéra—the first to use the newfangled string contrabass. He became widely known as a teacher, and his writings suggest that he was a good one. In 1709 he published his *Nouvelle méthode pour apprendre la musique* and, a couple of years later, one of the first violin methods. In 1716 the Opéra produced his first stage work, *Les Festes d'été (Summer Festivals),* one of the better opera-ballets. In 1721 he and a nephew, François Boivin, opened a music store in Paris, but in 1728 Montéclair got out of what eventually became a thriving business. His second and last stage work, *David et Jonathan,* was successfully produced in 1732. One of the more original French operas between Lully [517] and Rameau [675], it continued to play for thirty years. It was also the first biblical work to be staged at the Opéra and probably the first real opera of the kind to appear in Paris. It struck some as sacrilegious, including the Archbishop of Paris, who tried to get it banned.

Montéclair wrote *finis* to his teaching career with two more books. One was a method for teaching (in his words) children and even persons of more advanced age. The other was a four-volume summation of his musical knowledge, *Principes de musique,* in 1736, still a valuable reference for the musical thought and practice of the day. A year after it came out, Montéclair was pensioned off, and he died a little over two months later.

Little of Montéclair's religious music (some of it very ambitious) remains. Of his instrumental works, some *concerts* for one and two flutes and 3 orchestral suites *(Sérénades)* survive, the latter notable for sensitivity to mood and color and for clever instrumentation. Montéclair published several collections of *airs sérieux* and of *brunettes* (pastoral love songs), some of them arranged in dramatic sequences. Perhaps best of all are the *cantates* (3 volumes, 1709–28), marked by melodic inventiveness, harmonic acumen, and effective use of obbligato instruments. (We may regret the loss of "100 Minuets Old and New.") Obviously a composer of stature, and an influence on Rameau, Montéclair might be well worth reviving.

RECORDINGS: Little has appeared on records—a Christmas motet from Louis Frémaux, the *cantate Retour de la paix* from Claudie Sanéva, and a couple of *airs* from Edith Selig about sum it up.

[609] **ERNST LUDWIG, Landgraf von Hesse-Darmstadt** (Ărnst Lōōd'-vikh)
LUTENIST
BORN: Gotha, December 15, 1667
DIED: Jägersburg, November 12, 1739

In his latter years Ernst Ludwig made Darmstadt an important musical center— though one wonders what he would have thought of the avant-garde festivals that have made its name a byword in recent years. The third of the four sons of Ludwig VI (his mother was Elisabeth Dorothea of Saxe-Gotha), he succeeded to the title at the age of eleven, his elder brothers having died. He got his musical training from Kapellmeister Wolfgang Karl Briegel, his mother's old teacher, and studied lute with the court valet Johann Valentin Strobel, whose father and grandfather had been famous lutenists. The mandatory grand tour took the young Landgraf to Paris, where he saw the operas of Lully [517]—he produced *Acis et Galatée* back at Darmstadt in 1687 to mark his own wedding to Dorothea Charlotte of Brandenburg-Ansbach—and became a passionate opera buff. For the next several years the War of the Augsburg League, which forced the court to move to Giessen until 1694, put a crimp in his musical plans. After that he spent several more years traveling in Europe to see how it should be done. In 1709 he was ready. He hired Christoph Graupner [673], whom he had gotten to know in Hamburg, as *Kapellmeister*, rebuilt the opera house (previously destroyed by the French), hired a company of musicians, and from then on it was music, music, music!—mostly of the home-baked variety, including some by the Landgraf. (Sad to say, Ernst Ludwig overdid it and had to close the opera in 1719, but the court concerts went on.) Despite his extravagance, he was a better ruler than most: he built homes for orphans, did other charitable work, and opened his gates to religious refugees from all over. His other passion was hunting, and he breathed his last in one of his hunting lodges. He left some orchestral music for one of Graupner's operas, and some quite competent orchestral suites in the Germanized Lullyan mode. RECORDINGS: One of the orchestral suites has been recorded by Dietfried Bernet.

[610] JACQUET DE LA GUERRE, Elisabeth-Claude (Zhà-kā' də là Gâr, E-lês-à-bet' Klōd)
HARPSICHORDIST
BORN: Paris, c. 1667
DIED: Paris, June 27, 1729

There were women composers before Elisabeth Jacquet, but they have suffered general phonographic neglect and so do not appear in these pages. There is, however, nothing of the dog-walking-on-its-hinder-legs about Mademoiselle de la Guerre, as she was known ("Madame" being reserved at court for noble ladies). Member of a widespread family of harpsichord makers and musicians, daughter of the organist Claude Jacquet and sister of another, Pierre, she was a female Mozart at the age of five, playing and singing at sight, it was said, anything set before her. Presented at court, where she was known as *la petite merveille* (the small wonder), she was taken under the wing of Louis XIV himself, and Madame de Montespan, his morganatic wife, saw to it that she had a thorough education. When she was seventeen or eighteen, she married Marin de la Guerre, later organist at Ste. Chapelle and son of Michel de la Guerre, whose 1655 *La Triomphe de l'amour* has been called the first French opera. Elisabeth delighted the king with her 1685 ballet *Les Jeux en honneur de la victoire (The Games in Honor of Victory*—now lost), but her only opera, *Céphale et Procris,* produced nine years later, was not a hit. After her husband died in 1707 (their only child had preceded him), Mademoiselle de la Guerre turned to composition and to presenting concerts at her home. That year she published a second volume of exquisite and original keyboard pieces (the first one has vanished) and a set of 6 violin sonatas. These were followed by several collections of *cantates*—some on Old Testament themes; others drawn, with a sense of humor, from mythology. She also wrote a number of songs. In 1717 she moved to the parish of St. Eustache and went into virtually total retirement, emerging only to write a Te Deum (lost) in 1721 on the occasion of the young king's recovery from smallpox. She was buried in the parish church. RECORDINGS: Thurston Dart, Laurence Boulay, and a few others have recorded some of the keyboard pieces and Ettel Sussman an aria from *Céphale et Procris.* Jacques Somary has recorded two cantatas: *Samson* and *Le Sommeil d'Ulisse.*

[611] PEPUSCH, John Christopher (Pā'-poosh, Jon Kris'-to-fer)
VIOLIST, KEYBOARDIST, SCHOLAR
BORN: Berlin, 1667
DIED: London, July 20, 1752

Pepusch, known today chiefly for a work that he merely arranged, has long suffered a bad press because he was an intellectual and a thirster after knowledge. He was, of course, not always "John Christopher"; the son of a Lutheran pastor in Berlin, he was baptized Johann Christoph. A bright child, he had music lessons with unknowns named Klingenberg and Grosse but was largely self-taught—as he was in ancient Greek, which he learned in order to acquaint himself with classical theory. At fourteen he was employed by Elector Frederick William of Brandenburg, the Prussian ruler. In 1688 Frederick William was succeeded as elector by Frederick III, one of those rulers who helped give "Prussian" the connotation it has today. Pepusch was not disinclined to the conservative, but when, c. 1697, Frederick III had one of his officers decapitated without trial before the court assembled to impress on him the need for choosing one's words wisely, Pepusch decided things had gone too far and ran away at the first opportunity—or so the story goes. (Soon thereafter, in 1701, Frederick III became King Frederick I of Prussia.) Pepusch spent some time in Holland, then made his way to London (before 1704), where he became employed as violist and harpsichordist at Drury Lane Theatre and adopted the name of John Christopher. He was involved in stage productions there as early as 1707 and in the middle of the next decade wrote several successful masques for the theater. Around 1710, having continued to broaden and deepen his learning, he joined with several others, including violinist Henry Needler, oboist John Ernest Galliard (like himself, German-born), and the Royal Organ Tuner Bernard Gates, to found the Academy of Antient Musick, which—unusual for the era—gave concerts of old music. His fame brought him a D.Mus. from Oxford in 1713, the university perhaps overlooking the fact that his antiquarian inclinations led him to insist on the long-outmoded practice of sight-reading according to the hexachord (c-d-e-f-g-a, omitting the seventh step!). Before the decade was out, he had been appointed music director to the Duke of Chandos at Cannons—and thus, for a time, Handel's [683] superior. In the early 1720s he married the Drury Lane soprano Marguerite de l'Epine, who brought him affluence and gave him a son in 1724. He is said to have lost much of his wife's money shortly afterward in a scheme of Bishop George Berkeley, the eminent philosopher, to found a college in Bermuda. Supposedly Pepusch was shipwrecked on the way there. But the year given is 1724, and Berkeley did not get going until 1728, when he made his way to Rhode Island and spent three years there.

Whatever happened, it is a sure thing that Pepusch did not sail in 1728, for that was the year of *The Beggar's Opera*. Designed as a satire on both the politics of the day and the craze for Italian opera (with the attendant social phenomena), it was conceived by the poet John Gay and backed by the ex-dancer John Rich. In form the work was merely an extension of the musicals ("operas") popular in the English theater since the Restoration, but Gay's story had to do with a new subject, life in the London underworld, and the music was drawn from the popular songs of the day. These Pepusch arranged, and added a Lullyan overture, in part based on a song "Walpole the Happy Clown," aimed at the prime minister. The work was a wild success, making—as an old saw has it—"Gay rich and Rich gay." But the lord chamberlain, presumably inspired by the P.M., banned the sequel *Polly*, which did not get played for fifty years. *The Beggar's Opera* inaugurated a growing taste for "ballad opera," as the popular genre was called, but the old story that Handel and the Italians were crushed out of existence by it is demonstrably false.

Pepusch's career at Cannons ended about 1730 because of an austerity program there, and in 1735 he moved to a house in Fetter Lane and opened a music school for boys under the auspices of his sometime academy. Two years later he was appointed organist at the Charterhouse, the famous charity school. (He was now seventy.) Marguerite Pepusch died in 1746—their son had died some years before—and in that same year the old doctor was initiated into the Royal Society, on which occasion he read a learned paper on the types of music known to the ancients. He died at eighty-five, leaving many pupils—William Boyce [787] was one—and an impressive library that included the *Fitzwilliam Virginal Book*.

There was obviously something very thorough and methodical about Pepusch, and he is usually thought of as a pedant, largely thanks to his younger contemporary Charles Burney, who, noting that another composer had more system and less originality than anyone he could think of, added "always excepting Dr. Pepusch." Besides his theatrical works, he left odes, cantatas, anthems, sonatas, and concerti.

RECORDINGS: Recordings of some of the sonatas—e.g., an LP by flutist Maxence Larrieu—show them to be far less dreadful than reputed, and Pepusch's admirers think some of the cantatas delightful. Many recordings of *The Beggar's Opera* are in updated versions, though those by Denis Stevens and Max Goberman adhere to the antient musick.

[612] GORCZYCKI, Grzegorz Gerwazy
(Gôr-chits′-kĕ, G'zhe′-gōzh Ger-và′-zĕ)
PRIEST, TEACHER, CHOIR DIRECTOR
BORN: Bytom, c. 1667
DIED: Cracow, April 30, 1734

Born about fifty miles northwest of Cracow, in a town sometimes known as Beuthen, Gorczycki studied theology in Vienna and Prague, acquired a doctorate, and was ordained in Cracow in 1692, at which time he was cited for his musical attainments. He was then appointed rector to the school run by the Missionary Priests in Chelmno (about seventy miles south of Danzig), where he taught rhetoric and poetics and directed the chapel choir. After two years, however, he returned to the capital, and two years later succeeded Sebastian Jaroszewicz as director of the choir at Wawel Cathedral. During his thirty-six years there he also held other posts, both musical and priestly, at other local churches. The accounts of his death pose a medical puzzle. It is agreed that he caught cold while conducting the music for the coronation of the Saxon Elector August III as King of Poland, on January 17, 1734. But one story has him dying of tuberculosis at the end of April, an uncommonly rapid progression; and another says that he fought pneumonia for nearly four months, which seems highly unusual. However, it is obvious that he died of respiratory trouble. All his surviving music is for the church, and some of that is fragmentary. Regarded as the most important Polish composer of his generation, he wrote chiefly in a sort of neo-Palestrinan *a cappella* style, but also used a *concertato* approach which, in opposing a small body of singers to the full choir, seems to reflect the *concerto grosso* rather than the quasi-operatic coloration then taking hold elsewhere in Europe. RECORDINGS: Stanisław Galonski has recorded the Compline service, or *Completorium*, and Edmund Kajdasz the *Easter Mass.*

[613] LOTTI, Antonio (Lot'-tē, Àn-tōn'-yō)
ORGANIST, CHOIRMASTER, TEACHER
BORN: c. 1667
DIED: Venice, January 5, 1740

Matteo Lotti, Antonio's father, was *Kapellmeister* at the ducal court of Hanover in the early 1670s and possibly before, though the son is said to have been Venetian-born. At any rate, Antonio was in Venice from his middle teens, studying with Giovanni Legrenzi **[503]**, and joined the Venetian chapter of the Accademia di Santa Cecilia when it was inaugurated in 1687 at St. Mark's. Shortly afterward he was taken into the choir as a countertenor. To his singing duties were added those of substitute second organist in 1690, at a salary of 130 ducats a year. (One must remember that the ducat went farther then than now.) Two years later he was named number-two organist and had his first opera, *Il Trionfo dell'innocenza*, produced at the Teatro Sant' Angelo. Venetian theatergoers were to hear at least eighteen more in the next two decades. In 1704 he became the basilica's first organist, after which his upward progress there hit a snag. It must have been about this time that he married a well-to-do singer, Santa Scarabelli Stella. She brought a daughter with her, but the couple had no children of their own.

In 1712 Frederick Augustus, future Elector of Saxony, visited Venice, heard some of Lotti's music, took a great fancy to it, and eventually, with the promise of a splendid salary, persuaded him to bring a company of his own selection to Dresden and put on

some of his operas. In 1717 the composer got a leave from St. Mark's and set out with his wife and party for Saxony. Over the next two years he wrote and produced three operas, plus an entertainment for his patron's wedding. But by 1719 the authorities were demanding he get back to Venice or forfeit his job. The elector gave him a coach and four in which to make the trip. Lotti kept the coach as a valued memento and willed it to Santa. He never left Venice again.

For a time in the 1720s he taught the girls to sing at the Ospedale degli Incurabili. Around 1732 he had to take on some of the duties of *maestro di cappella* at St. Mark's because the incumbent, Antonio Biffi, was growing old and feeble. Biffi passed on in 1733. Lotti tried out for the vacancy, as did Antonio Pollarolo (1680–1746), son of Carlo Francesco **[569]**, and the Neapolitan opera composer Nicola Porpora **[690]**, who had settled in Venice. The vote was split, and Lotti was named director *pro tem,* until the mess could be straightened out. It wasn't for three years, during which time Porpora withdrew and was replaced by Giovanni Porta, later court *Kapellmeister* at Munich. In 1737 Lotti was finally declared the winner. He died of dropsy three years later.

Lotti represented a curious mixture of the old and the new. As church musician, he was a rigorous but brilliant contrapuntist. (His much admired *Miserere* was a standard part of the St. Mark repertoire for nearly a century.) In line with this musical puritanism, he ignored the orchestra in favor of organ accompaniments. At the same time, he was a brilliant and often daring harmonist and a dramatic composer in the line from Monteverdi **[333]** through Cavalli **[464]** and Legrenzi **[503]**. Among his pupils were Baldassare Galuppi **[768]** and Benedetto Marcello **[689]**. He was admired at first hand by Johann Adolf Hasse **[736]** and Handel **[683]**, and at a distance by Johann Sebastian Bach **[684]**. His best-known work is an aria "Pur dicesti" from an operatic pastiche, *Arminio.* RECORDINGS: The aria from *Arminio* has been frequently recorded. There are also a number of recordings of one or another of two *Crucifixus* settings from as many *Credos,* and at least one (an old one by the Harvard Glee Club) of the famous *Miserere,* but not much else.

[614] GILLES, Jean (Zhēlz, Zhàn)
CHOIRMASTER, CLERIC
BORN: Tarascon, January 8, 1668
DIED: Toulouse, February 5, 1705

The penalty for being Provençal and remaining provincial in the Sun King's day was obscurity. Until recently, few reference works have taken note of Jean Gilles, the son of a proletarian of Tarascon, a city the novelist Daudet later established as the Peoria of France. Young Gilles sang there at the church of Ste. Marthe and then, like so many of his southern contemporaries, moved on to St. Sauveur in Aix to study with Guillaume Poitevin [545]. At that time, 1679, he was described as frail and sickly. In 1688 he became Poitevin's assistant, but a year later he was so ill that his mother (listed as Madame Conchone on his birth certificate) had to be summoned to care for him. By 1693 he was well enough to succeed Poitevin, but after two years went AWOL to become master of music at Agde Cathedral. There he made such an impression on the Bishop of Rieux with one of his psalm settings that he apparently had the recently appointed Michel Farinel ousted from his post at St. Etienne in Toulouse to make way for Gilles, who was installed there by the end of 1697. There he performed his *Te Deum* for the Peace of Ryswick, which ended the War of the Grand Alliance; legend says that he wrote the work in a single night. Meanwhile his health continued to worsen, and he was apparently unable to accept a 1701 offer to head the *maîtrise* to Notre Dame des Doms in Avignon. His last known composition was a *Requiem*, commissioned by two local politicians in memory of a relative. But they balked at the price, and it was first heard at Gilles's own funeral a few months later. Fifty years afterwards it was suddenly the hottest requiem in France, and was played at the funerals of Rameau and Louis XV. If Gilles wrote in the approved (sacred) forms of the day (mostly big and little motets), he did not necessarily adhere to the approved style. His music is personal, often intimate, and splashed with the folk idiom of the Midi. RECORDINGS: Louis Martini and Louis Frémaux have recorded the *Requiem,* Laurence Boulay the *Te Deum,* and Georges Durans 3 motet-psalms.

[615] GASPARINI, Francesco (Gàs-pà-rē'-nē, Fràn-chās'-kō)
TEACHER, CHOIRMASTER, THEORIST
BORN: Camaiore, March 5, 1668
DIED: Rome, March 22, 1727

Except that he was born in a village near Lucca, nothing is known of Gasparini's parentage or childhood. He was apparently gifted, for he was made a member of the Accademia Filarmonica in Bologna when he was seventeen and at around the same time was studying with Legrenzi [503] in Venice. He moved on to Rome, where he remained for some years—doing what, is uncertain. Evidently he quickly made his mark, for he came to know Corelli [565], Pasquini [524], and Alessandro Scarlatti [583], became a member of the Accademia di Santa Cecilia in 1689, and produced his first opera, *Il Roderico,* at the Teatro Pace five years later. In 1701 he returned to Venice as chorus master (i.e., conservatory director) at the Ospedale della Pietà, where he soon became known not only as a superb administrator—Vivaldi [650] was on his staff—but as a fertile and successful composer of operas. An oft-repeated tale to the contrary, Gasparini was not in London during his period of employment in Venice. That was a violinist named Gasparo Visconti, known by the diminutive of his first name. But in 1713 Gasparini got a six-month leave of absence, took off for Rome, and stayed permanently. He was named *maestro* at San Lorenzo in Lucina in 1717 and eight years later at San Giovanni Laterano. But by then he was too ill to take up his duties and died less than two years afterward. He was married and had a daughter who was once engaged to the librettist Pietro Antonio Trapassi, who wrote as "Pietro Metastasio." Among his pupils were Benedetto Marcello [689], with whom he carried on a lifelong correspondence, Domenico Scarlatti [687], and Joachim Quantz [730]. In 1708 Gasparini published a method for realizing continuo parts for harpsichordists. Gasparini was strictly a vocal composer. Besides more than 60 operas (performed all over Italy), he wrote Masses, motets, oratorios, cantatas, and duets. Now forgotten, they were much admired in their time. Recordings offer only an aria or two (e.g., one by Peter Schreier).

[616] COUPERIN, François, Le Grand (Kōō-per-àn', Fràn-swà')
KEYBOARDIST
BORN: Paris, November 10, 1668
DIED: Paris, September 11, 1733

The "great" Couperin was the son of Charles Couperin *cadet,* the youngest brother of Louis Couperin [504] and his successor in 1661 at the organ of St. Gervais. (For how the *frères* Couperin came to Paris, see 463). Two months later he married Marie Guérin, daughter of a barber attached to the Royal Stables. François was their only child. When he was eleven, his father (age forty) died. François was already sufficiently skilled to be his successor, but the church board asked Delalande [576] to sit in for him until he had acquired more polish and at least seven more years. François continued to study under the court organist Jacques Thomelin, and, Delalande having moved on, received his appointment a year ahead of schedule. He held it for the rest of his life.

In 1689 Couperin married a lady called Marie-Anne Ansault, of whom we know little save that she bore him four children, two of each sex. The second daughter, Marguerite-Antoinette (1705–78), carried on the family tradition and was the first woman to hold the title of Clavecinist-in-Ordinary at the French court. In 1690, the king, at Delalande's behest, gave Couperin a permit to print and sell his two organ Masses (one "for the parishes," the other "for the convents"). Unfortunately Couperin could not afford the costs, and "publication" amounted to, at most, a few handwritten copies. About the same time, he began work on a set of six trio-sonatas in homage to those of Corelli [565]. (Some of them were first performed as by a fictitious Italian, whose name was an anagram of Couperin's.) In 1693 he succeeded his fatherly mentor Thomelin as one of the four court organists, the others being Nivers [518], Lebègue [515], and Jean-Baptiste Buterne; their duties were those of composers and directors more than of performers. Shortly afterward he became music master to the royal children, which "honest employment" (a provision made by the king) allowed Couperin to buy himself a patent of nobility in 1696. He was already known as the "Sieur de Crouilly" and, especially after being named a knight of the Lateran Order in 1702, he took to signing himself "le Chevalier Couperin." In 1697 he celebrated his good fortune by moving from the organist's apartment that overlooked the cemetery to one on the rue St. François.

By the turn of the century, Couperin had established himself as a musical power in everything but name (Delalande having hogged all the good appointments) and people were speaking of him as "le grand Couperin," which, being inclined to irony, he didn't seem to mind. He was turning out music for the Royal Chapel and for the Sunday concerts of the Royal Chamber, where he was often assisted by Antoine Forqueray [635], Jean-Féry Rebel [604], and by his own niece (Uncle François's girl), the remarkable soprano-clavecinist Marguerite-Louise Couperin. Having prospered, he took out a second publishing privilege in

1713 and brought out his first book of *Pièces de clavecin*. This was followed by the *Leçons de ténèbres*, 1714; his clavecin method *L'Art de toucher le clavecin*, 1716; and the second volume of keyboard pieces, 1717. In the last year he was named the official successor to the increasingly myopic Jean-Henri d'Anglebert, royal Clavecinist-in-Ordinary, whose duties he had been performing for more than a decade (see 520). The third clavecin book appeared in 1722 and included, as a second part, the four *Concerts royaux* which, said the composer, could be played with or without melody and/or bass instruments. In 1724 the Couperins, having made several shifts, settled in a mansion on the rue Neuve des Bons-Enfants (New Street of the Good Fellows). François, having inherited his family's inferior genes, was slowly failing; but, inspired by the reception of the first four, he brought out that year ten more "royal concertos" under the title of *Les Goûts Réunis (The Tastes* [French and Italian] *Reconciled)*. The last of these was *La Parnasse, ou l'apothéose de Corelli,* which, to keep things in balance, Couperin followed the next year with an *Apothéose de Lully.* In 1726 he got out three of his early trio sonatas, polished them up, added one more, appended a French dance suite to each, and published them as *Les Nations* (the nations being French, Spanish, Imperial, and Piedmontese). His final publications were the two suites for viols of 1728 and the fourth book of *Pièces de clavecin,* 1730. In the preface to the latter, Couperin wrote that he was too ill to go on and that year turned over his chapel post to one Guillaume Marchand and the expectation of his place in the King's Chamber—*Chambre du Roi* (d'Anglebert was still on the payroll)—to his daughter. She inherited it finally in 1737, but had to give it up on account of poor health four years later. Couperin willed that his family collect and publish his other music, but for some reason they did not. Apart from the works in the archives of the Royal Chapel, a few songs and the remaining early sonatas, it has all vanished. Couperin's oldest daughter became a nun and the boys died young, in the family tradition. Uncle François's heirs, who included at least five musicians of note, survived for four generations, dying out with the poverty-stricken Céleste-Thérèse in 1860. (It is said that J. S. Bach's [684] letters to Couperin were used by Madame Couperin to seal jam jars—or perhaps it was Frau Bach who used Couperin's.)

Couperin's extant output is not large—apart from the 231 short harpsichord pieces, it consists of 28 chamber works, about 30 religious compositions (mostly of small dimensions), and a few songs and other minor vocal pieces. Yet he is a pivotal figure in the history of French music—certainly the greatest composer between Lully [517] and Rameau [675], and arguably a giant in any terms. His triumph, as with so many artistic giants, was chiefly one of synthesis.

For some time there had been an increasing coterie of French lovers of Italian music, and Couperin was not the first to try to reconcile the tastes (e.g., see 544, 584, and 599). The process by which he effected the reconciliation, however, was not merely one of imitation, no rude forcing together of characteristics, no pointed setting off of Italian emotionalism against Gallic reserve. With uncanny prescience, Couperin chose precisely the trait that functioned perfectly and meaningfully in the place where he used it —no ornament where the added glint of color was extraneous, no chromaticism where passion or pain was not implied. Indeed it is this exquisite rightness, coupled with an impeccable sense of balance, that is the hallmark of Couperin's style. One finds it as early as the organ Masses (once credited to the elder François on the grounds that no one so young could have written them). Here plainsong fantasias embellished with French graces rub elbows with the *air de cour,* the legacy of the lutenists, the ballet, and the opera (from both sides of the Alps)—but never is the result frivolous or cheap. One finds much the same thing in the church music, together with a luminous transparency of texture. (Only three pieces call for choir—sparingly used—and only three for orchestra. The rest are, it might be said, vocal approximations of the sonata concept.)

But Couperin's chief fame lies—and justly!—in the harpsichord pieces. All 4 books presented them arranged in *ordres* (suites) according to key. In the first collection, these seem to be no more than loose pieces conveniently packaged, but later on each suite is an entity with its own color and mood. The roots of this music are easy to see: dances, pastoral songs, Corellian movements, programmatic or characteristic lute pieces, *tombeaux.* What defies description is the magic. It has been said that the *Pièces de clavecin* are Couperin's world in sonic microcosm. But if that microcosm includes such obvious and homely things as lovesick nightingales and chiming alarm clocks, it also includes impressions, essences, and evocations. Couperin's adaptation of the harpsichord to a means of expressing his own personal vision has been likened to Claude Debussy's [1547] of the

piano, and one may properly say that the instrument came of age here.

RECORDINGS: An integral recording of the clavecin music by Ruggero Gerlin has been superseded by a more musicologically accurate and more inspired one by his pupil Kenneth Gilbert. The organ Masses have been recorded in tandem by Marie-Claire Alain, Michel Chapuis, Pierre Cochereau, and Robert Noehren, and individually by several others. There is a recording of the complete *Concerts royaux* and the complete *Nouveaux Concerts* on Deutsche Grammophon Archiv, and many pieces have been done individually in various readings. There are recordings of *Les Nations* by the Alarius Ensemble, Thurston Dart, Jean-François Paillard, and the Quadro Amsterdam, and there are several recordings of the *apothéoses.* There are also several of the *Leçons de ténèbres* and an anthology of motets by Anthony Lewis.

[617] ECCLES, John (Ek′-kels, Jon)
COURT MUSICIAN
BORN: c. 1668
DIED: Hampton Wick, January 12, 1735

There were several musical Eccles (or Eagles) active in London in the late seventeenth and early eighteenth centuries (see 644), and their interrelationships have not yet been sorted out. John was once thought to have been the child of the eccentric Quaker musician Solomon Eccles (d. 1682), but he is now known to have been the only son of the elder Henry Eccles, a court violinist who died in 1711. A good deal of breath and paper was once wasted proving that because he wrote music for plays premiered c. 1681, John was either a prodigy or was born much earlier than the date given above. It turned out that he wrote the music all right but for later revivals. He seems to have begun his career at Drury Lane Theatre, writing music for the singing debut of the popular actress Anne Bracegirdle (c. 1674–1748). Her success was so great that she would permit no one else to write for her, providing Eccles with a marvelous foot in the door.

Over the next thirteen years, Eccles wrote music for more than sixty plays, including Congreve's *Love for Love* and *The Way of the World,* George Etherege's *The Man of Mode,* Nicholas Rowe's *The Fair Penitent* (which introduced "gay Lothario"), and works by John Dryden and Thomas Otway. In 1694 Eccles was also made an unpaid Musician-in-Ordinary to King William and was stepped up to a paying post two years

later. Meanwhile there had been an upheaval at Drury Lane in 1695. The actors
had struck against John Rich (see 611), and
had set themselves up at Lincoln's Inn
Fields. There Eccles was named musical director, and there, mostly for his protégée,
he produced most of his several masques
and operatic works. In 1700 he was named
Music Master at court and that same year
entered a contest for the best setting of Congreve's masque *The Judgement of Paris,*
along with three others; he came in second
to John Weldon [645]. The next year he and
Congreve delivered the annual St. Cecilia
ode, and Eccles wrote several other occasional odes for the court. Soon afterward
the Italian opera began seriously to threaten
the native musical theater. Eccles countered
with an opera of his own, *The British En-
chanters,* and then, more ambitiously, set
Congreve's *Semele* to music. But there were
no takers and, seeing his sun was set, Eccles
retired up the Thames to indulge his passion
for fishing. He died some seventeen years
later, leaving his three daughters a shilling
apiece. Eccles is regarded as the best and
last of the post-Purcell theater composers,
and his songs are highly regarded.
RECORDINGS: So far little has been recorded, although there is at least one song
by Alfred Deller.

[618] LÓPEZ, Miguel (Lō-páth', Mē-
      hwel')
MONK, ORGANIST, CHOIRMASTER,
      WRITER
BORN: Villarroya de la Sierra, February
      1, 1669
DIED: Zaragoza, 1723

At the age of nine or so López came from
his native hill country southwest of Zaragoza to Catalonia as a choirboy at the Benedictine monastery of Montserrat, where he
was taught by Cererols [491]. He joined the
order in 1684 and in 1689 went to Madrid,
where he served as organist in the monastery of San Martín and studied theology. He
returned to Montserrat in 1696 as *maestro
de capilla,* left to assume the post of organist
in the monastery at Valladolid, and came
back to resume his job ten years later. In
1722 he was delegated to the monastery at
Alcañiz, and died while on a visit to Zaragoza a year later. A writer, theorist, and
polemicist, he left a manuscript history of
Montserrat and a large collection of his religious music, *villancicos,* and organ pieces.
The sacred works show him a rather sobersided polyphonist aware of the current
trends. He is said to have been the first

Montserrat composer to have called for
orchestral parts; moreover, his are independent parts, not doublings. RECORDINGS:
The Montserrat Choir under Ireneu Segarra
has recorded an LP that surveys his work.

[619] MARCHAND, Louis (Mâr-shàn',
      Lōō-ē')
KEYBOARDIST, TEACHER
BORN: Lyons, February 2, 1669
DIED: Paris, February 17, 1732

Louis Marchand obviously lived a checkered life, but not so checkered as the various
hoary anecdotes about him would have it.
He seems to have been unrelated to the family of musical Marchands several of whom
held places in the royal court of Louis XIV
in his day (see 616). He was the son and
pupil of a Lyons organist, Jean Marchand,
and allegedly precocious, but it is doubtful
that he became organist at Nevers Cathedral at fourteen and quite untrue that he
took a similar post at Auxerre ten years
later. Paris archives show that in 1689 he
married (to his sorrow) a Mademoiselle
Marie Angélique Denis there. Two years
later he was organist for the Jesuits (who
did *not* rescue him from starvation in the
streets), and by 1703 he was also playing at
St. Bénoit, St. Honoré, and the church of
the Cordeliers (Franciscans). Meanwhile his
personal life had gone on the rocks. He was
ruthless in various intrigues (regularly unsuccessful) against his colleagues (see 586);
he drank, wenched, and beat his wife, who
left him in 1701. But his playing was of such
high repute that in 1708 he was selected to
replace Nivers [518] as one of the Royal
Chapel organists without his having to compete for the honor. Meanwhile his wife was
hounding him for money and eventually appealed to the king, who—so the story goes
—directed that half Marchand's salary be
directed to her. (This supposedly took place
in 1713). The next time he played a chapel
service, Marchand walked out in the middle, saying that Mademoiselle Marchand
could damn well finish it, or words to that
effect. The king is said to have ordered him
to leave the country. Marchand left and
went on a tour of the Germanies, where he
was made much of. In the autumn of 1717 he
and J. S. Bach [684] arrived in Dresden at
the same time, and it occurred to someone
that a playoff between the two great organists might prove interesting. Both agreed to
it, but when the time for the duel rolled
around, Marchand failed to show up, and it
was learned that he had left town around
daybreak that morning. Or so the German

accounts have it. The French ignore the whole thing, noting only that Marchand was suddenly overwhelmed by homesickness and hurried back to France. (Louis XIV was dead by that time.) He returned to his job at the Cordeliers and to teaching. (He taught organ to Daquin [717].) As a performer, he enjoyed the kind of popularity one connects with nineteenth-century virtuosi and today's rock stars.

Marchand left his manuscripts to his daughter Françoise, and what she did with them heaven only knows. He published 2 harpsichord suites, typical of their time; someone else (perhaps Françoise) published 12 organ pieces, forty-two other instrumental pieces, a cantata, 3 *cantiques spirituels*, and some songs survive in manuscript. The organ music fails to show the vaunted virtuosity of its composer, which was probably a matter of improvisation anyway. It also shows a decline—what with references to secular and popular elements—from the high-minded organ music of a generation earlier. At the same time, it is emotional, often to the point of anguish, and contains harmonic sequences that would have been deemed advanced 150 years later.

RECORDINGS: Various samples have been recorded—e.g., by Marie-Claire Alain and Michel Chapuis.

[620] BONONCINI, Giovanni (Bō-non-chē′-nē, Jō-vàn′-nē)
CELLIST
BORN: Modena, July 18, 1670
DIED: Vienna, July 9, 1747

Those versed in basic musical history may recall that Handel's [683] sometime London rival was Bononcini, but faced with the fact that there were several composers of that name, they will probably be hard put to say which it was. The problem is exacerbated by a long-standing confusion and misapprehension of Christian names and careless attribution of Bononcini compositions.

The famous Bononcini—he of the rivalry —was baptized simply "Giovanni," though for ages writers have insisted on calling him Giovanni Battista. He was a son of the former Anna Maria Prezii and her husband, Giovanni Maria Bononcini (1642–78), composer, violinist, and *maestro di cappella* of Modena Cathedral. He had a younger brother, a cellist and composer named Antonio Maria (1677–1726). When Giovanni was six, his mother died, and his father, very soon afterward, married again. Giovanni Maria died a year later, and an hour after he breathed his last, his wife bore a son

named Giovanni Maria but called "Angelo." Angelo became a violinist and composer too. (It should also be noted that Antonio Maria sometimes appears as "Marc′ Antonio.")

Doubts have been voiced about the correctness of Giovanni's birth date, on the grounds that he would have been a mere fifteen when he published his first book of trio sonatas. In fact he *was* fifteen and maintains in the publication that he was even younger. He had then been studying in Bologna with Giovanni Colonna [523] for five years and had just been made a member of the Accademia Filarmonica. By the time he began his *Wanderjahre* in 1689, he had been an all-purpose musician at San Petronio and choirmaster at San Giovanni in Monte, had written two oratorios and four Masses, and had published six sets of chamber works (including some Bolognese trumpet "sonatas"). After a couple of fairly footloose years, he settled down in Rome in the employ of the Colonna family (the old patrician one) and began a career of turning out stage works. One of them, the opera *Il Trionfo di Camilla* (formerly attributed to Antonio), premiered in Naples in 1696, became eventually the most popular Italian opera to be performed in London in the whole eighteenth century. A year later, Bononcini's patron died, and he found employment at the court of Leopold I [528] in Vienna, where he drew down 5,000 florins a year and enjoyed extraordinary favor, particularly from Joseph I [651], who succeeded Leopold in 1705. Later his brother Antonio joined him. In 1702 things got depressing in Vienna, owing to the War of the Spanish Succession, and the Bononcini brothers went to Berlin to serve in the Prussian court orchestra under the patronage of Queen Sophie Charlotte. There, in the summer of 1702, Giovanni's one-act opera *Polifemo* became the first Italian opera known to have played in Berlin; the queen herself supplied the harpsichord continuo. The next year Giovanni and Antonio returned to Vienna, where the death of Leopold in 1705 put a further crimp in their activities. Giovanni's Austrian career peaked under Joseph's reign, but he died in 1711 and Charles VI took less interest in music than his predecessors, so in 1713 Antonio returned to Modena and Giovanni to Rome, where he joined the household of the Austrian ambassador, Count Gallas. But Giovanni's bad luck in choosing patrons persisted, for the ambassador died six years later. (At some time during this period Giovanni had married one Margherita Balletti.

A daughter survived to the age of twenty-two, dying in 1743.)

Fortunately, the British Royal Academy of Music was in the market for Italian composers, and the Earl of Burlington found Bononcini willing to go to London and compose operas to be produced under Handel's management. His *Turno Aricino,* revised as *Almahide,* produced in London a decade earlier, is said to have been the first Italian opera sung there in Italian by Italians. By now the English had become acclimatized to, then dazzled by, the steady stream of immigrant Italian musicians, and the worship of *prime donne* of whatever sex was an established fact, at least among those who counted. Thus Bononcini was welcomed as a hero and his first two London seasons were the only two in which the academy wound up in the black. Audiences, for reasons more sociopolitical than musical, fixed on Handel and Bononcini as polar rallying points, occasioning the famous jingle by hymn writer and shorthand inventor John Byrom that begins, "Some say, compared to Bononcini,/That Mynheer Handel's but a ninny." But Bononcini unwisely accepted the patronage of adherents of the Stuart pretender, and his contract was dropped in 1722. He had to get by on occasional opportunities in France until 1724, when Henrietta, Duchess of Marlborough, hired him for life at 500 pounds a year. He had quarters at Blenheim Palace and freedom to write as he pleased, and there were weekly concerts of his music, performed by musicians imported from London. It all went to his head, and he is reported to have behaved abominably to his employer and her household.

Bononcini's final London opera, *Astianatte,* produced in 1727, culminated in the notorious hair-pulling clash onstage between the rival *divas* Francesca Cuzzoni and Faustina Bordoni, and a riot in the audience. The year before, he had joined John Christopher Pepusch's **[611]** Academy of Antient Musick, which became the locus of his ultimate disgrace. He laid claim to a madrigal introduced there about the time of *Astianatte.* In 1731 another member came across it in a collection of works by Antonio Lotti **[613]** and said so. Bononcini cried foul and then turned his back on the matter. Soon afterward Duchess Henrietta showed him the gate for dedicating a set of sonatas to her mother, the Dowager Duchess Sarah, whom she hated. Finding that his name in England was now *fango,* he shook her mud from his shoes and retired to the Continent. He was said at that time to own more gold than could be made by all the alchemists—a statement whose meaning depended on what one thought of alchemy. At any rate, one such—a self-styled Count Ughi—fastened onto him and took him for all he had. After playing cello briefly in the court of Louis XV and doing something in that of John V in Lisbon, Bononcini returned to Vienna and tried to resume his career. At seventy-one he petitioned Empress Maria Theresa to remember an old servant with a pension. She responded with enough to ease his last years.

Bononcini's music has been largely forgotten. He wrote religious and instrumental compositions, but his success rested on his enormous outpouring of dramatic music and cantatas. He obviously had genius, but he too often catered to public taste. His melodies are easy, his music attractive, but he lacks real profundity. His arias are short-winded, his emotionalism *galant* rather than heroic.

RECORDINGS: The only serious consideration of his operas on record is the set of excerpts from *Griselda* directed by Richard Bonynge. Michel Piguet and Ferdinand Conrad have both recorded a divertimento for flute and continuo, and Jean-François Paillard a few of the Bolognese *sinfonie.* (There is some expectable confusion in the labeling of Bononcini records.) Pastoral cantatas have been recorded by the Kuijken Ensemble.

[621] ALBICASTRO, Enrico (Ȧl-bē-kȧs'-trō, En-rē'-kō)
VIOLINIST, SOLDIER
BORN: Switzerland, c. 1670
DIED: c. 1738

A soldier of fortune both militarily and musically, "Albicastro" (cashing in on the rage for Italian musicians) was really Heinrich Weissenberg von Biswang, a native of the Simme Valley between Bern and the Bernese Alps. In 1686 he was registered as a student at the University of Leyden, at which time he already seems to have been using both names interchangeably. In the War of the Spanish Succession, which ramped through the Low Countries from 1701 to 1714, he reputedly served as a cavalry officer. Around the turn of the century he published 9 sets of sonatas and a set of *concerti a 4* (Op. 7). Though he called himself an amateur *(dilettante),* these show solid and often inventive musicianship. The violin works, which call for a dazzling technique, indicate that he must have been a virtuoso fiddler. His music was much admired by young Joachim Quantz **[730]**, who rated it with that of Bi-

ber [539] and Walther [680]. Denis Stevens
has recorded some of the Op. 7 *concerti.*

[622] BRUNCKHORST, Arnold
Melchior (Brōōnk'-hôrst, Âr'-nōlt
Melkh'-yôr)
ORGANIST
BORN: c. 1670
DIED: c. 1725

Very little is known of Brunckhorst or his
music. Even his middle name is uncertain—
it also appears as "Martin" and "Matthias."
From 1693 to 1697 he was a church organist
in Hildesheim and then was appointed municipal organist in Celle by Duke Georg
Wilhelm of Braunschweig-Lüneburg. He remained in Celle (where he may have met
J. S. Bach [684]) until 1720, when he became
court organist in Hanover. His only surviving compositions are 2 extended cantatas,
for Christmas and Easter respectively (recorded by Gerhard Rehm), a prelude and
fugue for organ (recorded by Jørgen Ernst
Hansen), and a harpsichord sonata.

[623] CAIX D'HERVELOIS, Louis de
(Kä Dârv-lwä', Lōō-wēē' də)
VIOLA DA GAMBA PLAYER
BORN: c. 1670
DIED: c. 1760

Evidence suggests that Caix d'Hervelois
was related to the several contemporaneous
viol-playing Caix from Lyons. He seems to
have spent a lifetime in Paris without ever
making it to the Big Time—a court appointment—though he was for a time patronized
by Philippe, Regent of France. He is said to
have been a pupil of the Sieur de Saint-
Colombe, that quixotic promoter of the
gamba who taught Marais [574]. It has also
been suggested that Caix was a pupil of
Marais. He published 6 books of music for
viols and 2 for flutes. His music shows the
French compactness and epigrammatic wit
of the day, wedded to an Italian harmonic
approach. At his worst, he becomes obsessed with ornament. With modern
regrowth of interest in the viola da gamba,
his music has been rediscovered. RECORD-
INGS: Examples have been recorded by John
Hsu, Paul Doktor (on viola), and Marie-
Thérèse Heurtier.

[624] CALDARA, Antonio (Kál-dä'-rä,
Än-tōn'-yō)
CELLIST

BORN: Venice, c. 1670
DIED: Vienna, December 28, 1736

Although he held an important musical
post, was incredibly prolific, enjoyed much
fame and influence in his time, and seems
presently to be having a small revival, Antonio Caldara remains an elusive figure. The
son of a Venetian violinist, he became a
choirboy at St. Mark's and remained there
as singer and instrumentalist until 1699. His
music seems to confirm the probability that
he was a pupil of Giovanni Legrenzi [503].
He wrote or had a hand in three operas produced in Venice during that time and published all his chamber music and a volume
of cantatas there. In 1699 he left Venice for
Mantua, to become general music director
for Duke Ferdinando Carlo. He held the
post apparently until the duke died (or was
killed) in 1708, though there is evidence that
he was at many other places during the period. He then went to Rome but, driven out
by a threat of invasion, he made his way to
Barcelona, where he was briefly in the service of Charles (second son of Emperor Leopold I), who as Charles III of Hungary
was laying claim to the throne of Spain. In
1709 he returned to Rome and entered the
service of Prince Ruspoli as his *maestro di
cappella.* Two years later he married one of
the court singers, Caterina Petrolli, who
later bore him two daughters. That same
year Emperor Joseph I died, and Charles
was summoned to take the Imperial throne
(a better bargain than that of Spain) as
Charles VI. Caldara, hoping to make hay
out of the old association, headed for Vienna and applied for the *Kapellmeisterschaft,* but it went to a certain Ziani, whose
second-in-command was Johann Fux [585],
and Caldara had to return to Rome. His
chance came when Ziani died in 1715 and
Fux was moved up, though the appointment
did not come through for two full years. In
his remaining nineteen years he turned out
at least 44 operas and other dramatic works,
24 oratorios, and a large number of religious
works, cantatas, arias, etc., for the court
(and moonlighted for other theaters in the
empire). He never became *Kapellmeister,*
though he often took over for the gouty
Fux. Nevertheless he ended up drawing a
much higher salary than his superior and
around 1730, on demand, was paid 12,000
florins in lieu of an annual pension. Oddly,
he died insolvent, though he is said to have
left 20,000 pages of manuscript in the
archives. Most admired in his day for his
flashy and tuneful operas, he was probably
at his best in the smaller vocal forms, where
he often exhibited a whimsical wit. Among

his operas are a number of pioneer settings of libretti by Pietro Metastasio, the leading Italian dramatist of the day. (Manfred Bukofzer has noted that a good deal of Caldara is dull—an opinion that has not been challenged.) RECORDINGS: Among recordings, René Clemencic and Edwin Loehrer have provided two LP samplers. Loehrer's includes the cantata *Il Giuoco del quadriglio,* representing the tittle-tattle of four female card players. (In the original performance Princess Maria Theresa and her sister took two of the parts.) The early Venetian sonatas have attracted various chamber groups, and Václav Smetáček has directed the festival *Mass* written in 1726 for the canonization of Jan Nepomuk. The Christmas cantata *Vaticini di Pace* has been recorded by the Württemberg Chamber Orchestra.

[625] DIEUPART, François (Dyö-pâr', Fräṅ-swà')
VIOLINIST, HARPSICHORDIST
BORN: c. 1670
DIED: London, c. 1740

That nebulous year c. 1670 produced its share of hazy characters among composers. Dieupart was probably the son of a Parisian chandler named François Dieupart. In 1701 he published in Amsterdam 6 *suites de clavecin* and an alternative version for melody instrument and continuo. These represent the first French-composed textbook models of the dance suite in its mature form: overture, allemande, courante, sarabande, modern dance(s), gigue. Shortly afterward he emigrated to London, where he became known as "Charles." In 1704 he worked for the first time with the French-born dramatist Pierre Motteux (translator of Rabelais and Cervantes), composing music for an interlude at Drury Lane. Later he entered into an opera-production scheme with Thomas Clayton and Nicola Haym (Handel's [683] compatriot and sometime librettist), but Handel's success in the field put an end to that. Dieupart is said to have furnished the continuo in Handel's orchestra for a time, later to have tried teaching, and eventually to have hit the skids and died in poverty. Some songs and fragments survive, apart from the suites. J. S. Bach [684] thought enough of the latter to copy two of them out and to use material from one in his first English suite. RECORDINGS: The several recordings from the collection (e.g., by Michel Piguet, Ferdinand Conrad) use the version for flute (or whatever) and continuo.

[626] FISCHER, Johann Caspar Ferdinand (Fish'-er, Yō'-hån Kås'-pâr Fār'-dē-nånt)
MUSIC DIRECTOR
BORN: c. 1670 (?)
DIED: Rastatt, March 27, 1746

Nothing at all is known of Fischer's early life—and not much more of the rest of it. He was *Kapellmeister* to the rulers of Baden—Markgraf Ludwig Wilhelm, his widow, the Markgräfin Franziska Sibylla Augusta, and their son, the Markgraf Ludwig Georg from at least 1692 to the end of his life. The French invasions had driven the household out of Baden and they had set up shop in a Bohemian castle called Schlackenwerth, where Fischer's children were born. In 1716 the court removed to Rastatt in Baden, where the composer died thirty years later. Other than this we know only that he was in charge of both sacred and secular music.

Fischer's legacy consists of only 7 published works. Two of these (the Op. 3 of 1701 and the Op. 5 of 1711) are religious choral works—*Vesper psalms* and the *Loretan Litany,* respectively. His first publication, *Le Journal du printemps (Spring Diary), Op. 1,* is his only orchestral work, a set of very French and very sophisticated dance suites for five-part string ensemble with trumpets ad lib. The 2 harpsichord collections, *Les Pièces de clavessin, Op. 2* of 1696 and the *Musikalischer Parnassus* of 1738 are again French suites, modeled on orchestral ballet suites, and are called the finest of their kind between Froberger [490] and J. S. Bach [684]. *Blumenstrauss (Bouquet,* 1732) contains 8 organ suites in the church modes, each consisting of a prelude and eight little fugues. The earlier *Ariadne musica, Op.* 4 of 1702, also consists of preludes and fugues cyclically arranged, but perhaps more interestingly. (The reference of the title is to the weaver of classical mythology transmogrified into a spider, a negotiator of complex webs.) Obviously with the meantone tuning reforms of Andreas Werckmeister of a decade earlier in mind, Fischer arranged his pairings according to the circle of fifths, moving from C major to C-sharp minor, omitting only five of the keys now familiar to us. The *Ariadne* almost certainly lies behind Bach's *Wohltemperierte Klavier,* and indeed Fischer exerted other influences on the younger composer as well.

RECORDINGS: The entire *Ariadne musica,* minus the five appended *ricercari,* has been recorded by Franz Haselböck, 4 of the harpsichord suites by Neil Roberts, and suites from the *Journal* by the Heidelberg Kammerorchester and by Louis de Froment.

[627] LEVERIDGE, Richard
SINGER
BORN: c. 1670
DIED: London, March 22, 1758

In his own time Richard Leveridge's musical fame was chiefly owing to his bass voice —a foghorn of immense power and profundity. He was evidently one of those "yo-ho-ho!" singers dear to the Anglo-Saxon heart, for contemporary accounts suggest that interpretation and finesse were not his long suits. Though he appeared in some Italian operas (Handel's [683] occasionally), he seems to have been happier in more plebeian stage works and in celebratory pieces, such as St. Cecilia odes. When he retired at Covent Garden in 1751, he had been appearing professionally for fifty-six years. On the side, he ran a London coffeehouse. In his last years he was supported by his friends on a subscription basis. As a composer, he turned out some quasi-operas and masques, and supplied music for a number of plays— notably *Macbeth,* in which he played the role of the witch-goddess Hecate. His songs (many of them for plays) were popular, and one, "The Roast Beef of Old England," remains a standard English song of good fellowship. RECORDINGS: His duet setting of Shakespeare's "Who Is Sylvia?" has been recorded by Wilfred Brown and Maurice Bevan.

[628] WILLIAMS, William
VIOLINIST
BORN: c. 1670 (?)
DIED: London, January 1701 (?)

Williams published some recorder duets in 1695 and was admitted, *sans* emolument, to the royal music the same year. Two years later he was placed on the payroll. He was dead, according to William Congreve, by January 28, 1701. Besides the pieces noted, and a few others like them, he left a flute sonata, 6 trio sonatas, and some songs. RECORDINGS: Ferdinand Conrad has recorded the "solo" sonata.

[629] DELLA CIAIA, Azzolino Bernardino (Del'-là Chà'-yà, Àd-zō-lē'-nō Bâr-nàr-dē'-nō)
ORGANIST, ORGAN BUILDER, SAILOR, POLITICIAN, PRIEST
BORN: Siena, March 21, 1671
DIED: Pisa, January 15, 1755

Like his exact contemporary Albinoni [630], Della Ciaia was an amateur who had no need to write music for a living. At seventeen, in Pisa, he joined the seafaring Cavalieri di San Stefano for sixteen years. He then became a city councillor in Pisa. In 1713 he left for Rome, where he worked until 1730 as secretary to the Colonna-Barbiglias. He then returned to his government post in Pisa. He was a dedicated and talented organ builder. His masterpiece was the magnificent instrument still in use in the church of San Stefano (that of his order), which he not only designed but helped erect. He gave up his post in 1734 to enter the priesthood and ended his career as prior of Urbino. Della Ciaia published some psalms and solo cantatas, and left Masses, other religious works, and organ pieces in manuscript. He is, however, chiefly known for a printed collection of 6 harpsichord sonatas (with some additional organ pieces). The sonatas (in four movements but otherwise unlike later sonatas) are very early examples of the keyboard species, and therefore important historically, but the old story that Della Ciaia pioneered sonata-allegro form does not hold water. The organ pieces are new expressive wine in old contrapuntal bottles. RECORDINGS: Clemente Terni and Konrad Philipp Schuba, among others, have recorded some of the organ pieces.

[630] ALBINONI, Tomaso Giovanni (Àl-bē-nō'-nē, Tō-mà'-zō Jō-vàn'-nē)
VIOLINIST, SINGING TEACHER
BORN: Venice, June 14, 1671
DIED: Venice, January 17, 1751

The musical fire that had burned so steadily in Venice for more than a hundred years was, like the Most Serene Republic itself, beginning to flicker, but with Albinoni's generation it flared up for one last time. Albinoni came into the world well provided for: his father, Bergamo-born Antonio, had established himself as a thriving paper merchant in Venice and had married a member of the patrician Fabris family. We know nothing of Tomaso's youth or musical training. The arguments that he studied with Corelli [565] or someone in Rome and that he hired out at the Mantuan court are based solely on early dedications and are untenable. In 1694 he launched an immensely successful operatic career with *Zenobia* at the Teatro San Zanipolo and published a set of 12 trio sonatas. (He modestly signed his works *"Musico di violino dilettante veneto"* —Venetian amateur fiddler.) A steady succession of operas carried his name abroad, and soon he was getting productions and premieres in other cities. In 1705 he married the singer Margherita Rimondi (c. 1684–1721), known as "La Salarina" (probably from her birthplace), who in the course of events, bore him six children. In 1708 Antonio Albinoni died, leaving one of his several shops to Tomaso but the bulk of the operation to his two younger sons. It was a hollow legacy in any case, for in examining the ledgers the heirs found they had inherited a mountain of debts so high as virtually to wipe them out. Tomaso dropped his self-deprecating signature and entered the ranks of the self-employed. His best source of income is said to have been the singing school that he opened—though when that was is not clear.

By 1722 he had published 8 collections of sonatas and concerti and one of cantatas—regarded as the Albinoni canon until recently. In that same year he was summoned to Munich—the only considerable journey of his lifetime—to present two of his stage works at the wedding of Elector Maximilian Emanuel II to the Archduchess Maria Amalia, daughter of the late Emperor Joseph I. Afterward he devoted himself almost exclusively to operas, his total reaching fourscore or so it is said. But the flood abated in the early 1730s and trickled out in 1741. Then there is silence so profound that the date given on his death certificate (which notes he had been bedridden for two years) has been questioned by some.

For the two and more centuries subsequent, Albinoni, even more than Antonio Vivaldi [650], has been the victim of ignorance, prejudicial judgments, and neglect. Even with the current revival of his music, we appear doomed never to see him whole, for of all his operas only three complete scores and some fragments are known to survive. So far there seems to have been little attention paid to the solo cantatas, and the few pieces of religious music are early and amateurish. This leaves the instrumental music, most of it published, as noted above. (Recently a hitherto unknown Op. 10 set of *Concerti a 5* has turned up in Sweden, where an impostor Albinoni visited in the 1720s, but even so there is no reason to think of these works as frauds.) The instrumental works show a composer of marked individuality (despite occasional tics), exquisite melodic invention, enormous technical skill, and exquisite and conscious taste that never permits him the ebullience and occasional vulgarity of Vivaldi. The *sonate da chiesa* are perhaps the least interesting of these works. The earlier specimens are heavily dependent on Corelli, though later Albinoni breaks free to a degree, notably in his use of fugal devices. The Opp. 3 and 8

balletti are more experimental and show his fine handling of counterpoint.

However, it is the concerti, each in five parts, that catch the attention. The fifth voice is not always so much a solo instrument as leader of the pack, but to all intents and purposes, these are solo concerti. We are told that Torelli [578] was probably the first to write such works, but Albinoni's seem to have been the first printed. With him and Vivaldi things are more uncertain, but in point of publication Albinoni's first two concerto opuses antedate Vivaldi's first one by twelve and five years, respectively. The Albinonian concerto is already cast in the soon-to-be-standard three-movement pattern of the operatic *sinfonia* (fast-slow-fast). (There are some manuscript works designated as *sinfonie.)* Despite the composer's tendency toward the epigrammatic, classical, and abstract, the concerti move toward the expressive and even the emotional. It appears also that in specifying on several concerti that the lead instrument be an oboe, Albinoni was the first to write such works for solo winds. (It must be noted that the most widely known work ascribed to Albinoni, an *adagio* for organ and strings, is really a confection by his modern biographer Remo Giazotto constructed with a cookie press over an isolated Albinoni continuo part.)

RECORDINGS: Claudio Scimone appears to have embarked on a project to record the entire published canon and to date has brought out Opp. 2, 5, 6, 7, 9, and 10; there are other complete recordings of Opp. 5, 7, and 9, plus innumerable individual concerti and sonatas. Claudio Scimone has recorded two operas—*Pimpinone* and *Le Triomphe de l'Aurore.*

[631] MANCINI, Francesco (Mȧn-chē'-nē, Fràn-chās'-kō)
ORGANIST, MUSIC DIRECTOR, EDUCATOR
BORN: Naples, January 16, 1672
DIED: Naples, September 22, 1737

Mancini was one of the most successful opportunists in the history of music. He studied organ at the Conservatorio della Pietà dei Turchini in Naples, and was the school organist to 1702, when he began his successful operatic career with his *Ariovisto* at the Teatro San Bartolomeo. He then applied to take the place of the errant Alessandro Scarlatti [583] as *maestro di cappella* at the Spanish viceregal court but succeeded only in becoming organist—third in rank to Gaetano Veneziano and Domenico Natale Sarro

[658]. Fortunately for him, the War of the Spanish Succession had broken out a couple of years earlier, and in 1707 the victorious Austrians came marching to take Naples over. Mancini gathered up friends and supporters and met them at Aversa, producing a victory *Te Deum* at the cathedral. Accordingly he was promoted to *maestro*. However, the next year Scarlatti returned and Mancini was demoted a step. By 1710 his reputation as a composer of operas had reached England and his *Idaspe*, premiered that year in London, became a tremendous hit—not least, one suspects, because it featured a fight between the castrato Nicolini and a lion (obviously not the real thing). In 1720 Mancini also became director of the Conservatorio di Santa Maria di Loreto, and in 1725 he succeeded Scarlatti. When in the War of the Polish Succession (the eighteenth century was marked by a succession of such wars), the invading French threatened his position, Mancini pulled the old Aversa trick again (in 1734) and was permitted to continue. However, it was his last gasp, for a stroke incapacitated him the next year, and Sarro had to deputize for him until Mancini's death in 1737. The successful composer of a score of operas, many smaller stage works, a handful of oratorios, and around 200 cantatas, Mancini is regarded as a transitional figure between the Baroque and the Classical. RECORDINGS: Jean-Pierre Rampal has recorded a chamber concerto attributed to him.

[632] DESTOUCHES, André-Cardinal
(Dä-tōōsh', Än-drä' Kär-dē-nàl')
SOLDIER, ADMINISTRATOR
BORN: Paris, c. April 6, 1672
DIED: Paris, February 7, 1749

"Cardinal" was a family name, not a title. The father of Destouches, as he came to call himself, was Étienne Cardinal, Seigneur des Touches et de Guilleville, a Parisian merchant. André-Cardinal was sent to the Jesuit school in Paris, and at fourteen sailed to Siam with Père Gui Tachard, one of his teachers. (King Phra Narai had been making overtures to Western Europe, and the French were vying with their neighbors for the trade and souls of the Siamese.) After two years Destouches came home and at twenty joined the Mousquetaires (of whom there were now more than three—several companies, in fact). During his six years of service, in which he saw action against the English at Namur, he took up the guitar and wrote some songs—an experience that decided him on a musical career. He studied

with Campra [584], who let him contribute three pieces to his opera-ballet *L'Europe galante*. Among Destouches's aristocratic friends was the musical amateur Antoine Grimaldi, later Prince of Monaco, who introduced, at a 1697 Fontainebleau concert, music from the opera *Issé*, which Destouches had set to a libretto by Antoine Houdar de La Motte, a former Trappist monk. Louis XIV found his jaded responses so stirred once again that he rewarded the composer with a purse, ordered the work produced at the Académie, and even made some suggestions for revision.

From then on, Destouches was accounted Campra's equal as a stage composer. Though he has been given credit for musical advances he did not originate, he understood how drama worked, and his 1712 *Callirhoë* enjoyed revivals for more than fifty years. In 1713 he became Inspector General of the Opéra, and in 1718 he was appointed Superintendent of the Royal Chamber. Three years later he produced his opera-ballet *Les Éléments* at the Tuileries; it was a failure owing (according to Destouches) to the amateurish dancing of some of the courtiers. (In 1725 Delalande [576] successfully reworked it.) At forty-two Destouches married Anne Antoinette de Reynold de la Ferrière. When Delalande died, he inherited the directorship of the Opéra but gave up both of his posts there in 1730. His last opera was *Les Stratagèmes de l'amour* in 1726. From then to the end of his life, he directed, at Versailles, the *concerts spirituels* sponsored by Louis XV's hapless Polish queen, Marie Leszczynska. He was buried in the church of St. Roch, next door to his mansion. He left 11 operas and some published *airs*. His small body of religious music has disappeared.

RECORDINGS: So far he has been given only small attention on records—orchestral suites from *Issé* (Raymond Leppard) and *Les Éléments* (J.-S. Béreau and Christopher Hogwood) and a few isolated songs and arias.

[633] BONPORTI, Francesco Antonio
(Bun-pôr'-tē, Frän-chäs'-kō Än-tōn'-yō)
PRIEST, VIOLINIST
BORN: Trento, June 11, 1672
DIED: Padua, December 19, 1749

Bonporti, like so many composers of his era, preferred to be thought of as an amateur. Not that he was preparing for some imagined musical Olympics: he had something more pragmatic in mind. The scion of a wealthy old family of Trent, once the site of one of the most important and prolonged church councils of modern times but now a mere stopover on the road from Verona to Innsbruck, Bonporti studied there and then took a Ph.D. at (i.e., graduated from) the University of Innsbruck. From 1691 to 1695 he was at the Collegium Germanicum in Rome preparing for his vocation, and studying music on the side. It has been said that Corelli [565] or Corelli's pupil Matteo Fornari taught him the violin, but who knows? At the end of his studies he was ordained and went home. The following year he published his Op. 1, a set of ten trio sonatas, in Venice, dedicating them to the local prince-bishop, and indicating himself to be a *gentiluomo di Trento* (i.e., a man who should be paid attention to). The result was a minor post in the cathedral that conveyed neither wealth nor importance. Envisioning a bleak future in the sticks for himself, Bonporti set about to write his way out. Over the next couple of decades he published 12 opuses in all—instrumental, save for a set of solo motets—replete with forelock-tugging dedications to whoever he thought might help him. Having heard that Italians were in demand in England, he tried George I. In effect he then attempted to bribe his way into the imperial court, but all he got was an empty title ("aulic familiar," meaning that the emperor would be happy to see him if he should visit Vienna). Later he indicated that he would be satisfied with a mere canonry in Trento. It was not forthcoming, and in 1740 he chucked it all and moved in with a priestly friend in Padua.

When Bonporti died, there were those who recognized his worth. Francesco Maria Veracini [705] had his Op. 10 Inventions for violin and continuo in his repertoire. Two hundred years later four of these pieces were included in the Bach Gesellschaft edition as works of J. S. Bach [684], who had merely copied them out. Henry Eccles [644] plagiarized from Bononcini. Bonporti shows his Corellian underpinnings and there is a whiff of Handel (probably not derivative) about him. But he was cut off from the great world and thus had to develop on his own, eventually showing an independence that some have termed "freakishness." He was also a master of melody. These qualities are especially obvious in the inventions and in the remarkable Op. 11 *Concerti a 4*. Why the *recitativo* movement from the fifth of these has not won the popularity of the Pachelbel [567] canon is a mystery.

RECORDINGS: The *recitative* movement was recorded by the Virtuosi di Roma. Recordings of other concerti from this opus have been made by I Musici, the Società Corelli, and Lee Schaenen.

[634] GRIGNY, Nicolas de (Grēn-yē', Nē-kō-làs' də)
ORGANIST
BORN: Rheims, c. September 18, 1672
DIED: Rheims, November 30, 1703

Organ playing was the Grigny family trade. Nicolas' grandfather played at the basilica of St. Pierre in Rheims, his Uncle Robert at St. Hilaire, and his own father at the historic cathedral. One assumes he got his first lessons at home. Later he went to Paris to study with Nicolas Antoine Lebègue [515], where he himself was organist at the abbey church of St. Denis from 1693 to 1695. In the latter year he married Marie-Magdeleine de France, a merchant's daughter, who became the mother, in rapid order, of his seven children. The first was born in Rheims a year later, and in 1697 Grigny succeeded his father at the cathedral. He published what he intended to be his first organ book in 1699 and in 1702 also signed on as organist of St. Symphorien. He died suddenly the following year, at age thirty-one. Marie-Magdeleine republished the now ironically named *Premier livre d'orgue* in 1711: the *Mass* and the 5 hymns it contains represent Grigny's entire known legacy. But a splendid legacy it is, however brief. Johann Sebastian Bach [684] must have recognized this, for he copied out the whole thing. Nowadays the book is held on the same level as François Couperin's [616] two organ Masses, as representing the acme of French Baroque organ music—a watershed between the polyphonic, decorative, and balletic traditions of the Grand Siècle, on the one hand, and the new expressivity, on the other. RECORDINGS: Marie-Claire Alain has provided an integral recording of the organ book.

[635] FORQUERAY, Antoine (Fôr-ker-ā', An-twàn')
VIOLA DA GAMBA PLAYER, TEACHER
BORN: Paris, c. 1672
DIED: Mantes, June 28, 1745

When Forqueray was ten, he played the now long obsolete bass violin before Louis XIV. The king was so tickled that he ordered the child be given lessons on the gamba at his expense, and seven years later, that having come to pass, made him a musician-in-ordinary to the Royal Chamber. Forqueray's duties were to amuse his employer at dinner (he aspired to and apparently acquired a technique that astonished virtuoso violinists) and to teach people who hung about the court. In 1697, apparently in a fit of irrationality, he married Henriette-Angélique Houssou, the daughter of an apparently rather sobersided church organist. In 1699 she bore him a son, christened Jean-Baptiste-Antoine, who eventually succeeded his father at court and had a remarkable playing and teaching career of his own. Forqueray not only played like the devil (see 574); he acted like him to his wife and son. With Henriette-Angélique there were thirteen dreary years of quarrels, recriminations, and separations, finally ending in a permanent split in 1710. For whatever reason, he treated the boy abominably, had him imprisoned in 1719 and exiled in 1725. Not long afterward, Antoine retired to Mantes on the Seine, but continued to draw his salary to the end of his life. He left a few pieces in manuscript and a couple more were transcribed for lute by his friend Robert de Visée [561]. Rather touchingly, in 1747 Jean-Baptiste published a volume containing 3 of his own pieces and 29 of his father's, gathered in 5 suites but rather severely trimmed to his own tastes. (He also published keyboard reductions.) The Italian bent is clear, and the pieces are technically demanding, but (no doubt thanks to Forqueray *fils*) rather tentative harmonically. RECORDINGS: John Hsu has recorded the whole collection.

[636] ALDROVANDINI, Giuseppe Antonio Vincenzo (Ȧl'-drō-vȧn-dē'-nē, Jōō-sep'-pā Ȧn-tōn'-yō Vēn-chānt'-sō)
DIRECTOR (?)
BORN: Bologna, 1672 or 1673
DIED: Bologna, February 9, 1707

A pupil of Giuseppe Antonio Perti (1661–1756), he had two oratorios performed for one of the local religious confraternities in 1691. He was elected to the Accademia Filarmonica in 1695. In his first opera (of perhaps 20) presented at the Teatro Formagliari in 1696, the low-class characters sang in the local dialect; it was one of the first comic operas in northern Italy. He also wrote a few more oratorios, and published collections of motets, cantatas (secular and sacred), and sonatas. On the evening of February 9, 1707, leaving a wineshop after a habitually large infusion of Lambrusco, he toppled into a canal and was drowned. (Perhaps the canals have been filled in, for none

show on maps, nor do present-day visitors recall encountering any.) RECORDINGS: Maurice André and Marcel Lagorce have recorded a *sinfonia* for two trumpets, and Janos Sebestyan and Clemente Terni some organ pieces, all credited to Aldrovandini.

[637] BRÉHY, Pierre-Hercule (Brā-ē', Pē-âr'-Ȧr-kül')
ORGANIST, TEACHER
BORN: Brussels, c. September 13, 1673
DIED: Brussels, c. February 26, 1737

Bréhy's entire life seems to have focused on the church of Ste. Gudule in Brussels. He was probably a chorister there, later served as an organist, and in 1705 was named to the post of singing master, which he retained until he died. He also taught, in his own phrase, the "English Benedictine ladies" in a local convent. His religious music, particularly his motets, shows that he knew what such big-time composers as Marc-Antoine Charpentier [544] and Delalande [576] were up to in Paris; his sonatas, on the other hand, seem to show the influence of Albinoni [630] and Vivaldi [650] (both of whose works were published in Amsterdam). RECORDINGS: Géry Lemaire has recorded a sonata (as *sinfonia-ouverture).*

[638] CLARKE, Jeremiah
ORGANIST
BORN: London, c. 1673
DIED: London, December 1, 1707

Clarke ranks high among well-known obscure composers, for many a graduate and lodge brother has marched to his *Prince of Denmark's March,* confident that they were hearing something called *Purcell's Trumpet Voluntary.* Nothing is known of his parentage or background, though it has been suggested that he was a Clarke of Windsor, not a Clarke of Oxenford. He sang in the Chapel Royal under John Blow [552] at the coronation of James II in 1685 and had graduated by 1691. Shortly after that, he became organist at Winchester College, where he played for three years. By the end of the decade he had moved on to St. Paul's Cathedral in London, by which time Sir Christopher Wren's new building, though still unfinished, was in business. When Blow vacated the posts of almoner and master of the children in 1702, Clarke succeeded him. Meanwhile Clarke and William Croft [652] in 1700 had become Gentlemen Extraordinary of the Chapel Royal until such time as an organist should leave and they could be made Ordinary. That happened with the death of William Piggott in 1704, and they were named to share his job. Clarke, who apart from the expectable church music had also provided songs and incidental music for the theater and some occasional odes, would thus appear to have been facing a bright future. But, even at his best, he seems to have been a morose fellow, and on December 1, 1707, he blew his brains out. The records blame a fit of madness. The balladeers of the day said it was unrequited love. Perhaps it was the holiday blues.

It was Clarke who in 1697 commissioned the poem "Alexander's Feast" from John Dryden for the annual St. Cecilia ode, but his setting of it has vanished, alas! He wrote other works, for the death of Henry Purcell [581], Marlborough's victory at Ramillies, and Queen Anne's birthday. The *Prince of Denmark's March* has nothing to do with *Hamlet*, but (originally for harpsichord) was one of several marches dedicated to visiting dignitaries.

RECORDINGS: *The Prince of Denmark's March* was later included in a suite for winds that has been recorded by Pierre Colombo as *Suite de Clark (sic)*.

[639] KEISER, Reinhard (Kī'-zer, Rīn'-härt)
ORGANIST, CONDUCTOR, IMPRESARIO
BORN: Teuchern, January 12, 1674
DIED: Hamburg, September 12, 1739

Nature is said to abhor a vacuum. And so, given an important figure about whom little is known, the lacunae are filled with all manner of odd tales. So with Reinhard Keiser. Widely known and deeply influential in his day, and hailed by the eighteenth-century composer and writer Johann Mattheson (1681-1764), his contemporary, as the world's greatest operatic composer, he emerged from the imagination of the nineteenth century as a lurid scapegrace who himself became the subject of a 1931 opera, *Der tolle Kapellmeister (The Mad Conductor)*, by Benno Bardi.

Egocentric Keiser certainly was and eccentric he may have been, but his history shows nothing that strikes one as mad. He was born in a Saxon village near Weissenfels, in which town his father, Gottfried, worked as an organist. Gottfried left home about the time Reinhard arrived, and the source of the latter's initial training, if any, is unknown. In 1685 Keiser was enrolled in the Thomasschule in Leipzig. Probably in 1692 he found a post in Braunschweig, at the court of the Duke of Braunschweig-

Wolfenbüttel, where the *Kapellmeister* was the much-traveled Johann Sigismund Kusser. Within the year he had an opera, *Der königliche Schäfer (The Kingly Shepherd)*, on the ducal stage, and when Kusser left for Hamburg in 1695, Keiser was elevated to *Kammerkomponist* (court composer). Having produced a couple more operas, he too went to Hamburg. Kusser had been conductor at, and probably director of, the Goose Market Opera, but by now he had taken off to tour the provinces with his own company, and Keiser, who had already had an opera produced in Hamburg, took his place. For the next twenty years, despite certain vicissitudes, it might have been said that Keiser *was* the Hamburg opera, for the theater in the Goose Market never shone so brilliantly before or after. Economic necessity forced him out of the directorship in 1707, but he continued to compose, often at the rate of three or four works a year. In keeping with the Hamburg tradition, they were determinedly German—in language (including excursions into the local *Plattdeutsch)*, in melody (if not in treatment of it), and sometimes in story. We know of more than 80, and it is conjectured that, including rewritings, he may have composed as many as 120. The Hamburgers went around humming Keiser tunes and, at the height of his fame, he swaggered about with a retinue of flunkies and yes-men, for all the world like a Hollywood mogul.

In 1700, Keiser instituted the Winter Concerts—something like a modern pops concert but intended for the *cognoscenti* and the social elite. Musical virtuosity and taste were taken for granted, but the performers also had to be good to look upon, and the whole was set off with the best food and wine to be had. In 1702 the Duke of Mecklenburg-Schwerin awarded him the title of *Kapellmeister*, though it amounted to little more than a merit badge. In 1703, partnered with a writer named Drüsicke, Keiser took over direction of the Hamburg opera house, but Drüsicke soon disappeared with the proceeds, leaving his colleague to struggle. Early in his directorate Keiser acquired a young Saxon second fiddler named Handel [683], who sometimes relieved him at the keyboard. One day Keiser handed him a dreadful libretto, *Almira*, that he himself had given up on. The result was premiered in 1705, the composer conducting, so successfully that Keiser found himself feeling uneasy. He thereupon whipped up a piece called *Nero* to spike his rival's guns. When it didn't, he wrote and produced his own version of *Almira*. But by that time Handel

273

had grown tired of the silly game and left for Italy with a wandering Medici. In 1709, noting that the Goose Market was lowering its standards (his own pastiches had not helped), Keiser shored up his fortunes with a prosperous marriage to a Fräulein Oldenberg. In 1717 the Goose Market, for all practical purposes, had ground to a halt, and Keiser began to explore court options by producing his operas at likely places. He may have tried Baden. He certainly tried Copenhagen but brought away only another *Papierkapellmeisterschaft*. He hung around Stuttgart for a year or two. In 1724 he seems to have reconciled himself to another round of operatic drudgery in Hamburg. Over the years he had also kept his hand in with oratorios and other religious music, and though Telemann's [665] presence blocked him from any meaningful church appointment, in 1728 he was made cantor of the cathedral and awarded a canonry there. The year before he died, the Goose Market, finally brought to its knees by the growing rage for Italian opera, closed its doors forever. Twenty-five years later it was pulled down in the interests of urban renewal.

It is probably safe to say that not one American musical layman in ten has so much as heard of Reinhard Keiser, yet it is hardly arguable that he was the greatest German opera composer before Gluck [803], always excepting the Anglicized Handel. It is true that he wrote too much and that he sometimes played to the mob, but he had that rarest of gifts among composers, a true sense of the dramatic. He also sensed that the simplest melody was the most beautiful (though he knew all the vocal gimmicks that paid off), and he was a brilliant orchestrator. In some of his big numbers there was sufficient Handelian grandeur for Handel to use them to his own ends.

RECORDINGS: Keiser has been shamefully neglected on records, the only significant recordings known to me being an LP side of excerpts from his opera *Croesus* and his *St. Mark Passion*, directed by Jörg Ewald Dähler.

[640] HOTTETERRE, Jacques-Martin
(Ut-târ´, Zhàk Mâr-taɴ´)
WIND-PLAYER TEACHER
BORN: Paris, September 29, 1674
DIED: Paris, July 16, 1763

The Hotteterres were a particularly numerous tribe of instrument makers and instrumentalists, and trying to sort out which one did what leads directly to the madhouse.

The patriarch Loys (d. c. 1620) was a woodturner in the Norman village of La Couture. He begat two daughters and six sons. Confusingly, two of the latter were named Louis and two Jean. The elder Jean (c. 1605– c. 1690) went into making instruments in Paris. He is supposed to have discovered that you could make a recorder better out of three pieces of wood than one, and to have been a virtuoso on the flageolet and the musette. His son Martin (c. 1640–1712) specialized in the latter instrument, to which he added a keyed chanter, and played in various royal outdoor bands. He was succeeded in the Poitou Hautbois et Musettes by *his* son Jean [662]. His only other known offspring was Jacques-Martin, who for unknown reasons was known as "the Roman." (He was baptized just plain Jacques, adding the Martin in 1712 in memory of his father.) Jacques-Martin's history is confused with that of a contemporary called Jacques-Jean (family connection unknown). At any rate, Jacques-Martin married Elisabeth-Geneviève Charpentier and had at least three sons whose musical contributions, if any, were negligible. He is variously said to have played the bassoon, the bass oboe, and the cello in the Grande Écurie, but he is best remembered for his connections with the transverse flute. He was apparently a virtuoso thereon, and, because he was a much-sought-after teacher, it is said that his espousal of it struck the death knell of the recorder in France. His 1707 manual was almost certainly the first ever written for the instrument (though it also dealt with the recorder and the oboe). He later wrote books on how to improvise preludes on *dessus* (melody instruments) and how to play the musette, and he published 9 opuses for flutes and the like, including sonatas and suites and many arrangements. RECORDINGS: Samples have been recorded by the Vienna Concentus Musicus, Le Rondeau de Paris, Ferdinand Conrad, Michel Piguet, James Pellerite, and others. (A duo played by Helmut Riessberger and Gernot Kury and ascribed to Louis Hotteterre [c. 1645– 1716], a cousin of Martin, is almost certainly by Jacques-Martin.)

[641] DUMAGE, Pierre (Dü-màzh´, Pē- âr´)
ORGANIST, CIVIL SERVANT
BORN: Beauvais, c. November 23, 1674
DIED: Laon, October 2, 1751

Dumage's name and fame rest chiefly on his *Livre d'orgue*, which he published in 1708. There he tells us that he studied with Louis

Marchand [619] and that he was presently organist of the collegiate church in St. Quentin (where he had been since about 1703). His father had been a musician at Beauvais Cathedral thirty-odd years earlier. Dumage left St. Quentin after 1710 for Laon Cathedral. There, however, he was unable to get along with the chapter and resigned in 1719 to take a government job. (Some accounts say that, with Clérambault [647] and Daquin [717], he inaugurated the new organ at Notre-Dame de Paris in 1733.) His organ book contains 8 pieces, his only known legacy, a second increment having disappeared. RECORDINGS: Selections have been recorded by Marie-Claire Alain and René Saorgin.

[642] DALL'ABACO, Evaristo Felice
(Dál Á-bá'-kō, Ā-vá-rēs'-tō Fā-lē'-chá)
VIOLINIST, CELLIST
BORN: Verona, July 12, 1675
DIED: München, July 12, 1742

A lawyer's son, Dall'Abaco grew up in the same town as the somewhat older Torelli [578], whom he must have known and possibly studied with. When he became a man, he took his cello and went to Modena, where he successfully freelanced for five years. After a brief hiatus in his history, he emerges in 1704 as a cellist in Maximilian II Emanuel's electoral court orchestra in Munich. It was, however, not a good year for emerging in Munich, for the elector, having cast his lot with Louis XIV, was electorally whupped on August 14 by the Duke of Marlborough at Höchstädt, Austria, in a battle generally called Blenheim. Maximilian hurriedly packed his bags and his musicians and repaired to Brussels, then to Mons two years later, and eventually to Compiègne in 1709, where circumstances were economically tight. Meanwhile Dall'-Abaco had taken a Netherlandish bride named Marie-Clémence Bultinck, who in 1710 bore him a son who was christened Joseph-Marie-Clément. (Joseph-Marie later became a noted cellist and a baron and died at ninety-five). In 1715 everybody went back to München, where the senior Dall'Abaco was appointed *Konzertmeister* and went on gradually getting more and more behind the times until he was retired in 1740 by Elector Karl Albrecht.

Between the first decade of the century and 1735, Dall'Abaco published 6 sets of pieces, 4 of them described as sonatas *da camera* and *da chiesa*, though there is little to choose between them formally. To his basically Corellian beginnings the composer's experience and peregrinations had given him a taste for French dances and abstract movements. His last two sets, designated as *concerti a più istrumenti*, are basically orchestral concerti featuring dynamic contrasts rather than opposing groups, though there is some rather timid experimentation with solo instruments.

RECORDINGS: Sonatas have been recorded by the Piacenza Ensemble and the Lugano Società Cameristica, and a concerto by Joseph Kraus.

[643] CORRETTE, Gaspard (Kôr-ret', Gàs-pàr')
ORGANIST
BORN: Delft, c. 1675 (?)
DIED: after 1712

Corrette's birthplace is indicated in a collection of music by him arranged for two melody instruments by his more famous son, Michel [779]. In 1703, when Gaspard Corrette published his only other known work, an organ *Mass* written for the use of local nuns, he was organist of the church of St. Herbland in Rouen. By 1712 he had married Marguerite Jourdain, become a father (in 1709), and taken on three other Rouen organs—at St. Pierre-le-Portier, St. Denis, and St. Jean. RECORDINGS: His *Mass*, recorded by Raymond Daveluy, is somewhat old-fashioned, showing Italian influence in its melody.

[644] ECCLES, Henry (Ek'-kels, Hen'-rē)
VIOLINIST
BORN: London, c. 1675
DIED: Paris, after 1735

Once, like John Eccles [617], said to be the son of the elder Solomon Eccles, Henry Eccles (the second of that name) now cannot be located on the family tree. All we know is that he had a violin-playing brother named Thomas, a few years older than he, who drank himself to death around 1745. He seems to have been a freelance around London and to have moved to Paris at some time between 1713 and 1720, the year in which he published his first set of violin sonatas there. The pronoun *his* is used advisedly, since more than half of the material in them was stolen direct from Giuseppe Valentini [664] and Francesco Bonporti [633]. Three years later he published a dozen more sonatas, which he may well have written himself. He was apparently for a time in the employ of the Duke of Aumont and was possibly later at Versailles. RECORDINGS:

Ferdinand Conrad has recorded (on recorder) a sonata from the second opus.

[645] WELDON, John
ORGANIST
BORN: Chichester, January 19, 1676
DIED: London, May 7, 1736

Weldon was an alumnus of the choir of Eton College, where he was trained by John Walter, the resident organist. After some lessons with Henry Purcell [581] in London, he replaced Richard Goodson (later Oxford Professor of Music) as organist of New College, Oxford University. At twenty-four he won first prize in a contest for setting Congreve's masque libretto *The Judgement of Paris* (for details see 603). This triumph brought him the then astronomical cash prize of 100 pounds; unhappily the music, save for a song or two, is lost. In 1702 he left Oxford for London, becoming organist at St. Bride's. When John Blow [552] died six years later, Weldon, already a Gentleman Extraordinary, was taken into the Chapel Royal as organist, and in 1715 was named one of the two official composers to that body. (William Croft [652] was his senior in both posts, if not in age.) In 1714 he was named organist of St.-Martin-in-the-Fields. One suspects that a decline of some sort set in not long after, for he seems to have composed very little after the middle of the decade. In 1727 Maurice Greene [727] was appointed Croft's successor, over Weldon's head, in the chapel, and the vestry at St. Martin's hired an assistant organist. By the time Weldon died, he had apparently ceased to function musically altogether; he was succeeded by William Boyce [787], who had been substituting for him for some time.

Weldon apparently wrote a good deal of dramatic music, little of which is extant. One regrets the loss of that for a 1716 revival of *The Tempest*, though one scholar argues that the score ascribed to Henry Purcell [581], for which no date is known, may be Weldon's. Otherwise his legacy consists of songs, instrumental airs, anthems, and a communion service.

RECORDINGS: A few songs have been recorded (e.g., by April Cantelo and Alfred Deller).

[646] BACH, Johann Bernhard (Bàkh, Yō'-hàn Bârn'-härt)
ORGANIST
BORN: Erfurt, November 23, 1676
DIED: Eisenach, June 11, 1749

Bernhard was the elder son of Johann Aegidius Bach, sometime director of the Erfurt town band and middle son of Johann Bach [470] and his wife, Hedwig, *née* Lammerhirt. He was thus doubly related to Johann Sebastian [684], whose father was Johann's nephew and whose mother was Johann's sister-in-law (some sort of second cousins, one supposes). Bernhard studied organ with his father and began his career at the Kaufmannskirche in Erfurt in 1695. He was evidently very good, for in a short time he had been lured away to a church in Magdeburg. In 1703, however, his father's cousin Johann Christoph [536], municipal organist and court harpsichordist in Eisenach, died, and Bernhard succeeded him in both posts, inheriting the fine new organ that Christoph had had built in the Georgikirche. Three years later the Duke of Eisenach acquired a new *Kapellmeister* in the person of Pantaleon Hebenstreit, the internationally known master of the pantaleon, a sort of dulcimer of his own invention. He injected class into the musical life of the town, which was, if anything, augmented by his successor, Georg Philipp Telemann [665], who was there from 1709 to 1712. After Telemann left, things slowly went back to normal and when, in 1741, Eisenach was incorporated into the Duchy of Saxe-Weimar, the orchestra was let go, though Bernhard kept his civic appointment and did rather well at it. Meanwhile, a score of years earlier he had married Johanna Sophia Siegler and their only child, Johann Ernst [822], became Johann Sebastian's pupil. On the other hand, Johann Gottfried Walther [680], Johann Sebastian's and Bernhard's relative through the Lammerhirts, was Bernhard's pupil.

Thanks to the industry of J. S. Bach and J. G. Walther, 4 of Bernhard's orchestral suites (copied by Bach) and 9 of his organ pieces (copied by Walther) have survived.

RECORDINGS: Franz Lehrndorfer has recorded some of the latter.

[647] CLÉRAMBAULT, Louis Nicolas (Klà-ràm-bō', Lōō-ē' Nē-kō-làs')
ORGANIST, VIOLINIST, TEACHER
BORN: Paris, December 19, 1676
DIED: Paris, October 26, 1749

From a long dynasty of court musicians, Louis was the son of a violinist, Dominique Clérambault, and the father of two organists, César-François-Nicolas and Evrard-Dominique. He learned the violin from his father, the organ from the Paris organist André Raison, of whom it was said "*Nulle* musique sans Raison" (No Music Without Judgment), and from whom J. S. Bach [684] borrowed the theme of his great C-minor passacaglia. His first job was with the Augustinians in 1707, but shortly afterward he went to Versailles to direct the concerts sponsored by Madame de Maintenon. It was no doubt through her that he came to assist Nivers [518] in his last months both at her academy for officers' daughters at St. Cyr and the church of St. Sulpice, and to succeed him in both posts when Nivers died in 1714. About the time of his first court appointment, he married Marie-Marguerite Grulé; they had seven children. In 1719 he succeeded his old teacher, Raison, as organist at the church of the Jacobins. Clérambault sometimes gave chamber music concerts in his home.

Though he was known as an organist, he left only a single livre d'orgue whose 2 suites have nothing to do with the devotional and seem to forecast the sweetness and frivolousness of the Rococo. There is also a book of harpsichord pieces and some early violin sonatas and three simphonies for two violins and continuo. But Clérambault was obviously happiest when putting music to words. His larger efforts in this area include motets, psalms, an oratorio, and some occasional or ceremonial effusions, but he is best —indeed superior—in his cantates. On mythological or (less often) biblical themes, these are carefully wrought dramatic scenes in which every note and every ornament seems calculated for its expressive effect. The Orphée (Orpheus) is said to have been the most popular example of the genre in the eighteenth century. There is also an attractive set of songs to some of La Fontaine's fables attributed to Clérambault.

RECORDINGS: Marie-Claire Alain and André Marchal have recorded the organ suites. Carlos Surinach has recorded an orchestral version of one of the simphonies, entitled Symphonia Quarta. The Orphée has been recorded by Dietrich Fischer-Dieskau, and the La Fontaine songs by Hugues Cuénod.

[648] BACH, Johann Ludwig (Båkh, Yō-
hán Lōōd'-vikh)
VIOLINIST, KEYBOARDIST, CONDUCTOR,
SCHOOLMASTER
BORN: Thal, February 4, 1677
DIED: Meiningen, c. February 27, 1731

The majority of the musical Bachs were descended from Johann [470], son of the legendary Veit. Ludwig, however, belonged to the branch of the family descended from Johann's brother, the carpetmaker Lips (i.e., Philippus). His great-grandfather and grandfather, both named Wendel, seem to have been peasants, but his father, Johann Jakob, got an education and became an organist. When he was eighteen, he eloped from Gotha with Anna Martha Schmidt. However, they were so strapped for money that they had to postpone domestic felicity for three years until Jakob nailed down the organist's job in Thal, where Ludwig was born and his mother died. Jakob subsequently became cantor in the Swabian villages of Steinach, Wasungen, and Ruhla, took three more (successive) wives, and sired a great tribe of children, of whom at least two became musicians of no great fame.

Ludwig was educated at the Gotha Gymnasium and had a fling with theology before he settled down in Salzungen as cantor. Meanwhile, in 1690 Ernst the Pius of Gotha had willed his holdings to his seven sons, of whom Bernhard, the third, was thus the first ruler of the pocket duchy of Saxe-Meiningen-Hildburghausen. Bernhard, who was every bit as pious and much more superstitious than his father, in 1699 hired Ludwig Bach to oversee the music for his religious services, of which there were many, and to keep the pages in line in the court. The job paid well enough and included board and lodgings, but Ludwig found his life cramped and depressing, and was trying to find a way out when his prince died in 1706. Ernst Ludwig, the new duke, was a less rigid type and relieved him of his more tiresome duties, gave him an orchestra to conduct, and provided him with a rental allowance, free meat, grain, and candles. Bach's nonmusical obligation was to teach painting to the princely children. Ludwig celebrated by marrying Fräulein Rust, daughter of the court architect. The duke fancied himself a poet and composer, and the two men enjoyed a splendid rapport. Unhappily, Ernst Ludwig died suddenly in 1724. His surviving heirs being minors, the state was put in charge of two of their uncles who hated each other. As a result of their feuding, Ludwig Bach was both neglected and unpaid, until after four years he demanded his salary.

Ludwig Bach was an important composer of cantatas and motets, and Johann Sebastian [684] made copies of some of them. The cantatas belong to the older type based on the scriptural lessons for the day but are marked by Italianate melody and expressiveness. Some of the motets pose a challenge to the performers. Two of his "Lu-

theran Masses" were once attributed to Sebastian.
RECORDINGS: One of the cantatas has been recorded by Uwe Gronostay.

[649] MORIN, Jean-Baptiste (Mō-ràn', Zhàn-Bà-tĕst')
COURT MUSICIAN
BORN: Orléans, 1677
DIED: Paris, 1754

Morin was educated in the choir school of Orléans Cathedral. His first post was with the Abbess de Chelles, the daughter of Louis XIV's nephew Philippe II, Duke d'Orléans, the future regent. Later he was in the service of Jean Séré, Sieur de Rieux, amateur poet and aficionado of the chase. Finally he became a musician-in-ordinary to the regent himself. It is generally agreed that Morin pioneered the French *cantate* (see 584, 599) using Italian models but adhering to French taste. His first volume, to texts by Jean-Baptiste Rousseau, who made a career of writing *cantates,* came out in 1706, but the contents had been in circulation for some years. The pattern was an alternation of *récitatifs* and *airs,* generally three of each. Two other volumes followed. Morin also published 2 collections of motets (now lost) and some songs, as well as various divertissements and occasional pieces. His favorite of all his works was the divertissement *La Chasse du cerf (The Stag Hunt),* a long programmatic affair detailing the progress of a typical hunt (in quasi-mythological terms, replete with horn calls and the French equivalents of "yoicks!" and "tally-ho!" RECORDINGS: There is a highly evocative and authentic recording by Jean-François Paillard that includes a rally of hunting horns.

[650] VIVALDI, Antonio Lucio (Vē-vàl'-dē, Àn-tōn'-yō Lōō'-chē-yō)
VIOLINIST, TEACHER, PRIEST, MUSIC DIRECTOR
BORN: Venice, March 4, 1678
DIED: Vienna, July 28, 1741

In his lifetime more honored abroad than in his own city, for the two hundred years after his death Antonio Vivaldi was remembered (when he was remembered) as a man who influenced Johann Sebastian Bach [684], and that only latterly. To be sure, a few of his instrumental works were beginning to be heard by the middle of this century, but usually in bits and pieces and in inaccurate arrangements. Moreover, these

excerpts came from the published works, for the vast repository of manuscript material (see below) had not yet become available. The turnaround seems to have come with the "discovery" and performance of the *Four Seasons* concerti around 1950, and the subsequent rage for Baroque music that came contemporaneously with the development of the high-fidelity long-playing record. Today Vivaldi is recognized as perhaps the most important figure in the early history of the solo concerto (though he thought of himself as an opera man), and a great, albeit sometimes prolix, composer in his own right.

As a child, Vivaldi's father Gianbattista (sometimes known as "G. B. Rossi" from his red hair) had come to Venice from his native Brescia, had mastered the violin, and had set up a barbershop that featured musical entertainment while one waited. In 1677 he had married Camilla Calicchio, a tailor's daughter, who bore Antonio, apparently prematurely, late the following winter. At least six siblings followed; two of the boys later made the police blotter for brawling, and one was temporarily exiled. Gianbattista, who was apparently a fine performer, gradually gave up the barbering business and became a violinist at St. Mark's, Venice. His pupil, young Antonio, is said to have made his first appearance there at ten.

Antonio was apparently destined for the priesthood early. He was tonsured at fifteen and given the bottom clerical rank of "porter." Whether because of poor health or a disinclination to his calling, it took him ten years to reach ordination. But his first attempt to say Mass brought on an attack of what he said was a lifelong affliction, involving chest pains, and thought to be perhaps asthma or angina. There is, anyhow, no basis for the silly story that he was forbidden further priestly activity because he kept interrupting the service to run out and write down themes that were occurring to him. But the image of Vivaldi (whicι he helped promote) as a helpless semi-invalid trapped in his seminary does not fit subsequent facts.

In 1704 the music director Francesco Gasparini [615] hired Vivaldi, who had already begun to make a name for himself as a soloist, to teach his instrument to the musically inclined girls of the Ospedale della Pietà. This was one of four such institutions in Venice that took in female "orphans"— mostly the bastard offspring of the citizenry. Vivaldi worked there, off and on, for thirty-five years, receiving a raise in 1708, tenure in 1711, the status of official composer on Gasparini's departure in 1713, and that of *mae-*

stro dei concerti in 1716. (But he was never *maestro del coro*—i.e., general music director—as he is often said to have been.) Given such laboratory conditions to try out his ideas, he composed prodigiously, conducted, taught, and did some local concertizing. Frederick IV of Denmark (the dedicatee of Vivaldi's Op. 2 violin sonatas) was one of those who came to hear him, and he drew other professional violinists as pupils —Pisendel [694] certainly, Heinichen [674], and Zelenka [656] probably.

Vivaldi apparently came to opera late, but once into it he made up for lost time. His first effort was *Ottone in villa:* he took a month off from the Pietà to get it on the stage in Vicenza. In the next five years he produced, in Venice, eight more operas, as well as the oratorios *Juditha triumphans* and *Moyses.* At the end of that period, he went off to Florence to produce his *Scanderbeg* (on the theme of the Albanian national hero). Instead of returning to his job, he entered the service of the Markgraf Philipp of Hesse-Darmstadt, commander of the imperial troops headquartered in Mantua. It was probably there that he met Anne Giraud (or Anna Girò "La Mantovana," as she was called), the pretty daughter of a French barber, who became his vocal pupil, protégée, and constant companion, and who later starred in his operas. Her sister Pauline (or Paolina) also joined his household as his "nurse." After producing his *Ercole sul Termodonte* in Rome in 1723, he returned to the Pietà with a new contract that gave him more freedom, requiring that he conduct the orchestra when on the premises and contribute two new concerti a month. (Eyewitness evidence suggests that Vivaldi was close to right when he said that he could compose faster than a copyist could make his manuscript practicable.) Anne made her debut the following year in an opera by Albinoni [630], and Vivaldi then took her to Rome to present her in two new works of his own, one of which enjoyed a command performance before the pope (presumably Innocent XIII, who died later that year). He was also commissioned to write a *Gloria* for the wedding, in France, of Louis XV and Marie Leszczynska. Vivaldi seems to have been absent from the Pietà for the next decade, but not necessarily from Venice, where he directed eleven new operas during that period. But he and his entourage were obviously on the road much of the time. In 1728 he met Emperor Charles VI, apparently in Trieste, and so fascinated him that the emperor neglected the current crises for several days to talk music with him, and gave him decorations, consider-

able money, and a knighthood. The next year, on Charles's invitation, he took his septuagenarian father along with his own womenfolk to Vienna and perhaps on to Münich.

In 1735 the prodigal returned to the Pietà. The authorities, who (not unreasonably) had grown impatient with him, insisted that he toe the line. But he continued to produce operas in the neighborhood and in 1737 he suffered a terrible blow to his pride. Contracted to produce an opera in Ferrara (now Papal territory), he was refused on the grounds that, as a priest, he refused to say Mass and consorted with women. A letter from this period shows Vivaldi desperately trying to justify himself to his Ferrarese patron. (A sketch by the dramatist Carlo Goldoni, depicting the composer around this time, shows him an irascible and untidy eccentric, interspersing his conversation with muttered scriptural tags. But it was written long after the fact, and a more immediate account by the playwright shows none of the grotesqueries.) In 1738 the sun shone briefly again when Vivaldi was called to Amsterdam (where his publishers Roger and Le Cène had made his name famous) to direct a music festival. On his return, however, the directors of the Pietà voted him out, and he was forced to live on the proceeds of his operas (he claimed to have written more than ninety) and to peddling concerti to whomever would buy. One taker was apparently the visiting Saxon prince Friedrich August, who late in 1739 heard Vivaldi's music performed at the Pietà and, to judge from the holdings of the Dresden library, took some back with him. A few months later, the directors of the Pietà, to build up their own library, agreed to seek out concerto manuscripts, notably from Vivaldi, whom they described as about to leave Venice; in May they paid him seventy ducats for twenty works.

It appears that Vivaldi, now sixty-two, planned to go to Vienna and capitalize on Emperor Charles's expressed admiration and friendship. About the time he arrived there, however, the emperor had died suddenly at a hunting lodge in Hungary after he had ingested a dish of mushrooms. Whether Vivaldi lacked funds to go farther or to return home, or whether he waited to see what might turn up, or whether his health had finally caught up with him, he remained in Vienna in quarters overlooking a cemetery. The next summer he developed a gastric ailment and died. Given the cheapest funeral that money could buy, he was buried in the adjacent cemetery, which has since vanished under the pavements of the city.

Vivaldi's published legacy runs to 14 collections—5 of sonatas and 9 of concerti. Of the sonata collections, one *(Pastor fido,* Op. 13) is of doubtful authorship and another (the 6 cello sonatas of Op. 14) was posthumously published.

A word must be said about the Vivaldi manuscripts. In 1926 a Turin musicologist, Alberto Gentili, who had vainly sought the lost material from the Pietà, was asked by the monks of the Collegio San Carlo (near Alessandria) to appraise some old music they wished to sell. Among it he found fourteen volumes of the missing Vivaldi material. These he traced back to the noble Durazzi of Genoa and put a genealogist named Faustino Curlo on the trail. It led to a cranky and reclusive last survivor, the Marchese Giuseppe Maria Durazzo, in whose library they found the rest of the collection. After being softened up for several years, the old man agreed to sell it for an exorbitant price, with impossible strictures on publication and performance—which took years of legal maneuvering to get around. The money was eventually forthcoming from two Turin industrialists, Roberto Foà and Filippo Giordano, who presented the collection to the Turin library in memory of their respective infant sons Mauro and Renzo. By the time the music was available the outbreak of World War II intervened, so that it was not until the era noted at the outset of this article that it was really possible to explore Vivaldi in depth. Since then, a number of other manuscript works have emerged, notably in Scandinavia. The works have been several times catalogued in the past forty years—notably by Antonio Fanna ("F" numbers), Marc Pincherle ("P" numbers), and most recently by Peter Ryom ("RV" or "R" numbers), whose system has now come into general use.

RECORDINGS: The concerti have been given an integral recording by Claudio Scimone (who seems on his way to doing all the rest of the orchestral material), and individual opuses and separate concerti have enjoyed a plethora of treatments. Of the operas, we now know the names of fewer than half of the vaunted total, and only about 20 are still extant. Of these there are recordings of *La fida ninfa,* 1732; *L'Olimpiade,* 1734; *Orlando Furioso,* 1727; *Tito Manlio,* 1720; *Catone in Utica,* 1737. There are at least two recordings of the surviving oratorio *Juditha triumphans,* and both Michel Corboz and Vittorio Negri have gone a long way toward recording the religious music. Finally, there

are innumerable recordings of isolated concerti, *sinfonie,* and sonatas. Only the solo cantatas have been seriously neglected.

[651] JOSEPH I, Holy Roman Emperor
BORN: Vienna, July 26, 1678
DIED: Vienna, April 17, 1711

Brought up in one of the great musical establishments of his time, and with a father and grandfather who were more than capable composers, Joseph I could hardly have escaped being musical. The product of Leopold I's [528] marriage to Eleanore of Pfalz-Neuberg (his third marriage; the others were brief and barren), Joseph was King of Hungary at nine and King of the Romans at twelve. In 1699 he married Wilhelmine Amalie of Braunschweig-Lüneburg. There were two children, both daughters—Maria Josepha born that same year, and Maria Amalia in 1701. After serving as an officer in the War of the Spanish Succession, Joseph succeeded his father in 1705. In his brief reign, marked by troubles with Hungary, triumph over Louis XIV, and a down-playing of Jesuitical influence in the government, he made himself generally popular. He played the harpsichord and, before he took the throne, frequently appeared in court performances as both singer and dancer. He died of smallpox at thirty-two and was succeeded by his younger brother Charles. RECORDINGS: He left a solo motet, *Regina coeli,* recorded by Rohtraud Hansmann and Wolfgang Gabriel, and some arias, two of which were recorded by Aida Poj.

[652] CROFT, William
ORGANIST, TEACHER
BORN: Nether Ettington, c. December 30, 1678
DIED: Bath, August 14, 1727

A Warwickshire lad, Croft studied with John Blow [552] while trebling in the Chapel Royal. He became the first organist on the new instrument at St. Anne's in Soho in 1700, holding the post for more than a decade. In the same year, he and Jeremiah Clarke [638] were named Gentlemen Extraordinary of the Royal Chapel (regular status to be conferred when one of the organists died. That melancholy action was taken by Francis Piggott in 1704. A year later Croft solemnized his nuptials with Mary George in the chapel; they produced no children. When Clarke killed himself in 1707, Croft had the organ all to himself. A year later he succeeded Blow in both his chapel posts—official composer and master of the children (Croft had to teach them the three R's as well as music)—and as organist at Westminster Abbey. In 1713 Oxford made him a D.Mus. on his submission of two odes. And so he went on, pursuing the tenor of his ways, which was so even as almost to be baritone. His contemporaries found him grave, decent, and dignified: in short, nice but not very exciting—terms that apply to much of his music. He wrote the standard Anglican burial service (among others), and many anthems, a number of which he published in score (an English first) in 1724 in *Musica Sacra* (2 vols.). They show the impact of late-Baroque Italian music, as do his sonatas. Those for violin, published in 1700 as by "Mr. Wm. Crofts & an Italian Mr.," are very early efforts in that genre for England. He also left some other odes, harpsichord pieces, and songs, dramatic and otherwise. He is best known today for the tune to "O God, Our Help in Ages Past," which he may or may not have written. RECORDINGS: There is an LP devoted to Croft, performed by various vocal and instrumental soloists with the harpsichordist Robert Elliott.

[653] ZUMAYA, Manuel de (Thōō-má'-yà, Má'-nōō-el dä)
ORGANIST, CHOIRMASTER, TEACHER
BORN: Mexico City, c. 1678
DIED: Oaxaca, spring 1756

One of the first important composers born in the New World, Zumaya got his training at the Mexico City Cathedral with choirmaster Antonio Salazar and organist José Ydíaquez. He was ordained and became an organist himself there in the first decade of the new century and was delegated to teach counterpoint in the choir school. He succeeded Salazar in 1711 on a provisional basis, and was confirmed in the post when Salazar died four years later. Meanwhile a new viceroy, the Duke of Linares, had arrived from Spain, full of the growing Spanish passion for Italian opera, and he persuaded Zumaya to set Silvio Stampiglia's 1699 libretto *Il Partenope*. (Handel [683] used a revised version in 1730.) Zumaya's work was produced in the viceregal palace that spring, and, so far as we know, was the first opera ever produced in North America. (Tomás de Torrejón's *La Purpura de la rosa* [542] was a decade ahead of it, but that was south of the Isthmus.) Twenty-eight years later, at the invitation of the Bishop of Oaxaca, Zumaya abandoned his post and settled in Oaxaca as

a parish priest. But three years later, during which period he had broken all ties with Mexico City, his sponsor died and his job dried up. The cathedral chapter then offered him the directorship of the choir, which he accepted. He left rather conservative religious music and a number of highly Italianate *villancicos*. RECORDINGS: One of the *villancicos* has been recorded by Roger Wagner.

[654] SCARLATTI, Pietro Filippo (Skär-làt'-tē, Pē-ā'-trō Fē-lēp'-pō)
ORGANIST, CHOIRMASTER
BORN: Rome, January 5, 1679
DIED: Naples, February 22, 1750

The eldest of Alessandro Scarlatti's [583] children, Pietro was the only son, other than Domenico [687], to survive to manhood, as far as we know. In 1705 he went to Urbino as choirmaster of the cathedral. While there he married Vittoria Glieri, who gave him three children, Domenico, Alessandro, and Anna. But Alessandro had more ambitious plans for him and in 1708 fetched him back to Naples. For a while Pietro served the court as a substitute organist and then in 1712 was given the full-time post. But that was it, for he never went any further. In 1728 he wrote his only opera, *Clitarco*, which has vanished. He left his family badly off. The children petitioned unsuccessfully that his son Alessandro be given his post. Anna is said to have been given a pauper's funeral. Pietro Scarlatti left 3 cantatas, a few bits and pieces, and a score of keyboard toccatas—one of which has been recorded by Luciano Sgrizzi.

[655] KAUFFMANN, Georg Friedrich (Kouf'-màn, Gä'-ôrg Frēd'-rikh)
ORGANIST
BORN: Ostermondra, February 14, 1679
DIED: Merseburg, February 24, 1735

After studying organ with Johann Heinrich Buttstädt [605] in Erfurt, Kauffmann continued with Johann Friedrich Alberti, organist of the cathedral in Merseburg, a city near his birthplace. In 1698 Alberti suffered a stroke, which robbed him of the use of his right hand, and Kauffmann substituted for him until Alberti died a dozen years later. He was then given Alberti's place in the cathedral and as court organist to the Duke of Saxe-Merseburg. (Some accounts call him the court *Kapellmeister.*) When Johann Kuhnau [582] died in 1722, Kauffmann was a finalist in the competition for his successor at the Thomaskirche in Leipzig, but he was eventually beaten out by Johann Sebastian Bach [684]. He wrote a manual for composers but apparently never found a publisher for it. He suffered from tuberculosis in his last years, and was working on the publication of his organ chorales when he died. His widow finished the job for him, the work as a whole being called *Harmonische Seelenlust (Harmonic Joy for the Soul)*. It is said to have been the first such collection in over a century. An oratorio and 4 cantatas have survived. His organ music is marked by interesting decorative and "programmatic" effects. RECORDINGS: Some of the organ preludes have been recorded by Franz Lehrndorfer, and in the composer-authorized versions for oboe and organ by Georg Meerwein and Wilhelm Krumbach.

[656] ZELENKA, Jan Dismas (Ze-leng'-kà, Yän Dēz'-màs)
CONTRABASSIST
BORN: Louňovice, Bohemia, October 16, 1679
DIED: Dresden, December 22, 1745

Jan (or Johann) Zelenka got his basic training from his father, Jiří, a village schoolmaster-organist. After some polishing at the Jesuit College in Prague, he went to work, c. 1709, for a Count Hartig or Baron von Hartwig, but was hired in 1710 to play contrabass in the remarkable Dresden court orchestra of the Elector Friedrich August. In 1715, though Zelenka seemed a perfectly capable composer and was already thirty-five years old, the elector let him go to Vienna to study with Fux [585]. The next year he went on an Italian junket with his employer, during which he is said to have studied with Antonio Lotti [613]; if he did, it was not for long, for he was back in Vienna by 1717. Two years later he returned to the Dresden court, where he became an assistant to Kapellmeister Johann David Heinichen [674], who was in poor health. But when Heinichen died in 1729, Zelenka was passed over in favor of the flashier Hasse [736]. He was paid a healthy salary and was given the rather meaningless title of Court Composer, but the whole thing depressed him and he wrote little after that.

Zelenka's music was admired by connoisseurs, including J. S. Bach [684], in its time, and his church compositions are said to have been kept in a special cabinet in Dresden Cathedral. The bulk of his output is religious, including several Masses and Mass movements, Magnificats, responsories, mo-

tets, and cantatas, in which he shows himself a master of counterpoint and harmony. He also wrote Italian oratorios, a festival opera, orchestral works, and chamber music. There is something of the glitter of Lully [517] and something of the fluidity of Corelli [565] in it, but Zelenka is very much his own man and has no temerity about experimenting with rhythm, tone color, dissonance, and even the use of Czech tunes or imitations thereof.

RECORDINGS: The record industry has been promoting a small Zelenka revival lately. The set of wind trio sonatas has been done by a group headed by Heinz Holliger, with individual examples by other performers; Nicholas Harnoncourt conducts a selection of orchestral pieces and Alexander van Wijnkoop directs the entire orchestral output, both including an overture called *Hypochondria*. There is also a *Lamentations* by Milan Munclinger.

[657] SCHIEFFERDECKER, Johann Christian (Shē'-fer-dek'-er, Yō'-hàn Krēst'-yàn)
ORGANIST, HARPSICHORDIST
BORN: Teuchern, November 10, 1679
DIED: Lübeck, April 5, 1732

Schiefferdecker is remembered with admiration as the man who married Buxtehude's [525] daughter. It happened in 1707 after better men than he—Handel [683] and Mattheson [668] and maybe even J. S. Bach [684]—had turned her down. She was four years older than he (and thus even older than they), but with her came the prestigious appointment as organist of Lübeck's Marienkirche. Schiefferdecker came from a village near Weissenfels, where his father, Christian, was organist-schoolteacher. From 1692 to 1702 he attended the Thomasschule and the university in Leipzig, and in his latter years there produced a couple of operas. That led into a job as keyboard accompanist at the Goose Market opera house in Hamburg in the palmy days of Reinhard Keiser [639], who produced three more Schiefferdecker operas. This brings us back to the Lübeck coup. There he continued Buxtehude's Advent concerts on Sunday evenings, up to his last two years there. We are not told how the marriage worked out. Most of Schiefferdecker's music is lost. There survive a *Missa brevis*, a few cantatas and arias, a set of concerti (or *ouvertures),* and a single chorale prelude (recorded by Jørgen Ernst Hansen).

[658] SARRO, Domenico Natale (Sär'-rō, Dō-mān'-ē-kō)
CONDUCTOR
BORN: Trani, December 24, 1679
DIED: Naples, January 25, 1744

Sarro went from his birthplace on the Adriatic coast northwest of Bari to study at the Neapolitan conservatory of San Onofrio when he was still a small child. One source says that he remained there as a student for nine years and then for several more as a teacher. In 1702 he produced a religious opera for a Neapolitan organization. On Alessandro Scarlatti's [583] defection from the viceregal court the next year, Sarro tried out for the directorship, but was defeated by Gaetano Veneziano. However, he was given the assistant director's post in 1704. In 1705 he married and shortly afterward launched what was eventually to be a highly successful, if local, operatic career. This, however, was postponed by military invasions and political jockeying in court musical circles (see Francesco Mancini, 631, for details). In 1718 he returned to his opera writing, and produced more than twenty between then and 1741, as well as many shorter dramatic works and a number of oratorios. Though he had lost his court post, he was reappointed in 1725 and made municipal music director to boot three years later. When Mancini was laid low by a stroke in 1735, Sarro became de facto chief of operations at court and inherited the title when Mancini died in 1737. Many of his stage works were comedies, and he was a pioneer in the movement toward putting primary emphasis on vocal melody to the detriment of the instrumental parts. Besides the works noted, he left a few pieces of religious music and a single flute concerto. RECORDINGS: Raymond Meylan has recorded the flute concerto, and Karl Ristenpart the Sonata in A minor for flute, strings, and harpsichord.

[659] LOEILLET, Jean-Baptiste, of London (Lwä-yā', Zhàn Bà-tēst')
FLUTIST, OBOIST, VIOLINIST, HARPSICHORDIST, TEACHER, CONCERT MANAGER
BORN: Ghent, November 18, 1680
DIED: London, July 19, 1730

The Loeillets managed to create more confusion in two generations about which was who and who wrote what than the Bachs did in eight. The chief problem rests with J.-B. Loeillet of London and J.-B. Loeillet of Ghent [697]. For a long time many insisted that they were one and the same, and

lumped their compositions together, but it is known now that the Gantois Jean-Baptiste (who lived in Lyons) was first cousin to the Jean-Baptiste of London (who was born in Ghent and who, after his emigration, was called "John"—and sometimes, to confuse the issue even more, "John Lully"). The latter Loeillet, the subject of this article, was the son of Jean-Baptiste-François Loeillet, a master surgeon, and his second wife, née Barbe Buys, who also produced the oboist-composer Jacques Loeillet [685], often carelessly confused with the other two.

Nothing else is known of the elder J.-B. Loeillet until after he crossed the Channel around 1705. He found work in the orchestra of the Drury Lane Theatre, then became solo wind player in the opera orchestra at the Queen's Theatre. On the side he began building up a clientele of people eager to pay good money to learn the harpsichord from a distinguished foreign musician. He is supposed also to have inaugurated the English craze for the transverse flute. In 1710 he was able to give up being a regular wage earner and devote himself to his more lucrative activity. He also began a series of weekly musical at-homes in which many of the participants were wealthy amateurs who paid well for the privilege of sitting in. (One of his concerts introduced Corelli's concerti [565] to England.) Not surprisingly, Loeillet died a rich man, with a large and valuable collection of musical instruments. He left a set of "lessons" (suites) for harpsichord and 3 of sonatas, Opp. 1–3, all published in London. The first two sets of sonatas are trio sonatas, the third being designated as "solos": they are for a variety of melody instruments (specified) with continuo. Loeillet was aware of English musical tradition and at his best exhibited a flair for Italianate melody.

RECORDINGS: There are many recordings, but one must beware of mislabelings and misattributions.

[660] COURBOIS, Philippe (Kōōr-bwä', Fē-lēp')
TEACHER
BORN: c. 1680 (?)
DIED: after 1730

About all that is known of Courbois is that he was music master at the court of Anne-Louise-Bénédicte de Bourbon, Duchess of Maine (see 599), in the first third of the eighteenth century. Apart from some isolated airs, his only surviving works are 7 fine cantates, of which Gérard Souzay has recorded the masterpiece, Dom Quichotte.

[661] DORNEL, Louis-Antoine (Dôr-nel', Lōō-ês' Ȧn-twȧn')
ORGANIST, THEORIST, TEACHER
BORN: c. 1680
DIED: Paris, after 1756

Nothing is known of Dornel before his less than triumphant victory over Jean-Philippe Rameau [675] in the competition for the organist's job at Ste. Madeleine-en-la-Vité. (Rameau refused to abide by the rules.) During his decade there, he published his three opuses, containing solo and trio sonatas and suites. In 1716 he began substituting for the organist André Raison at the royal abbey of Ste. Geneviève, and succeeded him there on his death in 1719 (as Clérambault [647] did at the Jacobins' church). In 1725 he was appointed, concurrently, to be music master to the Opéra, but was forced out by Jean-Féry Rebel [604] in 1742. Later he published a treatise objecting to keys with all those sharps and flats. Apart from his sonatas, Dornel left a few *cantates, airs,* and keyboard pieces. His work shows a leaning toward polyphony, a working knowledge of Corellian instrumentalism, and no great evidence of imagination. Rafael Tambyeff has recorded an organ *noël.*

[662] HOTTETERRE, Jean (Ut-târ', Zhȧn)
WIND-INSTRUMENT PLAYER
BORN: c. 1680 (?)
DIED: Paris, February 20, 1720

The third Jean Hotteterre was a grandson of the first, the younger son of Martin, and the brother of Jacques "le Romain" [640]. He was a member of the royal Grands Hautbois and of the Hautbois et Musettes de Poitou, though it is not clear what he played. He left a single work, a *Rustic Wedding* suite for melody instrument and continuo. RECORDINGS: This suite is performed (on recorder) by the Telemann Society and (on hurdy-gurdy) by Michèle Fromenteau.

[663] VALENTINE, Robert
FLUTIST
BORN: Leicester, c. 1680
DIED: c. 1735

Nothing is known of Valentine before 1708, when he published his Op. 2 recorder sonatas in Rome, where he was known as Roberto Valentini—though he was undoubtedly related to the several eighteenth-century musical Valentines in and from Leicestershire. He presumably remained in Italy until his return home in 1731. He was somehow connected with the Dresden court at one time. His compositions, mostly published (in Amsterdam and London as well as in Rome), are with few exceptions for recorder(s) and continuo—sonatas, suites, and airs. They reflect post-Corellian [565] Italian melody but are otherwise pretty average stuff. RECORDINGS: Ferdinand Conrad has recorded a sonata and the Cologne Musica Antiqua a Concerto in B-flat Major for flute.

[664] VALENTINI, Giuseppe (Vȧ-len-tē'-nē, Jōō-sep'-pē)
VIOLINIST, POET
BORN: Florence, c. 1680
DIED: after 1759

Not to be confused with his contemporary "Roberto Valentini" (see under 663), he was, to judge from his first eight (instrumental) opuses, in Rome at the same time. During part of this period he was in the employ of Prince Ruspoli there. In 1714–15 he produced two operas at Cisterna (between Rome and Naples) under the patronage of the Prince of Caserta, Michelangelo Caetani. He is said to have been at the Medici court in Florence in 1735, though his occasional compositions continued to be written for Rome into the 1740s. At the end of that decade, a "Signor Valentini" turns up in Paris, where he published 6 four-part "simphonies," and where he was listed as a violin teacher in 1759. To judge from his violin music, he must have been an expert fiddler, for he goes so far as to explore the then remote sixth position. Some of his publications have whimsical names—*Bizzarries, Chamber Ideas, Harmonic Vacation for Three,* or *Allurements.* The whimsy is farther at times: Valentini tells us in some of the sonatas that he has included extra allegros for people who can't handle the hard ones, and in one preface he notes that he has broken formal rules to please those who don't like to be hemmed in. His concerti follow the new paths being blazed by the Venetians. RECORDINGS: One concerto for oboe has been recorded by Silvano Prestini and (in trumpet transcription) by Maurice André.

[665] TELEMANN, Georg Philipp (Te'-le-mȧn, Gä-ôrg' Fē-lēp')
CONDUCTOR, PUBLISHER, MUSIC DIRECTOR, CONCERT PROMOTER
BORN: Magdeburg, March 14, 1681
DIED: Hamburg, June 25, 1767

When, around 1940, two or three Telemann recordings found their way into American catalogs, not one American music lover in ten had so much as heard of the composer. But in his own time—the era of J. S. Bach [684] and Handel [683]—he was the most prolific, most influential, and best-known musician in the Germanies. Influenced in some degree by the Italians and a passionate admirer of the French, he made "serious" music a popular art, saw to it that it was available to the householder, and, largely through public concerts, educated the public to enjoy it.

Telemann was the son of a clergyman and the grandson of clergymen. When he was four, his father Heinrich died, leaving his wife (née Anna Haltmeier) to bring up their surviving three children. The younger son, though there were no musical genes in his ancestry, proved musically precocious: at a very early age he had taught himself to play the cittern, the flute, and the violin, and was trying to compose. At ten he was attending the Old City School, where, as a matter of course, he had music lessons with the cantor, Benedikt Christiani. By the time he was twelve, he had written an opera, Sigismundus, in which he sang the lead. At this point his mother decided that the musical nonsense had gone far enough and ordered him to stop. However, like the young Handel and young Bach of legend, he continued to work at it under cover. When he was thirteen, Anna sent him off to Zellerfeld to study under the tutelage of the headmaster, Caspar Calvör, a onetime friend of his father, and a man noted for his educational pragmatism—a true Gradgrind by reputation. But it turned out that Calvör was a secret music addict. Delighted with his protégé's progress and talent, he gave him free rein to learn what he wanted, and in no time Telemann's music was being heard all over Zellerfeld—not a large theater, to be sure, but better than most of us can hope for, especially at age sixteen, unless we are rock stars. After four years, he moved on to the Gymnasium at Hildesheim, where the rector seized on his abilities to supply music for the school plays. Academically Telemann did well; musically he picked up the winds and strings he had not previously mastered, wrote for the local monks, and went frequently to performances in nearby Hanover.

Around 1700, Telemann promised to buckle down at last to a serious calling, and set out for Leipzig to become a lawyer. Even before he got there, a meeting with young Handel in Halle caused him to waver, and when he arrived, he found that

Fate had decreed he room with a music enthusiast. The roommate soon had the choir of the Thomaskirche singing Telemann, whose work so impressed the authorities that they commissioned him to compose for them on a regular basis. In 1701 the frail Kuhnau [582] had just been appointed cantor, and found his style cramped by the young upstart, who was being privately assured that he was next in line. It was not long before Telemann chucked all pretense of studying law and, abetted by other students, set himself up as a powerful musical force in Leipzig. Nicolaus Strungk, director of the local opera house, having died, Telemann took over in 1702 and began turning out operas. In that same year he organized a student Collegium Musicum which gave public concerts, and served both city and university. (It was later directed by J. S. Bach and is considered to have been the lineal ancestor of the Leipzig Gewandhaus Orchestra, which is still going strong.) In 1704, promising that if he got the job he would not ask for more money and would provide free Sunday concerts with his band, Telemann was appointed organist and Kapellmeister of the Neukirche. He also, as a result of Kuhnau's protests, agreed not to sing any more in his opera house.

A year later, however, Telemann found himself unable to resist an offer of a job as Kapellmeister to Count Erdmann von Promnitz, an aficionado of French music, at his estate at Sorau, Brandenburg (now Żary, Poland), about a hundred miles southeast of Berlin. Fearing the Swedish military activity thereabout, however, Telemann left, probably within the year, though the evidence is ambiguous. But before he went, he had become acquainted with, and used, Polish folk music, and had fallen in love with a local landowner's daughter named Amalie Louise Eberlin. His next stop, probably in 1708, was Eisenach, where he became the Konzertmeister at the court under the famous pantaleonist Pantaleon Hebenstreit (see 646). Before the year was out, Telemann was above him, and Hebenstreit left in a huff. While in Eisenach, Telemann became acquainted with Johann Bernhard Bach [646] and his cousin Johann Sebastian [684], for whose son Carl Philipp Emanuel [801] Telemann stood godfather in 1714. In 1709, after swearing a solemn oath not to dawdle along the way and above all to come back, he was allowed to return to Sorau to marry his Louise. Two years later she died in childbed.

Telemann afterward said that he grew up in Eisenach. No doubt this blow contributed to his maturation. Although the Duke of Eisenach admired his art passionately, Telemann chose to leave in 1712 to direct the choir of the Barfüsserkirche in Frankfurt am Main, and to be generally in charge of the city's music. Not long after his arrival there he was also choirmaster at the Katharinenkirche and director of the collegium concerts of a local but influential club, the Frauensteingesellschaft. In 1714 he married Maria Catharina Textor, the daughter of a local politician, who gave him ten children and lifelong misery. Meanwhile, he had kept up his relationship with the Eisenach court, sending back music for this or that occasion when it was needed, and in 1716 Duke Johann Wilhelm named him *Kapellmeister von Haus aus,* which meant that he was welcome to *meister* the *Kapelle* any time he was in the neighborhood. Meanwhile Duke Ernst of Saxe-Gotha was dangling a lucrative and prestigious offer and hinting that he might be able to have Telemann made overall *Kapellmeister* to all the little Saxe-princedoms. Telemann took this to the Frankfurt elders, who were delighted to make things more attractive there for him.

In 1721, however, Telemann faced them with what he said was a gratuitous bid from Hamburg for him to take over the cantorship of the Johanneum (a Latin school specializing in church music) and run the musical side of the five main churches. They were either unwilling or unable to match it, and he was installed in his new post in October of that year, to work at it for the remaining forty-six of his long life. In terms of productivity, it was terribly demanding. It required him to write a Passion, an oratorio, a serenata, whatever occasional pieces were needed, and 104 cantatas every year, as well as teach at the Johanneum (an activity he detested). Nevertheless, he was soon giving concerts with a collegium and working at the Goose Market Opera. This secular activity upset the city fathers, who threatened to order him to abstain. At that point, in 1722, old Kuhnau expired back in Leipzig and Telemann reminded the council of its ancient promise. Using this as a club, he got the local people to keep their hands off his activities and give him a raise as well. (The Leipzig post eventually went to his old friend J. S. Bach.) One cannot blame him for wanting to stay in Hamburg. What with his Eisenach salary and royalties for his cantata and Passion librettos, which by Hamburg custom were peddled at the performances, he was making *per annum* three times what Bach made in his best year. Nonetheless Hamburg left something to be desired. Prices were high and the politicians

were tightfisted, and he sometimes had to reach into his own pocket to secure the kind of performance he wanted. But he rode it out and was soon conducting the kind of concerts he had attained in Leipzig and Frankfurt, some of which included his church compositions, no doubt ensuring more libretto sales. Indeed most of the music he played was his own, designed to please rather than edify, and he charged people a pretty penny to hear it. In 1722, after Keiser [639] had failed at the Goose Market and apparently left for what he hoped would be greener fields, Telemann took over the opera and ran it until its ultimate collapse in 1738, producing along the way a number of works by Handel, with whom he kept up a correspondence. In 1728 he began publishing a musical periodical (it contained music for home performance) called *Der getreue Musikmeister (The Faithful Music Teacher),* often doing his own engraving. (He also published much of his other music under similar conditions, including the *Harmonischer Gottesdienst [Harmonic Divine Service],* a complete cycle of church cantatas.) He turned down an offer from the newly Westernized Russian court in St. Petersburg in 1729, but eight years later he fulfilled a lifelong dream by visiting Paris for eight months, joining enthusiastically in the musical life and making friends with the leading composers. Back in Hamburg, he continued to compose what he was supposed to compose and amused himself with his hobby of plant collecting, to which it pleased Handel to contribute rare specimens. The Goose Market Opera closed, and he no longer had to consider writing operas. In 1740 he went out of the publishing business and sold off the plates, saying that he meant to spend his spare time getting his ideas about music on paper, but the only serious evidence of such work was his 1752 *Neues musicalisches System,* which was largely a discussion of the nature of enharmonic tones. After all those children and years of nagging, his wife ran off with a Swede, which would have been a relief had not she left a mountain of debts which his friends chipped in to help him meet. As with his friends Bach and Handel, Telemann's eyes went bad in his last years. At eighty-six he succumbed to what was described as an acute chest ailment—probably pneumonia. Bach and Handel were long dead; Mozart was already eleven. Telemann's successor was his godson, C. P. E. Bach, though in the interim before he arrived from Berlin, Telemann's own grandson, Georg Michael Telemann, later cantor at Riga, filled in.

Telemann's output was enormous—over 1,500 church cantatas and numerous others for state and ceremonial occasions, Passions, oratorios, operas, Masses, orchestral suites, concerti, sonatas, songs, keyboard works, and others. It still remains for someone to sort out and impose order and a numbering system on this great mass of material.

RECORDINGS: It is thus difficult to talk about the spate of Telemann recordings that has poured out in the last thirty years, save to note that it has focused largely on every aspect of the instrumental music. The vocal music, on the other hand, has been barely skimmed. Of the operas there appear to be versions only of the comedies *Der geduldige Sokrates (Patient Socrates)* and *Pimpinone* the two-character forerunner of *La Serva padrona* by Pergolesi [782]. There is a scattering of cantatas, but probably no more than one or two percent of the whole. Of larger religious works one notes a Passion each according to Sts. Mark and Luke, the oratorio *Der Tag des Gerichts (Judgment Day)*, and a couple of Magnificats.

[666] PHILIDOR, Anne Danican (Fē-lē-dôr', Àn Dà-nē-kà*n'*)
OBOIST, CONDUCTOR, CONCERT PROMOTER
BORN: Paris, April 11, 1681
DIED: Paris, October 8, 1728

A feminist writer recently listed Anne Philidor in a rundown of Great Women Composers. Evidently she neglected to look at the musician's biography, which would have told her that this particular Anne was every bit as male as Marie-Joseph Canteloube [1722]. (The odd name came from his godfather, Anne, Duke of Noailles, who in the 1690s backed court productions of three pastorals by the teenage Philidor.) Anne was the son of the elder André Danican Philidor [549], and was the much older half-brother (by forty-five years!) of the chess-playing François-André Danican Philidor. He played in all the royal musical organizations—stable, chapel, and chamber. In 1725 he founded the Concert Spirituel, which until the Revolution offered religious and instrumental music to subscription audiences. He conducted these concerts during the last two years of his short life, and in 1727 also inaugurated the Concerts Français, which did not long survive him. He left a few manuscript religious compositions and 2 books of *pièces* for melody instrument and continuo, from which both

Michel Piguet and Jean-Pierre Rampal have recorded a D-minor sonata.

[667] PHILIDOR, Pierre Danican (Fē-lē-dôr', Pē-är' Dà-nē-kà*n'*)
FLUTIST, OBOIST
BORN: Paris, August 22, 1681
DIED: Paris, September 1, 1731

Pierre Philidor came into the world only four months after his first cousin Anne Danican [666] and outlived him by only three years, dying at fifty. He was one of the twelve children of the wind player Jacques Danican Philidor *cadet,* brother to André Danican [549], the tribal patriarch. Like Anne, he had a pastoral produced at court when he was only sixteen and played in the royal bands, both outdoors and in. He wrote duos and trios for melody instruments, with and without continuo. RECORDINGS: Pierre Pierlot has recorded a suite of his on the oboe.

[668] MATTHESON, Johann (Màt'-te-zōn, Yō'-hàn)
SINGER, KEYBOARDIST, LEXICOGRAPHER, TRANSLATOR, DIPLOMAT
BORN: Hamburg, September 28, 1681
DIED: Hamburg, April 17, 1764

Johann Mattheson was by no means the composer he felt himself to be, but he remains one of the most important musical figures in the Germanies of his time. The third son and namesake of a tax collector, he seems to have been as a child an unbearably forward as he was conceited and opinionated as an adult. He had, however, a right to be proud of himself, for there appears to have been very little that he could not do. He readily absorbed knowledge of all kinds, and was apparently obsessed with a need to impart it to others. He became fluent in several languages, ancient and modern, studied law, and was a notable dancer, singer, fencer, horseman, and dresser. A pupil of J. N. Hanff [601], he became a virtuoso organist before he reached puberty, was soloist with the Goose Market Opera from the age of fifteen, and for a time, until his father retrieved him, was the pampered darling of the Norwegian viceregal court. When he was eighteen he wrote his first opera—and guess who the star was!

When a Saxon fiddler named Handel [683], four years his junior, joined the Goose Market Opera orchestra in 1703, Mattheson took him under his personal wing. That same year the two went over to Lübeck to check out the opening for an assistant and possible successor to Buxtehude [525] at the Marienkirche but evidently decided that the spinster daughter who went with the position negatively outweighed the security it offered. (Schiefferdecker [657] was hungrier or more ambitious than they.) Mattheson afterward fondly recalled the journey as a time of liberation, however. But a year later the friendship nearly foundered. The Goose Market was playing Mattheson's new opera, *Die unglückselige Cleopatra (Unlucky Cleopatra)*, and, having breathed his last onstage as Anthony, the composer descended to the pit to spell Handel as harpsichordist-conductor. But Handel, perhaps piqued by the fact that Mattheson had stolen his pupil Cyril Wich, son of the English Ambassador or perhaps drunk with power, refused to budge. The ensuing struggle brought the opera to a halt. Furious, Mattheson invited Handel to step outside. Out came the swords and the thing might have ended tragically had not Mattheson, in a wild lunge, snapped his blade on one of Handel's large brass buttons. They eventually made up. There was a Lenten season years later during which Mattheson conducted Barthold Brockes's Passion in settings by Keiser [639], Telemann [665], himself, and Handel. Shortly before he died, he published the first German biography of his sometime friend, largely cribbed from one published in England the year before. (In his famous musicobiographical encyclopedia, however, the entry under "Mattheson" is four times longer than that under "Handel.")

Mattheson's singing career came to an end around 1705. As a result of his link with the Wiches, he became secretary to the ambassador a year later, and in the time between the death of Sir John and the appointment of Cyril in his place, served as acting representative of the British government in Hamburg. He became a devout Anglophile, mastered the language, and married Catharina Jennings, an Englishwoman, in 1709. His operatic career ended with *Boris Godunow* in 1710 and *Henrico IV* in 1711. (The latter deals not with the English king but with the hapless ruler of Castile.) In 1715 Mattheson was appointed *Kapellmeister* of the local cathedral, for which he wrote, over the next dozen years, a string of Passions and oratorios. Four years later he was given a similar title by the Duke of Holstein, which seems to have been largely honorary.

Meanwhile, his hearing was giving him serious trouble, and he was turning increasingly to writing. By 1728, when it became no longer possible for him to carry out his duties, he had already published ten books, most of them theoretical and involving slashing attacks on outmoded classical notions of music. He had also initiated the first German journal of music criticism, *Critica musica* in 1722. It survived for three years. Other works dealt with opera as drama and the validity elsewhere of the dramatic style, what the good *Kapellmeister* should know (a *tour de force* of learning), and most of all the 1740 *Grundlage einer Ehren-Pforte (Foundation for a Triumphal Arch)*, a dictionary of 149 composers. Not always trustworthy (though most of the living supplied their own material) nor without bias, it nevertheless remains an indispensable source book. Mattheson died at eighty-three (three years younger than his contemporary and fellow-citizen Telemann) and was buried with his wife in the Michaelskirche, toward whose restoration he had left his considerable fortune. He wrote an oratorio for his own funeral.

Besides the works noted, Mattheson left some Italian cantatas and other occasional secular pieces, and some instrumental pieces, including sonatas (one for two harpsichords was meant to be played by himself and Cyril Wich).

RECORDINGS: His most extensive representation on records in this country to date is an LP side of excerpts from his *Boris Godunow* conducted by Friedrich Brückner-Rüggeberg. There is also a sonata for three unaccompanied recorders by the Telemann Society.

[669] MOURET, Jean Joseph (Mōō-rā', Zhàn Zhō-zef')
MUSIC DIRECTOR, SINGER
BORN: Avignon, April 11, 1682
DIED: Charenton, December 22, 1738

It is probably safe to say that Mouret's music is known to more Americans than that of any French composer before the nineteenth century, for the opening movement of his 1729 *Fanfares* has long been the theme music for the television program "Masterpiece Theater." The son of a silk merchant who played the violin, Mouret first appears in three dimensions in Paris in 1707 as music teacher to the household of the Maréchal de Noailles. Soon after he was given charge of the music of Anne-Louise-Bénédicte de Bourbon, Duchess of Maine—she of the "Grandes nuits de Sceaux," to which he contributed the lyric comedy *Le Mariage de Ragonde,* an unusual genre so early in France. Earlier the same year the

Opéra had staged his opera-ballet *Les Festes et la triomphe de Thalie,* also full of comic and realistic elements. The prologue in which Thalia, Muse of Comedy, bests Melpomene, Muse of Tragedy, created such a scandal in those halls so long devoted to the ostensibly serious that Mouret was forced to omit the triumphal aspect of his title and add a scene criticizing the blasphemy. By this time he was also working as a conductor at the Opéra. At some point he married a lady named Marie Prompt, who promptly gave him a daughter. In 1716 he established ties with the Théâtre Français, and in 1717 with the Nouveau Théâtre Italien, where he was able to give full rein to his talent for comedy and popular melody. This theater pointed toward *opéra comique,* especially when in 1718 it turned from Italian to French. In 1720 Mouret was appointed a singer to the Chamber of the boy king Louis XV, and during the Regency years was one of the most popular composers in that world of Watteauesque *fêtes galantes.* Many of his melodies became popular songs. From 1728 to 1734 he was part of a troika managing the Concert Spirituel, but there was so much mismanagement that in the latter year the series was turned over to Jean-Féry Rebel [604] and Mouret was dropped. In rapid succession he also lost his posts at Sceaux (his employers died), and at the Théâtre Italien. Though highly placed friends came to his rescue, he went mad and was committed to the famous asylum at Charenton, where he died at the end of the same year. As noted he is chiefly remembered for his *Suites de simphonies,* of which the *Fanfares,* specifically scored for trumpets, oboes, violins, timpani, and continuo, is the first. RECORDINGS: Both suites have been recorded by Jean-François Paillard and others.

[670] RATHGEBER, Johann Valentin
(Rāt'-gā-ber, Yō'-hàn Fä'-len-tēn)
ORGANIST, SCHOOLMASTER, MONK,
CHOIRMASTER, EDITOR
BORN: Oberelsbach, April 3, 1682
DIED: Banz, June 2, 1750

The son of the schoolmaster-organist of a hill town in Lower Franconia, he studied theology at the university of nearby Würzburg. In 1704 he took up the paternal trade(s) in an orphanage in that city. After three years he got a job as valet and musician to Abbot Kilian Düring of the Benedictine monastery at Banz, just north of Bamberg. The monastery was wealthy, and Rathgeber evidently liked what he found there, for he joined the order before the year was out, underwent ordination in 1711, and was named *Kapellmeister* soon afterward. He brought a measure of fame to Banz, particularly through his religious music, whose tunefulness and simplicity recommended it to churches unable to afford professional-caliber musical organizations. He is said also to have entertained the brethren at refection with his songs. Despite all this popularity and success, he, like his Siberian counterpart in a well-known limerick, apparently found his life growing "drearier and drearier." Denied permission to travel, in 1721 he escaped from his cell and set out to see the world, especially as it was manifested in Swabia, Bavaria, and the Rhineland. He also began collecting, editing, and arranging popular songs, which he published anonymously in 1733 (Vol. 1) and 1737 (Vol. 2) as *Ohren-vergnügende und Gemüthergötzende Tafelkonfekt (Ear-Pleasing and Heart-Delighting Goodies).* But there was a warrant out for him, and in the latter year they caught up with him and brought him back to Banz. In Max Reinhardt's play *The Miracle,* the errant nun returns to the convent to find that the Virgin has substituted for her in her absence. Rathgeber was not so blessed. Instead he was locked in a dark hole beneath the kitchen and might have remained there had not his admirers clamored for his release. At length, after he was thought sufficiently to have abased himself (both in the basement and at the abbot's feet), he was restored to his old post. Apparently he composed no more sacred music, but he did turn out a collection of airs for keyboard and another volume of the *Tafelkonfekt.* He died just short of two months before J. S. Bach [684].

A number of years ago Max Friedländer (1852–1934) deduced from a cipher on the title pages of the *Tafelkonfekt* that the composer must have been Rathgeber, and since the publisher was an old friend of the renegade's, there is no reason to challenge his conclusion. (In the same way, Hans Joachim Moser [1889–1967] figured out that a fourth volume was by Johann Caspar Seyfert [733].) Meant purely for amusement, the contents are not great music, but it is lively and often charming, and represents a reawakening of interest in the *Lied* after a long dry spell.

RECORDINGS: Selections have been recorded by groups directed by Willy Spilling and Fritz Neumeyer.

[671] DANDRIEU, Jean-François (Dàn-drē-ö', Zhán Fràn-swà')
KEYBOARDIST
BORN: Paris, c. 1682
DIED: Paris, January 17, 1738

One of at least four children of a seed merchant named Jean d'Andrieu, Jean-François was the nephew of Pierre Dandrieu [586], organist of St. Barthélemy, in Paris, whom he succeeded eventually. He was musically precocious and recalled later playing for the queen when he was five. It would have been a good trick, for the queen was dead by then; the lady was the Electress of Bavaria, for whom his sister Jeanne-Françoise served for a time as harpsichordist. Both children studied with Jean-Baptiste Moreau, who taught at Madame de Maintenon's academy at St. Cyr. In 1705 Dandrieu became organist at St. Merry in Paris, and in 1721 he became one of the rotating organists of the Royal Chapel. Exactly when he took over from his uncle, who died in 1733, is not known—but take over he must have, for his sister succeeded him on his death.

Dandrieu's music (all that we know of it was published), which includes not only keyboard pieces but solo and trio sonatas, and a programmatic Caractères de la guerre for orchestra shows the changeover from the ornamented Baroque style to the plainer classicism, especially in his books of harpsichord pieces. The latter 3 (of 6) not only are in the newer style but show reworkings of some of the earlier pieces in the interest of simplification. A collection of organ noëls (for playing which he was famous) does the same thing with some of Uncle Pierre's pieces. The first organ book (of 1739) also contains noëls, among other works, and a warning to the user that the contents may be regarded as unsuitable for church use. RECORDINGS: Organ works have been recorded by, inter alias, Marie-Claire Alain, Michel Chapuis, and Raphael Tambyeff, and Eiji Hashimoto have given us an LP of the harpsichord pieces. The Caractères de la guerre has been recorded by Newell Jenkins.

[672] SCHICKHARDT, Johann Christian (Shik'-härt, Yō'-hàn Krēst'-yàn)
INSTRUMENTALIST (oboe and recorder)
BORN: Braunschweig, c. 1682
DIED: Leiden, March 1762

Schickhardt seems to have been a restless and elusive fellow. Brought up at the court of his native city, he spent his early career working for various Dutch nobles of, or linked with, the House of Orange. Early in the second decade of the new century, Schickhardt was in Hamburg, serving as agent for the Amsterdam music publisher Estienne Roger, but after a few years he was a musician to the courts of several German principalities, mostly in Saxony. After a shift to Scandinavia, he returned to Holland and was at the University of Leiden for his last seventeen years. He published more than a score of collections, mostly dance pieces and sonatas for recorders, generally quite popular, as well as methods for flute and oboe. RECORDINGS: Ferdinand Conrad has recorded a sonata.

[673] GRAUPNER, Johann Christoph (Group'-ner, Yō'-hàn Krēst'-ôf)
KEYBOARDIST, CONDUCTOR, TEACHER
BORN: Kirchberg, January 13, 1683
DIED: Darmstadt, May 10, 1760

Graupner was the son of a Saxon tailor of the same name. (Some sources list his birthplace as the village of Hartmannsdorf.) He showed musical talent early, and studied with the Kirchberg cantor Michael Mylius and with organist Nikolaus Kuster there and in Reichenbach. In 1696 he was accepted at the Thomasschule in Leipzig, where one of his teachers was Kuhnau [582], whom he served as secretary, and in 1704 he began legal studies at the university. But that came to an end two years later when Charles XII of Sweden arrived with his armies to punish Elector Frederick Augustus for allying himself with Charles's enemies. Graupner fled to Hamburg, where he found work in the place vacated by J. C. Schiefferdecker [657], playing harpsichord for the Goose Market Opera, where Reinhard Keiser [639] produced some operas for him. After two years, however, he made what turned out to be a permanent move to Darmstadt as vice-Kapellmeister to Landgraf Ernst Ludwig [609]. In 1711 he married Sophie Elisabeth Eckard, who bore him seven children, and a year later he became Kapellmeister. He indulged himself in operatic writing, sometimes in collaboration with his master, and usually to librettos by his brother-in-law, Pastor Lichtenberg, until the Landgraf closed his opera house in 1719. When his old friend Telemann [665] refused his appointment as Kuhnau's successor at the Thomaskirche, Graupner competed with J. S. Bach [684] for the post and won. However, the Landgraf frowned on the notion and raised his salary, so Bach won by default. Graupner remained at Darmstadt for the rest of his life. He was blind in his last years. He was, up to that point, an indefatigable worker. Before the Darmstadt Library was bombed in World War II, it contained the manuscripts of nearly 1,500 of his cantatas, as well as an enormous number of suites, *sinfonie*, concerti, sonatas, and keyboard pieces. Most of the operas have disappeared. Graupner, when he had nothing else to do, engraved plates of his music, which the Landgraf had printed. His manuscript, incidentally, was said to appear printed. He also copied out much music by others without identifying the source, which creates a problem of attribution. RECORDINGS: Though Graupner appears to have had a Telemann-like talent that moves toward the Rococo, his music has actually been little explored, as the paucity of recordings suggests. There are oboe concerti performed by Alfred Hertel, trumpet concerti by Maurice André, a bassoon concerto by the Ravina Chamber Ensemble, and a Concerto in D major for Viola d'amore, Viola, Strings, and Continuo by the Capella Clementina.

[674] HEINICHEN, Johann David (Hī'-ni-khen, Yō'-hàn Dā-fēt)
LAWYER, CONDUCTOR, THEORIST
BORN: Krössuln, April 17, 1683
DIED: Dresden, July 16, 1729

Born near Weissenfels, Heinichen followed in the steps of his preacher-father, David, in attending the Thomasschule and university in Leipzig, where he studied music with Kuhnau [582] and made friends with Christoph Graupner [673]. Unlike Graupner, being two years ahead of him in his studies and thus unaffected by the Swedish invasion, he completed his law degree and went back to Weissenfels to set up a practice, and he composed on the side. Influential friends spread the word of his prowess, and he found himself writing for the little courts of Saxe-Zeitz and Naumburg and for the Leipzig opera house. Moreover, he took over the concerts of Telemann's [665] Collegium Musicum in that city. In the summer of 1710 a Councillor Buchta offered him a chance to accompany him to Italy, and Heinichen threw away all his commitments and went. Italy must have suited him well enough, for he stayed there for six years, chiefly in Venice, where two of his operas were produced in 1713, making him the only German of the period other than Handel to have been so honored. He hobnobbed with Vivaldi [650] and other composers of the burgeoning solo concerto, as his own essays in the form demonstrate. He also met the visiting Saxon

Elector Friedrich August, who persuaded him to come to Dresden and share the duties of *Kapellmeister* with Johann Christoph Schmidt (father to John Christopher Smith [795]). He arrived there in 1717, the same year that Lotti [613] came from Venice. Evidently the Italian problem there had not abated since the days of Schütz [412], and soon Heinichen found himself at an impasse with the Italian opera house's *primo castrato*, Francesco Bernardi, alias "Senesino," who is said to have been an impossible person in any case. Things eventually came to such a pass that the elector terminated the Italian troupe. (At that point Handel [683], back from London to recruit singers, arrived on the scene and scooped up most of its members.) Heinichen devoted the few years left him (he suffered from tuberculosis) to sacred and instrumental music, and to rewriting his 1711 continuo manual, which turned out to be one of the most important on the subject. He died at forty-six. His music is determinedly eclectic, though not unexpectedly the Italian elements are the most pronounced. RECORDINGS: Roman Totenberg has recorded a violin concerto, Hans Reinartz a Christmas pastorale, and an ensemble directed by Kurt List one of the trio sonatas.

[675] RAMEAU, Jean-Philippe (Rà-mō', Zhàn Fi-lēp')
ORGANIST, CONDUCTOR, TEACHER, THEORIST
BORN: Dijon, September 25, 1683
DIED: Paris, September 12, 1764

Perhaps because his works have found no place in the usual concert and operatic repertoires, Rameau is little more than a name to most music lovers. But the fact is that he is, in several respects, one of the towering figures in the history of music. In a sense he was in France what his contemporary J. S. Bach [684] was in Germany: the culmination of the Baroque. Perhaps his most important work was the *Traité de l'harmonie* (Paris, 1722). Though composers had been thinking in harmonic terms for the better part of a century, it was Rameau who, with has keen rationality and innate musical instinct, laid out the whys and wherefores of harmonic practice, established harmony as the basis for music, and dealt with tonality in terms of the "circle of fifths." If in effect he was doing no more than sum up what his contemporaries were already doing, he at least codified it and provided an intelligible rationale for it, and he stressed its most progressive aspects. No matter that modern sci-

ence has rendered some of his pronouncements less than absolute or that his notion
of the relative expressivity of specific keys,
chords, progressions, and so forth were
largely subjective: his theories influenced
generations. In his keyboard music he
summed up the whole French tradition; in
his *Pièces de clavecin en concert,* for keyboard and two melody instruments, he
moved away from the trio sonata, with its
subservient continuo part, toward a genuine
partnership of the instruments. And in his
operas, wherein he considered himself a disciple of Lully [517] and his opponents considered him a traitor to French music, he
created genuine music drama, developed the
concept of ensemble numbers, and made the
orchestra a functional part of the musicodramatic effect.

Rameau himself remains something of a
shadowy and secretive figure. Whether by
design or bad luck, his career developed
very slowly. He was not, however, given to
blowing his own horn. People who knew
him report him brusque, laconic, and loud
—a rather unpleasant person; but his impatience with the outer world seems to have
come from his total preoccupation with music. He is also accused of having been a
pinchpenny, though again his spartan way
of life is almost certainly attributable to a
lack of interest in exteriority. He was born
to music—his father was a church organist
—and learned it early at the paternal knee.
His parent had dreams of making him a
lawyer, but when the boy was sixteen he
gave in and let him leave the Jesuit College
to go into music. In 1701 young Rameau
went off to Italy for polishing his musical
skills. But somehow the venture went sour,
for he got no farther than Milan, then took
a job with a touring opera company, and by
1702 was back in France, playing the organ
at Notre-Dame-des-Doms in Avignon and
taking pupils. Shortly afterward he was appointed cathedral organist in Clermont-Ferrand. Having established himself locally as
a composer of church music, he seems to
have thought himself ready for the Big
Time and betook himself to Paris, probably
in 1705. He remained there for three years,
supporting himself as organist and teacher
and in 1706 publishing his first book of
harpsichord pieces; but nothing promising
happened, so eventually he went back to Dijon to succeed his father. After six years he
got an offer from Lyons, but stayed there
only a few months and then returned to his
old job in Clermont-Ferrand.

All this time his ideas on harmony were
solidifying, and in 1722 he went back to
Paris to publish his book. It was greeted

with the expectable hoots from the entrenched theorists, but in 1724 the second
book of clavecin pieces finally won Rameau
not only attention but popularity among the
affluent as a teacher. Two years later, at the
age of forty-three, he at last took a bride—a
nineteen-year-old singer named Marie-Louise Mangot. Whatever the truth about his
personality, they seem to have been happy
and produced four children. That same year
he published another important theoretical
work, by way of introduction to the *Traité:
Nouveau système de musique théorique.* This
too was viewed at the time with great skep-
ticism. In 1727 he competed for the organist's post at the church of St.-Vincent-de-
Paul but was bested by Daquin [717]—
whether through political skulduggery, as
rumor had it, is not clear. Anyhow,
Rameau found a place at the less important
church of Sainte-Croix-de-la-Brétonnerie.

For several years Rameau lived in Paris,
teaching, writing keyboard music, playing
the organ, and writing pamphlets, but making no great splash. All the time he seems to
have been nursing an urge to write for the
stage, but his only efforts in that direction
were pieces contributed to plays and vaudevilles (light, comic stage shows). He also acquired a patron in the tax farmer La Riche
de la Pouplinière, a Maecenas to several
musicians, who put his personal orchestra
at Rameau's disposal, thereby affording him
a practical education in instrumentation.
During this time the composer had been
seeking a suitable libretto for his talents
from Voltaire and others. He and the philosopher actually whipped up a treatment of
the Samson and Delilah story, but the censors blocked it as sacrilegious—prophetic of
Saint-Saëns's [1343] troubles with his work
on the same subject 140 years later. Finally
Rameau's patron linked him with the septuagenarian Abbé Simon-Joseph Pellegrin, a
successful librettist and playwright in his
day. Pellegrin agreed to a treatment of
Racine's *Phèdre* on assurance of indemnity
against any monetary losses, and he produced *Hippolyte et Aricie.* After a private
viewing at La Pouplinière's, it reached the
stage of the Académie, with a hodgepodge
of old sets and costumes, six days after the
composer's fiftieth birthday. At best it was a
succès d'estime, eliciting outraged screams
from doctrinaire disciples of Lully, and
Rameau was so taken aback that he swore
his first opera would be his last. But the
piece caught on, ran for thirty-two performances, won the backing of so important a
musician as André Campra [584], and was
revived in 1742, 1757, and 1767. Despite the
paper war that raged between the "Lul-

listes" and the "Ramistes," Rameau soon found himself the most important opera composer in France, and held in honor by the greatest of his contemporaries elsewhere. In short order and with enormous success there followed *Les Indes galantes* in 1735; *Castor et Pollux* in 1737; and *Les Fêtes d'Hébé* and *Dardanus*, both in 1739.

After this there is an unaccountable lapse of five years, during which Rameau seems to have occupied himself with teaching, writing keyboard pieces, and conducting. In 1744, however, the association with Voltaire finally bore fruit in *La Princesse de Navarre*, produced at Versailles the next year for the nuptials of the heir presumptive (who died twenty years later, before his father did). In the nineteen years left him, Rameau wrote at least as many operas and ballets, most of which were produced at the Opéra or one of the royal palaces, though none had the success, the staying power, and probably the quality of his earlier masterpieces. In 1752, when it appeared that he had been accepted by all factions, the so-called "War of the Buffoons," occasioned by the successful performances of Pergolesi's [782] *La Serva Padrona* by an Italian troupe in Paris started the acrimony all over again, and Rameau was kept busy defending himself in print, being now cast in the conservative role! Early in the next decade, Louis XV granted him a patent of nobility. Late in his eighty-first year he was stricken with typhoid fever and, after fighting it for three weeks, died thirteen days short of his birthday. Until quite recent times most of his music had fallen into desuetude, and thirty years ago a historian of opera considered a Rameau revival an impossibility. But beginning with the postwar presentation of *Les Indes galantes* at the Paris Opéra, a number of enterprising producers have proved him wrong.

RECORDINGS: There are complete versions of *Hippolyte et Aricie, Zéphire, Les Boreades, Anacrèon, Zaïs, Naïs, Les Indes galantes, Dardanus, Castor et Pollux*, the comedy *Platée, Le Temple de la Gloire, Pygmalion, La Princesse de Navarre*, Act 3 of *Les Fêtes de Hébé*, the interlude *La Guirlande*, dance suites from several other stage works. The complete keyboard music. The *Pièces de clavecin en concert* are available in their original version and arranged as *Concerts en sextuor*. A few pieces of church music, cantatas, and songs have also been recorded. The tricentennial of Rameau's birth has seen the release of large numbers of new recordings, particularly on the French Erato label.

[676] **BOUVARD, François** (Bōō-värd', Frȧn-swȧ')
SINGER
BORN: Lyons, c. 1683
DIED: Paris, March 2, 1760

Bouvard came to Paris in the 1690s to sing as a treble at the Opéra, went to Rome to study when that gig was over, and returned shortly after the turn of the century. Two operas, *Médus* and *Cassandre* were performed successfully by the Académie, but he seems to have written no more after 1706. Up to about 1750 he continued to produce songs, *cantatilles* (recitatives-and-airs), and *cantates;* he also published a "first" book of violin sonatas. The only other facts that we have about him are that he was twice married, had at least one child (a daughter), was a Knight of the Lateran Order, and died broke and forgotten. RECORDINGS: Jacques Herbillon has recorded 2 drinking songs by Bouvard.

[677] **ČERNOHORSKÝ, Bohuslav Matěj** (Cher-nō-hôr'-skē, Bō'-hōō-sláv Mȧt'-yā)
PRIEST, ORGANIST, TEACHER
BORN: Nymburk, Bohemia, February 16, 1684
DIED: Graz, Austria, July 1, 1742

Černohorský is a tantalizingly obscure figure about whom little is certain—even the dates of his birth and death, which are traditional but undocumented. The son of a schoolteacher from a river town northeast of Prague, he graduated from the University of Prague in 1702, joined the Minorite Friars (Franciscans) the next year, and was ordained in 1708. Two years later he went to Italy and remained for a decade as organist first in Assisi and then in Padua. If he was "il Padre Boemo" at San Francesco in Assisi, then Tartini [714] studied with him. He returned to Bohemia in 1720 and was at the monastery of St. Jakub in Prague for the next seven years. Supposedly he taught the young Gluck [803] there, but since he left for Horaždovice some seventy-five miles to the south about the time Gluck arrived in Prague, it seems unlikely. He did, however, teach Josef Seger [807], who sang at St. Jakub in his youth. In 1731 Černohorský returned to his organ loft at Padua Cathedral and remained there for a decade. On the way home he was taken ill in Graz and died. Most of his music is said to have gone up in a fire at St. Jakub a dozen years after his death. Only a handful of surviving religious pieces are certainly his. RECORDINGS:

Organist Jiří Ropek has recorded a toccata and a fugue attributed to Černohorský, but the one is now considered spurious and the other highly suspect.

[678] DURANTE, Francesco (Dōō-ràn'-tā, Fràn-chās'-kō)
TEACHER
BORN: Frattamaggiore, March 31, 1684
DIED: Naples, September 30, 1755

Unusually for his time, Durante was a composer who devoted most of his life to teaching. And very good he obviously was at it too, for his pupils are a sort of who's who of the next Italian generation, including as they do Paisiello [914]; Pergolesi [782]; Piccinni, his favorite [848]; Sacchini [857]; and Vinci [712]. The seventh child of a wool comber who sang in the local church, Durante was born in a village ("Big Thicket") near Naples. When Gaetano Durante died in 1699, Francesco's uncle Don Angelo, rector of the conservatory of San Onofrio in the city, took him in and saw to his education. He left the conservatory in 1705, and for the next twenty-three years there is only sketchy information about him. He himself became a teacher at San Onofrio in 1710, but resigned for reasons unknown at the end of the year. He was again in Naples in 1714, when he married, to his eternal regret, the forty-two-year-old Orsola de Laurentis (he was thirty), perhaps because she reminded him of his mother (they had the same Christian name). The "cursed old woman" turned out to be a shrew and a compulsive gambler. She is said once to have sold all his manuscripts to support her habit, but he put up with her for twenty-seven years. Legend has it that Durante studied during this period with Giuseppe Pitoni, choirmaster of the Lateran in Rome, and with Pasquini [524]. Records show him to have been in that city in 1718. Later he is supposed to have traveled in the Germanies. When he finally emerged into the daylight again, it was as director of the Neapolitan Conservatorio dei Poveri di Gesù Cristo (of Jesus Christ's Paupers). He was appointed there in 1728, became an important figure in Neapolitan musical life, and resigned (again for unknown reasons) eleven years later. In 1741, his first wife died, and a year later Durante took the directorship of the Conservatorio di Santa Maria di Loreto, succeeding Porpora [690], who had gone off to Venice. Early in 1744 he was happily wed to Anna Furano, and a year later, his old enemy Leonardo Leo [718] having died, he returned to the Poveri. (The quarrel with Leo,

which spawned factions of "Durantists" and "Leists," seems now, like most such affairs, remarkably trivial. It appears, in a nutshell, to have had to do with whether the head or the heart should have primacy in church music, Durante espousing the latter position.)

Durante's connubial happiness with his Anna—she of the splendid figure—did not last long. She died in August 1747. He is said to have conducted her obsequies himself in his own house, placed her body in the coffin, and nailed down the lid. Four months later, the sexagenarian composer married one of his servants, Angela Anna Carmina Giacobbe, age twenty-two. He remained in charge of both conservatories for the rest of his life. From all accounts he must have been a lovable if slightly eccentric man. We catch a glimpse of him in old age, rumpled and dusty but in a gleaming white wig, threading his way through the stands in the marketplace, his inverted hat filled with fruit, which he loved. In fact that passion probably was fatal, for he is said to have died of diarrhea brought on by a surfeit of melons.

Curiously, but probably typically for him, Durante did not write operas, save for a few religious dramas. His forte, however, was vocal music, especially sacred, which, he prided himself, was "according to Palestrina" [201]—meaning, in the main, that it was a cappella. But he was not a throwback, and his later music is both "modern" and individual. Apart from the religious music he published an early set of keyboard sonatas (consisting of a fugal section followed by a "divertimento"), and other harpsichord pieces exist in manuscript. His quartet-concerti, for strings and continuo, with their splashes of Handelian majesty, are perhaps his best-known works, some of them having been recorded by, for example, Thomas Schippers, the Collegium Aureum, and the Virtuosi di Roma. His only harpsichord concerto (unusual for that time in Italy) has been recorded by Ruggero Gerlin. The "old Italian air" Danza, danza, fanciulla gentil, attributed to Durante, is really one of his vocal exercises outfitted with words and an accompaniment. Another song, "Inka Dinka Doo," is by a much later Durante.

[679] MANFREDINI, Francesco Onofrio (Màn'-frā-dē'-nē, Fràn-chās'-kō O-nō'-frē-ō)
CHOIRMASTER, VIOLINIST
BORN: Pistoia, June 22, 1684
DIED: Pistoia, October 6, 1762

Manfredini's name became briefly a byword a few years ago as a result of American musicologist H. C. Robbins Landon's article "A Pox on Manfredini," lambasting the proclivity of recording companies to publishing "the complete" whatever of obscure and unimportant Baroque composers. Manfredini was not really that bad, as A. J. B. Hutchings argues in *The Baroque Concerto.* What we know of his life is sketchy. His father played trombone in Pistoia. As a teenager, Francesco studied with the elder Perti and Torelli [578] in Bologna, then went to Ferrara as a church-orchestra violinist. He returned to Bologna when the orchestra was reassembled at San Petronio, succeeded Torelli as concertmaster, and was elected to the Accademia Filarmonica. After 1707 his whereabouts are obscure for twenty years. Between 1704 and 1718 he published 3 sets of sonatas *("concertini"* and *"sinfonie")* and concerti in Bologna, and in 1719–20 produced 2 oratorios there. It is said, however, that he served for a time in Monte Carlo as *maestro* to Prince Antoine I Grimaldi, to whom he dedicated the 12 concerti of 1718. (The dedication to "Antonio del Monaco," however, has misled some into locating him in Munich, where there was no Anton, and from which the reigning prince had fled to escape the Austrians.) Around 1727, wherever he had been, Manfredini came home to Pistoia to direct the music at the cathedral. Here he presumably married. He produced at least two sons there—the elder, Giuseppe, becoming a noted *castrato,* and the younger, Vincenzo [896], a composer and teacher. Francesco Manfredini's set of concerti *(concerti grossi)* have enjoyed a measure of popularity. RECORDINGS: All 12 concerti were recorded by Dean Eckertsen and a selection by I Musici.

[680] WALTHER, Johann Gottfried (Väl'-ter, Yō'-hán Got'-frēt)
ORGANIST, TEACHER, THEORIST, LEXICOGRAPHER
BORN: Erfurt, September 18, 1684
DIED: Weimar, March 23, 1748

Walther's father, Stefan, was in the cloth industry; his mother, Martha Dorothea, was born Lämmerhirt, as was Sebastian Bach's [684], Elisabeth. The two composers were, in fact, second cousins, rather complexly. Born just six months before Sebastian, Walther grew up in the same house that had sheltered Elisabeth in her girlhood. Moreover, his Erfurt organ teacher was Bernhard Bach [646], another second cousin of Sebastian's through both Bachs and Läm-

merhirts. (Bernhard and Sebastian each later stood godfather to one of the other's children.) Walther graduated from the local *Gymnasium* and entered the university to study law, but at about the same time, in 1702, he also became organist in Erfurt's Thomaskirche. Shortly he discovered that music was more fun than legal studies. He studied composition for a time with Buttstädt [605], and then, in 1706, with Wilhelm Hieronymus Pachelbel (see 567) in Nuremberg. In 1707 he was hired (it turned out) for life, as municipal organist in Weimar. There he had to play at the church of Sts. Peter and Paul and teach the offspring and young relatives of the puritanical Duke Wilhelm Ernst. (One of them was the talented but short-lived Johann Ernst, Prince of Saxe-Weimar [729].) Lo and behold, who should turn up there the next year but Cousin Sebastian, come to replace tottery old Herr Effler. (In 1707 the cousins had both tried out for the organist's job in Mühlhausen. Bach, to his later sorrow, won.) Relatives, of an age, and newly married, the two young musicians became very thick, what with daily kaffeeklatsches and borrowing flour and vying to reduce the latest Italian concerto to keyboard dimensions. Bach was godfather to Walther's first son in 1712 (there were eight children all together). When Bach bragged he could read any piece of music at sight, Walther spiked his guns with a puzzle canon. Since the organ in Walther's church was far superior to the one at court, Bach used to use it to test his compositions. In 1721, after Bach had moved on to Cöthen, Walther was elevated to Court Musician. It did not mean much, for there was no increase in salary or status, and as time went on, he had to sell off his library to make ends meet. Like Bach, Walther suffered from eye trouble and by 1745 he was unable to play. His son (later organist at the Ulm minster) substituted for him but was dismissed after his father's death, which occurred two years before Bach's.

Walther was a lifelong musical scholar and thinker. Around the time he came to Weimar, he wrote a *Praecepta der musikalischen Composition (Precepts of Musical Composition),* probably for a princely student, which is a measure of his knowledge. More important is his *Musikalisches Lexicon,* published in Leipzig in 1732, the first known combined dictionary of music and musicians. Of his music little remains save organ works—mostly chorale preludes and variations of the highest caliber, and concerto transcriptions.

RECORDINGS: There are recorded collections by Nicholas Jackson and Hans Christoph Schuster, Finn Viderø, and others.

[681] DAGINCOURT, François (Dà-zhân-kōōr', Frán-swà')
KEYBOARDIST
BORN: Rouen, 1684
DIED: Paris, April 30, 1758

Dagincourt was a pupil of the Rouen Cathedral organist Jacques Boyvin, and later of Nicolas Lebègue [515] at St. Merry in Paris. At seventeen he himself was appointed organist of the Paris church of St. Madeleine-en-la-Cité. On hearing of Boyvin's demise in 1706, he hurried back to Rouen, entered the competition for the job, won it, and played at the cathedral for over fifty years, as well as at the local churches of St. Ouen and St. Jean. At some point along the way, he married a lady named Anne Poisson. In 1714, after Louis Marchand [619] had stirred the king's ire, Dagincourt succeeded him as one of the organists of the Royal Chapel at Versailles, though that duty took only three months out of his year. Perhaps it was his having to be in two places that created the now-exploded belief that there were two Dagincourts, the other called "Jacques-André." He published a few songs and, in 1733, a book of harpsichord pieces, mostly imitation Couperin, though individualized by some harmonic experiments. However, a fellow-Rouennais, Père Pingré, copied out 46 organ pieces arranged by key in 6 suites. These are rather simple, roughhewn affairs, probably blueprints for the organist's own improvisations. RECORDINGS: Two of the organ suites have been recorded by Marie-Claire Alain.

[682] MARCELLO, Alessandro (Mär-chel'-lō, Á-les-sàn'-drō)
VIOLINIST
BORN: Venice, 1684
DIED: Venice, 1750

For 250 years (though not in his own day) Alessandro Marcello has stood in the shadow of his younger brother Benedetto [689], and this has inevitably resulted in some misattribution of works. The father of the two, Agostino, was a senator, a rich man, a descendent of doges, and an enthusiastic musical amateur; the mother, Paolina Capello, was a poetess and painter and a member of the family of that Bianca Capello who, after many vicissitudes, became Grand Duchess of Tuscany a century earlier. Neither of the sons made music for a living. Besides playing the violin and composing, Alessandro also sang, painted, wrote poetry, was conversant with mathematics and philosophy, and, with weekly concerts, made his home a center for music and the arts. A member of the prestigious Accademia dell'Arcadia, he issued all his publications—a set each of cantatas, solo violin sonatas, and concerti—under his Arcadian code name, Eterio Stinfalico. The 6 concerti, known collectively as La Cetra (The Cithara), are for oboe, strings, and continuo; they are not quite solo concerti and not quite concerti grossi—rich and sometimes audacious, harmonically speaking, and fit to be mentioned with Handel's [683]. RECORDINGS: Four concerti grossi have been recorded by I Musici. An isolated oboe concerto, known in a solo clavier transcription by J. S. Bach [684], has been attributed variously to Vivaldi [650], Benedetto Marcello, and "Anonymous" but has not been shown to be Alessandro's. It appears in several recordings, not always in the right key or attributed to the right composer.

[683] HANDEL, George Friderick (Han'-dəl, Jôrj Frē'-dâ-rik)
OBOIST, VIOLINIST, HARPSICHORDIST, ORGANIST
BORN: Halle, February 23, 1685
DIED: London, April 13/14, 1759

For more than two centuries patriotic Englishmen have claimed Handel as their country's greatest composer. He was actually German by birth (christened Georg Friedrich Händel) and Italian by musical inclination, and his presence probably did more to stifle the native product in England than any other force. But there is no question that he did his best work in England and that he was one of the supreme composers in the history of music.

Less than a month before J. S. Bach [684] and eight before Domenico Scarlatti [687], Handel was born to the barber-surgeon Georg Händel and his second wife Dorothea (née Taust) in the wineshop Zum Gelben Hirschen. Dorothea, whose first child had been born and died a year earlier, was about thirty-five. Her husband, a somebody in a town that was going nowhere and holder of a court appointment for the local duke, Augustus, was sixty-five and was to sire two more children. Old Georg, sour and strict, had no truck with impractical things like music, but somehow the child learned to play the keyboards. (The story of him secretly practicing the clavichord in the attic in the small hours of the night has been neither substantiated nor disproved.) At some point, under circumstances of which we know very little, he played the organ for the duke, who instructed old Georg to make a musician of him. Georg had meant his son for a lawyer, but, being a good German, he clenched his teeth and sent him to Friedrich Wilhelm Zachau [594], organist at the Lady-Church. Zachau worked with him for something over two years and, having exhausted his knowledge, turned young Handel loose in 1696. Shortly afterward the boy visited Berlin, where he was forbidden to accept a court appointment by his father, now in declining health. Shortly after the son came home, Georg Händel died. Georg Friedrich stayed in Halle for six more years, finishing his secondary schooling, inaugurating a lifelong friendship with Georg Philipp Telemann [665], playing the cathedral organ, and beginning his legal studies at the university.

In 1703, however, Handel suddenly chucked it all and took off for Hamburg, where he became a violinist in the Goose Market Opera orchestra. He made friends with the composer-singer Johann Mattheson [668], and in August the two traipsed over to Lübeck to check out the possibility of succeeding Buxtehude [525] at the Marienkirche, and both boggled at taking Fräulein Buxtehude with the job. Afterward, Handel moved in with the Mathtesons, and he and Johann vied in writing operas for Goose Market production. They soon fell out, however. One night, during a performance of Mattheson's Cleopatra, Handel refused to yield the keyboard to the composer when his singing stint was done, and there was an impromptu duel in the street, which ended when Mattheson lunged and broke his sword against one of Handel's jacket buttons. Shortly afterward Handel's first opera Almira, a macaronic German-Italian affair, had a great success. But his Nero did not a few weeks later, and in 1705 Handel gave up the Goose Market, which seems to have been on the skids anyway. Probably in the summer of the next year, perhaps inspired by acquaintance with a ne'er-do-well Italian drifter (whom fate later catapulted onto the Tuscan throne as the last of the Medici dukes!), Handel took off for Italy.

After a stopover in Florence to visit the other Medici, Handel reached Rome at the beginning of 1707 and promptly established himself as a virtuoso organist. But opera was in his mind, and opera had been banned in Rome as licentious, so he soon made his way to Venice, where public opera houses had been springing up like mushrooms for seventy years. There he got a production of his Rodrigo, met several important local musicians, and allegedly became good friends with his coeval Domenico Scarlatti, with whom he apparently returned to Rome. There Handel was for a time protégé of Prince Ruspoli, a friend of the Medici, and later of Corelli's [565] patron, Cardinal Pietro Ottoboni, who staged the famous Handel-Scarlatti keyboard duels. Later he traveled to Naples and, in 1709, returned to Venice, where his Agrippina became a smash hit, winning him the adoration of the Venetians ("our dear Saxon" they called him), and an offer from Elector Georg Ludwig (later George I of England) to be his court musician in Hanover. (There are various hoary yarns of Handel's love affairs in Italy. But as he never married, showed no interest in women or apparently in sexual activity of any kind, these are probably fiction.)

No sooner had Handel arrived in Hanover in 1710 than the Kapellmeister, Agostino Steffani, resigned, leaving the post to him. Oddly, Handel almost immediately got leave to go to London, where he went, perhaps circling through Halle, and certainly stopping at the Palatine Court at Düsseldorf, before reaching what was rapidly becoming a citadel of German and Italian music. Why he went is uncertain, but he quickly acquired a libretto from Aaron Hill, impresario at the Haymarket Theater, and in two weeks completed Rinaldo, which opened on February 24, 1711. It not only wowed the London public; it also introduced it, in the person of the singer Niccolò Grimaldi, called "Nicolini," to the first of the great cult castrati (though other castrati had sung there before him). That summer he reluctantly returned to Hanover, but in the fall a year later he went back to London for what, somewhat to his surprise, turned out to be a permanent sojourn. Nicolini had left and Hill had been succeeded by one MacSwiney, but Handel blithely set about producing his pastoral Il Pastor fido. The public didn't think it was much, but Nicolo Haym, a former enemy, did and collaborated with Handel on a new piece, Teseo, which drew such crowds to the Haymarket that MacSwiney lived up to his name and absconded with the receipts, leaving the troops unpaid. But another German, Jakob Heidegger, said to be the homeliest man in London, stepped into the breach, and if the composer did not get rich, at least he did not have to go to debtor's prison.

Meanwhile Handel had found a generous patron in the teenaged Earl of Burlington, who put him up at Burlington House.

Moreover by some clever politicking, he achieved performances of his *Birthday Ode* (for Queen Anne's forty-eighth) and the *Te Deum* (for the infamous Peace of Utrecht) that won him a royal annuity of 200 pounds. Handel was rather enjoying his affluence and resting on his laurels when Anne's death in 1714 brought the master whom Handel had forsaken to London as King of England.

For a while the two circled each other warily (though King George, accompanied by his retinue and "disguised" by a mask or a false beard or something, attended a revival of *Rinaldo* and the new spectacle *Amadigi* in the 1714–15 season). How the two were reunited is moot: Francesco Geminiani [693] says that he brought Handel to court as his accompanist and the king was so delighted he doubled the composer's pension; indomitable legend says that in the summer of 1715 Handel and a bargeload of musicians trailed the royal water party down the Thames, softening the royal heart with the famous *Water Music* (which evidence suggests was not written until 1717). At any rate, Handel went back to Hanover with the king on a visit in 1716, during which time he probably composed his only *Passion* to a text by a Hamburger named Barthold Brockes (also set by the rest of the old Hamburg gang: Reinhard Keiser [639], Mattheson, and Telemann). Handel visited his old mother and picked up his future secretary-companion, Johann Christoph Schmidt—later known as John Christopher Smith [795]. Returning to London, Handel found that his absence had snuffed out interest in opera and accepted a post as music director at Cannons, Middlesex, to the Earl of Carnarvon, soon to be Duke of Chandos. Here he wrote such domestic music as the Chandos Anthems and the harpsichord suites. But following the death of his sister Dorothea Sophia, Handel again went to Germany in 1719 to see his mother and to collect singers toward another operatic upsurge that began with *Radamisto* (libretto by Haym) late the following April at His Majesty's Theater. (This production eventually yielded in 1720 to *Narcisco,* a revision by Thomas Roseingrave [699] of an earlier work by Domenico Scarlatti. *Narcisco* was rather a flop.) The same period also saw the masques *Acis and Galatea* and *Haman and Mordecai* at Cannons.

The Royal Academy of Music, which functioned at His Majesty's, was a corporation born of the mania for stock companies that peaked and collapsed with the South Sea Company in 1720. In that year it produced *Astarto* by the newly arrived Gio-

vanni Bononcini [620], precipitating a wholly artificial "war" between his admirers and Handel's. Handel, in fact, seems not to have been much concerned, and indeed the two collaborated with a third composer (possibly Attilio Ariosti [606]) in 1721 in *Muzio Scevola,* which closed after eight performances. Adherency to one composer or the other was mostly a matter of larger political leanings, but Handel did his cause no good by imitating his rival in the 1721 *Floridante,* whereas Bononcini had palpable hits shortly afterward with *Crispo* and *Griselda.* Seeing things going in the wrong direction, Handel hit on the notion of bringing in an international star, Francesca Cuzzoni. The operation was successful, but the patient died. Cuzzoni, who turned out to be ugly, stupid, temperamental, and very expensive, drew crowds. Handel, perforce, discovered the star system, and Bononcini faded from there on. Later Handel added Faustina Bordoni (the future Frau Hasse (see 736), precipitating a prima donna rivalry among the fans that often turned riotous. But Italian opera in London was essentially a highbrow fad, and singers at 2,000 pounds a year were hard on the budget. Despite the successes of such Handelian operas as *Ottone, Giulio Cesare,* and *Rodelinda,* the Royal Academy of Music was in severe straits, and following the overwhelming success of John Gay's *The Beggar's Opera* (see 611), a lowlife parody, early in 1728, the academy quietly expired.

Meanwhile, in 1726, after sixteen years in London, Handel decided it was politically expedient to become officially an Englishman and was rewarded with a post as Composer to the Chapel Royal. He was able to put it to use the following autumn with four great anthems for the coronation of George II, the old king having died of a stroke while traveling through the Low Countries that summer. No sooner had the academy breathed its almost-simultaneous last than Handel got together with Heidegger and sank most of his capital in a New Royal Academy. Early in February he was off to Italy talent-hunting—and discovered the librettos of Metastasio, made to order for his kind of opera. In mid-journey, he was informed that his aged mother had also suffered a stroke, and went to Halle to do what he could. While there he was approached by a young man named Wilhelm Friedemann Bach [784] bearing an invitation to visit his father, a Leipzig *Kapellmeister* of some local repute, but Handel could not spare the time. He returned to England in midsummer and got the new venture off to a shaky start in the fall, and it was not until he hired

Senesino, the great *castrato* of the previous company, that things began looking up the next year, though the composer's joy thereat was tempered by his mother's death. Moreover, he was severely overworked and, a notorious trencherman, terribly overweight.

In 1732 the success of several non-Handelian performances of his *Haman and Mordecai* (revised and now called *Esther)* made Handel think about the notion of presenting works in English, which he soon tried with *Acis and Galatea* to forestall Thomas Arne [783], who had been making hay in the Haymarket with his own recension of it. Early in 1733 the new company had its first real success with *Orlando.* Then he followed it with the first of his real oratorios, *Deborah;* despite the attendance of the king and seats at doubled prices, the audience was puzzled and disappointed. Moreover, Handel was now increasingly the target of a mounting hostility, mostly politically inspired, and centering on Crown Prince Frederick, who was not about to admire a musician whom his parents liked; it culminated in the foundation of a rival company, the Opera of the Nobility, which wooed away Senesino and later brought in Farinelli, the ultimate *castrato* phenomenon. At the end of the 1733–34 season, Heidegger pulled out of the partnership, and Handel lost his lease on His Majesty's. He thereupon joined forces with John Rich, proprietor of the still-unfinished Covent Garden Theatre and erstwhile producer of *The Beggar's Opera*, with whom he had collaborated in 1732 on a production of Ben Jonson's *The Alchemist.* The first fruits of their collaboration were the Ariostan operas *Ariodante* and *Alcina*, among Handel's best, but the public reaction suggested that the long-predicted death of the genre was imminent. Against that catastrophe, Handel wrote instrumental pieces for publication and presented concerts in which he appeared as organ soloist. His health, both physical and emotional, gave way in the spring of 1736, and he went to Tunbridge Wells for a cure, which seemed to take. By now, the Prince of Wales had shifted his allegiance to Covent Garden and the King had thereupon withdrawn his support. Halfway through another desperate season of trying to please the public, Handel had a stroke that paralyzed his right arm. But he saw the season (his last in that venture) through, then went to Aachen, Germany, for several months to recover his health again.

He returned in the autumn in time to write a funeral ode for his former friend and patron, Queen Caroline. He found Heidegger also presiding over the obsequies of Italian opera, to which he contributed *Faramondo* and *Serse* (the source of "Handel's Largo" and his only comedy in 40-odd operas). That same spring he was honored—if that is the word—with a hideous portrait-statue in Vauxhall Gardens. Opera being now obviously no longer viable, Handel turned his talents to other things. Aided by his friend Charles Jennens, Jr., who pieced together the librettos, he wrote in quick order the great oratorios *Saul* and *Israel in Egypt*, which he presented in the first months of 1739. The public did not buy them. He then (financially strapped) took over a tiny theater in Lincoln's Inn Fields and had something of a success with a 1739 St. Cecilia's Day concert, featuring his setting of Dryden's ode for that occasion. But his two final operas, *Imeneo* (1740) and *Deidamia* (1741), ran for only two and three nights respectively; and so, nearly broke, Handel gave a farewell concert and "retired."

Almost immediately, however, he set to work on two new oratorios, *Messiah* and *Samson.* In November, at the invitation of Ireland's Lord Lieutenant, he set out on a seven months' visit to Dublin. After a series of concerts featuring some of his shorter works and his own organ-playing, he premiered *Messiah* on April 13, 1742; one critic reported it "the finest Composition of Musick that ever was heard," though the audience did not spontaneously rise to its feet during the "Hallelujah" chorus as it did at the London premiere. Oddly, however, London initially thought less of the work than it did of *Samson*, first sung at Covent Garden in February 1743. The next several years are a history of "oratorio seasons" at various theaters (some more or less successful, some not), more anti-Handel cabals, and more bouts of bad health. In 1746 he appeared in a concert with young Christoph Gluck [803], then a virtuoso on the musical glasses. Handel noted that Gluck knew no more counterpoint than Gustavus Waltz, his cook (who happened to be a musician). With *Judas Maccabaeus* of 1747, Handel's oratorios began to enjoy real success, though nothing like what the operas in their heyday had. In 1749 he was called on for music to accompany a fireworks display to celebrate the end of the War of the Austrian Succession, and came up with a suite for a large wind band. Unfortunately the fireworks got out of control while it was being played, and set fire to the wooden "temple" erected as part of the display—though a more successful performance was given a month later for the Foundling Hospital, one of Handel's favorite charities, to which he donated an organ that same year. In 1750 the composer, now sixty-five, made a will, and a last visit to Germany, where he was involved in a traffic accident. Early the next year he started *Jephtha*, his last oratorio, whose completion was postponed until late summer by another bout of illness. Long complaining of visual problems, the composer discovered in the autumn that he had incipient cataracts. There was some sort of dreadful operation, though whether it worked for better or worse is no more clear than Handel's vision. In any case, he seems to have been blind by 1753. Shortly afterward he had a falling-out on the streets of Tunbridge Wells with his faithful old companion John Christopher Smith, who abandoned him then and there. Handel summoned J. C. Smith, Jr., from France to take his father's place. For a while he continued to appear in concerts, but increasingly he stayed home, editing his music with Smith's help. By late 1758 he had, ominously, lost interest in food. Early the next year, however, he conducted an abbreviated oratorio season. Two days before Palm Sunday, after *Messiah*, he collapsed, and was put to bed. He remained there for a week, sometimes lucid, sometimes comatose, and died late on the night of Good Friday, as he had prayed he would. He was buried with great honor in Westminster Abbey—to the music of William Croft!

RECORDINGS: Although he was the supreme composer of religious oratorios and one of the greatest writers of opera, neither category has been by any means fully represented on records. Of the oratorios there are recordings of *Alexander Balus; L'Allegro, il Pensieroso, ed il Moderato; Belshazzar; Deborah; Hercules; Israel in Egypt; Jephtha; Joshua; Judas Maccabaeus; Messiah; La Resurrezione; St. John Passion; Samson; Saul; Solomon;* and *Theodora,* though not all in English or in optimum versions. The operas fare less well: *Alcina, Acis and Galatea, Almira, Apollo e Dafne, Ariodante, Giulio Cesare, Orlando, Partenope, Rinaldo, Rodelinda, Semele, Serse, Sosarme,* and *Tamerlano,* though there are many excerpts from others. The instrumental and orchestral works, on the other hand, have been almost entirely covered. There is good representation of the less ambitious choral works, less good of the solo cantatas, and very little of the minor vocal pieces.

[684] BACH, Johann Sebastian (Bàkh, Yō'-hàn Se-bàs'-tē-àn)
ORGANIST, VIOLINIST, TEACHER

BORN: Eisenach, March 21, 1685
DIED: Leipzig, July 28, 1750

The greatest of the musical Bachs, five generations removed from the legendary Veit and only two from the end of the line, also represents the culmination of Western music up to his time. He not only absorbs the chief national styles—German, French, Italian, even English—and synthesizes them; he is also the final word on the Baroque and the long contrapuntal tradition that began in the late Middle Ages. But he is an end, not a beginning; after him there was no School of Bach. As such he was seen by many in his own time—and not entirely improperly!—as old-fashioned, a fact that helps explain why he was generally regarded as one more provincial *Kapellmeister* rather than as a supernal genius. However, the notion that after his death he lay forgotten until Mendelssohn "discovered" him a century later is an exaggeration. His work (or some of it) was known and admired by many a solid musician, and there were even Bach enthusiasts. Mendelssohn's contribution was to make him popular (and, unintentionally, to deify him in some quarters).

Sebastian Bach was the son of Johann Ambrosius Bach, Eisenach *Stadtpfeiffer* and court musician, who had just failed to get permission to take a better post in Erfurt. Grandson of Johannes Bach and son of Christoph, Ambrosius was junior to Georg Christoph, cantor of Themar and later of Schweinfurt. Ambrosius' other brother, Johann Christoph (not to be confused with **[536]** or with J. S. Bach's oldest brother), town and court musician of Arnstadt, was his twin—so identical, it is said, that even their wives could not tell them apart—though this assertion has cast no doubt on Sebastian's paternity. In 1668 Ambrosius had married Elisabeth Lämmerhirt, a younger sister of the wife of his uncle Johann, who in due course bore him six sons and two daughters (of which several died young). Sebastian was not, incidentally, born in the "Bach Birthplace" that stands as a museum in Eisenach, though his father lived there earlier.

Bach got his musical basics from his father, and his organ grounding from his father's twin; he sang soprano in the choir of the Georgikirche. At the age of eight he entered the local Latin school for his academic education. Only a few months later his mother died. Toward the end of the same year, Ambrosius remarried, but himself succumbed before the winter was out. Sebastian and his brother Johann Jakob went to nearby Ohrdruf to live with their oldest brother Johann Christoph, who was town organist there, and probably continued their musical training. Sebastian transferred to the Ohrdruf Latin school, distinguished himself as a student, and graduated precociously at fourteen. On the strength of the boy's vocal prowess, one of his teachers who had connections recommended him to the Michaelsschule in Lüneburg, in whose prestigious Mettenchor he was expected to sing. He thereupon, in the spring of 1700, hiked the 200 miles to Lüneburg in company with another youth, Georg Erdmann (who later became Baron von Erdman, Russian minister in Danzig, though not as a result of his walk). Bach spent the next three years in Lüneburg, though, having discovered the joys of pedestrian locomotion, he was given to strolling over to Hamburg, a mere twenty-five miles away, to partake of its musical advantages, notably the organ playing of old Adam Reincken. He also made friends with a French dancing master attached to the court at Celle, 50 miles to the south, and went there with him to sample the French music that the duke affected. In Lüneburg he also came to know the organist-composer Georg Böhm and probably studied with him. Very early in his stay Bach found himself singing soprano-baritone octaves, and then his voice broke; but he was permitted to stay, perhaps because of his skill on the violin and organ.

In 1703, Bach took his first job as violin-playing servant to Prince Johann Ernst of Saxe-Weimar [729], a younger brother of the reigning duke. A few months later he was invited to test the new organ in the Neue Kirche in Arnstadt and played so stupendously that he was chosen organist on the spot, the usual competition being considered unnecessary. He was also entrusted with training the choir, and probably played in the local court orchestra. It was in Arnstadt that he ran into his second cousin Maria Barbara Bach, who was about his own age. She was the orphan daughter of Johann Michael [550], the son of old Heinrich Bach [488]. But conditions in Arnstadt were far from ideal (one of his singers, in a fit of pique, precipitated a fight with him one night in the streets), and Sebastian began again looking around. He asked for, and got, a month's leave to improve his base by attending the Buxtehude Advent concerts in Lübeck, though this time he probably did not walk the 230 miles, as legend claims him to have done. He overstayed his leave by three months, however, and seems to have returned only when faced with the necessity of marrying poor Fräulein

Buxtehude to become her father's successor. Finally, in 1707, partly through the machinations of Maria Barbara, he was invited to try out for the organist's post at the Blasius-kirche in Mühlhausen, 35 miles northwest of Arnstadt. Once more it was no contest, and Bach was told to name his own salary. Having settled into his new job, he came back in October to marry Maria Barbara. At first he was a success: an occasional motet written early in 1708 was printed with municipal financing, and the authorities agreed to having the organ enlarged according to Bach's specifications. But Bach's pastor was a supporter of the radical (and puritanical) Pietists, who found anything but the plainest music suspect, and Bach exacerbated matters by siding with the local orthodox Lutherans. Things were getting sticky when Weimar advertised for a court organist in early 1708. Bach, already known there, applied and was accepted; he handed in a rather snotty resignation in June, recommending his cousin Johann Friedrich Bach, son of Heinrich's Johann Christoph [536], as his successor. (Another cousin, Johann Ernst [822], followed him at Arnstadt.)

Just about the first thing the Bachs did in Weimar was to produce their first child, named Catherine Dorothea. She was followed at fairly regular intervals by Wilhelm Friedemann in 1710 (see 784), twins who died in infancy, Carl Philipp Emanuel in 1714 (see 801), and Johann Gottfried Bernhard in 1715. It was in the Weimar years that J. S. Bach came to the height of his powers as an organist (though he modestly claimed that his virtuosity was merely a matter of hitting the right notes at the right time). He also had many pupils, including his nephew Johann Bernhard Bach (not to be confused with [646]) and his young cousin Johann Lorenz Bach. Another relative, Johann Walther [680] was a colleague and close friend, who stood godfather to Friedemann and was teacher to Prince Johann Ernst, the previously mentioned talented and ill-fated son of Bach's first employer. Telemann [665] came over from Frankfurt to be Carl Philipp Emanuel's godfather. Despite certain puritanical strictnesses of his master, Bach seems to have found Weimar much to his liking—though in 1712 he considered taking the post in Halle left vacant by Handel's [683] teacher Friedrich Wilhelm Zachau [594]; but the duke more than matched the offer and Bach stayed. He was also elevated to be *Konzertmeister,* and since the *Kapellmeister,* Drese, was tottery, Bach looked forward to succeeding him. But when he died in 1716, the duke first offered the post to Telemann, and then gave it to Drese's son. Bach was understandably angry, and he and the duke ended up on nonspeaking terms. But intermarriage between the ruling families of Weimar and Anhalt-Cöthen (some fifty miles to the northeast) provided him with an avenue of escape, and in 1717, without waiting for his release, he signed on as conductor of the court orchestra in Cöthen.

Having gotten settled, Bach visited Dresden (where the abortive organ-playing contest with Louis Marchand [619] is supposed to have taken place), and then stopped by Weimar to wind up his affairs there. When the duke found him determined to leave, however, he threw him in jail for a month, and finally let him go with a dishonorable discharge. But Bach was probably happier in Cöthen than he ever was anywhere else. Since the court was Calvinist, he had no church duties and was able to devote himself almost wholly to instrumental music, producing much of his chamber and orchestral music during the period he was there. The orchestra had acquired many of the musicians released by the antimusical Frederick William I of Prussia and was probably the equal of any in Europe. Bach continued to take pupils, among them his own two elder sons, both of whom showed great talent. But in 1720 the idyll shockingly ended. In July Bach went to the health resort of Carlsbad (now the Czech town of Karlovy Vary) with Prince Leopold. When he returned, he was told that Maria Barbara had sickened and died so swiftly that it had been impossible to notify him, and had been buried without him. Shortly afterward Bach went to Hamburg to try for the organist's job at the Jakobikirche. One of the judges, who marveled at his performance, was the ninety-seven-year-old Reincken [498]; but flattered as he was, Bach balked at the subrosa stipulation that the winner had to come up with a cash "gift" for certain officials. Shortly afterward he wrote the six *Brandenburg Concerti* for the Markgraf of Brandenburg, the Prussian king's uncle (who apparently never used them) and began the *Well-Tempered Clavier* for Friedemann's use. (It is not certain whether Bach had in mind here our arbitrary division of the octave into twelve equal intervals or something more or less like it.) In December 1721 Bach took a bride, the twenty-year-old Anna Magdalena Wilcken, a trumpeter's daughter and herself a singer. (Bach wrote the famous *Notebook* for her.) When Prince Leopold married a flibbertigibbet (in Bach's opinion) a week later, the composer decided it was time to move on again, and the following year applied for the cantorship of the Leipzig Thomaskirche, left vacant by the death of Kuhnau [582]. Leipzig wanted, however, a big name (which Bach's was not) and at one time thought it had landed Telemann. But eventually the list was exhausted and Bach won by default. Not even the premature death of his princess kept him in Cöthen, which he left in mid-April 1723, though he kept up friendly relations with Leopold until the latter's death five years later.

Bach began at Leipzig on a sour note: his installation created a ruckus between church and civic authorities, and he discovered the Thomasschule in a state of anarchy, necessitating the exercise of strict discipline to bring the little savages into line, while he tried to get their conditions bettered. Among his onerous duties at the church was the composition of a new cantata for each Sunday and feast day—the total said to have reached 295, though some were certainly retreads or earlier works. And he was, in theory at least, musical overseer of the other Lutheran churches in Leipzig—four maintained by the city plus the university's Paulinerkirche. He severed personal connections with the last, however, when the university insisted on giving him half pay for double duty. Indeed, Bach was not on good terms with the professors, who deplored his lack of an academic education and did all they could to keep commissions out of his hands. Nor did he fare much better with the city fathers, who meddled in the school, nagged and carped about his work, probably disliked his highfalutin music, and in 1729 (the year of the great *St. Matthew Passion)* managed to cut his income. Meanwhile, birth control being what it was in those days, a new sequence of young Bachs was steadily increasing and demanding to be fed, clothed, and educated. In 1730 Bach seriously considered a new move, but the appointment of a friendly rector at the school and the acquisition of some talented pupils made things more bearable. In 1729 he had also become director of the Collegium Musicum founded by Telemann nearly thirty years before, whose concerts produced a number of secular cantatas and the several keyboard concerti among other things. In 1733 he turned out four cantatas marking the succession of Augustus III to the Saxon electorate and a *Lutheran Mass* for his ceremonial visit to Leipzig. Bucked up by these successes, Bach tendered his *Mass in B minor* for Augustus' coronation as King of Poland, but it was not used. However, the monarch in 1736 named Bach court composer to both his holdings. Meanwhile, things had gone bad again at the school. Bach's friend Rector Gesner accepted a professorship at the University of Göttingen in 1734, and was succeeded by a young man named Ernesti, who considered musical training a frivolity and Bach's views old-fashioned. The two men clashed over the appointment of a student-assistant to the cantor, who became violent about the matter, and in 1738 they successfully sought the intervention of his royal patron. But from 1740 Bach seems largely to have lost interest in his official posts and to have devoted most of his time to teaching. (Besides his own children and other young relatives, his most famous pupils were Johann Ludwig Krebs [798], Gottfried August Homilius [800], Johann Philipp Kirnberger [821], Johann Theophilus Goldberg, and Johann Gottfried Müthel [849].) In 1741 Bach went to Berlin to visit his son Emanuel, now court organist to Frederick the Great, who was away at the wars. Four years later Frederick, as enemy, was besieging Leipzig; naturally the two men did not meet then either. In 1747, however, Bach returned to Berlin, and when Frederick heard the news, he stopped his evening concert with the announcement, "Gentlemen, old Bach is here!" and went personally to welcome him. He made much of the old fellow, insisting that he try out all the organs, harpsichords, and Silbermann pianos at Sans Souci, Frederick the Great's palace. (Bach's feelings about this last newfangled instrument are not certain.) Legend has it that the composer performed prodigies of contrapuntal improvisation at the king's request, and it is certain that he took home a theme proffered by Frederick, on which he based the *Musikalische Opfer (Musical Offering),* one of the great contrapuntal feats of all time. That summer Bach, somewhat against his inclinations, joined the Leipzig Society for Musical Knowledge, founded by one of his pupils. His last years were spent editing the 18 great "Leipzig" organ chorales and working on the monumental *Art of the Fugue.* In 1749, however, his already weak eyes gave out, and there was open talk of a successor. Bach, however, held his own. When John Taylor, an English eye man of some repute, came to Leipzig late in the year, Bach underwent two barbarous operations that left him totally blind and impaired his health. He took to his bed in a darkened room. On July 18, 1750, he suddenly regained his vision, but the miracle was merely a prelude to a massive stroke, the aftereffects of which carried him off ten days later. Ninety-five years later the male line of descendants ran out with the death of his grandson Wilhelm

Friedrich Ernst, though Sebastian's genes still survive in the Colson family.

In his last years Bach must have sometimes felt himself the last of the dinosaurs. His music seemed needlessly complex and rhetorical to a public taken with the *galanterie* of a Telemann. And he must finally have closed his eyes with misgivings. *Art of the Fugue* was left uncompleted. Wilhelm Friedemann, the apple of his eye, seemed unable to get established. There was not much to leave to the others. Christian got some shirts and a couple of harpsichords. Anna Magdalena, left with two young daughters, a halfwit son, and a spinster stepdaughter from the earlier marriage, was given a half-year salary and evicted from the cantor's house. She sold off everything that was saleable and died in poverty at fifty-nine. Poor Gottfried was taken in by his brother-in-law, J. C. Altnikol. Catharina, the eldest unmarried daughter, died in 1774, Caroline in 1781—in what circumstances, no one knows. In 1800 Susanna was discovered to be facing starvation. A Breitkopf editor got up a small purse, the Beethoven circle a much larger one, and she survived for nine more years.

RECORDINGS: By the time these pages see print, two integral recordings of the surviving cantatas will be nearing completion. The concerti, the chamber music, the orchestral suites, the harpsichord works, and several cycles of the organ music have long been available, as well as all the major choral works and such anomalies as the *Musical Offering* and *Art of the Fugue* in various realizations. There are also "reconstructions" of various miscellaneous concerti, and of parts of the *St. Mark Passion,* as well as a *St. Luke Passion* that is almost certainly spurious.

[685] LOEILLET, Jacques (Lwä-yā', Zhàk)
WIND PLAYER
BORN: Ghent, July 7, 1685
DIED: Ghent, November 28, 1746

Jacques Loeillet is often confused with his brother Jean-Baptiste of Ghent [697] and his cousin Jean-Baptiste of London [659]. He joined the musical forces of the Bavarian Elector Maximilian Emanuel when that war-dispossessed ruler was sojourning in Brussels and eventually returned to Munich with him in 1726. A year later he had occasion to demonstrate his mastery of several instruments (including his ability to make funny noises with them) to Louis XV and was promptly appointed to both His Majesty's indoor and outdoor musics. In 1728 he published 6 solo sonatas and 6 trio sonatas as Opp. 4 and 5. The nature and whereabouts of their predecessors are unknown. RECORDINGS: A "reconstructed" Concerto in D Major, from an imperfect ms., has been recorded by flutists Jean-Pierre Rampal and Claude Monteux, and by trumpeter Maurice André.

[686] ALBERTI, Giuseppe Matteo (Àl-bâr'-tē, Jōō-sep'-pā Màt-tā'-ō)
VIOLINIST
BORN: Bologna, September 20, 1685
DIED: Bologna, 1751

Alberti appears to be unrelated to the slightly later Domenico Alberti [785], "inventor" of the Alberti bass. He is one of the last representatives of the Bolognese Baroque school. A violin pupil of locals named Manzolini and Minelli, he learned to compose from Floriano Arresti, son of Giulio Cesare [501]. He was a violinist at San Petronio, Bologna, from at least 1713, and was elected to the Accademia Filarmonica in 1714, serving six terms as president between 1721 and 1746. He published a set each of concerti, sinfonie, and violin sonatas. The concerti were performed at the home of Count Orazio Bargellini under Alberti's direction before publication. The rather bland four-part sinfonie won considerable popularity in England. There are also some manuscript works, including a couple of vocal pieces. RECORDINGS: Maurice André and Ludovic Vaillant have recorded an early sonata à 3, which may or may not have been intended for trumpet.

[687] SCARLATTI, Giuseppe Domenico (Scär-làt'-tē, Jōō-sep'-pā Dō-mān'-ē-kō)
KEYBOARDIST, TEACHER
BORN: Naples, October 26, 1685
DIED: Madrid, July 23, 1757

It may be, as has been argued, that the modern keyboard repertoire, from Haydn [871] to Boulez [2346], owes its very being to Domenico Scarlatti. It is possible—but not, in any meaningful sense, likely. Little more than a local celebrity for most of his mature life, he was, after his death, all but forgotten, save by a few composers isolated in Spain and Portugal. As a partial result, his career remains obscure. The sixth of Alessandro's [583] ten children, he was born eight months after Handel [683] (whom he came to know) and seven after J. S. Bach

[684] (of whom he probably never heard). He spent most of his early life in the shadow and under the thumb of his father, who appears to have been his only teacher. At fifteen he became organist of the Spanish viceregal chapel in Naples, which Alessandro directed. The next year the pair were given four months' leave to visit Florence, where Alessandro basked in the patronage of Ferdinando de' Medici. When he decided to test the viridity of the Roman grass, Domenico, like the good boy he was, trudged back to Naples. A year later he produced two operas of his own, Ottavia restituita al trono (Octavia Restored to the Throne) and Il Giustino, and in 1704 successfully retailored Pollarolo's [569] old Irene. Such success in his own personal bailiwick was evidently too much for Alessandro. Noting that Domenico's genius was wrong for Naples and that Rome was no place for an ambitious opera man, he shipped him, by way of Florence, off to Venice with the castrato Nicolini, who happened to be going that way.

Here legend takes over. Scarlatti is supposed to have studied in Venice with Gasparini [615]. Already a virtuoso at the keyboard, he allegedly encountered there another recently arrived virtuoso, the Saxon Handel. The musty story goes that during Carnival the disguised Scarlatti recognized the disguised Handel by his playing—"Either the Saxon or the Devil," he is supposed to have crowed. Soon afterward, the yarn goes, the two set out together for Rome. As a matter of fact, there is no support for any of this, save that both men got to Rome c. 1708. What Scarlatti did in the meantime remains a mystery.

In Rome Scarlatti seems to have been briefly in the orbit of Cardinal Ottoboni, under whose sponsorship the famous contest between Scarlatti and Handel may have taken place, if it took place at all. (Scarlatti was declared the better harpsichordist, Handel the better organist. For the rest of their lives, it is said, Handel's eyes would run over at the mention of Scarlatti's name, and Domenico would cross himself at the sound of Handel's.) Soon, however, the Italian was in the employ of Ottoboni's rival, Maria Casimira, widow of King John III Sobieski of Poland. The queen had her own private opera in the Palazzo Zuccari, and for it Scarlatti wrote, over the next five seasons, six operas (Silvia, Tolomeo e Alessandro, Tetide in Sciro, Ifigenia in Aulide, Ifigenia in Tauride, and Amor d'un ombra e gelsoia d'un'aura), and two oratorios. In 1713 he was also appointed vice-maestro di cappella to Tommaso Bai in the Cappella

Giulia, the choir of St. Peter's. The year following, Maria Casimira, unable to keep up the standard of living to which she had become accustomed, disappeared from Rome to take refuge from her creditors in a Loire château that had been provided for her by Louis XIV. Scarlatti made an almost equally rapid transition to the household of the Portuguese ambassador, the Marques de Fontes, and shortly afterward succeeded Bai, who had died. In 1717, only a decade after he turned twenty-one, he became his own man through a legal instrument that said in effect that he no longer had to obey his father if he didn't want to.

In 1719 Scarlatti gave up his appointment at St. Peter's—ostensibly, it is said, to visit London. That would have been on the instance of Thomas Roseingrave [699], who had known and admired him for some years in Rome, and who was later chiefly responsible for making Scarlatti's music known in England, where it had a certain vogue. Roseingrave said that he had met Scarlatti in Venice in 1709, which seems unlikely, Scarlatti having already left for Rome by then. Though Roseingrave produced his own version of *Amor d'un ombra* (as *Narciso)* in London in 1720, it is unlikely that its composer ever got there. Instead he seems to have gone directly to Lisbon as palace music director to John V, and music teacher to his daughter Maria Barbara, though the court records pertinent to such matters have vanished, and we know nothing for sure about his activities in Iberia until 1728. We *do* know, however, that he was in Rome in 1724, visited his dying father in 1725, and returned to Rome in 1728 to marry, at forty-three, Maria Caterina Gentile, twenty-seven years his junior; they had five children.

The next year, Princess Maria Barbara married the *infante* of Spain, Don Fernando, later sixth monarch of that name, and moved to Madrid, taking along her teacher. Just what his role was in the Spanish court is not clear. He had abandoned operas and oratorios back in Italy. He apparently gave up playing in public in Spain. (Gossip long had it that he grew too fat to play cross-handed at the keyboard, but portraits from his last two decades show that he kept in trim.) He appears in no official capacity on any list. Apparently he devoted himself mostly to turning out the hundreds of short sonatas—those miniature universes that he modestly termed "exercises"—on which his present fame rests. These were imitated by the next generations of Iberian keyboardists, notably Antonio Soler [854] and José Antonio Seixas [755], both of whom Scarlatti certainly knew and may have taught. In 1738 he was made a Knight of the Order of Santiago. A year later Maria Caterina died, a few days before her eleventh wedding anniversary. The widower was wed again three years later, at fifty-seven, to Anastasia Maxarti Jiménez, who bore him four more children. Four of his total brood made it to maturity, but none took up music as a livelihood. The legend persists that their father was a compulsive gambler, lost all of his money, and left his heirs (who were bailed out by the queen) in poverty. The queen followed him in death a year later, and the grief-stricken king sank into a deep depression.

RECORDINGS: The sonatas have enjoyed great popularity on records, not only played on the harpsichord, but also on everything from the piano to the guitar. There is, however, no integral edition so far, though Fernando Valenti did about twenty LPs worth of one before his sponsors went bankrupt. There is also a healthy selection by Ralph Kirkpatrick, whose catalog (K-numbers) has superseded that of Alessandro Longo (L-numbers). (Kirkpatrick has argued convincingly that the sonatas were conceived not singly but in groups of two or three.) Of the earlier and larger sonatas there are recordings of the opera *Tetide in Sciro (Thetis on Skyros),* the *Stabat Mater,* the *Salve Regina* (a very late work), at least one cantata, and a few orchestral *sinfonias.*

[688] GIUSTINI, Lodovico Maria (Jōōs-tē'-nē, Lō-dō-vē'-kō Mà-rē'-à)
ORGANIST
BORN: Pistoia, December 12, 1685
DIED: Pistoia, February 7, 1743

All that is known of Giustini's life, between the parentheses of his birth and death, is that he was the son of Francesco Giustini and succeeded him as organist of the Congregation of the Holy Spirit in Pistoia (then part of Tuscany). In 1732 he published a set of 12 sonatas for the pianoforte—the first known specified for the newfangled instruments that Bartolommeo Cristofori (1655–1731), curator of the grand duke's collection of instruments, had been turning out since 1709. RECORDINGS: Mieczysław Horszowski has recorded two thirds of the sonatas on a piano made by Cristofori in 1720.

[689] MARCELLO, Benedetto (Mär-chel'-lō, Bā-ne-dāt'-tō)
LAWYER, SATIRIST, POLITICIAN, POET

BORN: Venice, July 24 or August 1, 1686
DIED: Brescia, July 24, 1739

The youngest of the three sons of Senator Agostino Marcello (see 682), Benedetto passed his boyhood as the family klutz, exhibiting neither the talent nor the industry of his brothers. At about seventeen, however, he suddenly caught fire and for two years worked so hard at his music (or so the story goes) that eventually his father packed him off for a rest, forbidding him pen and paper, to forestall a collapse. (His teacher was Francesco Gasparini [615].) In 1705 he issued a savage satire of Antonio Lotti [613], with whom he may also have studied. Two years later his political career was launched when at twenty-one he was appointed to the Grand Council of the Most Serene Republic. He studied law (in Rome?) and was admitted to practice in 1711; about the same time (some think earlier), he was taken into the prestigious Accademia dell'-Arcadia (as "Driante Sacreo") and was elected to Bologna's Accademia Filarmonica on the strength of a Mass he wrote to celebrate the elevation of Giovanni Francesco Albani of Urbino to the Papacy as Clement XI. Around 1720 he published one of the most brilliant musical satires ever written, *Il Teatro alla moda*, a picture of what goes on behind the scenes at the opera. He also taught and in 1728 secretly married one of his pupils, Rosana Scalfi, a singer of proletarian background. (Much romantic nonsense has been written about their love.) That same year, while attending Mass at the church of the Santi Apostoli, Marcello felt the floor crumble beneath him, precipitating him into an old tomb. The experience struck him as a warning, and he supposedly turned away from secular writing as a result. He also began a long poem on the Redemption, which he never finished. He had served now for a time on the Council of Forty, and in 1730 he was dispatched across the Adriatic as *provveditore* of the Istrian city of Pola (now Pula). There he suffered from malaria and lung trouble brought on by the dampness. He was finally relieved in 1737 and sent to the other extreme of the republic as *camerlingo* of Brescia. But he continued to be unwell, and even a pilgrimage did not heal him; he died a year after he took office. His wife was responsible for his tomb, the inscription on which calls him "the Michelangelo of Music."

Marcello's reputation as a composer was great and widespread in his lifetime, largely because of his *Estro poetico-armonico*, a cantata-style setting of Psalms 1–50, issued in the mid-1720s. The texts are Italian verse

translations by his friend Ascanio Giustiniani, and the music sometimes incorporated Jewish chant and even ancient Greek music (as it was then understood). Much of Marcello's other music is vocal—oratorios, Masses, motets, *serenatas,* many cantatas, and shorter works, but only a single opera, and that highly suspect as to authenticity. Before 1720, however, he devoted himself chiefly to instrumental music, beginning with a set of *Concerti a 5* in the old *da chiesa* format. These were published in Venice in 1708 as Op. 1. A set of recorder sonatas appeared in London as Op. 1, however, and one of violin sonatas in Amsterdam. There were similar Op. 2 problems. There are also a number of keyboard sonatas from this period, said to be the earliest such works written in Venice, a couple of concerti, and some *sinfonie.*

RECORDINGS: Michel Corboz and Giulio Bertola have sampled the psalms on records. Angelo Ephrikian has recorded the *concerti a 5,* Carroll Glenn an isolated violin concerto, Janoz Scholz the cello sonatas, and Jean-Pierre Rampal two of the recorder/flute sonatas (which are really reworkings of the earlier concerti). Luciano Sgrizzi and Judith Norell have recorded some of the keyboard sonatas.

[690] PORPORA, Nicola Antonio (Pôr'-pō-rà, Nē'-kō-là Àn-tōn'-yō)
TEACHER, CONDUCTOR
BORN: Naples, August 17, 1686
DIED: Naples, March 3, 1768

Porpora's was in his day a name to conjure with, though in his present eclipse one would never guess it. His bookseller father, Carlo, sent him to the Conservatorio dei Poveri di Gesù Cristo when he was ten. After a couple of years he was placed on full scholarship, perhaps because of some financial reversal at home but most likely in recognition of his talent. A year or so after he left, his first opera, *Agrippina,* was produced in the viceregal palace to celebrate the name day of the Archduke Charles, the imperial claimant to the Spanish throne and later Emperor Charles VI (1708). From at least that time, Porpora was in the service of Landgrave Philipp of Hesse-Darmstadt, who was Emperor Josef's man in Italy. In his years there, the landgrave also employed Vivaldi [650] and Locatelli [721]. Though Porpora called himself Philipp's *maestro di cappella* as late as 1725, the title was perhaps honorary, since he remained in Naples when the landgrave left in 1713 and became imperial governor of Mantua. A year later

Porpora's *Arianna e Teseo* was performed in Vienna to celebrate the emperor's birthday and was followed by works performed both there and in Naples. However, Porpora himself remained in the latter city as singing teacher at the Conservatorio di San Onofrio until at least 1722. Among his notable pupils were the *castrati* Caffarelli *(né* Gaetano Majorano), Farinelli *(né* Carlo Broschi), Salimbeni, and Porporino *(né* Antonio Uberti). Hasse [736] gave him a try but preferred Alessandro Scarlatti [583]. In 1718 Porpora collaborated with Domenico Scarlatti [687] on *Berenice* (the latter composer's last operatic venture), which was produced in Rome, opening the door there for Porpora. And in 1720, for the emperor's birthday, he wrote a *serenata*, entitled *Angelica*, to a libretto by a sometime student, Pietro Trapassi, whose patron had dubbed him "Metastasio," and who would be the greatest librettist of the eighteenth century.

Around 1725, Porpora broadened his base of operations, producing operas in Milan and Reggio nell'Emilia, and possibly visiting Vienna, before settling in Venice in 1726. Here he taught at the Ospedale degli Incurabili, another haven for "foundlings," and established himself as an operatic composer of international rank. When the associate *Kapellmeister* at Dresden, David Heinichen [674], died in 1729, Porpora was considered as his successor, but not hired. A year later, upon the demise of Antonio Biffi, he competed for the post of *maestro di cappella* at St. Mark's. When a tie was declared between Porpora, Pollarolo [569], and Lotti [613], Lotti was named acting *maestro* until the thing could be decided. However, Porpora's interest became academic a few weeks later. In London, some of the Beautiful People, headed by Bononcini's [620] former patron, the young Duke of Marlborough, and encouraged by the Prince of Wales's expressed distaste for his father's favorite, Handel [683], formed the Opera of the Nobility to run the Saxon out of business. As chief attraction they hired Handel's onetime *primo uomo,* the great *castrato* Senesino, and they invited Porpora to become their composer-in-chief. He accepted, coming to London in 1733 for the premiere of his *Arianna in Nasso.* The company strove bravely for three years, stealing the King's Theatre from Handel, and topping Senesino with Farinelli. But when, in 1736, the fickle prince called on Handel to write the music for his nuptials, Porpora sensed the party was over and went back to the Incurabili. He did not, however, stay in Venice for long, returning to Naples in 1739 as chief conductor of the Conservatorio di

Santa Maria di Loreto. Evidently the job did not satisfy him, for on the pretext of having to oversee an operatic production, he returned to Venice and signed on at the Ospedale della Pietà in 1741, from which he resigned a little over a year later in favor of the Ospedaletto. There he heard of the death of Leonardo Leo [718], *maestro* of the viceregal chapel in Naples, and applied for his post, but missed it because he was unable to return for the required competition.

In 1747 Porpora went to Dresden as singing teacher to the Princess Maria Antonia. Things began there well enough, but he soon crossed metaphorical swords with his sometime pupil Hasse, who had established himself as Chief Musician to the Elector-King. When one of Porpora's vocal pupils threatened the fading star of Frau Hasse, the great Faustina Bordoni, the writing was on the wall. When Porpora was named *Kapellmeister* a year later, Hasse demanded and got that of *Oberkapellmeister.* Porpora was quietly pensioned off in 1752. He left soon after for Vienna, where he entered the service of the Venetian Ambassador, Pietro Correr (as his mistress's teacher). There he acquired a young Man Friday named Franz Joseph Haydn [871], whom he clearly taught a good deal. But old age and the outbreak of the Seven Years War made Porpora's situation increasingly alarming. In 1759, however, he was saved by a call back to his post at Santa Maria di Loreto in Naples (obviously a sinecure, since the place already had two *maestri),* and a year later he was also made *maestro* at San Onofrio. But he had to give up both posts in 1761. Virtually forgotten, he dragged out his last years in poverty and sometimes near starvation. He died a pauper, and friends and former students paid for his funeral.

RECORDINGS: Most of Porpora's music was for the stage (more than 60 operas and oratorios), and the church, and he knew better than most how to write for the voice. Perversely, this side of his work is represented on records by very little—e.g., a dull *Salve Regina* sung by Yves Tinayre. The cellist Thomas Blees has recorded a concerto (one of 2 for the instrument).

---

[691] WEISS, Silvius Leopold (Vīs, Zēl'-vē-ōōs Lā'-ō-polt)

LUTENIST

BORN: Breslau, October 12, 1686
DIED: Dresden, October 16, 1750

Weiss is something of a dinosaur—a lutenist long after that instrument's heyday. But he arrived at that state logically, for his father,

Johann Jakob (c. 1662–1764), was a famous lutenist at several German courts in his long day. At twenty he was in the employ of Karl Philipp, Count Palatine, in Breslau, and later (like his father) at the court of the count's brother, Elector Johann Wilhelm, in Düsseldorf. In 1708 he joined the retinue of Prince Alexander Sobieski, son of the late King John III of Poland, and spent six years in Rome with him, until the prince died in 1714. He then returned to Düsseldorf, after a brief stopover at Cassel and the court of Landgraf Charles. But while visiting Dresden in 1717, he was persuaded to join the stellar musical establishment of the elector, Augustus the Strong. The elector took him, Pantaleon Hebenstreit (1667–1750), Pisendel [694], and Zelenka [656] to show off when he visited Emperor Charles in 1718. Handel [683] remarked on his virtuosity when he stopped by Dresden the year following. Musical matters were as usual not very stable at the court, and Weiss's career was nearly terminated in 1722 when a berserk French violinist named Petit tried unsuccessfully to bite his thumb off. But by 1723 he was fully recovered and played (together with Quantz [730] and K. H. Graun [757]) at the premiere of Fux's [585] *Costanza e fortezza* in Prague, celebrating the emperor's coronation as King of Bohemia. Weiss was a friend of the noble lutenist Losy von Losymthal [558], for whose death in 1721 he wrote a *tombeau*, and he was the teacher of Baron [724]. He traveled widely with his employers, and was heard at various times in London, Münich, and Berlin, as well as in the cities already noted. In 1739, Wilhelm Friedemann Bach [784], then organist at Dresden's Sophienkirche, brought Weiss and his fellow-lutenist Kropfgans back to Leipzig for a month's stay with his father, and there is the expectable legend that Weiss and Johann Sebastian Bach [684] once engaged in a public lute duel in Dresden. By 1744 Weiss was the highest-paid musician at the Dresden court. He left a widow and a number of children (he had eleven all together) and more than 600 compositions. RECORDINGS: His works are arranged in seven-movement suites—each consisting of a prelude and six dances—a number of which have been recorded by lutenists and guitarists—e.g., Laurindo Almeida, William Matthews, Brigitte Zaczek. His other compositions have not survived in playable form.

[692] FESCH, Willem de (Fesh, Vil'-lem dä)
VIOLINIST, CHOIRMASTER

BORN: Alkmaar, August 26, 1687
DIED: London, January 3, 1761

Other than that he was the son of Louis and Johanna de Fesch (occupations and status unknown), there is no information on Willem de Fesch's early life and training. Around 1710 he began concertizing in the Lowlands as a violin virtuoso, and in 1711 he married Maria Anna Rosier, daughter of the Liègeois violinist Carl Rosier, then *Kapellmeister* at Cologne Cathedral. Fesch took the analogous post at Antwerp Cathedral in 1725 but was fired six years later for being unpleasant to the choristers, the chapter, the clergy, and just about everyone else in sight. He thereupon followed the then-current trend and emigrated to London, where he successfully pursued his concert career, taught (he was on the books as a "respectable professor"), and did orchestral work (he was Handel's first violinist one time). In 1748 he became conductor of the orchestra at Marylebone Gardens, one of the several burgeoning alfresco pleasure gardens in London, but nothing is heard of him after 1750, and even the date of his death is a subject for argument. He evidently tried to cash in on the Handelian rage in London with a couple of oratorios, but they have vanished, along with his few other large works. What remain are half a dozen books of songs from the London years, and a little over twice as many collections of instrumental works—mostly sonatas and concerti—about half published on the Continent and the rest in London. They show Fesch as a transitional figure, in the end strongly influenced by the new Italians. At its best Fesch's music is said to be sweet, clean, and (consumed in bulk) cloying. RECORDINGS: There is a concerto played on the trumpet by Maurice André and a trio sonata by the Los Angeles Baroque Players.

[693] GEMINIANI, Francesco (Jā-mēn-yä'-nē, Frän-chäs'-kō)
VIOLINIST, THEORIST, TEACHER, CONDUCTOR
BORN: Lucca, c. December 5, 1687
DIED: Dublin, September 17, 1762

Tartini's [714] epithet *furibondo* (wild) and Charles Burney's tale of how a Neapolitan orchestra could not follow his eccentric beat have transformed the Geminiani of legend into a raving loony. He seems at worst to have been a romantic born before his time, a conclusion that is supported by his own utterances on music as a vehicle of feeling. The facts of his early life are hazy. We now know definitely that he was born in Lucca (unless he was rushed there for baptism) and that he had lessons with the hunchbacked violinist Carlo Ambrogio Lonati, though we are not sure when or where. If Corelli [565] really had all the pupils credited to him, he would not have had a moment for himself, but that he taught Geminiani (who drank deep of his style) seems unarguable. Whether Alessandro Scarlatti [583] also taught him is another matter. Education past, Geminiani played in the Lucchese opera orchestra from 1707 to 1710, when he was fired for absenteeism. It was supposedly after this that the Neapolitan fiasco occurred.

In 1714, the tidal wave of Continental musical emigration washed him up in London. English fiddle playing being what it was, he was welcomed. There is an old story, which may well be true, at least in part, that he let it be known that at his English court debut he would have no other accompanist than Handel [683]. King George, to heal a rift between himself and his old retainer, saw to it. Geminiani then quickly established himself as a highly paid and much-lionized society violin teacher. He also won acclaim as a producer of concerts (in which he himself, however, rarely played). At one point he went into the art business, buying and selling paintings, and wound up in debtor's prison, from which a wealthy pupil had to bail him out. In 1733 he moved to Dublin, where he continued his pursuits for a couple of years, then returned to London. In 1737, however, he was back in Dublin, and for the two succeeding decades he operated not only between the two cities, but also on the Continent, though the story of a six-year sojourn in Paris beginning in 1749 seems unlikely. From 1749 to 1760 he seems largely to have devoted himself to writing and publishing theoretical and practical works, including how-to books on the violin, the guitar, harmony, and accompanying, and a study of musical taste (i.e., how to ornament correctly). Many of these sold for years. After 1760 he settled in Ireland for good. He had nearly completed another manual when a servant, according to him, stole the manuscript. The shock allegedly killed him.

The Art of Playing on the Violin of 1751, written in English like all of Geminiani's guides, is said to be the first such work published anywhere. Much of it is still valid, and all of it gives splendid insight into the musical thinking of the times. His music, which survives only in published form, is all instrumental and, apart from the Tassonian ballet of 1754, *Enchanted Forest,* and some keyboard pieces arranged from his other works, consists entirely of sonatas and concerti (the latter including *concerto-grosso* recensions of Corelli's Opp. 3 and 5 sonatas). If Geminiani is not a composer of alpine stature, his music is blessed by a Handelian richness and real passion. The later works, incidentally, show on the printed page not only what is to be played but how in terms of expression.

RECORDINGS: *The Enchanted Forest* (Claudio Scimone, Newell Jenkins); *concerti grossi:* Op. 2 (Paul Angerer, Dean Eckertsen); Op. 3 (Angerer, Christopher Hogwood, Rolf Reinhardt, and Hermann Scherchen); Op. 4, from sonatas (Angerer); Op. 7, after Corelli's Op. 5 (Eckertsen, Claudio Scimone, I Musici); cello sonatas, Op. 5 (William Pleeth); violin sonatas, Opp. 1, 4 (selection: Sonia Monosoff); a selection of sonatas for guitar, cello, and harpsichord from the collection *The Art of Playing Guitar* (various Hungarian artists).

[694] PISENDEL, Johann Georg (Pē'-zent-el, Yō'-hàn Gä-ôrg')
VIOLINIST
BORN: Cadolzburg, December 26, 1687
DIED: Dresden, November 25, 1755

Pisendel was the son of a cantor in a village just west of Nuremberg. He showed musical leanings early and accordingly at around ten was sent off to Ansbach to chirp in the chapel choir of the Markgraf of Brandenburg. The first violin there at the time was Torelli [578], who taught Pisendel to play well enough to take his place in the orchestra by the time he was in his mid-teens. In 1709, however, he decided that he needed an education and went to Leipzig, where he enrolled in the university. But he was soon soloing with the Collegium Musicum under the direction of Telemann's [665] successor, Melchior Hoffmann, whom he sometimes relieved as conductor. No doubt this sort of thing brought him to the attention of the musical powers at the Dresden electoral court of Augustus the Strong, and in 1712 he was hired as a violinist there. He took the opportunity to study composition with Heinichen [674]. Perhaps because of the fringe benefits it offered, however, he shortly transferred to the service of the heir-apparent, Friedrich August, who took him a-journeying to France, Prussia, and especially Italy. In Venice, Pisendel struck up a friendship with Vivaldi [650], and almost certainly took lessons from him. In 1730 he was appointed court *Konzertmeister* in Dresden, though he had actually filled the post for the two years previous. As the finest and most famous native violinist of his day, he attracted a number of pupils, including František Benda [776] and J. G. Graun [751], Vivaldi dedicated a concerto to him, and it is thought that Bach (whom he knew) wrote his unaccompanied violin sonatas for Pisendel. His extant musical legacy is small—7 violin concerti, a *sinfonia,* a few sonatas, and some concerti grossi arranged from other works. The violin concerti clearly reflect Vivaldi. RECORDINGS: Roman Totenberg has recorded one of the violin concerti.

[695] GALLIARD, Johann Ernest (Gàl-yärd', Yō'-han Er-nest')
WIND PLAYER, ORGANIST, TRANSLATOR
BORN: Celle, c. 1687
DIED: London, 1749

Galliard's father was a French wigmaker who settled in Celle, near Hanover, where people wore large wigs. His son went on the official records as "Johann Ernst," who learned oboe from a compatriot of his father's so well that he was playing it in the orchestra of the Duke of Lüneburg-Celle at the age of twelve. He also used to run over to Hanover for music lessons with the court *Kapellmeister,* Agostino Steffani [570], and another displaced Frenchman, Jean-Baptiste Farinel, who called himself "Farinelli," which might have been a name to conjure with, except that the great *castrato* who made it famous was not born until 1705, just one year before not only the Celle orchestra but also the duchy was dismantled. Galliard then joined the migration to London, where he became "John Ernst" and entered the service of that stodgy, asthmatic nonentity Prince George of Denmark, husband of Queen Anne. In 1710 he became organist at Somerset House, and from 1713 was solo oboist in Handel's [683] opera orchestra at the Queen's Theatre. Galliard, who seems to have had a fine knowledge of the language (he wrote on opera and translated a work on vocal music), had a rather quixotic faith in opera in English and produced an example of his own, *Calypso and Telemachus,* at the Queen's Theatre; it flopped. In 1717 he joined forces with John Rich, manager of the theater at Lincoln's Inn Fields (see 611), and with Lewis Theobald, the much-maligned Shakespearean scholar. After a few false starts, they found great success in pantomimes. These were mimed, musically accompanied playlets that mixed the classical with the popular, as the title of one, *Apollo and Daphne, or The Burgomas-*

ter Trick'd suggests. Galliard wrote another couple of unsuccessful English operas, then began one to an Italian libretto, which, unhappily, he did not live to finish. He also wrote some masques, some religious music, and some cantatas, of which one, a setting of the morning hymn from Canto IV of Milton's *Paradise Lost* enjoyed considerable popularity. On the whole Galliard's vocal music is not very interesting (it was he of whom Dr. Charles Burney said that only Pepusch was duller). But one would like to hear the lost Concerto for 24 Bassoons and Cello written for his 1745 benefit. Six surviving sonatas for flute and 6 for bassoon are, however, well regarded. RECORDINGS: Arthur Grossman has recorded the complete set of bassoon sonatas.

[696] FASCH, Johann Friedrich (Fàsh, Yō'-hän Frēd-rikh)
CONDUCTOR, ORGANIST
BORN: Buttelstedt, April 15, 1688
DIED: Zerbst, December 5, 1758

Not to be confused with his contemporary Willem de Fesch [692], Fasch was born in the vicinity of Weimar, studied with Johann Philipp Krieger [553] as a choirboy at the court of Saxe-Weissenfels, and from 1701 with Johann Kuhnau [582] at the Thomasschule in Leipzig, where he was befriended by the somewhat older Telemann [665]. He seems to have emulated Telemann in taking up the law at the university and later in conducting a student *Collegium musicum* to the general outrage of Kuhnau. (This was not the organization founded by Telemann, but apparently Fasch's own idea. It remained in existence until 1756. Some accounts suggest that he himself left Leipzig soon after.) By 1711 he was turning out operas under the sponsorship of the Duke of Saxe-Zeitz (none survive). There followed a period of *Wanderjahre.* In 1713 he was in Darmstadt studying with Christoph Graupner [673]. A year later he was a violinist in the court orchestra at Bayreuth, then municipal secretary at Gera. By 1719 he was holding down a similar post in nearby Greiz and doubling as town organist, and in 1721 he was at Count Morzin's little court in Lucaveč, Bohemia. His last post was as court *Kapellmeister* in Zerbst, forty miles north of Leipzig, where he settled in 1722. That same year he was invited to compete for the cantorial vacancy at the Thomaskirche left by Kuhnau's death, but declined, saying that he did not like teaching (not, as legend has it, that he thought Bach deserved the job). In Zerbst he produced a notable body of cantatas and other church music, which became quite famous, much instrumental music (concerti, suites, *sinfonie,* sonatas), and a son, Karl Friedrich Christian (1736–1800), who replaced C. P. E. Bach [801] as harpsichordist to Frederick II of Prussia, taught Carl Zelter [1008], and knew the young Ludwig van Beethoven [1063].

Johann Sebastian Bach [684] admired Fasch's music and copied out five orchestral suites. As an instrumental composer, he, it is argued, moves very close to classicism, but the chief impetuses seem to come from the Venice of Vivaldi [650] and Albinoni [630].

RECORDINGS: Trumpet concerti have been recorded by Maurice André, Edward Tarr, and Heinz Zickler, a lute concerto by Konrad Ragossnig, a concerto for two horns by the Paillard Orchestra, and bassoon sonatas by Robert Thompson and Helman Jung. The *Concerto Grosso* (Op. 3, No. 2) is recorded by members of the Hague Philharmonic. *Sinfonias* in G and A major have been recorded by Jean-François Paillard, and there are also scattered instrumental miscellanea.

[697] LOEILLET, Jean-Baptiste, of Ghent (Lwä-yä′, Zhän Bȧ-tēst′)

WIND PLAYER

BORN: Ghent, c. July 6, 1688

DIED: Lyons, c. 1720

Long confused with his cousin Jean-Baptiste, of London [659], and often thought to be identical with him, Loeillet of Ghent (both were actually born there) remains a shadow. His father was Pieter Loeillet (1651–1735), a violinist, his mother, Pieter's first wife, *née* Marte Nortier—uncle and aunt of the other Jean-Baptiste. He found employment in the household of the Archbishop of Lyons, where he died in his thirties. Between 1710 and 1717 he published 5 collections of recorder sonatas. RECORDINGS: Examples of the recorder sonatas have been recorded by Frans Brüggen, Jean-Pierre Rampal, and many others. There are also a number of arrangements for various instrumental groups.

[698] ZIPOLI, Domenico (Tsē′-pō-lē, Dō-mä′-nē-kō)

ORGANIST, MISSIONARY

BORN: Prato, c. October 16, 1688

DIED: Santa Catalina, Argentina, January 2, 1726

Zipoli, the son of Sabatino Zipoli, had his earliest training in Prato and Florence, where at twenty, he collaborated on an oratorio with twenty-three other composers, including Caldara [624] and Gasparini [615]. (Like his others, it is now lost.) He studied briefly in Naples with Alessandro Scarlatti [583], then in Bologna with a certain Vannucci, and finally with the valetudinarian Bernardo Pasquini [524] in Rome. In 1715 he became organist at the Gesù there, obviously preparatory to his joining the Jesuits the year following. He then went to Spain, and in 1717 embarked on a stormy voyage to Argentina, where he planned to undertake missionary work. He studied for the priesthood at the Jesuit university in Córdoba. But meanwhile he had contracted tuberculosis and died shortly after completing his studies without having reached either of his goals. He left a Mass and a couple of cantatas, but his musical reputation rests on the 1716 *Sonate d'intavolatura* for keyboards. These are not sonatas at all, but *(a)* organ pieces and *(b)* suites and variations for harpsichord. Brilliant little works, tonally very flexible, but tainted with the unproved rumor that they were stolen, at least in part, from Pasquini. RECORDINGS: Some of the pieces have been recorded—e.g., by Luciano Sgrizzi, Luigi Ferdinando Tagliavini, Karl Philipp Schuba. (Recordings of Zipoli works for trumpet and organ merely take advantage of his strong melodic line.)

[699] ROSEINGRAVE, Thomas

ORGANIST, TEACHER

BORN: Winchester, 1688

DIED: Dunleary, Ireland, June 23, 1766

Thomas Roseingrave was the son of Daniel Roseingrave, at various times organist of cathedrals in Gloucester, Winchester, Salisbury, and Dublin, who left him a legacy of five shillings (the bulk of his considerable property going to the younger son, Ralph). Thomas was taught by his father, attended Trinity College in Dublin, but dropped out, and in 1710 went off to study in Italy, with a small scholarship from St. Patrick's Cathedral. He met the Scarlattis (see 583 and 687) and became a satellite of Domenico in his remaining Italian years, and an apostle for his music thereafter.

By 1718 he was back in London, giving a public performance of music by Scarlatti and himself. He was probably responsible for the 1720 London production of Scarlatti's *Narciso,* to which he certainly added some numbers of his own (see 687). In 1725 he was chosen organist of St. George's

Church in Hanover Square. Greatly admired as an organist and especially as an improviser, he attracted flocks of pupils. According to a report of the day, he fell hopelessly in love with one young lady but was thwarted by her father, who felt marriage to a musician beneath his daughter. The experience is said to have unbalanced Roseingrave's mind. Certainly he was dismissed from the church around 1744, and certainly there are later reports of "fits of madness." But it is clear that he could also function at other times. After he went back to Ireland, probably around 1750, to live with his nephew William, he continued to concertize and produced his opera *Phaedra and Hippolitus* in 1753, to great applause. He apparently never married. (His instability may have been congenital, for his father was several times in trouble for displays of violent temper.) Besides the opera, Roseingrave left organ pieces (voluntaries, fugues), harpsichord pieces ("lessons"), and flute sonatas. Moreover, he published an edition of 42 sonatas by Domenico Scarlatti.

RECORDINGS: A recording of eight double fugues and twelve "lessons" has been made by organist Leonard Raver.

[700] TUFTS, John
MINISTER, SHOPKEEPER
BORN: Medford, Massachusetts, February 26, 1689
DIED: Amesbury, Massachusetts, August 17, 1750

Tufts is the first composer (if such he was) born north of the Mexican border to find a place in these pages. A Harvard graduate (class of 1708), he was ordained in Newbury in 1714. After pursuing his ministry for nearly a quarter century, he retired to Amesbury in 1738 and opened a store there. In 1721, he published his pioneering textbook, *An Introduction to the Singing of Psalm-Tunes*. The first extant copy, however, dates from 1726, when it had already gone through five editions. It was to enjoy at least six more. It contains 37 hymn tunes in three-part arrangements, presumably the handiwork of the Rev. Mr. Tufts. Though it is not certain that he actually composed any of them, *100 Psalm Tune New* is generally credited to him as the first original piece of sacred music written in the United States. RECORDINGS: This and other pieces from the collection have been recorded by Gregg Smith.

[701] AUBERT, Jacques, "Le vieux" (Ō-bâr', Zhàk)
VIOLINIST
BORN: Paris, September 30, 1689
DIED: Belleville (Paris), May 18 (?), 1753

Aubert's father was—as the son was to be—a member of the *24 Violons du Roy*. Young Jacques (later called "le vieux," the elder, to distinguish him from his son Louis [1693], studied with Tommaso Vitali's pupil Jean-Baptiste Senaillé, who left indelible Italian fingerprints on him. In 1719 he became concertmaster and general director of the Duke de Bourbon's household music. It was in 1727 that he briefly followed in his father's footsteps at court before joining the orchestra of the opera in 1728 for a lifetime career there. Aubert seems to have been popular in his day, contributing a number of works to the Concert Spirituel, though his music was, not without reason, generally considered lightweight. Apart from an opera, his output was chiefly instrumental. Five sets of violin sonatas show an almost slavish worship of Corelli [565] without real comprehension of his methods. A sixth book for two unaccompanied violins, however, reflects a new move from grandiosity to preciosity. His *Suites de concert de simphonie en trio* of 1730 provides, in terms of title, a challenge to classifiers of forms; according to the composer, these works may be played "orchestrally like concertos." Later he published 2 volumes of concerti for four violins, cello, and continuo (1734 and 1739), cast in the Italian three-movement form. These have rather intemperately (following their publisher's puff) been hailed as the first concerti written in France by a Frenchman; in fact Michel Corrette [779] published his Op. 3 concerti six years earlier. Nevertheless they provide examples of a genre that remained rare in France before 1750. It should be noted that with Aubert's pretty and graceful and rather vacuous music we have entered the pale sunlight of the Rococo. RECORDINGS: Jean-François Paillard has recorded one of the concerti (Op. 17, No. 6).

[702] BOISMORTIER, Joseph Bodin de
(Bwà-môrt-yä', Zhō'-zef Bō-dan' də)
BORN: Thionville, December 23, 1689
DIED: Roissy-en-Brie, October 28, 1755

Boismortier was a prodigiously facile composer and some of his music has attained a not undeserved popularity in recent years, but very little about the man himself has been turned up. He was born not in the shadow of the Pyrenees, as has been long supposed, but in the dreary flatlands of northeast France (or the Duchy of Lorraine, as it then was, in the days of the absentee Duke Charles). His father was a merchant and a man of some substance. Young Joseph next turns up in Metz, age thirteen, probably as a chorister and/or student. In his early twenties he was in Nancy and Lunéville, where the new Duke Leopold held court, though there is no evidence that he was ever a ducal employee. By 1720 he had migrated south to Perpignan (formerly supposed to be his birthplace), as shown by the records of his marriage to Marie Valette and of the birth of their daughter Suzanne in 1722. By 1724 he had heeded the siren call of Paris, and spent the rest of his highly productive life there. It seems also to have been a lucrative life, for some time after 1747 he retired to his estate, "La Gastinellerie," in the countryside east of Paris that gave us the Couperins and Brie cheese, where he lived out his days in apparent peace and comfort.

Boismortier obviously worked hard to satisfy the period's insatiable demand for new music. He is said to have published at least one hundred opuses, consisting mostly of sets of sonatas, suites, and suchlike chamber music. He was a pioneer in writing ensembles for unaccompanied wind instruments—e.g., bassoon duos and works for from two to five flutes. With Jacques Aubert [701] and Jean-Marie Leclair [732], he shares the distinction of being one of the few French writers of concerti before 1750; his are in the Italian three-movement form, though they do not always adhere to the fast-slow-fast formula. Boismortier also wrote religious music, including a Christmas motet, *Fugit nox,* that incorporated popular carols and was standard holiday fare at the Concert Spirituel for years. His 4 musical stage works include a treatment of *Don Quixote.* Of his handful of *cantates, Diane et Actéon* was thought until very recently to be by Rameau.

RECORDINGS: *Diane et Actéon* has been recorded by Charles Bressler. There are many recordings of the instrumental pieces, notably of flute works by Jean-Pierre Rampal and bassoon works by Robert Thompson. If Boismortier did not write supreme music, the evaluation by his younger contemporary Jean-Benjamin de LaBorde, that it, like an abandoned mine, contains enough gold dust to make an ingot, still seems to pertain.

[703] CAREY, Henry
  POET, PLAYWRIGHT

BORN: c. 1689
DIED: London, October 5, 1743

Much of Carey's fame rests on error. Born Henry Savile, he was an illegitimate grandson of George Savile, Marquis of Halifax. In 1708 he himself was legally bound to a Sarah Dobson in the Yorkshire village of Rothwell. A couple of years later the Saviles came to London and turned into Careys. Henry turned to writing, publishing a volume of verse in 1713 and producing a comedy, *The Contrivances,* at Drury Lane Theatre two years later. He set his poem *Sally in Our Alley* to music. It was such a hit that he took up the study of composition, with Geminiani [693], Thomas Roseingrave [699], and an obscure Swede called Olaus Westen Linnert. For a decade and a half, Carey worked as a theatrical hack, though by 1723 he was beginning to contribute songs to London musicals. A year later he published a volume of cantatas, designed, as he candidly owned in his preface, "to please my friends, to mortify my enemies, to get money and reputation." After having a go at pantomimes, he turned to ballad opera, wherein he shows himself a better librettist than composer. His greatest successes were the interlude *Nancy, or The Parting Lovers* (successfully revived and recorded by the Intimate Opera Company) and the burlesque *Chrononhotonthologos,* but such libretti for others as *The Dragon of Wantley,* for the imported Saxon John Frederick Lampe, became even better known. But around 1740 both opportunities and demand declined; Carey's income suffered, and his family was increasing, and in 1743 he hanged himself. His son George later insisted that his father had written the melody to "God Save the King," but although many songbooks still credit it to him, the notion has long since been exploded. Nor is the tune to which "Sally" is now sung Carey's. George Carey became a playwright and librettist, and was the grandfather of the actor Edmund Kean.

[704] STÖLZEL, Gottfried Heinrich
  (Shtölt'-sel, Got'-frēt Hīn-rikh)
  ORGANIST, CONDUCTOR, THEORIST
  BORN: Grünstädtel, January 13, 1690
  DIED: Gotha, November 27, 1749

With the rediscovery of Stölzel, one finds such formulae as "he lacked genius" being cautiously replaced with terms like "minor master." His contemporaries thought highly of him, and these included J. S. Bach [684], who transcribed a partita of his in the notebook he wrote for his own son Wilhelm Friedemann [784].

Stölzel's father was a Saxon village organist and gave him his first lessons. When he had taught him what he knew, he sent him off to Schneeberg, near Zwickau, to study with the local cantor, a man named Umlauff, a pupil of Johann Kuhnau [582]. In 1707, young Stölzel enrolled at the University of Leipzig, where soon the activities of the collegium musicum founded by Telemann [665] were occupying most of his time. Between 1710 and 1712 he was in Breslau, drumming up a clientele of affluent pupils and producing his first opera, *Narcissus*. It must have gone over well enough, for next season he turned out three more for the Naumburg Fair, a favorite showcase for south German opera composers. Late in 1713 he yielded to the lure of Italy and traveled to Venice, where his compatriot Heinichen [674] introduced him to the important composers. Later he went to Florence and Rome, where he came to know Domenico Scarlatti [687]. He returned to Mitteleuropa in 1715, spent three years in Prague (more operas), turned down a job in Dresden, and spent brief stints at the courts of Bayreuth and Gera (at the latter he was married to Christiane Dorothea Knauer). He went to Gotha late in 1719 and was named court *Kapellmeister* there in 1720—an appointment he held for the rest of his life.

Stölzel was nothing if not productive—a fact that is said to have damaged his mind toward the end of his life. Apart from his 18 known operas and 11 oratorios, he wrote a number of Masses, a thousand or so cantatas, and many concerti, sonatas, and other instrumental works. He also published a treatise on canon, and left one on recitative in manuscript.

RECORDINGS: The Eichendorff Wind Group has recorded a trio sonata, and Maurice André an oboe concerto (transcribed for trumpet). By all odds his most popular work on records is the D-major *Concerto grosso* for two groups of trumpets and timpani, woodwinds, strings, and continuo, which has appeared in readings by André Bernard, Philippe Caillard, Jörg Faerber, Sir Charles Mackerras, and others. Even better known, though, is the song *"Bist du bei mir,"* ("You Are With Me") usually credited to J. S. Bach.

[705] **VERACINI, Francesco Maria** (Vä-rä-chē′-nē, Frän-chäs′-kō Mä-rē′-ä)
VIOLINIST, CONDUCTOR

BORN: Florence, February 1, 1690
DIED: Florence, October 31, 1768

Veracini seems to have everyone's vote as the foremost violin virtuoso of the post-Corelli [565] generation. Certainly he would not have disagreed, for he said his creed was "One God, one Veracini!" One may see him either as a forerunner of the flamboyant performers of the next century or as decidedly paranoid—though the two estates are not necessarily mutually exclusive. Despite his article of faith, there were several Veracinis, including his grandfather, Francesco di Niccolò, who opened a music school in Florence, and his uncle Antonio, himself a noted virtuoso and composer, who later ran it. Francesco Maria's father, Agostino, apparently did not share the family interest; he ran an establishment that dealt in drugs and burials. ("If it does no good, sir, you'll remember whom to call.")

Veracini certainly studied with Uncle Antonio, and with other Florentine musicians. It is possible that he studied with Gasparini [615] when he went to Venice in 1711, but the legend that he was a Corelli pupil seems to have no basis in fact. Nor does there seem much likelihood that he taught Locatelli [721] in these years. After impressing the Venetians with several concerts, Veracini spent the better part of 1714 doing the same thing to Londoners. After spending 1715 at the electoral court of Johann Wilhelm of the Palatinate in Düsseldorf, he returned to Venice. Presumably it was then that his playing so shook up Tartini [714] that he took himself off to Ancona for a period of solitary meditation and restudy. It was certainly then that he caught the ear of Prince Friedrich August of Saxony, who invited him to Dresden as part of his private musical organization. At the end of 1717, Elector August the Strong, put him on his own payroll at a very high salary. Allegedly there developed serious friction between Il Fiorentino, as Veracini was known, and his German rival Johann Pisendel [694], and supposedly Pisendel humiliated him by making it appear (having secretly coached the man) that any old fiddler could toss off as difficult music as he at sight. In chagrin, the story goes, Veracini threw himself out of an upper window, doing himself permanent damage. Johann Mattheson [668] said he had driven himself mad studying alchemy. Veracini himself said darkly that they were out to get him.

Recovered as well as he ever would, Veracini returned to Florence in early 1723, and apparently remained in Italy until a decade later, when he went back to London, where

314

he became all the rage, and where he played at the Opera of the Nobility (see Nicola Porpora—690). In 1735 that company produced his *Adriano* (and repeated it many times) with an all-star cast that included Farinelli, Senesino, and Francesca Cuzzoni, called La Bastardella (The Little Bastard) because she was in both senses. Veracini wrote two more operas for the company before it folded in 1738, one of them a setting of Metastasio's *La Clemenza di Tito*, later more famously treated by Mozart [992]. After a last opera in 1744, a treatment of Shakespeare's *As You Like It* called *Rosalinda*, Veracini left England for good, suffering a nonfatal shipwreck crossing the Channel. By then his star had set: opera was out of fashion and so was he, having been superseded in the public's favor by Geminiani [693]. Indeed, for a long time his ultimate fate eluded historians. Some thought he had died in London; others said he retired to a hamlet near Pisa and died "c. 1750" in great poverty. We now know that he returned to Florence and spent his last twenty or so years directing the music of various churches and occasionally concertizing.

Veracini is remembered chiefly for his published violin sonatas, though he also left some Vivaldi-like concerti, a few manuscript cantatas, and some opera fragments. His earlier sonatas show him moving toward classicism, and thinking of the set as a unit—6 chamber sonatas in as many minor keys, 6 church sonatas in as many major. The "Academic" sonatas of Op. 2 follow the same plan but introduce imaginative and diversified movements, among which (the composer tells us) we may pick and choose to suit our own sense of symmetry and taste. A fourth set, unpublished until recently, recasts Corelli's Op. 5 to suit Veracini and the temper of the times.

RECORDINGS: For such a maverick Veracini has enjoyed rather scant representation on records, though Hyman Bress has recorded the whole Op. 1 and there are individual recordings of a few individual sonatas by various violinists, flutists, and a harmonica player. The indefatigable Maurice André has also recorded a trumpet transcription of a violin concerto.

[706] MUFFAT, Gottlieb (Moof'-fàt, Got'-lép)

ORGANIST, TEACHER

BORN: Passau, c. April 25, 1690

DIED: Vienna, December 9, 1770

Muffat's name often appears as "Gottlieb Theophil"—obviously in error, since "Theophil" is merely "Gottlieb" Hellenized. The son of Georg Muffat [566], Gottlieb was born during the time his father was *Kapellmeister* to the Bishop of Passau, and no doubt studied with him. In 1711 he was in Vienna studying at the imperial court with Fux [585]. At twenty-seven he was named official continuo player at the Hofoper, and harpsichordist to the Dowager Empress Wilhelmine Amalie, widow of Emperor Joseph I. He was also delegated to teach the little archdukes and -duchesses, including Maria Theresa. He was named second organist in 1729, but had to wait until 1741 to get the top spot. He was pensioned off at seventy-three, though he had apparently ceased to compose twenty-five years before. He wrote almost entirely for keyboard. Apart from his two publications, the 72 *Versets* of 1726 and the *Componimenti musicali* of perhaps fifteen years later, he left at least 200 works in manuscript, perhaps even twice that many. Shortly after the *Componimenti*, a set of tasteful French Baroque style pieces in suites, was published, Handel [683] raided it for ideas for his *St. Cecilia Ode*. RECORDINGS: Michael Thomas has recorded a suite from it on a hybrid instrument, the claviorganum.

[707] COLIN DE BLAMONT, François (Kō-lan' də Blà-mon', Frän-swä')

VIOLINIST, ADMINISTRATOR

BORN: Versailles, November 22, 1690

DIED: Versailles, February 14, 1760

François Colin, as he was born, was the son and pupil of Nicolas Colin, violinist to Louis XIV. When he was 17 he was taken into the establishment of the Duchess de Maine at Sceaux (see 576) and contributed to the famous Grandes Nuits. Here he caught the attention of Delalande [576] and became his pupil and protégé and prospered mightily. In 1719, with the ouster of the ineffectual Jean-Baptiste Lully *fils*, he was made one of the two *surintendants* of young Louis XV's Royal Chamber (Delalande being the other). In 1723 the Académie staged his opera-ballet (libretto by Louis Fuzelier) *Les Festes grecques et romaines* with great success. Colin claimed that it inaugurated a new genre—the *ballet héroïque*. The Chevalier spent the rest of his career trying to emulate it but never did. In 1726 he succeeded his mentor in the post of Music Master to the Royal Chamber. In 1750 he was ennobled, adding "de Blamont" to his name, and a year later was named a Knight of the Order of St. Michel. Not surprisingly, Colin rather closely imitated Delalande, and late in his life, at the height of the to-do over *opera buffa* versus *opèra comique (La Querelle des Bouffons)*, delivered himself of a diatribe defending the Good Old Ways. Besides his stage music, he left many *cantates, cantatilles,* and songs, and a few religious pieces. RECORDINGS: Jacques Herbillon has recorded a song.

[708] PACHELBEL, Carl Theodor
(Pákh'-el-bel, Kärl Te'-ō-dôr)
ORGANIST, IMPRESARIO
BORN: Stuttgart, c. November 24, 1690
DIED: Charleston, South Carolina, September 15, 1750

In the face of mounting affirmative evidence, scholars have concluded that Carl Theodor Pachelbel (a.k.a. "Percheval," etc.) was the son of Johann Pachelbel **[567]** by his first wife, born during his father's stint at the Stuttgart court. Undoubtedly Carl studied with his father, but his life, before he came to America, probably at around forty, is a closed book. In 1733 he became organist of a church in Newport, Rhode Island, having helped build the organ himself. (Earlier he had been in Boston.) Not long after, he moved to New York, where in 1736 he put on two public concerts, among the very earliest to be given in that city. Then he went to Charleston, South Carolina, and became organist at St. Philip's. In 1737 he advertised a concert to be given in his home there. Beyond that he drops out of sight until his death. Claims for Carl Pachelbel as an early American composer appear to be exaggerated, since his only known work, an eight-voice *Magnificat* was written before he left Germany. RECORDINGS: The *Magnificat* has been recorded by Alden Gilchrist.

[709] BARSANTI, Francesco (Bär-sàn'-tē, Fràn-chàs'-kō)
WIND PLAYER, TIMPANIST, VIOLIST
BORN: Lucca, 1690
DIED: London, 1772

Since Barsanti was a contemporary and fellow-townsman of Francesco Geminiani **[693]**, it is reasonable to assume that their acquaintance went back to childhood. Barsanti went to the University of Padua, ostensibly to study law, but when Geminiani set sail for London in 1714, Barsanti went along to seek his fortune in the musical world. He seems to have done rather well at first, playing oboe and flute (recorder?) in

Handel's orchestra and publishing three books of sonatas (the third arranged from Geminiani). In 1735, however, he moved to Edinburgh, built up a clientele of students, married a Scottish woman, and played kettledrums in the orchestra of the Edinburgh Musical Society. In 1742 he sold his drums and returned to London, where he found himself forgotten. He eked out his last thirty years as a sometime violist in the local theaters and pleasure gardens, and published a few more pieces of music. His recorder sonatas are much admired, and the *concerti grossi* (published in Edinburgh and featuring the timpani) deserve looking into. He also published some *concerti grossi* based on sonatas by G. B. Sammartini **[738]**, some motets, and (cashing in on the folk revival north of the border) *A Collection of Old Scots Tunes*. RECORDINGS: Ferdinand Conrad (among others) has recorded a couple of the recorder sonatas. Jörg Faerber and Maurice André together have recorded a *Concerto Grosso* in D major (Op. 3, No. 10). Other recordings include *Overture* for strings, Op. 9 No. 2; Concerto in D Major for 2 Horns (Kapp Sinfonietta); several other Op. 3 *concerti grossi;* and a few miscellani.

[710] NAUDOT, Jacques-Christophe (Nō-dō', Zhàk Krēs-tof')
FLUTIST
BORN: c. 1690
DIED: Paris, November 26, 1762

Though everyone seemed to have heard of Naudot in his time, very little factual information about him has filtered down to us. His name often appears as "Jean-Jacques" and sometimes as "Jean-Francisque"; on his publications it usually is simply "Naudot." But we know only the date of his death, the fact that he was a Freemason, and that he was in charge of music in his lodge from 1737. It appears that his entire career was spent in Paris, that he was patronized by the Count of Egmont, and that he played the vielle and musette. There is a general consensus that he was one of the great French flutists of his time. He published several sets of sonatas for flute (or other melody instrument) and was chronologically second to Vivaldi **[650]** in publishing concerti specifically for flute. His music is attractive if lightweight. RECORDINGS: Among recordings of his work are concerti performed by Jean-Pierre Rampal, Ferdinand Conrad, and oboist André Lardrot, and sonatas by Rampal.

[711] TESSARINI, Carlo (Tes-sà-rē'-nē, Kär'-lō)
VIOLINIST, PUBLISHER
BORN: Rimini, c. 1690
DIED: 1766 or later

Tradition calls Tessarini a pupil of Corelli [565] and Vivaldi [650]. The first is quite unlikely, the second possible, since he first turns up at about age thirty playing at St. Mark's in Venice, and a decade later as concertmaster of the Conservatorio di San Zanipolo. From the early 1730s he belonged (loosely, it would seem) to the musical forces at Urbino Cathedral. But he was frequently on leave—in the service of Cardinal Schrattenbach in Brünn (Brno) c. 1735–38, later in Rome, Paris, and the Netherlands. He and his brother Giovanni Francesco ran a music-publishing operation for a time in Urbino, and Carlo doubled as music director of the Accademia dei Anarconti in nearby Fano. He is last heard of in Urbino in 1757, after which he appears to have settled in Arnhem, Netherlands, where he was still appearing in concerts (without glasses, according to an admiring reviewer) just before Christmas in his seventy-sixth year. He published a violin method and 20 opuses—sonatas, concerti, suites, and *sinfonie*—mostly for strings. A product of Vivaldian Venice, Tessarini uses the three-movement *sinfonia* form for his sonatas, and exhibits a Rococo lightness. RECORDINGS: Maurice André has recorded a trumpet transcription of a violin concerto.

[712] VINCI, Leonardo (Vēn'-chē, Lā-ō-när'-dō)
CONDUCTOR
BORN: Strongoli, c. 1690
DIED: Naples, c. May 28, 1730

Unlike his great Renaissance near-namesake, a native of Vinci in Tuscany, Leonardo Vinci (no *da)* came from Calabria, though both the place and date of his birth are still debated. He enrolled at the Conservatorio dei Poveri di Gesù Cristo in Naples in 1708, and studied with Gaetano Greco, then municipal *maestro di cappella.* In 1719, the year in which he produced his first two comic operas, he was in the employ of Alessandro Scarlatti's [583] old patron, the Prince of Sansevero. When Scarlatti died, Vinci was named vice-*maestro* of the viceregal chapel; this was not his only brush with vice, according to tradition, as we shall see in a moment. In 1728 he was appointed music director at the Poveri, where Pergolesi [782] was one of his pupils. Sup-

posedly he compromised a noble lady, bragged in public about it, and was given a cup of poisoned chocolate by her vengeful brother. One contemporary account (there is no agreement on the exact day of his death) says that he died of a colic so sudden that he had no time to make confession (could have been poison or cholera), though other reports say that he signified confession or even took the Sacrament. Vinci was primarily an opera composer, at first of Neapolitan dialect comedies, and then (and more importantly) of *opera seria;* he was one of the composers who took the aria beyond the abbreviated Scarlattian form. He also wrote some cantatas and other odds and ends. RECORDINGS: A flute sonata has been recorded by René LeRoy (in the "78" era) and later by Michel Debost.

[713] WOODCOCK, Robert
BORN: c. 1690 (?)
DIED: before May 1734

The only solid fact we have about Woodcock's life is that he was active between 1720 and 1730 and dead by mid-spring 1734. At some point about halfway through that period, he published 12 attractive concerti, variously for recorder(s), flute, and oboe—among the first English wind concerti to be printed. RECORDINGS: Examples have been recorded by the Lucerne Festival Orchestra and the Telemann Society.

[714] TARTINI, Giuseppe (Tär-tē'-nē, Jōō-sep'-pā)
VIOLINIST, THEORIST, TEACHER
BORN: Pirano, April 8, 1692
DIED: Padua, February 26, 1770

One of the greatest of all violinists, Tartini also ranks high as a composer and theorist. He was the discoverer (or one of them) of the acoustical phenomenon known as differential tones—*terzi tuoni* in his phrase, a kind of harmonic produced when two other tones are sounded together. He wrote this up in his valuable treatise on harmony, published in 1754 though he had hit on it forty years earlier. He also made improvements in violin strings and the bow. His concerti and sonatas—the bulk of his output apart from a few sacred works—develop the Corellian forms to the verge of the Rococo; there his emphasis is as much on melody and sonic beauty as on structure.

Apart from a 1969 Russian study, the most recent treatment of Tartini's life seems to be a 1953 novel by the American violinist and sporting-goods heir Albert Spalding, *A Fiddle, a Sword, and a Lady.* If the title sounds like something by Rafael Sabatini, so does Tartini's biography as we know it. Much of it seems too good to be true, but although there have been some minor corrections, the basic outlines go back to the subject's own day and will have to stand until scholarship proves them wrong. Tartini's father is said to have been a Florentine of means, who moved to the north Dalmatian coast (then Istria), became director of the local saltworks, married in 1685, and sired four sons (of whom Giuseppe was the youngest) and a daughter. Iseppo, as the locals knew him, was slated for the church and sent to Capo d'Istria to study at the monastery school there. Apparently the rule of St. Francis was not to his taste, for at seventeen he persuaded the bishop (who persuaded his father) that he really ought to be studying law at Padua. Here the plot thickens. It seems that what the youth was really interested in was music and fencing, and that he even considered going to Naples (why Naples?) to open a fencing academy. But in 1713 he eloped (to his regret, both then and later) with Elisabetta Premazone, said to be a fellow student. (A girl? At Padua? In 1713?)

Cardinal Giorgio Cornaro forthwith swore out a warrant for Tartini's arrest. It used to be said that he was outraged because the girl was his cousin or his niece or perhaps even his daughter; it now appears that she bore some such relationship to his *cook,* who must have been a dandy. At any rate, Tartini, like Romeo, had to skip town after a too-brief honeymoon, clad in monastic garb, perhaps left over from his days with the Franciscans. After weeks, or maybe months, of wandering disconsolate, he found refuge, rather ironically, in the Franciscan mother-house in Assisi. There he whiled away the time improving his fiddling and studying composition with a Bohemian priest *(padre boemo),* whom a good many people suppose to have been Bohuslav Černohorský [677]. Others are less confident. It was at Assisi that Tartini had his famous dream, in which the devil appeared to him, playing like sin on a violin. The musician awoke and jotted down the piece which turned out to be the Sonata in G Minor, known as the "Devil's Trill." The tale was relayed by a French traveler fifty years later. Equally unlikely, but so far unrefuted, is the story of Tartini's ultimate return to grace: lest he be recognized, he was performing behind a curtain during a service one summer's day in 1715. A sudden gust of wind lifted the cloth, and some Paduan pilgrims in the congregation recognized him. They carried the story back to the cardinal, who forgave him and permitted him to come home and rejoin his bride.

The following year (goes yet another yarn), the city of Venice invited Tartini to vie before the visiting elector-apparent of Saxony with Veracini [705]. Whether by chance or design, Tartini heard Veracini play before the date appointed and was so appalled at his own shortcomings that he cut and ran for Ancona, taking only his violin, and spent many months bringing his performing powers up to snuff. In 1721 he was appointed first violin and director of concerts at Il Santo (the Basilica of San Antonio) in Padua, without having to undergo the ritual audition, and with freedom to fulfill outside engagements. He took rather rapid advantage of this last clause, going to Prague in 1723 and working for Graf Kinsky, the royal chancellor, until 1726. Yet another tale says that in actuality he was fleeing a pregnant landlady who was threatening to have the law on him. In any case, his marriage reportedly had turned out to be no idyll, for Elisabetta is said to have become a whining hypochondriac who forced his return in 1726 and kept him pretty much tied to Padua for the rest of her life. Certainly he turned down a number of lucrative offers. Shortly after he came back, he opened a violin school. Among his many pupils were Pietro Nardini [823] and Johann Gottlieb Graun [751]. He undertook an Italian tour in 1740 but somehow injured an arm in Bergamo. He continued to play at the Santo until 1767. The next year he suffered a stroke, from which he partly recovered, though he had complained of bad health for twenty years. His wife finally died in 1769. Tradition has it that Tartini developed cancer and was confined to bed. The faithful Nardini, hearing that his old master was in a bad way, came to Padua and ministered to him until he died. Evidence suggests he did no such thing and that Tartini died from a gangrenous injury to his foot.

RECORDINGS: Tartini is well represented on records in terms of violin sonatas, violin concerti, concerti grossi, and trio- and quartet-sonatas. Concerti for other solo instruments than the violin (e.g., flute, trumpet, cello) are adaptations.

[715] **WERNER, Gregor Joseph** (Vâr'-ner, Grä'-gôr Yō'-zef)
ORGANIST, CONDUCTOR
BORN: Ybbs-auf-der-Donau, January 28, 1693
DIED: Eisenstadt, March 3, 1766

There must have been scores of capable musicians like Werner, content to bloom unseen, unknown, in a reasonably cozy job on some rich man's estate. The rich man—or men, in this case—were Prince Pál Antal Esterházy and his brother and successor Prince Miklós Jozsef, and the estate was at Eisenstadt, twenty-five miles south of Vienna. Very little is known of Werner's life before he came there as *Kapellmeister* in 1728. He was born in a river town between Linz and Vienna. As a young man, he was organist at the great Benedictine Abbey of Melk nearby, and he was married in Vienna the year before he went to Esterháza. (A son later sang in the choir there.) For thirty-three years he conducted the musical forces and supplied them with music—chiefly religious, including a score of oratorios, though he also wrote instrumental music, and even published some trio sonatas and a *Neuer und sehr curios musicalischer Instrumental-Calendar (New and Quite Curious Musical-Instrumental Calendar*—Werner loved long titles). This orchestral work, whose movements cycle through the year, naively depicts such events as thunderstorms, frogs, lazy students, earthquakes, and Judgment Day. In 1761, the old fellow, to judge from the contract, was getting feeble or dotty, for Joseph Haydn [871], then twenty-nine, was hired as vice-*Kapellmeister*, with the understanding that he would be taking over most directorial duties. Werner, understandably, resented the young man's intrusion and made a good deal of trouble for him. Forty years later, Haydn, now himself an old man, issued a little volume of preludes and fugues that he had arranged for string quartet from Werner's oratorios. RECORDINGS: The *Calendar* has been recorded whole or in extensive excerpts by Edgar Seipenbusch and Paul Angerer. Vilmos Tatrai has recorded a *Pastorale* for harpsichord and strings. The Tatrai Quartet and the Sinnhofer Quartet have recorded some of the preludes and fugues. A Christmas cantata is directed by Herbert Froitzheim. There are also Hungarian recordings of a couple of *Pastorales* for organ and strings.

[716] LEMAIRE, Louis (Lə-mâr', Loo-ē')
BORN: c. 1693
DIED: Tours, c. 1750

Little seems to be known of Lemaire beyond publication and performance dates. He got his musical education at Meaux from Sébastien de Brossard [573], cathedral organist there, and then settled in Paris. Lemaire wrote some motets, a few instrumental

works, and a cycle of *cantates* on the seasons, but his specialty was the *air* and its extension the *cantatille*. RECORDINGS: Jacques Herbillon has recorded one of his songs.

[717] DAQUIN, Louis-Claude (Dà-kan', Loo-ē' Klōd)
KEYBOARDIST
BORN: Paris, July 4, 1694
DIED: Paris, June 15, 1772

Daquin's maternal great grand-uncle, for what it is worth, was François Rabelais, and his godmother was that pioneer woman composer Elisabeth Jacquet de la Guerre [610]. Daquin was a keyboard prodigy who wowed Louis XIV when he was only six. It is said that his first teacher was his godmother's husband, organist at the St. Chapelle. Later he studied with Nicolas Bernier [599] and Louis Marchand [619], whom he idolized. At twelve he became organist of the convent chapel of Petit St. Antoine, though he could have succeeded La Guerre had he so chosen. It is said that crowds fought to get into the chapel when he played. He was married in his early twenties; his son, known as Pierre-Louis D'Aquin de Château-Lyon, was born in 1720 and became a critic and biographer. In 1727 Daquin defeated Rameau [675], who admired his work, in the competition for the organist's post at St. Paul (since demolished). Five years later he succeeded his teacher Marchand at the Cordeliers (the Franciscan church—though, contrary to some accounts of his life, he did not join the order. In 1739, he followed Dandrieu [671] as one of the four Chapel Royal organists, and was appointed on a similar footing at Notre-Dame de Paris in 1755.

Though Rameau remarked that Daquin was ever mindful of the grace and majesty of the organ, it would appear that, like so many virtuosi, he frequently sacrificed musical integrity to flashy and programmatic effects. Of his 4 books of harpsichord pieces, only the imitative *Le coucou* is much heard, reputedly for good reason. Save for a single drinking song, his only other extant music is a collection of *noëls* with variations, *Nouveau livre de noëls*—for organ or harpsichord; also suitable for violins, flutes, oboes, etc.—charming, but lightweight.

RECORDINGS: The *noëls* have been recorded complete at the organ by E. Power Biggs and Gaston Litaize. The drinking song has been recorded by Jacques Herbillon.

[718] LEO, Leonardo (Lä'-ō, Lä-o-när'-dō)
TEACHER, CONDUCTOR, ORGANIST
BORN: San Vito degli Schiavi, August 5, 1694
DIED: Naples, October 31, 1744

Like his contemporary Nicola Antonio Porpora **[690]**, Leo was in his time one of the towering figures of Italian opera; and, like Porpora, he exists today chiefly as a name in the history books. He was born in a village (now known as San Vito dei Normanni) near Brindisi on the Adriatic side of the boot, and christened Lionardo Oronzo Salvatore di Leo. (One supposes that no one ever dared call him Leo Leo.) His parents, Corrado and Rosabetta (Pinto), were people of sufficient means to send him as a paying pupil to the Conservatorio della Pietà dei Turchini in Naples, where, between 1709 and 1713, he studied with Andrea Basso and Nicola Fago "il Tarantino," a successful composer of operas. Leo came up with his first opera when he was eighteen—an *opera sacra* on St. Clare (now lost) written for student production during the Carnival and produced again at the viceregal palace a month later. The following spring he was given the prestigious, if unpaid, job of steady extra organist there, and in the summer he married Anna Losi, age seventeen. Shortly afterward he made something of a hit with his first *opera seria*—*Pisistrato*. By 1718, when his *Sofonisba* established him as no flash in the pan, he was serving as *maestro di cappella* at Santa Maria della Solitaria and was receiving a regular salary from the court. In 1723 Leo produced *La 'mpeca scoperta (The Imbroglio Unraveled)*, the first of the many comedies in Neapolitan dialect that were to be his forte. On the death of Alessandro Scarlatti **[583]** in 1725, Leo (who by now was drawing down fourteen ducats a month as mere substitute) was appointed chief court organist.

Shortly Leo's operas were being produced in the chief Italian centers—Rome, Venice, Bologna—and in 1732 he took a successful foray into oratorio with *La Morte di Abele (Abel's Death)* and *Sant' Elena al Calvario (Saint Helen on Calvary)*. Two years later he was appointed Second Master at his old conservatory, a post he held until 1737 (in which year he was paid nearly 1,600 lire—then a considerable sum, now about two dollars—for his *Farnace*). It was also in 1737 that the new opera house, the Teatro San Carlo, was opened in Naples; Leo's *L'Olimpiade (The Olympiad)* was the second opera to play its stage. A year later,

under house arrest and watched by guards to see that he didn't nap, he wrote a Cupid-and-Psyche charade for the wedding of King Charles IV of the Two Sicilies (later Charles III of Spain) to the Saxon princess, Maria Amelie Walburga.

It was about this time that the celebrated quarrel (see 678) between Leo and Francesco Durante (or rather between their adherents) took place—something rather obscure about the place of polyphony in religious music. (Leo was a true master of the new polyphony based on harmonic principles.) In 1739 Leo wrote the *Miserere*, of which he was almost obsessively proud, and his most successful comedy, *Amor vuol sofferenze (Love Demands Tolerance)*; he was also made headmaster of the Conservatorio di San Onofrio. To this appointment he added the headmastership of the Turchini conservatory two years later and the directorship of the viceregal chapel (at last) in 1744. Six months later he was found slumped over his harpsichord, dead at fifty of a stroke. (At the chapel he had followed the succession of Leonardo Vinci **[712]**, Francesco Mancini **[631]**, and Domenico Sarro **[658]**.)

Leo was a compulsive worker and may well have, so to speak, died for his art. Despite the fact that he is said to have composed only in his spare time, he turned out more than 60 operas, 8 oratorios, 6 Masses, besides a large number of other religious works—7 concerti (6 for cello, one for four violins), harpsichord pieces, cantatas, and arias. Many of the operas have vanished. Of those that remain, the critical consensus is that the comic works still sparkle but that the serious ones are tedious.

RECORDINGS: Until the record producers give us more than the aria from the early *Zenobia in Palmira* (sung by Peter Schreier), we shall have to take the critics' word. There is, however, a recording of *La Morte di Abele* by Carlo Felice Cillario that will permit us some conclusions about the religious music, which is said better to exemplify Leo's strengths. On records the scant list of instrumental compositions has fared better. There are recordings of several cello concerti from such players as Thomas Blees, Giacinto Caramia, and Enzo Altobelli, and the four-violin concerto has been recorded by the Berlin Musikkreis and (on 78s) by a group led by Eddy Brown and Roman Totenberg.

[719] ROMAN, Johan Helmich (Rō'-mån, Yō'-hån Hel'-mikh)
OBOIST, VIOLINIST, CONDUCTOR

BORN: Stockholm, October 26, 1694
DIED: Haraldsmåla, November 20, 1758

Descended from the Raumannus family, long resident in Finland, Roman was the son of Johan Roman, *konzertmeister* to Charleses XI and XII, and himself joined the court orchestra at seventeen. The king's sister, Princess Ulrika Eleonora, took a shine to him and sent him to London for further training in 1714. (As heiress-presumptive to the throne, she perhaps saw him as a hope for Swedish musical life which, up to then, had not been much to brag about.) In England, Roman cultivated the musical luminaries, came to worship Handel [683], perhaps studied with Ariosti [606] and Pepusch [611], and is said to have worked for the Duke of Newcastle from 1717 to 1720. Meanwhile Charles XII had been slain by a Norwegian sniper in 1718. His sister succeeded him provisionally, but in 1720 her consort, Frederick of Hesse-Cassel, was elected king as Frederick I. Roman was then called home and made vice-*Kapellmeister* in 1721. As was expected, he improved the court musical situation enormously and was placed in full charge in 1727.

Roman married in 1730, but his wife died four years later. He received permission to go abroad for a while, and over the next two years visited most of the important European musical centers, collecting up literally trunkloads of new music. He returned to Stockholm in 1737, remarried the next year, and was elected to the newly established Academy of Science in 1740. Unhappily for him, the tide turned here. The political situation in Sweden was—and had long been—unstable, owing to a struggle between two factions known quaintly as the "Hats" and the "Caps." The Hats, then in the ascendancy, voted for a resumption of the endless wars with Russia. There was a humiliating Swedish defeat and near chaos. In the midst of all this, Queen Ulrika died childless, and in the maneuvering that followed, Adolphus Frederick, Duke of Schleswig-Holstein-Gottorp was named king. He brought his own musicians with him. In 1744 he married Luise Ulrike (or "Lovisa Ulrika" as the Swedes preferred) of Prussia. For the wedding, Roman composed a Handelian suite, *Drottningholmsmusique (Music for the Queen's Palace).* Queen Lovisa was, like her brother Frederick II, used to having her own way, and her musical tastes ran to Italian opera. Roman, ill and growing hard of hearing, and left widowed again that very year (with five small children) saw his usefulness at an end. The next year, supplanted by an Italian, he retired to an estate 200 miles to the south, returning only to oversee the musical arrangements for the old king's funeral and the new one's coronation in 1751.

Roman has been called "the father of Swedish music." Certainly he was the first composer of international stature of Swedish blood, and he was responsible for establishing a healthy musical life in Sweden. He translated and disseminated musical textbooks, made Swedish the language of the church music, and provided the impetus toward a national conservatory (which opened thirteen years after his death). He left a large body of compositions—much sacred music (including a vernacular *Mass!*), a number of occasional cantatas and other celebratory pieces, concerti, sinfonias, orchestral suites, sonatas, and songs. Not surprisingly, they are strongly influenced by the music he encountered in his travels, and not at all by the native cow calls and fiddle tunes.

RECORDINGS: The *Drottningholms* suite has been recorded by Ulf Björlin and by the Camerata Lutetiensis. Stig Westerberg has recorded *sinfonie* in D major and E minor, and there is a recording of another *sinfonia* (in B major) performed by members of the Stockholm Philharmonic. The Stockholm Philharmonic also provides the Concerto for Violin in D Minor, and the Concerto for Oboe in B Major is performed by members of the Stockholm Baroque Ensemble. Claude Genetay conducts a *Suite in D Major* for chamber orchestra, and there is also a recording of the *Swedish Mass.* Chamber music on records includes a trio sonata by the Prague Pro Arte Antiqua Ensemble and two harpsichord sonatas played by Eva Nordenfelt.

[720] **SAMMARTINI, Giuseppe** (Sàm-mär-tē′-nē, Jōō-sep′-pä)
OBOIST, TEACHER
BORN: Milan, January 6, 1695
DIED: London, November 1750

The two musical Sammartini brothers were among the eight progeny of Alexis Saint-Martin, an oboist from France, and his Milanese wife, Girolama de Federici, and appear also as San Martini or just plain Martini. The elder, baptized Giuseppe Francesco Gaspare Melchiorre Baldassare, was called "il Londinese," to distinguish him from his stay-at-home brother, Giovanni Battista "il Milanese" [738]. Two other brothers, Antonio and Carlo, seem also to have followed the musical trade. Giuseppe became a virtuoso oboist and first-desk man in the opera orchestra of the Ducal Theater in Milan. Quantz [730], who heard him there in 1726, praised him extravagantly, and his obituary said that he was "thought to be the finest performer on the hautboy in Europe." Around 1728 he emigrated to London where the action was and distinguished himself there as both soloist and orchestral musician. He played under the direction of both Bononcini [620] and Handel [683], and was soloist at Cambridge when Maurice Greene [727] received his doctorate in 1730. In 1736 he joined the household of Frederick, Prince of Wales (son of George II and father of George III), as music teacher to his wife the Princess Augusta and her children. Sir John Hawkins reported Sammartini still living in 1770, but in fact he died during the week ending November 23, 1750. He published at least 14 instrumental collections, including concerti grossi and concerti for keyboard and for oboe, and sonatas. A masque, some cantatas and arias, and other instrumental works exist in manuscript. There has been much careless confusion (on records and elsewhere) of Giuseppe's music with that of his brother. RECORDINGS: Oboe and flute concerti have been recorded by Frans Brüggen, Ferdinand Conrad, Sidney Gallesi, Hans-Martin Linde, David Munrow, and others, and there are scattered recordings of trio sonatas.

[721] LOCATELLI, Pietro (Lō-kä-tel'-lē, Pē-ä'-trō)
VIOLINIST, MERCHANT
BORN: Bergamo, September 3, 1695
DIED: Amsterdam, March 30, 1764

When Locatelli was sixteen, he left his job as a violinist in Bergamo's Santa Maria Maggiore and went to Rome to perfect his art. With whom he did it is not known. It almost certainly was not Corelli [565], as it was long said to be. A better case can be made for Giuseppe Valentini [664], whom Locatelli knew well. He stayed in Rome until at least 1723 and then may have been in Mantua, working for the Imperial governor, Philipp of Hessen-Darmstadt, sometime employer of Porpora [690] and Vivaldi [650], who in 1725 made Locatelli Chamber Virtuoso, whatever that title signified. By 1727 he had moved on to Germany, and a year later he visited Berlin in the entourage of the traveling Prince Frederick Augustus of Saxony. By 1729 he had settled down in Amsterdam, where he devoted himself to teaching, conducting an amateur orchestra, editing for Charles LeCène (successor to Estienne Robert, Vivaldi's and Albinoni's

[630] publisher), and printing his own chamber works. He still played occasionally, and though he no longer capitalized on his incredible virtuosity, an English tourist reported in 1741 that he played with sufficient fury to wear out a dozen fiddles a year, yet never needed to remove his jacket. In 1742 he advertised that, besides his music, he was selling strings for all kinds of instruments. There is an old tale that he was driven to this by his mistress-housekeeper, a demanding virago to whose tune he meekly danced. During the 1740s he supposedly enjoyed an extended visit from his French arch-rival, Jean-Marie Leclair [732].

Locatelli's authentic (and published) works consist entirely of concerti and sonatas. The most famous and least typical is the Opp. 3–4 set L'Arte del violino, consisting of 12 virtuoso violin concerti and 24 capricci. Op. 1 shows a profound, not to say slavish, admiration for Corelli, but the later concerti grossi (if that's what they are properly called) make significant advances on the convention. In the same way, the earlier sonatas are the more conventional.

RECORDINGS: The Op. 1 concerti are recorded by Dean Eckertsen, a selection from Op. 1 by I Musici, the Arte by Suzanne Lautenbacher, and there are many recordings of individual works. The Funeral Symphony alleged to have been composed for his wife's funeral (Locatelli apparently never had a wife) and recorded by Henry Swoboda is held to be spurious.

[722] BACH, Johann Lorenz (Bäkh, Yō'-hän Lôr'-ents)
ORGANIST
BORN: Schweinfurt, September 10, 1695
DIED: Lahm, December 14, 1773

Lorenz Bach was the son of Johann Valentin Bach, a municipal musician of Schweinfurt and son of Johann Sebastian Bach's [684] uncle Georg Christoph, who was the elder brother of the twins Johann Christoph and Johann Ambrosius (Sebastian's father). Lorenz was Sebastian's pupil during part of the Weimar period (1708–17), and his younger brother Johann Elias became Sebastian's secretary and the teacher of some of his children (including Johann Christoph Friedrich [872] and Johann Christian [886]) between 1738 and 1740. Lorenz became town organist at Lahm, assuming there is such a place. He left only a single organ work, Prelude and Fugue in D Major. RECORDINGS: Franz Lehrndorfer has recorded the fugue.

[723] MONRO, George
HARPSICHORDIST, ORGANIST
BORN: c. 1695 (?)
DIED: London, 1731

Monro is known to have been organist at the London church of St. Peter's, Cornhill, and harpsichordist at the Goodman Fields Theater for the last two years of his life. A prolific composer of songs, he is remembered largely by "My Goddess Celia," best known in Lane Wilson's arrangement as "My Lovely Celia."

[724] BARON, Ernst Gottlieb (Bä'-rōn, Ärnst Got'-lēp)
LUTENIST, THEORIST
BORN: Breslau, February 17, 1696
DIED: Berlin, April 12, 1760

Perhaps the last brief flareup of popularity enjoyed by the lute in the early eighteenth century is to be explained by the desire of petty German princes to ape the French court (as it had been a century earlier). Ernst Gottlieb Baron (who liked, like the younger Gottlieb Muffat [706], to spell his middle name "Theophil") learned it, while attending the Collegium Elisabethanum, from a Czech said to have been called Kohatt or Kohott or Kohaut. Deciding that he did not want to pursue the paternal trade of making gold lace (even though gold was not yet $600 an ounce), he hit the road with his lute, after studying law at Leipzig. He wandered restlessly for nearly twenty years over central and southern Germany, pausing at Jena for two years in 1720, and at the court of Saxe-Gotha from 1728 to 1732. In between he wrote and published a "historical-theoretical and practical investigation of the lute" in which he discusses lute playing and lutenists in his own time.

Meanwhile Prince Frederick of Prussia, who had alienated his Prussian sire by attempting to escape, had got back in the paternal good graces (see 791), and had built up a fine musical establishment on his estate at Rheinsberg, north of Berlin. In 1737 he hired Baron as his theorbo player. The only problem was that Baron neither owned nor played the theorbo, a kind of bass lute used for continuo parts in those days. However, he went off to Dresden and got one, together with a crash course in playing it from Silvius Leopold Weiss [691], and apparently lived happily ever after.

RECORDINGS: Guitarist William Matthews has recorded a lute suite transcription (very French), and members of the Brussels Pro Musica Antiqua one of several trios (some designated as "concerti") for violin, lute, and string bass.

[725] BLANCHARD, Esprit Joseph Antoine (Blän-shârd', Es-prē' Zhō-zef' Än-twän')
CHOIRMASTER
BORN: Pernes, February 29, 1696
DIED: Versailles, April 1, 1770

Esprit Blanchard was born in a village in the old Comtat Venaissin, which was later absorbed into the Department of Vaucluse. His father was a physician. Like so many young musicians in the region of Provence, he got his initial training from Guillaume Poitevin in the choir-school of St. Sauveur in Aix. At twenty-one he became director of the choir of St. Victor in Marseilles, and five years later began working his way northward as director of the cathedral choirs in Toulon, Besançon, and Amiens. In 1738 he was appointed, in Nicolas Bernier's [599] old place, as one of the *quadriga* of Surintendants de la Chapelle Royale, Louis XV having been overwhelmed by one of his motets. He seems to have been in minor orders, for he was called "Abbé," although it is said that this was merely a nickname deriving from the cassock he wore as choirmaster. At any rate, Louis also granted him an abbey to oversee and a pension. (But he had to abandon his priory when he married.) In 1748 he was also made Master of the Children of the Chapel Royal, but, having the right to do so, he sold the post nine years later. Eventually Louis named him le Chevalier Blanchard and decorated him (as he had Colin de Blamont) with the order of St. Michel.

Blanchard was best known for his *grand* motets which, though under the influence of Delalande's [576], show an orchestral independence of their own. They were long in the repertoire of the Concert Spirituel and have been successfully resurrected in modern times. They have been admired for their expressiveness and their avoidance of the bombast so often connected with the form.

RECORDINGS: Louis Frémaux has recorded the solitary *Te Deum*, thought to have been composed to celebrate Marshal Saxe's victory over the Duke of Cumberland in the War of the Austrian Succession at Fontenoy in 1745. Blanchard is said to have been the last significant French composer to use continuo parts in church music.

[726] VOGLER, Johann Kaspar (Fōg'-ler, Yō'-hàn Kàs'-pär)
ORGANIST, TEACHER, POLITICIAN
BORN: Hausen, May 23, 1696
DIED: Weimar, June 1, 1763

Vogler was Johann Sebastian Bach's [684] oldest pupil, having studied with him as a child at nearby Arnstadt. Later he studied with him for four years (1710–14) in Weimar. In 1721 he returned to Weimar as successor to the late Johann Martin Schubart, who on Bach's recommendation had been hired as organist when he left. Among the princelings he taught was Ernst August Constantin, who became Duke of Saxe-Weimar-Eisenach in 1755, and married Anna Amalie [905] of Braunschweig, herself no mean composer. In 1756 he appointed Johann Ernst Bach [822], son of Johann Bernhard [646], his *Kapellmeister*, with permission to improve the musical establishment within agreed-upon financial guidelines. J. E. Bach named Vogler his harpsichordist. Unhappily the duke succumbed two years later, not yet twenty-one, and the hard-pressed widow had to dismiss most of the orchestra, though Vogler remained. He published a collection of chorale-preludes. RECORD-INGS: Franz Lehrndorfer has recorded a sample of the chorale-preludes.

[727] GREENE, Maurice
ORGANIST, TEACHER, CONCERT PRO-MOTER
BORN: London, August 12, 1696
DIED: London, December 1, 1755

The son of a London clergyman, Maurice Greene got his first training as a choirboy in the newly finished St. Paul's Cathedral from Jeremiah Clarke [638]. Apprenticed in 1710 to Richard Brind, the organist there, Greene made rapid progress and in 1714 himself became organist at the church of St. Dunstan's-in-the-West; four years later he succeeded Daniel Purcell [603] at another Wren church, St. Andrew's Holborn. When Brind died in 1718, Greene gave up his other appointments to take over as cathedral organist. Organs being at a premium in post-Puritan London, and that at St. Paul's being shiny new, Greene let his friend Handel [683] practise on it. But when Handel found that Greene was buttering up his rival Giovanni Bononcini [620], he dropped him cold. It was Greene who in 1728 presented Bononcini's notorious plagiarized madrigal at the Academy of Antient Musick. When the truth became known, both were ostracized. Thereupon Greene took his adher-

ents, including his former pupil William Boyce [787], and founded the Apollo Academy, a rival concert organization which operated in a tavern called "the Devil." (Handel is supposed to have remarked that he was glad that Greene had gone to the Devil; one hopes he didn't.)

The year before his fall from grace, Greene succeeded William Croft [652] as organist-composer to the Chapel Royal. In 1730 he was granted a doctorate by Cambridge University and named Professor of Music—a title which involved neither teaching duties, committee work, or salary. Finally, in 1735, he was named Master of the King's Musick—a post whose chief function by then was to furnish New Year's and birthday odes to His Majesty (one of each, annually). (The previous incumbent was John Eccles [617].) In 1752 Greene was left the estate of his bastard cousin, the income from which made him independently wealthy. Though now in bad health (he had been partly crippled from birth), he devoted what was left of his life to collecting and transcribing what he considered the finest examples of Anglican church music, with a view toward publishing them. When he died, he willed the material to Boyce to bring the project to completion. His widow, *née* Mary Dillingham, survived him a dozen years; of their five children, however, only Katharine, now married to her father's old friend, the violinist Michael Festing, a Geminiani pupil [693] remained. Among Greene's notable students was Charles John Stanley [796].

Greene composed a few large works—3 oratorios, a pastoral opera, etc.—but his reputation rests chiefly on his church music—especially his anthems, still much in use and frequently recorded for the home folks in English choral anthologies. He also wrote many smaller works, mostly vocal, including a cycle of songs to Spenser's *Amoretti*. RECORDINGS: In addition to the previously mentioned choral anthologies, organ voluntaries are available in domestic recordings—e.g., by George Kent and Haig Mardirosian.

[728] WALTER, Thomas
CLERGYMAN
BORN: Roxbury, Mass., December 13, 1696
DIED: Roxbury, January 10, 1725

Together with the Reverend John Tufts [700], the Reverend Thomas Walter was a pioneer in combating the dreadful state of church music in the North American colo-

nies, both of them issuing correctives in
1721. Walter, son of a clergyman and
nephew to Cotton Mather, went to Harvard, where he seems to have enjoyed himself, emerging in 1713 with an M.A. Ordained five years later, he became his father's assistant in Roxbury. His initial publication, printed by Benjamin Franklin's
half-brother James, was a singing method,
*Grounds and Rules of Musick Explained
. . . Fitted to the Meanest Capacities* (i.e.,
accessible even to the stupid). It incorporated, in three-voice arrangements, 13 tunes
from the *Bay Psalm Book* (published eighty
years earlier), plus 11 others (the tune to
Southwel New being Walter's own). A year
later he published a sermon, *The Sweet
Psalmist of Israel,* exhorting musical reform. Walter died at twenty-eight. He and
Tufts are regarded as the fathers of musical
education in this country and especially of
the singing schools that soon sprung up. RE-
CORDINGS: Selections from Walter's book
have been recorded by Gregg Smith.

[729] JOHANN ERNST, Prince of Saxe-
Weimar (Yō'-hån Årnst)
VIOLINIST
BORN: Weimar, 1696
DIED: Frankfurt am Main, August 1,
1715

A nephew of the reigning duke, Wilhelm
Ernst, Prince Johann Ernst was eleven
when Johann Sebastian Bach [684] came to
Weimar. He had already had violin lessons,
and at about this time began keyboard studies with Bach's cousin, Johann Gottfried
Walther [680]. After attending the University of Utrecht, he returned to take up composition with Walther, and he possibly
worked with Bach. Unfortunately he died at
nineteen. Three years later, Telemann [665]
—with whom the prince had obviously been
in touch—published a collection of 6 violin
concerti. Three of these Bach transcribed
for keyboard (BWV 982, 984, and 987). RE-
CORDINGS: Reconstructions of these three
works have been recorded by Hans Kop-
penberg.

[730] QUANTZ, Johann Joachim
(Kvånts, Yō'-hån Yō-å'-khem)
FLUTIST, VIOLINIST, OBOIST, ETC.
BORN: Oberscheden, January 30, 1697
DIED: Potsdam, July 12, 1773

Besides being one of the very few composers
whose name begins with Q, Quantz is notable for having left an autobiographical

sketch. His father was a village blacksmith
in southern Hanover, and his dying wish
(made when the boy was ten) was that his
son confine his musical instincts to the an-
vil. At that time the lad was already playing
the "German bass fiddle" by ear at fairs.
After his father's death, he went to live with
his Uncle Justus Quantz, a *Stadtpfeifer* in
Merseburg, but three months later Justus
joined his brother, and his apprentices were
taken over by a colleague named Adolf
Fleischhack. He, according to Quantz, was
so lazy that the kids learned more from
each other than they did from him. Nevertheless Quantz mastered the violin, oboe,
trumpet, cornett, trombone, horn, recorder,
bassoon, gamba, and cello. On his own he
also learned from a relative named
Kiesewetter something about keyboard
technique and the basics of harmony. In
1714 he acquired journeyman status. His
journey ultimately took him to Radeberg, a
suburb of Dresden, where he became assistant to a *Stadtpfeifer* named Knoll. Unfortunately a few nights later lightning burned
the town to the ground, and after being
nearly roasted in the marketplace, Quantz
found a similar job in nearby Pirna, a more
fireproof place. He was already familiar
with much music by the established composers of the age, such as Corelli [565] and
Telemann [665], but now he encountered
for the first time Vivaldi's [650] concerti,
which changed his thinking about how music should go. After a further stint in Merseburg, a musical acquaintance summoned
him to Dresden, which had long been his
goal.

Hearing the famous Dresden orchestra of
Augustus the Strong (Augustus II) also
helped change his thinking. At that time it
was made up of more than thirty players,
including Pisendel [694], Veracini [705],
and Weiss [691]. Quantz had not known
that music could sound so well and saw little future for a musician so roughhewn as he
was. When a funeral halted musical festivities at court for a suitable mourning period,
Quantz took some lessons with Zelenka
[656]. In 1718 he was hired as oboist with the
newly formed "Polish *Kapelle,*" to serve
Augustus II in his role as King of Poland.
But he was not very successful as an oboist.
One of his colleagues, Marseilles-born
Pierre-Gabriel Buffardin, however, had just
blown in from a job in Constantinople,
where he played the newly fashionable
transverse flute. Seeing which way the wind
blew, Quantz took lessons from him and by
1723 was good enough to be delegated to
Prague to play at the premiere of Fux's

[585] *Constanza e Fortezza* for the Emperor Charles's coronation as King of Bohemia.

A year later, when Count von Lagnasco was sent as Polish ambassador to Rome, Quantz got permission to go along. In Rome he studied counterpoint with Gasparini [615]. The next year he went to Naples, accepted the hospitality of his compatriot Johann Adolf Hasse [736], met such luminaries as Francisco Feo (1691–1761), Leonardo Leo [718], and Francesco Mancini [631], and overcame old Alessandro Scarlatti's [583] distaste for wind players by playing for him. Then he did northern Italy, including Venice (where he heard Vivaldi and Giuseppe Sammartini [720], and got permission to visit France. In Paris he undoubtedly, and to his future benefit, learned Rococo musical graces, and there he figured out how to give the flute more flexibility by adding a second key. (It was still mostly a matter of fingerholes.) After a three-month visit to London, where he saw and heard Handel [683] in action, Quantz returned to Dresden in 1728 and was installed in the main orchestra. A concert appearance at the Prussian court in Berlin so pleased Crown Prince Frederick that he arranged for Quantz to come twice a year to give him lessons. There followed a long struggle between the Prussian and Saxon thrones for Quantz's services, during which he became so affluent that in 1737 he married a widow-lady named Anne Rosina Caroline Schindlerin, who turned out to be a holy terror. He also became unbearably conceited.

When the prince became King Frederick II (but not yet the Great) in 1741, he decided he must have Quantz for his court, airs and all. He then offered him a lifetime contract—base pay of 2,000 thalers a year, additional sums for each piece composed and each flute made, and other fringe benefits, not the least of which was that he would be answerable only to the king—who, as an aspiring flutist and composer, stood in awe of him. Emanuel Bach once explained why Frau Quantz's little dog was the most powerful being in the court: the king feared Herr Quantz, Herr Quantz feared Frau Quantz, and Frau Quantz feared the dog, whose temper was shorter than hers. Quantz spent the rest of his life coaching Frederick, checking out his compositions, playing duets with him, and conducting the evening musicales at Sans-Souci, whose star was none other than his pupil. He was the only person permitted to interrupt the royal performance with cheers, which he usually saved for those crises when the king was running out of breath. He was also permitted to tell his master when he was off-pitch,

which was fairly often. He reached something like a peak in 1752 when he remedied the pitch problems with a telescoping endjoint for the flute, and published his method, which has as much to do with embellishments and polite conversation as it does with flute playing.

Quantz wrote some songs, hymns, and arias, but his major output, including more than 250 sonatas and more than 300 concerti, was for the flute. He was probably of more consequence to the flute than to its music—a good honest composer on his way to Classicism—but the present resurgence of interest in the instrument has assured his revival.

RECORDINGS: Helmut Riessberger has devoted two LPs to a selection of sonatas, and John Wummer has paired Quantz and his royal pupil on another. There are numerous isolated concerto and sonata recordings.

[731] BOUTMY, Josse (Boōt-mē′, Zhōs)
KEYBOARDIST, TEACHER
BORN: Ghent, February 1, 1697
DIED: Brussels, November 27, 1779

Charles Joseph Boutmy, called "Josse," was perhaps the most distinguished representative of four generations of musicians. The son of Jacques Boutmy, organist at St. Nicolas in Ghent, he was the brother of the short-lived Jacques-Adrien Boutmy. Both men seem to have found their way to Brussels when in their early twenties. Jacques, the elder by sixteen years, was organist at St. Michel et St. Gudule from 1711 until his death in 1719. Josse arrived shortly after he had married Catherine Janssens of Osnabrück in 1721. Their sons Guillaume and Jean-Joseph, both of whom became notable musicians, were born there in 1723 and 1725, respectively. Boutmy became a citizen of Brussels in 1729. He took service with the Prince of Thurn und Taxis (of the family of postal fame) in 1736, and his eldest son did later both as musician and postal worker. In 1744, when the Empress Maria-Theresa appointed her brother-in-law, Charles of Lorraine, viceregent of the Austrian Netherlands (i.e., Belgium), Boutmy became court organist. After his wife died, he married again, and another son, Laurent-François, born in 1756 of that union, also made his name as a musician. (Forget an alleged son called Léonard Boutmy de Lisbon, whom we now know never existed.) Boutmy kept a written account of his life from his first marriage to Laurent's birth, which sticks strictly to domestic matters. The infirmities

of old age dictated his retirement when he
was eighty. He left 3 books of keyboard music which show an interesting meld of the
French, Italian, and German currents of the
day. RECORDINGS: Marie-Claire Alain has
recorded an air-and-variations.

[732] LECLAIR, Jean-Marie, L'aîné (Lə-
klâr′, Zhá*n* Má-rē)
DANCER, VIOLINIST, TEACHER
BORN: Lyons, May 10, 1697
DIED: Paris, October 23, 1764

Perhaps more than any other French composer of his era, Leclair has profited from
the renewal of interest in "Baroque" music.
He was born into a highly musical family.
His father Antoine, a good Lyonnais
lacemaker, was an amateur cellist, and his
mother, *née* Benoîte Ferrier is said to have
played the violin. At least six of their eight
children became professional violinists.
Jean-Marie is called "the elder" because he
was: in the curious way of earlier times, his
parents gave a younger brother (1703–77)
the same name, and he went on to make a
reputation for himself as both performer
and composer. The young years of the elder
Jean-Marie are obscure. He was slated to
enter the family business and indeed served
some time in it. But by the time he was
nineteen, he was dancing in the Lyons opera
and had married Marie-Rose Casthagnié.
Six years later he was at the Turin opera as
premier danseur, ballet-master, and choreographer. In 1723 he went to Paris to publish his Op. 1 violin sonatas, some of which
had been composed at least two years earlier. Returning to Turin, he studied with the
virtuoso Giovanni Battista Somis, an hon-
est-to-God pupil of Corelli [565]. He more
or less settled in Paris in 1728, published a
second collection of sonatas, and was the
star of the Concert Spirituel that season.
For two years he also played at the Opéra.
Concert engagements took him to, among
other places, Cassel, where he conducted a
musical "duel" with Pietro Locatelli [721],
who impressed him mightily. Now a widower (without children), he rather fore-
sightedly married, in 1730, a music engraver, Louise Roussel, who not only etched
the plates for his future publications, but
also taught their daughter Louise her trade.
The marriage contract was witnessed by
André Chéron, a pupil of Nicolas Bernier
[599] and organist of the Concert Spirituel,
with whom Leclair was studying at the
time.
In 1733 Leclair was appointed a first-desk
man in the King's Violins. He shared this

position with a Torinese, Giovanni Pietro
Ghignone, also a Somis pupil, now known
as Jean-Pierre Guignon. Between Guignon's
scheming and Leclair's temperament, it did
not work. Though they eventually agreed to
alternate in the role of leader, Leclai
walked out in 1737 rather than take second
place, however temporarily. Shortly afterward he seems to have given up public performance altogether. In 1738 he was invited
by Princess Anne of Orange to come to her
court; for the next five years he was there
for a quarter of each year and took the opportunity to renew his acquaintance with
Locatelli. In 1740 Leclair began remaining
in Holland, working the rest of the year in
The Hague as orchestra-director for a François Du Liz, whom the books describe as "a
strange Jewish adventurer." The adventurer, however, had a misadventure in 1743:
he went broke. Leclair went home.
For a while during the next year he was
in Chambéry, in the French Alps, at the
court of the Spanish prince, Don Felipe, but
he soon withdrew to an increasingly private
existence in Paris, taking in a few pupils,
among whom may have been the Chevalier
de Saint-Georges [908]. At forty-nine he
produced his first and only opera, *Scylla et
Glaucis,* ironically likening himself to
Rameau [675]. Indeed his career did enjoy a
brief revival in 1748, when he became director of the Duke of Gramont's private theater, for which he is known to have written
some *divertissements* and incidental music
in the next two or three years. But he seems
to have become ever more bitter, introverted, and reclusive. In 1758 he bought a
rundown house in the slummy *banlieue* of
La Courtille, just beyond the Porte du Temple, and abandoning his family, he went
there to live. Six years later, on the morning
of October 23, 1764, his body, the chest
punctured with three stab wounds, was
found just inside his door. The prime suspects were the gardener, a nephew (with
whom he had quarreled), Madame Leclair,
and the inevitable person or persons unknown, but it eventually went on the books
as an unsolved murder.
There is no mistaking Leclair's position
in his own century. By the time he was
thirty-five, he had been enshrined in J. G.
Walther's [680] dictionary, and various contemporaries ranked him with Telemann
[665], and even with Handel [683] or J. S.
Bach [684]. If present-day musicologists are
more cautious, they nevertheless find in his
music the influence of these great men and
others, such as Vivaldi [650] and Corelli.
That he was a supreme virtuoso is made
clear by the difficulty of his violin music,

which involves double, triple, and quadruple stops and forays into the eighth position. But Leclair was no mere virtuoso for virtuosity's sake. His figurations and "difficult" passages are part of the warp and woof of his music. It has been said that he, even better than François Couperin [616], really succeeded in "uniting the tastes." If, for example, the form taken by his concerti is that of the Italian *sinfonia,* and if their general outlines are Vivaldian, their tunes and rhythms come from French song and French dance. If he did not "create" the French concerto—Boismortier [702] apparently did that—he was unquestionably its greatest exemplar in his time and his Opp. 6 and 10 still attract violinists (not to say flutists and oboists). There are recorded anthologies by Claire Bernard, Huguette Fernandez, and Annie Jodry. Of the many sonatas—for violin, two violins unaccompanied, and "trios"—the first category includes some of the most remarkable of the era.

RECORDINGS: Collections have been recorded by Georges Alès, André Hadges, and flutist Christian Lardé. There is also a suite from *Scylla et Glaucis,* conducted by Raymond Leppard, and many individual works.

[733] SEYFERT, Johann Caspar (Zī'-färt, Yō'-hán Käs'-pâr)
ORGANIST, LUTENIST, MUSIC DIRECTOR
BORN: c. 1697
DIED: Augsburg, May 26, 1767

Probably from Augsburg, Seyfert studied there as a child with Philipp David Kräuter, cantor of the Church of St. Anna. Later he was a pupil at the Dresden court of Pisendel [694] and Weiss [691]. He returned to Saint Anna's to direct the choir in 1723 and succeeded Kräuter eighteen years later. He is said to have known and perhaps taught young Leopold Mozart [816] and was a friend of Valentin Rathgeber [670]. It was this last fact that led to Hans Joachim Moser's conclusion that it was Seyfert who authored the last volume of the *Tafelkonfekt* songs, which series Rathgeber inaugurated. Not everyone agrees with him. Most of Seyfert's other compositions have vanished, leaving him something of a cipher. RECORDINGS: See 670.

[734] FRANCOEUR, François, Le Cadet (Frán-kur', Frán-swä')
VIOLINIST, ADMINISTRATOR

BORN: Paris, September 21, 1698
DIED: Paris, August 5, 1787

Francoeur was a member of one of those musical families so common in this period. His older brother Louis ("the Elder" Francoeur) was also a violinist, who headed the 24 Violons du Roi before his premature death in 1745; his nephew, Louis-Joseph, followed in his uncle's footsteps. François became a member of the orchestra at l'Opera in 1710 and there met his lifelong buddy, François Rebel, who joined the violins in the place of his father Jean-Féry [604] in 1717, when he was thirteen. They are said to have traveled together to Prague in 1723 to see the Emperor Charles VI crowned and there to have met such musical luminaries as Fux [585] and Quantz [730]. Four years later they were made tandem chamber composers to Louis XV. For the next thirty years they turned out, apart from their cameral obligations, collaborative operas and ballets of stunning ordinariness. In 1746 they were made Inspectors of the Ópera, and three years thereafter were elevated to the joint directorship of that institution. In 1753 they were replaced temporarily, but returned in 1757. Francoeur was named Surintendant of the Royal Music in 1760, was ennobled in 1764, and decorated a year later with the Ordre de St. Michel. In 1766 the friends stepped down from their operatic directorship to make way for Pierre-Montan Berton and Jean-Claude Trial (brother of the singer Antoine, whose high, light baritone made his surname the generic term for that kind of peculiarly French singer). Rebel died in 1775. Francoeur resigned his superintendency in 1778, but lived on to be nearly eighty-nine.

Francoeur is chiefly remembered by his 2 books of violin sonatas, which show some interesting developments in violinistic technique. His music, in the conservative style that the court admired, includes pieces borrowed from Jean-Féry Rebel, Rameau [675], Mondonville [789], and others.

In the collaborations (which make up the bulk of Francoeur's output) no one has ever been able to figure out who wrote what—not that it apparently mattered much, since the works were mostly light music of a stunning ordinariness. The sort of thing I mean may be sampled in the 2 suites which were cobbled up in 1773 to celebrate the nuptials of Louis XV's grandson, Charles Philippe, Comte d'Artois, to Marie-Thérèse of Savoy. Rain spoiled the ceremonies and ruined the fireworks, causing the suicide of the *Maître des feux d'artifice,* or whatever the poor fellow was called. Half a century later the

Comte became Charles X. Francoeur also left some apparently uncollaborated early violin sonatas which are quite pleasant. The familiar *Sicilienne et rigaudon* is really one of Fritz Kreisler's [1664] "forgeries."

RECORDINGS: The 1773 wedding suites have been recorded by Jean-François Paillard.

[735] HARST, Coelestin (Härst, Che-les'-tin)
MONK, KEYBOARDIST
BORN: Sélestat (alias Schlettstadt), 1698
DIED: Ebersmünster, 1776

Born in the Alsatian Rhine Valley, Père Harst spent most of his life in the Benedictine monastery at Ebersmünster. He became famous as a harpsichordist and in 1744 was summoned to Strasbourg to play for the visiting King Louis XV. The year following he published his *Pièces de clavecin* and became prior of his monastery. His harpsichord music is as if by François Couperin [616] out of Rameau [675]. RECORDINGS: Huguette Dreyfus has recorded his third suite.

[736] HASSE, Johann Adolf (Häs'-sə, Yō'-hàn Ä'-dolf)
SINGER, CONDUCTOR, TEACHER
BORN: Bergedorf, March 25, 1699
DIED: Venice, December 16, 1783

Rivaled in his time as an operatic composer only by Handel [683] and Porpora [690], Hasse is scarcely more than a name today. A member of a widespread musical family, he was initially taught by his father Peter, an organist in a town near Hamburg. Blessed with good looks and a fine tenor voice, he made his debut at the Goose Market Opera when he was eighteen, thanks to a local patron and poet, Ulrich von König, who was soon to become a Dresden court official. By 1719 he was a court singer in Braunschweig and had his first opera, *Antioco*, staged there three years later. The consensus that he was strong on talent but weak in skill sent him to Italy, where he settled in Naples. He tried to study with Porpora, but the two did not get along, so he persuaded the aging and reclusive Alessandro Scarlatti [583] to take him on. (It was Hasse who introduced the touring Quantz [730] to the old fellow.) His composing career got a boost when the great *castrato* Farinelli sang in one of his *serenatas*. This resulted in a commission for an opera, and the result, *Il Sesostrate* of 1726, was not only a hit in Naples (Hasse wrote

six more before he left) but won him a European reputation.

In 1730 he left Naples to attend to the production of his *Artaserse* during the Carnival in Venice. It was then that he met the great alto Faustina Bordoni, whom he married that summer. Of noble birth and a protégée of the Marcellos (see 682 and 689), she was considered a past mistress of vocal technique, though at twenty-nine her voice was already beginning to show signs of wear. She had probably reached her peak in London under Handel's direction a couple of years earlier, though her onstage catfights with her rival Francesca Cuzzoni had hastened her exit. No doubt seeing how the wind blew, she linked her career with Hasse's, sensing him a winner, and fought thereafter to promote both. It was undoubtedly at this time that they were contracted to head up the opera at the extravagant court of Augustus the Strong in Dresden, though they did not go until the following year, having commitments to fill in Italy. Almost immediately they triumphed in Hasse's new (well, mostly new) *Cleofide*. But the old trouble with Italian musical intrigues still persisted in Dresden, and the Hasses found it politic to keep out of the way, save when needed. Thus there was a series of operas produced in Italy in the off-season, beginning with *Catone in Utica* in Turin and *Caio Fabrizio* in Rome that same winter. Dresden was closed down for mourning on the elector's death in 1733. It was probably then that Hasse was invited to London, presumably to head the Opera of the Nobility, but he evidently recognized that he might be painting himself into a corner—and besides, Handel was having a success with Hasse's music if in a somewhat adulterated form (e.g., the *Caius Fabricius* he presented was about seventy-five percent of Hasse's *Caio Fabrizio*. But that was also about how Hasse treated the libretti he used).

Hasse returned to Dresden in 1734, but when the new elector took his court off to his Polish realms that fall, the Hasses went back to Italy. From then to 1760 this became the pattern of their lives, which involved a certain monotony of operatic success. Early in this period Hasse became good friends with Pietro Metastasio, now imperial court poet. In setting Metastasio's libretti after that, Hasse became not only his chief prophet; he even made amends for his past sins by *resetting* those he had earlier mangled. In Dresden in 1747 there was a splashy wedding, Bavaria's new Elector Max III Joseph marrying Princess Maria Anna, and her brother, Crown Prince Frederick Christian, marrying the elector's sister, Maria Antonia. Hasse wrote a new opera, *La Spartana generosa,* and Pietro Mingotti's company, which had filled in during his absence, presented a *teatra festale,* written and conducted by a rising young musician named Gluck [803] and starring Mingotti's wife, Regina. Frederick Christian, a longtime Italophile, forthwith imported Porpora, Hasse's onetime teacher, who was named *Kapellmeister,* and Porpora forthwith hired La Mingotta as his prima donna. Naturally this did not sit well, but the Hasses moved diplomatically. In 1750 Hasse was promoted to *Oberkapellmeister,* and two years later, when Mingotta made trouble during rehearsals of his *Adriano in Siria,* she was fired with loss of pension, and Porpora beat a strategic retreat to Vienna in the train of the Venetian Ambassador. It was shortly afterward that Hasse's flute music caught the ear of Frederick II of Prussia, Saxony's enemy, who invited him to Potsdam on at least two occasions. Meanwhile, Hasse's employer, Elector Frederick II Augustus (Augustus III of Poland) offered to publish a complete edition of Hasse's music. But in 1756 the Seven Years War broke out, the elector moved to Warsaw, and Hasse to Italy. (Later, in 1762, Hasse went to Vienna, where he established a new base of operations.) In 1763, the war over, he came home to find his home, the royal library, and the opera house destroyed, and with them much of his music and the home of the *Gesamtausgabe.* On top of all this, the elector died the first week in October, and Frederick Christian a few weeks later (of smallpox). Under his successor, Frederick III Augustus, a minor, stringent economizing was in order, and the musical establishment had to go—Hasse's pension with it. The Hasses returned to Vienna, where the rigors of old age—gout and arthritis—seem to have done little to decrease his incredible productivity. In these years, however, he found a formidable rival in Gluck, and at the very end in a precocious adolescent named Wolfgang Mozart [992], who, the old man noted with uncommon percipience, "will cast us all in the shade." In 1773, at seventy-four, Hasse and his wife retired to Venice, where he went on writing. A financial crash wiped him out. Faustina died in 1781, leaving him grief-stricken. When he himself died two years later, only his daughter and a few admirers attended the funeral, and his grave went unmarked for forty years. In Dresden a few pieces of his sacred music were traditionally performed on specific occasions for more than a century, but for the rest his compositions were as dead as

their author—and even in these novelty-hungry times there has been no attempted revival. His output was enormous—a term that describes as well what survives: the undetailed listing of it occupies nearly six pages of fine print in *The New Grove's Dictionary.*

RECORDINGS: One would never know the size of Hasse's output from the record listings. There is a flute concerto played by Helmut Riessberger and one for mandolin by Jacob Thomas, a cantata *(L'Armonica)* conducted by Paul Angerer, a flute sonata by Jean-Pierre Rampal, and a few minor odds and ends.

[737] BLAVET, Michel (Blà-vā', Mē-shel')
FLUTIST, CONDUCTOR
BORN: Besançon, March 13, 1700
DIED: Paris, October 28, 1768

Michel Blavet might be thought of as the Jean-Pierre Rampal of his time. A performer on the newly popular transverse flute, he probably did much to hasten the demise (or long eclipse) of the recorder. At the age of eighteen, when he married Anne-Marguerite Ligier, he was already sufficiently remarkable to be invited to play in Paris. But he refused, feeling that his place was with his pregnant wife, who bore him his first son, Jean-Louis, the next year. He eventually made it to the capital in 1723, and became a chamber musician to Duke Charles-Eugène de Lévis. In the years that followed he became one of the reigning stars of the Concert Spirituel, where he was rated in the same class with the great violinist Leclair [732]. There is a persistent but unsubstantiated story that Frederick II of Prussia, while he was still crown prince, invited him to his Rheinsberger establishment. Since Frederick was mad for flutists and French culture, such an episode seems not impossible. But Frederick did not settle at Rheinsberg until 1733, and Blavet seems to have been quite busy at home during that period —at the Concert Spirituel until 1735, as *maître de chappelle* to the Comte de Clermont from 1731, and from around 1738 to his death a member of the Chambre du Roi. He was also first flutist at the Paris Opera. His contemporaries depict him as a modest and kindly man, unperturbed by his eminence and always willing to clear the path for talented rivals. His tone and technique (though he was left-handed) were legendary.

Blavet's music is strongly influenced by the Italians, and perhaps by Telemann

[665], some of whose music he performed while that composer was visiting Paris in 1746. Best known for his three books of flute sonatas, he also wrote some operas for the Comte de Clermont's private theater in suburban Berny in the 1750s. The most famous of these, *Le Jaloux corrigé (The Jealous Lover Chastised),* is really a pastiche of Italian arias and things, only parts of it being by Blavet.

RECORDINGS: *Le Jaloux carrigé* has been recorded by Jean-François Paillard. The 6 sonatas of Op. 2 have been recorded by Ransom Wilson, and individual sonatas have been recorded by innumerable prominent flutists.

[738] SAMMARTINI, Giovanni Battista
(Sảm-mär-tẽ'-nē, Jō-vản'-nē Bảt-tēs'-
tả)
ORGANIST, CONDUCTOR, TEACHER
BORN: Milan, 1700
DIED: Milan, January 15, 1775

For G. B. Sammartini's background, see the entry for his brother Giuseppe [720]. He was among the most important musicians in Milan in his time and an important one in the history of Western music, but despite a considerable Sammartini industry among recent musicologists, we know little more about him than his musical activity. Unlike his brother, he stuck close to home all his life (hence the sobriquet "di Milano"). By the time he married Margherita Benna in 1727, he was said to be highly renowned, though his fame then may have rested on his organ playing or choir directing, since he seems to have begun seriously to compose only shortly before that. In the course of his life he seems to have served as *maestro di cappella* to most of Milan's important churches, including the ducal chapel and San Ambrogio. At first he seems to have been content to write sacred music in acceptable late-Baroque style, but gradually he turned to instrumental composition. His earliest *sinfonie* were the usual three-movement Italian overtures, but in the mid-1730s he extended his concept to four movements with far-reaching results. It was in this period that he produced the first two of his 3 known operas, *Memet* in 1730 and *L'Ambizione superata dalla virtù (Ambition Overcome by Virtue)* in 1734. In 1730 he became a teacher at the Collegio de' Nobili. His most famous pupil was Christoph von Gluck [803], who came to him seven years later; he also taught Giorgio Giulini [808]. Sammartini's renown and his music quickly spread all over Europe, and his importance as an

orchestral composer seems to have been fully recognized in his time. His wife died in 1754, leaving at least one child, a daughter named Marianna Rosa, who was a professional singer. Sammartini remarried less than a year later. Among visitors who took note of him later in his life were the young Wolfgang Amadeus Mozart [992] and Mysliveček [890], who announced that he had discovered the source of Haydn's symphonies. Haydn snorted "Nonsense!" but modern research seems, at least in principle, to have borne the Czech's conclusion out.

Sammartini di Milano has been credited with upwards of 2,000 works, though modern scholars have proved a good many of them mistakenly attributed or spurious. (There was long great confusion between the Sammartinis, and between them and Padre Martini [767].) At least 68 symphonies have been definitely credited to Sammartini; at least as many more are deemed probably or possibly his. Once considered an interesting transitional figure, he is now regarded, if not as the father of the symphony, at least as its most important practitioner before Haydn. In his mature works—and this applies both to orchestral and chamber music —it may be said that diatonic melody and tonic-dominant harmony have come to stay. Sammartini's concern is for form and symmetry. Though the tendency does not originate with him, he illustrates admirably the slowdown of harmonic rhythm that (to oversimplify) permits the symphony to operate on a basis of contrasting keys and of an agon between primary and secondary themes.

RECORDINGS: Considering his importance, Sammartini has enjoyed relatively few recordings. Newell Jenkins, his chief modern spokesman, has recorded two discs of symphonies (which tend to be brief), and John Lubbock another. Antonio Abussi and Carroll Glenn have recorded violin concerti, and Ulrich Koch an unusual one for viola pomposa. Expectably Jean-Pierre Rampal has found some flute sonatas. From the church music, there are two cantatas led by Jenkins.

[739] TANS'UR, William (Tan'-ser)
ORGANIST, TEACHER
BORN: Dunchurch, 1700
DIED: St. Neot's, October 7, 1783

No one seems to know why Tans'ur spelled his name in that catchy fashion. He was the son of a Warwickshire laborer named Edward Tanzer, probably of German parentage or descent, and was baptized William

Tanzer on November 6, 1706, though he insisted that he was born in 1700. His father died when he was six, and his mother a few weeks later. Of the immediately ensuing years we know nothing, but William became an itinerant teacher of psalm singing at a fairly early age and acquired an education somehow, both musical and otherwise. He served as organist at churches the length and breadth of England, from 1735 published a number of collections of hymns *(The Royal Melody Compleat, Heaven on Earth, Sacred Mirth,* and *The Psalm Singer's Jewel),* for many of which he supplied not only the arrangements but the words and music as well. His *New Musical Grammar* (later *The Elements of Musick Displayed)* continued to be used for nearly a hundred years after its first publication in 1746. Tans'ur's collections were popular in the American colonies. RECORDINGS: The Berkeley Chamber Singers have recorded his "An Hymn: On Christ's Nativity."

[740] BODINUS, Sebastian (Bō-dē′-noos, Se-bàst′-yàn)
VIOLINIST
BORN: c. 1700
DIED: c. 1760

Bodinus left a good deal of music, mostly for chamber performance, but little vital data. His origins, other than vaguely "central Germany," are unknown; some have suggested that he may have been of Italian descent and originally Bodini. At eighteen he was a musical servant to the Markgraf of Baden-Durlach in the new capital of Karlsruhe, named after the Markgraf himself. Bodinus went to Stuttgart in 1723 to avoid being sent to the wars, became *Konzertmeister* at the Württemberg court, and married a singer. In 1728 they returned to Karlsruhe, but another war in 1733 broke up the *Kapelle.* In 1736 it was again in business, with Bodinus replacing Johann Melchior Molter as its *Meister,* but it was terminated two years later when the Markgraf died. Molter returned to run a very small operation under Karl Friedrich, the new ruler, and Bodinus wound up in Basle. When Karl Friedrich decided to rebuild his musical establishment in 1747, Bodinus came back once more, but left in 1752 and dropped out of sight. RECORDINGS: The Berlin Camerata Musicale has recorded a trio sonata of his, and Jean-Pierre Rampal and Mario Duschenes a sonata for two unaccompanied flutes.

[741] CHILCOT, Thomas
ORGANIST, MERCHANT, TEACHER
BORN: Bath, c. 1700
DIED: Bath, November 24, 1766

Chilcot was organist of the abbey church in Bath for his last thirty-eight years. He sold musical instruments and taught to help support his two (successive) wives and ten children. His most famous pupil was Thomas Linley, Sr. (see 995). He left 12 keyboard concerti, 6 harpsichord suites, and 12 songs, mostly to Shakespearean texts. RECORDINGS: Some of the songs have been recorded by, for example, April Cantelo and Wilfrid Brown.

[742] PLATTI, Giovanni Benedetto (Plàt′-tē, Jō-vàn′-nē Bā-nā-dā′-tō)
STRING, WIND, AND KEYBOARD PLAYER; SINGER; TEACHER
BORN: c. 1700
DIED: Würzburg, January 11, 1763

In recent years Platti has been resurrected from the darkest shadows, and with him has been raised the question of whether he was one composer or two. Obviously very little is known of him. He is said to have been born in Padua or Venice, and to have studied in the latter city, perhaps with Francesco Gasparini [615]. He came to the episcopal court in Würzburg with a contingent of Venetian musicians in 1722, and spent the rest of his life there. In 1723, in Mainz, he married a soprano named Therese Langprückner, who bore him at least two sons. And therein lies the crux of the alleged problem. Platti left a fair-sized body of works, including oratorios, Masses, motets, cantatas, and more than a hundred instrumental compositions, mostly concerti and sonatas. Among the latter are some keyboard sonatas in a fairly advanced idiom. The composer was certainly cognizant of the work of Carl Philipp Emanuel Bach [801], and one enthusiast sees him as a forerunner of Beethoven [1063]. Since much of his other music is of a piece with late-Venetian Baroque, why, asks the two-Platti faction, may these pieces not be the work of another Giovanni Platti—undoubtedly one of the sons, other traces of whom must have been destroyed in the destruction of Würzburg in World War II? More temperate scholars find the sonatas somewhat less adventurous than advertised, and see them as part of a perfectly logical musical development. RECORDINGS: Some of the sonatas have been recorded by Luciano Sgrizzi. Felicja Blumental has recorded two keyboard concerti, and Alain Marion one for flute (originally for oboe).

[743] LAVIGNE, Philibert de (Là-vēn′-yə, Fī-lē-bâr′ də)
BORN: c. 1700 (?)
DIED: after 1739

All that is known about Lavigne is that he was active in Paris c. 1730 and was musical director to the Comte d'Ayen toward the end of that decade. RECORDINGS: A sonata for oboe variously designated "La Barsan" or "La Persane" has been recorded by Michel Piguet and other flutists and oboists.

[744] SIMON, Johann Kaspar (Sē′-mōn, Yō′-hàn Kàs′-pär)
ORGANIST, TEACHER, MUSIC DIRECTOR, DRAPER
BORN: Schmalkalden, January 10, 1701
DIED: Leipzig, November 22, 1776

Born in the Thuringian town that lent its name to the Protestant Schmalkaldic League in the Reformation, Simon graduated from the University of Jena in 1727 and became *Kapellmeister* in what must have been one of the least important courts in Germany, Langenburg an der Jagst. From 1731 to 1750 he was organist and choir director at the Georgikirche in the pretty little city of Nördlingen. He then gave up his musical career to run his late brother-in-law's drapery business in Leipzig. However, he devoted enough time to music between 1749 and 1754 to publish 4 organ books, including some rather late chorale preludes and preludes-and-fugues. There are also a few cantatas in manuscript. RECORDINGS: Walter Supper has recorded one prelude-and-fugue.

[745] AGRELL, Johan Joachim (À-grel′, Yō′-hàn Yō′-ā-khēm)
VIOLINIST, MUSIC DIRECTOR
BORN: Löth, February 1, 1701
DIED: Nuremberg, January 19, 1765

Agrell shows the impact of Johan Helmich Roman [719] on Swedish musicians, though he qualifies as a Swedish composer only by birth and education. The son of a village parson in east-central Sweden, he learned violin and attended the University of Uppsala. Given the opportunity to play in the court orchestra of Hessen-Kassel and astutely reasoning that musical opportunities were better there for a serious musician, he

went. Tradition says his departure for Hessen-Kassell was about 1723; records show him there from 1734 to 1746. In the latter year, unable to collect back salary and beer money from his employer, he went to Nuremberg, became municipal chief of music, and married a singer named Margarethe Förtsch in 1749. Unhappily, she died four years later. A good deal of Agrell's instrumental music survives; interestingly for such a conservative composer, it includes a number of symphonies. The new expressiveness is alien to him, and he is supposed to have said deprecatingly that music is nothing but arithmetic. Nevertheless his music seems to have been popular. There were publications of it in London (which Agrell may have visited), and both Leopold Mozart [816] and Thomas Jefferson played it. RECORDINGS: A harpsichord sonata has been recorded by Eva Nordenfeldt. Sten Frykberg conducts the Nörrköping Symphony in the *Sinfonia* in F Major (Op. 1, No. 6).

[746] GÖRNER, Johann Valentin (Gör′-ner, Yō-hàn Fä′-len-tēn)
CHOIRMASTER
BORN: Penig, February 27, 1702
DIED: Hamburg, July 1762

Saxon-born Valentin Görner was a younger brother of Gottlieb Görner, Johann Sebastian Bach's [684] organist at the Thomaskirche and sometime musical rival, at whom he is said once to have hurled his wig in rage. After studying at the University of Leipzig, Valentin went to Hamburg, probably in the later 1720s and in 1756 became *Kapellmeister* of the cathedral there. He was apparently well regarded in his day, but his reputation now rests almost wholly on a long series of popular songs set to texts by Friedrich von Hagedorn (1708–54), one of the first considerable poets to emerge in Germany after the long literary hiatus that followed the Thirty Years War. RECORDINGS: Examples have been recorded by Benno Kusche in a record called (in translation) *The Greatest Hits of 1762*.

[747] EBERLIN, Johann Ernst (Ā′-berlin, Yō′-hàn Ânst)
ORGANIST, CONDUCTOR
BORN: Jettingen, March 27, 1702
DIED: Salzburg, June 19, 1762

The son of Baron von Stain's land steward on an estate in the vicinity of Ulm, Eberlin, setting a path for his younger colleague Leopold Mozart **[816]**, grew up in Augsburg and attended the seminary in Salzburg, before giving up the cloth for a musical career. He was made number-four organist at Salzburg Cathedral in 1726 and married a year later. (His daughter Maria Josefa married his successor at the Cathedral organ.) Taken into the service of Prince-Archbishop Franz Anton, Graf von Harrach, he rose to be *Kapellmeister* at both court and cathedral, and was given the honorary title of Court Steward in 1754. Leopold Mozart, who joined the *Kapelle* in 1743, admired Eberlin greatly (as did Mozart's son), copied out a great deal of his music, and, when Eberlin died, aspired vainly to his job. (He and his two prodigies were on tour when that melancholy event took place.) Eberlin was a sound contrapuntalist, as may be seen in the church music that forms the major part of his legacy. He also left oratorios, school plays, organ music, and 3 symphonies. Late in his life, he and the elder Mozart collaborated on a cycle of pieces for the *Hornwerk,* or mechanical organ, of Hohensalzburg, the great fortress that still broods over the town. RECORDINGS: The *Hornwerk* cycle has been recorded on a nonmechanical organ by Franz Haselböck.

[748] MAICHELBECK, Franz Anton
(Mī'-khel-bek, Frånts Ån'-tōn)
ORGANIST, TEACHER
BORN: Reichenau, July 6, 1702
DIED: Freiburg im Breisgau, June 14, 1750

Most of what we know of Maichelbeck (and that subject to interpretation) comes from his first and more interesting publication of 1736, the title of which translates literally as "the at-the-keyboard-playing-and-ear-delighting Cecilia." Born on the island at the western end of Lake Constanz, he went to Freiburg to study for the ministry but was sent to Rome for musical studies a few years later by some wealthy patrons. In 1727 he settled in Freiburg as cathedral organist and member of the operational staff. He says that he was also a professor of Italian, which probably means merely that he was available for lessons. He was very proud of his Italian culture and points out that the sonatas in the collection noted reflect it. But the evidence is pretty hard to come by, and the pieces are as much keyboard suites as sonatas, and Maichelbeck's importance in the early history of the keyboard sonata has been softpedaled of late. In 1737 he published a follow-up to his first work, a treatise on keyboard technique ("The at-the-

keyboard-studying Cecilia") which rather daringly counsels the passing under of the thumb. RECORDINGS: Franz Lehrndorfer has recorded a sample of Maichelbeck on the organ.

[749] SCHNEIDER, Johann (Shnī'-der, Yō'-hàn)
ORGANIST, VIOLINIST
BORN: Oberlauter, c. July 17, 1702
DIED: Leipzig, January 5, 1788

Not to be confused with a number of later musical Johann Schneiders, this one, a miller's son from the Coburg area, was trained to music from the outset, studying with, among others, Johann Sebastian Bach **[684]** at Cöthen, and Johann Gottlieb Graun **[751]** at Merseburg. In 1721 he became organist and conductor at the Kitzenstein in Saalfeld, where he had studied four years earlier with the *Kapellmeister.* He left in 1726 to become a violinist at the court of Saxe-Weimar. In 1729 the Nikolaikirche in Leipzig offered him the position of organist. He accepted and the following year began a stand of fifty-eight years there. When members of the rival collegia musica formed the Grosses Konzert, the direct forerunner of the Gewandhaus Orchestra in the 1740s, Schneider became a member. In Bach's lifetime, Schneider came to be known as the second-best organist in Leipzig; whether he reached first rank after 1750 is not reported. He left an overture and a few organ works that show the fingerprints of his master. RECORDINGS: Organist Wilhelm Krumbach has recorded a theme and variations.

[750] BESOZZI, Alessandro (Bā-sod'-zē, Ȧl-les-sàn'-drō)
OBOIST
BORN: Parma, July 22, 1702
DIED: Turin, July 26, 1793

Alessandro Besozzi represents the second of at least four generations of Besozzi musicians, most of whom played double-reeds. They originated in Milan, whence Cristoforo (1661–1725) went to Parma in 1701 and ten years later joined the band of the ducal Irish Guards (where he was no doubt enrolled as Christopher O'Besozzi). His three sons, Giuseppe, Alessandro, and Paolo Girolamo, joined him in alphabetical order. When Duke Francesco Maria died in 1727, his brother Duke Antonio promoted all three to chapel status. But Antonio died in 1731, leaving no heir, and the duchy was turned over to a cousin, the Spanish prince

Don Carlos, son of King Philip V. Thereupon Giuseppe Besozzi went to Naples, and
the other two found a home in the court of
Charles Emmanuel III of Savoy and Sardinia in Turin. The pair became quite famous (they played at the Concert Spirituel
in Paris in 1735), and in 1775 (the year in
which most references say he died) Alessandro was named first virtuoso of the royal
band and given charge of the instruments.
He lived four days past his ninety-first
birthday. He published at least 12 sets of sonatas for oboe and/or other melody instruments. Giuseppe's heirs went from Naples
to Germany and eventually to Paris, where,
in 1837, his great-great-grandson, Louis-Dé-
siré (1814–79), beat out Charles Gounod
[1258] for the Prix de Rome. RECORDINGS:
Various short works appear in recorded
anthologies.

[751] GRAUN, Johann Gottlieb (Groun,
    Yō'-hàn Got'-lēp)
    VIOLINIST
    BORN: Wahrenbrück, 1702
    DIED: Berlin, October 27, 1771

Johann Gottlieb Graun was the second of
the three musical sons of August Graun, a
tax collector in a Dresden suburb. The eldest, August Friedrich (c. 1698–1765), was
an organist and cantor in Merseburg. The
youngest son was the important operatic
composer Karl Heinrich [757]. The two
younger brothers were members, in childhood, of the famous Kreuzchor in Dresden,
where Gottlieb studied with Pisendel [694].
He entered the University of Leipzig in 1718,
and in 1723 he studied violin for a few
months with Tartini [714] in Prague, after
which time he was sometimes called "Giuseppe Amadeo." In the middle 1720s he followed his elder brother to Merseburg,
where he served until 1728 as the Konzertmeister, and taught young Wilhelm
Friedemann Bach [784]. A visit to the Prussian court that year created a good deal of
excitement, but no job, and Graun took service instead at that of Waldeck in Arolsen,
near Kassel. But in 1732 the Prussian crown
prince called him to Ruppin as part of the
nucleus of the all-star musical establishment
with which he was to surround himself.
There he was called on to teach young
František Benda [776] a year later. When
Prince Frederick went to Berlin as King
Frederick II in 1740, Graun went with him
as royal Konzertmeister. His immediate superior was his younger brother, Karl
Heinrich. (There is no truth to the story
that when Frederick considered hiring Karl

Heinrich in 1735, his bride, Elisabeth Christina, who had troubles enough of her own,
protested, saying that one Graun was sufficient, and to bring in another would provide
Grauns for divorce.)
    As with the Bendas, there has been a
problem of determining which Graun wrote
what. (Many of the mss. are simply signed
"Graun.") Since Johann Gottlieb published
some sonatas and Karl Heinrich made his
name on operas, the rule of thumb seems to
be: when in doubt, give the first the instrumental pieces and the second the vocal. To
J.G., then, are ascribed about 400 sinfonias,
concerti, and sonatas, of a somewhat old-
fashioned cast.
    RECORDINGS: In any case, very little of
this material has reached phonograph
records—e.g., a bassoon concerto played by
George Zuckerman, two for oboe by Hans
Holliger, one for oboe d'amore by Alfred
Hertel, one for violin and viola by the
Capella Clementina ensemble, a trio sonata
by the Stuttgart Chamber Ensemble, and a
cantata (O Dio Fileno) for soprano, gamba,
and strings.

[752] FIOCCO, Joseph-Hector (Fyok'-kō,
    Zhō-zef' Ek-tôr')
    KEYBOARDIST, CHOIRMASTER, TEACHER
    BORN: Brussels, January 20, 1703
    DIED: Brussels, June 22, 1741

Fiocco's father was either a Venetian or a
Veronese, who came to Brussels in his early
thirties and worked variously there as director of the ambitious but unsuccessful Opera
at the Hay-Wharf, conductor of the chapel
of the Austrian viceregal court, and choir
director of the Church of Notre-Dame du
Sablon. Shortly after his arrival, he married
a local girl, Jeanne de Laetre, who died in
1691. Of their three children, Jean-Joseph
(1686–1746) was a musician and succeeded
his father in 1714 at the church. A year after
his bereavement, the elder Fiocco wed
Jeanne-Françoise Deudon, daughter of the
Mons postmaster, who, made of tougher
material than her predecessor, bore him
eleven more children, of whom the eighth
was Joseph-Hector. J.-H. studied with his
father and half-brother, and joined the
court orchestra under the latter's direction
in 1725. A year later he married Marie-Car-
oline Dujardin. Before he left, he rose to be
second in command in the orchestra but resigned in 1731 to become, in succession to
Willem de Fesch [692], the last married layman to direct the choir of Antwerp Cathedral. But six years later he came home to
follow Hercule-Pierre Bréhy as maître de

335

chapelle at Sts. Michel et Gudule. He died a little over three years later at thirty-eight, leaving a widow and two children. Supposedly he taught not only keyboard instruments but also classical languages. His sole publication was a Couperin-inspired *Pièces de clavecin.* But he left in manuscript several Masses, motets, and offices for Holy Week, works that show more independence and a strong Italian influence. RECORDINGS: Géry Lemaire has recorded the impressive *Missa solemnis* (with missing parts "reconstructed") and one of the motets. Netania Davrath has recorded the *Lecons de ténèbres pour la semaine sainte* and *Lamentatio secunda.*

[753] SORGE, Georg Andreas (Zôr'-ge, Gä'-ôrg Àn'-drä-às)
ORGANIST, THEORIST, TEACHER
BORN: Mellenbach, March 21, 1703
DIED: Lobenstein, April 4, 1778

Born in a village in the Schwarzburg area of Thuringia, Sorge was lucky enough to get a good education, both academic and musical, from local people. Before he turned twenty, he found himself set for life as court organist to the Prince of Reuss-Lobenstein-Elersdorf, a pocket-size Thuringian state, and municipal schoolteacher-organist in Lobenstein. He chose to remain in these posts for the rest of his life, doubtless because they permitted him the leisure to write his twenty or more theoretical treatises. He, rather than Tartini [714], may have been the real discoverer of differential tones, which he described in his composition manual published in the mid-1740s. He was a promoter of harmony as a basic musical study, described the circle of fifths, the notion of key relationships, and the third as a basic chordal interval. None of these were necessarily original ideas—Rameau [675], for example, was on the same track, but they show that Sorge was keenly aware of what was going on in music. His music, mostly for keyboard, shows a similar awareness—e.g., the toccata in all twenty-four keys recorded by Franz Haselböck. Sorge won considerable notice for his work, and followed Johann Sebastian Bach [684] as the next new member admitted to the Society for Musical Knowledge in Leipzig. He is said also to have been conceited and querulous.

[754] TRAVERS, John
ORGANIST

BORN: c. 1703
DIED: London, June 1758

While he was a choirboy at Windsor, Travers attracted the attention of the Dean of St. Paul's, who arranged for him to do some serious studying with Maurice Greene [727]. Later Travers also worked with the learned Dr. John Christopher Pepusch [611], some of whose enthusiasm for musical antiquarianism he absorbed and a good deal of whose library he inherited. After serving as organist at the church of St. Paul's in Covent Garden (from 1725) and Fulham Church, he succeeded Jonathan Martin as organist of the Chapel Royal. His publications include a 3-volume setting of the Psalms for from one to five voices and continuo, and *18 Canzonets* to words by the poet Matthew Prior. He also contributed to a volume of organ voluntaries, which also included works by Greene and "other eminent masters." RECORDINGS: The authorship of the individual works has not been ascertained, but Haig Mardirosian has recorded one ascribed to Travers.

[755] SEIXAS, José Antonio Carlos de (Sä'-shàs, Zhōō-zâ' Àn-tōn'-yōō Kär'-lōōsh dǝ)
ORGANIST, TEACHER
BORN: Coimbra, June 11, 1704
DIED: Lisbon, August 25, 1742

Seixas studied with his father, the organist of Coimbra Cathedral, whose name was Francisco Vaz. How Seixas got to be Seixas remains a mystery. At fourteen he inherited his father's job, but two years later he became royal organist in Lisbon and remained royal organist for the rest of his short life. He was also highly regarded as a teacher of the harpsichord. Between 1721 and 1729 he was a colleague of Domenico Scarlatti [687], then at the Portuguese court as music tutor to Princess Maria Barbara. We know little more about the details of his subsequent life, save that King John V knighted him in 1738. Seixas was allegedly a very productive composer, but little of his work remains—a handful of motets, an overture, a sinfonia, a keyboard concerto (recorded by Ruggero Gerlin), and between 80 and 100 keyboard sonatas (not all of them certain). These last, the pieces by which he is best known, are one-movement affairs which incorporate the essence of Portuguese song and dance. Though Seixas is glibly spoken of as "the Portuguese Scarlatti," Scarlatti's influence on him is still a subject of debate. RECORDINGS: Discs of sonatas have been re-

corded by a number of harpsichordists—
e.g., Gerlin, Pamela Cook, Luciano Sgrizzi,
and Neil Roberts.

[756] TŮMA, František Ignác Antonín
(Tōō'-mä, Frän'-tyi-shek Ēg'-nach
Än'-tō-nyēn)
ORGANIST, VIOLA DA GAMBA PLAYER,
LUTENIST, MUSIC DIRECTOR
BORN: Kostelec nad Orlicí, October 2,
1704
DIED: Vienna, January 30, 1774

Admired in his time both for his musical
skill and his expressiveness, especially in his
religious music, Tůma represents a sort of
last blaze of the Baroque. He was first
taught by his father, a village schoolmaster-
organist in eastern Bohemia. Tradition has
it that he was later a pupil of Černohorský
[677], and he certainly studied in Vienna
with Fux [585], where his son was born in
1729. Soon afterward he was on the books as
Kapellmeister to Graf Kinsky, Chancellor
of Bohemia. When Kinsky died a decade
later, Tůma was hired to direct the *Kapelle*
of the Dowager Empress Elisabeth Christine, widow of Emperor Charles VI. At her
death in 1750, Maria Theresa, seeing that he
was out of step with the times, retired him
on a handsome pension. In 1768 Tůma lost
his wife and took up residence in the
Premonstratensian monastery at Geras in
Lower Austria, apparently on the urging of
former pupils who were now monks there.
He died in the hospital of the Brothers of
Mercy in Vienna in his seventieth year. Besides a considerable body of religious works,
Tůma left a number of instrumental suites,
sonatas, and sinfonias. RECORDINGS: Some
of the instrumental works have been recorded by the Prague Chamber Orchestra.

[757] GRAUN, Karl Heinrich (Groun,
Kärl Hīn'-rikh)
SINGER, CONDUCTOR
BORN: Wahrenbrück, c. 1704
DIED: Berlin, August 8, 1759

Karl Heinrich was the most famous of the
brothers Graun, and in Germany at least he
was rivaled as an operatic composer only by
Hasse [736]. Like his brother Johann Gottlieb [751], he sang—"starred" would be
more accurate—in the Kreuzchor in Dresden, in which city he was trained by several
musicians and acquired his taste for opera.
As a boy soprano he was named Singer to
the Dresden City Council and was writing
for the Kreuzchor while still in his early

teens. After his voice broke, he trained as a
tenor. In 1725 he was hired by the ducal
opera house in Braunschweig as a leading
tenor and was permitted to alter arias not to
his liking or to write new ones. Asked for a
work of his own, he responded with his first
complete opera, *Sancio und Sinilde*, in February 1727 and was rewarded with the post
of vice-*Kapellmeister* and with several more
commissions. One of these was for *Lo
specchio della fedeltà (The Mirror of Fidelity)*, played at the June wedding in 1733 of
Princess Elisabeth Christine (poor girl!) to
Frederick, Crown Prince of Prussia (later
known as King Frederick II, the Great).
Frederick, who had already begun building
his all-star *Kapelle*, began negotiations with
Graun, whose employer, however, would
not release him. But two years later said
employer, Duke Ludwig Rudolf, conveniently expired, and Graun joined his elder
brother at Ruppin—not as one of the boys
in the band, but as *Kapellmeister* (and operatic tenor).

When the old Prussian king, Frederick
William I, died in 1740, Graun wrote the
funeral music and then went off to Italy to
round up singers for the as yet unbuilt
Royal Opera (for Frederick wanted not the
best German opera company in Germany,
but the best Italian one). Graun visited the
Italian centers—not overlooking the chance
to establish himself there as a singer—and
came back with a not very distinguished
crew, which put on Graun's setting of
Handel's [683] old *Rodelinda* libretto in
temporary quarters at the end of 1741. By
1742 the new house was ready, opening on
December 7, 1742 with *Cesare e Cleopatra*.
Graun conducted from the harpsichord, as
he was to do for the rest of his life, and
wrote an average of 2 new works per season
—26 in all. The king often dictated changes
in words and music and added arias of his
own. For several of Graun's last operas—
*Silla, Montezuma, I Fratelli nemici (The
Feuding Brothers)*, and *La Merope*—Frederick wrote the libretti in French prose and
had them translated into Italian verse by
the court poet Tagliazucchi. (In a burst of
democracy, he decreed that any citizen who
was decently dressed might attend the
Royal Opera. The house survived—latterly
as the Berlin State Opera—until it was destroyed in air raids in World War II.) Graun
died at fifty-five, apparently of underwork,
the Opera having closed down so that Frederick II could discharge his military obligations in the Seven Years War. Graun's operas were soon forgotten—not apparently
unjustly, for though the man had considerable talent, he too often approached his task

as a mechanic and was perfectly happy to bend to the whims of his employer. RECORDINGS: Richard Bonynge recorded a disc of highlights from *Montezuma*, said to be Graun's best work, but otherwise he seems to have been phonographically neglected.

[758] PESCETTI, Giovanni Battista (Pās-shet′-tē, Jō-vàn′-nē Bàt-tēs′-tà)
CONDUCTOR, KEYBOARDIST
BORN: Venice, c. 1704
DIED: Venice, March 20, 1766

A pupil of Antonio Lotti [613], Pescetti entered the operatic sweepstakes in 1725 with a *Nero detronato (Nero Dethroned)*, and toward the end of the decade inaugurated an operatic collaboration with Baldassare Galuppi [768], a friend from the Lotti studio. At some time in the middle 1730s, he preceded Galuppi to London, where he succeeded Porpora [690] in 1737 as director of the foundering Opera of the Nobility. He managed to stage four of his works at the King's Theatre before the venture finally went under at the end of the season. Nevertheless Pescetti hung around London to produce several more operas and publish a collection of 10 keyboard sonatas, before returning to Venice in the mid-1740s. (He would certainly have picked up his old friendship with Galuppi, who was director at King's Theatre in 1741.) Pescetti remained at home the rest of his life, writing operas at least until 1761 and becoming second organist at St. Mark's Cathedral the year following. His sonatas are among the first for keyboard to appear in England and involve a succession of two to four contrasting movements. At his best, he is melodically interesting, harmonically *au courant*, and idiomatic in his keyboard writing. RECORDINGS: Luciano Sgrizzi has recorded three of the harpsichord sonatas.

[759] LEFFLOTH, Johann Matthias
(Lef′-lōt, Yō′-hàn Màt-tē′-às)
ORGANIST
BORN: Nuremberg, c. February 6, 1705
DIED: Nuremberg, c. October 31, 1731

Leffloth's first teacher was his father, J.M. Sr., a successful merchant who was organist at the Margaretenkirche. He is said also to have studied with Johann Pachelbel's [567] elder son, Wilhelm Hieronymus, at the Sebaldikirche. At eighteen he himself was appointed organist at St. Leonhard's, and the general opinion around town was that

he would have proved right royal had he been put on—but he died at twenty-six. He left a cantata and a few pieces of instrumental music. RECORDINGS: The Consortium Classicum has recorded a "concerto" for violin and harpsichord and a gamba sonata that was once attributed to Handel [683].

[760] DE CROES, Henri-Jacques (Də Krōōs, An-rē′ Zhàk)
VIOLINIST, CONDUCTOR
BORN: Antwerp, c. September 19, 1705
DIED: Brussels, August 16, 1786

In a translated sketch of his life that appears on a record jacket, one reads that De Croes's native village was Antwerp and that he later brought unprecedented musical acclaim to the Austrian village of Pays-Bas. At any rate the Belgians (or those who are interested in such things) consider him one of their greatest composers. Among most other nationalities the adjective is silent. He was first a violinist at St. Jacques in Antwerp, and then at twenty-five was hired by the postal magnate, the Brussels-based Prince of Thurn and Taxis (or "Tour and Taxi," as the sketch has it), and played in his band, mostly at Frankfurt-am-Main, for about fifteen years. In 1744 he took his place in the court orchestra of Charles de Lorraine, Governor-General of the Austrian Netherlands. Two years later the director, Jean-Joseph Fiocco (half-brother to Joseph-Hector [752]), died, but it was three years before they decided to promote De Croes to the directorship. He kept it until he himself died at eighty. In 1779, having got himself into a financial bind, he sold all of his manuscripts to his employer. Supposedly they were lost in a shipwreck. He did not, however, succeed in palming off his son Henri-Joseph (1758–1842) as his successor. What remains of De Croes's music includes some Masses (incomplete), motets, concerti (favorably compared with Jean-Marie Leclair's [732]), divertissements, and sonatas. RECORDINGS: Géry Lemaire has recorded a couple of the concerti and a motet. The Divertimento No. 5 in C Minor is recorded in the Musique en Wallonie series.

[761] KELLNER, Johann Peter (Kel′-ner, Yō-hàn Pā′-ter)
ORGANIST, TEACHER
BORN: Gräfenroda, September 28, 1705
DIED: Gräfenroda, April 19, 1772

Yet another Thuringian, Kellner studied from the age of twelve with the town cantor, whose name was Nagel, and later with one of the innumerable Johann Christoph Schmidt's (this one neither Karl Heinrich Graun's [757] teacher nor Handel's [683] amanuensis, but the church organist in nearby Zella.) At nineteen or twenty he found a job as cantor of a school in Frankenhain, but after three years he gave it up and became an assistant to his old teacher's son and successor back in Gräfenroda. The younger Nagel died in 1732, and Kellner worked happily as Gräfenroda cantor for the next forty years. His son Johann Christoph—later an organist, composer, and theorist of some note—was born there in 1736. Kellner adored the music of Johann Sebastian Bach [684] and Handel, both of whom he came to know, and made copies of some of Bach's, but his own music was in the style of his times. He is said to have whipped up a fine impromptu fugue on the (German) notes B-A-C-H (H being B-flat) when Bach once made a surprise visit to his church. Kellner published two collections of keyboard suites, and left some organ music, and perhaps some cantatas, in manuscript, though it is not always certain which Kellner wrote what. RECORDINGS: Wilhelm Krumbach has recorded an organ prelude.

[762] CHÉDEVILLE, Nicolas (Shā-də-vēl', Nē-kō-làs')
OBOIST, MUSETTE PLAYER, TEACHER
BORN: Sérez, 1705
DIED: Paris, August 6, 1782

The three musical *frères* Chédeville—Pierre, Esprit Philippe, and Nicolas—all masters of the musette (a small bagpipe), were close relatives of the Hotteterres (see 640 and 662), a name by which they too were sometimes confusingly called. All three played at the Opéra and at court, Esprit Philippe succeeding Pierre, who died young, and Nicolas succeeding Esprit Philippe on his retirement. This was the time when it amused the court to play at being peasants, and Nicolas was known as a teacher of the little bagpipe to royal princesses and other great ladies. Like his brothers, he also manufactured the instruments and published his own compositions and arrangements. He left the Opéra in 1748, after twenty-three years, but remained on call there and played at court until his very last years. He published at least 20 collections of sonatas, arrangements, and pieces for musette(s) (or, of course, for other melody instruments). Among the arrangements one finds Vivaldi's *Four Seasons* concerti. RECORDINGS: A sonata for two

musettes has been recorded by Helmut Riessberger and Gernot Kury, and by Jean-Pierre Rampal (who plays both parts), needless to say on flutes.

[763] CAPORALE, Andrea (Kà-pō-rà'-lā, Àn-drā'-à)
CELLIST
BORN: c. 1705 (?)
DIED: after 1757

Caporale made a big splash as a cellist in London, where he apparently arrived in the mid-1730s. He was soloist in Handel's [683] orchestra, and Handel wrote the cello obbligato in the first act aria of *Deidamia* for him in 1740. He may have left London about a decade after he came. Some accounts find him in Dublin giving concerts in the 1750s. In 1746 he published a volume containing 6 ornate solos (sonatas) for cello and continuo, together with cello transcriptions of 6 of the bassoon sonatas by Johann Ernst Galliard [695]. RECORDINGS: Cellist Albert Catel has recorded a movement from one of the sonata transcriptions.

[764] ROYER, Joseph-Nicolas-Pancrace (Roi-yā', Zhō-zef' Nē-kō-làs' Pàn-kràs')
HARPSICHORDIST, TEACHER, ADMINISTRATOR
BORN: Turin, c. 1705
DIED: Paris, January 11, 1755

Though Italian-born, Pancrace Royer was a Burgundian blueblood, his father being a military officer and official at the court of Savoy. When his father died broke, Royer moved to Paris in 1725, produced a couple of comic operas at the fairs, and set himself up as a teacher of voice and harpsichord. Thanks largely to his efforts on his own behalf, he became a musical Somebody in his time. In 1734 he became a teacher to the royal children and in 1746 became sole Music Master to them. Two years later he took over the staggering Concert Spirituel on a concession basis and made it work. In 1753 he was appointed chief composer and concertmaster at the Opéra, now being run by the municipality. He died at around fifty, though some accounts make him five years older. His eight or so operas are said to have been most effective, and the *Zaïde* of 1739 was in the repertoire for several decades. But Royer is now remembered, if at all, for his book of harpsichord pieces published in 1746, including transcriptions from the operas. RECORDINGS: This book has been recorded by William Christie.

[765] FIORENZA, Nicola (Fyō-rānt'-zà, Nē'-kō-là)
VIOLINIST, TEACHER
BORN: c. 1705 (?)
DIED: Naples, April 13, 1764

Very little is known about Fiorenza. In 1743, by the luck of the draw, he was appointed teacher of violin at the Conservatorio di Santa Maria di Loreto in Naples, the directors having been unable to decide among the applicants. They came to regret their choice and, after nearly twenty years, fired him for beating up the students. By then, he was number-one violin at the viceregal chapel, but he lived only a year and a half longer. He left in manuscript a number of concerti and symphonies. RECORDINGS: Raymond Meylan has recorded a flute concerto, with the Saar Orchestra conducted by Karl Ristenpart; this is coupled with the *Siciliana* in C Minor for strings.

[766] FRANKLIN, Benjamin
FOUNDING FATHER, POLYMATH
BORN: Boston, January 17, 1706
DIED: Philadelphia, April 17, 1790

Considering the modest musical achievements of Josiah Franklin's youngest and most precocious son, this is not the place to outline his rich life and his achievements as printer, bookseller, essayist, journalist, philosopher, self-taught scholar, scientist, inventor (the Franklin stove, the lightning rod), politician, diplomat, and practical joker. That Franklin was one of the chiefest of the founding fathers is axiomatic, and it should be added that without his efforts, especially in getting aid from France, it is unlikely that the American Revolution would have succeeded. But one should keep in mind that though he was considered a progressive, this Deist proponent of the Protestant work ethic was, like Raskolnikov, committed temperamentally to "evolution, not revolution," and supported the notion of change from within the system by legal means rather than by the violent overthrow of governments.
Franklin, however, had more strings to his bow than the one attached to his famous kite. He was a good musician and, as was expected of educated men of his day, knew something about music. No doubt, as an apprentice to his half-brother James, he checked the plates for the printing of the

Reverend Thomas Walter's [728] "revolutionary" songbook. He taught himself to play both the harp and the guitar, and tried to teach Mary Shewell, a Philadelphia Quaker girl, and later mother of the poet and music critic Leigh Hunt, to play it, but she was too shy. Also, like Mozart's Papageno, he used to carry about with him a little set of glass chimes called the *Sticado-Pastorale*. Fascinated by a performance on the musical glasses (goblets made to vibrate by running a wet fingertip around the rims), he ran an axle through the bottoms of a set of graduated glass bowls, and arranged it horizontally in a sort of trough with a little water in it to keep them moist. They were spun by a foot pedal, and the instrument, initially called the "glassichord" became popular as the glass harmonica. Many famous composers, including Wolfgang Amadeus Mozart [992] and Beethoven [1063], wrote pieces for it, and as late as 1835 Donizetti [1155] called for it in his *Lucia* mad scene.

As far as composition is concerned, some songs attributed to Franklin seem to have been no more than the adaptation of old tunes to new texts. A few years ago, however, there was found in Paris a sort of string quartet (really a dance suite for three violins and cello), said to be by "Benjamin Francklin." It is a trivial but ingenious piece; the instruments are specially tuned so that no fingering is necessary. It is the sort of thing Franklin might well have written. RECORDINGS: The string quartet has been recorded by the Kohon Quartet.

[767] MARTINI, Giovanni Battista (Mär-tē'-nē, Jō-vàn'-nē Bàt-tēs'-tà)
ORGANIST, CHOIRMASTER, THEORIST,
HISTORIAN, BIBLIOPHILE
BORN: Bologna, April 24, 1706
DIED: Bologna, August 3, 1784

This is Padre Martini, not to be confused with Martini il Tedesco, ("the German") [922], than whom he is more important, or with the Sammartinis [720, 738], than whom he was more influential. The son of a local violinist, Antonio Maria Martini, he studied strings with his father, keyboard with Angelo Predieri *(maestro di cappella* at the San Pietro Cathedral), singing with the *castrato* G. A. Riccieri, and composition with G. A. Perti (longtime choirmaster at San Petronio). His formal education, however, in which he focused on philosophy and theology, he got from the local Oratorians. Having elected the celibate life, he did his novitiate with the Franciscans at Lugo, a few miles down the Via Emilia, in 1721. The next year he returned to Bologna, became organist at San Francesco, took a cell in the monastery, and in 1725 began a lifetime appointment as choirmaster. He was ordained in 1729. But this did not mark the end of his education, which probably concluded only with his death. For example, he studied mathematics with a local man named Zanotti and frequently conferred with Perti on the finer points of church music. A voracious reader on all subjects, he amassed a library said to have run to around 20,000 volumes. Friends and admirers from all over Europe sent him additions that they thought he might like, and the bulk of the collection remains in the Liceo. He also collected portraits of musicians done by the famous painters of the day. His lifetime project was a definitive history of music up to his own time, but the 3 volumes he managed to complete do not go beyond antiquity.

Martini's enormous musical learning made him a lodestone. He was frequently called on to settle pedantic quarrels over matters of theory and practice. He drew innumerable students, and to pass an examination administered by the good father became a sort of sign of having arrived. Gluck [803] had his blessing. So did Grétry [919]. The thirteen-year-old Wolfgang Amadeus Mozart [992] fairly stunned the old man, but the admiration was mutual, and they kept up a correspondence. Martini was in the course of time elected to the Arcadian Academy, the Bolognese Academy of Science, and (by special dispensation, because he was a monk) the Accademia Filarmonica. In his last years he suffered from a urinary ailment, asthma, and an ulcerated leg, though he let these problems slow him down very little. When he died, his funeral featured a *Requiem* written by thirteen prominent composers, and a medal was struck in his memory.

As a composer, Martini was guided by Palestrinan principles, as they were then understood. His music is scrupulously correct but often more concerned with form and propriety than with freedom of idea. He left much sacred music, some intermezzi, cantatas, arias, sinfonias, concerti, sonatas, and a good deal of organ music.

RECORDINGS: Some organ music has been recorded by Marie-Claire Alain, Janos Sebestyan, and others; there is also a recording of *Duetti da Camera* for voices and continuo.

[768] **GALUPPI, Baldassare** (Gà-loop'-pē, Bàl-dàs-sà'-rä)
HARPSICHORDIST, CONDUCTOR
BORN: Burano, October 18, 1706
DIED: Venice, January 3, 1785

Thousands of English-speaking students have encountered Galuppi in Robert Browning's poem "A Toccata of Galuppi's" with only a hazy notion of who he was and never having heard a note of his music. This is in keeping with the poem, where the toccata stands as a symbol of a vanished world. (Browning, versed in music and an amateur composer, is said to have had no particular toccata in mind.) Galuppi, in fact, though he died rich and famous, was forgotten soon after. From his birthplace (an island in the Venetian lagoon) and his diminutive stature, he was known as *Il Buranello*—the little Buranese. (Burney describes him at sixty as an agile cricket of a man.) Like Vivaldi's, Galuppi's father was a barber who played the violin—but in theaters rather than in churches. He trained his son well enough for him to get an opera produced when he was sixteen. The curtain, however, was brought down before the audience turned violent, and the composer betook himself to Antonio Lotti [613] for more sophisticated lessons. There he encountered Pescetti [758], with whom he teamed up in 1728 to try again. Their second effort, *Dorinda,* launched Galuppi on a fabulously successful career, and from 1733 into the 1770s he turned out, on the average, at least two operas a year, and enjoyed premieres in Turin, Milan, Rome, Naples, Florence, Bologna, Padua, and Madrid, as well as on his home turf.

In 1740 he was placed in charge of musical education at the Ospedale dei Mendicanti, and before he left eleven years later, he had brought its conservatory (which it had not taken very seriously before) up to par with the other such schools in Venice. From 1741 he was, for two seasons, his friend Pescetti's successor as operatic director at the King's Theatre in London under the aegis of the Earl of Middlesex, who was giving the place one more try. He successfully premiered four operas there. Audiences took to him slowly, but he soon became a fixture in London opera houses, and Burney estimated that he had more impact on English music than any Italian of his time. Back in Venice he was named vice-*maestro* at St. Mark's Cathedral in 1748, and twelve years later *maestro di cappella.* By then his fame had reached even to Russia, and in 1765 he was permitted to go to St. Petersburg for three years to westernize court music for Catherine the Great. His chief impact was on religious music: he replaced traditional chant with Italianate compositions and taught several of the first generation of new-style Russian composers, such as Maxim Berezovsky [938] and Dmitri Bortniansky [976]. At the time appointed, he came home and devoted himself to the basilica and to teaching and conducting at the Incurabili. He left a widow, *née* Adriana Pavan, and three sons, of whom Antonio became known as a librettist.

Forgotten though he may be, Galuppi was an important operatic composer. He began with *opera seria*, setting, among others, most of the standard Metastasio libretti (anticipating Wolfgang Amadeus Mozart [992] with *Il Re pastore* and *La Clemenza di Tito*), reflecting as he progressed changes in form and attitude, including the revolt against opera as costumed concert or athletic contest and the turn toward musical drama. Midway through his career he picked up *opera buffa* from the Neapolitans and—especially with Carlo Goldoni as his librettist—made a brilliant success of his efforts. He is said to have developed the complex finales that characterize the comedies of Mozart and Rossini [1143], and his *Il Filosofo di campagna (The Rural Philosopher)* was played all over the world and is still occasionally revived. Galuppi also wrote oratorios and much sacred music, as well as keyboard sonatas and instrumental works. The keyboard sonatas, like Domenico Scarlatti's [687], are in cycles of from three to five movements. Simply conceived, they are melodically fertile, harmonically ingenious, and reflect Galuppi's own dictum that the three requisites of music are beauty, clarity, and good modulation. If they sometimes make one think of Mozart, one must remember that Mozart outlived Galuppi by only six years.

RECORDINGS: The short comic opera *L'Arcadia in Brenta* is recorded by Claudio Gallico. *Il Filosofo di campagna* has been recorded under the direction of Renato Fasano. He is also represented on records by instrumental works—some *Concerti a 4* by Ennio Gerelli and others, a flute concerto by Jean-Pierre Rampal, a trio sonata by the Berlin Camerata Musicale. A good deal of attention has been given to his keyboard sonatas (e.g. by Luciano Sgrizzi, Arturo Benedetti Michelangeli, Eugene List).

[769] LAMPUGNANI, Giovanni Battista
(Läm-pōōn-yá'-nē, Jō-vän'-nē Bät-tēs'-tä)
HARPSICHORDIST, CONDUCTOR
BORN: Milan, 1706
DIED: 1786 or later

Lampugnani, one of the better opera composers of his time, is an elusive figure. He had an exact namesake, a Florentine, who was attached to the staff of the papal nuncio in Warsaw in the 1690s and who wrote a couple of libretti, but there is nothing else to link them. The composer does not, in fact, appear on the stage of history until the production of his opera *Candace* at the Teatro Ducale in Milan in 1732. After several others premiered variously in Venice, Rome, Piacenza, Padua, and elsewhere in Italy, he went to London in 1743 to succeed Galuppi [768] at the King's Theatre, where he produced at least two new works. He can have stayed no more than two seasons, since his last opera there opened in 1744 and Gluck [803] took over in 1745. Where he was exactly for the next decade and a half is uncertain, though his new productions crop up every year or so here and there, mostly in Italy. In the latter 1750s he was definitely back in Milan, teaching voice, and now writing comic operas to Goldoni texts—perhaps on the example of Galuppi. In 1760 he became *maestro al cembalo* (i.e., he conducted from the harpsichord) at the Teatro Ducale, yielding his place to the sixteen-year-old Wolfgang Amadeus Mozart [992] for the first three performances of the latter's *Mitridate* in 1770. During the 1776 Carnival, the theater burned down and was replaced by the Teatro alla Scala, popularly known ever since as La Scala. When it opened in 1778, Lampugnani was back at his keyboard, and he is last heard of in 1786. Apart from operas, cantatas, and other vocal works, Lampugnani published some trio sonatas, and left others, as well as sinfonias and 3 keyboard concerti in manuscript. Thomas Jefferson owned two sets of sonatas. Music historian Charles Burney said the music was "light, airy, and pleasant," the work of a "gay man of the world." RECORDINGS: Newell Jenkins has conducted a pair of concerti *(sinfonie?)* for two flutes.

[770] OREJÓN Y APARICIO, José de
(Ō-rä-hōn' ē Ä-pä-rēs'-yō, Hō-zä' dä)
ORGANIST, CHOIRMASTER, PRIEST
BORN: Huacho, 1706
DIED: Lima, May 1765

Born in Peru, Orejón became a choirboy at Lima Cathedral and remained as a countertenor after his voice changed. He studied organ with Juan de Peralta and theory with Tomás de Torrejón y Velasco [542], the choirmaster, who may have been a relative on his mother's side. Torrejón was succeeded on his death in 1728 by an Italian named Ceruti, who tried to impose newfangled Italian ideas on the choir. Orejón, now a priest, did not cotton to this and sought a nonmusical appointment elsewhere but failed to find one. In 1742, however, a vacancy allowed him to become first organist at the Cathedral. His work was interrupted by a severe earthquake in 1746, but he seems to have used the hiatus to take a degree at the local university. In 1760 he followed Ceruti to the directorship and four years later in May 1765, as the result of an accident, to the grave. He left a Passion and about a score of motets and cantatas, of considerable beauty, dedicated to the Blessed Sacrament. RECORDINGS: Roger Wagner has recorded the duo-cantata *Mariposa*.

[771] CAPUA, Rinaldo di (Kà'-pōō-à, Rē-nàl'-dō dē)
BORN: c. 1706 (?)
DIED: after 1778

Though his career as an operatic composer (chiefly in Rome) between 1737 and 1778 is well documented, most of what we know of Rinaldo di Capua (if that is his name) is what was reported by music historian Charles Burney, who met him in 1771. Burney says he was a Neapolitan, the illegitimate child of an important noble, that he had been educated as a gentleman, but had wasted his substance and was presently on the verge of starvation in Rome. However, the dates Burney gives mesh neither with his report nor with other known facts, and one wonders how much credence to put in the whole narrative. We do know that Rinaldo wrote 30 or more operas, a number of oratorios, and some orchestral music, that some of his pieces, especially his comedies, were immensely successful and played all over Europe, and that he and his wife were hired away to Portugal in 1740 but did not stay long. We do *not* know whether Capua was his surname or his place of origin (an ancient town near Naples), or when he died. As an opera composer he was inclined toward intermezzi—one-act comedies to be inserted between the acts of serious works. He is said to have invented or at least perfected the device of punctuating arias with

instrumental passages to express passions too strong or inchoate for words. His most famous work was *La Zingara (The Gypsy Girl)*, like many of his operas partly reworked from earlier material, and which created a storm when it was presented in Paris in 1753 by the touring Bambini company, whose performances of Italian comedies precipitated the *Querelle des Bouffons* (Quarrel of the Buffoons) by igniting a rage for the genre. One of its claims to fame was that it was supposed to have been the first stage work to present a man in a bear suit. *La Zingara* has been recorded under the direction of Günther Kehr.

[772] PARADISI, Pietro Domenico (Pà-rà-dē'-sē, Pē-ā'-trō Dō-mā'-nē-kō)
TEACHER, HARPSICHORDIST (?)
BORN: Naples, 1707 (?)
DIED: Venice, August 25, 1791

Almost all reference books say that Paradisi was born in Naples in 1707, probably studied with Porpora [690], produced two operatic flops in Italy, went to London, and bombed again in 1747. After that he set up in England as a vocal teacher, proved a "bad influence" on a pubescent prodigy known as "Madam Mara," taught Thomas Linley Sr. (see 995) composition (probably in Bath), sold off his manuscripts, and went home to die at a respectable old age. He is often listed as "Paradies" on the grounds that this is how he usually signed himself. Fifty years ago the Italian musicologist Fausto Torrefranca made some interesting conjectures about Paradisi. Since Paradisis were uncommon around Naples and since there are no records of this one's being there, why not, he asks, assume that he was the son of one of two theatrical brothers, Pietro and Domenico Paradisi, active in Florence around the turn of the century? And since the London opera was dismissed as the work of a rank amateur, why not assume that the London man was another Paradisi, perhaps a failed *castrato* seeking a new career? Nevertheless this ingenious solution does not explain the publication by John Johnson in 1754 of Paradisi-Paradies' *12 Sonate di gravicembalo* or the presence of his manuscripts at Oxford. Nonetheless it is hard to reconcile the skillful and muchpraised sonatas with the reputation of the operas, especially the London-premiered *Fetonte (Phaeton)*. (Whether or not the sonatas show incipient sonata form seems still to be a vexed question.) RECORDINGS: There are occasional recordings of sonatas (e.g., by George Malcolm, Luciano Sgrizzi); and a highly inauthentic version of a movement from Sonata No. 6, known as "Toccata," has achieved a certain popularity. And if the operas were so bad, one wonders why such singers as Lily Pons, Renata Tebaldi, Hina Spani, and Igor Gorin have chosen to record arias from them.

[773] REUTTER, Johann Adam Karl Georg von, Jr. (Roi'-ter, Yō'-han Ä'-dàm Kärl Gä-ôrg)
ORGANIST, CONDUCTOR
BORN: Vienna, c. April 6, 1708
DIED: Vienna, March 11, 1772

Although at his best he seems to have been a reasonably good composer, Georg von Reutter the younger qualifies as one of the disaster areas of musical history. His father, Georg Sr., was a nice old man who had fifteen children, served as a sort of musician-of-all-work at the court of Joseph I and Charles VI, succeeded Johann Joseph Fux [585] as *Kapellmeister* of the Cathedral of St. Stephen, and was knighted by Count Francesco Sforza, who had inherited the papal privilege of knighting people. Young Georg was notable for his ambition and his laziness. He studied with Antonio Caldara [624] and won the implacable dislike of Fux. In 1720 his father gave him a job as the Cathedral organist. In 1731 he married Theresia Holzhauer, a court prima donna who knocked down 3,500 florins per annum. In that same year, having ingratiated himself with their imperial majesties, he was named court composer and in 1736 took over at the Cathedral from his aging parent, who died two years later. Early in 1739 he went on a choirboy hunt and stumbled on young Joseph Haydn [871]. Haydn couldn't trill, but when, on a few elementary suggestions, he quickly mastered the technique, Reutter gave him a big bunch of cherries and a contract. Haydn's father had, no doubt, told him never to accept cherries from a stranger, and he was right, for they were about the last thing Reutter ever gave the boy.

In 1740, one of the Austrian coregents, Francis Stephen or possibly his wife Maria Theresa, ennobled Reutter. (Unlike his father, he insisted on the title.) The next year his old enemy Fux died, and he assumed he would become *Kapellmeister*, but the job went to a Bolognese nonentity named Luca Antonio Predieri. Reutter then set about to maintain a high profile and was rewarded with the vice-*Kapellmeister's* post in 1747. Among his duties was to provide dinner music (the eighteenth-century counterpart of Muzak) for the empress, for which function he sometimes brought in his choirboys. Along with his various court and church salaries, Reutter was getting a free home and 1,200 florins from the city for housing and teaching six choristers. His notion of fulfilling this duty was to keep them on starvation rations and teach them (forcibly if necessary) only what they needed to know to keep up their trills. When one evening Maria Theresa gave Michael Haydn [894], who had joined his brother, twenty-four gold pieces for his solo performance, Michael gave them to Reutter to keep for him against hard times. He never saw them again. Meanwhile Joseph Haydn saw hard times staring him in the face, for at seventeen he was about to run out of useful voice. Reutter suggested that he might assure himself of a long and lucrative career by submitting to a minor operation, but to his credit Haydn's father vetoed that notion. In November 1749, angered by some prank, Reutter beat him and tossed him out on the street.

In 1751 (through what machinations, history does not say) *Kapellmeister* Predieri was retired and Reutter became his successor *de facto,* though he had to wait eighteen years for Predieri to die so that he could have the title. At this time, Maria Theresa (who had become Holy Roman empress in 1745) was on an economy kick. The court music was among the first (as such things usually are) to suffer budgetary cuts. Reutter apparently did not protest, and so, over the years, though he occasionally suggested that a little more money might help, the musical forces during his twenty-year intendancy were reduced by eighty percent. The opera suffered particularly, but Reutter successfully blocked an attempt to have Gluck [803] replace him in that quarter. At St. Stephen's Cathedral he had managed to win yet another cushy post as director of the musicians attendant on the *Gnadenbild*, a picture of the Virgin said to weep real tears, but that was merely another prestige appointment, and the cathedral music suffered almost as much as did the court's.

Reutter turned out, quite uncritically, whatever was needed for the stage (around 50 works, mostly occasional) and for worship (81 Masses and over 300 other pieces). He also left a few symphonies and concerti and some keyboard pieces.

RECORDINGS: He is represented on records by a dinner-music *Servizio di tavola* in performances directed by Theodor Guschlbauer and Günther Kehr.

[774] KÖNIGSPERGER, Bruder Marianus (Kö'-niks-pâr-ger, Må-rē-å'-nōōs)

MONK, ORGANIST, CHOIRMASTER
BORN: Roding, December 4, 1708
DIED: Prüfening, October 9, 1769

A native of eastern Bavaria, Johann Erhard Königsperger, as he was baptized, became a choirboy at the Benedictine monastery at Prüfening in the purlieus of nearby Regensburg, and remained there for the rest of his life as a member of the order. He was appointed organist and choirmaster in 1734 and at about the same time began publishing his sacred and instrumental compositions. He was much admired as a performer, and his music was known and used far and wide. His religious music was in the simple, singable vein popularized by Valentin Rathgeber [670]. His publisher said that Königsperger's work alone had accounted for his own success, and the royalties bought a new organ for the monastery and helped stock its library. Königsperger is also said to have written *Singspiels* (musical comedies), but none have survived. RECORDINGS: Franz Lehrndorfer has recorded an organ piece.

[775] AVISON, Charles

ORGANIST, TEACHER, CONCERT MANAGER
BORN: Newcastle-upon-Tyne, c. February 16, 1709
DIED: Newcastle-upon-Tyne, c. May 10, 1770

Charles Avison was the middle child of the nine born to Richard Avison, a municipal musician in Newcastle, and his wife Ann. He evidently went to London after some local training, to study, it is said, with Geminiani [693]. He turned down job offers from London, York, Dublin, and Edinburgh to return to Newcastle as organist of St. John's Church in 1736, and, in the fall of the same year, became organist of St. Nicholas'. He married Catherine Reynolds in 1737 and, like his own parents, they had nine children, though most of them died in childhood. He became head of the Newcastle Music Society in 1738 (it had been founded just before he came home) and was thus director of the community concert series. He also promoted concerts in Durham and taught the harpsichord in his home. As a composer, Avison is best known for his *concerti grossi* of which he wrote 60, sedulously but attractively in the style of Geminiani, as well as arranging another set of 12 from Domenico Scarlatti [687] sonatas. He also published 24

trio sonatas, the later ones much influenced by Rameau [675], and an edition of Benedetto Marcello's [689] psalms adapted to English texts. Avison appears to have served the local newspapers as music critic and in 1752 collaborated on *An Essay on Musical Expression,* which deals both with aesthetic theory and criticism of contemporary composers and performance practices. RECORDINGS: Emanuel Hurwitz has recorded some of the original *concerti grossi,* and Neville Marriner the Scarlatti transcriptions.

[776] BENDA, František (Ben'-då, Fràn'-tyi-shek)

VIOLINIST
BORN: Alt-Benatek, c. November 22, 1709
DIED: Nowawes, March 7, 1786

The Bendas—a musical dynasty that reaches down to the twentieth-century conductor Hans von Benda—came from the village of Old Benatek (now Staré Benátky) adjacent to New Benátky in northeast Bohemia. The patriarch was Jan Jiří (alias Hans Georg), a linen weaver who doubled as "beer-fiddler"; his wife Dorota came from another musical clan, the Brixis (see 870). František, better known as "Franz," was the oldest son among twelve children, three others of whom had musical careers, the most notable being Jiří, or "Georg" [824]. Much of what we know of Franz is owing to a charming autobiographical sketch he wrote in 1763. At nine he became a choirboy at the abbey church of St. Nicholas in Prague and was enrolled at the Jesuit school. Two years later, though the Jesuits tried to prevent him by taking away his coat, he ran away to join the Electoral Chapel in Dresden. But after some months, he grew homesick and tried to sneak home; he was caught but developed such a case of laryngitis that his career seemed over, and he was sent home anyhow. There he was cured with an infusion of alcoholic beverage and was sent to the Altstädter Seminary in Prague, with whose choir he sang in Fux's [585] *Costanza e fortezza* at Charles VI's royal coronation in 1723; but shortly afterwards his voice changed and he went home once more. Having fallen in love with the burgomaster's daughter, Benda petitioned the local count to be allowed to become a gingerbread baker (in order to be worthy of her). The count, however, paid his way back to Prague to study violin with a certain Koniček; Benda says he also learned a great deal by following around a blind Jewish street musician named Lebel or Löbel. After ten weeks of study, Benda's master told him he was ready for employment. He had no trouble finding it, but after shifting from one noble household to another without attaining true happiness, he and a fellow violinist named Georg Czarth ran off to Warsaw, with the gendarmes hard at their heels all the way to the border, and holed up in an abandoned palace. Eventually Benda and his friends (two others had joined them) were hired as the nucleus of a chamber orchestra by a provincial governor named Suchakwenski, with Benda as nominal *Kapellmeister.* After a couple of years, he was auditioned for a vacancy in the Warsaw *Kapelle* of Augustus II, the Strong, and accepted. Though his employer tried to retain him with threats and promises, he went to the court in 1732 and discovered to his dismay that he had lost money by so doing. The next year the king died, and Benda returned to Dresden as part of the household of Count Brühl, formerly viceroy in Poland. Soon thereafter, on the recommendation of his friend Quantz [730], he was summoned to Ruppin to be a violinist for Prince Frederick of Prussia. On his first day there, Frederick heard him practicing, ordered him to court, and accompanied him himself. He was immediately sent to study with the brothers Graun [751, 757] that he might compose with facility. He moved with the establishment to Rheinsberg in 1736 after the prince married. Meanwhile Frederick had been farming Benda out to his favorite sister Wilhelmine, Markgräfin of Bayreuth [781], and in her service he met one of the princess's attendants, Eleonore Stephein, whom he married in 1739. Their union got off to an inauspicious start when a fire in Rheinsberg destroyed their lodgings and all their possessions, but the next year they moved to Berlin when Frederick became king, and were established at Potsdam. There Frederick met Benda's visiting father, and, finding himself in Benatek while on campaign in 1742, invited the whole tribe to move to Potsdam at his expense. Two of Franz's sons became violinists at the Prussian court, and his daughter Juliane, a singer and composer, married Johann Friedrich Reichardt [980]. When his wife died, he married her sister Caroline. Franz's parents celebrated their golden wedding in 1756 at the Czech colony of Nowawes near Potsdam. When he wrote his autobiography, Benda estimated that he had accompanied his king in at least 10,000 concerts. In 1771 he was given the title of *Konzertmeister.* Supposedly gout, from which he suffered

many years, terminated his playing in the 1760s, but music historian Charles Burney, who visited the court in 1772, said his expressiveness brought tears to his (Burney's) eyes.

Benda, who came late to composition, and who must have had little time for it, left 17 symphonies, a score of concerti, and a number of sonatas and other chamber works. He notes also that a wealthy admirer of his music made it worth his while to withhold it from publication. All of his music is harmonically simple, and he himself laments his ignorance of counterpoint, but the charm lies in the singing quality and the wealth of free-flowing melody. The manuscripts of his sonatas often have the embellishments notated, providing a valuable insight into performance practice. Because many of the mss. are signed merely "Benda," it is not always easy to determine which brother wrote which piece.

RECORDINGS: Milan Munclinger has recorded ten of the symphonies. There is also a flute concerto played by Jean-Pierre Rampal, a violin sonata by Sándor Károlyi, and a piece for mechanical harp played by Franz Haselböck (on an organ).

[777] **RICHTER, Franz Xaver** (Rēkh'-ter, Frànts Eks-à'-ver)
SINGER, CONDUCTOR
BORN: December 1, 1709
DIED: Strasbourg, September 12, 1789

Though Richter apparently came from Bohemia, there is no record of him there; nor do modern Czech publications, always punctilious about such matters, list his name in a Czech form. In fact nothing concrete is known about him until 1740, when he became assistant *Kapellmeister* to the abbot of the old Benedictine monastery at Kempten in southern Swabia. In 1743, the year he married Maria Anna Josefa Moz there, some interesting things were taking place a hundred or so miles to the northwest, in Mannheim. Duke Karl Theodor had just become Elector Palatine and had set about immediately to build a first-rate musical establishment. The result was not only an opera company and chapel but also what amounted to the first modern symphony orchestra in Europe, directed initially by Richter's countryman J. W. A. Stamitz [810]. Richter was apparently hired there in 1747, though some accounts say that he was moonlighting up to 1750 when the abbot fired him for too many absences. It is also said that he served as a violinist, though one finds him listed only as a singer *(basso).* He was treated well, was permitted to travel, and was appointed court composer in 1768, but it is said that he was not happy with the avant-garde approach to music there and only a year later went to Strasbourg to spend his last two decades as director of the cathedral choir.

Richter was indeed conservative, though he was *au courant* to the tune of around 80 symphonies. His Baroque inclinations are shown perhaps most typically in his considerable body of church music (around 40 Masses alone). Though he sang in operas, he apparently did not write in the medium. But being where he was, he could hardly avoid being affected by the virtuosity of the instrumentalists with whom he was surrounded nor the currents that passed through the court from outside. Thus modern listeners seem to find his orchestral music fresher than did his contemporaries, nor can one overlook his 6 string quartets, which some think preceded Joseph Haydn's [871].

RECORDINGS: Some of the string quartets have been recorded by the Vienna Concentus Musicus, the New Music and Oistersek Quartets, and others. There are also recordings of symphonies by Boris Brott and Wolfgang Hofmann and of concerti by Jean-Pierre Rampal (flute), Maurice André (trumpet), and Lajos Lencses (oboe).

[778] HAMAL, Jean-Noël (Ä-mäl′, Zhàn Nō-el′)
MUSIC DIRECTOR
BORN: Liège, December 23, 1709
DIED: Liège, November 26, 1778

Hamal's father, Henri-Guillaume (1685–1752), himself a composer, was Master of the Boys at the Cathedral of St. Lambert, where Jean-Noël served as a choirboy. He studied with his father and with the choir director Henri Dupont, and later attended the local Jesuit college. In 1728 the chapter sent him to the Liège College in Rome, where he remained until 1731. Some accounts say that he was ordained there. At any rate, on his return he was given a benefice ànd resumed his place in the choir. One of his colleagues for a few months shortly afterward was a young *basso* named Ludwig van Beethoven, who later moved on to the electoral court at Bonn, where he became grandsire to a more famous namesake. In 1738 the younger Hamal was elevated to the directorship, which he held, despite a number of vicissitudes, for the next thirty-three years. At about the same time he and his father inaugurated a series of *concerts spir-*

ituels at the city hall. In 1745 Hamal was named an honorary Imperial Chaplain. Four years later, deciding he needed to update his musical knowledge or perhaps take a rest, he returned for some months in Italy, where he conversed with, among others, Niccolò Jommelli (1714–74) and Francesco Durante [678].

Such gallivanting did not, however, sit well with the authorities, who began to mutter about neglect of duty. It seems there was some justice on their side, for in devoting himself to composition, not all of it sacred, he had let the choir go to pot. In 1743 he had published a set of so-called *ouvertures,* which were really symphonies very close to the classical mold. Later (1757–58) he turned out 4 comic operas to libretti in the local Walloon dialect. In 1760 the chapter had him locked up in a monastery to reconsider. But within the year Hamal had got himself reinstated and relieved of irksome duties, no doubt to the joy of his townsmen, who were now calling him the "Pergolesi of Liège." In 1771 he retired in favor of his nephew Henri [932], but continued to write until a stroke felled him in 1778. Two years before, André Grétry [919] said that Hamal was the only important musician that Paris lacked. Besides the works noted, Hamal left a very large body of sacred music and some other instrumental works.

RECORDINGS: Géry Lemaire has recorded a symphony and a *grand* motet, *In exitu Israel.*

[779] CORRETTE, Michel (Côr-ret′, Mĕ-shel′)
ORGANIST, TEACHER
BORN: Rouen, 1709
DIED: Paris, January 22, 1795

Son of the organist Gaspard Corrette, Michel Corrette, some argue, was born at a later date than that given and at St. Germain-en-Laye. At any rate, he himself is said to have been organist at a Rouen church in 1725, but soon thereafter went to Paris where, in 1733, he saw his ballet *Les Âges* staged and married Marie-Catherine Morize. What else we know about him is largely limited to a chronology of jobs and publications. From 1737 he was successively organist to the Grand Prior of France, the Jesuit College in Paris, the Prince of Conti (Louis-François de Bourbon), the church of Ste. Marie-Madeleine, and the Duke of Angoulême. He seems to have been a tireless composer—or rather arranger, for much of his music is based on the hits of the day, and what isn't is not very interesting. Perhaps his best-known works are the 22 surviving *concerts comiques* for three melody instruments and continuo, which use popular song themes to construct real, if fairly simple-minded, concerti. In the same vein are some concerti based on *noëls* and the curious *Le Phénix* for four bassoons. His last set of violin sonatas offers a new and prophetic point of view to that genre: the keyboard is dominant, the violin subsidiary; it is instructed to observe that fact by playing at half volume. One of his organ books "in a new genre" contains pieces with titles like "The Seven-League Boots" and "The Taking of Jericho." During the American Revolution, Corrette produced a piano piece called *Les Échos de Boston,* and he wrote an orchestral imitation of the Rouen carillon to be appended to Jean Gilles's [614] *Requiem.* But Corrette is perhaps most important for his interestingly anecdotal methods for keyboards, strings, flute, oboe, bassoon, hurdy-gurdy, voice, etc., of which he published no fewer than 20. It is said that the popularity of his cello method spelled the doom of the viola da gamba. RECORDINGS: Extended samplings of the concerts comiques have been recorded by Jacques Roussel and by Jean-Pierre Rampal. Gérard Cartigny has recorded one of the carol-concerti and the ballet *Les Âges,* and there have been several versions of *Le Phénix.*

[780] SCHAFFRATH, Christoph (Shåf'-råt, Krēs'-tōf)
HARPSICHORDIST, ORGANIST
BORN: Hohenstein-am-Elbe, 1709
DIED: Berlin, February 17, 1763

Born in a village near Dresden, Schaffrath was, in 1733, one of the unsuccessful seekers after the organist's job in the Sophienkirche there. (It was won by Wilhelm Friedemann Bach [784].) At that time Schaffrath was in the employ of a Polish Prince Sangusko, doubtless as a consequence of the elector's having been made King of Poland ("Augustus the Strong") in the same year. Two years later, Schaffrath set off down a path that was well-trodden by Grauns, Bendas, and others: to wit, he joined the musical entourage of Crown Prince Frederick of Prussia at his Rheinsberg estate. Later they all went to Potsdam and lived happily ever after—though one supposes there must have been some rivalry between Schaffrath and Carl Philipp Emanuel Bach [801], who was also a harpsichordist. Though not one of the first-magnitude stars among Frederick's men, Schaffrath was a fairly prolific composer in most of the instrumental forms. In his latter years, he was in the particular service of the king's sister, Princess Amalie. RECORDINGS: Uwe Zipperling and Hugo Ruf have recorded an *Adagio* for gamba and continuo. There is also a recording of a *Duetto in D Minor* for two bass viols.

[781] WILHELMINE, Markgräfin von Bayreuth (Vil-hel-mē'-nə)
BORN: Berlin, 1709
DIED: Bayreuth, 1758

The daughter of Frederick William I of Prussia and Queen Sophie Dorothee, daughter of George I of England, Wilhelmine was older than her brother Frederick by three years. Nonetheless, she was his favorite sister, for not only did she share his love for music, she also detested her father's stuffy and tyrannical ways. Scheduled to marry her cousin, the Prince of Wales (George II's Frederick, who did not live to be king), she had the rug pulled from under her when her brother tried to arrange his own marriage with Frederick's sister. Later she went to Bayreuth to marry the Markgraf, and though it turned out to be 150 years too early to catch the Holy German Wagner Festival, she consoled herself by writing a very nice harpsichord concerto. RECORDINGS: Hilde Langfort has recorded the harpsichord concerto.

[782] PERGOLESI, Giovanni Battista (Pâr-gō-lā'-zē, Jō-vàn'-nē Bàt-tēs'-tà)
VIOLINIST
BORN: Iesi, January 4, 1710
DIED: Pozzuoli, March 16, 1736

There is probably more confusion about the life and works of poor Giovanni Pergolesi than over those of any other reasonably well-known composer. To start with, he had only slightly more claim to his surname than Giovanni Pierluigi did to Palestrina [201]. His grandfather, a shoemaker named Draghi, from Pergola, a town about twenty miles south of Pesaro, married a daughter of Iesi (or Jesi), about the same distance east of Pergola, and settled there. Insularity being what it is, his family was known to the natives as "I Pergolesi"—the people from Pergola. The composer's father, a surveyor named Francesco Andrea Draghi, and his wife, *née* Anna Vittoria di Pompilia Giorgi, produced two boys and a girl who went into the baptismal register as "Draghi" and died. Whether Francesco Andrea bowed to the inevitable or whether the registrar did what came naturally, the fourth and last child, sickly and with a deformed leg, was listed as "Giovanni Battista Pergolesi." This much of the story brooks no argument.

The history of Pergolesi's upbringing and education is, however, less certain. Various stories have him taught by various musicians and prominent citizens of Iesi, of purely local interest, and some of them may be right. Supposedly the boy showed almost Mozartian precocity and was duly sent down to Naples to study at the Conservatorio dei Poveri di Jesu Cristo, and there is reasonable evidence that a local Marchese Cardolo Pianetti footed the bill. There is no Pergolesi on the conservatory rosters for the period in question, but for 1729–30 there is a student listed as "Iesi," which is in keeping with the school's habit of identifying students by their place of origin. Assuming him to have gone there in his early to middle teens, he would have studied under directors Gaetano Greco, Leonardo Vinci [712], and Francesco Durante [678]. He was still a student in 1731 when his religious drama on the conversion of St. Guilhem of Aquitaine was produced at a Neapolitan monastery—apparently as a sort of senior thesis, since Pergolesi was on his own later that year, when he received a commission for an opera. Owing in part to the exigencies of production, the result, Salustia, flopped when it was put on at the Teatro San Bartolomeo the following February.

The composer's father died that same year (his mother had preceded him five years earlier), and his possessions were sold to cover his debts. Meanwhile, Pergolesi had become maestro di cappella to a court official, Prince Stigliano. In September he had an enormous success with a comedy Lo Frate 'nnamorato (The Monk in Love), but its run was interrupted for several months of atonement following a severe earthquake. His next new work was an opera seria entitled Il Prigionier superbo (The Haughty Prisoner) in the fall of 1733. It was, as they say, no big deal, but the two-character intermezzo that played between the acts, La Serva padrona (The Maid as Boss) was to make history. In 1734 Pergolesi was made maestro di cappella to the municipality—presumably as deputy to Domenico Sarro [658], who had been given the chief post in 1728. But at that point the Spanish arrived under Carlos de Bourbon to drive out the Austrians, who had seized Naples in 1707, and Pergolesi apparently left for Rome with his prince. There was a festival performance there of his Mass in F Major from which he emerged as music director to its sponsor,

the Duke of Maddaloni, and returned to Naples. There he produced another unsuccessful opera seria, entitled Adriano in Siria, for the queen mother's birthday, accompanied by another sparkling intermezzo, La Contadina astuta (The Wily Peasant Girl). The next winter he went back to Rome to produce L'Olimpiade (The Olympiad), but production difficulties pretty much negated its good qualities, and to add insult to injury, a member of the audience hit the composer in the head with an orange—or so the story goes. (The work was later successful elsewhere.)

Whether the orange contributed to Pergolesi's physical decline from that point is impossible to say. He returned to Naples, allegedly became organist to the Chapel Royal, produced a last comedy, Il Flaminio, in the autumn of 1735, turned over his belongings to his aunt, who kept house for him, and retired to Pozzuoli (later famed as Sophia Loren's birthplace) to a Franciscan monastery that was under the protection of his patron. There he died about two months later—tradition says of tuberculosis—at the age of twenty-six.

La Serva padrona soon began to gain currency as the little masterpiece it is. (Until the recent Monteverdi revival, it was the oldest opera regularly played.) Eventually performance in Paris by an Italian troupe in 1752 ignited the silly Querelle des Bouffons (Quarrel of the Buffoons) over Italian versus French again, which in the end made comic opera all the rage. It also made its composer legendary, and all sorts of music he had never heard of was offered as his. The so-called complete edition published at the outset of World War II contains more music than he could have written in good health and working a sixteen-hour day.

RECORDINGS: Much that appears on record under the name of Pergolesi is spurious. The opera Il Geloso schernito (The Jealous Man Mocked) is really by one Chiarini and Il Maestro di musica is a pastiche. As a rule, most of the instrumental works are suspect. The trio sonatas, of which there are several recordings, are later than Pergolesi, and are said to be by a Venetian, Domenico Gallo. A remarkable set of concertini is now known to be by Unico Wilhelm van Wassenaer (1692–1766). Neither are the flute concerti his, nor the two arias long claimed for him, "Tre giorni son che Nina" and "Se tu m'ami." On the other hand, most of the church music is genuine, though recordings of the Stabat Mater (for two sopranos and strings) often add a gratuitous choir. There are several recordings of the C-minor Salve regina, one by Angelo Ephrikian of the

Missa di gloria, one by Giulio Bertoia of motets, several of *La Serva padrona,* one by Ennio Gerelli of *La Contadina* (as *"Livietta e Tracollo"),* and one of the cantata *Orfeo* by Newell Jenkins.

[783] ARNE, Thomas Augustine
VIOLINIST, HARPSICHORDIST, FLUTIST
BORN: London, March 12, 1710
DIED: London, March 5, 1778

Thomas Arne was a good tunesmith. When one considers that his is the best-known name in English music between Purcell [581] and Elgar [1499], one gets a fair notion of the state of English music over a two-century stretch.

The son of a well-to-do Covent Garden upholsterer, Arne was sent to Eaton, and then, to suit his station in life, was placed in the office of a London solicitor for on-the-job law training. But he quickly learned that he preferred making music to soliciting, and followed that path deviously, in disguise (as a liveried servant in the gallery at the opera) and by subterfuge (practice on a muffled harpsichord and clandestine lessons with the German violinist Michael Festing, a Geminiani [693] pupil). Eventually the inevitable happened: Arne Senior encountered his son playing first fiddle at a private concert. The usual struggle followed, but the father soon gave it up, recognizing that his son had a real talent and a real vocation.

Thomas Arne's chief interest was the stage, and the performance of his works was sometimes a sort of family project. A younger brother appeared in his *Rosamond* of 1733 and in the title role of his 1733 musical setting of Henry Fielding's *Tom Thumb* (as *The Opera of Operas).* Arne taught his sister Susanna Maria to sing well enough to appear in several of his pieces, before she became, as Mrs. Cibber (daughter-in-law of Colley Cibber, the playwright), one of the great tragediennes of her time. In 1737 he married another singer, Cecilia Young, daughter of the organist of All Hallows, Barking-by-the-Tower. When her chronic ill health permitted, Cecilia appeared in some of his more famous pieces. (Arne is said, however, to have treated her wretchedly, finally abandoning her in Dublin in 1756, where she was later described as "an object of compassion." Arne's composer-son Michael [916] was apparently not her child. Late in their lives, however, the couple made up.)

Arne had his first great successes in 1740 with his setting of Congreve's masque *The Judgment of Paris,* and, a bit later that year,

with another such work, *Alfred,* a patriotic effusion whose finale was "Rule, Britannia," beloved of makers of films about the British Navy. Over the years Arne was connected with various London theaters (Drury Lane, the Haymarket, Covent Garden), turning out more than 50 operas and other "musicals," and supplying incidental music for many plays, including a number of Shakespeare's. He also furnished countless songs for entertainment in the popular pleasure gardens of Marylebone ("Marlybone"), Ranelagh, and Vauxhall ("Voxhall"). Among his stage pieces, one should note particularly the updated version of Milton's masque *Comus,* 1738; *Thomas and Sally,* 1760, a much-admired and much-imitated musical comedy of a jolly tar who rescues his sweetheart from a lecherous squire (libretto by Isaac Bickerstaffe); and two works from 1762—*Artaxerxes,* Arne's most successful excursion into virtuoso Italian opera; and a highly successful ballad-opera, *Love in a Village.* He also produced 2 oratorios, of which one, *The Death of Abel* (from the Metastasio text made famous by Leonardo Leo [718]) was premiered in 1743 on the first of his three stays in Dublin. As a Catholic, Arne is also said to have written some Masses, but they have vanished.

In 1759 the University of Oxford conferred on Thomas Arne an honorary doctorate, providing the reason why he has ever since been known as "Dr. Arne." And ten years later he set David Garrick's ode on Shakespeare for the 200th-birthday celebration (five years late) at Stratford. In 1777 he took poor, ailing Cecilia back to his bosom, but he died the next spring, a week before he would have attained the age of sixty-eight. He was buried at St. Paul's, Covent Garden, near his birthplace.

RECORDINGS: Apart from "Rule, Britannia," recorded by Peter Pears in its stirring but ultimately tedious original form, Arne is remembered chiefly for his Shakespeare songs, which, however inauthentic in style, are probably the most familiar of all such settings. There are innumerable recordings, though one should take note perhaps of a whole LP disc by Maureen Forrester and Alexander Young that includes a selection from the Garrick *Ode. Thomas and Sally* has been twice recorded—by the Intimate Opera Company under Frederick Woodhouse and by a group directed by Simon Preston. There is also a complete recording of the musical portions of *Comus* by Anthony Lewis, and such divas as Marilyn Horne, Beverly Sills, and Joan Sutherland have given us selections from *Artaxerxes.*

Two cantatas have been recorded by Robert Tear.

Of Arne's small body of instrumental music, Christopher Hogwood has recorded the 8 "overtures" (both Lullyan [517] and Italian in style), and Kenneth Montgomery the 4 symphonies (i.e., sinfonias), among the earliest English explorations of these forms. Hogwood, as harpsichordist, has also recorded the 8 "Sonatas or Lessons"—the earliest published examples of English keyboard sonatas.

[784] BACH, Wilhelm Friedemann (Bàkh, Vil'-helm Frē'-də-màn)
ORGANIST, VIOLINIST, TEACHER
BORN: Weimar, November 22, 1710
DIED: Berlin, July 1, 1784

It was apparently insufficient to the Fates that things should go badly for Wilhelm Friedemann Bach in his lifetime. Beginning with the generation that followed his, he was besmirched with irresponsible gossip and idle fabrication until the nineteenth century wrote him off for being that worst of sinners in the Victorian canon: a dissipator. (A dissipator was, as often as not, a respectable man caught having a drink in public.) In the twentieth century, the German composer Paul Graener (1872–1944) wrote an opera, *Friedemann Bach* (premiered in 1931), perpetuating these legends, including the one showing Bach as a tattered itinerant musician. And the cloud still hovers, though these days he is taxed with such things as egocentricity, individualism, and eccentricity.

Friedemann—or "Friede," as his father called him—was the oldest son of Johann Sebastian [684] and Maria Barbara (Catherine Dorothea was two years older, Carl Philipp Emanuel [801] four years younger). He had his earliest schooling at the gymnasium in Cöthen, in which city his mother died when he was ten. Perhaps this last fact intensified his father's concern and affection for him. In that same year Sebastian set about giving him a thorough musical grounding, at first making up a notebook of easy keyboard pieces for his practice and later writing such exemplary works for him as the *Little Preludes*, the inventions, and the *Well-Tempered Clavier*. When Sebastian made his move to Leipzig, it was partly with an eye to Friedemann's studying at the university. And, having graduated valedictorian from the Thomasschule, and taken a year out to study violin with J. G. Graun [751] in Merseburg, that is exactly what Friedemann did.

Father and son were very close, enjoying an easy intimacy that none of the other children seem to have shared in. When Sebastian traveled, Friedemann traveled with him—often to Dresden, for example, and in 1747 up to Berlin to visit Emanuel and the Prussian court. It was Friedemann that Sebastian sent to Halle to invite the visiting Handel [683] to come to Leipzig in 1729. (Family problems prevented his accepting.) Since Friedemann's life began seriously to fall apart after his father's death, it seems not unreasonable to think that he found himself helpless out from under the paternal umbrella. Not that he lacked the brains. Evidence suggests that Friedemann had the keenest intellect of all the young Bachs, and perhaps it was the curse of being able to see things as they really were that lay behind his increasing withdrawal and misanthropy.

But at first he found the runway greased for him. In 1733 he applied (in a formula drafted by Sebastian) for the organist's post at the Sophienkirche (Lutheran, naturally) in Dresden. The "competition" seems to have been a put-up job; he won without a struggle. Nor was the job a demanding one. It gave him a good deal of time to compose and to taste the cultural delights of Frederick August's glittering capital. And he quickly established himself as a demonic performer—contemporary hyperbole extends to—"the greatest organist who ever lived." But he was not satisfied—perhaps because as a Lutheran he was the odd-man-out in a fiercely Catholic city, or possibly because he did not have a clubbable nature. To be sure, his salary was small, but he was unmarried, and the lessons he gave (e.g., to Johann Gottlieb Goldberg for whom Sebastian wrote the famous variations) made up the deficit. But after thirteen years, learning that there was a vacancy in Halle at the Church of Our Dear Lady (Unserer Lieben Frauenkirche), the former bailiwick of Scheidt and Zachau, he applied. This time there was not even a pretense of a competition: he was hired forthwith.

Halle, however, was as narrowly Protestant as Dresden had been expansively Catholic, and Friedemann soon found himself on the wrong side of the elders—not for sins, but for lapses, such as staying too long in Berlin or going to Leipzig in 1750 to wind up his dead father's affairs. In 1751 he married at last. The bride was Dorothea Elisabeth Georgi, the spinster daughter of a local tax collector, and over the next five years she bore him three children. Only the last, Friederike Sophie, survived infancy. Meanwhile, Friedemann had competed for a vacancy in Zittau with Sebastian's favorite pupil Johann Ludwig Krebs [798], his own brother Emanuel, and their brother-in-law Johann Christoph Altnikol (1719–59): a fellow named Johann Trier got the job. In 1762 (Friedemann was now fifty-two) he was offered the late Christoph Graupner's [673] place as *Kapellmeister* to the court of Hesse-Darmstadt. No one knows just what happened; but, in the vernacular, he blew it. In 1764, with no clear prospects, he resigned the Halle post. (His longest stint, it won him the identifying sobriquet among Sebastian's sons as "the Halle Bach.") In his years there he turned out some interesting pupils, notably Friedrich Wilhelm Rust [904] and a distant cousin, Johann Christian Bach [886], known as "the Clavier Bach."

Then the drifting began. In 1771, having unloaded his wife's real estate in Halle, the Bachs moved, for reasons unknown, to Braunschweig. There was no job there and Friedemann was sixty-one. In June a Wolfenbüttel competition jury awarded him the post at the Aegidiuskirche, but he was rejected by the authorities because of his advanced years. In 1773, he sold off a number of Sebastian's manuscripts and eventually took his family to Berlin (which Emanuel had fled long before). There, for ten years, he led a wretched hand-to-mouth existence, and his desperate forgeries of his father's name on a few of his own manuscripts (and vice versa) should hardly be held against him (though they are regularly cited as testimony to his amorality). Like Emanuel, he died of a respiratory illness. Dorothea Elisabeth dragged on until 1791. Friederike eventually married a Johann Schmidt and died in 1801.

If Friedemann Bach won great fame as an organist in his lifetime, he did not do so as a composer. His very few publications (and his abortive announcements of a few more) seem to have elicited little or no interest. Even today, when he has his defenders, there is nothing wholehearted about their defense; and his modern detractors attack equally his alleged mechanistic and old-fashioned imitation of his father and his alleged overindulgence in emotionalism. Compared with the phonographic attention lavished on Emanuel and Christian, that directed to Friedemann seems puny indeed.

Part of the problem is that he was not very productive. The 21 church cantatas are his largest works—and, with one or two exceptions, among his most backward-looking. (An unfinished opera is lost.) Of the 5 and a fraction concerti for one clavier and orchestra, and the 1 for two (and orchestra), a couple show him at perhaps his best— quite *au courant* with the formal develop-

ments of his time. The 9 symphonies are a mixed bag, ranging from a one-movement prelude and a Lullyan [517] *ouverture* (adagio and fugue), through some rather unambitious affairs for strings, to a single work (in F major, F. 67) that shows a good understanding of the modern orchestra. Friedemann seems, however, happier with small forms. The so-called polonaises for piano and some of the duos for flute are clearly the work of an ingenious and superbly trained talent, and are real charmers. The keyboard fantasias and some of the double handful of keyboard sonatas show the *Empfindsamkeit* in which he could surpass even Emanuel in depth of feeling. The Sonata for two keyboards is perhaps his best and most forward-looking work in that form—it was long ascribed to Sebastian, it being known only from his manuscript. The little contrapuntal pieces show him his father's true disciple, but late fantasias and the viola duets and the very few other late works show him short on inspiration and long on inchoate babbling.

RECORDINGS: Various of the symphonies have been recorded by Raffael Adler, Louis de Froment, Günther Kehr, Karl Ristenpart, Kurt Redel, Helmut Müller-Bruhl, and others. Helma Elsner has recorded the polonaises, John Newmark some of the fantasias and fugues, Jean-Pierre Rampal with Samuel Baron (and Rampal with various others) have recorded some of the 5 trios for flutes and continuo. Karen Philips and Walter Trampler have recorded the viola duos. The Concerto for 2 Solo Claviers may be heard from Huguette Dreyfus and Luciano Sgrizzi, and from Arwed Henking and Herman Maihöfer. The Concerto in E-flat for Clavier and Strings is played by Daniel Pinkham, that in C minor by Robert Veyron Lacroix, and the two-clavier-and-strings work by the Concentus Musicus. A cantata, *Erzittert und fallet,* is performed under the direction of Helmut Rilling. There is also a two-record set of the complete organ music by Leo van Doeselaar.

[785] ALBERTI, Domenico (Àl-bâr'-tē, Dō-mā'-nē-kō)
SINGER (?), HARPSICHORDIST
BORN: Venice, c. 1710 (?)
DIED: Rome, 1740 (?)

The most reliable evidence we have for the existence of Domenico Alberti is his name on a set of popular keyboard sonatas published by John Walsh in London in 1748— and even this is open to question. The dates given for his birth and death are no more than scholarly deductions—these based on the somewhat romanticized notion that he died young (some would place his demise at age twenty-three). No mention of him during his supposed lifetime has ever been encountered. His "biography" consists of embroidery on a sketch written long after 1740. According to it, he spent most of his life, from adolescence, with the Venetian embassies in Spain and Rome. He played (they say) beautifully but sang even better. He had an untrained voice, and when he made his *passeggiata* at twilight through the Roman streets, caroling like a bird, great crowds followed him, and the professionals despaired lest he decide to try out at the opera. Some accounts tell us that he did, in fact, appear in some operas in Rome, but not that there was any ensuing explosion in the operatic world.

So all we have of Alberti is 14 more or less authentic two-movement keyboard sonatas (including the 8 that were published), and 10 single movements. To complicate the picture, around the time of Alberti's supposed death, a *castrato* called Giuseppe Jozzi was caught red-handed palming off some Alberti pieces as his own. Though he was run out of the country, he published some of them under his own name in Holland. Supposedly Walsh published his set at the request of a wealthy Venetian who owned most of the Alberti manuscripts, to rectify misapprehensions of their authorship.

What is all the fuss about? Well, depending on whom you talk with, Alberti had (or didn't have) a major role in the development of the keyboard sonata. To be sure, he was one of the earlier Italians to write keyboard sonatas. But too much has been made of the notion that he established a pattern of contrasting movements, or that by recapitulating the first section of some movements (A-B-A'), he heralded sonata-allegro form. More tenable perhaps is the argument that he promoted the "singing" allegro—i.e., that his fast movements were conceived in terms of melodic form. (The arguments against this view are too complex to be set forth here.) Finally there is the "Alberti bass." Some scholars, in a debunking mood, say that broken or arpeggiated chords in the left hand were by then old stuff. But no one seems to have found anyone before Alberti using that pattern in eighths or sixteenths familiar to all Mozart players: *ta-dee-tee-de* or, for example, C-G-E-G.

RECORDINGS: Luciano Sgrizzi has recorded two of the sonatas.

[786] **EXAUDET, André-Joseph** (Eks-ō-dā', Ản-drā' Zhō-zef')
VIOLINIST
BORN: Rouen, c. 1710
DIED: Paris, 1762

Exaudet rises full-blown in 1744 as concertmaster of the Rouen Opera orchestra and sometime violinist in orchestras of the Paris fairs. Five years later he was taken into the Opéra in Paris, and two years after that into the Concert Spirituel. At some time before 1758 he received a court appointment as well, and he was violin teacher to the household of the Prince de Condé. His 18 sonatas and 1 concerto suggest that he was as accomplished a violinist as he was said to be. Exaudet lives on through a piece known as the *Menuet d'Exaudet,* which exists in innumerable arrangements. RECORDINGS: The *Menuet* was often recorded, in the early days of the phonograph, by such singers as Charles Gilibert and Emilio de Gogorza, in a version by Weckerlin [1277]: it is really the finale of his first trio sonata from Op. 2.

[787] **BOYCE, William**
ORGANIST, EDITOR
BORN: London, c. September 1, 1711
DIED: Kensington, February 7, 1779

An exact contemporary of Thomas Arne [783], Boyce's career sometimes paralleled his and occasionally crossed it. If Arne was the most famous English composer between Purcell [581] and Elgar [1499], Boyce was, in the opinion of many, the best. Some of his forebears belonged to the Worshipful Company of Joiners (i.e., woodworkers). When, at twelve, young William was chirruping in the choir of St. Paul's Cathedral under the direction and tutelage of Charles King, his father was appointed beadle (or, as we would say, building superintendent) of Joiners' Hall, where Boyce is said to have lived until around midcentury. At fifteen or sixteen he was apprenticed to Maurice Greene [727], the Cathedral's organist, and himself became organist at Oxford Chapel in Cavendish Square in 1734. Two years later he was named composer to the Chapel Royal and appointed organist at St. Michael's, Cornhill. During this period he went through a course of study with the learned Dr. Pepusch [611], which immeasurably improved his feeling for old music, and taught the harpsichord at various schools. In 1737 he was made conductor of the so-called music meeting held annually by the cathedral choirs of Gloucester, Hereford, and Worcester; founded at least a dozen years earlier, and now called the Three Choirs Festival, this is the oldest music festival still extant in England.

Boyce's next big year seems to have been 1749, when he added the churches of All Hallows Great and Less, Thames Street, to his organ-playing responsibilities, composed the ode for the installation of the Duke of Newcastle as Chancellor of Cambridge University, and was awarded the degrees of B. Mus. and D. Mus. by that institution. During the 1740s and early 1750s, he also wrote a good deal of music for plays given at Drury Lane—where he seems, figuratively, to have trod on Arne's toes—and many songs for the London pleasure gardens. Around 1748 he took unto himself a wife, known to history only as Hannah, who presented him with a daughter and a son, born, in that order, fifteen years apart. In 1755 Greene, his old organ teacher, died, leaving him his collection of old "cathedral music," his post as conductor of the Sons of the Clergy Festival, and, after a two-year delay, his Mastership of the King's Music. In 1758 Boyce became one of the three organists of the Chapel Royal.

Between 1760 and 1778, Boyce brought out his monumental *Cathedral Music,* three volumes of works by other English composers, which, though it sold badly, has since been recognized as perhaps his most important achievement. In later life he suffered from gout, and from an increasing deafness that eventually forced him to give up all his jobs except those at the court. He died, of causes unknown to us, at sixty-nine and was buried in the middle of the cathedral. Those who knew him remembered him as modest, just, and kindly. His son and namesake was a contrabass player.

RECORDINGS: Some of Boyce's church music lived on in practical use, and a song or two remained popular. The phonograph, however, has been largely to thank for a renewed interest in his other works, particularly his interesting instrumental music. Forty years ago the late Max Goberman created a stir by recording for a small company the 8 "symphonies" (i.e., three-movement *sinfonias* for plays and odes), in a version taken from the manuscripts, not from Constant Lambert's [2074] "improved" edition. Others—such as Karl Haas, Jörg Faerber, Yehudi Menuhin, Antonio Janigro, and Neville Marriner—have since brought out more modern recordings. Anthony Lewis has turned his attention to some of the overtures and ceremonial odes, and Adrian Shepherd to three *concerti grossi* and all of the overtures. In addition, Denis Stevens has edited and recorded two *con-*

certi grossi. Some of the anthems are to be found in English record catalogues.

[788] HOLZBAUER, Ignaz Jakob
(Hōltz'-bou-er, Ēg'-nåts Yä'-kōp)
MUSIC DIRECTOR
BORN: Vienna, September 17, 1711
DIED: Mannheim, April 7, 1783

Holzbauer is rightly identified as one of the more important of the Mannheim symphonists, though he was not primarily a symphonist, and it took him more than half a lifetime to get to Mannheim. The son of a merchant, he bucked parental wishes and learned music, largely by working out with the choristers at St. Stephen's and by assiduously studying Fux's [585] *Gradus ad Parnassum.* Later he met its author, who cheered him on. On the old man's recommendation, he went to Venice, then took service briefly (in the mid-1730s?) as *Kapellmeister* to a Count Rottal at Holešov, Bohemia. There he married an opera singer named Rosalie Andreides in 1737 and went off to Vienna with her to seek their fortunes. After another, much longer stay in Italy (the precise chronology of Holzbauer's early years is lacking), they came back to Vienna, then moved on to Stuttgart, where Holzbauer was appointed court *Kapellmeister* in 1751. There he wrote *Ipermestra,* his first opera (of 17), which was produced in the Palatine Elector's opera house at Schwetzingen. It apparently won him immediate appointment in 1753 as the Mannheim *Kapellmeister* and the direction of the finest orchestra in Europe. Apart from 2 ballets that he added to Hasse [736] operas in Vienna, Holzbauer produced all of his known music there. After his wife died in 1755, he made several more trips to Italy to see his operas staged there. The twenty-one-year-old Mozart [992] came to know him when he visited Mannheim in 1777 and was much taken with both him and his music. During his stay he attended a gala performance of Holzbauer's most-admired opera, *Günther von Schwarzburg* of 1776, said to be the first on a German subject by a German; and later, in Paris, he contributed some extra numbers (now lost) for a Holzbauer *Miserere* sung at the Concert Spirituel. A year later, Prince Karl Theodor having become, for want of any more Wittelsbach heirs, also the Elector of Bavaria, he moved his court to Munich. Holzbauer, plagued by increasing deafness, saw his usefulness at an end and remained behind. A year before he died, he drew up a brief autobiography.

Holzbauer's chief area of productivity

was that of sacred music, but much of that and most of the operas have vanished. His present reputation, however, rests on his orchestral music, and especially on his 30 or so surviving symphonies in an increasingly Classical style.

RECORDINGS: There are token recordings of the symphonies (e.g., by Boris Brott, Wolfgang Hofmann), a Concerto for Flute by the ubiquitous Jean-Pierre Rampal, the Double Concerto for Viola, Cello, Strings, and Continuo by the Capella Clementina, quintets by the Concentus Musicus of Vienna and members of the Winterthur Baroque Orchestra, and *3 Notturni* by the Winterthur ensemble.

[789] MONDONVILLE, Jean-Joseph
     Cassanéa de (Mon-don-vēl', Zhàn
     Zhō-zef' Kȧs-sà-nā'-à dә)
VIOLINIST, ADMINISTRATOR
BORN: Narbonne, c. December 25, 1711
DIED: Paris, October 8, 1772

Mondonville came from a poor but proud musical family. Like his younger brother Jean (later violinist in the Chapel Royal and composer), he studied with his father, an organist. By 1733 he had made his mark as a brilliant violinist at the Paris Concert Spirituel. His whereabouts during the next five years is uncertain, though he was in Lille for at least part of the time. He then settled in Paris, where he pursued his career as soloist and saw the first of his series of *grand* motets performed at the Spirituel. These works, produced over the next twenty years, were much admired in their day and after, though they now seem rather empty—the last popularized gasp of an outmoded form. His first attempt at the stage, the heroic pastoral *Isbé* of 1742, was, however, a failure.

In 1744, Mondonville, having served in an accessory capacity there for four years, was appointed intendant of the Chapel Royal, and about the same time took on executive duties at the Opéra and the Concert Spirituel. Four years later, he married the harpsichordist Anne-Jeanne Boucon; he was thirty-seven, she was forty—and very rich. It was apparently a good formula: after he died, she said he had been the perfect husband. The next year their only child, a son named Maximilien Joseph, was born, and Mondonville had a success with his opera *Le Carnaval du Parnasse (Carnival of Parnassus)*. When, three years later, Bambini's troupe's performance of Pergolesi's [782] *La Serva padrona* unleashed the silly *Querelle des Bouffons* (Quarrel of the Buffoons), La Pompadour, the King's mistress, saw to

it that Mondonville directed the pro-French forces. He attacked with *Titon et Aurore (Tithonus and Aurora)* in January 1753, sending the court ladies into ecstasies of patriotism. Something over two years later he enjoyed another success with *Daphnis et Alcimadure*, which featured Provençal folksongs in the *langue d'oc*. From 1755 to 1762 he acquitted himself with real distinction as director of the Concert Spirituel.

Mondonville's earliest works are regarded now as his best, and he is of some consequence in the history of violin music. His first four published opuses are violin sonatas. Op. 4 involves harmonics and contains the first published instructions for producing them. Opp. 3 and 5 are *Pièces de clavecin* with violin (and voice [!] in Op. 5), the point being that the keyboard player is regarded as full partner in the sonatas. He also wrote three oratorios, a genre largely unheard of in France since Marc-Antoine Charpentier [544], but they have been lost. There is said to exist a parody *cantate* set to the text of the royal printing license.

RECORDINGS: Recordings include sonatas played by Lars Fryden and Gustav Leonhardt, and the motet *Cantate Domino* led by Louis Martini. *Daphnis et Alcimadure* is performed in the original Provençal dialect under the baton of Louis Berthelon.

[790] OSWALD, James
DANCING MASTER, SINGER, PUBLISHER
BORN: 1711
DIED: Knebworth, 1769

A Scotsman true-blue in an age of Gaelic musical nationalism, Oswald began his career as a dancing master in Dunfermline. In 1736 he moved to Edinburgh and published a collection of minuets. He remained there five years, singing, teaching, and writing or arranging "Scots sangs," which he published under the pen name of "David Rizzio," thereby creating great confusion concerning the musical achievements of the real Rizzio [206]. In 1741 he evidently felt ready to take on London. There he worked as an arranger, taught ladies to sing, and offered to make anyone proficient in playing "Scots sangs" on any instrument in just twelve lessons. He somehow gained the patronage of Frederick Louis, the Prince of Wales, and may have taught the prince's son, later George III. In 1747 he set up his own printery and music shop. Somewhere along the way he founded a secret society, the Temple of Apollo, of which Dr. Charles Burney, music critic and historian, became a member. Among its stipulated mysteries was the reason why Oswald published works somehow connected with it under a pseudonym. (Oswald's personae play hob with identifying his work.) In the late 1740s and '50s, he wrote several masques and pantomimes, which may have been produced in or by the Temple. A mock cantata, *The Old Woman's Oratory or The Dust-Cart Cantata* played at the Haymarket in 1751. Apart from his song collections, Oswald published several volumes of pieces for one or two melody instruments and continuo, notably the *Airs for the Four Seasons* of 1755–56, each named after a flower. In 1761 George III appointed him royal chamber composer. He died in Hertfordshire eight years later. RECORDINGS: Scottish violinist Edna Arthur has recorded four of the flower pieces (including "Deadly Nightshade") and some of the anonymous song-variations she plays may be Oswald's. *The Old Woman's Oratory* has been recorded by the Intimate Opera Company.

[791] FREDERICK II (Frederick the Great)

FLUTIST, WRITER, KING OF PRUSSIA
BORN: Berlin, January 24, 1712
DIED: Potsdam, August 17, 1786

Frederick, whose grandfather Frederick I had promoted himself from the electorship of Brandenburg to the monarchy of Prussia, was the third son of Frederick William I, but the first to live to maturity. The father was a straitlaced martinet whose tastes ran to soldiering, drinking, and hunting, and who believed that subjection to Prussian discipline (to coin a phrase) would give the boy something called character. Frederick William was particularly alarmed by his son's tendencies to write poetry and play the flute. He disciplined him, when young Frederick showed real enthusiasm for a proposed marriage with Princess Amelia, daughter of George II of England, by calling the whole thing off. He disciplined him even more severely when the young man, heartily fed up, ran away: he threw him into solitary confinement, and had Frederick's friend Lieutenant Katte, who had helped him, decapitated in his presence. (A similar beheading before the court assembled had supposedly sent Dr. Pepusch [611] flying to England.) From that point on, Frederick was quite tractable. Little by little the strictures were loosened, and three years later, in 1733, he was married off to Elisabeth Christine of Brunswick-Bevern. The couple was settled on a large estate at Rheinsberg, a little way from Berlin, and left alone.

The marriage was a disaster: Frederick did not like his bride, was impolite and sarcastic with her, and saw as little of her as possible (they remained childless), though he gave her a handsome allowance, most of which she donated to charity. But apart from that, the crown prince was happy at Rheinsberg. He immediately began to build up his splendid musical establishment, which began with Quantz [730], who had been his flute teacher for some years since they had met in Dresden, and who remained virtually musical dictator at court. Later came the Graun brothers [751, 757], the Benda brothers [776, 824], Emanuel Bach [801], Christoph Schaffrath [780], and many others. The whole aggregation moved to Berlin when Frederick succeeded his father in 1740. For a long time thereafter, until the similarly named palace was built following the Seven Years War, headquarters were a mansion called Sans-Souci ("Carefree") in suburban Potsdam.

When it comes to German rulers, we have a tendency to visit the sins of the children upon their fathers, and, moreover, it is easy to laugh (as Voltaire did) at Frederick's pretensions to Frenchified culture. Nor does one find his power-politicking on the international scene particularly admirable. But there is no denying the fact that he was a good ruler and a remarkable man. He actively supported the arts and sciences (though he was never convinced that there was such a thing as German literature.) He did much good work among his people and took a special interest and pride in seeing justice done at all levels. He made Prussia strong, both militarily and economically, and left an enormous surplus in the treasury. On the personal level, however, he had the acid tongue and scathing wit that so often goes with high intelligence, and his last years were lonely ones.

Music played an enormous—even obsessive—role in Frederick's life. As well as building up a crack orchestra, he founded one of the finest opera companies in Europe. Two segments of his well-regimented day were given over to playing. For an hour or so in midmorning, he tootled on the flute while thinking out problems of state. And every evening at seven, except when he was on campaign, there was a concert, at which he was the star performer, and poor Emanuel Bach his unprotesting accompanist. It is clear that his senses of rhythm and intonation were not of virtuoso quality, and his had a repertoire of about 300 pieces (mostly by Quantz or himself) that he played in rotation, year in and year out. The concerts, like his other social functions at court, seem to have been rather uncomfortable affairs at which the attendance of the ladies was not encouraged. He insisted on checking out and revising opera libretti, often writing his own arias to be substituted, and wrote a number of libretti for Carl Heinrich Graun and others to set. As a poet he does not rank high, and his magnum opus (in French on the Art of War) is said to be one of the most tedious pieces ever written. He read philosophy avidly and, of course, brought Voltaire to Potsdam, but they could not resist using their ironic wit on each other, and the honeymoon was short. Frederick was an interesting thinker on governmental affairs, a professed atheist, and a Freemason.

Frederick studied composition with the youngest Graun (he also studied lute with Sylvius Leopold Weiss [691] but seems not to have written for it). Perhaps his best-known composition is the "royal theme" that underlies Johann Sebastian Bach's [684] *Musikalische Opfer,* sent to the king after Bach's 1747 visit to Potsdam. But Frederick also wrote (besides the operatic contributions noted) over 120 flute sonatas, several flute concertos, and other instrumental compositions. To paraphrase Dr. Johnson, one might suppose that the wonder is that it was done at all. But, overlooking his formal conservatism, one finds many of these pieces well-made and pleasing to the ear.

RECORDINGS: There is a disc of sonatas played by Marianne Steffen, and many other flutists have had a recorded go at a sonata or two (John Wummer, Jean-Pierre Rampal, Hans-Martin Linde, Maxence Larrieu, etc.) Linde and Camillo Wanausek have recorded concerti, and there is a *sinfonia* conducted by Emil Seiler and by Hans von Benda, a latter-day representative of the Sans-Souci family; four symphonies are performed by the Munich Pro Arte Orchestra.

[792] KAYSER, Isfrid (Kī'-zer, Ēz'-frēt)
PRIEST, MUSIC DIRECTOR
BORN: Türkheim-an-der-Wertach,
    March 13, 1712
DIED: Marchtal, March 1, 1771

Son and pupil of the schoolmaster-organist in a village near Augsburg, Kayser later studied in Munich, and at twenty joined the Premonstratensian monks at Marchtal near Ulm. In 1741 he was named *Kapellmeister* but left the monastery around 1750 to serve as a priest in the vicinity. After a decade he returned and died there as Sub-Prior. Kayser was in the line of Bavarian monastic composers that began with Rathgeber [670],

who believed in writing and publishing practical music for church use. Kayser's works, however, were more ambitious and demanding than those of most of his predecessors. He published 7 opuses, of which the fourth, *Concors digitorum discordia,* consists of keyboard suites. RECORDINGS: Franz Lehrndorfer has recorded a selection of the keyboard suites.

[793] ROUSSEAU, Jean-Jacques (Rōō-sō', Zhàn Zhàk)
WRITER, POLITICAL THEORIST, MUSICAL THEORIST, ECONOMIC THEORIST
BORN: Geneva, June 28, 1712
DIED: Ermenonville, July 2, 1778

Space does not here permit the detailing of the puzzling biography of the man who was (and is) regarded as the catalyst of revolution, romanticism, and democracy. For that one must go to his *Confessions* and other autobiographical works, these being the only sources for many of the more astounding details of his life and alleged amours. A general education today will tell you about the "social contract"—his appealing, if flawed, notion that all government should be by the consent of the governed. His idea of back-to-nature or the "noble savage" touched a universal chord of guilt in civilized intellectuals that continues to produce esoteric overtones (such as those that would have the porpoise and the whale higher than man in the order of creation). For all his dabbling in such treacherous waters, it was as a musician that Rousseau liked to think of himself, and as a musician that he will be treated here.

A descendant of Huguenots who had fled to Geneva, Jean-Jacques developed a thirst for, and some knowledge of music, in the company of his musical aunt and his father, a part-time dancing master who, as dancing masters did, played the kit (a pocket violin). Reared by relatives when his father had to flee Geneva to escape being jailed, he himself cut and ran at the age of twenty, to escape his job as an engraver's helper. (He seems to have been allergic to regular work hours.) Just beyond the border he took up residence with a pretty little widow called Mme. de Warens or Vuarrens. He called her "Mama," but whether his role was that of son or lover remains questionable. About that time, he tried his hand at writing operas (partial libretti to two still exist). He also played recorder in the choir-orchestra of the local cathedral and took lessons in theory from a professional teacher. In the 1730s he is said to have been himself a professional performer in Chambèry in the French Alps, and the *Mercure de France* published one of his songs in 1737. Various journeys to Italy increased his admiration for the music of that country.

In 1741 Rousseau came to Paris with the intention of setting himself up as a music teacher. In 1742 he read his paper on a new form of musical notation to the Academy of Sciences. It got a negative vote, and moreover students were staying away from his door in droves. To subsist, he took a job as secretary to the French ambassador to Venice. There, inspired no doubt by the moonlight on the gondolas or whatever, he turned out an opera-ballet, *Les Muses galantes*. In October 1744 he quit and went back to Paris, where his piece got a private hearing and some lukewarm praise from Rameau [675]. While he tried to get it staged, Rousseau led a marginal existence as secretary and music copyist. In 1747 the Opéra agreed to produce *Les Muses galantes*. It got as far as the dress rehearsal, at which point the composer inexplicably withdrew it. Two years later he made his name as a philosopher with a prize-winning essay on the impact of science on morality (whose thesis is said to have been suggested to him by his sometime friend Denis Diderot, to whose *Encyclopédie* Rousseau contributed articles on music and political philosophy). That same year he was appointed to a lucrative civil service post but quit after a short time.

In 1751 Rousseau held the style of Italian operatic comedy to be superior to that of all French dramatic music, a view seconded in spades by the German writer, Friedrich Melchior Grimm. The following year a troupe directed by one Bambini gave their adherents a rallying point with its performances of Pergolesi's [782] *La Serva padrona* (a work that had been seen in Paris without incident twenty years earlier). In the slow-developing *Querelle des Bouffons* (Quarrel of the Buffoons) that followed, everyone awaited a blast from Rousseau. What came, however, was a little one-act intermezzo, *Le Devin du village (The Village Soothsayer),* produced that fall at Fontainebleau. It was really one of the first shots of the French Revolution, exemplifying, to music of stultifying simplicity, peasant virtue, unspoiled by science and high culture. It enjoyed enormous popularity until, long after the Revolution, someone tossed a nightcap onstage during a performance and that ended it. Upheld as the beginning of *opéra comique,* it really exemplified the Italian approach that Rousseau upheld again in print in 1753. But by then the war was nearing a French victory. Rousseau's fellow citizens did not like hearing that their beloved language was full of impure vowels and that France had no hope of producing real music. They hanged him in effigy and rescinded his pass to the Opéra.

Rousseau went on to publish his *Dictionnaire de musique* in 1768 and to issue other occasional articles, but his career as a musician had peaked. In 1770 he presented in Lyons a curious stage work, *Pygmalion,* supposed to demonstrate the only hope for French music drama: it was all spoken (by a single actor) with an overture and musical interludes, most of them by one Horace Coignet, a fact that Rousseau forgot to mention. At the time of his death he was working on an operatic version of *Daphnis et Chloe.*

RECORDINGS: There have been at least two complete recordings of *Le Devin du village* (by Louis de Froment and Roger Cotte) and several of excerpts. Edith Mathis has recorded a song, *"Écho."*

[794] SCHEIDLER, Christian Gottlieb
(Shīd-ler, Krēst'-yȧn Gȯt'-lēp)
GUITARIST, CELLIST, BASSOONIST
BORN: 1712
DIED: 1815

Scheidler was at first attached to the court of the Archbishop-Elector of Mainz. Later he moved to the Mainz cities, Aschaffenburg and Frankfurt, in that order. He seems to have been almost pathologically self-deprecating; though he was skilled both as performer and composer, soloing appalled him, and he made every effort to keep his publications out of publishers' hands.
RECORDINGS: A Sonata for Violin and Guitar has been recorded by Roman Totenberg and Rudolf Wangler.

[795] SMITH, John Christopher, the
younger
ORGANIST, COOK
BORN: Ansbach, 1712
DIED: Bath, October 3, 1795

Smith's father, Johann Christoph Schmidt, was a friend of Handel's [683] at the University of Halle and later went into the wool business. He did not prosper. When Handel found that out, he invited him to come to London and be his Man Friday. Schmidt arrived in 1716, brought over his family four years later, and they all became Smiths. Young J.C. studied briefly with Handel when he was around twelve and later equally briefly with old Dr. Pepusch [611]. Even later, he arranged to cook for Thomas Roseingrave [699] in exchange for music lessons. A sweet, gentle, modest man, Smith seems to have made friends everywhere. For a time, around 1730, he lived in the home of Dr. John Arbuthnot (1667–1735; creator of "John Bull") and hobnobbed with the members of the Scriblerus Club. Urged by Thomas Arne [783] and Henry Carey [703] to write an English opera *a la maniera italiana* for their company at Lincoln's Inn Fields, he produced *Ulysses* in 1733; it failed, leaving its composer apparently badly shaken. In 1736 Smith married a Miss Pakenham, who died six years later. During this period he wrote some short vocal works (several performed at Hickford's Rooms, London's chief concert hall), and published the first 2 of 4 books of keyboard suites. After his wife's death, he went abroad, wrote several Italian operas, for which there were no takers, and subsisted for a time as a paid companion to an invalid.

Around 1752, Handel, old, fat, crippled, and half-blind, had a row with his lifetime companion, the elder Smith, who walked off leaving him to shift for himself. The composer sent for J. C., Jr., who took over his father's duties. Handel willed him his harpsichord and *positiv,* his music, and 500 pounds; later he upped the financial legacy to 1,500 pounds. In Handel's last years, Smith helped the old man with his favorite charities, the Fund for the Support of Decayed Musicians and Their Families, and the Hospital for the Maintenance and Education of Exposed and Deserted Young Children, familiarly known as the Foundling Hospital. Smith became organist at the latter institution, and, together with John Stanley [796], kept up the benefit performances Handel had inaugurated until he retired to Bath around 1770; they added nearly 3,500 pounds to the 7,000 Handel had previously raised.

Smith's eighteenth-century biographer, Reverend W. Coxe, says that Smith was not particularly chummy with musicians, seeking his friends elsewhere. He had many, including Coxe's father, the royal physician, whose widow Smith married in 1760; Benjamin Stillingfleet, whose blue stockings, which he insisted on wearing to Lady Mary Wortley Montague's literary teas, gave her circles the nickname of "Bluestockings," and who wrote the libretto for Smith's 1760 oratorio *Paradise Lost;* and David Garrick, for whom Smith wrote his most famous works, the two Shakespeare operas *The Fairies* and *The Tempest,* of 1754 and 1756 respectively, as well as one of the earliest

"Turkish" operas, *The Enchanter,* in 1760. In 1762 Smith became music master to the Prince of Wales's widow. Later he was granted a royal pension, in return for which he left his Handel manuscripts to the Crown. The second Mrs. Smith died in 1785, and the old man, still active, spent his final years with her daughter.

RECORDINGS: Songs from the Shakespeare works have been recorded by such as April Cantelo, Mordecai Bauman, and John Brownlee (the last under the impression that they were Henry Purcell's [581]). *A Miniature Suite,* recorded by Arthur Fiedler, is really the work of American composer Harl MacDonald (1899–1955).

[796] STANLEY, Charles John
ORGANIST, CONDUCTOR
BORN: London, January 17, 1713
DIED: London, May 19, 1786

Stanley was blinded in early childhood in an accident. (Gainsborough's portrait of him shows heavy scarring on his brow and eye sockets.) When still quite young, he began studying music, chiefly with Maurice Greene [727]. At eleven he was the regular organist of All Hallows in Bread Street, at thirteen of St. Andrew's in Holborn, and at sixteen he was granted a B. Mus. by Oxford University. In 1734 he gave up his other appointments to become organist of the Temple Church, and it is said that when he played there the most important of his London colleagues flocked to hear him. Four years later he was married to the daughter of a wealthy officer of the East India Company, Sarah Arlond. His first extant composition is an anthem written in 1734, but from around 1740 he began composing more regularly, publishing 2 sets of sonatas, 3 of cantatas (mostly to texts by his friend and neighbor John Hawkins—later knighted and a notable historian of music), and 1 of concerti for strings. He became associated with Handel, who much admired his playing. However, when Handel's own eyes went and it was suggested that Stanley take over the organ for the annual oratorio seasons, the old man grimly quoted scripture regarding the blind leading the blind, and settled on John Christopher Smith [795] instead. However, when Handel died, it was Stanley who took charge. In these years, Stanley also tried his hand at some pieces for the stage, including an unproduced opera, and wrote 2 oratorios. In 1779 he was named to succeed Boyce [787] as Master of the King's Music, in which capacity he wrote the mandatory odes, all of which have disappeared. Nowadays Stanley is remembered chiefly for his instrumental works and particularly for the 3 volumes of voluntaries, which are still played by church organists. RECORDINGS: The "trumpet" voluntaries have elicited recordings involving such trumpeters as Edward Tarr and Hermann Sauter. Like much of Stanley's other music, the trumpet voluntaries show a musician who kept up with the musical changes of his time. His Concerti for strings, Op. 2 (recorded by Leslie Jones), are attractive but conservative and rather less Handelian than advertised.

[797] DAUVERGNE, Antoine (Dō-vârn', Án-twàn')
VIOLINIST, ADMINISTRATOR
BORN: Moulins, October 3, 1713
DIED: Lyons, February 11, 1797

Dauvergne—who, rather than Jean-Jacques Rousseau [793], is the real father of *opéra comique*—was the son of Jacques Dauvergne, first violinist of the Moulins orchestra, who undoubtedly taught him to play. Antoine held a similar post in Clermont-Ferrand before he went to Paris, where he is said to have studied with Rameau [675]. He was admitted to the royal chamber in 1739 and the orchestra of the Opéra five years later. In 1752 the latter institution produced his first stage work, the heroic ballet *Les Amours de Tempé (Love in Tempé)*. It was in the same year that the touring Bambini company unleashed the War of the Buffoons with its performances of Pergolesi's [782] *La Serva padrona* and other Italian *intermezzi* (see under Rousseau). At this juncture, Jean Monnet, director of the Opéra Comique at the Foire St. Laurent, exhibited the perspicacity that earned him the sobriquet of *le grand prophète*. He prepared a libretto based on a LaFontaine fable, and had Dauvergne set it in the Italian style but using spoken dialogue instead of recitative. Advertising it as the work of an Italian located in Vienna, he produced *Les Troqueurs (The Wife-Swappers)* in 1753. It was a howling success. Then he brought the real composer forward. Dauvergne's career was made, even though nothing he produced afterward lived up to his one triumph. In 1755 he succeeded François Rebel as director of, and composer to, the royal chamber, and seven years later he followed Mondonville [789] as a director of the Concert Spirituel, serving there for eleven years and writing much sacred music, all of which is lost. In 1769 he began the first of his three stormy terms as director of

the Opéra (the others date from 1780 and 1785), and a few years later he was named *surintendant* of the king's music. As an administrator he was notable for his attempts to block Gluck [803] at the Opéra and for perpetually making enemies. He was the last director there during the *ancien régime*. When the Revolution began to heat up, he retired to Lyons in 1790 and died there, forgotten, at eighty-three. He wrote nearly 20 stage works, most of them of no moment, and the last ones unperformed. He also left some published sonatas and chamber suites (or *concerts de simphonies*, as he termed them). RECORDINGS: Examples of the chamber suites have been recorded by Gérard Cartigny and Jean-François Paillard, and there is a single recording of *Les Troqueurs* by Jean-Louis Petit.

[798] KREBS, Johann Ludwig (Kreps, Yō'-hàn Lōōd'-vikh)
ORGANIST
BORN: Buttelstedt, c. October 12, 1713
DIED: Altenburg, January 1, 1780

Krebs's father, Johann Tobias, an organist from Heichelheim, had studied in nearby Weimar with both J. S. Bach [684] and Bach's cousin J. G. Walther [680], while serving in a church in Buttelstedt. In 1721 he established himself as schoolmaster-organist in Buttstädt. (His consecutive addresses must have given the postal service fits.) There he began teaching Ludwig, the eldest of his three sons. A year later, as a Bach alumnus, he shipped the boy off to the Thomasschule in Leipzig. Ludwig was soon followed by his younger brother Tobias. Bach distinguished them as "Krebs major" and "Krebs minor." He developed a special affection for Krebs major, who stayed with him until 1737, assisting him in various ways. Every account of their relationship quotes Bach's pun about Ludwig's being the only *Krebs* (crayfish) in the *Bach* (brook). In 1735 Krebs, having been thwarted in an attempt to obtain a post at Naumburg, matriculated at the university to obtain a degree in philosophy. Just in case, Bach gave him a letter of recommendation which said that he was skilled on the keyboards, lute, and violin, as well as in composition.

In 1737 Krebs found a rather poorly paid job as organist of the Marienkirche in Zwickau, where three years later he found a bride, Johanna Sophie Nackens, the daughter of a civil servant. The first of their several children, Johann Gottfried, was born in 1741. Curiously, when Ludwig was offered the prestigious appointment as organist of

Dresden's Frauenkirche, he turned it down. In 1743 he became castle organist at Zeitz, and in 1755 court organist at Altenburg. The petty courts paid no better than the petty churches, and Krebs qualified as a depressed area all his professional life. To make matters worse, his eyes, like his old teacher's, failed him in his last years. When he died, Gottfried, who expected to succeed him, was rebuffed for consorting with improper females and became the town organist instead, his younger brother Ehrenfried Christian Traugott getting the court post. Another brother, Carl Heinrich Gottlieb, was court organist in Eisenberg.

Admired in his day as a performer, J. L. Krebs left music that does credit both to him and to his teacher. He shows a firm grasp of both Bach's style and the new *galanterie.* The bulk of his output is instrumental, mostly for organ and harpsichord, but including some sonatas, *sinfonias,* and concerti.

RECORDINGS: Hubert Schoonbroodt has recorded the first of the 4 volumes of the *Clavier Ubung,* consisting of choralepreludes and variations. David Gooding has devoted an LP to organ pieces, and several of the chorale-preludes calling for obbligato oboe or trumpet have been recorded by Georg Meerwein, Maurice André, and Edward Tarr. A two-keyboard concerto is played by Huguette Dreyfus and Luciano Sgrizzi, and one written for lute is played on guitar by Konrad Ragossnig.

[799] ZWIERZCHOWSKI, Mateusz

(Zvězh-khou'-skē, Mà-te'-ōōsh)
ORGANIST, CHOIRMASTER
BORN: Wielkopolska, c. 1713
DIED: Gniezno, April 14, 1768

Andrzej Zwierzchowski, Mateusz' father, a violinist and organist, came in 1723 to Gniezno (a.k.a. Gnesen), an important musical center near Poznań, to play the organ and conduct the choir of the Gniezno Cathedral. He may well have been Mateusz' only teacher. In 1735, when Andrzej died, Mateusz took over as organist. He acquitted himself so well that when the directorship fell vacant again fifteen years later, he inherited that. In 1760 the cathedral burned down. The only music by Zwierzchowski to survive appears to have been 2 cantatalike *pastorelle* and a *Requiem* written in the year of the fire in memory of the cathedral cantor. With its high trumpet parts and its Baroque vocabulary, it might have been written forty years earlier, but it has melodic charm and appears to be influenced by Pol-

ish folk music. RECORDINGS: There is a recording of the *Requiem* by Zbigniew Chwedczuk.

[800] HOMILIUS, Gottfried August (Hō-mē'-lē-ōōs, Got'-frēt Ou'-gōōst)

ORGANIST, TEACHER, MUSIC DIRECTOR
BORN: Rosenthal, February 2, 1714
DIED: Leipzig, June 2, 1785

Though born in a Saxon vale of roses, the son of a Lutheran minister, Homilius soon moved with his family to Porschendorf. His father died when the boy was eight, and he spent the next dozen or so years at a school in Dresden, where he studied organ with the resident organist, a man named Stübner. In 1735 he went to Leipzig to study law, during which time he took lessons from J. S. Bach [684]. In 1742 he was appointed to play the fine new organ at the Frauenkirche in Dresden—the job Krebs [798] had turned down. He seems to have been not wholly satisfied with it, but after thirteen years he was made cantor of the Kreuzkirche (the subsequent fame of whose choir was deeply in his debt) and music director of both churches to which he was then attached and of the Sophienkirche—the three most important in Dresden. He was reckoned a fine teacher. His most famous pupil was Johann Adam Hiller (1728–1804). Unfortunately the Kreuzkirche was destroyed in the bombardments of the Seven Years War. Incapacitated by a stroke, Homilius was retired three months before he died. Like his teacher, he took his work as a mission and produced much sacred music of high quality, including Passions, a Christmas oratorio, motets, and cantata cycles. This music is largely in the new homophonic style, emphasizing accompanied melody rather than the interwoven melodies of polyphony, but it still attests to the thorough grounding Bach gave him. He also lef organ compositions. RECORDINGS: Some the organ works appear in recorded org recitals—e.g., by E. Power Biggs and Fr Lehrndorfer.

[801] BACH, Carl Philipp Emanuel

(Bàkh, Kärl Fē'-lip E-mà'-nōō-
KEYBOARDIST, THEORIST, CONDU
TEACHER
BORN: Weimar, March 8, 1714
DIED: Hamburg, December 15

Though Sebastian Bach's [684 music lived on among discernin his reputation was eclipsed a that of his third son. Beethoven [1063], thanks to Beethoven's father and teacher Neefe [954], was nurtured on Emanuel Bach. Mozart [992] remarked in all candor, "He is the father, we are all his children." Haydn [871], who once wore out the night playing a book of Emanuel Bach sonatas he had come upon, said that he owed all that he was to him. Charles Burney, who met and conversed with him, called him one of the greatest musicians of all time, and the great German poet Klopstock wrote a memorial ode to him. Generally Emanuel was "the Berlin Bach" or "the Hamburg Bach," but most often "the great Bach."

The fifth child of Sebastian and Maria Barbara Bach, Emanuel was preceded by Catherine Dorothea, Wilhelm Friedemann [784], and nameless twins who died at birth. "Philipp" and "Emanuel" came from his musical godfathers, Telemann [665], then at Frankfurt, and Adam Emanuel Weltzig or Weldig, a musician at the Weissenfels court. When the boy was three, and after his father had served a jail term for insubordination, the Bachs moved to Cöthen. There, during his seventh summer, while Sebastian was away with his employer, Emanuel's mother suddenly died. The next year, however, the widower remarried, and in 1723 packed his ever-growing family off to Leipzig where he became Cantor of the Thomaskirche.

Sebastian Bach's number-two son was obviously not the apple of his eye that Friedemann was. It was obvious, however, that he had musical talent to spare. He had a photographic memory, and once he had learned to read music, he needed only to glance at a page to be able to play it without ʌoking again. On the debit side, he was left-ʌded and could not be counted on to ʌr the gamba or the zink. Nevertheless ʌher gave him thorough grounding, ʌfessionally and paternally—the ʌng he ever had, Emanuel noted in ʌraphical sketch written years ʌsurface at least, Emanuel re- ʌer as a musician, imitating ʌ often performing his mu- ʌrg years. Nevertheless, ʌ remarks about dry-as- ʌllectualism. On the ʌvas pleased by his ʌwhen Emanuel ʌPotsdam, Sebas- ʌ"It's Prussian

was over, ʌal prod- ʌ study ʌmusic—he

published a minuet from plates he had engraved in 1731—he proceeded in 1734 to Frankfurt (the one on the Oder) for advanced legal training. In his four years there, however, he became deeply involved in the musical life of the town, teaching, participating in concerts, composing, and conducting the Collegium Musicum. In 1738, highly educated and thoroughly skilled, he went to Berlin, apparently to seek his fortune. His fortune first manifested itself in an opportunity to serve as companion to young Count von Keyserlingk, whose father, the Russian emissary to Saxony, was an old acquaintance of his own. The count was to tour Europe as a necessary part of his education. But before he took off, Emanuel was summoned to Rheinsberg by Prince Frederick of Prussia for a tryout. He seems to have pleased the prince well enough, but not sufficiently to elicit the kind of offer Bach had hoped for. But when the old king (Frederick William I) died two years later, he found himself on the way back to Berlin, and, on the evening after the coronation of Frederick II, joining his master in the first of those thousands of mandatory concerts through which he would have to suffer.

Four years later Bach seemingly locked himself in: he married Johanna Maria Dannemann, the twenty-year-old daughter of a local wine merchant, thereby becoming a Prussian citizen and wholly subservient to the king on every level. Despite the prestige it carried, his was not a wholly happy situation. For one thing, musically speaking, he was not part of the old Rheinsberg-Ruppin gang—Quantz [730], the Grauns [751, 757], and all. For another, he was paid poorly— less than a third of what the leading instrumentalists got. Moreover, he was incapable of fawning, and he was cursed with a comic view of life. Frederick did not care for Emanuel's music (he considered it too modern), a fact attested to by the latter's tiny output of flute pieces in the Berlin years. And Bach must have gotten dreadfully weary of having to hear, night after night, the endless sonatas and concerti of Quantz and his royal pupil, not to speak of the royal pupil's vagaries of rhythm and pitch, about which Bach complained privately. Nor, one supposes, was he always happy as second keyboard to the likes of Schaffrath [780] and Karl Friedrich Christian Fasch (1736–1800). Nevertheless he was a sanguine person, and seems to have been able to make the most of it, even in the mud and dust of raw Berlin. He got along with his colleagues, joined the Monday Club, made interesting friends (one was Lessing, the great

German playwright and critic), and gave concerts in his home (Bach had a gift for hospitality). Landmark occurrences in his life there were the births of his children— Johann August, in 1745; Anna Carolina Philippina, in 1746; and Johann Sebastian or "Hans," in 1748. There were also visits from his father in 1741 and 1747, his brother Christian's [886] four-year sojourn beginning in 1750, and Frederick II's wars. During the Seven Years War salaries dried up and only Emanuel's teaching kept his family afloat; even so, they had to flee the Russian advance and wound up living with the Fasches in Zerbst for several months.

However, it was not that Bach was a violet by a mossy stone, half hidden from the eye. His reputation as teacher and performer had spread throughout Europe; and his compositions, especially his keyboard manual (first published in 1753), were well known. And so he had kept an eye open for ways out. In 1750 he had applied for his late father's post, but it went to one Gottlieb Harrer. Nor did he have any luck in Zittau three years later. But in 1767, when his octogenarian godfather Telemann died, Bach beat out his half-brother Johann Christoph Friedrich [872] and several others for the appointment as cantor of the Johanneum (the Latin school) in Hamburg and music director of the city's five churches. With the aid of the king's musical sister Anna Amalie [828], who appointed him her *Kapellmeister von Haus aus* (i.e., *in absentia)*, he got grudging permission to go the following spring.

Hamburg was better than Berlin, if not ideal. Musically, it had already seen its great days, and musicians currently there were undertrained and overworked. (There were perhaps 200 concerts annually.) But Bach adapted readily to these conditions, throwing himself into his work with enormous energy and building up a fine musical organization for his own concerts at the Saal-auf-den-Kamp. He liked the city and loved to show visitors around it. He reveled in his freedom from capricious authority and debasing court etiquette. For a musician he was well paid; if he has been criticized for letting his stepmother live in poverty, he was only one of Bach's children, and he had a family of his own to care for. He kept open house, entertaining such out-of-towners as Dr. Burney and Baron von Swieten, as well as members of the brilliant Hamburg literary circle, including Lessing (again), Klopstock, Sturm, Claudius, and Gerstenberg. His contract relieved him of teaching duties, giving him time to rehearse,

compose, and take meticulous care of the church and school accounts.

Emanuel's later years were, however, marred by tragedy. His younger son, a greatly gifted painter, died a lingering death in Rome at thirty. The early 1780s carried off Emanuel's beloved sister Elisabeth and his brothers Friedemann and Christian. In 1782 he himself incurred a severe lung infection, which lingered (probably as tuberculosis), leaving him increasingly weak, killing him six years later. His elder son, a lawyer, survived him only a year. His daughter (unmarried) kept up the family music business until around 1804 when she vanished. There were no grandchildren.

With the rediscovery of J. S. Bach some decades later, Emanuel was forgotten and has only recently begun to get the renewed attention he merits. One of the problems with his music is its variety: he admitted that what he wrote to sell and what he wrote for himself were two very different things. In his later years he lived in that false dawn of Romanticism, the period of *Sturm und Drang* (storm and stress) when overt emotional displays were encouraged, and perhaps what one thinks of most readily about his music is its emotionalism *(Empfindsamkeit).* But that does not say that it was all "feeling"; Emanuel was not his father's son for nothing, and he was a master of polyphonic structure, Frenchified *galanterie,* and Italian form alike.

If the catalogue of Emanuel's music drawn up in 1906 by the indefatigable Belgian cataloguer Alfred Wotquenne (see Wq. numbers) does not approach the bulk of Sebastian's, it is still impressive. In vocal music it includes 2 impressive oratorios, *Die Israeliten in der Wüste* and the *Auferstehung und Himmelfahrt Jesu;* 2 Passions, a splendid *Magnificat,* more than a dozen church cantatas, other sacred music, 3 secular cantatas, and nearly 300 songs. These last are important to the history of the *Lied.* As for the instrumental music, which bulks larger, one thinks first of all of that for keyboard. Bach wrote more than 60 keyboard concerti (some with alternative versions for flute, violin, etc.; his instrument of choice was the clavichord. Emanuel Bach did not "invent" the keyboard concerto—his father has better claim, but he surely set it on the road that led to Mozart's and Beethoven's; the opening allegros are in basic sonata form, with exposition, development, and recapitulation. Certainly Emanuel is high among claimants to the paternity of modern keyboard music, notably in his numerous keyboard sonatas, including 6 collections and 1 sonata for harp. Many published in sets over the last 45 years of Bach's life. Without going into the moot question of whether he was responsible for "sonata form" or the "sonata-as-we-know-it," one may marvel at the variety, inventiveness, and imagination of these works, and especially at the depth of feeling in the slow movements (furthered by explorations of harmony and chromaticism). Late in his life, Bach produced 18 symphonies, conceived for "modern" orchestra—though it should be noted that by then Mozart and Haydn were far along as symphonists.

RECORDINGS: The oratorio *Die Israeliten in der Wüste* has been recorded by Mathieu Lange, and the *Auferstehung und Himmelfahrt Jesu* by Wilfred Fischer. The *Magnificat* is performed by Felix Prohaska, Adolph Detel, and Philipp Ledger, among others. There is an LP of songs by Dietrich Fischer-Dieskau. The keyboard concerti are well represented, though the phonographic traversal is by no means complete. Heinz Holliger has recorded an oboe concerto, and several flute concerti have been done by Jean-Pierre Rampal, Ingrid Dingfelder, and others. Some of the earlier symphonies have been committed to vinyl by Christopher Hogwood. The penultimate set of symphonies has been done by the Collegium Aureum and the final set by Helmut Koch, Raymond Leppard, and Leslie Jones. Recordings of all 3 cello concerti have appeared; the B-flat and A-major concerti are fairly common on discs. Louis Bagger, Siegfried Petrenz, Franzpeter Goebels, and Xavier Darasse have recorded several sets of sonatas, and the complete solo organ music is performed by Herbert Tachezi. There are also many albums of trio sonatas and miscellaneous chamber works.

AVONDANO, Pedro Antonio (A-dá'-nō, Pā'-drō Ăn-tōn'-yō)
?T, DANCING MASTER
?bon, c. April 16, 1714
?n, 1782

were musically active in
?he court, into the nine-
began with Pietro, Pe-
? violinist who settled
followed in his fa-
the cataclysmic
?ne of those who
Santa Cecélia,
?sicians, and
?f musical
?ecretary.
?d in the
?ed a highly

successful dancing academy, for which his several collections of minuets were written. Avondano did not, as accounts used to say, later become a monk; what he did was, for a suitable price, award himself the Order of Christ. Among his more ambitious works were an opera on Goldoni's *Il Mondo della luna (The World on the Moon)*, also set by Haydn [871] a dozen years later, 2 religious dramas, some oratorios, 2 symphonies, and 3 violin concerti. RECORDINGS: Ruggero Gerlin has recorded one of Avondano's keyboard sonatas.

[803] GLUCK, Christoph Willibald, Ritter von (Glŏŏk, Khrēs'-tōf Vil'-lē-bált)
CONDUCTOR, KEYBOARDIST
BORN: Erasbach, July 2, 1714
DIED: Vienna, November 15, 1787

As one who insisted, more than a century after Monteverdi [333], that opera was neither a play nor a musical form, but music drama, he stands as one of the pivotal figures in its history. Yet today one rarely hears the names, much less the sound of more than a tenth of his operatic output—and even that tenth, with a single exception, is rarely produced. Moreover, though he made some impact on the music of Cherubini [1019] and Spontini [1081], and on the thinking of Berlioz [1175] and Wagner [1230], there were no subsequent Gluckists.

Gluck was born of a line of foresters. His father, Alexander, was living at Erasbach, with his wife, whom history knows only as Maria Walburga, when their first known son arrived. The father, formerly a huntsman for Prince Eugene of Savoy, one of the victors at Blenheim, had apparently been stationed in this conquered Bavarian territory (south of Nuremberg) as a forester and customs officer. Over the next twenty years the couple produced at least eight more children, none of whom distinguished himself in music. After Erasbach was returned to Bavaria, Alexander Gluck took his family to Bohemia, improving his lot under various employers at various places until he settled at Eisenberg (now Železný Brod) about fifty miles northwest of Prague, as chief forester to one of the Princes Lobkowitz. There he acquired an estate of his own and retired. Of young Gluck's early years we know nothing specific. He and his father appear not to have agreed on his future, with the result that around 1727, or shortly thereafter, when his family moved to Eisenberg, he ran away to Prague. He evidently already had some musical education and some sort of academic grounding, for he supported himself by playing organ, and perhaps violin and cello, and registered at the university to study philosophy. He probably did not study with Černohorský [677] as legend has insisted he did, since the "Padre Boemo" left about the time he got there. Whatever he may have accomplished in Prague, he left at some time in the early to mid-1730s for Vienna, where he may have served briefly as a chamber musician to Prince Lobkowitz's son and heir. By 1737, however, he was in Milan in the service of Prince Melzi, the imperial administrator-general, and remained in that city until 1745. During the first half of that period, he almost certainly studied with G. B. Sammartini [738], whom for a time he imitated. In 1741 he tried his hand for the first time at opera—quite traditionally, a setting of Metastasio's *Artaserse*. It was so successful that Gluck was kept busy writing operas, not only for Milan, but for Venice and other cities as well.

After nine of these, Gluck was invited to London by the ever-hopeful Lord Middleton to assist, or perhaps supersede, Lampugnani [769] in the direction of his opera company at the Haymarket (King's) Theater. Since the house was closed for much of the year because of the Scottish uprising under the Young Pretender, Gluck must have gotten there toward the end of 1745. He hailed the Caledonian defeat several weeks prematurely with a quasi-Handelian serenata, a partly warmed-over piece called *La Caduta de' giganti (The Fall of the Giants)*, early in January. Its topical interest drew full houses. Handel is supposed to have snorted that Gluck knew no more about counterpoint than his (Handel's) cook. It was an ambiguous remark, if it ever got made, since said cook was a well-trained old-school musician named Walz, and in any case Handel was quite friendly to his fellow countryman. But Gluck's next offering, another patchwork, called *Artamene*, failed. Seeing no future for himself in London, he gave a couple of benefit concerts for himself in April, at which he played on musical glasses tuned with pure spring water, and took up his wanderings.

When he left and where he went are, like so much else in the first half of Gluck's life, not clear. By June 1747 he was in Dresden, where, at the double wedding of the Bavarian elector and the Saxon crown prince to each other's sisters, he conducted the opera troupe run by Pietro and Angelo Mingotti in *Le Nozze d'Ercole e d'Ebe (The Marriage of Hercules and Hebe)*, written for the occasion. Stopping off at Eisenberg to settle the estate of his recently deceased father, he

went on to Vienna to produce another new piece, *Semiramide riconisciuta (Semiramis Identified)* to open the Burgtheater on the birthday of the Empress Maria Theresa in 1748. It was probably his most successful work to date, running a full two months, but nothing solid came of it, and in August he rejoined the Mingottis in Hamburg and went on to Copenhagen (where he contracted the case of gonorrhea that probably rendered him sterile). Gluck apparently remained in Denmark at least until spring, but then disappeared, save for the Prague premiere of his *Ezio* at the end of the year, until his wedding in Vienna in September 1750 to Maria Anna Bergin, daughter of a wealthy merchant or banker, whose inheritance assured him of financial independence, and whose connections gave him an "in" at the court. In the autumn of 1752 the couple traveled to Naples, where Gluck set and produced *La Clemenza di Tito (Titus's Mercy)* to enormous acclaim.

On his return to Vienna, Gluck was appointed *Kapellmeister* to Feldmarschall Prinz Joseph Friedrich von Sachsen-Hildburghausen, in whose splendid musical organization he met and befriended young Carl Ditters, later von Dittersdorf [906]. In 1754 Count Durazzo, imperial intendant, hired Gluck as an arranger for the French company at the Burgtheater, where he soon also took over the conducting. At about the same time, Gluck's field marshal put on his *Le Cinesi* (one of the first ventures into oriental exoticism) for the delectation of their Imperial Majesties. The result was a number of commissions for occasional pieces from the court and increasing fame. The production of his *Antigono* in 1756 brought him the Order of the Golden Spur from Pope Benedict XIV. Two years later, Gluck began a series of eight *opéras comiques* for the Burgtheater, which included the still viable *Le Cadi dupé (The Cadi Tricked)* and *L'Ivrogne corrigé (The Reformed Drunkard)*, and culminated in *La Rencontre imprévue (The Unexpected Encounter)* in 1764. In 1761 he was released from his formal employment when the field marshall closed up shop in Vienna and went off to Thuringia to serve as regent for his great-grandnephew.

Gluck's first dramatic breakthrough—and his first association with the librettist Raniero Calzabigi—came in the autumn of that same year. The vehicle, however, was not an opera, but a *ballet d'action* entitled *Don Juan*, in which the story of that questionable hero was set forth in what amounted to a danced drama. It was both controversial and successful. The next Gluck-Calzabigi collaboration, premiered in

October 1762, was even more significant—in fact Gluck's most lasting monument. The partners, led by Calzabigi (and one must not exclude the choreographer Gasparo Angiolini) turned, no doubt unwittingly, to the Orpheus legend with which Monteverdi had begun. What emerged, in *Orfeo ed Euridice*, was not the stop-and-start parade of arias of *opera seria* but a "theatrical action" in which both story and music unfolded uninterruptedly, in which the music reflected both mood and action, and in which the dancing was an integral and logical part of the whole. The work was recognized immediately as something quite special by the more perceptive, among them the empress, who sent the composer a snuffbox filled with gold. However, Gluck did not proceed directly on the path indicated, but returned for the moment to *opéra comique* and to old-fashioned Metastasian formulae. Then in 1767 came *Alceste;* the librettist was again Calzabigi, working from Euripides' play. (It is possible that Gluck's taste for classical antiquity owed something to Johann Winckelmann, whom he had met earlier in Rome and who was helping change the taste of the era.) He dedicated the score to Maria Theresa, widowed two years earlier. (Her son Joseph II was now emperor.) The work was prefaced with an essay by Calzabigi, spelling out the nature of the reform they were undertaking. It reopened the Burgtheater, which had been closed in mourning for the Archduchess Maria Josefa, who had died after a month as Queen of Naples, on December 26, 1767, to disapproving notices. But it caught on quickly and ran for at least sixty performances. The last Gluck-Calzabigi collaboration, *Paride ed Elena (Paris and Helen)* of 1770, did less well—in fact it failed, owing to what was considered a curious treatment of the story. Perhaps Metastasio saw the handwriting on the wall or perhaps old age had caught up with him, but he gave up writing libretti at about this time. Though Calzabigi later wrote for Salieri [966] and still later for Paisiello [914], his career fizzled after the association with Gluck ended.

Gluck could have retired at this point, had he wished to. Apart from his wife's dowry and income, he had long been receiving regular court salaries as ballet composer and an annuity in token of his other services, as well as specific payments for various compositions. He also had taken on a domestic obligation: around 1760 he had adopted his late sister's baby daughter Marianne Hedler, whom he called "Nanette" and adored. Indeed for a time after 1770, he occupied himself with his own affairs. He

had been setting some of the poems of Klopstock and may have been toying with the notion of a German opera.

In 1772 he undertook the setting of a French libretto, however—*Iphigénie en Aulide (Iphigenia in Aulis)*, by the French diplomat François du Roullet (after Racine). It was presumably aimed at Paris, where an earlier opportunity for Gluck had been thwarted by a fire at the Opéra. With the influence of the Archduchess Maria Antonia (now the Dauphine Marie Antoinette), he got the work accepted there and arrived in Paris with his family in November 1773. Twenty years after the hubbub of the Italian-French *Querelle des Bouffons* (Quarrel of the Buffoons) had died down, here came a German proposing to show the French how to write *tragédie lyrique*. The authorities were not exactly thrilled, but Gluck used both pull and diplomacy, and the premiere on February 19, 1774, was the kind of triumph that even Gluck had not hoped for. (Unfortunately most modern performances are in Wagner's recension.)

Contracted to supply the Académie with five more operas, he fulfilled a fifth of that obligation with a rewrite of what became *Orphée et Eurydice*, with the male lead for tenor rather than *castrato* and an elaborate balletic finale. Having seen it successfully staged in August, he returned to Vienna. His triumphs increased his income by a 6,000-livre pension from the Dauphine, and a yearly salary from Joseph II as court composer. Gluck returned to Paris at the end of 1774, to produce a revised version of *Iphigénie* and his *opéra comique* entitled *L'Arbre enchanté (The Enchanted Arbor)*, presented as an *opéra-ballet*, then left for Vienna again, where illness prevented his further return until early 1776.

Meanwhile, the ambassador from Naples, eager to prove Italian operatic superiority had, in 1774, sold the Dauphine and Madame Dubarry on Niccolò Piccinni [848], composer of the hit *La buona figliuola (The Good Daughter)*. Gluck arrived in Paris in March 1776, started the French version of *Alceste* on a run that picked up from its disappointing beginnings, but was called back to Vienna by the death (from smallpox) of Nanette, age seventeen. Piccinni reached Paris on the last day of the year and was put to work on a setting of Du Roullet's *Roland* —the same libretto on which Gluck was at work—presumably to fan up a "war" between the two composers. When Gluck got wind of what was going on, he refused to play, dropping his own *Roland* then and there and writing the librettist a scorching letter—whose publication had precisely the desired effect. Gluck, however, proceeded with his next work, *Armide,* which was staged in September to applause by his admirers and criticism by his opponents. He remained in Paris long enough to see *Roland,* which, although it was cheered by the Piccinnists, seems to have been something of a botch. The much-heralded rivalry seems indeed to have been a teapot tempest. Piccinni never lived up to expectations and eventually died in poverty. In 1779 Gluck enjoyed a triumph with *Iphigénie en Tauride (Iphigenia in Tauris);* Piccinni had less luck with *his* version two years later. While rehearsing *Écho et Narcisse* that autumn, Gluck suffered a small stroke. This was followed by the opera's failure, and the composer returned to Vienna for good. He worked on his Klopstock opera, which came to naught, and talked of returns to Paris and London. But his health went from bad to worse. Another stroke paralyzed his right arm, and pneumonia debilitated him. His doctors limited his diet and forbade him alcohol. On November 15, 1787, lunching with friends from Paris, he sneaked a glass of liqueur. On the way home he incurred a massive stroke, and died at his house in Perchtoldsdorf. Many of his manuscripts were destroyed in the Napoleonic wars two decades later.

RECORDINGS: Save for many recordings of various versions of *Orfeo/Orphée,* Gluck has been neglected by the phonograph. There are two professional versions of the (Italian) *Alceste* (one with Kirsten Flagstad, the other with Jessye Norman), two of *Le Cadi dupé* in German, one of *Armide;* single old and inferior recordings of *L'Ivrogne corrigé* and *Iphigénie en Tauride* (plus a Cluytens-led disc of highlights of the latter); and the Wagnerian *Iphigénie en Aulide.* There are three recordings of *Don Juan,* but only that by Neville Marriner is up to modern standards. A few songs and a flute concerto of doubtful provenance, "arranged" by Hermann Scherchen, bring up the rear.

[804] WAGENSEIL, Georg Christoph
(Vä'-gen-zīl, Gā'-ôrg Krēs'-tof)
KEYBOARDIST, TEACHER
BORN: Vienna, January 29, 1715
DIED: Vienna, March 1, 1777

One of several composers suspected of the paternity of the Classical symphony, Wagenseil was the son and grandson of imperial courtiers and a Viennese all his life (though he published much of his music in Paris). His musical talent caught the ear of Fux **[585]**, who taught him and was largely

responsible for his appointment as court composer to Charles VI in 1739. After the emperor died the next year, he took on additional duties as the dowager empress' organist and later as music master to Maria Theresa's daughters. In 1762, when the prodigious six-year-old Mozart **[992]** played for the imperial family, Mozart imperiously ordered Wagenseil, himself a famous harpsichordist, to attest to the correctness of his performance. When sciatica and gout rendered him a semiinvalid, he went on composing, teaching, and welcoming such visitors as the ubiquitous Charles Burney. Among his pupils were F. X. Dušek **[867]**, Leopold Hofmann **[899]**, and Schenck **[982]**.

Generally speaking, Wagenseil was an eclectic who composed in most of the current genres. His output included some Metastasian operas, 16 Masses, a *Requiem,* much other religious music, secular cantatas, more than 80 symphonies, a number of concerti, a good deal of chamber music, keyboard pieces, and arias. His later instrumental pieces are his most original and interesting compositions. His keyboard *divertimenti* are really sonatas, which show melodic ingenuity and something approaching sonata form, though the left-hand parts are rather stodgy. (An Italian writer has termed them *sonate col pum-pum*—"boom-boom" sonatas.) The keyboard concerti are rather simply conceived, the symphonies much more interesting, especially as they develop from the Baroque to the pre-Classical.

RECORDINGS: On records there is a symphony led by Hermann Scherchen; a *sinfonia* (from his own opera, *La Clemenza di Tito,* of 1746) by Theodor Guschlbauer; concerti for cello (Enrico Mainardi), harp (Nicanor Zabaleta), and trombone (Concentus Musicus)—probably the first trombone concerto ever written! Oboists Alfred Hertel and Alfred Dutka have recorded a trio sonata.

[805] HELMONT, Charles-Joseph van
(El-mon', Shârl Zhō-zef' vàn)
ORGANIST, CHOIRMASTER
BORN: Brussels, March 19, 1715
DIED: Brussels, June 8, 1790

Helmont seems to have spent an uneventful existence in his native city. A pupil of Pierre Bréhy **[637]** and successor to Josse Boutmy **[731]** at the church of Ste. Gudule, he was appointed music master at Notre-Dame du Sablon and La Chapelle de Montserrat when he was twenty-two. Four years later he was appointed music director of Ste.

Gudule. In 1768 he inaugurated weekly public concerts in Brussels. In 1777 he retired in favor of his son Adrien-Joseph (1747–1830), who later founded the school that became the Brussels Conservatory. The elder Helmont wrote mostly religious music, including 12 Masses and an oratorio, *Judith.* There is also a published volume of *clavecin* pieces and some organ fugues. RECORDINGS: Géry Lemaire has recorded a motet *Accensa furore* from the oratorio. Of the instrumental music, he has recorded the D-major *Overture* (really a symphony for double orchestra).

[806] BISCOGLI, Francesco (Bēs-kōl'-yē, Frán-chās'-kō)
BORN: c. 1715 (?)
DIED: after 1740 (?)

It seems that the closer one comes to modern times, the more obscure previously as well as newly obscure composers become. Biscogli, if he ever existed, was allegedly responsible for a concerto for trumpet, oboe, bassoon, and strings, which survives in an ill-written ms. kept at the Paris Conservatory. Jean-François Paillard, who has recorded the work, wonders if "Biscogli" is a scribal error for Besozzi [750].

[807] SEGER, Josef Ferdinand Norbert (Zā'-ger, Yō'-zef Fâr'-dē-nánt Nôr'-bârt)
ORGANIST, VIOLINIST, TEACHER
BORN: Repin, c. March 21, 1716
DIED: Prague, April 22, 1782

Seger, encountered in orthographies that range alphabetically from "Czegert" and "Seeger" to "Zeckert," was born, probably of Germanic stock, in a village north of Prague. He went to Prague as a choirboy, studied with Tůma [756] and with Černohorský [677], played violin at St. Martin's, and took a Ph.D. at the university. In 1741 he became organist at Týn, about sixty miles to the south, but from 1744 he divided his time between there and the Crusaders' Church in the capital. He was admired both as performer and teacher, his numerous pupils including Koželuh [950], Kuchař [974], Mysliveček [890], and Pichl [923]. When the Emperor Joseph visited Prague in 1780, he was so taken with Seger's playing that he promised him a court appointment, but by the time the red tape was untangled, Seger was dead. Though he wrote a good deal of church music, what keeps his name alive is his organ composi-

tions. RECORDINGS: Some of his organ works have been recorded by Jiří Ropek and, in string transcriptions, by the Pro Arte Antiqua of Prague.

[808] GIULINI, Giorgio (Jōō-lē'-nē, Jôr'-jō)
ARCHAEOLOGIST, HISTORIAN, LAWYER
BORN: Milan, 1716
DIED: 1780

A wealthy nobleman (he bore the title of Conte), Giulini won a law degree from the university at nearby Pavia. He was interested in music from the first, studied with G. B. Sammartini [738] and perhaps with his brother Giuseppe [720], and moved in Milan musical circles, where he was accepted as a talented amateur. Later he became interested in the history of his native city and conducted researches into the leavings of its earlier times. Around 1780 he began publishing his history of Milan. He was rewarded by being made official municipal historian and was granted an annuity to go with the title. Giulini wrote an opera and other vocal and instrumental works, including a number of well-regarded sonatas. He is chiefly admired for his symphonies, however, the mandatory qualifier for which appears to be "interesting." RECORDINGS: One symphony, in F major, has been recorded by Newell Jenkins.

[809] MONN, Matthias Georg (Mon, Mát-tē'-ás Gā'-ôrg)
ORGANIST
BORN: Vienna, April 9, 1717
DIED: Vienna, October 3, 1750

The Monn boys, Johann and Johann Christoph (1726–1782), were the sons of Jakob Monn, a Vienna coachman. Both became keyboard players and composers. Johann also became Matthias Georg or sometimes Georg Matthias. It is sometimes hard to keep them apart since each liked to inscribe his compositions with just plain "Monn." The elder was a chorister at the monastery of Klosterneuberg and from his early twenties was organist at the Karlskirche, built in 1716 by Charles VI in thanksgiving for the end of a plague epidemic. He seems to have led a rather obscure life and died at thirty-three. (Johann Christoph is said to have died in dire poverty.) Matthias composed some Masses and other religious music, and among his chamber works, some string quartets. Both brothers wrote symphonies and concerti and keyboard sonatas. Matthias is especially forward-looking in his orchestral works, and composed the first known symphony in four movements with a minuet (between the slow movement and finale). None other than Arnold Schoenberg [1657] realized the continuo parts and edited works by both Monns, and arranged a curious cello concerto for Pablo Casals supposedly from a harpsichord concerto by Matthias. Casals never used it, and the work is probably more Schoenberg than Monn. RECORDINGS: The Schoenberg arrangement has been recorded by Lawrence Lesser, and Jacqueline Du Pré has recorded the *real* cello concerto, Janos Sebestyan an unarranged harpsichord concerto, and the Vienna Concentus Musicus the first quartet.

[810] STAMITZ, Johann Wenzel Anton
(Shtä'-mitz, Yō'-hån Vent'-zel Ån'-tōn)
VIOLINIST, CONDUCTOR, TEACHER
BORN: Deutsch-Brod (Německý Brod),
  c. June 19, 1717
DIED: Mannheim, March 27, 1757

Though Stamitz was baptized Jan Waclaw Antonín, there is no authority for current Czech insistence that his surname was really Stamic. The family came, two generations earlier, from what is now northwest Yugoslavia. The composer's father settled in what is now Havlíčkův Brod (located between Brno and Prague), became organist and choir director at the Dekanal Church, entered local politics, married Rozina Boëm, a politician's daughter, in 1714, and set about immediately producing eleven children, of whom Johann was the third. After giving him basic training, Anton Stamitz sent the boy to the Jesuit school in Jihlava, and then, at seventeen, to the university in Prague. At that point Johann drops out of sight, to reappear early in 1742 as a member of the Mannheim musical forces operative at the wedding of Prince Carl Theodor, who would succeed to the Palatine electorate the following year. By that time Stamitz had several strings to his bow, for he could solo not only on the violin, but also on the viola d'amore and the contrabass. With the new regime he was promoted to first violinist. The following year (1744) he married a Mannheim girl, Maria Antonia Lüneborn; their first son, Carl [937] became a musician of consequence, as did their fifth and last child Anton (1750–?). By the time he was given the title of *Konzertmeister* in the mid-1740s, Stamitz was the highest-paid musician at the court. In 1750 he was given charge of instrumental music. It was a highly appropriate post, for at Mannheim Stamitz had put together the prototype of the modern symphony orchestra. With pride of place given to strings, of course, it also boasted timpani and pairs of flutes, oboes, trumpets, horns, and (a novelty) clarinets; and its feats of precision and dynamic range from pianissimo to fortissimo made it the musical wonder of Europe. Just before this last appointment, the Stamitzes made a journey of several months back home. In 1754 Johann began a year in Paris, where his fame had preceded him through his music, pupils, travelers, and Baron von Grimm's 1752 satire *The Little Prophet from Böhmischbroda,* which depicted an itinerant Bohemian fiddler bringing the New Music to France. (In the context of the War of the Buffoons, the Stamitzean protagonist was supposed somehow to symbolize Pergolesi [782].) Stamitz was the guest of the wealthy tax farmer and music patron Jean Le Riche de la Pouplinière, whom he persuaded to update his private orchestra. The composer was lionized and conducted his music at both public and private concerts, including the Concert Spirituel. Nothing is known of the cause or circumstances of his early death two years later.

Though he was generally forgotten a century later, Stamitz's contemporaries recognized him for what he was worth. He was imitated by, for example, Johann Schobert [888], Gossec [879], and Maldere [852], and his style influenced that of Boccherini [927], Johann Christian Bach [886] and other early Classicists. Moreover, he left a number of influential pupils, such as Filtz [874], Cannabich [868], and his own son Carl. Charles Burney, in an excess of admiration, likened him to Shakespeare, a supernal genius coming from nowhere. Stamitz wrote some sacred music, including a *Mass* popular in its time, and some chamber music, but he is properly best remembered for his orchestral works. He wrote at least 60 symphonies, 35 concerti, and 10 orchestral trios, but there may be more because it is sometimes impossible, among the manuscripts of various Stamitzes (spelled with prodigal variety) and Steinmetzes, to tell who wrote what.

Stamitz is one of the most important figures in the development of the symphony. He moved it from the Sammartinian [738] development of the old operatic *sinfonia* to the four-movement-with-minuet form inherited by Haydn [871] and Mozart [992]. Thanks to the elector's generosity, he was able to develop an orchestra that enabled him to experiment, so that he could move

from the string symphony to one that was genuinely orchestral in the modern sense. The old assertion that Stamitz "invented" sonata-allegro form is now seriously in question, but in using contrasting primary-secondary, male-female themes in his opening movements, he came close to it.
RECORDINGS: There is a disc apiece of the orchestral trios from Dietfried Bernet and Milan Munclinger, various individual symphonies led by (for example) Carl Gorvin, Christopher Hogwood, and Henry Swoboda, three flute concerti played by Gerard Schaub, and the clarinet concerto by Jacques Lancelot and Jost Michaels.

[811] STRAUBE, Rudolf (Shtrou'-bə, Rōō'-dolf)
HARPSICHORDIST, GUITARIST
BORN: Trebnitz, 1717
DIED: London, c. 1780

Straube was a pupil of J. S. Bach [684], but not his most famous one. The son of a Silesian cantor, he also studied at the University of Leipzig from 1740. Though he specialized in the *clavier* while in Leipzig, he later turned to the lute and finally to the more fashionable guitar. He eventually settled in London in 1759 and lived there the rest of his life. RECORDINGS: Three sonatas for the rather unusual combination of guitar and continuo have been recorded by John Williams. Stephen Dodgson describes this music as being that of "a lesser Leopold Mozart." *Caveat emptor.*

[812] NICHELMANN, Christoph (Nēkh'-el-mán, Krēs'-tōf)
HARPSICHORDIST, THEORIST, TEACHER
BORN: Treuenbrietzen, August 13, 1717
DIED: Berlin, July 20, 1762

A native of a small town southwest of Berlin, Nichelmann was a chorister under Johann Sebastian Bach [684] at the Thomasschule in Leipzig. Bach, however, entrusted Nichelmann's keyboard and compositional training to his son Wilhelm Friedemann [784], who was seven years older than his pupil. At sixteen, Nichelmann, who wanted to write operas, went to Hamburg, where he alternately worked as a domestic musician and studied with the likes of Telemann [665] and Matthesson [668]. In 1739 he moved to Berlin for further training under Quantz [730] and with Karl Heinrich Graun [757]. He was also pretty clearly influenced by C. P. E. Bach [801], to whom

he became backup court harpsichordist in 1744. In 1755, as a consequence of the Italian-French quarrel, which had spilled over into Frederick's Gallicized bailiwick, Nichelmann published a pamphlet on the nature of melody, which elicited a counterblast by a pseudonymous Caspar Dünkelfeind (Caspar Enemy-of-Presumption), thought by some to have been C. P. E. Bach and resulted in a brief *Papierkrieg.* A year later, apparently for reasons of his own, Nichelmann resigned and spent the rest of his brief life eking out a living as a teacher in wartime Berlin. Nichelmann, a practitioner of the New Sentiment, was not prolific. His largest area of creativity was that of harpsichord music, including easy sonatas and smaller pieces for amateur consumption. He also left a setting of Metastasio's *Il Sogno di Scipione (Scipio's Dream),* a *Requiem,* some *Lieder,* and orchestral works, including 16 keyboard concerti. RECORDINGS: One concerto has been recorded by Günther Radhuber.

[813] CENNICK, John
BORN: 1718
DIED: 1755

Though he lived in England all his life, his importance is more to American music than to British. A religious "enthusiast," he began as a Quaker, but later, probably owing to the involvement of the Wesley brothers, became a member of the Moravian Brethren. (The remnants of the old pre-Reformation Hussites and perhaps of the Waldenses, they had been given new life and impetus by their patron and protector, Count Zinzendorf, who "refounded" the sect in 1727. Many members settled in Pennsylvania and North Carolina, where the Moravians remain active.) Cennick published 2 books of hymns—*Hymns for the Children of God,* 1741; and *Sacred Hymns,* 1743. The second work reflects the Moravian practice of segregating the sisters from the brethren in church, in that many of the selections are meant to be dialogued. Cennick's simple verses and catchy tunes are regarded as one of the chief bases of American spirituals, both white and black. The Leonard dePaur Chorus has recorded the most popular of them, "Jesus My All to Heav'n Is Gone."

[814] MUDGE, Richard
CLERGYMAN
BORN: Bideford, 1718
DIED: April 1763

Mudge, a musical amateur from Devon, followed professionally in the footsteps of his father, the Reverend Zachariah Mudge, a friend of Dr. Samuel Johnson. Richard's brother Thomas was a well-known clockmaker, and another, John, was a surgeon. Richard took a B.A. at Pembroke College, Oxford, in 1738 and an M.A. in 1741. In the latter year he was ordained and became a country curate at Great Packington, near Birmingham. He is assumed to be the "Rev. Mr. Mudge" who was musically active in Birmingham in the years he was in the vicinity. In 1749 a set of 6 concerti, followed by an *Adagio* for strings with added voices at the end, appeared in London. The composer is identified simply as "Mr. Mudge," and the more cautious are not wholly willing to grant our man their authorship. In 1756 he became rector of Bedworth in Warwickshire and presumably died there—some accounts give the date as April 3. RECORDINGS: The first concerto, which calls for a trumpet as well as strings, has inevitably been recorded by Maurice André.

[815] OXINAGAS, Joaquín de (Oks-ē-nà'-gàs, Hwà-kēn' dā)
ORGANIST
BORN: Bilbao, c. October 26, 1719
DIED: Madrid, October 24, 1789

One of the so-called Basque "Scarlattists," Oxinagas served as organist of the cathedrals of Burgos (from 1740), Bilbao (from 1742), and Toledo (from 1750), and of the Royal Chapel in Madrid from 1747 to at least 1749, the year in which he collaborated with José de Nebra (1702–68) and Sebastian Albero in a published treatise on the organ music of José Elías (c. 1715–51). He resigned from his Toledo post in 1754. He left a handful of keyboard pieces, including some fine fugues. RECORDINGS: Antonio Ruiz-Pipó has recorded a sonata.

[816] MOZART, Johann Georg Leopold (Mōt'-särt, Yō'-hàn Gā'-ôrg Lā'-ō-pōlt)
VIOLINIST, TEACHER
BORN: Augsburg, November 14, 1719
DIED: Salzburg, May 28, 1787

As Alfred Einstein has astutely noted, if Leopold Mozart had not been the father of Wolfgang [992], his music would probably lie gathering dust, like that of many another honest, mediocre musician of the time. But he was who he was, and his music has a

present currency quite out of keeping with its intrinsic value.

Leopold Mozart was the oldest of the six sons of the bookbinder Johann Georg Mozart (or Motzert) and his second wife Anna Maria, *née* Sulzer. The family home was (and is) a few blocks from the cathedral, where Leopold sang as a choirboy. When his father died in 1736, he was sent over the hills to Salzburg with a scholarship to study for the priesthood at the Benedictine University. He was granted a baccalaureate degree in philosophy in 1738 but found he had no taste for a clerical career and parted company with the university a year later. (There seems to be a question of whether he was kicked out or whether his guardians refused to support him.) Meanwhile he had learned to play the violin well enough to get a post as valet-musician in the household of one of the cathedral officials, the Count of Thurn-Valsassina and Taxis, a member of the family who ran the imperial postal service. Leopold, who always had a strong sense of his own worth, apparently decided that he would, as they say, write his way out of his flunkey job, and began turning out sonatas, church music, and dramatic pieces, and, sure enough, in 1743, he found himself playing fourth fiddle in the Prince-Archbishop's orchestra, and, a year later, also teaching his instrument to the cathedral choirboys. In 1747, after a long courtship, he married Anna Maria Pertl, twenty-seven, an orphan since childhood, and set up in an apartment (now a Mozart museum) in the Getreidegasse. An eyewitness calls them the handsomest couple in Salzburg. In the next nine years, they produced seven children, but only the fourth, Maria Anna Wallburga Ignatia, alias "Nannerl" (1751–1829) and the last, Wolfgang, survived.

Two years after Nannerl was born, Salzburg got a new ruler, Sigismund von Schrattenbach, who (as was common) had turned cleric to be eligible for the post. Three years after that, Anna Maria produced her remarkable son and Leopold the violin method that remained the standard for many decades and (children apart) was perhaps his most important contribution to music. In 1757 the archbishop—not, apparently, as a consequence of either achievement—named him court composer, for what it was worth. In 1758 Leopold moved up to the second chair in the orchestra. But from then on, his story is largely that of Wolfgang's successes and his own failures. In 1762, feeling it was time to exhibit his prodigies, he got permission to take them to Munich, where they played for the Elector Max III Joseph. In the autumn they drove to Vienna and performed privately for the imperial family. From Vienna they took a somewhat harebrained winter trip to Pressburg (then in Hungary; now known as Bratislava, Czechoslovakia) before returning to Salzburg. While all this was going on, *Kapellmeister* Eberlin died. Leopold, who had got on Eberlin's good side, assumed he would succeed him. But as it turned out, it was the vice-*Kapellmeister,* a nonentity named Lolli, who was promoted, Mozart being given *his* place—from which he never progressed. Six months after he came back, Leopold and his family were off for a much longer junket involving a grand tour of the Germanies, five months in Paris, more than a year in London, then a slow journey home through the Low Countries, France, and Switzerland. It was not until 1766 that they reached Salzburg.

There is no doubt that Leopold exploited his children. There is no doubt that he endangered their health and perhaps their lives (they were frequently ill during their travels). At the same time, he showed great concern for their welfare. Though he was not paid while on the road (or for the time spent away), he saw to it that they traveled by coach on the long hauls, and by sedan chair when the city weather was inclement. Archbishop Sigismund has been criticized for his stinginess and his failure to further Leopold's career, but the archbishop was not clairvoyant and one can hardly blame him. In 1769 he let father and son go again, this time for a tour of Italy. They came back in 1771 to find Sigismund dead and themselves in the employ of a very different sort of man. Hieronymus Colleredo was a believer in the dangerous new ideas emanating from France, a ruler who inspired dislike among his subjects and a man who had no particular interest in the fine arts. For a time he allowed the Mozarts a measure of freedom, but their absences redounded to Leopold's ambitions.

In 1773 Mozart bought a house on the Marktplatz, just across from the gardens of the Mirabell Palace, which Archbishop Wolf Dietrich had built for his mistress in the previous century. He was to live there the rest of his days. In 1777 matters came to a head. Father and son were denied permission to go to Paris. Wolfgang tendered his resignation, and the archbishop fired them both. Leopold managed to get reinstated. Wolfgang set off with his mother, who died in Paris in the summer of the next year. Three years later he left Salzburg to live in Vienna, and the story of Leopold's last years is one of loneliness, bitterness, and disappointment.

As a man, Leopold Mozart was an interesting and contradictory character. An adoring husband and father, he was nevertheless basically a misanthrope. Possessed of a keen, even brilliant mind, he saw through the sham and sloth around him, and both hated and feared the system that rated dolts and nobodies his betters. Yet he did not hesitate to bend the knee to his alleged superiors and attempt to butter up those who might improve his lot. His letters show him a highly articulate and observant man with many interests. But one has to rate him both professionally and personally as something of a failure.

Between 1740 and the years when his children began to occupy his time, Leopold Mozart wrote a great deal of music in most of the genres one might expect; then his output tailed off and had virtually dried up twenty years before he died. Perhaps his largest production was of sacred music, but he also wrote many symphonies and some concerti, as well as the sort of background music for outdoor and indoor entertainments that one would expect.

RECORDINGS: Of this last sort of thing there are recordings of the *Bauernhochzeit (Peasant Wedding)* by Wilhelm Jerger; the *Cassation* in G Major (the source of the so-called "Toy Symphony" mistakenly attributed to Joseph Haydn [871]), by Carl Gorvin and F. Charles Adler; the *Serenade* in D Major for trumpet, trombone, and orchestra, conducted by Ernö Sebestyen; and many of the *Schlittenfahrt (Sleighride).* A disc by the Concerto Amsterdam offers works for horns and strings, and every trumpeter worth his salt has had a go at the trumpet concerto. Both Karl Ristenpart and Ernst Märzendorfer have recorded one of the several G-major symphonies. Sacred music recordings include a *Missa solemnis* in C Major by Roland Bader and the *Litany of Loreto* in E-flat Major by Ernst Hinreiser.

[817] KRUMLOVSKÝ, Jan (Krum-lōv'-skē, Yàn)
VIOLA D'AMORIST, POLITICIAN
BORN: Tabor, 1719
DIED: 1763

One of the earliest Bohemian virtuosi on the viola d'amore, Krumlovský worked for a time at the electoral court in Dresden. Later he returned to Tabor (south of Prague) where he became burgomaster. His only surviving music consists of three suites and another piece for his instruments. RECORDINGS: One of the suites has been recorded by

Jaroslav Horak, accompanied on the viola da gamba by František Posta.

[818] SAVAGE, William
SINGER, ORGANIST, TEACHER
BORN: 1720
DIED: London, July 27, 1789

William Savage began his career as a youthful alto in several of Handel's operas and oratorios, and, having passed through a tenor phase, wound up as a basso. He studied with Geminiani [693] and Pepusch [611] and by the time he reached his majority, he was church organist at Finchley, Middlesex. Three years later he became a gentleman of the Chapel Royal, and in 1748 almoner, singer, and master to the boys at St. Paul's Cathedral. He taught a number of musicians well known in their day, including his daughter Jane, a successful harpsichordist and composer, and Joseph Battishill. Plagued by bad health, Savage had to give up his various appointments when in his middle fifties. His musical legacy consists primarily of anthems, songs, and catches. RECORDINGS: One catch has been recorded by the Deller Consort.

[819] AUFFMANN, Josef Anton (Ouf'-mán, Yō'-zef Àn'-tōn)
ORGANIST, MUSIC DIRECTOR
BORN: c. 1720
DIED: after 1773

What is known of Auffmann amounts to a chronology of some of his jobs. He succeeded Franz Xaver Richter [777] in 1750 as *Kapellmeister* to the Abbot of Kempten, was in Straubing from 1756, was a member of the court music at Donaueschingen at some later period, and is last heard of in 1773 as *Kapellmeister*-organist to the Bishop of Pruntrut (assuming such a place to exist) in Switzerland. He wrote a couple of symphonies, some lost incidental music, and works for organ, including concerti. RECORDINGS: Franz Lehrndorfer has recorded an organ sonata.

[820] BREMNER, James
ORGANIST, VIOLINIST
BORN: England, c. 1720
DIED: Philadelphia, 1780

Bremner was a close friend of Francis Hopkinson [895], who probably studied under him. He was organist at Christ Church in Philadelphia, where, in 1770, Hopkinson

substituted in his absence, and was a member of Hopkinson's amateur chamber orchestra. He was perhaps related to the publisher (Edinburgh and London), Robert Bremner (1713–89). Hopkinson wrote an *Ode* on the occasion of his death. RECORDINGS: Janice Beck has recorded a "trumpet air" for organ.

[821] KIRNBERGER, Johann Philipp
(Kērn'-bâr-ger, Yō'-hán Fē'-lip)
VIOLINIST, MUSIC DIRECTOR, THEORIST
BORN: Saalfeld, c. April 24, 1721
DIED: Berlin, July 27, 1783

Crotchety, irritable, learned, brilliant, stuffy, and often wrong-headed, Thuringian-born Kirnberger was better known for his musical writings than for his musical compositions and would certainly have been given an endowed chair had there been one. Like all Great Authorities, he attracted many students, but that Carl Friedrich Zelter [1008] and Karl Friedrich Fasch (1736–1800) seem to have been the best of them says something about him. His most passionate belief was that J. S. Bach [684] was the greatest of all musicians and that he, Kirnberger, was his prophet, and he maintained that his practical and theoretical works were chiefly designed to preserve Bach's musical thought and methodology. He devised an approach to harmony that reconciled very conservative thinking with those of the new radical theories that he could swallow and insisted on the virtue of applying mathematics to music. Accordingly, he published treatises on how to compose in a hurry that some modern musicologists have taken for parodies—but Kirnberger was not known for a sense of humor.

Initially trained at home, then by J. P. Kellner [761], Bach enthusiast and organist at Gräfenroda, he proceeded to Sondershausen c. 1738 to study violin with one Meil and organ with Heinrich Nikolaus Gerber, court organist and Bach pupil. It was Gerber who sent him on to Bach in 1739 and changed Kirnberger's life. He left Leipzig in 1741 for Poland, where, across a decade, he held various ecclesiastical and princely appointments, though one suspects that his frequent changes in employment reflect his prickly personality. In 1751 he went to Dresden, did some graduate study on the violin with a master named Zickler, and joined Frederick II's musical establishment in Berlin. He must have admired Kapellmeister K. H. Graun [757], for he later edited some of his music, but in 1754 he transferred to the *Kapelle* of Prince Heinrich. Four years later Princess Anna Amalie [828], who was especially kind to her brother's problem musicians, gave him a berth for the rest of his days. All of Kirnberger's known music and writing was done under her patronage. The former includes chamber and keyboard works, songs, and a small body of church music. It suffers, as might be expected, from an excess of theory and would have won the composer a foundation grant today. His meticulous counterpoint is seen at its best in the organ music.

RECORDINGS: A sample of the organ music has been recorded by Franz Lehrndorfer. Martin Gotthart Schneider has recorded some lightweight harpsichord pieces. A C-minor keyboard concerto, recorded by Luciano Sgrizzi, was long attributed to Wilhelm Friedemann Bach [784], but is now thought to be Kirnberger's.

[822] BACH, Johann Ernst (Bȧkh, Yō'- hȧn Ȧrnst)
ORGANIST, LAWYER, ACCOUNTANT
BORN: Eisenach, c. January 30, 1722
DIED: Eisenach, September 1, 1777

This Johann Ernst Bach was Johann Sebastian's [684] godson and the son of his double cousin, the Eisenach organist, Johann Bernhard [646]. (Another Johann Ernst [1683–1739], the son of Sebastian's Uncle Christoph, was an organist in Arnstadt.) The younger Ernst was sent to the Thomasschule in Leipzig but was eventually kicked out for cutting classes. However, he remained in Leipzig (probably with his relative) and began work on a law degree at the university. But he was not permitted to finish: when he was nineteen, Eisenach was absorbed into the Duchy of Weimar, terminating his father's court appointment. Bernhard called his son home to help out. Ernst persuaded the Eisenach fathers to let him practice law. But he found his profession not as lucrative as he had hoped and applied for an appointment as court counsel to no avail. At this point in 1749, his father died and he shelved his legal ambitions to take over his musical duties. A year later he married a parson's daughter, Florentina Katharina Malsch, who in time bore him seven sons and a daughter.

At about this same time, Bach had dedicated a collection of musical fables to the Weimar heir-apparent, Ernst August Constantin. In 1755 Constantin, himself a man of high culture, married Princess Anna Amalie of Braunschweig, niece of Frederick II of Prussia [791], and herself a composer

[905]. Wanting a suitable court musical organization, but with limited funds to support it, he posed the problem to Jiří Benda [824], court *Kapellmeister* at Gotha, and was told it was no-go. Then he applied to Bach, who put his training to use and came up with a plan that would work. When Constantin succeeded to the title he put it in operation and hired Bach as his *Kapellmeister* at 400 thalers a year, with permission to retain his Eisenach post. This last provision was probably a good thing, for two years later, in 1758, Constantin died, and in the interests of economy Anna Amalie reluctantly disbanded her band—but she let Bach keep his salary and title for the rest of his life. He wrote a funeral ode in memory of his prince, which seemed the least he could do. Thereafter, he devoted most of his energies to Eisenach, where he also became church accountant. When he died, his son Johann Georg (1751–94), the only one of his offspring trained in both music and law, succeeded him in both posts. Ernst left a *Passion,* a *Magnificat,* a few cantatas, violin sonatas, and keyboard pieces; they reflect talent and a certain puzzlement at the direction music seemed to be taking.

RECORDINGS: Franz Lehrndorfer has recorded an organ piece, and pianist Ray Lev a prelude and fugue. Helmut Rilling conducts the Bach-Collegium Stuttgart in the cantata *Die Liebe Gottes ist ausgegossen.*

[823] NARDINI, Pietro (När-dē'-nē, Pē- ā'-trō)
VIOLINIST
BORN: Livorno, April 12, 1722
DIED: Florence, May 7, 1793

Nardini was the greatest of the pupils of Tartini [714], with whom he was closely associated. At twelve he went from his native "Leghorn" to study with him in Padua, remaining there for some years before going home in or around 1740. The next twenty years of his life are obscure, but 1760 found him for a time in Vienna. He may also have visited Dresden before returning to Italy in 1762. Later that year he accepted a post in the court orchestra of Frederick Eugene of Württemberg in Stuttgart, where he played for a little over two years (with summers off for trips home). In 1765 he was briefly at the Brunswick court and perhaps did some touring in Germany before going back to Italy for good the next year. There he continued to concertize for a while and visited his aged teacher in Padua in 1769. (Recent research seems to have thrown cold water on the story of Nardini's hovering over his bed and ministering to his needs until he died the following year.) Nardini, in fact, seems to have returned to Tuscany in 1769 and to have settled down in Florence for the rest of his life, taking in pupils and performing at the court of the Grand Duke Leopold I (later the Emperor Leopold II).

Nardini was universally praised as a great, if lachrymose, violinist (Christian Schubart [1739–91] reports violinist and audience all weeping profusely as he played.) He left a handful of concerti, some *sinfonias* and "quartets," and over 60 sonatas. Most of these last are for violin and continuo, but there are some trio sonatas, four sonatas for piano, and an oddity called *Sonate enigmatique,* for solo violin with *scordatura* tuning. His music derives much from Tartini's (except real inspiration), but his emotionally songful slow movements are his personal hallmark. His representation on records is spotty: the E minor concerto by Mischa Elman, Peter Rybar, and Jan Tomasow, the A major by Herman Krebbers, a quartet by the Schäffer quartet, and a D major sonata by Eduard Melkus and Stephen Staryk, one (unspecified) by Erika Morini, an E-flat concerto by Melkus, and snippets by way of encore from several violinists.

[824] BENDA, Jiří Antonín ("Georg Anton") (Ben′-dȧ, Yēr′-zhē Ȧn′-tô-nyēn)
VIOLINIST, CONDUCTOR, OBOIST, KEYBOARDIST
BORN: Alt Benatek, c. June 30, 1722
DIED: Köstritz, November 6, 1795

Third son of the four sons of Jan Jiří Benda, linen weaver and tavern musician, and the brother of František [776], Jiří must have picked up some musical training at home before being sent off at thirteen to the Piarist school at Kosmonosy. In 1739 he went on to Jičín, northeast of Prague, to study at the Jesuit College there. When the War of the Austrian Succession broke out, Frederick II of Prussia, on campaign, found himself in Staré Benátky. František (Franz) Benda being one of his favorite musicians back in Berlin, the king looked up his family and invited them to move to Prussia, which they did in 1742. Stopping off in Jičín, they persuaded Jiří to join them. On the recommendation of František, he was placed among the second violins in the court orchestra. After seven years he was no longer content to play second fiddle, and applied for the *Kapellmeister's* post at Gotha left vacant by the death of Heinrich Stölzel [704]. He won it in the spring of 1750. In Gotha, Benda married, and eventually produced

seven children, several of them musical, especially the oldest, Friedrich Ludwig, who had a career as a stage composer and did the earliest German music for Beaumarchais' *Le Barbier de Seville.* In 1765 he took a sabbatical and visited Italy in company with young Friedrich Wilhelm Rust [904], a sometime pupil of his lifelong friend C. P. E. Bach [801] and his brother František.

Strangely, Benda's not unimpressive composing career did not begin in earnest until after he was fifty. (He published a set of keyboard sonatas as early as 1757.) Beginning with church music and 3 Italian operas, he went on to more original works— *Singspiele* (including a treatment of *Romeo and Juliet),* secular cantatas *(Lessing's Obsequies, Benda's Lament),* and especially his novel melodramas (or duo-dramas) for accompanied dramatic recitation. (Like Asplmayr [850], he was obviously acquainted with Rousseau's [793] work; he wrote one of his melodramas to a German translation of the latter's *Pygmalion.)* Mozart [992], who thought him the best of the *Kapellmeister* breed, especially admired his *Ariadne auf Naxos* and his *Medea.* In 1778 Benda retired from Gotha, visited Hamburg, Vienna, Mannheim, and Paris, apparently hopeful of a new post, and eventually stopped in Thuringia where he spent his last decade moving from small town to small town.

Some of Benda's dramatic works have had modern revivals but no recordings. His instrumental music includes, besides more than 50 sonatas, some symphonies, concerti, and chamber music. Extravagantly praised in his time, Benda is found often wanting in inspiration by modern critics and, at his worst, too heavy on "self-expression."

RECORDINGS: Five of the symphonies have been recorded by Libor Hlaváček, a keyboard concerto by Susana Ruzičkova, another by Lory Wallfisch, a piano sonata by Rudolf Firkusny, a flute sonata by Hans-Martin Linde, and a trio sonata by the Oistrakhs.

[825] LANG, Johann Georg (Láng, Yō′-hȧn Gä′-ôrg)
VIOLINIST, CONDUCTOR
BORN: Svojšin, 1722
DIED: Ehrenbreitstein, July 17, 1798

Lang probably studied in his native Bohemia, then became a musician to the Prince-Bishop of Augsburg when he was twenty-four. Between 1749 and 1752 he was in Italy, and studied in Naples with Francesco Durante [678]. He returned to Augsburg to become *Konzertmeister* in the Bishop's orchestra. In 1769 the bishopric went to Clemens Wenzeslaus, Elector of Trier, who moved his acquired musicians to his castle at Ehrenbreitstein on the Rhine. When the elector moved to his new capital in Koblenz across the river, Lang commuted to work. In 1794 the French drove Clemens Wenzeslaus out, thus terminating the electorate. Lang went on living at Ehrenbreitstein and was buried there. Besides some sacred music, he wrote symphonies, concerti, quartets, sonatas, and keyboard works. Christian Schubart (1739–91), a contemporary composer and critic, admired his music a great deal, particularly its melodiousness. Lang shows a real grasp of Classical form, and in his duo sonatas it is the keyboard that accompanies. RECORDINGS: The Mannheim Duo have recorded an aria and minuet.

[826] RUTINI, Giovanni Marco (Rōō-tē′-nē, Jō-vän′-nē Mär′-kō)
KEYBOARDIST
BORN: Florence, April 25, 1723
DIED: Florence, December 22, 1797

The history books used to speak of the Rutini brothers, Giovanni Placido and Giovanni Maria, but it turns out they were closer than Siamese twins, contained as they were in the skin of Giovanni Marco. As a lad of thirteen, he entered the Conservatorio della Pietà dei Turchini, where he studied with Leonardo Leo [718] and later served as a sort of teaching assistant. Between 1748 and 1758 he was active in central Europe, chiefly in Prague but also in Dresden and Berlin. In the latter year he traveled to St. Petersburg with an opera troupe operated by Giovanni Battista Locatelli (apparently unrelated to the violinist-composer). Rutini remained there two or three years, teaching keyboards to the nobility, including the future Tsarina Catherine the Great. In 1761, he returned to his birthplace, married, and settled down as a composer of operas and keyboard sonatas. In the former area he won popularity all over Italy. He was elected to the Accademia Filarmonica in Bologna and was made honorary *maestro di cappella* to the court of Modena. As a sonata writer, he is viewed by some as a spiritual ancestor of Wolfgang Amadeus Mozart [992], and there is no question that his works were admired by Mozart's father, Leopold [816]. His son Ferdinando (c. 1764–1827) was for a time a composer-about-Florence, and later worked in Ancona and other Italian cities. RECORDINGS: Luciano Sgrizzi

has recorded some of the elder Rutini's sonatas.

[827] GRAF, Christian Ernst (Gräf, Krēst′-yàn Ârnst)
VIOLINIST
BORN: Rudolstadt, June 30, 1723
DIED: The Hague, July 17, 1804

Graf was one of the six musical sons of the violinist Johann Graf or Graff, (1684–1750), who spent the latter half of his life as *Konzertmeister* and *Kapellmeister* at the court of Schwarzburg-Rudolstadt. C. E. Graf succeeded his father there, but in 1762 left for Holland to become *Kapellmeister* at the Dutch court during the minority of William V. There he became known as Christiaan Graaf. He is perhaps best remembered by the set of variations that the child Wolfgang Amadeus Mozart [992] wrote on a song of his when he passed through The Hague in 1765. RECORDINGS: The Sonata da Camera Ensemble has recorded one of his trio sonatas, and the Pleyel Quartet a quartet for flute and strings.

[828] ANNA AMALIE, Princess of Prussia (Àn′-nà À-mà′-lē-à)
HARPSICHORDIST
BORN: Berlin, November 9, 1723
DIED: Berlin, March 30, 1787

Not to be confused with her niece, Anna Amalie of Saxe-Weimar [905], Anna Amalie, sister of Frederick II, was the youngest child of Frederick William I and Sophie Dorothee. She got her musical grounding from her brother and from the local cathedral organist Gottlieb Hayne. She lived all of her life in Berlin and never married. In 1758, after he had left her brother's employ, she hired Kirnberger [821] as her *Kapellmeister* and studied counterpoint and composition with him. Later she facilitated C. P. E. Bach's [801] escape from Berlin, appointing him *Kapellmeister von Haus aus*. Like her teacher, she was a conservative composer with conservative tastes. Over a lifetime she collected a magnificent musical library, containing autograph scores by many important contemporary and earlier musicians, including more than a hundred by J. S. Bach [684], which found its way into the Royal Prussian Library. Her most ambitious composition was a setting of *Vom Tod Jesu (Of Jesus' Death)*, a Passion libretto by C. W. Ramler, better known from K. H. Graun's [757] slightly later treatment. Not unexpectedly, she also wrote flute sonatas. RECORDINGS: Dietfried Bernet has recorded four military marches by her.

[829] ABEL, Karl Friedrich (Ä'-bel, Kärl Frē'-drikh)
GAMBA PLAYER, CONDUCTOR, CONCERT
PROMOTER
BORN: Cöthen, December 22, 1723
DIED: London, June 20, 1787

K. F. Abel represents the fifth known generation of the Abel musical dynasty, and is its most famous member. His grandfather, the intriguingly named Clamor Heinrich, was a municipal gambist in Bremen when he died in 1696. His father, Christian Ferdinand, who played both gamba and violin, was a member of the Cöthen court orchestra under J. S. Bach [684]. Bach stood godfather to a daughter of his in 1720, and probably wrote the three gamba sonatas for him. An older son, Leopold August, and two of *his* sons, played in the orchestra of the Duke of Mecklenberg-Schwerin. Christian Ferdinand Abel died when Karl Friedrich was fourteen, but it is not certain whether the youth was sent to study with Bach at the Thomasschule. From 1743 until the Prussian invasion of 1757, he played at the Dresden court. Then he emigrated to London, where he made an impact in 1759 with a concert of his own music wherein he performed on the gamba, the harpsichord, and something called the pentachord. (He seems to have been able to play many instruments and is said also to have performed publicly on the French horn.)

When Johann Christian Bach [886] arrived in London, the two became fast friends, took living quarters together, and appeared in a joint concert in 1764. A year later they went into the concert business and were so successful that they were called upon for court performances (both were officially chamber musicians to Queen Charlotte) and in 1774 opened a splendiferous new hall in Hanover Square. Its cost, coupled with a general falling-off of public interest, undoubtedly hastened Bach's death in 1782. Abel held out to the end of that season and then went back to Germany for a time. But he returned to London and to the concert business in 1785. A kind and generous man, he helped many London musicians and taught some, including Johann Baptist Cramer [1067]. He was one of the last important musicians (at least until modern times) to elect the gamba as his instrument. In his later years he suffered from what is now called "a drinking problem."

His music—mostly symphonies, concerti, and sonatas—is properly termed Rococo: light, filigreed, and mildly conservative for its time.

RECORDINGS: Concerto Amsterdam has recorded a concerto for violin, oboe, clarinet, and orchestra. Wolfgang Amadeus Mozart [992] came to know Abel on his childhood visit to London and copied out one of his symphonies, which thus got into the books as "Mozart's Third Symphony" and, as such, has been recorded by Otto Ackermann and Erich Leinsdorf.

[830] AULETTA, Domenico (Ou-let'-tä, Dō-mā'-nē-kō)
ORGANIST
BORN: Naples, 1723
DIED: Naples, 1753

Domenico Auletta was the son of Pietro Auletta (c. 1698–1771), a successful opera composer, who is now known largely through *Il Maestro di musica,* a comic pastiche long attributed to Pergolesi, the bulk of whose music comes from Auletta's *Orazio.* Nothing is known of Domenico's life, save that he produced three sons who became professional musicians of no great moment. He left a few pieces of religious music and three concerti for keyboard and strings. RECORDINGS: One keyboard concerto has been recorded by Ruggero Gerlin.

[831] UTTINI, Francesco Antonio Baldassare (OOt-tē'-nē, Frän'-chäs-kō Ántōn'-yō Bàl-dàs-sà'-rä)
CONDUCTOR
BORN: Bologna, 1723
DIED: Stockholm, October 25, 1795

A pupil of Padre Martini, Uttini became a composer of operas, was elected to the Accademia Filarmonica in 1743, and served as its president in 1751. A year or two later he joined Pietro Mingotti's opera troupe in Germany and married the singer Rosa Scarlatti, thought to have been Alessandro's [583] niece. He conducted works of his own in Hamburg, Rostock, and Copenhagen. Queen Luise Ulrike of Sweden invited him to Stockholm in 1755 and persuaded him to stay and write operas for her theater at Drottningholm. He managed to write six before it burned down in 1762. It was rebuilt in 1766, and the following year he was appointed court *Kapellmeister.* Five years later, however, King Adolf Frederik died, and the widowed queen closed up Drottningholm and left it. The new king,

Gustav III, her son, retained Uttini. Bright, talented, and doomed (the king was originally the protagonist of Verdi's [1232] opera *Un Ballo in maschera)*, Gustav encouraged the arts and, responding to such a favorable atmosphere, Uttini produced the first two serious operas to Swedish libretti—*Thetis och Pelée (Thetis and Peleus)*, 1773; and *Aline, Drotning uti Golconda (Aline, Queen of Golconda)* 1776. In 1777 Gustav bought the Drottningholm Theater from his mother, but put J. G. Naumann in charge, Uttini having all he could handle (which reviews said was not a great deal) as conductor of the Royal Opera. He retired in 1788 and, now a widower, married a twenty-three-year-old singer, Sophie Liljegren. Apart from more than a score of operas and other dramatic works, he left 2 oratorios, cantatas, 3 symphonies, and some sonatas. RECORDINGS: Ulf Björlin and the present-day orchestra of the Drottningholm Theater have recorded the overture to *Il re pastore* of 1755.

[832] CIRRI, Giovanni Battista (Chēr'-rē, Jō-vàn'-nē Bàt-tēs'-tà)
CELLIST, TEACHER, CLERIC, CHOIR DIRECTOR
BORN: Forlì, October 1, 1724
DIED: Forlì, June 11, 1808

Cirri studied with his older brother, Ignazio, later cathedral organist and choir director in Forlì on the Via Emilia east of Bologna. At fifteen he began a religious vocation, which seems not to have burdened him much afterward. He went to Bologna, joined the orchestra of San Petronio, and became a member of the Accademia Filarmonica in 1759. In the middle 1760s he established himself as a much-admired soloist in London (he appeared with the child Wolfgang Amadeus Mozart [992]), served as a musician to Edward Augustus, Duke of York and Albany, whom he had met in Italy, and conductor to William Henry, Duke of Gloucester and Edinburgh, both younger brothers of King George III. In 1780, learning that his brother was ill, he went back to Forlì to help out, though he continued to play in Italy until he succeeded Ignazio in 1787. Cirri published more than a score of engagingly tuneful chamber collections, including two cello concerti. RECORDINGS: One cello concerto has been recorded by the Virtuosi di Roma, with Benedetto Mazzacurati.

[833] MÜLLER, Marian (Mül-ler, Märyàn)
PRIEST, ORGANIST
BORN: 1724
DIED: ?

Müller studied music in Milan and became organist in Bellinzona in southern Switzerland. He then entered the Benedictine order in Einsiedeln, was ordained, and became abbot of the monastery. RECORDINGS: A sonata for four organs has been recorded by Rudolf Ewerhart et al.

[834] BERTONI, Ferdinando Gasparo (Ber-tō'-nē, Fer-dē-nàn'-do Gàs-pà'-rō)
ORGANIST, CHOIRMASTER, CONDUCTOR
BORN: Salò, August 15, 1725
DIED: Desenzano del Garda, December 1, 1813

Bertoni's mature life was focused on Venice, a city he loved and one where he became the most popular composer of his time, save perhaps for his colleague and sometime collaborator Galuppi [768]. He was born (and died) on the shores of Lake Garda, became a pupil of Padre Martini [767] in Bologna when he was in his late teens, and had a smash hit with *La Vedova accorta (The Crafty Widow)*, premiered at the Carnival of Venice in 1745. He probably remained in Venice, producing a puppet opera, *Il Cajetto,* the next year, and several *serie* and oratorios in those immediately following (though *Ipermestra* was premiered at the Carnival of Genoa in 1748). In 1752 Bertoni won the appointment as first organist at the Basilica of St. Mark's, beating out Pescetti [758] among others. Five years later he also became choirmaster at the Ospedale dei Mendicanti. Though these jobs elicited reams of sacred music (much of it with orchestra) from him, they do not seem to have put a crimp in his operatic output, which eventually reached a total of at least 50 works, not counting a score of occasional pieces. Though many of them were produced in Venice, Bertoni was soon getting premieres all over Italy. One of his most successful and most curious operas was *Orfeo ed Euridice* of 1776, set to the libretto Calzabigi had written for Gluck [803], and penned, it is said, with Gluck's score open before the composer. (Curiously, Gluck was accused of stealing some of his own *Orfeo* music from earlier works by Bertoni.)
The success in Milan of Bertoni's *Quinto Fabio,* starring the *castrato* Gasparo Pacchiarotti, in 1778, won both an invitation

to London, where the composer conducted that work and a number of others, including *La Governante*, a treatment of Sheridan's *The Duenna* written for the occasion. He said goodbye with a concert performance of his *Orfeo* in 1780 but was brought back by popular demand for two more years in 1781. He then went home for good and succeeded Galuppi as *maestro* at the Basilica in 1785, after which he wrote only two more operas. The death of his wife a decade later and Venice's capitulation to Napoleon and Austria two years later shattered him, and he was retired in 1808. He died at the home of his nephew in Desenzano del Garda at the age of eighty-eight. Among his many pupils were his nephew Ferdinando Turrini [963], the male soprano Gasparo Pacchiarotti, Grazioli [944], and J. S. Mayr [1034]. For all his popularity in the field, Bertoni's operas are forgotten. His chamber music, however, gets some small attention. RECORDINGS: Luciano Sgrizzi has recorded one of his keyboard sonatas.

[835] DENCKE, Jeremiah (Denk, Je-re-mī'-à)
ORGANIST, CLERGYMAN
BORN: Langenbilau, October 2, 1725
DIED: Bethlehem, Pa., May 28, 1795

Unlike many of the religious dissidents who settled in America, the Moravian Brethren, descendents of the old Hussites, actively encouraged the use of music. The earliest Moravian composer to settle and practice here was Silesian-born Jeremiah Dencke. In 1748 Dencke became organist at Herrnhut, the refuge set up in Saxony for members of the flock by their leader and patron, Graf Zinzendorf. Dencke emigrated to Pennsylvania in 1761. Between 1772 and 1784, he was warden to the congregation in Bethlehem, and afterward was overseer of the married members. He is said to have been the first to write and perform sacred music with instrumental accompaniment (frowned on by the New England Puritans). His first known work is a hymn with strings and continuo that he wrote for the synodal convention in Bethlehem in 1766. He later wrote some more ambitious anthems and arias. RECORDINGS: One aria has been recorded by Rosalind Rees.

[836] CHIESA, Melchiorre (Kē-ā'-zà, Māl-kē-ôr'-rā)
HARPSICHORDIST, CONDUCTOR
BORN: c. 1725 (?)
DIED: 1799 or later

Considered in his day one of Italy's outstanding composers, Chiesa is now little more than a shadow figure. He was probably a Milanese by birth, though claims have been made for Florence, and he seems to have served as choirmaster of various Milanese churches, including Santa Maria alla Scala. By the time of the Mozarts' [816, 992] visit in 1771, he was serving as backup harpsichordist to Lampugnani [769] at the Teatro Ducale. When fire rendered that theater inoperative five years later, Santa Maria alla Scala was razed to make way for the Teatro alla Scala, where Chiesa and Lampugnani resumed their former posts. Chiesa is said to have written operas, but not even any record remains of them. Extant are some sacred works and orchestral and chamber pieces. RECORDINGS: Antonio Ballista has recorded one of the symphonies.

[837] LARRANAGA, José (Lär-rà-nà'-gà, Hō-zā')
CHOIRMASTER
BORN: c. 1725
DIED: Aranzuzu, September 1806

The influence of Domenico Scarlatti [687] long persisted in provincial enclaves in Spain. One of these was in the Basque country in the north, apparently focused on the Franciscan monastery of Aranzuzu. Padre José was choirmaster there at the time of his death. He left a fair number of compositions, mostly choral and keyboard works, the earliest dated 1746. As a follower of Scarlatti, he seems to have been one of the more considerable talents. RECORDINGS: Antonio Ruiz-Pipó has recorded five of his sonatas.

[838] PIAZZA, Gaetano (Pē-àd'-zà, Gī-tà'-nō)
CHOIRMASTER
BORN: c. 1725 (?)
DIED: after 1775 (?)

Gaetano Piazza served as *maestro di cappella* in various Milanese churches in the third quarter of the eighteenth century. Nothing else is presently known of him. RECORDINGS: Rudolf Ewerhart and Mathias Siedel recorded his Sonata for 2 Organs.

[839] WALOND, William, the elder
ORGANIST
BORN: c. 1725
DIED: Oxford, 1770

As of June 25, 1757, Walond held the post of *organorum pulsator* (striker of organs) at Oxford, which probably means that he played in one or more of the chapels there. He took a B. Mus. from Christ Church the following July, and a year later published what is thought to be the first complete setting of Alexander Pope's "Ode to St. Cecilia." He also published some keyboard voluntaries. He was presumably the father of three musical Walond brothers, William, Richard, and George. His namesake was for a time organist at Chichester Cathedral and later became a recluse. RECORDINGS: Haig Mardirosian has recorded three "cornet" voluntaries.

[840] ŠTĚPÁN, Josef Antonín (Shtyā'-pàn, Ân'-tô-nyēn)
HARPSICHORDIST, TEACHER
BORN: Kopidlno, c. March 14, 1726
DIED: Vienna, April 12, 1797

The recent claim that Štěpán was the missing link, so to speak, between the pre-Classics on the one hand, and Haydn [871] and Mozart [992] on the other has given him considerably more attention than he has had for two centuries. He was the son of the schoolmaster-organist of a village eastward of Prague. When the newly crowned Frederick II of Prussia unleashed the First Silesian War in 1741, Štěpán fled to Vienna and put himself under the protection of his absentee landlord, Count Šlik, in what was obviously a slick getaway. The count had him trained by his own *Kapellmeister* and by Wagenseil [804]. (Earlier critics were less exercised over Štěpán's influence on Mozart than about his debt to Wagenseil.) As Georg Anton Steffan, the young man became a much-praised harpsichordist and a much-sought-after teacher. He later became the count's *Kapellmeister* and in 1766 was appointed keyboard teacher to the Imperial Archduchesses Maria Carolina and Maria Antonia (later known in another context as Marie Antoinette). He probably suffered from hypertension, for he temporarily lost his eyesight in the 1770s and was pensioned off and died of a stroke at fifty-one. It is his sonatas and concerti that demonstrate such features as sonata-allegro opening movements and finales, song-form slow movements, and minor-key introductions. Štěpán also has some importance in the history of the art song. RECORDINGS: Janos Sebestyan has recorded one of his early keyboard divertimenti.

[841] BERTON, Pierre-Montan (Bâr-tōn', Pē-âr' Mōn-tàn')
SINGER, KEYBOARDIST, CELLIST, CONDUCTOR, IMPRESARIO
BORN: Maubert-Fontaines, January 7, 1727
DIED: Paris, May 14, 1780

Berton founded an operatic dynasty. His son Henri-Montan (1767–1844), who succeeded Étienne-Nicolas Méhul [1036] at the Paris Conservatory, wrote more than 40 operas, including *Les Rigueurs du cloître (The Tyranny of the Cloister)* of 1790, said to be the first "rescue-opera" and thus the prototype of Beethoven's [1063] *Fidelio.* Henri-Montan's illegitimate son Henri was a composer of *opéras comiques* and professor of voice and the Conservatory, and *his* son Adolphe sang at the Opéra Comique, in Nice, and in Algiers.

Pierre-Montan himself began as a singer. Born in a village equidistant from Rheims and Charleroi, he sang as a choirboy in the cathedral choir at Senlis. In 1743 he went to Paris, joined the choir of Notre-Dame as a tenor, gave the Opéra a try in 1745, but decided he was better adapted to playing cello in the orchestra. In 1746 he found his proper level at the Marseilles opera as a basso. From 1748 to 1753 he worked in Bordeaux as conductor and composer at the opera house and as organist to two churches. Then he came back to Paris, had an opera-ballet, *Deucalion et Pyrrha,* accepted by the Opéra in 1755, and then was appointed conductor there. In 1766 he and the Avignonese violinist Jean-Claude Trial were maneuvered into the directorship of the Opéra by Trial's patron, the Prince de Conti, displacing Francoeur [734] and François Rebel. The next year Berton also took charge of musical performances at Versailles, and in 1771 of the Concert Spirituel. In 1775 he reached the top of his success as General Intendant of the Opéra and Superintendent of the Royal Music. He gave up his post at the Concert Spirituel in 1773 and at the Opéra in 1778 but continued to conduct there.

As a composer, Berton was most successful as an opera-doctor. He updated a number of earlier works to contemporary tastes, providing ballets for several. His own contributions were not especially successful. He twice collaborated with Trial and once with J.-B. de LaBorde, who later lost his head in the Terror. It was Berton who was running the Opéra when Gluck [803] arrived, and saw most of his triumphs onto the stage.

RECORDINGS: On records Jean-Pierre Daniel conducts a Berton chaconne.

[842] HAINDL, Franz Sebastian (Hīn-dəl, Frǎnts Se-bást'-yǎn)
VIOLINIST, CONDUCTOR
BORN: Altötting, January 11, 1727
DIED: Passau, April 27, 1812

Haindl's grandfather, father (who died when the boy was five), and stepfather were all musicians in and around Munich. Haindl himself was a chorister in the pilgrimage town of Altötting, and a violin student in Munich. In 1748 he settled in Innsbruck, where he taught and directed the theater orchestra. He also worked in Bavaria and throughout the Tyrol. In 1785 he went to Passau where he worked for the bishop and again presided over the theater orchestra. He left a few pieces of sacred music, a flute concerto, and orchestral suite, and 2 symphonies. RECORDINGS: One symphony has been recorded by F. Charles Adler.

[843] BALBASTRE, Claude-Bénigne (Bal-bä'tr', Klōd Bä-nēn')
ORGANIST
BORN: Dijon, January 22, 1727
DIED: Paris, May 9, 1799

Called *"l' organiste des graces"* for his airy performance at the console, Balbastre studied with his father, the Dijon church organist Bénigne Balbastre. The Balbastres knew the Rameaus, and when Claude came to Paris in 1750 he studied composition with Jean-Philippe [675]. Five years later he had a triumph at the Concerts Spirituel with an organ concerto of his own devising. In 1756 he became organist at the church of St. Roch. It became a custom every Christmas Eve at midnight for him to give a concert of his own *noëls.* These became so popular that St. Roch's on Christmas Eve looked like Macy's during a January white sale. The archbishop, in the interests of religious propriety, public safety, and possibly national defense, put a stop to it in 1762, but afterward high society vied to see whose party Balbastre could be persuaded to appear at. In 1760 he also became one fourth of the Notre-Dame organist, the other three quarters consisting of Armand-Louis Couperin [844], Louis-Claude Daquin [717], and Nicolas Séjan. In 1776 he was appointed organist to the king's brother, the future Louis XVIII, and keyboard coach to Marie Antoinette. He was very popular as a teacher in diplomatic circles. Came the Revolution . . . We catch a glimpse of him, before he disappears into penurious obscurity, forced to play the *Marseillaise* on the Notre-Dame

organ. He reportedly invented a combination organ-harpsichord. Apart from a few pieces of chamber music and a song, his only extant works are for solo keyboard, including a book of *noëls.* RECORDINGS: The *noëls* have elicited selective recordings by such organists as Michel Chapuis, André Marchel, and Rafaël Tambyeff.

[844] COUPERIN, Armand-Louis (Kōō-per-àn', Ȧr-màn' Lōō-ē')
KEYBOARDIST
BORN: Paris, February 25, 1727
DIED: Paris, February 2, 1789

The son of Nicolas Couperin, first cousin of François le Grand [616] and organist at St. Gervais, Armand-Louis was left motherless in babyhood and fatherless at 21. At that point, he inherited his father's post, lodgings, and property. Four years later he married the organist Elisabeth-Antoinette Blanchet, daughter of an immensely successful harpsichord maker, who brought him a fortune. In addition to St. Gervais, Couperin came to preside over the consoles of no fewer than six other Paris churches, including Notre-Dame, the Ste. Chapelle, and the Chapel Royal. His wife was organist at Montmartre Abbey and both were successful teachers. During Couperin's forty-one-year tenure at St. Gervais, the church acquired a magnificent new organ built by François-Henri Cliquot, one of the greatest of builders. All three Couperin children, Pierre-Louis (1755–89), Gervais-François (1759–1826), and Antoinette-Victoire (c. 1760–1812) became successful organists. Armand-Louis, dashing from one post to another one wintry Sunday evening, was fatally struck down by a runaway horse, thereby providing a lesson for us all. He was buried, like his father and his eldest son, in St. Gervais; during the Revolution all three were dug up and dispossessed of their coffins, which were melted down for bullets. Armand-Louis' music, consisting mostly of keyboard works and duo and trio sonatas, show that he saw the direction music was then taking but not always that he had the finesse to follow it. RECORDINGS: A sonata has been recorded by violinist Marshall Moss and some keyboard pieces by harpsichordist Martin Pearlman.

[845] HARDOUIN, Henri (Ȧrd-wan', On-rē')
CLERIC, TEACHER, CONDUCTOR
BORN: Grandpré, April 7, 1727
DIED: Grandpré, August 13, 1808

At the age of eight, Hardouin came to the Rheims Cathedral Choir from his nearby village on the Aisne. He entered holy orders and by the time he was twenty-two was himself in charge of the choirboys. He was ordained in 1751 and for the next twenty years was also in charge of the weekly concerts at the *Hôtel de ville.* In 1775 he was selected to write, with the two François, Giroust [891] and François Rebel, a coronation Mass for the new King Louis XVI. The next year he was made a canon of the cathedral. Proscribed during the Revolution, he had to go into hiding but came back in 1794 and retired to Grandpré in 1801, turning his music over to the cathedral. It seems to have consisted entirely of religious material, and much of it is said to have been lost in the shelling of Rheims in World War I. He also published a method of learning to sing plainchant. RECORDINGS: Jean-François Paillard has recorded one *Magnificat* with (appropriately) the Rheims Cathedral Choir.

[846] GRAF, Friedrich Hartmann (Gräf, Frē'-drikh Härt'-màn)
FLUTIST, TIMPANIST, CONDUCTOR
BORN: Rudolstadt, August 23, 1727
DIED: Augsburg, August 19, 1795

A younger brother of Christian Graf [827], Friedrich studied with his father Johann, *Kapellmeister* at Rudolstadt. He became an army kettledrummer, was wounded and captured in Holland in 1747, and interned in England. He became a flutist, went to Hamburg in 1759, and until the mid-sixties deputized for old Georg Philipp Telemann [665] as director of concerts. Then he toured for a time as a soloist and spent the years 1769–72 with his brother in The Hague. In 1772 he was hired by the city of Augsburg to succeed Johann Gottfried Seyfert, son of Johann Caspar [733], as Protestant *Kapellmeister* there. Wolfgang Amadeus Mozart [992], passing through in 1777, heard some of his music and awarded him an "E" for Effort. Two years later, Graf inaugurated a subscription concert series there. In 1783 he went to London to supervise performances of some of his works by the Society of Antient Musick, even though they were not all that old. He stayed on through the next season to assume J. C. Bach's [886] place as director of the Professional Concerts, then went home to Augsburg. Oxford University gave him an honorary doctorate in 1789. RECORDINGS: The Concerto Amsterdam has recorded two of his flute quartets.

[847] HERTEL, Johann Wilhelm (Hâr'-tel, Yō'-hàn Vil'-helm)
VIOLINIST, KEYBOARDIST, CONDUCTOR, SECRETARY
BORN: Eisenach, October 9, 1727
DIED: Schwerin, June 14, 1789

Hertel's grandfather and father were both court musicians. At the time he was born, the latter, hight Johann Christian, was a string player to Duke Johann Wilhelm in Eisenach and five years later was appointed *Konzertmeister.* Johann Wilhelm Hertel had lessons with his father and a Bach pupil named Heil. In 1741 the duke died, Eisenach reverted to Weimar, and the *Kapelle* was discharged. Johann Christian found employment in the court orchestra of Mecklenberg-Strelitz at the new capital, Neustrelitz, and his son went to Zerbst to study with Karl Höckh before joining his parent in 1744. Not long after, he heard C. P. E. Bach [801] play in Berlin, made himself known to the court musicians, and had further training from František Benda [776] and K. H. Graun [757].

When Hertel's father's health began to fail, he substituted for him as *Konzertmeister.* But once again the duke died, and the orchestra was dissolved in 1753 (the year before Hertel's father also died). Hertel himself moved on to the court of Mecklenburg-Schwerin. But within two years, Duke Christian Ludwig died and was succeeded by his straitlaced son Friedrich, who promoted religious music, chiefly oratorios, but frowned on the secular variety. For a time Hertel was also church *Kapellmeister* and organist at Stralsund, some one hundred miles to the northeast, and in 1765 he became private secretary to the Dowager Duchess Ulrike in Schwerin. When Friedrich moved his court in 1767 to Ludwigslust, twenty-two miles away, he permitted Hertel to stay behind. In 1769 Hertel married one of his students, a harpist, but the pair separated in 1783. In 1770 the duchess elevated him to a privy councellorship. In his later years, Hertel suffered from failing eyesight and poor general health, which conditions account for his turning from the violin to the piano, which newfangled invention he came to prefer to the harpsichord.

Hertel wrote much (save for music for the stage), but he published little (2 volumes of *Lieder,* 1 of keyboard sonatas, and 6 symphonies), and even in his day it was said that his reputation was circumscribed by his rather remote place of business. He was an interesting composer of piano concerti and a fine orchestrator.

RECORDINGS: Some trumpet concerti have been recorded by, for example, Maurice André and Heinz Zickler, the Concerto in C Major for 8 Timpani, 2 Oboes, 2 Trumpets, and Strings by timpanist Werner Thärichen (Vernon Handley conducting), the Concerto in A Minor for Bassoon by Milan Turkovic, a symphony by Enrico Bartello, *Partita III* for oboe and organ by James Ostryniec, and some oboe sonatas and concerti by his lineal descendant Alfred Hertel.

[848] PICCINNI, Vito Niccolò Marcello Antonio Giacomo (Pit-chin'-nē, Vē'-tō Nik'-kō-lō Mâr-chel'-lō An-tōn'-yō Jà'-kō-mō)
ORGANIST, TEACHER, CONDUCTOR
BORN: Bari, January 16, 1728
DIED: Passy, May 7, 1800

Though his reputation in his day was undoubtedly inflated, few considerable composers have suffered such total eclipse as Niccolò Piccinni, now reduced to a footnote as "Gluck's unsuccessful rival" (see 803). He inherited musical genes from both parents, who, however, imagined him in ecclesiastical robes. But the Bishop of Bari, Muzio Gaeta, perhaps divinely guided, intervened and shipped him off to the Conservatory of San Onofrio in Naples when he was fourteen. There he fell into the hands of a sort of graduate assistant, who (typically) virtually destroyed his interest in music. Fortunately the director, Leonardo Leo [718], got wind of what was going on and took over the boy's education himself. When he died in 1744, Francesco Durante [678] returned and supplanted him in both roles. He was especially proud of Piccinni's success, and Piccinni later gave Durante most of the credit for it. (Some recent writers have tried to prove that Piccinni must have studied elsewhere and come to Naples only as a mature musician, but there seems to be little evidence to support them.)

Piccinni embarked on his long operatic career when he left the conservatory in 1754 with a comedy, *Le Donne dispettose (The Ladies Scorned)*, which won both production and triumph against seemingly insuperable political odds, for an even more forgotten composer named Nicola Logroscino (1698–1767), enjoying momentary popularity, had a virtual monopoly on the Neapolitan stage. Logroscino was quickly eclipsed, and over the next four years Piccinni gave Naples at least eight more operas. In the midst of his success, at twenty-eight, he married a pretty and promising vocal student, Vincenza Sibilla, who was half his age (effectively ending her career, what with her having to care for the seven survivors of their nine children). In 1758 Piccinni moved on to Rome with *Alessandro nell' Indie (Alexander in India)*, and followed its success with *La Cecchina (The Little Chatterbox, 1760)*. This work, perhaps the first to exploit the climactic and complex finales of which Wolfgang Amadeus Mozart [992] later availed himself, became, as *La buona figluola (The Good Daughter)*, not only Piccinni's greatest hit, but one of the greatest of the century. (Goldoni, the librettist, based it on Samuel Richardson's *Pamela* [1742], sometimes called the first novel.) A year later Piccinni followed it up with a setting of Metastasio's *L'Olimpiade (The Olympiad)*, which was regarded as the best in a field that included Galuppi [768], Hasse [736], and Vivaldi [650].

Piccinni was now the favorite opera composer in Rome. He was nothing if not productive: we know that he wrote more than 120 operas—18 between the carnivals of 1761 and 1763 alone!—and some early writers have given the figure of 300. He ruled the Roman stage until 1774, when the public suddenly (and forcibly) rejected his work in favor of that of Pasquale Anfossi (1727–97), a mediocrity now remembered chiefly because Mozart wrote some substitute arias for some of his operas. Piccinni fretted himself into a severe illness, shook the dust of Rome off his shoes forever, and went home (where he was second organist at court and *maestro di cappella* at the Cathedral).

It was at this point that Domenico Caracciolo, Neapolitan ambassador to Paris, persuaded Marie Antoinette to bring in Piccinni to play against Gluck. The composer was given travel expenses for himself and his family, a promise of 6,000 francs a year, and tempting, if vague, fringe benefits. He arrived at the very end of 1776 and was promptly plunged into a crash course in French (of which he was ignorant) by the dramatist Jean-François Marmontel, who had gone to work updating old Quinault libretti for him. The outline of what followed has been given in the article on Gluck. By the time Piccinni's *Roland* was at last ready (January 1778), the composers' names were fighting words, and it was feared that the Italian might be injured or killed at the premiere. But the alarm was groundless, the work a reasonable success, and the Piccinnists cried that *Orphée* was routed. The composer was rewarded with an Italian opera troupe to manage—and with a good deal of exploitation and welching on promises. In 1780 a real confrontation between the supposed rivals (Piccinni actually admired Gluck) was engineered, with the proposed presentation of their respective versions of *Iphigénie en Tauride*. Contrary to what the Opéra had given Piccinni to understand, however, Gluck's piece was played first. Its success seriously undercut that of Piccinni's quite respectable effort, nor was its reception helped by the fact that the prima donna was drunk on opening night. ("Iphigénie en Champagne," someone is supposed to have called out.) However, Gluck decamped afterward, leaving the Italian with a clear field. He enjoyed a brief popularity for a year or two. Then Sacchini [857] and Salieri [966] caught the public's fancy, and eventually he could not even get his operas produced. But he seems not to have had a mean bone in his body: when Sacchini died in 1786, Piccinni spoke his eulogy, and after Gluck's death the following year he tried to promote a series of memorial concerts. In 1791 the Revolution, and the resultant discontinuance of the pension, which had finally been granted him in 1783, drove him back to Naples. There he was at first lionized but was soon accused of revolutionary sympathies (his daughter had married a young hothead), and confined to his home for four years. In 1798 he was permitted to return to Paris, where he was feted and where his pension was restored—but not paid. His family's arrival was the last straw, and he suffered a stroke, though he partially recovered. Eventually, at Napoleon's behest, a special inspector's post was created for him at the conservatory. But his health was now in serious decline and was not improved by the botchery of his doctors. He moved to suburban Passy, where he died and was buried in a common grave. A son, Luigi (1764–1827), had a marginal operatic career as a composer and conductor.

Piccinni's eclipse is said to have resulted largely from his operas' being untransplantable from their own milieu. But he contributed not a little to the form, making the duet a functioning musicodramatic device, expanding the finale, writing musically admirable overtures, and orchestrating conscientiously and effectively.

RECORDINGS: Apart from a pirated version of *La Buono figluola*, he is, however, represented on records only by such scraps as an aria from that work sung by Joan Sutherland and the overture to *Iphigénie* conducted by Ernst Märzendorfer.

[849] MÜTHEL, Johann Gottfried (Mü'-tel, Yō'-hàn Got'-frēt)
ORGANIST, TEACHER
BORN: Mölln, January 17, 1727
DIED: Bienenhof, July 14, 1788

Müthel spent most of his life in his native Baltic area and, cut off from the mainstream of German music, made little impact on it. His father was a smalltown organist who sent him to nearby Lübeck to study with one J. P. Kuntzen, a successor of Buxtehude [525] at the Marienkirche. At nineteen he was appointed court organist to Christian Ludwig II, Duke of Mecklenburg-Schwerin. He also had to teach the princely children. Evidently he gave good service, for after seventeen years, the duke suggested in 1750 that he take a year's sabbatical and perhaps bring his musical knowledge up to date by taking some lessons from that fellow J. S. Bach [684] in Leipzig. Müthel thereupon went dutifully south and found the old cantor fading and blind, but still very much alive and willing not only to give him lessons but to put him up as well. They worked together until Bach was felled by a stroke in July; Müthel was one of those beside him when he died. Since his leave had nearly six months to go, he decided to put it to good use. First he went to Naumburg to study with Bach's son-in-law, Johann Christoph Altnikol (1719–59), who had married Anna Magdalena's oldest daughter Elisabeth two years before). Then on his way home he went around by Dresden to get some tips from Hasse [736], stopped off in Hamburg to visit Telemann [665], and spent some time with C. P. E. Bach [801] in Potsdam. In 1753 he, rather ungratefully, took employment with another German noble in Riga (then, as now, a Russian city), and after 1767 served as organist at the Church of St. Peter. He also established a reputation there as a fine teacher.

Dr. Charles Burney thought Müthel one of the most exciting keyboard composers of his time, and Burney's daughter Fanny, the novelist, noted that a duet for two keyboards was a favorite in her father's household. Published in Riga in 1771, it seems to be the first known work specified for the "fortepiano." It, like much of Müthel's piano music, is inventive, emotional, and reflects the *Empfindsamkeit* and *Sturm und Drang* of which C. P. E. Bach was chief apostle.

RECORDINGS: There is a recording of the duet by Ingeborg and Reimer Küchler. The organ music, which shows more clearly the influence of J. S. Bach, also looks in the direction of Beethoven **[1063]**. An example has been recorded by Wilhelm Krumbach. Müthel also published 2 interesting keyboard concerti, one of which is recorded by Eduard Müller.

[850] ASPLMAYR, Franz (Ås'-pəl-mīr, Frånts)
VIOLINIST
BORN: Linz, c. April 2, 1728
DIED: Vienna, July 29, 1786

Nothing is known of Asplmayr's early life except that he studied violin with his father. Around 1760, the year in which he married Elisabeth Reiss, he was secretary to the music-loving Count von Morzin, to whom Joseph Haydn **[871]** was then *Kapellmeister*. (Twenty years later, Asplmayr played Haydn quartets at the imperial court.) From 1761 to 1763 he served as official composer to the Kärntnertortheater, though none of his work there seems to have survived. Later he teamed up with the great French choreographer Jean-Georges Noverre (1727-1810) to become one of the most popular ballet composers in Europe. He seems to have anticipated Jiří Benda **[824]** in the field of melodrama (i.e., spoken text to musical accompaniment) and also became a writer of successful *Singspiels* (the German equivalent of *opéra comique)*. (It would be amusing to find his lost work on Montgolfier, the balloon ascensionist.) Like so many early musicians, Asplmayr died in poverty. Most of his stage music has disappeared, but a good deal of rather cautious but pleasant orchestral and chamber music has survived in print. RECORDINGS: The Oistersek Quartet has recorded one of Asplmayr's string quartets.

[851] GASSMANN, Florian Leopold (Gås'-mån, Flôr'-yån Lā'-ō-pōlt)
MUSIC DIRECTOR
BORN: Brüx, May 3, 1729
DIED: Vienna, January 20, 1774

Gassmann offers one more piece of evidence that the best eighteenth-century German composers were Bohemians. Aside from the fact that he was born in a town northwest of Prague that is now called Most and ran away from home rather than undertake a commercial career, his youth and training are a blank. He eventually arrived in Venice, took service with a Count Veneri, and saw his *Merope* successfully produced at the Teatro San Moisè in 1757. He went on to make a name for himself in Italy, and, following the success of Gluck's **[803]** *Don Juan,* he was invited to Vienna to help meet the demand for ballets. No sooner had he got there, however, than the theaters were closed in mourning for Emperor Franz, and he returned to Venice. There in 1766 he encountered a lively sixteen-year-old named Antonio Salieri **[966]** and brought him along to Vienna as protégé and pupil. The ballet matter seems to have come to naught, but Gassmann was put in charge of the Italian wing of the Burgtheater and produced half a score of his operas there. *Don Quischott* was a 1771 collaboration with Paisiello **[914]**. In 1771 he founded the Pensions-verein für Witwen und Waisen österreichischer Tonkünstler (Pension Association for the Widows and Orphans of Austrian Musicians), a pioneering venture for Vienna, and later better known as the Tonkünstler-Sozietät. Gassmann was first vice president —the presidency going honorifically to a noble patron—and Franz Asplmayr **[850]** was one of the directors. When the unspeakable Georg von Reutter, Jr. **[773]**, finally went to whatever his reward was in 1772, Gassmann succeeded him as *Hofkapellmeister* and set about repairing the damage he had done to the imperial *Kapelle.* Unhappily for everyone concerned, two years later he was accidentally thrown from a moving carriage and died as a result of his injuries. His two daughters, Maria Anna and Maria Therese (then still unborn and goddaughter of the empress), were taken in hand by Salieri and became successful opera singers.

Apart from the operas, which were generally admired everywhere, Gassmann wrote a good deal of sacred music, including a setting of Metastasio's *La Betulia liberata* (*Bethel Freed),* written in 1772, the same year as Mozart's **[992]**. Gassmann was particularly brilliant in his use of the orchestra, a fact that is made clear in his symphonies. RECORDINGS: The Vienna Concentus Musicus has recorded a string quartet.

[852] MALDERE, Pierre van (Mål'-der, Pē-âr' van)
VIOLINIST, CONDUCTOR, IMPRESARIO
BORN: Brussels, October 16, 1729
DIED: Brussels, November 1, 1768

Pierre van Maldere, one of three violin-playing brothers, crowded a considerable accomplishment into a brief life. From at least 1746 he was a violinist in the viceregal chapel in Brussels under Jean-Joseph Fiocco (see 752) and his successor Henri-Jacques De Croes **[760]**. There he caught the attention of Governor-General Charles of Lorraine, the Empress Maria Theresa's brother-in-law and one of the few foreign rulers to be remembered with affection in Belgium. Charles became his friend and sponsor. In 1751 he let him go to Ireland to conduct the Dublin Philharmonic Concerts for two years on full salary, and in 1754 to Paris to solo at the Concert Spirituel. In 1756 he took him back to Vienna, where his first two known *opéras comiques* were produced at Schönbrünn Palace. When the Seven Years War broke out, Charles took to the field and was unable to return to Brussels until 1758, after Frederick II of Prussia had humiliatingly defeated him at Leuthen. Back home, Charles promoted van Maldere to *valet de chambre,* allowing him to turn his musical duties over to his brothers and compose. But Charles's peripatetic life was not conducive to creativity and in 1762, to give himself a base of operations, van Maldere took over the directorship of the Grand Théâtre, where he served as general factotum—composer, conductor, regisseur, etc. The result was that he wore himself out, became ill, resigned in 1767, and died a year later.

Despite his concern with opera, he wrote only 5, all very lightweight. His instrumental music is more substantial stuff and was played far and wide. (There are examples in the American Moravian Archives.) His sonatas and trios, all involving violins, are well written but conservative. His chief importance, however, lies in his more than 30 symphonies, the most mature of which exhibit sophisticated use of the orchestra and a brilliant sense of form. Some of them were, in fact, once attributed to Haydn.

RECORDINGS: There has been an LP of examples from Op. 4 led by Jean Jakus, and duplications of a B-flat major symphony from that group by Géry Lemaire and Carlos Surinach. The Symphony No. 3 in E-flat Major and Symphony No. 4 in C Major are recorded in the Musique en Wallonie series. There is also a recording of a violin *siciliana* and *vivace* by Eugen Prokop.

[853] SARTI, Giuseppe (Sär'-tē, Jōō-sep'-pä)
ORGANIST, CONDUCTOR, ADMINISTRATOR
BORN: Faenza, c. December 1, 1729
DIED: Berlin, July 28, 1802

Until recently Sarti has been chiefly remembered as a composer quoted by Mozart [992] in *Don Giovanni* and the author of an "old Italian air" (*"Lungi dal caro bene"* from his opera *Giulio Sabino*). But two cen-

turies ago he was one of the most respected opera composers in Europe. His father, a jeweller and part-time violinist in Faenza, where they make faience-ware, had ten other children. Giuseppe's chief teacher was Padre G. B. Martini [767]. At nineteen he became organist of the cathedral in his hometown and acquitted himself so well that four years later he was made director of the local opera. He kicked off his administration with his maiden effort, *Pompeo in Armenia,* which won him an invitation to write another for the carnival at Venice in 1753. This, a setting of the ubiquitous *Il rè pastore,* was also a success, and, like Uttini [831], he became a conductor for Pietro Mingotti's opera troupe on its northern tour at the end of the year. This resulted in his being hired by Frederick V of Denmark as *Kapellmeister* to the crown prince and then as director of the Italian Opera. When circumstances forced its closing in 1763, Sarti was made court music director. Two years later the king sent him to Italy to shark up a new troupe. However, Frederick died soon thereafter, and then the illness and death of Sarti's mother delayed his return until 1768, during which time he taught at the Pietà in Venice.

The new king, Christian VII, was a homosexual and a psychiatric case. Sarti, however, was on the good sides of the queen and Denmark's gray eminence, Johan Frederik Streuensee, the king's physician and Svengali. Shortly after Sarti's return, Streuensee broke the back of the landholders' party and became the effective head of government. During this period Sarti ran the Royal Opera, married a lady named Camilla Passi, and sired two daughters. In 1772 a conspiracy of the dispossessed overthrew Streuensee (who was beheaded, drawn, and quartered), imprisoned the queen, and entrusted the reins to Christian's half-brother Frederik. Sarti, after being repeatedly threatened and humiliated, was dismissed in 1775. He and his family returned to Venice, where he succeeded the departed Antonio Sacchini [857] as music director at the Ospidaletto. In 1779 he became music director of Milan Cathedral, beating out an impressive field of applicants. One of his students—later his assistant there—was the young Luigi Cherubini [1019]. Sarti, by now the composer of fifty operas, reached the apex of his fame in the Milanese years, especially with *Giulio Sabino* and *Fra due litiganti il terzo gode (Between Two Litigants It Is the Third Who Profits).*

In 1784 Sarti was invited, with irresistible monetary bait, to come to St. Petersburg and take over Tsarina Catherine's court music. On his way he stopped over in Vienna, where the emperor turned over to him the proceeds of a performance of the *Litiganti*. It was this work that Mozart [992], who met him then, quoted in his opera *Don Giovanni* and in a set of piano variations (though some now argue that Sarti himself wrote these last). In the Russian capital, Sarti rode high for a time at least. He produced nine new operas, including one based on Russian history with a text by the tsarina herself. He also wrote a *Requiem* for the murdered Louis XVI of France and a *Te Deum* to celebrate a victory by the tsarina's current favorite, Prince Grigori Alexandrovitch Potemkin. In calling for cannons and fireworks, it looks ahead to Tchaikovsky's [1377] *1812 Overture;* the prince liked it so well that as Governor of the Ukraine he presented Sarti with his very own village there. It came in handy, for Sarti managed to offend Catherine's crony, the Portuguese prima donna Luisa Roza d'Aguiar Todi. As a result he was exiled there, where he managed to while away the time organizing a singing school that turned out some fairly important musicians. In 1793, after La Todi was long gone, Catherine forgave him, brought him back, and set up a brand-new conservatory for him to run. It was there that in the interest of standardizing pitch he invented the vibration-counting device that won him election to the Imperial Academy of Science. Catherine died in 1796, and her son and successor, Paul I, was assassinated in 1801. Sarti decided it was time to go home. One of his daughters had married Natale Mussini, *Kapellmeister* to the widow of Frederick William II of Prussia. On his way he stopped by Berlin to visit her. His gout caught up with him and he died there.

RECORDINGS: Most of the operas have survived on paper but not on the stage. Some of the sacred music held on until the end of the last century. Some sonatas, symphonies, and concerti are also extant. Newell Jenkins has recorded one of 3 *concertoni*—offshoots of the *concerto grosso*. Of more interest is Václav Smetáček's account of the Russian oratorio and a prayer from Sarti's setting of the Orthodox liturgy.

[854] SOLER RAMOS, Antonio Francisco Javier José (Sō'-lâr Rá'-mōs, Àn-tōn'-yō Fràn-thēs'-kō Hō-zā' Hàv'-yâr)

KEYBOARDIST, CHOIRMASTER, TEACHER, MONK, THEORIST

BORN: Olot, Geronia (?), c. December 3, 1729
DIED: El Escorial, December 20, 1783

Though he was born in Catalonia to a military musician, Marcos Mateo Soler, neither of Antonio Soler's parents were natives of the region. At the age of six he was admitted to the *escolania* of the Monastery of Montserrat. When he reached his majority, he was pronounced ready to conduct a choir and two cathedrals bid for his services, that of Lerida being his choice. But he had decided to take the cloth, and after he had entered minor orders in 1752, he began his novitiate in the Order of San Jeronimo at the Monastery of San Lorenzo el réal—part of the vast complex of the Escorial Palace, built nearly two centuries earlier by Philip II. In 1753 he was admitted to the Order. King Ferdinand VI and his court spent part of each year here until 1758, giving Soler a chance to meet the musicians and to study with Domenico Scarlatti [687]. In 1757 Soler was appointed the monastery's choirmaster. Besides writing sacred music (including more than 130 *villancicos)*, Soler was giving some serious thought to musical theory and in 1762 published, with the blessings of his order, his manual on how to modulate from any one of the twenty-four keys to any other. It occasioned a controversy and an exchange of tracts that went on for four years; it also gave rise to a protracted correspondence with Padre Martini [767], to whom Soler modestly refused his portrait. He was also working away during this period at the Scarlatti-inspired sonatas which are today his chief claim to fame. He wrote many of them for his pupil, the Infante Don Gabriel, who died in 1788 at thirty-six. In 1772 he gave twenty-seven of them to the visiting Lord Fitzwilliam, who published them back in London. Most of the rest gathered Spanish dust until this century.

Soler loved to work and even designed a desk that would enable him to write when he was sick in bed. (He also invented a gadget that allowed him to demonstrate microtones to Prince Gabriel, wrote a book on currency conversion, and was a notable authority on organs.) Most of his original manuscripts perished in the Spanish Civil War, but many copies of the keyboard pieces have been found. The sonatas show him not a mere Scarlattist but an individual musical thinker with real imagination and some surprisingly Romantic tendencies.

RECORDINGS: Among those who have recorded programs of the sonatas are Frederick Marvin (editor of a complete edition-in-progress), Alicia de Larrocha, Fernando Valenti, Igor Kipnis, and Rena Kyriakou. Genoveva Galvez and the Spanish National Chamber Ensemble have recorded the 6 quintets for keyboard and strings, and the 6 two-keyboard concerti have been done by organists Marie-Claire Alain and Luigi Ferdinando Tagliavini. Isidro Barrio is doing a complete recorded edition of 130 sonatas for EMI Spain. Finally, Gregg Smith has recorded four Christmas *villancicos.*

[855] POKORNÝ, František Xaver
   Thomas (Pō-kôr'-nē, Frán'-tyi-shek
   Eks-á'-ver Tō'-más)
COURT MUSICIAN
BORN: Mies, December 20, 1729
DIED: Regensburg, July 2, 1794

Born near Pilsen in a place now known as Stříbro, Pokorný studied with *Kapellmeister* Joseph Riepel of the court of Thurn and Taxis in Regensburg. He was then hired by Count Philipp Karl of Oettingen-Wallerstein, in Swabia. The count was ambitious to have a splendid *Kapelle* and sent Pokorný off to Mannheim to learn up-to-date approaches from the orchestral chiefs there. He returned in 1754 and was told that he would be promoted to choir director. When Philipp Karl died twelve years later, Pokorný noted, in a petition to the widow and regent, that he was still waiting. When nothing came of it, he went back to Regensburg and got himself placed in the court orchestra, where he spent the rest of his days. Two sons became musicians. Pokorný was quite prolific as an instrumental composer, writing innumerable symphonies and concerti, respectable examples of the music of their times. (It is not possible to say how many, since the woods then were full of composing Pokornýs who have not yet been sorted out.) RECORDINGS: Jacques Lancelot has recorded a clarinet concerto, and the Concerto Amsterdam one for flute.

[856] PASTERWIZ, Georg Robert von
   (Pás'-ter-vētz, Gā'-ôrg Rō'-bárt fun)
PRIEST, EDUCATOR, CHOIRMASTER
BORN: Bierhütten, June 3, 1730
DIED: Kremsmünster, January 28, 1803

A village boy from near Passau, Pasterwiz was educated at the Benedictine abbey in nearby Kremsmünster and took orders there at nineteen. He was sent to the University of Salzburg and while there undertook further musical studies with court Kapellmeister Johann Ernst Eberlin [747]. He

was ordained in 1755, the year of his first annual musical or opera or whatever it was for the brethren. From 1759 he taught mathematics, humanities, and sciences (both natural and social) at the monastery school. He was also choirmaster from 1767. But in 1785 the anticlerical and antimonastic policies of Joseph II became so worrisome that he was sent to Vienna as a sort of lobbyist. There he is said to have moved in the company of such luminaries as Haydn [871], Mozart [992], and their friends and enemies, though one would never know it from the standard biographies of most of them. At any rate, they are said to have converted him (musically) to Classicism. He returned to Kremsmünster after a decade as dean of the secondary school. His dramatic works and his large body of sacred music reposes in the Kremsmünster archives. He published 3 volumes of excellently conceived keyboard fugues and one of organ versets. RECORDINGS: Franz Lehrndorfer has recorded an example of the keyboard fugues.

[857] SACCHINI, Antonio Maria Gasparo Gioacchino (Sák-kē'-nē, Án-tōn'-yō Má-rē'-á Gás'-pá-rō Jō-ák-kē'-nō)
VIOLINIST, TEACHER
BORN: Florence, June 14, 1730
DIED: Paris, October 6, 1786

Modern research has destroyed the picture of Sacchini as the artless fisherboy, discovered caroling on the streets of Naples by Francesco Durante [678]. In 1734 the Infante Carlos of Spain handily retrieved Naples from the Austrians, and the elder Sacchini found employment as a cook in his court. Six years later young Antonio entered the conservatory of Santa Maria di Loreto, where he did indeed study with Durante *inter alias.* Durante took quite a shine to him and predicted that he would rival any and all of his other pupils—prophetic in the case of Niccolò Piccinni [848]. In his mid-twenties, Sacchini began writing successful *intermezzi* and became first a teaching assistant (unpaid) and then an assistant conductor (also unpaid) at the conservatory. With further successes (including his first *opera seria,* entitled *Andromaca)* he was promoted to associate *maestro* (paid) in 1761. Commissions now began to come in, and the following year he got leave to help produce two of them in Venice—and never came back. *Alessandro nell'Indie (Alexander in India)* and the immensely popular *L'Olimpiade (The Olympiad),* both from 1763, help underscore the parallel with Piccinni, who had set both of Metastasio's libretti (as who had not?). His success with *Semiramide* in Rome in 1764 attached him to the Teatro Argentina and the Teatro Valle there, where he had immense successes with such works as *Il Finto pazzo per amore (The Man Who Acted Love-Crazy)* and *La Contadina in Corte (The Country Girl at Court)*. In 1768 he went to Venice to take charge of music at the Ospedaletto. Except for a hiatus to see operas onstage in Stuttgart and Münich, he remained in that post until 1772.

In that year Sacchini decided to try his luck in London. At first it was immense. He became a popular composer of operas (10 in all), eclipsing Johann Christian Bach [886], and a successful teacher of singing (one of his pupils was Nancy Storace, Mozart's [992] first Susanna in *Le Nozze di Figaro*). But his high living and low morals made him enemies, and in 1781 he had to skip to Paris a few steps ahead of the bailiffs from debtors' prison. He arrived at the time that Joseph II of Austria, who admired his work, was visiting his sister, Queen Marie Antoinette, and so won royal patronage. Advertised as a backup for Piccinni and counted on to help administer the one-two to Gluck [803], Sacchini was already in trouble. Neither faction cared for *Renaud* (cobbled up from the 1780 *Rinaldo*, itself a reworking of the 1772 *Armida*). *Chimène* (a new version of the even earlier *Il gran Cidde [The Great Cid]*) ultimately was better received. Sacchini now set about to write, from scratch, a real French opera, according to his own lights. *Dardanus* was that—but it failed (though a revision did better at court in 1785). But the work he counted on to make his name in France, a treatment of Sophocles' *Oedipus at Colonus*, was not produced as scheduled—the queen admitted that she went back on her promise because of pressure from powerful 200 percent Frenchmen—and Sacchini was, not unreasonably, disappointed. Whether he went to bed and died of a broken heart is questionable. But he did go to bed and die of gout and other complications produced by his dissipations. He was fifty-six.

Sacchini was primarily an opera man (around 50, plus some oratorios). At his best—which too often he is not—he was an affecting melodist. His textures have been described as Mozartian and, especially in his later work, where he is clearly an ancestor of *grand opéra*, he shows both Classical and proto-Romantic leanings. But there is little around to demonstrate any of this.

RECORDINGS: On records his masterpiece, *Oedipe à Colonne* is represented by the overture (conducted by Franco Caracci-olo and Raymond Leppard), and a bass aria (Léon Rothier). Richard Bonynge has also recorded the overture to *La Contadina in Corte*. Of the sacred music there is nothing. From the small body of instrumental works (including 2 symphonies), Luciano Sgrizzi has recorded a keyboard sonata.

[858] MADLSEDER, Nonnosus (Måd'-əl-zā-der, Non-nō'-zōōs)

PRIEST, ORGANIST, TEACHER, MUSIC DIRECTOR
BORN: Meran, June 20, 1730
DIED: Andechs, April 3, 1797

Bruder Nonnosus was born in the Tirol at a place now known as Merano but apparently spent almost his whole life in south Germany. He was a convent choirboy and student in Hall, was trained in monasteries in Polling and Freising, and became himself a monk at the Benedictine monastery on the Andechsberg near the Ammersee, west of Munich. He was ordained in 1754 and appointed music director in 1757. He divided his time thereafter between Andechs and Lilienberg. Most of his work is sacred music of a somewhat operatic cast. His only known symphony was recorded by F. Charles Adler on a disc devoted to symphonists of the Innsbruck court. There is no explanation of why Madlseder is included or why his first name is given there as "Nonnonus."

[859] BOND, Capel

ORGANIST, CONDUCTOR
BORN: Gloucester, c. December 14, 1730
DIED: Coventry, February 14, 1790

A bookseller's son, Capel Bond, at twelve, became apprentice to Martin Smith, the local cathedral organist. Having discharged his seven years, he went to Coventry as organist of St. Michael and All Angels, the great Gothic church that would become Coventry Cathedral and be destroyed by a savage air raid in World War II. In 1752 he was also named organist of Holy Trinity and held both posts for the rest of his life. Bond inaugurated a music festival in Coventry in 1760 and eight years later conducted the first Birmingham Festival, an institution that, with interruptions, has survived until today. His music is limited to his two publications: 6 concerti of 1766, the first for trumpet, the sixth for bassoon, the others concerti grossi; and 6 anthems. The concerti are among the better English efforts of the century. RECORDINGS: Maurice André has inevitably recorded the one for trumpet.

[860] ANGLÉS, Rafael (Àn-glāz', Rà'-fà-el)
ORGANIST, PRIEST
BORN: Rafalés, 1730
DIED: Valencia, February 9, 1816

A native of Aragon, Padre Rafael was *maestro de capilla* at Alcañiz, about eighty miles due west of Tarragona. In 1761 he lost out in a competition for the job of organist at Valencia Cathedral, but the winner decamped a year later and Anglés had it for the next fifty-four years. His few surviving compositions consist chiefly of keyboard pieces, especially Haydnesque sonatas. RECORDINGS: Examples have been recorded by José Echaniz and Fernando Valenti, among others.

[861] BENNETT, John
ORGANIST
BORN: c. 1730
DIED: London, September 1784

The history of English music is punctuated by a series of obscure John Bennetts, however spelled (see 59, 372). In 1752 this one succeeded Charles Burney as organist of St. Dionis Backchurch in London when Burney's health collapsed. He composed 3 settings of Psalms paraphrased by Kit Smart and published a collection of organ voluntaries in 1758. RECORDINGS: Haig Mardirosian has recorded one organ voluntary.

[862] ECHEVARRÍA, Agustin de (Ā-chā-vär-rē'-à, À-gōōs'-tēn dā)
MONK
BORN: c. 1730 (?)
DIED: Aranzazu, June 11, 1792

The Basque Echevarrías have been musically active in Spain since at least the seventeenth century. How Padre Agustin is related to the others is unknown. He was a brother at the Franciscan monastery of Aranzazu from c. 1756 until his death and left a number of Scarlattiesque piano sonatas. RECORDINGS: One piano sonata has been recorded by Antonio Ruiz-Pipó.

[863] GAMARRA, Manuel de (Gà-mä'-rà, Má'-nōō-el dā)
CONDUCTOR

BORN: c. 1730 (?)
DIED: after 1786

One of the several "Basque Scarlattists" whose music has been preserved in northern Spain, Gamarra became *maestro de capilla* for the Royal Basque Society of Vitoria in 1753 and still held that post in 1786. The Society produced one of his operas, *The Miserly Doctor*, in 1772. The only other fact that we have about him is that he went once to Vergara with the Count of Penaflorida. RECORDINGS: Antonio Ruiz-Pipó has recorded one of his little keyboard sonatas.

[864] MARELLA, Giovanni Battista (Mà-rel'-là, Jō-vàn'-nē Bàt-tēs'-tà)
VIOLINIST, GUITARIST
BORN: c. 1730 (?)
DIED: after 1760

Marella's career, from the few hints we have of it, seems to have been pursued in Naples. In 1760 he published 6 suites for two guitars. RECORDINGS: One of the two-guitar suites has been recorded by the Duo Company-Paolini.

[865] PALMA, John
BORN: c. 1730
DIED: after 1757

It is uncertain where Palma was born. He was active in Philadelphia, where, in 1757, he gave the first public concert of which there is any record there. Legend also has it that he taught Francis Hopkinson [895]—a notion that seems to be borne out by the fact that Hopkinson copied out one of his keyboard "lessons." RECORDINGS: The keyboard "lesson" has been recorded by Janice Beck. The Berkeley Chamber Singers have recorded Palma's setting of "When Shepherds Watch'd Their Flocks by Night."

[866] PUGNANI, Giulio Gaetano Gerolamo (Pōōn-yà'-nē, Jōōl'-yō Gī-tá'-nō Jā-rō'-là-mō)
VIOLINIST, CONDUCTOR, TEACHER
BORN: Turin, November 27, 1731
DIED: Turin, July 15, 1798

Pugnani studied the violin in his native city with Giovanni Battista Somis (1686–1763), one of Corelli's [565] more important pupils, and carried on that master's teachings to the next generation. The old story that he combined it with that of Tartini [714], with whom he supposedly studied in

Padua, has too many holes in it to be believable. At the early age of ten, Pugnani was playing second fiddle in the orchestra of the Royal Opera, and, largely by winning fame as a concert performer elsewhere, worked his way up to the first desk of the section by the time he was twenty-one. From 1767 he, as a number of his compatriots had, became a conductor of the opera company at the King's Theatre in London, where he produced the first of his 8 operas, a comedy called *Nanetta e Lubino*. He was quite popular in England, but in 1770 he returned to Turin to become concertmaster of King Victor Amadeus III's orchestra and at the Teatro Regio. His colleagues included the Besozzi brothers (see 750) on oboe and bassoon. Charles Burney reported that Pugnani conducted a symphony every morning in chapel, during which the royal family said Mass silently, and that on special occasions he or the Besozzis did solo turns. In 1780 he and his star pupil Viotti **[988]** went off on a tour that took them as far as Russia and lasted for two years. After his return, Pugnani was also made inspector of military bands. Among the friends he acquired abroad were Johann Christian Bach **[886]** and Dittersdorf **[906].** In 1796 the new king, Charles Emmanuel IV was euchred into selling out to Napoleon. He disbanded his musical establishment and retired to Sardinia.

Despite his nodding acquaintance with vocal music, Pugnani was at his best as an instrumental composer. He left a number of symphonies, overtures, orchestral "quintets," chamber works (mostly sonatas), and an orchestral suite based on Goethe's popular and weepy novel *Werther*. Because of his inclination toward sonata form and his abandonment of continuo, he ranks as a pre-Classic.

RECORDINGS: Newell Jenkins has recorded a symphony and Jean-Pierre Rampal a violin sonata arranged for flute. The popular *Praeludium and Allegro* and *Tempo di Minuetto* are fakeries by Fritz Kreisler **[1664].**

[867] DUŠEK, František Xaver (Doo'-shek, Från'-tyi-shek Eks-á'-ver)
PIANIST, TEACHER
BORN: Chotěborky, c. December 8, 1731
DIED: Prague, February 12, 1799

The Dušeks seem to be a different tribe from the Dusíks, though both are frequently turned into Dusseks (see 1016). This one came from a small town about fifty miles southeast of Prague and was sent to the Je-

suit school in Hradec Králové by a local nobleman, Count Spork. Lamed in an accident, Dušek turned to music, and, after some study in Prague with a church *Kapellmeister* named Franz Habermann, he went to Vienna and became a pupil of Wagenseil **[804].** He became a superb pianist and, after he returned to Prague, became the man to study with there. One reads that he specialized in the music of C. P. E. Bach **[801].** Among his pupils was the composer Leopold Koželuh **[950]** and a soprano named Josefa Hambacher. Josefa was the mistress of a wealthy Count Clam-Gallas, and when the time came for their ways to part, the count settled a large sum of money on her and married her off to the obliging Dušek. She became one of the outstanding concert singers of her time. With her dowry, the couple bought a fine hillside retreat in the suburbs, called the "Bertramka." Josefa met Mozart **[992]** in 1777 when she visited her grandfather in Salzburg, and the Dušeks apparently went to a performance of his *Le Nozze di Figaro* in Vienna. It was in part owing to their efforts that Mozart went on to produce it in Prague. Soon afterward he returned to the Bertramka to finish up *Don Giovanni*. He wrote at least two of his concert arias for Josefa (K. 272, K. 528), and it was she who first sang Beethoven's **[1063]** *Ah, Perfido!* The Bertramka is now a Mozart museum.

As a product of the Viennese school, Dušek wrote about 40 symphonies, as well as concerti, string quartets, chamber suites, and sonatas and other pieces for keyboard. Some of his music is reminiscent of Mozart's, though it lacks the strength.

RECORDINGS: Both the Eichendorff Winds and the Prague Chamber Harmony Ensemble have recorded a wind suite, and János Sebestyan has recorded some sonata movements.

[868] CANNABICH, Johann Christian Innocenz Bonaventura (Kån'-nå-bĕkh, Yō'-hån Krĕst'-yån Ĕn'-ō-sents Bō-nå-ven-tōō'-rå)
VIOLINIST, CONDUCTOR
BORN: Mannheim, c. December 28, 1731
DIED: Frankfurt am Main, January 20, 1798

Cannabich seems to have been the only important musical Mannheimer who was a native. As a matter of fact, his father Martin Friedrich, a flutist (origins uncertain), was a court musician there long before Elector Karl Theodor (whom he taught) came to power and began upgrading his music.

Christian Cannabich was a pupil of the newly imported *Kapellmeister,* Johann Stamitz **[810]**, and at the age of thirteen was already sawing away in the ranks as an apprentice. The elector, liking what he heard, shipped him off to Rome for three years of study with Niccolò Jommelli (1714–74). Cannabich is also said to have studied for a time in 1754 with G. B. Sammartini **[738]** in Milan. Not long after Cannabich's return to Mannheim, Stamitz died, and Cannabich took his place in 1758. Early the next year he married a noble lady, Marie Elisabeth de La Motte, from the little ducal court of Zweibrücken near the Saar basin. She provided him with some clout in Paris (where he met the Mozarts) and with children. Rosine (b. 1764) charmed a sonata, K. 309, and a flurry of scatological verse from Wolfgang **[992]**, when he visited Mannheim in the winter of 1777–78. Carl (1771–1806) became *Konzertmeister* of the court orchestra, went to Frankfurt as an opera conductor when political conditions disbanded it, and returned to direct it in 1800. In 1774 Cannabich was given complete charge of the orchestra, and it was he who, with such innovations as uniform bowing, brought it to its peak. When the court moved to Munich, after Karl Theodor succeeded to the Bavarian electorate, Cannabich retained his post, at least nominally, until the end of his life. Unable, however, to collect his salary after 1796, he went on tour as a violinist. He died at sixty-five while visiting Carl. Carl died eight years later at thirty-four; Rosine's traces have vanished.

Cannabich fancied himself a symphonic composer. He is said to have written about 90 symphonies, about half as much chamber music, a few concerti, and 40 or so ballets. The last were more representative of his excellences than the symphonies and were much admired in their day, but his strengths were in conducting, teaching, and administration. RECORDINGS: Boris Brott has recorded a symphony, Wolfgang Hoffmann a *pastorella,* and Thomas Füri the *Sinfonia concertante* in C Major.

[869] WILLIAMS, Aaron
EDITOR, MUSIC ENGRAVER, TEACHER
BORN: 1731
DIED: London, 1776

Williams was probably a native Londoner. At any rate he conducted his professions there, and was clerk of the Scottish church in the London Wall. He wrote Psalm tunes and anthems, and published a number of

popular collections of such music, such as *The Royal Harmony.* RECORDINGS: Gillian Anderson's Colonial Singers have recorded the anthem "Lift Up Your Heads," as printed by Daniel Bayley in his *New Royal Harmony.*

[870] BRIXI, František Xaver (Brēks'-ē, Frän'-tyi-shek Eks-ä'-ver)
ORGANIST, CHOIRMASTER
BORN: Prague, c. January 2, 1732
DIED: Prague, October 14, 1771

The Brixis were a family that produced, in its various branches, a number of Czech musicians. F. X. Brixi was a cousin in some degree of Dorota Brixi, who became the mother of the Benda boys **[776, 824]**, and the son of Šimon Brixi, a prominent Prague organist and official composer for the celebration of St. Jan Nepomuk's Eve, during which hundreds of candles were set afloat on the Vltava. (The senior Brixi was married by Father Černohorský **[677]**.) František Xaver studied from the age of twelve at the *Gymnasium* run by the Pauline Congregation of the Mother of God (or Piarists) at Kosmonosy. His music teacher there was Father Simon à Sancto Bartholomaeo *(né* Václav Kalous), a prolific composer of Masses and offertories. He left in 1749, became successively organist of various Prague churches, and in 1757 became a successor to his father as composer of the St. Jan music. In 1759 he was appointed choir director of the Cathedral of St. Vitus (where, understandably, dance music was taboo). In his brief career, Brixi was a prodigious composer, turning out in two decades about 400 works, including at least 100 Masses, plus oratorios, school plays, cantatas, and other vocal works, and a few symphonies, concerti, chamber works, and keyboard pieces. Brixi died at thirty-nine of tuberculosis. RECORDINGS: Josef Veselka has recorded one of his folklike Nativity Masses, and there is an organ concerto from Franz Lehrndorfer and some harpsichord pieces from János Sebestyan.

[871] HAYDN, Franz Joseph (Hīd'-ən, Frånts Yō'-zef)
CONDUCTOR
BORN: Rohrau, March 31, 1732
DIED: Vienna, May 31, 1809

Haydn is one of those supreme composers who represent neither a summation nor a beginning. He worked in the forms and traditions he inherited from the Rococo and the *Sturm und Drang* composers; but he purified them of inconsequentiality and dross and, more than anyone else, is responsible for that period of exquisite musical form, logic, and balance known as the Classical. He has been accused of intellectualism at the expense of feeling. And indeed Haydn is not a passionate composer; he does not leave the hearer reeling as J. S. Bach [684] and Beethoven [1063] and even Mozart [992] can do. But there is emotion—perhaps a Wordsworthian emotion recollected in tranquillity and detachment, and often tinged with the humor born of retrospect. Though he sometimes indulged in programmatic effect, he is less concerned with message than with music—with making the art express itself in terms that owe nothing to the external world. Suffice it to say that though he did not invent them, he set the standard and the direction for the symphony, the string quartet, and even the sonata, and ranks among the greatest writers of Masses and oratorios. Even his operas, which he himself dismissed as merely achieving what they were supposed to achieve, have recently come in for a reevaluation.

Haydn was born in a squalid Austrian market village near the Hungarian border, the second of twelve children, half of whom survived to adulthood, and two others of whom (Michael [894] and Johann Evangelist) became musicians. Their father Mathias, of German lineage and variously described as a wheelwright and a wainwright, came to Rohrau from nearby Hainburg, built a make-do home, and prospered better than he is usually given credit for doing. A year later he married Maria Koller, formerly a cook for the local count and daughter of the village's chief magistrate, whose job Mathias inherited. There was no history of musical talent in the family, though Mathias had taught himself to play the harp after a fashion, and both parents enjoyed singing. Young Joseph, however, evinced musicality at a very early age, and when he was five he went to Hainburg to live and learn with a relative, schoolmaster Johann Mathias Franck. Haydn found the amenities and even the necessities scarcer there than in Rohrau, but he learned to sing and to play the harpsichord, the violin, and the kettledrums (the last because the local drummer died just prior to a state occasion). When he was around eight, he was auditioned by Karl Georg Reutter [773], Gluck's [803] rival at the Austrian court and choirmaster of St. Stephen's in Vienna, who was out recruiting choirboys, and, with parental permission, went to Vienna in 1740

to sing with what are now known as the Vienna Choirboys. The experience turned out to be no picnic. Reutter, an oddball if ever there was one, gave his charges the barest minimum—musically and physically —on which to survive, and Haydn literally found it often necessary to sing for his supper in the homes of the great, where the choristers were usually fed generously. Five years after his arrival, he was overshadowed as a soloist by his brother Michael, and soon his voice showed signs of breaking. Reutter's suggestion that he have himself castrated was forestalled by Mathias Haydn, and one day in November 1749, given a pretext for unloading him, Reutter actually threw him out on the streets. The boy was taken in by one of the older choristers, scarcely more affluent than himself, and, untrained to do anything well save sing soprano, which he could no longer do, he led a dreadfully precarious existence for some time.

About 1750, however, a man named Buchholz loaned him 150 florins with no strings attached, enabling him to get an attic room in the building where, incidentally, everyone's favorite librettist Pietro Metastasio had his quarters. He acquired a second-hand harpsichord, composed, gave lessons, and set about to teach himself real music, chiefly from the writings of Fux [585], Mattheson [668], and Kellner [761]; he also learned much from the keyboard music of C. P. E. Bach [801]. The deaths of his mother in 1754 and her mother in 1756 brought him small legacies and Metastasio hired him to teach his protégée, Marianne de Martinez, who was currently studying voice with Porpora [690], then riding high as an opera composer. Haydn persuaded the grumpy and slovenly Porpora to take him on as a body servant and, despite the indignities that went with the job, he met some important people (including Gluck) and learned something about composition. Soon he became music teacher to the young Countess Thun, a relative of Count Harrach of Rohrau, and found himself with his foot in the door leading to a more satisfactory way of living. One of the first fruits of this entrée was his being invited to Weinzierl, the country estate of one Karl Joseph von Fürnberg, where, for the proprietor's delectation, Haydn, the steward, the local priest, and a cellist named Albrechtsberger (probably the composer [889]) played string quartets, providing the occasion for Haydn's first tries at the form. He proved so satisfactory that Fürnberg sent him to a Bohemian noble, Count von Morzin, who hired him as his *Kapellmeister* at 200 florins a year plus food and lodging. Morzin had a chamber orchestra, for which Haydn wrote his earliest symphonies.

Some time before taking the post with the count, Haydn had fallen in love with one of his pupils, the younger daughter of a hairdresser named Keller, only to have her become a nun. Whether out of altruism, desperation, or stupidity, in 1760 (though his contract stipulated he be unattached), he married the elder Keller girl. Maria Anna Haydn was nearly four years older than her husband, and was plain, sterile, and a shrew. Haydn soon found he had bought an albatross. He also soon found himself unemployed, Morzin having fallen on hard times. But Prince Pál Antal Esterházy, one of the wealthiest men in the Empire, had taken a shine to the composer and took him on as his vice-*Kapellmeister* (tottery old Gregor Joseph Werner [715] being still nominally in charge of his music).

For the next thirty years Haydn was a servant to the Esterházys, based at Eisenstadt, about twenty-five miles south of Vienna. His most important duties were to provide (write, rehearse, conduct) music for the household and to keep the members of its musical establishment in line. He was obviously more than successful in the first regard: the preponderance of his vast output comes from the Esterházy years—eighty of the symphonies, most of the Masses, quartets, trios, concerti, divertimenti, and piano sonatas, and all but two of the operas. That he was also a master diplomat in his negotiations for his musicians is testified to by the sobriquet "Papa Haydn" that they gave him. When Haydn came to Eisenstadt, the forces he had to work with were skimpy but gradually increased and improved. Among the earliest recruits were his own brother Johann Evangelist (a tenor) and Luigi Tomasini, his longtime concertmaster. Within two years of Haydn's arrival, Prince Pál Antal, a rather tightfisted puritan, died and was succeeded by his brother Nikolaus (or Miklás). Nikolaus was a different order of person. A man of education, enlightenment, and taste, he aimed to make the Esterházys the cultural hub of the Empire, and to that end he built a magnificent new palace (he was known as *Nikolaus der Prächtig*—Nikolaus the Magnificent) called Esterház on the Hungarian side of the Neusiedler See. He summered there after its completion in 1766 (the year old Werner died and Haydn officially became the *Kapellmeister).* Esterház was the scene of many splendiferous parties, festivals, and state visits for which music was needed; music was also needed for its chapel, its opera house, and

its puppet theater. And, since Nikolaus was a passionate performer on the baryton, an odd relative of the viola da gamba, there was constant need for new baryton music, filled, at least in part, by nearly 150 divertimenti, duos, and other works from Haydn's pen.

Prince Nikolaus seems to have been a more liberal and lovable man than his brother. In 1771, however, the visiting spouses and children of his musicians at Esterház apparently annoyed him, and the following season he gave the command "No families." Haydn was probably delighted, but many of his charges grumbled loudly. When, in the autumn, Nikolaus showed no inclination to pack, there was talk of mutiny. Haydn wrote and played for his employer his Symphony No. 45 (now known as the "Farewell"), during whose last movement each player, as his part ended, snuffed his candle and left. Shortly afterward so did Nikolaus, having got the point. A few years later he decided not to use his authority on Haydn's account. Haydn had hired on trial in 1779 an elderly violinist named Antonio Polzelli and his young wife, a mediocre mezzo. Neither worked out very well (old Polzelli soon fell ill), but Haydn fell head over heels in love with Luigia, and they agreed to marry when at last they should be free. As it turned out, things had long since cooled, but at the time Nikolaus thought it wise to keep the couple on his payroll. Luigia produced a son in 1783 (her second in fact); everyone assumed it to be Haydn's, and he offered no argument to the contrary. He was equally kind to both boys and numbered them among his pupils.

Though he spent most of his mature life out in the Austro-Hungarian boondocks, Haydn was far from unknown. The great world beat a path to Esterház, and eventually he was dedicating quartets to grand dukes of Russia and kings of Prussia, supplying Ferdinand, the eccentric King of Naples, with concerti for the *lira organizzata* (a toy instrument he had mastered), and shipping off symphonies to the Loge Olympique Concerts in Paris and the orchestral *Seven Last Words of Christ* to Cadiz Cathedral. On annual visits to Vienna, he had acquired a circle of friends, including Wolfgang Amadeus Mozart [992]—perhaps through the agency of Michael Haydn, the latter's colleague at Salzburg—and Marianne von Genzinger, wife of the Esterházys' gynecologist, who became his closest friend and correspondent. His patron's claims on his compositions having been relaxed, he also acquired a publisher in the firm of Artaria. Early in 1790 the Emperor Joseph II and

Princess Maria Elisabeth Esterházy died within a few days of each other. Prince Nikolaus survived his wife by only six months, leaving his *Kapellmeister* an annuity of 1,000 florins. His successor, Prince Antal, boosted Haydn's salary, but, having no interest in music, dismissed most of his *Kapelle*. From then on, Haydn was essentially free, and he moved almost immediately to the capital. He had long been idolized in London and, hearing the news, the impresario Johann Peter Salomon swooped down on Vienna and persuaded him to come to England. They reached London on New Year's Day 1791. Haydn knew no English (he set about learning it immediately), but he encountered there many old friends who spoke his language—Adelbert Gyrowetz [1032], Muzio Clementi [977], Nancy and Stephen Storace (see 1025), and J. L. Dussek [1016], who kindly loaned him his piano. He was soon the social event of the season, and was guest in one great home after another, including that of the future George IV. In March Salomon's orchestra premiered the first of the "London symphonies" (No. 93), with the composer at the harpsichord; five others followed during that season. Haydn also composed his last opera, *L'Anima del filosofo* (or *Orfeo ed Euridice*), for an operatic venture that fizzled; the work had to wait 150 years to be heard. One of the symphonies commemorated his acquisition of an honorary doctorate from Oxford that summer. In the autumn a rival group, the Professional Concerts, spread a rumor that Haydn was growing too senile to carry on and brought in his pupil Ignaz Pleyel [1003]. Haydn took it with good grace and immediately invited Pleyel to dinner. But he was understandably flagging and demands were being made by his wife and Prince Antal back home; faced with an order from Salomon for six new symphonies, he reluctantly broke off an *amour* with Rebecca Schröter, widow of the Queen's music master (whom he later said he would have married if he could), and returned to Vienna in July 1792, where he could work in peace.

One of his first actions was to yield to his wife's importunings for a place where she could spend her widowhood (he outlived her by nine years) and buy a home in the suburb of Mariahilf. He also took on as a pupil Ludwig van Beethoven, whom he may have met in passing through Bonn. Haydn always cited Beethoven as the crowning success of his teaching career; Beethoven, who had really wanted to study with Mozart, found Haydn a disappointment and, in fact, depended on Johann Schenck [982] for

meaningful evaluations of the tasks Haydn assigned him. Beethoven also palmed off on him some old compositions, pretending that they were the fruits of their association. Haydn was shocked when he found out. He was more seriously shocked in 1793 by the sudden death of Marianne von Genzinger at thirty-eight.

The following January, despite the anguished protests of Prince Antal (who died a few days later), Haydn left again for London, where he remained, more popular than ever, until August 1795. His friend the Prince of Wales presented him to his father and mother, who begged him to make his home in England and become a great English composer. Shortly after his arrival, Salomon performed the first nine "London" symphonies in the course of a dozen concerts, but the next season he could not meet his obligations and gave up; the remaining three were premiered during the "Opera Conserts" run by Viotti [988] at the King's Theatre. (The "Surprise" Symphony [No. 94] was, incidentally, not designed to wake up the audience, and the "Miracle" [No. 96] was not being played the evening a falling chandelier left the audience unscathed.) Whether Mrs. Schröter played any part in this visit we don't know.

Back in Austria Haydn took up new, if sporadic, duties under Prince Nikolaus II Esterházy (who thought him rather passé); these involved largely the composition of Masses (the great final six). But the composer had been mightily impressed with Handelian oratorio as performed in England and set to work to carry on that tradition himself. *The Creation* (which took not six days but three years) was premiered before ecstatic and highborn audiences at the Schwarzenburg Palace at the end of April in 1798. After repeating it the following week, the composer went to bed exhausted. (Another spinoff of the English experience was a national anthem for Austria, with the innovative first line "God save the Emperor.") In 1797 Haydn had bought himself a suburban home of his own. In March of 1800 "the infernal beast," his wife, died while alleviating her chronic arthritis at Baden. A month later Haydn himself suffered an unrelated illness that left him weak for many months. But he recovered and went on turning out such works as the oratorio *The Seasons* and the Mass No. 9, or "Nelson Mass," for the visiting admiral and his lady, as well as an interminable series of "folksong" arrangements for the publisher George Thomson of Edinburgh, who also had Beethoven and Weber [1124] in his stable.

By 1801, however, Haydn realized he was running out of energy and made his will, leaving most of his 50,000 florins worth to his two musical brothers, but with bequests to Luigia Polzelli (who had given up and remarried) and Josephine Keller (his first love, turned out of her convent by religious reforms). In 1803 he arranged with Prince Nikolaus that his post would be turned over to brother Michael, but Michael turned out to be disinclined to leave Salzburg, and it went eventually to Hummel [1091]. In the same year Joseph Haydn apparently left off composing and went into a slow decline. In 1805 there were memorial observances of his death—at age ninety-seven (!) it was proclaimed—throughout Europe, but happily they proved premature. He last appeared in public for a performance of *The Creation* early in 1808, was borne into the hall in an armchair, and was greeted with a standing ovation. In his last years the old man received honors and presents from all over the world—save from his own government, which never gave him any official recognition in his lifetime. In the spring of 1809 the Napoleonic wars reached Vienna, as they had in the 1790s. Haydn suffered through the siege, but it was too much for him. On May 26 he dragged himself to the piano and played the Austrian anthem through three times; five nights later he died in his sleep. Michael Haydn's *Requiem* was sung at the funeral and Joseph was buried in the local cemetery, the wartime conditions preventing any more ambitious observation. In 1820 the Esterházys ordered the body reinterred at Eisenstadt, at which time it was found that someone had stolen the skull. The culprits turned out to be a household secretary named Rosenbaum and an accessory named Peter; they refused to give it up, and willed it to the Friends of Music. It was not reunited with the other remains until 1954.

RECORDINGS: The phonograph treated Haydn rather shabbily during its first fifty years, turning out mostly versions of the popular symphonies in corrupt editions. (There were no complete recordings of the oratorios, Masses, and operas until the LP era, and very few of the chamber works.) This has all been rectified fairly recently. At present there are two complete traversals of the symphonies (Antal Dorati's in the authoritative Landon edition and Ernst Märzendorfer's.) There are also one or more complete recordings of each of the quartets, the piano trios, and the piano music, and ongoing projects will soon complete the religious music and the operas. In fact only such minor things as the baryton music and the Thomson folksongs have not received saturation treatment, though they too are reasonably well represented.

[872] BACH, Johann Christoph Friedrich
    (Bȧkh, Yō'-hȧn Krēs'-tōf Frē'-drikh)
HARPSICHORDIST, MUSIC DIRECTOR
BORN: Leipzig, June 21, 1732
DIED: Bückeburg, January 26, 1795

Long overshadowed by his brothers, the Berlin Bach, the London Bach, and even the Halle Bach, the Bückeburg Bach seems latterly to have been recognized as something more than a mere *Kapellmeister*. Friedrich was the third of the children of Johann Sebastian [684] and Anna Magdalena to survive past childhood. (The eldest, Gottfried Heinrich, was not right in the head and died at forty-one; his sister Elisabeth married her father's pupil, J. C. Altnikol (1719–59), and lived until 1781.) It has been argued that Friedrich's musical education was in part owing to their live-in cousin, Johann Elias—Sebastian by then disapproving of the way the Thomasschule was being run—but Friedrich himself termed his father his only teacher. At seventeen or so, however, the boy was entered at the local university to become a lawyer. But soon word filtered down that there was an opening at the court of Schaumburg-Lippe up in Bückeburg (near Hannover), where the new Count Wilhelm was building a little cultural enclave. Old Bach was by now seriously ailing and, no doubt, was anxious to see his progeny provided for. At any rate, in 1750, Friedrich went to Bückeburg as the *Hofgräflicher Schaumburg-Lippischer Kammermusicus*, a title that meant he supplied the harpsichord continuo. In the orchestral hierarchy, he answered to two Italians, *Konzertmeister* Colonna and *Kapellmeister* Serini.

The Enlightenment and Friedrich of Prussia were then very much in the air, and Count Wilhelm strove, not at all unsuccessfully, to follow this trend. As a German prince should, he fancied himself a soldier, and, in the Seven Years War, rose to the commandership-in-chief of the Portuguese Army. But he also prided himself on his humanity and provided his people with something like social security and welfare—not to mention a military draft. Obviously blessed with both intelligence and sensitivity, he liked the company of artists and philosophers. Described as an Ichabod Crane of a man, he affected the studied disarray of an early Romantic. But he also had a very undemocratic sense of station: it was very well to play music with the servants, but one did not chat with them.

Five years after he came to Bückeburg, Friedrich Bach married a twenty-three-year-old court singer named Lucia Elisabeth Münchhausen, who brought her salary of 100 thalers to add to his of 200. Count Wilhelm threw in a fine garden as a wedding present. But in 1756 the war broke out, and music at Bückeburg suffered in consequence. The Italians, perhaps found to be luxuries, decamped, and Bach found himself de facto *Konzertmeister-Kapellmeister* to the somewhat reduced forces. In 1759 his only son, Wilhelm Friedrich Ernst [1012], whose name came from his godfather Count Wilhelm, was born. Probably Bach may have noted that 300 thalers was not much for a growing family (there were eventually eight daughters) for the count doubled his salary around that time. He also was officially appointed *Konzertmeister* (the other title went begging ever after). Things looked up when the count finally came marching home in 1763, but in 1766 his young friend, the philosopher Thomas Abbt, suddenly died, and music was hushed for a long mourning period. Friedrich applied for Telemann's [665] old job in Hamburg but was beaten out by his own brother Emanuel [801]. The count, however, eased the sting with another (small) salary raise.

Meanwhile the count, now in his forties, had fallen hopelessly in love with a portrait of a distant cousin who was called Maria Eleanore, and had brought the young woman home as a twenty-two-year-old bride. She was a bright and sensitive woman who adored music and poetry, and Bach seems to have worshipped her. Then in 1771, the count hired as court pastor a young man of twenty-seven called Johann Gottfried Herder. Herder was to become the mover and shaker of the German Romantic movement in later years, but his was already a mind and spirit to be reckoned with. He stimulated not only the count's mind but Bach's, for he was a poet and vitally interested in the relationship between words and music, and the two collaborated hand-in-glove on cantatas, oratorios, and other works—the countess like some muse urging them on. But this paradisal situation was too good to last. The countess, never strong, died on her thirty-third birthday. Herder, perhaps inconsiderately but understandably, went off to join Goethe at Weimar and to invent German culture. Count Wilhelm, with nothing left to live for, died a year later.

Friedrich Bach in the confusion that followed decided to take his only vacation in his entire sixty-three years. He packed up his son Ernst, stopped off at Hamburg to visit Emanuel, and then sailed for London, where Christian was setting the musical world afire and where Ernst was to study with him. After a few months of heady living in a world capital, Friedrich returned to a somewhat reduced salary, bringing a piano with him. Though things were not as stimulating at Bückeburg under Count Philipp Ernst, Friedrich kept the troops up to standard and honed their perceptions with new works by brother Emanuel and by Mozart. In 1787—the year in which he began publishing a music periodical which ran for only four issues—he lost a second master. But the widow, who ran the country for her two-year-old son, was extremely musical, letting him give her keyboard lessons and singing his cantatas, and Bach's last years seem again to have been sunny. He died in 1795 of pneumonia. His close friend, Councillor Horstig, wrote an obituary that reflects Bach's unassuming warmth and charm.

It is the modesty and warmth that is the hallmark of Friedrich Bach's music. He was not an innovator; the spirits of Sebastian and Emanuel—and later of Christian and Joseph Haydn [871]—hover over his compositions. There is also an almost naive simplicity. Though he was a demon performer, by all accounts it is clear that he meant much of what he wrote for amateur performers and not too sophisticated listeners. His most ambitious music, the vocal output —and especially the collaborations with Herder—has so far been the least investigated.

RECORDINGS: There is now a recording of the oratorio, *The Resurrection of Lazarus,* directed by Gerd Witte, that gives a good notion of Bach's sensitive word settings. There is also a cantata, *Ich lieg' und schlafe,* conducted by Uwe Gronostay and a motet, *Wachet auf,* by Helmut Rilling. Of the 20 symphonies, mostly of Bach's latter years, seven have been recorded by Helmut Müller-Brühl (but these include chiefly the early examples, save for the Haydnesque No. 20). Helma Elsner has recorded one of the several keyboard concerti, which obviously owe a good deal to his brother Christian. Many of the chamber works have been recorded, including an album of eight by the Freiburg Baroque Ensemble, but so far very little attention has been paid to the keyboard sonatas (solo or accompanied).

[873] DOW, Daniel
TEACHER, ETHNOMUSICOLOGIST

BORN: Perthshire, 1732
DIED: Edinburgh, January 20, 1783

Little is known about Dow's life. He himself taught the guitar in Edinburgh and his son John was a fiddler. Dow was one of the first collectors of Scots folk music and issued a collection of some of the instrumental fruits of his researches in 1776. He also produced 3 volumes of original dances, chiefly strathspeys and reels. One of the latter, "Sir Archibald Grant of Monemusk's Reel" attained great popularity in North America as "Money-Musk." RECORDINGS: There is an authentic recording of "Money-Musk" by the Smithsonian Social Orchestra.

[874] FILTZ, Johann Anton (Fēlts, Yō'-hȧn Ȧn'-tōn)
CELLIST
BORN: Eichstätt, c. September 22, 1733
DIED: Mannheim, March 12, 1760

Patriotic efforts have been made to convince the world that this composer was a Czech named Antonín Fils (as he appears on a number of records). But his birthplace is nearly 150 miles west of the Czech border, and his father, also a cellist, is on the books there as "Johann Georg Filtz." Little is known of the short-lived Johann Anton. He came to the Mannheim orchestra when he was eighteen, married three years later, and had a daughter. He evidently studied with the elder Stamitz [810]. Despite his obscurity as a person, he ranks extremely high among the Mannheimers as a composer, even if one discounts the overevaluation accorded him as a consequence of the Filtz legend (brilliant composer cut off in the first blush of youth, perhaps by dastardly deed— or suddenly vanished in the wilds of Bohemia). His numerous folksy, danceable symphonies are real charmers; if profundity is lacking, what can one expect by twenty-six —even from a Mozart or Schubert. RECORDINGS: An example in E-flat has been recorded by both Boyd Neel and Gabor Ötvos. There are also a few concerti, some sonatas and quartets, and three Masses. Josef Veselka has recorded one as an example of a typical Czech Christmas Mass.

[875] BEECKE, Notger Ignaz Franz von (Bā'-ke, Nōt'-ger Ēg'-nȧts Frȧnts fun)
SOLDIER, CONDUCTOR, PIANIST
BORN: Wimpfen im Tal, October 28, 1733
DIED: Wallerstein, January 3, 1803

Beecke came from a Neckar Valley town near Heidelberg, where his father was an official in a knightly order, and became a cavalry officer in the Bavarian army. The facts of his musical training are shaky. Some references say he studied with Niccolò Jommelli (1714–74)—quite possible since Jommelli was in Stuttgart at the right time; others cite Gluck [803] as his teacher. In any case he taught himself to play the piano and was reckoned a brilliant if highly unorthodox performer. In 1759, during the Seven Years War, he was stationed in Wallerstein, where Count Philipp Karl put him in charge of his court band and made him adjutant to his young son and heir, Kraft Ernst. Philipp Karl died in 1766. When Kraft Ernst reached his maturity seven years later and took over the government, it was largely Beecke's influence that caused him to turn the *Kapelle* into a virtuoso chamber orchestra, with Beecke (naturally) at the helm. Beecke was, along the way, moved up the ladder of military promotions, winding up in 1792 with the rank of major and a lifetime annuity. The count at least once afterward bailed him out of gambling-debt trouble. Beecke traveled a good deal and along the way came to know Gluck, Joseph Haydn [871], and Wolfgang Amadeus Mozart [992]. The first encouraged him to complete his maiden opera, *Roland,* produced in Paris in the 1770s. Those that followed were *Singspiels,* including an early setting of Goethe's *Claudine von Villa Bella.* He played a duet with Mozart, whom he had initially met in Paris twenty-four years before, in a concert in Frankfurt am Main celebrating the coronation of Emperor Leopold II, in 1790. Mozart privately noted that Beecke's piano music was "wretched," though it was quite popular. Haydn exerted a powerful influence on Beecke's later music. Beecke also wrote oratorios, cantatas, symphonies, concerti, chamber music, and songs. The consensus seems to be "useful but not particularly inspired." RECORDINGS: There is a *Romanze* for violin and piano by the Mannheim Duo.

[876] FISCHER, Johann Christian (Fish'-er, Yō'-hȧn Krēst'-yȧn)
OBOIST
BORN: Freiburg im Breisgau, 1733
DIED: London, April 29, 1800

Fischer was one of the most notable virtuoso oboists of his day, though he had his detractors. A pupil of Alessandro Besozzi [750], he found his way to the Dresden court orchestra at some point in the late

1750s or early 1760s. But what with the Seven Years War and the deaths of Frederick Augustus II and his successor Frederick Christian in 1763, it was an unsettled time in Dresden, and in about 1764 Fischer hit the road again. Mozart [992] encountered him in his travels and later wrote a set of piano variations on one of his minuets. Eventually he settled in London and made his concert debut at the same concert at which J. C. Bach [886] made his. After that, he starred regularly at the Bach-Abel concerts, performed at Vauxhall Gardens, toured, and in 1780 was appointed oboist to Her Majesty Queen Charlotte. The same year, over her father's objections, he married Mary Gainsborough, the painter's daughter. Thomas Gainsborough, though he liked Fischer and twice painted his portrait, obviously knew his man, for the couple soon broke up. In 1786, Fischer's bid to follow John Stanley [796] as Master of the King's Musick failed, and he retired to the Continent in a pet. But he rather quickly got over it and came back to London to die with his boots on—he suffered a stroke while playing before the king and queen. Fischer wrote an oboe method, several concerti (one the source of the minuet noted above), and sonatas, etc. for flute. RECORDINGS: There is a recording of an oboe concerto played by André Lardrot.

[877] GIORDANI, Tommaso (Jôr-dà'-nē, Tōm-mä'-zō)
KEYBOARDIST, IMPRESARIO, CONDUCTOR, TEACHER
BORN: Naples, c. 1733 (?)
DIED: Dublin, February 1806

There has long been much confusion about the two eighteenth-century musical Giordanis, Giuseppe and Tommaso. For a long time it was supposed that they were brothers, the sons of a Neapolitan organist called Carmine Giordani, and probably born no more than a decade apart. In fact they were separated in time by at least a generation and were probably unrelated, though the fact that Tommaso's father was named Giuseppe has not helped matters. That Giuseppe ran an opera troupe whose stars were himself, his wife Antonia, and three of their children, Francesco, Marina, and Nicolina. In the mid-1740s they left Naples in an apparently aimless northward tour that took them, by way of Austria, Germany, and Holland, to England, where they appeared at the Covent Garden Theatre in 1753 in Gli amanti gelosi (The Jealous Lovers) by Gioacchino Cocchi, paving the way for his

successful London career a few years later. They appeared there again three years later in Tommaso's first known work, Le Comediante fatta cantatrice (The Comedienne Turned Diva). Then they all drop out of sight for eight years, to turn up in Dublin in 1764 singing Gli amanti gelosi, this time with music written by Tommaso and borrowed from Galuppi [768].

Whatever became of his relatives, Tommaso remained in Dublin writing and producing operas, mostly to English libretti, until 1767. His proclivity for using other people's music and capitalizing on popular libretti apparently got him in trouble, and in 1768 he returned to London, where, for the next fifteen years, like so many of his compatriots before him, he conducted at, and wrote operas for, the King's Theatre. He also did a great deal of theatrical hackwork —which included, it should be noted, songs for the first production of Sheridan's The Critic in 1779. In 1783 he returned to Dublin to open an English opera house, which failed within the year. He remained, however, as a piano teacher and as a musical factotum around Dublin theaters, and in 1785 married a Miss Wilkinson, daughter of the manager of one of them. He became president of the Irish Music Fund in 1794 and gave up composition soon afterward. Giordani was a prolific composer of pretty, galant music, both vocal and instrumental (concerti and chamber works).

RECORDINGS: Carlo Bussotti has recorded a keyboard concerto, and Franz Haselböck and John Henry van der Meer a duettino for two keyboards.

[878] MATIELLI, Giovanni Antonio (Màt-yel'-lē, Jō-vàn'-nē Àn-tōn'-yō)
HARPSICHORDIST
BORN: c. 1733
DIED: 1805

Little seems to be known of Matielli other than that he was an Italian who settled in Vienna and studied with Wagenseil [804]. He published a couple of sets of attractive keyboard sonatas. RECORDINGS: Lily Laskine, the harpist, has recorded a movement from one of these.

[879] GOSSEC, François-Joseph (Gussek', Fràn-swà' Zhō-zef')
CONDUCTOR, TEACHER, ADMINISTRATOR
BORN: Vergnies, January 17, 1734
DIED: Passy, February 16, 1829

Gossec's family name was originally something closer to Gossé. His father was a Hainaut peasant. The child's obvious musicality led him, by way of some local choirs, to a place as a chorister in Antwerp Cathedral when he was still only eight. Along the road he learned the violin, and when his voice broke, after another eight years, he went off to Paris with a letter of introduction to the aging Rameau [675]. Gossec, who was one of the great survivors, so impressed the great man that he shortly found himself playing violin in the private orchestra of Rameau's patron La Riche de La Pouplinière, the millionaire tax farmer. (How you gonna keep 'em down on the farm after they've seen Paree?) Almost immediately he went to work composing chamber music for himself and his colleagues and, inspired by guest conductor Johann Stamitz [810], symphonies for the orchestra (whose direction he took on by mid-decade). In 1759 he married Marie-Elisabeth Georges, and his employers stood as godparents to the son who was born the following year. Gossec was becoming known for his clever orchestration and that same year created a sensation with the offstage brasses in his *Requiem*.

La Pouplinière died at the end of 1762. Gossec moved to Chantilly to direct the theatricals of Louis-Joseph de Bourbon, Prince de Condé, and four years later also took on duties with the prince's distant cousin, Louis-Francois de Bourbon, Prince de Conti, for whose theater he had written his first opera, *Le Périgourdin (The Man from Perigord)*, in 1761. For the next several years he tried, with remarkably little success, to produce a really successful *opéra comique*. In 1769 he gave up and founded the Concert des Amateurs, which, in contrast to the Concert Spirituel, was all orchestral and which elicited more symphonies from him. He gave up his post at Chantilly in 1770, and in 1773 he gave over his orchestra to the Chevalier de Saint-Georges [908] to direct (as part of a troika) the Concert Spirituel. Two years later he was named music master of the Opéra, and in 1777 he gave up his other posts to devote his time to that one and to writing serious operas. He made no waves there, but discovered that he had a talent for ballets. He rose steadily in his profession, becoming associate director of the Opéra (under Dauvergne [797]) in 1780 and codirector in 1782. In 1784 Gossec was named director of the newly founded École Royale du Chant, the immediate forebear of the Paris Conservatory.

Came the Revolution, and Gossec had no trouble exchanging his powdered wig for a liberty cap. Nor were his aristocratic associations apparently held against him. Appointed music director to the Garde Republicaine, he turned out endless hymns to Liberty, Equality, Humanity, and Jean-Jacques Rousseau [793], many of them for chorus and wind band. In 1795 he was appointed one of the five inspectors of the rechristened Conservatoire and served as professor of composition there until Louis XVIII suppressed it twenty-one years later, then virtually retiring from composing. Napoleon conferred the *Légion d'honneur* on him in 1804. When his job ended, he retired to Passy and died there at ninety-five. His son, Alexandre François Joseph, who had a career as a pianist and teacher, had died long before.

Gossec's stage music is largely hampered by the librettos he chose, and his Revolutionary stuff has the ephemerality of most such things. His reputation, such as it is, stands largely on his symphonies, and he and his contemporaries, Cherubini [1019], Maldere [852], and Méhul [1036] are viewed as the nucleus of a French Symphonic School. His innovations (not always tasteful) should perhaps be noted: he is said to have established the clarinets and the horns in the French operatic orchestra, and to have introduced the gong (in his music for Mirabeau's funeral). He was also apparently the first to conduct a Haydn symphony in France.

RECORDINGS: On records Carlos Surinach conducts a G-major symphony. Jacques Houtmann conducts three symphonies (two in F major and one in G minor) and a *Grand Messe des Morts*, Jean-François Paillard a concerto for two harps (which Gossec arranged from his ballet *Mirza),* and Desiré Dondeyne some of the patriotic pieces.

[880] ROSKOVSKY, Josef (Rōs-kōv'-skē, Yō'-zef)
ORGANIST, CANTOR, TRUMPETER, VIOLINIST, MONK
BORN: Stará L'ubovňa, March 10, 1734
DIED: Pest, March 27, 1789

Roskovsky was the son of Jakub Roszkowski, cantor at Stará L'ubovňa, a town in the Tatras, some sixty-five miles southeast of Cracow. He took a degree in philosophy at the university and then entered the Franciscan order at the monastery of St. Catharine near Trnava, in the Carpathians north of Bratislava. As Father Pantaleon he graduated in theology, probably in Bratislava and was ordained. Afterward he served as organist and choirmaster in monasteries at Nové Zámky, Trnava, Bratislava, and Pest. He composed church music and compiled anthologies of the same. RECORDINGS: On records he is represented by a curious mock vespers, called *Vesperae bachanales,* praising the wine god. It is directed by Ladislav Holasek.

[881] ALTENBURG, Johann Ernst (Ål'-ten-bōōrg, Yō'-hån Årnst)
TRUMPETER, ORGANIST
BORN: Weissenfels, June 15, 1734
DIED: Bitterfeld, May 14, 1801

Johann Ernst Altenburg came from an old musical family that went back to the sixteenth century. His trumpeter-father, Johann Caspar, served in the War of the Spanish Succession and in the Weissenfels court, and was known as a touring virtuoso. Johann Ernst studied with him, with J. T. Römhild, organist of Merseburg Cathedral, and with J. C. Altnikol, Sebastian Bach's son-in-law. He found, however, that the market for trumpeters was distinctly bearish, and his only professional employment in that field came in the Seven Years War when the French paid him to sound reveille and retreat. He spent his last thirty-two years as an underpaid organist in the aptly named hamlet of Bitterfeld north of Leipzig. About that time he wrote his magnum opus, a manual on ensemble music for trumpets and drums (or what we might call a drum-and-bugle corps). It is a pioneering effort of considerable interest, but, even so, it took Altenburg twenty-five years t⌐ get it published. He also wrote some piano sonatas. RECORDINGS: Philip Jones, Fritz Lehan, and the Freiburg Cathedral Brasses have recorded some of his ensemble pieces.

[882] PHILE, Philip
VIOLINIST, CONDUCTOR
BORN: Germany, c. 1734
DIED: Philadelphia, 1793

Phile's name, though it appears in many spellings, was probably originally "Pfeil." Around 1776 he began serving with the Pennsylvania German Regiment, was later transferred to the Invalid Regiment and was mustered out in 1783. He was thereafter active in Philadelphia and New York. He was for a time violinist-conductor of the orchestra of the Old American Company. In 1787 he replaced Alexander Juhan (fired in a quarrel) as first violin in the first concert of the Uranian Society (founded to teach poor children church music). Phile was a victim of the yellow fever that swept through Philadelphia in the late summer and autumn of 1793. His single memorable composition was "The President's March" which was later adapted to Joseph Hopkinson's text "Hail, Columbia!" RECORDINGS: Janice Beck has recorded "The President's March."

[883] NISLE, Johannes (Nēz-le, Yō-hån'-nes)
HORNIST, OBOIST
BORN: Geislingen, February 28, 1735
DIED: Sorau, May 22, 1788

Nisle was the progenitor of a tribe of horn players and, at the height of his fame, was known as the best second horn in Europe—a rather Gilbertian distinction! During the Seven Years War, he played oboe in a Württemberg regimental band and afterward became first horn under Niccolò Jommelli (1714–74) in Duke Friedrich Eugen's court orchestra at Ludwigsburg, just outside Stuttgart. His two elder sons, Johann Wilhelm Friedrich and Christian David, were born there. In 1773 he accepted the post of second horn in the crack little orchestra of Count Kraft Ernst of Oettingen-Wallerstein, where he was a colleague of the likes of Josef Fiala **[953]** and Josef Reicha **[978].** In 1777 he went to the court at Neuwied, near Koblenz, where his third son, Martin, was born. All three boys mastered the horn, and Nisle often toured with them (or so one reads, though Martin must have been unusually precocious, since he was only seven when his father died). Some accounts say that Nisle eventually returned to Stuttgart; others say that he worked later in Hildburghausen, Thuringia, and Meiningen. He died at fifty-three in what is now Zaŕy, Poland. RECORDINGS: Of his two known works, a septet and an octet, the Consortium Classicum has recorded the first.

[884] LYON, James
CLERGYMAN
BORN: Newark, N.J., July 1, 1735
DIED: Machias, Me., October 12, 1794

If we discount such arrangers of hymn tunes as John Tufts **[700]** and Thomas Walter **[728]**, James Lyon is the only composer herein treated who can seriously challenge Francis Hopkinson's **[895]** claim to be the first composer born in the thirteen colonies.

Both Hopkinson and Lyon are said to have written musical works as early as 1759, but only Hopkinson's is known. Lyon, son of Zopher Lyon, was orphaned at fifteen. His guardians sent him to the College of New Jersey (now Princeton University), and the composition in question was the ode that concluded his graduation ceremonies. Afterward he took a master's degree from the College of Philadelphia (now the University of Pennsylvania) while Hopkinson was there, and at the 1761 commencement they shared the musical billing, Lyon with an anthem, Hopkinson with a memorial ode to the late King George II. That same year Lyon published *Urania,* the first new collection of psalm tunes in forty years and the largest to date. It contained some standard melodies, both English and American, and some new ones, including examples by the compiler and by Hopkinson. By the time it was published, Lyon had become a Presbyterian minister and in 1765 he accepted a parish in Nova Scotia. But he found the pickings there too slim to raise a family on and eventually settled for another in Machias, in Down East Maine. Though his salary there looked better on paper, things turned out much the same, since it was usually in arrears, and he sometimes had to spend a good deal of time fishing in order to survive. In 1774 he paid New Jersey a visit and mentioned that he was working on another collection, which seems not to have seen the light of day. When the Revolution broke out, he offered General Washington what seems to have been a very sound plan for him (Lyon) to lead an expedition to capture Nova Scotia, but the general didn't buy it. Lyon remained at his post until he died. He is said to have been totally color-blind and to have once brought his wife several yards of red fabric for a new clerical outfit. RECORDINGS: The Gregg Smith Singers have recorded his psalm tunes and the ode "Friendship."

[885] HERBST, Johannes (Hârpst, Yō-hàn'-nes)
CLERGYMAN
BORN: Kempten, Swabia, July 23, 1735
DIED: Salem, N.C., January 15, 1812

Born in Swabia, near Liechtenstein, a member of the Moravian sect, Herbst was educated at Count Zinzendorf's Moravian refuge at Herrnhut in Saxony, and worked for around thirty years in various Moravian communities in Germany and England. He was married during this period and ordained in 1774. In 1786 he and his wife, leaving their children behind, went to Lancaster, Pennsylvania, where he had been sent as minister. With him he brought a library of more than a thousand pieces of religious music, which he himself had copied out. The year after he arrived, he participated in the dedication of Franklin College (now known as Franklin and Marshall), and became one of its trustees. In 1791 he was transferred as pastor to nearby Lititz, where he also ran the girls' school. Twenty years later he was made bishop and sent to Salem, where he succumbed shortly afterward. He was a close friend of J. F. Peter [941], who had preceded him there. A well-trained musician, Herbst left about 220 compositions, mostly anthems and hymns. His library remains intact in the Moravian archives in Winston-Salem. RECORDINGS: He appears on records in a survey of Moravian music conducted by Thor Johnson, in Gregg Smith's history of American song, and as composer of several hymns sung by Cynthia Clarey and Charles Bressler.

[886] BACH, Johann Christian (Bàkh, Yō'-hàn Krēst'-yàn)
ORGANIST, PIANIST, CONDUCTOR, TEACHER, IMPRESARIO
BORN: Leipzig, September 5, 1735
DIED: London, January 1, 1782

Christian Bach was the last son of Sebastian [684]; he had two younger sisters, Johanna Caroline and Regine Susanna, the latter of whom, poor thing, outlived the whole family, dying at the un-Bachian old age of sixty-seven. He was also about the last of the musically productive Bachs, save for Friedrich's son, Wilhelm Friedrich Ernst [1012]. He was born halfway into his father's fifty-first year. Sebastian was delighted with the musical talent the boy showed, and we can presume that he taught him his basics, though the name of cousin Johann Elias (1705–55) crops up supposititiously in this connection. But Sebastian's last years were marred by his ongoing quarrel with the rector of the Thomasschule, the recognition of the fact that his kind of music was not *au courant,* and his increasing blindness. He died when Christian was fifteen, leaving him three claviers, a supply of linen shirts, and thirty-eight thalers in cash.

Christian presented a problem to his womenfolk, who were not only unemployed but also had to take care of poor Gottfried, his oldest full-brother, who was mentally unsound, perhaps in punishment for not having been given the first name of Johann. Friedrich [872] had only just found a foothold in Bückeburg and God knows what Friedemann [784] was up to, so it was decided to ship him off, to be nurtured and educated in Berlin by his half-brother Emanuel [801], who had left home when Christian was five. As far as education was concerned, the solution was a good one, and Christian soon did the family name credit as a keyboard player. But he also found the Italian opera irresistible. King Frederick had decreed that anyone could enter the opera house who had decent clothes on, and Christian discovered that at least the shirt part of his father's legacy was a blessing in disguise. (We are not told what became of the three claviers.) He developed such a passion for the opera that he decided he must go to Italy or else . . . At twenty, over his brother's protests, he went—we are not sure how—and wound up in Milan. He must, even then, have had the looks, the talent, and the charm he showed later, for he was almost immediately taken up by a young Count Litta, who sent him for musical finishing to none other than Padre Martini [767] himself. Bach, who had a chameleonlike quality that, unluckily for him, was only skin-deep, renamed himself "Giovanni," and turned Catholic (having noted which way the musico-ecclesiastical wind blew). He was soon impressing everyone with his church music. In 1760, when Angelo Caselli, organist at the *duomo* in Milan, retired (pressured ever so slightly by Litta and his influential friends), Giovanni Bach was named to take his place.

But he had already gotten into the operatic act, and productions of his operas—in Turin and Naples—took and kept him away from his work, with the result that the cathedral authorities began to get testy and Count Litta nervous. But Providence, in the person of Signora Colomba Mattei, directrix of the King's Theatre in London (where Italian opera was "in" again), prevented an unpleasant crisis by inviting Bach to London as house composer for her company. Bach arrived in November 1762. He seems rather quickly to have overlooked his own Catholicism and to have changed his name from Giovanni to John. He found that, in terms of artists, he hadn't much to work with and that what he had were Italians with tenure, but he made the most of it, and the next February opened with *Orione,* which made such a hit that Their Majesties, George III and his bride Sophie Charlotte, came back the second night to see it again. Sophie Charlotte, age twenty and a very homesick import from Mecklenburg-Strelitz, latched on to her fellow countryman and employed him: (a.) to improve her

harpsichording; (b.) to accompany the King on that by now royal instrument, the flute; (c.) to teach music to a rapidly growing passel of princes and princesses. It was just as well she did too, for the Italians saw to it that the erstwhile Giovanni's contract at the theater was not renewed. Nevertheless, the house continued to produce his operas to great acclaim.

Bach basked in the glow of royal favor and himself became a great favorite around London. He knew and hobnobbed with everybody who was anybody. He wrote for other theaters, contributed songs and such to the pleasure gardens, and was an immensely fashionable teacher. In 1764 he was introduced to the visiting child Mozart, then eight years old, took a great shine to him, influenced him tremendously as a composer, and became his correspondent for life. The same year he and Karl Friedrich Abel [829], another protégé of the Queen and the son of a violinist who had played with Sebastian back in Cöthen, initiated what was to become a highly successful concert series and set up housekeeping together. By 1772 Bach's fame had filtered back to Mannheim, now the orchestral cynosure of all Europe, and he was asked to write an opera for the court theater there. He obliged with *Temistocle,* and went there to produce it, to rapturous applause. At thirty-seven, he also fell head over heels in love with the daughter of the orchestra's first flutist, in whose home he stayed while there. The lady was having none of it, but having apparently convinced himself of the blessedness of the married state, Bach went back to London and married a singer, Celia Grassi, with whom he had worked for years. They had no children. Four years later Bach returned to Mannheim with his *Lucio Silla,* but the climate had changed; German nationalism was in the saddle, and Italian operas were no longer popular. He had much the same reception in Paris in 1778 with his *La Clemenza di Scipione,* but here he was caught in the crossfire between "Gluckists" and "Piccinnists."

All this was only part of the ebbtide that suddenly appeared in Bach's fortunes. He found his popularity as London vocal teacher and London piano teacher suddenly vitiated and his place taken by others—in the latter instance by one who had once been his protégé. On top of all this, he and Abel and one Gallini had invested in a new hall for the concerts, on a scale consistent with Bach's rather lavish notions of how one should live. The venture did not pan out as he had supposed it would. Moreover, the fickle public seemed suddenly to tire of the Bach-Abel Concerts, and to add to the threat of calamity, Bach's housekeeper, in 1777, bilked him out of the modern equivalent of about $50,000. His adaptive mechanism was not built for this sort of thing. He fretted and fretted, and in 1781 he collapsed. As winter approached, he seems to have given up. He died on New Year's Day at the age of forty-six, leaving nothing but a mountain of debts. There were four mourners at the funeral, for which the Queen paid. (She also awarded the widow a lifetime pension, may her name be blest.)

With Christian Bach, there is less talk of "pre-Classics." He was not, as his brothers were, touched by the indelible ink of his father's style, which he had been too young to absorb. And his Italians had pretty much effaced whatever he may have absorbed of Emanuel's rhapsodizing and *Empfindsamkeit*. He cultivated the singing style in his instrumental music, which makes up the bulk of his work, within Classic forms. One can argue that his development sections are sometimes rudimentary and that there is not always the contrast of two opposing themes, but he clearly has the idea of "sonata form." Moreover, he liked to write in large forms, and there is little or no ambiguity about what he intends for chamber ensemble and what he intends for orchestra. It should be added that in the London phase of his career he espoused the piano over its various relatives, and his influence did much to establish its later primacy. He was particularly attracted to the symphony and the concerto, turning out about 50 of the first, 37 piano concerti, and almost as many *sinfonie concertante*, that hybrid form briefly popular in the 1770s. Besides his 13 operas, he produced a good deal of sacred music in Italy, and a miscellany of songs and cantatas in London.

RECORDINGS: The symphonies and concerti have been frequently, if not exhaustively, recorded, and there is no need to detail examples. The chamber music has been less explored, though Ingrid Dingfelder has done the complete flute sonatas, Rampal and Pierlot the Op. 11 quintets, and Jack Brymer the curious "symphonies" for wind sextet. Piano music is limited mostly to scattered sonata recordings, and the church music to the Collegium Aureum's treatment of the motet *Confitebor tibi*, the *Dies Irae* (by Helmut Rilling and Ruggero Maghini), and an excerpt from the *Requiem* (by Helmut Rilling). Elsie Morison and Jennifer Vyvyan recorded the Vauxhall songs, but treatments of the Italian operas are limited to occasional overture recordings and a disc of arias sung by Agnes Giebel.

[887] RÖLLIG, Karl Leopold (Kärl Lā'-ō-pōlt Röl'-lēkh)
HARMONICIST, CONDUCTOR, LIBRARIAN, INVENTOR
BORN: c. 1735 (?)
DIED: Vienna, March 4, 1804

Röllig's origins are obscure. He turns up in Hamburg in 1764 as conductor for a theater troupe run by a certain Ackermann, with which he worked, off and on, until 1772 or so. He later became known as a virtuoso on the glass harmonica, an instrument for which he tried to perfect a keyboard mechanism. Around 1795 he invented a harpshaped portable piano, to be slung about the neck or held in the lap—useful for picnics and canoeing parties, where the grand might prove an encumbrance. He called it *orphica* and wrote a method for it; it was in manufacture for about thirty-five years. Around the same time, he was given a post in the Imperial Library in Vienna but continued to concertize. In 1801 Röllig came up with the *xänorphica*, a piano sort of thing in which the strings were activated by little fiddle bows moved by keys and a treadle; it too had some currency, believe it or not. Röllig also wrote a glass harmonica method, other treatises and articles, an opera (lost), orchestral pieces, and works for the glass harmonica alone and accompanied or accompanying. RECORDINGS: Bruno Hoffmann has recorded his Quintet for Harmonica and Strings.

[888] SCHOBERT, Johann (Shō'-bârt, Yō'-hán)
BORN: c. 1735 (?)
DIED: Paris, August 28, 1767

Johann Schobert is not to be confused with various Schuberts and Schubarts, though claims have been made for relationship; he has enough identity problems of his own. In his brief day, he was a successful and influential composer, and is said, as a performer (on the piano?) to have put such popular keyboardists as Balbastre [843] and Jacques Duphly (1715–89) in the shade. Nevertheless no one knows for sure when he was born or where he came from (Alsace, Bavaria, and Silesia have all been offered as possibilities). It is likely that he arrived in Paris around 1760. There is a story that he became some sort of organist at Versailles but was fired. He married a Frenchwoman. He was on the staff of, or at least a protégé of, the Prince de Conti. He published and perhaps printed twenty opuses of his own sonatas and concerti. He wowed such connoisseurs as Dr.

Charles Burney and Baron Grimm. Little Wolfgang Amadeus Mozart [992] was much taken with him, borrowed a sonata movement for one of his early concerti, and showed his influence in a number of original pieces. However, the only relatively detailed data we have about Schobert have to do with his demise. One late August day in 1767, he found a handsome stand of mushrooms in the St. Germain woods. He took them home and may have invited in a friend or three for a mushroom dinner. (The story has perhaps been embroidered.) The maid is said to have finished up the leftovers. Everyone concerned, except the baby, who was presumably toothless, died in agony from amanita poisoning.

Schobert was not a great composer, though he is an attractive and often very spontaneous one and speaks with his own voice. There is the usual argument about how far he was ahead of his time and whether or not he had really got the hang of sonata form. Most of his duo and trio sonatas, incidentally, indicate that the string parts are incidental.

RECORDINGS: There is a keyboard concerto recorded by Anne-Marie Beckensteiner, the 6 Op. 14 sonatas (violin omitted) by Brigitte Haudebourg, and a disc of chamber works by Maria Bergmann and a string ensemble.

[889] ALBRECHTSBERGER, Johann Georg (Ál'-brekhts-bâr'-ger, Yō'-hàn Gä'-ôrg)
ORGANIST, TEACHER, CHOIRMASTER, THEORIST
BORN: Klosterneuburg, February 3, 1736
DIED: Vienna, March 7, 1809

This is probably the Albrechtsberger who played cello with Joseph Haydn [871] in his earliest quartet performances. Johann Georg received his earliest musical training as a choirboy in the Augustinian abbey at Klosterneuburg and the Benedictine abbey at Melk. At nineteen he went to Györ, Hungary (then called Raab) as an organist for two years, then worked for two more in a village called Mariataferl near Melk (where he also was employed as teacher to the children of a local magnate), and then in 1759 returned to the Benedictine abbey as organist. After six years he left, ostensibly for court service somewhere in Silesia. By the spring of 1768, however, he was back in the Melk area getting married. At some time soon thereafter, he settled in Vienna, where he became choirmaster at the Church of the

Carmelites. The Emperor Joseph II had been impressed by his playing at Melk years before and invited him to apply for a position as court organist if a vacancy should occur. It did, and he applied in 1772 and became organist to the Kapelle. Albrechtsberger remained in Vienna for the rest of his life and became known as a very great organist and, especially for his comprehensive knowledge of counterpoint, an equally great teacher. He summed up his teaching approach in 1790 in his Gründliche Anweisung zur Composition (Fundamental Composition Method). A year later he became assistant to Kapellmeister Leopold Hofmann [899] at St. Stephen's; his predecessor was his friend and admirer, Wolfgang Amadeus Mozart [992], who had willed him the post, so to speak. (Mozart's son Franz Xaver [1141] later became an Albrechtsberger pupil.) The year following, Hofmann died and Albrechtsberger took his place, giving up his other appointments. In 1794, when Joseph Haydn [871] returned to London, he sent him his not very satisfactory pupil Beethoven [1063]. In a year's time Albrechtsberger had grounded him in the mysteries of counterpoint, which Haydn had largely failed to convey to him. (Some of Beethoven's exercises for him have turned up and been recorded by Boris Brott.)

Albrechtsberger was incredibly prolific, turning out as he did over 700 compositions —Masses and other liturgical works, oratorios, cantatas, a few symphonies, concerti for such instruments as organ, trombone, harp, mandora, and jew's harp (!), divertimenti, sonatas, string quartets and other chamber works, and reams of keyboard music. As a rule of thumb, he seems to have been more inventive and flexible in his early years, more intellectual in his later ones (he was a compulsive writer of fugues). Most of his output waits to be heard. What has been unearthed suggests that further exploration might be rewarding.

RECORDINGS: Some works have made it to records—the Concerto for Trombone performed by György Zilcz, Concerto for 5 Instruments conducted by Harold Farberman, Concerto for Harp performed by Hedvig Lubik, Nicanor Zabaleta, and (on harpsichord) János Sebestyan; two concerti (in E major and F major) for Jew's harp, mandora, and orchestra conducted by Hans Stadlmair; the Sonata for Strings conducted by György Lehel, the Concertino for Trumpet performed by Armando Ghitalla, a partita (arranged) by the New York Harp Ensemble, and organ pieces by Alois Forer, Franz Lehrndorfer, and others.

[890] **MYSLIVEČEK, Josef** (Mis-lĕ′-ve-chek, Yō′-zef)
MILLER, VIOLINIST
BORN: Horni Šárka, March 9, 1737
DIED: Rome, February 4, 1781

Josef Mysliveček's life was the sort of rags-to-riches-to-rags saga that novels are made from, and indeed has inspired at least one. His father was a successful miller in the outskirts of Prague, and planned for Josef, his eldest, to take over the business. As a boy, Josef had sung in St. Michael's choir in the city under Jiří Benda [824], and later, as part of his education, his father let him study with Josef Seger [807] and Franz Habermann. In 1761 he was admitted to the guild as a master miller. But the Seven Years War had virtually bankrupted the family, and when the old man died a year later, Josef left his brother in charge and became a church violinist. By the end of 1763 he was able to go to Venice and study with Pescetti [758]. In 1764 he went to Parma to produce (successfully) his first opera, *Medea*, and to become involved with soprano Lucrezia Agujari—she of the incredible upward extension (an octave above high C) and the gimpy leg (supposedly mauled by a hungry hog when she was a child). His next opera, *Il Bellerofonte (Bellerophon)*, a Neapolitan commission premiered in 1767, made Mysliveček's name in Italy—a name that, because it posed insurmountable problems of pronunciation, became "Il Venatorini" (the Little Hunter—perhaps with a reference to his womanizing), alias "Il divino Boemo" (the divine Bohemian). It was probably on this trip to Naples that Mysliveček met the love of his life, singer Caterina Gabrielli. Gabrielli (she took her patron's name and may have been his daughter, though she was nominally the child of his cook) had an unsavory moral reputation and a talent for scandal, and may have contributed to the composer's ultimate downfall. But for the moment he was riding high.

Within the next fourteen years he had at least 25 operas produced in most of the major Italian cities from Rome northward. (There was also an unhappy Munich premiere, *Il Demetrio.*) In 1771 he gave his parodistic *Montezuma* in Florence and went on to Bologna to receive Padre Martini's [767] seal of approval, manifested in membership in the Accademia Filarmonica. In 1777 Carl Theodor, Elector of Bavaria (late of Mannheim), invited Mysliveček back to Munich to present one of his most successful operas *(Ezio,* first performed in Naples in 1775). While there, the composer was confined to the hospital with severe manifestations of advancing syphilis. Over parental objections, Wolfgang Amadeus Mozart [992], who had met him in Bologna, paid him a visit. It evidently provided him with an object lesson—between the disease and the physicians, Mysliveček had lost his nose—for Mozart wrote his father a few months later: "I am no Mysliveček; I am a Mozart —a young and pure-minded Mozart." The divine Bohemian recovered sufficiently to resume his career in Naples in the spring of 1778. In 1779 he went to Milan to produce his *Armida* at La Scala the day after Christmas, and it was there that he made the since-famous observation that Haydn's [871] symphonies were derived from G. B. Sammartini's [738]. *Armida*, however, was a disaster. High living had bankrupted him, and his disease was now taking its toll. He spent his last months in Rome, where two final operas failed, supported by an old pupil, Sir Edward Barry, who paid for his interment in the church of San Lorenzo in Lucina there.

Mysliveček coupled what seems to have been a natural gift for melody with his Italian operatic training, but he is also said by those who know to have absorbed Czech folksongs down by the old mill-stream. When the score of his oratorio (one of 6) *Abramo ed Isacco* turned up a few years ago, it was guessed by some to be a work by Haydn [871] or Mozart.

RECORDINGS: Peter Maag has recorded it. There are also on records a symphony conducted by Martin Turnovsky, two wind octets by James Bolle, three violin concerti played by Ernö Sebestyen and one by Eugen Prokop, a piano trio by the Gensler-Winkler Trio, and some vocal-orchestral nocturnes by the Prague Chamber Harmony Ensemble.

[891] **GIROUST, François** (Zhĕ-rōō′, Frȧn-swȧ′)
PRIEST, TEACHER, ADMINISTRATOR, DOORKEEPER
BORN: Paris, April 10, 1737
DIED: Versailles, April 28, 1799

After a turn as a chorister at Notre-Dame de Paris, Giroust took orders and was ordained when he was nineteen. In the same year he became music master at Orleans. His religious compositions enjoyed considerable popularity at the Concert Spirituel. He is said to have won both first and second prize there in 1768 for his two settings of the psalm "By the Waters of Babylon," one submitted anonymously. In the next year he moved to Paris to teach the choristers at Les Saints-Innocents. He was appointed one of the masters of the royal chapel in 1775, wrote a Mass performed at the coronation of Louis XVI, and between 1779 and 1785 produced four oratorios. In the latter year, having purchased the privilege, he succeeded to the superintendency of the royal chamber. But despite his close connection with the royal family, he adapted quickly to democracy when the Revolution broke out, and wrote many songs and hymns to the new order. He was rewarded by being made concierge of the liberated Versailles, though the post seems to have carried more honor than money. Giroust's major output was of *grand* motets. He also wrote some Masses and Masonic music. His few stage works either went unperformed or have been lost. RECORDINGS: His coronation Mass and one of his two psalm settings is conducted by Louis Martini; there is also a curious Masonic funeral ceremony, *Le Déluge*, by Roger Cotte.

[892] SCHWINDL, Friedrich (Shvin-dəl, Frēd'-rikh)
VIOLINIST, TEACHER
BORN: May 3, 1737
DIED: Karlsruhe, August 7, 1786

Schwindl is said to have been a German born in Holland, but the skimpy evidence suggests otherwise. The first known record of his existence indicates that he was married in Jungbunzlau, a town northeast of Prague now called Mladá Boleslav, around 1758; a daughter, Anna Christina, was born a year later. After a decade or so in small courts—in that of the Markgraf of Wied-Runkel in the Koblenz area, then in that of Hieronymus, Count Colloredo, later Archbishop of Salzburg and Wolfgang Amadeus Mozart's [992] nemesis—Schwindl settled in The Hague, c. 1770. There he taught and served as concertmaster in the orchestra of William V but concertized widely, especially in Switzerland. In 1780 he took an analogous post in Karlsruhe with the Markgraf of Bad Durlach, Karl Friedrich. Known and admired in his lifetime as a fine performer, Schwindl left some once-popular symphonies in the Mannheim mold, as well as chamber music, and religious works. His comic operas have been lost. Some of his marches remain in the repertoire of Dutch military bands. No one argues with Dr. Charles Burney's view that his music is "pretty." (Schwindl's daughter became a singer, married a wine merchant, and became the mother of composer Bernhard

Klein [1793–1832].) RECORDINGS: The Pleyel String Quartet has recorded one of his quartets.

[893] FLAGG, Josiah
BANDMASTER
BORN: Woburn, Mass., May 28, 1737
DIED: c. 1795

Mr. Flagg first enters on the scene as the compiler of *A Collection of the Best Psalm Tunes*, engraved by no less than Paul Revere in 1764. Two years later he brought out a collection of *Anthems and Psalm Tunes*, presumably of his own devising. At some point he became founder and director of the band of the 64th Regiment of the Boston Militia, thought to be the first such musical organization in the colonies. By 1771 they were honed sharply enough to present a concert of vocal and instrumental music that included J. S. Bach [684] and Handel [683]. In the autumn of 1773, Flagg celebrated his own departure with a Grand Final Concert at Faneuil Hall, featuring "upwards of fifty performers," the proceeds to help him on his way. He went to Providence, where he served as an officer in the Revolutionary Army. The year after his death there was a benefit concert in Boston that raised $102 to tide over Mrs. Flagg and her daughters, who apparently were done out of their heritage by Josiah, Jr., a surgeon-dentist. They afterward set up in business in Boston, specializing in repairing glassware and crockery, in needlework, and in riveting. RECORDINGS: The Berkeley Chamber Singers have recorded one of Flagg's anthems.

[894] HAYDN, Johann Michael (Hīd'-ən, Yō'-hán Mē'-khà-el)
ORGANIST, VIOLINIST, CONDUCTOR, TEACHER
BORN: Rohrau, c. September 14, 1737
DIED: Salzburg, August 10, 1806

If Michael Haydn has been overshadowed these two centuries by his elder brother Joseph [871], it was not always so. As a child he seems to have demonstrated more ability and promise than Joseph; he also seems to have been something of a pain at that time. After some rudimentary training in his native village, he joined his brother among the Vienna Choirboys of St. Stephen's. With his crystalline three-octave soprano, he was soon hogging all the solos. Moreover, he was so adept as an organist that he was permitted to deputize for the intendant of that post. Among his fellows, he invented a self-policing system to detect plagiarism in composition exercises. Once his singing so pleased Emperor Joseph that he awarded Haydn fifty goldpieces. Michael, like a good boy, gave half the sum to his peasant parents and the other half to Kapellmeister Georg von Reutter, Jr. [773], to hold for him against his "retirement." He never saw a penny of it again.

As a composer, Michael seems to have been largely self-taught, leaning heavily on Fux [585], which fact probably helps account for the somewhat conservative turn of a good deal of Michael's music. After leaving St. Stephen's in 1754, he appears to have wandered about Hungary for a while before settling down at nineteen or twenty as *Kapellmeister* to Count Firmian, Bishop of Grosswardein in Pressburg. (His brother Joseph was still looking for steady employment.) But the bishop had an even more prestigious relative, Sigismund, Count Schrattenbach, Archbishop of Salzburg; and by 1762 Michael was established as his *Konzertmeister* and conductor.

Six years after he arrived in Salzburg, Haydn married Maria Magdalena Lipp, daughter of the cathedral organist and a singer at the archbishop's court. (She created the title role in young Wolfgang Mozart's [992] *La Finta Semplice* a year later.) Magdalena presented Michael with a daughter in 1770. The child died a few months later, leaving Haydn in a black depression that prohibited any creative work and may have contributed to his love of the bottle, at which Leopold Mozart [816] cast puritan eyes. Poor Magdalena, who had no more children, turned odd, wearing a hairshirt and subjecting herself to regular self-administered beatings. On top of these tragedies, Archbishop Sigismund died in December of 1771. Haydn memorialized that melancholy event in a Requiem that Mozart greatly admired. Things did not get any brighter with the advent of Archbishop Colloredo, though Haydn, having already taken his lumps, found the situation more bearable than did young Mozart.

It should be noted here that Leopold Mozart considered Michael Haydn an exemplary composer, whatever his reservations about him as a person, and Wolfgang obviously liked him. There is the too often repeated story of how Mozart, upon arriving in Salzburg in 1783 with his bride, found Haydn ill and faced with a salary cut if he did not produce some string duos that had been ordered. Mozart came to Haydn's aid and filled the order himself. Mozart also occasionally borrowed musical ideas from

Haydn, and once outfitted a Michael Haydn symphony with an introduction, with the result that for decades the entire work was accepted as "Mozart's Symphony No. 37."

Otherwise, for Michael Haydn, things seem to have gone on their humdrum way in Salzburg, where he stayed put year after year. In 1798 he made a short visit to Vienna to see his now-famous brother (whom he had not seen for over thirty years). He was so excited about the capital that he kept a diary of his experiences there and delighted in rereading it back in Salzburg. But in 1800 the even tenor of his ways was seriously ruffled by the Napoleonic invasion, during which the French troops stripped him of everything they could carry away. But Joseph came to his financial rescue, and the Empress María Theresa (the Spanish wife of Francis II, not the great Hapsburg ruler) gave him contracts for some Masses. He conducted one of them in Vienna in 1801 with the Empress herself as soprano soloist. Moreover, Joseph's patrons, the Esterházys, offered him a vice-*Kapellmeisterschaft* at their palace in Eisenstadt. But habit proved too strong and in the end he decided to remain in Salzburg. In his last years he was honored with a membership in the Stockholm Academy. He died peacefully in 1805, four years before the brother who had made him his chief heir and twenty-two years before his own unhappy wife, who was, however, provided for by the empress, Prince Esterházy, and Joseph Haydn. He left a large quantity of church music—some of it old-fashioned, some of it spotty, and some of it very fine indeed. There were also some operas, mostly for local performance and thus not very demanding, some oratorios (often in collaboration with others), more than forty symphonies, a considerable amount of occasional music, chamber works, and part-songs.

RECORDINGS: Of the church music, the most significant representations on record are the *Requiem for Sigismund* and the *St. Hieronymus Mass* recorded by the musical forces of the University of Missouri, and the *St. Ursula Mass* by Alois Kirchberger. There are concerti for flute (Camillo Wanausek); violin (Robert Gerle and Arthur Grumiaux); horn (Barry Tuckwell); trumpet (Maurice André, Adolf Scherbaum); alto trombone (Armin Rosin); the Double Concerto for Viola and Harpsichord (Ernst and Lory Wallfisch); etc., and an increasing number of recordings of various symphonies (including the Mozart-doctored piece), as well as of *divertimenti* and chamber pieces. The dramatic music is represented by a suite from *Die Hochzeit auf der Alm.*

[895] HOPKINSON, Francis
LAWYER, POET, HARPSICHORDIST, STATESMAN
BORN: Philadelphia, September 21, 1737
DIED: Philadelphia, May 9, 1791

As a musician, Francis Hopkinson does not rank very high, but he is nonetheless a fascinating, and even important, figure. His father was a Philadelphia lawyer named Thomas Hopkinson. He was first president of the American Philosophical Society, which still thrives. Young Francis was the first student to be enrolled in what is now the University of Pennsylvania, an institution of which Thomas was a trustee and from which Francis graduated as a lawyer. (It awarded him an LL.D. the year before he died.)

Like most well-educated men of his day, Francis Hopkinson had several strings to his bow. He sketched and painted. He wrote poems and satires. He traveled. He led a busy social life. He held offices, private and public—as secretary to the Library Company in Philadelphia, as Collector of the Port of Newcastle, and as a member of the Provincial Council of New Jersey. (He had married Ann Borden of Bordentown, where he lived for a time.)

Of his musical education we know nothing save that he developed into a good harpsichordist. But it is generally agreed that he must have studied with the organist James Bremner [820], for whom he once deputized at Christ Church, and on whose death in 1780 he wrote an ode. He was an ardent member of an informal music club that met at one home or another to perform. In 1754 he wrote an *Ode to Music* and five years later the song by which he is best known, "My days have been so wondrous free," probably upholding his claim that he was the first native-born composer in America.

When the Revolution broke out, Hopkinson placed himself firmly on the side of the Revolutionists. He gave up all posts that linked him to the king, was sent to the Continental Congress, signed the Declaration of Independence, and is even supposed to have designed the flag. Later he was appointed the first Secretary of the Navy and attended the Constitutional Convention, some of whose members his literary satire, *The History of a New Roof,* strongly influenced. Among the founding fathers, he counted John Adams, Franklin, Jefferson, and Washington as his friends. In 1781 he made something of a stir in Philadelphia with his "oratorical entertainment," *America Independent, or The Temple of Minerva,* which, at one point, reduced Franklin's daughter Mrs. Bache to tears. Hopkinson wrote the text for sure; apparently he adapted music from other sources to it.

Besides a collection of psalm tunes provisionally ascribed to him, Hopkinson published a set of *Seven Songs for the harpsichord or forte piano.* This set of pieces, consisting of text with treble and bass lines to be fleshed out by the player was meant to consist of six songs, but (despite the title) the collection as published contains eight songs. The set was dedicated to George Washington, who, in acknowledging them, admitted his own total lack of musical talent. They are of a piece with the popular songs of Arne [916], Thomas Linley, Sr. (1733–95), and others of the time.

Hopkinson's other contributions to music were of a more practical nature: he invented a superior method of quilling harpsichords, a keyboard for Benjamin Franklin's [766] glass harmonica, and a sort of metronome that he called a Bell-Harmonic. He died of a stroke at fifty-three. His son Joseph, also a lawyer, won a measure of musical fame as author of the words to "Hail, Columbia!" His descendants, who have preserved the fine musical library of their ancestor, carry on the amateur musical tradition.

RECORDINGS: Margaret Truman, in her singing days, once recorded the eight songs, and Gregg Smith has included them in his first album of his survey of American song, along with Hopkinson's earliest song (noted above) and the "Toast" (to Washington). Gilian Anderson's Colonial Singers and Players has realized a performance of *America Independent,* based on a contemporary libretto that identifies most of the music used.

[896] MANFREDINI, Vincenzo (Mån-frä-dē'-nē, Věn-chänt'-sō)
TEACHER, THEORIST
BORN: Pistoia, October 22, 1737
DIED: St. Petersburg, August 16, 1799

In the time of Catherine the Great of Russia, civilizational advances there were attracting a trickle of Western musicians to St. Petersburg. One who went—not wholly to his profit—was Vincenzo Manfredini. He was a younger son of Francesco Onofrio Manfredini [679], born after his father had come home to Pistoia for good. After some paternal training, Vincenzo became one of the last pupils of old G. A. Perti in Bologna, and is also said to have worked in Milan with the Cathedral choirmaster, Giovanni Andrea Fioroni. His older brother Giuseppe, thanks to parental ambitions then common in Italy, was a *castrato* attached to the opera troupe operated in Central Europe by G. B. Locatelli. When Locatelli, largely to avoid his creditors and the Seven Years War, took it to St. Petersburg in 1757, Manfredini joined his brother for the ride. There he found employment as music director for Czarevitch Peter. Peter, though not as loony as Hollywood liked to depict him, was a psychological mess, a drunkard, a sadist, and a rotten violinist. When he ascended the throne in 1762, he appointed Manfredini as director of the Italian opera orchestra (Locatelli ran the company). That summer, the Czar's wife had him put away, and she became Catherine II. She didn't mind Manfredini's keeping his job for the time being, but when Galuppi [768] arrived three years later, she demoted him to part-time composer and teacher to her son Paul, who was no better than his putative father. Finally they gave him a pension in 1769, and he settled in Bologna. There he tried unsuccessfully to write operas, taught, turned out attacks on modern music, presumably married, and sired a daughter, Antonia Elisabetta, who became an opera singer. When his imperial pupil became Czar Paul I in 1796, he invited Manfredini back to Russia. Manfredini died a year after he returned. Paul survived him by a few months, and was, like Peter III, murdered. Most of Manfredini's music seems to date from the Russian years. In its day it was fashionable to denigrate it, but the instrumental works, at least, seem to be pleasant enough. RECORDINGS: Pianist Felicja Blumental has recorded his only known keyboard concerto.

[897] MEYER, Philippe-Jacques (Mā-yer', Fē-lēp' Zhàk)
HARPIST
BORN: Strasbourg, 1737
DIED: London, 1819

Originally a divinity student, Meyer studied harp in Paris with Simon Hochbrucker, the first great modern virtuoso on that instrument. Hockbrucker's virtuosity was facilitated by the pedal harp, which his father had invented in Donauwörth around the turn of the century. Meyer soloed at the Concert Spirituel in 1761, then was active as performer and teacher in Paris, Strasbourg, and London (where he introduced the pedal harp). He married in Strasbourg in the early 1760s, and finally settled in London in 1784,

where he was known as Philip James Meyer. Two sons, his namesake and Frederick Charles, followed his profession in England. Meyer wrote a harp method and published a number of sonatas, etc., for harp (solo and accompanied). RECORDINGS: Harpist Nicanor Zabaleta has recorded one of the solo sonatas.

[898] KOHAUT, Wenzel Joseph Thomas (Kō'-hout, Vent'-zel Yō'-zef Tō'-màs)
TRUMPETER, LUTENIST
BORN: Saaz, May 4, 1738
DIED: Paris, c. 1793 (?)

Kohaut was the son of a choirmaster in the city northwest of Prague now called Žatec. Impressed into the imperial forces as a trumpeter at the outset of the Seven Years War, he deserted, went to France, joined the Prince de Conti's orchestra, and, rather anachronistically, took up the lute. During the 1760s he wrote a number of successful *opéras-comiques,* beginning in 1764 with *Le Serrurier (The Locksmith).* During the same period he also published 14 trios (or *sonates)* for keyboard, harp, or lute and strings, and 6 symphonies (all lost). Nothing is known of Kohaut's activities after 1770, and the date given for his death is unsubstantiated. RECORDINGS: One of the *sonates* has been twice recorded as a "lute concerto" by guitarists Julian Bream and Alirio Diaz.

[899] HOFMANN, Leopold (Hōf'-màn, Lā'-ō-pōlt)
VIOLINIST, ORGANIST, CHOIRMASTER
BORN: Vienna, August 14, 1738
DIED: Vienna, March 17, 1793

The son of a court officer, Hofmann was taught by Wagenseil [804] whom he succeeded in 1769 as clavier-teacher to the imperial children. Before then he played at the Michaelskirche and conducted the choir of the Petrikirche. In 1772 he succeeded Reutter [773] as *Kapellmeister* of the Stefansdom and was named number-two court organist, but following the death of Florian Gassmann two years later, was frustrated in his attempt to become court *Kapellmeister.* In 1791, Mozart [992], then in desperate financial straits, wrung from the authorities an appointment as Hofmann's unpaid assistant, with the proviso that he should succeed him—when, as, and if. As it turned out, Hofmann outlived him by sixteen months. Haydn [871] had some nasty things to say about Hofmann for setting some song texts that he himself had used, criticizing

Hofmann for his arrogance. In his day Hofmann was an extremely successful composer in terms of his sacred, orchestral, and chamber music; his symphonies and concerti were particularly admired. RECORDINGS: On records he is represented by a flute concerto, ironically still attributed to Haydn (performances by Hans-Martin Linde, Camillo Wanausek, and others), and a *Sinfonia berchtesgadolensis (Berchtesgaden Symphony)* conducted by F. Charles Adler. (Obviously it has nothing directly to do with the late Hitler but is so called because it features musical toys, for which Berchtesgaden was a center of manufacture.)

[900] TAPRAY, Jean-François (Tảp-rā′, Zhản Frản-swả′)
ORGANIST, PIANIST, TEACHER
BORN: Gray, 1738
DIED: Fontainebleau, 1819

Tapray's father, Jean, was chief organist in Gray, a town east of Dijon. He initiated his son in music, then entrusted his further education to a pupil of Domenico Scarlatti [687], a M. Dancier. At fourteen he was appointed organist and instructor to the choristers at Dôle and nine years later, cathedral organist in Besançon. In 1768 he moved to Paris, where he was already known as a performer, and became a fashionable keyboard teacher. From 1776 to 1786 he was organist at the Royal Military Academy at St. Cyr. At, or shortly before, the onset of the Revolution, he retired to Fontainebleau, where later he was music director at the church of St. Louis. Almost all his published composition—concerti (by any other name), chamber music, and sonatas—focus on the keyboard. Much of his output, including several instruction books, was directed to his pupils and is rather conservative and simple-minded. But he was perhaps the first French composer to specify the piano, and wrote 4 concertante symphonies pitting it against the harpsichord. RECORDINGS: Gérard Cartigny conducts one concertante symphony on a record, along with an organ concerto, and a symphony (with solo keyboard). There is also a piano sonata, with accompaniment for violin and cello, played by André Krust and friends.

[901] BESOZZI, Carlo (Bả-sŏd′-zē, Kär′-lŏ)
OBOIST
BORN: Dresden, c. 1738
DIED: 1798 or later

Proceeding up the Besozzi family tree (see 750), we come to fourth-generation Carlo, son of Antonio (who became first oboe at the Dresden court in 1738) and great-nephew of Alessandro. Carlo, who dutifully took up the family trade, joined the orchestra in 1755. In the first years of the Seven Years War, father and son went to Paris and then worked briefly at the Stuttgart court before returning to Saxony in 1759. Antonio retired in 1774 and went to live with his uncles in Turin. When Paolo, the younger of them, died in 1778, Carlo went to Turin, performing in Salzburg en route; Leopold Mozart [816] thought his compositions as good as those of "our Haydn"—presumably he meant Michael [894]. Carlo's son, Francesco, joined the Dresden orchestra in 1792, and you can bet he was not playing saxophone. Carlo wrote 2 oboe concerti and 24 *divertimenti* for wind sextet. RECORDINGS: One *divertimento* has been recorded by the Eichendorff Wind Group.

[902] SELBY, William
ORGANIST, GROCER, TEACHER, IMPRESARIO
BORN: England, c. 1738
DIED: Boston, December 12, 1798

William Selby came to Boston around 1770 and was appointed organist of King's Chapel. He was a soloist in an organ concerto of his own composition at the first public concert given by Josiah Flagg [893] and appeared in other concerts directed by Flagg and his successor Justin Morgan [951]. On his own Selby created an enthusiasm for choral singing in Boston, and in 1773 he and Morgan presented a concert for band and choir that featured Handel's "Hallelujah Chorus." During the American Revolution, when there was no job for him at the chapel, he ran a store specializing in such necessaries as wine, tea, and logwood. He resumed his post, however, in the early 1780s and kept it for the rest of his life. In 1782 he embarked on a series of concerts to raise money for various charities and proposed the publication of a music magazine (based on a rather starry-eyed optimism about American music), of which nothing seems to have come. The concerts grew bigger and bigger until they collapsed of their own weight. In the last five years of his life, he seems to have withdrawn from productive musical activity. Not much of his music has turned up, though we know of various concerti, sonatas, odes, and songs. RECORDINGS: Janice Beck has recorded an organ voluntary.

[903] VANHAL, Jan Křtitl (Vàn'-hàl, Yàn Krzh'tē'-təl)

ORGANIST, VIOLINIST, TEACHER
BORN: Nové Nechanice, May 12, 1739
DIED: Vienna, August 20, 1813

There have been claims that the Vanhals were originally Dutch, and the name is sometimes therefore spelled "van Hall" or Vanhall; the Czechs spell it "Vaňhal." More frequently it appears in its German form "Johann Baptist Wanhal." Vanhal's father was, in effect, a serf, situated about fifty miles northeast of Prague. Vanhal himself learned the rudiments of music from local school-church musicians but seems to have been largely self-taught. He served in nearby towns as organist and choirmaster from 1757 and became a fine violinist. A local noblewoman took him to Vienna when he was in his early twenties and turned him over to Dittersdorf [906] for serious training. He went into teaching, developed an expensive clientele, and was soon able to buy his freedom. Toward the end of the decade, Vanhal began a forty-year period of prolific composition and publication. In 1769 a wealthy Baron Riesch, apparently with an eye to acquiring a first-class *Kapellmeister*, financed a trip to Italy for him, where in 1770 he produced his only known operas in Rome. Shortly after his return in 1771, however, Vanhal suffered a mental breakdown. Various of his patrons took care of him. Within a few months he had recovered well enough to function and went on to establish his total independence, living entirely on his creativity and his teaching. His music was known worldwide and was particularly respected by his Viennese contemporaries, as was the man himself. Michael Kelly [1028] once heard a string quartet in Vienna whose members were Haydn [871], Mozart [992], Dittersdorf, and Vanhal (on cello). It is estimated that Vanhal may have written more than a thousand works, at least three-quarters of which were published. Many of his symphonies invite comparison with Haydn's, though his concerti and chamber works tend to be in a lighter vein, from the evidence at hand. (No one, so far, has attempted a systematic study of his vast output.) RECORDINGS: On records he is represented by such things as his contrabass viol concerto (Thomas Lom, Roger Scott), a viola concerto (Ernst Wallfisch), an A-minor symphony (Karl Ristenpart), a G-minor symphony (Räto Tschupp), a string quartet (the Weller Quartet), and a clarinet sonata (Jerome Bunke, John Russo).

[904] RUST, Friedrich Wilhelm (Roost, Frē'-drikh Vil'-helm)

PIANIST, CONDUCTOR
BORN: Wörlitz, July 6, 1739
DIED: Dessau, February 28, 1796

Rust is an interesting composer, and his work might have attracted notice sooner had it not become the subject of a scandal of which both the composer and the music were innocent. Rust, who was born in Saxony near Dessau, was up to his knees in Bachs from the outset. His earliest teacher was his brother, Johann Ludwig Anton, who had been a violinist in Sebastian's Leipzig Collegium. The boy is said to have memorized the *Wohltemperierte Clavier* by the time he was thirteen. When he went off to Halle to major in law at the university, he continued his musical studies with Wilhelm Friedemann Bach [784]. Later, taken into the *Kapelle* of the local prince, Duke Leopold III of Anhalt-Dessau, he studied keyboard technique with Gottlieb Friedrich Müller, a pupil of the virtuoso Johann Gottlieb Goldberg, whom tradition calls a pupil of both Sebastian and Friedemann Bach. He also studied violin with Carl Höckh, who apparently had nothing to do with the Bachs. In 1763 Duke Leopold sent him off to Berlin for final polishing with Emanuel Bach [801] and František Benda [776]. Two years later, his employer took him on a junket to Italy, where he met the likes of Tartini [714], Padre Martini [767], Nardini [823], Pugnani [866], and the visiting Jiří Benda [824]. After that, he left Dessau only for occasional trips to other German cities, in the course of which he came to know Goethe, the composer J. F. Reichardt [980], and C. G. Neefe [954]—Beethoven's [1063] Bonn teacher, who would briefly succeed Rust in Dessau. Rust succeeded in bringing Dessau to life musically, and it was largely through his urging that the Duke built a theater-opera house in 1774. He was appointed *Kapellmeister* the next year. Rust married one of his pupils, a court singer named Henriette Niedhart. In 1794 their eldest son was accidentally drowned. Rust was so grief-stricken that he gave up composing and died two years later. Another son, Wilhelm Karl, was a successful pianist and teacher in Vienna and Dessau. A grandson, Wilhelm, studied with Wilhelm Karl and moved to Berlin, where in 1858 he was appointed editor-in-chief of the Bach Gesellschaft edition of J. S. Bach's [684] works. A musicologist who commanded the highest respect, he edited a volume of his grandfather's piano sonatas, calling attention to their striking anticipations of Beethoven, at which everyone marveled. Years later it was found that Wilhelm had doctored them to suit his theories.

F. W. Rust wrote a comic opera, *Der blaue Montag (Blue Monday)*, some other stage music, mostly having to do with MacPherson's faked Ossianic poems, and some cantatas and other vocal pieces, but his chief output was of chamber music and sonatas, including the Quartet for Nail Violin, 2 Violins, and Bass, and 3 sonatas for viola d'amore. The piano sonatas may not be pieces Beethoven forgot to write, but they are sterling examples of early Classicism. RECORDINGS: Hans Kann has recorded four of the undoctored piano sonatas. There are on records also an oboe-harp sonata played by Heinz and Ursula Holliger, and the lovely Sonata for Viola, 2 Horns, and Cello played by Joseph di Pasquale.

[905] ANNA AMALIE, Duchess of Saxe-Weimar (Än'-nä Ä-mä'-lē-ä)
BORN: Wolfenbüttel, October 24, 1739
DIED: Weimar, April 10, 1807

Anna Amalie, not to be confused with her Prussian namesake [828], was the daughter of Duke Karl of Braunschweig. As a child, she showed considerable musical talent and was educated accordingly. She came to Weimar as the sixteen-year-old bride of Duke Ernst August Konstantin, two years her senior. The duke also loved music and hired Johann Ernst Bach [822] to build up his *Kapelle*. When she was eighteen, Anna Amalie was the mother of two sons, a widow, and in charge of the state. Nevertheless she strove toward the ideal of Weimar as a cultural center, gradually attracting artists of stature there. In 1761, for example, she persuaded the composer Ernst Wilhelm Wolf (1735–92), passing through on his way to Italy from Leipzig, to stay and teach her boys. (She herself also took lessons with him and appointed him *Kapellmeister* in succession to Bach.) In 1772 she brought the poet Wieland there for the same reason. In the court opera house, she saw to the production of German operas by German composers, until it burned down in 1774. When her elder son Karl Ernst attained his maturity in 1775, she was able to devote herself full-time to her project. Goethe came to live in Weimar, followed by Herder, Schiller, and the rest. The duchess held court in the Wittum Palace, which came to be called "the Court of the Muses." She also turned to composition, writing, among other pieces, a setting of Goethe's *Singspiel* entitled *Erwin und Elmire*. RECORDINGS: Dietrich Fischer-Dieskau has recorded two airs from the *Singspiel*. There is also a recording, by Rosario Marciano, of a keyboard concerto attributed to the duchess.

[906] DITTERSDORF, Karl Ditters von (Dit'-ters-dôrf, Kärl Dit'-ters fun)
VIOLINIST, CONDUCTOR
BORN: Vienna, November 2, 1739
DIED: Rothlhotta, Bohemia, October 24, 1799

In his last months—in fact, on his deathbed —Dittersdorf dictated his autobiography to his son, so that we have a good deal of rather egocentric information about an interesting man who was also a prolific if minor composer. (Someone termed him the Telemann [665] of his day.)

He was born plain Karl Ditters. His father, a Danziger, was an embroiderer to the Imperial Court and Theater of Charles VI, his talents equipping him somehow to serve as an officer with a command of twenty cannon in the war with Bavaria that followed the emperor's death (as part of the War of the Austrian Succession). At the age of seven, young Ditters began violin study with a Herr König, who shortly passed him on to the violinist-composer Joseph Ziegler. When the boy was about eleven, Ziegler sent him around to the Schottenkirche to get permission to sit in with the orchestra. He proved his worth and in about a year's time was permitted by the first violinist to take one of his solos. Heard by one of the musicians of the retired music-loving Feldmarschall Friedrich von Sachsen-Hildburghausen, he shortly afterward found himself a page to that worthy in the Auersperg Palace, dressed in a gray suit with silver bindings and a red vest, a place at the princely table, and his own door key. He was treated almost as if he were his patron's own son and was given an education commensurate with such station. Besides having to accompany the prince's attempts at writing flute concerti and the singing of the great diva Vittoria Tesi, who was a permanent guest in the palace, he was called on to play the violin concerti of Domenico Ferrari (1722–80), now wholly forgotten but then all the rage.

In 1752, at the request of his master, Giuseppe Bonno, *Hofkomponist* and Ditters's composition teacher, brought Gluck [803] to court, where he was forthwith appointed *Kapellmeister*. The next summer but one at the prince's summer palace, Schlosshof, the youth witnessed (and reported) the lavish entertainments presented to the visiting Empress Maria Theresa, which included Gluck's first comic opera, *Le Cinesi (The Chinese)*. Two of Ditters's brothers were soon taken into the court orchestra, and it seems to have been under the prince's roof that he first met his lifelong friend Joseph Haydn [871]. In 1756, when the Seven Years War began, the prince once again took the field, carrying with him a *Kammerorchester* of fourteen that included the three Ditters boys. They made their way up into Thuringia, wintered at the family castle in Hildburghausen, and then marched back to Vienna. On the trip young Karl developed a taste for gambling that soon put him in desperate straits. Nor did the compositions he was just beginning to write help cover his debts. On top of all this, the prince was forced, in 1759, to go back to Thuringia as regent for his great-grandnephew. There being already a house orchestra at Hildburghausen, he broke up his Viennese establishment, securing for Ditters a post at the Imperial Opera, which necessitated more hard work than he had bargained for. In 1763 he feared he would not have the money to go with Gluck to Italy, but several court friends came to his rescue and advanced him the funds to make the trip possible. They got to Venice in time to see the Doge's funeral in the Piazza di San Marco, and went on to Bologna where Ditters wowed everyone with his playing—or so his account goes.

On his return, he discovered that the Italian violinist Antonio Lolli was the latest rage in Vienna; but with a single performance of one of his own concerti, to hear him tell it, he put a stop to that. In 1764 he, Gluck, and the *castrato* Gaetano Guadagni went to Frankfurt for the coronation of Archduke Joseph as "King of the Romans," and performed as part of the celebration. However, back in Vienna his situation at the Opera had become intolerable, and he therefore gladly accepted the invitation of Count Firmian, Prince-Bishop of Grosswardein to come to his palace in Pressburg (now Bratislava), to replace his former Kapellmeister Michael Haydn [894], who was leaving for Salzburg. Ditters impressed the bishop not only with his orchestral discipline but also with his economy. In fact he saved so much money that the bishop let him build a theater to his own taste. Here Dittersdorf really came into his own.

In 1769 Maria Theresa took offense at the lavish manner in which the bishop was living and ordered him to cut back. The *Kapelle* was among the first things to go. However, soon thereafter, he was picked up by Count Schaffgotsch, the ousted Prince-Bishop of Breslau who was living at Johannesburg in Silesia. Besides supplying that worthy with an orchestra, an opera company, and a repertoire of *Singspiele*, he served as *raconteur* and hunting companion. Accordingly he was awarded the Order of the Golden Spur by Pope Clement XIV in 1770, the title of Chief Forester of Neisse, and the magistracy of Freiwaldau (which required imperial ennoblement, occasioning the addition to Ditters's name of "von Dittersdorf" in 1773. Emperor Joseph let it be known in 1774 that the imperial *Kapellmeisterschaft* was vacant, but curiously Dittersdorf could not bring himself to "beg" for it, and the emperor refused to go so far as to demean himself by offering it. Several of his former associates from Pressburg joined him at Johannesburg, among them the tenor Renner, whose stepdaughter, Fräulein Nicolini, Dittersdorf married. The idyll at Johannesburg was temporarily interrupted by war, but afterward Dittersdorf lived in Freiwaldau and divided his time between the castle and Vienna, where he conducted concerts in the Augarten. The bishop died in 1795, leaving Dittersdorf a small pension, insufficient to his luxurious habits. Moreover, his health was on the wane. He was taken in by a Baron von Stillfried at his castle in Rothlhotta east of Prague, and after years of illness Dittersdorf died, just before his fiftieth birthday.

Dittersdorf is not a great composer. However, in spite of his tendency to pad, he is a sunny one, with a gift for grace and tunefulness. He was also ingenious, as his symphonies on tales from Ovid's *Metamorphoses*, his Concerto for Double-Bass, and his curious symphony-concerto in which all the instruments enter as soloists testify. He wrote well over 100 symphonies, about 35 concerti, a considerable number of sonatas (some of them arranged from symphonies and larger works), all sorts of chamber pieces and *divertimenti,* several oratorios, and nearly 30 operas. If he has any claim to innovative importance or influence, it is probably because of his *Singspiele,* produced in Vienna in the latter part of his career, which certainly hastened the offsplit of German opera from the Italian tradition.

RECORDINGS: Most of his *Singspiele* are now lost, but there is an abridged recording of the most famous, *Doktor und Apotheker,* by the forces of the Salzburg Mozarteum under Uli Weder. A couple of the 12 Ovidian symphonies (only half of them are extant) were recorded by Clemens Dahinden, and a disc by the Württemberg Chamber orchestra conducted by Jörg

Faerber includes the Concerto for Double-Bass, Concerto for Harp, and the *Sinfonia Concertante* for double-bass and viola. There are many other recordings.

[907] GOLĄBEK, Jakub (Gō'-lä-bek, Yä'-kōōb)
TEACHER, SINGER
BORN: Silesia, 1739
DIED: Cracow, March 30, 1789

Goląbek's exact birthplace has never been ascertained. His family came to Cracow when he was a child, and he lived the rest of his life there. He married in 1766 and had several children. In 1773, when Pope Clement XIV inclemently dissolved the Order of Jesus, Goląbek was teaching in a Jesuit school. The following year he was admitted to the choir of Wawel Cathedral and later taught in the school connected with that institution. While there he produced a number of Masses, motets, cantatas, etc. (many now lost), in the old-fashioned style cultivated by Polish churches. However, his symphonies, of which 5 are extant, are of interest as early examples of that form so far to the east. RECORDINGS: Three of the symphonies have been recorded by Robert Satanowski.

[908] SAINT-GEORGES, Joseph Boulogne, Chevalier de (Saη-Zhôrzh', Zhō-zef' Bōō-lôn'y', She-väl-yä' də)
VIOLINIST, CONDUCTOR, SPORTSMAN, SOLDIER
BORN: Guadeloupe, c. 1739
DIED: Paris, c. June 10, 1799

The Chevalier was perhaps the first composer of black African ancestry to make an impression on Western music. His father, M. de Boulogne, a politician from Metz, was stationed in Guadeloupe in the West Indies as comptroller-general. His mother was a black islander whom history remembers only as Nanon (which was probably her only name). His father accepted the responsibility of rearing him and had him baptized on his estate on San Domingo, whimsically taking the name "Saint-Georges" from a ship anchored in the harbor. From the age of ten, the boy grew up in France and spent six years as a student in the academy run by a certain La Boëssière that specialized in what we should now call "P.E." Saint-Georges came to be known as the finest fencer in Europe (and an opponent to be avoided in a duel), and also as a splendid dancer, horseman, swimmer, boxer, and skater. Remarkably handsome—to judge from a portrait that he termed frighteningly good—polished, and graceful, he apparently was a heartbreaker.

The facts of the Chevalier's musical upbringing are quite uncertain. Legend has it that a slave named Plato taught him the violin during the Caribbean years and that later he studied with Leclair [732]. That he studied with Gossec [879] seems more certain. He was in Gossec's orchestra in the Concert des Amateurs in 1769, made his solo debut there three years later (performing the first two of his own violin concerti), and took over the orchestra a year later. He apparently conducted as well as he did everything else—except for writing operas. He began writing *opéras comiques* with *Ernestine* in 1777, the year he entered the employ of the Duke of Orléans, and wrote at least 7 before the French Revolution, but none enjoyed success. In 1781 his orchestra was disbanded, but he soon replaced it with another, the Concert de la Loge Olympique. The name came from the Masonic lodge to which the founders belonged; the musicians played in cerulean coats with lace ruffling and swords at their sides. The Concert's most notable commission was the so-called "Paris" symphonies from fellow Mason Joseph Haydn [871]. The Chevalier acted as contact man and presumably conducted the premieres. When the duke died in 1785, Saint-Georges went to London for two years, appearing as an exhibition fencer.

With the upheaval of 1789, the orchestra disappeared forever, and the Chevalier went into voluntary exile with his late patron's son, the sixteen-year-old Duke of Chartres (later King Louis-Philippe), at first at a place called Villers-Cotterets, northwest of Paris, and later in England. Profligate with his money as usual, he was soon reduced to selling off his personal belongings. In 1790 he and the duke made their way back to France and cast their lot with the revolutionists. Saint-Georges attempted a concert tour of Picardy, then became a captain of the National Guard in Lille. In 1792 he organized what was intended to be an all-black regiment, which was named "Les hussards Américains et du Midi" and unluckily designated the "13th." One of the officers was young Thomas-Alexandre Dumas Davy de la Pailleterie, also from San Domingo, later to be a famous general and the father of the novelist Alexandre Dumas *père*. But in that paranoid climate and perhaps hampered by his flashy past, Saint-Georges was accused in 1793 of misappropriating regimental monies and was imprisoned for more than a year at Houdainville, a village north of Paris. Eventually he was cleared and released but was dismissed from the service. He made his way briefly back to San Domingo to participate in Toussaint l'Ouverture's struggle for black independence. In 1797 he came back to Paris, where he lived a hand-to-mouth existence, headquartered in a closet-size room whose walls he decorated with old love letters. Later he became director of a new musical organization, Le Cercle de l'Harmonie. But the effects of luxury, penury, and stress caught up with him, and he died of a stomach ulcer at sixty.

Saint-Georges's music, or what has survived of it—numerous violin concerti and *symphonies concertantes,* 2 symphonies, several string quartets, a harp-flute sonata, a couple of the operas, and some songs—is neither great nor adventurous. The concerted pieces, perhaps the most interesting, were clearly designed to show off his remarkable technique and in that respect look ahead to the virtuoso vehicles of the next century. The rest is pretty but unmemorable.

RECORDINGS: More perhaps because of who he was than of what he accomplished, the Chevalier is well-represented on records. There are the first two violin concerti played by Jean-Jacques Kantorow, the Op. 1 quartets by the Moldar Quartet, a *sinfonia concertante* conducted by Jean-François Paillard, and a disc in the Columbia Black Composers Series duplicating that work and the String Quartet No. 1 and adding the Symphony No. 1 in G Major and an aria from *Ernestine.* Paul Freeman conducts the London Symphony, and the Juilliard Quartet plays the string quartet.

[909] VERNON, Joseph
ACTOR, SINGER
BORN: Coventry, c. 1739
DIED: London, March 19, 1782

Born on the wrong side of the sheets, Vernon was a charity-school student, then a chorister at St. Paul's Cathedral, and a prepubescent actor in David Garrick's company at the Drury Lane Theatre. At around sixteen, he fell in love with an adolescent actress named Jane Poitier and was secretly married to her—but not as secretly as they assumed. The marriage was annulled, the minister and his assistant arrested, tried, convicted, and shipped off to the colonies. Vernon had testified as a thoroughly reluctant witness, and his action had so incensed the public that at his next performance he was hooted off the stage. Eventually he was

permitted to resume his career, if not his marriage, and later, almost by default, became the company's leading male singer. Though his voice was nothing to write home about, he succeeded through his acting skill and his musicianship. His few compositions are chiefly songs. RECORDINGS: Wilfred Brown has recorded his setting of "When that I was and a little tiny boy" from *Twelfth Night.* Vernon continued to perform until his last illness made it impossible for him to go on.

[910] LASCEUX, Guillaume (La-sö', Gwē-yōm')
ORGANIST
BORN: Poissy, February 3, 1740
DIED: Paris, c. 1831

Born near Paris, Lasceux became a church organist in the neighborhood in 1758, and four years later he went to Paris to study with the organist-harpsichordist Charles Noblet. In 1769 he succeeded his teacher at the Church of the Mathurins, and in 1774 also became organist at St. Étienne-du-Mont. Concurrently, from time to time, he held other posts. With the Revolutionists' attack on religion, he found himself unemployed and had to make do playing for the Theophilanthropists, who took over St. Étienne. Under Napoleon he was restored to his position there, retiring at the age of seventy-nine. What survives of his work includes one of his several *opéras comiques,* a couple of motets, a set of harpsichord-violin sonatas, a quartet with keyboard, a number of organ pieces, romances, and many keyboard arrangements of current songs (said to have been very successful with domestic musicians). RECORDINGS: Raphaël Tambyeff has recorded one of his *noëls* for organ.

[911] BELLMAN, Carl Michael (Bel'-mån, Kârl Mē'-kà-el)
POET, CIVIL SERVANT
BORN: Stockholm, February 4, 1740
DIED: Stockholm, February 11, 1795

In some ways Bellman qualifies as Sweden's Robert Burns. Sweden's most popular songwriter, he did not so much compose as pour new lyrics into old tunes, though those he was more apt to cull from popular operas and songbooks than from the folk. He was the oldest of the fifteen children of a public servant, who was, fortunately, rather well-off. Bellman himself attended the University of Uppsala, then at nineteen got a job in the Bank of Sweden. But his tastes did not that way lean, and he soon got so deeply into debt that he had to skip across the Norwegian border to avoid being locked up. After his return he worked in a customs post and in other not very remunerative jobs. He seems, however, not to have cared, so long as he could work at his poetry and sing as an entertainer. Some accounts have him accompanying himself on the lute, but the zither seems more likely. His first publication was a collection of fashionable ruminations on death, translated from the German. But his true bent was for satire, exemplified in his popular collections of 1790 and 1791, *Fredmans epistlar* and *Fredmans sånger*. (Fredman was a real character known in Stockholm taverns.) Not unsurprisingly Bellman's charm and talent recommended him to Gustavus III, that paragon of literary monarchs. He appointed Bellman to a royal secretaryship, which post seems largely to have required that he write for the king's private theater—a part of his Little Versailles, built no doubt, under the Frenchified inspiration of his Prussian uncle, Frederick II. But in 1792 the party ended when Count J. J. Anckarström, an old-regimist, drilled Gustavus in the back at the infamous Masked Ball. His protector gone, Bellman at last made it to debtor's prison, where he died three years later of exposure and malnutrition. RECORDINGS: In America, his songs are known largely through the recorded efforts of Aksel Schiøtz.

[912] EICHNER, Ernst Dieterich Adolph
(Īkh′-ner, Árnst Dēt′-er-ikh Á-dölf)
BASSOONIST, VIOLINIST
BORN: Arolsen, February 9, 1740
DIED: Potsdam, 1777

Born to a bassoonist of the Waldeck court, located in Arolsen (near Kassel), Eichner was probably trained by his father and his colleagues. In his late teens he married Maria Magdalena Ritter, who, a year or so later, bore him a daughter, Adelheid, slated for a promising singing career and an early death (at twenty-five). In 1762 Eichner joined the court orchestra at Zweibrücken for a ten-year stay, during which he became concertmaster. During this period he also toured as a bassoonist, appearing in Paris and London (at the Bach-Abel concerts). He then took service with Frederick William, the Prussian heir-presumptive, and died after four years at thirty-seven. As a symphonist, it appears he would have proved likely had he been put on, for his 30-odd examples show steady growth, culmi-

nating in full mastery of the Classic style but imitating no one. Almost as much can be said for his concerti and chamber music. RECORDINGS: Annie Challan and Nicanor Zabaleta have each recorded one of the 2 harp concerti.

[913] ANTES, John
WATCHMAKER, LUTHIER, INVENTOR, MISSIONARY
BORN: Frederick Township, Pa., March 24, 1740
DIED: Bristol, December 18, 1811

John Antes was the son of Henry Antes, a Lutheran minister who had a farm in Montgomery County, Pennsylvania. In 1740 he opened his home to Moravian refugees and during the next few months was instrumental in the founding of their settlements at Nazareth and Bethlehem. After the founding of the latter town at Christmas, 1741, the elder Antes moved there and became the first justice of the peace, but he resigned and went back to his farm in 1750 when a theocratic faction took over the government. There seems to be some disagreement about the place and date of his son's birth. It is agreed that he studied in the Moravian Boys' School in Bethlehem. However, this too poses an interesting problem, for the school had, in fact, been inaugurated on his father's farm and was moved to the town only in 1749. He evidently had musical ability then and built a violin, a viola, and a cello while he was still in the area. When he was twenty-four, he was sent back to the mother settlement in Herrnhut to become a missionary and was also taught watchmaking at Neuwied. In 1769 he entered his ministry and was dispatched to Egypt the following year. In 1779 a local official, supposing him rich, had him severely beaten, an experience from which he never entirely recovered. He went back to Germany in 1781 and was transferred to one of the settlements in England, where he spent the rest of his life. He seems to have regarded his musical activities as of no consequence and does not even refer to them in his little autobiography. They included a number of improvements for the violin and the piano, and a page-turning music stand. Aside from 3 string trios, his music consists of around 90 anthems and hymns. The trios for two violins and cello, written in Egypt, are the earliest extant chamber works by an American-born composer, and the church music includes some of the best from the Moravians. RECORDINGS: Examples of the church music, plus one of the trios, were included in the Columbia anthology of Moravian music recorded by Thor Johnson.

[914] **PAISIELLO, Giovanni** (Pī-zē-el'-lō, Jō-vàn'-nē)
CONDUCTOR
BORN: Roccaforzata, May 9, 1740
DIED: Naples, June 5, 1816

At the height of his career, the paranoid and fiercely competitive Paisiello probably succeeded in outstripping in reputation his two operatic rivals, Cimarosa [962] and Piccinni [848]. Mozart [992] thought him unequalled in light music. Rossini [1143] originally called his most famous opera *Almaviva ossia L'Inutile precauzione* "out of respect to Paisiello" (it later became *Il Barbiere di Siviglia*). And, in an entry for a biographical dictionary published near the end of his life, the composer himself noted that he had received the homage of his era and assured himself that of posterity—which, in a small way, is correct.

A veterinarian's son, young Paisiello sang for, and was schooled by, the Jesuits in nearby Taranto. His father wanted him to be a lawyer but was persuaded instead to send him to Sant' Onofrio in Naples in 1754, where he was one of the last pupils of old Francesco Durante [678]. He stayed at the Naples Conservatory until midsummer 1763, devoting most of his study to the composition of church music. Just before he left, however, the school produced an intermezzo by him (the name of the work is lost) which was so successful that it decided him on his future. His first full-length comedy was produced at Bologna the next year, and by 1776 he had written and staged around fifty works of varying length all over Italy, though his chief center of operations remained Naples.

Though an observer noted that she was bored by drama, lacked a sense of humor, and disliked music at heart, the Empress Catherine of Russia knew a good thing when she saw it and offered Paisiello all kinds of goodies if he would only come to St. Petersburg. He remained there for eight years, not always contendedly (he deplored the unavailability of good libretti). Whether Catherine liked the stage or not, she believed that the French had invented civilization and was properly admiring of a French production of Beaumarchais' *Le Barbier de Seville*. Paisiello, who had his eyes open, obtained a libretto from a priest called Giuseppe Petrosellini and produced the work in 1782. It swept everything before it and is still played occasionally today—though it is

low-key stuff compared to Rossini's version. Two years later Paisiello left St. Petersburg. In Vienna he bid for the attention of Joseph II with an opera and some symphonies but ultimately settled for Naples again, where he became *maestro de cappella* to rotten and eccentric King Ferdinand IV, son of Charles III of Spain, and husband to Marie Antoinette's sister. Paisiello continued to fill important contracts from elsewhere—one from London in 1791 and the house opener for the new Teatro La Fenice in Venice in 1792, for example. In 1797, Napoleon, who admired him inordinately, accepted his funeral march for the late General Hoche over that submitted by Cimarosa. Two years later with French aid, Ferdinand was overthrown, and the Parthenopian Republic was founded in Naples. Paisiello, like Cimarosa, blandly changed sides and accepted the title of *Maestro della nazione*. Ferdinand was shortly restored to power, and Paisiello found himself with no title at all. After two years of groveling, he was accepted back as court conductor. At this point Napoleon demanded his presence in Paris to head his *chapelle*. He was offered 12,000 francs a year, given 18,000 outright to cover expenses, and provided with a coach-and-four, and a daily catered dinner for twelve. But Paisiello soon discovered he had met his Machiavellian match in Cherubini [1019], and when his opera *Proserpine* failed (not without prompting from his rivals), resigned and went home. The Bonapartists had chased Ferdinand off to Sicily in 1806, so Paisiello served their representatives, Joseph Bonaparte and (later) Murat. With Napoleon's overthrow, Ferdinand returned once more. Paisiello was not only ousted; he lost his various pensions and had to subsist on his salary as chapelmaster alone. His sense of defeat was intensified by the death of his long-ailing wife in 1815. On the following February 20, Rossini's *Almaviva* was a disaster in its Rome premiere, thanks largely to the efforts of Paisiello's fans (probably stirred up by the old man himself). The next night it triumphed. Paisiello died less than five months later.

Paisiello left more than 100 operas. The best of them show taste, dramatic instinct, and a gift for both melody and expression (but there are no fireworks). There is also sacred music, cantatas, symphonies, and chamber music, all of superior workmanship. On records he has fared better, operatically speaking, than Piccinni or Cimarosa: there are complete recordings of his two best works, *Il Barbiere* (Renato Fasano) and *Nina* (Ennio Gerelli), as well as of the intermezzo *Il Duello* (Ugo Ràpalo) and *La*

Molinara (Franco Carracciolo), and "highlights" from *Semiramide in Villa* (Arturo Basile). Piano concerti are played by Carlo Bussotti and Felicja Blumental, a keyboard sonata by Luciano Sgrizzi, a "concerto a cinque" by Fasano, a military march for Napoleon by Desiré Dondeyne, and six *divertimenti* for flute, violin, viola, and cello by various Italian musicians. The *cantata comica* entitled *Il Maestro* is performed by the Hungarian State Orchestra and the Budapest Madrigal chorus.

[915] ARNOLD, Samuel
ORGANIST, CONDUCTOR, IMPRESARIO, EDITOR
BORN: London, August 10, 1740
DIED: London, October 22, 1802

Samuel Arnold was a nice, gregarious, well-meaning, hard-working, hard-drinking man, but the general level of his musical output shows the art had sunk in England by his time. He began his career as a choirboy in the Chapel Royal, where he was taught by Bernard Gates, a former Handelian *basso*, and by James Nares, Maurice Greene's **[727]** successor—neither of them exactly first-rate musicians. At twenty-four he became harpsichordist at Covent Garden, for which theater he began grinding out stage pieces. It is significant that his initial work, a treatment of novelist Samuel Richardson's *Pamela* called *The Maid of the Mill*, in 1765, was his most successful, for it was a pastiche of material by popular French, Italian, and even English composers, to which Arnold contributed 4 original songs. Most of the nearly 100 stage works that followed were pastiches, updatings, pantomimes, interludes, ballets, and afterpieces. At best Arnold's "operas" were the usual excuse for song smithing—though, interestingly enough, he frequently borrowed his tunes from English folksongs, apparently directly from the sources. He married Mary Ann Napier, a member of a famous and wealthy family, and was thus able to purchase Marylebone (pronounced "Marlybone") Gardens in 1769. One of several such London places of amusement or *al fresco* "pleasure gardens," it existed under that name from 1738 to 1776 and, like the others, provided various manifestations of music, as well as dancing, food and drink, fireworks, etc. Many of Arnold's short stage pieces were written for this enterprise. Consistent with the long illness that afflicted the English for a century and a half after Handel **[683]** died, Arnold was also turning out

oratorios, an activity which, in 1773, brought him a doctorate from Oxford.

Three years later he had to close down Marylebone, having been cleaned out by one of his staff, and went back to theatrical work, this time with a former colleague, the playwright George Colman, who had just taken over the Little Theatre in the Haymarket. The Little Theatre, a peculiarly estival festival, occupied him for the rest of his life. One of his first accomplishments there was a revision and production of the Gay-Pepusch ballad opera *Polly*, suppressed in 1729 (see 611). In his spare time Arnold succeeded Nares as Chapel Royal organist, inherited the Drury Lane oratorio performances from John Stanley **[796]** in 1786, and (with J. W. Callcott **[1047]**) founded, in 1787, a dining-and-singing society, the Glee Club, which survived for seventy years. In 1787 he also embarked on an ambitious complete edition of Handel. It eventually extended to 180 fascicles; though far from finished and not very accurate, it was more than anyone else did in that direction for another half century. In 1790 he published a four-volume revision of Boyce's **[787]** *Cathedral Music*. In 1789 he became conductor of the Academy of Antient Musick. In 1790 he founded another musical organization, the scholarly Graduates Meeting and a year later set up the philanthropic Choral Fund. He became organist at Westminster Abbey in 1793 and conductor of the annual benefit concerts for the Sons of the Clergy at St. Paul's in 1797. A year later Arnold toppled off a ladder in his library, was immobilized for months, and became permanently crippled. But he returned to musical activity and composed and conducted to the end of his life. He was buried in the Abbey. A son, Samuel James, managed the Lyceum Theater.

RECORDINGS: Apart from his stage works and oratorios, Arnold wrote anthems, psalms, hymns, and many popularly oriented songs and keyboard pieces. He is represented on records by a few examples from the last category (e.g., a sonata played by Esther Fischer).

[916] ARNE, Michael
ACTOR, SINGER, TEACHER, CONDUCTOR, IMPRESARIO, ALCHEMIST
BORN: London, c. 1740
DIED: London, January 14, 1786

It appears that Dr. Thomas Arne **[783]** had other amatory interests than his unfortunate Cecilia, for (at least according to Dr. Charles Burney) she was not Michael's mother. At the insistence of his paternal aunt, Mrs. Cibber, Michael debuted early as an actor, and, at the insistence of his father, was chirping away as a solo singing act in the theaters and pleasure gardens by the time he was ten. At fifteen, however, he wrote a hit song, "The Highland Laddie," and the road was opened to his true artistic career. He continued to write dramatic music for the rest of his short life. (Many of his efforts were collaborative, and most were by way of songs and other music for plays.) He entered into a brief marriage with the singer Elizabeth Wright in 1766, but she died less than three years later, after having produced a daughter, Jemima, who also had a singing career.

In 1767 Arne wrote the music for David Garrick's *Cymon,* which represents the highwater mark of his musical efforts. He soon became obsessed with the notion that he had the secret to the Philosopher's Stone (to transmute base metals into gold) and by 1770 had bankrupted himself in his efforts. He then took off for Germany, in the company of a singing pupil, Ann Venables, where he did some conducting, including the first presentation of Handel's *Messiah* in that country in 1772. The next year he and Miss Venables got married. They appeared together in *Cymon* at the Smock Theatre in Dublin in 1776 and became the stars of the moment. But his old obsession got the better of him again, and by 1777 he was in debtor's prison. A local wine merchant, Thomas Kelly, took pity on him, sent him a piano so that he might compose, and had him teach his own young Michael [1028], who was later also a composer and a friend of Mozart [992]. Eventually they sprung Arne, and he returned to London, where he continued sporadically to compose and conduct.

RECORDINGS: Long ago Roy Henderson recorded a song from *Cymon,* but Arne's enduring fame seems now to depend solely on a familiar tune, "The Lass with the Delicate Air."

[917] ATTERBURY, Luffman
CARPENTER, SINGER
BORN: c. 1740
DIED: Westminster, June 11, 1796

A one-time carpenter, Atterbury sang well enough to win himself a post as court singer to George III. In 1773 he produced the oratorio *Goliath,* but he was best known for his catches and glees, some of which were prizewinners at the Catch Club and some of which he published in 1790. Some time after

that, he got into debt and gave a series of benefit concerts to try to extricate himself; during the last one he dropped dead. RECORDINGS: He is immortalized on records by the Deller Consort's rendition of "Hot Cross Buns"—the one we learned at our mother's knee.

[918] ZEIDLER, Jozef (Zīd-ler, Yō'-zef)
BORN: Wielkopolsku region, c. 1740
DIED: c. 1809

Of Zeidler all that is known is that he was a Polish composer of sacred music and died in the early nineteenth century. His vesper service, in a manuscript copy dated 1787, was found at the cathedral of Gniezno. RECORDINGS: The vesper service has been recorded under the baton of Zbigniew Chwedczuk.

[919] GRÉTRY, André Ernest Modeste
(Grā'-trē, An-drā Ấr-nest' Mō-dest')
TEACHER
BORN: Liège, February 8, 1741
DIED: Montmorency, September 24, 1813

The Grétrys were a Walloon family traceable back to the mid-sixteenth century in a northeast Belgian village that bore their name. The composer's father was a musician—a teacher and first violin at the church of St. Martin in Liège. He married a pupil, Marie-Jeanne des Fossés, and later was first violin at the St. Denis church, where the child became a choirboy. Although he had to walk a mile each way for the three daily services, he was ruthlessly punished for tardiness and, to escape such brutality, used to make a point of arriving well ahead of time, often shivering on the steps for long waits on winter mornings. At the age of twelve, he was admitted to the choir school where he endured further cruelties from an impatient master, young C. F. Jalheau, and was finally tossed out as hopeless. But the bad effects were counteracted by an understanding teacher named Leclercq and by a visiting Italian opera troupe with whose presentations he fell in love. He soon redeemed himself at St. Denis by doing, by way of test, a solo presentation of a motet (written to a melody from an Italian opera). The result was that all the choristers were sent to learn by listening to Italian opera.

Without any theoretical training, he was soon trying to compose. He had no idea of what harmony was all about, but the church organist who was teaching him to play gave him the ground rules, and after the chapter had heard his first Mass (polished up a bit by Henri Moreau, choirmaster at the Collegiate Church of St. Paul, with whom he was now studying), they voted to send him to Italy for serious study. Accordingly in March 1759, he set out on foot across the Alps in a little party consisting of another student, a barber-surgeon, and an abbe (who soon dropped out); the leader was an old and experienced smuggler of laces. After the forbidding wilds of the Tirol, Grétry was (as so many have been) overwhelmed by Italy. He entered Rome on a Sunday by the Porta del Popolo (to which he often returned to recapture the moment) and spent days gawking about the city before he settled down at the College of Liège, where young *Liègeois* were permitted to spend five years pursuing whatever studies they had come for. As a teacher he hit on Giovanni Battista Casali, *maestro di cappella* of the Lateran, who, recognizing the inadequacy of his preparation, went back to basics and for two years drilled him on exercises in harmony and counterpoint. During that period, Grétry was elevated to some ineffable heaven by being taken to the studio of Piccinni [848], who was then riding his greatest wave of popularity. Finally Casali suggested that he go north and get the cachet of approval from Padre Martini [767] in Bologna. This he did, much to the surprise of some of his musical acquaintances. In 1766 he left Italy and set himself up in Geneva as a teacher of proper and well-healed young ladies. The "War of the Buffoons" (see 793) was over, and *opéra-comique* had triumphed, and when Grétry made its acquaintance, he knew that (even though he had written a successful intermezzo, *Le Vendemmiatrici* for the Roman Carnival in 1765) he was, at heart, a Frenchman, not an Italian. His first effort, *Isabelle et Gertrude,* had a moderate success in Geneva, and he was urged by Voltaire (now ensconced at Ferney on Lake Geneva) to seek his fortune in Paris. He went there in 1767, won some backing from the Swedish attache, Count de Creutz, and set about writing his first version of *Les Mariages samnites.* It was presented in the winter at the private theater of the Prince de Conti and flopped—Grétry was an unknown, the music was too floridly Italian, and the cast was lackadaisical. But *Le Huron,* presented at the Comédie Italienne six months later was a fair hit; *Lucile,* produced there the following January, established him as a popular favorite, and *Le Tableau parlant* (September 1769) as a composer to be reckoned with.

In 1770, while working on *Les Deux*

Avares, he fell gravely ill of a fever. His mother, widowed two years earlier, came to live with him and nursed him back to health, no doubt with her own recipe for *waterzooi* (Belgian chicken-vegetable soup). Meanwhile he had encountered a charming young lady artist from Lyon, a Mlle. Grandon, and, after beating down some opposition from her family, married her on July 3, 1771. It seems to have been a matter of locking the stable door after the theft of the horse, for the first of their three daughters, Jenny (Henriette-Marie-Jeanne) was born the previous year. Lucile (Angélique-Dorothée-Lucie) and Antoinette followed in 1772 and 1774. And Grétry went on, serenely turning out something like two operas a year, season after season. The occasional serious works tended to fail, the comedies to succeed. Among his most important hits were *Zemire et Azor* in 1771, *L'Epreuve villageoise* in 1784, and, above all, *Richard Coeur-de-Lion* (the same year). The Gluck-Piccinni war seems not to have touched him; he does not even mention it in his *Mémoires ou Essais sur la musique.*

What did touch him was his health and that of his daughters. He suffered repeated bouts of fever and often spit blood during the rest of his life. He clearly suffered from tuberculosis (possibly owing to those nights on the church steps), and all three daughters contracted it. Lucile, who had also inherited his talent and had had two operas produced, died at eighteen. The other two missed that span by two years. But Grétry went on writing, and when the Revolution came, he merely changed his subjects, writing now of William Tell and republican celebrations. One of the works of this period—a committee job, actually—was *Le Congres des Rois,* at the end of which the remaining monarchs of Europe were made to dance the Carmagnole. The aria "O Richard! O mon Roi!", from *Richard Coeur-de-Lion,* became, with appropriate words, a revolutionary rallying song.

No prophet, Grétry was repeatedly honored in his own country. In 1785 they named a Paris street "rue Grétry." A bust of him graced the Opéra Comique and a statue the Opéra. He was awarded a pension by the king, which, of course, he lost, but it was doubled by Napoleon and sweetened with the ribbon of the *Légion d'honneur.* He was named a councillor to the Bishop of Liège and was one of the five original inspectors of the new Conservatoire. But after 1792 his energy began to fail, and he found his new pieces attracting less and less interest. He bought Jean-Jacques Rousseau's "Ermitage" near Montmorency and retired there to write his *Réflexions d'un Solitaire.* (He had published his *Mémoires* earlier.) Unfortunately he was no more profound as a thinker, for all his quick intelligence, than he was as a composer, and the 8 volumes remained in manuscript until recent times. He became more and more withdrawn from the world, refused even to discuss music, and died at seventy-two. He was given what amounted to a state funeral. Louis XVIII entered Paris the following spring to the strains of the quartet from *Lucile,* "Where are things better than in the bosom of one's family?"

It is not true that Grétry was immediately forgotten. Some of his operas continued to be produced sporadically until early in this century. There are signs of a reawakening of interest in them. Grétry never mastered the rules, and his harmonic and contrapuntal texture is thin and sometimes "wrong." But he had an extraordinary gift for melody and a sense of what would work. He also understood that opera was a dramatic form and made more than one would have supposed he could from the escapist stuff he was given to set. A set of *Danses villageoises* arranged from the operas by the Belgian musicologist François-Auguste Gevaert has helped keep his name alive this past century.

RECORDINGS: The set of dances was available on shellac records in a reading by one F. Ruhlmann, and there is a modern version by Paul Strauss. Other snippets, both vocal and orchestral, have kept his name in the record catalogues. Complete recordings of *Zemire et Azor, Richard Coeur-de-Lion, L'Amant jaloux, Le Jugement de Midas,* and *Lucile* have been published in Europe. He wrote little else than the operas, but even two of his Roman string quartets have been recorded (as string symphonies) by Emanuel Koch. There are also recordings of the Concerto in C Major for Flute (by Michele Debost and Jean-Pierre Rampal); several overtures and the ballet music for *Céphale et Procris* (Paul Strauss); and the ballet music for *La Caravane du Caire* and *L'Epreuve villageoise* (Raymond Leppard).

---

[920] NAUMANN, Johann Gottlieb
(Nou'-mán, Yō'-hán Got'-lēp)
VIOLINIST, HARPSICHORDIST, CONDUCTOR
BORN: Blasewitz, April 17, 1741
DIED: Dresden, October 23, 1801

A Saxon peasant's son, Naumann had, for the nonce, to be satisfied with the musical education he got in Dresden's famous Kreuzchor. But while he studied to be a schoolmaster, he worked at his music, and became sufficiently expert on harpsichord to be taken on as accompanist by the Swedish violinist Anders Wesström (1720–81), embarking rather late on a solo career. They started out to tour Germany in 1756, but illness kept them in Hamburg for the better part of a year. In 1757 they went to Italy, where Wesström let Naumann cool his heels and take up the fiddle to pass the time while he himself studied with Tartini [714]. Eventually Naumann broke off the association and, with help from an English patron, took lessons with Tartini also. Later he studied with Padre Martini [767] in Bologna, winning his essential cachet of approval. In 1762, his first stage work, an intermezzo *Il Tesoro insidiato (The Seductive Treasure),* won the admiration of Hasse [736], on wartime leave from Dresden. Hasse sent him thither, where he was employed as subsidiary chapel composer in 1764 and a year later as the primary chamber composer; but he was also given a good deal of freedom to pursue his operatic career in Italy and elsewhere. In 1776 he was promoted to *Kapellmeister* and given a healthy raise, which helped him turn down an offer from Frederick II's Prussian court. But the next year, on the invitation of the musically inclined Gustavus III, he went to Stockholm to reorganize the disarrayed musical forces at court and get the Drottningholm Opera back on its feet. He returned in 1782 for a longer stay, opening the new Royal Opera with his *Cora och Alonzo* and, to a plot outlined by the king himself, producing *Gustaf Wasa* (still revered by the Swedes) in 1786. In the interim, he went to Copenhagen for similar therapeutic activities and produced there, a few days after *Gustaf Wasa,* the first important opera in Danish, *Orpheus og Euridice.* He was asked to remain but turned the offer down. This selfless act won him still another raise in Dresden and the position of *Oberkapellmeister,* long vacated by the late Hasse. Naumann went on to produce several more operas, including two in Berlin. At fifty-one, he married a Danish admiral's daughter, Catarina von Grodtschilling; by the end of the century, the couple had three sons. Two grandsons, Emil (1827–88) and Ernst (1832–1910), became musicians and scholars.

RECORDINGS: Of Naumann's 20-odd operas, *Gustav Wasa* lives on in Sweden and in a "pirate" recording. Of his considerable body of sacred music, everyone knows the "Dresden Amen" used in Wagner's **[1230]** *Tannhäuser* and *Parsifal* and in Mendels-

sohn's [1200] *Reformation Symphony*. In
1776 Naumann mastered the glass harmonica and wrote a number of pieces for it, several of which have been recorded by Bruno
Hoffmann.

[921] TOMASINI, Luigi (Tō-mà-sē'-nē,
    Lōō-ē'-gē)
VIOLINIST
BORN: Pesaro, June 22, 1741
DIED: Eisenstadt, April 25, 1808

Prince Pál Antal Esterházy discovered the
sixteen-year-old Tomasini in Italy and
brought him home with him as a servant.
(Tomasini's name often appears as Alois
Luigi or Aloysius Luigi, but since the two
are cognate, one assumes he was called
"Alois" at Eisenstadt.) The prince had Tomasini trained in Venice, and perhaps elsewhere, and made him first-desk violin in his
orchestra in or before 1761. After Joseph
Haydn [871] took over direction of the orchestra, Tomasini was named *Konzertmeister*. It is likely that Haydn wrote his 3 violin concerti and the first-violin parts of the
Esterházy quartet series for his particular
talents. Tomasini married one Josepha Vogl
and had twelve children by her. Four of
them later became Esterházy court musicians: Anton and Alois were violinists and
Joseph and Elisabeth, singers. In 1783 Tomasini considered defecting to the court of
Prince Széchényi, but its musical wing
folded before he could. When Prince Antal
Esterházy succeeded his father, Nikolaus
the Magnificent, in 1790, he dismissed his
orchestra, retiring Tomasini on a pension
and giving him a chance to tour. Frau Tomasini died three years later, and in 1797
twenty-four-year-old Barbara Feichtinger,
whom he got around to marrying two years
later, presented him with yet another son.
In 1794 Prince Antal died and was succeeded by his brother, Nikolaus II, who revived the orchestra and appointed Tomasini
Kammermeister in 1802. In the year of his
father's death, Alois Tomasini, who had
several times been reprimanded for his "unseemly levity," eloped with a singer named
Sophie Croll, and became *Konzertmeister* at
Neustrelitz, where he was succeeded by his
son Carlo. Luigi Tomasini left numerous
compositions for his baryton-playing employer, 21 string quartets, a number of violin
sonatas and duos, 3 symphonies, and 3 violin concerti. RECORDINGS: Eduard Malkus
has recorded one of the violin concerti.

[922] MARTINI, Johann Paul Aegidius,
    Il Tedesco (Màr-tē'-nē, Yō'-hàn Poul
    Ā-jē'-dyōōs)
ORGANIST, SOLDIER, TEACHER, EDUCA-
TOR, CONDUCTOR
BORN: Freystadt, August 31, 1741
DIED: Paris, February 10, 1816

For years it was carefully pointed out that
"Martini the German" was really named
Schwarzendorf. In fact, in his birthplace
southeast of Nuremberg, he was known as
Johann Paul Aegidius Martin, son of a local
organist. He studied in the Jesuit school at
Neuburg, near Ingolstadt, serving as organist from the age of ten. He took a philosophy degree at Freiburg-im-Breisgau, then,
using the name of "Schwarzendorf," he hit
the road for an apparently aimless existence. This step seems to have been precipitated by his dislike of his new stepmother
back home. Arriving in Nancy broke and
hungry in 1760, he found a place as a court
musician for good King Stanislaus, formerly of Poland and now compensatory
Duke of Lorraine. When the duke died in
1766, Martin, now calling himself "Martini"
and termed "il Tedesco" to distinguish him
from Padre Martini [767], went to Paris and
won a contest for a signature march for the
Garde Suisse. This won him overtures from
the Light Cavalry and an officership
therein.
    During the next few years he is said to
have reformed French military music. In
1771 he wrote the first of a number of successful operas, *L'Amoureux de quinze ans
(The Fifteen-Year-Old Lover)*, and, as a
more or less direct result, he was hired as
director of the Prince of Condé's orchestra
at Chantilly, and then of that of the Count
of Artois. Fearing for his life when the
Revolution broke out, Martini fled to Lyons, where he spent his time cribbing a vocal method from Johann Adam Hiller's
Anweisung der Singekunst of twenty years
earlier. He returned to Paris in 1794, resumed his operatic career, and was appointed an inspector of the new Paris Conservatory in 1798 and professor of composition there in 1800. In 1814 Louis XVIII appointed him conductor of the Royal Orchestra and decorated him with the Order of St.
Michel a little while before he died. About
the same time his Requiem for the slain
Louis XVI was performed.
    RECORDINGS: Some of Martini's operas
survived well into the new century but are
now, like his religious music, forgotten.
What hangs on are a few of his tuneful romances for voice and piano (said to be the
first to specify that instrument), especially

the still popular "Plaisir d'amour" (innumerable recordings); Regina Resnik has also recorded "Plainte de Marie-Stuart".

[923] PICHL, Václav (Pēk'-əl, Vä'-tsläf)
CONDUCTOR, VIOLINIST, WRITER
BORN: Bechyně, September 25, 1741
DIED: Vienna, January 23, 1805

An astonishingly prolific composer (nearly 1,000 works), Pichl has been all but forgotten. Born into a working-class family in a little town about fifty miles south of Prague, he studied with the local cantor, sang in the choir at the Breznice Jesuit School, and graduated in humanities from the University of Prague. He studied with Seger, his colleague at Týn, where he played violin. Dittersdorf [906] took him as his right-hand man to the court of the Bishop of Grosswardein in 1765, but when the empress commanded the bishop to cut out the ostentation, Pichl returned in 1769 to Prague and became Konzertmeister at the Imperial Opera the next year. It is said that the empress preferred him to Mozart [992]. In 1777 he was dispatched to Milan as Kapellmeister to Archduke Ferdinand, imperial governor of Lombardy. While there he won the approval of Padre Martini [767] and membership in the Bolognese Accademia Filarmonica (as well as the Mantuan one), and directed the opera company in Monza for a time. With the approach of Napoleon in 1796, Pichl and the archduke left for Vienna. There Pichl was friendly with Haydn [871] and Beethoven [1063]. Nine years later he expired while performing for Beethoven's patron, Count Lobkowitz. Pichl's literary works—Latin libretti, a Czech version of Schikaneder's play Die Zauberflöte, and a history of Bohemian musicians in Italy—are mostly lost or destroyed, as are his stage works. But most of his symphonies (nearly 100), concerti, divertimenti, quartets, trios, etc., are still extant and compare favorably with the work of the better Classical composers. RECORDINGS: The usually conductorless Prague Chamber Orchestra, has recorded the Symphony in D Major, "Mars."

[924] LEDUC, Simon (Lə-Dük', Sē-môn')
VIOLINIST, ADMINISTRATOR
BORN: Paris, January 15, 1742
DIED: Paris, January 22, 1777

Simon LeDuc was called "LeDuc l'ainé," to distinguish him from his younger brother (and pupil), Pierre LeDuc (1755–1826).

(Pierre became an important music publisher, but his house did not long survive the death of his son Auguste in 1823 and should not be confused with that founded by Alphonse Leduc [no relation] c. 1841 and still in business.) Simon LeDuc studied with the violinist Pierre Gaviniès and at seventeen became a second violinist in the orchestra of the Concert Spirituel. In 1763 he moved up to the first violins and appeared as a soloist but went out on his own the following year. In 1768 he was given a privilège (i.e., a sort of copyright) to publish his own compositions, and in 1770 Pierre appeared at the Concert Spirituel as soloist in some of them. When he inaugurated his business five years later, he became their sole publisher. In 1773 Simon again appeared as soloist with the orchestra, and became, with his old teacher and with Gossec [879], a member of a threeman directorate. LeDuc did much to rehabilitate the Concert Spirituel, which had got into a slump, and was very popular with its musicians, but he died suddenly a week after his thirty-fifth birthday. He left 44 compositions, most of them featuring the violin; but, inspired by the Mannheimers, he completed 3 interesting symphonies shortly before he died. Rehearsing the last of them shortly after LeDuc's death, the Chevalier de Saint-Georges [908] burst into tears, and the whole group became so overcome that the rehearsal had to be called off. RECORDINGS: The symphonies have been recorded by Bernard Wahl. Carol Lieberman has recorded three violin sonatas.

[925] KRUMPHOLTZ, Johann Baptist (Krōōmp'-holts, Yō-hàn Bàp'-tēst)
HARPIST, INSTRUMENT DESIGNER
BORN: Budenice, May 3, 1742
DIED: Paris, February 19, 1790

The greatest harpist of his time, Krumpholtz was born at a Bohemian crossroads near Zlonice, whose bells Dvořák [1386] was to celebrate in his first symphony. His younger brother Wenzel (c. 1750–1817) was a violinist and a close friend of Beethoven [1063], whose mandolin sonata was written for him. The father, a serf or bondservant of Count Kinský, was a horn player and taught the older boy to play. In 1758 his employer sent the latter to a horn tutor in Vienna. There he took up the harp, whose basics he is said to have gotten from his mother. Later he apparently joined the band of his uncle's regiment and was sent to the Netherlands, whence he found his way to Paris. (Some accounts have the father joining a French unit and taking both boys there, but that seems quite unlikely.) By 1771 he was back in Prague, where his harping caught the fancy of Pichl [923] and Dušek [867]. He went to Vienna, gave a concert in 1773, and wound up in Haydn's [871] Esterházy orchestra. (Wenzel also found employment there.) Three years later, he undertook a European tour. By now he was developing ideas for improving the harp and stopped in Metz to test them out in the workshop of a certain Christian Steckler. When he left for Paris, he took along Steckler's pubescent daughter as pupil. He settled in Paris and became Jean-Baptiste. In 1778 he married Marguerite Gilbert, daughter of a harp manufacturer, but she died giving birth to their first child. Meanwhile Anne-Marie was obviously developing very nicely, and soon her teacher married her and gave her a solo debut at the Concert Spirituel. By 1785 Krumpholtz had perfected the harp to his satisfaction (his model included pedal-operated shutters to dampen or direct the sound, got the nod from the French Academy, and put it into manufacture. It seems to have had considerable impact on the fad for using the harp as a means of having young ladies exhibit their charms, musical and otherwise. In 1789 Krumpholtz's young lady exhibited her independence by eloping to London with a lover, apparently that sometime Adonis of the piano, J. L. Dussek [1016]. She was a success there for a decade or so, then faded out, and disappears from the pages of history in 1824. She left a daughter (b. 1785) who was also a harpist. Dussek married someone else in 1792. The shock of the whole thing crumpled Krumpholtz, and, after some weeks of brooding, he threw himself into the icy Seine. All of his music involves his instrument, and includes 6 concerti, 2 *symphonies concertantes,* and a number of sonatas with ad-lib accompanying instruments. RECORDINGS: Lily Laskine has recorded the Concerto for Harp No. 6, and she and Nicanor Zabaleta have each recorded a sonata.

[926] SCHOENFELD, Johann Philipp
(Shön'-felt, Yō'-hán Fē'-lip)
MUSIC DIRECTOR, TEACHER
BORN: Strasbourg, 1742
DIED: Strasbourg, January 5, 1790

The short-lived Schoenfeld is of some importance in the history of the art song as one who was concerned to suit music to words. Originally a divinity student, he took up music and was employed as a teacher by a family named Münchhausen in Braun-

schweig, where he was acquainted with Friedemann Bach [784]. He returned to Strasbourg as assistant to the choirmaster at the New Church in 1777, was sent to Italy to study two years later, and returned to take over the choir and the municipal concerts. He developed radical plans for reforming the latter, but the Revolution threw a monkey wrench into them, and a year later he was dead. RECORDINGS: Edith Selig has recorded two of his songs.

[927] BOCCHERINI, Ridolfo Luigi
(Bōk-ker-ē'-nē, Rē-dol'-fō Lōō-ē'-gē)
CELLIST
BORN: Lucca, February 19, 1743
DIED: Madrid, May 28, 1805

Among dedicatees of chamber music there have been some small stirrings of interest in Boccherini recently, but the average musical layman knows him chiefly by a ubiquitous minuet, a pastiche cello concerto cobbled up by a nineteenth-century German virtuoso, and the silly tag, allegedly applied to him by the eccentric violinist Giuseppe Puppo: "the wife of Haydn." ("They were only good friends," quipped someone, who, one wishes, knew more about it—see below.)

Luigi Boccherini was the third child of Leopoldo Boccherini, a contrabassist in the Lucchese court orchestra who gave the boy his first lessons and then turned him over to Maestro Francesco Vanucci. The boy developed as a fine cellist and at fourteen was sent off to Rome for polishing his performance skills—probably with Giovanni Battista Costanzi, choirmaster at St. Peter's. Later that year, the Boccherinis went to Vienna, where Leopoldo and Luigi played in the opera orchestra, and three other children, Giovanni Gastone, Maria Ester, and Anna Matilda, embarked on ballet careers. Anna Matilda gave it up. Maria Ester was a success and later became the wife of one great dancer-choreographer, Onorato Viganò, and the mother of another, Salvatore Viganò. Giovan' Gastone also won success as a poet, as we shall see. In Vienna Luigi won the approbation of Gluck [803]. He and his father divided the next several years between Vienna and Lucca, where, in 1765, Luigi was appointed first cellist. That same year, both Boccherinis played concerts in Pavia and Cremona under the direction of G. B. Sammartini [738].

Shortly after his return to Lucca, Boccherini is said to have become a part of one of the first string quartets and perhaps the very first to concertize. Its membership was all-star: the violinists were Nardini [823] and Filippo Manfredi, who had studied both with him and Tartini [714]; the violist was *their* pupil Cambini [940]. The rumor persists that the group played in Paris, but, delayed by Barbary pirates, Cambini seems to have not got there before 1770, and Nardini seems never to have been there at all. But Boccherini and his fellow-Lucchese Manfredi arrived there in 1767 and played at the Concert Spirituel the following spring—with enormous or indifferent success, depending on whose review one reads. Encouraged by a patron, local publishers brought out some of Boccherini's trios and quartets. In the course of 1768, according to legend, the Spanish ambassador convinced the duo that fame and fortune awaited them at the court of the Prince of Asturias (the future Charles IV), and they had only to go and knock. At any rate they went and knocked—but nothing much seems to have happened. For one thing the prince already had a music director in the person of composer-violinist Gaetano Brunetti [934]. Brunetti has had an undeservedly bad press from Boccherini's proponents, but there is no way of telling whether he deliberately stood in his way. Nor were chances any better in the royal establishment. However, by 1770, Boccherini had found a home with the Infante Don Luis, the king's brother—a bachelor playboy and sometime cardinal. (No one seems to care what became of Manfredi.) For a time the Infantile household moved from *palacio* to *palacio,* while Boccherini composed and played when called upon. In 1771 he married Clementina Pelicho, who bore him two sons. In 1776 he lost his mother, who had apparently gone along to do his socks all those years. At about the same time, his employer married a commoner, and, in accordance with an agreement previously made with his brother, went into token exile at his estate near Avila, which he turned into a little cultural enclave. There Boccherini seems to have been happy and productive until 1785 when both Don Luis and the composer's wife died.

Just what happened next is obscure. Boccherini was granted a royal pension and promised a slot in the royal *capila.* As the result of some cello pieces dedicated to Frederick William II, the cello-playing King of Prussia, he was designated Prussian *Kammerkomponist.* But there is no credible evidence that he either played in the Spanish court orchestra or went to Berlin. We *do* know that in 1786 he was in the employ of the Duchess of Osuna, for whom he wrote his only stage work, a *zarzuela* that bore the

name of his late wife, *La Clementina.* A year later he was patronized by a certain Pacheco, a Portuguese, in whose home a visitor, the eccentric English novelist William Beckford, embarrassed him by dancing a fandango to one of his compositions. The Duchess of Osuna also commissioned a number of compositions from Joseph Haydn [871]. Whether Boccherini had anything to do with this would be hard to say. There is no concrete evidence that the two ever met or even corresponded. But each admired the other, and they shared a Viennese publisher often entrusted with friendly greetings. Moreover, it was Giovan' Gastone Boccherini who provided the libretto for Haydn's first oratorio, *Il Ritorno di Tobia (The Return of Tobias).*

In 1787 Boccherini married again—a cellist's daughter, Maria del Pilar Joaquina Porreti, who gave him three daughters. What we know of his last eighteen years seems quite gloomy, even if one allows for sentimentalizing. Over the next decade there is little information about his activities. His Prussian salary ended with the king's death in 1797; his last known patron left town a year later. He had financial troubles with his publisher. When Napoleon subverted the Spanish rulers, Boccherini hitched his wagon to the star of the First Consul's brother, Lucien, dispatched to Spain in 1800 as ambassador; but Lucien and his brother did not agree, and he was soon removed. Moreover Boccherini was suffering from tuberculosis. In 1802 two of his daughters died. A year later a visitor found the composer, his wife, and their remaining daughter living in a one-room apartment with a sort of attic that served as a study. In 1804 two more deaths left Boccherini alone, and he followed the next year. In 1927 his remains were disinterred and taken back to Lucca for burial.

Like Haydn, Boccherini was extremely productive, and, according to the most recent catalogue—Gérard, 1969—is credited with more than 550 compositions. But to see him as a sort of pale copy of Haydn is to do him a grave injustice. Both men were undoubtedly influenced by Mannheim, Vienna, and Paris, as well as by Italy. But it is tempting to think of Middle European peasant brusqueness in Haydn and polished Italian suppleness and grace in Boccherini—later colored by the feel of guitars and castanets. If Haydn was the Father of the String Quartet, Boccherini invented the string quintet, of which species he wrote more than 100 examples. He also wrote 20-odd fine symphonies, 11 cello concerti, a couple of oratorios, and some sacred music, but most of the rest of his output is for chamber-size ensembles.

RECORDINGS: Boccherini has been fairly well treated by the record companies, though recordings of his music seem to be as ephemeral as bubbles. More than half of the symphonies are represented—notably the six of Op. 35 from Angelo Ephrikian, six of Op. 12 from Raymond Leppard, and four from Op. 21 by Lee Schaenen. Anner Bylsma has recorded some of the cello concerti in their original form, and Ivan Polidori has conducted the *Stabat Mater*. EMI-Angel once ambitiously embarked on a complete survey of the quintets with the Quintetto Boccherini, but the project was abandoned after only a few discs were issued. Over the years, however, there have been sporadic appearances of the chamber works—too numerous to detail here.

[928] EGUIGUREN, Fernando (Ā-gē-goo'-ren, Fer-nȧn'-dō)
MONK
BORN: Eibar, March 17, 1743
DIED: Aranzuzu (?)

Fray Fernando was one of the Basque Scarlattists of northern Spain. Born in the hills near Bilbao, he joined the Franciscan Order at the monastery of Aranzuzu in 1759 and, apparently, spent his life there. He left 3 Masses, and some other church music, as well as keyboard pieces. RECORDINGS: One of the keyboard pieces has been recorded by Antonio Ruiz-Pipó.

[929] PETER, Simon
MINISTER, ADMINISTRATOR
BORN: Heerendijk, April 2, 1743
DIED: Salem, N.C., May 29, 1819

Not the Apostle, but the elder brother of the more famous Johann Friedrich Peter **[941]**. The biographies of the two men overlap until their emigration from Holland to Pennsylvania in 1770. Simon Peter preceded "John" to the Salem settlement by five years, in 1784, and spent the rest of his life there as a minister and later as a member of the governing board of the Moravian Church. He was only incidentally a composer but turned out some highly effective anthems. RECORDINGS: Two of the anthems have been recorded by Gregg Smith.

[930] GUGEL, Georg Anton (Gōō'-gel, Gā'-ôrg Ȧn'-tōn)
CONDUCTOR

BORN: Mainz, 1743
DIED: Stuttgart, 1802

The reference books overlook Gugel, though they list a 1901 opera, *Gugeline* by Ludwig Thuille **[1537]**. Gugel's career seems to have been spent as *Kapellmeister* to Duke Ludwig Eugen of Württemberg at his castles in Weiltingen and Bönnigheim. He wrote some symphonies and a good deal of chamber music. RECORDINGS: The Mannheim Duo has recorded a little keyboard-and-violin suite designated as *Ballo.*

[931] WOODWARD, Richard, Jr.
ORGANIST, SINGER
BORN: 1743
DIED: Dublin, November 22, 1777

Presumably Woodward was born in England, because when Christ Church Cathedral in Dublin hired his father for its choir in 1751, it paid out travel expenses for the boy, who was to serve as chorister. Young Woodward also sang at St. Patrick's. He returned to Christ Church as an organist and mature singer in 1765, and in the latter capacity to St. Patrick's five years later. In 1767 he published a collection of songs and catches and an occasional motet, and in 1771 a collection of anthems. In the latter year the University of Dublin awarded him a doctorate. He died at the early age of thirty-four and was buried in Christ Church. RECORDINGS: One of his songs has been recorded by the Worcester Cathedral Choir.

[932] HAMAL, Henri (Ȧ-mȧl', On-rē')
CHOIRMASTER
BORN: Liège, July 20, 1744
DIED: Liège, September 17, 1820

The son of a surgeon, Dieudonné Hamal, Henri studied with his paternal uncle, the composer Jean-Noël Hamal **[778]**, as a chorister in the local cathedral. In 1763 he took the road taken two years earlier by his fellow-townsman Grétry **[919]** over the hills to the Liègois College in Rome. He remained in Italy until 1769, studying part of the time in Naples with Sarti **[853]**. He returned to Liège to become his uncle's assistant and, in 1778, his successor (against some opposition from the chapter). During the nine years of their association, they collaborated on several compositions. Henri also had a three-act *opéra-comique* produced in Liège in 1775. In 1792 the French Revolutionaries overran the city, and in the summer of 1793 they had the cathedral demolished as a symbol of oppression. Later Hamal wrote a history of the fine arts in Liège. Besides a considerable body of religious music, he left a couple of symphonies, some keyboard sonatas, and a trumpet concerto long ascribed to Jean-Noël. RECORDINGS: The Concerto for Trumpet has been recorded by Maurice André.

[933] SECKENDORFF, Karl Siegmund, Freiherr von (Zek'-en-dôrf, Kärl Zēg'-mōont)
SOLDIER, COURT OFFICIAL, DIPLOMAT
BORN: Erlangen, November 20, 1744
DIED: Ansbach, April 26, 1785

Baron von Seckendorff studied at his hometown university. At seventeen, in the middle of the Seven Years War, he became an officer in the imperial forces. When it was over, he served nearly a decade under Charles Emmanuel III in Sardinia, leaving in 1774 after the king's death. The next year he came to Weimar when Duke Karl Ernst reached his maturity, and was appointed chamberlain and steward. He was part of the Dowager Duchess Anna Amalie's [905] "Court of the Muses," and was particularly thick with Goethe, several of whose poems he set to music before their publication. He also wrote stage pieces to libretti by Goethe, most of them (alas!) lost, translated *Werther* into French, orchestrated works by the duchess, and wrote plays. But he eventually got fed up with that kind of life and got himself an appointment as ambassador to the Margravate of Ansbach from Frederick II of Prussia in 1784. However, he died there the following spring, at forty. Besides his stage works, Seckendorff composed 3 volumes of "folksongs" (under Herder's influence), other songs, and some chamber music, including 12 string quartets and the first known piano sonatas for three hands. RECORDINGS: Dietrich Fischer-Dieskau has recorded one of his Goethe settings.

[934] BRUNETTI, Gaetano (Brōo-net'-tē, Gī-tä'-nō)
VIOLINIST, CONDUCTOR
BORN: 1744
DIED: Culminal de Orejo, December 16, 1798

In the seventeenth and eighteenth centuries there were a number of musical Brunettis who came from Italy. There is no evidence that Gaetano was or was not related to them, but they have made for some confusion with regard to his history. The Neapol-

itan violinist Antonio Brunetti, who succeeded Mozart [992] in the Archepiscopal Orchestra at Salzburg, for example, commonly appears in books on Mozart as "Gaetano." Nor was the real Gaetano the son of an apparently mythical Antonio Brunetti of Arezzo. His father was a Stefano Brunetti of Fano, who seems to have had no claim to fame of his own. Presumably his son was born in Fano on the Adriatic coast. For reasons unknown, the family moved to Madrid in 1762, where, five years later, Brunetti became a member of the *capilla* of Charles III. He also is said to have worked for the Duke of Alva, and was music teacher and music director to the Prince of the Asturias, who became king, after a fashion, as Charles IV in 1788.

It was once argued that Brunetti's music was unknown for so long because his patrons demanded proprietary rights over it, but there is no evidence to suggest any truth whatsoever in the story. He has also been called a mere imitator of Boccherini [927], who supposedly put him on the map, and to whom he proved a conniving ingrate. But Brunetti was already established when Boccherini arrived in Spain in 1768. He was married and had a daughter and a son, the latter a court cellist. After Charles IV took the throne, he appointed Brunetti as director of his up-to-date little orchestra. Charles, though he was a rotten ruler—he sold Spain out to Napoleon—was a connoisseur of the arts and a good violinist, the latter fact accounting for Brunetti's 64 violin sonatas and 44 string quartets, as well as a lot of other chamber music. (Brunetti also wrote for the royal performing horses.) Still another legend says that Brunetti died of shock when he encountered French soldiers in the streets. He apparently died suddenly, but whether his passing was caused by the invasion, his second marriage shortly before, both, or neither remains unknown. Brunetti is an uncommonly charming composer and was a quite prolific one; the official list of his works runs to more than 450 —mostly instrumental, but including 2 operas (lost), a Mass, and a few other vocal works. Perhaps most interesting are the 28 symphonies. RECORDINGS: About a third of the symphonies have been recorded, thanks to Newell Jenkins' quixotic espousal of them.

[935] CARVALHO, João de Sousa (Kâr-vä'-lyōo, Zhwoun dä Sō'-sà)
TEACHER, CHOIRMASTER
BORN: Estremoz, February 22, 1745
DIED: Alentejo, 1798

Recent research has resurrected the name and works of Sousa Carvalho, an important figure in eighteenth-century Portuguese music. Born some eighty miles east of Lisbon, he was sent as a child to the nearby Colégio dos Santos Reis Magos at the ducal palace in Vicosa. He showed so much ability that when he was fifteen the Patriarchate in Lisbon sent him to the Conservatorio di Sant' Onofrio in Naples, where he was a fellow student of Paisiello's [914] under Maestro Carlo Cotumacci and perhaps, as his later music suggests, studied with Porpora [690]. The first of his several operas, La Nitetti, was performed in Rome when he was twenty-one. A year later he came home to teach counterpoint in the Patriarchal Seminary, of which he was later director. Among his many pupils were Antonio Leal Moreira and Marcos Portugal. His comedy L'Amore industrioso (Busy Love) was performed in 1769, and between 1778 and 1785 he might have been described as "Carvalho industrioso," turning out ten operas. He also wrote some fine church music and some keyboard sonatas. RECORDINGS: The Gulbenkian Foundation Orchestra, under various conductors, has recorded the great Te Deum of 1792 and the overtures to L'Amore industrioso and Penelope. Ruggero Gerlin and János Sebestyan have recorded various harpsichord and organ pieces.

[936] DIBDIN, Charles
ENTERTAINER, IMPRESARIO, PUBLISHER, WRITER, ETC.
BORN: Southampton, c. March 15, 1745
DIED: London, July 25, 1814

If Dibdin is of little consequence to the history of music as an art form, he was a man of great ingenuity, multifarious talents, and incredible irascibility, and seems to foreshadow some aspects of P. T. Barnum and Tin Pan Alley. He came of middle-class stock—his grandfather, a merchant, had founded a village called Dibdin—though his father, a parish clerk, was hard put to make most ends meet, as sire of at least fourteen children, of whom Charles was the twelfth. Charles went to Winchester Cathedral as a choirboy at eleven and left three years later. Save for what music he learned there, he was an autodidact. At fifteen he was working in a music warehouse in London and singing in the chorus at the Covent Garden Theatre. He published his first collection of songs and cantatas (in score) when he was eighteen. A year later Covent Garden produced his first opera, The Shepherd's Artifice, starring Charles Dibdin, who also wrote the libretto; he quickly became a popular favorite, both as a singing actor and a composer. He had married at about eighteen but soon left his wife for a dancer named Harriet Pitt. They had two sons, Charles Isaac (1768–1833) who later became owner of the Sadler's Wells Theatre, and Thomas John (1771–1841), actor and dramatist.

In 1767 Dibdin began a highly successful partnership with the Irish librettist Isaac Bickerstaffe. A year later, he left Covent Garden in a huff and signed a contract with David Garrick at the Drury Lane Theatre, which gave him a good deal of freedom. For several summers, for example, he sang and directed the musical program at Ranelegh Gardens, and he published numerous of his "hits." In 1772 Bickerstaffe's fondness for young men forced his flight across the Channel, and his consequent reputation redounded on Dibdin, who, shortly afterward, abandoned Harriet for a singer known to posterity only as "Miss Wilde." Disgusted, Garrick refused to renew the contract, which was up in 1775, and, in 1776, with debtor's prison snapping at his heels, Dibdin took Miss Wilde and their new daughter and followed Bickerstaffe. From France, he supplied Thomas King, the owner of Sadler's Wells, with musical intermezzi called "dialogues" and at Drury Lane, Thomas Linley, Jr. [995], who had succeeded Garrick, made a hit of Dibdin's The Quaker. After two years it was possible for Dibdin to return unscathed and take a job as official composer to Covent Garden. But little came of it and three years later, 1781, he quarreled with the manager and quit.

With a partner and financial backing, Dibdin built the Royal Circus on the South Bank in 1782, opening it that fall. Part playhouse, part circus, it involved horses and clowns as well as singers, dancers, and actors. When it failed, the board fired him and had him jailed for debt at last. Later they rehired him, but he was so affronted to be thought an object of charity that he set out on a similar venture of his own. That ended when a storm blew down his half-finished theater, the Helicon. He determined that the grass must be greener in India and took ship in 1788, having raised the requisite passage money by a solo tour of the provinces. A few miles out of port, however, he was so afflicted by seasickness that he had to be put ashore. Heartened, however, by his successful tour, he decided to go it alone in London and began presenting what he called "table entertainments," wherein he served as impresario, master of ceremonies, narrator, script writer, singer, pianist, and composer. The first attempt, in January 1789, was disappointing, but the following December *The Oddities* was an enormous success. It contained a number of rousing sea songs, but the one that became a classic was the elegiac "Tom Bowling," written in memory of his own brother Tom, a sea captain. The table entertainments sustained Dibdin so well that he was able to open his own pocket-size Sans-Souci Theatre in 1792 and a larger version four years later. Meanwhile he was grinding out and publishing topical songs at a prodigious rate, and writing prose for publication, including autobiographical works, three novels, *A Complete History of the English Stage* (!), and do-it-yourself books on music. (Dibdin also painted, designed sets, and illustrated some of his books.) Dibdin retired on a government pension in 1805, but the government failed to come through, and he went back to the stage. Unable to make a go of it anymore, he sunk his savings in a music store, which went bankrupt, and for a while he, Miss Wilde, and their daughter subsisted on charity. He suffered a stroke and died a year later in a London slum.

Most of Dibdin's theater pieces have been lost, and all but a few probably had only historical value at best. What survives is an enormous body of songs, which contains a few pearls amidst the junk.

RECORDINGS: Besides "Tom Bowling," some of these used to be recorded by hearty baritones like Peter Dawson.

[937] STAMITZ, Carl Philipp (Shtä'-mitz, Kärl Fē-lēp')
STRING PLAYER
BORN: Mannheim, May 7, 1745
DIED: Jena, November 9, 1801

Carl Stamitz was the more famous of the two sons of Johann Wenzel [810], the younger son being Anton (1754–?). Carl's father died when he was eleven and his musical education was continued by Richter [777] and other members of the Mannheim organization. At seventeen he himself became a second violin in the orchestra, where he was joined by his young brother two years later. Both followed Richter to France in 1770 and wound up in Paris. Anton remained there for twenty years as teacher and court violinist; then he disappears from the records. Carl appeared solo and with his brother as a virtuoso (on violin, viola, and viola d'amore) and became music director to Louis, the Duke of Noailles and Marshal of France. But shortly he began leading

what has been described by some as "the life of a touring virtuoso" and by others as an irrepressible inability to stay in one place. Such activity may have occasioned the break with the duke that seems to have occurred in 1777 when Stamitz went to London. At the time Mozart [992] described Stamitz to his father [816] as shiftless and dissolute. Be that as it may, after two years or so, Stamitz moved on to The Hague, where, in one of his concerts he appeared with a pre-adolescent pianist named Ludwig van Beethoven [1063]. By mid-decade he was back in Germany, where he moved about restlessly for another five years. Toward the end of that period, he married a Maria Josepha Pilz and alit in Greiz, between Leipzig and the Bohemian border. Her two difficult confinements (producing a son and a daughter) and subsequent bad health trapped him there, and he seems to have existed by writing music for various courts and by very occasional concerts. After fruitless attempts to find a post, he finally got one as a university music director and teacher in Jena. Two more sons were born there, but none of the children reached maturity. Stamitz is said to have spent his last years dabbling in alchemy. He was about to embark on a concert tour to Russia when he died. He left about 150 orchestral works (mostly symphonies, *sinfonie concertante,* and concerti), even more chamber compositions, and a few vocal works. His 2 known operas are lost. His compositions are perhaps shallower than his father's but are more lyrical and show a masterly grasp of orchestration. RECORDINGS: There are many recordings of Stamitz's "orchestral quartets," concerti, and *sinfonie concertante,* as well as a few chamber works (notably duos)—in fact too many to specify here.

[938] BEREZOVSKY, Maxim Sozontovich (Byā-rā-zōv'-skē, Mȧk-sēm' Sō-zon-tō'-vich)
SINGER
BORN: Glukhov, October 27, 1745
DIED: St. Petersburg, April 2, 1777

After the westernization of the Russian court by Peter I, the *desideratum* was Western music, and no attempt was made to create a Russian music on folk roots or on the *znamenny* chant of the Orthodox liturgy, itself a victim of subsequent upheavals within the church. Peter's niece, the Czarina Anna, in 1734 imported the Neapolitan composer Francesco Araja (1709–70), to give her court an Italian opera company, orchestra, and so forth, and for several decades the subsequent history of Russian music of consequence was a history of the comings and goings of foreigners.

Berezovsky was the first of the significant native aspirants. Born in the Ukraine in the general vicinity of Kiev, he was educated in a church school in that city, and brought to St. Petersburg to study with Galuppi [768] and sing in the Czarina Elisabeth's chapel. At fourteen he sang the *(castrato)* lead in one of Araja's operas. Later he developed a fine tenor. In 1765, the new czarina, Catherine the Great, sent him to Bologna to study with Padre Martini [767]. After acquiring the now virtually inevitable membership in the Accademia Filarmonica and producing an opera—the first on an Italian stage by a Russian (in Livorno)—he returned after a decade to St. Petersburg. Unhappily for him, the Italian musicians at court did not encourage interlopers, and after months of trying to win notice, he cut his throat (or perhaps shot himself) at thirty-one. All that survives is a few liturgical pieces of more than historical interest.

RECORDINGS: Alexander Yurlov has recorded the best of the liturgical pieces, a "concerto" setting of Psalm 41.

[939] LONBIDE, Juan Andres (Lōn-bī'-dā, Hwản Ản'-dres)
ORGANIST, CHOIRMASTER, MONK
BORN: Elgueta, November 14, 1745
DIED: ?

Another of the "Basque Scarlattists," Lonbide was for a time organist and choirmaster at the Franciscan Monastery of Aranzazu and at the Cathedral of Calahorra. Among his other productions was a book on organ technique, no longer extant. RECORDINGS: Antonio Ruiz-Pipó has recorded one of his keyboard sonatas.

[940] CAMBINI, Giuseppe Maria Gioacchino (Kảm-bē'-nē, Jōō-sep'-pā Mả-rē'-ả Jō-ảk-kē'-nō)
VIOLINIST
BORN: Livorno, February 13, 1746
DIED: after 1810

One of the great benefits of modern scholarship is to demonstrate that fiction is almost always stranger than truth. The Cambini biography is a case in point. For years it read like something by Byron or an opera libretto. After studying violin with Nardini [823], Manfredi, and Polli (whoever he may have been), he went to Bologna for season-

ing with Padre Martini [767]. In 1766, apparently after the all-star quartet tour (see Boccherini [927]), he went to Naples to see his first opera on the stage. When it flopped, he took ship as the quickest way back to Livorno, either to escape the outraged audience or to get married. Once at sea, the vessel was attacked by Barbary pirates and Cambini was taken back to North Africa and put on the block as a slave. As luck would have it, one of the buyers was a Venetian who, disliking to see a fellow Italian in trouble, bought him and set him free. He followed his friend Boccherini to Paris, was a hit at the Concert Spirituel in 1773. He became a musical power in that city, and it was he that blocked the scheduled performance of Mozart's [992] *Sinfonia Concertante* for winds and string orchestra, K. Anh. 9, at the Concert Spirituel. But his star faded after the Revolution. He took up hackwork, and even produced some Boccherini forgeries in his desperation. Finally, around 1815, he was committed to the poorhouse, where he died wretched and alone in 1825.

Out of all this material, the only verifiable fact now seems to be that he played at the Concert Spirituel in 1773, though it is conceded that he may have studied with Manfredi and even Nardini. (Even his birthdate is in doubt.) After he got to Paris, he wrote a number of operas, mostly for the Théâtres Beaujolais and Louvois, where he seems to have conducted. He also wrote vast amounts of other music, mostly orchestral and instrumental (e.g., c. 150 string quartets and 110 string quintets). During the Revolution he wrote a lot of the mandatory jingoistic garbage. Afterward he slowly fades out. He may have died in Holland. His music is neither as important nor as bad as it has been said to be. He seems to have been a thoroughly capable musician who wrote to please in an age when pleasure was a *desideratum.*

RECORDINGS: There are a few recordings —a concerto directed by Renato Fasano; a *sinfonia concertante* and a cantata by Newell Jenkins; wind quintets by the Soni Ventorum, Oberlin, and Philadelphia Quintets; and quartets by the Carmirelli Quartet and the Quartetto Italiano.

[941] PETER, Johann Friedrich (Pā'-ter, Yō'-hản Frē'-drikh)
MINISTER, TEACHER, ORGANIST, MUSIC DIRECTOR
BORN: Heerendijk, May 19, 1746
DIED: Bethlehem, Pa., July 13, 1813

J. F. Peter and his brother Simon [929] were the sons of a German minister of the Moravian Church stationed in Holland, and both were educated there and in Germany to follow in their father's steps. The elder Peters were sent to Bethlehem, Pa., in 1760 and the boys arrived a decade later. Johann—or "John" as he became—worked in Nazareth, Bethlehem, and Lititz, before going to Salem, N.C., where he served as music director. He appears to have gained his knowledge of composition largely from copying scores for his own use, though he doubtless had some practical training. He brought with him a large library of such manuscripts, which is said to contain unique copies of works by Haydn [871] and the younger Bachs. During his decade in Salem, 1779–89, he married and wrote 6 Haydnesque string quintets that are thought to be the first chamber works written in America. After further transfers to Maryland and New Jersey, he returned to Bethlehem and spent the rest of his life as organist at the Central Moravian Church. Though he left more than 100 compositions (mostly religious), he evidently, like so many of his kind, considered his musical activities a matter of course and scarcely mentions them in his manuscript autobiography. RECORDINGS: The anthems and hymns are represented in the various recordings of Moravian music. The Fine Arts Quartet (plus one) recorded the quintets, and there is one in an orchestral version conducted by Howard Hanson.

[942] CRAMER, Wilhelm (Krä'-mer, Vil'-helm)
VIOLINIST, CONDUCTOR
BORN: Mannheim, c. June 2, 1746
DIED: London, October 5, 1799

Wilhelm Cramer is known to have been musically precocious, but the conjecture in the New Grove Dictionary of Music and Musicians that he entered the Mannheim Orchestra, where his father Jacob was a violinist, in 1752 seems a bit extreme. The date given by most other references, 1757, is difficult enough to believe. He was a pupil of both the elder Stamitz [810] and Cannabich [868]. Toward the end of the next decade, he began to concertize, appearing in Paris and London beginning in 1769. He must have married about this time, for his sons Johann Baptist ("Glorious John") [1067] and Franz, a violinist and later Master of the Queen's Musick, were born in Mannheim in 1771 and 1772, respectively. Once in London in 1772, Wilhelm decided to remain

and brought his family over a couple of years later. He was extremely highly regarded as a performer in England and was named chamber musician to the king. He was concertmaster to the Concert of Antient Music, one of the founders of the Professional Concerts in 1783 (superseding the Bach-Abel Concerts). He was also first violin of the opera orchestra at the Pantheon (which, unhappily, burned down in 1792 after one season). He was also called on to conduct two of the annual Handel Commemorative Concerts at the Abbey—a particular honor. He wrote several violin concerti and sonatas, 6 string quartets, and some other chamber music. RECORDINGS: The Mannheim Duo has recorded the Adagio for violin and piano.

[943] HOOK, James
ORGANIST
BORN: Norwich, June 3, 1746
DIED: Boulogne, 1827

Rotund, affable, easy-going, witty James Hook was one of the most prolific and successful songsmiths of his time (more than 2,000 numbers). A cutler's son, he was born severely and doubly club-footed, but a series of operations enabled him to hobble about. His precociousness, if not his talent, was Mozartian. He could play the harpsichord at four, made his debut at six, and turned out his first stage work at eight. He had lessons with the local cathedral organist but was otherwise largely self-taught. Left fatherless at eleven, he undertook to support the survivors by teaching at a girls' school and by advertising his services as a tutor for keyboards, guitar, violin, and flute, and as composer, copyist, and tuner. Six or seven years later he set out for London, where he became the equivalent of a cocktail organist in a fashionable teahouse. Within two years he had worked his way into the concert and theater world, and married the beauteous Miss Madden, an officer's daughter, who contributed to the family budget by painting miniatures and who furnished her husband with several libretti (by "H. H. Hook"). Their first son, James, Jr. (1772–1828), became the Dean of Worcester. Their second, Theodore (1788–1841), multitalented, became a playboy, a colonial official, a newspaperman, a highly successful novelist, and a practical joker of genius. (It was Theodore who invited several hundred London tradesmen to come to a certain residence to display their wares at staggered intervals throughout a specified day.)
Shortly before 1770 Samuel Arnold [915]

got James the post of organist-composer to Marylebone Gardens, and in 1776, when Marylebone went broke, he moved over to Vauxhall, the most popular and prestigious of the species. He was also a church organist and a piano teacher who counted his annual income from that source in the hundreds of pounds. On top of all this, he turned out lightweight stage pieces, popular instrumental music (including pieces for the "garden" concerts), and piano instruction books. Mrs. Hook died in 1795, and the widower remarried a few years later. We know little or nothing of his second wife. He up and retired one day in 1820 and died at a French coastal resort at age eighty-one.

At its best, Hook's "serious" music is charming, in the manner of lesser J. C. Bach [886]; at worst, it is a pastiche of current clichés.

RECORDINGS: He is represented on records by such once enormously popular songs as "Doun the Burn," "The Lass of Richmond Hill," "Within a Mile o' Edinbro Town," and "The Willow Song," but there is also a recording by the Intimate Opera Company of a Vauxhall "dialogue," *The Musical Courtship*.

---

[944] GRAZIOLI, Giovanni Battista Ignazio (Gràd-zē-ō'-lē, Jō-vàn'-nē Bàt-tēs'-tā Ēn-yàdz'-yō)
ORGANIST, CHOIRMASTER
BORN: Bogliaco, July 6, 1746
DIED: Venice, c. 1820

Grazioli came from the shores of Lake Garda in the Lake District, but was a Venetian from childhood. He studied with, and sometimes deputized for, Ferdinando Bertoni [834], first organist at St. Mark's. He himself became second organist in 1782 and succeeded Bertoni when he was promoted to choirmaster three years later. He resigned or was fired in 1789, and, save that he had a son named Alessandro who was also a composer, little is known of his final thirty years. He left 13 Masses, many other religious works, and 3 books of high-Classic keyboard sonatas. RECORDINGS: One keyboard sonata has been recorded by Luciano Sgrizzi.

---

[945] STICH, Johann Wenzel (Giovanni Punto) (Shtēkh, Yō'-hàn Vent'-sel)
HORNIST, VIOLINIST
BORN: Žehusiče, September 28, 1746
DIED: Prague, February 16, 1803

Johann Wenzel (or Jan Václav) Stich was the first great horn player, and perhaps the greatest before the present era. (One has to remember that the instrument then had no valves or keys, and that notes outside the natural harmonic series were produced by lipping and inserting the hand in the bell.) Stich came from the estate of Count Thun about forty miles southeast of Prague. Sensing the boy's potential, the count sent him to the best horn players in Prague, Munich, and Dresden to learn their methods. In return, Stich was obligated to play in the count's orchestra, which he began doing when he was no more than seventeen. In 1766, tired of what struck him as a kind of slavery, he fled Bohemia and turned into "Giovanni Punto," a name that more-or-less translates his real one (John Puncture or perhaps Jack Point). Afterward, he was based at various courts—Hechingen, Mainz, Würzburg, and Paris (in the music of the Count of Artois, later Charles X), but spent much of his time touring. Punto was one of the first of the flamboyant virtuosi, traveling in his own expensive coach-and-four, and playing a custom-made silver horn. He was the genuine article, however. Mozart [992], who remarked, "Punto blows *magnifique*," wrote the horn part of the K. Anh. 9 *sinfonia concertante* for him. Beethoven's horn sonata was cut to Punto's measure, and the composer was at the piano when he premiered it [1063]. Caught in Paris by the Revolution, Punto rode it out as concertmaster of the Théâtre des Variétés Amusantes, then went back to concertizing in 1799. In 1802 he toured with his fellow Bohemian, J. L. Dussek [1016]. That autumn he fell ill and died the following February. He left concerti, duos, trios, quartets, and quintets featuring the horn, a few other pieces of chamber music, and a couple of libertarian hymns. RECORDINGS: Hornists James Stagliano and Gustav Neudecker have recorded an F-major quartet and Barry Tuckwell four of the horn concerti.

---

[946] BILLINGS, William
TANNER, TEACHER, CONDUCTOR
BORN: Boston, October 7, 1746
DIED: Boston, September 29, 1800

William Billings was an American original in the tradition of Charles Ives [1659]. The son of a shopkeeper, Billings's education seems to have been sketchy, and he was early apprenticed to a tanner, which trade he conducted by and by, at least nominally. It is possible that he had some local musical instruction, but most of what he knew he got from reading such treatises as William Tans'ur's [739]. He grew up to be an ugly, unkempt little man with one eye and a bad limp. His business—and consequently his family and he himself—suffered as a result of his wild enthusiasm for music. In 1770 he published a collection of his compositions entitled *The New England Psalm Singer*, which he fondly termed "Reuben" (his first-born). In its preface he proclaimed that he had learned that rules were made to be broken. Among its contents were examples of what he called "fuging-tunes" (fuguing tunes), which involved something like canonic imitation but no real fugue. He did not invent this notion but did become famous for it. Though he thought his church music much more stimulating than the usual stuff one heard in church, others found the contents of "Reuben" too insipid. In his second work, of 1778, *The Singing-Master's Assistant* (afterward popularly known as "Billings' Best"), he attempted to rectify his failure by rewriting a number of pieces. He also included one work called "Jargon" which was so determinedly cacophonous that someone hung two cats by their tails to his shingle in protest.

Billings published four more volumes, of which the most important was *The Continental Harmony*, 1794. Many of his pieces—"Chester," "When Jesus Wept," "I am the Rose of Sharon," for example—became known all over the country, and he was regularly included in new choral anthologies. He was an ardent patriot during the Revolution, and "Chester," to new militant lyrics, became the great hit of the day. In 1786 his singing school became the Stoughton Musical Society, which still survives. He introduced the pitch pipe into choirs, forcing them to observe concord, the focus of a grave problem up to then. He seems to have fallen on hard times in his last decade, and one finds various efforts being made to raise money for him, his family, and his musical projects. There was not enough, however, to provide him with a decent burial. His grave, said to be on Boston Common, is unmarked. Twentieth-century composers such as Henry Cowell [1934] and William Schuman [2158] have helped spark a revival of interest in Billings and have incorporated his tunes in their works.

RECORDINGS: Compositions by Billings appear in most recorded anthologies of American choral music. There is a whole disc by the Gregg Smith Singers devoted to his music. E. Power Biggs has recorded several pieces arranged for organ.

[947] CASANOVAS, Narciso (Kä-zä-nō'-väs, När-thē'-zō)
MONK, ORGANIST
BORN: Zabadell, February 17, 1747
DIED: Viña-Vieja, April 1, 1799

Apart from the vital statistics noted, all we know of Padre Casanovas is that he was born near Barcelona, studied in the *escolania* of Montserrat Abbey, where he was admitted to the order in 1763 and where he won much fame as an organist. His keyboard pieces are "Scarlattian" to begin with but later show Viennese influence, as do his sacred compositions. RECORDINGS: Ireneu Segarra and the Montserrat Choir have recorded a motet, and examples of the keyboard music are found in numerous organ and harpsichord anthologies (e.g., by Paul Bernard, François Chapelet, Albert De-Klerk, and Fernando Valenti).

[948] HÄSSLER, Johann Wilhelm (Häs'-ler, Yō'-hän Vil'-helm)
PIANIST, ORGANIST, HATTER, TEACHER
BORN: Erfurt, March 29, 1747
DIED: Moscow, March 29, 1822

Hässler (no relation to the Renaissance Hassler tribe) was, in musical descent, of the second generation from J. S. Bach [684], his teacher having been his uncle, Johann Christian Kittel. Kittel (whose dates are precisely Haydn's [871]) was one of the cantor's last pupils and, according to Bach's biographer Forkel, the last survivor of them all. Kittel treasured a portrait of his teacher and left an account of Bach's teaching methods. By the time he was fourteen, Hässler was deemed sufficiently competent to be named organist at the Barfüsserkirche in Erfurt. But a musical career was not in the thinking of his father, who insisted on his preparing to carry on the family business. For a while, young Hässler was a traveling salesman and met many important musicians, including C. P. E. Bach [801], who seems to have decided him on his own future. The senior Hässler died in 1769 and for a few years the son specialized in selling hand muffs, the while he concertized and taught. In 1779 he married Sophie Kiel, one of his students and apparently a talented singer. The following year he gave up his business career and began a series of winter concerts in Erfurt, in which Sophie participated. He wrote a little autobiography in 1786, which he published with some sonatas. In 1789 he seems to have begun a concert tour that took him as far as England. He played for the court in Potsdam, "competed" on organ and piano with Mozart [992] in Vienna (Mozart had his usual snide things to say), and performed under Haydn in London. All in all, however, his musical career seems to have been a struggle. In 1792 Hässler pulled up stakes, abandoned his family, and moved to St. Petersburg, then to Moscow, where he seems to have considered himself to be taking up a new life. (His first Russian publication is marked "Op. 1.") In any case he enjoyed a popularity and a success such as he had not known before and was the most popular teacher of his time in Moscow (where Field [1104] may be said to have succeeded him). Hässler's music is chiefly for piano and shows, over its span, an awareness of musical changes from pre-Classic to pre-Romantic. RECORDINGS: On records he is represented by a sonata played by Luciano Sgrizzi and one for three hands (!) done by Eugene List and Gary Kirkpatrick.

[949] SCHULZ, Johann Abraham Peter
(Shōōlts, Yō'-hàn Àb'-rà-ham Pā'-ter)
ORGANIST, MUSIC DIRECTOR
BORN: Lüneburg, March 31, 1747
DIED: Schwedt an der Öder, June 10, 1800

Perhaps the first musical Schulz not to be a Praetorius, this one was a baker's son slated for the ministry. However, music lessons from a Lüneburg organist named Schmügel, who had studied with Telemann [665], gave him other ideas. Convinced that Berlin was, in musical terms, the earthly paradise, he ran away from his parents at fifteen and went there and knocked on the door of J. P. Kirnberger [821]. Kirnberger sent him home, but three years later he was back and was taken on as a student. In 1768 Kirnberger got him a job as accompanist and musical companion with a Polish princess, who took him around the Continent with her for five years. Returning to Berlin in 1773, Schulz joined Kirnberger in writing the musical portion of the encyclopedia *General Theory of the Fine Arts* got out by the Swiss aesthetician Johann Georg Sulzer (1720–79). In 1776 he was appointed conductor at the French Theater and two years later at the private theater of Princess Luise, wife of the future Frederick William III. In 1780 he went to Rheinsberg as *Kapellmeister* to the crown prince's brother, Prince Heinrich. But Schulz's avant-garde tastes did not sit well, and in 1787 he went to the court of Prince Frederik of Denmark as general music director. (Frederik was standing in for his half-brother Christian VII

who was mentally not up to it.) There he created a number of reforms, some of them socially advanced, but the climate did not agree with him, and in 1795, ill with tuberculosis, he accepted a pension, and sailed for Portugal to recover his health. But a storm cast him ashore in Norway, and, after some months, he found his way back to Rheinsberg. He died at a spa east of Berlin.

Schulz wrote a number of stage pieces for the Hohenzollerns and for the Danish Royal Opera, as well as the usual sorts of sacred and secular music required of a court composer, and a handful of instrumental things. His chief importance, however, lies in his several collections of songs. He was one of the first to turn to folk music as the archetype, and he wrote a treatise on the influence of music on ethnic cultures. Though simplicity and "familiarity" were important *desiderata* in his songs, he insisted on first-rate lyrics and on the music's function in underlining their content. He was especially influential in Denmark.

RECORDINGS: Though there may be scattered songs on imported labels, Schulz appears to be represented on records only by his *Largo* for glass harmonica, played by Bruno Hoffmann.

[950] KOŽELUH, Jan Antonín ("Leopold") (Kö'-zhe-lōōkh, Yàn An-tō-nyēn')
PIANIST, PUBLISHER, ARRANGER, TEACHER
BORN: Welwarn, June 16, 1747
DIED: Vienna, May 7, 1818

The town now called Velvary, near Prague, produced two notable composers named Koželuh: Jan Antonín (1738–1814) and his younger cousin Jan Antonín, who, understandably, took the name of Leopold. The elder Koželuh, a pupil of Gluck [803], Hasse [736], and Gassmann [851], taught the younger in Prague, and turned him over to Mozart's [992] friend Dušek for keyboard training. All the while the young man was supposed to be studying jurisprudence at the university, but when he found himself getting produced as a ballet composer, he quit and in 1778 went to Vienna, where there was a demand for ballet. There he was appointed teacher to the Archduchess Elisabeth and was soon the darling of high society and turning a pretty pfennig. After Mozart left or was ejected from the Salzburg court, the archbishop offered Koželuh the post of court organist; Koželuh politely declined it, noting privately that he could hope for no respect in a place that would let such a musician go. In 1784 he opened his own publishing company, which he eventually put in charge of his brother Antonín Tomáš. Mozart reported (incorrectly, it turned out) that it was publishing his latest set of quartets in 1789. Yet in personal encounters, Koželuh is said to have treated Mozart with condescension if not contempt. He also had no use for Beethoven [1063] and once, when someone played him a new work by that composer, he snatched the music off the stand and hurled it to the floor. Beethoven had a word for Koželuh: *miserabilis*. In 1792 the Czech succeeded Mozart as imperial court composer (i.e., for court balls) but was also given the title of *Kammerkapellmeister* (and twice Mozart's salary). He was one of those commissioned by George Thomson of Edinburgh to arrange folksongs from Scotland, Ireland, and Wales. (His stablemates included, at various times, Pleyel [1003], Haydn [871], Beethoven, Weber [1124], Hummel [1091], and Bishop [1123].) Among Koželuh's musical relatives was his daughter Catherine (1785–1858), a pianist known under her married name of Cibbini.

Koželuh was a Classicist verging on the Rococo at one end of his career and the Romantic at the other. He turned out reams of music in practically every genre and by 1800 was being called the most important composer in Europe. By 1830 he was virtually forgotten.

RECORDINGS: Felicja Blumental has recorded one of his 22 piano concerti. Eliahu Inbal and Claudio Scimone conduct the *Sinfonia Concertante* in E-flat major for mandolin, trumpet, contrabass, piano, and orchestra; Scimone has also recorded the Concerto for Piano (four hands) in B-flat Major.

[951] MORGAN, Justin
TEACHER, TAVERN OWNER, HORSE
   BREEDER, POLITICIAN
BORN: West Springfield, Mass., 1747
DIED: Randolph, Vt., March 2, 1798

A writer of hymn tunes, Morgan subsisted in the various ways noted, winding up his career as town clerk in Randolph. He conducted singing schools here and there but apparently published no singing manual. His name (if not its source) is widely known from the breed of horse known as the Morgan, which he developed. Among his more popular pieces were the hymn tune "Amanda" (said to be named after his wife), the fuguing tune "Montgomery," and the more ambitious "Judgment Anthem."

RECORDINGS: These pieces have been recorded variously by the Western Wind Ensemble and the Gregg Smith Singers.

[952] PALUSELLI, Stefan Johann Adam
(Pȧl-ōō-sel´-lē, Shtef´-ȧn Yō´-hȧn Ȧd´-ȧm)
MONK, TEACHER, CHOIRMASTER
BORN: Kurtatsch, January 9, 1748
DIED: Stams, February 27, 1805

A native of the south Tyrol where Italian and German cultures and politics overlap, Paluselli was a scholarship student and choirboy at the church of the University of Innsbruck, at which institution he later probably studied. In 1770 he entered the Abbey of Stams in the upper Inn River valley, where he was ordained four years later. In 1791 he was placed in charge of the school and choir. He wrote musicals for student performance, sacred music, occasional cantatas, and some lighter-hearted and less conservative instrumental music. RECORDINGS: F. Charles Adler conducts a *divertimento* on records.

[953] FIALA, Josef (Fē-ȧ´-lȧ, Yō´-zef)
OBOIST, VIOLA DA GAMBA PLAYER, MU-
   SIC DIRECTOR
BORN: Lochovice, February 3, 1748
DIED: Donaueschingen, July 31, 1816

Fiala was a dependent of a Countess Netolická, who divided her time between her estate at Lochovice (between Prague and Pilsen) and Vienna. She had him trained in the latter city and took him into her domestic orchestra. For some reason Fiala found his work or that of his employer not to his taste, tried to run away, and was jailed for two years until the Empress Maria Theresa herself sprung him. Or so goes the old tale. In 1774 he was added to the jim-dandy little orchestra Count Kraft Ernst was building himself at the Oettingen-Wallerstein court. But he caught the ear of Elector Max Joseph and was brought to Munich three years later. There Mozart [992], out job hunting, met him through the dinner-music group Fiala had trained for a local tavern, took an uncharacteristic fancy to him, and did more to find work for the Czech than he did for himself. Thus when the new elector moved his Mannheimers to Munich in 1778, Fiala found a place in the Archbishop's orchestra in Salzburg. He moved on to Vienna in 1785, where Mozart is said again to have helped him, though how is not clear. A year later Fiala went to

St. Petersburg to play at the Russian court for five years. He returned to Germany in 1790, demonstrated (successfully) his string prowess before the cello-playing Frederick William of Prussia, and then became director of another crackerjack small-court orchestra, that of the Fürstenburg princes at Donaueschingen, where he spent the rest of his life. His son Franz became an orchestral violist. Joseph Fiala published some string duos and quartets and left much more chamber music, as well as symphonies, concerti, and pieces for wind ensembles, in manuscript. RECORDINGS: On records, Heinz Holliger plays his concerto for *cor anglais*, Ab Koster and Jan Schröder that for two horns, and the Prague Chamber Harmony Ensemble a partita for horns (two French, two English) and bassoon.

[954] NEEFE, Christian Gottlob (Nā'-fe, Krĕst'-yàn Got'-lōp)
CONDUCTOR, ORGANIST, TEACHER
BORN: Chemnitz, February 5, 1748
DIED: Dessau, January 26, 1798

Once regarded as one of the most important composers in Germany, Neefe is now remembered only as the man who taught Beethoven **[1063]**. His father was a struggling tailor in what is now Karl Marx Stadt. The boy had a fine soprano voice, became a chorister in the town's principal church, and received what education the area could give him. After a few years of supporting himself as a teacher, he entered the University of Leipzig in 1769 and took a law degree. While there he kept up his music and attracted the attention of Johann Adam Hiller, a leading spirit in the *Singspiele* movement, later first conductor of the Gewandhaus concerts and cantor of the Thomasschule, and then musical director of a theatrical company run by a man named Seyler. Hiller gave Neefe lessons, published some of his music in his own periodical, and in 1776 resigned his post in his pupil's favor. Neefe traveled with the Seyler company for about three years, during which time he married one of its members, a Fräulein Susanne Zink, sometime *Kammersängerin* to the court of Saxe-Gotha, and a foster daughter of Jiří Benda **[824]**. In 1778 the company undertook what proved to be a disastrously unsuccessful season in Frankfurt am Main. Faced with ruin, Seyler and his wife decamped. Neefe had smelled trouble and was already negotiating with one Bondini, in Dresden, for a similar job. But since Bondini kept shuffling his feet, Neefe went down the Rhine to Bonn, where he

was taken on by his old Seyler-colleague Grossmann, now director of the Prince-Archbishop Maximilian's theater company. However, when the Bondini contract finally came through, Grossmann had Neefe's belongings confiscated, and by the time things were ironed out, the contract had expired. The blow was softened by Neefe's official appointment in 1781 as court organist, succeeding the ailing Gilles van den Eeden. He also inherited Eeden's pupil, the eleven-year-old apprentice keyboardist Ludwig van Beethoven. In short order he had the boy playing the *Wolhtemperierte Klavier*, and it was not long before he was officially appointed as Neefe's assistant and replacement. The relationship was on the whole friendly and fruitful, and Beethoven was properly grateful later on. Meanwhile, Neefe went on playing, composing, and having children (three of his daughters were professional singers and his son Hermann was a set designer). In 1796 the court dissolved under threat from Napoleon's advancing troops. Neefe was taken on as musical director of the Dessau court opera and died there less than two years later. Besides operas, *Singspiele,* and other vocal works, he wrote keyboard pieces, including sonatas and a piano concerto. RECORDINGS: He is represented on records by a song to a Goethe text, sung by Dietrich Fischer-Dieskau.

[955] SHIELD, William
VIOLINIST, VIOLIST, CONDUCTOR
BORN: Whickham, March 5, 1748
DIED: London, January 25, 1849

Evidence suggests that Shield could have been a composer of real stature, given different opportunities from those offered by the England of his time. He was the son of a Durham County singing master, though whether he was born in Whickham or Swalwell is a matter of debate. Orphaned at nine, he was apprenticed to a shipwright in a town coincidentally named South Shields. His term up, however, he found means to study with Charles Avison **[775]** in Newcastle and became a professional violinist, making his living playing in theaters and concerts in the area. It was under such conditions that someone of importance—various accounts name violinists Luigi Borghi and Felice Giardini and oboist J. C. Fischer **[876]**—discovered him and gave him letters of introduction. In 1773 he found a place as violinist at the King's Theatre but was soon promoted to first violist. Though he had been composing for some time, it was not until the later 1770s that he set to it in earnest, publishing a group of violin duets in 1777 and a collection of songs in 1778. In the latter year Shield had a considerable hit at the Little Theatre with his first stage work, an afterpiece called *A Flitch of Bacon*, in which he introduced some popular (or folksongs). This triumph won him a contract with the Covent Garden Theatre, for which, over the next thirty years, he turned out nearly 50 operas, pantomimes, and afterpieces. Among the more notable (both afterpieces) were *Rosina* and *The Farmer*. The latter produced a runaway hit song, "The Ploughboy"; whether the other was responsible for the popularity of "Auld Lang Syne," whose tune it quoted, is debatable. His long friendship with the scholar-republican Joseph Ritson undoubtedly fanned his interest in the music of the people, which he collected and often quoted in his works. In the late 1780s he married (or took up residence with) a woman named Ann Stokes. In 1791 Shields broke for the time being with Covent Garden and traveled to Paris with Ritson to view republicanism on the hoof, then proceeded over the hills to Rome. After he came home, he continued to write for Covent Garden fairly regularly until 1797, but after that he seems to have done only one stage work a decade later. He was sufficiently well-known and well-to-do to rate a visit and a dedication from Joseph Haydn [871]. Shield died at eighty, leaving his property, including a splendid musical library, to his "beloved partner, Ann," save for his viola, which he willed to the Crown. He was buried in the cloisters of Westminster Abbey. Apart from the works mentioned, Shield left some interesting string trios and quartets. Though his stage vehicles are ephemeral, he was a fine melodist, a knowledgeable musician, and a sometimes daring orchestrator. RECORDINGS: Richard Bonynge has recorded a performance of *Rosina*.

[956] SCHACHT, Theodor von (Shàkht, Tä'-ō-dôr fun)
MUSIC DIRECTOR
BORN: Strasbourg, 1748
DIED: Regensburg, June 20, 1823

It is not clear just why Schacht went to the court of Prince Alexander Ferdinand of Thurn und Taxis in Regensburg for his musical basics, but it turned out to be a useful move. In 1766 he moved on to Stuttgart for five years, studying with Niccolò Jommelli until the latter left for Italy in 1769. Schacht returned to the Regensburg court in 1771 as a gentleman-in-waiting. When the new and

musically gifted prince, variously designated as Carl Anselm or Carl Alexander, succeeded to power in 1773, he put Schacht in charge of music, apparently with *"carte de crédit blanche."* The first thing Schacht did was to open an Italian Opera for which he wrote Italian operas. When that had to be abandoned for whatever reason in 1778, he opened a German Opera for which he wrote such German operas as the 1779 *Romeo und Julie*. When it was closed in 1784, he turned his attention to building up the orchestra (it included various Pokornýs [see 855]).

In 1805, Schacht left for Vienna, beating the disbanding of the orchestra by one year and the destruction of the town by five. In Vienna he became part of the musical circle (which included Beethoven [1063]) around Archduke Rudolf. The triumphant Bonaparte, who never thought small, commissioned him to write 6 Masses for him when he arrived in 1809. In 1812 Schacht retired to a Thurn und Taxis property in Württemberg, and seven years later he went back to Regensburg to finish out his life. Besides his operas, Schacht wrote a good deal of sacred music, contatas, part songs, 84 amusing canons published as (in Italian) *Diversion for the Fair Sex for a Stay in Baden*, 33 symphonies (one long attributed to Haydn), 45 concerti, and much other instrumental music. He was one of those (the most famous was Beethoven) commissioned to set the poem *"In questa tomba oscura"* ("In this Dark Tomb") by Giuseppe Carpani in 1806.

RECORDINGS: The Concerto Amsterdam has recorded a clarinet concerto.

[957] LAW, Andrew
MINISTER, TEACHER, THEORIST
BORN: Milford, Conn., March 21, 1749
DIED: Cheshire, Conn., July 13, 1821

At a time when many American musicians were little more than "rude mechanicals," Andrew Law stood for the intellectual aristocracy. Indeed he openly sneered at clumsy amateurs. He was the grandson of a governor of Connecticut, took an M. A. from what is now Brown University in 1778, was given another by Yale in 1786, and was ordained a year later. He held ministries in Philadelphia and Baltimore but spent most of his life in New England. Imbued with a determination to improve choral singing so that it might be "decent, chaste, and solemn," he published the first of his choral collections, *A Select Number of Plain Tunes* around 1775 (authorities differ on the dates) and followed it with several others, the most notable being his *Select Harmony* of 1778. In this he used a system of "shape-notes" without staves or bars, the notion being that all the important information lay in the shapes. He strove mightily to promote this system, even getting the backing of some academic authorities, but with no real luck. Oddly, two Philadelphians, William Smith and William Little, had copyrighted a remarkably similar system (with staves) two years earlier, and it caught on in the frontier. Law also wrote several influential pedagogic manuals, which were used for a long time. Perhaps his chief contribution to American hymnody was placing the tune in the soprano rather than in the tenor line of his harmonizations—a device that had long been familiar in Europe. He also wrote a volume of musical criticism in 1814. Shortly before his death, he was awarded an honorary LL.D. from Allegheny College. RECORDINGS: Some of Law's arrangements are included in recorded anthologies of early American music (e.g., those by the Western Wind and by Gregg Smith)—usually the tunes "Archdale" and "Bunker Hill," which it is now generally agreed he did not compose.

[958] SOSTOA, Manuel (Sō-stō'-à, Mån'-wel)
MONK
BORN: Eibar, March 23, 1749
DIED: Aranzazu, after 1802

One of the last of the "Basque Scarlattists," Fray Manuel was six days less than six years younger than his fellow townsman, Padre Fernando Eguiguren [928]. He joined the Franciscans at Aranzazu in 1754. Besides keyboard pieces, he wrote a good deal of church music. RECORDINGS: Antonio Ruiz-Pipó has recorded a piano sonata.

[959] EDELMANN, Johann Friedrich (Â'-del-mån, Yō'-hån Frē'-drikh)
PIANIST, POLITICIAN
BORN: Strasbourg, May 5, 1749
DIED: Paris, July 17, 1794

With a law degree from Strasbourg University, Johann Friedrich—a.k.a. Jean-Frédéric—Edelmann came to Paris after some travels in Germany and Italy and by 1775 was established as a fashionable keyboard teacher. Though he also played the harpsichord, he liked the piano, and the instructions for playing some of his keyboard pieces show that he had a Romantic's appreciation of its expressive possibilities.

While he was in Paris, he published a good deal of instrumental music, mostly of chamber scale. He also wrote some stage works, including the successful short opera of 1782, *Ariane dans l'isle de Naxos (Ariadne on Naxos)*, which he dedicated to Dr. J. I. Guillotin. Mozart [992], in his year in Paris, was sufficiently taken with some of Edelmann's music to mention it to his father. With the coming of the Revolution, Edelmann went back to Strasbourg, where he joined the radical forces and was given charge of eastern Alsace. This resulted in a political clash with his former friend Philippe-Frédéric Dietrich, Mayor of Strasbourg. A trial ensued, and as a result of Edelmann's testimony, Dietrich lost his head. A year later Edelmann and his brother, an organist, followed him to Dr. Guillotin's fatal instrument. A full pardon for crimes uncommitted did not help since it came some years later. Among Edelmann's students was Méhul [1036]. RECORDINGS: A violin sonata has been recorded by the Mannheim Duo.

[960] VOGLER, (Abt or Abbé) Georg Joseph (Fōg'-ler, Gā-ôrg Yō'-zef)
CLERIC, ORGANIST, TEACHER, THEORIST, SCHOLAR
BORN: Pleichach, June 15, 1749
DIED: Darmstadt, May 6, 1814

Like Galuppi [768], Vogler is probably better known today as the subject of a Browning poem than as a composer—and indeed, as a composer, his repute has never been very high. (The "musical instrument of his own invention" of Browning's subtitle was the orchestrion, a kind of small portable organ. His octochord measured intervals.) Nonetheless he was a gifted, influential, and interesting musician. He grew up in Würzburg, where his father was a violinist to the prince-bishop. He graduated from the local university in humanities and law (class of 1767), spent three more years acquiring a theological degree from Bamberg, and in 1771 was hired by the Elector Palatine Carl Theodor in that capacity for the Mannheim court. But his little opera, *Der Kaufmann von Smyrna (The Smyrna Merchant)* so impressed his employer that he packed him off to Italy for Real Musical Training with Padre Martini [767]. But Vogler found Martini too dry for his taste and moved on to Padua, where he was considerably more excited by the harmonic theories of Padre F. A. Vallotti (1697–1780). To fulfil a vocation that had nagged him since childhood, he went to Rome to be ordained in 1773. He also managed to get himself elected to the Arcadian Academy and in time to be made a papal knight and chamberlain, and an apostolic prothonotary.

When he returned to Mannheim in 1775, the elector made him his vice-*kapellmeister* and chief spiritual adviser, and funded a music school where Vogler taught a compositional system of his own, based on his conviction that the triad (the root, third, and fifth) is the scientific basis of all chords. (He also developed, like the musical Marx brothers, unorthodox fingerings for keyboard instruments, which he advocated as shortcuts. When Carl Theodor went to Munich to become Elector of Bavaria, Vogler stayed behind to run the school but caught up with his master in 1786. By now, however, concert work was occupying much of his time. He was recognized by most as a brilliant performer and improviser, though Mozart [992] flatly, if privately, termed him a phony. (Vogler delighted in the kind of sound effects that would manifest themselves in such later popular Romantic pieces as Charles Grobe's [1254] *The Fall of Sebastopol.*) In 1788 he left Munich for a lucrative long-term contract at the Swedish court of the hapless Gustavus III. In 1792 he visited various Mediterranean areas to examine native musics. (Vogler may properly be regarded as an early ethnomusicologist.) During his absence, Gustavus was assassinated, but his successor, Gustavus Adolphus IV, honored the contract. During his Swedish years Vogler wrote an opera to a Swedish libretto, *Gustavus Adolphus och Ebba Brahe,* premiered in 1788, and opened another school. Reports of his travels to Russia and Greenland appear to be unfounded, though he continued to concertize widely. He left Sweden, as agreed, in 1797. He came to rest temporarily in Vienna in 1804, where he produced another opera, *Samori,* and engaged in an improvisatory duel with Beethoven [1063], in which he seems to have "won." In 1805 he moved on to Salzburg, then back to Munich, where in 1806 he furnished the music for the wedding of Napoleon's stepson, Eugène de Beauharnais and Princess Augusta of Bavaria. Eventually, at fifty-eight, he settled down in Darmstadt as *Hofkapellmeister* and spiritual adviser to Landgraf Ludwig X, with various emoluments befitting his reputation and his opinion of himself. (Gustavus Adolphus had inconveniently terminated his Swedish pension the year before. However, the Swedish king was dethroned in 1809 and it served him right.) In Darmstadt Vogler opened his third music school, where he taught his two most prestigious pupils, Meyerbeer [1142]

and Weber [1124]. In 1812 he made a final tour to Munich and Vienna. Five weeks before his sixty-fifth birthday he died of a stroke. Besides turning out numerous theoretical works, mostly on his harmonic and acoustical beliefs and on ways to improve organs and organ-building, Vogler left a great deal of music of most of the current genres.

RECORDINGS: There is a recording of the piano-orchestral variations on "Malbrouck" (i.e., "The Bear Went Over the Mountain") played by Felicja Blumental and a piracy of *Gustavus Adolphus.*

[961] DUPORT, Jean-Louis (Dü-pôr', Zhàn Lōō-ē')
CELLIST
BORN: Paris, October 4, 1749
DIED: Paris, September 7, 1819

The cello-playing Duport brothers, Jean-Pierre *l'aîné* (1741–1818) and Jean-Louis *le jeune,* are thought to have been the sons of an otherwise anonymous Duport who played cello in the chamber of Louis XV. (The story that they were sons of a dancing master and that Jean-Louis was *premier danseur* at the Opéra is the result of a confusion with other Duports.) The younger boy was the pupil of the older, and the two appeared together as, respectively, soloist and accompanist at a 1768 Concert Spirituel. In 1773 Jean-Pierre became Frederick II's first cellist in Berlin-Potsdam and taught the heir-presumptive, Frederick William, who became a fair cellist. With the coming of the Revolution in 1789, Jean-Louis joined him. In 1796 Beethoven [1063] and Jean-Pierre introduced the former's first two cello sonatas to Frederick William, the dedicatee, though some think Beethoven had the more brilliant Jean-Louis in mind. In 1806 Jean-Louis came back to Paris. He gave a highly successful concert with the soprano Isabella Colbran, later Rossini's [1143] wife, but nothing substantive turned up, so he went to Marseilles to work for the exiled King of Spain, Charles IV. He came back to Paris once again in 1812, caught the attention of the Empress Marie-Louise, and wound up in the Imperial Chapel. A year later he also became a professor of cello at the Conservatory. He lost that post after Napoleon's fall but continued in his court appointment until his death. The contemporary Russian cellist-conductor Mstislav Rostropovitch owns his Stradivarius. Duport was perhaps the greatest virtuoso cellist of his day. His cello method was to that instrument what Leopold Mozart's [816] was to the violin. He also wrote concerti, sonatas, and other works featuring the cello. RECORDINGS: Cellist Klaus Storck has recorded a G-minor sonata for cello and harp.

[962] CIMAROSA, Domenico (Chē-mà-rô'-zà, Dō-mā'-nē-kō)
ORGANIST, TEACHER, CONDUCTOR
BORN: Aversa, December 17, 1749
DIED: Venice, January 11, 1801

In the late eighteenth century, until the triumph of Rossini [1143], two composers of Italian comic opera towered in respect and popularity over all the rest, including Mozart [992]: they were Paisiello [914] and Cimarosa. The writer Stendhal, who died in 1842, wanted inscribed on his tombstone that he had loved Cimarosa, Mozart, and Shakespeare (in that order).

Domenico Cimarosa was born into the family of a stonemason in Aversa, just north of Naples. Hearing there was work to be had in the latter city where the Capodimonte Palace was being built, he took his family there. The move turned out to be fatal, for he fell from a wall on the job and was killed. In order to carry on, the widow became a laundress, and the neighborhood Minorites, in exchange for clean habits, undertook her son's education. He acquitted himself so well in music that they sent him, as a charity student, to the Conservatorio di Santa Maria di Loreto when he was around eleven. His teachers seem to have been mostly men of no great importance, though Sacchini [857] and Piccinni [848] are said by some to have been among them. In 1772 his first opera, *Le Stravaganze del Conte (The Count's Eccentricities)*, was put on during the annual Carnival, but he did not really begin to make his mark until the latter 1770s, after Piccinni and Paisiello had left for foreign parts. From 1777 to 1787 he turned out more than forty operas—mostly comedies, but some *serie*—at first chiefly in Naples and Rome, but later all over Italy. For a time he taught at the Ospedaletto in Venice, and in 1785 he was given the (largely honorary) post of second organist to King Ferdinand.

Cimarosa's fame won him an invitation from Catherine the Great in 1787 to replace Sarti [853], who had been exiled to the Ukraine, as court music director. Since both Sarti and Paisiello had encountered trouble there, Cimarosa should probably have been more wary, but he went. During his four years there, the Empress pulled the rug from under him, so to speak, and he wound up with no musical establishment. In 1791 he

left for home—taking with him a piano, token of Catherine's esteem. His path, however, led him through Vienna, where Mozart lay dying and where Leopold II had succeeded to the imperial throne the year before. Supposedly Leopold and Cimarosa had met when the former was Grand Duke of Tuscany, and Leopold's theater music director Salieri [966], who did not see eye to eye with him, had resigned the post when he came to the throne (though he retained the position of *Hofkapellmeister*). Apparently Cimarosa was chosen over Salieri's pupil Joseph Weigl to fill the slot, though accounts are hazy on the subject. At any rate, in February 1792, the Burgtheater produced his greatest triumph, *Il Matrimonio segreto (The Clandestine Marriage*, after Garrick), an opera that is still viable. But Leopold died a month later, and the composer deemed it advisable to hasten his homecoming. He was given a hero's welcome in Naples and in 1796 was promoted to the status of first organist for the abominable Ferdinand. In 1798 Cimarosa underwent a serious illness but had sufficiently recovered by 1799 to help celebrate with an appropriate hymn to Liberty, the overthrow of his patron and the establishment of a "Parthenopean Republic" on the fashionable French model. But a few months later Cardinal Fabrizio Ruffo and his ruffians ended it, with some help from Admiral Nelson; Ferdinand returned and, ignoring Cimarosa's proffered hymns to monarchy, tossed him in the clink. He was sprung after four months by influential friends, including Emma, Lady Hamilton (Nelson's mistress). Older accounts suggest that he was rescued by soldiers from the Russian embassy and that he was carried in triumph through the streets, whereupon he decided to return to Russia, where he was appreciated. But in fact he returned to Venice, took sick, and died within a few months. It was bruited about that he had been poisoned by a Neapolitan fiat (probably the *gasolio*-burning kind). An autopsy was ordered, but it revealed that he had been suffering from (apparently) an intestinal cancer. He was twice married and twice widowed; there were no children.

Besides his operas (somewhere between 75 and 100), Cimarosa wrote oratorios, a good deal of religious music, cantatas, 2 concerti, a few chamber works, and many charming one-movement keyboard sonatas which, like Domenico Scarlatti's [687], may have been intended to be played in groups of two or three.

RECORDINGS: His only opera on commercial recordings appears to be *Il Matrimonio segreto* (with Nino Sanzogno and Daniel Barenboim conducting), though a one-man intermezzo (cantata?) entitled *Il Maestro di cappella (The Conductor)* has been repeatedly recorded (thrice by Fernando Corena alone). (There are also, of course, scattered arias and overtures. His *Requiem* (for the wife of the Neapolitan ambassador to Russia) has been recorded by Vittorio Negri; a Concerto for Harpsichord by Elzbieta Lucowicz; *sinfonie* taken from several operas by Richard Schumacher; the Concerto for 2 Flutes by Franco Caracciolo, Jörg Faerber, Claudio Scimone, and others; and two flute quartets by the Amphion Quartet. There are several collections of the sonatas (e.g., by Robert Veyron-Lacroix, Luciano Sgrizzi, and M. G. Schneider). A ubiquitous "oboe concerto" is really an orchestration by Sir John Barbirolli of four sonatas.

[963] TURRINI, Ferdinando (Too-rē'-nē, Fâr-dē-nàn'-dō)
ORGANIST
BORN: Salò, c. 1749
DIED: Brescia, c. 1812

Like his uncle Fernando Bertoni [834], by whose surname he was sometimes called, Turrini came from the Lake Garda country. He was taught in Venice by Bertoni, and was working there when he went blind in 1772. However, he took a job as organist at the Church of San Giustiniano in Padua, where he worked for twenty-eight years, until the danger of the French invasion sent him to Brescia. He is ignored by most of the standard musical dictionaries, and of the several sonatas he is known to have published, only a few have surfaced. These, however, show an independent mind and a Romantic temperament that looks far ahead into the next century. RECORDINGS: Luciano Sgrizzi has recorded a single example of the sonatas.

[964] SPERGER, Johann Mathias (Shpâr'-ger, Yō'-hàn Mà-tē'-às)
CONTRABASS PLAYER
BORN: Feldsberg, March 23, 1750
DIED: Ludwigslust, May 13, 1812

Sperger was born and grew up in what is now Valtice, just across the Czech border north of Vienna. He studied in the latter city with Albrechtsberger [889], and then supposedly played at the Esterházy court for a time. (Some of Haydn's [871] trickier bass fiddle parts are said to have been written for him.) By 1777 he was definitely at the archepiscopal court in Pressburg (alias Bratislava). From there he went into the service of Count Erdödy, near the Hungarian border about seventy-five miles south of the capital. From 1786 to 1789 Sperger was unable to find a post following his employer's death and lived in Vienna as a copyist. He finally found a place in the orchestra of the Mecklenburg-Schwerin ducal court, where he was a colleague of Rössler (see 972), and where he spent his last twenty-three years. Known as a virtuoso player, Sperger wrote a number of concerti and sonatas for his instrument, but also many symphonies, string quartets, etc. Ludwig Streicher has recorded a sonata dedicated to Joseph Haydn at "Città di Ferro" (i.e., Eisenstadt).

[965] TÜRK, Daniel Gottlob (Türk, Dàn'-yel Got'-lōp)
TEACHER, THEORIST, VIOLINIST, ORGANIST, ADMINISTRATOR
BORN: Clausnitz, August 10, 1750
DIED: Halle, August 26, 1813

Türk (né Türcke) was more important as a pedagogue and writer on music than as a composer. His *Klavierschule* of 1789 in particular holds a high place in the history of keyboard manuals. He was the son of a household musician of southern Saxony who doubled as a hosiery manufacturer, for which trade the boy was slated. However, as a chorister at Dresden's Kreuzkirche, he attracted the attention of Bach [684] pupil Homilius [800], who, when Türk moved on to the University of Leipzig, recommended that he study with his (Homilius') pupil, J. A. Hiller (1728–1804). Hiller was then director of the Grosses Konzert (the direct ancestor of the Gewandhaus Orchestra) and appointed Türk his first violinist. By the time Türk was ready to leave Leipzig in 1774, he was committed to music and with Hiller's help became cantor at the Ulrichskirche in Leipzig and a teacher in the *Gymnasium*. In short order he became the most influential musician in Halle. He was appointed to the faculty of the university in 1779 as music director, and in 1787 he became organist-*Kapellmeister* at the wealthy Liebfrauenkirche. From that time on, he devoted much of his time to writing his theoretical works, which, apart from the *Klavierschule,* included treatises on organ playing, continuo, systems of tuning, and various other keyboard manuals. He also wrote in those years the bulk of his large output of teaching pieces for piano. He also conducted the local concert series. In 1806 he was awarded an honorary degree by the university and promoted to professor of music. In 1808 his wife of twenty-five years died, and soon after his own health began to decline. In 1810 he took the fourteen-year-old choirboy Carl Loewe [1152] into his home as his protégé; Loewe became probably his best-known pupil. Besides his keyboard music, Türk composed a two-character opera (lost), a few symphonies, cantatas, and songs. RECORDINGS: Pianist Luciano Sgrizzi has recorded one of his sonatas.

[966] SALIERI, Antonio (Säl-yâr'-ē, Àn-tōn'-yō)
CONDUCTOR, TEACHER
BORN: Legnago, August 18, 1750
DIED: Vienna, May 7, 1825

For nearly 200 years Antonio Salieri has been depicted as a musical nonentity of Machiavellian ruthlessness who not only blocked Mozart's [992] career but even terminated Mozart's life with poison. Alexander Pushkin depicted the murder in a little play, *Mozart and Salieri*, which was later turned into an opera by Rimsky-Korsakov [1416]. A novelist named David Weiss, in his *The Assassination of Mozart*, has depicted the event as part of a larger political conspiracy. Most recently, Peter Shaffer, in his international hit drama *Amadeus*, has broadened public awareness of the legend. But there seems no shred of concrete evidence for any of it, save that Salieri, considering his power position at the time, undoubtedly took care of himself.

Born near Verona, he was the youngest son (of five) of a successful merchant. An elder brother, Francesco, who had studied with Tartini [714], gave him his first music lessons, and he then studied with the town organist, Giuseppe Simoni, who had been a pupil of Padre Martini [767]. Both parents had died by the time the boy was fifteen, and a family friend, a scion of the old ducal house of Mocenigo, took him to Venice, where he continued his studies with the aging Pescetti [758] and a singer named Pacini. A year later he fell into the good graces of the visiting Florian Gassmann [851], who carried him back to Vienna and took him into his own family. There Salieri acted as an aide to his foster parent and often filled in for him. Gassmann, in turn, smoothed his path for him, introducing him to such important theater men as Metastasio, Calzabigi, and Gluck [803], and winning him the patronage of the Emperor Joseph. Salieri wrote his first opera at eighteen and two years later had his first hit *(Le Donne letterate [The Lettered Ladies])* at

the Burgtheater, following it with eleven more works by 1775. When Gassmann died in 1774, Salieri succeeded him as *Kammerkomponist* and conductor of the Hofoper. He also undertook to bring up Gassmann's two young daughters, both of whom became successful singers. In 1775 he married Theresia Helferstorfer, who provided him with eight children of his own. Early on, he had also won the fatherly friendship of Gluck, who in 1778 sent him to Milan to provide an opera for the opening of the newly built Teatro alla Scala—*L'Europa riconosciuta (Europa Recognized).* With the emperor's permission he remained in Italy, turning out pieces for various theaters for two years.

His next new work for Vienna was *Der Rauchfangkehrer (The Chimneysweep)*, produced by the emperor's newly founded (and short-lived) German company at the Burgtheater. The next year he wrote a one-act *Semiramide* for Vienna. Then Gluck put opportunity in his way again: incapacitated by a series of strokes, he gave Salieri the commission from Paris for *Les Danaïdes (The Danaids)*. It was produced in 1784 as Gluck's or as a collaboration with Gluck, but after its success Gluck disclaimed any connection. Salieri returned to Paris in 1786 with *Les Horaces*, and in 1787 with his greatest triumph and most original opera, *Tarare*, to a libretto by Caron de Beaumarchais, the dramatist of *Le Barbier de Séville* and *Les Noces de Figaro.* On returning to Vienna (where Gluck had died in the interim), Salieri had Lorenzo da Ponte (librettist of Mozart's *Figaro, Don Giovanni,* and *Così)* rewrite the libretto while he himself "Italianized" the music and produced it in 1788 as *Axur, Re d'Ormus.* That same year Salieri became *Hofkapellmeister* and the politically most powerful musical figure in the empire. But his ascendancy was brief, for two years later Joseph II died and was replaced by Leopold II, who was no friend of the Italian's. Salieri resigned from the opera, though he maintained his more prestigious post. He continued for a time to write operas—one notes a *Falstaff* in 1799 and a final *Die Neger (The Negroes)* in 1804. But Salieri had outlived both his friends and his era and was no longer popular. In the latter year he wrote his *Requiem* for himself and retired, devoting himself to the promotion of music and musicians (through vigorous activity in the Tonkünstler Sozietat [Gassmann's brainchild], the Musikfreunde Gesellschaft, and the Conservatory), and to teaching. (His pupils included Beethoven [1063], Schubert [1153], Liszt [1218], Hummel [1091], Czerny [1137], and a host of lesser lights.) He died at seventy-four, full of honors, and was very quickly forgotten as a composer. He wrote, besides the operas, a great deal of religious music and other vocal works, as well as some concerti, serenades, ballet pieces, etc.

RECORDINGS: Few of the operas have reached records—one notes the overture to *Axur, Re d'Ormus* from Thomas Schippers and that to the 1772 *La Fiera di Venezia (The Fair at Venice)* from Richard Bonynge. Instrumental works include a symphony led by Bonynge and Ernst Maerzendorfer, two symphonies and 26 *Variations on "La Follia di Spagna"* by Zoltán Peskó, two piano concerti by Aldo Ciccolini, and numerous recordings of a flute-oboe concerto conducted by Jörg Faerber and others.

[967] BLASCO DE NEBRA, Manuel
(Bvlàs'-kō dä Nāb'-vrà, Mån-wel')
ORGANIST
BORN: Castile, 1750
DIED: Seville, September 12, 1784

Famous in his day as a keyboard player, Blasco de Nebra was a pupil of his more famous uncle, José Melchor de Nebra Blasco (1702–68), organist of the Spanish royal chapel. He himself spent most of his mature life as organist of Seville Cathedral. His only known compositions—many are lost—is a published set of piano sonatas, the only such works published in Spain in his century. RECORDINGS: Two piano sonatas have been recorded by Luciano Sgrizzi.

[968] ALMEIDA MOTTA, João Pedro de
(Ȧl-mā'-ē-*th*à Mō'-tȧ, Zhwou*n* Pā-*th*rōō dä)
BORN: c. 1750
DIED: after 1790

Almeida Motta is one of the mystery men of music. The very fact of his existence hinges on a fine setting of Metastasio's *La Passione di Gesù Cristo*. Experts peg it as a product of the last quarter of the eighteenth century, and it may be the work of that title published anonymously in Rome in 1790. It is clearly the work of a skilled and confident composer, but of his life there seems to be no record. RECORDINGS: The Metastasio setting has been recorded by Gianfranco Rivoli in the Archiv series devoted to monuments of Portuguese music.

[969] BLANCO, José (Blàn'-kō, Hō-zā')
ORGANIST, HARPIST

BORN: c. 1750
DIED: ?

Blanco was an organist of the cathedral at Cuenca, in central Spain, and perhaps at Ciudad Rodrigo near the Portuguese border, in the late eighteenth century. RECORDINGS: Walter Opp and Wilhelm Krumbach have recorded his Concerto No. 1 for 2 Organs.

[970] DUPORT, Pierre Landrin (Dü-pôr', Pē-âr Là*n*-dra*n*')
DANCING MASTER
BORN: France, c. 1750
DIED: United States (?)

Duport was a popular representative of his profession in the early United States, and apparently was something of a character. His daughter Anna married Alexander Reinagle in Baltimore in 1803. It is not known what his relationship (if any) was to Louis Antoine Duport, *premier danseur* at the Paris Opéra, or to the composing Duports (see 961). RECORDINGS: Janice Beck has recorded two minuets of his authorship.

[971] PELISSIER, Victor (Pe-lē'-syä, Vik'-tôr)
HORNIST, ARRANGER
BORN: France, c. 1750
DIED: after 1811

An indefatigable concocter of musical plays and spectacles, Pelissier came to Philadelphia in 1792 and joined the Old American (theater) Company as horn player the next year. Eyewitness descriptions suggest that he looked something like, and possessed the sunny personality of, the nearsighted Mr. Magoo. Despite several proponents of the view, it is demonstrably untrue that his *Edwin and Angelina* was the first "opera" written in America—though just what was is debatable. His patriotic extravaganzas, *The Launch, or Huzza for the Constitution* and *The Fourth of July,* already have the smell of Barnum and deMille about them. More artistically ambitious were *Ariadne Abandoned, The Castle of Otranto* (after Horace Walpole), and *Robinson Crusoe*. Between 1794 and 1800, Pelissier is credited with at least 30 musical productions, though for many of them he served as no more than arranger of tunes borrowed from elsewhere. In 1811 he published a collection of *Columbian Melodies*. He also left a string quartet. RECORDINGS: A waltz from the 1811 collection has been recorded by Janice Beck.

[972] ROSETTI, Francesco Antonio (Rō-zet'-tē, Fràn-chās'-kō Àn-tōn'-yō)
CONTRABASSIST, MUSIC DIRECTOR
BORN: Leitmeritz, c. 1750
DIED: Ludwigslust, June 30, 1792

Antonio Rosetti—not to be confused with Antonio Rosetti (1744–after 1780)—was born north of Prague in the Vltava town now called Litoměřice of German stock and baptized Franz Anton Rösler (not to be confused with a local shoemaker, Franz Anton Rössler, born a few years earlier). At thirteen he joined the Jesuits to prepare for a priestly career, but by the time he had completed his education a decade later, he decided that was not the life for him and withdrew from the order. Within a matter of weeks, he had been employed by Prince Kraft Ernst of Oettingen-Wallerstein as contrabass player in his crack orchestra, where he was a colleague of, among others, Johannes Nisle [883] and Josef Reicha [978]. He married, made several successful concert tours, became vice-*Kapellmeister* in 1780 and *Kapellmeister* in 1785 when Reicha left for the Rhineland. Four years later, however, he assumed the same post at the Ludwigslust court of Friedrich Franz of Mecklenburg-Schwerin, where the salary was much higher and he was safe from his creditors. In 1791 he wrote a *Requiem* as a memorial to Mozart [992], and spent some time (by invitation) at the Prussian court in Berlin. A year later he died at forty-two. An attractive composer, he has been called "the German Boccherini." He seems to have been influenced by Haydn [871] and in turn to have influenced Schubert [1153]. He composed in most genres save opera. RE-CORDINGS: Three of his concerti for horn have been recorded (by Hermann Baumann, Erich Penzel, and Pasqualino Rossi), and one for two horns (by the Sörensens). There are also a symphony (Enrico Bartoletti), a *notturno* (Musici Pragenses), a wind quintet (members of the Southwest German Radio Orchestra), a string quartet (the Oisterseks), a harp sonata (Nicanor Zabaleta), and the six harp sonatas of Op. 2 (Susann McDonald).

[973] LASERNA, Blas de (Là-sâr'-nà, Blàs dà)
CONDUCTOR, COPYIST, TEACHER
BORN: Corella, c. February 4, 1751
DIED: Madrid, August 8, 1816

Laserna was a specialist in Spanish popular stage forms, notably the *tonadilla,* which, shortly before, had developed from an *en-tr'acte* song into a dramatic (usually comic) intermezzo. He also wrote *sainetes* (after-pieces) and other theater music. He came to Madrid in his early twenties from his Navarrais birthplace, married, and became an extremely popular theater composer, turning out somewhere in the vicinity of 1,000 compositions. In 1788 he became conductor of the Teatro de la Cruz, where the tenor Manuel Garcia (Rossini's [1143] Almaviva in *Il Barbiere di Siviglia* and father of Maria Malibran and Pauline Viardot) was for a time his assistant. Laserna's longest-lived piece was *La Gitanilla por amor (The Gypsy for Love),* but a song *"La tirana del Tripoli"* became an international hit and was quoted by Mercadante [1148] in the overture to his *I due Figaro* and by Granados [1588] in his *Goyescas.* Senora Laserna died in 1793 and the widower married a singer named María Pupilla. He often had to eke out a living as a copyist and teacher of musical basics. He also conducted for a time at the Teatro Principe. A song, *"El jilguerito con pico d'oro,"* from his *Los amantes chasqueados* of 1779 has been recorded by Victoria de Los Angeles and Ninon Vallin in an arrangement by Joaquín Nin [1721].

[974] KUCHAŘ, Jan Křtitel (Koo'-chärzh, Yàn Krzh'tē'-təl)
KEYBOARDIST, CONDUCTOR, MANDO-LINIST, GLASS HARMONICIST
BORN: Choteč, March 5, 1751
DIED: Prague, February 18, 1829

Educated in Jesuit schools in Königgrätz and Gitschin (now Hradec Králové and Jičín), Kuchař (alias Johann Baptist Kucharz) studied organ with Seger [807]. In 1772 he began eighteen years of service as organist of St. Jindřich's in Prague, after which he spent the rest of his life as organist of the Strahov Monastery. From 1792 to 1800 he was also musical director of the Italian Opera in Prague. His compositions are mostly for organ and for church choirs. He also produced vocal scores of the last four operas (exclusive of *La Clemenza di Tito*) of Mozart [992]. Organ pieces have been recorded by Jiří Ropek and Franz Lehrndorfer.

[975] MICHAEL, David Moritz (Mē'-khà-el, Dà'-fēt Mō'-rētz)
OBOIST, HORNIST, VIOLINIST, CONDUC-TOR
BORN: Kienhausen, October 27, 1751
DIED: Neuwied, 1827

Born near Erfurt in Thuringia, Michael, in his early years, was a windplayer in opera orchestras and military bands in Germany. A member of the Moravian sect, he migrated to Nazareth, Pennsylvania, in 1795, where he directed the Collegium Musicum. In 1804 he came to Bethlehem and joined the Philharmonic Society (founded in 1780), which had already performed many works by C. P. E. Bach [801], Haydn [871], and their contemporaries. Michael wrote a good deal of music, including pieces for the church and the first works for wind ensemble written in this country. Among the latter was a sextet for clarinets, horns, and bassoons, called *Die Wasserfahrt (The Water Journey)* to be played from a barge floating on the Lehigh for strollers along the shore. In 1811 Michael directed the first American performance (in Bethlehem) of Haydn's oratorio *The Creation*. At the end of his life, he went home to die in a small Rhine town near Koblenz. RECORDINGS: One of his anthems has been recorded by Thor Johnson.

[976] BORTNIANSKY, Dmitri Stepanovich (Bôrt-nyȧn'-skē, Də-mē'-trē Styȧ-pȧ-nō'-vēch)
MUSIC DIRECTOR
BORN: Glukhov, 1751
DIED: St. Petersburg, October 10, 1825

Save for the hapless Berezovsky [938], Bortniansky qualifies as the first internationally known Russian native composer (if one overlooks the fact that both men were Ukrainians). Tradition says that he was a choirboy at the imperial court under Galuppi [768] and went to Italy to study with him after Galuppi had returned there in 1768. Certainly Bortniansky went there in 1769 and remained for a decade, winning some success with several Italian operas. (Among these, *Quinto Fabio* and *Alcide* survive.) On his return to St. Petersburg, the Czarina Catherine II put him in charge of the imperial choir, where he wrought prodigies of ensemble. In 1796 Paul I elevated him to the position of court music director. In 1786–87 Bortniansky wrote and produced four *opéras-comiques*. He wrote music of other kinds as well but is best known for his quite Italianate church music, which was edited in 1881 by none other than Tchaikovsky [1377]. Two decades after Bortniansky's death, Berlioz [1175] could still marvel at his effect on Russian choral singing. RECORDINGS: Various church compositions have appeared on records, some going back nearly fifty years.

[977] CLEMENTI, Muzio (Klä-mān'-tē, Mōōdz'-yō)
PIANIST, CONDUCTOR, PUBLISHER, MANUFACTURER
BORN: Rome, January 23, 1752
DIED: Evesham, March 10, 1832

Now known to most piano students as the composer of a few inconsequential sonatinas, Clementi, in his day, was ranked with Haydn [871] and Mozart [992], exerted a great influence on Beethoven [1063], taught half of the successful pianists of the next generation, and helped to establish the piano as essential to any household with pretensions to culture. Baptized "Mutius Philippus Vincentius Franciscus Xaverius," he was the first child of Nicola Clementi, a Roman silversmith, and his second wife, Magdalena *(née* Kaiser). He was trained by several now forgotten musicians—Antonio Boroni (a Martini [767] pupil), a *castrato* named Santarelli, an organist named Cordicelli, and Gaetano Carpani (choirmaster at the Gesù), and shortly before his fourteenth birthday was appointed organist of San Lorenzo in Damaso. At that time Peter Beckford, a fox-hunting country cousin of the novelist William Beckford, heard him and evidently decided he would make an interesting ornament for his Dorsetshire estate at Steepleton Iwerne. Accordingly, he negotiated with the elder Clementi, who was feeling the pinch of a recession in the religious-silverware trade, and "bought" the boy (i.e., acquired him as an indentured servant) for a seven-year period.

At Beckford's estate music seems to have been considered essential only to occasional social gatherings, so that Clementi's servitude was not onerous, in and of itself. But he subjected himself to an extremely rigid program of musical self-improvement, reading and practicing ten hours daily the works of such composers as Domenico Scarlatti [687], Handel [683], and assorted Bachs. He also composed sporadically. In 1774 he moved to London. His term was up, to be sure, but there are hints that other circumstances sped his departure—especially Beckford's fulminations against music masters, who, he declared in print, should all be castrated. Contrary to legend, Clementi did not "descend like a thunderbolt" on the capital. He seems to have begun quite obscurely as an accompanist, was keyboard-conductor (i.e., harpsichordist) at the King's Theatre for a while and evidently from time to time played in public the sonatas he was publishing.

Both they and he began to make a stir, and in 1780 he undertook the first of his many Continental tours. He spent a year in Paris, where he claims to have played before Marie Antoinette. He went on to entertain such other luminaries as the Duke of Zweibrücken in Strasbourg and the Elector Karl Theodor (late of Mannheim) in Munich. In December he was invited by the French queen's brother, Emperor Joseph II, to play on Christmas Eve for the visiting Russian crown prince, Grand Duke Paul and his wife Maria Fedorovna (née Sophia Dorothea of Württemberg). To his surprise, Clementi found himself pitted in a "duel" against Mozart. The latter, to hear him tell it, won in a walk, but for months afterward he fumed about his rival, calling him a charlatan and a *mechanicus*. Clementi (who seems deliberately to have been given a defective piano to emphasize the superiority of the home folks) reported drily that he had met Mozart and had had the honor of performing with him before the crowned heads.

Clementi remained in Vienna for another five months, spent some time in Lyons, and came back to London late in 1783. There he took on his first important pupil in the person of J. B. Cramer [1067], son of the violinist Wilhelm Cramer [942], and, as a concert performer, Clementi began making the musical public take notice. But he had lost his heart in Lyons to a young lady pupil, Marie-Victoire Imbert-Colomés, and in the spring of 1784 he precipitately returned there to claim her as his bride. But her wealthy father wanted no part of it and thwarted their elopement before they could reach the Swiss border. For a while Clementi lay low in Bern, nursing his wounded heart. By the summer of 1785, however, he was back in London, having stopped off to commiserate with his newly widowed father in Rome. He seems to have borne the scars of his unhappy romance for a long time. However, he throve otherwise. He became head of the Grand Professional Concerts in Hanover Square (where his symphonies were first played), switched to the LaMara-Salomon Concerts in 1787 (where he ran into devastating competition from Haydn, and returned to Hanover Square in 1789 (but only as solo performer). After 1790 he to all intents and purposes retired from the stage. He continued to conduct for a time, though he was obscured at first by Haydn and then by Viotti [988]. And Clementi went on teaching—sixteen hours a day, says one contemporary report—and became very rich from it. Some of his wealth he sank in the piano factory operated by John Longman and Francis Fane Broderip. He lost it when the firm went bankrupt in 1798 but quickly produced his own company from

the ashes, running it in various partnerships for the rest of his life. It also produced printed music as well as pianos, much of it composed by the owner. A compulsive money maker by nature, he was delighted to the point of obsession by his success. Nevertheless he was apparently an attractive (if volatile and notably absent-minded) companion, with considerable learning (he spoke several languages and was interested in math and astronomy) and with great charm and wit (though Samuel Wesley [1045] objected to his constant puns).

In 1802, disregarding the instability of international politics, he embarked on another European tour, taking along his favorite pupil, the graceless but talented Irishman John Field [1104]. His peregrinations lasted for eight years, taking him as circumstances permitted to the major cities of France, Germany, Austria, Switzerland, Russia, and Italy. Much of this activity was designed to sell pianos and music. Field found the 1802 visit to St. Petersburg quite satisfactory and remained behind. The next year Clementi, then fifty-one, met the eighteen-year-old Caroline Lehmann, the daughter of a church musician, and suddenly it was spring again. Despite mutterings about dirty old men, her parents approved the match, and Clementi came back in 1804 to marry her. A year later she gave birth to a son and died. The disconsolate widower left the baby, named Carl, with his in-laws, and took to the road again, though after that he seems hardly to have played at all, even privately. One of his chief objects was to acquire publishing rights to Beethoven's music. But negotiations with both the composer and his publishers Breitkopf and Härtel turned out to be more complex than anyone had expected, and the project did not really come to fruition until after Clementi returned to London in 1810. A year later he married a placid Englishwoman, twenty-six-year-old Emma Gisborne, whom he had perhaps met in Rome a few years earlier. She bore him two sons and two daughters, all of whom survived him. In 1813, lacking an orchestra to play his newest symphonies, he became one of the founders of the Philharmonic Society. The orchestra (not to be confused with the present-day London Philharmonic) opened its first season in March with music by Haydn, Beethoven, and Cherubini [1019]. The impresario J. P. Salomon (killed in a riding accident two years later) was first violin, and Clementi (who retained the post until 1816) was harpsichordist-conductor. Later associates here were Viotti, who took Salomon's place, and two German pupils, Alexander Klengel and Ludwig Berger **[1088]**, later Mendelssohn's **[1200]** teacher. In 1814 the Swedish Royal Academy elected Clementi to fill the place left empty by Grétry's **[919]** death.

In 1816 Clementi went to Paris to conduct some of his symphonies (with no great success) at the revived Concert Spirituel. He remained abroad for a time, visited Frankfurt am Main, and was home by 1818, where he accepted his first son Carl into his family. Carl, who seems to have had some musical talent, shot himself "by accident" a dozen years later. With little regard for his advancing age, Clementi continued to visit Europe to conduct and attend to business matters, but interest in his music gradually waned, as it came increasingly to be viewed as old-fashioned. In 1822 he was felled by a vicious attack of sciatica but fought his way back to conducting the Philharmonic one more time. But—perhaps not coincidentally after hearing Liszt's **[1218]** London debut— he gave up both writing and performing in 1824. He visited Vienna in 1827, the year Beethoven died, and in 1828 published a study of Palestrina **[201]** and was persuaded to make a final appearance at the helm of the Philharmonic. Later that year at a party, Walter Scott coaxed him into playing the piano. In 1830 he acquired a home in Lichfield, Staffordshire, but in 1831 settled at Evesham in Worcestershire, where he died the following winter at eighty. He was buried in Westminster Abbey as befitted a hero of the arts and free enterprise. His tombstone calls him "the father of the pianoforte," though in fact he was more an opportunist than a pioneer. Despite his very real achievements elsewhere, Clementi undoubtedly yearned to be remembered as a great symphonist. Unhappily, according to his grandson, most of his symphonic scores were burned by a careless housemaid.

RECORDINGS: The two earliest examples (Op. 18) survive in print and have been recorded by Alberto Zedda (No. 2 also by Sergiu Commissiona and Renato Fasano). Recently, however, the mss. of four later examples from the Library of Congess have been "reconstructed" by Pietro Spada and recorded, with considerable hoopla, by Claudio Scimone. The only extant piano concerto is played on records by Felicja Blumental and by Gino Gorini, and there are some trios (out of a handful of chamber works) by the Trio di Bolzano. What is left is the piano music. This is a mixed bag, but most of it is worth hearing and it contains some of the finest sonatas of the period. There are various recordings, notably by Artur Balsam, Sidney Foster, Vera Franceschi, Robert Goldsand, Lazar Berman, and Vladimir Horowitz, though they are by no means exhaustive. Three sonatas for piano, four hands, are recorded by Genevieve Chinn and Allen Brings; and there are several recordings of music for two pianos. The Trio Fauré has recorded several trios.

[978] REICHA, Josef (Rī'-khà, Yō'-zef)
CELLIST, CONDUCTOR
BORN: Chuděnice, March 13, 1752
DIED: Bonn, March 5, 1795

The Czechs spell his name "Rejcha," and his birthplace, south of Pilsen (Plzeň), is near Klatovy (then Klatau). He studied in Prague and at twenty-two became first cellist and colleague of Fiala **[953]** and Rosetti **[972]** in the orchestra of Count Kraft Ernst of Oettingen-Wallerstein. Five years later, in 1779, he married a Lucie Certelet, from Lorraine, who spoke only French. Shortly afterward the couple adopted Reicha's runaway orphan nephew, Antonín **[1059]**, who to his advantage was taught not only music but French and German in the household. In 1785, a year after becoming Archbishop-Elector of Cologne, the Austrian Archduke Max Franz summoned Josef Reicha to Bonn to be his first cellist (Antonín, now "Anton," played violin and flute in the orchestra). Before the year was out, he had succeeded Cajetano Mattioli as director of the court orchestra, and in 1789 he was named conductor for the newly built opera house. A year later he became general music director, but his eminence proved to be only temporary. The approach of the French in 1794 forced Max Franz to flee, and Reicha died the following winter. He left 6 symphonies, 5 *sinfonie concertante,* 4 concerti, some chamber suites, and string duos. He was an unquestionable influence on his nephew, with whose music his has become confused, and perhaps taught Beethoven **[1063]** a trick or two. RECORDINGS: Anner Bylsma has recorded one of the two cello concerti, and Roseline Piveteau and Jan Stegenga one of the duos.

[979] KNECHT, Justin Heinrich
(K'nekht, Yōōs'-tēn Hīn'-rikh)
ORGANIST, CONDUCTOR, THEORIST
BORN: Biberach, September 30, 1752
DIED: Biberach, December 1, 1817

Born near Ausgburg, Justin Knecht's career was, like that of his younger contemporary C. L. Dieter **[1002]**, determinedly provincial. His tutor was the poet Christoph Martin Wieland, but he got what music he had from other locals. Mostly, it is said, he learned it on his own. Supposedly the Biberach school produced a *Singspiel* that he wrote at twelve. He developed as a fine organist and at nineteen was appointed by the city fathers as municipal organist and *Kapellmeister.* He became an enthusiastic promoter of the harmonic system advocated by "Abt" Vogler [960] and from the middle 1780s produced a series of theoretical works and an organ method. One of his more than a dozen operas (and another link with Dieter) was a setting of Gottlob Stephanie's *Die Entführung aus dem Serail,* used by Mozart [992] five years earlier. In 1807 he was invited by Duke Friedrich II to become his *Kapellmeister* in Stuttgart, where Dieter was still a member of the orchestra. His two-year stay there seems to represent his only time away from Biberach. Besides stage pieces, Knecht wrote some choral works, a programmatic ensemble piece on country matters (possible influence on Beethoven's [1063] "Pastoral" symphony has been discounted), and organ music. RECORDINGS: A sample of the organ music has been recorded by Franz Lehrndorfer.

[980] REICHARDT, Johann Friedrich
(Rīkh'-ärt, Yō'-hản Frē'-drikh)
POLYMATH
BORN: Königsberg, November 25, 1752
DIED: Giebichenstein, June 27, 1814

An odd and prickly figure, Reichardt, for a variety of reasons, was disliked by some factions in his time, upheld by others, and stands today as an important, if still little-known, pioneer in the early history of German Romantic music. He was born in the city now known as Kaliningrad, the son of Johann Reichardt, a lutenist, who taught him not only that instrument, but also singing. From other locals, he learned violin and the keyboards, as well as a smattering of theory, and embarked at ten on a career as a solo violinist. Five years later he began a three-year studentage at the town university and then hit the road as a touring performer. The world tour he envisioned in fact embraced only parts of Germany and Bohemia, but he made the most of it, meeting whatever important musicians were available, taking in operas and concerts, and studying briefly en route with Kirnberger [821] and Homilius [800]. After three years he returned to his home and became a civil servant, and set about writing up his travels and impressions. But he was already also composing seriously, and when Johann Friedrich Agricola, director of the Royal

Prussian Opera in Berlin, died at the end of 1774, Reichardt, not yet twenty-three, sent Frederick II an application for the vacancy, accompanied by the score of his *Le Festi galanti* (a deliberate exercise in old-style writing), and was given the job.

Within a year of his arrival in Berlin, Reichardt had married Juliane Benda (1752–83), the daughter of František [776] and herself a composer and singer. Their daughter Luise (1779–1826) became a successful teacher and choral director, but her personal life was tragic; she wrote many songs that remained popular, notably *"Hoffnung"* ("Hope," known here as "In the Time of Roses" or "When the Roses Bloom.") After Juliane's death, Reichardt married a widow. Berlin turned out to be a mixed blessing. Reichardt had sat at Kant's feet in Königsberg, identified with the avant-garde, and was an intimate of such leading figures of the German artistic upsurge as Goethe, Schiller, Herder, and Moses Mendelssohn (leader of the Jewish emancipation and grandfather of the composer [1200]). Yet, as *Kapellmeister* of the opera, he found himself having to cater to the king's tastes, which were never very daring and were now decidedly mouldy. He was quite unable to get any official notice taken of his own melodramas and *Singspiele,* though there were productions elsewhere. Moreover, he made enemies who gave him trouble (though there is some evidence that at least part of the opposition had justice on its side, since, if we can believe Mozart [992], Reichardt was not a very good conductor). Nevertheless he was given frequent leaves of absence to travel, which ameliorated the situation. In 1783 he inaugurated a concert series based on the Parisian Concert Spirituel, wherein he presented much new music (including his own) for which he wrote the program notes. While he was in Paris in 1786, the old king died. His successor, Frederick William II, put Reichardt in full charge of the Royal Music. The composer celebrated with a production of *Claudine von Villa Bella* to a libretto by his friend Goethe. (Several other collaborations ensued.) But the changes Reichardt made in personnel and procedure provoked an open rebellion, and he got leave to take again to the road until things should have cooled off. While in Paris, just before his return in 1792, he proclaimed his sympathy with the Jacobins. Word got back to his enemies, and two years later Frederick William summarily fired him. His hoity-toity self-righteousness had also alienated his friends, and he retired to a country place near Halle. Later everyone forgave him,

Frederick William made him director of the Halle salt mine, and his home became a gathering place for the young Romantics. But with the French invasion in 1806, Reichardt fled with his family to Altona, near Hamburg. After Jerome Bonaparte, the French emperor's brother, was installed as King of Westphalia in Kassel, he ordered Beethoven to appear as his *Kapellmeister,* but Beethoven refused. He then turned to Reichardt, who, Republican or not, acceded when Jerome threatened to appropriate his estate. But Jerome's transfer to the Russian front seems to have forestalled the appointment, and instead Reichardt found his way to Vienna. In 1809 he returned to Halle to find it and the Giebichenstein property in ruins. For two years he lived by his pen, then survived until his death on a small pension.

Reichardt wrote copiously in most musical genres, but he is of more interest as an influence than as a composer, and in that respect chiefly in opera and song. His music is deliberately folksy and simple, if not simple-minded. But his *Singspiele* convinced people that German-language opera had a future for the Germans and paved the way for Weber [1124]. However, it is as a songwriter that he looms largest. With Zelter [1008] Reichardt was a prime favorite of Goethe (who had his own notions about how a song should be written—i.e., the music should take a back seat to the verse), and was thus influential. Reichardt found all sorts of ingenious ways to observe Goethe's dictum. He had a strong sense of word meanings and usually managed to give them impact; his impact on Schubert [1153] is incalculable. Reichardt, incidentally, set *all* of Goethe's lyrics written up to 1811 and published them in 4 volumes.

RECORDINGS: Dietrich Fischer-Dieskau has recorded a representative sample of the Goethe lyrics and other Reichardt songs, Bruno Hoffmann has recorded a glass harmonica piece. There are also recordings conducted by Ernö Sebestyen of two *sinfonie,* a violin concerto, and the Double Concerto for Harpsichord, Violin, and Orchestra. Gerd Albrecht conducts the *Funeral Cantata on the Death of Frederick the Great.* (Note should also be taken of Reichardt's writings, which cover music, theory, performers, biography, autobiography, current events, politics, and some stabs at the fictional.)

[981] STADLER, Anton Paul (Shtăt'-ler, Än'-tōn Poul)
CLARINETIST

BORN: Bruck an der Leitha, June 28, 1753
DIED: Vienna, June 15, 1812

Stadler, remembered chiefly for his friendship with Mozart [992], must not be confused with Abbé Maximilian Stadler (1748–1833), who was also a member of the Mozart circle and who copied out the *Requiem.* Anton Stadler and his younger brother Johann, also a clarinetist, came to Vienna from their birthplace just to the southeast in the early 1770s, working as a team in various situations until they were given contracts as court musicians in 1782. They became the first clarinetists to be regularly employed in the court orchestra. Anton was a Masonic lodge brother of Mozart, and a close enough friend to get the impossible pet name of Natschibinitschibi, though he was not above taking unfair advantage of the younger man. It was for him and his "basset-clarinet" of his own design that Mozart wrote the quintet, the concerto, and a number of orchestral parts. Stadler retired from the Hoforchester in 1799 and from solo playing in 1806. His compositions are, expectably, mostly for clarinets and basset horns (a kind of alto clarinet). RECORDINGS: Heinrich Fink, through electronic magic, has recorded a terzet for three basset horns.

[982] SCHENCK, Johann Baptist (Shenk, Yō'-hán Báp'-tist)
TEACHER
BORN: Wiener Neustadt, November 30, 1753
DIED: Vienna, December 29, 1836

Today Schenck is remembered as the composer of a still viable one-act *Singspiel* entitled *Der Dorfbarbier (The Village Barber)* and as a man who taught Beethoven [1063]. He was, as a matter of fact, of some significance in the development of German opera. He was not born in Vienna, as some references carelessly indicate, but in its namesake to the south, where Maximilian I lies buried and which was razed by fire two years before Schenck died. Nor was he born in 1761, as his own autobiographical letter maintains. He became a choirboy in the Austrian spa of Baden, where a visiting archbishop took note of him and turned his education over to Wagenseil's [804] father confessor, Canon Schneller, who quickly passed him on to that gouty old musician in 1774. Wagenseil, who believed in teaching by example, acquainted him intimately with Palestrina [201], then much in fashion; J. S. Bach [684]; Hasse [736]; Galuppi [768]; and especially Handel [683]. Depressed by Wagenseil's death three years later, Schenck was aroused by a Mass composed by a fellow pupil and wrote one of his own for the installation of Father Schneller as canon of the Magdalenakirche. It was conducted by Leopold Hofmann [899], won approval from a number of musicians including Haydn [871], and brought in commissions for other sacred works.

In the 1780s Schenck branched out, undertaking symphonies and concerti and sharpening his dramatic skills. His first two commissioned *Singspiele,* entitled *Die Weinlese (The Vintage)* and *Die Weihnacht auf dem Lande (The Country Christmas)* were given anonymously, at the composer's request, by the Leopoldstädt Theater in 1785 and 1786. Schenck took off the mask in 1787 with *Im Finstern ist nicht gut tappen (It's No Good Groping in the Dark)* and went on to turn out nearly a dozen more such works, several of them quite successful. The greatest hit was *Der Dorfbarbier* of 1796, which remained in the regular German repertoire for decades and still enjoys revivals.

The connection with Beethoven [1063] dates from 1793. Beethoven had come to Vienna to study counterpoint with Haydn and was apparently making slow headway. It is likely that Schenck, as he seems to say, offered his services as a tutor rather than as a replacement, but it seems unquestionable that he facilitated the younger man's progress. He was also a friend of Mozart's [992]. After 1802 Schenck suffered a nervous breakdown and, save for a couple of cantatas, composed little or nothing else, devoting his time to teaching in his home.

RECORDINGS: Schenck is represented on records by a variation for piano commissioned by Diabelli [1100] on his own famous theme, and (rather improbably) by a guitar suite recorded by Siegfried Behrend.

[983] WIKMANSON, Johan (Vēk'-màn-sōn, Yō'-hàn)
ORGANIST, VIOLIST, CELLIST, BUREAU-CRAT
BORN: Stockholm, December 28, 1753
DIED: Stockholm, January 16, 1800

As a child, Wikmanson studied piano, but in adolescence he was packed off to Copenhagen to study mathematics and other "practical" matters. These he liked even less than he thought he would, so he became a struggling piano teacher until they finally let him come home. In 1772 he became a cashier for the National Lottery and eventually worked up to the post of financial man-

ager. But he also kept his hand in music as organist of various Stockholm churches. He was popular in both musical and commercial circles, numbering among his close friends the Grills, who were in shipping, and such musicians as Joseph Martin Kraus [998]; Abt Vogler [960], whose Swedish Wikmanson corrected in his writings; and the cellist Pihlmann, who persuaded him to give up the viola for that instrument. In 1796 Wikmanson was named educational director at the Stockholm Academy of Music, and a year later he was appointed professor of harmony and counterpoint, which goes to prove that one does not need a university degree to succeed. Wikmanson's largest compositions were three string quartets dedicated to Haydn [871], who liked them; but he also wrote music for the cello, 3 sonatinas for the zither(!), and some piano sonatas and other keyboard pieces. RECORDINGS: Stig Ribbing, using period instruments, has recorded several keyboard pieces, including the famous "henhouse" finale from the B minor sonata. The Chilingirian Quartet has recorded the Quartet No. 2 in E Minor.

[984] GIORDANI, Giuseppe (Jôr-dà'-nē, Joo-sep'-pä)
CHOIRMASTER
BORN: Naples, c. 1753
DIED: Fermo, January 4, 1798

As noted in the entry for Tommaso Giordani [877], the myth of the Giordani brothers of Naples has been exploded: he and Giuseppe were probably quite unrelated. Giuseppe is thought to have been the son of Carmine Giordani (c. 1685–1758), deputy organist at the Neapolitan court. He studied at the Conservatory of Santa Maria di Loreto, where he was a classmate of Cimarosa [962]. From about 1771 he turned out operas and oratorios for twenty years, then became choirmaster of the Cathedral at Fermo on the Adriatic coast south of Ancona. He is traditionally credited with the old Italian air *"Caro mio ben."* RECORDINGS: The air has been much recorded.

[985] HOFFMEISTER, Franz Anton (Hof'-mīs-ter, Frànts Àn'-tōn)
HARPSICHORDIST, PUBLISHER, EDITOR
BORN: Rottenburg am Neckar, May 12, 1754
DIED: Vienna, February 9, 1812

Anyone who knows modern American music publishers is likely to be surprised to encounter one who can perform music and stunned at the notion of one writing it. Franz Anton Hoffmeister (not to be confused with his sometime employee, the Leipzig publisher Friedrich Hofmeister) did both—the first well enough to concertize, the second well enough to meet the demands of the public. Born in Rottenburg (just south of Stuttgart and not to be confused with the one south of Regensburg or with Rothenburg ob der Tauber), Hoffmeister passed his bar examination in Leipzig before casting his lot with music. He began publishing his own music when he was around thirty and by 1785 had established a firm. Though rather eccentrically run, from a businessman's view, it prospered and published not only Hoffmeister but many important Viennese composers, including Haydn [871], Mozart [992], and Beethoven [1063], as well as some earlier masters, including J. S. Bach [684]. It is said that Hoffmeister was one of the few musicians whose friendship Mozart cultivated—though the fact that Hoffmeister could be counted on not only for publication but also for loans may have had something to do with it. Beethoven was on intimate terms with him.

Over the years the business went through a number of changes what with the opening and closing of branches and with changes of administrators and partners. In the decade of the 1790s, Hoffmeister turned out a number of operas and *Singspiele* for Emanuel Schikaneder, the original producer of Mozart's *Zauberflöte*. In 1798 he went to England with a flutist named Franz Thurmer on a highly successful concert tour. A year or so later, going to Leipzig to perform, he fell in with one Ambrosius Kühnel and with him opened the firm called Bureau de Musique in 1801. Hoffmeister operated both businesses (it is not certain how) until 1805, when he returned to Vienna. But a year later he gave up his publishing career and retired to compose. The Bureau de Musique eventually became C. F. Peters which, now headquartered in New York, still flourishes.

An able craftsman who understood the taste of the times, Hoffmeister wrote prodigiously. His chief output was chamber music intended for home consumption, but he also wrote nearly 70 symphonies. Some of his quartets were once ascribed to Haydn. He was especially productive of flute music, which may account in part for today's small Hoffmeister revival.

RECORDINGS: A piano concerto has been recorded by both Felicja Blumental and Wilhelm Neuhaus; a viola concerto performed by the Philharmonia Hungarica;

several flute concerti variously by Jean-Pierre Rampal, Ingrid Dingfelder, and Hans-Jürgen Mohring; a trio by the Trio Helvetica; the Op. #14 flute sonata by the Bryan-Keys Duo; and a violin-viola duo by Arthur Grumiaux and Arrigo Pelliccia.

[986] FRENCH, Jacob
TEACHER
BORN: Stoughton, Mass., July 15, 1754
DIED: Simsbury, Conn., May 1817

A pupil of William Billings [946], French fought in the Continental Army during the Revolution and himself became a music teacher. He published 3 volumes, mostly devoted to hymn tunes: *New American Melody*, 1789; *The Psalmodist's Companion*, 1793; and *The Harmony of Harmony*, 1802. The last-named includes some basic theory (in catechistical style) and various original compositions, characterized as anthems, odes, and fuguing pieces. RECORDINGS: The Abbey Singers have recorded the ode *The Death of General Washington.*

[987] WINTER, Peter von (Vin'-ter, Pā'-ter fun)
VIOLINIST, CONTRABASSIST, CONDUCTOR
BORN: Mannheim, c. August 28, 1754
DIED: Munich, October 17, 1825

Born in the great days of the Mannheim Orchestra, Winter profited by his environment and joined the string section at age ten. When his employer became the Elector of Bavaria and moved his forces to Munich in 1778, Winter became conductor, specializing in German-language operas. Contact with the genre made him eager to distinguish himself in it, though he met with indifferent success at first. In 1781 a concert tour took him to Vienna, where Mozart [992], whom he had met earlier, was just getting settled in. Mozart complained to his father [816] that Winter had been mongering all manner of rotten stories about him and his relations with Constanze, though it is now thought that such behavior was mostly in Mozart's head. But Winter *does* seem to have been an unpleasant sort, to judge from the reactions of others to him. At any rate, while he was in Vienna, he took time to pick up some pointers from Salieri [966]. In 1787 the elector appointed him vice-*Kapellmeister*. After that Winter was given a good deal of time off to try to get his operatic career off the ground, which he finally succeeded in doing at Vienna in 1796; however, he never evoked much interest in Munich in that area, and his popularity was spotty elsewhere. In his capacity as a practical musician, nevertheless, he continued to rise, being appointed court music director in 1798 and winning ennoblement in 1814. In his final years he devoted himself chiefly to religious music. He was gifted with a turn for melody but lacked both solid technique and profundity of feeling. Besides the works noted, Winter produced a good deal of chamber music, some concerti, and a few symphonies. RECORDINGS: Karl Ristenpart, with Jost Michaels and Irene Güdel, has recorded a *sinfonia concertante* for clarinet and cello that shows the tuneful attractiveness of the music and its leanings toward Weberian [1124] Romanticism.

[988] VIOTTI, Giovanni Battista (Vē-ot′-tē, Jō-vàn′-nē Bàt-tēs′-tà)

VIOLINIST, CONDUCTOR, IMPRESARIO, WINE SELLER
BORN: Fontanetto da Po, May 12, 1755
DIED: London, March 3, 1824

Before the advent of long-playing records, Viotti was thought of chiefly as a perpetrator of a method and wearying exercises for young violinists. In historical fact, he was the greatest violin virtuoso between Tartini [714] and Paganini [1106], and a composer of important violin concerti involving symphonic principles. His origins are bemisted in legend. Supposedly his father was a horn-playing blacksmith in a riverside hamlet near Vercelli in the foothills of the Alps. Exactly how he is supposed to have become a musical prodigy is not clear, but by the age of eleven he found himself ensconced in a *palazzo* in Turin, the companion and fellow pupil of the young Prince Alfonso del Pozzo della Cisterna, whose father, the Marchese di Vogliera, footed the bills for his education and upkeep. His most important teacher was Pugnani [866], who instilled in him the Corellian tradition (see 565). When he was twenty, Viotti was given a post in the orchestra of King Victor Amadeus III. But the salary was minimal and the court was a mess, and five years later he took off with Pugnani on a tour that took them to Geneva, Dresden, Berlin, Warsaw, and St. Petersburg. Viotti was billed as "a pupil of the celebrated Pugnani." On the way back, Viotti decided that he was tired of playing second fiddle and struck off on his own. When he arrived at Paris in the spring of 1782, he got himself booked at the Concert Spirituel, and sure enough he got loud huzzas without even breathing Pugnani's name.

In fact he was so pleased that although he had intended Paris as the start of a solo tour, he decided to stay. But toward the end of 1783, he suddenly gave up public performances. Several explanations for this behavior have been advanced, but the most likely one is that he found working for Marie-Antoinette and her court friends more lucrative and less taxing. In 1788, sponsored by the Count of Chartres (the future Louis XVIII), Viotti and the queen's *parfumier,* M. Autié, known as "Léonard," founded a new opera company which had temporary quarters in the Tuileries and was called the Théâtre de Monsieur. As conductor, Viotti hired his old friend Cherubini [1019] with whom he had shared quarters (and even a few sous) earlier in Paris. In 1790 the company had its season at the Foire St. Germain and the next year took up residence in the newly built Salle Feydeau. Viotti strove to produce the best Italian opera performances possible, even dressed in his National Guard uniform as the Revolution went into high gear. But with the Terror, he feared that his royal connections and his foreign background would do him in and so fled to England.

For a time in London Viotti was the toast of the town, playing in the Salomon concerts, managing the King's Theatre, and conducting there and at the opera concerts. With the backing of a Mr. and Mrs. William Chinnery, he also went into the wine-importing business. But ironically, having had to get out of France as a suspected royalist, his French connections in 1798 got him ordered out of England as a suspected revolutionary. For some months he was taken care of by English friends in northern Germany, then was allowed to return to London. From then on, he devoted his time to his wine business, playing only rarely and then usually in small private gatherings. He lent his name to the list of founders of the London Philharmonic Society in 1813. Five years later, even with financial infusions from his friends, his business failed. The next year Viotti was appointed director of the Paris Opéra by his old patron, Louis XVIII. But when the king's nephew, the Duke of Berry, was murdered the following winter as he left the building, Viotti was unable to cope with the ensuing tensions and resigned. He returned to London in 1823, still deeply in debt to his friends and in low spirits. When Mrs. Chinnery took him in, he willed her everything he owned and died a few months later.

Viotti's most important works are his 29 violin concerti and 2 *sinfonie concertante,* though he also wrote quartets, trios, duos, and sonatas for strings, a handful of piano pieces, and a few songs. Several of the concerti exist in piano arrangements, many of them by other hands.

RECORDINGS: Some of the violin concerti have been recorded in the original versions —e.g., No. 3 (Giuseppe Prencipe), No. 4 (Antonio Abussi), Nos. 16, 24 (Röhn), and No. 22 (Isaac Stern, Arthur Grumiaux, Peter Rybar, Suzanne Lautenbacher, etc.). There are also piano arrangements (Felicja Blumental, Eugene List), and *sinfonie concertante* (C. A. Bünte, Claudio Scimone), and two quartets (Baker Quartet).

[989] MOLLER, John Christopher
KEYBOARDIST, VIOLIST, CONCERT MANAGER, PUBLISHER
BORN: Germany, 1755
DIED: New York, September 21, 1803

Originally Johann Christoph Möller, Moller came to America by way of London, where by 1785 he had published a set of string quartets, two of accompanied keyboard sonatas, and a number of "lessons" for young players. He arrived in New York in or before 1790. In that year he gave a harpsichord recital there, then moved to Philadelphia, where he joined Reinagle [994] in running the City Concerts, in which he performed, sometimes together with his young daughter. He also served as organist at Zion Church and became famous for his mastery of Benjamin Franklin's [766] glass harmonica. In 1793 he gave up the concert business to join forces with Reinagle's former partner, Henri Capron, in a business that both published and purveyed music. They also published a musical periodical, *Monthly Numbers,* and ran a music school on the premises. A year later Capron accepted a job as principal of a French boarding school, and in 1796 Moller returned to New York, where he played at Trinity Church and re-entered the concert business, in which he later failed. In America he published various odds and ends of his own composing. RECORDINGS: Organist Janice Beck has recorded a *sinfonia* from the first issue of Moller's magazine.

[990] PALOMINO, José (Pà-lō-mē'-nō, Hō-zā')
VIOLINIST, TEACHER, CHOIRMASTER
BORN: Madrid, 1755
DIED: Las Palmas, April 9, 1810

A pupil of the Spanish operatic pioneer Antonio Rodríguez de Hita (c. 1724–87), Palo-mino was playing violin in the Capilla Real in early adolescence and composed a very successful *tonadilla,* entitled *El Canapé,* when he was only fourteen. In 1774 he moved to Lisbon, joined the musicians' guild, and became a successful teacher and a much-admired performer in the royal orchestra. In 1785 he wrote an opera, *Il Ritorno d'Astrea in terra (Astrea's Return to Earth)* for a Portuguese-Spanish royal wedding (though sung in Italian) that brought him all sorts of goodies in the way of rewards. In 1807, when Napoleon's troops appeared on the horizon, he flew to the Canary Islands, where he spent his last days as choirmaster of the cathedral. He wrote various dramatic intermezzi in both Spanish and Portuguese, and left a piano quintet and a few other miscellaneous works. RECORDINGS: Victoria de Los Angeles has recorded an air from *El Canapé.*

[991] ALBÉNIZ, Mateo Antonio Pérez de (Ál-bā'-nēth, Mà-tā'-ō Án-tōn'-yō Pā'-reth dā)
ORGANIST, TEACHER
BORN: c. 1755
DIED: St. Sebastian, June 23, 1831

Albéniz probably came from a musical family in northwest Spain, for a monk named Pedro Albéniz was his organist at Logroño and St. Sebastian, where Mateo functioned as *maestro de capilla.* St. Sebastian was his base of operations, the Logroño period, 1795–1800, being occasioned by the invasion of French Republican troops. Albéniz was, somewhat unusually for the time and place, a married layman. His son Pedro (1795–1855) studied with Herz [1170] and Kalkbrenner [1118], and became organist of the Capilla Real and a professor at the Madrid Conservatory. Mateo, who wrote an *Instrucción metodica,* was up on the latest in keyboard music and obviously trained him well. RECORDINGS: Mateo was best known in his time for his church music but survives on records through the little Sonata in D Major for Piano (Fernando Valenti, Eugene List, guitarist Julian Bream [a transcription], etc.)

[992] MOZART, Wolfgang Amadeus (Mō'-tsärt, Volf'-gàng Á-mà-dā'-oos)
PIANIST
BORN: Salzburg, January 27, 1756
DIED: Vienna, December 5, 1791

Mozart is perhaps unique among all the great figures of western music. He not only founded no school: he summed none up. His music is archetypally of its time (innumerable lesser composers "sound like Mozart"—superficially). But if his genes were German, his music was not—no more than it was Italian, French, or English; and it was in some degree all of these. From infancy he absorbed musical impulses as most children absorb linguistic ones. "I write as the sows piss," he once said quite characteristically. To be sure, he advanced the vocabulary of his art but in no such imitable way as, say, Schoenberg [1657] or even Monteverdi [333]. If he found the concerto as brick and left it as marble, so to speak, on what form or genre did he not work some similar magic? He was equally comfortable with voices and instruments. Who will say his operas are greater than his symphonies or his Masses greater than his string quartets? His music was recognizably Mozartian from his sixth year (from which the first examples stem) and masterful by the time he attained early adolescence. Yet his only formal instruction was what he got from his father. As a human being, he remains something of an enigma. Peter Shaffer's play *Amadeus* presents him as childish, willful, conceited, testy, and foul-mouthed; it is merely stressing characteristics that were there. More charitable eyes have seen him as a rebel against the system, a prophet of democracy, a champion of human rights, an upholder of the brotherhood of man. Such views are also supportable. But his letters and history suggest that though he was as intelligent as most of us, intellect was not his long suit. Undeniable though his genius was and is, he was never able to find a job that recognized the fact, and ultimately could not support himself and his family.

Mozart, *né* Johannes Chrysostomus Wolfgangus Theophilus (the Greek of the last element gave way to the Latin "Amadeus" for German "Gottlieb"), was the seventh and last child of Leopold [816] and Anna Maria Mozart. Of his siblings, only his sister Anna Maria Walburga, called "Nannerl," had survived. She was five years older and on her way to becoming a fine harpsichordist by the time her brother was three. He seemed even then determined to catch up with her. Soon he was sight-reading at the keyboard and on a pint-sized fiddle, and attempting to write out compositions of his own. Two years later his father noted down the minuet that cataloguer Ludwig Koechel designated K. I. It was not long before Leopold began to suspect that his children were a valuable asset. Early in 1762 he took them on a trial run to Munich to play for the elector; the financial return

confirmed his suspicions. A few months later, it was down the Danube to Vienna, with way stops. The pilgrims stayed for three months (no one has ever satisfactorily explained Archbishop Sigismund's tolerance), during which period they played for, and were feted by, Viennese high society. The children played repeatedly for the imperial family. Wolfgang sat on the lap of the Empress Maria Theresa, ordered the emperor off the piano bench to make room for Wagenseil [804], who would turn his pages, and proposed marriage to his coeval, the future Queen of France. Later he was very ill with what turned out not to be scarlet fever. After a six-months rest in Salzburg, the Mozarts began a grand tour that, moving northwesterly through the Germanies and the Netherlands, brought them to Paris in November 1763. Their reception there was good, if not overwhelming. Louis XV gave them an audience at Versailles, and Wolfgang was impressed by the piano music of Johann Schobert [888], as he had been en route by the orchestral music of the Mannheimers. Hearing that across the English Channel the fields were greener, the Mozarts proceeded to London the following April. Hearsay proved truth, and they remained for more than a year. During that time, young Wolfgang became a pet of the childless Christian Bach [886], who profoundly influenced him. In the summer of 1765 the family moved on to The Hague, where both children were struck down by near-fatal typhus, which cost Leopold a price of fourteen Masses back home and a delay of six months. Recovered, they returned briefly to Paris, then went east through Burgundy, the Franche-Comté, and Switzerland, to reach Salzburg on the last day of November 1766. Less than a year later it was back to Vienna, where, during a sojourn that lasted into 1768, both children survived smallpox.

Wolfgang now stood on the brink of adolescence, and Leopold foresaw that the little dance pieces and monkey tricks of performance (e.g., playing on a cloth-covered keyboard) would soon no longer be salable. To be sure, by then Wolfgang had written several symphonies, some duo sonatas, and even a couple of stage works for student performance. Now, in 1768, Leopold launched Wolfgang on his operatic career with *La Finta semplice (The Feigned Idiot,* after Goldoni), but the promised Viennese production was thwarted by zealous locals. However, that autumn, Dr. Anton Mesmer, a fashionable astrologer who had discovered the therapeutic use of hypnotism ("mesmerism"), gave a private showing of its immediate successor, *Bastien und Bastienne* (a spin-off of Rousseau's [**793**] *Le Devin du village).* The same period also produced the first Masses, which were performed in Vienna.

After almost a year in Salzburg, Leopold and Wolfgang inaugurated a sixteen-month tour of Italy late in 1770. It embraced visits to Venice, Bologna, Milan, Turin, Florence, Rome, and Naples, and encounters of some consequence with G. B. Sammartini [**738**], Padre Martini [**767**], Nardini [**823**] and his protégé Thomas Linley, Jr. [**995**], Paisiello [**914**], Niccolò Jommelli, and Mysliveček [**890**]. There were the usual impressive awards and honors—e.g., a commission for a Milanese opera, membership in the Bolognese Accademia Filarmonica (rules of minimum age were waived), and the Order of the Golden Spur First Class from Pope Clement XIV (which entitled the fourteen-year-old to be called Signor Cavaliere—Sir Wolfgang, so to speak—though he eschewed that honor). On the road Mozart managed to whip up an *opera seria* entitled *Mitridate, Re di Ponto (Mithridates, King of Pontus)* and, foiling the expectable intrigues, saw it onstage at Milan's Ducal Theater in December. Its success was enormous, and Mozart returned in October 1771 for the wedding of the Austrian Archduke Ferdinand and a Modenese princess with the festivities' *pièce de résistance*, the celebratory opera *Ascanio in Alba.* The triumphant Mozarts returned to Salzburg again in December in time to see Archbishop Sigismund breathe his last.

The travels had a purpose over and above the immediate returns: Leopold was looking for a place for his son worthy of his talents and had directed his considerable powers of press-agentry to that end. (It has been suggested that such feats attributed to Wolfgang as his "instant" memorization of the sacrosanct *Allegri Miserere* at St. Peter's in Rome were rigged because, in this instance, clandestine copies were in circulation in Austria.) Much admiration was expressed, but unfortunately there were no offers. Now Leopold had a new employer in Salzburg—Hieronymous Joseph von Paula, Count Colloredo, formerly Prince-Bishop of Gurk, a hard-nosed rationalist and efficiency expert —and things were about to change. Wolfgang welcomed Colloredo with an operatic morality play, *Il Sogno di Scipione (Scipio's Dream),* and was rewarded with a salary of 150 florins to suit the title of *Konzertmeister* (which he had held paylessly for three years). At first the situation seemed relatively unchanged. Father and son returned to Milan in the autumn of 1772 for the premiere of *Lucio Silla (Lucius Sulla),* bought

a house in Salzburg, visited Vienna again in 1773, and late in 1774 went to Munich to produce his opera *La Finta giardiniera (The Fake Gardener-Girl),* which the elector had commissioned. There was an unwontedly long period in Salzburg after that, during which Wolfgang wrote prodigally—*Il Re pastore (The Shepherd King)* for the visit of Archduke Max Franz (later of Cologne and Bonn), symphonies up through No. 29, concerti, Masses, and a great deal of background music for Colloredo's social occasions. But his future still offered nothing more than drudgery in a backwater. In 1777 Leopold applied for leave for himself and Wolfgang to conduct another tour—and was turned down flat. Wolfgang, who disliked the archbishop intensely, offered his resignation. Colloredo countered by demanding Leopold's as well. Leopold groveled a bit and managed to stay on, but Wolfgang was now bent on seeking his fortune. Even though he had reached his maturity, his mother went along as chaperone. In Munich the elector regretted that there were no openings. In Augsburg, the paternal home, Wolfgang began a flirtation with his cousin Thekla (called *die Bäsle*—"little cousin"), who seems to have relished the outrageously scatological letters he wrote her. In Mannheim he fell in love with the orchestra and a fifteen-year-old soprano, Aloysia Weber, one of the four daughters of an impecunious copyist. Accordingly he wasted time, resources, and his mother's patience waiting to be asked to stay on. Finally, in the spring of 1778, his parents persuaded him to go on to Paris, where surely he would find his chance. But Paris turned out to be a bitter disappointment. Though Mozart managed to find some pupils and to have a new symphony (No. 31, "Paris") played at the Concert Spirituel, he produced no stir. Moreover both he and his mother found they liked neither the city nor its people. Late in June Anna Maria came down with a fever. On July 3 she was dead. Wolfgang, unable to handle the fact, wrote his father only that she was ill, but Leopold somehow sensed what had happened and was ready for the news when friends brought it to him.

Later that summer Colloredo's court organist died, and Leopold, seeing nothing else for him to do, won the job for his son. Wolfgang dawdled his way home, stopping again in Mannheim, where Aloysia gave him the cold shoulder, and Munich, and not reaching Salzburg until mid-January 1779. His new post was, as they say, a living but not much to his taste, especially since Colloredo looked on his musicians as mere servants. But he could not refuse this particular one permission in 1780 to return to Munich to produce a new opera for the new elector (late of Mannheim). The work was *Idomeneo*, now regarded as Mozart's first masterpiece in the genre—and one of the last of his *opera seria*. But when he overstayed his leave by several months, Colloredo peremptorily ordered him to join his entourage in Vienna forthwith. Finding his freedom there severely circumscribed, Mozart, when he felt the occasion warranted it, simply ignored the strictures. When on May 9, 1781, he told his employer he had no intention of returning to Salzburg at that time, he was dismissed. The now-widowed Frau Weber had meanwhile moved with her three daughters to Vienna (Aloysia having married Joseph Lange, a painter who left an unfinished portrait of his sometime rival), and Mozart took lodging with her. A month later he went to the archbishop's to demand that Colloredo accept his resignation in writing. In demanding to see him, Mozart got so testy with a court official, Count Arco, that the latter literally kicked him into the street, thereby terminating his history as a meaningfully salaried employee.

For a time Mozart lived on his connections and his reputation. Unable to resist women in close proximity, he made eyes at Constanze Weber, giving her ambitious mother grounds to engineer a shotgun engagement toward the end of 1781, around the time of the court round of dueling keyboards with Clementi [977]. The following summer, the emperor's ephemeral German theater produced his first completed German-language opera, *Die Entführung aus dem Serail (The Flight from the Harem).* Other commissions came in (notably one for a serenade for the Haffner family to celebrate a wedding in Salzburg); he was concertizing frequently; he had many pupils: to him, the future looked rosy. Meanwhile Frau Weber's nagging had driven both Wolfgang and Constanze out of the house, and on August 4, 1782, without the consent of either parent, they were hastily married at St. Stephen's. Mozart wrote his *Mass* (in C minor)—or part of one—to be played in celebration of the event when they visited Leopold in Salzburg. But the journey had to await the birth of their first son the following June. When it was over, they came back by Linz, where Mozart produced the symphony (No. 36) known by that name. When they reached Vienna, they found that the child, left with a nurse, had died. They were to lose four more (out of six) in the time left them. They were a compatible pair but childlike and impractical. Constanze was a

poor housekeeper, and Wolfgang spent money as fast as he got it. For a time, things seemed hopeful, however. Pupils continued to come. In 1785 Mozart impulsively took little Hummel [1091] into his home. In 1787 he auditioned Beethoven [1063] and possibly gave him a few lessons. But he was headed for the economic skids and virtual pauperdom. Meanwhile, his music was becoming deeper, more subjective, and more daring—all of which may have contributed to his waning popularity. ("Too many notes!" chided Emperor Joseph after *Entführung.)*

Late in 1784 Mozart became a Freemason —as much from conviction as from fashion —with considerable effect on his music. Joseph Haydn [871] became a lodge brother, and they sometimes met to play together, with the likes of Dittersdorf [906] and Vanhal [903], making one wish that Edison had been born a century sooner. That same year Karl Thomas Mozart was born (he was later a civil servant), and his Aunt Nannerl married the Count of Sonnenberg (she outlived her brother by thirty-eight years). Leopold visited his son in the new year and left satisfied that he was on his way at last. About the same time the set of great quartets dedicated to Haydn appeared. But Wolfgang still yearned to be a successful operatic composer—though he had junked his most recent attempts almost as soon as they were begun. Though in fact they had met earlier, fate now threw Lorenzo da Ponte in his path. The Abbé da Ponte was an operator—a converted Venetian Jew, a friend and would-be imitator of Casanova, who had conned the emperor into appointing him court poet (i.e., librettist), though he had never written a libretto in his life. But that did not bother da Ponte, who *was* blessed with talent as well as gall. In 1785 he and Mozart embarked on a version of Caron de Beaumarchais' inflammatory comedy *Les Noces de Figaro (The Marriage of Figaro).* It was da Ponte who persuaded the emperor that the opera would be fangless—and indeed he removed the more overt attacks on the *ancien régime*. After the usual vicissitudes, *Le Nozze di Figaro* opened at the Burgtheater on Mayday, 1786. It proved to be revolutionary in more ways than one— notably in its use of credible flesh-and-blood characters—but the audience loved it. (In the cast were Nancy Storace, sister of Mozart's Anglo-Italian pupil Stephen [1025], and his Irish billiards partner Michael Kelly [1028].) Politics, however, closed it after nine performances. Early in 1787, however, Mozart was invited to repeat it in Prague (then itself in a revolutionary ferment). He became an overnight hero there and was commissioned thereupon to give Prague another opera. Before he could begin it, his father died (on May 28, 1787).

When the collaborators got down to business, da Ponte suggested the Don Juan legend—perhaps inspired as much by a recent treatment by Giovanni Bertati (from which he cribbed liberally) as by his own interests. What would be one of the greatest—and most enigmatic—works ever written for the stage was, typically, put together in a few months. It premiered on October 29 and made sufficient splash for the emperor to ask to see it the following year. But the first Vienna performance was chaotic, and the work was soon dropped. Meanwhile, Mozart had at last got a court appointment, though it was not exactly what he had had in mind: he was named imperial *Kammerkomponist* at 800 florins a year—his job was to write dances for court balls. From here on, it was all downhill. His concerts failed to draw, and he gave them up. Forced to borrow money to pay his rent, he moved his family to smaller, cheaper suburban quarters. Constanze's health broke down, and she had to go to Baden several times for rehabilitation. Mozart was reduced to producing whatever might sell—minuets, contradanses, updated orchestrations of Handel for Count von Swieten (who fancied oratorios and wrote the libretto for Joseph Haydn's *Creation*). In 1789 a former pupil, Prince Lichnowsky, invited Mozart to accompany him to the court of Frederick William II in Berlin. They stopped by Dresden where Mozart appeared at the Saxon court and played the Thomaskirche organ (Swieten had taught him to admire J. S. Bach [684]). The Prussian king offered to make him his *Kapellmeister*. Inexplicably, Mozart turned him down (some say out of patriotism) and returned to further misery in Vienna. There he and da Ponte set to work on an "original" comedy, *Così fan tutte (All Women Do It)*, said to have been based on a local scandal that had amused the emperor. It opened with fair success early in 1790, but a month later Joseph II died and the theaters were all closed in mourning. Mozart pawned the silverware and went, uninvited, to the coronation of Leopold II in Frankfurt, hoping that somehow it would pay off. The gesture merely left him deeper in the hole, though he and Constanze and Karl had moved again to still more spartan quarters in the city.

By 1791 Mozart was busier and more desperate than ever. He was working on both a German fairytale opera for Emanuel Schikaneder, who ran a comedy troupe, and

the Metastasian *La Clemenza di Tito (Titus' Mercy)* for the Prague coronation of Leopold as King of Bohemia. A mysterious stranger had also commissioned a *Requiem*. The stranger was, in actuality, the mayor's son, acting for a Count Walsegg who liked to palm off his commissions as his own work; but Mozart, weary and ailing, saw the hand of God in the matter. *Tito*, though admired by the *cognoscenti*, was a loser from its premiere early in September. *Zauberflöte (The Magic Flute)* got off to a slow start later that month but was soon playing to s.r.o. audiences (as the first great German opera should have). Even Salieri [966] was enthusiastic. But Mozart was now a very sick man. Late in November he took to his bed but continued to work at the *Requiem*. On the night of December 4, he rolled over on his side and went to sleep. He never woke again. He was not yet thirty-five. Constanze, with a mountain of debts and two sons to support (Franz Xaver Wolfgang [1141] had arrived in July), had to settle for a pauper's funeral. A small handful of mourners, including Salieri and Swieten, attended the service. The day was cloudy and unusually mild, and the story of their being kept from the cemetery by a violent storm is romantic legend. No one knows where the body was laid—or what Mozart died of. Chronic hypertension seems indicated, but the old story that Salieri did his rival in does not bear up. Contanze later remarried and profited rather well from the manuscripts. Franz Xaver took to calling himself "Wolfgang, Jr.," and became a moderately successful composer.

RECORDINGS: Save for some juvenilia, fragments, and doubtful pieces, every scrap of Mozart's music seems to have been recorded, most of it many times over, and even sketchy listings would be impossible here.

[993] VOGEL, Johann Christoph (Fō'-gel, Yō'-hán Krēs'-tōf)
HORNIST
BORN: Nuremberg, c. March 18, 1756
DIED: Paris, June 28, 1788

The scion of a family of violin makers, Vogel studied in Regensburg with Joseph Riepel, *Kapellmeister* to the Prince of Thurn and Taxis. At twenty Vogel emigrated to Paris, where he played horn in private orchestras. Hearing Gluck's [803] revolutionary operas, he was inspired to write one of his own, *Le Toison d'or (The Golden Fleece*—on the Medea theme). He dedicated it to his idol, who found it good, causing

Vogel to go around telling everyone that Gluck was his only teacher. However, it took some years for the piece to get a performance, at which the public was less impressed than the dedicatee had been. Nevertheless Vogel was encouraged to write *Démophon,* but not sufficiently to finish it before Cherubini [1019] had presented his own treatment of the subject. We are told that his "irregular habits" (a phrase that usually refers to someone who drank) slowed him down, but they did not prevent him from turning out a respectable number of symphonies, concerti, and chamber pieces, which often make interesting use of the winds. At any rate, by the time *Démophon* was premiered (successfully), Vogel had been dead more than a year. A grandson, Charles-Louis-Adolphe (1808–92) wrote operas and operettas. RECORDINGS: The Consortium Classicum has recorded quartet for clarinet and strings by Vogel. Jaap Schroeder and Concerto Amsterdam have recorded a *Symphonie Concertante* in B-flat major for six winds and strings.

[994] REINAGLE, Alexander (Rī'-nȧ-gəl,
   Al-eg-zan'-der)
PIANIST, IMPRESARIO
BORN: Portsmouth (England), c. April
   23, 1756
DIED: Baltimore, September 21, 1809

In Philadelphia, where his career chiefly unfolded, Alexander Reinagle was regarded as a gentleman, a classification in which musicians were usually not included. He was probably the first fine pianist this country ever heard, and he, by his imposing presence, brought class to the music hall and the theater. His father was an Austrian trumpet player who had emigrated to England. The family moved to Edinburgh sometime after 1770, and there Alexander (it is assumed) studied music with Raynor Taylor, later director of the orchestra at Sadler's Wells in London, and after that a colleague of his former pupil in America. As a pianist and sometime violinist, Reinagle went to London with his brother Hugh, who was a cellist. In London he was strongly influenced by Christian Bach [886]. In 1784 the brothers went to concertize in Lisbon—successfully but tragically, for Hugh, already ill with tuberculosis, died there. Alexander, it would appear, continued to tour for a time, apparently going as far as Hamburg, where he struck up a friendship with Emanuel Bach [801]. A year after he returned to England, he suddenly took ship for America,

landing in New York in mid-1786. He made an unsuccessful stab at a concert career there and moved to Philadelphia.

There concert life was in abeyance, owing to a hassle between the three chief entrepreneurs. In September Reinagle participated in a benefit for one of them, Henri Capron, a French emigré. After a successful concert of his own, Reinagle effected an understanding between Capron and William Brown, the interloper who had caused the original trouble. The third impresario, John Bentley, went off to New York, and the other three joined forces with Alexander Juhan, a pianist-composer-conductor of rather misty origins, to resume the City Concerts. In 1787, in a benefit for Juhan, he and Reinagle played a four-hand sonata by Haydn [871], said to have been the first piano duet played publicly in this country. The audience included George Washington, who became a loyal fan of Reinagle, and in turn Reinagle dedicated some of his music to him. Shortly afterward, Reinagle became associated with the "clandestine" Old American Theater Company (Philadelphia had a not very strictly enforced prohibition against theaters) and in 1788 went with it for performances in New York, where he and Capron injected new impetus into the flagging concert life there. Meanwhile Philadelphia got rid of its puritanical statute, and Reinagle and the Old American Company returned to step into the daylight at the Southwark Theater. With various partners, he also continued to run his concert series there. In 1791, together with a former colleague in the acting company, Thomas Wignell, Reinagle set about building a new theater on Chestnut Street. Though the opening was delayed by a fierce epidemic of yellow fever in 1793, the venture soon proved so successful that the Old American Company decamped in 1794, leaving the field to the New Company. In 1894 Reinagle also opened a theater in Baltimore, and nine years later settled there and married Anna Duport, daughter of Pierre Landrin Duport [970].

Reinagle turned out at least 30 comic operas and other stage pieces, but these, together with some of his other music, went up in flames with the New Theater in 1820. What survives are some songs, piano pieces, and four sonatas, said to be the first pieces written for piano in the United States, and perhaps the first American sonatas of any kind.

RECORDINGS: Three of the piano sonatas have been recorded by Jack Winerock, and one of those by Eugene List.

[995] LINLEY, Thomas, Jr.
VIOLINIST
BORN: Bath, May 5, 1756
DIED: Grimsthorpe, August 5, 1778

Thomas Linley, Sr., (1733–95), composer, conductor, teacher, and impresario, was a man singularly blessed: of the twelve children born to him and his wife, the former Mary Johnson, eight became successful musicians. None had more promise, however, than his namesake, a wonder child like his close contemporary, the poet Thomas Chatterton (1752–70). (For composers 1756 was an ill-starred year: of those born in it, Linley, Mozart [992], Vogel [993], and Kraus [998] did not live to see forty.) Young Linley was already playing violin concerti at seven when he began study with his father's old teacher William Boyce [787], and made his operatic debut in London at eleven. At twelve he was sent to Florence to study with Nardini [823], and made friends there with the visiting Mozart. From 1773 until his death he played first violin at the Drury Lane Theatre, which was managed by his father and John Stanley [796]. In 1775 he and his father collaborated on the music for *The Duenna* by his brother-in-law, Richard Brinsley Sheridan. (In a celebrated scandal, Sheridan had eloped with Elizabeth Linley (1754–92), a brilliant singer, to France. He was later the senior Linley's partner at the theater.) Young Thomas also wrote other stage music, choral works, at least 20 violin concerti, and some sonatas. In the summer of 1778 he went vacationing with his family to the Lincolnshire estate of the Duke of Ancaster. While he was boating, his boat capsized, and he drowned. Tragically, almost all of his important music has vanished. RECORDINGS: April Cantelo has recorded a song from his incidental music for Shakespeare's *The Tempest.*

[996] ŻYWNY, Wojciech (Zhiv'-ni, Voi'-chekh)
PIANIST, TEACHER
BORN: Bohemia, May 13, 1756
DIED: Warsaw, February 21, 1842

Żywny is known by the Polish form of his name, though in his birthplace he was called Vojtěch or Adalbert Živný. There he studied with Kuchař [974]. At some point he was taken to Poland by Prince Kazimierz Sapieha as his court pianist. After three years, perhaps as a consequence of the political upheavals of the day, he went to Warsaw and set up as a piano teacher. In that capacity, the Chopin family, who lived

in his neighborhood, employed him in 1816 to teach their young Frédéric [1208]. Żywny was a kindly and self-deprecating man. He affected a reddish yellow wig, kneeboots, and green waistcoats—made, he claimed, from the trousers of the late King Stanisław August Poniatowski—and was addicted to snuff and vodka. He became a fixture in the Chopin household, until 1822, when he announced that he had nothing more to offer his pupil. Among the things he had offered him was an introduction to the music of J. S. Bach [684], which Żywny worshiped. Chopin was very fond of the old man and, when Żywny died, thought seriously of trying to get back to Warsaw from Paris as a sort of tribute. RECORDINGS: Virtually all of Żywny's music has disappeared, but pianist Lidia Kozubek has turned up a folksy little polonaise to record.

[997] HÜLLMANDEL, Nicolas Joseph (Hüll'-mån-del, Nē-kō-làs' Zhō-sef')
PIANIST, THEORIST, TEACHER
BORN: Strasbourg, May 23, 1756
DIED: London, December 19, 1823

Hüllmandel, like his fellow Strasbourgian Edelmann [959], was a pianistic pioneer in Paris, and, again like Edelmann's, his career was radically affected by the Revolution. His father and a maternal uncle were violinists, and he received musical training as a choirboy at Strasbourg Cathedral. At fourteen he played under the direction of Christian Bach [886] in London, but it is highly unlikely that—as legend has it—he was ever a pupil of Emanuel Bach [801]. Subsequently he traveled for a time, spending at least six months in Milan, then settled in Paris in 1776. He was taken up by the Beautiful People, who were particularly enchanted by his performances on the glass harmonica. In 1778 the visiting Mozart [992] gave his father a favorable report of Hüllmandel's (and Edelmann's) pianistic prowess. Among Hüllmandel's pupils one counts Auber [1103], Onslow [1115], and Hyacinthe Jadin [1058]. In 1787 he married the wealthy Camille Aurore Ducazan, niece of the receiver-general. When the Revolution began to loom two years later, the couple fled to London, where their son Charles Joseph (1789–1850), one of the pioneers of lithography, was born. (A daughter Evalina became a piano teacher and composer.) Hüllmandel continued to teach in England but abandoned composition entirely. His entire output consists of music (mostly sonatas) for piano, much of it with optional violin. Hüllmandel also published a *Princi-*

ples of Music, and wrote the *"clavecin"* article for Diderot's Encyclopedia. RECORDINGS: The Mannheim Duo has recorded one of Hüllmandel's sonatas.

[998] KRAUS, Joseph Martin (Krous, Yō'-zef Mär-tin')
MUSIC DIRECTOR, WRITER
BORN: Miltenberg am Main, June 20, 1756
DIED: Stockholm, December 15, 1792

Kraus is sometimes called the Swedish Mozart—not because he was particularly Mozartian or ethnically Scandinavian, but because he was an almost exact contemporary of that short-lived genius [992]. He came, in fact, from a small town between Heidelberg and Würzburg, and graduated in law from the University of Göttingen in 1778. Among his music teachers he numbered Abt Vogler [960] in Mannheim. When he went to Hamburg after graduation to meet Emanuel Bach [801], a fellow student from Sweden, Carl Stridsberg, persuaded him to come to Stockholm where, under Gustavus III, things were looking up for artists. He found employment conducting at a Stockholm theater, where he was promoted to music director three years later. After he had produced his opera *Proserpina* in 1781 to a libretto conceived by the king himself, Gustavus took him under his wing, and paid his way for five years of musical study in Europe. In the first year, 1782, Kraus visited Rome, Florence, Paris, and London. In 1783 he was in Vienna, where both Gluck [803] and Haydn [871] certified him as a genius. In 1785 he returned to London for the Handel [683] centenary celebrations. In 1787 he returned to Stockholm where, on Uttini's [831] retirement the following year, he became court music director and the focus of musical activity in the capital. His masterpiece was the opera *Aeneas in Carthage,* the plot again outlined by the king, whose assassination eight years earlier prevented his attending the 1799 premiere. Kraus did not live to see it either, having died of tuberculosis only nine months after his monarch died. He survived long enough, however, to write a splendid funeral cantata in Gustavus's memory. Besides operas and other stage works, Kraus left sacred music, various cantatas (some occasional), symphonies, a violin concerto, quartets, and smaller works. RECORDINGS: The funeral cantata has been recorded by Newell Jenkins, the *Trauersymphonie* (extravagantly praised by Haydn) by Jenkins and Gabor Ötvos, the overture to Kellgren's play *Olympia* by Richard Bonynge, and a violin sonata by the Mannheim Duo.

[999] ÅHLSTRÖM, Olof (Ōl'-ström, OO'-lôf)
ORGANIST, TEACHER, EDITOR, PUBLISHER
BORN: Aletorp, August 14, 1756
DIED: Stockholm, August 11, 1835

A particularly successful songwriter, Åhlström was an important force in the growth of Swedish music in the early nineteenth century. A native of east-central Sweden, he studied with a local organist as a child and at sixteen was admitted to the Academy of Music in Stockholm, where he studied with its founder and director, the younger Ferdinand Zellbell. At twenty-one he entered the civil service and also became organist at the church of St. Mary. For the next forty-seven years, he pursued both his official and his musical careers with considerable success. He worked his way up through the ranks in the Treasury, then transferred to the War Office, where he became an important figure. Meanwhile he had been appointed music teacher to the Crown Prince in 1786 and three years later succeeded the pioneering J. Ödberg as Sweden's foremost (and only) music publisher. That year he inaugurated a musical journal, *Musikalikst tidsfördrif,* which he kept up until he was seventy-eight. He also published Swedish folksongs and dances, works by Carl Michael Bellman [911], and music by Swedish composers, including his own. In 1792 he became organist of the church of St. James and was made a member of the Academy. From 1803 to 1805 he directed its educational program. He retired from the War Office in 1824 but continued most of his other activities to the end of his long life, dying three days before his eighty-second birthday. Besides his songs, many of which remain popular, he wrote a good deal of piano and chamber music. His larger works, including 2 operas and some incidental music, did not succeed. He also popularized, by means of piano and vocal transcriptions, works by such masters as Haydn [871] and Mozart [992]. RECORDINGS: Elisabeth Söderström has recorded some of his songs, Stig Ribbing some of his keyboard music.

[1000] BRÉVAL, Jean-Baptiste Sébastien (Brā-vàl', Zhàn Bà-tēst' Sā-bás'-tyan)
CELLIST, TEACHER
BORN: Paris, November 6, 1756
DIED: Colligis, March 18, 1823

Not much is known of Bréval's youth, except that he was probably a pupil of Jean-Baptiste Cupis, violinist, champion horseman, and peach farmer. By the time he was twenty-one, he was already himself established as a cello teacher. He first appeared as soloist at the Concert Spirituel in 1778 and later played in its orchestra (1781–91), and subsequently in those of the Théâtre Feydeau (1791–1800) and the Opéra (to c. 1814). Apart from a single opera, *Inès et Léonore*, his compositions consist of concerti, *symphonie concertante*, chamber music, and songs—the instrumental pieces almost all involving violin and/or cello. He also wrote a cello method. RECORDINGS: Samuel Mayes has recorded a cello sonata.

[1001] ROLLA, Alessandro (Rōl'-là, Á-les-sàn'-drō)
VIOLINIST, VIOLIST, TEACHER, CONDUCTOR
BORN: Pavia, April 6, 1757
DIED: Milan, September 15, 1841

Rolla is said to have begun as a keyboard student and then to have switched to violin. Aspects of his career have been confused with those of another violinist, Giacomo Conti, with whom he is supposed to have studied. When he was twenty-five, Rolla joined the court orchestra at Parma as first viola. The story has been persistently repeated that the young Paganini [1106] came to him for lessons and that Rolla either taught him or told him that there was nothing left to teach him; it apparently has no basis in fact. However, like Paganini, he was very fond of the viola and helped establish it as a solo instrument. In 1792, nevertheless, he took over the first desk in the violin section. Later he was appointed conductor. His son and pupil Antonio was born in Parma in 1798 and later became *konzertmeister* of the Dresden Royal Opera. In 1803 the senior Rolla moved to Milan to become violinist-conductor at La Scala, and a few years later, under the patronage of Eugène de Beauharnais, Napoleon's stepson and viceroy, he was appointed professor of violin at the Milan Conservatory. Among his many pupils were Luigi Arditi [1283], conductor and composer of the once-popular waltz song *"Il Bacio,"* and Cesare Pugni [1168], indefatigable composer of pieces for the Imperial Russian Ballet. Rolla himself wrote ballets, though they have vanished. He played at La Scala until 1833 and was one of the rare instrumentalists to give solo performances there. He left the conservatory two

years later. In published form and in manuscript, he left a number of attractive, if conservative, symphonies, concerti, and chamber works, as well as a good deal of teaching material. RECORDINGS: Salvatore Accardo and L. A. Bianchi have recorded a pair of violin-viola duos; Susanne Lautenbacher performs the Concerto in A Major for Violin, with Jörg Faerber conducting.

[1002] DIETER, Christian Ludwig (Dē'-ter, Krēst'-yàn Lōōt'-vikh)
VIOLINIST
BORN: Ludwigsburg, June 13, 1757
DIED: Stuttgart, May 15, 1822

Dieter's career provides a warning that patronage may not always be desirable. He was born in the village surrounding the favorite stronghold of the Dukes of Württemberg. To properly train his courtiers, Duke Karl Eugen had inaugurated nearby (in a place rather forbiddingly known as "Solitude") a school that copied the strictest Prussian military models. (It was later moved to Stuttgart.) When Dieter was orphaned at thirteen, the duke offered him a free education there—as a painter!—if he would swear to devote the rest of his life to his service. It was soon agreed, however, that Dieter's talent and interests lay in music and he was trained by various members of the *Kapelle*. In 1779 he delighted his patron with the first of his several *Singspiele*, entitled *Der Schulz im Dorf (The Village Mayor)*. But confinement was getting to him, and a year later (as Friedrich Schiller in similar circumstances was to do) he headed for the hills. The ducal military apprehended him forthwith and jailed him as a deserter. The duke, after letting him fidget for a few months, made him promise to adhere to his oath and appointed him his first violinist. Dieter was as good as his word and remained at the court for the rest of his life, overworked and underpaid, and trying to support an increasingly large family that peaked at eleven. His chief historical importance is as one of the promoters of German-language operas. Among his *Singspiele*, his *Belmont und Konstanze, oder Die Entführung aus dem Serail*, based on the text used by Mozart [992] in his like-named work, was so popular that it precluded a performance of the Mozart piece in Württemberg for many years. Kotzebue's libretto to Dieter's final *Singspiel*, entitled *Des Teufels Lustschloss (The Devil's Pleasure Castle)* was later set by Franz Schubert [1153]. Dieter also produced an Italian opera, *Le Feste della Tessaglia (The Thessalian*

Celebrations) in collaboration with three other composers. He retired five years before he died. He also wrote unassuming church music and instrumental works. RE-CORDINGS: On records he is represented by his *Concerto Concertante* in D Major for two flutes, played by Jean-Pierre Rampal and Ransom Wilson.

[1003] PLEYEL, Ignaz Joseph (Plī-yel, Ĕg'-nätz Yō'-zef)

PIANIST, CONDUCTOR, ENTREPRENEUR
BORN: Ruppersthal, June 18, 1757
DIED: Paris, November 14, 1831

Ignaz (or Ignace, as he later spelled it) Pleyel was, in his day, both immensely popular and immensely productive. The productivity was, in fact, somewhat inflated by the appearance of certain works, or parts thereof, in alternative forms—not always made by the composer or with his sanction. Mozart [992] thought that Pleyel might one day become a new Haydn [871]. So did Pleyel, apparently, which perhaps explains his relative lack of originality. The twenty-fourth child of a village schoolmaster in Lower Austria (found in the upper part of the map), he supposedly studied with Vanhal [903] in Vienna, where, at fifteen, he attracted the attention of Count Erdödy, a relative of the Esterházys, who sent him to Haydn for training. He lived with Haydn for several years and became the most famous of his pupils, if one excludes Beethoven [1063], who hardly belongs in that category. Pleyel's apprenticeship completed, his patron took him on as his *Kapellmeister.* But by the 1780s Pleyel was in Italy and seems to have returned to Austria only briefly in 1781. In 1783 he went to Strasbourg as assistant choirmaster to Richter [777] at the cathedral. It was during the Strasbourg years that he wrote the most and best of his works, which eventually included 40 symphonies, 6 *symphonie concertante,* 9 concerti, 17 quintets, 89 quartets, 65 trios, 62 duos, 2 operas, 2 Masses, a *Requiem,* and much miscellaneous material. When Richter died in 1789, Pleyel succeeded him.

Meanwhile the Revolution (of which Strasbourg was one of the hot spots) had erupted and meanwhile the promoter Salomon had brought Haydn to London for his concert series. Salomon's chief rivals, the Professional Concerts, strove mightily to win Haydn away. Having failed, they invited Pleyel—almost certainly without letting him know their motive—to conduct a series for them. When he had signed the contract, the promoters noised it about that

Haydn was now senile and that better things could be expected from his favorite pupil. The two composers, however, maintained friendly relations, although there was a certain tenseness in the situation. Pleyel promised a "new" work every concert; Haydn, with no virgin stock to draw on, sat up late writing the "London" symphonies. While Pleyel was on British soil, he was approached by that great Scots opportunist George Thomson about making some folk-song settings for him. Pleyel at least partly completed the project, and Thomson paid him a sum of money; both later complained that they had been had, but they maintained cordial relations.

In May 1792, Pleyel returned to Alsace and bought a château in the environs of Strasbourg. Just what happened next is not clear. Since the cathedral was closed, he had no function there. There has long been a story that he was arrested and jailed for a time as an enemy of the Noble Cause. But there is no record of it, and he turned out several of the revolutionary effusions expected of a loyal composer, including a mammoth forerunner of Tchaikovsky's *1812 Overture,* performed in the former cathedral, replete with cannons and bells. A couple of years later he moved to Paris, where he became a very successful publisher of, and dealer in, music. Among his important publications was a complete edition of Haydn's string quartets, containing the first known miniature scores. In 1800, the Opéra proposed a series of Haydn concerts such as London had had in the previous decade and sent Pleyel off to Vienna to deliver the official invitation. But the Viennese, certain he was spying for Napoleon, refused him admission to the city. He returned, however, in 1805 to visit the old man and was distressed to find him so feeble.

In 1807 Pleyel opened the piano-and-harp factory that continued in operation for 154 years; the German-born Jean-Henri Pape, who designed many improvements for pianos, helped him get the firm into operation. When he left to set up his own company in 1815, Pleyel took his son Camille (1788–1855) into partnership. (The elder Pleyel had four children by the former Gabrielle Lefevre, whom he married in 1788. Camille was a pianist who wrote fashionable potpourris, etc., for the instrument. He married the pianist Marie Moke, Berlioz's [1175] beloved, while Berlioz was in Rome. Berlioz, in female attire, left Rome posthaste to do them both in, but fortunately the project collapsed en route. The happy couple separated after four years.) Two years before his death, Pleyel also took

Kalkbrenner **[1118]** into the firm. Once the factory got into production, Pleyel pretty much gave up composing, which was probably just as well, since he had apparently run out of anything new to say.

There has been some confusion over the authorship of certain pieces attributed to Haydn and Pleyel respectively. One yarn tells how Haydn allegedly quieted an importunate publisher with some Pleyel quartets submitted as his own, and how, when the unwitting Pleyel published them elsewhere, he was accused of plagiarism. We know that Haydn did not write the so-called "St. Anthony" wind divertimento from which Brahms took the theme of his *Variations on a Theme of Haydn;* it is now fairly certain that Pleyel, long thought to be its real author, was not.

Pleyel's music, particularly the earlier stuff, is unfailingly pleasant, if not profound. There is a *Symphonie périodique* recorded by Roger Delage, *symphonie concertante* by Louis de Froment and Daniel Barenboim, a clarinet concerto conducted by Paul Angerer, three wind sextets by the Consortium Classicum, a wind sextet and a serenade by the Strasbourg Philharmonic Wind Octet, four flute trios by the Northwest German Chamber Trio, and various other chamber works.

[1004] READ, Daniel
SINGING TEACHER, MANUFACTURER, PUBLISHER, ETC.
BORN: Attleboro, Mass., November 16, 1757
DIED: New Haven, December 4, 1836

Daniel Read is an early example of the American self-made man. He began as a farmhand, worked as a mechanic and surveyor, fought as a private in the revolutionary forces, and wrote hymns on the side. After a period in New Stratford, he settled in New Haven around 1780. He ran a singing school there for about a year and fell in love with a young woman called Jerusha Sherman, whose father opposed the match because Read could not support her in the manner to which Mr. Sherman wanted her accustomed. With one Amos Doolittle as partner, Read went into the book business and later became a successful producer of ivory combs. True love prevailed in proper fashion, and he and Jerusha embarked on a marriage that produced four little Reads, one of them baptized George Frederick Handel. In 1785 Daniel published his *American Singing Book,* whose entire contents he had composed by hand and which went

through five editions in the next decade. The next year he inaugurated the first known American musical journal, *The American Musical Magazine,* which survived for twelve issues. Other publications were the Socratic manual *An Introduction to Psalmody* and the collection *The Columbian Harmonist,* its three sections devoted to newly composed hymn tunes, established hymn tunes, and anthems. Read did not live to finish *Musica Ecclesia.* He largely gave up composing after forty, though some late compositions appear in *The New Haven Collection of Sacred Music* of 1818. By then he had gotten self-conscious about his rough-and-ready style and was endeavoring to imitate the best imported models. In the pristine state, however, he was a real original in the mold of Billings **[946]**. By the end of his life he was a stockholder in a banking firm and a director of the New Haven Library. Many of his tunes, such as "Newport" and "Sherburne," became a standard part of American hymnody and appear in recorded anthologies of such.

[1005] WESLEY, Charles, Jr.
ORGANIST
BORN: Bristol, December 11, 1757
DIED: London, May 23, 1834

The elder son of the Reverend Charles Wesley (and the nephew of the Reverend John Wesley who founded Methodism) appears to present a classic case of the child prodigy who burned himself out. He was picking out tunes on the harpsichord ("in just time") before he was three, and, not much later, tied into his chair to prevent his tumbling out, he was harmonizing them. The Reverend Charles, sensing a miracle, had him play for everyone he could think of. He found the situation perplexing, however, for, like his brother, he thought music frivolous. Yet he let the boy study with Joseph Kelway, organist at St. Martin-in-the-Fields, and Joseph Worgan of Vauxhall Gardens ("Hear Worgan at the organ."). But he would not countenance his singing in the Chapel Royal (Anglican, you know), though it appears that had a patron put himself forward, Wesley might have smiled on him. The boy received advice and encouragement from William Boyce **[787]**—and, surprisingly, a set of the latter's *Cathedral Music* from Uncle John. Charles Wesley even let young Charles and his brother Samuel **[1045]** appear in public in duo concerts, arguing, in effect, that it kept them off the streets. Wesley, Jr., wrote a set of jejune string quartets at around twenty and continued to compose sporadically until he was sixty or so—anthems, keyboard pieces, and songs, but also 6 keyboard concerti and a cantata *Caractacus.* Anglican church posts were closed to him, though he found work in nonconformist chapels. Always indolent, he became increasingly withdrawn as he grew older, and, according to report, turned into something of a slob, appearing with his waistcoat buttoned crooked, his wig at an angle, and his shoelaces untied. His condition would probably now be diagnosed as clinical depression. RECORDINGS: Examples of his organ music appear in recorded anthologies (e.g., a voluntary played by Franz Haselböck).

[1006] BLASIUS, Matthieu Frédéric
(Blàz'-yōōs, Màt-yö' Frä-dä-rēk')
VIOLINIST, WIND PLAYER, CONDUCTOR, TEACHER
BORN: Lauterbourg, April 24, 1758
DIED: Versailles, 1829

A member of a musical family from an Alsatian town just across the Rhine from Karlsruhe, Blasius first made his career as a violinist, though he was also a brilliant wind player (flute, clarinet, bassoon). He was concertmaster and then conductor at the Comédie-Italienne from 1788. In that year he produced there the first of his 3 *opéras-comiques*, entitled *La Paysanne supposée (The Presumed Peasant Girl).* During the Revolution he wrote the required patriotic and propagandistic stuff, including the opera *Le Pelletier de Saint-Fargeau (The Furrier of St. Fargeau,* a piece about a Republican hero) and much band music. He also participated in that curious communal stage piece *Le Congrès des rois (The Kings' Congress)* with Grétry [919], and others. In 1795 he became the first professor of winds at the Conservatoire, and in 1799 director of the Garde Consulaire band. When the Comédie-Italienne merged with the Théâtre Feydeau in 1801 as the Opéra-Comique, Blasius was its chief conductor until he retired to Versailles in 1816. His two elder brothers, Pierre, a violinist, and Ignace, a bassoonist, also taught at the Conservatoire. Matthieu Blasius wrote a clarinet method, a *symphonie concertante,* several concerti, about 20 string quartets, much other chamber music, and several collections for band. RECORDINGS: Desiré Dondeyne has recorded a suite from one of these, the *Harmonie militaire.*

[1007] SWAN, Timothy
FLUTIST
BORN: Worcester, Mass., July 23, 1758
DIED: Northfield, Mass., July 23, 1842

Timothy Swan began his career as a hatter's apprentice. His formal musical education was limited to three weeks in a singing school. After serving in the Continental Army, where he learned to play the flute, he settled in Suffield, Connecticut, from which vantage point he published 2 or 3 books of hymn tunes. Several of these—notably "Poland," "China," and "Ocean"—were widely used for a century and a half all over America. In 1807 Swan went back to Massachusetts to live in Northfield, where he died on his eighty-fourth birthday. RECORDINGS: Several of his tunes have been recorded by Gregg Smith.

[1008] ZELTER, Carl Friedrich (Tsel'-ter, Kärl Frē'-drikh)
MASTER MASON, VIOLINIST, CONDUCTOR, TEACHER, WRITER
BORN: Berlin, December 11, 1758
DIED: Berlin, May 15, 1832

Zelter's father was a mason but not the sort that Mozart [992] would have clasped to his bosom in fraternity. When the boy was twelve, his parents took him to the opera, and it hit him like a ton of bricks. What he appreciated most was that it was totally unintelligible linguistically (being in Italian), and he became a life-long opponent of opera in the vernacular. This stance was unpopular in Germany, but in Anglo-Saxon countries it proved an idea whose time had come. Zelter's father sent him to the local *Gymnasium,* where he was quite unpopular with his peers—though it is not certain whether his proletarian origins or his addiction to practical jokes weighed the more heavily against him. So he transferred to a private school run, as a sideline, by the gymnasium organist. Then he returned to the *Gymnasium,* and subsequently the private school. At seventeen he was felled by smallpox, and, during his recovery, became proficient on the piano and even more so on the violin. (Presumably the moonlighting organist had provided some basics.) Now his father decreed it was time for him to lay some bricks, so for five years or so he laid them, though his heart wasn't in it. He was frustrated in his wish to travel because of his lack of money, and he fell in love with a Jewish girl, which was not *comme il faut* at the time but which introduced him to the Mendelssohn family (see 1200). In his spare time he participated in various musical activities, both as a performer and listener. In 1779 he had a viola concerto performed, and three years later the choir of the Georgikirche sang one of his cantatas. Dissatisfied with everything he heard on these occasions save the applause, he sought training from Emanuel Bach's [801] friend and pupil K. F. C. Fasch and from Kirnberger [821]. In 1787 he was hired by the publisher Johann Karl Friedrich Rellstab, father of the poet Ludwig Rellstab, to direct the Berlin Amateur Concerts, which, however, soon failed. That same year Zelter married a widow, Sophie Flöricke, who brought him three ready-made children. In 1790 Fasch founded a chorus that eventually became the Berlin Singakademie and the next year took Zelter on as his assistant. It was Fasch who introduced Zelter to the music of Sebastian Bach [684], to which he became fanatically devoted. Sophie Zelter having died in the interim, the widower married Juliane Pappritz, a singer, in 1796.

Around 1799 Goethe heard some of Zelter's settings of his lyrics and was quite taken with them. Zelter, like Reichardt [980], seemed to agree with the poet that the words should dominate the music, and a correspondence developed that ripened into close friendship. Indeed it is said that Zelter was the only male whose intimacy Goethe encouraged after Schiller died. It was an odd pairing, for the composer, who was actually a clever and sensitive man, loved to play the clod—loud, bumptious, philistine, and obscene. He did not delete the expletives in his letters to the poet; he added them for shock effect.

The long-ailing Fasch died in 1800, and Zelter became in name what he had for some time been in fact: director of the Singakademie. What had been little more than a private club became, under his hand, a moving force in Berlin musical life and a means whereby the best local composers could try out their works. In 1806 Zelter was given the title of Assessor and named to the Royal Academy of Fine Arts—and widowed again, now with a large brood to rear. A year later he added to the Singakademie an orchestra known as the Ripienschule, which eventually became the Berlin Philharmonic. In 1809 he organized the Liedertafel, forerunner of all those *Männerchöre* and *Liederkränze* and indeed of the male chorus tradition. The same year saw his appointment as professor of music at the University of Berlin and the birth of Felix Mendelssohn [1200]. In 1818 the Mendelssohns asked Zelter, now the musical oracle of Berlin, to teach their young genius. It was love

at first sight, and the old man trained the boy with the most scrupulous concern, encouraging him every step of the way. Zelter took Felix to visit Goethe, who was so pleased that he kissed the child a lot, when he wasn't busy kissing his daughter-in-law's sister.

Zelter collected compositions by Bach and at one point acquired the *St. Matthew Passion*, which he planned to "correct"; fortunately he was too busy to get around to doing so. In the meantime, Mendelssohn's grandmother gave him a copy for his fourteenth birthday. Zelter was miserly with his Bach treasures, which he kept in a locked cabinet for private gloating, but his pupil finally persuaded him to condone a performance of the Passion. In the end, Zelter threw all his considerable power into the project, and the work got its first modern hearing from his forces in 1829.

In 1822 Zelter founded what became the Royal Institute for Sacred Music. He also instituted the Department of Music in the Royal Library. Two years before his death, the university gave him an honorary doctorate. Among his important pupils were Jakob Beer, later called Giacomo Meyerbeer [1142]; Carl Loewe [1152]; and Otto Nicolai [1212]. The bulk of his musical output consisted of choral works for the Singakademie and songs. The latter in many instances point the way to Franz Schubert [1153].

RECORDINGS: A handful of the songs has been recorded by Dietrich Fischer-Dieskau; more attention to them is in order. The viola concerto (Zelter's only orchestral work) is played on records by Georg Schmid.

[1009] BURNS, Robert
FARMER, POET, TAX COLLECTOR
BORN: Alloway, January 25, 1759
DIED: Dumfries, July 21, 1796

Robert Burns deserves only passing mention here for, though his songs are world famous, he was not a composer but a lyricist who poured new whiskey into old Scotch bottles. Every educated English-speaking person is acquainted with the brief lifetime of grinding poverty, romantic frustration, exploitation, and lack of recognition, winding down into alcoholism, failing health, and death at thirty-seven. Most of the songs were written for his sometime friend George Thomson, the Scottish folksong addict, who conned Beethoven [1063] and Haydn [871], among other famous musicians, into doing arrangements for him. For his hundred-odd lyrics, Burns got a shawl for his wife, a painting, and five pounds cash, not to mention a healthy (or, in his case, unhealthy) mistrust of the capitalistic system. RECORDINGS: In an earlier and more innocent age, "Comin' thro the Rye" was recorded by every major singer worth his or her salt who could sing, or approximate, the language.

[1010] DEVIENNE, François (Dəv-yen', Frȧn-swȧ')
FLUTIST, BASSOONIST, TEACHER
BORN: Joinville, January 31, 1759
DIED: Charenton, September 5, 1803

It has been said that Devienne was the only significant French composer born between the death of Rameau **[675]** in 1764 and the birth of Berlioz **[1175]** in 1803. The argument is supportable if we do not insist too strongly on the meaning of "significant." He was born into the family of a harness maker in a small town on the Marne and probably learned the rudiments of music from his older brother. Legends of his precocious achievements as a professional may be safely discounted. At twenty he was installed as a lowly bassoonist in the orchestra of the Paris Opéra. There he learned the flute and took service with Cardinal de Rohan, to whom he dedicated some of his early compositions. He was soon appearing frequently both as flutist and bassoonist at the Concert Spirituel, and in the latter capacity was regarded as especially soulful. In 1784 he joined the orchestra of the masonic Loge Olympique and participated in the premieres of his fellow Mason Haydn's **[871]**, "Paris" symphonies. Devienne served as bassoonist at the Théâtre Feydeau from 1789 until its 1801 merger with the Comédie-Italienne as the Opéra-Comique. Shortly after the Revolution began, he joined the band of the Garde Nationale and was soon put in charge of its music school, which, in 1795, became the Paris Conservatoire, where he served as the first professor of flute. In 1790 he produced his *Le Mariage clandestin (The Clandestine Marriage)*, the first of the several comic operas for which he was chiefly famous in his day. His most successful stage effort was the 1792 *Les Visitandines*, wherein a nunnery is mistaken for an inn; it was frequently performed for the next thirty years, and revived later with the setting changed to a girls' school. He also contributed to the collaborative group effort *Le Congrès des rois (The Kings' Congress)* with Blasius **[1006]** and others. In the early 1790s he married and subsequently produced five children. In 1803 he was committed to the madhouse at Charenton (of *Marat-Sade*

fame). It was said that his collapse had been occasioned by "sorrows experienced during the Revolution," but it was almost certainly paresis. Devienne wrote an important flute method and scads of quite sophisticated instrumental music, almost all of it involving winds. RECORDINGS: Jean-Pierre Rampal has recorded several flute concerti, Michel Debost some of the flute sonatas, and both George Zukerman and Gerhard Hasse a quartet for bassoon and strings.

[1011] PARADIS, Maria Theresia von (Pä'-rȧ-dēs, Mä-rē'-ȧ Tä-rāz'-yȧ fun)
PIANIST, SINGER, TEACHER
BORN: Vienna, May 15, 1759
DIED: Vienna, February 1, 1824

If attitudes to the performances of "La Paradis" have a smack of Dr. Johnson's dog-walking-on-its-hinder-legs, one need make no excuses for the lady herself, for she had brains, talent, and courage. She was the daughter of an imperial court councillor and was named for the empress, who stood as godmother at her baptism. At the age of five she was permanently blinded, but this handicap did not stand in her way. Among her several teachers were Jan Antonín Koželuh **[950]**, Salieri **[966]**, and "Abt" Vogler **[960]**, and she became a fine pianist, as well as a singer, organist, and composer. (To be sure her way was smoothed by a handsome annuity from the empress.) Mozart **[992]** is said to have written her a concerto, though she rather specialized in those of his rival Koželuh. In 1784 she embarked on a European concert tour, playing in Paris for the royal family and at the Concert Spirituel, following a similar pattern in London (where she accompanied the future George IV in a cello recital) and winding up with a triumphal progression through Belgium and the Germanies. Shortly afterward she began composing, using a system of notation especially invented for her. Several of her operas and other stage pieces were produced in Vienna. Later on, she founded a conservatory for young ladies and devoted most of her energies to teaching. Her music is sometimes confused with that by the Italian Domenico Paradisi **[772]**. Besides her operas there are chamber works, keyboard pieces, and songs—including a setting of August Bürger's gothic ballad "Lenore," which so fetched the early Romantics. RECORDINGS: She seems to survive on records solely through a little *Sicilienne*, generally played in modern arrangements.

[1012] BACH, Wilhelm Friedrich Ernst
(Bákh, Vil'-helm Frē'-drikh Ârnst)
PIANIST, MUSIC DIRECTOR, TEACHER
BORN: Bückeburg, May 23, 1759
DIED: Berlin, December 25, 1845

And so we come to the last musical Bach and the end of the line. J. C. F. Bach [872] had three children. The elder daughter, Anna Philippine Friederike, married a Lieutenant Ernst Carl Colson, and their descendants are still living. The younger daughter, Christine Luise, died an old maid at ninety. The middle child, the subject of this piece, left two daughters who never married. Wilhelm, as he was called, showed talent as a child and was taught by his father, briefly by his Uncle Emanuel [801] in Hamburg, and then by Uncle Christian [886] in London. When the latter died after his nephew had been with him for three years, Wilhelm returned to the Continent and survived for a while as a strolling performer. In 1786 he became *Kapellmeister* to the little princely court at Minden, about five miles from his birthplace. When Frederick William II of Prussia came visiting in 1788, Bach pleased him with a celebratory cantata. The king invited him to Berlin where he was appointed court music master and *Kapellmeister* to Frederick the Great's widow, Queen Elisabeth Christine. When she died, he fulfilled the same duties for the new queen, Luise, wife of Frederick William III. Among his pupils was the brilliant and ill-fated Prince Louis Ferdinand [1073].

A year later, in 1798, Bach married a young and pretty girl, the mother of his daughters, who died at twenty. He soon married again, quite happily, though the marriage produced only one child, a son who died in infancy. When Bach's father died in 1795 he applied, as a matter of course, for the Bückeburg appointment but was turned down. He retired from his court duties in 1811 and lived quietly in Berlin with his wife for his last thirty-four years. In 1843 the aged couple, whose very existence had been forgotten outside their circle, turned up in Leipzig, much to the delight of the other participants, to help dedicate a monument to Frederick William's grandfather.

RECORDINGS: Wilhelm Bach turned out a lot of perfectly competent but not very thrilling music. He had a sense of humor, which informs his recorded compositions— *Die Musikanten*, a cantata for baritone and toy instruments, sung by William Chapman; and *Das Dreyblatt*, a composition for three pianists, one male and two female, played by Garrick Ohlsson, Gina Bachauer, and Alicia de Larrocha. (The male player,

seated between the other two, plays the extremes of the keyboard, which necessitates encircling the waists of his partners.) There is also a recording by Helmut Rilling of *Vater unser* for tenor, bass, choir, and orchestra, and one of a trio for two flutes and viola (Jean-Pierre Rampal, Eugenia and Pinchas Zukerman).

[1013] KROMMER, Franz Vinzenz
(Krôm'-er, Frânts Vēnts'-ents)
VIOLINIST, CONDUCTOR, TEACHER
BORN: Kamenice u Třebíče, November 27, 1759
DIED: Vienna, January 8, 1831

The son of an innkeeper in a village west of Brno, Krommer was baptized Franciscus Vincentius Kramarz (for František Vincenc Kramář). The Czechs now like to have it both ways with "Krommer-Kramář." He was partly taught by his paternal Uncle Anton, a choirmaster at Turăn, and partly by his own efforts. He went to Vienna in 1785, but the conditions were not yet propitious for his success there. Instead he got bogged down for a decade in the wilds of Hungary. For a while he was violinist, then *Kapellmeister*, to the Duke of Styrum-Limburg at Simontornya, some fifty miles south of Budapest. In 1790 he went even farther south to be choirmaster at the Cathedral of Pécs (then Fünfkirchen). In 1793 he took over direction of the regimental band of a Count Karolyi. But the count soon died and the band was disbanded, and Krommer became *Kapellmeister* to a Prince Grassalkovics, headquartered at Gödöllö near Budapest. But the mortality rate for Hungarian princes apparently proved discouraging, and in 1795 Krommer gave Vienna another try. There the smile of fortune slowly broke into a wide grin. Having established himself as a teacher, he found employment with Duke Fuchs three years later. In 1810 Krommer was appointed ballet conductor at the Burgtheater, and in 1815 he was made imperial doorkeeper, though his duties involved the keeping of no particular doors. The Emperor Franz I took a shine to him, and took him all over in the signing of post-Napoleonic treaties and such. When Koželuh [950] died in 1818, Krommer became the last imperial court composer. In the course of events, Krommer's music became immensely popular all over the Western world, he was spoken of in the same breath with Haydn [871], Mozart [992], and Beethoven [1063], and he was the recipient of innumerable international honors. He wrote some church music, but most of his output was

instrumental. He has been particularly admired for his concerti and string quartets.
RECORDINGS: A clarinet concerto has been
recorded by Jack Brymer, Bohuslav
Zahradník, and David Glazer; an oboe concerto by Jiří Mihaule; a symphony by František Vajnar; and three wind partitas by the
Netherlands Wind Ensemble.

[1014] RODRIGUEZ, Felipe (Rod-rē'-
gez, Fā-lē'-pā)
ORGANIST, PRIEST, TEACHER
BORN: Madrid, 1759
DIED: Madrid, May 1814

A pupil of Padre Narciso Casanovas [947],
Rodriguez became a monk and organist at
the monastery of Montserrat in Catalonia.
He was ordained in 1778. Later he returned
to Madrid as organist of the Montserrat
church there, where he also taught. He left
some keyboard sonatas of the Soler [854]
ilk. RECORDINGS: Examples appear in recorded anthologies of early Spanish keyboard music—e.g., by Fernando Valenti and
José Echaniz.

[1015] SCHLICK, Johann Conrad (Shlik,
Yō'-hän Kōn'-rät)
CELLIST
BORN: Münster, 1759
DIED: Gotha, 1825

A virtuoso cellist, Schlick began his career
in the orchestra of the Prince-Bishop of
Münster but soon made a permanent transfer to that of the Duke of Saxe-Coburg-Gotha. He made, however, frequent concert
tours that led him as far afield as Italy,
Hungary, and Russia. In 1785 he married
the beautiful Italian violinist Regina
Strinasacchi (1764–1823), for whom Mozart
[992] wrote his K. 454 sonata, and with
whom he played before the Emperor Joseph
II. The pair made beautiful music together,
concertizing as a duo until 1809. Though
Schlick wrote a good deal of instrumental
music, most of it has disappeared. RECORD-
INGS: On records he is represented by a divertimento for two mandolins and continuo,
played by Elfriede Kunschack and Vinzenz
Hladky. Perhaps the composer was taking
advantage of the brief craze for the mandolin, which inspired even Mozart and Beethoven [1063], though he may have written
the piece for Regina, who is known to have
been a fine guitarist.

[1016] DUSSEK, Jan Ladislav (Dōō'-sek,
Yän Lä'-dē-slaf)
PIANIST, PUBLISHER
BORN: Čáslav, February 12, 1760
DIED: St.-Germain-en-Laye, March 20,
1812

An upper-class Bohemian, Dussek is sometimes viewed as the first professional touring virtuoso, though his life-style sometimes
appears that of a lowercase bohemian. He
was the son of Jan Josef Dussek, the leading
musician of Čáslav, and the former Veronika Štěbetová, a harpist, and was baptized
Wenceslaus Johannes. Of his seven siblings,
two became notable musicians, Veronika
(1769–1833) and Franz (1766–?) both of
whom left some compositions. Jan, after
having lessons from his father, became a
chorister in the Minorite church in Iglau
(now Johlava), some thirty miles to the
southward, and stayed to study at the Jesuit
school there. He was then briefly organist at
another Jesuit school in Kutná Hora, closer
to home, and finally went to Prague to
study theology, with the intention of becoming a priest in one of the monastic orders. However, his playing acquired him a
patron in the person of an army officer,
Count Männer, who perhaps needed a pianist for his Männerchor, and he gave up
school in 1779 for a trip with Männer to the
Low Countries. For some months he served
as organist and taught in Malines/Meche-
len, moved on to Bergen-op-Zoom on the
Dutch coast, then to Amsterdam, and finally to The Hague, where for a year he
taught the children of the Stadholder William V. Then he began his wanderings in
earnest. In Berlin he met and probably studied with Emanuel Bach [801]. By 1783 he
was in Russia, where he played for the czarina but had to flee when he was accused of
conspiracy against her, and wound up in the
service of the then-current Prince Radziwill
in Lithuania. When a year had passed, he
descended on Berlin again late in 1784 and
took the town by storm.
As a pianist, Dussek was chiefly admired
for his remarkable singing tone. But he was
also one of the first players to make studied
and systematic use of the pedals and to play
the new longer keyboard, extended from
5½ octaves to 6 at his urging. And he was
the first modern musical superstar: handsome, in a rather girlish way, he was proud
of his profile, and so instead of sitting with
his back or his face to his audience, he sat
sideways, the raised lid of the instrument
projecting the sound into the room—since
his time the standard recital pose.
In Germany Dussek took up the glass

harmonica and toured the country (or countries) demonstrating it at the behest of its manufacturer. In 1786 he found his way to Paris, played for Marie-Antoinette, and settled down to teach, though he interrupted his stay once to visit his brother Franz in Milan. The queen dangled all sorts of lucrative offers before him, but the outbreak of the Revolution in 1789 drove him across the Channel to London. In 1790 he performed at the Salomon Concerts and then put down something like roots for a whole decade. He continued to take pupils, became involved in concert promotion, lent the visiting Haydn [871] his piano, and married the Edinburgh-born Sophia Corri (1775–1847), daughter of a Neapolitan conductor and publisher, Domenico Corri. She was a brilliant musician (singer, harpist, pianist) and appeared in concert with her husband. They had a daughter, Olivia. Dussek joined his father-in-law in the publishing firm of Corri, Dussek, and Company. Neither man had the slightest notion of business, and the enterprise was soon headed for disaster. They tried to forestall it by taking into the partnership Lorenzo da Ponte, Mozart's [992] sometime librettist, but bankruptcy arrived in 1799. Corri was thrown into debtor's prison (but soon released). Legend has it that Dussek was spirited away by a beautiful Scandinavian princess who became his mistress, but in reality he fled ignominiously by night to Hamburg, abandoning his wife and child for good.

In Germany Dussek resumed his concertizing. In 1802 he returned to Bohemia to visit his parents, whom he had not seen since he left for Prague a quarter century earlier, and it was then that he toured with the horn virtuoso Giovanni Punto (see 945). The next year, in Magdeburg, he met the young and musical Hohenzollern prince, Louis Ferdinand [1073], who made him part of his household collection of prominent musicians (Spohr [1112] was a member for a time). Dussek became not only the prince's *Kapellmeister,* but his bosom friend and carousing companion, which must have been difficult, since the prince arose at 6 A.M. to practice. But the idyll ended with Louis Ferdinand's premature death in the battle of Saalfeld, which plunged Dussek into a depression from which he never recovered. Despite his busy life, he was fundamentally sloppy, and he now began to go to seed. After a short stint as *Kammermusikus* with a Prinz von Isenburg, he was taken on by the great Charles Maurice de Talleyrand-Périgord, Prince de Benevent (known to history as Talleyrand) as a sort of kept artist with no special duties. He

taught occasionally, but his heart was not in it. He became enormously fat—a great blubbery baby, according to a late portrait —and often spent whole days wallowing in bed. His unwillingness to act brought on pangs of guilt, and he tried stimulating draughts of port and brandy; this only intensified his problems, which also included gout. At fifty-two he died, probably of alcoholism.

Dussek wrote an opera of sorts, a *Mass,* other odds and ends, and a good deal of pianistic claptrap for parlor use, but in his serious works, concerti, sonatas, and chamber works (almost all involving piano or harp) he was almost as important a composer as his popularity in his time might have suggested, looking ahead as he does to the Romantics of the next generation.

RECORDINGS: The piano sonatas have been phonographically touched on by such as Rudolf Firkusny, Edward Gold, Frederick Marvin, and Vladimir Pleshakov. Rena Kyriakou has recorded a concerto for piano, and the Grünschlag sisters one for two pianos. There are six harp sonatas from Susann McDonald, two violin sonatas from Paul Kling, and a piano trio from the Pittsburgh Trio.

[1017] BÜHLER, Franz (Bü'-ler, Frånts)
PRIEST, ORGANIST, CHOIRMASTER
BORN: Schneidheim, April 12, 1760
DIED: Augsburg, February 4, 1824

Born in a Bavarian village, Bühler entered the Benedictine order at the nearby Heiligenkreuz Monastery at eighteen and received ordination seven years later. He was thereafter called Pater Gregorius or Abt Bühler. But the cloistered life did not agree with him, and he was released from his vows in 1794. He went to the Tyrolean city of Bozen (now Bolzano) and became organist at the collegiate church there, but in 1801 he returned to Bavaria as *Kapellmeister* at Augsburg Cathedral, where he spent the rest of his days. Though he wrote a good deal of church music, he was a composer of no great profundity and was chiefly popular for his pleasant compositions for the parlor.

RECORDINGS: The Consortium Classicum has recorded a *Grande Sonate* for piano, with wind and string accompaniment.

[1018] ROUGET DE L'ISLE, Claude Joseph (Hrōō-zhä' də Lēl, Klōd Zhō-zef')
SOLDIER, ENGINEER, POET, VIOLINIST, SINGER

BORN: Lons-le-Saulnier, May 10, 1760
DIED: Choisy-le-Roy, June 27, 1836

A native of the Jura country, Rouget graduated from l'Ecole Royale du Génie at Mézières in 1784 with the rank of aspirant-lieutenant. He eventually made first lieutenant in 1790 and was stationed in Strasbourg with a regiment of engineers. There he amused himself by writing texts for musical plays and the like, and singing and playing at the officers' mess. In 1792 he wrote a song that he called *"Le Chant de guerre de l'armée du Rhin,"* intended simply as a marching song. Revolutionaries from Marseilles, marching on the capital, took it up, and it became known as *La Marseillaise.* Revolution was far from Rouget's intent. He was brought up a conservative royalist and refused to go against the monarchy. As a result he was stripped of his rank and jailed. He escaped in 1794 and for the next several years turned out the kind of propagandistic works demanded by that heady period of self-congratulation. Under Napoleon he returned to soldiering, was seriously wounded in battle, mustered out, and retired to private life. He lived alone, forgotten, and horribly poor at Montaigu near Nantes until the return of the monarchy in 1815. Circumstances forced him to go to Paris, where he was granted a small pension and taken care of by old friends. When Rouget was around seventy, Berlioz [1175] paid him homage with an all-stops-out arrangement of the *Marseillaise.* The old man wrote to thank the "young volcano," admitting sadly that his own fires were out. He offered Berlioz a libretto for an *Othello,* but Berlioz was about to go on tour and could not accept it. Rouget died at the home of his friends the Voiarts in suburban Paris, where he had been sheltered for some years. He published a book of songs in 1825. Over the past century the music of the *Marseillaise* has been claimed for Pleyel, a certain Grisons, and an anonymous German, among others. RECORDINGS: Jean-Pierre Jacquillat recorded the Berlioz arrangement.

[1019] CHERUBINI, Luigi (Carlo Zanobi
    Salvatore Maria) (Kā-rōō-bĕ'-nē, Lōō-
    ē'-jē)
    CONDUCTOR, TEACHER, ADMINISTRA-
    TOR
    BORN: Florence, September 14, 1760
    DIED: Paris, March 15, 1842

At the height of his career in Paris, Cherubini, like his earlier compatriot Lully [517],

was the Grand Pooh-Bah of music i: France, nor was the effect of his own com positions exactly negligible. Yet, like s many such figures, he was, after his deatl quickly reduced to an entry in the histor books, and it has only been very recentl that public hunger for novelty and the el forts of influential performers like Arturc Toscanini and Maria Callas have given u: some notion of what all the shouting was about.

Cherubini's father, Bartolomeo, conducted from his harpsichord at the Teatro della Pergola, then Florence's chief opera house. The boy studied with him and with various local musicians of no great consequence and, as he entered adolescence, began turning out Masses, motets, and other works at an impressive rate and level. While he was still in his teens, Leopold, the Austrian Grand Duke of Tuscany (latterly and briefly the Emperor Leopold II) took a fancy to him and sent him off to study with Sarti [853], who was in the process of becoming *maestro di cappella* at Milan Cathedral. Cherubini stayed with him about three years, serving as his assistant, and learning strict "Palestrinan" counterpoint. In 1779 Cherubini's first full-length opera *Quinto Fabio* (he had previously written two or three intermezzi) was produced at Alessandria della Paglia without shaking the Apennines. But after the composer returned to Florence in 1781, he continued to pursue operatic fame (mostly with *opera serie)* and was soon being produced all over the peninsula. In 1784 he went to London to seek his fortune and was commissioned to write a new work for the King's Theatre. This, *La finta principessa (The Feigned Princess),* an *opera buffa,* was a considerable success and won him the patronage of the future George IV and the title of Composer to His Majesty.

In 1785 Cherubini went to explore Paris for the summer, made friends with his compatriot Viotti [988], and liked what he saw in Paris. After returning to London to produce the revised *Quinto Fabio,* and going to Turin (his last trip to his homeland) for the new *Ifigenia in Aulide,* he settled permanently in Paris in 1788. Paris, of course, was still ringing with echoes of the Gluck [803]–Piccinni [848] fracas, and Cherubini determined to suit his work to *le goût français.* His first attempt, *Démophon,* in which he adopted Gluckian methods, suffered from librettitis and had little impact. A year later, however, Viotti and his partner Léonard, entrusted him with the directorship of the orchestra in the new company soon to be known as the Théâtre Feydeau. There Cherubini enjoyed his first French triumph with *Lodoiska* in 1791. But the Terror made further efforts seem worthless and, save for his part in the committee-composed *Le Congrès des rois* and a two-act comedy *Eliza*, he left opera alone for six years. In fact, for some months he left Paris alone until the worst was over. Then he returned to marry a musician's daughter, Cécile Tourette. The theater had closed down, and the only job available was that of a triangle player in a band. However, when the Garde Nationale's music school began to turn into the Paris Conservatory, he was made an inspector and found himself (at least for the nonce) in on the ground floor. His next opera, *Médée (Medea)* was his first real masterpiece—a forerunner of Beethoven's [1063] *Fidelio* in its study of feminine psychology and its use of the *opéra-comique* (spoken dialogue) format. (Modern performances are usually done in the Italian-edition-with-recitatives made by Franz Lachner [1171].) Three years later, in 1800, Cherubini produced another important work, *Les Deux Journées* (translated as *The Two Days* although the title was *The Watercarrier* for the English premiere), a "rescue" opera about ordinary people commenting on democratic values that also had an impact on Beethoven.

Cherubini's success helped keep him where he had gotten to but did nothing to promote him, since Napoleon, now in charge of things, had taken a strong dislike both to the composer and his music. In 1805 the "other" emperor, Francis II (last of the Holy Roman Emperors, a.k.a. Francis I of Austria) invited Cherubini to Vienna. He got there in time for the unsuccessful premiere of Beethoven's *Fidelio* and added his own uncomplimentary remarks to the general chorus. (If he was a musical revolutionary, it was against his conscious will.) While he was there, getting ready for the premiere of his *Faniska*, who should arrive with all his merry men but Napoleon. Meeting a fellow Parisian on foreign soil seems to have made a difference to him, for he requested Cherubini to direct concerts for his party and wished him well. But Cherubini was unconvinced that he meant it and, on returning to France, gave up music altogether and turned his attention to botanizing and painting. Eventually he decided to go back to writing religious pieces and slowly returned to his musical career. With Napoleon's exile in 1814, he wrote a coronation Mass for Louis XVIII (former patron of the Feydeau), who conferred on him the *Légion d'honneur* and made him Superintendent of the King's Music. He tried his hand at a few

more operas, mostly pastiches, collaborations, and retreads, though in *Les Abencérages* of 1811 he tried to come to terms with the all-out sort of thing that would become *grand-opéra*. In 1816 he wrote his *Requiem* in C Minor in memory of the slain Louis XVI which came to be regarded as one of his greatest works, though the Church later protested its use of female voices. That same year, Cherubini and Jean-François Le Sueur (1760–1837), one of his chief rivals, were appointed directors of the royal chapel.

In 1822 Cherubini began his twenty-year reign as director of the Paris Conservatory and thereafter devoted himself chiefly to the demands of the job and the needs of his students (which included the publication of various manuals and a course in counterpoint). He became something of a mandarin —or a sort of museum piece. Like Lully, he became 200 percent French, barring foreigners from his institution. He was consulted by musical visitors as if he were an oracle. Abraham Mendelssohn brought young Felix [1200] to him for assay; Cherubini pronounced him *très riche*, which certainly described his economic position. Le Sueur's pupil, Hector Berlioz [1175], in his memoirs, depicts the old fellow as a ridiculous stuffed-shirt standing in the way of musical progress (mostly represented by Berlioz). Among his pupils, however, Cherubini counted some of the most influential French composers of the next generation, including Auber [1103], Boieldieu [1084], and Halévy [1157]. Six years before he died, he wrote his remarkable *Requiem* in D Minor, insuring that it would not be opposed at his own obsequies by calling for male voices only.

As a result of Maria Callas's espousal of *Medée*, two official and several unofficial recordings of the work have appeared, and indeed the underground market now offers versions of virtually all of Cherubini's considerable operas. Newell Jenkins has recorded the *Solemn Mass* of 1816, and there are several recordings of both Requiems and of the lone symphony commissioned by the London Philharmonic Society in 1815. Vera Franceschi has recorded the six early keyboard sonatas of 1780, and the Melos Quartet performs the six string quartets. Organ pieces have been recorded by Arturo Sacchetti, and the Quintetto Boccherini offers a string quintet and the *Souvenir pour cher Bailot* for string quartet.

[1020] GAVEAUX, Pierre (Gà-vō', Pē-âr')
SINGER, PUBLISHER

BORN: Béziers, October 9, 1760
DIED: Charenton, February 5, 1825

Born in southern France, Gaveaux was a singer for most of his active life, beginning as a choirboy in the local cathedral at the age of seven. After his voice changed, he went to Bordeaux to sing tenor at the church of St. Seurin. There he studied with the transplanted Mannheimer Franz Beck and began composing. Up to then Gaveaux was planning to become a priest, but when he discovered opera he gave the notion up. He began his operatic career there, moved to Montpellier in 1788, and when the Théâtre de Monsieur was organized in Paris a year later, under the direction of Viotti [988], and the queen's *parfumier,* he was called there as a leading tenor. After the company settled in at the Théâtre Feydeau, in 1792, he began trying his hand at *opérascomiques,* of which he ultimately turned out more than 30. He often took a cue from Cherubini [1019], in whose *Lodoiska* he created a leading role, in using the form for serious music drama. His most important work, historically, was the 1798 "rescue" opera, *Léonore, ou L'amour conjugal,* whose libretto by Jean-Nicolas Bouilly provided the basis for *Leonore* by Paër [1069] and *Fidelio* by Beethoven [1063]. After the company merged to become the Opèra-Comique, Gaveaux, now in his forties, became a *comprimario.* Three years later, in 1804, he was appointed to Napoleon's chapel. From 1793 until 1812 he ran a music shop with his brother Simon on the side. In the latter year, he suffered a mental breakdown, but soon returned to the business. In 1819, however, he had to be committed to the notorious Charenton madhouse, where Devienne [1010] had died some years before. Gaveaux also wrote religious music and songs—all, like the operas, now forgotten. RECORDINGS: Regina Resnik has recorded an aria from his *L'Enfant prodigue (The Prodigal Son)* of 1811.

[1021] GIULIANI, Giovanni Francesco
(Jōōl-yä′-nē, Jō-vän′-nē Frän-chä′-skō)
CONDUCTOR
BORN: Livorno, c. 1760
DIED: Florence, after 1818

This Giuliani appears to have been unrelated to the guitar virtuoso Mauro Giuliani [1099] and his family. He was a pupil of Nardini [823] and spent all of his mature life in Florence, where for a time he was conductor at the Teatro degli Intrepidi. He wrote a large number of instrumental works which seem to have been quite popular. Though the name is given on a record jacket as "Francesco Giovanni Giuliani," he apparently wrote a quartet for mandolin, violin, viola, and lute. RECORDINGS: The quartet has been recorded under the direction of Vinzenz Hladky.

[1022] NEUBAUER, Franz Christoph
(Noi′-bou-er, Frånts Krēs′-tōf)
VIOLINIST, CONDUCTOR
BORN: Hořín, c. 1760
DIED: Bückeburg, October 11, 1795

Another floating Czech. As his name indicates, Neubauer was a peasant's son. The village schoolmaster-organist liked the cut of his jib and gave him music lessons, including fiddle training. After some further study in Prague, the young man took to the road, playing for his supper and a bed. In the course of his travels, he met some important musicians and formed some bad habits. He was in Munich in 1784 and then in Vienna, where Emanuel Schikaneder produced his *Singspiel* entitled *Fernando und Yariko* in 1788. In 1789 Neubauer was in Heilbronn conducting his program symphony, *La Bataille de Martinestie,* celebrating an Austro-Russian defeat of the Turks. Shortly afterward he tried to settle down as *Kapellmeister* to the Duke of Nassau-Weilburg, but revolutionary rumblings from France shut the court down, and Neubauer moved on to Minden, where he succeeded Wilhelm Friedrich Ernst Bach [1012]. After a short time he went to nearby Bückeburg, where Wilhelm's father, J. C. F. Bach [872], gave his music a hearing. Much to Bach's alarm, Neubauer was invited to stick around. When Bach publicly attacked his competence, Neubauer proposed a musical duel. Bach responded by falling ill and dying. His worst fears were realized, for Neubauer, not son Wilhelm, got his job. Moreover he was right about his successor, for shortly afterward Neubauer's carousing caught up with him and he died in his mid-thirties. A facile composer, he left symphonies, chamber music, and choral works. RECORDINGS: Newell Jenkins has recorded the battle symphony.

[1023] VRANICKÝ, Antonín (Vrå-nēch′-kē, Ån-tō-nyēn′)
VIOLINIST, CONDUCTOR, TEACHER
BORN: Neureisch, June 13, 1761
DIED: Vienna, August 6, 1820

In his day, Vranický was more commonly known as Anton Wranitzky, and his birthplace is now called Nová Říše. His father doubled as innkeeper and farmer. He learned his ABC's, or whatever Czechs have, at the Latin school of the local monastery, and his violin training from his elder brother Pavel, alias Paul. (Paul Wranitzky [1756–1808] was a pupil of J. M. Kraus [998] and Joseph Haydn [871], worked under the latter at the Esterházy court, and was conductor at the Imperial Opera for twenty-three years. Paul wrote many stage works, including a pioneer treatment of Wieland's *Oberon,* and was an important symphonist.) Antonín majored in law at Brno, went to Vienna in 1783, where he worked as a choirmaster and studied with Haydn, Albrechtsberger [889], and Mozart [992]. He then went to work for Prince Lobkowitz, Beethoven's [1063] patron, and by 1797 had become his *Kapellmeister.* Under Lobkowitz's patronage, he succeeded his brother at the Imperial Opera, and later was also conductor of the Theater an der Wien. He was the most important violin teacher of his day in Vienna and published a method. He wrote 15 symphonies on the Classical model and as many more adventurous concerti, mostly for violin, as well as a good deal of chamber music. His daughter Caroline Seidler, one of his four musical offspring, created the role of Agathe in Weber's [1124] *Der Freischütz,* the year after her father's death. RECORDINGS: The Netherlands Wind Ensemble has recorded ten clever little marches.

[1024] GALLES, José (Gä'-yez, Hō-zā')
PRIEST, ORGANIST
BORN: Casteltersol, 1761
DIED: Vich, 1836

Of José Galles we know that he was born in a Catalan village, became a priest, and served as organist of the cathedral at Vich (between Barcelona and the French border). He left 23 rather simple-minded keyboard sonatas rooted in Domenico Scarlatti [687] in manuscript. A couple have been recorded by Fernando Valenti, one of them also by José Echaniz.

[1025] STORACE, Stephen John Seymour
VIOLINIST, PUBLISHER
BORN: London, April 4, 1763
DIED: London, March 19, 1796

Mozart [992] died at thirty-four; his English friend Stephen Storace outlived him by five

years and died at thirty-three. Stephen's father, originally called Stefano, a contrabassist, had come to Dublin from Italy, prospered, moved on to London, become conductor at Marylebone Gardens, and married his boss's daughter, Elizabeth Trusler. Their only other surviving child was a daughter Nancy (1765–1817). Stephen early showed talent both as painter and musician (a prodigy violinist), and so his father shipped him back to Naples to attend the Conservatorio di San Onofrio in 1776. Two years later his family dropped in on him, decided he was wasting his time and their money, and brought him home. Still torn between his talents, he composed fitfully but at last struck gold when he published two piano quintets and a sextet in 1784. By that time Nancy was in Vienna, singing soprano leads at the Court Opera. Soon her brother had a commission from there for a comedy, which turned out to be *Gli sposi malcontenti (The Dissatisfied Bridegrooms).* He went there to get it on the stage—at the Burgtheater in June 1785—and set up housekeeping with Nancy. She had caught Mozart's [992] roving eye, so that he was a frequent visitor and probably gave Stephen some pointers. Nancy and their Irish-tenor friend Michael Kelly [1028] sang in the premiere, and exactly eleven months later were Susanna and Don Curzio in the first performance of *Le Nozze di Figaro.* It was at the Storaces' that the famous quartet session featuring Mozart, Haydn [871], Dittersdorf [906], and Vanhal [903] took place. Having entered into that charmed circle, Stephen got another libretto—this time from Lorenzo da Ponte, *Gli equivoci (The Ambiguities,* after Shakespeare's *The Comedy of Errors),* which once more featured Nancy and Michael in its year's end premiere. Then the three Britishers went home.

In London Nancy found a place at the King's Theatre, to which in 1788, the year he married Mary Hall, Stephen contributed *La Cameriera astuta (The Clever Chambermaid).* But the house was in the hands of real imported Italians, who wanted, ironically, no part of Englishmen, and the piece was decried as "too modern." Perhaps by way of divine retribution, the theater burned to the ground a year later. Meanwhile Stephen was busy publishing his *Collection of Original Harpsichord* [read "Piano"] *Music*—works he had found in Europe, including some by Mozart and three trios of his own. Nancy soon joined Richard Brinsley Sheridan's company at the Drury Lane, which put on Stephen's dialogue-opera *The Haunted Tower* with great success. Over the next six years, he wrote thirteen stage works (many with copious borrow-ings, including some from himself) and managed the 1792 opera season. His 1792 *Pirates* also enjoyed real success. In 1796, ill with "gout," he insisted on overseeing rehearsals of his *The Iron Chest*, caught cold, and died. Nancy and Kelly pieced out his unfinished *Mahmoud* in which the great tenor John Braham [1079] made his debut a month later. Storace was survived by his wife and a son, Brinsley John, named after Sheridan, who died at nineteen.

RECORDINGS: Arias and duets from *The Pirates* and *The Siege of Belgrade* have been recorded by Bethany Beardslee and by the team of Sasha Abrams and Dan Klein.

[1026] GARAT, Dominique Pierre Jean
(Gȧ-rá', Dō-mē-nēk' Pē-âr' Zhȧn)
SINGER
BORN: Bordeaux, April 26, 1762
DIED: Paris, March 1, 1823

Garat was one of the most remarkable singers in history—a baritone with a high tenor extension that enabled him to sing almost anything written for voice. Like Pierre Gaveaux [1020], he studied in Bordeaux with Franz Beck, who had come there from Mannheim to escape the consequences of winning a duel. At twenty, at his father's insistence, he went to the University of Paris to study law, where he found more interesting things to do. He fell in with the Count d'Artois, who introduced him to Marie Antoinette. She saw to it that he need not work for a living and even paid his debts when his extravagance got him into a hole. In the Great Upheaval, he found his connections an embarrassment and moved to Rouen, where he was promptly jailed as a Royalist. He escaped to Hamburg with his fellow townsman, the violinist-composer Pierre Rode (1774–1830). He sang in Germany, the Lowlands, and England until the worst was over in Paris. He was soon established as the Sinatra of his day there. (He sang operatic material only on the concert stage but specialized in popular romances.) He taught voice at the Conservatoire from 1796 until his death and in 1817 married one of his pupils, a Mlle. Duchamp. Part of his attraction seems to have been his avant-garde attire. Garat wrote many romances of his own which are typical of the genre. RECORDINGS: Two romances have been recorded by Bernard Kruysen.

[1027] HOLYOKE, Samuel Adams
TEACHER, CLARINETIST

BORN: Boxford, Mass., October 15, 1762
DIED: Concord, N.H., February 7, 1820

Samuel Holyoke was better educated (he graduated from Harvard in 1789) than Oliver Holden [1041], his collaborator on *The Massachusetts Compiler* (a collection of hymn tunes with musical theory thrown in) but was not necessarily a more gifted musician. The son of a minister, Holyoke was self-taught and wrote his most famous tune "Arnheim" when he was sixteen. In 1793, after his graduation, he founded a school, the Groton (later Lawrence) Academy. Like Holden, he wrote a piece memorializing George Washington (and prior to that another honoring the general while yet living). In 1800 he moved to Salem, Massachusetts, where he taught and was active in various musical organizations, both vocal and instrumental. He published several collections. The first, a volume of hymn tunes called *Harmonia Americana* of 1791, contains a foreword attacking fuguing tunes as improper to worship. His largest collection, *The Columbian Repository*, included settings of all of Issac Watts's sacred lyrics. The two-volume *The Instrumental Assistant* is basically a manual for orchestral performers. For all his enormous productivity, Holyoke died broke. RECORDINGS: The Berkeley Chamber Singers have included "Arnheim" in an anthology.

[1028] KELLY, Michael
SINGER, ENTREPRENEUR
BORN: Dublin, December 25, 1762
DIED: Margate, October 9, 1826

The tenor Michael Kelly, known as "Mick" to his friends and as "Michele Ochelli" in his Continental years, was the first Don Basilio and Don Curzio in Mozart's [992] *Le Nozze di Figaro* and the author of voluminous *Reminiscences* that, however dependable, cast considerable illumination on the era. He was the son of a wine merchant who, Michael tells us, officiated as "Master of Ceremonies at the Castle." Michael's vocal efforts were encouraged from his fourth year, and he was given lessons by the best teachers around, including Michael Arne [916]. Somewhat fortuitously, he was soon appearing on Dublin opera stages. He saved up the apparently substantial fruits of his labors and in the spring of 1779 sailed for Naples, the wellspring of operatic training. There he fell in with Nancy Storace, who had come to visit her brother Stephen [1025] and remained behind to try her luck at a singing career. The two (not necessarily ensemble) made names for themselves at various Italian opera houses and in 1783 were hired for the Imperial Court Opera in Vienna. The history of Kelly's career there has been covered above in the account of Storace.

Back in England in 1787, Kelly became a very popular performer, with the stress apparently on "popular." He made his operatic debut in London that same year at Drury Lane in *Lionel and Clarissa*, by Dibdin [936]. His leading lady was Anna Maria Crouch (née Phillips), and he soon became part of a *ménage à trois* at the Crouches. When Lieutenant Crouch moved out in 1791, Kelly stayed with Anna Maria until she left London and her career ten years later. In 1793 he became stage manager at the King's Theatre, where he worked until shortly before his death. Having helped Nancy Storace complete her brother's last opera in 1796, he began grinding out stage musicals, of which he produced more than sixty in the next twenty-three years. Kelly (when he was not lifting his material from other sources) was at best a good tunesmith. He opened a music store in 1801 but mismanaged it and went bankrupt. He then turned to the paternal trade. Sheridan, his director at Drury Lane, said that his sign should read "composer of wines and importer of music." Told by his friend Lord Howth that the key to a long life was "good punch by night and copious gargles of old port by day," Kelly enthusiastically followed the recipe. The *Reminiscences*, published in the year of his death, were ghost-written by Theodore Hook, son of the composer James Hook [943]. Kelly died of gout at sixty-three.

RECORDINGS: Some of his songs have been recorded by Sasha Abrams and Dan Klein, and by the Gregg Smith Singers.

[1029] JANIEWICZ, Feliks (Yàn-yā'-vich, Fā'-lĕks)
VIOLINIST, CONDUCTOR, ENTREPRENEUR
BORN: Wilno, 1762
DIED: Edinburgh, May 21, 1848

Janiewicz's birthplace is now the Soviet city of Vilnius. At fifteen he was already a violinist in the court orchestra of Stanisław II Poniatowski of Poland. But Poland was being whittled away by the Great Powers, and around 1784 he moved to Vienna, where he hobnobbed with Mozart [992] and perhaps studied with Haydn [871]. After a long concert tour of Italy, he went on to Paris, played at the Concert Spirituel late in 1787,

and became a protégé of the Duke of Orléans. After the outbreak of the Revolution, we lose track of him until 1792, when he turns up in London. He played there and in the provinces, settled in 1800 in Liverpool, married a Miss Eliza Breeze, called himself "Felix Yaniewicz," and (with various partners) conducted a publishing business and music store. He was a founder of the London Philharmonic Society in 1813. Two years later he moved to Edinburgh, where he taught, performed as soloist and concertmaster with the local orchestra, and was a mover and shaker in the musical life of the city. He retired in 1829. His daughters Paulina and Felicia became known as a harpist and pianist respectively. Janiewicz's most important compositions are his violin concerti and his chamber works. RECORDINGS: One of his trios has been recorded by Fritz Rikko in an orchestral transcription by Andrzej Panufnik [2226].

[1030] WAŃSKI, Jan (Vàn'y'-ski, Yàn)
VIOLINIST
BORN: Wielkopolski, 1762
DIED: after 1821

Very little is known of Jan Wański, who survived the agony of the partitions that wiped independent Poland off the map. He lived for a while in Poznan, and played in Pomeranian orchestras. His son Roch (1780–1810) was a cellist in Poland. Another son, Jan Nepomucen (1782–1840), was a violinist and composer who settled in France near the end of his life. Among Wański's scattered musical remains are a *Requiem*, an offertory, some dances, and 3 symphonies. RECORDINGS: Two symphonies, drawn from the lost operas *The Shepherd of the Vistula* and *The Peasant*, have been recorded by Robert Satanowski.

[1031] FERNÁNDEZ, Hipolito (Fär-nàn'-deth, Hē-pō'-lē-tō)
PRIEST, ORGANIST
BORN: Valencia, c. 1762
DIED: ?

As with so many of his keyboard-playing compatriots and contemporaries, Padre Fernández has left only scattered traces. He went to Majorca around 1791, served there as organist, and taught the children of the governor. After that he drops out of sight completely. RECORDINGS: He left a single Scarlattesque sonata, recorded by organist Fernando Valenti.

[1032] GYROWETZ, Adalbert (Jē'-rō-vets, Ád'-àl-bârt)
VIOLINIST, CONDUCTOR
BORN: Budweis (now České Budějovice), February 20, 1763
DIED: Vienna, March 19, 1850

Though his name appears as above in most standard reference sources, the Czechs insist that this amiable Budweiser was really Vojtěch Matyáš Jírovec. They have a point, for at the lowest ebb in Czech cultural history he took pride in his origins and spoke the language, which was "infra dig" among the educated. (He even set some Czech lyrics.) He got his musical background from his choirmaster father, then went to Prague to study law. There, wiped out financially by illness, he found a good angel in the person of Count Franz von Fünfkirchen, who took him on as his secretary. Since the count was a dedicated music lover, he insisted on musical employees, which was fine with Gyrowetz, who was thus able to get on-the-job training. He was soon up to writing symphonies and dedicated his first six to his employer in 1783. Deciding that he needed more sophisticated training, he went to Vienna where a certain Hofrat von Kees introduced him to the likes of Albrechtsberger [889], Mozart [992], who featured a Gyrowetz symphony on one of his programs, and Joseph Haydn [871], whose impact Gyrowetz never quite got over.

Gyrowetz' secretarial experience stood him in good stead in Vienna, for he found a place in that capacity with a Prince Ruspoli, who took him to Italy, where he had wanted to go all along. After seeing the important towns of the north, he took off on his own for Naples, where he studied with Nicola Sala, a pupil of Leo [718], and perhaps with Paisiello [914]. There King Ferdinand commissioned him (as he had Haydn) to write him some pieces for the toylike lira organizzata, to which he was addicted (perhaps his only admirable trait). In 1789 Gyrowetz decided that his education was reasonably complete and went to Paris. He was pleased to find some of his symphonies in the orchestral repertoire there but was less pleased when he found them credited to Haydn. The Parisians, however, pointed out that it was a natural mistake and that the comparison was flattering. Meanwhile Gyrowetz found himself disinclined to sit around and watch the Revolution develop, so he went to England, which was already sinking from the weight of refugee musicians. According to Gyrowetz himself, he found the air of freedom unbelievably heady

and the bad taste of the English unbelievable. But his music was performed to applause, he got commissions from Salomon, and had the privilege of showing Haydn the sights when he arrived in 1791. Later that same year he wrote his first opera, *Semiramis*, for the Pantheon Theatre, which had just been turned over to that sport. But just before its opening, the Pantheon burned down and *Semiramis* went with it. Soon afterward Gyrowetz found that the heady air was also chill and dank and gave him the sniffles, and retreated to Vienna where he settled. Apparently the government saw something useful in his cosmopolitan experience, for it used him as a sort of diplomatic courier on and off for the next decade. Appointed composer to the Hoftheater in 1804, he largely gave up other forms of composition in favor of opera and ballet. Between then and 1834, he wrote more than fifty such works. One is intrigued by such titles as *Ida die Büssende (Ida the Penitent), Das Winterquartier in Amerika (Winterquarters in America),* and *Der Augenarzt (The Eye Doctor,* his most successful work); but one also takes note of *Il finto Stanislao (The Fake Stanislas)* to the same libretto that Verdi used for his disastrous *Un Giorno di regno (King for a Day)* thirty years later, and *Hans Sachs im vorgerückten Alter (Hans Sachs in Old Age),* the first opera using the protagonist of Wagner's *Die Meistersinger.* Gyrowetz, who musically went on sounding like Haydn, came to be regarded as an anachronism, but he was a dear old thing, so no one told him. He retired in 1831 and lived out his eighty-four years on CARE-packages supplied by friends. Toward the end he wrote his memoirs, which he insisted on casting in the third person.

Gyrowetz was amazingly prolific. Besides the stage works, he left some 40 symphonies, 3 *sinfonie concertante,* 2 piano concerti, nearly 50 quartets, as many piano trios, and so on. Despite the confusion with Haydn, he had individuality and imagination. However, he awaits revival.

RECORDINGS: The Prague Chamber Orchestra has recorded the overture to the ill-fated *Semiramis* and a very early symphony.

[1033] DRAGONETTI, Domenico Carlo Maria (Drà-gō-net'-tē, Dō-mā'-nē-kō Kär'-lō Mà-rē'-à)
CONTRABASSIST
BORN: Venice, April 10, 1763
DIED: London, April 16, 1846

Sometimes called the "Paganini of the double-bass" (and by Alexander Thayer, the biographer of Beethoven [1063]), "the greatest contrabassist known to history," Dragonetti was certainly the first of the infrequent virtuosi on that unwieldy instrument. His father has been variously described as an orchestral musician and a barber. The boy supposedly learned the guitar and either the contrabass or the violin (the latter seems more reasonable!) on his own. At any rate, when he was twelve, he studied contrabass with Michele Berini, the first-desk man at St. Mark's. At thirteen he was taken into the orchestra of the Teatro San Benedetto, and five years later Berini made way for him at the Basilica. During this period he also played in an opera orchestra in Vincenza, where, supposedly, he discovered his beloved Gasparo da Salò instrument under a pile of rubble. He was soon offered a handsome sum to come to St. Petersburg, but the authorities at St. Mark's managed to outbid the czarina.

In 1794, however, Dragonetti was unable to resist an invitation to London, where he settled. People were thunderstruck at his playing, and he was hired immediately as first bass at the King's Theatre. He shared a desk with the brilliant first cellist Robert Lindley, with whom he enjoyed a close life-long friendship, and with whom he frequently concertized. Later Lindley's son William, also a cellist, sometimes appeared with them. He also made friends with the visiting Haydn [871], who learned much about the potential of the instrument from him. Unhappily, the concerto that Haydn wrote for him has disappeared. Dragonetti returned the visit after Haydn went home. In Vienna he also met Beethoven [1063] and Simon Sechter, who arranged some of his music. Much to Beethoven's delight, Dragonetti played his G minor cello sonata at sight. Dragonetti regularly transposed both cello and violin compositions to his own use; he and Lindley liked to play Viotti's [988] violin duos together on their respective instruments. Dragonetti was in Vienna as the guest of Prince Staremberg when the city was taken by the French in 1809. Convinced that they would drag him back to Paris, he hid out under an assumed name. Back in London he became a member of the Philharmonic Society. Socially, he was very popular and something of a bon vivant. He was addicted to snuff and had an admirable collection of snuffboxes, but he also collected musical instruments, furniture, pictures, and costume dolls, and left a handsome music library to the British Museum. When he played, his dog always lay

at his feet. At the age of eighty-two he was in the orchestra at Bonn for the unveiling of the Beethoven memorial. When he died a year later, he ordered his beloved Gasparo da Salò given to St. Mark's. His compositional output includes concerti, string quintets, songs, and miscellaneous pieces.

RECORDINGS: Thomas Lom and Mario Anastasio have recorded two concerti, and Ludwig Streicher an *Andante and Rondo.*

[1034] MAYR, Johannes Simon (Mī'-er, Yō-hàn'-es Sē'-mōn)
KEYBOARDIST, CONDUCTOR, TEACHER
BORN: Mendorf, June 14, 1763
DIED: Bergamo, December 2, 1845

As "Giovanni Simone," Mayr was easily the most successful opera composer in Italy in the generation before Rossini, but there is no truth in the claim that he was of Italian blood. He studied music with his father, the schoolmaster-organist of a village near Ingolstadt, and demonstrated superior talent. He also had a fine voice, which got him into the Jesuit school in Ingolstadt when he was eleven. But at about the same time, Pope Clement XIV, decided (as he put it) to cut the mast to save the ship and disbanded the order. Without much parental encouragement, Mayr went on with self-education in music, mastering most of the standard orchestral instruments. At eighteen, however, he bowed to his father's wish that he become a priest and entered the university as a theology major. When the authorities took note of his abilities, they appointed him as university organist. In 1786 he published a book of *Lieder,* his only known compositions in his native language. Shortly afterward, he fell in with a Baron Thomas de Bessus from eastern Switzerland, who persuaded Mayr to accompany him to Italy. The baron turned him over to Carlo Lenzi, choirmaster of Santa Maria Maggiore in Bergamo. This proved to be a poor move, for Mayr soon realized that he already knew as much as Lenzi. Then Count Pesenti, one of the canons, stepped in and financed his way to study with Ferdinando Giuseppe Bertoni, *maestro di cappella* at St. Mark's in Venice. Mayr arrived there in 1789 and became a violist at the Teatro La Fenice, when it opened three years later.

At first Mayr met success with oratorios, but in the early 1790s the visiting Peter von Winter [987] persuaded him to try his hand at opera. In 1794 La Fenice successfully staged his maiden effort, *Saffo,* and by the time the next decade had passed, thirty-five of his operas had been produced, increasingly internationally. In 1796, Mayr married one of his students, Angiola Venturali, but she died a year later giving birth to her first child. In 1799 he began his successful connection with La Scala and in 1802 went back to Bergamo to succeed Lenzi. Two years later, he married his sister-in-law, Lucrezia. From his return, he had gone to work building up the *cappella,* which was in sad shape. Then he turned his attention to the choir school, which in 1805 became the Lezioni Caritatevoli di Musica (roughly, Charity School of Music) and, long after, the Bergamo Conservatory. Mayr's most famous pupil there was Gaetano Donizetti [1155], whose name it now bears. Another was the legendary tenor Giovanni Battista Rubini. In 1809 Mayr took on the direction of the Teatro Sociale, and in 1822 founded the Società Filarmonica. Failing eyesight increasingly limited his work after 1820, and he was completely blind six years later. In 1838 he returned briefly to Mendorf where his sister still lived. His wife died in 1844. His great pupil followed him in 1848. In 1875 Mayr's and Donizetti's bodies were reinterred in the church.

Besides his 68 operas, Mayr wrote an enormous amount of sacred music, as well as cantatas, songs, and a few instrumental works. In opera he was influenced by Gluck [803] and by the Vienna-Mannheim approaches to orchestration and is a vital link between the time-honored Neapolitan tradition and that of the so-called nineteenth century *bel canto* school.

RECORDINGS: His masterpiece of 1813, *Medea in Corinto,* is conducted on records by Newell Jenkins. Maria Littauer has recorded one of his 2 piano concerti, Gianfranco Plenizio conducts two *divertimenti.*

[1035] DANZI, Franz Ignaz (Dánt'-sē, Fránts Ég'-nàts)
CELLIST, CONDUCTOR
BORN: Schwetzingen, June 15, 1763
DIED: Karlsruhe, April 13, 1826

Innocente Danzi, an Italian of uncertain origins, joined the Mannheim orchestra in 1754 as a cellist, married the dancer Barbara Toeschi, daughter and sister respectively of two of his colleagues, and produced three musical children, Johann Baptist, a violinist; Franziska (later Lebrun), a singer; and Franz. Franz was appointed to the cello section in 1778. Within a matter of weeks, however, his employer succeeded to the Bavarian electorate and moved his orchestra to Munich. Young Danzi, however, chose to

stay behind to study with Abt Vogler [960], play in the German opera house the elector had established, and try his own hand at the stage medium. When Innocenz Danzi, as Innocente was now known, retired in 1783, Franz went to Munich to take his place. In 1790 he married the prima donna Margarethe Marchand, who had lived with the Mozarts for five years and studied with Leopold [816]. They left Munich to tour and found a place in the touring company run by Domenico Guardasoni, who had originally produced *Don Giovanni* and who featured the Mozart [992] operas. (Danzi became his conductor.) In 1796 Frau Danzi joined the Munich Opera, and two years later her husband was appointed second-in-command to Peter von Winter [987]. But he was so desolated by her premature death in 1800 (at thirty-two) that he resigned and absented himself from all public performance for seven years. In 1807, however, he got himself together and took the post of *Kapellmeister* at the Stuttgart court of King Frederick II of Württemberg. Doubtless there were times when he wished he hadn't, for Frederick, a disciple of his Prussian namesake, was a despot of the mediaeval stripe. However, Danzi encountered there the secretary to the king's brother, young Carl Maria von Weber [1124], and the two, despite the generation that lay between them, became close friends. In their correspondence, Weber, for reasons best known to him, addressed Danzi as "Rapunzel," and signed himself "Krautsalat." In 1810, two years after Frederick's gendarmes exiled Weber for his father's debts, Danzi quit to become *Kapellmeister* to the Grand Duke Karl of Baden, Napoleon's stepson-in-law, at Karlsruhe, where he spent the rest of his life building up the musical forces on the Mannheim model and promoting Weber's operas. Danzi, a prolific and considerable composer in all forms and a fine orchestrator, exerted a strong influence on Weber. Danzi was a pre-Romantic with both invention and skill.

RECORDINGS: There has been a recent minirevival of his work on long-playing records—e.g., the Concerto in E Minor for Cello played by Thomas Blees and Wolfgang Boettcher; a flute concerto by Raymond Meylan; four flute concerti by András Adjorán; wind quintets by the New York Woodwind Quintet, the Boehm Quintet, and the Soni Ventorum; several quartets for bassoon and strings by Arthur Grossman; horn sonatas by Franz Koch and Barry Tuckwell; and a sonata for two organs by Walter Opp and Wilhelm Krumbach.

[1036] MÉHUL, Étienne-Nicolas (Mã-ül',
Ā-tyen' Nē-kō-làs')
ORGANIST
BORN: Givet, June 22, 1763
DIED: Paris, October 18, 1817

Méhul is an important figure in the development of opéra-comique and might have
loomed larger in the history of music had
not his health and French politics prevented. His birthplace was in a backwoods
village just up the Meuse from the Belgian
city of Dinant. Legend has it that his father
was an impecunious cook, but he was, in
fact, steward to the Count of Montmorency
and later went into the wine business. The
boy studied with the blind organist of the
local Franciscan monastery, the Couvent
des Récollets, and allegedly succeeded him
there at the age of ten. Two years later the
Abbot of Lavaldieu, about seventeen miles
south of Givet, brought back from Württemberg a crackerjack organist named Wilhelm Hanser (not Hauser, as many accounts have it). Stories differ about how
Méhul became his pupil. Some have him
trudging the weary distance back and forth
between home and lessons. Others have him
importuning Abbot Lissoir to admit him as
a novice. Whatever happened, he eventually
became a helper in the monastery gardens,
and finally Hanser's assistant. Inevitably an
influential   and   oh-so-musical   stranger
chanced by, and, noting his talent, insisted
that he go to Paris.

Arriving in the capital in 1778, Méhul betook himself for lessons to J. F. Edelmann
[959], whose career was later cut short by
the guillotine. Supposedly he paid his way
by giving lessons himself. Whatever he did,
he found economics in Paris a tough course.
Legend has it that he managed to take in
the premiere of Gluck's [803] Iphigénie en
Tauride in 1779 and saw that writing operas
would be his fate. Eventually he found a patron in a Mme. de Silly, who took him into
her home. Shortly afterward, in 1782, his
Ode sacrée was performed at the Concert
Spirituel, and he published his 3 attractive
piano sonatas. He also began practicing opera writing, and eventually the Opéra asked
him to set a libretto called Alonso et Cora.
He finished it just in time for the Revolution. By the time the company had got itself
sorted out, he had had the immensely successful Euphrosine performed at the Théâtre
Favart in 1790. Cora, as it was now called,
was staged in 1791. It was followed by
Stratonice, in a severe vein that he soon
abandoned, and by national madness. The
watchwords were sink or swim, and Méhul
gave himself over to band music, republican

hymns, and the committee-composed Le
Congrès des rois, as well as operas on edifying themes. It all paid off. He was granted
an annuity in 1794, was elected to the Institut (the newly founded official pantheon
of French intellectual and artistic leaders)
and to the directorate of the Conservatoire
in 1795, and was invited by Napoleon himself to the Battle of the Nile in 1797. (Méhul
declined on grounds of health.) In fact, for a
time, he enjoyed Bonaparte's patronage and
the commissioning of self-congratulatory
cantatas and such, for which he was
awarded the Légion d'honneur in 1804. In
1800 Méhul married, but his wife left him
shortly afterward. His most successful opera, and one that is still occasionally revived, was the biblical Joseph of 1807. But as
time went on, he found his brand of French
music being replaced (again!) by the influence of Italy, and his refusal to knuckle under lost him support at the Opéra. Of his
nearly 40 operas, only five were written after Joseph. Moreover, never healthy, he was
increasingly debilitated by tuberculosis. By
1816 he could no longer work. They sent him
to Provence to restore his health, but he was
too far gone and a few months later came
home to die. An unfinished comic opera,
Valentine de Milan, was completed by his
nephew and adopted son, Louis-Joseph
Daussoigné-Méhul (1790–1875), and was
produced by the Opéra-Comique in 1822.

Save for some of the overtures espoused
by various conductors—Les Deux Aveugles
de Tolède (The Two Blind Men of Toledo),
by Marcel Couraud; Timoléon, by Thomas
Beecham; and Le juene Henri (Young
Henry), by Thomas Beecham and Raymond
Leppard—and snippets from Joseph, mostly
from half a century and more ago, Méhul's
operas still await phonographic attention.
There are recordings of the first of his 2 interesting symphonies (by Rolf Kleinert), a
piano sonata (by Luciano Sgrizzi), and two
Napoleonic pieces for chorus and band (by
Desiré Dondeyne).

[1037] DEMAR, Johann Sebastian
(Dem'-är, Yō'-hàn Se-bàst'-yàn)
ORGANIST, CONDUCTOR, PUBLISHER
BORN: Gauaschach, June 29, 1763
DIED: Orléans, c. 1832

Demar came from a Bavarian village to
Strasbourg to study with Franz Xaver Richter [777]. Then he went back to become organist at Weissenburg for a time, before embarking on travels that led him to Austria,
to Italy, and back to France, where he settled in Paris just before the Revolution, dur-

ing which he was metamorphosed into Se-
bastien Démar. After the turn of the century, he moved to Orléans, where he organized the Grand Concert d'Amateurs and
became a music publisher. He wrote concerti and chamber music and a number of
instrumental methods. RECORDINGS: He
seems to be represented on records only by
some fantasias for two flageolets (recorder-
like instruments) on popular operatic airs
played by Roger Cotte.

[1038] GEBAUER, Michel Joseph (Ge-
bou'-er, Mē-shel' Zhō-zef')
OBOIST, VIOLIST, BANDMASTER
BORN: La Fère, 1763
DIED: Russia (?), 1812

The Gebauers are said to have come to
France from Saxony. The father of the tribe
(first name unknown) became a member of
the band of the Garde Suisse at Versailles,
as did his two eldest sons, Michel Joseph,
an oboist, and François René [1075], a bassoonist. Two others, Pierre Paul (1775–?)
and Étienne François (1777–1823), played
horn and flute respectively in Paris orchestras. Michel Joseph was born in a village
near Laon, began his band career in 1777,
and six years later joined the royal chapel as
a violist. An accident sent him back to the
oboe, which he played in the Garde Nationale band and in theater orchestras, and
taught at the Conservatoire from 1795 to
1800. He then became director of Napoleon's own Garde Consulaire band and a
member of his chamber music group. He
wrote music for vaudevilles and small ensembles but was chiefly celebrated for his
military music. RECORDINGS: Desiré
Dondeyne has recorded selections from his
first suite of Fanfares and Marches for four
instruments and kettledrums. It includes
the march La Victoire, which Gebauer had
his boys play as the emperor entered smol-
dering Moscow. He disappeared on the way
home.

[1039] INGALLS, Jeremiah
CHOIRMASTER, TEACHER, TAVERNER,
COOPER, FARMER
BORN: Andover, Mass., March 1, 1764
DIED: Hancock, Vt., April 6, 1828

Ingalls, who had only a rudimentary education, moved around Vermont a good deal
(Newbury, Rochester, Hancock) in his efforts to make a living at his various professions. His large family constituted a sort of
domestic orchestra. His only publication,

The Christian Harmony, is unusual in that it
includes revival hymns and adaptations of
dance tunes and other secular music. Needless to say, it won little popularity in New
England, where sterner stuff was wanted.
His fuguing tune "Northfield," once known
widely, he supposedly made up by way of
complaint when his dinner one day took
longer than he liked to be put on the table.
RECORDINGS: "Northfield" is included in a
recorded program of early hymn tunes by
the Western Wind Ensemble.

[1040] FIORAVANTI, Valentino (Fē-ôr-à-
vàn'-tē, Và-len-tē'-nō)
CONDUCTOR
BORN: Rome, September 11, 1764
DIED: Capua, June 16, 1837

Fioravanti, who wrote no fewer than 75 operas between 1784 and c. 1820, has been
called the most important composer of opera buffa born after Paisiello [914] and before Rossini [1143]—though he also wrote
dramatic works. He studied with Giuseppe
Jannaconi, a "Palestrinan" and later, appropriately, director of the Cappella Giulia in
St. Peter's. After that he studied in Naples
with the theorist Nicola Sala. He began his
theatrical conducting career in Rome in 1781
and produced his first opera, an intermezzo,
there three years later. He had his first hit in
Naples in 1788 with Gl' inganni fortunati
(The Lucky Deceptions), and thereafter divided much of his time between the two cities. In 1799 he produced his masterpiece Le
Cantatrici villane (The Rustic Divas) in Naples and a son, Vincenzo, who became a
composer of some note, in Rome. From 1801
to 1805, Fioravanti was the conductor of the
Teatro San Carlos in Lisbon but left for
Paris with the outbreak of the Peninsular
War. There he wrote I virtuosi ambulanti
(The Strolling Virtuosi) for the French Théâtre-Italien, before returning to Italy. In
1816 Jannaconi died of a stroke, and Fioravanti was named his successor. There he
turned increasingly to sacred music and
gave up opera altogether. RECORDINGS: The
1951 revival of Le Cantatrici villane, performed in Rome under the baton of Mario
Rossi, was committed to records.

[1041] HOLDEN, Oliver
CARPENTER, MERCHANT, TEACHER,
PREACHER, POLITICIAN
BORN: Shirley, Mass., September 18,
1765
DIED: Charlestown, Mass., September 4,
1844

Holden published a number of collections of hymn tunes and the like. One of his own melodies, "Coronation," is familiar to many modern churchgoers as "All Hail the Power of Jesus' Name." After serving as a youthful marine in the Continental forces, Holden settled in Charlestown in 1787 where he worked as a carpenter and held the office of justice of the peace. Later he opened a music store, where he gave music lessons. In 1792 he published his first book, the little *American Harmony*, and shortly afterward announced that he was about to issue a monthly musical magazine. Evidently little interest was evinced, and the project seems never to have got past the planning stage. In 1795, together with Samuel Holyoke [**1027**] and a Dane named Hans Gram, he put out *The Massachusetts Compiler*, a combination hymnal and theory text of some historical importance. Later he became a preacher and for fifteen years, 1818–33, represented his district in the Massachusetts legislature. He left about 250 compositions, including some ambitious anthems and a couple of memorial pieces to George Washington. RECORDINGS: The Berkeley Chamber Singers have recorded "Coronation" as Holden wrote it.

[1042] OGIŃSKI, Michał Kleofas (Ō-gin'-skē, Mē'-khȧlw Klȧ'-ō-fȧs)
DIPLOMAT, WRITER, PIANIST, VIOLINIST
BORN: Guzów, September 25, 1765
DIED: Florence, October 15, 1833

Ogiński was the son of Prince Andrzej Ogiński, Governor of Troki, and the nephew of Prince Michał Kazimierz Ogiński, military commander of Lithuania, harpist, violinist, and canal builder. Born on the family estate near Warsaw, he studied the violin with Józef Kozłowski, who, shortly afterward, created a scandal by defecting to Russia. Like his uncle, he is also supposed to have had lessons with Viotti [**988**]. After serving in diplomatic posts in Holland and England, Ogiński was appointed treasurer of Lithuania in 1793. But following the final partition of Poland, the Russians seized his property, and he was forced to flee for his life. He went to Constantinople, the Turks having refused to admit that Poland no longer existed, and there dreamed of freeing his country. He applied to Napoleon for aid, and in 1799 wrote his only opera, *Vélis et Valcour*, subtitled "Bonaparte in Cairo," but it didn't help his cause. Eventually he gave up, successfully sought a pardon from the czar, and returned to Poland, where he became a senator. Following the post-Napole-

onic "final solution" in 1815, however, he left Poland and politics for good and, after some wanderings, settled in Florence, where he published his memoirs in 1827. His musical output consists mostly of songs and piano pieces. RECORDINGS: Hans Kann has recorded the corpus of 19 polonaises, which, though by no means so grandiose as Chopin's, show the form handled with artistry. Half a dozen songs have been recorded by Eugeniusz Sasiadek.

[1043] DUVERNOY, Frédéric Nicolas (Dü-vârn-wȧ', Frā-dā-rēk' Nē-kō-lȧs')
HORNIST, TEACHER
BORN: Montbéliard, October 16, 1765
DIED: Paris, July 19, 1838

Frédéric Duvernoy is not to be confused with Victor Duvernoy (1842–1907), the author of a set of piano exercises known as the *École de mécanisme*, or with the several other Duvernoys of French musical history. This one, an autodidact, came from the Franche-Comté to Paris where he reigned for twenty years as one of the star performers in all music. In effect, he was the first modern horn player. Before him, hornists specialized either in the high register *(cor-alt)* or the low *(cor-basse)*. Even the great Stich [**945**] was a *cor-basse*. Duvernoy wanted the best of both possible worlds and invented the technique known as *cor mixte*. He played in the orchestras of the Comédie-Italienne and the Théâtre Feydeau and in the Garde Nationale band, and also concertized, before coming to the Opéra in 1796. Three years later he was promoted to the anomalous position of solo horn, independent of the orchestral quartet. He had already become first professor of horn at the Paris Conservatoire the previous year. Napoleon later made him first horn in the imperial chapel. Duvernoy was given the *Légion d'honneur* in 1815. He retired from the Conservatoire a year later and from the Opéra the year after that but kept his chapel appointment until 1830. He published a horn method and wrote concerti and chamber works featuring the horn. RECORDINGS: Désiré Dondeyne has memorialized him on records with a march from his pen.

[1044] STEIBELT, Daniel (Shtī'-belt, Dȧn'-yel)
PIANIST, TEACHER, ADMINISTRATOR
BORN: Berlin, October 22, 1765
DIED: St. Petersburg, September 20, 1823

Dussek's [1016] greatest rival at the box office was Steibelt. Biographers regularly dismiss him as a fraud; it is clear that Steibelt had the instincts of a Barnum, but he was not without talent. The son of a manufacturer of keyboard instruments, he supposedly studied with Kirnberger [821]. (Since Kirnberger was primarily a violinist, perhaps this explains the weaknesses in Steibelt's technique.) His early years are not well documented. For example, in 1784 we find him a deserter from the Prussian army —which there is no record of his joining. After a time spent concertizing, mostly in the Germanies, he settled in Paris in 1790. There his good looks, his hyacinthine curls, and his romantic dress probably did as much to make him popular as did his playing. In 1792 he completed his first opera, *Roméo et Juliette*. It had been slated for the Paris Opéra, but was finally produced a year later by the Théâtre Feydeau and was rapturously received. But Steibelt's life-style was not calculated to charm everyone. He is said to have been a kleptomaniac, and he was often dishonest. When, in 1796, two Paris publishers discovered that he had sold them both exclusive rights to the same compositions, he left hastily for Holland.

Steibelt arrived in London before the year was out and began appearing in fashionable concerts there the following spring. In 1798 he made an enormous hit with his third concerto, whose third movement was one of those musical evocations of storms soon to become so popular. He also produced an opera, *Albert and Adelaide*, at the Covent Garden Theatre, to which his own musical contributions were minimal. About this time, he married ("without benefit of clergy," whispered the gossips) a reportedly very sexy-looking young woman, whose great talent was shaking her tambourine. For ensuing concerts he wrote some "bacchanales" for piano and tambourine, which the pair performed together to the wild delight of the audience.

The Steibelts returned to Germany in 1799. There, though the Prussian government had apparently officially wiped his military desertion from the books, he played the role of an outlander of mysterious origins who knew no word of German. He ignored or abbreviated orchestral rehearsals, which, when he remembered them, he held behind locked doors so that his rivals would not steal his "special effects." (One was the tremolo beloved of barroom pianists ever since.) He was often late for performances and indeed showed much of the laudable independence of a modern rock superstar. He was scheduled for two orchestral concerts

in Berlin, but the first was such a farce that the orchestra refused to play the second. His virtuoso playing was (if one ignored the limping left hand) apparently very flashy, but he was no good in lyrical passages— facts which showed up embarrassingly when he insisted on "dueling" Beethoven [1063] in Vienna in 1800. He fled back to Paris, which, apparently, had also forgiven him his sins. For Napoleon he put on a performance of Haydn's [871] *The Creation*, which he himself had "corrected" and emended, and which caused a scandal. For the next six years, however, he worked in both Paris and London, chiefly as a writer and producer of ballets and a composer of (salable) piano music. But in 1808, with his creditors snapping at his heels, he skipped town again, this time for good. He finally came to rest in St. Petersburg. Fortuitously, soon afterward, Boieldieu [1084] gave up the directorship of the Imperial French Opera, and Alexander I named Steibelt his successor. Steibelt was increasingly occupied with his duties, with teaching, and with writing operas and ballets, and retired from playing in 1814. Six years later he emerged for a one-time-only appearance as soloist in his eighth and last concerto, which terminated in a "bacchanalian rondo" with chorus. He died a lingering death, and when he was gone, outsiders had to support the poor tambourine lady and her children.

Steibelt, who correctly gauged public taste, turned out reams of piano music (nearly 400 sonatas alone), the majority of it meretricious potpourris, fantasias, variations, and dances. It was such things, along with his character, that for more than a century obscured his good qualities. Modern scholars, reviewing his music, have been surprised to find much that is interesting among the dross, and some have gone so far as to call him a forerunner of Chopin. He was a fine orchestrator, and his small body of chamber music is said to be worth taking seriously. Most of the big works are no longer available, but *Roméo*, which was published, is said to have its points.

RECORDINGS: The pieces that appear on record, however, show his popular side, for the most part—some bacchanales (with tambourine!) from Raymond Lewenthal, and a battle piece, *La Journée d'Ulm* from Valda Aveling. Duo organists Walter Opp and Wilhelm Krumm, however, tackle one of the seriously intended sonatas.

[1045] WESLEY, Samuel
ORGANIST

BORN: Bristol, February 24, 1766
DIED: London, October 11, 1837

Like his elder brother Charles [1005], Samuel Wesley embarrassed his father by being a musical prodigy. Though it took him three months longer to get the hang of the piano, he turned out to be even more brilliant, at least for a while. If his reverend parent may be trusted, Samuel learned to read music by poring over a score of Handel's [683] *Samson,* and then mastered writing it on his own, with no coaching from the sidelines. Fortified with some lessons from a local organist, he completed his first oratorio, *Ruth,* when he was eight, and presented it to Dr. Boyce [787], who vowed to preserve it as "the most curious product of [his] musical library." Like Charles, Samuel was trotted out to play for visiting musical celebrities—though he balked at performing for William Crotch, nine years his junior, for fear of mortifying him. He concertized for a time with Charles and acquired considerably more formal education than he. But at seventeen, apparently in a rebellious gesture, he converted to Roman Catholicism, much to the distress of his aged father, and celebrated by writing several Masses, one of which he shipped off to Pope Pius VI. (Later he became disillusioned and gave up the faith.) When he was twenty-one, coming home after a social evening, he fell into an excavation and knocked himself silly. His later fits of depression and odd behavior were said to have resulted from the accident, but it is more likely that he was born eccentric.

In 1793 Samuel married one Charlotte Louisa Martin. The union produced three children but was otherwise not a success. The Reverend Martin Madan, author of some familiar hymns and the tract *Thelyphthora (Down with Women),* had inoculated Samuel with some radical ideas about the blessings of polygamy. Since Charlotte proved an unenthusiastic bedfellow and soon let herself run to obesity, Samuel accordingly sought solace in their housekeeper, Sarah Suter, with whom he lived in unholy matrimony after Charlotte left him. Sarah bore him several children, including Samuel Sebastian [1213], perhaps the most gifted of all the musical Wesleys.

Around 1800, Samuel heard the fifteen-year-old George Frederick Pinto (who died six years later, "a martyr to dissipation") play something by Sebastian Bach [684]. It was a revelation, and Wesley became a torch-eyed zealot for the Bachian cause. He descended on the aged Dr. Charles Burney to try to change his unfavorable opinion of the composer, and he cursed his brother Charles for a miserable Handelian, led astray by God knows what evil forces. He became a voice crying in the wilderness. Long before the Bach Gesellschaft was formed, he projected a complete works, and got as far as publishing the organ trios, the *Well-Tempered Clavier,* and Forkel's (translated) biography. In 1811 he became organist-conductor of the Birmingham Festival and in 1824 organist of Camden Chapel, though his work was several times interrupted by his "spells." In 1834 he conducted his memorial anthem to his brother, "All Go unto One Place," at the concert of the Sacred Harmonic Society, and retired from further public activity. That September the *Messiah,* in the person of Felix Mendelssohn [1200], who in Germany had raised Bach from the dead, arrived in England. The old man went to hear him play. Afterward he tried to slip away quietly, but someone spotted him and introduced him to the young genius, who insisted that he play for him. When Mendelssohn praised his performance, he said sadly, "You should have heard me forty years ago." He died a month later.

Unlike Charles Wesley, Samuel was extremely prolific. Besides the Masses (and motets) and the expectable voluntaries, variations, songs, and hymns (more than 600 of these), he produced services, anthems, concerti, symphonies, and chamber works. Writing as he did in the Dark Age of English music, he has long been ignored, but recent investigations suggest that he may have been the most considerable composer of the post-Arne [783] generation.

RECORDINGS: On records Gordon and Grady Wilson play an early organ duet. Of much more interest, however, is the Symphony in D Major recorded by Kenneth Montgomery.

[1046] DOCHE, Joseph Denis (Dōsh, Zhō-zef' Də-nēs')
STRING PLAYER, CONDUCTOR
BORN: Paris, August 22, 1766
DIED: Soissons, July 20, 1825

Doche's forte was the vaudeville—by this time a sort of musical comedy, though with no aspirations to sophistication. He was a choirboy-student at Meaux Cathedral, just outside eastern Paris, and at nineteen was appointed choirmaster at Coutances Cathedral in Normandy. In 1794 he joined the orchestra of the Théâtre du Vaudeville in Paris, playing (though not simultaneously) viola, cello, and double-bass. Around 1799 he began writing music for the works produced there and in 1810 was appointed director. He retired to Soissons in 1823. In 1828 his son Alexandre Pierre Joseph (1789–1849) began a twenty-year stint as conductor at the Vaudevilles. The elder Doche also wrote a few *opéras-comiques,* some sacred music, and songs, but was best known for his vaudeville tunes, an anthology of which appeared three years before he died. RECORDINGS: One of the tunes has been recorded (as it might very well have been played then in the boondocks) by Michele Fromenteau on a hurdy-gurdy.

[1047] CALLCOTT, John Wall
ORGANIST, OBOIST, WRITER
BORN: London, November 20, 1766
DIED: Bristol, May 15, 1821

Callcott, the son of a prosperous bricklayer-turned-contractor, was probably the foremost writer of his time of those curiously English phenomena, the glee and the catch. A brilliant student academically, he gave up dreams of becoming a physician at an early age when he became ill watching his first operation. He was largely (and inadequately) self-taught in music. At seventeen he was appointed second organist of the church of St. George the Martyr in Bloomsbury and what Local 802 terms a "steady extra oboist" at the Antient Concerts. He was granted a B.Mus. degree by Oxford University and that same year won three of the four prizes offered by the Catch Club, and went on winning them until the club decided that it was no longer any fun. In 1787 he joined Samuel Arnold [915] and the elder Thomas Linley in founding the Glee Club, a sort of chowder-and-singing society that flourished for seventy years. He was elected to the Royal Society in 1788, received important performing and teaching appointments, and was given an honorary doctorate by Oxford in 1800. An officer of the Kensington Volunteers, he founded their band in 1801, supplying the music and instruments and teaching the players himself. Despite some lessons with Haydn [871] when the latter visited London, Callcott never really mastered instrumental writing. After 1797 he became increasingly involved in a projected dictionary of music. Meanwhile he published his *Musical Grammar,* long popular as a basic theory book, in 1806. A year later he suffered a mental breakdown and had to be institutionalized. He recovered in 1812 well enough to proceed with his work, but suffered an irreversible relapse five years later. He left *A Dictionary of Musicians* complete through "O" and thirty-six volumes of notes for his more comprehensive project. RECORDINGS: Glees have been recorded by the Scholars and by Ian Partridge.

[1048] ADDISON, John
CONTRABASSIST, CONDUCTOR, ENTREPRENEUR
BORN: London, c. 1766
DIED: London, January 30, 1844

Not to be confused with his twentieth-century English namesake [2298], this John Addison is said to have been the son of a humble mechanic. Since mechanics are usually anything but humble, this probably means that Addison, Sr., was an unskilled laborer. Having taught himself to play several instruments, John found a job as a cellist at Vauxhall Gardens. When he was in his latter twenties, he married a Miss Willems who had vocal aspirations. It occurred to them that they could make beautiful music together, and they went to Liverpool to prove their point. It was apparently there that Addison switched to the contrabass. Then Addison found a place in Dublin as a conductor and arranger in a private theater. In 1796 Mrs. Addison debuted at Covent Garden and stayed for the season. Perhaps the reviews were not satisfactory, for the next year she went to Bath for further study. Subsequently they returned to Dublin for three years. By the time the term was up, Addison had convinced himself he could get rich faster as a capitalist than as a musician, and so he went to Manchester and became the proprietor of a cotton mill. He found he was wrong: he got poorer. Returning to London, he became a partner in Michael Kelly's [1028] music firm, which failed in 1811. Between 1805 and 1817, he wrote and produced several comic operas and the like, and an oratorio, while he continued to serve as an orchestral musician. He also published songs and a singing manual. RECORDINGS: John Whitworth has recorded his setting of Shakespeare's "Fie on Sinful Fantasy."

[1049] CALL, Leonhard von (fun Kol, Lä′-ōn-hârt)
CIVIL SERVANT, GUITARIST
BORN: Eppan, March 19, 1767
DIED: Vienna, February 19, 1815

Born in a Tyrolian village, Call worked in Vienna as a minor court official. As a composer, he represents the taste of the so-called "Biedermeier" or *petit-bourgeois* period. He was noted for his parlor songs, for his pieces for the increasingly popular male choral societies, and for his more than 100 chamber works involving the guitar, which was enjoying a period of great popularity. RECORDINGS: Leo Witoszynskij has recorded one of his guitar sonatinas.

[1050] NUNES GARCIA, José Maurício
(Nōō′-nēsh Ger-sē′-à, Zhōō-zâ′ Mou-rē′-tsyō)
CONDUCTOR, TEACHER, PRIEST
BORN: Rio de Janeiro, September 22, 1767
DIED: Rio de Janeiro, April 18, 1830

Nunes Garcia appears to have been the first Brazilian composer of real stature. His father, Apolinário, who died when the boy was six, was an army lieutenant. His mother, Victoria Maria, was a descendant of slaves brought from Portuguese Guinea. Just how he was educated remains uncertain, but it is clear that he had both brains and talent. Supposedly he financed his music lessons by singing and dancing for coins on the streets. He also had a fine academic upbringing and ultimately mastered six languages. At seventeen, he was a founder of the Brazilian branch of the musical guild, the Fraternity of St. Cecilia. In 1791 he entered the monastic order of São Pedro dos Clérigos and was ordained the following year. Some time thereafter he opened a free music school. In 1798 he was also placed in charge of music at the cathedral. In the face of the Napoleonic invasion of Portugal in 1807, the regent, Dom João, moved his government to Brazil, then a Portuguese colony. Dom João named Nunes Garcia *mestre de capela* on the strength of his by-then reputation as the finest composer in the country. In 1811, however, Marcos Portugal, a tireless writer of operas and known all over Europe, followed his leader, and by adroit maneuvering (despite suffering a stroke in the year of his arrival), he had soon replaced Nunes Garcia at court. But the latter continued with his other duties and interests, despite steadily declining health. He conducted the first performances in Brazil of Mozart's **[992]** *Requiem* and Haydn's **[871]** *Creation*. Political events recalled Dom João (since 1816, King João [John] VI) back to Lisbon in 1821, appointing his son and heir Dom Pedro his viceroy. Under severe pressure, Dom Pedro declared Brazil independent that fall and was crowned emperor. Subsequent chaos put a damper on musical life in Rio, and in

1824 Nunes Garcia's mind began to fail. He died at sixty-two in extreme poverty. He wrote over 400 works, including a single opera; of these, nearly 250—mostly religious —are known to be extant. His masterpiece is said to be the grandiose *Requiem* (one of 4) that he wrote in 1816 in memory of Dom João's predecessor, the mad Queen Maria I. RECORDINGS: The 1816 *Requiem* has been recorded by Paul Freeman. There have also been numerous other recordings of choral and orchestral works on the Brazilian EMI-Coronado label, but these are not generally available domestically.

[1051] ROMBERG, Bernhard Heinrich
(Rōm′-bârk, Bârn′-härt Hīn′-rikh)
CELLIST, CONDUCTOR, TEACHER
BORN: Dinklage, November 11, 1767
DIED: Hamburg, August 13, 1841

Bernhard Romberg, the outstanding cellist of his day, was unrelated to the later Hungarian-born Sigmund Romberg **[1821]**, author of such operettas as *The Desert Song* and *The Student Prince*. His father and teacher, Bernhard Anton Romberg, later played bassoon in the *Kapelle* of the Bishop of Münster, as did his younger son, Anton. Bernhard Anton's brother, Gerhard Heinrich, who played clarinet and violin, was also a colleague there. *His* son and pupil, Andreas Jakob, who became a fine violinist, was just six months older than his cousin, Bernhard Heinrich, and the pair debuted *en duo* in Münster at the age of seven. They were virtually inseparable for a quarter of a century thereafter. (The story of the twin brothers Anton and Heinrich Romberg of Bonn who lived together and dressed and behaved exactly alike is almost certainly a garbled version of facts about the Rombergs generally.) After concertizing throughout Europe with great success for some years, the cousins entered the court orchestra at Bonn in 1790, where they were colleagues of Beethoven **[1063]**, Neefe **[954]**, Antonín Reicha **[1059]**, Ries **[1116]**, and the future publisher Simrock, among others. The French invasion of 1793 put an end to that brief idyll, and the cousins escaped to Hamburg, where they were employed in a theater orchestra for some months before going on an Italian tour. While they were visiting an old Bonn colleague in Rome, the French shadow began to darken that city, and so they moved on to Vienna. There they put up at Beethoven's. Bernhard played one of the cello sonatas with the composer at the keyboard, and the two played again in a benefit. The

Rombergs then returned to Hamburg, where both married—an action that was perhaps in part responsible for the parting of their ways. In 1801 they went to Paris. Bernhard stayed on to teach at the Conservatoire. Andreas returned to Hamburg where the wars wiped him out financially. In 1815 he succeeded Spohr [1112] as *Kapellmeister* at Gotha but fell ill and died in straitened circumstances. Two of his sons became court musicians in Russia.

Bernhard soon left Paris for Berlin, where he became a member of the *Kapelle* of Frederick William III, but the military situation forced him once again to flee in 1806. Eventually he went to Moscow, where in 1812 playing Beethoven's first "Rasumovsky" quartet for the first time, he became so upset by its modernity, that he supposedly hurled its part to the floor and jumped up and down on it. Shortly afterward, Moscow also became too warm for him, and he moved on to London. By 1815 he could return to Berlin as court *Kapellmeister,* but when Spontini [1081] was brought in as his superior three years later, he quit, moved back to Hamburg, and spent two lucrative decades touring as a soloist. Of his children, a daughter became an opera singer and a son, like his second cousins, a Russian court musician. There has been some confusion over which Romberg wrote what. (Both failed as opera composers.)

RECORDINGS: Andreas seems to have been the more substantial of the two, but I have traced nothing of his on records. Flute concerti by Bernhard have been recorded by John Wion, Peter Martin, and Jean-Pierre Rampal, and Wion has recorded a flute quintet. The Sonata for Harp and Cello has been recorded by Helga and Klaus Storck.

[1052] VEDEL, Artemiy Lukyanovitch
(Vā'-del, Ȧr-tā'-mē Look-yȧ-nō'-vitch)
CHOIRMASTER
BORN: Kiev, 1767
DIED: 1806

Vedel, about whom not much information is at hand, was a Moscow choirmaster for a while but went back to Kiev and entered the Perchersky Monastery as a novice. He found the strict life not to his taste and ran away to become a wanderer. He was arrested and spent most of the rest of his brief life in jail. Choral compositions of his are extant. RECORDINGS: Alexander Yurov has recorded one of them, a rather ambitious choral concerto.

[1053] BACKOFEN, Johann Georg Heinrich (Băk'-ō-ven, Yō'-hȧn Gā'-ôrg Hīn'-rikh)
CLARINETIST, HARPIST, FLUTIST, TEACHER
BORN: Durlach, July 6, 1768
DIED: Darmstadt, July 10, 1839

The "Bakeoven" family (as the name translates) was originally a musical one in Nuremberg. J.G.H. and his brothers Ernst and Gottfried, who became a bassoonist and a violinist-clarinetist respectively, were, however, born near Karlsruhe, but were sent back to Nuremberg for training. Having mastered the harp and established himself as a virtuoso on the clarinet and basset horn, J.G.H. came back to Nuremberg to study the flute. He settled in Gotha in 1802 and joined the court orchestra four years later. One of his harp pupils, Dorette Scheidler, married Spohr [1112] while the latter was *Kapellmeister* there. In 1811, during the Napoleonic Wars, Backofen moved permanently to the court of Hesse-Darmstadt. The date of his death is sometimes given as 1830. He wrote methods for both harp and clarinet and wrote a good deal of unassuming instrumental music. RECORDINGS: The Concerto Amsterdam has recorded a *sinfonia concertante* for two clarinets and orchestra, the Heidelberg Chamber Players a *concertante* for basset horn, harp, and cello, and the Consortium Classicum a quintet for clarinet and strings.

[1054] CARR, Benjamin
ORGANIST, SINGER, PUBLISHER, ETC.
BORN: London, September 12, 1768
DIED: Philadelphia, May 24, 1831

Benjamin Carr was one of the most energetic figures in the early history of American music. A pupil of Samuel Arnold [915] and Charles Wesley [1005], he had already made a name for himself in London when he sailed for Philadelphia in 1793. There he opened a music firm, Carr's Musical Repository, apparently the second oldest such business in this country. (Muller and Capron's beat it by a few weeks.) His father, mother, and brother followed him a year later and opened a plant in Baltimore where, some years later, "The Star-Spangled Banner" was first published. Carr also established a branch in New York, but sold it to James Hewitt in 1797. Benjamin Carr became organist of two Philadelphia churches, appeared occasionally as a pianist, and frequently as a singer. He made his operatic debut in Thomas Arne's [783] *Love in a Village.* He joined forces with Alexander Reinagle as an impresario and was associated with him in the Old American Company. In 1820, together with Reinagle's friend and teacher Raynor Taylor and others, Carr organized the Musical Fund Society to help support "decayed" musicians and to improve the state of musical art in America. Whether its orchestra or A. P. Heinrich's [1097] in the wilds of Kentucky gave the American premiere of Beethoven's fifth symphony is moot.

Carr published the musical periodicals *Carr's Musical Miscellany* and *The Gentleman's Amusement,* wherein he showed taste and enterprise in admitting both imported and homegrown compositions. *Gentleman's* was the first to publish Philip Phile's [882] *The President's March,* which was fitted to the younger Hopkinson's text "Hail, Columbia!" later on, and Carr's own *Federal Overture* (for flute duo), a medley that includes the first known musical appearance of "Yankee Doodle." He did notable service in arranging important European works for the forces locally available. His own compositions include stage pieces *(The Archers* was a forerunner of Rossini's [1143] *Guillaume Tell),* church music, songs, and piano pieces.

RECORDINGS: The *Federal Overture* has been recorded by members of the New York Flute Club.

[1055] JADIN, Louis Emmanuel (Zhà-dàn', Lōō-ēs' E-mà-nü-el')
PIANIST, CONDUCTOR, TEACHER
BORN: Versailles, September 21, 1768
DIED: Paris, April 11, 1853

Jadin's father and uncle played violin and bassoon respectively in the royal chapel at Versailles, and he himself began his career as a chorister there. His younger brother Hyacinthe [1058] supposedly taught him the piano. He debuted on that instrument at the Concert Spirituel in 1789 and was appointed second keyboardist at the Théâtre de Monsieur. When it became the Théâtre Feydeau, he moved up to make way for his brother. His opera *Joconde* was produced by that company in 1790 (two others had preceded it elsewhere) and by 1812, when he seems to have given up the stage, more than 35 such works by him had been performed. (Almost all are lost.) During the height of the Revolution, he joined the Garde Nationale for whose musical forces he wrote propaganda pieces, and was one of the committee of eleven (it seems more!) who whipped up *Le Congrès des rois.* From 1796 to 1816 he

taught at the Conservatoire in various capacities. In 1814 Louis XVIII put him in charge of the boys of the royal chapel. When he was ousted in the 1830 revolution, he also gave up the concertizing that made him in his day perhaps the most famous native-born pianist in France, and retired to his estate at Montfort l'Amaury. He died in his eighty-fifth year, virtually forgotten. His music—orchestral, concerted, chamber, keyboard, sacred, etc.—is pleasantly romantic. His songs have some historical importance. Lily Laskine and Robert Veyron-Lacroix have recorded a movement from a harp-piano duo as well as a *Fantasie Concertante* for harp, piano, and orchestra, and Bernard Kruysen two songs, including the once famous *"La Mort de Werther,"* inspired by Goethe's lachrymose novel.

[1056] OVSIANKO-KULIKOVSKY, Nikolai Dimitrievitch (Ōfs-yànk'-ō Kōō-lē-kof'-skē, Nē'-kō-lī Dē-mē-trē-yā'-vich)
BORN: c. 1768
DIED: c. 1846

When Ovsianko-Kulikovsky's twenty-first symphony, apparently written for the opening of the Odessa Theater in 1809, turned up in 1948, there was general rejoicing among the cultural commissars. Here was proof positive that Mother Russia, in the face of all those czarist-imported Italians and Frenchmen, could produce a symphonist of Haydn's [871] stature—or nearly. Furthermore this symphonist was no slavish imitator, but a true patriot who had ended his work with a Cossack dance. (Never mind that the composer and dance were technically Ukrainian.) Yevgeni Mravinsky was rushed to the recording studios to make this wonder available to the skeptical world. Alas! A few years later Mikhail Goldstein, a Jewish composer from Odessa (b. 1917), announced that he was Ovsianko-Kulikovsky and the whole thing had been a ruse to get published, his own works having been turned down by the state publishing house. For making such an outrageous and self-seeking claim, he was branded a liar, an opportunist, and a traitor to Russian culture. Ovsianko-Kulikovsky lives! So, when last heard of, did Goldstein—in Hamburg.

[1057] ASIOLI, Bonifazio (Àz-yō'-lē, Bō-nē-fàts'-yō)
HARPSICHORDIST, TEACHER, CONDUCTOR, ADMINISTRATOR

BORN: Coreggio, August 30, 1769
DIED: Coreggio, May 18, 1832

The Asioli musicians, from the Po Valley town that lent its name to the great Renaissance painter, are traceable back to the seventeenth-century guitarist, Francesco Asioli. Bonifazio was a prodigy and an autodidact, who had already written "adult" music by the time he was eight. In his early adolescence he toured as a harpsichordist and taught the instrument. The home folks produced his first operas for him when he was sixteen and appointed him municipal *maestro di cappella*. For some years he worked in Turin, Venice, and Milan for the Gherardini family. Eugène de Beauharnais, Napoleon's stepson and viceroy in Milan, put him in charge of his court music in 1803 and appointed him the first director and professor of composition at the Milan Conservatory. Meanwhile Asioli's elder brother Luigi, a singer, had moved to London, where he published some sonatas. Some sonatas that appeared there under Bonifazio's more famous name are now suspected to be Luigi's.

In 1810 Bonifazio accompanied the viceroy to Paris to see the latter's mother supplanted by the new empress, Marie-Louise of Austria. Four years later, when Lombardy was parceled out to the victorious Austrians, Asioli, now an alien, was dismissed. He returned to Coreggio, where he and another brother, Giovanni, ran a music school for the rest of their lives. (Giovanni died in 1831.) Bonifazio also set up the Conservatory in nearby Reggio Emilia, of which he was made honorary president. Among his pupils was Karl Mozart, Wolfgang's [992] elder son, back in Milan. Asioli published a dozen theory texts and methods, and his *Principi elementari di musica* was long a standard work in Italy. He wrote a few operas, and a good deal of sacred and instrumental music.

RECORDINGS: His piano sonatas have been cited as examples of high Classicism tilting toward the Romantic. Vladimir Pleshakov has recorded two piano sonatas.

[1058] JADIN, Hyacinthe (Zhà-da*n*, Hē-à-sant')
PIANIST
BORN: Versailles, 1769
DIED: Paris, September 1802

The younger brother of Louis Emmanuel Jadin [1055], and allegedly his teacher, was a pupil of Hüllmandel [997]. He made his solo debut at the Concert Spirituel in 1789

and succeeded his brother as number-two keyboard player at the Théâtre Feydeau. He came to be greatly admired as a performer and was named first professor of piano when the Conservatoire opened in 1795. Unhappily he died at thirty-three. Among his surviving works are 3 piano concerti, string quartets, and sonatas. RECORDINGS: Robert Veyron-Lacroix has recorded one of the sonatas, and Bernard Kruysen a romance.

[1059] REICHA, Antonín (Rī'-khà, Àn'-tō-nyēn)
FLUTIST, TEACHER, THEORIST
BORN: Prague, February 26, 1770
DIED: Paris, May 28, 1836

Nephew of Josef Reicha [978], colleague and friend of Beethoven [1063], teacher of many important composers, Antonín (later Anton, then Antoine) Reicha became notable for his sophisticated compositions for winds and for his startlingly advanced musical thinking. The son of a municipal musician who died shortly after the boy's birth, he got some training as a choirboy but not enough to suit him. At eleven he stowed away in the boot of a stagecoach to find a better life with his grandfather in Glatow (now Klatovy), a little mountain town near Pilsen. It quickly proved a step in the wrong direction, and he ran away to Wallerstein and his Uncle Joseph, a court cellist there. His Aunt Lucie spoke only French, and the locals spoke only German, so he learned both languages along with the piano, violin, and flute. In 1785 Uncle Joseph became first cellist and then *Kapellmeister* of Elector Max Franz's court orchestra at Bonn, where Anton was installed as a flutist. When Joseph discouraged his wish to write music as well as play it, the young man taught himself by reading Kirnberger [821] and such, and analyzing scores. Eventually his uncle gave in and helped him. Anton took up conducting in 1787 and matriculated at the local university two years later. When the French invasion scattered the court in 1794, he fled to Hamburg, where he abandoned playing and conducting for good, and became a teacher and composer. He also continued his researches, giving himself a thorough grounding in mathematics, which he always said afterward was the foundation of his musical understanding.

Ambitious to break into the world of opera and with a couple of scores in hand, Reicha moved on to Paris in 1799. His instrumental music was well received, but his operas were ignored, and after two years he went to Vienna. There he got at least private performances of two of his operas. (One, commissioned by the Empress Maria Theresa [Franz II's wife] starred that eminent lady.) He studied there, like his friend Beethoven, with Albrechtsberger [889] and Salieri [966], and had advice from Haydn [871], whom he had known in Bonn and Hamburg. He wrote treatises and exemplary manuals on variation and fugue. Breitkopf and Härtel bought and published about fifty of his compositions. In 1806 he visited his mother in Prague, and, despite past disagreements, there were tears and swoonings. He went on to Leipzig on business, but the Battle of Jena shut the town down, and it was four months before he could get back to Vienna. But by 1808, as he remarked, the boom of cannon had begun to strike him as quite unmusical, and he went back to Paris for good.

In Paris Reicha became an increasingly important factor in the musical life. He had three operas produced there—not really successfully, but he was satisfied. In 1817 he succeeded Méhul at a Conservatoire already dominated by his own pupils. In the fall of 1818, he married Virginie Enaust, who later provided him with two daughters. Though he wrote prodigally in all forms, it was at about this time that his wind quintets became the admiration of Paris. Reicha became a French citizen in 1829, was decorated with the *Légion d'honneur* in 1831, and succeeded Boieldieu in the Institut five years later. As his musical thinking progressed, he became the Conservatoire's token modernist and attracted such young Turks as Berlioz [1175], Liszt [1218], Gounod [1258], and Franck [1284]. He worked them hard and thoroughly but was astute enough to deal with each student as an individual. Those he taught had only good to say of his methods, though they did not always agree with his ideas. He experimented with folk tunes, odd meters, and strange combinations of instruments, and predicted that some day quarter-tones would be a common feature of the musical language. He and his adherents considered his *36 Fugues* (for piano) a breakthrough in a form long considered dead, though his opponents thought otherwise. His most important theoretical works were his 1814 treatise on melody as it relates to harmony, his composition course (which was the standard at the Conservatoire from 1818), and his treatise on advanced composition, which was his most controversial, far-seeing, and ultimately influential work. Perhaps his most famous advice to students was that they should never take up composition to get rich or even to make a living.

RECORDINGS: His 24 wind quintets continue to be performed and recorded, though most of the rest of his vast output has been neglected. But recordings do also include a funeral march for band (Desiré Dondeyne), the Quartet for 4 Flutes (Jean-Pierre Rampal), a symphony (Prague Chamber Orchestra), and some horn trios. Heinz Holliger performs a *Scena* for English horn and orchestra.

[1060] CARULLI, Ferdinando (Kà-rōōl'-lē, Fâr-dē-nàn'-dō)
GUITARIST, TEACHER
BORN: c. February 1770
DIED: Paris, February 17, 1841

Carulli was the first of the great nineteenth-century guitar virtuosi and the father of the modern "classical" guitar school. He supposedly studied cello with a Neapolitan priest but was self-taught on the six-string guitar. Arriving unheralded in Paris in 1808, he created a furor and remained the unrivalled performer and teacher until Sor [1090] arrived there in the mid-1820s. Carulli composed prodigiously and wrote a popular guitar method. His son Gustavo (1801–1876) followed successfully in his footsteps. Forgotten until recently, save by specialists, he is now represented by a number of recordings by such guitarists as Karl Scheit (a concerto), Siegfried Behrend, Julian Bream, Konrad Ragossnig, Mario Sicca, Spyros Thomatos, and John Williams.

[1061] HEWITT, James
VIOLINIST, CONDUCTOR, IMPRESARIO, PUBLISHER
BORN: Dartmoor, June 4, 1770
DIED: Boston, August 2, 1827

It is a curious fact that Hewitt was Beethoven's [1063] exact contemporary, his life bracketing the German's by five months at either end. He is supposed, like his father (who also emigrated to America), to have served in the Royal Navy and later to have been a court musician. (Hewitt owned a cello given him by the Prince of Wales.) He is also said to have studied with Viotti [988], but there is no documentation of any of this. He is known to have played in an orchestra in a London theater just before he left for New York—an action apparently triggered by the loss of his young wife and baby. He reached Manhattan in 1792 and found enough former colleagues to arrange a benefit concert for himself. It was sufficiently heartwarming to persuade Hewitt and three of the other participants—the violinists Gehot and Bergmann, and the flutist Young—that there was gold in the concert business. However, that enterprise was at the time considered the private preserve of a family called von Hagen. While Hewitt was jockeying for position, Gehot and Young defected to Philadelphia and were replaced by a cellist named Philips. (Young later killed a bailiff sent to take him to debtors' prison and was executed.) The concert series eventually got off the ground in 1793 with the first American performance of Haydn's [871] *Seven Last Words*. In 1794 Philips went over to the von Hagens, and Hewitt and Bergmann took on Reinagle's [994] old partner Capron. A year later the rivals saw the light and merged, but shortly afterward Hewitt bowed out to become concertmaster for the Old American Company, which had moved to New York after Reinagle opened his theater in Philadelphia. In the years that followed, Hewitt was also organist at Trinity Church and conductor of a pleasure-garden band. In 1795 he married Eliza King, the daughter of a wealthy British army officer; she had once been a prisoner in the Bastille. Together they had six highly musical children. (The oldest son, John Hill, was a journalist, poet, and composer of popular songs, notably the Civil War hit "All Quiet Along the Potomac Tonight.") In 1804 Captain John Hewitt, the composer's father, was killed in a traffic accident at a spry 101.

Hewitt's New York career was punctuated by productions of several of his stage works, some of them very successful. The first, an "opera" called *Tammany,* was commissioned by the Sons of St. Tammany, who stood in opposition to the Federalists. It created a sensation, and the Federalists argued in effect that they should have gotten equal time. (Tammany was, by the way, allegedly an Indian chief who exhibited the Rousseauan ideals of the Noble Savage.) Other Hewitt subjects were Robin Hood, William Tell, and the explorer Pizarro.

Hewitt had also developed interests in Boston and moved his family there for five years in 1811. After they returned to New York, James led a peripatetic existence that took him as far afield as Georgia. At some point he left his wife and apparently his manuscripts, a possibility that is said to explain the relative scarcity of his works today. In 1826, ill with cancer, he resigned from the management of the Park Theater. Letters shortly afterward speak feelingly of some sort of barbarous operation to remove

part of his face. In January he resigned himself to the inevitable.

RECORDINGS: Hewitt is now remembered chiefly for his programmatic piano sonatas, *The Fourth of July* and *The Battle of Trenton.* The first has been recorded by organist Richard Elsasser and the second by the Goldman Band in a transcription by Jonathan Elkus [2395]. Janice Beck has recorded the *Nahant Waltz,* surely a very early example of that dance form in America.

[1062] WITT, Jeremias Friedrich (Vit, Yā-rā-mē'-ås Frē'-drikh)
CELLIST, CONDUCTOR
BORN: Niederstetten, November 8, 1770
DIED: Würzburg, January 3, 1836

Friedrich Witt was a reasonably competent and fairly prolific provincial composer, who attained a measure of modern fame by way of the back door. Born in a Württemberg village, he became a cellist (some accounts say a violinist) in the court orchestra of Oettingen-Wallerstein when he was nineteen. He resigned five or six years later, then led a peripatetic life until he became *Kapellmeister* to the Prince-Bishop of Würzburg in 1802. When the *Kapelle* was broken up in 1814, he took a similar post in the municipal theater for the rest of his days. As a good *Kapellmeister* should, he wrote operas, oratorios, Masses, cantatas, concerti, band music, chamber works, and symphonies. In 1906 musicologist Fritz Stein found a manuscript copy of a symphony at Jena, whereon the name "Beethoven" was written. The work accordingly became Beethoven's "Jena" Symphony in C Major—date and provenance unknown. In 1957, however, H. C. Robbins Landon found another copy which identified the composer as Witt (who, incidentally, did not like Beethoven's music). Robbins Landon, a Haydn [871] scholar, soon discerned that it was really half-Witt, a good part of it having been borrowed from Haydn. RECORDINGS: The "Jena" Symphony was several times recorded by Frieder Weissmann, Werner Janssen, Robert Heger, Rolf Kleinert, and others. Recent recordings by Wolfgang Hoffman and Friedrich Reichert credit the work to Witt. Records also offer a septet by the Consortium Classicum and the Concerto for 2 Horns conducted by Helmut Winschermann.

[1063] BEETHOVEN, Ludwig van (Bā'-tō-ven, Loōt'-vikh fàn)
PIANIST, CONDUCTOR, TEACHER

BORN: Bonn, c. December 17, 1770
DIED: Vienna, March 26, 1827

Of all the great composers, Beethoven still seems to loom largest in the consciousness of the general public and perhaps even in that of musicians, including the prophets of pop and the radical avant-garde. Nor, one ventures to say, has any later claimant to musical leadership—Wagner [1230], Stravinsky [1748], or Schoenberg [1657], for example—spoken to so many so compellingly. And yet he was a musician of his time, using the same forms and the same basic language as his older contemporaries, Haydn [871] and Mozart [992]. But he realized the possibilities of both as no one else ever had and left us with the uneasy feeling that to depart from them was somehow to betray the art of music.

The Beethovens of Mechelin (Malines) in Belgium go back at least to the sixteenth century. The composer's grandfather Lodewijk (later Ludwig), born in 1712, was the son of a prosperous master baker who paid for his organ lessons. He became a fine basso in churches in Leeuven (Louvain) and Liège. The bishop of the latter city, who was also Archbishop-Elector of Cologne, took the twenty-one-year-old into his private *Kapelle* at Bonn, where he became Ludwig, soon thereafter the bridegroom of Maria Josepha Poll, the father of Johann (c. 1740), and eventually (in 1761) *Kapellmeister*. Maria Josepha fared less well: she became a sodden alcoholic and was finally institutionalized in a local convent.

Johann van Beethoven followed in his mother's footsteps. A hyphen between his father and his famous son, he was a tenor of sorts in the *Kapelle* at a salary that never rose above the subsistence level. At twenty-seven he married a young widow, Maria Magdalena Laym, daughter of the Elector of Trier's chef. (It was in Trier in 1761 that old Ludwig's first employer, Clemens August, had died at a ball; his successor was Maximilian Friedrich of Königsegg-Rothenfels.) In April 1769, a year and a half after her wedding, Maria Magdalena bore a son, christened Ludwig after his grandfather. He soon died. When a second boy arrived a year later, he was given the same name. (Beethoven was later to insist that it was the other Ludwig who was born in 1770 and that his own birthdate was 1772.) Of several other children, only Carl Caspar and Johann survived. Grandfather Ludwig, who became a mythic figure to his namesake, died when the latter was three.

Johann set about to see to his son's carrying on the family tradition. Already a

hanger-out in taverns in the evenings, he is said often to have come home late with a crony to haul the boy out of bed and make him play. But details of Beethoven's early education are obscure. He undoubtedly worked with various of the court musicians and was permitted to complete grammar school. In 1779 Christian Gottlob Neefe [954] arrived with a traveling opera troupe and remained to succeed Heinrich van den Eeden as court organist in 1781. Beethoven, who may have been his predecessor's pupil, became Neefe's and was proficient enough the next summer to sit in for him when Neefe was out of town. By 1782 Beethoven was also conducting opera rehearsals from the harpsichord and had published a set of variations and three piano sonatas (not included in the official canon of 32).

Johann van Beethoven had a half-baked notion that he had produced another Mozart, who would bring him affluence and reflected glory. But Ludwig was neither as precocious nor as cute, and by now Johann was on the skids, often publicly drunk. When the Archduke Max Franz, brother to the Emperor Joseph and Marie-Antoinette, became Elector in 1784, Johann's job was in jeopardy; Ludwig, however, got a raise, and there was talk of giving him Neefe's post. Meanwhile he was studying violin and viola, and in 1787 the elector sent him to Vienna for an audition, and possible study, with Mozart himself. On hearing him, Mozart is supposed to have said, "That young man will make a noise in the world one day"—and there may indeed have been a few lessons, but soon Beethoven was called back to Bonn to be with his long-consumptive and now dying mother. Two years later, by then a violist in the *Kapelle* under Josef Reicha [978], he asked to be named head of his family and given half of Johann's salary in addition to his own. Max Franz acceded and retired the now useless Johann. (When Johann succumbed in 1792, shortly after Ludwig had moved to Vienna, the elector rather callously noted the sudden drop in liquor revenues.)

In his remaining time in Bonn, Beethoven inaugurated lifelong friendships with the brothers Romberg (see 1051), Anton Reicha [1059], Franz Ries (see 1116), and the young Count Waldstein, and became an intimate of the family of Hofrat von Breuning's young widow. He took on pupils and continued to compose—mostly in small forms, but one should note the cantata in memory of the Emperor Joseph and the music for a court ballet. He came to know Haydn [871], who stopped by on his way to and from England, and it was agreed that he must go to Vienna and study with him. He made his move in November 1792 and found initial quarters in the proverbial attic; but soon afterward he came down to ground level and then was taken in by an occupant of the same building, Prince Karl Lichnowsky, a sometime Mozart pupil and a patron of music. (But all of his life Beethoven moved restlessly from one address to another.)

Beethoven's studies with Haydn seem to have been uncomfortable. The focus was counterpoint, and Beethoven felt that Haydn moved too slowly, so he studied in secret with Johann Schenck [982], and, hoping to get an increased allowance from the elector (who was not fooled for a moment), palmed off on Haydn some old Bonn compositions as evidence of his productivity. Ultimately, though the two composers remained cordial, Beethoven refused to call himself Haydn's pupil. Haydn's return to London after a year effectively resolved the problem, and Beethoven went on to study with Albrechtsberger [889] and less formally with Salieri [966].

Such connections did Beethoven's career no harm in Vienna. Neither did the fact that he was sponsored by a member of the imperial family and had such friends as Waldstein and Lichnowsky. As a result he was welcomed in many noble households and found himself with more pupils than he wanted. In such private surroundings, he quickly became known as a formidable pianist, and so his concert debut in 1795, at which he played the piano concerto now known as his second, was a great success. Thus even though history had put an end to the Bonn court and his allowance in 1794, he was able to support a horse (given him by Count von Browne-Camus in the imperial Russian service) and a manservant, and could help his brothers get settled in the city. Publication of his works added to his income. He began with small things—mostly songs and piano pieces—but by the end of the decade, he had added the early piano trios, the first (mature) piano sonatas, sonatas for violin and for cello, and other chamber works. In keeping with his character, however, Beethoven was already beginning to resent being asked by his hostesses to play for his dinner and as a teacher did not suffer fools gladly.

Many of Beethoven's pupils were young ladies who, as the times demanded, were being rendered marriageable with "accomplishments." Though he was far from handsome, he had, we are told, a great appeal to women and at this stage was always in love with one or another. Later on, some of his flames emerge from anonymity—Goethe's

innamorata Bettina von Brentano, the Countess Giulietta Guicciardi, the Countess Therese von Brunsvik, her sister Josephine (who, some claim, bore him a child), and Antonie Brentano. Some were already spoken for; others rejected him for whatever reason. It has been suggested that Beethoven did not want marriage, perhaps because the ideal woman did not exist or because he was seeking a replacement for his mother or because he enjoyed being the unfulfilled third side of a triangle. Whatever the truth, he had neither wife nor mistress, save on a short-term basis.

For the time being, Beethoven lived a highly gregarious life, moving easily in society, and performing publicly and privately with visiting musical celebrities such as Dragonetti [1033], the Rombergs, Stich [945], and Steibelt [1044]—the last of whom, nettled by his arrogance, he wiped out in a drawing room improvisational battle. He made brief concert tours, trips to Berlin and Dresden proving highly rewarding both in remuneration and acquaintances. He frequently played and conducted his own music at home, winning enormous popular favor and resultant sales in spite of the tut-tutting of certain critics. Moreover his noble admirers saw to it that he should not want. Prince Lichnowsky provided an annuity of 600 florins and presented him with a quartet of valuable stringed instruments, including two Guarnieris and an Amati. Later, in 1809, the Princes Lobkowitz and Kinsky and the Archduke Rudolph (Beethoven's composition pupil) contracted to provide him with 4,000 florins a year until some court should hire him at a like or greater salary. Such affluence enabled Beethoven to forego the aspiring young-lady pianists for wealthy amateurs and youngsters with obvious talent. Of the latter (save for his nephew Karl), the closest to his heart were Ferdinand Ries [1116] and Carl Czerny [1137]. (Karl van Beethoven was the son of Carl Caspar, born three months after his marriage to Johanna Reiss. Carl Caspar handled his brother's business affairs for a time and became quite swellheaded about it.) Money and relative independence also permitted the composer to initiate a habit of spending his summers in the country or the suburbs, where he could work without interruption and commune with nature on long walks.

All, however, was not as rosy as one might think. There were problems of health. Beethoven was plagued for most of his adult life by abdominal troubles, which seem to have begun as colitis. Much to his horror, he found himself, from 1799, growing deaf.

The cause remains a mystery. Legend attributes it to a chill incurred while sitting shirtless before a window after a hike on a hot day. A doctor thought it an aftereffect of typhus (date unknown). Beethoven once said it began when he banged his head on the floor in a rage at a singer. Evidence suggests that initially he made more of the problem than was warranted. He kept it to himself for about four years, growing withdrawn, morose, and taciturn in the process. But he was still able to function musically for several years and in his last decade could still hear some sounds, including speech on good days, though after 1818 he depended more and more on written communication (the "conversation books," many of which were no more than pieces of scrap paper). The lowest ebb in his midlife crisis came at his retreat in the Heiligenstadt suburb in the early autumn of 1802, as demonstrated by the tragic-theatrical "Heiligenstadt testament," allegedly meant for his brothers, but almost certainly as a message to the world. After that he seems to have come to terms with his life, at least for a time.

But Beethoven's self-enforced solitude was also productive. It saw the completion of twenty of the piano sonatas, all the violin sonatas but one, four of the 7 mature trios, seventeen of the 20 sets of piano variations, and many other works. In 1800 he completed his first set of (six) string quartets and the first of the symphonies (on which his greatest fame depends). It has been suggested that Haydn's development of both forms in the 1790s spurred Beethoven on; certainly he began where Haydn left off and went on to unforeseen heights. Symphonically, he found his own voice in his third try, the so-called "Eroica" (Heroic), to which much myth adheres. Beethoven, like many intellectuals of his time, had seen in Napoleon, the republican leader come from humble origins, a classic hero figure, and had planned to subtitle the work the "Bonaparte symphony." His later substitution of "To the memory of a great hero" for the name is supposed to reflect his democratic passion. But at the time he was writing the work, he was making noises about moving to Paris to escape Hapsburg tyranny, and the original title may have been intended to make him welcome there, just as the revised one may have been calculated to please Vienna, where he decided to remain.

In 1801 Emanuel Schikaneder, Mozart's Zauberflöte librettist, had opened the Theater an der Wien, the largest and most modern in Vienna. Two years later, he hired Beethoven as house composer, with quar-

ters there. Beethoven announced, in effect, his arrival there in April 1803 with a concert featuring the first two symphonies, the third piano concerto, and the premiere of the oratorio *Christus am Ölberge (Christ on the Mount of Olives)*. Toward the end of the year, he began to work on a Schikaneder libretto, *Vestas Feuer (The Vestal Fire)*, but preoccupation with the still unfinished "Eroica" soon caused him to drop it. However, enthusiasm for the "rescue" operas of Cherubini [1019], perhaps abetted by a flareup of his passion for the now-widowed Josephine von Brunsvik, turned his attention to the libretto *Léonore, ou l'Amour conjugal*, once written by Bouilly for Pierre Gaveaux [1020], which he had Joseph von Sonnleithner (who had succeeded Schikaneder) translate for him. (Paër [1069] was, by coincidence, working on an Italian version, presented in Dresden the year following.) Changes on the theater management and Beethoven's connection with it delayed matters, but *Fidelio*, as it came to be called, was finally performed in November 1805. Unfortunately, Napoleon's troops had occupied the city shortly before; consequently attendance was sparse, and many of those who came knew no German. Those who understood it complained that it was too loose. Beethoven reworked it, added a new overture (the one now known as *Leonore No. 3*, and presented the new version the following March. But the directorship was maddeningly indefinite about repetitions, and when they suggested that the composer direct it to the gallery, he balked and withdrew the opera. The year 1806 also saw the completion of the "Razumowsky" quartets, the fourth piano concerto, the violin concerto, and the 32 variations for piano. 1807, however, was less fruitful. Some of it was taken up with the C-major *Mass*, commissioned by Prince Esterházy for his wife's name-day. On that occasion the hearers were puzzled; when the prince indicated as much, Beethoven, in a kind of action that was to become typical, walked out in a huff. The next year produced the fifth and sixth symphonies, the two penultimate piano trios, the third cello sonata, and the *Fantasia* in C Minor for piano, chorus, and orchestra.

By 1809 inflation and international politics had affected Beethoven's income. He continued to talk of leaving Vienna, and when Jerome Bonaparte, King of Westphalia by his brother's grace, offered to make him his *Kapellmeister*, it appeared that Beethoven might carry out his threat. It was then that Kinsky, Lobkowitz, and Archduke Rudolf arranged his annuity. (Beethoven had broken with Lichnowsky over playing for his French guests.) Later in the year, when the returning French bombarded the largely deserted city, the composer sweated out the attack in Carl's basement, a pillow over his head to save what was left of his hearing. The absence of Archduke Rudolf elicited the sonata known as "Les Adieux," and the year also brought forth the final (fifth) piano concerto ("The Emperor") and the Op. 74 String Quartet No. 10. Toward year's end, Beethoven fell ill and was in poor health for some months afterward.

At forty he seems to have decided to make a real effort to find the elusive woman of his dreams. It was while he was writing the music for Goethe's *Egmont* that he saw much of the poet's friend Bettina Brentano, but she married Achim von Arnim in 1811. He proposed to his doctor's young niece, Therese Malfatti, without any luck. Within this same period occurred the grandest of his passions: that for the "immortal Beloved," as he hailed an otherwise anonymous lady in a famous letter. She has since been identified as Antonie Brentano, Bettina's half-sister-in-law. When she left Vienna in 1812, Beethoven seems to have resigned himself to his single state, though he evidently took out some of his frustration on his brothers. He had never approved of Carl Caspar's marriage, and when the latter had Johanna arrested for embezzlement in 1811, he seems to have been gratified. Meanwhile the other brother, Johann, had settled in Linz with his mistress, Therese Obermeyer. When, overflowing with righteous wrath, Beethoven descended on them in 1812 with demands that the trollop be thrown out, Johann married her. (She later openly cuckolded him.)

No doubt partly because of his personal turmoil, Beethoven's output began to fall off not only in volume but also for a time in quality. The most important works of the period 1809–14 were the seventh and eighth symphonies, completed around 1812. One should also note the final violin sonata and perhaps the incidental music for the plays *Die Ruinen von Athen (The Ruins of Athens), König Stefan (King Stephen),* and *Tarpeja.* And it was in these years that the composer began devoting considerable time to arranging "folksongs" for George Thomson of Edinburgh. (The eventual total came to more than 150.) The low ebb for the moment came in 1813, with the *Tarpeja* pieces; the so-called "Battle Symphony" entitled *Wellingtons Sieg (Wellington's Victory),* for a music machine devised by J. N. Maelzel, the inventor of the metronome; three songs; and a canon. By then Beethoven faced financial problems, especially with regard to

the annuity. Kinsky was dead, Lobkowitz temporarily insolvent, and only the archduke was holding up his end of the bargain. But 1814 brought what must have been a heartening change. At the beginning of the year, the directorship of the Kärntnertortheater decided to give *Fidelio* another try. Beethoven made a third revision and wrote a fourth overture, *Fidelio;* "Leonore No. 2" was for a proposed Prague production that never materialized. Though his hearing was now bad, the composer conducted the triumphant first performance that established the opera as a masterpiece. The same year he played the piano part in the first performance of the "Archduke" trio but made such a botch of it that he never played in public again. The year 1814 also produced the Sonata for Piano No. 27 and some negligible pieces celebrating the Congress of Vienna. By the end of the year, Beethoven's finances were looking up: Kinsky's heirs had agreed to continue his part of the bargain, Lobkowitz had recovered his money, and sales and royalties were doing very well.

Meanwhile Carl Caspar Beethoven was losing a struggle with tuberculosis. When he died in November 1815, he left his wife and his brother to be co-guardians of his son Karl—the boy to remain with Johanna. Beethoven, who had envisioned the lad as a prop for his old age, brought suit against Johanna, charging that she was morally unfit because of her earlier arrest at the instigation of her husband. This action initiated a struggle that went on for the rest of the composer's life, wearing him down and badly interfering with his work. At first the courts found in his favor, and in 1816 he took over Karl's upbringing. Predictably the boy, the chief sufferer in the matter, fared badly: he was a poor student, ran away from home, and was expelled from one school. Meanwhile, Johanna harmed her chances by taking on a lover and bearing him a daughter. In the course of the wrangling, Beethoven was humiliated when the court discovered his "van" was not an indicator of noble origins, and remanded the case to a lower court. (He had done nothing to counter the widespread rumor that he was a bastard son of Frederick II of Prussia.) To add injury to insult, the new court found in favor of the natural parent. But Beethoven found subterfuges to keep Karl from her, and in 1820 he at last was given sole custody.

In Beethoven's final decade, though he produced his supernal masterpieces—the last four piano sonatas, the ninth symphony, the *Missa Solemnis,* and the final quartets—he produced them slowly and wrote very little else. This was generally an unhappy and unfortunate period. His deafness, now almost total, caused him for a considerable time to avoid contact with the rest of humanity, though he could be approached by those who had the temerity to do so. (Later, when he became reconciled to his condition, there was a flow of pilgrims from all over the world.) His health, especially his abdominal trouble, was generally bad. His living quarters, wherever they might be, were chaotic. He became more violently irascible and frequently exploded in violent rages. Pitifully, out of his obsessive attachment to Karl, he kept the young man (whom he sent to school and to the university) on a short tether, allowing him no freedom of action or choice in such matters as friends, pleasures, and career. Once again he fell on hard times, which he made no better by putting the bulk of his money in bank shares as an inheritance for his "son." This situation caused him to play fast and loose with publishers, setting one against another, and promising works (e.g., two Masses, an oratorio, a tenth symphony) that never existed save in his plans. There was endless talk of traveling or emigrating, especially to London, but Beethoven seemed quite unable to summon up the will for any such major move.

In 1819 the Archduke Rudolph was made a cardinal and appointed Archbishop of Olmütz (now Olomouc). Beethoven was sufficiently excited to promise a Mass for his investiture in 1820. But the work grew far beyond the scope the composer had foreseen, and he was interrupted by illness and took time out to write the "variation" on a waltz theme requested by its author, Diabelli [1100]. This in turn grew into a set of thirty-three variations so enormous that it had to be published separately from the other contributions to the project. When the investiture had come and gone, Beethoven paused again to write the final three piano sonatas and so did not finish work on the Mass until the end of 1822. Much of 1823 was taken up with work on the long-postponed symphony and with a scheme to get the crowned heads of Europe to subscribe to autographed copies of the Mass. Toward the end of the year, Beethoven insisted on conducting a revival of Fidelio; but, quite unable to hear, he made a mess of a rehearsal and fled the theater in humiliation. Around this same period, brother Johann, now a man of property and some means, reentered Beethoven's life, serving self-importantly and apparently not always trustworthily as his agent. Beethoven no doubt took some

satisfaction in his sister-in-law's living up to his predictions by bringing her lover into the household.

Evidently Beethoven was still hurting from the experience of the Fidelio debacle, for in 1824 he began trying to arrange a Berlin premiere for the Mass and the new symphony. But his friends rallied around, and instead it took place in the Kärntnertortheater on May 7. The concert included the symphony, the Weihe des Hauses Overture, and three movements of the Mass, the inclusion of the whole Mass having proved impracticable. The concert was a triumph, but Beethoven, who was mentally following with the score of the symphony, was unaware of the triumph until one of the singers turned him around to see the applauding crowd.

Meanwhile Beethoven had returned to the string quartet medium, impelled by a commission for three from a wealthy Russian amateur, Prince Nikolai Galitzin. It was fulfilled by the end of 1825, though later Beethoven found the fugal conclusion of the third quartet too much for most performers and replaced it with a new ending. (The matter ended rather badly, for Galitzin had gone temporarily bankrupt and was unable to meet his obligation in the composer's lifetime.) The next year, interrupted by spells of severe illness, Beethoven completed two more quartets—his last compositions of any consequence. Meanwhile the struggle with Karl, who had decided to become a soldier, grew more intense. Eventually Karl "attempted suicide"—aiming two pistols at his head, he missed entirely with one and grazed his scalp with the other. But Beethoven did not recognize the melodrama and began to fall apart. Two months later he and Johann took Karl to Johann's country place in Gneixendorf for what was meant to be a brief stay before the young man joined his regiment. But they lingered through November, Beethoven, though ailing, putting the finishing touches on the final quartet and walking in the countryside, where his eccentric gestures and shouting to himself puzzled and amused the peasantry. On a bitter December 1, uncle and nephew returned to Vienna in an open vehicle, stopping in a wretched inn overnight. By the time they reached home, Beethoven was ill and feverish and took to his bed. He survived what appears to have been pneumonia, but his greatly swollen belly had to be tapped to relieve the pressure of the fluids therein, and the procedure had to be repeated several times. He was cheered by the receipt of forty volumes of Samuel Arnold's [915] Handel edition sent him as a gift from

London, for he admired Handel above all composers. (Cherubini was his favorite contemporary.) In early January Karl left for the army at last; the two were not to meet again. By the end of February the doctors lost hope, for the liver was no longer functioning. In his last days someone brought the great man a selection of Schubert's **[1153]** songs, over which he marveled. He had now resigned himself to the inevitable, and on March 23 remarked in Latin to a friend, "Rejoice, for the comedy is over." Next day he took communion and soon lapsed into delirium. According to an eyewitness, a thunderstorm broke out on the afternoon of the twenty-sixth. After a great lightning flash, the dying man opened his eyes and seemed to shake his fist at the elements; then he sank back and died. At the funeral the pallbearers and torchbearers included Gyrowetz **[1032]**, Hummel **[1091]**, Conradin Kreutzer **[1096]**, Czerny, and Schubert, and more than 10,000 people lined the streets for the procession. The obituary was written by Franz Grillparzer and delivered by the great actor Heinrich Anschütz. The body was interred in the Währing Cemetery; in 1888 it, together with Schubert's, was removed to the Central Cemetery, where both now lie. (Karl left the army and married in 1832. Later he inherited his Uncle Johann's estate and lived at ease until his death in 1858. His only son, Ludwig, became involved in some crooked dealings and is said to have emigrated to America. *His* only son, Karl, died without issue in Vienna in 1917.)

RECORDINGS: Beethoven's major works —the symphonies, quartets, trios, Masses, mature sonatas, *Fidelio*, etc.—have, of course, proved a staple for the recording industry. But oddly some of the minor works —choral pieces, songs, "folksong arrangements," and various juvenilia—seem so far to have been overlooked.

[1064] DUPUY, Jean-Baptiste Edouard (Düp-wē', Zhán Bà-tēst' Ed-wärd')
PIANIST, VIOLINIST, SINGER, TEACHER, SOLDIER
BORN: Corcelles, c. 1770
DIED: Stockholm, April 3, 1822

It has perhaps been the derring-do of Dupuy's life that has misled some into calling him a Navarraise rather than a Swiss. His early life is in any case obscure. He was supposedly a pupil of Dussek **[1016]** in Paris in 1783 or so, but Dussek seems not to have been there at that time. Two years later he was concertmaster at Rheinsberg in

the theater orchestra of Prince Heinrich of Prussia, a son of Frederick William II— quite an accomplishment for a fifteen-year-old. Having gotten himself into some sort of scrape, he was fired, free-lanced for a time, and then joined the court musical establishment at Stockholm as a violinist, singer, and composer. Between 1793 and 1797, he wrote ballets for the Arsenal company, and was elected to the Academy. But he was suspected of political intrigue and run out of the country in 1799. His next stop was Copenhagen. When, in 1806, it proved impossible to acquire the music for a scheduled performance of Méhul's **[1036]** *Une folie* at the Royal Theater, Dupuy provided a new score for a Swedish translation of the libretto *(Ungdom og galskap)* and sang the baritone lead himself. A year later he created Mozart's **[992]** *Don Giovanni* for Denmark. Appointed music master to the Princess Charlotte Frederike, young wife of the future Christian VIII, the relationship became more romantic than musical. Both were ordered to get out in 1809 and the marriage was annulled. Shortly afterward King Gustavus Adolphus IV was toppled in Sweden, and Dupuy was invited back as director of the Royal Theater, where he worked for the rest of his life. He wrote many stage works, a good deal of occasional music, and some instrumental things. RECORDINGS: Johan Hye-Knudsen has recorded the overture to *Ungdom og galskap*.

[1065] FLIES, Bernhard (Flēz, Bârn'-härt)
PHYSICIAN (?)
BORN: Berlin, c. 1770
DIED: Zerbst, date uncertain

Flies is one of those composers who is unknown for his most famous composition. In fact almost nothing is known of him at all. He is said to have been a physician. He had an opera produced in Berlin in 1798 and published some songs and a set of piano variations on themes from Mozart's *Don Giovanni*. Among the songs is a lullaby beginning "Schlaf, mein Prinzchen." It was early accepted as a work of Mozart's and, despite solid evidence to the contrary, still turns up on records and on concert programs as "Mozart's *'Wiegenlied.'* "

[1066] HOFFMANN, Giovanni (Hôf'-màn, Jō-vàn'-nē)
MANDOLINIST
BORN: c. 1770
DIED: ?

Hoffmann left a number of mandolin compositions in the archives of the Gesellschaft der Musikfreunde in Vienna. Some published duets bear the date 1799, suggesting that he cashed in on the mandolin craze of the turn of the century. It is assumed that "Giovanni" was an Italianization of "Johann," but nothing else is known of him save that he was not one of several other known Johann Hoffmanns. RECORDINGS: Elfriede Kunschack has recorded a mandolin concerto and a quartet "arranged by Vinzenz Hladky."

[1067] CRAMER, Johann Baptist (Kră'-mer, Yō'-hän Bäp'-tĕst)
PIANIST, TEACHER, PUBLISHER
BORN: Mannheim, February 24, 1771
DIED: London, April 16, 1858

Enveloped in a cloud of snuff and vitriol, Cramer may have sometimes shocked the respectable, but he was famous enough to be mentioned in Jane Austen's novel *Emma*, and his appellation "Glorious John" betokened genuine admiration, for as a performer he was ranked with Mozart [992] and Clementi [977], and commanded Beethoven's [1063] real respect. When he was three, his mother brought him and his younger brother Franz (later Master of the Queen's Musick, 1837–48) to London to join their father Wilhelm [942]. "John" studied with his father and others, but most notably for a year with Clementi. He made his solo debut at ten and in 1784 appeared with his great teacher in a two-piano recital. He was nurtured on the music of Haydn [871]; Mozart; Domenico Scarlatti [687]; and, consistent with the trend of the times, J. S. Bach [684], for which last he developed a passion. Though he had some lessons with Abel [829], he was largely self-taught in theory and composition.

Cramer toured Germany and France in 1788, and was in Paris when the Revolution began. He returned to London in 1791 and settled down as performer and teacher. In 1799 he made another tour, proceeding as far as Vienna, where he was introduced to Beethoven. One morning, visiting that composer, he heard him improvising. Letting himself in, he listened for a long time before tiptoeing out again, to report that no one had ever improvised so well. A gregarious man, Cramer seems to have known everyone in the musical world, and he provided a sort of link between the previous generation of Classicists and the upcoming Romantics.

In 1804 Cramer issued the first of the 2 volumes of piano studies by which his name

has chiefly survived (the other came in 1810). A year later, with a certain Keys, he went into the publishing business. There were several changes in partnership, but the company (which once also manufactured pianos) has lasted down to the present day. He helped initiate the Philharmonic Society and the Royal Academy of music. At one point he was promoting a finger harness called the chiroplast, guaranteed to keep the pianist's hands properly positioned, but it was no great success. He published some works by Beethoven, whom he idolized, and supposedly dubbed the fifth piano concerto "the Emperor."

After Clementi retired, Cramer was regarded in England as the foremost virtuoso of his time. In 1831 he and young Liszt [1218], aspirant to that title, played together. Afterward Liszt said he had felt like a poisonous mushroom sitting beside an antidotal glass of milk. At a later date, Cramer said that in his day pianists had been *fort bien* (really good), but that now they were *bien fort* (awfully loud). He gave his final concert in London in 1835 and spent most of the next decade on the Continent. He returned to England and died there at eighty-seven. He was twice married.

RECORDINGS: Besides the famous etudes, Cramer wrote 9 piano concerti, more than 125 sonatas (with and without "accompaniment"), some chamber music, and numerous smaller or less ambitious piano works, mostly designed for quick sale to amateurs. Akiko Sagara has recorded the fifth concerto.

[1068] LINLEY, William
BUREAUCRAT, IMPRESARIO
BORN: Bath, February 1771
DIED: London, May 6, 1835

The youngest and perhaps least musically gifted of the musical progeny of the elder Thomas Linley (see 995), William was trained by his father and by Abel [829]. He got his formal education at Harrow and St. Paul's, and at nineteen went to Madras in India as a cog in the colonial government. From 1796 he was comanager with his brother-in-law Richard Brinsley Sheridan of the Drury Lane Theatre, where Linley aspired to operatic composition. His aspirations having come to naught, he returned to India in 1800. He retired in 1807 and came home to lead a life of leisure, amusing himself by writing songs, glees, and fiction. His magnum opus is his two-volume anthology, *Shakespeare's Dramatic Songs*. Where he could find no settings for lyrics, he supplied his own. RECORDINGS: April Cantelo has recorded one setting, "Now the Hungry Lion Roars."

[1069] PAËR, Ferdinando (Pä'-er, Fär-dē-nän'-dō)
CONDUCTOR, TEACHER
BORN: Parma, June 1, 1771
DIED: Paris, May 3, 1839

Paër was the first important writer of *opere semiserie,* a sentimental compromise between *opere buffe* and *opere serie* that dealt with the problems of ordinary people. As such he was probably Mayr's **[1034]** greatest operatic rival, and he certainly influenced Beethoven **[1063]**, whom he knew. His now-forgotten teachers Giovanni Francesco Fortunati and Gaspare Ghiretti were once big Parmesan cheeses. He began his career with a local production of his *Orphée et Euridice* when he was twenty-one and made something of a splash the following year with *Circe* in Venice and *Le Astuzie amorose (The Ruses of Love)* back home, after which he won several commissions and the honorary Parmese court title of *maestro di cappella.* After the French took over Parma, Paër moved to Venice and married the soprano Francesca Riccardi. In 1797 she was invited to sing in Vienna, and her husband became music director of the Kärntnertor Theater. There Paër was strongly influenced by the Viennese understanding of the orchestra, and his first real masterpiece—*Griselda, Camilla,* and *Achille* —date from the Vienna years. In 1801 he was invited to Dresden as court *Kapellmeister* to Frederick Augustus I, replacing the late J. G. Naumann **[920]**. It was there that he produced *Leonora,* his version of Bouilly's *Léonore, ou l'Amour conjugal* in 1804, a year before Beethoven's **[1063]** *Fidelio* reached the stage. In 1806, when the triumphant Napoleon came marching in, he had little trouble persuading Paër to accompany him on the campaign and to succeed Paisiello **[914]** as his chief musician in Paris.

Among his early assignments was the composition of the wedding marches for the emperor and his new empress, Marie Louise of Austria (who would later become the duchess of Paër's native Parma). The emoluments of the post included the directorship of the Opéra-Comique and a guaranteed 12,000 francs a year. As titular singing master to the emperor, Paër did not want for affluent pupils. In 1812 he took over the Théâtre Italien from Spontini **[1081]**, who was fired for "financial irregularities." (It should be noted that Spontini had taken the side of the discarded Empress Josephine.) With Napoleon's fall, Paër was stripped of most of his posts but continued at the Théâtre Italien. In 1821 he produced what has proved his hardiest work, the two-act farce *Le Maître de chapelle.* In 1824 he was slated to be replaced with Rossini **[1143]**, against whom he had reputedly long intrigued, but Rossini magnanimously insisted on sharing the management. However, two years later Paër was dropped for "financial irregularities"; he had, in fact, been a rotten manager, though Rossini proved not much better. All was later forgiven, and he was awarded the *Légion d'honneur,* elected to the Académie, and put in charge of Louis Philippe's personal music. He wrote at least 55 operas, oratorios, Masses, cantatas, symphonies, etc.

RECORDINGS: There are recordings of *Leonora* (Peter Maag), *Le Maître de chapelle* (Jean-Paul Kreder), two of the imperial wedding marches (Desiré Dondeyde), the overture to the 1803 *Sargino* (Richard Bonynge), and songs (Giulietta Simionato, Suzanne Danco).

[1070] BELKNAP, Daniel
FARMER, MECHANIC, SINGING MASTER
BORN: Framingham, Mass., 1771
DIED: Pawtucket, R.I., 1815

When he was not occupied with homelier duties, Belknap served as one of many itinerant New England singing masters. As a writer of music, he was primarily an anthologist of hymn tunes, producing such collections as *The Harmonist's Companion,* 1797; *The Evangelical Harmony,* 1800; and *The Village Compilation of Sacred Music,* 1806. His own sacred music is influenced by Billings **[946]**. His most famous work is *Belknap's March.* RECORDINGS: The Gregg Smith Singers have recorded his *Songs of the Seasons.*

[1071] FÜRSTENAU, Caspar (Fürst'-e-nou, Kàs'-pär)
FLUTIST
BORN: Münster, February 26, 1772
DIED: Oldenburg, May 11, 1819

Representing at least the second generation of a musical dynasty, Caspar Fürstenau studied oboe with his father. He was, however, orphaned young and was taken in hand by a colleague of his father, Bernhard Anton Romberg, father of the cellist-composer Bernhard Romberg **[1051]**. Romberg insisted on Fürstenau's taking up *his* instrument, the bassoon, but the boy discovered the flute and was soon playing in local bands and then at the court of the local ecclesiastic. He married and sired a son, Anton Bernhard (1792–1852), before he was twenty, and taught him the flute when he was very young. In 1794 Fürstenau became music master to the future Grand Duke Paul of Oldenburg and performer in the court orchestra. He frequently toured as a soloist—after 1800 in company with his son. The perils of war brought an end to music at the Oldenburg court in 1811. After Napoleon's defeat, the duchy was restored and raised to a higher power. Caspar Fürstenau, in failing health, returned there to die. Anton joined the orchestra in Frankfurt am Main in 1817 and in 1820 became first flute in the Dresden court orchestra under Carl Maria von Weber [1124]. He was joined there by his son Moritz (1824–89) in 1842, who later distinguished himself as a conductor, professor, and historian of music. Though Caspar Fürstenau wrote 2 concerti, most of his output consists of *Hausmusik.* RECORDINGS: Poul Birkelund and Ulrik Neuman have recorded some little pieces for flute and guitar.

[1072] DALVIMARE, Martin Pierre (Dàl-vē-màr', Màr-ta*n* Pyâr)
HARPIST, TEACHER
BORN: Dreux, September 18, 1772
DIED: Paris, June 13, 1839

"Dalvimare," as he called himself professionally, was born d'Alvimare to an old and wealthy Norman noble family; he learned the harp as a gentleman should. When the Revolution wiped out his fortune, he turned to music as a livelihood. He became harpist at the Opéra in 1800. He attracted Napoleon's attention and became chamber harpist to the emperor in 1806 and music master to Empress Josephine in 1807. In 1812 the family estate was restored to him, and he retired there to his private interests. It is said that he liked to pretend that the musical interlude had never occurred. His only opera, *Le Mariage par imprudence* of 1809 was a disaster; wits said the chief imprudences came from the composer and the librettist. Dalvimare's chief output was of popular harp-accompanied romances. RECORDINGS: Bernard Kruysen has recorded one of the romances with Lily Laskine. Mme. Laskine has also recorded a set of variations.

[1073] LOUIS FERDINAND, Prince of Prussia
SOLDIER, PIANIST
BORN: Friedrichsfelde, November 18, 1772
DIED: Saalfeld, October 13, 1806

Handsome, dashing, impetuous, heroic, a bit wild, Louis Ferdinand might have stepped out of a romantic novel. The fifth child of Prince August, a younger brother of Frederick II, he was baptized Friedrich Christian Ludwig, the name by which he was known being a result of the Gallicized Berlin court. Nothing is known specifically of his musical training, but he developed into a superb pianist. Beethoven [1063] not only praised his playing but dedicated his third piano concerto to him. Scarcely out of his teens, the prince was an important force in the Berlin intellectual ferment dedicated to developing a German art. By that time he had already distinguished himself as a soldier and officer. In the decade that bridged the turn of the century, when he was unable to indulge his military passion, he built up a domestic musical organization that included both Spohr [1112] and Dussek [1016]. The latter became devoted to him and went to seed after Louis Ferdinand died leading his men into battle against the French near Weimar. The prince published 13 opuses, all for piano, mostly with other instruments. RECORDINGS: Hélène Salome and Robert Spillman have each recorded the F-minor piano quartet, said to be his best work. Spillman has also committed to vinyl the *Rondo* in B-flat Major for piano and orchestra. In addition there is a six-record set on the German Thorofon label containing Louis Ferdinand's complete output, utilizing various performers. (Note: This Louis Ferdinand is not to be confused with a later one [2115], the composer-son of the infamous "Kaiser Bill" of World War I.)

[1074] PUCCINI, Domenico Vincenzo Maria (Pōō-chē'-nē, Dō-mā'-nē-kō Vēn-chänt'-zō Mà-rē'-à)
CONDUCTOR
BORN: Lucca, 1772
DIED: Lucca, May 25, 1815

There were five generations of important musical Puccinis in Lucca, the Alpha and Omega of the tribe being named Giacomo. Domenico was the grandson of one and the grandfather of another. His father Antonio was an organist, conductor, and composer. At twenty-one, Domenico collaborated with him on a *tasca* entitled *Spartaco. (Tasche* were a Lucchese phenomenon. They were, in essence, democratic cantatas and were entered in a triennial contest held in connection with municipal elections. The generic name came from *tasca*, a ballot box in Lucchese slang.) Domenico studied with his father and mother, *née* Caterina Tesei, an organist, and later in Naples with Paisiello [914]. He became assistant *maestro di cappella* at the cathedral under his father in the mid-1790s. In 1805 Elize Bonaparte was appointed Duchess of Tuscany by her imperial brother and was headquartered in Lucca. She disbanded the ancient Cappella Palatina, which Antonio Puccini had directed, and organized her own orchestra, for which Domenico served as conductor. When she decided to get rid of it in 1809, Domenico, with a wife and four children to support, came to her on bended knee and won the conductorship of the Cappella Municipale, which had risen from the Palatina's ashes. Between 1800 and his death, Puccini wrote several operas, of which the 1810 *Quinto Fabio* was much praised; he was even hailed as the new Cimarosa [962]. After Napoleon fell, Lucca was occupied by the Austrians, and Domenico came under suspicion of harboring revolutionary ideas. He died suddenly at forty-three, under what were said to be suspicious circumstances. It was whispered that his sherbet, the gustatory fad of the day, had been doctored. His father outlived him by seventeen years. Domenico also wrote sacred music and a few instrumental pieces. RECORDINGS: Eugene List has recorded his sole keyboard concerto. There is a piracy of his opera *Il Ciarlatano.*

[1075] GEBAUER, François René (Ge-bou'-er, Fràn-swà' Hren-ā')
BASSOONIST, TEACHER
BORN: Versailles, March 15, 1773
DIED: Paris, July 28, 1845

The second eldest of the musical Gebauer brothers (and the longest-lived) studied, like his two younger siblings, with the oldest, Michel Joseph [1038]. François was also a pupil of Devienne [1010]. He played in the bands of the Garde Suisse and the Garde Nationale, in several theater orchestras (including the Opéra, c. 1800–26), and in the imperial and royal chapels. He was first professor of bassoon at the Conservatoire, where he taught off and on from 1795 to 1838. He wrote a bassoon method, and a good deal of instrumental music focused on his instrument. RECORDINGS: Desiré Dondeyne has recorded a couple of his band marches.

[1076] CATEL, Charles-Simon (Kà-tel', Shärl Sē-mōn')
TEACHER, THEORIST, HORTICULTURIST
BORN: L'Aigle, June 10, 1773
DIED: Paris, November 29, 1830

Born in a Norman village, Catel came as a child to the École Royale du Chant in Paris, where his most important teacher was Gossec [879]. At the height of the Revolution, Catel turned out reams of propaganda music for the Garde Nationale and worked as the Opéra as a rehearsal conductor. In 1795 he became professor of harmony and counterpoint at the Conservatoire, which provided a basis for the harmony text he published in 1802 and which was long a favorite. In that same year he began his career as an operatic composer with *Sémiramis.* It and his 1807 comedy *L'Auberge de Bagnères* were both successful, and *Les Bayadères* of 1810 remained in the repertoire. His only ballet, *Alexandre chez Apelle,* first performed in 1808, is said to have been the first work at the Opéra calling for the *cor-anglais* (English horn). He was named an inspector at the Conservatoire in 1810 but fell out with his *confrères* and resigned in 1816. A year later he was elected to the Académie. But, apparently discouraged by the reception of his last operas, he heeded Voltaire's *Candide* and spent his last decade working in his garden. Besides the works noted, he left a few instrumental compositions. RECORDINGS: Marcel Couraud has recorded an orchestral suite from *L'Auberge de Bagnères* and Desiré Dondeyne a military march.

[1077] MATIEGKA, Wenzel Thomas (Mà-tēj'-kà, Vent'-zel Tō'-màs)
PIANIST, GUITARIST, LAWYER
BORN: Choceň, c. July 16, 1773
DIED: Vienna, January 19, 1830

After serving as a choirboy in Kremsier (now Kroměříž), Matiegka studied law and piano in Prague. After serving as a law clerk to Prince Kinsky, he decided he preferred music and went to Vienna, where he was caught up in the guitar craze and was soon making a living teaching that instrument and publishing compositions and arrangements for it. His keyboard training stood him in good stead, for he also served as organist at the Thomaskirche and at the parish church in suburban Leopoldstadt, where he established a home and family. He is remembered, rather accidentally, by a quartet for flute, violin, guitar, and cello, often credited to Schubert [1153], who added the cello part. RECORDINGS: The quartet has been several times recorded. Leo Witoszyn-skyj has also recorded a set of Matiegka's guitar variations.

[1078] WEYSE, Christoph Ernst Frie-drich (Vī'-ze, Krēs'-tōf Ârnst Frē'-drikh)
PIANIST, ORGANIST, TEACHER
BORN: Altona, March 5, 1774
DIED: Copenhagen, October 8, 1842

Weyse studied organ with his grandfather, C. B. Heuser, in Altona, then a Danish border town. When the aged and ailing Emanuel Bach **[801]** refused to take him on as a student, he went to Copenhagen, where he was both taught and housed by Hofkapellmeister J. A. P. Schulz **[949]**. At twenty he was named principal organist of the Reformed Church and nine years later became organist of the Fruekirke for the rest of his life, performing for Liszt **[1218]** there in 1831. Around the turn of the century, Weyse was rejected by a young woman with whom he had fallen in love, and he remained a bachelor. He was a pioneer in developing a Danish school of opera, beginning with his *Sovedrikken (The Sleeping Potion)* in 1809, and later was especially admired for his songs, many of which have been recorded by such Danish singers as Aksel Schiøtz and Lauritz Melchior. Schumann **[1211]** hailed his piano études, but then Schumann was a rather indiscriminate hailer. Most of Weyse's instrumental music might have been written a generation earlier. He was, however, the leading Danish musician of his time. In 1816 he was named professor of music at the University of Copenhagen, and court composer in 1819. In the last year of his life, he was awarded an honorary doctorate.

[1079] BRAHAM, John
SINGER, TEACHER, ENTREPRENEUR
BORN: London, March 20, 1774
DIED: London, February 17, 1856

Braham's father, a Jew whose real name is said to have been Abraham, died when his son was a child, and legend has the boy selling pencils in the streets. His clear treble won him the protection of a co-religionist named Meyer Leon or Lyon, who sang as "Michael Leoni." Leoni, possibly a relative, put him on the musical stage as a treble, and another member of his congregation paid for his piano lessons. Eventually Braham's soprano career came to an end, and Leoni took a synagogue post in Ja-maica. Braham taught piano until his voice, a tenor, ripened, and then he went to Bath to study with Venanzio Rauzzini, a *castrato* who was the most sought-after vocal teacher in England. In 1796 he made his new debut at Drury Lane in Stephen Storace's **[1025]** last opera *Mahmoud,* which had been finished by Michael Kelly **[1028]** and Storace's sister Nancy, who was not incidentally a pupil of Rauzzini's. Though Braham was nine years younger than Nancy, and she was still technically married to John Abraham Fisher (1744–1806), the two fell in love and soon embarked on a Continental tour together. It lasted nearly four years, two of them spent in Milan, where Braham and Nancy appeared together at La Scala. In Venice the ailing Cimarosa **[962]** embarked on *Artemisia* for Braham but died in January 1801; the finishing touches were made by others so that it could be premiered at that winter's carnival. The pair came back to London later that year for Braham to make his first appearance as a tenor at Covent Garden. The work in which he appeared was such a disaster that he afterward reserved the right to select or compose the music for his own roles. A short, bandy-legged man, he was no actor, but his power, range, technique, and expressiveness won him acclaim as one of the supreme singers of his day. He was Max in the first London production of Weber's **[1124]** *Der Freischütz* and created the role of Huon in the same composer's *Oberon.* He also loved to play to the gallery with sentimental claptrap.

In 1802 Nancy bore Braham a son named Spencer, who later became an Anglican cleric as "Spencer Meadows." But Braham did not make an honest woman of her when Fisher died, and in 1816 he threw her over to marry Frances Elizabeth Bolton, by whom he had six legitimate children. The heartbroken Nancy died a year later. By 1830 Braham was quite wealthy and sunk his money in the St. James Theatre and the Colosseum. He lost everything but his nether garments and went on singing until he was in his seventies. In his later operatic appearances he essayed baritone roles. In 1840 he embarked on a two-year tour of America where his reputation drew full houses. Later he went back to London and retired from singing in 1852. He wrote many songs, mostly in connection with his stage roles.

RECORDINGS: His 1811 song "The Death of Nelson" (its protagonist had been his friend) has been recorded by such English tenors as Robert Tear and Walter Widdop.

[1080] TOMÁŠEK, Václav Jan Křtitel
(Tō-má'-shek, Vä'-tsláf Yán Krzh'tē'-təl)
PIANIST, TEACHER
BORN: Skuteč, April 17, 1774
DIED: Prague, April 3, 1850

Wenzel Tomaschek, as history usually lists him, loved to rattle on, and so has put us in his debt for his gossipy views of Beethoven **[1063]** and other great musicians of his time. Tall, erect, topped with an ill-fitting wig, witty, gregarious, loquacious, opinionated, hungry for praise (but not so eager to give it), he spent his mature life as a sort of object of musical pilgrimage in Prague. The youngest of thirteen children of a once-affluent weaver who had fallen on hard times, he managed to study the violin and in 1787 was accepted as a chorister by the Minorites at Jihlava. Given access to a piano in the monastery, he taught himself to play and read whatever theory texts he could get his hands on. From the age of sixteen, he was able to support himself as a piano teacher while attending the gymnasium in Prague. In 1794 he matriculated at the university there and wound up taking a law degree. While Tomášek was contemplating a legal or civil-service career, a Count Bucquoi von Langueval proposed that he become his personal composer at a handsome salary. Tomášek was not even required to live-in; in fact the count gave him a house of his own.

Though Tomášek was perhaps his own most devoted fan, he was highly self-critical as a composer. His first encounter with Beethoven in 1798 almost decided him to give up writing music. In 1811 his first opera, *Seraphine*, was successfully premiered in Prague, but the composer was so dissatisfied that he refused to let a later effort be produced. He visited Beethoven again in 1814, and the two had a wonderful time lambasting that upstart Meyerbeer **[1142]**. At forty-nine Tomášek married a Fräulein Wilhelmine Ebert, of whom history says little. He was probably the most important teacher in Prague in his time, and his pupils include Voříšek **[1138]**, Dreyschock **[1260]**, and the critic Eduard Hanslick (who thought him superior to Wagner **[1230]**). As a composer for the piano, Tomášek also had considerable impact on Schubert **[1153]** and Robert Schumann **[1211]**. But Clara Schumann **[1267]**, then still Clara Wieck, visited him in 1837 and was unimpressed, perhaps because the old fellow got into a rage about her opinion of Gluck **[803]** and walked out on her. Berlioz **[1175]** met him later and was amused to find at a Prague concert that thirty-one of the thirty-two selections pro-

grammed were by Tomášek. From 1845 to 1850 Tomášek serialized his memoirs. Though he wrote choral, orchestral, and chamber works, he is chiefly important as a composer of free-form piano pieces and pre-Romantic songs.

RECORDINGS: A piano concerto has been recorded by Peter Toperczer, an eclogue by pianist Rudolf Firkusny, and a fantasia for glass harmonica by Bruno Hoffmann.

[1081] SPONTINI, Gaspare Luigi Pacifico (Spôn-tē'-nē, Gàs'-pà-rā Lōō-ē'-jē Pà-chē'-fē-kō)
CONDUCTOR, ADMINISTRATOR
BORN: Majolati, November 14, 1774
DIED: Majolati, January 24, 1851

Of all the major nineteenth-century operatic composers, Spontini is now perhaps the least performed. But he was not prolific, and once he found himself his rate of production was so slow that his really considerable operas come to only a handful.

The son of a peasant from the Marches, young Spontini was sent to nearby Jesi to live with a priestly uncle and get ready for a clerical career. When he found the uncle had no sympathy with his musical leanings, he ran away to another in a village in the locality, who got him some training that uncovered signs of talent. Not to be robbed of the fame that might accrue from sponsorship, *Lo zio padre* reclaimed him and found him some even better instruction. At nineteen Spontini won a scholarship at the Conservatorio della Pietà dei Turchini in Naples, where he studied under the octogenarian Nicola Sala and the *secondo maestro* Domenico Tritto, and where, a couple of years later, he won, or did not win the post of *maestrino*. Whatever the case, it made little difference, for he got himself into some kind of trouble and went AWOL in October 1795.

However, he was in luck: a Roman impresario, having heard some of his work, commissioned a one-act comedy, *I Puntigli delle donne (The Ladies' Punctilios)*, which, performed at the 1796 Carnival, won him further commissions from Venice and Naples. Supposedly the Neapolitan effort won him the friendship and tutelage of Cimarosa **[962]**. In 1798 King Ferdinand, having declared war on France, deemed it discreet to remove himself and his court to Palermo. Legend says that he took Spontini instead of Cimarosa, but the record shows Spontini producing comedies in Naples up through the summer of 1799. He produced two more in Palermo in 1800, returned to Naples the following year, and took off for Paris in 1802. It was a fairly risky thing to do, for Spontini had no international reputation and even in Italy was regarded as an also-ran. He managed to get a successful production of his *La Finta filosofa (The Sham Philosopher-Lady)*; and, apparently convinced that he had the Parisians eating out of his fine Italian hand, he followed it with an *opéra-comique, La Petite Maison*, which the audience stopped in mid-performance. At this point, the playwright Etienne de Jouy walked into his life, and things took an upturn. Their first collaboration, the one-act *Milton* of 1804, shows Spontini in a less frivolous vein. But what Jouy had in mind was a lyric tragedy, *La Vestale*. He had previously worked with Boieldieu [1084] and Catel [1076] and was to collaborate with Rossini [1143] on *Moïse* and *Guillaume Tell*. As soon as Spontini got something called *Julie, ou Le Pot de fleurs* out of the way, he set to work, completing *La Vestale* in 1805. In the meantime, the Empress Josephine had become his patroness. It is not clear whether the delay in production resulted more from recalcitrance at the Opéra or from Spontini's continued tinkering with the score, but it finally reached the stage in 1807 and became the hit of the day.

The next Spontini-Jouy collaboration, *Fernand Cortez*, reached the stage only two years later but satisfied neither the public nor the composer. In 1810 Spontini married Céleste Érard, daughter of the harp manufacturer who was also Spontini's publisher, was awarded the prize for the best opera of the decade, and was entrusted with the managership of the Théâtre Italien. Soon after he attempted to resuscitate the long-moribund Concert Spirituel. But his opposition to Napoleon's divorce and remarriage and his refusal to mix politics with art got him fired in 1812. When Louis XVIII took the throne two years later, he placed Spontini in charge of the music of the royal chamber and restored him to his theatrical post. But from then on, having caught the attention of Frederick William III of Prussia, Spontini played both ends against the middle. He quickly peddled the management of the Théâtre Italien to the soprano Angelica Catalani and devoted himself to producing works praising the Bourbons. Meanwhile he had been banging away for years at *Cortez*, bringing in a new librettist whose changes included the addition of Montezuma (!) to the cast. (Jouy, a republican, had boggled at Spontini's self-serving royalism.) The new version, though costly and spectacular—close to what would be termed *grand opéra*—was triumphant. But

Spontini's next effort, a treatment of Voltaire's *Olympie* (more costly and more spectacular) fell flat.

But when it did, Spontini had already concluded successful negotiations with the Prussian king, having got around the opposition posed by Count Brühl, intendant of the Royal Opera. In 1820 he went to Berlin as the grand panjandrum of his majesty's music, taking precedence in fact if not in name over the still-dangerous Brühl. He produced the following spring an even more grandiose version of *Olimpie* (now *Olympia*). (The libretto was the work of E. T. A. Hoffmann [1086].) But Spontini's contract contained a rake-in-the-grass, which, given his record over the preceding fifteen years, was bound to smite him in the face: it required that he turn out two new operas a year. This was hardly consistent with his increasing perfectionism, which, for example, demanded three months' rehearsal for *Olympia*. Moreover Brühl had cast his lot with the rising musical nationalism in the Germanies, and the brilliant premiere of Weber's [1124] *Der Freischütz* in Berlin five weeks later played right into his hands.

But though Spontini's star was fading (in Paris as well as in Berlin), this by no means spelled the end. There was *Nurmahal* in 1822 (based on Thomas Moore's [1093] *Lalla Rookh*, for a dramatic treatment of which he had written the music a year earlier). There was *Alcidor* for the Princess Luise's wedding in 1825. And there was *Agnes von Hohenstaufen*, which, what with partial representations, revisions, and revisions of revisions, dragged on for a dozen years and succeeded in none of its manifestations. Then there was endless talk and dither and sabbaticals to expand *Milton* into a major work, perhaps to be called *Das verlorene Paradies*, but nothing came of any of it. And there were some occasional cantatas and a thin trickle of songs, choral works, and band pieces. To be sure, Berlin benefitted from Spontini's sojourn. He, with his ebony-and-ivory drum-major's baton, was in fact a true conductor in the modern sense, with a no-nonsense approach to impeccable ensemble performance. He also had a dramatic genius and, recognizing that successful opera was "total theater," he approached it accordingly—though his repertoire was limited to his own works and a few masterpieces by Gluck [803] and Mozart [992]. He also conducted orchestral concerts, wherein he introduced Beethoven's [1063] fifth and seventh symphonies to Berlin and parts of J. S. Bach's [684] B-minor *Mass*. Despite the increasing instability of the ground he walked on, he also continued to play the role of the musical autocrat. (His arbitrary decisions were frequently defensible: when, over Spontini's opposition, the Mendelssohn family [see 1200] "bought" the opera house to produce young Felix's first opera for public consumption, it was Felix who walked out first on the ensuing debacle.) As things got worse, Spontini took increasingly desperate measures to shore up his position. The crisis came with the death of Frederick William III in 1840. Spontini chose this moment to take his feud with the opera management to court, and was injudicious enough to attack the new king, Frederick William IV, in print. Convicted of sedition, he was sentenced to nine months in jail. The king generously pardoned him, but Spontini had gone too far. He was dismissed as honorably as is conceivable: he was granted his full salary in perpetuity, an outright gift of 6,000 thalers, and the right to use his title as long as he lived. He returned to Paris in 1842, a broken man. He was heaped with honors and invitations to conduct—he even made a triumphant visit to Berlin five years later—but he soon became too deaf and feeble to work. He retired to his native village, devoted his last years to good works, and died there at seventy-seven. Childless, he left his goods to the local poor. Despite the advocacy of such as Berlioz [1175] and Wagner [1230], Spontini seems not to have been a very great musician. His importance lies in his sense of theater and his influence, for better or worse, on the French school of grand opera that followed.

RECORDINGS: A few great singers (Rosa Ponselle, Maria Callas) have made *La Vestale* work for modern audiences, but the sole commercial recording (of a routine radio performance conducted by Fernando Previtali) barely sustains the interest. Apart from a scattering of songs and arias, the only other notable recording are piracies of *Agnes von Hohenstaufen* and *Fernand Cortez*.

[1082] CRUSELL, Bernhard Henrik
(Krōō-zel', Bârn'-härd Hen'-rik)
CLARINETIST, CONDUCTOR, POET
BORN: Nystad, October 15, 1775
DIED: Stockholm, July 28, 1838

Crusell is the first Finn to be treated in these pages, his birthplace on the southeast coast of Finland now being known as Uusikaupunki. When he was a child, his family moved to Nurmijärvi, just north of the capital, where he learned the clarinet and at twelve joined a military band. There

he became the protégé of a Swedish officer, Major Wallenstjerna, who saw to it that he had lessons with Abt Vogler [960] in Stockholm. Crusell became first clarinetist in the Royal Orchestra and was placed in charge of military music in Stockholm. He traveled widely as a performer and studied for a time with Gossec [879] in Paris. He returned to Finland only once, for a concert in 1801. He was a notable translator of opera libretti for the Stockholm theaters and had something of a hit with his own opera, *Lilla Slafvinna*, in 1824. He was also noted as a songwriter, but his most enduring works are for the clarinet. RECORDINGS: Gervase De Peyer has recorded a clarinet concerto in F minor, and Thea King has recorded clarinet concerti in E-flat major and B-flat major, as well as three quintets for clarinet and strings (with the Allegri Quartet), and the Frankfurt Sestetto da Camera performs a quintet for oboe and strings.

[1083] ISOUARD, Nicolas (Ēz-wärd', Nē-kō-läs')
BUSINESSMAN, ORGANIST, PUBLISHER
BORN: Malta, December 6, 1775
DIED: Paris, March 23, 1818

The first Maltese composer of consequence, Isouard wrote as "Nicolò de Malte" or simply "Nicolò," in deference to his father, a prominent merchant and government official. He was educated as a military engineer in Paris, where he took piano lessons on the side. When the outbreak of the Revolution put an end to his plans for soldiering, he returned to Malta to enter the commercial world. Having made himself a popular salon pianist, he took further lessons in Valletta, then in Palermo, where he pursued his mercantile career, and finally in Naples, where he worked as a banker. His first operas, *L'Avviso ai maritati (Advice to Husbands)* and *Artaserse (Artaxerxes)* were successfully produced in 1794, in Florence and Livorno respectively. Isouard then abandoned business entirely, much to his father's distress, and became organist and music director to the Knights of St. John in Valletta. When the French seized the island in 1799, he took a job as secretary to the French governor and so found his way back to Paris. There he found an éntree to the operatic stage by collaborating with the violinist-composer Rodolphe Kreutzer, and in 1802 had the first of his many successes at the Opéra-Comique with *Michel-Ange*. That same year he and Kreutzer went into the publishing business with Boieldieu [1084] Cherubini [1019], Méhul [1036], and the violinist-composer Pierre Rode. It folded nine years later. In 1812 he was wedded to Claudine Berthault, and his father, having seen that success extended beyond the business world, was among the guests. Two years later Claudine bore a daughter, who, as Ninette Nicolò, had a career as a pianist. As a composer of *opéras-comiques*, Isouard was rivaled only by his sometime friend Boieldieu, with whom he broke in 1817 when the latter was named to fill a vacancy in the Institut. Isouard had a gift for easy melody and an understanding of public taste, and several of his essentially lightweight works, notably *Joconde*, held the stage for many years. Toward the end of his life, he allegedly took to drink, and, like many another in that crowded urban age, died of tuberculosis. RECORDINGS: On ancient records one finds a few excerpts, mainly from *Joconde*.

[1084] BOIELDIEU, François-Adrien
(Bwáld-yö', Frán-swá' A-drē-an')
KEYBOARDIST, IMPRESARIO
BORN: Rouen, December 16, 1775
DIED: Jarcy, October 8, 1834

As he stands before his piano, in Boilly's portrait in the Rouen Museum, frockcoated, waistcoated, cravatted, tightly pantalooned, and Hessian-booted, his hair in a "Brutus crop," Boieldieu is very much a man of the new age; not unsurprisingly then his stage works foreshadow the whole *opéra-comique* tradition of the nineteenth century. His beginnings, however, (apart from the divorce of his parents) are remarkably conventional. His father was an usher in the Rouen archiepiscopal court; his mother was a fashionable milliner. Gifted with a remarkable ear and a good strong treble, the boy became a chorister at the great cathedral, where he was taught by the music master Urbain Cordonnier and later by the organist Charles Broche, who had once studied with Padre Martini [767] and who was by then chiefly notable for his boozing. From 1791 until the Revolutionists shut down the churches, Boieldieu served as organist at St. André. By then he was already writing songs and piano pieces and now embarked on setting a sentimental libretto, *La Fille coupable (The Guilty Daughter)* written by his father. The local boy made good when it was produced in 1793 in Rouen, though a sequel was not so successful two years later. By then, however, Boieldieu was being published in Paris, and seeing no special future for himself in the provinces, he went upriver in 1796 to seek his fortune in the capital.

One of the first important people he met there was the great tenor Garat [1026], who not only took up his romances, but also introduced him to Louis Emmanuel Jadin [1055], who, in turn, procured him entrée to the fashionable salons of Sébastien Erard, wealthy manufacturer of harps and pianos. The next year three of his one-act *opéras-comiques* were produced prestigiously and to great applause. The year 1798 saw the success of the full-length *Zoraïme et Zulnar*, in which one of the leads was the high baritone Jean-Blaise Martin, who lent his name to a peculiarly French voice still known as a *baryton-Martin*. That same year Boieldieu was appointed to a professorship at the Conservatoire. In 1800 he turned out an even more successful Oriental confection, *Le Calife de Bagdad* (the overture is still played). According to the composer, at the triumphant end of the premiere, Cherubini [1019] told him that one so ignorant of music did not deserve such success and offered to instruct him. One doubts that it happened, however, for the two composers had collaborated on *Emma* the year previous.

Shortly afterward Boieldieu fell in love with a beautiful ballerina named Clotilde Mafleurai (or Malfleuroy) and married her in 1802. Nine months later he gave birth to *Ma tante Aurore*. For some reason there was a cabal against it, and all hell broke loose at the Opéra-Comique during the performance. J. F. Reichardt [980] recalled strolling out on the stage to observe the riot, unnoticed either by performers or audience. Two nights later it established itself as one of the composer's greatest successes. By that time La Mafleurai, whose reputation for sleeping around Boieldieu had ignored, had proved a *fleur du mal*. The heartbroken composer left her to her own devices, of which she had a good many, and went off to St. Petersburg, at the invitation of Czar Alexander to succeed Sarti [853], who had left two years before.

Boieldieu was put in charge of the French Opéra, where his first offering was *Aline, reine de Golconde* in the spring of 1804. The prima donna was Jeanne (or "Jenny") Phillis-Bertin, who had been recently widowed, and it was not long before the two sufferers found solace in a longtime *ménage à deux*. Boieldieu remained in Russia for another seven years, during which time he should have, according to his contract, written twenty-one operas to libretti selected personally by the czar. But the czar was too busy or something to deliver them, and Boieldieu was forced to fall back on whatever old stuff was in the library. As a result he produced only ten works all told, of which only *Les Voitures versées (The Overturned Carriages)*, rewritten in 1820, was worth much. In 1811, seeing stormclouds on the international horizon, he gave up his 4,000 rubles a year and took his Jenny back to Paris. There they were not as lucky as Boieldieu's parents had been, for liberalism was again out, and he was denied a divorce. (Still, the informal relationship left him obviously with a measure of freedom, for in 1815 a singer named Thérèse Louise Antoinette Regnault bore him a son, listed as Adrien Louis Victor, who became an opera composer of sorts and a writer of popular songs.

In 1812 Boieldieu *père* produced his first new opera for Paris in almost a decade, *Jean de Paris*. Years later Robert Schumann [1211] cited it as the composer's best work, and Richard Wagner [1230] thought it had all "the vivacity and natural grace of the French." After that, however, his production was spotty, dotted with trifles and collaborations—with old hands like Cherubini [1019], and such contemporaries and juniors as Berton [841], Catel [1076], Isouard [1083], and Hérold [1136], individually and collectively. But he had made his mark, and the Establishment took notice. The new king, for example, appointed him court composer in 1815, and, to the chagrin of his old friend Isouard, Boieldieu was named to fill the dead Méhul's [1036] place in the Academy of Fine Arts. A year later, in 1818, he delivered himself of his penultimate success, *Le Petit Chaperon rouge (Little Red Riding Hood)* and retired to. the country, where he occasionally wrote one-acters or parts of collaborative works.

Boieldieu's greatest hit came late in 1825 with *La Dame blanche (The White Lady)*, which became one of the keystones of *opéra-comique*. Its Gothic plot, borrowed from Sir Walter Scott, was worked into a libretto by Eugène Scribe, whose dramatic works ultimately filled seventy-six volumes, and the opera, written to counter the Rossini craze [1143] that had seized the Parisians, may be seen as in many ways the French counterpart to Weber's *Der Freischütz*—the archetypal Romantic opera. Some months afterward, Boieldieu's long-estranged wife died, and in early 1827 he married Jenny, with Cherubini and Catel present as witnesses. A little over two years later, what was to prove his last opera, *Les deux nuits (The Two Nights)* won critical acclaim at the Opéra-Comique but drew so poorly that it was soon dropped. It was Boieldieu's most ambitious effort, and in the opinion of some his most worthy one. He had been suffering from tuberculosis for some time, and the

failure of his opera set him back seriously. On medical advice he went south and spent nearly four years in the Pyrenees, Provence, and Italy. By 1834 he was unable to speak. He had lost his court appointment in the Revolution of 1830 and was now unable to accept the professorship tendered him by the Conservatoire. Since he composed melodies by singing them, he was also forced to give up composition, but in his final silence he indulged in his considerable talent for painting, some of the products of which may be seen in the Rouen Museum. In September he dragged himself to Paris for the opening of *Le Chalet* by his pupil Adolphe Adam [1172]. When he got home, he went to bed and never got up again. When he died, he was honored with a state funeral, and later they named a little street near the Opéra-Comique after him.

RECORDINGS: There is a complete recording of *La Dame blanche* conducted by Pierre Stoll (and a wealth of excerpts), and an abridged one of *Ma tante Aurore* by Marcel Couraud. There are also several recordings of various opera overtures. Some of his pretty instrumental works are also on records—the harp concerto (Lily Laskine, Nicanor Zabaleta, and others), the Concerto for Piano (Martin Galling), a piano trio (Krust-Gendre-Bex), and six piano sonatas (Hans Kann).

[1085] **MOLINO, Francesco** (Mō-lē′-nō, Fràn-chäs′-kō)
GUITARIST, VIOLINIST
BORN: Florence, 1775
DIED: Paris, 1847

One of the many virtuoso guitarists spawned by this renaissance of plectrum instruments, Molino was also a fine violinist and concertized throughout Europe. He wrote a guitar concerto and many other works for that instrument. RECORDINGS: Spiro Thomatos has recorded several of his guitar preludes.

[1086] **HOFFMANN, Ernst Theodor Amadeus** (Hof′-mán, Árnst Tä′-ō-dôr Á-mà-dä′-ōōs)
JURIST, FICTION WRITER, CRITIC, CONDUCTOR, PAINTER, ETC.
BORN: Königsberg, January 24, 1776
DIED: Berlin, June 25, 1822

Best known for his fantastic tales that provided the impetus for Offenbach's [1264] opera, as well as for Schumann's [1211] *Kreisleriana* and Tchaikovsky's [1377] *Nut-*

cracker, Hoffmann was also an important music critic—one of the first to try to approach the subject from an objective viewpoint. And though he was trained for the law and worked as a government official, he yearned to be remembered as a composer.

His father was a beer-swilling, womanizing lawyer who in middle age married his neurotic, bovine, teenage cousin, Lovisa Albertina Doerffer. When the elder Hoffmann (who also fancied himself musical, though he had a tin ear) was given a judgeship in the boondocks of Prussia two years after his son was born, he won legal sanction to abandon his family. Ernst Theodor Wilhelm (he later exchanged the final element of his name for "Amadeus" in honor of Mozart [992]) and his mother went to live with the Doerffers. The Doerffer household, which might have been created by Dickens in a dark mood, consisted of: (1) a gigantic grandmother, obsessed by religion; (2) a diminutive maiden aunt called Sophie, who played the harp and with dolls; (3) a bachelor uncle named Otto Wilhelm, who was a failed lawyer and a fanatic for system and order, and who was known as "Onkel O Weh"; (4) poor Frau Hoffmann, who mostly sat and stared. Upstairs lived a Frau Werner, convinced that her little son Zacharias represented the Second Coming. (She convinced Zacharias for a time too; after being a cult leader, he ultimately became a civil servant and then a Catholic priest. He also became a poet of some note. Schubert [1153] set some of his verses and Verdi's [1232] opera *Attila* was the basis of one of his plays.) "Onkel O Weh" saw to it that the boy had an education at the Burgschule, where his salvation (then and later) was a schoolmate, Theodor von Hippel, who understood and shared his artistic interests.

At sixteen the dwarfish, ugly lad with the oversized head was entered in the local university to become a lawyer. When he graduated in 1795, he had to serve a term as an unpaid law clerk in the Königsberg courts. Having studied both music and art on the side, he supported himself by giving piano lessons and painting landscapes. He fell violently in love with a pupil, a married woman named Johanna Dorothea Hatt, whom he called "Cora" after a favorite novelistic heroine; but, apparently before the affair had got beyond the glazed-eyeball stage, Cora's husband put an abrupt stop to her lessons. Hoffmann was so upset that he wrote a novel, tried to write several more, and made a setting of Gretchen's church scene from Goethe's *Faust.* After fighting nosebleeds and dizzy spells, he fled in 1796 to Glogau in Silesia, where he became apprentice to his maternal uncle Johann Ludwig, a court official. Having learned nothing from his parents' marriage, he soon got himself engaged to his cousin Mina, a relationship that dragged on, however, for nearly five years. In 1798 the family moved to Berlin, where in due course Hoffmann passed his bar exams. In the process he managed to get in some music lessons with Reichardt and to begin composing (notably a *Singspiel* entitled *Die Maske [The Masks]*). The authorities told him that following the usual probationary period, which he would fill at Posen in Prussian Poland, he could serve on any high court in the country.

He went to Posen in 1800 and, on his own for the first time in his life, proceeded to kick up his heels. His high-jinks included drawing unflattering cartoons of local bigwigs, which early in 1802 got him sent off to help govern Plock, a little town whose inhabitants spoke only Polish. Later that year he assuaged his need for conversation by breaking his engagement to Mina and marrying Michaelina Rorer, a girl he had met in Posen. He spent two wretched years in Plock, writing and composing without even a nod from a publisher and seeking nepenthe in the local taverns in the evenings. At last, through Hippel, now a Somebody, he got himself transferred to Warsaw. There Hoffmann found things more to his liking, and two kindred spirits among his court associates: Eduard Hitzig, who had studied under A. W. von Schlegel and was *au courant* in literature, and none other than the onetime Messiah, Zacharias Werner. Then he got in with a group of young Poles, who persuaded him to help them start an academy of music. They redid the crumbling old Mniszek Palace, which Hoffmann decorated with his own murals, and began a series of concerts in which Hoffmann appeared as conductor, pianist, singer, and composer. But Napoleon's arrival in 1806 scattered the membership, and the whole thing ground to a halt. Hoffmann became so ill that he claimed his body glowed in the dark. He sent his wife and their daughter Cäcilie back to Posen and tried to emigrate to Vienna. Denied a passport, he went to Berlin, where he was unable to find work. Word came to him that Cäcilie was dead and Michaelina gravely ill. In desperation, he advertised that he was available as a music director. Count Soden, intendant of the theater in Bamberg, made him an offer which he accepted, and stopping by Posen to pick up his now-recovered wife, he reached Bamberg in the fall of 1808.

Much to Hoffmann's chagrin, he found

Soden out of office and his replacement unenthusiastic about having him do more than supply music for the theater. Within a year the theater was bankrupt, and Hoffmann was keeping his head above water with teaching, reviewing, and, still fruitlessly, trying to get published. In 1810 Bamberg got a new intendant in the person of one Franz von Holbein, an old Berlin acquaintance who hired Hoffmann to do everything except sing, play, and conduct. About this time he was suffering the pangs of unspoken (and of course unrequited) love for a sixteen-year-old pupil, Julia Marc, whom in his writings he designated as "Katherina," after another literary heroine, but most usually as "Ktch." Meanwhile he had found a patron in a merchant, C. K. Kunz, who was, however, interested only in Hoffmann's prose writings, which he began publishing in 1814. Production of these pieces naturally interfered with composition, which Hoffmann still considered all-important to him. By 1813 the unwitting Julia was married, Holbein had quit the theater business, and Hoffmann had been saved from starving by a small legacy from "Onkel O Weh." In April, however, he was employed by Josef Sekonda, who operated a touring opera company out of Dresden, as conductor and *repetiteur*. In what spare time he had away from his duties and his writing, he worked furiously on his opera *Undine*, based on the famous story by Baron de La Motte-Fouqué, who had been persuaded to supply the libretto. Though he did not get on well with Sekonda, Hoffmann felt stable at last. In February 1814 he turned down an offer to direct in Königsberg. Four days later Sekonda fired him. At Hoffmann's darkest hour who should turn up, like a fairy godparent, but Hippel, who persuaded him to return to Berlin and the calm waters of the civil service.

He did so in 1814, hoping for a flunkey job that would give him time for music, but his reputation as a crack lawyer betrayed him. Nevertheless *Undine* was triumphantly produced under the baton of Bernhard Romberg [1051] in 1816—and then shelved. But, now famous both as an author, composer, and high government official, Hoffmann was lionized by Berlin hostesses. He drank too much at their *soirées*, behaved abominably, and finally abandoned them for evenings at Lutter-und-Wegener, a tavern that provided the model for "Maître Luther's" in the prologue to Offenbach's opera. He drove himself unmercifully, trying to come up with a new opera and with a fantastic novel, *Kater Murr*, with his own pet tomcat

as protagonist. In 1819 he suffered a severe attack of "arthritis," and the doctors forbade him booze. But his health degenerated, and when the real Kater Murr died, Hoffmann took to his bed. There, ravaged by syphilis, he slowly turned to stone and withered away to the size of a child. At the point where he no longer had any sensation from the neck down, he told his physician that he thought the worst was over. It was. He died the next day, at forty-six.

Though he was greatly gifted, Hoffmann was a far greater writer and critic than composer, and anyone who expects from his music the imagination and individuality of the prose will be largely disappointed. The music is of its time, but what *outré* qualities it shows result more from lack of skill than from intent. (Much of it has been lost.) However, *Undine* and *Aurora*, premiered in 1812, are important predecessors of Weber [1124] and Wagner [1230] and have been successfully revived. There survive also orchestral and chamber works, some piano sonatas, a Mass, etc.

RECORDINGS: The Trio à Cordes Français has recorded a piano trio and the harp quintet. A piano sonata has been recorded by Annie Gicquel. The Symphony in E-flat Major is performed under the baton of Tamás Sulyok. Roland Bader conducts the *Miserere* in B-flat Minor. A piracy of *Undine* is in the works.

[1087] KÜFFNER, Joseph (Küf'-ner, Yō'-zef)

BANDMASTER, VIOLINIST
BORN: Würzburg, March 31, 1776
DIED: Würzburg, September 9, 1856

Küffner, who had studied to be a lawyer, found his direction changed when he was offered a post as violinist in the court of the local prince-bishop in 1797. But in 1803 the city was annexed to Bavaria, a fact that was nailed down in 1815 after a ten-year period in which Ferdinand, ex-Grand Duke of Tuscany and son of the Emperor Leopold II, reigned as Grand Duke of Würzburg. From 1803 to the end of his days, however, Küffner served as state bandmaster. He seems to have been purely a local celebrity. His only 2 operas were produced in Würzburg and, apparently nowhere else. He also wrote symphonies and chamber music and expectably a good deal of band music. RECORDINGS: Records offer a slight *Rondo* for guitar and piano, played by Mario Sicca and Rita Maria Fleres.

[1088] BERGER, Ludwig (Bâr'-ger, Lōōd'-vikh)
PIANIST TEACHER
BORN: Berlin, April 18, 1777
DIED: Berlin, February 16, 1839

Berger is now remembered, if at all, as one of Felix Mendelssohn's [1200] teachers. He was also the chief exemplar of the Berlin school of *Lieder* in the period from Reichardt [980] and Zelter [1008] to his own famous pupil. Berger was composing at an early age and in 1799 began taking lessons with one Gürrlich. When Clementi [977] arrived in Berlin a few years later, he was so taken with Berger's playing that he took him back to St. Petersburg with him as protégé and companion. Berger met Field [1104] and Steibelt [1044] there and decided to stay. He married there but was widowed within the year. With Napoleon's armies on the horizon, he moved to Stockholm in 1812 and thence to London. Though he renewed his ties there with Clementi and made friends with Glorious John Cramer [1067], and though he quickly won public affection as a performer, he went home for good in 1815. There he taught not only Mendelssohn but also the latter's sister Fanny [1186], Taubert [1216], and many others. (It is doubtful that Henselt [1237] was, as has often been claimed, one of them.) Berger suffered increasingly from hypochondria, lost the use of an arm in 1817, and gradually shut himself off from the world. He had some success with his music for the burgeoning choral societies, but his only opera, *Oreste,* went unproduced. His piano studies became classics; his sonatas show the impact of Beethoven [1063]. Typical of the Berlin School, his songs are largely strophic. He was the first to set poems from Wilhelm Müller's *Die schöne Müllerin* (seven years before Schubert [1153]). RECORDINGS: There is a recording of his treatment of Goethe's *Trost im Tränen* by Karl Markus.

[1089] FUSZ, János (Fōōs, Yä'-nōsh)
KEYBOARDIST, TEACHER, CONDUCTOR
BORN: Tolna, December 16, 1777
DIED: Buda, March 9, 1819

Fusz, also known as Johann Evangelist Fuss, was born and educated down the Danube from Budapest, and worked as a piano teacher in Pozsony (alias Pressburg, alias Bratislava). Around the turn of the century, he moved to Vienna, where he hobnobbed with such as Albrechtsberger [889], Beethoven [1063], and Haydn [871]. He

wrote several operas and melodramas and was well known as a concert pianist. He also wrote chamber music and songs. He retired to Hungary for reasons of health in 1817. RECORDINGS: The Heidelberg Chamber Players have recorded his Op. 2 Quartet for Basset Horn and Strings.

[1090] SOR, Josep Fernando Macari (Sôr, Hō'-sep Fâr-nàn'-dō Mâ-kà'-rē)
GUITARIST, ORGANIST, CIVIL SERVANT, SOLDIER, TEACHER
BORN: Barcelona, c. February 14, 1778
DIED: Paris, July 10, 1839

Sor was probably the most important player and teacher of, and composer for, the guitar in its nineteenth-century Golden Age. He was a choirboy at the monastery of Montserrat and studied there with Anselmo Viola. He is reported to have written a Mass while he was there. Later he returned to Barcelona to study at the military academy and to produce his first opera at nineteen, *Telemaco nella isola di Calipso (Telemachus on the Isle of Calypso).* (Another opera, *Don Trastullo,* was probably unfinished and is in any case lost.) After that, he held various governmental posts and was court organist to the Duchess of Alva and music teacher to her children. In 1808 he served as an officer in the Spanish army against the invading French. But when they triumphed, he accepted a post in the occupation government. Having thus compromised himself, there was nothing to do but accompany the invaders when Wellington drove them back over the Pyrenees in 1813. Arriving in Paris, he established himself as a concert guitarist and won the support of Méhul [1036] and Cherubini [1019].

In 1815, however, he settled in London, where he was patronized by the Earl of Sussex, a son of George III, and where there was a fad for his songs and guitar pieces. He also became a successful ballet composer, and his *Cendrillon* of 1822 became one of the most popular ballets of its time; it was the first work performed at the Bolshoi Theater in Moscow a year later, with the composer in attendance. Sor remained in Russia for three years, then returned to Paris to spend the rest of his days there. Some accounts maintain that he had been forgotten there in the interim and died in poverty, but the tally of his publications support the story that from then on he concentrated on the guitar as teacher and performer. Most of his other music, which included symphonies, string quartets, and a Mass, has vanished.

RECORDINGS: The guitar pieces, which include 2 large sonatas and run to 63 opus numbers, have been well represented on records by most important guitarists over the last forty years.

[1091] HUMMEL, Johann Nepomuk
(Hoom'-mel, Yō'-hån Ne'-pō-mook)
PIANIST, CONDUCTOR, TEACHER
BORN: Pressburg, November 14, 1778
DIED: Weimar, October 17, 1837

Hummel is a composer whose musical reputation has ridden a roller-coaster over the years. Favorably compared with Beethoven [1063] in his lifetime, he was described forty years after his death in *Grove's Dictionary* as "a respectable mediocrity." A revival of some of his music recently suggests that the truth lies somewhere in between. He was born in that bordertown now known to the Czechs as Bratislava, the son of Johannes Hummel, director of the Royal School of Military Music. That institution closed down in 1785, and the elder Hummel—his son already a piano prodigy—moved to Vienna, where he became music director of the suburban Freihaus Theater, scene of the premiere of Mozart's [992] *Zauberflöte*. Hummel took the boy around to Mozart, who, with the understanding that he would not take him on as a pupil, agreed to listen to him. However, young Hummel's performance so charmed him that he took him into his own home until 1788. At that point the Hummels started off on a tour that began in Prague, went on through the Germanies to Denmark, then across the sea to Edinburgh. After three months they proceeded through various English cities to London, where they remained until late 1792, waiting for the French Revolution to subside. When it didn't, they continued the tour through Holland and more German towns, reaching Vienna in 1793. There young Hummel sought out Albrechtsberger [889] and Salieri [966] for some serious training in composition and later took some organ lessons from Haydn [871]. He also met the newly arrived Beethoven, and despite their wariness of each other as rivals, the two became friends.

By 1803 Hummel, who had been pretty much out of the limelight for ten years and who had slaved away as a teacher, was a pockmarked and decidedly unprepossessing young man, uncelebrated for personal tidiness. Despite support by Haydn, he was rejected as archepiscopal *Kapellmeister* at Salzburg but a year later succeeded Haydn in everything but title at the Esterházys' in Eisenstadt. The shoes were perhaps too large for him to fill, and moreover he spent too much time in Vienna and elsewhere. In 1808 he was fired, rehired shortly afterward, and then let go for good in 1811. He settled back to his old ways in Vienna and in 1813 married a singer, Elisabeth Roeckel, who, sensing correctly that his future financial needs would be larger (they had two children), persuaded him to take up playing again. In 1816 Hummel was, however, appointed court *Kapellmeister* at Stuttgart. But he found he disliked Stuttgart, and the court found him a decidedly rough diamond, so two years later he chucked the job for its analogue in Weimar, where the cultural environment and the working conditions were much more to his taste. There he became a friend of the septuagenarian Goethe, autocrat of the ducal theater, and an increasingly large frog in that small pond. (Like Dussek [1016], Hummel became terribly obese, and an old story has it that a semicircle had to be cut at his place in the dining table to allow him to reach his plate.) His contract called for him to be in place for only nine months out of the year, and he resumed touring, going to Russia, Poland, Paris, and London, among other places. In the early 1830s, perhaps because of his size, he abandoned the piano for the podium. In Weimar he had a number of important pupils, including Ferdinand Hiller [1219], Thalberg [1220], and Henselt [1237]. In 1827 he took Hiller to visit the dying Beethoven and to see the house where he had lived with the Mozarts. Hummel was a pallbearer at the funeral and played a memorial concert. After 1835 he was afflicted with a serious and painful illness and retired from musical activity. His son Eduard had a career as a pianist. Though Hummel wrote much for the piano, he was enormously productive in virtually all fields save that of the symphony. Some of his output was catchpenny stuff for quick sale, which has helped give his serious music a bad name.

RECORDINGS: Of the latter there are recordings of at least four piano concerti; the concerto for violin and piano; the concerti for mandolin, for bassoon, and for trumpet (many versions); the *Rondo* for piano and orchestra; the *Variations* for oboe and orchestra; the two chamber septets; several piano sonatas, sonatas for cello and for violin; a Mass; and many other chamber and piano works.

[1092] SHAW, Oliver
SINGER, CLARINETIST, ORGANIST,
TEACHER

BORN: Middleboro, Mass., March 13, 1779
DIED: Providence, R.I., December 31, 1848

To call the mature Shaw a blind ballad singer, or even a blind organist, would be perhaps to sell him short. He lost his right eye playing with his wee penknife as a child. Later, emulating his father, he became a naval officer and burned out the other "shooting the sun" after an attack of yellow fever. Unable to pursue his calling further, he took organ lessons with a blind organist from Newport named John Berkenhead. Then he studied in Boston with an immigrant German oboist and music dealer, Gottlieb Graupner—apparently unrelated to Christoph Graupner [673] but a former orchestral musician under Haydn [871]. He also had lessons from a clarinetist, Thomas Granger. In 1807 he established himself as a music teacher in Providence, being guided to his pupils' homes by a seeing-eye boy. Two years later he founded the Psallonian Society, which, for the next sixteen years, improved Providential taste by performing European masterpieces. In 1812 Shaw married a Miss Sarah Jencks and subsequently fathered at least seven children. As a composer he wrote chiefly hymns and sentimental songs, which last he was often called on to perform. (He sang "Mary's Tears" for President Monroe in 1817.) He was also one of the founders of the Handel and Haydn Society in Boston in 1815. Shaw published 4 books of hymn tunes, 1815–35; a piano method; and anthologies of piano and chamber music, such as For the Gentlemen of 1807. RECORDINGS: The New York Flute Club has recorded a selection from this last anthology, and E. Power Biggs a tiny keyboard jeu d'esprit entitled A Trip to Pawtucket.

[1093] MOORE, Thomas
POET, SINGER, SATIRIST
BORN: Dublin, May 28, 1779
DIED: Near Devizes, February 26, 1852

Thomas Moore has more right to be called a composer than his Scottish counterpart Robert Burns. He did in fact write songs and part-songs—and was an immensely popular singer around London—though his best-known efforts are, like Burns's, popular tunes fitted to lyrics of his own making. Like Michael Kelly [1028], with whom he collaborated on The Gypsy Prince in 1801, Moore was the son of a Dublin wine merchant. In his late adolescence, while he was

at Trinity College, he became involved with the United Irishmen, a group of militant young patriots, and Robert Emmet's execution later on reverberated through his poetry for a long time. After studying law in London, he got an appointment at the admiralty court in Bermuda in 1803. But Bermuda was not then what it is now, and a year later Moore turned his job over to a deputy and came back to England by way of the United States and Canada. He was soon well known and popular as a songwriter (his contract obligated him to advertise his creations by singing them wherever he might be heard) and as a satirist. In 1806 he went back to Dublin for a (much-interrupted) three-year sojourn. While there, he met and fell in love with Elizabeth ("Bessie") Dyke, an actress, whom he married in 1811. In 1807 he was approached by a music publisher named William Power with the proposition that he contribute verses to a projected edition of Irish Airs, with lyrics by various hands (in flagrant imitation of the Thomson-Burns collection). As it eventuated, Moore did all of the lyrics. The first volume appeared in 1808; nine more and a supplement followed between then and 1834. The first eight volumes were harmonized by Sir John Stevenson, the rest by Sir Henry Bishop. With these two collaborators, Moore also produced a collection of Sacred Songs, 6 collections of popular national airs, and a collection entitled Evenings in Greece. For his Irish tunes, Moore did not exactly do fieldwork: he simply raided recent collections by one Edward Bunting. The charge that he attempted to avoid being charged with plagiarism by distorting the melodies has, however, been discounted.

Moore, as lyricist and patriot, was grossly overvalued in his time. Berlioz [1175] set him beside Shakespeare and repeatedly recurred to Moore texts. "The Last Rose of Summer," as "Letzte Rose," became the theme song of Flotow's [1222] Martha. His Oriental romance Lalla Rookh elicited operatic and choral settings from such as Félicien David [1209], Spontini [1081], and Robert Schumann [1211]. Schumann, Mendelssohn [1200], Weber [1124], and Adolf Jensen [1349], among many others, made their own settings of his lyrics. And of course such Irish melodies as "Believe Me If All Those Endearing Young Charms," and "The Harp That Once Through Tara's Halls" came to grace the repertoire of every Irish tenor and every book of "old home songs."

Despite such success, Moore's later years were sad. Soon after he published Lalla Rookh, in 1817, he was told he was responsible for his Bermuda deputy's embezzlement of 6,000 pounds—then an enormous sum, which Moore saw no way of raising. He went abroad and remained on the Continent until 1822, when his publishers effected a settlement. While there he met Lord Byron, who entrusted him with his memoirs. These Moore sold for much-needed cash, but after Byron died Moore was able to buy them back. When Byron's heirs blocked their publication, however, Moore burned them. By 1845 his last child had died. He himself slipped into premature senility and dragged out a wretched last few years. In 1895 Sir Charles Villiers Stanford [1467] brought out a "corrected" version of the Irish airs, though doubts about his emendations are even graver than those about Moore's original versions.

RECORDINGS: There are numerous, widely scattered recordings of Moore's songs.

[1094] TASKIN, Henri Joseph (Täs-ka*n*, Än-rē′ Zhō-zef′)

COURT PAGE
BORN: Versailles, August 24, 1779
DIED: Paris, May 4, 1852

Taskin's great-uncle Pascal (1723–93), born in Liège, became a trial Walloon in Paris, apprenticed to the harpsichord maker François Étienne Blanchet, father-in-law to Armand-Louis Couperin [844]. Pascal later took over the business and was a notable maker of harpsichords and later of pianos. His nephew and protégé Pascal Joseph Taskin (1750–1829) married another of Blanchet's daughters. When Louis XV asked the elder Taskin to become Keeper of the Royal Musical Instruments, Taskin got him to accept the nephew instead, which explains how Henri Joseph came to be born at Versailles. Louis XVI was charmed by the child and made him a Royal Page. Henri Joseph studied first with his mother and then with his aunt Mme. Couperin. After the Revolution he became a dedicated Freemason. He published chamber music, a piano concerto, keyboard pieces and songs. His three operas never saw the stage or print. He also left unpublished Masonic pieces. His grandson Émile Alexandre Taskin (1853–97) was a famous operatic baritone. RECORDINGS: H. J. Taskin's *Masonic Funeral March* has been recorded by Roger Cotte.

[1095] BERNER, Friedrich Wilhelm (Bâr′-ner, Frē′-drikh Vil′-helm)

ORGANIST, CLARINETIST
BORN: Breslau, May 16, 1780
DIED: Breslau, May 9, 1827

Berner is perhaps chiefly remembered for saving the life of his friend Carl Maria von Weber [1124] when the latter accidentally mistook a bottle of engraving acid for one of wine. Berner was the son of the Elisabethskirche organist, with whom he studied and whom he succeeded in 1810. He also mastered several other instruments and as a youth was the clarinetist in the pit of the Stadttheater. In 1810 Weber made him a member of his secret society for the advancement of music, the Harmonische Verein. Two years later the Prussian government entrusted Berner and Weber's old rival, the conductor-composer Joseph Schnabel, with the promulgation of choral societies in Breslau on the Zelter [1008] model, and in 1815 they founded a conservatory there. Berner was also entrusted with cataloguing the music from the local monasteries, which had been closed down. He was a noted theorist and teacher, but most of his output, both literary and musical, has been lost. RECORDINGS: Franz Haselböck has recorded a set of his organ variations.

[1096] KREUTZER, Conradin (Kroit′-zer, Kōn′-rȧd-in)

MUSIC DIRECTOR
BORN: Messkirch, November 22, 1780
DIED: Riga, December 14, 1849

Konrad Kreutzer, as he was born (he later adopted the name Conradin), was unrelated to the violinist Rodolphe Kreutzer, dedicatee of Beethoven's [1063] famous sonata. The son of a miller who lived near the northern tip of Lake Constance, he became a composer of music (mostly operatic), tailored to Biedermeier tastes, and a wanderer. He received his basic musical training as a choirboy at Zwiefalten Abbey. At eighteen he went off to Freiburg im Breisgau to study law, but a student production in 1800 of his maiden stage effort, a *Singspiel* called *Die lächerliche Werbung (The Silly Courtship)* (with the composer singing the tenor lead), went to his head, and he cast his lot with music. His next decade is obscure, though he spent part of it in Vienna, where he is said to have had lessons from Albrechtsberger [889], and where he had a couple of one-acters produced. At the end of that period he went out on a demonstration tour for a sort of music box called the "panharmonicon" and wound up in Stuttgart. In 1812 he produced two operas there, *Konradin von Schwaben* and *Feodora.* They went over so well that when Franz Danzi **[1035]**, the court music director, defected to Karlsruhe at about the same time, Kreutzer was given his job. Kreutzer celebrated by getting married, but his rejoicing was premature, for things turned out to be difficult and unrewarding, and in 1816 he resigned and moved to Schaffhausen in northern Switzerland. In 1818 he accepted an invitation from Prince Karl Egon von Fürstenberg to take charge of his music in Donaueschingen, but this proved even more of a backwater than Stuttgart, and in 1822 Kreutzer went back to Vienna for the longest sojourn of his mature life. Save for an interruption by a trip to Paris, where he produced two *opéras-comiques* in 1827, he served as *Kapellmeister* at the Kärntnertor Theater from 1822 to 1832, where his *Libussa* was a great success in the first year of his intendancy. (Smetana's **[1291]** came fifty-nine years later in 1881.) In 1833, Franz Pokorny, who operated the Josephstadt Theater in the like-named suburb, lured him thither. There the winter of 1834 saw his most enduring successes, the Romantic opera *Das Nachtlager in Granada (The Bivouac in Granada)* and the musical play *Der Verschwender (The Spendthrift).* Both still enjoy occasional revivals in Germany and Austria. (A year earlier Kreutzer's setting of Grillparzer's *Melusina,* originally meant for Beethoven **[1063]**, had been premiered in Berlin. Mendelssohn **[1200]** was so put off by it that he wrote an overture of his own to show how the music ought to be.)

Kreutzer divided his time between the two houses until 1840, then went on a concert tour with his singer-daughter Cäcilie. This time he came to rest in Cologne where he stayed until 1842 as municipal music director. Then he took to the road again, eventually as accompanist to the child of his second marriage, Marie, who was also a singer. By then he was almost completely out of fashion as a composer for the stage. Eventually he and Marie settled in Riga in 1848, where Kreutzer suffered a stroke and died a year later. Besides his fifty or more stage pieces (nearly all forgotten), Kreutzer wrote religious music, very popular male choruses, songs, 3 piano concerti, and a number of chamber and instrumental works.

RECORDINGS: There is a complete recording of *Das Nachtlager in Granada* issued by Preiser of Vienna, and several recordings of an attractive instrumental septet and a number of other chamber works.

[1097] HEINRICH, Anthony Philip
VIOLINIST, ORGANIST, CONDUCTOR
BORN: Schönbüchel, March 11, 1781
DIED: New York, May 3, 1861

One contemporary hailed him as "the Beethoven of America." Another dismissed him as a harmless nut. Everyone knew him affectionately as "Father Heinrich." Controversy still continues as to the real worth of his music, though we can no longer regard him as a "primitive" or a *"naïf."* Self-taught he may have been, but he understood the European music of his time at a sophisticated level. If he thought at times like a showman and had the egotism of a Whitman, he was in both respects in the tradition of the American maverick, and no one can take away from him the fact that he was the first American composer to win the respect of European musicians and scholars.

Born "Anton Philipp" in Bohemia, Heinrich was reared by a wealthy uncle, and no doubt had musical training in accordance with his status. He began his adult career as a Hamburg bank official and, as such, was required to travel a good deal. In Malta he found a Cremona violin, in Boston a wife. The adventures of Napoleon and their aftermath bankrupted him. His wife died in 1814, leaving him with an infant daughter, whom circumstances forced him to farm out to a relative. He settled briefly in Philadelphia, where he conducted at the Southwark Theater. Perhaps reasoning that there might be more demand for his talents in a less established area, he walked to Pittsburgh and sailed down the Ohio River to Kentucky. He managed to put together an orchestra in Lexington, and to conduct it in the first North American performance of a Beethoven symphony late in 1817. Then he pushed on fifty miles farther west and holed up in a cabin in Bardstown, where by 1820 he had produced a collection of vocal and instrumental pieces, *The Dawning of Music in Kentucky,* Op. 1, which was published in Philadelphia in 1820. This was followed immediately by *The Western Minstrel,* Op. 2 and, three years later, by *The Sylviad,* Op. 3. Having eked out a living as a music teacher in Louisville, he somehow managed to get passage to England in 1826, where he is said to have buckled down to serious study. He returned to the States in 1831 and became organist at the Old South Church in Boston, and finished his first known orchestral work, an Indian fantasy called *Pushmataha.* (Numerous other "Indian" works followed.)

By 1834 Heinrich was back in London playing his fiddle at Drury Lane. Then he spent three years on the Continent, apparently to promote his work. He discovered that his daughter and her guardians had vanished. He was repeatedly ill and spent time in the hospital in London, Budapest, and Vienna. In Graz he managed to get a performance of his magnum opus, a symphony called *The Ornithological Combat of Kings* (having to do mostly with a condor). But the playing was scornfully perfunctory, and the listeners (including Heinrich) were bored. On his way home he was robbed in Bordeaux and spent some time in wretched straits before he could get passage. Soon after landing, he found that his daughter was looking for him in America, though it still took time for them to get together. Now Heinrich settled in New York, where he won recognition, though it did little to improve his material situation. His music provided the chief focus for a "Grand Musical Festival" in New York in 1842, and that same year he chaired the meeting that initiated the New York Philharmonic Society. However, he soon withdrew from that organization when it failed to give his music an airing soon enough to suit him. Shortly afterward he went to Washington to play for President Tyler. Halfway through a performance of one of his rhapsodic fantasies, the President announced that he would prefer to hear a reel. The experience is said somewhat to have soured Heinrich's faith in the efficacy of democratic elections. Other Heinrich concerts were given in New York and Boston in 1846, and there was a "Grand Valedictory" eight years prematurely in 1853. In 1850 he tried unsuccessfully to win the advocacy of the visiting Jenny Lind with a divertissement called *Jenny Lind and the Septinarian* (sic!) and other appropriate pieces. He continued to compose voluminously until his health broke in 1858. He died at eighty, poor as always. Some of Heinrich's music has been lost, but the majority remains, though it is neglected. One would like to hear, for example, such symphonies as *The Columbiad* (on the migration of the passenger pigeons) or *The Mastodon* (dedicated to "the spirit of Beethoven").

RECORDINGS: Fortunately for us Christopher Keene has recorded *The Ornithological Combat*, and Neely Bruce at least two LPs of piano and vocal pieces, including *The Western Minstrel*.

[1098] DAUPRAT, Louis François (Dō-prá´, Lōō-ē´ Frá*n*-swä´)
HORNIST, TEACHER

BORN: Paris, May 24, 1781
DIED: Paris, July 17, 1868

The modest, self-effacing Dauprat was the greatest horn player in France in the generation after Frédéric Nicolas Duvernoy's [1043]. He sang as a boy soprano at Notre Dame de Paris, served in the band of the Garde Nationale, and studied at the Conservatoire, winning first prize for horn in 1798. The next year he joined the Band of the Garde Consulaire and was with Napoleon at Marengo (where the famous chicken recipe was concocted). He then returned to the Conservatoire to study with Catel [1076], Gossec [879], and Antonín Reicha [1059]. In 1802 he was given an honorary appointment as assistant professor there. After serving as solo horn player at the Bordeaux Opera for two years, he joined the orchestra of the Paris Opera. In 1811 he was taken into the emperor's chapel and remained in the analogous position under the next three kings. In 1816 he was appointed professor of horn at the Conservatoire, and a year later succeeded the legendary Duvernoy as soloist at the Opéra. He helped in 1838 to found the Paris Conservatory Orchestra, which survived until 1967. In 1831 he was unable to see eye to eye with the new director of the Opéra and resigned his post there. In 1842 he retired from all of his duties and went to live with a daughter in Egypt, where he edited Reicha's wind quintets. He was a notable teacher and wrote a standard method. His more ambitious compositions (including operas and symphonies) were apparently never performed. RECORDINGS: His 6 little sextets for horns have been recorded by the Cors d'Esprits.

[1099] GIULIANI, Mauro Giuseppe Sergio Pantaleo (Jōōl-yà´-nē, Mou´-rō Jōō-sep´-pä Sâr´-jyō Pàn-tà-lä´-ō)
GUITARIST, CELLIST
BORN: Bisceglie, July 27, 1781
DIED: Naples, May 8, 1829

Save for Fernando Sor [1090], Giuliani was the most important guitarist and guitar composer of his time. Though his birthplace is variously given as Barletta and Bologna, it was really a small town near Bari. He was initially trained as a cellist (and later played as such in the first performance of Beethoven's [1063] seventh symphony in 1813). He migrated to Vienna in 1806 with his family, having already won a reputation as a touring virtuoso. He was much admired by both the public and his fellow musicians. Beethoven arranged some of his songs for him, and he concertized *en trio* with the violinist Mayseder and the pianist Hummel [1091], who was later replaced by Moscheles [1146]. However, he went to Rome to escape his creditors around 1820. In 1823 he concertized in London and created such a sensation that his fans brought out a short-lived magazine, *The Giulianiad,* to report his doings. Afterward he became a sort of unofficial court guitarist in Naples. His son Michele became professor of voice at the Paris Conservatoire, and his daughter Emilia was a guitar virtuoso in her own right. Mauro Giuliani's 1808 Concerto for Guitar (the first of 3) is said to have been the first such work performed. RECORDINGS: The first guitar concerto has been recorded by most of the important present-day guitarists, and Pepe Romero has recorded its two successors. There are also records of a sonata for flute and guitar (Jean-Pierre Rampal and René Bartoli), one for violin and guitar (Itzhak Perlman and John Williams), one for two guitars (Hugh and Thomas Geoghegan), the Rossini fantasias "Rossiniane" (Julian Bream, Angel Romero), and many solo works by various performers.

[1100] DIABELLI, Anton (Dē-à-bel'-lē, An'-tōn)
PIANIST, GUITARIST, TEACHER, PUBLISHER
BORN: Mattsee, September 6, 1781
DIED: Vienna, April 7, 1858

The musical embodiment of that Austrian petit-bourgeois phenomenon known as the *Biedermeier,* poor old Diabelli has gotten a worse name than he deserves from underpaying Schubert [1153] for his compositions. But his father saved him from an even worse one when he Italianized his surname, which was Dämon or Demon. Born in Salzburg country, young Anton was a choirboy in a local monastery and at Salzburg Cathedral. Supposedly he had lessons with Michael Haydn [894]. He began a monastic career in 1800 at Raichenhaslach in Bavaria. But shortly afterward Bavaria was defeated by Napoleon, who in the ensuing negotiations took the monasteries (including Raichenhaslach) from the Church and gave the property to the state, which turned the monks out. In 1803 Diabelli arrived in Vienna, where he quickly established himself as a teacher of piano and guitar, and also worked as proofreader for a publisher and composed on the side. By 1817 he was in the publishing business for himself, and a year later he joined forces with an art dealer

named Cappi. Cappi and Diabelli specialized in popular music for amateurs. In 1821 Diabelli hit on an idea worthy of Madison Avenue thinking: envisioning an anthology capitalizing on post-Napoleonic patriotism, he submitted to every Austrian composer he could think of a waltz tune of his own composition, requesting variations on the same. By 1824 he had had fifty-one responses. He published in a single volume fifty of these by famous musicians like Schubert, Czerny [1137], Tomášek [1080], and the eleven-year-old Liszt [1218], as well as obscure ones like Huglmann, Panny, and Umlauff. Missing was the fifty-first, Beethoven's [1063] offering, which had expanded to thirty-three variations and had to be published under separate cover. In 1821 Diabelli began his formal association with Schubert, bringing out his first published compositions, the songs *"Erlkönig"* and *"Gretchen am Spinnrade."*

The firm became Anton Diabelli et Cie. on Cappi's retirement in 1824. Thereafter the proprietor went on enlarging his empire by buying out smaller publishers. Schubert quarreled with him in 1823, but after Schubert's death Diabelli bought many manuscripts from his brother Ferdinand. Diabelli retired in 1851, but the business went on under various names until 1876, when it was taken over by the Hamburg publisher August Cranz (whose name the firm still operates under). By that time it had brought out nearly 25,000 works. As a serious composer, Diabelli was chiefly interested in church music, and his simple but charming Masses are still sung in rural Austria. RECORDINGS: A *Christmas Mass* in F Major has been recorded by Ernst Ehret. Diabelli also wrote some stage pieces, including a sequel to Schenck's [982] *Der Dorfbarbier,* but his largest output was of popular piano and guitar pieces, of which there are many samples on records. There are also recordings of the fifty variations by Hans Kann and by Rudolf Buchbinder. Michael Dittrich conducts the Bella Musica Ensemble in a selection of Viennese dances.

[1101] BLANGINI, Giuseppe Marco Maria Felice (Blàn-jē'-nē, Joo-sep'-pā Màr'-kō Mà-rē'-à Fā-lē'-chà)
SINGER, MUSIC DIRECTOR, TEACHER
BORN: Turin, November 18, 1781
DIED: Paris, December 18, 1841

Felice Blangini began his musical studies as a chorister in Turin Cathedral. By the time he was twelve, he was proficient as organist and cellist, and was already composing. His family moved with him to Paris in 1799, and his performance of his own songs soon made him the darling of the salons, and in 1802 the first of his 30 or so lightweight operas was staged at the Théâtre Feydeau. In 1805 he was invited to Munich to serve as *Kapellmeister* to Duke Franz of Saxe-Coburg-Saalfeld (grandfather of Queen Victoria's Prince Albert), who had been displaced by the wars. When he died the following year, Blangini returned to Paris and soon found himself *maître de chapelle* and resident lover to Napoleon's free-and-easy sister Pauline, Princess Borghese and Duchess of Guastalla. When her brother Jerome, King of Westphalia, was unable to persuade Beethoven to be his *Hofkapellmeister*, Napoleon in 1809 killed two birds with a single stone by sending him Blangini. When the emperor's downfall ended that, Blangini, by adroit playing of his cards, wound up back in Paris as court composer and *maître de chapelle* to Louis XVIII, and professor of voice at the Conservatoire. He lasted through the reign of Charles X, married for money, and was awarded (as who was not) the *Légion d'Honneur*. After 1830 he was both out of office and out of fashion. His music was almost entirely vocal. Besides the operas, he produced church compositions, including 4 Masses, but was most successful as a writer of songs and duets, and is said to have invented the vocal nocturne (a form that Berlioz [1175] uses so beautifully in his *Béatrice et Bénédict*). RECORDINGS: Long ago Nellie Melba and Charles Gilibert recorded a Blangini duet.

[1102] NADERMANN, Jean François Joseph (Nà'-dâr-màn, Zhàn Fràn-swà' Zhō-zef')
HARPIST, TEACHER, PUBLISHER
BORN: Paris, 1781
DIED: Paris, April 3, 1835

The son of the publisher and harp manufacturer Jean Henri Nadermann (1735–1799), François-Joseph studied with his father's partner Krumpholtz [925]. He became known as the finest harpist in France and was appointed to the chapel of Louis XVIII with the Restoration in 1815. (The Viscount of Marin was said to be better, but since he refused to play save for his friends, he hardly counts. Neither does Nadermann's rival Bochsa [1131], whose ethics removed him from the scene by 1817.) His music suggests that he was more show-off than serious musician. For the last ten years of his life, he was professor of harp at the Conservatoire, and shortly before he died, he pub-

lished a method. After the death of his father, he helped his brother Henri run the business, which seems to have come to an end when both died in the same year. François-Joseph left 2 harp concerti, some chamber music, and many pieces for solo harp. RECORDINGS: Marie-Claire Jamet has recorded two sonatas, and Lily Laskine a *rondolette*.

[1103] AUBER, Daniel François Esprit (Ō-bâr', Dàn-yel' Fràn-swà Es-prē')
ADMINISTRATOR
BORN: Caen, January 29, 1782
DIED: Paris, May 12, 1871

Stellar Italian and German operatic composers continued to rise and set on the Parisian scene, but for fifty years (1820–70) Esprit Auber lit it with the first-magnitude light of his *opéras-comiques* and grand operas. It was by his work that others were measured. But it has been said that the French do little honor to the memory of their great musicians, and Auber (assuming that he qualifies) seems to offer proof, for since 1914 his *oeuvre* has been almost totally neglected.

Though his birthplace is listed as Caen, Auber was actually born en route there in a stagecoach. The event was ironic for one who later said that the pictures on his walls gave him all he needed of rurality and that the locales of his operas satisfied his curiosity about the world beyond Paris. It was also appropriate for one whose grandfather, Daniel, had painted the decor on royal coaches. Auber's father, also named Daniel, served as an officer in Louis XVI's hunt until the Revolution left him at leisure, whereupon he opened an art shop that became a gathering place for the artistic elite of Paris. Young Esprit studied piano, violin, and voice, as a gentleman should, and had taken to composing when he was shipped off to London in 1802 to learn business methods at the fountainhead. He seems to have focused his studies chiefly on horses, parties, and the folkways of the affluent. But after two years, the political winds veered, and as an enemy alien he had to hurry home.

For the next several years, Auber devoted himself mostly to instrumental composition, producing, among other things, 4 pseudonymous cello concerti and 1 for violin. His one venture onto the stage, a setting of an old libretto *L'Erreur d'un moment (The Error of a Moment)*, bore unexpected fruit, however. Cherubini [1019] saw the (amateur) performance given it, took Auber under his wing, and retrained him from scratch. He also introduced him to some useful people, notably the future Prince de Chimay, who produced Auber's next opera, *Jean de Couvin,* at his Belgian château in 1812. It was politely applauded, and Auber, greatly encouraged, got his next work, *Le Séjour militaire (The Military Encampment),* produced by the Opéra-Comique. It went so badly that he gave up opera for six whole years.

The catalyst was the bankruptcy of Auber senior, who had been supporting his son in the style he liked. Cherubini came to the rescue with some viable libretti, and on his second try, in 1820, Auber came up with a palpable hit in *La Bergère châtelaine (The Shepherdess as Chatelaine).* Two or three years later Auber teamed up with Eugène Scribe in what became one of the most successful composer-librettist associations in history. (Scribe, prophet of the "well-made play," was probably the most productive of all dramatic writers, though much of his output was done on an assembly-line basis.) Their first effort was the Rossinian *Leicester* of 1823, but with the highly successful *Le Maçon (The Mason)* they found themselves two years later. From then until 1850 they turned out, on the average, somewhat more than an opera a year, replete with happy peasants, handsome brigands, and the other familiar appurtenances of Romantic opera. By the time Scribe died in 1861, he had supplied or collaborated on thirty-seven libretti for Auber.

After nine *opéras-comiques,* the pair embarked on a big serious work, *La Muette de Portici (The Dumb Girl of Portici)* or *Masaniello.* Based on the abortive Neapolitan revolution of 1647, it was itself revolutionary in more than one sense. Not only did it deal with common folk from modern history; it also indulged in a kind of epic theatricality, culminating in the eruption of Vesuvius, and is generally regarded as the first grand opera. An extraordinary triumph, it quickly won performances all over the world. In Dutch-controlled Belgium, it struck King William as too risky to present, and he forbade further showings. When the ban was lifted in 1830, the work occasioned a riot in Brussels that resulted in the creation of an independent Belgium.

Two years later, Auber had another howling success with the comedy *Fra Diavolo,* which proved his most durable work, even furnishing the basis of a film for Laurel and Hardy before being put on the shelf. *Gustave III,* of 1833, based on the assassination of that Swedish monarch, furnished Verdi [1232] twenty-six years later with the basic libretto for his *Un Ballo in*

maschera. Other notable successes were the Oriental fantasy *Le Cheval de bronze (The Bronze Horse),* 1835, later converted into a ballet; *Les Diamants de la couronne (The Crown Diamonds),* 1841; *Haydée,* 1847; *Marco Spada,* 1852, also balletized; and *Manon Lescaut,* 1856. The composer was, in the course of time, showered with honors: he succeeded Gossec [879] in the Académie in 1829, and succeeded Cherubini as director of the Conservatoire in 1842; he was given the honorary post (he disliked conducting) of *maître de chapelle* to Napoleon III in 1852 and in 1861 was made a grand officer of the *Légion d'honneur.*

Auber, a tiny man, was so self-conscious about his music that he refused to perform it and even to attend performances of it. A lifelong bachelor, he was a fixture of the salons, a mordant wit, and a playboy into old age. He said the things he loved most were women, horses, the boulevards, and the Bois de Boulogne. The 1871 war did not drive the old man from his beloved city, nor did the ensuing horror of the Commune. He went on trying to pretend that things were normal (we catch an unwonted glimpse of him playing piano duets with Massenet [1396] at a party). But when they commandeered his beloved horses to feed the starving citizenry, he took to his bed and, on a May morning in his ninetieth year, died in the arms of his pupils Weckerlin [1277] and Ambroise Thomas [1217].

Considering some other operas that are as persistent as pokeweed, it is hard to say why Auber has suffered such total eclipse. The problems of spoken dialogue and preposterous plots are hardly enough. Someone has said they were written when their genre was supposed to be fun, and perhaps the modern priestly view of the arts has something to do with it. (Auber also wrote a Mass and other religious music, ballets, chamber music, and songs.)

RECORDINGS: Auber fares better on records than one might expect. There are three recordings of *Fra Diavolo* (in as many languages), one (by Jean-Pierre Marty) of *Manon Lescaut,* and an "underground" account of a somewhat cut *Muette de Portici* performed by Opera Rara. Early records offer a fair number of operatic excerpts, and some recordings of overtures continue to survive. Richard Bonynge has recorded the ballet version of *Marco Spada,* and Jascha Silberstein the only cello concerto that survives complete.

[1104] FIELD, John
PIANIST, TEACHER

BORN: Dublin, July 26, 1782
DIED: Moscow, January 23, 1837

Nowadays John Field is remembered
mostly as the man who invented the piano
nocturne. If his essays in that genre have
something of the same relationship to
Chopin's that Ogiński's [1042] polonaises
have to his fellow Pole's, they still have a
fragile poetry that sorts ill with their creator. Son and grandson of Irish theater musicians, Field was so determinedly drilled in
the art as a child that he once ran away
from home—but returned when he found
piano practice more bearable than starvation. At nine he was turned over to Tommaso Giordani [877] and a year later created a stir when he debuted in a concerto
performance. In 1793 the senior Field
moved his family to London, where he
found employment at the Haymarket. Clementi [977], for 100 guineas, took young
John on as an apprentice. Apart from practicing, which he did compulsively and joy-
lessly, Field was supposed to demonstrate
pianos in the Clementi warehouse. In his
treatment of the youth, Clementi has been
presented as both exploiter and benefactor.
Apparently he published some Field piano
pieces—but anonymously—and supposedly
he prevented his public performances.
Spohr [1112] describes the Field he met at
Clementi's as a gangling, morose lout, clad
in ill-fitting clothes, half-starved and overworked. But Field dedicated his first sonatas to his benefactor, who took him on his
Continental tour in 1802.

By that time Field had already won a
name for himself in London as both a composer and performer, and he continued to
win applause in Europe, though there are
suggestions that Clementi kept a tight rein
on him. Field became noted for his singing
tone and his expressivity, and probably
qualifies as the first Romantic pianist. The
travelers reached St. Petersburg in 1803.
There Field found a patron in a General
Marklovsky and decided to stay. He quickly
became a fad and was soon giving the most
expensive piano lessons in Russia to the
wealthiest Russian ladies. As a teacher he is
said to have been ineffectual and unimagina-
tive, and moreover his students had to put
up with his gloomy and sarcastic personality. He demanded that he be supplied with
champagne during lessons and later bragged
that he had often slept while his students
played. He took one of them, a French actress named Adelaide Percheron, as a bedfellow in 1808. He made it official two years
later, but his vows do not seem to have
stopped his womanizing, for in 1815 another

pupil, a Mlle. Charpentier, bore him a son
named Léon, whom his father tried to set
on the same thorny path that he had been
forced to tread. Four years later Adelaide
presented him with an official heir, christened Adrien. Having done her duty, she
traipsed off to Smolensk, and the couple
were divorced two years later.

Adelaide can hardly be blamed. Not only
had she had to put up with her husband's
bearishness and his infidelities, the champagne had caught up with him as well. He
grew fat and blowsy and was seldom sober.
(He was distinguished from "Glorious
John" Cramer [1067] as "Drunken John"
Field.) He insisted on performing (when he
could play) in a vast bearskin cloak and was
uniformly rude to everyone. He had no use
for competitors: he was suspicious of Chopin [1208], said Beethoven [1063] was a
fraud, and at a Liszt [1218] concert asked
his neighbor if the performer bit. By 1831 he
was nearly broke and suffering from a rectal
fistula. He came back to London for an operation, then went on tour to recoup his
losses. But he was out of practice and favor,
and the venture was not successful. In Italy
people stayed away in droves. He reached
Naples in 1834, too ill to go on, and spent
nine months in the hospital. He was rescued
by Russian friends, who took him back to
Moscow. He stopped over in Vienna for
some concerts, which proved to be his last
hurrah. Played out and used up, he died
eighteen months later.

RECORDINGS: All of Field's compositions,
which include 7 concerti, 4 sonatas, and
some chamber works, are for piano. There
have been several complete and partial recordings of the nocturnes, but very few of
the other solo piano pieces (rondos, variations, dances, etc.). There are recordings by
various hands of the first three piano concerti, and all the piano concerti have recently been recorded by Irish pianist John
O'Conor with the New Irish Chamber Orchestra conducted by Janos Fürst. Frank
Merrick performs the four sonatas, and one
of the *divertimenti* for piano and string
quartet is included in the RCA History of
Music series. One should note also Sir
Hamilton Harty's [1725] arrangement of
four piano pieces for orchestra as *A John
Field Suite* (conducted by Malcolm Sargent,
Neville Dilkes, and Bryden Thompson).

[1105] MAZAS, Jacques Féréol (Mȧ-zȧs',
    Zhȧk Fā-rā-ōl')
VIOLINIST, TEACHER
BORN: September 23, 1782
DIED: August 26, 1849

Neither the place of Mazas' birth nor that of his death is certain. He came from south-central France—both Béziers and Lavour (Lavaur?) are offered as birthplaces—studied at the Paris Conservatoire under Pierre Baillot, a violinist trained by a Nardini [823] pupil, and won a first prize for his playing in 1805. Auber [1103] wrote his only violin concerto for him. After playing in the pit at the Odéon for several years, Mazas embarked on increasingly wide-ranging concert tours. After fluctuations of failure and success, he returned to Paris in 1829 to find himself forgotten. After teaching for a while in Orléans, he directed a conservatory in Cambrai from 1837 to 1841. After that he is reported to have lived quietly in Bordeaux, where he probably died. Apart from a couple of operas (one produced at the Opéra-Comique in 1842) and a few minor vocal works, he wrote mostly for the violin. His études and method are still in use. RECORDINGS: A set of twelve little violin duets have been recorded by Eimar Oliveira and Regis Iandiorio.

[1106] PAGANINI, Niccolò (Pà-gà-nē'-nē, Nik'-kō-lō)
VIOLINIST, CONDUCTOR
BORN: Genoa, October 27, 1782
DIED: Nice, May 27, 1840

The greatest violin virtuoso of his century, Paganini attracted gossip. Thus what has long passed for biographical information about him is in great part fiction, causing the man himself to be seen through distorting lenses. But when all the varnish is peeled away, he remains a fascinating figure and the archetypal virtuoso. We can dismiss the charges of grasping avarice and nameless crimes, just as we can dismiss tales of pacts with the devil, but we cannot ignore his great attraction to and for women. Lanky, cadaverous, and even grotesque he was, but he was also warm and friendly. He was perhaps his own worst enemy, making apologies where none were required, and standing haughtily aloof when a word would have set things right. His total command of the violin led him to indulge in cheap tricks, such as imitating animal cries and deliberately breaking strings when he played to demonstrate that four or even three were not required for him. His many compositions were primarily designed to show off his own prowess and have little value except to show what that prowess must have been, though they do have an easy melodic charm. He had a dazzling career and a wretched life.

Paganini's father came from a mountain village called Carro on the Ligurian coast. He became a waterfront laborer in Genoa and, owing to the international situation, was unemployed during Niccolò's childhood. His wife was a Genoese named Teresa Bocciardo, and there was an older son, Carlo. Legend has it that he taught both boys to play the fiddle, but in fact nothing is really known of Niccolò's beginnings save that he was sickly. As he grew, he studied with several local violinists of no moment but was most strongly motivated to take matters seriously when he attended a concert by Auguste Durand, a virtuoso born in Poland and therefore billed as Duranowski. At thirteen Paganini gave a concert in Genoa to finance his studying with Rolla [1001] in Parma. The story goes that on first hearing Rolla declared that there was nothing he could teach the lad and turned him over to Paër [1069] for some solid theoretical grounding. At any rate Paganini remained in Parma for a year and, during the latter part of it, did study with Paër. Then, following a serious bout of pneumonia, he returned to Genoa and began sporadic concertizing. He also took up the guitar. In 1801 he and Carlo went to play in Lucca and made such an impression that Niccolò wrote his father that he was now his own man and intended to settle there. He found employment in the Cappella Palatina and as a teacher.

In 1805 Napoleon turned Lucca over to his sister Élise and her husband Felix Baciocchi. The princess promptly disbanded the established orchestras in favor of one of her own, in which Paganini was installed as second-desk violin, under the direction of Domenico Puccini [1074]; later he became concertmaster. In 1808 she junked it for a string quartet, which included the Paganini brothers. It was more easily portable and moved from one dwelling to another with Élise, now Grand Duchess of Tuscany. Paganini's duties also included conducting operas and playing quartets with Baciocchi. The grand duchess once gave him a diamond ring, though whether in gratitude for his musical or his amatory services is not clear. Within a year, however, the relationship(s) had become strained: Élise taxed Paganini with insubordination and he, apparently gratefully, resigned.

For nearly twenty years he pursued a concert career, though only in Italy and not always with approbation. In 1812 he was run out of Ferrara for insulting the audience, who had been rude to another performer on the program. A year later he was such a hit in Milan that he had to play eleven concerts before they would let him go. In his spare time he seems to have led a life of dissipation, chasing women and gambling, though history shows no record of the long incarceration he is supposed to have endured for his sins. The political upheavals of 1814, however, interrupted his progress and sent him home. There he became involved with a slum girl, Angelina Cavanna, persuaded her to elope on a promise of marriage, got her pregnant, attempted (apparently) to abort the fetus by doctoring her wine, and, having failed, abandoned her. Her father had him arrested and won a judgment against him of 3,000 lire a couple of years later. Meanwhile Paganini continued his touring and his erotic adventures. In Trieste he spent some time, for "auld lang syne," with the now-ousted Grand Duchess Élise and met such celebrities as Rossini [1143], Spohr [1112], and Lord Byron. In 1819 Paganini conquered Rome, where during the Carnival he, Rossini, and their friends disported themselves on the streets as blind female beggars. He moved on to Naples, where there was talk of his marrying, but nothing came of it. Not unexpectably, his never robust health began to deteriorate. Plagued by colitis and a hacking cough, he discovered, seeking treatment, that he was also afflicted with syphilis in a fairly advanced stage. He subjected himself to rounds of barbarous cures, which he kept up for much of the rest of his life—cathartics and emetics in alternation, milk diets, and large doses of laudanum and mercury, which later rotted his teeth out and gave him a breath that would have felled a hippo.

Nevertheless in 1824 he found solace in a singer named Antonia Bianchi, from Como —to his later sorrow. By the next January she was pregnant, and in Palermo she was delivered of a son, whom they named Achilles Cyrus Alexander. (His descendants are very much alive today.) In 1828 Paganini at last headed for Vienna to open the door to the outside world, taking his family with him. His reception in Vienna was overwhelming, and marked the first stage in a triumphal European progression that would make him a legend. Since the unsanctified liaison with Antonia Bianchi was not working out, he dropped her there—though he kept his son, who became very dear to him. (Shortly afterward, Antonia found another husband.) Despite a painfully ulcerated mouth and resultant bone infection, the violinist resumed his tour—to Prague, Dresden, Leipzig, Berlin, Warsaw, Breslau, and the Rhineland. Wherever he went, however, ugly rumors preceded him; nor did he aid his cause when he cancelled concerts without explanation (he was often too ill to play) or refused to play for some bigwig's favorite charity. In 1830 he headquartered himself for the nonce in Frankfurt am Main, while continuing to play in various German cities. In Nuremberg he fell in love with the Baroness Helene von Dobeneck. She divorced her husband for him, but by then he had lost interest and left the country. She carried a torch for him the rest of her life, dying nearly sixty years later, a recluse in Treviso.

Paganini's next stop was Paris, where he resumed his friendship with Rossini and became a cynosure of the musical life there. His first concerts created a kind of madness akin to that reserved today for grubby young men playing electric guitars. Later, however, another piece of poor diplomacy gave the press the excuse it wanted to "expose" the foreign charlatan. When he reached London a few months afterward, the local paper picked up the hue and cry, charging him with being a sort of vampire come to bleed the national treasury white. But high society and intelligent musicians like Moscheles [1146] welcomed him, and his concerts proved successful. Moving on into the provinces, which included Scotland and Ireland, he put management of his affairs into the hands of one John Watson—another mistake, as he was soon to find out. Returning to Paris in 1832, he found a cholera epidemic raging there. He himself fell ill, but the sickness turned out to be another manifestation of his syphilis and he recovered. That same year a deposed German princeling, Frederick IV of Salm-Kyrburg, awarded Paganini the title of baron, on which the musician afterward insisted, though the title was as empty as his violin. About the same time, he took up the viola and brought some sunlight into Berlioz's [1175] spartan existence by commissioning what turned out to be Harold in Italy— which also turned out not to be what its sponsor wanted.

In 1834 Paganini went on tour again, this time in the Low Countries, but an injured finger limited his effectiveness, and Charlotte Watson, his manager's daughter and a singer, filled in for him. Again Paganini set up a plan for an elopement, but in the event it was Watson himself who turned up at the rendezvous and spirited his errant child off to America. Paganini sent them word that he was serious, but by then Charlotte had become engaged to a Mr. Bailey. Paganini returned to Paris where he was viciously attacked (for parsimony) by a rising journalist named Jules Janin, who was nettled because Paganini had refused to contribute to flood relief for Janin's native city, St. Étienne. Paganini had had enough and sought refuge in Italy at the Villa Gaione near Parma. While he was there, a court councillor of the Duchess Marie Louise, the late Napoleon's sometime empress, persuaded Paganini to lend him a large sum of money, in turn urging his employer to retain the violinist to revitalize the *cappella*. Paganini assumed that he was in full charge of the orchestra and set about hiring and firing. He was horribly embarrassed when the duchess let him know she had authorized nothing.

Paganini's health now took a nosedive. His tuberculosis manifested itself in a frightening pulmonary hemorrhage, his syphilis was destroying his vocal cords (he was quite speechless in his final years), and he was suffering the pains of *tabes dorsalis*. Nevertheless he returned to Paris, where he was sucked into a grandiose scheme for a pleasure palace involving a casino, concert halls, and other places of amusement. The scheme collapsed, his associates sued him, he lost the case and a whopping sum of money, appealed the decision, and had the sum increased. Nevertheless it was at this same time that he saw fit to bestow on Berlioz a gift of 20,000 francs, eliciting a public apology from Janin for his own previous behavior. Soon afterward, Paganini moved to Marseilles, then to Genoa, and finally, in 1839, to Nice. There he spent six months dying a slow and agonizing death. He steadfastly refused absolution and was so denied burial for five years until Marie Louise arranged for his remains to be interred at the Villa Gaione. Thirty years later they were transferred to the municipal cemetery.

RECORDINGS: Paganini's most substantial works were the 6 violin concerti, which—some of them "reconstructed"—have been recorded in an integral edition by Salvatore Accardo. (There are also numerous individual recordings, especially of the first two concerti.) Ulrich Koch has recorded the sonata for large viola and orchestra. Accardo, with Charles Dutoit conducting, has further recorded numerous miscellaneous works for violin and orchestra. There are also various accounts of string quartets, chamber works with guitar, and violin sonatas. There have been many recordings of the 24 caprices for solo violin, a veritable catalogue of Paganinian technique (including transcriptions for viola, cello, brass quintet, and flute). Paganini was a collector of instruments, and the Stradivarius instruments played latterly by the Paganini Quartet all once belonged to him.

[1107] COOKE, Thomas Simpson
SINGER, INSTRUMENTALIST, CONDUCTOR, ENTREPRENEUR, ETC.
BORN: Dublin, 1782
DIED: London, February 26, 1848

In its general outlines, Tom Cooke's career resembles those of Michael Kelly **[1028]** and Henry Bishop **[1123]**, though neither possessed his versatility. He studied with his father Bartlett Cooke, an oboist, and with Tommaso Giordani **[877]**. From the age of fifteen he was concertmaster of a Dublin theater orchestra and from eighteen, proprietor of a music store. Assuming, as a sort of lark, the lead in a benefit performance of Stephen Storace's **[1025]** *The Siege of Belgrade,* Cooke surprised everyone, including himself, with his success and in 1815 became the first tenor at Drury Lane in London, where at times he also served as conductor, concertmaster, and composer. Between 1815 and 1842 more than fifty of his stage pieces were presented there, including *Shakespeare vs. Harlequin, The Magpie* (on the same story as Rossini's **[1143]** *La Gazza ladra), Coriolanus, Frederick the Great, Peter the Great,* and, in 1826, an *Oberon* intended to counter Weber's **[1124]**. Like Bishop, he cooked up mangled versions of such current hits as Boieldieu's **[1084]** *La Dame blanche,* Auber's **[1103]** *La Muette de Portici,* and Halévy's **[1157]** *La Juive,* and was a director at Vauxhall Gardens, the Philharmonic Society, and Covent Garden. He was Bishop's concertmaster in the final seasons of the Antient Concerts. On occasion Cooke also appeared as soloist on all the strings but the viola, the standard woodwinds, and the piano. He was regular tenor soloist at the chapel of the Bavarian Embassy and taught many younger singers, including the great tenor Sims Reeves. He wrote many glees and some songs for Shakespeare revivals. RECORDINGS: Two of the Shakespeare songs are included in the Caedmon anthology of Shakespeare songs.

[1108] GEIJER, Erik Gustaf (Gī'-yer, Ā'-rēk Gōōs'-tàf)
HISTORIAN, TEACHER, POET, ESSAYIST
BORN: Ransäter, January 12, 1783
DIED: Stockholm, April 23, 1847

Though Geijer is firmly lodged in the history of Swedish song, he was a musical amateur whose chief achievements were elsewhere. He took piano lessons and picked up some basic theory in childhood. He went to the University of Uppsala, where he developed a great interest in medieval culture.

After teaching there briefly following graduation, he took a job in the public record office in the capital. He and some friends with similar interests founded the Gothic Society and published a magazine, to which he contributed articles and folklike lyrics, some of which he set to music. In 1801 he wrote the first of several sonatas, which show familiarity with Mendelssohn [1200] and Beethoven [1063] and the Classical composers but also have individual touches. He was called back to Uppsala and in 1814 was appointed professor of history there. He wrote (or at least began) several seminal studies on early Scandinavian history and legend, and edited a number of early literary works. He also contributed philosophical and other essays to various journals. Failing health forced his retirement in 1846, and he died the following year. Many of Geijer's c. 120 vocal pieces (songs and choruses) remain popular in Sweden. RECORDINGS: Erik Saedén has recorded two of the songs, and Stig Ribbing a couple of small piano pieces.

[1109] WALMISLEY, Thomas Forbes
ORGANIST
BORN: Westminster, May 22, 1783
DIED: London, July 23, 1866

The son of an official in the House of Lords, Thomas Forbes Walmisley was a choirboy at Westminster Abbey and studied with Thomas Attwood. In 1810 he was appointed assistant organist at the Female Orphan Asylum, giving up that job in 1814 to begin a forty-year engagement as organist at St. Martin-in-the-Fields. In that same year his son was born; Thomas Attwood stood as godfather to the son and gave him his name. Young Thomas Attwood Walmisley became professor of music at Cambridge and a notable composer of church music. He died at forty-two, January 17, 1856, and his father edited and published his works. T. F. Walmisley was, as a composer, the writer of popular songs and glees. RECORDINGS: One of the best-known of his glees is included in the Purcell Singers' recorded album of Victorian parlor music.

[1110] BEALE, William
ORGANIST
BORN: Landrake, January 1, 1784
DIED: London, May 3, 1854

The career and output of such as William Beale provide some notion of the state to which musical composition in England had sunk in his time. A Cornwall lad, Beale was a choirboy at Westminster Abbey and a midshipman on a captured frigate in the Napoleonic wars. After that he was successively a Gentleman of the Chapel Royal, and organist of Trinity College, Cambridge, and of two London churches. His music consists mostly of what he called "madrigals," which were really the male-voice glees so popular at the time. For some of these, he won prizes from various choral societies. RECORDINGS: The most popular glees were "Awake, Sweet Muse" and "Come, Let Us Join the Roundelay"—the latter recorded by the Partridges in a program of Victorian domestic music.

[1111] FÉTIS, François-Joseph (Fā-tēs, Frän-swä′ Zhō-zef′)
THEORIST, CRITIC, WRITER, JOURNALIST, ADMINISTRATOR, TEACHER, ETC.
BORN: Mons, March 25, 1784
DIED: Brussels, March 26, 1871

The leading musical tastemaker of his times, Fétis looms much smaller in composition than he does in his other activities, notably musicology, which he virtually invented. Pedantic and dogmatic he may have been (he put too much stock in Comtean positivism and thought he could make musicology an exact science), but we have much to thank him for. He introduced comparative study as the means by which music should be evaluated, and he enunciated the then-heretical theory that the art of composition did not improve but merely changed. This notion he objectified in a series of "historical" concerts that did much to implant the notion of "classical" music (i.e., music of the past that is worth hearing). His *Biographie universelle* is a goldmine of facts about musicians that Fétis really knew about and—alas!—the source of many continuing misapprehensions about others.

The son of a professional organist-violinist-conductor, Fétis initially studied with his father, Antoine, was precocious as a composer, but a rather ordinary student at the Paris Conservatoire, where he studied with Boieldieu [1084] *inter alias*. At twenty-two he married a rich child of fourteen, Adelaïde Catherine Robert. Five years later dreams of scholarly ease vanished with Adelaïde Catherine's fortune. The couple retired to the Ardennes, then to Douai, where Fétis kept his head above water as a teacher and church organist. In 1818 they returned to Paris, where Fétis managed to get half a dozen extremely old-fashioned *opéras-comiques* staged, and ground out piano music designed for quick sale. In 1823 he became professor of counterpoint and fugue at the Conservatoire and in 1826, librarian. In the latter year he inaugurated his Historical Concerts and his influential journal, the *Revue Musicale* (later the *Revue et Gazette Musicale).*

In 1833 he returned to newly independent Belgium as music director to King Léopold I and as first head of the Brussels Conservatoire. He published innumerable articles (many of them opinionated and controversial), and at least 25 theoretical and biographico-historical works under separate cover, and was one of the most influential musical thinkers of the century. In 1846 he was named to the Belgian Royal Academy. Toward the end of his long life, Fétis returned to instrumental composition, producing, among other things, 2 symphonies, a flute concerto, and 3 string quintets. His son Édouard was a musical scholar and teacher; another son, Adolphe, was a pianist and composer. Fétis died the day after he turned eighty-seven.

RECORDINGS: The Brussels String Quartet participates in a recorded performance of one of the string quintets and performs a quartet written when Fétis was twelve.

[1112] SPOHR, Louis (Shpôr, Lōō′-ēs)
VIOLINIST, CONDUCTOR
BORN: Braunschweig, April 5, 1784
DIED: Kassel, October 22, 1859

The music-hall singer attends a series
Of masses and fugues and "ops"
By Bach, interwoven
With Spohr and Beethoven,
At classical Monday Pops.

In fitting the punishment to the crime, W. S. Gilbert's *Mikado* gives us a notion of Spohr's status a hundred years ago. That in his day he was one of the great violinists—the antithesis of the pyrotechnician Paganini [1106]—we must take on faith. As a composer—a would-be Mozartian with a narrow definition of form and a gift for pretty but sentimental melodies—he appears to have been oversold. Moreover, he had a curious case of musical astigmatism: he was baffled by Beethoven [1063], worried by Weber [1124], but oddly he hailed Wagner [1230] as the savior of music.

Spohr was the grandson of a parson and the son of a doctor, who moved his family to Seesen, between Braunschweig and Kassel, in 1786. Ludwig, as he was then known, grew up in a musical atmosphere (both parents were gifted amateurs), demonstrated

musical leanings, studied with local professionals, and at the age of five was sawing away on a miniature fiddle quite creditably. Eventually he was sent to study in Braunschweig, where he continued his violin studies and got some basic theory, though most of his training in the latter area was derived from his own reading of scores. At fourteen he set out for Hamburg as a virtuoso, but the audience laughed when he stood up beside the piano, and soon, his pockets empty, he had to hike the eighty miles back to where he had started from. There his teacher, the *Konzertmeister* of the court orchestra, got him a place in that body. The duke took a shine to the young man and paid for lessons with Franz Eck, whose amorous adventures had made him a fugitive from his native Mannheim. Eck instilled the ways of Mannheim in his pupil, and took him off to St. Petersburg for the winter (perhaps not having heard of Florida). On his travels Spohr met Clementi [977] and Field [1104] and was given a Guarnerius violin by a wealthy Russian. Spohr was also so dazzled by the playing of Pierre Rode, who performed in Braunschweig soon after his return, and readjusted his sights accordingly. This got him an equally dazzling rise in salary. In 1804 Spohr started off to Paris to concertize, but someone stole his violin. The good duke found him another, and he was soon being applauded in major German cities, notably Berlin where he was accompanied by a thirteen-year-old named Beer, who later won fame under the name of "Meyerbeer" [1142].

In 1805 Spohr became *Konzertmeister* at the Gotha court and a year later married a young harpist, Dorette Scheidler. He now turned seriously to writing music, turning out operas, concerti, and other works, including (expectably) pieces involving violin and harp for his frequent appearances with his wife. His tours soon established him as the leading German violinist, and he also became known as a conductor. In 1810 he led Haydn's [871] *The Creation* at what was the earliest German music festival, at Frankenhausen. There he conducted with a piece of rolled-up paper instead of his violin and later graduated to a wooden baton. In 1812, after a smashing success in Vienna, he became orchestral director of the Theater an der Wien (Dorette was hired as harpist), but, unable to see eye to eye with the management, he resigned three years later. The Spohrs then, by way of Alsace and Switzerland, went to Italy, where they remained for nearly two years. There Louis received enthusiastic support from an anti-Paganini faction, which he viewed as a mixed blessing.

He and Paganini eventually ran into each other there; Paganini made much of Spohr's performance but refused to play for him. Spohr was also introduced to Rossini [1143], of whose newfangled operas he did not think much. During his absence, his own *Faust* was premiered in Prague, in 1816. Based not on Goethe, but on the old legend, it was perhaps his most important opera and exerted a considerable influence on Wagner.

In 1817 Spohr again paused, this time to direct the opera in Frankfurt am Main. There he himself produced *Faust* and in 1819 premiered another success, *Zemire und Azor*. But again he clashed with the management and resigned. In 1820 he conducted the Philharmonic Society in London, frightening the members when he whipped out his baton (though they soon took to this new approach). The next year he went to Dresden. There Weber suggested that Spohr be considered for the opening as court *Kapellmeister* at Kassel. (Spohr liked Weber himself; it was the music that bothered him.) Spohr settled for a handsome lifetime contract, with attractive fringe benefits that included a couple of months off annually and a guaranteed pension when and if he should retire. In 1822 he made what proved to be his last move, establishing permanent residence in Kassel. The new elector, Wilhelm II, turned out to be a petty autocrat, and his generosity was counterbalanced by his dictatorial attitudes. Nevertheless a topnotch opera company and a symphonic-size orchestra (fifty-five members) were not to be easily tossed aside, and Spohr, as composer, made the most of the advantages. The year 1822 saw the premiere of his most successful opera, *Jessonda*. Later he turned to the production of oratorios.

In 1832 political upheavals caused the elector to close down the opera house for some months, which no doubt fueled Spohr's increasingly liberal political inclinations. Two years later, Dorette, long in poor health, went to make harp music in a higher sphere. In 1836 Spohr married a pianist named Marianne Pfeiffer, with whom he also appeared in joint recitals, and who outlived him by thirty-three years. Spohr had always been successful in England, and now the English passion for oratorios made him one of the chief festival drawing cards in that country. In 1842 the elector refused to let him fulfill his commitment to conduct at the Norwich Festival, but the next year Spohr went for a very satisfying tour, during which he managed to please, if not amuse, Queen Victoria and her musical consort. He returned to England in 1844 (and twice thereafter), and conducted the Beethoven

Festival at Bonn in 1846. His thinking was further radicalized by the political explosion of 1848, and two years later, when he was refused his annual leave, he took it anyway. The opera management sued him and won. In 1853, against strong opposition, he produced Wagner's *Tannhäuser* (he had already conducted the *Fliegende Holländer* there a decade earlier), but his attempts to follow it with *Lohengrin* were balked. Meanwhile Spohr was growing a bit tottery, and in 1857, over his loud protests, he was retired. Shortly afterward an arm fracture put an end to his violinistic career. However, he continued to conduct occasionally until 1858.

The operas (save for an air from *Zemire)*, the oratorios, the 10 symphonies (some with intriguing titles) appear to be largely a dead issue. The concerti (15 for violin, 4 for clarinet, and several for various combinations) show more vitality.

RECORDINGS: There are numerous recordings of concerti (especially the so-called *"Gesangszene"* Concerto for Violin No. 8). The Symphony No. 3 in C Minor has been twice recorded by Tamás Sulyok and Gerd Albrecht, and there is a new recording of the 1826 oratorio *Die letzten Dinge (The Last Judgment)* by Siegfried Heinrich. A *Potpourri* for violin, cello, and orchestra, based on themes from the opera *Jessonda*, has been recorded under the direction of Aloys Springer. Other recent or pending releases include the *Jessonda Overture* (Albrecht) and Concerti for Clarinet Nos. 1–4 (Karl Leister). The chamber music, often interesting because of Spohr's experiments with unusual combinations, has also attracted some interest. There are several recordings of a *Grand Nonet* and of a double string quartet, the Op. 69 String Quintet, three sonatas for harp and violin by Susan MacDonald and Louis Kaufman, a number of recordings of various string quartets etc. But the surface of that vast output has barely been scratched.

[1113] AGUADO Y GARCIA, Dionisio
(A-gwá'-dō ē Gär-thē'-à, Dē-on-ēs'-yō)
GUITARIST
BORN: Madrid, April 8, 1784
DIED: Madrid, December 29, 1849

Next to his friend Sor [1090], Aguado was, outside of Spain, probably the best-known Spanish guitarist of his time. He was once said to have studied with the tenor-guitarist Manuel Garcia, but he probably didn't. Owing to the political upheavals of the time, the first forty years of his life were spent in Spain. He arrived in Paris in 1825, fortuitously during Sor's absence, and was well established as a performer and teacher by the time Sor returned. Though they differed in their views on how the instrument should be played—Aguado liked to (ugh!) pluck it with his nails—they often appeared in concert together. Aguado is said to have become an intimate of both Rossini [1143] and Paganini [1106], but the standard English-language biographies ignore him. In 1838 he returned to Madrid, where it is said the home folks hailed him as a conquering hero. He wrote an important guitar method and much music for the instrument. RECORDINGS: A sample of his guitar music is played on records by Spiro Thomatos.

[1114] MORLACCHI, Francesco Giuseppe Baldassare (Môr-làk´-kē, Frànchäs´-kō Jōō-sep´-pä Bàl-dàs-sá´-rä)
CONDUCTOR
BORN: Perugia, June 14, 1784
DIED: Innsbruck, October 28, 1841

Once one of the most successful operatic composers of his time, Morlacchi is now remembered only as Weber's [1124] Dresden rival. Musically precocious, he studied in Perugia and was already composing when in 1803 he went to Niccolò Zingarelli, then choirmaster of the Santa Casa in Loreto and later teacher of Bellini [1164] and Mercadante [1148]. But the two did not get on, and a year later Zingarelli went to Rome and Morlacchi to Bologna, where he completed his training. Having already written a good deal of sacred music, Morlacchi turned to opera in 1805, and in 1808 scored his first triumph with *Il Corradino* in Parma. A cantata written in 1810 for a relative of the Saxon ambassador to Milan won him an invitation from King Frederick Augustus "the Just" to direct the Italian Opera in Dresden for a year. He succeeded Franz Anton Schubert (1768–1827), father of that Franz Schubert [1196] who wrote a violin piece called *The Bee* (beloved of the late Jack Benny). Morlacchi gave such satisfaction that after a year he was appointed *Kapellmeister* for life, with fringe benefits that might even satisfy a modern union worker. During the next few years, however, what with Saxony being on the losing side in the international struggle, things did not go well for him. When Frederick Augustus was run out by the Allies, Morlacchi lay low. But when he was threatened by the occupying Russians with exportation to Siberia, he wrote a cantata for Czar Alexander's birthday. This proved a wise capitulation, for soon thereafter he was able to convince the czar that it would not be in

keeping with his image to dismantle the Dresden musical organization. In the next few years, in fact, Morlacchi did wonders with it. He also produced a string of successful operas, including *Il nuovo Barbiere di Siviglia (The New Barber of Seville,* following hard on the heels of Rossini's [1143] old one), that were praised for a true sense of theater. Pius VII named him a papal count, and he was showered with other honors.

In the midst of all this success, the king brought Weber in to direct the German Opera, beginning in 1817. The resultant infighting between Italians and Germans was like the days of Schütz [412] all over again. Morlacchi didn't mind so much when Weber was merely a *Musikdirektor* and he was *Königliche Kapellmeister,* but he was piqued when Weber got the same title. He retaliated by alternately hamstringing his rival by refusing him needed facilities or by going off to Italy leaving his duties to Weber. After nine years, Weber went to London to die, and Morlacchi was left in lonely grandeur. His productivity fell off, but he continued to make Dresden an important showcase for operas and concerts. But the climate must have been bad for musicians, for Morlacchi, like his rival, suffered from tuberculosis. In 1841 he started to Italy to try to regain his health but died on the way.

RECORDINGS: There are perhaps scattered operatic snippets on record, but I trace only a song sung by Suzanne Danco.

[1115] ONSLOW, George
CELLIST
BORN: Clermont-Ferrand, July 27, 1784
DIED: Clermont-Ferrand, October 3, 1853

An English gentleman born in the Auvergne backwoods in Napoleonic times? Well, yes and no. Onslow got his surname and his money from his father Edward, a cadet son of the first Lord Onslow, self-exiled after being involved in some naughtiness back home. But his mother, Marie de Bourdeille de Brantôme, was decidedly and decisively French, and her son went into the books as "André Georges Louis," of the Catholic faith. But he was educated in the ways of his class in London, which regimen involved his being placed before a keyboard and instructed in how to manipulate it by, at various times, Cramer [1067], Dussek [1016], and Hüllmandel [997]. He indicated no more interest or talent than might have been expected of most English gentlemen. Certified to move in Good Society, he returned to the French hinterlands, where he found precious little of it. What there was of it was curiously addicted to making music. Not to be left out, Onslow took up the cello and found he liked it. After a bit he journeyed to Vienna, where for several months he was subjected to a good deal of music. He tried writing some of his own, but it did not appeal to his taste, which had been pronounced "Good" by the proper authorities, so in 1808 he began studying in Paris with the newcomer Antonín Reicha [1059]. He also married a young person of Good Family called Charlotte Françoise Delphine de Fontanges, and what with her inheritance and his, they eventually became very rich. Onslow devoted some time each year to Paris, where three operas and three symphonies were performed with considerable success, and where he was taken seriously by the musical establishment. In 1829, while he was hunting, a stray bullet creased his scalp, impairing his hearing in one ear, but doing no more serious damage; Onslow commemorated the miracle in the so-called "ball" quintet, Op. 38. A year later he became the second honorary member of the London Philharmonic Society (the first was Mendelssohn [1200]). In 1842 he was elected to succeed Cherubini [1019] in the Institut, beating out Auber [1103] and Berlioz [1175]. Onslow, had, incidentally, been a longtime supporter of Berlioz, who, rather typically, suspected his motives. Onslow's chief importance lies in his chamber music, of which he was the largest producer in France in his day (35 string quartets, 34 string quintets, and 20-odd other works). Carefully tailored for home music making, they enjoyed great popularity. RECORDINGS: There are recordings of a few—e.g., the Op. 79 Sextet for Piano and Winds; the Op. 81 Quintet for Winds; and the Op. 7 Duo for Piano, four hands.

[1116] RIES, Ferdinand (Rēs, Fâr′-dē-nànt)
PIANIST, VIOLINIST, CELLIST, CONDUCTOR, COPYIST
BORN: Bonn, c. November 28, 1784
DIED: Frankfurt am Main, January 13, 1838

Eminently successful and influential in his lifetime, Ries is now remembered largely because he knew Beethoven [1063] and told about it. He came from a family of Bonn court musicians. His father, Franz Anton, befriended the Beethovens and was a prop in their bad times. Like Kuhlau [1121], Ferdinand lost an eye in childhood—because of smallpox, however, rather than an accident.

He was scheduled from the start to carry out the family calling. Franz Anton drilled him in keyboard and violin technique, and Bernhard Romberg [1051] taught him cello. After the French broke up the court in 1794, the family stayed on. In 1797 a friend took Ferdinand to Arnsberg in Westphalia for finishing studies with a local organist, but somehow the tables got turned and Ferdinand taught the organist to play the violin. Four years later Ferdinand took himself to Munich, set up as a copyist, and studied with Peter von Winter [987] until he had saved up enough to get to Vienna to work with Beethoven [1063].

Though Ries's recollections of their early relationship there appear to be confused, Beethoven took him on gratis, laconically noting that he owed a debt to Franz Anton. For composition lessons, however, he sent him to Albrechtsberger [889], who was not so charitable: when Ries's money ran out, he dropped him. Generally Beethoven was quite kind to his fellow townsman, introducing him to the Vienna musicians—Ries and Beethoven's "other" pupil Carl Czerny [1137] became friends—and to potential patrons, and helping tide him over numerous financial crises. It was Ries who, on a pastoral walk with his master, noted a shepherd's piping which the horrified Beethoven realized he himself could not hear. But the two also had their quarrels. On hearing Beethoven play the so-called Andante favori for the first time, Ries stopped by Prince Lichnowsky's and played his recollection of it for him. Lichnowsky in turn played his version for Beethoven, claiming to have written it himself. Beethoven refused ever to play for Ries again and ordered him out of the house before he played the Fidelio score for other visitors. When Beethoven turned down Jerome Bonaparte's invitation to be his Kapellmeister, Bonaparte offered the post to Ries. Beethoven accused Ries of undermining him, and by the time they had gotten things straightened out, the job had gone to Spohr [1112]. At the other extreme, Beethoven dedicated his third piano concerto to his pupil and let him premiere it with his own cadenzas.

In 1805 Ries heard that his name was on the French conscription list. Lacking coach fare, he walked to Coblenz headquarters, where he discovered that one-eyed men were exempt. When the French retook Vienna in 1809, Ries took to the road and established himself as a popular performer throughout northern Germany and Scandinavia. Deciding that what he had heard of opportunities in Russia was worth investigating, he took a ship for St. Petersburg but was captured by an English gunboat crew and imprisoned on a Baltic island for a week. He reached his goal in 1811 and, with his old teacher Romberg to run interference for him, he prospered as he had been told he would. Pushing on to Moscow the next year, he arrived to find that city in ashes. He returned to Sweden and went on to London in the spring of 1813. There he found another valuable intermediary in the person of the impresario J. P. Salomon, his father's onetime violin teacher. He settled down, became a member of the Philharmonic Society, concertized, taught, composed, and acquired fame, money, and a charming wife named Harriet Mangean. He also served as Beethoven's London agent and one of his chief apostles. After eleven years—an unwontedly long sojourn for Ries —he bought an estate at Bad Godesburg, a spa near Bonn, and retired there, bringing his father into his household. But he could not remain idle, so in 1827 he moved to Frankfurt. During his last years he was involved with the Lower Rhine Music Festival (presented alternately at Aachen, Cologne, and Düsseldorf) in a directorial capacity. From 1834 to 1836 he headed the conservatory and conducted the orchestra in Aachen. His Beethoven memoirs were published in the year of his death. His father outlived him by eight years, dying nine days before his ninety-first birthday. A younger brother Joseph, a musical amateur, was a colleague of Charles Lamb's at East India House. Another, Hubert, was an important violinist, and his three sons were professional musicians. The heirs of the youngest, Franz, still operate the publishing firm of Ries and Erler in London. Ferdinand Ries, who composed prodigiously in all forms then current, has long been considered a pallid imitator of Beethoven, but investigation, especially of his orchestral and chamber music, shows a talented musician writing in the musical dialect of his times.

RECORDINGS: So far, his major recorded representations seem to be his second piano concerto (played both by Felicja Blumental and Maria Littauer), a flute sonata (played by Louise and Virginia DiTullio), a horn sonata (two recordings), and two cello sonatas (Klaus Storck and Alfons Kontarsky).

[1117] KURPIŃSKI, Karol Kazimierz (Koor-pin'-shki, Kả'-rōl Kả-zē'-myesh)
ORGANIST, VIOLINIST, CONDUCTOR, TEACHER, ADMINISTRATOR
BORN: Włoszakowice, March 6, 1785
DIED: Warsaw, September 18, 1857

A significant figure in the nineteenth-century revival of Polish music, Kurpiński also offers an archetypal success story. Son of a village organist, he held a similar post himself at the age of twelve and at fifteen was playing second fiddle in a nobleman's house orchestra. He settled in Warsaw in 1810, found work in a theater orchestra, and saw his opera The Palace of Lucifer produced a year later. He founded a theater school in 1812. Józef Elsner appointed him second conductor of the Warsaw Opera, and he was appointed Kapellmeister to the Polish court in 1819. (The "king" was Czar Alexander I of Russia wearing a different hat.) Kurpiński moved up to the chief conductorship when Elsner left the opera in 1824, and it was he who conducted the concerts in which Chopin [1208] premiered his piano concerti. He married one of the singers in the company, Zofia Brzowska. In 1835 he founded a vocal academy. During his years at the opera house (he retired in 1840), Kurpiński wrote and produced more than 20 operas, ballets, and melodramas. He also wrote several Masses, and other vocal and instrumental works, and manuals for the clavichord and the study of harmony. RECORDINGS: Lidia Kozubek has recorded some of his piano pieces. There is a Polish Muza disc of Henry VI Hunting, an opera reconstructed by Jerzy Dobrzański using musical excerpts from several other Kurpiński operas and a libretto previously used for an unsuccessful opera by one of Kurpiński's contemporaries (one Bogusławski).

[1118] KALKBRENNER, Friedrich Wilhelm Michael (Kảlk'-bren-ner, Frē'-drikh Vil'-helm Mēkh'-à-el)
PIANIST, TEACHER
BORN: near Kassel, first week of November 1785
DIED: Enghien-les-Bains, June 10, 1849

Kalkbrenner was in the vanguard of the showoff keyboard virtuosi of the nineteenth century. There is no doubt that he was a brilliant performer—he would have told you so—or that, when he put his mind to it, he was at least a capable composer. But he was so inclined to make an ass of himself that he got a bad press from his peers, from which his reputation still suffers—though Chopin [1208], fresh from Warsaw, thought well of him, as did Clara Schumann's [1267] father, himself a bit of a stuffed shirt. Once deemed beyond redemption, some of his music has been played and recorded in recent years.
Like his contemporary Auber [1103], Kalkbrenner was born in a stagecoach—en

route to Berlin. His father Christian was a respectable musician who had "kapellmeistered" for various Hohenzollerns and directed the Paris Opéra Chorus. Christian soon suspected that he had not only been blessed with progeny but also with a prodigy and duly enrolled his *Wunderkind* in the Paris Conservatoire in 1798. The prodigy studied there for a couple of years (piano with Louis Adam, Adolphe's [1172] father, and harmony with Catel [1076]), took first prizes in both subjects, and secretly plotted an heroic military career under the emperor. Feeling that such might be dangerous to his musical future, Christian took him to Vienna, where he reputedly studied with Albrechtsberger [889] and met Haydn [871]. He began his concert career in Germany in 1805. The next year Christian moved back to Paris and died, and his son retired to a rural cottage with a mistress. Eight years later the idyll and Napoleon's reign ended, and Kalkbrenner went to London, where he quickly established himself as a popular performer. Besieged by pupils, he "improved" and used on them the chiroplast, a sort of torture device for positioning the fingers, the invention of a compatriot named Logier.

In 1824, after a couple of tours, Kalkbrenner settled for good in Paris. There he continued to win admirers and also made enemies with his constant name-dropping and self-congratulation, though he seems basically to have meant no harm. He involved himself with Pleyel [1003], whose future wife he taught and who took him into his piano business as a sort of living testimonial to the efficacy of the product. He is said to have sold one of the instruments to Chopin but failed to sell him his three-year master course. (Mendelssohn [1200] convinced Chopin that he already played at least as well as Kalkbrenner.) Though stories of his pomposity and possible fraudulence continued to circulate, they did not prevent the Kalkbrenner mansion from becoming a gathering place for the elite or its owner from becoming very, very rich. To his colleagues he represented the bourgeois spirit triumphant, a sellout of talent for money. He wrote voluminously, and much of his output was indeed tailored to the needs of husband-hunting young ladies. But he had listened to and no doubt learned from the likes of Clementi [977], Cramer [1067], and Hummel [1091], and possibily Beethoven [1063], and if his serious works, which include 4 piano concerti, 13 sonatas, and a good deal of chamber music, were not pathbreaking or profound, they are the work of a man who understood both his art and his audience. During his last fifteen years, he

suffered bad health and was carried away by a cholera epidemic.

RECORDINGS: Hans Kann has recorded the first piano concerto, Adrian Ruiz the *grande sonate* of 1845, Mary Louise Boehm the Op. 81 piano quintet and the solo *Effusio musica* (Kalkbrenner's own favorite of his works).

[1119] SCHNYDER VON WARTENSEE, Franz Xaver (Shnī'-der fun Vár'-tenzā, Fránts Eks-á'-ver)
INSTRUMENTALIST, TEACHER, SCIENTIST, WRITER, CIVIL SERVANT
BORN: Lucerne, April 18, 1786
DIED: Frankfurt am Main, August 27, 1868

Schnyder's father intended him for a government career, but having tried it (the job was supposed to be its own reward, there being no salary), he chucked it. His passion was music, in which he was on the practical side mostly self-taught. After participating in the first Lucerne festivals, he then moved to Zürich in 1810. Having come into some money of his own, he went to Vienna and later to Baden. When, in 1812, his home there burned, he returned to Switzerland to lead a life of cultured leisure, eventually in his own lakeside castle. However, when his father died in 1815, Schnyder discovered that all he had left was debts, owing to his proclivity to good works, and found that he would have to make a living for himself and his family (he was twice married). At first he headed the music department in the experimental school Johann Heinrich Pestalozzi had set up at Yverdun on Lake Neufchâtel. But internal dissension there drove him to Frankfurt a year later, where he taught in a girls' school for a time, then taught privately, and became one of the last glass-harmonica virtuosi, as well as an admired pianist. Spurred on by Pestalozzi's notions and by those of Hans Georg Nägeli on the essential humanity of song, he founded the Frankfurt Liederkranz (choral society) in 1828. He spent the remainder of his life between Frankfurt and Lucerne, composing, writing, and dabbling in science. In 1847 he set up in Zürich the foundation that still bears his name, devoted to the promotion of the arts and sciences. Schnyder wrote a few operas, 5 symphonies, chamber music, and much choral and other vocal material. RECORDINGS: On records, Bruno Hoffmann and Fritz Neumeyer play Schnyder's *Der durch Musik überwundene Wüterich (The Despot Conquered by Music)* for glass harmonica and piano.

[1120] HORN, Charles Edward

SINGER, CONDUCTOR, IMPRESARIO, MERCHANT
BORN: London, June 21, 1786
DIED: Boston, October 21, 1849

Horn offers another example of the horrid state of English music in his day: though he had a mediocre voice (at best) and little inspiration, he was one of the leading singers and stage composers of his day. His father, Karl Friedrich, Saxon-born, was Queen Caroline's music master and Charles Edward's chief teacher. The younger Horn, whose chief vocal virtue was a range that enabled him to sing most male parts from bass to tenor, took some lessons in Bath with Rauzzini and made his debut in 1809. His first "opera," *Tricks upon Travellers,* was performed the following year, and he had a hand in more than forty more such works. He sang the role of Caspar in the first London performance of Weber's **[1124]** *Der Freischütz* (much "arranged"). In 1827 he went to the United States, where he spent more than two years singing and producing some of his stage pieces, and spent the rest of his life between London and New York. An illness forced him to give up his vocal career in 1835, a year which, however, saw him become (it is said) the first to write an oratorio, *The Remission of Sin* (a.k.a. *Satan)* on American soil. Horn was one of the founders of the New York Philharmonic Society in 1847, and from that year until his death was conductor of the Handel and Haydn Society in Boston. His son and namesake had an operatic career as a tenor. Despite his serious efforts (most of them now lost), Horn was essentially a second-rate songwriter who managed a few hits. His most popular one, "Cherry Ripe" (beloved of early recording artists), was introduced in a musical called *Paul Pry* in 1826. He was promptly sued for plagiarism by Thomas Attwood, who had studied with Mozart **[992]** and written his own setting, but the court found in favor of the defendant.

[1121] KUHLAU, Daniel Friedrich Rudolph (Kōō'-lou, Dán'-yel Frē'-drikh Rōō'-dolf)

PIANIST
BORN: Ülzen, September 11, 1786
DIED: Copenhagen, March 12, 1832

Like so many early "Scandinavian" composers, Kuhlau was actually a foreigner. He was born in Germany near Hannover two months before Weber **[1124]**, and, like Weber, was to die prematurely of tuberculosis. His father was an army bandmaster, and the family was shifted wherever the regiment was stationed. As a child, Friedrich lost an eye in an accident. Having somehow mastered the piano, he went to Hamburg around 1800 and gave lessons to support his theoretical studies with Cantor Christian Friedrich Gottlieb Schwenke, a pupil of C. P. E. Bach **[801]** and Kirnberger **[821]**. (Some accounts call Kuhlau a pupil of C. P. E. Bach, but Bach died when Kuhlau was not yet two.) Kuhlau was doing well enough as a concert pianist and composer when the French arrived in 1810 and issued a list of locals eligible for military service which included his name. Unwilling to find out whether monocularity qualified him for exemption, he fled to Copenhagen, where he hid out under an assumed name. But the need to exist forced him to play a concert, which blew his cover and ultimately resulted in his appointment as a royal chamber musician as "Frederik" Kuhlau. (Sometimes known as "the Beethoven of the flute," he wrote many works for the instrument, but contrary to frequent statements he was never first flute in the royal orchestra and did not even play the instrument.) As a pianist he concertized widely throughout Scandinavia. He also wrote a great deal of stuff for quick sale, having to support his parents and other relatives who came to spend their old age with him. (He never married, perhaps for economic reasons.) For a time he was chorus master at the Royal Theater, where he produced a number of stage works. The most successful was his incidental music to J. L. Heiberg's romantic drama *Elverhøj (Elf-Hill),* which has enjoyed more than a thousand performances in Denmark. Perhaps the highpoint in his life came in 1825 when he spent an evening with Beethoven in Vienna, strolling, making up canons—Beethoven did one on the punning text *"kühl nicht lau"* (cool not lukewarm)—and drinking a great deal of champagne. Both of them confessed in letters afterward that they had no recollection of how it ended. In 1830 Kuhlau lost everything he owned in a fire. Shortly afterward his parents died, and he gave up the struggle himself. RECORDINGS: He is rather well represented on records—twice by the *Elverhøj* music (conducted by Johan Hye-Knudsen and John Frandsen) and the overture to the play *William Shakespeare* (by Hye-Knudsen), the first piano concerto (Felicja Blumental), piano sonatinas (Philippe Entremont), a violin sonata (Palle Heichelmann and Tamás Vetö), and numerous other chamber works involving the flute.

[1122] TULOU, Jean-Louis (Tü-lōō′, Zhàn Lōō-ē′)

FLUTIST, TEACHER, MANUFACTURER
BORN: Paris, September 12, 1786
DIED: Nantes, July 23, 1865

Many people considered Tulou the greatest flutist of the age—though he had stiff competition from his younger compatriot Louis Drouet and the Englishman Charles Nicholson **[1149]**. His father, bassoonist Jean-Pierre Tulou, who died in 1799, got him into the Paris Conservatoire in 1796. Three years later everyone was betting on Tulou's winning first prize, but it was withheld until 1800 "because of his age." After playing for a time at the Théâtre Italien, he succeeded his master, Jean-Georges Wunderlich, at the Opéra in 1813. Three years later Tulou made an enormous hit with his onomatopoeic "contests" with the prima donna in a piece of operatic fluff *Le Rossignol (The Nightingale)* by Louis-Sebastien Lebrun, a sometime tenor turned composer. Tulou then fully expected to be rewarded with the professorship just vacated by Wunderlich, but his wisecracks about the monarchy did not sit well with the recently enthroned Louis XVIII, who blocked his appointment. In pique Tulou left the Opéra and took up painting, but returned in 1826 and got his professorship three years later. In 1831 he opened a flute factory where he turned out old-fashioned flutes stamped with a nightingale, resisting to the bitter end the improved instrument invented by Theobald Boehm. At seventy he retired from his various activities and spent his last years in Nantes. His salonesque compositions were for the flute. RECORDINGS: Michel Debost has recorded a "grand solo"—i.e., a sonata.

[1123] BISHOP, (Sir) Henry Rowley

CONDUCTOR, ADMINISTRATOR, TEACHER
BORN: London, November 18, 1786
DIED: London, April 30, 1855

Born propitiously on the same day as Weber **[1124]**, Bishop lived to be regarded as the one English composer of his time likely to be remembered. His memory persists through a handful of decreasingly well-known songs of an Italianate and quasi-Handelian cast once beloved of prima donnas. The son of a haberdasher, he began writing music early and was publishing songs at fourteen. He set out to make a living as a jockey but was apparently too large for the role. However, the trial gave him a patron, who sent him to study with the Cremonese Francesco Bianchi, the composer of nearly a hundred operas, who committed suicide a few years later, though apparently not because of Bishop. After getting a few ballets produced, Bishop had his first "opera," *The Circassian Bride,* accepted by the Drury Lane. Starring Sarah Lyon, it premiered successfully on February 23, 1809. The next day the theater was destroyed by fire, taking the score but fortunately not Miss Lyon, whom Bishop married two months later. (She bore him three children before dying in 1831.)

In 1810 Bishop took over direction of the Covent Garden Theatre, which he operated for fourteen years, during which time he lent his name to nearly eighty works performed there. In 1813 he was (as who was not?) one of the founders of the London Philharmonic Society. In 1816–17 he also conducted at the King's Theatre, in 1819 at the Lenten Oratorio Concerts, in 1820 in Dublin (where he was given the keys to the city). The year 1823 saw the production of his *Clari* (to a libretto by the American expatriate John Howard Payne) whose haunting theme song was "Home, Sweet Home." The melody was a runaway hit (for more than a century no ball could end until it was played), and Bishop was accused of having stolen it. He had— from himself, for he had used similar tunes at least twice before—but he was exonerated of the charge. (Later he used it again in a sequel called *Home, Sweet Home* in 1829, and Donizetti **[1155]** used something remarkably like it in *Anna Bolena* of 1830.) Despite such success, quarrels with the management and offers from the rebuilt Drury Lane caused Bishop to defect to that house, where his first major project was *Aladdin,* which was supposed to crush Weber's soon-to-be-premiered *Oberon* (it didn't). In 1830 Bishop succeeded Tom Cooke **[1107]** as director of Vauxhall Gardens, then already on its last legs, though it survived another twenty-nine years.

Shortly after Sarah Bishop died the next year, the bereaved married another singer, a twenty-one-year-old soprano named Anne Riviere, who afterward sang as Anna Bishop and often appeared with her husband and the harpist Bochsa **[1131]**. Having had some part by then in perhaps 150 stage works, Bishop seems to have been about ready to rest on his laurels: *The Doom Kiss,* produced in October 1832 was his last such work save for some arrangements. Having been turned down for a couple of posts he had sought, he acquired a B.Mus. at Oxford in 1839, the ceremonies being accompanied with a sort of Bishop festival. Perhaps this took some of the sting out of his marital catastrophe, for that August Anna eloped to Germany with

Bochsa. (She had a long and adventurous career and died in New York forty-five years later.) Two years later Bishop was appointed professor of music at the University of Edinburgh, and in 1842 he was knighted. A year later, having demonstrated a severe and chronic distaste for lecturing, he had to resign his professorship, but he was soon appointed to the analogous post at Oxford, which institution awarded him the D.Mus. in 1853. From 1840 until it closed down in 1848, he conducted the Concerts of Antient Musick. He died at sixty-eight of cancer.

Bishop, like most of his ilk, was not an opera composer in any real sense, but a songwriter. Many of the works with which he is credited included only a few musical numbers. Many were adaptations (for which term read "travesties"): these included *The Libertine* (after Mozart's [992] *Don Giovanni*), *Hofer, the Tell of the Tyrol* (after Rossini's [1143] *Guillaume Tell*), and *The Demon* (after Meyerbeer's [1142] *Robert le Diable*). He was also called on to provide music for what passed for Shakespearean revivals, and he had a special fondness for works based on Sir Walter Scott. He treated the Masaniello story two years before Auber [1103], that of the Sicilian Vespers thirty-two years before Verdi, and supplied music for Byron's *Manfred* nineteen years before Schumann [1211]. Apart from his songs and glees, his other music is negligible.

RECORDINGS: Such pieces as "Lo, Here the Gentle lark," "My Pretty Jane," "Should He Upbraid," "Echo Song," "Pretty Mocking-Bird," and "The Dashing White Sergeant" once enjoyed frequent recording.

[1124] WEBER, Carl Maria von (Vä'-ber, Kârl Mà-rē'-à fun)
CONDUCTOR, PIANIST
BORN: Eutin, November 18, 1786
DIED: London, June 5, 1826

Carl Maria von Weber did not invent German opera or even German Romantic opera (Mozart [992] and Beethoven [1063] have prior claims), but, impelled by the contemporary currents of nationalism, nature worship, and antiquarianism, he set the direction for both German opera and European musical Romanticism. If his own operas sometimes demand more suspension of disbelief than the will can manage, they embrace the archetypal Romantic mix of the idealized rural, the imagined mediaeval, the supernatural, the heroic, and the amatory, and their music is a mirror of their emotions and a director of ours. Moreover, Weber was

perhaps the first modern conductor: he conducted from a podium with a baton, arranged his men as orchestras have been generally arranged ever since, and exercised dictatorial authority over them. Both as composer and performer—he was also one of the first of the roving virtuosi—he probably understood the piano better than most of his predecessors and contemporaries (though poor health and other exigencies telescoped a playing career that would in any case have been shortened by a lamentably early death).

The petit bourgeois Webers had for some generations aspired to higher estate. The "von" was an invention of Weber's father, Franz Anton, an ex-soldier who, until he was pensioned off in 1768, had managed an estate for the Elector-Archbishop of Cologne. The uncle of Constanze Weber Mozart and her singing sisters, he was a passionate musical amateur and at the time of his son's birth was serving as *Kapellmeister* to the Prince-Bishop of Lübeck in Eutin. A little over a year before, recently widowed, he had married, on a visit to Vienna, a singer named Genovefa Brenner, She was tubercular, and Carl was born frail and crippled in one hip. In 1787 Franz Anton, who had few scruples, little common sense, itchy feet, and vast dreams, made his wife and some relatives the nucleus of a covey of strolling players that he called the "Weber Opera Company." Thus the child, who had some early music lessons from his father, took in the feel of the theater with his mother's milk. But her declining health and the wars necessitated a halt in Salzburg in 1797, and there the child got to study with Michael Haydn [894], and published a set of fughettas. The next year Genovefa Weber died, and the rest of the family settled in Munich where Carl studied with several teachers and wrote his first opera, *Der Macht der Liebe und des Weins (The Power of Love and Wine)*, whose score was destroyed by a fire before production could even be contemplated.

Looking for a cheap way to get his prodigy's music published, Franz Anton apprenticed him to Aloys Senefelder, who had invented lithography a short time before and who held a royal monopoly on the process. When he was satisfied that they were ready to go into the business independently, Franz Anton took Carl to Freiberg in Saxony, where the boy soon gave up printing for writing a new opera, *Das Waldmädchen (The Woodland Maiden)*, which a local company produced in 1800. (Its score has also vanished.) A year later the Webers were back in Salzburg, where the burgeoning composer turned out a Mass and *Peter Schmoll und sein Nachbarn (Peter Schmoll and His Neighbors),* which last, after some delay, was produced in 1803 in Augsburg, where his half-brother Edmond was an opera conductor. (The overture is still occasionally played.) A few months later Carl went to Vienna in order to study with Joseph Haydn [871], but when that plan fell through, Weber found a teacher in "Abt" Vogler [960]. It was in this period that the youth fell in love with folksongs, which he loved to sing to his own guitar accompaniment, especially by way of serenade.

In the spring of 1804, in his eighteenth year, Weber was made *Kapellmeister* at Breslau (Wroclaw). His youthfulness, opposed to entrenched musical interests, made the job impossible—especially since he insisted on radical methods of dealing with the orchestra and in overseeing (as he was to do thenceforward) all aspects of operatic production with which he was involved. Nevertheless he hung on for three years. One night in 1806 while working alone at home, he, feeling thirsty, took a swig from a wine bottle, unaware that his father had been puttering with his printing equipment and had filled it with nitric acid. He was saved by his friend Berner [1095], who, chancing by, found him unconscious. Weber eventually recovered (though his voice did not) and, seeing the handwriting on the wall, he resigned his post. Pulling some strings, he managed to become a sort of domestic protégé of the Duke of Württemberg-Öls, to whom he dedicated his only two symphonies. But by February 1807 he was off again, and, after some months of wandering, found a place as private secretary to Duke Ludwig of Württemberg, a younger brother of King Frederick II of that state. The job was little more than menial, but Weber found much intellectual and social stimulus in Stuttgart, fell in love (a chronic weakness) with a girl named Gretchen Lang, lived irresponsibly, and was eventually needled back to a sense of his vocation by Franz Danzi [1035]. He wrote incidental music for Danzi's production of Schiller's *Turandot* and reworked the *Waldmädchen* as *Silvana.* In 1809 his feckless father caught up with him, and managed to get hold of 800 gulden with which Carl's employer had entrusted him. Carl covered the loss by borrowing the money from an acquaintance who got the notion that the gesture would somehow keep his boy out of the army. When it failed to, he had Weber arrested for treason and the theft of two silver candlesticks. Though the charges were dropped, other creditors immediately had Weber re-arrested for debt. In February 1810 both Webers were ejected from

Württemberg and told not to come back unless they wanted to be imprisoned.

After spending some weeks between Mannheim (where he played in concerts sponsored by the unrelated Gottfried Weber) and Heidelberg (where he played a sort of student-prince *manqué),* Weber tried Darmstadt, where he was reunited with Vogler and his sometime fellow student Johann Gansbächer, and where he made friends with young Jakob Beer, scion of a wealthy Berlin Jewish family, who was himself to make an operatic splash as "Giacomo Meyerbeer" [1142]. In September 1810, after several delays, *Silvana* was produced at Frankfurt am Main. Gretchen Lang sang the second female lead; Caroline Brandt (ironically, as we shall see) sang the first. Despite the concomitant ascent in Frankfurt of a lady balloonist, the work had a fair success, caught on, and became Weber's first internationally known opera. By then the composer was already at work on a new one, an "oriental" comedy called *Abu Hassan.* Premiered in Munich the following summer, 1811, it was a hit, though productions were circumscribed by its one-act format. In the meantime Weber had left Darmstadt on a concert tour. But when he got to Munich, he broke it off to write a concerto for the great clarinetist Heinrich Bärmann and to oversee the production of his opera. Rejecting a conducting post in Wiesbaden on account of the salary, he next headed for Switzerland. En route, he carelessly wandered into Württemberg, where the authorities made good their threat and threw him in the brig. After a few days, however, they ferried him across Lake Constance and dropped him off in Switzerland with further warnings. There he concertized and roamed the Alps until fall, when he returned to Munich, only to take to the road again, this time with Bärmann. They gave a successful concert in Prague, were feted by the eccentric Duke of Saxe-Gotha (he refused to have an army and preferred dressing in female costume), met Goethe in Weimar, and wound up staying with the Beers in Berlin. It was during this period that the now-senile Franz Anton Weber died and that his son experienced the first symptoms of "rheumatism of the chest." In July Berlin saw a successful production of *Silvana* under its composer's baton. Bärmann having already gone home by August, Weber took his leave then and spent the autumn in Gotha helping Spohr [1112] keep the duke amused.

After further travels, Weber returned to Prague in January 1813 and was offered the intendancy of the opera house. The terms overcame his hesitancy, and he appointed

Gänsbacher as his aide. Part of his task was to rebuild the company, and one of the first singers he hired was Caroline Brandt. A veritable frenzy of work at the theater and more concert appearances forced him to take to his bed in the spring, and during his convalescence he learned Czech to understand the remarks hurled at him by his men, unused to his kind of martial discipline. Shortly before Fräulein Brandt arrived, Weber became involved in a rather sordid affair with a singer-dancer named Therese Brunetti, eventually living with her in a house that also contained her husband and five children. But after Caroline made her debut (in Isouard's [1083] *Cendrillon),* he increasingly turned to her for stability and reassurance.

In the spring of 1814, again ailing, Weber took some time off. He returned to Berlin (where he was nearly run over in the tumult celebrating Napoleon's defeat), then went on to Leipzig, Weimar, and Gotha. In September he was called home to tide the opera company over a crisis. Offers of similar posts in Königsberg and (very temptingly) Berlin increased the tension. On top of all this, Weber's production of *Fidelio* (November 1814), which he had counted on to create an appetite for German operas, failed, and he began to think seriously of getting out. Shortly afterward he proposed to Caroline. But when he indicated that he expected her to give up her career, they quarreled, and he spent a miserable summer alone in Munich. Back home in September, he conducted the first performance of his "Waterloo" cantata *Kampf und Sieg (Battle and Victory)* during a terrible snowstorm just before Christmas. The impact of Prague winters on his now seriously failing health made him more than ever determined to move on. In January 1816 he took lodgings in the home of the widow Brandt, and the following October, having resigned at the opera house, he took her and Caroline with him to Berlin. Shortly afterward, as the sun, with admirable cooperation, emerged from a total eclipse, Carl and Caroline officially announced their engagement. On Christmas Day, in another happy coincidence, Weber concluded negotiations with Dresden (a city then under a cloud for having been perforce on the French side in the recent hostilities) by signing a contract that made him director of the Royal German Opera.

Dresden was to be the focus of Weber's life for his last nine years. But the job turned out to have its drawbacks. The real operatic power was Francesco Morlacchi [1114], director of the Royal Italian Opera, who outranked his German colleague. Although he was diplomatic about it, he made things difficult for Weber at every turn. Nevertheless Weber's attention to detail and his discipline were so evident in his first Dresden production (Méhul's [1036] *Joseph)* that he was promptly elevated to at least nominally equal status with Morlacchi and was given tenure for life. (His new eminence also had its penalties, for during Morlacchi's frequent absences, Weber had to run both companies.) On November 4, 1818, Weber married Caroline in Prague. They concertized their way back to Dresden, where they took a flat. For the remainder of their time together, Caroline suffered through a succession of difficult pregnancies, miscarriages, and infant deaths, though eventually the household included two sons, a daughter, and a menagerie of pets. Things were made more pleasant with the acquisition of a vacation home in the suburbs, but no easier, since all their belongings had to go with them both ways. Perhaps understandably, Weber's health steadily worsened, and in the spring of 1819 illness forced him to give up work on an opera called *Alcindor*—a project that was terminated when the commission for the work was canceled and the German Opera, thanks to Morlacchi's machinations, staggered to a virtual halt. However, no longer harassed by the sense that the show had to go on, Weber turned with relief to composition, for which he had had little time recently.

Shortly after he came to Dresden, Weber, working with the poet Friedrich Kind, began an opera based on an old tale of black magic and devilish trafficking in the German forests, but had had to put it aside. Now he was able to return to it. (He first called it *Die Jägersbraut [The Hunter's Bride],* but it soon became *Der Freischütz [The Freeshooter]* and, as such, the prototype of the German Romantic opera *par excellence.)* He completed it in the spring of 1820 in the Dresden suburb of Antonstadt, where he and his family had taken a cottage, and immediately plunged into writing music for Pius Alexander Wolff's play *Preciosa* (after Cervantes) and a comic opera on a Spanish theme, *Die drei Pintos (The Three Pintos). Freischütz* was scheduled for a Berlin premiere, but the burning of the opera house delayed it for a year. In the interim Weber concertized and took on as a pupil the sixteen-year-old Julius Benedict, who became very close to him and was later his biographer. *Preciosa* opened in Berlin in March 1821 and proved popular. After more delays, *Freischütz* reached the stage on May 14. It puzzled the audience at first, but the evening ended in a triumph, though afterward there was some critical sniping.

Dresden apparently took no notice. Nothing was said about producing the new opera, but Weber was told that the *Pintos* could not be mounted in the foreseeable future. (He gave it up; sixty-odd years later Gustav Mahler [1525] completed and produced it.) For a time he hoped for an appointment at Kassel, but it went to Spohr. On top of all this—or perhaps because of it—Weber suffered his first pulmonary hemorrhage. Soon, however, Domenico Barbaja, the new director of the Imperial Opera in Vienna was requesting a *"Freischütz*-like" opera for his company. A literary lady called Helmine von Chézy (whom Weber came to refer to as "Das Chez") offered her services in writing a libretto for an old French romance, *Gérard et Euriant*. Weber accepted. As those who dealt with her could have told him, Das Chez should have been declared a disaster area; talentless and demanding, she gave him no end of trouble, and produced one of the worst libretti ever foisted on a major operatic composer, *Euryanthe*. While she was writing it, Weber managed to let Dresden hear *Freischütz* in January 1822. Then he went off to Vienna, feeling so horribly ill that he left a sealed farewell note to Caroline, to be opened in case . . . The trip did not kill him, but it wore him down, as did the resumption of his duties in Dresden, work on the opera, and new fatherhood. Aware that his days were numbered, he completed *Euryanthe* with grave misgivings. For the Vienna premiere on October 25, 1823, the theater was so packed that Das Chez, who arrived late, had to be passed to her seat over the heads of those already in place. Much to Weber's amazement, the piece was wildly applauded. But shortly attendance began to fall off, and two weeks later the composer went home, convinced that he was a failure. He devoted the next several months largely to trying to stay alive.

The English actor-producer Charles Kemble revived him by requesting a work for Covent Garden. Terrified that he might die and leave his family beggars, Weber, against his doctors' advice, jumped at the chance. Waiting for further word from Kemble, he set about teaching himself English, which he did so well that he could tell the librettist James Robinson Planché that a translation would not be necessary. It was about this time that he also joined George Thomson's stable of all-star folksong arrangers, which included Haydn [871], Beethoven [1063], Pleyel [1003], and Hummel [1091]. Despite numerous interruptions, including useless visits to spas, he had completed two acts of

Oberon by the end of 1825. Six weeks later he set out for London, despite Caroline's fears that she would never see him again. Accompanied by the flutist Caspar Fürstenau [1071], he eventually reached Paris, where he met all the important musicians save Berlioz [1175], whom he was unable to find, and arrived in London on March 4. He was received as a hero and feted beyond the limits of his strength. He rehearsed the new opera and conducted concerts, at which the much-demanded *Freischütz* overture became gall and wormwood to him. All the while he was running a fever, suffering from diarrhea, and spitting blood. The first night of *Oberon* was well attended, despite the efforts of rivals to draw the audience away, and won Weber an ovation. Somehow he managed to get through the twelve performances called for by his contract. Determined to live until June 6, when he had passage home, he managed to hang on and even to make a few more concert appearances. He tried to keep his true condition from Caroline, though he could barely control his pen in his last few letters. On the morning of June 5, he did not answer his door. Finding it locked, his callers forced it and found him dead in bed. His body was placed in a lead coffin, which was sealed and stored in the Catholic chapel at Moorfields. Eighteen years later, thanks to his Dresden successor Richard Wagner [1230], Meyerbeer, Benedict, and Weber's son Max, he was taken home and buried in the Catholic Cemetery in Dresden.

RECORDINGS: Many of Weber's works were occasional or ephemeral so that representation of it on records appears spotty. But there are recordings of all the operas from *Abu Hassan* through *Oberon,* including Mahler's *Drei Pintos;* the 2 mature Masses; *Kampf und Sieg;* the piano and clarinet concerti and most of the minor concerted works; the 2 symphonies and the 2 concert overtures; the flute trio and clarinet quintet; the 6 little violin sonatas and the pieces for clarinet and piano; the 4 piano sonatas and most of the other pieces for piano solo and four-hands; several collections that account for most of the songs and duets and all of the Scottish folksongs. The only seriously neglected area is that of the choral works and partsongs.

[1125] ALYABIEV, Alexander Alexandrovitch (Ăl-yāb'-yef, Ăl-yek-săn'-der Ăl-yek-săn-drō-vĕch)
SOLDIER, GENTLEMAN
BORN: Tobolsk, August 15, 1787
DIED: Moscow, March 6, 1851

Though he was one of the first Russian composers to attempt anything beyond songs and religious pieces, Alyabiev has been remembered mostly for a song "The Nightingale," which, with someone else's variations, long served as a showpiece for sopranos. Born, to his later regret, a thousand miles east of Moscow, he was the son of the governor of the district, a man of unusual taste and culture. During the Napoleonic invasion he became an officer in the czar's cavalry and was among the first to enter Paris when the emperor was overthrown. Alyabiev left the military in 1823, shortly after composing his first opera, *The Moonlight Night,* and lived in St. Petersburg. Two years later, on what may have been a trumped-up charge of murder—the alleged victim died, it was maintained, following a fight with Alyabiev over a game of cards—he was jailed and in 1828 was exiled back to Tobolsk. He seems to have whiled away the time composing. In 1831, for reasons of health, he was permitted to go south, a trip which resulted in a collection of Ukrainian folksongs. In 1836 he settled in Moscow, where four years later he married a widow, Ekaterina Alexandrovna Ofrosima, a member of the Rimsky-Korsakov [1416] family. During his last years he was ill much of the time. He left much stage music (vaudevilles, music for Pushkin's *Rusalka* and Shakespeare's *Merry Wives of Windsor,* operatic treatments of *The Tempest* and *A Midsummer Night's Dream,* 4 symphonies, 3 string quartets, and many songs. RECORDINGS: There is a recording of the piano quintet by Emil Gilels and the Borodin Quartet—and dozens of "The Nightingale."

[1126] GRUBER, Franz Xaver (Grōō'-bâr, Frânts Eks-â'-ver)
ORGANIST, CHOIRMASTER, TEACHER
BORN: Unterweizburg, November 25, 1787
DIED: Hallein, June 7, 1863

A village organist-schoolmaster in the Salzburg district, Gruber was the son of a peasant weaver, who opposed his musical dreams. The boy, however, managed to get lessons from the organist at Burghausen. He became schoolmaster in Arndorf when he was twenty and organist of the Nikolaikirche in Oberndorf when he was twenty-eight. Two years later, in 1818, the curate, Joseph Mohr, asked Gruber on Christmas Eve if he could put music to a *Weihnachtslied* that he had written. Gruber obliged with a setting for two solo voices, choir, and —because the organ was out of whack—a

guitar. It was sung at midnight Mass with the authors taking the solo parts. Its title was *"Stille Nacht"* ("Silent Night"). It was picked up by others, made its way into the Tyrol, and became known worldwide as a Tyrolian folk carol. Gruber moved to Berndorf in 1829 and settled permanently in Hallein in 1833. In 1854 he laid formal claim to his song, largely because it had become known in a melodically corrupt version. Gruber wrote a few other church works. RECORDINGS: There is a recording of a couple of Masses, and the original version of *"Stille Nacht"* has been recorded by Elisabeth Schwarzkopf (singing both solo parts).

[1127] ETT, Kaspar (Et, Kàs'-pär)
ORGANIST
BORN: Eresing, January 5, 1788
DIED: Munich, May 16, 1847

For most of his adult life, Ett was organist of the Michaelskirche in Munich. He was also a pioneer musicologist, who spent much time digging out and studying sacred music from the Renaissance and early Baroque. He attempted to imitate it in many of his nearly 300 church works, few of which saw publication in his lifetime. RECORDINGS: One of his church works, a motet, sung by Felicie Hüni-Mihacsek and other stars of the Third Reich Munich Opera was recorded from a broadcast. Alois Kirnberger and the Musica Bavarica Ensemble perform *Ave vivens hostia* for soprano, violin, and organ.

[1128] PIXIS, Johann Peter (Pēk-sis, Yō'-hàn Pä'-ter)
PIANIST, TEACHER
BORN: Mannheim, February 10, 1788
DIED: Baden-Baden, December 22, 1874

Pixis was one of the five stellar pianist composers who collaborated with Liszt [1218] on the *Hexaemeron* (the six days of the Creation!), a series of variations on a march from Bellini's [1164] *Puritani.* Pixis had a musical father and older brother both named Friedrich Wilhelm. The brother (1785–1842) played violin, and the father, an organist, trotted the pair around Europe in 1796 on a prodigy tour. Ten years later, when the only thing still prodigious about Peter was his nose, the family moved to Vienna, where he studied with Albrechtsberger [889] and established himself as a significant part of musical life there. (Two of his four operas were produced in Vienna.) In 1823 he went on to Paris, where he was equally successful, especially as a teacher. Though he never married, and despite his colossal nose, Pixis had an eye for the girls. In 1828, he took the lovely singer Henriette Sontag (his brother's pupil) to London. Three years later Chopin [1208] found him living with a pretty fifteen-year-old pupil, whom Pixis mumbled something about marrying. This was almost certainly Francilla Göhringer, whom he adopted and who became a famous operatic contralto. (She moved Robert Schumann [1211] to tears in a Donizetti [1155] performance and created the title role in Pacini's *Saffo.)* In 1840 Pixis moved to Baden-Baden, where he spent his last thirty-four years teaching. A prolific composer, mostly in instrumental forms, he has been largely forgotten. RECORDINGS: Besides his contribution to the *Hexaemeron* (at least two recordings), he is represented phonographically by the Concerto for Piano, Violin, and Strings played by Mary Louise Boehm and Kees Kooper.

[1129] SECHTER, Simon (Zekh'-ter, Sē'-mōn)
ORGANIST, TEACHER, THEORIST
BORN: Friedberg, October 11, 1788
DIED: Vienna, September 10, 1877

Even in his own time Sechter was best known as a teacher; he is now remembered as the man who taught Bruckner [1293] and with whom Schubert [1153], just before he died, was planning to study counterpoint. Sechter came to Vienna from his native Bohemia in 1804 to complete his musical studies. During the French occupation he became friends with the great contrabassist Dragonetti [1033] for whose concerti he wrote piano parts. In 1810 Sechter won a teaching post at the Institute for the Blind; and in 1824, with the backing of Mozart's [992] old friend, the Abbé Stadler, he was appointed second organist at the imperial court. A year later he succeeded Voříšek [1138] as first court organist. The Emperor Ferdinand decorated Sechter for one of his Masses. Among the well-known musicians whom Sechter taught were Henselt [1237], Thalberg [1220], and Vieuxtemps [1270]. He was named professor of counterpoint at the Vienna Conservatory in 1851. When he retired in 1863, Bruckner succeeded him. In his last years Sechter fell on hard times. Inasmuch as his philosophy seemed to be that writing a fugue a day was the way to good musical health, he composed an inordinate number of compositions; he also published a number of theoretical works and manuals. He wrote 35 Masses and much other religious music, including 2 oratorios. Only one

of his 4 operas, *Ali Hitsch-Hatsch,* was performed, and many of his compositions were never finished. RECORDINGS: Franz Haselböck has recorded an LP side of Sechter's organ pieces.

[1130] SILCHER, Philipp Friedrich (Zil'-kher, Fē'-lip Frē'-drikh)
TEACHER, CONDUCTOR
BORN: Schnaith, June 27, 1789
DIED: Tübingen, August 26, 1860

Silcher is still popular in Germany as the composer of male-chorus songs, and is known worldwide for his setting of Heine's "*Die Lorelei*" (which, however, often appears anonymously as a "folksong"). In short, he is not regarded very highly, and it is therefore surprising to find that he was once an important figure in German musical education. He came to that eminence honestly and late. His father, Johann Karl, was schoolmaster-organist of a Württemberg village, though he died when Friedrich was only six. The boy got some music lessons from his stepfather and from the local school inspector Mayerlen, who took him on as his assistant in 1803. After three years, during which time he substituted in the local school, Silcher went to nearby Fellbach as assistant to the schoolmaster-organist Nikolaus Ferdinand Auberlen, who gave him his first serious musical training. Soon he was playing for some of the church services, for which Auberlen, in the nationalistic spirit of the times, used the music of J. S. Bach [684] and other early German composers.

Soon afterward, Baron Johann Friedrich von Berlichingen, chief magistrate of the neighboring town of Schorndorf, hired Silcher to teach his daughters. Silcher acquitted himself so well that in 1809 the baron got him a place with a girls' school in Ludwigsburg. There he became friends with Prince Ludwig's personal secretary, Carl Maria von Weber [1124]. It was Weber's influence that caused him in 1815 to give up schoolmastering and go to Stuttgart for some serious study. His teachers there were Conradin Kreutzer [1096] and Hummel [1091]. A year later an encounter with Johann Heinrich Pestalozzi converted him to the latter's views on folksong as the proper basis for musical education. In 1817, promoted by his friend J. F. Bahnmeier, professor of theology at Tübingen, he was appointed music director and teacher there. In his forty-three years there, he founded the Liedertafel and the Oratorio Choir (still active), and in 1851 was awarded an honorary doctorate. He died a few months after he retired.

RECORDINGS: Besides innumerable recordings of *"Lorelei,"* Silcher is represented on records by several LP discs of popular choral pieces and by one of variations for soprano and/or flute and piano. Oddest to us moderns, perhaps, are the song versions of various Beethoven [1063] instrumental themes, of which Cathy Berberian has recorded a few tongue-in-cheek and Hermann Prey an LP side as seriously as they were intended.

[1131] BOCHSA, Robert Nicolas Charles
(Bōkh'-sà, Rō-bâr' Nē-kō-làs' Shärlz)
HARPIST, TEACHER
BORN: Montmédy, August 9, 1789
DIED: Sydney, January 6, 1856

Though he is said to have played all the standard orchestral instruments well, Nicolas Bochsa was particularly admired as a harpist in a harp-happy era. He also exhibited the kind of amorality that gives musicians a bad name. His father was a Bohemian musician who later went into the retail music business. Nicolas was born in a small town north of Verdun, but spent his youth in Lyons and Bordeaux, in which latter city he studied with old Franz Beck, who, a generation earlier, had taught Gaveaux [1020] and Garat [1026]. By the time his family moved to Paris in 1806, he had already written an oratorio and had had an opera and a ballet produced. In that same year he was enrolled in the Paris Conservatoire, where he studied with Catel [1076] and Méhul [1036] and took up the harp with Nadermann [1102]. By 1809 Bochsa had surpassed his teacher in technique, and in 1813 he became personal harpist to Napoleon himself. The job proved a brief one, but, thanks to the success of the impressive *Requiem* written for the reburial of Louis XVI, he was taken on by Louis XVIII. Meanwhile, though Bochsa had enjoyed considerable success in Paris as a composer of operas, he had also engaged in some more dubious activities, and a year later, in 1817, he moved rather precipitately to London, abandoning his wife. The following February he was tried in absentia, found guilty of forgery, and sentenced to a long prison term, a heavy fine, and branding should he ever fall into French hands.

In London, however, he throve as a performer and teacher, married a woman named Amy Wilson, and in 1822 was appointed secretary and professor of harp at the newly opened Royal Academy of Music. Two years later he went bankrupt. In 1826,

by pulling strings, he became music director of the King's Theatre, and though he held on there for four years, he was dismissed from his Royal Academy posts as morally unfit to hold them. After 1830, Bochsa devoted his time to concertizing and to private teaching. (His most famous pupil was the brilliant but short-lived Parish-Alvars [1194].) With increasing frequency he appeared with Sir Henry Bishop [1123] and his young wife Anna, a singer. In 1839 he crowned his dubious career by running off to Germany with her. (He was then fifty and, to judge from his portrait, no Adonis when he was younger.) For the next seventeen years they wandered uneasily, but successfully, all over the world until death caught up with Bochsa in Australia, seven months after it felled Bishop. Now free both officially and unofficially, Anna married an American millionaire named Schultz.

RECORDINGS: Bochsa was primarily a brilliant if superficial composer for the harp. Lily Laskine has recorded one of his 5 concerti, and the Holligers a *Nocturne* for harp and oboe.

[1132] TADOLINI, Giovanni (Tà-dō-lē'-nē, Jō-vàn'-nē)
TEACHER, CONDUCTOR
BORN: Bologna, October 18, 1789 (?)
DIED: Bologna, November 29, 1872

A minor composer of operas, Tadolini was overshadowed by his more illustrious associates. He was a classmate of Rossini [1143] under Padre Mattei at the Liceo in Bologna, then went to Paris in 1811 as Spontini's [1081] chorus master at the Théâtre-Italien. After three years he returned to Italy where he taught voice and composed (all 8 of his operas come from this period). His best-known pupil was Eugenia Savonari, whom he married, and who, as Eugenia Tadolini, created roles in Donizetti [1155] and Verdi [1232] works. In 1829 he returned to the Théâtre-Italien as chief conductor. After nine years he returned to Bologna, where he ran a vocal academy. It is sometimes said that he completed Rossini's *Stabat Mater.* This needs qualification. The work was commissioned by a Spanish priest named Varela. After writing about two thirds of it, Rossini was incapacitated by illness. In order to get Varela off his back, he had Tadolini set the missing sections and sent the work off to Spain. Later Rossini filled in the blanks himself, and what we know today is all his. Tadolini's chief compositional success was as a writer of songs. RECORDINGS: Suzanne Danco has recorded one of his songs.

[1133] SZYMANOWSKA, Maria Agata
(Shē-mȧ-nôf'-shkȧ, Mȧ-rē'-ȧ Á'-gȧ-tȧ)
PIANIST, TEACHER
BORN: Warsaw, December 14, 1789
DIED: St. Petersburg, July 24, 1831

Maria Wołowska, as she was born, studied in
Warsaw. One of her teachers is said to have
been Franz Lessel, a pupil of Haydn [871].
In 1810 she married a landowner, Theophilus
Jozef Szymanowski, and made successful de-
buts in both Warsaw and Paris as a concert
pianist. The marriage seems to have been a
rather casual affair, for Szymanowska continued to play all over Europe, and the two
were divorced in 1820. After hearing her in
Weimar in 1821, Goethe wrote a poem to her,
and the next year she replaced John Field
[1104], who had moved to Moscow, as Russian imperial court pianist. She is said to
have taken some lessons from Field and was
sometimes called "the female Field"—which
sounds odd in English. Szymanowska continued to tour until 1828, when she settled
down to teach in St. Petersburg. She was a
victim of the great cholera epidemic that
swept across Europe from India in the 1830s.
Her remarkable collection of celebrity autographs is preserved in the Mickiewicz Museum in Paris. Her compositions consist
mostly of songs and piano pieces, including
preludes, polonaises, mazurkas, nocturnes,
and waltzes. Chopin heard her play in his
youth and probably played some of her music himself. RECORDINGS: Lidia Kozubek
has recorded a set of dances.

[1134] VACCAI, Nicola (Vȧk-kȧ'-ē, Nē'-
kō-lȧ)
TEACHER
BORN: Tolentino, March 15, 1790
DIED: Pesaro, August 5, 1848

As an operatic composer, Vaccai enjoyed a
brief moment of popularity in the gap between Rossini's [1143] defection to France
and the rise of Bellini [1164]. Born in the
Marches, he grew up in Pesaro and began
his career in his teens as a dramatic poet. At
seventeen he went to Rome to study law but
became caught up in music and took a degree in 1811 from the Accademia di Santa
Cecilia. After some further work with
Paisiello [914] in Naples, he wrote his first
opera, *I solitari di Scozia (The Scottish Her-
mits),* which was produced there with moderate success. The Bourbon restoration sent
him to Venice, where he had some success
with ballets but none with operas. He became, however, immensely in demand as a
vocal teacher, a calling he pursued later

(1821–23) in Trieste. A commission from
Parma in the latter year turned him back to
opera, and he reached his peak with *Giulietta e Romeo,* premiered at the Teatro Ca-
nobbiana in Milan in 1825. After that, his
star rapidly faded, and he returned to teaching, spending the years 1830–33 in Paris and
London. He returned to Italy in 1833, married, and became director of the vocal wing
of the Milan Conservatory. Between 1836
and 1845 he produced four more operas, all
unsuccessful. A quarrel with the higher authorities at the conservatory caused him to
resign in 1844 and return to Pesaro.
Vaccai's greatest successes were with his
songs and his singing method of 1832, which
is still in use. As an opera composer he survives on records by accident. His *Giulietta e
Romeo* was quickly supplanted by Bellini's *I
Capuleti e i Montecchi (The Capulets and
Montagues).* But the singer Maria Malibran
did not like Bellini's final scene and substituted Vaccai's, which has been generally
used ever since.

[1135] LEGNANI, Rinaldo Luigi (Lȧn-yȧ'-
nē, Rē-nȧl'-dō Lōō-ē'-jē)
VIOLINIST, SINGER, GUITARIST, LUTHIER
BORN: Ferrara, November 7, 1790
DIED: Ravenna, August 5, 1877

Legnani studied violin with a view to becoming an orchestral musician but made his
first public appearance at seventeen as a concert tenor. Twelve years later he embarked
on a career as a concert guitarist in Milan
and had a very successful career in Italy and
central Europe. In 1836 he, Paganini [1106],
and Mercadante [1148] met by chance in
Turin and amused themselves by playing as
a trio. Paganini, who played the guitar himself, considered Legnani the greatest
guitarist he had ever heard and arranged to
tour with him, but the plan came to naught,
probably owing to the great violinist's declining health. After 1840 Legnani manufactured violins and guitars in Ravenna. He
wrote many works for guitar. RECORDINGS:
Spiro Thomatos has recorded one of his caprices.

[1136] HÉROLD, Louis-Joseph-Ferdinand
(Ā-rōl, Lōō-ē' Zhō-zef' Fȧr-dē-nȧn')
PIANIST, TEACHER
BORN: Paris, January 28, 1791
DIED: Paris, January 19, 1833

Once one of the more successful and talented composers of *opéra-comique,* Hérold
has been virtually forgotten. His Alsatian fa-

ther, François Joseph, was a onetime pupil of Emanuel Bach [801] and a respectable composer himself. He passed on to Ferdinand his musical knowledge and his tuberculosis. Young Hérold, at fifteen, enrolled at the Paris Conservatoire, where he studied with, among others, Méhul [1036], Catel [1076], and Jean-Louis Adam, father of Adolphe [1172]. Hérold took the first prize for his pianism in 1810 and two years later became the first composer of note to win the Prix de Rome in its ten-year history. But his health permitted his spending only a few months in Rome. He sought a more hospitable climate in Naples, where he taught the daughters of the French-born Neapolitan king, Joachim Murat, and served as pianist to Queen Marie Caroline, Napoleon's sister. In 1815 he saw his first opera, *La gioventù di Enrico Quinto, (The Youth of Henry V),* successfully produced there. Afterward he returned to Paris by way of Rome and Vienna. As luck would have it, Boieldieu [1084] had run out of steam on his opera *Charles de France,* composed for the nuptials of the future Charles X, and persuaded Hérold to write the second act (of two).

Hérold accepted the post of pit keyboard player at the Théâtre-Italien. His first Parisian success was *Les Rosières (The May-Queens),* which was premiered at the Opéra-Comique in January 1817 and was followed by the even more successful *La Clochette (The Little Bell)* later that year. But Hérold was always plagued by an inability to find good libretti, and he did not have any real luck with his operas for nearly a decade thereafter. Finally, in August 1826, he had a real hit with *Marie* (which became one of the most popular operas of the era) at the Opéra-Comique, where, at the end of that year, he was appointed vocal coach. Among his duties there was the composition of ballets. One such effort, *La Somnambule (The Sleepwalker),* provided the plot for Bellini's [1164] opera *La Sonnambula* four years later, in 1831; another, in which Hérold incorporated popular songs, *La Fille mal gardée (The Poorly Guarded Girl),* has survived to this day.

In 1827 Hérold married Adèle Élise Rollet. Four years later he produced one of his finest and, ultimately, most enduring works, *Zampa ou La Fiancée de marbre, (Zampa, or The Marble Bride*—not inspired by Mme. Hérold, who bore him three children). Unfortunately, economic necessity shut down the Opéra-Comique for reorganization shortly afterward, and the composer was not permitted to see the work's real triumph. Almost immediately he began work on *Le Pré aux clercs (The Dueling-Ground),* but by the

time it was finished political and financial upheavals forestalled its production. It was finally premiered with great success in December. A month later Hérold died, nine days before his forty-second birthday. On his deathbed he remarked that he was just beginning to understand what opera was all about. Fromental Halévy [1157] completed his *Ludovic,* which, however, made no waves. *Zampa* disappeared from the repertoire after fifty years; *La Pré* remained popular until the turn of this century. Besides his operas, Hérold wrote 4 piano concerti, 2 symphonies, 3 string quartets, and much piano music, all of which still awaits possible revival.

RECORDINGS: The overture to *Zampa* may still be featured at concerts-in-the-park and has been frequently recorded, but little else from that opera has reached records, save for one of the protagonist's arias which survives in a remarkable rendition by Mattia Battistini. Early singers sometimes waxed numbers from *La Pré aux clercs,* and there is a modern but undistinguished record of highlights. John Lanchbery has recorded his own adaptation of *La Fille mal gardée,* and Jean-François Paillard conducts a brief *Caprice* for piano and strings.

[1137] CZERNY, Carl (Chär'-nē, Kärl)
PIANIST, TEACHER, WRITER
BORN: Vienna, February 21, 1791
DIED: Vienna, July 15, 1857

Any piano student subjected to the Czerny études would be hard put to imagine their composer as an interesting person—and indeed, though his friends found him warm, there was more than a little of the mechanic and pedant about him. Yet his influence on the pianistic art (to the present!) is incalculable, and he was a more considerable composer than one might have guessed. His Czech father, Wenzel or Václav, came to Vienna in 1750 and set up as a piano teacher. Shortly after Carl, his only child, arrived, the elder Czerny took his family to Poland, where he had been hired as piano teacher to a noble family. But the foreign invasions that led to the second partition of Poland soon drove them back to Vienna, where Carl developed remarkable pianistic skill under his father's tutelage. In 1801, Czerny *père* persuaded the violinist Wenzel Krumpholtz, brother of the harpist [925], to introduce him and Carl to Beethoven [1063]. Years later, Carl recalled climbing endless stairs, a slovenly servant, a messy room with lots of musical people sitting around it, and an unshaven Beethoven who somehow made him think of Robinson Crusoe. After tossing off a Mozart [992] concerto, the boy (carefully coached in advance) delighted the great man with a performance of his "Pathétique" sonata, and a rendition of the song "Adelaide," with Wenzel Czerny providing the vocals.

Beethoven enthusiastically accepted Czerny as his student, and he was closer, perhaps, only to Ferdinand Ries [1116]. He worked him through Emanuel Bach's [801] method and through endless exercises. Czerny also profited by hearing Hummel [1091] play, and, later, by getting to know Clementi [977]. Beethoven marveled at his eidetic memory: in 1805, for example, having heard Beethoven play large chunks of Gluck's [803] *Iphigénie en Tauride* for guests one day, Czerny played them back to him on the next. But Beethoven also deplored his failure to use written scores when performing. In 1804, however, teacher and pupil agreed that the latter was ready to take on Europe, and Czerny mapped out an extensive tour. But the military-political situation did not permit it even to start, and though he played occasionally in concert in Vienna and gave musical at-homes, he soon decided that he was not constitutionally suited to the life of a virtuoso.

Czerny was soon able to pick only those students he considered promising. Among them were Heller [1229], Alfred Jaëll ("our good fat Jaëll," Bülow [1310] dubbed him), Theodor Kullak, Thalberg [1220], and Theodor Leschetizky. Leschetizky in turn became one of the most successful of all piano teachers and, through his pupils, passed on the Czerny heritage right down to today. Czerny continued to live with his adored parents. He never married, and his chief social outlet was a daily walk to Diabelli's [1100], to pick up the latest musical news and gossip. Though he became wealthy, he was not much interested in money and often traded Diabelli his own compositions for other music. His lessons occupied him from early morning until late evening. In 1820 Adam Liszt brought him his nine-year-old son Franz [1218] from Hungary. Czerny was so impressed by the child's raw talent and so depressed by the bad training he had had from his father that he took him on for free. Since he felt that Liszt merited special attention, he scheduled his lessons for last in his teaching day so that they could be expanded when necessary.

At the same time, in the interstices of his life, Czerny was composing like mad. The opus numbers eventually ran to nearly 900, the individual compositions allegedly to around 2,000. He is said to have operated a

sort of assembly line: in his studio, several desks each held a work in progress. Completing a page of one, he would move on to the next, and so on. By the time he got back to desk No. 1, the ink would have dried, and he could turn the page. Beyond the general round of activities, the notable events of his life were few. In 1827 he carried a torch at Beethoven's funeral. Nine years later he left Vienna for the first time since childhood, to visit Leipzig, and in 1837 he ventured to London and Paris (where he found Liszt's mature virtuosity "wild"). By the early 1840s he was having problems with his health, which may account for a journey to Italy in 1846. After his parents died, he shared his home with an ever-growing pride of cats. By 1850 he was semi-invalid. Before his death at sixty-six, he methodically divided up his wealth among various charities and musical organizations.

Though he wrote music in most of the current instrumental forms (plus some choral works), made innumerable arrangements and editions, and published several theoretical and musico-historical books, Czerny is now chiefly known for his many piano exercises, which are still used. (Note: The publisher Josef Czerný, who (like Carl) also contributed a variation to the collection Diabelli invited on his waltz theme, seems not to have been related.)

RECORDINGS: Vivian Harvey Slater has done Czerny particular homage by recording the *Schools of Velocity* and *Finger-Dexterity* as well as some individual piano pieces. There is also a disc of such works from Hans Kann, and a set of concerted variations on Haydn's Austrian hymn from Felicja Blumental. Hilde Somer offers a rendition of the Op. 7 piano sonata and the Op. 377 *Fantasie et Variations*. Other recordings include a Concerto in C Major for Piano, four hands (Jean and Kenneth Wentworth) and *Divertissement* for piano and orchestra (Michael Ponti).

[1138] VOŘÍŠEK, Jan Václav (Vôr'-zhi-shek, Yàn Vä'-tslâf)
PIANIST, CONDUCTOR, LAWYER, CIVIL SERVANT
BORN: Vamberk, May 11, 1791
DIED: Vienna, November 19, 1825

Johann Hugo Worzischek (as he came to be known) was the third and youngest of that trio of forgotten Czechs—the other were J. L. Dussek [1016] and Tomášek [1080]—who influenced the First Vienna School and the Romantic movement generally. The son of a village schoolmaster-organist, he became a child prodigy in his homeland. He served as organist at the Prague Gymnasium from 1810 to 1813, then took up the study of law at the university, while he took private lessons with Tomášek and became known as a pianist around Prague. After graduating, he went to Vienna, drawn by his admiration for Beethoven [1063], in the peripheries of whose circle he moved thereafter. His knowledge of law got him a clerkship in the War Office, and he underwent further studies with Hummel [1091], whose student clientele he inherited when Hummel left on tour in 1816. In 1818 he was appointed conductor of the Society of the Friends of Music, founded five years before by Josef Sonnleithner, and it was probably as a member of the Sonnleithner circle that he exerted an impact on Schubert [1153] and vice versa. In 1822 he left the War Office to become assistant court organist, and moved up to the top spot the year following. By then he was already quite ill with tuberculosis, which he perhaps acquired during his student years in Prague. Neither a vacation at Graz nor the ministrations of Beethoven's personal physician helped his condition, and he died at thirty-four. He was buried (without music, as he had specified) in the Währing Cemetery, which, in 1925, was dug up to make Franz Schubert Park. Voříšek did not write a great deal. Apart from a Mass, a few motets, and one symphony, his music involved the piano. RECORDINGS: There are recordings of the Symphony in D Major by Sir Charles Mackerras and by the conductorless Prague Chamber Orchestra. Václav Snitil has recorded the Rondo and the Sonata for Violin and Piano, Vladimir Pleshakov a piano sonata, and Rudolf Firkusny one of the piano impromptus.

[1139] GABRIELSKI, Johann Wilhelm (Gà-brē-el'-skē, Yō'-hàn Vil'-helm)
FLUTIST
BORN: Berlin, May 27, 1791
DIED: Berlin, September 18, 1846

The son of a Polish couple, Gabrielski played flute in the Prussian court orchestra from the age of twenty-five until his death. After 1825 he shared his music stand with his younger brother and pupil Julius (1806–78). He wrote sonatas and concerti for flute. RECORDINGS: F. Charles Adler has recorded his *March and Trio* for toy instruments and orchestra, which Gabrielski intended as an addition to "Haydn's" (that is, Leopold Mozart's [816]) *Toy Symphony.*

[1140] MÜLLER, Johann Peter (Mü'-ler, Yō'-hàn Pä'-ter)
CHORAL DIRECTOR, CLERIC
BORN: Kesselstadt, June 9, 1791
DIED: Langen, August 29, 1877

Peter Müller came from a Hessian village near Darmstadt which attained a measure of notoriety when an alleged death mask of Shakespeare turned up there. Müller was known for his popular male chorus pieces, but he also wrote chamber and keyboard music. At forty-eight he became the village parson in nearby Staden. He died thirty-eight years later in Langen, a few miles from his boyhood home. RECORDINGS: The Richards Quintet has recorded three of his wind quintets.

[1141] MOZART, Franz Xaver Wolfgang (Mōt'-zart, Frànts Eks-à'-ver Vulf'-gàng)
PIANIST, TEACHER
BORN: Vienna, July 26, 1791
DIED: Carlsbad, July 29, 1844

When Wolfgang Amadeus Mozart [992] died, he left two children—Karl Thomas (age seven) and Franz Xaver Wolfgang (age four months). Karl Thomas studied with J. L. Dussek [1016] and Asioli [1057] but did not pursue a musical career. His brother, who came to be known as "Wolfgang Amadeus," studied with several teachers, including Albrechtsberger [889], Hummel [1091], and (oddly) his father's supposed rival Salieri [966]. When Franz Xaver was not yet sixteen, he went to Lemberg (now Lwów or Lvov) to teach the children of a noble Polish family and later established a private clientele there. In 1819 he went on an extended concert tour of central Europe, returning in 1822. He founded the St. Cecilia Choral Society at Lemberg in 1826. Twelve years later, however, he removed permanently to Vienna, where he received several honors. He was well regarded in his day as both a performer and composer, though his adoption of his father's name has perhaps stood in his way since. RECORDINGS: Recordings show him a better than average composer of his time. They include the first of 2 piano concerti (by Marylène Dosse), the Op. 1 piano quartet (Genser-Winkler Quartet), and the *Grande Sonate,* Op. 19, for violin (Gidon Kremer) or cello (George Neikrug).

[1142] MEYERBEER, Giacomo (né Jakob Liebmann Beer) (Mī'-er-bâr, Jă'-kō-mō)
PIANIST
BORN: Vogelsdorf, September 5, 1791
DIED: Paris, May 2, 1864

Grand opera, a subgenre that aims at large-scale theatricality and is said to have begun with Auber's *La Muette de Portici* [1103] in 1828, found its chief successful exponent in Meyerbeer, without whom Wagner [1230] probably would have not developed in the way he did. Yet for all his success, Meyerbeer had many detractors in his own day (chiefly because he was Jewish and rich) and latterly has suffered great neglect. (Efforts to revive him, however, have, even with heroic measures, proved largely unsuccessful.) Ironically, Meyerbeer came to opera in a roundabout way, produced surprisingly few examples, and did not particularly care for it.

Meyerbeer's father Jakob was a successful capitalist who was, as they say, "in sugar." His mother, Amalia, was the daughter of the banker Leibmann Meyer Wulf, who was in charge of the Prussian national lottery. Like that of the Mendelssohns [1200], their Berlin home was a place where the elite met, including members of the royal family, whose piano teacher Franz Lauska became young Jakob's. The boy began playing in public at eleven and won the approval of the visiting Clementi [977]. Three years later he began composition lessons with Zelter [1008] but in 1807 switched to Bernard Aloysius Weber (unrelated to Carl Maria [1124]), successful writer of operas, sometime virtuoso on the xänorphika, and at the time *Kapellmeister* of the Royal Theater. After producing his pupil's maiden ballet, *Der Fischer und das Milchmädchen (The Fisherman and the Milkmaid)* in 1810, Weber shipped him off to Darmstadt for finishing by his own teacher, Abt Vogler [960].

At this point in his career, composition was only a secondary consideration to the young musician. His pianistic prowess had inspired his maternal grandfather to settle on him a lifetime annuity of 300,000 francs, with the sole *proviso* that he add the name "Meyer" to his own. (The two elements were at first hyphenated.) In Darmstadt he lived in Vogler's home and found several lifetime friends among his fellow pupils, including Carl Maria von Weber. But he was impatient to get on with his career, and, after a little more than a year and a half, left for Munich. There his first opera, *Jephthas Gelübde (Jephtha's Sacrifice)*, all full of Voglerian learning, was performed at the

end of 1812 and not repeated. A *Singspiel* entitled *Wirt und Gast (Host and Guest)*, premiered in Stuttgart three weeks later was, if anything, less successful. Shortly afterward, Meyer-Beer, thanks to Vogler, discovered that he was officially composer to Ludwig X of Hesse-Darmstadt—a title long on prestige and short on responsibility. It did not, however, save the revised *Singspiel*, produced in Vienna in the fall of 1814 as *Die beiden Kalifen (The Two Caliphs)*. Another, *Das Brandenburger Thor (The Brandenburg Gate)*, written the previous spring, was not even produced, having reached Berlin too late for the victory celebration in which it was supposed to be featured. Depressed about his own playing after hearing Hummel's [1091], Meyerbeer had reached the lowest ebb of his career.

After visiting Paris and London, Meyerbeer betook himself to Naples in 1816 to collect folksongs and experience Italian music on the hoof. A year later, however, *Romilda e Costanze*, an attempt at *opera seria*, won sufficient success in Padua to persuade him to stay on for nine years as a composer of Italian operas (during which period he became "Giacomo"). It was his most productive period, resulting in six operas. (At least three more were unfinished or unproduced.) The climax came with *Il Crociato in Egitto (The Crusade in Egypt)*, written for Giovanni Battista Vellucci, the last of the great castrati, and premiered in Venice in 1819. It was quickly picked up in major European capitals and established Meyerbeer as an important opera composer. In 1825 he went, for the French premiere, to Paris, which was to be the scene of his subsequent triumphs. A month later his father died, leaving him even wealthier. In May 1826, following the success of his (revised) *Margherita d'Angiù*—the original dates from 1820—Meyerbeer married his cousin, Minna Mosson. (Their only children, a boy and a girl, both died shortly after birth.)

With success—and perhaps immortality—virtually assured, Meyerbeer encountered the first of his several fallow periods. *La Nymphe de Danube*, planned as a vehicle for his greatest (Italian) hits, never got off the ground. He was unable to make anything of the fragments of Weber's *Die drei Pintos*, with whose completion his late friend had entrusted him. An *opéra-comique* to be called *Robert le diable* refused to jell, and a gallicization of the *Crociato* came slowly. The consecutive successes of Auber's *La Muette* and Rossini's [1143] *Guillaume Tell* convinced Meyerbeer that he was barking up the wrong tree. The public had developed a taste not only for grand opera, but also for the supernatural, replete with vampires, willies, and necrophilia. To suit that taste, Meyerbeer converted *Robert le diable* into a through-composed grand opera. Its debut in November 1831 elicited a hysteria such as Paris had never seen; some years later Heine told Meyerbeer that he thought it a major turning point in musical history. The composer was awarded the *Légion d'honneur,* and was elected to the Institute and to the Prussian Academy. But *Robert* proved a hard act to follow. He quarreled with the Opéra management and Scribe over the form of *Le Portefaix (The Stevedore)* and abandoned it. He quarreled with Alexandre Dumas, the scheduled librettist for *Les Brigands* and did not start it. He plugged away at *La Saint-Barthélemy (The Saint Bartholomew's Massacre),* was unable to meet his 1833 deadline (in part because of health problems that were to prove chronic), and was fined 30,000 francs (which was later returned to him by Director Véron when he discovered that the Opéra was about to dispense with his services). After further tinkering with the libretto and some skirmishes with the censors, Meyerbeer finally completed the piece in 1835, and in February 1836, as *Les Huguenots,* it enjoyed one of the greatest of all operatic triumphs. Meyerbeer may not have liked opera, but he was a connoisseur of singers, and he tailored the work to his cast, which included the tenor Adolphe Nourrit (who committed suicide three years later) and the soprano Marie-Cornélie Falcon (whose remarkable voice broke down when she was not yet twenty-five).

Paris had to wait thirteen years for a *Huguenots* successor. After discussing an *opéra-comique,* to be entitled *Cinq-Mars,* Scribe and Meyerbeer settled on *Le Prophète,* having to do with the Anabaptist uprising in Holland in the 1530s. This they soon put aside for *L'Africaine,* loosely based on the story of the explorer Vasco da Gama, intended for La Falcon. But the sudden end of her career left them in limbo. In 1839, while sea bathing at Boulogne for his health, Meyerbeer encountered Richard Wagner, come to France to find a producer for his as-yet-unfinished *Rienzi* and without a franc to his name. The older man, who had ignored his epistolary importunings, was friendly, opened doors for him in Paris, and lent him money. But when he failed to win immediate acceptance, Wagner undertook a campaign of scurrility about the rich Jew. Meyerbeer, getting wind of it, terminated the relationship—though privately he spoke well of Wagner's operas as long as he lived.

In 1842 the Prussian crown prince, a ha-

bitué of the Beer home in his youth, became Frederick William IV and chose Meyerbeer to succeed Spontini [1081] as his chief music director. The composer was honored with a production of *Les Huguenots,* which had theretofore been banned as anti-royalist. The following year, the Royal Opera burned down, and Meyerbeer was asked to write a new work for its reopening. The result was *Ein Feldlager in Schlesien (An Army Camp in Silesia),* premiered in December 1844. The plot was Scribe's, the librettist Meyerbeer's sometime enemy, the critic Ludwig Rellstab, some of whose lyrics Franz Schubert [1153] had set in his last year. The star was Jenny Lind. The determinedly "German" work succeeded nowhere but in Germany (it appeared, much revised, in Vienna, as *Vielka* in 1847). But the Berlin appointment produced little else, and, on the losing end of a power struggle, Meyerbeer resigned in 1848.

Meanwhile another proposed collaboration with Scribe, *Noëma,* came to nothing. What finally sent Meyerbeer back to the long dormant *Prophète* was the remarkable contralto voice of Pauline Viardot, the younger daughter of Manuel Garcia, Rossini's original Count Almaviva. Though he had actually finished the opera sometime since, he revised it for her, greatly enlarging the role of Fidès, the prophet's mother. It reached the stage of the Opéra in April 1849 and was another unqualified triumph—though some complained at the idea of having a religious fanatic for the protagonist. (Though his major operas were few, they made the composer even wealthier with each increment, and there were few private citizens in his time who had more money than he.)

It took Meyerbeer only five years to produce his next work, *L'Étoile du Nord (The North Star)*—largely because it was a re-working of the *Feldlager* music to a new "Scribretto." Even so, the composer dawdled, returning now and again to the interminable *Africaine.* Though, when it was finally played in February 1854, the new work seemed almost as successful as its predecessors, it remained the least known of Meyerbeer's Paris operas. Once it was out of the way, he acquired a new libretto, *Judith,* from Scribe, but almost immediately he put it aside to work on an *opéra-comique* to a libretto by Jules Barbier. This emerged in 1859 as *Le Pardon de Ploërmel (The Pilgrimage of Ploërmel,* popularly called "Dinorah"), another colossal hit. Meyerbeer then returned once more to *L'Africaine,* but again veered off to write music for a play about Goethe which never got played. While he was occupied with that in 1861, Scribe died; a year later, Scribe's widow collected 10,000 francs from him as a penalty for his failure to complete *Judith.*

By 1862 Meyerbeer's health was in serious decline. Nevertheless, hearing that Verdi [1232], his most formidable rival, was to conduct a new work (the *Inno delle nazioni)* at the Crystal Palace Exposition in London, he cobbled up a *Festival Overture* and went thither to conduct it. Urged on by the Emperor Napoleon III, he now settled down in earnest to complete *L'Africaine,* and by the spring of 1864 it was in rehearsal. But soon after rehearsals started, he was suddenly taken ill and died. There were state funerals in both Paris and Berlin, and a year later there was a final triumphant Meyerbeer premiere. Most of his mature operas continued to hold the stage into the first decade of this century, then faded out. Whether modern producers can successfully overcome their fustian plots and their playing to the gallery remains to be seen. (Meyerbeer's manuscripts disappeared after his death.)

RECORDINGS: Only two Meyerbeer operas, *Prophète* and *Huguenots,* have received commercial recordings, though excerpts have always been plentiful, especially from earlier singers. There are, however, "private" versions of everything from *Il Crociato* on, with the exception of the *Feldlager.* Dietrich Fischer-Dieskau has enterprisingly recorded an LP of some interesting Meyerbeer songs.

[1143] ROSSINI, Gioacchino (Rōs-sē'-nē, Jō-äk-kē'-nō)
CONDUCTOR, IMPRESARIO
BORN: Pesaro, February 29, 1792
DIED: Paris, November 13, 1868

It appears that Rossini was a very complex man. But though we know a good deal about his life, the facts that we have tantalize and frustrate rather than illuminate. His maturity falls into three clearly defined periods: (1) the productive era—not quite twenty years—for which the outstanding data are a catalog of the operas; (2) a time of illness, both physical and mental, about which such information as we have (much of it clinical) asks as many questions as it answers; (3) resurgent old age, the time when Rossini was the musical Buddha of Paris, the period when the real man is largely obscured by the anecdotes. Repeated attempts to explain the early retirement at the height of a spectacular career have never entirely succeeded. Though there is ample evidence that Rossini was thoughtful, generous, and magnetic, his relations with those closest to him remain an

enigma. One senses a person of penetrating intelligence who saw the absurdity of human existence with painful clarity and countered it with wit—or withdrawal. There is no doubt that, for better or worse, he revolutionized opera—gave it the modern orchestra, dictated the ornaments previously left to the improvisation of the singers, insisted that the genre was drama, provided much of the impetus for "grand opera," and helped make Paris the world center of opera it became in the mid-nineteenth century. But one suspects that, like Thomas Mann, he saw his talent as chicanery and was half ashamed of it. Yet the persistent image one retains is that of the late portraits—the Roman-nosed, wry-mouthed Falstaff, his wiglet perched precariously on the top of his head, basking, tolerantly amused, in his affluence and popularity.

There is a legend that the Rossini ancestors were both affluent and noble, but the known family tree dead-ends with his great-grandfather, a laborer of Fano. Rossini's father, something of a conman and known as "Vivazza" (Peppy), finagled his way into the job of Pesarese town trumpeter and maintained it by some political legerdemain that gave him a reputation as a revolutionary in revolutionary times. He took quarters in the home of a baker, Domenico Guidarini, who had two daughters. The younger daughter had got on the police blotter for soliciting, and by the fall of 1791 Vivazza had got the older one, Anna, in the family way, and married her. Five months later (on leap day), Gioacchino was born. Within six years he was playing triangle in the town band and his parents had embarked on an operatic career of sorts. The father, Antonio, played horn in the orchestras of ephemeral companies, and Anna, a seamstress by trade and a musical illiterate, sang secondary roles. When they toured, the boy stayed behind with the Guidarinis and attended the local school. There boredom led him to mischief, for which he was often sentenced to blowing up the forge for a local blacksmith. Then for a time he was apprenticed to a butcher in Bologna, where he picked up a grasp of keyboard playing from a certain Prinetti, famous for sleeping bolt upright in dark street corners. When he was ten, Rossini's family moved back to Fano, where two wealthy canons gave him voice lessons and the run of a fine musical library. Two years later, after Anna had lost her voice, the Rossinis settled in Bologna, where the fourteen-year-old Gioacchino was admitted to the Liceo Musicale to study with Padre Mattei and elected to the Accademia Filarmonica. He soon began to pick up loose change as a soprano both in churches and theaters (but turned down a chance to become a castrato) and as a continuo player. (By the time he entered the Liceo, he had already turned out a number of compositions, including the 6 enchanting *sonate a 4.)* In 1807 he first heard, at a concert, the Spanish soprano Isabella Colbran (age twenty-two), who was later to become his wife. In the same year, he met the singing Mobelli family, which commissioned from him an opera, *Demetrio e Polibio,* which he wrote piecemeal but was not performed until 1812. Two years prior to that date, despite Padre Mattei's pleadings, Rossini decided he had enough musical book learning and quit school.

Soon afterward, the manager of the Teatro San Moise in Venice found himself in dire need of a one-act piece. Rossini forthwith turned out a farce, *La Cambiale di matrimonio (The Marital Bill of Sale),* which brought him success and 200 lire. For another year he plugged away as continuo player and coach, and then in October 1811 he enjoyed another Venetian success with *L'Equivoco stravagante (The Strange Misunderstanding).* Some imagined naughtiness in the libretto got it quickly closed down, but it provided, with minor changes, an overture that did for *Aureliano in Palmira, Elisabetta,* and *Il Barbiere di Siviglia (The Barber of Seville).* During the next year, in which he turned twenty and probably picked up the case of gonorrhea that plagued him for much of the rest of his life, Rossini turned out no fewer than 6 operas, the climax coming with the triumph of *La Pietra del paragone (The Touchstone)* at La Scala, Milan, in the summer. Three others were fair successes—*L'Inganno felice (The Happy Deception), Demetrio e Polibio,* and *L'Occasione fa il ladro (Opportunity Makes the Thief);* the others—*Ciro in Babilonia (Cyrus in Babylon)* and *La Scala di seta (The Silken Ladder)* failed. The year 1813 began with the brilliant farce *Il Signor Bruschino* in Milan, and proceeded a month later to *Tancredi* in Venice. Like most of Rossini's initial serious efforts, this one got off to a slow start but within a short time caught on; and one aria, "*Di tanti palpiti,"* became the rage of all Italy. (The fact that Rossini's melodies were infectious did not hurt his popularity.) His first real runaway success came in Rome in May with *L'Italiana in Algeri (The Italian Girl in Algiers).* The Italians hailed him as their foremost operatic composer; the Germans thought him next only to Mayr [1034]. Rossini was twenty-one. But the next three works—*Aureliano in Palmira* and *Il Turco in Italia* in Milan and especially *Sigismondo* in Venice—were failures. In April 1815, in-

spired by Joachim Murat's futile attempt to unite Italy, Rossini wrote a hymn to independence for performance in Bologna; it made him a target for the Austrian secret police for many years thereafter.

Soon, however, Domenico Barbaja, a noted impresario and the current lover of Isabella Colbran, had lured him to Naples—against strong opposition to "the northerner"—to be director of the Teatri San Carlo and del Fondo. One of his chief tasks there was to write two *serie* a year for Colbran. His first such effort, *Elisabetta, regina d'Inghilterra (Elizabeth, Queen of England)* —in which, incidentally, he abandoned *secco* recitative—managed to disarm even his harshest opponents. In December (still in 1815) Rossini went to Rome for the opening of his *Torvaldo e Dorliska,* for which the Romans didn't much care. While there, the composer signed a contract for a new comedy for the Teatro di Torre Argentina. After some vacillation, he settled on a treatment by Cesare Sterbini of Beaumarchais' *Le Barbier de Séville.* In a letter he begged old Paisiello's [914] blessing and, to avoid confusing the public, advertised his own version as *Almaviva.* (It became *Il Barbiere di Siviglia* when it was premiered in Bologna in summer 1816.) Rossini dashed the score off in two weeks. The omens were unpropitious— the San Carlo burned down back in Naples, and the manager of the Torre Argentina was felled by a stroke. On February 20, 1816, the house was packed with people hostile to Rossini or to his encroachment on Paisiello's territory; in the course of the performance one of the bassos incurred a nosebleed in a fall, a cat made an unscheduled entrance and refused to leave, and Rossini angered the audience by ostentatiously applauding the singers (he had to escape by a back door). The following night's performance established the piece as a masterwork. Rossini stayed away, and when a crowd of well-wishers came after the show to serenade him, he thought they had lynching in mind.

Back in Naples in September *La Gazzetta (The Newspaper),* largely a pastiche of *Il Turco* and other pre-Naples operas, was a dismal failure. It was counterbalanced by the success of *Otello* (written for Colbran) in December. Audiences had more reservations about the tragic ending than they did about the Marchese Berio's mangling of Shakespeare. Rossini's third act showed significant progress toward a unified musicodramatic structure, and the work held the stage until it was ousted by Verdi's [1232] version seventy years later. Immediately after the premiere, Rossini returned to Rome to produce another comedy, about which he had not even thought. But by the start of the new year, 1817, with some more self-plagiarism and the help of one Luca Agolini, he had *La Cenerentola (Cinderella)* well in hand. Like *Il Barbiere*, it survived a stormy first night on January 21 and went on to great success. It was Rossini's last *opera buffa*. (Though *La Gazza ladra [The Thieving Magpie]*, which opened in Milan four months later, nominally qualifies, it really belongs to the *semiseria* genre later cultivated by Bellini [1164].) Back in Naples the oddly Gluckian *Armida*, performed in November in the rebuilt Teatro San Carlo, failed because it did not offer the expected "numbers" ("too German!"); the next month *Adelaide di Borgogna* failed in Rome because, thrown together in a hurry, it deserved to. But in March Rossini redeemed himself with *Mosè in Egitto (Moses in Egypt)* one of his most powerful operas.

After that, Rossini went back to Pesaro for a festival in his honor in the newly rebuilt theater. The trip was a disaster. The promoter went bankrupt, Rossini affronted the castoff Charlotte, Princess of Wales, now a local resident, by turning down her invitation to a *soirée*, he was accused of appropriating his host's wife (an odd lady), and he came down with a throat infection so serious that it was widely reported that he had died. But he recovered to write, on the commission of the Lisbon chief-of-police's son, a farce entitled *Adina;* production, for whatever reason, was, however, delayed eight years, and Rossini never saw the work. *Ricciardo e Zoraide*, hamstrung by a dreadful libretto, was a surprise hit in Naples in December, and *Ermione* a surprise failure the following March. But in April *Edoardo e Cristina*, a mishmash of snippets from earlier Rossini operas, went over well in Venice, where they had not been heard. Then, much taken with Walter Scott's *The Lady of the Lake* and with Isabella Colbran, whom Barbaja had turned over to him as mistress, he wrote for her *La Donna del lago*, which, after a decidedly qualified reception in September, soon caught on. As a Christmas present, in 1819 Milan got another pastiche, *Bianca e Falliero*. After that, the pace of Rossini's output began to slow. His only opera in 1820 was *Maometto II;* moving toward grand opera, with much use of chorus and ensemble, it was not to the taste of Neapolitan connoisseurs of vocal athletics. *Matilde di Shabran*, a patchwork *semiseria* and the only operatic offering in 1821 (February), occasioned fisticuffs in the Teatro Argentina during that Carnival in which the plump Rossini and the cadaverous Paganini [1106] went masquerading as beggarwomen.

That December Barbaja was appointed manager of the Kärntnertortheater in Vienna and left Rossini to his own devices. In February 1822 Rossini said goodbye to Naples with *Zelmira*. Then he and Colbran took off for Vienna, pausing near Bologna on March 16 to legalize their union. She brought him a dowry worth a quarter of a million dollars by modern standards. (Soon afterward her voice began to go, she turned into a compulsive gambler and a nag, and the marriage went sour.) In Vienna Rossini heard Weber [1124]—who detested Rossini's music—conduct the *Freischütz*. Rossini conducted several of his own operas there and was accorded the frenzied reception of some latter-day "superstar." He met Beethoven [1063], who urged him to stick to comedy. The Rossinis spent the autumn, at the behest of Metternich, in Verona, amusing the crowned heads gathered there for the Congress of Europe. Rossini made a great hit as a singer. He had a pleasant light baritone, and his *pièce de resistance* was Figaro's *"Largo al factotum"* from *Il Barbiere*. He also got together in Bologna with the librettist Gaetano Rossi to work on *Semiramide*. First sung at the Teatro la Fenice in Venice in February 1823, it was to be his last and probably his greatest opera for Italy.

Having signed a contract to write a new work for London—it never materialized—the Rossinis went to Paris in November. Though he had enemies there (the French-Italian operatic war was far from over), Rossini was again greeted like a hero. However, the London expedition was a failure, so far as opera was concerned. For one thing, Colbran's singing was disastrous; for another the theater (King's) went bankrupt. But the visitors were handsomely rewarded for entertaining privately in the homes of the wealthy. Back in Paris by August 1824, the composer signed a 40,000-franc contract with the Ministry of the Royal Household to write two new operas. He and his wife then returned to Bologna for the summer. During their vacation, Louis XVIII died, and on their return Rossini was appointed director of the Théâtre-Italien. To celebrate the coronation of Charles X, he cobbled up the pageantlike *Il Viaggio a Reims (The Trip to Rheims)*, produced in June 1825. Older works, most notably *Cenerentola* and *Semiramide*, produced enormous enthusiasm in Paris, and a good deal of chauvinistic hostility. In his directorial capacity, Rossini imported the greatest Italian singers of the era—e.g., Lablache, Malibran, Rubini, and Tamburini—but by 1826 he had had enough and resigned. In recompense he was given the empty titles of Composer to the King

and Royal Inspector of Singing, with an annual salary of 25,000 francs. That October
his *Le Siège de Corinth,* a reworking of
Maometto II that had grand opera very
clearly in sight, stood Paris on its ear, as did
Moïse et Pharaon (a revision of *Mosè in
Egitto),* the following spring. Even a hostile
press was pleased. It may be said that these
works established in Paris the supremacy of
the Rossinian orchestral concept and mark
the triumph of Italian melody over French
declamation.

Anna Rossini died in February 1827, and
the bereaved Vivazza came to visit his son.
By then, the latter was already making
noises about retiring. What was to be his last
comedy, *Le Comte Ory* (which used much of
the music of the *Viaggio),* was first played in
August 1828 and soon conquered the initially
puzzled public. Then, having rejected
Scribe's libretti—*Gustave III,* later set by
Auber [1103]; and *La Juive (The Jewess),*
later set by Halévy [1157]—he fastened on
Étienne Jouy's treatment of Schiller's *Wilhelm Tell*—though he had it reworked by
Hippolyte Bis and Armand Marrast. While
he was working on it, he negotiated a new
contract that gave him 15,000 francs for each
new opera and a 6,000-franc annuity for life.
After some delay, *Guillaume Tell* was triumphantly produced on August 3, 1829. It remains one of the monuments of grand opera
(as a genre) and is clearly a basis for the
work of the mature Verdi. Rossini was
thirty-seven, and he never wrote another opera. He was awarded the *Légion d'honneur*
and took Colbran back to a new *palazzo* in
Bologna. There was some talk of a new
work, but when, after the Revolution of
1830, the Paris Opéra went into private
hands, Rossini disclaimed all obligation to
write for it. He did, however, sue to keep his
annuity and won in 1835. This necessitated
that he come back to Paris, and when he did
so, he left Colbran, who was becoming impossible, with his father. He did not return
to Bologna for four years. In 1831 he vacationed in Spain with his banker, Aguada,
and while there agreed to compose a *Stabat
Mater* for a cleric named Varela. But after
finishing only about half of it, he farmed the
rest out to Tadolini [1132]. The result was
performed in Madrid in 1833 and then retired. By the end of the year, Rossini's recurrent urethritis was undermining his health,
both physical and emotional. Nevertheless it
was around this time that he found a replacement for the absent Colbran in a demimondaine called Olympe Pelissier.

This Parisian stay also saw the production
of the series of charming songs known as the
Soirées musicales, and Rossini's return to the

Théâtre-Italien as part of a directorial
troika. At one point, for a young woman
named Louise Carlier, he collected an autograph album of songs by his notable contemporaries (recorded by Suzanne Danco as *Album de musique).* In the summer of 1836 he
visited Germany and made friends with Felix Mendelssohn [1200]. That fall he returned to Bologna, and a few months later
Olympe joined him in Milan, though they
maintained separate residences until Colbran's death. The aged Vivazza died in 1839.
Shortly afterward, his son, though plagued
by his chronic ailment, hemorrhoids, depression, and general debility, took on the directorship of the Liceo Musicale in Bologna.
Then, threatened with a performance of the
resurrected mongrel *Stabat Mater,* he rallied
to rewrite the Tadolini-composed segments
himself. After a triumphant performance in
Paris, Rossini persuaded Donizetti [1155] to
conduct the Italian premiere in Bologna but
could not persuade him to accept a post at
the conservatory.

The next few years were largely empty
ones, given over to physical illnesses and a
sort of paralysis of the will. Ironically Rossini was inundated with honors—a Prussian
knighthood, another from Greece, a bust at
the Liceo, a plaque over the door of his
birthplace in Pesaro, etc. By mid-1843 he
was forced to seek medical help in Paris;
three months of intensive treatment provided some relief from pain, but the lassi-
tude remained. Rossini returned to Bologna
when his wife died in 1845 and married
Olympe ten months later. But in the turmoil
of 1848, libelous statements by nationalist
hotheads hounded the couple out of Bologna. They perched uncertainly in Florence
for several years, and there in 1855 the composer reached his lowest ebb. It was then
that Olympe persuaded him to return to
Paris for good—in both senses of the word,
it turned out.

Soon, miraculously, Rossini began to recover. He began to see visitors, and, with the
help of a grateful government, bought an estate near the Bois de Boulogne, though his
real headquarters remained the apartment
on the Rue de la Chaussée d'Antin. After
two years, he began to compose again—
mostly the little pieces that he called the
"sins of old age" that occupied him for the
rest of his life. The Rossinis' Saturday evenings (always terminated at ten o'clock
sharp) came to be the focus of Parisian musical and social life—though some of the visitors had reservations about Rossini's
vaunted cuisine. Among those who came
there in 1860 were Richard Wagner [1230]
and his arch-foe, critic Eduard Hanslick. In

1863, to inaugurate the private chapel of the Count and Countess Pillet-Will, Rossini wrote his last major work, the ironically named *Petit Messe Solennelle*, a little solemn Mass that lasts for nearly two hours. In 1866–67 he orchestrated the instrumental parts, originally for two pianos and harmonium. That winter he was bothered by a persistent cough, but by March he was well enough to attend the premiere of Verdi's *Don Carlos* and to write a *Hymne* honoring Napoleon III. But he began to fail again the next winter and then went into a precipitous decline. An operation in the autumn revealed a rectal cancer. Shortly before he died, he gave his blessing to a composer named Costantino dall'Argine, who wanted to compose a *Barbiere di Siviglia*. Despite strong protests from Olympe, Verdi, and others, the city of Florence claimed his body and buried it in Santa Maria Novella.

RECORDINGS: Until recently, most people knew Rossini chiefly from corrupt performances of *Barbiere* and church-choir representations of the *Stabat Mater*. As of now, all the comedies have been recorded commercially save *Adina*. Of the serious works there have been commercial versions of *Tancredi, Elisabetta, Torvaldo, Otello, La Gazza ladra, Mosè, Semiramide, Siège de Corinth,* and *Guillaume Tell,* and piracies of some of these and *Armida, Donna del lago, Matilde Shabran,* and *Zelmira.* There are also recordings of the *Stabat Mater,* the *Petite Messe* (both versions), the 1820 *Mass,* and generous representations of the minor works, both early and late.

[1144] ALMQVIST, Carl Jonas Love
(Alm'-kvist, Kärl Yō'-nàs Lōō'-ve)
WRITER, SCHOOLMASTER
BORN: Stockholm, November 28, 1793
DIED: Bremen, September 26, 1866

Almqvist is one of the odder figures in the history of music—a highly educated and intelligent person who insisted on remaining a musical primitive on moral and aesthetic grounds. His father was a professor of theology at the University of Uppsala, where the son took a degree in philosophy before becoming a civil servant. But Almqvist was already full of the radical social thinking that was eventually to undo him. At thirty he chucked it all and went off with a group of friends to find a communal utopia in the wilderness. He did not find it and returned to the capital in 1828 to teach in an elementary school, of which he was made headmaster the following year. In 1832 he began writing his novel-cycle (if that is the proper term),

Törnrosens Bok (Thornrose's Book), a landmark in Swedish literature. A sort of attempt at a *Gesamtkunstwerk,* it is interspersed with lyrics set to Almqvist's own unaccompanied melodies—songs still beloved in Sweden. He also wrote articles on various subjects and lectured, while moving fitfully from one job to another. In the late 1840s he published 11 volumes of *Free Fantasies* for piano. (Two more were never published owing to the turn his career took shortly afterward.) For these he sought some help from his friend Adolf Fredrik Lindblad [1160], though he refused to have anything to do with formal musical theory on the grounds that it would pervert the free flow of melodic inspiration. Meanwhile he was becoming increasingly vehement in his preachment of socialism and was beginning to alienate people who had formerly admired him. Suddenly in 1851 he was convicted of forgery and charged with murder.

Almqvist managed to escape and fled to the United States, where he lived in St. Louis for over a decade. On a trip through Texas he lost the trunk containing his manuscripts to a thief. It was never recovered, though Almqvist eventually made a direct appeal to Abraham Lincoln. At the end of the Civil War, he returned to Europe, but as his status in Sweden remained unchanged he was forced to remain in Germany where he died a year after his return. Now, of course, he is among the most honored of Swedish artists. His music, a gush of water from a mountain spring, ranks him with such quasi-folk musicians as Stephen Foster.

RECORDINGS: Elisabeth Söderström has recorded some of the songs and Stig Ribbing a number of the fantasies.

[1145] HÜNTEN, Franz (Hün'-ten, Frànts)
PIANIST, TEACHER
BORN: Koblenz, December 26, 1793
DIED: Koblenz, February 22, 1878

The names of "François" Hünten and his younger friend "Henri" Herz [1170] were once household words wherever a parlor held a piano. They were also execrated by such serious musicians as Robert Schumann [1211]. Schumann's wife Clara [1267] recalled her father shredding some Hünten variations he found her playing in lieu of the prescribed Czerny [1137] etudes. Hünten's father Daniel was court organist in Koblenz, and two brothers, Wilhelm and Peter, were successful piano teachers in Germany. Daniel gave Franz lessons but forbade him a musical career. When he was twenty-six,

however, Herz talked him into studying at
the Paris Conservatoire. His teachers there
included Hyacinthe Jadin's [1058] successor,
Louis-Barthélmy Pradher, Reicha [1059],
and Cherubini [1019]. Hünten spent two
years there, then became a teacher—a calling he vastly preferred to concertizing, perhaps because it involved no travel and assured him of a more regular income. In fact,
having quickly established himself as the
darling of the salons, he became very rich.
He ground out potpourris, variations,
dances, and other ephemeral pieces suited to
the taste of the era by the yard, getting up to
200 francs a page. He also produced a piano
method that was very successful with musical governesses and the like. In 1848 he was
able to retire permanently to Koblenz and
watch the Rhine flow by for the thirty years
that remained to him. RECORDINGS: Frank
Cooper has recorded an LP side of his confections.

[1146] MOSCHELES, Ignaz (Mō'-she-les, Eg'-nátz)
PIANIST, CONDUCTOR, TEACHER
BORN: Prague, May 23, 1794
DIED: Leipzig, March 10, 1870

Beethoven's epistolary salutation, "Good,
kind Moscheles," typifies the usual reaction
to the man. Popular from the start as a piano virtuoso of the old school, Moscheles
later faded before the new fire-eaters but
continued to enjoy the deepest respect as a
conductor and teacher. A gifted child, he became the pupil and protégé of Bedřich Diviš
("Dionys") Weber, soon after the founder
and director of the Prague Conservatory.
Weber, to protect him from corruption by
modern music, forbade him access to the library, but Moscheles sneaked in anyhow,
discovered, copied, and learned Beethoven's
[1063] "Pathétique" sonata, and was forever
after its composer's apostle. At sixteen he
migrated to Vienna, where he taught piano
and studied with Albrechtsberger [889] and
Salieri [966]. In 1814 he was assigned to
make the piano score of Fidelio, on which he
worked under the composer's supervision.
(His diary reports Beethoven hopping out of
bed to scan the latest increment before an
open window, unaware of the crowd gathering below to observe his deshabille.)
For the next dozen years, Moscheles
toured as a performer, making a particular
hit with his flashy variations on something
called the Alexander March; it is said that he
came to loathe them much as Rachmaninoff
[1638] did his own C-sharp minor prelude.
Moscheles was especially popular in Lon-

don, where he was hailed by Clementi [977]
and appeared en duo with "Glorious John"
Cramer [1067]. In Berlin, in 1824, Moscheles
was one of the cultural lions invited to the
Mendelssohn soirées (his origins too were
Jewish) and there began a lifelong friendship
with Felix [1200], even though the latter was
less than half his age. He volunteered to
teach the youngster but soon discovered that
Mendelssohn was beyond his powers.
In 1825 Moscheles married Charlotte
Embden (posthumously his biographer) and
then settled in London, where he remained
at the center of its musical life for twenty
years. He taught, concertized, and played in
the fashionable salons (where he often insisted on playing the late Beethoven sonatas.
Acquainted with most of the leading musical
lights of Europe, Moscheles became a sort of
one-man welcoming committee. Early a
member of the Philharmonic Society, he
served as its co-director for a time and specialized in conducting Beethoven. It was at
Moscheles' behest that the Society sent Beethoven a gift of 100 pounds in 1827. Two
years later, Moscheles was able to tender an
enthusiastic welcome to his sometime pupil,
Mendelssohn, on the first of several visits. In
London the two sometimes appeared in concert together. This time Mendelssohn noted
the fun they had rehearsing his Concerto in
E Major for 2 Pianos "in Clementi's piano
factory," devising exploitive cadenzas and
betting how long the applause would last. At
another concert, some years later, the participants in a Bach three-keyboard concerto
were Moscheles, Mendelssohn, and Clara
Wieck, who was not yet Clara Schumann
[1267]. After 1840, however, Moscheles,
finding himself regarded as old hat, made
few concert appearances.
When Mendelssohn, in 1843, put the
wheels in motion that produced the Leipzig
Conservatory, he chose Moscheles to be his
professor of piano. The Moscheles settled
there in 1846. One October afternoon the
next year, they took Mendelssohn, who was
complaining of feeling "gray on gray," for a
walk. That night he was felled by a stroke
and died less than a month later. Grief-
stricken, Moscheles made the success of the
Conservatory his particular responsibility,
and turned it into the most influential such
institution in Europe in his time there.
Among his early pupils was the first winner
of the Mendelssohn Prize, Arthur Sullivan
[1397].
A transitional figure—a Classical throwback in a Romantic world—Moscheles had
some curious blindspots. He, of course,
adored Beethoven and became a great proponent of Schumann [1211]; he deplored

Chopin [1208], at least until he heard him play his own music, and was mystified by Liszt [1218]. His own music ranges from parlor bonbons to seriously intended studies, concerti (8), and sonatas (6).

RECORDINGS: Michael Ponti has recorded the G-minor concerto, Mary Louise Boehm that in C major, the Consortium Classicum a sextet and a septet (both designated as "grand"), and the Boehm sisters the four-hand piano sonata (which Moscheles and his daughter Emilie played before King Louis Philippe). There are also recorded programs of piano pieces by Ponti, Noël Lee, and Philip Challis.

[1147] MARSCHNER, Heinrich August
    (Marsh'-ner, Hīn'-rikh Ou'-goost)
    PIANIST, CONDUCTOR
    BORN: Zittau, August 16, 1795
    DIED: Hannover, December 14, 1861

To judge from a mid-life portrait, Marschner, the chief link between Weber [1124] and Wagner [1230], looked more perhaps like a prosperous grocer than a self-styled Romantic or a man whose life was dogged by hard luck and tragedy. His petit bourgeois father came to Zittau from Bohemia and there indulged his love of music by playing the flute and the harp and conducting the local band. Young Heinrich sang in the *Gymnasium* choir, learned to play the piano, and was soon happily composing, with only instinct to tell him musical right from wrong. An early attempt at opera, *Die Kindsmörderin (The Child Murderess,* now lost), indicated the direction he would take. At last, sensing that he knew very little about the science of composition, he took lessons from one Karl Hering, music master of the Zittau teachers' college. By the time he went off to Leipzig in 1813 to study law, he was good enough to attract the attention and aid of the Thomasschule cantor, J. G. Schicht. When his bagatelles for guitar won publication, Marschner opted for music and took off on a concert tour as a pianist.

In his travels Marschner encountered a Count de Varkony, a Hungarian Maecenas, who sent him off to Vienna to meet Beethoven [1063]—in whose presence Marschner said he felt like a hick encountering Cologne Cathedral. In 1816, through Varkony, he was employed by a Count Zichy to teach his children in Pressburg (Bratislava), where he became *Kapellmeister* to a Prince Krasatzkowitz. Imagining himself at last on solid financial ground, he married his fiancée, Emilie von Cerva, in 1817; she died before the year was out. Two years later he married

Franziska Jäggi, herself a pianist and composer, and shortly afterward Weber produced Marschner's *Heinrich IV und d'Aubigné* in Dresden. The composer settled there in 1821 but, unable to find a post, he began negotiations in 1824 with the Amsterdam Opera. Fearing to lose him, the Dresden officials, over Weber's protests, offered him Morlacchi's [1114] job. While the question was in abeyance, Franziska died in 1825, followed by Weber a year later. Though Marschner had been serving as the latter's deputy, he suddenly found himself passed over.

Assuaging his domestic loneliness by marrying the soprano Marianne Wohlbrück, Marschner again hit the concert trail until, in 1827, he found a place at the Leipzig Opera. The following year he successfully produced his first important opera, *Der Vampyr* (libretto by his brother-in-law, Wilhelm August Wohlbrück, after the Gothic tale by John Polidori). The 1829 London production ran for sixty nights. *Vampyr* is said to have been the first important opera featuring an accursed protagonist, which device relates it to Wagner's *Fliegende Holländer*. In 1829 the brothers-in-law drew from Walter Scott's *Ivanhoe* for another great success, *Der Templar und die Jüdin (The Templar and the Jewess),* in which Marianne created the female lead. Two years later the great baritone, Eduard Devrient, ruined his voice by attempting to sing the Berlin premiere while suffering from laryngitis. That year Marschner became director of the court opera in Hannover. Devrient, who apparently did not hold his misfortune against the composer, offered him a libretto, *Hans Heiling* (which Mendelssohn [1200] had turned down), and in 1833, to the enthusiastic welcome of an audience that included Mendelssohn, it was produced in Berlin with Devrient's brother, Emil, in the title role. (He survived.) This work in particular influenced Wagner and still holds the stage in Germany.

Hans Heiling's success and offers from other places, notably Copenhagen, helped smooth over Marschner's quarrels with the Hannover officials and gave him a long-term contract. He became immensely popular, especially for his male choruses, songs, and other *Hausmusik,* but despite his passionate and effective promotion of the German musical stage, his operatic output declined. (He was to write only five more such works, none of which have lasted.)

Up to 1837, Hannover had remained the realm of the Hannoverian kings of England, but when William IV was succeeded in that year by Victoria, law forbade a woman's rule, and Ernest Augustus, a younger son of

George III, took over. His regime refused to support Marschner's rather lavish ways, and, as he repeatedly pointed out to his master, he now qualified as the lowest-paid royal *Kapellmeister* in the Germanies. He grew sour and cynical and, when a superior was placed over him, he resigned, in 1852. At that point the king gave in and gave him a lifetime appointment. That year Marschner produced his *Austin;* the libretto was by Marianne, who, unhappily, died two years later. Marschner was for a time immobilized by grief and an eye infection. But a few months later he fell in love with a beautiful young singer, Therese Janda, and married her in 1855. Though she cheered him up, he was unable to deal with the new management, and the next year he was "retired"—i.e., kicked upstairs for insubordination. In 1860 he went to Paris to try to produce *Sangeskönig Hiarne (Hiarne, King of Song).* He got the backing of Rossini [1143], but before anything concrete could be done, the debacle of Wagner's *Tannhäuser* made the production of another German opera impossible. Marschner, increasingly embittered and withdrawn, went home and died of apoplexy a few months later. *Hiarne* was staged in 1863 at Frankfurt am Main.

RECORDINGS: On commercial records, Marschner was until recently represented mostly by operatic snippets. There have been piratical versions of *Der Vampyr* and *Hans Heiling,* and recently a commercial recording of *Der Vampyr* (Günter Neuhold conducting) was released.

[1148] **MERCADANTE, Giuseppe Saverio Raffaele** (Mâr-kà-dàn'-tä, Jōō-sep'-pä Sà-vä'-rē-ō Râf'-fà-ä'-lä)
FLUTIST, VIOLINIST, CONDUCTOR, EDUCATOR
BORN: Altamura, c. September 17, 1795
DIED: Naples, December 17, 1870

Between the death of Donizetti [1155] in 1848 and the 1860s, Saverio Mercadante was Verdi's [1232] only serious operatic rival in Italy. Fifty years later he counted as little more than a footnote in the history books—though a latter-day effort to revive him has come in on the coattails of the *bel canto* resurrection. His birthplace near Bari (named after its high mediaeval walls) now has a Mercadante Institute and a sporadic Mercadante Festival. He was begotten on an unwed servant girl by a local miller and was baptized on the date noted above. Luca de Samuele Cagnazzi, a local cleric whom one source describes as "a well-known economist and madrigalist," took his musical edu-

cation in charge. The elder Mercadante, his son in tow, became a customs official in Naples in 1806, and two years later the boy was enrolled in the new Royal Conservatory as "Francesco Mercadante, Neapolitan, age eleven"—fictions perpetuated by his Neapolitan memorial. He proved to be a remarkably clever instrumentalist, founded a student orchestra, and wrote pieces for it to play, including symphonies and concerti. He became the pride and joy of the institution's director Zingarelli, and there is apparently no truth at all in the story that in a fit of anger Zingarelli expelled him.

Mercadante turned to opera in 1819, getting his maiden effort, *L'Apoteosi d'Ercole (The Apotheosis of Hercules)* produced by the Teatro San Carlo. Nearly 60 others would follow in the next forty-seven years. His reputation was made with the production of *Elisa e Claudio* at La Scala in 1821. In 1824 he had premieres in Rome and Turin and three in Vienna. Between 1826 and 1831, Mercadante seems to have spent most of his time in Iberia, where some new works were produced, but where, in spite of promises, he found no permanent post. On returning to Italy, he found that he had to rebuild his reputation there, which he managed to do with *I Normanni a Parigi (The Normans in Paris)* at Turin in 1832. He celebrated by marrying Sofia Gambaro that summer in Genoa; she later gave him two sons and a daughter. In the winter he accepted the post of choirmaster of the cathedral at Novara in the Piedmont. Here he worked (when not overseeing operatic productions) for seven years, producing a great deal of once-popular sacred music and losing the sight of one eye in an accident. In 1836 he went to Paris, on Rossini's [1143] invitation, to conduct the opening of his *I Briganti* (based, like Verdi's *I Masnadieri* on Schiller's *Die Räuber)* at the Théâtre-Italien. Up to then, he had pretty much followed the *bel canto* tradition, but his Paris encounter with the *grand-opéra* caused him to rethink his approach. With *Il giuramento (The Oath)*—based like Ponchielli's [1334] *La Gioconda* on Hugo's *Angelo*—which opened at La Scala the following March, his new foci were on the dramatic requirements of the text and on the orchestra. (His orchestration later earned him the inappropriate name of "the Italian Beethoven.")

Zingarelli died in 1837, and King Ferdinand dithered over naming his successor. Donizetti thought himself a shoo-in, and in 1839 Mercadante accepted the directorship of the Liceo in Bologna. But when the king unexpectedly named him a few months later, he resigned without ever having taken office.

He ran the Naples Conservatory until he died thirty years later. His operatic output now slowed down. He was to complete only ten more operas, the last in 1857, though among them were two of his most successful, *Il Reggente* (on the theme of Auber's [1103] and Verdi's *Masked Ball)* in 1843, and *Gli Orazi ed e Curiazi* in 1846. Many stories and a good deal of evidence indicate that despite Verdi's friendly and respectful treatment of him, Mercadante did much to block productions of his work in Naples. (A contemporary cartoon shows a chunky, grinning, chin-whiskered Mercadante, wearing an oversized topper, introducing an apprehensive Verdi to a crowd of hostile students.) In 1862 Mercadante went totally blind but continued to dictate (nonoperatic) compositions. He was the first person Verdi asked to contribute a movement to the projected memorial *Mass* for Rossini, and there is no denying his influence on Verdi.

RECORDINGS: On commercial records, Mercadante is represented by recordings of several flute concerti (mostly Jean-Pierre Rampal), a horn concerto (Domenico Ceccarossi and Thomas Bourgue), a clarinet concerto (Thomas Friedli), an overture for Rossini's *Stabat mater* (Claudio Scimone), and various snippets, but only one opera, *Il Bravo.* However, the pirate underground has accounted for several more, including *Il Reggente, Elisa e Claudio, Le due illustri rivale (The Two Famous Rivals), La Vestale,* and *Gli Orazi ed e Curiazi.*

[1149] NICHOLSON, Charles
FLUTIST
BORN: Liverpool, 1795
DIED: London, March 26, 1837

Nicholson's father, also named Charles, was a professional flutist and taught his son all he knew, which was apparently a good deal. He also invented an improved flute, whose manufacture and sale kept the younger Charles rather comfortably off. The latter eventually came to be first flutist of the Philharmonic Society and most of the first-rank London theaters, and was first professor of flute at the Royal Academy of Music from 1822. He was noted for his power and breath control, though he was not much admired outside of England. Nicholson wrote pieces and methods for his instrument. RECORDINGS: Ransom Wilson has recorded his variations on *"Ah! Vous dirais-je, Maman."*

[1150] PANSERON, Auguste-Mathieu
Pàn-ser-o*n'*, Ou-güst' Màt'-yö')
TEACHER, PIANIST
BORN: Paris, April 26, 1796
DIED: Paris, July 29, 1859

After having instructed young Auguste in the basics of music, his father, who had helped Grétry [919] with his orchestrations, sent him toddling off to the Paris Conservatoire when he was eight. Having studied there with Gossec [879] and others, he was awarded the Prix de Rome when he was seventeen, which may suggest the scarcity of candidates. He spent more than the allotted time in Italy, including a period with Padre Mattei in Bologna, and then visited central Europe and Russia. Around 1819 he returned to Paris and a post as accompanist at the Opéra-Comique. He had made himself authoritative on voice in Italy, and became very successful as a vocal teacher. After having had some frothy pieces produced at the Opéra-Comique, in 1826 he was appointed professor of *solfège* at the Conservatoire. In 1831 he was named professor of vocalization, and in 1836 professor of voice. His *solfège* manuals and vocal studies are still in use. As a composer, he was most successful with his songs. RECORDINGS: Suzanne Danco recorded one of his songs.

[1151] BERWALD, Franz Adolf (Bâr'-vàld, Fràns Ád-ulf)
VIOLINIST, BUSINESSMAN, PHYSICAL THERAPIST, INVENTOR
BORN: Stockholm, July 23, 1796
DIED: Stockholm, April 3, 1868

Now universally recognized as Sweden's most important nineteenth-century composer, Berwald offers the kind of example of long-deferred appreciation that gladdens the heart of every neglected avant-gardist today. Because Swedish musical taste had gotten mired in the legend of Gustavus III, it was fifty years behind the times, and so the Swedish public ridiculed Berwald's music when they didn't ignore it. Owing to such neglect, all of the facts of the composer's life and output are still not certain.

Berwald's was a musical family going back to his Prussian grandfather. His father, Christian Friedrich Georg, studied with František Benda [776] and played in the Swedish Royal Orchestra; his younger brother, August, who later directed Stockholm Conservatory, and an uncle, Georg Johann Abraham, were also Royal Orchestra musicians, and a cousin, Johan Fredrik, became its director. Franz had lessons from his father and conductor DuPuy [1064], and played in the orchestra, off and on, from 1812 to 1828. During this period he made some solo appearances, toured with his brother, and produced some large-scale works, including a symphony, concerti, and an opera, *Gustaf Wasa*, in 1827. The works occasioned little interest, and have since mostly disappeared. After several fruitless attempts, he won a scholarship for foreign study and went to Berlin, where he fancied that there were more civilized and sophisticated people. Instead he did not even get an opportunity to perform, and his music, including two more operas, gathered dust. But he was a resourceful person, and, having evolved some obviously sound notions about orthopedic therapy, he inaugurated a practice. By 1835, using machines of his own invention, he was able to open his own institute, which prospered.

In 1841 Berwald and Mathilde Schorer, who worked for him, went to Vienna and were married. He spent a year there, where he received more attention and encouragement than he had elsewhere, including the endorsement of Liszt [1218]. However, he found he could not live on such things and returned to Stockholm. There his reception was tepid at best, though at least he was given a hearing. In 1846 Berwald went abroad again but once more found encouragement only in Austria, where his compatriot Jenny Lind appeared gratis in one of his 5 cantatas, and he was made an honorary member of the Mozarteum in Salzburg. But when he returned to Sweden in 1849, he was unable to get serious consideration for either the conductorship of the orchestra, from which Cousin Johan Fredrik had just retired, or the vacant directorship at the University of Uppsala.

Discouraged, Berwald became manager of a glass factory in the northern boondocks, and prospered so well that he was able to buy into the firm and to establish a sawmill. However, he continued to compose and won publication and favorable critical notices in Germany. In 1864 he was made a member of the Royal Academy, which had turned down his application for a teaching position two years earlier and which rather grudgingly gave him one in 1867, when the first choice proved unable to accept. Berwald died of pneumonia the following spring.

Berwald was the typical Romantic individualist—to a great degree self-taught and stylistically his own man, though some influence from Beethoven [1063] and Berlioz [1175] is obvious. (He is sometimes called "the Swedish Berlioz.") He left some works unfinished, others were lost, and the com-

poser in 1829 disowned all his previous output. There remain 5 operas, 4 symphonies (one of them reconstructed from the short score), concerti for piano, for violin, and for two violins, a few other orchestral pieces, several chamber compositions, choral pieces, songs, and some mostly trivial keyboard pieces.

RECORDINGS: The orchestral works have received most attention on records, notably in the collection conducted by Ulf Björlin, which includes the symphonies, the symphonic poems, the piano and violin concerti, and two opera overtures. Robert Riefling has recorded the 2 piano quintets; the Vienna Octet and the Nash Ensemble, the septet; and the Phoenix Quartet, the 3 string quartets.

[1152] LOEWE, Johann Carl Gottfried
(Lö'-və, Yō'-hän Kärl Got'-frēt)
SINGER, KEYBOARDIST, TEACHER
BORN: Löbejün, November 30, 1796
DIED: Kiel, April 20, 1869

Chronologically the first of the great *Lieder* composers, Carl Loewe preceded Schubert [1153] into the world by only two months and was the only songwriter of that generation worthy of comparison with him. Oddly, his much admired setting of Goethe's *Erlkönig* was, like Schubert's, his Op. 1 (or part of it), and when he visited Vienna in 1844, he was hailed as "the German Schubert." But outside of German-speaking lands, his eminence, save with a few dogged admirers, has been virtually invisible. It is not easy to say why. To argue that his music "does not travel well" is to beg the question. To be sure, it shows a jingoistic streak, but only in a relatively small number of rather inconsequential songs. Perhaps he is neglected because his biography is so unromantic—he was neither poor nor rebellious nor too-early-dead. Or perhaps it is because his more ambitious works (8 operas, 15 oratorios, 2 symphonies, 2 piano concerti, 5 string quartets, etc.) have no currency even in his homeland (though again one must ask why).

Born in a village (now East German) between Halle and Cöthen, Carl Loewe was the twelfth and last child of the town cantor. Neither he nor his father seems to have had any reservations about his becoming a musician, for from a very early age he studied at the paternal knee, if not on it. His mother appears to have been a flowing spring of fairytales, and the sufficiently unspoiled countryside where he roamed gave him a feeling for the mysteries of nature. At ten he became a choirboy in Cöthen where the spirit of Sebastian Bach [684] may still have hovered after ninety years. At the appropriate time Loewe was enrolled in the *Gymnasium* at Halle and in 1810 was taken into the choir of the Marktkirche, where his talent so struck the *Kapellmeister,* Daniel Gottlob Türk, trained by Homilius [800], Reichardt [980], and J. A. Hiller, that he took him into his home as his pupil. Türk brought him to the attention of Jerome Bonaparte, King of Westphalia, who decreed him an annuity of 300 thalers. However, with Türk's death and the French defeat at Leipzig in 1813, the free ride came to a jarring halt. Nevertheless his headmaster managed to get him a scholarship at the local university, where he majored in theology and philosophy, and joined the newly founded Singakademie. By then he had already written some songs and an opera.

Loewe left Halle to travel in 1819. He met en route Goethe, Hummel [1091], and Weber [1124], for which last he arranged a Halle concert in 1820. In that year he was invited to apply for a teaching post at the *Gymnasium* and seminary in Stettin (now Polish Szczecin), the port city of Berlin. After passing the tests, which included preaching a sermon, he won the blessings of Zelter [1008] and the job, at which he spent the rest of his working days. A year later he was elevated to the royal and municipal music directorship, became organist at the Jakobikirche, and married his college sweetheart, the beautiful and talented Julie von Jacob. Having presented him with a namesake daughter, she died in 1823. After three years Loewe married Augusta Lange, a singer from Königsberg, who helped popularize his songs.

The year 1824 saw the publication of Loewe's "real" Op. 1, consisting of *Erlkönig* and two other *Balladen.* (Premature Opp. 1–2 had been disowned.) The *Ballade,* or narrative song, which reflected the growing interest in such folksongs, was not Loewe's invention, but it became his particular province (though it is improper to lump all of his songs under that head, as is sometimes done). Loewe's *Balladen* appear to have a folklike simplicity, but the best examples are highly ingenious musical structures and most effective in performance. Their chief advocate was the composer himself, who possessed a fine voice (variously described as a high baritone or tenor) and a commanding stage presence.

In 1834 Spontini [1081] successfully produced Loewe's opera *Die drei Wünsche (The Three Wishes)* in Berlin; it was his only opera staged during his lifetime. But Loewe be-

came a favorite of two Frederick Williams in the capital, where he was elected to the Prussian Academy three years later. He took up concert touring in the 1840s, appearing in Vienna, in 1844; London, in 1847; Scandinavia, in 1851; and Paris, in 1857. The Viennese were, as noted, impressed, and he found an admirer in London in the person of his fellow songwriter Prince Albert [1266], but otherwise he seems to have made no deep impression. Back in Stettin, he lapsed into a coma in 1864 and did not emerge from it for six weeks. Afterward it was obvious that he was not up to his duties, and the king retired him on a pension. Loewe moved to Kiel, where four years later he died of apoplexy.

RECORDINGS: Loewe has enjoyed steady representation on records, which seem, however, not to sell very well and to disappear quickly. In recent decades such singers as Theo Adam, Wolfgang Anheisser, Dietrich Fischer-Dieskau, Ferdinand Frantz, Hermann Prey, William Warfield, and a number of others have contributed significantly to the Loewe song discography.

[1153] SCHUBERT, Franz Peter (Shōō'-bârt, Frånts Pä'-ter)
TEACHER
BORN: Vienna, January 31, 1797
DIED: Vienna, November 19, 1828

Schubert is now ranked with the greatest composers; with Haydn [871] and Beethoven [1063] he is the third member of the Trinity of the First Vienna School. Yet in his day his was little more than a local celebrity, and that was restricted largely to a circle of friends and admirers. His brief existence was neither very successful nor eventful. And most of his greatest music derives from the last few months of his life.

Schubert was the twelfth of the eighteen known children of Franz Theodor Florian Schubert, a Viennese schoolmaster whose hobby was playing the cello. The mother, Elisabeth (*née* Vitz), a sometime cook, had produced fourteen of the brood when she died in Schubert's sixteenth year. His elder brother Ferdinand, who took up the paternal calling, was also a decent composer. In 1801 the elder Schubert bought a building known as "Zum schwarzen Rössl" (At the Sign of the Black Pony), which served both as a schoolhouse and family living quarters. There for seven years Franz studied academic subjects as well as piano and violin, on which he was soon performing in the local church and in domestic *musicales* as part of a string quartet that included his two elder brothers and his father. At eleven he became a chorister (a "Vienna choirboy") in the Imperial Kapelle, which position entitled him to a free education at the Konvikt —an abbreviation that signified nothing more sinister than a state-operated boarding school, though there were uniforms and rather strict regimentation. The Konvikt offered superior musical training, from which Schubert quickly profited. He became a second violin in the student orchestra organized by Josef von Spaun, a student from the university who entered into what was to be a lifelong friendship with the boy and promoted him to the position of *Konzertmeister,* which enabled him to serve as a substitute conductor. (He was also librarian, a title that carried more work than honor.) His teachers soon found him to be way ahead of them, and Schubert was turned over to Kapellmeister Salieri [966] himself.

In 1812, the year of his mother's death, Schubert's voice broke, but he was permitted to remain at the school until autumn 1813, by which time he was composing regularly and envisioning a musical career for himself. (The first six string quartets date from this period.) But his father had more "practical" plans for him; and, coming home to find his mother's successor, *née* Anna Kleyenböck, installed, he was immediately enrolled in a teacher-education program. Normally, he would have had to undergo military service at this time in his life, but the examiners rejected him for his stumpiness (4′11½″) without even considering his myopia. In 1814 he became an assistant to his father at roughly five cents a day (by modern standards!). At the same time he fell in love with a homely little soprano named Therese Grob, who was soloist in his first Mass that year. The affair ended three years later, when Therese's schoolmaster-father decided that Schubert would never be able to support his daughter in the style to which he felt she should become accustomed. Thereafter—certain operettas to the contrary—Schubert's love life seems to have been limited to one-night stands with chance acquaintances.

It was in 1814 that Schubert wrote his first great *Lied,* a setting of *"Gretchen am Spinnrade"* ("Gretchen at the Spinning Wheel") from Goethe's *Faust.* It was the forerunner of an incredible flood of songs turned out over the next three years and one of a total output that surpassed 600. In attempting to convey the mood and meaning of the text through music, Schubert, to all intents and purposes, invented the art song. Toward the end of the year, he made friends with Johann Mayrhofer, a dour poet and civil servant (he later killed himself), who became one of his chief lyricists. In the spring of 1815, he entered into an even closer friendship with Franz von Schober, a Swede, who also furnished him with texts—and later, in 1822, with the libretto to *Alfonso und Estrella,* one of Schubert's 2 completed full-length operas. Encouraged by a growing circle of admirers, Schubert made 1815 his most productive year, completing, besides the *Lieder,* two symphonies, Masses, other church music, a quartet, and piano sonatas. He also wrote three *Singspiele,* none of which had any more luck than some unfinished predecessors, and the Goethe song *Erlkönig,* his first great success, which in 1821 became his first published work.

Though teaching frustrated him, Schubert applied in the spring of 1816 for a schoolmastering job in Laibach (now Ljubljana) but was turned down. After that he gradually drifted away from his profession. Toward the end of the year, he left the paternal roof for rooms in the home of Schober's mother. There he was introduced to the great operatic baritone Johann Michael Vogl who, for all his self-importance, could not resist Schubert's songs and became their chief prophet in the Vienna salons. (They did not fare so well elsewhere. Spaun sent some of the Goethe settings to the poet, who did not even bother to acknowledge them. He also submitted *"Erlkönig"* to the publishers Breitkopf and Härtel of Leipzig, who, confused by the composer's name, sent it to court contrabassist Franz Schubert in Dresden. He shipped it back with a letter full of moral outrage at his name being attached to such rubbish.)

Schubert continued to teach under his father—since early 1817 in a new establishment in the Rossau sector—until the summer of 1818. That July he left to take what was to be his only musical job, teaching Marie and Caroline Esterházy at the family "château" at Zseliz in the Hungarian countryside (now Zeliezovce in Czechoslovakia). The girls' father, Count Johann, was a lesser member of the family that had employed Haydn [871] for so many years. Schubert's status was that of a servant, and he was treated accordingly. Though he had plenty of time to compose, he was often bored and lonely. He seems to have found some solace in a fellow servant called Pepi Pöckelhofer, and he apparently carried the torch for a while for Princess Caroline, though his cause, as he knew, was hopeless. In November the Esterházys came back to Vienna for the winter and, his father not having forgiven him for his defection, Schubert moved in with Mayrhofer.

Having apparently abandoned all hope of any serious employment, Schubert settled into a routine of concentrated writing during his mornings and later socializing in one way or another with his constantly growing circle of friends. Evenings they often got together to hear him play or to help perform his music, and such chance gatherings developed into the famous weekly Schubertiads. On less formal occasions, Schubert seems to have been happy just to sit at the piano, improvising for the dancing couples and drinking wine—of which he often partook too freely, and sometimes he had to be poured into bed. In the summer of 1819, Vogl impulsively took him on vacation to Upper Austria, which produced the "Trout" quintet, commissioned by a citizen of Steyr who loved the song that gives it its name. The following June, in 1820, Vogl managed to get the Kärntnertortheater to produce Schubert's one-act *Singspiel* entitled *Die Zwillingsbrüder (The Twin Brothers)*, but even Vogl's espousal of the title roles did not make it succeed. Nor did the music for the play *Der Zauberharfe (The Magic Harp)* save that work in August. Then the theater went bankrupt before Schubert could collect the little that was coming to him. The next year he forsook the Mayrhofian gloom for quarters of his own. It was in the course of 1821 that some of his friends decided, after Vogl's masterly performance of *"Erlkönig"* at a public concert drew no offers, that Schubert had gone unpublished too long, and took up a subscription that financed Diabelli's **[1100]** publication of twenty songs. That summer the composer vacationed with Schober at Atzenbrugg and in the autumn they holed up together in a castle, owned by a Schober relative, near St. Pölten, to begin work on their opera. It was finished by February, and Schubert showed it to the visiting Weber **[1124]**, who promised to try to get it a Dresden production. But nothing came of the offer, and the Hoftheater (now under Barbaja) rejected it. (It was first performed at Weimar in 1854.) In the course of that same year, 1822, Schubert wrote—or at least began—a symphony in B minor, his eighth attempt in that form (No. 7 was left largely unscored). It was intended for the Graz Musikverein (which later made him an honorary member). He turned the manuscript over to Josef Hüttenbrenner as a gift to Josef's brother and Schubert's friend Anselm, who was the Musikverein's president. Nearly half a century later Arthur Sullivan **[1397]** and George Grove talked Anselm Hüttenbrenner out of it. The manuscript ends a few bars into the third movement. There is solid evidence that Schubert left it in this state, though no one knows why.

At the end of the year, Schubert returned to his family and shortly after fell seriously ill, grew steadily worse, and wound up in the hospital in May. He suffered blinding headaches and attacks of vertigo. Afterward he lost his hair and had to wear a wig for a time. It has been suspected that the problem was syphilis, but the diagnosis is by no means certain. On top of all this, he found that Diabelli was exploiting him and switched to another publisher. By the end of May, on the mend, he began work on his second serious opera, *Fierabras*, part of which was written on vacation in Linz and Steyr. Though the Hoftheater had commissioned it, Barbaja found it so impossible that he rejected it without payment. Schubert followed it in the autumn with music for Helmina von Chézy's (Weber's *Euryanthe* nemesis) *Rosamunde*, which was removed from the boards after two performances. It was his last completed dramatic piece.

On his return from vacation, Schubert had moved in with another friend, Josef Huber, Schober having inherited a fortune that enabled him to go to Breslau to try his hand at acting. Between further bouts of illness, he completed *Die schöne Müllerin (The Pretty Miller Maid)*, the first of his great song cycles. The next year the Schubertiads collapsed of their own weight, having become intimate gatherings no longer, and Schubert added loneliness to the difficulties of declining health. That was intensified when, undoubtedly lured by need for money, he returned to the Esterházys in the summer for another six months of tutorial work. In October he returned briefly to the Schubert schoolhouse, then moved into rooms with his friend the painter Moritz von Schwind. In May 1825 he undertook yet another vacation in Linz (where he was a corresponding member of the Musikverein), Steyr, and the spa at Gastein, where he wrote another symphony. There has been a great deal of romantic twaddle about this apparently lost work, which was probably the "Great" C major (No. 9), long buried in the archives of the Vienna Friends of Music. During this time, Schubert rejected the post of second imperial organist—some say because his legs were too short to negotiate the pedals. At the end of the tour, Vogl took off for Italy, where he ended a bachelorhood of fifty-eight years by marrying one of his pupils.

On his return to Vienna in October, Schubert found Schober in residence again, and their night-owling began all over. Once more they set up housekeeping together—wherever the mercurial Schober was moved to hang his hat. Still desperately poor, Schubert grubbed for publication and saw his widening reputation bring in some small returns. By the end of 1826, however, Schubert was once again living by himself. After Salieri died in 1825, the composer waited in vain to be offered his court post. He *was* offered a conductorship at the Kärntnertortheater, but he wrecked his chances during his audition when he refused to knuckle under to the prima donna. This happened shortly after the death of Schubert's hero Beethoven, whom he may have known slightly, and in whose funeral procession he was a torchbearer. No doubt he did not view this last action symbolically, but he does in fact seem to have taken up Beethoven's torch, for in the twenty-three months left him he wrote music of transcendent beauty, beginning with the song cycle *Die Winterreise (The Winter Journey)* and including the *Mass* in E-flat, the final three piano sonatas, the E-flat piano trio, and the C-major quintet. In the early summer he spent some time in the suburban village of Dornbach, and was at last elected a member of Vienna's Gesellschaft der Musikfreunde. In September he at last had an opportunity to visit Graz, where he spent a happy three weeks, returning to Vienna on the twentieth. It was soon obvious that something was wrong. His headaches and dizzy spells recurred, he was gloomy and withdrawn, and he worked like one possessed. On March 26, 1828, the Musikfreunde presented an all-Schubert concert; a partisan audience cheered, but the critics all went to hear Paganini [1106] instead.

In the summer there was neither time nor money for a vacation. When his symptoms did not mitigate, his doctor persuaded him to go live with his brother Ferdinand in the suburb of Neue Wieden. The next month Ferdinand took him on a three-day hike to Eisenstadt, but his health continued to deteriorate. His stomach began to trouble him, and on the thirty-first he found he was unable to eat the dinner he had ordered in a restaurant. Five days later, still unable to eat, he began counterpoint lessons with Sechter [1129]. On November 11 he took to his bed, where he occupied his time reading Fenimore Cooper and correcting the *Winterreise* proofs. His disease was diagnosed as typhus, though there are those who are convinced that it was yet another manifestation of syphilis. Delirium set in, and he raved about Beethoven and about being buried alive. On the afternoon of the nineteenth he died. Ferdinand persuaded his father to have him buried in the Währing Cemetery, as near Beethoven's grave as possible. Schubert's friends chipped in for a monument, for which the poet Grillparzer wrote the famous epitaph: "Here Music has buried a rich treasure, but far fairer hopes." Sixty years later, with great pomp and ceremony, both bodies were transferred to the Central Cemetery. By then, Schubert's friends and such younger admirers as Sullivan and Schumann [1211] had firmly established him as a great composer.

RECORDINGS: With the exception of the opera *Fierabras,* all of Schubert's major works have been recorded, many of them several or numerous times. There are integral sets of the symphonies (Karl Böhm, Peter Maag, Herbert von Karajan, etc.), the quartets (Vienna Konzerthaus, Melos Ensemble), the piano sonatas (Friedrich Wührer, Rudolf Kempff, Paul Badura-Skoda, Walter Klien, etc.), and the dances for piano (Jacques Abrams). Between them, Dietrich Fischer-Dieskau, Janet Baker, and Gundula Janowitz have single-handedly accounted for most of the songs, and the teams of Noël Lee and Christian Ivaldi and of Paul Badura-Skoda and Jörg Demus much of the four-hand piano music. What gaps there are lie mostly in the realm of choral music.

[1154] LOVER, Samuel
PAINTER, NOVELIST, POET, PLAYWRIGHT, SINGER
BORN: Dublin, February 24, 1797
DIED: St. Heliers, Jersey, July 6, 1868

The son of a stockbroker, Samuel Lover's first musical success came at twenty-one, when he sang an original song at a Dublin dinner for Thomas Moore [1093] and won the latter's praise. However, he opted for miniature painting as a means whereby to earn a livelihood. In 1827 he married a Miss Berrill; their daughter Fanny was the mother of Victor Herbert [1513]. A year later he was elected to the Royal Hibernian Academy and was named its secretary in 1830. In his spare time he tried his hand at writing. In 1831 he published his *Legends and Stories of Ireland* and the next year an opera (using Irish popular tunes) was produced to his libretto *Grana Uile.* That same year he painted a much-praised miniature of Paganini [1106]. In 1835 Lover moved permanently to London, where he was even more successful. As a singer he became an attraction at the *soirées* given by his compatriot, Marguerite, Lady Blessington. He published a successful novel, *Rory O'More* (after one of his songs) in 1836 and turned it into an even more successful play a year later. At about the same time he was associated with Charles Dickens, fresh from the triumph of *Pickwick Papers,* in the publication of *Bentley's Miscellany,* and had a whole series of musical stage works produced. Another popular novel, *Handy Andy*, appeared in 1842. Of his many songs, "The Low-Back'd Car," "The Girl I Left Behind Me," and "Molly Bawn" became "standards." When deterioration of his eyesight affected his productivity after 1844, he toured the British Isles and the United States as the star of Irish revues. At sixty-seven he retired, spent the remainder of his life in Dublin, and died on the Isle of Jersey. RECORDINGS: The songs previously noted have been many times recorded by popular Irish tenors.

[1155] DONIZETTI, Domenico Gaetano Maria (Dŏn-it-set′-tē, Dō-mā′-nē-kō Gà-ā-tà′-nō Mà-rē′-à)
CONDUCTOR
BORN: Bergamo, November 29, 1797
DIED: Bergamo, April 8, 1848

Only a few decades ago, Donizetti was represented on the opera stage largely by the then-much-derided *Lucia di Lammermoor*, and bid fair to slip into the limbo of the forgotten. But since World War II, thanks to singers able and willing to tackle his vocally and stylistically demanding music, he has been once again elevated to the pantheon of nineteenth-century Italian opera composers as party of a trinity with Rossini [1143] and Bellini [1164]. Such was his outpouring of music that it is difficult to imagine that he could have remained long overlooked. His detractors rather rudely called him (behind his back) "Maestro Orgasmo"—a name all too grimly appropriate in the light of his medical history. Indeed, so wholly engrossed was he in his art that the story of his life is primarily a record of his operas.

Gaetano Donizetti was the fifth and penultimate child of Andrea Donizetti, janitor of the municipal pawnshop, and Domenica Nava, his wife of eleven years. Giuseppe, Gaetano's eldest brother, eventually became, as Donizetti Pasha, music director of the Turkish military; another brother, feeble-minded Francesco, was a drummer in a local band. When he was nine, Gaetano became a pupil in the Lezioni Caritatevoli di Musica, the charity school that Giovanni Simone Mayr [1034] had just fashioned from the academy for the cathedral choristers. A throat problem kept the child from the choir, but he became Mayr's chief pet and worshipper, though later he was able to appear in at least two school operas. (Still later he became a basso.)

When Donizetti turned eighteen, Mayr pulled some strings and got him support for

two years of study with Padre Mattei, sometime teacher of Rossini [1143], Morlacchi [1114], Giovanni Pacini (1796–1867), and Tadolini [1132], in Bologna. There he seems to have exhibited the single-mindedness that characterized his career: he wrote music by the yard, including two operas. (The first, *Il Pigmalione*, was first produced at Bergamo in 1960; there is no record of a performance of the other, *L'Ira d'Achille [The Wrath of Achilles].)* He is said to have had little social life there, but the case of syphilis that he picked up did not come from manuscript paper. On his return to Bergamo in 1817, he got, thanks to Mayr, a contract to write four operas for an impresario named Zancia. Two, *Enrico di Borgogna (Henry of Burgundy)* and *Una Follia* were produced in Venice toward the end of 1818, the first being credited to Maestro Donzellati; it was afterward produced in Bergamo, but neither work had much effect. The fourth, *Il Falegname di Livonia (The Livonian Carpenter*, on the same plot as Lortzing's [1163] *Zar und Zimmermann)*, premiered in Venice a year later, was taken up by several Italian houses. Donizetti returned to the story with *Il Borgomestro di Saardam* in 1827.

This relative success stood Donizetti in good stead, for it prompted a Bergamese lady to buy his way out of military service in 1818. In 1821 Mayr got him a contract for an opera at the Teatro Argentina in Rome. *Zoraide di Granata* ran into difficulties in rehearsal when the tenor burst a blood vessel and died, but it won an ovation when it reached the stage the following January. Invited to Naples by the impresario Barbaja, Donizetti soon made it his headquarters, becoming, in effect, Rossini's successor there. His first work for Naples was *La Zingara (The Gypsy Girl)*, and thereafter he held a contract to write for the Naples theaters. In the ten years before he abrogated it, he turned out around thirty operas. Among the early ones, *L'Aio nell' imbarazzo (The Tutor in Trouble)*, premiered in Rome in 1824, was the most successful. In 1825 Donizetti briefly took over the musical directorship of the Teatro Carolino in Palermo, where he was beset by all the troubles attendant on provincial opera houses.

A year later the composer fell in love with an eighteen-year-old Roman girl, Virginia Vasselli, the sister of his friend and lifelong correspondent "Toto" Vasselli. They were wed in Rome in 1828, despite opposition from Donizetti's father, now risen to the eminence of pawnshop usher, and returned to Naples to an apartment close to the San Carlo Theater. During this period Donizetti suffered some ominous spells of illness, and thirteen months after the wedding Virginia gave birth to a misshapen son who survived only two weeks. Two later children were stillborn. But matters operatic were brighter: in 1830 Donizetti had his first grand success with *Anna Bolena* at the Teatro Carcano in Milan, and it was soon being played internationally. (It is the earliest of the Donizetti operas to have recaptured the stage, thanks to the initial efforts of Maria Callas.) Oddly, on the same night Bellini's [1164] new *La Sonnambula* opened the La Scala season. But the next year brought the onset of the great cholera epidemic, the first upheaval of pan-Italian patriotism (with which the composer did not hold), and the sneers of the visiting Mendelssohn [1200] at his supposedly uncritical facility.

After breaking with Naples to permit himself more latitude, Donizetti began the long string of his most notable successes at Milan in 1832 with *L'Elisir d'amore (The Elixir of Love,* a bucolic romp that even at the lowest ebb of Donizetti's subsequent fame, kept a parlous hold on the repertoire. It was immediately followed by such works as *Il Furioso all'isola di San Domingo (The Madman on the Isle of San Domingo),* Rome 1833; *Parisina d'Este,* Florence 1833; *Torquato Tasso,* Rome 1833; and *Rosamunda d'Inghilterra,* Florence 1834. It was in 1834 that Donizetti, somewhat reluctantly, despite Mayr's urging, became a professor at the Royal College of Music in Naples and also contracted to write an opera a year for the San Carlo. He was again in bad health, and with his first effort under the new contract, *Maria Stuarda (Mary Stuart),* he locked horns with the censors, who forced him to redo it as *Buondelmonte.*

At the beginning of the new year, 1835, Donizetti went to Paris on Rossini's invitation, to produce a new opera at the Théâtre-Italien. He arrived in time to catch the premiere of Bellini's *I Puritani,* a sensation and Bellini's last opera. He was much taken with it, but neither Bellini nor anyone else (at the time) liked his own *Marino Faliero.* However, back in Naples the following September, Donizetti produced *his* greatest hit, *Lucia di Lammermoor*—three days after Bellini's untimely death. In December Donizetti's involvement in the Milan premiere (the real one) of *Maria Stuarda* made it impossible for him to attend his father's funeral in Bergamo, and the following March, while getting *Belisario* ready for production in Venice, he heard for the first time that his mother had died a month before. On his return to Naples, he discovered that the cholera had set in there in earnest. By the fall of 1837, some 14,000 Neapolitans had succumbed to it. In between, he ironically had successes with two lovely comedies, *Il Campanello (The Night Bell)* and *Betly,* but by the time of *L'Assedio di Calais (The Siege of Calais)* in November 1836, much of the potential audience was avoiding public places. It was followed in February by *Pia de' Tolomei,* produced at the Apollo in Venice, La Fenice having as yet failed to rise from the ashes of the fire two months earlier.

In May the Donizettis moved to a more imposing apartment—as luck would have it, on the day of Conservatory director Zingarelli's death. Donizetti temporarily took his place, assuming that he would soon be confirmed in it. A month later Virginia bore a third child (dead), developed a rash (variously diagnosed), became feverish and delirious, and died after six weeks. She was twenty-nine. Donizetti was inconsolable and for the rest of his life found it difficult to return to places he connected with her. He submerged his grief in work and in short order had turned out two more works—*Roberto Devereux,* at Naples, October 29, 1837; and *Maria di Rudenz,* at Venice in the now-resurrected La Fenice, January 30, 1838. On going home he found that the shillyshallying King Ferdinand had decided to give the Conservatory appointment to Mercadante [1148] and tried vainly to resign his professorship. On top of that, the censors flatly refused to let him put on his new *Poliuto,* on religious grounds. At this point, with contracts for two more Paris operas in hand, Donizetti decided he needed no more of Naples and left for France in October.

This break with Italy also marked a break in Donizetti's production. Though he gave the Parisians several of his previous successes, including a revised *Lucia,* there was nothing new until *La Fille du régiment (The Daughter of the Regiment)* in February 1840. He quickly became a favorite in Paris, albeit a homesick one. Having observed the grand-opera style, he applied it to the orphaned *Poliuto,* which emerged in April as *Les Martyrs* and won a tumultuous reception. He was summoned to court to present the dedication to Queen Marie-Amélie (daughter of Ferdinand IV of Naples), and he also profited rather handsomely from each repetition of the opera. But on learning that the Neapolitan authorities had censored all news of his success, he resolved never to go back. After brief vacations in Switzerland and Bergamo, he returned to Paris to rework his 1839 *L'Ange de Nisida (The Angel of Nisida),* unperformed because of the bankruptcy of the theater that had commissioned it; the result was premiered in December as *La Favorite.* (The old story that Donizetti wrote the last act in an evening is bunk, though he may have revised the material that he used for it in a short time.) The Act Two ballet, starring Carlotta Grisi, marked the beginning of the great age of nineteenth-century Parisian ballet, though the opera itself found favor slowly. (A year later, making transcriptions of it helped Wagner [1230] survive in Paris.)

The year 1841 saw the none-too-successful premieres of *Adelia* in Rome in February and of *Maria Padilla* in Milan the following December. The next spring, en route to Vienna, Donizetti stopped off at Bologna, at the composer's request, to conduct Rossini's at-long-last-completed *Stabat Mater*. In Vienna, a city that overwhelmed him, he presented his new *Linda di Chamounix* in May and, to the horror of patriotic Italians, accepted the post of imperial *Hofkapellmeister*. But while his public successes moved from triumph to triumph, his private life was beginning to deteriorate. Though it is all very hush-hush, Donizetti appears to have increasingly suffered from the satyriasis that often accompanies the latter stages of syphilis. We hear whispers of nights spent cruising parks and back alleys, of women preying on his weakness, of orgies. His letters from this period seem to take an increasingly obscene turn, though he was always earthy, but otherwise they show him his old witty, modest self. He continued to compose, and by the end of 1843 had completed four more operas—*Don Pasquale* (Paris, January); *Maria di Rohan* (Vienna, June); and *Dom Sébastien* (Paris, November). *Caterina Cornaro,* the earliest of the quartet, waited until January 1844 for its premiere at the San Carlo. (*Le Duc d'Albe,* which he had left unfinished in 1839, was eventually completed by others and premiered in 1882.) Around the end of this period, Donizetti was behaving strangely and losing his ability to concentrate. In the summer of 1845, though not yet fifty, he aged alarmingly and began to grow incoherent. Physicians were summoned. They applied leeches and subjected the patient to other indignities without salutary result. He lost his sense of balance and even kept falling out of bed. By a ruse his nephew Andrea got him into a sanitarium in the suburbs, where Donizetti wept constantly, under the impression that he had been jailed. By fall he was barely mobile, had lost control of his excretory functions, and could speak only in monosyllables. Finally total paralysis set in. It was proposed that he be taken back to Bergamo, but the police refused permission on the odd notion that the trip might kill him. In September 1847 the permit finally

came through. Seven months later, after repeated bouts of fever and a stroke, he died.

Though he wrote a vast amount of other music—sacred works, chamber music, concerti and other orchestral pieces, piano music, songs, and duets—Donizetti's importance is as a composer of operas, nearly 70 in all, in a career that lasted only twenty-five years. If he was largely an imitator of Rossini at the beginning of his career, after 1830 he developed into a tragedian and comedian of both power and individuality.

RECORDINGS: Though there is little representation on records of the early works—*Il Pigmalione* and *Le Convenienze ed inconvenienze teatrali* appear to be the only examples—about eighty percent of the mature works from *Anna Bolena* on have been made available, though perhaps half of those exist only in pirated versions. There are also a good many scattered recordings of songs, and a few of string quartets, concerti, and religious pieces.

[1156] VERSTOVSKY, Alexei Niko-laievitch (Ver-stōv'-ski, Ȧl-yeks-ā'-ē Nē-kō-lī-yā'-vich)
ADMINISTRATOR
BORN: Seliverstovo, March 1, 1799
DIED: Moscow, November 17, 1862

Russia was, in the heady days after Napoleon's defeat, so anxious for a composer of major stature of her own that when Verstovsky hove on the scene, he was greeted as if he had been the Messiah. Actually he was not much more than a clever tunesmith, though he had an ear for Russian characteristics. His father, a wealthy landowner in the Tambov District, shipped him off to St. Petersburg to become a military engineer. Verstovsky left school at eighteen, having devoted much of his time to private music study—including piano lessons with both Steibelt [1044] and Field [1104]. Within a couple of years, having tasted success with the songs he wrote for some retreaded French vaudevilles, he turned to music as a profession. In 1823 he moved to Moscow, where in 1825 he was appointed inspector of theaters. After some more vaudevilles, he embarked on a *Singspiel* called *Pan Tvardovsky;* the libretto was after the Polish poet Mickiewicz, but the opera (premiered in 1828) was strongly influenced by Weber [1124]. His one real hit (out of six tries) was *Askold's Tomb* which, first played in 1835, remained in the Russian repertoire until the October Revolution. In 1842 Verstovsky was put in full charge of all the Moscow theaters, where he was an effective and popular director. In 1851 he married the great actress Nadezhda Remina. Unhappily Verstovsky lived to see himself eclipsed by Glinka [1179]. He retired two years before his death. RECORDINGS: There are a few recordings of arias from *Askold's Tomb,* mostly from the early decades of this century.

[1157] HALÉVY, Jacques-François-Fromental-Élie (Á-lā-vē′, Zhák Frán-swá′ Frō-mon-tál′ Ál-ē′)
TEACHER
BORN: Paris, May 27, 1799
DIED: Nice, March 17, 1862

Some older references give the impression that Halévy was called Jacques, but he preferred Fromental; his parents at the time of his birth were still officially Lévy. His father Elias, a Bavarian Jew, migrated to France, where he married Julie Meyer of Lorraine. He was devout and a Talmudic scholar to boot—a direction his son eschewed. As a child, Fromental was sufficiently gifted to be admitted to the Conservatoire in 1809, where, in the next two years, he won prizes in *solfège* and harmony. Then, for five years more, he learned all there was to know about counterpoint under Cherubini's [1019] eye. In 1816 he entered the Prix de Rome competition and came in second but perhaps took comfort in the fact that no one came in first. The next year, however, he was bested by Désiré-Alexandre Batton, later a manufacturer of artificial flowers and inspector of the Conservatoire's subsidiary schools. Probably discouraged, Halévy did not compete in 1818, when there was also no winner. When he finally succeeded in 1819, he had to share his prize with one Massin-Turina, whose career seems to have been even more obscure than Batton's. Before Halévy could begin his mandatory pilgrimage, the Duke of Berry was murdered at the Opéra, and Halévy took time out to write a memorial psalm to a Hebrew text—one of his few musical nods toward his heritage. (This was during the fifteen-year period in which French Jews were denied the rights they had won in the Revolution; later Halévy seems to have felt it expedient not to call attention to his origins.)

Though he is said to have profited musically by his stays in Rome and Vienna, Halévy seems to have turned out nothing of substance there. Though his talents were obviously recognized, he had no success with his several attempts at opera, until 1827, when the Opéra-Comique mounted his one-act *L'Artisan.* It did not set the bells of Paris ringing, but shortly afterward he was ap-

pointed professor of harmony and accompaniment at the Conservatoire and was called upon to celebrate the achievements of Charles X (no mean task), which he attempted in another one-acter, *Le Roi et le bâtelier (The King and the Ferryman).* A year later the Théâtre-Italien produced his full-length *Clari,* starring the great Maria Malibran, to no particular effect. He was vocal coach there at the time but in 1829 took the analogous post at the Opéra. In the latter year he had his first considerable hit at the Opéra-Comique with the one-act *La Dilettante d'Avignon*—libretto by his younger brother Léon, *un dilettante de Paris* and father of the dramatist Ludovic Halévy. Over the next five years, during which he succeeded Fétis [1111] as professor of counterpoint and fugue, his ballets *Manon Lescaut* and *La Tentation* were danced at the Opéra, but he had little luck with his *opéras-comiques.*

Both his admirers and his detractors spoke of Halévy as a generous and modest man but not a very energetic creator. The truth of this charge seems to have been in part owing to indifferent health and in part a means of keeping overwrought nerves in check. After completing Hérold's [1136] unfinished *Ludovic* in 1833, Halévy at last felt himself ready to tackle his first grand opera, *La Juive (The Jewess).* The effort kept him physically ill during most of the time he worked at it. It was unveiled at the Opéra on February 23, 1835, with a starry cast that included the tenor Adolphe Nourrit and Cornélie Falcon, the Maria Callas of her time, and was an enormous success. Regarded in some quarters today as a "Jewish" opera, it qualifies only in name and outline, since Halévy's music makes no effort to be "ethnic," and Scribe shows no special insight into Jewish culture.

Hard on the heels of this mammoth effort came *L'Éclair,* a four-character comedy that stands as Halévy's other most successful opera. He was duly rewarded for his contributions to French culture by his election to the Institut (to fill Reicha's [1059] place) in 1836. But he seems to have been, for a time, creatively drained, for fifteen months went by before he completed *Guido et Ginevra* in 1838, and he had no further important success until *La Reine de Chypre (The Queen of Cyprus)* in 1841. (Based on the story of Caterina Cornaro, this piece, by a curious coincidence, appeared at the same time that Donizetti [1155] and Franz Lachner [1171] were working on the same libretto.) Two years later, at the age of forty-three, Halévy married the twenty-one-year-old Léonie Rodrigues-Henriques, the daughter of a Sephardic banker. In due course she bore him two daughters—Esther, who died before she could marry her cousin Ludovic, and Geneviève, who became the wife of Georges Bizet [1363]. Later Léonie grew decidedly peculiar, nearly bankrupted her husband with her wild spending sprees, and several times had to be institutionalized.

Part of Halévy's creative troubles derived from a bad case of "Meyerbeeritis," which made him keep trying to make of an essentially lyric and intimate talent a melodramatic one. *Charles VI,* produced in the spring of his nuptial year, had some success in that direction. (A persistent legend maintains that it had to be retired because during a particular aria whomever the singer's eyes happened to rest on in the audience fell dead!) Among his later comic operas, the most notable were *Les Mousquetaires de la reine (The Queen's Musketeers)* of 1846; *Le Val d'Andorre (The Valley of Andorra)* of 1848; and *Jaguarita* of 1855. Halévy gave up his duties at the Opéra in 1845. In 1850 he took his family to London for the premiere of *La Tempestà*—the libretto was translated from Scribe's treatment of Shakespeare's play. On the whole, however, Halévy had grown not only uncritical of his libretti (a life-long failing) but also of his own work, and not even the series of Delacroix paintings based on some of the later operas could save them.

In 1854, nevertheless, Halévy was honored again by being elected secretary of the Académie des Beaux-Arts. In 1857 he published a textbook for sight-reading classes and two volumes of attractively written essays and sketches, *Souvenirs et Portraits,* 1861–63. In 1858 he finished *La Magicienne,* the last opera he was to complete. (Bizet later completed *Noé,* but it was not produced until ten years after *he* died, and then at Karlsruhe as *Le Déluge.)* By then Halévy was not only exhausted by his too-many duties, his composition, and his domestic troubles, but he was also suffering from tuberculosis. In 1861 he moved his household to Nice and a warmer climate, but the effort seems to have taken his last strength. In the late winter of 1862, he slipped out of life so quietly that among those at his bedside only his doctor was aware of his passing. The body was returned to Paris and buried with proper pomp in the Montmartre cemetery. Mme. Halévy, for some weeks again resident at a sanitarium, was not in attendance.

Though he continues to occupy a prominent spot in the histories of opera, Halévy has dropped out of the active repertoire, and even *La Juive* is revived only for an occasional tenor who wants to emulate Caruso in the role of Eléazar. Other than his stage works, he left only a few songs and choral pieces and less than a handful of instrumental works—all forgotten.

RECORDINGS: On records there is a fair sampling of arias from *La Juive* and a few from other operas (most of them pre-electric), but no adequate complete recording of *La Juive* has yet appeared. (There was a jackleg version made by a transitory company and starring one Miklos Gafny; later there was a piracy of Richard Tucker's New Orleans performance, and an RCA album of highlights, also featuring Tucker.)

[1158] WERNER, Heinrich (Vâr´-ner, Hīn´-rikh)

BORN: Kirchohmfeld, October 2, 1800
DIED: Braunschweig, May 3, 1833

Not to be confused with his priestly namesake of seventy years earlier, who specialized in church music, this short-lived Heinrich Werner wrote parlor songs, male quartets, and salonesque piano pieces. He is remembered chiefly for his setting of Goethe's *"Heidenröslein,"* almost as popular in Germany as Schubert's. RECORDINGS: Recordings have been made by Johanna Gadski and others.

[1159] BREE, Johannes Bernardus van (Brā, Yō-hàn´-nes Bâr-när´-doos vàn)

VIOLINIST, CONDUCTOR, TEACHER
BORN: Amsterdam, January 29, 1801
DIED: Amsterdam, February 14, 1857

Son and pupil of a music teacher, Bree was assisting his father by the time he was twelve, and became a violinist in the orchestra of Amsterdam's Théâtre Français at eighteen. Two years later he left to make appearances and tours as a soloist, but from 1828 he turned more and more to conducting, both of choral and orchestral groups. In 1830 he took charge of the Felix Meritis orchestral concerts (founded in 1777), and he had much to do with the establishment in 1829 of the Association for the Promotion of the Art of Music. He became director of its Caecilia Orchestra in 1841, its president from 1849 to 1850, and director of its conservatory from 1853 until his death. Bree had a passion for German music and introduced many of its eighteenth- and nineteenth-century masterpieces to Dutch audiences, though his own compositions were French-derived. He produced 3 operas, 2 symphonies, 5 violin concerti, and much choral music. RECORDINGS: Neville Marriner has recorded his best-known work, an *Allegro* for four four-part string groups.

[1160] LINDBLAD, Adolf Fredrik (Lind'-blåd, Å'-dolf Fred'-rēk)
TEACHER
BORN: Skänninge, February 1, 1801
DIED: Löfvingsborg, August 23, 1878

An adopted child, Adolf Lindblad was unrelated to his contemporary, Otto Jonas Lindblad (1809–64), a choral composer of some note. He soon abandoned the business world, for which he was intended, and eventually studied music at the University of Uppsala. One of his first pupils was Jenny Lind (1820–87), though the fact that her voice broke down early in her career and had to be retrained does not seem to speak well for him. After two years of travel, during which he became friends with Felix Mendelssohn **[1200]**, Lindblad settled down in Stockholm as director of a music school, which was attended by various members of the royal family. When she was sixteen, Lind played a role in his only opera *Frondörerna (The Frondists)*. Though he won the support of such important musicians as Spohr **[1112]** and Mendelssohn, who conducted Lindblad's symphony in Leipzig, his fellow countrymen found him too avant-garde. He gave up his school in 1861 and devoted the rest of his life to writing the songs on which his reputation now chiefly rests. Faithful Jenny sang them whenever she could, and after the composer died they were published in an integral edition. RECORDINGS: A number of the songs have been recorded, most recently by such singers as Elisabeth Söderström and Erik Saedén.

[1161] KALLIWODA, Johann Wenzel (Käl'-i-vō-då, Yō'-hån Vent'-sel)
VIOLINIST, CONDUCTOR
BORN: Prague, February 21, 1801
DIED: Karlsruhe, December 3, 1866

Although he answered to "Jan Křtitl Václav Kalivoda," this composer is best known by his German name. He became, in 1811, one of the first students at the Prague Conservatory, where he studied violin with the elder Pixis (see 1128), and five years later joined the orchestra of the opera house under Weber **[1124]**. A fine, though not flashy, violinist, he left to tour in 1821 and soon afterward ran into Prince Karl Egon II von Fürstenberg, whose castle at Donaueschingen was already a citadel of high culture and

who persuaded him to join his household as chief musician. In Donaueschingen, Kalliwoda married the *prima donna* Teresa Brunetti; their son Wilhelm (1827–93) later dominated musical life in Karlsruhe. In his years at Donaueschingen, Kalliwoda made it one of the most important musical centers in Germany. Given free rein, he produced many important operas and symphonic works there, and attracted the cream of the virtuosi. The upheavals of 1848 and a fire that destroyed the theater made his work at first difficult and then impossible, and he eventually retired to Karlsruhe on a handsome pension. Kalliwoda wrote fairly prodigally in all forms (2 operas, 7 symphonies), but only his early work is said to do his talent justice. RECORDINGS: Jindřich Rohan has recorded his first symphony, and Hermann Baumann an *Introduction and Rondo* for horn and orchestra.

[1162] LANNER, Josef Franz Karl (Lån'-ner, Yō'-zef Frånts Kärl)
VIOLINIST, CONDUCTOR
BORN: Vienna, April 12, 1801
DIED: Oberdöbling, April 14, 1843

Whether Lanner "invented" the waltz is arguable, but it was certainly he and his sometime partner, the elder Johann Strauss, who made it the dance craze of the century. The son of a glovemaker, Martin Lanner, he was born within the confines of the Vienna wall. He is said to have mastered the violin and the art of composition mostly from observing others. In 1813 he joined the dance orchestra of Michael Pamer, a generally amiable drunk who specialized in *ländler*, and who, in his cups, was given to fits of rage. After five years of putting up with him, Lanner decided he could do as well on his own, and with two coevals, the Drahanek brothers, who played violin and guitar respectively, began playing dances on streetcorners and in parks for whatever groschen (Austrian coins) people might offer. Within the year he had taken on a violist of fourteen named Johann Strauss **[1177]**, and later added a cellist. The pickings were at first slim, and for a time Lanner and Strauss (later known as Johann, Sr.) roomed together to cut costs and even shared clothes. But gradually people began to take notice— Franz Schubert **[1153]** heard them and approved—and the contrast between the blond poetic-looking Lanner and the dark, explosive Strauss particularly attracted feminine attention. In the evenings Lanner sketched out new pieces, which he later scored in meticulous script. Shortly he found a publisher

in the canny Diabelli **[1100]** and later in Tobias Haslinger. It is said that he sometimes
used Strauss compositions (he being the
"boss") without credit, as Pamer had previously used his.

By 1824 the quintet had become a string
orchestra that performed sometimes in the
Prater and sometimes in night spots. But demand continued to rise, wind and percussion
instruments were added, and the organization split down the middle, with Lanner
conducting one group and Strauss the other.
Lanner's pieces were characterized by their
romantic lyricism, Strauss's by their rhythmic verve, and soon their admirers chose up
sides. The usual irresponsible gossip sprang
up, in which it appeared that Strauss was
not getting his due. One night in 1825 at the
Schwarzer Bock, Strauss thought Lanner
had insulted him, and when the smoke
cleared, the instruments and the glassware
were in shards. That ended the partnership,
and though they later resumed their friendly
relations, Strauss, in getting off on his own,
did not hesitate to raid Lanner's personnel.
But in 1828 Lanner married Franziska Jahns
and a year later was unexpectedly appointed
imperial *Hofballmusikdirektor*. He held this
high post until one night, somewhat the
worse for wine, he suggested that the
Archduchess Sophie feel how wet his shirt
was. He was summarily dismissed, though
he continued to hold a post as director of the
Second Viennese Regimental Band. He died
of typhus and overwork two days after his
forty-second birthday, in a Vienna suburb.
His son August bid fair to carry on the waltz
tradition but died of tuberculosis at twenty-
one; his daughter Katti became a well-
known ballerina.

RECORDINGS: Lanner left over 200 dance
pieces and marches. After years of being discounted as inferior to Strauss's, they have
more recently been seen as masterful poetic
miniatures. LPs devoted entirely to Lanner
have appeared from Willy Boskovsky and
Kurt Rapf, and his music appears increasingly in Vienna dance anthologies.

[1163] LORTZING, Gustav Albert (Lôrt'-
zing, Gōōs'-tȧf Ȧl'-bȧrt)
ACTOR, SINGER, CONDUCTOR
BORN: Berlin, October 23, 1801
DIED: Berlin, January 21, 1851

Though several Lortzing *Singspiele* remain
staples in Germany, they are rarely played
elsewhere (though this writer once knew a
singer who had done them in Milwaukee). It
is said that they do not "travel"—are too
German, too provincial, too silly. Yet, on

records at least, they seem perfectly delightful. Granted that they follow the *opéra-
comique* formula, exhibit at times a sort of
Teutonic heartiness, and invite pratfall acting, none of these are characteristics that
have stood in the way of other more successful comic operas.

Albert Lortzing's life reads like an opera
—a *semiseria*. His parents, having refined
his grandfather's occupation of dealing in
hides, sold leather goods. His mother, *née*
Charlotte Sophie Seidel, but of French parentage, was musical and probably gave him
his first lessons, though he studied more formally with local professionals. In the turmoil of 1812, the shop went broke, and the
Lortzings became, in effect, strolling players,
beginning with a six-month engagement in
Breslau. For nearly a dozen years they appeared all over Germany. Albert, who was
learning his métier through independent
study and astute observation, played occasional juvenile roles and wrote music, sometimes for the vehicles in which his family
appeared. In 1817 they joined a touring company operated by a Tyrolese, Josef Derossi.
While it was playing Cologne in 1823, Lortzing married one of the actresses, Rosina
Ahles, two years older than he was, and
wrote his first opera, *Ali Pascha von Janina*.
The couple also shortly began producing
children, who eventually, living and dead,
totaled eleven. In 1826 they joined the court
theater at Detmold, which that winter premiered *Ali Pascha* to tempered applause at
Münster. Lortzing was now occasionally appearing as an operatic tenor and as an actor,
though at first he was not liked. (He and his
wife were, by the way, Romeo and Juliet, in
the 1825 premiere of Friedrich Schlegel's
now-standard translation of Shakespeare's
play.)

After seven years at Detmold, during
which Lortzing turned out several *Singspiele*
that were essentially pastiches, the couple
rejoined Lortzing's parents at the
Stadttheater in Leipzig, where one of their
colleagues was Richard Wagner's **[1230]** sister Johanna. There, in 1835, Lortzing completed his first full-length opera, *Die beiden
Schützen (The Two Marksmen)*, but even
though he was no Wagner, it was at first ignored. Finally two years later, with its composer in the lead, it was produced by the
Leipzig company and was a great success.
Not only was it taken up by other theaters,
but Lortzing was urged to produce a successor. That turned out to be *Zar und Zimmermann* (in which his mother played Widow
Browe), a fiction about Czar Peter the
Great's apprentice years in Holland, a yarn
which had already attracted the likes of Gré-

try [919] and Donizetti [1155]. It seems not
to have lived up to the Leipzigers' expectations, but two years later its Berlin premiere
started it on its way to becoming its composer's most popular and enduring work. The
several works that followed it, however, including the 1840 Hans Sachs, a forebear of
Wagner's Meistersinger, made no special impact. But with Der Wildschütz (The
Poacher), Lortzing hit again on New Year's
Eve, 1842. His career soon reached its brief
peak: early in 1844, with a change of management in the theater, he was named Kapellmeister. He had bids from several theaters for his newly completed Undine, based
on the romantic novel by Baron de La
Motte-Fouqué that had once attracted
E. T. A. Hoffmann [1086]. The contract
went to Hamburg, but delays saw it put on
first at Magdeburg, though its success was
not assured until the Hamburg performance
with Lortzing at the helm. But beyond this
pinnacle of success yawned the abyss.

As a conductor in Leipzig, Lortzing had
alienated powerful members of the company, and when he returned from Hamburg
he found the door closed to him. Early the
next year, 1846, however, he was taken on as
conductor by the Theater an der Wien in
Vienna, where he premiered his Der Waffenschmied (The Armorer) in May. Though
it later became a favorite in Germany, the
Viennese took an instant dislike to it, and
the theater refused his next opera, Zum
Grossadmiral (At the Sign of the Admiral of
the Fleet). Soon Lortzing found himself having to share his post with Franz von Suppé
[1262]. Misreading the potential of the 1848
revolution, Lortzing filled his next effort,
Regina, with revolutionary sentiments, and,
the revolt having failed, was unable to get it
produced anywhere. Meanwhile the theater
had fallen on hard times, and by September
he was again among the unemployed.

Once again fate seemed to smile when yet
another new Leipzig management invited
him to replace Berlin-bound Julius Rietz
[1227] as conductor. Lortzing successfully
produced his Rolands Knappen (Roland's
Pages) there, but then Rietz reclaimed the
conducting post. Asked to remain in a
flunkey job, Lortzing quit. For some months
he was forced to return to his old strolling
life. Fatigue and worry began to impair his
health, and his hearing began to go. In April
1850 he gratefully accepted a job with a
small Berlin theater that paid him 50 thalers
a month. (Because of the nonexistence of
copyright, his operas were played all over
Germany while his family was literally
starving.) His benefit night in Berlin did not
even cover expenses, and at year's end he

was given a month's notice. He became ill
and finally had to go to bed. On the night of
January 20, while his last opera, Die Opernprobe (The Opera Rehearsal) was being premiered in Frankfurt am Main, he suffered a
stroke and died the next day.

RECORDINGS: The operas Opernprobe,
Undine, Waffenschmied, and Wildschütz
have all been recorded by Electrola (EMI).
Hans Sachs, conducted by Max Loy, is
available on a Melodram recording, and
there are three or four versions of Zar und
Zimmermann and innumerable excerpts
from these and some of the other operas.

[1164] BELLINI, Vincenzo (Bel-lē'-nē,
Vĕn-chänt'-zō)
BORN: Catania, November 3, 1801
DIED: Puteaux, September 23, 1835

Bellini, with Rossini [1143] and Donizetti
[1155], one of the three cornerstones of the
modern Italian operatic repertoire, was the
youngest, the least productive, and the
shortest-lived of the three. Moreover what
we know of him suggests that his life was the
least interesting. When we have discounted,
as we must, most of the Bellini legends, we
find neither a great lover nor a remarkable
personality. Obsessed with his music and
avid of success, he turns out often to have
been selfish, egocentric, and paranoid, for all
his friends' bestowal of labels like "pure"
and "noble" on him. Tall and handsome he
may have been ("a sigh in dancing pumps,"
said Heine), but the several portraits and
busts that survive are so different that it is
hard to see him as he must have been. As an
opera composer, Bellini was deeply concerned with dramatic effect, mostly through
vocal means, and was scrupulous enough to
train his singers to produce it. But the chief
impression that his music leaves on the modern listener is as an outpouring of melody
paramount to all other musical considerations—an approach that was to affect not
only opera composers but such instrumental
writers as Chopin [1208].

Though born in Sicily, Bellini did not fit
the swarthy stereotype. His paternal grandfather, Vincenzo Tobia Bellini, a conservatory-trained musician, had, in fact, come
there from the Abruzzi, and had served as a
maestro di cappella for both noble families
and churches. His eldest son, Rosario,
Vincenzo's father, took up his calling. But
Vincenzo's blond hair and blue eyes came
from his mother, a native of Catania, baptized Agata Ferlito. Vincenzo, the oldest of
her seven children, was the only one with
any strong response to music. Catania, flat-

tened by an earthquake a century earlier, was a cultural backwater, so he probably owed his musical interest chiefly to his home environment. For all the rumors of his *Wunderkind* prowess, we really know very little of his childhood. His first serious teacher was apparently his grandfather, and there remain some early religious compositions and songs probably written under the grandfather's tutelage. Obviously, however, Vincenzo made a local impression, for in 1819, prompted by the new governor, the Duke of San Martino, the Catanian city fathers raised money to send him to the Royal College of Music in Naples.

There, despite his advanced years and attainments, Bellini was placed in basic courses. In his eight years at the college, he made friends with, among others, the brothers Ricci [1183, 1205], Mercadante [1148], and Francesco Florimo, later to be the school's librarian and Bellini's most intimate correspondent. He also fell in love with a girl named Maddalena Fumaroli, but her father barred their marriage. Later, when Bellini had left and won a measure of fame, Signor Fumaroli advised him that he had suffered a change of heart, but by then Bellini had lost interest. Maddalena died, supposedly of a broken heart, a year before her father did. Meanwhile, back at the college, Bellini had been forced publicly to eat crow for an unseemly exhibition of democratic sentiments during the constitutional upheaval of 1820. But he had also won a scholarship and admission to the class of Nicola Zingarelli, the school's director, who introduced him to the music of Mozart [992] and Haydn [871]. Bellini rose to the status of *maestrino* (the equivalent of graduate assistant), and late in 1824 completed his first opera, *Adelson e Salvini*. Presented in the college theater that winter with a student (all male!) cast, it was so successful that it was repeated nearly every Sunday for the rest of the term and won its composer a commission for the Teatro San Carlo.

The result was *Bianca e Fernando*. After some delays it was played before the queen on May 30, 1826, the name day of the once and future kings named Ferdinando, the title being temporarily changed, in deference to that fact, to *Bianco e Gernando*. Though applause was considered rude when the royal family was present, it broke out spontaneously. The upshot was that Domenico Barbaja, Italy's most powerful impresario, who had a finger in the La Scala pie, invited Bellini to write a work for that theater. When Bellini arrived in Milan in mid-April, Mercadante introduced him to the poet Felice Romani, to whom his operatic fortunes

were to be linked for most of his career. Romani was one of the most prolific librettists of the age, set by more than 100 composers (the notable exception was Verdi [1232]). The immediate result of their collaboration was *Il Pirata (The Pirate)*, which got a thunderous ovation on its first night, when it starred the tenor Giovanni Battista Rubini and the baritone Antonio Tamburini, whose stunning careers had their origin in Bellini's music. (They set standards for Italian singing, no small thanks to the composer, who trained them to do what his music demanded.)

Bellini, unlike Rossini and Donizetti, worked slowly and fussily (he violently disapproved of those who did otherwise), and his next opera was not forthcoming for eighteen months. Meanwhile, on April 7, 1828, the revised *Bianca e Fernando* (the original title restored) opened the new Teatro Carlo Felice in Genoa, before the Sardinian king for whom the theater was named. Despite Bellini's conviction that Donizetti had plotted its failure, the work was a success again. In June the composer signed a contract with Barbaja for a second La Scala opera for the next winter's carnival. Bellini and Romani found their subject in a French novel, *La Solitaire*, though, as noted, the resultant *La Straniera* came slowly. During this period Bellini met a wealthy young matron named Giuditta Turina, wife of a capitalist. He spent much time on the Turina estate and those of the Cantùs, her relatives, and soon made her his mistress. *La Straniera* finally opened on February 14, 1829, two months late. Again featuring Tamburini, it was another smash hit.

By then, Bellini was already discussing with Parma a work to open the new opera house there. By demanding too much money and rejecting a libretto by a local literary light, he managed to make enemies among the directorate and disaster was being predicted. Romani was summoned, and the two settled on Voltaire's *Zaire*. Then, quite typically, the librettist stalled until the Parmese threatened to abrogate the deal. Consequently, when the opera (with the Italian title *Zaira*) reached the stage on May 16, 1829, such a reservoir of bad feeling had built up (a 2 A.M. final curtain did not help) that it was written off as a failure. Failure was alien to Bellini's experience, and the subsequent triumphs of works by his rivals Giovanni Pacini *(Il Talismano)* and Rossini *(Guillaume Tell)* rendered him particularly tetchy. Toward year's end Bellini went to Venice to oversee a production of *Il Pirata* and to arrange for a new opera for La Fenice. He agreed, if Pacini defaulted on such a work as it appeared he would, to treat the Romeo and Juliet legend. Romani duly supplied the text for *I Capuleti e i Montecchi* (a far cry from Shakespeare's version). This time it was Bellini, his health affected by the dank Venetian winter, who dragged his feet. But when the curtain fell on March 11, 1830, he knew he was back on track, and signed a contract for another new work for the following season (turning down a request from Turin).

Bellini's health remained bad—probably the first signs of the amoebic dysentery that would from then on recur every summer and finally kill him. However, he contracted for another new opera at La Scala for 1831 and yet another with a new Milanese management. By now he had seen in the great soprano Giuditta Pasta the kind of female voice he wanted, and the two agreed with Romani on a setting of Victor Hugo's *Hernani* for the new company. But by December threats of wholesale deletions by the censors forced them to give it up. Instead, Bellini wrote *La Sonnambula.* Starring both Pasta and Rubini, it was a sensation at the Teatro Carcano on March 6, 1831. Then Bellini and Romani began work on *Norma* for La Scala. Bellini, despite his nervousness over the approaching cholera epidemic, completed the music in November. In rehearsals, Pasta balked at the *"Casta diva"* aria, and the composer had to browbeat her into singing it. (She later admitted she had been very wrong to question it.) On December 26, *Norma* opened a La Scala season that would also include Pacini's *Il Corsaro* and Donizetti's *Anna Bolena.* To Bellini's horror, the first-night audience was baffled. He immediately smelled a conspiracy, but the work's power soon asserted itself.

His reputation now secure, the thirty-year-old Bellini went on vacation, visiting friends in Naples and making a triumphal progress through Sicily. (Catania had struck a medal in his honor a year or so earlier.) He caught up with Giuditta Turina in Rome and, after spending some time with her, went on to produce *Norma* in Bergamo— Donizetti country! By September he got around to thinking about the La Fenice commission. After weeks of discussion, he and Romani decided on a piece about Queen Christina of Sweden. But it failed to develop, and instead they set to work on *Beatrice di Tenda.* Despite the growing suspicions of her husband, la Turina had followed her lover to Venice, causing increasing gossip. Moreover, Romani, who had taken on more work than he could handle, failed to uphold his end, and eventually Bellini called on the authorities to intervene. By cutting corners,

he managed to get *Beatrice,* whose failure he correctly predicted, onstage by March 16, 1833, the tail end of the season. Its fiasco occasioned a paper war in the journals that drove a wedge between the composer and librettist—permanently, as it turned out.

That April Bellini traveled to London by way of Paris, to honor a long-standing commitment to the King's Theatre. *Norma* and *Il Pirata* were enormously successful there, though the English understandably thought less of *I Capuleti.* Afterward Bellini produced *La Sonnambula* with the great Maria Malibran at Drury Lane. He returned to Paris in August and settled in. In the meantime Turina had discovered Bellini's letters to his wife and had thrown her out of the house. When she offered to come to her lover in Paris, Bellini coldly rejected her on the grounds that she had been unfaithful to him. He intended to stay there only long enough to firm up a contract with the Opéra, but the deal fell through. However, through the good offices of Rossini (whom Bellini persisted in seeing as the enemy), the Thé-âtre-Italien produced *Il Pirata* and *I Capuleti* and commissioned a new work from him. The libretto (a long way after Walter Scott) was entrusted to Count Carlo Pepoli, the exiled poetical amateur who had furnished Rossini with some song lyrics, including that of *La Danza.* The work was set in Commonwealth Plymouth and called, with admirable illogic, *I Puritani di Scozia (The Scottish Puritans).* Bellini wasted a good deal of time buttering up Rossini and fretting because the theater had also commissioned a work from Donizetti. He did much of the actual composing in suburban Puteaux at the home of a young English Jew named Samuel Levys or Lewis, while being bombarded with offers from all over. A brilliant *Sonnambula,* with Giulia Grisi and Rubini, at the Théâtre-Italien whetted the public's appetite for *I Puritani,* which opened on January 24, 1835. The stars were Grisi, Rubini, Tamburini, and the rotund basso Luigi Lablache, forever after known as "the Puritani quartet," and there have been few such triumphs in the history of opera. A week later the composer was awarded the *Légion d'honneur,* and shortly afterward presented the score to the queen. Then he rested on his laurels. There were desultory negotiations with this house and that, and some talk of getting married, though there seems to have been no particular bride in view. In lieu of a new opera for the San Carlo in Naples, Bellini revised *Puritani* but missed the deadline. He continued to stew over the "Donizetti menace."

In May he moved out to Puteaux again

for the summer. By August his chronic malady had returned, eventually forcing him to go to bed. Levys and his wife suspected cholera, which had been rife for some time, and tried to keep him isolated, though a few visitors managed to elude them. Bellini's physician was optimistic; then suddenly the patient took a bad turn, and on September 22 he suffered convulsions and went into a coma. The next day a friend, Baron Aymé d'Aquino, riding in the neighborhood, stopped by to visit, but was refused admission. On his way home that evening, a thunderstorm caught him in Puteaux, and he sought refuge at Levys'. He found the doors open and the house deserted—save for Bellini's corpse, already grown cold. The autopsy did not bear out rumors of poison, though medical science did not then understand the cause of his death. The pallbearers at Les Invalides included Rossini, Cherubini [1019], and Paër [1069]. The body was interred at Père Lachaise, then moved to Catania forty-one years later. The Catania opera house is now the Teatro Bellini.

RECORDINGS: Bellini's nonoperatic works are of no moment, though there are recordings of some pretty songs and an early oboe concerto (Heinz Holliger). *Il Pirata, I Capuleti, La Sonnambula, Norma, Beatrice di Tenda*, and *I Puritani* have all received commercial recordings, and the others exist in pirated versions.

[1165] VARLAMOV, Alexander

Yegorovich (V är´-là-mof, Ål-yek-sàn´-der Yā-gō-rō´-věch)
TEACHER, CHOIRMASTER
BORN: Moscow, November 27, 1801
DIED: St. Petersburg, October 27, 1848

Scion of a noble Moldavian family, Varlamov took to music early, teaching himself several instruments. At ten he became a choirboy at the court of Alexander I and a pupil and protégé of the director Bortniansky [976]. In 1819 he was sent to Holland, where the czar's sister Anna Pavlovna had married Crown Prince Willem, to direct the Russian Embassy choir. After four years he returned to St. Petersburg to teach voice, violin, and guitar. Early in 1832 he went to Moscow as music director of the imperial theaters. There he became enormously successful as a composer of songs on the Alyabiev [1125] model, only a few of them with any ethnic pretensions. He also wrote ballets and incidental music and a vocal method. He spent his last three years in St. Petersburg, dying of a heart attack a month before his forty-seventh birthday. RECORDINGS:

The songs are still sung and turn up in various recorded anthologies. One, "The Red Sarafan," has long passed as a folksong.

[1166] GHYS, Joseph (Gēs, Zhō-zef´)

VIOLINIST, TEACHER
BORN: Ghent, 1801
DIED: St. Petersburg, August 22, 1848

Ghys was a pupil of the French violinist Charles Philippe Lafont, himself a pupil of Conradin Kreutzer [1096] and Pierre Rode (and, in 1839, the victim of a traffic accident). Ghys became a violin teacher in France, and then in the 1830s began to make concert tours to various parts of Europe. He wrote a number of pieces for his instrument, including chamber works and a concerto, but his name survives chiefly through a salon trifle called "Amaryllis." RECORDINGS: There is a piano recording by Hans Kann.

[1167] NIEDERMEYER, Abraham Louis

(Nē´-der-mī-er, Á´-brà-hàm Lōō-ēē´)
EDUCATOR
BORN: Nyon, April 27, 1802
DIED: Paris, March 14, 1861

In 1817 Louis Niedermeyer went from his Swiss home on Lake Geneva to Vienna, to study with Moscheles [1146], then to Rome to study with Valentino Fioravanti [1040], and finally to Naples to study with Nicola Zingarelli. With the assistance of Rossini [1143], who befriended him, he began his notably unsuccessful operatic career there with a trifle called *Il Reo per amore (Guilty of Love)* in 1820. He then returned to Geneva, where he had some success as a teacher of piano and composer of songs, but moved on to Paris in 1823. There, again on Rossini's recommendation, he got the Théâtre-Italien to put on his one-act *La Casa nel bosco (The House in the Woods)*. Its resounding failure made him forswear opera for nearly a decade. In the middle 1830s he taught at a school in Brussels but returned to Paris to produce his *Alessandro Stradella* (a disaster) in 1837. He had no more luck with *Marie Stuart* in 1844. Two years later, with Rossini's blessing, he raided the latter's *La Donna del lago (The Lady of the Lake)* for *Robert Bruce*. It was as close as he came to operatic success in Paris, though the critics—notably Berlioz [1175]—panned it. After *La Fronde* went down for the count in 1853, Niedermeyer abandoned opera for sacred music and songs, for both of which genres he had a talent. He took over the moribund Institution Royale de Musique

Classique et Religieuse and renamed it L'École de Musique Religieuse Classique, though it came popularly to be known as L'École Niedermeyer. Aided by government subsidy, it throve under his direction. (Its most famous product was probably Gabriel Fauré [1424].) In 1857 he inaugurated a journal *La Maîtrise,* dedicated to sacred choral music. Besides being a successful song composer, Niedermeyer was an important figure in the restoration of Gregorian chant. Other Niedermeyer pupils were Audran [1376], Boëllmann [1549], Gigout [1417], and Messager [1474]. When Berlioz was finally admitted to the Institut, one of his first duties was to conduct a Niedermeyer *Mass*—ironic, for Niedermeyer had several times gotten more votes than he. RECORDINGS: The much-recorded "old Italian air" *"Pietà, Signore"* ("Mercy, Lord"), once assigned to Stradella [541] and later to Rossini, is now agreed to be Niedermeyer's. In an earlier age, many singers also recorded his *"Le Lac"* ("The Lake").

[1168] PUGNI, Cesare (Poon'-yē, Chā'-zà-rā)
VIOLINIST, PIANIST
BORN: Genoa, May 31, 1802
DIED: St. Petersburg, January 26, 1870

Pugni, once thought to be a Milanese by birth, was trained at the Milan Conservatory —by Alessandro Rolla [1001] and Bonifazio Asioli [1057], among others. After having a ballet, *Elerz e Zulmida,* successfully produced at La Scala in 1826, he embarked on an increasingly unsuccessful operatic career. In 1834, after five operas and two years at the keyboard in the La Scala orchestra, he gave up the quest. La Scala also gave him up, owing to what are mysteriously described as his irregular ways. After nearly ten years of a hand-to-mouth existence in Paris, he returned to ballet in collaboration with the choreographer Louis Perrot. After successes in London, Paris, and Milan, Pugni was made imperial ballet composer in St. Petersburg in 1854. There he often collaborated with Marius Petipa. In all, he is said to have written or contributed to as many as 300 ballets—good danceable music that, like so much of its ilk of that day, has little to say apart from its function. Pugni also wrote a good deal of sacred music (many Masses) and a few orchestral pieces. RECORDINGS: Richard Bonynge has recorded excerpts from his ballet *Esmeralda.*

[1169] MOLIQUE, Wilhelm Bernhard (Mō-lēk', Vil'-helm Bârn'-härt)
VIOLINIST, CONDUCTOR
BORN: Nuremberg, October 7, 1802
DIED: Cannstadt, May 10, 1869

Molique's father was a municipal bandsman in Nuremberg and taught the boy several instruments. He showed, however, remarkable aptitude for the violin. Spohr [1112] heard him while in Nuremberg in 1815 and was sufficiently impressed to give him some lessons. The following year, with financial aid from King Maximilian I himself, Molique went to Munich to study with Pietro Rovelli, the royal *Konzertmeister.* In 1818 he was taken into the orchestra of the Theater an der Wien in Vienna but was called back to Munich two years later to take Rovelli's place. Shortly afterward he began making concert tours through Germany and wowed audiences from Nuremberg to Berlin with his phrasing, intonation, and cantabile. In Munich he was particularly friendly with the first flutist, Theobald Boehm, the inventor of the modern flute, who sometimes toured with him, and for whom Molique wrote several compositions. In 1826 he accepted the post of Music Director at the court of William I of Württemberg in Stuttgart. In the next several years his tours and fame became international. When the 1848 Revolution turned nasty in Stuttgart—what with the granting and rescinding of a constitution and all—Molique fled to England, where he was both popular and successful. In 1860 he contributed *Abraham* to the insatiable Victorian hunger for oratorios. He made his public farewell six years later and retired to Cannstadt, near Stuttgart. Besides the oratorio, he left a couple of Masses, a symphony, several concerti, and a good deal of chamber music. RECORDINGS: Molique is represented on records by the Concerto for Flute (for Boehm), Quintet for Flute and Strings, the Concertino for Oboe, and some pieces for concertina and piano.

[1170] HERZ, Henri *(né Heinrich)* (Ârts, On'-rē)
PIANIST, TEACHER, MANUFACTURER
BORN: Vienna, January 6, 1803
DIED: Paris, January 5, 1888

Like Franz Hünten [1145], Herz was idolized in the Paris salons for his glittering technique and composed frothy stuff that the public bought by the yard. The likeness is not accidental: after the elder Herz had given his son some basics, he took his family to Coblenz where the boy became a pupil of

Daniel Hünten. When he turned sixteen, he showed such promise that his father trotted him off to Paris and entered him in the Conservatoire, where, like Hünten, he studied composition with Antonín Reicha [1059]. Despite a first prize in piano three years later, Herz disliked the style and technique he had been taught, and set about deliberately to imitate those of Moscheles [1146]. Then he settled into a cozy niche in Paris, composing for publication, concertizing, and teaching—at very high fees. His romantic good looks and his fashion-plate attire irritated the press but did nothing to hinder his success. A series of tours with the violinist Charles Philippe Lafont, begun in 1831, ended in 1839 when the latter was killed in a road accident at Tarbes. Herz appeared in London in 1833–34, where he sometimes played duets with Moscheles and Cramer [1067]. Shortly afterward he bought into a piano factory operated by one Klepfer, but the venture went bankrupt, necessitating Herz's return to the road. In 1842 he was appointed professor of piano (appropriately) to the female students at the Conservatoire.

In 1845 Herz toured the Caribbean and Mexico, then spent the next six years crisscrossing the United States, his way prepared by a self-appointed publicity man named Ullmann ("Ph.D., Vienna Imperial Polytechnic Institute"). Ullmann persuaded him to react to American "bigthink" with a piece for eight pianos, but Herz drew the line at appearing with Jenny Lind under the auspices of Phineas T. Barnum. Reviews were not always favorable; one journalist, groggy from the knees-and-elbows pianism of Leopold de Meyer, "the lion pianist" then touring the states, likened Herz's traceries to patterns drawn by "frost-fairies on the window-pane." (Herz and de Meyer dueled briefly in the Baltimore papers, when the latter left the stage littered with pianos before a Herz concert.) Herz later published a memoir of his tour, in which, typically, he views himself with wry amusement. On his return to Paris, he went into manufacturing pianos on his own and won a first prize at the 1855 Paris Exposition. He also built the Salle Henri Herz (now vanished) and, with his brother Jacques Simon, founded the École Spéciale de Piano for ladies. He retired in 1874 and died on the eve of his eighty-fifth birthday.

RECORDINGS: Frank Cooper has devoted an LP side to his music, and Earl Wild has recorded variations on a Rossini aria.

[1171] LACHNER, Franz Paul (Làkh'-ner, Frànts Poul)
ORGANIST, CONDUCTOR, TEACHER
BORN: Rain am Lech, April 2, 1803
DIED: Munich, January 20, 1890

Franz Lachner was half-brother to Munich court organist Theodor Lachner, and brother to conductor Ignaz Lachner [1192] and organists Vinzenz, Thekla, and Christiane Lachner. On the death of the father and teacher of the brood, a poor Bavarian village organist, Franz went to Munich, where he lived shakily for a year. In 1823 he won an organist's post at a Viennese church and there studied with the Abbé Stadler and Simon Sechter [1129]. He also became a friend and drinking companion of Franz Schubert [1153], to whose biography he later contributed much information. (He and brother Ignaz appear in the left foreground of Moritz von Schwind's well-known drawing of a "Schubertiad.") By 1825 Lachner was acting as a coach at the Kärntnertortheater and worked his way up to *Kapellmeister* in 1829. It was he who engineered Schubert's unsuccessful conducting tryout there. After three years at the Mannheim Opera, he came back to Munich in 1836 and joined the Royal Opera of Ludwig I. By 1852 he had become *Generalmusikdirektor* at court and the chief musical power in the city. His high ideals and exacting standards gave Munich a first-class musical establishment. Lachner promoted the music of his contemporaries, including that of Wagner [1230], which he did not care for. Nor did he get along with Wagner. When the accession of mad Ludwig II gave the Wagnerians the upper hand, Lachner was sent on vacation and supplanted with Bülow [1310]. Lachner was retired in 1868. In 1873, however, at his suggestion, Brahms [1329] and Wagner received the Royal Order of Maximilian, and ten years later he was granted the freedom of the city. An important teacher, he numbered Josef Rheinberger [1368] among his most successful pupils. Lachner was a tireless, if derivative, composer, turning out, among other things, 4 operas, an oratorio, 8 Masses, a Requiem, 8 symphonies, 3 concerti, and much other instrumental and vocal music. He is perhaps best known today, however, for the recitatives he wrote for Cherubini's [1019] *Medea* (i.e., *Medée*, formerly in the *opéra-comique* format). RECORDINGS: James Bolle has recorded the Lachner wind octet.

[1172] ADAM, Adolphe-Charles (À-dàn', À-dolf' Shàrl)
TEACHER, CRITIC, IMPRESARIO

BORN: Paris, July 24, 1803
DIED: Paris, May 3, 1856

Adam was blessed with melodic inspiration and a fragile charm, and cursed with an inability to view his work critically. As a result his large *oeuvre*, which includes 70 operas, 14 ballets, and much other music, has left scarce any wrack behind—though everyone knows his Christmas song *"Cantique de Noël"* ("O Holy Night"), and the ballet *Giselle* has reestablished itself recently (not always as Adam wrote it) as a sort of ultimate test for prima ballerinas. (It is, by the way, the oldest in the repertoire.)

Adolphe Adam was the son of the important Alsatian-born piano teacher Jean Louis (or Johann Ludwig) Adam (1758–1848). Oddly Adam *père* was dead set against Adolphe's becoming a musician, refused to teach him, and denied him lessons from others. But the boy was eager, and finally, at seventeen, he was permitted to enroll at the Conservatoire on condition that he would eschew the musical stage. He soon became a sensation in the salons for his wild improvisations at the harmonium. Boieldieu [1084], however, recognized his talent and took him in hand, ultimately, abetted by some counterpoint training from Reicha [1059], getting him to the point in 1825 where he could entrust him with the composition of the overture (on Boieldieu themes) for his own masterpiece *La Dame blanche*. By then Adam had already been grinding out vaudevilles and other trifles for some of the smaller Paris theaters for some time. Having linked up with the ubiquitous playwright-librettist Eugène Scribe, he made a successful debut at the Opéra-Comique with *Pierre et Catherine* in 1829. The flood of works that followed was stemmed by the aftermath of the 1830 revolution, and Adam spent some time in London, where he produced his full-length ballet *Faust* at the King's Theatre in 1833.

A year later, back in Paris, came the one-act *Le Chalet*, Adam's first major success (it ran up a thousand performances at the Opéra-Comique in forty years). Adam's beloved mentor, Boieldieu (of whom he later wrote a memoir), though dying, attended. Later, Adam's friend Donizetti [1155] used a translation of the libretto for his own *Betly*. It was followed in 1836 by *Le Postillon de Longjumeau (The Coachman of Longjumeau)*, whose high-lying "postillion song" is still beloved of tenors and which continues to survive, at least in Germany. (In the United States it provided a vehicle for Barron Berthald, a real coachman-turned-singer.) In 1841 *Giselle*, a result of Théophile Gautier's infatuation with Ger-

man folklore as filtered through Heinrich Heine, was one of the greatest successes of the ballerina Carlotta Grisi. (Its current good health is owing to the Russians, who preserved it.) Another Grisi-starring role was in *Le Diable à quatre (The Devil to Pay)* two years later.

The year 1844 was crucial for Adam: he was elected to the Institut, produced his first grand opera, *Richard en Palestine* (unsuccessful), and was barred from the Opéra-Comique following a quarrel with the new management. Buoyed by his popularity, however, he plowed his capital and a good deal of borrowed money into an opera house of his own, the Opéra-National, dedicated to promoting the output of likely new composers. It opened in 1847. But the revolution came, and it closed forever, leaving Adam deeply in debt. An honest and kindly man, he directed that all his royalties be turned over to his creditors, and plunged into a frenzy of composing, teaching (he now had a Conservatoire post), and reviewing (for which he had considerable talent). Of his later operas, the 1852, *Si j'étais roi (If I Were King)* still gets an occasional hearing, and *Le Toréador* of 1849 includes a set of popular coloratura variations on the nursery tune we know as "Twinkle, Twinkle, Little Star." Having a long-lived parent failed to counteract the effects of overwork: Adam died in his sleep at the age of fifty-two.

RECORDINGS: Apart from excerpts, there is a German recording of *Le Postillon* and another of highlights from *Si j'étais roi*. Richard Bonynge has recorded *Le Diable à quatre* and the most authentic of the several *Giselles*. Albert Wolff conducts the overture to *Si j'étais roi*.

[1173] BERG, Isak Albert (Bârg, Ē-zȧk' Al-bârt')
SINGER, CONDUCTOR, TEACHER
BORN: Stockholm, August 22, 1803
DIED: Stockholm, December 1, 1886

Berg was one of the first Swedish singers to become internationally known. After graduating from the University of Uppsala in 1824 and passing a civil service test, he spent two years studying voice with Giuseppe Siboni, who was then director of the Royal Opera and the Academy of Music in Copenhagen. Concert tours in the next two years took him to Vienna, where he met Schubert [1153], who supposedly learned from him the Swedish melody he used in his E-flat major piano trio. Berg first sang in opera at Venice in 1828. He came home in 1830 to take over leadership of the Harmonic Society

Choir, which he conducted for seventeen years. The following year he was elected to the Swedish Academy and was appointed court singer and singing teacher to the Royal Theater. Among his pupils were members of the royal family but most notably Jenny Lind, who popularized many of the songs he wrote. RECORDINGS: Elisabeth Söderström has recorded one or two of the songs.

[1174] GURILEV, Alexander Lvovich
(Gōō'-ril-yof, Al-ek-sàn'-der Lyə-vōf'-ĕch)
VIOLINIST
BORN: Moscow, September 3, 1803
DIED: Moscow, September 11, 1858

Alexander Gurilev was the son of Sarti's [853] pupil Lev Stepanovich Gurilev, a serf belonging to Count Orlov, whose all-serf orchestra he conducted. The younger Gurilev played in the orchestra until the family was freed in 1831. He then settled in Moscow, where he became known for his piano transcriptions and his pretty salon songs. In his last years, Gurilev was incapacitated by paresis. RECORDINGS: Many of his salon songs turn up in recorded anthologies of Russian romances.

[1175] BERLIOZ, Louis Hector (Ber-lyōz', Lōō-ē' Ek-tôr')
CRITIC, CONDUCTOR
BORN: Côte-Saint-André, December 11, 1803
DIED: Paris, March 8, 1869

Writers of *opéras-comiques* aside, Berlioz was the first significant composer born in France in more than fifty years and the only one to make a mark there until the emergence of Gounod [1258] a decade before his death. Regarded by many as the ultimate musical Romantic, he was firmly rooted in Classicism and, as a critic and reviewer, served as a sort of musical conscience (often unheeded) for his times, urging attention to unfrivolous music and demanding respect for the composer's intentions. His music, like the man himself, was so individual that no convenient pigeonhole could be found for it, and Berlioz was not really established as a popular composer (if that is the term) until this century.

Hector Berlioz was born in a Dauphinois village between Grenoble and Vienne. His father, Louis, was a native of the place, its physician, and briefly its mayor—a man of not only considerable medical skill but also

of great intelligence and broad culture. Hector's mother was pious and flighty. There were three sisters and two brothers, but only two of the sisters survived adolescence. After trying his son in a local school, stressing (in the spirit of the times) jingoism, the military arts, and Catholicism, Dr. Berlioz took over his education himself and gave him a thorough and effective grounding in the humanities and sciences. Hector was stirred by music from the first, and when he unearthed his father's old flageolet, he was shown how to play it and was then given a real flute and a real music teacher—a violinist named Imbert, who taught him the guitar. The boy was soon attempting composition and playing for private musicales and public functions. At the turn of his teens, he fell wildly in love with Estelle Duboeuf, a pink-shod young woman from the neighborhood seven years his senior, who became the focus of his creative efforts. Through reading and listening, Berlioz improved his musical skills until at fifteen he elected to send off some of his compositions to a Paris publisher—without results.

But music was not in his parents' plans for him. In 1821 he acquired the requisite B.A. by examination and that May set out for Paris and medical school. He did not mind the lectures and disguised his natural horror of the dissecting room in outrageously cynical behavior. But he quickly discovered the Opéra, and not long afterward the library of the Conservatoire (where he had a run-in with Cherubini [1019] and successfully defended his right to use it.) Both places began to take more and more of his time. Discovering the gap between music as written and music as performed in Paris, he became a very vocal member of the audiences and, as a result, the acknowledged leader of the claque at the Opéra. After a year, fate played into his hands, for the government closed down the medical school as a supposed hotbed of opposition. An acquaintance introduced him to the composer Lesueur, who was a sort of throwback to the now-out-of-favor Gluckist school. After some hesitancy, he took Berlioz on as a pupil, and the two turned out to be a happy combination. It was at about this same time that Berlioz embarked on his career as a critic with a defense of Gluck [803] against the Rossinians [1143]. He was soon ambitious to have something performed and, after fooling about with a couple of opera libretti, wrote a cantata, *The Crossing of the Red Sea*, for which he rounded up some 200 volunteers, including a conductor from the Opéra. But the production failed to come off because many of the volunteers did not turn up and the parts proved indecipherable.

Berlioz finally, in 1824, had to let his family know that he was not going to be a doctor. His perplexed father cut off his support, relented, stopped funds again in a yo-yo pattern that lasted for some time. Berlioz gave lessons, wrote, nearly starved, and, for want of money, operated on his own ulcerated throat. Bound and determined to be heard, he borrowed funds to produce in 1825, a performance of his new *Mass.* It was successful, but further trouble erupted when his creditor went to his father for reimbursement, and his mother became so upset that she laid her curse on him. He had a try at the Prix de Rome competition but was rejected. In 1827 he was accepted, but his cantata *La Morte d'Orphée* won no award, owing mostly to the incompetence of the pianist. (The winner was the immortal Jean-Baptiste Guiraud, whoever he may have been—not to be confused with Ernest Guiraud [1352].) That same year Berlioz was introduced to Goethe's *Faust,* in Gérard de Nerval's translation, and to the plays of Shakespeare through an English company led by Charles Kemble. This company included an Irish actress of considerable beauty and talent, named Harriet Smithson, and Berlioz, thitherto apparently virtually celibate, fell painfully in love with her as a sort of *Ewigweibliche* projection of the playwright. Determined to catch her attention, when she failed to reply to his passionate messages, he decided on an all-Berlioz concert. By pulling some strings he secured the hall at the conservatory over Cherubini's protests. The concert, which included the *Waverly* overture and that to the opera-in-progress, *Les Francs-Juges,* was a success with almost everyone in the small audience, but not with Miss Smithson, who was riding the brief crest of her fame and apparently did not notice. While she was touring the provinces, Berlioz gave the Prix de Rome another try and won second prize, which brought him nothing, but convinced his father that perhaps the boy might yet amount to something. Shortly afterward the composer completed his *8 Scenes from "Faust"* and published the work at his own expense. Early in the new year, encouraged by rumors from her friends, he took lodgings across the street from Harriet, only to see her, a few days later, move out on her way to Holland and home.

Once more, in 1829, Berlioz entered the prize competition, the set subject being *La Mort de Cléopâtre.* He was now teaching in a school for girls and writing a good deal, though he was still making the barest of living; but he had high hopes, it being generally agreed that the prize jury could deny him first place only if he went out of his way to flout them. But, owing to infighting and a poor performance by a substitute singer, they did, choosing to give no award at all. While waiting for his next chance to roll around, Berlioz became increasingly disenchanted with the absent Harriet, who he felt had treated him like dirt, and transmuted the whole affair into the *Symphonie fantastique;* he also found solace in a pretty and flirtatious young pianist, Camille Moke, to whom he actually became engaged with some coaching from her mother. In July he was again shut up with the Prix de Rome contestants to write his cantata *(La Mort de Sardanapale)* and so, though he was the first to finish, missed the July Revolution that overthrew Charles X. This time he was unanimously voted the Grand Prix winner —though the previous year's prize was awarded simultaneously to one Montfort.

At the tail end of 1830, Berlioz kissed Camille goodbye, stopped by to see his parents, and, hampered by a sea storm and visa troubles related to the shaky political climate, arrived in Rome three months later. Barely had he gotten settled when there came a letter from Mme. Moke announcing Camille's imminent marriage to the piano manufacturer Pleyel [1003], then in his late fifties. In perhaps the most Berliozian episode of his life, Hector sent his belongings home, his scores to the conductor Habeneck at the conservatory, equipped himself with a female disguise, two pistols, and some poison, and set out posthaste to wipe out the Mokes and himself. Frustrated once again in Turin by the visa people, he made a feeble attempt at drowning himself, then got as far as Nice before the rage in his heart burned itself out. The Academy kindly overlooked the whole business, and he returned to spend his two years composing, roaming the Italian countryside, making an uneasy friendship with Mendelssohn [1200], who thought him a wild man, and affirming his dislike for what passed for music in Italy.

In the fall of 1832 Berlioz was back in Paris, quartered—doubtless not fortuitously —in Miss Smithson's old apartment. And who but Miss Smithson herself turned up at his subsequent concert of his new music, which included the "melologue" *Lélio,* a sequel to the *Symphonie fantastique,* in which an actor spelled out the source of inspiration in case the lady had missed it in the symphony (also performed). The next day the ill-starred pair met for the first time. By now Harriet's brief heyday was on the wane and, with a mother and sister dependent on her, she was in trouble. Berlioz was supposed to go to Germany to carry out the unfulfilled terms of his prize, but he canceled his trip to propose to his *idée fixe*. She accepted him conditionally in a sort of open-end engagement. In the interim she managed to break her leg, and both parties were increasingly negatively pressured by their relatives. After other dramatic highlights, including another "suicide attempt" by Berlioz, they were married in October, with Liszt [1218] as witness, in a civil ceremony. She bore him a son, Louis, in the summer of 1834, but the marriage was, predictably, a disaster. Harriet's career was done, and she brought her husband a mountain of debts. She grew fat, quarrelsome, insanely jealous, and alcoholic. In 1841 Berlioz took a live-in mistress in the person of a singer of sorts named Marie Recio, and three years later he left his wife. After a series of strokes, she died in March 1854. (Ten years later, in a macabre scene, Berlioz was required to identify her remains when it was necessary to move the coffin for legal reasons.)

For a while it seemed as if Berlioz was about to succeed. His *Scène heroïque* (a reworking of an earlier piece) was to be featured in a vast public concert under Habeneck—which was canceled. Paganini [1106], then at the peak of his fame, asked for a viola concerto which Berlioz turned into *Harold in Italy*. This was not, Paganini said, what he had in mind (though its premiere attracted most of the chief figures of the artistic avant-garde). Berlioz was good-naturedly parodied, by Adam [1172] and others, in a piece called *Episodes in the Life of a Gambler*. Most importantly, perhaps, he became critic for the influential *Journal des débats*—though his unfaltering honesty and his undisguised attempts to change Parisian musical life for the better probably did his compositional career little good. His influence in the selection of a new director of the Paris Opéra seemed about to bear fruit in the tentative acceptance of his first completed opera, *Benvenuto Cellini—Les Francs-Juges* was never completed, and the parts were cannibalized—but the government intervened and canceled the arrangement, though Berlioz did succeed in getting a production of *La Esmeralda* by his protégée, Louise Bertin, the crippled daughter of the publisher of the *Débats*.

However, in 1836, friends in the government commissioned Berlioz to write a *Requiem* to pay tribute to the martyrs of the 1830 revolution. There was the usual backing and filling, the memorial affair being eventually canceled, but the death of a general in the ongoing Algerian adventure produced the excuse to perform the piece in Les Invalides during December of 1837. To fill the vast space, Berlioz demanded 190 players, 210 choristers, and 4 brass-and-percussion ensembles in the four corners of the hall to signal the crack of doom. The performance was a triumph, although Berlioz tells us that he himself had to cue in the four bands, Habeneck having thoughtlessly paused for a pinch of snuff. (Until it became readily available on records to disprove the charge, the *Requiem* was long cited, however, as evidence of Berlioz's pointless noisiness.) Soon afterward Berlioz got a commitment at the Opéra for his *Benvenuto Cellini*. After the usual delays and the mutilation of the libretto by the censors, the work was premiered in December 1838; the occasion was an unmitigated disaster, owing largely to an audience that wanted to be heard more than the music. Ensuing performances were more temperate but ill-attended, and the work had to be written off as a failure (though it enjoyed some success in Germany later, thanks to Liszt). Berlioz became ill. Further tragedy struck a few weeks later when his nineteen-year-old brother Prosper, studying in Paris, died.

Still ailing, Berlioz had an unexpected windfall to lighten his heart when Paganini bestowed 20,000 francs on him in token of his esteem, and his lot was further improved when he was made curator of the conservatory library (from which he had once been threatened with eviction). He was also awarded the *Légion d'Honneur* and was recommended for a vacancy in the Institut, but he deferred to Spontini [1081]. His good fortune spurred him to complete his so-called dramatic symphony *Roméo et Juliette*, which he performed for enthusiastic (if biased) audiences. Stymied by the librettist Scribe in his plans for another opera, *La Nonne sanglante*, which never got off the ground, he set to work on a fourth symphony, later called *Funèbre et triomphale*, to be performed in the course of a mammoth outdoor veterans' commemoration in late July 1840. As it happened, it was impossible to hear the music (which, considering the general disorganization, was probably just as well, though the work was later admired in concert).

Still unable to make a real living from his efforts, Berlioz spent the next several years running in place, so to speak. He composed. He conducted his music as often as possible. When Paris lost interest, he went abroad, where he found more appreciation, now usually accompanied by Marie Recio. When Cherubini died in 1842, Berlioz's name was not even put in the running to succeed him in the Institut. Soon thereafter he made a conducting tour through Belgium and Germany, making new acquaintances, such as with Schumann [1211], and renewing old ones, as with Mendelssohn. As usual, he had to foot many of his expenses, but the tour was a success. In 1844 he concertized in the French provinces, and he published his still authoritative orchestration manual (Berlioz thought orchestrally as no one before him had). He set to work on an expansion of his early *Faust* pieces, at which he labored during another heartening Central European tour in 1845, during which he turned down a chance to become imperial *Kapellmeister* in Vienna. The journey lasted some months, but in late 1846 Berlioz was back in Paris rehearsing the newly completed *Damnation de Faust* at the Opéra-Comique. But France was in a recession and on the edge of revolution, and the two performances were ill-attended. The venture left the composer broke. With financial help from friends, he paid off his debts and set out for Russia, where the wretched traveling eventuated in successes in St. Petersburg and Moscow that paled his receptions elsewhere. He came home in 1847, visited his now-dying father, and went on to London to take a lucrative post as conductor of an opera company organized by the eccentric impresario Antoine Jullien. But the English winter affected his health, and Jullien's habit of thinking too big doomed the venture. On top of that, France rose in open revolution, the Chartist upheaval shook England, and Berlioz was caught in the middle. He got back to Paris on Bastille Day, 1848, and for a time had to scratch merely to survive. His father died two weeks later, but he was unable to attend the funeral. Eventually the new government reconfirmed his library post and three years later made him head librarian.

In the years immediately following, Nanci, Berlioz's elder sister died of cancer, his son Louis joined the Merchant Marine, abandoned it, and was persuaded to return, and Harriet suffered cholera and a series of strokes. Frustrated at the red tape required to get his and other new music performed, Berlioz promoted a Philharmonic Society, which achieved his purpose but soon expired for lack of funds. In 1851 the government unwittingly saved the composer from going down with his ship by dispatching him to London to help judge the musical instruments displayed at the Crystal Palace Exhibition. The job was a chore, but he made valuable connections there and returned the following year to conduct the recently organized New Philharmonic Orchestra in a very successful series of concerts, wherein he was

enabled to play music by Beethoven [1063], one of his great idols. About the same time he published *Evenings with the Orchestra,* a collection of fugitive pieces that enjoyed a surprisingly good sale, especially because of his remarkable literary style—which also makes his *Mémoires* one of the monuments of autobiography. Orchestral politics saw to it that Berlioz was not invited back to conduct the orchestra, but late in 1852 Liszt feted him with a celebratory week in Weimar, where he met many of the young Turks of German music who saw him as their spiritual father. His popularity in England eventuated in an 1853 production of *Benvenuto Cellini,* at which the audience, primed by Berlioz's enemies and the usual gossip, behaved worse than the audience had in Paris. The performers offered to give a free concert to make up for the failure, but he turned them down as being not to blame.

The operatic failure was followed by another series of German concert engagements which turned out to be a sort of triumphal procession in which the composer was showered with gifts and honors. It was then that Peter Cornelius [1294] invented the notion of the three titanic B's of music—Berlioz being the third. (Brahms [1329], who made a favorable impression on Berlioz, was only on the threshhold of his career.) Shortly after returning to Paris, Berlioz lost his wife and his employer at the *Débats.* The heirs, however, kept him on the staff of the magazine, and he entered into a legalized union with Marie Recio that proved not much happier than that with Harriet. In 1854 he was once more turned down for the Institut in favor of a hack named Clapisson. Much to his surprise, he achieved an enormous success with his oratorio *L'Enfance du Christ,* part of which he had earlier successfully foisted on the public as a newly discovered piece from the Baroque age. About the same time he was offered the conductorship of the London Philharmonic, but a legal tangle prevented him from taking it, and eventually it went to Richard Wagner [1230], now one of his chief journalistic antagonists. The two, however, were reconciled the following year when Berlioz went to London to conduct concerts of the New Philharmonic, though privately he thought Wagner a miserable batonist.

Soon after this, Berlioz turned (as he was doing in other matters) to an early passion, Virgil's *Aeneid,* as the source of what was to be his operatic masterpiece. It went surprisingly rapidly, though there was faint hope of a production. While he was working at it, Adolphe Adam died, and, on the fourth ballot, Berlioz was voted into his place in the

Institut. In the spring of 1858, he completed his mammoth score, which he had decided to call *Les Troyens;* it had taken nearly six years. He first performed an excerpt—the love duet—at Baden, where he was invited regularly to conduct in the summers. In 1859 Carvalho, the director of the Opéra, surprisingly asked him to produce Gluck's *Orpheus,* with Pauline Viardot in the title role; Berlioz admitted no tampering with the score, and the results were so successful that it ultimately eventuated in a scholarly edition of Gluck.

Meanwhile Richard Wagner had come to Paris with his now-legendary *Tannhäuser* and was knocking at the door of the Opéra himself. Nevertheless Berlioz, *Les Troyens* still in abeyance, set to work on what was to be his last piece, an operatic treatment of Shakespeare's *Much Ado About Nothing.* The famous *Tannhäuser* fiasco in 1861 made production of another large "experimental" work more unlikely than ever. All the while the composer had been suffering increasingly from general bad health. In 1862 Marie Berlioz died of the last of a series of heart attacks. (Her old mother kept the house of the composer for the rest of his life.) For a while there was a romance with a young woman he encountered while visiting the cemetery, but shortly she too died. That summer Baden provided the premiere for *Béatrice et Benedict*—successful, but largely ignored in Paris. After interminable vacillation, the Opéra accepted *Les Troyens* for a December 1863 premiere. The production was jackleg, the musicians puzzled and uneasy, the score mutilated in the name of economy, but surprisingly it ran for more than twenty performances before being put in cold storage. A bit later, visiting his home (his other sister had meanwhile died), Berlioz went to see the pink-shod Estelle of his youth; thereafter they corresponded and saw each other occasionally, but there was no fairytale ending. With the completion of the *Mémoires* in 1865, Berlioz's productive life was over. Ever sicker, he continued to tilt at windmills and fulfilled a conducting engagement in Cologne in the late winter of 1867. The next summer, worried about not hearing from his hapless son, he learned that he had succumbed to yellow fever in Havana early in June. It was the last straw. Ill most of the time, wholly unable to sleep, he wanted only to die. But at an invitation from Grand Duchess Helen of Russia, he somehow got himself together and made the endless journey to St. Petersburg and Moscow, where he conducted for the last time. In 1868 his doctor told him that his end was only a matter of time. Berlioz sought the sun in Nice, but

two severe falls from the seaside rocks sent him back to his bed in Paris. He sank slowly for the better part of a year and died quietly in Mme. Recio's arms. During his funeral procession, the horses drawing the hearse inexplicably bolted and reached the cemetery well ahead of the mourners.

RECORDINGS: Though the hindsight of recent years has seen to it that all of Berlioz's major works have been committed to record, it is almost expectable that some of the minor things—mostly choral pieces and songs —still go untouched.

[1176] FREYER, August (Frī'-er, Ou'-gōost)
ORGANIST, TEACHER
BORN: Mulda, December 15, 1803
DIED: Pilica, May 28, 1883

Born in Saxony and initially educated there, Freyer moved to Warsaw in his teens. There he studied with Chopin's teacher, Josef Elsner, at the conservatory he had recently founded. He soon became a much-admired virtuoso organist and gave free lessons to talented pupils. One such was Stanisław Moniuszko, who became the "father of Polish opera." In 1861, the violinist Apolinary Kątski (or "Apollinaire de Kontski" as he styled himself) became director of the new conservatory and appointed Freyer to teach harmony and counterpoint there. Besides textbooks on organ playing and harmony, Freyer wrote songs, choral works, and many organ pieces, the most popular of which was a set of concert variations. RECORDINGS: Organist Feliks Raczkowski has recorded the final fugue from the concert variations.

[1177] STRAUSS, Johann Baptist (Shtrous, Yō'-hàn Bàp'-tēst)
VIOLINIST, CONDUCTOR
BORN: Vienna, March 14, 1804
DIED: Vienna, September 25, 1849

Johann Strauss's great-grandparents came from all over—Luxembourg, Bavaria, Italy, Lower Austria, and even Vienna—but the pair that bore the family name, Wolf and Theresia Strauss, were Hungarian and Jewish. This last fact was discovered in the 1930s, to the unspeakable chagrin of the Nazis, who had held up the Strausses' music as a typically German phenomenon, and they went to great lengths to suppress it. Wolf's son, Johann Michael, converted. *His* son Franz ran a low-class riverside tavern in Vienna with his wife Barbara, and their son was born in the living quarters upstairs. Barbara Strauss died in 1811, and Franz remarried in 1812. When Johann was eleven, they fished his father's body out of the Danube; no one knows how it got there. His stepmother, Katharina, acquired a new husband, a man remembered only as Golder, who, noting the boy's fascination with music, bought him a cheap fiddle, on which he learned to play after a fashion. At twelve, Johann, barely literate, was apprenticed to a bookbinder named Lichtscheidl, who reportedly beat him. At any rate he ran away about five years later and was taken in by a family friend named Polischansky, who taught him to handle the violin well enough to get a job playing for a bibulous but popular danceband leader named Michael Pamer. There he made friends with another young fiddler, Joseph Lanner [1162], age seventeen. Eventually they broke away and formed their own street-corner ensemble, roomed together to cut costs, became codirectors of the most popular dance orchestra(s) in Vienna, and in 1825, after a spectacular fight, they went their own ways (see 1162 for more details.)

The breakup came on September 1. Not quite two months before, Strauss had married Anna Streim, twenty-four, the black-haired daughter of a prosperous innkeeper. Not a moment too soon, either, for their first child, named after his father, was born on October 25. Five others followed: Josef, in 1827; Anna, in 1829; Therese, in 1831; Ferdinand, in 1834; and Eduard, in 1835. (Ferdinand died a baby.) For a while Strauss struggled to make ends meet by teaching, but by the end of winter he was leading a fourteen-man band at the sign of the Two Pigeons and soon at many other signs. It may have been about then that he began to take clandestine lessons with Ignaz von Seyfried and Leopold Jansa, to improve his composition and violin technique. In the style of the times, he led the band while playing, through a sort of body language. Lanner had, no doubt, "created" the Viennese waltz by syncopating the rhythm of the peasant *Ländler,* a clod-hopping dance in three-quarter time. But the verve and vitality of Strauss's approach drove the Viennese mad *en masse.* Literally thousands danced in the parks and taverns and dance halls at night, and the repressive Metternich government approved, for it kept their minds off other matters. Strauss, during Paganini's [1106] visit, was the only musician in Vienna who could claim equal attention, and in the plague years a frightened young Richard Wagner braved the mobs repeatedly to hear him. The orchestra grew and split in two to meet the demand, Strauss spending part of

an evening with one group, part with another. Later, in a pattern followed by popular dance entrepreneurs ever since, it became four "Johann Strauss orchestras." In 1829 Strauss was engaged by Sperl, Vienna's most popular night spot (where Pamer had once performed), for six years at a very high salary.

In 1833 Strauss was smitten by a young woman named Emilie Trambusch (or Trampusch) and at about the same time began touring with his band. The two facts are probably not unrelated, for two months after Anna had produced the last of her six children, Emilie produced the first of hers. The initial tour was only within Austria, but in 1834, the year in which he was also appointed bandmaster to the First Vienna Militia, Strauss went to Berlin, where he performed before the King of Prussia, and was (with his whole band) "kidnapped" one night to play for the visiting czar and czarina. On the way back to Vienna, Strauss picked up a new dance called the *polka* in Prague and popularized it back home. The next year he went on a more extended tour of Germany, in 1836 as far as the Low Countries, and in 1837 to Paris. Though the usual French intrigues against him had been prepared, he swept everything before him and found allies in those who were prepared to be his enemies. Berlioz, as critic, was particularly taken with his music and his orchestration, and said so. By Christmas, Strauss's men, despite being put up in the best hotels and fed in the best restaurants, were getting homesick, but Strauss stayed on until April, when he announced they were going to London. The players suspected that, given his domestic problems, he had no wish to go back to Vienna. After a bad start in London (stolen funds and a suit for debt), the triumph continued. Victoria and Albert danced to Strauss's conducting, he had to play at every important mansion, and having exhausted the capital for the moment, he invaded the provinces. In November, however, the strain caught up with him. He caught cold, became increasingly sicker, and finally, against doctors' advice, went home to Vienna (he thought) to die. But by 1839 he was back at Sperl, offering a new discovery from Paris, the quadrille.

By now the situation with Anna was growing intolerable. Strauss first moved into his own rooms in the family house, but in 1844 Anna sued for divorce. In that year, the younger Johann, against his father's orders, struck out on his own as conductor and composer. Johann, Sr., was at last appointed *Hofmusikballdirektor* in 1845. In 1846 the divorce was granted, and a year later Strauss moved in with Emilie in a slum apartment and cut his legal family off without a groschen.

The 1848 revolution caused a further split, especially with Strauss's eldest. Johann I sided with the imperial faction, Johann II with the rebellious students. Both, having served the government as military bandmasters, produced appropriate marches. When the uproar was over, the elder Strauss found himself regarded in some quarters as a representative of the Bad Old Days. To escape the unpleasantness, he again took his men on tour, finally once more reaching London. But all across Europe he was hooted by the clamorous young, and in England he played to half-empty houses. When he returned to Vienna in July 1849, however, he found the atmosphere less hostile. In the fall he was asked to do a concert for Field Marshal Radetzky, home from his victories over the Italian upstarts. While Strauss was writing the music, Emilie's brood came down with scarlet fever and passed it on to him. It went into meningitis, and he died during the night of September 24–25. Emilie bolted, taking with her everything she could carry, including the bedclothes, and leaving the door wide open. A delivery boy found the naked corpse on the bedroom floor the next morning. Two days later a hundred thousand mourners came to the funeral at St. Stephen's. Johann Strauss I left more than 250 compositions—mostly dances.

RECORDINGS: A few favorite compositions, such as the *Radetzky March,* have been much recorded, but on the whole he has been neglected and eclipsed by his sons, though lately Viennese specialists such as Willy Boskovsky and Kurt Rapf have paid him some serious attention.

[1178] FARRENC, Jeanne Louise (Fär-ránk', Zhàn Lōō-ēz')
PIANIST, TEACHER, EDITOR
BORN: Paris, May 31, 1804
DIED: Paris, September 15, 1875

The wife of the publisher and musical scholar Aristide Farrenc (1794–1865), Louise Farrenc was herself an important figure in nineteenth-century French musical life, though she has been much neglected until the modern feminist movement brought her again to attention. She came of an important artistic family. Her father Jacques-Edmé DuMont and her brother Augustin-Alexandre were third and fourth in a line of prominent sculptors. Her sister's child (later Louise's pupil) was the composer Ernest Reyer [1289]. She soon showed musical tal-

ents far beyond the "accomplishments" expected from young women of good family and at fifteen took up the study of composition with Antonín Reicha [1059]. Hummel [1091] and Moscheles [1146] were both struck with her playing and gave her advice. At seventeen she married Farrenc, then a flutist, and accompanied him on a tour of France. In 1826 her freedom was curtailed by the arrival of a daughter, Victorine, and she spent her spare time composing, writing much piano music, chamber works, and 3 symphonies, all of which attracted considerable favorable attention. (Victorine Farrenc became a promising pianist, but her career was foreshortened by chronic illness and death at thirty-two.)

In the early 1830s the Farrencs attended Fétis's [1111] historical concerts and were greatly excited by their implications. They became ardent promoters of old music, and Aristide worked with Fétis on the *Biographie universelle.* In 1842 Auber [1103] named Louise Farrenc professor of piano at the Conservatoire—the only woman in her century to be so honored; she filled the post brilliantly for more than thirty years. In 1861 the Académie des Beaux-Arts awarded her the Prix Chartier for her chamber music. In the same year the Farrencs began putting together their great historical anthology of piano music, *Le trésor des pianistes.* Aristide died after the eighth volume; Louise added fifteen more volumes after his death, the last appearing the year before her own. In 1869 she was again the recipient of the Prix Chartier. Louise Farrenc was no great innovator as a composer, but her work is soundly crafted in the Classical tradition, and rich by contrast with the salonesque norm of the times.

RECORDINGS: The New York Lyric Arts Trio has recorded an LP of her music, including the D-minor piano trio and some piano pieces. The Bronx Arts Ensemble performs her *Nonetto,* Op. 38.

[1179] GLINKA, Mikhail Ivanovitch (Glin'-kà, Mēkh'-à-il Ē-và-nō'-vich)
CIVIL SERVANT, CHOIRMASTER
BORN: Novospasskoye, June 1, 1804
DIED: Berlin, February 15, 1857

There had been Russian composers (in our sense) before Glinka, but he was the first to make international waves, the first consciously to create a synthesis of Russian and Western music, and the pathfinder for those of his musical countrymen who followed. And yet he succeeded in spite of himself. Pampered, lazy, self-indulgent, lecherous, hypochondriac, a malcontent, and a misfit, he turned out, in his mature years, a couple of operas, a handful of short orchestral works, and some songs and piano pieces. Yet the best of these were clearly the work of a genius—if not always a self-critical one.

Glinka was the son of a wealthy landowner of the Smolensk district. He was reared mostly by an invalid grandmother, and Fräulein Klammer, a German governess, who essayed to teach him piano. But the first real impetus was his uncle's band of serfs, which his father occasionally borrowed; later Mikhail would be permitted to conduct them in music that included symphonies by Haydn [871], Mozart [992], and Beethoven [1063]. In 1817 he was packed off to an exclusive boys' school in St. Petersburg but was allowed to study piano with another German, Karl Meyer, and violin with yet another named Böhm. (Piano lessons with John Field [1104] ended abruptly when Field left for Moscow, which was perhaps just as well.) Some ineffectual attempts at composition led to some spotty theoretical studies. When Glinka graduated at eighteen, however, he found his father adamant against his embarking on a musical career. In the ensuing battle, he sank into the first of the spells of vague illness that plagued him most of his life, and was sent to a spa in the Caucasus and then home to recuperate. In 1824 his father found him a post in the ministry of communications. He did not like it on principle, but since it involved only short spells of tangling red tape, he found himself free to pursue his interests—socializing, music, and women. He lolled about the fashionable drawing rooms, collected birds (with and without feathers), took singing lessons, wrote some vapid songs and chamber music (most of which he later disavowed), made friends with Pushkin and Zhukovsky, and was briefly brushed by the taint of the Decembrist plot against the czar.

By 1830 Glinka was again feeling unwell and, on medical advice, headed by a circuitous route for Italian sunshine. He settled in Milan, where he attended the premieres of Anna Bolena and La Sonnambula, which works reduced him to a jelly, and later went to Naples, where he met their composers. But even a succession of beautiful Italian women could not stem his growing nostalgia for the motherland. However, he took a circuitous route home in 1833—through Baden (for the waters) and Berlin, where at last he availed himself of a thorough theoretical grounding under Siegfried Dehn. This was interrupted, however, in the spring of 1834 by the death of his father, which necessitated his going home. Shortly afterward he

met and fell in love with a pretty flibbertigibbet named Maria Petrovna Ivanovna and by the following spring had acquired a wife and a pushy German mother-in-law, neither of whom turned out to be to his taste.

Meanwhile, casting about for a subject for an opera, he had taken the suggestion of his poet-friend Zhukovsky that he do one on the legendary peasant-hero Ivan Sussanin, who had saved the czar from the invading Polish armies by getting them lost in the Russian forests. It was a subject that had been used a generation earlier by an Italian immigrant, Catterino Cavos, now an official of the Imperial Opera. Cavos was delighted with it, and as a result A Life for the Czar (as it had become in deference to Nicholas I) was successfully premiered before the imperial family on December 9, 1836. As a result, Glinka was named music director of the opera. Shortly afterward Pushkin was killed in a duel, casting a temporary pall over Glinka's plans to use his Russlan and Ludmila for a new opera. Nor, in the absence of even a scenario, did the work proceed very rapidly, and its progress was further hindered by continual dissension in the Glinka household, which was aggravated in 1839 by his falling in love with a girl named Ekaterina Kern. The scenario was finally forthcoming one drunken evening from someone named Bakhturin, and the libretto, a patchwork from several hands, eventually grew out of it. In 1841 Glinka at last caught poor Maria Petrovna two-timing him and sued for divorce, a proceeding that ground through the courts for several years. The following December, a badly mutilated, badly produced Russlan was played before a puzzled audience, with disastrous results. (Whereas in his earlier opera Glinka had gingerly used Russian melody in a framework that was basically Italian, here he displayed a remarkable eclecticism that brought together his Russian, German, and Italian musical experiences, and dabbled in Oriental scales and modality.) Despite its failure, Russlan became a source for later Russian composers to drink from.

Frustrated and disappointed, Glinka went abroad, moving about from one European capital to another, and pursuing women as though they were an endangered species. (He also acquired syphilis, which helped undermine his already frail health.) Renewed acquaintance with Berlioz [1175] in Paris (they had met in Italy years before), bolstered the self-confidence of both men and fanned an interest in orchestral music in the Russian, who, in 1845, took himself off to Spain for two years to absorb local sounds and colors. He was delighted with both and even tried flamenco dancing, but found himself inept with castanets. The trip produced 2 brilliant "Spanish Overtures." In 1847 he returned to Novo Spasskoye but there was nothing to keep him there—the divorce had been granted the previous year, and he had long since lost interest in Ekaterina—so he moved on to Warsaw and set up housekeeping with several birds, two rabbits, and a girl named Angélique, who probably was not very. There he wrote his last important work, a fantasia on a Russian wedding tune, *Kamarinskaya*. After that, it was all downhill. He began several projects with which he got nowhere, started once more for Spain but bogged down in Paris, suffered pangs of patriotic guilt when the Crimean War broke out, and returned to St. Petersburg. But he was soon back in Paris and then in Berlin. In 1855, at the insistence of his adoring younger sister Ludmila—who moved heaven and earth after his death to preserve his memory —he began his memoirs. A year later, possessed by a curiosity about the modes of *znemanny* chant, he again returned to Dehn in Berlin. While there he caught cold at a concert and died unexpectedly three weeks later.

RECORDINGS: There are Russian recordings of the operas, and a Western one, conducted by Igor Markevitch, of *A Life for the Czar*. There also many recordings of the overture to *Russlan and Ludmila* and several recordings of most of the orchestral works *(Jota Aragones, Summer Night in Madrid, Kamarinskaya, Valse-Fantaisie,* the incidental music to *Prince Kholmsky)* by the likes of Ernest Ansermet, Aldo Ceccato, and Jonel Perlea. Boris Christoff, who sings the role of Sussanin in it, also recorded a disc of the songs, and Thomas Hrynkiv has devoted another to piano pieces and the *Trio Pathétique*.

[1180] BENEDICT, (Sir) Julius

CONDUCTOR, PIANIST, TEACHER, EDITOR
BORN: Stuttgart, November 27, 1804
DIED: London, June 5, 1885

As his title (conferred by Queen Victoria in 1871) indicates, Benedict was one of the most admired musicians in nineteenth-century England, and, with Balfe [1195] and Wallace [1221], whose best operas he conducted, one of the most successful operatic composers. But latter-day national self-consciousness has neglected the output of this German Jew who wrote Italian music. The son of a Stuttgart banker, he studied with Hummel

[1091], and, on the recommendation of the latter, became Weber's [1124] first pupil at fifteen. Weber took a shine to him and boarded him as a member of his family for three and a half years, during which Benedict attended the premieres of *Freischütz* and *Euryanthe*. In Vienna for the latter, Benedict bumped into Beethoven [1063] in a music shop and was invited out to Baden with the whole Weber entourage. A year later, in 1824, he left Weber (of whom he later wrote a valuable memoir) to conduct, under the auspices of Domenico Barbaja, first at the Kärntnertortheater, and then, from 1825 to 1834, at the two royal theaters in Naples, where he produced his first two operas. When he left, he went after some indecision to London, where he was to spend the rest of his career.

Following two years as conductor of the Opera Buffa at the Lyceum, Benedict spent a decade at the helm of the Drury Lane orchestra, which he led in the premieres of *The Bohemian Girl* and *Maritana*. His own most successful offering there, of three, was his first, *The Gypsy's Warning*, in 1838. In 1845 he began a thirty-five-year intendancy as conductor of the Norwich Festival. Three years later he conducted the London premiere of Mendelssohn's [1200] oratorio *Elijah*, made friends with the soprano soloist, Jenny Lind, and served as her accompanist on her American tour in 1850–51. In 1852 he was appointed conductor at Her Majesty's Theatre and in 1855 inaugurated choral concerts at the Crystal Palace. In 1858, during Cattle Show Week, he conducted three concerts at St. James Hall; though in themselves unsuccessful, they spawned the "Classical Monday Pops" at which Benedict appeared for many years. In 1860 he revised Weber's *Oberon* for a revival at Her Majesty's, adding recitatives of his own. Two years later Covent Garden produced his *The Lily of Killarney*, one of the most successful English operas of the era. At seventy-two, Benedict took over direction of the Liverpool Philharmonic. In his last years, he fell on hard times. He died at eighty of a heart attack and was buried, like Balfe, in Kensal Green Cemetery. His home is now a public monument.

RECORDINGS: A composer of parts for both voice and piano (though he often succumbed to publishing claptrap), Benedict is represented on records mostly by soprano display pieces—*"La Capinera,"* "The Gypsy and the Bird," and the immortal variations on "The Carnival of Venice." Uel Deane has recorded selections from *The Lily of Killarney*.

[1181] BERTIN, Louise-Angélique (Bâr-tan', Loo-ēz' An-zhā-lēk')
POET
BORN: Les Roches (near Paris), February 15, 1805
DIED: Paris, April 26, 1877

Louise Bertin was crippled by a birth defect, her femininity, and the fact that her father, Louis-François, her uncle, and her brothers published and edited the controversial and important *Journal des débats,* of which her friend Hector Berlioz **[1175]** was music reviewer. She studied with Fétis **[1111]**, who, when she was twenty, directed a private performance of her first opera, *Guy Mannering.* This was followed by a one-acter, *Le Loup-garou (The Werewolf),* at the Opéra-Comique. Next she tackled nothing less than Goethe's *Faust,* the result *Fausto* meeting with some success at the Théâtre-Italien in 1831. But *Esmeralda,* to a libretto by Victor Hugo after his own *Notre-Dame,* was a dismal failure at the Opéra in 1836. (A whispering campaign said it was written by Berlioz, who had promoted it, but who protested that he contributed not a note.) Crushed, Bertin turned to vocal and instrumental works for private performance, most of which remain unpublished. RECORDINGS: Suzanne Danco recorded one of her songs.

[1182] HARTMANN, Johann Peder Emilius (Härt'-mán, Yō'-hàn Pā'-der Ā-mēl'-yoos)
LAWYER, ORGANIST, TEACHER, ADMINISTRATOR
BORN: Copenhagen, May 14, 1805
DIED: Copenhagen, March 10, 1900

Hartmann, the father of Danish musical Romanticism, represents the third generation of a musical dynasty. His grandfather, Johann Ernst (1726–93), had come, by a series of coincidences, to be *Kapellmeister* of the Danish Royal Orchestra. His father, August Wilhelm, played violin in it and was later organist at the Garrison Church, when Johann Peder succeeded him in 1824. At the time, the youngest Hartmann was studying law at the city's university and, on graduation four years later, he pursued that calling in the civil service until 1870. The year after he graduated, he married Emma Sophie Amalia Zinn, herself a composer of songs (as "Frederik Palmer"), who, in 1836, bore him a son, Emil (d. 1898), who also became a composer of stature. Their daughter, Emma Sophie, was the first wife of Niels Gade **[1248]**.
    Hartmann did not let his profession curb his musical activities. From the age of twenty-two, he taught at the Royal Conservatory. Five years later he produced his first opera, *The Raven,* to a libretto by Hans Christian Andersen, followed by *The Corsairs* in 1835. In 1836 he helped found the Music Society, which, until 1931, was the chief musical force in Copenhagen. He was associated with the university's Student Singing Society from 1839, organist at the cathedral from 1843, and co-director, with Gade, of the Copenhagen Conservatory from its foundation in 1867. His third, last, and most enduring opera (still in the Danish repertoire), *Liden Kirsten (Little Christina)* was first produced in 1846, and in an expanded version twelve years later. Hartmann was decorated by his government, given an honorary doctorate and a professorship by the university, and generally revered by his people. Though travels introduced him to most of the important European composers of his time, his music never caught on outside of Denmark—probably because it is so insistently Danish. He was active up to the time of his death, two months short of his ninety-fifth birthday. Besides the operas, Hartmann wrote ballets (he was a close friend of the great choreographer August Bournonville), incidental music, 2 symphonies, a violin concerto, cantatas, and much music in smaller forms.
    RECORDINGS: On records, he is represented by songs, choral works, the full-length ballet *A Folk Tale* (a collaboration with Niels Gade **[1248]** conducted by John Krandsen), Symphony No. 1 (Mogens Wöldike), a string quartet (Copenhagen Quartet), a piano sonata (Arne Skjøld Rasmussen), selections from *Liden Kirsten,* and a few other instrumental pieces, mostly from Danish artists.

[1183] RICCI, Luigi (Rēt'-chē, Loo-ē'-jē)
CONDUCTOR, TEACHER
BORN: Naples, July 8, 1805
DIED: Prague, December 31, 1859

Luigi Ricci was the elder brother and sometime teacher and collaborator of Federico Ricci **[1205]**. Neither the exact date nor the place of his birth is certain. From 1814 to 1823 he was a student (and, in the latter years, instructor) at the Royal Conservatory in Naples, where he studied with Zingarelli and was a close friend of Bellini **[1164]**. Like Bellini's, Ricci's first opera was successfully produced by his fellow students there in his final year. He was to write twenty-six more, but, though he was a sound musician, he was usually too hasty, too uncritical, too conservative, and too formulaic. He was best at comedy, though his first real success, *Chiara di Rosemberg*, premiered at La Scala in 1831, was a *semiseria*. In 1835 he first joined forces with his brother in *Il Colonnello (The Colonel)*—Federico's maiden effort, by the way. A year later, he became music director of the cathedral in Trieste, to which post he devoted most of his time after the 1838 failure of his *Le Nozze di Figaro* in Milan. But he also conducted at the Teatro Grande, where he encountered the singing twin sisters Fanny and Lidia Stolz (sisters of the more famous Teresa, whom he later taught.) Although only sixteen, they became his mistresses and traveled with him to Russia and Scandinavia. He married Lidia in 1849; she bore him a daughter, Adelaide, whose operatic career was cut short by her death at twenty-one. In 1852 Fanny bore him a son, Luigi, who operated as a conductor under the name of Ricci-Stolz. In between children, Luigi collaborated with Federico on a fourth jointly written opera, *Crispino e la comare (Crispin and the Fairy Godmother)*, which opened in Venice in 1850 and was for many years a repertoire staple. (It was performed at the Metropolitan Opera by the resident company [with Luisa Tetrazzini] in 1908 and by the Chicago Opera [with Amelita Galli-Curci] in 1919.) By the time of Luigi Ricci's last opera, *Il Diavolo a quattro (The Devil to Pay)* in 1859, he was beginning a rapid syphilitic decline. He was committed to an asylum in Prague, where he died of paresis at the end of the year. There are scattered old recordings of excerpts from *Crispino* and a piracy of the whole work.

[1184] SAINT-LUBIN, Léon de (San-Lü-ban', Lā-on' də)

VIOLINIST

BORN: Turin, July 5, 1805
DIED: Berlin, February 13, 1850

Saint-Lubin was born of a French family resident in Italy, and spent most of his career in Germany and Austria. A pupil of Spohr's **[1112]**, among others, he was a member of the orchestra of the Josephstadt Theater in Vienna in 1829–30 and of that of the Königstadt Theater in Berlin from 1830 to 1847. He wrote 2 operas *(King Branor's Sword, Dr. Faust's Cousin)*, 5 violin concerti, 19 string quartets, other chamber music, and many pieces for violin. RECORDINGS: Ruggiero Ricci has recorded his *Fantasy on the Sextet from Lucia di Lammermoor*.

[1185] MARLIANI, (Count) Marco Aurelio (Märl-yå'-nē, Mär'-kō Ou-rāl'-yō)

TEACHER, DIPLOMAT, SOLDIER

BORN: Milan, August 1805
DIED: Bologna, May 8, 1849

A man of wealth and position, Marliani cast his lot and his fortune with the revolutionists in Italy. By 1830, when he received his doctorate in philosophy from Siena, he was broke and fled to Paris. A talented musical amateur, he supported himself there as a voice teacher and was taken under the wing of Rossini **[1143]**. Beginning with *Il Bravo*, he produced 4 operas in Paris; he also wrote a ballet *La Gipsy* with Ambroise Thomas **[1217]**. For a time he served as Spain's consul general. He went back to Italy in 1847, distinguished himself as an officer in the abortive uprising of 1848, and died of wounds incurred in a skirmish with Marshal Radetsky's men near Bologna. RECORDINGS: Suzanne Danco recorded a Marliani song.

[1186] MENDELSSOHN-BARTHOLDY, Fanny Cäcilie (Men'-del-sōn Bär-tōl'-dē, Fä'-nē Sä'-sē-lē)

PIANIST

BORN: Hamburg, November 14, 1805
DIED: Berlin, May 17, 1847

Fanny Mendelssohn was the granddaughter of the philosopher Moses Mendelssohn, the oldest child of banker Abraham Mendelssohn and his wife Leah, and the beloved sister of Felix Mendelssohn **[1200]**. When the French occupied Hamburg in 1811, the Mendelssohns fled to Berlin, where their home became a center of intellectual and artistic life. The children, provided with the best tutors, had admirable liberal educations, and, in 1816, were baptized into the Lutheran Church; that same year Fanny and Felix studied with Mme. Bigot in Paris. Fanny, like her brother, was both talented and brilliant. Both were stimulated by the visitors to their home; both took part in, and contributed music to, the family Sunday musicales; both played leading roles in the Shakespeare plays put on by the Mendelssohn children. Fanny grew up to be a rather plain-looking woman, her ripe figure slightly warped by a spinal curvature—though Heine praised her beautiful eyes. She was a superb pianist, though her father objected to a concert career for her as being unsuited to a nice middle-class ex-Jewish girl. Likewise, her brother disapproved publication of her compositions on the grounds that the commercial side of music was too sordid for young women. At seventeen she fell in love with

Wilhelm Hensel, a struggling painter, who reciprocated her feelings. But her parents separated them for six years, finally giving in when Leah's eccentric brother, who called himself Jakob Salomon-Bartholdy, made Hensel curator of his vast art collection.

At the time of the wedding, Felix was recovering from an accident in London. Fanny's letters to him at the time indicate that she felt that the move was somehow a betrayal of their relationship, but the marriage turned out a happy one. The newlyweds moved into the family compound, where a studio had been built for Wilhelm. Fanny kept up with her music and became director of the home musicales. A son, Sebastian, survived to write the first biography of the family, relying heavily on his mother's diary. In 1839–40 the Hensels stayed in Rome, where Fanny exerted special musical influence on young Charles Gounod [1258]. In the mid-1840s she began to be troubled by recurrent nosebleeds. On May 16, 1847, playing the piano at a rehearsal of her brother's cantata *Die erste Walpurgisnacht,* she felt her hands go numb, and a few moments later was felled by a massive stroke, of which she died the next day. Felix followed her six months later. Felix published some of her songs under his own name, and the piano trio and some *Songs Without Words* were printed after Fanny's death. But her more ambitious pieces remain in manuscript.

RECORDINGS: Piano pieces have been recorded by Judith Alstadter, the trio by the Macalester Trio, and a few songs by various singers.

[1187] ARRIAGA Y BALZOLA, Juan Crisóstomo Jacobo Antonio (Där-ri-á'-gá ē Bál-thō'-lá, Hwán Krē-sō'-stō-mō Yá-kō'-bō Án-tō'-nyō)
VIOLINIST
BORN: Rigoitia, January 27, 1806
DIED: Paris, January 17, 1826

Arriaga, for a long time forgotten, has been resurrected in recent years by his fellow Basques, as "the Spanish Mozart." This title arises in part from his musical precocity, in part from wishful thinking, and in part from the coincidence that he was born (near Bilbao) on Mozart's [992] fiftieth birthday. One source adds that both composers died young —of tuberculosis, which will be news to Mozart scholars. Arriaga is now memorialized in Bilbao by an Arriaga theater and an Arriaga museum.

The boy indeed evinced remarkable talent at an early age. At ten he was playing string quartets regularly with three adult musi-

cians, and at fourteen, supposedly with no technical musical training, he saw his first opera, *Los Esclavos felices,* produced to huzzahs in Bilbao. This success inspired his family to bundle him off to the Paris Conservatory, where he studied violin with Pierre Baillot and composition with François-Joseph Fétis [1111], and soon had Cherubini [1019] himself calling his works "masterpieces." In a brief time he wrote another opera, a Mass, a symphony, 3 quartets, various works for the church, a number of solo cantatas, and some keyboard and chamber music. But his career was hardly more than half the length of Mozart's, for he died ten days short of his twentieth birthday. (Various sources give the cause of his death as "galloping consumption" and "decline"; one notes quaintly that it was "what probably has been tuberculosis," but offers no help as to what it may now be.

RECORDINGS: There have been several recordings of the very fine Haydnesque quartets (Chilingirian and Phoenix quartets), the symphony (Jésus Maria Arambarri, Cobos), and several other works.

[1188] GORDIGIANI, Luigi (Gôr-dē-ja'-nē, Loō-ē'-jē)
BORN: Modena, June 21, 1806
DIED: Florence, May 1, 1860

If Arriaga [1187] was the Spanish Mozart, Luigi Gordigiani, a prolific songwriter, was the Italian Schubert to his contemporaries. Luigi was the son of Antonio Gordigiani, a prominent operatic baritone, and the younger brother of Giovanni Battista Gordigiani, professor of voice at the Prague Conservatory and himself a composer. Luigi seems to have had minimal formal training, but enough talent to make a living turning out hackwork under various aliases. He attracted wealthy backers, and eight of his operas were produced, mostly in Florence, though with no permanent impact. His more than 300 songs and duets are based on, or imitative of, Italian tunes and were once popular worldwide. RECORDINGS: Suzanne Danco recorded an example, and there are doubtless others on early records.

[1189] COSTE, Napoléon (Kost, Nà-pō-lā-on')
GUITARIST
BORN: Doubs, June 26, 1806
DIED: Paris, February 17, 1883

Coste was among the last of the nineteenth-century guitar virtuosi and probably the greatest born on French soil. His chief teacher seems to have been his mother. He lived and worked in Paris from 1830 and was there associated with Carulli [1060] and Sor [1090], among others of his ilk. He wrote a great deal of music for his instrument, most of which he had to publish himself, commercial houses having lost interest in the field. His playing career ended when he broke his arm at the age of fifty-seven. RECORDINGS: Coste compositions appear in various recorded guitar recitals.

[1190] BURGMÜLLER, Johann Friedrich Franz (Bōōrk'-mül-ler, Yō'-hán Frē'-drikh Fránts)
PIANIST, TEACHER
BORN: Regensburg, December 4, 1806
DIED: Beaulieu, February 13, 1874

Friedrich Burgmüller was the eldest son of the former Baroness von Zandt and Johann August Franz Burgmüller, a conductor active in Düsseldorf and founder of the famous Lower Rhine Music Festival. He was also the elder brother of the hapless Norbert Burgmüller [1207]. Friedrich studied with his father and later with Spohr [1112] in Kassel. In his mid-twenties he emigrated to Paris, where he became popular as a salon musician and a teacher. (He numbered some of the royal family among his students.) His most ambitious composition was the ballet La Péri, a follow-up to Adam's [1172] Giselle, which was wildly applauded at its premiere (featuring Carlotta Grisi and Lucien Petipa) on February 22, 1843. The next year, Burgmüller collaborated with Flotow [1222] on another ballet, Lady Harriet, which generated Flotow's opera Martha. He also wrote a waltz and peasant pas de deux for Giselle that are still frequently used in it. He gave up writing music at forty and devoted himself to teaching. RECORDINGS: Richard Bonynge has recorded La Péri.

[1191] RUNG, Henrik (Rōōng, Hen'-rēk)
CONDUCTOR
BORN: Copenhagen, March 3, 1807
DIED: Copenhagen, December 13, 1871

Henrik Rung was the founder and leader of the Cecilia Society in Copenhagen and wrote many popular choral pieces and songs. He was the father and teacher of Frederik Rung (1854–1914), conductor at the Royal Opera, and himself the composer of operas, ballets, incidental music, and other works. RECORDINGS: The tenor Aksel Schiøtz recorded some of Rung's songs.

[1192] LACHNER, Ignaz (Làkh'-ner, Ēg'-náts)
ORGANIST, CONDUCTOR
BORN: Rain am Lech, September 11, 1807
DIED: Hannover, February 24, 1895

Ignaz, youngest but one of the musical and long-lived Lachner brood, was a classmate of the Count of Saint Leu (later better known as Napoleon III) at the Augsburg Gymnasium. After further study in Munich, he succeeded his brother Franz [1171] as organist of the Lutheran church in Vienna, and his assistant at the Kärntnertortheater. Later he held Kapellmeister posts in various degrees at the Vienna Court Opera, the Munich Court Opera, the Hamburg Opera, the Royal Swedish Opera, and the opera at Frankfurt am Main. He himself produced 3 operas (one to a libretto by the parson-poet Eduard Mörike) and other stage works, and was almost as productive of chamber music and songs as his brother. RECORDINGS: Emanuel Vardi has recorded a "toy" symphony.

[1193] COSTA, (Sir) Michael Andrew Agnus
CONDUCTOR
BORN: Naples, February 4, 1808
DIED: Hove, April 29, 1884

Baptized Michele Andrea Agniello, Costa was ultimately of Spanish descent. He studied with his father, the composer Pasquale Costa and his maternal grandfather, Giacomo Tritto, court maestro di cappella in Naples. At the conservatory he was a contemporary of Bellini [1164] and the elder Ricci [1183], and a special favorite of the director, Zingarelli. By the time he was twenty, he had written and heard performed operas, church works, and symphonies, and in 1829 Barbaja commissioned from him Malvina for the Teatro San Carlo. That same year Zingarelli dispatched him to England to conduct a psalm of his ordered up by the Birmingham Festival. The Birminghamers said there must be some mistake, he was obviously too young, and made him tenor soloist instead. Costa had studied singing but was no singer, as the result seems to have demonstrated. Nevertheless he took to England and remained, becoming keyboardist in the pit of the King's Theatre in 1830 and director in 1832. He thereupon adopted the newfangled method of conducting with a baton from a podium and was soon known as an effective disciplinarian and orchestra builder throughout England, though more demanding Continental musicians such as

Berlioz [1175] felt he left something to be desired. He took most of his men with him to Covent Garden in 1846, the year he also became chief conductor of the London Philharmonic Society. In 1868 he returned to Her Majesty's Theatre (as it became known in 1837) and served again as director there until 1881. He was knighted in 1869. Costa was also a noted oratorio conductor at various English festivals. He wrote operas and ballets, but had most success (which is not saying much) with his own oratorios. (He is not to be confused with a popular Neapolitan songwriter, Mario Costa.) RECORDINGS: Costa survives on records through a few songs.

[1194] PARISH-ALVARS, Elias (Pár'-ish Ál'-vàrs, A-lē'-às)
HARPIST
BORN: Teignmouth, February 28, 1808
DIED: Vienna, January 25, 1849

In an era when the harp was largely an instrument on which young ladies plunked in the parental drawing room and Berlioz [1175] tore his hair out for want of someone able to play his orchestral harp parts, Parish-Alvars was a rarity—a harp virtuoso of a younger generation. Descended from a Jewish family that had moved to England from Portugal in the Renaissance, he was fortunate to come along when London could boast three great international harp teachers: Robert Nicolas Charles Bochsa [1131], he of dubious ethics; François-Joseph Dizi, inventor of the perpendicular harp; and Theodore Labarre, later professor of harp at the Conservatoire in Paris. Parish-Alvars availed himself of the services of all three. From 1831 he concertized with great success consecutively in Germany and Italy, before settling in Vienna in 1836, where he himself did some teaching. After two years he and his harp set sail for the Orient, where he noted down Eastern tunes and incorporated his experiences in a memoir. In 1842 he returned and spent some time concertizing again in Central Europe. Berlioz delightedly encountered him in Dresden and dubbed him "the Liszt [1218] of the harp," noting with approval the advances he had made in harp technique and the effectiveness of such of his compositions as his fantasies and variations on themes of Rossini [1143] and Weber [1124]. After a journey to Naples in 1844, Parish-Alvars came to Leipzig and worked with Mendelssohn [1200] for a time. He returned to Vienna for good in 1847, won an appointment as harpist to the emperor, and married a pupil, but died broke two

years later. RECORDINGS: Nicanor Zabaleta has recorded one of his 4 harp concerti.

[1195] BALFE, Michael William
VIOLINIST, SINGER
BORN: Dublin, May 15, 1808
DIED: Rowney Abbey, October 20, 1870

The Irish Balfe was the first British composer to attain real international stature in more than a century. In his own day that fact inflated his reputation at home. More recently a talent that often went no farther than pretty Italianate tunes and an affinity for impossibly corny libretti have reduced him to a figure of fun. He probably deserves something better.

The son of a dancing master, Balfe moved with his parents to Wexford in 1810, began music lessons with his father, studied with other locals, was helping with the parental classes at the age of seven, and appeared as a violin soloist at nine. When the elder Balfe died in 1822, young Michael went to London to seek his fortune, which he had little difficulty finding. He studied with the Horns (see 1120)—son and father, in that order—concertized, and was soon an assistant conductor at Drury Lane. When his voice had changed to a promising baritone, he tried it out in what purported to be a production of Weber's [1124] Der Freischütz in Norwich but found the test premature. By 1825, however, his talent had struck a Count Mazzara, who took him to Italy and treated him to lessons. A year later Balfe had a ballet, La Pérouse, produced at La Scala. He then went to Paris, won the admiration of Rossini [1143], and sang for a time at the Théâtre-Italien, notably as Figaro in Il Barbiere di Siviglia, Rossini's favorite of his own roles; but illness terminated his activity there, and he returned to Italy. In 1829 he sang for a season in Palermo, where his first opera, I Rivali di se stessi (Their Own Rivals), was produced. Further Italian engagements occupied him for the next three years. He married a Hungarian soprano, Lina Rosa or Roser, with whom he sang in Bologna, and at last got a La Scala commission (Enrico IV) in 1833.

After that peak, Balfe returned to London where, in 1835, he had a success with The Siege of Rochelle unprecedented by any operatic composer from the British Isles. This was at the Drury Lane, where three years later he created the role of Papageno in Mozart's Zauberflöte for England. Further successes with his own operas, including a notable Falstaff (to an Italian text) in 1838, persuaded him to take a flyer in 1841 in the impresario business, but his company had fallen apart within a few months, and Balfe had fled to Paris. There he wrote two French works with Scribe in 1843 and 1844. In between, however, his ballad opera, *The Bohemian Girl,* opened at the Drury Lane. It proved his most enduring piece, becoming for a time part of the standard repertoire, and contributing several hit songs, such as "I Dreamt I Dwelt in Marble Halls" and "Then You'll Remember Me." In 1846 Balfe replaced Michael Costa as conductor at Her Majesty's Theatre until it closed six years later. Having already won acclaim and princely favor in Berlin on an 1849 visit, when he left the theater, he decided to try his luck in St. Petersburg. It held, for he was treated there as a major celebrity. He remained abroad until 1854. Shortly after his return, his daughter Victoire made her operatic debut and later became a favorite singer of Queen Victoria's. After writing another half dozen operas, mostly for Covent Garden, Balfe purchased Rowney Abbey in Hertfordshire, and settled down to play the gentleman farmer and dabble in chamber music composition. Five years later, in 1869, he revised *The Bohemian Girl* for Paris. He did not live to complete *The Knight of the Leopard,* which he wanted to be his masterpiece, though Costa pieced it out for a production in 1874. Balfe succumbed to lung trouble and was buried in Kensal Green. Lina Balfe lived to 1888.

RECORDINGS: The largest representation of Balfe's works on records is of his popular drawing-room songs and duets and of selections from the major operas—chiefly *The Siege of Rochelle* and *The Bohemian Girl.* No commercial recording of the latter has been forthcoming, though there are a couple of piracies, and there is a recording of the 1844 opera *The Daughter of St. Mark* from a small English company.

[1196] SCHUBERT, Franz or "François"
(Shoo'-bârt, Frànts)

VIOLINIST
BORN: Dresden, July 22, 1808
DIED: Dresden, April 12, 1878

This Franz Schubert is often called "François" to distinguish him from his more famous namesake [1153]. His father, Franz Anton (1768–1824) was a contrabass player, composer of church music, and Morlacchi's [1114] predecessor as director of Dresden's Italian Opera; it was he to whom Breitkopf and Härtel sent the rejected Schubert song *"Erlkönig,"* sending him into a fury that he should be thought the source of such junk.

François studied with him and proved talented enough to win a royal scholarship to study in Paris with Charles-Philippe Lafont, a violinist whom Paganini [1106] admired. He returned to join the Dresden orchestra, of which he was appointed *Konzertmeister* in 1861. His wife Maschinka *(née* Schneider) and their daughter Georgine were both important operatic sopranos. Though François Schubert wrote other music, his memory depends almost wholly on a bagatelle for violin and piano, *L'Abeille (The Bee),* the *pièce de résistance* of the late comedian Jack Benny. RECORDINGS: *The Bee* has been recorded in a number of collections of violin encores.

[1197] CROUCH, Frederick William Nicholls

CELLIST, TRUMPETER, SINGER, TEACHER, ENGRAVER, SALESMAN, ETC.
BORN: London, July 31, 1808
DIED: Portland, Me., August 18, 1896

An orchestral cellist at the age of nine, Crouch came from a line of musicians. As a youth, he ran away to sea, but after two years he returned to London, where he played at Drury Lane, and was a chorister at St. Paul's and Westminster Abbey. He entered the Royal Academy of Music shortly after it opened and studied there with ex-prodigy William Crotch and with the younger William Linley [995]. After serving in various other theater orchestras and in Queen Adelaide's private band, he moved to Plymouth in 1832. There he led a precarious existence as a traveling salesman and sometime singer, which did not prevent him from marrying and siring sixteen children. One of them, Eliza Elizabeth [1836–86], deflowered at thirteen by a diamond merchant, became "Cora Pearl," the most famous demimondaine in Napoleon III's Paris, said to have danced the cancan on a carpet of orchids and bathed in champagne to amuse her dinner guests. Among her lovers she numbered two Murats, Jerome Bonaparte, and the Crown Prince of the Netherlands. Clad in blue plumes, diamonds, and several square feet of bare skin, she sang Cupidon in Offenbach's [1264] *Orphée aux enfers,* but her musical talents did not match her others, and she was hissed off the stage. Driven from Paris after the Franco-Prussian war, she wandered the Continent for fourteen years before being permitted to come back to die (of cancer).

Crouch's later career was, if anything, even more dismal than Cora's. In 1849, having taken on a mistress, he skipped with her to New York. For a time he was cellist at the Astor Place Opera House. Then he moved to Portland, where he gave chamber music concerts, unsuccessfully. He conducted in Philadelphia, opened an ill-starred music school in Washington, D.C., and, during the Civil War, joined Stonewall Jackson in Richmond as an army trumpeter. Crouch's memoirs were lost when, in a retreat, Jackson ordered all baggage destroyed. Afterward he taught voice in Baltimore and worked there in a factory before returning to Portland. (During a brief stint as a publisher before he left England, Crouch invented the printing process known as zincography.) He left a couple of operatic scores and many songs.

RECORDINGS: His song "Kathleen Mavourneen," recorded by John McCormack and others, was justifiably enormously popular.

[1198] KLOSÉ, Hyacinthe Eléanore (Klō-zā', Ē-à-sant' El-ā'-à-nôr)
CLARINETIST, BANDMASTER, TEACHER
BORN: Corfu, October 11, 1808
DIED: Paris, August 29, 1880

Despite his misleading Christian names, Klosé was male. After playing as a youth in the band of the Garde Royale in Paris, he enrolled at the Conservatoire in 1831 and served there as professor of clarinet from 1839 to 1868. He was also a military bandmaster. In the late 1830s, with the instrument maker Auguste Buffet, he applied to the clarinet the adaptations Theobald Boehm had made in the keying and fingering of the flute. The result, popularly called the "Boehm" clarinet, is still standard, as is the method Klosé wrote for it. Later he also took an interest in the newly invented saxophone (patented by Adolphe Sax in 1846). He wrote studies and solo pieces for both instruments, some of which have probably been preserved on records of didactic intent. RECORDINGS: There is, in a collection of Victorian parlor music, an air and variations for ophicleide (a brass instrument which was a forerunner of the tuba) played by Alan Lumsden.

[1199] YRADIER, Sebastián (Ē-rad'-ē-âr, Sā-bvàs'-tē-àn)
TEACHER
BORN: Sauciego, January 20, 1809
DIED: Vitoria, December 6, 1865

Spanish musical composition fell on hard times after the eighteenth century, but Yradier's salonesque confections passed widely for the real thing. In 1851 he went to Paris as vocal coach to the Spanish-born Eugénie, wife of President Louis Napoleon and soon to be Empress of France. He also taught at the Madrid Conservatory and spent much time in Cuba. An anthology of his songs, *Fleurs d'Espagne,* published the year before he died, was immensely popular. Georges Bizet heard someone singing his *"El Arreglito,"* jotted down the tune, and revised it for the *habañera* in his *Carmen,* assuming it to be a Spanish folktune. He was stunned to find it wasn't even a Cuban folktune! Yradier also wrote some zarzuelas. RECORDINGS: The perennial favorite for recording was *"La Paloma"* ("The Dove"), but notable singers (e.g., Adelina Patti and Emma Calvé) also recorded others of his songs.

[1200] MENDELSSOHN-BARTHOLDY, Jakob Ludwig Felix (Men'-del-sōn Bàr-tōl'-dē, Yā'-kop Lōōt'-vikh Fā'-lēks)
PIANIST, VIOLINIST, CONDUCTOR
BORN: Hamburg, February 3, 1809
DIED: Leipzig, November 4, 1847

The Fates seem to have favored Felix Mendelssohn with everything except a long life. Born to wealth and position, he enjoyed every opportunity to foster his talents. He grew up to be handsome, brilliant, and magnetic. He was a first-rate pianist, perhaps the first great podium conductor, a fine draughtsman, an accomplished linguist, a good writer. He knew everyone who was anyone. He married a stunningly beautiful woman. He had a happy family life. He built one of the great symphony orchestras and founded what was in its day the most successful conservatory in Europe. He called attention to and enhanced the reputations of many other composers, both living and dead. He was himself, from an early age, one of the most admired and influential of all composers. For all that, his background, his own weaknesses, his imitators, and widespread misunderstanding of what he represented (Classicism rather than Romanticism) have in this century reduced him to something less than Olympian stature.

His paternal grandfather was Moses, the son of a Jewish teacher and scribe from Dessau named Mendel and known as Mendel Dessau. German Jews in that era being denied surnames, Moses became Mendelssohn. Though sickly and hunchbacked, he had a brilliant mind, obtained a remarkable education of his own, became a wealthy man, a famous philosopher, a key figure in the new

German intellectualism, and, like his namesake, a liberator of his people and an unwitting reformer of their religion. Abraham, Felix's father, was his third child and second son. In 1803, when he was twenty-seven, Abraham went to Paris—he supposed permanently—to become a banker. Before the year was out his sister Henrietta introduced him to her friend Leah Solomon, on a visit from Berlin. Abraham saw fit to accompany her home and married her forthwith. Leah's family was both important and wealthy and protested having their daughter taken so far away, so Abraham arranged to work in his elder brother Joseph's bank, just opened in Hamburg, instead. There the first three of their four children were born—Fanny in 1805, Felix two years later, and Rebecca in 1811. By the last year the Mendelssohns, who had defied Napoleon's attempted blockade by engaging in smuggling, found it the better part of discretion to pack themselves back to Berlin, under cover of darkness. They settled on the New Promenade, resumed the business (they had managed to bring its assets with them), and in 1813 produced a fourth and last child, Paul. Abraham became a major contributor to the war effort against Napoleon and a city councillor. Both of the senior Mendelssohns had education, culture, and taste, and their home became a gathering place for artists, intellectuals, and important people in all fields.

Not unexpectably, the Mendelssohns wanted the best for their children, and saw to it that they had it, with a vengeance. They were parents who would have not been out of place in today's affluent society; if Little League Baseball had been invented, Felix would have played Little League Baseball. His upbringing was basically that of his siblings. From the age of four, except on Sundays, he was rousted out of bed to begin the business of the day. His earliest lessons came from his parents, his mother starting him off at the piano and overseeing his practice. When he was six, that aspect of his training was turned over to Ludwig Berger, a protégé of Clementi [977] and John Field [1104], and he made his concert debut three years later. He also had tutors for academic subjects, painting, and violin. On Sundays the family (all of the children made music) and their friends gathered for morning musicales, to which Felix was later chief composer.

Leah Mendelssohn had an odd brother, who made a career in the diplomatic service in Italy, and who, troubled by his Jewishness, converted to Protestantism in 1805, taking the name "Bartholdy" from a Berlin estate he had acquired. He urged his sister and brother-in-law to follow his example. When in 1816 they had their four children baptized as Lutherans (they themselves held out for six years more), Bartholdy further insisted that they substitute his chosen name for Mendelssohn. Abraham compromised by *adding* it. When he recognized that his son was to be an international figure, he tried to persuade him to become Felix M. Bartholdy, but Felix refused.

It was in 1816 that Abraham, entrusted with collecting war reparations, took Fanny and Felix with him to Paris, where they studied with Marie Bigot de Morogues, a pianist admired by Haydn [871], Beethoven [1063], and Cherubini [1019]. In 1819 Felix began studying theory and harmony with Carl Friedrich Zelter [1008], director of the Berlin Singakademie, bosom friend of Goethe and an admirer of the music of Sebastian Bach [684]. By the time Zelter took him on a visit to Goethe in Weimar two years later, Felix had already written a piano trio, several symphonies for strings, a wedding cantata, and many smaller pieces. Though Goethe was not noted for his musical taste, he could not get enough of young Felix, who reciprocated his admiration. For the rest of Goethe's life, the two remained close, and the old man exerted a powerful influence on the younger.

By 1822, when the Mendelssohn family made an extensive tour of Germany and Switzerland, Felix had written two piano concerti, a piano quartet, several of his short comic operas, and some large choral pieces. In 1825 he returned with his father to Paris, where Cherubini overcame his scorn for aliens and gave him his cachet as a promising musician. That same year Abraham Mendelssohn bought a magnificent estate on the prophetically named Leipzigerstrasse, which became the focal center of the Berlin upper-class world. There the children liked to produce plays, among them some of Shakespeare's in the German translation of August Wilhelm von Schlegel (with whose brother Friedrich their Aunt Dorothea had taken up an adulterous relationship and later married.) Out of these performances there came, in 1826, the *Midsummer Night's Dream Overture*, which, together, with the string octet of the previous year, proclaimed the composer's arrival at musical maturity. (According to Bernhard Marx, a musician who was a family friend, it was his criticisms and suggestions that shaped the overture as we now know it; the first public performance was directed by Carl Loewe [1152] in Stettin a year after its completion.) In 1820–23 Mendelssohn wrote five short operas for home consumption: *Ich, J. Mendelssohn . . . ,*

1820; *Die Soldaten Liebschaft (The Soldiers' Sweetheart),* 1820; *Die beiden Pädagogen (The Two Pedagogues),* 1821, *Die wanderten Komödianten (The Traveling Comediens)* 1822; *Der Onkel aus Boston (The Uncle from Boston),* 1823. In 1827 familial influence secured a public premiere in the Berlin Schauspielhaus for his two-act *Die Hochzeit des Camacho (The Marriage of Camacho),* after Cervantes, but for several reasons it went so badly that the composer himself left before it was over. Mendelssohn's wish to write a successful opera was never realized. He completed only one more work in the genre, *Die Heimkehr aus der Fremde (The Soldier's Return from Abroad),* a one-act comedy written for his parents' twenty-fifth wedding anniversary on his return from his first trip to England. *Lorelei,* his only attempt at a major operatic work, was left in fragmentary form.

In 1827 Mendelssohn was admitted to the University of Berlin, where he studied under the philosopher Friedrich Hegel (a family friend), among others. About this time a groundswell of interest in J. S. Bach was slowly making itself felt. Zelter, who collected Bach manuscripts (real and purported), some of which had been given him by Abraham Mendelssohn, had aroused his young charge's interest, and for Felix's fourteenth birthday his grandmother Solomon had given him a copy of Zelter's copy of the *St. Matthew Passion.* In 1828 he and the singer-actor Eduard Devrient, who coveted the role of Jesus in the work, decided to promote what would be the first performance since the composer's death. They rounded up other notable soloists, a 156-voice choir, and members of the amateur Philharmonic Society, plus professional first-desk men, and, for the benefit of a sewing school for poor girls, Mendelssohn conducted it at the Singakademie the following March. In so doing he dispelled the myth that Bach's major works were unperformable and introduced Bach's music to a general public, some of which, however, was to continue to resist it as stuffy and antiquated for some time to come.

Shortly afterward Mendelssohn, at his father's urgings, set out to broaden his mind, in the approved way, by seeing the civilized world. He first set out for London. The Mendelssohns were Anglophiles, Felix spoke the language extremely well, and he had friends there in the poet Karl Klingemann, then in the diplomatic service, and the pianist Ignaz Moscheles **[1146],** with whom he had studied briefly, and Sir George Smart, a founder of the London Philharmonic Society who had paid the Mendelssohns several

visits in 1825. He chose to sail from Hamburg. The voyage was stormy and took eleven days, and Mendelssohn was wretchedly seasick, but London made up for the experience. He was excited by its size and vitality. He indulged himself in girl watching, apparently a favorite pastime with him. He heard Malibran sing Rossini's **[1143]** Desdemona and saw Charles Kemble as Hamlet. English society made much of him; he was, after all, one of them, not some beggarly musician scheming to get their money. After some delay, the Philharmonic let him conduct his so-called first symphony (really his thirteenth). The concert was a triumph. So was the piano recital he gave shortly afterward. Neither held a candle, however, to the benefit concert he gave for Silesian flood victims, which included Malibran, Henriette Sontag (the two reigning divas of the day), Moscheles, and several other stars. After it, he and Klingemann toured Scotland (which was to inspire the *Hebrides* overture and the third symphony) and introduced themselves to Sir Walter Scott, the most popular novelist of the era. In September, four months having passed since he left home, Mendelssohn decided it was time to go and returned to London. There, however, his carriage overturned when a horse bolted, severely injuring his knee and putting him to bed for two more months, causing him to miss the wedding of his adored sister Fanny.

No sooner was he home than, largely inspired by Goethe (who knew the land), he was off, by a roundabout road, to Italy. He stopped by Weimar to see the old man on what was to prove their last visit together. In Munich he apparently fell in love with a young pianist named Delphine von Schauroth; if he did, it was his first serious romantic involvement. Then he traveled southeast to Vienna and Budapest and finally to Venice, moved on to Bologna and Florence, to settle early in November at No. 5 Piazza di Spagna, beside the Spanish Steps. Like most Germans he was ravished by Italy, but felt, probably rightly, that he was regularly bilked by the Italians. In this attitude, he had something in common with Berlioz **[1175],** whom he met in Rome. He liked the Frenchman, though, in his highbrow way, he found him roughhewn and his music (by his own Classical standards) a mess; Berlioz, typically, adored him. In the spring Mendelssohn continued his travels as far as the sub-Neapolitan south, then returned to Florence and, after soaking himself again in its art, moved on to Milan and then to Switzerland for the summer. During this time, he was working on the compositions noted, as well as on the fourth symphony (the "Italian"), the *Songs Without Words*, and a "first" piano concerto for Delphine. He got back to Munich in September and performed it at a festival concert before the king a month later. Though he did not like Paris, he decided he must make his name there. He arrived in December 1831, played and was played, had his so-called fifth symphony rejected by the Conservatory Orchestra, renewed acquaintances with Chopin [1208], Liszt [1218], Ferdinand Hiller [1219], and others, and, as he was about to leave early in the spring, was touched by the cholera, then raging throughout Western Europe. He finally left in late April, on a second and much briefer trip to London never to return.

In March Goethe had died; on the Ides of May, Zelter followed him. The following month Mendelssohn finally went home, where his parents argued him into entering the competition for Zelter's post at the Singakademie. Mendelssohn was then but two years past his majority, and his conducting experience had been sporadic; moreover, though a practicing Christian, he was a Jew's grandson. Consequently the post went to Zelter's assistant Rungenhagen by a wide majority. But he was more acceptable elsewhere: the London Philharmonic commissioned a symphony (the still unfinished "Italian"), an overture *(Die schöne Melusine)*, and a choral work, and he was asked to conduct the following spring's Niederrhenische Musikfest at Düsseldorf. The latter appointment eventuated in Mendelssohn's accepting the post of municipal *Kapellmeister* in that city. The festival, where he conducted, among other things, Handel's *Israel in Egypt* in its original form and was pelted with flowers by the singers, was more successful than the long-term job. He found the town provincial and musically backward. After a carefully prepared performance of Mozart's [992] *Don Giovanni* proved more trouble than it was worth, he resigned as opera intendant, ruffling a good many feathers. Though he came back to the area for the spring festivals (he premiered his first oratorio *St. Paul* there in 1836), he gave up his Düsseldorf post after a year to take a much more promising one with the Leipzig Gewandhaus Orchestra.

Taking its name from the old Drapers' Hall where it played, the Leipzig orchestra was even then one of the oldest and best in Europe. Mendelssohn was something new as a conductor. He did not conduct from the piano or with his violin bow or with a rolled-up sheet of music. He used a baton, not merely to beat time but to interpret the music. He had a photographic memory and knew precisely what he wanted to hear (when he conducted without music, it made people nervous, so he always kept a score before him and flipped the pages). In Leipzig he built up an already fine orchestra to a membership of fifty, raised salaries, and brought in top-rank leaders like the violinist Ferdinand David. The orchestra became "his" in the sense that the Philadelphia was Stokowski's or the NBC Symphony Toscanini's. And he used it to perform not only great music (e.g., Beethoven's) but also contemporary music (e.g., Schumann's [1211] and even Berlioz's [1175]).

The first season was marred by the sudden death of Abraham Mendelssohn in November 1835. Felix completed *St. Paul* as a sort of memorial. After the premiere, he was summoned to Frankfort to conduct another performance when the scheduled conductor became sick. There he met and fell deeply in love with the beautiful Cécile Jeanrenaud, daughter of a Swiss Huguenot pastor. It may be true that his deep attachment to his sister Fanny had inhibited his love life, but it did not do so here. At first he seems to have been frightened and left Frankfort for a Dutch resort. But he soon made his mind up, became engaged in September, and married Cécile the following March. Of their five children, Felix died in childhood, Paul founded the firm now known as Agfa, and several other descendents have had distinguished careers, but none of them in music.

Shortly after Frederick William IV came to the Prussian throne in 1840, he invited Mendelssohn, at a steep rise in salary, to come to Berlin to direct the Royal Opera, the Cathedral Choir, the Royal Orchestra, and the projected Royal Academy. The composer hesitated, but, providing himself with an escape valve, with the Leipzig orchestra, he finally went, leaving David, then Ferdinand Hiller, and finally Gade [1248] to conduct in his place. He immediately found himself entangled in bureaucratic red tape, putting out maximum effort with minimum result. In 1842 he offered to resign, but the king wheedled him into staying with promises, reduced responsibilities, and the title of *Generalmusikdirektor*, the longest he had at hand. The Berlin Academy having been shelved, Mendelssohn in 1843 opened his own conservatory in Leipzig. Staffed with the best teachers he could find (most of them of his musical mind), it became the most important music school in Germany for the rest of the century. Meanwhile in Berlin things went from bad to worse, and in 1844 Mendelssohn resigned for good. (His mother's death in 1842 gave him one less tie to the city.) The chief musical product of the experience was the rest of the incidental music for *A Midsummer Night's Dream.*

Over the years Mendelssohn had returned to England several times. In 1842 he had met Victoria's Prince-Consort, Albert, himself a minor imitator of Mendelssohn, and then the queen herself. She sang for him, he dedicated the "Scotch" Symphony to her, they became fast friends, and accordingly Mendelssohn became a new foreign model, which inhibited the development of English music and inspired all those dreadful hymntuney pieces. In 1846 he capped his English influence with *Elijah* at the Birmingham Festival, which he was asked to direct. It was to star Jenny Lind, who appeared with the Leipzig orchestra, to which Mendelssohn had returned the year previous, and had also sung in the 1846 Lower Rhine Festival, in Haydn's [871] *Creation.* The relation between the two musicians was a close one, but for whatever reason she withdrew from the oratorio, and it cooled. *Elijah* convinced the English that religious oratorio represented the highest level of musical art, and for years they tried unsuccessfully to prove it.

On the way home Mendelssohn was so exhausted that he had to make three layovers between London and Leipzig. He returned to England the next spring but was obviously unwell. In May his sister Fanny died of a stroke. Mendelssohn collapsed at the news. Cécile took him to Switzerland for the summer to rest. Back in Leipzig, he became ill in October. For three weeks his health was up and down. Then, on October 28, he had some sort of attack (probably cardiac), went to bed, and died a week later. Germany and England both went into mourning, and he was buried with a state funeral in Berlin. Cécile died of tuberculosis six years later, leaving her orphaned children to be reared by her mother and Mendelssohn's brother Paul.

RECORDINGS: All of the orchestral works (including juvenilia), the chamber and keyboard music, the two great oratorios, the operas *Die Heimkehr aus der Fremde* and *Die beiden Pädagogen* have been recorded. There still remain severe gaps in the lesser vocal works.

[1201] ALBERT, Charles Louis Napoléon d' (dàl-bâr', Shärl Loo-ē' Nà-pō-lā-on')
DANCE TEACHER
BORN: Nienstedten, February 25, 1809
DIED: London, May 26, 1886

Descended though he was from a line of important Italian composers named Alberti, Charles d'Albert's father was a French army officer, stationed in what is now a western suburb of Hamburg. He died when the boy was seven, and the mother, who had given the latter some preparatory piano lessons, took him to London where he became a pupil of Kalkbrenner [1118] and studied composition with Samuel Sebastian Wesley [1213], eighteen months his junior. D'Albert gravitated toward the dance and served as ballet master at the Paris Opéra and at various London theaters before embarking on a highly successful freelance career as a dancing teacher. For a time he lived in Newcastle-on-Tyne, where, in 1863, he married a German wife. The immediate fruit of the union was a son baptized Eugene Francis Charles [1562], who was to eclipse his father's fame. Charles later returned to London. His compositions consist almost entirely of popular dances for piano. RECORDINGS: These dances have been recorded in various collections of period dance music.

[1202] PROCH, Heinrich (Prōkh, Hīn'-rikh)
VIOLINIST, TEACHER, CONDUCTOR
BORN: Böhmisch-Leipa, July 22, 1809
DIED: Vienna, December 18, 1878

A native of what is now Česká Lipa in Czechoslovakia, Proch came to Vienna to study law, but took up the violin, made a name for himself as a performer, and in 1837 was accordingly appointed conductor at the Josephstadt theater, and three years later also at the Hofoper. His most important compositions were mostly by way of incidental music for plays at the Josephstadttheater, though he produced 4 comic operas of no consequence in the 1840s. He was highly esteemed as a vocal teacher; among his many famous pupils were Therese Tietjens and Amalie Materna (who created Wagner's [1230] Brünnhilde and Kundry). Proch was pensioned off in 1870 but came out of retirement in 1874 to direct the orchestra of the Komische Oper (which soon failed). RECORDINGS: Today he is remembered almost exclusively for a set of coloratura variations that every florid soprano once felt impelled to record. He also provided the recitatives for Nicolai's [1212] *Lustigen Weiber von Windsor* when it was eventually premiered in Vienna after the composer's death.

[1203] HESSE, Adolf Friedrich (Hes'-sə, Ád-olf Frē'-drikh)
ORGANIST
BORN: Breslau (Wroclaw), August 30, 1809
DIED: Breslau, August 5, 1863

Once a name to conjure with in European organ circles, Hesse is all but forgotten now. His father was an organ builder by profession and taught the boy all he knew, which gave him considerable insight into his instrument. He later studied with Weber's [1124] friend Friedrich Wilhelm Berner, and the Breslau organist Ernst Köhler. His talent so impressed the city fathers that they subsidized him to travel about Germany performing and studying the great organs. In 1831 he was appointed organist of the Bernhardinkirche in his native city, which in the ensuing thirty years became a sort of pilgrimage spot for European organists. He was also chief conductor of the local symphony orchestra. In 1844 he was invited to Paris to inaugurate the new organ at the church of Saint Eustache, and later performed in London at the Crystal Palace Exhibition of 1851. Though he wrote in other genres, it was his organ pieces that preserved his name for some time after his death. The Wilson twins have recorded one of his fantasias for two organs and Franz Haselböck a set of variations on a Christmas carol.

[1204] HATTON, John Liptrot
ENTERTAINER, ORGANIST, CONDUCTOR
BORN: Liverpool, October 12, 1809
DIED: Margate, September 20, 1886

Though Hatton had a good many strings to his bow, he was chiefly noted as a composer of drawing-room songs. The son of a violinist, he began his career in his teens as a church organist and a performer on the Liverpool stage. In 1842 he became choral director at the Drury Lane Theatre in London, where he produced his first opera that same year. Two years later he went to Vienna for the premiere of his second, Pascal Bruno, and studied with Simon Sechter [1129] while there. He soon began doing one-man shows, with which he successfully toured North America at mid-century. In 1853 he sang a concert performance of Mozart's [992] Don Giovanni in Dublin with a number of important singers. Later in the decade he was musical director for Charles Kean, for whom he wrote much incidental music. He spent some time during his latter years in Germany and then retired to the coastal towns of Aldeburgh and Margate. Though he wrote a good deal of choral music and a few instrumental pieces, it was the songs that survived. RECORDINGS: Sir Charles Santley, in his seventieth year, made a fine record of "To Anthea," and other recordings of the acoustical era also exist. (Some of Hatton's pieces were published under the pseudonym "Czapek," supposedly a Czech or Hungarian term having to do with hats.)

[1205] RICCI, Federico (Rē'-chē, Fā-dā-rē'-kō)
BORN: Naples, October 22, 1809
DIED: Conegliano, December 10, 1877

Federico Ricci studied at the Royal Conservatory in Naples with Zingarelli, as well as with his older brother Luigi [1183] and Vincenzo Bellini [1164], both advanced students there. Federico was a more careful and less prolific composer than Luigi, with whom he collaborated on 4 operas, beginning with Il Colonello (The Little Colonel) in 1835. Federico's own maiden voyage was with Monsieur de Chalumeaux in Venice later that year, but his first—and perhaps greatest—success was in Trieste in 1838 with La Prigione d'Edimburgo (The Edinburgh Prison, after Walter Scott). Other successes were Luigi Rolla e Michelangelo, Florence 1841; Corrado d'Altamura, La Scala 1841; the final Ricci-brothers collaboration Crispino e la comare, Venice 1850. (The Griselda of 1847 is chiefly interesting for the plot twist at the end, which sends the long-suffering heroine back to her father in disgust.) After the enthusiastic reception of his comedy Il Marito e l'amante (Husband and Lover) in Vienna in 1852, Federico went to St. Petersburg as musical director of the imperial theaters, a sinecure which he held until 1869, during which period he turned out nothing but trifles. He was one of the composers who contributed to the synthetic Requiem got up by Verdi [1232] for Rossini [1143]. In 1869 Ricci had such a triumph in Paris with an Offenbachian farce, Una Follia a Roma (A Roman Folly), that he remained to mine the same vein for a few years, but without further success. He retired in 1876 to Conegliano in the Alpine foothills north of Venice. RECORDINGS: Little of Ricci survives save old recordings of excerpts from Crispino and the barcarolle "Sulla poppa del mio brick" ("On the poop of my brig") from La Prigione d'Edimburgo.

[1206] BULL, Ōle Bornemann (Bool, Ō'-lə Bôr'-nə-mán)
VIOLINIST

BORN: Bergen, February 5, 1810
DIED: Lysøen, August 17, 1880

Owing partly to political circumstances, Norwegian musical life, beyond the folk level, did not begin to develop until the latter eighteenth century. Thus it is not surprising that Ole Bull was the first Norwegian composer to win international fame, though he was in fact better known for his playing than for his music. In many ways the archetypal Romantic virtuoso, he appears to have been part genius, part *naif*, and part charlatan; but his biography has been much distorted, and most of his music seems to need serious evaluation. A druggist's son, he was musically precocious, first appearing with the Bergen Harmonic Society (which had to waive its rules for him) as soloist at the age of nine. He was taught by local musicians, but also learned much from country fiddlers, and developed a violin, a bow, and a technique that were all his own.

At eighteen he followed the paternal injunction to go to Christiania (now Oslo) and study theology. But, having failed to qualify, he accepted the just-vacated posts of conductor at the Lyceum and the town theater. He spent the summer of 1829 in Denmark and Germany, where he was probably *not* rejected as a pupil by Spohr [1112], who may have been on vacation, and where he seems *not* to have fought the duel with which he has been credited. An unsuccessful concert tour of Norway was followed by an equally unsuccessful Parisian venture, though his introduction of the Hardanger fiddle (the traditional Norwegian folk instrument with sympathetic strings) caused some comment. Poverty led to serious illness, which he survived thanks to Mme. Villeminot, his landlady. Then, inspired to feats of virtuosic derring-do by hearing Paganini [1106], his increasingly successful concerts in Italy in 1834 culminated in an all-out triumph in Bologna, where he was given membership in the Philharmonic Academy. In 1835 he returned a conqueror to Paris, where he performed at the Opéra (a privilege granted previously only to Paganini among violinists), and where he married Félicie Villeminot, granddaughter of his good angel. England gave him the kind of reception it had denied even Paganini, and he performed there nearly 300 times before returning to Norway in 1838. The next several years were crammed with concert dates all over Europe. (Bull played Beethoven [1063] with Liszt [1218] in London and chamber music with Mendelssohn [1200] in Leipzig.) In 1843 he made his first American tour, inau-

gurating a mutual love affair with the American people, who fanned the fiercely democratic flame that burned in him.

This proclivity and his patriotism made him an important figure in the Norwegian nationalistic-republican movement, if not always an effectual one. (He was in part the model for Henrik Ibsen's *Peer Gynt.*) In 1849 he established a Norwegian National Theater in Bergen to give plays in Norwegian (the official language was Danish). Ironically, one of the first playwrights whose cause he espoused was Ibsen, whom he left in charge when it became clear that his own concert tours would have to support the venture. Now envisioning a utopian community for Norway's poor, he returned to America in 1852 to buy some 11,000 acres of forest wilderness in north central Pennsylvania, which tract he named "Oleana." But Oleana turned out to be a mistake, and though Bull recouped his investment, he went deeply into debt to take care of those who had tried to settle there. Nor did an abortive attempt at establishing an opera house in New York improve his situation.

Back in Bergen, he replaced Ibsen (who had gone to the capital) with Bjørnstjerne Bjørnson, Norway's other burgeoning playwright, and helped Edvard Grieg [1410] get a start on a musical education. But his plans for establishing a national conservatory collapsed before they ever got off the ground in 1862. That same year, Félicie Bull died. From 1870 Bull made annual trips to the United States, spending much time in Wisconsin, where he presented the university with a collection of Scandinavian literature and married a senator's young daughter. He celebrated his seventieth birthday in America but died shortly afterward on his estate near Bergen.

RECORDINGS: Bull's compositional output includes concerti and many programmatic pieces, not to mention a string quartet for solo violin (!). But he is remembered today chiefly for a much-recorded song, *"Saeterjentens Søndag"* ("The Herd-Girl's Sunday"), actually an adaptation from a piece for strings. Recently, however, the Norwegian government has produced a record that includes the latter and several other Bull concerted works.

[1207] BURGMÜLLER, August Joseph Norbert (Bōōrg'-mü-ler, Ou'-gōōst Yō'-zef Nôr'-bârt)
PIANIST
BORN: Düsseldorf, February 8, 1810
DIED: Aachen, May 7, 1836

Norbert Burgmüller, the younger brother of
Friedrich [1190], was a sickly (apparently
epileptic) genius, who evinced enormous
musical talent in childhood. He studied with
his father and then in Kassel with Spohr
[1112] and the latter's friend Moritz Hauptmann. Afterward, apparently unable to find
a post, he lived obscurely, his music known
only to a few. (It was promoted by Schumann [1211].) An epileptic seizure carried
him off at twenty-six. Schumann completed
the second of Burgmüller's 2 symphonies (in
B minor, like Schubert's [1153] "Unfinished"). He also left a piano concerto, sonatas, and a string quartet. RECORDINGS: Pianist Adrian Ruiz has recorded the F-minor
sonata.

[1208] CHOPIN, Frédéric François (Shō-
pan', Frā-dā-rēk' Frän-swà')
PIANIST, TEACHER
BORN: Żelazowa Wola, March 1, 1810
DIED: Paris, October 17, 1849

Chopin was born a few months past the centenary of Bartolomeo Cristofori's first piano.
The instrument had begun to assert its primacy in the last decades of the eighteenth
century and by 1810 was not only dominant,
but was in fact the domestic symbol of economic success. For half a century there had
been composers who wrote specifically for it,
and more recently virtuosi to show what it
could do. But recalling that it occupies an
important place in all his compositions, we
may say that Chopin was the first major
composer (and probably the only one) to
write for it exclusively. Moreover, no other
more fully realized its possibilities, affected
the way in which it is played or contributed
more importantly to its repertoire than he.
Yet his music is very much a product of his
time—the Romantic age—drawing as it does
from the Bellinian [1164] notion of melody,
national pride (the polonaises and mazurkas), apotheosized popular forms (e.g., the
waltz), and virtuosic embellishments.

Chopin's French father Nicolas had, for
whatever reason, made his way to Poland at
seventeen, fought for the patriots in the 1788
uprising, and settled down as a tobacconist's
bookkeeper. In 1794 he was again in the military, this time as an officer, then became a
teacher of French (the second language of
the aristocracy) and found a place at Żelazowa Wola, some forty miles from Warsaw, as tutor to the children of Countess
Skarbek, in 1802. Four years later, he married the housekeeper, twenty-four-year-old
Tekla-Justyna Krzyzanowska, said to be a
poor relation of the Skarbeks. Their first

child, Louise (or Ludwika), arrived ten
months later. After a three-year hiatus, she
was followed by their only son, officially
listed as "Frederyk Franciszek." Six months
later Nicolas moved his family to Warsaw,
where he took a job at the Lyceum, and,
having providently salted away his salary
during his years in service, bought a home,
in which he boarded select male students.
Two more daughters, Isabella and Emilia,
were born in 1811 and 1813 respectively, and
their father accordingly took on additional
teaching duties at two local military schools.

Despite the eternal precariousness of life
in Warsaw, the Chopins throve and soon
took an apartment in the palace that housed
the Lyceum. Both parents were musical, and
by the time Frédéric was three, it was clear
that he was too. After some lessons from his
mother and Louise, he was turned over to a
bibulous eccentric, Adalbert Żywny, who finally threw up his hands in 1822, having
overstepped his limited knowledge. Though
subject to frequent colds and more intelligent than most, Chopin seems to have led a
normal and happy childhood. (Small-boned,
he eventually attained an average height for
his day but never weighed as much as a hundred pounds.) Though he wrote music early
—he had a polonaise published when he was
seven—he was far from prolific. In 1818 he
played a movement from a Gyrowetz [1032]
concerto in public, and he performed fairly
frequently for various nobles and celebrities.
(The singer Angelica Catalani gave him an
engraved watch that he treasured all his
life.) Having imbibed the classics, notably
Mozart and Bach, from Żywny, in 1822 he
began study with Józef Elsner, founder of
the newly opened Warsaw Conservatory and
a composer of some stature. Shortly afterward he was enrolled in the Lyceum to complete his academic studies. He made many
friendships there, including an almost passionate one with Tytus Woyciechowski, son
of a squire in the Ukraine, who boarded with
the family and acquitted himself brilliantly
enough to make the local newspapers. En
passant he played before Czar Alexander I,
attended the opera, enrolled in the Conservatory, and, after his graduation from the
Lyceum in 1826, took the waters at Reinertz
(now Dusziki) in Silesia. The following year,
in which he decided to forego the university
for music, his youngest sister died, ominously, of tuberculosis.

In 1829 Elsner certified him as a genius, an
opinion that, based on his variations for piano and orchestra on Mozart's Don Giovanni duet, "La ci darem," was to be more
reverberantly echoed in print by Robert
Schumann [1211], age twenty-one ("Hats

off, gentlemen! A genius!"). Having visited Berlin (where he did not perform) in 1828, Chopin now set out for Vienna, where he gave two highly successful recitals, returning to Warsaw by way of Prague and Dresden. He fell romantically and inarticulately in love with a young soprano, Konstancja Gladkowska, over whom he mooned for many months and about whom he did nothing. In March 1830 he presented his first concerto in a Warsaw concert (confusingly, it is now known as the second because of the sequence of publication), and after vacationing on Tytus' farm followed it with the second (or first) in October, in which concert he shared the stage with Miss Gladkowska. Three years later, still all unwitting, she married someone else. Meanwhile, finding his career circumscribed by the provincialism of Poland, Chopin was eager to get out into the big world, but typically he shuffled his feet until he at last got up the will to set out early in November for Vienna, where he had tasted success. Much to his surprise he discovered that Vienna had forgotten him and was not anxious to renew the acquaintance. After six months he decided to move on to Stuttgart. No sooner had he gotten there than he learned that the latest Polish uprising had been put down by a Russian invasion that had taken Warsaw and brutally treated the population. Since there was no turning back, he went on to Paris in September, just in time for the great cholera epidemic, which fortunately he escaped. He found digs on the Right Bank and introduced himself to Ferdinando Paër [1069], who in turn introduced him to Cherubini [1019], Rossini [1143], and Kalkbrenner [1118], the musical powers of the city. Early the following year he gave a concert in the little Salle Pleyel—a critical success if a financial failure—enabled by Kalkbrenner, with whom he studied briefly. It took only one more concert to establish Chopin. Pupils began to arrive—mostly titled ladies—and he was soon able to pick and choose (his selectivity abetted by his native snobbishness). He moved in the highest levels of both the social and the artistic world. His taste was exquisite, his sensibilities ultra-refined, his dress up to the minute, his grooming immaculate. He disapproved of the aggressiveness, the brusqueness, and the rough edges of such of his acquaintances as Berlioz [1175] and the exiled Polish poet Adam Mickiewicz. He became a close friend of the short-lived Bellini, whose feel for melody had so much impact on both his composition and his playing (he saw the piano as a singing instrument, not a percussive one). Scrupulous of what was *comme il faut,* he

spent most of the considerable amount he took in on appearances (he had nine different addresses in his eighteen Paris-based years). He concertized remarkably little and preferred the private salon to the public hall. Regarded as a remarkable, if unorthodox teacher, he left no piano method—and no student of any real importance.

He was besieged by would-be lovers of both sexes, but for a long time his sex life, if any, was apparently minimal. On a trip to see his parents at Karlsbad, he visited his old friends the Wodzińskis, exiled Polish nobles, in Dresden in 1835 and worked up a tepid enthusiasm for their daughter Maria. He was with them again the following summer in Marienbad, proposed, and was accepted. But the Wodzińskis recovered their status and lands and returned to Poland, and the whole thing died quietly. Before, during, and after this feeble affair there may have been something more substantial with a Polish beauty named Delfina Potocka in Paris; but our knowledge of it (which shows an atypically randy Chopin) is largely based on a series of letters announced, but produced only in photocopy, by a Polish woman musicologist (who later committed suicide). Late in 1836, at an intimate party, he was introduced to the cigar-smoking, trousers-clad feminist, Mme. Aurore Dudevant, better known by her novelistic *nom de plume* "George Sand." It was distaste at first sight on both sides, but Sand discovered that Chopin held a fascination for her and later invited him to join Liszt [1218] and his mistress Marie d'Agoult at her home in Nohant the following spring. Chopin was overworked and beginning to ail—he had suffered at least one small pulmonary hemorrhage—but he ignored this chance for a vacation and its tenderer. She returned to Paris in the summer of 1838 and set to work, and —to avoid the details—Chopin capitulated and agreed to go with her to Mallorca in October. The affair is generally cited as one of the great love stories; it is certainly one of the oddest of that genre. Sexually Sand was eager and aggressive but suffered a severe trauma from her wedding night and was, as a result, frigid. Chopin was delicate, feminine, passive, weak of will, possibly a virgin, perhaps impotent. Nor was the Mallorcan idyll exactly that. It began in impossibly noisy and cramped quarters in Palma, moved to a leaky-roofed house in the country, where in the cold and damp Chopin's disease throve alarmingly, and wound up in a pair of cells in an old monastery in the hills. Chopin had to work with a dilapidated piano until a decent one could be imported. Both suffered from the disapproval of the intensely moral native population. They left in February, Chopin suffering another hemorrhage on the journey. Sand and her two children, who had been underfoot the whole time, were also decidedly unwell. They spent the summer recuperating at Nohant—where supposedly Liszt, playing in a romantically darkened room, fooled everyone into thinking him to be Chopin (everyone except Chopin, that is)—then returned to Paris, where eventually they set up living quarters in the Rue Pigalle.

The relationship kept on a relatively even keel for several years. Despite his unpredictable health, Chopin continued to teach, was highly productive, and gave an occasional concert (he played several times before Louis-Philippe, whom he despised, by royal command). The couple continued to summer at Nohant. Among those who joined them there was the painter Delacroix (Chopin liked him but not his work), the Polish poet Witwicki (who supplied the texts for most of Chopin's songs), the great contralto Pauline Viardot (Gounod's [1258] sometime patron-mistress), and Chopin's older sister Ludwika (who, with her husband, came to console Chopin after their father died in 1844). But the fabric eventually began to unravel. A chief point of contention was Sand's daughter Solange, whom, in feminine jealousy apparently, she thwarted at every opportunity and whose side Chopin often took. The rift came when Sand palmed Solange off in marriage to an adventurer, a sculptor named Clésinger. The newlyweds visited Nohant, and it is hard to say which behaved more abominably toward Solange's mother. Chopin felt sorry for the girl and acted accordingly. In July, in an excess of self-justification, Sand told him in effect to get lost—though she let it be generally known that she was the one who had been inexplicably abandoned.

Deprived of both companionship and support, Chopin, despite his seriously declining condition, gave over what time and strength he had to teaching. In February 1848, now too weak to negotiate stairs by himself, he took part, in the Salle Pleyel, in what was to be his last concert appearance in Paris. Two days later came the revolution that toppled Louis-Philippe and a simultaneous uprising in Poland that had the usual dire results there. Chopin had thought of going home, or perhaps to Germany, but in the end decided on London, where he was taken in hand by his sometime pupil Jane Stirling and her sister, a Mrs. Erskine. He, with his distaste for large halls, refused to appear with the Philharmonic but played in the salons of a number of members of high society;

the expected royal command never came. Unhappy and bored, he let Jane Stirling (who wanted him for her very own) to hale him to Scotland. He gave concerts in Manchester, Glasgow, and Edinburgh, and endured the amateur "accomplishments" of innumerable hostesses. He grew steadily worse (he had written little or nothing during the past year). He was quite sick when he reached London at the end of October, and left for Paris three weeks later. There he had good days and bad ones and obviously knew he could not live much longer. He destroyed some of his manuscripts in May, moved to the edge of town where breathing might be easier, and in June summoned his sister Ludwika, who was, however, not able to get out of Poland until August. His money was now gone, and his friends were supporting him. The Clésingers moved to the neighborhood to look after him. Jane Stirling came from Scotland. From out of the past Titus Woyciechowski proposed a visit but was denied a passport. In September Chopin made a last move to an apartment in the Place Vendôme, where he took to his bed. The room was literally crowded with visitors. (Mme. Viardot said sarcastically that all the ladies in Paris came there to faint.) Chopin, long estranged from the Church, made his confession. Delfina Potocka volunteered to sing for him on October 15. He lost consciousness the next day and died early the following morning. His body was buried in the Père Lachaise cemetery, his heart in the Church of the Holy Cross in Warsaw.

RECORDINGS: By now virtually every scrap of Chopin's music has been recorded, much of it by the greatest pianists of the century (though this author has never encountered a record of the childhood march).

[1209] DAVID, Félicien-César (Dá-vēd', Fā-lē-sē-àn' Sā'-zär)
CONDUCTOR, PIANIST
BORN: Cadenet, April 13, 1810
DIED: St.-Germain-en-Laye, August 29, 1876

An archetypal Romantic and the father of latter-day French musical Orientalism, Félicien David now languishes in obscurity, as he did for much of his life. Born in the Vaucluse and orphaned at an early age, he became a chorister at St. Sauveur in Aix-en-Provence when he was eight. From 1825 to 1828 he attended the Jesuit college there. When it closed, he found work as a theatrical conductor, then as a law clerk, and finally as choir director at St. Sauveur. In 1830 he gave it up and went to Paris, where he studied briefly at the Conservatoire under Fétis [1111] and others. A year later David's uncle withdrew the pittance he had grudgingly granted him to live on. David suddenly found that he agreed with the preachments of the late Count Saint-Simon, a sort of proto-Marxist, and joined the commune at Ménilmont that the Saint-Simonians had founded after the 1830 revolution. He grew his hair long and dressed in cerulean blue, according to the rules of the order, until a fearful government broke it up in 1832. With a remnant of the group and accompanied by his faithful piano, he went to Marseilles where they took ship on an idealistic mission to the Near East. David finally settled in Cairo, where he supported himself with music lessons and soaked up the exotic atmosphere, returning to France in 1835. Having published unsuccessfully and at his own expense some *Mélodies orientales* for piano, he retired to Igny, about twenty miles from Paris and devoted himself to composition. His music at last began to draw some notice, and in 1844 he moved back to Paris, where his sprawling symphonic ode *Le Désert* created a sensation. (Recent revivals have won it much praise, but so far it has gone unrecorded.)

David then spent some time in Germany and returned to mine the *Désert* lode for several years without further notable success. In his first opera, *La Perle du Brésil (The Pearl of Brazil)* of 1851, he substituted South American for eastern exoticism. Of his five later operas, only *Lalla-Roukh*, 1862, can be called successful. His acceptance, however, was signalized that same year when he was awarded the *Légion d'honneur*. In 1867, when he had virtually given up composition, the Académie awarded him a prize of 20,000 francs, and two years later he was elected to the Institut to fill the place of his champion, Berlioz [1175]. Besides the operas and symphonic odes, David left 3 symphonies, chamber music, choral works (many of them for the Saint-Simonians), piano pieces, and a large number of songs.

RECORDINGS: A single much-recorded aria, *"Charmant oiseau"* ("Charming bird"), seems to about cover David's phonographic representation.

[1210] LUMBYE, Hans Christian (Loom'-bi, Hàns Krēst'-yàn)
TRUMPETER, VIOLINIST, CONDUCTOR
BORN: Copenhagen, May 2, 1810
DIED: Copenhagen, March 20, 1874

It is hardly accidental that Lumbye became "the Waltz King of the North," since the music for which he is known was directly inspired by the elder Johann Strauss [1177]. The son of a soldier, Lumbye studied violin as a child and then entered the military himself. He became a trumpeter in the garrison band at Odense and was promoted to the post of first trumpet in the Royal Horse Guards in the capital. There he was able to continue his musical education and began composing. In 1839 he heard a visiting Viennese orchestra in an "all-Strauss" program and was infected on the spot. He organized a dance band of his own and began writing for it in Viennese style. In 1843 it was installed in the dance hall of the newly opened Tivoli Gardens, an amusement park that remains one of the landmarks of Copenhagen. Shortly the government began promoting tours by the band to various European capitals, where Lumbye was universally hailed as a master of his craft. At home he furnished some of the music for ballets by the great Danish choreographer, August Bournonville. After nearly thirty years as one of the chief attractions at Tivoli, Lumbye was forced by increasing deafness to retire. Like Strauss, he founded a family dynasty. His sons Carl Christian and Georg August both produced a good deal of light music. RECORDINGS: His grandson Tippe has made several records of Hans Christian's music.

[1211] SCHUMANN, Robert Alexander (Shōō'-màn, Rō'-bârt À-lek-sàn'-der)
CONDUCTOR, TEACHER
BORN: Zwickau, June 8, 1810
DIED: Endenich, July 29, 1856

If Weber [1124] represents one side of the Romantic creative impulse, Schumann represents the other. To oversimplify, one might say that Weber draws from objective impulses—nature, history, folklore—and Schumann from subjective—his own personality. Schumann's chief "subject" is his own emotions, feelings, and reactions. He exemplifies the "germinal" view of Romanticism, which argues that form is not to be imposed from outside because the creative work, like any other growing organism, will assume the form that is proper to it. It is not surprising then that Schumann was happiest in the small forms (notably his piano pieces and songs). His success with the larger forms is often a tempered success, representing as it were a compromise between powerful emotions and a keen intellect—one aspect of the composer's lifelong duality. And whereas with opera Weber had his greatest success, Schumann was at his weakest. His influence as both a critic and artist was enormous; in the second instance it was also often unfortunate, for generations of musicians, lacking Schumann's peculiar genius, imitated his subjective approach and wound up with musical antimacassars and mustache cups.

Schumann was the son of a dilettante writer, Friedrich August Gottlieb Schumann, who slaked his thirst for literary fame by opening a bookshop in Zwickau, from which he issued his own hackwork. (His greatest success was an illustrated dictionary of the "Greatest Men of All Time," to which his youngest son contributed a few biographies.) The elder Schumann was highly strung and at about the time of Robert's birth fell prey to the "nervous ailment" that killed him sixteen years later. His wife, Johanna Christina, daughter of a surgeon named Schnabel, was a flighty and emotional woman who had already borne him three sons and a daughter. All four died too young, the girl Emilie, ominously, insane and a suicide.

As a child Robert seems to have been sunny and extroverted, except for his passion for reading which the bookshop fed. At six he was sent to a local private school, where he was no standout. A year later he began piano lessons with a Herr Kuntsch, a self-taught organist of decidedly limited talents and ability. Nevertheless the boy took to the piano as though it were his native element—especially after hearing Moscheles [1146] in concert in 1819. He spent much time improvising and was soon composing for himself and a group of musical friends. Shortly before his tenth birthday, he entered the local Gymnasium. Over the next several years, he made himself increasingly well known locally as a pianist, both publicly and in the home circle of a musical Maecenas named Carus, where he played chamber music. There he made friends with his host's nephew, a doctor, and especially Dr. Carus's wife Agnes, whom he found a kindred spirit. It was they who kindled in him his great passion for the music of Schubert [1153], whom he once thought of visiting in 1827, and whose great C-major symphony he was to discover. (Oddly, however, Schumann was more strongly influenced by his other musical passion, J. S. Bach [684].)

In 1825 Schumann's father arranged for him to study with Weber, but the plan fell through; a year later both Weber and the elder Schumann were dead. No doubt the loss of both father and sister within a few weeks helped turn Schumann into the introverted youth he became—though for most of his life he vacillated between the roles of the hearty German burgher and the brooding poet, the "Florestan" and "Eusebius" personae of his later musical writings. It was at about this time that he came almost obsessively under the spell of the extravagant romances of Jean Paul (Johann Paul Richter). Having graduated from the *Gymnasium* in 1828, he acceded (unenthusiastically) to his mother's demand that he study law, and headed for the University of Leipzig by a devious route that took him to Bayreuth to see where Jean Paul had lived and to Munich to meet Heinrich Heine, whose musical prophet he would later become. In Leipzig he took an increasing distaste to his studies and, abetted by the Carus couple (the doctor was now teaching there), occupied himself with his and other people's music. The Caruses introduced him to the great piano teacher Friedrich Wieck, with whom Schumann was soon studying and with whose nine-year-old daughter Clara [1267] he became acquainted for the first time. The following year, however, he pulled up stakes and transferred to Heidelberg for a year on the grounds that he wanted particularly to study with certain law professors there. By then, in line with his student persona, he had developed a fondness for cigars and champagne, neither of which he could always afford and the second of which was to pose a threat to his future happiness. It was in Heidelberg that he began what were to be his first published compositions (for piano, though he also worked on an operatic treatment of *Hamlet* that came to nothing). In the summer Romantic patriotism took him on a pilgrimage down the Rhine, and later he made the mandatory journey to Italy (through Switzerland), visiting Milan and Venice, where the money ran out. By the following July Schumann decided that he had had it with law and, after his mother had received assurance that her son had musical promise from Wieck, returned to Leipzig to live with his teacher.

At this point Schumann presents a familiar picture of rebellious youth. He was smoking, drinking, and, probably, wenching too much. He was living beyond his means. He was openly critical of Wieck and talked loudly of going to Hummel [1091]. And he had so far resisted any study of musical theory because he regarded it as dry as dust. When Wieck insisted that he go to the Thomaskirche cantor, Christian Theodor Weinlig, for lessons, Schumann perversely went instead to the opera director, Heinrich Dorn, only six years his senior. Though he made progress in counterpoint, he seems to have disliked it as much as he thought he would, and by the time Dorn left Leipzig in 1832, they had come to a parting of the ways.

Meanwhile in 1831 Schumann had published his *Variations on A-B-E-G-G,* Op. 1 (named after a friend's sweetheart), and his *Papillons,* and had seen his first review (of Chopin) printed. That same year Wieck had taken Clara, now a piano virtuosa of twelve, on an extended European tour. Schumann, left on his own, became impatient with a fourth finger that seemed unwilling to do what he demanded of it and created a device to strengthen it. Instead it did the digit such severe damage that he had to abandon all notion of a pianistic career. The experience proved not as catastrophic as it might have been, but it sobered Schumann noticeably.

In November 1832 the Zwickau orchestra gave a concert featuring movements of a symphony by Schumann and Clara Wieck as pianist. Schumann reworked the piece for the Leipzig Gewandhaus orchestra but eventually shelved it. In 1833, impatient with the musical journals of the day, he and his forward-looking musical friends founded their own, the *Neue Leipziger Zeitschrift für Musik* (New Leipzig Musical Times), of which Schumann was soon to become the enormously influential editor and, as such, the force behind German Romanticism as a conscious movement. (He and his colleagues became the *Davidsbund,* appearing under imaginative aliases as the opposition to cultural Philistinism.) Late in 1833 Schumann left the Wiecks' home for rooms of his own. Shortly afterward, he was stunned by the consecutive deaths of a favorite sister-in-law and his brother Julius. The shock occasioned the first manifestations of real emotional instability—dizziness, insomnia, hyperventilation, then deep depression culminating in a suicide attempt—though, mostly by sheer will, he shook it off by the new year.

Schumann had long had a brotherly affection for Clara, who, now fifteen, found herself falling in love with him. But early in 1834 she made the mistake of introducing him to Ernestine von Fricken, whose guardian and adoptive father, Baron von Fricken, had brought her from Asch in Bohemia to study with Wieck. To Clara's consternation, it was love at first sight, and the pair (officially or unofficially) were soon engaged. Schumann assumed her to be nobly born, wealthy, and bright. (Moreover, his doctor had recommended marriage as a therapeutic release for his overwrought emotions.) But Ernestine turned out a disappointment—a girl of limited intellect, small financial hopes, and the bastard of a Bohemian bourgeois and a Countess Zedwitz—and the engagement burned lower and lower and flickered out in early 1836. (Ernestine married an

elderly cousin six years later, was widowed in a few months, and died herself at twenty-eight.)

During this period Schumann had met and established friendships with Mendelssohn [1200], Chopin [1208], and Moscheles [1146]. On the heels of the Ernestine affair, his friendship with Clara, though he seems not to have realized it at first, was ripening into something more. Clara was by now recognized as a brilliant pianist on the threshold of a great career. Wieck, who had invested a good deal of time, effort, and money in developing her talent, took note of the increased cuddling and kissing. Deciding to nip matters in the bud, he shipped Clara off to Dresden and forbade the young people to write each other. The move had the opposite effect from what he wanted: Schumann slipped off to Dresden, poured out his love to a highly receptive Clara, and returned to Leipzig to ask for her hand. Wieck, beside himself with anger, not only refused, but through threats, insults, cajolery, and whatever other means he could find, set about to erect a permanent barrier. He almost succeeded: Schumann, hearing rumors of Clara's interest in her vocal teacher (apparently not entirely unfounded) attacked her in his journal with thinly veiled satire, and gave himself up to an orgy of riotous living. He also let it be known that he was considering marrying someone else (identity, if any, still obscure). Clara, on the other hand, feared that she was going the way of Ernestine. Meanwhile Schumann was concentrating his emotions in his compositions (all for piano), which gushed from him in an increasingly steady stream. In August 1837 Clara gave a Leipzig concert in which she played the F-minor sonata, which Schumann had dedicated to her the previous year. The action resulted in a reconciliation, and, despite Wieck's opposition, the two pledged their love, vowing to wait, if need be, until Clara was of age. A month later he faced her father with the fact, pointing out that he was now an accepted musician with an apparently secure future—to no avail. During a further separation Clara temporarily had another attack of cold feet, plunging her fiancé into despair. They weathered that storm, but then Wieck set to work in earnest against the union. He threatened to back Ernestine in a breach-of-promise suit, he offered Clara's hand to another, and he kept her on the road as much as possible. At one point Schumann went off to Vienna with a view to moving there if he made an impression, but the plan did not work out, and he returned to Leipzig, providing Wieck with an opportunity to triumphantly label him a failure. (The impetus for his return was actually the death of his brother Eduard and the subsequent disposal of the bookshop.) In the summer of 1839, the year Clara was to turn twenty, the lovers asked the courts to force Wieck's hand. Wieck replied with countercharges, the most stubborn of which was that Schumann was an alcoholic and could not support a family. The case dragged on for months, during which anxiety almost dried up Schumann's creative vein. Early in 1840 the court dismissed all of Wieck's objections, save the charge of drunkenness, which he was given the task of proving. Schumann responded to this relief with an outpouring of new compositions—but now songs, a medium in which he could express his feelings more explicitly. (Nearly half his total *Lied* output, including the great cycles, date from this one year.) In July, Wieck having failed to produce the required evidence, the court told Clara and Schumann that they were free to do as they wished. Having gone through the necessary legalities and amenities, they were married on September 12, the eve of Clara's twenty-first birthday.

The marriage is always upheld as an ideal in the history of music. But it had its drawbacks. Schumann, increasingly conscious of his insecurity as a wage earner and of his emotional immaturity, veered from overcompensation to childish dependence. He had, to bolster his self-esteem, acquired a doctorate from the University of Jena in 1840, not without some finagling. Now he continued his orgy of productivity, following the "song year" with an orchestral one that turned out the first and "fourth" symphonies, the *Overture, Scherzo, and Finale,* and the beginning of the Concerto for Piano. This he followed with a chamber-music year, and all the while he kept up the journal. Clara concertized when she could, between babies—Marie, 1841; Elise, 1843; Julie, 1845; Emil, 1846; Ludwig, 1848; Ferdinand, 1849; Eugenie, 1851; Felix, 1854. When she was away, Schumann fretted and abandoned his work; when she was home, she fretted at the abridgment of her career, albeit mostly to herself. And, though Schumann and Wieck made up, after a fashion, in 1843, the older man maintained a point of tension in the couple's life together.

By late 1842 Schumann had worked himself into such a state of nerves and fatigue that he was unable to compose for some weeks. However, in the spring of 1843 he took up the compositon of the cantata *Das Paradies und die Peri* (after Thomas Moore's [1093] *Lalla Rookh),* his first major choral work, successfully performed in December.

While it was taking shape, Mendelssohn opened his conservatory and gave Schumann his first real job there as professor of piano, composition, and score reading. By now, however, Florestan had been ousted by the diffident, tongue-tied Eusebius, and Schumann proved as ineffectual as a teacher as he later proved as a conductor. Early in 1844 Clara embarked on a long-planned five-month Russian tour. Her husband, feeling like a fifth wheel, accompanied her. Though there were pleasant interludes, including a reunion with Henselt [1237], he was generally miserable and often sick. On their return he began an opera on Byron's *The Corsair* and a setting of part of Goethe's *Faust.* In August, however, he suffered a more severe breakdown than that of 1842–43—anxiety, sleeplessness, phobias, auditory problems, and fear of death. He had resigned his editorship in June. A vacation in the Harz Mountains did more harm than good. Schumann and Clara (who had been also teaching there) quit the Conservatory and moved, at first temporarily, then permanently, to Dresden. By spring Schumann, still by no means well, was able to return to his work, writing several pieces including the last two movements of the piano concerto. At first he welcomed the low-key musical life of Dresden, as it was then, but later it came to irritate him. He found solace in Hiller's [1219] circle, in which he was thrown with Richard Wagner [1230], whose *Tannhäuser,* which he had not liked on paper, he found surprisingly effective in the theater. Hampered by hallucinations of musical tones, Schumann dragged out the composition of the second symphony over most of 1846. The next year he returned to *Faust* and began his only completed opera, *Genoveva.* There was a Schumann festival of sorts in Zwickau that summer, but the year was saddened by the deaths of Mendelssohn and little Emil Schumann. Toward year's end, Hiller left for Düsseldorf, and Schumann inherited his male *Liedertafel,* which so fired him up that he also founded a mixed choir of his own. In 1848 he began to pick up the pace of his composition again, returning to piano music, writing the music for Byron's play *Manfred,* and completing *Genoveva.* The revolutions of that year excited him, at least to the point of writing some patriotic pieces, but when the shooting actually began in Dresden in May 1849, Schumann ignominiously skedaddled with Clara and Marie, leaving the former to return in the middle of the night for the other children. Despite all this, and some low emotional troughs, 1849 was Schumann's most productive year since early in the decade. *Genoveva* was accepted for performance in Leipzig but was repeatedly postponed. Meanwhile, tired of being a nobody in a nothing town, Schumann had been job hunting, and in 1850 he accepted Hiller's offer of the Düsseldorf post (despite the presence there of a madhouse, one of his phobias). After a concert tour with Clara early in 1850 and the premiere of the opera that summer (it was unsuccessful, owing to a botched libretto and Schumann's lack of feeling for the stage), the Schumanns moved to Düsseldorf in September.

Though he found the town noisy and provincial, Schumann was welcomed with open arms by the Düsseldorfers and was enchanted to be in the Rhineland. The result was another burst of composition that included the third ("Rhenish") symphony, the concert overtures, the Concerto for Cello, the completion of the *Faust* scenes, and much music for his choral forces. But the honeymoon soon ended. The musicians began to find their conductor ineffectual, and the press began to say as much. Unable to bring himself to fight back, Schumann suffered another breakdown in mid-1852, which involved more alarming symptoms. On his return to work that winter, some hotheads demanded his resignation but later apologized. In the spring of 1853, he played second fiddle to Hiller at the Lower Rhine Festival, where the revised fourth symphony was played and where he made friends with the violinist Joachim [1321], who introduced him to young Brahms [1329] that September. Schumann wrote his Concerto for Violin for Joachim (which went unplayed until 1937), and he, Brahms, and Schumann's pupil Albert Dietrich collaborated on a violin sonata. (Schumann later replaced the young men's movements with two of his own.)

In February 1854 the final breakdown came, though Schumann's mental condition had been parlous for some time. He heard angels singing, then a hellish cacophony. After days and nights of agony, he rushed out on the stormy morning of the twenty-seventh and threw himself off the Rhine bridge. Fishermen dragged him out, but he now had to be institutionalized. Clara mercifully chose not the local sanitarium but a private one near Bonn. There he slowly sank into paresis and, after nearly two and a half dreadful years, died in his sleep, at the age of forty-six. He was buried, in a private funeral, at Bonn.

RECORDINGS: The orchestral, piano, and chamber music have, by now, been pretty thoroughly covered. (Jörg Demus has made the most comprehensive recording of the piano pieces, and there is at least one version of the early incomplete symphony.) It appears that some of the *Lieder* and duets may still await attention. There is a single professional recording of the opera and at least two of *Manfred*. The greatest lacunae are in the partsongs and choral works, though there are versions of *Das Paradies und die Peri* and the other big cantata *Der Rose Pilgerfahrt*, the *Mass*, and the *Requiem*.

[1212] NICOLAI, Carl Otto Ehrenfried
(Nē'-kō-lī, Kärl O'-tō Ā'-ren-frēt)
KEYBOARDIST, SINGER, CONDUCTOR
BORN: Königsberg, June 9, 1810
DIED: Berlin, May 11, 1849

Otto Nicolai hoped, as a composer of opera, to find a middle ground between the Italians' overemphasis of music and the Germans' of idea. To judge from his masterpiece, *Die lustigen Weiber von Windsor (The Merry Wives of Winsdor)*, he might have succeeded, had not fate—as it did his contemporary Albert Lortzing [1163]—cut him down at the threshold of his musical maturity.

Nicolai was the product of a broken home. When his parents split up, he remained with his father, a musician, who gave him his earliest training and little else save perhaps a conflicting personality. The senior Nicolai, in fact, proved so violently unreasonable that Otto, in his mid-teens, cut and ran. He soon found a patron, however, who sent him to Zelter [1008] in Berlin for further training and saw to it that he got an academic education. Nicolai specialized in church music, then for a time lived a precarious existence in Berlin, grubbing as a teacher, organist, and singer (bass). During this period (1830–33) he began composing songs and choral pieces, and proceeded to a symphony, a *Te Deum*, and a *Mass*—all successfully produced. In 1833 he caught the attention of Frederick William III, who sent him to Rome as chapel organist to the Prussian embassy. An admirer of the German classics, he had no time for what he considered modern Italian trivia and buried himself in the study of old Italian polyphony. Since his duties at the embassy were not taxing, he soon found himself (not unaided by his good looks) the pianistic darling of the Roman salons and much in demand as teacher by the daughters of the diplomatic set. He also impressed the ambassador, a Freiherr de Bunsen, who paid for his lessons with the Palestrina [201] scholar Giuseppe Baini and groomed him as the potential future head of a Prussian state conservatory in Berlin. Though Nicolai seems to have skirted the German artist colony in Rome, he found an amiable crony and drinking companion in Bertel Thorwaldsen, the Danish sculptor, who was nearly forty years his senior.

Despite his snobbishness, however, Nicolai was eventually bitten by the opera bug and quit his post in 1836 to embark on an operatic career as a composer. But his first effort, *Rosmonda d'Inghilterra (Rosamund of England)*, failed to get even a nibble. However, he accepted, in 1837, the offer of the directorship at the Kärntnertortheater in Vienna. A brilliant and demanding conductor, he was successful with the audiences, but not with the management, and was let go at the end of the year. Returning to Italy, he got a production of *Rosmonda* (retitled as *Enrico II)* in Trieste in 1839. It was a great success, as was *Il Templario (The Templar,* after *Ivanhoe)* in Turin the year following. Reviews suggest in fact that he was thought to have few rivals among the natives, to whom Nicolai took a very superior attitude, singling out for special opprobrium the neophyte Verdi **[1232]**.

Curiously, Nicolai rejected the *Nabucco* libretto, which underlay Verdi's first step on the stairway to Italian operatic primacy, in favor of one called *Il Proscritto,* which Verdi had turned down. Nicolai's *Odoardo e Gildippe* fizzled in Genoa in 1841, but he determined that *Il Proscritto* would crown his career to date and, to insure that it would, gave his fiancée Erminia Frezzolini the soprano lead. The premiere was a disaster, and so was Frezzolini; Nicolai ditched her, walked out on his contracts, and went back to Vienna to produce *Il Templario* so well that he received appointment as *Hofkapellmeister.* Under such auspices he inaugurated a concert series in 1842 that represented the beginning of the Vienna Philharmonic Orchestra. He greatly improved the level of orchestral performance. For a time he dickered for a post in Berlin, but in the end he decided to stay where he was. A new version of the *Templario* (as *Der Tempelritter)* and a production of the *Proscritto* (as *Die Heimkehr des Verbannten)* were both successful, and he was asked to write a new German comedy. Having decided on the *Merry Wives* after a good deal of hesitation, he had trouble with the librettists, and his deadline slipped past. He thus played into the hands of his rival Balochino, director of the Italian season, who refused to make room for it. Nicolai resigned in a huff. Luckily at this point Frederick William III came through with the combined directorships of the Berlin cathedral choir and court opera, which was just what Nicolai had been asking for all along. With Jenny Lind as soloist in excerpts from the new opera, he gave the Viennese a preview of what they would be missing and left for Berlin. There the work was premiered in March 1849. But, young as he was, Nicolai had worn himself out, and two months later he suffered a massive stroke and died, thirty days before his thirty-ninth birthday.

RECORDINGS: There are at least five recordings of *Die lustigen Weiber* and innumerable excerpts, as well as a scattered few excerpts from other operas. There are also recordings of the *Te Deum* and some songs and duets.

[1213] WESLEY, Samuel Sebastian
ORGANIST, CONDUCTOR
BORN: London, August 14, 1810
DIED: Gloucester, April 19, 1876

Irascible and quixotic about his calling, Wesley, as a church composer, is a monadnock in the dreary waste of nineteenth-century English music, albeit an anomaly on the context of European Romanticism. The usual assertion that he was the illegitimate son of Samuel Wesley **[1045]** needs qualification. Samuel was no rake. When his wife forsook his roof, he, as a fairly confirmed convert to polygamy, entered into a union with his housekeeper, Sarah Suter. They lived as man and wife, producing several children. Samuel Sebastian, the eldest, had his middle name and much of his musical credo from his father's hero, Johann Sebastian Bach **[684]**. As a child he was accepted in the Chapel Royal, studied with the master of the boys, William Hawes, became solo soprano, in which capacity he was awarded a gold watch and a ride in the royal carriage by George IV. At fifteen he became organist at St. James's in Hampstead Road and, by 1832 when he went to Hereford Cathedral, had served in the same capacity at three other churches. He is also listed as having conducted a performance of Mozart's **[992]** *Così fan tutte* at the Theatre Royal.

Hereford, like most English churches of the day, had a makeshift musical wing and paid only 60 pounds a year, forcing Wesley to make ends meet by teaching, which he detested. Nevertheless he stayed on for three years and conducted the Three Choirs Festival in 1834. At the end of the period he eloped with Dean Merewether's sister (some accounts say daughter), Mary Anne, and took a job at Exeter Cathedral, where things seem to have been even worse. Looking for advancement, he qualified for both a B. Mus. and a D. Mus. at Oxford in 1839, but his aspiration to the professorships there and at Edinburgh were frustrated by the appointments of H. H. Pierson at the one and Sir Henry Bishop [1123] at the other. In 1842, after seven years, he took what looked like a step downward, to the parish church at Leeds. But the vicar was a great supporter of choral music; he had had the church rebuilt to be musically effective, had installed a fine choir and organ, and had offered Wesley 200 pounds a year. Despite a promising honeymoon, which inspired his Anglican service and several other fine pieces, Wesley's fault finding soon got to his proponents there. In 1847, while fishing (he was a passionate angler all his life), he injured a leg so badly that he was permanently lame. Two years later he issued a scathing pamphlet, *A Few Words on Cathedral Music* (not his first attack on the establishment), in which he notes that the painter Edwin Landseer commanded a thousand pounds for a picture of a horse, whereas the Church of England would not give a thousand farthings for the greatest of church compositions).

That same year Wesley decamped for Winchester as the cathedral (and later college) organist—largely because he could get his sons educated there free and because the fishing was said to be especially good. When the new cathedral organ (from the Crystal Palace Exposition) was installed in 1854, Wesley had a stair built to the loft by which he could enter and exit unseen. After fifteen years—though he must have mellowed, considering the unusual length of time—his irascibility and absenteeism got to the cathedral chapter. He evidently sensed his time was up: asked to recommend candidates for the analogous post at Gloucester, he recommended himself, concurrently with Winchester's demand for his resignation, and was accepted. Though Gloucester offered him the chance to conduct four Three Choirs Festivals (at one of which he introduced Bach's *St. Matthew Passion)* in the next decade, he was no happier there than elsewhere. He declined a knighthood from Her Majesty Queen Victoria, who nevertheless awarded him a pension in 1874. He had long been conducting a running battle with an arch-conservative clique at Worcester, which he particularly offended that year by playing the dead-march from Handel's [683] *Saul* after a sermon by one of its representatives. Injury being added to insult when it failed to get a cut of the 1874 festival proceeds, Worcester threatened to secede unless its musical demands were met, and the 1875 festival was, as a result, a wasteland of dreary contemporary *a cappella* stuff. Wesley, in a physical decline, retired that December and died four months later. For his time and place, Wesley was a formidably

learned musician, conversant not only with Bach, but with the giants of polyphonic music of even earlier times. (Even there, he execrated English music, mostly because it tended to be small-scale.) If his own services and anthems do not measure up to the work of his heroes, they are still head and shoulders above anything else written in England in his day.

RECORDINGS: There are at least two LPs devoted to Wesley's church music, in addition to numerous isolated examples in choral anthologies.

[1214] ERKEL, Ferenc (Er'-kel, Fer'-enk)
PIANIST, CONDUCTOR, IMPRESARIO
BORN: Gyula, November 7, 1810
DIED: Budapest, June 15, 1893

Little known outside his native country, Erkel is regarded by the Hungarians as the counterpart of Glinka [1179], Weber [1124], and Verdi [1232]: the fountainhead of their national opera. The second of ten children, Erkel came from a line of professional musicians. His father, schoolteacher and choirmaster of Gyula (in the southeast corner of modern Hungary), gave him his first music lessons, and he was playing the church organ at the age of ten. Three more years of study in the cosmopolitan center of Pozsony (now Bratislava, Czechoslovakia) made him a fine pianist and prepared him to become, at seventeen, music master to the family of a Count Csáky in Kolozsvár (now Cluj, Rumania), where he became involved with the local opera company. In 1834 he was hired away to Szemeréd by a Countess Stainlein-Sallfeld. En route thither he gave a recital in Pest with such happy results that by 1835 he was settled in the capital as a theater conductor. A year later he crossed the Danube to Pest as associate conductor of the German Opera there, and two years later became music director of the newly founded national theater, which he inaugurated with the Hungarian premiere of Bellini's [1164] *La Straniera.* Shortly afterward, seeing little point in competing with Liszt [1218], he gave up his pianistic career.

A national theater in those heady days of growing ethnic self-consciousness necessitated national opera. Already one of the first to use folk themes (albeit of the dubious kind adopted by Liszt) in his music, Erkel came up with his first effort, *Báthory Mária (Mária Báthory:* the Hungarian language places surnames first) in 1840; though it leaned heavily on Western European models, some of the music was recognizably Hungarian, notably the slow-fast *verbunkos* (a military dance whose pattern underlies many of Liszt's *Hungarian Rhapsodies).* Real triumph came, however, with *Hunyadi László* in 1844, a work that was taken up all over the country and is still the cornerstone of Hungarian opera. About the same time, Erkel wrote music for a number of plays, but soon his conducting duties and the demands of a large and growing family were taking up all his time. (His 1844 choral *Hymnusz*, by the way, was adopted as the national anthem.) He was named director of the bi-city musical association that was to become the Budapest Philharmonic Society. In 1846 he welcomed the visiting Berlioz [1175], for whom, in the course of events, he played the traditional *Rákóczy March*—which Berlioz incorporated in his *La Damnation de Faust*, whose locale he changed to Hungary to justify it.

It was not until 1857 that Erkel wrote a third opera, *Erzsébet*, a collaboration with the brothers Doppler [see 1276]. This was followed, however, four years later, by a second huge success, *Bánk-Bán*. Much of its orchestration was by his sons Gyula (1842–1909) and Sándor (1846–1900). (Gyula collaborated with his father in all six of his subsequent operas, and in the penultimate one, *Névtelen hösök [Unknown Heroes]*, was joined by his brothers Sándor, Elek, and László.) Though, with the exception of *Bánk-Bán*, performed ritually every March 15, the later works were not successful, they show continued growth, both in musical idiom and the use of folk music. (Lászlo Erkel [1844–96] was, not incidentally, an early teacher of Bartók [1734].) Ferenc Erkel retired from the opera in 1874 and became director of the Academy of Music a year later. He continued to make occasional appearances as conductor and even returned to piano performances—the last when he was eighty. There are recordings of *Hunyadi László*, *Bánk-Bán*, and the *Festival Overture* of 1887.

[1215] GUNGL, Joseph (Gōōng'-əl, Yō'-zef)
SCHOOLMASTER, OBOIST, CONDUCTOR
BORN: Zsámbék, December 1, 1810
DIED: Weimar, January 31 or February 1, 1889

A Hungarian weaver's son, Gungl taught school in Budapest while he studied music. He entered the army at eighteen, became oboist in a regimental band six years later, and its bandmaster soon after. A successful composer of marches and dances, he became well known in central Europe. In 1843 he

resigned to form an orchestra à la Strauss [1177] in Berlin, with which he toured the world. A successful American visit in 1849 produced such works as *Klänge von Delaware (Sounds from Delaware).* During summer stints in Pavlovsk near St. Petersburg, the orchestra drew the admiration of the young Borodin [1331]. In 1858 Gungl returned to the Austrian military as the imperial chief bandmaster. After six years, however, he formed another orchestra. He retired in 1870 but continued to guest-conduct for a few years. His daughter Virginia was an operatic prima donna in the 1870s. (The composer's surname usually appears—wrongly—as "Gung'l.") RECORDINGS: Gungl's more popular pieces turn up in recorded anthologies of Viennese light music.

[1216] TAUBERT, Carl Gottfried Wilhelm (Tou'-bârt, Kärl Got'-frēt Vil'-helm)
PIANIST, CONDUCTOR
BORN: Berlin, March 23, 1811
DIED: Berlin, January 7, 1891

Son of a government official, Wilhelm Taubert came from the same musically conservative background as Felix Mendelssohn [1200], with whom he shared Ludwig Berger [1088] as teacher. He became a court musician at twenty, after leaving the university the year previous. Soon after, he sent Mendelssohn some of his songs for evaluation, initiating a correspondence. Mendelssohn suggested that the music lacked individual profile. About the same time, Taubert conducted the first of his 4 symphonies. His first opera, *Die Kirmess (The Carnival)*, was produced in January 1832. He worked under Mendelssohn during the latter's court intendency in Berlin, became the *Kapellmeister* at the Royal Opera in 1845 and *Hofkapellmeister* later. He left the opera in 1869, but continued to conduct the orchestra and to teach at the Royal Academy. Though Taubert wrote a number of large works, he won his chief successes with salonesque piano pieces and more than 300 songs. RECORDINGS: Some of his songs were recorded in an earlier day.

[1217] THOMAS, Charles-Louis Ambroise (Tō-mås', Shärlz Lōō-ē' Ambrwàz')
PIANIST, EDUCATOR
BORN: Metz, August 5, 1811
DIED: Paris, February 12, 1896

Ambroise Thomas's representation on early phonograph records (excerpts from his most popular operas) might have led one to conclude that he was among the top rank of composers. And indeed in the France of his day he was a power to be reckoned with. Today, however, attempts to restore him to the active repertoire have so far proved unsuccessful, although his gift for easy melody is admired.

Like his younger contemporary Gounod [1258], Thomas demonstrated uncommon musical ability in childhood, but unlike Gounod (or most other composers, for that matter), he found life an oiled chute to success. He was sent to the Conservatoire in Paris when he was seventeen and immediately won the approbation of its director Cherubini [1019]. Again like Gounod, he studied piano with Zimmermann (later Kalkbrenner [1118]) and composition with Jean François Le Sueur (1760–1837). Though he won first prize for his playing at the end of his freshman year, he was too jittery ever to attempt a concert career. A year later he won a first in harmony and in 1832 the Grand Prix de Rome (following Eugène Prévost and preceding the even more anonymous Thys). Thomas spent the required time in Rome where he was a favorite of the painter Ingres, then in charge of the prizewinners, and turned out the required compositions, which so pleased the judges that they were published forthwith. Back in Paris after three years, Thomas began churning out frothy opéras-comiques, beginning with La Double Échelle (The Double Ladder) premiered at the Opéra-Comique in 1837. After four such pieces, he reached l'Opéra with the ballet La Gipsy in 1839 and followed it with two two-act operas before returning to the smaller house, where he was more at home. He was sufficiently well regarded by 1845 to win the Légion d'honneur. During the 1848 revolution he served in the National Guard. A year later he returned to the Opéra-Comique with his most successful effort to date, an Oriental spoof called Le Caïd (The Cadi), whose coloratura bass aria is still occasionally essayed by enterprising bassos. It was followed in 1850 by the curious Le Songe d'une nuit d'été (A Midsummer Night's Dream), which is Shakespearean only in that it involves a tipsy Shakespeare, Queen Elizabeth, and Falstaff. The Raymond of 1851 survives through an overture beloved of Sunday-afternoon park bandmasters.

That same year Thomas was picked to succeed Spontini [1081] in the Institut and not long afterward was appointed professor of composition at the Conservatoire. The five operas he turned out between 1853 and 1860 showed little originality and met with

little success, though their composer was elevated to an officership in the Légion d'honneur in 1858. Increasingly mired in his pedagogical duties and feeling burned out (especially after Gounod's revolutionary Faust in 1859), Thomas withdrew from operatic composition for five years. When he returned with Mignon (like Faust, after Goethe) in 1866, it was obvious that he had learned a good deal from Gounod's example and, despite its rather feeble treatment of its ostensible subject, the work held the stage for nearly a century. When Gounod countered the next year with his Shakespearean Roméo et Juliette, Thomas responded with a Hamlet, 1868, that he intended to be his monument. It wasn't, though it is the only other Thomas opera still occasionally to be heard. (The title role, originally for tenor, was rewritten for the great baritone Jean-Baptiste Faure [1311] when no tenor of comparable stature could be found.)

Though there were two later operas and a ballet, Hamlet was in effect Thomas' last operatic gasp, for by the 1870s he was already being regarded as old hat. When Auber [1103] died in 1871, Thomas was named to succeed him as director of the Conservatoire. In that post he made some useful changes in the curriculum and helped the economic plight of the faculty, but he was too much a member of the establishment to do much about the internal rivalries that had for some time made the school a laughing stock among serious musicians. Two years before he died (at eighty-four), Thomas was awarded the Grand Croix of the Légion d'honneur on the occasion of the one-thousandth performance of Mignon at the Opéra-Comique.

RECORDINGS: Both Mignon and Hamlet, together with innumerable excerpts, enjoy commercial recordings.

[1218] LISZT, Franz (List, Frânts)
PIANIST, CONDUCTOR, TEACHER
BORN: Raiding, October 22, 1811
DIED: Bayreuth, July 31, 1886

If Liszt was one of the chief representatives of the cult of "genius" that has helped divide art music from popular music, it was not entirely his fault. Since no one now living ever heard him play and since he died even before Edison's representatives promoted his recording machine in Europe, we must take it on faith that he was the greatest pianist who ever lived (a dubious assumption). To that donnée have attached themselves such other articles of faith as that he was a charlatan, a diabolist, a saint, an orgiast, a savant, a sexual phenomenon, and a composer of fustian. Recent re-evaluation has cleared his name on the last count, placing him as one of the most daring innovators and experimenters of his century, for all the flashy pianistic stuff he turned out in his early career. There is no evidence of any unholy pacts, and his religiosity or mysticism appears to have been less self-dramatization than the result of a somewhat neurotic temperament coupled with the search of an essentially lonely man for meaning in his life. If women fainted when he took the stage and fought over his cast-aside cigar butts, it was partly that he was handsome, partly that he had an innate sense of the theatrical, and partly that he was known to understand the needs (especially the sexual needs) of women. Such things no doubt account also for a lifelong string of mistresses, but there is absolutely nothing but hoary rumor (abetted by a recent film) to suggest that he was better endowed, more insatiable, or kinkier than the typical middle-class male of his day.

The records indicate that Franz Liszt was the only child of Adam Liszt and his bride of a year, born Anna Läger, the daughter of an Austrian draper. His birthplace, now called Doborján, was in the Hungarian boondocks, where Adam, a good musician and an aspirant to the finer things, was enjoying the dubious rewards of good service to Prince Nikolaus Esterházy as manager of one of his farms. Though Franz entered the local records as "Liszt Ferenc," his parents spoke German. Adam claimed his ancestors were noble Hungarians, but evidence suggests they were peasants. "Liszt" is a common Hungarian name, but it may be that these Liszts were really Germanic Lists, the "z" inserted to forestall the Hungarian pronunciation "Lisht."

Young Liszt was a sickly child, given to fevers and convulsions. Of his academic training we know only that he learned to write and read, both of which skills he practiced almost compulsively. When he showed early evidence of musical talent, Adam saw in it the road to affluence and set about turning the boy into a concert prodigy. (Whether he brutalized him in the process, as the story later had it, is highly uncertain.) When the boy was nine, his father decided he was ready for the big time. When the prince failed to come through with an offer of support, Adam got up a subscription from some other magnates through a concert at Poszony (alias Pressberg, now Bratislava), and in 1821 took his family to Vienna. There Czerny [1137] took the boy on as a pupil, scheduling him last in his long teaching day

so that he could get extra attention. It was probably through Czerny that he was asked to contribute a variation to Diabelli's [1100] famous set. Beethoven [1063] is supposed to have bestowed a kiss of blessing on him after hearing him play, though by then Beethoven could hear little or nothing. Liszt had some composition lessons from Salieri [966].

After two years, Adam gathered up his family and proceeded to Paris, where Cherubini [1019] refused Franz admission to the Conservatoire on the grounds that he was not French. (Neither was Cherubini.) So the boy took some more private composition lessons, this time with Antonín Reicha [1059], and was set about making the family fortune. Soon the darling of the salons, he was taken on tours of France and England, and, with the "help" of Paër [1069], wrote his only opera, a one-acter called *Don Sanche* that flopped at the Opéra in October 1825. At home Liszt sulked a good deal and talked darkly of the priesthood. His mother, fed up with the whole business, returned to Vienna. He himself began to show signs of an incipient emotional collapse. That he might recover, his father took him to Boulogne and promptly died, supposedly warning him against the wiles of women with his last breath. Liszt, now nearly sixteen, miraculously recovered his health, returned to Paris, recalled his mother to keep house, and devoted himself to teaching the piano. Wealthy young ladies beat a path to his door. With one of them, Caroline de Saint-Cricq, daughter of a cabinet minister, he fell in love. When the fact became obvious, her father terminated the lessons and the affair, if affair it was. Liszt sunk into a depression (real or romanticized) so deep and made himself so scarce (until the gunfire of the 1830 revolution awakened him) that he was reported dead in the press; he seems indeed to have treasured the memory of his first love to the grave, including her in his will.

Liszt began his lifelong friendship with Berlioz [1175] on the eve of the premiere of the *Symphonie fantastique*, a work that exerted enormous influence on him. (He transcribed it for piano solo and later adapted its monothematic method for his orchestral tone poems.) He first heard Paganini [1106] the next year and was impressed, but the story that he thereupon resolved to become the Italian's pianistic counterpart and the one that he became his disciple in *diablerie* both appear groundless. (They may even never have met.) That same year Liszt was introduced to Saint-Simonism—some accounts say by the violinist Christian Urhan, others by Félicien David [1209]. Though he later denied any affiliation with the movement, it is obvious that its view of the artist as a person above the vulgar herd appealed to him. Not long after, Liszt became a favorite disciple of the Abbé Lamennais, a Catholic mystic so far to the right that he had been rejected by Rome; it was largely from Lamennais that Liszt got his notion of the artist as priest—and, one is tempted to say, the priest as artist. And it seems to have been Lamennais who inspired Liszt to turn to compositions more "serious" than the virtuoso pieces he had been sporadically turning out, beginning with the *Harmonies poëtiques et religieuses* of 1834.

Meanwhile Liszt's amatory life ill-sorted with all this religiosity. In the winter of 1832, he enjoyed several snowbound weeks in a Swiss castle with the Countess Adèle de Laprunarède, whose husband was too senile to care. Shortly afterward—again accounts differ widely—he began a much more serious affair with the Countess Marie d'Agoult. A blond beauty, she was the daughter of the Royalist Viscount of Flavigny and Elisabeth Bethmann, a Frankfurter of Jewish ancestry. Marie, decidedly neurotic and no brighter than need be, had married Charles d'Agoult, a battle-lamed nobody ten years her senior, by whom she had had two children. (She, on the other hand, was six years older than Liszt.) Though the affair lasted nearly a decade, the course of true love ran even less smoothly than usual. To begin with, Marie was a puritan at heart, who liked to suffer. She suffered bitterly in 1834, when her neglected little daughter suddenly sickened and died. It was a year when she also had to share Liszt with Lamennais. Matters became even more confused when George Sand (i.e., Mme. Dudevant) injected herself into the relationship, for a time living with the couple, though whether she shared Liszt's bed or fell in love with Marie remains ambiguous.

In March 1835 Marie found herself pregnant and, without telling Liszt, talked him into running away to Switzerland with her. They settled in Geneva where Liszt taught at the Conservatory, where a daughter named Blandine was born in due course, and where the lovers were bored to death. A vacation at Chamonix (that included Sand and others) helped break the monotony, but in the spring of 1836 Liszt returned to France to concertize and, ostensibly, to tangle with Thalberg [1220], who supposedly threatened his reputation. As it eventuated, Thalberg turned up missing. The famous duel at Princess Belgiojoso's finally took place in March 1837, by which time Marie was staying with Sand at Nohant. It was declared a draw, but everyone knew Liszt had won. It was at

about this time that the press began to come down hard, however, on his outrageous get-ups and his irregular life. A summer spent at Nohant seems to have permanently ended the *ménage à trois,* whatever it may have been. (The next year Sand began her affair with Chopin [1208]). Liszt and Marie (pregnant again) returned to Switzerland and passed on to Italy. (These peregrinations provided the basis for the first parts of the *Album d'un voyageur.)* They settled at Bellagio on Lake Como, where a second daughter, Cosima, was born in December.

The couple spent a good deal of time in Italy playing the role of tourist and pontificating about "great art." Economic necessity forced Liszt to give concerts, at which he soon discovered that the flashy gimmickry he had abandoned paid off. While in Venice, hearing of the disastrous Danube floods up north, he went to Vienna to give two charity concerts. There he was welcomed as a returning hero, and his stay was stretched to cover ten. The enormous sums that he raised revealed to him that he could get rich as a pianist. But when Marie, left behind in Venice, discovered that he had mapped out an imminent German tour, she turned on the tears until he gave it up. Instead they moved to Rome, where their last child, Daniel, was born in 1839. But Liszt was rapidly finding the *ménage* a burden, and soon afterward he sent it back to France and embarked on the postponed tour, which at the end of the year brought him triumphantly back to Hungary. He had not seen Hungary since his boyhood, and he was inspired to write a fantasia on Hungarian folk tunes, the first of his "Magyar" compositions.

Thus began the eight-year period that saw the flood tide of Lisztomania, as the poet Heinrich Heine dubbed it. Women literally became orgasmic when Liszt appeared on the platform; men wept and grew incoherent when he played. (Such reactions were, however, not universal: Mendelssohn [1200] strongly disapproved of both Liszt's playing and his music. Schumann [1211], to his surprise, did not really take to him when they met in Leipzig in 1840, and Clara [1267] decided that he was "immoral"—a view largely echoed in Victorian England. Others took issue with his theatricality—the shoulder-length hair, the heavenward-rolled eyes, the Hungarian sword of honor worn onstage.) He liked to have more than one piano available, so when the strings of one snapped under the onslaught, he could move on to the next. But it must not be forgotten that behind the panache he was a musician apart. He could sight-read anything at the piano, including full scores, and his musical memory was photographic. He is said to have been the first to perform without music and the first to give an all-whoever recital.

Liszt did not return to Paris until autumn 1840, when he met Wagner [1230] for the first time. Though he stayed the next three summers with his mistress and their children on an island in the Rhine, he spent the rest of the time on the road and relations between him and Marie were rapidly moving toward the freezing point. (The children were usually farmed out to Liszt's mother or whoever would take them.) Liszt took the first steps toward settling down as *Kapellmeister* in Weimar, Marie her first toward an authorial career (as "Daniel Stern."). Meanwhile Liszt was conducting rather flamboyant affairs with various women—most notably the dying demimondaine Alphonsine ("Marie") Duplessis, soon to be memorialized as the younger Dumas' *Dame aux caméllias* and Verdi's *Traviata,* and the dancer Lola Montez, whose later amours would force Ludwig I of Bavaria from his throne. The final break came in 1844, but the problem of the hapless children lingered. It appeared they would go to the loser. As it turned out, they were shunted about among various third parties and institutions. Liszt himself did not see them from 1845 to 1853. Blandine married five years later and died in childbed in 1862. Her brilliant and neglected brother succumbed to tuberculosis in 1859. Cosima, of course, married Hans von Bülow [1310], and soon gave him up for Richard Wagner, who was two years Liszt's junior.

Liszt was by now sick of the footloose life and anxious to develop his talents in other directions. The opportunity, as he saw it, lay in Weimar, which he decided to make once again an important musical center. But his contract called for a minimum of time in residence there, and the tours continued until 1847, taking him that year to Russia. There he met the Polish-born Princess Carolyne Sayn-Wittgenstein, a dumpy, tactless, cigar-smoking religious enthusiast—and moved in with her at her Ukrainian estate until it was time to return to Weimar. (That same year, Marie, writing as "Daniel Stern," produced a *roman à clef, Nélida,* which purported to tell all and made Liszt's name mud in Paris.) The following year, after some fancy footwork owing to the revolutions that rocked the continent (and crushed the Hungarians), the two, with Carolyne's daughter, settled in at Weimar, at first with separate propriety, but later together in a villa called the Altenburg. For the next several years there was talk of a divorce, but, though Prince Wittgenstein

was more than willing, the legal and religious barriers were too complex.

In Weimar, true to his intention, Liszt built up the musical establishment, became a conductor to be reckoned with, and made it (and himself) the goal of pilgrims from all over. A coterie of pupils and acolytes, known for whatever reason as the "Murls," passed through the Altenburg. They include Bülow, William Mason [1305], Carl Tausig [1389], Joachim Raff [1282], and Peter Cornelius [1294]. He devoted much of his musical program to airing the works of neglected composers, mostly contemporary. Shortly after he settled in, he produced Wagner's *Tannhäuser* and gave *Lohengrin* its premiere two years later. Thus encouraged, Wagner fastened like a leech on Liszt and, true to form, dealt with him outrageously. (When Wagner took Cosima from her husband, Liszt broke with them, though later made it up.) It was at Weimar that Liszt produced nearly all of his orchestral music, including all but the last of the symphonic poems and the *Faust* and *Dante* symphonies. (Raff, who helped with the orchestration of some of the early pieces, later claimed much fuller responsibility.) There was also considerable writing about music, including the misguided *The Gypsies and Their Music in Hungary* of 1859. (What Liszt took to be folk music and used in his Hungarian rhapsodies was mostly popular stuff that Gypsy musicians had picked up and adapted for café use.)

The Weimar years effectually came to an end late in 1858 when the premiere of Cornelius' *Der Barbier von Bagdad* was booed, perhaps by a cabal. Liszt (whom Cornelius ungenerously blamed), resigned, though he stayed in Weimar until 1861. Carolyne, who had been granted a civil divorce in 1855, had gone to Rome to square it with the pope. Her marriage to Liszt was scheduled for October 22, 1861. Liszt, apparently dragging his feet (he had maintained at least one spare mistress in the interim), arrived a couple of days before. Hours afterward, the Church rescinded its permission. The pair maintained separate establishments. Four years later Prince Wittgenstein died, but Liszt, encouraged by the pope's enthusiasm for his turn to religious music, responded negatively by taking holy orders, assuming appropriate costume, and becoming forever afterward the Abbé Liszt. For the next several years, barring some travels and pilgrimages, he worked quietly at such big pieces as the oratorio *Christus,* the *Requiem,* and the *Coronation Mass.*

In 1869 Liszt was invited back to Weimar and given a house known as the *Hof-*

gärtnerei (the home of the former ducal gardener), to which pupils would flock until the end of his life. (Many Liszt "pupils" were no more than observers.) The following year he conducted a festival in Weimar and also took up his duties as director of the Royal Academy of Music in Budapest. In between the demands of his two official posts, he lived in virtual retirement in Rome (there were occasional guest-conducting stints), writing the stark works of his final period that are only now beginning to be understood. There was a stormy affair with a Russian pupil, the Countess Janina, which ended with her attempt on his life, thwarted by her own collapse in 1871. The next year Liszt and the Wagners were reconciled at Bayreuth, resulting in a deeper rift between him and Carolyne. Marie died of pneumonia in 1876, Wagner (who had dedicated his *Parsifal* appropriately to Liszt) seven years later. Saddened, ailing, and weary, the old man continued to keep up an astonishing round of activities. In 1886 he embarked on a grand tour performing mostly his own music (he had given up public piano-playing in 1847!). On his way to Bayreuth that summer, he came down with a cold but insisted on attending a performance of *Tristan*. Pneumonia developed, and he died a week later.

RECORDINGS: Serious phonographic attention to Liszt's music has, together with the reestablishment of his reputation as a composer, come late. Though such things as the symphonic poems and larger orchestral works have been accounted for, some of the smaller ones have escaped the net. There is a piracy of the lone opera. The Hungarians have a complete choral music in progress. The small bodies of organ and chamber music have been accounted for. There is no integral recording of the songs, though the majority of them have appeared singly and in groups. Even a purportedly "complete" set of piano works has passed up early manifestations of those compositions that were several times revised, as well as a good deal of the vast body of transcriptions. Of especial interest are some of the late piano works: *Csárdas macabre, Am Grabe Richard Wagners, Unstern, Schaflos, R.W.-Venezia,* and *Bagatelle sans tonalité.* These are generally short, cryptic, and amazingly advanced for their time.

[1219] HILLER, Ferdinand von (Hil'-ler, Fär'-dē-nànt fun)
PIANIST, TEACHER, CONDUCTOR, WRITER

BORN: Frankfurt am Main, October 24, 1811
DIED: Cologne, May 10/11, 1885

It is an oddity that the decade 1810–20 produced composers named Hiller, Heller [1229], and Hullah [1223], none of whom led very exciting lives. (Augustin Holler, who came earlier, and Michael Haller, who came later, are unfortunately outside the province of this book.) Hiller (unrelated to the earlier Johann Adam Hiller) came from an affluent Jewish family and was at first educated to other ends than music. In early childhood, however, he studied violin and then took up the piano, under the tutelage of Alois Schmitt, making his Frankfurt debut in a Mozart [992] concerto at the age of ten. At the urging of the sixteen-year-old Mendelssohn [1200], the Hillers broke down and sent their fourteen-year-old son to Weimar to study with Hummel [1091]. (Hiller afterward recalled that he was more impressed with Fanny Mendelssohn [1186] than with her brother.) Hummel was very tough with his pupil, but Hiller bore up bravely and was soon composing away like mad. (Mendelssohn later bullied the publisher Simrock into bringing out some of his pieces.) In 1827 Hummel took his pupil with him to Vienna to visit the dying Beethoven [1063], of which experience Hiller later wrote an account.

Shortly afterward, Hiller moved to Paris, where he lived and played until 1835. He came to know everyone who was anyone in the musical world, of which his salons became a focal point, especially for the younger Turks. Hiller was particularly close to Berlioz [1175], for whom he even gave up his lady love Camille Moke. A conservative himself, Hiller insisted that Paris listen to the German masters and was the first to perform Beethoven's "Emperor" concerto there. In 1836 he returned to Frankfurt to conduct the Cäcilienverein but a year later went to Italy for an extended stay. He saw his first opera (unsuccessful, like its five successors) produced at La Scala in 1839, though a year later his first oratorio, *Die Zerstörung Jerusalems (The Destruction of Jerusalem)*, which he conducted in Leipzig at Mendelssohn's invitation, won approval. He returned to Germany for good in 1842 and deputized for Mendelssohn with the Leipzig orchestra the following season. Meanwhile he cultivated the acquaintance of German musicians as assiduously as he had those in Paris, providing himself with much material for his later writings on music. In 1844 he settled in Dresden, where he married a singer named Antolka Hogé and became once more the focus of a town's musical life.

(His presence there was a godsend to the Schumanns [1211, 1267].)

In 1847 Hiller took the post of municipal music director (once held by Mendelssohn) in Düsseldorf. Having built up the musical forces and standards there, he turned the job over to Schumann and took the analogous one in Cologne. He conducted the symphony concerts, oversaw the Lower Rhine Music Festivals, founded and directed (for more than thirty years) the Conservatory, and served as critic for the *Kölnische Zeitung*. In his last two decades he published a number of books on music, including an edition of Mendelssohn's letters. Hiller wrote symphonies, concerti, and chamber music, but the bulk of his work (and the best of it) lies mostly in smaller pieces (for chorus, solo voice, and piano). As he grew older, he became increasingly conservative and openly opposed the new wave. Among his pupils, one should note Max Bruch [1358].

RECORDINGS: Michael Ponti has recorded Hiller's Concerto No. 2 for Piano.

[1220] THALBERG, Sigismond Fortuné François (Tàl'-bârg, Sē-zhēs-mōnd' Fôr-tü-nā' Frà*n*-swà)
PIANIST
BORN: Pâquis (Geneva suburb), January 8, 1812
DIED: Posillipo, April 27, 1871

Strikingly handsome, the ultimate in polish, witty and articulate in several languages, and Liszt's [1218] most noted pianistic rival, Thalberg was not hurt in his career by being a mystery man—as he remains today. Rumored to be of noble but illegitimate birth, the records show that he was, in fact, fathered by one Joseph Thalberg of Frankfurt am Main on a Genèvoise named Fortunée Stein, who gave him the not especially romantic name of Louis. Nevertheless he was reared from the age of ten in Vienna by Count Moritz von Dietrichstein, a crusty martinet and amateur composer who had contributed a variation to Diabelli's [1100] famous project of 1819. Dietrichstein was also the guardian of the short-lived *Aiglon*, Napoleon's son (the Count of Reichstadt). He sent both young men to the Polytechnic Institute, envisioning a diplomatic career for Thalberg; there the strenuously inclined, if fragile, young count almost persuaded his co-protégé of the glories of soldiering. But Thalberg was even then studying music with the court bassoonist, August Mittag, and made such progress that he was at last permitted to follow his musical bent. He studied composition with Sechter [1129] and briefly took piano lessons from Hummel [1091], although he was already well known in Vienna society as a pianist, before embarking on a concert career at eighteen. (Thalberg later had a few lessons from J. P. Pixis [1128], Moscheles [1146], and Kalkbrenner [1118]). In 1834 he was named imperial *Kammervirtuos* in Vienna, to which effrontery Liszt responded with a scathing article. By 1836 Thalberg had further exacerbated Liszt by establishing himself as a favorite in Paris, where sides were quickly chosen up. Thalberg's erect, seemingly immobile pose at the piano (said to have been acquired by smoking a hubble-bubble with a short hose while practicing) was the very antithesis of the Hungarian's athleticism, and drove *his* female admirers just as wild. Thalberg's trick of producing a "ghost voice" by dividing the melody between his thumbs and festooning it with embellishments in the treble and bass also produced Dionysiac responses and won him the name of "Old Arpeggio." His worshippers showered him with gifts, including a mansion in Vienna. In 1837 the Princess Belgiojoso forced the issue by persuading the rivals to duel it out in her drawing room (at the piano, of course). The princess pronounced it a draw with the famous dictum "Thalberg is the greatest pianist in the world, but Liszt is the only one."

Thalberg continued to tour Europe for the next several years. In 1844 he married a Mme. Boucher, daughter of the great basso Luigi Lablache and widow of a painter (but not of the painter of the pneumatic pink female nudes, who died in 1770). Thalberg toured Brazil in 1855, and a year later, in the vanguard of the great invasion of European virtuosi, went to the United States, where he stayed for nearly two years. There he tried his hand (with Maurice Strakosch, Adelina Patti's brother-in-law) at operatic management, toured with the violinist Vieuxtemps [1270], and gave over fifty concerts in New York alone—one of them in tandem with Gottschalk [1306]. After a second visit to Brazil in 1863, Thalberg retired to his villa at Posillipo, near Naples, gave up all musical activity, and amused himself with grape growing. As a composer, Thalberg was a piano virtuoso. His 2 operas were disasters. Though he wrote a Concerto in F Minor for Piano, a couple of chamber works, and some songs, the bulk of his output was for the solo piano, most of it consisting of the variations and fantasias so much in demand in his day.

RECORDINGS: In the wake of the so-called "Romantic revival," Thalberg has received some notice on records. See especially the

Concerto for Piano (Michael Ponti), the Trio for Violin, Cello, and Piano (Mirecourt Trio), the "duel" pieces, and Thalberg's contribution to the *Hexaemeron* (Raymond Lewenthal).

[1221] WALLACE, William (Vincent)
VIOLINIST, PIANIST, TEACHER
BORN: Waterford, March 11, 1812
DIED: Château de Haget, October 12, 1865

Like Balfe [1195], Wallace was one of the few natives of the British Isles to write operas with any staying power. He was even better at producing blarney: though his relatively short life contained marvels enough, much of his account of it seems to have been embroidery or downright fabrication.

Wallace was one of three musical children of an Irish bandmaster who gave them their initial training. The elder Wallace retired to Dublin in 1825, where William became a violinist at the Theatre Royal three years later. In 1830 he was appointed organist at Thurles Cathedral, Tipperary, and music teacher to the young ladies of the school run there by the Ursulines. He was forthwith smitten by one of his pupils, a harpist named Isabella Kelly. When her family opposed the match on religious grounds, Wallace turned Catholic and was baptized "Vincent" after Isabella's nun-sister, Sister Vincent, who had been especially disapproving. The couple returned to Dublin, where Wallace returned to his theater job. A month or so later, in 1831, he heard Paganini [1106] and decided to emulate him. Wallace's virtuoso performances won him applause both at home and abroad, and enough engagements to undermine his health. Supposedly to recover, he and Isabella took ship for Australia in 1835. (His sister, the singer Eliza Bushelle, had already preceded him.)

Wallace was successful in Australia both as a violinist and pianist. In 1836 he settled in Sydney, where he, his wife, and his sister opened a music school for girls. After that the trail becomes obscure. He may have also run a music shop and is said to have tried his hand at sheep ranching for a while. Early in 1838 he abruptly sailed from Sydney without his wife and son—ostensibly on a whaling expedition, but more probably to escape his creditors. Years later he spun for Berlioz [1175] a yarn about his subsequent wanderings, involving a punitive attack on some cannibals, and doe-eyed native girls who followed him like llamas. Berlioz was inclined to believe it, for he said Wallace was too lazy to lie. Whatever else he did, Wallace wound

up in Valparaiso, Chile, where he was taken up by the cultural elite. For the next six years, he wandered slowly northward through the Americas, concertizing, reaching the United States in 1841 and New York in 1843. After a year of great success there, he went on to London, where an old friend introduced him to the Irish dramatist Edward Fitzball (by coincidence at a ball). Taken with the flamboyant fellow, Fitzball offered him a libretto, *Maritana*, on which he was working. Wallace accepted it, wrote the music in a few weeks, and enjoyed a smash hit with it when it was unveiled in October 1845 at the Drury Lane. It was taken up all over the world and held the stage until the present century, and the air "Scenes that are brightest" enjoyed popular-song status. But Wallace's next opera, *Matilda of Hungary*, was a failure in 1847, and *Lurline*, scheduled for 1848, was not even produced.

In 1848, Wallace, suffering from an eye disease, went to Brazil on the suggestion of his doctors. The prescription effected an apparently complete cure, but while he was there the piano company in which he had sunk his money failed, leaving him bankrupt. Instead of going home, he headed for New York again. On the way, his ship's boiler exploded (a common occurrence in those days), but Wallace survived. In New York, where he decided to become an American citizen, he fell in love with a debutant pianist named Hélène Stoepel. Finding a lawyer willing to invalidate his marriage to the hapless Isabella (on the grounds that Wallace had been too young to make the religious decision involved), he took Hélène to wife. The pair concertized for a time in America, but by the late 1850s they were in Germany. In 1860 Covent Garden finally put *Lurline* on. It was successful and proved almost as hardy as *Maritana* for a while. However, by then Wallace had sold the rights to it for ten pounds, which he gave to charity. (Covent Garden netted 50,000.) His later operas were failures or went unproduced.

For half a dozen years Wallace had been suffering from degenerative heart disease. In 1864, just arrived from France, he collapsed in London. He returned to his home in Passy. When his condition failed to improve, Hélène took him to the Château de Haget in the Haute-Pyrénées, where he died a month later. Operas aside, Wallace was a glib and prolific composer of virtuoso and sentimental piano pieces and a writer of songs.

RECORDINGS: The two successful operas are represented on records by excerpts, mostly of early vintage.

FLOTOW [1222] HULLAH [1223]

[1222] FLOTOW, Friedrich Adolf Ferdinand, Freiherr von (Flō'-tō, Frē'-drikh Ä'-dolf Fâr'-dē-nȧnt fun)
IMPRESARIO
BORN: Teutendorf, April 27, 1812
DIED: Darmstadt, January 24, 1883

Even though he was Richard Wagner's [1230] exact contemporary (though eleven months older), Friedrich von Flotow had little in common with him, save that they were both Germans who wrote operas. Though usually found in lists of "great opera composers," Flotow is essentially a one-work man *(Martha)*. But the work is rarely heard nowadays, and its two perennial hits come from elsewhere—*"Letzte Rose"* from Thomas Moore [1093] and *"Ach, so fromm!"* from Flotow's own *L'Âme en peine (The Soul in Pain)*.

The son and heir of an old noble family, Flotow was born on the ancestral estate in Mecklenburg and was reared to be a diplomat. Sent at sixteen to Paris for polishing, he was drawn into the artistic whirlpool of the time. Already having had music lessons, he studied piano with Pixis [1128] and theory with Antonín Reicha [1059]. The 1830 revolution sent him home for a time, but he soon returned and set about to write operas. Between 1835 and 1837 he completed nine, the first produced as *Peter und Kathinka* (a treatment of the Peter-the-Great-in-Holland story) back home, some of the later ones in France, all without much impact. In 1838, the year in which he also wrote cello duos with Offenbach [1264], Flotow began ghost-writing numbers for his old Reicha-stablemate Albert Grisar (1808–69). This activity produced *Le Naufrage de la Méduse (The Wreck of the Medusa)*, for which Flotow composed the two last acts (the first was by one Pilati)—a sound success in 1839. Three years later Flotow rewrote the work to a libretto by Friedrich Wilhelm Riese as *Die Matrosen (The Sailors)* when the original was destroyed by fire. Its 1845 Hamburg premiere was preceded in 1844 by another collaboration of Flotow and "W. Friedrich," as the librettist signed himself—*Alessandro Stradella*, the only other Flotow opera still to show signs of life. That same year, in Paris, Flotow collaborated on a ballet, *Lady Harriette*, which provided the plot for *Martha*, premiered with great success in 1847 at the Kärntnertortheater in Vienna and immediately taken up all over the world. (The erring and errant wife of Sir Henry Bishop [1123] sang the title role in the New York premiere in 1852.)

The 1848 Revolution drove Flotow out of Paris again. A year later he married Elise von Zadow, who died after giving birth to a son in 1851. The boy followed her, and Flotow moved in with a friend, Heinrich Gans zu Putlitz, who provided several libretti and plays to which Flotow attached music. In 1853 the composer married Anna Theen, a dancer half his age, who gave him two sons that lived to maturity. Their headquarters were in the Vienna suburb of Sievering, but in 1855 Flotow became director of the court theater in Stettin, a post he held for eight years. From 1863 he divided his time between Vienna and Paris, where he was elected to the Académie and where, in 1870, *L'Ombre (The Shadow)* became the first of his 30 operas to win more than ephemeral success. By then he had divorced Anna and had married (in 1868) her younger sister Rose. In 1873 he returned to the Flotow estate but spent his final years, from 1880, in Darmstadt. He wrote instrumental and vocal music apart from the stage works, but most of it has disappeared.

RECORDINGS: There have been several recordings of *Martha*, one of *Stradella*, and a sprinkling of pieces from other operas.

[1223] HULLAH, John Pyke
ORGANIST, EDUCATOR, EDITOR
BORN: Worcester, June 27, 1812
DIED: London, February 21, 1884

John Hullah, long remembered for his settings of Charles Kingsley's poems "The Three Fishers" and "Oh That We Two Were Maying," was more important as a force in the rebirth of English music than as a composer. A product of the Royal Academy, he wrote a successful opera, *The Village Coquettes*, when he was twenty-four—libretto by his exact contemporary, Charles Dickens. Unhappily the score went up in flames. The following year he was appointed church organist at Croyden and soon became deeply interested in new Continental methods of teaching sight-singing *en masse*. Having investigated these, he got government backing and began such classes at Battersea in 1840. A year later he began classes for schoolteachers and the general public in London. Unfortunately, his espousal of the "immovable *do*" system, in which that syllable always represents the note "C" regardless of the key, confused more students than it enlightened. Nevertheless, with continued backing, he stubbornly continued it until he retired. In 1847 he was named professor of voice at King's College, University of London, and got similar appointments there at Queen's and Bedford colleges when they opened. His concerts tracing the development of English music won him a concert hall at Long Acre erected in 1853 by his admirers; unhappily it burned down in 1860. In 1870 he became director of student concerts at the Royal Academy and in 1872 was appointed inspector of training schools for the kingdom. His many musical manuals included several choral collections for amateur groups. RECORDINGS: The two songs noted previously were recorded by English singers early in this century.

[1224] KNIGHT, Joseph Philip
CLERGYMAN, ORGANIST
BORN: Bradford-on-Avon, July 26, 1812
DIED: Great Yarmouth, June 2, 1887

Born in an ancient Wiltshire town (the Avon of the town's name is not Shakespeare's), Knight studied in his youth with the organist of the cathedral in Bristol, a few miles downstream. A few years later he embarked on a career as a writer of popular songs, at first as "Philip Mortimer" and then under his own name. One of the earlier ones, written with Haynes Bayley, who was his preferred lyricist, was "She Wore a Wreath of Roses," but many others were immensely popular. In 1839–40 he visited the United States, where he wrote his all-time hit "Rocked in the Cradle of the Deep." (Generally treated as a display piece for bass notes, it was first sung by the tenor John Braham.) Later he took orders, and for two years he was vicar and organist of the church on the tiny Isle of St. Agnes in the Scillies off Cornwall. Evidently he found the cradle of the deep not as soothing as he had imagined for he left, got married, and lived abroad for some years. RECORDINGS: There are many recordings of his more popular songs.

[1225] DANNSTRÖM, Johan Isidor
(Dàn'-ström, Yō'-hàn Ē'-zē-dôr)
SINGER, TEACHER, CRITIC, ENTREPRENEUR
BORN: Stockholm, December 15, 1812
DIED: Stockholm, October 17, 1897

Isidor Dannström underwent a long musical education, interrupted several times out of economic necessity, during which periods he worked as a civil servant and taught guitar and flute. Among his vocal teachers were Rubini and Garcia, and, like Glinka [1179], he studied theory with Dehn in Berlin. He made his operatic debut in Stockholm in 1841 and sang several times with Jenny Lind, who often performed his songs in concert. He be-

came a very successful vocal teacher, conducted the Harmonic Society, served as critic for several Stockholm newspapers, and was elected to the Academy in 1851. Two years later he went on a concert tour of America. On his return he opened a musical-instrument business. He wrote some operettas, but his chief source of compositional fame was his songs and duets, many of them in a Swedish folk vein. RECORDINGS: His songs and duets often appear on records by earlier Scandinavian singers. He published a vocal method and an autobiography.

[1226] RUSSELL, Henry
MONOLOGIST, SINGER, SOCIAL CRUSADER
BORN: Sheerness, Kent, December 24, 1812
DIED: London, December 8, 1900

Russell's was the time not only of the emergence of wildly successful writers of popular songs, but also of the escape from the ghetto. Russell's people were French Jews originally called Roussel. As a child of three, he made his stage debut in something called *Panzarro*. He took up piano at five and became a chorister at eight. He joined a traveling juvenile theatrical troupe, met Edmund Kean (and his pet lion), and was jounced on the knee of George IV. At thirteen he went to Italy to study voice. According to his (not always reliable) memoirs, he studied there with Rossini [1143] and/or Bellini [1164], was on good terms with Donizetti [1155], and palled around Italy with Balfe [1195]. Returning to England as a baritone, he added to his string of acquaintances the soprano Maria Malibran and the violinists Charles-Auguste de Bériot and Paganini [1106] but found no special call for his services. Anticipating a better reception in the New World, he went to Toronto in the early 1830s and in 1835 found acceptance in Rochester, New York, as an organist at the First Presbyterian Church and teacher at the Academy of Sacred Music.

Taken with the oratory of Henry Clay, Russell began to appear as a monologuist on the lecture circuit. But, still conscious of himself as a singer, he decided to stud his act with songs, which he wrote himself. The first was "Wind of the Winter Night," 1836; this was followed by dozens of others before his American stay ended, including "Woodman, Spare That Tree" in 1837 and "A Life on the Ocean Wave" in 1838. It is said that Russell was the best-selling songwriter in America during this period; he was certainly one of the most popular entertainers, drawing huge crowds from the East Coast and the frontiers of the Middle West alike. From 1840 he specialized in "protest" songs—against such ills as gambling, alcoholism, slavery, and the maltreatment of Indians. As a performer he had perfect diction, a good voice, and flair—though more serious reviewers taxed him with bad taste and labeled him a fraud.

In 1841 Russell returned in triumph to England. He undertook one more American tour in 1843, then confined his appearances to his native land, retiring in the early 1860s. His social interests in later life took concrete form, for he enabled many poor people to begin new lives in Australia and New Zealand. Married and with five children, he abandoned his family in his late middle age for the young daughter of a Portuguese painter named de Lara, who took the name of Ronald. They lived and traveled together for some years, finally being enabled to marry in 1883. In 1871 the first of two sons was born to the couple. He was registered as Henry Russell, and went on to become the flamboyant impresario of the Boston Opera Company. A second son, born two years later, was known as Landon Ronald; he became Melba's accompanist, and later, as *Sir* Landon Ronald, conductor of the New Symphony Orchestra (and of many recordings). Russell died two weeks before his eighty-eighth birthday. He left innumerable songs, though his claim to have composed more than eight hundred has been doubted.

RECORDINGS: Clifford Jackson has reconstructed a "Russell evening" on a record.

[1227] RIETZ, August Wilhelm Julius
(Rēts, Ou'-gōōst Vil'-helm Yōōl'-yōōs)
CONDUCTOR, CELLIST, ADMINISTRATOR
BORN: Berlin, December 28, 1812
DIED: Dresden, September 12, 1877

Julius Rietz (or Ritz) was yet another *Kapellmeister* who profited from the Leipzig seal of approval. His father, Johann Friedrich Rietz, was a musician to Frederick William III of Prussia. His talented elder brother, Eduard, was a violinist, composer, and conductor, who died of tuberculosis at twenty-nine. Julius studied with both. Among his other teachers in Berlin were Zelter [1008] and the cellist Bernhard Romberg [1051]. He became a fine cellist and in 1828 he was accepted into the opera orchestra at Königsstadt. At twenty-two he was called to Düsseldorf as assistant conductor of the opera house, where his brother's close friend Felix Mendelssohn [1200] had just assumed charge. When Mendelssohn left in 1835, he saw to it that Rietz succeeded him,

and a year later Rietz became general music director of the municipality. During his twelve years there he wrote a great deal of incidental music (for plays by Shakespeare, Goethe, and Calderón, among others) much choral music, a symphony, and three concert overtures. The overture in A major of 1839 was performed by Mendelssohn at the Niederrheinische Music Festival and was hailed by Schumann [1211] as a masterpiece. (Rietz was, of course, on the Zelter-Mendelssohn axis as a composer.) When Mendelssohn died, Rietz turned the Düsseldorf functions over to Hiller [1219] and headed for Leipzig (though he returned sporadically to conduct the festivals). In Leipzig Rietz became conductor of the opera and the Gewandhaus Orchestra, director of the Singakademie, and professor of composition at the Conservatory. In 1859 he was given an honorary Ph.D. by the Conservatory, which did not prevent his defection to Dresden the next year to run the royal operatic and ecclesiastical music, the Conservatory, and eventually, in 1874, the whole musical life of the court and city. Rietz was an excellent scholar and edited important works of Bach [684], Handel [683], Mozart [992], and Beethoven [1063], and the collected works of Mendelssohn. Rietz performed operas were failures, but the *Concert Overture* and the second symphony managed to survive for some decades. RECORDINGS: The *Concert Overture* (in A major) has been recorded by Jorge Mester.

[1228] DARGOMIZHSKY, Alexander
Sergeyevitch (Där-gō-mēzh'-kē, Ál-yek-sàn-der Sâr-gā'-yə-vich)
CIVIL SERVANT, TEACHER
BORN: Troitskoye Tula, February 14, 1813
DIED: St. Petersburg, January 17, 1869

Dargomizhsky, even today little known outside of Russia, represents the link in Russian vocal music between Glinka [1179] and Mussorgsky [1369]. Born into a well-to-do family (like Glinka, on a country estate), he was slow to develop in childhood, and grew up stunted and ugly. Like most children of his class, he was taught to play instruments (the piano and violin) but was given no theoretical instruction. He was schooled in the capital and in 1831 took a job in the Ministry of Justice. At the time he was writing amateurish songs and salon pieces. In 1834 he met Glinka and became convinced that music was his vocation. He borrowed the notebooks that Glinka had used in his Berlin studies with Dehn and devoured them. These represent the only theoretical training he had. He quit the ministry and set to work on an opera, using as his libretto the *Esmeralda* which Victor Hugo had drawn from his own *Notre-Dame de Paris* for Louise Bertin [1181]. He completed it in 1839 and submitted it to the Imperial Opera for consideration, but the board put it aside for future reference. In 1843 he began a cantata to a Pushkin text, *The Triumph of Bacchus*. A visit to Paris in the winter of 1844–45, however, gave him pause about his musical direction, which was intensified by the unsuccessful production of *Esmeralda* (imitative of the current French style) in 1847. He converted *Bacchus* into a sort of opera-ballet but had to wait nineteen years to see it produced.

The new direction evidenced itself in *Russalka*. Though set to a Pushkin text, it drew from Russian folklore, and in its recitatives Dargomizhsky had already begun to experiment with his notions of musicoverbal expressivity. It was premiered in St. Petersburg in 1856 but was not well-liked (though a decade later it entered the repertoire and remains Dargomizhsky's one unqualified operatic success). Its initial failure discouraged him, and he abandoned operatic composition for the time. Instead he wrote songs and his only three orchestral pieces, all fantasies on Russian themes. In 1864 he went again to Western Europe and heard some of his music performed in Brussels. (It was there that he wrote a piano duet, *Tarantelle slave*, with a one-note *secondo* part for a pretty ballerina, who could not otherwise play. Dargomizhsky adored women and accepted only female students, but he never married.)

Back in Russia, Dargomizhsky was swept up in the nationalistic movement being nurtured by Balakirev [1348] and further developed his notions of supplanting operatic set pieces with a sort of dramatic recitative that emphasized word meanings. To demonstrate them, he elected to set, in through-composed fashion, Pushkin's Don Juan playlet, *The Stone Guest*. Mussorgsky, who sang Leporello in some readings of it, was fascinated and later adopted Dragomizhsky's principles for his own operas. By now, Dargomizhsky's frail body was aching and racked with pain and his health was failing, and he died before he could complete the work. César Cui [1337] finished up the vocal score and Rimsky-Korsakov [1416] orchestrated it, and it was eventually produced in 1872, with a first-rate cast. Predictably, it was a dismal failure.

Dargomizhsky's greatest successes were his songs. He explored oriental modes, indulged his considerable sense of humor, and, for all practical purposes, invented the graceful "romance" which borrowed from both Italian opera and the German *Lied*. There are about 90 songs plus a number of part-songs. Two additional operas, *Rogdana* and *Mazeppa*, barely got off the drawing board.

RECORDINGS: Excerpts from *Russalka* are about all that has been committed to Western-produced records, but direct imports and various repressings from the Soviets have made available complete versions of *Russalka* and *The Stone Guest*, a collection of orchestral snippets and fragments (the *Chukhon Fantasy, Kazachok, Baba Yaga*, etc.) and a generous sampling of the songs.

[1229] **HELLER, Stephen** (*né* **Jakob**)
PIANIST, CRITIC
BORN: Pest, May 15, 1813
DIED: Paris, January 14, 1888

Called the equal, if not the superior, of Chopin [1208], both as player and composer in his day, Stephen Heller is now remembered mostly as the writer of workaday studies for tyro pianists. Though he was clearly a remarkable performer and an interesting musician, he was temperamentally unfit for the kind of life that usually goes with such a calling. Self-effacing and shy, he had the greatest reverence for the leading romantics; but he also had his own notions—some of them important—about what music should be.

Heller's Jewish parents converted when he was eleven, and he was then baptized István, a name he later westernized. He studied from an early age with local keyboard players of no importance, and played his first concert at nine. Convinced of his talent, his parents sent him to Vienna to study with Czerny [1137], but Czerny turned out to be out of his economic range and he settled for someone named Anton Halm. When he was fourteen, he was deemed ready to join virtuosic ranks and set out on a tour, but in 1830 he collapsed in Augsburg and had to remain there for a long convalescence. A wealthy lady of the town came to his rescue, and later one of the Fuggers underwrote his education. Here he began composing in earnest, and in 1836, thanks to the intervention of Schumann [1211], who had become a pen pal, began to be published. Two years later Heller set out to Paris to study with Kalkbrenner [1118] but again found he could not afford the man and settled down there quietly for the rest of his life. He was friendly with the important musicians there—Berlioz's [1175] memoirs include a long letter to Heller written in Leipzig—but rarely appeared in public. Though he had written music for other media in the Augsburg days, he limited his composition entirely to piano music from now on. He was a dedicated promoter of Romanticism, but eschewed tone painting for the re-creation of emotional reactions. Some of his music is said to presage the later Liszt [1218] and even Janáček [1478]. In 1862 he went to London and played at the Crystal Palace with his friend Charles Hallé. In his last years he suffered from failing eyesight, but friends (including Robert Browning) saw to it that he had enough to live on.

RECORDINGS: The pianist Gerhard Puchelt has devoted a record to a sampling of Heller's music.

[1230] WAGNER, Wilhelm Richard (Vȧg'-ner, Vil'-helm Rēkh'-ärt)

WRITER, CONDUCTOR
BORN: Leipzig, May 22, 1813
DIED: Venice, February 13, 1883

If ever genius existed, it must have been Richard Wagner. Writer, philosopher, poet, visionary, actor, director, he changed, largely through his own determination in the face of behemothian opposition, the direction of music and the theater—for better or worse. But no artist ever had to carry such a weight of blame, during his lifetime and after. It was probably Wagner's unconquerable estimate of his own worth that led all too many people to view the artist as superhuman and his work to be approached as a religious manifestation brooking no criticism. Though in music Wagner's roots were deeply conservative (he insisted that melody was the paramount element!), it was perhaps his innovations, especially those that led away from tonal harmony, that led ultimately to the dead-end fatuity of the insistence that each composer must reinvent the art in his own image. It may have been Wagner who unwittingly inspired the trend toward gigantism that daily threatens opera with extinction on both economic and artistic grounds. But there is nothing in the man's history or character to say that he would in any way have approved such developments. Elsewhere he also has a good deal to answer for. Though there can have been few human beings more charismatic than he, there is no blinking at his almost megalomanic egoism, his sense of *génie obligé*, his manipulativeness, and his arrogance. Whether he can be blamed for the development of Nazism is another matter. He was passionately nationalistic because he believed that German salvation lay in the unifi-

cation of that people; but he deplored the jingoism and militarism that followed the event. He attacked the Jews in the press (at a time when anti-Semitism was the norm in the so-called Christian world), but he numbered several Jews—Carl Tausig [1389], Hermann Levi, Joseph Rubinstein, Heinrich Porges—among his closest and most trusted associates, and he refused, after unification, to sign an anti-Jewish petition to the Reichstag. Recent studies have in fact tended to mitigate and even disprove some of the more damning charges brought against him.

Wagner was born in Leipzig, a few months before Napoleon's catastrophic defeat there, the ninth child of Johanna Wagner, *née* Pätz, fifteen years wed to Karl Friedrich Wilhelm Wagner, a stage-struck police actuary. (Johanna, officially the child of a Weissenfels baker, was rumored to be the daughter of Prince Constantin of Weimar, who in fact paid for her education but who was only sixteen when she was born.) Karl Friedrich succumbed to typhus six months after Richard's birth. The following August Johanna married the actor Ludwig Geyer, a longtime family friend, and bore him a daughter seven months later. That curious circumstance has led many to believe that Geyer was also Richard's father—a notion that Richard encouraged. It is true that Geyer was more than kind to the boy; there was also a facial resemblance, but young Wagner looked even more like Karl Friedrich's brother Joseph. There is, despite many assertions to the contrary, no evidence at all that Geyer was Jewish.

Richard's brother Albert became an important tenor and producer and his sister Rosalie a successful actress. Richard himself made a few juvenile stage appearances, but Geyer, though he fostered his interest in the theater and music, was determined that he would not make the stage his life. But Geyer died when the boy was nine. Johanna took in roomers—one was Spohr [1112]—and Richard attended the Kreuzschule in Dresden, demonstrating a thirst for knowledge, especially Classical, and an antipathy to work. He had some piano lessons but preferred to play by ear. He wrote a prize-winning poem on the death of a schoolmate, momentarily raising his mother's hopes that he might, after all, amount to something. In 1827 the family moved back to Leipzig where Richard found a kindred spirit in his Uncle Adolf, and, not finding the Nikolaischule to his taste, dropped out (keeping his mother in the dark for six months) and worked at a "Shakespearean tragedy" called *Leubald*. (His destruction of forty-two characters by the last act necessitated the return of several as ghosts.) Already fascinated in opera by a performance of Weber's *Freischütz* that Geyer had taken him to, he discovered Beethoven [1063] when he heard Wilhelmine Schröder-Devrient sing *Fidelio* and decided he must study music to add that element to his play. Though he got the publisher Schott at least to consider his piano reduction of the ninth symphony, efforts at self-education finally convinced him he needed help, and finally he found a satisfactory and sympathetic teacher in C. T. Weinlig, the ailing cantor of the Thomaskirche.

In 1831 he began a year as a special student at the university but distinguished himself chiefly in drinking, wenching, dueling, and getting into debt. Then he visited Vienna, was enchanted by the waltzes of Johann Strauss, Sr. [1177], and ran up more debts. Returning through Prague, he persuaded Dionys Weber to give an orchestral reading of the symphony he had written, and embarked on his first opera *Die Hochzeit,* which he soon abandoned. In 1833 he became chorus master at the Würzburg theater, where brother Albert was an important figure, and so escaped the Saxon military callup. Despite the press of duty and a still free-wheeling social life, he completed his opera *Die Feen (The Fairies,* in the style of Marschner [1147]), which, however, went unproduced until five years after his death. Shortly afterward, having rejected the Germanic approach for the pure melody of Bellini [1164], which he tried applying to his next effort, *Das Liebesverbot (The Ban on Love).*

The Würzburg job lasted only a season. Invited to try out as conductor with the decrepit Magdeburg company, Wagner decided to take the post against his better judgment when he encountered the leading actress, Minna Planer. A few years his senior, she possessed good looks, a rather dull mind, a string of lovers, and a ten-year-old daughter, Natalie, who passed as her sister. Wagner laid siege to her heart until she fled, ultimately to Königsberg. He remained long enough to see the shabby production of his opera and the subsequent collapse of the company in the spring of 1836, then followed her, and married her in November. In April he was appointed *Kapellmeister* in Königsberg but gave up the job to pursue Minna, who had skipped to Dresden with a lover. Wagner was reunited with her, found a conducting post in Riga for the fall, but had to go there alone in July 1837, since Minna had run off again. He hired Minna's sister Amalie as one of his leading singers; when she arrived in October, she had his penitent wife in tow.

Wagner did not get along with the Riga administration and was let go in 1839. By then he had been infected by Meyerbeerian [1142] grand opera, and was writing such a work based on Bulwer-Lytton's *Rienzi, the Last of the Tribunes.* Convinced that Paris was the only place for such a work, he let Minna raise money by returning to the stage and then selling off her costumes and their furniture. With their Newfoundland "Robber," the first of Wagner's many adored pets, they set out for what appeared to be a vacation in the country. But, by devious paths and a good deal of skulking, they managed to reach the Baltic port of Pillau and take ship for a storm-tossed voyage to London that was later to contribute to *Der fliegende Holländer (The Flying Dutchman).* From London they went to Boulogne, where they found Meyerbeer vacationing. Richard read him the *Rienzi* libretto, showed him the score of the first two acts, and acquired some letters of introduction that turned out not to be the keys to instant fame and fortune. He got the conductor Habeneck to take his orchestra through his *Columbus Overture,* which did his cause more harm than good. The Wagners had been reduced to pawning their wedding rings when Meyerbeer secured a promise of a production of *Das Liebesverbot* for early 1840. Without reading the fine print, Wagner promptly took a lease on a posh apartment—and almost as promptly the theater went bankrupt. Songs and other salon pieces failed to sell, and Wagner subsisted on hackwork procured by Meyerbeer from the publisher Schlesinger. In the autumn he was taken to debtors' prison. Eventually his release was effected, the apartment was sublet, and the Wagners moved to suburban Meudon early in 1841. *Rienzi* was now completed, and Wagner had written a one-act libretto on the Dutchman legend. The latter, thanks to Meyerbeer again, he sold to the director of the Paris Opéra, Léon Pillet. Pillet, unwilling to gamble on an unknown composer, had it set, as *Le Vaisseau fantôme,* by a nonentity named Dietsch. (It sank without a trace; ironically it was Dietsch who was assigned to conduct the Paris premiere of *Tannhäuser* in 1861).

Having given up on Paris, Wagner shipped *Rienzi* back to Dresden, where it was accepted for a future date (unspecified). Having expanded the *Holländer* to three acts, he wrote the music at white heat, and, again using Meyerbeer's clout, got it accepted in Berlin. In April 1842 he and Minna, having won the backing of his family, returned to Dresden.

While waiting for the production of *Rienzi* (October 20, 1842), Wagner, inspired by his reading about the *Minnesingers*, began work on *Tannhäuser* (like the *Dutchman*, a tale of redemption by pure love), which occupied him until 1845. Despite the composer's fears that *Rienzi* would prove beyond the attention span of the audience (he offered to make cuts), it won an ovation, and soon after, following the death of Morlacchi [1114], he was appointed to share the *Kapellmeister*-ship with Reissiger for life. Berlin having dropped the *Holländer*, it too first saw the light in Dresden (January 2, 1843). Despite the presence of the great Schröder-Devrient as Senta, the audience was puzzled, and in fact neither opera got more than local attention. Meanwhile, in his official capacity, Wagner wrote *Das Liebesmahl der Apostel (The Apostles' Love Feast)* for a choral congress, an ode on the king's return from London, and a funeral piece for the reburial of Weber's remains. Despite his increasing debts, he had already adopted the luxurious lifestyle he had felt necessary to his muse and had even published his scores at his own (?) expense.

The Wagner jinx struck again at the *Tannhäuser* premiere on October 19, 1845. The tenor, Tichatschek, had laryngitis; Mme. Schröder-Devrient, miffed at having to take second place to Wagner's adoptive niece Johanna, was a blowsy and ineffective Venus; and the scenery had failed to arrive. The audience slept through much of it, though later, under more favorable circumstances, the Dresdeners gave the work a grudging thumbs-up. By then Wagner was hard at work on *Lohengrin*, yet another version of the pure-love theme with quasi-religious overtones and a romanticized medieval setting. Completed in 1847, it moved much farther than any of its predecessors toward the Wagnerian ideal of "endless melody." (Influenced by his own philosophy, Wagner, with the concurrence of Minna's physician, forsook her bed in the supposed interests of her health and a "pure" relationship.)

As he continued to shape his self-image and his world view, these had a profound effect on his position. He indicated, for example, that he was underpaid, and he urged a shakeup of the orchestra in the interests of quality rather than seniority. Such stances not only made him dangerous enemies but led to his involvement in other, even more volatile areas. The revolutionary democratic tides sweeping Europe caught him up, and he became concerned with the need for a German national identity and with the way in which Christian doctrine had been distorted (around this time he projected an opera on the life of Christ, as well as one on the

national epic, the *Nibelungenlied*). He made a proposal for a German National Theater, to be sponsored by King John and to be run by someone very like Richard Wagner, which outraged some of his associates and superiors. Wagner was, meanwhile, finding friends among the political radicals, including the nihilist Mikhail Bakunin. In the fall of 1848 he was informed that *Lohengrin* was canceled. The following May, revolt erupted in Dresden. Wagner's precise role in it remains obscure, but he had sufficiently compromised himself to make it necessary for him to get out with the radical leaders when the uprising collapsed. Somehow he got separated from them and so avoided arrest. He made his way to Weimar, where Liszt [1218], with whom he had a casual acquaintance, was rehearsing *Tannhäuser*, lay low there for a short while, urging his protector to take up his banner, got across the Swiss border to Zürich one night, and, rather unpredictably, went on to Paris. Finding nothing there to encourage him, he settled in Zürich in July 1849. Minna, true bourgeoise that she was, did not care for the prospects and could not be persuaded to join him for some months.

There followed a quarter of a century in which Wagner had no permanent employment and no income save the charity of friends and admirers—which he did not hesitate to use to promote the luxurious lifestyle to which he wished to become accustomed. For all the difficulty and uncertainty, Wagner produced his most important literary utterances and much of his mature composition in the first part of this period. He abandoned the Christ opera, *Wieland der Schmied*, and a sketched Achilles tragedy; of the projected Nibelung drama, he had written the libretto for *Siegfrieds Tod* before he left Dresden. Immediately on settling in Zürich, he turned out two prose tracts central to the development of his thinking. The first was *Art and Revolution*, which, deploring art as a toy for the monied few, urged a return to something like Athenian drama which would express the ethos of the "folk" (the German folk being understood.) The second, *The Art-Work of the Future*, argued that that soul could be best expressed in a theatrical blend of music, poetry, and dance operating on equal terms and supported by painting, sculpture, and architecture. (Later he came to feel that music must be paramount.) In 1851 he completed *Opera and Drama*, which set forth his theory of "music drama." In human development, he argued, the primal scream, the expression of raw emotion, had been supplanted by intellectualized verbal utterance. (Vowels had, as expressive devices, been weakened by consonants.) The music drama aimed to undo some of the damage through a compromise, wherein words would be subject to "endless" melody against an orchestral background that would provide a connotative context through the interweaving of associational *leitmotivs* or musical cells, each identified with some important element of the drama as a whole. (The period also produced the infamous article "Jewishness in Music," basically an attack on the operas of Meyerbeer, who Wagner felt had only pretended to support him.) Up to now Wagner had been much influenced by German Classicism and the mystical humanism of Ludwig Feuerbach. Soon, however, he would come under the spell of Arthur Schopenhauer, particularly as regarded his rejection of materialism and his advocacy of renunciation of the will and the self. These ideas were further bolstered by an exploration of Buddhism. (Almost to the end of his life Wagner planned a Buddhist opera to be called *Die Sieger [The Victors]*).

Meanwhile Minna was insisting that Wagner realize his talents in a meaningful (i.e., money-producing) way. Both she and Liszt insisted that this could only be done in Paris, so back he went in early 1850, only to find the place more depressing than even he had thought. At the suggestion of his Dresden friend and patron Frau Julie Ritter, he went to Bordeaux to visit a young English admirer, the former Jessie Taylor, who had persuaded her wealthy husband M. Laussot that Wagner was a worthy cause. Wagner promptly fell in love with her, got her to agree to flee with him to the Near East, notified Minna that he would not be back, and hurried to the rendezvous in Geneva. But Jessie stood him up, and in the end he meekly went back to Zürich and Minna. Shortly afterward Liszt premiered *Lohengrin* in Weimar. Barred from Germany, Wagner sat it out in a local pub with Minna, checking off the presumed action on his watch. He was not to see the work for eleven years.

Though he was involved in musical life in Zürich, Wagner never held an official post there. He recommended Frau Ritter's son Karl as an opera conductor there. When Ritter proved not up to it, Wagner took over a number of performances, until Bülow [1310], who he also suggested could step in. (Bülow later quarreled with the management and was replaced by Abt [1268].) Meanwhile Liszt's championing of *Tannhäuser* and *Lohengrin* had aroused some interest in those works—though all too often Wagner spent, in anticipation, royalties that never materialized. To relieve some of the

financial pressure, he now offered Liszt first-performance rights to *Siegfrieds Tod* for a cash advance, which Liszt gave him. But Wagner soon realized that his plot—a paragon destroyed by a crass world wholly alien to his nature—needed something to explain it. He therefore conceived a forerunner, to be called *Der junge Siegfried*, which was suggested to him by a fairytale about a boy who set out to find what fear was. By autumn of 1851 the plan had expanded to include *three* operas, with a fourth as prologue—in short, the tetralogy *Der Ring des Nibelungens* much as we know it. This, as Liszt agreed, would be impossible for Weimar—or any other existing stage, and Wagner dreamed of a special theater where the four operas could be given seriatim in a sort of festival of German art. By the end of 1852 he had written all four libretti and was worn out, pausing for several rest cures along the route.

In February 1853, Wagner's friends, led by Mathilde and Otto Wesendonck, a Zürich couple, staked him to a Wagner festival of his own, in which he conducted soloists, chorus, and orchestra and heard some of his own music for the first time. The following August, stymied by the musical demands of his operas, he went rather aimlessly to Italy. There, drowsing in a fit of fever in a La Spezia hotel, he hallucinated endless permutations of an E-flat-major chord and suddenly realized that he had not only the opening of his prologue *Das Rheingold (The Rhine Gold)* but the germ of the entire gigantic work. After a brief visit to Paris with Liszt (where, fatefully, he met Liszt's sixteen-year-old daughter Cosima), he settled in in November to compose. *Rheingold* was sketched in six weeks and completed in May 1854. *Die Walküre* was begun a month later. By then, however, Wagner's creditors were turning nasty. He raised money to placate them by ceding to Otto Wesendonck future performance rights to *Tannhäuser* and *Lohengrin*. By then, as Otto seems to have been aware, Wagner and Mathilde were deeply in love—though the precise nature of their relationship remains obscure. Influenced by Schopenhauerian doctrine, Wagner found himself increasingly drawn to making a statement about the affair in an opera on the Tristan and Isolde legend, which would present union in death as the only solution for mortal passion. Nevertheless he plugged on with *Walküre*, completing the sketch by the end of the year.

Having overthrown no thrones for some time, Wagner began to dream of a pardon from King John. In September Minna, not wholly unselfishly, went to Dresden to try to obtain one, but without any luck. The following January there was another "Wagner festival" in Zürich, and its honoree was invited to come to London to conduct the Philharmonic Society in the late winter and spring. He appeared in eight concerts, impressed Queen Victoria, saw something of Berlioz [1175], but for the most part spent the time in frustrated boredom. On his return to Zürich a stubborn skin ailment (which he called *Rotlauf* [erysipelas] and his doctor "nerves," and which modern medicine would probably see as an allergy) slowed his progress, as did his emotional involvement with Mathilde. However, he managed to complete *Walküre* by March 1856, but did not turn to its sequel (now simply *Siegfried)* for six months, after going for a "cure" (successful for the time being).

Meanwhile the Wesendoncks were building a new home at the lakeside with (ostensibly) a guest cottage that Mathilde insisted they offer to the Wagners so that Richard could work in quiet. The Wagners accepted, dubbed the house "Asyl" and moved in in April 1857. He had gotten to the middle of Act Two of *Siegfried* when the Wesendoncks occupied the house next door in July. Mathilde's proximity proved too much, and *Siegfried* was shelved for a decade in favor of *Tristan und Isolde*. The pair were thick as thieves. There was continual visiting back and forth. Mathilde wrote poems, and Wagner set them to music. Otto was phlegmatic, suspecting a phase that would pass. Minna too was unusually tolerant. (Wagner often complained, with some justice, that she did not understand him.) But eventually she intercepted a letter to Mathilde that suggested matters were not so Platonic as they appeared. She went into fits of rage eventually so affecting her already ailing heart that in the spring of 1858 she was persuaded to return to Germany for medical aid. Her abuse of Mathilde and the fact that Wagner had kept their love from his wife burst Mathilde's bubble. In August, Wagner gave up his Siegmund role for that of Lohengrin, renounced his great love, and took off for Venice with Karl Ritter. There he spent several months in a dank and drafty *palazzo* working at *Tristan*. Eventually, the Saxons having put pressure on the Austrians to get rid of him, he left on his own, winding up in Lucerne at the end of March 1859. There he quickly gathered momentum and finished *Tristan* in August.

Paris having shown some interest in his work, Wagner went there, hoping to get a production of his new opera. Optimistically taking a three-year lease on a house, he sent for Minna, who appeared to be in a forgiving mood but was soon nagging him endlessly.

Though he found many friends in artistic circles, the press remained hostile. Though the audience was ecstatic at the concert he gave at the Théâtre-Italien early in 1860, the reviewers excoriated it almost to a man. He made friends with the poet Charles Baudelaire and even spent a happy afternoon with old Rossini [1143], whom he had once deplored. But hope of a *Tristan* premiere soon flickered out, and the whole Paris experiment was looking increasingly more hopeless when an angel in the person of Marie Kalergis, Princess Nesselrode, suddenly appeared with 10,000 francs. In thanks, Wagner sang her (and Berlioz) the whole second act of *Tristan,* abetted by Pauline Viardot and by Klindworth at the piano.

Efforts to get *Tannhäuser* put on at the Opéra seemed fruitless when Napoleon III —thanks in part to Bülow's efforts—decreed its production. Wagner had the libretto translated into French rhymed verse (by several hands) and somewhat grudgingly wrote the mandatory ballet—but for the first act, "Venusberg," rather than for the second act, "Songfest," as had been advised. Espousal of his cause by the emperor brought a partial amnesty from Dresden. (Wagner could visit those states whose governments officially requested his presence.) But the production forced him to turn down a lucrative offer from St. Petersburg, Baron Haussmann's rebuilding program forced him out of his house with two years to go on the lease, and he was felled by typhoid. Nor could he persuade the Opéra management to let him supplant the ineffectual Dietsch (of *Vaisseau fantôme* obloquy) on the podium. *Tannhäuser's* fate was sealed by the Jockey Club, a clique of wealthy young bucks, whose operatic interest focused on the female legs of the second-act ballets, for which they were wont to arrive in the nick of time. At the first performance they merely shouted and guffawed; they drowned out the next two with silver whistles ordered up for the occasion, and Wagner withdrew the opera. Though the boxoffice sales set a record, so did the 164 rehearsals, and Wagner did not receive a sou.

But a trip to Vienna after the catastrophe enabled him at last to see *Lohengrin* and seemed to promise *Tristan's* realization at the Hofoper. But bad luck pursued him and, after various delays and other snags, the possibility fizzled out. Meanwhile, Wagner had returned to a project that he had sketched as early as 1845: an opera about the mastersingers of Nuremberg. As it now developed, it had two heroes, both modeled on Richard Wagner: Walther, the young musical revolutionary who must adapt to the needs of the "folk" and Hans Sachs, the wise old *Meister,* who knows that the new must grow from the old (and who unselfishly renounces love in his rival's favor). Having completed the libretto, Wagner peddled *Die Meistersinger* to the publisher Schott in Mainz and, in February 1862, settled in nearby Biebrich. Minna, who had returned to Germany for her health, joined him, only to be outraged immediately when she found that he and Mathilde were still corresponding. She packed her bags and returned to Dresden. Wagner was left to draw inspiration and solace from another young Mathilde, hight Maier. There was talk of divorce, of which Minna would not hear. In fact she managed to obtain complete amnesty for her husband, apparently hoping that he would now become settled down in Dresden and cut out the foolishness. But he only stopped by on his way to Vienna (he was traveling with a pretty actress, Friederike Meyer), where he read the *Meistersinger* to an audience that included his longtime enemy, the critic Eduard Hanslick, and conducted, for the first time, music from *Der Ring.* There were further conducting dates (in Prague and St. Petersburg) before the composer came to rest in suburban Penzing (in lieu of the elusive rose-covered cottage he had sought on the Rhine). But continued engagements as a guest conductor did little to lower the mountain of debts (each new domicile had necessitated a heavy outlay for decorating and furnishing), and early in the spring of 1864 he fled back to Zürich, a jump ahead of his creditors and the police. After a month he moved on to Stuttgart, where there appeared a *rex ex machina.*

On April 30 Wagner found a calling card from an emissary of Ludwig II who, at eighteen, had ascended the Bavarian throne a few weeks before. Though apprehensive about royal emissaries, Wagner met the visitor on the next day and received a ring and a letter pledging his undying devotion. (Ludwig, who had a fixation about swans among other things, thought *Lohengrin* the *ne plus ultra* of opera.) When the king and composer met a few days later, Ludwig gave him money, a temporary home beside the Starnberger See, and notice that Wagner's wish was his command. In the future, he said, there would be a Wagner theater, an adjunct conservatory, and a propagandizing newspaper. After he settled in his new home, Wagner invited Mathilde Maier to become his resident muse. She turned him down. Instead, in June, there arrived Cosima Bülow *(née* Liszt) and her children. The Bülows had been frequent guests of the Wagners since their marriage seven years earlier—a

marriage that had not gone well despite outward appearances. By the time Hans arrived a month later, preparatory to becoming *Kapellmeister* and conservatory director in the new regime, Cosima was carrying Wagner's child. (Born in April 1865 and christened Isolde, her true parentage was mentioned by no one.)

The scheduled premiere in Munich of *Tristan* on May 15 was at the last minute postponed, owing to the illness of Malvina Schnorr von Carolsfeld, scheduled to sing the heroine opposite her rotund real-life spouse Ludwig, Wagner's "ideal tenor." The opera at last reached the stage on June 10 and had four performances. Ludwig was ecstatic, but many of Wagner's old friends (e.g., Liszt, Peter Cornelius [1294], Mathilde Wesendonck) failed to show up, and the rather sparse audiences were largely baffled. Only a few recognized that they were hearing a turning point in music. It was, in fact, the first of Wagner's operas to let the world see his musicodramatic theories realized. Moreover, it exhibited a chromaticism that often teetered on the edge of atonality. The disappointing reception apart, the production seemed to spawn yet one more catastrophe: Ludwig Schnorr succumbed, six weeks later, to something called "galloping gout"; he had just turned twenty-nine.

Next on the schedule was the still unfinished *Meistersinger.* Wagner and King Ludwig and Cosima, whom Ludwig chose to view as Wagner's muse, were even closer than before. Ludwig was a homosexual, but if he was in love with Wagner, there is no evidence that Wagner reciprocated or even encouraged his feelings. All the same he was treading on dangerous ground: not only were there those who resented what they deemed his raids on the treasury, but he also had become an unwitting pawn in the struggle between pro-Prussian and pro-Austrian factions at court. (His sympathies lay with the former, but the latter was in the saddle.) Drawn into recommending in print the replacement of certain powerful ministers, he precipitated a crisis that forced the reluctant Ludwig to order him out of the country "until it should blow over." Wagner, sensing that his luck had gone sour again, left for Geneva, vowing never to return. For the first weeks of 1866 he sought a refuge in southern France, where, on January 26, he received a telegram reporting Minna's death. (Shortly before this she had published a notice in the paper, to counter rumors of Wagner's shabby treatment of her, saying that her husband, however much they disagreed, had always seen that she was provided for.) Wagner returned to Geneva and finished the first act of *Meistersinger*.

In March Cosima came to stay for three weeks. No sooner had she left than Wagner found a house to his liking at Triebschen on Lake Lucerne. He invited the Bülows to join him; Cosima came with the children, but Hans was "too busy." At about the same time, Wagner had a distraught letter from Ludwig, threatening to abdicate so that they might be together again. The letter was followed a week later by Ludwig himself, but after two days, Wagner persuaded him that his duty was to his country. Six weeks afterward war broke out between Prussia and Austria, Bavaria siding with the latter. After a disastrous defeat, however, Ludwig heeded some of Wagner's suggestions and replaced some of his chief ministers. Still denied entry to the kingdom, Wagner continued to operate as a power behind the throne. Ludwig, on his part, opened the promised conservatory and inaugurated the *Süddeutsche Presse*. But Wagner's articles for the paper again fired dissension, and he had to be told shortly to withdraw.

In February 1867 Cosima bore a second Wagner daughter, Eva, at Triebschen. Bülow, who was quite aware of the affair but who preferred to keep up appearances, attended the accouchement and offered his "forgiveness." Ludwig, however, increasingly assailed by gossip on the matter, began to smell a rat, and it took some fancy footwork on the part of the lovers (including Cosima's return to Hans in Munich) to convince him they had been dreadfully maligned. Hans was considered essential to the success of *Die Meistersinger*, which Wagner completed on October 24. He celebrated with a trip to Paris, then returned to Munich to visit the Bülows and to see his king again. Things went smoothly. The premiere of the opera, catching the rising tide of nationalism with its panegyric to "Holy German Art," was a triumph on June 21, 1868. Wagner was summoned to the royal box during the first act, sat with the king for the rest of the performance, and took two bows from that exalted vantage point. But the two were not to meet again until the king came to the first Bayreuth Festival eight years later.

Wagner and Cosima apparently saw no point in continuing the subterfuge, both now being able to dispense with Bülow. (Wagner had found his replacement in Hans Richter.) The couple, with a lame excuse about Cosima's health, went on an Italian vacation in September. It was marred by torrential rains and floods that made their journey home a nightmare, but it enabled them to make some decisions. Cosima told Hans that she wanted a divorce. He agreed, and she moved in with Wagner for good in November. (Ludwig was appalled and bitter at this flaunting of immorality by his Lohengrin and Elisabeth.) Wagner got out the almost-forgotten *Siegfried* and went to work on it. Early in June 1869 Cosima gave birth to Wagner's last child, a boy whom they named Siegfried. Two weeks later, having by Ludwig's order conducted a performance of *Tristan* that Wagner forbade, Bülow left Munich for good. But the king went on with his plans to produce *Das Rheingold*, which, by the terms of an earlier agreement, was his right. Wagner's friends warned him that a disaster was in the making. Unable to persuade Ludwig to call it off, he tried to take over the rehearsals but was turned away, and the work was left to Franz Wüllner (later *Kapellmeister* of the court opera). The premiere took place on September 22 before a distinguished audience. The press gave the spectacle good marks but deplored the music; the inner Wagnerian circle considered the production a travesty. The great friendship was further strained when Ludwig announced his intention to put on *Die Walküre*, which he did on June 24, 1870. On July 18 the Bülows' divorce was handed down; a day later, when a delegation of French admirers, including Saint-Saëns [1343] and Duparc [1442], arrived in Triebschen, France declared war on Prussia, which, this time, found an ally in Bavaria. On the twenty-fifth Wagner and Cosima were married. To prevent Ludwig's depredations on *Siegfried*, he shelved it again and turned to *Die Götterdämmerung*.

Wagner, who had many friends and supporters in France, was placed in something of a bind by the war. Whether his utterances (some of them clearly misinterpreted by his biographers) indicate a savagely anti-Gallic bias rather than an enthusiasm for a show of German unity is another of those matters about which there seems to be little agreement. His farce, *Eine Kapitulation*, written at this time, has, for example, been called both a gloat over the starving Parisians under siege and a lampoon of German attempts to imitate French operetta.

On another note, on Christmas morning 1870, Cosima was awakened by the sounds of an orchestra playing the tender *Siegfried Idyll*—her present from her husband. The following April Wagner, as a member of the Berlin Academy, took her to pay homage in that city to the new Emperor of Germany, William I. On the way, they visited Bayreuth on a hunch that the theater might serve the composer's purposes. It did not suit, but the town did, and plans were soon set in motion to build not only a *Festspielhaus* but also a permanent domicile for Wagner there. This plan was laid before Carl Tausig **[1389]**, whom Wagner had known since the pianist was sixteen, during the Berlin visit. Tausig agreed to become business manager for the upcoming Festival. Shortly afterward, at the suggestion of the publisher Heckel, and the *Meister*'s concurrence, he began the organization of local Wagner Societies dedicated to helping finance the venture. But a malign fate once again intervened: Tausig contracted typhoid in July and died at the age of twenty-nine.

Meanwhile Wagner had finally completed *Siegfried* in February 1871, and despite such interruptions as having to conduct a benefit for the Mannheim Wagner Society that December, had outlined the music for *Götterdämmerung* by April 1872. Later that month the family moved (for the last time) to Bayreuth, where, on his fiftieth birthday, May 22, Wagner laid the cornerstone of the new theater. Ludwig telegraphed his blessing but no funds. The building of both the theater and the home proceeded but in the face of grave difficulties. The most immediate was money—the Wagner Societies had not responded with the tangible enthusiasm that had been predicted, and no angels had materialized. Moreover Wagner continued to be an object of criticism and mockery in the press. Nor did it prove easy to round up personnel for the festival, now projected for 1875. Just when Wagner had reached the nadir of despair and exhaustion (and even so passionate an admirer as Nietzsche **[1422]** was giving up on him), Ludwig came through with a loan of 100,000 talers, to be paid off from a chunk of the patronage shares (which, ominously, were still not on the bestseller list). The following month, April 1874, the Wagners moved into their new home, christened Wahnfried (roughly "Escape from Madness"), where the composer finished *Götterdämmerung.* There Wagner set up a corps of assistants, including the young conductors Anton Seidl and Felix Mottl, to do the copying and other essential grubbing. (They were dubbed the "Nibelung Chancellery.") Richter was delegated to make a final selection of personnel, and by summer singers were already visiting for preliminary coaching. The set designs were entrusted to Joseph Hoffmann, a painter long known to American Sunday-schoolers for his depiction of the adolescent Christ. Their realization was entrusted, however, to theatrical professionals. (The results were a terrible disappointment even to Wagner's most rabid supporters.) Much of

early 1875 was devoted to money-raising concerts, the proceeds going to support the orchestral rehearsals that began in August. There was trouble with singers: Albert Niemann, the scheduled Siegmund in *Walküre,* left in a huff; the Vienna Hofoper refused to release Amalie Materna, slated to sing all three Brünnhildes, unless Wagner would come and prepare its productions of *Tannhäuser* and *Lohengrin,* a task that occupied six weeks of the late fall (during which he saw and approved Bizet's **[1363]** *Carmen.)* The year 1875 came and went without any festival, and the prospects did not look sanguine for 1876. Wagner begged Emperor William for aid in the name of the new Germany, but the request was strangled in red tape. There was, however, a successful benefit performance of *Tristan* in Berlin and a $5,000 commission from Theodor Thomas for a march to mark the American centennial. (In later hours of discouragement, Wagner's fantasy of America caused him seriously to consider emigrating.) By June, however, momentum had reached a point of no return. Ludwig came for the dress rehearsals in August, as did the disenchanted Nietzsche, plagued by continual headaches. (Bülow was ill and in a nursing home.) The emperors of Germany and Brazil were among the brilliant audience for the first of the three cycles; Ludwig returned for the third. For the most part the reception was ecstatic, though Wagner himself saw all too many flaws and failures. When it was all over and the money had been counted, the deficit was found to be nearly 150,000 marks.

Drained, Wagner took his family to Italy for a vacation. They stayed for about a month in a rainy Sorrento (where Wagner and Nietzsche met for the last time), spent another in Rome (where Wagner met Sgambati **[1385]** and persuaded Schott to publish him), paused briefly in Florence, and returned to Munich for Christmas. Wagner had thought of his festival as symbolic of Germany's discovery of her national identity and assumed that his country would offer him material thanks. Instead it offered him louder and shriller attacks. Nevertheless he turned to *Parsifal,* which, with its summation of his religious views, he had had in mind for many years. To makes ends meet and pay off his debts, he began negotiating with various theaters about productions of the *Ring,* only to run afoul of the ever more eccentric Ludwig, who insisted that he was the sole owner of the rights.

In 1877 Wagner agreed to conduct twenty concerts at the Royal Albert Hall in London. Assuming they sold out, he was told he should clear 10,000 pounds. When he got there in April, it eventuated that the house was only available for eight concerts and that the 2,000 choicest seats were privately owned and would bring in nothing. In the end, Wagner paid his soloists out of his pocket and netted only 700 pounds, all of which he used to start a subscription to pay off the Bayreuth debt. A group of Londoners, mortified by his bad luck, raised another 500 pounds. The Germans launched another salvo of near-libelous attacks. It was not until Ludwig renegotiated his loan in March 1878, providing that it might be repaid through royalties from the operas, that Wagner was able to breathe easier.

Sensing that he was now in a race with time, the composer devoted most of the next three years to *Parsifal*, though he also contributed some articles to the new *Bayreuther Tageblatt*, which was, in effect, the organ of the Wagner Societies. There was at the outset of this period a last brief amatory flareup in a sort of epistolary romance with Judith Gautier, daughter of the poet Théophile Gautier and ex-wife of Catulles Mendès. Cosima seems to have known it would flicker out harmlessly. Then Wagner's health began to go—a digestive ailment that had plagued him for some years and then signs of a failing heart. In 1880 and again in 1881, he took his household south to Italy and Sicily for the winters. He found himself increasingly disenchanted with the direction that was being taken by the new Germany. He (a lifelong animal lover) also devoted some time to campaigning against vivisection.

Parsifal was completed at last in Palermo on January 13, 1882, and Wagner came home in May. Once more thanks to King Ludwig, performances were assured, and the premiere came on July 26. There were seventeen subsequent performances that summer, during the last of which the composer took over the podium from the ailing Levi. In the end, Ludwig turned over to Wagner and his heirs all rights to the work. In September the Wagner household returned to Italy, this time taking over the Palazzo Vendramin in Venice. For Cosima's birthday-Christmas present, Wagner arranged a performance at the Teatro La Fenice of his early C-major symphony. The following February 13, after a day of vague indisposition, he suffered a major heart attack at his desk and died in her arms. He was buried, as he had planned from the time he had laid out Wahnfried, in the garden there. Cosima held out for nearly fifty years as the guardian of the Bayreuth Festivals, abetted by her son Siegfried (1869–1930), who also became a (minor) composer, primarily of operas.

RECORDINGS: Curiously, no single Wagnerian opera was recorded complete before the invention of long-playing records. Since then, all the standard ones have each had a number of recordings. *Rienzi*, however, has only appeared once in a commercial version (not particularly well performed). There are excellent "unofficial" representations of *Die Feen, Das Liebesverbot*, and even the *Hochzeit* fragments from BBC broadcasts. Nonoperatic works are represented by the symphony, the *Polonia* and *Faust* overtures, the Weber *Trauermusik*, the *Siegfried Idyll*, the *Centennial, Kaiser*, and *Huldigungs* marches, *Das Liebesmahl der Apostel*, all of the surviving piano music, and most of the songs. Some of the choral music remains unrecorded. (There are several recordings of Siegfried Wagner's instrumental music, notably the 1915 Concerto for Violin.)

[1231] FRY, William Henry
JOURNALIST, CRITIC LECTURER
BORN: Philadelphia, August 10, 1813
DIED: St. Croix, Virgin Islands, September 21, 1864

After a period of relative quiescence, American music returned to life with William Henry Fry. The son of the publisher of the successful *National Gazette,* he had a classical academic education at Mount St. Mary's School, Emmitsburg, Maryland, where he began composing. (He had managed to learn piano by eavesdropping on his brother's lessons.) He then studied with Leopold Meignen, a Philadelphia music publisher with credentials from the Paris Conservatoire. When he embarked on a newspaper career at nineteen, he had written three orchestra overtures, one of which had been played by a local orchestra. In 1844, having abandoned one attempt at an opera and seen another through, he became editor of the *Public Ledger.* In June 1845 Seguin's opera troupe put on his third attempt, *Leonora* (libretto by Fry's brother, after Bulwer-Lytton), at the Chestnut Street Theater. It enjoyed twelve performances and was later revived in New York; it was apparently the first opera by an American to be staged publicly. (Fry was a great one for vernacular opera.)

In 1846 Fry went to Europe as a foreign correspondent, chiefly for the New York *Tribune.* He participated in European musical life, continued to compose, found a friend in Berlioz [1175], but discovered that money would not buy a production there of *Leonora.* After six years he came home and settled in as the *Tribune's* music critic. In November 1852 he inaugurated, at his own expense, an ambitious lecture series in Metropolitan Hall that covered nothing less than the whole history of music, illustrated by "a corps of principal Italian vocalists; a grand chorus of one hundred singers; an orchestra of eighty performers; a military band of fifty performers." At the then-enormous price of five dollars a seat, the house sold out. The final lecture was a stirring attack on the musical establishment for giving native composers a raw deal, which won sympathy from some and ruffled the feathers of others. A year later, when P. T. Barnum brought over Berlioz's sometime partner Louis Antoine Jullien and his orchestra, Fry got them to perform his symphonies *Santa Claus* and *A Day in the Country,* which drew journalistic thunderbolts from the opposition, and gave rise to a brisk little paper-war. (Fry's other symphonies include *The Breaking Heart, Childe Harold, Niagara,* and *Hagar in the Wilderness.)* A final opera, *Notre Dame of Paris,* had a showing in Philadelphia in May 1864. By then Fry was mortally ill of tuberculosis, to which he succumbed that December in the Virgin Islands, where he had sought a cure. Fry, though no great composer, proved an encouragement to later Americans. Much of his music—alas!—has vanished.

RECORDINGS: On records Ivan Davis plays his only known piano piece, *Adieu.* The Society for the Preservation of the American Musical Heritage once recorded the *Santa Claus Symphony.*

[1232] VERDI, Giuseppe Fortunino Francesco (Vâr'-dē, Jōō-sep'-pā Fôr-tōō-nē'-nō Frán-chäs'-kō)
BORN: Le Roncole, October 9/10, 1813
DIED: Milan, January 27, 1901

From the fadeout of Donizetti [1155] to the advent of Puccini [1511], Giuseppe Verdi bestrode the Italian operatic scene like a colossus. After his death it became briefly fashionable to sneer at much of his work as being best suited for barrel organs, but he is now seen as the apex of the nineteenth-century Italian tradition and the greatest Italian music dramatist since Monteverdi [333]. Endowed with superb melodic invention, passion, and a sense of the theatrical, he learned how, without slighting his singers or breaking with the basic conventions, to weld all parts of his creations (and not least the orchestra) into powerful dramatic statements about human life.

Verdi was a very private man, and there is much we shall never know about him; moreover his own accounts of himself are not always to be trusted. For example, whatever their ultimate origins, his immediate forebears were small freeholders rather than the simple peasants he made them out to be. His father, Carlo, inherited his home and place of business from *his* father. Situated in isolation from the village, at the intersection of roads to Parma and Busseto, the Verdi home served the neighborhood as a sort of corner grocery and wine shop. Carlo's wife, *née* Luigia Uttini, whom he had married in 1805, was the daughter of another such entrepreneur. Since Verdi was born on an autumn evening and it was often customary to consider the new day begun at nightfall, the actual date of his birth remains ambiguous. The community being under French occupation, the official records list him as "Joseph Fortunin François." Save for a younger mentally retarded sister, who died in her teens, he was an only child.

It was soon seen that the child was musical, and he was given lessons by the village organist, Pietro Baistrocchi. To facilitate his practice, his parents found him an old spinet which a neighbor put in running order. On Baistrocchi's death in 1822, Verdi took over his church duties, which he kept up after being sent, a year later, to live in Busseto and study at the local *ginnasio,* walking the not-very-great distance (9 km. round-trip) every Sunday and feast day. Once, in the dark and mist of a winter morning, he fell into one of the irrigation ditches that lace the plain, and had to be rescued. Though the priests at the school tried to talk him into a clerical commitment, the call of music was too strong, and he was soon studying with Ferdinando Provesi, who ran a music school and conducted the "philharmonic society" (town band) in Busseto. By 1829 he was acting as Provesi's assistant and composing. Two years later he was taken into the home of Antonio Barezzi, a prosperous wholesale grocer and patron of things musical in Busseto, where he tutored Barezzi's lovely elder daughter Margherita. When the two inevitably fell in love, Barezzi approved but insisted that Verdi complete his musical education before he married.

Barezzi, in fact, agreed to support him as a student at the Milan Conservatory. When that institution, however, refused in 1832 to accept him (they said he was too old and not a Lombard citizen), Barezzi upped the ante to permit him to study privately with Vincenzo Lavigna (1776–1836), a composer of old-fashioned operas. A year later Provesi died, but before Verdi could claim his place, the church faction managed to bring in one of their own named Ferrari, and open war raged (even to a fistfight in the church) between Verdists and Ferrarists. Meanwhile in Milan, called on in an emergency to direct a rehearsal of Haydn's **[871]** *Creation,* Verdi had proved so impressive that he had been asked to conduct the public performance and so won a measure of fame there. He came home in 1835, to become—after the government had intervened and Ferrari had beaten a retreat—civic *maestro* at 657 lire a year. He and Margherita were married in May 1836.

Though there is a mystery about its possible predecessors, Verdi's earliest surviving opera is *Oberto, conte di San Bonifacio.* He had apparently contemplated its production in one of the smaller Milan theaters, but he was suddenly approached by Bartolomeo Merelli, director of La Scala, who wanted it for the spring of 1839. One of the scheduled singers was the soprano Giuseppina Strepponi, then at the height of her brief career. She was much taken with the score, but the illness of another singer necessitated that the work be postponed until fall, when she was no longer available. Unveiled finally on November 13, *Oberto* was a sufficient success to win publication by Giovanni Ricordi and a commission for three more operas from Merelli.

In the meantime, Margherita had borne Verdi two children—Virginia in March 1837 and a son, Icilio, sixteen months later. When Virginia sickened and died in August, Verdi resigned his job and moved the rest of his family to Milan. There, three weeks before the *Oberto* premiere, Icilio followed his sister. No doubt the composer was saddened, but infant mortality was common, and he had a new opera, a light comedy called *Un Giorno di regno (A One-day Reign)* to write. But in the process, he himself suffered a severe bout of sickness. Then in May 1840 Margherita took to her bed with a mysterious "brain fever" that took an alarming turn. In mid-June Barezzi was summoned and arrived on the eighteenth just in time to see her die. The despairing Verdi returned to Bussetto and somehow managed to finish his composition in time for its September 5 premiere. It failed dismally, for whatever reason, though it has since proved viable, if not a masterpiece. Verdi is supposed to have declared that he was through. If he thought so, Merelli was determined otherwise. In any case Verdi returned to Milan, where he rejected a proposed *Il Proscritto,* later taken up by Nicolai **[1212]**. Merelli pressed on him *Nabucodonosor (Nebuchadnezzar,* better known today as *Nabucco),* a libretto by the flamboyant playwright and composer Temistocle Solera, who had contributed something to *Oberto.* (Oddly, Nicolai had rejected this

work). The legend goes that Verdi's eye happened to fall on the chorus of captive Hebrews, *"Va, pensiero, sull' ali dorate"* ("Go, my thoughts, on golden wings"), and he became so inspired that he began working at white heat. Evidence, however, suggests that it was a matter of weeks or months before he seriously involved himself with the task.

Whatever the truth, *Nabucco,* premiered on March 9, 1842, was a simon-pure triumph. The chorus, in whose homesick longing for freedom and the fatherland the Austrian-ruled Lombards saw their own feeling reflected, became a rallying cry. Strepponi was cast in the taxing role of Abigaille; but her voice was going, and her career petered out in the provinces, despite Verdi's efforts to help, four years later. They seem to have met for the first time during rehearsals. Her affair with the tenor Napoleone Moriani— by whom she bore a son, Camillino, and another child who probably died in infancy— had ended shortly before, but there seems to be no hint of any personal liaison with Verdi at this time.

Verdi's next effort for Merelli was *I Lombardi alla prima Crociata (The Lombards at the First Crusade).* The text, again by Solera, was based on a poem by Tommaso Grossi, a friend of the great novelist Alessandro Manzoni. *I Lombardi* was Verdi's first opera to deal openly with Italians united in a common cause and, incredibly, his only one from an Italian literary source. Objections, however, came from the Church rather than the civil authorities. Hearing that a baptism (a sacrament) was to be enacted on the stage, the local archbishop demanded an investigation. But the police chief was an opera lover, and he passed it with only a few token changes. *I Lombardi,* which opened on February 11, 1843, was received with the wildest enthusiasm.

Merelli seems to have been both a tightwad and a conman, and, having fulfilled his obligation to him, Verdi turned to the Teatro La Fenice in Venice, agreeing to oversee *Lombardi* (which, to everyone's surprise, was not liked) and write a new work. For this, he jettisoned Solera, who liked to have his own way, and turned to Francesco Maria Piave, an amateur whose chief asset, in Verdi's eyes, was his willingness to do what he was asked. When a Walter Scott spinoff, variously called *Allan Cameron* and *Cromwell,* failed to take shape, the composer happily seized the suggestion of the Fenice's impresario, the Marchese Mocenigo, that they try Victor Hugo's play *Hernani,* whose initial tempestuous performance in Paris thirteen years earlier had ushered in the era of romantic drama. *Ernani*, as the opera became known, had to do some fancy footwork to get through a gantlet of censors, a disapproving Hugo, and a Venetian operatic public in a belligerent mood, but it triumphed on March 9, 1844, and was soon announcing its composer's arrival around the world.

When the Roman censors rather predictably rejected a *Lorenzino de' Medici* proposed for the Teatro Argentina (Lorenzino assassinated his relative, the despotic Duke Alessandro), Verdi returned to Byron's *The Two Foscari*, which he had considered for the Fenice earlier. (It deals with the Richard Nixon of Venice, the only doge ever forced to resign.) The audience, miffed over an unannounced rise in ticket prices, did not receive *I due Foscari* (Verdi's title) very well when it opened on November 3. Verdi was stunned, but later blamed himself for writing too gloomy an opera. In the meantime, however, he had yielded to Merelli's importunings for one for the road and was again collaborating with Solera, this time on a work about Joan of Arc. Though Solera knew Schiller's play, he claimed his treatment of the story was his own idea, which it probably was. In spite of a shabby production and an inferior cast, the public cheered the resultant *Giovanna d'Arco* on February 15, 1845. But the Milan critics were patronizing, and when Merelli and Ricordi arranged publication without consulting the composer, Verdi, tired and ailing, swore never to return to La Scala.

His next commission took him to the Teatro San Carlo in Naples—a theater that would also give him trouble. When the house librettist Salvatore Cammarano (author of Donizetti's *Lucia di Lammermoor)* suggested they work on Voltaire's problematic *Alzire*, a play about the Incas (thought a joke by some), Verdi atypically agreed without protest. The *Alzira* libretto was so brief that the management had to ask for an overture (not in the original contract) to make an evening of it. Verdi's current poor health forced a postponement, but there was little enthusiasm on the opening night (August 12), and less at the Rome and Milan productions. Again the composer was hurt, and again he later took the blame ("really ugly," he called the work—and *Alzira* remains his least-known opera). It was, in fact, not recorded commercially until very recently.

These may have been "years in the galley," as Verdi termed them, but though he was perhaps writing too much too fast, he had become world-famous. Around this time he sold the Paris production rights to his operas to Léon Escudier, and those for

London to Benjamin Lumley (who was pleading for ten new works for that city). Meanwhile something else had to be written for La Fenice. He had hit on a German romantic drama *Attila,* by Zacarias Werner, E. T. A. Hoffmann's [1086] odd friend, and entrusted the libretto to Solera. When that worthy decamped to Spain without warning, leaving his final act in draft, Verdi, in the edgy and half-sick state he had learned to expect with each new creative effort, called in Piave. Solera was outraged and the association ended right there. The play was radically changed to appeal to rising Italian patriotism. One sees, for instance, the founding of Venice by refugee monks, and the assassination of the invader by a fiery-eyed Italian beauty. Poorly sung, the premiere (March 17, 1846) was less triumphant than later performances, which fanned audiences to a frenzy, especially at the point where the Roman general, Ezio, tells the Hun, "You may have the universe, but leave Italy to me!"

Shortly afterward Giuseppina Strepponi retired and went to Paris to open a vocal studio, leaving her surviving child in Milan under the eye of Giovannina Lucca, wife of the publisher Francesco Lucca, a rival of the Ricordis. Aggressive and ambitious, Signora Lucca (who, as a widow, took over the business and scored a great coup by acquiring the Italian rights to Wagner's [1230] operas) had decided that her husband should be Verdi's publisher and set about to hound the composer into agreeing. Ricordi's alleged treachery in the *Giovanna d'Arco* affair played into her hands: Verdi signed *Attila* over to Lucca and promised him two more operas. However, instead of setting to work, he produced medical evidence that he was ill and marched off to a spa with the poet Andrea Maffei, who had just separated from his wife, the Countess Clarina Maffei, a longtime patroness of the composer. Verdi found himself not so sick as he had thought. Bored, he talked Maffei into working up Schiller's *Die Räuber (The Bandits)* for Lucca and for the Teatro della Pergola in Florence, and went home to Milan to begin work. But it turned out that the Pergola did not have appropriate singers. A lifelong devotee of Shakespeare, Verdi had been discussing the possibilities of *Macbeth* with Maffei, but it was Piave he now called in to work on the play.

Undoubtedly, Verdi knew what he was doing. Piave was a good craftsman with words, but Verdi was increasingly sure of his dramatic needs and from now on was to make constant and sometime stringent demands on the timid and pliable poet. Here Verdi himself dictated the action and characterizations and, apparently, when Piave could not please him, called in Maffei. He was particularly proud of his conception of "Lady," as he called Mrs. Macbeth, and he bullyragged his cast through innumerable rehearsals at the Pergola in the winter of 1847. After the March 14 premiere, he was called out for twenty-five curtain calls. The next morning, however, he was outraged to read that he did not understand Shakespeare! He was also outraged by Lucca's high-handed dealings with *Attila* and the upcoming Schiller opera, and turned *Macbeth* over to Ricordi, who, once the Lucca contract was met, was to remain his publisher.

The Schiller piece, now transmogrified into *I Masnadieri,* had meanwhile been promised to Lumley and was to involve Verdi's first foreign premiere. He finished it within a few weeks and set out for London with his secretary, factotum, and sometime pupil, Emanuele Muzio. Verdi stopped in Paris and sent Muzio ahead to scout what had been reported as major impediments to the production. But, told that all was in order, he himself reached London on June 3. He was delighted with everything but the summer heat. Lumley had rounded up a cast that included Jenny Lind and Luigi Lablache, the basso of the great *Puritani* quartet and Queen Victoria's voice teacher. The queen and her consort headed the glittering audience that thronged Her Majesty's Theatre on July 22 and gave the opera an ovation. But the critics were not enthusiastic —one called it the worst opera of his experience—and interest quickly waned. But Lumley and Verdi were satisfied, and Verdi contemplated the offer of the musical directorship of the theater: a new opera once a year, eight months of conducting and administrative work, and an enormous salary. But insurmountable problems (not the least of them Lucca) prevented his acceptance.

His immediate obligations discharged, Verdi returned to Paris at the end of July, where finally, after several false starts, he was slated to deliver up an opera in the fall. Pleading lack of time, he agreed to overhaul *Lombardi* (for the price of a new work). Alphonse Royer and Gustave Vaëz (authors of Donizetti's *Favorite)* whipped him up a new libretto, *Jérusalem,* which had only the crusades in common with its predecessor, necessitating a radical reworking of the music. The successful production on November 26 caused King Louis-Philippe to order an encore (two acts only) at the Tuileries and won the composer membership in the *Légion d'honneur* (of which he eventually became a grand commander).

Ricordi dedicated the *Jérusalem* score to Giuseppina Strepponi, whose presence in Paris undoubtedly kept Verdi there. To rid himself of the incubus of Lucca, he worked on *Il Corsaro,* the libretto that Piave had derived from Byron's *The Corsair*—and which Verdi had earlier rejected in favor of *Macbeth.* That winter, 1847–48, he persuaded his father-in-law to visit him. Happily, Barezzi was delighted with "Signora Peppina." Forced to stay on into the spring by a heavy cold, Verdi was mildly amused by the revolution that erupted in Paris. But he was not at all amused by the uprising in Milan and the Venetian breakaway that followed, and hurried back to Busseto in March. A few years before, he had bought a *palazzo* there and some land near Le Roncole. This last he now traded in on the Villa Sant' Agata, an estate between Busseto and Cremona. Meanwhile political events had forced a postponement of the Trieste production of *Corsaro,* but the revolt was looking more and more like a lost cause. In late May Verdi returned to Paris and took a house with Peppina in suburban Passy (an augury of Alfredo and Violetta in *La Traviata).* That summer Italian resistance to Austria collapsed. The *Corsaro* premiere, directed by Luigi Ricci [1183], occurred on October 25. Verdi did not attend, which was probably just as well, since the thing was a disaster and the work closed after only three showings.

Because of the stringent censorship there, Verdi had put off writing a new work requested by the San Carlo in Naples, and when, following the 1848 revolution, the house acquired a new management, he decided that he had no further obligation. Instead, he and Cammarano turned to Joseph Méry's play *La Bataille de Toulouse,* for a work which Verdi proposed to let Ricordi peddle where he might. The result was *La Battaglia di Legnano,* which, in depicting the defeat of a German emperor by Lombards, was an out-and-out incitement to Italian nationalists. Its success was assured when it opened on January 27, 1849 in a Rome on the verge of declaring its short-lived republican independence. Though it owes something to Rossini's [1143] *Guillaume Tell, Legnano* foreshadows Verdi's middle-period maturity. Meanwhile the Neapolitans had turned nasty and were threatening to jail poor Cammarano (who had a brood to support) for breach of contract. Avoiding the impulse to follow with another patriotic piece, Verdi and his collaborator agreed on Schiller's *Kabale und Liebe (Intrigue and Love).* Though it has to do with small-time tyranny, *Luisa Miller* (as the opera became known) is the first of

Verdi's serious operas to focus on ordinary people of reasonable contemporaneity (though it has something of the "happy peasant" syndrome of, say, Bellini's [1164] *Sonnambula).*

At the end of July Verdi and Peppina left Paris for Italy—he to settle in Busseto, she to find a home for Camillino in Florence (where he probably died a few years later). Then, to the horror of the Bussetani, she moved into Verdi's *palazzo.* Her fellow townspeople made it clear in every way that she was not welcome. It is argued that she refused to regularize the union because she was ashamed of her past and felt herself unworthy of the man she adored; considering her superior intelligence, one finds it hard to believe. In October she went to Parma to stay with her mother while Verdi and Barezzi went to Naples for the rehearsals. The *Luisa* premiere on December 8 was a fair success, though the audience did not care for the final act. But the work was not recognized as one of Verdi's most accomplished efforts thus far until the present day. Even so, it fared much better than its successor. Verdi was determined to make up to Trieste for the black eye inflicted by the *Corsaro.* Though he was eager to get at the *King Lear* of which he had been dreaming for some time (and never wrote), he and Piave eventually settled on a French play, *Le Pasteur (The Pastor,* also called *Stiffelius)* by Émile Souvestre and Eugène Bourgeois, which deals with a German Lutheran pastor who forgives his adulterous wife. Though *Stiffelio* reflects the new Verdian "realistic" bent (and perhaps his own feelings), it was a strange choice for an Italian Catholic audience. The censors agreed and forced changes that made nonsense of the opera. As a result, *Stiffelio's* reception, at its November 16 premiere, was not enthusiastic, and it enjoyed little subsequent production.

In deciding on this work, Verdi had reluctantly rejected Hugo's *Le Roi s'amuse (The King Is Amused),* a melodrama about a hunchbacked jester's attempted revenge on his master, François I, for the rape of his daughter. Now he decided it was just what he wanted. Though the Paris authorities had banned the play after its first performance (and did not permit it for fifty years), those in Venice passed Verdi's proposal. But as the scheduled time approached, they suddenly rescinded the permit on the grounds of immorality and obscenity—though what was really at issue was a question of *lese majesty.* There was a long hassle, which was finally resolved when Verdi agreed to changes, the most important of which involved moving the scene to Mantua and making the king a

duke (identity ambiguous). Further problems of casting and rehearsal delayed the opening until February II, 1851. Perhaps what captivated the audiences were the melodrama and the tunes (Verdi had kept *"La donna è mobile"* under tight wraps until the premiere.) The critics, for the most part, disapproved. But what ensured the continuous success of *Rigoletto* is its taut musicodramatic inevitability, and everyone is now agreed that it signaled Verdi's coming of age.

Since they had settled in Busseto, Peppina and Verdi had been virtually isolated from the citizenry, who took the moral stance of Verdi's last two operas as evidence of his depravity. Even Barezzi at one point seems to have sided with the opposition. Shortly after the *Rigoletto* premiere, they gave it up and moved to Sant' Agata, where Verdi could be assured of uninterrupted time for composing and where he devoted his free hours to improving the land. Having found his own voice and established his artistic position, he could now afford to create more carefully. He had agreed with Cammarano in principle that the source of their next work was to be the ultraromantic *El Trovador (The Troubadour)* by a contemporary Spaniard, Antonio García Gutiérrez. Verdi was fascinated by the character on whom the plot hinges, a half-mad old Gypsy woman driven equally by mother love for her son and the need to avenge the death of her own mother. (A parental motif runs through many of Verdi's operas, perhaps stemming from his own childlessness; in this case it perhaps also reflected the death of his mother in 1851.) Cammarano balked at the suggested treatment of the material (it was customary to give the librettist top billing in Italy), but Verdi, as he was to do from now on, got his way and virtually dictated his wishes to his collaborator. But Cammarano, as he usually did, dragged his heels, and the composer probably had to work even more slowly than he had intended. In the winter of 1851–52 he and Peppina returned to Paris, where he contracted another new opera for some future date. There he was much excited by a new play, *La Dame aux caméllias (The Camellia Lady),* a *pièce à clef* by the younger Alexandre Dumas based on his unhappy affair with the young demimondaine "Marie" Duplessis. Verdi had already been moved by its novelistic prototype—and he almost certainly saw something of Peppina in the female protagonist's anomalous social position. At any rate he began rethinking the story in operatic terms. In March the pair returned to Sant' Agata. They were by now reconciled with Barezzi, and there were frequent visitors from elsewhere, though

Muzio, so long a part of Verdi's existence, had gone to Brussels to direct the Italian opera.

In the middle of the summer Verdi was aghast to read in a magazine that Cammarano was dead. *Il Trovatore,* though still incomplete, was scheduled for a premiere at the Teatro Apollo in Rome. He called in a young poet, Leone Bardare, to put the final touches on the libretto, and the work reached the stage on January 19, 1853. The house was sold out, and Verdi enjoyed one of the most unequivocal triumphs of his entire career. Though the work has since been a target for jokes about silly opera plots, it has held on steadily, and over its first hundred years there must have been few in the Western world who could not recognize at least one of its tunes.

While *Trovatore* was taking final shape, Verdi and Piave were already hard at work on the Dumas opus, now designated as *La Traviata (The Errant Woman* or *The Sinner),* scheduled for La Fenice in March. It fared by no means so well as its predecessor. To begin with, its basis—a sympathetic treatment of a contemporary courtesan dying of tuberculosis—was touchy. Oddly most people seem to have been more put off by her contemporaneity and her disease than by her morals. Much to Verdi's disgust, the Fenice decided to set the production in the early eighteenth century. On the first night, March 6, the baritone was out of voice, and the chubby soprano gave no illusion of frailty. The audience sat on its hands. Verdi, who believed in the work, shrugged and saw it redeem itself a year later at the Teatro San Benedetto. A remarkable development of the old-fashioned "numbers" opera, *Traviata* continues to delight musically, but all too often it fails to capitalize on its inherent drama.

By the time of the San Benedetto performance, the composer and his lady were back in Paris to begin the long-promised French work, whose libretto would be, inevitably, by Scribe. Nothing, however, had been decided by midsummer save that it would be a grand opera in five acts. Verdi then decided to force the issue. He rejected Scribe's offer of *Le Duc d'Albe* (which the late Donizetti had failed to complete), countering with "something Sicilian." The result was *Les Vêpres siciliennes (The Sicilian Vespers),* loosely based on the 1283 Sicilian revolt against the Angevins—for whose libretto Scribe borrowed rather heavily from *Le Duc d'Albe.* The struggle over the book was followed by a struggle with the cast. The venture almost collapsed when the prima donna took an unannounced vacation with her

lover and Verdi threatened to go home. Thus matters dragged on until June 6, 1855, which date happily coincided with a World's Fair in Paris and assured an audience. Verdi had made his piece with a format that he found uncomfortable, but the French liked the product. However, such a subject was, of course, unthinkable in Italy, and the opera played there in a bowdlerized form as *Giovanna di Guzman* until after the unification. Though there have been repeated revivals, it has yet, however, to become a popular favorite.

Once again bypassing *King Lear,* Verdi and Piave decided in 1856 to turn to another García Gutiérrez play, *Simon Bocanegra,* about a patriotic pirate who became, to his undoing, doge of Genoa—this, using the spelling *Simon Boccanegra,* also for La Fenice. Hardly had they begun work when the composer had to go back to Paris to try to deal with piracy of another kind: unauthorized and distorted productions of his operas by the Théâtre Italien. The most positive result was a commission from the Opéra for a French version of *Trovatore* (with, of course, a ballet). Meanwhile he was dissatisfied with the work that Piave was submitting and, detained in Paris, he had the exiled poet Giuseppe Montanelli reshape the *Simon Boccanegra* libretto. He then sent it to Piave, saying that if he wished to claim authorship there would be no objections. Piave was wounded, and it took Verdi a while to patch matters up. In the end it was probably the libretto as much as anything else that was responsible for the work's failure both in Venice, on March 12, 1857, and two years later at La Scala.

Deciding to give the *Stiffelio* music another chance, Verdi now had Piave cobble up a completely new libretto, based on Edward Bulwer-Lytton's 1848 novel *Harold, the Last of the Saxon Kings,* about the Harold who died at Hastings in 1066. Set in "Kenth" and near "Loch Lomond," its likeness to its model appears mostly coincidental. *Aroldo* was successfully premiered in Rimini on August 16, 1857, but it soon fell on hard times from which it has never really recovered. Meanwhile Verdi was convinced that he had found, in the Venetian playwright Antonio Somma, just the man for *Lear,* and, by dint of much coaching from the sidelines, got a libretto out of him. A production was planned at the San Carlo in Naples, but the opera once again failed to develop. To fulfill the contract, Somma agreed to rework Scribe's *Gustave III ou Le bal masqué* (about the assassination of that Swedish monarch), which Auber [1103] had set twenty-five years earlier. As usual, obtaining just the libretto he had in mind gave the composer trouble, but oddly the Neapolitan authorities approved it. But while the opera was in the making, attempts to kill King Ferdinando and the visiting Napoleon III changed the picture, and demands were made for wholesale changes, including the deletion of the crucial ball scene. Verdi thereupon offered the work to the Teatro Apollo in Rome. Suit and countersuit followed, but the public vociferously sided with the composer, and the San Carlo let him go. The demands of the Roman censors proved not insurmountable. What the first-night audience saw on February 17, 1859, was the assassination of an English governor of a highly unlikely eighteenth-century Boston. Though there was some grumbling about the "Wagnerian" orchestration, *Un Ballo in maschera* was Verdi's first considerable success since *Trovatore* and has retained its popularity and effectiveness.

In the meantime the political situation in Italy was moving to a climax. The Sardinian premier, Count Cavour, convinced that his king, Vittorio Emanuele, presented the only possible focus for Italian freedom and unity, won military backing from Emperor Napoleon III (if not from his people). Soon after Verdi and Peppina had returned to Sant' Agata, he enticed the Austrians to invade Piedmont on April 29. By the twenty-fourth of June they were demoralized. At that point, Napoleon III, frightened by Prussian rumblings and finding himself upstaged by Vittorio Emanuele, secretly made a treaty with Austria, giving Lombardy to Piedmont but allowing them to retain Venice. The Italians were furious, and Cavour retired in protest to Switzerland. A republican at heart, Verdi was also a pragmatist and had backed him all the way. Perhaps it was prescience that caused him late in August to slip away with Peppina to Savoy, near the Swiss border, and marry her. On September 3 Busseto elected Verdi to the new Parmese-Modenese Assembly, which dispatched him to Turin to request union with Piedmont. The king acceded, recalled Cavour, ceded Nice and Savoy to France, and took the Papal States into the new Italian kingdom—to the outrage of Pius IX, who locked himself in the Vatican and excommunicated everybody. Cavour persuaded Verdi (who protested that he was only a musical farmer) to run for the chamber of deputies. He was elected by a three-to-two margin and took his seat on February 18, 1860. He regularly voted with Cavour. But the premier died unexpectedly in June, and Verdi withdrew from further participation in the legislature and eventually resigned in 1865.

Politics and a large and costly program of improvements at Sant' Agata had kept Verdi from his music for two years. Now, in the summer of 1861, he agreed to write an opera for Enrico Tamberlik, leading tenor of the Imperial Opera at St. Petersburg. Verdi said that his choice was Hugo's *Ruy Blas.* The Russian censor said it wasn't his, and they finally settled on another Spanish melodrama, *Don Alvaro,* by the Duke of Rivas. Piave was again the nominal librettist, though Verdi once more got help from others, notably Maffei. Verdi completed the piano score in November and took Peppina to St. Petersburg for the preparations. But in February the prima donna fell ill, necessitating a postponement until fall, and the Verdis left for London, where he was to represent his country with a composition for the International Exhibition. (Others invited were Auber, Meyerbeer **[1142]**, and William Sterndale Bennett **[1246]**.) Verdi's offering was a patriotic cantata, *Inno delle Nazioni (Hymn of the Nations),* to a text by young Arrigo Boito **[1393]**, for tenor, chorus, and orchestra. But as it happened not only did Michael Costa **[1193]** refuse to conduct the piece, on the grounds that a march was what was wanted, but he also refused to lend Tamberlik, the intended soloist, for a substitute performance at Her Majesty's. (Verdi had to settle for a soprano.)

At summer's end the Verdis returned to Russia and saw *La Forza del destino* onstage on November 10. It was applauded, but everyone thought it too long and the audience was puzzled by the choppy alternation of melodrama and genre scenes, with an admixture of comedy. Verdi was displeased with the ending in which the three principals died; and, with Antonio Ghislanzoni as librettist, Verdi rewrote it for La Scala in 1869. But *Forza* continues to be butchered for the sake of brevity, and only recently has anyone attempted to stage what Verdi originally had in mind. After the premiere the Verdis went to Spain for a production in Madrid, did some sightseeing, and went home. A year later Verdi returned to Paris to prepare a revival of *Vêpres.* But the Paris Opéra's orchestra balked at rehearsals. The regular conductor Dietsch—who had presided over the *Tannhäuser* massacre in 1861—called them unnecessary. Verdi, furious, ostentatiously decamped after the first performance. However, he had promised Léon Carvalho to revise *Macbeth* for the Théâtre Lyrique. The sweeping changes resulted in the opera largely as we now know it. But Verdi refused to go back for either rehearsals or public presentation (April 19, 1865). It was just as well. The Parisians did not care for it, and it lasted only fourteen performances. Instead the composer attended to domestic affairs and established the custom of wintering, with his wife, in the Riviera climate of Genoa. There was a rift with Boito when the latter, in an ode to his friend Francesco Faccio, a rising conductor and composer, said unkind things about the Old Guard. In 1864 the Paris Opéra came, hat in hand, to suggest that Verdi set *Judith*, a libretto which the late Meyerbeer had not got around to. Verdi snorted in disbelief. But the door had been reopened, and Escudier, visiting in midsummer 1865, rekindled his interest in Schiller's *Don Carlos*, a work he had considered fifteen years earlier. In November Verdi went back to Paris to be near his librettists, Joseph Méry and Camille du Locle. Work went slowly. Verdi suffered from sore throat and the other psychosomatic symptoms that usually accompanied his composing. Méry, terminally ill, had to give it up. In March Verdi went home, where his work was made uneasy by the mutters of war from the north (which eventually cost Austria Venice). After a brief return to Paris in July, he settled in Cauterets, a French spa in the Pyrenees, to finish his opera. Once rehearsals got under way, there were endless changes and the usual quarrels with the singers. In January 1867 Verdi took time off to mourn his father who had died (at eighty-one) in his absence. Though the *Don Carlos* that was revealed to the world on March 11 was a very long work, much had been trimmed from it. A powerful if diffuse statement about the tyrannies of State and Church, it is now considered by many to be one of Verdi's greatest works. It did not so strike Parisians that first night, some of whom took their cue from the Empress Eugénie, who pointedly turned her back in protest at the Grand Inquisitor scene. This scene was quickly dropped—though in London, in June, Michael Costa [1193], who had once written a *Don Carlo* himself, made a success of it. (Verdi went on tinkering with it. In 1884 he lopped off the first act and tightened up other parts for La Scala, producing the version most commonly played until quite recently.)

Back in Busseto, Barezzi had taken to his bed. He died on July 21 as Verdi softly sang the *Nabucco* chorus to him. The composer was desolated. On the positive side, that summer the Verdis adopted a little girl, Filomena Verdi, the daughter of a poor relation, whom they called "Maria." But tragedy struck again in December: Piave was felled by a stroke and vegetated for eight years before dying. As he had done with Cammarano's, Verdi helped take care of Piave's family. Early in 1868 *Don Carlos* tri-

umphed at La Scala. The conductor was Angelo Mariani, Verdi's recent conductor of choice and a bosom friend; the Elisabeth of Valois was Mariani's mistress Teresa Stolz, of whom more will be said later. Later that spring Verdi went to Milan to meet one of his real-life heroes, the novelist Alessandro Manzoni, whose historical novel *I promessi sposi* had given Italians a sense of Italianness. It was the first time Verdi had been there since he fell out with Merelli. Verdi was stunned to find that in the interim the graves and remains of Margherita and Icilio had vanished. In the summer, after another series of tensions with the Bussetani, the town tried to make up for its treatment of its favorite son by opening the little Teatro Verdi (for which the composer helped pay).

In November old Rossini died in Paris. Verdi had attended his salons, had corresponded with him, and respected him profoundly. He therefore called on a number of his Italian colleagues to contribute to a *Requiem* in Rossini's memory, for which he himself was writing the final movement, the "Libera me." Others involved were Bazzini [1256], Pedrotti [1252], Petrella [1234], Federico Ricci [1205], and several others beyond the purview of this volume. In the end the work was neither performed nor published. While this was going on, he permitted La Scala at last to produce *La Forza del destino* (somewhat revised), which work until then he had withheld from Italian performance. The prima donna was again Teresa Stolz, who had become identified with Verdi's operas—and, in the yellow press, with their composer. (Verdi and Mariani later became estranged—but whether over her and whether she and Verdi were really lovers are questions that, despite assiduous digging, remain unanswered.)

Meanwhile Camille du Locle, now impresario of the Opéra-Comique, wanted again to collaborate with Verdi. While the latter was mulling over various possibilities (works by Sardou, Nero, Molière's *Tartuffe*), he received and rejected an invitation from the (Turkish) Khedive of Egypt to write an ode celebrating the opening of the Suez Canal. But the khedive seems not to have been discouraged: when the French Egyptologist Auguste Mariette suggested a celebratory opera on a plot he had cooked up, the khedive suggested that he take it up with du Locle, a passionate Egyptophile. Du Locle wrote a scenario and sent it to Verdi (who somehow got the idea it was the khedive's work). He was sufficiently taken with it to agree to turn it into an opera—for 150,000 francs. The khedive did not even blink, and the contract was signed in mid-1870. The librettist was to be Ghislanzoni, who had made the revisions in the *Forza* libretto; in the end, it might be said, Verdi guided his pen for much of the time. Since the composer had no intention of going to Cairo, most of the preparations were made at Sant' Agata and in winter quarters in Genoa. The aftermath of the Franco-Prussian War, however, trapped scenery and costumes in Paris, and the production of *Aida* had to be postponed. Both Stolz and Mariani priced themselves out of it. In the latter instance Verdi was willing to forgive and forget, but Mariani's mortal illness put him out of consideration. Muzio, the next choice, managed to offend the khedive, and Verdi settled for the great contrabass player Bottesini [1278]. Shortly before the premiere, Verdi attended *Lohengrin,* his first encounter in the theater with Wagner, in Bologna. The Cairo performance went smoothly on Christmas Eve 1871, winning the composer a Turkish decoration, but the more important premiere was the one in Milan the following February 7, in which the conductor was Boito's friend, the brilliant Faccio. Stolz, now estranged from the dying Mariani and personally coached by Verdi, was the Aida. Verdi replaced the brief prelude with an overture, which he withdrew as soon as he heard it played. The opening night was one of Verdi's greatest triumphs. *Aida,* the acme of Italianized grand opera, remains a sure-fire favorite, especially where conditions lend themselves to spectacularity, though the music makes it equally welcome in Aachen and Plzeň. But as a matter of fact, the circumstances of its reception, especially in Italy, turned its composer off from further operatic creation for more than a decade. The critical fraternity, much to his disgust, set up a howl of "Wagnerism." Impresarios here and there began to play fast and loose with the structure of the work. And, on the other hand, Verdi's popularity was so great that he was mobbed everywhere he went—and the Stolz "scandal" became the preoccupation of the day. After supervising a few early productions of the new work, he largely retired to his farming.

One such production was in Naples in 1873, where *Aida* was to be premiered in rotation with *Don Carlos.* But in late winter Stolz fell ill, and Verdi and Giuseppina were, so to speak, stuck in their hotel. To while away the time, Verdi wrote a string quartet, which he had performed privately for a small group of friends. He, however, insisted it was only a trifle, and it was three years before Ricordi finally won his permission to publish it.

In May of that same year Alessandro Manzoni died as the result of a fall. Verdi was both deeply moved and outraged at the journalistic sneers at the "old revolutionary." With the *"Libera me"* of the aborted Rossini memorial as a foundation, he proposed to write a Requiem Mass for the first anniversary of Manzoni's death, the music to be copied and printed at his expense, the production paid for by the city of Milan. He wrote most of the rest of the work in Paris in 1873–74, and conducted the premiere at the church of San Marco in Milan on May 22; this he followed with the first of three performances at La Scala. (The others were conducted by Faccio; Stolz was the soprano soloist on all four occasions, and, in fact, gave her farewell performance in a benefit production of the work in 1879, again under Verdi's direction.) Though the *Requiem* was a success (if that word may be used in this context), there were (and still are) those who thought it too secular. (Some of these, such as Hans von Bülow [1310], later changed their minds.) If one accepts it, as one must, as a dramatic commentary on death and the ultimate fate of humanity, perhaps the charge is true; but the sobriquet "Verdi's greatest opera" is not far off the mark.

To all intents and purposes, the Requiem seemed to mark the end of Verdi's creative career. He occupied himself with the farm, oversaw the 1878 wedding of Maria Verdi to his own lawyer's son, Alberto Carrara, and wintered with Giuseppina in Genoa. In 1875 he accepted a largely decorative appointment as a senator in Rome; he shortly resigned it. However, in 1880 he returned to his music, producing additional ballet music for the Opéra's *Aida,* a *Pater noster* for chorus, and an *Ave Maria* for soprano and strings. At a dinner party that same year, Giulio got to talking about the possibilities of Shakespeare's *Othello* as an opera. Seeing that Verdi was listening intently, he sent Faccio around the next day with Boito, who just happened to have a scenario at hand. Verdi read it and said, noncommittally, that it might make a libretto, which Boito, in his methodical way, eventually produced. But instead of embarking on setting it, Verdi enlisted Boito in a complete overhaul of *Simon Boccanegra,* perhaps to see if they could work together. Boito's chief contribution was the magnificent scene in the council chamber that closes Act One. Faccio conducted the successful premiere at La Scala on March 24, 1881, with the French baritone Victor Maurel in the title role and the heroic tenor Francesco Tamagno as Gabriele. The work did not, however, really come into its own for fifty years.

After the *Boccanegra* revision Verdi

seemed again to have forsaken composition, busying himself with the farm and various local philanthropies, including the building of a small hospital. In the interest of their health, the Verdis now began spending part of each summer at the baths of Montecatini. In 1883 the composer roused himself to shorten *Don Carlos* for the La Scala revival and even attended some rehearsals, but it was not until a year later, when he was seventy-one, that he began seriously to consider *Othello,* or *Otello* as it was known in Italian. Shortly afterward, however, a reporter wrote that Boito had said in Naples that he thought he could make a better setting of his libretto. Verdi replied that he was welcome to it and laid his pen down until Boito persuaded him (correctly) that he had been misinterpreted. Soon afterward Verdi had caught the old rhythm again. He found that he had a collaborator who was an artist that would not be bullied and whose ideas were always worth considering. By November 1, 1886, the score was completed. Despite the strictest secrecy, news of the project had leaked and anticipation was electric. The La Scala premiere under Faccio the following February 5 was one prolonged alleluia to the composer. Tamagno's trumpet voice set a standard for the Moor, and Maurel's great dramatic ability brought Iago to vivid life (though Maurel was bitter that it had been decided not to call the opera *Iago).* Some of the critics were their patronizing selves, talking about the substitution of Wagnerian dazzle for loss of inspiration. But most intelligent auditors recognized the work as Verdi's dramatic masterpiece—an opinion that time seems only to confirm.

Verdi, however, found himself depressed —not at the reception, but at the thought that his career was done. Boito went off in romantic pursuit of Eleonora Duse, and Verdi soon settled back into his domestic routine. But the collaboration had excited him, and he began to think that if time permitted he might have a last word to offer the world. Steeped again in Shakespeare, the man who all his life had, upper lip taut, faced the ultimate meaninglessness of existence, found in Falstaff someone who took another view. In 1889 he let Boito know he was willing, but that they must not undertake such a project seriously or publicly. The libretto, to his surprise, took the poet nearly a year to complete. Verdi lost momentum after finishing the first act. But after four months of doing very little, he went into high gear and completed the opera before the end of 1891, finishing the orchestration in the fall a year later. Maurel, for all the impossible demands he made, was inevitable

for the title role. Faccio had in the meantime succumbed in a Milan mental hospital to paresis. Owing to a change of management, there had been doubts about La Scala, but it was there that *Falstaff* saw the light seven years and four days after *Otello.* Its triumph was perhaps more ceremonial than real: the public was not prepared for the subtle masterpiece it got, and even today *Falstaff* remains largely a connoisseur's delight. Verdi's last word was the final fugue for the entire cast on "The world's a joke and man is born a jokester."

Falstaff was in fact the end. In 1894 Verdi wrote a ballet for the Paris premiere of *Otello.* To a *Laudi alla Vergine Maria* for women's voices and a choral *Ave Maria* (on an "enigmatic scale" published in a Milan newspaper), which he had written in 1888, he appended in 1896–97 a big *Te Deum* and a *Stabat Mater* for chorus and orchestra. Though not originally intended as the *4 Sacred Pieces* that they have become, they were first so presented in 1899 at La Scala by Arturo Toscanini, who had played cello in the *Otello* premiere. In 1895, to plans by Boito's brother Camillo, Verdi began the erection, on a piece of Milanese land he had bought in 1889, of a rest home, the Casa di Riposo, for aged musicians. He called it his best composition. It still functions. He suffered in January 1897 what appears to have been a stroke, but he quickly recovered; it was Peppina who went first, dying that November (at eighty-two) of pneumonia. She was his match in everything but creative genius, and her going told on him. Increasingly he found Genoa and Milan more tolerable than Sant' Agata. He spent Christmas 1900 at his hotel in the latter city with Maria Carrara, Teresa Stolz, Boito, and Ricordi. Less than a month later, on January 21, he had a massive stroke but hung on for six more days. Silent crowds waited for the inevitable on streets whose traffic sounds had been deadened with straw. When the end came, by his own wish his body was taken before dawn on January 30 for interment in the Milan cemetery beside Peppina's. A month later both, carried through streets lined with vast mourning crowds, were reburied at the Casa di Riposo to the sound of 800 voices conducted by Toscanini in the *Nabucco* chorus.

RECORDINGS: Only *Jérusalem* lacks a commercial recording. But it, together with the early versions of *Forza, Boccanegra,* a French-language *Vespri,* and *Macbeth,* and a virtually uncut French *Don Carlos* are available "privately." There are also recordings of all of the post-juvenile nonoperatic material save perhaps a few minor vocal pieces, as well as of the added opera ballets, the

Aida overture, and some optional arias. It should also be noted that Tamagno and Maurel left recordings from the two works they created.

[1233] ALKAN (né MORHANGE), Charles-Henri Valentin (Ăl-kăn', Shärl On-rē' Vă-lon-tan')
PIANIST, TEACHER
BORN: Paris, November 30, 1813
DIED: Paris, March 29, 1888

Alkan remains an enigma. In his lifetime he was, through every fault of his own, neglected, and after his death he was forgotten. In this century, interest in him has been kindled by the advocacy of such as Bernard van Dieren [1786] and Kaikhosru Sorabji [1867] and through performances by the likes of Isidore Philipp, Busoni [1577], Egon Petri, Ronald Smith, and Raymond Lewenthal. Together with the variations, fantasias, and salon trifles that were the common coin of his era, he turned out titanic pieces that challenge the ultimate resources of both piano and pianist. His language is individual and sometimes prophetic, but whether his music has staying power remains to be seen.

Alkan came from a Jewish family that, for whatever reason, adopted the name "Alkan." His father ran a school for children of the faith, and most of his own progeny became musicians. Charles Valentin exhibited such prodigious talent that he was enrolled at the Conservatoire at the age of six. Like Thomas [1217], Franck [1284], and Gounod [1258], Alkan studied piano with P. J. G. Zimmermann, and, until he reached early manhood, was a feature of Parisian salons. At twenty he visited London but apparently never left Paris again. He taught part-time at the Conservatoire until 1836. Brilliant and extraordinarily well-read, he numbered Hugo, Liszt [1218], and Delacroix among his friends, as well as such neighbors in the Place d'Orléans as Chopin [1208], George Sand, Alexandre Dumas, and Pauline Viardot. But after 1838 he became increasingly reclusive, hypochondriacal, and housebound. He emerged in 1844–45 for a few concerts, at one of which he, Chopin, Zimmermann, and Pixis [1128] played an eight-hand arrangement of Beethoven's [1063] seventh symphony.

There were other concerts in 1853. For the rest of the time in the quarter century he spent in isolation, he composed much (but published little) and studied (chiefly the Talmud, it is said). He took a few pupils. He never held a steady job or an official post but yearned for recognition by way of a decora-

tion. However, as the story goes, when a delegation arrived unheralded to announce his appointment to the *Légion d'honneur,* it was told to go away because M. Alkan was occupied with digesting his dinner. In 1873 he began giving an annual concert series that ran to the end of his life—and, typically, largely ignored his own music. Tradition has it that in attempting to pull down a Talmud from a top shelf, he toppled the bookcase and was crushed beneath it, but there is no evidence that this story is true. Alkan left a son (illegitimate) and disciple, Élie-Miriam Delaborde (1839–1913), who became well known as a concert pianist.

RECORDINGS: Several pianists in the last few years have devoted LPs to Alkan's music, including such blockbusters as the Symphony for Piano, the Concerto for Piano Solo, the *Quasi-Faust,* and *Le Festin d'Ésope.* (His treatment of "The Eddystone Light" *[Romance du phare d'Eddystone]* is, unhappily, no longer extant.) Also recorded are the Op. 30 Piano Trio, *Sonate de Concert* for cello and piano, and the *Concerto da Camera No. 2* for piano and strings.

[1234] PETRELLA, Errico (Pā-trel'-là, Âr'-rē-kō)
TEACHER
BORN: Palermo, December 10, 1813
DIED: Genoa, April 7, 1877

Forgotten today, Petrella was once one of Verdi's [1232] most formidable rivals (though Verdi thought little of his music). The secret of his success and subsequent eclipse was that he composed à la mode (a rather outmoded mode even then), producing old-fashioned "number" operas with surefire set pieces. Rather precocious, he was yet another product of Zingarelli at the Naples Conservatory, where he also studied with Bellini [1164] and Michael Costa [1193]. His first opera, the comedy *Il Diavolo color di rosa (The Rose-Colored Devil)* was played in Naples when he was only fifteen, winning him applause and expulsion from school. He went on writing comedies until 1839, when he fell out with the theater management and, in pique, retired from the arena to teach voice. However, he came back to opera in 1851 with *Le Precauzioni (The Precautions)*—a great success—and produced 15 more operas before he died. His most durable work was *Jone,* after Bulwer-Lytton's *The Last Days of Pompei,* produced at La Scala in 1858. Eleven years later his *I Promessi sposi (The Betrothed)* from Manzoni's great novel profited briefly from an early example of press agentry, being premiered in Lecco, the chief scene of the book, with the revered author in attendance. Despite his Midas touch, Petrella died in poverty. RECORDINGS: Selections from some of his works (e.g., *Jone, La Contessa d'Amalfi*) may be found on various early vocal records. Recently a complete *Jone* has appeared.

[1235] OESTEN, Theodor (Ös'-ten, Tā'-ō-dôr)
INSTRUMENTALIST, TEACHER
BORN: Berlin, December 31, 1813
DIED: Berlin, March 16, 1870

Oesten grew up in Fürstenwalde, some twenty miles east of Berlin, where one of the municipal musicians taught him proficiency on several instruments. He also began to compose dances and salon pieces during this period. Later he returned to Berlin and underwent more formal training, his teachers including Carl Friedrich Rungenhagen and W. F. E. Bach [1012]. Oesten became a fashionable piano teacher and mass-produced little piano pieces of the variety intended for not very talented young women to please prospective husbands with. RECORDINGS: Hans Kann has recorded one or two of these.

[1236] ERNST, Heinrich Wilhelm (Ârnst, Hīn'-rikh Vil'-helm)
VIOLINIST
BORN: Brno, May 6, 1814
DIED: Nice, October 8, 1865

Ernst studied composition at the Vienna Conservatory with Mozart's [992] old friend, Ignaz Xaver Seyfried. His violin teachers were Joseph Böhm (who also taught Leopold Auer and Joseph Joachim [1321]) and later Joseph Mayseder, the emperor's court violinist. In 1828 Ernst attended one of Paganini's [1106] initial concerts in Vienna and was so impressed that on his concert tours for the next few years, he followed Paganini around Germany, learning from him by observation. Ernst settled in Paris in 1832 for six years, then concertized throughout Europe for another six. He was regarded as Paganini's logical successor in technique, and his superior in tone. Berlioz [1175] devotes several pages of his memoirs to Ernst, whom he admired equally as a man, musician, and composer; they performed Berlioz's *Harold in Italy* together in St. Petersburg. Ernst settled in London in 1855, but shortly afterward failing health terminated his career. Like his idol, he died af-

ter a long illness in Nice. Most of his compositions are showpieces for the violin, though he and Stephen Heller [1229] wrote some piano duets together. RECORDINGS: Aaron Rosand has recorded Ernst's violin concerto, and Ruggiero Ricci his variations on themes from Rossini's *Otello* and on *The Last Rose of Summer*—the last set of variations is dedicated to Antonio Bazzini [1256].

[1237] HENSELT, (Georg Martin) Adolf von (Hen'-zelt, À'-dolf fun)
PIANIST, TEACHER
BORN: Schwabach, May 9, 1814
DIED: Warmbrunn, Silesia, October 10, 1889

Robert Schumann [1211] hailed Henselt the composer as the long-sought German hope who would match all the Poles, Hungarians, Frenchmen, and (yes!) Englishmen then riding high. About 125 years later pianist Arthur Loesser suspected that when the dust had cleared some bright young scholar still might find something to admire in Henselt's long-scorned music. As a performer, Henselt, whose classically based, from-the-fingers virtuosity was in a class by itself, was thought the equal of both Liszt [1218] and Chopin [1208]. But a quirk of personal psychology allowed very few people ever to test that notion.

Henselt was born near Nuremberg, but his family moved to Munich soon afterward, and he studied there with a Frau von Fladt. When he was seventeen, Ludwig I of Bavaria provided him with a grant to study with old Hummel [1091] in Weimar. The two did not hit it off at all, and Henselt went on to Vienna to study theory with Simon Sechter [1129]. Henselt was a compulsive practicer, working away at the keyboard for ten hours a day, using a dummy when he was traveling. He undertook a German concert tour in 1836–37, but, even more than Heller [1229], he found himself unsuited to the virtuoso career. He suffered from such stage fright that going on stage made him physically ill, and he was even self-conscious playing before friends. (Supposedly he had forgotten one of his pieces during his debut concert and lived in dread of undergoing such humiliation again, but one suspects an irrational perfectionism to have been the root problem.) In 1838 he played, however, in St. Petersburg, and so impressed the czar that he made him court pianist and teacher to the imperial family. There Henselt stayed, save for holiday trips, for the rest of his career. He also served as inspector of music to the Imperial Ladies' Seminaries. His teaching was quite in keeping with his personality: he was a drill sergeant, quite intolerant of the slightest weakness, and as a result seems to have paralyzed his students. The last of the great Romantic finger busters, he died in Silesia. His compositional output was small. He also did arrangements of works by Weber [1124] and Cramer [1067], and edited Weber's piano music.

RECORDINGS: His most considerable works were a piano concerto (recorded by Raymond Lewenthal and Michael Ponti) and a piano trio (recorded by the Mirecourt Trio). Of his piano pieces, the two sets of "characteristic" études (recorded by Ponti and by Daniel Graham) are the most praised.

[1238] MOSONYI, Mihály (Mō-zōn'-yē, Mē-hàl'y')
CONTRABASSIST, TEACHER, WRITER
BORN: Boldogasszonyfalva, September 4, 1814
DIED: Budapest, October 31, 1870

Little known outside Hungary, save perhaps as the dedicatee of a memorial piece by Liszt [1218], Mosonyi is there regarded as one of the pioneers of true Hungarian art music. Officially Michael Brand, of German descent, he first saw the light at what is now Frauenkirchen in eastern Austria. Largely self-taught in music, he had some lessons in Pozsony (now Bratislava) with a pianist named Turányi in the early 1830s. This got him a job as piano teacher with a wealthy Hungarian family, with whom he visited Vienna and other centers. During this period he studied Antonín Reicha's [1059] theoretical works and began composing sound but conservative music. In 1842 he moved to Pest, where he supported himself and his creative endeavors by teaching and playing the double bass in orchestras. In 1846 he married Paulina Weber and two years later took part in the abortive Hungarian bid for independence. Paulina died after only five years of marriage, plunging Brand into a deep depression for many months, during which he was unable to compose at all. In 1856 he attracted the attention of Liszt, who wrote a contrabass solo for him in his "Graner" Mass, and asked him to provide music for the Gradual and the Offertory appropriate to the day. As it turned out, however, the Church authorities saw fit to use music by a local composer. Liszt also made noises about producing Brand's first opera, Kaiser Max auf der Martinswand, but he never got around to it—and neither did anyone else.

In 1857 Brand decided that he must write true Hungarian music henceforth, and Magyarized his name to the one he is best known by, Mosonyi (meaning "Michael from the Moson district"). He turned to Hungarian melodic conformations and the slow-fast pattern of the verbunkos and csárdás adopted by Liszt in his rhapsodies. He also wrote much on Hungarian music, mostly for the journal Zenészti lapok. The rising tide of nationalism both made him a popular figure and inspired him. He plugged for universal musical education in Hungary and the development of a national style that would need to take a back seat to no other, though unhappily his own efforts were hampered by his ingrained classicism. His second opera, Szép Ilonka, a piece of determinedly Magyaresque Wagnerianism, was produced in Pest in 1861, but did not replace Erkel's [1214] Italianate successes. Among his other works are 5 Masses, 7 string quartets, 2 symphonies, a piano concerto, and a good deal of vocal and piano music.

RECORDINGS: Jerome Rose has recorded the piano concerto.

[1239] VENZANO, Luigi (Vānt-sà'-nō, Lōō-ē'-jē)
CELLIST, TEACHER
BORN: Genoa, 1814
DIED: Genoa, January 26, 1878

Venzano, who played in the orchestra of the Genoa opera and taught at the conservatory, wrote at least one opera and one ballet, but is known almost exclusively for a once-popular vocal waltz, sometimes included in the lesson scene of Rossini's [1143] Il Barbiere Siviglia (as what hasn't been).

[1240] ALARD, Jean-Delphin (Á-lärd', Zhàn Del-fan')
VIOLINIST, TEACHER
BORN: Bayonne, March 8, 1815
DIED: Paris, February 22, 1888

Delphin Alard's fellow townspeople were sufficiently affected by his playing to ship him off to Paris where he studied at the Conservatoire and won first prize for violin when he was fifteen. A year later he was being hailed as a virtuoso. From 1840 he served as an orchestral violinist at the French court, rising shortly to the post of concertmaster. He was professor of violin at the Conservatoire for thirty-two years (1843–75) and numbered Pablo de Sarasate [1415] among his many pupils. He wrote an important violin method and edited an anthology of old violin pieces. He wrote concerti and concertant symphonies, but only small works (e.g., études) seem to have made it to recordings.

[1241] VOLKMANN, Friedrich Robert
(Fōlk'-mån, Frē'-drikh Rō'-bårt)
TEACHER
BORN: Lommatzsch, April 6, 1815
DIED: Budapest, October 29, 1883

Robert Volkmann, a composer once spoken of in the same breath with Brahms [1329], but now neglected, was the son of a schoolmaster-cantor in a village near Meissen. He learned the rudiments of the keyboard from his father and of the strings from a neighbor, and then went off to Leipzig to get a real musical education. While there, he quite naturally came into the orbit of Robert Schumann [1211], who said nice things about his music. Between 1839 and 1841 he served a noble family in Prague as tutor. From the latter year to 1854 he taught and worked in Budapest, then moved to Vienna for four years, before returning to Budapest as professor of composition at the National Academy, where he remained the rest of his life. The bulk of Volkmann's output is in small forms—pieces for piano, choral works, songs, and chamber music (including 6 string quartets and 2 piano trios). He wrote incidental music for Shakespeare's *Richard III*, 2 Masses, 2 symphonies, 3 serenades, 2 overtures, a *Konzertstück* for piano, and a concerto for cello. RECORDINGS: The last two works have been recorded by Jerome Rose and Thomas Blees, respectively, and Vilmos Tatrai has recorded *Serenade No. 2*.

[1242] FRANZ, Robert (Frànts, Rō'-bårt)
ORGANIST, CONDUCTOR, EDITOR
BORN: Halle, June 28, 1815
DIED: Halle, October 24, 1892

In point of publication chronology, Franz was, after Loewe [1152], Schubert [1153], Mendelssohn [1200], and Schumann [1211], the fifth of the great nineteenth-century German *Lieder* writers. Once ranked as a near-equal to his predecessors, he is now all but forgotten, perhaps because the intimacy of his songs does not lend itself to the concert hall.

Franz's father, Christoph Franz Knauth, was in the family salt business. Around 1800, because people kept mixing him up with his brother, he changed his name to Christoph Franz. (The old story that the composer took his names from Schumann and Schu-

bert is thus nonsense.) Robert's bourgeois family looked askance at his musical interests, but with the compliance of his mother he learned to play the keyboards well enough to accompany the local singing societies. At twenty he won approval to pursue his art professionally and studied for two years with Hofkapellmeister Friedrich Schneider in Dessau. Finding no regular demand for his services in Halle, he whiled away the next four years in self-education, musical and otherwise. Then he was given the post of organist at the Ulrichskirche and appointed conductor of the Singakademie. In 1843 he sent off his first set of songs to Schumann. Both Schumann and Mendelssohn were taken by them and, to Franz's surprise, got them published. (Later, he said, their interest cooled when he failed to develop as they thought he should.) Though he wrote some choral music in connection with his official functions, his creative career was devoted almost wholly to *Lieder*, of which he left nearly 300 published examples. At best they are exquisite miniatures, highly conscious of form and exemplary of the organic approach, but also highly attentive to word meanings. Wagner [1230] and Liszt [1218], who wrote a book about him, came to consider him as a prophet of "the music of the future," and Wagner once showed the doubting Franz that the only composers he admitted to the shelves of his music library were J. S. Bach [684], Beethoven [1063], and himself (Franz). Franz was not especially flattered at being placed among the avant-garde. Himself a Bach scholar, he regarded himself as a radical in the true sense and argued that the Wagnerian-dramatic approach was precisely what he eschewed in his own music.

Franz married Maria Hinrichs in 1848 and was the father of three children. He was particularly treasured in Halle, where he produced a series of successful music festivals. But his increasing deafness and a series of breakdowns forced him into retirement and a reclusive existence. Admirers of both sides of the Atlantic raised enough money so that he could live out his life in relative comfort. Among his many honors was knighthood conferred by Maximilian II of Bavaria.

RECORDINGS: His songs now turn up occasionally in recorded *Lieder* recitals, and Hilde Rössl-Majdan has given him a whole LP.

[1243] WILHELM, Karl Friedrich (Vil'-helm, Kärl Frē'-drikh)
PIANIST, CONDUCTOR

BORN: Schmalkalden, September 5, 1815
DIED: Schmalkalden, August 26, 1873

A native of the small Thuringian city that figured so prominently in Reformation history, Karl Wilhelm is now remembered solely for his patriotic song *"Die Wacht am Rhein"* ("The Watch on the Rhine"), written in 1854. Educated at home, in Kassel, and in Frankfurt am Main, he was from 1841 director of the singing societies in Krefeld. After twenty-five years his drinking problem forced his resignation, but six years later Bismarck granted him a pension in token of his government's esteem for his help in awakening the German national spirit. RECORDINGS: Many early (pre–World War I) recordings exist.

[1244] KJERULF, Halfdan (Kyå´-roolf, Hålf´-dàn)
CONDUCTOR, TEACHER
BORN: Christiania, September 15, 1815
DIED: Grefsen, August 11, 1868

One used to find in second-hand music shops innumerable collections of Kjerulf's songs, testimony to a popularity for which such Scandinavian singers as Jenny Lind and Christine Nilsson were largely responsible. Kjerulf was the son of a civil servant and a member of a gifted if lamentably short-lived family. He studied law but was forced by the onset of lifelong bad health to give it up and seek a more temperate climate. Having tasted the musical life of Paris, he was hooked and began writing songs. Shortly after his return to Norway in 1840, his father and two older siblings died, and he turned to journalism to support what was left of his family. Concurrently he studied music on his own and by 1845 was sufficiently competent to be entrusted with the directorship of a local male choir. He also gave up journalism to set up as a piano teacher. Though he disliked the calling, he was apparently quite good at it, for he turned out a number of good pianists, notably Agathe Backer-Grøndahl **[1440]** and Erika Lie, both of whom became known internationally. About this time his doctors told him that he had advanced tuberculosis and should put his affairs in order. However, he managed to survive more than twenty years. Terribly self-conscious about his lack of formal training, he began in 1848 taking lessons with Karl Arnold, the recently appointed conductor of the Christiania Philharmonic, and the next year he won a government fellowship to study abroad. Despite his illness, he went to Copenhagen to meet and work

with Gade **[1248]**, whose music had influenced his own, and then to Leipzig to study with Ernst Friedrich Richter, author of standard theory texts. On his travels he became acquainted with many orchestral masterpieces, some of which he introduced to Norwegian audiences on his return. Kjerulf's compositions are limited to vocal works (mostly songs and male choruses) and piano pieces. At the time he was writing, Norway was still part of Sweden, but in his use of folklike material he clearly reflects the growing nationalistic fervor. He also made settings of the Norwegian poet Bjørnstjerne Bjørnson, and exerted a powerful influence on Grieg **[1410]**, both of whom honored him with obituaries. He was knighted by the king in 1863 and was made a member of the Swedish Academy two years later. RECORDINGS: Gerald Robbins has recorded an LP side of his piano pieces, and some of the songs still show up in recital records. The Norwegian government has recently issued several records: piano works (Jan Henrik Kayser) and two volumes of songs (baritone Olav Eriksen and soprano Hallgerd Benum Dahl).

[1245] EMMETT, Daniel Decatur
MILITARY MUSICIAN, BLACKFACE MINSTREL, BANJOIST
BORN: Mt. Vernon, Ohio, October 29, 1815
DIED: Mt. Vernon, Ohio, June 28, 1904

Probably the first to organize a blackface minstrel show, Dan Emmett was also a popular song composer in the middle of his century, though some of his "compositions," such as "Ol' Dan Tucker" and "Turkey in the Straw," were almost certainly arranged from traditional tunes, and there are those who would even deprive him of "Dixie." Born in rural Ohio, he worked in his teens as printer for a newspaper, then spent his nineteenth year in the army, which taught him to play the fife and the drums. Afterward he spent several summers playing in circus bands, during which time he worked up a blackface song-and-banjo routine. In 1842 he joined forces with Frank Brower, a virtuoso on the bones (played as castanets), and a year later they and two others presented the first known minstrel show in New York City. As the Virginia Minstrels they attained immediate success both here and in England. Later Emmett worked with White's Serenaders and in 1858 joined the most popular of the many troupes, Bryant's minstrels. He wrote "I Wish I Was in Dixie's Land" for a walkaround (finale) in 1859 and copyrighted it a year later, after others had claimed authorship. It caught on all over the country and was played at Jefferson Davis's inaugural as President of the Confederacy, whose unofficial anthem it became. Emmett moved to Chicago in 1867, where his career went steadily downhill for the next twenty years. He lost everything he owned in 1871, thanks to Mrs. O'Leary's cow, and apart from occasional token appearances in minstrel shows, he subsisted by fiddling in bars. Several benefits and some more substantial minstrel work eased his plight in the 1880s, and in 1888 he went back to Mt. Vernon, where he worked as a handyman until the Actor's Fund came to his aid with a pension. He made his last tour in his eightieth year. RECORDINGS: Such divas as Emma Calvé and Emma Eames did not hesitate to record "Dixie," still a rallying point in the American South.

[1246] BENNETT, (Sir) William Sterndale
PIANIST, CONDUCTOR, TEACHER
BORN: Sheffield, April 13, 1816
DIED: London, February 1, 1875

Sterndale Bennett would appear to have been one of the few major musical talents to appear in England between Purcell [581] and Elgar [1499], though unhappily he bloomed only briefly. Orphaned by the time he was four, Bennett was reared and trained by his paternal grandfather, a choir singer at Cambridge, who introduced the boy, in 1824, into the King's College Choir. Two years later, tuition and board assured by his musical promise, young Bennett was sent off to the Royal Academy of Music, founded just a year before in London. (Its first enrollee was named Kellow Pye.) There he was trained in violin and piano, and studied composition with the successive principals, William Crotch and Cipriani Potter. Until his voice broke, he also sang at St. Paul's, but it was as a pianist that he really began to win notice. In 1832 his first piano concerto not only got him a command performance before William IV and Queen Adelaide but also so attracted Mendelssohn [1200] that the two became lifelong friends. In 1833 Bennett was appointed organist of St. Ann's, Wandsworth, and in two years began his association with the Philharmonic Society by playing his second piano concerto with the orchestra. Two concerti later, he made his first trip to Germany in 1836 and returned a few months later for a year-long sojourn in Leipzig. There he enjoyed the backing of Mendelssohn and Schumann [1211], both of

whom considered him a compositional equal. (Bennett, basically conservative, privately thought Schumann's music "eccentric.")

Back in London in 1837, Bennett joined the faculty of his alma mater, and, perhaps because of the drain on his energies, began to write less and less. He made two more trips to Leipzig in 1838 and 1841, but his marriage in 1844 to his pupil Mary Wood necessitated an end to such frivolities. He ran a concert series of his own and continued his association with the Philharmonic until he quarreled with its conductor Michael Costa [1193] in 1848. A year later he founded the Bach Society, and in 1853, for whatever reason, he reluctantly turned down the conductorship of the Leipzig orchestra. In 1854 he led the first English performance of J. S. Bach's [684] *St. Matthew Passion,* and a year later succeeded Wagner [1230] as Philharmonic conductor. In 1856 he was elected professor of music at Cambridge (he had been turned down at Oxford twelve years before). Almost totally unproductive for fourteen years, he returned to composition in 1858 with a cantata, *The May Queen,* and followed it with some occasional odes, a second symphony, and the oratorio *The Woman of Samaria*—none of which works fulfilled the early promise. Bennett was named principal of the Royal Academy in 1868 and knighted in 1871. He is now neglected save by amateur English choral groups.
RECORDINGS: James Sykes has recorded his Sonata No. 1 for Piano.

[1247] BAZIN, François Emanuel Joseph (Bà-zan', Fràn-swä E-mà-nü-el' Zhō-zef')
CONDUCTOR, TEACHER
BORN: Marseille, September 4, 1816
DIED: Paris, July 2, 1878

Emanuel Bazin was a product of the Paris Conservatoire, where he was a classmate of Gounod [1258] under Halévy [1157]. In 1840 he won the Prix de Rome with a cantata, *Loyse de Montfort,* which seems to have been better than most such efforts and which was sung by Rosine Stoltz, later mistress to the Emperor of Brazil. He wrote several religious works, including a *Mass,* and produced his first *opéra-comique* (of 7) in 1846 (*Le Trompette de M. le Prince*). He became professor of singing at the Conservatoire in 1844 and later professor of harmony. In 1860 he was appointed director of the Orpheon (male choral society of the Left Bank). When Ambroise Thomas [1217] was made director of the Conservatoire in 1871, Bazin succeeded him as professor of composition. His most successful operas were *Madelon,* 1852; *Le Voyage en Chine,* 1865; and especially *Maître Pathelin,* which remained in the repertoire for some time. RECORDINGS: Occasional excerpts from Bazin's operas are encountered among recordings by older French singers.

[1248] GADE, Niels Wilhelm (Gä'-de, Nēls Vil'-helm)

VIOLINIST, ORGANIST, CONDUCTOR, TEACHER
BORN: Copenhagen, February 22, 1817
DIED: Copenhagen, December 21, 1890

Niels Gade has even more claim to the paternity of modern Danish music than his father-in-law J. P. E. Hartmann [1182]. His own father was a joiner who moved from furniture to stringed instruments without making any notable improvement in the family's limited budget. Not unreasonably, however, young Gade began fooling about with a violin and at fifteen managed some lessons with a violinist named Wexschall from the Royal Orchestra. The lad made his debut a year later and was soon himself a member of the orchestra. He studied theory with the composer Andreas Peter Berggreen (1801–80), best known as a folklorist, who inculcated in him a passion for Danish music and literature. In the orchestra, however, he became acquainted with the music of Mendelssohn [1200], and his first abortive compositions were in a Mendelssohnian vein. In 1840 his overture *Echoes of Ossian,* an eleventh-hour entry, won first prize in a composition contest sponsored by the newly founded Copenhagen Music Society, and subsequent publication, as Op. 1, by Breitkopf and Härtel. (One of the judges was Spohr [1112].)

Heartened by his success, Gade shipped his first symphony off to Mendelssohn in Leipzig. The puzzled Copenhagen Music Society had rejected it, but it delighted Mendelssohn, who conducted it successfully at the Gewandhaus in 1843, thereby inspiring the Danish government to vote Gade a substantial traveling fellowship. He immediately headed for Leipzig to meet his idol and was permitted to conduct the orchestra there in public. Gade went on to Italy and Mendelssohn to Berlin, leaving the orchestra in Hiller's [1219] charge. But in 1844 Gade was called back to take the place of Hiller, who had moved to Dresden. Gade was chosen Mendelssohn's successor on the latter's death three years later, but the outbreak of war in 1848 necessitated his return to Denmark. He was organist at the Holmenkirk in Copenhagen until he became director of the Music Society in 1850, under whose auspices he organized regular orchestral concerts. (Like his English contemporary Bennett [1246], he was the first to present J. S. Bach's [684] *St. Matthew Passion* to his compatriots.) In 1852 he married Hartmann's daughter, Emma Sophie, and the following year he and Hartmann collaborated on the ballet *A Folk-Saga* for August Bournonville. The same year marked the premiere of Gade's most successful large work, the cantata *Elverskud* (on the tale of Sir Oluf abducted by fairies on his wedding night). His wife died only three years after her marriage, and in 1857 Gade married Mathilde Staeger, who outlived him by a quarter of a century. He was briefly associate conductor at the Royal Theater in 1862, and in 1866 he and Hartmann were appointed to the directorial troika at the new Academy of Music, where he also taught. (One of his pupils was Carl Nielsen [1571].) His duties limited his composing periods to the summers, but he managed to find time for occasional guest-conducting appearances.

It is true that Gade was often imitative of Mendelssohn, and in his later years his music tended to grow perfunctory and stodgy, but early on the admixture of Danish folk themes and a certain personal verve individualized it. The bulk of his music was, as noted, for chorus and/or orchestra. There were at least 16 cantatas and a good deal of occasional music. Gade wrote 8 symphonies (eschewing a ninth, it is said, out of deference to Beethoven [1063]), several overtures, and a violin concerto. Like Grieg [1410], whom he influenced, he wrote a suite after the dramatist Ludvig Holberg (but Grieg did it first). Gade's son, Axel Willy (1860–1921), was a violinist, conductor, teacher, and composer, like his father, but far less notably. Niels Gade is, incidentally, not to be confused with Jacob Gade (1879–1962), the author of *Jalousie.*

RECORDINGS: *Elverskud,* the first symphony, and *Echoes of Ossian* have all been recorded by the Royal Danish Orchestra under Johan Hye-Knudsen. Other orchestral works recorded include the fourth and eighth symphonies (by Bengt Nilsson and John Frandsen, respectively), *Spring Fantasy* (Frandsen), *Novelettes* for strings (Jiří Stárek), the ballet *A Folk Tale* (Frandsen)— a collaboration with J. P. E. Hartmann. Many of these are part of the ongoing Danish Music Anthology series. A new release on the Paula label features the Concerto for Violin and the *Capriccio* in A Minor performed by Anton Kontra with Carl von Garguly and Frandsen conducting. (There are also dubious piracies of the third and fifth symphonies by a pseudonymous orchestra and conductor.) Of the chamber works, two violin sonatas, two quartets (played by the Copenhagen String Quartet), a string quintet, and some of the *Novelettes* for piano trio have reached records. There are two LP discs by Bengt Johnsson and Adrian Ruiz that do a fair job of covering the salonlike piano pieces.

[1249] MAILLART, Louis (Mī-yär´, Lōō-ē´)
BORN: Montpellier, March 24, 1817
DIED: Moulins, May 26, 1871

There seems to be some disagreement as to whether Maillart was named Louis-Aimé or Aimé-Louis or just plain Louis, but the fact remains that he was known as Aimé. After some basic study in Moulins, he was admitted, at sixteen, to the Paris Conservatoire, where his instrument was the violin and his composition teacher Halévy [1157]. He carried off the Grand Prix de Rome in 1841. Later he aspired to opera, but he was not terribly energetic and his first try, *Gastibelza*, was not forthcoming until 1847. (It opened the Théâtre National, the idealistic venture that bankrupted Adolphe Adam [1172].) *Gastibelza*, and five of the six Maillart operas that followed it enjoyed some success but showed no staying power. Only *Les Dragons de Villars (The Dragoons of Villars)* of 1856 was a solid hit, in part because its gleaming helmets and other military dress-ups were faddish at the time. It survived in the French repertoire for decades and (as *Das Glöckchen des Eremiten—The Hermit's Little Bell*) remained popular in Germany even longer. Maillart also wrote a few choral pieces, but largely abandoned composition in favor of a life of leisure after 1860. RECORDINGS: Selections from *Les Dragons* were once quite common on records, and the overture occasionally still turns up.

[1250] LEYBACH, Ignace Xavier Joseph (Lī´-bȧk, Ēg-nȧs´ Eks-ȧv-yä´ Zhō-zef´)
PIANIST, ORGANIST
BORN: Gambsheim, July 17, 1817
DIED: Toulouse, May 23, 1891

Half a century ago every dime-store anthology of Piano Music the Whole World Loves included Ignace Leybach's now-forgotten fifth nocturne. The production of nocturnes

marked him as a pupil of none other than Chopin [1208], though he also studied with Kalkbrenner [1118] and Pixis [1128]—all in Paris. In 1844 he was appointed organist of Toulouse Cathedral, and lived and taught in Toulouse for the rest of his life. He wrote methods for both piano and organ. As a composer he specialized in small forms, both vocal and instrumental, but was best known for his salonesque piano pieces. RECORDINGS: Hans Kann has recorded the nocturne noted.

[1251] WENNERBERG, Gunnar (Ven´-ner-bâr'y, Goon´-när)
WRITER, POLITICIAN, TEACHER
BORN: Lidköping, October 2, 1817
DIED: Läckö, August 22, 1901

The son of a parish priest, Wennerberg took a Ph.D. at Uppsala and embarked on a teaching career. An amateur musician, he sang in various choral societies and taught himself to compose, achieving some local success as a writer of songs and choruses, for which he often also provided the lyrics. In 1843, while still working on his degree, he joined a student musical club called "The Juvenals," for whom he wrote *Gluntarne (The Boys)*, an attractive series of vocal duets (male) about student life. In 1850 he made a tour of Sweden, reciting and singing his own music. In later life he became a politician, advancing in 1876 from the lower to the upper house of the parliament, where he continued to serve for the next twenty-five years. He served two terms (1870–75, 1888–91) as minister for cultural affairs, and was elected to the Academy in 1867. Though Wennerberg wrote some more ambitious works, he is remembered mostly for his psalms for amateur groups and for *Gluntarne*. RECORDINGS: The latter has been most recently recorded by Ingvar Wixell and Erik Saedén.

[1252] PEDROTTI, Carlo (Pä-drōt´-tē, Kär´-lō)
CONDUCTOR, TEACHER, ADMINISTRATOR
BORN: Verona, November 12, 1817
DIED: Verona, October 16, 1893

Pedrotti was another of those forgotten operatic composers once considered serious rivals of Verdi [1232]. As a youth he taught himself to compose and to conduct an *ad hoc* chamber orchestra; later he studied with a local musician named Domenico Foroni. After a couple of false operatic starts, a Veronese production in 1840 of his *Lina* won him a measure of fame and the production of a second opera, procuring him a post as conductor of the Italian Opera in Amsterdam, which house produced his next two operas. He returned to Verona in 1845 and remained there for twenty-three years, conducting and teaching. During that time he composed ten more works, of which the 1856 comedy *Tutti in maschera (Everyone Disguised)* was, for the nonce, an international hit. In 1868 Pedrotti was called to Turin to run the conservatory and conduct the Teatro Regio orchestra. There he pioneered weekly "pop" concerts, with the aim of introducing the Torinese to the symphonic repertoire from all over. He also took pains to produce unknown and foreign operas; it was under his baton that Bizet's **[1363]** *Carmen* first caught on with Italian audiences. Recognizing that his own style of composition was behind the times, he produced only one new Pedrotti opera, *Il Favorito*, in Turin, and thereafter refused to let his works be revived. In 1882 he took over direction of the new Liceo Rossini in Pesaro, but, sick both physically and emotionally, he resigned ten years later after directing the celebrations for Rossini's hundredth birthday. He returned to Verona where, a month before his seventy-sixth birthday, he drowned himself in the Adige. RECORDINGS: Excerpts from a few of his operas appear on old vocal records.

[1253] LEFÉBURE-WÉLY, Louis James Alfred (Lǝ-fā-bür′ Vā-lē′, Lōō-ē′ Zhàm Àl-fred′)
ORGANIST
BORN: Paris, November 13, 1817
DIED: Paris, December 31, 1869

The family name was originally Lefébre, but Louis's father Antoine, an organist, changed it to Lefébure-Wély. Louis was Antoine's pupil from a very early age, and was substituting for his father at St. Roch in Paris by the time he was eight. When Antoine died in 1831, Louis succeeded him as regular organist there—probably a testimony to his reputed brilliance, but one also to how seriously people took church organ-playing in those years. A year later he was admitted to the Conservatoire, studied composition under Halévy **[1157]** and Henri-Montan Berton (1767–1844), and won first prizes for organ and piano in 1835. In 1847 he was appointed organist of the Madeleine, which post he held for eleven years. He was made a chevalier of the *Légion d'Honneur* in 1850. After 1858 he free-lanced until 1863, when he

became organist of St. Sulpice. He died at fifty-two of tuberculosis. RECORDINGS: Though Lefébure-Wély wrote such large-scale things as an opera, Masses, and symphonies, he was chiefly celebrated for his piano pieces of a stylish salon cast. RECORDINGS: One of the most popular pieces, *Les Cloches du monastère*, is recorded by Hans Kann. There are also scattered French recordings of other piano and organ pieces.

[1254] GROBE, Charles
TEACHER, MERCHANT
BORN: Saxe-Weimar, 1817
DIED: Pennington, N.J., 1880

All that is known of Grobe's early life is that he was the son of a German Lutheran minister and was probably christened Karl. He emigrated to the United States when he was about twenty-two and settled in Wilmington, Delaware, where he taught in a girls' school from 1841 until the mid-1860s and ran a music store from 1845 to 1871. In 1872 he joined the faculty of the Pennington School, and he is thought to have died there eight years later. He was an indefatigable source of salon music for piano, specializing in variations. His published works run to at least Op. 1995. He had taken to heart every cliché of the genre and applied them with machine-like regularity. During the Civil War he tried his hand at onomatopoeic battle pieces— e.g., *The Battle of Roanoke Island: Story of an Eye Witness*, though by then his extraordinary and inexplicable popularity seems to have waned. (Op. 1350 appeared in 1865.) RECORDINGS: Ivan Davis has recorded his *United States Grand Waltz* (an early work, numbered Op. 43.)

[1255] SAUMELL REBREDO, Manuel (Sä′-ōō-mel Rä-brä′-dō, Mà′-nōō-el)
PIANIST, CELLIST
BORN: Havana, 1817
DIED: Havana, August 14, 1870

Latter-day Castroan nationalism has raised the shade of Manuel Saumell, an early example of native talent in a world dominated by imports from Europe and North America. Saumell was an autodidact, though later he took some lessons. He seems to have been a sort of musical factotum in Havana, working as teacher, performer, arranger, etc. His favorite musical form appears to have been the *contradanza* (the Cubans have termed him *el padre de la contradanza*). RECORDINGS: Some of these simple but charming pieces have been recorded (in guitar arrangements) by Leo Brouwer, Turibio Santos, and Oscar Caceres.

[1256] BAZZINI, Antonio (Bàd-zē'-nē, Àn-tōn'-yō)
VIOLINIST, TEACHER
BORN: Brescia, March 11, 1818
DIED: Milan, February 10, 1897

Bazzini, who studied in Milan, was admired as a violinist by Paganini [1106], who urged that he tour. Between 1840 and 1852 he was heard in most of Central and Western Europe and then settled in Paris for a dozen years, continuing to play and tour. However, he gradually became more interested in composing and in 1864 went home to Brescia to devote himself to it. He wrote an opera *Turanda,* based on Gozzi's play *Turandot,* which was unsuccessfully produced at La Scala in 1867, but by 1873 he was thought so well of that he was appointed professor of composition at the Milan Conservatory, of which he became director in 1880. His later compositions, which include sonatas and other more ambitious chamber works, cantatas, and orchestra overtures on Shakespeare's *King Lear* and Vittorio Alfieri's *Saul* are highly spoken of as interesting mixtures of Germanic formalism and Italian lyricism, but all are neglected. RECORDINGS: A little violinistic tour-de-force, *Le Ronde des lutins,* is frequently played and recorded.

[1257] JOSEPHSON, Jacob Axel
ORGANIST, CONDUCTOR, TEACHER
BORN: Stockholm, March 27, 1818
DIED: Uppsala, March 29, 1880

More important as a force in nineteenth-century Swedish music than as a composer, Josephson came from an immigrant Jewish family but converted to Lutheranism at the age of twenty-three. He graduated from the University of Uppsala, where he came under the influence of E. G. Geijer [1108]. Though his degree was in philosophy, he was already active in music as a teacher, choral conductor, and writer of songs. Some of the last caught the attention of Jenny Lind, who helped pay for his further musical education in Rome and Leipzig. ("They were more than friends," coos a gossipy liner note for a recorded Jenny Lind recital.) Josephson's idol was Mendelssohn [1200], and one of his teachers was Niels Gade [1248]. On his return he was identified chiefly with Uppsala where he served as music director, cathedral organist, and professor of music history. He was particularly influential in the performance and reform of church music. The bulk of his compositions consists of choruses and solo songs, many of which remain popular in Sweden. RECORDINGS: A number of the songs appear in recorded song recitals by Swedish singers.

[1258] GOUNOD, Charles François (Gōō-nō, Shàrl Fràn-swà')
ORGANIST, CONDUCTOR
BORN: Paris, June 17, 1818
DIED: Paris, October 18, 1893

Charles Gounod has perhaps been the victim of overexposure (chiefly through his *Faust,* which had its thousandth performance in Paris right after his death, and earned the early Metropolitan Opera the sobriquet of *Faustspielhaus).* At any rate, for many he represents all that was wrong with the nineteenth century. True, his music can be saccharine, sentimental, and pseudo-religious. (Like Sullivan [1397], he wanted to be thought of as a great religious composer, and his Masses and oratorios considerably outnumber his operas.) But as an operatic composer he had more seriousness, depth, and—yes!—musical inspiration than any Frenchman of his day, always excepting Berlioz [1175], though Gounod had vastly more influence.

Gounod's paternal forebears came to Paris in the eighteenth century, probably from the Franche-Comté, and his great-grandfather was officially the cutler to Louis XV. Gounod's father was an academic painter of no great gifts who was officially the drawing master to the royal pages and court artist to the Duke of Berry. At forty-eight he married a twenty-six-year-old Rouennaise, Victoire Lemachois, a fine pianist, who forthwith presented him with a son named Louis Urbain. Their second child, the composer-to-be, waited eleven years to appear. Left fatherless at the age of five, he was supported by the proceeds from the piano lessons given by his mother, of which he naturally partook. His talent astounded such musicians as the singer Gilbert Duprez, with whom Gounod studied from the age of seven, and Louis Jadin [1055], a family acquaintance. But his mother, who wanted him to be a notary, was more interested in his academic education, and in 1829 she entered him as a resident student on partial scholarship in the Lycée St. Louis. He performed well, but his chief interest was still music, and his introduction to opera when he was thirteen made up his mind about what he wanted to do. His schoolmaster knew a good thing when he saw it and sided with Gounod. Mme. Gounod took her son to Antonín Reicha [1059], by then one of the leading teachers in Paris, hoping that his hard-nosed approach to musical education would kill the boy's interest; after a year, Reicha told her that he was destined for music. In 1836 he was admitted to the Conservatoire, where he studied with Halévy [1157], Henri-Montan Berton (1767–1844), Jean-François Lesueur (1760–1837), and Paër [1069]. After Lesueur died, Gounod's memorial *Agnus Dei* won him the praise and friendship of Berlioz.

After two unsuccessful tries, Gounod took the Grand Prix de Rome in 1839. At the Villa Medici he became the protégé of the director, the painter Ingres, who painted his portrait. Discovering that Gounod had also inherited graphic talent, Ingres had him draw copies of his pictures and offered to procure him the Prix de Rome for painting if he wanted it. Like many of his compatriots, Gounod was disappointed with Roman music, but he discovered Palestrina [201] there. He developed a passion for that composer, which fed the religious enthusiasm inspired in him by his friend Charles Gay and by Père Lacordaire, the leader of a sort of born-again Catholic movement. He thought seriously of entering the priesthood—a notion that he kept in the back of his head for much of his life—but was eventually dissuaded by his brother and his adored mother. Spontini [1081], sitting in judgment on the Rome students back in Paris, found Gounod's Palestrina-influenced *Te Deum* preposterous, but on his mandatory tour of the Germanies, the young composer so impressed Vienna with his *Mass* and *Requiem* that he was given a commission for another such work. After visiting Mendelssohn [1200], whose sister Fanny [1186] had been a good friend in Rome, Gounod returned to Paris in 1843 to become organist-choirmaster at the Church of Foreign Missions.

Gounod took his quasi-religious mission so seriously as to sign himself "l'Abbé Gounod." For five years he struggled to convert the congregation to Bach and Palestrina but gave up in 1848. A year later he was introduced to the great contralto Pauline Viardot, sister of La Malibran and daughter of Manuel Garcia. He became her devout admirer, and probably shared her, as lover, with her husband and the novelist Turgenev; they seem, at any rate, to have had a cozy arrangement, for Gounod and the Russian lived amicably in the Viardots' country home while Gounod worked at the opera Pauline had promised to star in for him. *Sapho* was duly premiered at the Opéra in April 1851; the audience generally approved,

but the reviewers found it too "modern," and it survived only thirteen showings.

About the same time Gounod's former Conservatoire piano teacher Pierre Zimmermann had rediscovered him and taken him into the bosom of his family. There Mme. Zimmermann cleverly contrived to engage him to their daughter Anna, whom he dutifully married (to his eternal regret) in 1852. (They made him return the bracelet La Viardot sent the bride. It was Zimmermann, by the way, who noted down the melody Gounod improvised to the first prélude from Bach's *Well-Tempered Clavier* that was to become the infamous *Ave Maria* which made the composer's name a household word.) Shortly after his wedding, Gounod became director of the chorus l'Orphéon de la Ville de Paris, where he presided for eight years, and for which he wrote many works, including the official imperial anthem of Napoleon III. During this period he worked with the young Saint-Saëns [1343] on the incidental music to a play, *Ulysse*, by François Ponsard (a flop), and encouraged the even younger Bizet [1363], whom he had make piano transcriptions of his compositions. His second opera, *La Nonne sanglante*, to a Scribe libretto that had been rejected by Berlioz, Halévy [1157], Meyerbeer [1142], and Verdi [1232], among others, had a temporary success in 1854 but showed even less staying power than its predecessor. In the next year, following another attack of piety, the so-called *St. Cecilia Mass* won him the *Légion d'honneur,* and he was considered as Adam's [1172] successor in the Institut, though in the end the honor was given Berlioz. A third opera, *Ivan le Terrible,* was aborted. Pressured by his duties, the deaths of a daughter and M. Zimmermann, and the birth of a son, Gounod collapsed in 1856 and had to spend some time in a sanitarium—a pattern that was to be repeated.

Having recovered, Gounod, spurred by his friend the playwright Jules Barbier, began to have visions of turning Gounod's *Faust* into an opera. He managed to sell the idea to Léon Carvalho, impresario of the Théâtre-Lyrique (and husband of its imperious prima donna). But Carvalho quickly shelved the plan, having learned that another theater was about to produce a *Faust* with music. He persuaded Bizet and his librettists, Barbier and Michel Carré, to set Molière's *Le Médecin malgré lui* instead. The censors, incredibly, found the vehicle too racy, but Gounod's newest patroness Princess Mathilde, a cousin of the emperor, waved her wand, and the work, which opened in mid-January 1858 was Gounod's first real theatrical success. Meanwhile

Carvalho decided to risk *Faust* after all. Having overcome struggles with Mme. Carvalho and the censors (who thought it might offend the Pope!), *Faust*, somewhat altered from Gounod's original vision, took the stage on March 19, 1859. Though such considerable figures as Berlioz and Meyerbeer admired it, others were puzzled by its break with the usual notion of grand opera, and it caught on only slowly. (Gounod, incidentally, sold it outright to the publisher Choudens, and so did not profit as he might have by the later mania for the work.) Meanwhile Gounod was working on another less raucous comedy, *Philémon et Baucis*, for Baden-Baden. Carvalho, however, persuaded the Germans to let him have it and offered it eleven months after the first night of *Faust*. The critics approved, but the public and Mme. Carvalho did not, and it had to wait even longer than its predecessor for acceptance. In recompense, Baden-Baden got *La Colombe*, based on a LaFontaine fable, that summer (starring the inevitable Mme. Carvalho.) The vacationers liked it, but Paris did not when it opened there in 1866, and it is now largely forgotten. Having waited in vain (but not very long) for the ballet plot promised him by the Empress Eugénie when he visited the royal family in 1860, Gounod next embarked on *La Reine de Saba*, which had invitingly religious overtones. There was dissension among the performers from the start. The February 1862 premiere ran much too long, the emperor (who attended) smelled sedition, and the critics scented Wagnerism (the *Tannhäuser* scandal at the Opéra was fresh in their minds), and it lasted but fifteen performances. Disappointed, Gounod went with his family to Italy, where he took up the guitar (he was much admired as a self-accompanying singer of his own salon songs, of which he wrote dozens).

After a period of indolence, during which he decided not to compose *Le Cid* and *Mignon*, earning the later gratitude of Massenet [1396] and Thomas [1217], Gounod settled on "Mirèio," a Provençal poem by Frédéric Mistral, later a Nobel laureate. On the poet's invitation, Gounod came to the Provençal village of St. Rémy to work on it, thinly incognito as "M. Pépin." The effort of this work, the London premiere of *Faust*, and the arrival of a daughter caused another breakdown. Despite the first-act irrelevant waltz-song insisted on by Mme. Carvalho, *Mireille*, as the opera was retitled, premiered in 1864, but it did not please. ("Too gloomy!" people said.) Under pressure, Gounod telescoped it to three acts and gave it a lovers'-clinch ending, in which distorted form it

survived for seventy-five years. Following a bout with gout, incidental music to a play blocked by the censors, and a fiasco at setting Schiller's *Fiesco*, Gounod settled in St. Raphaël on the Riviera to write *Roméo et Juliette*. Overwork and humidity produced a third breakdown, and Gounod went to his suburban estate at St. Cloud (inherited from Zimmermann), to recover. He completed the score in August of 1866. Shortly afterward he was elected to the Institut. After a number of hassles with the Carvalhos, which produced yet another waltz-song, Gounod got the work onstage the following April and enjoyed his only uncontested triumph.

Next the Opéra demanded that *Faust* be equipped with recitatives and a ballet for production there. Gounod at first tried to argue Saint-Saëns into providing them but finally wrote them himself, around another visit to Rome and the inception of the oratorio *Rédemption*. He was once again feeling pious and was affecting a sort of clerical costume and a skullcap. After the successful premiere of the new *Faust*, in March 1869 Gounod began a treatment of Corneille's *Polyeucte*. It was interrupted by another emotional crisis, followed by the outbreak of the Franco-Prussian War. Gounod, who was immensely popular in England, where he had visited before, moved his tribe to Blackheath and then established himself in London, where he wrote the patriotic oratorio *Gallia* for Novello and was the social hit of the season as singer of his own songs. In the winter of 1871 he met Giorgina Weldon, a married singer of thirty-three, who swept him off his feet. It turned out that she wanted him in bed to nurse rather than to love. Gounod moved into the Weldon menage, and, after conducting Giorgina in the Parisian premiere of *Gallia*, returned there suffering yet another breakdown, complicated by eczema, dysentery, influenza, hemorrhoids, swollen glands, and rheumatism. This permitted Giorgina and her husband to mother him, as desired. Recovering in the spring, Gounod notified Anna that he was through and would live in England henceforth. But the idyll soon dissolved. Opposition from patriots forced him to give up the choir he had formed at the Royal Albert Hall. In a quarrel over terms, Novello's sued him for libel and won damages of two pounds, which Gounod refused to pay, demanding to be jailed instead. After months of situation comedy with Giorgina, there was a severe breakdown, and he was hauled back to Paris by his physician in person. Giorgina sued him for failure to deliver monies allegedly promised her for a school for orphans and held the score of *Polyeucte* hos-tage. He was forced to rewrite it, since a return to England would have resulted in his arrest. Meanwhile the triumphant Anna reclaimed him as her own.

Gounod's last operas—*Cinq-Mars,* 1877; *Polyeucte,* 1878; and *Le Tribut de Zamora,* 1881—all failed in one way or another. He turned more than ever to "religious" music and to writing articles on such things as faith, beauty, and breast-feeding. In 1880 he was made a grand officer of the *Légion d'honneur.* He was permitted back in England in 1882 to conduct a performance of *Rédemption,* but two years later the courts at last found for Giorgina to the tune of 11,640 pounds, failure to pay which barred him from responding to a royal invitation in 1885 to conduct his latest mystical pronouncement, *Mors et vita.* Meanwhile in 1879 he had built himself a Parisian mansion, and increasingly he spent his time there or at St. Cloud, welcoming pilgrims. He played the organ at a local church on Sundays, argued points of theology with whomever wished to do so, and attempted the salvation of Sarah Bernhardt. He took on a protégé and amanuensis in the person of young Henri Büsser (who died only in 1973 at 101). Even an offer of a million francs for a tour of America failed to dislodge him. By 1891 his eyesight was dimming, he suffered from sciatica and chronic bronchitis, and his vascular system was failing. In 1893 he produced a *Requiem* for his grandson Maurice. Shortly after he and Büsser had discussed arranging it for organ, he died while thumbing through the manuscript. He was given a state funeral and buried in the Auteuil cemetery.

RECORDINGS: Gounod survives largely through *Faust, Roméo et Juliette,* the *Petite symphonie* for winds, and the *St. Cecilia Mass,* all of which have had a number of recordings. (The operas were among the earliest to be recorded in reasonably complete versions.) There are also commercial recordings of *Mireille,* the last *Requiem,* the *Fantasy on the Russian National Hymn* for piano and orchestra, symphonies in D major and E-flat major, the A-minor string quartet, a fair representation of the songs, and a handful of other smaller pieces. The piratical underground boasts readings of *Sapho, La Reine de Saba, Philémon et Baucis,* and possibly several of the other operas, but most of the omissions would appear past resuscitation—though that is a risky thing to say in the present climate.

[1259] LITOLFF, Henry Charles
PIANIST, CONDUCTOR, PUBLISHER

BORN: London, August 7, 1818
DIED: Colombes (?), August 5, 1891

In his day, Henry Litolff was known, because of his pianistic virtuosity, as the English Liszt [1218], though he had almost as many wives as Liszt had mistresses. He is also remembered for his yellow-bound inexpensive Editions Litolff that made the classics available to the man-in-the-street and for the scherzo from his fourth piano concerto. His father was a Napoleonic recruit from Alsace, who was brought to England as a prisoner from Spain, married a Scotswoman, and became a professional violinist. Young Henry was his pupil and later a piano student of Moscheles [1146]. As a twelve-year-old prodigy, he made his solo debut in 1832, though he was only fourteen. Three years later he eloped to the Continent with Miss Elizabeth Etherington, a year his junior, and led a peripatetic life there as a touring concert artist. He left Elizabeth in 1839 and settled in Germany in 1844, where he became one of the teachers of Hans von Bülow. [1310].

In 1845 he returned to England to obtain a divorce, but wound up in jail, from which he managed to flee to Holland and thence to Braunschweig. There he finally got his divorce and in 1851 married Julie Meyer, widow of his friend the publisher Gottfried Meyer, whose firm he thus came into possession of. (He also adopted Julie's son Theodor, who succeeded him as head of the business, which operated until it was absorbed by C. F. Peters in 1940.) In 1855 he became *Kapellmeister* to Ernst II, Duke of Saxe-Coburg-Gotha (and brother to Queen Victoria's consort). Three years later he divorced Julie, turned Henry Litolffs Verlag over to Theodor, and moved to Paris, where he married Louise, Countess of Larochefoucauld in 1860. When she died in 1873, Litolff, who had a long history of poor health, married his nurse (age seventeen). The Paris suburb in which he died is variously listed as Bois-les-Combes, Bois-Colombes, and Colombes. Litolff wrote 7 operas, an oratorio, orchestral and chamber music, and songs.

RECORDINGS: Litolffs most significant and representative works are his 4 *concerts symphoniques* for piano and orchestra and his solo piano music. *Concerts Symphoniques Nos. 3 and 4* have been recorded by Michael Ponti and Gerald Robbins, respectively; a fifth has disappeared. One of his 3 piano trios has been recorded by the Mirecourt Trio.

[1260] DREYSCHOCK, Alexander (Drī'-shok, Á-lek-sán'-der)

PIANIST, TEACHER
BORN: Zak, October 15, 1818
DIED: Venice, April 1, 1869

Bohemian-born, Dreyschock studied with Tomášek [1080] from 1833 to 1838. It is said that in his determination to master every possible pianistic problem, he practiced sixteen hours a day. He spent fourteen years on the concert trail. From the outset Mendelssohn [1200] and Moscheles [1146] were bowled over. Cramer [1067] credited him with two right hands, Theodor Kullak (1818–82) called him more brilliant than Liszt [1218], and the critic Eduard Hanslick proclaimed him the ultimate virtuoso. (The poet Heine, however, found him noisy and said that he was aptly named, for he sounded like *drei Schock* [three times threescore] pianists.) In 1862 he was invited to St. Petersburg to profess piano in the new Conservatory and was later made director of the School of Theater Music and imperial court pianist. But the Russian winters ruined his health; a trip to Italy in 1868 to recover it ended in his death there. Most of his 140 compositions were designed to show off his technique. (Dreyschock's younger brother Raimund, a violinist, concertized with him and was professor of violin at the Leipzig Conservatory; Raimund's son, Felix, was professor of piano at the Stern Conservatory in Berlin.) RECORDINGS: Frank Cooper has recorded his *Konzertstück* for piano and orchestra.

[1261] CAMPANA, Fabio (Kàm-pá'-ná, Fàb'-yō)

TEACHER
BORN: Livorno, January 14, 1819
DIED: London, February 2, 1882

A product of the Bologna Liceo, Campana aspired, without much luck, to be an opera composer, though late in his career Adelina Patti's infatuation with his *Esmeralda* won it sporadic performances. Around mid-century he went to England and became a successful vocal teacher in London. RECORDINGS: He wrote innumerable drawing-room songs, some of which were recorded by singers in the first decades of this century.

[1262] SUPPÉ, Franz von (Zōō-pā', Frànts fun)

FLUTIST, SINGER, CONDUCTOR
BORN: Spalato, April 18, 1819
DIED: Vienna, May 21, 1895

We think of Vienna and operetta as virtually synonymous. It therefore may come as a shock for some to learn that Viennese operetta had a beginning and that its beginning was not with a Strauss, but with a Belgian-Italian-Yugoslav acting in emulation of Offenbach [1264], his exact contemporary. The composer's full name was Francesco Ezechiele Ermenegildo, Cavaliere Suppé-Demelli, and he was born in what is now Split. His father's people had originally emigrated to Cremona from Belgium, where they had intermarried with Donizetti's [1155]; his mother was *echt* Viennese. After the family had moved to Zara, Suppé mastered the flute, wrote a *Mass* at thirteen, and, lest he become a musician, was hustled off to Padua to study law, which he didn't very much. In 1835 his father died and his mother brought him to live in Vienna, where he was encouraged to study medicine. Apart from his linguistic difficulties (he retained a strong Italian accent all his life), he found cadavers no more appealing than torts and turned to full-time music study with Simon Sechter [1129] and with Mozart's [992] old friend Ignaz Seyfried. In 1840 he was taken on at the Josephstadt Theater as an unsalaried flutist-conductor. Apparently around this time he had some lessons from his cousin Hofkapellmeister Donizetti, and in 1841 the theater produced his Donizettian *Singspiel* entitled *Jung lustig (Merry in Youth)* to favorable reviews. It was the predecessor of literally unnumbered Suppé farces, plays, *Singspiele*, and operettas—perhaps as many as 300. His boss, Franz Pokorny, liked what he heard, and Suppé soon became known in Pressburg (Bratislava) and Baden, where the company had spring and summer seasons—not only as composer and conductor but also as a buffo-basso. In 1845 Pokorny took over the Theater an der Wien, where, with time out for revolutions, Suppé served as associate *Kapellmeister* (with Lortzing [1163] *inter alias*) until 1862.

It was in 1846 that Suppé wrote the famous *Dichter und Bauer (Poet and Peasant)* overture for a now-forgotten play, but he did not have his first real hit until *Das Mädchen vom Lande (The Country Girl)* a year later, nor one on a more than local scale until *Paragraph 3* in 1858. That was the year Offenbach set Vienna on its ear and inspired Suppé to write the one-act *Das Pensionat*, premiered in 1860 and regarded as the first Viennese operetta. (To detail the gradations between *opéra-comique*, *Singspiel*, operetta, etc. would demand more space than is possible here; let us say that operetta is perhaps frothier, more popularly aimed, and more irreverent.) After three years at the

Kaitheater, where he produced in 1863 *Die flotten Burschen (The Lively Lads,* forerunner of the *Student Prince* model of operetta), Suppé settled in at the Karltheater in 1865, where he remained until his retirement in 1882, though he continued to write until he died. Other successes were *Die schöne Galathée (Pretty Galatea* of 1865), *Die leichte Kavallerie (The Light Cavalry* of 1866—whose overture must have been transcribed for every possible instrument or combination), and *Fatinitza* of 1876. In 1879 (five years after Strauss's *Fledermaus)* Suppé produced his masterpiece, *Boccaccio,* which even won performances at the Metropolitan Opera. Suppé wrote operettas on Schubert [1153] and Haydn [871]. He also wrote parodies of Wagner [1230], *Lohengelb;* and of Meyerbeer [1142], *Dinorah, oder die Turnerfahrt nach Hütteldorf—The Gymnastic Meet at Hütteldorf).* Besides the stage works, he left a *Requiem* for Pokorny, at least one symphony, some string quartets, and a number of other nondramatic pieces. An easygoing, friendly man, Suppé preferred to compose, bundled up to the top of his egg-bald head, in an unheated studio. He died of cancer at seventy-six. His home in Vienna has been preserved as a monument.

RECORDINGS: On records he is represented by complete recordings of *Boccaccio* (Willi Boskovsky) and *Die schöne Galathée* (Kurt Eichhorn), and many overtures.

[1263] MONIUSZKO, Stanisław (Mon-yōōsh′-kō, Stă′-nē-slwăf)
ORGANIST, CONDUCTOR, TEACHER
BORN: Ubiel, May 5, 1819
DIED: Warsaw, June 4, 1872

Hailed (mostly by his compatriots) as "the Polish Verdi" [1232], the resemblance lies chiefly in the fact that Moniuszko pioneered nationalistic opera in Poland. His father owned the Lithuanian estate where he was born; his mother sang him Polish songs and taught him the rudiments of piano technique. Both parents were all for encouraging his obvious talent and, when he was eight, settled in Warsaw where he was able to study with August Freyer, a pupil of Joseph Elsner, who may have instilled in him Elsner's conviction that the Polish musical Messiah would write operas. Stanisław was the last male heir of the Moniuszko line, but, as a result of legal snarls, he failed to inherit his uncles' properties; furthermore by 1830 his father had managed to lose the Ubiel estate. Economy thereupon dictated a retreat to Minsk, where prices were lower. However, Moniuszko continued his studies there,

and by 1837 circumstances had sufficiently improved to enable him to proceed to Berlin for two years with Ringenhagen, Zelter's [1008] successor at the Singakademie. During that time he was influenced not only by German music but perhaps even more by the Italian operas he encountered. He soon was publishing songs and writing a *Singspiel,* entitled *A Night in the Apennines,* which was produced in 1839 in Wilno (now Vilnius). In 1840 he married his sweetheart Aleksandra Müller and settled in Wilno, making ends meet for his growing family as church organist, teacher, and sometime theater conductor. He also founded a choral society and kept busy grinding out *Singspiele* (several of them now lost). One of them, *The Lottery,* was sufficiently successful to win a Warsaw production in 1846, at which time Moniuszko met, among others, the poet Włodzimierz Wolski. The two began work soon afterward on an opera *Halka,* which was given an amateur concert performance in Wilno in 1848. Six years later the local theater staged it with considerable success.

Seeing a way out of poverty, Moniuszko importuned the Warsaw Opera, then a bastion of Italianism, to produce his piece, while he worked at others. *(Betly* in 1852 was set to the libretto used by Donizetti [1155] and, even earlier, as *Le Chalet,* by Adam [1172].) A shakeup in the operatic administration finally won *Halka* a hearing in a much-revised and expanded version. The premiere on January 1, 1858, exactly ten years to the day after the work was first sung, marks a turning point in Polish operatic history. *Halka* is still revered as *the* Polish opera. A series of Moniuszkan successes ensued—*The Raftsman* that September, *The Countess* and *Verbum nobile* in 1860, and *The Haunted Manor* (probably Moniuszko's finest opera) in 1865. But *Paria* in 1869 and the operetta *Beata* in 1872, his last completed efforts, were both failures and are said to have hastened the death of the harried composer, who, since 1864, had also been teaching at the Music Institute to help support his ten children, despite declining health. His funeral occasioned a great patriotic outpouring.

Though he wrote other music (chiefly choral), Moniuszko was primarily a stage composer (of ballets and incidental music as well as operas). However, his several books of simple *Songs for Home Use* continue to be used in Poland.

RECORDINGS: There are complete (Polish) recordings of *The Raftsman, The Haunted Manor, Verbum nobile, The Countess,* and *Halka* (which last has also enjoyed a Russian recording), numerous operatic selections in recorded Polish vocal recitals, the String Quartet No. 1, a few piano pieces, and at least two LP discs of the songs.

[1264] OFFENBACH, Jacques (né Jakob)
(Of'-fen-bàkh, Zhàk)
CELLIST, CONDUCTOR, IMPRESARIO
BORN: Cologne, June 20, 1819
DIED: Paris, October 5, 1880

Jacques Offenbach was the clown who wanted to play Hamlet. Blocked in his wish to become a successful writer of operas, he invented and thrived on the operetta, that delicious, effervescent, naughty commentary on the hypocritical mores of the Second Empire and on the whole operatic genre. Contrary to frequently printed misinformation, Offenbach's surname was never Eberst, much less Cohen. His father, Isaac Juda Eberst, an amateur poet trained as a bookbinder, had preferred the life of a traveling fiddler and cantor. Born in Offenbach (near Frankfurt am Main), he worked the Rhineland, where he was known as *der Offenbacher* (the man from Offenbach). When he settled in 1802 in Deutz, near Cologne, he was known as Isaac Offenbach. There he married Marianne Rindskopf and set about producing a family of ten children, of which Jakob was the seventh. In 1816 the family moved into Cologne.

The Offenbach children had music lessons as a matter of course. Julius showed considerable talent as a violinist and Isabella as a pianist, but Jakob outstripped both. He was trained in the violin but mastered the cello on his own in secret, announcing the fact to his startled family when he stepped into a parlor string-quartet performance when the expected cellist failed to show up. Isaac forthwith saw that he had commensurate training with a couple of local musicians—the lessons paid for in part by performances in Cologne taverns with Julius and Isabella. (Jakob was advertised as being two years younger than his real age, a circumstance that confused him for many years thereafter.) In 1833 Isaac took the two boys to Paris and somehow overcame Cherubini's [1019] bias against foreigners, winning admittance to the Conservatoire for Jakob. After the boys had spent a wretched year in the proverbial Montmartre attic (they were now "Jules" and "Jacques"), Jacques quit school to try to make some money. After free-lancing for a time, he found a place in the orchestra of the Opéra-Comique. The routine bored him, and he and his desk mate, Hippolyte Seligmann, found ingenious ways to make the time pass—such as alternating the notes in the cello parts—which often got Offenbach fined. Attracted by the music of Halévy [1157], in the premiere of whose *L'Éclair* he participated, Offenbach introduced himself to the composer and won his friendship and advice. It was probably Halévy who was instrumental in getting his sometime pupil Louis Antoine Jullien to conduct some of Offenbach's dances at the Jardin Turc, the pleasure spot where he officiated. But this link ended in a quarrel in 1838, the year that Offenbach quit the orchestra. Shortly afterward he was taken up by Flotow [1222], who helped him write some suitable cello pieces and introduced him to the salons, where he became an immediate hit as the "Liszt of the cello." One suspects that some of the attraction lay in Offenbach's ability to do barnyard imitations on the instrument. At any rate, for some time he pursued a career as a virtuoso and composer of salon songs, while he importuned the Opéra-Comique to let him do a work for its stage. The failure of his first dramatic effort, a vaudeville called *Pascal et Chambord* at the Palais-Royal in 1839 did not bode well, and the Opéra-Comique did not heed his pleas for another eight years. Meanwhile Offenbach was a name that was increasingly recognized in Parisian musical circles, and its owner could claim appearances with such accompanists as Gottschalk [1306], Rubinstein [1309], and Liszt [1218].

In 1843, as a result of an encounter with a theater manager named John Mitchell, Offenbach turned up, invited but unannounced, at Mme. Mitchell's salon and promptly fell in love with one of Mitchell's two stepdaughters, Herminie de Alcain. When, soon afterward, he voiced his honorable intentions, the family set two conditions: (1) he should test his concert appeal in London, and (2) he should convert from Judaism to Catholicism. He fulfilled the first with great success in May 1844 (Londoners termed him the "Paganini of the cello"); never particularly devout, he seems to have managed the second condition without a qualm. (Curiously, as he grew older, Offenbach seems perversely to have emphasized his Semitic features and, in the French press, was depicted as something like the quintessential Jewish caricature.) Beginning in 1845, the marriage was blessed five times with issue—four daughters and a son.

The Opéra-Comique finally, in 1847, agreed to let Offenbach adapt a one-act comedy, *L'Alcove,* but then it shuffled its figurative feet so long that the composer produced it on his own. At that point salvation seemed to arrive in the person of Adolphe Adam [1172], proprietor of the new Théâtre-

Lyrique, who commissioned a three-act opera in 1848. But came the Revolution and Adam's bankruptcy, and the bubble burst. Then in 1850, shortly after Isaac Offenbach died, Arsène Houssaye hired his son to reshape and direct the orchestra of the Comédie-Française at a salary of 6,000 francs. Despite hostility from both musicians and public, Offenbach succeeded there in sufficient measure to make the music noticed and win himself the patronage of such important people as Jerome Bonaparte (known as "Plon-Plon"), the playboy cousin of Louis-Napoleon who had declared himself the Emperor Napoleon III in 1851. After the Opéra-Comique had turned up its figurative nose at three more Offenbach efforts, he got a hearing in 1855 at the Folies-Nouvelles, a little theater run by one Florimond Ronger, who as "Hervé" had been delighting Paris with his musical farces. The work, about cannibals and called *Oyayaie*, was sufficiently successful to inspire Offenbach, with the help of Plon-Plon and the Count of Morny (the Emperor's bastard brother), to acquire a rickety theater of his own on the Champs-Elysées, which he revamped and christened the Bouffes-Parisiens. It opened with a triple all-Offenbach bill on July 5. Of the three works, *Les Deux Aveugles (The Two Blind Beggars)* was an instant hit and ran for a year, during which time the Bouffes-Parisiens moved to more watertight quarters in the Passage Choiseul, which for the rest of Offenbach's life would see the premieres of most of his more than a hundred stage works. One of the librettists of the prologue was a young civil servant, Ludovic Halévy (nephew of the composer), who would work with Offenbach until the end of his days. The last night in August saw the debut of the mistress of one of the stars of the *Aveugles*, a young woman from Bordeaux named Hortense Schneider, who would at a later date be Offenbach's most famous and most expensive vocal exponent. (Offenbach's original concertmaster was his brother Jules, who, by odd coincidence, afterward went *to* Bordeaux to end his career as an opera conductor.)

The new theater opened at the end of December with a new four-character (regulations would allow the composer no more!) Meyerbeer [1142] spoof *à la chinoise*, entitled *Ba-ta-clan*, which became the runaway hit of Paris. Offenbach began to branch out, producing—mostly unsuccessfully—operas by Mozart [992], *Der Schauspieldirektor;* Rossini [1143], *Il Signor Bruschino;* and Rousseau [793], *Le Devin du village.* He also set up a contest for new composers of *opérabouffe* of the dimensions to which he was limited. The first winners, for their settings of Ludovic Halévy's [1157] *Le Docteur Miracle*, were Georges Bizet [1363] and Charles Lecocq [1322]. Meanwhile the company enjoyed a command performance before the emperor and a successful London season in 1857, in the course of which even Queen Victoria was amused. But poor management and a hot summer brought the theater to the verge of bankruptcy. Added to this, Offenbach was already feeling the twinges of the gout that would incapacitate him regularly as long as he lived. ("For his health," he several times escaped his creditors to visit spas.) And Hortense had left in a huff over salary.

A turning point came on October 21, 1858, with the premiere of Offenbach's most perennially successful work, the irreverent *Orphée aux enfers (To Hell with Orpheus).* The plot was anonymously by Halévy, who as recently appointed secretary for Algerian affairs feared compromising himself. Receipts spiraled ever upward, and nine months later Offenbach retired the work because the cast was too weary to go on. (It was revived by imperial command after a year and was regularly trotted out whenever the company was in dire straits; in 1874 it was expanded to four acts from the original two.) *Orphée* was followed by the very successful *Geneviève de Brabant* in 1859. (Offenbach also took a whack at Wagner [1230] with the skit *Le Musicien de l'avenir [The Musician of the Future]*, which made his name mud with the Wagner crowd.) All this notoriety brought him at long last notice from not only the Opéra-Comique but also from the Opéra itself. For the latter, Offenbach wrote a ballet, *Le Papillon (The Butterfly).* Choreographed by the great ballerina Taglioni, it became the *pièce de resistance* of a young *danseuse* named Emma Livry. But two years later the poor butterfly's tutu brushed a candle flame, and the work (literally) died with her. The Opéra-Comique number (libretto by Scribe) was called *Barkouf* (the protagonist was a dog) and sank like lead. But Offenbach countered with *Le Chanson de Fortunio (Fortunio's Song)*, which continued the forward impetus of his career—as did *M. Choufleuri restera chez lui (Mr. Cauliflowery Will Be at Home)* six months later. (There was no small curiosity value here in the libretto, the brainchild of Morny—now a duke—himself, pseudonymously identified as "M. de Saint-Rémy). But despite the successes, Offenbach was again in financial hot water and was forced to resign as impresario of the Bouffes-Parisiens in 1862. To add to his difficulties, his beloved summer home, the Villa Orphée at Étretat on the Normandy coast, burned to the ground. (They nearly saved the piano, but as it was being eased out of a window, someone lost control and it crashed.) On the brighter side, Herminie presented her husband with a fifth and last child, a son christened Auguste-Jacques.

No longer tied to the Bouffes-Parisiens, Offenbach premiered *Les Bavards* at his favorite watering place, Bad Ems, in 1862. It was later the site of other Offenbach premieres, but none so successful. Within six months *Bavards* was playing Vienna, and in an expanded Parisian version it soon went round the world. In 1863 Offenbach himself went to Vienna, met Johann Strauss, Jr. **[1295]**, and wrote *Die Rhein-nixen (The Rhine-Nixies)*. The Viennese did not take to it, but they adored the French Offenbach, who inspired Suppé **[1262]** to create Viennese operetta.

With *La Belle Hélène (Pretty Helen)*, a send-up of the Trojan War in the manner of *Orphée*, Offenbach began in 1864 a period that saw the height of his popularity. Ludovic Halévy had found the perfect partner in Henri Meilhac—with whom he wrote such succeeding hits as *Barbe-Bleue (Bluebeard)*, 1866; *La Vie parisienne (Parisian Life)*, 1866; *La Grande-Duchesse de Gérolstein*, 1867; and *La Périchole*, 1868. *La Belle Hélène* served to lure back *la belle* Schneider back to the fold (at outrageous wages) and made her the Offenbachian prima donna *par excellence* until her retirement a decade later. The works named, on a scale too large for the Bouffes-Parisiens, were produced in bigger houses, chiefly the Théâtre des Variétés. (There was also a hearteningly successful return to the Opéra-Comique with *Robinson Crusoe* in 1867, but *Vert-Vert* chalked up another flop there two years later.) However, the good years came to an end with the Franco-German War in 1871. Though he loudly protested his patriotism (he had become a citizen in 1860), he never quite recovered from the stigma of "German Jew" that the jingoes marked him with.

The world of the Third Republic was also a different one. Sober and chauvinistic, it neither provided fuel for, nor appreciated, Offenbach's kind of satire and turned instead to the blander works of Lecocq. Convinced that spectacle was the answer, Offenbach became an impresario once more, sinking a fortune in redoing the Théâtre de la Gaité. But his offerings only sank him deeper into debt until, early in 1874, he beefed up *Orphée*. In less than a year it brought in over two million francs. But the ensuing grandiose production of Victorien Sardou's play *La Haine* ate up the profits and had to be replaced once more with *Orphée*. In 1875 Offenbach withdrew from the theater again. That same year he persuaded Schneider, now a blowsy forty-two, to return to the stage in *La Boulangère a des écus (The Baker's Wife Has Money)*. But the audience did not buy her, and she gracefully retired. Meilhac and Halévy, seeing the handwriting on the wall, defected to Lecocq.

In 1876 Offenbach, though ailing, was persuaded to go to the United States (where three of his sisters had settled) in the hope that Centennial appearances might relieve his mountainous debts. The voyage was dreadful, and he was not well-received at first; but later, when it was perceived that the Americans wanted to hear the operetta tunes, he attracted enormous crowds in New York and Philadelphia and went home with heart and pockets full. However, on the homeward voyage he fell afoul of a 200-percent Frenchman, a senator, who stirred up the old charges all over again. Later he had relative successes with *Mme. Favart* in 1878 and *La Fille du tambour-majeur (The Drum Major's Daughter)* in 1879. Then he turned to the opera he had always wanted to write. *Les Contes d'Hoffmann* had been inspired thirty years before by a play by Jules Barbier, librettist of Gounod's **[1258]** *Faust*. It was based on tales by E. T. A. Hoffmann **[1086]**, and in the mid-1870s Offenbach had persuaded Barbier to adapt it for him. The work was, as Offenbach sensed, a race against time—and one that he did not win. In September 1880 his gout put him permanently to bed, and early in the morning of October 5 his heart stopped. One of his comedians, Léonce, came to visit after the day had broken and was told that the composer had died in his sleep. *"Tant pis!"* said Léonce. "He'll be quite vexed when he finds out."

The *Hoffmann* score was completed to his satisfaction by Ernest Guiraud **[1352]**, and it was produced in 1881 at the Opéra-Comique with the Venetian scene omitted, to considerable applause. But at the Vienna premiere that December, the Ringtheater went up in flames with considerable loss of life. Six years later the Salle Favart, home of the Opéra-Comique, also burned, destroying the manuscript.

RECORDINGS: In recent years there has been a small industry devoted to "reconstructing" the opera, which is reflected in some of its many recordings. There are also commercial recordings of *Barbe-Bleue, Orphée, Hélène, Périchole, Le Pont des soupirs, Mesdames de la Halle, Brigands, Chanson de Fortunio, Croquefer, Deux aveugles, Madame Favart, Pomme d'api, Vie parisienne, Lischen et Fritzchen, La Grande-Duchesse, Violoneux, Ba-ta-clan, Les Bavards, Papillon, Monsieur Choufleuri,* and some of Offenbach's early cello duos. Among the innumerable excerpts are several synthetic ballets, the most notable of which is Manuel Rosenthal's *Gaité parisienne.* Recordings by Julie Simon-Girard, Offenbach's last leading lady, including an air from *Mme. Favart,* whose *protagoniste* she created, have been transferred to LP. Piracies include performances of *Pépito, La Leçon du chant (The Singing Lesson), Robinson Crusoe,* and *Pomme d'api (Lady-Apple).*

[1265] LISINSKI, Vatroslav (Li-sin'-skē, Vä'-trō-slàf)

TEACHER, CLERK
BORN: Zagreb, c. July 8, 1819
DIED: Zagreb, May 31, 1854

The Turkish occupation of the Balkans effectively removed Croatia from the history of Western music for three centuries. Lisinski represents the first glimmer of the rebirth of a national musical culture. His life, however, stands as a paradigm for the traditional tear-jerking operetta composer's biography—almost too tragic to be believed. He was born Ignacije Fuchs. Though he had some musicial training in his youth, his first employment was as a law clerk (a learner without salary). Meanwhile he wrote music and in 1846 his *Love and Malice* (the first known Croatian opera) was produced in Zagreb. Encouraged by its reception, Fuchs proceeded to Prague to study at the Conservatory. But the Conservatory told him he was beyond the age limit, and he had to content himself with a year or so of private lessons. Imbued with nationalistic fervor, he changed his name to Vatroslav Lisinski and returned to Zagreb, where he tried to make a living as a piano teacher. Though pupils were few and though he was harassed by the Austrian authorities, he continued to compose, completing a second opera, *Porin,* by 1851. He also wrote several overtures, though the bulk of his output consists of dances, choral pieces, and songs. A year before his untimely death, he gave it all up and went back to clerking. His music remained largely undiscovered until *Porin* was produced in 1897 and was quickly elevated to the status of "Croatian national opera." RECORDINGS: Selections from *Porin* have been recorded by various Yugoslav singers.

[1266] ALBERT, Prince-Consort of England

STATESMAN
BORN: Rosenau, August 26, 1819
DIED: London, December 14, 1861

Francis Charles Augustus Albert Emanuel, Prince of Saxe-Coburg-Gotha, was the second son of Ernst I of Saxe-Coburg-Saalfeld (he later traded Saalfeld for Gotha). A graduate of the University of Bonn, he had a thorough classical education, which included the arts and athletics (he was a brilliant fencer). Both Albert and his elder brother (later Ernst II) were passionate about music. Ernst became an indefatigable, if negligible, composer of operas. At fourteen Albert set aside four hours a week for music study, exclusive of practice. He developed into a good drawing-room singer, and, according to all reports, was a highly qualified keyboard player. In 1840, through the machinations of their uncle Leopold I of Belgium but with the enthusiastic consent of both participants, Albert married his first cousin and exact coeval, Queen Victoria. Brilliant and energetic, he gradually became the queen's chief adviser (in effect, the power behind the throne), yet he maintained a marriage that was happier than most. Though he had little time for composition in his new life, he continued to cultivate both music and musicians. Felix Mendelssohn [1200], whose music was sometimes close in spirit to Albert's own, was always a welcome guest in the royal household. As a foreigner Albert was at first looked on with suspicion by the Britishers, and when he proposed to the Society of Arts what would be the great "Crystal Palace" Exhibition of 1851, there was a howl that the visiting foreigners would take over and ruin the nation. But as it turned out, it was an enormous cultural and commercial success, and the profit went to found what is now the Victoria and Albert Museum. It was the inspiration of "Albert the Good" that also led to the founding of other cultural and educational institutions. In 1861, Albert contracted typhoid. It was misdiagnosed as influenza, and he died of a combination of complications and overwork. Albert's compositions, save for a cantata *Invocazione all'armonia* completed in 1845, were mostly pleasant Mendelssohnian songs to German texts, written before his marriage. RECORDINGS: The Purcell Consort of Voices has devoted an LP to his songs.

[1267] SCHUMANN, Clara Josephine

(*née* Wieck) (Shoō'-màn, Klá'-rà Yō-
ze-fē'-nə)

PIANIST, TEACHER

BORN: Leipzig, September 13, 1819
DIED: Frankfurt am Main, May 29, 1896

Though the general public perhaps thinks of
her chiefly in her relationships with Robert
Schumann [1211] and Brahms [1329], Clara
Schumann was a composer in her own right
(if expectably derivative), an important piano teacher, and a performer who ranked
with the best of her contemporaries of whatever sex. She was the sister of the pianist
Alwin Wieck (1821–85) and the half-sister of
the pianist Marie Wieck (1832–1916). Her
mother forsook her family (not without
cause) when Clara was five and married a
Berlin piano teacher named Adolf Bargiel.
Her father Friedrich had begun his career as
a successful preacher, but apparently his
musical leanings combined with his materialism, and he operated (successfully) a musical lending-library (used by young Wagner
[1230] among others) and a piano factory
until his teaching of piano and voice began
to occupy all his time. He developed his own
no-nonsense piano method and taught it
brilliantly, something in the manner of a
Prussian top-sergeant. Besides his own offspring, he numbered among his noteworthy
pupils Bülow [1310], Fritz Spindler (1817–
1905), and Merkel [1301].

Clara, who demonstrated her unusual talent from early childhood, was not exempt
from Wieck's hardboiled approach. However much genius the man had, he was short
on imagination and tenderness. Moreover he
felt that in Clara he was onto a good thing
that, rightly handled, promised them both
financial independence and even wealth.
Among her other gifts was a prodigious musical memory, and when later she performed
without music—unheard of!—she was regarded as a showoff. She made her debut in
Leipzig as an assisting artist at someone
else's concert in 1828, the year that Robert
Schumann, a law student, met Friedrich
Wieck. The next year Schumann, then
nearly twice as old as Clara, became Wieck's
pupil and boarder. He got along well with
the talented little girl, who amused him. She
made her Gewandhaus debut in 1830 and a
few months later published her first music—
four polonaises. Her repertoire at the time
consisted mostly of the virtuosic salon pieces
of the day, but Friedrich considered her
ready for the Big Time by 1831. She concertized in several German cities, stopped by
Weimar to play some Herz [1170] for old
Goethe (who said some nice bland things

about her performance), and wound up in
Paris, where the cholera epidemic kept the
people away from her debut there in droves.
By the fall of 1832 the Wiecks were back in
Leipzig, and Clara was playing Moscheles
[1146] with the Gewandhaus Orchestra,
with which she continued to appear.

In late 1835 Clara and Robert Schumann
became aware that they had fallen in love
and sealed the discovery with a kiss—or a
series of them, which was serious business in
those days. When they announced their discovery to her father, however, he protested
that he could not afford to lose Clara now,
for she was at the threshold of the great career he had foreseen for her. (It was just before this that Clara had premiered her piano
concerto at the Gewandhaus and had played
Beethoven's [1063] "Appassionata" in concert.) Wieck emphasized his point by keeping the two apart, taking Clara on concert
tours and putting out the "Not In" sign for
Schumann. In Vienna in 1837 Clara was
named "imperial chamber virtuoso". When
the affair persisted, Wieck turned ugly,
spread slanderous gossip about both, and finally disinherited Clara. (Not that the long
wait was quite the rapturous affair it has
sometimes been painted; both lovers found
other interests, and at one point Schumann
seems to have thought of venting his wrath
and frustration on Clara herself.) In 1839 the
question of Clara's rights was taken to court,
and after many months Wieck lost the case
and the lovers were married on the eve of
Clara's twenty-first birthday in 1840.

Clara's life, for the next sixteen years, is
largely indistinguishable from Robert's. She
bore him seven children—Marie, Elise, Julie, Emil, feeble-minded Ludwig, Ferdinand,
Eugenie, and Felix—but still managed to
concertize occasionally. She played in St.
Petersburg on their visit there in 1844, premiered Robert's concerto in Dresden in 1845,
and played in Vienna, Prague, and Berlin
the next year. (In Vienna she was "assisted"
by her lifelong friend Jenny Lind, whom she
had met in Altona.) She supported her husband through his illnesses and decline. In
1853 they were visited by young Brahms,
who seems to have fallen in love with her on
the spot. Clara played in London shortly before Robert's death. After that she and her
children lived with her widowed mother in
Berlin for some seven years, while she took
up her career again. Her association with
Schumann had made her taste uncompromising: besides the music of Schumann, and
his friends Chopin [1208] and Brahms, she
specialized in the Classics and was a notable
Beethovenist. But whereas she had espoused
the new Romanticism, she could not abide

"modernism." She came to dislike Liszt [1218], with whom she had formerly performed, found Bruckner [1293] undisciplined, and loathed Wagner [1230]. Her concerts were a repeated memorial ritual; she always appeared clad in black, bent over the keyboard as if in prayer. In 1863 she moved to the vicinity of Baden-Baden, and in 1878 she was appointed chief piano teacher at the Hoch Conservatory in Frankfurt, where she lived out her life.

Clara's relationship with Brahms was ambiguous. Early on he addressed her as "Frau Mama," and his adoration was as much filial as romantic. But when Brahms seemed about to marry someone else, Clara helped break up the possibility. In 1891 they quarrelled over which version of a Schumann symphony was best but eventually made it up. In her last years Clara was plagued by headaches and growing deafness (which forced her retirement in 1892), and she was at times mobile only in a wheelchair. She left 20-odd compositions. Save for the piano trio and the piano concerto, they are piano pieces and a few songs, all influenced by Robert.

RECORDINGS: A number of recordings have been issued, including all the major works.

[1268] ABT, Franz Wilhelm (Àbt, Frànts Vil'-helm)
CONDUCTOR
BORN: Eilenburg, December 22, 1819
DIED: Wiesbaden, March 31, 1885

Franz Abt, both at home and abroad, was one of the most popular songwriters and choral composers of his century. He was the son of a musical parson from the vicinity of Leipzig. His father did not mind his studying music seriously so long as he took up the paternal calling, so he pursued both courses at the Thomasschule and the University of Leipzig, where he became acquainted with such musical Leipzigers as Schumann [1211], Lortzing [1163], and Mendelssohn [1200]. He gave up the ministry when his father died, married Rosalie Neumann (they had gone steady for years), and, after a time as conductor in a Bernburg theater, was hired by the Akazientheater in Zürich in 1841. He remained there for eleven years, during the course of which time he acquired the exiled Richard Wagner [1230] as a colleague. Among the duties he took on were the direction of the Harmonic Society and the Allgemeine Musikgesellschaft concerts. In 1852 he accepted an appointment as the Hofkapellmeister at the Braunschweig

court, which he held until he retired to Wiesbaden in 1882. In 1872 Abt, together with Johann Strauss, Jr. [1295], was invited to Boston to participate in the Boston Peace Festival, a Barnumesque extravaganza supposedly celebrating music's contribution to world peace. By then Abt's songs were sung in every parlor, and his choral works were done by every college gleeclub, and he was received as the great celebrity that he was, much to his amazement and delight. He also performed in Washington, Philadelphia, Baltimore, Buffalo, Chicago, Cincinnati, Evansville, and St. Louis, and went home several thousands of thalers richer. RECORDINGS: His greatest hit was *"Wenn die Schwalben heimwärts ziehen"* ("When the Swallows Homeward Fly"), later set by Hugo Wolf [1521]. It and others of his folksonglike tunes were recorded by turn-of-the-century singers.

[1269] SEROV, Alexander Nikolayevich (Syā'-rof, Àl-yek-sàn'-der Nē-kō-là-yā'-vich)
CIVIL SERVANT, JURIST, CRITIC
BORN: St. Petersburg, January 23, 1820
DIED: St. Petersburg, February 1, 1871

As Wagner's [1230] most vocal supporter, Serov was a storm center in Russian musical circles. Nevertheless he was amazingly successful as an operatic composer, though he never caught on outside his homeland. Born into a governmental family, he was reared to uphold its traditions. He went to law school in the capital, where he made friends with Vladimir Vassilievich Stasov (1824–1906), later the chief spokesman for the nationalistic school of the arts. Their common interest gave Serov the notion of becoming a musician, though he had had little or no training. After taking a civil-service job in 1840, he learned cello and piano and wrote some salon pieces. He also attempted (unsuccessfully) an opera based on Shakespeare's *Merry Wives of Windsor*. In 1845 he was given a high-sounding but unimportant judicial post in the Crimea and whiled away the time with a counterpoint-by-mail course and an affair with a colleague's wife. After three years he quit the job and was promptly railroaded to more of the same in Pskov. There he worked on an opera based on Gogol's *The May Night*, not to be confused with Rimsky-Korsakov's [1416] later work. In 1851 he decided that music was really what he wanted to do and returned to St. Petersburg to eke out an existence as a critic. In that role he rather intemperately fawned all over the Central European avant-gardists and savaged most of his musical country-men. But when Stasov told him that his op-era was no good, Serov destroyed it and be-came Stasov's implacable enemy for life. Economically his existence was not all that painful, since he found a generous patron in the Grand Duchess Helena, Czar Nicolas' sister.

In 1858 Serov took a trip to Germany, met Wagner, and came home to preach the new gospel. In 1863, with the Grand Duchess's backing, he produced his next opera, *Judith,* on the biblical story. Surprisingly it was more Meyerbeerian [1142] than Wagnerian; in any case, despite the antagonism of the musical establishment, it became a hit, won Serov a government pension, and brought in enough money to enable him to marry sev-enteen-year-old Valentine Semyonova Berg-mann, a talented pianist and (later) Russia's first significant woman opera composer. (She died in 1927.) In 1865 Serov produced *Rogneda,* on a Russian historical theme, which was even more successful and more Meyerbeerian, although it made consider-able use of Russian folk-style music. He was at work on an opera called *The Power of Evil* when a heart attack killed him a few days after his fifty-first birthday; the piece was completed by his wife and Nikolai Soloviev and produced in May 1871. Although they made fun of Serov, he exerted considerable influence on the younger generation of Rus-sian composers, notably Mussorgsky [1369] and Tchaikovsky [1377].

RECORDINGS: Selections from *Judith, Rogneda,* and *The Power of Evil* have been recorded by various Russian singers.

[1270] **VIEUXTEMPS, Henri** (Vyö-tȧn', Än-rē')
VIOLINIST
BORN: Verviers, February 17, 1820
DIED: Mustapha, June 6, 1881

Now remembered chiefly as the author of a warhorse concerto, Vieuxtemps was better known in his own day as a violin virtuoso. He was born in Walloon country near Liège in what was then still the Netherlands. His father, a onetime military man, tuned pianos and made instruments. Having taught Henri his musical basics, he turned him over to a local violinist named Lecloux-Dejonc, who soon found he had a prodigy on his hands. Lecloux-Dejonc presented the child in con-cert in various Belgian cities. In Brussels Vieuxtemps came to the attention of the great violinist Charles de Bériot, who took his further training in hand and announced him ready for the Big Time with a Paris con-cert in 1829. The Belgian revolt of 1830 lost Bériot his Dutch court appointment and made it necessary for him to go on a long concert tour, after persuading King Leopold to support his pupil. In 1833 the latter em-barked with his father on what was to be-come a life of ceaseless, not to say obsessive and exhausting, wandering, beginning with the Germanies. He paused in Vienna to study with Sechter [1129], made his way to England in 1834, and then went to Paris to study with Reicha [1059] the following year.

It is not necessary to detail all the tours, which, with ever increasing acclaim, took him from Russia to the United States and back. He seems to have begun composing seriously in the early 1840s, though one of his 7 violin concerti dates from 1836. Most of his other output, largely violinistic, consists of the expectable showoff and salon pieces, but he also wrote 2 cello concerti, a viola sonata, and 3 string quartets. In 1844 he married Josephine Eder, a pianist, and bought a home in Frankfurt am Main. Two years later he was appointed violinist to Czar Nicolas I, and lived and taught in St. Petersburg until 1851. Then he returned to his wanderings, making a memorable (sec-ond) tour of America in 1857 with Sigismond Thalberg [1220]. The roving came to a halt in 1868 with the deaths of his father and his wife. Knowing only one way to find surcease from sorrow, Vieuxtemps again took to the road, covering Europe, then America again, this time with the soprano Christine Nils-son. On his return in 1871, he accepted a post at the Brussels Conservatory, where he taught master classes. In 1873, following his election to the Belgian Academy, he (like Bériot before him) was partially incapaci-tated by a stroke. He lived and taught then in Paris. He gave it all up in 1879 and retired to North Africa, where he died in a suburb of Algiers.

RECORDINGS: There are many recordings of Vieuxtemps' fifth concerto (a contest piece), fewer of the more original fourth and the *Fantasia appassionata,* and even fewer of the very early second. Some of the smaller pieces, including the viola sonata, have also been recorded.

[1271] **FESCA, Alexander Ernst** (Fes'-kȧ, Äl-ek-sȧn'-der Ärnst)
PIANIST
BORN: Karlsruhe, May 22, 1820
DIED: Braunschweig, February 22, 1849

Alexander Fesca was the son of the violinist-composer Friedrich Ernst Fesca, who was a court musician at Oldenberg, Cassel, and

Karlsruhe, and died of tuberculosis at thirty-seven. Though he is credited with Alexander's early musical training, it could not have proceeded far, since he died two days after the boy's sixth birthday. Later young Fesca studied in Berlin with Carl Friedrich Rungenhagen (1778–1851), Zelter's [1008] successor, after having made his concert debut as a pianist at eleven. His other teachers included Wilhelm Taubert [1216], Julius Schneider (1805–85), and organist August Wilhelm Bach. After a successful round of concerts in 1839, Fesca was employed by the Mycaenas of Donaueschingen, Prince Karl Egon von Fürstenberg, and in 1842 he settled in Braunschweig. Two of his 4 operas, *Der Troubadour* and *Ulrich von Hütten,* were produced there. His other compositions were mostly songs and chamber compositions (some of which Schumann [1211] praised). Fesca's career was more promise than fulfillment, for he died at twenty-eight. RECORDINGS: The Collegium con Basso has recorded one of his 2 septets.

[1272] ROOT, George Frederick
TEACHER, SINGER, PUBLISHER
BORN: Sheffield, Mass., August 30, 1820
DIED: Bailey's Island, Me., August 6, 1895

In his autobiography of 1891, George F. Root notes that he had never meant to be a great composer (he wasn't) or a successful one (his name became a household word in American parlors). He was born into a farm family whose womenfolk were musical in a pious way. In 1826 they moved to North Reading, where the father taught Root to toot the flute. This and his experience of church music convinced the boy that he wanted a musical career, and at eighteen he took a sort of janitorial job in nearby Boston to finance lessons there with one Artemas Johnson. He gravitated to Lowell Mason (1792–1872), studied voice with George J. Webb, joined the Handel and Haydn Society, and soon found himself working as Mason's assistant. In 1846 Root was hired to teach music to the select young ladies of Abbott's School in New York City. His reputation grew swiftly, and he was soon teaching in half a dozen schools and conducting the choir of the Church of the Strangers. Root, his wife, and his sister and brother formed a vocal quartet to practice part-songs, and began giving concerts, including some with the New York Philharmonic Society. Finding no suitable material for his girl choristers, he published his own collection, *The Young Ladies' Choir.* Feeling that he lacked the last word in

polish, Root sailed for Paris in 1850 to acquire some from Jules (alias Giulio) Alary, whose greatest claim to fame is that the Paris Opéra staged one of his works in 1861 to make use of the scenery left over from Wagner's [1230] *Tannhäuser* disaster. When Alary invited his pupil to attend a rehearsal of one of his operas, Root's Puritan conscience acted up so at the idea of his entering a theater that he changed teachers. After imbibing as much Parisian musical experience (in concert halls) as he could, he came home with wider horizons and a cannier notion of what his public would accept. One of his first efforts was *The Flower Queen* in 1852, a pioneering tableau-cantata for girls. Encouraged by the success of Stephen Foster [1299], Root asked Fanny Crosby, a former pupil at the state Institution for the Blind, to write him some song lyrics. His first efforts were published under the Germanized pseudonym of "G. Friedrich Würzel." Later he offered a batch to a Boston publisher for a hundred dollars each but had to settle for a royalty arrangement, from which he ultimately made a good deal of money. In 1853 he and Mason opened the Normal Musical Institute for the estival training of schoolteachers—an enormous success which won Root the reputation of being one of the best choral teachers on either side of the Atlantic. In 1856, commissioned by Mason, he wrote his most ambitious work, the dramatic cantata *The Haymakers,* composed on location (the Root family farm).

Meanwhile, G. F. Root's brother E.T. had gone to Chicago and joined forces with C. M. Cady in a music-publishing venture, Root and Cady. The composer joined the firm in 1859. When the Civil War erupted, he turned (unsuccessfully at first) to writing patriotic songs. Then one day (or so the story goes), inspired by reading a Lincoln proclamation, he dashed off "Battlecry of Freedom" on the premises, pressed it on a customer to sing at a rally, and made history. Other Root wartime hits were "Tramp, Tramp, Tramp," "Just Before the Battle, Mother," and "The Vacant Chair." Both Root and his company prospered until 1871, when Mrs. O'Leary's cow reduced the latter to ashes. (Among the successful songwriters the company had promoted was Henry Clay Work [1326].) Not long after, the University of Chicago awarded Root an honorary doctorate. He continued to teach until his death.

RECORDINGS: There have been many recordings of the more popular songs, and the North Texas State University Choir has devoted an LP to the second part of *The Haymakers.*

[1273] ECKERT, Karl Anton Florian (Ek'-ert, Kärl Ȧn'-tōn Flôr'-yản)
PIANIST, VIOLINIST, CONDUCTOR
BORN: Potsdam, December 7, 1820
DIED: Berlin, October 14, 1879

As a small boy Karl Eckert showed such obvious musical talent that the historian and dramatist Friedrich Christoph Förster staked him to a thorough musical education. After turning out his first opera at ten and his first oratorio at thirteen, he studied briefly with Mendelssohn [1200] in 1839. A second oratorio, *Judith,* was sung in Berlin two years later, so pleasing Frederick William IV that he sent Eckert on a two-year tour of Italy. Eckert's *Wilhelm von Oranien* was well received at Berlin in 1846 and at The Hague in 1848. He took a post as accompanist at the Théâtre-Italien in Paris in 1851 and, in the same capacity, toured the United States with Henriette Sontag in 1851–2. In succession he served as conductor at the Théâtre-Italien in 1852, the Vienna Hofoper from 1853 to 1860, and the Stuttgart Hofoper from 1860 to 1867. He resigned in the last year but two years later was called to Berlin as *Hofkapellmeister.* Besides his operas and oratorios, Eckert left a symphony, a cello concerto, and a good deal of other music. But, like so many of his contemporaries, he is remembered only for a single song, the *"Norwegisches Echolied,"* which used to be a favorite recording vehicle for lyric sopranos.

[1274] DUPONT, Pierre (Dü-po*n*', Pē-âr')
LABORER
BORN: Rochetaillée, April 23, 1821
DIED: St. Étienne, July 25, 1870

Born into a working-class family in a village near Lyons, Dupont had little or no education. He took a job in a silkmill. Then, having developed a sort of mystical-socialistic credo, he drifted to Paris where, at Père Fricaud's tavern in the Rue Guénégaud, he sang proletarian songs, for which he made up both music and lyrics. There he attracted the interest of Gounod [1258], who, together with his friend Reyer [1289], wrote the songs down and provided them with accompaniments. Eventually the government decided that Dupont was too potentially dangerous and ordered him deported. Dupont made a direct appeal to Napoleon III, who reversed the order, whereupon Dupont reversed his politics and sang *hommages* to the emperor. He died, poor and neglected, a year before the Empire did. Several of his songs (notably *"Les Boeufs"* ["The Oxen"]) were popular with early French recording artists.

[1275] ZAREMBA, Nikolai Ivanovich (Zȧ-rem'-bȧ, Nē'-kō-lī Ē-vȧ-nō'-vich)
TEACHER, ADMINISTRATOR
BORN: near Vitebsk, June 15, 1821
DIED: St. Petersburg, April 8, 1879

Like many Russian musicians of his time, Zaremba was German-trained. More specifically, as a pupil of Adolf Bernhard Marx, he espoused the ultra-conservative views of the Berlin School, originated by Zelter [1008]. No shining light as a composer, he was a successful teacher of theory, whose most famous pupil was Tchaikovsky [1377]. He joined the staff of the Conservatory in St. Petersburg when it opened in 1862 and became its director when Anton Rubinstein [1309] left in 1867. After five years, illness forced his resignation, and he spent most of the remainder of his life in the West. He was utterly intolerant of any music that smelled of "modernism." RECORDINGS: A few songs show up on records by Russian singers.

[1276] DOPPLER, Albert Franz (Dop'-pler, Ȧl'-bârt Frȧnts)
FLUTIST, CONDUCTOR
BORN: Lemberg, October 16, 1821
DIED: Baden, July 27, 1883

Franz Doppler and his brother Karl (1825–1900), the sons of a musician and born in what is now Lvov (Lwów), began their careers in a brother act *(verdoppelt)* as virtuoso flutists. Then they played in the orchestras of first the German Theater and then the National Theater in Pest. They also got in on the ground floor of the Hungarian Philharmonic Orchestra in 1853. Karl also conducted at the National Theater and, from 1865 until his retirement in 1898, served as court *Kapellmeister* in Stuttgart. Franz moved to Vienna in 1858, where he played and conducted (ballet) at the Imperial Opera and taught at the Conservatory. He died at the Austrian spa at Baden. The brothers collaborated on a number of compositions. Franz produced 7 operas and a number of ballets. RECORDINGS: There are recordings of some of the flute pieces, and a comprehensive collection of these is in progress. Franz Doppler is even better known as the orchestrator of some of Liszt's [1218] *Hungarian Rhapsodies,* but recent findings indicate that the work is really Liszt's, who paid homage to Doppler for some earlier attempts by crediting him as a collaborator.

[1277] WECKERLIN, Jean-Baptiste-Théodore (Vek-er-làn′, Zhàn Bà-tēst′ Tā-ō-dôr′)
LIBRARIAN, TEACHER, CONDUCTOR
BORN: Guebwiller, November 9, 1821
DIED: Trottberg, May 20, 1910

Weckerlin's Alsatian father ran a prosperous dye works and was dying to have Jean-Baptiste succeed him. But the latter became hooked on music, and when he turned twenty-one left home for Paris, where despite his age and inexperience he wangled his way into the Conservatoire. There he studied singing and was a composition pupil of Halévy's [1157]. However, he flunked his final examinations, and for the next several years supported himself by teaching and choral conducting. In 1853 his first opera, a one-act comedy called *L'Organiste dans l'embarras (The Lady Organist in Difficulties),* had a very successful run at the Théâtre-Lyrique; but its eleven successors (some in Alsatian dialect) enjoyed no such luck. In 1863 Weckerlin was appointed archivist and librarian to the newly founded Société des Compositeurs de Musique. Six years later Auber [1103] gave him a post in the library of the Conservatoire, where he succeeded Félicien David as head librarian in 1876. At heart a musicologist, he made vast improvements in the library's holdings and functioning. In his eighty-eighth year he retired to a village near his birthplace. As a composer he specialized in songs and choral music, but he is best known for his many arrangements of early songs, most of which he himself dug out of obscurity. RECORDINGS: A few generations back these songs enjoyed many recordings.

[1278] BOTTESINI, Giovanni (Bot-tā-sē′-nē, Jō-vàn′-nē)
CONTRABASSIST, CONDUCTOR
BORN: Crema, December 22, 1821
DIED: Parma, July 7, 1889

In the line of great contrabassists from Dragonetti [1033] to Koussevitzky [1655], Bottesini was perhaps the supreme master of his instrument, though, like the latter, he also became a notable conductor. The son of a clarinetist, he was musically precocious. By the time he was fourteen, he was so expert on the violin that his father took him to Milan in the hope of getting him a scholarship at the Conservatory. But they found there were only two remaining vacancies—one for a bassoonist, the other for a contrabassist. Thereupon young Bottesini applied himself to the latter instrument and by mid-autumn passed the entrance exams and was admitted as a pupil of Luigi Rossi. (Bottesini's composition teacher was Vaccai [1134].) Four years later, in 1839, having obtained a first prize for performance and an instrument of his own, he began a parlous decade as a free-lance musician. (Legend persists that he found his contrabass, a small "chamber" model by the old Milanese master C. G. Testore, under a pile of rubble in an abandoned theater. He used three strings only, tuned a tone higher than normal, and was easily able to adapt much of the cello repertoire to it.) In 1846 Bottesini and his friend Luigi Arditi [1283] sailed for Havana, where he became first bass in the orchestra of the Teatro Tacon, which produced his first opera—appropriately titled *Cristoforo Colombo*—a year later. Before returning to Europe, he toured the United States, where he was a sensation (and where an enterprising jeweller got rich peddling pins in the likeness of Bottesini). He found a firm friend in Verdi [1232], who encouraged his conducting aspirations. He returned to America in 1850 and again in 1853, when he conducted in New Orleans. He was chief conductor at the Théâtre-Italien in Paris from 1855 to 1857, producing his *L'Assedio di Firenze (The Siege of Florence)* there. From 1861 to 1863 he held the same post at the Teatro Bellini in Palermo, where his *Marion Delorme* (libretto by Antonio Ghislanzoni, author of Verdi's *Aida)* was premiered. In the decade of the 1870s he reached his peak of success as both a composer and conductor. His *Vinciguerra il bandito,* a one-acter, had a considerable run in Paris in 1870, as did his *Alí Babà* in London, at the Lyceum Theatre, where he was conductor for the 1870–71 season. On Christmas Eve 1871 he conducted the premiere of *Aida* in Cairo. (Verdi's first two choices of conductors were for one reason or another unavailable.) Bottesini's most successful opera was *Ero e Leandro (Hero and Leander),* premiered in Turin in 1879. His *Requiem Mass* was first heard there in 1880, and he wrote an oratorio, *Gethsemane,* for the 1887 Norwich Festival in England (where he was known as "the Paganini of the double-bass"). That same year Verdi wrote the solo bass part in *Otello* for him and later got him the directorship of the Parma Conservatory (where he served only a few months until his death.) Despite his more serious works, Bottesini is now remembered almost wholly for his virtuoso contrabass pieces. RECORDINGS: The 2 contrabass concerti, the *Grand Duo* for violin, contrabass, and orchestra, two of the early duos, and a number of smaller pieces have enjoyed recordings.

[1279] GAZTAMBIDE Y GARBAYO,
Joaquín Romualdo (Gåth-tåm-bē'-*thä*
ē Gär-bī'-yō, Hwå-kēn' Rōm-wål'-dō)
CONDUCTOR
BORN: Tudela, February 7, 1822
DIED: Madrid, March 18, 1870

Joaquín Gaztambide, who was a Navarraise of Basque blood, was an important figure in the resuscitation of the *zarzuela,* that peculiarly Spanish musicotheatrical form. (The name comes from *zarza,* meaning "bramble bush," but it probably traces back to an inn called *La Zarzuela,* the locale of a seventeenth-century ancestor of the genre.) Orphaned in childhood, Gaztambide was a chorister in Tudela, then studied in Pamplona, and, like his later collaborator Francisco Barbieri [1287], at the Madrid Conservatory with Ramón Carnicer and pianist Pedro Albéniz. After a year as chorus master of an Italian opera company in Madrid, Gaztambide went in 1846 to Paris to conduct the ballet. Two years later he came back to make a name for himself as musical director of several Madrid theaters and as a composer of *zarzuelas,* many of which he wrote with Barbieri. With the latter and Arrieta [1288], he formed a society to promote the form. In the 1860s he became conductor of the Conservatory orchestra, which became the Madrid Concert Society in 1868. In 1869 Gaztambide organized a *zarzuela* company to tour Latin America. After a series of failures and successes—one performance somehow precipitated a revolution in Havana— Gaztambide fell seriously ill in Mexico in 1870 and had to be taken home, where he succumbed to an operation. Some of his 40-odd *zarzuelas* still hold the stage. RECORDINGS: Selections have been recorded by various Spanish singers.

[1280] STRAUSS, Franz Josef (Shtrous,
Frånts Yō'-zef)
HORN PLAYER, VIOLIST, CONDUCTOR
BORN: Parkstein, February 26, 1822
DIED: Munich, May 31, 1905

Born in a little town in the Fichtelgebirge of northeast Bavaria, Franz Strauss was apparently unrelated to the Viennese Strausses. His father was a policeman, but his mother, *née* Walter, came from a musical family. (One of her relatives was Benno Walter, a violinist and founder of the Walter String Quartet.) Franz Strauss came to be one of the greatest horn virtuosi since Stich [945]. He was solo horn with the court opera orchestra in Munich and professor of his instrument at the Royal School of Music. In 1853 a cholera epidemic killed his wife and children. Later he married Johanna Pschorr, the daughter of a Munich brewer, who bore him two more children, Richard [1563] and Johanna, and brought him sufficient wealth that he never had to worry about money again. Franz Strauss suffered from asthma, which became so serious that he had to give up the horn. But he continued his musical life as a string-quartet violist and as the conductor of a highly reputable amateur orchestra called "Wilde Gungl." For all his talent, he was a musical reactionary who loathed modernism. He particularly detested Wagner's [1230] music and got into frequent screaming matches with Wagner, who always managed to smooth things over, since he valued what Strauss could do with the solo horn parts in his scores. Bülow [1310], with whom he also had set-tos, called him "the Joachim of the horn." Franz Strauss was immensely proud of his son Richard's prowess and did not hesitate to use his influence to get his son's music produced, though that music soon became too modern for him. "It makes me feel as though my pants were full of junebugs," he told Richard of the *Salome* score. RECORDINGS: Franz Strauss's own few compositions, mostly for horn, would not have made Mendelssohn [1200] wince. Barry Tuckwell has recorded the Concerto for Horn. John Cerminaro offers the Op. 7 *Nocturno* for horn and piano.

[1281] MASSÉ, Victor (Màs-sā', Vēk-tôr')
CONDUCTOR, TEACHER
BORN: Lorient, March 7, 1822
DIED: Paris, July 5, 1884

Massé's chief problem was that he could never accept the fact that he was incapable of musical profundity. Born in Brittany (and christened Félix-Marie), he entered the Paris Conservatoire at twelve. There, like so many of his generation, he studied composition with Halévy [1157] and piano with Zimmermann. After winning first and second prizes in several of his fields, he took the Grand Prix de Rome in 1844. (Actually he had to share it with Alfonse Charles Renaud de Vilbac, later a salon composer and an organist of some note, but since no prizes were awarded in 1843 or 1845, he had no room for complaint.) In Rome he wrote a *Mass* and possibly his Italian opera *La Favorita e la schiava (The Favorite and the Slave),* which was not, however, produced until 1855. After some success with songs (he later published several volumes of them), he produced his one-act *La Chambre gothique (The Gothic Room)* at the Folies-Dramatiques in 1849.

He had more success with *La Chanteuse voilée (The Veiled Singer)* in 1850 and *Galathée (Galatea)* in 1852, and his career reached a climax with *Les Noces de Jeannette (Jeannette's Wedding)* in 1853. But his ensuing efforts—six in as many years—either failed or enjoyed only ephemeral popularity. ("Moments of great charm, but no depth" was the consensus.) His 1860 appointment as chorus master at the Paris Opéra slowed down his output, and in 1866, when he succeeded Aimé-Ambroise-Simon Leborne as professor of composition at the Conservatoire, it came to a virtual halt. His second opera, *La Mule de Pédro,* appeared in 1863. The second, *Paul et Virginie,* appeared in 1876 and for a time won productions outside of France, but it was quickly forgotten. By that time he was suffering from a terminal illness, which forced his resignation from the Conservatoire. He dragged on for eight painful years, working when he could on *Une Nuit de Cléopâtre (A Night with Cleopatra),* which he intended to be his monument. Produced posthumously in 1885, it proved not to be. Massé was an officer of the *Légion d'honneur* and was elected to succeed Auber [1103] in the Institut. RECORDINGS: A 1921 recording of *Les Noces de Jeannette,* starring Ninon Vallin, has been transferred to LP. Selections from various operettas appear on early records.

[1282] RAFF, Joseph Joachim (Răf, Yō′-zef Yō-á′-khēm)
SCHOOLMASTER, COPYIST, ARRANGER,
SECRETARY, ADMINISTRATOR
BORN: Lachen, May 22, 1822
DIED: Frankfurt am Main, June 25, 1882

The bad luck that dogged Joachim Raff most of his life seems to have followed him in death. Once touted as one of the great composers of his time, he was soon forgotten, and his reputation has so far resisted efforts to pump it up again. He was born on the shores of the Zürich See in Switzerland, whither his father (a Württemberg organist) had fled to avoid being made a member of Napoleon's army. He learned, largely on his own, to play violin and piano, and to compose, meanwhile distinguishing himself as a student of humanities at the local Jesuit school. Unable to afford further education, he became a schoolteacher, devoting his spare time, such as it was, to further self-improvement. On a whim he mailed one of his compositions off to Mendelssohn [1200], who obtained for him Schumann's [1211] notice in print and a publishing arrangement

with Breitkopf and Härtel. In 1845 Raff walked to Basel to meet Liszt [1218], who took him under his wing. A job with a music store in Cologne did not work out, and he moved to Stuttgart. In 1846 he arranged to study with Mendelssohn, who inconveniently died before Raff could get to Leipzig. A job with the publisher Mechetti in Vienna failed to materialize for exactly similar reasons. Raff's opera, *König Alfred,* was promised a Stuttgart production, which was canceled by the 1848 Revolution. Liszt got Raff a job as an arranger with the Hamburg publisher Schuberth and then, when he settled in Weimar, took him on as his own musical Man Friday.

Being, in effect, Liszt's protégé and taken up by such futurists as Wagner [1230] and Bülow [1310], Raff began to get a swollen head. He let it be known that it was he who taught Liszt to orchestrate and who had himself scored most of the symphonic poems. (There appears to be no evidence for his claims.) He also took on himself a mission to help re-create Holy German Music by synthesizing its main tendencies, past and present, in his own compositions. This notion was chiefly manifested in 11 programmatic symphonies written between 1860 and 1876. Though their intent had some impact on younger composers, such as Richard Strauss [1563], they cannot hide the fact that Raff's inspiration was that of a salon miniaturist.

In his five years in Weimar, Raff fell in love with Doris Genast, the daughter of a prominent theater man. He followed her to Wiesbaden, where he taught and where he married her in 1859. In 1877 he became director of the Hoch Conservatory in Frankfurt, where he taught Edward MacDowell [1529] and where he died at sixty of heart disease. Of his 6 operas, only *König Alfred* and *Dame Kobold* were produced (both in Weimar). His most ambitious work lies in the areas of orchestral and chamber music; his largest output was for the piano.

RECORDINGS: The third *(Im Walde)* and fifth *(Lenore)* symphonies have been recorded by Richard Kapp and Bernard Herrmann, respectively. The *Sinfonietta* for ten winds has been recorded by Leopold Casella. Both Frank Cooper and Michael Ponti have recorded the Concerto for Piano, and Adrian Ruiz the piano *Suite in D Minor.* The Octet in C Major and the *Grand Quintet* are recorded by the Kammermusiker Zürich and the Zürich Piano Quintet (respectively). However, Raff is best known for a *Cavatina* for violin and piano, recorded in its original form and in numerous arrangements.

[1283] ARDITI, Luigi (Är-dē'-tē, Lōō-ē'-jē)
CONDUCTOR
BORN: Crescentino (Italy), July 16, 1822
DIED: Hove (England), May 1, 1903

Remembered now as the composer of a few insipid salon songs, Arditi was, in his day, one of the most respectable of operatic conductors. A product of the Milan Conservatory, where he studied violin with Rolla **[1001]** and composition with Vaccai **[1134]**, he wrote his first opera *I Briganti (The Brigands)* for student production there in 1841. Two years later he made his professional conducting debut at Novara. In 1846 he and Bottesini **[1278]** decided to try the New World and sailed to Havana. He worked in the United States and Latin America for the next ten years, then, after a time in Constantinople, came to London in 1858 as conductor at Her Majesty's Theatre. For the next twenty years he seems to have been chiefly connected with London, though he also conducted in Vienna and St. Petersburg. After 1878 he spent most of his time between London and the United States, where he was chief conductor for "Colonel" Mapleson, who toured the sticks annually with a company that featured such stars as Adelina Patti and Emma Nevada. Among the operas Arditi premiered in London were: *Cavalleria rusticana,* 1891; *La Forza del destino,* 1867; *Hänsel und Gretel,* 1894; and *Mefistofele,* 1880. Arditi's best-known composition is the often-parodied waltz-song, *"Il Bacio"* ("The Kiss"). Noodling around one evening at the piano, he hit on its theme which, at the urging of the singer Marietta Piccolomini, he jotted down. Some years later, when she begged him for a song, he remembered it and set it to words by the baritone Gottardo Aldinghieri (who created the role of Barnaba in Ponchielli's **[1334]** *La Gioconda.)* Other Arditi songs frequently recorded a couple of generations past were *"Parla!"* ("Speak!"), *"Se saran rose"* ("There Will Be Roses" or "The Melba Waltz"), and the bolero *"Leggiero invisibile"* ("Airy, Invisible").

[1284] FRANCK, César Auguste Jean Guillaume Hubert (Fránk, Sä-zär' Ō-güst' Zhàn Gē-yōm' Ü-bâr')
ORGANIST, PIANIST, TEACHER
BORN: Liège, December 10, 1822
DIED: Paris, November 8, 1890

Among the French composers of his century, Franck is a virtual anomaly. Primarily an instrumental composer, he belonged to no school; as an eclectic, however, he turned more readily to German sources, past and contemporary, than to French. Nor, though he had many admiring disciples, did he create a school. His worst works, which are in the majority, tend to be marzipan-sweet; his best, written after he had attained middle age, harness his natural emotionalism with a remarkable sense of form. If he borrowed his chromaticism from Wagner **[1230]** and his cyclic notions from Liszt **[1218]**, he made them peculiarly his own. (Franck's so-called "cyclic form" is an "organic" process by which the shape and continuity of the whole is based on the transformations of a germinal theme.)

The Liège of Franck's birth was French. How much of his Germanic tendency was inherited is still a subject for debate. His mother came from the Rhineland. His father's forebears had long lived in Wallonia, but the name Franck appears to be German. (No link with Melchior **[388]** or J.W. **[538]** has ever been traced, however.) At the time César was born, the father was an out-of-work bank clerk. When both César and his little brother Joseph (1825–91) indicated musical talent, visions of sugar plums danced in his head, and he hurried to enroll them in the local conservatory, preparatory to lucrative concert careers. In 1835 he moved his family to Paris, where the action was said to be. César studied with Zimmermann and old Antonín Reicha **[1059]** while waiting for the red tape that barred him from the Conservatoire to be cut. Admission came in 1837, and subsequently he won several prizes, including a Grand Prix d'Honneur for piano. The second place he took in organ playing is said to have resulted from his puzzling the judges by playing the two test pieces simultaneously, but the tale remains unsubstantiated. (Joseph eventually became a church organist and a minor composer.) In 1842, however, the father, again in a monetary bind, said in effect to hell with the Prix de Rome and hurried César back to Belgium (as it had become) to make them all rich. He didn't do this, and the next year the entourage returned to Paris, where the boys helped make ends meet by teaching.

By then César had written a number of works (including a symphony) of no moment and was embarked on *Stradella,* the first of his 4 operas—none of which was produced in his lifetime and all of which are said to be unstageworthy. However, a set of three *trios concertants* for piano, violin, and cello won publication through the backing of the most important composers in Paris, including Chopin **[1208]** and Liszt. But when the oratorio *Ruth,* the first of his big horsehair-stuffed religious pieces, was performed at the Conservatoire early in 1846, the heavens failed to open, as Franck, Sr., had imagined they would. Furthermore the pianistic career having produced little more than poor health on the part of its protagonist, it was increasingly apparent that César was unlikely ever to become a Liszt (or even a Chopin). Finally, when he announced that he wanted to marry Félicité Saillot Desmousseaux, an actor's daughter, he and his father came to the parting of the ways, and César set forth to support himself as church organist and free-lance teacher. When the guns of the 1848 Revolution began to bark, he and Félicité made their way over the barricades to be married at Notre-Dame-de-Lorette.

Franck, a devout Catholic, who reminds one in several ways of Bruckner [1293], was an indefatigable and willing slave to duty. He got up at 5:30 every morning to begin his long day's teaching and performing, in order to support a growing family. (His son Georges became known as a professor of fine arts.) For the two decades following his marriage he composed little, save for things of a practical nature for church use. In 1851 he was named organist at St. Jean-St. François au Marais and in 1853 choirmaster at Ste. Clothilde, whose organist was Lefébure-Wély [1253]. Five years later Franck himself transported to the organ loft, where in 1859 he inaugurated the vast Cavaillé-Coll instrument for which he produced the remarkable (if flawed) pieces that revitalized French organ composition.

In the 1860s Franck acquired a number of devoted pupils, led by Henri Duparc [1442], who set about to see that he won deserved recognition. Franck was something of a *naïf* who never fathomed the deviousness of his fellow men nor understood that saying what one thought was not always politic. Nevertheless in 1872 he was appointed, despite some strong opposition, professor of organ at the Conservatoire. But despite the post-Auberian [1103] efforts of Ambroise Thomas [1217], that institution remained largely devoted to opera and operatic politics. Thus Franck did not endear himself to his colleagues when he started branching out into the teaching of serious composition, notably in the long-neglected instrumental areas. To add to the friction, he was a charismatic teacher who got on best with the young (the roster of his pupils (Chausson [1484], Guilmant [1351], Guy Ropartz [1564], d'Indy [1462], Pierné [1555], Vierne [1616], etc.) reads like a who's-who of the next French generation). Through them, Franck's no-nonsense approach came eventually to permeate French music teaching—

though some, such as d'Indy, held it in such veneration that a later generation came to regard its innovations as establishment techniques.

Franck's own style did not really ripen until the 1880s, the period that produced the quintet, the quartet, the violin sonata, the symphonic poems, the greatest of the keyboard pieces, and the symphony (the first true French symphony to enter the repertoire, though Gounod [1258], Bizet [1363], and Saint-Saëns [1343] had by then made interesting essays in the form.) Franck's creative vitality seemed to grow with his art, despite continued public resistance to that art. But in May 1890 he was struck down by a horse-drawn omnibus. He shook off the injury, refused to see a doctor, and went about his business. However, complications set in and he died in November. The diagnosis was "pleurisy"—though one wonders if the trouble may not have been a lung cancer.

RECORDINGS: All the late instrumental works have been recorded many times over. The youthful effusions have been almost universally ignored, as has much of the vocal material, save for a few songs, the oratorio *The Beatitudes* (Jean Allain), and the *Mass* (which has appeared in a recording by the Welch Chorale). There is a piracy of the 1885 opera *Hulda,* sung in Italian.

[1285] ROCKSTRO, William Smith
PIANIST, TEACHER, MUSICOLOGIST, THEORIST
BORN: North Cheam, January 5, 1823
DIED: London, July 2, 1895

Surrey-born Rockstro was originally, like the hero of *H.M.S. Pinafore,* named Rackstraw. A pupil of William Sterndale Bennett [1246], he naturally gravitated to Leipzig in 1845, where he was a special pet of Mendelssohn [1200]. (It was perhaps German pronunciation rather than Gilbertian association that caused him to respell his name.) For more than a decade afterward he was active in England concertizing, composing, teaching, and accompanying at the London Wednesday Concerts. But in 1860 his health went bad, and with his invalid mother he moved to Torquay on the Devonshire coast. Though he served as organist at nearby Babbacombe, he spent the next thirty years in musical research and writing. His special fields of interest were in Gregorian chant and other mediaeval church music, in which areas he did some pioneering work. He also made some excellent piano reductions of operas. His popular biographies of Mendelssohn and Handel [683] contributed no little to the English deification of those composers. In 1876 he converted to Roman Catholicism. In his last four years he taught in London at both the Royal College and the Royal Academy. His songs and piano pieces are Mendelssohnian. RECORDINGS: Some piano pieces have turned up in recorded collections of Victoriana (e.g., that by Neely Bruce).

[1286] LALO, Victoire-Antoine-Édouard
(Là-lō′, Vĕk-twär′ AN-twăn′ A-dwär′)
STRING PLAYER, TEACHER
BORN: Lille, January 27, 1823
DIED: Paris, April 22, 1892

Like César Franck [1284], Lalo distinguished himself as a writer of instrumental music in a country still almost totally committed to opera. And like Franck it took him a long time to get off the ground. When he did, he was hooted for being "too German," and until recently at least his name has survived primarily through one work, the *Symphonie espagnole* for violin and orchestra.

The Lalos came to Flanders from Spain in the Renaissance. Édouard's family sent him to the local conservatory to learn violin and cello, but balked when he announced that he planned to be a musician. Thereupon in 1839 he ran off to Paris, where he studied with the conductor Habeneck and other more obscure musickers. He survived as an orchestral violinist and by teaching, and in the late 1840s brought out a few songs, which the books describe as "competent," and a handful of violin pieces. In 1853 he published two piano trios, and two years later became violist of the newly formed Armingaud-Jacquard Quartet, which for some years served as chamber-music missionary to the Gauls. Lalo, who wrote a quartet for this ensemble in 1859, later became second violinist, and eventually the group became a chamber orchestra known as the Société Classique.

Discouraged by the lack of interest in his music, Lalo largely gave up composing until after his 1865 marriage to his pupil Julie de Maligny, who persuaded him to return to it. In 1867, prodded by the government, the Paris opera houses announced a contest for a new opera. Lalo submitted his *Fiesque* (after Schiller's play *Fiesco*). In 1869 the jury pronounced it *magnifique*—and gave it third prize, behind the work of persons called Phillipot and Canoby. The librettist, Charles Beauquier, a journalist, demanded a recount, whereupon the Théâtre Lyrique volunteered to produce the work—at its convenience. But the director's resignation and

the outbreak of the Franco-Prussian War ended that. Two years later *Fiesque* had actually gone into rehearsal in Brussels when another administrative shakeup ended Lalo's hopes for good. He published the vocal score at his own expense and later used much of the music for his orchestral *Divertissement* of 1872 and the pantomime *Néron (Nero)* of 1891.

Despite the setbacks, Lalo now began to hit his stride. The great Spanish violinist Pablo de Sarasate [1415] had success with the Concerto for Violin No. 1 in 1873 and even more in 1874 with the *Symphonie espagnole,* also for cello and orchestra, which met the current French taste for musical exoticism. These works were followed by the Concerto for Cello, the *Norwegian Rhapsody,* and the *Concerto russe* for violin and orchestra. (Inspired by his wife's singing, he also produced some highly individual *lieder* that are now almost wholly neglected.) It may be said that in general Lalo was admired by the progressives (e.g., Gounod [1258], Massenet [1396], some of the Impressionist painters) and scorned by the conservatives. His admirers were especially taken with his brilliant orchestration. His cause was aided by the 1871 foundation of the Société National de Musique, devoted to the performance of French music, especially instrumental music.

Lalo completed his second opera, *Le Roi d'Ys (The King of Ys)* in 1881, but the Paris Opéra turned it down. Instead they commissioned him to write a ballet *à la Hindoue.* However, they gave him so little time that he pressured himself into a partial stroke. Gounod, who had striven manfully against the fiasco of *Fiesque,* orchestrated the ballet, now called *Namouna,* from its composer's dictation. But by the time it reached the stage in March 1882, a whispering campaign had ensured its failure. (It was said to be "German" and undanceable.) The nineteen-year-old Debussy [1547] protested its reception so vigorously that he was ejected from the theater. Lalo salvaged much of the music in a pair of orchestral suites that proved successful. In 1886 he produced his only symphony and in 1889 his only piano concerto. Meanwhile he had finally got a commitment from the Opéra-Comique for a production of *Le Roi d'Ys,* which had a triumphant premiere in May 1888, winning him the ribbon of the *Légion d'honneur.* He died four years later, leaving an unfinished opera *La Jacquerie* and a son, Pierre (1866–1943), who became an important critic and musical administrator.

RECORDINGS: Apart from the *Symphonie espagnole* and the Concerto for Cello, Lalo has had rather infrequent representation on records, though most of the mature orchestral and chamber music has been recorded at one time or another. (Louis de Froment conducts a boxed set of the concerted works.) Of the operas, *Le Roi d'Ys* has enjoyed many excerpted recordings but so far only one *intégrale* (by André Cluytens).

[1287] BARBIERI, Francisco Asenjo
(Bärb-yā'-rē, Fràn-thēs'-kō Ā-sän'-khō)
CLARINETIST, SINGER, PIANIST, MUSICOLOGIST
BORN: Madrid, August 23, 1823
DIED: Madrid, February 17, 1894

Even more than his friend Gaztambide **[1279]**, Barbieri was a power in the revival of Spanish music. His paternal grandfather was Italian and danced with his wife at the Teatro de la Cruz. He took the boy in charge after the latter's father was slain in the Carlist wars of the 1830s. At fourteen young Barbieri entered the local conservatory where, like Gaztambide, he studied with Mateo Albéniz's **[991]** son Pedro and the composer Ramón Carnicer. Later he became a wandering musician, playing or singing wherever the jobs were. In 1846 he decided to go straight and came back to Madrid to compose and to dig into early music. His ambition was to become a creator of opera in the Italian vein, but his only attempt did not even get a production. In 1850 he turned to the *zarzuela*. After a palpable hit with his first try, he joined with Gaztambide and others to open the Teatro del Circo, which was to be devoted to the genre. When Gaztambide's initial offering flopped, Barbieri hastily wrote *Jugar con fuego (Playing with Fire)* and enjoyed a triumph. In all he turned out nearly 80 stage works (some in collaboration with Gaztambide), of which several—notably *El Barberillo de Lavapiés (The Little Barber of Lavapiés)* of 1874—are still popular. As a musicologist he was notable for his edition of Spanish Renaissance songs, though his proposed history of Spanish music never saw the light. He was also instrumental in founding the orchestra of the Madrid Concert Society. Barbieri died within a week of his friend Arrieta **[1288]**. RECORDINGS: Recordings from the two *zarzuelas* noted are common.

[1288] ARRIETA Y CORERA, Pascual Juan Emilio (Är-yā'-tä ē Kō-rā'-rà, Pàs'-kwàl Hwàn Ā-mēl'-yō)
TEACHER, ADMINISTRATOR

BORN: Puente la Reina, October 21, 1823
DIED: Madrid, February 11, 1874

With Barbieri **[1287]** and Gaztambide **[1279]**, Arrieta was the third of the founding trinity of the modern *zarzuela*. His music was certainly the most infected by Italian opera—with some reason. A Navarraise, he studied under Vaccai **[1134]** at the Milan Conservatory, which mounted his first opera, *Ildegonda*, in 1845, his last year there. On his return to Madrid, he was appointed singing teacher to Isabela II. A second opera, *La conquista di Granada*, was produced there in 1850 and later as *Isabel la Católica*. In 1853 Arrieta, encouraged by Barbieri, turned to *zarzuela*, enjoying a smash hit with his first attempt, *El dominó azul (The Blue Cape)*. In 1855 he produced his two-act *Marina*, which became his most popular work. Two years later he was appointed professor of composition at the Madrid Conservatory, whose direction he took over in 1868. In 1871 he upgraded *Marina* to operatic status by adding recitatives and another act. It became the first opera in Spanish to be produced at the Teatro Real. All told, Arrieta wrote about 50 *zarzuelas*. Another opera, *San Francesco da Siena* appeared in 1883. Among his pupils was Ruperto Chapí **[1461]**. RECORDINGS: *Marina* has been corded in both its versions. (The operatic cording dates from the early days of electrical recording and features such front-rank singers as Mercedes Capsir, Hipolito Lazaro, and José Mardones.)

[1289] REYER, Louis-Étienne-Ernest (Rā-yā', Lōō-es' Ā-tyen' Er-nest')
CRITIC, CONDUCTOR
BORN: Marseilles, December 1, 1823
DIED: Le Lavandou, January 15, 1909

Reyer, who like his idol Berlioz **[1175]** has perhaps suffered for his honesty and his originality, was born Louis-Étienne Rey. (There is no indication that he was related to the musical Reys of Tarascon of a generation earlier.) He took advantage of the free music school in Marseilles but demonstrated no particular genius, and in 1840 he became a civil servant in Algiers, where his uncle worked. However, he continued to dabble in music and even wrote and produced a festival mass to welcome home the Duke of Aumerle, the governor-general. The 1848 upheaval brought Reyer back to France, where, against family wishes, he went to Paris to study with his aunt, the composer Louise Farrenc **[1178]**. He made friends with such young literary lions as Flaubert and Gautier and, through them, found acceptance in various journals as a music critic. (It is suspected that he had something to do with some of the music criticism that appeared under Gautier's byline; Reyer also, like Gounod [1258], wrote down and harmonized some of the songs of the illiterate peasant composer and political agitator Pierre Dupont [1274].)

Reyer was much taken by the taste for exoticism then popular among the Paris aesthetes, and several of his early works—the "symphonic ode" *Le Sélam*, 1850; the ballet *Sacountale*, 1858; and the opera *La Statue*, 1861—were based on oriental themes. The successful one-act opera of 1854, *Maître Wolfram*, was not. In these endeavors, the composer won high praise from Berlioz. Reyer's opera *Erostrate* was premiered in the summer of 1862, just two weeks after Berlioz's *Béatrice et Bénédict*, at Baden-Baden. It was Berlioz too who suggested to Reyer the composition of an opera after Flaubert's *Salammbô*.

In 1866 Reyer was appointed librarian of the Paris Opéra, and critic of the *Journal des débats*, where Berlioz had so long served. (Reyer was the last person Berlioz visited before taking to his deathbed and was one of those who saw him through his final days.) Reyer became a passionate defender of the musical rebels, such as Gounod, Bizet [1363], Franck [1284], Lalo [1286], Liszt [1218], and especially Wagner [1230]. He was also among the first to recognize Verdi's [1232] true greatness. During this period he wrote his *Sigurd*, an opera derived from the *Nibelungenlied* but, save in basic subject matter, quite unrelated to Wagner's epic. It was not, however, until 1884 that he could get a performance—in Brussels. It was a great success—though the first Paris performance a year later was so atrociously cut that Reyer walked out on it. Six years later, Brussels had another winner with *Salammbô*, Reyer's last opera. *Sigurd* has managed a precarious hold on the French repertoire ever since.

RECORDINGS: A splendid recording of *Sigurd* from the French Radio circulates in the underground; it shows an immensely dramatic work, whose music owes something to Berlioz, and perhaps a little to Wagner, but derives its strength mostly from its composer's own instincts. Up to thirty years ago, excerpts were common on French-derived records, which also produced occasional snippets from *Salammbô* and *Maître Wolfram*. (Note: The *Salammbô* scene in the film *Citizen Kane* is not from Reyer's opera but a composition of Bernard Herrmann [2175].)

[1290] KIRCHNER, Theodor Fürchtegott (Kērkh'-ner, Tā'-ō-dôr Fürkh'-te-got) ORGANIST, CONDUCTOR, ADMINISTRATOR
BORN: Neukirchen, December 10, 1823
DIED: Hamburg, September 18, 1903

Kirchner is one more representative of the mighty army of Schumannists that swarmed over the Germanies in mid-century. He came from a Saxon village to Leipzig, where he studied with the organist Karl Ferdinand Becker (1804–77), with Mendelssohn [1200], and with Schumann's [1211] colleague Julius Knorr (1807–61). Later Kirchner completed his studies in Dresden with the organist Johann Schneider, whom Mendelssohn greatly admired. In 1843 Kirchner was appointed organist in Winterthur, Switzerland. After holding that post for nineteen years, he conducted in Zürich and taught at the conservatory there for another decade. An appointment as director of the Würzburg Conservatory did not work out, and he quit after two years. After that he lived again in Leipzig and from 1890 in Hamburg. His final years were marred by illness and poverty. Kirchner is chiefly noted for his imaginative, if Schumannesque, character pieces for piano. He also wrote some chamber music and songs (in Schumann's vein). RECORDINGS: A few of his songs have been recorded by Dietrich Fischer-Dieskau.

[1291] SMETANA, Bedřich (Smā'-tà-nà, Be'-der-zhikh)
PIANIST, CONDUCTOR, TEACHER
BORN: Litomyšl, Bohemia, March 2, 1824
DIED: Prague, May 12, 1884

There had been many composers of Czech descent in Bohemia prior to Bedřich Smetana. But they were on the whole Czech composers only in that sense, for they came from a Germanized middle or upper class and wrote music in the approved international style. Indeed, after the short-lived attempt of the Bohemians to get out from under the Austrian yoke that ended in the flight of Frederick V, the "Winter King," in 1620, most evidence of a national culture had been ruthlessly trampled down, and what traces were left of it, including song and dance, were to be found among the peasants in the backwoods. But political events in the nineteenth century bred hope and increasing national spirit, and Bedřich Smetana, the first important composer to identify himself with it, can properly be regarded as the father of Czech art music. It must be said, however, that though he fought hard to create a national music, it was against dreadful odds and the opposition of a powerful segment of his own kind, and he was not to know of his true success in his tortured lifetime.

Smetana's father František had risen from gamekeeper's assistant to the status of master brewer, one that enabled him to hobnob with a high social level and to live comfortably (though he later fell on hard times). Twice widowed, in 1820 (when forty-three) he had married the twenty-eight-year-old Barborá Lynková, a coachman's daughter who was to bear him the last ten of his twenty children. The third of these, after twelve girls all told, was a boy, quasi-Germanically christened Fridrich. At the time František was running the brewery at Litomyšl, about one hundred miles north of Vienna. The boy grew up speaking German, and, oddly, never really mastered Czech. In 1831 the family moved to the estate of Count Czernin at Jindřichův Hradec, east of Brno (Brünn), where František took a position as the count's brewer and became independent enough to buy a farm near Čechtice, some miles to the northwest, which was to prove his financial downfall. Bedřich was first enrolled in the *Gymnasium* at Jihlava, and then in that at Havlíčkův Brod, where some of his teachers began to take note of his musical leanings. In 1839 he persuaded his father to let him go to Prague, where he was shortly enrolled in the Classical Grammar School. But he became increasingly engaged in matters musical, perfecting his pianism, studying scores (both mostly on his own), playing in a string quartet (for which he arranged music), and attending concerts. (He was influenced for life by one of Liszt's [1218].) Eventually he quit school. When his father found out, he decided to make a farmer of him, but his Uncle Josef Smetana, a teacher at the Premonstratensian School in Plzeň (Pilsen), decided to take him under his wing, with salutary educational results.

In Plzeň, Smetana won fame as a gifted pianist, became acquainted with the national dances that, in the somewhat liberalized atmosphere, were becoming all the rage, and wrote several himself, including polkas, which were the fad of the day. He also fell in love with Kateřina Kolárová, then sixteen, a childhood acquaintance and herself a fine pianist, and boarded with her family until they moved to a village near Prague in the summer of 1843. At that point Smetana felt himself sufficiently educated and, with the blessing of his now impecunious father, set out for Prague to make his fortune. Though he found lodgings with a cousin, it was touch

and go for a time. Nevertheless he managed to wangle piano and theory lessons from the blind theorist Josef Proksch, Kateřina's piano teacher, who employed him for accompanying stints at his student concerts and eventually found him a place as music master to the children of Count Leopold Thun und Hohenstein in 1844. As part of the princely household, Smetana found himself with leisure time, which he put to good use furthering his musical knowledge. It was at this time that he heard Berlioz [1175] conduct in Prague and found one of the chief models for his own creative career. (The others were Liszt and, to a much lesser degree, Wagner [1230].) In 1846 he turned his post over to Kateřina and set out on a concert tour of Bohemia. It flopped at the outset, and he soon found himself again down and out in Prague.

He managed to survive with musical odd jobs, and eventually began to attract a student clientele sufficient to allow him to think of opening his own "academy" in 1848. Just as that hope was about to be realized, he became somehow involved in the revolution that broke out that year and fled the city early in June. On his return in July he opened his school, though the building lacked the simplest amenities and he was unable to afford decent pianos for the use of his students. Nevertheless, it then being thought necessary for nubile young ladies to play the instrument and there being no conservatory in Prague that admitted them, the institution throve in spite of itself, and on August 27, 1849, he was able to risk marrying his Kateřina. The next year, thanks to Proksch, he became court pianist to the deposed (and flighty) Ferdinand I of Austria, now resident in Prague, with whom he was required to struggle through piano duets. He also began to win attention for his inventive student concerts, for his writings on music, and for his piano compositions, a few of which began to see publication. For the wedding of the Emperor Franz Joseph to Elisabeth of Bavaria, he wrote and submitted a *Triumphal Symphony,* based on the Austrian anthem, but it was ignored. To get it a hearing, Smetana went to great effort and expense to arrange a concert of which it would be the main feature on February 26, 1855. As it turned out the concert conflicted with a production of Wagner's *Tannhäuser* that drew on both audience and performers, and proved to be much too long, with the result that the symphony had to be reckoned a failure. (Later, retitled as *Festive Symphony,* it proved better than he remembered it.)

Meanwhile things were not going well for Smetana on the domestic front. Kateřina, who had by now borne him three daughters —Bedřiška, Gabriela, and Zofie—was exhibiting unmistakable symptoms of tuberculosis. In 1854 Gabriela died, followed a little over a year later by Bedřiška, his favorite, in whose memory her father wrote his G-minor piano trio. A fourth girl, named after her mother, was born in 1855 but lived only eight months. In 1856 Smetana's best friend Karel Havlíček died in an Austrian prison, where he had been held for "treasonable" activities. Fired up by reports from the pianist Alexander Dreyschock **[1260]**, and anxious to escape the tragedy that seemed to pursue him, Smetana left in October to seek a better career in Göteborg, Sweden. This was to be the chief focus of his activity until 1862. Having established his credentials with a recital, he opened a school that was quickly overenrolled and within the year was conductor of the chorus of the Harmonic Society. In truth the musical level of Göteborg was not a very sophisticated one, and in trying to improve it Smetana was hampered by his apparent inability to learn Swedish. Nevertheless he seems to have been both popular and happy. In the summer of 1857 he went home in time to be informed of the death of his father and to find both his wife and remaining child ill. Despite the climatic dangers to Kateřina, he took them back with him that fall. Kateřina was sick and alone most of the time, and her husband had become rather deeply involved with a student, a Mrs. Fröjda Benecke, to whom he dedicated several compositions. Having begun and abandoned various ambitious projects, he completed in 1858 *Richard III,* a Lisztian symphonic poem (though he did not think of it in those terms), and followed it immediately with another, *Wallenstein's Camp.* By the time he completed it, early in 1859, Kateřina's condition was very grave indeed. Her mother came to attend to her, and at the end of March they decided to take her home. On the way she collapsed and died in Dresden. Smetana turned Zofie over to Mme. Kolárová and for several weeks wandered aimlessly around Bohemia. At the end of May he accepted an invitation from Liszt to come to Leipzig for the twenty-fifth anniversary of the *Neue Zeitschrift für Musik.* After a salutary fortnight with the apostles of the New Music, he returned to Bohemia to stay with his younger brother Karel, a forester. There he met Barbara ("Betty") Ferdinandi, age nineteen, a young woman of considerable intellectual prowess, and shortly afterward proposed to her. She at first (wisely) rejected him but soon yielded to please her parents. That fall he returned to Göteborg, where he was even more successful than before but was made unhappy by the shadow of the past.

In July Smetana and Betty were married in Bohemia, and they returned to Sweden in September, where the following January he completed his third symphonic poem, *Hakon Jarl.* That year, however, his clientele fell off for whatever reason. Betty disliked Göteborg (and Mrs. Benecke), quarreled often with her husband, and nagged him to get out of the small puddle and make something of himself. Concerts in Stockholm and Norrköping turned out disappointingly, however, and in April 1861 the Smetanas pulled up stakes and went home for good. (In the spring of 1862, on the invitation of the city, the composer went back for two months, but never again.) They returned to a Prague in which significant concessions by the Austrians had created a nationalistic ferment, and Smetana began learning his ancestral language, which was now allowed to be used.

Finding himself, however, a forgotten man for whom no opportunities loomed, he set out to pursue them elsewhere. (He now had another daughter, Zdenka, to figure into the budget.) There proved to be nothing in Leipzig, nothing in Cologne, Rotterdam, The Hague, Amsterdam, or Bonn. Returning to Prague, he gambled on an orchestral concert that would introduce the first two symphonic poems—and lost. He did no better with a piano recital a couple of weeks later, but, after his last hurrah in Göteborg, he settled in Prague for good. Now burning to somehow spark a national music, he found his first opportunity in the choirmastership of the Hlahol, a Czech choral society, for which he composed and arranged a number of pieces. What he really yearned for was the conductorship of the Czech Provisional Theater, founded to serve Czech drama and opera until a National Theater could be built. It opened in November 1862, but Smetana's dream went unrealized then, for the conservative powers mistrusted him and gave the post to a hack named Jan Nepomuk Maýr. Meanwhile Smetana went back to playing four-hands with dotty old Ferdinand. In 1863 he was to his delight elected president of the music section of the newly founded Arts Society, dedicated to the community of the arts and professions. This honor was partly owing to the success of the overture he had written the previous December for the Society's presentation of the puppet play *Doktor Faust* by Matěj Kopecký. A year later he provided another for Kopecký's *Oldřich and Božena* (which seems to have provided the name for Betty's second daughter, Božena, born in February

1863). That October he became director of the Hlahol, which in May 1864 produced a three-hundredth-anniversary celebration of Shakespeare's birth that included a performance of Smetana's *Shakespeare March.*

Meanwhile Smetana was entrusting his hopes of the opera conductorship to the Czech press, chipping away at the shortcomings of the current administration, which were many. He also coveted the directorship of the Prague Conservatory, but when it fell vacant, it was given to another conservative bumbler. (Smetana was particularly and understandably incensed at the Prague Opera's promotion of a one-legged dancer as a drawing card.)

Back in 1861 a Count Harrach had offered a prize for a true Czech opera. Smetana thought himself the man to succeed there but was unable to find an idea for a libretto. Around the first of the next year, he met a poet and journalist named Karel Sabina, who volunteered a libretto in a Czech historical subject having to do with the medieval invasion of Bohemia by Otto of Brandenburg. The deadline was September 1862, by which time Smetana had not finished Act One of *The Brandenburgers in Bohemia.* But no one else was farther along, and so Harrach extended the grace period for a year. By then Smetana had two competitors, Adolf Pozděny and the ineffable Maýr. The intendant of the Provisional Opera was all ready to produce Smetana's piece, but, not unexpectably, Maýr vetoed it. Eventually he was overruled and the work went into rehearsal. But it got little cooperation, and Smetana himself had to oversee and conduct it from the outset. Premiered on January 6, 1866, it won both the Harrach prize and popular approval, and got eleven performances by March. But apparently its detractors were in a majority and it soon faded.

While all this was going on, Smetana and Sabina had completed a second opera, a peasant comedy in two acts called *The Bartered Bride.* Smetana insisted it was a mere bagatelle, though ultimately it came to be the work in which he captured the essential Czech spirit. Not at first, however. The Provisional Theater, after the success of *The Brandenburgers,* was eager to stage it and did so on May 30. Unfortunately the day was a national holiday and stifling hot to boot. Attendance was therefore sparse, and those who came were not pleased. It would eventually become the most successful of all Czech operas internationally, but it went through four revisions over a period of years before Smetana was really satisfied with it. Seventeen days after the premiere, the Prussians marched into Prague, and Smetana,

fearing reprisals for his portrayal of their ancestors, the Brandenburgers, again fled the city. When he returned, he was surprised and overjoyed to be elected chief conductor of the Provisional Opera, where he first appeared in that role on September 28, leading Weber's **[1124]** *Der Freischütz.* During his tenure there, Smetana strove not only to further Czech opera, but to give the company a well-rounded repertoire as well sung and played as was possible.

Before either of his other operas were realized, Smetana had begun on another, *Dalibor,* based on an old legend and set to a libretto by Josef Wenzig, a German poet and history teacher. (It was later translated into Czech.) Smetana decided it would mark the laying of the cornerstone of the National Theater on May 16, 1868. The premiere at the New Town Theater climaxed the day and was preceded by the *Festive Overture* that Smetana had written for the occasion. The occasion had all the earmarks of a major success, but there was little enthusiasm for the five subsequent performances of *Dalibor,* after which it was shelved. It also gave rise to a nattering chorus, which cried "Wagnerite" and "Teutonophile," implying "traitor to our national cause," though there was nothing notably Wagnerian or German about the work.

Though deeply disappointed, Smetana went ahead with plans for a new opera, for which Wenzig provided an outline as early as 1866. It was to be based on the legend of the supposed Bohemian queen Libuše, who was said to have founded Prague. It was a tale that had been the basis for more than one opera, most notably perhaps for Johann Joseph Fux's **[585]** *Costanza e fortezza,* performed for the coronation of the Emperor Charles VI as King of Bohemia in 1723. Smetana conceived of his work also as a ceremonial piece, a great historical pageant to be performed only on state occasions. In fact he meant it for the Bohemian coronation of Franz Joseph, and when the latter refused the crown, Smetana, against all advice, withheld it until 1881, when he had it played to celebrate the opening of the National Theater. (It was also meant to celebrate the nuptials of Archduke Rudolf and Stephanie of Belgium, but at the last minute the bride reneged. Moreover the National Theater had to be closed shortly afterward owing to damage from a fire.)

What all this meant was that six years elapsed before a new Smetana opera was unveiled after *Dalibor.* The antipathy of Smetana's enemies to that work found new fuel in his continued silence, and they took every opportunity to attack him. Their chief spokesman was František Pivoda, founder of the Prague Singing School and a former supporter of Smetana, who had turned rabidly against him, largely to foster his own ends. To make matters worse, an aural deterioration that had begun as a high-pitched sound in his ears had rendered the composer virtually stone-deaf by 1874, and the hue and cry was now for his resignation from the Opera. Musical Prague was divided into two camps, his supporters being nearly as loud as his enemies.

In the meantime Smetana was feeling the urge to write another opera and suggested to a young member of his chorus, Eliška Krásnohorská, then making a name for herself as a poet, that she whip him up something relatively frothy. In late April 1871 she had worked up a scenario, *Sebastian and Viola,* based on Shakespeare's *Twelfth Night.* In the end they could not agree on it, but meanwhile Smetana had found a French farce by Jean Pierre Félicien Malfille called *Les deux veuves (The Two Widows)* that caught his fancy. He worked out a libretto with one Emanuel Züngl, which made a Czech parlor comedy out of the play. Smetana completed the score in a little more than six months, and it was first played at the National Theater on March 27, 1874, as a benefit for its composer. The public liked it, but his opponents did not, and Pivoda attacked him in print as a "pathological idiot," this phrase being a reference to his deafness.

At more or less the same time Smetana had been working on a cycle of tone poems reflecting various aspects of his country. Beginning probably in 1872 with *Vyšehrad* (a crag above the city of Prague, frequently mistranslated as *The High Castle),* it was followed by *Vltava (The Moldau), Šárka* (a legendary Czech Amazon), and *From Bohemia's Meadows and Forests,* the last two completed in 1875. But he came to feel that he had not said all he wanted to say on the subject, and in 1878–79 he added *Tábor* (named after the stronghold of the Hussites) and *Blaník* (after the mountain fastness from which the Hussites will supposedly one day emerge to save their country.) These works, among Smetana's most popular, represent his most mature orchestral writing.

By late 1874 his hearing had failed so completely that he was forced to give up his conductorship. That was insufficient for his tormentors, however, for they acquired the rights to his operas on the most demeaning and parsimonious terms and then failed to pay him even the little they had agreed upon. To his physical misery—he suffered acutely from the noises in his head and aged rapidly—was added that of poverty again.

In desperation in 1875 he submitted himself to a Dr. Zoufal, who kept him for a month in a dark room, smearing him with foul-smelling ointments, none of which treatment had any effect whatsoever. Later he returned for equally unsuccessful "electric-shock therapy." That same year he went back to his Shakespeare opera, whose librettist called to his attention a novel by Karolina Svetlá, an idyll of village life called *Hubička (The Kiss).* Smetana was taken by its simple sentimental story (a fiancée refuses her lover a kiss until they are married) and shortly had a libretto from Krásnohorská. There were the usual disagreements and vicissitudes, but the opera was ready for a November 7, 1876, premiere under Adolf Čech's baton. It proved an unexpected success and gave its composer one of his last happy moments.

By then, he and Betty had moved in with his daughter Zofie and her husband, Josef Schwartz, a forester in Jabkenice. Betty was now exhibiting something very like hatred toward him and had denied him her bed. Furthermore he had submitted himself to the barbarities of a self-styled Russian doctor named Klima whose ministrations had left him feeling worse than ever. Nevertheless he was so elated by his triumph that he returned to Krásnohorská for a new libretto, and they settled a sort of fairytale about a hidden treasure (which turns out to be the *protagoniste)* called *Tajemství (The Secret).* Smetana's parlous health made for slow going, but the collaborators worked with wonderful unanimity, and Čech was able to ring up the curtain on the finished product on September 18, 1878. The first-night audience was ecstatic, but thereafter interest rapidly cooled and the work came to be regarded as little more than a failure.

During this period Smetana had returned to piano writing, producing among other things, the cycle *Rêves (Dreams)* and a set of Czech dances in answer to Dvořák's **[1386]** *Slavonic Dances,* with whose authenticity of spirit he took issue. He also continued to write choral works, the most considerable of which was the cantata *The Czech Song.* Once again he toyed with the work that was now called *Viola,* rejected another Krásnohorská proposal, and finally settled on a scenario that was to become *Čertova stěna (The Devil's Wall),* a title that refers to a rock barrier across the Moldau, supposedly hurled there by the Devil. The plot, which involved nothing less than a struggle between the forces of Christianity and those of Hell, Smetana decided he wanted handled as a comedy. Krásnohorská, rather uncertain about all this, obliged—whereupon he decided to treat it with the utmost seriousness. She protested vehemently, asking to be permitted to add a disclaimer to the score, and in the end they parted company. By dint of heroic effort, Smetana completed the score in mid-April 1882, and it was played first on October 29. The audience did not understand it, and it was an abject failure. Crushed, the composer retired inside himself and out of the depths of his anguish brought his first string quartet, in E minor, which he called "From My Life."

Now he began to suffer serious hallucinations which culminated in something like a partial paralysis, leaving his features contorted. Other dreadful symptoms ensued, yet with unbelievable doggedness and against medical orders he managed somehow to produce a second quartet as well as some lesser pieces. Then he again turned to *Viola*. He made some progress, but failing memory and confusion made for increasing chaos. In February 1884 his mind gave way completely, and he grew more and more demented, violent, incoherent, and uncontrollable. Literally pursued by demons conjured up by his own brain, he sank into a quivering lethargy and died in the late afternoon of May 12.

RECORDINGS: Smetana's music, with a few exceptions *(The Bartered Bride,* the quartets, the *My Country [Má Vlast]* cycle) does not "travel" well, but the Czechs have given it its due on records. All of the completed operas have appeared, as has the complete piano *oeuvre.* As much goes for the extant chamber music, most (if not all) of the orchestral material, and many of the choral pieces and songs.

[1292] REINECKE, Carl Heinrich Carsten (Rī'-nek-e, Kärl Hīn'-rikh Kär'-sten)
PIANIST, VIOLINIST, CONDUCTOR, EDUCATOR, WRITER
BORN: Altona, June 23, 1824
DIED: Leipzig, March 10, 1910

Tremendously productive and greatly influential, Carl Reinecke, though he lived well into the present century, was little more than a name in the fifty years after his death, save perhaps as the composer of standard cadenzas for many standard concerti. Born in a suburb of Hamburg, he was the son of Johann Peter Reinecke, a musician and teacher, who gave him a sound and historically based musical education. Carl developed into a good orchestral violinist and a virtuoso pianist. Having appeared in public from the age of eleven, he undertook a suc-

cessful tour of Scandinavia at eighteen and met Gade [1248] in Copenhagen. This last fact may have helped inspire his move to Leipzig in 1843. There he worked both with Mendelssohn [1200] and with Schumann [1211], who once said that Reinecke understood him better than most people did. The following year Reinecke toured the Baltic area with the violinist Joseph von Wasielewsky, a Mendelssohn pupil and future biographer of Schumann. Shortly afterward he settled in Copenhagen for a couple of years as court pianist to Christian VIII. On the death of that monarch in the violent year of 1848, Reinecke found his way back to Leipzig, where he set out on a tour of Italy and France with another violinist from the Conservatory, Otto von Königslow. Reinecke spent some time in Paris and then, in 1851, was called by the Cologne Conservatory to teach piano and counterpoint. After three years he took over the directorship of the concert society in Barmen (near Düsseldorf) and there established himself as one of the up-and-coming conductors in Germany.

In 1860 Reinecke came into his own at the age of thirty-six. Julius Rietz [1227], Mendelssohn's successor as conductor of the Gewandhaus Orchestra, became royal *Kapellmeister* in Dresden, and Reinecke was called to succeed him. He was also made professor of composition at the Conservatory. For his last fifty years, he was to be at the center of European musical life there in Leipzig, a refuge for those who deplored "modernism," though he continued to make occasional concert tours until 1872. Among his pupils in one area or another were Isaac Albéniz [1523], Edvard Grieg [1410], Christian Sinding [1488], Johan Svendsen [1379], Felix von Weingartner [1552], the musicologist Hugo Reimann, and the American pianist Ernest Hutcheson. Reinecke turned the orchestra over to Artur Nikisch in 1896 but remained at the Conservatory (where he was named director in 1897) until 1902.

In his playing, his composition, and his ideas, Reinecke was a throwback, who had no patience with the "new music." To be sure he was influenced by Brahms [1329] and the early Wagner [1230], but the real Reinecke came from his Classical training, shored up by his admiration for the best of Mendelssohn. Given these limitations, his music is sound as a whistle, extremely attractive, and surprisingly inventive. His operas (one would like to know more of *Kathleen und Charlie)* are probably a lost cause, as are the large occasional choral pieces, but one may hope for a revival of his cantata treatments of some of the less-Grimm fairytales, and perhaps of the 3 symphonies (the third is numbered Op. 227!).

RECORDINGS: There are recordings of the 2 piano concerti (Gerald Robbins, Michael Ponti), the harp concerto (Lily Laskine, Nicanor Zabaleta), the flute concerto (James Galway, Raymond Meylan, and Jean-Pierre Rampal), the *Toy Symphony* (Emanuel Vardi, Raymond Lewenthal), and the "Undine" flute sonata (Rampal and others), as well as other works for chamber ensembles and for piano. (It should be noted that much of Reinecke's creative effort went into music for home consumption—i.e., salon music at its best.)

[1293] BRUCKNER, Joseph Anton
(Brook'-ner, Yō'-zef Ân'-tōn)
ORGANIST, VIOLINIST, CONDUCTOR, TEACHER
BORN: Ansfelden, September 4, 1824
DIED: Vienna, October 11, 1896

Anton Bruckner, one of the towering figures of the post-Romantic era, suffered in his lifetime from the machinations of Wagner's [1230] enemies and his own friends and from being generally misunderstood both as a composer and man. The reverberations have not yet died away.

Bruckner, though ultimately of peasant stock, was the son of the schoolmaster and organist of Ansfelden, a village in Upper Austria. His mother sang soprano in the choir, and by the time he was four the child was scratching out hymn tunes on a small fiddle. Noting his son's proclivity, the elder Anton gave him keyboard instruction and, by the time the boy was ten, his father could depend on him to fill in for him at church. In 1835 Anton was sent to live and study with his godfather, Johann Baptist Weiss, organist of Hörsching, another village in the area. But at the end of the following year, Bruckner's father, worn out with the overwork needed to support his large family, fell ill, and died six months later. Though young Anton was virtually superannuated, his mother talked Father Michael Arneth, prior of the nearby Augustinian community of St. Florian, into taking him on as a choirboy (as a result of which he would get a free education). He received especially valuable training from organist Anton Kattinger, widely admired as a performer. In 1840, Bruckner having elected to follow in his father's path, was sent to the educational preparatory school in Linz, the provincial capital. There his music teacher was August Dürrnberger, whom Bruckner so much admired that he later adopted his theory text for his own

classes in Vienna. Having attained certification as an assistant teacher, Bruckner was sent to the border village of Windhaag, where his superior treated him as a sort of slave. After a year and a half, by mutual consent, Bruckner was relieved of his duties and sent to the hamlet of Kronstorf—where his superior treated him like a son. A neighbor supplied him with a spinet, he studied the music of J. S. Bach [684] from Leopold von Zenetti, choirmaster in adjacent Enns, was befriended by the priest of nearby Steyr, Joseph Plersch (who let him use the church organ), and played duets with Karoline Eberstaller, a former keyboard partner of Franz Schubert [1153]. By now Bruckner was also composing fairly regularly, though his juvenilia (mostly choral works) are generally only of academic interest.

In 1845 Bruckner passed his examination, permitting him to take elementary-school jobs as a full-fledged teacher, and he was hired to teach at St. Florian, where he spent the next decade (and whither he often returned when the pressures became too much.) Gradually his reputation as a composer and virtuoso organist spread beyond the walls, and he received occasional commissions, which his detractors argued interfered with what he was being paid for. Nevertheless Bruckner was happy with his work, his creation, and his continuing studies, except for a persistent sense of loneliness. He desperately wanted to marry, and he fell passionately in love with the headmaster's teenage daughter, who rejected him. This was a pattern that pursued him all his life—infatuation with and rejection by girls (usually in their late teens), the torment surely aggravated by Bruckner's high-minded espousal of extramarital chastity.

When Father Arneth died in 1854, however, Bruckner at the age of thirty was apparently beginning to find St. Florian's too constraining. Buoyed up by the success of the *Mass* he wrote for the installation of Arneth's successor, he sent the score to Simon Sechter [1129] in Vienna and was told he must come and study with him. Meanwhile he had had his hands slapped for applying elsewhere for a job as an organist, and when the competition for that post at Linz Cathedral came up, Bruckner assumed his participation would be improper and stayed away. However, Dürrnberger euchred him into sitting in on the auditions, and, when the other candidates failed, into taking the test, which he passed handsomely. The authorities at St. Florian blessed him.

In Linz, Bruckner took his duties very seriously (as he always did). He was responsible for the organ music both in the cathedral and in the parish church, gave lessons, and both practiced and studied assiduously. Unable to afford Vienna, he took lessons with Sechter by correspondence, visiting the capital yearly for a test under his teacher's eye. In 1861, shortly after Bruckner had been granted the directorship of the Linz Liedertafel, Sechter pronounced him ready for all musical eventualities. In Linz Bruckner also acquired many friends, none of them more valuable than Bishop Franz Joseph Rudigier. Bruckner composed for the choral society as well as for the church, and whipped his charges into a prizewinning body. However, in 1861 he resigned. As a joke, some of the members had arranged a phony attempted seduction of Bruckner by a waitress on whom he had cast worshipful eyes. Bruckner did not find it funny. Later that year, seeking certification as a conservatory teacher, he went to Vienna and was asked to improvise for a jury consisting of Sechter, Joseph Hellmesberger, Felix Otto Dessoff, Johann von Herbeck, and Becker. Some quirk persuaded them to give him a theme they all thought impossible. Bruckner, without blinking, turned it into an introduction and fugue that left them gasping. (It has been suggested that Bruckner's remarkable improvisational prowess explains why he wrote down no important organ pieces.)

Ever the perfectionist, Bruckner was still not satisfied with his progress, and applied to Otto Kitzler, a Linz orchestral cellist, for lessons in orchestration. It was Kitzler who in 1864 introduced him to Wagner's music, of which he had not previously heard a note. Bruckner was stunned at how far one could diverge from the rules he had been taught to treasure and was henceforth a worshipper (but by no means an imitator) of Wagner.

The combination of favorable circumstances produced a violent release of creativity, and between 1863 and 1869 Bruckner produced the orchestral overture, the 3 great Masses, and the first three of the 11 symphonies (including the later-rejected F-minor work and the one in D minor that Bruckner numbered "0"), as well as the *Germanenzug* and other choral pieces. In 1865, to his great delight, he had a personal invitation from Wagner to attend the premiere of *Tristan und Isolde* in Munich. There he met his hero and many of his followers, including Hans von Bülow [1310]. In the same year Bruckner also met the Viennese critic Eduard Hanslick, who was helpful at first but who later turned against him. During the same period he suffered a succession of heartbreaks from thwarted love (which made him contemplate emigrating to some exotic place like Mexico or London). By the spring of 1867 such upheavals, coupled with overwork and his own innate sense of insecurity, resulted in depression, panic anxiety, and an obsession with counting things, and he spent the summer in a mental hospital recovering.

The year 1868 began with Bruckner's reappointment to the directorship of the Liedertafel, an association that he climaxed four months later by unveiling for the first time anywhere the finale of Wagner's *Die Meistersinger,* with the composer's concurrence. Meanwhile Bruckner's teacher and friend Sechter had died, and he was offered the latter's professorship at the conservatory (though what he had coveted was the post of court organist). He was hesitant to forego the equity he had built up in Linz, but in the end he and his spinster sister "Nani," who had moved in with him a couple of years earlier, left for Vienna in July. He proved to be a brilliant teacher—uncompromising as to standards, but so enthusiastic and lucid that none of his students minded. While the authorities made up their minds about Sechter's successor at the Hofkapelle organ, Bruckner served there on a provisional basis without pay. This activity won him an invitation to dedicate a new organ in Nancy in 1869, to play at Notre-Dame de Paris, and to give some concerts in London at the new Albert Hall. In 1870 Nani died; some months later he hired a housekeeper, Frau Kachelmayr, who remained with him until his own death.

The history of the rest of Bruckner's life is largely the history of the symphonies. He completed Nos. 2–6 between 1871 and 1876, in which latter year he visited Bayreuth for the premiere of the Ring operas. (Bruckner seems to have had little interest in opera except as music. He studied *Tristan* from a textless score, and at the end of *Walküre* someone had to explain to him that Wotan had not cremated Brünnhilde.) In 1873 he had dedicated the third symphony to Wagner, who had become his staunch friend, much to the displeasure of Hanslick and Brahms [1329]. But they were unable to prevent his being appointed to a newly created professorship at the University of Vienna in 1875, or occasional performances of one and another of the symphonies. In 1877 he was forced to conduct the Philharmonic himself in the premiere of the third, Herbeck having suddenly died; the results were such that most of the audience had left by the end. In 1881, however, he was so pleased with Hans Richter's performance of the fourth that he tipped him a thaler to buy himself a beer. In 1886, downcast because Brahms had received an honorary doctorate and he hadn't, he applied to the Universities of Cincinnati and Pennsylvania for one—unsuccessfully. But two years later, after a decade without pay, he finally was made court organist. He was also named by the emperor to the Order of Franz Joseph. By then there was no doubt as to Bruckner's place in the scheme of things, and his music was being heard all over the world (though he never heard a performance of the gigantic fifth symphony). The seventh and eighth symphonies and the *Te Deum* were products of the 1880s. The ninth was incomplete at his death.

In 1889 admirers of the two men got Bruckner and Brahms together for a dinner. They chatted amiably, but no friendship resulted. The university gave Bruckner his doctorate in 1891, the year that saw his last abortive love affair, with a Berlin chambermaid. He suffered increasingly from circulatory troubles and in his last year had occasional brushes with senile dementia. When he could no longer negotiate the stairs to his apartment, the emperor installed him in the gatekeeper's lodge at the Belvedere. There he was working on the last symphony the morning of his death.

As has been noted, Bruckner was a perfectionist, and the original versions of the symphonies usually underwent thorough revisions consistent with his very clear notions of what their form and structure ought to be. But too often, to get them performed he let himself be swayed by the urgings of acolytes and well-wishers (who sometimes made "improvements" themselves). All this has resulted in endless research and eternal argument as to just what the true version may be.

RECORDINGS: Though all of the symphonies have been recorded (most of them many times), various versions have been used. Only Bruckner's youthful and minor works have been done less than justice on records, though such things as the *Requiem,* the *Mass* in C Major, the cantata *Helgoland,* the quartet and quintet, and some of the church works have in recent years become available.

[1294] CORNELIUS, Carl August Peter
(Kôr-nāl′-yoos, Kärl Ou′-gŏ͞ost Pä′-ter)
POET, TEACHER
BORN: Mainz, December 24, 1824
DIED: Mainz, October 26, 1874

Peter Cornelius (not to be confused with his uncle the painter) had a fragile but genuine talent for both music and poetry, as he himself knew. But it was only partially realized, for, as he also recognized, he allied himself with more forceful and charismatic figures who drained him. The son of actors, he trained for the stage, absorbing music and literature along the way. But he found that he lacked the self-confidence for the profession. (His looking like a drowned rat can't have encouraged him!) He then turned to music, living with Uncle Peter in Berlin and studying with the theorist Siegfried Dehn until he was twenty-eight. Identifying with the moderns, he gravitated to Weimar, where Liszt **[1218]** employed him to translate his own French-language articles (mostly, it would appear, the handiwork of Carolyne von Sayn-Wittgenstein, Liszt's mistress, who rode herd on Cornelius in his labors). Shortly after his arrival, he began turning out *Lieder,* to his own lyrics, which won Liszt's approval. In the course of his first year at Weimar, he was also introduced to Wagner **[1230]**, who suggested that they ought to take up housekeeping together, "like man and wife!"

In 1855 Cornelius began work on what was to be his masterpiece, the comic opera *Der Barbier von Bagdad (The Barber of Bagdad).* Liszt undertook to premiere it three years later. As it turned out, all hell broke loose in the theater; directed at Liszt by a person or persons unknown for reasons that remain obscure, the demonstration ruined what was to be the only performance of the work in the composer's lifetime. Liszt resigned, and though his resignation was turned down, he abandoned opera at Weimar and left three years later. The disenchanted Cornelius moved to Vienna in 1859, where he lived a marginal existence for the next six years, and wrote *Der Cid,* which was produced in non-Lisztian Weimar in 1865. Meanwhile its composer had cemented his friendship with Wagner, who persuaded Ludwig II to pay Cornelius a salary as his rehearsal coach. Toward the end of May, Cornelius went to Weimar to see his opera onstage and so missed the premiere of *Tristan.* Wagner told him that if he could not keep his commitments, he should resign, but Cornelius did not resign, and two years later he was given a teaching post, in theory and rhetoric, at the Royal School of Music. That same year he married Bertha Jung (age thirty-three) from his hometown. By then, his creative vein had about run dry. A final opera, of Wagnerian aspirations, *Gunlöd,* was left unfinished. (It was later completed by Waldemar von Baussnern, but made no impact when it was produced in Cologne in 1906.) Cornelius also wrote a good deal of songs and choral music.

RECORDINGS: There are many recordings of his songs and at least three of *Der Barbier.*

[1295] STRAUSS, Johann, Jr. (Shtrous,
Yō'-hán)
CONDUCTOR, VIOLINIST
BORN: Vienna, October 25, 1825
DIED: Vienna, June 3, 1899

The second Johann Strauss neither invented
the waltz nor made it the paramount dance
craze of the nineteenth century. Some anonymous peasant did the former; Johann's own
father [1177] did the latter, if anyone did it
singlehandedly. But the son (and his brothers, to a degree) apotheosized and immortalized it, turned a bawdy dance-form into a
vehicle for symphonic poetry. Moreover, his
life (almost exactly coeval with that of Franz
Josef I) brackets, as it were, the great days of
the Austrian Empire and its capital. (Schubert [1153] and Beethoven [1063] were still
alive when he was born; he outlived Brahms
[1329] and Bruckner [1293] by only three
and two years respectively.) One learns early
to link Strauss and Viennese gaiety, but (as
with present-day Vienna) the gaiety of the
man is a false superimposition of the mind,
for he was in fact morose, shy, inarticulate,
and introverted.

Johann Strauss, Jr., the eldest son of his
father, was one of five whom he got on his
wife, née Anna Streim. (His mistress provided him simultaneously with another family, which did not inherit his talent.) Young
Johann was born two and a half months after his parents' wedding, when his father
was twenty-one (and on the rise) and his
mother was twenty-four. Johann, Jr., was
slated for a commercial career and was educated accordingly, though his father
grudged him piano lessons. He yearned,
however, to play the violin, and his mother
arranged for secret study with Franz Amon,
concertmaster of the Strauss orchestra. At
fifteen, having gotten through the *Gymnasium,* he was sent to a business school but
was ejected two years later in a row precipitated by his absentmindedly singing in class.
When Johann begged, in the name of helping to support his mother, that he be allowed to become a musician, his father (who
had left home) gave in. The young man then
continued his violin lessons with one Johann
Anton Kohlmann, ballet master at the
Kärntnerthor Theater, and studied theory
and composition with Josef Drechsler, soon
to be *Kapellmeister* at the cathedral. Pronounced fit for service by his teachers,
Strauss in 1844 took out a musician's license
and hired an orchestra. Together they made
their debut on October 15 at Dommayer's
Casino, across the way from the Schönbrunn
Park in the suburb of Hietzing. Widespread
curiosity provided a full house, and the ven-

ture was a triumph. From then until the father's death five years later, the two Johann
Strausses were competitors, though much of
the younger's repertoire came from the elder's pen. The split became most pronounced during the 1848 uprising, when Johann, Sr., sided with the government and Johann, Jr., who got into trouble by playing
La Marseillaise on the public streets, sympa-
thized with the student revolutionaries.
Nonetheless the younger man always retained a great respect for the father he had
never really known.

After the Viennese got over the loss of the
first Johann Strauss, they accepted the second as his successor—the Waltz King in every way but one. Labeled as a dangerous
radical because of the *Marseillaise* episode,
he had to wait fourteen years to achieve the
title of *Hofballmusikdirektor.* He was now
able, with some judicious weeding, to combine his own orchestra with his father's and
was from then on in nonstop demand both
as a conductor and composer. There was little or no time for any sort of private life
(though his first wife noted that he had had
at least thirteen serious affairs). In 1854, going home from work in the small hours one
spring night, he collapsed and was shipped
off to a sanitarium at Bad Gastein in the
Styrian Alps. There he had an offer from a
Russian railway magnate, involving 20,000
rubles a season (later doubled!) and a villa of
his own, to perform summers at Pavlovsk, a
resort which the fellow was promoting on
the new railway south out of St. Petersburg.
Leaving the orchestra, or most of it, with his
brother Josef [1300], who had proved his
worth during Johann's hospitalization, he
went there the following summer. People
from the capital, including the czar and
Grand Duke Constantine, flocked thither;
the railway and Strauss prospered; and
Pavlovsk claimed him for the next eleven
seasons. Early on, he entered into a passionate affair with a Russian girl named Olga
Smirnitzki, but when he proposed, her father turned him down. Finally in 1862, he
abruptly wed pudgy, forty-four-year-old
Jetty Treffz, née Henriette Chalupetzky, the
common-law wife of Baron Moritz Tedesco
and mother of his two daughters. The baron
took her defection gracefully and provided
her with a handsome dowry that enabled her
to buy and furnish a fine home in Hietzing,
near the scene of her husband's first triumph.

Shortly after his marriage Strauss turned
the orchestra over to his brothers and devoted himself chiefly to composition. Many
of the great waltzes come from this period—
Artist's Life (to give them their familiar En-

glish names), *Tales from the Vienna Woods, Wine, Woman, and Song,* and *The Blue Danube.* The last, commissioned by a *Männerchor* and sung in a vocal arrangement, was regarded as a flop until Strauss used it to fulfill a commission from the 1867 Paris World's Fair, where, in orchestral dress, it became the hit of the century. He occasionally conducted, in part to fill court obligations, and sometimes to exercise his talents as a symphonic conductor, which he had begun to explore a decade earlier. (It was Strauss who, in 1861, first introduced to Vienna music from the then-unperformed *Tristan und Isolde,* specially arranged for him by the composer. Strauss and Wagner [1230] had a lifetime mutual-admiration society.) Strauss had gone to Paris for the World's Fair in 1867, and five years later with grave misgivings, he embarked to conduct at the World Peace Jubilee in Boston. There, where the promoters thought big, he found himself leading, with the aid of a hundred assistants, twenty thousand singers and instrumentalists in *The Blue Danube.* He reported that it was the most incredible bedlam he had ever heard, but that everyone finished together.

If the waltzes of Strauss took Paris by storm, the operettas of Offenbach [1264], Parisian by adoption, set Vienna on its ear, from his first appearance there in 1858. The vaunted Viennese operetta, in fact, derived its impetus from Offenbach. In the mid 1860s he is supposed to have suggested that Strauss try to emulate him. Strauss, distrustful of words in whatever form, demurred until Max Steiner, director of the Theater an der Wien convinced him how singable his melodies were. Strauss agreed to give it a try, and Steiner had one of his people jerrybuild a libretto called *Die lustigen Weiber von Wien (The Merry Wives of Vienna).* But there was so much arm-twisting applied by various would-be participants that Strauss refused to go on and accepted instead a piece of Steiner's own cobbling called *Indigo und die vierzig Räuber (Indigo and the Forty Robbers,* a.k.a. *Ali Baba).* It was scheduled for October 1870, but the Franco-Prussian War forced its postponement until the following February. Despite its four-hour length, it enchanted the first-nighters; however, the critics recognized its theatrical flaws and it quickly died. It was followed by another such concoction, *Der Karneval in Rom,* which opened on the eve of the 1873 Vienna World's Fair. The tourist trade kept the theater full for a time, but in May the stock market, temporarily buoyed by the French defeat in 1871, collapsed. Many people were wiped out financially, and things

looked grim for the exposition. However, both it and the operetta survived the season.

For his next effort, Steiner secured the services of the conductor-lyricist Richard Genée and the playwright Karl Haffner to convert into a libretto a French farce entitled *Le Réveillon* by sometime librettists Meilhac and Ludovic Halévy. The result, premiered on April 5, 1874, was *Die Fledermaus (The Bat);* it got mediocre reviews but survived nearly seventy performances. Later productions in New York, Berlin, London, and Paris, however, firmly established it as the most stageworthy and probably the best of Strauss's 16 operettas—though *Der Zigeunerbaron (The Gypsy Baron)* of 1885 has proved almost as lasting, and *Eine Nacht in Venedig (A Night in Venice),* a drastically revised *Indigo* (as *Tausend und eine Nacht [A Thousand and One Nights]),* and the posthumous pastiche *Wiener Blut (Vienna Blood)* still hold the stage in Austria and Germany.

The Strauss marriage was by this time in serious trouble. A son of Jetty's from a liaison preceding that with Tedesco had injected himself into the *ménage* unannounced and had proved so demanding that Strauss threw him out. The Hietzing establishment may have been another bone of contention, and he began building a mansion in town on what is now the Johann Strauss Gasse. One April night in 1878, he went home to find that Jetty had suffered a stroke. She died a few hours later (discount the yarn about his having stumbled over her dead body in the dark), and Strauss, morbid and hypochondriac all his life, dumped the funeral arrangements in the lap of his brother Eduard and took the next train to Italy. That seems to have solved nothing, and he soon returned and took rooms in the Hotel Viktoria. There he met Angelika Dittrich, called "Lili," a would-be singer half his age, and married her in September. Lili had it all over Jetty in looks, but the marriage was a disaster. Unable to understand this morose, laconic, undemonstrative elderly man, she soon became involved with the ineffable Max Steiner and walked out. In 1881 Strauss met a young widow, Adele Strauss, whose father-in-law had been a friend (but no relation) of his own father. Love—apparently quite genuine—eventuated (Adele was as least as attractive as Lili). Lili's affair did not pan out, and she made scenes. Strauss was determined to divorce her and marry Adele. But divorces in Austria were hard to come by and precluded remarriage—and besides, Adele was Jewish and Strauss was Catholic (whatever his ancestors may have been), which made for a legally unbridgeable gap. But Strauss had a few cards up his sleeve in the persons of some highborn admirers. Early in 1887 he became a citizen of Saxe-Coburg-Gotha, which had no such marriage laws. In July the musically inclined Prince Ernst II (brother of Victoria's Prince Albert [1266]) personally handed down the divorce decree, and a month later in an operetta finale the two Strausses were married in the Royal Chapel. It was a happy union; Adele survived Johann by more than thirty years and devoted the whole period to seeing that he was properly remembered and honored.

Three years before his marriage, he had his one unequivocal stage success with *Der Zigeunerbaron,* which he later went to Russia to conduct (taking his bride-to-be along). It is the progenitor of the innumerable and indistinguishable Viennese-Hungarian operettas that followed. Encouraged perhaps by his success in the Magyar vein, he later embarked on a full-fledged opera, *Ritter Pasman,* based on a Hungarian narrative poem. It was introduced at the Hofoper on New Year's Day in 1892 and was received respectfully, as were the four operettas that followed it; all have been forgotten. Forgotten too (indeed, never published) is the ballet *Aschenbrödel (Cinderella),* commissioned by Gustav Mahler [1525] but not produced until a decade after its composer died. In his last years Strauss, who suffered from neuralgia and fits of black depression, became less productive and even more private than before. Obsessed with a fear of dying in poverty, he salted his money away in real estate. Though he became an object of pilgrimage (his final visitor was Mark Twain), he enjoyed most playing cards or billiards with a few close friends, among whom he numbered Brahms, Goldmark [1315], and the conductor Hans Richter. There is a persistent legend that Strauss sometimes spent an afternoon with the emperor (whose jubilee he marked with the *Kaiserwalzer)* at the home of the actress Kathi Schratt, the mistress with whom the empress had thoughtfully provided her husband.

Mahler had honored Strauss by including *Fledermaus* in the Hofoper repertoire. While conducting it in May 1899, Strauss suffered some sort of seizure and had to be taken home. After several days of indifferent health, he became quite ill and was found to be suffering from pneumonia. Soon afterward he died in his sleep. Word of his illness had spread throughout the city. When the conductor Eduard Kremser, who was conducting a charity concert in the Volksgarten (where Strauss had first played the *Tristan* music), was handed a note that Strauss was dead, he stopped the music and began the shimmering pianissimo introduction to The

Blue Danube. The audience, to a man, stood up, heads bowed, and filed out. On June 6 the body was carried in procession through the streets to its resting place near that of Brahms in the Central Cemetery. In 1923 the beautiful *art-nouveau* statue of Strauss was erected in the park on the Ring. The house on Johann Strauss Gasse is now a museum. In 1906 the unpredictable Eduard Strauss burned innumerable manuscripts, said to be arrangements by himself and Josef, but probably containing many works by Johann.

RECORDINGS: There are recordings of all the operettas noted, except the original *Indigo* and *Ritter Pasman.* The popular waltzes, polkas, quadrilles, etc. have been realized in a myriad of versions, including many abbreviations and other arrangements, and there are many of lesser-known works, but so far no systematic attempt to present the entire canon has been undertaken.

[1296] BRISTOW, George Frederick
VIOLINIST, KEYBOARDIST, TEACHER, CHOIRMASTER
BORN: Brooklyn, December 19, 1825
DIED: New York, December 13, 1898

Bristow has a niche in musical history not only as one of the first American orchestral composers, but also as a champion of the native product. His father, an English singing teacher and conductor named William Richard Bristow, settled in Brooklyn a year or so before his son was born. Young George obviously had talent because he was sawing away at his violin in the orchestra of the Olympic Theater when he was eleven. He studied music with the German-born Henry Timm (later president of the New York Philharmonic Society) and with the English-born G. A. MacFarren. In the course of his career, Bristow served as organist in various New York churches. A year after the founding of the Philharmonic Society in 1842, he took his place among the orchestra's first violins and later became a member of the board of directors. In 1850 P. T. Barnum hired him for the orchestra that played at the American debut of the fabled Jenny Lind. A year later he began his twelve-year directorship of the New York Harmonic Society, a chorus, which premiered his oratorio *Praise to God.* His duties, however, did not stand in the way of his performing in various orchestras, conducting church choirs, and teaching music in the New York schools.

In 1853, when W. H. Fry [1231] launched his attack against those who ignored American composers, the usually docile Bristow publicly charged the Philharmonic with such neglect. His E-flat overture, he said, was the only American piece the orchestra had ever played, and that was a matter of accident; if the Society did not shape up, he would resign. It did not, and he did. (Ironically, the eccentric French conductor Louis Antoine Jullien, under whom Bristow played around this time, made a point of playing American music on his tour.) Finally they made up the quarrel, Bristow resumed his chair (which he held for nearly thirty years longer), and the Philharmonic eventually played four of his 5 German-derived symphonies, including the "Arcadian" and the "Niagara." His career reached its climax in 1855, when his opera *Rip Van Winkle* (the first such American work to play in New York) had a month's run at Niblo's Gardens. Among Bristow's other "American" works were the overture *Columbus,* the cantata *The Pioneer,* and the choral ode *The Great Republic.* He also wrote a *Mass* and 2 string quartets. His music has mostly historical interest, though it shows his awareness of European currents, if somewhat belatedly.

RECORDINGS: A few keyboard pieces have been recorded (e.g., by pianist Ivan Davis and organist Janice Beck). The Society for the Preservation of the American Musical Heritage has issued three discs containing Bristow symphonies.

[1297] STRAKOSCH, Maurice, *(né Moritz)* (Shtrá'-kôsh, Mō-rēs')
PIANIST, TEACHER, IMPRESARIO
BORN: Gross-Seelowitz, 1825
DIED: Paris, October 9, 1887

Strakosch (of the brothers Max and Moritz) is variously said to be a native of Poland or Moravia. He studied at the Vienna Conservatory (with Sechter **[1129]**, among others.) In 1849 he came to the United States, where he made his debut as a pianist in New York. His repertoire appears to have consisted mostly of his own fantasias and variations on popular arias and patriotic songs; he once offended (as too popular!) with variations on "Nelly Bly." (Arthur Loesser thinks he was the subject of a contemporary cartoon of a hairy virtuoso called "Herr Smash.") Shortly afterward he married Amalia Patti and took in charge the training and exploitation of her prodigious eight-year-old sister Adelina. In 1855 he withdrew her from circulation for further training, then shipped her off to Havana with Gottschalk **[1306]** for a test run in 1857. Meanwhile he had continued occasionally to concertize but now gave it up for management. He formed an opera

company, which performed for a time in New York and then went west in 1859 to give Chicago the most brilliant opera season it had ever had. (Amalia Strakosch, a contralto, was one of the stars.) After that Maurice turned over his managerial interests to his brother Max and returned to Europe. He himself wrote an opera, which he produced in New York. RECORDINGS: His piano salon pieces (an example has been recorded by Neely Bruce) were his chief successes, if that is the word.

[1298] MINKUS, Léon Fedorovich
(Mink'-oos, Lā-on' Fyā-dō-rō'-vich)
VIOLINIST, CONDUCTOR, ADMINISTRATOR
BORN: Vienna, March 23, 1826
DIED: Vienna, December 7, 1917

One thinks of ballet music as frothy; that by Minkus, a highly successful ballet composer in his day, makes most standard nineteenth-century ballet scores (e.g., those by Delibes **[1344]**, Tchaikovsky **[1377]**, or Glazunov **[1573]**) sound positively profound. Despite a recent revival of interest in some of his long-forgotten ballets, there is much about the man that remains obscure. His ethnic origins and his very name remain uncertain (Austrian records list him as "Alois Ludwig"). The precise dates of his birth and death have been ascertained only recently. Early in his career he was probably in Paris, for he had a hand in *Paquita,* first performed there in 1846. But he was in Russia by the early 1850s, where he concertized, gave violin lessons, and for a time directed a nobleman's private orchestra in St. Petersburg. In 1862 he was named conductor at the Bolshoi Theater in Moscow, to which duties he added those of professor of violin at the conservatory and imperial orchestral inspector. In his spare time he wrote ballet music for the Paris violinist-turned-choreographer Arthur Saint-Léon *(né Michel)*—e.g., for *Fiammetta* in 1864. In 1866 Minkus and the neophyte Delibes each contributed two acts of music for *La Source (The Fount);* the press noted that the newcomer's music easily surpassed that of the old hand (described as "vague, indolent, and melancholic"). In 1869, however, in the first of his many collaborations with Marius Petipa, Minkus had a triumph with *Don Quixote* at the Bolshoi. (The music sounds as though it were written by the yard—a process which would have exactly suited Petipa, who liked to order by the measure.) *Don Quixote* has been recently revived in the West, as has *La Bayadère* of 1877, thanks to Russian defectors who have preserved the tradition. In 1872 Minkus gave up his other posts to become officially the imperial ballet composer. In the same year he was asked to collaborate with the *kuchka* (or "the Mighty Five") in the committee-composed opera *Mlada;* it came to nothing, though he used his offering for an independent ballet. Other successful Minkus scores were *Camargo,* 1872; *Zoraiya,* 1881; *Night and Day,* 1883; and *Kalkabrino,* 1891. Minkus retired at sixty-five in the last year—a date given in many references as that of his death. Nothing at all is known of his final twenty-six years. RECORDINGS: Charles Mackerras has recorded his own recension of *Don Quixote.* Richard Bonynge and John Lanchbery offer excerpts from *Paquita* and *La Bayadère.*

[1299] FOSTER, Stephen Collins
CLERK, FLUTIST
BORN: Lawrenceville, Pa., July 4, 1826
DIED: New York, January 13, 1864

Modern writers who consider the "real" American music rough stuff from downtrodden minorities and bullheaded eccentrics sneer at Foster as a representative of the European-derived tradition they call "genteel." In his own day, what he termed "the opera-mongers" complained that his were mechanical tunes designed for thoughtless whistling. But the fact remains that America has probably never produced a more universally popular composer, and in 1940 he was the first such artist to be named to the American Hall of Fame. If his melodies owed more to Italian opera and European dance forms than to the blues, it must be remembered that that was the case with most popular music of the day.

Foster was born on the fiftieth anniversary of American independence (on which John Adams and Thomas Jefferson breathed their last). His father, Colonel William Barclay Foster, had come west to Pittsburgh, had worked on the frontier for a mercantile firm of that city, had been made a member of the partnership, had grown rich and founded Lawrenceville and, in the year of Stephen's birth, went temporarily bankrupt. His mother, Eliza Tomlinson of Wilmington, Delaware, was the well-educated product of a long-established family. The pair had adopted a boy, whom they named after the colonel; he was followed by nine natural children, all but two of whom survived infancy. Stephen was the penultimate one. After losing the Lawrenceville farm, the family lived for a while in Harmony (both geographically and metaphorically) and, from 1832, in Allegheny. There was a piano in the house, and the girls learned to play it in the interest of future marriageability. The brothers all went into successful business careers connected with the advancement of civilization and trade in the West. Stephen showed no such inclination, being given to "dreaming" and amusing himself with a toy drum, his sister's guitar, a flageolet, and eventually a clarinet, though he was denied music lessons as unsuitable to a boy child in a macho society. He was, however, the star of a family theater in which he and his siblings put on shows. He went off eventually to live with his oldest brother William and to attend the Athens Academy at Towanda but was an almost-immediate dropout at Jefferson College. At Athens he wrote his first known piece, "The Tioga Waltz."

He came home in 1843 and the colonel, now mayor of Allegheny, despairing of educating him further, found him a job in a river warehouse in Pittsburgh. He apparently took some music lessons with one Henry Kleber. That same year Stephen published his first song, "Open Thy Lattice, Love." Two years later he went to work as a bookkeeper for Irwin and Foster (in which firm his brother Dunning was a partner) in Cincinnati, where, finding a willing publisher, he began writing songs in earnest. It was during this period that he first turned out his "Ethiopian melodies" (as the current euphemism had it), though his knowledge of American blacks at close range was limited to a servant at home and occasional attendance at religious "meetings." He wrote his own lyrics in his notion of black dialect. It was not until the early 1850s that he made a trip (his only one) down the Mississippi, though there is no record of his studying black music in the field. He seems, in fact, to have had higher aspirations and to have been ashamed of his ventures into this area. He gave his infectious polka tune, "Oh! Susanna," to a publisher on request and was delighted to get 100 dollars in return. Later he was equally cavalier with other such works. His all-time hit, "Old Folks at Home," he sold to E. P. Christy of the famous minstrel company, giving Christy full right to advertise it as his own (though Foster later tried, unsuccessfully, to break the contract). At any rate, according to his own statement, the success of "Oh! Susanna" convinced him to turn pro, and he actually made what might have been a reasonable living at it, if he had not spent it.

In 1850 Foster married Jane Denny McDowell, daughter of a local M.D., whose light brown hair was almost certainly hymned in "I Dream of Jeanie." Why else he dreamed of her remains obscure. Though she is said to have been an amateur singer, the unhappy record of their marriage shows her apparently uninterested in music. After the birth of their only child, a daughter called Marion, the relationship became increasingly shaky. It broke up temporarily in 1853. Stephen went to New York, but by the next year they were back together, living in Hoboken. In 1857, the struggling composer sold his soul to a New York publisher: Firth, Pond, and Company. After that the slide began. The family moved to Manhattan in 1860, but in 1861 Jane and Marion went to live with relatives. Whether Foster was a drunk by then (or ever) is arguable, but he was running with a fast set in New York, and no one denies that he had developed a taste for rum. He gave up his "plantation songs" for sentimental ballads, in the hope of a quick hit, but eventually Firth, Pond, and Company refused to publish them. After other attempts to shore up the marriage, Jane supported herself as a telegraph operator in a Pennsylvania village. Stephen entered into a partnership with a lyricist named George Cooper. On the morning of January 9, sick and suffering from a severe burn from an overturned spirit lamp, he fell in his Bowery hotel room, damaging his head on the china chamber pot. Cooper took him to Bellevue and called the family. Foster went into a coma and died five days later. He was buried in Allegheny.

RECORDINGS: Foster left over 150 songs—many of them perennial favorites, many more recently resurrected on lovingly reconstructed recorded recitals by such as Jan De Gaetani, Leslie Guinn, and the Gregg Smith Singers. Foster's largest body of instrumental music (also recorded by Smith) is *The Social Orchestra,* a collection of pieces of his own (and Kleber's) and arrangements of dances by Strauss and Lanner and operatic medleys by Donizetti [1155] and Bellini [1164].

[1300] STRAUSS, Josef (Shtrous, Yō'-zef)
ENGINEER, CONDUCTOR
BORN: Vienna, August 20, 1827
DIED: Vienna, July 22, 1870

The second son of the senior Johann Strauss [1177] was obviously gifted and intelligent from the start, though shy and introspective. His father wanted him to be an army officer, but he said that he didn't like killing people. His mother thought he should follow the family trade, but he said he was too ugly (portraits suggest a ski-jump nose and a Hapsburg chin). He wrote poems and painted pictures, and when he finished his necessary school, imbued with the notion of Progress, he entered the Vienna Polytechnic to become a civil engineer and architect. By 1850 he was working under the municipal architect and later became a factory chief engineer. He made the design for a waterworks, published a book of useful mathematical formulae and tables, and invented a mechanical street sweeper that was bought by the city.

When, in 1853, Johann, Jr. [1295] collapsed from overwork, he flattered and cajoled his brother into taking over the band at Sperl's. His was such an unexpected success that largely in the name of family loyalty, Josef took a crash brush-up on music from Johann's former teachers and at the end of August introduced his maiden composition, categorically entitled "First and Last Waltzes." It created such a demand that he was forced to respond with the "First Waltz After the Last." Johann came back to work in September, but by then the die was cast. Josef was the regular substitute at home and abroad (changes of cast were covered by advertising the conductor as "J. Strauss.") Though he had not previously studied, he was playing the violin by 1856. The next year he married his longtime sweetheart, Karoline Pruckmayr, to whom, uncharacteristically for a Strauss, he remained devoted the rest of his life. He was a homebody and today would be called a workaholic. He worked at his music, his poetry, his painting, and his drama furiously, with little sleep and too many cigars. He resented the road trips and swore he would cut them out. Overwork and his mother's death in 1870 left him enervated, depressed, and subject to blackouts. In April, playing in Warsaw, there was a contretemps with a disgruntled orchestral player. Strauss suffered one of his spells, took a terrible fall, and landed on his head. He lingered for three months, then asked to go home. He died there, a month short of his forty-third birthday, not long after his arrival. Josef Strauss's music consists of nearly 300 waltzes, polkas, and the like. The waltzes tend to be gentler and more melancholy than Johann's, the polkas more snappy.

RECORDINGS: His output is well, if not generously, represented on records.

[1301] MERKEL, Gustav Adolf (Mârk'-el, Gōōs'-tàf À'-dolf)
ORGANIST, CHOIRMASTER, TEACHER
BORN: Oberoderwitz, November 2, 1827
DIED: Dresden, October 30, 1885

Gustav Merkel, a famous and influential organist, made his whole career in Dresden, to which he came as a twenty-one-year-old schoolmaster. There he turned the presence of such teachers as Friedrich Wieck, Robert Schumann [1211], and Carl Gottlieb Reissiger (1798–1859) to his advantage. Merkel became an organist successively at the Waisenkirche, the Kreuzkirche, and the Hofkirche. He also taught at the Dresden Conservatory and for a time directed the Singakademie. He was a prolific composer of songs, keyboard pieces, and choral works. RECORDINGS: The Wilson twins have recorded one of his organ duets and Hans Kann a representative salon piece for piano.

[1302] COTTRAU, Teodoro (Kot'-trō or Kot-trä'-ōō, Tä-ō-dō'-rō)
PUBLISHER
BORN: Naples, December 7, 1827
DIED: Naples, March 30, 1879

The Cottraus were at least the godparents, if not the progenitors, of that minor subgenre, the Neapolitan popular song. The patriarch Guillaume (later Guglielmo) (1797–1847), came from his native Paris to Naples, where in 1828 he became manager of the publishing firm of B. Girard & C., which had first dibs on the work of such local celebrities as Rossini [1143], Bellini [1164], Donizetti [1155], and the Riccis [1183, 1205]. Guglielmo, who became director in 1835, published in that year *Passatempi musicali (Musical Pastimes)*, an influential collection of Neapolitan songs arranged by him (from which Liszt [1218], among others, borrowed themes). He turned the firm over to his elder son Teodoro in 1846. A friend of many of the important Italian composers of his day (if not of publishers!), he also composed piano pieces and songs, sometimes as "Eutalindo Martelli." As the latter, his greatest and most enduring success was *Santa Lucia*. His brother Giulio (1831–1916) wrote both songs and operas. (Note: Authority to the contrary, it is unlikely that Teodoro was an influential friend to Bellini, who died when Teodoro was eight.) RECORDINGS: Some of the songs have been recorded.

[1303] GEVAERT, François Auguste (Zhə-vârt', Frä*n*-swà Ô-güst')
MUSICOLOGIST, EDUCATOR, ORGANIST, CONDUCTOR
BORN: Huysse, July 31, 1828
DIED: Brussels, December 24, 1908

Though he was highly successful as a composer (especially of operas), Gevaert is now remembered for his researches in, and revival of, old music. He was born into the family of a baker in the western part of what would two years later become Belgium. When his father became convinced that his creativity lay elsewhere than in the oven, he entered him in the conservatory of nearby Ghent, where he studied composition under the director, Martin-Joseph Mengal. At fifteen he became organist at the local Jesuit church and at nineteen carried off the Prix de Rome (Belgian section). He is said to have been permitted to postpone his mandatory travels for two years because of his youth, which seems odd. His first operas, *Hugues de Zomerghem* and *La Comédie à la ville*, were produced in Ghent within the next two seasons, after which he went to Spain by way of Paris. He sent back informative reports of the musical ferment there and had performed an orchestral fantasy on Spanish tunes that won him the Order of Isabela la Católica. After making the circuit of Italy and Germany, he was back in Ghent by 1852. He then returned to Paris, where, over the next dozen years, he produced eight operas and *opéras-comiques*, nearly all of them successful and all of them now wholly forgotten. A cantata on the silver anniversary of the Belgian monarchy brought him the Order of Leopold. He became chorus master at the Paris Opéra in 1867, but the Franco-Prussian War sent him home, where in 1871 he succeeded Fétis [1111] as director of the Brussels Conservatory. Gevaert was an immensely successful administrator, thoroughly revising the educational program and making the institution something of a model. Not the least in importance of his ventures there were the historical concerts that he conducted. He was elected to the French Academy on the death of Mercadante [1148] in 1873. Toward the end of his life, he was given the title of "Baron" by his government for his *Congolese National Anthem* (a work that is also no longer heard). Besides operas, Gevaert wrote a *Requiem*, various cantatas, other choral works, songs, etc. RECORDINGS: Some of the smaller works occasionally turn up on records, but there his name is perhaps more familiar from arrangements and editions of older music. (e.g., his Grétry [919] suite). His many important studies include works on ancient music, Gregorian chant, Italian Baroque music, and textbooks on harmony, theory, and instrumentation.

[1304] WARREN, George William
ORGANIST
BORN: Albany, N.Y., August 17, 1828
DIED: New York, March 17, 1902

Warren, like so many early American musicians, was self-taught. He became a church organist in Albany at eighteen, played there for fourteen years, and then played in Brooklyn for another decade before settling down in 1870 at the console of St. Thomas's in Manhattan. His chief monument is *Warren's Hymns and Tunes as Sung at St. Thomas's Church,* which contains the tune of the well-known processional "God of Our Fathers." Curiously this conservative religionist was an intimate friend of the swashbuckling Louis Moreau Gottschalk [1306] and caught from him a fervor for native music. His "marche di bravoura" (sic!) *The Andes,* based on a painting by Frederick Church, was written in response to an attack on American music. RECORDINGS: *The Andes* has been recorded by Ivan Davis.

[1305] MASON, William
PIANIST, TEACHER
BORN: Boston, January 24, 1829
DIED: New York, July 14, 1908

As a concertizing American pianist, Mason did not have the wild success that Gottschalk had in Europe a few years earlier, but there is no doubt that he helped establish concert conventions in his native land. He was the youngest son of Lowell Mason (1792–1872), a sometime banker who became rich on his collections of hymn tunes and who, as a Pestalozzian, revolutionized public-school music teaching. William was the younger brother of the publishers Lowell Jr. and Daniel, and of the piano manufacturer (Mason and Hamlin) Henry, and the uncle of the composer Daniel Gregory Mason [1648]. His obvious musical talent was encouraged from an early age. He studied with Henry Schmidt, but his method was largely his own, evolved from observation, experimentation, and study of the muscles involved in playing. After making a start in Boston as church organist and with some recitals, he sailed for Europe in 1849. En route he met Schuberth, the Hamburg publisher, who established a liaison for him with Liszt [1218]. When the revolutionary turmoil in Leipzig cleared, Mason went there to work with Moscheles [1146] and with Hauptmann, and later studied in Prague with Dreyschock [1260]. He gave some concerts and in 1853 screwed up his courage to visit Liszt, who had actually been expecting him

for some years. He spent more than a year in Weimar in a kind of informal situation in which he was treated rather as a member of the family than as a student. While there he met such luminaries as Berlioz [1175], Brahms [1329], and Rubinstein [1309]. He had already come to know Schumann [1211] and Wagner [1230] in Leipzig.

Immediately on coming home, Mason became engaged to a Miss Webb, the daughter of his father's partner. Then, full of missionary zeal, he set out on a concert tour that extended to Chicago. He was probably the first American to play solo recitals and the first to use an advance man. The outward trip was discouraging, but in the same cities, homeward bound, the halls were full. However, after this, Mason married and settled in New York, where he became one of the most successful and influential teachers in the American history of the piano. He was also filled with a zeal to force the masterpieces down the throats of American audiences. To that end, he teamed up with Theodore Thomas and others in a chamber ensemble that from 1855 to 1868 valiantly played to small audiences in Manhattan and nearby communities. He published an interesting autobiography.

RECORDINGS: As a composer, Mason wrote mostly piano pieces in the salon-virtuoso style of the day. A few have been recorded—e.g., by Ivan Davis.

[1306] GOTTSCHALK, Louis Moreau
(Got'-shôk, Lōō-ē' Mō-rō')
PIANIST
BORN: New Orleans, May 8, 1829
DIED: Tijuca, Rio de Janeiro, December 18, 1869

Moreau Gottschalk, as his family called him, was certainly the first great international American musical performer and probably our first considerable international composer. He, at his best, wrote as well as most of the virtuosi—Liszt [1218] and Chopin [1208] always excluded—and his material was certainly more "original." It seems odd that from his death to the recent rediscovery of his music, he was remembered only by a couple of stickily sentimental effusions (still sold in dimestore music departments in my youth) that represented his weakest side.

Edward Gottschalk, the father of Moreau and half a dozen siblings, was a cultured, educated, and reckless English Jewish businessman. The boy's adoring mother, the beautiful Aimee de Bruslée, came from a French governmental family that had been run out of San Domingo by the turn-of-the-century black revolt. Moreau showed the usual signs of prodigal genius at an extremely early age, and at seven he substituted at Mass one Sunday for the organist who was his teacher. When he was thirteen, over the protests of his mother, his father shipped him to Paris to become a virtuoso and help support the family.

Moreau's reception at the Conservatoire was unexpected: Zimmermann, professor of piano (and later Gounod's [1258] father-in-law), refused to see him on the grounds that America was a nation of savages and mechanics and did not produce musicians. Not to be stopped, Gottschalk studied piano with Karl Hallé (future founder of the Hallé orchestra) and then with Camille Stamaty (a pupil of Kalkbrenner [1118] and Mendelssohn [1200]). He also took lessons in theory and composition with one Pierre Maledan. Among his fellow pupils, he made friends with Bizet [1363] and Saint-Saëns [1343]. But Gottschalk was no kind of animal if not a social one, and he made friends with dozens of others—among the people who counted, the cream of Parisian society and the stars of the artistic community. Chopin singled him out as the great pianist of the future. Berlioz [1175] became his ardent supporter and a lifelong correspondent. Theophile Gautier and Victor Hugo made poetic pronouncements about him. The salon set went mad over his jazzy pieces based on the polyglot music of New Orleans, and its feminine members went mad over the slight and soulful performer. Offenbach [1264] transcribed Gottschalk for the cello, and some of his music seems even to have been ground through the Czerny [1137] mill in Vienna.

In 1847 Gottschalk's mother called an end to her marriage and brought her brood to Paris. Two years later her son made his formal concert debut there. His success was overwhelming. For the next two years he divided his time in concertizing between Paris, other French towns, and Switzerland—in which last place he became the pampered protégé of the old Grand Duchess Anna of Russia. She showered him with jewels—the first of his innumerable trophies that included a nine-inch gold medal from the city of San Francisco and a home-baked cake from the sister of the King of Spain. He had his pick too of the forerunners of today's groupies. One particularly athletic young woman is said to have swept him off the bench, tossed him into her carriage, and disappeared with him for a week.

In 1851–52 Gottschalk's chief theater was Spain where he became the darling of both the public and Queen Isabela II, then in her early twenties. He was swamped with medals and honors, and his public progress was that of a champion matador, lacking only the traje de luz. He wrote two operas there—lost, alas!—and inaugurated the "monster concerts," for which he became famous, with such pieces as The Siege of Saragossa (for ten pianos; later, with American tunes replacing the Spanish ones, it became Bunker's Hill). At the end of 1852 Gottschalk returned to the United States, where his first New York concert was a considerable letdown. He soon found that American audiences wanted not the exotica the Europeans liked, but the claptrap operatic fantasies, the inspirational treacle, and something distressingly akin to barroom piano style. But he also made clever and sometimes quite original use of American popular tunes. By the time Thalberg [1220] arrived five years later, Gottschalk was such a popular favorite that the two wisely joined forces in duo concerts. Not unexpectedly, considering their spiritual kinship, P. T. Barnum tried to talk Gottschalk into touring with Jenny Lind, but instead Strakosch [1297] persuaded him to go to Havana with the teenage Adelina Patti that same year. It was also in 1857 that Gottschalk's father died, rather ostentatiously blessing his son in seven languages (a superfluity that may account for Moreau's early demise); the son immediately freed the slaves he inherited.

Gottschalk found himself entranced by the Caribbean and stayed on, composing a good deal, concertizing when he felt like it, and pursuing the dolce far niente that the climate and the culture invited. He apparently sinned immoderately with the native girls, charmed by the fact that they saw no link between sex and guilt. (Not that the link had stopped him on the mainland, where his amatory exploits were as celebrated as his playing: Ada Clare, an emancipated woman journalist, with whom he left a bastard son, wrote up her affair and published it.) But the outbreak of the Civil War, and the fact that his resources were running out, not to mention guilt of his own over his "wasted life," sent him home as a declared citizen of the United States rather than of the Confederacy (where his French accent made him seem out of place). He wrote patriotic pieces, concertized nonstop the length and breadth of the country, and became as much of an attraction in Washington as he had been in Paris. But he topped his San Francisco triumph, where gold pieces were thrown on the stage, with a wretched piece of bad judgment: he kept a young inmate of a select ladies' seminary out past hours and unchaperoned, and escaped lynching only by stowing away on a ship for South America. There he spent the rest of his life, dying in Rio at forty of what has variously been called cholera, yellow fever, and a ruptured appendix—aggravated by an orgy of combined overwork and dissipation.

RECORDINGS: Despite the loss of manuscripts, publication of Gottschalk's piano pieces has permitted access to large numbers of them, which have been copiously recorded, the largest collection to date being a four-record LP album by Alan Mandel. Some of the larger works (often lovingly "reconstructed"), including the *Gran Tarantella* for piano and orchestra as well as the two programmatic symphonies, *A Night in the Tropics* and *A Montevideo*, have been preserved in an album overseen by Eugene List. One should perhaps also note Hershy Kay's [2294] ballet *Cakewalk*, orchestrated from Gottschalk pieces (recorded by Arthur Fiedler and Eugene Ormandy).

[1307] PINSUTI, (Cavaliere) Ciro (Pēn-soo͞'-tē, Chē'-rō)
PIANIST, TEACHER
BORN: Sinalunga, May 9, 1829
DIED: Florence, March 10, 1888

Though he aspired higher, Pinsuti was as a composer of drawing-room ballads almost as popular in Anglo-Saxon countries as his younger compatriot, Paolo Tosti [1429]. He came from a Tuscan village, where he was taught musical basics by his father. He developed into a fine pianist, making public appearances by 1839; as a result, he was made an honorary member of the Philharmonic Society in Rome. There he was taken in tow by the English banker and politician Henry Drummond, a founder of the Catholic Apostolic (or "Irvingite") Church. Drummond took him back to London, cared for him for six years, and had him trained by Cipriani Potter and others. In 1845 Pinsuti went back to Italy, studied at the Bologna Liceo for two more years, and then studied privately with Rossini [1143], its director, for another two. He then returned to England where he taught voice in London and Newcastle until 1856, when he was contracted to teach singing at the Royal Academy. When his native state was joined to the new Italian kingdom in 1859, he was asked to write the ceremonial *Te Deum*. In the decade from 1873 to 1882, he had 3 operas produced—in Bologna, Milan, and Venice, respectively. He was knighted by King Umberto in 1878. Most of the international Italian opera singers regarded him as a splendid vocal coach. Apart from his operas, which were quickly forgot-

ten, he produced some piano pieces and over 300 songs and part-songs, some still popular in the early decades of this century. RECORDINGS: There are scattered older recordings of some of the piano music and songs.

[1308] BRAGA, Gaetano (Brä'-gà, Gī-tà'-nō)
CELLIST, VOCAL COACH
BORN: Giulianova, June 9, 1829
DIED: Milan, November 21, 1907

Not to be confused with such later Brazilian Bragas as Francisco and Ernani, Gaetano was an Abruzzese, born on the Adriatic shore. A pupil of Mercadante [1148] at the Naples Conservatory, he became an international concert cellist, eventually making his headquarters in Paris and London. His cello method was admired; his 8 operas were not. He also wrote a few ambitious orchestral and choral works, but his immortality was ensured almost entirely by a salon effusion, *Leggenda valacca (Wallachian Legend)*, for voice, cello, and piano, which enjoyed enormous popularity, especially as "The Angel's Serenade." RECORDINGS: "The Angel's Serenade" is oft recorded.

[1309] RUBINSTEIN, Anton Grigorievitch (Roo͞'-bēn-stīn, An'-tōn Grē-gôr-ē-yä'-vich)
PIANIST, TEACHER, ADMINISTRATOR
BORN: Vikhvatinetz, November 28, 1829
DIED: Peterhof, November 20, 1894

Challenged only by Liszt [1218] as a pianist, Anton Rubinstein would have preferred to be esteemed as a composer. Some of his innumerable works had a vogue in his day, but most seem to have faded past hope of resurrection (though resurrection has been attempted).

Rubinstein's parents were Jewish. His father Grigori was an unwilling farmer in the Ukraine. His mother Kaleria was born Clara in Prussian Silesia; she was well-educated and a good pianist. Anton was the second of five children; his younger brother Nicolas (1835–1881) was also to become a great pianist and to found the Moscow Conservatory. A little less than two years after Anton's birth, the entire Rubinstein clan, sixty strong, gathered in Berdichev to convert to Christianity to escape the brutal anti-Jewish laws. In 1834 Grigori and his brothers moved their families to Moscow, the farm having been lost in a suit. There they established a pencil factory, also doomed to ultimate bankruptcy. When young Anton was five, his mother began teaching him piano. In three years she exhausted her pedagogical resources and turned to a Moscow-born French pianist, Alexandre Villoing. Villoing soon recognized that he was dealing with an extraordinary talent. After the boy had created a stir in Moscow with a concert a few months before his tenth birthday, Villoing persuaded the parents to let him take him on a European tour, culminating in study at the Paris Conservatoire.

As it happened, Rubinstein, as a foreigner, was refused even an audition at the Conservatoire, but after Villoing had carefully cultivated the *salon* set, Anton made a triumphant appearance at the Salle Érard late in 1841. There followed a tour of all the European capitals, in the course of which Anton met Mendelssohn [1200], Liszt, and other musical giants of the day. Early in 1843 the travelers capped the journey with a concert in St. Petersburg before the czar and czarina, which resulted in an invitation to play at the palace. There followed a short Russian tour to raise money for the serious musical study in Berlin recommended by Liszt. In May 1844 Anton, Nicolas, and their mother settled down in Berlin, where Anton studied theory with Siegfried Dehn. But in 1846 Grigori Rubinstein suddenly died, leaving his wife saddled with a mountain of debts. Kaleria returned to Moscow to take a job in a school. Anton headed for Vienna. But, now seventeen and no longer suited to the role of soulful-eyed boy genius, he found himself reduced to living in an attic and giving piano lessons at one pfennig each. A concert attempted in 1847 was a disaster, and Rubinstein set out to raise money to emigrate to the United States, but the 1848 Revolution, which caught him in Berlin, turned him homeward again. Unaware that he needed a passport, he was detained in St. Petersburg, lost his manuscripts, and escaped prison and possible Siberian exile only by calling on some of his powerful admirers.

By dint of strenuous practice, Rubinstein regained his technique, which he had allowed to lapse (though all of his career he was as famous for the notes he missed as for those he struck). He was now composing steadily and had two of his 5 piano concerti in his repertoire. The 1852 premiere of his first opera, *Dmitri Donskoi* won him the patronage and lifelong friendship of the Grand Duchess Helena, the czar's German sister-in-law, who installed him in her palace at Kamenoi-Ostrov as her *Kapellmeister*. But after two years, his feet began to itch and he took to the road, again on a four-year European tour. Though he played his own music and the mandatory trivia, it was at this point

that he began making a case for what have become the keyboard classics—especially the music of Beethoven [1063]. Rubinstein, incidentally, was not above capitalizing on his physical likeness to that composer. In 1855 a Berlin orchestra played his second symphony, "The Ocean," making it the first Russian symphony to be heard in Western Europe. But it was hardly Russian in concept, and an article attacking the whole notion of a national Russian music, which the composer published at about this time, made him the focus of attacks by the burgeoning nationalist school back home, which labeled him "German" and "Jew." In the summer of 1856, however, the grand duchess called Rubinstein to Russia for the coronation of Czar Alexander II, and with her he proceeded to Nice for the winter. When she returned in the spring, Rubinstein went on to further triumphs in Paris and critical failures in London, where animosity to Russians and Jews ran high.

In 1858 Rubinstein settled down with his mother in St. Petersburg. Early the next year, at the Grand Duchess's behest, he founded the Russian Musical Society to sponsor concerts which became a reality the following winter. An offshoot of this project was a national conservatory—the counterpart of that in Paris, which was set in operation in 1861, with financing from the grand duchess and with Rubinstein as director. Rubinstein brought in the best talent he could find for his faculty—Dreyschock [1260] and Leschetizky for piano, Wieniawski [1340] for violin, Davidov [1360] for cello, and so on. One of the first pupils was the young Tchaikovsky [1377], who eventually studied orchestration with the director, whom he idolized and who took a dislike to him. The school throve in spite of strong and loud opposition from Balakirev's [1348] men, who set up a rival Free School. (Concurrently in 1860 Nicolas Rubinstein founded the Moscow Musical Society, and, soon thereafter, the Moscow Conservatory, in which Tchaikovsky became professor of harmony.)

In 1865 Anton Rubinstein married the Princess Vera Alexandrovna Chekuanov, who, in the course of time, gave him a daughter and two sons (the elder of whom died young of tuberculosis) and spent his money almost as fast as he made it, which was pretty fast. By 1866 the Moscow Conservatory had been chartered, and in 1867 it graduated its first class. But Rubinstein was dissatisfied—he wanted to play; he wanted even more to write operas, vast biblical epics, and to conduct them. (His opera *Paradise Lost* had already been gathering dust for more than a decade.) At the end of the 1867 academic session, both Rubinstein and Wieniawski resigned. The pianist embarked on another marathon tour, in whose interstices he worked on a new opera, *The Tower of Babel*. In 1871–72 he took over the conducting of the Vienna Philharmonic concerts and in the spring conducted a concert performance of the new opera at Düsseldorf.

In August 1872 Rubinstein and Wieniawski sailed for New York. Rubinstein hoped to make enough in the New World to offset his wife's expenditures. It was a dangerous venture, for he had been preceded only by charlatans and finger-busters such as Leopold Meyer, Herz [1170], and Gottschalk [1306], who had made no effort to acculturate the "savages." Rubinstein suffered wretchedly from seasickness on the long passage. Though his concerts involved not only Wieniawski but also the other usual supernumeraries, and had the usual carnival atmosphere, Rubinstein insisted on playing (much to the apprehension of his manager, Maurice Grau, future general manager of the Metropolitan Opera) "heavy" music—Beethoven, Liszt, Schumann [1211]. But the public loved it and showered him with gifts and tributes. He soon found the weight of the gold coins he had demanded in payment an embarrassment and willingly agreed to have them converted to something more portable. Relations with Wieniawski began to sour, and in January 1873 the pair played their last joint concert with the Theodore Thomas Orchestra in New York. Then Rubinstein did a daring thing: he gave a one-man concert, of the kind of music *he* wanted to play. It was a triumph, and once again he went on tour, concluding with seven one-man New York concerts in which, for the first time, he undertook a historical survey of keyboard music. His impact on America was overwhelming. He changed American musical taste. He inspired the foundation of Leopold Damrosch's New York Symphony and the Peabody Conservatory in Baltimore. He was hailed affectionately in the boondocks as "Ruby"—and he took home the then-enormous sum of $60,000.

When Rubinstein got home, he built in suburban Peterhof the villa his wife had been demanding. He produced several of his beloved operas—*Feramors* at La Scala, *Paradise Lost* in Düsseldorf, *The Maccabees* in Berlin, and *The Demon* in St. Petersburg. In 1877 he was granted the rank of Hereditary Nobleman and was awarded the *Légion d'honneur* in Paris. In March 1881, however, his brother Nicolas died unexpectedly at forty-five in Paris, in the arms of the novelist Turgenev. Anton claimed the body and took it home for burial. (Ten days before, Czar Alexander had been murdered by a nihilist bomber and was succeeded by the paranoid and Jew-hating Alexander III.)

In 1885 Rubinstein put together a series of seven historical concerts, and toured Europe with them, beginning in Berlin. The tour lasted only a few months, but by the time it ended, the pianist was already exhibiting symptoms of heart disease. Ignoring these, he set out again in the spring, then returned in the summer of 1886 to embark on yet another epic, *Moses*. By that time the Conservatory had deteriorated so badly that he accepted in 1887 an invitation to direct it once again. He ruthlessly cleared out deadwood, both students and teachers—among the latter, Davidov, for a liaison with a student. (Rubinstein then had glass doors installed on all the rooms.) Despite the czar's distaste for his origins, he granted Rubinstein the title of state councillor in the new year. That fall the composer inaugurated a series of illustrated lectures on the history of the piano. The excitement they aroused inspired the czar to grant him the old Bolshoi Theater for the Conservatory. Virtually in ruins, it proved a white elephant, and Rubinstein said as much to the czar. The result was the banning of his opera *The Merchant Kalashnikov* on the grounds of sedition. However, during the Rubinstein jubilee in 1889, Alexander rather grudgingly awarded him a token pension of 3,000 rubles. By then Rubinstein's heart was giving him serious trouble—though he refused to consult a doctor—and his memory was becoming fallible; moreover, the government was unleashing a series of pogroms against the Jews. After inaugurating his International Musical Competition in 1890 (wherein Busoni [1577] won the composition prize), Rubinstein again withdrew from the Conservatory, where he found himself no longer able to function effectively, in the spring of 1891. Once again he went abroad to concertize and to produce *Moses* in Prague. He lost his mother and then his older son, Alexander, in 1893. Six weeks later Tchaikovsky poisoned himself. Rubinstein came home from his self-imposed exile at Christmas, gave a farewell concert in January, and then played once more in Vienna in April at the request of Leschetizky. In June he conducted the premiere of his final opera *Christus* in Stuttgart and went home, as he told his intimates, to die. He succumbed to a midnight heart attack eight days before his sixty-fifth birthday.

For all his importance as a force for music and as a performer, Rubinstein is most likely to be remembered by his salon pieces such as the *Melody in F* and the "Angelic Dream" from *Kamenoi-Ostrov*. The *Demon* alone of his 19 operas still keeps a tenuous hold on the stage in Russia, and an occasional adventurous pianist drags out one of the concerti, but the music seems too inflated and derivative to ever enjoy any real life.

RECORDINGS: *The Demon* (the opera conducted by Alexander Melik-Pashaiev and the ballet music conducted by Heribert Beissel; piano concerti (No. 1 by Michael Fardink, No. 3 by Robert Preston, No. 4 by Raymond Lewenthal and Michael Ponti, and No. 5 by Adrian Ruiz); symphonies (No. 2 by Richard Kapp and No. 6 by Beissel); the *Konzertstück* for piano and orchestra (Felicja Blumental); all of the violin sonatas and cello sonatas; various piano pieces; songs; and selections from other operas.

[1310] BÜLOW, Hans Guido, Freiherr von (Bü'-lō, Håns Gwē'-dō, Frī'-hâr fun)
PIANIST, CONDUCTOR
BORN: Dresden, January 8, 1830
DIED: Cairo, February 12, 1894

Bülow got off to a slow start, evincing, it is said, no interest in music until he underwent a serious childhood illness, which apparently unclogged the musical conduits. Indeed he made up for lost time, for he developed not only a scrupulous musicianship, but also a fantastic memory that enabled him to conduct without a score and to memorize a piece simply by reading it.

He began his musical studies in Leipzig with no thought of a career. His piano teacher was Friedrich Wieck, Schumann's [1211] reluctant father-in-law. His chief composition teacher was the Hegelian Moritz Hauptmann, who also taught Arthur Sullivan [1397], and was greatly admired for his music in his time. At nineteen, at his parents' insistance, Bülow entered the University of Leipzig, but continued his musical studies. But he soon came under the spell of Liszt [1218] and of the leftist movement that followed the 1848 Revolution. He became a polemicist (and a brilliant one, with a gift for the memorable phrase) for the new politics and the new music. The Weimar premiere of *Lohengrin* brought him to Zürich to sit at Wagner's [1230] feet—and begin his conducting career. After a return to Weimar to perfect his pianism under Liszt, he concertized from 1853 to 1855, then became professor of piano at the Stern Conservatory in Berlin, though he continued to tour as both a pianist and conductor. His repertoire in both fields was catholic, but he steadily plunked for the new German music, and he became Wagner's most ardent spokesman, both verbally and musically.

In 1855 Liszt saw fit to take his daughters Blandine and Cosima away from their mother in Paris. His current mistress, the Princess Carolyne von Sayn-Wittgenstein, got the curious notion that they should be placed with Mme. von Bülow in Berlin, no doubt overlooking the fact that that lady had an eligible son. Bülow was knocked breathless—more perhaps by their pianistic talent and resemblance to their sainted father than by anything else. The night Cosima sat waiting for him after the concert in which he fainted as a result of a bad reception of the *Tannhäuser* overture, he proposed to her. Liszt, with apparently some second thoughts, forbade the marriage for two years.

In 1864, at Wagner's urging, Ludwig II of Bavaria took Bülow on as court pianist. While winding up his affairs in Berlin, Bülow sent Cosima and the children on ahead to stay with Wagner, and right there was where he made his big mistake. Bülow became conductor of the Royal Opera (conducting the premieres of *Tristan* and *Meistersinger)* and director of the Royal Conservatory. By then, Wagner's relations with Cosima had resulted in two (and possibly three) children, and the idyll came to an end. Bülow divorced his wife and resigned his posts, and Ludwig turned his back on Wagner and went off to build his castles in the air. Between that time and 1878, when he became director of the Hofoper at Hannover, Bülow made his home in Florence and concertized worldwide. (He premiered the Tchaikovsky [1377] Piano Concerto No. 1, which Nicolas Rubinstein had rejected, in Boston in 1875). After two years in Hannover, he moved on to Meiningen, where his genius with an orchestra came to be especially noted. In 1882 he married one of the local actresses, Marie Schanzer. In 1885, after taking on a young assistant named Richard Strauss [1563], he suddenly resigned. He continued to concertize and held teaching posts in Berlin and Frankfurt am Main. In his later years, though he continued to be a Wagnerian apostle, he was much taken by the music of Brahms [1329]. It was Bülow who formulated the "three B's." (Another memorable Bülow phrase had made his name anathema in Munich: in discussing the removal of a row of seats in the opera house to permit enlargement of the stage, he remarked that he didn't think another thirty or so skunks in the audience made any difference.) Bülow settled in Hamburg in 1888, in increasingly poor health. All his life he was the stereotypical Prussian—chauvinistic, anti-Semitic, arrogant, and perhaps a bit mad. When Kaiser Wilhelm II announced that those who did not like his regime could wipe the German dust from their shoes, Bülow ostentatiously did just that at the conclusion of a concert, and went to Egypt, where he died.

RECORDINGS: Bülow left a few orchestral pieces and a number of rather Lisztian piano works, one of which Werner Genuit has recorded.

[1311] FAURE, Jean-Baptiste (Fôr, Zhàn Bà-tēst')
SINGER, CONTRABASSIST, TEACHER
BORN: Moulins, January 15, 1830
DIED: Paris, November 9, 1914

Faure (not to be confused with the *accent aigu* Fauré), an operatic baritone, was one of the great singing actors of his day and only incidentally a composer. His father, a member of the Moulins Cathedral choir, moved with his family to Paris in 1833 and died there four years later. Jean-Baptiste served a turn as a chorister at the Madeleine, and played contrabass in the orchestra at the Odéon. He studied at the Conservatoire and made his debut at the Opéra-Comique in 1852. There he remained for nine years, during which time he debuted in London, in 1860, and taught voice at the Conservatoire. Then he moved on to the Opéra, where he created several roles—notably Nelusko in Meyerbeer's **[1142]** *L'Africaine,* Rodrigue in Verdi's **[1232]** *Don Carlos,* and Hamlet in Thomas' **[1217]** opera. (Thomas rewrote the part for him when he could not find a suitable tenor to sing it.) He was a notable Don Giovanni and Méphistophéles. He was also a member of the Brussels Opera in 1870–72, serving concurrently as overseer of vocal instruction in the Brussels Conservatory. He left the Opéra in 1876 but sang in Vienna in 1878 and concertized for some time thereafter. In the late 1890s he made a cylinder recording of an aria from Donizetti's *La Favorita* which has been transferred to LP on the Rococo label. His son Maurice was known as a painter. RECORDINGS: Faure published a number of rather sentimental religious songs, of which *"Les Rameaux"* ("The Palms," said to be the late President Dwight D. Eisenhower's favorite piece of music) has shown remarkable longevity and has been recorded. A duet, "Crucifix," was once also very popular on records.

[1312] BRONSART VON SCHELLENDORF, Hans August Alexander (Brōn'-zärt fon Shel'-len-dôrf, Hàns Ou'-gōōst À-lek-sàn'-der)
PIANIST, ADMINISTRATOR
BORN: Berlin, February 11, 1830
DIED: Munich, November 3, 1913

Hans von Bronsart (as he was called) was yet one more musician who held an important place in his day and has been almost wholly forgotten, presumably for lack of any real individuality in his music. He had his first training in Danzig and then worked with Theodor Kullak (1818–82) and the great theorist-teacher Siegfried Dehn at the University of Berlin. At twenty-four he was accepted by Liszt **[1218]** as a pupil at Weimar, where he remained until 1857. Liszt thought especially highly of him and gave Bronsart the privilege of premiering his own second piano concerto, which he dedicated to him. Hans von Bülow **[1310]** thought Bronsart's second concerto the best one produced by the younger generation at Weimar and programmed it often. In the five years that followed his Weimar experience, Bronsart concertized all over Europe, from St. Petersburg to London. In 1861 he married the brilliant pianist-composer Ingeborg Starck (1840–1913), a pupil of Henselt **[1237]** and Liszt, and three years later followed Bülow as director of the Berlin Society of the Friends of Music. In 1867 he was given the charge of the theater in Hannover, and twenty years later he became general music director at Weimar. On his retirement in 1895 Bronsart was made a privy councillor. He devoted his last years (he lived to be eighty-three) to composition. He survived his wife by only five months. His compositions are not numerous: they include an opera, *Der Corsar,* a Christmas cantata, a choral symphony, other orchestral works, and a piano trio (also admired by Bülow). RECORDINGS: Michael Ponti has recorded the Op. 10 Concerto for Piano in F-sharp Minor.

[1313] HEISE, Peter Arnold (Hī'-ze, Pā'-ter Àr'-nōld)
ORGANIST, TEACHER
BORN: Copenhagen, February 11, 1830
DIED: Ny Tårbaek, September 12, 1879

A follower of Niels Gade **[1248]**, Heise wrote many songs that are still popular in Denmark. Gade urged him to study in Leipzig, which, after some work with Andreas Berggreen in Copenhagen, he did. Heise's teacher was Moritz Hauptmann, a Mendelssohn **[1200]** protégé who also taught Bülow

[1310] and Sullivan **[1397]**. After a year Heise returned to Copenhagen in 1854 to conduct the Student Singing Society. Then from 1857 to 1865 he taught at the conservatory at Sorø and served as organist there. Having married into money, he settled down in Copenhagen to devote himself to composition. Besides the songs, he wrote some chamber music and several stage works—incidental music, a ballet, and 2 operas: *The Pasha's Daughter* in 1869 and *King and Marshal* in 1879. The latter is regarded as a kind of monument in Denmark. RECORDINGS: A complete recording by John Frandsen of *King and Marshal* was recently released as a part of the Danish Music Anthology series. There are also recordings of many of the songs from Danish singers.

[1314] LASSEN, Eduard (Làs'-sen, Ed'-wärd)
CONDUCTOR
BORN: Copenhagen, April 13, 1830
DIED: Weimar, January 15, 1904

To judge from their incidence on early recordings and in second-hand music stores, Lassen's songs once enjoyed great popularity, though even they are now forgotten. The Lassen family moved to Brussels in Eduard's childhood. There he entered the Brussels Conservatory at the age of twelve, won several prizes, and in 1851 trekked off to Italy as the recipient of the Belgian Prix de Rome. Afterward he continued to roam, finally alighting in Weimar in 1857, where Liszt **[1218]** kindly staged his first opera *Le Roi Edgard (King Edgar)* as *Landgraf Ludwigs Brautfahrt (Landgrave Ludwig's Bridal Trip)*. When Liszt resigned the following year, Lassen was given his appointment which he held until he retired at sixty-five. He wrote two other operas (neither successful), a pair of symphonies, a piano concerto, and incidental music. He was one of the very first to stage Wagner's *Tristan*, and in 1877 he conducted the world premiere of Saint-Saëns' **[1343]** *Samson et Dalila*. RECORDINGS: Some songs have been committed to disc.

[1315] GOLDMARK, Karl (Gōlt'-märk, Kärl)
VIOLINIST, TEACHER, CHOIRMASTER
BORN: Keszthely, May 18, 1830
DIED: Vienna, January 2, 1915

Born into a German-speaking Hungarian Jewish family on the shores of Lake Balaton, Goldmark was one of a vast brood of children. The father, a cantor and sometime notary, was barely able to provide the necessities for them. He moved his tribe to Deutsch-Kreuz (now Sopronkeresztur), a primitive village near the Austrian border, when Karl was four. There the children largely ran wild. Karl is said to have learned the alphabet only when he was about twelve, thanks to a brother-in-law. Somehow at about the same time, his father managed to get him into the music school operated by the local music society in nearby Ödenburg (Sopron), only a four-hours' walk away. He soon reached sufficient violinistic proficiency to be accepted as a pupil by Leopold Jansa in Vienna. But there was no money to keep up the lessons, and for some time Goldmark existed on handouts from kindly people; one winter, according to his memoirs, his diet was cucumbers and curds. For a time he roomed with his brother Joseph, a medical student. In 1847 he was at last admitted to the Conservatory to study with the Hungarian violinist Joseph Böhm, who had taught Joachim **[1321]**. The 1848 Revolution put an end to such frivolities. Brother Joseph fled to the United States, where his son Rubin (1872–1936) attained a measure of fame as a composer and teacher. Jansa, who was concertizing in England, played a benefit for the revolutionaries, had a price put on his head, and remained there the rest of his life. Karl found work in an orchestra in Györ. There he was arrested by the imperial forces, condemned as a dissident, and stood before a firing squad; before the guns could be fired, someone convinced the soldiers that he was merely a harmless fiddler. Goldmark's formal training, such as it was, was over. As an orchestral musician he made his way back to Vienna, where he wound up playing at the Karlstheater and taught piano (!) on the side. He devoted assiduous study to the scores he played and soon began composing, at first in small forms and then orchestrally. In 1858 he managed an all-Goldmark concert, which, however, was praised with faint damns. Discouraged, he moved to Budapest, redoubled his efforts as self-education, and gave a much more successful retrospective there in 1859. That convinced him to give up the orchestral drudgery and return to Vienna. Within a few years he had established himself as a composer to be reckoned with. He was welcomed into important musical circles and formed a close friendship with Brahms **[1329]**, who liked to needle him and with whom he hiked the Vienna woods. Goldmark did some reviewing and came out in favor of Wagnerian **[1230]** reforms, a position that seems not to have turned his more conservative friends against him.

Around 1873 Goldmark jumped aboard the current biblical-oriental opera bandwagon and began writing his first stage work, *Die Königin von Saba (The Queen of Sheba)*, aided by a grant from the Hungarian government. Premiered in March 1875, it was his greatest success and for a while enjoyed international currency. (The cast included Amalia Materna, Wagner's first Brünnhilde, in the title role.) Goldmark was afterward known as "Composer to Her Majesty the Queen of Sheba." The next year produced the so-called *Rustic Wedding Symphony*, which has demonstrated more staying power than any other Goldmark work. Between 1886 and 1908 the composer unveiled five other operas, of which *Das Heimchen am Herd (The Cricket on the Hearth*, after Dickens) and *Ein Wintermärchen (A Winter's Tale)* also had some success, however brief. In his later years Goldmark was the recipient of many honors. In 1897 he was a pallbearer at Brahms's funeral. He himself lived well into his eighty-fifth year. Though his concept of opera was essentially Wagnerian, his music, which demonstrates melodic ability and coloristic sense, was, though not very daring, his own.

RECORDINGS: There are several recordings of the *Rustic Wedding*, and rare ones of the violin concerto and the overtures *Sakuntala, In Italy,* and *Im Frühling (In Springtime)*. Early vocal recordings represent *Die Königin von Saba* well and touch on some of the others. There have been two full recordings of *Die Königin*, one of them commercial, the other a piracy.

[1316] DURAND, Marie-Auguste (Dü-rän', Mȧ-rē' O-güst')
PUBLISHER, ORGANIST, CRITIC
BORN: Paris, July 18, 1830
DIED: Paris, May 31, 1909

Born a few days before the revolution that toppled Charles X, Durand studied organ with François Benoist at the Paris Conservatoire together with Franck [1284] and Saint-Saëns [1343], and played in a number of important Parisian churches. He was also a well-known reviewer. In 1870 he entered the music-publishing business in partnership with one Schönewerk; the house is now Durand et Cie., and Auguste's son Jacques is famous as Debussy's [1547] publisher and adviser. Auguste composed largely salonesque pieces of which occasional examples—e.g., the *Valse in E-flat* and the *Chaconne*—appear on records.

[1317] LANGE, Gustav (Lȧng'-ə, Gōōs'-tȧf)
PIANIST
BORN: Schwerstedt, August 13, 1830
DIED: Wernigerode, July 19, 1889

This Thuringian studied in Berlin with the organists August Wilhelm Bach (not one of *the* Bachs) and Eduard August Grell and their pupil Albert Löschhorn. He made most of his career in that city. Some of his hundreds of pretty little salon pieces were once very popular with amateur pianists and have been preserved in museum-piece recordings of the taste of those times (e.g., by Hans Kann).

[1318] RADECKE, Robert (Rȧ'-dek-e, Rō-bȧrt')
CONDUCTOR, TEACHER
BORN: Dittmannsdorf, October 31, 1830
DIED: Wernigerode, June 21, 1911

Radecke studied in Leipzig and eventually became a musical power in Berlin. He was conductor at the Imperial Opera there from the time of the unification until 1887 and later was a professor at the Royal Institute for Church Music, where he was very popular with his students. His elder brother Rudolf (1829–93), also Leipzig-trained, was a successful composer, conductor, and teacher in Berlin. Robert wrote an opera and a symphony and other ambitious compositions, but his name has been preserved largely through a song *"Aus der Jugendzeit,"* often taken for a folksong.

[1319] MARCHETTI, Filippo (Mär-ket'-tē, Fē-lēp'-pō)
TEACHER, ADMINISTRATOR
BORN: Bolognola, February 26, 1831
DIED: Rome, January 18, 1902

After some music lessons in his birthplace in the Marches near Macerata, Marchetti, at nineteen, went to the Naples Conservatory to study with Carlo Conti, who had once taught Bellini [1164]. After four years he went back to Bolognola, and, with his brother Raffaele as librettist, wrote a first opera, *Gentile da Varano*. Produced in Turin in 1856, it was such a hit that the impresario commissioned a successor. But that was such a failure that Marchetti couldn't get anyone even to look at his third attempt. Defeated, he took up teaching voice and writing songs in Rome. In 1862 he moved to Milan, and, with many misgivings, yielded to the importunings of a certain Marcelliano

Marcello to set his libretto *Romeo e Giulietta.* It was premiered in Trieste three years later, but not much came of it until the Milanese Teatro Carcano decided to run it in 1867 in opposition to Gounod's [1258] treatment of the story, which was playing at La Scala, whereupon the natives decided they preferred the home-grown product. The same sort of thing happened with Marchetti's next opera, *Ruy Blas:* the La Scala premiere in 1869 was a near-failure, but a subsequent performance in Florence set it on the road to international success that lasted half a century. However, two further operas made no impact at all. By 1881, when he became head of the St. Cecilia Academy in Rome, Marchetti had abandoned the stage for good. He ended his career as director of the Liceo Musicale in Rome, retiring in 1901, and dying (of tongue cancer) a few months later. RECORDINGS: Selections from *Ruy Blas,* recorded by such singers as Celestina Boninsegna and Mattia Battistini, suggest a composer who knew all the proper gestures but offered little that was memorable.

[1320] HOFFMAN, Richard
PIANIST, TEACHER
BORN: Manchester, May 24, 1831
DIED: New York, August 17, 1909

A member of a large musical family, Richard Hoffman was born on Queen Victoria's (twelfth) birthday, a fact that he observed regularly in later life by breaking out the Union Jack and playing the national anthem. Though he was said to have studied with the Great Pianists of Europe, his only traceable teachers are his father and Leopold de Meyer, the eccentric "Lion Pianist" (for his ferocious pounces on the keyboard). At sixteen Hoffman emigrated to New York, where, after a successful recital, he was invited to play a Mendelssohn [1200] concerto with the Philharmonic. Here he was so well-liked that he was invited back repeatedly. In 1849 he toured the Far West with a young Irish violinist named Joseph Burke—a pioneering venture that took him to remote places like Milwaukee, where the pair had often to provide their own piano moving. Back in New York, his name and fame reached P. T. Barnum, who engaged him for Jenny Lind's debut there, and then, as assisting artist, for her two-year tour of the country. When that was over, William Vincent Wallace [1221], in his managerial phase, teamed him with Gottschalk [1306]. The two played each other's music and Gottschalk's duets, and became close friends. In 1854 Hoffman introduced the Chopin [1208]

E minor concerto to New York with the Philharmonic, of which society he was forthwith made a member, despite the fact that he retained his British citizenship. In 1862 he resumed his association with Gottschalk, self-resurrected from the tropics, and wrote an *In Memoriam L.M.G.* after the latter's death. Thanks in part to Gottschalk's performance of his music, Hoffman became a popular and expensive teacher but is said never to have turned down a talented youngster for lack of money. In 1892 the Philharmonic chose him as soloist for its fiftieth-anniversary concert, and fifteen years later Hoffman's many friends honored him with a concert observing his own fiftieth anniversary in America. His memoirs were published posthumously. Hoffman wrote some vocal music, but his output was chiefly for the piano—both arrangements and original material of great competence. RECORDINGS: Examples are included in recorded anthologies by Neely Bruce and Ivan Davis.

[1321] JOACHIM, Joseph (Yō'-ā-khēm, Yō'-zef)
VIOLINIST, TEACHER
BORN: Kittsee (Köpecsény), June 28, 1831
DIED: Berlin, August 15, 1907

Though he wrote music heavily influenced by Schumann [1211] and his friend Brahms [1329], Joachim was perhaps *the* great violinist of his time—one who made music paramount to virtuosity. Born in eastern Austria (near what is now Bratislava) to Hungarian-Jewish parents, he was a child prodigy. He studied from the age of five with Stanisław Serwaczynski, "the Polish Paganini," who was theater *Konzertmeister* in Pest, and at ten went to Vienna, where his teachers were Miska Hauser, *his* teacher Georg Hellmesberger, Sr., and *his* teacher, old Josef Böhm. Joachim made his official debut as a performer in Leipzig in 1843, as assisting artist at a concert of Pauline Viardot's; his accompanist was Felix Mendelssohn [1200]. Joachim remained in Leipzig for seven years, with time out for a few appearances in London, occasionally performing but mostly drinking deep of the sacred waters blessed by Mendelssohn and Schumann. He performed in the Gewandhaus orchestra for a time as assistant concertmaster to Ferdinand David.

At eighteen Joachim himself became *Konzertmeister* at Weimar under Liszt [1218]. But Joachim developed a great distaste for Liszt and his music—he particularly abhorred Liszt's proclivity to monkey around with piano accompaniments—and in 1853 took a similar post in Hannover. There he first met the twenty-year-old Brahms, then on tour with the violinist Remenyi, and was much taken with his music. (Brahms had heard Joachim play earlier in Hamburg.) A great friendship sprang up between the two, and Brahms wrote several works, including the violin concerto, for Joachim, whom he called "Yussuf." In 1860 they issued their famous manifesto against the New German Music, notably that of Liszt and Wagner [1230]. Late in his Hannover stay, Joachim married a well-known contralto, Amalie Weiss. He had a wide streak of paranoia in him, and the union was not a happy one. He gave up his Hannover post in 1866 and in 1868 became director of a branch of the Royal Academy in Berlin, the High School of Applied Music (Hochschule für ausübende Tonkunst). The following year he founded the Joachim String Quartet (all-Stradivarius), which quickly became world-famous and set a model for string-quartet behavior and repertoire. During the summer of 1881, in Vienna, the marriage reached the breaking point. Brahms rather perversely took Amalie's side, and the friendship too came to a parting of the ways. Later they made it up when Brahms composed the double concerto to placate Joachim. At seventy-two Joachim made a few recordings in Berlin, including the first two Brahms *Hungarian Dances* and his own *Romance in B-flat*. Besides solo violin music, Joachim wrote some orchestral overtures, and 3 violin concerti, of which the best-known is No. 2, the "Hungarian Concerto."

RECORDINGS: The second violin concerto has been recorded by Charles Treger and, in a truncated version, by Aaron Rosand. The third has been committed to disc by Takako Nishizaki. Other recordings include the *Nocturne in A Major* and *Variations in E Minor*, both for violin and orchestra, and the *Overture in Memoriam Heinrich von Kleist.*

[1322] LECOCQ, Alexandre Charles (Lə-kōk′, Ál-eks-àn'dr′ Shärl)
TEACHER, PIANIST
BORN: Paris, June 3, 1832
DIED: Paris, October 24, 1918

Though he had higher aspirations, Charles Lecocq ranks highest as a composer of operetta—one who increasingly eclipsed Offenbach [1264] after the collapse of the Empire in 1871. Crippled by a congenital hip deformity and poor, he found solace in music from the hoots of his coevals. At seventeen he won admission to the Conservatoire,

where he studied with the familiar crew (Halévy [1157], Benoist, Bazin [1247]), but had to leave after five years to bolster the family income by teaching piano and playing for dances. In 1856 he set the libretto *Le Docteur Miracle,* by Léon Battu and Ludovic Halévy for a competition arranged by Offenbach. So did his sometime classmate Georges Bizet [1363]. Both were declared the winners, though Lecocq later said that the jury had been rigged by the elder Halévy to favor his pet pupil and future son-in-law Bizet. Offenbach, on the other hand, did not think as much of Lecocq's contribution as its composer did, but he was scrupulously fair and gave each work eleven performances at the Bouffes-Parisiens.

After that, Lecocq found himself right back where he was before. Between 1859 and 1868, he had seven more pieces—mostly one-act curtain raisers—performed in various theaters without attracting much notice. He finally had a significant hit with *Fleur-de-thé (Tea Flower).* Forty-odd other stage works followed. His successes came mostly in the decade of the 1870s. During the war years he moved to Brussels where he remained until 1874 and produced *Les Cent vierges (The Hundred Virgins* of 1872) and *Giroflé-Girofla,* in 1874, as well as his most famous and longest-lasting operetta *La Fille de Mme. Angot (Mme. Angot's Daughter)* in 1872. *Plutus,* his one attempt at serious opera, failed dismally in 1886. Lecocq also wrote a ballet, *Le Cygne (The Swan),* a violin sonata, a few chamber and orchestral pieces, some religious music for nuns (a collaboration with Louis-Desiré Besozzi, the last of that clan), and many songs and piano works (for some of which he used the pen name "Georges Stern.")

RECORDINGS: Plentifully excerpted on old vocal records, his operettas are still occasionally represented by "highlight" recordings in France, and an orchestral suite, *Mme. Angot,* has several times appeared here.

[1323] SÖDERMAN, Johan August (Sö′-der-màn, Yō′-hàn Ou′-goost)
CONDUCTOR, ARRANGER, EDITOR
BORN: Stockholm, July 17, 1832
DIED: Stockholm, February 10, 1876

Söderman's father, Johan Wilhelm, was a theatrical conductor and composer, but the child showed no particular interest in music, and went to sea at eleven—as a cabin boy, one supposes. Discovering himself too frail for such an existence, he returned to Stockholm to follow the paternal path. He was partly self-taught but managed to put in three years at the Academy of Music. At nineteen he was hired as conductor of a traveling theater company run by one Edvard Stjernström and spent two years in Finland, where Söderman wrote his first stage music. The Stjernström troupe then took up residence in Stockholm. Söderman took a year off in 1856 to study with E. F. Richter in Leipzig, where he discovered the music of Schumann [1211]. In 1860 he was hired by the Royal Swedish Opera as chorus master and assistant conductor, posts that he held until his last illness. In 1869 he was awarded a Jenny Lind Fellowship and went on a tour of Denmark and Germany, finding to his surprise that his fame had preceded him. An encounter with Edvard Grieg [1410] in 1871 led to the foundation of a journal, *Nordiske Musikblade,* for which they served as joint editors. Söderman died prematurely (at forty-three) but left a large body of work that included 4 operas or operettas and incidental music for some eighty plays. (The music for Ibsen's *Peer Gynt,* which that author suggested he write, mysteriously vanished before it could be performed.) The stage music had a strong effect on the next generation of Swedish composers, as did the cantata-ballads (a genre that seems to have been original with Söderman). There is very little independent instrumental music. RECORDINGS: There are recordings of *Swedish Festival Music* (by Göran Nilsson and by Bjorn Hallman), some songs, and the *Fantasies after Almqvist* by pianist Stig Ribbing.

[1324] WYMAN, Addison P.
VIOLINIST, EDUCATOR
BORN: Cornish, N.H. (?), June 23, 1832
DIED: Washington, Pa., April 15, 1872

The sole reference *(Baker's Biographical Dictionary of Musicians)* gives Wyman's birthplace and the arena of his activities as New York, but surely New Hampshire is meant. Cornish is in the southwest part of the state, near the Vermont border. Wyman was a violin teacher, and founded a music school in 1869 in Claremont, a few miles to the south. He was the composer of many popular and trivial piano pieces—some recorded in recent anthologies of salon music.

[1325] ZAJC, Ivan (Zà'ik, Ē'-van)
CONDUCTOR, TEACHER, ADMINISTRATOR
BORN: Fiume (Rijeka), August 3, 1832
DIED: Zagreb, December 16, 1914

The son of a bandmaster in the Austrian army, Zajc studied at home and then at eighteen entered the Milan Conservatory, where he produced his first opera, *La Tirolese* in 1855. He then returned to Fiume where he himself became band director. In 1863 he produced his *Amelia* (like Verdi's *I Masnadieri,* based on Schiller's *Die Räuber).* In 1862 he went to Vienna to seek his fortune and was quite successful turning out (as "Giovanni von Zaytz") German-language operettas. In 1870 he returned to his native land and his proper name as conductor of the Zagreb opera company and director of the Conservatory, in both of which posts he was eminently successful. In these years he promoted opera in the vernacular—he wrote at least 15 Croatian operas himself (the most famous is *Nikola Šubrić Zrinski* of 1876) and produced Lisinski's [1265] *Porin.* Zajc was an extraordinarily prolific (if eclectic) composer: he turned out over 1,000 works in virtually all forms and is regarded as the true founder of modern Yugoslav music. RECORDINGS: Selections from the operas have been recorded by various Yugoslav singers. There is also a Yugoslav recording of an *Andante* for six violins and one of *Nikola Šubrić Zrinski* by the Croatian National Opera under Milan Sachs.

[1326] WORK, Henry Clay
PRINTER, EDITOR
BORN: Middletown, Conn., October 1, 1832
DIED: Hartford, Conn., June 8, 1884

Famous (or infamous) as the author of "Marching Through Georgia," Work was one of the most popular song writers to succeed Stephen Foster [1299]. His father Alanson was so committed to the cause of abolition that he took his family to Illinois when Henry was three to help slaves escape northward. In 1841 he was caught and imprisoned for four years, after which he went back home, leaving Henry to stay with friends. Subsequently Henry taught himself music and learned the printer's trade. In 1857 he married and moved to Chicago, where he practiced his profession. Having published a couple of songs, he entered into an arrangement with Root and Cady, which firm remained his publisher for many years. In 1863, George Root [1272] asked him to assume the editorship of the firm's magazine, *The Song Messenger of the Northwest.* Work, who was not only a dedicated abolitionist and temperance advocate, but also a rather doctrinaire Christian, proceeded immediately to attack the likes of such hymn writers as Root's friend Lowell Mason and had to be relieved of his duties.

In 1866 Work's wife suddenly suffered a mental breakdown and had to be sent to an asylum. Work, stunned, farmed the children out and moved to Philadelphia, where he boarded with a family and returned to printing. He fell hopelessly in love with one of the girls in the house, for whom he carried a torch for more than a decade. His last years were lonely and chaotic. He composed only infrequently and tried real estate and inventing. In 1882 he moved to Bath in southwestern New York. A year later, his wife, still insane, finally died. He suffered a fatal heart attack the next year at the age of fifty-one. Apart from his celebration of Sherman's Georgia depredations, Work is universally remembered for "Grandfather's Clock" and the temperance tear-jerker "Come Home, Father!" ("Father, dear father, come home with me now").

RECORDINGS: Joan Morris and Clifford Jackson have recorded an attractive selection of Work songs.

[1327] LABITZKY, August (Là-bĕts'-ki, Ou'-gōōst)
CONDUCTOR, VIOLINIST
BORN: Petschau (now Bečov), October 22, 1832
DIED: Reichenhall, August 28, 1903

August Labitzky was one of the musical offspring of Josef Labitzky, who, as director of the dance orchestra at Carlsbad, the fashionable spa (now known as Karlovy Vary) and composer of dances, bid fair to rival the Strausses [1177, 1295] at one time. August's brother Wilhelm, also a violinist, emigrated to Canada; their sister was an opera singer at Frankfurt am Main. August was a product of the Conservatories of Prague and Leipzig, where he studied violin with Ferdinand David. He became his father's assistant and later successor. He wrote some salon piano pieces. RECORDINGS: One of the salon pieces has been recorded by Hans Kann.

[1328] MONTERO, José Angel (Mōn-tä'-rō, Hō-zā' Án-hel')
ORGANIST, FLUTIST, CONDUCTOR, EDUCATOR
BORN: Caracas, late 1832
DIED: Caracas, August 24, 1881

Most references give Montero's birthdate as 1839, but the recording of his opera Virginia, issued by the Venezuelan Ministry of Culture, disagrees. Montero was one of at least three musical sons of a church musician, José María Montero, who was his only teacher. Angel quickly learned to play strings and keyboards, but preferred the flute, on which he is said to have been a virtuoso. In his adult years, he worked as bandmaster, theater conductor, and from 1875 choirmaster at the Cathedral of St. Iglesias. He founded the first conservatory in Venezuela a year later. The Cherubinian Virginia, to a libretto by an Italian Garibaldino named Domenico Bancalari, was produced in Caracas in 1873 and is said to be the first opera ever written by a Venezuelan.

[1329] BRAHMS, Johannes (Bràmz, Yō-hàn'-nes)
PIANIST, CONDUCTOR
BORN: Hamburg, May 7, 1833
DIED: Vienna, April 3, 1897

It was Hans von Bülow [1310] who elevated Brahms to the holy trinity of German music with J. S. Bach [684] and Beethoven [1063], "the three B's". There is no doubt that Brahms represents the culmination of several traditions—formalism, Schumannesque [1211] introspection and lyricism, the impact of the folksong, and middle-class coziness. Eighty years after his death, he remains extremely popular, with his orchestral works, chamber music, piano pieces, and many of the Lieder more than holding their own as repertoire staples. In his day he was touted—especially by the influential Viennese critic Eduard Hanslick—as the savior of all that was good in German music against the rising tide of modernism (i.e., Wagner [1230]). As there were dissenters from that position, there are dissenters now—those to whom Brahms represents the worst of inflated Victorian sentiment, a composer who thought small and wrote big. The late Benjamin Britten [2215] is said to have played a Brahms record (or read through the scores of the works—the stories differ) once a year to remind himself how bad the man was. There are others, like the present writer, who can take delight in the more intimate or personal works—the horn trio, the Alto Rhapsody—but who find the overstuffed, churning symphonies and concerti all but insufferable. Apparently the doubters and the dislikers still remain in a minority.

Brahms's father, Johann Jakob, of petit-bourgeois stock, had resisted his family's opposition and moved to Hamburg (from Holstein) at twenty to earn a living of sorts as a contrabass player in night spots and theaters. At twenty-four he married Johanna Nissen, age forty-one, an ugly, gimpy little woman who ran a notions shop and sewed well. They made a home in a warren in a slum district (the Gangeviertel) and there their second child Johannes was born, not quite three years after their marriage. (He had been preceded in 1831 by a sister, Elisabeth Wilhelmine, and was followed in 1835 by a brother, Friedrich, alias "Fritz," who was to become a workaday piano teacher.) Very early, young Johannes began collecting tin soldiers (a lifelong hobby) and taking a shine to music. When he was seven, his father turned him over to one Otto Cossel for lessons on the piano. By the time the boy was ten, he was playing so professionally that an itinerant promoter offered to take him off to the United States where child geniuses could get rich quickly. Cossel resisted and instead turned the child over to his own master, Eduard Marxsen, for advanced training—without charge. Marxsen, who indoctrinated him in the music of Bach, handled him with extreme care, letting him attempt nothing, either in the way of performance or composition, until he considered him ready.

In between lessons and practice, Brahms was making his way through grammar school and *Gymnasium,* actually acquiring a better education than most youngsters of his times. But, considering the family circumstances, all this was lagniappe, and he was expected to pay his own ticket. He did this in part by giving piano lessons to local children at a pittance. He also did it by playing in what were euphemistically called "dance halls" in and around the Gangeviertel. This district was analogous to the present-day Reepersbahn, and Brahms's evening milieu was where the whores and the sailors just off the ships in port conducted their business. The boy under these circumstances played mostly by ear, while conning some favorite book of poetry propped up on his music rack. But he could not help seeing and hearing a side of humanity—especially female humanity—that shocked him and disgusted him. Moreover the women often used him (at the most sexually excitable point of adolescence) as a come-on—Cupid in the lap of Dido, as it were. The result was severe emotional crippling and a schizophrenic view of women. Like a good bourgeois gentleman, he idolized the "good" ones but could not imagine physical contact with them and found sexual release only in the whorehouses. No doubt such childhood experiences had something to do with the headaches and general ill health he experienced. But the summers of his fifteenth and sixteenth years gave him a break and a taste for freedom in the natural world when a Herr

Giesemann, who had struck up an acquaintance with the senior Brahms, invited Johannes to his country home for several weeks. (In gratitude, he later educated Giesemann's granddaughter.)

Meanwhile Marxsen had been proceeding at his usual cautious rate. He had allowed the public a glimpse of his prodigy as a participant in a couple of concerts, but not until Brahms was sixteen did he appear in a solo recital. Brahms was also now composing (and doing some arranging for pay), but he later destroyed all his early work as juvenilia. His "serious" work began in 1851 with the E-flat minor *Scherzo* (Op. 4), followed within the next two years by the first two piano sonatas (in reverse order).

In 1848 the uprisings in Hungary had driven a horde of refugees across its borders. Among those who reached Hamburg was Eduard Hoffmann, a violinist in his early twenties who patriotically renamed himself Eduard Reményi and specialized in "Hungarian Gypsy" music—which was fast becoming fashionable in Germany. He met Brahms, liked him, and persuaded him to accompany him (in both senses) on a pedestrian concert tour of nearby cities. In the course of it, they met a greater Hungarian violinist, Joseph Joachim [**1321**], in Hannover. Joachim, who was to be Brahms's lifelong friend, gave them letters of introduction to Liszt [**1218**] at Weimar and Schumann at Bonn. With the former, Brahms was standoffish, and, according to Reményi, snored through Liszt's playing of his own sonata. Whatever the truth, it was Reményi who left precipitately and Brahms who stayed for several weeks. But in the end he and Liszt found they did not see eye to eye, and, after visiting and concertizing with Joachim in Göttingen, Brahms set off down the Rhine, eventually to meet Robert and Clara Schumann.

Despite the slum kid's apprehension at meeting the most influential musician in Germany, the Schumanns not only welcomed him, but made a great to-do over him and took him in as their guest. While there, Brahms even collaborated with the *Meister* and Schumann's pupil Albert Dietrich on a violin sonata as a gift for Joachim, who joined them later. Schumann sent his young visitor off with what amounted to an order to Breitkopf and Härtel to publish his music, and followed him with a paean of praise in the *Neue Zeitschrift für Musik* in which he fairly wrapped his own mantle about the (still) slender shoulders of the young Hamburger. But in the winter of 1854, when Brahms was visiting Joachim in Hannover (where the Schumanns had earlier joined them for a time), and two were shocked to read in a newspaper of Schumann's mental collapse and suicide attempt. Brahms rushed to Bonn to do what he could—and remained as Clara's chief support. When it became clear that Schumann would not recover, he joined Clara and Joachim on a fund-raising tour in 1855, in the course of which he made his first (not-very-successful) concert appearance in Hamburg since he had risen to national fame. In the course of his association with Clara (who was almost as much older than he [fourteen years] as his own mother had been than his father), he fell deeply in love with her and eventually let her know it. But it was a chivalrous (if not filial) passion at best, and he probably could not have consummated the union had he wanted to; but the dogged devotion lasted long after Robert's death. In 1857 Clara took her children to Berlin, and Brahms divided his time chiefly between Hamburg and the court at Detmold where for three seasons he served a four-month term as a sort of musical factotum.

During this period, composition—mostly for the piano, plus a few sets of songs and some choral pieces for the groups he was conducting in his two places of residence—went slowly, for Brahms was a merciless self-critic. He tried his hand at a symphony but gave it up, cannibalizing what he had done for other works. After working at it for four years, he completed the first of his 2 piano concerti in 1858. By the end of the decade he had written the 2 orchestral serenades and the first of the 2 string sextets. (In this last work, he memorialized thematically (A-G-A-H[B]-E) his love for Agathe von Siebold of Göttingen, who in 1858 had taken his mind off of Clara, but whom he dropped when marriage came into question.)

In 1857 Brahms had injured some other feelings when he and Joachim came out publicly against the Liszt-Wagner axis. The new piano concerto, which was applauded when premiered in Hannover and was a raving success later in Hamburg (with the elder Brahms in the orchestra) was cold-shouldered by the public and critics in Leipzig, and Brahms suddenly found his Leipzig publishers were no longer interested in him. (His long association with the house of Simrock was a direct result of this estrangement.) Nor was he in particular demand as a pianist, and his choral ladies in Hamburg hardly seemed the way to fame. He had at last given up the parental roof for a room in the home of a Dr. Rösing (female) in the suburb of Hamm. His chief hope was that he might succeed Friedrich Wilhelm Grund, the founder, in 1828, and conductor of the

Philharmonic Society. Rather than wait around in what was otherwise a musical backwater, he decided to go to Vienna, where the action was, and try to add luster to his name. Whether, in terms of the Philharmonic, that was a good or bad decision is hard to say, for in 1863 Grund turned the orchestra over to Julius Stockhausen, a singer (and a chief proponent of Brahms's songs). Later the same year, by a narrow vote, Brahms was appointed director of the Vienna Singakademie.

In Vienna he found a number of old friends and quickly made new admirers, such as the conductor Otto Dessoff, the pianist-composer Tausig [1389], and Joseph Hellmesberger, the violinist, whose quartet (with the pianist Julius Epstein) soon gave the first readings of the 2 piano quartets and the quintet. Various of his works were played and sung in public concerts—one, in April 1864, an all-Brahms affair which he put on with the help of his Singakademie. Reviews were not enthusiastic at first, and this applies particularly to those of Hanslick, an arch-conservative who was inclined to like what he knew. The more he came to know Brahms's work, the more he liked it, and he gradually became a one-man cheering section. (Brahms admired Wagner's music. It was Hanslick who insisted on the dichotomy until Wagner attacked Brahms in print and the enmity became real.) In Vienna, Brahms also established himself as a piano teacher and was generous of his time with talented students who could not pay. In the earlier years of his stay there, he continued to concertize a good deal, often with Joachim and others, but by the end of the decade he was making only occasional appearances, which may have been just as well, for the word was out that there were better pianists around.

Back in Hamburg the lusty senior Brahms had gradually discovered that he was married to a frail little old lady. In 1864, at long last, he was appointed to the Philharmonic. But the necessary practice this entailed drove the little old lady to exile him to the attic, and, despite the efforts of their elder son, the marriage collapsed. On January 31, 1865, Johanna Brahms died at seventy-six. (A few months later, in a *volte face*, the sexagenarian widower married a woman of forty-one.) Deeply grieving, Brahms turned back in February to a choral work he had once contemplated as a memorial to Schumann and wrote the *German Requiem* (a sort of large-scale funeral cantata to Biblical texts in the vernacular). Three numbers were performed in Vienna in 1867, but the complete work was premiered (in Leipzig under Carl Reinecke [1292]) only in February 1869. Meanwhile Brahms was still hoping to find a suitable post back home. He had given up the Singakademie as a bad job after a season but was still deluding himself that he could marry only if he held a respectable post. But when Stockhausen left the Philharmonic to pursue his career in 1867, Brahms was apparently not even considered. In 1870, the Vienna Gesellschaft der Musikfreunde offered him the direction of its concerts, but he turned down the job and it went to Anton Rubinstein [1309]. When Rubinstein gave it up in 1872, the year Brahms's father died, Brahms reconsidered and took it. However, convinced once for all that he was not a first-class conductor, he resigned three years later.

The decade had been marked by much composing with increasing success. The only orchestral work had been the *Haydn Variations* of 1874, which was immensely successful, but almost all the big choral works—the *German Requiem,* the cantata *Rinaldo,* the *Alto Rhapsody* (for Joachim's wife, the contralto Amalie Weiss), the *Schicksalslied,* and the rather infamous *Triumphlied* (a gloat over the French defeat in 1871)—had been completed. So had half of the *Lieder,* most of the vocal duets, and many of the part-songs. The output of chamber music had temporarily slowed, producing only the second sextet, the first cello sonata, the horn trio, the last piano quartet, and the first two string quartets. Curiously, during this period Brahms virtually stopped writing for the piano, producing nothing for the solo instrument after the foray into variation form in the late 1850s and early 1860s save the waltzes for piano duet and the sonata and *Haydn Variations* transcribed for two pianos. In passing, Brahms was becoming quite comfortably off and a power to be reckoned with in musical circles. (It was in the 1870s that Brahms helped swing the State Scholarship to Antonín Dvořák.) Such works as the first two volumes of *Hungarian Dances* (based on what amounted to cabaret Gypsy songs, though Brahms thought the sources real folk music) had made him world-famous even among laymen—and had made Simrock very rich. Brahms, who could put away vast quantities of food and wine, was also beginning to *look* prosperous, thought he was not yet the familiar Santa Claus figure. When he was not working, he was vacationing—in Switzerland, in Italy, in Bavaria.

He could not see, however, going to England, and he rejected an honorary doctorate from Cambridge on such grounds in 1876 and again in 1892. Late in 1876 he completed the long-delayed symphony which Dessoff

premiered in November at Karlsruhe. He completed the second symphony only a year later. Joachim premiered the violin concerto in Leipzig in 1879, and the composer himself premiered the second piano concerto in Stuttgart in 1881. In between, he had been tapped for an honorary doctorate by the University of Breslau. Discovering that he was expected to respond with an orchestral work, he did so with one of his few essays in overt musical humor (though he had a broad comedic sense). The *Academic Festival Overture* was based on four familiar student songs and delighted the students at Breslau. (To counterbalance the levity, he wrote the *Tragic Overture* at the same time.) The last two symphonies followed in 1883 and 1885; the last major orchestral essay, the Double Concerto, appeared in 1887. But for the most part, the late years were devoted chiefly to smaller forms—chamber music (the 2 string quintets, the piano trios, the violin sonatas, the works with clarinet inspired by the virtuoso clarinetist Richard Mühlfeld); a return to the piano that produced most of the character pieces; songs and part-songs; at the very end, the organ chorale-preludes and the third and largest collection of folksong settings.

Compared with, say, Liszt or Verdi [1232] or Wagner, Brahms led a remarkably uneventful life after his earliest struggles. His personal goal seems to have been *Gemütlichkeit,* which he attained reasonably soon. He fell in love repeatedly with conveniently unattainable women; he was pursued by others who did not interest him. He had a wide coterie of friends; besides those mentioned (and innumerable lay-persons who need not detain us here) he was close to such Viennese luminaries as Goldmark [1315], Brüll [1434], and the younger Johann Strauss [1295]. For the most part, he was kind, warm, and generous. He set his father's sickly stepson up in business and sent his sister a monthly check. But he had a streak of crudity and often offended people whom he loved. He got on the outs with Clara Schumann (a notably stuffy lady) early. Around 1881 he intervened in a quarrel between the Joachims on Amalie's side and quite alienated Joseph. Though in both instances relations were patched up after a fashion, they remained gingerly. He had violent antipathies to other composers—notably Bruckner [1293] and Hugo Wolf [1521], as well as the Wagner crowd. Curiously, however, one of his greatest champions was Bülow, who, after the rupture with Wagner and the acceptance of the *Kapellmeister*-ship at Meiningen, put his orchestra at Brahms's disposal. (Brahms, though he befriended

Grieg [1410], showed very little interest in non-German music and composers.)

In due course, he received the expectable decorations—one from Prussia in 1887, another from his emperor in 1889, and, in the same year, the freedom of the city of Hamburg. By the mid-1880s he began to slow down, both creatively and physically. (His *embonpoint* clearly must have curtailed his passion for hiking.) But, though only in his fifties and apparently in robust health, he already looked twenty years older. He had decided to retire in 1890, but Mühlfeld's clarinet so fascinated him that he returned for a curtain call. His final musical statement was the moving and skeptical *Serious Songs,* written in 1896. Late that year he was found to have an advanced hepatic cancer. Swearing to defeat it, he kept up social engagements and attended concerts until March 26, 1897. Then he took to his bed, telling his friends he needed rest. His last words were *"Ja, das ist schön"* ("Yes, that's lovely") after being given a glass of Rhine wine by his doctor. He died the next morning.

RECORDINGS: In 1890 an emissary of Edison came through Vienna with a cylinder recording machine and persuaded Brahms to wax an abbreviated rendition of the first *Hungarian Dance.* Rediscovered in this century, what is left of it has been transferred to a commercial LP by the International Piano Library. One can plainly hear the composer introducing himself in his hoarse tenor, but the piano—alas!—is little more than a faceless blur. (About the same time Brahms indicated to an American visitor that he should like to investigate ragtime. The imagination reels.) Joachim made disc recordings of two of the *Hungarian Dances* in 1903. As for more modern exemplars, the orchestral, chamber, piano, organ, and major choral music has all been recorded innumerable times. In 1983 Deutsche Grammophon brought out, to celebrate Brahms's 150th birthday, a "complete recorded works" on more than sixty LPs.

[1330] RITTER, Alexander (Rit'-ter, Ä-lek-sän'-der)
VIOLINIST, MERCHANT
BORN: Narva, June 7, 1833
DIED: Munich, April 12, 1896

Nowadays Alexander Ritter is remembered, if at all, for a programmatic poem he wrote for Richard Strauss's [1563] tone poem *Tod und Verklärung.* Indeed his chief importance was probably as an influence on Strauss. Though born in Estonia, he came of a German family and made his career in Ger-

many. At eight he moved to Dresden with his parents and studied violin with the "other" Franz (a.k.a. François) Schubert [1196], composer of *The Bee.* The Ritters were early admirers of Wagner [1230]. At sixteen he began two years of study at the Leipzig Conservatory with Ferdinand David (1810–73) and E. F. Richter (1808–79). In 1854 Ritter married a young actress, Franziska Wagner, the daughter of Richard's brother Albert, and accepted the post of number-two violinist in Liszt's [1218] Weimar orchestra. Despite his idolatry of Liszt, two years later Alexander accepted the musical directorship of the Stettin Theater, where Franziska was also hired. But Ritter seems not to have been cut out for stardom, and after holding orchestral posts in Dresden and Schwerin, he and his wife found employment in Würzburg, where he opened a music store to bolster the family exchequer. In 1882 his old friend Hans von Bülow [1310] took over the Meiningen orchestra and hired Ritter as associate concertmaster. It was in Meiningen that Ritter met young Strauss. As the composer of some Lisztian tone poems himself, Ritter persuaded Strauss to try his hand at the genre. Later he urged Strauss to do an opera in the Wagnerian style. The result was *Guntram,* but when Strauss refused to resolve the plot in religious terms, the devout Ritter was shocked, and the friendship cooled. Ritter himself wrote 2 operas (and the libretto for Ludwig Thuille's [1537] *Theuerdank),* but as a composer he remains little more than a footnote. RECORDINGS: Dietrich Fischer-Dieskau, however, gives him a nod in his recorded survey of the post-Schumann [1211] *Lied.*

[1331] BORODIN, Alexander Porfirievitch (Bô-rō-dēn', Ä-lex-àn'-der Pôr-fē-rē-yä'-vich)
PHYSICIAN, SCIENTIST
BORN: St. Petersburg, November 12, 1833
DIED: St. Petersburg, February 27, 1887

Considering the popularity of Borodin's colorful music, one is always surprised when reminded just how little he was able to produce in a busy and abbreviated life. He was the bastard son of the elderly Georgian Prince Luka Semeonovitch Gedeanashvili (who was, understandably, usually called Gedeanov). His mother, the young wife of a military doctor, is variously listed as Avdotia, Antonova, and Eudoxia Kleinecke. Whoever she was, she had taste, education, and money, and she saw to it that he had broad, if isolated, schooling from her and various domestics. (Borodin, by the way, was officially registered, as was a common custom in such cases, as the son of one of his real father's serfs, Porfiry Borodin.) The boy became multilingual, able to make his way in French, German, Italian, and English, as well as in Russian. He showed an intense interest in music, learned to play the flute, picked up the rudiments of piano apparently on his own, began composing at the age of eight without instruction, and in his teens taught himself to play the cello. In the later 1840s he had the company of a boarder of his own age named Shchiglev, with whom he played piano duets and chamber music, some of it of his own devising.

Having dabbled in chemistry and other sciences (attaining sufficient learning to make his own fireworks), Borodin decided that he was cut out to be a physician and was duly admitted to the Academy of Medicine and Surgery in his native city. He managed to distinguish himself as a student, despite a lamentable tendency to spend more time than he could spare on performing and writing music, and became a dedicated laboratory chemist. He graduated in 1856 with high honors and served for two years as a teaching assistant at the Academy, during which time he presented an imposing research paper at a professional conclave (and published it) and at the end of which he was awarded his M.D. He was then dispatched to Heidelberg for postdoctoral work, with side excursions over the next two years to such places as Amsterdam, Genoa, Rome, Paris, and Switzerland. In 1861 an attractive, musical, and frail Russian girl, Ekaterina Sergeyevna Protopopova, in Germany for her health, took a room in Borodin's pension. They fell in love, and in 1862 journeyed to Italy together, where they spent some months at Viareggio and where Borodin composed his piano quintet.

At the end of that year, Borodin came back to St. Petersburg, where he was made adjunct professor at the Academy, and where he fell in with the Balakirev circle (he had met Mussorgsky [1369] some years earlier). The next year he married Ekaterina, began chemical lectures at the School of Forestry and the translation of scientific books, and was given an apartment in the recently completed laboratory of the Academy, in which building he lived and plugged away at his research for the rest of his life. His musical composition had largely to be set aside for vacation times. However, under the goad of Balakirev [1348], he completed his first symphony in 1867 (Balakirev conducted it in public two years later) and some songs. He also embarked on an opera called

The Bogatyrs, intended as a satire on non-Russian music (especially that composed by such Russians as Serov [1269]). But, having got a commitment from the Bolshoi to produce it, he was unable to meet the deadline so that much of the work is a cut-and-paste job from the composers supposedly lampooned. Borodin was clever enough not to lend his name to the work, which, premiered in November 1867, was a disaster.

Borodin's marriage survived under the most extraordinary pressures. His hours were shockingly irregular. The apartment was a gathering place for all sorts of people who passed through the halls of the laboratory. Ekaterina's asthma at times was so bad that she had to go away on extended trips (no doubt the resident pride of cats and the conditions under which she otherwise lived did not help). And Borodin, who was surely more monogamous than the next man, was the constant target of adoring females. The Viareggio idyll had been complicated by a certain Giannina Centoni, who trotted doe-eyed at his heels. And in 1868 there was the onslaught of Anna Kalinina, who, in her frustration at being held at arms' length, developed all sorts of grotesque psychosomatic ailments. Borodin was quite puzzled at his wife's outrage when he told her about this relationship. The next year, however, the adoption of a daughter seemed to help matters.

In the late 1860s, Borodin worked hectically and sporadically on a second symphony and on operas based on Mey's The Czar's bride and (at Stassov's suggestion) on the heroic poem The Lay of Igor's Campaign. The Mey piece came to nothing. Borodin became so dissatisfied with the other opera that he cannibalized it for the symphony. This confusion was further interrupted by the commission for the opera Mlada, to be written by the Balakirev quintet in collaboration (with ballet music by Minkus [1298]!). This collapsed of its own weight, leaving Borodin with more music to be converted to one of his other enterprises. Meanwhile increased teaching duties at the Academy (he had been a full professor since 1864) cut into his time, but he managed to complete the symphony, to rethink Prince Igor, and to write his first (surprisingly un-Russian) quartet by 1879. Notified that the symphony would be played in 1876, he discovered that he had irretrievably lost the score of the first and last movements and had to do them over again. In 1877, while on a professional trip to Germany, he visited Liszt [1218], in whom he found a sympathetic and kindred spirit; three years later he paid him homage with the symphonic poem

In the Steppes of Central Asia. By 1879 the famous *Polovetsian Dances* for *Prince Igor* were finished and performed, but from then until shortly before Borodin's death *Prince Igor* lay dormant again.

In the late 1870s Borodin turned out a number of amusing trifles as well, most notably the so-called *Variations on "Chopsticks"* (i.e., *Tati-tati)* to which Cui [1337], Rimsky-Korsakov [1416], and Liadov [1485] contributed. The 1880s were a grimmer period. Driven and overworked, Borodin suffered several heart attacks and survived a bout of cholera. Ekaterina's declining health forced her to live in Moscow, where twice, in 1886, her life was despaired of. On the brighter side, Borodin's music began to be performed all over Europe, and he completed the second quartet, the *Petite Suite* for piano, and some songs. He also began a third quartet and a third symphony, and worked out in his head several more sections for *Prince Igor,* including the overture, which he played for his friends. On the evening of February 26 he attended a costume ball for the Academy faculty, clad as a Russian peasant, and just after midnight in mid-conversation with a group of friends, he fell dead. He had just turned fifty-four. The third symphony remains a playable fragment. The opera was completed by Rimsky-Korsakov and Glazunov [1573], using the material noted down, and what they recalled of Borodin's playing. In performance, the brief third act is often omitted as being chiefly Glazunov's, but recent studies show that much more of it is Borodin's than was previously assumed.

RECORDINGS: *Prince Igor,* though not a repertoire staple in the West, has enjoyed several recordings, not only from Russia but also from Yugoslavia and Bulgaria. All of the orchestral music and the mature chamber music, and most of the songs and piano pieces have also been recorded, most of them several times.

[1332] ZABEL, Albert Heinrich (Tsä'-bel, Äl'-bârt Hīn'-rikh)
HARPIST, TEACHER
BORN: Berlin, February 22, 1834
DIED: St. Petersburg, February 16, 1910

Zabel was one of the noted harp virtuosi of the nineteenth century. He was trained in Berlin and won international fame when he toured Europe and America in the late 1840s with Joseph Gungl's [1215] orchestra. He was thereafter harpist with the Berlin Hofoper and, from 1855, with the Imperial Ballet in St. Petersburg, where Anton Ru-binstein [1309] appointed him his harp man when he opened the Conservatory in 1862. Zabel wrote a harp method, a concerto, and many solo pieces for his instrument. RECORDINGS: Some of his solo harp pieces may be found in recorded harp recitals.

[1333] REUBKE, Friedrich Julius (Roib'-ke, Frē'-drikh Yōōl'-yus)
KEYBOARDIST, TEACHER
BORN: Hausneindorf, March 23, 1834
DIED: Pillnitz, June 3, 1858

Prussian-born Julius Reubke was the eldest son of Adolf Reubke, a noted organ builder. His brother Emil took up the paternal calling; another brother, Otto, also a keyboard player and composer, settled in Halle where he was right-hand man to Robert Franz, [1242], and later music director to the university. Julius was first trained in nearby Quedlinburg and then went to the Berlin Conservatory to study with Theodor Kullak and A. B. Marx. He graduated *cum laude* and went on to study with Liszt [1218] in Weimar in 1856. (Reubke dedicated his piano sonata to Liszt.) In 1857 Reubke moved to Dresden but was soon incapacitated by what is vaguely described as "a nervous ailment," and died the following spring at twenty-four. He is remembered today almost solely for his big organ sonata based on Psalm 94. RECORDINGS: The Psalm 94 sonata has had many recordings.

[1334] PONCHIELLI, Amilcare (Pon-kyel'-lē, Ä-mil-cä'-rä)
CONDUCTOR, ORGANIST, TEACHER
BORN: Paderno Fasolano, August 31/ September 1, 1834
DIED: Milan, January 17, 1886

Today Ponchielli's name survives almost entirely through his opera *La Gioconda,* which, despite a plot that sometimes seems a grand parody of romantic Italian opera, refuses to budge from the repertoire. (Actually the libretto is by Boito [1393], disguised as "Tobia Gorrio," after Victor Hugo.) His teachers and colleagues saw him rightly as a composer of great promise, but it was a promise that remained largely unfulfilled because of his timidity and perfectionism. He was essentially a small-town boy at heart.

His particular small town, rechristened Paderno Ponchielli in his memory, was a hamlet on the Emilian plain near Cremona. His father was a schoolmaster who doubled as organist by tradition and as shopkeeper out of necessity. Having taught the boy all he knew, he got him into the Milan Conservatory as a scholarship student in 1843. There, despite his diffidence, he was overwhelmingly successful and when, in 1856, he graduated with all sorts of prizes and honors, everyone expected him to set the musical world afire. Instead he went back to Cremona and subsisted there as music teacher and organist of the Church of Sant' Hilario. Though he had done nothing so far in the operatic medium except a few numbers contributed to a collaborative student farce, *Il Sindaco Babbeo (The Idiot Mayor)*, at the Conservatory, he undertook a treatment of Manzoni's epic novel *I promessi sposi (The Betrothed)*. Thanks to the director of the local theater, it was performed to the great delight of the Cremonese in 1856; but a success in Cremona is like a success in Peoria. A second opera, *Bertrando dal Bormio*, got some rehearsal in Turin but was dropped. *La Savoiarda (The Girl from Savoy)*, produced in Cremona in 1861, also did nothing to advance Ponchielli's name and fame. That same year he became conductor of the National Guard band in nearby Piacenza, where he produced—again to no avail—his *Roderico, re dei Goti (Roderick, King of the Goths)* in 1863. The following year he came back to Cremona as director of *its* National Guard band. Toward the end of the decade, he applied for an opening at the Milan Conservatory. He was judged remarkably well-fitted, but the job went to Franco Faccio, six years younger and, no doubt, considered good for more mileage. Ponchielli took the slap with good grace and set his sights on becoming a sergeant-major in the National Guard.

Though he had by then all but abandoned composition, he had been tinkering with the score to *I promessi sposi*, and in 1872 (he was now thirty-eight) he got a production of it in the new Teatro dal Verme in Milan. It was an unexpected success and won him a contract with the publisher Ricordi. (Verdi [1232], however, thought the opera too little and too late.) After successfully producing two ballets in Milan—one new, one old, Ponchielli was commissioned to set *I Lituani (The Lithuanians)*, a big historical drama devised by *Aida*-librettist Antonio Ghislanzoni from Adam Mickiewicz's *Konrad Wallenrod*. The composer hemmed and hawed, murmuring that it was all too grand for the likes of him, but he finished it by 1874, and it was cheered at La Scala that March (though Ponchielli typically revised it for the next season). In September his memorial cantata to Donizetti [1155] was sung at the entombment of that composer's remains at Bergamo Cathedral. Meanwhile

Ponchielli was winding up his work on *La Gioconda*, beset more with reservations and self-doubts than usual. (The story goes that Tito Ricordi salvaged the tenor aria *"Cielo e mar"* from the trash basket.) Unveiled at La Scala on April 8, 1876, the opera was an enormous triumph; even today the passion of the music makes one forget the blood-and-thunder plot. Ironically the conductor was Franco Faccio, and the composer was hailed by the press as the dormant Verdi's successor. It was not to be. In 1877 he produced a revision of *La Savoiarda*, now called *Lina*, at the Teatro del Verme to no particular acclaim. *I Mori di Valenza (The Moors of Valencia)* got no farther than the piano score; it was completed by Ponchielli's son Annibale and produced in Monte Carlo in 1914. (Ponchielli had married Teresa or "Teresina" Brambilla, star of the revised *Promessi sposi* and niece of Verdi's first *Rigoletto* Gilda in 1874; they also had another son and a daughter.) In 1880 Ponchielli was named professor of composition at the Conservatory; among his pupils were Puccini [1511] and Mascagni [1559]. The same year La Scala premiered his biblical *Il Figliuol prodigo*, and in 1881 he was given the additional post of *maestro di cappella* at Bergamo Cathedral. His last opera, *Marion Delorme*, appeared at La Scala in 1885. Nine months later Ponchielli contracted pneumonia and died at fifty-one.

RECORDINGS: Expectably *Gioconda* is represented on commercial records by several complete recordings and innumerable excerpts, but there are only a few numbers from the most successful of the other operas. (There is a pirate version of *I Lituani.*) There is also sparse representation of his many songs and instrumental pieces (most of them in a decidedly popular or utile vein; of the works for band one would especially like to hear the flügelhorn concerto.) The Syrinx Ensemble has recorded a collection of short chamber pieces.

[1335] **BLODEK,** Vilém (Blō'-dek, Vil'-âm)
PIANIST, FLUTIST, TEACHER, CONDUCTOR
BORN: Prague, October 3, 1834
DIED: Prague, May 1, 1874

A piano pupil of Alexander Dreyschock [1260], Blodek later specialized in the flute at the Prague Conservatory and became known as a fine performer on both instruments. After a couple of years as music tutor to a wealthy Polish family, he returned to Prague and set up as a teacher. There he began writing incidental music for plays (more than 50 in all!) He also served for a time as one of the conductors of the Hlahol (the local male chorus). When Smetana [1291] made his first official appearance as head of that organization in 1864 with a three hundredth-birthday Shakespeare tribute, Blodek wrote the music for six of the *tableaux*. (He had, by then, joined the Conservatory faculty as professor of flute.) In 1865 he married one of his students, Marie Doudlebská. Two years later, Smetana, now director of the Provisional Theater, premiered Blodek's little folk opera *In the Well (V Studni)*, which was a tremendous hit and still holds the stage in Czechoslovakia. Blodek, rather ungratefully, allowed some of Smetana's enemies to convince him that he was Smetana's logical successor—the sooner the better. He was working on a more ambitious opera, *Zitek*, in 1870 when his mind gave way. *Zitek* was completed by F. X. Vana and premiered October 3, 1934. He died, under conditions horribly prophetic of Smetana's end a decade later, at thirty-nine. Beginning as a Mendelssohnian [1200], Blodek bid fair to become a nationalist composer of striking originality but did not live to more than hint at what he might have been. RECORDINGS: There are recordings of his flute concerto, a *Fantasy and Caprice* for flute and orchestra, an orchestral suite *Music for Shakespeare*, and various excerpts from the folk opera.

[1336] BĄDARZEWSKA-BARANOW-
SKA, Tekla (Bôn-där-zef'-skà Bà-rà-
nof'-skà, Tek'-là)
BORN: Warsaw, 1834
DIED: Warsaw, September 29, 1861

About all that seems to be known of Bądarzewska is that she was an amateur who wrote around 35 little salon pieces for piano and died of tuberculosis at twenty-three (1834 was not a good year for composers to be born in, though there is some disagreement about this one's birthdate). Tekla's biggest—indeed only—hit was *La prière d'une vierge* (better known here as *The Maiden's Prayer*), first published in 1856, but given worldwide impetus when it was printed in a French magazine in 1859. Pianist Arthur Loesser remarked in *Men, Women, and Pianos* that "a poorer specimen of an attempted music . . . would be hard to conceive." Nevertheless it became an all-time bestseller. Poor Tekla spent her declining years trying to cash in on its success with the expectable sequels *(The Maiden's Second Prayer, Answer to the Maiden's Prayer*, etc.),

though she never specified what the maiden was praying for. RECORDINGS: Hans Kann, among others, has recorded her masterwork.

[1337] CUI, César (Kwē, Sä'-zär)
ENGINEER, GENERAL, WRITER
BORN: Wilno (Vilnius), January 18, 1835
DIED: Petrograd, March 26, 1918

Of the fingers of the "mighty fist" of Russian musical nationalism, Cui was decidedly the pinky. His father, a French army officer who named his other sons "Alexander" and "Napoléon," had thought better of following his emperor home from Moscow. He settled in Lithuania, married a native, Yulya Gutzevich, and taught his native language at the Wilno *Gymnasium*. An amateur pianist and composer, he saw that his son had piano lessons. Later the boy tried his hand at composing, and received some help from Moniuszko [1263], then resident in Wilno. But at sixteen he gave up music for fortifications, distinguishing himself as a student at the Academy of Military Engineering at St. Petersburg. He joined its staff on his graduation in 1857 and became an authority in his field, eventually rising to the rank of general. Before that date, however, he had been introduced to Balakirev [1348] and gotten caught up in the avant-garde swirl around him. He became Balakirev's disciple and wrote his first opera, *A Prisoner in the Caucasus*, under his eye. (It was not, however, produced for nearly a quarter of a century.) In 1858 he married another Balakirev disciple, Malvina Bamberg, for whose amusement he wrote an operatic comedy, *The Mandarin's Son*. It was produced in the Cui parlor with César, Malvina, and Mussorgsky [1369] in the leading roles and Balakirev at the piano. But Cui's first serious essay at opera came with the premiere at the Maryinsky Theater of his *William Ratcliff* (after Heine) in 1869. Despite the fact that it was diametrically opposed to Cui's nationalist stance in the press, the nationalists praised it to the skies—though Rimsky-Korsakov [1416] privately thought it could stand reorchestration (preferably his own). It has rarely been heard from since. His chief later operas include *Angelo*, 1876, after the Victor Hugo play that inspired Ponchielli's [1334] *La Gioconda* in the same year; *Le Flibustier*, premiered in Paris in 1894; *The Saracen*, 1903, after Dumas; *Mam'zelle Fifi*, 1903, after Maupassant; *Matteo Falcone*, 1908, after Merimée; only the Pushkin-derived *A Feast in Plague Time* of 1901 and *The Captain's Daughter* of 1911 drew from Russian sources, and even there the music is not notably Russian. Toward the end of his career, Cui did some fairy-tale operas for children.

In 1864 he began his work as a part-time music critic, proclaiming the ideals of the *kuchka* but not always reserving his vicious diatribes for the opposition. He was on active duty in the Russo-Turkish War of 1877 and was appointed professor at the Academy the year following. He also wrote 4 orchestral suites, some choral music, and chamber pieces, salonesque piano music, and songs.

RECORDINGS: Boris Christoff has recorded an LP of the songs, for which Cui had a considerable gift. There are a few other small pieces on records, of which the *Orientale* for violin and piano was once popular; Jonel Perlea once recorded the 1859 orchestral snippet, *Tarantella.*

[1338] FERNÁNDEZ CABALLERO, Manuel (Fâr-nán'-deth Kâb-vàl-yā'-rō, Màn'-wel)
CONDUCTOR
BORN: Murcia, March 14, 1835
DIED: Madrid, February 26, 1906

The youngest of eighteen children, Fernández Caballero began his musical career as a choirboy. He somehow learned to play instruments (violin, piccolo, flute, piano) well enough to qualify for a place in the school band at the age of seven. Later he undertook formal study of the violin and at fifteen entered the Madrid Conservatory, where in his final year he carried off the composition prize. He then became a professional theater violinist and drifted into conducting. In that capacity he was well-known both in Spain and Cuba, where he once directed a company for seven years. He wrote some operas and some sacred music, but was (and is) chiefly famous for some of his approximately 200 *zarzuelas,* the most famous of them being *Gigantes y Cabezudos* (1898). In his last years he was blind, but this affliction did not stem his composition, which he dictated. (One source claims that he persuaded the great *castrato* Farinelli to come out of retirement to sing in one of his works. If so, it was a remarkable feat, for Farinelli died fifty-three years before Fernández Caballero was born!) RECORDINGS: There are recordings of *El Cabo primero, El Duo de la Africana, Gigantes y Cabezudos,* and *La Viejecita,* and of many excerpts.

[1339] STRAUSS, Eduard (Shtrous, Ed'-wärd)
VIOLINIST, HARPIST, CONDUCTOR

BORN: Vienna, March 15, 1835
DIED: Vienna, December 28, 1916

Eduard was the youngest and least gifted of the sons of Johann Strauss, Sr. **[1177]**, born when his father was already presiding over two households. As a result, he was reared by his mother and his brothers. The former wanted him to enter governmental service; he wanted to be a writer (he seems to have had even less talent there!); his oldest brother saw to it that he became a musician. He is said to have been a good violinist, and he studied harp with the English virtuoso Parish-Alvars **[1194]**. He also learned to compose from the ubiquitous Simon Sechter **[1129]**. In 1859 the three brothers led three dance orchestras in their own and each others' compositions, individually and collectively, including some collaborative pieces, at the Sofienbad in Vienna. From about 1864 he and Josef Strauss **[1300]** were, in effect, the conductors of the Strauss Orchestra and, on Josef's ultimately fatal accident in 1870, Eduard became sole proprietor. He seems to have been highly efficient, not to say dictatorial, though not inspired. The public, however, could not tell the difference, and he was an enormous success all over the world. He was handsome, inordinately vain, and terribly conscious of his musical inferiority. Therefore he sought official approval wherever he could find it. He was not only Imperial Court Ball Director (from 1870), but also *Hofkapellmeister* to the Emperor of Brazil, and held (and wore) decorations from Austria, Spain, France, Russia, and Persia, to name only some sources. (His chest, in full regalia, would have put Idi Amin's to shame.) He played regularly in Vienna and made several tours, including one to England in 1885 and one to the United States in 1890. At one point in the last decade of the century, while he was away, his wife and children sank virtually his entire fortune in some wild investment deal and wiped him out. That was enough to sour any man, but Eduard had a wide streak of jealousy and suspicion all his life, chiefly directed at his eldest brother. Long after the latter's death, Eduard, in 1906, immolated hundreds of his papers, allegedly on Johann's orders. Many people suspect that irreplaceable manuscripts went up in smoke and that it was an act of revenge, conscious or not. After Eduard's death, the family orchestra continued to be directed by his descendents, variously called Eduard, Johann, and Joseph. Eduard II, who took over in 1949, has made many records. Eduard I wrote well over 200 dances, most of which at least go through the proper motions. RECORDINGS: There are sufficient recordings of his output.

[1340] WIENIAWSKI, Henryk ("Henri")
(Vĕn-yov'-skĕ, Hen'-rik)
VIOLINIST, TEACHER
BORN: Lublin, July 10, 1835
DIED: Moscow, March 31, 1880

A graceful and popular composer for his own instrument, Henryk Wieniawski was, by all accounts, one of the most remarkable of all violin virtuosi. His father Tadeusz was an army surgeon, but his mother Regina was a splendid pianist, and her brother Edouard Wolff, a friend and imitator of Chopin [1208], was a well-known professional in Paris. Henryk's younger brother Jozef became an admired pianist, teacher, and composer as well; he accompanied Henryk early in his career, studied with Liszt [1218], and was coinventor of the two-keyboard Piano-Mangeot. Henryk began violin lessons as a small child with Jan Hornziel, concertmaster of the Warsaw opera orchestra, and studied later on with Stanisław Serwaczynski, one of Joachim's [1321] teachers. At eight he was sent to his uncle in Paris so that he might study at the Conservatoire. After a year he was promoted to the advanced violin class under Lambert-Joseph Massart, a Rodolphe Kreutzer (1766–1831) pupil who also taught Sarasate [1415] and José White [1375]. He astounded his teacher by playing the Paganini [1106] caprices. At eleven he won the first prize for violin and was rewarded by the Emperor Nicholas with a Guarnerius instrument when he played in St. Petersburg in 1848. There he also won the support of court violinist Vieuxtemps [1270]. After further study (mostly theory and composition) at the Conservatoire, the Wieniawski brothers spent three years concertizing in Russia. In 1853 Henryk created a great impression in Leipzig with the first of his 2 violin concerti and went on concertizing throughout Europe for the next several years. In London in 1859, he fell in love with an English girl, Isobel Hampton, and married her a year later. (Their daughter, Irene Regine [1880–1932], later Lady Dean Paul, studied with, among others, Vincent d'Indy [1462] and published her compositions under the pseudonym of "Poldowski." Her impressionistic songs were once highly praised.)

In 1860 Wieniawski was appointed imperial chamber virtuoso to the czar, a post whose duties did not put a crimp into his concertizing. Two years later his close friend Anton Rubinstein [1309], with whom he fre-

quently appeared, named him professor of violin at the Conservatory in St. Petersburg. It was Henryk's prestige that saved his Uncle Jules, a leader in the Polish 1863 uprising, from execution. In 1872 he and Rubinstein embarked on a marathon tour of the United States. Wieniawski, like some modern rock stars, was given to appearing at his concerts only when it suited him; on this venture his contract not only gave him only half the fee commanded by his pianist, but also threatened whopping fines for nonappearances. To add insult to injury, Rubinstein got by far the most attention and the partnership eventually went sour, the two going their separate ways. Wieniawski continued to tour America, going all the way to California, and losing his entire take on the stock market. However, in 1875 he was called back to Europe to take over at the Brussels Conservatory for the ailing Vieuxtemps. But Wieniawski was now exhausted, and his health began to fail. Heart disease forced his resignation two years later, but he went on concertizing. In Berlin in 1878 he became ill while playing his Concerto No. 2 for Violin of 1862. Calling for a chair, he tried to go on, seated, but could not. Joachim, who was in the audience, borrowed his violin and played the Bach [684] unaccompanied *chaconne*. Wieniawski recovered, but economic necessity (brought on by his proclivity to gambling and making poor investments) forced him to stay on the road, despite several more attacks. When he suffered one in Moscow in the winter of 1880, he was rushed to a hospital, where it was discovered that he was penniless. Peter Tchaikovsky's [1377] Egeria, Nadezhda von Meck, thereupon took him into her own home, saw to it that he had medical care, and promoted a benefit concert for him, but he died a few weeks later, not yet forty-five. He left only 30 published compositions.

RECORDINGS: Most of his works remain popular with violinists and have been recorded.

[1341] GOBBAERTS, Jean-Louis (Gobârts', Zhàn Lōō-ē')
PIANIST
BORN: Antwerp, September 28, 1835
DIED: Saint-Gilles, May 5, 1886

A product of the Brussels Conservatory, Gobbaerts was a one-man salon-music factory. He turned out hundreds of featherweight piano pieces, many of them under such pseudonyms as "Lèvi," "Ludovic," and the palindromic "Streabbog." The *Little Fairy Waltz* is said to have been featured in

President Truman's repertoire. RECORD-INGS: Hans Kann has recorded the Streab-bogian *La Violette.*

[1342] DRAESEKE, Felix August Bernhard (Drā'-ze-ke, Fā'-lēks Ou'-gōōst Bârn'-hart)
TEACHER, WRITER
BORN: Coburg, October 7, 1835
DIED: Dresden, February 26, 1913

It might be said that Felix Draeseke was cut from the whole cloth, since his forebears on both sides were churchmen and he himself was originally slated for the ministry. The first half of his life was singularly unlucky. His mother died as a consequence of giving birth. Having argued for a time with his father, preacher to the Coburg court, over vocation, he managed to get into the Leipzig Conservatory at seventeen, from which he was ejected a few years later as an incorrigible musical radical, having become a devotee of Wagner [1230]. However, he continued to study with Julius Rietz [1227], who had been his composition teacher there, and some of his work won Franz Liszt's [1218] approval. He was drawn into the Weimar circle and proselytized for the "new music." (Later on he published works on Liszt and Cornelius [1294].) However, at the Weimar Festival of 1861 two of his compositions were hissed, and the German Prince Konstantin von Hohenzollern-Hechingen, to whom a third was dedicated, had its performance canceled. Discouraged, Draeseke destroyed several of his creations and recast them.

In 1862 he moved to Switzerland where, after a wretched time as a piano teacher in Vevey (no pupils), and Yverdon (no life), he settled in Lausanne, where he developed a following. At some point during this period, he fell in love with one of his pupils, Louisa de Trey, and became engaged to her. In 1865, attending the premiere of *Tristan* in Munich, he was told by a physician that he was going deaf. (There was apparently no cause-and-effect relationship here.) In 1870 the elder Draeseke died and Louisa's father terminated the engagement. By 1876, having been refused a teaching appointment at the Geneva Conservatory and lost what money he had in unfortunate investments, Draeseke found himself facing the wall and left Switzerland for Dresden.

At this point, the bad times ended with the death of a wealthy godmother (apparently not supernatural). Fixed for life, Draeseke returned to composing and lived on his own terms until 1884, when he was asked to succeed Franz Wüllner as professor of composition at the Conservatory, where by 1894 he had risen to the eminence of court councillor. Grown conservative, he deplored such modernists as Richard Strauss [1563].

Draeseke was a fairly prolific composer and much admired at the height of his career. Of his 6 operas, however, only two reached the stage in his lifetime. He had more luck with his oratorio-cycle *Christus,* which was well-received the year before his death. There are several other big choral works, 4 symphonies, overtures, concerti, quartets, a quintet, sonatas (including 2 for the viola alta), piano pieces, and songs.

RECORDINGS: A recording of the third symphony *(Symphonia Tragica),* conducted by Hermann Desser, suggests that a reevaluation may be in order. There is also a recording of the 1881 *Requiem* by Udo Follert.

[1343] SAINT-SAËNS, Charles Camille (San-Sàn, Shàrl Kà-mēl')
PIANIST, COMPOSER, WRITER, ETC.
BORN: Paris, October 9, 1835
DIED: Algiers, December 16, 1921

An out-of-step conservative in his own day (but admired as a brilliant performer), Saint-Saëns has doggedly held on in the sixty years since he died through that charming *jeu d'esprit* entitled *Le Carnaval des Animaux,* the Third Symphony and what may be the most stultifying opera in the standard repertoire, *Samson et Dalila.* Within the past decade, however, he seems (at least on records) to be making a strong comeback.

Camille Saint-Saëns' father, born in Dieppe of Norman peasant stock, was a tubercular civil servant in Paris. On December 31, 1834 he married a young and sketchily educated *bourgeoise,* Clemence Collin. Nine months later she bore him a son. On December 31, 1835 she became a widow. Fearful that the child would succumb to his father's disease, she sent him to nurse in the countryside for two years and moved back in with her aunt Charlotte Masson, who had sheltered her in earlier years. Clemence was mad about music and wanted her son to become a musician. Charlotte was a pianist and teacher. According to his memoirs, Camille started distinguishing between notes from the time he could sit up, and Charlotte began training him before he was three. At five he was writing pieces his hands were too small to play. At seven he was entrusted by Charlotte to Camille-Marie Stamaty, a student of Mendelssohn [1200] and Kalkbrenner [1118], and Gottschalk's [1306] teacher, who taught him the precise finger articulation that is regarded as

"French style" (Stamaty shared with Saint-Saëns the same odd name, early loss of a father, and rearing by women.) In 1846 the boy made his public debut in the Salle Pleyel. (As an encore, he is said to have offered to play any Beethoven sonata on request.) Afterward he did a command performance for King Louis Philippe. Following a course in harmony with Pierre Maleden, and a sound foundation in classics, science, and mathematics, he entered the Paris Conservatoire in 1848 where, like so many of his contemporaries, he was trained by Fromental Halèvy [1157] and by the organist Benoist. In these early years he was a friend of Gottschalk, Bizet [1363], and Guiraud [1352], and won the notice and approbation of several older musicians, including Rossini [1143] and Liszt [1218], who was a strong influence on him. He became a protégé of Berlioz [1175], who found in his clearheaded musical thinking a great help in the revision of the Gluck [803] scores on which he was working. Gounod [1258], who is said to have been the first to call him *"le Beethoven français"* (because, atypical of Frenchmen, he wrote symphonies), took a great shine to him, and called on him often for help (among other things, to play back his completed compositions to him). For all this, Saint-Saëns did no better than well at the Conservatoire, and both his attempts at the Prix de Rome miscarried.

However, his first mature large-scale composition, an *Ode à Ste. Cécile,* won the competition sponsored by the St. Cecilia Society in 1852. The next year Saint-Saëns left the Conservatoire and was appointed organist at St. Merry. In 1853 too his Symphony in E-flat (officially "No. 1" but preceded by a student work in A major) was premiered in Paris. (It was this work that wowed both Berlioz and Gounod). At St. Merry, the dedication of a Mass to the *curé* won Saint-Saëns a trip with him to Rome, which perhaps accounts for the code name *"Urbs Roma"* under which (by requirement) Symphony in F Major (another unnumbered symphony, the third that he wrote) was anonymously submitted for the 1856 Bordeaux St. Cecilia contest. It won, and the composer made his conducting debut with it in Bordeaux. In 1858, when Louis Lefébure-Wély [1253] took the organist's post at St. Sulpice, Saint-Saëns succeeded him at the Madeleine, at 3,000 francs annually. In 1861 he also took on a professorship at the Niedermeyer School. Among his pupils he numbered Gabriel Fauré [1424], Messager [1474], and the organist Gigout [1417], but he did not care for teaching and gave up after four years. That was also the year in

which he met Richard Wagner [1230], who hailed him as the greatest living French composer. Despite his classical leanings, Saint-Saëns became an outspoken supporter of Wagner, Liszt, and the New Music—which stance did not help his own career.

In 1864 he was beaten out for the *Prix de Rome* (his last try) by none other than Victor Sieg, future inspector of singing for Paris schools, and began his largely frustrating career as an operatic composer with *Le Timbre d'argent (The Silver Bell),* which did not get a performance until 1877. The year 1867 saw him the winner of a competition connected with the Paris World's Fair for the cantata *Les Noces de Prométhée (Prometheus' Wedding).* In 1868 he led a series of concerts with Anton Rubinstein [1309], with whom he had earlier established a fast friendship. For these, Saint-Saëns dashed off the second of his 5 piano concerti. During the Franco-Prussian War, he donned a uniform like a good patriot and laid plans for the foundation of an organization to encourage French composition. The Société Nationale de Musique was duly chartered in 1871, but at that point the Commune forced the composer to flee to England for some weeks. After that he concertized regularly in London. (During one engagement he fell through a trap door just before his performance and found himself quite unable to bow after it.)

In 1868, with his cousin Ferdinand Lemaire as librettist, Saint-Saëns began work on *Samson et Dalila* (whose music shows the influence of Berlioz' *Les Troyens*) but did not complete it until 1874. Meanwhile the Opéra-Comique had produced, without stopping the Earth in its revolution, the one-act *La Princesse jaune (The Yellow Princess)* in 1872. But no one in France would touch the Biblical work, and, at Liszt's suggestion, it finally had its premiere (as *Simson und Delila* under Eduard Lassen [1314] at Weimar on December 2, 1877). It was not performed in Paris until 1890 and then at a subsidiary theater, and it did not reach London in stage form until 1909, owing to the strictures against sacrilege imposed by the Lord Chamberlain. Saint-Saëns went on to write nine more operas *(Étienne Marcel, Henry VIII, Proserpine, Ascanio, Phryné, Les Barbares, Hélène, L'Ancêtre,* and *Déjanire),* but not one survived much beyond its first performances.

The 1870s also saw the composition of the Lisztian symphonic poems *Danse macabre* (developed from a song), *Le Rouet d'Omphale, Phaëton,* and *La Jeunesse d'Hercule,* and of the officially designated Symphony No. 2 in A Minor (actually the fourth). In 1875 Saint-Saëns, not noted for his pursuit of women, married Marie Truffot, age nineteen. She bore him two sons. One fell from an open window and was killed in 1879. The other died at the age of seven months. Blaming Marie's negligence, the composer put on his hat and walked out forever. There was no divorce. Marie died in 1950 at ninety-five. Meanwhile Saint-Saëns had attracted the attention of Henri Le Libon, director of the post office, who, feeling that he should devote his career to creation, willed him 100,000 francs on condition that he would give up his post at the Madeleine and write a *Requiem* in his memory. On his deathbed in 1876, Le Libon canceled the second requirement as vain, but the composer carried it out anyhow. From then on, he was entirely independent and spent a great deal of his time traveling and concertizing around the world. (At some point in the late 1870s we have the ravishing image of Saint-Saëns and Tchaikovsky [1377] dancing, at a party, the title roles in *Pygmalion et Galathée*, a ballet of their own concocting—alas, lost!).

For all that, Saint-Saëns seems to have been a very private man. On one vacation, he took such pains to preserve his anonymity that the secret police were ordered to keep an eye on him. In his younger days he was short and slight, with curiously shallow-set eyes peering past an enormous nose that made people liken him to a parrot. In late life he might have doubled for King Edward VII. His intellectuality and his energy did not stop at his music. He was a published poet and philosopher, wrote a book on the archaeology of the Roman theater and scholarly articles not only on music but also on botany. Likewise, he hurled journalistic diatribes at his pet hates, which included Jules Massenet [1396], unions, and (from 1914) the Germans. His preferred companions were cats and dogs. He resigned from the Société when d'Indy [1462] wanted to internationalize it.

After the 1880s (which produced the influential Symphony No. 3) Saint-Saëns became increasingly conservative and outmoded. But he was still admired as an indefatigable performer and won many honors—all possible degrees of the *Légion d'honneur*, a place in the Institut, an honorary doctorate from Cambridge, etc. He gave to the nation his memorabilia and art treasures in the Saint-Saëns Museum in Dieppe. At eighty he conducted his *Hail California* as official emissary of the French government at the Panama-Pacific Exposition in San Diego. Five years later he was at the Athens Festival as both conductor and pianist, and he last

played in Dieppe in 1921, before going to Algiers for the winter. He was not to return alive.

After Berlioz, Saint-Saëns represents the first important impetus to instrumental music in France. His own writing is clear, melodic, formal, often sensuous or witty, almost never profound—in a word, "French." He probably wrote too much (169 opus numbers, plus many works without), though he is said to have ruthlessly destroyed many pieces that did not please him.

RECORDINGS: On records, save for Jean-Gabriel Gaussens' performance of the *Requiem* and Donald Hunt's of the Op. 4 *Mass*, the large body of choral music has been mostly ignored. The operas are represented by a few recordings of *Samson* (one each, by my count, from Germany and Rumania, and at least two from France), and rare snippets of some of the others. On the other hand, all of the important concerted works have been made available, Jean Martinon made an *intégrale* of the 5 symphonies, and the symphonic poems and *Le Carnaval des Animaux (Carnival of the Animals)* in its various recensions, are common. There is a fairly complete account of the piano music by Marylène Dosse and Annie Petit, and there are some recordings of the not very large body of organ music. The chamber music and songs have been dealt with only sporadically.

[1344] DELIBES, Clément Philibert Léo
(De-lēbz', Klā-mon' Fē-lē-bâr' Lā-ō')
ORGANIST, PIANIST, CONDUCTOR,
TEACHER
BORN: St. Germain du Val, February 21, 1836
DIED: Paris, January 16, 1891

The name of Delibes is one of those commonly inscribed on the proscenium arches of opera houses; it is therefore somewhat surprising to realize that his fame rests on so few works. Nevertheless the only one of his operas that still holds the stage is much better than its reputation, and his ballets set a musical standard for that genre which had seldom been attained before.

The son of a postal official, Delibes was born in a village near Le Mans. His mother was musical and numbered several professional musicians among her immediate family. Her husband died when his son was eleven, and the next year she moved with her children to Paris where Léo was admitted to the Conservatoire. He studied organ with François Benoist; his harmony and composition teachers included François Bazin **[1247]**, Félix Le Couppey (1811–87), and particularly Adolphe Adam **[1172]**— staunch conservatives all. For a time he also sang treble in the choir of La Madeleine and doubled as a chorister at the Opéra. In 1853 he became organist at the Church of St. Pierre de Chaillot and rehearsal pianist at the Théâtre-Lyrique. Three years later, at the Folies-Nouvelle, an operetta theater run by Florimond Ronger, known as "Hervé," he inaugurated a successful if ephemeral career as a composer of light operas with *Deux sous de charbon (Two Cents' Worth of Charcoal,* described as an *"asphyxie lyrique").* Over the next thirteen years, he turned out nearly twenty of these little pieces, which appear to have had considerable charm, though most of them are forgotten. For *Les Musiciens de l'orchestre* of 1861, he had several collaborators, among them Offenbach **[1264]**, whose Bouffes Parisiens staged many of Delibes' operettas. Two of his pieces were premiered at the spa at Ems, and in 1863 the Théâtre-Lyrique mounted a one-acter, *Le Jardinier et son seigneur (The Gardener and His Master).* And in 1864, under considerable pressure, Delibes stepped in to write the fourth and final act of *Marlbrough s'en va-t-en guerre (Marlbrough's Going to War),* begun by Bizet **[1363]** and taken up by two other composers in the interim.

In 1858 Delibes took a brief fling at writing reviews (using the pseudonym of Eloi Delbès). Six years later he moved, as chorus master, from the Théâtre-Lyrique to the Opéra, which post he resigned in 1871 to marry and to free-lance for a decade. He first made a really strong musical impression with the ballet *La Source,* produced at the Opéra in 1866. In it he was supposed to play second fiddle to the inexhaustible Léon Minkus **[1298]**, but it was Delibes' contribution that caught the ear. In 1870 he reached his musical maturity and lasting fame with the full-length ballet *Coppélia,* based on a tale by E. T. A. Hoffmann **[1086]**, and followed it with the equally admirable *Sylvia* six years later. If a debt to Adam is discernible in Delibes' music, so is the influence of such as Gounod **[1258]** and Bizet—and what he contributed to later ballet music, such as that of Tchaikovsky **[1377]** and Glazunov **[1573]**. In between, the Opéra-Comique produced the most considerable of his comic operas, *Le Roi l'a dit (The King Has Spoken),* and in 1880 it mounted his full-length *Jean de Nivelle,* the problem with which is that Delibes can't seem to decide whether he wants to be serious or funny. (He is described by those who knew him as something of a fussbudget, self-conscious and deferential, albeit a smart cookie.) In 1881 he

became professor of composition at the Conservatoire. One of his more intransigent students was Claude Debussy **[1547]**, who had the temerity to take over the class one day in 1884 when Delibes was absent, with predictably chaotic results. Delibes' operatic masterpiece *Lakmé* was premiered at the Opéra-Comique in 1883. Often dismissed as a mere display piece for twittery coloraturas, it is in fact one of the more effective specimens of the pseudo-oriental exotic school then in fashion. At the time of his premature death, Delibes was working on a four-act opera, *Kassya,* which was completed and orchestrated by Massenet **[1396]** and produced in 1893. Delibes also left a good deal of choral music, some piano pieces, and some songs (including the popular bit of Spanishry *"Les Filles de Cadiz").*

RECORDINGS: There are several complete recordings of *Lakmé, Coppélia,* and *Sylvia* and many recordings of excerpts from the two ballets. Other recordings include the suite from *La Source,* incidental music to *Le Roi s'amuse,* the overture to *Le Roi l'a dit,* a handful of songs, and a piano piece or two.

[1345] HOPKINS, Charles Jerome
ORGANIST, TEACHER
BORN: Burlington, Vt., April 4, 1836
DIED: Athenia, N.J., November 4, 1898

Charles *(not* Edward) Hopkins seems to have been one of the great oddballs of American music, which has produced its share. He was mostly self-taught but was good enough to perform professionally at the keyboards. He attended the New York Medical College and then became organist at various churches in the city. At twenty he founded the American Music Association for the advancement of native composers. It seems to have devoted some concerts to the likes of Gottschalk **[1306]**, Bristow **[1296]** and Warren **[1304]**, but its chief object was clearly the promotion of Hopkins. He was given to wheedling, cajoling, and threatening commitments from whomever he thought could benefit him, and of bombarding with scurrilous missives those whom he deemed to have failed him. From 1868 to 1885 he edited the *New York Philharmonic Journal,* which he founded. In 1880 he completed a stage piece, *Taffy and Old Munch,* which he claimed to be the first musicianly and scientific *Kinder-Oper,* whatever that may have signified. After 1886 he ran free schools devoted to "singing and opera." In 1889 he went to lecture in England, advertising himself fearlessly as the first "American Operatic Oratorio Composer and Pianist" to bring the New World musical gospel to the heathen English and behaved so outrageously that he was sued for libel by the Church of England. In his last years he was, not unexpectedly, subject to fits of depression. He wrote a good deal of choral music and some piano pieces, most of his output being, unhappily (according to report), rather lumpy and mediocre. RECORDINGS: Pianist Ivan Davis has recorded Hopkins' storm piece *The Wind Demon* (alias *The Cyclone*).

[1346] RYDER, Thomas Philander

ORGANIST, TEACHER, CONDUCTOR, ORGAN BUILDER

BORN: Cohasset, Mass., June 29, 1836
DIED: Somerville, Mass., December 2, 1887

A pupil of the Vienna-born composer Gustav Satter, T. P. Ryder began his church-organist's career in Hyannis and later played at the Tremont Temple in Boston (from 1879). He doubled as choirmaster and teacher, and put together anthologies of partsongs, both sacred and secular. In his day he was popular as a composer of hymns and parlor piano pieces. RECORDINGS: The *"Nearer My God to Thee" Fantaisie* recorded by Neely Bruce combines both interests.

[1347] GOMES, Antônio Carlos (Gō'-mās, An'n-tō'-nyōō Kár-lōōs)

ADMINISTRATOR

BORN: Campinas, July 11, 1836
DIED: Belém, September 16, 1896

Carlos Gomes was the first native Brazilian composer to enjoy international success, though his music is more Italian than Brazilian. His parents were Portuguese immigrants. His father, a bandmaster who sired twenty-five children on four wives, taught him to play several instruments. He began composing and concertizing in his teens to contribute to the family budget, but, dissatisfied with his work, he left home in 1859 and got himself into the state conservatory in Rio de Janeiro. A year later he won a prize for his cantata *A última hora do Calvário (The Final Hour on Calvary)*. A public performance of his first opera, *A noite do castelo (A Night at the Castle)*, in Rio was loudly applauded in 1861, and his *Joanna de Flandres* of 1863 won him a government stipend to study at the Milan Conservatory, where his chief teacher was Lauro Rossi, the director of the school. After producing a couple of farces there in 1867 and 1868, he struck oil

with a full-length opera, *Il Guarany*, based on a novel about Brazilian Indians by José de Alencar and using some actual Guarany Indian tunes (which was about as close as Gomes ever came to musical nationalism). Produced with great success at La Scala in 1870, it looked for a while as though it would find a place in the standard international repertoire. Three years later, after a quick trip hime to put on *Guarany* as a token of gratitude to the Emperor Dom Pedro, he followed it up with *Fosca* at La Scala. Hooted down by the anti-Wagnerites, who did not even bother to listen to hear if it was Wagnerian (which it wasn't), it failed. But in a different venue (Genoa) *Salvator Rosa* was a decent success in 1874, and four years later Gomes redeemed himself at La Scala with a revised version of *Fosca* (not to be confused with Puccini's [1511] *Tosca*). After the Milan production of his *Maria Tudor* in 1879, the composer returned to Brazil, where he was hailed as a conquering hero. But it was a decade before he completed his next opera, *Lo schiavo (The Slave)*, in which he finally returned to a Brazilian subject—and which he wrote mostly in Italy. After its premiere in Rio, Gomes was promised the directorship of the conservatory, but before the promise could be realized, the republicans ousted the emperor and put an end to the composer's governmental support. He returned to Milan in 1891 to see his final opera, *Condor*, onstage. For the four hundredeth anniversary of the discovery of America, he wrote a cantata, *Colombo*, for which the Brazilians did not care much (he had also contributed such a work, *Il saluto del Brasile*, to the American centennial in Philadelphia in 1876). After that, he seems to have mostly sat around smoking cigars, which was probably ill-advised. In 1895 he was given the directorship of the new conservatory in Belém, but shortly after taking it over, he developed a tongue cancer and died a few months later. RECORDINGS: Snippets from *Il Guarany, Lo schiavo,* and *Salvator Rosa* were fairly common in record catalogs sixty years ago. Complete recordings of *Fosca* and *Il Guarany*, an orchestral *Sonata for Strings*, and miscellaneous overtures and operatic excerpts are recorded on imported labels. There is also a wretched piracy of *A noite do castelo* and better ones of *Il Guarany, Lo schiavo,* and *Salvator Rosa*.

[1348] BALAKIREV, Mily Alexeyevich (Ba̍-là'-kē-ref, Mē'-lē Ăl-yek-sā'-ye-vich)

EDUCATOR, CONDUCTOR, PIANIST

BORN: Nizhni-Novgorod, January 2,
1837
DIED: St. Petersburg, May 29, 1910

One writer, who termed Balakirev *un personnage invraisemblable*, was perhaps being hyperbolic, but another, who speaks of his "long periods of mystical self-communing," is obscuring the fact that the man was, at times, loony. Though blessed with genius, his influence on the next generation of Russian composers is probably more significant than is his own music. He was born in the ancient city of Great Novgorod, the son of an obscure civil servant whose ancestors had once been somebodies at the Russian court. Started at the piano by his mother, he was sent to Moscow when he was ten to study with Alexander Ivanovich Dubuc (or Dubuque, as some insist), pupil and biographer of John Field. But after ten lessons, the money ran out and he had to return home. There he found another teacher in the person of a German named Karl Eisrich, at the Alexandrovsky Institute. Eisrich introduced him to his patron Alexander Uliybiyshev, a wealthy and capable musical amateur who had his own orchestra. Uliybiyshev, recognizing talent when he saw it, took the boy on as a sort of musical handyman, giving him the run of his establishment and the use of his extensive library, and eventually letting him rehearse the orchestra. At sixteen, having completed his secondary education, Balakirev spent the next two academic years in Kazan, sitting in on mathematical and scientific courses at the university but also keeping up his ties with Uliybiyshev. In 1855 the latter took him with him to St. Petersburg, where Balakirev met Glinka [1179] and made up his mind to pursue a musical career, if not to become the self-appointed messiah of Russian music. He remained in the capital, eking out a marginal living by playing the piano and giving lessons. In 1858 his friend and patron died, leaving him, among other things, his music library. He found a kindred spirit in the scholar Vladimir Stassov, received help in composing from Glinka, came to know Dargomizhsky [1228], and between 1857 and 1862 drew four musical young military officers—Cui [1337], Mussorgsky [1369], Rimsky-Korsakov [1416], and Borodin [1331]—into his orbit. Amateurs all, they were open-mouthed at Balakirev's grasp of music, despite his lack of formal credentials. Most of them even accepted his notion that it was application, not education, that produced a musician. Stassov labeled the five "the mighty kuchka," a word meaning "handful," and by extension "bunch" or "gang." In the West the phrase

was misinterpreted, and the group—the van of the Russian nationalist avant-garde—became The Five. Turned off by the Italian and German leanings that had long infected Russian music, they proposed to create an indigenous school of their own.

In this last regard, Balakirev became an enthusiastic folksong hunter, using some of his findings in his two *Overtures on Russian Themes* (the second later retitled simply *Russia*), and in 1866 publishing a collection of them. To counter the Germanized conservatories (the Rubinstein-Rubinstein axis), he and the conductor-composer Gavriyl Yoakimovich Lomakhin inaugurated the Free School of Music in 1862 in St. Petersburg. Not only was the tuition free, but the pupils were also supposed to be free to do their own thing. This, naturally, produced a nasty little paper war between Balakirev and the conservatives. In 1867, as apostle to the Slavs, Balakirev went to Prague to produce the two Glinka operas at the Provisional Theater. (Among his other enterprises was the editing of Glinka's musical legacy.) He took such a dislike to Smetana [1291], who was to conduct them, that he insisted on the Czech's removal from the project. (When, later on, *The Bartered Bride* failed in St. Petersburg, Smetana was sure that Balakirev had rigged the audience.) That same year the Russian took over the concerts of the Russian Music Society, which Anton Rubinstein [1309] had given up, and in 1868 he became sole director of the Free School. His total lack of diplomacy forced his resignation from the first post in 1869. Meanwhile the school was losing money, and Balakirev himself was burdened by having to support his sisters, his father having died. In 1870 he gave a concert in his hometown to raise money for the school, and hardly anyone attended.

At this point Balakirev cracked up. He had survived an attack of encephalitis a dozen years earlier and had suffered migraines ever since. As he had spread himself ever thinner, he left projects (especially compositions) unfinished, and he became increasingly tactless and irascible. He now gradually abandoned his friends, his teaching, and his music, and eventually took a menial job as a railway freight agent. With his usual talent, he also assumed the role of the holy fool, fasting and praying continually, mumbling to himself, and depending for advice on a young female medium, who, to complicate matters, fell in love with him. After six years he began to act more normally and in 1882 returned to the Free School again. By then Mussorgsky was dead, and the *kuchka* was no longer an entity. A year later, by now a tiresome Christian dogmatist, he was made director of the Imperial Choir. He took his duties there very seriously—he was not noted for levity under any circumstances. He also continued to conduct and occasionally to play until he retired in 1895. His last fifteen years were given over to composition; he wrote a good many songs and piano pieces and completed the 2 symphonies. (Much else remained unfinished or disappeared.)

RECORDINGS: Recordings include the first symphony (Thomas Beecham, Yevgeny Svetlanov), the second symphony (Gennady Rozhdestvensky), the first (fragmentary) piano concerto, (the second piano concerto Michael Ponti), *Islamey, Tamar,* and the two overtures (numerous versions), and the incidental music for *King Lear.* Boris Christoff devoted an LP to Balakirev songs. Piano music has been recorded by Louis Kentner, Vladimir Pleshakov, and others.

[1349] JENSEN, Adolf (Yen'-sen, À'-dōlf)
PIANIST
BORN: Königsberg (now Kaliningrad),
January 12, 1837
DIED: Baden-Baden, January 23, 1879

Jensen had a grandfather and an uncle who were musicians of some standing. Accounts differ as to whether his parents did or did not countenance his musical training, but it is clear that he received a sufficiency from such local musicians as Köhler and Marpurg (not, however, to be confused with better-known bearers of those surnames). He was writing songs by the time he was twelve and at nineteen served as music tutor to a family in Russia, intending to save up enough money to be able to study with Schumann **[1211]**, one of his idols. But Schumann's death that same year put an end to that faint hope. For the next several years he taught, concertized, and conducted, and found a kindred spirit in Gade **[1248]**, whom he met in Copenhagen. Early in 1861 he became co-director of the conservatory in his native city, but resigned after only a year. He continued to live and work in Königsberg, where, in 1863, he married Friederike Bornträger, a union that brought him relative financial security. In 1865 he joined the pilgrims to Munich to attend the premiere of Wagner's **[1230]** *Tristan* and completed his own opera *Die Erbin von Montfort (The Heiress of Montfort),* which, however, went unperformed in that guise. (Jensen's daughter Elsbeth wrote an entirely new libretto—*Turandot*—to the opera, and Kienzl **[1496]** adapted it for a Leipzig premiere in 1888, but

it was not successful.) In the next year Carl Tausig **[1389]** gave him a professorship in his School of Advanced Piano Playing in Berlin. But Jensen had long been suffering from pulmonary tuberculosis, and in 1868 he resigned to live in Dresden. He survived another decade, seeking a cure or mitigation of his ailment in various spas and more southerly residences, and died eleven days after his forty-second birthday. Though Jensen had a true talent, he is, like so many of his generation, overshadowed by Schumann. Though he wrote a few orchestral and choral works, he was happiest in piano music and, especially, in the *Lied,* of which he was at least a minor master. RECORDINGS: Examples of the songs turn up in recorded *Lieder* recitals, and Adrian Ruiz has recorded the only piano sonata.

[1350] DIAZ DE LA PEÑA, Eugène Émile (Dē-àz də Là Pen'-yà, Ö-zhen' À-mēl')
BORN: Paris, February 27, 1837
DIED: Coleville, September 12, 1901

Of Spanish descent, Eugène Diaz was the son of the Barbizon painter Narcisse Virgil de la Peña (1808–76). He studied at the Paris Conservatory with Henri Reber and the inevitable Halévy **[1157]**. In 1865 the Théâtre-Lyrique produced his opera *Le Roi Candaule.* In 1873 his *La Coupe du roi de Thulé (The King of Thulé's Cup)* won a prize in manuscript but no applause at the Opéra. What lasting fame he has resides in a single aria from *Benvenuto Cellini* of 1890. RECORDINGS: The aria is still occasionally recorded by adventurous baritones.

[1351] GUILMANT, Félix Alexandre (Gēl-mán', Fä-lēks' À-lek-sàn'dr')
ORGANIST, TEACHER, MUSICOLOGIST
BORN: Boulogne sur Mer, March 12,
1837
DIED: Meudon, March 29, 1911

Famous and influential as a recitalist, Guilmant was the first to popularize the big symphonic organs of the latter part of his century. His father, Jean-Baptiste (who lived to be ninety-six), was organist of St. Nicolas in Boulogne and trained his son so well that Alexandre was substituting for him before reaching puberty. By the time Alexandre was twenty, the young man was conducting the choir and, though he had had only a few formal lessons in musical basics, was teaching in the local conservatory. Three years later he went to Brussels for some brief polishing by Nicolas Lemmens, professor of organ at the conservatory there, and then headed for Paris, where he played at St. Sulpice and Notre-Dame, before settling in, in 1871, for a thirty-year term at Ste. Trinité. He gave regular recitals at the Trocadéro and made concert tours all over the world. Having fallen in with Vincent d'Indy [1462], Guilmant helped him and Charles Bordes organize the Schola Cantorum in 1894. He was professor of organ there for two years, before inheriting the analogous post at the Conservatoire from Widor [1414]. Among his many notable pupils were Nadia Boulanger, Joseph Bonnet, and Marcel Dupré [1806]. For much of his life, Guilmant explored old French organ music, of which he brought out several scholarly collections. He wrote many works for organ (including 8 sonatas) and some for organ and orchestra (including a symphony), as well as a good deal of choral music. RECORDINGS: Some of the briefer organ works appear in recorded anthologies, and there have been at least two recordings of a *Morceau symphonique* for trombone and orchestra.

[1352] GUIRAUD, Ernest (Gē-rō', Ernest')
TEACHER, ARRANGER
BORN: New Orleans, La., June 23, 1837
DIED: Paris, May 6, 1892

There are few music lovers who could tell you that the most-performed American operatic composer is Ernest Guiraud. The performances, however, have rarely been of his own II operas; they are owing rather to the fact that he wrote, for Vienna in 1875, the standard recitatives for Bizet's [1363] *Carmen*, and completed and in part orchestrated Offenbach's [1264] *Les Contes d'Hoffmann*. Guiraud's father, Jean-Baptiste, was a contemporary of Berlioz [1175] and beat him out of the Grand Prix de Rome in 1827. Later, disgruntled at his failure to capture the operatic stage in Paris, he emigrated to New Orleans, where he became municipal director of music and where he taught his young son all he knew. When Ernest was about fifteen, his first opera, *Le Roi David (King David)*, was premiered at the New Orleans Opera. He then went to Paris, studied at the Conservatoire with Halévy [1157], made friends with Bizet, and followed him to Rome in 1859, having, like his father before him, taken the Grand Prix. Easy-going and phlegmatic, he did not reach the Paris stage until 1864, and then with a one-act trifle, *Sylvie*. Five years elapsed between that and an equally frothy piece, *En*

prison, followed in 1870 by yet another, *Le Kobold*. After seeing active service in the Franco-Prussian War, he returned with the two-act *Madame Turlupin* and a successful ballet, *Gretna Green*, both in 1874. After reworking *Carmen*, following Bizet's death, he had his chief success in *Piccolino* in 1876. He was thereupon appointed professor of harmony at the Conservatoire, where his pupils included Dukas [1574] and Debussy [1547]. He was awarded the *Légion d'honneur* in 1878. Two other operas, both unsuccessful, followed. When he died (at fifty-four), he left unfinished *Frédégonde*, his only attempt at a serious work. Completed by Dukas and Saint-Saëns [1343] and produced in 1895, it made no impact. Apart from his stage pieces, Guiraud left a few choral works and songs, a piano sonata, and some interesting orchestra works. RECORDINGS: Jorge Mester has recorded the orchestral *La Chasse fantasque (The Fantastic Hunt)*.

[1353] ŻELEŃSKI, Władysław (Zhel-en'-shkē, Vlwȧ-di'-slwȧf)
TEACHER, ADMINISTRATOR, THEORIST
BORN: Grodkowice, July 6, 1837
DIED: Cracow, January 23, 1921

Żeleński was the son of Marcjan Żeleński, a musical amateur who lived on the family estate near Cracow. The boy was orphaned at an early age. He attended a secondary school in Cracow, where he studied with Franz Mirecki, a pupil of Cherubini [1019] and Hummel [1091]. Then he majored in philosophy at the University of Prague but took piano lessons there with Dreyschock [1260] and studied composition with Josef Krejčí, director of the Prague Organ School. Between 1866 and 1871 he studied in Paris, with Henri Reber among others. After a year back in Cracow, he was appointed professor of theory at the Warsaw Conservatory in 1872 and in 1878 became director of the Warsaw Music Society. But, imbued with a desire to bring music to the Philistines of his native city, he returned there in 1881 and founded the Cracow Music Society. In 1885, the first of his 4 operas, *Konrad Wallenrod*, was produced in Lwów (Lvov). Two years later he inaugurated the Cracow Conservatory. He both directed it and taught piano, organ, and theory there. Among his first graduates was the great pianist Sigismund Stojowski. Cracow saw the premiere of Żeleński's *Goplana* in 1896. The following year he published textbooks on theory and harmony (the latter with Roguski). His other operas, *Janek* (in 1900) and *Stara baśń* (in 1907), were both premiered in Lwów. In

1912 Cracow gave him the keys to the city. His other compositions include 2 symphonies, a piano concerto, 2 Masses, much other choral music, chamber works, songs, and piano music. RECORDINGS: Several contemporary Polish singers have recorded excerpts from the operas, which remain in the repertoire in Poland.

[1354] BEHR, Franz (Bär, Frànts)
BORN: Lübtheen, July 22, 1837
DIED: Dresden, February 15, 1898

Lübtheen's gift to music was an Old Faithful of the kind of innocuous piano pieces that nice girls were taught to play in an earlier time. He published some of them under such pseudonyms as Francesco d'Orso, William Cooper, and Charles Morley—perhaps because he thought it ostentatious to appear so wantonly productive. RECORDINGS: Hans Kann has preserved several of the piano pieces in virgin vinyl.

[1355] MOLLOY, James Lyman
BORN: Cornalour, August 19, 1837
DIED: Wooleys, February 4, 1909

Born in Offaly County (alias King's) in central Ireland, Molloy became a successful writer of lightweight operettas. He also published collections of Irish tunes, but lives on through two of his many songs, "The Kerry Dance" and "Love's Old Sweet Song," both of which have been recorded. He died in Buckinghamshire, England.

[1356] DUBOIS, François Clément Théodore (Dü-bwà', Fràn-swà' Klä-mon' Tä-ō-dôr')
ORGANIST, CHOIRMASTER, TEACHER, ADMINISTRATOR
BORN: Rosnay, August 24, 1837
DIED: Paris, June 11, 1924

Chronic winner of awards, prizes, and honors, colleague of, and successor to, everyone who was anyone in important musical posts, prolific composer in all forms, Theodore Dubois is remembered today largely for a pallid *Seven Last Words* beloved of provincial choirs. Born in a Marne village, he studied in nearby Rheims, then entered the Paris Conservatoire, where he studied piano with Antoine-François Marmontel, organ with François Benoist, and composition with Ambroise Thomas [1217], carrying off one first prize after another and climaxing his student career with the Grand Prix de Rome

in 1861. After his mandatory travels he became choirmaster at Ste. Clothilde, where César Franck [1284] was organist and where he produced the oratorio noted above in 1867. He then became Saint-Saëns's [1343] colleague at the Madeleine in the same capacity and succeeded him at the organ in 1877. Meanwhile he had made a name for himself as a teacher and had been appointed professor of harmony at the Conservatoire in 1871.

In 1878 he won a prize offered by the city for his oratorio *Paradis perdu (Paradise Lost),* performed at the expense of the taxpayers. He had been dabbling in opera since his student days and had nominal successes with a couple of bits of the then fashionable orientalia: *La Guzla de l'emir,* 1873; and *Aben-Hamet,* 1884—both in smaller theaters, for he never got a hearing at the Opéra, save for the ballet *La Farandole* in 1883. In the last year he was inducted into the *Légion d'honneur* and eleven years later took Gounod's [1258] place in the Institut. In 1896 he was elevated to the directorship of the Conservatoire in succession to his teacher Thomas. The Conservatoire, which had long been largely a battlefield for operatic politics, probably sank to its lowest ebb under his ineffectual leadership. D'Indy [1462] and his associates opened the Schola Cantorum as an alternative the year Dubois took up his duties, and he was finally ousted in 1905, largely thanks to the crusading efforts of Gabriel Fauré [1424]. He produced little after that point but lived to almost reach his eighty-seventh birthday, dying just five months before Fauré. In his era he was better known for his watery religious pieces than for his operas and orchestral works.

RECORDINGS: There are recordings of the *Seven Last Words* (by the Welch Chorale, New Jersey Oratorio Chorus), some occasional organ pieces, and on early records a snippet or two from the operas.

[1357] WALDTEUFEL, Charles Émile (Vàld'-toi-fel, Shärl Ā-mēl')
PIANIST, CONDUCTOR, TEACHER
BORN: Strasbourg, December 9, 1837
DIED: Paris, February 12, 1915

Waldteufel's waltzes are still popular, though, designed chiefly for dancing, they are not in the same league with those of the Strausses. His family name was originally Lévy. His mother came from Bavaria. His father was a violinist and taught at the Strasbourg Conservatory. His elder brother Léon was also a musician. In 1849 the Waldteufels moved to Paris so that the boy could attend the Conservatoire. He sat in on Marmontel's class and then was admitted to Laurent's, but his family suffered serious financial reverses, and young Waldteufel had to sell newspapers on the streets to help make ends meet. Then he took a job in a piano factory and moonlighted by playing for parties. Once, we are told, while testing a piano at work, he heard a woman's voice in song from a nearby window and began accompanying it. Supposedly that is how he met Célestine Dufau, whom he married in 1868.

Meanwhile, in 1865, the Empress Eugénie had heard Waldteufel play at a *soirée* and had been so impressed that she got him appointed official court pianist. This led, a year later, to his elevation to the directorship of the court balls. He went on active service in the Franco-Prussian War, and when it was over, so was his job. He went back to freelancing. In 1874 he published two waltzes, *Joies et peines (Joys and Sorrows)* and *Manola,* at his own expense. The same year, Charles Coote, court band director to H. M. Queen Victoria, played Waldteufel's *Vergissmeinnicht (Forget-me-not)* at Buckingham Palace and created something of a stir. A month later the Prince of Wales heard its composer direct *Manola* at a Paris reception, made a point of meeting him, and saw to it that Waldteufel's music graced royal functions back home. Coote, who had bought the controlling interest in the publishing firm of Hopwood and Crew, signed Waldteufel to an exclusive contract in 1875— a lucrative arrangement for both, though foreign publishers were later permitted a slice of the cake.

Waldteufel continued to appear at state functions in France and took his band on a European tour in 1885. He played in Berlin in 1889, but he preferred not to travel and turned down a promising American offer in 1882. After the turn of the century, he faded, the waltz having fallen out of favor. Of his 300 or so dances, examples like *Les Patineurs (The Skaters), Estudiantina,* and *España* (after Chabrier [1382]) have remained perennial favorites.

RECORDINGS: Recently Willy Boskovsky has embarked on a series of records that explore the territory more adventurously.

[1358] BRUCH, Max Karl August
(Brōŏkh, Măks Kärl Ou'-gōŏst)
CONDUCTOR, VIOLINIST, TEACHER
BORN: Cologne, January 6, 1838
DIED: Friedenau, October 2, 1920

Though Max Bruch continues to appear in Little Lives of Great Composers, etc., his name is in fact meaningfully kept alive only by a handful of concerted pieces of declining popularity. The son of a civil servant, he first studied with his mother, a singer. (It is often said that the Bruchs were Jews because in 1880 Max wrote a *Kol Nidrei* for cello and orchestra, but the work was merely a fortuitous commission from the Jewish community in Liverpool.) After some theoretical training from a certain Breidenstein in Bonn, the boy took up composing, and when he was fourteen, a symphony won him a four-year scholarship from the Mozart Stiftung of Frankfurt, on which he studied with such Cologne notables as Ferdinand Hiller [1219] and Reinecke [1292]. His first opera, *Scherz, List, und Rache (Jest, Ruse, and Revenge)* was staged in Cologne when he had just turned twenty. After teaching there for a while, he embarked on a couple of German *Wanderjähre* and then settled in Mannheim in 1862. There he produced *Frithjof,* the first of the big choral numbers for which he became noted, and his second opera, *Die Loreley,* set, with the poet's blessing, to the libretto Emanuel Geibel had written for Mendelssohn [1200]. In 1865 he took the post of director of the Concert Institute in Koblenz but gave it up two years later to become *Kapellmeister* to the prince of Schwarzburg-Sondershausen in Thuringia. In 1870 he moved on to live independently in Berlin, which saw his third and last opera, *Hermione,* two years later. He moved back to the Rhineland in 1873 and lived in Bonn for five years, then returned to Berlin to succeed Julius Stockhausen as director of the Sternscher Gesangverein. After he had guest-conducted in London (accompanying Sarasate [1415] in the first violin concerto), he accepted the directorship of the Liverpool Philharmonic Society as successor to Benedict [1180] in 1881, the year of his marriage to the soprano Clara Tuczek. Humorless, arrogant, egotistical, and a martinet, he did not warm the hearts of his players and left in 1883 to take an analogous job in Breslau, where he, untypically, stayed for seven whole years. He then received a professional appointment at the Berlin Hochschule, where he taught a master class in composition for nearly twenty more, during which he was showered with honors from all over. He retired to a Berlin suburb in 1910 and died there at eighty-two, a year after his wife.

Bruch's chief compositional effort was, as indicated above, applied to his choral music, both secular and sacred. Many of his choral works, like the oratorios *Moses* and *Arminius,* the *Frithjof* cantatas, and the Homeric works *(Achilles* and *Odysseus)* were quite ambitious and once enjoyed considerable admiration, but now they appear to be dead issues. Bruch also wrote 3 mature symphonies, 2 string quartets, and various smaller orchestral and chamber works, as well as some songs and piano pieces. He is now chiefly remembered, however, for the first of his 3 violin concerti, the *Scottish Fantasy* for violin and orchestra, and the *Kol Nidrei* for cello and orchestra, all of which exhibit the melodic gift that is his chief charm.

RECORDINGS: Apart from numerous recordings of the compositions previously noted, Salvatore Accardo has done a survey of all of the music for violin and orchestra. Wolfgang Balzer has recorded the first symphony and short orchestral pieces; Jorge Mester the second symphony; Martin Berkofsky, with two different partners, as many versions of the long-lost Concerto for 2 Pianos (as well as a selection of piano pieces); and Rudolf Irmisch the Concerto for Clarinet, Viola, and Orchestra. There are several versions of the Op. 83 Trios for Clarinet, Viola, and Piano. Other chamber works on records include *8 Pieces* for clarinet, viola, and piano, and the string quartets. Few of the vocal-orchestral works seem to have been recorded. A recording of *Scherz, List, und Rache* has recently appeared.

[1359] LACÔME, Paul-Jean-Jacques (Lakōm', Pōl Zhàn Zhàk)
CRITIC
BORN: Le Houga, March 4, 1838
DIED: Le Houga, December 12, 1920

Born Paul-Jean-Jacques Lacôme d'Estaleux in a village north of the Pyrenees, Lacôme must not be confused with Paul Lacombe (1837–1927) of Carcassonne, who studied with Bizet **[1363]** by mail and became a chevalier of the *Légion d'honneur*. Educated locally, our man went to Paris in 1860, became a reviewer, and was more or less successful with a score of operettas on the Lecocq **[1322]** model: *Le Beau Nicolas; Jean, Jeannette, et Jeannot; Ma mie Rosette; Myrtille; Pâques fleuries; Toussaint;* and others. A few excerpts from these appear on old records. The melody of Lacôme's vocal duet *Estudiantina* was made famous by Waldteufel's **[1357]** waltz based on it.

[1360] DAVIDOV, Karl Yulyevich (Dà-vē'-dof, Kärl Yōol-yä'-vich)
MATHEMATICIAN, CELLIST, TEACHER, ADMINISTRATOR

BORN: Goldingen (Kuldiga), March 15, 1838
DIED: Moscow, February 26, 1889

Latvian-born Davidov majored in mathematics at the University of Moscow, and then, at twenty, decided he would prefer to be a composer. (He was already proficient on the cello.) Enrolled at the Leipzig Conservatory to study with Moritz Hauptmann, he found himself, willy-nilly, appointed first cello in the Gewandhaus Orchestra and professor of cello at the school at the age of twenty-one. Such responsibilities were alien to his nature, but he was trapped. Three years later, he was called back to St. Petersburg to take up similar duties at the Conservatory and the Italian Opera. In 1876 he was elevated to the directorship of the Conservatory. He proved the worst of a succession of incompetents. Far too soft-hearted, he could not bear to see students fail and graduated hopeless cases because he thought they deserved a chance. Anton Rubinstein **[1309]** was persuaded to come back in 1888 and take over, returning Davidov to teaching. When Davidov refused to terminate an affair that he was carrying on all too publicly with a Turkish female student, Rubinstein fired him and put glass doors on the studios. The cellist died the following year at fifty-five. His compositional ambitions remained largely frustrated, though he managed 4 concerti, and some chamber works. RECORDINGS: On records he is represented mostly by cello encore pieces.

[1361] SALOMON, Hector (Sàl-ō-mo*n*', Ek-tôr')
CONDUCTOR
BORN: Strasbourg, May 29, 1838
DIED: Paris, 1906

Salomon studied at the Conservatoire in Paris with Émile Jonas (cantor at the Portuguese Synagogue), Antoine-François Marmontel, Bazin **[1247]**, and Halévy **[1157]**. From 1870 he served as the deputy choirmaster, and later as director of singing, at the Paris Opéra. He himself wrote some operas, but his music survives through a few songs recorded early in the century.

[1362] BARNBY, (Sir) Joseph
ORGANIST, CHOIRMASTER, CONDUCTOR
BORN: York, August 12, 1838
DIED: London, January 28, 1896

With Barnby, English church music, which, despite the efforts of such as S. S. Wesley

[1213], had fallen into a state of almost total neglect, did an about-face. Trained by his organist father and as a chorister in York Minster, he was playing church organs and directing local choirs by the time he was twelve. At sixteen he enrolled at the Royal Academy of Music, where he studied with Cipriani Potter and was beaten out for the first Mendelssohn Scholarship by Arthur Sullivan [1397]. After holding posts at a number of London churches, he became choirmaster at St. Andrew's in Wells Street, which had espoused high-church reforms and fielded a professional choir. Under Barnby it became noted for its grandiose choral services, including vernacular Masses. He also served as adviser to the publisher Alfred Novello, who specialized in choral music. In 1867 Novello presented him with his own concert choir, popularly known as "Barnby's Choir," which featured magnificent, if overstuffed, performances of great choral masterpieces. In 1871 he gave the first church performance in England of Bach's [684] *St. Matthew Passion* at Westminster Abbey, putting the seal on Bach's sanctification in that nation. The same year, Barnby moved from St. Andrew's to St. Anne's in Soho, where he worked until 1886 and where the choral services came to be jokingly known as "the Sunday Opera." There he gave the first English performance of the *St. John Passion* with orchestra and repeated it as an annual event. In 1872 he amalgamated his own choir with the one organized at the Albert Hall for Gounod [1258], whom Barnby revered. In 1875 he was named precentor at Eton, where he turned what had been perfunctory chapel duties into a full-fledged musical program. Barnby's own combined choirs (which became the Royal Choral Society in 1888) premiered Dvořák's [1386] *Stabat Mater* in 1882 and gave a concert performance of Wagner's [1230] *Parsifal* a year after the composer's death. In 1887–88 he directed the concerts of the Royal Academy. Knighted in 1892, he gave up his Eton post to become principal of the Guildhall School. He died suddenly at fifty-seven. His large output of choral music, once very popular, is now regarded as too Victorian. His one surviving work is his setting of Tennyson's lullaby, *Sweet and Low* (not to be confused with the sugar substitute of the same name). RECORDINGS: *Sweet and Low* has been recorded.

[1363] BIZET, Georges (Alexandre-César-Léopold) (Bē-zā', Zhôrzh)
PIANIST

BORN: Paris, October 25, 1838
DIED: Bougival, June 3, 1875

Blessed with a great talent, Georges Bizet was rarely able to realize it to its fullest, owing mostly to circumstances beyond his control, as the phrase has it, and for most people will remain the composer of a single operatic masterpiece, *Carmen*.

Bizet was officially named Alexandre-César-Léopold, but when he was baptized eighteen months after his birth, he was called Georges. His father, Adolphe Armand Bizet, had opened a vocal studio shortly before his only child's birth, having previously been a hairdresser. His mother, Aimée Delsarte, came from a musical family which, according to unsubstantiated and improbable legend, was descended from the painter Andrea del Sarto. Georges, who early showed signs of uncommon musicality, was taught by his parents and by his uncle François Delsarte, one of those singers with no voice but exquisite artistry, who had a splendid reputation as a vocal teacher. Both parents intended their son to be a professional musician and managed to get him admitted to the Conservatoire two weeks before his tenth birthday, he having been allowed to sit in on Antoine-François Marmontel's piano class for some months previous. The following spring young Bizet carried off the first prize in *solfège* and the retiring Pierre-Joseph Zimmermann was so impressed that he offered him private lessons in counterpoint and fugue in his home. There he encountered Zimmermann's soon-to-become son-in-law Charles Gounod [1258], then in his early thirties, who became his lifelong friend and benefactor. As a piano student Bizet was a first-prize winner in 1852 and remained a brilliant pianist, though he resolutely refused all his life to concertize. (Years later, when Liszt [1218] was showing off at a *soirée*, he proclaimed that only he and Bülow [1310] could play the piece he had just performed. At the prodding of a friend, Bizet reproduced a segment of it from memory and then played through the whole piece flawlessly from score). Later in his Conservatoire career, Bizet studied organ with François Benoist, acquiring another first prize, and, after Zimmermann died, composition with Halèvy [1157], who treated him, prophetically, like a son.

Before he left the Conservatory, Bizet wrote a number of pieces, including a one-act comic opera *La Maison du docteur (The Doctor's House)* and an orchestral overture. In 1855 Gounod asked him to make piano-duet reductions of his opera *La Nonne sanglante (The Bloody Nun)* and his second symphony. The latter so impressed Bizet that he wrote a symphony of his own, using Gounod's as a model; this was the delightful Symphony in C, which did not see performance until 1933, having been rediscovered only three years before. In 1856 he competed for the Prix de Rome, but the usual hassle occurred and he was given a second, the judges being unable to decide on a Grand-Prix winner. That summer Offenbach [1264] announced a competition for a setting of an opéra-comique entitled Le Docteur Miracle. Bizet shared the prize (1,200 francs and production) with Charles Lecocq [1322], became something of a celebrity at Offenbach's soirées, and was invited to a Rossini [1143] at-home (soirée). With an autographed photo of that great man as talisman, he entered the Prix de Rome competition again the next spring and won, though not handily, with his cantata Clovis et Clotilde.

Bearing letters of introduction from Gounod and Rossini, Bizet set out for Rome on the first day of winter, taking a train to Lyon, proceeding by stagecoach to Toulon and by carriage to Savona. He stopped over briefly in Florence, was delighted by its art but not by Verdi's [1232] I Lombardi, and attained the Villa Medici five weeks after his journey began. Despite his uncompromising artistic standards, a talent for bluntness, and a violent temper, he generally endeared himself both to his fellow students and the director, the painter Victor Schnetz, who had succeeded Ingres. He seems to have spent more time socializing and traveling than he did composing, and when he had to get down to work, he found it hard to keep up his interest. Moreover he was frequently incapacitated by violent attacks of tonsilitis. In his first year he wrote a Te Deum, hoping to win the Rodrigues Prize, but it went to Adrien Barthe, the only other entrant. Faced with the necessity of sending his first envoi back to Paris (to demonstrate his competence as a prizewinner), he wrote an opera buffa entitled Don Procopio. In the spring of 1859, after a winter of illness, he made a southward tour, eventually reaching Naples (which he detested) and Pompeii (at which he marveled). Although Bizet had won a name for himself at the Villa Medici with his parody of the music of Clapisson, who had been preferred to Berlioz [1175] for the Académie, the judges from that august body found his opera one of the best works ever submitted from Rome. Later, however, Ambroise Thomas [1217] wrote him that he should have submitted a religious work, which he must now do. Bizet was at the time working on a symphonic ode, Vasco da Gama, based on Camoës' epic poem Os Lu-

siados, which he decided would pass. Meanwhile he had requested and gotten permission to spend a third year in Rome, to replace the usual German tour. During the latter part of that period, he met and befriended the latest prizewinner, Ernest Guiraud [1352], who later would write the recitatives for the grand opéra version of Carmen.

In the summer of 1860 Bizet broke off an impassioned but stubbornly anonymous love affair and began to make his slow way home through the cities of northern Italy, frequently, to judge from his letters, stopping to assuage his heartbreak in a survey of the bawdy houses. Understandably, considering his rather bohemian ways, he was not anxious to live under the parental roof and had already begun agitating for a place of his own. When he arrived in Paris, however, he discovered his mother, whom he knew to have been ailing, to be beyond medical help; she died a few months later. In the meantime his ode had been enthusiastically accepted, and he was working on an Italian symphony (ultimately the foreshortened Roma) and an opera, La Guzla de l'Emir, as the submissions he still owed the Academy. The symphony did not jell as such, and instead he offered its scherzo, a funeral march, and an overture, which were accepted. The first part of 1862 he spent helping Gounod get La Reine de Saba ready for its premiere; after its failure he was entrusted with making the piano score. Next he aided Reyer [1289] with his Erostate, scheduled for Baden-Baden in the summer. It took longer to complete than Reyer had foreseen, and the premiere was postponed until the end of August. The two composers were in attendance. During their visit Bizet became angry with the librettist, Emilien Pacini, for a supposed slight to Gounod and challenged him to a duel, but clearer heads prevailed. In the course of the summer, the Bizet family maid was delivered of a son whom everyone supposed was his bereaved father's, but on her deathbed fifty years later she admitted that he really was Georges's. Toward the end of 1862 the completed opera was accepted as Bizet's final obligation to the Academy.

Early in the new year Jules Pasdeloup conducted Bizet's scherzo in one of his orchestral concerts; later Bizet conducted it himself with the orchestra of the recently founded (and short-lived) Société National des Beaux-Arts, and three weeks later followed it with the premiere of Vasco da Gama. The scherzo was approved by the press, which, however, found the ode noisy and trite. A production of La Guzla de l'Emir was in the works at the Opéra-

Comique, and Bizet was already at work on another opera, *Ivan IV* (for which he cannibalized parts of the ode), when Léon Carvalho chose him to set for his Théâtre-Lyrique the three-act *Les Pêcheurs de perles (The Pearl Fishers)*. Carvalho was in financial trouble and had accepted 100,000 francs from the Ministry of Fine Arts to produce a full-length opera by a previously unproduced Rome laureate. Neither he nor Bizet could refuse, and so the other opera was withdrawn—and the score ultimately lost. (Apparently everyone concerned conveniently forgot *Le Docteur Miracle!)*

Bizet composed *Pêcheurs* at white heat. No sooner was it done than he entered into a prolonged set-to with the publisher Choudens, who suddenly reneged on the terms he had offered. The work went into rehearsal in August (as *Leïla)* for a September 14 opening, but as it turned out the prima donna was ill, and the date was moved back to the twentieth. Despite the silly libretto, the public liked it and got a bow from the composer. This for some reason rankled with the reviewers, who, with few exceptions (which included Berlioz and Halévy), came down hard on it, accusing Bizet of Wagnerism among other sins. It lasted only eighteen performances and was then dropped. In 1864, while helping rehearse Berlioz's *L'Enfance du Christ* and doing a run-through of Gounod's new *Mireille* at the keyboard in tandem with Saint-Saëns [1343], he returned to *Ivan IV,* for which Carvalho planned a production, date indefinite. In May he moved into a one-room cottage on the estate his father had bought at Le Vésinet, about twelve miles outside Paris. There he began the long-range tutoring of Edmond Galabert, who lived in Montauban, but who visited Paris annually. He was to become one of Bizet's closest friends. Bizet also drudged endlessly, to live, at hackwork, such as popular piano transcriptions and even a piano course for children. Gounod procured him entrée into the salon of the Princess Mathilde, daughter of Jerome Bonaparte and erstwhile fiancée of Napoleon III, who got him invited to play at an official reception in the Louvre, and there were occasional small commissions, but the pickings were slim. However, his new quarters provided him with a sympathetic friend in his neighbor, the former Céleste Vénard. The bastard daughter of a laundress and successively a prostitute, dance-hall girl, and circus rider, she had become the dowager Countess de Moreton de Chabrillan and a respected novelist. The close relationship with Bizet was apparently purely intellec-

tual, but it is thought that he drew something of his Carmen from her.

Meanwhile Carvalho, ever in deeper financial trouble, asked Bizet to put aside *Ivan IV* and set a new libretto, *La jolie fille de Perth,* based, at some remove, on Sir Walter Scott's *The Fair Maid of Perth.* Despite having simultaneously to cope with a mountain of hackwork, he completed it in six months. About this time he acquired two more friends, both composers—Paul Lacombe, whom, like Galabert, he taught by mail, and Jules Massenet [1396], who had his first stage production, *La Grand'-tante (The Great-Aunt),* in the spring of 1867. Meanwhile, waiting for the production of his own opera, Bizet entered a competition for a hymn and a cantata. After the submissions were all in, the judges canceled the hymn contest and granted the cantata prize to Saint-Saëns, with second place going to Massenet and third to Weckerlin [1277]. After the usual vicissitudes—including the defection of Christine Nillson in favor of Thomas's [1217] new *Hamlet—La jolie fille* went into rehearsal in September, and, after several postponements, opened the day after Christmas. Despite its weak libretto, the work got fine notices, but it did not draw, and after eighteen performances Carvalho retired it in favor of Clapisson's popular *La Fanchonette.* Two weeks previously, the Athenée had premiered the operetta *Marlbrough s'en va-t-en guerre (Marlbrough's Going to War),* a collaborative effort to which Bizet had contributed the first act and Delibes [1344] the last; Bizet disowned his part and it has disappeared.

It was in 1867 that Bizet fell in love with Geneviève Halévy, the younger daughter of his old teacher (and later Marcel Proust's model for the Duchess of Guermantes). Geneviève had problems because her mother, who was certifiably insane, had blamed Geneviève irrationally for the death of her twenty-year-old sister Rachel in 1864 and had farmed her out to relatives, refusing to see her. As a result, Geneviève was an emotional mess, but Bizet married her anyway in June 1869 in a civil ceremony. (It was Geneviève whose background was Jewish, not Bizet's as is so often asserted.) In the meantime, Carvalho had finally declared bankruptcy in early 1868, ending hope of his producing *Ivan IV.* During a renewed attack of his old throat trouble, Bizet set about finishing his Italian symphony, which, as *Roma,* Pasdeloup introduced the following February. He also, in the interests of familial amity, completed Halévy's unfinished *Noë,* eking out his work with large swatches of his *Vasco da Gama* ode. (It was eventually performed at Karlsruhe ten years after Bizet's death.) Against his better judgment he also entered a contest for a setting of a prizewinning libretto *La Coupe du Roi de Thulé (The King of Thulé's Cup)*. Of the forty-two scores submitted, Bizet's made it to the finals, but was beaten out by that of Eugène Diaz de La Peña [1350], a gentleman-composer and the son of a successful academic painter. Only fragments of Bizet's score are extant.

In 1869 the newlyweds had moved to Montmartre. Bizet's vast plans—mostly operatic—were there thwarted a year later by the Prussian siege of Paris and the ensuing Commune. He managed to pack Mme. Halévy off to her brother in Bordeaux, but Geneviève refused to go—an arrangement that set up unbearable tensions. Bizet, discovering a patriotism he did not know he had, served in the National Guard. Eventually, yielding to his mother-in-law's pleas, he managed to get his wife to Bordeaux, but the reunion with her mother was so traumatic that she had to be brought back to Paris. They found it expedient to sit out the troubles at Le Vésinet, and, with the end of the Commune, returned to Montmartre three days after their second wedding anniversary. Mme. Halévy continued to play sadistic games with Geneviève, much to the latter's detriment, and to meddle in Bizet's affairs. Despite her, he now managed to be appointed *chef de chant* at the Opéra, but he firmly rejected her various attempts to get him onto the Conservatoire faculty because he disapproved strongly of that then very feeble institution.

In 1871 Camille du Locle, a director of the Opéra-Comique and original scenarist of Verdi's *Aida,* asked him to set a libretto derived from de Musset's *Namouna.* He also managed to finish that summer, in spite of further throat trouble and a mother-in-law who was becoming a classic case, *Jeux d'enfants (Children's Games)* in both its four-hand and orchestral versions. In November he was replaced in his post at the Opéra, in which he had never actually served. The new opera, *Djamileh,* a one-act bit of oriental exoticism, went into rehearsal the following March and opened in May. The critics who counted approved, but, hampered by a poor cast, it sank after ten showings. The management was sufficiently heartened, however, to commission a three-act opera, libretto to be written by Henri Meilhac and Geneviève Bizet's first cousin Ludovic Halévy. (There was also an invitation from L'Opéra.) And in June, Geneviève presented her husband with a son, christened Jacques, who was later to found the

first auto-rental agency in France and commit suicide at fifty-one. At the time Bizet was already hard at work on incidental music for Daudet's new play *L'Arlésienne,* commissioned by Carvalho, who was back in business at the Vaudeville Théâtre. The work was conceived as a melodrama in which music played a functional role. It opened in October, out of season and largely unadvertised, in a production in which its rural proletarians were dressed in taffeta and velvet. The audience bridled at the musical "interruptions," only two music critics covered it, and, after twenty-one nights of diminishing houses, it closed.

By 1873, in which year Édouard Colonne introduced the orchestral *Jeux d'enfants,* Bizet and his collaborators had decided to make an opera of Prosper Mérimée's novella *Carmen.* But Du Locle's codirector, Adolph de Leuving, refused to tolerate such filth on his stage; after months of stalemate, he resigned. Discouraged, Bizet started an opera *Don Rodrigue,* on the legend of El Cid, for Jean-Baptiste Faure [1311], and got as far as setting down the vocal parts before dropping it. He also wrote the overture *Patrie* for Pasdeloup before returning to *Carmen.* It went into rehearsal on September 1, 1874, and proceeded, stormily, all fall. Many changes were made and many more urged, mostly in the interest of propriety. In January Choudens contracted to publish the score for 25,000 francs. A month later Bizet was awarded the *Légion d'honneur.* Otherwise he whiled away the time by auditing César Franck's [1284] organ classes, in preparation for writing an oratorio, *Geneviève de Paris.* *Carmen* opened at last on March 3, in its original version with spoken text instead of recitatives. The all-star audience cooled steadily as the performance went on and sat on its hands at the end. Various of its members heard all sorts of borrowings; among the offended was Gounod, who was sure he had been pillaged wholesale. Later performances went better, and most of the younger composers recognized the work's validity, but the reviewers lambasted it. Yet it continued to be performed on and off all spring. But its composer was severely wounded and deeply depressed. His old malady returned, accompanied by bizarre auditory symptoms. He had violent attacks of a rheumatic ailment that was also chronic and complained of finding breathing difficult. He blamed the "bad air" of Paris and toward the end of May moved out to Bougival on the Seine. The next day he went swimming in the river (he was addicted to icy water and cold showers). This action apparently produced an even more severe rheumatic attack and fever that culminated in a coronary spasm on June 1. Bizet recovered but suffered another attack the next day. He seemed to have weathered this one too, but during the night the faithful maid Marie (mother of his other son) found him dead in bed. Celeste Galli-Marié, Bizet's chosen Carmen, had played the opera that evening in a state of angst she could not explain, and she became severely ill next day when she heard the news. The body was buried in the Montmartre cemetery on the fifth after a moving and impressive funeral. That night the cast of *Carmen* could barely get through the work, often weeping openly. In the fall, it became a great hit in Vienna (later with Guiraud's recitatives) and by 1878, though dropped by the Opéra-Comique, was on its way to becoming the most popular of all operas.

RECORDINGS: Of the operas, only *Carmen*, *Pêcheurs*, and *Le Docteur Miracle* seem to have had commercial recordings, though there are also excerpts from *Ivan IV.* "Underground" sources have offered *La Jolie fille de Perth*, *Ivan IV*, and *Djamileh*. There is a complete recording of Daudet's *L'Arlésienne* with the incidental music, as well as many of the orchestral suites derived from operas. Other recordings include numerous versions of the 2 symphonies, *Jeux d'enfants*, *Patrie*, the *Te Deum*, and a scattering of piano pieces and songs.

[1364] THAYER, Whitney Eugene
ORGANIST, TEACHER
BORN: Mendon, Mass., December 11, 1838
DIED: Burlington, Vt., June 27, 1889

Though not to be confused with his Massachusetts contemporary Alexander Wheelock Thayer, Beethoven's biographer Eugene Thayer was also a member of a prolific and talented family that had come there from England in 1636. He took up the organ at fourteen, became a church organist in Worcester, and inaugurated the new organ of the Music Hall in Boston in 1862. Three years later he went abroad for concertizing and further study, then returned as the regular organist of the Music Hall, where he gave free concerts. He also served as conductor of the Boston Choral Union and the New England Church Musical Association, edited *The Organist's Journal* and *The Choir Journal*, and published *The Art of Organ Playing* in five volumes, 1874. In 1875 he opened a studio equipped with an instrument of his own design. He was an immensely successful teacher. Thayer moved to New York in 1881 as organist of the Fifth

Avenue Presbyterian Church. Eight years later he resigned and settled in Connecticut. That summer he died on vacation at fifty-five. He left a *Mass*, a *Festival Cantata*, 4 organ sonatas, and other choral and organ pieces. RECORDINGS: Organist Richard Morris has recorded his *Variations on a Russian Hymn*.

[1365] TOURS, Berthold (Tōōrs, Bertôld')
VIOLINIST, ORGANIST, EDITOR
BORN: Rotterdam, December 17, 1838
DIED: London, March 11, 1897

Not to be mistaken for a travel agency, Berthold Tours was the son of the Laurentskerke organist, Barthélemy Tours, in Rotterdam. He learned to play the organ from his father, and the violin from the conductor-composer Johannes Verhulst (1816–91), a friend of Mendelssohn [1200]. After rounding out his education at the conservatories in Brussels and Leipzig, Tours was taken to Russia for two years by Prince Yuri Galitzin. He settled in London in 1861 as an orchestral violinist and church organist (at the Swiss Church in Holborn) and married there. His son Frank (1877–1963) was a successful composer of musicals in London and on Broadway, wrote several popular drawing-room ballads (notably *Mother o' Mine*), was a conductor for RCA Victor, and served as music director for Paramount Pictures. Berthold's church music (he also wrote songs and piano pieces) caught the attention of Alfred Novello, the publisher, who took him on as editor in 1878. RECORDINGS: Some of his songs have been recorded.

[1366] PAINE, John Knowles
ORGANIST, CONDUCTOR, TEACHER
BORN: Portland, Me., January 9, 1839
DIED: Cambridge, Mass., April 25, 1906

At least in terms of his influence on the next generation, John Knowles Paine was the Patriarch of American Music—a composer who commanded honor and respect. His family, which traces back to fourteenth-century England, settled in America three hundred years later. Paine's paternal grandfather began his career as a cooper, turned to instrument making, and wound up as an organ builder. He had several musical offspring, but it was the composer's father Jacob who inherited the family enterprises. He married Rebecca Downes in 1833, and they produced five children. The parents entrusted John Knowles's musical training to

Portland's leading musician, a German refugee called Herman Kotschmar, who had been sponsored by Cyrus Curtis, later of Curtis Publishing Company fame. By the time he was sixteen, Paine was giving organ concerts, whose proceeds, added to a contribution from his older sister Helen, a music teacher and singer, enabled him to make the then-mandatory trek to Germany when he was nineteen. He studied at the Berlin Hochschule, was baptized with the Mendelssohn-Schumann influence, and rejoiced in the then-current Bach [684] revival. Having proved himself as a keyboard player, he came home in 1861 and found New England audiences ready for him if not for Bach. In 1862 he became organist of Harvard's Appleton Chapel and offered the university a non-credit music course for free. Since it would not count toward graduation, there were too few registrants to make it worth his while.

Though by then Paine had written such ambitious things as a string quartet and two piano sonatas, most of his composition of the period was Harvard-connected—ceremonial choral works and japes like his opera *Il Pesceballo (The Fishball),* whose librettists were James Russell Lowell and Francis James Child, the great ballad scholar. By 1866, however, he had completed his impressive *Mass in D* (impetus uncertain—he was not a Catholic). He went back to Germany to conduct the Berlin Singakademie in a performance of it (February 1867); it won justified praise on both sides of the Atlantic. In 1869 Paine married Mary Elizabeth Greeley and wrote a hymn for the inauguration of his friend Charles William Eliot as President of Harvard. The next year Eliot cleared the way for the lecture series he had proposed almost a decade before. The venture was successful, and Eliot, over the howls of a faculty enraged at having a mountebank as a colleague, made him in 1871 Harvard's first (assistant) professor of music. It was Paine who organized the first department of music in a major American university, and he was made full professor in 1875, though he enjoyed the scorn of some of his fellows for the rest of his long career. His work also led to the foundation of the American Organists' Guild and the formation of the Boston Symphony. He taught at the New England Conservatory and Boston University as well. Among his many famous pupils were such composers as Carpenter [1682], Converse [1618], Foote [1471], Hill [1632], and D. G. Mason [1648]. In 1873 his other magnum opus, the oratorio *St. Peter,* was simultaneously premiered in Boston and Portland. A discerning critic declared it superior to anything by Michael Costa [1193] or Sterndale

Bennett [1246]. Among other admired works by Paine was his music for Sophocles' *Oedipus tyrannus* and Aristophanes' *The Birds,* 2 symphonies, and several symphonic poems. He bitterly regretted that his only serious opera, *Azara,* for which he also wrote the libretto, never got a hearing. Basically a Germanized Classic-Romantic, he dabbled later on in Wagnerian [1230] chromaticism. Despite his position and popularity, however, there was nothing remotely "American" about his music. At sixty-five, laden with honors and weary of work, he retired to devote himself to creation but survived only a few months.

RECORDINGS: Recordings include the overtures to *Oedipus* (Howard Hanson) and *As You Like It* (Richard Korn), the *Mass* (Gunther Schuller), and a number of organ pieces. The symphonies have been recorded by the Society for the Preservation of the American Musical Heritage.

[1367] BUCK, Dudley, Sr.
ORGANIST, CONDUCTOR, TEACHER
BORN: Hartford, Conn., March 10, 1839
DIED: West Orange, N.J., October 6, 1909

Dudley Buck's father was in the shipping business and took little note of his son's interest in music until the boy's piano studies with W. A. Babcock, begun when he was sixteen, showed him to be truly gifted. After Dudley had studied for two years at Trinity College, his father sent him in 1858 to the Leipzig Conservatory, where his teachers included Moscheles [1146], Moritz Hauptmann, and Julius Rietz [1227]. He spent 1860 in Dresden, under the tutelage of the organist Johann Schneider, and 1861 in Paris soaking up culture; then he returned to Hartford to make his living as a teacher and church organist. He grew popular as a composer of church music and became known as a recitalist who played "difficult" music. In 1869—a year that saw the birth of Dudley, Jr., later a singer and voice teacher—Buck went to Chicago as organist of the Church of St. James. But Mrs. O'Leary's cow both ended the appointment and destroyed some of his manuscripts. In 1872 he moved to Boston, where he taught at the Conservatory and played at St. Paul's. Three years later the conductor Theodore Thomas took him on as his assistant for the Central Park Garden Concerts (founded in 1868) and the Cincinnati Biennial Music Festival (founded in 1866). Buck then made his home in Brooklyn, where he was organist at Holy Trinity. At Thomas's behest, he and the poet Sidney

Lanier collaborated on *The Centennial Meditation of Columbus,* a cantata that was performed to open the Centennial celebration in Philadelphia in 1876. (In his day, Buck was best known for his big cantatas to texts by popular poets such as Longfellow, Washington Irving, and Sir Edwin Arnold.) As a teacher, Buck turned out a number of pupils who made names for themselves in church and choral music. It was Buck who taught Charles Ives [1659] to play the organ. Besides the works noted, Buck wrote a couple of operas and some instrumental music. RECORDINGS: Richard Morris has recorded his *Grand Sonata* in E-flat for organ (featuring "Hail, Columbia!") and Jorge Mester and E. Power Biggs have recorded two pieces (one orchestral, the other for organ) based on the national anthem.

[1368] RHEINBERGER, Joseph Gabriel
(Rīn′-bâr-ger, Yō′-zef Gä′-brē-el)
KEYBOARDIST, CONDUCTOR, TEACHER
BORN: Vaduz, March 17, 1839
DIED: Munich, November 25, 1901

Rheinberger has the distinction of being indisputably the greatest composer born in Liechtenstein—if not the only one. He was also a notable teacher with a particular impact on American music. His father, the state treasurer, recognized his extraordinary talent and had him trained from the age of five. At seven Joseph became organist of the parish church in Vaduz, for which he wrote a *Mass* a year later. At nine he demonstrated that he had perfect pitch and was sent to nearby Feldkirch (in Austria) to live and study with Philipp Schmutzer, the town *Kapellmeister.* During his two years there, he made the twenty-mile hike every Sunday to discharge his duties in Vaduz. By 1851 it was clear that he was ready for the Big Time, which in Liechtenstein meant Munich, so he went there to spend the rest of his life. For the next three years he studied, at first at the Munich Conservatory, and then, on an informal basis, with Franz Lachner [1171], supporting himself by teaching and with church jobs. In 1857 he was appointed royal organist. Two years later, when his former piano teacher at the Conservatory, Julius Leonhard, left town, Rheinberger was named to succeed him; in the same year he became organist of the Michaelskirche and published his Op. 1, which consisted of four piano pieces—rejecting as juvenilia the many works he had produced earlier. At the Conservatory he was soon also assigned to teach harmony, counterpoint, composition, and music history. As if all this were not

enough, he took on the task, in 1864, of directing the municipal choral society.

Meanwhile, Wagner [1230] had arrived to unveil his grandiose schemes to King Ludwig, and in July 1865 the Conservatory was shut down to make way for the new Royal Music School. In the interim Rheinberger worked with Wagner as rehearsal coach at the opera and was himself inspired to operatic composition, producing two works in 1869 and 1873 that had local and ephemeral success. In 1867 he married Franziska von Hoffnaas, age thirty-five, a widow of rank and education, a singer, and a poetess, who wrote most of the texts her husband set from that time on. In the same year, Bülow [1310], director of the new conservatory and an ardent admirer of Rheinberger's teaching, had him named royal professor there, in charge of composition and organ courses. Ten years later, Rheinberger turned down a tempting offer from the Hoch Conservatory in Frankfurt and was then appointed to the post of *Hofkapellmeister,* succeeding Franz Wüllner, who had conducted the premieres of Wagner's first two *Ring* operas and had succeeded Rietz [1227] in Dresden. Among his other honors were a papal knighthood, an honorary doctorate from the University of Munich, and a patent of nobility in 1894 from the regent, Prince Luitpold.

Rheinberger's health was increasingly bad during his last thirty years. In 1892 he was shaken by Franziska's death and was never able to bring himself to hear a performance of his popular Christmas cantata, *Die Stern von Bethlehem (The Star of Bethlehem),* whose text she had written shortly before. He died nine years later at sixty-two. Among his European pupils were Humperdinck [1480], Kienzl [1496], Wolf-Ferrari [1679], and Furtwängler [1803]; among the Americans were Chadwick [1483], Converse [1618], Henry Huss (1862–1953), Homer [1568], and J. Fred Wolle, founder of the Bethlehem (Pennsylvania) Bach Festival.

As a composer, Rheinberger was quite gifted, but he wrote too much and played to the tastes of his day, a practice that found him increasingly out of fashion. He produced an enormous amount of choral music, including 18 Masses, 4 Requiems, and 5 Stabat Maters. There are also 2 symphonies, a piano concerto, 2 organ concerti, overtures and symphonic poems, chamber works, songs, and much for piano and organ.

RECORDINGS: The 20 organ sonatas have been recorded by a relay of British organists, the organ concerti by E. Power Biggs, the Concerto for Piano and a sonata by Adrian Ruiz, the *Mass* in E-flat and *Angelis suis* by Rolf Thomas, and the Christmas cantata by

Robert Heger. There is also a recording of the Nonet in E-flat Major (by Jaap Schroeder, the Danzi Quintet, et al.).

[1369] MUSSORGSKY, Modest Petrovich (Mōō-zôrk'-skē, Mōd-yest' Pyā-trō'-vich)
PIANIST, CIVIL SERVANT
BORN: Karevo (Pskov), March 21, 1839
DIED: St. Petersburg, March 28, 1881

Long considered greatly talented but woefully ignorant of the musical proprieties, Modest Mussorgsky is now recognized as the most original composer to emerge from the Russian musical upheaval of the nineteenth century. His one completed opera, *Boris Godunov,* and his 60-odd songs are rightly regarded as landmarks in the history of Western music. But for all that, his sadly abbreviated career is strewn with the remains of unfinished projects—some no more than sketchy ideas, some mighty torsos—to the degree that in the century since his death second-guessing what he might have done with them has become a veritable industry with other composers. (It is almost as large an industry as that of discovering what he actually did by stripping away the well-intended additions and changes imposed by his editors.) There are those who see Mussorgsky as a victim of circumstances, and one must agree that he had a hit-or-miss musical education and that the currents of history undermined his economic position. But he seems to have been his own worst enemy—rarely able to carry anything to completion, increasingly hampered by drinking bouts, and at best a sort of holy fool who imagined the world a more perfect and reasonable place than it was.

The Mussorgskys were an aristocratic family whose roots supposedly went back to the ninth-century Viking leader Hrörekr ("Rurik"), who established in Novgorod the beginnings of modern Russia. The name itself comes, however, from a sobriquet "Mussorga," meaning something like "the scurrilous," bestowed on a fifteenth-century ancestor. Two centuries later the Mussorgskys came into possession of a considerable estate in the Pskov district, which afterward expanded. By the time the composer was born, they counted their wealth both in land and in "souls" (serfs). On one of the latter Modest's grandfather had accidentally begotten a son, called Peter Alexeivich. He afterward married the mother and legitimized the boy. In due time Peter wed Yulya Chirikova, the daughter of another local landowner, and together they produced four sons, of whom Modest was the last. (Only he and his immediate forerunner, Filaret, lived to maturity.)

Very little is known of the composer's childhood. Supposedly his nurse, a repository of traditional tales and songs, gave him his subsequent identification with the common people and their art—though one suspects that it owes a good deal to his later reading on social matters. According to his own not very reliable autobiographical sketches, he began to make up tunes on the piano at an early age, had lessons from his mother and a governess, and soon gave evidence of a fairly prodigious talent. Intending both his sons for military careers, Peter Alexeivich took them to St. Petersburg in August 1849 and enrolled them in the School of Sts. Peter and Paul, the best secondary school in the city. To further his younger son's musical education, he entrusted him to a pianist named Anton Herke, a successful concert artist who had studied with Henselt [1237]. Modest was soon delighting salons with his playing, and in 1852 he wrote a polka called *Porte enseigne (Ensign Bearer)* which, on Herke's recommendation, got published. (It has since wholly vanished).

Meanwhile, the year previous, Mussorgsky had been transferred to an establishment run by a certain Komarov and designed to prepare candidates for the Cadet School of the Guards, which he entered in August 1852. Little is known of his education there save that it probably taught him to be fluent in French and German and that it involved no formal musical training. According to those who passed through it, the school's chief function seems to have been the kind of social polishing offered today by many college fraternities: how to wench, gamble, and drink. Mussorgsky, who was squeamish about sexual matters, probably did not indulge in the first of these activities, but it has been suggested that it was here that he acquired his fatal addiction to alcohol. (He later maintained that his red nose came from doing guard duty in freezing weather.)

In 1856, a handsome, dapper, and slightly affected young officer, Mussorgsky joined the Regiment of the Preobazhensky Guards to which his grandfather had belonged, and —totally untrained in theory and composition—began work on an opera, of which no trace remains. That same year, by chance, he met Alexander Borodin [1331], then a fledgling officer like himself. But his real introduction to St. Petersburg musical circles began in 1857 with his acquaintance with Dargomizhsky [1228], and through him with César Cui [1337], Balakirev [1348], and Alexander Stasov, who later, as critic, would champion the new Russian music. Soon Mussorgsky knew he must compose and persuaded Balakirev to give him lessons, which consisted chiefly of playing and analyzing works by Beethoven [1063], Schumann [1211], and other admired composers of the day. The two got on famously at first. Later Mussorgsky grew restive at the restraints Balakirev placed on him, whereas Balakirev became disappointed in his pupil's failure to (as he saw it) progress. (A good deal of blame for the latter's failures and supposed shortcomings has unjustly been laid at Balakirev's door.)

Meanwhile in 1858 Mussorgsky suffered some sort of breakdown. Whether it was mental, emotional, or perhaps even alcohol-related remains uncertain, but it forced him to resign his commission. Nor was he really well again for some three years, though there were periods when he composed. All that remains extant in finished form is a handful of songs, a like number of little piano pieces, and a scherzo orchestrated from one of the latter. A projected opera, *Oedipus in Athens*, came to nothing; the cantata *Shamil's March* remains fragmentary; two piano sonatas have disappeared (if they ever existed); a symphony never got off the drawing board.

In 1861 Czar Alexander II freed the serfs. However beneficial this act may have been for them, it spelled economic disaster for the Mussorgskys. Modest spent most of the next two years helping Filaret with the estate. On his return to the capital, he partially solved his financial problems by joining a "commune," which meant that he shared an apartment, reading, and ideas with five other rather starry-eyed young intellectual progressives. It was they who introduced him to Flaubert's novel *Salammbô*, for which, by the end of the year, 1863, he was making operatic sketches. But his living arrangements did not meet his need for an income, and in December he took a job as a clerk in the ministry of communications, where he enjoyed two promotions in as many years. He continued to produce piano pieces and songs, some of which last begin to show his conviction that song is a heightened form of speech. *Salammbô*—some of it cannibalized from the *Oedipus* sketches—went slowly, finally grinding to a halt around 1866.

In 1865 Mussorgsky's beloved mother died. Whatever the previous history of his drinking, he drowned his grief to the point that he incurred a horrendous attack of delirium tremens that necessitated Filaret's fetching him away from the "commune" to recover in his apartment, where he remained until 1868. (The correspondence regarding this lapse attributes it to "nerves," like the earlier breakdown.) Recovered, he returned to the composition of songs, which were now chiefly in the vein of "realism" or "artistic truth"—miniature dramatic portraits of very Russian characters, most of them from the lower social strata. The year 1867 also brought forth some larger works—the choral-orchestral *Destruction of Sennacherib*, the *Intermezzo in modo classico* (orchestrated from an earlier piano piece), and *St. John's Eve on the Bare Mountain*—better known, in the somewhat misguided recension by Rimsky-Korsakov [1416] as *A Night on Bare (or Bald) Mountain*. (The last-named work may originally have been conceived as early as 1858 in connection with a projected opera on Gogol's *St. John's Eve* or in 1860 when Mussorgsky claimed to be writing music for a play, *The Witches*, by a Baron Mengden. The 1867 version was excoriated by Balakirev and never performed in Mussorgsky's lifetime. Nor was the version with chorus that he arranged in 1872 for the opera-ballet *Mlada*, a projected collaboration by members of the "Mighty Handful," as Balakirev and his disciples had come to be known. *That* version Mussorgsky finally proposed as an intermezzo in the opera *Sorochintzy Fair*, which he did not live to complete.) A symphonic poem begun that same year, *Poděbrad of Bohemia*, was aborted.

This increased production was a byproduct of an important change in the composer's life: financial retrenchment in the ministry deprived him of further employment there in April 1867. At least that was the excuse given, though it is clear that he found the work dreary and performed it little short of incompetently. In any case he had been poorly paid, and now he imagined he could survive on musical odd jobs.

In 1868 Mussorgsky had his first experience of the music of Wagner [1230] through a performance of *Lohengrin*. Far more influential on him, however, was *The Stone Guest*, which Dargomizhsky had finished that same year. In this work the composer has set Pushkin's play verbatim in a sort of song-speech. Mussorgsky was in on the first read-through around Dargomizhsky's piano, taking the part of Leporello. He was ecstatic: this was the sort of breakthrough he had dreamed of. Almost immediately he set out to do a similar treatment of Gogol's comedy *The Marriage*. He worked furiously for a month in midsummer and completed his first act in piano score. It was eventually given a reading at Cui's, where it generated little enthusiasm—and that was the end of that. (Long afterward Ippolitov-Ivanov [1517] set the rest of the play.)

No doubt his associates' reaction to the work cooled Mussorgsky's interest, but that had in fact been diverted by a friend, Vladimir Nikolsky, a history professor who had introduced him to Pushkin's drama *Boris Godunov.* Meanwhile what was left of Filaret Mussorgsky's holdings had evaporated. He had to give up his apartment and move to the country. Modest took another clerical job in the government, this time with the forestry department, and found shelter with the Opichinins, whom he had met long ago through Dargomizhsky. For the next year he seems to have worked with a sustained intensity uncommon with him and completed his first version of *Boris Godunov* in 1869. This work focused exclusively on the rise and fall of the czar. (The composer had written his own libretto, backing up Pushkin's play with material from Karamzin's *History of the Russian Empire.)* In 1870 he submitted the score to the imperial theater people, and while casting about for a new operatic subject—he toyed for a moment with something called *Bobil, or The Landless Peasant*—completed several songs of the cycle called *The Nursery,* based on his memories of his childhood, and a lampoon of his musical enemies called *The Peep-Show,* a sort of extended song or cantata.

Early in 1871 the committee in charge of such matters turned *Boris* down. Apart from projected difficulties with the censors, its members were puzzled by a work that had no arias, no prima donna, no ballet, and sounded very odd to boot. Mussorgsky, apparently not much perturbed, set out to redo the opera. Besides cutting out episodes that might seem to smack of *lèse-majesté* (chiefly the scene at St. Basil's Cathedral), he added a good deal, including the folksy byplay of the nurse and the royal children in Act One, the final scene of the populace in revolt, and the entire "Polish" act—which supplied a prima donna and dancing of sorts. In recent months Mussorgsky and Rimsky-Korsakov had grown thick as thieves, and during the process of revision they shared living quarters. Various portions of the opera were performed both privately and publicly, while the theater committee again deliberated. Despite growing evidence that the work was viable, it was again rejected in the fall of 1872. In the course of that year Gedeonov, director of the imperial theaters, had commissioned what was left of the Mighty Handful (Balakirev having temporarily removed himself from musical life) to collaborate on the opera-ballet *Mlada,* which died a-borning. Now he took it upon himself to produce

three scenes from *Boris* during a benefit for the stage manager at the Maryinsky Theater. They were received with, on the whole, great enthusiasm, and the following winter (February 1874) he went over the heads of the committee and gave the whole an all-out production, which played ten times that season and was then shelved. When the opera was revived in 1896, it was in the version of Rimsky-Korsakov, who carefully removed all the fingerprints of Mussorgskian individuality, which he took to represent ineptitude and ignorance. In that version it has come to be recognized as the greatest of Russian music dramas and the supreme vehicle for a great bass singing-actor. In 1940 Dmitri Shostakovich [2094] reorchestrated the opera, but only in very recent years has there been a successful effort to return to the original—of which at this writing only a single, rather indifferent recording has appeared.

In 1872 Rimsky-Korsakov had moved out to get married, and the following year Mussorgsky shared quarters with his relative Count Arseny Golenishchev-Kutusov, a poet of some talent who provided the lyrics for the song cycles *Sunless* of 1874 and *Songs and Dances of Death* (of which the composer completed only four songs). Mussorgsky had also begun work on another big historical epic, *Khovantschina,* set in the time of Peter the Great. Not very long after he did so, however, his attention was directed toward a new idea, a treatment of Gogol's folktale *Sorochintzy Fair.* He completed neither.

It is difficult to say just when it happened, but Mussorgsky's drinking, by his own tacit admission, had gotten the better of him. (He admitted that he loved to drink but insisted it had nothing to do with the periods of mental aberration from which he suffered.) For a time in 1874 he seems to have been sobered by the unexpected death of a friend, the artist Victor Hartmann, on some of whose drawings he based the memorial piano cycle *Pictures at an Exhibition.* When Count Golenischev-Kutusov left to get married in 1875, the deterioration seems to have proceeded rapidly. There are dark reports of his selling off his furniture to support his habit, and one night he came home to find himself locked out for nonpayment of rent. He was taken in by a sometime naval officer, Paul Naumov. Naumov, estranged from his wife, was living with his sister-in-law and was something of a *bon vivant.* Mussorgsky's friends had misgivings about the atmosphere, but he remained there for several years. During this period his employers in the Forestry Department showed remarkable tolerance, even making him chief clerk in 1875 and boosting him a rank higher in

1878. A few months later, however, the handwriting was on the wall. The critic Stasov read it clearly and managed to get his friend transferred to an artificially created stopgap in another governmental department, whose director, a man named Filippov, was a devotee of music. In the early autumn of 1879, with Filippov's blessing, Mussorgsky acceded to the request of Darya Leonova, a singer who had created the role of the Innkeeper in *Boris,* that he accompany her (in both senses) on a tour of the south. The experience seems temporarily to have pulled him out of his tailspin and inspired him to some piano pieces and his last (and perhaps most famous) vocal piece, a setting of Goethe's "Song of the Flea" from *Faust.* Back at work, however, he relapsed and had to be let go at the end of the year. Filippov got him a monthly pension of 100 rubles. Other friends added more. Darya Leonova took him into her school to accompany, teach, and compose for the students (he managed some vocalises and folksong arrangements), and lent him her country home that summer, 1880. He completed an orchestral march, *The Capture of Kars,* and wrote his friends that *Khovantshina* was finished, save for the scoring. But back in the capital the deterioration continued apace. On a February night in 1881 he erupted into Leonova's house shouting incoherently about having to beg on the streets, underwent a seizure of some sort, and passed out. He was placed in a military hospital through the finagling of some influential well-wishers and recuperated slowly over the next several weeks, during which the painter Repin did the best-known portrait of him, haggard and disheveled in a rumpled bathrobe. On the eve of what Mussorgsky assumed to be his forty-second birthday—he had the date wrong all his life—a member of the hospital staff unwittingly presented him with a bottle of brandy. He died at 5 A.M. the next morning and was buried on March 30 in the Nevsky cemetery.

For better or worse, Rimsky completed and orchestrated *Khovantshina,* but the *Sorochintsk Fair* was left in fragments. Golenishchev-Kutusov finished the libretto. Various composers, including Cui and Liadov [1485], had a hand in putting Humpty-Dumpty together again, and Nikolai Tcherepnin [1642] produced a practical version of the whole. Maurice Ravel made the most famous of the numerous orchestrations of *Pictures at an Exhibition* (others were by Sir Henry Wood as "Klenovsky," Lucien Caillet, and Mikhail Tushmalov—all recorded) and is reputed to have had a hand in that for the single act of *The Wedding.*

The fragments of *Salammbô* have been assembled sufficiently to fill up two LP records.

RECORDINGS: The five salvageable operas and operatic fragments have all been committed to records. What remains of the piano music has had several integral recordings. Among the many versions of the songs and song cycles, one should note Boris Christoff's reasonably complete one. Most of the orchestral and choral pieces seem to have received at least some attention.

[1370] ROGUSKI, Gustaw (Rō'-gōōs'-kē, Gōōs'-tàv)
TEACHER, THEORIST
BORN: Warsaw, May 12, 1839
DIED: Warsaw, April 5, 1921

Roguski studied in Germany with Adolf Bernhard Marx and Friedrich Kiel (1821–85) and reportedly in France with Berlioz [1175]. He then returned to Warsaw and spent the rest of his life as professor of harmony and counterpoint at the Conservatory. (One of his pupils was Paderewski [1527].) He collaborated with Żeleński [1353] on a harmony text, translated Ebenezer Prout's treatise on orchestratio.1, and wrote, on his own, a pocket dictionary of composers (for emergencies on the tram). He wrote in most forms other than the operatic, and is particularly admired for his organ music. RECORDINGS: An example of the organ music has been recorded by Feliks Raczkowski.

[1371] SMITH, Alice Mary
HOUSEWIFE
BORN: London, May 19, 1839
DIED: London, December 4, 1884

Alice Mary Smith took composing seriously, despite the facts that she was of a good family and a Victorian woman. She studied with Sterndale Bennett [1246] and G. A. Macfarren (1813–87). At twenty-seven she married the Honorable Frederick Meadows-White, a future jurist, but went right on composing. She turned out 2 symphonies, 4 overtures, a clarinet concerto, 5 cantatas, several quartets, as well as the expectable salon pieces. It being difficult to pretend that she did not exist, she was made a female associate of the Philharmonic Society and an honorary member of the Royal Academy. RECORDINGS: There are recordings of some of her smaller vocal pieces, notably the long-popular duet setting of Charles Kingsley's *O That We Two Were Maying!*

[1372] SMITH, Edward Sydney
PIANIST, TEACHER
BORN: Dorchester, July 14, 1839
DIED: London, March 3, 1889

Sydney Smith was unrelated to his name-sake, the English humorist and divine (1771–1845), or to the composer Alice Mary Smith [1371] born two months before him. He was taught piano basics at home and then in 1855 was sent off to Leipzig where he spent three edifying years with Moscheles [1146], Rietz [1227], and the rest of the usual Leipzig crew. He afterward established himself in London as a fashionable and expensive teacher, and specialized in writing quasi-virtuoso pieces that would make his students sound brilliant even if they weren't. RECORDINGS: Some of them have been recorded as examples of the wretched taste of the times—e.g., by Neely Bruce and Malcolm Binns.

[1373] GERNSHEIM, Friedrich (Gârns'-hīm, Frē'-drikh)
TEACHER, CONDUCTOR, PIANIST
BORN: Worms, July 17, 1839
DIED: Berlin, September 11, 1916

Respected and admired as a teacher, Gernsheim wrote music that has been obscured by the fact that it owes too much to his friend Brahms [1329] and his idol Schumann [1211]. After beginning his career as a child prodigy (pianist, violinist, composer), he settled down at the Leipzig Conservatory in 1852 to hear the approved gospel from Moscheles [1146], Rietz [1227], Hauptmann, and Ferdinand David. He then went on to Paris in 1855 for further piano work with Marmontel and became part of the ebullient musical life there, getting to know most of the big names personally. In 1861 he went to Saarbrucken as a conductor. Four years later he was appointed professor of piano, counterpoint, and fugue at the conservatory in Cologne, where he taught and conducted until 1872. His most famous pupil, in the Cologne period, was Humperdinck [1480]. He then moved to Rotterdam as theater and choral conductor, and wound up in 1880 at the Stern Conservatory in Berlin, where he was active until 1907. Among his 90-odd opuses are 4 symphonies, a concerto apiece for violin and piano, choral works, keyboard pieces, and songs. He was reputedly best as a chamber music composer.
RECORDINGS: Gayle Smith has recorded one of his 2 cello sonatas.

[1374] NÁPRAVNÍK, Eduard (Ná-pràv'-nēk, Ed'-wärd)
CONDUCTOR
BORN: Beist (now Býšt'), August 24, 1839
DIED: Petrograd, November 23, 1916

A highly successful operatic composer (as well as a great conductor), Nápravník has never received his due outside of Russia, of which country he was not a native. He was born in a village northeast of Prague, where his father was schoolmaster, and had his first music lessons from the paternal assistant. When the family moved to another village, his uncle Augustin Svoboda took over. Orphaned at fourteen, he managed to get admitted to the Prague Organ School. He then taught while studying privately with Wagner's [1230] friend Friedrich Kittl, director of the Prague Conservatory. He began to attract attention as a composer and critic, which led to his hiring by Prince Yussupov to conduct his private orchestra in St. Petersburg, where he settled in 1861. The orchestra consisted of serfs, and with their general emancipation in 1863 there went the job. But Nápravník found work with Konstantin Liadov, father of the composer [1485] and director of the imperial theaters, who took him on as organist and répétiteur at the Maryinsky. He was advanced to the post of assistant conductor and, when Liadov died two years later, in 1869, Nápravník succeeded him. He also conducted several series of orchestral concerts over the years. As an operatic conductor, he presided over the premieres of many of the important Russian operas during the last third of the century, as well as the Russian premieres of such works as Gluck's [803] *Orfeo ed Euridice*, Beethoven's [1063] *Fidelio*, and Wagner's [1230] *Ring*.

Nápravník's own first-produced opera was *Nizhegorodtsiy (The People of Nizhegorod)*, at the Maryinsky in 1868. It was followed by *Harold* in 1886, *Dubrovsky* in 1895, and *Francesca da Rimini* in 1902. The third of these still holds the Russian stage. Nápravník was essentially an eclectic, affected by his early training and by Glinka [1179] and Tchaikovsky [1377] more than by the Wagnerians or the nationalists. He also wrote 4 symphonies and other orchestral and chamber pieces of magnitude.

RECORDINGS: Besides the usual operatic excerpts, there is a complete Russian recording of *Dubrovsky*, and Jorge Mester has recorded a *Festive March*.

[1375] WHITE, José Silvestre de Dolores
(Hwīt, Hō-sā′ Sēl-vās′-trā dā *Thō-lō′*-
rās)
VIOLINIST
BORN: Mantanzas, 1839
DIED: Rio de Janeiro (?), 1914

José White (later called "Joseph") was the
son of a French father (Charles) and a black
Cuban. He learned the rudiments of the violin from his father and later studied with
Cuban professionals. He made his first public appearance at sixteen accompanied by
Louis Moreau Gottschalk **[1306]**. On the
latter's urging, he soon thereafter set sail for
Paris. He was admitted to the Conservatoire
where he studied under Jean-Delphin Alard
[1240]—Pablo de Sarasate **[1415]** was a
classmate—and a year later took first prize
for violin. (White received a personal letter
of congratulations from Rossini **[1143]**.)
Soon afterward White's father became mortally ill and his son was forced to go home to
Cuba. He concertized there and did some
composing, and returned to Paris in 1861. He
spent 1863 in Spain, where he was decorated
by Queen Isabella, and returned to Paris to
substitute for Alard at the Conservatoire until 1865. He spent the next ten years there.
His return to Cuba was brief, for he was ordered out after an 1875 concert precipitated
a nationalist disturbance. The rest of his career is sketchy. In 1876 he played with the
Theodore Thomas Orchestra in New York
and gave a recital in Boston, where one
critic preferred him to Ole Bull **[1206]**,
Vieuxtemps **[1270]**, and Wieniawski **[1340]**.
The next several years found him concertizing in Central and South America, where he
eventually settled in Rio de Janeiro. There
he helped found the local Concert Society
and taught music to the children of Emperor
Pedro. White's compositions (mostly for his
own instrument) are not numerous, but they
include a string quartet and a violin concerto. RECORDINGS: The Concerto for Violin
has been recorded by Aaron Rosand.

[1376] AUDRAN, Edmond (Ō-drā*n*′, Ed-
mo*n*′)
ORGANIST
BORN: Lyons, April 12, 1840
DIED: Tierceville, August 17, 1901

Audran was one of the more successful operetta composers to follow Offenbach **[1264]**
and was perhaps Lecocq's **[1322]** chief com-
petitor. He was the son of Marius-Pierre
Audran, a leading tenor at the Paris Opéra-
Comique and later director of the Marseilles
Conservatory, to which city he moved his

family in 1861. Edmond, then two years out
of the Niedermeyer School (see 1167), found
a position there as organist at St. Joseph,
and the following year produced his first operetta, *L'Ours et le pacha (The Bear and the
Pasha)* in a Marseilles theater. Paris heard of
him by way of a *Mass* performed there in
1873, but it was not until the Marseilles success of *Le grand mogol (The Grand Mogul)*
in 1877 that he had a chance to attain the
Paris stage. He hit immediately with *Les
Noces d'Olivette (Olivette's Wedding)* in 1879
and *La Mascotte (The Mascot)* in 1880, the
latter work quickly winning worldwide attention. Other successes were *Gillette de
Narbonne*, 1882; *La Cigale et la fourmi (The
Grasshopper and the Ant)*, 1886; a revival of
Le grand mogol, first performed in Paris in
1884; and *Miss Helyett*, 1890. After *Monsieur
Lohengrin* in 1896, Audran became a victim
of paresis. He also left some sacred music
and salon pieces. RECORDINGS: Early
French vocal recordings include many selections from the operettas, of which he wrote
around 30.

[1377] TCHAIKOVSKY, Piotr Ilyich
(Chī-kôf′-ski, Pyō′tr Ēl′-yich)
TEACHER, REVIEWER, CONDUCTOR
BORN: Votkinsk, May 7, 1840
DIED: St. Petersburg, November 6, 1893

Tchaikovsky (the anglicized spelling, however inaccurate, is traditional) has been in
twentieth-century America perhaps the
most broadly popular of all the great composers, appealing even to people who have
little taste for other serious music. This phenomenon is owing no doubt to his great melodic facility and his sometimes rather unbuttoned (if not actually self-indulgent)
emotionalism. As a result, highly successful
popular songs (when such songs were permitted to have a musical content) were constructed on Tchaikovsky themes. This sort
of thing did his reputation no good among
the musical tastemakers, who viewed his
music as at best flimsy (as in the ballet
scores—among the finest ever written), and
at worst sentimental and incoherent. It is
true that (especially in his piano pieces)
Tchaikovsky wrote a certain amount of
salonesque stuff, but the fact remains that he
was the first (some would say the only) considerable Russian symphonist and that,
whatever his emotional problems, he wrote
usually with firm formal control and consciousness of what he was doing. Yet in his
own time these characteristics actually mili-
tated against him, for the Russian nationalists—the *Kuchka* and their adherents—

viewed him as a sellout, a "German" of the Anton Rubinstein [1309] stripe.

Piotr Ilyich Tchaikovsky was the second son and fourth child of Ilya Petrovich Tchaikovsky, a mining engineer then in charge of the iron works in Votkinsk, an industrial town in eastern Russia (presently in the Udmursk S.S.R.) about halfway between Kazan and Perm, in the Ural Mountains. The boy's mother, Ilya's second wife (eighteen years younger than he), née Alexandra Andreyevna Assier, was the granddaughter of a French émigré. The first marriage had produced a daughter, Zinaida; in the second Piotr had been preceded by Ekaterina (who had died) and Nikolai and was followed by Alexandra ("Sasha"), by Ippolit, and then after a hiatus by twin brothers, Anatoly and Modest, who were to be his favorite siblings.

Tchaikovsky's childhood, despite such promising circumstances, was not a particularly happy one. He was tetchy and oversensitive, like his mother's people. Though he was deeply attached to that parent, she seems not to have been outwardly affectionate. He appears to have been even more devoted to his governess, a young French woman named Fanny Dürbach. A crisis of sorts came in 1848 when Ilya (then fifty-three) retired and took his family to Moscow, where a new job awaited him, a move which did not, much to Piotr's grief, include Fanny. But the promised employment failed to materialize, and a chaotic period followed. There was a second move, to St. Petersburg, where the child was put into a school that he hated and where, shortly afterward, he nearly died of measles. In the spring Ilya found work as manager of a foundry in Alapayevsk, on the Siberian side of the Urals north of Sverdlovsk, and it was back to the sticks for the Tchaikovskys.

For reasons that are still not clear the family had decided by 1850 that legal training was the thing for their ten-year-old and arranged for him to enter the preparatory department of the School of Jurisprudence in the capital. His mother took him there and, as he felt, abandoned him. Within a few weeks an outbreak of scarlet fever closed the school. No sooner had some family friends, the Vakars, taken him in for the duration than their own son contracted the disease and died, a tragedy whose guilt Tchaikovsky bore the rest of his life. In 1852, after two unhappy years of mediocre scholarly performance, he was admitted to the upper school and, to his joy, Ilya having resigned his job, his family came to settle in St. Petersburg. But his happiness was short-lived, for two summers later his mother contracted cholera and died. In 1858 Ilya lost all his money in

an unwise investment venture but soon won an appointment as director of the Institute of Technology.

Piotr Ilyich graduated in 1859 at nineteen. No one in his family had been especially musical, and his own musical training, despite his evidencing considerable aptitude, had been sporadic. In his childhood a former female serf had given him some rudimentary piano lessons. He had been a chorister in the school, had been taken by relatives and friends to an occasional opera or ballet and in recent years had indulged himself in some vocal training and some more advanced piano lessons. He had also done some tentative composing—a piano waltz and a couple of songs, one of them published around 1865. However much he may then have fantasized a musical career, he forthwith took a post in the ministry of justice, and was stepped up two grades within the year. At that time, though he won something of a reputation as a scatterbrain, he seems to have led the normal life of a young man-about-town, including dances and, apparently, some heterosexual flirtations.

His work seems not to have been very demanding. In the summer of 1861 he got three months off to accompany a paternal acquaintance (in the role of interpreter) on a business trip to Germany, Belgium, England, and France—the first of a long series of wanderings. It was around this time that, encouraged by his father, Tchaikovsky began serious study of musical theory with Nikolai Zaremba [1275] of the Russian Musical Society, which organization, sponsored by the Grand Duchess Elena and directed by Anton Rubinstein, became the St. Petersburg Conservatory the next year. It was at that juncture that Tchaikovsky became a composition pupil of Rubinstein's. In 1863, disappointed in his expectations at the ministry, he resigned to enter the conservatory as a full-time student. The decision was not an easy one: he no longer had an income, and Ilya had just resigned his directorship. Piotr Ilyich subsisted on what he could glean from giving piano lessons (he had somehow become a more than competent pianist), and it was not long before he began to look like Raskolnikov (without the hatchet). Nevertheless he gave himself over wholeheartedly to his chosen career, using whatever spare time he could find to plug the rather alarming gaps in his musical knowledge.

Having tried his wings with the usual sort of compositional assignments (now mostly lost), he spent the summer writing an overture to Alexander Ostrovsky's play *The Storm* (also the literary source of the opera

Katya Kabanova by Janáček [1478]). Rubinstein turned his thumbs down, finding it too "modern," but he approved Tchaikovsky's translation the following summer of the orchestration text by Gevaert [1303] and saw to its publication. It was a trying year for Tchaikovsky. In the course of it his father took unto himself a third wife, and Piotr Ilyich was shunted about among friends and relatives. His health was poor; nor was it improved by the graduation project assigned him by his disapproving teacher: to write a cantata on Schiller's *An die Freude (To Joy)*, which was also the basis of the last movement of Beethoven's [1063] ninth symphony. (In the end Tchaikovsky could not bring himself to attend his own graduation in January 1866, further enraging Rubinstein.) Nevertheless 1865 had its pleasant moments. Johann Strauss's [1295] band gave a public performance of Tchaikovsky's *Characteristic Dances* at the Pavlovsk amusement park, and Anton Rubinstein's younger brother, Nikolai, hired him to teach harmony at his own newly founded Moscow Conservatory the following year, Alexander Serov [1269] having turned the job down.

The move to Moscow, however, seems further to have exacerbated Tchaikovsky's problems. His salary was minuscule, and, his clothes being so tattered, Rubinstein demanded that he blow most of his first paycheck on some decent apparel (which included an oversized frock coat once the property of Wieniawski [1340]). On the other hand Rubinstein gave him lodgings in his own quarters, though almost immediately Tchaikovsky took a strong dislike to him (later Tchaikovsky's feeling was reversed). A loner and misanthrope at heart, Tchaikovsky quickly found teaching an agony. In the way of his class and times, he drowned his sorrows in liquor, tobacco, and cards.

It was around this time that he seems to have had to come to terms (as best he could) with his homosexuality. No doubt numerous other composers have been homosexual, but few seem, as Tchaikovsky did, to have borne their state as a lifelong curse. Vera Davidova, sister of his own sister Sasha's husband Lyev Davidov, fell in love and threw herself at him, and he was forced to admit that he found her importunings repellent. (Later, in 1868, there was a curious liaison with the singer Desirée Artot, but the attraction was certainly more artistic than sexual.)

Meanwhile, despite the almost universally poor reception given his more ambitious works to date (two overtures in addition to those works already noted), Tchaikovsky embarked on the first of his 6 completed symphonies. Having been heard piecemeal, and not encouragingly, before, it got a complete and relatively successful reading under Nikolai Rubinstein's baton in 1868. Two years earlier the composer had been commissioned to do a patriotic overture for the visit to Moscow of the Czarevich Alexander and his Danish bride (who had been willed him, in effect, by his elder brother). As it turned out the work went unperformed, but the prince sent him a pair of jeweled cuff links, which he promptly pawned.

What Tchaikovsky chiefly yearned to do, however, was to become a successful composer of operas. Having become friends with Ostrovsky, he persuaded the latter to librettize his *Dream on the Volga* (as *The Voyevoda*). The progress of the composition was rough. Somehow the composer lost the text for the first act. Ostrovsky rewrote it but contributed no more, and Tchaikovsky had to do the rest himself. The opera was staged in Moscow early in 1869. He himself was wildly enthusiastic, but hardly anyone else was, and he later destroyed or cannibalized what he had written. Something similar happened with his symphonic poem *Fatum* of 1868, though the score has since been reconstructed.

Meanwhile that curious Svengali Mily Balakirev [1348] had met Tchaikovsky and had decided to shape him up. In 1867 he succeeded Anton Rubinstein as head of the St. Petersburg Conservatory, and in March 1869 he conducted *Fatum* there, sending the composer a blistering critique afterward. Shortly afterward he persuaded Tchaikovsky to write the *Romeo and Juliet* fantasy-overture, providing the program himself and overseeing the writing. After it had laid an egg at its 1870 premiere, Balakirev counseled the revisions that gave us the piece as most of us know it now. By then, however, his career was on the wane, and he faded out of Tchaikovsky's life for the time being.

In 1869 Tchaikovsky, undaunted by his first opera's failure, composed a second, *Undine*, to a libretto written for an earlier unsuccessful composer and based on one of de la Motte-Fouqué's *Märchen*. He had high hopes for it, but the Imperial Opera in St. Petersburg sat on it until too late to produce it that season and then rejected it. This action hit him hard, and he made false starts on two other such works before settling on *The Oprichnik*, for which he himself wrote the text after a play by Ivan Lazhechnikov. (The *oprichniki* were the hired bodyguards of Ivan the Terrible.) He began it in 1870, but it went slowly, being interrupted in the summer by a trip to Paris and Germany and a rest in Switzerland to stave off a possible breakdown. He laid it aside again to write the first of his 3 string quartets for a concert of his own works in March 1871 and again for a commissioned cantata for the two hundredth birthday of Peter the Great the next spring. The quartet was his first real success, mostly because of the *andante cantabile* movement, based on a rather saccharine Russian folksong he had collected. He deplored that fact, but among those greatly taken by the movement were Ivan Turgeniev and Lyev (Leo) Tolstoy, a particular hero of the composer's.

In 1871 Tchaikovsky finally discontinued his living arrangement with Rubinstein and acquired his own apartment. Neither the growth of his salary nor his income from the publication of the harmony text he completed that summer made this any less than a luxury, and so he took up reviewing for a Moscow journal, which suspended publication a few months later. But his increased eminence brought him, somewhat to his surprise, proposals for productions from both the St. Petersburg and Moscow opera houses and a contract from Bessel for prior publication of the score. Nápravník [1374] conducted the premiere in the former city in April 1874, and it was hailed as a success. But typically the composer took a strong dislike to the work and withheld it for the rest of his days.

While he was preparing the opera for performance, Tchaikovsky was working on his second symphony, a folksy affair since dubbed the "Little Russian." It was first performed by Rubinstein in Moscow and then by Nápravník in the capital to great acclaim, even winning the approval of the nationalists. But once again the composer found his work not to his taste and seven years later subjected it to radical revision. The original version was followed in rapid order by incidental music for Ostrovsky's play *The Snow Maiden* (cast into limbo nine years later by Rimsky-Korsakov's [1416] opera), the orchestral fantasia on Shakespeare's *The Tempest* (suggested in outline by Tchaikovsky's supporter, the critic Vladimir Stasov), and, early in 1874, the second string quartet. Following the production of the opera that spring, he embarked on a first visit to Italy. He had by then been in Western Europe several times. He did not find Italy much to his liking—Venice depressed him, Rome bored him, it was wet in Naples, and only the ruins of Pompei aroused his interest. After a couple of months he returned to Russia to set Yakov Polonsky's libretto on Gogol's "Christmas Eve."

This had been commissioned by the Grand Duchess Elena for Serov. When the latter had died shortly after embarking on the project, she had established a cash award for the winner of a contest for a satisfactory setting. Finding himself with no serious competition and unaware that the terminal date had been moved back several months, Tchaikovsky had the score ready by January 1875. Entries were supposed to be anonymous, but he made no effort to disguise his handwriting, which several of the judges knew. Realizing that his error about the dates meant no performance in the current season, he tried to withdraw the score for consideration by the Imperial Opera. That failing, he had Nikolai Rubinstein (one of the judges) conduct excerpts at a concert and discussed the work in detail with Rimsky-Korsakov (another judge). Of course the work won, and it was performed as *Vakula the Smith* at the Imperial Opera in December 1876. To the composer's intense disappointment, it received only a lukewarm reception. Ten years after completing it, he virtually rewrote it (as *The Slippers*), but that version fared no better.

To return to 1874: having gotten the opera out of the way, Tchaikovsky set to work, for reasons that are not clear, on a piano concerto. He completed it at the beginning of the new year and played it over for Nikolai Rubinstein. Rubinstein, apparently assuming himself slated to premiere it, lambasted its "mistakes," much to Tchaikovsky's dismay. Later Rubinstein told the composer that if certain changes were made, he would consider it, but by then the latter was furious and refused to alter a note. Instead (the whys are again obscure) he sent the score to Hans von Bülow [1310], who triumphed with it in Boston in October. Not long afterward Taneyev [1492], Tchaikovsky's favorite pupil and his successor at the conservatory, gave it a successful Moscow premiere. The conductor was Rubinstein, who had evidently thought better of it and who afterward played it often.

During the summer of 1875, staying with various friends and relatives, Tchaikovsky wrote his third symphony, inappropriately known as the "Polish" because of the final *polacca* movement, and began working on the ballet *Swan Lake.* Commissioned by the Imperial Theaters, this work had had its inception in an entertainment he had written, staged, and choreographed one summer for Sasha's children. (When Saint-Saëns [1343] visited Moscow that December, he, Tchaikovsky, and Rubinstein cooked up an impromptu ballet, *Galatea and Pygmalion,* in which the two composers danced the respective title roles.) His work was interrupted by his taking his brother Modest on a trip to Paris, in the course of which he was bowled over by the new opera *Carmen* by the recently deceased Bizet [1363] and began writing his third and last quartet, which he completed at the beginning of March. He then returned, somewhat reluctantly to the ballet, which went into rehearsal in April. The production a year later was a triumph of theatrical ineptitude, yet the score was so far superior to most such scores that it managed to survive to ultimate popular acceptance.

Although increasingly recognized as an important composer, Tchaikovsky of late had grown steadily more neurotic and despondent. He hated his conservatory work. He was overburdened by his reviewing commitments, which his economic condition had necessitated he keep up. He was rendered guilt-stricken, emotionally overwrought, and lonely by his sexual drive—not to be discussed or admitted in the puritanical atmosphere of nineteenth-century Russia, however much it might be fulfilled in secret. By 1876 all this was manifesting itself in endless restlessness and in bouts of serious, if undiagnosable, illness. The mood also doubtless manifested itself in the passion and hysteria of the symphonic fantasia *Francesca da Rimini*, originally planned as an opera, which he completed in November (and which was received with acclaim). (Earlier, having just returned from the first Bayreuth Festival, where Wagner's [1230] music largely appalled him, he had dashed off the *Marche slave*, moved by sympathy for the current Balkan War with Turkey).

It was at this juncture that he shocked Modest, whose sexual leanings were like his own, by confiding in him that for his own good he meant to wed. It is perhaps symptomatic of his distraught state that he intended to follow *Francesca* with an operatic treatment of *Othello*, though what was forthcoming in December was surprisingly the detached and quasi-Classical *Rococo Variations*, written for his conservatory colleague, the cellist Wilhelm Fitzenhagen.

To further confuse the atmosphere, it was precisely at this time that Nadezhda von Meck entered Tchaikovsky's life. The widow of an engineer who had made a fortune as a railway magnate, she was the mother of a large brood and something of a recluse. Her passion was music—she was a good pianist —and she gathered musicians about her (one was the young Claude Debussy [1547]) to join her in performance. When she applied to the conservatory for a violinist, Rubinstein sent Josef Kotek, a sometime pupil of Tchaikovsky's and a devoted admirer of

his music. Mme. von Meck seized the opportunity, being herself a like aficionado, and, with Kotek as go-between, offered the composer a handsome sum to make violin-piano arrangements for her. So began that extraordinary relationship, conducted by mutual agreement entirely through letters in which the two virtually bared their souls to each other for fourteen years. (They never formally met, and their only chance encounter, when they were independently strolling in the woods, reduced both to incoherent embarrassment.) Having for a time plied him with lavish commissions, mostly for potboilers, she eventually, in 1878, settled on him an annuity that enabled him to give up his employment and live independently.

Tchaikovsky's resolve to marry found a sudden and unexpected fulfillment. In the spring of 1877 he was left feeling particularly lonely by the marriage of Vladimir Shilovsky, with whom he had spent much time in the preceding several years. Shortly afterward he plunged into work on a fourth symphony and, when he felt he had that in control, on a new opera—this one based on Pushkin's verse novel, *Eugene Onegin*, which he felt properly expressed the love theme he wanted to deal with. In the midst of this activity (in May) he received a passionate letter from a certain Antonina Ivanovna Milyukova, age twenty-eight, who claimed that they had met at the conservatory and that she had loved him ever since. (She had indeed been briefly a conservatory student and had made a singularly bad impression on her teachers.) Subsequent hysterical threats of suicide panicked the composer, who did the gentlemanly thing and called on the woman to explain that he was flattered but could not take her kind offer of marriage. However, the pressure increased, not only from her but from his aged father. Finally, warning her that he might not prove the ideal husband, he talked himself into the fatal step on moral and romantic grounds. There was a private ceremony on July 18. (Three days before he had broken the news to Mme. von Meck, assuring her that his would be a loveless marriage; he wrote it to Shilovsky on his wedding day.) The bride and the terrified bridegroom then set out for St. Petersburg. His fears and loathing were somewhat allayed when Antonina assured him she would make no demands on him. But he soon found her—flighty, emptyheaded, and unmusical—an incompatible companion as well. He used all sorts of ruses to avoid being alone with her, but two months later (September 23) he arrived in the apartment she had set up for them in Moscow. After about a week he decided to end it all and waded out, up to his waist in the Moscow River, hoping thereby to contract fatal pneumonia. Failing to develop even the sniffles, he had his brother Anatoly wire Antonina that he had been suddenly called back by Nápravník to the capital. There he collapsed. Nikolai Rubinstein and Anatoly went to the bride, and the former explained in words of one syllable that her husband would not be back. Having convinced her, they persuaded her to go to Odessa at their expense.

Tchaikovsky was not only a shattered man: he and his family feared that he would be, in the aftermath, stripped naked before his countrymen. Within the week Anatoly had accompanied him to Switzerland, where they paused for a time at Clarens near Montreux. In such bracing surroundings the composer was able to return to work on his symphony and his opera. It was at this point that Mme. von Meck, jubilant over the turn of events, dispelled another cloud by making him financially independent. He found himself humming "No more lessons, no more books, no more students' dirty looks." There followed a journey to Paris and then to Italy, Anatoly at last going home from there. Tchaikovsky found himself quite disinclined to represent Russian music at the 1878 Paris Exposition (the ostensible purpose of his junket) and eventually came to rest at San Remo with brother Modest and the latter's charge, a deaf-mute boy named Kolya. There he completed the symphony in January and the opera a month later, before the *ménage* set out for further wanderings in Italy. On March 9 it settled in Clarens, where Tchaikovsky went to work on a concerto for Kotek, whom he summoned to oversee it. He finished it before the month was out. (The symphony, dedicated "to my best friend" [i.e., Mme. von Meck] with a privately communicated quasi-autobiographical program, had been premiered by Rubinstein a month earlier and had not gone over well, even with its composer's admirers.)

The concerto out of the way, Tchaikovsky returned to Russia and to several years of trying to wring a divorce from the eccentric Antonina that sapped his strength and his creative powers and turned him back to the bottle. He no longer felt able to wear his emotions on his musical sleeve, and some of the immediate products of the new era were such impersonal pieces as the second piano sonata, the *Liturgy of St. John Chrysostom,* both of 1878, the first of the 4 orchestral suites (stand-ins for symphonies over the next nine years), and the 1879 *Maid of Orleans,* perhaps the least interesting of the mature operas. (Its title is sometimes incorrectly translated as *Joan of Arc.*) In the end the concerto was, rather surprisingly, dedicated to Leopold Auer, who, to Tchaikovsky's disappointment and outrage, canceled the 1879 premiere for reasons of his own. (It was finally performed by Adolf Brodsky and the Vienna Philharmonic under Hans Richter in 1881.) As for *Onegin,* the composer, feeling it too intimate for the big houses, held out for a performance at the Moscow Conservatory. This materialized, with expectable amateurishness in March 1879, but the critics liked the work and it went on to become one of the most popular of Russian operas. (Tchaikovsky had resigned from his teaching post the previous autumn.)

Antonina rejected a settlement of 10,000 rubles (made secretly available by Nadezhda). Tchaikovsky even offered to play the role of adulterer, which only produced further vacillation. Finally in 1881 it was discovered that the poor woman had borne a child, making a divorce a fairly simple matter. But until 1884 Tchaikovsky felt himself pursued by the furies. When he was in Russia, he avoided the cities where he was known, and he spent most of his time abroad, even absenting himself from the premieres of some of his works. His fears that he was viewed as a loathsome monster were largely groundless: he had become with the public a respected and even a popular composer. So great was the applause at the first performance of *The Maid of Orleans* that he left the theater (and the country) under the illusion that he had achieved a great success —and was stunned when he read the reviews and had them corroborated by his friends. Indeed the music of this period was with some justice not generally highly regarded. Even the violin concerto met with a hostile reception at its Vienna premiere later that year, 1881, though it was a success back home.

In March, while in Nice, Tchaikovsky was dismayed to be told of the grave illness and subsequent death of Nikolai Rubinstein in Paris. He went there for the funeral and saw the body off on the train. Shortly afterward he himself returned to Russia, where he began a new opera, *Mazeppa*. He interrupted it in Rome in the autumn to write, as a memorial to Rubinstein, a piano trio—curious, in that he had turned down a commission for such a work from Mme. von Meck on the grounds that the instruments were acoustically incompatible. It is regarded by some as his best work of this period—which, considering how rarely it is heard, tells one something about the period. The following March Taneyev and Anton Rubinstein premiered the second piano concerto, which had been awaiting the event since 1880. The consensus was that it was much too long for its rather unexciting contents, and it is now usually played in an abridgment by Alexander Siloti. The *Festival Overture 1812*, commemorating Napoleon's Russian defeat, was performed in August after a similar delay. (One critic termed it "much ado about nothing.")

Save for the harmonizations of liturgical pieces for the *Vesper Service*, some songs and piano pieces, and the editing of the sacred works of Bortniansky [976], Tchaikovsky was occupied by *Mazeppa* and the second and third orchestral suites over the next two years. Thanks to the interest of the new czar, Alexander III (Alexander II had been assassinated in 1881), the opera won productions by the imperial operas of both St. Petersburg and Moscow (February 1884). The composer paused long enough to attend the latter and immediately went back to the West, to the considerable surprise of his emperor, who summoned him back to bestow on him the Order of St. Vladimir.

In this gesture, and in his election to the presidency of the Russian Musical Society in Moscow, Tchaikovsky read his redemption and soon afterward acquired a home of his own in a Moscow suburb. In 1882 a rehabilitated Balakirev had surfaced again, this time with an outline of a four-movement symphony on Byron's closet drama *Manfred,* which Tchaikovsky duly produced; it was voted the best new work of the season when it was performed in 1886. Despite the fact that his last two operas had been dismissed as failures—in fact only *Eugen Onegin,* of all his operatic attempts, had taken a firm hold on the stage, and that not without some initial struggle—hope apparently sprang eternal, and he not only reworked *Vakula* (as noted previously) but also began a completely new work, *The Enchantress,* based on a Russian quasi-historical play by Ippolit Shpazhinsky, who turned it into a libretto. The composer was by now sufficiently sure of himself to undertake the conducting of both premieres, in January (Moscow) and in November (St. Petersburg) 1887, respectively. If the first was tepidly received, the second, much to the composer's dismay, was virtually a total loss, though once again he was misled by the enthusiasm of the initial audience. Three weeks later he conducted an all-Tchaikovsky concert in Moscow, which included the premiere of his fourth and last orchestral suite, *Mozartiana,* consisting of free transcriptions of Mozart's [992] works. (Tchaikovsky adored Mozart all his life but had a dim understanding of his music.)

In mid-December the composer began a European tour as a conductor, beginning in Germany. In Leipzig he met Brahms [1329] and found to his own surprise that he liked the man almost as much as he disliked his music. He was even more taken with Grieg [1410]. At the New Year he learned that the czar had granted him a lifetime pension of 3,000 rubles a year. The concerts in Germany were successful, those in Prague even more so. In between Tchaikovsky heard for the first time works by Richard Strauss [1563] (which he described as "empty rhetoric!") and Busoni [1577] (which he termed "promising"), and saw a performance of the new *Otello* by Verdi [1232] ("no comment!"). But in Paris, where his musical heart was, he was triumphant—though the reviewers thought his compositions "too German." The trip ended with a brief, but again propitious, stand in London.

Returning to Russia in the spring of 1888, Tchaikovsky moved into a new house and began work on a new symphony—the fifth (and his first true symphony in a decade). While an American promoter dangled an offer of $25,000 for a tour of the United States, the work went quickly forward and was finished in August. It overlapped the fantasy overture on *Hamlet,* which was completed three months later. The composer directed the first performance of the symphony in mid-November and unveiled the overture a week later (St. Petersburg). Both works won the hearty approval of his friends and the audiences, though the reviewers caviled again. A month later Tchaikovsky had convinced himself the symphony was a jackleg work and deserving of failure.

The next year, largely devoted creatively to the ballet *The Sleeping Beauty,* was a repeat of the one before: it began in Germany with a conducting tour that terminated in London in April. The rest of it was spent in composing and in administrative and conducting chores with the Russian Music Society in Moscow. The ballet, of which he thought highly, was finished in September, but at the January gala dress rehearsal the czar could say only that it was "very nice," again throwing Tchaikovsky into a fit of depression. He almost immediately went abroad, and after some small vacillation settled in Florence to compose a new opera on Pushkin's *The Queen of Spades (Piquedame),* commissioned by the tenor Nikolai Figner (to whom Tchaikovsky was much attracted) and his wife, the Italian soprano Medea Mei. It was finished in June and was immediately followed by his last chamber work, the string sextet *Souvenir de Florence.* On the way home he stopped by Tbilisi (Tiflis in Russian) Georgia, where he had spent some time in each of the immediately previous years, to visit Anatoly. There he wrote his last symphonic poem, *The Voyevode* (which has nothing at all to do with the earlier opera). During this time Mme. von Meck abruptly broke off relations, with a flimsy story about being bankrupt. Tchaikovsky saw through it and was of course deeply hurt, but things might have been worse for by then he was financially well off. (The woman was in fact in poor health and died a little over three years later.)

The opera was first offered in St. Petersburg in mid-December 1890 and was performed in Kiev a few nights later. It was an unquestionable triumph with the audiences, but the critics were more than usually harsh, and the composer convinced himself that the czar had hated it. However, contrary word from the palace and a commission from the Imperial Opera for a new opera and a new ballet helped to ease his mind. Before starting on the new tasks, he cobbled up some incidental music for a February production of *Hamlet*, mostly reworked from earlier stuff and little to his taste. He was about to accept at last the American proposal, but a problem with the nerves in his right hand forced him temporarily to give up all conducting engagements. This affliction may have been indicative of a more general emotional problem indicated by growing depression. Nevertheless in April he began his journey. While he was en route to Le Havre, his brother Modest, then in Paris, had word that their sister Sasha had died after a long illness. He intercepted Piotr Ilyich but on seeing his state of mind could not bring himself to tell him the news and returned to Russia. Instead of proceeding to his destination, Tchaikovsky went to Paris, where he encountered the obituary in a Russian newspaper. As if this were not enough, on the voyage one of the passengers threw himself overboard and was lost, and the trip across was largely a stormy one, meteorologically speaking. Tchaikovsky was in a terrible state of apprehension and homesickness when he got to New York on the twenty-seventh and, though he was grateful for the kindness of his hosts, spent much of his time in lonely fits of tears. He was wined and dined at Delmonico's, introduced to such people as Walter Damrosch [1540], Andrew Carnegie, and Gustav Schirmer, opened the new Carnegie Hall, was taken to see all the mandatory sights (including Niagara Falls), concertized in Baltimore and Washington, and was inundated with requests for his autograph. He was surprised on the eve of his fifty-first birthday when a newspaper piece

reported him to be in his sixties: he in fact looked it. The homeward voyage at the end of May was as unpleasant as its counterpart had been.

Back in Russia, Tchaikovsky settled down to complete the ballet begun in February. Based on the elder Alexandre Dumas' recension of the tale "The Nutcracker" by E. T. A. Hoffmann [1086], it was choreographed by Marius Petipa, who specified in exact times how much music of what kind he needed for each number. Despite such restraints the composer succeeded in producing one of his most popular scores, though not one of his greatest. Concurrently he worked on the one-act opera *Iolanta*, which he finished in December, and orchestrated *The Voyevoda*. This proved such a disaster when it was played in November that he tore up the complete score, though Siloti salvaged the parts for posterity.

At the end of December Tchaikovsky set forth on another conducting tour. He led a performance of *Eugen Onegin* in Hamburg, where *Tannhäuser* under a young conductor named Gustav Mahler [1525] almost overcame his strong reservations about Wagner's music. But he soon became so depressed and homesick that he canceled the trip and returned to Russia, where he arranged a suite from the new ballet and began a new symphony (listed as the seventh and eventually realized by Semyon Bogatiryev). In May he settled in a new house in the village of Klin. That summer he went to Vichy for a cure of a stomach ailment and hated the place as much as he had during a stay there years before. On December 17 the new works, in tandem, were performed in St. Petersburg. (Tchaikovsky had offered his young admirer Sergei Rachmaninoff [1638] the premiere of his *Aleko* with *Iolanta*, but that proved infeasible.) Despite the presence of the Figners in the opera and an all-out production of the ballet, enthusiasm did not run high. About the same time he gave up on the symphony and began turning the materials into a third piano concerto. On the brighter side he was elected a corresponding member of the French Academy and heard unexpectedly from his beloved old governess Fanny Dürbach, whom he had long supposed dead. He hurried to Switzerland to visit her.

Otherwise the new year was marked by illness (violent headaches) and fits of uncontrollable weeping. In mid-February he was suddenly and strongly inspired to write yet another symphony (the sixth) on a vague program having to do with life, death, love, and frustration. His work was interrupted in May when he went to Cambridge, England, to accept an honorary doctorate together with Bruch [1358], Boito [1393], and Saint-Saëns [1343]. The symphony received its premiere on October 28. It was not well received (people thought it too gloomy), but this time the composer remained convinced that it was one of his finest efforts.

On November 2 Tchaikovsky, according to Modest, complained of an upset stomach. When he grew worse, a physician was called who diagnosed the ailment as cholera acquired from drinking a glass of polluted water. Four days later the composer was dead.

So goes the official account of his death. But eighty-five years later Alexandra Orlova, a Soviet musicologist who had emigrated to the United States and who had worked at the Tchaikovsky Museum at the house in Klin, revealed that she had learned from Alexander Voytov, a 1914 graduate of Tchaikovsky's own School of Jurisprudence, that matters had been quite otherwise. It had long been rumored that the composer had poisoned himself. In 1913 the widow of Nikolai Jakoby, a classmate of Tchaikovsky's who in 1893 had been a high official in the legal wing of the government, had told Voytov that her husband had been entrusted with an official complaint to the czar that Tchaikovsky was involved in a liaison with the nephew of a Russian duke. Fearing that the revelation would reflect badly on the school, Jakoby set up a kangaroo court of prominent alumni, summoned the presumed malefactor, and ordered him to remove himself from the scene or else. Mrs. Orlova has offered a considerable body of substantiating evidence, which many prominent scholars have accepted. But others have not, and at the moment the matter of Tchaikovsky's death is still the subject of violent controversy. (The Soviet composer Boris Tchaikovsky [1925–] is apparently not a descendant.)

RECORDINGS: Considering Tchaikovsky's enormous popularity over the past eighty years, it should surprise no one that his music has received commensurate attention from the record makers. There have been systematic recordings of the piano music, songs, chamber music, symphonies, orchestral works, and ballets. Even all the surviving operas, thanks to the assiduity of the Soviets, have been made available save (perhaps—who can be sure?) the "reconstructed" *Voyevoda* and *Vakula* in its original form. Yet there remain gaps. The *Hamlet* incidental music, the early version of *Romeo and Juliet,* and the *Serenade* for Rubinstein's name day have only recently appeared, and the choral music (some of it admittedly occasional) remains rather neglected. (It might be noted that the Figners made records—she even left a few remarkable microphoned pieces—but apparently not from the Tchaikovskian roles they created.)

[1378] STAINER, (Sir) John
ORGANIST, EDUCATOR, WRITER, MUSICOLOGIST
BORN: London, June 6, 1840
DIED: Verona, March 31, 1901

Although his music was mostly in the watered-down Mendelssohnian [1200] vein that passed for pious in Victorian England (and he knew it!), Stainer was a gifted and influential musician during the early stirrings of English musical reform. The son of a London schoolmaster, he was taught to play the organ and to sight-read by his father. (The latter attainment may have been more difficult for him than for most, since he had lost his left eye to a childhood accident.). At eight he became a chorister at St. Paul's and eventually rose to solo rank. Six years later he was appointed organist and choirmaster at the church of St. Benedict and St. Peter on the waterfront, and afterward also served as substitute organist at the cathedral. In 1856 he became first chapel organist at the new St. Michael's College at Tenbury in Worcestershire. After three years he matriculated at Christ Church College, Oxford (he was still just nineteen), was appointed organist of Magdalen and took his B.Mus. in 1860, became university organist a year later, and acquired three more degrees by 1866, in which year he debuted as founder-conductor of the Oxford Philharmonic Society. In 1872 he returned to St. Paul's as successor to Sir John Goss, organist there since 1838, and was instrumental in upgrading the cathedral's music to a professional level. He remained there until 1888 (the year of his knighting), when impaired vision in his good eye forced his resignation.

Stainer was also an important figure in the history of English musical education. He held various overseer positions at the three major universities (Cambridge, Oxford, and London), succeeded Sullivan [1397] in 1881 as principal of the National Training School, and Hullah [1223] in 1882 as inspector of elementary school music. In 1889 he was appointed professor of music at Oxford. He was one of the first important English musicologists: among his several books is a seminal one on *Dufay and His Contemporaries,* and with his daughter Eliza Cecilia and his son John he brought out in 1901 an edition of mediaeval English music in the Bodleian Library. He died at sixty while on a tour of Italy. His music—all sacred—which he deplored in later life, was immensely popular in English and American churches, and some of it is still in use today.

RECORDINGS: His Easter oratorio *The Crucifixion* is commonly performed, and there are several recordings of it.

[1379] SVENDSEN, Johan Severin
(Svent'-sen, Yō'-hån Se'-ve-rin)
VIOLINIST, CONDUCTOR
BORN: Christiania (i.e., Oslo), September 30, 1840
DIED: Copenhagen, June 14, 1911

Next to Grieg [1410], his friend Svendsen was the most important composer to emerge from the musical ferment in nineteenth-century Norway. The two were quite different in their music; Svendsen was the more conservative (but no imitator), the less nationalistic, and did his most important work in the orchestral medium. His father was a bandmaster in the Swedish Army (Sweden still being in charge in Norway), and, with his help, the boy learned to play several instruments. By the age of nine he was picking up dance jobs and was writing music for them by the time he was eleven. Later he did a hitch in the army, during which he became solo clarinet in a band. Afterward he returned to the violin, his instrument of choice, and played in Ibsen's Norwegian Theater, in a dance studio, and in a symphonic concert series. Around 1860 he began to do some conducting; then in 1862 he started out on an unstructured concert tour through northern Europe. Finding himself stone-broke in Lübeck, he went to the local consul to try to borrow enough to pay his way home. The consul became interested in his plight and got him instead a royal fellowship to study at the Leipzig Conservatory. He went there in 1863 to study violin with Ferdinand David, but having developed a chronic neuritic condition in his fingering hand, concentrated on composition with Reinecke [1292] and others. Before he left in 1867, he had completed his first five opuses, including the first symphony and the string octet, which latter work won him a first prize and a contract with the publishing house of Breitkopf and Härtel.

Back home that year he gave an all-Svendsen concert that included the symphony, but the audience sat on its hands. Discouraged, he resumed his roaming, winding up in Paris in 1868, where he supported himself as a free-lance orchestral musician. He performed some of his own works in concert, wrote music for Sara Bernhardt's production of Coppée's *Le Passant (The Passer-By)* and a violin concerto, and fell in love with an American girl named Sarah Levett. But the outbreak of war in 1870 caught him in Weimar and sent her home. Svendsen went on to Leipzig, where he was slated to conduct the Euterpe concerts but found they had been canceled. After performing his symphony with the Gewandhaus Orchestra (the Leipzigers were enthusiastic), he took ship for America to retrieve his girl, whom he married in New York in 1871. They returned to Leipzig, where Svendsen got to conduct the promised series finally. The next year he played the Beethoven [1063] ninth symphony under Wagner's [1230] direction during the cornerstone-laying ceremonies for the Bayreuth Festspielhaus. Around this time, Sarah Svendsen, a Jew, decided to convert, and the Wagners, always happy to save a Jewish soul, stood godparents to her.

That fall the Svendsens settled in Christiania, where he became joint conductor with Grieg in the concerts of the Music Society and established himself as a teacher. In 1874 Grieg resigned, and the Parliament voted Svendsen a lifetime annuity. But in 1877 he took to the road again, visiting Leipzig and Munich, wintering in Rome, and going on to London and finally, thanks to the offer of his residence from Sarasate [1415] to Paris, where he was happy from 1878 to 1880, when he returned to Norway. Guest-conducting engagements took him to Stockholm and then to Copenhagen, where, despite opposition from some of the native musicians, he became *Kapellmeister* at the Royal Opera in 1883. From then on, until his health would no longer permit it, he devoted himself to conducting and administration, and composed only the occasional works his post demanded. His marriage eventually went on the rocks, and in 1901 he married a dancer named Juliette Vilhelmine Haase. He retired seven years later and lived out his life in Denmark. A devout patriot to the end, despite his disenchantment with the cultural level in Norway, he retained his citizenship, even at the cost of a Danish pension; but the Norwegians generously reinstated his annuity. His major works include 2 symphonies, a violin concerto, a cello concerto, 4 Norwegian rhapsodies, several tone poems, a string quartet, quintet, and octet, and some festival cantatas.

RECORDINGS: Some of the Svendsen orchestral works once circulated here on the old Mercury label; more recently a government-sponsored series from Norway has covered most of the significant orchestral and chamber works.

[1380] GOETZ, Hermann Gustav (Götz, Här'-mån Gōōs'-tàf)
ORGANIST, PIANIST, CONDUCTOR
BORN: Königsberg (now Kaliningrad), December 7, 1840
DIED: Hottingen, December 3, 1876

Goetz did not live long enough to develop the remarkable promise shown by his few mature works. Intended for the ministry, he seems to have had no musical training to speak of in childhood. He took up piano study in 1857 with the noted pedagogue Louis Köhler. A year later he entered the local university to major in mathematics and science, but he became increasingly involved with music both as performer and conductor, and, after two years, he transferred to the Stern Conservatory in Berlin, determined to make a career of it. There his piano teacher was Bülow [1310], who took a shine to him and touted him to the Weimar crowd. He also studied conducting with the school's founder and director, Julius Stern, and composition with Hugo Ulrich. In 1863, Goetz seized the opportunity to succeed Theodor Kirchner [1290] as organist and choirmaster of the Municipal Church in Winterthur, Switzerland, in the hope that the Alpine air might alleviate the tuberculosis from which he had been suffering for a decade. Whatever the air might have done was probably negated by Goetz's workaholic tendencies, for he voluntarily added to his church duties piano concerts, theater and festival conducting, and the operation of a choral society. In 1865 Brahms [1329] paid him a visit; at first put off by Goetz's egoism, he soon became his fast friend. After much soul searching, considering the precarious nature of his health, Goetz married a local girl, Laura Wirth, in 1868. A year later they moved to Zürich, and in 1870 they settled in suburban Hottingen; however, he continued to return to his duties in Winterthur until 1872, when he was too weak to keep it up. To stay busy, however, he wrote reviews for the Zürich papers. In 1874 Ernst Frank, later executor of Goetz's musical estate and then court music director at Mannheim, produced Goetz's opera *Der Widerspenstigen Zähmung (The Taming of the Shrew),* his masterpiece. It was taken up by opera houses all over the world, and its present-day neglect is incomprehensible. Goetz was two acts into a successor, *Francesca da Rimini,* when death caught up with him four days before his thirty-sixth birthday; Frank

completed and produced the work. Among other major mature works, Goetz left a symphony, a piano concerto, a violin concerto, an overture, a trio, quartet, and quintet (all with piano), as well as choral works and piano pieces. (Frau Goetz, for whatever reason, burned another earlier symphony.)

RECORDINGS: The symphony and overture have been recorded by Edouard van Remoortel, the piano concerto by both Michael Ponti and Paul Baumgartner, the piano pieces by Adrian Ruiz, the chamber works by a group centered around pianist Gerald Robbins, and *The Taming of the Shrew* appears in a recording from wartime German radio tapes.

[1381] HORNEMAN, Christian Frederik Emil (Hôr'-ne-mån, Krēst'-yån Fred'-er-ik Ā'-mil)
CONDUCTOR, TEACHER, PUBLISHER
BORN: Copenhagen, December 17, 1840
DIED: Copenhagen, June 8, 1906

C. F. E. Horneman's father and first teacher was Johan Ole Emil Horneman (1809–70), a composer who, first with one partner and then another, ran a music-publishing company from 1844 to 1859. In 1858 the younger Horneman began two years of study at the Leipzig Conservatory, where he studied with Moscheles [1146] and others, and met his younger Scandinavian contemporary Edvard Grieg [1410]. When he came back to Copenhagen in 1860, he opened his own publishing house, with his father in charge; it published some of Grieg's music as well as their own (much of it pseudonymous forays into the popular realm). Young Horneman, however, also produced more serious works under his own name. Having quarreled with Gade [1248] and Hartmann [1182], the standard bearers of Danish music, he founded the Euterpe Society with Grieg, to counter them with performances of modern music. Under its auspices in 1865, he conducted his *Aladdin* overture, his most popular work. The venture soon failed. In 1874 Horneman organized the Musikforeningen, with himself and Otto Malling as conductors, but his irascible nature made it necessary for him to be replaced in 1879. He then opened a conservatory which was successful and lasted until 1920. In 1888, to celebrate Christian IX's twenty-fifth year of reign, he added an opera to his overture; though it took some time to establish itself, *Aladdin* is now regarded by the Danes as a classic. The same year its composer was given a sinecure as professor of music with the University of Copenhagen. He also wrote incidental music and choral works. RECORDINGS: The Copenhagen String Quartet has recorded the Quartet in G Minor. His *Aladdin Overture* is performed on records by Johan Hye-Knudsen.

[1382] CHABRIER, Alexis-Emmanuel
(Shäb-rē-ā', Á-lek-sē' E-mà-el')
CIVIL SERVANT, CHORUS MASTER
BORN: Ambert, January 18, 1841
DIED: Paris, September 13, 1894

Frustrated at every turn of his musical career, regarded during most of it as a negligible amateur—a clown, even—Chabrier turns out to have been the spiritual ancestor of Satie [1578] and Les Six. At a time when French music was dominated by frivolity, sentimentality, and melodrama, Chabrier's music was displaying terseness, wit, energy, and insouciance—the very qualities we now think of as "Gallic." Yet if he was outwardly a clown, he was of the genus Pagliaccio, for inwardly he was both deeply sensitive and always longing, so to speak, to play Hamlet.

Born in the shadow of that abrupt volcanic monadnock, the Puy de Dôme, in the Auvergne, Emmanuel Chabrier was the son of a locally prominent and successful lawyer. In the course of his tutoring, he got lessons in sight-singing and piano from two refugee Spaniards, Manuel Zaporta and Mateo Pitarch, who had fled the Carlist Wars about the time of his birth. But he was slated for the law or a governmental career, and music was not then considered for him more than a mandatory frill, though he obviously had talent. At eleven he went to the Lycée Blaise Pascal in nearby Clermont-Ferrand, where his musical training continued under one Tarnowski, who insisted on his playing dance music—a training that influenced his own later compositions. After five years or so the Chabriers moved to Paris so that Emmanuel might obtain the best possible advanced education. He spent a year there in a Lycée and then took up the study of law at the university. Completing his course in 1861, he took a desk job at the Ministry of the Interior that was to eat up more than half of his remaining life. Meanwhile he continued to study music—piano with the Pole Édouard Wolff (adulator of Chopin [1208] and uncle of Wieniawski [1340]), counterpoint and composition with Théophile Semet (a Halévy [1157] pupil and the Opéra's percussionist) and Aristide Hignard who won the Prix de Rome in 1848 and had the bad luck to finish his *Hamlet* in the year that Ambroise Thomas [1217] finished his.)

In these early years in Paris, Chabrier found himself happiest with the artistic icon-oclasts—the burgeoning Impressionist painters and literary Symbolists. Two of his closest friends were Édouard Manet and the poet Paul Verlaine. Chabrier composed little in this period. We have a couple of piano pieces and some fragments—two vaudevilles for which Verlaine wrote the texts, and an opera about Janos Hunyadi (see Erkel's [1214] *Hunyadi László*). His musical friends were Gabriel Fauré [1424], Charles Lecocq [1322], and the Franckians—d'Indy [1462], Chausson [1484], and especially Duparc [1442]. In 1873 Chabrier married Marie Alice Dejean, by whom he had two children. Two years later he joined Saint-Saëns's [1343], Société National de Musique and began to compose more seriously. His first known orchestra works, *Lamento* and *Larghetto,* date from this time. In 1877 Chabrier was surprised and delighted to have his operetta *L'Étoile* produced at the Bouffes-Parisiens. But in 1879 a superior piece, *Une Éducation manquée,* got only a single, piano-accompanied performance at a small theater. The same year Duparc dragged him off to Munich to hear Wagner [1230] in his native habitat. Chabrier was never the same again. Though he, tongue in cheek, wrote a set of quadrilles on tunes from *Tristan,* he returned to his office (from which he had neglected to get leave) only to tender his resignation. His family might starve, but he was going to be a musician—a French Wagnerian. In 1881 the firm of Enoch brought out his *10 Pièces pittoresques* for piano, and Charles Lamoureux, the conductor and founder of the Concerts Lamoureux, hired him as secretary and choral director. A junket to Spain produced the rhapsody *España,* which Lamoureux played in 1883 and had to repeat. This, the double handful of songs, the subsequent piano pieces, and the *Joyeuse marche,* contain the essential Chabrier. But a cantata, *La Sulamite,* produced unsuccessfully in 1884, was full of pseudo-Wagnerian heavings. Lamoureux's production of *Tristan* early the next year increased Chabrier's illusion that this was his cup of tea. He occupied much of his time with his "Wagnerian" opera *Gwendoline,* which won a Brussels production in 1886 and, predictably, had some success in Germany. His finest and most typical stage work, *Le Roi malgré lui,* was a success at the Opéra-Comique in 1887, but two nights after the premiere the house burned down, effectively terminating its run. There was little else. The cantata *Ode à la musique* appeared in 1890, and Chabrier began work on another big opera, *Briséis.* It remains only a fragment. In early 1892 Chabrier began to show symptoms of paresis, and his decline was precipitous. He attended the Paris premiere of *Gwendoline* at the Opéra in 1893 but did not recognize the music or understand the applause. He was dead less than a year later, at fifty-three.

RECORDINGS: There are recorded surveys of the piano music (Rena Kyriakou-Walter Klien, Pierre Barbizet-Jean Hubeau, and Annie d'Arco. Many recordings also exist of *España,* the *Joyeuse marche,* and the orchestral suite from the piano pieces. A complete set of songs has been recorded by baritone Bruno Laplante and pianist Janine Lachance. Mason Jones recorded the *Larghetto* for horn and orchestra, and Jean Fournet the *Ode.* There are excerpts from the operas and three complete operas: *Une Education manquée* (Charles Bruck conducting), *L'Étoile* (John Eliot Gardiner), and *Le Roi malgré lui* (Charles Dutoit).

[1383] NESSLER, Victor Ernst (Nes'-ler, Vēk'-tôr Ârnst)

CONDUCTOR

BORN: Baldenheim, January 28, 1841
DIED: Strasbourg, May 28, 1890

A native of French Alsace, Victor Nessler died there (at forty-nine) after it had become German. Initially intending to enter the ministry, he was thrown off that straight track by the success of an opera *Fleurette* in Strasbourg in 1864. He moved to Leipzig, where he worked as a choral conductor and wrote several more operas, with no conspicuous success. In 1870 he was appointed chorusmaster at the Stadttheater, and in 1879, conductor at the Caroltheater. There in the same year his *Der Rattenfänger von Hamelin (The Pied Piper of Hamelin)* was a hit and was carried to other theaters on a wave of German nationalism. In 1884 he had a greater and more lasting success with a setting of Viktor Scheffler's already popular *chante-fable* of German student life, *Der Trompeter von Säckingen.* It became almost talismanic in pre-War Germany, and the echoes of its sentimental but catchy tunes have not yet faded. RECORDINGS: The chief baritone aria has been repeatedly recorded by German lyric baritones; there is at least one, more extensive recording of excerpts featuring Hermann Prey.

[1384] PEDRELL, Felipe (Pä*th*'-rel, Fä-lē'-pä)

CONDUCTOR, MUSICOLOGIST, TEACHER

BORN: Tortosa, February 19, 1841
DIED: Barcelona, August 19, 1922

However much such composers as Albéniz **[1523]**, Falla **[1688]**, and Granados **[1588]** may have been responsible for Spain's twentieth-century musical renaissance, the impetus behind them was their teacher, the Catalan Felipe Pedrell. His only formal musical training seems to have been what he got as a choirboy in Tortosa Cathedral. Nevertheless by the time he had attained his thirty-fourth birthday, he was second in command of a light opera company in Barcelona, and had had two operas performed in that city. After a couple of years of travel in Italy and France and a flirtation with Madrid, he returned, discouraged, to Barcelona, and (apart from a couple of operettas, *Eda* and *Little Carmen,* written for a New York friend) he largely abandoned composition to devote himself to research, convinced that the hope of Spanish music lay in a knowledge of its history and its folklore. To that purpose, he founded and edited several journals, all of which came to a quick end for want of support. He also reviewed for a Barcelona newspaper. Toward the end of the decade, he returned to composition, reaching a climax in his nationalistic quasi-Wagnerian operatic trilogy *Los Pirineos (The Pyrenees),* eventually produced in 1902 in Barcelona. Meanwhile in 1894 he had moved to Madrid, where he was honored with professorships at the Conservatory and the Athenaeum and with election to the Academy, and where he devoted his energies to the musical life of the city. Eventually, however, embittered at the nonreception given his music, he returned to Barcelona, where he taught privately and published a number of important treatises and editions (e.g., the works of Victoria **[258]**). Besides operas and zarzuelas, he wrote works for orchestra, chorus, solo voice, and piano. RECORDINGS: One finds no significant representation on records, though the "Pedrelliana" movement of 1938 from Falla's *Homenajes* is built on Pedrell themes. There is also a recording of Roberto Gerhard's **[1926]** brief unnumbered symphony of 1941, *Homenaje a Pedrell.*

[1385] SGAMBATI, Giovanni (Sgàm-bä'-tē, Jō-vàn'-nē)

PIANIST, CONDUCTOR, TEACHER, CRITIC

BORN: Rome, May 28, 1841
DIED: Rome, December 14, 1914

Sgambati was an important force in opening Italy up to instrumental music, after the long total dominance of opera there. His father was a lawyer and a man of high culture. His mother was the daughter of an English sculptor, Joseph Gott, who had taken up residence in Rome. Young Giovanni let it be known by the time he was five that he was going to be a musician. He studied with one Amerigo Barbieri, and at seven he was giving salon performances at the piano, singing in a church choir, and "conducting little orchestras"—whatever that signifies. While all this heady activity was going on, the senior Signor Sgambati died. The mother remarried and moved to Trevi, where salons and little orchestras must have been few. Nevertheless he was able to continue his studies. When he was nineteen, Sgambati returned to Rome and began concertizing, playing both "ancient" and "modern" music, the like of which most Romans had never heard. He was instrumental in getting people together for chamber music. In 1862, the Abbé Liszt [1218], newly ensconced in his Roman monastery quarters, heard him in the Hummel [1091] Septet, and was so impressed that he took him on as a pupil on a twice-weekly basis. Shortly afterward, with Liszt's aid and encouragement, Sgambati organized an orchestra (a big one, this time), and began giving concerts (in a pioneering way) in the Sala Dante. Here he introduced Rome to German orchestral music, giving many Italian premiere performances, including some of major Beethoven [1063] works. In 1867 Sgambati broke another path when he inaugurated the Società Romana del Quartetto, to which he contributed his best-known works—2 piano quintets and a string quartet. In 1869 Liszt took him to Munich, where he became infatuated with the music of Wagner [1230], who later persuaded Schott to publish Sgambati's chamber music.

In 1839 Pope Gregory XIV had reconstituted the old Cecilian congregation as the Accademia di Santa Cecilia. Sgambati and his friend the violinist Ettore Pinelli were members, and after some years of effort got permission to give free classes in piano and violin at its headquarters. The experiment eventually became the famous conservatory or Liceo Musicale. In his later years, Sgambati became known all over Europe as a pianist and conductor. He declined the directorship of the Moscow Conservatory in 1881. In 1886 he succeeded Liszt as a member of the French Institut. His *Requiem* of 1896 was ordered to be performed at all future royal funerals in Italy (of which there have been few of late). He retired from public life in 1904.

Sgambati was not a prolific composer. Besides the works noted, he wrote symphonies and a few other orchestral pieces, a piano concerto, a motet, some admirable piano miniatures, and some songs.

RECORDINGS: The Concerto for Piano has been recorded by Jorge Bolet.

[1386] DVOŘÁK, Antonín Leopold
(Dvôr´-zhàk, Ȧn´-tō-nyēn Lā´-ō-pōlt)
VIOLINIST, CONDUCTOR
BORN: Mühlhausen (Nelahozeves), September 8, 1841
DIED: Prague, May 1, 1904

Together with Smetana [1291] and Janáček [1478], Dvořák is one of the most important composers to come out of what is now Czechoslovakia; yet it is difficult to say precisely wherein his importance lies. In a day of nationalism, he is the least nationalistic of the three; in maturity he spoke well the musical *lingua franca* which was the language of conservative Germans. But he did not materially affect or change it, and though he has an individual voice, it is not easy to say what characterizes it. Perhaps the closest term would be "sweetness": once he found himself, he spoke with a lyricism, something like that of the mature Schubert [1153], that was an expression of his own being. (Though he wore one of the world's fiercest beards, Dvořák was a kind and gentle man.) His other most telling musical attainment is his universality: he attempted every important genre of his time (save the ballet) and succeeded in all of them.

Dvořák's village birthplace lies less than twenty miles downriver from Prague. His grandparents were born peasants. His father František ran a shop that dispensed beer, meat (of his own butchering), and other comestible necessities, and in his spare time he played the fiddle and the zither. His mother was the daughter of an overseer for the local magnate, Prince Lobkowitz. Antonín was the first of fourteen children, none of the rest of them notably musical. During the celebration following his appearance, the family establishment caught fire, and he had to be moved across the street until the blaze was taken care of. From the age of seven he was taught by the local schoolmaster-organist Josef Spič (or Spitz) until he was sent in 1853 to live with relatives and study in Zloniče, a few miles westward. The point was that, as required by law, he should learn German; but his new master, Antonín Liehmann, who combined the usual dual functions of Czech schoolmasters, was so taken with his musicality that he concentrated on such things as violin, viola, keyboards, and harmony. A year later František Dvořák moved his family to Zloniče, persuaded that opportunities were greater there for his line of work. Dissatisfied with his son's progress, he promptly shipped him off to a German settlement now called Česka Kameniče, where he was permitted to deputize at the village organ and learned German perforce. The paternal venture having proved less advisable than advertised, however, Antonín was soon brought home to help tend the store. He was now able to contribute to the musical life of the village, and, bowing to the inevitable, the family scraped enough money together to send him, at sixteen, off to Prague to the Organ School. He lived again with relatives, picked up a serviceable but hardly forward-looking education at the school, and got some practical experience playing violin in an amateur orchestra run by the St. Cecilia Society, where he shared a stand with the future conductor Adolf Čech. He graduated after two years, took a free room at an aunt's, and joined the "pops" orchestra of Karel Komzák [1454] as a violist. The threat of military service was dispelled when he was rejected on medical grounds (nature unknown) in 1862. When the Provisional Theater, the forerunner of the National Theater, opened that same year, the Komzák orchestra initially did duty there, and Dvořák remained to play under Smetana until 1873. In 1864 he tried living independently with some other young men but soon went back to his relatives. Now eking out his income by teaching, he fell in love with a pupil, Josefa Čermáková, the disdainful adolescent daughter of a jeweller. Making no headway with her, he directed his affections toward her sister Anna, an opera singer of small attainments. Anna proved willing, but her parents did not.

It is probable that Dvořák had composed since childhood, but he was given to destroying works that did not satisfy him, and the first work of his that is known is a string quintet from his twentieth year, originally labeled Op. 1. It was followed by a quartet, and then, after a fallow period of nearly three years, a symphony in C minor (now designated as No. 1), which he called, for reasons that are not obvious, "The Bells of Zloniče." This was followed in quick order by another symphony (in B-flat, now known as No. 2) and a cello concerto (not the famous one but an early work for cello and piano, later orchestrated by other hands). By now Dvořák had acquired a mild case of Wagnerism [1230], and in 1870 he turned out a grand tragic opera, Alfred, dealing with Alfred the Great of England or an unreasonable facsimile thereof, which he seems not even to have tried to produce. It was followed in 1871 by a comedy, King and Collier, which went through a few rehearsals at the Provisional Theater before it was tabled. (He completely rewrote it three years later; despite an apparently successful premiere, it soon fizzled.) The first work that really called Dvořák's name to public attention was a patriotic cantata, Hymnus, sung by the Hlahol in 1873. That was the year that jeweller Čermák died, and, the widow having blessed the union and offered shelter to the couple, Dvořák and Anna were married that November.

At this point, Dvořák left the orchestra and became organist at St. Adalbert's Church. In March the Dvořáks moved into private quarters and Smetana conducted a symphony in E-flat (now known as No. 3), written the year before. The reviews were so disapproving the Dvořák withdrew the work, but he thought enough of it to submit it in competition for the Austrian State Prize. (The fourth symphony in D minor—originally unnumbered like its three predecessors—although written in 1874, had to wait eighteen years to be heard.) In the autumn Otakar Dvořák was born, and his father completed a second comic opera, The Pigheaded Peasants (disastrously premiered in 1881). The next year's opera, a tragedy called Vanda, earned its 1876 failure, however, on its own lack of merit. But the fifth symphony (in F, first published as "No. 3") showed Dvořák at thirty-four finally finding his own voice, and the prize committee, headed by Brahms [1329] and Eduard Hanslick, considered it worth 400 florins to its composer. (Afterward Brahms became a good friend.) Dvořák won the prize again the next year, and once more in 1877—the last time on the strength of the Moravian Duets (for soprano and alto), his first publication, partially financed by an admirer.

Dvořák was at last beginning to be noticed. The duets attracted attention, the Symphonic Variations were applauded in Prague in 1877, the comic opera The Peasant a Rogue early in 1878, though the Stabat Mater had to wait until 1880 for performance. But 1877 was also marked by personal tragedy, for it took away both the Dvořáks' children—Otakar and the year-old Růžena (another daughter had died at birth). Yet the composer's emotions, as usual, scarcely shadow the limpid surface of his music. Meanwhile Brahms had persuaded his publisher, Simrock of Berlin, to take on Dvořák. Simrock, having made a pile on the Brahms Hungarian Dances (for some of which Dvořák later provided orchestrations), persuaded his new client to write a set of Slavonic Dances, which shortly made his name a household word around the world (albeit not one always correctly spoken). Within two years Dvořák had signed a contract to let Simrock publish anything he might write in the future. Since he already had obligations to other publishers, this necessitated a considerable amount of back-dating and back-opussing of compositions, accounting in part at least for the dreadful confusion of Dvořák opus numbers.

With the birth of a third daughter, Otilie, in 1878, the Dvořáks began a new family, which eventually ran to six. Late that year the composer went to Vienna to meet Brahms at last (he had missed him on an earlier visit). It was Brahms who directed him to Joachim [1321], who inspired the violin concerto completed in 1880, the year in which Dvořák first summered in Vysoká, south of Prague. (His hostess was the Countess Kounicová, his first love and now his sister-in-law.) He was so taken with the area that a couple of years later he bought a tract and built a cottage on it where he could indulge his passion for raising pigeons. (Dvořák's other lifelong hobby was train watching.) In 1881 he wrote a new opera, *Dmitri* (about Boris Godunov's successor), for the new National Theater, which promptly burned down. The work was produced in another theater but did not have any real success. In the same year his former deskmate Adolf Čech premiered the sixth (in D major, originally known as the first) symphony.

The same symphony soon reached London, where Dvořák had already picked up an enthusiastic following—especially so for a man who had pulled himself up by his bootstraps. In 1884 he accepted an invitation to go to London and spent a glorious two weeks in the banquets and receptions the English traditionally reserved for foreign musicians. He came home with a contract from Novello for another symphony. He was back in England in September to conduct the sixth and the *Stabat Mater* at the Three Choirs Festival in Worcester, and again the following spring to deliver his manuscript (Symphony No. 7 in D minor, originally known as No. 2) to Novello, and to conduct his piano concerto and *Hymnus* in London. Other visits followed—to the Birmingham Festival in August in order to premiere the secular cantata *The Specter's Bride,* and the Leeds Festival (with his wife) in October 1886 to introduce the oratorio *St. Ludmila.* After that, he laid low for several years, rather tired out. He also turned out mostly small pieces of no great significance, though 1889 saw the premiere of his most successful opera to date, *The Jacobin* and the completion of the eighth symphony (in G, formerly regarded as No. 4). But early the next year the round of travels began

again when the Dvořáks spent a couple of weeks in Moscow with Tchaikovsky [1377], whom they had met in Prague in 1888. Then it was on to London to conduct the new symphony, which he had again contracted to Novello, ignoring Simrock's howls—doubtless on the grounds that that publisher had sufficiently profited at his expense. He was back in England the following June to receive an honorary doctorate from Cambridge, and yet again in the autumn to conduct the recently completed *Requiem* at the Birmingham Festival (which he had chosen to set rather than the suggested *Dream of Gerontius,* much to the later relief of Edward Elgar [1499]).

Two years previously the Prague Organ School and the Conservatory had merged, and at the beginning of 1891 Dvořák had, after at first demurring, accepted the professorship of composition there. Enter Jeanette Thurber, wife of a wealthy New York grocery wholesaler and patroness of the arts. After a disastrous attempt at opera-in-English, she had opened the National Conservatory of Music, headed by Jacques Bouhy, a fine voice teacher and Bizet's [1363] original Escamillo in *Carmen.* But homesickness overcame Bouhy in 1889 and, after mulling over the possibilities, Mrs. Thurber offered the post to Dvořák. Unable to ignore the $15,000 she was offering—a fortune in those days—Dvořák got leave, and on September 26, 1892, arrived with his family and the newly completed *Te Deum,* written in celebration of Columbus' arrival not quite 400 years before. The family found an apartment on East Seventeenth Street near the Conservatory. Dvořák taught composition students, struggled with the Conservatory orchestra, gave occasional concerts, and, early the next year, embarked on what was to be his ninth and last symphony, the so-called "From the New World" in E minor (old No. 5), whose purported native inspirations have been moot ever since. He considered going home for the summer but settled instead on Spillville, Iowa, a village of Czech immigrants about eighty miles northwest of Dubuque. The train ride thither must have been one of the high points in Dvořák's life! Before returning to New York he made a point of visiting the Columbian Exposition in Chicago and touring the American heartland. Back in the city he saw the new symphony through its first performance at the Philharmonic, attended the Metropolitan Opera, drank beer with conductor Anton Seidl, and struggled vainly with an operatic version of *Hiawatha* (his patroness' idea). The Dvořáks went home for the summer of 1894. The composer was by now reluctant to return to

America and did so only in November. He completed his second cello concerto and left for good in April. (He was succeeded at the Conservatory successively by Emil Pauer, Vassily Safonov, and, nominally, Engelbert Humperdinck [1480], who quit before he started; after that the school closed down.)

Dvořák, now in his mid-fifties, plunged back into an undiminished whirl of activity. He continued teaching composition at the Prague Conservatory, though he rejected the blandishments of Brahms to come teach at the Vienna Conservatory. He went to London in the spring of 1896, for what turned out to be his last visit there, to conduct the new cello concerto, and made several appearances. His government continued to ply him with honors—a lifetime seat in the upper house of the Parliament, the top professorial salary, membership in the commission that had once gotten him through three years of hardship. In 1901 he became director of the Conservatory, though the position was largely honorific. He continued to compose—the last two string quartets, the rather Wagnerian symphonic poems, and the best of his operas—the roistering *The Devil and Kate* and the haunting fairytale *Rusalka*, whose failure to win a place in the international repertoire is one of the great mysteries. The final opera, *Armida*, suffered from libretto trouble and a curious retrogression of style. But by then Dvořák was ailing from hardening arteries and resultant kidney damage. In fact, he collapsed during the premiere and had to go home to bed. He recovered but shortly afterward caught a severe cold while train watching and was confined to his bed for some weeks. On May Day, 1904, he was thought well enough to join the family at dinner. Halfway through, he became ill, was taken back to bed, and died of a stroke shortly afterward. Anna survived him by twenty-seven years, but his favorite child, Otilie, who had married his pupil, the composer Josef Suk [1651], followed her father a year later.

RECORDINGS: Thanks in part to Czech patriotism and in part to the insatiable LP appetite for novelty, Dvořák is well, but not exhaustively, represented on records. All 9 symphonies are now at least several times recorded. There is at least one version of each of the chamber works, the concerti and other concerted works, the symphonic poems, all but the very early overtures, and most of the minor orchestral pieces (a curious omission is the first of the 3 *Slavonic Rhapsodies*). Many of the choral works have been recorded, including *The Specter's Bride*, the *Stabat Mater*, the *Requiem*, and *The American Flag*. The solo piano pieces

have by now probably been accounted for, but there are minor gaps in the duets, songs, and part-songs. Of the operas only the last four—*The Jacobin, The Devil and Kate, Rusalka*, and *Armida*—have reached records in complete form (the last in a German radio-dubbing only). A disc of excerpts from *Dmitri* was recently released.

[1387] MATTEI, Tito (Mȧt-tä'-ē, Tē'-tō)
PIANIST, CONDUCTOR
BORN: Campobasso, May 24, 1841
DIED: London, March 30, 1914

Born near Naples, Mattei studied in that city with Thalberg [1220] and others. He became a prodigious pianist, was made an honorary professor of the Academy of St. Cecilia in Rome at eleven, was decorated by the Pope, and appointed court pianist to Victor Emmanuel II, first king of modern Italy. Apparently seeing no more possible conquests in Italy, he, like his contemporaries Denza [1426], Pinsuti [1307], and Tosti [1429], took the road to London. There he became an opera conductor, and wrote a number of forgettable operas, mostly to English-language libretti. RECORDINGS: He is remembered for some songs, notably *Non è ver'*, recorded by such as John McCormack and John Charles Thomas.

[1388] WEINZIERL, Max, Ritter von (Vīn'-zērl, Mȧks Rit'-târ fun)
CONDUCTOR
BORN: Bergstadtl, September 16, 1841
DIED: Mödling, July 10, 1898

Born in a Bohemian hamlet, Weinzierl became a theater conductor in Vienna and, in his latter years, the chorusmaster of the Männergesangverein. His 6 operas, written between 1879 and 1893, were produced in Vienna, Prague, and Berlin. He also wrote an oratorio *(Job)* and much other choral music. RECORDINGS: There are recordings of a song or two.

[1389] TAUSIG, Carl (Tou'-zikh, Kärl)
PIANIST, TEACHER
BORN: Warsaw, November 4, 1841
DIED: Leipzig, July 17, 1871

Carl Tausig, one of the most brilliant of the Liszt [1218] pupils, was the son and student of Bohemian-descended, Thalberg [1220]-trained, Aloys Tausig (1820–85), himself a fine pianist and keyboard composer. In 1855 he was brought to Weimar, where he played for Liszt and his chums. His approach combined Thalbergian "cool" with a personal explosiveness, and his performances knocked them all off their pins. Three years later, at seventeen, Tausig made his debut in Berlin at a concert conducted by Bülow [1310]. The opinion was that Tausig could indeed play but lacked discipline—which apparently also described other aspects of his life. Liszt sent him off to Zürich to meet Wagner [1230], who took him into his home, where Tausig behaved as if he owned the place. His thunderous practicing eventually got to Wagner, and he had to arrange for the young man to practice in off-hours at the local tavern. Tausig then moved to Dresden and concertized throughout Germany to mixed reviews. His attempt in Vienna in 1862 to educate "the Philistines" with demanding orchestral concerts failed, and for a time he seems to have floundered. During the Vienna period he became a friend of Brahms [1329] and was an assisting artist at his debut there. In 1864 Tausig married the pianist Sophie von Vrabely, who seems to have settled him down. They returned to Berlin in 1865, where Tausig's playing was now hailed without reservation. He set up a school for advanced pianists there and concertized virtually nonstop, all of which produced an erosive effect on his health. He interested himself in Wagner's Bayreuth project and suggested the subscription basis on which it was eventually financed. (Earlier he had generously backed Wagner at his lowest financial ebb—and heard the latter explain why champagne was essential to his welfare.) From the beginning of his concert career, Tausig had been composing virtuoso pieces that obviously owed something to his great teacher. He also made many brilliant transcriptions and published a book of functional studies. By 1870 he seems to have become dissatisfied with his composition. He published two concert etudes which he designated as Op. 1, intending to disown most of what came before. But there was no Op. 2, for he succumbed to typhoid at the age of twenty-nine. RECORDINGS: Michael Ponti has recorded an LP of Tausig pieces.

[1390] LAMMERS, Thorvald (Làm'-mers, Toor'-vàl)
SINGER, CONDUCTOR, TEACHER
BORN: 1841
DIED: 1922

The Norwegian Lammers (not to be confused with his older Leipzig contemporary Julius Lammers [1829–88]) was chiefly known as a singer and choir director. He

was sufficiently prominent to be awarded an annuity by the government. RECORDINGS: A few of his songs have been recorded (e.g., "Silver" by Carl Hague).

[1391] LANIER, Sidney Clopton
FLUTIST, WRITER, POET, TEACHER
BORN: Macon, Ga., Feburary 3, 1842
DIED: Lynn, N.C., September 7, 1881

It is not generally recalled that Lanier, one of the more considerable postwar poets to come out of what Mencken called "the Desert of Bozart," was also a fine musician. As a child, he developed proficiency on several instruments—keyboards, flute, violin, and guitar. In 1856 he entered Oglethorpe College, from which he graduated and where he taught until the Civil War broke out. He served in the Confederate forces for the entire time, and when he was mustered out in 1865, he was already suffering from tuberculosis. He directed a choir in Montgomery, Alabama, wrote a novel based on his experiences, and entered his father's law firm. Declining health forced him to seek a better climate in Texas in 1872, but he was unable to remain there. The year following he was appointed first flutist of the Peabody Concerts in Baltimore (performed by an orchestra connected with the Peabody Institute of Music and then directed by one Asger Hamerik). In 1876 he was commissioned to collaborate (as librettist) on the official *Centennial Cantata*, for which Dudley Buck [1367] wrote the music. His first book of poems was published in 1877, and in 1879 he was appointed as lecturer in English Literature at Johns Hopkins. In subsequent years he published studies of English prosody and the novel. He also wrote music criticism. In 1881, no longer able to work, he went to a camp in North Carolina, where he died a few months later. He left some works for flute, songs, and other small pieces. RECORDINGS: Some of the flute compositions have been recorded.

[1392] KLING, Henri Adrien Louis
(Kling, On-rē' À'-drē-àn Lōō-ē')
HORNIST, ORGANIST, CONDUCTOR, TEACHER
BORN: Paris, February 14, 1842
DIED: Geneva, May 2, 1918

Half-French, half-German, Henri Kling grew up in Karlsruhe and became a Swiss citizen. His father was a trombonist and contrabassist, who took his family back to Germany in 1844. There his wife died soon after. Henri, clearly musical from the start, became proficient on both violin and horn, and joined the grand duke's orchestra in Karlsruhe. But he had never been happy in that city, and in 1861 he emigrated to Geneva, where he was first horn of the symphony and at the Opera for many years. He also was a church organist, conductor of a military band and the casino orchestra, and a teacher of singing at the High School for Young Ladies. In 1866 he became professor of Solfege and Horn at the Conservatory, and functioned in these posts for over fifty years. His son Otto went to London, where he became head of the publishing firm of J. W. Chester. Kling wrote prolifically (hundreds of published works). The majority of his compositions were *Gebrauchsmusik,* but he had 4 operas produced in Geneva and turned out a symphony, a *David Livingstone Overture* (in which Henry Stanley's arrival is momentous), and other ambitious pieces— all long since forgotten. RECORDINGS: Pianist Raymond Lewenthal has rescued him from oblivion with a recording of his *Kitchen Symphony,* Op. 445, involving wine glasses, saucepans, bottles, funnels, and piano.

[1393] BOITO, Enrico ("Arrigo") (Bō-ē'-tō, Än-rē'-kō)
POET, LEGISLATOR, CIVIL SERVANT
BORN: Padua, February 24, 1842
DIED: Milan, June 10, 1918

Arrigo Boito's story is a familiar one in our time. Essentially it is that of a person of brilliant promise who paralyzes himself by too much thinking. Boito (or Boïto) was the younger son of Josephine Radolinska, a Polish noblewoman, and Silvestro Boito, a painter who specialized in miniatures. Silvestro found responsibility and domesticity unsuited to his free spirit and skedaddled when Enrico was still a child. We know little of the latter's childhood save that the family had no money and Silvestro had not heard about child support—and that Enrico showed good musical ability, which his mother did not discourage. In 1854 she took him to Milan and, by wringing the hearts of the authorities at her penury and sacrifice, got him into the Conservatory on scholarship and tolerance. His composition teacher was Alberto Mazzucato (1813–77), a violinist who a generation earlier had written such operas as *La Fidanzata di Lammermoor* and *Hernani.* (He quit when he saw that others did them better.) Boito found in Milan enough to satisfy his voracious appetite for knowledge. He read as though books were

going out of style and worked assiduously to remedy his defects. He mastered several languages. He wrote dance pieces and a symphony. He developed a lofty taste in literature—his touchstones were Shakespeare, Goethe, and Dante. He became Pythias to the Damon of Francesco Faccio, the future conductor, who was two years older than he. As young Italian patriots, they collaborated on two inspirational cantatas (texts by Boito) called *Il quattro giugno* ("June 4, 1859," celebrating the victory over the Austrians at Magenta) and *Le Sorelle d'Italia (Italy's sisters*—meaning Poland and Greece). The pair were eventually graduated with honors. Bucked up by success and letters of recommendation, they told the ministry of education in Turin that they should be tangibly encouraged in their art. They were, to the tune of 2,000 gold francs apiece, earmarked for their musical perfection, which they chose to seek in Paris. Now known as "Arrigo," Boito set out with his friend.

In Paris they met Berlioz [1175], were regular guests of the Rossinis [1143]—and the butt of some of the old man's wit—and were introduced to Verdi [1232] on his way to the London Exhibition of 1862, for which he was to supply a cantata. Finding Boito to be a poet, Verdi commissioned from him the text *Inno delle nazioni.* Later Boito alienated Verdi with some public scorn at the state of Italian opera and, it is said, with a polka arrangement of *"La Donna è mobile"* from his student days. Boito went on to Poland alone to visit relatives, then swung back through Germany, Belgium, and England, before going home.

Back in Italy, Boito identified himself with a young, ragtag, "intelleckshul," anti-Establishment set called *i scapigliati* (or roughly, "the bums"), given to general rowdiness and nose thumbing. Shortly after his return, he and another young poet, Emilio Praga, provoked a near-riot in Turin with their play *Le Madri galanti (The Sexy Mothers).* Two years later he and Faccio collaborated on a version of *Hamlet*—a figure with whom Boito has something in common. In 1866 they heard their country's call and joined Garibaldi against the Austrians. Their request that they not be separated was honored. They were assigned to a headquarters company and saw duty no more active than what standing guard required. The bohemian phase ended here.

In Paris Boito had conceived the notion of operas based on Nero and on Goethe's *Faust,* and had even begun the latter. What its relationship was to the *Mefistofele* premiered at La Scala on March 5, 1868, was, we don't know. The latter work, an attempt to deal with Goethe's whole vast masterpiece, shows German but not Wagnerian **[1230]**, influence and embodies Boito's overriding belief in the cosmic struggle between creative and destructive principles. The opera, whose prologue was applauded, dragged out for six hours and precipitated a fight between Boito's supporters and the antimoderns who spilled out into the square. The second performance was done on two consecutive evenings, and the work was then abandoned, by police order. The experience seems to have taken the heart out of Boito. Though he began work on *Nerone,* and revised *Mefistofele* drastically for a successful performance in Bologna in 1875, his career as a composer was effectively over. He continued to publish criticism and other writings—on which career he had embarked some years earlier—and busied himself with the concerts of the Quartet Society in Milan. In 1865 he had written a long poem, *Re Orso (King Bear),* that has drawn comparisons with Poe and Baudelaire. Ten years later he followed it up with a collected volume of verse. (This caused Benedetto Croce, years after, to call Boito the only Italian Romantic.) But this activity soon sputtered out. He wrote libretti (sometimes as "Tobia Gorrio"). *La Gioconda,* for Ponchielli **[1334]**, was a success. He wrote a few pages of music himself for *Ero e Leandro,* gave it to Giovanni Bottesini **[1278]**, whose setting was produced in 1879, and then to Luigi Mancinelli (1848–1921), who had somewhat more success in 1897. Cesare Dominiceti's (1821–88) *Iràm,* Constantino Palumbo's *Pier Luigi Farnese,* and Luigi San Germano's *Semir* never got a showing. *Basi e bote* did not even find a composer until nearly a decade after Boito's death. Boito was a real magician with words, and his libretti were usually far superior to the music set to them. Otherwise, now something of a dandy in dress and grooming, he began to settle into premature middle age.

Boito had had second thoughts about Verdi as an operatic composer, but Verdi, for the reasons noted and because he was skittish about "German" composers, avoided him. But others—notably their publisher Tito Ricordi and Faccio, now Italy's leading conductor—saw in their mutual understanding of Shakespeare the stuff of a happy marriage. In 1879 they connived to get Boito and the "retired" Verdi together and an iffy commitment to a Shakespearean opera by the latter. Three days later Boito produced, as if by magic, a scenario for *Otello.* But the course of true love never did run smooth. Though Boito revised the *Simon Boccanegra* libretto for Verdi in 1881, it was eight years

before the opera was finally born, after a near miscarriage and a hard labor. (Boito insisted on calling it *Iago,* after its denying spirit, and supposedly told his friends that he could do a better job with the music. Verdi, piqued when the news reached him, quit at one point.) In the end, of course, it was an enormous triumph, and Verdi gave Boito full credit as his artistic equal. (By now *Mefistofele* was established in the Italian repertoire.)

During the frenzy of the premiere, Boito, now nearly forty-five, encountered the actress Eleonora Duse, almost twenty years his junior, whom he had met a year or so earlier. This meeting, however, generated unexpected sparks. Boito made no move, but at 3 A.M. a few nights later Duse appeared at his window demanding to be let in. For two years—Boito was very discreet about it—a passionate affair ensued before she finally drifted away, eventually to become the mistress of Gabriele d'Annunzio (who translated Shakespeare for her use). Rejuvenated by love and success, it was Boito who bulldozed the aging Verdi into doing *Falstaff,* which they were also very discreet about until it was clear that the composer would live to finish it. It was the capstone of both their careers.

After Verdi's retirement, Boito puttered. He tinkered with *Nerone.* (It almost came to production once, but he got cold feet.) He wrote criticism. He conducted the *Mefistofele* prologue at Cambridge in 1893—apparently his only time on the podium since the work's initial presentation. He was awarded degrees and other honors. He was named chief inspector of conservatories for Italy in 1892 and was elected as a senator in 1912. In 1914 his health began to fail, and, having fiddled too long while Rome burned in Act IV, he abandoned *Nerone,* the fifth act unset. Felled by a chill in November 1917, he was found to be suffering from advanced heart disease and placed in a nursing home. He seemed on his way to recovery but suddenly died. Toscanini produced the truncated *Nerone* at La Scala in 1924, more than sixty years after Boito began it. Though it has its passionate defenders, it has never been successful.

RECORDINGS: *Mefistofele,* though uneven, is immensely theatrical and, in such terms, perhaps the best of the Faust operas. There have been several recordings. At least two piracies of *Nerone* have turned up, and the first commercial recording (a Hungarian production conducted by Eve Queler) was recently released. Claudio Scimone has recorded the juvenile symphony.

[1394] NEUPERT, Edmund

PIANIST, TEACHER
BORN: Christiania (Oslo), April 1, 1842
DIED: New York, June 22, 1888

Edmund Neupert studied with his father and with Theodor Kullak (1823–62) in Berlin. He taught at various conservatories in Berlin, Copenhagen, and Moscow before emigrating to New York in 1883. There, for the last five years of his life, he was a much sought-after teacher. He is best known for his etudes, but he wrote other piano pieces, songs, and so forth. RECORDINGS: Carl Hague recorded his song "Sing Me Home."

[1395] MILLÖCKER, Karl (Mil'-lök-er, Kärl)

FLUTIST, CONDUCTOR
BORN: Vienna, April 29, 1842
DIED: Baden (Austria), December 21, 1899

When Suppé [1262], the younger Johann Strauss [1295], Zeller [1399], and Millöcker all died within a few months of each other, the first and greatest age of German operetta ended. Millöcker has not exported well, and is largely unknown to non-German audiences. His father expected that he would follow him in the jewelry business, but his obvious musical talent led him to the Vienna Conservatory at thirteen, and a post as flutist in the Josephstadt Theater five years later. With the support of Suppé, he went to Graz in 1864 as theater conductor. During his year there he produced his first two operettas (Offenbachian [1264] trifles) and entered on the first of his two marriages. He returned to Vienna to a job that did not pan out at the Theater an der Wien, and then conducted at the Harmonietheater instead, until it folded. He then went to the German Theater in Pest in 1868, and the following year he returned to the Theater an der Wien, where he remained until bad health forced his retirement fifteen years later. His first real success there was Gräfin Dubarry (Countess Dubarry, now best known in Theo Mackeben's recension La Dubarry). Three years later came his masterpiece, Der Bettelstudent (The Beggar-Student), followed in 1884 by the almost as successful Gasparone. Among his more enduring later works were Der Feldprediger, also in 1884; Der Viceadmiral, 1886; and Der arme Jonathan (Poor Jonathan), 1890. Besides a score of operettas, Millöcker wrote much incidental music, and some individual songs and dances. RECORDINGS: On records there are innumerable excerpts and at least one complete recording of Bettelstudent (with Nicolai Gedda). Gasparone has been recorded under the baton of Heinz Wallberg.

[1396] MASSENET, Jules (Émile Frédéric) (Mas-nä', Ā-mēl' Frā-dā-rēk')

TEACHER
BORN: Montaud, May 12, 1842
DIED: Paris, August 13, 1912

There have been other operatic composers whose works were immensely successful in their lifetimes—Piccinni [848], Paisiello [914], Meyerbeer [1142], for example—only to fall into desuetude or obscurity afterward. Massenet is merely the latest, but there are many people alive today who can remember when opera guides still included seven or eight of his works as belonging to the standard repertoire, though by the 1930s (at least outside of France) one was likely to hear only Manon with any regularity. Even that has long been out of the repertoire of the major American opera houses—though a combination of guilt and jaded tastes has recently brought about revivals even of works that were omitted from the opera guides—Esclarmonde and Cendrillon, for instance.

There is no doubt that Massenet was a skilled and talented musician or that he had an unerring instinct for the theatrical. What has worked against him in this cynical century is his proclivity toward sentimental stories, mauve harmonies, and patchouli-scented melody. He came along at the time that opera was playing increasingly to a vast middle-class public with no special pretensions to musical education or literary taste, and he knew what pleased it. In fact he was, sociologically speaking, one of that public—an unpretentious, methodical, hardworking man obsessed with being successful and, in virtually everything he did, playing the role of Mr. Average Niceguy—being agreeable to everyone, rarely pulling rank, infrequently showing anger, and keeping as much as possible to his desk, whither he repaired every morning at four o'clock. The bulk of his output was dramatic—27 completed operas, 4 oratorios or sacred dramas, 3 ballets, and incidental music for 14 plays. Except for a large number of salonesque songs, he wrote comparatively little else—7 orchestral suites, a piano concerto, a few lesser orchestral pieces, a double handful of piano compositions, a Requiem, and some smaller choral works and part-songs. He also completed the opera Kassya, left by his friend Delibes [1344].

Massenet's father Alexis was the son of a Strasbourg history professor. Formerly an army officer and trained as an engineer, on Napoleon's defeat, he founded a scythe factory in Toulouse. When it succeeded beyond his hopes, he moved it, in 1838, to more modern quarters in a suburb of the dreary industrial city of St. Étienne just southwest of Lyons. His first wife having died, after bearing him eight children, he took a new one, Éléonore Royer de Marancourt, a sometime protégée of the Duchess of Angoulême, the daughter of Louis XVI. She produced four more, a girl and three boys, the last being the future composer. They named him "Jules," a name he detested all his life, preferring to be called simply "Massenet." In 1847 Alexis, scenting big trouble, packed the family off to Paris, unloaded the business, and joined them there after the 1848 Revolution. Massenet's mother undertook the spindly little boy's education herself; it included the piano, at which she was clearly no slouch, for when he was nine he played at the Conservatoire for an august committee, headed by Auber [1103] and including Fromental Halévy [1157] and Ambroise Thomas [1217], and was forthwith admitted as a student. Within a year or two, however, Alexis Massenet fell ill and in 1854 moved his family (including Jules) to Chambéry in the Savoian Alps, for reasons of health and (no doubt) economy.

Frustrated and bored to tears, the budding musician cut and ran, reaching Paris on foot and finding shelter with his married sister. He returned to his piano study at the Conservatoire, giving his first solo recital in Tournai when he was sixteen and winning first prize for piano in 1859. At about this time he took shabby quarters of his own in what was then an eastern suburb of the city, making ends meet by serving as a percussionist at the Théâtre Lyrique. In 1860 he embarked on broader musical studies. Ejected from Bazin's harmony class as a musical radical, he found a teacher in Napoléon Henri Reber. Later he studied composition with Thomas, who took a shine to him. After failing in 1862 (the year his father died), he won the Prix de Rome in 1863, thanks in large part to the advocacy of Berlioz [1175] and Thomas.

Massenet spent a good deal of time during his Rome stay acquainting himself with Italy. At the Villa Medici he heard, met, and caught the attention of the Abbé Franz Liszt [1218], now domiciled in the city. The abbé asked him to take over a young lady pupil, Constance de Sainte-Marie, who, to Massenet's delight and wonderment, turned out to be the same young woman who, on the steps of the Church of Ara Coeli, had caught his eye shortly before. A few months later he was asking her affluent parents for her hand. Expectably they turned him down until his prospects became more promising. He thereupon plunged into fulfilling his Prix de Rome commitments. Among the works he produced to that end were an overture and the *Requiem*. According to the terms of the prize, he dutifully toured Germany and settled for a time in Budapest. Then he returned to Rome and shortly afterward left for Paris, where he settled in Montmartre. There the cornettist Joseph Arban gave a performance of the suite *Pompéia,* and there, fortuitously, Massenet found a publisher in the tyro Georges Hartmann, who immediately made a success with his little song cycle *Poème d'Avril,* and a patroness in a wealthy American woman, Mrs. Charles Moulton. After a close shave with an attack of cholera (Thomas lent him his own physician), he published a set of piano pieces which contained the first version of the epidemically popular *Élégie.* Late in 1866, his prospects apparently being seen as brighter, he married his Constance (better known as "Ninon") in the village church of Avon, just outside Fontainebleau. Their only child, Juliette, was born two years later.

Recalling that the Prix de Rome entitled him to have a one-act opera produced gratis by the Opéra-Comique, Massenet began casting about for librettists, of which Thomas kindly provided him with two, who turned out a comedy called *La Grand'-Tante (The Great-Aunt).* Thanks in part to the casting of the popular tenor Victor Capoul as the male lead, the work was well received and ran for seventeen performances. Encouraged, the composer set to work on a treatment of Byron's *Manfred,* which he soon abandoned for *Méduse (Medusa).* That was broken off by the eruption of the Franco-Prussian War, in which Massenet underwent the siege of Paris as an infantryman. Afterward, he occupied himself with an "oratorio" called *Marie-Magdeleine* (a prostitute-with-a-heart-of-gold opera in a religious habit), which, completed, was rejected out of hand by the conductor-entrepreneur Jules Pasdeloup. The sting was, however, somewhat mitigated by commissions for a four-act opera from the Opéra-Comique, and music for Leconte de Lisle's play *Les Érinnyes (The Eumenides)* from Hartmann. The opera, *Don César de Bazan,* after Victor Hugo, had only a small success. (Later the score was accidentally burned, though Massenet afterward "re-created it.") The *Érinnyes* served to popularize the *Élégie* which Massenet had borrowed from himself for the libation scene.

Massenet's first big break came through

Pauline Viardot. Daughter of Manuel Garcia, Rossini's [1143] first Almaviva in *Il Barbiere di Siviglia*, and younger sister of the legendary singer Maria Malibran, Mme. Viardot, herself a singer (she created the role of Fides in Meyerbeer's *Le Prophète* and was Orfeo in Berlioz's famous revival of Gluck's [803] opera), composer (operas and songs), and admired vocal teacher, was a mover and shaker in French musical circles. When at a dinner party she asked Massenet to play some of his music for her, he obliged with pieces from the hapless *Marie-Magdeleine*. Viardot was so taken with them that she forthwith decided to break her retirement and appear in the premiere, which she persuaded Éduard Colonne to conduct in the spring of 1873. Though the composer was so apprehensive that he went home before the performance was over—typical behavior for him at premieres—the oratorio was a huge triumph with both public and critics.

After a trip to Italy with his family, the composer returned to write an overture for Racine's *Phèdre*, commissioned by the once-sneering Pasdeloup, and two orchestral suites entitled *Scènes pittoresques* and *Scènes dramatiques*, the latter "after Shakespeare"; a *Scènes hongroises*, the product of the Budapest sojourn, had preceded them two years earlier. He then turned his attention to another oratorio about an erring woman, this one called *Ève*. It enjoyed a reception commensurate with that of its predecessor. Massenet allowed himself to be hailed onstage from a nearby café to be honored. Stepping into the wings, he was summoned to his mother's sickbed to learn that she had died at precisely that moment.

In 1875, the year of *Ève*, Charles Garnier's imposing new Paris Opéra—the one that is still in use—opened. Anxious to capitalize on his present eminence, Massenet set about to write a work for it. After considerable effort he permanently shelved *Les Templiers (The Templars)*, and turned to a five-act work in the currently fashionable "oriental" mode, *Le Roi de Lahore (The King of Lahore)*. It was accepted without question, given an all-out production, and presented to an all-star audience on April 27, 1877. (The cast included Josephine de Reszke and Jean Lasalle.) Massenet had arrived: the work entered the repertoire at the Opéra and was soon playing in all the important opera houses.

The following year, again thanks to Ambroise Thomas, Massenet succeeded the irascible François Bazin [1247] as professor of composition at the Conservatoire at a not inconsiderable salary. Over the next thirty years he trained such successful composers

as Alfred Bruneau [1497], Gustave Charpentier [1524], Hahn [1672], Koechlin [1592], Gabriel Pierné [1555], Rabaud [1647], and Florent Schmitt [1615]. About the same time he also beat out Saint-Saëns [1343] for a vacancy in the Institut, for which feat the older composer broke off their friendship; ironically it was again Bazin whom he replaced.

A third oratorio, *La Vièrge (The Virgin)*, was an abject failure at the Opéra in 1880, perhaps because its subject had less implication of scandal about it. However, Massenet set to work on another "biblical" work, an opera about Salome and John the Baptist called *Hérodiade (Herodias)*. Having been stung once, the management of the Opéra flatly rejected it. But a fortuitous boulevard encounter between the composer and the director of the Théâtre de la Monnaie in Brussels found it a stage where it opened in December 1881. It drew people from all over, was a huge success, and won Massenet a decoration from King Leopold of Belgium. It was forty years before the Paris Opéra got around to it, however. Massenet followed it with the last and most popular of his orchestral suites, *Scènes alsaciennes* (which had been preceded in 1864 and 1876 by Neapolitan and fairy scenes, respectively).

One day Henri Meilhac, co-librettist of Bizet's *Carmen*, arrived on Massenet's doorstep saying, "Have *I* got a libretto for you!" Massenet read it and didn't like it. He returned it, explaining vaguely that he had something else in mind. "What?" asked Meilhac. "Oh, *Manon Lescaut*," replied the composer, picking a title out of the air. Meilhac was puzzled: Auber's treatment of the Abbé Prévost's sentimental romance was still around, but he went home and wrote, overnight, the first two acts. Massenet was delighted with them and set to work. In the end the libretto was a collaboration of Meilhac's and Philippe Gille's, with more than a little aid (and interference) from the composer. The work was finished in the summer of 1883 and accepted by the Opéra-Comique, but problems of casting held up production. The title role finally went to Marie Heilbronn, who had sung the premiere of Massenet's first opera and who identified with the part from experience. (She died in 1886.) *Manon* opened in January 1884, and despite cavils from some critics was an immense popular success—which it remained for more than half a century.

Eighteen months later *Manon* was followed by *Le Cid*, starring Jean and Édouard de Reszke. It was based on Corneille's heroic play. Heroics were not Massenet's stock in trade, but the piece was well received and played frequently into the new century. During rehearsals Massenet returned to Hungary for a semiofficial visit with a cultural delegation led by Ferdinand de Lesseps, builder of the Suez Canal, and including Delibes.

In 1887 at a dinner party given by an American hostess, Massenet was introduced to a beautiful (and wealthy) American girl named Sybil Sanderson, who sang for him. He was captivated and wrote his next opera, *Esclarmonde*, especially for her. He arranged for her to appear in the Dutch premiere of *Manon* at The Hague in 1888 and spent the summer in Switzerland with her and her mother, ostensibly working on the opera. Massenet appears in the history books as a notable womanizer, but he was scrupulously discreet about such matters and fiercely defensive of his wife's good name, so that there is some room to doubt that Miss Sanderson—and later Lucy Arbell—were in fact his mistresses. The spectacular and romantic *Esclarmonde* drew crowds initially—some perhaps motivated by a hint of scandal—but prior to the revival for Joan Sutherland nearly ninety years later, it enjoyed very few performances, much to its composer's annoyance. *Le Mage (The Magus)*, an opera about Zoroaster, premiered in March 1891, was even less successful, surviving only six months.

Meanwhile on a joint visit to Bayreuth in 1886, Hartmann had whetted Massenet's interest in Goethe and especially in his lachrymose novella *Die Leiden des jungen Werthers*. While *Le Mage* was on its way to oblivion, Massenet was writing his *Werther*. It was slated for the Opéra-Comique, but when fire destroyed that house the composer offered the work to the Imperial Opera in Vienna, which was delighted to accept and gave it a smashingly successful premiere in February 1892, with the Dutch tenor Ernest van Dyck as the lead. Despite prior predictions of doom and gloom, it has proved, next to *Manon*, the hardiest and most viable of the Massenet operas. Curiously it spawned a ballet *Le Carillon*, proposed to the composer by Van Dyck and produced in Vienna five weeks after *Werther*. In the midst of all this Hartmann went bankrupt, but Massenet's music was all taken over by Henri Heugel, whose establishment continued to publish him thereafter.

With Sybil again in mind as its titular heroine, Massenet now set to work on another excursion into the exotic-erotic, *Thaïs*, based loosely on Anatole France's novel about the Alexandrian courtesan and the Cenobitic monk. Work was interrupted by the task of completing Delibes's opera *Kassya*—which was a failure. Nor was it facilitated by Ninon's now open hostility to La Sanderson. Premiered inauspiciously on March 16, 1894, the third anniversary of *Le Mage*'s premiere, *Thaïs* was not a success, though it later caught on (thanks in some degree to its championing by Mary Garden) and now ranks as the third most successful Massenet opera. It was followed by an odd and nostalgic one-acter in May, *Le Portrait de Manon (Manon's Picture)* which, to whiffs of the earlier music, tells us what happened to Des Grieux (played by the indestructible Lucien Fugère, who was regularly associated with future Massenet operas). Next came another one-act work, *La Navarraise (The Woman of Navarre)*, Massenet's first dip into the waters of *verismo*. A gory little tale of derring-do and failure in the Carlist Wars in Spain, it opened at Covent Garden in London with the greatest of Carmens, Emma Calvé, in the title role. It was so successful that Queen Victoria requested and got a performance at Windsor. The Italian premiere in 1895 took Massenet to Milan, where he hobnobbed with Leoncavallo [**1498**], Giordano [**1589**], Mascagni [**1559**], and Cilea [**1580**], and took a side trip to Genoa to meet the octogenarian Verdi [**1232**].

Calvé had so impressed the composer that he wrote his next full-scale opera, *Sapho*, for her. This is not about the Lesbian poetess of antiquity but is drawn from a "realistic" novel by Daudet—a switch on the prostitute-with-golden-heart theme. While Massenet was at work on it, Thomas died and he was offered the directorship of the Conservatoire, but when his own terms were rejected he resigned. That same year, 1896, he was named commander of the *Légion d'honneur*. His *Sapho* opened in late November 1897 at the Opéra-Comique (temporarily quartered in the Théâtre Lyrique), was welcomed, and has enjoyed sporadic revivals ever since. The Opéra-Comique moved into its present house, the newly built Théâtre Favart, a year later and offered Massenet's next work the following May. This took a rather new direction. It was *Cendrillon (Cinderella)*, based on Charles Perrault's immortal fairy tale, and is marked by a delicate imagination not often found to such an extent in Massenet's operas. Starring Julie Guiraudon and Fugère (as her father), it was delightedly received. But taste for Massenet's pastel sentimentality was beginning to wane, and the work had little subsequent history until its recent revivals.

But the composer's eminence remained high, and in the first year of the new century he was named a grand officer of the *Légion*. At about the same time he bought an ancient house in Egreville, near Fontainebleau, where he spent about half his time. That March brought a final oratorio, *La Terre promise (The Promised Land)* for which there proved to be no demand at all. It was also in 1900 that Massenet had his first bout with the kidney ailment that carried him off a dozen years later. While recuperating he worked on *Grisélidis*, a witty handling of the Patient Griselde story with a *sainte ex machina* resolution. Under the baton of André Messager [1474], it first saw the light at the Opéra-Comique in November 1901 (Fugère sang the farcical role of the Devil). The work, as usual with Massenet, drew well initially but has not been much heard since.

Grisélidis marked Massenet's farewell to the Opéra-Comique. His next opera, the quasi-religious *Le Jongleur de Notre Dame (Our Lady's Juggler)*—again after Anatole France) called for an all-male cast (though Garden later took the title role unto herself) and frightened the Parisian impresarios. Massenet at last found a savior in the flamboyant Raoul Gunsbourg, director of the Monte Carlo Opera, who produced it in February 1902. It was the last Massenet opera to enjoy anything like subsequent success until the present-day reawakening of interest in the composer. The next year Massenet was shattered by the death (at thirty-eight) of Sybil Sanderson, by then the widow of a wealthy Cuban, Antonio Terry. Perhaps he had also seen the handwriting on the wall in Debussy's [1547] *Pelléas et Mélisande*, unveiled the year before. At any rate he wrote nothing but some music for a dramatic production of Dickens's *The Cricket on the Hearth* and a short ballet score, *Cigale*, in 1904. But he was back again in Monte Carlo in 1905 with *Chérubin*, featuring Garden, Lina Cavalieri, and Maurice Renaud. A sort of sequel to *The Marriage of Figaro* (Whatever Happened to Cherubino?), it had the usual first-night success, was taken over by the Opéra-Comique a few months later, and then vanished. That summer Massenet attempted something more grandiose: *Ariane (Ariadne)*, with an ambitious libretto by Catulle Mendes, a man for whom the composer had little liking. It opened at the Opéra in the autumn of 1906 and, surprisingly, enjoyed seventy performances before World War II. In a secondary role was a young soprano called Lucy Arbell *(née* Georgette Wallace), who was henceforth to be Massenet's new muse. For her he next wrote one of his most original works, the two-act *Thérèse*, based on an actual episode in the French Revolution. After its initial ecstatic reception in Monaco, its success was, however, limited—in part by the fact of its

odd-length brevity. (It shared its Paris premiere with the first production of Ravel's [1666] *L'Heure Espagnole (The Spanish Hour)*; in Monaco in 1908, it was coupled with *Espada*, Massenet's last excursion into ballet, which was stillborn.)

For some reason Heugel cajoled Massenet and Mendes into writing *Bacchus*, a sequel to *Ariane*, in part based on the Sanskrit *Ramayana (!)*, over which the collaborators nearly came to blows. Mendes, probably a suicide, was killed by a train three months before *Bacchus* opened at the Opéra, for the first of its six performances, in May. Massenet's sun was definitely setting: no one had a good word to say about the work. The composer's shock was exacerbated by another spell of illness, but he improved the hours by working at an opera for Arbell and Feodor Chaliapin, based at some remove on Cervantes' *Don Quixote* and more directly on a play by Jacques Le Lorrain, a cobbler (assisted by several more experienced authors) who had expired shortly after its 1904 premiere. At the Monte Carlo opening of the opera, Chaliapin created one of his great stage portraits and Massenet was buoyed up by the work's success. (It has enjoyed occasional revivals for notable singing actors.) Shortly afterward he was ill again. This time he touched up *Amadis*, which he had given up on nearly fifteen years earlier; in the end it failed to please him again and was not given until 1922, when it failed. However, as though he knew time was short, he was working frantically on three other operas: *Roma*, a classical tragedy; *Panurge*, a farce after Rabelais; and *Cléopatre*. By autumn 1910, as its oldest member, he became president of the Institut, and, worn out by his official duties, went back to bed, where he occupied his time by writing his memoirs. In 1911 they gave him a gala at the Opéra, and *Roma* went into rehearsal at Monte Carlo. Very tottery, he went there to oversee them. The ovation it received on opening night (February 17, 1912) brought on his onstage collapse. (The work had only twenty subsequent performances.) Thereafter his health fluctuated. His condition was not improved by Lucy, who tried to wrest from him a lifetime monopoly of "her" roles, and finally brought on an irreparable split between them. Massenet died of uremia four hours after the end of his seventieth birthday and was buried in Egreville. *Panurge* was produced in Paris, with Vanni Marcoux and the fledgling Giovanni Martinelli, in April 1913, *Cléopatre* in Monte Carlo ten months later. Neither survived. Ninon Massenet did until 1938.

RECORDINGS: Jaded tastes or a renewed

interest in Massenet has resulted in a spate of recordings in recent years. Complete versions of *Le Roi de Lahore, Manon, Le Cid, Esclarmonde, Werther, Thaïs, La Navarraise, Sapho, Cendrillon, Le Jongleur de Notre Dame, Thérèse, Don Quichotte,* the music for *Les Érinnyes,* and the ballet *Cigale* have been released by commercial companies, as have the orchestral suites, the Concerto for Piano, the complete piano music, and many of the songs. *Hérodiade, Le Portrait de Manon, Grisélidis* and *Chérubin* have all been accounted for by tapings from broadcasts.

[1397] SULLIVAN, (Sir) Arthur Seymour
ORGANIST, CONDUCTOR, TEACHER, ADMINISTRATOR
BORN: London, May 13, 1842
DIED: London, November 22, 1900

The life of Arthur Sullivan is full of paradoxes. He possessed a superb musical talent which was shortchanged by the taste of his times. He viewed himself as one destined to uplift the race through his inspirational (i.e., religious) compositions but is remembered chiefly for a frothy series of operettas. The only quasi-religious pieces that have persisted are a few hymns (notably "Onward, Christian Soldiers") and the maudlin "The Lost Chord," said to have been inspired by his brother's death. As a composer of operettas, he has become inseparable in people's minds from his librettist—Gilbertandsullivan. Long viewed as a saintly example of Victorian rectitude, he turns out to have been, in his prime, a sexual athlete who had at least three mistresses (apparently at the same time) and kept score of his successful and more-than-frequent encounters in his diary.

Sullivan is often cited as an Irish composer; genetically this is true, but he was a Londoner born and bred. His father, no ignorant bog trotter, had joined Her Majesty's forces and served as bandmaster at Sandhurst from 1843 to 1856, and then as professor of band at the Royal Military School of Music. Arthur's mother was also Irish, but her lineage was part Italian. By the time he was eight, he is said to have had a sound grasp of all the standard wind instruments. At twelve he was accepted as a chorister in the Chapel Royal, where he, of course, received musical training and a year later published an anthem of his own devising. In 1856 he competed for and won the Mendelssohn Scholarship, established by that composer's [1200] friends and admirers some years earlier but not activated until that year. (The next winner-but-one was William

Shakespeare!) The terms were that the winner would study at the Leipzig Conservatory, though Sullivan delayed his departure until his voice broke in 1858. In Leipzig he studied with such familiar figures as Moscheles [1146], Rietz [1227], and Ferdinand David (1810–73), and made them all very proud of him. He returned to London in 1861 and became organist at St. Michael's.

By that time he had written several works, notably three overtures, a piano sonata, and some choral works, but he first came to public attention in 1862 with a very Mendelssohnian set of pieces for Shakespeare's *The Tempest,* which was played several times within a few weeks. About the same time he began a lifelong friendship with George Grove, civil engineer, editor, litterateur, journalist, critic, and musical lexicographer, who was twenty-two years his senior and a powerful influence on him. Another friend was the reviewer Henry Chorley, who wrote the libretti to Sullivan's 1864 masque *Kenilworth* and his abortive first opera, *The Sapphire Necklace.* Also in 1864, Sullivan visited his parents' homeland, an experience that resulted in the *Irish Symphony,* premiered in 1866, the year that produced the Concerto for Cello. Earlier that year Sullivan had become professor of composition at the Royal Academy of Music, and in September his father had died, which event he lamented in the overture *In Memoriam.* (At some point in these post-Leipzig years, Sullivan had seriously courted Rachel Scott Russell, but her parents found his ardor beyond the bounds of Victorian propriety and closed their door to him. He never married.)

In 1867, the year in which Sullivan and Grove went Schubert [1153]-hunting in Vienna and found treasures beyond their wildest dreams, the former began his stage career in two comic collaborations with Francis Burnand, later the editor of *Punch.* The first, *Cox and Box,* was first performed privately but soon after had a decent run. The longer *Contrabandista* was to return as *The Chieftain* in revised form in 1894 but never made much impact. The early 1870s were mostly taken up with religious works, with one exception. In 1870 Sullivan met William Schwenk Gilbert, six years his senior and already celebrated as author of *The Bab Ballads.* They first joined forces in *Thespis,* which was performed the following December. It remains the forgotten stepchild of the collaboration. (Most of the music is lost.)

The union of Gilbert and Sullivan was not exactly made in heaven. The bluff Gilbert, the very physical model of a Victorian *boulevardier,* was in fact rather a prude. A former lawyer, he took his standing as a playwright, fictionist, and versifier almost as seriously as Sullivan took his as a musician. The history of their relationship was marked by jealousies, dissensions, and downright fallings-out. Their real joint career began in 1875, by which time Sullivan had written the two oratorios, *The Prodigal Son* and *The Light of the World,* by which he had set so much store, was conducting several concert series and festivals, and had received an honorary doctorate from Cambridge. Enter the third member of the trinity, Richard D'Oyly Carte (1844–1901), a musician turned producer, who was planning a season of operetta. He commissioned a one-act farce, *Trial by Jury,* from Gilbert and Sullivan (their only piece without spoken dialogue). Produced in March 1875, with Sullivan's brother Frederick as the Judge, it was such a success that the next year Carte set up a corporation to produce "operas" by his two associates. This marked the beginning of the famous company that midwifed the 12 operettas of the canon and preserved the traditions until recently.

While all this was getting under way, Sullivan turned out one more non-Gilbertian farce, *The Zoo,* and reluctantly took on the directorship of what was to become the Royal College of Music. The first production of the D'Oyly Carte Company was *The Sorcerer* in November 1877, which had a remarkable run of 175 performances. But the following year the success of *H.M.S. Pinafore* was absolutely unprecedented—a run of nearly two years, plus performances (mostly piratical) all over England and America (where a parody of one of the choruses gave us "Hail, Hail, the Gang's All Here!). After *Pinafore,* the corporation, which had proved intractable, was dissolved, and thereafter the operettas were produced by the trio of principals. The first under the new arrangement was *The Pirates of Penzance,* for which copyrights were carefully assured both in England and America and which opened in 1880, the same year that the composer and librettist came up with something completely different in the form of a cantata, *The Martyr of Antioch,* for the Leeds Festival. In 1881, the year of *Patience,* Sullivan impatiently gave up his post at the college, and Carte oversaw the building of the Savoy Theater. *Patience* was transferred there to complete its run and was followed by *Iolanthe* in November 1882. In 1883 Sullivan, who had meanwhile acquired the *Légion d'honneur,* the Order of Saxe-Coburg Gotha, and an honorary doctorate, was knighted. Gilbert, some of whose wit had not amused the queen, was not knighted,

and the omission did not sit well with him. *Patience* was followed in 1884 by the Tennysonian spoof *Princess Ida,* which ran less than a year and was followed by one of the most successful operettas of all, *The Mikado,* in 1885, the year Sullivan became conductor of the London Philharmonic Society. In 1886 there was no need for a new operetta, and Sullivan produced the most successful of his nondramatic works, *The Golden Legend* (a cantata after Longfellow) which, however, did not long survive. Then came *Ruddigore, The Yeomen of the Guard,* and *The Gondoliers,* in 1887, 1888, and 1889, respectively. By now the partnership was beginning to fray. Shortly Gilbert and Sullivan quarreled with Carte over business matters, and then Gilbert quarreled with Sullivan for waffling, and the three ceased to communicate. (It should be noted that Sullivan, who considered his part in the operettas something of a chore, had a stable of assistants that were called on to orchestrate and arrange overtures.)

During the breach, Sullivan (who was beginning to fail and who at fifty was prematurely aged) set to work to fulfill his platonic vision of himself with a grand opera, and Carte built the New English Opera to showcase it. *Ivanhoe* was premiered at the end of January 1891, received praise, ran for five months, and expired. After another stab at operatic production, Carte unloaded the theater. Following the unsuccessful *Haddon Hall* of 1892, Sullivan and Gilbert were officially and publicly reunited, and went on to produce *Utopia Limited* in 1893 and *The Grand Duke* in 1896, but neither enjoyed the popularity of their predecessors. Sullivan proceeded to write two more operettas, of which *The Rose of Persia* was the more successful. In obvious pain, he conducted the Leeds Festival of 1898. He was taken ill in November 1900 and died of a heart attack a few days later. He was only fifty-eight. Carte survived him by less than six months. Gilbert lived to be knighted eventually by Edward VII in 1907. Four years later, at the age of seventy-four, he drowned while attempting to rescue a young female swimmer. *The Emerald Isle,* left incomplete at Sullivan's death, was completed by Edward German [1541] for a posthumous premiere in 1901.

RECORDINGS: The operettas (with and without dialogue), from *Trial by Jury* to *Gondoliers,* have been repeatedly recorded by the D'Oyly Carte Company, and occasionally by others (a notable series under Malcolm Sargent, for example). The last two works, *Utopia Limited* and *The Grand Duke,* have made their disc debut only recently in both "authentic" and semiamateur performances. There are recordings by Royston Nash of *Cox and Box* and *The Zoo*. Recent recordings of *The Emerald Isle* and *Haddon Hall* have also appeared. *Ivanhoe,* the other operettas and operas, and the big religious works have appeared only in excerpts, most of them of an earlier day. Of the incidental music, there have been suites from *Henry VIII* (F. Charles Adler), *The Merchant of Venice* and *The Tempest* (Sir Vivian Dunn), and a complete recording of the *Tempest* music (Adler.) Dunn has also recorded the *In Memoriam Overture* and Charles Groves the *Irish Symphony*. There have been several recordings of the *Di Ballo Overture*. A suite from Sullivan's ballet *Victoria and Merrie England,* has been recorded by Royston Nash. Charles Mackerras has arranged and recorded *Pineapple Poll,* a latter-day ballet utilizing Sullivan's nonballetic music. There are a number of songs on record, especially by earlier English singers.

[1398] CZIBULKA, Alphons (Chĕ-bool'-kȧ, Ȧl-fonz')
CONDUCTOR, BANDMASTER, PIANIST
BORN: Szepes-Várallya, May 14, 1842
DIED: Vienna, October 27, 1894

A writer of Viennese operettas, the Hungarian-born Czibulka was more successful as a prolific composer of dances and other salon pieces. Beginning as a touring pianist in his teens, he conducted at theaters in several of the larger Austrian towns before settling in Vienna as conductor of the Karltheater in his mid-twenties. Later he served as bandmaster to the 17th and 25th Infantry Regiments, then returned to Vienna in the 1880s to turn out his operettas and conduct outdoor concerts of popular music. RECORDINGS: His best-known compositions are the much-anthologized *Stephanie-Gavotte,* Op. 312 and *Liebestraum nach dem Balle,* Op. 356 *(Love's Dream After the Ball).*

[1399] ZELLER, Carl Johann Adam (Tsel'-ler, Kärl Yō'-hȧn Ȧd'-ȧm)
LAWYER, CIVIL SERVANT
BORN: St. Peter-in-der-Au, June 19, 1842
DIED: Baden, Austria, August 17, 1898

The fourth of the Austro-German first-generation operetta quartet—the others were Suppé **[1262]**; Johann Strauss, Jr. **[1295]**; and Millöcker **[1395]**—Carl Zeller was the son of a country doctor in Lower Austria. In childhood he got a basic musical education as a Vienna Choirboy. Later he studied with Sechter **[1129]**, but the direction of his formal studies was legal, and he emerged from the University of Graz in 1869 with a doctorate of law. In 1873 he took a post in the Ministry of Education and Culture, where he eventually rose to the rank of privy councillor. Three years later he brought out his operatic comedy *Joconde* and followed it with two operettas, *Die Carbonari* in 1880 and *Der Vagabund* in 1886. The embarrassed government hemmed and hawed but finally said that such behavior was permissible if Dr. Zeller himself would agree not to appear on the stage in person. Zeller's greatest success was *Der Vogelhändler (The Birdseller)* in 1891, though it was hardly less successful than *Der Obersteiger (The Overseer)* of three years later. Shortly afterward, however, he became strange in the head and had to be retired. On top of that, the government brought perjury charges against him and convicted him, though it later relented and issued a pardon. His *Der Kellermeister (The Wine Steward)* was produced in 1901 after his death at fifty-six. RECORDINGS: Besides many recorded excerpts from the operettas, there is a complete recording of *Der Vogelhändler* led by Willy Boskovsky.

[1400] DUVERNOY, Victor Alphonse (Dü-vâr-noi', Vĕk-tôr' Ȧl-fons')
PIANIST, TEACHER, CRITIC
BORN: Paris, August 30, 1842
DIED: Paris, March 7, 1907

Victor Duvernoy seems to have been unrelated to several earlier musical Duvernoys. Hoping to become a concert performer, he studied with Marmontel at the Conservatoire and took first prize for piano when he was thirteen. But somehow his career did not develop, and he turned to promoting chamber music concerts, composing, reviewing, and teaching. He was, for more than a decade, professor of piano at the Conservatoire. Several of his compositions won prizes, and he was awarded the *Légion d'honneur*—as who wasn't? Besides works for voices, orchestra, chamber groups, and piano, he wrote 2 operas—*Sardanapale* in 1882 and *Hellé* in 1896—and a ballet, *Bacchus,* in 1902. RECORDINGS: An aria or two from *Hellé* may be found on old records.

[1401] MALASHKIN, Leonid Dimitrievitch (Má-làsh'-kēn, Lā'-ō-nēd Dē-mē-trī-yā'-vich)
BORN: Russia, 1842
DIED: Moscow, February 11, 1902

Malashkin wrote an opera, *Ilya Murometz,* and some other ambitious works but is important chiefly as a collector and arranger of folk songs. Popular with, and recorded by many Russian bassos from Chaliapin on, is an original song known in English as "Oh Could I But Express in Song." (There is an apocryphal legend of an English music clerk who took down this title from a phone order, and was found later vainly hunting for "Kodály: *Buttocks-Pressing Song.*")

[1402] TAYLOR, Franklin
PIANIST, TEACHER
BORN: Birmingham, February 5, 1843
DIED: London, March 19, 1919

Franklin Taylor made his name chiefly as a performer and pedagogue. As a child he studied with locals, was substituting as an organist at Litchfield Cathedral when thirteen, and, shortly afterward, was named organist of the Old Meeting-House in Birmingham. In 1859 he joined Arthur Sullivan [1397] at the Leipzig Conservatory, where he too studied piano under Moscheles [1146]. In 1861 he stopped off in Paris long enough for some lessons with Clara Schumann [1267], then established himself in London as a concert artist at the more prestigious concerts and as a successful teacher. He was also organist of several London churches, notably at St. Michael's in Chester Square, where he succeeded Sullivan. He spent his last thirty-seven years as professor of piano at the Royal College of Music. As a composer, he is known chiefly for his teaching pieces and didactic works. RECORDINGS: Raymond Lewenthal has recorded a part of his *Toy Symphony.*

[1403] SUDDS, William F.
BANDMASTER, VIOLINIST
BORN: London, March 5, 1843
DIED: Gouverneur, N.Y., September 25, 1920

An émigré to America in childhood, Sudds served in the Union Army in the Civil War, directing a band. Afterward he studied violin in Boston. He turned out dozens of compositions, mostly for keyboard or church choir, to *petit-bourgeois* tastes, and a violin method. RECORDINGS: Neely Bruce has recorded a couple of his piano pieces.

[1404] SVEDBOM, Per Jonas Fredrik Vilhelm (Svād'-bôm, Pâr Yōō'-nás Frā-drik Vil'-elm)
PHILOLOGIST, TEACHER, ADMINISTRATOR
BORN: Stockholm, March 8, 1843
DIED: Stockholm, December 25, 1904

Vilhelm Svedbom came to music late. In fact he had acquired a Ph.D. from Uppsala in philology and had been teaching literature there when, in the mid-1870s he decided on a musical career. After studying for a time in Berlin, he toured other European capitals to size up the musical situation. He organized a concert series in Stockholm, was elected to the Swedish Academy in 1876, and became director of the Stockholm Conservatory in 1901. As a composer he was by instinct a Romantic throwback, but he also made considerable use of Swedish folk music. Most of his works were vocal—cantatas, choruses, songs, and folksong arrangements. RECORDINGS: There are recordings of a piano piece or two and songs and snippets by Swedish vocal artists.

[1405] GREGH, Louis (Greg, Lōō-ē')
PUBLISHER
BORN: Philippeville, March 16, 1843
DIED: St. Mesme, January 21, 1915

Algerian-born Louis Gregh was a successful composer of operettas in Paris in the last years of the nineteenth century. His chief work was *Une Lycée de jeunes filles (A Highschool for Young Girls).* He later went into music publishing, giving his company his son's name, Henri Gregh et fils. RECORDINGS: There are a few early recordings of his songs.

[1406] ZIEHRER, Karl Michael (Tsēr'-er, Kärl Mē'-khà-el)
PIANIST, CONDUCTOR, EDITOR
BORN: Vienna, May 2, 1843
DIED: Vienna, November 14, 1922

In his heyday, Ziehrer bid fair to rival the Strausses [1177, 1295] in popularity. Beginning as an accompanist in a dancing school, he moved to dance-band conducting when he was twenty. Then he was successively bandmaster of the 55th and 76th Imperial Infantry Regiments. In the mid-seventies he founded and edited his own journal, the *Deutsche Musik-Zeitung,* which, under various names, ran until 1902. He left military service in 1878 and raided Eduard Strauss's orchestra to found his own, but returned in

1885 to head the now-famous Hoch-und-Deutschmeister Band. His operetta career began shortly afterward with *Ein Deutschmeister* (what else?) in 1888 and reached its height with *Der Landstreicher (The Hobo)* in 1899. In 1907 he followed the Strausses (at one remove) as *Hofball-musikdirektor* and was the last person to hold that office, which ended with the Empire. RECORDINGS: Ziehrer's waltzes and marches are fairly common on records.

[1407] MARQUÉS Y GARCIA, Pedro Miguel (Mär-kāz' ē Gär-thē'-à, Pā*th*'-rō Mē-gel')

VIOLINIST, TEACHER

BORN: Palma de Mallorca, May 20, 1843
DIED: Palma de Mallorca, February 25, 1925

Marqués studied violin with Alard [1240] at the Paris Conservatoire, and privately with Berlioz [1175]. At twenty-four he returned to Madrid for further study at its conservatory with Jesús de Monasterio, its director. He then taught at the Colegio de la Inclusa and served as inspector of conservatories. He wrote a number of popular zarzuelas, notably *El anillo de hierro* of 1878, from which excerpts have been recorded.

[1408] PESSARD, Émile-Louis-Fortuné (Pes-särd', Äm-ēl' Lōō-ē' Fôr-tü-nä')

EDUCATOR

BORN: Paris, May 29, 1843
DIED: Paris, February 10, 1917

The son of a musician, Émile Pessard was a product of the Paris Conservatoire, where he studied composition with Michele Carafa de Colobrano. Pessard won the Grand Prix de Rome in 1866, just one year after Charles Lenepveu and two after the otherwise anonymous Sieg. Shortly after his return to Paris, he began turning out a series of about 12 operettas and *opéras-comiques,* some reasonably successful but now all forgotten. He was professor of harmony at the Conservatoire from 1881 and held other educational posts and sinecures. He also wrote instrumental and choral music (mostly in small forms), but was best known for his songs, a few of which appear on records. (Because Debussy [1547] in his youth once copied out Pessard's *La Chanson d'un fou [A Madman's Song],* it was published as Debussy's after his death.) Pessard's most famous pupil was Maurice Ravel [1666].

[1409] NEUENDORFF, Adolf (Noi'-en-dôrf, Ä'-dolf)

CONDUCTOR, IMPRESARIO, VIOLINIST, PIANIST

BORN: Hamburg, June 13, 1843
DIED: New York, December 4, 1897

Neuendorff's family emigrated to New York when he was eleven. He studied violin and piano there, played both instruments in concert, and toured South America as a violinist. In 1863 he settled in Milwaukee, then virtually a German colony, where he conducted operas and operettas and wrote several of the latter. In the 1870s he was back in New York, where he conducted the American premieres of Wagner's [1230] *Lohengrin* (Stadt Theater, 1871) and *Die Walküre* (Academy of Music, 1877). In the latter year he brought Heinrich Conried, later general manager of the Metropolitan Opera, to America to assist him in a theatrical venture he had undertaken with Oscar Hammerstein. For part of the next decade he was in Boston, where in 1885 he inaugurated the Music Hall Promenade Concerts, the forerunner of the Boston Pops. The next year, he joined an "unauthorized" German company, sharked up from the Metropolitan by Maurice Grau, in a tour to the Midwest. Later Neuendorff's wife, Georgine von Januschowsky, sang with the authorized Met company. When she was hired by the Vienna Hofoper in 1893, he went with her. He returned in 1897 (one reads) to succeed Anton Seidl as conductor of "the Metropolitan Permanent Orchestra." (Seidl left the Met in 1891 for the Philharmonic, from which he resigned in 1897, but it seems unlikely that that body would have considered a jackleg like Neuendorff.) Whatever it was, he died before he could enter upon his duties. RECORDINGS: He is remembered chiefly for a wonderfully sentimental song from his *Der Rattenfänger von Hameln (The Pied Piper of Hamlin)* recorded by such tenors as Fritz Wunderlich and Karl Jörn.

[1410] GRIEG, Edvard (Grēg, Ed'-värd)

PIANIST

BORN: Bergen, June 15, 1843
DIED: Bergen, September 4, 1907

Edvard Grieg was by no means the first Scandinavian composer, nor did he—a miniaturist by nature—produce more than a handful of major works. Yet through his use of folk materials and his development of a characteristic musical vocabulary, he had an enormous impact on at least three ensuing generations of northern composers. He himself was basically of the school of Schumann [1211], via Niels Gade [1248], but his particular development owed much to Halfdan Kjerulf [1244] and to the ill-fated Rikard Nordraak (1842–66).

Grieg was a great grandson of Alexander Greig (sic!), a Scots fisherman who had settled in Bergen in the 1760s and built a thriving business there. Edvard's father (also Alexander) played the piano, and his mother, née Gesine Hagerup, was highly musical and literate. Of his four siblings, his brother John became a fine amateur cellist. (Most reference works to the contrary notwithstanding, young Grieg was not christened or generally called "Edvard Hagerup.") Grieg went to school in Bergen and apparently hated every moment of it, his teachers and fellow students being more materialistically oriented than he was. On the side he studied piano with his mother and began to compose. In the spring of 1858 the great violinist Ole Bull [1206], who had settled nearby, visited the Griegs and, hearing what the boy could do, urged that they send him to the Leipzig Conservatory. He went the following autumn and, despite his later dismissal of the experience as worthless, he seems to have profited at the hands of such teachers as Richter, Hauptmann, and especially Moscheles [1146]. In 1860 he was felled by an attack of pleurisy that necessitated his going home to convalesce and left him with permanent lung damage, but he returned to graduate, giving his farewell concert in the spring of 1862.

After an attempt to establish himself in Bergen, and trips to Paris and London, Grieg settled in Copenhagen in 1863, where he turned out a symphony (later discarded) at Gade's insistence. In Denmark he encountered his cousin, the singer Nina Hagerup, later to be one of his music's prime interpreters, and became engaged to her in 1864. That autumn he met at the Tivoli Gardens (where Lumbye [1210] had conducted his symphony) Rikard Nordraak (whose fervent nationalism is evidenced in his name change from Richard Nordraach). Nordraak, who composed as the birds sing and had little patience with training or discipline, was bent on creating a true Norwegian music and conveyed his enthusiasm to Grieg, whose own music soon began to show a trend away from Schumannesque imitation. The next year Nordraak went to Berlin to study, if he could stand it, with the proviso that later he and Grieg would go to Italy. No sooner had Grieg joined him, however, than Nordraak was put to bed with what proved to be terminal tuberculosis, and Grieg left without him. In March 1866

Grieg, in Rome, had word that his friend was dead. Grief-stricken, he commemorated him with his Funeral March and always blamed himself as somehow responsible for Nordraak's death. Grieg, who found the state of music in Italy as bad as had Berlioz [1175] before him, came home in the autumn of 1866 and this time settled in Christiania (later Oslo). The following year he and Nina were married, and Grieg took over the conductorship of the Christiania Philharmonic (actually an amateur orchestra). He found several staunch supporters there, notably Johan Svendsen [1379] and Kjerulf; unhappily the former soon decamped for greener fields and the latter died in 1868. He also developed a close friendship with the writer Bjørnstjerne Bjørnson (age thirty-three), who had come to Christiania to manage the theater in 1865, and the two frequently collaborated on songs, cantatas, and theater pieces. In April 1868 the Griegs' only child, Alexandra, was born; she died the next year. Before that happened, however, the family spent a happy summer in a vacation cottage in Denmark, where the composer finished the most successful of his larger works, the Concerto for Piano.

During his vacation a year later, Grieg discovered the collection cf Norwegian folktunes gathered by the organist Ludvig Lindeman that opened his eyes to the real possibilities of native music in Norway; Grieg published a collection of arrangements for piano in 1870. The same year in Rome Grieg met Liszt [1218], who gave him his seal of approval and inaugurated his association with Henrik Ibsen. Before that bore fruit, however, there were several years of close work with Bjørnson that in 1873 seemed about to culminate in an opera, Olav Trygvason, whose germ had been the brief 1872 cantata Landkjenning (Land sighting). But after composing several segments and waiting impatiently for the poet to deliver more, Grieg decided to accede to Ibsen's request that he write music for a revival of Peer Gynt. Bjørnson was furious, gave up the project, and broke with Grieg for sixteen years. Peer Gynt was a time-consuming project and did not reach the stage until February 1876. It was successful, but unhappily the theater burned down after thirty-seven showings. Grieg later several times expanded the score; it was not until 1888 and 1891, however, that he extracted the two popular orchestral suites.

Meanwhile Grieg had beefed up his orchestra to professional standing, and Svendsen had returned to be his co-conductor. There were also increasingly frequent concert tours. Toward the end of the decade, the

Griegs began spending their summers in the Norwegian mountains, where once again the composer's feeling for the native idiom was reinforced. It was also reinforced, oddly, by his attendance in 1876 at the Bayreuth premiere of Wagner's [1230] *Ring,* in which he sensed the whole Scandinavian ethos, making him once again yearn to express himself dramatically. But attempts to find a subject and a libretto—lukewarm at best—came to naught. In 1880 Grieg yielded to a call from Bergen to come be the town conductor and moved there to find that, as in Christiania, he had to build from virtually nothing. But the work was more than he had bargained for, and he resigned two years later. In 1883 he went on a long European tour, ending in an Italian vacation. Two years later he and Nina moved into their new home, Troldhaugen, overlooking the Bergen fjord, and that autumn there were two all-Grieg concerts in Christiania, signifying that the composer had prematurely won honor in his own country, and a musically expanded *Peer Gynt* in Copenhagen. By now Grieg's output consisted almost entirely of the little piano pieces and songs that captured his essence best.

The history of the rest of Grieg's life is largely one of concert tours and travels. He never came to America, having no taste for the sea journey, but he became much loved throughout Europe. Privately he is said to have been, like many artists, "difficult," but in public—a diminutive man with twinkling eyes and a squeaky voice—he charmed people. In Leipzig in 1888 a New Year's party began friendships with both Brahms [1329] and Tchaikovsky [1377]. In England he was able to persuade young Frederick Delius' [1539] father that his son was cut out to be a musician, not a businessman. He renewed old friendships—with Bjørnson and with Ibsen, from whom he had drifted during the opera-libretto search—and made new ones —with the poet Holger Drachmann and the young Australian pianist Percy Grainger [1749], who became another of his preferred interpreters. Bergen, and indeed all Norway, celebrated the Griegs' silver wedding in 1892. In 1898 there was a grand national music festival in Bergen, to which Grieg, without consultation, invited Willem Mengelberg and the Amsterdam Concertgebouw Orchestra, thereby bruising a good many Norwegian toes; nevertheless the event was a smashing success. In 1899, infected by Bjørnson's outrage at the Dreyfus case, Grieg refused to play in Paris; when he appeared there four years later, he had to ride out a storm of protest in the concert hall, and a journalistic attack by Debussy [1547], dis-

paraging one piece as "a pink bonbon stuffed with snow," and faintly praising him as "an adroit musician, more concerned with effects than with real art."

Always frail, Grieg found the concert life strenuous and increasingly complained of fatigue and illness. He lived to see Norway independent of Sweden in 1905. He visited Holland and England once more the next year. In the summer of 1907, although he seemed fit, he sensed that he had not long to live. At the beginning of September, he took a hotel room in Bergen to sail for England again, but became ill, lapsed into a coma, and died two days later. At his request, Johan Halvorsen [1561] conducted the Nordraak *Funeral March* at the obsequies; Grieg's ashes rest today in a grotto at Troldhaugen.

RECORDINGS: Grieg recorded a double handful of his piano pieces in Paris in 1903 and also made some piano rolls. The orchestral, chamber, and piano pieces have all received modern recordings, including the symphony (which was recently revived). There are also versions of the complete music for Bjørnson's *Sigurd Jorsalfar,* for Ibsen's *Peer Gynt* (the version by Per Dreier for Unicorn is the only one that is absolutely complete), and what is left of the abortive *Olav Trygvason.* Much of the choral music remains untouched, and though most of the songs have been recorded, there is so far no inclusive edition.

[1411] **POPPER, David** (Pop'-per, Dä'-fĕd)

CELLIST, TEACHER
BORN: Prague, June 16, 1843
DIED: Baden (Austria), August 7, 1913

Trained by Julius Goltermann at the Prague Conservatory, Popper began his concert career when he was twenty and came to international prominence at the Karlsruhe Festival of 1865. Hans von Bülow [1310] was especially taken with his talent, accompanying him in several recitals and getting him named *Kammervirtuos* to one of the Hohenzollern princes. Three years later he joined the Hofoper in Vienna as first cellist and soon afterward became a member of the Hellmesberger String Quartet. In 1872 he married the pianist Sophie Menter and a year later returned to the road with her as his accompanist. The marriage was not a success: in the early 1880s Sophie took a teaching post at the St. Petersburg Conservatory, and in 1886 the union came unglued. Ten years later Popper became professor of cello at the Budapest Conservatory; in that city he succeeded László Hegyesy as cellist of the Hubay Quartet. (Popper, Hubay [1509], and Brahms [1329] are said to have played trios together.) Popper ranks as one of the great cellists. He wrote 4 concerti, a string quintet, and many short pieces, the most popular of which were encore pieces for his instrument. At a time when his popularity had waned, American composer-author Marion Bauer (1887–1955), on hearing one of them played in concert, remarked that it sounded more like "Grandpopper music." RECORDINGS: Jascha Silberstein has recorded the E minor concerto, and Jascha Bernstein a whole LP disc of short pieces, including the *Requiem* for three celli and piano. There is also a disc of music for cello and piano on the Genesis label.

[1412] PINELLI, Ettore (Pē-nel′-lē, Et-tō′-rā)
VIOLINIST, TEACHER, CONDUCTOR
BORN: Rome, October 18, 1843
DIED: Rome, September 17, 1915

Pinelli studied the violin in Rome, embarked on a concert career at an early age, and then studied some more with Joachim [1321] in Hannover. He became second violin in the Quartetto Romano, founded by his uncle and teacher Tullio Ramacciotti, which in 1866 became the Quintetto Romano with the addition of the pianist Sgambati [1385]. Lifelong friends, he and Sgambati were the organizers and founders of the Liceo Musicale of the St. Cecilia Academy. They also founded the Società della Musica da camera and conducted the Court concerts. In 1874 Pinelli founded his own orchestra, the Società Orchestrale Romano, which he conducted until 1898. His largest works were a symphony, a string quartet, and an overture. RECORDINGS: On records he is represented only by a few songs.

[1413] BERNICAT, Firmin (Bâr-nē-kà′, Fēr-maɴ′)
BORN: 1843
DIED: 1883

Having made for himself a name of sorts as a deviser of music-hall vaudevilles, Bernicat began to set his sights higher. In 1882 he had a success in Brussels with a full-length operetta, *Les Beignets du Roi (The King's Fritters,* later produced in Paris as *Les premières armes de Louis XV—Louis XV's First Weapons).* Encouraged, he set out on a second operetta, *François-les-bas-bleus (Francis Bluestocking)* but died suddenly (at forty) before

he could finish it. It was completed by Messager [1474] in 1883, successfully launching Messager on his stage career. RECORDINGS: A few excerpts from these works are on early records.

[1414] WIDOR, Charles-Marie-Jean-Albert (Vē-dôr′, Shärl Mà-rē′ Zhàɴ Àl-bâr′)
ORGANIST, TEACHER, CRITIC, CONDUCTOR
BORN: Lyons, February 21, 1844
DIED: Paris, March 12, 1937

Charles-Marie Widor was among the most important of the first generation of modern French organists. His grandfather, of Hungarian descent, had been an organ builder in Alsace. His mother was descended from the balloonist Montgolfiers. His father was organist of the church of St. François in Lyons, and his first teacher, whom he succeeded at fifteen. He undertook further organ study in Brussels with Jacques Lemmens and at the same time studied composition with Fétis [1111]. In 1870 he became organist at the great Cavaillé-Coll organ in St. Sulpice in Paris. The first of the 10 organ symphonies followed within two years. This genre, which Widor invented, has less to do with form than with the resources of the big "orchestral" organs. His stage works date from 1880 and consist of a ballet, 3 operas, and incidental music for 2 plays; in three of these stage works he collaborated with the poet François Coppée. He became critic for *L'Estafette* (he was a very stylish writer and was also fluent in Latin and Greek), conductor of the Concordia Oratorio Society, a member of the *Légion d'honneur,* and permanent secretary of the Academie. His musical cronies included Gounod [1258], Delibes [1344], Massenet [1396], and Saint-Saëns [1343]. On the death of Franck [1284] in 1890, Widor became professor of organ at the Conservatoire, and when Dubois [1356] took over the directorship on Thomas's [1217] death in 1896, Widor moved up to the professorship of composition. Among his students he numbered such organists as Marcel Dupré [1806], Albert Schweitzer, and Louis Vierne [1616], and composers and teachers such as Nadia Boulanger, Honegger [1861], and Milhaud [1868]. A lifelong devotee of J. S. Bach [684] (he also worshipped Mozart [992]), it was Widor who persuaded Schweitzer to undertake his great Bach study. He himself wrote on orchestration and on the links between Gregorian chant and ancient Greek music. He is said to have been an irresistibly charming and witty man. After sixty-three years he retired from St. Sulpice but kept up his composition and practiced at the organ in his home until his death at the age of ninety-three. (He is the earliest composer mentioned in this book whose obituary this writer recalls reading in the news.) Widor wrote in all fields—there are 2 orchestral symphonies, other large works for orchestra, concertos, chamber music, choral works, much keyboard music, and songs. RECORDINGS: On records he is chiefly represented by the organ symphonies. (There is at least one integral recording as of this date—by Pierre Labric.) There are also recordings of a *Romance* for flute and orchestra (Raymond Meylan) and several versions of the Suite for Flute and Piano.

[1415] SARASATE Y NAVASCUÉZ, Pablo Martín Melitón de (Sà-rà-sá'-tē ē Nà-vàs'-kwōō-āth, Pàb'-vlō Mär-tēn' Mel-ē-tōn' dä)

VIOLINIST
BORN: Pamplona, March 10, 1844
DIED: Biarritz, September 20, 1908

Next to Paganini [1106], whose music he eschewed playing, Sarasate was probably the best-known violinist, worldwide, of his century. His father, a military bandmaster, gave him his first lessons, and he made his debut at La Coruna at the age of eight. He was brought to the attention of Queen Isabella II, who generously gave him a Stradivarius (a Spanish trophy from Naples) and paid his way to study with Alard [1240] at the Paris Conservatoire when he had reached the age of twelve. He became Alard's star pupil and won several prizes during his three-year stay. At first he meant to concentrate on composition, but soon gave in to the call of the road, on which he set out in 1859. For forty years he was heard all over the world, touring almost nonstop. A somewhat flamboyant figure, he was not fond of musical fireworks but was regarded as a performer of great taste (a tendency underlined by his refusal to play the Brahms [1329] concerto). Many important composers—e.g., Saint-Saëns [1343], Bruch [1358], Lalo [1286]—wrote major works for him. His long-popular violin works are catchy but superficial. RECORDINGS: The best known and most often recorded is the *Gypsy Airs,* published in Leipzig as *Zigeunerweisen,* but many others have also been often recorded. Around 1904 Sarasate himself made a series of records for the Gramophone Company.

[1416] RIMSKY-KORSAKOV, Nikolai Andreyevich (Rim'-skē Kôr'-sà-kôf, Ni'-ku-lī Àn-drā'-ye-vich)

TEACHER, ADMINISTRATOR
BORN: Tikhvin, March 18, 1844
DIED: Liubensk, June 21, 1908

Of the "mighty handful" of Russian nationalist composers (as critic Vladimir Stasov had dubbed them) Rimsky-Korsakov was the youngest, the most productive, the most directly influential, and ultimately the best-trained. He was a particularly successful composer of operas, but although most of them are still reverently performed in Soviet Russia, only one, *Le Coq d'Or (The Golden Cock),* has ever obtained so much as a toehold in the West. There he enjoys considerable popularity for a handful of brilliantly scored orchestral pieces which, however—and the composer would have agreed—are not much concerned with profundity. In some quarters such popularity has not exactly increased his reputation in any favorable sense. Nor have his revisions and completions of the fragments left by his friends Borodin [1331] and Mussorgsky [1369] done his cause any good, eliciting as they have in recent years loud cries of "Desecration!" Apart from one opera, several orchestral works, and a few of the songs, most of his large and very uneven output has remained little known from the outset. Yet the fact remains that he was an enormously important figure in the history of Russian music, and that he had, especially as an orchestrator, a significant impact outside his homeland.

Nikolai Andreyevich Rimsky-Korsakov spent his childhood in his birthplace, a river town some one hundred miles east of St. Petersburg. His father, Andrei, a former provincial governor, then retired, was a man of some affluence and culture who had a musical ear, by whose dictates he could play the piano. Save for the choir at the local monastery church there was little other music in Tikhvin. The boy showed some musicality at an early age—indeed, he was more than ordinarily bright in other respects—and was, in the usual way of children of good families in those days, put to studying piano with the town women who imagined themselves piano teachers. Despite their ministrations, he did rather well, but he was far more interested (from his voracious reading and from the fact that his much-older brother Voyin was a naval officer) in the sea. Accordingly, in 1856 he was sent off to the Naval Academy at St. Petersburg. Although the Academy seems to have exhibited most of the horrors common to boys' schools then, Rimsky adapted readily and performed well initially. Soon, however, he found other, more interesting diversions and settled, as we might say, for a "gentleman's C." He returned to piano study, spent summers on his brother's ship, and increasingly steeped himself in opera performances and orchestral concerts. He was particularly taken with Glinka's [1179] music, notably *Russlan and Ludmila,* and idly dreamed of composing, knowing perfectly well that he had no idea what that involved. In 1860 he took up with Theodore Canille, a piano teacher with some real claim to the title. Canille introduced him to non-Russian music by important composers, gave him some very rudimentary theory, and soon had him writing music, after a fashion. A year later Voyin, considering his brother sufficiently musically cultured for a naval officer, withdrew his funding of the lessons, but Canille kept them up anyhow. In 1861 Rimsky elected to conduct a volunteer cadet chorus, and that fall Canille took him to call on Balakirev [1348].

In the Balakirev milieu, which dazzled him in all respects, Rimsky made friends with Cui [1337], Mussorgsky, and Stasov, and became a favorite of its presiding genius, who began "training" him in his sporadic fashion, demanding almost immediately that he write a symphony. (Rimsky managed an opening movement rather quickly, but, ironically, was totally baffled about how to orchestrate it.) But all this soon came to an end. The following March Andrei Rimsky-Korsakov died (at seventy-eight), and a month later his younger son graduated as a midshipman and was detailed to a clipper ship, *Almaz,* under the command of one Zelyony, a bullying and pusillanimous captain. After some months of tedious duty in Baltic ports (during which he fell in love for the first time), Rimsky's ship took him to London for her refitting, remaining there nearly four months. After a return to the Baltic in 1863 to intercept vessels running arms to the Polish revolutionaries, the *Almaz* set sail for New York. The voyage was a long and rough one, involving a brush with an Atlantic hurricane. She made port in October and remained some six months, during which Rimsky-Korsakov attended Gounod's [1258] *Faust* (then new in America) and visited Niagara Falls, Annapolis, and Baltimore. In April 1864 Zelyony received orders to proceed westward around the world. He sailed slowly and reluctantly to Rio de Janeiro, and after a few days stay he went on. Shortly, to the captain's delight, the ship sprang an apparently not very consequential leak and had to return to Rio long enough for the global trip to be canceled.

The ship returned to Europe and spent the winter paradisally on the French and Italian Riviera until she was ordered in April to escort the body of the Czarevich, who had just died in Nice, back to Russia.

During all this time, Rimsky-Korsakov had given his music no serious attention. Stationed again in St. Petersburg in 1865, however, he was soon back with the Balakirev circle, wherein that autumn he initiated a lifelong friendship with Borodin. Balakirev nagged him into completing his symphony and played it at one of his Free School concerts, where it shared the program with the Mozart [992] *Requiem.* It was decently received and the composer was satisfied, though later he was aghast at his own naivety and temerity. Mostly, however, he led a life of *dolce far niente.* His naval duties were minimal. Risking Balakirev's displeasure, he polished his piano playing (mostly to wow his fellow officers) and wrote an *Overture on Russian Themes,* which Balakirev, disapprovingly, eventually conducted. That same year, 1866, Rimsky had his first publication—four songs. In 1867 he was, much to his hero-worshiping delight, taken into the circle of Glinka's sister Liudmila Shestakova, became firm friends with Mussorgsky (with whom he spent hours discussing music free of Balakirevian authority), and (contrary to the attitudes of most of his musical friends) found a good deal to admire in Tchaikovsky [1377], who was just beginning to come to notice. For a Balakirev concert of pan-Slavic music, he wrote a *Serbian Fantasy* and also composed songs for a soprano named Zotova and *Sadko,* an orchestral fantasy based on the story of the Novgorod merchant—an idea turned over to him by Mussorgsky, who had typically never gotten around to it. (It is musically unrelated to the later opera *Sadko.)* To his disappointment, Balakirev failed to introduce him to the visiting Berlioz [1175], then already in bad health. Rimsky also began a new symphony but abandoned it when he found that, in terms of formal considerations, he was out of his depth—and that of his friends.

In the spring of 1868, he began to frequent the home of three musical sisters, the Purgolds, one of whom, Nadezhda, he was eventually to marry. He set to work on a programmatic piece based on an oriental tale, *Antar,* which officially became Symphony No. 2. That completed, he began with some trepidation his first opera, *Pskovityanka (The Maid of Pskov),* based on a quasihistorical play by Mey. Operatically speaking, it was a heady time, for concurrently Borodin was writing *Prince Igor,* Mussorgsky *Boris Godunov*, and the ailing Dargo-myzhsky **[1228]** was at work on *The Stone Guest*. In 1869 the last-named died, be-queathing the scoring of that work to Rim-sky. (Rimsky had won the name of a master orchestrator among the members of his cir-cle, though in truth it was a case of the pur-blind leading the blind since his notions of procedure were based on outmoded texts. Most of his early work, in fact, he later sub-jected to radical revision.) To interrupt this interruption, there came a request from the Maryinsky that the *kuchka* (without Balaki-rev) collaborate on a sort of opera-ballet called *Mlada*. Rimsky did not get very far with *his* assignment, and the whole project eventually collapsed. Nor did the other works develop apace, in part owing to crises in the composer's private life. In December Nadezhda Purgold's mother died, followed the next autumn by Voyin Rimsky-Kor-sakov. In between, despite his lack of any serious training, Nikolai Andreyevich was offered the professorship of composition and orchestration at the Conservatory. After some hesitation, he accepted, spurred on by his own brash self-confidence and the urg-ings of Balakirev (who wanted to get even with the musical establishment, which was cramping his style). Three years later, know-ing nothing of harmony or counterpoint, he also undertook the teaching of those sub-jects. And he conducted the orchestra class, though he had earlier admitted that con-ducting was an unfathomable mystery to him. Somehow he bluffed his way through (as so many have) until guilt forced him to teach himself what he was professing to teach.

In the fall of 1871, Rimsky and Mussorg-sky began sharing an apartment. That ar-rangement was, however, not to last long. In December, after going to Italy to see that Voyin's body was sent home and to bring his relicts back with him, he announced his en-gagement to Nadezhda, whom he married with Mussorgsky as best man the following summer. *The Stone Guest* opened and closed at the Maryinsky in February. *Pskovityanka* (which would pass through several meta-morphoses in the next thirty years) was completed, and, after undergoing some revi-sions at the demand of the censor (in which the Grand Duke Constantine intervened positively), was premiered on the same stage in mid-January of 1873. It won nine repeti-tions that season. Rimsky rewrote it three years later but was dissatisfied with that ver-sion. A third and final version, based on the first, was played in 1895, and three years later Rimsky detached the prologue from

version two and presented it as a separate opera called *Boyarinya Vera Sheloga*.

By now Balakirev had for the nonce with-drawn from circulation, and Rimsky-Kor-sakov was increasingly thinking for himself musically. His naval post had become little more than a sinecure, and early in 1873 the department created for him a civil-service office as inspector of navy bands. The some-what demanding duties turned out to be of enormous benefit to him: not only did he get to hear at close range what modern wind instruments (a major stumbling block in in-strumentation for him) could and could not do; he also had laboratory conditions in which to try out experiments of his own in arrangements and original compositions. Shortly after his appointment, he completed a third symphony, and in August Nadezhda presented him with a son, Mikhail Niko-laievich. The following February Rimsky had an appointment in Samara where he made his public debut as a conductor, di-recting *inter alias* the premiere of the third symphony. It was at about this time that he took up the serious study of counterpoint and harmony; one of his texts was written by the outcast (to the *kuchka)* Tchaikovsky. One of the first fruits of his labors was a string quartet which, apparently, no one liked, and which remains largely unknown.

In the autumn of 1874 on the request of a delegation from the moribund Free School, Rimsky succeeded Balakirev as its director and shocked his friends by presenting its or-chestra in concerts of Renaissance (!) and Classical music. Small wonder that the pe-riod brought forth no major compositions, for he was also busy with his inspectorship, his conservatory professorship, his rigorous studies, and a growing preoccupation with native folk music. To add to all this, Nadezhda's birthing of a daughter, Sonya, left her very ill and bedridden for months. As if he did not have enough to do, Rimsky, at the urging of Balakirev (who had sud-denly surfaced again), took on a number of private pupils. Moreover Mme. Shestakova had asked Balakirev to edit for publication her brother's (Glinka's) works, and he dragooned Rimsky and Anatol Liadov **[1485]** into assisting him, the task taking two years. Thus the only works of signifi-cance (if that is the word) to appear in the later 1870s were a string sextet and a wind quintet, written for a chamber music compe-tition. (The prize went to Nápravník **[1374]**; the sextet got an honorable mention. Balaki-rev told Rimsky it served him right.) Rim-sky found himself in an embarrassing situa-tion apropos of a choral competition at about the same time: he was appointed a judge and had to consider his own entries (anonymously submitted like the rest). He somehow managed to be absent when they came up—and were declared prizewinners.

Rimsky next turned to an operatic setting of Gogol's *The May Night*, which his wife had long ago urged him to make. He completed it in 1879 (with a dedication to her); it was immediately accepted by the Imperial Opera and was premiered with qualified success at St. Petersburg in January 1880. The composer, who combined in it the fruits of his studies, his devotion to folksong, and a new self-confidence based on knowledge, considered it his declaration of independence. While it was being written, he collaborated with Liadov, Cui, and Borodin in a *jeu d'esprit:* a series of piano variations on a "Chopsticks"-like polka theme by the last named (which was christened "Tati-tati" by Stasov). In October 1878 a second son, Andrei—later a well-known musicologist—was born. Rimsky followed *May Night* with a string quartet on Russian folk melodies and an orchestral *Skazka (Fairy Tale)*, then set to work on an operatic version of Ostrovsky's play *Snegurochka (The Snow-Maiden)*, which embodied a Russian sun myth with which he was fascinated at the time. Around 1880 Balakirev introduced him to a potential young genius named Alexander Glazunov [1573], who became Rimsky's favorite pupil.

In 1881 Mussorgsky, who had long been sinking in the slough of alcohol, died. Out of enormous respect for his genius and for old times' sake, Rimsky-Korsakov took on the gigantic (and ultimately thankless) task of bringing some kind of order to the musical remains. Again the job cost him nearly two years of his time. To help effect it, he gave up another thankless task, the directorship of the Free School, which he had kept afloat with great effort, turning it back to Balakirev, who had been unsubtly nagging him to do so for some time. *Snegurochka*, to be sure, was completed, and produced at the Maryinsky, in 1881. (The reviewers, noting folksong references again, proclaimed that the composer had no melodic invention.) Predictably there was a long creative hiatus. True, during this period Rimsky revamped a number of his early works, but the single composition of any scope between 1881 and 1887 was a piano concerto in a single movement, on a Russian theme but much influenced by Liszt.

With the ascension of a new czar (Alexander III) to the throne, Rimsky found himself appointed as Balakirev's assistant in the direction of the imperial chapel, a post that involved the general musical education of the choristers. That same year he was drawn into the musical circle of Mitrofan Petrovich Belaiev, amateur violist, and wealthy patron and publisher of Russian music, who sponsored Friday *musicales* in his home. Somewhat to Rimsky's displeasure (for the effect of the action on navy music), the government abolished the inspectorship the next spring, 1884. In June Nadezhda bore a second daughter, named for her. In 1885, having gained full confidence and an enviable reputation as a teacher of harmony, Rimsky published a harmony manual, which went into a second edition a year later. The year 1886 produced a *Fantasy on Russian Themes* for violin and orchestra, and 1887 a work that was to have been its "Spanish" counterpart, but emerged, as the orchestral *Caprice Español (Spanish Caprice)*. However, at the beginning of the latter year the sudden death of Borodin once again left Rimsky with the task of picking up the pieces—in this instance those of the opera *Prince Igor*, which he and Glazunov completed and orchestrated. Increasingly—especially as the focus of the Belaiev coterie—Rimsky was finding himself chief arbiter of Russian music.

For a while it appeared as though the composer's productivity would at last shift into high gear. In 1888, for example, he wrote the two works by which he is best known: the symphonic suite *Scheherazade*, based on tales from the *Arabian Nights*, and the *Russian Easter Overture*. He then turned again to the aborted *Mlada* project and in 1889–90 wrote his own version. But 1890 posed severe difficulties on the domestic scene: Rimsky's aged mother died, Andrei was seriously ill, Nadezhda was sick off and on for most of the year, and a baby son was born and died. These anxieties and sorrows, no doubt coupled with the effects of twenty-five years of overwork, sent the poor man into a tailspin, which evidenced itself in a total disaffection for music, as well as in alarming physical and mental problems. He read almost compulsively and tried writing theoretical articles, which he found mostly chaotic. During this period *Prince Igor* reached the stage, and late in 1892 the much-postponed *Mlada*, which was not well received. After that, Rimsky's health took a turn for the worse, and he determined to resign his chapel post, though out of consideration for Balakirev he postponed that action until 1895. In May 1893 he went to Yalta, where Nadezhda had taken their ailing five-year-old daughter Maria. He found the child worse than when they had departed and settled in to await the inevitable, whiling away the time writing his memoirs (published posthumously in 1909 as *Chronicle of My Musical Life*). He was on his way back to St.

Petersburg in August when he got word that the little girl had died and returned for her funeral. His wife was unable to bear returning to their former home, so they moved into a new one on Zagorodny Prospect. In December Rimsky was stunned by news of the sudden death of Tchaikovsky, to whom he had grown quite close. (It gave rise to all sorts of rumors, he tells us significantly.)

The shock seems to have aroused him from his lethargy. He pulled himself together sufficiently to conduct a memorial concert in mid-December in the Russian Symphony Concert Series, at whose helm he remained for the rest of the season. And he again found himself in a creative vein. Casting about for an operatic subject, he hit on Gogol's "Christmas Eve." Doubtless he was attracted, as he says, by its strong mythic and folkloric elements, but it is hardly coincidental that it had provided the basis long ago for Tchaikovsky's *Vakula,* to which Rimsky had helped award the prize. He wrote furiously and had completed the work —not wholly to his satisfaction—within a twelvemonth. This marked the beginning of his most fertile period of composition, which lasted to the end of his life.

Rimsky had not completed the orchestration of *Christmas Eve* before he began work on a new opera, *Sadko,* a subject urged on him by a correspondent, and one with which he had already had some dealing. Meanwhile *Christmas Eve* had run afoul of the censor, who insisted that everyone knew its anonymous czarina was really Catherine the Great and that therefore it could not be presented in light of an imperial decree prohibiting stage representation of Romanovs. Approached (unsuccessfully) by a court minister about taking over the chapel in succession to Balakirev, who had resigned, Rimsky seized the opportunity to pull strings and thus got the show back on the road. The premiere was, in fact, to be a grandiose court-sponsored affair. But at the dress rehearsal in early December 1895, two of the grand dukes took umbrage at seeing what they took to be their ancestor onstage and banned performances unless radical changes were made. In the end the problem was resolved by having the alto czarina supplanted by a baritone Serene Highness, and the premiere took place on the tenth. But the work was offered under a cloud and had little initial success.

Meanwhile Rimsky had briefly interrupted *Sadko* to sketch a *Barber of Bagdad,* which ultimately went nowhere, except to provide some music for the later *Golden Cock.* A further interruption was provided by the now-infamous reorchestration of *Bo-*

ris Godunov. By 1896 Rimsky was teetering on the edge of another breakdown and could barely force himself to complete *Sadko.* However, on finishing it, he felt that he was at the peak of his musical powers. He followed this work almost immediately with a setting, reminiscent of Dargomizhsky's *Stone Guest* style, of Pushkin's one-act, two-character *Mozart and Salieri,* completed in 1897—a year that also saw the composition of more than half of his not inconsiderable output of songs. That fall he and Felix Blumenfeld read through *Sadko* for the directors of the Maryinsky. Rimsky was hoarse and Blumenfeld diffident, and the director hemmed and hawed and said, "Well, maybe—" The case was closed when the czar sent word that he wanted no more of that stuff. But, not entirely unfortuitously, the composer was visited by Savva Mamontov, a Moscow tycoon who ran an independent opera house and who volunteered to shelter *Sadko.* (He had already mounted the final version of *Pskovityanka* in 1896.) The first performances were badly flawed (January 1898), but that spring things went much better when Mamontov brought his company to the capital and the composer conducted not only *Sadko* but also *The May Night* and *Snegurochka.* For the nonce, the troupe was entrusted with the production of all new Rimsky-Korsakov operas. At the end of the year it gave the first performances of *Vera Sheloga* (see previously) and *Mozart and Salieri.* In the latter the great young basso Fedor Chaliapin established himself once and for all as a major singing-actor in the role of Salieri **[966].** (He had created the role of Ivan the Terrible in *Pskovityanka.)* The following November, 1899, the company gave a first hearing to *The Tsar's Bride,* a full-length opera distantly related to *Pskovityanka.* By then, however, Chaliapin had defected to the Bolshoi, and the following year Mamontov was jailed for his part in a commercial scandal. The company went on under the management of a committee, but its last important Rimsky premiere was *The Tale of Tsar Saltan,* another folkloristic work, to a libretto by Vladimir Bielski, who had also provided that for *Sadko.* To the composer's surprise, Belaiev refused the work on the ground that he had found opera publication uneconomical, and so their business relationship came to an end.

By the end of the century revolutionary fervor, especially among students, was beginning to build in Russia, and so the Rimsky-Korsakovs sent their son Andrei to the University of Strassburg. His presence abroad gave them an excuse to spend the next several summers in Germany and Switzerland. Meanwhile the imperial operas had been making friendly gestures, and Rimsky had set to work on a new piece, *Servilia*, set in ancient Rome, in which he set aside nationalism for his notion of Classicism, which he admitted had Italian and Greek roots. It was during this time that he finally gave up his regular role as conductor in St. Petersburg. In 1902 the Maryinsky Theater, having successfully mounted *Sadko*, premiered *Servilia*, which had little success after the opening night. But, having completed it, its composer was already at work on two new operas, the one-act *Kashchei the Immortal* and the "Polish" *Pan Voyevoda (The Commander)*, intended as a tribute to Chopin [1208]. The first was produced by the former Mamontov company, in tandem with Tchaikovsky's *Iolanta*, a little more than two months after the *Servilia* premiere. Just a year later Belaiev died of a heart attack while recuperating from an operation, and Rimsky conducted a specially composed orchestral piece, *At the Grave*, in a concert in his memory. (Most of the other orchestral works of his last years consist of suites or fantasias from the operas.) *Pan Voyevoda*, seemingly doomed from the start, was first played in 1904 at the St. Petersburg Conservatory, and hardly at all afterward.

A few months later, early in 1905, there was a particularly atrocious slaughter of dissident students by the Cossacks, causing an upheaval among those at the conservatory. The matter was poorly handled by the directorship, causing Rimsky to come out publicly on the side of the students. This action split the faculty and resulted in his summary dismissal and the closing of the school. Rimsky, rather to his surprise, found himself a symbolic figure for the dissidents. In his honor they planned a concert which was to begin with a performance of *Kashchei*. In the event, however, after the opera had been sung, the participants got out of hand with inflammatory speeches. The police were called. They closed the theater before the concert proper could take place and banned all performances of Rimsky's music—though that prohibition was soon lifted. On vacation that summer, too shaken to compose, Rimsky began writing his treatise on orchestration and returned to his memoirs. In the fall he attended the professional premiere of *Pan Voyevoda*, conducted by Rachmaninoff [1638] at the Bolshoi, but whatever its merits, the strikes and riots preceding the December revolution dictated its swift demise.

Despite the social conditions, Rimsky-Korsakov was reinstated at the conservatory, where he found conditions chaotic, re-signed, and was persuaded by Glazunov [1573] to stay on at least until the end of the academic year. During the time following completion of the last opera, he had been working at a new one, called *The Tale of the Invisible City Kitezh and the Maiden Fevronia* (libretto by Bielski), and had completed it in the late winter of 1905. By the time it was produced at the Maryinsky (February 1907), he was already well into what was to be his final opera, *The Golden Cock*, for which Bielski had made a text from Pushkin's poem. Full of satire of monarchy, the latter work predictably met strong resistance from the censors, and before it could finally be put on (at the Bolshoi in October 1909), the composer had succumbed to the heart disease that had plagued him for some time. Among the many composers of the next generation on whom he left a direct imprint as their teacher were (besides Glazunov and Liadov), Arensky [1536], Ippolitov-Ivanov [1517], Grechaninov [1567], Miaskovsky [1735], Nikolai Tcherepnin [1642], Prokofiev [1851], and Stravinsky [1748]. His grandson Georgi (1901–65), little known today, was a disciple of Scriabin [1625] and an early exponent of microtonal and electronic music.

RECORDINGS: There has been a proliferation of records of the popular orchestral numbers over the last half century, and most of the others have been in and out of the catalog. Thanks largely to the industry of the Soviets, there have been one or more recordings of each of the operas, save for (apparently) *Servilia* and *Pan Voyevoda*. On the other hand, outside of Russia at any rate, minimal attention has been paid to the chamber music, piano works, and choral compositions. Songs have appeared in various "recitals," and there is an LP by Boris Christoff of a representative selection.

[1417] GIGOUT, Eugène (Zhē-gōō′, Ö-zhen′)
ORGANIST, TEACHER
BORN: Nancy, March 23, 1844
DIED: Paris, December 9, 1925

Gigout was one of the more important figures in the nineteenth-century renaissance of French organ music, often in his music returning to an earlier tradition. He began his career as a choirboy and sometime organist at Nancy Cathedral, then entered the École Niedermeyer [1167] in Paris at thirteen, to study with, among others, the young Saint-Saëns [1343]. In 1863 he was appointed professor of organ there, married the daughter of the recently deceased founder, and also became organist at St. Augustin, where he held forth at the Cavaillé-Coll for sixty years. In 1885 he left the school, was appointed an officer of public instruction, and, backed by the government, opened his own organ school. He returned to Niedermeyer in 1900, and in 1911 his old classmate Fauré [1424], now director of the Conservatoire, appointed him to succeed Guilmant [1351] as professor of organ. Gigout received the *Légion d'honneur* and other tokens of recognition. He was also a reviewer and writer on musical subjects. The bulk of his musical output is for organ, running to some 400 works; much of it is primarily for liturgical use. RECORDINGS: Examples appear in various recorded anthologies of French organ music.

[1418] VARNEY, Louis (Vàr-nā', Lōō-ē')
CONDUCTOR
BORN: New Orleans, May 30, 1844
DIED: Paris, August 20, 1908

A prolific and successful composer of theater music, Varney wrote curiously old-fashioned music which faded quickly. His father, Pierre Joseph Alphonse (1811–79), a pupil of Antonín Reicha [1059], was himself a composer and a peripatetic theater conductor. From 1840 he directed the opera in New Orleans, where he married Jeanne Aimée Andry, returning to Paris a decade later. He was his son's chief teacher. Louis became conductor at the Théâtre de l'Athenée, for which he wrote revues, vaudevilles, and the like. In 1880 he had a solid hit at the Bouffes Parisiens with his *Les Mousquetaires au couvent (The Musketeers at the Convent)*, a full-length operetta. From then on until illness halted him, he turned out about two such works a year—30-odd in all. He spent his last years in the Pyrenees, trying vainly to regain his health. RECORDINGS: There are recorded excerpts of his works, mostly from an earlier day.

[1419] GRAMMANN, Karl (Gràm'-màn, Kärl)
BORN: Lübeck, June 3, 1844
DIED: Dresden, January 30, 1897

Karl Grammann, like just about everyone else of his day, studied at the Leipzig Conservatory. He lived for a while in Vienna, then settled in Dresden. Considering his rather brief life span, he was a fairly prolific composer. He wrote 8 operas; six of them were produced, and all have been wholly forgotten. There were other vocal compositions, symphonies, chamber music, and songs. RECORDINGS: One or two of the songs got recorded back in the early days of sound recording.

[1420] PALADILHE, Émile (Pà-là-dēl', À-mēl')
BORN: Montpellier, June 3, 1844
DIED: Paris, January 8, 1926

Though Paladilhe was prominent in his day —an era within the memories of many now living—there seem to be no detailed accounts of his life. He studied the organ in Montpellier before entering the Paris Conservatoire at nine. He worked there for seven years under the standard team of Halévy [1157], Marmontel, and Benoist, won first prizes for both piano and organ, and capped his youthful career with the Grand Prix de Rome in 1860. (He later suppressed his winning cantata.) But twelve years went by before he came up with his little opera *Le Passant (The Passer-By)*, based on François Coppée's playlet, in which he incorporated his very successful song "Mandolinata." He had a fair success in 1878 with *Suzanne*, but none with the two operas that bracketed it: *L'Amour africain (African Love)* in 1875 and *Diana* in 1885. In 1886, however, his one serious opera *Patrie (Fatherland)*, to a libretto by Victorien Sardou after one of his own plays, attracted international attention and was widely played for a time. But his only other dramatic effort was a religious spectacle, *Les Saintes Maries de la mer (The St. Marys of the Sea)*, presented in his native city in 1892. He also wrote 2 Masses, other religious works, a symphony, and a number of smaller works, notably songs. He won the *Légion d'honneur* in 1888 and succeeded Guiraud [1352] in the Institut in 1892, after which time he seems to have produced little. RECORDINGS: Paladilhe is represented on records chiefly by selections from *Patrie* and two songs, "Mandolinata" and "Psyché."

[1421] TAFFANEL, Claude Paul (Tàf-fà-nel', Klōd Pōl)
FLUTIST, CONDUCTOR, TEACHER
BORN: Bordeaux, September 16, 1844
DIED: Paris, November 22, 1908

Taffanel was the most important and influential flutist of his day. His father was a Bordeaux music teacher, who started him on the instrument at an early age. He later studied with Dorus, one of the first to espouse the new Boehm flute, who took him with him when he was appointed professor of flute at the Paris Conservatoire. There he studied composition with Henri Reber, Halévy's [1157] successor. In 1864—a year before he graduated with the first prize for flute—he began a long association with the Paris Opéra Orchestra, at first as chief flutist and then as conductor. In 1879 he founded the Société des quintettes pour instruments à vent (for which Gounod [1258] wrote his *Petite Symphonie*. In 1890 Taffanel was made conductor of the Conservatoire Orchestra and three years later succeeded his old teacher there. He also collaborated with Gaubert on an important method. Taffanel's pupils were a Who's Who of early twentieth-century French flutists, including Georges Barrère, Philippe Gaubert, and Marcel Moyse. RECORDINGS: Taffanel's Wind Quintet has had several recordings.

[1422] NIETZSCHE, Friedrich Wilhelm (Nēt'-shē, Frē'-drikh Vil'-helm)
PHILOSOPHER, TEACHER, POLEMICIST
BORN: Röcken, October 15, 1844
DIED: Weimar, August 25, 1900

A descendent of a double line of Protestant parsons, Nietzsche himself originally intended to carry on the tradition. Brought up on good German bourgeois values, he developed a love for both literature and music, and began composing when he was around ten. A decade later he went to Bonn to study theology, but there he discovered the writings of Schopenhauer, which caused him to give up both his studies and his faith. He graduated in philology and, in 1868, went to Switzerland to teach at the University of Basel. He met Richard Wagner [1230], for whose views Schopenhauer had prepared him, in Lucerne and promptly became Wagner's most passionate disciple and chief propagandist. He had already evolved a theory of two conflicting human impulses to creativity: the Apollonian (intellectual) and the Dionysian (emotional). In *The Birth of Tragedy* of 1871 he announced that Wagnerian music drama represented a return to the Dionysian wellsprings of Attic tragedy. But as time passed he grew increasingly disenchanted with his hero, and, in 1888, recanted in *Der Fall Wagner (The Wagner Case)*, saying that he had mistaken neurosis for inspiration. He finally decided that it was Bizet's [1363] *Carmen* that represented musicodramatic health. For similar reasons he also rejected religion and traditional ideals, which, he argued, blocked mankind from self-realization in the Superman. In 1889 he became insane and died at fifty-five. Afterward his

sister, to sell him as a prophet to the Nazis, forged documents limiting his antipathy to religion to Judaism alone. He published a piece for chorus and orchestra in his lifetime; in recent years many manuscripts of other choral works, songs, and piano pieces have been edited and published. RECORDINGS: Dietrich Fischer-Dieskau has recorded some of the songs.

[1423] BUNGERT, August (Boon'-gert, Ou'-gōost)
PIANIST, CONDUCTOR
BORN: Mülheim, March 14, 1845 (?)
DIED: Leutesdorf, October 26, 1915

Even August Bungert's songs, once very popular and occasionally recorded, seem to have been forgotten, but he was also noted (if not entirely admired) for more ambitious productions. Born in the Ruhr near Essen, he studied piano with Ferdinand Kufferath, the youngest of three brothers who put Mülheim on the musical map. Perhaps because his father opposed his choice of careers, Bungert seems never to have been sure that he was properly trained. Between 1860 and 1869 he studied, first at the Cologne Conservatory and then privately in Paris. Then he took a directorial post in Bad Kreuznach in the Palatinate, but by 1873 he seems to have felt himself still lacking and went to Berlin for eight more years of study. Toward the end of this period, he won a prize with a string quartet. In 1881 he moved to the Italian Riviera. Three years later he had his first operatic success (in Leipzig) with a comedy, *Liebe Siegerin, oder die Studenten von Salamanka (Dear Victress, or the Students of Salamanca)*. Later he became badly infected with a species of Wagnerian elephantiasis, in which he was abetted by his great and good friend, Queen Elisabeth of Rumania, a patroness of the arts and polyglot poetess, who wrote (and recorded) as "Carmen Sylva." He planned to do nothing less than a double tetralogy on the Homeric epics and to enshrine them in a Bungertian Bayreuth on the Rhine. The Odysseus cycle—*Kirke, Nausikaa, Odysseus' Heimkehr (Odysseus' Homecoming)*, and *Odysseus' Tod (Odysseus' Death)*—was realized, its elements generating more heat than light at their Dresden premieres between 1896 and 1903. The Iliad cycle never got off the drawing board, and the *Festspielhaus* remained a dream. However, Bungert did move to a Rhine town four years before he died. Other works include music for Goethe's *Faust*, a religious mystery *Warum? Woher? Wohin? (Why? Whence? Whither?)*, and a symphony *Genius triumphans: Zeppe-lins erste grosse Fahrt (Genius Triumphant: Zeppelin's First Great Flight)*. Record companies should take notice! RECORDINGS: At present only a few songs have been recorded.

[1424] FAURÉ, Gabriel Urbain (Fô-rā', Gá-brē-el' Ür-ban')
ORGANIST, CHOIRMASTER, TEACHER, ADMINISTRATOR
BORN: Pamiers, May 12, 1845
DIED: Paris, November 4, 1924

Something of a law unto himself, Gabriel Fauré is one of the first and greatest composers of the French art song and one of the few remarkable French composers of piano music in his century. He should, by the way, never be confused with his elder contemporary Jean-Baptiste Faure [1311], who had neither accent nor compositional genius. Fauré was born in the foothills of the Pyrenees, twenty-odd miles north of Andorra, the sixth child of Toussaint-Honoré Fauré, a school inspector. The home being overcrowded, he was farmed out to a family in a nearby village until his parents moved south to Verniolles, near Foix, in 1849. The history of Fauré's early musical development is hazy, but when he was eleven Louis Niedermeyer [1167] was so impressed by him that he offered him a full scholarship at his school in Paris. There he became acquainted with Gregorian chant and the music of J. S. Bach [684] and, from 1860, profited by the teaching (and friendship) of Camille Saint-Saëns [1343], only ten years his senior. Having published three *Songs Without Words* for piano and written at least some of his first twenty songs (all of which date from this general period), he completed his schooling in 1865. In January 1866 he secured a job as organist at St. Sauveur in Rennes, Brittany; he was relieved of it four years later, when one Sunday morning he reported for duty in full dress, having just arrived from an extended party. He returned to Paris, where he was hired at Notre-Dame de Clignancourt but shortly afterward joined the infantry to defend his country against the Boche. After a brief exile at Rambouillet (southwest of Versailles) during the Commune, he became organist at St. Honoré d'Eylau and then second organist (to Charles-Marie Widor [1414]) at St. Sulpice. A year later, in 1872, he returned to the École Niedermeyer to teach. And in 1877 he succeeded Théodore Dubois [1356] at the Madeleine, the latter having been elevated by the departure of Saint-Saëns. That was the year that Marianne Viardot, daughter of the great con-

tralto Pauline, terminated an engagement into which Faure had entered after some years of apparently rather timorous courtship, and it was the year he met Liszt [1218] in Weimar. In all this time he seems to have composed little—two choral pieces, two vocal duets, an orchestral suite (which, save for one movement, *Allegro symphonique*, he later disowned) and the first violin sonata.

Fauré returned to Germany in 1878 and 1879 to hear Wagner's *Ring* operas. He was mightily impressed, but shows in his own music almost no impression of that of Germany, either from the new or the old schools. The sonata was premiered in Paris in 1878 and was followed by publication of the first piano quartet. In 1883 he married Marie Fremiet, a sculptor's daughter. There seems to have been no hint of a grand passion. They produced children and remained on amiable terms, but Fauré often spent long periods away from home, living and composing in hotels or apartments rented for the purpose. Though he was regarded as an easy and friendly man, he seems to have preferred privacy. The 1880s saw his composition begin in earnest—several choral works, the *Requiem* (for his father), the piano-and-orchestra *Ballade*, the incidental music to *Caligula* and *Shylock*, the second piano quartet, about a third of the piano music, and another twenty-odd songs. He also heard performed his only symphony, which he never published.

When Ernest Guiraud [1352] died in 1892, Fauré was named his successor as inspector of conservatories. Four years later Dubois moved from the Madeleine into the directorship of the Paris Conservatoire, Ambroise Thomas [1217] having died. Fauré succeeded him at the organ and was at last brought into the Conservatoire (a move stoutly opposed in the past by Thomas on account of Fauré's "modernity.") There he taught such notable musicians as Ravel [1666], Charles Koechlin [1592], who scored much of his orchestral music for him, Florent Schmitt [1615], Georges Enesco [1738], Roger-Ducasse [1639], Alfredo Casella [1767], Louis Aubert [1693], Raoul Laparra [1685], and Nadia Boulanger. The 1890s saw the completion of the incidental music for Maeterlinck's *Pelléas et Mélisande* and Fauré's first opera *Prométhée*. Early in the new century he found himself growing deaf. In 1905 he succeeded Dubois for a fifteen-year reign as director of the Conservatoire. Long contemptuous of that institution's preference for operatic politics to sound musical education, the mild-mannered Fauré adopted such stringent measures that he came to be called "Robes-pierre" behind his back. (Fauré could be forceful. At one point there was a terrible clash with Marguerite Long, professor of piano and one of his apostles. When he ignored Sarah Bernhardt's announcement that she could not come for music lessons at 10 A.M. because she was not up so early, she savagely attacked him in the press, to no effect.)

In his last years, despite his affliction, Fauré wrote the opera *Pénélope* (much admired but rarely played), the bulk of his important chamber music, and the several song cycles. He especially encouraged the young baritone Charles Panzéra, for whom he wrote, in 1924, *L'Horizon chimerique,* the year he died after recovering from a near-fatal siege of pneumonia.

Fauré was essentially (in keeping with his nature) an intimate composer, happiest in music for the drawing room. It sounds disarmingly simple, pleasantly tuneful, almost always reserved. He preferred propriety and good taste to extravagance and display, and deplored performers who tried to go beyond his directions in an effort to "interpret." His is a subtle art, saved from what might become blandness by delicate touches of modality, dissonance, and syncopation.

RECORDINGS: Several complete sets of the songs, piano pieces, and chamber works have appeared on records, as well as many recordings of the *Requiem.* The choral music, song cycles, the incidental music, concerted works, and other orchestral pieces have good representation, save for the score for Georges Clemenceau's *Le Voile du bonheur* and the early symphony. Two recordings of *Pénélope*—one commercial, one pirated—have recently appeared.

[1425] IVANOVICI, Iosif (Ē-vä-nô-vēch'-ē, Yō'-sēf)
BANDMASTER
BORN: Banat (?), 1845 (?)
DIED: Bucharest, September 28, 1902

Neither the place nor the date of Ivanovici's birth have been confirmed, though he was almost certainly born in what is now western Rumania. He became a woodwind player in a military band in Galatz (now Galaţi), which he was directing by 1880. That was the year he wrote the one work by which his name still lives, *Valurile Dunării*—better known as *Donauwellen* or *Danube Waves.* (Described as originally a fanfare, it is more familiar as a waltz.) He moved on to Bucharest, was a prizewinner at the 1889 Paris Exposition, and was appointed chief inspector of military music for Rumania in

1900. He wrote numerous marches, dances, piano pieces, and songs.

[1426] DENZA, Luigi (Dent'-sà, Lōō-ē'-jē)
TEACHER
BORN: Castellammare di Stabia, February 24, 1846
DIED: London, January 26, 1922

Like his contemporary Paolo Tosti **[1429]**, Denza spent most of his career in England. Born in a nearby town, he studied in Naples at the Conservatory with Mercadante **[1148]** and Mercadante's pupil Paolo Serrao. The Teatro San Carlo staged his opera *Wallenstein* in 1876 without provoking Vesuvius to eruption. Having visited England and liking what he found there, he settled in London about a decade later. There he pursued a successful career as a teacher and particularly as a composer of parlor songs—more than 500 to texts in three languages. He was a director of the now-defunct London Academy of Music and became professor of singing at the Royal Academy in 1898. Such songs as *"Occhi di fata"* ("Fateful Eyes") and *"Si vous l'aviez compris"* ("If You Had Understood")—not to mention some with such laconic and peremptory titles as *"Se . . ."* ("If . . ."), *"Torna!"* ("Come Back!"), and *"Vieni!"* ("Come!")—were enormously popular with the first generations of recording singers. But Denza's greatest hit was a Neapolitan number *"Funiculi-funicula,"* which takes its title from the funicular railway built to take tourists up Vesuvius. Casella **[1767]** used it in his orchestral rhapsody *Italia* and Rimsky-Korsakov **[1416]** arranged it for orchestra. Thinking it a folksong, the young Richard Strauss **[1563]** incorporated it in his orchestral *Aus Italien* and was embarrassed to find it copyrighted.

[1427] FLÉGIER, Ange (Flā-zhā', Ȧnzh)
BORN: Marseilles, February 25, 1846
DIED: Marseilles, October 8, 1927

Flégier studied at the Marseilles Conservatoire and, save for three years, 1866–69, at its Parisian counterpart, he lived all of his life in his birthplace. There his *opéra-comique* entitled *Fatima* was produced in 1875. He also wrote a couple of large-scale cantatas and some orchestral pieces, but was known best, outside his habitat, for his songs. RECORDINGS: A special favorite with recording bassos was his setting of Alfred de Vigny's *"Le Cor"* ("The Horn").

[1428] VALVERDE, Joaquín (Bvàl-bvâr'-thā, Hwà-kēn')
FLUTIST, CONDUCTOR
BORN: Badajoz, February 27, 1846
DIED: Madrid, March 17, 1910

A band musician from his earliest teens, Valverde later distinguished himself at the Madrid Conservatory as a student in the late 1860s—though not as a teacher in the early 1880s! In 1871 he began conducting theater orchestras, often in his own zarzuelas, of which he composed some 30, both alone and with various collaborators. His greatest success was *La Gran vía (The Highway)* in 1886, written in collaboration with Federico Chueca [1430]. It has been performed all over the Spanish-speaking world and in other countries as well. The story that Valverde was a mere tunesmith and that the composition was all owing to Chueca is a vile canard, for Valverde wrote prizewinning orchestral works as well as stage pieces and songs and was, in fact, orchestrator of the work. (His *Clavelitos [Carnations]* is particularly well known.) However, there are those that say his zarzuelas show a qualitative decline from the great days—a slide that was continued by his son Quinito (1875–1918). There are complete recordings of the *Gran vía* music.

[1429] TOSTI, (Sir) Francesco Paolo
(Tôs'-tē, Fràn-chās'-kō Pà-ō'-lō)
SINGER, TEACHER
BORN: Ortona sul Mare, April 9, 1846
DIED: Rome, December 2, 1916

Tosti was by far the most successful of the Italian-born drawing-room balladeers—nor has there been his like post-Tosti. Born on the Adriatic coast just south of Pescara, he went, at the age of twelve, to the Naples Conservatory to study violin. His chief composition teacher was Mercadante [1148]. Slaving away at a graduate assistant's wages, he suffered a breakdown and had to go home to recuperate. There he served as organist and choirmaster in the twelfth-century cathedral, and began his songwriting career—rather unpropitiously at first. Hoping for better luck, he moved to Rome where Sgambati [1385] took a fancy to him and helped him put on a vocal recital (Tosti had a fine bass-baritone voice), to which he added a song of his own, written for the occasion. Crown Princess Margherita was in the audience and was so delighted that she appointed Tosti her singing teacher. As with Denza [1426], visits to England increasingly delighted the composer, and he settled in

London in 1880 as music master to Queen Victoria's brood. His songs became so popular that the publisher Chappell offered him 10,000 lire apiece if he would write a minimum of four per year. In 1888 he married an Englishwoman, Bertha Pierson, and became a citizen in 1906. He was knighted in the birthday honors list of 1908 by King Edward VIII but spent his last four years back in Italy. There have been dozens of recordings of "Good-Bye," "Ideale," "Marechiare," "L'Ultima canzone" ("The Last Song"), and "La Serenata," to name only a few. Tosti also wrote a couple of interesting cycles to texts by his fervent admirer Gabriele d'Annunzio—the *Canzone di amaranta (Song of Amaranth)*, recorded by Margherita Carosio, and *Consolazione*, recorded by Edward Hain de Lara.

[1430] CHUECA Y DURÁN, Federico
(Chōō-ā'-kà ē Thōō-ràn', Fāth-er-ī'-kō)
CONDUCTOR
BORN: Madrid, May 5, 1846
DIED: Madrid, June 20, 1908

Chueca was extremely popular for his operetta-weight zarzuelas. While a medical student at the university, he and his friends organized a dance band, for which he wrote music in the popular vein. Some of it attracted Francisco Barbieri [1287], who programmed a set of waltzes with the Madrid Concert Orchestra. This caused Chueca to abandon medicine for music, and he began a career of producing zarzuelas (with the frequent help and collaboration of Valverde [1428]) that capitalized on his knowledge of and feel for the popular idiom. His greatest success was *La Gran vía*, 1886. Chueca also served as a theater conductor. RECORDINGS: There are recordings of *La Gran vía*, as well as of *Agua, Azucarillas, y Aguardiente* of 1897 and *La Alegria de la Huerta* of 1900.

[1431] KORBAY, Ferenc (Kōr'-bī, Fe'-rents)
SINGER, PIANIST, TEACHER
BORN: Budapest, May 8, 1846
DIED: London, March 9, 1913

Korbay's parents were musical amateurs, sufficiently respected in Hungarian circles that they could call on Liszt [1218] to stand godfather to their son. He studied piano with Mosonyi [1238] and Volkmann [1241], and voice with Gustav Roger. He elected an operatic career and became a tenor at the Budapest Opera in 1865. But he did severe damage to his voice and, on Liszt's advice, became a concert pianist. His tours took him to New York in 1871, where he remained (as Francis Alexander Korbay) for twenty-three years. There he taught both piano and voice, and, having repaired the damage to his vocal cords, took up his singing career as a concert artist. He also lectured. He wrote a few orchestral pieces and a number of songs but became immensely popular through his arrangements of Hungarian Gypsy songs, notably one called "Had a Horse." Korbay moved to London in 1894 as professor of voice at the Royal Academy. RECORDINGS: Some of the arrangements have been recorded.

[1432] VISETTI, Alberto Antonio (Vē-zet'-tē, Ál-bâr'-tō Án-tōn'-yō)
PIANIST, CONDUCTOR, VOCAL TEACHER
BORN: Salona, May 13, 1846
DIED: London, July 10, 1928

Born in what is now Solin on the Yugoslav coast (near Split), Visetti won scholarships at the Milan Conservatory, where he studied with Alberto Mazzucato and was a friend of Boito [1393]. He went to France as pianist and conductor, was appointed chamber musician to the Empress Eugénie, and wrote an opera on *Les Trois Mousquetaires (The Three Musketeers)* to a libretto written for him by that work's author. It and his patronage went up in smoke during the upheavals of 1870–71. Visetti then settled in London, where he became known as Albert Anthony Visetti, and was a succesful singing teacher. He was on the faculty of the Royal College of Music and taught at several other schools. For twelve years, beginning in 1878, he conducted the Bath Philharmonic, which he in part supported. He was decorated in 1880 by King Umberto I. He translated a number of English musical works into Italian. As a composer he was known chiefly for some songs, notably the waltz-song "Diva," written for Patti. RECORDINGS: "Diva" has been recorded by the falsettist Michael Aspinall.

[1433] DRIGO, Riccardo (Drē'-gō, Rik-kär'-dō)
CONDUCTOR, TEACHER
BORN: Padua, June 30, 1846
DIED: Padua, October 1, 1930

A product of the Venice Conservatory, Drigo spent the next dozen or so years teaching and conducting in his hometown, where he produced an opera, *Don Pedro di Portogallo*. In 1879 he found his niche in St.

Petersburg, where for seven years he conducted the Italian Imperial Opera orchestra. After that he served as conductor and composer for the Imperial Ballet until the 1917 Revolution. His scores, like those of Minkus [1298] were, for the most part, efficient and forgettable, though two numbers, the "Serenade" and the *"Valse Bluette,"* from *Harlequinade* (or *Harlequin's Millions)*, were enormously popular. Others of his ballets were *The Magic Flute* (unrelated to Mozart's [992]), *The Talisman, The Pearl,* and *Flora's Awakening.* Drigo conducted the premieres of Tchaikovsky's [1377] *Nutcracker* and *Aurora's Wedding* (a one-act condensation of *Sleeping Beauty)* and of Glazunov's [1573] *Raymonda.* He also revised and added numbers to older ballets. Discovering that the Bolshevists were not for him, he returned to Padua in 1920 and died there at eighty-four. Just before his death, another of his operas, *Il Garofano bianco (The White Carnation),* was premiered there. (He also wrote an operetta listed as *Flaffy Raffles* and some piano music.) RECORDINGS: Besides the perennial favorites noted, there are recordings of a *pas de trois* from their source ballet, and *pas de deux* that Drigo added to Adam's [1172] *Le corsaire* and Pugni's [1168] *Esmeralda,* all led by Richard Bonynge. Nicolas Flagello [2373] has recorded a piano piece.

[1434] BRÜLL, Ignaz (Brül, Ēg'-nàtz)
PIANIST
BORN: Prossnitz, November 7, 1846
DIED: Vienna, September 17, 1907

Ignaz Brüll was born in what is now Prostějov in central Czechoslovakia. When he was three, his parents moved to Vienna, where he spent the rest of his life. He studied piano with Julius Epstein and composition with Epstein's teacher Johann Rufinatscha and with Otto Dessoff. He began composing early, and in 1861 Epstein volunteered to play his first piano concerto in public. (Epstein did not like to concertize.) The work was given its American premiere by Richard Hoffman [1320] and Theodore Thomas in 1880. Brüll himself became recognized as a fine pianist around Vienna and occasionally performed abroad. In 1864 his *Serenade* was a great success in its Stuttgart premiere, and his first opera *Der Bettler von Samarkand (The Beggar of Samarkand)* was well received in Vienna. He was a welcome crony of the Viennese composers, was a good friend of Goldmark's [1315], and was especially close to Brahms [1329]. Brahms preferred him as a hiking companion. (They must have made quite a picture—the lion-maned Brahms and the egg-bald Brüll, both with beards flowing to their midriffs!) The two also delighted in playing four-hand music together. Brüll became a teacher in the Horak School in 1872 and its director in 1881. His greatest success as a composer was the opera *Das goldene Kreuz (The Cross of Gold)*, produced in Berlin in 1875 and taken up by other opera houses. Brüll went to London to play in 1878 and made such a hit that he had given twenty concerts by the time he left. He married in 1882. (Brahms was also very fond of Marie Brüll, and especially of her cooking.) After that he gave up traveling altogether and led a rather uneventful life. He produced eight more operas (all forgotten) and was at work on another when he died at sixty. His other works (not numerous) include a second piano concerto, a violin concerto, a symphony, an overture to *Macbeth*, chamber music, piano pieces, and songs. RECORDINGS: Until recently he was represented on records only by an operatic excerpt or two (chiefly the bass aria from *Das goldene Kreuz*), but in the 1970s Zsolt Deáky recorded the *Macbeth* overture and (with Frank Cooper) the Concerto for Piano No. 2.

[1435] ROTOLI, Augusto (Rō-tō′-lē, Ou-gōōs′-tō)
CONDUCTOR, TEACHER
BORN: Rome, January 17, 1847
DIED: Boston, November 26, 1904

Rotoli was a pupil of Lucchesi, whoever he may have been. In 1876 he founded, as its conductor, the Società Corale de' Concerti Sagri. Two years later he replaced the errant Tosti **[1429]** as singing master to Queen Margherita and was named *maestro di cappella* of the Royal Chapel in Turin, his first offering being a *Requiem* for the late Victor Emmanuel II. He was subsequently knighted by King Umberto. In 1885, however, he settled in Boston as a professor at the New England Conservatory and died there. RECORDINGS: Some of his songs enjoyed recordings in the early days.

[1436] EULENBURG-HERTEFELD,
(Prince) Philipp zu (Oy′-len-bōōrg Hȧr′-tə-felt, Fē-lēp′ tsōō)
SOLDIER, DIPLOMAT
BORN: Königsberg, February 12, 1847
DIED: Liebensberg, September 17, 1921

Philipp, Count of Eulenburg, came from a distinguished Prussian family. He fought in the Austrian War of 1866 and the French War of 1870–71. In the latter, he was awarded the Iron Cross for conspicuous bravery. He then studied law at Leipzig and Strasbourg, and entered the diplomatic service in 1877. Appointed third secretary of the German Embassy in Paris, he became a close friend of Prince Bernhard von Bülow, the second secretary and later German chancellor. He was transferred to Munich in 1882, became Prussian representative to, successively, Oldenburg, Württemberg, and Bavaria, and in 1893 was offered his choice of ambassadorships to England, France, or Austria. He took the last, remaining until 1902, when ill health forced him to resign. In 1900 he was raised in rank to prince, given the additional name of Hertefeld, and made an hereditary member of the upper chamber of the parliament. It was Eulenburg who used his friendship with William II to get the chancellorship for Bülow. In the aftermath of the attacks on the morality of the court by the journalist Maximilian Harden, Eulenburg was accused of homosexuality and spent the rest of his life in disgrace on his estate. An amateur fictionist and composer, his *Rosenlieder* were once extraordinarily popular. RECORDINGS: A few recordings exist of the *Rosenlieder* and other songs.

[1437] SCHARWENKA, Ludwig Philipp (Shär-ven′-kȧ, Lōōt′-vēg Fē-lēp′)
TEACHER
BORN: Samter (now Szamotuly), February 16, 1847
DIED: Bad Nauheim, July 16, 1917

The elder of two once-famous musical brothers, Philipp Scharwenka was the son of an architect and born in a city associated with one of the earliest Polish composers, Wacław z Szamotuły **[200]**. The family moved to Posen (Poznan), where Philipp studied at the *Gymnasium* in 1859, and then to Berlin in 1865, where both Philipp and Xaver **[1448]** were promptly enrolled in the Kullak Academy. Three years later Philipp became an instructor there. In 1880 he married the violinist Marianne Stresow, and a year later she and the brothers opened their own music school, the Scharwenka Academy, with Xaver as director—Philipp taking over when he was absent on tour, which was frequently. At its height, the institution boasted about a thousand pupils, a faculty of sixty-two, and forty-two soundproof studios, and it inaugurated a New York branch in 1891. In 1895 it absorbed the Klindworth Academy. The school was especially fashionable in New York. Philipp Scharwenka was a prolific composer in a Schumannesque [1211] vein; his works include 3 symphonies, a violin concerto, symphonic poems, suites, cantatas, chamber music, songs, piano pieces, and an unperformed opera, *Roland.* RECORDINGS: There is a recording of a violin sonata by Robert Zimansky.

[1438] ANDERSEN, Anton Jörgen (Ản'-der-sen, Ản'-tōn Yer'-gen)

CELLIST, TEACHER

BORN: Kristiansand, October 10, 1847
DIED: Stockholm, September 9, 1926

Born on the south coast of Norway, Andersen became an orchestral cellist at a relatively early age. In 1867 he betook himself to Stockholm to study at the Conservatory, and he remained to play in the Royal Orchestra and teach at the school. He was also a member of the Royal Academy. He wrote symphonies, chamber music, choral works, and songs. RECORDINGS: Lauritz Melchior recorded some of the songs.

[1439] KLUGHARDT, August Friedrich Martin (Klo͞ok'-härt, Ou'-go͞ost Frē'-drikh Mär'-tin)

CONDUCTOR

BORN: Cöthen, November 30, 1847
DIED: Rosslau, August 3, 1902

After studies in Dresden, Klughardt spent a couple of peripatetic years as a theater conductor before settling down in Weimar in 1869 for four more—enough to bring him into the Liszt [1218]-Wagner [1230] orbit. After nine years in a similar post in Neustrelitz, he became *Kapellmeister* in Dessau, in 1882. His 4 operas, in which he tried to combine Wagnerian and Classical features, were produced in the cities where he was working between 1871 and 1886. He also wrote oratorios, symphonies, concerti, cantatas, and a good deal of chamber music. RECORDINGS: His wind quintet has been recorded both by the Boehm Quintet and the Norwegian Chamber Soloists. The Op. 28 *Schilflieder* for piano, oboe, and viola has also been committed to disc.

[1440] BACKER-GRØNDAHL, Agathe Ursula (Båk'-er Grön'-dål, Ȧ-gȧ'-tə O͞Or'-soo-là)

PIANIST, TEACHER

BORN: Holmestrand, December 1, 1847
DIED: Christiania (Oslo), June 4, 1907

Born on the shores of Oslo Fjord, Agathe Backer studied piano from childhood, and began composing when she was about thirteen. Her teachers included Kjerulf [1244] in Oslo, Theodor Kullak (1818–82) in Berlin, Liszt [1218] in Weimar, and Bülow [1310] in Florence. In 1872 she returned to Christiania and taught, with time out for frequent tours. She came to be regarded as one of the important concert pianists of her day. In 1875 she married O. A. Grøndahl, a singing teacher. Their son Fridtjof was also known as a pianist and composer. The year of her marriage, she was elected to the Swedish Academy. She was a close friend of Grieg [1410], who survived her by exactly three months. She wrote mostly piano works in a Mendelssohnian [1200] vein and songs, some of them still admired. RECORDINGS: Doris Pines has recorded an LP-side of her piano pieces, and there have been scattered recordings of songs. The Norwegian government has recently sponsored a recording of songs with soprano Kari Frisell and pianist Liv Glaser.

[1441] HOLMÈS, Augusta Mary Anne (Ōl-mes')

PIANIST, POETESS

BORN: Paris, December 16, 1847
DIED: Paris, January 28, 1903

To judge from her portrait, Augusta Holmès (as she was born) may have been the most beautiful of all composers. Her parents came from Ireland, though her nominal father, a retired military officer, held English citizenship, and her mother was part Scottish. They had been married twenty years when she (their only offspring) was born. Persistent rumor had it that her godfather, the poet Alfred de Vigny, was her real father, and Augusta did nothing to squelch it. She grew up in Versailles and was given the usual schooling toward the "accomplishments" expected of young women of good breeding but was not permitted to develop her artistic learnings. However, when her mother died in 1857, there was no stopping Augusta. She got some basic theory from her organ teacher, Henri Lambert, and, as she blossomed, she became a familiar figure in the salons, playing and singing her own songs, some of which she published under the pseudonym of "Hermann Zenta." Later she got a practical education in orchestration from Hyacinthe Klosé [1198]—though some thought her handling of the orchestra rather unladylike. In 1869 she attended the premiere of Wagner's *Das Rheingold* and was never the same afterward, but only one of her 4 operas ever got a hearing, which did not establish it in the repertoire. In the Franco-Prussian War, she served as a nurse and became a French citizen a year after it ended. In 1875 she studied with César Franck **[1284]**, her other chief musical influence. In Parisian artistic and literary circles she held her own as one of the boys, despite her extraordinary looks. Saint-Saëns **[1343]** once proposed to her, but she was a free spirit and spent many years in a free association with the poet Catulle Mendès, to whom she bore at least three children. She twice won prizes in the City of Paris competitions, though neither was a first; but in 1881 Pasdeloup chose to program her second-place dramatic symphony *Les Argonautes* in preference to Duvernoy's **[1400]** blue-ribbon piece. To escape the damning label of "female composer," she thought big: there is a Berliozian **[1175]** cast to her major works. In later life she became increasingly obsessed with her "Irishness," and in 1900, at the behest of an Irish priest, she became a Roman Catholic and had herself baptized "Patricia," after Ireland's patron saint. She died six weeks after her fifty-fifth birthday. RECORDINGS: Only some of her songs seem to have been recorded.

[1442] DUPARC, Marie Eugène Henri Fouques (Dü-pärk′, Má-rē′ Ö-zhen′ On-rē′ Fōoks)

BORN: Paris, January 21, 1848
DIED: Mont de Marsan, February 12, 1933

With his slightly older contemporary Fauré **[1424]**, Henri Duparc ranks as one of the two great pioneers of the modern French art song, wherein text and music are treated as equals. As a person, he also presents one of the most curious cases in musical history. It was César Franck **[1284]** who discovered his talent in his time as a teacher at the Collège du Vaugiraud, and Duparc became one of the first of his disciples. Hypersensitive, the young man destroyed many of his early compositions (as well as his later—and only —opera, *Rousalka)* and even tried to recall three of his first five published songs. In 1869 he and Chabrier **[1382]** made the great pilgrimage to Munich to hear Wagner's **[1230]** *Tristan* and *Die Walküre,* and met Liszt **[1218]**, by both of whom Duparc was influenced. After the Franco-Prussian War, Duparc became secretary to the Société National, which premiered his orchestral *Suite de valses* and *Poème nocturne* in 1874 and *Lénore* in 1875. Again Duparc destroyed the first two, though he revised the first move-

ment of the *Poème,* entitled *Aux étoiles.* The remainder of his output consists of a handful of instrumental pieces and transcriptions left in manuscript, a motet, a vocal duet, and ten other songs. In 1885 something snapped. He put his music on the shelf, retired with his family to the countryside, kept up his intellectual interests, was sociable, did watercolors, and never composed a note again, so far as anyone knows. In his later years he slowly went blind, was paralyzed, and died in his Swiss retreat at eighty-five. RECORDINGS: There are recordings of *Lénore* by Arthur Winograd and Antonio de Almeida, and a plethora of recordings of the "official" songs.

[1443] PARRY, (Sir) Charles Hubert Hastings

TEACHER, WRITER
BORN: Bournemouth, February 27, 1848
DIED: Rustington, October 7, 1918

The British tend to sanctify Parry (perhaps more in the breach than in the observance) as the progenitor of the latter-day musical renaissance in England, though elsewhere he seems not even to have been accorded the initial steps to beatification. Hubert Parry's father, Thomas, was a well-to-do Gloucestershireman, who, unusually for his time and place, loved the arts and amused himself by doing church frescoes. When Hubert entered Eaton at thirteen, he had already developed his musical tastes and skills and, concurrently with his prepping, worked toward a B.Mus., which he was awarded the year he entered Exeter College, Oxford. There he continued his academic studies and made a name for himself in sports, though he studied on the side with Sterndale Bennett **[1246]** and G. A. Macfarren (1813–87), spent a musical summer in Leipzig, and was instrumental in founding the Oxford Musical Club. On acquiring his B.A. in 1870, he went to work for Lloyd's of London. In the capital he continued to work at his music under the eye of Edward Dannreuther, an Alsatian-born pianist and champion of the moderns (Wagner **[1230]**,) who encouraged his composing and had his chamber music performed at his regular domestic *musicales.* In the mid-seventies Parry gave up insurance to concentrate on his art. Dannreuther effectively proclaimed his maturity with a performance of his piano concerto in 1880 at the Crystal Palace. That same year the Gloucester Festival programmed his quasi-Wagnerian *Scenes from Shelley's Prometheus Unbound.*

From the start (and rather expectably,

given the aesthetic climate of England then), Parry made his name with his choral works and was hailed as the new Handel [683]. He was not quite that, nor was the Mendelssohnian [1200] heritage far to seek beneath the "modern" gloss, but he had a feel for words and good taste in texts. In the wave of Tennysonian Arthurianism, he wrote a single opera, *Guinevere,* but much incidental music, notably for several Aristophanic comedies. His limited catalogue of orchestral music was generally perceived as forbidding and heavy, but he *was* among the first Englishmen to write symphonies on the contemporary German model. He wrote 5 of them. His 3 string quartets and 3 piano trios date back to the Dannreuther days, but there is a mature string quintet, a nonet, and a sonata each for violin and cello. Of his many songs, a few achieved considerable popularity. A unison chorus, on Blake's "Jerusalem," became a sort of unofficial national anthem.

Financially independent, Parry did not have to work, but he remained a mover and shaker in the musical world. In 1894, he succeeded his friend Sir George Grove (to whose *Dictionary of Music and Musicians* he contributed many articles) as director of the Royal College of Music (where he had taught for a decade) and devoted much of his energy to the job until he died. He also succeeded Stainer [1378] as Oxford Professor of Music in 1900, but resigned after eight years. He received honorary degrees from Oxford, Cambridge, Durham, and Dublin, and was knighted by the Queen in 1898 and elevated to a baronetcy in 1903.

RECORDINGS: Parry's music—a mixture of wit, moral uplift, skill, and plum-pudding—has long been out of fashion, but some of the major stuff has begun to appear on records recently, notably from the late Sir Adrian Boult: the third and fifth symphonies, the *Symphonic Variations,* the *Elegy to Johannes Brahms,* the *English Suite, Lady Radnor's Suite,* the *Overture to an Unwritten Tragedy,* and the cantata *Blest Pair of Sirens.* Among the more plentiful representations of smaller pieces may be numbered an LP of piano music performed by John Parry (no relation) and a collection of choral part-songs directed by Richard Hickox. The *Songs of Farewell* are performed by the Louis Halsey Singers, and the choral-orchestral *Ode on the Nativity* is performed under the baton of David Willcocks.

[1444] PLANQUETTE, Jean Robert
(Plán-ket', Zhán Rō-bâr')
PIANIST

BORN: Paris, July 31, 1848
DIED: Paris, January 28, 1903

After a short whirl through the Paris Conservatoire, Planquette set out to make a living writing popular songs and playing in bistros. His most famous song was *"Le Régiment de Sambre-et-Meuse,"* which unfortunately he sold without copyright. In 1872 he turned out a one-act farce, *Méfie-toi de Pharaon (Look Out for Pharaoh),* for a music hall and followed it with others. Then in 1877 his three-act *Les Cloches de Corneville (The Bells of Corneville,* played in England and America as *The Chimes of Normandy)* hit at the Folies-Dramatiques and ran for 400 performances before embarking on its worldwide popularity. Competing with the like of Lecocq [1322] and Audran [1376], the nearest Planquette came to duplicating his success was with *Rip van Winkle* (premiered in London, in 1882; later performed as *Rip-Rip* in Paris—on the whole, he was luckier in London). He seems not to have cared, the rewards from his one triumph having been considerable. He built himself a beach villa in Normandy, named it *Les Cloches,* and went into local politics. RECORDINGS: There have been at least two complete recordings of *Les Cloches de Corneville.*

[1445] GODARD, Benjamin Louis Paul
(Gō-där', Ban-zhá-man' Lōō-ē' Pōl)
VIOLIST
BORN: Paris, August 18, 1849
DIED: Cannes, January 10, 1895

In his day Godard enjoyed a prominence based chiefly on a gift for pretty tunes and apparent promise that was not fulfilled. He began as a child prodigy violinist (one of his teachers was Henri Vieuxtemps [1270]), and was accepted at the Conservatoire when he was fourteen. His composition teacher there was Halévy's [1157] successor, Napoléon-Henri Reber (1807–80). At sixteen he published a violin sonata and spent the next several years devoting himself largely to this field, both as creator and performer (on the viola). He was a recipient of the Prix Chartier for chamber music. His first success in orchestral music was his orchestration of Schumann's [1211] *Kinderszenen,* premiered in 1876. Two years later he made a great splash as cowinner, with Dubois [1356], of a municipal prize for his cantata, or "dramatic symphony," *Le Tasse.* The year 1878 also saw the production of his first opera, *Les Bijoux de Jeannette.* There followed a series of ambitious orchestral works, including 5 symphonies—four of them programmatic and some involving vocal parts. In 1884 his second opera, *Pedro de Zalamea*, was a total flop. That was the year that Jules-Étienne Pasdeloup abandoned the orchestral concerts he had been running for over twenty-five years. Godard, seeing what seemed to be a golden opportunity, stepped into the breach with a series dedicated to contemporary music: it lasted only one season and barely skinned by that. In 1888, however, the opera *Jocelyn*, with the great tenor Victor Capoul, was a smash in Brussels and was played internationally for a time. Only the lovely *Berceuse* survives (Capoul's only recording is of this piece). The opera *Dante* was also a success two years later. But Godard suffered from tuberculosis which was aggravated by overwork, and he died at forty-five. Two posthumous operas, *La Vivandière* (completed by Paul Vidal) and *Les Guelphes* were quickly forgotten. RECORDINGS: The only extensive works by Godard to be recorded seem to be the *Concerto romantique* for violin and orchestra (Aaron Rosand) and the Piano Trio in G Minor (Göbel Trio), though there are also salon pieces, songs, and (on older records) excerpts from the operas and symphonies.

[1446] IVANOV, Mikhail Mikhailovich (Ē-vȧn'-of, Mē-khȧ'-il Mē-khī-lȯ'-vich)
WRITER, CRITIC
BORN: Moscow, September 23, 1849
DIED: Rome, October 20, 1927

Ivanov started out to be a mechanical engineer, but after graduating from the St. Petersburg Technological Institute he returned to Moscow to study with Tchaikovsky [1377] for a year in 1869. He then moved on to Rome to be instructed by Sgambati [1385] and to hobnob with Liszt [1218]. In 1875 he came back to St. Petersburg and launched his career as a musical journalist, becoming first-string critic for *Novoye Vremya* in 1880 and holding the post for thirty-seven years. An arch conservative, he attacked the nationalists with malice, relish, and wit. Even so he managed to get at least two operas, *Zabava Putyatishna* and *Potemkin Holiday*, successfully staged. He also wrote a ballet, a *Requiem*, a symphony, orchestral suites, and songs in a Tchaikovskian vein. He published a history of Russian music, a study of musical treatments of Pushkin, and a translation of Hanslick on aesthetics. When the Bolsheviks arrived, he left for Italy, where he lived for the rest of his life. RECORDINGS: Dmitri Smirnov once recorded an aria from

Zabava, and there may be a few other representations.

[1447] HILDACH, Eugen (Hēl'-dȧkh, Oi-gȧn')
SINGER, TEACHER
BORN: Wittenberge am Elbe, November 20, 1849
DIED: Zehlendorf, July 29, 1924

Eugen Hildach began his career in the building trades. When he found he had a fine baritone voice, he went to Berlin in 1873 to study with Elisabeth Dreyschock, the sister-in-law of Alexander Dreyschock [1260]. He married Anna Schubert, a prominent soprano. Both were on the faculty of the Dresden Conservatory, and they often concertized as a duo. In 1904 they founded their own vocal academy in Berlin. Some of Hildach's pleasantly romantic *Lieder* have been recorded.

[1448] SCHARWENKA, Franz Xaver (Shär-ven'-kȧ, Frȧnts Eks-ȧ'-ver)
PIANIST, TEACHER, CONDUCTOR
BORN: Samter, January 6, 1850
DIED: Berlin, December 8, 1924

Xaver Scharwenka was the younger and more flamboyant brother of Philipp [1437], whose career his parallels at several points. Taken under the wing of Theodor Kullak, he made his piano debut at the Singakademie in 1869. After a brief spell of teaching in Kullak's conservatory, he was called up for military service in 1873. His real concert career began the next year, and he was soon hailed all over Europe. In Berlin he promoted a regular series of chamber concerts, and he was the moving spirit behind the foundation there of the Scharwenka Academy in 1881. It throve remarkably, and in 1891 the Scharwenka brothers went to New York to open an American branch. Xaver was so taken with the city that he sent for his family and took up residence there, though he returned to the Continent for annual tours. In 1898 he removed to Berlin but remained a favorite with American audiences, who particularly admired his Chopin [1208]. The eternal woes of Poland seem to have been a trading card with him; photos often show him in national costume and sporting huge mustaches. His music (notably the series of once-popular *Polish Dances* for piano) is also more consciously nationalistic than his brother's. His only opera, *Mataswintha*, was premiered at Weimar in 1896. When the outbreak of war in 1914 put an end to his touring, he inaugurated a series of master classes in Berlin. Besides much piano music, he left a symphony, 4 piano concerti, a sonata apiece for violin and cello, 2 for piano, other chamber music, and songs. RECORDINGS: Earl Wild has recorded the first concerto, Raymond Lewenthal and Michael Ponti the second, and Robert Zaimansky the Sonata for Violin and Piano. Evelinde Trenkner and Ponti have recorded a disc and half a disc, respectively, of piano pieces. Scharwenka himself made recordings, including a few of his own compositions.

[1449] HENSCHEL, (Sir) George (Hen'-shul, Jôrj)
SINGER, PIANIST, CONDUCTOR, TEACHER
BORN: Breslau (Wroclaw), February 18, 1850
DIED: Aviemore, September 10, 1934

Henschel's parents, Polish Jews, named him Isidor Georg. He began his musical career very early as a member of a children's piano octet. His parents converted to Christianity, and he became solo treble with the Breslau University Choral Society. He gave his first piano recital at twelve. Five years later he entered the Leipzig Conservatory to study with Moscheles [1146], Reinecke [1292], and others. Having as a singer explored the bass range (and, some accounts insist, the tenor), he settled down to being a concert baritone, though early on he sang the role of Hans Sachs in an 1868(!) Leipzig performance of Wagner's [1230] Die Meistersinger. In 1870 he transferred to the Royal Conservatory in Berlin. At the Lower Rhine Festival in Cologne in 1874, he was a soloist in the St. Matthew Passion; the conductor was Brahms [1329], who became Henschel's close friend and of whom Henschel left a Personal Recollections.

Henschel's English career began in London in 1877. At a concert there in 1879 he met the debutant Lillian June Bailey, a young soprano from Columbus, Ohio, and married her two years later. Together they went to Boston, where he had just been named the first conductor of the Boston Symphony and where they remained for three years. They had a daughter, Helen, who emulated her father's vocal-pianistic career. Back in England Henschel became plain George, and in 1886 founded the original London Symphony Orchestra. The same year he succeeded Jenny Lind as professor of voice at the Royal College, remaining in that post for two years. In 1891 he added a chorus to his orchestra and in 1893 also took on

conducting the Scottish Orchestra in Glasgow. (He gave that up in 1895 and the London orchestra in 1897.) In 1899 he made his only dramatic appearance when he substituted for an ailing baritone in his own third (and last) opera Nubia in Dresden. (The other operas were Friedrich der Schöne and Hamlet.)

When Lillian Henschel died prematurely (at forty-one), Henschel retired to Aviemore in Scotland. But by 1905 he was back at work, teaching voice at the Institute of Musical Art in New York. There, in 1907, he married one of his pupils, Amy Louis. Their daughter, Georgie, became a well-known radio personality in England. In 1908 the Henschels returned to London, where he resumed his singing career. He was knighted in 1914 and retired from the stage later that year. But he continued to conduct guest shots.

RECORDINGS: He made a number of records in his guest-conductor capacity, and at the age of seventy-eight recorded some Lieder of Schubert [1153] and others, accompanying himself as he frequently had onstage. As a singer he was an extraordinary interpreter; as a conductor, he saw himself as a missionary and educator. A few of his own songs were recorded by others.

[1450] GEORGES, Alexandre (Zhôrzh, À-lek-sàn'dr')
ORGANIST, TEACHER
BORN: Arras, February 25, 1850
DIED: Arras, January 18, 1938

Georges seems to have thought of himself chiefly as a dramatic composer, but posterity sees him as the author of a few well-crafted art songs. He was a product of the Niedermeyer School in Paris, where he won all sorts of awards and later taught. He also served as organist of several Paris churches. His most notable operas were Le Printemps, 1888; Poèmes d'Amour 1892; Charlotte Corday, 1901; Myrrha, 1909; and Sangre y sol 1912. But only Miarka of 1905 had any real success. He also wrote oratorios, symphonic poems, incidental music, and chamber works. RECORDINGS: A few songs (e.g., "Le Flibustier," "La Pluie") have been recorded.

[1451] HEUBERGER, Richard Franz Josef (Hoi'-bâr-ger, Rē'-khärt Frànts Yō'-sef)
ENGINEER, CONDUCTOR, CRITIC, TEACHER
BORN: Graz, June 18, 1850
DIED: Vienna, October 27, 1914

Trained to make an honest living as a civil engineer, Richard Heuberger abandoned the profession when he was twenty-six to study, in his hometown with Wilhelm Mayer (alias W. A. Rémy). Soon after he went to Vienna as conductor of the Akademischer Gesangverein, moving in 1878 to the Singakademie. In 1881 he became full-time critic of the *Wiener Tageblatt*. His career as a stage composer began with a comic opera, *Das Abenteuer einer Neujahrsnacht (A New Year's Eve Adventure)*, premiered in Leipzig in 1886. There ensued several "serious" operas of no particular moment. In 1896 he succeeded Hanslick for five years as critic of the *Neue Freie Presse*. Two years later he tried his hand at operetta with resounding success: *Der Opernball (The Opera Ball)* still keeps his memory green in central Europe. Its several successors were not so lucky. In 1904 Heuberger became critic of the *Neue Musikalische Presse*. He published a study of Schubert **[1153]**, a book on opera, and a memoir of Brahms **[1329]**, and edited a musical journal, *Musikbuch aus Österreich*, for three years. RECORDINGS: Recorded excerpts from *Der Opernball* are common, and conductor Jiří Stárek offers the *Night Music* for string orchestra.

[1452] SITT, Hans (Zit, Hànts)
VIOLINIST, VIOLIST, CONDUCTOR, TEACHER
BORN: Prague, September 21, 1850
DIED: Leipzig, March 10, 1922

Bohemian-born, German-descended Hans Sitt was a product of the Prague Conservatory, where he concentrated on the violin. He served his apprenticeship as concert master, and sometimes as conductor, in theaters in Breslau (Wroclaw), Chemnitz (Karl Marx Stadt), and Prague (Praha), before making Leipzig his home from 1881. There he served as conductor of the Bachverein, ran a concert series, played viola in the Brodsky Quartet, and taught at the conservatory, where he became quite famous. His didactic compositions still have considerable currency, though he wrote a good deal of other music, including concerti for violin, viola, and cello, chamber works, and songs. RECORDINGS: The Göbel Trio has recorded the little Trio in G major for piano and strings.

[1453] THOMÉ, Joseph François Luc (Tō-mā', Zhō-zef' Frán-swà' Lük)
TEACHER
BORN: Port Louis, October 18, 1850
DIED: Paris, November 16, 1909

Thomé, who preferred to be called "Francis," is probably the most notable composer produced in Mauritius, once the habitat of the dodo. He came to Paris in childhood, was taken into the Conservatoire, and studied piano with Marmontel and theory with Jules-Laurent Duprato, famed for writing French recitatives for Balfe's **[1195]** *La Bohémienne*. Graduating at twenty with a first prize for counterpoint, he established himself as a fashionable piano teacher and composer of much rather flimsy salon stuff. Though he wrote operas and ballets as well (or as badly), his most notable achievement is said to have been the "mystery" *L'enfant Jésus (The Child Jesus)*. RECORDINGS: On records his *Simple aveu*, a salonesque gem, was a longtime surviver with Palm Court ensembles and the like.

[1454] KOMZÁK, Karel, Jr. (Kōm'-zàk, Kär'-el)
VIOLINIST, BANDMASTER
BORN: Prague, November 8, 1850
DIED: Baden, April 23, 1905

The elder Karel Komzák (1823–93) progressed from being a village schoolmaster-organist to playing in the Church of St. Catherine in Prague to conducting his own orchestra, which he founded in 1854 and which provided the nucleus for that of the Provisional Theater initially directed by Smetana **[1291]**. When that happened, he became an army bandmaster. Karel, Jr., was his pupil, later studying at the Prague Conservatory. He conducted the orchestra of the municipal theater in Linz in 1870; then, like his father, he went into the military. From 1893 to the end of his life, he conducted the orchestra at Baden, the health resort near Vienna. He appeared, like Scott Joplin **[1602]**, at the St. Louis World's Fair with his own band in 1904. RECORDINGS: Like his father, with whom he often collaborated, Komzák wrote many dances and marches, of which the *Sturm Galop* turns up on recorded Viennese anthologies.

[1455] THOMAS, Arthur Goring
BORN: Ratton Park, November 20, 1850
DIED: London, March 20, 1892

Though Sussex-born Goring Thomas fooled about with music in his youth—he and his brother plugged away for some time at an opera called *Don Braggadocio*—he went through Haileybury College with an eye to the civil service. But when he was 23, he went off to Paris and studied for two years with Émile Durand, then professor of harmony at the Conservatoire. He continued his education in London at the Royal Academy with Arthur Sullivan [1397] and Ebenezer Prout, and saw a portion of his first completed opera, *The Light of the Harem,* produced there in 1879. In the early part of the next decade he took advantage of Max Bruch's [1358] presence in England to study orchestration with him. The opera performance elicited a commission from Carl Rosa *(né* Rose), impresario of the most important touring opera company in England, dedicated to opera in the vernacular. The result was *Esmeralda,* a rather aqueous version of Victor Hugo's *Hunchback of Notre-Dame,* brilliantly premiered in 1883 and launched on its way to brief international success. Thomas followed it with *Nadeshda* two years later, also with happy results. The fact seems to be that the man had a fine lyric gift, but (as all too often apparent with would-be opera composers) little dramatic understanding. He was working on a comedy, *The Golden Web,* when he committed suicide in 1892. It was completed by S. P. Waddington and premiered in Liverpool. Thomas's output also includes a *suite de ballet,* some cantatas and vocal *scenas,* a number of songs, and a few instrumental pieces. RECORDINGS: Some of the songs and a few arias from the two operatic hits have appeared on records.

[1456] LANGE-MÜLLER, Peter Erasmus (Làng'-e Mü'-ler, Pã'-ter E-ràz'-moos)
CONDUCTOR
BORN: Frederiksborg, December 1, 1850
DIED: Copenhagen, February 25, 1926

Born near Copenhagen, Peter Lange-Müller studied piano in his youth. Attempts at university and conservatory training were, however, thwarted by a mysterious eye ailment that incapacitated him all his life with severe headaches. As a result he tended to be reclusive and thus formed his own ideas about how music should go. His Op. 1, the *Songs of Sulamith,* attracted favorable attention to its publication in 1874. An apparent remission of his condition allowed him to undertake choral conducting from around 1877, and in 1879 he founded his own concert choir, but had to give it up by 1884. Fortunately he inherited money so that he could work at his own rate. He married in 1892 and went to live on a rural estate. Lange-Müller fancied himself an opera composer, but his four efforts in that genre did not succeed. He also wrote incidental music to several plays, including Ibsen's *The Feast at Solhaug;* in this he was luckier. In fact his

music for Holger Drachmann's *Det var engang (Once Upon a Time)* is still popular in Denmark, and its concluding "Midsummer Song" is sung there traditionally on St. John's Eve. He also wrote some choral music, a symphony, a violin concerto, 2 orchestral suites, a piano trio, and smaller instrumental works. But his forte was the song, and there he remains the quintessential Danish romantic *Lieder* writer. Despite his shortcomings, he was a hero among his people, and his seventy-fifth birthday was nationally celebrated. He died shortly afterward as the result of being run down by a car. (With typical self-effacement, he identified himself to the police as "Müller, a musician.") RECORDINGS: Johan Hye-Knudsen has recorded the *Det var engang* music, and a number of songs are on records. As part of the Danish Music Anthology series, pianist Mogens Dalsgaard offers an ample selection of piano works: *7 Forest Pieces, Fantasy in C Minor, Dances,* and *Intermezzi.*

[1457] FIBICH, Zdeněk (Fē'-bikh, Zden'-yek)
TEACHER, CONDUCTOR
BORN: Všeboriče, December 21, 1850
DIED: Prague, October 15, 1900

The Czech musical establishment continues to try to convince the rest of the world that Fibich ranks with Smetana [1291] and Dvořák [1386] as one of the patriarchs of Czech music. But the rest of the world appears to remain unconvinced, chiefly one suspects because he doesn't fit the mold, his rather personal style having more to do with Leipzig than, say, Brno. His father was an official in the forestry service. His mother taught him to play the piano and, while completing his academic education, he worked for a year in a private music school in Prague. From 1865 to 1867 he was at the Leipzig Conservatory, studying with Moscheles [1146] and E. F. Richter (1808–79). Then he spent a year in Paris and another in Mannheim under the tutelage of Vincenz Lachner (1811–93), brother of Franz [1171] and Ignaz [1192] and conductor of the opera there. In 1870 he finally came home to devote himself to composition (he had already written two symphonies—now lost— and some piano pieces and songs). Three years later he married Růžena Hanušová and accepted a teaching post in Vilna (Vilnius, Wilno). Then multiple tragedy struck. In January 1874 Růžena was delivered of twins. Her sister, who had come to help, died, followed shortly by one of the children, a boy. The mother was left in such poor shape that Fibich took her and the remaining child (a girl) back to Prague, where Růžena died before the year was out. The daughter lived only a little over a year afterward. Meanwhile, however, Fibich had married another of his wife's sisters, Betty Hanušová, a singer at the Provisional Theater, where she appeared in several of his operas and where he now took a job as chorus master and conductor. A son, Richard, was born to them in 1876. In 1878 Fibich, having found the theater too demanding, gave up his post for one in the local Russian church, but after three years he turned to private teaching as his only source of income other than his music.

Up to that time Fibich had seen the first two of his mature operas, *Bukovín* and *Blaník*, both somewhat imitative of Smetana, staged. But he had also written several melodramas for musical recitation—a form he was to make particularly his own—as well as incidental music, some Smetana [1291]-like symphonic poems and overtures, and much of his chamber output. The year 1884 saw the premiere of *The Bride of Messina*, arguably his finest and certainly his most individual opera, in which he paid scrupulous attention to the demands of the libretto and demonstrated a debt to Wagner [1230]. After that Fibich spent more than five years on his melodrama trilogy *Hippodamia*, in which he brought that orphan-child form to its height and anticipated Schoenberg [1657] in his treatment of recitation. During this same period he acquired a girl pupil named Anežka Schulzová. He fell madly in love with her and finally left his family for her. She came to dominate not only his life but his music. She was responsible for the feminist orientation of his last four operas, for the last three of which she wrote the libretti. Of them *Šárka* of 1897 remains Fibich's most successful opera, in part because of its patriotic associations. The others tend to be patchworks of material drawn from his *Moods, Impressions, and Reminiscences*, a pianistic journal of the affair with Schulzová that he kept from 1892 to 1899. In 1899 he returned to the (now) National Theater as a producer but succumbed a year later (at forty-nine to a kidney infection).

RECORDINGS: Outside of Czechoslovakia, Fibich's name has survived largely through a pretty *Poème*, originally for piano solo, but much transcribed. His countrymen, however, have recorded *Šárka* and all 3 of the mature symphonies, as well as the Piano Trio, the Piano Quintet, some of the shorter orchestral works, and excerpts from *The*

Bride of Messina, The Tempest, and *Hippodamia.* Pianist Jarmila Kozderková and four declamationists (i.e., speakers) perform the short melodramas *Christmas Eve, The Vengeance of Flowers, Eternity, The Water Sprite, Queen Ema,* and *Hákon.*

[1458] BRETÓN Y HERNÁNDEZ, Tomás (Brā-tōn' ē Hâr-nán'-deth, Tō-más')
VIOLINIST, CONDUCTOR, TEACHER
BORN: Salamanca, December 29, 1850
DIED: Madrid, December 2, 1923

Though Tomás Bretón holds a firm place on the Spanish musical stage as a composer of zarzuelas, he tried hard, under the influence of Barbieri [1287] to create a real Spanish opera. Left fatherless at the age of two, he managed to win admittance to the local School of Fine Arts when he was eight and four years later was paying his own way as a theater-orchestra violinist. He then went on to Madrid, where he spent several years at the Conservatory, while continuing to freelance as a violinist and, increasingly, as a conductor. It was at this time that he encountered Barbieri as conductor of the Madrid Concert Orchestra. Bretón studied composition with Arrieta [1288]. In 1872 he graduated with the prize for exceptional merit in composition and won a government scholarship for study abroad, which took him to Italy, Austria, and France. His first opera, *Guzman el bueno (Guzman the Good),* was produced in Madrid in 1875 without incident. He went on to found his own orchestra, which he devoted to introducing contemporary music. His second and more ambitious opera, *Los Amantes de Teruel (The Lovers of Teruel),* premiered in 1889, outraged the native conservatives, who knew what they liked and that that wasn't it. In *La Dolores* of 1895, however, he gave them what they wanted, and it was quite successful—though it has not attained the solid popularity of *La Verbena de la Paloma (The Feast of the Dove),* a rowdy zarzuela first staged the previous year. Bretón also served as professor and director at the Conservatory, and as conductor of the Madrid Symphony Orchestra. Apart from his 7 operas and 40 zarzuelas, he wrote a violin concerto and other orchestral works, an oratorio, and a good deal of chamber music. RECORDINGS: There have been several recordings of *Dolores* and *La Verbena,* a few of the orchestral suites entitled *Escenas Andaluzas,* and excerpts from other stage works.

[1459] RUDNICK, Wilhelm (Rōōt'-nik, Vil'-helm)
ORGANIST, CONDUCTOR
BORN: Damerkow, December 30, 1850
DIED: Damerkow, August 7, 1927

Rudnick studied at Theodor Kullak's Neue Akademie in Berlin, but made his whole career in Galicia, mostly in Landsberg and Liegnitz (now Gorzów Wielkopolski and Legnica). He wrote an opera and a couple of oratorios but was chiefly noted for his organ music. RECORDINGS: Franz Haselböck has recorded a *Fantasia on Christmas Songs*.

[1460] SURZYŃSKI, Józef (Sōōr-zin'y'-skē, Yō'-zef)
ORGANIST, VIOLIST, CONDUCTOR, TEACHER, MUSICOLOGIST, EDITOR, PRIEST
BORN: Śrem, March 15, 1851
DIED: Kościan, March 5, 1919

The eldest of three musical brothers—the others were Stefan and Mieczysław [1585]—Józef Surzyński was born near Poznan. After two years of musical study in Leipzig, he went to Rome to study theology in 1874, completing his doctoral work in 1879. He obtained some further musical training at the School of Church Music in Regensburg, then returned to Poznan as organist and choirmaster of the cathedral. He was an important figure in the restoration and reformation of church music in Poland, and from 1884 to 1902 served as editor of the journal *Muzyka kościelna (Church Music)*. He also published a collection of early Polish religious music. From 1894 to the end of his life, he was stationed in Kościan (thirty miles to the south) as a priest. As well as scholarly and didactic works, he produced some compositions—chiefly pieces for choir and for organ. RECORDINGS: Feliks Raczkowski had recorded a *Prelude and Fugue* for organ.

[1461] CHAPI Y LORENTE, Ruperto (Chä'-pē ē Lō-ren'-tä, Rōō-pâr'-tō)
CORNETIST, CONDUCTOR
BORN: Villena, March 27, 1851
DIED: Madrid, March 25, 1909

Blessed with a talent for both melody and comedy, Chapi was one of the best and most prolific of the later zarzuela writers. His admirers have likened him variously to Schubert [1153] and Bizet [1363], and have hailed him, rather hyperbolically, as the father of modern Spanish music. A barber's son, he was born in Alicante Province

(southeastern Spain) and learned to play piccolo and cornet. He was conducting the local band at the age of fourteen, and at sixteen he became a pupil at the Madrid Conservatory, supporting himself, after a fashion, as a theater cornetist. At twenty-one he was made music director for the Spanish Artillery forces. His first zarzuela, *Abel y Cain*, was performed in 1873, and his first opera, *La Naves de Cortés (Cortez's Ships)*, starring the great tenor Enrico Tamberlik, had its premiere at the Teatro Real a year later. It won him government support to study in Italy and France for three years. After a few more tries at opera, Chapi reverted to the zarzuela, turning out at least 150 examples between 1880 and February 1909. *La Tempestad (The Tempest)* of 1882 firmly established his reputation. RECORDINGS: *La Tempestad* has been recorded, as have these other Chapi hits: *La Bruja (The Witch)*, 1887; *El Punao de rosas*, 1902; *El Rey que rabió* (1891); *La Revoltosa (The Mischievous)* of 1897, his most famous work; and *El Tambor des granaderos (The Grenadier's Drum)*, 1894—with such notable performers as Teresa Berganza, Pilar Lorengar, Manuel Ausensi, and the conductor Ataulfo Argenta. There are also innumerable recorded excerpts. Besides his stage works, Chapi wrote orchestral pieces and string quartets.

[1462] INDY, Paul Marie Théodore Vincent d' (Dan-dē', Pōl Må-rē' Tä'-ō-dôr Van-son')
TEACHER, CONDUCTOR
BORN: Paris, March 27, 1851
DIED: Paris, December 2, 1931

Vincent d'Indy is a paradoxical figure. Musically influential and revered, he is largely unperformed. Though German-inspired, he was a jingoistic patriot. A devout Catholic, he wrote no important religious music. A stoic and ascetic, he wrote sensuous compositions. Outspokenly anti-Jewish, he was careful not to let matters of belief influence his dealings with colleagues and pupils.

D'Indy was born into an old noble family from the Cevennes Mountains in southeastern France. Left motherless at birth, he was reared by his paternal grandmother, a matriarch who enforced a strict code of behavior. Fortunately for the future, she was musical, and her older son Wilfrid was a composer of sorts, so Vincent grew up in a congenial milieu. After taking lessons from his grandmother, he studied piano with Marmontel and Diémer and became a remarkable pianist. Later he studied harmony with Albert Lavignac. His friendship with Henri Duparc

[1442] led to a study of masterpieces, and he began composing at about this time. An attempt at an opera, *Les Burgraves du Rhin,* was permanently interrupted by the declaration of war on Germany in 1870. As was befitting for one of his station, he enlisted in the 105th Battalion of the Garde Nationale and was decorated for bravery. (After the war he published a history of his outfit's participation in it.)

It having already been agreed that he was to become a musician, he then involved himself with the Parisian musical world with the total commitment he brought to everything he did. He became the youngest member of the new Société Nationale de Musique in 1871, and a friendship with the conductor Jules Pasdeloup shortly enabled him to hear what some of his orchestral music sounded like. Duparc urged him to submit his work to Franck **[1284]**, who shocked him by telling him that it was amateurish. Swallowing his considerable pride, he went back to basics. He enrolled in Franck's organ class at the Conservatoire, which of course meant that he was taught music from a Franckian viewpoint. Having gained some practical experience, he became, in 1873, timpanist of the newly organized Concerts Colonne. Fascinated by German music, he traveled to Germany and Austria that summer, visited Liszt **[1218]** in Weimar, met both Wagner **[1230]** and Brahms **[1329]**, and came away enlightened. The proof, the overture *Les Piccolomini* (later called *Max und Thekla* as the first element of the *Wallenstein* orchestral trilogy), was unveiled the next January.

D'Indy spent the summer of 1874 at the family estate in the Cevennes, where he fell in love with his cousin, Isabelle de Pampelonne—a romance that seven years later, he commemorated in the piano piece *Le Poème des montagnes.* There was considerable family resistance, but in August 1875 the couple was married. In the same year d'Indy took over the post of organist at the Church of St. Leu la Forêt and served as prompter for the unhappy premiere of Bizet's **[1363]** *Carmen,* whose composer he had known in Franck's class. In the summer of 1876 d'Indy went to Bayreuth for the first performances of Wagner's *Ring* cycle and vowed he would make this the new direction of French music.

D'Indy had been tinkering with operatic projects of his own for some time, but his first public unveiling of his Wagnerian self was orchestral. In 1875, after hearing his symphony *Jean Hunyade,* he wished that he hadn't written it and withdrew it. (It is not among his 3 numbered symphonies.) Now, in his new vein, he produced *Harald,* best

known as *La Forêt enchantée (The Enchanted Forest),* after a poem by the German poet Uhland. When his operatic debut came in 1882, it came not with the expected blockbuster, however, but with a little comedy, *Attendez-moi sous l'orme (Wait for Me Under the Elm Tree).* But it was not until his 1883 Schiller-derived dramatic cantata *Le Chant de la cloche (The Song of the Bell)* had won the City of Paris Prize in 1885 and a performance by Lamoureux in 1886 that d'Indy was recognized as a new sort of French composer and a force to be reckoned with. Surprisingly to many, however, in the *Symphonie Cévenole (Symphony on a tune from the Cevennes)* for orchestra and piano (not among the numbered symphonies), premiered in 1887, he declared himself a dedicated patriot, whatever his musical leanings. (Still he worked as chorus master to Lamoureux that same year in the riotous French first performance of *Lohengrin.*)

D'Indy's most fertile source of inspiration was nature and the mountains, and in the Ardèche, between Grenoble and Le Puy, he built his summer home. When Franck died in 1890, d'Indy inherited not only his pupils but also the presidency of the Société Nationale (which he had effectively run as secretary since 1876). Called on in that capacity to help reform the Conservatoire, the target of a growing attack, he came up with solutions that were rejected as too radical. Disgusted with the state of official French musical education, he, Charles Bordes, and Alexandre Guilmant **[1351]**, founded in 1894, largely with d'Indy's money, a school of their own, which systematized the Franckian Classical approach and which ultimately took Franck's name. As the first modern conservatory, it influenced music schools all over the world, not the least because many of its graduates left it to do just that. As a result of his leadership of the institution, d'Indy edited and made available much old music that is now taken for granted (e.g., the operas of Monteverdi **[333]** and Rameau **[675]**), wrote a monumental composition method, and became a globe-trotting apostle for his ideas.

The year 1897 finally saw the premiere of a major d'Indy opera (in Brussels). This was *Fervaal,* which took its story from a Swedish poem and had been in the works since 1878 (as *Axel*) but was chiefly inspired by *Parsifal,* its composer's notion of the perfect opera. Like *Parsifal, Fervaal's* theme is religious—the triumph of Christianity over darker forces. Though it was admired and still enjoys occasional revivals, it marks the beginning of a split with the progressive musical forces in France. *Fervaal* was succeeded in 1903 (the year of *Pelléas et Mélisande*, which d'Indy deplored) by *L'Étranger*—less mystical and less Wagnerian, though by then the myth of the Wagnerian pseudo-seer had been established. The same year brought the most popular of the 3 numbered symphonies, the second. (No. 1, *Italienne*, was not published.) In 1905 d'Indy completed another relatively popular work, the *Jour d'été sur la montagne (Summer Day on the Mountain)*, and went to Boston to conduct two concerts of the Boston Symphony. (Though he never formally headed an orchestra, he was in great demand as a guest conductor.) A year later an idyllically happy marriage of thirty-one years ended with Isabelle's death; d'Indy commemorated it in the orchestral poem *Souvenirs.*

Though he had previously rejected offers from the Conservatoire, d'Indy took over the ensemble course there in 1912, in which same year he became a grand officer of the *Légion d'honneur* (of which he had been a member since 1892). From 1908 to 1915 he was chiefly occupied with what he evidently intended to be his *magnum opus,* the opera *La Légende de St. Christophe.* The wartime conditions (perhaps fortunately) postponed its first performance. In 1918 he celebrated the end of the war with a third symphony (subtitled *"De Bello Gallico"),* which showed a shocking decline of his compositional powers. *St. Christophe* was produced at last by the Paris Opéra in June 1920. Though the music was praised, the libretto —a pro-Catholic, anti-Jewish polemic— doomed it, even in those days. After the war his second wife, Caroline Janson, persuaded him to move his summer home from the mountains to the Mediterranean beaches at Agay. There the Provençal light and warmth seem to have penetrated his music —which in his last years included another comic opera, *Le Rêve de Cinyras (Cinyras' Dream),* the orchestral *Poème des rivages (Beach Poem)* and *Diptyque méditerranéen,* the Op. 89 Concerto for Flute, Cello, Piano, and Strings, and some of his best chamber music—all of which seem to reject Wagner for a sort of Classical French luminosity. Shortly before his sudden death (at eighty), he returned to arranging French folksongs, which he had been collecting for much of his mature life. He also wrote choral works, both sacred and secular, songs, keyboard pieces, and didactic music, completed works by Chausson [1484] and Lekeu [1610], and did much writing on music and musicians.

RECORDINGS: Apart from a few relatively popular works, d'Indy has been much neglected on records. There are no commercial recordings of the operas (there is a pirate recording of *Fervaal)* and none known to this writer of the choral music. There have been many versions of the *Symphonie cévenole;* the *Istar Variations;* the *Fervaal Prélude;* as well as scattered versions of the Op. 89 Concerto for Flute, Cello, Piano, and Strings; *La Forêt enchantée; Karadec;* the complete *Wallenstein* (d'Indy himself made a recording of *La Camp); Tableaux de voyage;* Symphony No. 2; the *Andante cantabile* for horn and strings; the *Sarabande et Menuet* for wind quintet and piano; the *Suite for Trumpet, 2 Flutes, and Strings;* and the *Jour d'été.* Also recorded are the *Chansons et danses* for wind ensemble; the Sonata for Piano; the *Suite dans le style ancien;* the Sonata for Violin and Piano; the Trio for Clarinet, Cello, and Piano; the Piano Quartet in A Minor, miscellaneous piano works (a few by the composer on acoustical records and piano rolls), and a handful of songs and folksongs.

[1463] FERRARI, Gabrielle (Fe-rär-rē', Gà-brē-el')
PIANIST
BORN: Paris, September 14, 1851
DIED: Paris, July 4, 1921

Initially Mlle. Ferrari studied with the Hungarian pianist Henri Ketten (1848–83) and with a minor composer named Jules-Laurent Duprato (1828–92). At fourteen she made her concert debut in Naples and then spent some time at the Milan Conservatory. On returning to Paris, she became a pupil of Gounod [1258]. She worked mostly in small forms as a composer but later took up opera writing. Of her several efforts, the most successful was *Le Cobzar,* premiered in Monte Carlo in 1909, and revived several times afterward, notably (in an expanded version) in Paris in 1912. RECORDINGS: Some of her songs turn up on early records.

[1464] COWEN, (Sir) Hymen Frederic
PIANIST, CONDUCTOR, WRITER
BORN: Kingston, Jamaica, January 29, 1852
DIED: London, October 6, 1935

As a composer, Frederic Cowen (as he preferred to be called) had been virtually forgotten by the time he died, though he began with rare promise and became one of the first important English conductors (even though he was technically foreign born). He arrived on the ancestral soil when his family returned in 1856, his father becoming treasurer to the Royal Opera and secretary to

William Humble Ward, Earl of Dudley. Young Frederic was put to study with Henry Russell [1226], had his *Minna-Waltz* (for piano) published when he was six, and at eight wrote an operetta, *Garibaldi, or the Rival Patriots*, to a libretto by his sister. Around that time he became the pupil of Sir John Goss, organist at St. Paul's, and Sir Julius Benedict [1180]. He began his pianistic career at twelve, and a year later was awarded the Mendelssohn Scholarship to study at the Leipzig Conservatory. His parents, fearful of what might happen to their young hopeful alone in an alien world, turned it down and took him to Leipzig on their own, where in 1866 he initiated study with Moscheles [1146], Reinecke [1292], and other members of the establishment there. But this was all shortly terminated by the outbreak of the Austro-Prussian War. A year later he went to Berlin and studied at the Stern Conservatory with Tausig [1389] and others. He returned to London in 1868, took up his pianistic career, and was hailed as a composer when the first of his six symphonies and his only piano concerto were performed in 1869 (Cowen was then seventeen). He worked for several years as *répétiteur* in various opera companies, emerging as a conductor in a series of concerts with the Philharmonic Society in 1884. He was so admired that when Arthur Sullivan [1397] retired in 1888, Cowen succeeded him. That same year Cowen went to Melbourne to conduct at the Centennial Exposition for a fee of £5,000 (perhaps $100,000 in present-day terms). He broke with the Philharmonic management in 1892 but was lured back in 1900 and remained for seven years. At various times he was regular conductor of the Hallé Orchestra, the Liverpool Philharmonic, the Scottish Orchestra, and various festival organizations. The Universities of Cambridge and Edinburgh awarded him honorary doctorates, and the recently crowned George V knighted him in 1911. By then he had virtually given up composition. His 4 mature operas—*Pauline*, 1876; *Thorgrim*, 1890; *Signa*, 1893; and *Harold*, 1895—all received London productions. *(Signa* was, however, premiered at the Teatro dal Verme in Milan.) Cowen fancied his symphonies as his best work; one reads good things about some of his odes and his serious songs. RECORDINGS: He is represented on records solely by a few drawing-room ballads, mostly waxed half a century and more ago.

[1465] BAYER, Josef (Bī'-er, Yō'-zef)
VIOLINIST, CONDUCTOR

BORN: Vienna, March 6, 1852
DIED: Vienna, March 12, 1913

Josef Bayer was a product of the Vienna Conservatory, where his teachers included Bruckner [1293], the violinist Georg Hellmesberger, and the latter's son Josef. For a time he functioned as a violinist in the Hofoper orchestra but turned increasingly to conducting, making many guest appearances. He came to New York in 1881 to conduct the American premiere of his *Der Chevalier von San Marco*, one of his several successful but ephemeral operettas. His specialty, however, was ballets, of which he wrote more than twenty. He was chief ballet conductor at the Hofoper for thirteen years, 1885–98. His most successful dance scores were *Die Donaunixe (The Danube Sprite)* and especially *Die Puppenfee (The Doll Fairy)*, which is still popular in Central Europe. RECORDINGS: There is a recording of *Die Puppenfee* conducted by Peter Falk.

[1466] GRÜNFELD, Alfred (Grün'-felt, Ȧl'-fret)
PIANIST
BORN: Prague, July 4, 1852
DIED: Vienna, January 4, 1924

Immensely popular as a performer in his day, Grünfeld has (apparently with considerable justification) faded into oblivion both as a player and as a composer. He studied piano in Prague with Josef Krejči (1821–81) and others, and then at the Kullak Academy in Berlin. His younger brother Heinrich, a fine cellist, later taught at the latter school. Alfred settled in Vienna and in 1876 was named imperial *Kammervirtuos*. He toured widely in Europe, wrote a couple of light operas, and was admired for his compositions and arrangements for piano. He has been described as a sort of proto-Liberace—a salon pianist *in excelsis*. RECORDINGS: He made many recordings, including several of his own works.

[1467] STANFORD, (Sir) Charles Villiers
TEACHER, ORGANIST, CONDUCTOR
BORN: Dublin, September 30, 1852
DIED: London, March 29, 1924

It is a tenet of modern British music that Stanford is one of its patriarchs. The fifth edition of *Grove's Dictionary* accorded him no fewer than eight pages, and though its successor has halved that, it is still loud in its advocacy. He was a prolific and ambitious composer and an effective (if intolerant) teacher through whose hands passed a sort of Who's Who of the first generation of the twentieth-century English musical renaissance. The fact remains, however, that he is not much performed these days on his home grounds, and his name is scarcely known outside them.

Like so many nineteenth-century "English" composers, Stanford was an Irishman, but no bog trotter. His father was an eminent, affluent, and cultured lawyer and reared his son with every advantage, including music lessons from various Dublin notables and boxing lessons from the butler. The child began composing at a Mozartean age and playing in public not long afterward. After some study with Ernst Pauer in London, he matriculated at Queen's College, Cambridge, in 1870, to read classics. He had a scholarship there as a choir singer from the beginning and later functioned as organist of Trinity College and conductor of the University Music Society. After taking his B.A. in 1874, he went to Germany to study music, at first in Leipzig (with Reinecke [1292] among others) and then in Berlin with Friedrich Kiel. He was soon making a name for himself in British musical circles as a composer, and in 1876 his incidental music for Tennyson's play *Queen Mary* brought him to general attention. Up to this point John James Stanford had supported his son's inclinations, even when Charles foreswore the paternal profession for music; but in 1878, when he married Jennie Wetton without asking permission, his parent cut him off.

However, Stanford, a man of great drive, seems to have had little trouble making his own way. By the end of the decade, he had completed (and won a prize with) the first of his 7 symphonies, 2 oratorios, and an opera, *The Veiled Prophet of Khorassan.* This (the first of 9), was premiered in Hannover in 1881 and later produced at Covent Garden. When the Royal College of Music opened in 1883, Stanford was its professor of composition. In the same year Oxford bestowed an honorary doctorate on him. In 1885 he began a seventeen-year intendancy as conductor of the London Bach Choir. In 1887 he was named professor of music at Cambridge, which institution conferred another doctorate on him the next year. Among his important pupils were Benjamin [1887], Bliss [1854], Boughton [1702], Bridge [1713], Coleridge-Taylor [1674], George Dyson 1883–1964, Eugene Goossens [1878], Gurney [1839], Holst [1658], Howells [1870], Ireland [1719], Jacob [1911], and Vaughan Williams [1633]. Essentially a kindly man, Stanford was famous for his irascibility, quick to

explode with rage or laughter, and quite contemptuous of what he did not understand. (He went out of his way to further Elgar's [1499] career but was so overbearing and tactless in his relations with him that after 1904 Elgar steered clear of him except where encounters were professionally and diplomatically essential.)

Stanford received other honors from the Universities of Durham and Leeds, and was knighted by Edward VII in 1902. He remained energetically active until his health began to fail in 1921, when he had to give up conducting. To his distress, his reputation as a composer had begun to fade by the second decade of the century. He suffered a stroke on St. Patrick's Day, 1924, and died twelve days later. He is buried in Westminster Abbey. He left a daughter, Geraldine, and a son, Guy.

Of Stanford's large works, his church music, highly regarded in England, has been most successful. Only his "Irish" opera, *Shamus O'Brien* of 1896, managed to survive its earliest performances. The symphonies and concerti (2 for violin, 3 for piano) gather dust.

RECORDINGS: Some of the simpler songs and part-songs have received recordings. John Parry has done an LP side of piano pieces—rather unassuming works. Stanford himself, late in life, recorded a few works— the overture to *Shamus O'Brien,* the masque from the opera *The Critic,* abridged versions of the *Suite of Ancient Dances* and the first of the 6 *Irish Rhapsodies,* and the song cycle *Songs of the Fleet* (with baritone Harold Williams)—all transferred to LP. There is a recent English recording of the Concerto for Clarinet by Thea King, and English catalogs offer a fair sprinkling of choral works (e.g., part-songs performed by the Louis Halsey Singers). *Songs of the Sea* has been recorded by baritone Benjamin Luxon with Norman Del Mar conducting. Del Mar has also recorded the Symphony No. 3 ("Irish").

[1468] HOLLMAN, Joseph (Hōl'-màn, Yō'-zef)
CELLIST
BORN: Maastricht, October 16, 1852
DIED: Paris, January 1, 1927

Dutch-born Hollmann was a pupil of the great French cellist Adrien François Servais at the Brussels Conservatory and later of Léon Jacquard at the Paris Conservatoire. He lived in Paris after that and concertized all over the world, winning many honors and decorations. Saint-Saëns [1343] dedicated the Concerto for Cello No. 2 to him.

He made a number of recordings both in Europe and America, including some of his encore pieces which have also been recorded by other cellists.

[1469] TÁRREGA Y EIXEA, Francisco
(Târ'-rä-gà ē Äk-sä'-à, Frän-thēs'-kō)
GUITARIST, TEACHER
BORN: Villareal, November 21, 1852
DIED: Barcelona, December 15, 1909

Tárrega was almost singlehandedly responsible for the rebirth of interest in the guitar, an instrument whose popularity had been all but obliterated by the piano craze. Though he was trained in the latter instrument, Tárrega took up the guitar when he was ten years old and, after a broader grounding in music at the Madrid Conservatory, made his living and his fame concertizing on the instrument and teaching it. He demonstrated its range and scope with transcriptions of both Classical and contemporary piano pieces. His friend the composer Isaac Albéniz [1523] is said to have preferred some of Tárrega's versions of his compositions to his own. A stroke in 1906 virtually ended the guitarist's performing career. He also wrote many original pieces for his instrument. RECORDINGS: A number of his guitar pieces may be found in recorded guitar anthologies.

[1470] HILLEMACHER, Paul Joseph
Guillaume (Ēl'-mà-shä, Pōl Zhō-sef' Gē-yōm')
BORN: Paris, November 29, 1852
DIED: Versailles, August 13, 1933

Musically speaking, Paul Hillemacher is virtually inseparable from his younger brother Lucien (Joseph Édouard), who was born in Paris on June 10, 1860, and died there June 9, 1909. The sons of a painter, they not only shared a middle name, but for the most part composed jointly as "Paul-Lucien Hillemacher." Both studied at the Paris Conservatoire—Paul with François Bazin [1247], Lucien with Massenet [1396]. Both won the Grand Prix de Rome (respectively in 1876 and 1880), each after having been runner-up in a previous year. As collaborators they specialized in vocal music, producing 7 operas, some incidental music, 2 oratorios, briefer choral works, and a number of songs; there were also a few orchestral works, chamber, and keyboard pieces. Paul produced a few compositions under his own name, but after Lucien died (a day shy of his forty-ninth birthday) he seems largely to have dried up. RECORDINGS: There are recordings of a few songs. (One, *"Ici-bas"* ["Down Here"], was long credited to the young Debussy [1547].)

[1471] FOOTE, Arthur William
ORGANIST, PIANIST, TEACHER
BORN: Salem, Mass., March 5, 1853
DIED: Boston, April 3, 1937

Senior by a year to George Chadwick [1483], Arthur Foote, if he had been as influential or as colorful, might well stand as the Grand Old Man of the New England Classicists. His family had previously claimed no musicians, and he showed, as a child, no special interest in the art. As a practical matter of education, he was given piano lessons and found that he liked them. After some harmony training with Stephen Emory of the New England Conservatory, however, he entered Harvard in 1870 to prepare for a business career. There he discovered John Knowles Paine [1366] and took his music courses. He also became conductor of the Glee Club. After graduation, he took some keyboard lessons with Benjamin Johnson Lang, a Liszt [1218] pupil who served as organist to the Handel and Haydn Society. Lang convinced him that he had the talent to make a living in music. In 1875 Harvard awarded him the first musical M.A. ever given an American, and he hung out his shingle as a teacher in Boston. Though he was one of the few professionals of his day who could not claim European training, his heroes were Brahms [1329], Wagner [1230], and Liszt, in that order. He did, however, make the pilgrimage to the initial Bayreuth Festival in 1876. In 1878 he began thirty-two years as organist at the First Unitarian Church. He helped found the American Guild of Organists, serving as its president from 1909 to 1912. He also promoted chamber-music concerts around Boston and, mostly in the early years of his career, was frequently heard there as a pianist. He was married (from 1880) to Kate Grant Knowlton and had a daughter named Katharine. In 1910 he retired to Newton Center, where he occupied himself with composing, gardening, and writing. He composed little after 1918 but returned to teaching at the New England Conservatory in 1920. On his eightieth birthday Serge Koussevitzky conducted the Boston Symphony in a concert in Foote's honor; the old man was there to take a bow. He succumbed to pneumonia at eighty-four. Despite his taste for what had been the German avant-garde, Foote described himself as a conservative. He wrote no operas, no oratorios, no symphonies. His largest compositions are 3 Longfellow cantatas and some orchestral works. Most of his music was published, and some of his songs enjoyed considerable popularity. RECORDINGS: Works recorded include the tone poem *Francesca da Rimini* (Jorge Mester), the *Suite in E Major* for Strings (Howard Hanson, Serge Koussevitzky), the *Suite in D Minor* for orchestra (a Society for the Preservation of the American Musical Heritage release), the *Night Piece* for flute and string quartet (Julius Baker, Diane Gold) or flute and string orchestra (Louis Lane conducting), the Sonata for Violin and Piano (Eugene Gratovich, Joseph Silverstein), the Sonata for Cello and Piano and other cello pieces (Douglas Moore), String Quartet No. 3 (Kohon Quartet), the Piano Quintet (M. L. Boehm), piano pieces (George Bennette), the Piano Trio No. 1 Op. 5 (Macalester Trio) and the Piano Trio No. 2 Op. 65 (Joseph Silverstein, Jules and Virginia Eskin).

[1472] SJÖGREN, Johan Gustaf Emil
(Syö'-gren, Yō'-hàn Gus'-tàv Äm'-il)
ORGANIST, TEACHER
BORN: Stockholm, June 16, 1853
DIED: Stockholm, March 1, 1918

Emil Sjögren, essentially a musical miniaturist, has been called "the Swedish Grieg" **[1410]**, though he more closely resembles the Dane Lange-Müller **[1456]** and was chiefly influenced by Schumann **[1211]**. When he was about fifteen, he took up piano with a teacher named Ludvig Ohlson and soon afterward spent five years studying at the Stockholm Conservatory, where he specialized in piano and organ. After leaving in 1874, he took a job with a wholesaler of musical instruments. His employer recognized his talents and joined with Ohlson to send him to Berlin in 1879 for a further year of keyboard study with Friedrich Kiel (1821–85) and the organist Karl August Haupt. In 1881 he became organist of the French Reformed Church in Stockholm. Two years later his piano suite *Erotikon* won an all-Scandinavian competition, and his prize enabled him to return to Germany and to visit Vienna and Paris the next year. In 1886 he became a piano teacher in Richard Andersson's academy. The only other one at the time was Andersson, but later the institution became more flourishing, though Sjögren left in 1888. In 1891 he transferred to the organ loft of the Johanneskyrka. He also made concert tours. He married the pianist Bertha Dahlman in 1897. Sjögren's largest compositional efforts are some choral-orchestral

pieces and several sonatas (5 for violin, 2 for piano, one for cello). His best and most enduring works, however, are some of his more than 200 songs. RECORDINGS: Some of his songs have been recorded by such Scandinavian singers as Elisabeth Söderström and Nicolai Gedda. Gerald Robbin and Ingrid Lindgren have recorded the *Erotikon,* and Lindgren the *Serenata in D Minor.* Mats Persson has done the Sonata No. 1 for Piano, Mona Nordin the Sonata No. 2 for Violin and Piano and Guido Vecchi the Sonata for Cello and Piano.

[1473] NICODÉ, Jean-Louis (Nē-kō-dä', Zhàn Lōō-ē')
PIANIST, CONDUCTOR
BORN: Jerczig, August 12, 1853
DIED: Langebrück, October 5, 1919

Nicodé was born in what is now Jerczik, near Poznań, Poland. His mother was Polish; his father, a German, presumably of French descent, was a passionate amateur musician and his first teacher. When the child was three, the family moved to Berlin where he studied with an organist named Hartkäss and entered Theodor Kullak's (1818–82) academy at sixteen. On completing his studies, he became a concert pianist, establishing a series of concerts in Berlin under his own name and setting up a teaching studio. The great Belgian soprano Desirée Artot (1835–1907) took him along as her accompanist and assisting artist on a tour of southeast Europe. In 1878 he was named professor of piano at the Royal Conservatory in Dresden, then directed by Franz Wüllner (who had conducted the premieres of the first two operas of Wagner's **[1230]** *Ring* in Munich). But political machinations drove Wüllner out in 1883 and forced Nicodé to resign his post. Having already become a splendid conductor, he rallied the disbanded orchestra of the Royal Kapelle two years later and served as director of the Philharmonic Concerts until 1888. In 1893 he returned to conduct (again) a series of "Nicodé" concerts and later served as director of a choral society until 1900. At that time he retired to suburban Langebrück and spent the rest of his life writing music. Nicodé was a serious composer, and critics speak of his music (in the abstract) as "interesting." It includes two gigantic choral works, *Das Meer (The Sea)* and *Gloria!* (described as a "storm-and-sunlight song"), a symphony, symphonic poems, sonatas, and many smaller works. RECORDINGS: Nicodé seems to be represented on records only by the lightweight orchestral *Faschingsbilder (Carnival Scenes).*

[1474] MESSAGER, André Charles Prosper (Mes-sà-zhā', Àn-drā' Shârl Prôs-pâr')
CONDUCTOR, ADMINISTRATOR, CRITIC,
PIANIST, ORGANIST
BORN: Montluçon, December 30, 1853
DIED: Paris, February 24, 1929

The last important practitioner of the nineteenth-century French light-opera tradition, André Messager was born into an affluent civil-service family in central France. His parents found him more than they could handle and in 1860 farmed him out to relatives who saw to it that he had piano and violin lessons. In the aftermath of the Franco-Prussian War, the Messagers lost most of their money. Faced with having to shift for himself, André decided to become a musician. Getting himself admitted to the École Niedermeyer in Paris, he studied with Saint-Saëns [1343] and Gigout [1417]. He also became a friend of Gabriel Fauré [1424], whom he succeeded at St. Sulpice in 1874 as number two organist. (Widor [1414] was number one.) He won a gold medal with his only symphony in 1876, and a silver medal with a cantata a year or so later. In 1881 he took a less demanding and less lucrative organ post at the church of St. Paul-St. Louis and a year later became choirmaster at Ste. Marie des Batignolles. Meanwhile he had been conducting ballets (including some of his own) at the Folies-Bergère and had spent the 1880 season at the Eden Théâtre in Brussels as chief conductor.

The year 1883 was an important one for Messager. During its course he married Edith Clouet, made the pilgrimage to Bayreuth with Fauré (with whom he collaborated on a series of *Souvenirs de Bayreuth,* a quadrille for piano duet), and was asked to complete Bernicat's [1413] *François-les-basbleus (Francis Bluestockings).* The success of this last piece got him a production two years later of his own first operetta, *La Fauvette du temple (The Temple Warbler).* This was followed within the month by *La Béarnaise* at the Bouffes-Parisiens, a work that was soon to have a considerable success in London. In October 1886 the Opéra produced his ballet *Les Deux Pigeons (The Two Pigeons),* which remains one of his most popular scores. After *Les Bourgeois de Calais (The Burghers of Calais)* in 1887, the "fairy-spectacle" *Isoline* in 1888, and *Le Mari de la reine (The Queen's Husand)* in 1889, Messager struck international gold

with *La Basoche (The Legal Fraternity),* premiered at the Opéra-Comique in 1890 and soon afterward a great hit in London and New York. Late January of 1893 produced a failure in *Miss Dollar* and another big success in *Madame Chrysanthème* (based on a Pierre Loti tale that is often likened to the story of Puccini's [1511] *Madama Butterfly).* Meanwhile Messager's popularity in London had brought him a commission for a new work to open there at the Savoy. Called *Mirette,* it was at least a partial collaboration between the Frenchman and Dotie Davis, an Irishwoman who composed as "Hope Temple," and who married him (Edith having been divorced) in 1895. Both the work and the marriage seem to have been only fair successes. After a couple of more tries, Messager hit again with *Les p'tites Michu (The Michu Kids)* of 1897 and especially with *Véronique* in 1898, which again attained great popularity in England.

With his appointment as conductor at the Opéra-Comique in 1898, Messager established himself increasingly as one of the truly distinguished baton men of his time. He subsequently served (under various titles) at Covent Garden, the Paris Opéra, the Opéra-Comique (again), and with the Lamoureux and Paris Conservatoire orchestras. He directed a number of premieres, including that of Franco Leoni's [1566] *L'Oracolo* at Covent Garden in 1905, but the most famous was of Debussy's [1547] *Pelléas et Mélisande,* whose score the composer dedicated to him. (According to the first Mélisande, Mary Garden, Messager laid violent siege to her heart, Hope Temple or no.) His conducting and managerial duties curtailed his composition to a degree, but he still managed nine more stage works between 1905 and 1928. Among the more notable were *Fortunio* of 1907, source of the song *"La Maison grise"* ("The Gray House"); *Monsieur Beaucaire* of 1919, after a Booth Tarkington novel and written for Maggie Teyte, who recorded excerpts from it; and *L'Amour masqué (Love in Disguise)* for Sascha Guitry and Yvonne Printemps. He was already ill when he wrote his last work, *Coup de roulis,* 1928, and died five months after it opened.

Besides his 23 operettas, *opéras-comiques,* and musical comedies, his 10 ballets, and some incidental music, Messager wrote a number of songs and a few miscellaneous vocal and instrumental works, and did a good deal of arranging.

RECORDINGS: Of the stage works there seem to be no complete recordings, but there are innumerable excerpts, some with "original casts." There are also recordings of suites from *Isoline* and *Les deux pigeons* (Jean-Pierre Jacquillat), an orchestral *Suite funambulesque (Tight-Rope Suite* (Paul Godwin), and the *Souvenirs de Bayreuth* (piano duet of Christian Ivaldi and Noël Lee).

[1475] LISHIN, Grigori Andreievich (Lē-shēn', Grē-gôr'-ē Ăn-drä-ye'-vich)
PIANIST, CRITIC
BORN: St. Petersburg, May 5, 1854
DIED: St. Petersburg, June 27, 1888

Lishin studied piano with his mother, then was a pupil of Rimsky-Korsakov [1416] and Nikolai Soloviev at the St. Petersburg Conservatory. Afterward he worked as an accompanist and reviewer. He wrote 2 operas and other works of some magnitude, but is now remembered only for a song, "She Laughed," recorded by Feodor Chaliapin and others.

[1476] WAILLY, Louis Auguste Paul Warnier de (Vĭ-ye', Lōō-ē' Ô-güst' Pōl Värn-yä' də)
LAWYER, WRITER
BORN: Amiens, May 16, 1854
DIED: Paris, June 18, 1933

Paul de Wailly began his career as a lawyer. Though he had taught himself music, he did not take up formal study until he encountered César Franck [1284] when he was twenty-seven. He idolized Franck and imitated him sedululously in his compositions, which included symphonies, choral works, chamber music, and songs; he also wrote a book about him. RECORDINGS: His little *Aubade* has been recorded by members of the Philadelphia Orchestra.

[1477] CATALANI, Alfredo (Kä-tä-lä'-nē, Ăl-frä'-dō)
TEACHER
BORN: Lucca, June 19, 1854
DIED: Milan, August 7, 1893

Puccini's [1511] fellow townsman, Catalani was his chief rival while he lasted. He obviously had extraordinary musicodramatic gifts, but fate allowed them too little time to develop. His two successful operas cling to the Italian repertoire by their fingernails. Though it is customary to link them with *verismo*, the Italian version of operatic so-called "realism," they are—inspired both by Bellini [1164] and the German Romantics—difficult to pigeonhole.

Catalani had his first lessons from his fa-ther, an organist, and his advanced training at the local Liceo Pacini. At fourteen he wrote a *Mass* that was sung at the Cathedral of San Michele. At eighteen he went to Paris and is said to have studied composition with Bazin [1247] at the Paris Conservatoire, though the records do not include his name. Returning to Italy, he spent two years in fairly normal student poverty at the Milan Conservatory, where he was a pupil and protégé of Bazzini [1256]—note the curious resemblance of that name to Bazin's! There he identified with the *scapigliati* (unkempt), a determinedly Bohemian group that advocated the overturn of everything, including traditional Italian music. Here he found a friend in Boito [1393] who wrote the libretto for Catalani's graduation exercise, a pastorale called *La Falce (The Sickle)*, which received high marks when it was performed in the summer of 1875. It called him to the attention of Wagner's [1230] representative and Verdi's [1232] albatross, the publisher Giovannina Lucca, who retained him at a monthly salary to write an opera for her catalog. The result was *Elda,* a version of the Lorelei tale. Catalani completed it in 1876, but it was not staged until 1880 (in Turin), and it managed only nine performances. Its successor, *Dejanice,* did even worse at La Scala in 1883.

Catalani was now nearly thirty. The tuberculosis that eventually killed him was already undermining his constitution and his hair had turned white. Moreover he was tormented by guilt over what turned out to be a lifelong affair with Teresa Junck, the wife of his closest friend, an Alsatian-descended composer named Benedetto Junck (who, incidentally, commissioned a highly romantic portrait of Catalani which now hangs in the Museo Civico in Turin). In 1886 he achieved a measure of musical success with *Edmea* (libretto by Antonio Ghislanzoni, librettist of *Aida*) at La Scala, and was appointed to succeed the dead Ponchielli [1334] as professor of composition at the conservatory. *Edmea,* in revised form, was even more successful a few months later at the Teatro Carignano in Turin, where it was conducted by the nineteen-year-old Arturo Toscanini, in his first Italian appearance after his meteoric rise to fame as a last-minute substitute, hoisted from the orchestral cellos in Rio de Janeiro. *Edmea* made Toscanini Catalani's friend and, for the rest of the conductor's long life, his dogged champion. Toscanini even named his daughter "Wally" (later Mrs. Vladimir Horowitz) after the composer's last operatic heroine.

At this point Catalani's career was threatened by another crisis: Giovannina Lucca sold out to the Ricordis, who were touting his rival, Puccini, and were not interested in a man whom Verdi had written off as a nobody. (Verdi changed his mind, too late.) Catalani reworked *Elda* as *Loreley* (or *Lorelei)* and submitted it, without any result. Finally, in 1890, he maneuvered a production in Turin, where the work triumphed. (It is still sung in Italy today.) His next and last work was *La Wally,* to a libretto by Giuseppe Illica (later Puccini's librettist) to a German story Catalani had discovered in a newspaper. This won a star-studded premiere at La Scala in January 1892 and seemed to signal the composer's arrival at last among the operatic greats of his time. (The singers included Hariclea Darclée, later Puccini's first *Tosca;* Adelina Stehle, the first Nedda in Leoncavallo's **[1498]** *Pagliacci* and the first Nannetta in Verdi's *Falstaff;* and Virginia Guerrini, the first Meg in the latter work.) Vacationing in Switzerland a year later, Catalani suffered a massive pulmonary hemorrhage. He was brought back to Milan and died within the week, at age thirty-nine.

Apart from the operas, Catalani's major work was the symphonic poem *Ero e Leandro,* though he wrote some smaller orchestral pieces and a number of piano pieces and songs.

RECORDINGS: There is a commercial recording of *La Wally* (Fausto Cleva), an excellent piracy of *Loreley* (Gianandrea Gavazzeni) and a new commercial recording of *Loreley* (another Italian production, with Napoleone Annovazzi conducting), as well as many excerpts. Luciano Rosada has recorded two little pieces for strings, *A sera* (later incorporated in *La Wally)* and *Serenatella.* Ondrej Lenárd has also recorded the *Serenatella* together with *At Evening* for strings.

[1478] JANÁČEK, Leoš (Yä'-nà-chek, Lā'-ōsh)
CONDUCTOR, TEACHER, ADMINISTRATOR, THEORIST
BORN: Hukvaldy, July 3, 1854
DIED: Moravská Ostrava, August 12, 1928

Leoš Janáček is, with Smetana **[1291]** and Dvořák **[1386]**, now recognized as one of a trinity of remarkable composers born out of the nationalistic ferment that arose in the old kingdom of Bohemia in the nineteenth century. There are those who would call him the greatest of the three, and certainly he was the most daring and original. Yet he was past forty before he developed his own style

and past sixty when he at last came to international attention. Whereas one identifies the other two composers with the nineteenth-century Romantic movement, Janáček seems clearly to belong to the twentieth century, and is the first composer, perhaps, to appear in these pages whose music some listeners find still too "modern."

Janáček was born in what is now north-central Czechoslovakia (the province of North Moravia), where linguistic inflections and folksongs differ strongly from those to the west. He was the tenth of fourteen children of a schoolmaster-organist, Jiří Janáč, who kept bees to keep his mind off his troubles. The children were taught music as a matter of course, but only Leoš showed any real proclivity toward the art, and so in 1865 he was sent off to grace the choir of the Augustinian Abbey in Brünn (Brno), where Brother Gregor Mendel had, without reward, just discovered genetics. For three years Leoš studied there under Father Pavel Křížkovský (1820–85), the choirmaster, a choral composer and collector of folksongs. From 1869 to 1872 he prepared to follow in his father's footsteps in a Brno *Gymnasium* and in the teachers' college, where he did apprentice teaching for two years. In 1872 Křížkovský was transferred, and Janáček was summoned to take his place by (now) Abbot Mendel; soon he was also leading a local male chorus (for which he wrote and arranged some music). However, he was uncomfortable about his lack of preparation and took leave to study in Prague. There he was admitted to the organ school, where he studied with František Skuherský (1830–92), a composer of some prominence. Despite having to lead a virtual starvation existence, he did well, but his departure was hastened by his refusal to tolerate Skuherský's sloppy conducting. He went back to Brno in 1875, and took up where he left off, a year later giving up his glee club for a larger one which he turned into a quite formidable mixed choir. His successes brought him to the attention of Dvořák, and the two men became friends. Still dissatisfied with his shortcomings, however, he went to Leipzig for a stiff course of study with one Leo Grill in late 1879, and to Vienna in the spring, where he worked, less satisfactorily, with Franz Krenn (1816–97), Mahler's **[1525]** teacher. In May he returned to Brno for good, to be licensed as a music teacher by the Teachers' College and to become engaged to the fourteen-year-old daughter of the school's director, Zdenka Schulzová, whom he married a year later.

Though he was now doing a good bit of composing, Janáček had no more confidence in the results than he had had in his teaching and conducting. As a consequence he destroyed much of what he wrote, though two works for strings, *Suite* and *Idyll*, from 1877 and 1878, respectively, and some small instrumental and choral works have survived. Nor was the time particularly conducive to creation. A daughter, Olga, put in her appearance. In 1881 the composer founded an "organ school," with himself at the helm, in Brno. The following year the marriage went sour, and Janáček and Zdenka separated. In 1884 (when they were reunited) the new National Opera opened in Brno, and the composer inaugurated a journal (with himself as editor-in-chief) to review its offerings. During most of the period he seems to have written no music at all, and one can't blame him. In 1886 he also took up classes at the *Gymnasium*. In 1888 Zdenka bore him a son, named Vladimír, who died two years later (Olga died at twenty).

In the midst of all this activity, the composer was inspired (perhaps by the proximity of an opera house) to try his hand at an opera. He lit on a libretto *Šárka*, based on Czech legend, that one Julius Zeyer had written to tempt Dvořák. Janáček completed the work in 1888 (the year he gave up the journal) and was stunned to find that: (1) he needed the author's permission to get it produced and (2) that the author would not give it to him. (Fibich's [1457] successful treatment of the same theme did not help his cause, and it was thirty-seven years before the piece reached the stage.) At about this same time a confrere got him interested in folksong collecting, notably back on his Moravian home grounds, and this activity bore fruit not only in some arrangements of his findings, but also in their direct use and (more importantly) influence in his own compositions. A second opera, *The Beginning of a Romance*, a one-acter incorporating a good deal of folk music, *did* get a production at Brno in 1894 but made little impact. However, the story, borrowed from Gabriela Preissová, turned him to her further work, and he became fascinated with her stark drama of village life, *Her Foster Daughter*. Adapting it himself, he began work on the opera that is better-known in the West as *Jenůfa*.

It was nearly ten years before he completed *Jenůfa*. The man had enormous musical curiosity and a mind that ceaselessly combined and recombined the bits of musical information he stored in it. It was during this period that his credo took shape, based on two chief ideas: (1) that what satisfies the ear is paramount to all the supposed "laws" of music; (2) that music derives from natural sounds and, more particularly, from the pitches and rhythms of speech (which in turn reflect emotional states). From this latter theory he concluded that his own music should most naturally derive from the Slovak dialect he had been reared speaking and that the Rosetta Stone was the folksong of his native district. It appears that for such reasons he destroyed the first version of his opera and rewrote most of it from a new point of view. He submitted it to the National Opera in Prague, but it was rejected by Karel Kovařovic, the current intendant —whose own earlier operatic efforts had, perhaps not incidentally, suffered from Janáček's forthright reviews. The work was, however, accepted at Brno, and, despite a jackleg production, delighted the locals, who no doubt enjoyed seeing their world reflected in it.

Janáček had, during the past twenty years, continued to write utilitarian, mostly choral pieces, his one other major composition being the cantata *Amarus*, which he finished in 1897 but revised twice, in 1901 and 1906, before he was satisfied with it. For the next several years, he flirted with other operatic subjects—*The Angel Sonata*, Preissová's *The Housewife*, Tolstoy's *Anna Karenina*, but the work he settled on was called *Fate (Osud)*, a sort of *verismo* piece for which he and a girl pupil concocted a libretto. It was accepted for production by a Prague theater, but the plan fell through and it was not staged until thirty years after its composer was dead. In 1908 he embarked on what became *The Excursions of Mr. Brouček*, an odd work, based on a fantastic novel by Svatopluk Čech, whose two episodes take the slightly fuddled *petit-bourgeois* title character to the moon and to fifteenth-century Bohemia. Like *Jenůfa* it went very slowly. While it was doing so, Janáček also turned out his few mature piano pieces, and some of his most magnificent choral works, as well as a few pieces of chamber music and his symphonic poem *The Fiddler's Child*.

The composer, who had shaken off poverty and given up all his teaching duties save those connected with his burgeoning school, was, when war broke out in 1914, sixty years old, a hero in Brno, and hardly known elsewhere. When his male singers were called up for service, he settled for a women's choir, for which he wrote several works. Meanwhile in Prague his admirers had been urging Kovařovic (who *had* attended the premiere) to give *Jenůfa* a chance. In 1915 he capitulated, on condition that he might make some cuts, with the composer's approval. He conducted it himself the following May, and its success seems at last to have given its composer the confidence in himself that he needed. His final decade was his most productive and his greatest. (No doubt he was also heartened by the arrival of Czech independence.) He finished *Brouček* in 1917 (it was produced in Prague three years later), and soon thereafter completed the orchestral *Taras Bulba* and *Ballad of Blaník* (the latter in celebration of the republic) and the violin sonata. Four operas—his most radical and effective—followed: *Kát'a Kabanová*, 1921; *The Cunning Little Vixen*, 1924; *The Makropoulos Affair*, 1926; and the Dostoievskian *From the House of the Dead* of 1927–28, which he did not live to see produced. The year 1921 also brought the remarkable song cycle, *The Diary of One Who Vanished*, allegedly to lyrics by a young man who had run off with a Gypsy girl.

Janáček seems especially to have been rejuvenated in his last years by a passionate affair with Kamilá Stösslová, a married woman nearly half his age. She clearly influenced his three late woman-oriented operas and directly inspired his second (really his third—he rejected the first) string quartet of 1928, which he subtitled "Love Letters." Other important products of this happy Indian summer were: the *Glagolitic Mass*, to an Old Church Slavonic text, 1926; the curious *Nursery Rhymes* for voices and instruments, including an ocarina and a toy drum, 1927; the two concerted works for piano and chamber ensembles—the *Concertino* of 1925 and the *Capriccio* of 1926—and the orchestral *Sinfonietta* (really a sort of symphony), 1926.

Curiously the ill-sorted marriage held to the end, and indeed the passion, as far as Kamilá was concerned, seems to have been mostly on Janáček's side. In July 1928, however, she and her family came, on his invitation, to spend some time at his summer home in Hukvaldy. One night her little boy wandered off and Janáček caught a chill while helping look for him. The child was found, but the old man developed a cold which quickly turned to pneumonia; he died a few days later in a nearby hospital. At his funeral in Brno, the final scene of *The Cunning Little Vixen*, a revelation of the immortality of life in nature, was performed. The Brno theater now bears his name. In recent years his music has developed worldwide popularity, and his operas have been revealed in major houses as magnificently effective both as music and as theater.

RECORDINGS: Thanks to the diligence of the Czech recording arm, most of Janáček's music has been made available in idiomatic performances. The most important omission is the early opera *Šárka*, but on the credit

side Sir Charles Mackerras has been editing the mature works, returning them to the composer's intentions (all too often distorted by performance traditions) and recording them with major performers in up-to-date sound—which they require. Mirror gaps in the Janáček discography were recently filled with new recordings of *Beginning of a Romance* and the *Elegy on the Death of Olga* for tenor, chorus, and piano.

[1479] MOSZKOWSKI, Moritz (Mos-kōv'-skē, Mō'-rits)
PIANIST, TEACHER, CONDUCTOR
BORN: Breslau (now Wroclaw), August 23, 1854
DIED: Paris, March 4, 1925

Best known as a virtuoso performer, Moszkowski was, as a composer, once admired for his *Spanish Dances* (which owe more to the salon than to Seville) and long remembered for an innocuous and ubiquitous little *Serenade*. His heritages were Polish and Jewish, and he was proud of both. He is sometimes listed as "Maurycy," and he countered Bülow's **[1310]** remark that beside Bach **[684]**, Beethoven **[1063]**, and Brahms **[1329]** all others were cretins with the riposte that beside Mendelssohn **[1200]**, Meyerbeer **[1142]**, and Moszkowski, all others were Christians. Pianistically precocious, he began his studies in early childhood in Breslau and Dresden. During this time he is supposed to have shaken hands with Chopin **[1208]**, but it must have been done in an earlier incarnation. He went to the Stern Academy in Berlin and then transferred to Theodor Kullak's Neue Akademie. There he struck up a friendship with the brothers Philipp and Xaver Scharwenka **[1437, 1448]**. He made his concert debut in Berlin in 1873, became one of Kullak's staff, and made the city his base of operations for nearly a quarter of a century. He toured frequently, both as a pianist and conductor, and became rich and famous. He played duets with the aging Liszt **[1218]**, was Cécile Chaminade's **[1502]** brother-in-law, helped Paderewski **[1527]** find a publisher, and gave Thomas Beecham tips on orchestration. (But he never taught Josef Hofmann **[1680]**, whom he claimed as a pupil.) Though the critics did not regard Moszkowski's music highly, it was popular with the public and was programmed by his fellow pianists. He composed in large as well as in small forms. Having won a reputation for understanding the Iberian psyche, in 1892 he wrote a Moorish opera, *Boabdil der letzte Mauernkönig*, which won productions in major opera houses (including New York's Metropolitan) before being shelved.

In 1897 Moszkowski gave up his concert career and retired to Paris, where he acquired a couple of mansions and gave very expensive lessons to young Americans. A chronic digestive ailment and musical "modernism," however, made him more and more reclusive, and he eventually gave up all participation in music. His wife and daughter died, his son was drafted in 1914, and, having sunk his money in German and Russian securities, he found himself by 1918 ill, alone, and broke. In 1921 musical friends in New York staged a monster benefit for him, featuring fourteen piano virtuosi with Walter Damrosch [1540] in charge. The $10,000 it raised eased his last years.

RECORDINGS: There have been LP recitals devoted to Moszkowski's piano music by Michael Ponti, Ilana Vered, and Hans Kann. Michael Ponti and David Bar-Illan have each recorded the Concerto for Piano and there are versions of the *Suite No. 3* for orchestra and the Concerto for Violin conducted by Jorge Mester, with Charles Treger on violin. Itzhak Perlman and Pinchas Zukerman perform a *Suite* for two violins and piano. The *Spanish Dances* are conducted by Ataulfo Argenta.

[1480] HUMPERDINCK, Engelbert
(Hoom'-per-dink, Eng'-el-bârt)
CONDUCTOR, TEACHER
BORN: Siegburg, September 1, 1854
DIED: Neustrelitz, September 27, 1921

Humperdinck is usually credited with being the only successful "Wagnerian," though what he got from Wagner [1230] was largely a matter of orchestral texture, and his success rests mostly in a single opera. (He is quite unrelated to the pop singer Englebert Humperdinck, whose real name is Arnold Dorsey. Dorsey borrowed the name and was forced for a time by the Humperdinck family to give back the surname.)

The real Engelbert Humperdinck was the musically precocious son of a *Gymnasium* director (or high school principal) in a town near Cologne. He was slated for architecture until, at eighteen, he was persuaded by Ferdinand Hiller [1219] that music had need of him. He spent four years at Hiller's conservatory in Cologne, and then, on winning the Mozart Prize awarded by Frankfurt am Main in 1876, he moved on to Munich, where he studied with Rheinberger [1368] and Franz Lachner [1171], and got caught up in the fervor of Wagner [1230] worship. In 1879 Berlin awarded him the Mendels-

sohn Prize, which took him to Italy, where he met Wagner the following spring. Wagner summoned him to Bayreuth, where he became young Siegfried's teacher, and where he helped with the musical preparation of *Parsifal.* (Under Wagner's guidance, he extended the transformation scene in Act I to meet the practical demands of the staging. He also wrote the concert ending for the "Rhine-Journey" music from *Götterdämmerung.*) Using the proceeds of the Meyerbeer Prize, awarded him in Berlin in 1881, Humperdinck moved to Paris, though he kept up his ties with Wagner until the latter died early in 1883.

By then, apart from some juvenile operatic forays, Humperdinck had to his credit mostly choral works and songs, plus two string quartets, a piano quintet, and some minor orchestral pieces. The next several years were restless and unproductive. He visited North Africa and Spain in 1883, returning to Barcelona in 1885 for what turned out to be an unsatisfactory teaching post. He conducted briefly at the Cologne Opera, served almost as briefly in the household of the senile "cannon king" Alfred Krupp, spent a year teaching at his alma mater at Cologne in 1887, worked for two more years editing for Schott in Mainz, returned to his pupil Siegfried Wagner (1869–1930) in Bayreuth in 1889, and finally in 1890 settled in Frankfurt as a teacher at the Hoch Academy and in the vocal institute founded by Brahms's [1329] singer-friend Julius Stockhausen. He also served, as he had in Cologne and Mainz, as a reviewer.

In 1890 Humperdinck's sister, Frau Adelheid Wette, worked up a version of the Grimms' *Märchen* "Hansel and Gretel" for her children to perform and asked her brother to set four songs for it. The collaboration was performed in the Wette parlor that May. The composer was so taken with the project that he decided to make a *Singspiel* of it. This in turn developed into the opera as we know it, which, whatever one may say about the "heavy" orchestration, approaches sheer magic about as closely as the musical theater can. The premiere at Weimar (December 23, 1893) was conducted by Richard Strauss [1563], who correctly predicted a brilliant future for the piece. A second Grimm collaboration with Frau Wette, *Die sieben Geislein (The Seven Kids),* completed in 1895, did not however, proceed beyond the play-with-songs stage. (This period was the time of an uneasy friendship with Hugo Wolf [1521], for whom Humperdinck had earlier found a publisher in Schott and whom he introduced to people who might further his career.)

In 1894 Heinrich Porges, a fellow-Wagnerite, asked Humperdinck to write some songs for a fairy play, *Die Königskinder,* by his daughter Elsa Bernstein (who wrote as "Ernst Rosmer.") The composer decided, for whatever reason, that the whole play should be set as a melodrama. Having won his point, he scored the vocal lines in a manner anticipatory of Schoenbergian [1657] *Sprechstimme* (pitched speech). During the rehearsals for the Munich premiere at the Hoftheater, however, he took such a dislike to what he had done that he tried (in vain) to get his name removed from the programs. The work was produced in January 1897 to good reviews but was soon forgotten. A year previously Humperdinck had been named to the professorship at the Hoch Academy, but now he decided that he wanted to devote the rest of his days to composition and retired to Boppard on the Rhine south of Koblenz. In 1900, however, he was called to Berlin to teach master classes and was elected to the Academy there. (Among his Berlin pupils were the American Charles T. Griffes [1783] and Kurt Weill [1978].) The year 1902 produced another fairy-tale opera, *Dornröschen (The Sleeping Beauty),* and in 1905 there was a comedy after Dumas, *Die Heirat wider Willen (The Forced Marriage),* to a libretto by his wife, Hedwig. By the latter date Humperdinck had entered into a theatrical association with the great producer Max Reinhardt, and provided him, over the next several seasons, with music for plays by Aristophanes, Maeterlinck, and Shakespeare. In 1908 he returned to *Königskinder* to flesh it out as an opera. It was accepted by the Metropolitan Opera in New York for its world premiere in the 1910–11 season. Humperdinck arrived there in time to see another world premiere: Puccini's [1511] *La Fanciulla del West.* His own work opened on December 28 with a cast that included Geraldine Farrar, Hermann Jadlowker, and Otto Goritz as the principals. The public and the American press were ecstatic; the German reviewers were cautious, and indeed the work virtually vanished in a few years. Humperdinck followed it with a pantomime, *Das Mirakel,* and two *Singspiele—Die Marketenderin (The Camp Follower)* and *Gaudeamus.* Ill during his last years, he finally retired for good in 1920 and died a year later.

RECORDINGS: Incredibly *Hänsel und Gretel* had to wait until after World War II for a complete recording, though several now exist. So does a commercial one of *Königskinder,* at last. Apart from excerpts from these works and from *Dornröschen,* Humperdinck is represented on records by the *Moorish Rhapsody* for orchestra, a string quartet, and a handful of songs.

[1481] GIMÉNEZ Y BELLIDO, Jerónimo (Hē-mä′-neth ē Be-lē′-*thō,* Hā-rō′-nē-mō)
VIOLINIST, CONDUCTOR
BORN: Seville, October 10, 1854
DIED: Madrid, February 19, 1923

A violin prodigy, Giménez played in the municipal theater orchestra in Seville from the age of twelve and was conducting operas there at seventeen. A scholarship took him to the Paris Conservatoire, where he studied composition with Ambroise Thomas [1217] and violin with Delphin Alard [1240], graduating in 1877 with several prizes. In 1885 he settled in Madrid, where he eventually became conductor of the Teatro de la Zarzuela and the Madrid Concert Society. An important conductor and a "serious" composer, he made his name as a writer of (mostly one-act) *zarzuelas.* After an early collaboration with Chapi [1461], he wrote nothing more until *El Esclavo (The Slave)* in 1887, but between then and 1920 he turned out (sometimes with collaborators such as Amadeo Vives (1871–1932), but more often alone) more than 100 such works. RECORDINGS: There are recordings of *La Tempranica* of 1900 and *La Gatita blanca* (written with Vives) of 1906, and excerpts from *El Mundo comedia, La Boda de Luis Alonso, El Barbero de Sevilla, La Torre del oro,* and probably others.

[1482] SOUSA, John Philip
VIOLINIST, BANDMASTER
BORN: Washington, D.C., November 6, 1854
DIED: Reading, Pa., March 6, 1932

There is an old story that when a family named So, of some exotic origin, reached Ellis Island in the middle of the last century, an immigration officer, seeing "So U.S.A." on their baggage, entered them as "Sousa." But it just isn't *so.* Variously spelled, Sousa is a common Portuguese name, and the March King's paternal grandparents were Portuguese. His multilingual father was born in Seville and married Elisabeth Trinkhaus, a Bavarian. Their son was born in exotic southwest Washington near the Navy Yard, and there, in a school run by one John Esputa, took up several brass instruments and the violin. By the time he was thirteen, he had his own dance band, and a year later, to ensure that he would remain close to home, his father attached him to the U.S. Marine Band as a sort of gofer and extra cymbal player. (He had been making noises about running off with a circus.) In 1864–67 Sousa took further lessons from George F. Benkert, the leader of the Washington Orchestral Union, and was soon composing. In 1872, the year the Marine Band made him officially its first trombonist, he published a set of waltzes and over the next several years turned out a steady succession of songs and dances. (A big *Te Deum* that he supposedly wrote in 1877 has vanished.) Feeling himself destined for successes larger than the band could offer, he pulled some political strings to get his contract invalidated and went into local theater work. He was shortly sent out on tour with a road-show musical, and when he returned, he was hired as conductor for *Matt Morgan's Living Pictures,* which consisted of "historical" nude tableaux.

In 1876, when Jacques Offenbach [1264] came to America to conduct, Sousa was taken on at the Philadelphia Centennial Exposition as a violinist in his orchestra. It was while there that he heard Patrick Gilmore's remarkable band. After his employment ended, he stayed on in Philadelphia to freelance. Among the jobs he found was one as conductor of a Gilbert and Sullivan [1397] troupe. It inspired him to try his own hand at the musical stage. His first effort, an 1880 operetta called *Our Flirtation,* was adjudged worth sending out on the road with its composer in charge. But toward the end of the year he yielded to overtures from Washington and accepted the conductorship of the Marine Band. Fearing that he looked too young to control the hard-boiled veterans in the organization, he grew a fierce black beard, borrowed Gilmore's Prussian attitude, and had soon turned the band into a crack musical unit.

Since military bands thrive on marches, Sousa found himself writing marches for his. The earliest went largely unnoticed, but in 1886 *The Gladiator* created a stir in band circles. After several other successes, he had a mammoth hit in 1889 with *The Washington Post* (which also introduced the two-step). Up to then Sousa had been selling his compositions to publishers at a flat fee. Slowly, however, it began to dawn on him that they were getting rich on his work while he subsisted on a government pittance. In 1893 he made a royalty deal with the John Church Company, and then the money began to roll in. His 1897 march *The Stars and Stripes Forever* alone brought him in more than $300,000—an enormous amount for the time. Meanwhile he had left the Marine Band in 1892 and organized his own outfit,

which was first heard in Plainfield, N.J. It soon came to be regarded as the nonpareil of bands. In 1893 it was featured at the Columbian Exposition in Chicago, and it toured Europe four times between 1900 and 1905. In 1910–11 Sousa took his men triumphantly around the globe.

Despite his fame as a writer of marches, Sousa continued to write in other forms. Indeed he would have preferred to be remembered as a songwriter—he often wrote his own lyrics—but only those examples which he converted into marches attracted any real notice. However, with operettas he had more success. In 1884 *Desirée* launched De-Wolf Hopper on his long musical-comedy career, and it was Hopper who later commissioned the 1896 *El Capitan,* probably Sousa's stage masterpiece. (It has enjoyed a number of recent revivals.) When Sousa was not conducting or composing, he was writing: he was an indefatigable versifier and he published three novels. He continued to conduct literally to the end of his days: he died suddenly, at seventy-seven, in Reading, where he had gone to lead a concert. (James A. Michener's quasi-autobiographical novel, *The Fires of Spring,* features the aged Sousa as one of the characters.)

RECORDINGS: The Sousa Band made many recordings of his marches, though often with a subsidiary at the helm. None of his more ambitious works have been recorded. (He set great store by his symphonic poems, which, however, are said to be closer to the level of *The Battle of Prague* than to those of Liszt [1218].) Frederick Fennell once set out to record the entire corpus of marches, but after several invaluable discs had appeared, the project was abruptly terminated.

[1483] CHADWICK, George Whitefield
TEACHER, ORGANIST
BORN: Lowell, Mass., November 13, 1854
DIED: Boston, April 4, 1931

George Chadwick is generally regarded as the patriarch of the New England "Classical" school and thus the logical successor to John Knowles Paine [1366]. Strongly influenced by the later German Romantics, he was an energetic and capable composer whose music sometimes transcends the merely skillful.

Chadwick's mother died when he was born. His father, a self-made man on the rise, placed him with relatives until he himself remarried three years later. When George was six, the family moved to Lawrence, where Mr. Chadwick inaugurated what became a lucrative insurance business. An amateur conductor, he believed that music was a proper accomplishment for a successful businessman. From an older brother, George learned the keyboard well enough to substitute as organist at the local Congregational Church and later had weekly lessons with Eugene Thayer [1364] in nearby Boston. He also got some basic theory at the New England Conservatory. When he graduated from high school, however, he went directly into the family business. But when he was twenty-one, his response to an advertisement landed him the professorship of music at Olivet College in Michigan. For a year he hoarded his salary and then, against strong paternal opposition, took ship for Germany. After a turn with the organist Karl August Haupt in Berlin, he migrated to Leipzig, where he studied with Salomon Jadassohn, a conservative theorist, and then at the conservatory with Reinecke [1292]. After two years there, during which his compositions attracted some notice, he toyed with going to Paris to study with Franck [1284] but settled instead for Rheinberger [1368] in Munich.

Back in Boston in 1880, he opened a studio, through which passed such future composers as Horatio Parker [1556], Sidney Homer [1568], and George Whiting (1840–1923) —all in preparation for the requisite encounter with Rheinberger. That same year Chadwick conducted the orchestra of the Handel and Haydn Society in his *Rip Van Winkle Overture.* He was named organist at the South Congregational Church and in 1882 joined the staff of the New England Conservatory. He devoted the remainder of his life to his duties and his art. He became director of the Worcester (Massachusetts) Music Festival in 1889. Eight years later his career reached something of a climax with the awarding of an honorary M.A. from Yale and his appointment as director of the Springfield Festival and head of the conservatory. In the latter role he introduced many innovations in the curriculum and was justly regarded as one of the leading music educators in the country.

Chadwick was one of the first American composers to have some of his major works published, and to be paid (poorly!) for the use of his music. In his day he was highly regarded as a composer of big choral works and was commissioned to write the ode for the opening of the Columbian Exposition in Chicago. Of his 5 operas, *Judith* got a concert performance under his baton at Worcester in 1901, and the jazzy *Tabasco* a single performance at Boston in 1894. For all of his worship of his German and French prede-

cessors, Chadwick was not afraid to give a distinctly American flavor to some of his music. After having gathered dust for decades, it seems to be reawakening some interest.

RECORDINGS: Recordings include the 4 *Symphonic Sketches* (Howard Hanson and others), the *Euterpe Overture* (Jorge Mester), *Tam o'Shanter* (Max Schoenherr), and the String Quartet No. 4 of 5 (Kohon Quartet), as well as some songs and keyboard pieces.

[1484] CHAUSSON, Amédée-Ernest (Shō-sôn', À-mā-dā' Àr-nest')
LAWYER
BORN: Paris, January 20, 1855
DIED: Limay, June 10, 1899

The third (and ultimately only surviving) son of a successful contractor, Ernest Chausson was sedulously educated in the fine arts and brought up in an adult world that practiced and understood them. Though he showed talent in several directions, he entered at his father's urging into the study of law when he was twenty. Two years later, having passed his bar exams, he gave it up. At twenty-four he enrolled at the Paris Conservatoire, where he officially studied with Massenet [1396] but found more to his taste in auditing Franck's [1284] course. He spent summer vacations in Germany soaking up Wagner [1230]. During this period he wrote some songs, some piano pieces (which he later recalled), and a few choral works. (A perfectionist, he took endless pains with whatever he composed and was rarely satisfied with it.) In 1883 he married Jeanne Escudier and settled down to being a paterfamilias (they produced five children), a musician, and a sort of hub of the arts in Paris. He patronized and collected pictures by the Impressionist painters and helped Debussy [1547] get his start. In 1886 he was elected secretary to the Société Nationale de Musique, occupying the post for ten years. Though he had written a piano trio, the symphonic poem *Viviane,* and two operas *(Les Caprices de Marianne* and *Hélène)* earlier, it was not until the latter half of the 1880s that he seriously undertook the larger forms. Of these, the most important were the opera *Le Roi Arthus (King Arthur),* which occupied him for nearly a decade (to 1895) and the B-flat major symphony (he completed the latter in 1890 but did not conduct its premiere until 1898). When he was not traveling, he wintered in Paris and summered near Mantes, downriver from the capital. There, on June 10, 1899, he mounted his bicycle to meet visitors at the railway station. Riding down his driveway, he lost control of the vehicle, crashed headfirst into a stone wall, and died on the spot.

Apart from some early unpublished pieces, the Chausson output amounts to 39 opuses. Beside the works noted, there are some incidental music, chamber works, the *Poème* for violin and orchestra, another symphonic poem *(Soir de fête—Festival Evening)*, and a considerable body of vocal music—mostly songs with piano or orchestra. Chausson's compositions show the Franckian and Wagnerian stamps but also a sort of *fin-de-siècle* nervous passion.

RECORDINGS: The symphony, *Viviane*, the song cantatas *Poème de l'amour et de la mer (Poem of Love and the Sea)* and *Chanson perpetuelle (Perpetual Song)*, the *Poème*, the Op. 21 *Concert for Violin, Piano, and String Quartet*, Quartet for Piano and Strings, the Piano Trio, and the String Quartet have all been recorded, most of them repeatedly. There is a piracy of *Le Roi Arthus* (and an upcoming commercial release on French Erato). A handful of the nearly 50 songs and duets have appeared regularly on records, but the rest have been so far ignored.

[1485] LIADOV, Anatol Constantinovich
(Lyá'-dŏf, Á'-nȧ-tŏl Kŏn-stán-tē-nŏ'-vich)
TEACHER, CONDUCTOR,
ETHNOMUSICOLOGIST
BORN: St. Petersburg, May 11, 1855
DIED: Polinovka, August 28, 1914

Psychological problems prevented Anatol Liadov from realizing his potential as a composer, though just what they were remains obscure. His grandfather had conducted the St. Petersburg Philharmonic Society, and his father (his first teacher) was employed in the same capacity at the Maryinsky Theater. Anatol was accepted at the St. Petersburg Conservatory when he was fifteen. His most important teacher there was Rimsky-Korsakov [1416]. Rimsky was impressed with his talent but threw him out for repeated unexplained absenteeism. In 1878, however, he was readmitted for graduation examinations, which he passed handily. He was forthwith hired to teach theory there. He is said to have been a brilliant teacher, despite his almost pathological shyness, diffidence, and lack of belief in himself. He dreamed of writing large works, but apart from his piano pieces, songs, and a few trivial choruses, he completed only about a dozen short orchestral works. An opera, *Zoryushka*, occupied him for many years but produced only the familiar orchestral *The Enchanted*

Lake and *Kikimora*. A ballet, *Leila and Adelai*, remains a fragment. He was friendly with the Balakirev circle and a close associate and adviser to the publisher Belyayev. In 1901 he was made professor of counterpoint at the St. Petersburg Conservatory and in 1906 professor of composition. Around the turn of the century he collected Russian folksongs under the auspices of the Imperial Geographical Society, publishing 120 of his findings in his own arrangements. (The experience seems strongly to have colored his music.) Among his pupils was Sergei Prokofiev [1851], who detested his otherworldliness. In 1913 a great banquet was given to honor Liadov; typically, he failed to show up. He died a year later on his estate (which came to him through his marriage in 1884) near Novgorod. RECORDINGS: Recordings include several versions of the symphonic poems *Baba Yaga, Fragments from the Apocalypse, The Enchanted Lake*, and *Kikimora*, an orchestral *Scherzo*, and the *8 Russian Folksongs* (also for orchestra). There are also a few trifles, such as the *Musical Snuffbox*, the collaborative variations on "Chopsticks" *(Tati-tati)*, piano pieces, and some fanfares for the Rimsky-Korsakov jubilee.

[1486] WHITE, Maude Valérie
TRANSLATOR
BORN: Dieppe, June 23, 1855
DIED: London, November 2, 1937

Both of Maude White's parents were English, although she was born in France. She was a pupil of Rockstro [1285] and later of Sir George MacFarren (1813–87) at the Royal Academy. In 1879 she was the first woman to be awarded the Mendelssohn Prize, but the chronic illness that dogged her all of her long life prevented the study in Leipzig that should have been hers. However, she did obtain some advanced training from Robert Fuchs in Vienna four years later. Afterward she lived for a time in Florence and finally settled in London. She worked as a translator of books and also published two volumes of memoirs. She composed a ballet, some incidental music, choral numbers, and piano pieces, but was best known for her large output of songs. RECORDINGS: A number of her songs were recorded in earlier times.

[1487] MARTUCCI, Giuseppe (Mär-tōō'-chē, Jōō-sep'-pä)
PIANIST, CONDUCTOR, TEACHER
BORN: Capua, January 6, 1856
DIED: Naples, June 1, 1909

Older readers may recall that Toscanini liked to program works of Giuseppe Martucci, one of the few significant Italian composers of the nineteenth century to eschew opera. Martucci was the son and pupil of a bandmaster in Pozzuoli, near Naples. He made his first public appearance as a pianist when he was eight. Three years later he entered the Naples Conservatory to study composition with Paolo Serrao, a Mercadante [1148] pupil from Filadelfia, and Beniamino Cesi, a Thalberg [1220] protégé. When he was fifteen, his father withdrew him and sent him out on the road, where he appeared both as soloist and as partner to the cellist Alfredo Carlo Piatti, who was nearly thirty-five years his senior. In 1880 he returned to the conservatory as professor of piano and the following year inaugurated a successful and important career there as a conductor. His son Paolo was born in 1883 and himself enjoyed a long career as a pianist. Both at the keyboard and on the podium, the elder Martucci was dedicated to educating his audiences by performing for them the best works of the past and the present from all over the western world. He carried such progressive tendencies to the Bologna Liceo Musicale, of which he was appointed director in 1886. (Two years later, for example, he conducted the Italian premiere of Wagner's [1230] *Tristan und Isolde* in Bologna.) In 1902 he returned once more to Naples, this time to direct the conservatory there, where he remained until he died. Much of Martucci's output is parlor stuff for piano, and his best-known is his orchestral transcription of one of his *Notturni*. He also wrote 2 symphonies, 2 piano concerti, sonatas, piano trios, a piano quintet, a *Mass*, an oratorio, and many smaller works. RECORDINGS: His most-recorded works are the *Notturno* transcription and a similarly derived *Noveletta*. The Symphony No. 2 was once recorded by Antonio Guarnieri. A recent Czech Opus recording conducted by Ondrej Lenárd offers the *Momento musicale*, and *Momento musicale e Minuetto*. Renata Tebaldi recorded a song cycle, *La Canzone dei ricordi—The Song of Memories*.

[1488] SINDING, Christian August (Sin'-ding, Krist'-yàn Ou'-goost)
PIANIST, TEACHER
BORN: Kongsberg, January 11, 1856
DIED: Oslo, December 3, 1941

Of the Norwegian composers who immediately followed Grieg [1410], Christian Sinding is perhaps most universally known, if

only for a piano bonbon, *Frühlingsrauschen (The Rustle of Spring)*. Born in a mining town on the River Laagan, sixty miles southwest of the capital, he had sufficient training in his youth to allow him to enter the Leipzig Conservatory at eighteen, with a view toward becoming a violinist. He studied with Reinecke [1292] and Jadassohn and gradually drifted toward composition. When some of his music was performed on his return home in 1881, he won a government stipend and returned to Germany for further studies in Dresden, Berlin, and Munich. During that time, with his brother Otto as librettist, he embarked on a Wagnerian opera, *Titandros*, but when news of its progress aroused no interest, he gave it up.

Though he later played, taught, and wrote in Oslo, Sinding spent nearly half his life in Germany, mostly with support from his government. He was granted an annual pension of 4,000 kroner in 1910. In 1914 a second opera, *Der heilige Berg (The Sacred Mount)*, was a failure in Dessau. Norway celebrated his sixty-fifth birthday with a present of 30,000 kroner. That same year, 1921, he joined the newly organized Eastman School in Rochester, N.Y. as professor of theory and composition but remained for only two semesters. His seventy-fifth birthday was hailed with a production of *Der heilige Berg*, whose cast included a little-known soprano named Kirsten Flagstad. Sinding died a few weeks short of his eighty-sixth birthday. Though he was perhaps most popular for his songs and piano pieces, he was a considerable composer in the Lisztian tradition. RECORDINGS: Recently there have been domestic recordings of the Concerto for Piano (Rolland Keller), the *Suite for Violin and Orchestra* (Itzhak Perlman, Ruggiero Ricci), and some pieces for violin and piano. An LP side of piano pieces is recorded by Adrian Ruiz. A series sponsored by the Norwegian Cultural Fund, or NKF, has made available the first two (of 4) symphonies and the *Rondo infinito* for orchestra, surprisingly powerful works. NKF has also recently issued recordings of the Concerto No. 1 for Violin, the *Legende*, and another version of the violin suite with Arve Tellefsen on violin and Okko Kamu and Kjell Ingebretsen conducting. Various solo and chamber works have also been released: two volumes of songs, one for mezzo-soprano (Edith Thallaug), the other for baritone (Knut Skram); the Sonata for Piano (Kjell Baekkelund); and the *Variations in E-flat Minor* for two pianos (Baekkelund and Robert Levin). There are many recordings of *The Rustle of Spring*.

[1489] WAGNER, Josef Franz (Våg'-ner,
Yō'-zef Frånts)
BANDMASTER
BORN: Vienna, March 20, 1856
DIED: Vienna, June 5, 1908

J. F. Wagner was unrelated to Richard
[1230]. He served as bandmaster of the 47th
and 49th Imperial Regiments. His efforts at
musical theater were unmemorable, but he
was quite successful as a writer of dances
and marches, and one of the latter, *Unter
dem Doppeladler (Under the Double Eagle)*
of 1893 is among the best-known marches in
the world.

[1490] STRONG, George Templeton, Jr.
TEACHER, PAINTER
BORN: New York, May 26, 1856
DIED: Geneva, June 27, 1948

Strong was brought up in an atmosphere of
affluence and culture. (His father, a prominent lawyer, was for a time president of the
New York Philharmonic Society.) With no
real formal musical training, he traipsed off
to Leipzig when he was twenty-three. Having already begun to compose, he studied
counterpoint with Jadassohn, had some lessons in orchestration, and took up the horn.
Unlike his father, he doted on the new music
and was soon a member of the Liszt [1218]
circle in Weimar. He struck up friendships
with Raff [1282] and Edward MacDowell
[1529], the latter of whom he was very thick
with in Wiesbaden between 1886 and 1888.
By that time he had a considerable body of
music to his credit, including symphonic poems, cantatas, songs, and piano pieces.
Eventually he came home and, with the help
of MacDowell, was appointed to the staff of
the New England Conservatory in 1891. But,
disenchanted with the state of culture in his
native land and discouraged at the chances
for American music, he shook the dust of
the United States from his shoes a year later
and settled in Switzerland, where he took up
painting. Eventually he returned to composing and was well known to many important
European musicians throughout the rest of
his long life. Toward the end of it, some interest was evinced in his music in America
(Toscanini broadcast an orchestral suite, for
example.) RECORDINGS: Only the *Chorale
on a Theme by Hassler* (conducted by Howard Hanson) seems to have reached records.

[1491] SCHÜTT, Eduard (Shüt, Ed'-wärt)
PIANIST, CONDUCTOR

BORN: St. Petersburg, October 22, 1856
DIED: Obermias, July 26, 1933

Born in Russia, of Germanic lineage, Schütt
studied with Theodor Stein at the St. Petersburg Conservatory, graduating with honors
at twenty. After two years at the Leipzig
Conservatory, with Reinecke [1292], Jadassohn, etc., he studied piano in Vienna with
Theodor Leschetizky, and then succeeded
Felix Mottl there as conductor of the Academic Wagner Society. His opera, *Signor
Formica*, was produced in Vienna in 1882.
Schütt also wrote 2 piano concerti and some
chamber works but is best known for his
salonesque piano pieces, notably one called
À la bien-aimée (To the Beloved). He died in
the Alps on vacation near Merano.

[1492] TANEYEV, Sergei Ivanovich (Tà-
nā'-yof, Sâr'-gā Ē-và-nō'-vich)
PIANIST, TEACHER, ADMINISTRATOR
BORN: Vladimir district, November 25,
1856
DIED: Dyudkovo, June 19, 1915

Not to be confused with his cousin, the composer Alexander Sergeivich Taneyev (1850–
1918), Sergei Taneyev was the son of Ivan
Ilyich Taneyev, an educated and reasonably
affluent civil servant. A fast starter at the
keyboard, he was admitted to the Moscow
Conservatory at nine for polishing his skills.
After a year his parents, having no special
wish to foster a professional musician in the
family, sent him to a prep school. Eventually, however, the conservatory convinced
them they were making a mistake, and he
returned to study with Tchaikovsky [1377]
and later with Nicolai Rubinstein. Despite
Taneyev's sometimes brutally frank criticisms of Tchaikovsky's music, he was a lifelong favorite of Tchaikovsky. (Taneyev was
the first to play Tchaikovsky's first two piano concerti publicly in Russia, and he completed the unfinished third.) In studying
counterpoint with Nikolai Hubert, he laid
the foundation for his later encyclopedic
knowledge of the subject. He graduated in
1875, the winner of the first gold medal to be
awarded by the school.
    After some traveling and a Russian tour
as partner to the violinist Leopold Auer,
Taneyev returned in 1876 to the conservatory, on the insistence of Tchaikovsky, who
had resigned, to teach orchestration and
harmony. In 1881 he succeeded Rubinstein
and in 1883, Hubert. Eventually, in 1885, he
was named director. For a decade and more,
he had been in essence a closet composer,
showing his works (which included two

symphonies and several string quartets) only to Tchaikovsky and other cronies. Though his Pushkin cantata had been performed at the unveiling of a statue to that poet in 1880, Taneyev did not feel himself ready to publish until he took over the conservatory. His Op. 1 was a cantata on the subject of St. John of Damascus, and shortly afterward he conducted his third symphony (he had disowned the first two.) Next he buckled down to his only attempt at opera, a treatment of Aeschylus' *Oresteia* which finally reached the stage of the Maryinsky Theater in 1895. (It is remarkable musically, though rather ineffective dramatically.) That same year he became a frequent visitor at Yasnaya Polyana, Count Leo Tolstoi's home. A handsome bachelor, he inadvertently and apparently unwittingly set fire to Countess Tolstoi's heart. It smoldered painfully for many years, ultimately inspiring (if that is the word) Tolstoi's bitter story "The Kreutzer Sonata."

Taneyev had resigned his directorship in 1889, and when in the aftermath of the 1905 Revolution the administration dealt out stringent punishment to student sympathizers, he gave up teaching. Though he continued to perform as a pianist, he retired to a small house (innocent of all modern conveniences, save his Amazonian old nurse-housekeeper) in the Moscow suburbs. There he led a Spartan and would-be misanthropic existence. Friends, admirers, and students, however, paid no attention to the "not in" sign on the door and were usually welcomed warmly. In 1909 he completed his great counterpoint manual and embarked on another on canon, which he did not live to complete. In his last years he was given a great testimonial dinner in Moscow and was terribly embarrassed by all the encomia. In April 1915 he stood in the rain at the funeral of his pupil Alexander Scriabin [1625], caught pneumonia, and died of a heart attack two months later. Among his other pupils were Glière [1662], Liapunov [1518], Medtner [1727], and Rachmaninoff [1638], and after his retirement he served as mentor and guide to the young Prokofiev [1851].

Taneyev was, for Russia, an atypical composer—an eclectic and a classicist (he is sometimes called "the Russian Brahms"), making no effort to be "national"—though he collected and arranged folksongs. He wrote (or began) 4 symphonies, but most of his large-scale compositions are chamber works (11 string quartets, several quintets and trios for various combinations, etc.) He also produced many choral works and songs.

RECORDINGS: Recordings include the op-

era *Oresteia,* the second and fourth symphonies, the *John of Damascus* cantata, the *Suite de Concert* for violin and orchestra, at least eight of the string quartets, the String Trio, the 2 string quintets, the Piano Trio, the Piano Quartet, the Piano Quintet, short choral works, and songs—many but by no means all of them (especially recently) originating in the USSR. Of his work on Tchaikovsky's behalf, there are recorded versions of the Concerto No. 3 for Piano and his reconstruction of the love duet from the aborted *Romeo and Juliet* opera.

[1493] KASTALSKY, Alexander Dimitrievich (Kás-tál'-skē, Ál-yák-sán'-der Dē-mē-trē-yā'-vich)
CONDUCTOR, TEACHER, ETHNOMUSICOLOGIST
BORN: Moscow, November 28, 1856
DIED: Moscow, December 17, 1926

His studies interrupted by military service, Kastalsky was already thirty-seven when he graduated from the Moscow Conservatory, where his most important teachers had been Tchaikovsky [1377] and Taneyev [1492], who was only three days older than he was. By that time he had already had considerable experience as a choir director and had been teaching and conducting for six years at the Synodal Academy. By 1910 he had been made director of its choir, with which he toured Europe. He was a profound student of ancient church music and directly influenced Rachmaninoff [1638] in the composition of his *Vesper Service* (or *All-Night Vigil).* As early as 1906 he exhibited tendencies that would later make him acceptable to the Bolsheviks when he took up teaching in the People's Free Conservatory. He was also a notable collector and student of Russian folk music. After the October Revolution he was retained in his post at what became the People's Choral Academy. Enthusiastic about the promise of the new regime, Kastalsky became active in the Proletarian Culture Movement until Lenin, fearing that it invited an independent stance among workers, abolished it. Later Kastalsky worked for the propaganda wing of the state publishing house and contributed to the glory of the New Russia—an *Agricultural Symphony,* hymns to various aspects of sovietism, and a "railway-train" piece reflecting the short-lived mechanical-realism movement. His Lenin cantata was performed at that hero's funeral. Though he tried his hand at opera *(Clara Milich,* which was premiered in 1907) and other forms, Kastalsky is best known for his fine religious choral works. RECORD-

INGS: Some of his choral works have been recorded, e.g., the *Russian Nuptial Mass,* conducted by Winfried Pentek.

[1494] GALKIN, Nikolai Vladimirovich (Gál-kēn′, Nē′-kō-lī Vlád′-ē-mir-ō-vich)
VIOLINIST, CONDUCTOR, TEACHER
BORN: St. Petersburg, December 6, 1856
DIED: St. Petersburg, May 21, 1906

A student of (among others) Leopold Auer, Henryk Wieniawski **[1340]**, and Joseph Joachim **[1321]**, Galkin became well known throughout Europe as a concert violinist. Later he conducted in St. Petersburg and taught at the Conservatory from 1880 until his death. He composed some pieces for violin and piano, one or two of which turn up in recorded violin recitals.

[1495] ROHDE, Friedrich Wilhelm (Rō′-də, Frē-drikh Vil′-helm)
VIOLINIST
BORN: Altona, December 11, 1856
DIED: Gentofte, April 6, 1928

Born in a Hamburg suburb, Wilhelm Rohde put in some years at the Leipzig Conservatory under the likes of Ferdinand David, Julius Röntgen, and E. F. Richter. Later he emigrated to Chicago. After a season (1885–86) in the Boston Symphony under Wilhelm Gericke, he returned to Germany and settled in Schwerin. When war erupted in 1914, he moved to Copenhagen and spent his last years there. Though he essayed orchestral and choral works, he is remembered (if at all) for a few salon piano pieces. RECORD-INGS: His salon piece *The Marionettes* has been recorded by Hans Kann.

[1496] KIENZL, Wilhelm (Kēnt′-sel, Vil′-helm)
CONDUCTOR, ADMINISTRATOR, WRITER
BORN: Waizenkirchen, January 17, 1857
DIED: Vienna, October 19, 1941

Of the self-proclaimed Wagnerians, Kienzl was, save for Humperdinck **[1480]**, probably the most successful, though he has remained a purely Germanic phenomenon and his operas are perhaps closer to Weber's **[1124]** than to Wagner's **[1230]**. He was born near Linz in a market town on the Inn River, where his father had a law practice. When he was three, the family moved to Gmunden on the Traunsee and then settled in Graz a year later in a house called "Paradise," once

inhabited by the astronomer Kepler. The elder Kienzl, an amateur singer, flutist, and guitarist, served as mayor of Graz for a dozen years from 1873. Brought up in a musical atmosphere, Wilhelm had violin and piano lessons—some of the latter with a Chopin **[1208]** pupil. He was ready for *Gymnasium* at nine and composed his first song at twelve. At the local university he read philosophy, science, and literature and studied composition with W. A. Rémy (i.e., Wilhelm Mayer). Acquaintance with Adolf Jensen **[1349]** got him excited about Wagner. In 1876 he studied for a time at the University of Prague and went to Bayreuth in the summer for the premiere of the *Ring.* After some further study in Leipzig and with Liszt **[1218]** in Weimar, Kienzl went to Vienna and in 1879 wrote his doctoral dissertation under the direction of Wagner's old enemy, Eduard Hanslick.

In 1881, he toured Germany and Hungary as accompanist and assisting artist to the violinist Richard Sahla and the soprano Aglaia Orgeni. Two years later he accepted an appointment as music director of the German Opera in Amsterdam. But that institution folded in 1884, and he returned to Graz, where before the year was out he finished his first opera, *Urvasi.* It was successfully premiered in Dresden in 1886 and had some subsequent currency. In that same year, Kienzl, who had regularly summered in Bayreuth, married Lili Hoke, a singer he had met there, and took over directorship of the Styrian Musical Association. In this post he served as director of the conservatory and concert manager in Graz. In 1890 he was briefly director of the Hamburg Opera, and in 1892 of the Munich Royal Opera, where he premiered his *Heimar der Narr (Heimar the Fool),* but in both instances he found Graz more to his taste. In 1894, at his summer hideaway at Aussee, he completed his third opera, *Der Evangelimann (The Evangelist).* Premiered at Berlin in May 1895, it became a runaway success, remaining popular in the Germanies until after World War II. Not so its successor, *Don Quixote* of 1898, which was a flat failure. Kienzl did not return to the stage until 1907, with a one-act Christmas fantasy, *In Knecht Ruprechts Werkstatt (In Santa Claus's Workshop),* produced in Graz. But in 1909 he had another great hit at the Vienna Volksoper in *Der Kuhreigen (The Cowherd's Dance).* It was followed in 1916 by *Das Testament,* whose music has been praised, but whose Styrian-dialect libretto limits its performances.

In 1917 Kienzl finally left Graz (with an honorary degree from the university) to settle in Vienna. There his wife died two years later. In that same year he was asked to compose a new national anthem to a text by Karl Renner, the chancellor. It was used for a decade until popular demand brought back the old Haydn [871] imperial tune. In 1921 the composer married Henny Bauer, who wrote the libretto for *Hassan der Schwärmer (Hassan the Visionary)*, his last full-length opera, which did not survive its 1925 premiere in Chemnitz. She also was responsible for the texts of the melodrama *Sanctissimum* (Vienna 1925)—a form in which Kienzl had experimented several times before—and the text of *Hans Kipfel*, a 1926 *Singspiel* premiered in Vienna. At that point, feeling himself outmoded, Kienzl withdrew from the stage, though he continued to write choral pieces and songs, to conduct, and to lecture. Increasingly plagued by poor health, he lost an eye in 1931 and retired completely five years later. He lived, however, to be eighty-four and, with his long white hair and beard, presented an odd figure in a close-cropped world.

RECORDINGS: Kienzl also wrote some orchestral and chamber music, but on records he is chiefly represented by a recording of *Der Evangelimann* (Lothar Zagrosek conducting) and many excerpts from that work and from *Der Kuhreigen*.

[1497] BRUNEAU, Louis Charles Bonaventure Alfred (Brü-nō', Lōō-ē'- Shärl Bon-à-vàn-tür' Ál-fred')
CELLIST, CONDUCTOR, CRITIC
BORN: Paris, March 3, 1857
DIED: Paris, June 15, 1934

Though hardly a note of his music is heard today, Alfred Bruneau is spoken of with such admiration and respect by historians of opera that one hopes we shall have a chance to reevaluate it. He was clearly the first (perhaps the only) French *verismist* and a disciple, but not an imitator, of Wagner [1230].

Bruneau was born to parents who were artistic amateurs: his mother was a painter and pianist, his father a violinist. Naturally he was taught cello to make up a trio. Later he studied it seriously at the Conservatoire with Auguste-Joseph Franchomme and took the first prize in 1876. His composition teacher was Massenet [1396]. While attending the Conservatoire, he also played cello in the Pasdeloup Orchestra, where he was exposed to "modernism." This last was probably considered a Bad Thing, for his Prix de Rome entry was given only a second place because of its radical tendencies. In the 1880s Pasdeloup performed several orchestral works by Bruneau—the *Ouverture héroïque*,

the symphonic poems *La Belle au Bois dormant* and *Penthésilée*, and the choral symphony *Leda*. But after the production of his first opera, *Kérim*, in 1887, Bruneau cast his lot wholly with the lyric stage. He had become fascinated by the novels of Émile Zola and his next effort was based on that author's *Le Rêve*. Bruneau's *Le Rêve* was premiered at the Opéra-Comique in 1891 and played at Covent Garden a few months later. Its "modernism" elicited horrified cries from some auditors, but it was clearly effective. In 1892 Bruneau began his career as a reviewer and music critic, working successively for *Gil Blas*, *Le Figaro*, and *Le Matin*. (He later published several works of musical history and studies of Fauré [1424] and Massenet.)

In 1893 Bruneau had his most enduring success with another Zola-based opera, *L'Attaque du Moulin*. (Set in 1870 it was prudently moved back to 1792 so as not to inflame the audience.) One result of its success was that the great novelist elected to supply Bruneau with further libretti—written in prose! The partnership was a mixed blessing. Zola, in particular, was enchanted by the new experience. But meanwhile, because of his quixotic espousal of the cause of Captain Alfred Dreyfus, framed on a treason charge largely inspired by anti-Semitism in high places, Zola's name had become a fighting word. Nevertheless, the collaboration produced *Messidor* in 1897, *L'Ouragan (The Hurricane)* in 1901—said by many to be Bruneau's masterpiece—and *L'Enfant-roi* in 1905. (Zola did not live to see the last work completed, having been asphyxiated by a faulty stove in 1902.)

Bruneau went on writing operas (mostly to his own libretti) until two years before he died. Three were based on Zola—*Lazare* and *Naïs Micoulin*, both in 1907, and *Les Quatre Journées* in 1916. (He also wrote incidental music to *La Faute de l'Abbé Mouret*). One of his last operas was a treatment of Hugo's *Angelo, Tyran de Padoue*, a work that had inspired Ponchielli's [1334] *La Gioconda* fifty-two years earlier. In general the late works seem not to have been so successful as the earlier ones. Bruneau, incidentally, frequently conducted his operas, both in France and elsewhere. The other operas were: *Le Tambour*, 1916; *Le Roi Candaule*, 1920; *Le Jardin du Paradis*, 1923; and *Virginie*, 1931. There were also 2 ballets, *Les Bacchantes* and *L'Amoureuse Leçon*, an admired *Requiem*, *Le Navire* for voice and orchestra, a few chamber pieces, a couple of short choral works, and songs, many to texts by Catulle Mendès.

RECORDINGS: Up to about forty years ago

there were occasional recordings of some of the songs and of selections from the operas. Bruneau himself conducts the orchestra in Georges Thill's version of an aria from *L'Attaque au moulin*.

[1498] LEONCAVALLO, Ruggero (Lā-ōn-kä-väl'-lō, Rōōd-jä'-rō)

PIANIST, LIBRETTIST
BORN: Naples, April 23, 1857
DIED: Montecatini Termi, August 9, 1919

Although he was a leader of the *verismo* (roughly "realism") movement in opera, and although his *Pagliacci* holds its place as a mainstay of the repertoire, Leoncavallo has so far attracted no major published study, and so certain corners of his life remain ambiguous or obscure. For example, his first name is usually given incorrectly as "Ruggiero," and he claimed March 8, 1858, as his birthdate. (Recent reference works continue to show fairly consistent disagreement on this last matter.) His ancestors had come from Apulia by way of Bari and had been educated professional people for several generations. His maternal grandfather, Raffaele d'Auria, in whose home he was born, was well known as a painter in Naples, and his mother, Virginia, was Donizetti's [1155] goddaughter. His father Vincenzo, a lawyer and magistrate, published novels and short stories. After some early piano lessons, young Ruggero was admitted to the conservatory before he was ten on a day-student basis. His teachers included the pianist Beniamino Cesi and the opera composer Lauro Rossi. On graduation he migrated to Bologna, ostensibly to study law (in which he later claimed to have a degree, though it was in fact in literature). He was particularly taken by the lectures of the poet Giosuè Carducci and by his encounters with Wagner's [1230] music. (He apparently met the composer himself at the 1876 Bolognese production of *Rienzi*.) Thus inspired, he finished his *Chatterton*, which he had begun in Naples, and scraped together enough money for a production. But the money and producer vanished together overnight.

Though he had his degree by 1878, a political upheaval in Naples had left his father unable to support him, so Leoncavallo decided to live by his art. A paternal uncle, a political exile, had become a *bey* in Egypt, so he went to Cairo and found a place as conductor to the new Khedive Tewfik. But an Anglo-French military intervention having to do with the operation of the Suez Canal forced his exit. He sailed for Marseilles and settled in Montmartre in 1882 as a Bohemian

songwriter and bistro pianist. He is said to have written and produced *Une Songe d'un nuit d'été (A Midsummer Night's Dream)*, but no trace of the work or performance has been found. He spent his spare time on a grandiose scheme for an operatic Wagner-style trilogy *Crepusculo (Twilight)* on the subject of Renaissance Florence and completed the libretto of *I Medici*, its first leg. He struck up a friendship with the baritone Victor Maurel, Verdi's [1232] first Iago and Falstaff, who sent him to the publisher Ricordi. Ricordi gave him a contract for his two operas but did nothing with them. Instead he asked Leoncavallo to provide Puccini [1511] with a libretto for *Manon Lescaut*. But the two did not get along and Puccini fired him.

Frustrated and hungry for success, Leoncavallo discarded for the nonce his lofty ambitions to out-Wagner Wagner and took cognizance of *Cavalleria rusticana*, the little low-life shocker with which Pietro Mascagni [1559] had triumphed in 1890. Drawing on one of his father's cases—the murder by a strolling player named d'Alessandro of his two-timing wife—he dashed off *Pagliacci (The Buffoons)* and sent it to Ricordi's rival (and Mascagni's publisher) Sonzogno. Sonzogno arranged a premiere in the Teatro dal Verme in Milan on May 21, 1892, with Toscanini conducting and Victor Maurel as the hunchbacked Tonio. It had precisely the effect Leoncavallo had hoped for, and his name was made. Unfortunately, that meant he had to live up to it, preferably with more *Pagliaccis*. *I Medici*, which reached the stage eighteen months later, was not one of them and failed. (The proposed trilogy ended there.) The premiere of *Chatterton*, radically revised for the occasion, fared no better in 1896.

About the time of the *Medici* fiasco, Leoncavallo, who was well acquainted with the basic material from life, decided to make an opera of Henri Murger's *Scènes de la vie de Bohème (Scenes from Bohemian Life)*, a work based on the author's own experiences in the garrets of Paris. Again the details of what happened are obscure. Perhaps it was coincidental that Puccini's librettist, Luigi Illica, hit on the same notion at the same time. Perhaps Leoncavallo mentioned to Puccini what he was up to. There seems to be some evidence that he outlined his plot to his rival, or read him parts of the libretto (his own work). At any rate, in 1894 he discovered that Puccini, with Ricordi's blessing, was hard at work on *La Bohème*. Outraged he threatened suit, but found he had no legal redress. Puccini beat him to the stage by fifteen months, and though Leoncavallo's *La Bohème* was admired when it at last opened in 1897, it has always stood (justifiably) in the shadow of its predecessor. (Leoncavallo's work, by the way, focuses on the painter Marcello and his Musetta, rather than on Rodolfo and Mimi, as Puccini's does.)

Zazà, another opera involving theater people, was even more successful when Toscanini conducted its premiere in Milan in 1900, and it received a measure of notoriety when Geraldine Farrar, a popular idol of considerable magnitude, chose it as her retirement vehicle at the Metropolitan Opera in 1926—but it has had only sporadic currency since. Meanwhile in Berlin Wilhelm II ("Kaiser Bill") had (unlike others) been so impressed by *I Medici* that he had commissioned from the composer a Teutonic epic, *Der Roland von Berlin.* It took time to translate the libretto into Italian and then back into German, and so it was 1904 before Berlin saw the work. Despite the official hoopla about it, it was quickly *spurlos versenkt.* (It was in that same year that Leoncavallo wrote the first work for the phonograph—the song *Mattinata,* designed for Caruso to put on a ten-inch disc, which he did with the composer at the piano. Three years later, with *Pagliacci,* Leoncavallo became the first composer to record his own opera whole.)

Having (at least temporarily) abandoned dreams of music drama for something less (and more negotiable), Leoncavallo descended yet another step. On a promotional visit to America in 1906, he unveiled his first operetta, *La Jeunesse di Figaro (Figaro's Youth).* The fact that it did not add to his immortality seems not to have discouraged him, for in 1910 he produced another, *Malbrouck,* in Rome with some temporary success. But the seriously intended *Maia,* which had opened there four days earlier, failed (as had the re-revised *Chatterton* in 1905). The year 1912 brought another negligible operetta, *La Reginetta delle Rose (The Little Rose Queen)* in Rome, and his last reasonably successful opera, *Zingari (Gypsies),* after the same Pushkin piece that inspired Rachmaninoff's [1638] *Aleko)* in London. He returned to that city a year later with an English-language operetta, *Are You There?* Failure, ill-health, and the onset of war in 1914 turned the composer increasingly bitter and cynical. Several operatic attempts were abandoned, and instead there was a stream of trivial fluff—*La Candidata (The Lady Candidate)* in 1915; *Prestami tua moglie (Lend Me Your Wife)* and *Goffredo Mameli,* both in 1916. *A chi la giarrettiera? (Whose Garter?)* was produced in Rome two months after the composer's death. His final opera

Edipo re (King Oedipus), a marmoreal but ultimately unsuccessful treatment of Sophocles' tragedy, was produced by the Chicago Opera in 1920. A one-act operetta, *Il Primo Bacio,* was staged in 1923 at the spa where Leoncavallo died, and *La maschera nuda (The Naked Masquerade)* was completed by Salvatore Allegra and staged in Naples in 1925. Besides the stage pieces Leoncavallo wrote many songs, and a few piano pieces, choral, and orchestral works.

RECORDINGS: Besides innumerable recordings of *Pagliacci* there is a commercial one of *La Bohème* (Heinz Wallberg) and a few representations of songs, as well as a plethora of operatic excerpts. There are also piracies of *Zazà, Zingari,* and *Edipo re.*

[1499] ELGAR, (Sir) Edward William
CONDUCTOR, VIOLINIST, ORGANIST, BASSOONIST, CELLIST
BORN: Broadheath, June 2, 1857
DIED: Worcester, February 23, 1934

Sir Edward Elgar was the first English-born composer after Purcell [581] to win any real measure of international notice and probably was the real progenitor of the English musical renaissance of the twentieth century. There was nothing especially English about his music, save perhaps its sturdiness, and non-Englishmen are inclined to wonder if he has not been overvalued by his compatriots. If the least of his compositions are not far removed from the period-salonesque and if modern sensibilities tend to become impatient with the big oratorios, the best of his work (which means chiefly the larger orchestral pieces) stands on an equal footing with anything of the kind being written in his day.

Born in a suburb of Worcester, Elgar was the fourth child (of seven) of William and Anne Elgar, both converts to Roman Catholicism. William ran a music shop in the city, was organist at St. George's Catholic Church, played violin in the Three Choirs Festivals, and served as piano tuner to Dowager Queen Adelaide. Anne had more musical ability than the norm demanded of young *bourgeoises* and communicated her taste to her son. Edward, whose two elder brothers had died in childhood, was a bookish loner. By the time he was enrolled at Littleton House in 1868, a local boys' school, he was playing piano and violin and composing. Though he had set his mind on a career as a violinist, a low ebb in his family's finances necessitated that he become a solicitor's clerk when he graduated four years later. However, thanks to the resources of his father's shop, he continued to educate himself in music. He began to get engagements as both a violinist and organist and soon became general factotum and eventually conductor of the Worcester Glee Club. In 1879 he also became concertmaster of the Worcester Philharmonic and conductor of the band at the County Lunatic Asylum at Powick. On the side he taught, arranged, and sat in on local chamber-music performances as cellist or bassoonist. In 1878 he wrote an overture for a minstrel show—his first publicly performed composition. But around the same time he began to turn out church music, dances for his asylum band, and other works, some of which he later thought good enough to save.

By the early 1880s he was doing well enough to travel, and he sampled music and musical life in London, Paris, and Leipzig. In 1884 Sir August Manns, conductor of the Saturday Concerts at the Crystal Palace, introduced Elgar to his audiences with a performance of his *Sevillana,* and in the same year Elgar played under Dvořák's direction in a Worcester concert. However, the decade was for the young composer one of struggle and depressingly slow progress. In the course of it he seems also to have fallen in love several times, once fairly traumatically. But in 1886 he found the real thing in Caroline Alice Robert (called by her middle name), one of his pupils. She was eight years his senior and, as a general's daughter, out of his social class; when she announced shortly after receiving her not-very-large inheritance that she was marrying an impecunious Catholic musician, there was consternation in her family. But the marriage took place in 1889, and the couple settled in Kensington, where they lived rather beyond their current means. Their only child, a daughter named Carice (from her mother's Christian names), was born there a year later. By then Elgar had achieved something of a hit with his salon trifle, *Salut d'amour,* and had had a local triumph when in 1889 his overture *Froissart* was premiered at the Worcester Festival. Even so Kensington proved too much for the Elgars, and in 1891 they returned home, where Edward took up his old life. A cantata, *The Black Knight* (after Longfellow), received little notice at the 1893 festival but then began to catch on with local choirs. Seeing some hope there, Elgar composed furiously and soon had good luck with a second Longfellow cantata, *Scenes from the Saga of King Olaf,* which got a hearing and good reviews in London. But the breakthrough came—ironically and expectably—with nothing so lofty. The catalyst was the *Imperial March* for the queen's

1897 Diamond Jubilee. At this time began Elgar's long association and friendship with August Jaeger (punningly "Nimrod" in the *Enigma Variations),* a German-born editor for Novello and Company. In 1898, commissioned to write a cantata for the Leeds Festival, Elgar produced *Caractacus;* despite a poor presentation at the premiere, some important reviewers recognized the worth of the music—though today the text makes it more a curiosity than a masterpiece. (Elgar had written the first and least of his oratorios, *Lux Christi* [or *The Light of Life]* two years before that.)

By now Elgar had already assumed the role of the mustachioed, whimsical, tweedy, golfing, hunting, gardening, kite-flying Edwardian country squire who stares out of the old photographs. But he was also, publicly, still a musician. In 1898, for example, he founded the Worcestershire Philharmonic, which he devoted largely to contemporary music, and whose conducter he was for six years. But behind the facades, he was inexplicably bitter, cynical, and pessimistic, and remained so for all of his life. *Enigma Variations,* his most popular serious piece, which he completed early in 1899, reflects both sides of him. The variations—not very enigmatic portraits of his wife and friends, thinly masked by initials or nicknames—are tender, humorous, and rock-solid; the hidden countertheme, implied but never stated, has never been identified, though the composer said anyone would recognize it if played. First conducted by Hans Richter in London, the work was an immediate success and marked the arrival of Elgar's full maturity.

At that time Elgar was busy with the work that would establish his importance worldwide: an oratorio after Cardinal Newman's *The Dream of Gerontius,* a copy of which work he had received as a wedding present. Its premiere on October 3, 1900, at the Birmingham Festival was anything but propitious: Richter had failed to study the score sufficiently, two of the three soloists proved inadequate, and most of the choir singers were baffled. But several percipient people, including Richter, recognized its worth, and its success at Düsseldorf late in 1901 and again at the Lower Rhine Festival the following spring showed their faith was not misplaced. After the festival performance, Richard Strauss **[1563]**, later to become his friend, toasted Elgar as the herald of a new English music. But owing to religious and musical politics, *Gerontius* had been sung all over Europe and the United States before it was heard in England again. Still there were important tokens of recognition. In 1901 the composer was awarded an honorary doctorate by Cambridge, and King Edward knighted him in 1904. Moreover with that monarch's accession there was a new mood in London, and the Elgars now found themselves accepted by the movers and shakers of London society. It was during this decade of triumph that Elgar began his famous series of *Pomp and Circumstance Marches*, the first example of which, from 1901, with its brilliant main section and its stately trio, seems the perfect statement of the imperial confidence of the era. (The trio, set to a text beginning "Land of hope and glory," was incorporated in an ode written for Edward's coronation, but it went unperformed because the king came down with an attack of appendicitis.) By 1907 Elgar had acquired five more honorary degrees, including two from the United States. The one from the University of Birmingham required that he occupy a professorial chair there endowed in his name; his intendancy quickly convinced him and a good many students that lecturing was not one of his strengths. During 1905 he had toured England, conducting the London Symphony in performances of his own works. All this activity resulted in a slowdown in composition, an increase in nervous tension, persistent eye problems, and illness. In 1908 he resigned his professorship to relieve pressure.

Shortly after completing *The Dream of Gerontius*, Elgar had embarked on an oratorio trilogy calculated to be his masterpiece. It is arguable whether he was all that religious *(Falstaff* and a projected *Rabelais* may have been closer to his real nature), but such stuff was expected from him, particularly by Lady Alice. The first two elements of the trilogy were premiered again at the Birmingham Festival—*The Apostles* in 1903, *The Kingdom* in 1906. After that, however, for reasons that remain obscure, Elgar gave the whole idea up, though for a long time he talked of returning to it. It is perhaps just as well, for the two oratorios noted have dated sadly. Instead of becoming a second Handel **[683]**, he returned to the orchestra, for which, besides *Enigma, Froissart,* the overtures *Alassio* and *Cockaigne,* the *Serenade,* and the *Introduction and Allegro,* he had so far written mostly small and trivial pieces. In short order he arranged some of his very early pieces as the two *Wand of Youth* suites, and composed the 2 symphonies, the Concerto for Violin, and the big symphonic poem *Falstaff.* The first symphony of 1908 was immediately hailed as the first such English composition worthy of the name. Fritz Kreisler **[1664]** played the first performance of the violin concerto under Elgar's baton at

Queen's Hall in 1909. In 1911, the year of the second symphony (which did not catch on until after World War I), Elgar succeeded Richter as conductor of the London Symphony—but refused pay because it was in financial difficulties. Since the post required his presence in London, the Elgars moved into a handsome house in Hampstead.

From *Falstaff* onward, however, these new duties, the anxieties caused by the hostilities, persistent poor health, and perhaps the attrition of time, brought a decided falling-off in Elgar's creativity. The death of Jaeger in 1909 also took something out of him, for Jaeger had been a rock in times of self-doubt and despair. The ensuing years produced some patriotic stuff, some incidental stage music, and drawing-room potboilers. At the end of the fighting there was a brief upsurge of energy that produced the Sonata for Violin and Piano, the String Quartet, the Piano Quintet, and the Concerto for Cello. By the time he completed the last work, Lady Alice was failing. Her death in April 1920 produced a two-year drouth. (His own health remained shaky; he had been especially tormented by labyrinthitis and the vertigo it produced.) In 1921 he left the Hampstead house. In 1924 he was named Master of the King's Musick and was later made a baronet. There were a few more compositions—music for Laurence Binyon's *King Arthur* and Matthews' *Beau Brummel,* the *Severn Suite* for band, and the *Nursery Suite* (for the Princesses Elizabeth and Margaret Rose). But the impetus was gone; the old man saw that the period thought of him as a musical dinosaur. He amused himself with the horse races, motoring, and listening to the phonograph. In 1933 he flew to France and met the bedridden Delius **[1539]**. Later that year an operation to ease his sciatica uncovered advanced cancer. He died four months later and was buried beside his Alice. He left a few sketches for a piano concerto, a third symphony, and an opera.

RECORDINGS: Juvenilia apart, most of Elgar's theater music, the oratorios, the cantata *Caractacus,* the ode *The Music Makers,* the orchestral, and chamber works have been recorded, as well as some of the songs, smaller choral works, and piano pieces. Elgar firmly believed in the phonograph and recorded his own works, as conductor from 1914 to the year of his death. Most have been transferred to LP. Among the major microphones recordings made by Elgar are the two symphonies, *Falstaff, Cockaigne, Alassio, Enigma, Pomp and Circumstance,* the Concerto for Cello (with Beatrice Harrison), and the Concerto for Violin (with the adolescent Yehudi Menuhin).

[1500] TIERSOT, Jean-Baptiste Élisée Julien (Tēr-sō', Zhàn Bà-tēst' Zhül-yàn')
LIBRARIAN, MUSICOLOGIST
BORN: Bourg-en-Bresse, July 5, 1857
DIED: Paris, August 10, 1936

Julien Tiersot's life bears a superficial resemblance to that of Berlioz [1175]. He too was born in the shadow of the French Alps, and he too studied medicine in Paris. Like his predecessor he was drawn to the Paris Conservatoire, where his teachers included Augustin Savard (who also taught Edward MacDowell [1529]), Massenet [1396], and César Franck [1284]. Like Berlioz he became the institution's librarian, joining the staff in 1883 and serving as its head from 1910 until he retired in 1921. He wrote voluminously and authoritatively on many musical subjects, among them Hector Berlioz. He was a noted ethnomusicologist and published many collections of French folksongs, including the multivolume *Mélodies populaires des provinces de France* and one of songs from the Vivarais with d'Indy [1462]. His history of French popular song won the Académie's Bodin Prize in 1885. Tiersot was also a tireless delver into old music and did much to promote its performance. Though he wrote some original compositions—a folksong rhapsody, the cantata *Hellas,* a symphonic poem *Sire Halewyn,* etc.—he is best known for his song arrangements. RECORDINGS: There are many recordings of, for example, *L'Amour de moy [My Love]* and *Tambourin.*

[1501] DELLINGER, Rudolf (Del'-ling-er, Rōō'-dolf)
CONDUCTOR
BORN: Graslitz, July 8, 1857
DIED: Dresden, September 24, 1910

Dellinger was born in what is now Kraslice in extreme western Czechoslovakia. His father was a professional instrument maker. The son studied at a local musical school and then at the Prague Conservatory. An orchestral clarinetist, he was by 1880 assistant conductor at the municipal theater in Brno. He became known throughout the German world and in 1883 was hired as a conductor at the Carl Schulze Theater in Hamburg. There two years later his career as composer peaked with the performance of his *Don César,* a Viennese-style operetta that

verges on the operatic. In 1886 he married the soprano Anna Maria Eppich. He followed his one hit with six more tries, none of them really successful. (*Don César* and *Lorraine* both reached Broadway in the mid-1880s and flopped.) In 1893 Dellinger was called to Dresden to conduct at the Residenztheater. His failure as a composer and mounting debts led to a collapse in 1909 and his death a year later. RECORDINGS: There are recorded excerpts from *Don César.*

[1502] CHAMINADE, Cécile Louise Stéphanie (Shà-mē-nàd', Sā-sēl' Lōō-ēz' Stā'-fà-nē)
PIANIST
BORN: Paris, August 8, 1857
DIED: Monte Carlo, April 18, 1944

Known worldwide as a concert pianist—on which career she embarked at eighteen—Chaminade was also one of the few women composers of her time to win popularity. She did it mostly through her salonesque piano pieces, though she wrote some serious music too—an opera *La Sévillane (The Woman of Seville),* a ballet *Callirhoë,* a big choral symphony *Les Amazones,* a *Mass,* concerti, chamber music, etc. Her composition teacher was Godard [1445]. She made her American debut in 1908 with the Philadelphia Orchestra under Karl Pohlig. When she died at eighty-six, however, she was all but forgotten. RECORDINGS: There are recordings of the Piano Trio No. 1 (Macalester Trio), the Concertino for Flute (James Galway et al., with varying accompaniment of orchestra, wind ensemble, or piano), the *Concertstück* (sic!) for piano and orchestra (Rosario Marciano), and the Sonata for Piano and other keyboard pieces (Doris Pines). A number of songs were recorded in earlier times.

[1503] SMYTH, (Dame) Ethel
CONDUCTOR, WRITER
BORN: Marylebone, April 22, 1858
DIED: Woking, May 9, 1944

As a woman musician in a man's world, Ethel Smyth was a tough cookie, and the almost total neglect of her music today is a disgrace to her memory. She was born in Middlesex, the daughter of a general (her brother also attained high military rank), and no doubt absorbed some of the family militancy. She appears to have been introduced to music by her nurse, who played Beethoven on the piano in her spare time. Her interest was further fostered by a paternal friend, Lieutenant Colonel Alexander Ewing (1830–95), who won fame for his hymn, *Jerusalem the Golden*, but little notice for his more ambitious efforts. She enrolled in the Leipzig Conservatory when she was nineteen but considered the teachers there fuddy-duddies and took up private study with Heinrich von Herzogenberg, whom she followed to Berlin. She introduced herself to many of the important composers of the day, who treated her as a potential equal. She wrote a good deal of music during this period, making a considerable impression in Leipzig with her string quintet, which appeared as her Op. 1 in 1884. Returning to England in 1888, she began soon to get works performed in London concerts and eventually made a great impression with a *Mass,* which Sir Joseph Barnby [1362] conducted in 1893. (It was noted that one would not have guessed it was written by a woman.)

At about that time Miss Smyth decided to turn to opera. Her first effort, *Fantasio* (to her own libretto, after Alfred de Musset's play), found a production in Weimar in 1898, but it was botched, and she later disclaimed the work as immature. She had better luck with *Der Wald (The Forest),* premiered at Berlin in 1902, in London later that year, and at the New York Metropolitan Opera in 1903 (with Johanna Gadski, Georg Anthes, and David Bispham). By then she was finding champions in the likes of Hermann Levi, Gustav Mahler [1525], Bruno Walter, and (a bit later) Thomas Beecham. In 1906 she had a triumph with *Strandrecht* (originally written for Paris as *Les Naufrageurs* and best known, after the 1909 London premiere led by Beecham, as *The Wreckers.*

In 1910, at the beginning of a period that produced a number of choral works and songs, she was awarded an honorary doctorate by the University of Durham. By then she was deeply involved in the suffragist movement, and at the all-Smyth concert she conducted at Queen's Hall the next April she introduced the march that became the feminists' musical theme. *The Boatswain's Mate,* which Beecham premiered in 1916, had a feminist orientation and used the march as a motif. This work established itself in the English repertoire for a number of years. Her last two operas were both in one act—a fantasy, *Fête galante* (Birmingham, June 4, 1923), and a farce, *Entente cordiale* (Bristol, October 20, 1926). During the 1920s she frequently appeared as a conductor. She became a Dame of the British Empire in 1922. In 1927 Aubrey Brain played the first performance of her horn concerto under Sir Henry Wood's direction, and four years later

Adrian Boult introduced her choral symphony *The Prison*. Some call it her greatest work; others feel that it shows a decided decline. At any rate, increasing deafness made further musical endeavor impossible. Dame Ethel had by then published four successful prose works, all based on her own experiences, and she now turned to writing, bringing out five more in the same vein.

RECORDINGS: She left composer-conducted recordings of the overture to her two most successful operas, and there are original-cast excerpts from *The Boatswain's Mate,* some pieces from the two last operas, and a fanfare, *Hot Potatoes.* The only modern recording seems to be one of the overture to *The Wreckers* led by Sir Alexander Gibson.

[1504] TIRINDELLI, Pier Adolfo (Tir-in-del'-lē, Pyer Ȧ-dol'-fō)
VIOLINIST, CONDUCTOR, TEACHER
BORN: Conegliano, May 5, 1858
DIED: Rome, February 6, 1937

Born near Venice, Adolfo Tirindelli studied at the Milan Conservatory and with the organist Carlo Bonoforti before taking a conducting job in Gorizia. After three years there, he undertook further studies at the conservatories of Vienna and Paris, and then became professor of violin at the Liceo Benedetto Marcello in Venice, in which city his opera *L'Atenaide (The Atheniad)* was performed in 1892. In 1895 Tirindelli took a job as violinist in the Boston Symphony, but after a year he joined the faculty of the Cincinnati Conservatory, where he taught until 1922 and conducted the orchestra. He then returned to Rome. A second opera, *Blanc et noir (Black and White),* was premiered in Cincinnati in 1897. He was knighted in 1894 by King Umberto I. RECORDINGS: As a composer Tirindelli is best known for his once popular drawing-room songs, of which several (most notably *"O primavera!"* ["O Spring!"]) were recorded.

[1505] HÜE, Georges Adolphe (Ü, Zhôrzh Ȧ-dolf')
TEACHER
BORN: Versailles, May 6, 1858
DIED: Paris, June 7, 1948

Winner of the Grand Prix de Rome in 1879, Georges Hüe was a product of the Paris Conservatoire, where he studied with Henri Reber (1807–80), Paladilhe [1420], and Franck [1284]. He was later a successful teacher in Paris and had a number of stage works—5 operas, pantomimes, ballets, and incidental music—performed there. He also wrote a symphony, other orchestral and concerted works, choral pieces, and songs. He was elected to the Académie on the death of Saint-Saëns [1343]. RECORDINGS: Some of his songs have been recorded. Flutist Karl-Bernhard Sebon has recorded his *Fantaisie* for flute and orchestra.

[1506] TRNEČEK, Hanŭs (Trə'-ne-chek, Hán'-ōōsh)
HARPIST, PIANIST, TEACHER, ADMINIS-
TRATOR
BORN: Prague, May 16, 1858
DIED: Prague, March 28, 1914

A product of the Prague Conservatory, Trneček played harp in the orchestra of the Mecklenburg-Schwerin ducal court from 1882 to 1888. He then came back to Prague as the conservatory's first professor of harp. He also taught piano. In 1904 he founded the first music festival in Bohemia. He wrote 3 operas, symphonies, concerti, and chamber music, but is chiefly known as a composer for the harp and the piano. RECORDINGS: His arrangement of Smetana's [1291] *Vltava* for solo harp has been recorded by Bedřich Dobrodinsky.

[1507] YSAŸE, Eugène Auguste (Ē-zī'-yə, Ü-zhen' O-güst')
VIOLINIST, CONDUCTOR, TEACHER
BORN: Liège, July 16, 1858
DIED: Brussels, May 12, 1931

The old catalogs of Columbia Records (for which company he recorded both as a soloist and conductor) unreservedly proclaimed Eugène Ysaÿe "the world's greatest violinist." Be that as it may, he was admired and idolized by most of the younger violinists of his time. His father Nicolas, who was a theater conductor in Liège, was his first teacher. His younger brother Théophile (1865–1918), also a composer and teacher, was to become his accompanist and rehearsal conductor. Eugène made his concert debut and entered the Liège Conservatory in the year Théophile was born. Unable to get along with his teacher, a certain Désiré Heynberg, he withdrew in 1867 but returned five years later to study with Rodolphe Massart. Ysaÿe won several prizes and a scholarship to the Brussels Conservatory, where he studied in 1874 with Wieniawski [1340]. In 1876 he moved to Paris for three years of further work under the direction of the now-crippled Vieuxtemps [1270]. In 1879 he

toured the Rhineland as assisting artist to the soprano Pauline Lucca and then went to Berlin as concertmaster of Benjamin Bilse's orchestra (from which later sprang the Berlin Philharmonic). After an 1882 tour of Scandinavia and Russia with Anton Rubinstein [1309], Ysaÿe settled in Paris, where he became an intimate of most of the important composers of the day. César Franck's [1284] violin sonata was a wedding present to Ysaÿe, who premiered it at his wedding to Louise Bourdeau in 1886. That same year he went to Brussels as professor of violin at the Brussels Conservatory. There he organized the Ysaÿe String Quartet and the orchestral Concerts Ysaÿe in 1894. He did much to promote contemporary music. Debussy [1547] (who originally conceived his *Nocturnes* as a vehicle for Ysaÿe) wrote his string quartet for him, and Chausson [1484] his *Poème*. International tours began to take up more and more of his time, and he left the conservatory in 1898, though he continued to live in Brussels until the outbreak of war in 1914 forced him to seek refuge in London. He had earlier refused the conductorship of the New York Philharmonic (in succession to Anton Seidl), but now he was developing a marked tremor in his bow hand, and in 1918 he accepted an appointment as director of the Cincinnati Symphony. After four years, however, he relinquished his baton to Fritz Reiner and returned to Brussels to revive his own orchestra. His first wife having died, he married Jeannette Dincin, a Brooklyner of twenty-five, in 1927. Two years later he lost a foot to a long battle with diabetes but returned to the podium. In 1930 he completed his only opera, *Piér li Houïeu (Pierre the Miner,* in Walloon dialect), but was too ill to conduct the premiere and died two months afterward. Most of his other compositions, including 8 concerti, involved the violin. RE-CORDINGS: Ruggiero Ricci, Gidon Kremer, Oscar Shumsky, and William Castleman have recorded the sonatas for solo violin, tailored to the talents of Josef Szigeti, Jacques Thibaud, Georges Enesco [1738], Fritz Kreisler [1664], Ysaÿe's quartet mate Mathieu Crickboom, and the brief-careered Manuel Quiroga. There are also many individual recordings of the sonatas. Aaron Rosand performs the *Chant d'hiver,* Ulf Hoelscher the *Caprice After Saint-Saëns' Étude en forme de valse*—both for violin and orchestra. Robert Silvester offers the Op. 28 unaccompanied cello sonata.

[1508] DE LARA, Isidore (Dā Lä'-rä, I'-zi-dôr)
SINGER, CONDUCTOR

BORN: London, August 9, 1858
DIED: Paris, September 2, 1935

Born Isidore Cohen to an English father and a Portuguese mother, De Lara (as he dubbed himself) became a successful composer of French *opéra lyrique* and strove mightily on behalf of British music. He studied piano in London with one of the numerous Aguilars, voice in Milan with Lamperti and Mazzucato (who once composed an opera, *La Fidanzata di Lammermoor [The Sweetheart of Lammermoor])*, and had some final polishing in Paris from Lalo [1286]. He became known as a recitalist and composer of salon ballads, some of them very popular. After producing some operettas in London, he had a considerable success with his *Messaline* in 1899 at Monte Carlo, where he had a patroness in the Princess of Monaco. But, like the rest of his stage works, it proved a flash in the pan. During World War I he returned to London, where he conducted concerts of British music, featuring a number of premieres. RECORDINGS: Older records offer a few excerpts from *Messaline* and songs.

[1509] HUBAY, Jenö (Hoo′-bä-ē, Yen-ö)
VIOLINIST, TEACHER
BORN: Budapest, September 15, 1858
DIED: Budapest, March 12, 1937

A virtuoso of international rank and a successful composer, Hubay was also one of the most important violin teachers of his day. His father was Karl Huber, professor of violin at the Budapest Conservatory and concertmaster at the National Opera. The son was listed at birth as "Eugen Huber," but the family later changed its name for patriotic reasons. Jenö was a pupil of his father and made his concert debut at eleven. In 1871 the government paid his way to Berlin to put in five years of study with Joachim [1321]. In 1878 he made a successful debut in Paris, where he undertook further study with the partially paralyzed Vieuxtemps. He was with the elder violinist when he died and later edited his music. In 1882 he was appointed to the professorship at the Brussels Conservatory that Vieuxtemps once held. There he and the cellist Joseph Servais organized a notable string quartet, but Servais died two years later at thirty-five. In 1886 Hubay was called back to Budapest to succeed his father, leaving his Brussels post to his fellow Vieuxtemps pupil Eugène Ysaÿe [1507]. In Budapest he organized a second Hubay Quartet, which at one time included the great cellist David Popper [1411]. He soon also became well known as a composer,

particularly in Hungary. He produced 8 operas, other stage works, 4 symphonies, 4 violin concerti, and a number of works in other genres. In 1894 he married the Countess Rosa Cebrain and was himself ennobled by the Emperor Franz Josef in 1907. He was promoted to the directorship of the conservatory after Hungary received her independence and retired at seventy-five in 1933. Among his pupils were Jelly d'Aranyi, Eddy Brown, Josef Szigeti, Emil Telmanyi, and Franz von Vecsey. His music is romantic and Hungarian in the Lisztian sense. His best-known works are the *Czardas Scenes* (originally for tableaux) and encore pieces. RECORDINGS: Hubay himself recorded some of these encore pieces in the microphone era. Aaron Rosand has recorded the Concerto No. 3 for Violin and the *Hejre Kati* for violin and orchestra, and there was once a record of a movement from Symphony No. 2. Violinist Tibor Varnay and pianist Hadassa Schwimmer recently recorded a selection of pieces—the *Sonate romantique,* the *Carmen Fantasie,* and several others.

[1510] MUGNONE, Leopoldo (Moon-yō′-nā, Lā-ō-pōl′-dō)
CONDUCTOR, PIANIST
BORN: Naples, September 29, 1858
DIED: Capodichino, December 22, 1941

Though he showed early promise as a composer, Leopoldo Mugnone (not to be confused with the Brazilian Francisco Mignone [1941]) became one of the most admired conductors of his day. The son of an opera-house contrabassist, he wrote his own first opera, *Il Dottor Bartolo Salsapariglia (Doctor Bartolo Sarsaparilla)* when he was twelve. He studied at the Naples Conservatory, chiefly with Paolo Serrao, and at sixteen was conducting at the little Teatro La Fenice in his native city. The following year saw the premieres of two operettas. For a time he served as accompanist to the contrabass virtuoso Bottesini [1278] but was soon at the helm of the Rome Opera orchestra, where in 1890 he conducted the premiere of Mascagni's [1559] *Cavalleria rusticana.* By 1900, when he introduced Puccini's [1511] *Tosca,* Mugnone was known internationally. He gave the foreign premieres of several Italian operas, and made a special point of conducting French and German operas in Italy. Later he also conducted symphony orchestras. He successfully produced two more operas—*Il Birichino (The Street-Urchin)* in 1892 and *Vita bretonna (Breton Life)* in 1905. RECORDINGS: An excerpt or two from *Vita bretonna* was recorded in its day, and there are also versions of some of Mugnone's popular Neapolitan songs.

[1511] PUCCINI, Giacomo Antonio Domenico Michele Secondo Maria (Pōōt-chē'-nē, Já'-kō-mō Ȧn-tōn'-yō Dō-mā'-nē-kō Mē-kā'-lā Sā-kōn'-dō Mȧ-rē'-ȧ)
BORN: Lucca, December 23, 1858
DIED: Brussels, November 29, 1924

The current Italian operatic repertoire began with Rossini [1143]; it ends with Giacomo Puccini, who died sixty years ago. There are those who feel that it should have died earlier—that Puccini represents a debasement of both inspiration and taste, that he caters to the mob. What is at issue is his musical emotionalism, his blows to the solar plexus, his ability to jerk tears willy-nilly. Those who feel that the head should rule the heart decry his cheap little shockers and insist that he gets by on a single "Puccini tune." But the fact remains that no major operatic composer, save perhaps Wagner [1230], has as high a percentage of his work currently active. And the work *does* bear looking into, for whether one likes it or not Puccini was a superb, imaginative, and scrupulous artist.

Giacomo represents the last of five consecutive generations of musical Puccinis to emerge in Lucca. All of his predecessors were significant to the musical life of that city. The first Giacomo (1712–81) was probably a pupil of Padre Martini [767] and served as cathedral organist and director of the orchestra, which for a time included Boccherini [927]. His son Antonio and his grandson Domenico [1074] followed in his exact footsteps. His great-grandson Michele also studied in Bologna, and then with Donizetti [1155] and Mercadante [1148] in Naples. Michele married Albina Magi, the sister of one of his pupils, Fortunato Magi, and sired on her eight children before dying in 1864 at fifty-one. Giacomo, five years old at his death, was the fifth child and the second son. (The first died in infancy; the third, Michele, was born three months after his father died, grew up to become a music teacher, emigrated to South America, and succumbed to yellow fever at twenty-nine.)

The elder Michele in effect willed the succession to Giacomo, whose education was entrusted to his Uncle Fortunato, then director of the local conservatory and later of the Conservatorio Benedetto Marcello in Venice. Giacomo showed little inclination to study or practice, and the two got on quite badly; as a result Magi gave him up and turned him over to his colleague Carlo Angeloni, under whose tutelage things took an upward turn.

At ten the boy was singing in the choirs of the cathedral and the Church of San Michele. At fourteen he was playing for services in various churches and picking up a few centesimi at the piano in local dives. It was at this time that he acquired the tobacco addiction which probably killed him. At sixteen he took on a pupil of his own age—one of two about whom we know in his lifetime, since he found teaching not at all to his liking. Among the Lucchese his penchant for practical jokes won him the reputation of a bad boy. (He was once hauled into court on a charge of being accessory to a bogus suicide!)

Puccini was already composing utilitarian stuff for his church duties, but his vocation seems to have come with Verdi's [1232] *Aida* (then five years old), which he and two friends walked the forty miles to Pisa and back to see in 1876. That same year he produced his first orchestral piece, a *Preludio sinfonico* and submitted a cantata, *Juno*—which the judges declared illegible—to a local competition. Two years later he got a performance of a *Motet* and a *Credo*, and in 1880 his *Mass* (improperly known as the *Missa di gloria*), in which he incorporated them, made him the talk of the city. That same year, with a small royal scholarship and a loan from his maternal great-uncle Niccolò Cerù (both importuned by his mother), he went to Milan and, passing the entrance exams with the top score, entered the Milan Conservatory, where he studied with Bazzini [1256] and Ponchielli [1334]. He lived an expectably (and perhaps expectedly) Spartan existence, sharing a room (on one occasion with his brother Michele, on another with Pietro Mascagni [1559]), and apparently living mostly on soup, with beans in olive oil as a luxury. He also made friends with Catalani [1477], though the friendship (like those with Mascagni and Leoncavallo [1498]) soon succumbed to rivalry. Puccini graduated in 1883, offering as proof of his expertise a *Capriccio sinfonico*, performed at the school under the direction of Franco Faccio and praised by the critics. (Puccini later mined it for *Edgar* and *La Bohème.*) At about the same time the burgeoning publisher Edoardo Sonzogno announced the first of his competitions for one-act operas. Puccini was eager, and Ponchielli found him a librettist in a self-important young journalist, Ferdinando Fontana, who decided, on God knows what grounds, that Puccini needed a Gothic romance and produced a book on the *Giselle* theme.

The composer went back to Lucca to set it and submitted his first-draft manuscript within a hair's breadth of the year's-end deadline. Since his hand was notoriously bad, the judges probably did not seriously consider *Le Villi;* certainly it won no notice whatsoever, the prizes going to Zuelli and Borelli, whoever they may have been. But thanks to Fontana's not disinterested efforts, Puccini got to play part of the score at a Milan *soirée,* where he won the support of Boito [1393]—and, through him, the publisher Giulio Ricordi—and thereby a production at the Teatro dal Verme the following May. Advertised as a loser in Sonzogno's contest, the opera had a real triumph, won several other productions, and got Puccini a contract with Ricordi for its publication and for a new opera.

But before he could get to the latter, his private life underwent some major tremors. He had fallen in love with Elvira Gemignani, the wife of a onetime schoolmate and mother of two children. In July 1884 Puccini's own beloved mother died (at fifty-three), and shortly afterward Elvira eloped with him to Milan, taking her daughter Fosca with them. The Puccini family (and all Lucca) was outraged and Great-Uncle Niccolò demanded his loan back—as he would continue to do for some time to come. Moreover Puccini was having to help his hapless emigrant brother as best he could. On the credit side, Fontana had produced a libretto of sorts, *Edgar* (after Musset), and that same summer of 1884 Ricordi had started paying the composer 300 lire a month against future revenues. But the situation was not helped by the birth of Puccini's son Antonio in 1886. (His parents were unable to marry for eighteen more years, when Narciso Gemignani died.) *Edgar* was not completed until 1888. It was premiered at La Scala under Faccio's baton the following April. The cast included Romilda Pantaleoni (three years later Verdi's [1232] Desdemona in the first *Otello)* and Giovanni Battista de Negri (himself later a great *Otello),* but the reception was lukewarm, in part owing to the wretched libretto. Nevertheless Ricordi kept the faith and refused to let his board jettison his protégé—who, however, rid himself of Fontana for good. (Puccini revised *Edgar,* cutting out a whole act, and it enjoyed further productions. He was particularly optimistic about the one at Madrid in 1892, which featured Tamagno and Luisa Tetrazzini, but the work never became popular.)

Meanwhile Puccini had fallen in love with the Abbé Prévost's *Manon Lescaut,* probably through Massenet's [1396] setting. But now there was libretto trouble of a different kind. First Ricordi recommended Leoncavallo, but Puccini did not like his treatment. Next he tried a playwright, Marco Praga, untested in opera, who brought in an equally untried poet, Domenico Oliva. In the summer of 1890 Puccini took *their* version on vacation to Vacallo, on the Swiss frontier (where Leoncavallo was, incidentally, working on *Pagliacci).* In the spring of 1891 he went back to Lucca and finally found a spot to his liking at Torre del Lago (now Torre del Lago Puccini), a fishing village on Lake Massaciuccoli, between Lucca and the sea, where he could indulge his mania for hunting. In the meantime he was finding the libretto increasingly unsatisfactory. Praga refused to have anything more to do with it; Oliva, at first amenable to making changes, finally also quit in frustration. Ricordi then called in the popular playwright Giuseppe Giacosa, who suggested a young colleague, Luigi Illica. But by 1892 both men were contributing, and the opera, now called *Manon Lescaut,* to distinguish it from Massenet's, was completed in October. After much head scratching over how the librettists should be listed, all mention of them was omitted when the work was published. It was premiered in Turin (Ricordi was skittish about Milan for Puccini) on February 1, 1893, with Cesira Ferrani (later the first *Bohème* Mimi) in the title role, and, despite the composer's gloomy prognostications, it was a total triumph, assuring his fame and fortune.

Having finished *Manon,* Puccini embarked on *La Lupa (The She-Wolf)* after a story by Giovanni Verga; he even journeyed to Sicily to discuss it with him. But he was in part put off it by a chance meeting with Hans von Bülow's [1310] daughter, Countess Blandine Gravina, who was horrified by its sordidness and sacrilege. Moreover, he was increasingly involved with Henri Mürger's quasi-autobiographical *Scènes de la vie de Bohème (Scenes from Bohemian Life),* to which his attention may have been called by Leoncavallo, who was planning an opera based on it. Leoncavallo had later probably even shown him his libretto. When, in 1894, he discovered that Puccini was writing his own *La Bohème* (libretto by Illica and Giacosa), however, he was outraged, and the tenuous friendship ended. Things were not going smoothly for Puccini nevertheless, and in the end he and his librettists had to compromise, each sacrificing some cherished ideas. The work was finished at Torre del Lago on December 10, 1895, by the composer, by his own admission, bawling like a baby over Mimi's death. Whatever he may have originally intended, what he had produced was one of the most formally perfect operas in the repertoire—in essence a four-movement vocal symphony, but also a sure-fire dramatic vehicle (save for people with no hearts). With extraordinary diplomacy, Ricordi engineered the first production, again in Turin, with a cast chosen for aptitude rather than for box-office appeal and with a young man named Arturo Toscanini at the helm. Puccini was wary of the singers but absolutely dazzled by the conductor. The reception of the premiere (February 1, 1896—exactly three years after *Manon Lescaut)* was equivocal. In general the public approved, but the critics did not—not in all cases for relevant causes. The public won out—the theater was sold out for the rest of the month, and in Palermo, in April, the conductor Leopoldo Mugnone [1510] was forced, in the small hours of the morning, to encore the entire final act. Shortly afterward Puccini and his still unofficial family moved into the house they had built on the lakeside at Torre del Lago.

As the work on *Bohème* drew to an end, the composer seriously considered new possibilities, all from across the Alps—works by Louÿs, Maeterlinck, Zola, something about Marie Antoinette—but in the end he settled on *La Tosca*, a lurid piece that the popular playwright Victorien Sardou had written for Sarah Bernhardt. The only problem was that Illica was already committed, under the Ricordi aegis, to librettize it for Alberto Franchetti [1526], another of Puccini's old Lucca schoolmates. Ricordi, however, smelled higher profits from a Puccini setting, and so completely convinced poor Franchetti that the thing would not work that Franchetti tore up his contract—whereupon Ricordi signed one with his rival! By then Giacosa had rather convinced himself in the same negative fashion, and for a time the matter was at an impasse. When that was cleared, Sardou began making outrageous demands about abridgments of his play (unavoidable!) and the fee he should get (unheard of!). When *he* was placated, Ricordi blew up over the last act, which he predicted would be a disaster but to which Puccini stuck fast. Appropriately for its Roman *mise-en-scène*, the premiere was slated for the Teatro Costanzi in Rome. The conductor was once again Mugnone; the principals were the soprano Hariclea Darclée, the tenor Emilio de Marchi, and the baritone Eugenio Giraldoni—an all-star cast. The first night, January 14, 1900, there were rumors of bomb threats (whether musically or politically inspired was not clear); and poor Mugnone was in such a state that when latecomers tried to batter a door open in the first act, he ran for cover. However, no bomb exploded—but then, neither did the audience. *Tosca*, in fact, rather duplicated

the history of *Bohème*, with critical vituperation and twenty nights of sold-out houses. And worldwide acceptance followed quickly, though even today it remains, from the intellectual viewpoint, Puccini's most maligned major work. But its effectiveness is inescapable.

While in London later that year for the *Tosca* premiere there, Puccini (who spoke no English) went to see David Belasco's one-act play *Madame Butterfly* and was much taken with what he saw. Setting aside the various other possible subjects with which he had been toying—*Tartarin, Cyrano, Adolphe,* etc.—he began plugging for *Butterfly*. His librettists were unenthusiastic (Giacosa was ailing), Ricordi was hostile, and in any case Belasco played the prima donna and refused permission until he finally gave in, in September 1901. For the next year, despite unspecified domestic troubles at Torre, things went swimmingly. Then Puccini decided to telescope his second and third acts, making it necessary to placate Giacosa and Ricordi all over again. Puccini steeped himself in *japanaiserie*, reading voluminously, collecting recordings of Japanese music, conferring with the wife of the Italian ambassador to Japan, and listening to a Japanese actress speak her native language.

Puccini's use of recordings is one indication that he was a man of the twentieth century. The mechanical fascinated him, and for some time he had been buying bicycles and motorboats. During the composition of *Butterfly* he bought his first automobile, a Buire. In the midwinter of 1903 he drove Elvira and their son to Lucca, where he had a medical appointment regarding a persistent throat problem (ominous in the light of his later history). On the way home in the fog, he went off the road and down a steep embankment, breaking his leg. During his convalescence he was found to be diabetic. He was in a cast and then in a wheelchair for months and walked with a limp for the rest of his life. Nevertheless the opera was finished at year's end and was scheduled for La Scala the following February, with Rosina Storchio (Toscanini's current *innamorata),* Giovanni Zenatello, and Giuseppe de Luca in the cast, and Cleofonte Campanini on the podium. The rehearsals all pointed to a triumph. Instead, for whatever reason (memories of *Edgar,* anti-"Wagnerism," a conspiracy), the premiere on February 17 was a total disaster—pandemonium in the house and a witches' sabbath in the press. Puccini, who loved this opera above all his others, was deeply hurt and profoundly puzzled. But he revised it immediately, and the new version, with the Polish soprano Salomea Krusciniski *(née* Kruszelnicka) replacing Storchio (then in South America), began its triumphal progress in Brescia on May 28.

Shortly afterward, while Puccini was visiting London, Paolo Tosti **[1429]** introduced him to Sybil Seligman, the attractive wife of a banker. There was a brief and passionate affair that ripened into a lifelong friendship in which she (his "Cumaean Sybil") gave him much astute advice. At this time she suggested a number of operatic possibilities to him, of which Oscar Wilde's *A Florentine Tragedy* got serious and prolonged consideration. (So did *Parisina,* suggested by its author Gabriele d'Annunzio, and Pierre Louÿs's *La Femme et le pantin* [to be titled *Conchita]*; the libretti were ultimately set by Mascagni and Zandonai **[1766]** respectively.) Attracted by a considerable sum of money, the composer and his wife spent the summer of 1905 in Buenos Aires attending a festival of his operas and returned to London (and Sybil) in the fall. He still had no real work to occupy his time. The next year Giacosa died (at fifty-nine); between then and 1912 Puccini put Illica to work on several ultimately aborted projects but never used another libretto by him. It was in 1906 too that the Puccinis, for $8,000, were lured to New York to see Giacomo's four most popular works at the Metropolitan Opera. Elvira was seasick, and the voyage was delayed two days by fog. She also hated New York, though Puccini was dazzled by its modern air. He bought another motorboat and shipped it home. He disliked Geraldine Farrar's celebrated Butterfly and thought Caruso (whose early career he had furthered) a lazy conceited ass. But a visit to the theater to see Belasco's *The Girl of the Golden West* (which he had previously read) convinced him that it was what he was looking for, and by July 1907 he and the playwright had signed the contract. (There is a recording, with huzzaing, toasts, and speechmaking by the principals celebrating the Puccinis' return to Italy from this trip.)

For his horse opera (it required eight horses onstage) Puccini entrusted the libretto to one Carlo Zangarini, who could be presumed to know the territory since his mother was a Coloradan. When he proved dilatory, he was given a collaborator in Guelfo Civinini in the spring of 1908. But that autumn other matters slowed up composition to a crawl. Elvira's almost pathological (if not unfounded) jealousy had long made Puccini miserable, and only his fear of living alone held the marriage together. In 1903, when he was laid up, the couple had hired a local sixteen-year-old girl, Doria Manfredi, as a nurse. Five years later Elvira suddenly became obsessed with the notion that Puccini and Doria were two-timing her and began turning the young woman's life into a living hell, browbeating her and making all sorts of horrid charges about Torre. Early in the New Year Doria fled to her home, poisoned herself on January 23, and died horribly five days later—a virgin, according to the coroner's report. Elvira in turn fled to Milan. The Manfredis, however, sued her for slander, and in November she was found guilty, fined, and sentenced to five months in jail. While an appeal was pending, Puccini bought the Manfredis off, and the whole matter was dropped. The couple eventually reconciled and developed a workable *détente* in their final years together. By mid-1909, the composer was able again to devote his attention to his opera, which he completed in early August 1910. Translating the title unambiguously and meaningfully had proved a problem; it was Sybil who found the polyglot solution, *La Fanciulla del West.*

Given the American subject *("addio, mia California!"),* the premiere was naturally entrusted to the Metropolitan, and set for December 10, with Toscanini conducting, and Emmy Destinn, Caruso, and Pasquale Amato as the principals. Puccini attended; Elvira stayed home. Belasco helped direct the action. The horses appeared on cue. There were more than fifty curtain calls, and the press went wild. Puccini—as he always did—pronounced his newest opera his best one. But it has never caught on in the way its immediate predecessors did.

There followed the inevitable period of searching for a new focus. Puccini found a compatible librettist in Giuseppe Adami, a thirty-three-year-old playwright, and talked of an evening of one-acters from each of the three sections of Dante's *Divina commedia.* He talked of other ideas as well and led Adami to work on *Anima allegra (The Happy Soul)* by the Quintero brothers but dropped it after a year (the libretto was later set by Vittadini **[1778]**). Then he reverted to the one-acters (having apparently jettisoned the Dante notion) and lit on *La Houppelande (The Cloak),* a grisly piece of *verismo* by Didier Gold, in 1913. The assigned librettist, the aged Ferdinando Martini, dragged his feet, however, until Puccini turned the project over to Adami instead. (The eventual result was the opera *Il Tabarro.)* Meanwhile Giulio Ricordi had died in 1912, and Puccini did not get along with his son and heir Tito, who was plugging Zandonai as the new Puccini. In 1914 Puccini decided that he really wanted to set *Two Little Wooden Shoes* by Ouida (Louise de la Ramée). Problems immediately arose. Mascagni claimed it (it eventually emerged from his desk in 1917 as *Lodoletta*), and afterward it became clear that no one knew who owned the rights. The courts then whimsically ordered that they be sold at auction. By the time Ricordi had won them for 4,000 lire, Puccini had lost interest.

One thing that had deflected it was a commission from Vienna, a city he loved. When he had gone there in the fall of 1913 for the premiere of *Fanciulla*, he had been approached by the directors of the Carltheater to write a dozen numbers for an operetta, for a staggering amount of money. A year later he returned for Maria Jeritza's first *Tosca* and, having recently suffered further slings and arrows from Tito Ricordi, signed the contract independently of that firm. There was, as so often, foot shuffling, but finally in July 1914 he had something he thought he could work with; it became *La Rondine (The Swallow)*. War broke out a month later, shocking and horrifying him. When he returned to work late in the fall, he found he hated the whole thing. Adami, who had translated the work, thereupon turned it into a full-fledged opera—which pleased everyone concerned. But Italy entered the war in May 1915, and by the time the work was completed there was no hope of putting it on in Vienna. When Tito hemmed and hawed about publication, Puccini sold the score to his rival, Sonzogno. (In 1919 the Ricordi board of directors ousted Tito for good.) Despite the fact that his Viennese contract was still in force, the composer had *La Rondine* premiered in Monte Carlo (with Gilda dalla Rizza and Tito Schipa, Marinuzzi conducting). Despite the hosannas of public and press and the several productions that immediately followed, the work remains the least known of all of Puccini's mature operas. (Although his son was serving in the Italian army and he himself was a known patriot, his abhorrence of war and the Austrian connection brought howls of "treason" in the war years, especially in France.)

Puccini had also completed his first one-act opera, *Il Tabarro (The Cloak)*, in November 1916. Meanwhile he had met a one-time singer-turned-playwright, Giovacchino Forzano, who came up with an acceptable idea for a second—a work (wholly for women) about a young nun, encloistered by her family for producing a love child, who poisons herself (ah, Doria!) when she hears of his death. Puccini had a sister who had taken the veil and who provided insights into convent life. In the meantime Puccini himself seems to have reverted to Dante and to have suggested a comedy based on a line

(!) in the *Inferno* about one Gianni Schicchi who, at the behest of the heirs of one Buoso Donati, forged the latter's will—to his own benefit. Forzano whipped off a libretto, and Puccini worked on both operas at top speed, finishing *Suor Angelica (Sister Angelica)* by mid-September 1917 and *Gianni Schicchi* seven months later. The three pieces were dubbed *Il Trittico (The Triptych)*. (It has been said that they have no real interrelationship, but in fact they are all three about people trapped—by poverty, by mores, by greed.) The premiere was again given to the Metropolitan for December 14, 1918. The starry casts included Farrar (as Angelica), Claudia Muzio (as Giorgetta in *Tabarro*), Florence Easton as Lauretta (in *Schicchi*), Giuseppe de Luca as Schicchi himself, and Giulio Crimi as the tenor lead in the first and last works. Only *Schicchi* pleased, and for many years it was the only survivor, though recently opera houses have taken (successfully) to presenting the series as the composer intended. (Because ocean travel, so close to the armistice, was out, Puccini was unable to be present.)

The next year, on request, Puccini wrote a Roman anthem, *Inno a Roma*, which Mussolini later adopted as a Fascist marching song. (Puccini, who believed in strong leadership, welcomed the arrival of Il Duce, who named him a senator-at-large in 1924, though whether he espoused Fascist ideals is debatable.) Following the *Trittico*, there was the usual subject hunt. Puccini set Forzano to work on the Christopher Sly story implied by Shakespeare's prologue to *The Taming of the Shrew (Sly* was eventually set by Wolf-Ferrari [1679]), and Adami on Dickens' *Oliver Twist (as Fanny!)*; neither came to anything. In the summer of 1920 at a luncheon conversation, Simoni suggested they consider the eighteenth-century dramatist Carlo Gozzi, and from this Puccini came up with Gozzi's *Turandotte*, a combination of *chinoiserie* with *commedia dell'arte*. Adami and Simoni had a scenario ready by fall and a first act by January 1921. But the composition proceeded slowly, and several times Puccini cursed himself for undertaking it. Meanwhile a peat factory had gone up next door to the villa at Torre, and, unable to stand the smoke, the Puccinis moved to a new house in Viareggio in December. The year 1922 passed relatively uneventfully, save that on vacation in Bavaria that summer the composer had to have a swallowed fragment of bone removed from his throat. In the winter of 1923 Toscanini, with whom Puccini had been on the outs over the conductor's harsh criticism of the *Trittico*, led a magnificent revival of *Manon Lescaut* at La Scala, and the friendship was restored.

At about that time, Puccini began to be troubled with a persistent sore throat and what he took to be an aggravation of his smoker's cough. Two different physicians found nothing. But the ailment continued, and in August Sybil Seligman, visiting Viareggio, began to suspect the worst and confided her suspicions to Tonio, who, without telling them to his father, persuaded him to see a local throat specialist. He too found nothing but irritation from too much smoking, and counseled giving it up. But Puccini, now very uneasy, went privately to yet another specialist in Florence, who found a papilloma—a word the composer did not understand. Nor did Tonio, who sought clarification and learned that his father had terminal cancer. Despite the bleak outlook, they rushed Puccini to a Brussels clinic for radium treatment. He arrived on November 4, 1924, by which time he was bleeding from the throat. On the twenty-fourth he underwent an operation, after which the prognostication was optimistic. But four days later he suffered a heart attack and died early the next morning. The funeral took place in Milan Cathedral on December 3. Toscanini conducted the La Scala orchestra in music from *Edgar*. There was national official mourning. The body was interred in the Toscanini mausoleum in Milan, and two years later removed to Torre. In the same year *Turandot*, the final act pieced out by Franco Alfano [1683], was premiered under Toscanini's baton at La Scala, with Rosa Raisa, Maria Zamboni, and Miguel Fleta. In Act III on opening night, at the death of the pathetic slave-girl Liù, Toscanini turned to the audience, tears streaming down his face, said, "Here the maestro died," and called down the curtain.

RECORDINGS: All of the Puccini operas, even the lesser known ones, have by now seen from at least two to more than a score of commercial recordings. The *Mass*, the few instrumental pieces, and several of the few songs have also been made available. A great curiosity, however, is that so few of the singers who created Puccini roles sang excerpts from them for the phonograph. Cesira Ferrani left arias from *Manon Lescaut* and *Bohème*. Hariclea Darclée is known to have owned test copies of a couple of excerpts from *Tosca*, but for all practical purposes none exist now. Emilio de Marchi was captured briefly in performance at the Metropolitan on Lionel Mapleson's wax cylinders recorded from the catwalk in 1901—now barely audible. Krusciniski twice recorded an aria from *Butterfly* and Zenatello the love

duet. Incredibly not even Caruso recorded from *Fanciulla*. Florence Easton left her aria from *Gianni Schicchi;* Zamboni left Liù's two scenes from *Turandot*. The rest is silence.

[1512] ILYINSKY, Alexander Alexandrovich (Ēl-yēn'-skē, Ăl-yek-săn'-der Ăl-yek-săn-drō'-vich)
TEACHER, WRITER
BORN: Tsarskoye Selo [Russia], January 24, 1859
DIED: Moscow, February 23, 1920

A native of the old imperial summer resort, since rechristened "Pushkin," Ilyinsky went to Berlin to study piano with Theodor Kullak (1818–82) and composition with Woldemar Bargiel (1828–97), who was Clara Schumann's [1267] half-brother. Later a graduate of the St. Petersburg Conservatory, he taught for twenty years, 1885–1905, at the school of the Moscow Philharmonic Society. From 1905 to the end of his life he taught at the Moscow Conservatory. Among his books are manuals on harmony and orchestration, a composer dictionary, and studies of Wagner [1230], Beethoven [1063], Glinka [1179], and Dargomizhsky [1228]. He wrote an opera, other stage music, cantatas, a string quartet, miscellaneous orchestral pieces, etc. RECORDINGS: A few piano pieces have been recorded.

[1513] HERBERT, Victor August
CELLIST, CONDUCTOR
BORN: Dublin, February 1, 1859
DIED: New York, May 26, 1924

Like a number of early popular composers in America, Victor Herbert was an import. Amiable, mustachioed, roly-poly, a lover of good food and drink, he spoke with an Irish brogue tinged with German overtones. And for the first half of his career he was a "serious" musician.

Herbert lost his father when he was three, and his mother took him to England to live with *her* father, the novelist-composer Samuel Lover [1154]. Not long thereafter, she married a German doctor, Wilhelm Schmid, who took her and Victor, now seven, to live in Stuttgart. There the boy studied at the *Gymnasium*, then went to Baden-Baden to study the cello with Bernhard Cossmann. After two years he became a peripatetic orchestral cellist, and for a short time played in Eduard Strauss's [1339] orchestra in Vienna. In 1881 he returned to Stuttgart as a member of the court orchestra and took composition lessons from Max Seifriz (1827–85), a local violinist and conductor. Within four years the orchestra had premiered his Op. 3 *Suite for Cello and Orchestra* and his Concerto No. 1 for Cello, both with the composer as soloist. In the course of his duties in the opera house he met the soprano Therese Förster (not to be confused with her contemporary Berthe Foerster) and married her in the summer of 1886. At about the same time Mme. Förster signed a contract with the Metropolitan Opera in New York, on the condition that her husband be taken into the orchestra. (She was the Metropolitan's first Aida that November—in German!) The following season Herbert played his concerto with the New York Philharmonic under Theodore Thomas. Herbert continued to be heard as soloist with this and other orchestras, performed in chamber groups, and conducted—a pickup orchestra in New York, the Boston Festival Orchestra (ancestor of the "Pops"), the Worcester Festival Orchestra, and the 22nd Regiment Band (as successor to W. P. Gilmore). In 1889 he was appointed by the patroness Jeannette Thurber to teach cello in her newly founded National Conservatory, where he was later to become a colleague and friend of Dvořák. In 1894 he premiered his fine Concerto No. 2 for Cello with the Philharmonic under Anton Seidl.

For some time the Bostonians, a light-opera company, had been looking for a hit of the magnitude of Reginald De Koven's [1515] *Robin Hood,* which had put them on the map. Why they thought Herbert might supply it is not clear, but they asked him anyway and he came up, in 1894, with *Prince Ananias,* which did not quite live up to their hopes, though they gave it fifty-five times. Though he continued to write more ambitious works occasionally, he averaged better than one operetta a year for the rest of his life. The following year, working with Harry B. Smith, De Koven's librettist, he had a solid hit with *The Wizard of the Nile.* Among his most notable and enduring successes were: *The Fortune Teller,* 1898; *Babes in Toyland,* 1903; *Mlle. Modiste,* 1905; *The Red Mill,* 1906; *Naughty Marietta,* 1910; *Sweethearts,* 1913; and *Orange Blossoms,* 1922. Though the infectiously lyrical music was too often hamstrung by inane libretti, Herbert was in popularity the American counterpart of the younger Johann Strauss [1295], Offenbach [1264], and Sullivan [1397]. That many of the Herbert premieres occurred in towns like Wilkes-Barre and Atlantic City does not indicate eccentricity but rather the growth of the tryout system. Though even the best of the operettas have, in a self-consciously sophisticated age, gath-

ered dust for a time, there have been recent signs of their renewed viability.

Meanwhile Herbert was also busy with other pursuits. From 1898 to 1904 he served brilliantly as conductor of the Pittsburgh Symphony (founded 1895). After that, he returned to New York and organized his own orchestra (devoted to "light" music), with which he made many records for the Victor Company. In 1911 he momentarily forsook operetta (a term he did not like) to write the "American Indian" grand opera *Natoma.* Premiered in Philadelphia by the Chicago-Philadelphia company, and played afterward in Chicago and New York, it boasted a brilliant cast headed by Mary Garden, John McCormack, and Mario Sammarco. But suffering from Herbert's lack of real dramatic feeling and from such lines as "No country can mine own outvie" and "I list the trill of golden throat," it quickly disappeared. Nor did the one-act *Madeleine,* produced by the Metropolitan three years later, fare even as well. In 1913 Herbert became one of the founders of ASCAP, and served as its vice president until he died. On several occasions he supplied music for the Ziegfield Follies, for Paul Whiteman's orchestra, and for the marionettist Tony Sarg, and in 1916 he wrote one of the first symphonic scores for a (silent) film, *The Fall of a Nation.*

RECORDINGS: Save for at least two recordings of the Concerto No. 2 for Cello (Bernard Greenhouse, Georges Miquelle), Herbert is represented on records by lightweight orchestral pieces and by innumerable excerpts from the operettas and a few from the two operas. He also himself made a few cello recordings, including two little pieces of his own and transcriptions of two of his grandfather's songs. Oddly there seems to be, to date, no complete recording of any of the stage works. (*Naughty Marietta* has just been announced by the Smithsonian Institute.)

[1514] BEMBERG, Herman (Bản-bârg', Ăr-màn')

BORN: Paris, March 29, 1859
DIED: Bern, July 21, 1931

Born to wealth and thus a gentleman-composer, Bemberg was one of the *fin-de-siècle* exquisites. He studied with Franck [1284] and Massenet [1396] at the Paris Conservatoire but seems to have learned most from Théodore Dubois [1356]. He was awarded the Rossini Prize in 1885, produced a cantata, *La Mort de Jeanne d'Arc (The Death of Joan of Arc),* in 1896 and a little opera, *Le Baiser de Suzon (Suzy's Kiss),* two years later. He owes his immortality, such as it is, to the great soprano Nellie Melba, to whom he attached himself. (Most modern references omit him; one that includes him lists him as "Henri.") Melba said that, had it not been for his money, he would have become famous as either a composer or a clown. (The two delighted in playing dreadfully juvenile practical jokes on each other, falling just short of pie-in-the-face.) Melba thought enough of Bemberg to essay his opera *Elaine* (she usually stuck with the tried-and-true). She not only achieved a premiere for it at Covent Garden in 1892 with the De Reszke brothers and Pol Plançon but brought it to New York to the Metropolitan Opera two years later. Bernard Shaw dismissed the work as "inanely pretty," which term might also be applied to the composer's flaccid songs. RECORDINGS: Melba recorded a scene from *Elaine*. She also recorded a number of the songs, with the composer at the keyboard, and others inevitably took them up. Long forgotten, Bemberg died five months after his idol. Their entire collaboration has been transferred to LPs.

[1515] DE KOVEN, Henry Louis Reginald (Dā-kō'-ven, Hen'-rē Lōō'-is Re'-ji-nǝld)
CONDUCTOR, CRITIC
BORN: Middletown, Conn. April 3, 1859
DIED: Chicago, January 16, 1920

At one time it seemed positively indecent to wed in America if one did not do so to the strains of "O Promise Me," a song popularized by (but not written for) Reginald De Koven's operetta *Robin Hood*. De Koven was the son of a minister who moved to England with his family in 1872. After graduating from Oxford seven years later, the young man studied music variously in Stuttgart, Frankfurt-am-Main, and Florence, but perhaps most significantly with Suppé **[1262]** and Richard Genée in Vienna and with Léo Delibes **[1344]** in Paris. In 1882 he returned to Chicago and entered a business career. But marriage gave him affluence and leisure to devote his time wholly to music. In 1887 his first operetta, *The Begum*, was performed in New York. Though it boasted characters named Howja-Dhu and Myhnt-Juleep, it failed to catch on, though it did rather well in Chicago, where De Koven was Somebody. In 1889 he began his career as a reviewer with the *Evening Post* and had his *Don Quixote* accepted by the touring Boston Ideal Opera Company, popularly known as "The Bostonians." It did not do very well and was quickly dropped. Meanwhile, noth-

ing daunted, De Koven and his librettist Harry B. Smith produced *Robin Hood* successfully in Chicago in June 1890. The Bostonians gingerly took it up and gave it a production that cost $109.50. By the time they got it to Broadway in 1891, it had become an enormous hit and the staging was improved commensurately. ("O Promise Me," one of De Koven's many independent songs, had been a last-minute addition.)

So successful was *Robin Hood* that De Koven need never have written another operetta. As a matter of fact, he wrote more than twenty, most of them disasters. Unlike his exact contemporary Victor Herbert **[1513]**, De Koven was cold and humorless, and neither his fragile lyric talent nor his lack of dramatic sense could overcome the flaws of his libretti. In 1902 he fulfilled another ambition by founding his own symphony orchestra, the Washington (D.C.) Philharmonic, which survived for two seasons. He abandoned operetta in 1913 but shortly afterward embarked on a "grand opera," *The Canterbury Pilgrims*, which was duly premiered at the Metropolitan Opera in the spring of 1917. Its modest virtues were not enhanced by having imported Germans sing the important roles of Chaucer and the Wife of Bath (the libretto was Percy Mackaye's adaptation of his own play); a month later America entered the war, the Germans were sent home, and the opera abandoned. The "folk opera" *Rip van Winkle* (book also by Mackaye) made even less impact in Chicago in 1920, where the cast was largely Russian and French. De Koven died two weeks after it opened.

RECORDINGS: De Koven is memorialized on older records by excerpts from *Robin Hood* and a few songs.

[1516] MASCHERONI, Edoardo (Màs-ker-ō'-nē, Ed-ō-är'-dō)
CONDUCTOR, WRITER
BORN: Milan, September 4, 1859
DIED: Ghirla, March 4, 1941

Edoardo Mascheroni was the younger of two musical brothers. (Angelo [1855–1905] was a successful conductor who is remembered for a much-recorded song, *"Eternamente,"* often sung in English as "For All Eternity.") Edoardo came late to music. Having studied mathematics, he helped found an avant-garde literary magazine, *La vita nuova (The New Life)*, in Milan. Urged by his friends to cultivate his obvious musical leanings, he studied with a local choir director named Boucheron. He made his conducting debut in 1880 and four years later was conductor at the Teatro Apollo in Rome, where two years later, incredible as it may seem, he led the Italian premiere of Beethoven's [1063] *Fidelio*. He became particularly well known as a Wagnerian conductor and conducted a number of local first performances of the Wagner operas in Italy. After the death of Franco Faccio, Verdi [1232] chose Mascheroni to lead the initial performance of *Falstaff* and set great store by him afterward. He conducted at La Scala for a few years thereafter, then devoted his time to free-lancing and to composition. A memorial *Requiem* to united Italy's first king, Victor Emanuel II, brought him a commission from the royal family for another for its private use. Mascheroni conducted a number of operatic premieres of ephemeral works but got no support from the post-Verdian establishment and retired at sixty-five. Among his other compositions were 2 fairly successful operas: *Lorenza*, 1901, and *La Perugina*, 1909. RECORDINGS: *Lorenza* drew a few recordings in its day.

[1517] IPPOLITOV-IVANOV, Mikhail Mikhailovich (Ip-pō'-lē-tof Ē-vä'-nof, Mē-kil' Mē-ki-lō'-vich)
TEACHER, CONDUCTOR, ETHNOMUSICOLOGIST
BORN: Gatchina, November 19, 1859
DIED: Moscow, January 28, 1935

The son of a mechanic who worked at an imperial palace near St. Petersburg, Mikhail Mikhailovich Ivanov understandably appropriated his mother's family name, Ippolitov, so as not to be mistaken for the critic-composer Mikhail Mikhailovich Ivanov [1446]. As a child he studied the violin and sang as a chorister. He entered the St. Petersburg Conservatory in 1875 and studied there under Rimsky-Korsakov [1416]. On graduating in 1882 he went to Tbilisi (formerly Tiflis) in Georgia as director of the conservatory and served as such for a decade. During that time he became interested in the local ethnic music, collected many melodies, and later wrote authoritatively on the music of the region. In 1893 he accepted a professorship at the Moscow Conservatory. When the dictatorial and unpopular Vassily Safonov left in 1905 to head the New York Philharmonic, Ippolitov-Ivanov succeeded him as director. He managed to weather the Bolshevik Revolution but not the factionalism in the school that ensued, and he resigned his post on grounds of ill health in 1922. Though he continued to hold his professorship, he returned to Tbilisi to teach in 1924–25. From 1899 until the 1917 Revolution, he

had been an important and influential conductor at Savva Mamontov's "private" opera house in Moscow and then at its successor run by Sergei Zimin. In 1925 he became a conductor at the Bolshoi Theater. (He was married to an operatic singer, Varvara Zarudnaya.) In his latter years as a composer, he attempted to hew to the Soviet line, whatever it may have been: the official watchdogs alternately accused him of being too old-fashioned and praised him for "preserving the true Russian values" (i.e., those of the previous century). He wrote 6 operas —most of them, like much of his other music, on Near Eastern themes—and the last three acts for Mussorgsky's [1369] unfinished *The Marriage*. He also produced orchestral, choral, and chamber pieces, and an autobiography. RECORDINGS: He continues to live on records chiefly through his popular orchestral *Caucasian Sketches* (many versions), though there are recordings of a few other works, including an *Armenian Rhapsody*, the hybrid *The Marriage*, and the 1927 orchestral *From the Songs of Ossian*, based on supposed Celtic legendry.

[1518] LIAPUNOV, Sergei Mikhailovich (Lyà-pōō'-nof, Sâr'-gā Mē-ki-lō'-vich)
PIANIST, EDUCATOR, CONDUCTOR, ETHNOMUSICOLOGIST
BORN: Yaroslavl, November 30, 1859
DIED: Paris, November 8, 1924

Born 150 miles northeast of Moscow into the family of a school director, Liapunov evinced musicality early and was taught piano by his mother. At fourteen he entered the *Gymnasium* at Nizhni-Novgorod. Nicolas Rubinstein heard him perform and steered him to the Moscow Conservatory in 1878. He studied with Karl Klindworth (1830–1916), Tchaikovsky [1377], and Sergei Taneyev [1492], but finding the Germanic diet too suety, he left in 1884. After teaching for a while, he moved to the capital and became a disciple of and acolyte to Balakirev [1348]. In 1893 they, together with Liadov [1485], went gathering folksongs at the behest of the Imperial Geographical Institute. Liapunov later published two volumes of his own arrangements. A year later he took over the ailing Rimsky-Korsakov's [1416] post as assistant director of the imperial chapel. In 1902 he resigned to serve as an official of the Elena School and, from 1905 to 1911, as director of the Balakirev-founded Free School. From 1910 until the Revolution he taught at the conservatory. He also occasionally toured as conductor and virtuoso pianist. Liapunov discovered that he did not see eye to eye with the Soviets and defected to the West. In his last year he ran a music school for Russian *emigrés* in Paris. The bulk of his compositions consists of piano pieces and songs, though he left concerti (2 for piano, 1 for violin), symphonic poems (including one called *Hashish),* and other orchestral works. His music is a mix of folksong, Balakirev, and nineteenth-century virtuosity (notably Liszt's [1218]). RECORDINGS: There are recordings of the second piano concerto (Alexander Bakhchiev) the *Rhapsody on Ukrainian Themes* for piano and orchestra (Michael Ponti), Symphony No. 1 (Alexander Gauk), Symphony No. 2 (Yevgeny Svetlanov), and the very Lisztian *12 Transcendental Etudes* (Louis Kentner).

[1519] STATKOWSKI, Roman (Stȧt-kōv′-ski, Rō′-mȧn)
LAWYER, TEACHER
BORN: Szczypiórna, December 24, 1859 (?)
DIED: Warsaw, November 12, 1925

Statkowski was born in what is now central Poland. (Other sources give the date as January 5, 1859 or 1860). He went to Warsaw to take a law degree at the university, had lessons with Żeleński [1353], and then became a student at the Conservatory in St. Petersburg, under Anton Rubinstein [1309], among others. From 1890 to 1904 he taught in Kiev. In 1903 and 1905, respectively, his operas *Filenis* and *Maria* won international competitions. In between, he was invited back to Warsaw to teach at the conservatory. He left some orchestral pieces, 6 string quartets, and a good deal of piano music, generally progressive by contemporary Russian and German standards. RECORDINGS: *Maria* remains in the Polish repertoire and has drawn a few recordings of excerpts.

[1520] FOERSTER, Josef Bohuslav (För′-ster, Yō′-sef Bō′-hoos-lav)
ORGANIST, CHOIRMASTER, TEACHER, WRITER
BORN: Prague, December 30, 1859
DIED: Nový Vestec, May 29, 1951

J. B. Foerster is one of the most interesting of the Czech postromantics and one of the least known outside of Czechoslovakia. One might guess that such neglect has to do with his insistence on the close relationship between words and music, but such an attitude has not seriously hampered Janáček's [1478] acceptance. Foerster's father, Josef, was a composer and theorist who played the organ

and directed the choir at St. Vitus's Cathedral and taught at the Prague Conservatory. The son was educated in Prague at the Modern School, the Polytechnic Institute, and the Organ School. When Foerster was eighteen, he lost his mother, to whom he had been very close. On graduating in 1882 he succeeded Dvořák as organist at St. Vojtěch's (some accounts say he succeeded his Uncle Antonín at St. Adalbert's). He taught at two suburban *Gymnasiums* and held a deputy professorship at the Organ School. In 1888 he married a nineteen-year-old soprano, Berta Lauterová (known to record collectors as "Berthe Foerster-Lauterer"), who made her debut that year at the National Theater as Agathe in Weber's [1124] *Freischütz.* Shortly afterward, Foerster became choir director at Our Lady of the Snows. He was also critic for *Národní listy.* In 1892, on the death of his sister Marie, he wrote his second symphony in her memory.

The year 1893 was a banner year for the Foersters. It saw the premiere not only of Josef's second symphony but also of his first opera, *Deborah,* at the National Theater. Then Berta won a contract from the Hamburg State Opera, and the couple moved to that city, where they began a close friendship with the current opera director, Gustav Mahler [1525]. Josef taught at the conservatory and reviewed both for the *Hamburger Nachrichten* and his hometown journal. In 1897 Mahler became director of the Hofoper in Vienna, to which he summoned Berta in 1902. Josef of course went along and continued his career as teacher at the Neues Conservatorium and as reviewer for *Die Zeit.* A son was born to the couple in 1906, and Berta retired seven or eight years later. In 1918 Josef mourned the death of his brother in a cantata, *Mortuis fratribus.* Shortly afterward his newly independent homeland summoned him to serve as professor of composition at the Prague Conservatory. In 1921 his son died and was memorialized in the third piano trio. The next year Foerster transferred to the faculty of the graduate school. He retired in 1931 but served as president of the Academy until the onset of World War II. Berta died in 1936, and he later married Olga Dostálová-Hilkenová. Foerster not only survived the horrors of the war years but continued to compose and teach until he died at ninety-one. He was named a National Artist in 1945.

Foerster's musical language was in line of descent from that of the great Czech nationalists of the previous generation. Though it speaks with a personal accent, it was largely unaffected by the trends of the modernists.

Foerster developed into a mystic optimist who saw God and Music as the chief manifestations of the Good. He is perhaps at his most individual in his choral music, which includes 4 Masses, a *Stabat Mater*, an oratorio, and 6 cantatas. He wrote the libretti for four of his 6 operas and texts for many of his songs. He also wrote incidental music for many standard plays, 5 symphonies, 2 violin concerti, a concerto for cello, symphonic poems, suites, and overtures, 4 string quartets, 3 piano trios, violin and cello sonatas, and many small works.

RECORDINGS: Foerster has been fairly well represented on Czech records, including early examples from which he may be heard playing accompaniments to his songs and melodramas. Among the important works on modern discs are the fourth or "Easter" symphony (Václav Smetáček), the orchestral *Cyrano de Bergerac* (Břetislav Bacala), the cantata *May* (Zdeněk Košler), the 2 piano trios (Foerster Trio), and the Op. 95 wind quintet (Boehm Quintet). There was an early LP on Supraphon containing the symphonic song cycle *Clear Morning* (Zbyněk Vostřák conducting), the Concerto No. 2 for Violin, and the *Capriccio* for flute and orchestra (Václav Jiráček conducting). Berta Foerster made a few now very rare recordings in 1903 for the Gramaphone and Typewriter Company, all but two with tenor Leo Slezak and/or alto Hermine Kittel.

[1521] WOLF, Hugo Filipp Jakob (Vulf, Hōō'-gō Fē-lēp' Yä'-kōp)
CRITIC
BORN: Windischgraz, March 13, 1860
DIED: Vienna, February 22, 1903

Hugo Wolf was the last and perhaps the greatest of the nineteenth-century *Lied* composers. He composed little other than songs, but each of those produced in his too brief maturity was a carefully wrought and sometimes almost uncanny rendering of the lyric on which it was based. Wolf's Styrian birthplace is now the Yugoslav village of Slovenj Gradec. He was the fourth of eight children, of whom the next, Gilbert, was also musical. The father Philipp had desperately wanted to be a musician but was saddled with running the family tannery, which, along with his home, burned or was torched when Hugo was seven. Thereafter things were never really financially easy for the Wolfs.

Philipp Wolf, who had picked up reasonable proficiency on a number of instruments, insisted on teaching his children to play at least one. Hugo got the basics in piano and violin and mastered the Jew's-harp himself.

He then continued with a couple of local musicians, while he got his primary academic training in the village school. At ten he was sent off to *Gymnasium* in Graz. Within the year he flunked out, and by 1875 he had acquired similar distinction at two other schools. That September his father packed him off to Vienna to live with an aunt and attend the Vienna Conservatory—the thing he had been angling for all along.

Wolf was even then regarded as an oddball. Moody and sensitive, whimsical and pigheaded, he was given to almost obsessive enthusiasms and towering rages. The teacher with whom he seems to have gotten along best at the conservatory was Robert Fuchs, whose harmony instruction he shared with his coeval Gustav Mahler [1525], with whom he was briefly to room a few years later. He was sucked into the Wagner [1230] worship (with all the tics that implies) then rampant in Vienna, and when Wagner visited there late in the year, Wolf managed to get admitted to his hotel room to show him some of his compositions, which the master brushed aside. The following year Hugo took quarters of his own, which he soon found too confining or too noisy or otherwise oppressive to his sensibilities, and so moved to new ones. This nomadic pattern accounted for more than a score of addresses over the next forty-odd months. Something else that got on his nerves was his teachers at the conservatory, and he behaved so high-handedly that in the spring of 1877 he was thrown out and told not to come back. After some months at home, he got permission to return to Vienna and seek his fortune. He had already had some pupils and played some dance jobs, but he never managed to build up sufficient clientele to make a go of it and survived largely on the generosity of friends and money from his father. Having tried his compositional hand unsuccessfully at various large projects, he was now concentrating mostly on songs but was having no success in getting them published. Though as a devout Wagnerite he loathed everything Brahms [1329] stood for, he visited him in 1878. Brahms told him his work was immature and suggested a teacher, which reaction added more fuel to Wolf's hatred of him.

That same year Wolf fell painfully in love with Vally Franck, who lived in an apartment atop the home of his friend and patron Adalbert von Goldschmidt. One of the first fruits of what was to be a stormy relationship was one of those bursts of songwriting that were to become so characteristic of the composer. During this same period—though no one now knows when, where, or from whom—Wolf acquired the syphilis that would incapacitate and eventually kill him. But he spent a happy summer in 1880 in the village of Maierling working on his quartet; he was to try to reduplicate it again until the 1889 suicide of the crown prince there caused the emperor to destroy much of the place. The following February Vally, then in Provence, wrote him that she was through, plunging him into a depression that temporarily halted his creativity. (When a friend later brought the pair together again without warning Wolf, he fled without a word.) In the autumn of 1881, through Goldschmidt's influence, Wolf was hired as choral director at the Salzburg Opera under Karl Muck (only six months older than he was). Shortly after he got there, he was promoted to vice-*Kapellmeister,* but by the first of the year he had talked himself out of the post, seeing a conspiracy to keep him mired in operetta rehearsals. He then apparently bowed for a few months to the military duty which had been several times postponed but was back in Vienna (and then Maierling) in the spring. His total and overwhelming conversion to Wagner came with his visit to Bayreuth that summer to hear the new *Parsifal,* though he was unable to see his idol face to face.

In early 1884 Wolf, unable to make ends meet with his other musical pursuits, became a reviewer for the *Wiener Salonblatt,* a weekly journal of limited but prestigious circulation. He wrote for it until 1887, thumping the tub for his favorites (Wagner, Liszt [1218], Berlioz [1175], Weber [1124], and Meyerbeer [1142]), proclaiming the virtues of the great German Classicists, and attacking his pet hates (Brahms in particular and Italian opera in general). He found two generous and more than tolerant friends in the Köchert brothers, Theodor and Heinrich, court jewellers, and the other great love of his life in the latter's wife Melanie. In 1885 the Rosé String Quartet, led by the concertmaster of the Philharmonic, rejected the quartet. The following year the orchestra, after a perfunctory runthrough led by Hans Richter, who had seemed friendly until then, rejected the symphonic poem *Penthesilea.* Wolf was angry and disappointed, but it was perhaps just these reactions that spurred the first series of great songs, the settings of poems by Joseph von Eichendorff, written from December 1886 to March 1887, at about which latter date he gave up his post with the *Salonblatt,* presumably to devote his time to composition. In May he was summoned home just in time to have his father (of whose illness he had not been told) die in his arms.

Oddly at this point Wolf's fortunes took a change for the better. A friend backed publication by a small press of a dozen songs. The possibility of becoming known and accepted, however small, triggered in Wolf one of the most incredible periods of first-class creativity in the history of music. In January 1888 he moved into the unheated, waterless summer home of his friends the Werners in Perchtoldsdorf and, despite the discomfort, began almost obsessively setting poems by Eduard Mörike, a half-forgotten Swabian parson. He completed forty-three before leaving for the summer (during which he wrote the final thirteen songs to Eichendorff texts, mostly at a villa near Salzburg), and by mid-October he had added eleven more Mörike settings. Returning to Vienna toward the end of the month, he turned to Goethe's poetry and had finished all but one of the fifty *Goethe-Lieder* by spring. After a pause to breathe, he plunged in October 1889 into translations of Spanish poems by Emanuel Geibel and Paul Heyse (later a Nobel laureate), and by the end of April he had written all forty-four songs of the *Spanisches Liederbuch.*

By now Wolf had acquired a number of effective champions—Joseph Schalk, brother of the future director of the Vienna State Opera and director of the Wagner Verein; Ferdinand Jäger, a Bayreuth tenor; Elizabeth Fairchild, an American who helped finance publication—and as a result he was beginning to be heard and even bought. In 1890 Schalk published an admiring article that attracted widespread interest, and Engelbert Humperdinck [1480], then a reader for the publisher Schott in Mainz, recommended that his firm should take over Wolf's output. All was not roses, however. Members of the Wagner Verein, resentful of Schalk's and Jäger's promotion of their protégé within the association, countered with calumnies and efforts to dislodge their director. Most of the critics, being of the Brahmsian faction, effectively blocked public performances. And Wolf himself, with his almost maniacal insistence on perfection, made things very difficult for his publishers.

In the late spring of 1890 Wolf produced six settings of the Swiss poet Gottfried Keller and in the fall began the first volume of the Heyse *Italienisches Liederbuch,* which, however, he did not complete until the end of the following year. In the meantime he occupied himself with orchestrating and arranging some of his older songs and contemplated possibilities for an opera, among which were Shakespeare's *The Tempest,* the story of Pocahontas, and Pedro de Alarçon's *El Sombrero de tres picos.* The chief interruption, however, was a tour of Germany in October and November, during which he met his publishers and many other well-wishers, including Humperdinck, the poet Detlev von Lielienkron, Felix Weingartner [1552], the singer Eugen Gura, and Emil Kauffmann, director of music at the University of Tübingen. Back in Vienna he set about to fulfill a commission from the Burgtheater for music for Ibsen's *The Festival at Solhaug,* which task he came to detest and which was indeed not wholly completed. (Years earlier he had abandoned writing music for Kleist's *Der Prinz von Homburg.)* In the spring he made another visit to Germany which ended in a bad emotional and physical sag. Early the next year he went to Berlin for a concert, but the illness of the singers forced its postponement for several weeks. He returned to Vienna in March and collapsed again. For many months Wolf fooled around with plans for operas, dreamed of big self-promoting concerts in Berlin or Vienna, and produced nothing but the orchestration of the *Italian Serenade,* written for string quartet in 1887 (two other movements were left in fragmentary form). Early in January 1894 he and old Bruckner [1293] took the same train to Berlin to hear works of theirs performed by the Philharmonic under Siegfried Ochs. On the way home, Wolf met, at a concert of his songs in Darmstadt, a pretty young soprano named Frieda Zerny; they set out on an impromptu tour together, by the end of which they were deeply involved with each other. When he returned to Vienna, therefore, he was decidedly not happy to be met by the faithful and adoring Melanie Köchert and her understanding husband. Fräulein Zerny soon visited him in Vienna and sang his songs there. The emotional juggling act and his continued musical infertility began to tell on him, and he talked of emigrating to America, but by mid-June 1894 the affair seems effectively to have subsided.

Some years before, Rosa Mayreder, a friend and amateur poetess, had tried her hand at the Alarçon story in terms of a libretto. Wolf had at first sneered at it, but early in 1895 he suddenly decided it was what he had wanted all along and set furiously to writing what was to be his only completed opera, *Der Corregidor.* Friends supported him in his Perchtoldsdorf hideaway, and he wrote the whole work in fourteen weeks. By Christmas he had orchestrated it. There were nibbles for production from Berlin, Mannheim, Vienna, and Prague. While waiting, he returned once more to Perchtoldsdorf to complete the *Italienisches Liederbuch,* which work left

him ill and exhausted. Meanwhile Mannheim had scheduled the opera and rehearsals were going badly. Wolf's arrival there seems to have exacerbated matters. After several postponements the premiere occurred on June 7. It won applause but not the composer's, who behaved badly toward the performers. After a single repetition, it was dropped as unstageworthy. (Though the music does credit to Wolf, the judgment was probably correct.)

On his eventual return to Vienna in July 1896, Wolf at last settled in an apartment of his own. It was shortly afterward that his friend and patron Dr. Potpeschnigg accidentally recognized in his eyes the symptoms of incipient paresis. There would be a few more songs, including the final Michelangelo *Lieder,* but now Wolf was set on doing another opera. Frau Mayreder provided a libretto based on Alarçon's *Manuel Venegas* in May 1897, but it proved hopeless, and Wolf elicited another from his friend Moritz Hoernes, on which he immediately began work. Meanwhile Mahler, now director of the Imperial Opera, had evinced interest in *Der Corregidor,* but he and Wolf had had a violent run-in, leaving the latter seething. In mid-September Wolf became convinced that he himself had been appointed director and, rounding up some appalled friends, set off to turn Mahler out. Eventually they managed to lure the sick man into a private insane asylum in Vienna. After the first of the year he was well enough to be released, but in September he attempted suicide in the Traunsee, and begged to be reinstitutionalized. There were other remissions, but the decline was irreversible. Wolf became violent, then helpless, and finally died in convulsions shortly before his forty-third birthday. He was buried during *Fasching* in the Central Cemetery near Schubert [1153] and Beethoven [1063]. Melanie Köchert sank into a deep depression and a week after Wolf's forty-sixth birthday threw herself from a window.

RECORDINGS: Wolf's handful of orchestral and chamber works have been recorded, and there is a version of *Corregidor* from German wartime radio tapes. All the mature songs have been amply treated, and there are readings of what are probably the best of the juvenilia. The incidental music seems to have been ignored, and little of the choral music (in part song-arrangements) has been much dealt with.

[1522] REZNIČEK, Emil Nikolaus von
(Rez'-ni-chek, Ā'-mil Nē'-kō-lous fun)
CONDUCTOR, TEACHER

BORN: Vienna, May 4, 1860
DIED: Berlin, August 2, 1945

A prolific composer of operas, Rezniček shared his birthyear with Isaac Albéniz [1523], Mahler [1525], and Hugo Wolf [1521], and his chief teacher with Busoni [1577], Kienzl [1496], and Weingartner [1552]; yet he remains known only for a single lightweight overture. A law student at the University of Graz, he met and studied with Wilhelm Mayer, who operated under the anagram of W. A. Rémy and who also held a law degree. In 1881 he married Milka Thun, a relative of Weingartner's, gave up his legal studies, and enrolled at the Leipzig Conservatory. After three years he became a peripatetic theater conductor in Central Europe, finally settling down in 1888 as a military bandmaster in Prague. His first four operas were produced in that city, the last and most successful being *Donna Diana* of 1894, the overture of which is the one noted above. Two years later he became *Kapellmeister* at Weimar—a successor to Richard Strauss [1563]—and then in Mannheim. After three years in Wiesbaden, during which period he returned to opera writing with *Till Eulenspiegel,* premiered in January 1902, he moved to Berlin later in 1902, where he conducted and taught. In 1906 he began a three-year stint at the Warsaw Opera, then settled down in Berlin for good, conducting at the Komische Oper until it shut down in 1911. During his years on the podium, he had found little time for composition (the first two of his 4 symphonies were the chief products of the period), and in 1912 he decided to return to composition uninterrupted. He continued until the early 1930s—though he taught for a time at the Berlin Hochschule in the 1920s—turning out a dozen stage works, a *Requiem,* a jubilee *Mass,* a violin concerto, and 3 string quartets, among other things. RECORDINGS: He himself left recordings of the *Donna Diana* overture and of his *Comoedia* concert overture; there are also many modern recordings of the former. Robert Heger has recorded the orchestral *Theme and Variations,* and Jiří Stárek the *Serenade in G Major* for strings. Gordon Wright conducts the Symphony No. 3 and the Concerto for Violin, Michael Davis soloist.

[1523] ALBÉNIZ, Isaac Manuel Francisco (Ál-bā'-nēth, Ē'-zák Mán'-oo-el Fràn-thēs'-kō)
PIANIST, TEACHER
BORN: Camprodón, May 29, 1860
DIED: Cambô-les-Bains, May 18, 1909

Although Spanish music had, at least in the popular theaters, been showing some signs of life before he arrived on the scene, Isaac Albéniz was the first Iberian composer of modern times to become widely known outside his own country and to enter the international repertoire. It is not known whether he was related to earlier musical Albénizes [991]—he maintained, with typical panache, that his ancestry was Moorish. He was born in northeastern Catalonia, near the French border, where his father, Angel, was serving as a tax official. He showed alarming signs of musical precocity and studied the piano with his older sister, Clementine, with whom he, at the age of four, played his first concert, at the Teatro Romea in Barcelona. (Some of the audience insisted that he must be a midget.) Angel Albéniz, sensing that there was gold in those little fingers, thereupon began driving the boy unmercifully. When Isaac was six, his mother took him to Paris to study with Antoine-François Marmontel, but he was refused admission to the Paris Conservatoire because he was too young (and had moreover broken one of its windows playing ball while he waited to learn his fate). In 1869 the Albénizes moved to Madrid, where Isaac studied with teachers called Ajero and Mendizábal at the Madrid Conservatory. He was by then giving frequent concerts, which included such displays as sitting with his back to the keyboard and playing with the backs of his fingers.

Fed up with living under such pressure, Albéniz hopped a train out of Madrid when he was ten and for the next two years survived by his art and his wits. Eventually apprehended, he was sent home under police escort. But he stayed only long enough to collect up a change of clothes, ran off to Cádiz, and stowed away on a ship bound for the New World. When, far from land, he was discovered, the passengers chipped in to buy him a one-way ticket to Buenos Aires. There he courted starvation until someone who knew the ropes heard him playing in a café and arranged a concert tour of Brazil for him, which provided him with enough money to get to Cuba. But Spain (Cuba was still Spanish) had an all-points bulletin out on him, and he was immediately seized and taken to Havana where his father was now stationed. Angel shrugged his shoulders and let him go his way, which led to New York and further hard times. Eventually, however, he was booked for a concert tour that took him to San Francisco and sufficient affluence to buy passage home in 1873. But he did not stay: after a trip to England, he concertized his way to Leipzig, where he settled down to acquire mature knowledge at the Leipzig Conservatory under Reinecke [1292] and other. When his funds ran out at last, he went back to Madrid, where he drew the attention of Guillermo, Count Morphy, secretary to Alfonso XII, who procured him a royal scholarship

Albéniz' windfall took him to the Brussels Conservatory in 1877, where for that part of the next two years not occupied with concertizing in the Americas, he studied with Gevaert [1303] and the pianist Louis Brassin. Having acquired a piano first prize in 1879, he conceived the notion of studying with Liszt [1218], to whom he introduced himself in 1880 and whose footsteps he dogged for a time. Exactly what the "study" amounted to is apparently uncertain. At any rate he was soon off to America again. In 1883 he returned to Barcelona, where he came under the spell of Felipe Pedrell [1384], who was to have a great influence on his composition. He also took up teaching, and though he did not enjoy teaching, it brought him a wife in his pupil Rosina Jordana. (They had a son and two daughters.) In 1885 they moved to Madrid, where Albéniz continued to teach. He had been composing prodigally since childhood, but Pedrell's nationalistic approach had given him a new impetus, and he had rejected most of his earlier output as catchpenny junk (which a good deal of it was). Feeling that he now had enough worthwhile material, he essayed an all-Albéniz concert in Paris with heartening results. Pausing there to study briefly with Dukas [1574] and d'Indy [1462], he moved on to London in 1890. At a London concert he attracted the attention of a poetaster and important banker appropriately named Francis Burdett Money-Coutts, who offered to support him if he would remain in London and devote his time to composing operas to his (Money-Coutts's) libretti. Albéniz agreed and gave up his concert career. (Photos of the period show him pince-nez'ed, bearded, mustachioed, cigar puffing, and so fat that he can barely reach the keyboard, so perhaps it was just as well.) But the commission was not successful. Albéniz *did* stage an opera— *The Magic Opal,* 1893—in London, but the book was by Arthur Law. Money-Coutts had his heart set on an Arthurian cycle à la Wagner [1230], an approach wholly alien to Albéniz' temperament. He managed to complete the vocal score of *Merlin* and did some work on *Lancelot,* but neither was ever produced, and he suffered guilt pangs for his failure to do so for the rest of his life. The only ripe fruits of the collaboration were *Enrico Clifford* and *Pepita Jiménez* (the latter

successful), produced in Barcelona in 1895 and 1896 respectively.

Meanwhile in 1893 Albéniz and his family settled in Paris for a decade, where he became an important part of the musical life. (It was he who, without the composer's knowledge, had Chausson's [1484] *Poème* published.) In 1894 his zarzuela *San Antonio de la Flórida* appeared. But by 1898 his health was beginning to go bad, and he was found to be suffering from Bright's disease. In 1903 he moved to Nice, where he spent his last years working on what was to be his monument, the four books of *Iberia,* one of the great musical evocations of Spain, for piano. He completed it in the beginning of 1909, before moving to a spa in the Basses Pyrénées, where death overtook him eleven days before his forty-ninth birthday. Several piano works, left unfinished at his death, were completed by Enrique Granados [1588] and Déodat de Sévérac [1644].

As a composer, who shows both the impact of Liszt and pioneering "impressionist" tendencies, Albéniz is best represented by his strongly nationalistic piano music from his two final decades.

RECORDINGS: The best of his piano music has been recorded by innumerable great pianists (Rena Kyriakou has surveyed the whole output on ten LPs). As for the stage works, except for an intermezzo from *Pepita Jimenez,* there seems to be no representation on records. Felicja Blumental has recorded the sole piano concerto (other concerted works survive only in piano transcriptions), and there are recordings of a few of the songs. There are also many recordings of the orchestral transcriptions of Fernández Arbós (1863–1939). Guitar music has been recorded by Julian Bream and others.

[1524] CHARPENTIER, Gustave (Shärpon-tyä', Güs-táv')
BORN: Dieuze, June 25, 1860
DIED: Paris, February 18, 1956

Gustave Charpentier's name and fame rests almost solely on a single work, his 1900 opera *Louise,* which has proved remarkably hardy despite its denigration by the intellectual progressives over the years. Born in a village between Metz and Strasbourg, Charpentier was the son of a musical baker, who provided him with some rudimentary training. (A younger brother, Victor, became a cellist and conductor.) The German invasion of 1870 uprooted the family, and when the dust settled, so did they, in Tourcoing near Lille. There the fifteen-year-old Gustave was employed in a factory, where he worked his way up to an accountancy. Meanwhile he studied clarinet and violin and was so successful at passing his mastery of the latter on to his employer that the employer paid for his full-time training at the local conservatory. Later a subscription gotten up by his fellow citizens took him to Paris, where he settled (permanently, it turned out) in the bohemian quarter in Montmartre. He adopted bohemianism as a matter of faith and so irritated his Conservatoire violin teacher, Lambert-Joseph Massart (a Rodolphe Kreutzer pupil), that he was ejected. He returned to study with Pessard [1408], left again for military service, and finally came back in 1885 to study with Massenet [1396]. Two years later he carried off the Grand Prix de Rome.

Loath to give up his beloved Paris, Charpentier kept making unauthorized returns but eventually met his Roman commitments. The pressure seems to have been good for him, for—as he was wont not to do later on—he completed the work he undertook, chiefly the orchestral suite *Impressions d'Italie* (probably modeled on Massenet's series of *Scènes),* and a choral-orchestral effusion, *La Vie du poète (The Life of a Poet),* about which more later. After his return to Montmartre, he produced another orchestral suite (which was accidentally burned up), several sets of songs, and some further choral-dramatic experiments: *Sérénade à Watteau* and *La Couronnement de la Muse (The Coronation of the Muse).* He also worked on *Louise,* the beginnings of which are obscure. It was reportedly begun in Rome, but the poet Max Jacob says that the scenario was developed one night in his presence in a Paris bistro and that Paul Roux (alias Saint-Pol-Roux) had more than a little to do with the libretto, usually credited solely to the composer. The story is said to have been inspired by a Paris seamstress named Louise who was briefly Charpentier's mistress. Whatever the truth, the opera was a long time a-borning and seems to have undergone at least one complete rewriting. In the course of its growth, it incorporated *La Couronnement* as part of its third act, the titular heroine becoming the Muse.

Taken up by Albert Carré, the new director of the Opéra-Comique, *Louise* opened on February 2, 1900. Despite complaints about its "sordid realism" (Louise moves in with her lover), it was a solid hit. The title role was created by a debutante soprano, Marthe Rioton, who, shortly felled by illness, was replaced by another tyro, the Scotswoman Mary Garden, who became forever identified with the part. (Rioton retired to domesticity two years later.) Musically the work

owes something to Massenet, a little to Bruneau [1497], and perhaps a bit to Wagner [1230], but its success depends chiefly on its passionate evocation of the magic of Paris —though in 1900 Louise's exit from the paternal prison must have reverberated as loudly as had Nora Hellmer's in Ibsen's *A Doll House* twenty years before. And the impact of its depiction of the generational struggle is still powerful.

Charpentier quixotically practiced what he preached: in 1902 he opened his Conservatoire Populaire Mimi Pinson, which for more than thirty-five years offered free musical training to the seamstresses of Paris. In 1912 the composer succeeded his master, Massenet, in the Académie, and a year later the Opéra-Comique premiered his *Julien, ou La Vie du poète,* a sequel of sorts to *Louise,* based in part on the earlier work that shares its name. It was rather successful initially and was taken up by the Metropolitan Opera (with Caruso) a few months later, but it soon disappeared, apparently for good. And that for all practical purposes was the end of Charpentier's productive career. He fiddled interminably with his completed scores, and there was desultory talk of other operatic plans, of which nothing performable came. Dressed in his long-outmoded bohemian uniform, he hung around Montmartre as a sort of amiable museum piece, though in the last of his nearly ninety-six years he grew increasingly reclusive. In 1951 he conducted a slightly delayed fiftieth-anniversary celebration of his triumph in the square before Sacré-Coeur.

RECORDINGS: In 1936 Charpentier oversaw a film version of his masterpiece, starring Grace Moore, Georges Thill, and André Pernet, and a phonographic album of excerpts in which Ninon Vallin replaced Moore. But a complete recording—it is said the old man drove a hard bargain—had to wait until after his death, though there are now at least three. There are modern recordings of the *Impressions d'Italie,* which the composer also conducted for the microphone, together with the *Couronnement,* the early *Vie du poète,* and some orchestral songs.

[1525] MAHLER, Gustav (Mä'-ler, Goos'-täf)
CONDUCTOR, IMPRESARIO
BORN: Kalischt, Bohemia, July 7, 1860
DIED: Vienna, May 18, 1911

Mahler is a composer who should give heart to those creative artists who feel themselves neglected. Today his music is not only taken for granted as part of the standard repertoire but enjoys enormous popularity. However, it only began (very tentatively and in large part thanks to the efforts of his disciple Bruno Walter) to attain to such status around fifty years after the composer's premature death. Prior to that time Mahler was (except among a circle of devotees) shrugged off as "Wagnerian" [1230] or "Brucknerian" [1293], or dismissed as long-winded, disorganized, and "vulgar." Such attitudes were to a considerable degree born of unfamiliarity and a heritage from the influential enemies he made during his lifetime, not always on musical grounds.

Family background and birthplace notwithstanding, Mahler was an Austrian, and more specifically a Viennese, composer, a direct descendent of the "First Viennese School" inaugurated by Haydn [871], Schubert [1153], and Beethoven [1063]. If his music is full of Beethovenian aspiration, it is also characterized by melody and such popular dance rhythms as those of the *Ländler*. His forms of choice were the *Lied* and the symphony, both of which he often stretched to the breaking point. In fact he is generally regarded as representing the last blaze deriving from that century-old spark. But he is pivotal: it is just as easy to think of him as the forerunner of the "Second Viennese School." Mahler pushed tonality to where it tottered on the brink of the abyss. Moreover, though he frequently called for a super-Wagnerian orchestra that included odd instruments like mandolins and cowbells, his delicate scoring seems to look ahead toward the chamber groups of the Schoenbergians. Though Mahler did not always understand what they were up to, he supported that group with both financial and moral backing. With Schoenberg [1657], thirteen years his junior, there was a sort of father-son, love-hate relationship; but Alma Mahler (1879–1964), the composer's wife *(née* Schindler), says unequivocally that Mahler exerted an enormous influence on the younger man.

Mahler's birthplace was a village now called Kalište about sixty miles southeast of Prague. The composer was born to Jewish parents, the second of their fourteen progeny, seven years before the imperial government granted civil rights to such minorities. On the records he was listed as illegitimate, since the majority of Jewish marriages were not recognized. Though his parents seem to have adhered to their religion, far too much has been made of Mahler's Jewishness and his supposed guilt at having forsaken it, for there is little evidence that either concerned him very much (save for the Jewishness that

was thrust upon him by the virulent anti-Semites of the day). Religion aside, his father, Bernhard, was a man of brains, ambition, and violent temper. A few months after Gustav was born, Bernhard moved to the nearby town of Iglau (now Jihlava on the Bohemian-Moravian border), where he parlayed a distilling business into sufficient affluence to provide his family with a house and grounds and with middle-class respectability. He was a month short of his thirty-third birthday when his most notable son was born. His long-suffering wife, then twenty-three, was the frail, lame, timid Maria Hermann. Exactly half of their children did not survive infancy. Ernst, the third, died at fourteen, Leopoldine, the fourth, at twenty-six. The seventh, a boy, seems to have gone by several names; a scapegrace, he emigrated to Chicago where he worked as a baker. Justine, the eighth, long Gustav's housekeeper, and Emma, the thirteenth, married respectively the violinist Arnold Rosé and his brother, the cellist Eduard Rosé, and survived their famous sib by more than twenty years. The twelfth child, Otto, the only other one to show real musical talent, seemed on his way to a career as conductor and composer when he suddenly ended his life at the age of twenty-one.

Gustav Mahler himself appears to have taken notice of music from his cradle. His first instrument (when he was three) was a tiny accordion. Not long afterward his mother's father presented him with his own piano, and lessons with various local musicians followed. When the time was ripe, he became a choirboy in the neighborhood Catholic church and had harmony lessons from Herr Fischer, the choir director, who had encouraged his interests for years. The child was introspective and private, deriving his chief pleasures from the exercise of an imagination fueled by music and books. He is said to have written his first composition (a funeral march and polka!) when he was six, and he gave a piano recital in Iglau at ten. He also developed a taste for opera at the local theater, thanks to the offices of various teachers and well-wishers.

Before Mahler reached adolescence, he had tried teaching piano and found he could not tolerate his student's lack of talent and interest, a trait that marked his professional dealings all of his life. Nor did he take kindly to academic education. In fact his marks at the Iglau Gymnasium were so mediocre that in 1871 his father packed him off to Prague to study at a more demanding institution. He was housed with a large musical family named Grünfeld, one of whose sons, Alfred [1466], later became a notable pianist. But Gustav's marks did not improve, and he fared so badly in his new home that after a few months his father came and took him back to Iglau.

In the mid-1870s a local man of means, Gustav Schwarz, discovered Mahler's musical talent and was so impressed that he got him an audition in Vienna with Julius Epstein, friend of Brahms [1329] and professor of piano at the Vienna Conservatory. Bernhard Mahler had planned that his eldest surviving son would take over the family business, but Epstein convinced him that Gustav's was a talent that must be nurtured. Accordingly the youth, promising that he would attend to academic subjects sufficiently to acquire an equivalency certificate from the Gymnasium, entered the conservatory in the fall of 1875. He survived on an allowance sent by Bernhard and on the sometimes erratic payments of students directed to him by Epstein, who taught him piano. At that point Mahler supposed he would make his career as a performer on that instrument. He also studied harmony with Robert Fuchs and composition with one Franz Krenn (1816–97), who later taught him counterpoint. (Of Mahler's earliest compositions, which included starts on an opera and a symphony, only a piano-quartet movement has survived.) His closest friends among the students were Rudolf Krzyzanowski, Hugo Wolf [1521], Hans Rott, and Anton Krisper—all of whom later went mad and died insane. Even so early, Mahler already was known for his arrogance, impatience, puritanism, and fanatic perfectionism. Moreover he did not get along with the director, the anti-Jewish Joseph Hellmesberger the elder, and was in hot water more than once. For a while during these years Mahler committed himself with a certain passion to Wagner, vegetarianism, and socialism.

After a year in Vienna Mahler began taking some classes at the university. Initially he signed up for Anton Bruckner's harmony course. Mahler had apparently met the older man when he had been recommended to him to make a piano reduction of the latter's third symphony, with which Bruckner was delighted and which was published. The names of the two composers, as noted above, have been traditionally linked, but Mahler himself said that he was never Bruckner's pupil. Apparently he attended some of his lectures but did not complete the course as such. However, the two had a warm relationship, often walking to and from the university together and occasionally stopping off for a beer.

At the conservatory Mahler gradually abandoned plans for a pianistic career for one as a composer. In the summer of 1877 he managed to squeak through his Gymnasium examinations (having to repeat several of them) and obtained the certificate that enabled him to enroll formally at the university, where he read art history, literature, and philology. At the beginning of July 1878 he won his diploma from the conservatory, where, however, he had won no major prizes. He spent the next two years composing—in Vienna, at home, and with friends. In the summer of 1879 he fell in love with Josefa Poisl, daughter of the Iglau postmaster, who had come to him for lessons. Her interest quickly waned, however; and, after several months of increasingly passionate importunings, Mahler was told by the postmaster that any such union was impossible and that he should cease and desist. It was at this time that the musician began experimenting with various styles of facial foliage ranging from a rather luxuriant beard to a modest mustache. In the spring of 1880 he resumed his studies at the university, but soon decided that it was time to embark on a career and accepted a post as conductor at a summer operetta theater at Hall (or Bad Hall), a few miles southwest of Linz. The theater was little more than a shed (it now houses poultry), the company was tiny, the repertoire frivolous, and the salary minuscule, but after a month Mahler knew what he wanted to do with his life and began looking for a more permanent and promising post.

Meanwhile he had been planning an opera Rübezahl, for which he wrote a libretto that ended the friendship with Wolf, who claimed Mahler had stolen the idea. That work went no further, but in October he completed his first major work, the cantata Das klagende Lied (The Lamenting Song), based on a grim German folktale. He had high hopes for it, but twenty-one years passed before it was premiered, shorn of the first of its three sections, which Mahler had meanwhile decided was too much of a good thing.

The story of Mahler's next thirty years—the rest of his life—is primarily that of Mahler the conductor, composition being squeezed into summer vacations when possible. After Bad Hall, he, for reasons that are not clear, turned down a job at the Iglau Theater and returned to Vienna until the early fall of 1881, when he was hired as Kapellmeister of the district theater at Laibach (now Ljubljana, Yugoslavia). Then thoroughly provincial, it still had better facilities and more ambition than the Bad Hall house, including in its repertoire that year nearly a dozen operas along with the inevitable operettas. Though Mahler's efforts to impose high standards of performance did not sit well with some of the musicians, the public appreciated the improvement and gave him an ovation on his final evening. However, in April he returned to his humdrum existence in Vienna, summering in Iglau, until the second week in January 1883. At that point he was summoned to Olmütz (now Olomouc or Olomuč) in Moravia to replace the chief conductor of the municipal theater, who had left suddenly after a quarrel with the impresario. The appointment was something less than half a step up from that at Laibach in terms of prestige. Moreover accommodations were unsatisfactory, the theater was on the edge of bankruptcy, the critics were initially hostile, and Mahler was unhappy. Nevertheless he had a similar impact on the public there to what he had had in Laibach. However, he left in mid-March to fulfill an engagement as chorus master at the Carltheater in Vienna, which was putting on a short season of Italian opera featuring the Hungarian soprano Etelka Gerster.

The Olmütz engagement, however, bore unexpected fruit when the recommendation of an official of the Dresden Court Opera who had heard him there won him a three-year contract at Kassel after a week of tryouts in May. There that fall he took over the subordinate post of *Musikdirektor*, which introduced him to red tape he'd not dreamed of. He was also assigned, to his disappointment, most of the lightweight repertory, and the reviewers, though increasingly favorable, objected to his mannerisms on the podium. He might have left even sooner than he did, had he not fallen in love with a soprano named Johanna Richter, to whom he wrote poems that became the texts for the song cycle *Lieder eines fahrenden Gesellen (Songs of a Journeyman),* which he dedicated to her in 1885. There were other compensations in these years—e.g., a trip to Bayreuth to hear *Parsifal* in 1883, the summer after Wagner died, an opportunity in 1884 to hear Hans von Bülow [1310] conduct, which experience had an enormous impact on him. And there were occasional opportunities for him to conduct works that really interested him. But there were also unpleasant tasks. For example, in 1884 he had to compose music for a quasi-dramatic presentation of J. V. von Scheffel's popular *Der Trompeter von Säkkingen*—a work he detested and one which, set as an initially very successful if unoriginal opera by Viktor Nessler [1383], dogged his heels for years; he destroyed the score and parts after productions at Kassel and Wiesbaden. And at every turn he was called on the carpet for breaking petty rules and flouting hoary tradition. Even love did not make such things bearable, and by early 1885 he was sending out feelers in all directions. These bore fruit in a six-year engagement with the Leipzig Opera, to begin in 1886. Learning that his Kassel contract would be terminated as of September 1, 1885, because of his "insubordination," he tried to get the date moved up, and was in effect fired, though he was required to remain until July. In June, however, just as he had gotten used to the notion of a year of unemployment, he heard that Angelo Neumann at the German Opera in Prague wanted him immediately as co-*Kapellmeister* with Anton Seidl.

Neumann was an astute businessman who sensed that conductors in this post-Wagnerian world were about to have their day. Both he and Seidl were immediately taken with Mahler's effectiveness, and, along with the inevitable *Trompeter,* he was increasingly assigned major works, such as Mozart's [992] *Don Giovanni* and Beethoven's *Fidelio,* working up to uncut performances including the *Ring.* Substituting for Karl Muck at a concert in February 1886, he also conducted for the first time Beethoven's ninth symphony. On April 20 he led a benefit concert that included the first public performance of his own music—three of the *Lieder und Gesänge aus der Jugendzeit (Songs of Youth)* for voice and piano, sung by soprano Betty Frank, with whom he seems to have had a more successful affair than his previous ones.

Understandably Mahler was very happy at first and tried desperately to get out of his contract with Max Staegemann at Leipzig. But Staegemann and Neumann were mortal enemies and the former refused to budge. It was probably just as well, for inevitably Mahler overstepped his authority at Prague, Neumann tried to discipline him, there was a horrid row, and, one way or another, Neumann made it clear that his presence would not be required after this one season. Though he had had to take the usual critical sniping, the reviewers agreed when Mahler left that he was on his way up.

At the New Municipal Opera in Leipzig, a first-rank house, Mahler was subordinate to Artur Nikisch. In other words, under one roof Staegemann had perhaps two of the first great virtuoso conductors. Though the choice repertoire was divided between them (Mahler of course got the *Trompeter*), Mahler's worries about the rivalry seemed at first to be groundless, though certain pro-Nikisch reviewers made it clear that he was not welcome. However, when, contrary to his expectations, Mahler found that Nikisch would conduct the entire *Ring,* he threatened to resign and began once more to look for employment elsewhere. But that winter Nikisch was unexpectedly rendered *hors de combat* by a severe illness, and Mahler had the field to himself—onstage as well as in the pit, making small but radical changes in staging and presentation—and decided to stay on.

Nor was romance absent from his life in Leipzig. Staegemann had introduced him to Captain Karl von Weber, the grandson of Carl Maria [1124], who had succeeded in persuading him to complete that composer's comedy *Die drei Pintos*—at which task Meyerbeer [1142] and Franz Lachner [1171] had failed. While working on this project, he developed a passion for the captain's wife Marion to the degree that at one point he thought of eloping with her, but it soon cooled to a "platonic" relationship. During this time Mahler became acquainted with several important people in the musical world, including Richard Strauss [1563], Cosima Wagner, and Tchaikovsky [1377]. The opera, which was a success, brought him his first international fame and a lucrative contract for its publication that enabled him to send a thousand marks to his now ailing parents. Such success spurred him to further composition, and he began work on the official first symphony, the songs to texts from *Des Knaben Wunderhorn*, and the cantata *Totenfeier (Exequies)* that would become the basis for the second symphony.

The idyll, however, came to an end in May 1888. Mahler, feeling his authority challenged, had a violent quarrel with Albert Goldberg, the stage manager. Staegemann stood by Goldberg, and Mahler resigned. Neumann, who had been waiting for something like this to happen, invited him back to Prague to conduct some summer performances, but the two quarrelled over the staging of Peter Cornelius' [1294] *Der Barbier von Bagdad*, and Neumann summarily dismissed him. But once again luck was on his side: he literally ran into the famous cellist-composer David Popper [1411], who had come to Prague for *Die drei Pintos*, which encounter led directly to his being appointed director of the Royal Budapest Opera at an annual salary of 10,000 florins, plus expenses and four months of vacation.

The Royal Budapest Opera was ultramodern in terms of technical facilities and, in that day of nationalistic turmoil, ultra-Hungarian. It did not sit well with many in Budapest when they heard that the new director was (1.) an outsider, (2.) a Jew, and (3.) under thirty, and he was received with frigid hostility. Determined to give the Hungarians an institution they could be proud of, he be-

gan by decreeing that all performances would be in the national language; the critics hooted at the temerity of this German-speaking foreigner. Nothing daunted, Mahler set about imposing his kind of discipline on the company and by beginning to hire or bring in as guests first-line personnel. Many toes were, of course, bruised. He absented himself from the podium until late January 1889, when he felt his production of the first two operas of the *Ring* was ready. Despite a small stage fire on opening night and personal concern for his father's steadily declining health, the result was unqualified triumph on all fronts.

In mid-February Bernhard Mahler died, and Gustav was preoccupied with family problems for much of the spring. In the summer he himself underwent a painful hemorrhoidectomy from which recovery was slow. On top of this his mother began seriously to fail, his sister Leopoldine ("Poldi"), married and the mother of two children, began to manifest the first symptoms of a brain tumor, and his chief conductor Sándor Erkel (son of composer Ferenc Erkel [1214]) tried to resign to take a better job. The new season had barely gotten on track when Mahler was called to Iglau, where his mother was ostensibly dying. When she rallied, he returned to Budapest to learn that Poldi was dead. (Marie died two weeks later, and Mahler brought his sister Justi to live with him.)

Meanwhile Mahler had long since completed his first symphony, which Bülow had refused to conduct as "incomprehensible." Mahler himself led the Budapest Philharmonic in the premiere on November 20, 1889, presenting the piece, with the later-excised *"Blumine"* movement, as a symphonic poem. The audience sat on its hands; even Mahler's admirers among the critics had little good to say about it.

The honeymoon was now rapidly drawing to a close. Despite his efforts to adapt, Mahler felt himself increasingly a stranger in an alien land. And increasingly the natives were displeased with his failure to work miracles. The repertoire was too limited and too German; the ensemble was still wanting; there were too few star-quality singers; etc. Increasingly too the director clashed with the Hungarian singers, who showed their displeasure by sudden "indispositions," necessitating unsatisfactory cast changes and even the replacement of a scheduled work. At one point, two singers, unhappy at his tone of voice toward them during a rehearsal, walked out and threatened to challenge him to one or more duels. Guest appearances by the great Lilli Lehmann, the delight of Johannes Brahms [1329] at a performance of *Don Giovanni* (which he had been tricked into attending), and the first production outside of Italy of Mascagni's [1559] new *Cavalleria rusticana,* did little to stem the erosion. The breaking point came early in 1890 with the appointment of the super-patriot Count Zichy (a jackleg composer) as general administrator; Zichy immediately made it clear who would be the boss in the future and, after several run-ins with Mahler, bought up his contract in March for 20,000 florins.

There was no longer much likelihood that Mahler would find himself jobless: at thirty he was accepted as a proven conductor and impresario. He was immediately hired by the Hamburg Opera, another major house. Since 1874 it had been run by a former baritone named Bernhard Pohl, who had Italianized his surname to "Pollini." Pollini had the showmanly instincts of a Barnum: he knew what his public would buy and operated to meet the demand. He was sure Mahler would do that because Mahler was a star and Pollini believed in the star system (to the detriment of the rest of the company). Mahler made his debut with *Tannhäuser* and proved his employer right (though there had been no rehearsal). One who was knocked off his pins was the previously unapproachable Bülow, who now became the younger man's champion, though he continued to be appalled by his music. On a "guest" status Mahler had several more triumphs that spring, 1891, before taking a prolonged vacation that included a Scandinavian tour.

By the next season relations with Pollini were already beginning to grow abrasive—though Mahler was to spend seven seasons in Hamburg. In the course of the winter he turned again to composition and completed five more *Wunderhorn* songs, one of them later incorporated in the third symphony. In May he went to London (he had spent some months learning English) to conduct a short Wagnerian season at Covent Garden and Drury Lane, under the aegis of Sir Augustus Harris; it would give the city only its second opportunity to see and hear the *Ring.* (Many of the singers were from Mahler's own company.) The venture was enormously successful, but despite enticements from Harris, Mahler refused to give up his summers to do it again.

The opening of the 1892 Hamburg season was delayed because of an outbreak of cholera; the cautious Mahler hung back even after Pollini decided to get on with it and was threatened with a fine of almost a year's salary. On December 12, while Mahler was conducting an orchestral concert for the ailing Bülow in Hamburg, Amalie Joachim was premiering two of the new songs in Berlin; the press roasted him in the one instance for his gall in "imitating" a greater conductor, in the other for his "incoherence." The following summer was the first of several spent in virtual seclusion at Steinbach on the Attersee near Salzburg, where he was joined by his sisters Justi and Emma, his brother Otto, and Natalie Bauer-Lechner, a devoted friend and confidante since conservatory days. There he worked on more songs and on the earlier movements of the second symphony.

Back in Hamburg and recovered at last from the wounds of his Budapest experience, Mahler dared include six of the *Wunderhorn Lieder* and the symphony (now called "The Titan: A Symphonic Poem") in a Hamburg concert on October 27. The public responded warmly, even enthusiastically; the critics did not—nor did the songs go well when they were performed in Wiesbaden shortly afterward. Later that winter he introduced his public to Verdi's [1232] *Falstaff* and Smetana's [1291] *Bartered Bride.* In the course of preparing the latter, he established a friendship with the composer Josef Bohuslav Foerster [1520], through the latter's wife, the soprano Bertha Foerster-Lauterer. He also struck up a warm correspondence with Richard Strauss, then at Weimar. Mahler's contract was up for renewal and he was seriously considering moving on when Strauss announced that Pollini had invited him to Hamburg. When Pollini tendered Mahler a new contract that met all his demands, he signed it in the belief that he would be joined by his friend, only to discover that the whole Strauss business had been a red herring. A week later Bülow died in Egypt, where he had gone as a last expedient, and on February 26 Mahler, standing in for Strauss, who had finally declined, conducted a subscription concert in his memory, in the course of which the choir sang the "Resurrection" chorale, to a text by Friedrich Klopstock. Stymied for a finale to his second symphony, Mahler immediately recognized that this text was what he wanted. He set to work sketching the movement immediately, and completed the symphony the following summer. But before doing that he went to Weimar for a music festival that included the premieres of Strauss's *Guntram* and Humperdinck's [1480] *Hänsel und Gretel,* and the first local performance of his own *Titan,* which received a mixed reception and a bad press.

Mahler completed the new symphony at the end of June 1894 in the cabin he had had built at Steinbach to escape noise—an enemy that was responsible for his constant shifting of living quarters wherever he went. Following a visit to Brahms at Bad Ischl and a command appearance before Cosima Wagner in Bayreuth, he returned to Steinbach and completed the scoring. Back in Hamburg, he found a new rehearsal coach added to the staff, eighteen-year-old Bruno Schlesinger, who, as Bruno Walter, was to become his most devoted disciple, and in whom Mahler quickly learned to place his musical trust. That season Mahler inherited the subscription concerts from Bülow, which won him enemies in the local press. On March 4, 1895, thanks to Strauss, he conducted the Berlin Philharmonic in the first three movements of the second symphony. The public stayed away in droves, but the fragment that came was mostly enthusiastic. The critics again were less so, though they acknowledged the effectiveness of the orchestration. Mahler was further depressed by the outrageous reviews of his Hamburg concerts, which were having a deleterious impact on attendance. In the midst of all this, the feckless Otto, who, after living for years on his brother's generosity, had obtained a post in Leipzig with Staegemann, shot himself to death in a friend's apartment after a discussion of Dostoievski with her. Subsequently Gustav took both of his remaining sisters under his roof.

By the end of the season, he and Pollini were so at odds that Mahler tendered his resignation, of which action Pollini took no notice. The summer, apart from another visit to Brahms, was devoted to sketching out a new symphony. He returned to Hamburg to find a crisis in the company precipitated by the defection to America of a prima donna and her conductor-husband. The latter would be replaced eventually by Schlesinger-Walter, but for the moment Mahler had to do double duty on the podium. The crisis had another more personal effect on him. To replace the soprano, Pollini had brought in Anna von Mildenburg, a twenty-three-year-old student recommended by Rosa Papier of Vienna. She and Mahler met one day when she was rehearsing. She was at first terrified; he was mesmerized by the beauty of her voice. Immediately he assumed proprietorship over her career, and shortly he was passionately in love with her. She reciprocated, but she had a more permanent arrangement in mind and eventually her possessiveness cooled his ardor. Meanwhile he had decided to venture a complete performance of the second symphony in Berlin, which he would pay for himself. He conducted it, suffering from a blinding head-

ache, on December 13, 1895. This time the impact on the audience was overwhelming, and its members went out of the hall to spread the gospel despite the usual critical disapproval. As the season proceeded Pollini's declining health helped smooth Mahler's path, but the affair with Mildenburg kept him off balance. A follow-up concert in Berlin, including the local premiere of the *Titan,* was a financial disaster, leaving the composer deeply in debt.

In Hamburg matters were coming to a head. Walter was moving on at the end of the season and Pollini's death appeared imminent. Mahler began to look around for a new post and realized that his religious background was increasingly a hindrance. The summer added to his frustrations, for at Steinbach he found he had left his symphony behind and it was nearly a month before it caught up with him. Work went well, and he had the time to pay Brahms what turned out to be a final visit. By mid-July he had completed the vast first movement. By now he was hopeful of a position at the Vienna Imperial Opera, though he discovered that Cosima Wagner was one of those who was trying to insure that no such thing would happen. After his return to Hamburg, he found that Pollini was not only still alive but also apparently determined to make life unbearable for him there, giving him poor casts and inferior operas and preferring Mahler's conservatory chum Krzyzanowski, whom he had hired over the summer. However, in Berlin in November Nikisch conducted the second movement of the new symphony to wild applause and—*mirabile dictu!*—critical acclaim, and the piece was even more successful under Felix Weingartner's baton a month later. (Some reviewers began to have second thoughts about the earlier works.) As relations with Pollini deteriorated, the light began to brighten on the Vienna front. But early in 1897 he was told the company could never hire a Jew. Though he claimed to friends that he had turned Catholic in the Budapest years, he officially converted on February 23. In his defense it must be said that he had not practiced his father's religion since childhood and that his mysticism was as suited to Catholicism as to any other creed. Negotiations with Vienna, however, dragged on agonizingly, and it was not until April that he was appointed *Kapellmeister,* with the understanding that the directorship of the company would soon be his. He conducted for the last time in Hamburg on the twenty-sixth and arrived in Vienna the next day.

At this point, Mahler was one of five conductors. The most admired was Hans Richter. The others were J. N. Fuchs, brother of his old harmony professor; Pepi Hellmesberger, son of his old enemy; and Wilhelm Jahn, the nearly blind and retiring house director. Mahler's debut on May 11 was an unqualified success, even the powerful anti-Jewish press voicing approval. Shortly afterward he was felled by a severe throat infection that necessitated an operation and a subsequent unproductive convalescence in the mountains. However, his directorial appointment, which had faced many stumbling blocks, became assured *de facto* by August and was confirmed on September 8, Jahn having finally retired.

Mahler found himself in charge of a self-indulgent company in which trimming scores and humoring the "stars" was the order of the day. His ultimately successful efforts to change all this inevitably made him unpopular with company and public alike. (He also introduced such tyrannical innovations as refusing to admit latecomers during performances.) A considerable faction resented his getting a job they felt should have gone to dear old easygoing Richter. And when Mildenburg used Mme. Papier's influence to wangle her way into the company, it was whispered that Mahler had himself brought in his mistress—though by now the relationship was growing ever more distant as far as he was concerned. It was also held against him that he did not see fit to kowtow to Viennese high society and even went so far as to abolish the complimentary tickets traditionally available to dignitaries.

Mahler had one aim in mind: to make his the finest opera company in the world—and in his ten tempestuous seasons there he probably succeeded. He increased the emphasis on Mozart and Wagner (uncut)—and made the public like the latter, whose work it had previously tended to avoid. He introduced and made standard additional repertoire, both old (Lortzing **[1163]**, Smetana **[1291]**, Bizet **[1363]**, etc.) and new (Puccini **[1511]**, Leoncavallo **[1498]**, Richard Strauss, Pfitzner **[1606]**, Hugo Wolf, etc.). He brought in new singers—e.g., Leo Slezak, Marie Gutheil-Schoder, Selma Kurz—whose names would become legendary. He honed orchestral and choral performances to a razor edge. He presented operas as music *dramas*, abetted by carefully conceived and imaginative productions, thanks in considerable part to acquisition of specialists. In short he created the modern opera house.

During Mahler's first season in Vienna, his fellow Iglauan and university acquaintance Guido Adler, the musicologist, got him a grant to have the first three symphonies printed. (The third had recently been completed; in the spring of 1898 he also completed the revision of *Das klagende Lied.*) Despite conflicts on a personal level, he ended the season on an immense wave of popularity. In June his sister Emma left his household to marry Eduard Rosé and go to Boston. In August Richter, who was also conductor of the Vienna Philharmonic Concerts, received a leave of absence "for reasons of health," which became permanent when he decided to make his further career in England. At the request of the orchestra, Mahler took over the concerts in addition to his other duties. But this invitation represented only the will of the majority; a hostile minority took upon itself to make things as difficult as possible, in part through the anti-Jewish press, which was soon using every opportunity to attack him for whatever reason, sound or baseless. For better or worse, his own music was beginning to be played all over Europe, and in April 1899 he conducted the Vienna Philharmonic in his second symphony—an event that produced further attacks even before it came to pass. For all that, the performance was unexpectedly a triumph with the overflow audience. The reviews, however, were pretty much as usual.

For some time now, Mahler had been looking for a more satisfactory summer refuge. The spa at Aussee where he went in May was not it. Yet while there he wrote *"Revelge"* ("Reveille"), the penultimate *Wunderhorn* song, and then at white heat made such progress on the fourth symphony that he was able to finish it the following year. In late August he joined Justi and Natalie in Carinthia on the lake called the Wörthersee and was so enchanted that he made plans to build there even before he knew whether the land could be had. Mildenburg, who conveniently happened along, supplied the architect. By the following summer the cabin was completed and the villa was on its way. In the spring of 1900, Mahler spent Easter in Venice with Justi, Natalie, and Selma Kurz, his latest love interest. He ended the season with a few days of Italian opera (with Italian singers), an unsuccessful venture. In June under protest he took the Vienna Philharmonic to play at the Paris exposition, where he found himself billed as "M. Malheur" (disaster). The concerts were at least a *succès d'estime,* but the orchestra ran out of money and Mahler had to twist Baron Albert Rothschild's arm to provide it with trainfare home. He then hastened to his cabin and completed his symphony on August 5.

In the fall Mahler attracted considerable attention with a revival of the then neglected *Così fan tutte* of Mozart on a revolving stage, though more for the facility than the opera. He also won a battle with the opera administration that left him with almost free rein. He conducted a performance of the second symphony in Munich with enormous success (even with the critics) but had no such luck when he introduced the first to Vienna. Over Christmas and New Year's he got the fourth symphony ready for publication. In February he presented the much revised *Klagende Lied* for its first outing. The small audience liked it, the reviewers damned it as immature and unvocal.

Over a long period Mahler had had attacks of rectal bleeding, and a week after the premiere he suffered one so severe that he nearly died. Soon afterward he underwent a major operation, followed by a long convalescence, at first in a Viennese convalescent home and then at an Adriatic resort. His place in the Vienna Philharmonic concerts was filled by Hellmesberger and Franz Schalk, whom the newspapers praised to the skies. Using his health as an excuse, Mahler decided not to fight conditions there any longer, and the conductorship went to the innocuous Hellmesberger. For the summer Mahler went, as he would repeatedly to his now completed place at Maiernigg on the lake.

Whether it was the peace of the setting, his improving health, or freedom from the pressure of the orchestra, Mahler had in 1901 one of his most productive summers, completing the final *Wunderhorn* song, the five songs to texts by Friedrich Rückert, and the first two *Kindertotenlieder (Songs on the Death of Children).* (Contrary to the old story these obviously have nothing to do with the demise of his own children.) He also wrote two movements of the fifth symphony. In the fall Bruno Walter joined his staff to take the place of Fuchs, who had died two years earlier. After considerable dickering with Richard Strauss, who wanted to premiere either the third or the fourth symphony, Mahler himself presented the latter, played by Weingartner's Kaim Orchestra, to an uncomprehending Munich public, after which Weingartner played it on tour throughout Germany, equally puzzling most of his auditors.

Earlier that month, at a dinner party, Mahler had encountered a dazzlingly beautiful young woman of twenty-three, Alma Schindler, daughter of an important landscape painter who had died nine years earlier. As talented as she was beautiful, she had won the hearts of both her art teacher, Gustav Klimt, and her composition teacher, Alexander von Zemlinsky [1621]. When Mahler tried to dismiss her with sarcasm,

she stood up to him and showed him she had a mind to be reckoned with. He found himself drawn to her, despite the disparity between their ages. He sent her poems and candy and tickets to the opera. She soon found herself equally smitten, and there were passionate exchanges of letters. Two days before Christmas they announced their engagement. By February Alma was pregnant (she insists in her memoirs that Mahler was a virgin before their union), and they were married On March 9. The day after, Arnold Rosé and Justi, who had been fearing her brother's wrath in this matter for years, were also joined in holy matrimony. Mahler and Alma's honeymoon, such as it was, was a trip to St. Petersburg, where he had a conducting engagement.

It was an expectably odd marriage. Alma, bold and brassy toward Mahler when they were both single, found herself overawed by her husband. He turned his money over to her and told her to get rid of his mountain of debts. The old puritanical outlook persisted. There were few amenities; their life was Spartan. He forbade Alma any further composition and instructed her to avoid unpleasant matters in their conversation. She gave up, she says directly, will and self for him and his work, which was his sole concern. In this curious relationship Alma was not blameless. She disliked Mahler's friends and apparently drove them away, was highly intolerant of Justi, and suspected Mildenburg's every overture. On the other hand, she encouraged new acquaintances who clearly admired her—for example Pfitzner, who dedicated a string quartet to her, and the pianist Ossip Gabrilowitsch, who told her he was in love with her. And she drew Mahler into the circle of her painter-friends, members of the Art-Nouveau "Secession" movement. One of these was Alfred Roller, who sneered at the *Tristan* sets then in use and was hired by Mahler to design a new production, though he had never had anything to do with such matters before. Roller, who remained at the opera for thirty years, assumed enormous power there, became a tyrant, overspent his budget, and became one of the reasons for Mahler's eventual downfall.

Another was Mahler's ever more frequent guest-conducting engagements. As his music continued to gather more aficionados and stir more curiosity, he was in frequent demand. In the summer of 1902 he and Alma went to Krefeld to premiere the third symphony (at last) with the Gürzenich Orchestra of Cologne. He soon found such work more to his taste than the eternal struggle of putting on operas in Vienna, and the company began to fall into decline to the delight of his enemies, who were increasingly venomous in their criticism of him.

This situation—and doubtless Alma's staunch support—brought on a period of intense creativity. He completed the fifth symphony during the first summer of the marriage and scored it over the Christmas holidays, devoting four hours a day to the work. On November 3 Alma gave birth to the first of their two daughters; she was christened Maria after Mahler's mother but was called "Putzi." Anna (nicknamed "Guckerl") arrived on June 15, two years later, following which event her father completed the sixth symphony, begun the previous summer. Prophetically he also finished the *Kindertotenlieder*. And he began the seventh symphony, which he completed in the summer of 1905. He conducted the premieres of the three, respectively, at Cologne in 1905, Essen in 1906, and Prague in 1908; all for orchestra without voices, they are sometimes viewed as a sort of trilogy. Early in 1905 he unveiled the *Kindertotenlieder* and the *Songs from Rückert* at a concert in Vienna given by the Society of Composers. On the first day of his 1906 vacation, fearing loss of inspiration, he was suddenly struck by a memory of the medieval hymn *Veni creator spiritus (Come, Creating Spirit)*, which became the frame for the first movement of the vast eighth symphony; using the final scene of Goethe's *Faust* for the second, he completed in two months what may be the most magnificent failure in all music (its reach exceeds its grasp).

Then the hammer blow of fate depicted so graphically in the sixth symphony struck. In January 1907 a physical examination revealed a heart murmur, which news Mahler took fatalistically. At the opera Roller was reprimanded by the imperial chamberlain, Prince Montenuovo. Mahler defended Roller, the prince blamed Mahler's absences for severe box-office problems, and Mahler resigned on March 31. He was not only weary of the fight; he had lost interest and felt that repertoire opera had had its day. The following January he was succeeded by Weingartner. Emperor Franz Josef conferred a more than generous pension and other privileges on Mahler. But fate was not through. During a visit to Rome later in the spring of 1907, Alma developed a throat problem that required an operation. This had to be postponed, however, because on their return Guckerl came down with scarlet fever. When both were on the mend, the three of them went to their summer home, taking Putzi, who had been with Alma's mother. Three days later she too developed

scarlet fever complicated by diphtheria. It was a losing battle. Despite heroic measures taken, the child was dead in two weeks. Mahler, who had adored her, was inconsolable. Alma's mother came to be of what aid and comfort she might. When she saw the coffin being loaded into the hearse, she suffered a heart attack. She recovered but Alma was prostrated. A doctor was summoned. Mahler, to relieve the tension, suggested his heart be checked too. The physician complied, looked very grave, and urged him to see a specialist. The specialist told him that the streptococcal infection which had manifested itself in sore throats and abscesses over the years had attacked his heart. There were no wonder drugs in 1907, and Mahler knew what this meant. For a time all the life went out of him. The family left the Wörthersee forever and fled to the Tyrol, where the composer, when not resting or brooding, read from a collection of Chinese poems translated by Hans Bethge, which a friend had sent him. He had to return to the opera to prepare for Weingartner's takeover. He conducted *Fidelio* to a half-empty house on October 15; it was his last performance there.

Meanwhile he had signed a lucrative contract with Heinrich Conried to conduct at the Metropolitan Opera in New York. He bade farewell to the Imperial Opera on December 7 (someone ripped his message from the bulletin board and tore it to pieces) and set out with Alma two days later, leaving the surviving child with her grandmother. He found the Met at the height of perhaps its most authentic Golden Age, offering him a choice of some of the greatest singers in the world—and he had no longer to fight government flunkeys, make out budgets, and plan seasons. He debuted on New Year's Day, 1908, in *Tristan und Isolde* with Heinrich Knote and Olive Fremstad in the title roles. The other operas he conducted were *Don Giovanni, Die Walküre, Siegfried,* and *Fidelio,* all works for which he was famous. He did not even protest the standard cuts in the Wagner works and gave a greater semblance of sociability than he ever had before.

The Mahlers came home in May and summered in the Dolomites at a place called Toblach. At first Mahler did little but wait for the Grim Reaper to strike, as he was convinced he would. When that did not happen, he began to set some of Bethge's translations in what he insisted was an orchestral song cycle, which he tentatively called "The Jade Flute." (It was, in Mahlerian terms, a ninth symphony, but, recalling Beethoven and Bruckner, he did not dare tempt fate.)

He finished it the following summer but did not live to hear it performed. Back in New York in the fall, he found himself odd man out. The moribund Conried had stepped down to be replaced by Giulio Gatti-Casazza. Gatti had brought his own super-star in the person of Arturo Toscanini, who would play second cello to no one and who had demanded *Tristan* as his by divine right. Between January 13 and March 5 Mahler conducted *Le Nozze di Figaro, The Bartered Bride, The Queen of Spades,* and one last incandescent performance of *Tristan.* He also conducted three concerts of Walter Damrosch's **[1540]** New York Symphony. Even before his appearances at the opera, he was asked to take over the ailing New York Philharmonic the next season and do whatever it needed to make it again a major orchestra. Before setting sail for Europe, he made two guest appearances with it to get the feel of it.

In Europe that summer Mahler stopped by Paris to sit for Auguste Rodin's famous portrait bust, mended some fences, completed what had become *Das Lied von der Erde (The Song of the Earth),* and began the official ninth (actually, the tenth) symphony. Alma, a nervous wreck, went to a spa in the Trentino. Back in America once more, Mahler put together a much-revised orchestra and began his concert season on November 4. He conducted forty-six programs, including a Brooklyn series, and took the aggregation on a brief tour of the American Northeast. Only two of his own works—the first symphony and the *Kindertotenlieder*—were featured; they were not liked.

At Toblach in the summer of 1910, a long-building crisis came to a head. Alma, still ailing, entered a rest home. At a dance she met a young architect, Walter Gropius (whom she married in 1915). He fell madly in love with her. When she returned to Toblach in midsummer, he wrote her a passionate letter which by accident or intent he addressed to Mahler. When the latter in fury faced her with it, all her loneliness, sexual frustration, and self-sacrifice of the last nine years came pouring out. Mahler, who had never been made to look at himself before, was appalled at what he saw and horribly guilt-stricken. He even sought the advice of Sigmund Freud, who told him that Alma was seeking her lost father in him and that he had tried to turn her into his dead mother. Mahler, realizing that love was not a one-way street, did an about-face and did everything in his power to make it up to her, including encouraging her composing and promoting her songs.

On September 12 Mahler conducted the triumphant premiere of the eighth sym-

phony (with at least 1,000 performers). Accompanied by Alma and the little girl, he then returned to New York suffering from a recurrence of the old throat trouble. This year he was slated to present fifty-five programs. But problems again were growing. The public found his choice of music too "heavy." There was dissension in the orchestra, exacerbated by a self-appointed informer whom Mahler refused to discharge. The sore throat returned in December. The ladies of the board, in true American fashion, tried to dictate what he should play. Finally in early February the board took matters into its own hands, fired the offending musician, and in effect hamstrung the conductor. He fell ill again, and after the concert of February 21, 1911, gave up, turning the rest of the season over to Theodore Spiering, the concertmaster. The doctors found the infection general and dangerous. No remedies alleviated it. Alma sent for her mother, but eventually a nurse was also needed. Finally it was decided that the sick man must return to Europe, where bacteriology was more advanced. In Paris he seemed briefly better, but then relapsed and was placed in a nursing home. He grew steadily worse and was taken to Vienna, where he was put in the care of the most noted physician in the field, a Dr. Franz Chvostek. Chvostek soon saw that the case was hopeless. According to Alma, Mahler's last word was "Mozart." He died that night, May 18, at midnight during a thunderstorm, not yet fifty-one. His body lies in the Grinzing Cemetery beside his daughter's. Bruno Walter premiered the "song cycle" in a memorial concert on November 20 and the ninth symphony the following June. The late Deryck Cooke made two versions of the complete tenth symphony, of which Mahler left two movements *(Adagio* and *Purgatorio)* and many sketches.

RECORDINGS: As of 1950 there existed single recordings of the three song cycles, of the first, second, fourth, fifth, and ninth symphonies, and of some individual songs. Now it seems that every important conductor wants to leave for posterity his views on the ten symphonies; all of the Mahler canon has been repeatedly recorded, and there are even versions of *Die drei Pintos,* the piano-quartet movement, and Mahler's reorchestration and reworking of two of Bach's **[684]** orchestral suites into a single *Suite for Orchestra After J. S. Bach.*

[1526] FRANCHETTI, (Baron) Alberto
(Fràn-ket'-tē, Ál-bâr'-tō)
ADMINISTRATOR

BORN: Turin, September 18, 1860
DIED: Viareggio, August 4, 1942

The son of an old aristocratic family, Alberto Franchetti used his wealth to help assure him a success as an operatic composer that time has not fostered. He studied in Venice with Niccolò Coccon and then in Lucca with Puccini's [1511] maternal uncle, Fortunato Magi *(not* with Michele Puccini, Magi's predecessor as head of the local conservatory). Later, under the spell of Wagner [1230], Franchetti went to Dresden to become a pupil of Draeseke [1342] and finished off his training with Rheinberger [1368] in Munich. His first opera, the spectacular *Asrael,* was produced in Reggio Emilia in 1888 and impressed Verdi [1232], among others. Franchetti followed it with the even more successful *Cristoforo Colombo,* intended as a commemorative work and first staged in Genoa in 1892. Settling in Milan, Franchetti was regarded as one of the young rebels of the day (now usually improperly lumped as practitioners of *verismo).* During this period he got permission from the playwright Victorien Sardou to make an opera of his *La Tosca,* a project that Ricordi talked him out of in order to gain the piece for Puccini. In the meantime Franchetti had seen unsuccessful productions in Milan of his *Fior d'Alpe (Alpine Flower)* in 1894 and of *Il Signor di Pourceaugnac (M. de Pourceaugnac)* in 1897. In 1902 his career took an upward turn with *Germania,* produced at La Scala with an all-star cast that included Enrico Caruso, Mario Sammarco, and Amalia Pinto. *Germania* was taken up by other important theaters, including the Metropolitan Opera (with Caruso again, Emmy Destinn, and Pasquale Amato). La Scala gave *La Figlia di Iorio* similar treatment in 1906 but with considerably less success. After that Franchetti's reputation quickly faded: *Notte di leggenda (Fabulous Night),* 1915; *Giove a Pompei (Jove in Pompei),* a collaboration with Giordano [1589], 1921; and *Glauco,* 1922. These works made only small ripples, and after that there was silence. In 1926 Franchetti became director of the Florence Conservatory but left after two years. Besides the operas he wrote orchestral music (including a symphony), chamber works, and songs. RECORDINGS: In his heyday excerpts from his more successful operas were rather frequently recorded, by members of the original casts among others. More modern recordings of selections from *Cristoforo Colombo* and from *Germania* (pirated) suggest that Verdi's admiration was not wholly misplaced.

[1527] PADEREWSKI, Ignacy Jan (Pà-de-ref'-skē, Ig-nàt'-si Yàn)
PIANIST, STATESMAN
BORN: Kuryłówka, November 18, 1860
DIED: New York, June 29, 1941

For the rural American South of this writer's youth there was only one pianist, a foreign gentleman called "Patterooski," and Victrola shelves that did not contain at least one of his records marked the owner as a barbarian. The famous Burne-Jones portrait that shows a pale, handsome, and poetic face in an aureole of flame-colored hair explains part of the man's popularity; the unabashed and often wayward romanticism of his playing explains the rest of it.

Born in a village in Russian Poland *(The New Grove Dictionary* gives the date as November 6), Paderewski came from an educated and artistic family. His mother Polixena died while he was still in infancy. He had some piano lessons at home but was largely self-taught as a young pianist and would-be composer. At twelve he was sent to the Warsaw Conservatory, where he had a succession of piano teachers, none of whom seems to have been able to curb the bad habits he had acquired for himself. For the sake of the student orchestra, he was ordered to concentrate on the trombone. He finally blew up at the administration and was forthwith expelled. A disastrous tour in 1877 with a violinist made him rethink his position and get himself readmitted to the conservatory. He graduated the following year and was retained as a piano teacher. His first marriage, in 1880, to Antonina Korsakówna ended tragically the following year when she died bearing a son. Downhearted and discouraged that his career was failing to advance, he went to Berlin, where he studied first with Friedrich Kiel (1821–85) and then with Heinrich Urban (1837–1901). Much of Paderewski's piano music dates from this period. In 1884 he encountered the great Polish actress Helena Modjewska (actually Modrzejewska), who urged him to study with Theodor Leschetizky in Vienna and arranged a benefit concert to enable him to do so.

Leschetizky was so appalled at his would-be pupil's faulty playing that he candidly urged him to follow some other career and refused to take him on. Paderewski found a teaching post in Strasbourg and immersed himself so determinedly in practice that in 1886 Leschetizky relented. By 1888 the pianist was pronounced rehabilitated and made a second debut in Vienna. Legend has it that he had worked up only a single program and that when success came, as it did within two years, and he was faced with the problem of being held over, he had to sweat to ready others. (It was during this interim that he wrote his piano concerto, the most popular of his few large-scale works, which was premiered in Vienna by Anna Esipova, Leschetizky's wife.) Having established himself as a popular favorite with English audiences, he went on to America and struck gold. (The reviewers were by no means so enthusiastic as the lay concert goers, causing an almost pathological stagefright in the pianist.) His popularity quickly brought him a fortune, with part of which he financed competitions and the like for young musical aspirants and with part of which he bought an impressive estate in Switzerland on the shores of Lake Geneva. The year he purchased it, 1898, he married the Baroness Von Rosen.

Not content to be the idol of the crowds, however, Paderewski really wanted to be remembered as a great composer. Even though his *Minuet in G* had assured his immortality (if not his greatness), he embarked on an opera, *Manru*. It was premiered in Dresden in 1901 to great publicity, was taken up by other major houses, including the Metropolitan in 1902, and then was heard no more. His only symphony, inspired by the sorrows of captive Poland (which more and more occupied his mind) suffered a similar fate after its 1909 premiere in Boston. In the same year Paderewski was made director of the Warsaw Conservatory. The following year he donated $60,000 to the Chopin Memorial Hall, and $100,000 for a statue to the Polish liberator Wladislaw II Jagiełło. However, in 1913 he and his outsize entourage settled on a ranch in Paso Robles, California. The outbreak of war the next year cut him off from his homeland, but in the Russian defeats he began to see hope for Poland and devoted all his time to fund raising in her behalf, becoming the unofficial spokesman for American Poles. In 1917 he financed a training camp in Canada for Polish expatriates. Finally he was able to return to Warsaw where, despite considerable opposition that included an assassination attempt, he formed an independent government, in which he served as premier and foreign secretary. He signed the Versailles Treaty on Poland's behalf, but in 1920 he stepped down to return to his musical career, which went on much longer than his digital ability. In 1936 he appeared (as himself) in the very successful film *Moonlight Sonata,* which documents his personal charm if not his keyboard skills. With the outbreak of a new war, he returned to America and fund raising, dying in harness at eighty. He was a highly intelligent, kindly, and generous man who richly deserved the many honors showered on him, but as a pianist he rarely satisfied purists of any stripe, though his poetic touch and his willful romanticizing cast a spell of their own. (He left a fair number of recordings, both acoustic and microphoned.) As a composer, he was a romantic throwback. His largest output was of piano pieces, mostly small scale, but including a sonata.

RECORDINGS: Of the few larger works there are recordings of the Sonata for Violin and Piano, the *Fantaisie polonaise* for piano and orchestra, the Symphony, the Concerto for Piano (several versions), and a few excerpts from *Manru.* There is a scattering of recorded piano pieces, including some by the composer himself.

[1528] EWALD, Viktor (Ā-vȧlt', Vēk'-tôr)
ENGINEER
BORN: St. Petersburg, November 27, 1860
DIED: Leningrad, April 26, 1935

A talented amateur and ardent folksong collector, Ewald spent most of his life as a professor of civil engineering, both before and after the 1917 Revolution. On the side, he played cello and horn and sometimes performed in the chamber-music concerts sponsored by the publisher Belaiev. His daughter Zinaida Ewald Gippius was also a folklorist of note. RECORDINGS: There have been several recent recordings of Ewald's brass quintets.

[1529] MACDOWELL, Edward Alexander
PIANIST, TEACHER
BORN: New York, December 18, 1860
(Grove gives 1861)
DIED: New York, January 23, 1908

Edward MacDowell was perhaps the first native-born American composer to be taken seriously on an international basis, and, until well into the twentieth century, was held up as our greatest one. In recent years his reputation has been in limbo. The reasons are not far to seek: though he was a greatly talented musician, he was overvalued; his work (for all its American programmatic references) is German-Romantic, and such salonesque piano effusions as *To a Wild Rose* have been unfairly held against him. Moreover his productivity was limited by overwork and the short lifespan that oddly cursed so many significant composers born in 1860.

MacDowell's parents were well-to-do Scotch-Irish Quakers. When he demonstrated infantile musical proclivities, they hastened to furnish him with a piano teacher in the person of Señor Juan Buitrago, a Colombian. Buitrago introduced him to the budding piano virtuosa Teresa Carreño, whom it sometimes amused to oversee his practice, giving rise to the legend that he studied with her. When he was fifteen, MacDowell was taken to Paris to study with Antoine-François Marmontel. Because he was also a promising graphic artist, he was tempted by offers of free training in painting, but by 1877 he had been taken into the Conservatoire on scholarship. A concert by Nicolas Rubinstein, however, left him so dissatisfied with what the French were offering that he defected to the Stuttgart Conservatory and Siegmund Lebert *(né* Sigmund Levi), a pupil of Václav Tomášek [1080]. That proved even less satisfactory, and he moved on to Wiesbaden, where he studied with Louis Ehlert, a disciple of Mendelssohn [1200] and Schumann [1211]. Finally in 1879 he found happiness at the Hoch Conservatory in Frankfurt, studying with Joachim Raff [1282], its director, and Karl Heymann, its piano professor. After a year, however, he left and set himself up as a teacher. One of his first pupils was an American girl, Marian Nevins, with whom he was soon in love. When Heymann left the Hoch Conservatory in 1880, MacDowell applied for his post but failed to get it. Then he was taken on by the Darmstadt Conservatory early in 1881, but the work and the commuting proved too much for him and he quit after a year. Meanwhile he was winning a sound reputation as a pianist. In 1882, at Raff's urging, he went to Weimar to meet Liszt [1218], who had heard him play before, and to play his first piano concerto for him—assisted by Eugen d'Albert [1562]. Liszt was impressed, got him a publishing contract with Breitkopf and Härtel, and told him that he should devote his energies to composition. Raff's sudden death, however, cast a pall over the causes for rejoicing.

In 1884 MacDowell returned briefly to New York to wed his Marian and carry her back to Germany, which he now preferred to his homeland. Denied professorships at Würzburg and Edinburgh, despite his growing fame, MacDowell decided to give himself over to composing, and the couple settled down in a cottage in Wiesbaden—which soon began to attract numbers of American musical pilgrims. Many of them tried to persuade the composer that he was desperately needed back home. In 1888 he gave in, and he and Marian took ship for Boston. There he became both a musical stimulus and an annoyance. Young American hopefuls were heartened by the Boston Symphony's performances of his music (which was also taken

up by other American orchestras). The Old Guard was appalled by his "modernism" and his attacks on their philistinism. In addition to composing, he continued to teach, edited, and concertized.

In 1896 MacDowell agreed to become Columbia University's first professor of music. He went with high hopes and loftier aims and tried hard to realize both. However, for the next two years, he was in effect the department of music, with all the honors, privileges, backbreak, and heartbreak appertaining thereto. On the side, as if all that were not enough, he served concurrently for a time as conductor of the Mendelssohn Club. Despite his tremendous enthusiasm and his handsome glow of well-being, it was all a terrible strain, for he was basically a very shy and private man. Later he acquired a couple of assistants and in 1902 was able to take a year off, to tour Europe and visit his old friend George Templeton Strong [1490]. Just before he left, however, the university had acquired a new president in the person of Nicholas Murray Butler. On his return MacDowell discovered that Butler had radically altered the arts program and that all he had worked for was about to go up in smoke. After worrying for some months, he handed in a diplomatic resignation. But then he made the mistake of telling two student reporters that Butler had sold out to material interests. There were recriminations hurled back and forth and a formal reprimand from the trustees. MacDowell, already nervous and exhausted, began to lose sleep over what he felt was the denigration of his character and soon showed clear signs of mental illness. A traffic accident made things worse, and a medical examination showed advanced paresis. Though he had lucid moments (during which he conceived the idea of the MacDowell Colony for artists at his summer place in Peterborough, New Hampshire), he spent most of his last years playing uncomprehendingly with toys. After his death Marian oversaw the colony until her own demise in 1956 at the age of ninety-nine.

MacDowell is often called the American Grieg [1410]. If, like Grieg's, much of his output consisted of songs and piano pieces, he thought bigger and stronger. If his 4 piano sonatas, for example, are not (as Lawrence Gilman thought) the greatest since Beethoven's [1063], they are full of passion and grandeur that is not mere rhetoric. If he liked programmatic titles, they are obviously meant to evoke moods rather than images. Here, like Grieg, he was most successful in smaller forms. The big symphonic poems— *Lancelot and Elaine; Hamlet and Ophelia;*

and *Lamia*—are upholstered in fustian and stuffed with horsehair.

RECORDINGS: The three symphonic poems just mentioned have been recorded by Karl Krueger, though they are rarely if ever performed in concert today. But the two piano concerti have survived very well and have been several times recorded. Ditto the *Second Suite* for orchestra (on Amerindian themes), though the *First Suite* has been recorded only once to date (by Howard Hanson). There are also recordings of the sonatas and such piano works as the *Sea Pieces*, the *Woodland Sketches*, the *Virtuoso Studies*, the two *Modern Suites*, etc. The vocal music has been largely ignored, though there is a small selection by soprano Alexandra Hunt.

[1530] LOEFFLER, Charles Martin
(Tornow)
VIOLINIST
BORN: Mulhouse, January 30, 1861
DIED: Medfield, Mass., May 19, 1935

Born in Alsace (then still French), Loeffler became an American citizen when he was twenty-six and spent his entire productive career in the United States. He is therefore categorized as an American composer. But in his music one hears no cowboy songs, no Indian laments, little jazz. It is rather the work of a twentieth-century cosmopolitan, an eclectic who drew from both the geographical range of his experience and the chronological range of his musical studies. If his choice of subjects sometimes links him superficially with the French Impressionists, his taste for the mystical, the supernatural, and even the diabolic makes him something of a law unto himself.

Loeffler's blood was German, but he came to detest the Germans, who imprisoned his father for protesting the less savory aspects of the Prussian government, and insisted on his Frenchness. His father, Dr. Karl Loeffler, was an agronomist who wrote *Plattdeutsch* novels and poetry under the pseudonym of "Tornow," taken from the hamlet where he grew up. (Loeffler later added it to his own name.) There were other children, two of whom also became professional musicians. Not long after Charles's birth, Dr. Loeffler took a post with the provincial government of Kiev in Russia and took his family there to the village of Smyela, where, in his ninth year, the boy began to study the violin. Around the end of the decade Dr. Loeffler was appointed to a professorship at the Royal Hungarian Agricultural College and thereupon transferred his household to Debrecen (Debreczen). The Loefflers were,

however, only briefly there; they moved to Switzerland in 1873. Two years later Charles went to Berlin to study violin under Eduard Rappoldi and then under Joachim [1321], of whom he became a particular favorite. He also became a pupil of Friedrich Kiel and of Woldemar Bargiel (half-brother to Clara Schumann [1267]). Finding himself not wholly sympathetic with the German approach to music, Loeffler proceeded to Paris to work with Massart and with Guiraud [1352]. He played in the Pasdeloup Orchestra (engaged in a vain struggle for survival), and then was hired as violinist to the plutocratic Baron Paul von Derwies, a Russian with a German name and Dutch ancestors. The baron, who divided his time between Lugano and Nice and required three trains to move his entourage, had a symphony orchestra (conducted by Karl Müller-Berghaus and previously by Hans Sitt [1452]), an opera company, and a Slavic choir to officiate in his Orthodox chapel. But this remarkable experience was terminated in less than two years by the baron's death. Very shortly afterward, in 1881, Loeffler, armed with recommendations from Joachim, set sail for New York. He was immediately taken on by Leopold Damrosch to play not only in his orchestra but also in the string quartet that officiated at his Sunday at-home musicales. In the course of the next few months, Loeffler also played under Damrosch's chief rival, Theodore Thomas. In 1882, however, on the advice of Wilhelm Müller-Berghaus, who was brother of Baron von Derwies's *Kapellmeister* and was a Boston Symphony cellist, Loeffler was hired to share the concertmaster's desk in that orchestra with Fritz Kneisel. There he was joined by his own brother Erich, also a cellist, and there he remained until 1903, when he retired to devote his time to composing. Seven years later he moved to an estate in Medford, where he led the life of a connoisseur of the Good.

Though he had written music earlier, Loeffler's serious composition dates from the mid-1880s, and he had completed a good deal of his not-very-large *oeuvre* before he retired. This included several unpublished chamber works, more ambitious pieces for solo instruments and orchestra—*Nights in the Ukraine* (violin), *Fantastic Concerto* (cello), *Divertimento* (violin), *La Mort de Tintagiles* (viola d'amore), *La Villanelle du Diable* (organ), *Divertissement espagnole* (saxophone)—and songs. His exquisite orchestration, his use of medieval modes, and his espousal of such literary sources as Verlaine, Baudelaire, and Maeterlinck won him a reputation for "decadence"—a label intended as complimentary but suspect in Boston. Loeffler was elected to the French Academy in 1906 and received numerous other honors, both here and abroad. In 1911 (at fifty) he married Elise Burnett Fay, long his business manager. Much of his later work was vocal, but his orchestral *Memories of My Childhood* (subtitled "Life in a Russian Village" and again evoking the Ukraine) won a prize in 1926.

RECORDINGS: The orchestral version of *A Pagan Poem,* the 2 rhapsodies for oboe, viola, and piano, and the *Music for Four Stringed Instruments* have each enjoyed more than one recording. Also represented on records are *Memories of My Childhood,* the orchestral *Poem: "La Bonne Chanson"* after Verlaine, the 1894 string quintet, the *Partita* for violin and piano, and some songs (most notably a full LP by mezzo-soprano D'Anna Fortunato). But Loeffler has not received the attention he deserves.

[1531] BRÉVILLE, Pierre Eugène Onfroy de (Brā-vēl′, Pē-âr′ Ō-zhen′ Ôn-frwä′ də)
TEACHER, CRITIC
BORN: Bar-le-Duc, February 21, 1861
DIED: Paris, September 24, 1949

Pierre de Bréville is one of those composers who is highly spoken of but little performed. He originally planned to go into the foreign service and had completed his legal studies before he enrolled at the Paris Conservatoire to study with Théodore Dubois **[1356].** However, he soon abandoned Dubois for César Franck **[1284],** of whom he became a dedicated supporter. He later (1898–1904) taught at the Schola Cantorum and the Paris Conservatoire and served as music critic for the *Mercure de France* and other journals. He helped d'Indy **[1462]** and Chausson **[1484]** piece together Franck's opera *Ghisèle* after the master's death. His own opera, *Eros Vainqueur (Love Victorious),* which he considered his best work, won much favorable comment when it was premiered in Brussels in 1910 but had to wait an incredible twenty-two years before being heard in Paris. (It succeeded despite the delay and a weak libretto, but appears now to have been forgotten.) Bréville was a director and sometime president of the Société Nationale de Musique, which gave the first performances of many of his compositions. He wrote some incidental music and a fair amount for solo instruments and chamber ensembles but little for orchestra. The bulk of his output is vocal, including many fine songs. RECORDINGS: A few of his songs have been recorded.

[1532] GASTALDON, Stanislas (Gàs-tàl′-dōn, Stàn′-ēs-làs)
CRITIC
BORN: Turin, April 7, 1861
DIED: Florence, March 7, 1939

Gastaldon had already published a good deal of salon music by the time he reached his majority and continued to do so all his life. Between 1890 and 1913 he wrote a string of operas, beginning with *Mala Pasqua (Bad Easter),* some of which had a temporary success. He spent much of his life in Florence, where he was critic for the *Nuovo Giornale.* He was best known for his songs. RECORDINGS: One of his songs, *Musica proibita (Forbidden Music),* was recorded by Enrico Caruso and others of his day.

[1533] MEYER-HELMUND, Erik (Mī′-er Hel′-mōōnt, Ā′-rik)
SINGER
BORN: St. Petersburg, April 25, 1861
DIED: Berlin, April 4, 1932

Known chiefly as a composer of popular salon songs, Meyer-Helmund was German, despite his Russian birthplace. He first studied with his father, then went to the Stern-Akademie in Berlin, where he was a pupil of the great *Lieder* singer Julius Stockhausen and of Friedrich Kiel. He toured widely and successfully for some years as a concert singer before settling in Berlin in 1911. His large-scale compositions include 5 operas, 2 operettas, and a ballet. Of these, the most successful was the opera *Der Liebeskampf (The Battle of Love),* premiered at Dresden in 1892. RECORDINGS: Some of the songs appear on early records.

[1534] BOSSI, Marco Enrico (Bos′-sē, Mär′-kō En-rē′-kō)
ORGANIST, CONDUCTOR, TEACHER, ADMINISTRATOR
BORN: Salò, April 25, 1861
DIED: At sea, February 20, 1925

Enrico Bossi was perhaps the first internationally acclaimed organist to appear in Italy since the Classical era. He was born on the western shore of Lake Garda and studied with his father Pietro (1834–96), who became organist at Morbegno on the River Adda, near Lake Como and the Swiss border. (Enrico's brother, Costante Adolfo (1876–1953), who also became a composer, was born there.) In 1871 Enrico entered the Liceo in Bologna and two years later became a pupil of Ponchielli **[1334]** at the Milan

843

Conservatory. The year of his graduation, 1881, his first opera, *Paquita,* was produced in Milan. Immediately afterward he became cathedral organist at Como, back in the lake country, and remained there for nearly a decade. Another opera, *Il Veggente (The Prophet),* had a premiere (unsuccessful) in Milan in 1890, the year he moved to Naples to teach at the Royal Conservatory San Pietro. In 1895 he was appointed director of the Liceo Benedetto Marcello in Venice, where he also taught and conducted. In 1902 he came full circle back to the Liceo Musicale in Bologna, where he was director through 1911. After devoting five years to concertizing (he was admired both as an organist and pianist), he took over the direction of the Accademia di Santa Cecilia in Rome until 1923. He died two years later while returning from an American concert tour. Bossi's later operas went begging, but he wrote a number of large choral works—Masses, two Requiems, the "vocal symphonic-poem" *Il Paradiso perduto (Paradise Lost),* the "mystery" *Giovanna d'Arco (Joan of Arc),* cantatas, and smaller pieces. He was perhaps more important as a leader of the Italian instrumental school of his day, producing orchestral and chamber works as well as much keyboard music. His son Renzo (1883–1965) won some note as a composer and completed his father's unfinished opera *Malombra.* RECORDINGS: Enrico Bossi is represented on records by organ pieces and his organ concerto.

[1535] JONES, James Sidney
CONDUCTOR
BORN: London, June 17, 1861
DIED: London, January 29, 1946

Sidney Jones—like the Jones who became Edward German **[1541]**—was one of the more successful aspirants to the operetta throne left vacant by the abdication of Sir Arthur Sullivan **[1397]**. Jones's father was a bandmaster who later became a musical factotum in Leeds, where Sidney grew up and learned his trade. At first a clarinetist, he turned to conducting and toured (as far as Australia) with various light-opera companies. Eventually he settled in at the Prince of Wales' Theatre in London, where his first two musical comedies, *A Gaiety Girl* and *An Artist's Model,* were produced in 1893 and 1895 respectively. In 1896, *The Geisha,* first performed at Daly's Theatre, became a runaway hit, and is said, on a worldwide basis, to rank as the most successful of all British operettas. Jones never matched this success, alone or in the various collaborations he undertook—with Lionel Monckton **[1538]**,

Paul Rubens (1875–1917), and others. In 1905 he was appointed conductor of the Empire Theatre. He retired in 1916 and virtually gave up composing. Besides the operettas he wrote a couple of ballets and many songs. RECORDINGS: Some of the songs have been recorded, and there are innumerable excerpts from *The Geisha* in several languages.

[1536] ARENSKY, Anton Stepanovich
(Á-ren'-shkē, Án'-tōn Styá-pà-nō'-vēch)
TEACHER, CONDUCTOR, PIANIST
BORN: Novgorod, July 12, 1861
DIED: Terioki, February 25, 1906

The son of a cello-playing physician, Arensky could not heal himself, and a promising career was cut short by illness and early death. He grew up with music, studying with his parents and with local musicians in childhood and composing by the time he was nine. At eighteen he went off to study at the St. Petersburg Conservatory, where Rimsky-Korsakov **[1416]** was his admiring mentor. Though he acquitted himself admirably as a student, the bright lights of the capital proved irresistible, and a regimen of drinking, gambling, and partying undermined his health. In 1882, while still a student, he produced a successful piano concerto and the first of his 2 symphonies, and was awarded a gold medal on his graduation later that year. He was thereupon called to the Moscow Conservatory to teach harmony and counterpoint, and he included Rachmaninoff **[1638]**, Scriabin **[1625]**, Grechaninov **[1567]**, and Glière **[1662]** among his students.

At the conservatory he was powerfully influenced by Tchaikovsky **[1377]**, who took an almost proprietary interest in him. In 1888 he became director of the Moscow Choral Society, and in 1889 one of the overseers of the Synodal School of Church Music. In 1891 his first opera, *A Dream on the Volga,* was premiered successfully at the Bolshoi Theater. It was followed by *Raphael,* produced in 1894 at the conservatory. The next year Arensky returned to St. Petersburg to succeed Balakirev **[1348]** as director of the imperial chapel. In the course of time he discovered that he had tuberculosis and retired on a pension when he was forty. He continued to conduct and to concertize for a time but died five years later in a Finnish sanitarium. He never married and seems to have had few close friends. Undoubtedly talented and highly skilled, he wrote attractive music, at its best in small forms. An eclectic, chiefly in the central European Romantic tradition, he often seems a poor man's Tchaikovsky.

RECORDINGS: Works on records include the Concerto for Piano (Maria Littauer); the Concerto for Violin (Aaron Rosand); the *Fantasy on a Themes of Ryabinin* for piano and orchestra (several versions); the orchestral *Silhouettes* (several versions); the ballet suite *Egyptian Nights* (Boris Demchenko); the orchestral *Suites Nos. 1, 2;* the cantata *The Fountain of Bakhchisarai* (Alexander Melik-Pashayev); the *Variations on a Theme of Tchaikovsky* (many versions); Symphonies Nos. 1, 2; Piano Trio No. 1 (several versions); the one-act opera *Raphael;* numerous piano pieces; songs; and a few miscellaneous vocal and orchestral selections from the operas.

[1537] THUILLE, Ludwig Wilhelm Andreas Maria (Too̅-e̅'-le, Loo̅t'-vikh Vil'-helm Ȧn'-drā-as Mȧ-rē'-ȧ)
TEACHER, CONDUCTOR
BORN: Bozen, November 30, 1861
DIED: Munich, February 5, 1907

A Tyrolese of French descent from what is now the Italian city of Bolzano, Ludwig Thuille was the son of a timber merchant. The elder Thuille, who was also a musical amateur, gave the child his first lessons but died before they had proceeded very far. Frau Thuille followed him shortly, and Ludwig went to Kremsmünster (between Linz and Salzburg) to live with a step-uncle. The latter, far from being wicked, placed him in the choir of the local monastery and saw to it that he had an education, musical and academic. When he was fifteen, a well-to-do widow (of a musician) paid his way to study with Joseph Pembaur (1848–1923), a pupil of Bruckner [1293] and Rheinberger [1368] in Innsbruck. (Thuille was later to teach Joseph Pembaur, Jr. [1875–1950].) After four years, Pembaur, Sr., sent him on to Munich to study with Rheinberger and with Karl Bärmann, a piano pupil of Liszt's [1218], at the Royal Conservatory. He graduated in 1882 and, after teaching privately for a year, joined the staff of the conservatory, where, in 1890, he became professor of theory and composition. (Ernest Bloch [1729] was one of his pupils.) His approach to composition was strongly influenced from 1886 by Wagner's [1230] brother-in-law Alexander Ritter [1330] and his disciple Richard Strauss [1563], who settled in Munich that year. Ritter wrote the libretto to the first of Thuille's fairytale operas, *Theuerdank,* premiered there in 1897. Its successor, *Lobetanz,* produced a year later at Karlsruhe, created a brief sensation and even had five performances at the Metropolitan Opera in New York in 1911. (The third, *Gugeline,* premiered at Bremen in 1901, was not so lucky.) The rest of Thuille's small output includes a symphony, chamber works, choral pieces, and many songs. RECORDINGS: There are recordings of bits and pieces, including an aria from *Lobetanz* sung by Johanna Gadski, who created the leading soprano role at the Metropolitan. The Sextet for Piano and Winds has been recorded several times.

[1538] MONCKTON, John Lionel Alexander
LAWYER, JOURNALIST
BORN: London, December 18, 1861
DIED: London, February 15, 1924

A successful writer of show tunes, Monckton was a collaborator for most of his career, turning out only one or two musicals on his own. His father, Sir John Monckton, served as town clerk of London. Lionel went to the Charterhouse School and to Oxford, where he frequently appeared in plays and where he graduated from Oriel College. He began his legal practice in 1885 and wrote theatrical and musical reviews for several London papers. In the 1890s he began contributing songs to other composers' operettas—including several by Sidney Jones [1535]—and adapting foreign hits to the English stage. In 1896 he began a long partnership with the Belgian-born Ivan Caryll (né Félix Tilkin, 1861–1921). His first independent work was *A Country Girl,* produced when he was forty-one; his most successful one was *The Quaker Girl,* 1910. The greatest Caryll-Monckton hit was *Our Miss Gibbs* in 1909. That same year, however, he began a new collaboration with the New Yorker Howard Talbot (né Richard Munkittrick, 1865–1928) with the almost equally successful *The Arcadians.* Monckton's wife was the singer Gertie Miller, who after his death became the Countess of Dudley. RECORDINGS: Many of Monckton's songs have been recorded.

[1539] DELIUS, Frederick (né Fritz Theodore Albert)
WOOL DEALER, ORANGE GROWER, TEACHER
BORN: Bradford, January 29, 1862
DIED: Grez-sur-Loing, June 10, 1934

Frederick Delius, "the English Impressionist," has always been something of a cult figure. His particular brand of sensousness appeals to some more than to others. The sole English composer of stature between Elgar

[1499] and Vaughan Williams [1633], he refused to sound English and was moreover an expatriate by choice for most of his life. His popularity was created, almost singlehandedly, by Sir Thomas Beecham, who not only insisted on performing his music in concert, but also on committing it to phonograph records—and Delius has had no such advocate since Beecham's death. Delius was an Impressionist in that he attempted to reflect his emotional reactions to things in his music. But he was not of the Debussyan [1547] school; his style has in fact been described as Wagner [1230] leavened with Grieg [1410], though at his best he spoke in his own voice. His best music was rhapsodic and chromatic (in terms of color as much as of tonality), and his original freshness has been dimmed by the impact of too many feeble pseudo-Delian film scores. Such individual utterance was for him a relatively late achievement and was unhappily limited by broken health. When he attempted the traditional-formal, he was apt to hamstring himself.

Delius was the fourth of the fourteen children of a German couple, Julius and Elise Delius. They had emigrated from Bielefeld to a market town in the West Riding, where Julius had set up a branch of his brother's Manchester-based wool business. Though he was a hardboiled Victorian *paterfamilias,* Julius Delius was no barbarian, and there was music in the home. Young Fritz showed a bent toward it and was put to learning the violin. But he evinced no interest in, or aptitude for, matters academic, so he was eventually sent to a business school to prepare him for the family enterprise. He was admitted into the latter in 1881 and sent to Gloucestershire as an agent. There he performed so well that he was dispatched to Chemnitz (now Karl Marx Stadt) for further commercial seasoning. There he studied the violin with Hans Sitt [1452], and was so distracted by the musical opportunities in nearby Leipzig and Dresden that he neglected his duties, got a bad report, and was ordered forthwith to return to Bradford. Then his father sent him to Norköpping, Sweden, as a sales representative. He did well enough until he discovered the delights of the Scandinavian countryside and of Stockholm. Once more he was abruptly uprooted and shipped to St. Étienne in France, where there were (and are) no distractions whatsoever. Provided with only enough money for necessities, he skipped to Monaco, parlayed it into a considerably larger amount, and was discovered several weeks later basking on the Mediterranean sands. Striking while the iron was hot and his

father in despair, Delius and John Douglas, another Bradford black sheep, persuaded Delius' father to back them in an orange-growing venture in Florida. They leased a plantation at Solano Grove, just south of Jacksonville, where Douglas was shortly stricken with malaria. Delius went into town to fetch a doctor, ran into a visiting Brooklyn organist named Thomas F. Ward, and became so engrossed in conversation that he forgot to carry out his mission. Douglas, perhaps understandably, pulled out, and the elder Delius bought the plantation, leaving his son to make a go of it. But Frederick (as he had become known) spent most of his time studying with Ward and absorbing the music of the local blacks, which he was later to put to use. Toward the end of 1884 his elder brother Ernst arrived, disenchanted with sheep farming Down Under, and the following February Frederick abandoned the grove to him and moved to Jacksonville, where he eked out a subsistence by giving music lessons and singing in a synagogue choir. Shortly, however, he found a post in Danville, Virginia, tutoring the daughters of a Professor Ruckert, and soon thereafter found himself as Professor Delius on the faculty of the Roanoke Female College. He left in the spring of 1886, but by then a prominent Danvillean had persuaded his father that he should resign himself to his son's vocation, and Julius called him home with an offer of study at the Leipzig Conservatory, all expenses paid.

At that institution, where he enrolled in August, Delius resumed his association with Sitt and also studied under the likes of Reinecke [1292] and Salomon Jadassohn (1831–1902), but he chiefly profited from exposure to the rich musical life of the town. He also began composing seriously, his most ambitious work of the period being the *Florida Suite,* performed in 1888. He made friends with Grieg and spent time with him in Norway in 1887. When Julius Delius' beneficence came to its stipulated end after eighteen months, Frederick, feeling that he was making no progress in Leipzig anyhow, moved to Paris (again with parental support, thanks to Grieg, and with a larger handout from an indulgent uncle). There he fell in with the bohemian set and adopted official bohemian ways and uniform, affecting a beard and tattered garments and hanging out in low dives. He dabbled in alchemy with the playwright August Strindberg and took up vegetarianism. He returned to Norway in the summer of 1890 to visit Grieg and Christian Sinding [1488], who had persuaded Leipzig to issue Delius a diploma. He began work on *Irmelin,* his first opera, which occupied him for two years—and was not produced until almost nineteen years after his death. His Ibsen-inspired symphonic poem *Paa Vidderne (On the Mountain Peaks)* got a hearing in Oslo in 1891 and, thanks to his friend the composer Isidore De Lara **[1508]**, a second hearing in Monte Carlo two years later, winning him the advocacy of the Princess Alice. A second opera, *The Magic Fountain,* was finished in 1893; *it* had to wait seventy-two years for a premiere (by the BBC and duly commercially recorded).

In January 1896 Delius was introduced to Jelka Rosen, a young German painter from Belgrade, and the two were soon in love. She was not the first woman in Delius' life (he had in fact been infected with syphilis in Florida), and indeed she had a persistent rival at the time. Not long after their meeting Delius had to return to Jacksonville to dispose of the plantation (which Ernst had long since abandoned) and discovered far out at sea that the other woman was on board disguised as a sailor. In the meantime, when the estate at Grez-sur-Loing (about forty miles south of Paris) where Jelka liked to vacation was put up for sale, she borrowed the money to buy it. It was near the home of C. F. Keary, librettist for Delius' new opera *Koanga,* and so on his return from America Frederick moved in. The year 1897 saw the completion of the opera, as well as of the Concerto for Piano and the orchestral *Over the Hills and Far Away.* That October Delius went to Oslo to conduct his music for Gunnar Heiberg's play *Folkeraadet* (also known as the *Norwegian Suite* in concerts) and was driven from the podium by students outraged at what they took to be a parody of the Norwegian national anthem. At about the same time, however, he found support in Elberfeld, where the conductors Hans Haym and Fritz Cassirer took a liking to his music. From Elberfeld also came Alfred Hertz (later of the Metropolitan Opera and the San Francisco Symphony), who conducted the concert of Delius' music which the conductor had set up at Queen's Hall, London, in 1899. The audience was polite and the critics tolerant, but the event attracted no publishers for the music and left the composer deeply in debt. By then his allowance had long since dried up. Moreover he was still saddled with the Florida property, whose grove had been ruined by a freeze and leveled by a hurricane. In 1901 Julius Delius died after serious financial reverses, leaving no will. Frederick garnered only about 500 pounds from the estate. (Incidentally, neither parent apparently ever heard a note of their son's music.)

It was in 1901 that Haym premiered the orchestral *Paris,* regarded as the first truly Delian composition (its composer was nearing forty). In it German audiences discerned a third alternative to the polarities of Wagner and Brahms **[1329]**. But in 1902 the one-act opera *Margot la rouge* got nowhere in the annual Sonzogno competition that had discovered Mascagni's **[1559]** *Cavalleria* and Leoncavallo's **[1498]** *Pagliacci* a decade earlier. A year later Delius and Jelka (whose painting had by then won some notice and the praise of Auguste Rodin) were married. In 1904 the Elberfeld premieres of the opera *Koanga* and the orchestral *Appalachia* (the latter based in part on a Negro melody from the Florida days and utilizing a chorus in its final movement) further enhanced the composer's growing reputation. Though offers from the English conductor Henry Wood came to nothing at the time, Delius found a publisher at last in Harmonie Verlag in Berlin. The year 1906 saw the premiere of the choral-orchestral *Sea Drift* (to a Walt Whitman text) in Essen, with further positive reactions (some consider it his peak performance). Meanwhile Delius was working on what *he* considered his magnum opus, the *Mass of Life* (based on fragments from Nietzsche **[1422]**), and Cassirer was preparing *A Village Romeo and Juliet,* completed in 1901, for the new Komische Oper in Berlin. After the premiere in February 1907, it was agreed that the work was probably better than the production, which did not travel with the company to London, where its production of Offenbach's **[1264]** *Les contes d'Hoffmann* was deemed insufficiently *komisch.* However, arrangements were made for performances of the piano concerto, *Sea Drift,* and *Appalachia* in that city. It was also at this time that Delius and Beecham first met and that Delius was named second officer (to Elgar) in the League of Music, an organization set up to promote the performance of English music, which it did not manage to do very successfully.

Beecham and Delius became close friends. They went off to Norway together for a summer hike in the mountains (Grieg was now dead), and Beecham premiered the *Mass* in Queen's Hall in 1909. The next year he presented *Romeo and Juliet* at Covent Garden, but it was eclipsed by Richard Strauss's **[1563]** *Elektra,* the other novelty of the season. In 1910 Delius completed what was to be his last opera, *Fennimore and Gerda.* By then he was suffering severe digestive upsets and back pains, both manifestations of his disease, and was unsatisfactorily in and out of sanitariums. Nevertheless he continued to compose, producing such pieces as *On Hearing the First Cuckoo in*

Spring, 1912; *A Song of the High Hills* and *An Arabesk,* both 1911; and the *North Country Sketches,* 1913–14. His music was now giving him a small but steady income, and the death in 1913 of a rich aunt had left him comfortably off. However, the outbreak of war the following summer not only put a crimp in the progress of his career but actually endangered him. His nationality made his music no longer welcome in Germany; moreover the couple had to bury their valuables and flee ignominiously in a manure cart before the German advance. They returned to Grez after the Battle of the Marne but moved to London in 1915, where Delius was too upset to write for a time. When he returned to musical creation it was in a more abstract and formal vein, producing in 1916, the String Quartet, the Sonata for Cello and Piano, the Concerto for Violin, and the Double Concerto for Violin and Cello— none of them up to the best of the earlier work. The Deliuses went back to Grez in 1916 but continued to move about restlessly. (At one point their house was occupied and vandalized by troops.)

In 1919, after the war, the Frankfurt Opera premiered *Fennimore and Gerda* as a goodwill gesture, with the composer and his wife in attendance, but the reception was only so-so. A year later Delius sold, for 3,000 pounds, a Gauguin painting he had long ago bought in Paris for 20 pounds, and the French government reimbursed him handsomely for the damage to the house. But for much of 1922 he was confined to a sanitarium in Wiesbaden. Treatment produced some mitigation of his condition, and in September 1923 he was able to attend the opening of James Elroy Flecker's play *Hassan,* for which he had written the incidental music. The couple spent the winter at Rapallo on the Italian Riviera and the following spring discovered a German physician who promised a complete cure. For a while it appeared that he was making good, but in 1925 the composer suddenly took a turn for the worse and was soon blind and paralyzed— for the rest of his days, it turned out, though his mind and speech remained unimpaired.

In 1928 Delius was introduced to Eric Fenby (1906–), a Yorkshire musician who greatly admired his music and thought he might be able to help him produce more. He moved into the Grez estate and spent the next six years taking down scores from the composer's dictation. These included *A Song of Summer,* the *Irmelin Prelude,* the *Songs of Farewell, Idyll,* the Sonata No. 3 for Violin and Piano, and a number of small pieces. In 1929 Beecham directed a big Delius festival, during the course of whose six concerts

most of the composer's important nondramatic output was performed. In spite of his incapacities, Delius managed to attend. Five years later Jelka was found to be suffering from a terminal cancer. Shortly afterward, however, Frederick took another bad turn and died. He was buried at first in the village cemetery, but because he had expressed a wish to lie in English soil, Jelka arranged in 1935 for the wish to be carried out. Accompanying the coffin across the English Channel, she caught a cold which went into pneumonia and killed her a few days later.

RECORDINGS: All of the operas, the *Hassan* music, a portion of the early works, and most of the mature orchestral, choral, and chamber music have been recorded in reasonably up-to-date versions. Beecham left recordings of a generous selection, including *A Village Romeo and Juliet,* and EMI has released a set of the late works conducted by Eric Fenby. Only the songs have been neglected, though there is spotty representation even of these.

[1540] DAMROSCH, Walter Johannes
CONDUCTOR, IMPRESARIO
BORN: Breslau [Wroclaw], January 30, 1862
DIED: New York, December 22, 1950

For sixty-five years Walter Damrosch was an enormous influence on music in the United States, and in his latter years he was a German-accented grandfather figure to a whole generation, which he led to an enjoyment of good music via his radio broadcasts. Music was in his blood: his mother Helene *(née* von Heimburg) was a singer; his father Leopold and his brother Frank were conductors of stature. The family came to New York when Walter was nine, Leopold having been hired to direct the Arion male chorus there. Two years later he organized the Oratorio Society. He conducted the New York Philharmonic for a year and in 1878 founded the New York Symphony Orchestra. After the Metropolitan Opera's disastrous opening season, he reorganized the house as a German opera company in 1884, with Walter (who had meanwhile returned to Germany to study with Bülow **[1310]** and Draeseke **[1342]**) as his assistant. When Leopold died suddenly in 1885, Walter took over his chorus and orchestra and remained at the opera house as Anton Seidl's assistant. In 1894 Walter organized an opera company of his own (later known as the Damrosch-Ellis Opera Company); it brought several important German singers (e.g., Johanna Gadski and Milka Ternina) to America, and it toured the country for five seasons. In 1899 he returned to the Metropolitian Opera as conductor of the German wing. He left in the spring of 1902 but was seriously considered the next year to succeed Maurice Grau as general manager. However, Heinrich Conried was chosen, and Damrosch instead took over the Philharmonic for a season. His own orchestra had gone bankrupt in the previous decade, but in 1904 he revived it and led it for twenty-four more seasons until it merged with the Philharmonic (which then became officially the Philharmonic-Symphony).

The Damrosch Company had premiered its leader's first opera, *The Scarlet Letter,* at Boston in 1896, and his only operetta, *The Dove of Peace,* was premiered in Philadelphia in autumn 1912. Neither work caught on. Nor did the more ambitious opera *Cyrano de Bergerac,* produced at the Metropolitan the following February (with Pasquale Amato, Frances Alda, and Riccardo Martin, Alfred Hertz conducting). In 1917 Damrosch, at the request of General Pershing, turned to training military bandmasters in France, and when the shooting was over, he helped found the American Conservatory at Fontainebleau. In 1926 he pioneered the first coast-to-coast symphonic broadcast over the NBC Network, which appointed him its musical adviser the next year. After the merger of the orchestras, Damrosch devoted his activities entirely to radio, but in the mid-1930s also returned to composition, producing the cantata *An Abraham Lincoln Song,* the operas *The Man Without a Country* (in which Helen Traubel made her Metropolitan Opera debut in 1937), and the one-act *The Opera Cloak.* In 1943 he wrote another cantata, *Dunkirk.* He published an autobiography, *My Musical Life,* in 1923 (a second edition appeared in 1930).

RECORDINGS: On records he is represented by a few songs, notably his setting of Rudyard Kipling's "Danny Deever," a favorite vehicle for American baritones.

[1541] GERMAN, (Sir) Edward
VIOLINIST, CONDUCTOR
BORN: Whitchurch, February 17, 1862
DIED: London, November 11, 1936

Sir Edward German began life as a Shropshire lad named Edward German Jones. The son of an organist, he learned the keyboards at the paternal knee but taught himself the violin well enough to play in a local orchestra. An illness forced him to drop out of school in adolescence, but a local musician prepped him for the Royal Academy of Music, and he was admitted in 1880. He spent seven years there, majoring in violin and winning all sorts of awards. By 1884 he was teaching his instrument there and elsewhere, and in 1886 his first operetta *The Two Poets* (later revised as *The Rival Poets)* was given a successful London production and toured the provinces. He also had several nonoperatic works performed publicly, culminating in his first symphony the year of his graduation. It was during his Royal Academy period that he dropped his surname to avoid confusion with a like-named fellow student.

After leaving school, German continued to teach and to perform as an orchestral player. Within the year he was conductor of the orchestra at Richard Mansfield's Globe Theatre, where his incidental music for Shakespeare's *Richard III* won him notice shortly after his arrival there. Thereafter he was in great demand for such scores, writing music for several Shakespearean plays (notably *Henry VIII),* as well as contemporary works (e.g., playwright-librettist Anthony Hope's *Nell Gwyn*—the author was really Sir Anthony Hope Hawkins and the play was originally titled *English Nell).* In 1900 he was tapped to finish Sullivan's **[1397]** *The Emerald Isle* from very sketchy sketches. Though it was produced by D'Oyly Carte, it seems to have proved that Sullivan was past revival. But in 1902 German's own operetta *Merrie England,* though light-years from the Savoyard standard, won him a popularity that has lasted on his home turf. In 1903 *A Princess of Kensington* was somewhat less successful, but *Tom Jones,* premiered 1907, has also proved hardy. His least successful operetta was *Fallen Fairies,* a collaboration with W. S. Gilbert, who had vainly tried to get just about everyone else to accept the libretto. After that (though he wrote the march for George V's coronation) he decided—like his contemporary Lionel Monckton **[1538]**—that his day was over. Though he continued occasionally to conduct, he primarily amused himself as a country gentleman bachelor. He was knighted in 1928. German fancied himself a "serious composer," but what has lasted is the best of his stage music—although he cast most of it in a quasi-archaic style that has been described as "Olde Englyshe Tea-Shoppe."

RECORDINGS: Dances from the incidental music, the *Welsh Rhapsody* for orchestra, and selections from the operettas have been frequently recorded. Geoffrey Heald-Smith has recorded the Symphony No. 2 "Norwich."

[1542] GANNE, Gustave Louis (Gàn,
Güs-tàv′ Loo-ē′)
CONDUCTOR
BORN: Buxières-les-Mines, April 5, 1862
DIED: Paris, July 14, 1923

Remembed chiefly for two of the most stirring French marches, the *Marche Lorraine*
and *Le Père de la Victoire (The Father of
Victory)*, Louis Ganne died appropriately on
Bastille Day. Despite excellent training and
sound musical instincts, he devoted himself
exclusively to light music. Born in central
France near Moulins, he was a student and
prizewinner at the Paris Conservatoire under the tutelage of Théodore Dubois [1356],
Massenet [1396], and Franck [1284]. His
successful career began when he was twenty
with the production of his extravaganza *Les
Sources du Nil (The Source of the Nile)* at
the Folies-Bergère. Later dance pieces were
Au Japon (To Japan), Phryné, and *Kermesse
flamande (Carnival in Flanders)*. His first
comic opera, *Rabelais,* was produced at
Paris in 1892; but *Les Saltimbanques (The
Acrobats)* of 1899 and *Hans, le joueur de flûte
(Hans the Flutist)* of 1906 proved hardier.
(There were three others.) *Hans* was premiered in Monte-Carlo, where Ganne was
conductor of the casino orchestra. He also
conducted the opera balls in Paris, and
many of his dance pieces, such as the ma-
zurka *La Czarine,* won great popularity. He
also wrote many piano pieces. RECORDINGS:
There is a recording of *Les Saltimbanques*
and quite a few representations of the
marches and dances.

[1543] STERN, Leopold Lawrence
DRUGGIST, CELLIST, TEACHER
BORN: Brighton, April 5, 1862
DIED: London, September 10, 1904

Composing was only incidental to Leo
Stern's brief but spectacular career as a cellist. His German-born father, a violinist,
conducted the Brighton Symphony in which
young Leo served as percussionist. The boy
went to London to study apothecary science
when he was fifteen but took cello lessons on
the side. After following his chosen profession in Scotland for three years, he chucked
it and enrolled at the Royal Academy of
Music. He studied cello there with Alfred
Carlo Piatti, and was afterward a pupil of
Carl Davidov [1360] in Leipzig. He made
his solo debut in London in 1886 and thereafter appeared onstage with the sopranos
Emma Albani and Adelina Patti and with
Paderewski [1527]. Queen Victoria was
much taken with him and entrusted him

with improving the cello playing of her son-
in-law, Prince Henry of Battenberg (uncle of
the late Lord Mountbatten). In 1891 Stern
married a violinist, Nettie Carpenter. Four
years later, owing to a scheduling conflict
for the dedicatee Hanuš Wilhan, Stern premiered the Dvořák [1386] Concerto in B
Minor with the London Philharmonic Society, delighting the composer. He toured
North America in the 1897–98 season and in
the latter year married the pretty American
soprano Suzanne Adams. But his health began to deteriorate so badly that he had to
give up playing and died at forty two. The
widow, whose voice was already in a state of
decline, took her bereavement as a good opportunity to retire. She afterward opened a
laundry that catered successfully to the London carriage trade. RECORDINGS: In 1902
and 1903 she recorded a couple of his songs,
as did other singers of the period.

[1544] EMMANUEL, Marie-François
Maurice (Em-màn′-wel, Mà-rē⁷ Fràn-
swà′ Mō-rēs′)
MUSICOLOGIST, TEACHER, CRITIC
BORN: Bar-sur-Aube, May 2, 1862
DIED: Paris, December 14, 1938

Maurice Emmanuel was an extraordinarily
learned man and a productive scholar. He
was also a brilliant composer, but, like many
people who know too much, he was cautious
about evaluating his own work, and in the
end he rejected all but thirty of his creations.
Born in northeastern France near Troyes, he
grew up in the Burgundian wine center of
Beaune, where he was bowled over by the
modal melodies sung by the vineyard workers. He completed his secondary education
in nearby Dijon and at eighteen was enrolled
at the Paris Conservatoire. Here he studied
with Théodore Dubois [1356], Delibes
[1344], and perhaps most importantly with
the Hellenophile music historian Louis-Al-
bert Bourgault-Ducoudray. His history of
frustrations began at the Conservatoire
when Delibes took issue with some of his
experiments, banned the performance of his
music, and forbade him to compete for the
Prix de Rome. Emmanuel later studied with
Ernest Guiraud [1352] in Paris and with
Gevaert [1303] in Brussels. He also studied
art history at the Louvre and took a degree
in literature from the Sorbonne. His doctorate was granted for studies in ancient Greek
music and dance, on which he became one
of the great authorities of his time. (His two
operas, *Prométhée enchainé [Prometheus
Bound]* and *Salamine,* were derived from
tragedies by Aeschylus.) Powerful admirers

tried to get him appointed professor of music history at the Collège de France, but the minister of public instruction put the kibosh on that plan, and Emmanuel was forced to make a living by casting his pearls before high school students. His espousal of Gregorian chant as rehabilitated by the researches of the previous half-century at Solesmes Abbey got him fired from his directorship of the choir at Ste. Clothilde. But finally in 1909 he was appointed to succeed his mentor as professor of music history at the Paris Conservatoire. In the course of his career, he published works on sacred music, Greek music, and Baroque embellishments, studies of César Franck [1284] and Antonín Reicha [1059], and pieces on his beloved Burgundy. His music includes (besides the operas) 2 symphonies, incidental music, a string quartet, 6 sonatinas for piano, a sonata for bugle (!), and choral works. The unfamiliarity and neglect of his music owes less to its adventurousness than to the composer's reticence about having it heard. RECORDINGS: The soprano Madeleine Grey recorded some of his Burgundian folksong arrangements. The second symphony was recorded by the ORTF for the Barclay-Inédits label. Pianist Mireille Saunal performs the Sonatina No. 2.

[1545] LEHMANN, Liza

SINGER, TEACHER
BORN: London, July 11, 1862
DIED: Pinner, Middlesex, September 19, 1918

Elizabeth Nina Mary Frederika Lehmann was unrelated to other more famous singing Lehmanns, though her father, Rudolf, a painter, was German-born. Her mother, née Amelia Chambers, was the daughter of Robert Chambers, the self-educated Edinburgh encyclopedist and publisher, and, as "A.L.", was a writer of popular drawing-room songs. Liza, who had a remarkable if small soprano voice, studied singing at home and abroad (one of her teachers was Jenny Lind) and was a composition pupil of Hamish MacCunn [1595]. She made an immediate hit with her debut at the Monday Pops when she was twenty-three, but, probably wisely, eschewed the operatic stage. In 1894 she married Herbert Bedford (1867–1945), a successful miniature painter who turned increasingly to composition, retiring thereafter to domesticity. Having tried her hand at songs, she now began to occupy her leisure with more serious efforts. Almost immediately she had a great and lasting success

with *In a Persian Garden,* a cycle for four voices and piano drawn from Edward FitzGerald's popular *Rubáiyát of Omar Khayyám,* first sung at a private party in 1896 with an all-star cast—Emma Albani, Hilda Wilson, Ben Davies, and David Bispham. She was one of those that W. S. Gilbert tried to interest in his libretto *Fallen Fairies* (eventually set by Edward German [1541]), but in 1904 her operetta *Sergeant Brue* was kindly received. *The Vicar of Wakefield* was even more successful in 1906, and Thomas Beecham produced her one-act opera *Everyman* in 1915. There were also several cantatas, and further song cycles, some of them showing Lehmann's sense of humor in her treatment of such versifiers as Lewis Carroll and Hilaire Belloc. Later she returned to the stage to give recitals of her own songs, self-accompanied. Toward the end of her too-brief life, she taught voice and the Guildhall School. One wonders whether she intended such bits of Victorian kitsch as "There Are Fairies in the Bottom of Our Garden" seriously, for, no innovator, she had taste and a sense of what was musically appropriate. RECORDINGS: There are recordings of the *Omar Khayyám* cycle and of a number of songs.

[1546] BOND, Carrie Jacobs

PUBLISHER
BORN: Janesville, Wisc., August 11, 1862
DIED: Glendale, Calif., December 28, 1946

Whether we admire her sentimental tunes and pallid verses, Mrs. Bond should stand as an inspiration to us all. A small-town midwestern housewife with the degree of musical training that implies, she amused herself from childhood writing songs and painting. In 1895 she was left virtually penniless when her husband died after the collapse of his investments. On top of that she was injured in a fall on an icy street. She tried submitting some of her songs to publishers but was told they were too "Classical" to sell. Nothing daunted, she decided to publish them herself, designing the pastel-tinted covers with her own brush. In 1901 she found a market with "Just A-wearyin' for You" and in 1906 "I Love You Truly" became a bestseller. (Fifty years later it was still in demand as a wedding song.) Yet another triumph was "A Perfect Day" in 1910. Mrs. Bond later published an autobiography and a collection of her lyrics with critical commentary by the poetess. RECORDINGS: Many recordings exist.

[1547] DEBUSSY, Claude Achille (Du-büs-sē', Klôd A-shēl')
PIANIST, CONDUCTOR
BORN: St. Germain-en-Laye, August 22, 1862
DIED: Paris, March 25, 1918

For better or worse Claude Debussy must be seen as perhaps the most influential figure in twentieth-century music. Time will tell whether he represents a giant step forward in musical progress or one into the primrose path that led to a dead end. He clearly marks a crucial stage between Wagnerian [1230] chromaticism, the point of no return of the diatonic system, and such later phenomena as the Schoenbergian [1657] disavowal of tonality, Varèse's [1774] concept of music as patterned sound, and Cage's [2192] theories about the roles of chance and silence in the art. Though Debussy never broke entirely with the Western tradition of music, he fought against such ideas as tonal relationships, prescribed forms, and rhythms constrained by bar lines, and availed himself of antique and alien devices (e.g., church modes, oriental scales). His goal was to set music free of the fetters imposed by custom, time, and systems so that the composer might choose the sounds and colors his instinct dictated. In particular he wanted to break loose from the dead hand of the Classical school, which, as he became increasingly aware of his French musical heritage, he came to see as a Germanic tyranny. In 1910 Gabriele d' Annunzio hailed him as "Claude de France," and toward the end Debussy was adding to his signature the words "musicien français." Much to his chagrin, his imitators were many; but few of them managed much more than imitation, and within fifty years his "liberation" of music seemed to have led to more confining systems or to chaos.

Attempts to label Debussy have proved controversial and largely futile. The favorite tag has been "Impressionist." Borrowed from painting, this term was contemptuously coined by an art critic reviewing an exhibition by a group of young dissidents in 1874, deriving it from Claude Monet's picture "Impression: Sunrise." Impressionism has been variously defined as the recording of sense impressions rather than objects, the presentation of light instead of form, or a preoccupation with color and light. Insofar as such formulae can apply to music, it might be said that Debussy, in some of his works, is concerned with color and that he similarly is wont to deal with clumps of sound and fragmentary themes considered for their own sakes. But the term is applied with almost equal frequency to the Classical Ravel, and probably to most minds it indicates little more than a certain harmonic "feel." Debussy has also been termed—borrowing the term from literature—a "Symbolist." The poet Paul Verlaine summed up the Symbolist aim in a phrase which, translated, goes, "No color, only tinge" (or "suggestion"). Debussy, of course, set, or drew from, the poetry of some of the most important Symbolists, and his best-known music is surely a matter of nuances—but the term does not suffice for the whole range of his work, which runs from the salon-sentimental to the near neo-classical.

The Debussys—or de Bussys or de Bussis—have been traced back to seventeenth-century Burgundy, where they were peasants (despite the composer's sometime pretension of noble lineage). By the nineteenth century the family had become ubanized craftsmen and small tradesmen. Debussy's paternal grandfather was a carpenter and ran a wineshop at one time. He had nine children, one of whom, Jules-Alexandre, emigrated to England and became a music teacher in Manchester—the only other known exemplar of musical ability in the connection. The composer's father, Manuel-Achille, after a seven-year hitch in the army, married his mistress, Victorine Manoury, nine months before their son was born in the quarters above the little china shop Manuel was then operating. The couple subsequently produced four other children. Manuel became successively a traveling salesman, a printer's assistant, a clerk, and a soldier again (in the Franco-Prussian War), before joining the Paris communards in 1871 and winning a sentence of four years in prison for his efforts (suspended after he served one). Afterward he worked off and on as a bookkeeper and died in 1910.

The child, outwardly normal in all respects save for his large cranium and bulging forehead, was not baptized until nearly two years after his birth. The name given him was "Achille-Claude," and for a long time, to his displeasure, he was called "Achille." His godparents were his paternal aunt Clémentine, who called herself "Octavie de la Ferronière," and her lover of the moment, a stockbroker named Achille Arosa. Though the couple soon went their separate ways and married other partners, young Achille certainly spent some time in Cannes with his aunt, and it is likely that Arosa contributed to his godson's educational needs.

The details of Debussy's childhood remain obscure. Shortly after the baptism the family moved to Clichy, then a suburb of Paris, and three years later into the city itself. Manuel wanted his son to become a sailor. But during the Commune, the father became friends with Charles de Sivry, half-brother of Paul Verlaine's child-bride Mathilde Mauté. Sivry introduced the Debussys to his mother, a pianist named Antoinette Mauté de Fleurville. Mme Mauté recognized unusual musicality in the child, and took him on as a pupil. She claimed to have been a pupil of Chopin [1208]—and left Debussy certain all his life that the story was true, though the records do not show that it was. That she was a good teacher, however, is evident, for in little more than a year, in October 1872 (despite severe domestic troubles in the Mauté household occasioned by Verlaine's abandonment of Mathilde for Arthur Rimbaud), the boy was accepted into the Paris Conservatoire as a pupil of Antoine-François Marmontel (1816–98).

At first Debussy gave virtuoso promise. Within two years he could offer a performance of a Chopin concerto to the Conservatoire, and make his first public concert appearance at Chauny in northern France. Concurrently he studied theory with Albert Lavignac, who introduced him to Wagner's music. Later he took harmony lessons with Émile Durand and score reading with Auguste-Ernest Bazille. In 1877 he won a second prize for piano but was thereafter overlooked. Presumably he had lost interest in making a career as a performer. Or perhaps his revolutionary view of things displeased old Marmontel, for the more experienced Debussy became, the more he openly flouted and mocked the rules. Of the teachers least sympathetic to the rules, César Franck [1284] was the most notable; Debussy sat in on his organ classes and perhaps had informal hints on composition from him. Certainly Debussy had already begun writing songs (rather ordinary) during this time.

In the summer of 1879, probably aided by Marmontel, Debussy got a job as a chamber musician at the great château of Chenonceaux in the Loire Valley. His employer was a Scottish heiress, Marguerite Wilson-Pelouze, currently the mistress of the French president, Jules Grévy. (Her spendthrift brother, a cabinet minister in 1887, forced the latter's resignation through various malfeasances.) Debussy's chief function at Chenonceaux was to play the insomniac Marguerite to sleep. The following summer, doubtless with excellent recommendations, he was hired as a member of her resident piano trio by Nadezhda Filaretovna von Meck, the wealthy patroness and idolator of Piotr Ilyich Tchaikovsky [1377]. He traveled with her and her household in France,

Switzerland, and Italy, winding up in Fiesole in October.

On his return to the Conservatoire, Debussy began formal composition studies with the American-born Ernest Guiraud [1352], now barely known (if at all) for his completion of Offenbach's *Contes d' Hoffmann* and his recitatives for Bizet's [1363] *Carmen*. The easy-going and tolerant Guiraud was fascinated by his pupil's novel ideas but managed to keep him in check where conservatism counted. Debussy again spent the summer and fall with Mme. von Meck, this time in Russia, as he did the following year. By that time he had written a good deal—a piano trio and a symphony, as well as many songs and piano pieces. Some of the songs saw publication within the decade, and the *Danse bohémienne* of 1880 was his first piano composition to survive.

The Russian connection ended in 1882, and Debussy was forced to scratch for his existence. He gave piano lessons where he could, accompanied the Concordia Chorus, and played for a vocal teacher. In the last role, he became fascinated by one of the pupils, a Mme. Blanche Vasnier, to whom he dedicated several songs and who was the first to sing any of them (the composer accompanying). For nearly four years he spent much of his time in the Vasniers' winter and summer homes.

Though Debussy had taken no important prizes at the Conservatoire, Guiraud wanted him to compete for the Prix de Rome. In 1882 the candidate's submissions—a mandatory fugue and a piece for women's voices and orchestra called *Printemps*—did not get past the preliminaries. The next year he squeaked by them, but his setting of the cantata *Le Gladiateur* won only a second place to Paul Vidal's [1554]. In 1884, however, his *L'Enfant prodigue (The Prodigal Son)* took the grand prize. Debussy arrived at the Villa Medici for the required Roman sojourn the following February, heartsick at the separation from the Vasniers, who seem to have filled a parental role for him. He detested the place even more than he expected to. He found the situation artificial, the students pretentious, the villa ugly, and Rome a bore. His chief pleasure there seems to have been in discovering the music of the great Renaissance polyphonists sung at one of the churches. Twice in 1885 and once in 1886 he made unauthorized escapes back to Paris. One of the few high points of his stay was his acquaintanceship with the septuagenarian Liszt [1218], whom he heard play on occasion.

A perfectionist as a composer, Debussy found it difficult to write music on demand,

and the *envois* required by the Rome Academy came very hard. In the summer of 1885 he retired to a villa in Fiumicino, a beach resort near Rome, put at his disposal by Count Primoli, a grandson of Joseph Bonaparte, and set to work on a choral cantata, *Zuleima,* after a play by Heine. He came to dislike it intensely, but, probably under the urging of M. Vasnier, he submitted it something over a year later; the Academy turned it down. Late in 1886, having abandoned an opera based on Flaubert's *Salammbô* and a half-completed setting of Theodore de Banville's comedy *Diane au bois (Diana in the Woods),* he dashed off another *Printemps* (his third) for humming chorus and orchestra. A fire at the bindery destroyed the orchestral score, though it was rewritten twenty-six years later by Henri Büsser [1627] under the composer's supervision on the basis of the score for piano four hands. The Academicians grudgingly accepted this offering, noting that they had hoped for better.

It was now February 1887. Debussy had forwarded two thirds of what was required and put in the minimum two years residence. He happily forewent the third and the continental travel and headed back for Paris. He moved in with his family, only to be plunged into an economic crisis when his father was fired. (He remained unemployed for nearly eight years.) Though Debussy himself had no income to speak of, thanks to a wealthy friend he visited the Bayreuth Festival in the summers of 1888 and 1889, attending two performances each of *Parsifal* and *Meistersinger,* and one of *Tristan und Isolde.* Up to this time, he had been, like most trendy young French musicians of the day, a passionate, even doctrinaire Wagnerian. Within five years, however, the wind had veered to a different quarter. During this time he published the Verlaine songs later called *Ariettes oubliées (Forgotten Ariettas),* worked on the set of Baudelaire songs, and wrote, premiered, and published the *Petite Suite* for piano duet. Still owing the Academy an *envoi,* he completed and submitted the cantata for female voices and orchestra *La Demoiselle élue (The Blessed Damozel,* after the poem by Dante Gabriel Rossetti).

In 1889, the year in which the cantata was completed, there was a World's Fair on the Champ de Mars in Paris, overlooked by the newly erected Eiffel Tower. There Debussy discovered the art of the Far East and was mesmerized by the Indochinese theater, dancers, and Balinese *gamelan* music, which last he took very much to heart.

In due course, the Rome academicians looked on Debussy's most recent cantata, found it reasonably good, and proposed that it be presented in concert, together with the *Fantaisie* for piano and orchestra, which Debussy had completed in 1890. But, they told him, such a concert required an overture which he must deliver. Debussy was not of a mind to produce an overture; he flatly refused to produce, and the whole thing was called off. A year earlier he had joined the Société National de Musique, which now offered to premiere the *Fantaisie* (which had been accepted and printed by the publisher Choudens), under the baton of Vincent d'Indy [1462], with the composer as soloist. Following the first rehearsal, however, Debussy withdrew the piece, and it was not published until two years after he died. His reasons are obscure: the piece is not particularly characteristic, sounding more like Massenet [1396] than Debussy, but it is certainly not a bad work. Meanwhile, perhaps at the demand of his parents that he do something to bolster the family exchequer, he was plugging drearily away at an opera, *Rodrigue et Chimène,* to a libretto by the poet-critic Catulle Mendès, a leading drumbeater for the Wagner cult. After a couple of years, he gave it up, leaving an incomplete vocal score.

The fact is that at thirty Debussy was still little more than an obscure bohemian *musiker.* His meaningful output at the time consisted mostly of songs and miscellaneous piano pieces, many of them as yet unpublished. (Mendès had paid for the abortive publication of the *Fantaisie;* the Baudelaire songs were limited to a subscription of 150 copies.) There lay behind him (and ahead!) a path strewn with fragments of abandoned projects. Nor did he move in circles calculated to insure his fame as a composer. He delighted in hanging around the "sporting" crowd in bistros. He hobnobbed with painters (e.g., Whistler, Blanc) and with writers (e.g., Mallarmé, Regnier). In the latter group, he struck up one of his most intimate friendships in 1893 with the poet Pierre Louÿs, which lasted until their respective marriages at the end of the decade, and during which they once considered sharing quarters. There were few musicians of consequence. An acquaintance with Paul Dukas [1574] from Paris Conservatoire days ripened into little more than that. A warm friendship with Ernest Chausson [1484] was abruptly broken off in 1894. The relationship with Erik Satie [1578] would have profited him nothing at that period. In 1890, however, he was taken under the wing of Georges Hartmann, publisher and initial backer of the Concerts Colonne, who not only brought out Debussy's works but settled an annuity on him.

Nevertheless Debussy was about to take center stage. The year 1893 may be seen as the turning point. In its course he produced the *Proses lyriques,* songs for which he wrote his own texts and which then had little impact. But he also wrote his "first" (and only) string quartet (mysteriously designated as "Op. 10") which, played at a concert of the Société National by the Ysaÿe Quartet in December, created a mild sensation. More importantly, he was working on what was to be a "Prélude, Interlude, and Concluding Paraphrase" for Stephan Mallarme's poem *"L'Après-midi d'un faune"* (The Afternoon of a Faun") and began an operatic setting of Maurice Maeterlinck's Symbolist drama *Pelléas et Mélisande.* He had seen the play in a single unsuccessful production in May and had recognized it as the piece he had been waiting for. Introduced by Regnier, Debussy and Louÿs visited the playwright in Ghent and got his permission to do what was necessary with the text. The music was essentially completed by 1895, but Debussy took another seven years to orchestrate it and to make endless revisions.

For the Mallarmé work, only the *Prélude* was forthcoming. Ysaÿe [1507] scheduled it for an all-Debussy concert which he presented in Brussels the following March, but it was not yet ready. The concert included the quartet, songs, and *La Demoiselle élue,* which had been premiered in Paris by the Société National eleven months before. The latter organization played the *Prélude* at the end of December, conducted by the Swiss composer-conductor Gustave Doret [1582]. The enthusiastic audience recognized in the free treatment of themes and the wispy development something new and effective, and the work was quickly taken up by other conductors. However, despite this success the next several years were essentially barren, apart from work on the opera (accepted in 1897 by the Opéra-Comique for performance, when, as, and if) and work on the pieces that would eventually become the three *Nocturnes.* The only music that Debussy completed between 1894 and 1899 was the *Chansons de Bilitis,* three songs to texts by Louÿs for soprano and piano. (A year or two later he also composed a melodrama with the same title for narrator, two flutes, two harps, and celeste.)

Debussy's personal life during this decade was often stormy. Twice he thought of moving, like his uncle, to England. (He visited London several times in his life and had an affection for things English.) Once a wealthy patron tried to get him an engagement in New York. Probably in 1889, Debussy acquired a live-in mistress, a Norman woman four years his junior, named Gabrielle Dupont but preferring to be called Gaby Lhéry. The liaison lasted until 1898, with frequent upheavals and interruptions; Gaby afterward charged these to quarrels over money or lack of it, but there were obviously other women whom Debussy took more or less seriously. He and Auguste Rodin were at one time paying court to Paul Claudel's sister Camille. At another time he was enamored of Mallarmé's daughter Geneviève. Around 1893 he proposed to Catherine, the daughter of the painter Alfred Stevens, who rejected him for an admirer who could support her. In February 1894 he was accepted by Thérèse Roger, who premiered two of the *Proses lyriques* in the Brussels concert the next month. The engagement, however, was broken off on account of Gaby. Early in 1897 Gaby found an incriminating letter in Debussy's pocket, kicked up a row, and, according to reports, was hospitalized after shooting herself, though no records substantiate this. The letter was perhaps to the fashion model Rosalie ("Lily") Texier, with whom he took up living the next year. That idyll shortly went on the rocks. Debussy, broken-hearted, begged Lily to come back. On Gaby's advice she refused. This time it was Debussy who threatened suicide. He and Lily were married in a civil ceremony (being unable to afford anything better) on October 19, 1899, with Satie and the newlywed Louÿs among the official witnesses. Debussy had to leave the group and give a music lesson in order to pay for the wedding breakfast at a local *brasserie.*

Debussy's modest artistic success had not improved his financial situation; not only was he deeply in debt, but Hartmann's unexpected death in 1900 cut off his only regular income and made him liable for advances on unwritten works. On top of this, Lily had to undergo an operation that August. By then the *Nocturnes* had almost reached their final completion. These had started out, around 1892, as *Trois scènes au crépuscule (Three Twilight Scenes)* for orchestra, based on likenamed poems by Henri de Regnier, the first and third of which would feature a wordless female choir. By 1894 Debussy was converting these materials into a violin concerto which he had promised to Eugène Ysaÿe but which never materialized. In the final upshot the first two pieces, *Nuages (Clouds)* and *Fêtes* were purely orchestral, whereas the third, *Sirènes,* retained the chorus (and, performance costs being what they are, consequently remains the least-performed of the three). The title *Nocturnes* owes more to

Whistler than it does to Chopin. The first two were first heard at the Concerts Lamoureux under the direction of Camille Chévillard on December 9; *Sirènes* was added to them at a similar concert the following October. They met with immediate success; one critic called them "pure music," expressive of only what music alone can say. Debussy had arrived. Despite his lack of academic education (his orthography remained problematic), he became, between these two concerts, music critic of *La Révue blanche,* the 1901 equivalent of a "little mag." (It retained Toulouse-Lautrec to do its advertising posters.) Debussy's pieces were witty, attacking *en passant* the things he hated in the French musical world. In the course of writing he invented an alter-ego for himself, "M. Croche, the dilettante hater" (obviously patterned after Paul Valéry's M. Teste). But by the end of the year he had resigned, pleading spent nerves and overwork. During 1903 he wrote a weekly column for the daily *Gil Blas.* After that he contributed sporadically to various journals, from 1906 to 1914.

The year 1902, perhaps the climactic one in Debussy's rise to fame, began on January 11 with the premiere of the suite *Pour le piano* by the Spanish pianist Ricardo Viñes, who would later give the first performances of a number of Debussy's other great piano works: *Estampes (Prints),* 1904; *Masques* and *L'Ile joyeuse (The Joyous Isle)* both 1905; both sets of *Images,* 1906–08; several of the *Préludes;* and others. More significantly, it was the year in which *Pelléas* was finally staged. The final contract with the Opéra-Comique had been signed the previous year, but there was some delay because it had been deemed essential for the composer to write orchestral interludes to cover the many scene changes. Then ensued an unexpected contretemps with Maeterlinck. The management had chosen the Scottish soprano Mary Garden, who had attained stardom when she had taken over two years earlier for the creatrix of the role of Louise in Gustave Charpentier's **[1524]** new opera of that title. Maeterlinck had somehow gotten it into his head that the part would go to his mistress, the *diseuse* Georgette Leblanc (often billed as "Mme. Maeterlinck"), who later maintained she had actually rehearsed it with Debussy. Maeterlinck spoke of a duel, and there was a confrontation involving a cudgel or a walking stick, but nothing came of it all except protests from the playwright that his masterpiece had been butchered. (Eighteen years later he at last saw the opera and wrote Garden to apologize for his errors on all counts.) The invited dress-rehearsal audience was rude and noisy, that of the premiere on April 30 scarcely less so, and the critical reception was at first negative. But the work was overpowering and quickly established itself. It is perhaps the most perfect welding of words and music for the stage ever written—a true music drama in which the elements never get in each other's way, the music (and the silences) always supportive of the text. It paved the way—alas!—for numerous imitations, most of which are merely boring.

The emulations began almost immediately, and Debussy found himself, much to his chagrin, the unwilling "leader" of a school of Debussyists. Nor did his triumph work entirely to his own benefit: he repeatedly returned to projects for the operatic stage that sapped his time and energy and resisted completion. At one time he signed an open-end contract with the Metropolitan Opera for three works, two based on stories by Edgar Allan Poe—*Le Diable dans le beffroi (The Devil in the Belfry)* and *La Chute de la maison Usher (The Fall of the House of Usher*—and *La Légende de Tristan.* He managed some considerable progress on the first two (a reconstructed fragment from the second has been performed in recent years) but apparently made none on the third. He also had plans to write an opera based on Poe's "Masque of the Red Death." In February of 1903, to please his parents, he allowed himself to be enrolled in the *Légion d'honneur.* Shortly afterward the two *Danses sacrée et profane* for harp and string orchestra were introduced at the Schola Cantorum.

By 1903 a major crisis had arisen in the composer's tenuous marriage. He had met and fallen in love with Emma Bardac *(née* Moyse), a fine amateur singer and the wife of a wealthy banker. He left Lily the following spring and spent August and September at the seaside with Emma. On October 14 Lily tried to kill herself with (curiously but undoubtedly symbolically) two bullets in the groin. The story, thinly disguised, made the papers, and many of Debussy's few friends abandoned him. Both Debussy and Emma were divorced by their respective partners, and in 1905 she bore him a daughter, named Claude-Emma but called "Chouchou" by her adoring father. After the legal grace period they were married in 1908. Emma had enough money to buy them an apartment, where they lived until Debussy's death. They had counted on a legacy from Emma's rich uncle, but when he died she found he had cut her off without a sou. The upshot of the legal actions taken by Hartmann's heir was that Debussy lost all rights to his works published by that firm. He tried to hold on to *Pelléas*, but further debts and the cost of the divorces forced him to sell it outright to the publisher Jacques Durand, with the proviso that the latter have an option on all his future compositions. In fact debts and further lawsuits necessitated Debussy's undertaking a concert career, as pianist and conductor, at a time when such efforts were increasingly hard on him, for in 1909 he exhibited the first symptoms of the rectal cancer that finally killed him a decade later. (From all reports Debussy was a mediocre conductor but a remarkable pianist who—the formula has it—played as though the instrument had no hammers. Unfortunately, his only known recordings, dating from 1904 and dim of sound, are limited to four sides in which he accompanies Mary Garden in three of the *Ariettes* and the "tower" scene from *Pelléas*.) It should perhaps also be noted that in these years of upheaval Debussy came to a parting of the ways with two musicians who admired him: Paul Dukas, for treading on his turf in setting Maeterlinck's *Ariane et Barbe-bleue (Ariadne and Bluebeard)*, and Maurice Ravel [1666] for a number of peccadillos, real or imagined.

It is not surprising that Debussy suffered a creative dry period for a time after this; what *is* remarkable is that at the height of his troubles he produced as much as he did. Apart from the works noted above, he completed two sets of songs—the second *Fêtes galantes* and the *3 Chansons de France*—in 1904, and two orchestral pieces for a production of Shakespeare's *King Lear* (as well as a new orchestration of *L'Enfant prodigue)* in 1905. On October 15 of the latter year, Chévillard introduced at the Concerts Lamoureux what has come to be seen as probably Debussy's most characteristic and remarkable orchestral work, *La Mer (The Sea)*, on which he had worked since 1903. In defending it, he himself invoked the term "Impressionism." The public and most of the critics had apparently been expecting tonal seascapes in the descriptive manner, which of course they did not get. Moreover Chévillard seems to have done something of a botch job. Many were outraged and said so, and from this time on Debussy was a highly controversial figure. On January 19, 1908 he inaugurated his career as conductor with this same work at the Concerts Colonne, repeating it a week later and officiating at the London premiere immediately afterward. These concerts marked his first public appearance in six years and were like a Resurrection for his adherents; especially at the second performance there was a noisy and prolonged clash between supporters and detractors. In December Harold Bauer played the first performance of the *Children's Corner (sic!)* for piano. It was also in 1908 that Debussy completed the choral *Trois Chansons de Charles d'Orléans*, begun in 1898. And he continued to work on the orchestral *Images*, finishing *Ibéria* in piano score.

Besides the usual unrealized projects, one might here mention two that had a curious history. At some point Elise Hall, an affluent Boston matron who had taken up the saxophone on the advice of her physician, commissioned Debussy to write her a concerto. He was unfamiliar with the instrument and not much interested in the project, and so put it aside. In the midst of his divorce Mrs. Hall turned up to collect her piece. By 1908 he had cobbled up a piano score of a "Moorish Rhapsody," which he shipped off to her, indicating that the orchestral version would follow. It didn't, and it was not until 1919 that Jean Roger-Ducasse [1639] produced one based on a few sketches. It became known as the *Rapsodie* for saxophone and orchestra. Again, in 1911, when Debussy needed every franc he could get, he accepted a commission from another woman, the accomplished English dancer Maud Allen, for an "Egyptian" ballet, *Khamma*. Here he grew pressed for time and his interests were drawn elsewhere. At one time he suggested to Charles Koechlin [1592] that *he* write it over Debussy's signature. In the end he left it to Koechlin to orchestrate. It went unperformed in the composer's lifetime.

The year 1910 was the beginning of nearly five years of intense activity. Debussy was now an international figure, chiefly thanks to *Pelléas*, which had met with general success everywhere save in Germany and Italy, where it was not immediately liked or understood. The composer was increasingly called on to conduct—at various times in London, in Vienna and Budapest late in 1910, in Italy in 1911, in Russia in 1913, in Rome and the Netherlands in 1914, war and ill health precluded further travel. He also of course performed in Paris—in this capacity and as pianist and accompanist (to Maggie Teyte and Ninon Vallin). He dined with Richard Strauss [1563] and Mahler [1525] and seems not to have been very *simpatico* with either. He struck up a friendship with Stravinsky [1748], who came to Paris with the Diaghilev ballet in 1910, but within five years it had obviously cooled—though both men profited from the relationship.

In 1910 the "Spanish" and "French" movements—*Ibéria* and *Rondes de printemps (Spring Rounds)*—of the orchestral

Images were completed. The first, presented by Gabriel Pierné [1555] at the Concerts Colonne on February 20, evoked considerable applause, but a proffered encore was prevented by loud protests. *Gigues* (alias *Gigues tristes)*, the "English" segment, gave Debussy considerable trouble and was not heard until January 26, 1913. (André Caplet [1708] had made a previous four-hand arrangement and probably helped with the orchestration.) It produced puzzlement and hostility and has never won real popularity. Otherwise 1910 was a relatively fertile year. Debussy finished the first book of *Préludes* for piano, which were variously premiered by Viñes and the composer himself. There were also two separate piano pieces, *D'un cahier d'esquisses (From a Sketchbook*—first played by Ravel, despite the tension between the two men) and the little cocktail waltz, *La plus que lente (The More-Than-Slow)*. For tryouts at the Paris Conservatoire, Debussy turned out a *Petite pièce* for clarinet and piano, and an optimistically titled *Première rapsodie* for the same combination but orchestrated soon afterward. Finally he wrote two important sets of songs: *Le Promenoir de deux amants (The Stroll of Two Lovers)*, one of whose three songs was borrowed direct from the *Trois Chansons de France*, and the *Trois Ballades de François Villon*. These were first sung early in 1911, the former by Jane Bathori, the latter by Paule de l'Estang (and in March in orchestral dress by a baritone named Clarke).

The most demanding project of this period—the one that made the composer despair of finishing *Khamma*—was the music requested by Gabriele d'Annunzio for a sort of decadent mystery play, *Le Martyre de Saint Sébastien (The Martyrdom of St. Sebastian)*. D'Annunzio—Prince of Monte Nevoso, swashbuckler, hedonist, poet, soldier of fortune, pioneer aviator, playwright, and *poseur*—had been run out of Italy by his creditors, a fact that did little to curb his flamboyance in Paris, where he had sought refuge. He made contact with Debussy late in 1910 and pressured him into having the music ready for the first performance on May 22 of the following year. Caplet, who conducted it, had again been pressed into service, certainly as orchestrator and perhaps as author of parts of it. When he heard of the project, the archbishop of Paris was mortally offended (a male saint portrayed in a theater by a female dancer!), threatened the faithful who attended with excommunication, and proscribed the poet's published works *en masse*. The dress rehearsal had to be canceled because of the accidental death of the war minister. In any case the work,

which is neither fish, flesh, nor fowl, did not succeed and has never done so. As for the music, it was of a Gregorian chastity, stylistically speaking—some reviewers thought immediately of Wagner's *Parsifal*—and it drew the customary mixed reaction. It has since been successful in concert arrangements, with or without a narrator.

In 1912 Debussy grudgingly countenanced Diaghilev's request that he be permitted to offer a ballet version of *L'après-midi d'un faune*, to be choreographed by Nijinsky, who would dance the title role. Debussy did not care for the result, muttering to himself apropos the *premiere danseur*, "You are ugly! Get off the stage!" Much of the audience was distressed by the angularity of the dancing and shocked by the suggestiveness of the faun's actions. But this experiment produced others. The English dancer Loie Fuller, for example, presented a solo version of *Nuages* and *Fêtes* the next year. And Diaghilev commissioned a new Debussy-Nijinsky work based on a love triangle and a tennis game, and called *Jeux (Games)*. The initial scenario was frankly silly, and Debussy took the project on only because it offered him 10,000 francs. However, he became much involved in the music itself and had the score ready for the opening performance on May 15, 1913. Seeing it on the stage, the composer hated it all over again and walked out midway through. Some of the public was put off by seeing dancers in white ducks and tennis skirts, and there was little enthusiasm. Two weeks later the riotous premiere of *Le Sacre du printemps*—Debussy is said to have consulted Stravinsky on the orchestration of *Jeux*—put the latter work out of mind. Though some recognized that its harmonies, its development, and its shape represented a step forward in its composer's progress, it was generally (until recently) viewed, as were most of his late works, as the product of the flagging energies of a dying man. In 1913, however, the latter still had the strength to complete the second and last book of *Préludes,* to write *Syrinx* for solo flute, for use in the play *Psyché* by his old friend Gabriel Mourey, and to compose three songs to texts by Mallarmé. Finally there was yet another ballet project, *La Boîte à joujoux (The Toy Chest)*. This was a ballet for children proposed by a painter named André Helle, who had illustrated a children's book by this title. With his own little girl in mind and assuming the work would be danced by children (not Helle's intention), Debussy wrote a charming and simple piano score.

It was not so much his health as world events that brought Debussy up short. In

1914 he began orchestrating the ballet. That summer he produced the set of piano duets, *Épigraphes antiques*, though these were in fact arrangements of music for a chamber ensemble written fourteen years earlier to accompany recitations of some of Louÿs' *Chansons de Bilitis*. (Pierre Boulez **[2346]** has reconstructed the earlier work from the incomplete ms. It has also been orchestrated.) But the outbreak of war in August so affected Debussy that his creative skills were quite paralyzed. (The little ballet was eventually finished by Caplet but was not produced—with adult dancers—until after its composer's death.) In the autumn Debussy managed a *Berceuse heroïque (Heroic Lullaby)* based on the Belgian national anthem, in response to a request from the London *Daily Telegraph* that he write something for a book in homage to King Albert; he orchestrated it the following year. His depression was further aggravated by the death of his mother in March 1915. His publisher, to give him something to take his mind off his troubles, asked him to edit a new edition of Chopin, to whom Debussy considered he had a direct pipeline through his old teacher. (Pianists who know Chopin think differently.) By summer, however, Debussy was enjoying what proved to be a last flareup of compositional activity. Staying at the seaside in Normandy, he completed the three pieces for two pianos called *En blanc et noir (In Black and White)* and wrote the remarkable and demanding set of abstract piano *Études*. Patriotically inspired, he looked back to the old clavecinists and proposed a set of six chamber sonatas for various instrumental combinations. Before the year was out he had completed one for cello and piano, and another for flute, viola (originally oboe), and harp. Late in the fall, moved by the devastation in northern France, he wrote a little song to his own text, *"Noël des enfants qui n'ont pas plus de maison"* ("Carol of the Homeless Children"). By then his illness had progressed so far that in December he had to submit to a colostomy operation. During 1916 he was able to do very little, especially in the early months when he was undergoing radium therapy and was sedated with morphine. It was not until October that he found the strength and will to begin the third of the sonatas, this one for violin and piano. (A fourth, for oboe, French horn, and harpsichord, never got beyond the talking stage and the remaining two not even that far.) At the winter solstice he returned to the Paris concert stage for a concert for war relief, in the course of which he and Roger-Ducasse played *En blanc et noir*. He also began, to a

text by his friend Louis Laloy, a choral cantata, *Ode à la France,* but left it in a fragmentary state; it was completed after his death by the pianist Marius-François Gaillard. In the spring of 1917 he was again strong enough to complete the violin sonata and to edit (without enthusiasm) the violin sonatas of J. S. Bach **[684]** at the behest of Durand. He also made several more concert appearances. Those that attended them could not mistake the gravity of his physical state. On May 5 he accompanied Gaston Poulet in the premiere of the sonata; they played it again in September at St.-Jean-de-Luz, where Debussy was summering. It was his last concert. When he returned to the apartment on the Avenue du Bois de Boulogne, he took to his bed for good. After weeks of pain, he succumbed on March 25, 1918, while Paris was under bombardment from German planes and the famous monster cannon "Big Bertha." Three days later he was laid to rest in the Père Lachaise Cemetery on the Left Bank, during a fearsome shelling that killed several worshipers in the Church of St. Gervais. Newspapers being severely limited, there were no local obituaries. Later the body was moved to the cemetery in Passy. A year later Chouchou contracted diphtheria and followed her father. Her mother survived him by sixteen years, Lily Texier-Debussy by fourteen.

RECORDINGS: All of the official Debussy canon has been recorded, most works many times. Most of the unpublished and fragmentary works remain untouched, exceptions including the melodrama *Chansons de Bilitis*, the Büsser reorchestration of the 1887 *Printemps*, the four-hand arrangement of the allegro of the early symphony, the two-piano *Lindaraja* of 1901, the surviving movement of the 1880 Trio in G Major, and a few immature songs. Of historical interest are selections from *Pelléas* by Hector Dufranne, the first Golaud, and by Maggie Teyte, as well as songs by such creators as Teyte, Jane Bathori, and Vallin. A recording of the *Usher* fragment has just been released.

[1548] DIEPENBROCK, Alphons Johannes Maria (Dēp'-en-brok, Ál'-fons Yō-han'-nes Mà-rē'-à)
CLASSICIST, TEACHER, CRITIC
BORN: Amsterdam, September 2, 1862
DIED: Amsterdam April 5, 1921

Alphons Diepenbrock is regarded as the Grand Old Man of Post-Renaissance Dutch music. Though he had violin and piano lessons in childhood, he took a doctorate in classical languages at the University of Amsterdam and taught them for a time, first in the public schools and then privately. He learned to compose largely by reading and by analyzing scores. To learn to write religious music properly (as he saw it), he studied the work of the great Netherlands polyphonists. More modern influences came from Wagner [1230], Berlioz [1175], his friend Gustav Mahler [1525], and his almost-exact contemporary Debussy [1547]. The bulk of his composition was vocal, including church music (a *Mass*, a *Te Deum*, and shorter works) and songs in Dutch, French, and German. His most original efforts in this area are his several pieces for solo voice(s) and orchestra—*Les Elfes* (soprano, baritone, and women's chorus); 2 *Hymnen an die Nacht* (one for soprano, one for contralto); *Vondels Vaart naar Agrippine, Im grossen Schweigen*, and *Lydische Nacht* (baritone); and *Hymne aan Rembrandt* (soprano, women's chorus). His orchestral output consists chiefly of his incidental music for plays—e.g., Aristophanes' *The Birds*, Goethe's *Faust*, Sophocles' *Elektra*, Verhagen's *Marsyas*, and Vondel's *Gijsbrecht van Aemstel*. Many works were left unfinished. His articles on music have been collected. RECORDINGS: Eduard van Beinum recorded two movements from *Marsyas* and Elly Ameling a few songs. Dutch CBS recently included three songs in an anthology of twentieth-century Dutch songs. Dutch sources have also provided recordings of *Im grossen Schweigen*, both *Hymnen an die Nacht*, the *Elektra Suite*, the vocal-chamber work *Wenn ich ihn nur habe*, and some piano pieces.

[1549] BOËLLMANN, Léon (Bwel'-màn, Lā-on')
ORGANIST, TEACHER, CRITIC
BORN: Ensisheim, September 25, 1862
DIED: Paris, October 11, 1897

Born into a large family in an Alsatian village between Colmar and Mulhouse, Boëllmann was taken to Paris when the Germans appropriated the province in 1871. He was enrolled in the Niedermeyer School, where he studied with Niedermeyer's [1167] sons-in-law Gustave Lefèvre and the organist Eugène Gigout [1417]. He acquitted himself with distinction and on graduating in 1881 became assistant organist at St. Vincent de Paule and then organist. He married Lefèvre's daughter Louise in 1885, took quarters in Gigout's home, and taught in the school Gigout founded. He also served as critic for a Paris journal, *L'Art musical*. He died at thirty-five, leaving a body of work

that included music for orchestra (notably a symphony), choir, and chamber combinations, as well as songs and piano pieces. However, he is remembered chiefly for his organ music. RECORDINGS: Recordings of the organ music include the *Suite gothique* (several versions) and exerpts from *Heures mystique*, a collection of 100 pieces for harmonium.

[1550] NEVIN, Ethelbert Woodbridge
PIANIST
BORN: Edgeworth, Pa., November 25, 1862
DIED: New Haven, Conn., February 17, 1901

Ethelbert Nevin was the fifth of the eight children of a writer who lived near Pittsburgh. Both of his parents were musical, and his younger brother Arthur (1871–1943), who also composed, became a successful musical educator. Ethelbert had piano lessons with local teachers from the time he was ten and had some lessons with Leipzig-trained Franz Magnus Boehme when he visited Germany with his parents in 1877. But his family did not countenance his taking up music professionally and sent him to college to learn business methods. In 1880 he took an office job with the Pennsylvania Railroad but detested it so that his father finally broke down and let him go his way. It led at first to Boston and further study with B. J. Lang and Stephen Emery. After two years he returned to Pittsburgh to try to survive as a teacher and performer. He soon realized that he was not ready and in 1884 enrolled in the Klindworth Academy in Berlin, from which he graduated *summa cum laude*. He also studied briefly with Bülow [1310]. He came home again in 1886, pleased the Pittsburghers with a solo recital, and then settled in Boston, where he brought his hometown bride, Anne Paul, two years later. They sailed for Europe in 1891 and remained there for six years, chiefly in Italy. But Ethelbert's health began to deteriorate, and they came back to the States in 1897. He opened a studio in Carnegie Hall in New York. It was there that he wrote "The Rosary," a song damned by some for rampant sentimentality, by others for irreverence, but a runaway bestseller. By the summer of 1898, however, Nevin caved in and went home to try to recuperate. He did improve sufficiently for him to settle in New Haven in 1900, where he wrote another very popular song, "Mighty Lak' a rose." But he suffered a relapse and died at thirty-eight. Nevin wrote a pantomime *(Lady Florian's Dream)* and a cantata, but most of his work consisted of songs and graceful piano pieces. His Op. 13, *Water Scenes* for piano, contains "Narcissus," which, published in 1891, became so ubiquitous that he cursed the day he wrote it. RECORDINGS: Besides recordings of his more popular songs, there is an LP side of piano music played by Paulina Drake.

[1551] BLUMENFELD, Felix Mikhailovich (Bloo'-men-felt, Fā'-liks Měk-hī-lō'-vich)
PIANIST, TEACHER, CONDUCTOR
BORN: Kovalevka, April 19, 1863
DIED: Moscow, January 21, 1931

A native of the southern Ukraine, Blumenfeld, after some preliminary piano instruction, went to the St. Petersburg Conservatory, where he studied composition with Rimsky-Korsakov [1416] and from which he graduated in 1885. He was retained on the faculty and named professor of piano two years later. From 1895 he doubled as chorus master at the Imperial Opera and was eventually made conductor there. The upheaval of the Conservatory attendant on the 1905 Revolution forced him out, but he returned in 1911 (giving up his conductorship), remaining until the next revolution. Thereafter he spent four years at the Kiev Conservatory (where Vladimir Horowitz was one of his pupils), and then spent the rest of his life, 1922–1931, at the Moscow Conservatory. He was a notable concert virtuoso and also on occasion accompanied Feodor Chaliapin and other famous artists. Though he wrote a symphony and similarly ambitious works, he was known as a composer chiefly of songs and piano pieces. RECORDINGS: A few of the piano pieces have been recorded.

[1552] WEINGARTNER, Paul Felix (Vīn'-gärt-ner, Poul Fā'-liks)
CONDUCTOR, PIANIST, ADMINISTRATOR, WRITER
BORN: Zara, June 2, 1863
DIED: Winterthur, May 7, 1942

Felix Weingartner yearned for immortality as a composer but is remembered as a legendary conductor, especially of Beethoven [1063]. Born in what is now Zadar, Yugoslavia, to a German mother and a minor Viennese nobleman, he inherited the latter's title at the age of four. His first important music teacher was Wilhelm Mayer ("W. A. Rémy") in Graz. By the time he was sixteen, he already had several musical publications. In 1880 he entered the University of Leipzig

to take a philosophy degree. However, Brahms [1329] had been impressed by some of his music, and helped get him admitted to the conservatory there, where he studied with Reinecke [1292], Salomon Jadassohn (1831–1902), and the rest of that familiar coterie. He was awarded the Mozart Prize on graduation, and then went to Weimar to study with Liszt [1218]. There Liszt arranged the production of Weingartner's first opera *Sakuntala* in 1884, the year its composer began his peripatetic directorial career in Königsberg. In 1885 he moved on to Danzig and in 1887 to Hamburg. There he created a teapot-tempest by trying to show up Bülow's [1310] poor—as he considered it —interpretation of Bizet's [1363] *Carmen*. He left Hamburg for Mannheim in 1889 and stayed until 1891. A handsome man and (initially) a podium showman, Weingartner was immensely attractive to women, five of whom he married (in succession). The first was Marie Juillerat, whom he wed on becoming imperial *Kapellmeister* in Berlin. But at the Berlin Opera he was considered too radical—an adept of astrology, he had foreseen the worst—and he resigned that post in 1898 to Richard Strauss [1563], though he hung on to the concerts of the court orchestra until 1907. During the first years of this period he also conducted the Kaim Orchestra in Munich and appeared as pianist of the Weingartner Trio. In 1903 he married the Baroness Feodora von Dreifus.

When Mahler [1525] left the Austrian Imperial Opera in 1908, Weingartner was named his successor. He was immediately sued by Berlin for breach of contract (Weingartner was always involved in legal proceedings). Moreover his wholesale changes and his high-handedness at the Berlin Opera made him decidedly *non grata* there, and he was forced to resign in 1911—though he held on to the Vienna Philharmonic concerts for sixteen more years. One bone of contention had been the plummy roles that went to his mistress, the American soprano Lucille Wasself, who called herself Lucille Marcel, and whom he married in 1911. In the next few years they were connected with the Hamburg and Boston operas, and Weingartner conducted the New York Philharmonic. During World War I he was *Kapellmeister* at Darmstadt, then returned to Vienna to direct the Volksoper for five years before going to Basel to run the Basel Conservatory. He directed the Vienna State Opera again for a season in 1935 but in his latter years was increasingly on the road as a guest conductor. He founded his own conducting school at Interlaken in Switzerland. His last two wives were Roxo Bertha Kalisch, a poetess, and Carmen Studer, a pupil.

Weingartner's reputation as a conductor is unchallenged, attested to as it is by his many recordings, including the nine Beethoven symphonies. He was an important editor, assisting in the complete editions of Berlioz [1175] and Haydn [871], and he wrote voluminously and well—not only on music but also in such areas as drama, satire, and autobiography. His energy must have been enormous, for besides all this, he managed to compose 8 operas (some of them briefly successful), 7 symphonies, 5 string quartets, and much other music.

RECORDINGS: Save for his orchestrations of Beethoven's "Hammerklavier" sonata and Weber's [1124] *Aufforderung zum Tanz (Invitation to the Dance)*—he recorded both —he survives on records as a composer only through a handful of songs, of which the most popular was *"Liebesfeier"* ("Celebration of Love"). He recorded some of his songs with his third wife, Lucille Marcel.

[1553] SOMERVELL, (Sir) Arthur
EDUCATOR
BORN: Windermere, June 5, 1863
DIED: London, May 2, 1937

Perhaps his birth in the English Lake District gave Arthur Somervell his instinct for romantic poetry. He was a graduate of King's College, Cambridge, where he studied with Stanford [1467]. After two years in Berlin with Friedrich Kiel and Woldemar Bargiel, he enrolled at the Royal College of Music in 1885 and left in 1887. After private study with Parry [1443], he returned there to teach in 1894. In 1901 he became an inspector of musical education and eventually rose to be chief inspector to the national board. He received a D.Mus. from Cambridge in 1903 and was knighted by King George V in 1929 for his services to the nation. Somervell's music began to receive notice in the 1890s, and he produced a number of large-scale works—a symphony, concerti, Masses, a *Passion*, and cantatas to texts by major nineteenth-century English poets. But he was most successful with "practical" music for church choirs and most notable for his song cycles and songs. Though these last are musically unadventurous and unfailingly diatonic, they are written with sensitivity and effectiveness. RECORDINGS: There are recordings of the cycles *Maud* (after Tennyson) and *A Shropshire Lad* (after Housman) and of many individual songs.

[1554] VIDAL, Paul Antonin (Vē-dȧl', Pōl Ȧn-tō-naṅ')
TEACHER, CONDUCTOR
BORN: Toulouse, June 16, 1863
DIED: Paris, April 9, 1931

Conductor in chief at the Paris Opéra and then at the Opéra-Comique, professor of composition at the Paris Conservatoire, Paul Vidal was a pupil of Massenet [1396] at that institution, where he was several times a prizewinner. In 1883 he preceded his friend Claude Debussy [1547] by a year as winner of the Grand Prix de Rome. He joined the Opéra when he was twenty-six as assistant choral director and inaugurated the Concerts de l'Opéra there six years later. Along with his various duties he taught free evening courses for years in the Paris slums. His brother Joseph (1859–1924) was also a conductor as well as a musicologist and a writer of operettas. Paul Vidal's chief output was for the stage and included 2 (unsuccessful) operas (including *Guernica* of 1895), 3 operettas (including *Éros* of 1892), pantomimes, ballets, and incidental music (largely for religious works). He was most successful as a composer of ballets. RECORDINGS: Sir Thomas Beecham has recorded a selection from the 1906 ballet *Zino-Zina.*

[1555] PIERNÉ, Henri Constant Gabriel (Pēr-nā', On-rē' Kon-stȧn Gȧ-brē-el')
ORGANIST, CONDUCTOR
BORN: Metz, August 16, 1863
DIED: Ploujean, July 17, 1937

A fertile composer, whose bright surface sometimes masks hidden depths, and an important conductor, Gabriel Pierné is largely forgotten today. When he was seven, he and his family fled to Paris before the advancing Germans and settled there. The senior Piernés were themselves musical and did not oppose his aspirations. He was admitted early to the Paris Conservatoire, where he studied with Durand, Lavignac, Marmontel, Massenet [1396], and Franck [1284] and won several prizes. In 1882 he shared the Grand Prix de Rome with Eugène Marty (1860–1908). (None had been awarded in 1881.) When Franck died in 1890, Pierné succeeded him and served for eight years as organist of Ste. Clothilde. By the time he left, he had established himself firmly as a composer; in fact he had produced more than half of his total output. What slowed him down was his appointment in 1903 as second-in-command to Édouard Colonne, founder of the Concerts Colonne, whom he succeeded in 1910. He conducted the orchestra for twenty-four years thereafter in nearly fifty concerts a year (and made a number of recordings with it). Both popular and respected, he did much to advance the cause of modern music, though as a composer he was a conservative. He also served on the curriculum committee of the Paris Conservatoire. His *oeuvre* includes 8 operas (the first three never produced), 10 ballets, a piano concerto, overtures and suites, incidental music, a sonata each for violin and cello (the former also transcribed for flute), cantatas and oratorios, keyboard music, and songs. Pierné was awarded the *Légion d'honneur* in 1900 and elected to the Académie des Beaux Arts in 1925. In 1934 he turned his baton over to Paul Paray [1808] and retired to Brittany. RECORDINGS: Pierné left records of his own ballets *Cydalise et le chèvre-pied, Impressions de music-hall,* and *Giration* (composed for the phonograph), and music for Pierre Loti's play *Ramuntcho.* In his day there were also recordings of chamber works, songs, and operatic excerpts. After long neglect there has recently been a surge of Pierné recordings: the 1907 oratorio *Les Enfants à Bethléem (The Children at Bethlehem); Cydalise,* 1923; the 1932 *Divertissement sur un thème pastoral* for orchestra; the 1903 *Concertstück* (sic!) for harp and orchestra; the Concerto for Piano; *Ramuntcho Overture,* 1908; the 1935 ballet *Images;* and the 1920 *Paysages franciscains (Franciscan Landscapes).* Chamber and instrumental works on records include piano pieces; a Sonata for Violin and Piano as transcribed for flute by Jean-Pierre Rampal; *Introduction et variations sur une ronde populaire* for saxophone quartet; and *Solo de concert* for solo bassoon.

[1556] PARKER, Horatio William
ORGANIST, CONDUCTOR, TEACHER
BORN: Auburndale, Mass., September 15, 1863
DIED: Cedarhurst, N.Y., December 18, 1919

Within his limits Horatio Parker was one of the most important and influential American composers of his time, and today even his detractors admit that he was gifted. He was not always, however, interested in music. His parents, of colonial English ancestry, settled in a western suburb of Boston, where his father worked as an architect and his highly literate mother played the organ in a church. Horatio, a good red-blooded American boy, thought music was sissy until he reached puberty, when he developed an insatiable thirst for it. Thanking Providence,

Mrs. Parker thereupon set out to teach him to play, and when he was fifteen, he was up to composing fifty Kate Greenaway settings in two days. A year later he too was regularly playing in church (at Dedham) and writing music for the choir. Meanwhile he continued his keyboard studies with John Orth in Boston, learned harmony from Stephen Emery, and in 1880 became one of the first composition pupils of George Chadwick [1483], a former Emery student. Chadwick found Parker musically skeptical and irreverent (odd for one who was later to bridle at the irreverence of Charles Ives [1659]) but a demon worker. In 1882 the young man made the then-mandatory pilgrimage to Germany, where for three years he studied at the Munich Conservatory with Rheinberger [1368]. From among his fellow students he also took a wife, Anna Plössl, the daughter of a Bavarian banker, who was his most devoted supporter throughout his career.

Back in America Parker settled in New York, where he made a living teaching in a Garden City school and playing the organ in various churches. When Antonín Dvořák [1386] was brought over to head Mrs. Jeannette Thurber's National Conservatory, Dvořák chose Parker as his counterpoint teacher. In 1893, when the conservatory announced a competition for cantatas, he submitted two. *The Dream King and His Love* took first prize; *Hora Novissima,* on which the composer was betting and which is generally considered his masterpiece, did not even win honorable mention. However, after he premiered it that spring with the Church Choral Society, it was quickly taken up by choirs all over the country; it was also performed at the Three Choirs Festival in England in 1899, winning Parker other English commissions. At the end of 1893, he returned to Boston as music director of Trinity Church, but a year later he joined the Yale faculty and was named dean of the music school in 1904, two years after being awarded an honorary doctorate by Cambridge University. Among his notable students, besides Ives, were Elliot Griffis (1893–1967), Quincy Porter [1932], David Stanley Smith (1877–1949), and Roger Sessions [1931]. At Yale Parker organized a symphony orchestra and chorus, which he directed and which drew a handsome gift for a concert hall where they could function properly. When in 1910 the Metropolitan Opera offered a $10,000 prize for an American opera, it was Parker's *Mona*—whose plot suggests that of Bellini's *Norma* [1164]—that won the prize and became the second native American opera produced by that house (see Converse [1618]). Despite a fine cast (Louise

Homer, Riccardo Martin, and Herbert Witherspoon), three laurel wreaths presented the composer at the curtain of the premiere, and good notices, it survived only four performances. A second opera, *Fairyland,* won the award of the National Association of Women's Clubs and six performances in Los Angeles in 1915. About this time Parker's health, always frail, began to deteriorate, and he succumbed to pneumonia at fifty-six.

A serious, not to say idealistic, composer who did not suffer musical fools gladly, Parker showed his German training and his English turn of mind in the body of choral compositions that represent him at his best. Most of his few orchestral works (a symphony, etc.) and chamber works (a string quartet and quintet) remain unpublished, and his songs and piano pieces are of no special moment. At moments his music, largely conservative, shows flashes of the old American maverick.

RECORDINGS: Parker is badly represented on records: apart from small pieces and a couple of orchestral excerpts from *Mona* (by Howard Hanson), the chief examples are a pickup Viennese group's reading of *Hora novissima* (conducted by William Strickland) and a Society for the Preservation of the American Musical Heritage recording of the *Northern Ballad.*

[1557] LEROUX, Xavier Henry Napoléon (Lə-rōō′, Eks-à-vyā′ On-rē′ Nà-pō-lā-on′)
TEACHER, EDITOR
BORN: Velletri, October 11, 1863
DIED: Paris, February 2, 1919

Born of French parents near Rome, Xavier Leroux became a pupil of Massenet's **[1396]** at the Paris Conservatoire. After a couple of near-misses, he took the Grand Prix de Rome in 1885. Primarily a stage composer, he had his first opera, *Évangeline* (after Longfellow), produced in Brussels at the end of that year. He wrote at least a dozen others, including *William Ratcliff* (on Heine's plot) and *Le Carillonneur,* which features a carillon-playing competition. *La reine Fiammette* of 1903 was produced in 1919 by the Metropolitan Opera, and the Chicago Opera Company presented *Le Chemineau (The Vagabond)* there; both demonstrated that Leroux did not travel well. He also wrote incidental music, a *Mass,* and songs. He edited the journal *Musica* and taught harmony at the Paris Conservatoire for the last twenty-five years of his life. His music is now wholly forgotten. RECORDINGS: A few songs (e.g., *"Le Nil")* survive on records.

[1558] SAMARA, Spiro (Sà-mà′-rà, Spē′-rō)
BORN: Corfu, November 29, 1863
DIED: Athens, April 7, 1917

Samara—Spyridon Filiskos Samaras in reality—was the first modern Greek composer to win international attention. The exact day and year of his birth are uncertain. After preliminary studies on Corfu, he was admitted in his middle teens to the Athens Conservatory, where he studied with one Enrico Stancabiano, with whom he collaborated on an opera, *Olas.* In 1882 he went to Paris and studied with Delibes **[1344]** at the Paris Conservatoire. Four years later his *Flora Mirabilis,* one of the earliest *verismo* operas, was premiered in Milan. He followed it with half a dozen others in the same vein, with considerable (if ephemeral) success. A visit to Athens in 1889 won him a hero's welcome. He moved back there in 1911 and wrote several operettas for local consumption. Among his other works are a *Chitarrata* for a plectrum orchestra and the official *Olympic Hymn,* commissioned for the first modern Olympic games in 1896. RECORDINGS: The *Olympic Hymn* and a few selections from the operas have appeared on records.

[1559] MASCAGNI, Pietro (Màs-kàn′-yē, Pē-à′-trō)
CONDUCTOR, ADMINISTRATOR
BORN: Livorno (Leghorn), December 7, 1863
DIED: Rome, August 2, 1945

It is generally thought that Mascagni was a run-of-the-mill composer who happened to hit it lucky with a single work, the opera *Cavalleria rusticana (Rustic Chivalry).* A more correct view is probably that he was one who had unusual musico-dramatic talent but was a decade behind the times. He was the son of a Livornese baker who envisioned for him a future, at a more prestigious social level, as a lawyer. But young Mascagni pursued the archetypal plotline for the struggling would-be composer. Though his musical bent was ignored or suppressed at home, he somehow mastered the basics sufficiently to gain admittance to the local Istituto Luigi Cherubini without his parents' knowing it. He studied there with Alfredo Soffredini (who later edited the *Gazzetta musicale* and who had eight operas produced). Parental discovery of the subterfuge got Pietro tossed out of the family nest, but he was taken in and his direction was supported by an understanding uncle. His symphony and a *Kyrie* were performed at the Istituto, and in 1881 his cantata *In Filanda* won honorable mention in a Milanese competition. Such evidence of promise brought the senior Mascagni around, and Pietro was allowed to go home when his uncle suddenly died. (Afterward he reworked the cantata into an opera, *Pinotta,* for which he only managed to get a production fifty-one years later at San Remo.) His setting of Schiller's *Ode to Joy,* sung in Leghorn, won him the patronage of a local Maecenas, Count de Larderel, who paid his way to the Milan Conservatory.

Mascagni arrived there in 1882 and studied with Ponchielli [**1334**]. He also initiated an uneasy friendship with Ponchielli's star pupil, Giacomo Puccini [**1511**], with whom he roomed briefly. Another classmate, Vittorio Gianfreschi, introduced him to Andrea Maffei's translation of Heinrich Heine's play *William Ratcliff,* which he began setting to music. But he was more interested in bohemian student life than in meeting his academic obligations, and he was dismissed after two years. His own version of the story is that he was unable to resist the five lire a day offered him by a roving operatic impresario named Forlì to serve as his assistant conductor. Be that as it may, Mascagni joined him in Cremona in the spring of 1885. But after some months of crisscrossing Emilia, the director suddenly announced that he could not put up with the raffish ways of the members and left. Mascagni spent several ignominious months at home, until Forlì surfaced in Naples at the Teatro del Fondo, and invited him to join him. When Forlì vanished again, Mascagni stayed on with his replacement, Sconamiglio. Then it was back on the road again—Genoa, Alessandria, Modena, Ancona, Ascoli Piceno, until finally Duke Cirella, yet another intendant at the Fondo called him back again. Once more "dissoluteness" brought the venture to a halt. For some months Mascagni subsisted on a plate of unsauced spaghetti a day, until finally he was taken into a touring company run by one Maresca. It must have been a real Pagliacci troupe, for it played mostly in the small towns of southern Italy. At the end of 1886 it arrived in Cerignola, across the boot from Naples, and paused there. Mascagni was tired of roaming, his mistress Lina (Argenide Marcellina Carbognani) was far gone in pregnancy, and he liked the place. Maresca, smelling treachery, cajoled and threatened, but Mascagni, with the con-

nivance of local confederates, hid his *Ratcliff* manuscript and one night after the show escaped with Lina to a cottage in the countryside. When the smoke had cleared, he settled down in Cerignola at 100 lire a month as its *maestro di suono e canto* and made as honest a woman of Lina as he could.

Despite some cynicism about such matters, Mascagni was persuaded to try his luck in the second one-act opera competition run by the Milan publisher Sonzogno. Mascagni had an old friend in the Livornese poet Giovanni Targioni-Tozzetti, whom he asked to work Nicola Misasi's *Marito e sacerdote (Husband and Priest)* into a libretto for him. But before he had gone very far with it, the poet was greatly taken with a performance of Giovanni Verga's play *Cavalleria rusticana,* a Sicilian village tale of betrayal and vendetta. Mascagni liked the idea, but by now time was of the essence. Targioni called in a literary friend, Guido Menasci, to help him, and Mascagni worked at white heat, in the end literally going without sleep. The opera was completed at the end of May 1889. Not quite a year later, Sonzogno announced that it was one of the three finalist works and that they would be performed at the Teatro Costanzi in Rome on May 17, 1890. With Roberto Stagno and his wife Gemma Bellincioni in the leads, and Leopoldo Mugnone [**1510**] conducting, *Cavalleria* was the second of the three works on the program. It was one of the great spontaneous triumphs of operatic history. Taut, compact, aimed for the gut, and seething with melody, it is an undoubted masterpiece. It won Mascagni the first prize, a publishing contract, a knighthood, and undying fame. It also set him a standard that he never again lived up to—partly because he did not want to repeat himself.

His next effort, staged at the Costanzi in the autumn of 1891, was *L'Amico Fritz (Friend Fritz),* a gentle, humorous piece. The libretto by P. Suardon (really N. Daspuro) was drawn from a novel by the Alsatian writers Émile Erckmann and Alexandre Chatrian, who wrote as "Erckmann-Chatrian." It was fairly well received and is still produced occasionally, but the public was disappointed because it did not exert the raw power of its predecessor. *I Rantzau,* from the same authors, and librettized by the *Cavalleria* team fared much less well in Florence at the end of 1892. Then thirty months went by while the composer set his beloved *Ratcliff* in order for its La Scala premiere. He conducted it, and Giovanni Battista de Negri sang the title role, but the audience found it too static, too dark, too intellectual, and insufficiently rustic or chivalrous. Its February opening was followed by that of *Silvano* (also at La Scala) in March. At Sonzogno's bidding, this work had set out to be another *Cavalleria,* but there were difficulties with Alphonse Karr, who wrote the source work, *Romano,* and in the end it pleased no one.

That same year, 1895, Mascagni was appointed to the directorship of the Liceo Musicale in Pesaro. It was there, a year later, that he produced his next opera, *Zanetto,* an odd little work based on Coppée's *Le Passant (The Passerby),* and scored for two women's voices, offstage chorus, strings, and harp. Within the school his progressive notions did not sit well with the staff and there were troubles from the outset, climaxing in his ouster in 1897 and his reinstatement by the Minister of Fine Arts himself. In 1899 the Costanzi staged *Iris,* which dealt with a Japanese theme five years before Puccini's *Madama Butterfly* did. Despite its symbolistic leanings and the adverse critical reaction, it has remained precariously in the repertoire in Italy. It was followed by an interesting but unsuccessful foray into operatic *comedia dell' arte,* entitled *Le maschere (The Masks).* Without precedent, its premiere (January 17, 1901) was scheduled for six cities simultaneously—Genoa, Milan, Naples, Turin, Venice, and Verona. Naples had to postpone the premiere because of cast illnesses, and it was booed off the stage in Genoa.

After writing a score for Hall Caine's play *The Eternal City,* Mascagni was lured into making an American tour, conducting his own works with his own company. But the singers were unknown outside of Italy, the rehearsals were inadequate, and in the end the composer was arrested in Boston for unpaid debts. In his absence he also lost his post in Pesaro. After his return to Italy, he set to work on a French libretto for Monte Carlo, *Amica,* written by the publisher Paul Choudens (as "Paul Bérel"). It opened on March 16, 1905, but despite the presence of such stellar singers as Maurice Rénaud and Geraldine Farrar in the cast, it failed and remains among the least-known of Mascagni's operas. Six years elapsed between it and *Isabeau*—the Lady Godiva story to a symbolist libretto by Luigi Illica. Mascagni conducted a premiere in Buenos Aires in June 1911 that had all the earmarks of a triumph and remained to tour the continent. Owing to an impasse between rival claimants, there was another double first-night in Italy (Venice and Milan). The Milan performance marked the debut of the tenor Bernardo de Muro, on whose shoulders the lon-

gevity of the work chiefly rested (he sang it 382 times).

Mascagni considered *Parisina,* written to a d'Annunzio libretto and first performed in Milan on December 15, 1913, to be his masterpiece. Some later admirers have agreed, but the public did not. However, it thought rather better of *Lodoletta* (Rome, April 30, 1917), the setting of which devolved on Mascagni after Puccini had won the rights to Ouida's sentimental novel *Two Little Wooden Shoes* and then lost interest. *Si,* which followed in 1919, was another failure, but *Il Piccolo Marat* received an ovation at the Costanzi on May 2, 1921. The work did not last though, and it was in effect his last opera worthy of mention. In the twenties he cast his lot with the Mussolini government, whose display musician he became. When Arturo Toscanini resigned from La Scala in 1929, after refusing to play the Fascist anthem, Mascagni replaced him. There in 1935 he produced his fustian *Nerone,* a sort of tribute to Il Duce, the premiere of which was not saved by the presence of such singers as Aureliano Pertile, Apollo Granforte, Margherita Carosio, and the composer's current mistress, Lina Bruna Rasa. (The music came largely from *Vistilia,* an opera at which he had worked unsuccessfully for twenty-five years.) There was a great celebration in 1940 of the golden anniversary of *Cavalleria* with Bruna Rasa and Beniamino Gigli. Soon afterward the soprano became schizophrenic, attempted suicide, and had to be institutionalized. By the end of World War II, Mascagni, broke and alone, was living in a cheap hotel in Rome, *non grata* in the new democratic atmosphere. He died there at eighty-one. Apart from opera, Mascagni wrote choral music, a few orchestral pieces (a piece for a film, a movement for a collaborative ballet), and a number of songs.

RECORDINGS: Mascagni recorded the anniversary performance of *Cavelleria,* as well as *L'Amico Fritz* and a separate earlier version of the *Cavalleria* prelude with the Croatian tenor José Riavez. Besides innumerable versions of the masterpiece, there are commercial versions of *L'Amico Fritz* and *Il Piccolo Marat,* and piracies of all the others but *Amica, Pinotta,* and *Si.*

[1560] BACHELET, Alfred Georges (Bàshə-lā', Ăl-fred' Zhôrzh)
CONDUCTOR, ADMINISTRATOR
BORN: Paris, February 26, 1864
DIED: Nancy, February 10, 1944

A pupil of Ernest Guiraud [1352] at the Paris Conservatoire, Bachelet was the 1890 winner of the Grand Prix de Rome. Thereafter his chief compositional efforts were directed to the stage. His most successful operas were: *Scémo,* 1914; *Quand la cloche sonnera (When the Bell Rings),* 1922; and *Un Jardin sur l'Oronte,* 1931—the first and third were premiered at the Paris Opéra, where he conducted during World War I. In 1919 Bachelet followed Guy Ropartz [1564] as director of the Nancy Conservatoire. Late in his life, in 1939, he became a member of the Institut. He also wrote some ballets, choral, and concerted works and songs. RECORDINGS: One of the last, *"Chere nuit,"* has been frequently recorded.

[1561] HALVORSEN, Johan (Hàl-vôr'-sen, Yō-hàn')
VIOLINIST, CONDUCTOR
BORN: Drammen, March 15, 1864
DIED: Oslo, December 4, 1935

Johan Halvorsen was born in a city to the southwest of Christiania (Oslo) in Norway and studied at the Stockholm Conservatory. On graduation he became concertmaster of the orchestra in Bergen, where he came to know and admire Edvard Grieg [1410], whose niece he afterward married. After more study with Adolf Brodsky in Leipzig, he played for a while in Aberdeen, then taught in Helsinki. Following still further study with Adolf Becker in Berlin and César Thomson in Liège, he came back to Bergen as conductor in 1892. In 1899 he assumed that post in the Norwegian National Theater in Oslo. He was strongly influenced as a composer both by Grieg and by Norwegian folk music (which he collected). He wrote a good deal of incidental music, 3 symphonies, a violin concerto, suites, 2 *Norwegian Rhapsodies,* choral and chamber music. RECORDINGS: Of his larger works, the music to Eldegard's play *Fosse-grimen,* Symphony No. 2 ("Fatum") the *Suite ancienne No. 1,* and the *Rhapsodies* have been recorded, mostly under the auspices of the Norwegian government, which has also sponsored a recent anthology of brief orchestral pieces and concerted works—*Norwegian Fairy Tale Pictures, Danse visionaire,* and others. There is also a recording of the *March of the Hallingdal Battalion* for brass band. More ubiquitous are a *March of the Boyars* and an arrangement for violin and cello of a Handel [683] passacaglia.

[1562] ALBERT, Eugen d' (Dàl'-ber, Oi'-gän)
PIANIST, TEACHER

BORN: Glasgow, April 10, 1864
DIED: Riga, March 3, 1932

His paternal ancestors were Italian; his father, the dancing master and composer Charles d'Albert [1201], was born in Germany of French parents and reared in England. Eugène Francis Charles d'Albert, as he was baptized, was born in Scotland to a German mother, though he was legally English since his parents were living in Newcastle-on-Tyne. Until the age of twelve, he studied with his father, then won a scholarship to the National Training School in London. His teachers there included Ernst Pauer (a pupil of Franz Xavier Mozart [1141]), Sir John Stainer [1378], Ebenezer Prout (1835–1909), and Arthur Sullivan [1397]. He was precocious, both as a performer and a composer, and, in the latter capacity drove Sullivan, who did not want to read through all those pieces, up the wall. He appeared in public concerts from the time he was sixteen and played the premiere of his first piano concerto (of 2) a year later. In 1881 he was awarded a Mendelssohn Scholarship and went to Vienna to study with Hans Richter.

In the German lands d'Albert found himself at home. He became a German chauvinist, changed his name to Eugen, and before he was twenty he proclaimed his contempt for England and everything English in the press. Late in 1881 Liszt [1218] heard him play, pronounced him the most brilliant young pianist known to him, and took him under his wing at Weimar. (He jokingly called him Albertus Magnus—Albert the Great: d'Albert was very small, though he sported an enormous mustache.) D'Albert was no mere fireworks dispenser, however; he could apparently play everything, from Bach [684] to Debussy [1547], and his Beethoven [1063]—he edited the sonatas—was especially admired. In 1892 he took, as the second of his six wives, the great pianist-soprano Teresa Carreno, an Amazonian woman who was entering into her third of four marriages. A yarn claims that Eugen was once heard complaining to Teresa that "your child and my child are fighting with our child," but since the union lasted only three years, this seems unlikely. Though his performing career had made him internationally famous (he toured America with Sarasate [1415] in 1889), he had ambitions as an opera composer and eventually virtually gave up the keyboard.

Albert left 19 completed operas, the first of them being *Die Rubin (The Ruby)* of 1893. His first moderate success was 1898 with his fourth effort, a one-act comedy *Die Abreise*

(The Departure). Five years later he had his only real triumph with *Tiefland (Lowland),* set in a Pyrenéan village; the work was hailed as Germany's answer to *verismo.* It is still played in Germany but has never done well elsewhere. Of the rest, *Die toten Augen (The Dead Eyes)* created a mild stir in 1916, though less than d'Albert himself did in England when he declared himself wholly sympathetic to the Kaiser's cause. His mature compositions include little else than the operas—a concerto for cello as well as those for piano, 2 string quartets, a symphony, some incidental music, 2 overtures, an orchestral suite, a piano sonata, a few other pieces for piano, choruses, and songs. D'Albert was working on a twentieth opera, *Mister Wu,* when he died; it was completed by Leo Blech (1871–1958).

RECORDINGS: There have been four recordings of *Tiefland* two pre-stereo versions, a recent issue conducted by Hans Zanotelli derived from an early-1960s television film, and a new digital recording conducted by Marek Janowski, one of *Die Abreise,* a few excerpts from *Die toten Augen,* the Concerto No. 2 for Piano (Michael Ponti), Concerto for Cello, and a few piano pieces and songs. The composer made recordings and piano rolls, apparently long after he had given up playing in public.

[1563] STRAUSS, Richard Georg
(Shtrous, Rē-khart Gā-ôrg)
CONDUCTOR
BORN: Munich, June 11, 1864
DIED: Garmisch-Partenkirchen, September 8, 1949

If his friend Gustav Mahler [1525] looked ahead to a world of music that would break with long-established traditions, and if his sometime acquaintance Claude Debussy [1547] had perhaps already entered it, Richard Strauss represented the end of those same traditions. Beginning as a rather typical late Romantic, he was in the period of his orchestral tone poems and early operas regarded as the standard bearer of Wagnerian [1230] progress, but by the end of his long life, he was viewed with tolerant amazement as a sort of miraculously preserved living brontosaurus.

Though at the height of his career, he had many admirers, it is probably safe to say that he influenced few composers of importance, and it is certainly true that throughout most of his career he attracted a considerable measure of scorn and opprobrium. He was regarded, not without reason, as an incurable bourgeois. His obsession with money

turned even his friends off. He was (and is) accused of unforgivable lapses of musical taste, and the eroticism and perversity of some of his operas shocked more than the ultrafastidious. During half a century when musical intellectualism was the order of the day, his undisguised assaults on his hearer's emotions were considered beneath contempt. And it was long taken as fact by many critics that the work of his last fifty years amounted to mere note spinning, devoid of inspiration and vitality. Yet the major orchestral works have steadfastly held their place in the standard repertoire, and in recent years the late-period operas have increasingly enjoyed a popularity approaching that of the perennials of the turn of the century.

For all his love of complexity, Strauss was an unregenerate melodist—and grew more so as he aged. He was a great composer of *Lieder* in the Romantic tradition, and the best of his efforts in that genre are characterized by an upward striving toward a radiantly ecstatic climax. Something of the same sort of thing occurs on a larger scale in the operas. In *Der Rosenkavalier,* for example, each act moves from clever but faceless busyness toward increasing lyricism, which in turn culminates in the great finale of the last scene. But it is a lyricism that also involves the emotions by playing on the listener's expectations of the aural orgasm. For example, in the final scene of the same opera's first act, the solo violin endlessly pursues a tonal resolution that comes only with the final note.

Unrelated to the Viennese Strausses, Richard's father, Franz Strauss [1280] was a minor composer, a strong musical reactionary, and first French horn in the Munich Court Orchestra. When his first wife and their children had died in a cholera epidemic, he had married Josephine Pschorr, daughter of George Pschorr, a wealthy Munich brewer. They had one other child, a daughter Johanna, three years younger than Richard. The latter exhibited a taste and talent for music early. His initial training was at the hands of his father and his father's colleagues, notably his cousin, the orchestra's concertmaster Benno Walter. Later he had lessons in theory, harmony, and composition from Friedrich Wilhelm Meyer, one of the orchestra's conductors. However, he was already composing by that time, his maiden effort having been a piano polka in 1871. This was followed by a stream of songs, more piano pieces, and gradually by more ambitious works. In 1876, the year after he began work with Meyer, he wrote his first orchestral piece, a *Festmarsch* dedicated to his maternal Uncle Georg, who, in admiration and gratitude, paid Breitkopf and Härtel to publish it as his nephew's official Op. 1 in 1880. Meanwhile in 1874 young Strauss entered the Ludwigsgymnasium, where he studied until 1882, and where several of his choral pieces were performed. In 1880 he completed a string quartet and a symphony. Walter's quartet played the former the next year, and it was deemed good enough for publication (by a small firm) as Op. 2. As for the symphony, it was presented by the Court Orchestra under Hermann Levi, after which occasion the composer withdrew it as unworthy. Other publications of the period included a piano sonata and two sets of pieces for that instrument, Strauss's only official output for solo piano.

On graduating in 1882, Strauss entered the local university, where for a year he studied literature, art history, and philosophy before giving up formal education for good. Shortly before, he had written a one-movement *Serenade* (Op. 7) for thirteen wind instruments, which was premiered by Franz Wüllner and the winds of the Dresden Court Orchestra—an organization that would loom large in Strauss's future. The work was picked up by other conductors and repeated, and came under the purview of Hans von Bülow [1310], who was enthusiastic about it. Meanwhile Strauss had completed a violin concerto, a cello sonata, and a very difficult French horn concerto dedicated to his father (who had to struggle with it). Having left the university, the young man made his first pilgrimage to Bayreuth in 1883, then spent the winter in Leipzig, Dresden, and chiefly Berlin. There he heard Bülow conduct the Meiningen Court Orchestra in the *Serenade;* after the performance he met the conductor, who urged him to write a suite for the same instrumental combination. During that winter Strauss finished a second symphony, which his father called to the attention of the visiting Theodore Thomas, who took it back to New York and premiered it with the New York Philharmonic. Thus it may be said that at the age of twenty, young Strauss was already an international celebrity.

In the course of 1884 Strauss composed his piano quartet and completed the wind suite, although he and Bülow differed on just what it should consist of. It too was premiered in Dresden, but soon afterward Bülow programmed it in Munich. When he arrived with his orchestra, he decided the composer would conduct his own piece. It proved a trying debut, for Strauss was allowed no rehearsal and Bülow, suffering a flareup of rage at the city that had treated him so ill, absented himself from the auditorium. Nev-

ertheless he was sufficiently sure of his man to hire him as his assistant at Meiningen for the next season. Strauss arrived at the beginning of October and made his debut on the fifteenth as both piano soloist (the Mozart [992] C-minor piano concerto) and composer-conductor (the second symphony). Brahms [1329], who was in the audience, told him the latter was "very nice." When Bülow suddenly resigned in November, Strauss became de facto *Kapellmeister.* In January he played the first performance of the quartet before his approving ducal employer. But when the duke later announced that he was reducing the orchestra to chamber proportions, Strauss rejected a three-year contract and left at the end of the season. His duties had not permitted him much creative leisure, and his only important works of the period were a choral-orchestral setting of Goethe's *Wanderers Sturmlied (Wanderer's Storm Song)* and a scherzo for piano and orchestra that he shelved in disgust. (It later became the *Burleske.)* Up to now Strauss's music, though highly competent, was basically conservative and deeply indebted to the German Romantics, chiefly Mendelssohn [1200] and Brahms. At Meiningen, however, he became friends with Alexander Ritter [1330], then a member of the orchestra, who was a convinced disciple of Liszt [1218] and Wagner. Ritter preached the gospel of modernism to Strauss, and it took. On Brahms's suggestion, when Strauss left Meiningen, he headed south on the Italian tour required of every German aesthete since Goethe. The practical result was a four-movement programmatic work, *Aus Italien (From Italy)*—sometimes called the first of the Straussian tone poems—in which he tentatively played with some of the new formulae. (He also wove into the last movement Luigi Denza's [1426] Neapolitan hit of the moment, "Funiculi-Funicula," which he had mistaken for a folksong.)

Having established himself as a conductor, Strauss returned to Munich to begin a three-year stint with the Court Orchestra as second assistant to Levi. He premiered the new work there in March 1886 and was delighted that it elicited as many boos as cheers. In 1887 he bade farewell to the old ways (and to chamber music) with the violin sonata, in whose premiere he accompanied Robert Heckmann the following March. At the same time he wrote the first (and least-known) of his neo-Lisztian "tone poems," *Macbeth.* Bülow pronounced it garbage, and the composer set it aside until 1890, when he revised it and conducted it at Weimar. Meanwhile he was furiously writing songs, which he would do for the next decade and was becoming ever more widely known as a formidable conductor through guest appearances. He was also apparently winning something of a reputation as a skirt chaser. In the summer of 1887, however, while summering with his Uncle Georg on the Starnberger See, he fell in love with a young singer, Pauline de Ahna, the daughter of a musical general. It is questionable whether this affair inspired his next tone poem, *Don Juan,* based on a work by Nikolaus Lenau. This he completed in 1888, but, still unsure of himself, he set it aside and composed a third, *Tod und Verklärung (Death and Transfiguration).* (This work inspired Ritter to write a poem, which Strauss had printed with the score.)

A devotee of opera since childhood, Strauss had been yearning to be an opera conductor. When in 1889 such a post fell vacant at the Weimar Opera, Bülow recommended him to the *Kapellmeister* Eduard Lassen [1314], who enthusiastically hired him for the next season. During the summer Strauss was at Bayreuth as a rehearsal conductor and won the approval of Frau Wagner. On November 11 in Weimar he conducted the first performance of *Don Juan* and found himself hailed as Germany's most important new composer, the rightful heir to Wagner himself. Strauss unveiled *Tod und Verklärung* at a festival concert at Eisenach the following summer, 1890, and the revised *Macbeth* at Weimar in October. Weimar gave Strauss ample opportunity to acquaint himself with the operatic repertoire, and since it was a stronghold of the "music of the future," thanks to Liszt's intendancy there, he had his fill of Wagner. To his delight Pauline joined the company in 1891 and made her debut as Isolde in 1892 under his direction. In the meantime Strauss had told himself that he must write an opera and was working on the libretto of *Guntram,* an *echt*-Wagnerian concept.

But Strauss had been driving himself too hard, and not only his composing but his health was suffering. In the spring of 1891 he came down with a near fatal case of pneumonia, and a year later fell ill again with bronchitis. A clash of wills with the intendant Hans Bronsart von Schellendorf [1312] had no doubt not helped matters. At any rate he asked for and received a leave of absence for reasons of health, and it was granted. Taking his opera with him, he stayed first in Athens, then in Cairo, and finally in Sicily, where his hostess was the Countess Gravina, daughter of Bülow and Cosima Liszt-Bülow-Wagner. He finished *Guntram* in the Bavarian Alps in the summer of 1893. (Uncle Georg had footed the

bill for his travels.) By now Levi was dangling a tempting offer before him, to which Strauss played hard-to-get until Frau Wagner ordered him to cut it out and accept. Nevertheless he had powerful enemies too and had to return to Weimar for another season.

One of the attractions of a return to Munich had been the dream of putting *Guntram* on at the Court Opera, a major house. Felix Mottl attempted to do the honors at Karlsruhe but gave up when his lead tenor balked; Mahler's efforts to present it at Hamburg did not get that far. Though many of his singers were unqualified for such difficult music, Strauss finally undertook the premiere at Weimar, with Pauline in the female lead. (Once, during the hectic rehearsals, she threw the score at him.) It was not a great success. (A new opera that *was* successful was *Hänsel und Gretel* by Engelbert Humperdinck [1480], first conducted by Strauss two days before Christmas, in 1893.)

The premiere of *Guntram* took place in May 1894. Strauss and Pauline had had a row at an earlier date during a rehearsal of *Tannhäuser.* Cursing him in no uncertain terms, she had stomped off to her dressing room, followed by Strauss. After things had calmed down, the orchestra sent a delegation to apologize; it was told congratulations were in order: the couple had become engaged. They were married the following September, just before Strauss returned to Munich. (The previous season he had filled in, unsuccessfully, for the dying Bülow at the Berlin Philharmonic concerts.) Levi's declining health gave Strauss increasing authority, and in 1895 he attempted *Guntram* again. This time his singers of choice and the orchestra all refused. The latter group had to be ordered to play by the intendant. The performance was expectably a disaster. Strauss, who was planning an opera on the folktale of the rogue Till Eulenspiegel, was so wounded that he gave up the plan and converted the ideas to a new and highly successful tone poem in rondo form, *Till Eulenspiegels lustige Streiche (Till Eulenspiegel's Merry Pranks).* It was first conducted by Wüllner in May 1895.

The next year Levi retired and Strauss succeeded him as *Hofkapellmeister.* That November he introduced Frankfurt to his newest tone poem, *Also sprach Zarathustra,* after the philosophical work by Friedrich Nietzsche [1422], setting forth the notion of the *Übermensch* (superman). This grandiose attempt to portray abstract philosophical ideas musically was seen by some as evidence of a decline in Strauss's powers and remained (partly because of its need of a huge orchestra) one of the lesser-played tone poems until its opening measures were used in the soundtrack of the science fiction film *2001: A Space Odyssey*, since when it can scarcely be avoided. *Zarathustra* was followed a year later by the highly pictorial *Don Quixote*, a theme-and-variations involving a concerto-caliber part for solo cello, and in 1898 by *Ein Heldenleben (A Hero's Life)*, in which it was clear that the hero was one R. Strauss—his previous works are copiously quoted—and his enemies, the critics. (Strauss's bent for musical autobiography was also held against him as evidencing monumental egotism, which it probably did.)

In 1897 Pauline bore Strauss a son (their only child) who was christened after his father. Strauss was away at the time on a conducting tour. That year too he wrote piano music for a reading of Tennyson's poem *Enoch Arden* (in German translation), which he performed several times and at several places with the dedicatee, Ernest von Possart. In 1898 he left Munich to succeed Felix Weingartner [1552] at the Imperial Opera in Berlin, where he conducted for twenty years.

Shortly before his departure Strauss fell in with a satirical writer, Ernst von Wolzogen. He was still sore from the debacle of *Guntram*, and together the pair conceived a new work, *Feuersnot (The Need for Fire)*, based on an old Flemish legend but transferred to medieval Munich, to get back at the composer's detractors. Strauss had been toying with several operatic projects, but Wolzogen fanned his enthusiasm for this one, notably by showing how he (Strauss) might model the hero (a magician) on himself, thus making the story's application doubly clear. The composer completed the score in Berlin in 1901. Both Vienna and Dresden bid for the premiere, the latter winning. The successful production on November 21 marked the beginning of a long series of Strauss opening nights there. Some people were offended by what they considered the work's grossness, not the least of them the German empress, who persuaded the Kaiser to ban it after the first performance, though he relented shortly afterward. As the saying goes, such people hadn't seen *anything* yet!

Strauss offended in a different way with his next tone poem, which was separated from *Feuersnot* by a big orchestral cantata, *Taillefer*, premiered at Heidelberg in 1903. The work in question was the *Symphonia domestica*, which was finished the last day of that year. The composer chose to unveil it in New York in March 1904 during his American tour. The *Symphonia* depicts nothing less than a day in the life of the Strauss family, with gushing relatives, quarreling parents, "Bubi" (Franz) being bathed, and Richard and Pauline in bed. The critics to a man lambasted it.

In 1903 Strauss saw Max Reinhardt's Berlin production of Oscar Wilde's experiment in dramatic decadence, *Salome*. Strauss had already been alerted to the possibilities of the work by a poet named Anton Lindner. Instead of having it librettized, however, he used the translation Reinhardt had used, done by Hedwig Lachmann (the grandmother of comedian-director Mike Nichols), abridging it where necessary. He completed it early in 1905, the famous "Dance of the Seven Veils" being left to be dashed off at the last. Strauss played part of the score to his father, who complained that it made him feel as though he had ants in his pants. The experience was not connected with his demise on May 31. *Salome* was assigned also to Dresden. Marie Wittich, the chubby soprano chosen for the title role, refused it on moral grounds and had to be cajoled and warned. Much to everyone's surprise, the opera opened on December 9, the date originally agreed upon. With its more than intimations of incest, nudity, and perversions of several kinds, it became a worldwide scandal that audiences clamored for. Archbishop Piffl of Vienna got it banned there for the duration of the Austro-Hungarian Empire. The Metropolitan Opera removed it from its schedule after one dress rehearsal to test the waters. Strauss managed to get it performed in Berlin by personally manipulating Kaiser Wilhelm. In a short time it had paid for the new villa in Garmisch, which Strauss called home for the rest of his life.

Before 1903 had ended, Strauss had returned to Reinhardt's theater to see the latter's production of *Elektra* by the Austrian playwright Hugo von Hoffmannsthal. Hoffmannsthal had been introduced to the composer three years earlier and had already proposed a ballet scenario to him. Hearing that Strauss had liked his play, he now suggested that they make it into an opera. After hemming and hawing, the composer finally, swearing his collaborator to secrecy, agreed. Thus began an operatic partnership perhaps equalled in effectiveness only by those of Mozart and da Ponte and of Verdi [1232] and Boito [1393]. In 1907, shortly before the work was completed, Strauss was asked to take over the Berlin Philharmonic Concerts from Weingartner (who was to replace Mahler at the Vienna Opera) and was given the title of *Generalmusikdirektor*. The new opera was finished by early September 1908 and was produced in Dresden the following January 25. Again the singers complained about the enormous demands placed on them, and some of the public complained about the cacophony. But the drama was basically Sophocles' tragedy overlaid with quasi-Freudian motivation, and so there was not the *frisson* of nastiness and the reception was at first disappointing, though of course the work is now a standard one and a sort of ultimate test for dramatic sopranos.

Strauss was happy with both Hoffmannsthal's literary acumen and his pliability. For their next collaboration, Strauss decided he wanted a comedy. The playwright set to work on a piece involving Casanova, but it turned into a play that went to Reinhardt. Then, amused by the resemblance he saw between an earlier team of creators and his own, he began to play with the outlines of *Le Nozze di Figaro*. The work started out in Paris as a Molièrean comedy, moved to eighteenth-century Vienna as *Ochs von Lerchenau* (after its ostensible protagonist), and finally, as *Der Rosenkavalier (The Knight of the Rose)*, it focused on the doomed love of a princess no longer young for a boy half her age. Not only did Hoffmannsthal find it hard to keep up with Strauss, who was writing at white heat; it was the musician, with his instinct for the theater, who shaped the play into what it became. Strauss knew that this time he had struck gold, and he placed heavy demands on the Dresden Opera for the premiere (e.g., it was to keep all his operas in the repertoire). In the end he had to settle for compromise, but he got Reinhardt as director and Alfred Roller of Vienna as designer. This concession caused trouble with their Dresden counterparts, and ultimately Strauss could not get all the singers he had hoped for, Carl Perron as the lumpish Ochs being especially unsatisfactory, particularly when he developed a cold for the dress rehearsal. Nevertheless the premiere was all the composer had hoped for. The listeners found themselves surprised: the orchestra exhibited an almost Mozartean transparency, there was a wealth of melody and especially of infectious (if anachronistic) waltz tunes. Moreover the characters were not driven by obsessions and abnormal lusts, though the overt adultery, the naughty language, and the suggestiveness of the love scenes between a woman and a boy played by a woman were sufficient to bring condemnation from puritans worldwide. Comedy there was in plenty, but the work is also a poignant comment on the frailty of the myths we live by and has asserted itself as one of the great operas. Though Strauss went on, as he had planned, to become a

millionaire, he never had another success like it.

Der Rosenkavalier was presented on January 26, 1911. Strauss's mother had died the previous May, and he had stepped down from the directorship of the Berlin Opera in November. He had found a perfect partner in Hoffmannsthal, if an odd one. The two men were secretly in awe of each other, tiptoed warily in their dealings, and rarely met in person; yet, with one exception, Strauss wrote no operas without Hoffmannsthal until the latter died. Moreover in the future it would be the playwright who called the tune, substituting intellectual ingenuity for the eroticism that was Strauss's native element—in music if not in real life. Also for all practical purposes the composer would until his old age give himself entirely to the stage: save for the final tone poem, *Ein Alpensinfonie (An Alpine Symphony)*, at which he worked sporadically from 1911 to 1915, he wrote little instrumental music for the next thirty years.

Inspired by his brush with Molière, Hoffmannsthal now proposed a Reinhardt production of *Le Bourgeois gentilhomme* (as *Der Bürger als Edelmann)*, culminating in a one-act opera, *Ariadne auf Naxos,* which contains a sort of "play-within-a-play" combining an *opera seria* and an *opera buffa* played simultaneously at the behest of M. Jourdain, the play's protagonist, in the interest of getting more quickly to the fireworks display. Strauss cobbled up some incidental music for the play and wrote the opera in a sort of neo-classical style. But his notion of a chamber orchestra did not fit the Reinhardt Theater, so the whole troupe descended on the Stuttgart Opera for the production, creating a good deal of animosity there. Strauss conducted the premiere on October 25, 1912. The play lasted 2½ hours before the opera could begin. The opera crowd was bored during that time, the playgoers afterward, and *Ariadne* had to be accounted a failure. The next collaboration was scarcely more successful. This was a full-length ballet, *Der Josephslegende,* based on the biblical story of the attempt of Potiphar's wife to seduce Joseph. It was commissioned by the Diaghilev Ballet as a vehicle for Nijinsky. Unfortunately the latter chose this moment to get married, alienating his sometime lover Diaghilev, so the role went to the young Leonid Massine at the Paris premiere in May 1914, which the composer conducted. The next month Strauss went to London for the English premiere and received an honorary doctorate from Oxford. But his heart was not in this work and it remains little known.

Right after the completion of *Der*

Rosenkavalier, Hoffmannsthal became interested in a German fairy tale, "The Cold Heart," whose protagonist sells his heart (replaced by a stone) for money and power. He soon dropped this scheme but turned to a closely related one, involving a peri whose mortal husband will turn to stone if she does not acquire humanity by conceiving a child within a year of their marriage. To do so, she buys the shadow of a mortal woman who denies children to her own husband. The playwright conceived of this as a grand exercise in symbolism. The more he worked at it, the more complex it became, and in the end he had to write concurrently a novelized version to explain to himself what he meant. Thus he had completed only two acts of what was to become *Die Frau ohne Schatten (The Woman Without a Shadow)* when war broke out in 1914 and he was called into military service. Strauss, who could not remain idle, finished the *Alpensinfonie* without much enthusiasm. (He was surprised when he finally heard it that it was as good as it was.) After the failure of the Molière hybrid three years earlier, Hoffmannsthal had proposed that the opera be excised and provided with a prologue involving the supposed neophyte composer of the *opera seria* and M. Jourdain's household. With nothing now to do, Strauss indicated he was ready, and the new version of *Ariadne auf Naxos,* with two acts, was completed in May 1916 and was premiered in Vienna the following October 4, with Lotte Lehmann singing the role of the Composer. It was not a howling success at the time, but it supplanted the original version completely and has gradually come to be virtually a repertoire work. Then to take his mind off his troubles (Bubi was eligible for the army, though in the end he was rejected), Strauss decided to salvage the other half of the failed project by doing a more serious job on the incidental music for the play (as revised by Hoffmannsthal); it is from this version that the relatively familiar *Bourgeois gentilhomme* orchestral suite derives.

It was just before he took on this task that Strauss got the notion he would like to do an Offenbachian **[1264]** farce. With this Hoffmannsthal wanted nothing at all to do and sent the composer to his colleague Hermann Bahr. Having conceived a domestic comedy based on an incident in his own life (a love letter addressed by mistake to him and opened by Pauline), Strauss approached Bahr. When it became clear that the play was to be purely autobiographical (it would concern Albert and Christine Storch, Strauss's addiction to *Skat* (a card game), and Pauline's terrible temper, among other matters), Bahr suggested that Strauss write the libretto himself, which he did forthwith. In the meantime *Die Frau ohne Schatten* was back on track and finally saw the light at the Vienna State Opera on October 10, 1919. Despite a fine cast (Lotte Lehmann, Maria Jeritza, Richard Mayr) the demands of the drama were not done justice, and though Strauss considered it his greatest work (the parallels with Mozart's *Zauberflöte* are inescapable), it languished until recent times, when it took a new lease on life, though controversy still rages as to whether it is a superlative work or hokum.

Nothing of scope was forthcoming from Strauss's pen until 1922, when he completed another ballet, *Schlagobers (Whipped Cream).* Well-titled in more than one way (it has to do with goings-on in a Viennese confectionary), it did not survive its premiere (May 9, 1924). By now Strauss had identified himself with Vienna, having left Berlin in 1919 to become codirector (with Franz Schalk) of the Vienna State Opera. The ballet was given in connection with the celebration of Strauss's sixtieth birthday, in the course of which the city presented him with a plot of land near the Belvedere, where he had a mansion built. But he and Schalk did not get along, and Strauss resigned his post later that year—though he returned shortly as conductor.

Meanwhile he had completed his autobiographical domestic farce, *Intermezzo,* which, conducted by Fritz Busch, was performed in Dresden on November 4. Light, if scarcely Offenbachian, it made no great impact and is rarely heard today. The year 1924 also saw a curious reworking of Beethoven's **[1063]** incidental music to *Die Ruinen von Athen (The Ruins of Athens)* with new text by Hoffmannsthal. The next year Strauss wrote the concerted *Parergon to the Sinfonia domestica* (on a theme from that work) for the one-armed pianist Paul Wittgenstein (for whom he also composed the *Panathenäenzug* three years later). At the same time, he was working on a new opera which Hoffmannsthal had proposed when Strauss returned from a conducting tour of South America in 1923. This was *Die ägyptische Helena (The Egyptian Helen),* based on the legend that when Paris absconded with her, the real Helen of Troy had been spirited off to Egypt and a similitude substituted for her. The opera involves the reconciliation of the true Helen with Menelaus (or "Menelas") and includes, among other oddities, a singing prophetic clam. Again Hoffmannsthal became entangled in his own literary complexities and the partners disagreed on whether the work was to be lightweight or serious, so that it did not reach the stage until 1928. Busch conducted the premiere in Dresden on June 6, and the composer led the Vienna production on June 11. It reached the Metropolitan Opera in November. Everywhere it was accounted a failure. After the librettist died, Strauss and Lothar Wallerstein, who had overseen the Vienna version, reworked the second act, but their ministrations did little to increase the work's acceptance. (In 1931 Wallerstein and Strauss again worked together, this time on a recension of Mozart's *Idomeneo,* which they put on at the Vienna State Opera.)

In the face of declining interest in his work, Strauss decided he must somehow return to the *Rosenkavalier* formula. Hoffmannsthal was of a similar mind and wove two of his own earlier works—one about the Coachman's Ball in Vienna, the other about a noble but impecunious family that disguises the younger daughter as a boy to better the elder's chances for a husband—into a libretto set in the Vienna of the "other" Strausses. He completed the revisions Strauss asked for during the first ten days or so of July 1929. On the thirteenth his son committed suicide; two days later the distraught father died of a stroke. Strauss's work was delayed by shock and then by the Mozart project, and he did not complete the music until October 1932. He dedicated the score to Fritz Busch and Alfred Reucker, who were in charge of the scheduled Dresden premiere. But early the next year the Nazis came to power, and both were ousted. Strauss attempted to withhold *Arabella* until they were reinstated, but it was premiered on July 7 under the baton of Clemens Krauss. Though there was grousing about "*Rosenkavalier II,*" it was a considerable success and has grown in popularity since.

The events of 1933 mark a phase in Strauss's life for which some refuse to forgive him. After Hoffmannsthal's death, he had found a satisfactory librettist in Stefan Zweig, who provided him with a text, *Die schwiegsame Frau (The Silent Woman),* based on Ben Jonson's comedy. With the Nazi takeover, however, Zweig, a Jew, had fled to Switzerland and, much to his partner's surprise and annoyance, refused to return. Strauss willingly took over the remaining concert of the Berlin Philharmonic season when Bruno Walter was dismissed and conducted at Bayreuth that summer when Toscanini refused to appear there. In the autumn he was surprised but not displeased to hear that the Hitler government had named him head of the governmental musical bureau *(Reichsmusikkammer).* Strauss was no admirer of the Nazis. Nor did he take their

anti-Semitism as more than rhetoric. What is most probable is that he was quite unable to see beyond the end of his own nose and assumed that he could get around, or accommodate himself to, the minor inconveniences posed by the new rulers. He was put out when Dr. Goebbels announced, as though it were a criminal act, that he, Strauss, was coauthoring a new opera with a Jew, but he got the assurance of the *Führer* himself that the work would be allowed. He continued happily and uncircumspectly to write to Zweig. He had promises that both Hitler and Goebbels would attend the *Frau.* He protested when he found Zweig's name omitted from the posters. The premiere took place at Dresden on June 6, 1934, under Karl Böhm's direction. The following performances were summarily canceled "for lack of attendance," and the work was then proscribed. Just a month later the Gestapo descended on Strauss, faced him with his *verboten* letters, and ordered him to resign from the *Reichsmusikkammer* on a plea of poor health. A groveling letter to Hitler did nothing to mitigate his position.

Strauss was stunned and for the moment rendered helpless. He was seventy years old. He could see no future for himself. Moreover there was a real danger: Franz, his son, had in 1924 married Strauss's secretary, Alice Grab, who was Jewish and who had since borne Franz two sons. The old man had assumed his prestige would protect them. Clearly it would not. Again he sought refuge in work. He had discussed several projects with Zweig, notably at the Salzburg Festival that summer, and the latter had outlined a scenario for a drama, *1648,* having to do with the end of the Thirty Years' War. But Zweig had steadfastly refused to write the libretto and had recommended one Joseph Gregor, a Viennese theatrical historian. As luck would have it, Strauss had arranged to see Gregor the day after his own humiliation. Gregor, an academic to his fingertips, had been overawed at the idea of working with such a titan and came bearing libretti and deference. One text was a working model of the story in question; another was based on the Apollo-Daphne myth, which Strauss and Hoffmannsthal had once toyed with. Strauss found Gregor's offerings impossibly stiff and said so. Gregor quivered with gratitude and turned himself inside out to please the "Great Man." He was given quarters in the Garmisch villa, and *Friedenstag (Day of Peace),* as it was dubbed, was completed in June 1936 (the year in which, to his great distaste, Strauss had to furnish an *Olympic Hymn* for the Olympic Games in Berlin). Meanwhile the composer had had his eager librettist writing and rewriting his florid verse drama *Daphne*. As soon as he was done with *Friedenstag*, Strauss pronounced *Daphne* acceptable enough to start on. In the end he rejected the grandiose cantata with which Gregor wanted him to end the piece and substituted the scene of Daphne's metamorphosis—the high point of the opera. It was completed in December 1937. Gregor had intended the works as counterparts (on the themes of peace among men and in nature) and was shocked when he heard that Strauss was considering the first alone for the Munich Festival, thanks to Clemens Krauss. Krauss got his way (the premiere was July 24, 1938), though the two were played together when Karl Böhm presented *Daphne* in Dresden on October 15. *Daphne* still has some currency; *Friedenstag* is almost never played, though ironically it was very popular in Nazi Germany.

Strauss as usual needed to keep busy, though he was not anxious to continue with Gregor, whose obsequiousness and lack of talent brought out the worst in him. Then he remembered: back when he was seeing himself as a new Offenbach, Hoffmannsthal had written him a scenario that, distantly related to *Orphée aux Enfers*, brought together Midas (of the golden touch), Danaë (of the golden seduction), and Zeus's other conquests by metamorphosis. He set Gregor to work realizing this. After bullying the librettist brutally, he was still unhappy with the text but set to work anyhow; and, with much backing-and-filling and help from Krauss, he completed the opera at about the time France capitulated to Hitler's troops. Promising it to Krauss when conditions should be more propitious, he set it aside.

When Gregor had submitted the more or less approved libretto of *Die Liebe der Danaë (Danaë's Love)*, Strauss had resurrected another project, loosely based on an eighteenth-century libretto by Abbé G. B. Casti, *Prima la musica, poi le parole (Music First, Then Words)*, through which he wanted to deal with the eternal problem of which art, in musical settings, should be foremost: the concept was that the *protagoniste* must choose between the author of a sonnet written to her and the composer who has put it to music. But Strauss liked none of Gregor's offerings, and when Krauss made more sense of the thing than anyone had, Strauss asked him to write the libretto. What had been conceived as a curtain raiser—and was modestly termed a "conversation piece"— grew into *Capriccio*, a one-act opera as long as Wagner's *Rheingold*. It was offered on October 28, 1942, under the librettist's direction at the Munich State Opera and was wildly acclaimed, though the applause was doubtless more for the seventy-eight-year-old composer than for the work, whose intimacy is not calculated to please crowds. It was Strauss's farewell to the theater, and he could not have made it more poignantly than in the autumn-colored closing scene.

Krauss used this success as leverage to get Strauss to let *Danaë* be heard at the Salzburg Festival in the summer of 1944. It did in fact receive a public dress rehearsal, but by then the opera houses of Munich, Dresden, and Vienna were rubble, the German armies were in retreat on three fronts, and, following the discovery of the "generals' conspiracy" against Hitler, all theaters were ordered closed. The official premiere had to wait precisely eight years and two days.

In 1941 the Strausses had resolved to remain in their Vienna home for the duration. Having completed his last opera, the old composer thought of returning to tone poems but instead wrote a mellow second French horn concerto. In the ensuing winter and spring he and Pauline were both ill, and understandably he felt a cold hand on his shoulder. At the end of the year, while writing a piece for the Wiener Trompetercorps as a result of being awarded the Beethoven Prize, he remembered those early wind pieces of sixty years before, and wrote a second "sonatina" of rather formidable dimensions for sixteen winds, subtitled "From an Invalid's Workshop." Before he completed it, Vienna had become too risky, and he had taken his family back to Garmisch. There, in the autumn of 1943, as he watched his world fall apart, the Nazis demanded that he house "war victims" in his home. Strauss told them in effect to go to hell. The news reached Martin Bormann, who had him declared an outlaw and warned him that his grandchildren were pawns. On top of this Strauss was now near penniless, his funds having either been seized by enemy nations or vanished in the dissolution of Germany. When he was not composing—he encapsulated his grief in a memorial waltz to the city of Munich and the remarkable *Metamorphosen* for twenty-three strings—he was copying out by hand the scores of his tone poems with a view to selling them. One day in the spring of 1945 there was a knock on the door. He opened it to American soldiers. "I am Richard Strauss, composer of *Der Rosenkavalier,*" he told them and added, "Leave me alone!" One of them was John De Lancie, later first oboist of the Philadelphia Orchestra; Strauss afterward wrote the oboe concerto for him.

Since he was regarded by the occupying forces as a Nazi, Strauss was not permitted to work in Germany, nor could his accrued royalties reach him there. By autumn he and Pauline had allowed themselves to be persuaded to move to Switzerland. There, moving restlessly from one place to another, he scored the concerto, and in 1946 heard it and the second wind "sonatina" (subtitled "From a Happy Workshop") performed. That spring he was operated on for the removal of his appendix but bounced back, and in the autumn of 1947 he was well enough to go to London on invitation to attend a festival in his honor arranged by Sir Thomas Beecham, long a Strauss apostle. It was there that he identified himself as a "first-class second-rate composer." Back in Switzerland, though his health was now beginning to fail, he wrote the *Duet-Concertino* for clarinet, bassoon, harp, and strings. He even entered again into negotiations with Gregor, but not surprisingly they came to naught. However, between May and September 1948 he wrote *4 Last songs* for soprano and orchestra on valedictory texts by Hermann Hesse and Joseph von Eichendorff. Perhaps no composer has ever written so beautiful and peaceful a farewell to the world. Shortly after he had completed them, he was hospitalized for a recurrent bladder infection, which required another operation. But in the spring of 1949, having been declared free of Nazi taint, he and Pauline returned once more to Garmisch, where he celebrated his eighty-fifth birthday and accepted an honorary degree from the University of Munich. A few days later he went to Munich to see a performance of *Der Bürger als Edelmann* put on at his request. In July, however, he took to his bed. Several weeks later he told his daughter-in-law that dying was just as he had described it in *Tod und Verklärung*. He slipped away a few days later. Pauline survived him by only eight months.

RECORDINGS: Expectably Strauss's popular works have had a plethora of recordings; the others have been treated rather spottily. Of the operas, for example, no commercial recordings have appeared to date of *Friedenstag* or *Die Liebe der Danaë*. (There are piracies of both.) There are versions of the two ballets and of virtually all of the orchestral music except some juvenilia and the *Panathenäenzug*. Only the published piano and chamber works seem to have been attended to. Exclusive of very early examples, about ninety percent of the songs have appeared on records, most of them in a vast album made by Dietrich Fischer-Dieskau. The choral works seem largely to have been ignored, but *Enoch Arden* has enjoyed at least two recordings. Strauss himself made a

number of recordings as a conductor, and most of the tone poems are extant in one or more readings by him. He also appears on record as accompanist for his songs as sung by several singers.

[1564] ROPARTZ, Joseph Guy Marie
(Rō-pärts', Zhō-zef' Gē Mȧ-rē')
EDUCATOR, CONDUCTOR, POET
BORN: Guingamp, June 15, 1864
DIED: Lanloup-par-Plouha, November 22, 1955

Guy Ropartz—or Guy-Ropartz, as he came to be called—a Franckian by training, made a point of reflecting his native Brittany in his music. He studied literature and law in Vannes, Rennes, and Angers. Then in 1885 he went to the Paris Conservatoire, where he worked for a time with Théodore Dubois **[1356]** and Massenet **[1396]**. His encounter with César Franck **[1284]** a year later decided his musical direction, however, and he became a devout apostle of Franck's cyclic form. His first important compositions were the orchestral works dating from 1887–89: *La Cloche des morts (The Death Knell)*, the Breton-inspired *Les Landes, Marche de fête, 5 pieces brèves*, and *Carnaval*. In 1894 he was named director of the Nancy Conservatory (at thirty, the youngest such intendant in France). In his term he raised it to a high estate among French music schools. The year 1895 saw the first of his 5 symphonies. In 1912 he premiered in Nancy his Breton opera *Le Pays (The Country)*, which won a production at the Opéra-Comique later on. In 1919 he was called to Strasbourg to rehabilitate the conservatory there and to conduct the local symphony. In 1929 he retired to his ancestral home in Brittany but continued to compose for many years thereafter. (His sixth string quartet dates from 1951.) He died at ninety-one. After 1918 he pretty much abandoned his romantic and folkloristic leanings for a trim, even ascetic "classical" style. His musical output was large, running to around 200 publications, which included incidental music, a ballet, Masses, motets, much orchestral music, 2 cello sonatas, 2 violin sonatas, 6 string quartets, and other chamber works, piano pieces, organ music, and songs. He was also a published poet and playwright. RECORDINGS: To date, his phonographic representation appears to be limited to keyboard music, some chamber pieces (notably *Deux Pièces* recorded by the Boehm Wind Quintet and the *Prélude, Marine, et Chanson* for flute, violin, viola, cello, and harp by the Melos

Ensemble with harpist Osian Ellis), and songs.

[1565] NEPOMUCENO, Alberto (Ne-pō-moo-sä'-nŏŏ, Äl-ber'-tŏŏ)
CONDUCTOR, CELLIST (?), PIANIST
BORN: Fortaleza, July 6, 1864
DIED: Rio de Janeiro, October 16, 1920

Born in a city on the northeast coast of Brazil, Nepomuceno was reared farther down the coast in Recife (then Pernambuco), where his father taught school. Mostly home- and self-trained, he was conducting a local cabaret orchestra before he was twenty. After his father died, he migrated to Rio de Janeiro, where he formed a trio with the violinist José White **[1375]** and the future publisher Arthur Napoleão. He attracted a patron who financed his study beginning in 1890 at the Liceo di Santa Cecilia in Rome. After further training in Berlin and Paris, he came home in the mid-1890s and established himself as a composer and pianist. Shortly afterward he began using Brazilian themes in his music—the first known "serious" composer to do so. After some years as professor of organ at the National Conservatory, he was made its director in 1902. He had also made a name for himself as conductor of the Sociedade de Concèrtos Populares, and in 1910 the government sent him as cultural emissary to the Brussels Exposition to present concerts of Brazilian music. He conducted in other European capitals as well. Nepomuceno left 3 operas *(Artemis, Abul,* and the unfinished *O Garatuja),* a very popular orchestral *Suite Brasileira,* a symphony, a concerto, and many other works in various genres. RECORDINGS: The third string quartet has been recorded by the Brazilian Quartet. There are also numerous recordings on Brazilian labels, not readily available in the United States: an LP of piano pieces (Roberto Szidon); a boxed set of the complete piano music (Miguel Proença); *6 Songs* for soprano and orchestra (soprano Maria Helena Buzelin, conducted by Alceo Bocchino); an LP of short orchestral works (Souza Lima conducting); and a recording by the Radio MEC String Quartet featuring the first and third quartets.

[1566] LEONI, Franco (Lä-ō'-nē, Frän'-kō)
BORN: Milan, October 24, 1864
DIED: London, February 8, 1949 (Critic Max de Schauensee gives November 11, 1937)

Ignored by many standard reference books, remembered for the last forty years only as the composer of two or three encore songs, Franco Leoni aspired to be known as an opera composer of the veristic persuasion—and succeeded (barely!) in a single instance. Educated at the Milan Conservatory, he studied under the forgotten Cesare Dominiceti (1821–88) and under Ponchielli **[1334].** At twenty-four he saw his first opera, *Raggio di luna (Moonbeam),* produced in his native city. In 1892, however, he went to London and took up residence there. Following *Rip Van Winkle,* in 1897, and *Ib and Little Christina* in 1901, Covent Garden premiered his Chinese horror story *L'Oracolo (The Oracle)* in 1905. The baritone Antonio Scotti, who created the role of the villain Chim-Fen, found it dear to his heart and, as an international star, kept the work alive. The Metropolitan Opera produced it for him ten years later, Ravinia in 1919, and he elected to make his retirement appearance in it at the Met in 1933. It has attracted rare revivals here and there for other singing actors. Leoni followed *L'Oracolo* with five more operas, all premiered in France or Italy and none with any staying power. The last, *La Terra del Sogno (Dreamland),* was produced in 1920 at Milan, to which city he had returned a few years earlier. He later came back permanently to London. Besides his operas and songs, Leoni wrote cantatas, an oratorio *(The Gate of Life),* and some incidental music. RECORDINGS: *L'Oracolo* has been recorded as a vehicle for Tito Gobbi and Joan Sutherland, and the recording, conducted by Richard Bonynge, includes a side of incidental music for J. B. Fagan's 1904 play *The Prayer of the Sword.*

[1567] GRECHANINOV, Alexander Tikhonovich (Gre-chá'-nē-nof, Äl-yek-sän-der Tē-khō-nō'-vich)
TEACHER, ETHNOMUSICOLOGIST, PIANIST
BORN: Moscow, October 25, 1864
DIED: New York, N.Y., January 3, 1956

By the end of his long life, Grechaninov (also sometimes transcribed as Gretchaninoff) attracted interest chiefly as a sort of last dinosaur, a survivor from the great age of Russian music. He was in fact only a minor composer, but he *was* a link. In early youth he dabbled in music but did not take it up seriously until 1881, when he left school and, on his own, enrolled at the Moscow Conservatory. After he had been there for nine years, however, Arensky **[1536]** told him that he was wasting everyone's time.

Nothing daunted, Grechaninov went to St. Petersburg where, at the analogous institute, he found a willing teacher in Rimsky-Korsakov [1416] and was soon getting public performances of his music. He settled in Moscow in 1896, and his opera *Dobrinya Nikitich* was produced there at the Bolshoi Theater in 1903, starring Feodor Chaliapin. Grechaninov was connected with various schools in the city and taught composition at the Moscow Conservatory from 1906 until 1922. During these years he produced a considerable amount of music, including scores for several plays, three of his 5 symphonies, three operas for children, and a second "mature" opera, *Sister Beatrice*. (Grechaninov had great difficulty getting a production, and when one was effected in 1912 the Orthodox Church closed the work down as sacrilegious.) He was perhaps most successful with his religious music, which won him an imperial pension in 1910 but met with more opposition from the Church because he insisted on an orchestra with some of his more ambitious pieces. He also studied and arranged Russian folk music.

After the October Revolution, Grechaninov tried to adapt to the new regime, but he discovered there was little demand for liturgical composition in the New Russia, and he was shortly tarbrushed as a bourgeois-reactionary. The patronage of an American admirer enabled him to get out. Based in Paris from 1922, he taught and concertized as pianist and conductor. With the onset of World War II, he emigrated to New York and became an American citizen. He died there at ninety-one. One of his last important compositions was his *Missa Oecumenica,* combining musical aspects of several major religions, which Serge Koussevitzky [1655] premiered with the Boston Symphony in 1944. (It is Op. 142 of 200.)

RECORDINGS: Grechaninov is today remembered for a handful of effective songs and appears on records accompanying Nina Koshetz and Maria Kurenko in some of them. There are also selections from the successful opera and choral works. Of the instrumental compositions there is an old recording of a *Russian Rhapsody,* a Soviet recording of the Symphony No. 4 conducted by Algis Žiuraitis, and some piano pieces played by Sondra Bianca.

[1568] HOMER, Sidney
TEACHER
BORN: Boston, December 9, 1864
DIED: Winter Park, Fla., July 10, 1953

Sidney Homer's parents, George (a customs agent) and Anna Maria *(née* Swift), were both deaf. After undergoing a (to him) highly unsatisfactory education at the Boston Latin School and Andover, he persuaded them to let him go to London. There he discovered music and came home to study with George Chadwick [1483], who eventually directed him to Rheinberger [1368] in Munich. Homer had planned to go on to Vienna as a pupil of Brahms [1329], but the death of his father placed the burden of his mother's and sister's support on his shoulders, and he (with Chadwick's help) set up a studio in Boston. One of his pupils was a struggling young singer, a contralto named Louise Beatty from Pittsburgh, whom he married in 1895. He took her career in hand and, as Louise Homer, she became one of the most admired opera stars of her day. Of their several children, Louise's namesake had a brief singing career as Louise Homer Stires and made some records with her mother. Sidney Homer was also a strong influence on his wife's nephew Samuel Barber [2149], who later edited an anthology of his uncle's songs. Though he wrote some instrumental pieces, Homer's chief reputation was as a composer of well-crafted drawing-room songs that sometimes come close to qualifying as *Lieder.* Homer devoted the last two years of his long life to editing his output and died in his sleep the night that he completed the project. RECORDINGS: In their day his songs were quite popular and frequently recorded.

[1569] LONGO, Alessandro (Lon'-gō, Ā-les-sàn'-drō)
PIANIST, TEACHER, EDITOR
BORN: Amantea, December 30, 1864
DIED: Naples, November 3, 1945

Though he wrote much music, Longo is now remembered chiefly as the pioneering editor of Domenico Scarlatti's [687] keyboard sonatas and the source of the "L" numbers long attached to them, before they were supplanted with Ralph Kirkpatrick's less-arbitrary "K" numbers. Born on the rugged Italian coast south of Naples, Longo studied at the Naples Conservatory with Paolo Serrao (1830–1907) and Beniamino Cesi (1845–1907), a piano student of Thalberg's [1220]. He spent much of his life teaching keyboards there, retiring in 1934 but being called back as director when the city was liberated a decade later. His passion for Scarlatti led to his founding the Cercolo Scarlatti, and to the great edition, completed in 1910. He was also pianist of the Società del Quartetto, and founder-editor of the journal *L'arte pianistica* (1914–26). His son Achille (1900–54) was known as a teacher, composer, and critic. Alessandro Longo's own neo-classical compositions include chamber works, piano pieces, and songs. RECORDINGS: There is a recording of a suite for clarinet (substituting bassoon!) and piano.

[1570] MAGNARD, Lucien Denis Gabriel Albéric (Màn-yärd', Lüs-yon' De-nēs' Gäb-rē-el' Ȧl-bä-rēk')
TEACHER
BORN: Paris, June 9, 1865
DIED: Baron, September 3, 1914

Albéric Magnard took the name by which he was called from a godfather, not from the saturnine Nibelung in Wagner's *Ring*. But he might well have, for the two had misanthropy in common, and the present obscurity of Magnard's music owes not a little to his nature. His father Francis was a well-to-do newspaperman. His mother died when he was four. The boy had piano lessons as a matter of course, but it was assumed that he would take up a profession. By the time he finished secondary school, his father was editor of the powerful *Le Figaro*. Albéric went off to England to study at Ramsgate Abbey and have his upper lip stiffened, did a tour of military duty, and acquired a law degree. By 1886 he was his own man at last and, determined to be beholden to his father for nothing, he enrolled at the Paris Conservatoire to embark on a musical career. He studied with Théodore Dubois [1356] and Massenet [1396] and demonstrated that he had talent. But he found both too lax for his tastes, and, a passionate admirer of Franck [1284] and Wagner [1230], he turned to d'Indy [1462], with whom he worked for four years (1888–92). During that period he completed the first of his 4 symphonies and a one-act opera, *Yolande*. The latter was produced in Brussels in 1892, and the former in Angers in 1894. It was whispered that both were done only because the elder Magnard applied pressure. Whatever the truth, he died in 1894, and neither work was performed again.

Albéric mourned his father in the orchestral *Chant funèbre* (which was not played for a decade). It was a typical gesture. Naturally sensitive—even tender-hearted—he held the world at bay with a curmudgeonly mask. It is said that he was afraid to love—at least openly. Nevertheless in 1896, when he took up teaching counterpoint at the Schola Cantorum (Déodat de Sévérac [1644] was a pupil), he married Julia Creton, for whom he wrote the piano suite *Promenades*,

memorializing places in Paris they had enjoyed together. They later had two daughters. As an artist, Magnard was a Platonist who saw the mature Beethoven [1063] as his ideal. Rather than be falsely represented by publishers bent on making sales, he chose to print and distribute his own work. Since he had no head for business, this procedure won him little notice. And though his music found advocates in the likes of Ysaÿe [1507], Guy Ropartz [1564], and Busoni [1577], the concertgoing public did not take to it. Magnard grew increasingly distrustful and withdrawn. In the Dreyfus affair he was so disgusted with the military's blatant display of anti-Semitism that he resigned his commission.

On top of all this, he found he was going deaf. In 1904 he moved with his family to a country house at Baron near Beauvais and avoided Paris as much as he could. He completed a second opera, *Guercoeur*, in 1900 but in his lifetime was able to get only two concert performances of as many individual acts. *Bérénice*, completed in 1909, failed at the Opéra-Comique two years later. A little over a month after the Germans invaded France in 1914, a party of German marauders appeared on the lawn at Baron. Magnard opened fire from inside the house. What was left of him was found later in the smoking ruins. *Yolande*, a new set of songs, and much of the orchestral score of *Guercoeur* went with him. Guy Ropartz reorchestrated *Guercoeur*, which was eventually staged in 1931 starring the American baritone Arthur Endréze *(né* Krackman).

RECORDINGS: Endréze recorded two numbers from *Guercoeur*. Other recordings include the Symphony No. 3 (Ernest Ansermet), the Symphony No. 4 (Michel Plasson), *Promenades* (Jean Doyen), and two cello sonatas (James Lyon). His severe, classical, lofty music has its supporters and may be biding its time.

[1571] NIELSEN, Carl August (Nēl'-sen, Kärl Ou'-goost)
VIOLINIST, BRASS PLAYER, CONDUCTOR, TEACHER
BORN: Sortelung, June 9, 1865
DIED: Copenhagen, October 3, 1931

Carl Nielsen almost certainly ranks on the world stage as Denmark's most important composer. Not that he is known internationally as a particularly "Danish" composer. His songs and choral pieces are founded in the folk music of his country, but that had far less impact on his instrumental music, with which his major reputation rests. There he moves from a throwback classicism to a language that is very much his own and fairly resistant to imitation. Nor did he enjoy worldwide fame in any great degree during his lifetime; that was to come, in part thanks to the phonograph, after 1945.

Nielsen was the seventh of the large brood produced by Maren Kirstine and Niels Jørgensen. (By old Scandinavian tradition, children take their surnames from their father's Christian name. The practice persists in Iceland, where the telephone directory is alphabetized by first names.) He was born in a village on the island of Fyn (or Funen), where his father made a living painting houses and playing (fiddle and cornet) at local social events. Needless to say, the living was inadequate. At four Carl evinced his musical leanings by constructing for his amusement a sort of xylophone from scrap lumber. When, at six, he began fiddling with his father's violin, Niels gave him some basic instruction, then passed him on to the local schoolmaster. In the meantime his education was sporadic, being interrupted by stints at sheepherding or cutting bricks in the local brickyard. He eventually joined his father in his professional musical activities. When he was thirteen, his formal education ended and he was apprenticed to a grocer. The grocer, however, shortly went broke, and Nielsen went to Odense to try out for a military band, wherein he was accepted to play the cornet, the bugle horn, and the trombone. He settled in the town, acquired a piano, and taught himself to play it. Introduced by friends to the German Classicists, he began to compose seriously, if amateurishly. Eventually affluent acquaintances shipped him off to Niels Gade [1248], then director of the Copenhagen Conservatory. He reached Copenhagen concurrently with the Czar of all the Russias, and his audition was postponed until Gade was through with whatever his official duties were. However, when he looked over Nielsen's compositions, he admitted him to the school on full scholarship. There he studied with both Gade and J. P. E. Hartmann [1182], though his chief composition teacher was Orla Rosenhoff.

Nielsen completed his conservatory training in 1886, though he continued to study with Rosenhoff for some time thereafter. In 1888 the orchestra at the Tivoli amusement park unveiled a *Little Suite* for strings by "the unknown Mr. Nielsen," who did not remain unknown for long after that. A year later he was playing second violin in the Royal Danish Symphony Orchestra, under the baton of Johan Svendsen [1379], and was trying to write a symphony. In 1890 he received a government grant to study in Germany. After six months he went on to Paris. There, touring the galleries, he met a compatriot, a talented young sculptor named Anne Marie Brodersen. Friendship proceeded to marriage and they honeymooned in Italy. Returning to Denmark and his post after not quite a year away, Nielsen continued to compose, trying to shake off the influences of the Mendelssohn [1200] school and Svendsen and find his own voice. For a time he was affected by the music of Brahms [1329]. Over the next decade he completed his Symphony No. 1, wrote the official String Quartets Nos. 2 and 3 (there were also some youthful efforts), piano pieces, songs, and incidental music. In 1902 the mature Nielsen began to show with the Symphony No. 2, subtitled "The Four Temperaments," and especially in his monolithic opera *Saul og David*, premiered at the Royal Opera in November of that year.

In 1903 the publishing firm of Wilhelm Hansen agreed to pay the composer an annual stipend for the rights to his works, two years later he resigned from the orchestra to give full time to his composition. The chief product of his new leisure was his charming comic opera *Maskarade*, his only other work in that form. But in 1908 he was asked to succeed Svendsen at the Royal Opera, as second in command to Frederik Rung (1854–1914). However, he was not happy there and resigned after six years. (He afterward said that if he had known what drudgery his earlier years would entail, he would have become a laborer.) But he managed to complete the magnificent Symphony No. 3 *(Sinfonia Espansiva)*, the Concerto for Violin, the *Saga Dream* overture, as well as the mandatory celebratory choral works and stage music. On leaving the theater, Nielsen assumed the conductorship of the concerts of the Copenhagen Music Society, which he led until 1927. From 1915 to 1919 he was professor of composition at the Copenhagen Conservatory, and a member of its governing board from 1914. During the war years (marred also by marital difficulties which at last blew over), he wrote Symphony No. 4 ("The Inextinguishable") and Symphony No. 5, hymns to the human spirit's ability to prevail against chaos. (In the fifth the full orchestra, having found its tonality at last—a Nielsenian hallmark—drowns the rattling of a snare drum gone mad in great billows of music.) From 1918 until Stenhammar [1619] returned in 1922, Nielsen spent much time in Göteborg, Sweden, relieving him on the podium. In his largely calmer final decade, Nielsen produced such highly individual works as the clarinet and flute concerti, the Symphony

No. 6 ("Sinfonia Semplice"), the Wind Quintet, and the small body of organ music. In 1926, however, he suffered a heart attack while conducting in Odense—the first of many. Nevertheless he took on the directorship of the conservatory in 1931. His ailment killed him that fall.

RECORDINGS: Nielsen has by now been well represented on records. There is a complete survey of the orchestral music by Herbert Blomstedt, almost all of which has also been repeatedly recorded in single increments. (Blomstedt even includes the 1888 *Symphonic Rhapsody*, until recently considered lost.) The two operas have recently been committed to records—*Saul og David* in English (of a sort). There are also complete recordings of the piano music and the organ music, and individual readings of the chamber works and many of the songs. So far the incidental music seems to be represented chiefly by the scores for Oehlenschlager's *Aladdin* and Rode's *Moderen (The Mother)*, the choral music by the 1929 *a cappella* motets and three choral-orchestral works: *Hymnus amoris, Sleep,* and the song cycle *Fynsk Forar (Spring in Funen)*. Such occasional works as the cantata for the anniversary of the Danish Cremation Union appear unlikely to be resurrected.

[1572] GILSON, Paul (Zhēl-son', Pōl)
TEACHER, THEORIST, CRITIC
BORN: Brussels, June 15, 1865
DIED: Brussels, April 3, 1942

Paul Gilson grew up in Ruysbroeck, a suburb of Brussels, where he learned to play the organ and had some theory lessons. After that he spent much time studying scores, and on reaching his majority he was already a practiced composer. In 1887 he began a two-year course of study with Gevaert [1303] at the Brussels Conservatory, at the end of which he captured the Belgian Prix de Rome. In 1892 his impressionistic orchestral work *La Mer (The Sea)* created a great stir in Belgium, where its composer was hailed as a sort of musical messiah. The novelty, however, was mostly in the orchestration (of which art he was a master), for Gilson was at heart a dyed-in-the-wool conservative whose god was Beethoven [1063] and to whom Wagner [1230] represented modernism. Moreover his creativeness did not measure up to his energy and his ambition. Though he composed feverishly, usually with literary inspiration, and turned out operas, oratorios, cantatas, and large amounts of music for orchestra, band, small

ensembles, and solo instruments, he never had another success like his first one. Early in the new century he held professorships at the conservatories of Brussels and Antwerp but gave them up for private teaching and a governmental inspectorship. He taught many of the next generation of Belgian composers—e.g., Marcel Poot [1992] and Jean Absil [1889]. Gilson wrote music criticism for *Le Soir* and (later) for *Le Diapason* and *Le Midi*, and founded the *Revue Musicale Belge*. He plugged manfully for modern music, most of which he did not understand. Among his books are manuals on harmony, intervals, orchestration, and military music, and an autobiography published in the year of his death. RECORDINGS: There are recordings of *La Mer* and *Valse symphonique* conducted by Louis Weemaels. (French composer Henri Sauguet [1994] has written a bittersweet *2 mouvements à la memoire de Paul Gilson* for string orchestra, recorded by Sauguet.)

[1573] GLAZUNOV, Alexander Constantinovich (Glä'-zōō-nof, Ăl-yek'-sàn'-der Kon-stàn-tē-nō'-vich)
TEACHER, ADMINISTRATOR, CONDUCTOR
BORN: St. Petersburg, August 10, 1865
DIED: Paris, March 21, 1936

The last of Balakirev's [1348] discoveries, Glazunov was perhaps the most precociously gifted. In the end, however, he turned out to be more eclectic than nationalistic. If some people saw him as a "little Glinka" [1179], others called him "the Russian Brahms" [1329]—and Stravinsky [1748] referred to him as "Karl Philipp Emanuel Rimsky-Korsakov." Still others find in him the influences of Liszt [1218] and Wagner [1230] or even a determinedly abstract classicism. At the end of his life, among the likes of Schoenberg [1657] and Bartók [1734], he seemed a relic of another world.

The son of a well-to-do publisher, Glazunov early exhibited signs of unusual musical genius. He had piano lessons from a certain Yelenovsky and was soon composing on his own. When he was fourteen, he caught the attention of Balakirev, who forthwith turned him over to Rimsky-Korsakov [1416] at the St. Petersburg Conservatory. Rimsky set about to impose some shape and order on his undisciplined musical thinking and found him an apt pupil, blessed with perfect pitch and an eidetic memory. Glazunov immediately absorbed whatever was thrown at him and at sixteen heard his first symphony conducted by his sometime sponsor at Balakirev's Free Concerts. (But he rewrote it four times after that before he was satisfied.) The powerful music publisher Mitofan Belaiev took him under his wing, and he became a leader of the Belaiev circle, devoted to the furtherance of Russian music. Under the publisher's aegis he met Borodin [1331], Scriabin [1625], Liadov [1485], and Liszt, among other important musicians. When Borodin died, Glazunov and Rimsky took it upon themselves to render playable all that was salvageable. The focus was chiefly on the opera *Prince Igor,* for which Glazunov reconstructed from memory the overture and most of the third act. (It was his only operatic essay.)

Glazunov began his conducting career in 1888 and was first heard on the international scene at the Paris World's Fair in 1889. By 1899, when he was appointed professor of orchestration at the St. Petersburg Conservatory, he had written six of his 8 completed symphonies, his ballets *Raymonda, The Ruses of Love,* and *The Seasons,* seventy-five percent of his large body of miscellaneous orchestral works, five of his 7 string quartets, and the majority of his songs, cantatas, chamber works, and piano pieces. When, as a result of the 1905 Revolution, Rimsky was dismissed for his liberalism, Glazunov resigned his post, but at the end of the year he accepted the will of his former colleagues that he take over the directorship of the school. To the detriment of his composition (or perhaps because his inspiration was flickering), he threw himself into his job with a passion. He not only made important innovations but took the progress and welfare of each student as a personal concern. He managed to weather the October Revolution and retained his directorship, though he suffered considerable personal deprivation. (Nevertheless in 1919 he helped support young Dmitri Shostakovich [2094] at the conservatory.) But conditions in the school, as well as in the two cramped rooms where he lived with his old mother, began to gall him. He wrote less and less and is said frequently to have shut himself up in his office with a case of champagne. In 1928 he was delegated to Vienna to represent the Soviets at the Schubert centenary. He did not return to Russia. For a while he guest-conducted all over the world. Married late, he settled in Paris with his wife and her daughter (a pianist who appeared as Yelena Glazunova) in 1932 and died there four years later. His body was reinterred in Leningrad in 1972. (One movement of a projected Symphony No. 9 was completed in piano score.)

RECORDINGS: Shortly before his death Glazunov conducted *The Seasons* for records. Recently returned to favor in his native country, he has enjoyed considerable phonographic attention there, and the completed symphonies have by now all been recorded several times. A recent Melodiya release is a boxed set of the complete symphonies under the baton of Vladimir Fedoseyev; Japanese RCA has issued an audiophile-quality pressing of the same set. The Russian Shishlov Quartet has also recorded several of the numbered string quartets and miscellaneous works in that medium. In the West his most popular works have been the ballets, *Raymonda* and *The Seasons* having been recorded several times. (That they are watered-down Tchaikovsky [1377] without the Tchaikovskyan charm is typical of Glazunov.) There have been sporadic recordings of numerous briefer orchestral works, and recently there has been one of the music for the Grand Duke Constantine's play *The King of the Jews* and one of the *Solemn Cantata for the Pushkin Centenary,* as well as what appears to be a start of a traversal of the piano music (not extensive) by Leslie Howard. Of the concerti, that for violin has enjoyed considerable popularity, and there are recordings of the Concerto No. 2 for Piano and the Concerto for Saxophone (Glazunov's last work). The Op. 109 Quartet for Saxophones has been several times recorded.

[1574] DUKAS, Paul (Abraham) (Dü-kà′, Pōl Á-brà-àm′)
TEACHER, EDITOR, CRITIC
BORN: Paris, October 1, 1865
DIED: Paris, May 17, 1935

Born into a Jewish banking family, Paul Dukas lost his mother, a fine pianist, when he was five. Piano lessons set him to writing music, and in 1881 he entered the Paris Conservatoire where he studied with Théodore Dubois [1356] and later with Guiraud [1352]. (He was in the same class as Debussy [1547].) Vincent d'Indy [1462] accepted him as a friend despite his background, and like d'Indy he served as an orchestral percussionist. He made four tries for the Prix de Rome but did no better than a second prize in 1888. After failing again in 1889, he quit and put in his military obligation. In 1892 his overture for Corneille's *Polyeucte* was performed at the Concerts Lamoureux, and shortly afterward he took on the orchestration of what Guiraud (who died that year) had completed of his opera *Frédégonde.* (Saint-Saëns [1343] composed the rest.) About the same time Dukas began his career as a reviewer and editor. His next work to be heard was his only completed symphony, which did not delight its first audiences in 1897. But *L'Apprenti sorcier (The Sorcerer's Apprentice)*, first performed in May of the same year, did, and it has been delighting listeners ever since—even without the help of Walt Disney's *Fantasia*.

The Sorcerer's Apprentice was followed in 1901 by the piano sonata and in 1902 by the *Variations, Interlude, and Finale on a Theme of Rameau*, for the same instrument. (Dukas was one of the editors of the complete editions of Rameau [675] and François Couperin [616].) There followed a five-year hiatus before the premiere of his only opera, *Ariane et Barbe-bleue (Ariadne and Bluebeard)*, a work more praised than performed. Between 1906 and 1909 he also composed three small pieces—a *Villanelle* for horn and piano, a piano prelude, and a vocalise. In 1910 he became professor of orchestration at the Paris Conservatoire and in 1913 professor of composition. He later also taught composition at the École Normale de Musique. (Among his pupils was Olivier Messiaen [2129].) Dukas' last major work was the ballet *La Péri*, completed in 1910 and premiered in 1912. At fifty he married Suzanne Pereyra; they had a daughter in 1919. In his final twenty-three years he published only two pieces—one for piano, the other a song. In 1934 he was elected to the Académie to take the place of Bruneau [1497]. He died at sixty-nine of a heart attack. Dukas was a perfectionist and a very private person. He would not permit pictures of him to be published, and shortly before his death he told Enesco [1738] that he had burned all his manuscripts. Besides early works and 3 unfinished operas, these are known to have included a second symphony, a violin sonata, and a ballet. Apart from his Prix de Rome cantatas in the archives of the Conservatoire, the catalogue includes only the works noted above.

RECORDINGS: The orchestral and piano pieces have been recorded, and there are two recordings of *Ariane*—a new version by Armin Jordan and a pirated version from a radio broadcast, Tony Aubin conducting.

[1575] SIBELIUS, Jean Julius Christian
(Sē-bāl-yoos, Zhàn Yōōl'-yoos Krēs'-tyàn)
VIOLINIST, TEACHER, CONDUCTOR
BORN: Tavastehus, December 8, 1865
DIED: Järvenpää, September 20, 1957

When Jean (as he called himself) or Jan (as much of the Western press incorrectly termed him) Sibelius died at almost ninety-two, he was widely hailed as the last of the musical titans. A leftover from another age he certainly was, but his magnitude has been moot ever since. That he was the greatest composer to have emerged from Finland up to that time is certainly unarguable but not very meaningful. Outside of his native land he was held in high esteem mostly in the British Isles and the United States; and even there, it has been said, his reputation was pumped up by a handful of highly placed conductors and critics and collapsed after they left the scene. Whatever his worth, it depends largely on the symphonies, tone poems, and the violin concerto, much of the rest of his large output sloping off steeply toward the salonesque and the utilitarian. In his best work he speaks with an individual (if conservative) voice, in which past and contemporary influences are obscure; but whether he brought a radical approach of form to the symphony or merely lucked-out with a basic rhapsodicity is not clear.

Sibelius was born in the town now called Hämeenlinna, about sixty miles north of Helsinki, the second of the three children and the first son of Dr. Christian Sibelius, a physician, and his wife Maria Charlotta (*née* Borg). The family name was a Latinization of Sibbe, which was adopted from that of his farm by Dr. Sibelius' grandfather, who was originally called Martinpoika. Whether his forebears were Swedes called Mårtensson, as is sometimes alleged, is not provable. But Jean Sibelius' mother was second-generation Swedish, and Swedish was the language spoken in the home; the boy had to learn Finnish in school and is said never to have spoken it idiomatically. He was, incidentally, baptized Johan; he said he took the French form after inheriting his Uncle Johan's calling cards, which used it in the interest of international trade (he was a skipper).

The life of Sibelius, for all its length, was a relatively placid one. He lost his father quite early and was reared in the homes of his two grandmothers. A rather shy and introverted child, he was blessed with imagination. All three children were musical and formed a piano trio, of which Jean was the violinist. At fifteen he began serious study with the leader of the local army band, though he maintained that he got the basics of composition from poring over Adolf Bernhard Marx's 1847 treatise. In 1885 he went to Helsingfors (Helsinki) to study law at the university, but soon switched to the recently opened Music Institute, where he continued his violin studies and was soon made second fiddle of the faculty string quartet. His chief theoretical instructor was Martin Wegelius (1846–1906) the school's founder, a Leipziger

by training and a Wagnerian [1230] by inclination. Among his close friends were Ferruccio Busoni [1577], then a young instructor at the Institute, and Armas Järnefelt
[1608], a fellow pupil. At this time Sibelius
scarcely resembled the monolithic figure of
the late portraits: he was slender and handsome, with a mop of unruly hair and a luxuriant moustache that made him look like one
of the bohèmes of the Strindberg and Munch
crowds; if he was not a flaming radical, he
was at least a habitué of the coffee houses
and bars and led a fairly untidy existence
that included an overfondness for drink. He
was already composing fairly steadily, but
there was nothing prophetic about the early
music, most of which he later disowned.

In 1889 Sibelius won a government scholarship for study abroad, which was sweetened with another from the Nyland Student
Corporation. He went to Berlin, where he
soaked himself in music and studied counterpoint with Albert Becker (1834–99), an
old-line drill sergeant, for the better part of a
year, then came home and got himself engaged to Aino Järnefelt, his friend's sister.
He proceeded to Vienna, where Robert
Fuchs (1847–1927) took him on. Later he had
a few lessons with Goldmark [1315]. He
tried several times to meet Brahms [1329],
but that composer was always out. If he absorbed any special influence from his experiences, it was that of Bruckner [1293]. By the
time he got home again in 1891, the Russians
had abandoned their laissez-faire attitude toward their Finnish dependency and were in-
stituting increasingly repressive measures,
which produced a correspondingly increasing growth of Finnish nationalism. Sibelius
joined a group of patriotic esthetes and intellectuals known as the "Young Finns," who
in the spring of 1892 sponsored an all-Finn-
ish concert. Sibelius contributed his first big
work to this concert—the so-called Kullervo
Symphony, really a sort of cantata based on
part of the Kalevala, the national epic which
had been taken down from oral tradition less
than half a century before. Sibelius conducted his own work with the Helsinki Orchestra Association, founded and regularly
led by Robert Kajanus (1856–1933), himself a
composer and later a champion of (and
probably, to a degree, a collaborator with)
the younger man. Kullervo was an enormous
success, though its composer soon set it
aside as immature (the press notices, though
favorable, were not overwhelmingly so); at
least it seemed to assure his future as a musician, and shortly afterward he married his
fiancée (who later bore him five daughters
and kept respectfully in the background)
and was appointed as a part-time teacher at

his alma mater. The couple honeymooned
upcountry in Karelia (now a part of Russia),
where he heard his first Finnish folksongs on
the hoof; he is said to have been delighted
that he had the idiom in his blood, even
though he never borrowed from the wellsprings.

Over the next several years Sibelius produced music which was increasingly "Sibe-
lian," including the original versions of En
Saga and the Lemminkäinen symphonic poems (4 Legends from the Kalevala). There
was a good deal of occasional nationalistic
stuff: the accompaniment for a series of patriotic tableaux in 1893 eventually became
the Karelia Suite and three choral pieces of
1894, written for a competition, were reworked as the string-orchestra (with
percusssion) Rakastava. There was talk of a
full-length opera, but the project was soon
abandoned, and Sibelius' only venture in
that form, the one-act Maid in the Tower of
1896, he refused to publish.

In 1896 there was an opening for a professor of music at the university. Sibelius and
Kajanus were finalists in the competition.
Neither distinguished himself in the mandatory trial lecture, but Kajanus plagiarized
his, and the appointment went overwhelmingly to Sibelius. Kajanus, however, complained to the Russians that he had seniority, so to speak, and the vote was reversed.
The sting was mitigated by a government
annuity for Sibelius in the amount of 3,000
marks, the equivalent of the salary he would
have gotten, which was made a lifetime pension (for an unexpectable forty years!) in
1907. (It was probably just as well: Sibelius
had no feel for academia and was by his own
admission a lousy teacher.) At any rate he
could devote more time to composition, and
in 1899 he conducted the premiere of the first
of his 7 symphonies. Later that year he produced music for another group of nationalistic tableaux, which yielded the first set of the
Historical Scenes and more notably Finlandia—perhaps (with Valse triste, part of
the music for an unsuccessful 1903 play by
his brother-in-law Arvid Järnefelt with the
forbidding title of Death) Sibelius' only universally popular work.

In 1900 Kajanus took his orchestra on a
tour of northern and western Europe, culminating in a pair of concerts at the Paris Exposition. Sibelius went along as nominal associate conductor, and his music figured
largely in the programs, with the result that
he got himself known outside his own country (or city, to be more accurate). Following
the 1902 premiere of the second symphony
and the 1903 premiere of the violin concerto
(which he was later to revise), he moved his

family to a log cabin at Järvenpää, a lakeside village just outside Helsinki, which was to be his home for the remainder of his life. Following a trip to Berlin to conduct, thanks to Busoni, the new symphony, Sibelius yielded to the urgings of Granville Bantock **[1600]** and went to Liverpool in December 1905, where he conducted another concert. His interpreter was Rosa Newmarch, a writer on music (especially on that of Russia) who became a staunch friend and supporter, which relationship she memorialized in a 1939 memoir. This visit was the beginning of Sibelius' popularity in England. He dedicated the third symphony to Bantock and premiered it in London in 1908. On his return to Helsinki, his doctors discovered a malignancy in his throat and removed it; the operation was successful, but he suffered for a time from the ban on alcohol imposed on him.

For the next several years, the record of Sibelius' life is largely the record of his compositions. In 1911 Finland, the rest of Scandinavia, England, and America were successively puzzled and disappointed by the craggy fourth symphony, later to be regarded as one of his greatest works. Early the next year the composer received an unexpected offer from the Vienna Akademie of a post as professor of composition, which he used to jack his pension up to 5,000 marks. In the spring of 1914, he accepted an invitation to appear at the Norfolk (Connecticut) Festival. He was entertained and adulated in a manner commensurate with his rather lavish tastes, introduced to most of the luminaries of American music, driven to various points of interest, and given an honorary doctorate by Yale. He agreed to return the following year, but the outbreak of general war in Europe blocked him. In fact for the next several years, Sibelius' activities were generally confined to Scandinavia. Nevertheless 1915 was an important year for him; his own country went all out to celebrate his fiftieth birthday and showered him with honors (a procedure that was to be repeated every decade for the next forty years). The composer responded by introducing his fifth symphony (which, however, he continued to work on until 1918). The next year he was made an honorary professor by Czar Nicholas.

Owing to Finland's isolated position, the latter years of the war brought severe food shortages. The Russian Revolution was followed by Finland's declaration of independence, a takeover by the Communists, and a civil war. Though their home was searched, the Sibeliuses got off easy; however, they moved into Helsinki for safety. With the aid of the Germans, the conservative faction finally won, though in the end the nation became a republic instead of the monarchy the conservatives had planned. In 1919 Sibelius was in Copenhagen with an all-star cast of Scandinavian composers for the Festival of Nordic Music. The next year he signed a contract to teach at the newly created Eastman School of Music. The authorities blinked at his demand for a $20,000 salary but agreed to meet it with certain strings attached. In the end, however, Sibelius backed down, pleading his own distaste for teaching. In 1921 he made an extended conducting tour of England—the last of five appearances there—during which he appeared in a London concert with his old friend Busoni. In 1923 he premiered the sixth symphony in Helsinki and in 1924 a piece called *Fantasia sinfonica* in Stockholm. Shortly afterward he decided that the latter work was really Symphony No. 7. It was followed by the extensive incidental music for Shakespeare's *The Tempest* and *Tapiola* in 1926. After that, save for a few little pieces, there was nothing for more than thirty years. He in effect retired to Järvenpää, received important visitors, listened to his own music on radio and records, and basked in the innumerable honors showered on him, the while he built up the mythology of the enigmatic Giant of the North (he was actually about 5' 9"). The world waited breathlessly for the eighth symphony and other great works which he was said to be holding back until his death. Well into his ninety-second year, he suffered a stroke and died. There proved to be no eighth symphony or anything else.

RECORDINGS: The major works—the symphonies, the tone poems, the Concerto for Violin, *Karelia, Rakastava, King Christian II, The Tempest, Finlandia, Valse triste,* and the string quartet ("Voces Intimae") have all been amply recorded, as have the majority of the songs. Available on disc but less often treated are the *Andante festivo Luonnotar, Kullervo, Swanwhite,* the *Historic Scenes,* and *Kuolema* (exclusive of the ubiquitous *Valse Triste),* and the lesser concerted works for violin and orchestra. There is a complete traversal of the piano music by Erik T. Tawastjerna and samplings of the works for violin and piano. Save for one or two pieces (e.g., *The Origin of Fire)* the large body of choral music seems to have attracted no attention, at least outside of Finland. Two recordings of *The Maid in the Tower* have recently been issued: a pirated live performance conducted by Jussi Jalas and a studio recording conducted by Neeme Järvi. Much of the incidental music remains unrecorded.

[1576] KALINNIKOV, Vassily Sergeivich

(Kå-lēn′-nē-kôf, Vå-sē′-li Sâr-gā′-e-vich)

CONDUCTOR, TEACHER, BASSOONIST

BORN: Voina, January 13, 1866
DIED: Yalta, January 11, 1901

Poor Kalinnikov might have been a character out of Dostoievsky. His father was a policeman in a village about 150 miles south of Moscow, and the family was terribly poor. The boy showed musical ability at an early age and studied at a seminary on scholarship. In 1884 he made his way to Moscow, where he was admitted to the conservatory but soon had to give it up for lack of funds. However, the free music school operated by the Moscow Philharmonic Society offered him an alternative, and he studied there under Alexander Ilyinsky [1512] and others. But there was still the matter of subsistence to which he clung through pickup jobs in local orchestras, giving lessons, and copying music. However, he acquitted himself brilliantly as a student, and when he graduated in 1892, salvation seemed at hand in the form of an assistant conductorship at the Moscow Italian Opera. He began in the 1893–94 season, but shortly after he started, he began to suffer pulmonary hemorrhages. The doctors found him to be in an advanced state of tuberculosis and ordered him to cease all activity and seek a warmer climate. With his wife, he moved to Yalta on the Black Sea where, undoubtedly conscious of the hopelessness of his situation, he plunged into a frenzy of composing. The most important of his few works were written there, in desperate economic circumstances, during his last few years. The first symphony (in G minor), premiered in 1897, quickly became popular worldwide. A second (in A major) followed a year later, and Kalinnikov's music for Alexei Tolstoy's *Tsar Boris* was performed at St. Petersburg in 1899. But no publisher accepted any of these pieces. However, Rachmaninoff [1638], on vacation in Yalta, took it upon himself to see that justice was done and used his influence to obtain him a lucrative contract. Six months after it went into effect, Kalinnikov was dead, two days short of his thirty-fifth birthday. His widow offered Rachmaninoff his manuscripts as security for a loan to buy a tombstone. Much to the pianist's surprise, the publisher Jurgenson offered her a handsome sum for them, noting astutely that the composer's early death would assure good sales. RE-CORDINGS: Apart from the symphonies, which have been recorded a few times each, Kalinnikov is represented on records by choral pieces and songs.

[1577] BUSONI, Ferruccio Dante Michelangiolo Benvenuto

(Bōō-zō′-nē, Fer-rōōch′-yō Dån′-tā Mē-kel-an′-jyō-lō Ben-vā-nōō-tō)

PIANIST, CONDUCTOR, TEACHER, WRITER

BORN: Empoli, April 1, 1866
DIED: Berlin, July 27, 1924

A titanic pianist, an intrepid conductor, and a first-rate musical thinker, Busoni remains isolated and enigmatic as a composer, for all the lip service done his music. Much has been made of his Latin-Teutonic genetic and cultural polarities, but it does little to explain the monolithic quality of his masterpieces or their failure really to be accepted. Busoni's father Ferdinando, a handsome, bibulous, womanizing fellow whose ancestors probably came from Corsica, was a virtuoso (and peripatetic) clarinetist. In 1865 in Trieste he found himself on the stage with a twenty-two-year-old half-German pianist, Anna Weiss, who decided then and there to marry him and did so soon after, over implacable opposition from her father. The following spring in Empoli she produced, with considerable difficulty, their only child. Eight months later the parents took to the road. In the late 1860s they contemplated settling in Paris, but war clouds drove them back across the Alps. Anna and Ferruccio took refuge in her father's home in Trieste; Ferdinando, still *non grata* there, went his way. Under his mother's eye, Ferruccio learned his letters and the keyboard. A chance encounter at a puppet show in the winter of 1872–73 reunited the parents, who thereupon took rooms in Trieste. Ferdinando, seeing his son a potential Mozart [992], made him practice four sequential hours every day (surprisingly feeding him Bach [684] and other German composers) and had already presented him twice in concert by the time he turned eight. In 1875, feeling the prodigy ready for the Big Time, Ferdinando took him off to Vienna where, short of funds, he sometimes had to beg. But he got the boy an audition with Anton Rubinstein [1309] and early in 1876 a concert engagement in which he not only played a man-sized program but also demonstrated his brilliant improvisatory ability. It was a huge success and won young Busoni the public approval of Eduard Hanslick, Vienna's most influential critic, and the patronage of the Baroness Todesco. Anna joined her husband and son the following winter. In the fall of 1877, on Rubinstein's advice, the family moved to Graz, where Ferruccio took up study with W. A. Rémy *(né* Wilhelm Mayer), who also taught

Heuberger [1451], Kienzl [1496], Rezniček [1522], and Weingartner [1552], among others. (Rémy's antipathy to Wagner [1230] and devotion to Berlioz [1175] and Cherubini [1019] undoubtedly left their mark on his pupil.) Busoni, who had been composing since he was ten or so, made unusually rapid progress. In 1881 he "graduated" with a concert that included several pieces of his own. Less than a year later, still only fifteen, he was inducted into the Reale Accademia Filarmonica in Bologna (which had similarly honored his father eighteen years before).

In 1883 father and son took on Vienna again, but the Vienna Philharmonic, after a read-through, rejected the orchestral composition Ferruccio submitted. Two years later in Leipzig, however, his first string quartet was played in concert by the Petri Quartet (whose leader's son, Egon Petri, was to become Busoni's most famous piano pupil.) That November the young composer broke away from his father and returned to Leipzig, where he came to know Delius [1539], Grieg [1410], Mahler [1525], Sinding [1488], and Tchaikovsky [1377], and where he acquired Lesko, a huge Labrador retriever (later succeeded by Giotto, a behemothian St. Bernard). He kept busy concertizing, composing (now for publication), and, in the current fashion of young intellectuals, attending socialist meetings. Then, in 1888, Carl Reinecke [1292] recommended him to the newly founded Helsinki Conservatory in Finland as a piano teacher. Busoni took the job. Meanwhile he had turned from a lumpy and brooding child into a darkly handsome, bearded young man, and no sooner had he arrived than he attracted the attention of a young pianist, Gerda Sjöstrand, the daughter of a Swedish sculptor. After several encounters, Busoni invited her to a concert of his in March 1889. A couple of evenings later, over dinner, he proposed. Gerda accepted, her father acquiesced, and Busoni sealed the engagement with a gift of the Brockhaus Encyclopedia (which his fiancée said he wanted at least as much as she did). But when they visited Signora Busoni, she raised such an outcry (the first duty of children was to care for their parents, and besides Gerda's hairdo was all wrong) that the bride-to-be tried (unsuccessfully) to call it all off.

In 1890 Busoni's Konzertstück for piano and orchestra took top prize in Anton Rubinstein's first international competition in the amount of 5,000 francs. Busoni proceeded to Moscow to teach at the conservatory there. Gerda followed in September, just in time for a hurry-up wedding ceremony (she hadn't the opportunity to unpack her wedding dress) necessitated by the officiating clergyman's imminent vacation. But, as he so often did, Busoni found his surroundings not to his liking and the following year accepted a post at the New England Conservatory in Boston. That city did not please him either, and in May, shortly after the birth of Benvenuto, the first of his two sons, he moved to New York City. There he began to have idyllic memories of a visit to Berlin, and in 1894 he settled there with his family, his second son Rafaello (later a noted artist) being born there the next spring.

From then on, save for a wartime hiatus in Switzerland, Busoni was a resident of Berlin. But the fact is that much of the rest of his life was spent on the road, both in Europe and abroad, as a pianist and conductor. In 1900 and again in 1901 he gave master classes in Weimar. In 1907 he accepted an offer from the Vienna Conservatory to spend 280 hours there over the next ten months doing the same sort of thing. But owing to other commitments and a growing distaste for the work, he fell far behind and was therefore dismissed in the spring. In 1913 he took over the directorship of the Liceo Musicale in Bologna but resigned at the end of his first term. Finally in 1919 he inaugurated a series of master classes at the Prussian Academy in Berlin, which he kept up for the rest of his life. (Among the pupils who attended them were Kurt Weill [1978], the American Louis Gruenberg [1782], and Philipp Jarnach, who completed Busoni's unfinished opera Doktor Faustus).

Meanwhile, in 1902, as both impresario and conductor, Busoni had begun a seven-year series of Berlin Philharmonic concerts devoted both to new music and older works that were being neglected. Representatives of modernity included not only such relatively accepted figures as Debussy [1547] and Sibelius [1575] but also exemplars of the avant-garde such as Bartók [1734] and Schoenberg [1657]. (However, Busoni had his doubts about the directions the latter musicians were taking.) Many of the new works were conducted by their composers. At a 1904 concert—at which Busoni appeared for the first time beardless—he played his own vast piano concerto under Karl Muck's baton. Later, perhaps taking his cue from Rubinstein, he toured with a series of historically conceived piano concerts. Around 1907, the year in which he published his Entwurf einer neuen Ästhetik der Tonkunst (Outline for a New Esthetics of Music), he disowned the whole body of his earlier composition—the songs, most of the chamber music, over half of the piano pieces, the early opera *Sigune,* the 1897 Concerto for Violin, the *Konzertstück,* etc.—as immature and romantic. In 1911 he wrote incidental music for Carlo Gozzi's fantastic play *Turandot;* this spawned several other *Turandot* pieces, and eventually, in 1917, an opera.

Busoni several times made long concert tours of North America. On the last of them, in 1915, Benvenuto, exercising his birthright, chose to remain as a United States citizen. (He served in the American military in World War I and later lived in seclusion in Berlin.) The elder Busonis, whom Ferruccio had long supported, both died in 1909. In 1915, at odds with the war, he found asylum in Zürich, where in the spring of 1916 he completed his third opera, *Arlecchino,* a one-act *commedia dell'arte* piece to his own libretto. (The second, *Die Brautwahl [The Bridal Lottery]* after E. T. A. Hoffmann [1086], had been premiered in Hamburg four years before.) He returned to Berlin in 1920 to find his home, his library, and his art collection intact. But soon afterward a kidney ailment began to sap his health, and he aged rapidly. Moreover the postwar inflation ruined him in terms of accessible money. He did not live to complete his masterwork, a monumental operatic treatment of the Faust legend based more on the old *Faustbuch* than on Goethe's play. After Busoni died, Gerda had to sell most of their belongings to meet expenses. Ill and blind, she moved to Sweden in 1943 and died there at ninety-one. The Berlin house was destroyed by a bombing in World War II.

RECORDINGS: Recordings include all four mature operas *(Doctor Faustus* by Ferdinand Leitner and *Arlecchino* by John Pritchard; *Turandot* and *Die Brautwahl* in piracies, the concerti for violin (Adolph Busch, Joseph Szigeti) and piano (John Ogden), the *Konzertstück* for piano and orchestra (Frank Glazer), the Concertino for Clarinet (Walter Triebskorn), the *Lustspielouverture* (a piracy), the *Rondo arlecchinesco* (two versions, by C. A. Bünte and Jascha Horenstein), the *Berceuse élégiaque* (Frederick Prausnitz), the two orchestral studies for *Dr. Faustus* (Daniell Revenaugh), the *Divertimento* for flute and orchestra (Hermann Klemeyer), the *Indianischer Fantasie* for piano and orchestra (Marjorie Mitchell), the *Tanzwalzer,* the two violin sonatas, many piano pieces (including the *Fantasia contrappuntistica,* the *Elegies,* and the *Sonatinas),* the songs, and various transcriptions.

[1578] SATIE, Erik Alfred Leslie (Sà-tē', Ā-rĕk' Ăl-fred' Les'-li)
ECCENTRIC
BORN: Honfleur, May 17, 1866
DIED: Paris, July 1, 1925

In the cultural upheaval of the late 1960s, Erik (as he preferred to spell it) Satie came to be venerated as a sort of patron saint of the abnegation of established values. As a result most of his musical output was enthusiastically (and opportunistically) recorded, some of it many times over. There is no doubt that he had an important impact on composers of at least two generations, but whether he himself qualifies as a major creator remains to be seen.

When Satie was born, his father, a Frenchman, was working as a ship's broker in Honfleur, across the Seine estuary from Le Havre. His mother, born Jane Leslie Anton in London, was a Scot. In 1872, after she had in rapid sequence borne Erik's two siblings, Olga and Conrad, and after the family had moved to Paris, she died. The children returned to Honfleur to live with their paternal grandparents, and Erik went to school there and took some lessons from an organist named Vinot. Six years later he joined his recently remarried father in Paris. His stepmother was also an organist—she had studied with Guilmant [1351]—and set about continuing his musical education, but he took a dislike to her and the lessons had a largely negative effect. However, in 1879 he entered the Paris Conservatoire as a preparatory piano student. There he distinguished himself by failing his examinations for three years in a row and being consequently ejected as a hopeless case. In 1885 he was readmitted as a regular pupil to study with Georges Mathias (1826–1910), a former Chopin [1208] student. But after a year he was dropped again.

By now Satie had won himself a reputation as a young man-about-town, though hardly in its approved quarters. Typically he affected an antibohemian getup, which included a high collar and pince-nez. He had also taken to composing. His father, now a stationer and printer, published some of his early efforts, and a year or so later a real music publisher brought out two piano compositions, *Ogives* and *3 Sarabandes.* In 1886 Satie made one more stab at the Conservatoire, but that December, faced with military service, he took advantage of his student status and volunteered for a year (otherwise he would have had to serve four). A few weeks later, having deliberately brought on a heavy cold that seemed to threaten pneumonia or tuberculosis, he was mustered out. Caught *in flagrante delicto* with his stepmother's housemaid, he was dismissed from the family's bosom, moved into a cubicle in Montmartre, and became a habitué of a bistro called Le Chat Noir. He developed a passion for things medieval, including Gregorian chant, and wrote several works, such as the *Gnossiennes* and the *Gymnopédies,* that in their modality seemed almost static. During this period he encountered Joséphin Péladan, author of the bestselling *Le Vice suprême.* As "Sâr Merodack," Péladan was then founder and self-appointed head of the Rose + Croix du Temple et du Graal, a mystic sect that attempted to reconcile Catholicism and Rosicrucianism (with Wagnerian [1230] overtones). Péladan, in 1891, appointed him its official composer. But Satie found that, un-Wagnerlike, he did not agree that music was a counterpart of the emotions, and his scores for presentations by the sect courted instead stasis and chastity.

He had been playing piano at Le Chat Noir, but around this time he quarreled with his employer, quit, and took a job at the Auberge du Clou. There he met Claude Debussy [1547]. The two became fast friends, and it is obvious that Satie's esthetic contributed much to Debussy's concept of his opera *Pélleas et Mélisande.* Soon afterward, Satie moved on to the Café de la Nouvelle Athens, where he met Maurice Ravel [1666], who was later to help promote his music and put him on the map. Satie was horribly self-conscious about his lack of knowledge and his menial place as a musician and so took on the role of a self-deprecating clown with overweening pretensions. When Ernest Guiraud [1352] died in 1892, Satie proposed that he be elected to his place in the Académie and went through the ceremonial ritual of visiting all the members, some of whom must have been astounded. Of course he got no farther than he did when he later claimed the seats vacated by Gounod [1258] and Ambroise Thomas [1217]. Meanwhile he had entered into a wild love affair with Suzanne Valadon, the mother of the painter Maurice Utrillo. For a while they lived in adjoining rooms, Satie's being too tiny to accommodate two.

In 1892 Satie broke with Péladan. Pursuing his own mystical views, he wrote, with his friend Contamine de Latour, a "Christian ballet" called *Uspud.* When the director of the Opéra refused to look at it, Satie forced him to by sending a formal challenge to a duel. The Opéra did not produce it. Satie also founded a sect of his own, the Metropolitan Art Church of Jesus Conductor, of which he appears to have been the only member. From his own cramped quarters,

dubbed "Our Abbatial," he issued pontifical bulls, mostly attacking musical stuffed shirts. The death of his father left him 7,000 francs which supported such work and also provided him with twelve identical gray corduroy suits, which became his uniform, replacing the bohemian garb he had affected for some years.

This change perhaps reflected a change in his musical esthetic. With the *Pièces froides (Cold Pieces)* of 1897, he went into creative hibernation, though he continued to set down both music and ideas in his notebooks which he always kept at hand. A year later he inexplicably wheelbarrowed his few worldly possessions to even more Spartan quarters over a café in the then working-class suburb of Arcueil, where his existence became (if that were possible) even more marginal. Daily he trudged the several miles between his room and his work in Montmartre. The only pieces he seems to have set down over the next several years were a ballet, *Jack-in-the-Box* (sic!), and a puppet "opera," *Geneviève de Brabant,* both in piano score; neither, however, saw the light in his lifetime, having slid behind a piece of furniture to await discovery by Milhaud [1868] in 1925. In 1903 Satie completed the piano duet *3 Morceaux en forme de poire (3 Fragments* [or *Bites!] in the Form of a Pear),* the result of Debussy's charge that the composer ignored form.

At forty Satie decided to do something serious about his lack of technique and accordingly enrolled at the Schola Cantorum, where his chief teacher was Albert Roussel [1605], three years his junior. He also studied with d'Indy [1462]. Despite his pupil's eccentricities (Satie was by now well on his way to becoming an alcoholic), Roussel admired his nerve and his fresh approach, and in 1908 Satie was given a diploma. But it was not his new learning that after 1910 suddenly brought him to notice; rather it was the performances of his music by Ravel, Ricardo Viñes, and even Debussy. These won him publication, inspired him to a new outpouring of composition, and eventually attracted Jean Cocteau, who made it his business to preach the Satiean gospel as representative of the new century's rejection of Romanticism in favor of light, air, and wit.

Satie's revolutionary tendencies were not confined to his music and his lifestyle. He was a dedicated socialist and agitated in Arcueil for art for the masses. (Later he espoused communism.) His first great impact on the general public came in 1917, when in association with Diaghilev, Picasso, Cocteau, and Leonid Massine, his ballet *Parade* was presented in Paris. The deliberate ab-

surdism of the book, Picasso's cubist costumes, and above all Satie's scoring for type-
writers and pistols as part of his orchestra,
created an uproar. Reviews were insulting if
not libelous. Satie replied in the press that
one of his critics was "not only an asshole,
but an unmusical asshole," and was given a
jail sentence for it, which gave his friends
much trouble to get revoked. About this
time he also received a commission from the
Princesse de Polignac (heiress to the Singer
sewing-machine millions) for an opera on
the death of Socrates. The result was the
drame symphonique of 1918, *Socrate*—stud-
iedly unemotional, cool settings of three relevant passages from Plato for one or more
voices and strings (or piano).

Despite the upswing of his career, Satie's
drinking and the approach of old age (which
terrified him) affected his personality and
made him querulous. He broke with many
old friends. In 1918 he wrote Debussy, from
whom he had long been estranged, a brutally
sarcastic note and was later horrified to hear
that it had deeply hurt the dying man. But
he also acquired many new friends—especially the so-called *Les Six,* who adopted
him as their patron. In 1920 a concert of
their music was given in Paris, to which Satie provided a score to be played during the
intermissions. He labeled it *Musique
d'ameublement (Furniture Music),* intending
it to be the sort of impersonal background
one now hears in dentists' offices and eleva-
tors. When the audience paused to listen, he
ran about the house urging them to talk. In
1924 another Satie-Picasso-Massine ballet,
*Les Aventures de Mercure (The Adventures
of Mercury),* in "three plastic poses" precipitated another scandal—and a quarrel with
Auric [1962] and Poulenc [1960]. It was followed by perhaps the most outrageous work
of all, *Relâche,* whose title means roughly
"no performance." It was a surrealistic ballet with cinema, a collaboration with the
painter Picabia and the filmmaker René
Clair. When the audience arrived, it found
the theater indeed closed (actually the lead
dancer was ill) and an invitation to come
back next week. At the opening Satie took
his bows from a miniature automobile which
he drove onstage. The whole thing was
roundly damned. Shortly afterward his liver
gave out, and the decline in his health was
aggravated by a lung ailment diagnosed as
"pleurisy." He insisted on dragging about as
long as he had the strength to walk. When
that failed, his friends installed him in a hotel room until at last he had to be taken to a
hospital, where he succumbed.

Virgil Thomson [1928], an admirer and
disciple, has called Satie's esthetic the only
real twentieth-century musical one in the
western world. Satie's music, he says, exhibits "quietude, precision, acuteness of auditory observation, gentleness, sincerity, and
directness of statement," and is based on its
composer's conviction that "the only
healthy thing music can do in our century is
to stop trying to be impressive." In its rejection of both thought and feeling, it is reminiscent of certain Oriental musics, and for
some time it seemed to offer a direction for
an age weary of being asked to think and feel
beyond human capacity. Apart from the
stage pieces and the choral *Messe des
pauvres (Mass for the Poor),* it consists almost entirely of piano pieces and a few
songs.

RECORDINGS: The most extensive recording of the piano music is by Aldo Ciccolini,
and Frank Glazer has recorded a substantial
portion. *Parade* and the two Debussy-
orchestrated *Gymnopédies* have been recorded many times. There was a single recording of the other *Gymnopédie* as orchestrated by someone named Jones. Most of the
stage works, two-piano works, and miscellaneous pieces (e.g., orchestrations of the piano pieces by the likes of Milhaud, Manuel
Rosenthal, John Lanchbery, and Roger
Désormière) have been recorded one or
more times. The *Messe de pauvres* has been
done several times.

[1579] WOOD, Charles
TEACHER, CONDUCTOR
BORN: Armagh, June 15, 1866
DIED: Cambridge, July 12, 1926

Charles Wood's father was a member of the
Armagh (Ireland) Cathedral choir, and the
son's first teacher was the organist there. In
1883 he went to London to study with Stanford [1467] at the Royal College of Music,
where he became harmony teacher five years
later, at which time he also began work toward degrees at Cambridge. From 1889 he
was organist of Gonville and Caius College
there and conducted the university musical
society and the band. He received his M.A.
and D.Mus. in 1894 and was named a fellow
of the college. He became lecturer in counterpoint and harmony in 1897, and succeeded Stanford as professor of music for the
last few months of his life. Wood was chiefly
a vocal composer, turning out a one-act opera, *Pickwick Papers,* and many cantatas and
songs, though he also wrote 6 string quartets
and some orchestral pieces. He is, however,
chiefly celebrated for his music for the
Anglican Church, which includes several
services, anthems, psalms, and a *St. Mark*

Passion. RECORDINGS: Samplings appear in recorded choral anthologies. He also published arrangements of hymns and carols.

[1580] CILÈA, Francesco (Chē-lä'-à, Frán-chäs'-kō)
TEACHER, PIANIST, ADMINISTRATOR
BORN: Palmi, July 26, 1866
DIED: Varazze, November 20, 1950

Francesco Cilèa, one of the last Italian opera composers to get a handhold—albeit a precarious one—on the standard repertoire, was prodigious neither in terms of age or output. The son of a lawyer who had his practice in a little city at the toe-tip of the Italian boot, he had no music lessons until he was nine. At that point Francesco Florimo, Bellini's **[1164]** old friend, now librarian of the Naples Conservatory, detected his musical proclivities and urged that he study. Cilèa was thereupon sent to Naples to a teacher and shortly admitted to the conservatory, where his composition mentor was Paolo Serrao (1830–1907) and where he became an excellent pianist. He wrote his first opera, *Gina,* while still a student, and its production in 1889, the year of his graduation, won him a contract with the publisher Sonzogno, which resulted in a second effort, *La Tilda.* This, produced in Florence in 1892, was an effort to get on the *verismo* bandwagon. It won him no fame. He soon afterward returned to the conservatory to teach piano, transferring to its counterpart in Florence in 1896. He had more luck with his next opera, *L'Arlesiana (The Woman of Arles),* based on the Daudet play for which Bizet **[1363]** had earlier written his famous score. It was produced in 1897 at the Teatro Lirico in Milan; the leading male role was created by Enrico Caruso, then at the very outset of his career. Much revised by its composer over the years, the piece is still heard occasionally in Italian theaters.

Caruso also sang in the premiere of Cilèa's next work. This was *Adriana Lecouvreur,* based on a famous Scribe play about a real eighteenth-century French actress. It was first heard in 1902 and had a general success before disappearing. However, after World War II, the composer persuaded the soprano Magda Oliviero that the lead was her dish, and she had such a success with it that other sopranos (Renata Tebaldi, Montserrat Caballé, Renata Scotto, etc.) have given the work new life on the international scene. *Adriana* was followed by *Gloria* in 1907. Produced at La Scala under Toscanini's baton, it was a failure. Cilèa

never wrote another opera. In 1913 he took over the directorship of the Palermo Conservatory and three years later returned to his alma mater in the same capacity. He remained there until he retired in 1935. His small compositional output also includes 2 orchestral suites, choral works, chamber music, piano pieces, and songs.

RECORDINGS: There are several versions of *Adriana Lecouvreur,* most recently productions with Renata Tebaldi and Renata Scotto. *L'Arlesiana* has also been recorded.

[1581] AULIN, Tor Bernhard Vilhelm (Ou'-lin, Tôr Bârn'-härd Vil'-helm)
VIOLINIST, CONDUCTOR
BORN: Stockholm, September 10, 1866
DIED: Saltsjöbaden, March 1, 1914

As a violinist, Aulin was considered in Scandinavia the successor to Ole Bull **[1206].** He graduated from the Stockholm Conservatory in 1883, then went to Berlin to study composition with Philipp Scharwenka **[1437]** and violin with Émile Sauret (one of pianist Teresa Carreño's several husbands). In 1886 he returned to Sweden as an orchestral musician and shortly afterward formed his own string quartet, which functioned for twenty-five years. From 1889 to 1902 he was concertmaster of the Swedish Royal Orchestra. He also appeared frequently as soloist, both at home and abroad. Around 1900 he turned to conducting and in 1902 became director of the orchestra of the Stockholm Concert Association, which he helped found. From 1909 to 1912 he led the Göteborg Symphony. He was a zealous missionary for Swedish music, performing it at every opportunity. He wrote 3 violin concertos, music for Strindberg's *Master Olof,* a string quartet, a violin sonata, and numerous works in small forms. Aulin's sister Laura was a well-known pianist and teacher and herself a composition student of Gade **[1248],** Godard **[1445],** and Massenet **[1396].** RECORDINGS: The Concerto for Violin No. 3 was recorded in the pre-LP era and more recently by violinist Arve Tellefsen, with Leif Segerstam conducting. The *4 Aquarelles* and *Dances from Grotland* have also been done by Tellefsen, with pianist Göran Nilson.

[1582] DORET, Gustave (Dō-rā', Güstàv')
VIOLINIST, CONDUCTOR, CRITIC
BORN: Aigle, September 20, 1866
DIED: Lausanne, April 19, 1943

Born on the banks of the Rhone near its entry into Lake Geneva, Doret divided his life between France and Switzerland. A pupil of Joachim [1321], he went to the Paris Conservatoire at twenty-one to study with Théodore Dubois [1356] and Massenet [1396]. He stayed in Paris as assistant conductor of the Concerts d'Harcourt and rose to be musical director of the Société Nationale. He was a close friend of Debussy and led the Société's orchestra in the successful premiere of his *Prélude à l'après-midi d'un faune* in 1894. He later held posts in Switzerland and at the Paris Opéra-Comique, and was a popular guest conductor. Doret wrote a dozen stage works, the most successful of them being a series of musical plays or operettas written with René Morax for a theater in Mézières. He was music critic for several Swiss newspapers, where he plugged (as on the podium) for French-style music. He received the *Légion d'honneur* and was named to the Académie in France and given other honors and awards in his native country. Apart from an orchestral suite, a string quartet, and a clarinet quintet, his music is mostly for voice. RECORDINGS: One is most likely to encounter him on records as a composer of songs and part-songs, some of which have become part of daily life in Switzerland.

[1583] LINCKE, Carl Emil Paul (Link'-e, Kärl Ā'-mil Poul)
BASSOONIST, CONDUCTOR, PUBLISHER
BORN: Berlin, November 7, 1866
DIED: Clausthal-Zellerfeld, September 3, 1946

Paul Lincke was the chief progenitor of the "Berlin operetta," a form (if that is the word) that demonstrates the degeneration of the genre from dramatic vehicle to quasi-revue. At the outset of his career he played several instruments—chiefly bassoon—in theater orchestras, eventually becoming conductor at the Apollo in Berlin. He tried his hand at song writing and was so successful that he opened his own publishing company, named after the theater. He also served as conductor at the Folies-Bergère in Paris for a short time. His most successful operettas, beginning in 1897 with *Venus auf Erden (Venus on Earth)*, were produced at the Apollo and include his two greatest hits, *Frau Luna* and *Im Reiche des Indra (In the Kingdom of Indra)*, both from 1899. In 1902, however, *Lysistrata* provided the piece by which he is best known here, the "Glowworm Idyll," popularized by the dancer Anna Pavlova and sung by American children to a parody

text ("Glow, little glowworm, glimmer, glimmer, I got a gal that's slimmer, slimmer . . ."). He virtually gave up composition with World War I, but he was, *faute de mieux*, espoused by the Nazis and wrote a last-gasp, *Ein Liebestraum (A Dream of Love)*, for the state radio in 1940. The postwar West German government seems to have forgiven him his associations, for it issued a postage stamp in his memory. Gervase Hughes describes his work as "prone to vulgarities which it might not be unfair to describe as Teutonic." RECORDINGS: He also conducted some of his music for records in the Nazi era.

[1584] BURLEIGH, Henry Thacker
SINGER
BORN: Erie, Pa., December 2, 1866
DIED: Stamford, Conn., September 12, 1949

Harry T. Burleigh was perhaps the first black American composer to be taken seriously. One of five children, he lost his father very early, and his mother took service in Erie with a wealthy family named Russell. Harry showed an interest in music from childhood, and Mrs. Russell let him act as doorman at her musicales so that he could listen in. When his voice changed to a fine baritone, he began appearing as a soloist with local church choirs. Eventually admirers got up a purse to enable him to study at the newly founded National Conservatory in New York, headed by Dvořák [1386]. He attracted the Czech's interest and was a frequent guest in his home, where Dvořák delighted in hearing him sing spirituals. Later he was appointed to teach voice in the National Conservatory. In 1894 he was named soloist at St. George's Episcopal Church in New York. At first there was opposition, but he weathered it and remained there, a greatly beloved figure, until he retired fifty-two years later. He toured extensively, both in America and Europe, and once sang a command performance for Edward VII of England. In the late 1890s he began publishing successful drawing-room ballads and concert songs. In 1900 he took on an additional appointment as soloist at Temple Emanu-El and in 1911 became an editor for the publishing firm of Ricordi. In 1916 he began (with "Deep River") his pathbreaking and influential series of concert arrangements of spirituals (whose style, it must be said, owes more to European Romanticism than to any native tradition). The 1916 Spingarn Medal of the NAACP and several honorary degrees testified to the estimation in which he came to be held. Though he wrote some few instrumental pieces, the bulk of his output consists of songs and choral works. RECORDINGS: Some of Burleigh's songs and many spirituals have been recorded.

[1585] SURZYŃSKI, Mieczysław (Sōōr-zin'y'-skē, Mye'-chi-slwáf)
ORGANIST, TEACHER
BORN: Środa, December 22, 1866
DIED: Warsaw, September 11, 1924

Born near Poznan, Mieczysław Surzyński was a younger brother of the composer-organists Józef **[1460]** and Stefan Surzyński. He first studied in Berlin with Ludwig Bussler and the Marienkirche organist Otto Dienel, then with Salomon Jadassohn (1831–1902) in Leipzig, and finally at the School of Church Music in Regensburg. After playing and teaching in various Polish and Russian cities, he became professor of organ at the Warsaw Conservatory in 1906 and organist at that city's cathedral in 1918. He was admired as a virtuoso performer, and wrote very successful instruction books. He composed mostly for organ and for choir. RECORDINGS: Feliks Raczkowski has recorded one of his organ toccatas.

[1586] LEVA, Enrico de (Lā'-và, En-rē'-kō dē)
TEACHER
BORN: Naples, January 19, 1867
DIED: Naples, July 28, 1955

An immensely popular songwriter in his day, Leva studied piano and composition in Naples. His teachers included the father of Guido Pannain **[1857]**, the theorist and minor opera composer Nicola d'Arienzo (1842–1915), and people named Rossomondi and Puzone. His first hit song won him a contract with Ricordi and a commission (for a cantata) from Queen Margherita. He went on producing songs prodigally for most of his long life. He was also a skilled vocal teacher, both of soloists and choirs. His only opera, *La Camargo*, was premiered in 1898. Nine years later he succeeded Arienzo as director of the Istituto di SS. Giuseppe e Lucia. RECORDINGS: Some songs are recorded.

[1587] PETERSON-BERGER, Olof Wilhelm (Pā'-ter-sōn Bâr'-ger, Ō'-lōf Vil'-elm)
CRITIC, LIBRETTIST, STAGE DIRECTOR, TEACHER

BORN: Ullånger, February 27, 1867
DIED: Östersund, December 3, 1942

A lyrical late Romantic, motivated by nationalism and a love of nature, Wilhelm Peterson-Berger has, outside of Sweden, been known best as an effective writer of songs. Born in the northern part of the country, he was schooled in Umeå on the Umeälv River, near the Gulf of Bothnia. At nineteen he undertook three years of study at the Stockholm Conservatory, then went to Dresden for a year, where he worked with Hermann Scholz (a Louis Plaidy-Bülow **[1310]**-Rheinberger **[1368]** pupil) and Hermann Kretzschmar (1848–1924), the court organist. From 1890 to 1892 he taught in the school at Umeå and then returned to Dresden as a music teacher. From 1894 to 1895 he lived at Frösö in central Sweden's lake country. In the latter year he came to Stockholm as a critic for *Dagens Nyheter,* a post he held for thirty-four years, fearlessly attacking what he considered to be fools and showoffs. Beginning in 1908 he served the Swedish Royal Opera for two years as stage director and producer. Among the works he put on there was Wagner's **[1230]** *Tristan,* in his own translation. He himself wrote 5 operas, produced between 1903 and 1927 in Stockholm, all to his own libretti and all much influenced by Wagner. The third, *Arnljot,* is revered as the Swedish national opera. He spent 1920–21 in Italy and his final dozen years back in Frösö. He wrote a number of orchestral works, including 5 symphonies and some chamber music (mostly in small forms), but most of his music is for voice or voices. He also published several books on music and made translations from Nietzsche and of Wagner's writings. RECORDINGS: Until fairly recently he has been represented on records only by occasional songs. However, since the late 1960s his countrymen have begun to take phonographic notice of him and have brought out recordings of such things as the opera *Arnljot,* Symphony No. 2 ("Journey to the South"), Symphony No. 3, the first movement of Symphony No. 4, some of the choral cycles, and several LPs devoted to the songs. Chamber and solo works committed to disc include the *Suite* and *Frösöblomster* for violin and piano, as well as the piano cycles *Earina* and *Anakreontika.* A number of short piano works have also been recorded, both in their original forms and in orchestral transcriptions.

[1588] GRANADOS Y CAMPIÑA,
Pantaléon Enrique (Grà-nä'-*th*ōs ē
Kâm-pēn'-yà, Pän-tà-lä'-ōn En-rē'-kä)
PIANIST, TEACHER
BORN: Lérida, July 27, 1867
DIED: at sea, March 24, 1916

Spanish music returned to international currency with Granados and his slightly older contemporary Isaac Albéniz [1523]. Though Granados was born in Catalonia, his father, an army officer, was a Cuban, and his mother came from Santander on the Bay of Biscay. As a small child he got some basic musical training from one of his father's colleagues. When the family moved to Barcelona, he was enrolled at the Barcelona Conservatory to study piano with Joan Baptista Pujol. He gave his first concert at ten and six years later won the Concurso Pujol. Meanwhile he had taken up the study of composition at the Madrid Conservatory under the great pioneering Hispanist Felipe Pedrell [1384]. In 1887 a patron provided funds for him to study at the Paris Conservatoire. Unfortunately he was ill when the entrance examinations came up and so failed to qualify. However, Charles Wilfride de Bériot, a Thalberg [1220] pupil and son of the great violinist-composer Charles Auguste (1802–70), offered to teach him privately. During his stay in Paris he roomed with his countryman Ricardo Viñes, who was later to premiere many piano works by Debussy [1547], Ravel [1666], and Satie [1578]. Granados enjoyed musical life there and indulged in a bit of hell raising. He went back to Barcelona in 1889 and stunned his fellow citizens with his mature debut in 1890.

For the next several years Granados concertized in Europe, often appearing with such partners as Pablo Casals [1690], Joan Manén [1762], and Jacques Thibaud. He also did some teaching, and though that activity did not delight him, he founded a school of his own, the Academia Granados, in 1901. (After his death it was run by his pupil Frank Marshall.) In 1892 he married Amparo Gal; they had six children, of whom the short-lived Eduardo (1894–1928) showed promise as a conductor and composer. In the latter role Enrique Granados first won attention with his *Danzas españolas* and in 1898 had a real success with his *zarzuela grande* entitled *Maria del Carmen,* but its several successors seem to have had little impact. There were also a few orchestral compositions (e.g., the symphonic poems *La Nit del Mort* and *Dante)* and chamber works (including a piano quintet), but he was chiefly known for his piano music and songs. Probably his greatest work was the

piano suite *Goyescas* after scenes by the painter Goya (Granados was himself an accomplished graphic artist). When he played it in an all-Granados concert at Paris in 1914, it won him the *Légion d'honneur* and a contract with the Opéra for an opera based on it.

Granados went to Switzerland to write the requested work, but the outbreak of war stymied the production. However, the Metropolitan Opera offered its facilities, and late in 1915 Granados and his wife sailed to New York to oversee the premiere. The first Spanish work produced in that house, it opened on January 28, 1916, with a cast that featured Anna Fitziù, Giovanni Martinelli, and Giuseppe de Luca. The reviews were enthusiastic, but it survived for only five performances. Just as the couple were about to embark for Spain, Granados was summoned to the White House to play for President Woodrow Wilson. The delay forced them to take a boat for England instead. From there they took the English ship *Sussex* across the Channel. A German torpedo got it in mid-Channel. Granados was rescued but drowned trying to save Amparo. Six weeks later the Metropolitan mounted an all-star benefit on behalf of the orphaned children; the participants included Maria Barrientos, John McCormack, Julia Culp, Casals, Kreisler [1664], and Paderewski [1527].

RECORDINGS: There is a recording each of the opera *Goyescas* (Ataulfo Argenta) and the symphonic poem *Dante* (Jorge Mester). Marylène Dosse has recorded all the piano music (some of it of no special merit) and Alicia De Larrocha, Frank Marshall's pupil, has recorded the best of it (of which there are many other versions). There is also a number of representations of the songs, notably the *Tonadillas* and most of the *Canciones amatorias* accompanied by De Larrocha and sung by the sexagenarian Conchita Badìa, who studied with Granados. Several of the *Danzas españolas* were orchestrated by Juan Lamote de Grignon (1872–1949) and have been recorded by Carlos Surinach, Enrique Jorda, and others.

[1589] GIORDANO, Umberto (Jôr-dà'-nō,
ŌŌm-bâr'-tō)
CONDUCTOR
BORN: Foggia, August 27/28, 1867
DIED: Milan, November 12, 1948

With the remote exceptions of Zandonai [1766] and Menotti [2177], Giordano was the last-born Italian to place an opera *(Andrea Chenier)* in the standard international repertoire. His Jewish father was a pharmacist in the Apulian town of Foggia, across the boot from Naples, and meant for his son to take up his profession. But the boy was seduced into music by Gaetano Briganti, a local inventor of automatic musical instruments who taught him his basics. He was also severely bitten by the theater bug and indulged his taste as an unpaid prop boy and scenery pusher in the Teatro Duano. Winning a stipend to study at the Naples Conservatory, he went thither in the autumn of 1880, only to fail his entrance exams. However, he attracted the attention of Paolo Serrao (1830–1907) who coached him until he was acceptable. Giordano spent eight years there. After the first four years his symphonic poem *Delizia (Delight)* was performed at a public concert. In 1889 he submitted a one-act opera, *Marina,* to the competition announced by the publisher Edoardo Sonzogno. It came in sixth behind the winner, Mascagni's [1559] *Cavalleria rusticana* but won him a contract from Sonzogno for another effort. Having graduated with a first prize in 1890, Giordano completed the new work two years later. Called *Mala vita (Bad Life)* and involving a consumptive and a whore, it was *verismo* with a vengeance. The Roman premiere featured the husband-and-wife team of Roberto Stagno and Gemma Bellincioni, who had created the *Cavalleria* leads. When they sang it in Naples, however, the reception was scandalous. Giordano tried to apologize two years later by offering an old-fashioned melodrama, *Regina Diaz,* to the Neapolitans, who liked it little better—because, Giordano later said, Sonzogno had interfered fatally with the production.

Sonzogno, considering Giordano hampered by inferior librettists, introduced him to the rising Luigi Illica. The pair agreed that Victorien Sardou's popular play *Fedora* was what they wanted, but Sardou made so many demands that they shelved the idea. After toying with Lamartine's *Jocelyn* and works by Turgenev and George Sand, Alberto Franchetti [1526], who had taken a shine to the younger composer, then offered him *Andrea Chenier,* a libretto about the French Revolutionary poet that Illica had been writing for him—for a consideration. Giordano bit and immediately moved to Milan to begin work on it. But Illica proved a refractory partner with ideas of his own, and refused to accede to certain of the neophyte's wishes. Having reached an impasse, Giordano forced him to back down at gunpoint and then handed him the gun, which proved to be a toy. Once completed, the score was vetoed by Sonzogno's reader. Giordano called on Mascagni, the house's hottest composer, to apply pressure and at last got a performance date at La Scala. The 1895–96 season there proved full of unpropitious disasters, and the rehearsals went so badly that the tenor assigned the lead walked out—thereby giving the then virtually unknown Giuseppe Borgatti, later ranked as Italy's greatest *Heldentenor,* his big chance. The opera was paired with Tchaikovsky's [1377] *Sleeping Beauty* ballet on the interminable opening night but was an unqualified triumph. In short order it won its composer a lucrative long-term contract with his publisher, a knighthood, and the hand of Olga Spatz-Wurms, a hotel heiress. The opera quickly won worldwide acceptance (though New York's Metropolitan Opera took twenty-five years getting around to it).

Chenier's success also made Sardou more pliable, and in 1897 Giordano finally embarked on *Fedora*—not, however, with Illica, who was too busy, but with Arturo Colautti. He completed it a year later and produced it at the Teatro Lirico with the now-widowed Bellincioni in the title role and young Enrico Caruso subbing for Fernando de Lucia, who had proved too temperamental. Despite some initial audience hostility, the piece was a success and remains the only other Giordano opera to keep a tenuous hold on the stage.

Having embarked on a comic operetta, *Giove a Pompeii (Jove in Pompeii)* with Franchetti, Giordano abandoned it in 1901 to work on *Siberia* with Illica. Full of "Russian atmosphere," it created considerable excitement at La Scala in 1903 (with Rosina Storchio, Giovanni Zenatello, and Giuseppe de Luca), even spawning some "original cast" recordings, but it dropped out of sight after a few years. *Marcella,* premiered at the Lirico in 1907, did not do that well, nor did the one-act *Mese mariano (The Marian Month),* a curious foreshadowing of Puccini's [1511] *Suor Angelica,* produced in Palermo in 1910. *Mme. Sans-Gêne,* a historical comedy based on another Sardou work, received another grand sendoff, largely because of its being premiered at the Metropolitan Opera in 1915 with Geraldine Farrar in the title role and Toscanini at the helm. It lasted three seasons before disappearing. *Giove a Pompeii* finally reached the stage in Rome in 1921 and was even more quickly forgotten. In 1924 *La Cena delle beffe (The Jokesters' Supper),* the libretto by Sem Benelli adapted from his own play, famous in America as *The Jest* played by the three Barrymore siblings, enjoyed a brief popularity. In 1928 Giordano wrote a ballet, *L'Astro magico (The Magical Star)* which went begging. It was succeeded a year later by the slight *Il Re (The King)*, which survived until the eve of World War II as a vehicle for such high sopranos as Pagliughi, Carosio, Toti dal Monte, and Bidú Sayão. In 1942 Giordano revised *Fedora* for a movie version, but for the most part he was silent in his last years. After his death Foggia honored him with a magnificent sculptured memorial.

RECORDINGS: There are several commercial recordings of *Andrea Chenier*, at least three of *Fedora*, and, oddly, one of *Mese mariano*, as well as selections from these and other operas, and a few songs. There are also pirated versions of *La Cena delle beffe*, *Mme. Sans-Gêne, Il Re*, and *Siberia*.

[1590] BEACH, Amy Marcy Cheney
(Mrs. H. H. A.)
PIANIST
BORN: Henniker, N.H., September 5,
1867
DIED: New York, N.Y. December 27,
1944

Forty years ago, when the older generations of American composers were fashionably beneath contempt, Mrs. H. H. A. Beach, as she insisted on being called, produced snickers from the ignorant at her presumption. Nowadays, aided by the actions of time and feminism, she is recognized as one of the more considerable native composers of her time and place—not to say sex. Born in a village near Concord, she was descended from early settlers. Her mother was musical, and the child showed extraordinary musical sensitivity from childhood. It is said that such sentimental effusions as Gottschalk's [1306] *Last Hope* so distressed her that they were played to her when punishment was in order. At six she began piano lessons with her mother and made such progress that at the end of two years she was taken to Boston for professional training. Her several teachers included Ernst Perabo and Junius Welch Hill, both pupils of Moscheles [1146], and Karl Baermann. Though Hill gave her some basic harmony lessons, she mostly taught herself to compose by analyzing scores. She also translated the Berlioz [1175] and Gevaert [1303] orchestration manuals in writing. Though she had given recitals in Henniker as a child, Amy Cheney made her formal debut (in her first formal dress) playing the Moscheles concerto with the Boston Symphony. That was in 1883 and she was sixteen. The reviewers predicted a major career for her. But two years later she married a Boston surgeon, Dr. Henry Harris Aubrey Beach. Though he loved music and indulged

his wife, she happily settled down to be Mrs. Beach, finding her musical outlet in composing. In 1892 the venerable Handel and Haydn Society performed her *Mass*—claimed to be the first such work in history by a woman. That same year the New York Philharmonic reached a similar milestone with her concert aria *Eilende Wolken (Flying Clouds)*. In 1896 she produced the first symphony known to have been written in America by a woman and three years later completed a powerful piano concerto.

In 1910 Dr. Beach died. There had been no children, and so Mrs. Beach went to Europe, where for the next four years she made a solid impact both as a pianist and composer. Returning home in 1914, she made her headquarters in a New York hotel, summering at the MacDowell Colony or in England and making frequent concert tours. (No one of course thought to record her.) She was quite popular and had fan clubs all over the country. She continued to compose until she died at seventy-seven. There is nothing "American" about her music, though atypically she had no training abroad. Though she was influenced by German Romanticism, she was a deliberate eclectic. She liked to use folk themes whatever their origin but did not write "folksy" music. She also anticipated Messiaen [2129] and John La Montaine [2299] by collecting birdcalls in the New England woods for thematic use. Mrs. Beach wrote in most genres (there is even a one-act opera, *Cabildo*), though her largest and most popular output was in the areas of piano music and songs.

RECORDINGS: There are recordings of the concerto and piano quintet (Mary Louise Boehm), the string quartet, the piano trio, the violin sonata (Joseph Silverstein), and a collection of piano pieces (Virginia Eskin), as well as scattered songs and other small works.

[1591] WEBBER, Amherst
PIANIST, CONDUCTOR
BORN: Cannes, October 25, 1867
DIED: London, July 25, 1946

Of English parentage, Webber graduated from Oxford, then pursued musical studies with Nicodé [1473] in Dresden and Guiraud [1352] in Paris. Known as "Squib" to his friends and charges, he served as rehearsal pianist and vocal coach at Covent Garden and the Metropolitan Opera and was an assistant to Jean de Reszke at his school in Paris. He wrote an opera, *Fiorella*, produced in London in 1905 and a symphony that once had some currency, but he is best remembered for his songs. RECORDINGS: Some of his songs have been recorded.

[1592] KOECHLIN, Charles Louis Eugène (Kesh'-la*n*, Shärl Lōō'-ē Ö-zhen')
TEACHER, THEORIST
BORN: Paris, November 27, 1867
DIED: Le Canadel, December 31, 1950

Though the French are noted for neglecting their composers until forced to recognize them, it is generally agreed that they (and everyone else) have overdone it in the case of Charles Koechlin. Even today, when the past is being assiduously combed for viable musical works, one looks almost in vain for representation of his vast output. Yet his neglect is explicable. His life was free of scandals and eccentricities (though in his later years one could scarcely overlook the flowing silver mane and beard and the black cloak). He allied himself with no faction or school and avoided competitions. The necessity of his making a living as teacher and writer took the focus away from his composition, which he did little to promote in any case. A simple person with a mystical view, he preserved a low profile. He developed slowly and methodically, was always an eclectic (though he acquired a highly individual style), and evolved his ideas of what music should be from what it had been. He believed that its paramount element was melody and that the symphony orchestra was its most expressive medium—ideas that in his day were deemed passé.

Of Protestant Alsatian descent, Koechlin came from a wealthy family in the textile trade. He pursued an engineering degree at the Polytechnique in Paris but contracted tuberculosis and had to go to Algeria to recover. There he decided that he preferred to be a musician and in 1890 was admitted to the Paris Conservatoire. There he studied with Massenet [1396], but was more impressed by his counterpoint teacher André Gédalge (1856–1926), and especially by Gabriel Fauré [1424], who exerted a powerful influence on him and with whom he continued to work after graduating in 1897. At the outset of his career, he was chiefly known for his finely crafted songs, though he was soon cautiously experimenting with chamber music and even with orchestral works. In 1903 he married Suzanne Pierrard. Apparently the family fortune dried up, for he soon had to turn to teaching, reviewing, and other such tasks to keep afloat. He became internationally known as a teacher, and his many articles and books on music (especially its theoretical aspects) won him

great respect. He was also in demand as an orchestrator: among his orchestrations are Fauré's *Pelléas et Mélisande* incidental music, Debussy's [1547] ballet *Khamma,* and Cole Porter's [1853] ballet *Within the Quota.* A dedicated (but critical) proponent of new music, he was in 1909 a cofounder of the Société Musicale Indépendante and later president of the French branch of the International Society for Contemporary Music. He thrice came to the United States as a lecturer (in English)—in 1918, in 1928 (to Berkeley), and in 1937 (to San Diego). A proponent of communism (though not a Communist), he was also president of the Fédération Musicale Populaire from 1937. Belgian critic Paul Collaer was among the first to call attention to Koechlin's music.

Wilfred Mellers has neatly summed up the characteristics of Koechlin's mature style as involving "nonmetrical rhythms, polymodal lines and polyharmonic textures that fuse mediaeval with oriental principles." He drew inspiration from everywhere —especially nature (both terrestrial and cosmic), literature, and films. His most impressive orchestral work is a series of suites based on Rudyard Kipling's *The Jungle Book.* He not only wrote film scores but also much music evoked by film stars, such as the orchestral suite entitled the *Seven Stars Symphony* (with movements for Douglas Fairbanks, Lilian Harvey, Greta Garbo, Clara Bow, Marlene Dietrich, Emil Jannings, and Charlie Chaplin), the *Epitaphe de Jean Harlow* for saxophone, and the *Danses pour Ginger.* The stage, however, did not attract him, producing only a one-act Biblical pastoral *(Jacob chez Laban),* some pastiche-ballets, and a few pieces of incidental music. His total output runs to more than 225 opuses—mostly orchestral, choral, chamber music, songs, and educational material.

RECORDINGS: Koechlin's representation on records is minuscule: one traces the Kipling piece *Les Bandar-log* (Antal Dorati), the orchestral 5 *Chorals dans les modes du moyen age* and *Partita* (Jorge Mester), a woodwind trio (Bennington Trio), two piano suites (Boaz Sharon), the Harlow *Epitaphe* and four of the *Études* for saxophone and piano, (Jean-Marie Londeix), several pedagogical works for clarinet with accompaniments, and two recordings of the *Seven Stars Symphony*—a pseudonymous and badly recorded piracy and a new digital recording by Alexandre Myrat coupled with the 1919 *Ballade* for piano and orchestra (with pianist Bruno Rigutto). There is also an archival recording of a 1937 performance by Roger Désormière of the orchestral *Les Eaux vives* on a disc which also contains modern performances of the wind septet and the *Song of Kala-Nag* for chorus, tenor, and piano. Just released is a recording of Koechlin's Sonata for Violin and Piano and Sonata for Cello and Piano.

[1593] LANG, Margaret Ruthven
BORN: Boston, November 27, 1867
DIED: Boston, May 29, 1972

Miss Lang, a fixture at Boston Symphony concerts for more than eighty-five years, was the daughter of Benjamin Johnson Lang (1837–1909), a pianist, organist, conductor, teacher, and pillar of Bostonian musical activity. He was her first teacher. She also studied in Leipzig and with George Chadwick [1483] and Edward MacDowell [1529]. She wrote some overtures and other orchestral works, and some large-scale choral pieces but was best known as a songwriter. Her *Irish Love Song* enjoyed particular popularity and was often recorded. She apparently abandoned composition in her fifties but remained active in local musical circles. She died in her 105th year.

[1594] AGUIRRE, Julián (Ä-gwē'-rä, Hōōl-yán')
TEACHER, PIANIST, FOLKLORIST
BORN: Buenos Aires, January 28, 1868
DIED: Buenos Aires, August 13, 1924

Aguirre was taken to Spain at the age of four. When he was fourteen, he entered the Madrid Conservatory, where his composition teacher was Arrieta [1288]. He returned to Argentina four years later and began a career as a concert pianist. He became interested in folk music during trips to the interior and was the first Argentinian musician to collect and arrange it (in 4 volumes of *Aires nacionales argentinos* for piano). He soon settled in the capital, where he became known as a teacher and provided a central focus for the city's musical life. Apart from an orchestral suite, *De mi pais (Of My Country),* he wrote in small forms—mostly songs and piano pieces. His daughter married the conductor-composer Juan José Castro (1895–1968), who orchestrated some of them. RECORDINGS: His works appear in anthologies (e.g., by Andrés Segovia).

[1595] MACCUNN, Hamish
CONDUCTOR, TEACHER
BORN: Greenock, March 22, 1868
DIED: London, August 2, 1916

If Hamish MacCunn sounds like a comic character in a Walter Scott novel, he tried earnestly, if not wholly successfully, to override that handicap. He seems to have thought of himself as the Scots national composer, a figure for which Scotland appears not to have been ready. His father was a shipowner who abetted his son's musical inclinations. At fifteen Hamish went to London as one of the first scholarship students at the Royal College of Music, where he studied (as who did not?) with Parry [1443] and Stanford [1467]. Two years later the college performed his cantata *The Moss Rose,* and Sir August Manns conducted his overture *Cior Mhor* at the Crystal Palace. The success of three more overtures on Scots programs by 1888 (in which year, at twenty, he became professor of harmony at the college) led to a whole succession of "Scottish" works. The next year the Carl Rosa Opera Company commissioned an opera from him. He responded with *Jeanie Deans,* which was premiered in 1894 and continued to be performed for several years. MacCunn joined the company as conductor in 1898 and soon in considerable demand in that capacity. He later conducted for the Moody-Manners and Beecham Companies and directed Edward German's [1541] most successful operettas at the Savoy. In 1889 he married the daughter of the Scottish artist John Pettie, who painted a coy picture of the couple called *Two Strings to Her Bow.* In 1912 MacCunn joined the staff of the Guildhall School. In 1897 a second opera, *Diarmid,* was unsuccessful. After 1900 his output fell off and by the time he died at forty-eight his compositions had for the most part been shelved. RECORDINGS: Alexander Gibson has recorded his second overture, *Land of the Mountains and the Flood.*

[1596] SILVER, Charles (Sēl-vâr', Shärl)
BORN: Paris, April 16, 1868
DIED: Paris, October 10, 1949

Silver studied at the Paris Conservatoire with Massenet [1396] and Théodore Dubois [1356] and won the Grand Prix de Rome in 1891. He wrote a number of orchestral works and half a dozen operas. The most successful of the latter was the first, *La Belle aux bois dormant (The Sleeping Beauty),* which he wrote for his wife, the former Georgette Bréjean-Gravières *(née* Georgette-Amélie Sisout), who recorded selections from it.

[1597] SCHILLINGS, Max (von) (Shil'-lings, Mäks)
CONDUCTOR, ADMINISTRATOR
BORN: Düren, April 19, 1868
DIED: Berlin, July 24, 1933

Born into a wealthy family in the Rhine Valley between Aachen and Cologne, Schillings came to be better known as a conductor and opera-house director than as a composer—he was a rather doctrinaire Wagnerian [1230]. Schooled in Bonn, Schillings studied violin with the Cologne *Konzertmeister*, Otto von Königslöw, and composition with Joseph Brambach (1833–1902), a pupil of Ferdinand Hiller's [1219]. By the time he left for university studies in Munich, he had written and conducted some orchestral works. He intended to become a lawyer, but in Munich Richard Strauss [1563] urged him to take up music, which he did. From 1892 he worked on and off at Bayreuth, becoming chorus master there in 1902. The following year he was appointed to a professorship at the Royal Conservatory in Munich, and in 1908 he became conductor and *régisseur* at the Stuttgart Opera, where he was elevated to the general directorship in 1911 and ennobled in 1912, thus becoming Max *von* Schillings. During World War I he served as a medical orderly and at its close gave up his Stuttgart post. Shortly afterward he was summoned to Berlin to run the Berlin State Opera, where he remained until his resignation in 1925.

Schillings's first three operas—*Ingwelde,* 1894; *Der Pfeifertag (The Piper's Day),* 1899; and *Moloch,* 1906—were all seen as rather slavish imitations of Wagner. His most successful work was the melodramatic *Mona Lisa,* first performed at Stuttgart in 1915. In 1923 Schillings wed (in a second marriage) the soprano Barbara Kemp, who made something of a specialty of the work, singing its American premiere under his direction at the Metropolitan Opera in March of that same year. After ending his Berlin appointment, he guest-conducted for several years and made many records with the orchestra of the Berlin Municipal Opera. In 1933 he was appointed director of that house but died before he could take office. Besides the operas he wrote some incidental music, symphonic poems, and other orchestral works, a string quartet, a piano quintet, choral music, and songs.

RECORDINGS: Schillings conducted for records a few of his own shorter works, including selections from the opera with his wife. Helmut Krebs has recorded the song cycle *Glockenlieder,* and there is a piracy of *Mona Lisa.*

[1598] ERLANGER, (Baron) Frédéric d' (Âr'-làng-er, Frā-dā-rēk' də)
BANKER, IMPRESARIO
BORN: Paris, May 29, 1868
DIED: London, April 23, 1943

In terms of nationality and professionalism, the baron is a hard man to classify. Parisian-born, he had a German father and an American mother. After studying with a certain Anselm Ehmant, he went to London, where the family conducted a banking business and eventually took out English citizenship. Some of his early compositions appeared under the pseudonyms Ferdinand Regnal and Federico Ringel. He wrote several operas that enjoyed some success—*Jehan de Saintré,* 1893; *Inès Mendo,* 1897; *Tess* (after Thomas Hardy), 1906; and *Noël,* 1909. Other music included the ballet *Les Cent baisers (The Hundred Kisses),* a violin concerto, a piano concerto, a *Requiem,* chamber music, and songs. Erlanger was a director of the Covent Garden Opera House. He is not to be confused with the French operatic composer Camille Erlanger (1863–1919). RECORDINGS: Some of the songs appear on early recordings, and Antal Dorati once recorded the ballet.

[1599] MERIKANTO, Frans Oskar (Mā-rē-kàn'-tō, Fràns Ōs'-kär)
CONDUCTOR, ACCOMPANIST, ORGANIST
BORN: Helsinki, August 5, 1868
DIED: Hausjärvi-Oitti, February 17, 1924

Three years younger than Sibelius, Oskar Merikanto was also influential in the rise of musical activity in Finland. After first studying in his native city, he completed his education in Leipzig and Berlin, then returned to Helsinki as organist in St. John's Church. His first opera, *Pohjan neiti (The Girl from the North)* of 1908, is said to be the first ever composed to a Finnish libretto. It was succeeded by two others, *Elinan surma (Elina's Death)* of 1910 and *Regina von Emmeritz* of 1920. During the period of the last two, 1911–22, Merikanto served as head conductor of the Finnish National Opera. He wrote some incidental music, choral pieces, organ music, and manuals for that instrument, but was most successful with his songs. His son Aarre [1882] also became a composer. RECORDINGS: Some of his songs have been recorded, and pianist Izumi Tateno offers an album of piano music.

[1600] BANTOCK, (Sir) Granville
CONDUCTOR, EDUCATOR

BORN: London, August 7, 1868
DIED: London, October 11, 1946

Bantock was an extraordinarily prolific composer (the list of his works occupies nearly ten pages in the fifth edition of *Grove's Dictionary of Music and Musicians*) and was considered an important one in England earlier in the century. But his music has dated badly and is little heard now. He was a physician's son and trained for the Civil Service in India. But at twenty-one, having had basic musical training, he entered the Royal College of Music, where he held the first Macfarren Scholarship. He wrote some big choral works, and his first opera *Caedmar* was performed there in 1892. The following year, his studies behind him, he founded and edited the *New Quarterly Musical Review*, which survived nearly three years. He also conducted in theaters in the provinces and went on a world tour with an operetta company. In 1896 he began a dynamic advocacy for contemporary music with a financially disastrous London orchestral concert dedicated to recent British composers. The following year he became director of the band at New Brighton; this he developed into a symphony orchestra and created the New Brighton Choral Society as an adjunct. In 1898 he married Helen von Schweitzer, who, as Helen F. Bantock, wrote many of the texts he later set.

In 1900 Bantock became director of the Birmingham and Midland Institute School of Music. For all his public dedication to modernism, he insisted not only on a depth of background but also on a broadly humanistic education for his students. He was named Elgar's **[1499]** successor as professor of music at the University of Birmingham in 1908. He held that post until his retirement twenty-six years later, receiving a knighthood from King George V in 1930. Afterward he lived in London and taught at Trinity College. In 1938 he took another world tour. He died of pneumonia eight years later.

Much of Bantock's music suffers from post-Wagnerian elephantiasis and lack of self-criticism. He had a taste for the exotic—or pseudo-exotic—and the literary, often in combination. His "oriental" side is mostly by way of Thomas Moore **[1093]**, Robert Southey, Edward FitzGerald, and their ilk. He also went through a "Hebridean" phase, inspired by the folksongs collected and translated by Margery Kennedy-Fraser, who provided him with a libretto for his 1924 opera *The Seal-Woman*. A good deal of his instrumental music is programmatic, deriving from works by Dante, the Greek tragedians,

Browning, Shelley, and others. (He once planned a cycle of twenty-four symphonic poems to be based on Shelley's "The Curse of Kehama.") Some of his songs still remain in use.

RECORDINGS: In pre-LP times his publisher Paxton brought out a series of Bantock records that included orchestral pieces. Sir Thomas Beecham left a recording of the Browningesque symphonic poem *Fifine at the Fair;* Norman Del Mar performs the *Comedy Overture* and *The Pierrot of the Minute;* Geoffrey Heald-Smith has recorded the *Hebridean Symphony,* the *Macbeth Overture,* and the *Sapphic Poem* for cello and orchestra; and there is a piracy of the *Pagan Symphony.*

[1601] GILBERT, Henry Franklin Belknap
VIOLINIST, TEACHER, CRITIC
BORN: Somerville, Mass., September 26, 1868
DIED: Cambridge, Mass., May 19, 1928

Henry F. Gilbert was a determined maverick—a nationalist who had no patience with the German music that passed for American in his time and place. Hence his work went largely ignored in his lifetime—a fate that continues to pursue it. Gilbert came from an old New England family. He was born a "blue baby"—a condition then incurable—and confounded the doctors by outliving their gloomy prognoses by more than a quarter of a century. He studied briefly at the New England Conservatory and was Edward MacDowell's **[1529]** first American pupil. After trying his hand at fiddling in dance and theater orchestras, he variously tried real estate, silkworm raising, and factory work. While working in a bakery establishment at the Chicago Columbian Exposition, he encountered a Russian friend of Rimsky-Korsakov's **[1416]**, who got him thinking about the Russian nationalistic approach (i.e., the use of folksong). In 1895 Gilbert came into an inheritance that enabled him to give up working and to travel. His interest in French literature drew him to Paris; in 1901 he worked his way back there on a cattle boat to hear Charpentier's *Louise,* which decided him once and for all to become a composer. He had already experimented with the music of American blacks in his *Negro Episode* of 1896, and now for fifteen years it was to provide his chief orientation. The sort of music that resulted did not win him many friends. His *Comedy Overture on Negro Themes* struck a 1911 Boston Symphony audience as being in bad taste, and the conductor Karl Muck dismissed *The Dance in the Place Congo* as "nigger music." A projected *Uncle Remus* opera was abandoned. The vocal piece (not Negro-derived) *Salammbo's Invocation to Tänith* received a single performance by the Russian Symphony Orchestra in New York. (Russian interest in Gilbert's music came to naught with World War I and the subsequent 1917 Revolution.) During this period he was known chiefly for his "Pirate Song," sung by David Bispham, and taken up by other baritones. Gilbert's one important hearing came in 1918, when the Metropolitan Opera elected to do the *Dance in the Place Congo* as a ballet (under Pierre Monteux) in tandem with Cadman's **[1741]** opera *Shanewis*. Shortly after the turn of the century, Gilbert became a friend of another maverick, Arthur Farwell **[1629]**, whose Wa-Wan Press published some of his compositions. Gilbert did not limit himself to Negro folk music but also drew from other folk sources, including Irish and South American music. He continued composing, though hampered by his infirmity, up to the time of his death at sixty. RECORDINGS: On records he is little represented—two versions of *Dance in the Place Congo* (Calvin Simmons, Werner Janssen), the *Humoresque* and *Nocturne* (in Karl Krueger's American music series), a piano piece or two, and several recordings of the "Pirate Song," including an early one by David Bispham.

[1602] JOPLIN, Scott
PIANIST, CORNETIST, TEACHER
BORN: Texarkana, Texas, November 24, 1868
DIED: New York, N.Y., April 1, 1917

Scott Joplin claimed to have invented ragtime, but both the history and the definition of ragtime remain clouded. In its heyday the term seems to have been loosely applied, no doubt to capitalize on its sales appeal. What Joplin meant was specifically the piano rag, a form that counterposes a peculiarly syncopated right-hand (melodic) part to a non-syncopated left-hand (rhythmic) part. Rags differ from jazz chiefly in that they are written out, not improvised, and that the harmonies tend to be diatonic rather than "blue." They have been linked with such earlier phenomena as banjo music, the quadrille, and the cakewalk. Whether or not Joplin "invented" them, he is now acknowledged to have been their Chopin **[1208]**.

Joplin's father Giles, a former slave, had learned the fiddle, which he had played at parties up at the big house. The mother,

Florence, born free, was adept at the banjo and sang. Several other children also contributed to the family music. Accounts differ as to the boy's training, but he appears to have been essentially self-taught. Some sources say that his father bought him a second-hand square piano, others that he practiced at a neighbor's. The latter story seems more credible, for Giles Joplin, fed up with what seemed a hopeless struggle, disappeared early, leaving his wife to support the children as a domestic. Somehow Scott fell in with a German pianist who is said to have introduced him to the beauties of the standard repertoire. The boy eventually set out on his own, working his way north as a honky-tonk pianist in black ghettoes. By 1885 he had reached St. Louis, where he became house musician of the Silver Dollar Saloon, run by Honest John Turpin.

Ragtime is said to have made its first great impact at the Columbian Exposition in Chicago in 1893, where Joplin and other ragtime pianists performed. If so, the pieces must then have been improvised or played by ear and memory, for none has survived. After that, Joplin settled for a time in Sedalia, Missouri, supporting himself as pianist at the Maple Leaf Club. He also played cornet in the Queen City Band and toured with the Texas Medley Quartet, an eight-man vocal group. He managed to get in some formal music study at George R. Smith College, a black school run by the Methodist Church. By mid-decade he had published a couple of songs and three piano pieces. The title of one of the latter, the *Great Crush Collision March*, was perhaps their most interesting feature. In 1897 William H. Krell, a white band leader, published a *Mississippi Rag*, whose claim to the generic title is slight. Later that same year Tom Turpin, the rotund black proprietor of the Rosebud Café in St. Louis, brought out *Harlem Rag*. Allegedly Joplin committed his first two rags to paper around or before then and sold them to Carl Hoffman for publication. But it was 1899 before Hoffman got around to printing *Original Rags*, and he rejected the *Maple Leaf Rag*. A sexagenarian Sedalia music dealer named Joseph Stark decided, however, to gamble on the latter piece. It was an instantaneous success and for many years after Joplin's death was his only composition generally remembered. As a result of his windfall, Stark decided that ragtime was here to stay and devoted the rest of his life to promoting it.

In 1900 Joplin married Nelly Hayden, with whose brother (also named Scott) he collaborated on some new rags. The marriage was an unhappy one. Stark moved to

St. Louis and Joplin followed. In 1902 Joplin offered him a sort of ballet called *The Ragtime Dance,* which Stark staged. It was a failure, and Stark turned down his opera, *A Guest of Honor* (now lost). Convinced of its worth, Joplin somehow got a company together and produced it, probably in 1903, but it did not catch on. In 1905, the year in which Stark took his business to New York, the Joplins' daughter (their only child) died, and the marriage collapsed. (Nelly Joplin died within a year or two.) Scott went to New York in 1907, settled on West Forty-seventh Street, remarried, and finally moved to Harlem. He played, took in pupils, and worked feverishly, if not obsessively, on a new opera, *Treemonisha,* which he completed in 1911. Unable to rouse any interest in it, he published the vocal score on his own, then set about orchestrating the work. Finally, again largely out of his own slim resources, he offered a public "rehearsal" of parts of it in a Harlem hall in 1915. It made no impression. Already manifesting advanced symptoms of syphilis, Joplin came unhinged. He was committed to Manhattan State Hospital late in 1916 and died the following spring in his forty-ninth year. Like much of his music, the orchestral score of *Treemonisha* disappeared.

RECORDINGS: In the early 1970s a recording of Joplin rags by pianist-musicologist Joshua Rifkin touched off a spontaneous Joplin revival. Rifkin and others made several more records, and composers such as William Bolcom [2425] and William Albright [2433] tried their hands at the rag form. This rise in interest was intensified when Joplin music was used as the score for the hit film *The Sting,* and there was even a ballet, *The Entertainer.* In 1972 the Atlanta Symphony commissioned an orchestration of *Treemonisha* from composer T. J. Anderson (1928–). The production aroused so much interest that the work came to Broadway (reorchestrated by Gunther Schuller [2354]), where it had a short but successful run and was recorded by Deutsche Grammophon.

[1603] DRDLA, František Alois (Dird'-là, Frän'-tyi-shek À'-lois)
VIOLINIST, CONDUCTOR
BORN: Žďár nad Sázavou, November 28, 1868
DIED: Bad Gastein, September 3, 1944

Born in Moravia, Franz Drdla (as he came to be known) studied composition with Foerster [1520] at the Prague Conservatory and (rather incredibly) with Bruckner

[1293] at its Viennese counterpart, where his violin teacher was the younger Joseph Hellmesberger (1855–1907). He won a first prize for his fiddling and joined the strings of the Imperial Opera Orchestra in 1890. Four years later he was made *Konzertmeister* and conductor at the Theater an der Wien. He left in 1899 to concentrate on performing and later played in the United States for two years, 1923–25. He wrote a violin concerto, 2 operettas, and other large works but was most successful as a composer of light music. RECORDINGS: His violin encore piece *Souvenir,* once much-recorded, was his most popular work.

[1604] LEVADÉ, Charles Gaston (Le-vàdä', Shärlz Gàs-to*n*')
BORN: Paris, January 3, 1869
DIED: Paris, October 27, 1948

A product of the Paris Conservatoire, where he was one of the innumerable pupils of Massenet [1396], Charles Levadé took the Grand Prix de Rome at the ripe old age of thirty and not long afterward began his career as a writer of operas with *Les Hérétiques,* 1905. *La Rôtisserie de la Reine Pedauque (Queen Pedauque's Cook Shop)* of 1920 was popular enough to win revival, and *Le Peau de chagrin (The Sharkskin)* of 1929 also met with considerable success. Levadé also wrote instrumental works and was particularly admired for his songs. RECORDINGS: A few of his songs survive on records.

[1605] ROUSSEL, Albert Charles Paul Marie (Ro͞os-sel', Àl-bâr' Shärlz Pōl Mà-rē')
NAVAL OFFICER, TEACHER
BORN: Tourcoing, April 5, 1869
DIED: Royan, August 23, 1937

Because of his late flowering and long productivity, one is inclined to think of Roussel as the last of the giants of what has been called France's third musical Golden Age. He was in fact six years older than Ravel [1666] and six years younger than Debussy [1547]. Born in a northern industrial town near the Belgian frontier, he was the son of a wealthy carpet manufacturer. His mother played the piano and gave him his initial lessons but died before she could see their effect. Her husband soon followed her, and Albert, age eight, went to live with his grandfather, Charles Roussel-Defontaine, mayor of Tourcoing, who saw to it that he got an academic grounding. When the mayor too succumbed, the boy, now eleven, went to live with his mother's sister, Mme. Félix Requillard and her husband. It was they who recognized his interest and fostered it. However, having developed a passion for the sea from vacations on the coast and a taste for adventure from the novels of Jules Verne, Roussel decided to become a sailor and in 1884 entered the Collège Stanislas in Paris to train for the Navy. There he kept up his musical studies with one Jules Stoltz, who taught there and was organist at the Church of St. Ambroise. Three years later he entered the naval academy, from which he graduated in 1889, sixteenth in a class of more than 500. The ensuing year was taken up with a cruise to Indo-China on the frigate *Melpomène* and other ships; his experience of the East—to which he returned in 1893—imprinted itself indelibly on him. Later, on the gunboat *Styx*, of which he was an officer, he saw one of the men swept overboard and drowned in a Mediterranean storm; he suffered nightmares long afterward and memorialized the event in the prelude to his F-sharp piano suite. In his five years as a naval officer he served on several other ships, suffered a spell of bad health from which he recovered in Tunis, and was stationed in Cherbourg, where to pass the time he began to compose. Persuaded to get a professional opinion, he took his works to Julien Koszul, the head of the conservatory at Roubaix, near his birthplace, and was urged to devote himself to music.

Accordingly Roussel resigned his commission in 1894 and went to Paris to study with Eugène Gigout [1417]. Later, however, acquaintance with Vincent d'Indy [1462] persuaded him that Impressionism was the wrong course for him, and he became one of d'Indy's first pupils at the Schola Cantorum. During these early years his compositions were few and small-scale. In 1902 (still nominally a student) he became professor of counterpoint at the Schola and soon thereafter began to blossom: his first major composition was his piano trio, premiered in 1904, and it was followed two years later by the first symphony. In 1908 he married Blanche Preisach and took her to the Far East on a honeymoon cruise, whose immediate product was the *Evocations* for orchestra and voices. This was preceded by the incidental music to Jean-Aubry's *Le Marchand de sable qui passe (The Sandman Goes By)* of 1908, and the 1913 ballet *Le Festin de l'araignée (The Spider's Feast)*—works that show a coalescence of Roussel's Impressionistic tendencies with d'Indy's hard-nosed views. Roussel came into his own with his "opéra-ballet" *Padmâvatî*, based on an In-

dian tale and using as its basis Indian ragas and rhythms. It was interrupted, however, by the outbreak of the 1914 war. Dropped from the naval reserve because of persistent poor health, and now forty-five years old, Roussel became a driver for the Red Cross. A year later he was accepted as a transport officer for the artillery. Eventually he became ill and was released ten months before the Armistice. He settled down on the Breton coast to finish his opera, which was completed that same year—though it had to wait until 1923 for production at the Paris Opéra.

After completing a second symphony, he and his wife acquired a house on the Norman coast near Varengeville, where Roussel spent the rest of his life. The history of that period is largely a chronology of his major works—the ballets *Bacchus et Ariane* and *Aenéas* of 1930 and 1935; the 1936 opera *Le Testament de Tante Caroline (Aunt Caroline's Will);* two more symphonies; the 2 orchestral suites; and a number of chamber works and songs. The third symphony was commissioned by Serge Koussevitzky, and Roussel was in Boston for its 1930 premiere. By 1920 Roussel had developed his characteristic style—a neo-classical approach that makes much use of polyphony, polytonality, and orchestral color and is marked by a motoric energy. What he retained from Debussy and d'Indy was their aristocratic view: he wrote not for the crowd but for musical connoisseurs. As a result, though he became sufficiently famous to be honored with a Roussel Festival in Paris in 1929, he was never a drawing card—nor is he today.

Despite steadily declining health—notably a bad heart—in his later years, Roussel worked untiringly, overseeing music at the Paris Exposition in 1936 and serving as an officer of the ISCM. Finally in 1937 his doctors told him that the Atlantic climate was likely to prove fatal. Accordingly he moved to Royan on the Gironde Estuary, where his heart gave out a few weeks later.

RECORDINGS: *Padmâvatî* exists in a good pirated recording (from French Radio), and recently a commercial recording was made, directed by Michel Plasson with Marilyn Horne. Most of the major works, and many of the minor ones, have appeared on commercial recordings over the years, though Roussel's output has by no means been treated exhaustively. (The first symphony and *Le Testament de Tante Caroline,* for instance, seem to be lacking.) One new release of especial interest is Alain Raes's two-disc traversal of the complete piano works.

[1606] PFITZNER, Hans Erich (Fits'-ner, Hánz Â'-rikh)
CONDUCTOR, TEACHER, WRITER, POLEMICIST
BORN: Moscow, May 5, 1869
DIED: Salzburg, May 22, 1949

Dwarfish, sharp-tongued, conservative, and not a little paranoid, Hans Pfitzner was perhaps his own worst enemy. But his pronouncements have been misread and his intentions misconstrued, and certain puzzling aspects of his life have been held against him, so that thirty-five years after his death he remains an unjustly neglected figure.

Though Pfitzner was born in Moscow, his parents (as he never tired of proclaiming) were *echt deutsch,* his father Robert being employed there as a violinist. Robert Pfitzner was also his son's first music teacher. Soon the family moved to Frankfurt am Main, where the father had been appointed director of the municipal theater. There Hans was enrolled at the Hoch Conservatory in 1886, where his chief teachers were the Russian-reared Iwan Knorr and the Dutch-born James Kwast. Afterward Pfitzner fell in love with Kwast's daughter Mimi, who, on her mother's side, was a descendant of Ferdinand von Hiller [1219]. His studies completed, he took a job in 1890 as *repetiteur* and vocal coach at the Koblenz Opera, teaching in the local conservatory on the side. Three years later he had produced enough music—a cantata, the cello sonata, an orchestral scherzo, and some 50 fine songs—to give a one-man concert in Berlin. In 1895 his first opera, *Der arme Heinrich (Poor Henry)*—watered-down Wagner [1230]—won extravagant praise on its premiere in Mainz, where its composer served for a season as assistant conductor. He then joined the faculty of the Stern Conservatory in Berlin. The Kwasts having steadfastly opposed his marriage to Mimi, he eloped with her to Canterbury in 1899. Two years later his second opera, *Die Rose vom Liebesgarten (The Rose from Love's Garden),* was successfully premiered at Elberfeld and taken up all over Germany (for a time). By 1903 he was chief conductor at the Theater des Westens in Berlin. In 1906 he went to Munich as director of the Kaim Orchestra, and there Felix Mottl conducted his Christmas opera, *Das Christ-Elflein (The Little Christmas Elf).* A year later Pfitzner was called to Strassburg (Strasbourg) to serve as civic musical director and head of the conservatory, and he became intendant at the opera house there in 1910.

During these busy years Pfitzner, never very productive, had written little more than

the operas, save for his first string quartet, the piano quintet, incidental music, and songs. But he had already begun to develop his curious notions about the artist's need for isolation from the world and the undesirability of musical "progress." These were not so bad as they sound: he essentially felt that the artist's duty was as an intermediary between the great dead of his art and the living—close to Wagner's position in *Die Meistersinger.* Such notions began to manifest themselves in an essay on music drama and in a furious attack on Busoni's [1577] "new" esthetic. More importantly they were incorporated into Pfitzner's opera *Palestrina* (his masterpiece), whose libretto he wrote himself. In it that Renaissance composer (a projection of Pfitzner himself) "purifies" music in the face of all sorts of external pressures and turmoil. The work was premiered in Munich in 1917, with Karl Erb in the title role, accepted as a sort of Holy German Work and enshrined in the German repertoire—for all the wrong reasons. Elsewhere it has been ignored, which is a pity, for it is a very great work.

In 1920 Pfitzner went back to Berlin to teach a master class at the Academy of Fine Arts. A year later he produced the cantata *Von deutscher Seele (Of the German Spirit)* which has been taken as evidence of his Nazi leanings; the texts are in fact by the Romantic poet Joseph von Eichendorff (1788–1857). Otherwise the decade was rather infertile until 1929, when he produced another important cantata, *Das dunkle Reich (The Dark Kingdom).* In 1926 Mimi Pfitzner died. In 1930 Pfitzner went to the Munich Academy "for life."

Pfitzner remained in Germany throughout the Third Reich. Much has been made of this, and though a postwar court pronounced him clear of official taint, the record remains clouded. In 1934 his "lifetime" appointment was terminated on the argument that at sixty-five one should retire. It is true that he was by then ailing and half blind. He continued, however, to conduct and compose. When Richard Strauss [1563], an old rival and enemy, fell from grace, the official press touted Pfitzner as a superior musician whose music expressed real German virility. Evidence suggests that though initially he agreed with the stated aims of the Nazis, he was ultimately bitterly disillusioned. In the course of the war his home was bombed, and at its conclusion he was discovered, totally without funds, in a crowded Munich old-people's home. A subscription got up by the Vienna Philharmonic Society enabled him to move into a house of his own in Salzburg, where he died three weeks after his nationally celebrated eightieth birthday.

RECORDINGS: In the 1930s and 1940s, Pfitzner recorded his second symphony, some orchestral selections from the stage music, and, as accompanist to baritone Gerhard Hüsch, some of his *Lieder*. More recently there have appeared a splendid recording of *Palestrina* (Rafael Kubelik) and a piracy of *Das Christ-Elflein,* as well as modern and/or archival readings of all three symphonies, *Das dunkle Reich* (Alois Hochstrasser), the Concerto for Violin (Suzanne Lautenbacher), *Von deutscher Seele* (Joseph Keilberth), the string quartets, and most of the songs. A new eight-record boxed set on the Da Camera Magna label contains the complete chamber music by various performers. Dietrich Fischer-Dieskau and Wolfgang Sawallisch have recorded a scene from *Der arme Heinrich* and a selection of six orchestral songs.

[1607] DIACK, John Michael
PUBLISHER, EDITOR, VOICE TEACHER
BORN: Glasgow, June 26, 1869
DIED: London, February 2, 1946

Michael Diack was president of the London music publishers Paterson and Company. He is chiefly known for some effective singing manuals and for choral music and folksong arrangements. RECORDINGS: Some of his parodistic nursery-rhyme settings were recorded by such bassos as Alexander Kipnis and Owen Brannigan.

[1608] JÄRNEFELT, Armas (Yâr'-ne-felt, Ár'-màs)
CONDUCTOR
BORN: Viipuri, August 14, 1869
DIED: Stockholm, June 23, 1958

Armas Järnefelt was the brother of Aino Järnefelt, whom Jean Sibelius [1575] married in 1892, and of Arvid Järnefelt, for whose play *Kuolema* Sibelius wrote music, including the popular *Valse triste.* He was a product of the Helsingfors Music College, where his chief teachers were its founder Martin Wegelius (1846–1906) and Ferruccio Busoni [1577]. After further study with Albert Becker (1834–99) in Berlin, he went to Paris for a year's polishing by Massenet [1396]. In 1892 he returned to Finland to marry the singer Maikki Pakarinen. After working as conductor and coach in Magdeburg and Düsseldorf, he was appointed director of the Viipuri Orchestra in 1897. Upon making himself known as a guest conductor, he was hired in 1907 by the Royal Opera in Stockholm, where he worked for twenty-five years. He and his wife were divorced shortly after he moved there. She later married the composer Selim Palmgren [1703], and Järnefelt married another singer, Liva Edström. In 1910 he became a citizen of Sweden, was appointed court *Kapellmeister,* and was made musical director of the opera in 1923. Nine years later he was called back to Helsinki (as it had become known) as director of the National Opera, a post he held for four years. During World War II he was conductor of the Helsinki Philharmonic for a season, 1942–43. Otherwise he remained in Stockholm, where he died in his eighty-ninth year. Järnefelt wrote for plays and films and composed some orchestral and choral works of some scope but was happiest in small forms. RECORDINGS: His most recorded works are the *Praeludium* and the *Berceuse,* both for small orchestra.

[1609] DAVIES, (Sir) Henry Walford
ORGANIST, CHOIRMASTER, EDUCATOR
BORN: Oswestry, September 6, 1869
DIED: Wrington, March 11, 1941

A fairly prolific and popular composer in his youth, Davies made his greatest impact as a church musician and an educator who combined a gift for teaching with the new electronic media to reach a mass audience. A Shropshire lad, he was apprenticed to the great organist Sir Walter Parratt at Windsor, where he was initially a choirboy. In 1890 he won a scholarship to the Royal College of Music, where he was a pupil of Stanford [1467], Parry [1443], and Rockstro [1285]. He succeeded the last as counterpoint teacher in 1895. After taking a doctorate at Cambridge and serving in other London churches, he began a notable twenty-year career as organist and choirmaster at the Temple Church in 1898. Here he showed remarkable imagination in his choice of music for the services and set supernal standards for choral singing and organ playing. In 1903 he left his teaching post to conduct the Bach Choir and to free-lance at choral festivals. During the 1914–18 war he at first busied himself with music for and among the troops, and later, as Major Davies, became director of music for the Royal Air Force. In 1919 he was given an endowed chair at the University of Wales, from which he made musical policy for the Welsh schools. Knighted in 1922, he was named Gresham Professor of Music (in London) two years later. On April 4, 1924, he made his first educational broadcast to the schools and afterward became a familiar and popular radio figure. He was made musical adviser to the BBC in 1927, the year he returned to Windsor as an organist. The school broadcasts ran for a decade, at the end of which he succeeded Elgar [1499] as Master of the King's Musick. From 1926 he broadcast another educational series for adult listeners and in 1934 inaugurated still another series on English church music. He also recorded a set of lectures on melody. He died in Somersetshire. As a composer, Davies, expectably, looms largest in the choral area, and his setting of *Everyman* and his oratorio *The Temple* were once well known. He also wrote some orchestral and chamber music. Today, however, except for a few pieces for worship, he is remembered for his *Solemn Melody* and his official march for the Royal Air Force. RECORDINGS: All of the works mentioned have been recorded.

[1610] LEKEU, Guillaume Jean Joseph Nicolas (Lə-kö', Gē-yōm' Zhàn Zhō-zef' Nē-kō-làs')
BORN: Heusy, January 20, 1870
DIED: Angers, January 21, 1894

Guillaume Lekeu was undoubtedly a remarkably gifted young man, though his too-early death has perhaps confused promise with fulfillment. His parents were Belgian. In 1879 they moved from their village near Verviers to Poitiers in France, where Guillaume attended the Lycée. When he was fourteen, an encounter with some music of Beethoven [1063] excited his interest, and he set about to analyze the string quartets. This led to his trying his hand at composition. At eighteen he went to Paris to take a degree in liberal arts. There he met the young Polish musicologist Théodor de Wyzewa, who sent him to Gaston Vallin for some serious formal training. After Vallin had given him a grounding, he passed him on to César Franck [1284], whom Lekeu idolized. But Franck died shortly, and Lekeu's further education was entrusted to Vincent d'Indy [1462]. D'Indy urged him to enter the Belgian Prix de Rome competition in 1891. Lekeu complied but took only a second prize. However, Eugène Ysaÿe [1507] was so impressed with his work that he commissioned what remains Lekeu's masterpiece, the Sonata for Violin and Piano. Lekeu continued to write as if there were no tomorrow. There wasn't: he contracted typhoid and died on the day after his twenty-fourth birthday. RECORDINGS: Lekeu is memorialized on records by some songs, several readings of the Sonata for Violin and Piano as well as the Sonata for Cello and Piano, the Piano Trio, the Quartet for Piano and Strings, and the *Adagio for String-Quartet.* Orchestral works and records include the *Fantasy on Angevin tunes,* the *Adagio for Strings,* the symphonic etudes *Hamlet* and *Ophelia,* and the *Fantaisie contrapunctique sur un cramignon liègois.*

[1611] TOURNEMIRE, Charles Arnould (Tōōrn-mēr', Shärlz Àr-nōōld')
ORGANIST, TEACHER
BORN: Bordeaux, January 22, 1870
DIED: Arcachon, November 3, 1939

Nine months older than his fellow pupil and rival Louis Vierne [1616], Charles Tournemire outlived him by thirty months and died almost as dramatically as he did. Tournemire was the more precocious, becoming organist at the church of St. Pierre in Bordeaux at the age of eleven. Like Vierne he studied with Franck [1284] and Widor [1414] at the Paris Conservatoire, taking first prizes in organ and improvisation. Later he was a pupil of d'Indy [1462], and in 1898 he succeeded Gabriel Pierné [1555], who had succeeded Franck, at Ste. Clotilde. Tournemire played there for the rest of his life, winning especial admiration for his improvisations. He was appointed to a professorship at the Conservatoire in 1919. A quiet man with a wide streak of unworldliness, Tournemire was a tireless composer. He is best known for his organ music, especially the monumental *L'Orgue mystique,* a vast cycle based on Gregorian melodies and including music for every Sunday in the year. But he wrote much more. A big cantata, *Le Sang de la sirène (The Siren's Blood)* won the City of Paris Prize in 1904, and the Paris Opéra produced his *Les Dieux sont morts (The Gods Are Dead)* in 1924 (twelve years after its completion), but most of his output went unnoticed and remains unpublished. It includes three other operas, 8 orchestral symphonies, a number of large-scale choral works (including a trilogy on Faust, Don Quixote, and St. Francis, many chamber works, and songs. Early on November 4, 1939, Tournemire's body was found on a side street in Arcachon, a town near his birthplace. He had been dead for several hours. RECORDINGS: Tournemire recorded some of his compositions and improvisations at Ste. Clotilde. (His pupil Maurice Duruflé [2010] has noted down the improvisations from the records and made recordings of them himself.) Among other records of organ pieces, one should note Georges Delvallée's of the *Chorals-poèmes,* Op. 67 (on the *Seven Last*

Words) and a generous selection from
L'Orgue mystique.

[1612] GODOWSKY, Leopold (Gō-dov'-
skĕ, Lā'-ō-pōld)
PIANIST, TEACHER
BORN: Soshly, February 13, 1870
DIED: New York, N.Y., November 21,
1938

For Leopold Godowsky, composition was
largely an extension of playing the piano,
which most of his great piano-playing contemporaries agreed he did better than any of
them; some of his pieces, however, contain
some of the greatest challenges to piano
technique ever put on paper. A doctor's son,
he was born near the Polish-Lithuanian city
of Vilna (Wilno, Vilnius) and lost his father
when he was four years old. According to
legend, his talent had by then already manifested itself, and his mother had set him to
studying violin. But his superiority at the piano soon became clear and, though he had
had little and sporadic training, he gave his
first public recital at the age of nine. Subsequently he went on a middle-European tour
and attracted the attention of a Königsberg
banker named Feinburg, who sent him to
the Berlin Hochschule in 1883. There he
studied briefly with Woldemar Bargiel (1828–
97), Clara Schumann's **[1267]** half-brother,
and with Ernst Rudorff (1840–1916), a friend
of Brahms **[1329]**. But by 1884 he was touring the United States and Canada—the latter with the violinist Ovide Musin, who later
settled in New York. On his return to Europe, Godowsky stopped off in Paris to
study with Saint-Saëns **[1343]**, whose "lessons," according to Godowsky, consisted
mostly of listening to him play.
    In 1890 the pianist returned to the United
States, became a citizen, and married Frieda
Saxe. (A son was coinventor of the Kodachrome color-film process; a daughter married Godowsky's pupil, the gifted David
Saperton.) For five years Godowsky taught
at the New York College of Music and, after
one year at the Broad Street Music School in
Philadelphia, in 1895 he became head of the
Chicago Conservatory. But in 1900 he returned to Europe to play and settled in Berlin. By then his reputation had become
legendary, and his initial concert (in Berlin)
included almost everyone who was anyone
in the piano world in its audience. He was
hailed as the greatest pianist of the day, and
many of his most formidable rivals became
his admiring friends. In his intimate circle,
he was known as "Popsy." It is reliably reported that no one ever really heard Godow-

sky play who did not hear him play infor-
mally for his cronies. On stage he seems to
have been hampered by a combination of
perfectionism and stage fright, as he certainly was before the recording microphone.
He stayed in Berlin until 1909, then taught at
the Vienna Academy until war broke out in
1914. He thereupon returned to America, settling for a time in California. While recording the Chopin **[1208]** *Nocturnes* in London
he suffered a stroke which cost him the use
of his right arm and thus his career as a performer, though he went on composing until
he died.
    Apart from a few violin pieces and songs,
Godowsky wrote for the piano, and most of
his work in that medium was intended di-
dactically. The difficulties of his Strauss
waltz paraphrases are legendary, but they
pale before his 53 paraphrases of the Chopin
études, a *tour de force* of piano writing and
polyphonic thinking. Saperton, whose career
was cursed, recorded a number of them, but
the earlier and more comprehensive set went
unissued, and the masters were melted down
in the 1940s to aid the war effort. Other
works included the *Triakontameron* (30
pieces in 3/4 time), the *Java Suite* (on oriental scales, the fruit of an Eastern tour), and
the *Miniatures* (46 piano duets, the *secondo*
parts written for beginners).
    RECORDINGS: Godowsky recorded a few
of his own pieces, and Hans Kann has devoted an LP to him. The complete *Triakontameron* has been recorded by Benno
Schmidbauer for Micula, a small German label, and other pieces are scattered through
various recorded anthologies.

[1613] STRAUS, Oscar (Shtrous, Ōs'-kär)
CONDUCTOR
BORN: Vienna, March 6, 1870
DIED: Bad Ischl, January 11, 1954

Straus studied at the Vienna Conservatory
with the pianist Adolf Prosniz, a pupil of
Tomásek **[1080]**, and with Bruckner's **[1293]**
successor Hermann Grädener (1844–1929).
He then, in 1891, became a pupil of Max
Bruch **[1358]** in Berlin for a couple of years.
On the advice of Johann Strauss, Jr. **[1295]**
—Oscar Straus had shed the final *s* of his
name to avoid identification with other musical Strausses, to whom he was unrelated—
he became a peripatetic theater conductor.
In 1900 he was hired as conductor by the
avant-garde Überbrettl cabaret in Berlin—
where Arnold Schoenberg **[1657]** tried his
hand at pop songs. Though previously
Straus had had serious aspirations—he had
produced some orchestral music and the op-

era *Die Waise von Cordova (The Orphan Girl of Cordova)*—he made his first real compositional success as a songsmith. In 1904 he returned to Vienna and embarked on his operetta career. After a couple of Offenbachian [1264] farces—*Die lustigen Nibelungen (The Merry Nibelungs)*, 1904; *Hugdietrichs Brautfahrt (Hugdietrich's Bridal Journey)*, 1906—he hit in 1907 with *Ein Walzertraum (A Waltz Dream)*, one of the most successful Viennese operettas of the day. He followed this a year later with *Der tapfere Soldat* (based on Bernard Shaw's *Arms and the Man*, and popular in America as *The Chocolate Soldier*). Later he had lesser successes with works written for the Viennese operetta star Fritzi Massary and with *Les trois valses* for Yvonne Printemps. The latter was, however, a pastiche of pieces by the "other" Strausses, and indeed for most of the rest of his career, Oscar Straus ground out self-imitations and catchpenny "jazz" musicals. Under the Nazi threat he moved first to Paris and then to the United States. Already expert as a writer of film scores, he found employment in Hollywood. His most successful such score, *La Ronde*, however, was written after his return to Austria in 1948. He continued to conduct into his eighties. RECORDINGS: There is a recording of a *Serenade* conducted by Jirí Stárek as well as numerous recordings of excerpts from the operettas.

[1614] **LEHÁR, Franz** (Lā'-här, Frántz)
VIOLINST, BANDMASTER, CONDUCTOR
BORN: Komáron, April 30, 1870
DIED: Bad Ischl, October 24, 1948

One automatically thinks of Lehár, exact contemporary of Oscar Straus [1613], and the most renowned operetta composer since the second Johann Strauss [1295], as Viennese. But his childhood tongue was Hungarian, and his people came from what is now Czechoslovakia, where they spelled the name "Lehar." The father, also Franz, was a longtime military bandmaster, and his son's first teacher; the mother, Christine, was Hungarian-born. Young Franz went in 1882 to Prague to study; his composition teachers were Josef Foerster, father of the composer [1520], and Zdeněk Fibich [1457]. In 1888 he went to work as a theater violinist in Barmen-Elberfeld, Germany, but he was drafted into the military shortly afterward and became first a musician in his father's band and then embarked on a career as bandmaster. When the Leipzig Municipal Theater accepted his first full-length opera, *Kukuška*, in 1896, he resigned his post. The work was,

however, a failure—nor did it fare better eight years later as *Tatiana*—and, after rejoining the service in Trieste, he took over his father's band in Budapest. He also embarked on a long and happy marriage about this time. In 1899 he was transferred to Vienna, where he at last had some success with his music. Encouraged, he again resigned in 1902 and shortly afterward became a conductor at the Theater an der Wien, where his operetta *Wiener Frauen (Viennese Women)* had a mild success later that year. A month later the Carltheater produced his *Der Rastelbinder (The Tinker)*, which definitely put him on the map. However, his next two outings *Der Göttergatte (The Gods Married)* and *Die Juxheirat (The Phony Marriage)*, staged at the same two theaters in 1904 (in reverse order), were not liked. (The first reappeared in 1911 as *Die ideale Gattin—The Ideal Mate.)*

In 1905 Richard Heuberger [1451], slated to set a libretto that Victor Léon and Leo Stein had based on a French farce, *L'Attaché*, failed to produce. Léon, librettist of the two failed works just noted, was on the outs with Lehár but finally, in desperation, turned the piece over to him. It (still untitled) was scheduled for the Theater an der Wien for December 30, 1905. This unpropitious date—the eve of New Year's Eve—was apparently arranged by Heuberger, a power in Viennese music who also blocked Lehár's application for the conductorship of the Vienna Tonkünstler concerts. The title of the operetta was the result of a mistake; the relict of some high official had been bothering the management about free tickets. Hearing someone refer to the *lästige Witwe* (annoying widow), Lehár thought he said *lustige Witwe* (merry widow) and immediately appropriated that phrase for his operetta or so goes the tale. Though everything went wrong right up to the rise of the curtain, the piece was a triumph and has remained one of the most popular and enduring of all operettas.

But the next several Lehár offerings came nowhere near equaling *The Merry Widow*, and it was not until 1909 that he had a comparable success, this time with *Der Graf von Luxemburg (The Count of Luxembourg)*. He kept up that standard with *Zigeunerliebe (Gypsy Love)* the next year and, to a lesser degree, with *Eva* in 1910. But there ensued a fallow period of several years in which Lehár wrote relatively little and turned out nothing of consequence until 1922, when *Frasquita* caught the public fancy. It was followed by an oriental tale, *Die gelbe Jacke (The Yellow Jacket)*, which did not. But another successful period began when the great tenor Richard Tauber [1865] took over the title role in *Paganini*. Tauber knew how to put over a Lehár song, and Lehár knew how to write for the Tauber voice, and they capitalized on these abilities in *Der Zarewitsch (The Czarevich)* of 1927, and *Friederike*, 1928. The apex of the association, however, came surprisingly with *Das Land des Lächelns (The Land of Smiles)*, which was nothing more than *Die gelbe Jacke* revised—though the additions included *"Dein ist mein ganzes Herz,"* ("Thine is my whole heart," or, as the standard translation has it, "Yours is my heart alone.") The operetta became an enormous money maker; Tauber brought a revival to Broadway a year or so before he died. Lehár's last great success was *Giuditta*, produced with enormous fanfare at the Vienna State Opera in 1934, and more an opera than an operetta. In the 1930s he also wrote several film scores. Although his wife was Jewish, Lehár remained in Austria for the duration of World War II. Afterward he moved to Zürich for a time, and, like Straus, made some LP recordings in his old age. Like Straus too, he finally lived and died in Bad Ischl. Lehár has perhaps been underrated. He was a highly knowledgeable and sophisticated musician, whose technical acumen was balanced by a gift for easy melody, together with wit and verve. However unlikely his libretti, he took them seriously as drama, and much of his success is owing to his sense of theater.

RECORDINGS: His best operettas have enjoyed complete recordings—*Die lustige Witwe* several—and the others are mostly well represented by excerpts.

[1615] SCHMITT, Florent (Shmit, Flôr'-ent)
ADMINISTRATOR, CRITIC, CONDUCTOR, PIANIST
BORN: Blâmont, September 28, 1870
DIED: Neuilly-sur-Seine, August 17, 1958

Schmitt, who had German forebears, was born in a small Lorraine town between Nancy and Strasbourg. Schmitt, Sr., an enthusiastic amateur keyboard player, gave lessons to his son, who did not share his enthusiasm until he reached his teens and became infatuated with the music of Chopin [1208]. After two years of study at the municipal conservatory in Nancy, he transferred to its counterpart at Paris in 1889. But two years later he was called up for army service, which he carried out as a band flutist. On his return to the conservatory, he studied composition with Massenet [1396] and then with Gabriel Fauré [1424]. In 1896 he failed in a try for the Prix de Rome.

Three more attempts won him only a single second place. Finally he triumphed at the age of thirty. After his three-year stay in Rome and two more years of travel, he came back to Paris, where late in 1906 an all-Schmitt concert was presented to sharply divided critical opinion, the majority impression being that here was another of those wild men. (The most important piece performed was the choral-orchestral *Psalm 47*, one of his Rome *envois* and now regarded as one of his masterpieces.)

Schmitt was in on the formation of the Société Musicale Indépendante and active as a board member for a number of years. In 1907 he unveiled a fashionably decadent ballet, *La Tragédie de Salomé*, for the English dancer Loie Fuller, already noted for her work with gauzy scarves. The symphonic poem (same title) that he fashioned from the music is perhaps his best-known composition today. The same period brought forth the much-admired and very difficult Piano Quintet of 1908.

A fairly prolific composer for all of his long life, Schmitt made his biggest splash in these early years. He wrote ballets, incidental dramatic music, and film scores, but no operas. In other areas he tended to eschew Classical forms. He liked to think big and was a master orchestrator. Though he encouraged such avant-gardists as Stravinsky [1748] and Satie [1578], he espoused no school, and writers have trouble trying to pigeonhole him, calling him a conservative, a neo-romantic, and a polyphonist, among other things. It is perhaps this difficulty that has prevented wider acceptance of his music.

Schmitt appeared occasionally, as pianist and conductor, in his own works. (He played, for example, the premiere of his first symphony, the *Symphonie concertante* for piano and orchestra, at Boston in 1932 under the baton of Koussevitzky [1655].) For two years, 1922–24, he headed the Lyons Conservatory and served for the decade before World War II as music critic for *Le Temps*. He was elected to the Académie in 1936 following the demise of Paul Dukas [1574]. Most of his life was, however, devoted to his composition. *Janiana* for string orchestra, which he called his second symphony, appeared in 1941. He remained active up to the end, attending the premiere of his Op. 137 symphony (actually his third symphony) in Strasbourg two months before his death.

RECORDINGS: Schmitt himself recorded the second movement of the quintet with the Calvet Quartet and, as conductor, two movements of his orchestration of the four-hand piano suite *Reflets d'Allemand (German Reflections)*. There have been several recordings of *La Tragédie de Salomé*. Others include *Dionysiaques* and *Sélamlik* for band, *Chant élégiaque* for cello and orchestra or piano; the string symphony *Janiana; Rapsodie viennoise* for orchestra; the 1904 orchestral piece after Poe, *Le Palais hanté (The Haunted Palace); Ronde burlesque* for orchestra; the choral-orchestral *Psalm 47; A contre-voix* for mixed chorus; the String Trio; *Sonatine en trio* for violin, cello, and piano; Quintet in A Minor for Piano and Strings; *Suite en rocaille* for flute, harp, and string trio; *Soirs* for piano; and a number of songs. There may be additional small pieces scattered in various anthologies.

[1616] VIERNE, Louis Victor Jules (Vĕrn, Lōō-ē′ Vĕk-tôr′ Zhülz)
ORGANIST, TEACHER
BORN: Poitiers, October 8, 1870
DIED: Paris, June 2, 1937

The parallels between the lives of Louis Vierne and Charles Tournemire [1611] have been noted above. Vierne's father was a journalist. The boy was born blind and on the advice of his uncle Charles Colin, a musician, was directed toward a musical career from earliest childhood. After being introduced to the organ by Colin, he studied at the Paris Institute for Blind Children and then entered the Paris Conservatoire. There he studied with César Franck [1284] for a few weeks. Though Franck died shortly after Vierne's matriculation, he not only left his imprint on Vierne's style but also taught him to compose away from his instrument. The young man completed his studies under Widor [1414] and became his lieutenant at St. Sulpice. In 1900 he applied for the vacancy at Notre Dame and, though he had eighty-eight rivals, he was selected unanimously. He remained there for thirty-seven years, with time out for tours and for operations on his eyes. The latter, which he underwent between 1916 and 1920, were performed by a Dr. de Wecker and were sufficiently successful that afterward Vierne was able to recognize faces and even read large print. He became professor of organ at the Schola Cantorum in 1912 and was renowned as a teacher. Among his products were Nadia Boulanger (1887–1979, Marcel Dupré [1806], Joseph Bonnet, and Maurice Duruflé [2010], who also studied with Tournemire. Vierne made a tour of the United States in 1927. In his sixty-seventh year, while playing a concert for Les Amis de l'Orgue at Notre Dame, he fell dead. He is best known for his organ music (he himself left some recordings), especially the 6 organ symphonies. RE-

CORDINGS: There is at least one complete recorded traversal of the organ symphonies, by Pierre Labric, and there are numerous recordings of individual works. Vierne's only orchestral symphony and four songs from the Verlaine cycle *Spleens et détresses* have also been recorded by Georges Tzipine. The *Messe solennelle* for chorus and two organs has been recorded by Pierre Cochereau and Jacques Marichal, and cellist Reinhold Buhl has recorded the Sonata in B Minor.

[1617] NOVÁK, Vítězslav Augustín Rudolf (Nŏ′-vák, Vĕ′-tyez-slàf Ou′-goos-tyin Rōō′-dolf)
TEACHER
BORN: Kamenice nad Lipou, December 5, 1870
DIED: Skuteč, July 18, 1949

Together with Janáček [1478] and Suk [1651], Novák represents the best of the second generation of Bohemian composers. Born in a village south of Prague (near the present border), he was the son of a country doctor who died when the boy was twelve. Vítězslav had been given music lessons as a child and hated every moment of them. In 1883 the family, desperately poor, moved to Neuhaus (now Jindřichův Hradec), where he was put to study in the *Gymnasium*. Previously a listless and backward student, he suddenly caught fire. More remarkably, the music teacher, one Vilém Pojman, so interested him in the art that he developed into a fine pianist and decided to make music his profession. A scholarship to study law at the university got him to Prague, where he spent most of his time taking classes at the conservatory. Naturally timid and retiring, he was cowed by his teachers and lost what little self-confidence he had. However, study with Dvořák [1386], who insisted that he stick to his goal, helped buoy him up. He graduated in 1892 and completed his studies (now in philosophy) at the university three years later but did not take the degree.

Novák won a state grant and a publishing contract which barely covered the support of his ailing mother and his siblings which devolved on him. He also began to take in pupils. But he was terribly dissatisfied with his music, which he thought imitative. (It was. His models were first Mendelssohn [1200] and Schumann [1211], then Grieg [1410] and Tchaikovsky [1377], finally Berlioz [1175] and Liszt [1218].) In 1896 a summer vacation in the backwoods awakened him to Slovak folk music, which directly influenced several compositions—the overture to a play *Maryša*, the early chamber works, choral pieces, and songs—and which became part of his own musical vocabulary. There was afterward a brief flirtation with Impressionism, but Novák soon developed a style of his own incorporating the influences of both the folk and art music of his country and reflecting his passionate love of nature, perhaps first exhibited maturely in the symphonic poem, *In the Tatras* of 1902 and culminating in such things as *Pan* for piano and the cantata *The Storm*, both in 1910.

At last Novák found both happiness and recognition. In 1910 he took the place once held by Dvořák as teacher of the master class at the Conservatory. Three years later he married his former student Marie Prašková, who bore him a son. But his euphoria was short-lived. In the postwar atmosphere the modernists moved to the fore, and Novák found himself regarded as a relic of the dead past. Nevertheless he bore it with equanimity and continued to teach with great success (his most famous pupil was perhaps Alois Hába [1879]). He also started writing for the stage, turning out four operas and two ballets between 1914 and 1929. With the exception of the opera *The Lantern*, still occasionally performed in Czechoslovakia, none was very successful. Novák, atypically, laid the blame at the feet of Otakar Ostrčil (1879–1935), director of the National Theater, but the real reason seems to be his own lack of a theatrical sense.

RECORDINGS: With the rise in patriotic sentiment during World War II, Novák enjoyed a revival of popularity that has lasted until today and is evidenced by the considerable number of Novák records issued by Supraphon in recent years. These include the orchestral works *Maryška Overture*, the *Slovak Suite*, *In the Tatras*, *The Eternal Longing*, the *South Bohemian Suite*, *De profundis*, the cantata *The Storm*, *Tomon and the Wood Nymph*, *Ballads on Moravian Folk Texts*, the string quartets and other chamber works, piano pieces, songs, and a few operatic excerpts.

[1618] CONVERSE, Frederick Shepherd
TEACHER
BORN: Newton, Mass., January 5, 1871
DIED: Westwood, Mass., June 8, 1940

Frederick Converse is not to be confused with his older Massachusetts contemporary, the lawyer Charles Crozat Converse (1832–1918), who wrote such familiar hymns as "What a Friend We Have in Jesus" and "The Ninety and Nine." The youngest of seven children, he studied piano from 1881. At Harvard he took courses with John

Knowles Paine [1366] but embarked on a business career when he graduated in 1893. He continued to compose, however, and a few months later, after his violin sonata had won approval in a concert, he gave up the struggle and went to Carl Baermann for piano lessons and to George Chadwick [1483] to learn to compose better. On the latter's urging, in 1896 he went to Munich to study at the Royal Academy with the inevitable Rheinberger [1368]. Converse's Symphony in D Minor was premiered there at the time of his graduation two years later. Meanwhile Chadwick had become director of the New England Conservatory, and now he hired his former pupil to teach harmony there. In 1902 Paine took him on as an instructor at Harvard; later he was promoted to an assistant professorship but found that his duties there got in the way of his composing and resigned in 1907. By that time he had written several good-sized works, including the 1907 oratorio *Job*, several orchestral and choral pieces inspired by Keats, the 1905 *Night and Day* for piano and orchestra, two string quartets, the orchestral fantasy *The Mystic Trumpeter*, and an opera, *The Pipe of Desire*. This last, produced in Boston in 1906, became on March 18, 1910, the first native opera ever staged at the Metropolitan. The cast included Louise Homer, Riccardo Martin, and Clarence Whitehill, but it did not survive its first season. In 1911 Converse became vice president of the ambitious but short-lived Boston Opera, which produced his second opera, *The Sacrifice*, with a polyglot cast that included Alice Nielsen, Ramón Blanchart, and Florencio Constantino. (It also did its own version of *The Pipe of Desire.*) In World War I Converse served as an officer and was a member of the committee overseeing music in the camps. He became professor of theory at the New England Conservatory in 1920 and dean of the faculty in 1931. In 1933 he was awarded an honorary doctorate by Boston University and four years later was elected to the American Academy of Arts and Letters. He retired in 1938. In addition to the works already noted, Converse left two more operas (unperformed), at least four more symphonies (some sources suggest five or six), other orchestral pieces, chamber works, and instrumental compositions. He also wrote a score for *The Scarecrow*, a silent film by his friend Percy MacKaye. In his later years, Converse tried to become more "American," as is evidenced by such titles as *California*, *American Sketches*, and *Flivver Ten Million* (a salute to the Ford automobile). RECORDINGS: *Flivver Ten Million*, *The Mystic Trumpeter*, and *Endymion's Narrative* have all been recorded, the first and last works by Jorge Mester, the second by Max Schoenherr.

[1619] STENHAMMAR, Karl Wilhelm Eugen (Sten'-håm-här, Kärl Vil'-elm Oi'-gen)
PIANIST, ORGANIST, CONDUCTOR
BORN: Stockholm, February 7, 1871
DIED: Stockholm, November 20, 1927

Regarded by his countrymen as one of their most representative composers, Wilhelm Stenhammar was the son of the architect Per Ulrik Stenhammar (1828–75), himself a successful composer of songs and choral pieces. Music was taken as a matter of course in his home, and Wilhelm grew up playing the piano. Though he had some sporadic keyboard lessons and a bit of theoretical training, he was essentially self-taught. He wrote small pieces during his adolescence and qualified as an organist in 1890. In 1892 he went to Berlin for a year's piano polishing with Heinrich Barth. He completed the first of his 2 piano concerti in 1893 and his first opera, *The Feast at Solhaug,* that same year. His first two string quartets followed by 1896. In 1897 he made his first podium appearance, conducting his overture *Excelsior!* and thereafter frequently directed in Stockholm. A second opera, *Tirfing,* was commissioned by the Royal Opera in 1898. Neither of his stage efforts—both mixtures of Wagner and Swedish folk influences—was a success, and he did not try again. In 1902 he made his pianistic debut with the Royal Swedish Orchestra and played for the first time with Tor Aulin's **[1581]** quartet, of which afterward he was virtually a fifth member. Four years later he became the first permanent conductor of the Göteborg Symphony, a post he held with justifiable acclaim until 1922. Afterward he conducted at the Royal Opera until shortly before his death at the age of fifty-six. Stenhammar moved from quite imitative late Romanticism to an increasingly clean formalism, at first neo-classical and later, after exhaustive self-training in counterpoint, to something more personal. He is highly regarded in Sweden for his fine songs. RECORDINGS: These include Symphonies Nos. 1, 2; Concerti for Piano Nos. 1, 2; the overture *Excelsior!;* the orchestral *Serenade; Florez och Blaniflor* for orchestra; the 1921 cantata *Sången (The Song);* the song cycle *Visor och Stämmingar;* piano sonatas in G minor and A-flat major; the complete string quartets; *Sentimental Romances* for violin and orchestra; Sonata for Violin and Piano; the orches-

tral *Chitra Suite* of incidental music to a play by Rabandranath Tagore; a few piano pieces; and numerous songs.

[1620] LIE, Sigurd (Lē, Si'-goord)
VIOLINIST, CONDUCTOR
BORN: Drammen, May 23, 1871
DIED: Vestre Aker, September 30, 1904

One of the most promising of the generation of Norwegian musicians after Grieg **[1410]**, Lie died too young to accomplish what he might have. He was born not far from Christiania (Oslo) but grew up in Christiansand on the south coast, where he had his initial music lessons from the local organist. Later he studied with Iver Holter (1850–1941) in Christiania and played violin in a theater orchestra there. At twenty he enrolled at the Leipzig Conservatory, where he was a pupil of Reinecke **[1292]**. The subsequent performance of his piano quintet in Christiania in 1894 won him a grant that enabled him to put in another year of study in Berlin with Heinrich Urban (1837–1901), who also taught Paderewski **[1527]**. On its completion he became conductor of the Bergen Orchestra and later of its choral society as well. In 1901, however, he was found to have tuberculosis and spent several months in a sanitarium, during which time he called in his old teacher, Holter, to help him complete his symphony. He was able to return to work in 1903 but collapsed after a concert the following year and died at thirty-three. Besides the works noted, he left an orchestral suite, a string quartet, a violin sonata, a cantata, and many smaller works. But he is best known for his songs, notably *"Sne"* ("Snow"). RECORDINGS: *"Sne"* has been several times recorded.

[1621] ZEMLINSKY, Alexander (von) (Zem-lin'-skē, À-lek-sàn'-der)
CONDUCTOR
BORN: Vienna, October 14, 1871
DIED: Larchmont, N.Y., March 15, 1942

Until recently Zemlinsky has figured in musical history mostly as a footnote to the Second Viennese School, even though Schoenberg **[1657]** had called him "a great composer" and the source of his own compositional knowledge. Zemlinsky graduated from the Vienna Conservatory, where he was a pupil of the Fuchs brothers, who were members of the Brahms **[1329]** circle. By 1895 he had completed the first of his 3 numbered symphonies, his opera *Sarema* (produced in Munich in 1897), and a number of songs and chamber works. Brahms himself went to bat for him to persuade the publisher Simrock to publish the Op. 3 piano trio. In that year Zemlinsky began conducting Polyhymnia, a Viennese amateur orchestra in which Schoenberg played cello. It was then that he gave some counterpoint lessons to the younger man, and their relationship blossomed for a time into close friendship. In 1901 Schoenberg married Zemlinsky's sister Mathilde, and three years later the two men founded the Society for Creative Musicians, dedicated to the performance of new music.

The honorary president of this organization was Gustav Mahler [1525]. Mahler had produced Zemlinsky's second opera *Es war einmal (Once Upon a Time)* in 1900, and was planning the premieres of the third, *Der Traumgörge* and the ballet *Das gläserne Herz (The Crystalline Heart)* when circumstances forced his resignation. Zemlinsky regarded Mahler with enormous admiration and later patterned his *Lyrische Symphonie* on Mahler's *Das Lied von der Erde*—despite the fact that Mahler had alienated the affections of Zemlinsky's pupil-mistress Alma Schindler. (To judge from portraits and eyewitness descriptions, Zemlinsky was physically surpassingly ugly, but Alma's diaries make it clear that the relationship was reciprocal.)

In 1906, following some guest appearances there, Zemlinsky became chief conductor of the Vienna Volksoper, where he was able to stage his comedy *Kleider machen Leute (Clothes Make the Man)* in 1910. He also conducted at the Hofoper for a single season, 1907-8. In 1911 he took over the operatic wing of the German Theater in Prague and remained there for sixteen years. During this period he continued to teach and for a time directed a new music society of his own founding. In 1927 he went to Berlin as chief conductor at the Kroll Opera, under the direction of Otto Klemperer [1794] and as professor at the Musikhochschule. After the closing of the opera in 1931, he continued to live in Berlin until the Nazi triumph forced his return to Vienna in 1933.

Of necessity Zemlinsky had been at best a part-time composer during the preceding three decades. Since 1910 he had produced three operas—*Eine florentinische Tragödie (A Florentine Tragedy), Der Zwerg (The Dwarf),* and *Der Kreidekreis (The Chalk Circle)*—as well as the *Lyrische Symphonie,* music for Shakespeare's *Cymbeline,* the second and third (of his 4) string quartets, and some songs. He now decided to seek no new permanent post, but to attend to his composition. But the *Anschluss* of 1938 drove him

first to Prague and then, just after the outbreak of war in 1939, shattered and ill to the United States, where he died two and a half years later.

Nurtured on Brahms, converted to Wagnerism [1230], a conservative who looked with admiration and even envy on the innovations of his friends, Zemlinsky remained an eclectic whose music is saved from mere imitation by the impress of a powerful intellect and a highly individual personality. RECORDINGS: There are several recordings of the *Lyrische Symphonie* as well as one apiece of *Eine florentinische Tragödie, Der Zwerg,* the complete string quartets, the Piano Trio, the *Sinfonietta,* and many songs.

[1622] VIVES, Amadeo (Vē'-vez, Ȧ-mȧ-dä'-ō)
TEACHER, WRITER
BORN: Collbató, November 18, 1871
DIED: Madrid, December 1, 1932

A Catalonian, born near Barcelona, Vives first studied music as an acolyte in a church. According to Carl van Vechten, his early years were peripatetic if not picaresque. He wandered about Spain as an itinerant orchestral musician, a conductor, and a reviewer, surviving as a street peddler when nothing else was available. Less romantic accounts have him a pupil of Felipe Pedrell [1384] and at twenty a cofounder (with Luis Millet) of the famous Orféo Català Choir in Barcelona. His conducting career ended abruptly with a shoulder fracture exacerbated by an attack of polio. In 1895 his first opera *Artus (King Arthur)* was successfully produced, and he settled in Madrid, where he wrote four more and nearly a hundred zarzuelas and other lighter works. He also taught composition in the Madrid Conservatory. In 1929 he wrote a stage play that was also successful. He is regarded as one of the best of the Spanish composers for the musical stage. RECORDINGS: There are complete recordings of *Doña Francisquita* of 1923 (his greatest success), the 1904 *Bohemios,* and *Maruxa* from 1913, as well as innumerable excerpts.

[1623] HADLEY, Henry Kimball
CONDUCTOR, TEACHER
BORN: Somerville, Mass., December 20, 1871
DIED: New York, September 6, 1937

Once ranked among the more important American composers of his generation, Hadley is virtually forgotten now. Even in his day there were those who, admitting his great skill, thought him too glib in an assumed German dialect. Initially he was taught by his father, who was in charge of music in the Somerville Schools. Later he matriculated at the New England Conservatory in nearby Boston, where he was a pupil of Stephen Emery (1841–91) and George Chadwick [1483], both German-trained. In 1892 Walter Damrosch [1540] directed an overture of his, and the following year Hadley signed on as conductor of the touring opera troupe that the legendary "Colonel" Mapleson had put together for his bride, the soprano Laura Schirmer. But in 1894, feeling that he had not yet drunk music at the source, the young man trekked off to Vienna for one year of study with Eusebius Mandyczewski, editor of Schubert [1153] and Brahms [1329]. From 1895 to 1902 he taught at St. Paul's School in Garden City, New York. During this period he wrote his first two symphonies, subtitled respectively "Youth and Life" and "The Four Seasons"; the latter won the Paderewski Prize in 1901. In 1904 he returned to Europe as a peripatetic conductor. His last year there (1908–9) he spent at the Mainz Opera, which produced his one-act Safié.

Hadley's growing reputation won him the conductorship of the Seattle Symphony in 1909, and two years later he was named director of the infant San Francisco Symphony, which post he held for five years. By the time he left, he had completed two more symphonies (the fourth of the series subtitled "North, South, East, West") and symphonic poems with titles—Salome, Lucifer, The Ocean—that give one a feeling of déjà vu. In 1916 he embarked on a full-length opera called Azora, Daughter of Montezuma. Cursed with a wretched libretto, it survived three performances under its composer's baton at the Chicago Opera, 1917–18, before heavily papered houses. In 1918 another opera, Bianca, won a prize (that included a performance) from the Society of American Singers. In 1920 Hadley was named associate conductor of the New York Philharmonic, where he rubbed figurative elbows with Mengelberg and Toscanini. The same year the Metropolitan Opera produced his Cleopatra's Night, starring Frances Alda and Orville Harrold; it hung on for two seasons. Hadley continued to guest-conduct at home, in Europe, and in South America, and at the end of the decade he founded his own orchestra, the Manhattan Symphony, dedicated to native music; it survived until 1932. In 1934 he conducted, in Stockbridge, Massachusetts, the first concerts of what became the Berkshire Music Festival. Hadley's last

opera, A Night in Old Paris, was commissioned a year earlier (and performed) by NBC Radio. A fifth and last symphony resulted from a commission for the Connecticut Tercentenary in 1935, a year that also produced the Scherzo Diabolique, dedicated to the American automobile maniac. After his death, the National Association for American Composers and Conductors dedicated a library of American music (now part of the New York Public Library) to his memory. RECORDINGS: There are recordings of the Concertino for piano and orchestra, the piano quintet (Isabelle Byman and the Kohon Quartet), and the Scherzo Diabolique (Richard Korn).

[1624] WILSON, Henry Lane
SINGER, PIANIST, ORGANIST
BORN: Gloucester, England, 1871
DIED: London, January 8, 1915

Lane Wilson came from a musical family: his sisters Agnes and Hilda were both well-known singers, and he himself made many records as a baritone. These included a number of drawing-room ballads of his own composing, as well as some of his popular arrangements of "Olde Englishe" songs.

[1625] SCRIABIN, Alexander Niko-
layevich (Skrē-à'-bin, Ál-yek-sàn'-der Nē-kō-là-yā'-vich)
PIANIST
BORN: Moscow, January 6, 1872
DIED: Moscow, April 27, 1915

Hailed by his admirers as part of the wave of the future, Scriabin bears certain resemblances to another such composer—his contemporary Cyril Scott [1720]. Both promoted their own music as concert pianists, both led unorthodox lives, both became deeply involved in mysticism, and the music of both suffered a long period of neglect before being "rediscovered." Of the two, however, Scriabin was the more dynamic, the more interesting, and the more important, though both his innovations and his messianic beliefs turn out to have pointed to a dead end rather than to the future.

Scriabin was the son of a government official in the foreign service whose duties kept him abroad much of the time. The boy's mother, a capable pianist, died of tuberculosis a little more than a year after his birth. Scriabin, Sr., remarried, and Alexander was farmed out to various relatives. While at his grandmother's home, he was given piano lessons by an aunt and quickly demonstrated a true ear, a remarkable musical memory, and great learning ability. It was, however, deemed best that he make a career in the army, so at the age of nine he was enrolled for officer training at the Cadet School in Moscow. Not long afterward, he began private piano lessons with Georgi Conus (1862–1933), brother of the composer-violinist Julius Conus (1869–1942). Then he moved on to work with Nikolai Zverev, proprietor of a musical boarding school that at the time housed young Rachmaninoff **[1638]**. In 1888 Scriabin abandoned his military career for the Moscow Conservatory (he had already written several very Chopinesque **[1208]** piano pieces). He studied first with Vassily Safonov, who later in his career as conductor was to be an important drum-beater for his pupil. Determined to be a virtuoso of virtuosos, Scriabin worked on the most difficult pieces he could find, overpracticed, and lost the effectiveness of his right hand for a time (hence the several early left-hand pieces; from childhood he had been given to various neuroses and psychosomatic ailments, and one account speaks of an earlier broken right collarbone). Taneyev **[1492]** was his counterpoint teacher at the conservatory. Then he set about to study fugue and composition with Arensky **[1536]**. But the two prima donnas did not hit it off, and Scriabin quit without a diploma. (Among his student friends were Josef Hofmann **[1680]** and the conductor Modest Altschuler.)

In 1892 Scriabin published a waltz and followed it with several other piano pieces. In the spring of 1894 the publisher Belaiev heard him play some of his compositions, and bought the "first" sonata (there are two other earlier unnumbered ones) and several other pieces for a fairly handsome sum. Belaiev continued to finance him for the next decade, both openly and through anonymous awards. In 1895–96 Scriabin went on a concert tour that culminated in a triumphant recital in Paris in January of the latter year. (Accounts of his playing vary wildly, some indicating him to be a brilliant performer, others finding him decidedly sloppy.) In 1897, the year in which Safonov premiered Scriabin's sole piano concerto in Odessa, he married the pianist Vera Isakovitch (d. 1920). It soon became clear that what supported one would not do for two, much less three, and when Paul Schloezer, professor of piano at the conservatory, died in 1898, Scriabin gladly accepted his post, though he did not care much for teaching and was apparently not very good at it. That same year his first child, a daughter Rimma, was born; though she lived only briefly, she was soon joined by two sisters,

Yelena and Maria, and a brother, Lyov. In 1899 Scriabin's brief orchestral piece, *Rêverie*, was completed.

Pictures of Scriabin in maturity show a very small man who seems to have made up for lack of stature with an enormous mustache and high stiff collars that make Herbert Hoover look unbuttoned by contrast. By this time he was beginning to develop his "mystic" philosophy, which would somehow combine diabolism, pantheism, synaesthesia, a belief in the life force, and the promise of the redemption of mankind through some sort of cosmic upheaval brought about by the arts. The basis for this murky thinking seems to have been such seers as Goethe and Wagner **[1230]**, the popular mystic tracts of the day, and brushes with the doctrines and such of Mme. Blavatsky, Maurice Maeterlinck, and the Symbolists. The choral finale (text by Scriabin) to his first symphony, premiered in 1902, represents a first public announcement of these beliefs.

In 1903 the 2,400-ruble annuity granted him by a patroness, a Mme. Morozov, enabled him to quit the conservatory and settle in Switzerland, where he proposed to build a temple for his developing faith. About the same time, he fell in love with Tatiana Schloezer, niece of his conservatory predecessor and sister of his good friend, the critic Boris Schloezer. In 1905 he left Vera to live with her in Italy, and she presented him with a daughter named Ariadna. Scriabin, having lost his outlet through Belaiev's death in 1903, had of necessity to do some financial fast-stepping and returned to concertizing. In 1906 his old friend Altschuler, conductor of the Russian Symphony, invited him to New York, where Safonov was conductor of the New York Philharmonic. The American tour ended suddenly, when Scriabin decided that the authorities were about to crack down on him for traveling with a woman to whom he was not married. The couple's return was celebrated with a great retrospective concert in Paris, organized by Diaghilev.

Scriabin, whose roots were originally in the music of Chopin **[1208]**, Liszt **[1218]**, and Wagner, had always exhibited a fondness for *outré* tonalities. By 1908, the year his son Julian was born, he had virtually abandoned conventional tonality altogether and began to base his music on a "mystical" whole-tone chord, which he argued was a natural succession of overtones (unhappily untrue for the modern piano.) The first major composition to exhibit this characteristic was the orchestral *Poem of Ecstasy* (sometimes known as SymphonyNo. 4), which

Modest Altschuler premiered in New York in 1908. In the same year Scriabin found a new publisher in Serge Koussevitzky [1655], who supported him to the tune of 5,000 rubles a year. As a conductor, Koussevitzky became his new champion, taking Scriabin along as a soloist on his Volga cruise in 1910 and premiering the *Prometheus* (sometimes known as Symphony No. 5) a year later. This work was supposed, in accordance with Scriabin's synaesthetic notions, to involve a color-organ (c.f. the modern "light-show"), but this proved impracticable. Shortly afterward the two men quarreled over Scriabin's playing fees, broke off relations, and never spoke again. In the next two years a last daughter, Marina, was born, and Lyov, the son of his legitimate union, died. Scriabin's final years were spent in concertizing and in working at a grandiose "happening" to be called *Mysterium*, which would set forth all of his ideas and presumably bring the world to rights. It would involve bells hanging from skyhooks over the Himalayas, a complex of sounds, colors, odors, and tastes, and would take seven days (like the Creation) to perform. When war broke out in 1914, he saw it as the beginning of his personally directed apocalypse. But in the spring of 1915 a pimple on his lip unexpectedly developed into blood poisoning, and in a few days he was dead at forty-three. His family had little better luck. Julian, who showed great musical promise, died on a river accident in 1919. His mother followed him three years later, and Ariadna was shot by the Nazis in France in 1941. Marina (who spells her last name Scriabine) settled in Paris, studied with René Leibowitz, and became a composer and scholar.

RECORDINGS: Of mature large works, Scriabin left 3 symphonies, the piano concerto, the *Rêverie*, and the 2 symphonic poems noted; all the rest, save for a single song (unpublished) was for piano. After a long drought, almost all of this has been committed to records (the symphonies by Svetlanov, the complete piano music by Michael Ponti). There is even a version of *Universe*, part one of the *Preliminary Act* to *Mysterium*, as "reconstructed" by Soviet composer Alexander Nemtin (1936–). (This was premiered in Moscow on March 16, 1973; Nemtin claims to have enough sketches to "reconstruct" the remainder of the *Preliminary Act*, but more than a decade later this has apparently not appeared.)

[1626] GRAENER, Paul (Grä'-ner, Poul)
CONDUCTOR, TEACHER, ADMINISTRATOR

BORN: Berlin, January 11, 1872
DIED: Salzburg, November 13, 1944

Forty years ago Paul Graener's interesting *Lieder* had some currency even outside of Germany, where they were often recorded by singers like Heinrich Schlusnus and Gerhard Hüsch. Today they seem to be totally forgotten—whether owing to the composer's political associations, his stylistic unclassifiability, or a change in tastes is hard to say.

Though he sang in the Berlin Cathedral choir as a child, Graener took no serious interest in music until after high school. He enrolled in a Berlin music school at sixteen, found lessons not to his liking, and learned the art largely by osmosis. Having gotten some experience as a theater conductor, he emigrated to England and in 1896 became conductor of the Haymarket Theatre in London. The job did not last long, but he remained in that city teaching—for part of the time at the Royal Academy. In 1908 he moved to Vienna and taught at the New Conservatory. In 1910 he began a three-year term as director of the Mozarteum in Salzburg. After some further *Wanderjähre*, he made Munich his home until 1920, when he was called to the Leipzig Conservatory to fill the professorial chair left vacant by Max Reger's [1637] death. That same year he was elected to the Berlin Academy of Arts and five years later was given an honorary degree by the Leipzig Conservatory, from which he then resigned to return to Munich. In 1930 he was appointed head of the Stern Conservatory in Berlin. With Hitler's triumph, Graener took over master classes at the Berlin Academy and was named vice president of the Reichsmusikkammer. However, he resigned in 1941. Graener was a prolific, if conservative, composer, but even in his heyday his choral, orchestral, and chamber music was not much performed. He had better luck with his 9 operas. RECORDINGS: A few excerpts from his most famous opera, *Friedemann Bach*, were recorded. But his chief fame, such as it is, rests on his clever songs, notably his many settings of the oddball verses of Christian Morgenstern.

[1627] BÜSSER, Paul Henri (Bü'-sä', Pōl On-rē')
CONDUCTOR, TEACHER, WRITER, ORGANIST
BORN: Toulouse, January 16, 1872
DIED: Paris, December 30, 1973

Among composers, Henri Büsser was among the longest-lived, dying two weeks short of his 102nd birthday. He began his musical study as a chorister at his local cathedral, began composing almost immediately, and at thirteen was shipped off to Paris to study with Alexandre Georges [1450]. Four years later he was admitted to the Paris Conservatoire, where he studied with Franck [1284], Widor [1414], and Guiraud [1352]. While there he picked up spending money ghost-writing music for a politician who found it necessary to display artistic attainments. Gounod [1258] took a fancy to him and procured him a job as organist in a church near his home in St. Cloud. Büsser became an intimate and disciple and was in fact the last person to talk with the old man. (On his way to the train after a conference with Gounod, Büsser met a hurrying priest and learned that he had been summoned to administer last rites, Gounod having suffered a stroke within the interim.) In 1893 Büsser was declared cowinner (with André Bloch [1873–1960]) of the Grand Prix de Rome. His studies over, he returned to Paris to conduct, joining the staff of the Opéra-Comique in 1902. Two years later he also began teaching at the Paris Conservatoire, and in 1905 was appointed conductor at the Opéra. He also taught at the École Niedermeyer and in 1931 succeeded Paul Vidal [1554] as professor of composition at the Paris Conservatoire. In 1938, soon after the death of Gabriel Pierné [1555] Büsser was elected to the Académie and served for a time as its president. At eighty-six he married the former singer Yvonne Gall (then seventy-three).

Büsser's most successful original music was for the stage. His first opera, *Colomba,* 1921, was his most successful; his last, *La Vénus d'Ille,* was completed when he was ninety-two. He also wrote a good deal of orchestral and choral music, including 6 Masses, but his most lasting efforts were on behalf of others. It was he who restored Gounod's *Mireille* to its original form after it had been mangled by the management of the Opéra, and completed Bizet's [1363] *Ivan IV.* He also made the standard orchestration of his friend Debussy's *Petite Suite* and reconstructed *Printemps* under that composer's supervision. He realized Dukas's [1574] edition of Rameau's [675] *Les Indes galantes* for the great 1952 revival at the Opéra. Among his writings are a manual of orchestration based on Guiraud's and a biography of Gounod.

RECORDINGS: As a conductor he recorded his 1905 ballet *La Ronde des saisons,* his *Pièce de concert* for harp and orchestra (with Lily Laskine), his own *Petite Suite,* and his version of Debussy's similarly titled work.

He also directed the first microphoned version of Gounod's *Faust* (with the sexagenarian Marcel Journet as Méphistopheles).

[1628] VASSILENKO, Sergei Nikiforovich (Vȧ-sēl-yenk'-ō, Sȧr'-gā Nē-kē-fō-rō'-vich)
CONDUCTOR, TEACHER
BORN: Moscow, March 30, 1872
DIED: Moscow, March 11, 1956

A carryover from imperial days but a dedicated *apparachnik,* Vassilenko came to have the stature of a musical patriarch under the Soviets. After some study with such teachers as Grechaninov [1567] and Georgi Conus (1862–1933), he read law at the University of Moscow. In 1895 he entered the Moscow Conservatory, where he was a pupil of Taneyev [1492] and Ippolitov-Ivanov [1517]. After his graduation, he became briefly a conductor at Mamontov's Opera House, which in 1902 produced his first opera, *The Legend of the Great City of Kitezh and the Calm Lake Svetovar*—five years before the appearance of Rimsky-Korsakov's [1416] on the same subject. Imbued with socialistic idealism from the outset, Vassilenko initiated in 1907 a series of historical concerts priced for the proletariat, and continued them until the October Revolution. That same year he was given a professorship at the conservatory, which he held, with occasional interruptions, for nearly half a century. As a composer he was initially influenced by Russian liturgical music; then, after a brief flirtation with Impressionism, he turned to "people's music," working with folk themes from all over—the more exotic, the better, apparently. No doubt as a result of this fact and his dogmatic adherence to Stalin's policies, he was detailed to organize musical activities in Tashkent, where in 1938 he helped a local musician named Ashrafi construct the first Uzbek opera, *The Snowstorm.* He was accordingly several times honored by his government. His innumerable compositions range over the whole spectrum. RECORDINGS: A few recordings have been available here—e.g., the Concerto for Balalaika, the *Springtime Suite* for flute and orchestra, and the Op. 138 *Suite on Chinese Themes* (Alexander Gauk).

[1629] FARWELL, Arthur
ETHNOMUSICOLOGIST, PUBLISHER, CONDUCTOR, TEACHER
BORN: St. Paul, Minn., April 23, 1872
DIED: New York, January 20, 1952

A maverick among his fellows and a force in American music, Farwell seems only now to be coming into his own. As a child he was taught to play the violin in the interest of rounding him well, but, like F. Scott Fitzgerald, he found little in St. Paul to satisfy whatever artistic needs he may have felt. After high school he was shipped off to Boston to get into electrical engineering on the ground floor at MIT. There he heard a symphony orchestra (under Artur Nikisch) for the first time and discovered what he had been missing. Thereafter he attended the symphony concerts weekly, found a mentor in one Rudolph Gott, discussed his chances in the field with George Chadwick [**1483**] and Edward MacDowell [**1529**], and, on graduating in 1893, took up serious study with one Homer Norris. After the New York Philharmonic had accepted and programmed his *Suite for Grand Orchestra*, he heeded Norris's advice and in 1897 sailed for Europe, where he put in more than a year with Humperdinck [**1480**] and Pfitzner [**1606**], had a few lessons with Guilmant [**1351**], and came home to a job teaching music history at Cornell. But he found the academic world constraining and quit after two years to devote more time to collecting folk music, which he did mostly among the cowboys, Indians, and Chicanos of the American West. In 1901 he set up his own press, called the Wa-Wan Press after an Indian ceremony, designed to fill not only his own needs but those of other American composers neglected by the publishing establishment. He supported this venture by lecturing tirelessly all over the country, and wherever he went he urged the formation of local music clubs to advance the art in the boondocks. In 1904 his orchestral version of his Indian fantasy *Dawn* was performed at the St. Louis World's Fair; it was one of the more ambitious of his numerous Indian pieces, but he was by no means merely an "Indianist."

In 1909 Farwell went to New York as critic for *Musical America;* a year later W. J. Gaynor, just elected major of that city, appointed him supervisor of municipal music. Farwell was a great believer in music as a communal activity, and this job was right down his alley: he organized community choruses and turned park bands into orchestras. In 1912, feeling that the Wa-Wan Press had made its contribution (it had published four volumes a year containing music by nearly forty composers all told), he turned it over to the publishing house of G. Schirmer. With Mayor Gaynor's demise in 1913 the municipal appointment came to an end, and Farwell left the magazine a year later. How-

ever, in 1915 he succeeded David Mannes as director of the Music School Settlement, a school for black children. One of Farwell's interests was musical pageants (or "community drama," as he saw them), and in this area he had his first success with his music for Percy MacKaye's *Caliban,* produced in the Lewissohn Stadium to mark Shakespeare's three hundredth deathday. He followed this in 1917 with a Christmas "masque," *The Evergreen Tree.* In 1918 he began a year as chairman of the music department of the University of California at Berkeley. Later he was at UCLA. In Los Angeles he contributed music for C. W. Stevenson's *The Pilgrimage Way,* produced another masque, *The Grail Song,* and was one of the founders of the Hollywood Bowl. During this period he also wrote audience-participation works such as *March! March!* and the *Symphonic Song on "Old Black Joe."* In 1927 he began twelve years of teaching at Michigan State College, where he again returned to publishing his own hand-printed music. Among the several works he wrote while there was the *Rudolph Gott Symphony* on themes by his old friend. After his retirement he lived in New York, dabbling in mysticism and composing in an increasingly advanced idiom. Among his later works were a series of songs to Emily Dickinson texts, several chamber and piano works, and a memorial to General George Patton. His final composition was the Sonata for Cello and Piano.

RECORDINGS: The cello sonata is played by cellist Douglas Moore. Other recordings include the fine Piano Quintet, the orchestral suite from *The Gods of the Mountains* (for Lord Dunsany's play), and an LP that includes some of his Indian pieces among the works of other Indianists.

[**1630**] ALFVÉN, Hugo Emil (Ålf'-vin, Hōō'-gô Ä'-mil)
CONDUCTOR, VIOLINIST
BORN: Stockholm, May 1, 1872
DIED: Falun, May 8, 1960

Hugo Alfvén remained an unreconstructed and unashamed late-romantic painter of musical landscapes—and, more particularly, seascapes—for all of his long life. He entered the Stockholm Conservatory at fifteen, spent four years there, and then made his living as a violinist in the Royal Opera Orchestra while studying composition with Johan Lindegren and trying to decide whether to become a painter or a musician. Music won out when a government scholarship in 1896 (renewed the following year) enabled him to study with the violinist César Thomson in Brussels. He wrote his first two symphonies (of 5) in 1897 and 1898. The second brought him the Jenny Lind Prize, which stipend he used to study conducting with Hermann Ludwig Kutschbach in Dresden. In 1904 he took over the directorship of the Siljan Choir, a regional organization in Dalecarlia (west central Sweden), which he headed for fifty-three years. In 1910 he was named musical director of Uppsala University and began a thirty-seven-year conductorship of the Initiates of Orpheus, another mixed chorus. He appeared all over Europe as a choral conductor and also guest-conducted his own orchestal works. He continued actively both as performer and composer far into his old age. Between 1946 and 1952 he published an autobiography in four volumes, entitled *First Movement, Tempo Furioso, In Major and Minor,* and *Finale.* His Symphony No. 5 was premiered in 1952, but he disliked the work and withdrew all but one (long) movement. He died a week after his eighty-eighth birthday.

The bulk of Alfvén's output (which runs to nearly 225 opus numbers) is choral; there are a few big pieces with soloists and orchestra, but most, not unexpectably, are practical works for amateur choirs, and so are not well known outside Sweden. Neither are his attractive songs, with one or two exceptions, nor his rather slight chamber works. This leaves the orchestral works—something over a score, including music for films and occasional pieces. Alfvén's name is known worldwide for the first of 3 *Swedish Rhapsodies, Midsummer Vigil*—no musical monument but absolutely irresistible.

RECORDINGS: Alfvén himself recorded *Midsummer Vigil* (along with many other conductors) as well as several of his other works. The first four symphonies and the surviving first movement of the fifth are on record, plus the second rhapsody *Uppsala,* the third rhapsody *Dalecarlia, Festival Music* for orchestra, a suite of incidental music to *Gustav II Adolf,* the symphonic poem *A Tale of the Skerries, A Boat of Flowers* for baritone and orchestra, the suite *Synnöve Solbakken,* the cantata *The Lord's Prayer,* suites from the ballets *The Mountain King* and *The Prodigal Son,* Sonata for Violin and Piano, songs, choral pieces, and solo piano music.

[1631] FUČIK, Julius Arnošt Vilém (Fōō'-chik, Yōōl'-yōōs Är'-nōsht Vil'-em)
BASSOONIST, BANDMASTER
BORN: Prague, July 18, 1872
DIED: Berlin, September 25, 1916

Though he wrote waltzes and other pieces, Julius Fučik is known chiefly for his marches, for which he is regarded as a sort of European Sousa [1482]. A gifted and serious musician, he was a pupil of Dvořák at the Prague Conservatory. On graduating in 1891 he became a bassoonist in the regimental band directed by Josef Franz Wagner [1489]. After a period in theater orchestras, notably the opera houses of Prague and Zagreb, he returned to the military as a bandmaster. As such he became increasingly well known and was in considerable demand. In 1913, after sixteen years, he retired to Berlin, married, organized his own orchestra, and opened a music publishing house. Shortly afterward, however, he developed cancer and died at forty-four. Fučik wrote some serious music (e.g., his *Requiem Mass)* but is remembered entirely for his lighter efforts, notably the march *The Entry of the Gladiators,* that staple of circus bands.
RECORDINGS: There is an LP devoted to his music conducted by Václav Neumann.

[1632] HILL, Edward Burlingame
TEACHER
BORN: Cambridge, Mass., September 9, 1872
DIED: Francestown, N.H., July 9, 1960

A reviewer once called Hill "a man who has learned to be brilliantly normal." Perhaps it is the normalcy of his music that accounts for his neglect in recent abnormal times. Born in Harvard's backyard, so to speak, he came from a Harvard dynasty, his grandfather Edward Hill having been president of the school in the 1860s and his father Henry B., a professor of chemistry there. Inevitably E.B. became a Harvard man, majored in liberal arts, studied with Paine [1366], and graduated *summa cum laude* in 1894. He then settled down to serious music study with Arthur Whiting, Benjamin Lang (father of Margaret Ruthven Lang [1593]), George Chadwick [1483], and Frederick Field Bullard (1864–1904), another Rheinberger [1368] pupil. Hill, however, withstood the European magnet, though he spent one summer studying with Widor [1414] in Paris. He set up in Boston as a music teacher but was recalled to Harvard as an instructor in 1908. At ten-year intervals he was promoted to associate professor and full professor. He then was made head of his department and in 1936 was named to the Ditson Chair. He retired four years later, much honored both at home and abroad, and divided his last two decades between New Hampshire and a home in Florida called

"Hill and High Water." One of his more famous pupils was Leonard Bernstein [2282].
Hill was one of the first Americans to take
his inspiration from France rather than Germany. At first he was inclined to the
programmatic—*The Fall of the House of
Usher, The Parting of Lancelot and Guinevere,* the *Stevensoniana Suites* (all orchestral)
—but as his style matured he turned to pure
abstraction. Though his idiom was admittedly conservative, it often showed the impact of Impressionism and jazz, and it is
characterized by wit. Among his larger
works are 3 symphonies, 2 sinfoniettas, a
concerto apiece for piano and violin, and
several sizable chamber works.

RECORDINGS: The very few recordings include the Sextet for Piano and Winds and
the orchestral *Prelude* of 1953 (conducted by
Leonard Bernstein).

[1633] VAUGHAN WILLIAMS, Ralph
VIOLINIST, VIOLIST, ORGANIST, CON-
DUCTOR, TEACHER
BORN: Down Ampney, Gloucestershire,
October 12, 1872
DIED: London, August 26, 1958

People can argue endlessly—and probably
will—over whether it was Sullivan [1397],
Parry [1443], Stanford [1467], or Elgar
[1499] who kicked off the latter-day English
musical renaissance, but they will unanimously agree that Ralph Vaughan Williams
was its first composer to speak a language
that was unmistakably English. It was no
accident that he did. He came to music with
an intuitive taste for the old modes that
characterize the popular musical tongue. He
steeped himself in folk music (he was the
first English musician of stature to collect it
in the field) and in the work of the great
composers of the Tudor period. It was out of
a deep-seated belief that an artist should
speak to his countrymen that he fashioned a
synthesis that was unmistakably (but not
slavishly) national and utterly personal. Yet
he did so not through a ready-to-hand talent
but through hard work and not from an
ivory tower but through associating with
Englishmen from every walk of life.

The Williamses—as they were originally
—were ultimately Welsh but had settled in
England in the late eighteenth century,
where they had produced a succession of notable lawyers and jurists. Ralph's father, Arthur Vaughan Williams, had married in 1868
Margaret Susan Wedgwood, one of the pottery Wedgwoods and closely related to the
evolutionary Darwins and had settled in as
vicar of a West Country village. He died

when Ralph, the youngest of his three children, was two. Margaret Vaughan Williams
then went to live with her sister at a family
estate, Leith Hill Place, in Surrey, where the
children grew up. They were left comfortably off, and in fact Ralph was able to live
on his income for most of his long life. When
he early evinced an interest in music, his
mother fostered it by paying for violin lessons and buying him an organ (which one of
the servants had to pump when it was in
use). His preliminary lessons in harmony
and theory came, however, from his Aunt
Sophie. At ten he was enrolled in a school in
Rottingdean, on the English Channel near
Brighton, where he pursued his violin studies, took up piano, and developed a flair for
ancient Greek. Five years later he moved on
to the Charterhouse, thirty-five miles to the
northeast, where he studied viola and organ,
and heard his Trio in G Major played in a
school concert. By then he had made up his
mind what he wanted to do with his life, and
in 1890 he accordingly began studies at the
Royal College of Music under the organist-
composer F. E. Gladstone (1845–1928). Later
he was handed over to Parry, whose name
had drawn him there in the first place. In
1892 he entered Trinity College, Cambridge,
where he majored in history. He found the
intellectual atmosphere just to his taste; he
had notable music teachers in Charles Wood
[1579] and Stanford; he won baccalaureate
degrees both in history and in music, but his
performance was such that no one gave him
much of a chance for a successful career.

Accordingly he returned to the Royal
College for further work. He put the finishing touches on his organ playing under the
tutelage of Sir Walter Parratt and got a job
(which he detested) as organist in a South
Lambeth church. He made friends with
Thomas Dunhill [1691] and John Ireland
[1719], but particularly with Gustav Holst
[1658], who, until Holst's death in 1934, was
his closest and most sympathetic musical acquaintance. Throughout the relationship
two men had regular "field-days" (as they
termed them) going over and criticizing
each other's music. Vaughan Williams also
met and fell in love with Adeline Fisher, a
talented musician and a beauty. He married
her in 1897, quit his organist's job, and went
on a honeymoon to Berlin, where they might
(and did) hear Wagner's *Ring* uncut. (The
marriage lasted fifty-four years, but tragically Adeline was afflicted by an irreversible
arthritic condition that gradually turned her
into an invalid.) After the opera, Vaughan
Williams decided to remain in Berlin for a
while and study with Max Bruch [1358]. In

1891 he was granted his Mus.D. by Cambridge.

Although he was keeping busy with lecturing, writing, and editing, he had still to get off the ground as a composer. (Apart from the disowned juvenilia, his output to date consisted mostly of songs and part-songs—none of it especially original.) In 1904, the year in which Cecil Sharp announced that ethnomusicology was more profitably pursued among the folk than in the study, Vaughan Williams joined the English Folk Song Society, founded six years earlier. He had already for some months been following Sharp's dictum and between 1903 and 1906 had collected a considerable body of folksongs, mostly in Essex, Norfolk, and Sussex. Some of these he put to use immediately in the 3 *Norfolk Rhapsodies* for orchestra (the last two of them were withdrawn); the contemporaneous *In the Fen Country* found him writing in folk-song style.

In 1904, Percy Dearmer, on the recommendation of Sharp, had talked the composer into doing a new Anglican hymnbook, for which he and others had collected the texts and for which Vaughan Williams was to find tunes. Dearmer assured him that it would take no more than two months and might cost five pounds for research and materials. Two years and two hundred and fifty pounds (spent by the composer) later, the *English Hymnal* was finished—cleansed of all dross and fustian, the texts relevant to the Anglican rite and creed, the tunes sturdily English, drawn from earlier composers and from folk music or provided by Vaughan Williams and his friends; over the next fifty years five million copies were sold. With the same collaborators, he later compiled *The Oxford Book of Carols and Songs of Praise.* Though Parry had introduced his choral-orchestral *Towards the Unknown Region* at the 1907 Leeds Festival, Vaughan Williams was still uncertain about his composing and the next year went off to Paris for a crash course with Maurice Ravel [1666], three years his junior, from whom he learned something about orchestration.

Whether or not Ravel provided the catalyst (which is doubtful), Vaughan Williams came into his own in 1909 with the first ("Sea") symphony for soprano, baritone, chorus, and orchestra and the incidental music to Aristophanes' *The Wasps* but more characteristically with the song cycle *On Wenlock Edge* for tenor, string quartet, and piano (later orchestrated) to Housman poems (Housman loathed it), and the *Fantasia on a Theme by Thomas Tallis* (on a psalm tune Vaughan Williams had used in the

hymnal). He had just completed his first opera, *Hugh the Drover* (not to reach the stage for a decade), when Germany invaded Belgium. Though he was already a few weeks shy of his forty-second birthday, he, true to his beliefs, enlisted—as an orderly in the medical corps. Along with his more menial duties, he brought music into whatever unit he was serving with, directing community sings, playing organ and piano and, when these were not available, the harmonica. With his longtime army roommate Henry Steggles, he formed the piano-half of a music-hall duo that became well known both during the war and after it at veterans' get-togethers. Following considerable home duty, Vaughan Williams served for the last six months of 1916 in an ambulance corps in France, and then spent six more in Salonika, Greece, before being sent to an officers' training school. He finished out the war as an administrative lieutenant in France and returned to join the faculty of the Royal College (with Holst) under the intendency of Hugh Allen, a former classmate who had succeeded Parry.

In April 1920, five months before joining the college faculty, he had assumed conductorship of the Bach Choir from Allen, who could no longer afford the time. In May Albert Coates conducted the revised second ("London") symphony in Queen's Hall, the original having been premiered by young Adrian Boult, later Vaughan Williams' chief orchestral spokesman, while its author was still serving in France. The early 1920s produced such landmarks as the third ("Pastoral") symphony (also premiered by Boult and containing wordless vocalization for soprano), the *English Folk Song Suite,* and the oratorio *Sancta Civitas.* In 1923 the Vaughan Williamses were invited to the music festival at Norfolk, Connecticut, where he conducted the new symphony, but four years later they had to move into a single-story house in Surry because Adeline was no longer capable of negotiating stairs. In July 1924 the so-called "folk-opera," *Hugh the Drover,* finally got a production under Malcolm Sargent's direction at His Majesty's Theatre in London. Though there had been insufficient rehearsals, it was deemed good enough to be taken on a short tour of the provinces and to be recorded in abridged form. (A complete recording, however, had to wait more than half a century.) It was succeeded in fairly short order by three other operatic ventures: *Sir John in Love* (a "Falstaff" opera), *The Poisoned Kiss* (an operetta), and *Riders to the Sea* (a setting of Synge's one-act play). Though *Sir John* had a 1929 showing at the Royal College, it got no professional production until 1946, and the others were also delayed, though not quite as long. The period of theatrical composition also included the 1931 ballet *Job*, originally intended for Diaghilev, who died in 1929, but ultimately first danced by the Camargo Society, ancestor of today's Royal Ballet.

In 1932, the year in which he finished the Synge opera, Vaughan Williams returned to the United States (this time alone) as Flexner Lecturer at Bryn Mawr, during which time he turned sixty. Rumpled, ponderous, and flat-footed, but beginning to replace his shyness with a modest awareness of his artistic and intellectual stature, the composer was now only just coming into his own. The year 1934 brought the powerful and bitter fourth symphony. (Supposedly when Vaughan Williams finished the rehearsal, he said to the orchestra, "Gentlemen, if that's modern music, you can have it!") The year also brought the irreplaceable loss of his friend Holst. In 1935, having typically rejected a knighthood because he felt he could not live up to the responsibilities it entailed, he was awarded the Order of Merit by King George V. With Elgar, Delius, and Holst gone, Vaughan Williams was now the elder statesman of English music. The year 1936 brought the swaggering and sensitive 5 *Tudor Portraits* on poems by John Skelton and the oratorio *Dona nobis pacem*, which expressed the terrible apprehension of the era. In 1938 he accepted the Shakespeare Prize from the University of Hamburg in the vain hope that a community of arts and letters might yet prevail; and at the same period he headed up a committee to help the refugees from the Nazis then flooding England. That summer, having passed his sixty-fifth birthday, he retired from the Royal College. Too old to serve his country militarily again when the 1939 war broke out, he had to content himself with small patriotic contributions until in 1940, London Films, having enjoyed a success with Arthur Bliss's **[1854]** score for *Things to Come*, asked Vaughan Williams to provide one for a Lawrence Olivier picture called *Forty-Ninth Parallel* (shown in the United States as *The Invaders*). Afterward he found satisfaction in writing music for a number of wartime documentaries and propaganda films. He also helped with concerts for the troops, chaired a government committee to deal with the problems of nominally enemy immigrant composers, and continued with his own private composition. In 1942 his seventieth birthday was celebrated nationwide, and the BBC devoted a week to his music. In the summer of the next year, he con-

ducted the premiere of his fifth symphony at the Proms. His Concerto for Oboe and Strings was premiered at Liverpool in 1944. At the war's end he supplied the BBC with *A Thanksgiving for Victory* for soprano, speaker, chorus, and orchestra.

Though he required a hearing aid and a copyist, old age hardly slowed him down at all. In the decade from 1948 until the year of his death he produced four more symphonies (it had taken three times as long to progress from the first to the fifth), the Concerto for Tuba, the choral-orchestral *Sons of Light* and *Hodie (This Day)*, choral and chamber works, the *Romance* for harmonica and orchestra (for Larry Adler), the film score for *Scott of the Antarctic*, and his operatic masterpiece *Pilgrim's Progress*, at which he had worked off and on for thirty years. He was showered with honorary degrees and other tokens of admiration. In 1951 the crippled Adeline died at the age of eighty, and two years later Vaughan Williams moved into London after his marriage to Ursula Wood, a longtime friend, much younger than he. Just before his eighty-second birthday, he returned to America as visiting professor at Cornell and then made a grand tour of the country, conducting at Buffalo, lecturing at Yale, Michigan, Indiana, and UCLA, and satisfying a lifelong ambition to see the Grand Canyon. Meanwhile, since the advent of long-playing records, Boult had been methodically recording the symphonies. At the end of Boult's first recording of the sixth the composer may be heard thanking the men of the London Philharmonic "and the lady harpist." The ninth was premiered at the beginning of April 1958; on the August morning on which he was to oversee Boult's first recording of it, he unexpectedly died. He was buried in Westminster Abbey.

RECORDINGS: Vaughan Williams left few recordings of his own conducting—a reading of the fourth symphony from the middle 1930s and acoustical versions of the ballet *Old King Cole* and the overture to *The Wasps*. There are complete recordings of all the operas except *The Poisoned Kiss*. The major choral and orchestral works have also been recorded, thanks in great part to Adrian Boult and André Previn. There are good representations of the chamber works and songs but only spotty examples of the minor and utilitarian vocal works and not much of the large body of incidental stage and film music.

[1634] PEROSI, (Dom) Lorenzo (Pā-rō'-zē, Lō-rent'-sō)
CHOIRMASTER

BORN: Tortona, December 20, 1872
DIED: Rome, October 12, 1956

Perosi's father was cathedral choirmaster at Tortona, a town in the southeast Piedmont, and taught both of his musical sons (Marziano, the younger, also became a church musician and composer). Lorenzo spent a year, 1892-93, at the Milan Conservatory and the following year at the School of Church Music in Regensburg. Rapidly thereafter he moved from being organist at Montecassino Abbey near Naples to the directorship of the cathedral choir at Imola and then to that of the choir of San Marco in Venice. Meanwhile he had been preparing to enter the priesthood and was ordained in 1895. In 1896 Pope Leo XIII, following the retirement of the castrato Domenico Mustafà, appointed him director of the Sistine Chapel Choir.

Soon Perosi was arousing considerable excitement as a composer of church music, especially with a series of oratorios on the Passion, the Resurrection, the Assumption, and the raising of Lazarus. In 1902 his appointment was renewed "in perpetuity"—which was perhaps not a good thing, as it turned out. He found a friend in Cardinal Giuseppe Sarto. When, as Pius X, the latter succeeded Pope Leo in 1904, Perosi became the force behind his sweeping reforms in liturgical music, notably in the restoration of Gregorian chant as cleansed by modern scholarship. But the musician operated under considerable strain, and in 1915, disheartened by the ongoing war and by his father's death, he found himself unable to function and took a leave. However, his health continued to deteriorate, and in 1922 he was for some months committed to a mental hospital. He returned to the Vatican a year later, but though he was able at times to fulfill his duties, he continued to suffer lapses until the end of his life. He last directed the choir in his eightieth year.

The music, a compendium of Gregorian chant, Renaissance and Baroque polyphony, and late-Romantic opera, is now recognized to have been overrated, but at least some of the religious works (of which Perosi left nearly 400 examples in all forms) are still performed in Italy. His considerable body of instrumental music—several concerti; 8 orchestral works, each bearing the name of an Italian city; 18 string quartets; etc.—has never had much currency.

RECORDINGS: The Angelicum Company in Milan has published several LPs of the most important works.

[1635] RASSE, François Adolphe Jean Jules (Ràs, Fràn-swà' À-dulf' Zhàn Zhülz)
CONDUCTOR, CRITIC, TEACHER, ADMINISTRATOR
BORN: Helchin, January 27, 1873
DIED: Brussels, January 4, 1955

Born in Hainaut near Ath, François Rasse studied at the Brussels Conservatory with its director Gevaert [1303] and with the great violinist Ysaÿe [1507]. He won the local variety of the Prix de Rome in 1899. From 1902 he conducted in opera houses and concert halls in France and the Low Countries—Toulouse, Brussels, Ghent, Spa, Ostend, Amsterdam, etc. He became director of a music school in the Brussels suburb of St.-Josse-ten-Noode in 1910, and a decade later was made professor of harmony at the Brussels Conservatory. He gave up both posts in 1925, when he was selected to direct the Liège Conservatory. He also served as critic for the Belgian newspaper Le Soir. In 1933 he was elected to the Belgian Academy. He virtually gave up conducting after the early 1930s and retired in 1938. His music—which includes 2 operas, a ballet, 3 symphonies, concerted works, several tone poems, chamber compositions, and many songs—owes a good deal to his German contemporaries.
RECORDINGS: There is a recording of his 1906 Concerto for Violin.

[1636] FALL, Leopold (Fàl, Lä'-ō-pōlt)
VIOLINIST, CONDUCTOR
BORN: Olmütz (Olomouc), February 2, 1873
DIED: Vienna, September 16, 1925

Czech-born Leo Fall represents a late blooming of the so-called "Viennese-Hungarian" operetta. He was educated in Lwów (Lvov), where his father, a military bandmaster, was stationed, and learned from him to play the violin. Then he went to Vienna to study at the conservatory with its future director (and imperial Hofkapellmeister) Johann Nepomuk Fuchs and with the latter's brother Robert. After a short period in an army band—which also featured Franz Lehár and was conducted by Lehár's father—Fall moved to Berlin, where his family now lived. For the next several years he conducted and played in theaters and cabarets there, in Hamburg, and in Cologne. His one-act opera Paroli was performed in Hamburg in 1902, and the full-length Irrlicht (Will-o'-the-Wisp) in Mannheim in 1905; both failed. In the latter year, however, Vienna produced his first operetta Der Rebell with sufficiently salutary results to cause him to settle there. It was followed in 1907 by two enormous successes, *Der fidele Bauer (The Faithful Peasant)* in Mannheim and *Die Dollarprinzessin (The Dollar Princess)* in Vienna; the latter was soon being played all over the world (the Broadway premiere, starring Valli Valli, came in 1909). In 1911 Fall wrote *The Eternal Waltz* to an English libretto for London, and early the next year he had considerable success with *Der liebe Augustin (Der Rebell* in new clothes). In 1916 *Die Rose von Stamboul (The Rose of Istanbul)* made a great impact, as did *Mme. Pompadour* in 1922. Altogether Fall wrote more than twenty stage works. A last opera, *Der goldene Vogel (The Golden Bird),* failed in Dresden in 1920, even though it starred Elisabeth Rethberg and Richard Tauber [1865]. Fall died at fifty-two; his final operetta, *Jugend im Mai (Youth in May),* was produced posthumously. RECORDINGS: There are recordings of innumerable excerpts from the more popular works.

[1637] REGER, Johann Baptist Joseph
Maximilian (Rā'-ger, Yō'-hȧn Bȧp'-tēst
Yō'-zef Mȧk-si-mēl'-yȧn)
BORN: Brand, March 19, 1873
DIED: Leipzig, May 11, 1916

Max Reger is, in the books, regularly classed with such great postromantics as Wolf [1521] and Richard Strauss [1563], but his music is seldom heard. For many people, he is not easy to like. His compositions, for all his formidable mastery of technique and form, sound thick, lumpy, and sometimes maudlin. In his day he was often dismissed as too "modern"; in fact he was stylistically a classicist and emotionally a romantic, and his modernity is often more the result of impatience with cliché procedures than of intent. Personally he was myopic, fat, blubberlipped, rumpled, foulmouthed, aggressive, neurotic, and alcoholic; for all that, he loved children, made many devoted friends, was a splendid teacher, performer, and conductor, and a much too indefatigable worker.

Reger, whose immediate ancestors were peasants, was the son of a Bavarian village schoolmaster-organist, Joseph Reger, who settled in Weiden (near the Czech border) shortly after Max was born. Joseph acquired a junk organ, rebuilt it, and taught the boy to play it (and the violin) so that he might join in the family music making. After a while Max caught the attention of the local church organist, Adalbert Lindner, who took him in hand. Lindner not only polished his playing but also acquainted him (often

through transcriptions) with the standard repertoire. At thirteen he was subbing for Lindner at the church and was already writing music. Two years later, having attended the Bayreuth Festival, he decided that he must become a musician and turned out a Wagnerian tone poem *(Héroïde funèbre).* To further his purpose, he enrolled at the local teachers' college, expecting to follow in his father's footsteps, which action his parents approved. Lindner, however, suspected he was cut out for something more imposing and sent some of Max's music to Hugo Riemann, the great musicologist, who in 1890 was briefly teaching at the Sonderheim Conservatory in Thuringia. The elder Regers, alarmed, took their son to Rheinberger [1368]. Rheinberger's reaction was, however, discouraging, whereas Riemann's was positive. Accordingly Max went to Sondershausen, and a few weeks later followed Riemann to the Wiesbaden Conservatory, where he became his assistant and taught organ and piano.

He stayed on after Riemann left for Leipzig in 1895 and a year later, in spite of his myopia, was drafted. He took to drinking heavily and in 1898 suffered a total collapse after his release. His sister came to his aid and took care of him until he was able to return to Weiden. There he spent three years recuperating and composing furiously, chiefly for the organ. By now some of his music had been published, though it had not brought him any great fame (and his publisher kept telling him he was not in business for his health). In 1901, recovered and feeling that he could no longer postpone his career, he moved to Munich, where a year later he married his Wiesbaden sweetheart, Elsa von Bercken (formerly Bagenski). The couple later adopted two children. Reger spent the next several years composing and touring with a number of important artists as an accompanist and chamber musician, chiefly in central Europe but at times as far afield as Russia and England. However, he made implacable enemies of some of the Munich establishment—partly because they did not approve of his music and partly through his own bellicosity and his refusal to suffer fools at all. (The most famous of Reger stories involves a letter to a critic, which purportedly began: "I am sitting in the smallest room in my house. Your review is before me; soon it will be behind me.)

Finding it impossible to support his family through such sporadic and uncertain employment, Reger joined the faculty of the Royal Academy in 1905 and became director of a choral society. At the school he was the target of constant hostility and gave back as good as he got. He lasted a year. In 1906 the performance of his *Sinfonietta* (his first orchestral work since adolescence) created an uproar. Fed up with Munich, Reger went the following year to serve the University of Leipzig as professor of composition and director of music. He gave up the directorship soon afterward, but was very popular and successful as a teacher there and kept up the association for the remainder of his life, even though later he had to commute.

In 1911 Duke Georg II of Saxe-Meiningen invited Reger to become his *Kapellmeister* and rebuild his musical establishment, which had deteriorated since the palmy days of Bülow [1310] and Richard Strauss. Already experienced at guest-conducting orchestras, Reger carried out his task in short order. It was in the Meiningen years that he wrote most of his brief list of orchestral works—brief because his stay was brief. In 1914 Georg II died; his successor disbanded the *Kapelle*. For a while the sympathetic Reger held it together and gave public concerts to help the musicians. In 1915, however, he moved to Jena, where he devoted himself to composition, but he continued to commute to Leipzig once a week. There, on May 10 of the following year, he suffered chest pains while visiting friends and returned to his hotel. The next morning he was found dead in bed there, where he had been correcting proofs of his Op. 138 motets. He was only forty-three. After the war Reger Societies were formed in Germany and Austria, and thirty-one years after Max died, Elsa opened the Reger Institute in Bad Godesberg near Bonn.

The Reger opus numbers run to nearly 150, but they give little notion of the extent of his output. For one thing, there is much material that is unnumbered. For another, many opuses are made up of many smaller works—for instance, Op. 76 contains sixty *Lieder* alone, and Op. 57 consists of fifty-two chorale-preludes. The bulk of his output consists of keyboard music (both organ and piano), songs, and chamber works, but there is also choral and orchestral music. He wrote a concerto apiece for piano and violin, but no symphonies and no operas. His lyric impulse was essentially romantic—he worshipped Schumann [1211] and Brahms [1329] but was equally fond of Mendelssohn [1200] and came, after initially rejecting him, to love Mozart [992]. At the same time he was a master of counterpoint and has been called the greatest (certainly the most prolific) German organ composer since Bach [684], who stood at the top of his pantheon. Wagner [1230], however, left his mark on Reger's harmonies and orchestration.

RECORDINGS: Reger himself left no recordings except for a few Welte piano rolls. Until recent years he went virtually ignored on records, but within the past decade or so, spurred in part by the centenary, virtually his entire output has become available, thanks particularly to some enterprising small companies.

[1638] RACHMANINOFF, Sergei Vassilievich (Ràkh-mà´-nē-nof, Sâr´-gā Và-sil-yā´-vēch)
PIANIST, CONDUCTOR
BORN: Semyonovo, April 1, 1873
DIED: Beverly Hills, Calif., March 28, 1943

Though his music contains Slavic elements, Rachmaninoff (he spelled it thus after he came to the United States) was the last great Russian practitioner of the international Romanticism espoused by Tchaikovsky [1377], whom he idolized. Several of his works enjoyed enormous popularity from the outset —a sin for which some, especially in England and America, never forgave him, dismissing him as vulgar and trivial. Today hindsight has done a good deal to elevate his rank as a composer—and even as a pianist.

Rachmaninoff's paternal grandfather, Arkady Alexandrovich, was a student of John Field [1104] and had, against the grain, become an army officer. Rachmaninoff's father, Vassili Arkadievich, also studied piano and took up a military profession. He seems to have been an unpleasant sort—a wastrel, a compulsive gambler, a pathological liar, and a skirt chaser. He married Lyubov Petrovna Butakova, the daughter of a wealthy general, who provided him with five estates and six children. Sergei was born on one of the estates, called Oneg, near Novgorod. Owing to the liberation of the serfs (the former measure of Russian wealth) and Vassili's improvidence, it was soon the only property left. The child had piano lessons from his mother and showed such promise that on Arkady's orders Vassili fetched a conservatory graduate, Anna Ornatskaya, from St. Petersburg to teach him. By 1882 the family was bankrupt and moved into a flat in the capital. The boy, however, was able to go to the conservatory on scholarship. But shortly after their arrival he, his older brother, and his sister Sophia came down with diphtheria. Sophia died, and Vassili, with the approval of most of his family, left for parts unknown. No doubt as a result of such traumas, Sergei quit practicing, got failing marks in school, and was faced with the loss of his scholarship. To top it all off, his older sister Yelena, having won a contract to sing at the Bolshoi Theater the next season, also died.

At this point Rachmaninoff's first cousin, the pianist Alexander Siloti, arranged for his own teacher in Moscow, Nikolai Zveryev, to take him. Highly successful (and very expensive) as a pedagogue, Zveryev, a pupil of Henselt [1237], was commonly likened to Liszt [1218] in more than facial features—though, it is said, no one could remember hearing him play. However, for talented children from poor families tuition was free. Moreover they lived in his own home, where they followed a Prussian training routine six days a week. (At that time Rachmaninoff was one of three such charges.) But however tough, Zveryev was also kind: he took the children to as many concerts as could be squeezed in and to his vacation home in the Crimea in summers. On Sundays he held open house; the musical great came, and they and the boys held court. It was under these circumstances that Rachmaninoff met Tchaikovsky.

When the boy was thirteen and in his second year with Zveryev, he began the study of harmony with Arensky [1536]. Shortly thereafter he made a piano-duet arrangement of Tchaikovsky's *Manfred* and in 1887 wrote a scherzo for orchestra. He spent Easter of the following spring with his cousins, the Satins, and that same year was promoted to the advanced section of the conservatory, where his piano teacher (not wholly to his approval) was Siloti and where he (as a classmate of Scriabin [1625]) studied composition with Taneyev [1492]. Musical creation now absorbed him, but he found that having to share the piano at Zveryev's hampered him. When he asked if he might have a studio of his own, he got into a fierce argument with Zveryev, who finally struck him, whereupon Rachmaninoff read him off. Zveryev gave him the silent treatment for a month. The young man then packed his bags and moved in with a fellow student until summer, when he returned to the Satins' place at Ivanovka, two hundred miles to the south. There he fell in love with Natalya Satin's best friend, Vera Skalon, whom he called his "little psychopath" because he liked the sound of the phrase, and for whom, at eighteen, he wrote what became one of his most popular songs, "In the Silence of the Night" (or "When Night Descends"). However, they were peremptorily separated when they were caught snuggling and were forbidden even to write each other.

Back in Moscow, Rachmaninoff gave piano lessons, conducted a chorus, heard his initial string quartet played, and went to St.

Petersburg for Tchaikovsky's new opera *Pique dame*. In the spring of 1891 Siloti, unable to get along with Safonov, who had replaced Taneyev as director of the conservatory, resigned. Rachmaninoff, a year prematurely, petitioned to take his piano finals before his teacher left, and, rather to everyone's surprise, won honors. He was now free to work at his composition full time. He returned to Ivanovka for the summer and completed his first piano concerto. But after going swimming at his grandmother's, he became very ill and was laid up for much of the autumn. However, by spring he had finished a symphonic poem entitled *Prince Rostislav,* an orchestral suite (lost), and his *Trio élégiaque* in G Minor (not to be confused with the one in D minor—see below). In March he was handed the project for his composition finals —the libretto to *Aleko,* a one-act opera derived from Pushkin's dramatic poem *The Gypsies.* By now he was sharing an apartment with his errant father, who had surfaced again. Excited by the project, he ran all the way home, only to find the place full of guests. Bursting into tears in his frustration, he shut himself in his room. Vassili, sensing a crisis, gently dismissed the visitors, and Sergei went to work. He finished the piece in full score in little more than two weeks. Early in May he played it for the examining committee, which awarded it a fiveplus (the highest possible mark) and its composer the third gold medal ever bestowed on a conservatory graduate. To top all this, Zveryev forgave him, presented him with his own watch, and arranged for him to play the score for Tchaikovsky. The publisher Gutheil signed a contract with the young composer, paying 500 rubles for the opera, the two Op. 2 pieces for cello and the six Op. 4 songs. The Bolshoi Theater accepted *Aleko,* then dragged its heels until some adroit maneuvering by Siloti got the thing into rehearsal. Tchaikovsky, who had hoped it could be premiered on the same bill with his new *Iolanta* in St. Petersburg, was in attendance and led the applause at its successful premiere in May 1893. Not unsurprisingly, his sudden death the following fall shook Rachmaninoff badly, and he wrote the second *Trio élégiaque* (in six weeks) as a memorial.

Lonely and depressed, Rachmaninoff eked out a living for some time by giving piano lessons, until he was hired by the Maryinsky School for Girls and once again moved in with the Satins. A tour in the winter of 1894–95 with a lady violinist turned out to be not worth the effort, and he skipped out. Most of the new year was taken up with his first completed symphony, based on Russian liturgical chants. The publisher Belyaiev, hopeful of a client, promised to have Glazunov [1573] conduct it at a concert. It boded well, especially since, under the same auspices, Glazunov, in January 1896, premiered Rachmaninoff's symphonic poem *The Rock* (together with Ippolitov-Ivanov's [1517] *Caucasian Sketches)* with considerable success. But when he got around to the symphony in March, it was an utter disaster. The fault seems to have been Glazunov's, who was reportedly drunk. The composer fled the hall, the reviews were brutal, and Rachmaninoff said afterward that he was unable to create for three years. He destroyed the score, but the parts were discovered years later.

Convinced that he (or anyone else for that matter) could do better on the podium than Glazunov, Rachmaninoff offered his services to Savva Mamontov, who ran a private (i.e., not government-subsidized) opera house in Moscow. There Rachmaninoff renewed his association with the great basso Feodor Chaliapin, who had created the title role in *Aleko;* the two inspired each other, became close friends, and later gave joint recitals. In his new role, Rachmaninoff was a brilliant success, but his compositional frustrations were beginning to undermine his well-being. In 1898 Siloti played in London his piano Prelude in C-sharp minor that Rachmaninoff had written in 1890 and set musical England on its ear. Nothing would do but that its composer should appear there and play it himself. (The piece was to become the bane of his existence, and he later referred to the work as "It.") Rachmaninoff went in April and appeared both as a pianist and conductor. Asked to return and play his piano concerto, he glibly promised to bring a new and better one. However, back in Russia he found himself still blocked and began to sink into a depression. At this point the Satins got him to a Dr. Nikolai Dahl, a psychiatrist who was experimenting with hypnosis. Under Dahl's treatment, Rachmaninoff's state of mind improved rapidly. In the spring of 1900 he and Chaliapin took a trip to the Crimea, where they renewed their friendship with Anton Chekhov, and where the composer eased the last days of the dying Kalinnikov [1576] by persuading publishers to pay him a proper sum for his music. When Chaliapin was invited to sing at La Scala in Milan, Rachmaninoff accompanied him to Italy, where the two took a house on the Riviera. There the singer worked on his role in Boito's [1393] *Mefistofele,* and the composer began producing sketches for the long-delayed concerto and for the opera *Francesca da Rimini,* over the libretto of which

he had haggled with Modest Tchaikovsky for some years. On November 9, 1901, the second piano concerto was premiered by the Moscow Philharmonic, with Rachmaninoff as soloist and Siloti as conductor.

The success of this work broke the dam, and others followed swiftly—the cello sonata, the second two-piano suite, the cantata *Spring*—all within a matter of months. Meanwhile Rachmaninoff had, at long last, found himself in love with his cousin Natalya Satin, herself a good pianist. First-cousin marriages were forbidden in Russia, but the law was set aside (it is said, by the intervention of the czar himself) and the pair were wed in May of 1902. They honeymooned in Austria, Italy, and Switzerland, attended the Bayreuth festival, finished the summer in Ivanovka, and settled in a flat in Moscow. There Irina, the elder of their two daughters, was born a year after the wedding. When, in 1904, Rachmaninoff signed a contract to conduct at the Bolshoi, he was working on two operas, *Francesca* and *The Miserly Knight,* of which he hoped to make a double bill in the upcoming season. It was, however, not to be: *Francesca* was finished by the time he first conducted in September, but the other work had to wait until the following summer. Before 1904 was out, however, the composer was, by the terms of Belyaiev's will, awarded a 500-ruble prize for his concerto. He marked the revolutionary year of 1905 by signing a manifesto demanding basic reforms in the arts. On January 24, 1906, he introduced his operas as he had planned. Chaliapin has been scheduled to sing the leads but was unable to learn them in time; instead they did much to further the career of Georgi Baklanov (later "Georges Baklanoff"), who took them over. At the finish of that season, however, Rachmaninoff, at odds with factions within the company, resigned and took his family to Florence, where both Natalya and Irina were sick in bed for several weeks. There he toyed with an operatic version of Flaubert's *Salammbô.* With the aborted *Monna Vanna* a year later, his operatic career, both as composer and conductor, ended.

Toward the end of 1906, finding urban Russia too much for him, Rachmaninoff took a house in Dresden, though he continued to summer at Ivanovka. At about the same time he won another prize for *Spring.* Meanwhile he had daringly embarked on a second symphony, whose successful premiere he led in St. Petersburg early in 1908; it won him yet another prize. Meanwhile in May 1907, under the aegis of Sergei Diaghilev, he, Scriabin, Rimsky-Korsakov [1416], and others went to Paris to show the

West what contemporary Russian music was like. That summer his second daughter, Tatiana—he had hoped for a son—arrived. Rachmaninoff wrote his first piano sonata in 1907, but performing demands had become so great that all he was able to manage the next year was a musical letter congratulating Stanislavsky on the tenth anniversary of his theater company. In 1909 he wrote the symphonic poem *The Isle of the Dead* inspired by a postcard reproduction of one of Arnold Böcklin's four paintings on that theme. He was bone-weary by the time he arrived at Ivanovka that summer but drove himself to begin a third concerto for his upcoming American tour (his first). He reached the United States early in November and concertized for nearly three months, both in recital and with the orchestras of New York, Boston, Philadelphia, Cincinnati, and Chicago. He was lonely, and neither the tour nor America pleased him. The critics, on the other hand, were not much impressed either by the second concerto or the new one. He was, in passing, offered the conductorship of the Boston Symphony temporarily vacated by Karl Muck but rejected it. On his return to Russia his uncle, Alexander Satin, deeded Ivanovka to him, and there, over the next few years, it was his pleasure to breed racehorses. Despite continuing demands on his time, Rachmaninoff managed a good deal of composing. Besides a number of piano pieces (including the second sonata) and songs, he wrote the *Liturgy of St. John Chrysostom* in 1910, a major choral work. In the late winter of 1913, quite exhausted, he canceled his remaining concerts and took his family on an extended vacation, during which he wrote his "choral symphony" *The Bells* (after Edgar Allan Poe) and the girls survived an attack of typhoid fever. In 1915 he completed another liturgical work, the *All-Night Vigil.* It was to be his farewell to Russia.

Depressed by the outbreak of war in 1914, Rachmaninoff dedicated the first performance of the *Vigil* (or *Vesper Service)* to war relief. When Scriabin died in April 1915, his former classmate and sometime rival swore on his grave to honor his memory with a series of concerts of Scriabin's music, which he did to the considerable distress and anger of some of Scriabin's admirers. In the summer of 1916 Vassili Rachmaninoff came to Ivanovka. The composer happened to be at a spa, and by the time he got home his father was dead. In February 1917, on the very afternoon when Czar Nicholas was dethroned, Rachmaninoff gave what was to be his last solo recital in Russia, dedicating the proceeds to freed political prisoners and

soldiers. In March he played (again for charity) an orchestral concert in Moscow, then took his family to Yalta, where he made a last orchestral appearance in September. Over the summer he had tried to find a way to emigrate, but nothing had eventuated. Three weeks after the October Revolution, however, opportunity presented itself by way of an invitation to play in Stockholm. Carrying only what they could get into their suitcases, the family traveled across Finland to Sweden in December. They eventually settled in Copenhagen, and a series of concerts provided them with enough money to scrape by on. Offers came in from America —to give a recital series, to conduct in Boston and Cincinnati—but, remembering his previous experiences, Rachmaninoff turned them down. However, he soon realized that if he was ever to be solvent again, the handwriting was on the wall. In November he borrowed passage money and took Natalya and the girls to New York, where on their first night they were frightened awake by the noise of the Armistice celebration.

By the time he left Russia, Rachmaninoff had already ended his career as a writer of stage works, chamber music, and songs. During the twenty years remaining to him he would produce 3 Russian folksong settings for chorus and orchestra and a fourth piano concerto (both from 1926), a set of piano variations on a theme by Corelli **[565]** in 1931, the *Rhapsody on a Theme by Paganini* of 1934, a third symphony in 1936, and the *Symphonic Dances* of 1940. For the most part, however, the time was taken up with performances, including a whole series of records for Victor (later RCA). For a time the Rachmaninoffs made their home in the United States. Spurred by a letter from a longtime correspondent, who argued that the composer could not divorce himself from Russia, he attempted to replicate the life of Ivanovka in New Jersey but found he was happier abroad. In Germany, September 1925, Irina married Prince Peter Wolkonsky; he was dead before their daughter was born a year later. To help her, her father established his own publishing company and decided to sell his American home and settle in Europe. He continued, however, to concertize in the New World. There the fourth concerto received a bad press—as did the third symphony, premiered by the Philadelphia Orchestra under Stokowski a decade later. Late in 1930 the Rachmaninoffs bought a Swiss villa on Lake Lucerne, which they christened "Senar" (an acronym of their first and last names). The next January, the composer cosigned a letter to the New York *Times* protesting the Bengali poet

Rabindranath Tagore's praise of the Soviets which, it maintained, ignored the blood on their hands. The Russian government thereupon pronounced Rachmaninoff a "violent enemy" and banned his music. (The ban was lifted two years later.) In 1932 Tatiana married Boris Conus, son of her father's old friend Julius Conus. The *Paganini Rhapsody* was the most immediately successful of Rachmaninoff's later works, and in 1937 he collaborated with the choreographer Mikhail Fokine in turning it into a ballet. In August 1939, Rachmaninoff played at the Lucerne Festival, and then, war clouds again boiling up, he took Natalya back to America —for good. Late that fall the Philadelphia Orchestra staged a Rachmaninoff festival under Ormandy, the composer leading the third symphony (which he recorded) and *The Bells* at the final concert. In 1942 he bought a home in Beverly Hills, and that fall he hit the concert trail again. Plagued by a bad back, arthritis, and exhaustion, he meant this to be a farewell tour. It was. By midwinter his lungs were bothering him. The diagnosis was "pleurisy," and he was permitted to go on. After a concert in Knoxville, Tennessee, in mid-February, he collapsed and had to be taken back to California. There it soon became clear that he was in a terminal phase of cancer. He became comatose and died a month later.

It is now generally agreed that Rachmaninoff was one of the supreme pianists and of scarcely less rank as a conductor. As a composer, he stands in retrospect as one of the last great Romantics, unafraid to express powerful emotions through such outmoded means as sweeping melodies and rich harmonies.

RECORDINGS: In 1973, his centenary year, RCA issued fifteen LPs containing all the records he made under RCA and Victor auspices, including the 4 piano concerti, the *Rhapsody,* the third symphony, *The Isle of the Dead,* and the Grieg [1410] and Schubert [1153] violin sonatas with Fritz Kreisler [1664]. (Rachmaninoff—alas!—never recorded with Chaliapin or with Nina Koshetz, who introduced so many of the songs.) Except for juvenilia and perhaps a few choral works there are modern recordings of most of the canon, including all 3 completed operas. Both Ruth Laredo and Michael Ponti have done comprehensive surveys of the piano music, and Elisabeth Söderström and Vladimir Ashkenazy have issued a five-record traversal of the songs.

[1639] ROGER-DUCASSE, Jean-Jules Aimable (Rō-zhā'-Dü-kȧs', Zhȧn Zhülz Ȧ-mȧb'l')
TEACHER, CIVIL SERVANT
BORN: Bordeaux, April 18, 1873
DIED: Le Taillan-Médoc, July 19, 1954

Roger-Ducasse studied at the Paris Conservatoire with Charles-Wilfride de Bériot (1833–1914), Gédalge (1856–1926), and Pessard [1408] but chiefly with Fauré [1424], who made a strong impact on his early compositions. In 1902 he was beaten out for the Prix de Rome by one Kunc. From 1909 he served as superintendent of vocal teaching in the Paris schools. Later he taught an ensemble course at the Paris Conservatoire and in 1935 was named to succeed Paul Dukas [1574] as professor of composition. When France fell to the Germans in 1940, he resigned and did not return, spending the remainder of his life in the Bordeaux country. Though not prodigally productive, he developed a quite individual style, influenced not only by Fauré but also by Impressionism and J. S. Bach [684], whose music he greatly admired. Among his compositions are a mime-ballet, *Orphée (Orpheus,* staged at the Paris Opéra in 1926), a successful 1931 comic opera *Cantegril,* a Faust cantata *Au jardin de Marguerite (In Marguerite's Garden),* 2 string quartets, some once-popular orchestral works, songs, and piano pieces. RECORDINGS: One or two small things have been recorded—e.g., a *Barcarolle* for harp by Marcel Grandjany [1855].

[1640] LETOREY, Omer (Lǝ-tō-rā', Ō-mȧr')
CONDUCTOR
BORN: Chalon-sur-Saône, May 4, 1873
DIED: Paris, March 21, 1938

Letorey studied at the Conservatoire with Émile Pessard [1408], and won the 1895 Grand Prix de Rome for his cantata *Clarissa Harlowe.* He became music director of the Théâtre-Français, where he supplied incidental music for plays by Shakespeare, Ibsen, Molière, and others. His opera *Le Sicilien* was successfully produced at the Opéra-Comique. RECORDINGS: A few of his songs are on record.

[1641] PICKA, František (Pēts'-kȧ, Frȧn'-tyi-shek)
ORGANIST, CONDUCTOR
BORN: Strasice, May 12, 1873
DIED: Prague, October 18, 1918

The son of a schoolmaster-organist in a village between Prague and Plzen, Picka went to the Organ School in Prague and graduated in 1890. He then worked as an organist and choirmaster, winding up in that post at the Dominican monastery in Prague. He also conducted opera at the National Theater. He wrote mostly church music, including 9 Masses and 2 Requiems, but he had an opera, *The Painter Reiner*, produced unsuccessfully in 1911. RECORDINGS: A few of his songs found their way onto records in his day.

[1642] TCHEREPNIN, Nikolai Nikolaievich (Chã′-rep′-nēn, Nē′-kō-lī Nē-kō-lī-yã′-vich)
PIANIST, CONDUCTOR, TEACHER
BORN: St. Petersburg, May 14, 1873
DIED: Issy-les-Moulineaux, June 26, 1945

A pupil of Rimsky-Korsakov **[1416]** and teacher of Prokofiev **[1851]**, Nikolai Tcherepnin was the founder of a musical dynasty that includes his son Alexander **[1961]** and his grandsons Serge (1942–) and Ivan (1943–). Originally a law student, Nikolai was twenty-two when he entered the St. Petersburg Conservatory. He quickly made a name for himself as a pianist and conductor. He graduated in 1898 and by the turn of the century was conducting the Belyaiev Concerts and at the Maryinsky Theater in the capital. He taught at the conservatory from 1905 to 1908, put in a year conducting at the Imperial Opera, then went to Paris as conductor of Diaghilev's Ballets Russes. The company featured two of his own ballets, *Le Pavillon d'Armide (Armida's Pavilion)* and *Narcisse et Echo*. Tcherepnin remained with it until 1914. After the October Revolution he was sent to Tiflis (Tbilisi) in Georgia to head both the conservatory and the opera company. But Soviet life did not agree with him, and he and his family fled to Paris in 1921. There they settled. Tcherepnin continued to write ballets (some for Anna Pavlova) and to appear as a conductor. He was also, off and on, director of the Russian Conservatory in Paris. In the 1930s he wrote two operas, *Swat* and *Vanka*, preceded in 1923 at Monte Carlo by his "reconstruction" of Mussorgsky's **[1369]** unfinished *Sorochintsy Fair*. Tcherepnin also wrote orchestral, choral, and chamber music and songs. His style moves from eclecticism to a sort of nostalgic Russian nationalism. RECORDINGS: There are a few small things on records, notably a suite for horn (or trombone) quartet.

[1643] RONALD, (Sir) Landon *(né* Landon Ronald Russell)
PIANIST, CONDUCTOR, EDUCATOR
BORN: London, June 7, 1873
DIED: London, August 14, 1938

Landon Ronald, as he called himself, was the second son of singer-songwriter Henry Russell **[1226]**, born of the latter's then still-unsanctified union with Senhora de Lara. (Ronald's elder brother, also named Henry (1871–1937), was a notable operatic impresario.) After acquiring an academic education in London and Margate, Landon studied, from a very early age, at the Royal College of Music under Stanford **[1467]**, Parry **[1443]**, Franklin Taylor (1843–1919), and Walter Parratt (1841–1924). When he was eighteen, the conductor-composer Luigi Mancinelli (1848–1921) hired him as his assistant and rehearsal pianist at Covent Garden. The following year he began fourteen years as Nellie Melba's regular accompanist. He played for all of her early records and for the first series made by the legendary Adelina Patti. In the same year, 1892, Sir Augustus Harris, manager of Covent Garden and the Drury Lane Theatre, sent him on tour with his Italian opera troupe. Ronald made his conducting debut at Covent Garden in 1894 in Gounod's **[1258]** *Faust*. After Harris's death in 1896, Ronald conducted operetta at the Lyric Theatre and summer concerts at Blackpool. With the formation in 1904 of the London Symphony Orchestra (by renegades from the Queen's Hall Orchestra), he got a chance to show what he could do with a symphony orchestra and was soon in demand all over Europe. In 1909 he succeeded Thomas Beecham as director of the New Symphony Orchestra (later the Albert Hall Orchestra), which he continued to lead for the rest of his career. Concurrently, from 1910, he was principal of the Guildhall School of Music. In 1916 he also began a four-year conductorship of the Scottish Orchestra in Glasgow. King George V conferred a knighthood on him in 1922.

Apart from his accompanying, Ronald was a pioneer in recording. He made his first record—a piano transcription of the *Liebestod* from Wagner's **[1230]** *Tristan*—in 1900. A year later he began his lifetime service as musical adviser to the Gramophone Company, to which he brought many important performers. In 1910 he conducted his orchestra for Wilhelm Backhaus in the Grieg **[1410]** concerto—the first concerto record ever made. He followed this with some symphonic recordings, and just before the introduction of the microphone, he directed some of the first uncut symphonies on record.

RECORDINGS: Though he wrote some orchestral and stage music, Ronald was chiefly noted, as a composer, for some pretty parlor songs. He accompanied Melba in several for the phonograph, and other singers of the day also recorded them.

[1644] SÉVÉRAC, Marie Joseph Alexandre Déodat de (Sä-ver-àk', Má-rē' Zhō-zef' À-lek-sàn'dr' Dā-ō-dât' də)
ORGANIST, TEACHER, CRITIC
BORN: St. Félix de Caraman en Lauragais, July 20, 1873
DIED: Céret, March 24, 1921

Born in a small town in the foothills of the Pyrenees, located between Toulouse and Carcassonne, Déodat de Sévérac came from old Languedocian nobility. His father, a painter and amateur musician, taught him his musical ABCs but planned for him to become a lawyer. Having completed his secondary schooling in Toulouse, the young man matriculated at the university there, but in 1893 he succumbed to the lure of music and switched to the Toulouse Conservatory. After three years he transferred to the big one in Paris. This he found a vast disappointment, and within a matter of weeks he moved on to the Schola Cantorum. There he studied with d'Indy **[1462]**, Magnard **[1570]**, and Guilmant **[1351]**; his piano teacher was Albéniz **[1523]**. On the side he gave music lessons and wrote reviews. His circle of friends included many of the avant-garde painters of the time. In 1900 he became Albéniz' assistant. Two years later the Société National de Musique (of which he was later an officer) presented his E-minor suite for organ, and in 1905 the Schola Cantorum put on an all-Sévérac concert, at which some of his piano music was played by Ricardo Viñes and Blanche Selva, both afterward his staunch apostles. (Selva later made a couple of recordings of Sévérac pieces. Some sources list her as one of his teachers at the Schola—hard to believe, inasmuch as she was only twelve when he came there.) Sévérac hated Paris and what it represented —his graduation thesis was an argument for the decentralization of French music—and on leaving school in 1907 he hurried back to the southern landscape that was in his blood. On his return he was elected to the town council in St. Félix. He was much loved by his countrymen, found his identity among them and their music, and became a sort of unofficial composer-laureate of Languédoc. He returned to the capital only

when it was absolutely necessary to do so, as for the premiere of his first full-length opera, *Le Coeur du moulin (The Heart of the Mill)* in 1909. But the next one, *Héliogabale (Heliogabalus)*—into which he wrote a part for a *cobla,* as the local *sardana* bands are called —was given the following August on his home grounds in the arena at Béziers before an overflow crowd. That same year he settled in Céret on the Catalan border. There he married; a daughter, Magali, was born in 1913—the year in which another opera, *La Fille du terre (The Daughter of the Earth),* was produced in Coursan (near Narbonne). That work virtually marked the end of Sévérac's musical career. When war broke out a year later, he volunteered but was turned down for poor health. However, he became a medical aide and worked in hospitals until 1919. By then he was seriously ill. A course of treatment at Aix-les-Thermes did not help, and he died of uremia at forty-eight.

Sévérac's music shows the impacts of both d'Indy's formalism and Albéniz' color, but it also bears traces of the Romantic and the Impressionistic. A final opera, *Les Princesses d'Hokifari,* went unperformed. There are some symphonic poems and some incidental dramatic music, but Sévérac lacked ambition and a number of major works were lost, unfinished, or never written out. His reputation today rests mainly on his piano music, highly evocative of his world, and his 20 or so songs.

RECORDINGS: The complete piano music has been recorded by Aldo Ciccolini, and there are numerous selections of piano music by the likes of Monique Müller, Pierre Huybreghts, and Grant Johannesen. Annie Petit and Marylène Dosse have recorded *Le Soldat de Plomb* for two pianos. Most of the songs are also on records.

[1645] SJÖBERG, Svante Leonard (Shö'-bârg, Svàn'-te Lā'-ô-nàrd)
ORGANIST, CONDUCTOR
BORN: Karlskrona, August 28, 1873
DIED: Karlskrona, January 18, 1935

Sjöberg is remembered exclusively for a popular and much-recorded song, *"Tonerna"* ("Music"). The question is what Sjöberg wrote it. Most references give this one. He was born in a Swedish port on the south coast, studied at the Stockholm Conservatory, and had some postgraduate lessons in Berlin with Max Bruch **[1358]**. Others, however, ascribe the song to an amateur musician, Carl Leopold Sjöberg (1861–1900), who was a physician in Hedemora in central Sweden. (There are also songs by a Birger Sjöberg, 1887–1929.)

[1646] SERRANO SIMEÓN, José (Ser-rä'-nō Sē-mä-ōn', Hō-zä')
CONDUCTOR
BORN: Sueca, October 14, 1873
DIED: Madrid, March 8, 1941

José Serrano was the son and pupil of the Valencian composer Emilio Serrano (1850–1939). For a time he studied at the Valencia Conservatory, but he left before graduating and went to Madrid, where he had lessons and help from Tomás Bretón [1458] and Ruperto Chapí [1461]. In 1900 his zarzuela entitled El motete was a great hit, and he devoted the rest of his life to that form, in which he was eminently successful. His catalog of zarzuelas runs to over 100 items. For a time he was director of the Teatro de la Zarzuela in Madrid. Serrano refused to have his only opera, La venta de los gatos, produced, though it was staged after his death. RECORDINGS: There exist recordings of: La reina mora, 1903; Alma de Dios, 1907; La canción de olvidó, 1916; Los de Aragón, 1927; Los claveles, 1929; La dolorosa, 1931; and innumerable excerpts—especially the jota from El trust de los tenorios, 1910.

[1647] RABAUD, Henri Benjamin (Ra-bō', On-rē Ban-zhà-man')
CONDUCTOR, TEACHER
BORN: Paris, November 10, 1873
DIED: Paris, September 11, 1949

Henri Rabaud's maternal grandfather was a prominent flutist, and his own father, Hippolyte Rabaud, was professor of cello at the Paris Conservatoire. Not surprisingly Henri attended that school, where he was a pupil of Massenet [1396] but not for long: at the end of three years, in 1894, he won the Grand Prix de Rome. Previously an uncompromising reactionary, in Rome and Germany he came to admire modern music, particularly that of the opera composers. Between his last year at the Conservatoire and 1900, he wrote (among other things) two symphonies, a string quartet, La Procession nocturne (The Nocturnal Procession, after Lenau's Faust—his most popular orchestral piece), and some large choral works. In 1904 he tried his hand at opera with La Fille de Roland (Roland's Daughter, produced at the Opéra-Comique) and followed it in 1908 at Bézièrs with Le Premier Glaive (The First Broadsword). In this same period he began to win a reputation as a conductor and

joined the staffs of both the Opéra and the Opéra-Comique in 1908. During 1909 he appeared in the United States. In 1914, the Opéra-Comique produced, with great success, his comedy Marouf, Savetier de Caïre (Marouf, the Shoemaker of Cairo), still played in France. (Later Rabaud rewrote the baritone title role for the American tenor Mario Chamlee, who made it peculiarly his own. In its original version, with Giuseppe de Luca, it was heard for three seasons at the Metropolitan and was later revived for Chamlee.) When in 1918 Karl Muck, conductor of the Boston Symphony, was jailed and deported for refusing to play The Star-Spangled Banner, Rabaud was picked to succeed him. He remained only one season, however, and was replaced by Pierre Monteux. In 1918 Rabaud also became a member of the Académie. On Gabriel Fauré's [1424] resignation in 1922, Rabaud succeeded him as director of the Conservatoire. In 1938 he toured South America. He retired from his post in 1941. Rabaud wrote four more operas, incidental music for several plays, and scores to accompany two silent films. RECORDINGS: He conducted recorded performances of La Procession nocturne, his Eclogue and his Divertissement sur des chansons russes; these three works have also more recently been recorded by Pierre Derveaux. There is a commercial recording of Marouf (conducted by Jesús Etcheverry) and at least one piracy, and selections from it, La Fille de Roland, and Roland et le mauvais garçon (Roland and the Naughty Boy) from 1933.

[1648] MASON, Daniel Gregory
TEACHER, WRITER
BORN: Brookline, Mass., November 20, 1873
DIED: Greenwich, Conn., December 4, 1953

Daniel Gregory Mason represents the epitome of what has been called the genteel tradition in American music. He believed that American music was, like the nation, a melting pot, which should draw from the best European traditions. These, however, excluded such radicals as the French Impressionists but also the ilk of Liszt [1218] and Wagner [1230]. For a time he was willing to admit folk influences and even tinkered with them; but, like his friend John Powell [1753], he eventually came to believe that the lesser breeds (notably blacks and Jews) represented a corrupting influence that should be discouraged at all costs.

Mason came by his musical aristocracy

honestly. His grandfather was the hymnologist Lowell Mason (1792–1872), his uncle the pianist-composer William [1305], and his father Henry the founder of the piano manufactury of Mason and Hamlin. Inevitably Daniel went to Harvard for a proper liberal arts education. While there he tried on John Knowles Paine's [1366] classes for size but found them too confining. After graduating, however, he studied with George Chadwick [1483] in Boston, then went on to New York to work with Percy Goetschius and Arthur Whiting. From 1902 on he wrote a veritable stream of books and articles on music appreciation and musical history. In 1905 he joined the music faculty at Columbia University. In 1913 he studied privately in France with Vincent d'Indy [1462], in whose social views he doubtless found a kindred spirit. In 1929 he was named to the Mac-Dowell Chair at Columbia and served as the head of the department until 1940. He retired in 1942. He held honorary degrees from Oberlin, Eastman, and Tufts. Mason turned out some forty opuses, including 3 symphonies, other works for orchestra, and a good deal of chamber and piano music. RECORDINGS: His most-recorded work is, ironically, the *Quartet on Negro Themes* (Kohon Quartet, among others). Other recordings include the clarinet sonata; the *Pastorale* for violin, clarinet, and piano; the *Three Pieces* for flute, harp, and string quartet; the *Country Pictures* for piano (George Bennette); the *Chanticleer Overture* (Dean Dixon conducting); and the *Prelude and Fugue* for piano and orchestra (Mary Louise Boehm-Kooper).

[1649] JONGEN, Joseph Marie Alphonse Nicolas (Zhôn'-gen, Zhō-zef' Mà-rē' Àl-fons' Nē-kō-làs)
TEACHER, PIANIST, ORGANIST, CONDUCTOR
BORN: Liège, December 14, 1873
DIED: Sart-lez-Spa, July 12, 1953

The elder brother of Léon Jongen [1776], Joseph Jongen was perhaps the best-known composer internationally to come out of Belgium after César Franck [1284]. The son of a cabinetmaker devoted to music, he was a choirboy at Liège Cathedral and was taken into the conservatory at the age of seven. By the time he reached his teens he was composing, and he carried off first prizes year after year. His Op. 1 (later, like almost half of his output, disowned) was a big Franckian piano concerto. His Op. 3, a string quartet, won first prize in a competition in 1894. In 1897 he was awarded the Prix de Rome and

spent the next four years traveling and composing—chiefly in Berlin, Munich, Rome, and Paris. He returned to the conservatory as professor of harmony in 1902. The German invasion in 1914 drove him to London, where he spent the war years concertizing with a string quartet that included the violinist Desiré Defauw (later conductor of the Chicago Symphony), the great violist Lionel Tertis, and the cellist Émile Doehaerd. When the fighting was over, he returned to his post but in 1920 was hired away by the Brussels Conservatory. In the capital he also conducted the Concert Spirituel (devoted to the music of devotion) until 1925, when he assumed the directorship of the conservatory. He retired in 1939 to be succeeded by his brother Léon. Among the many honors bestowed on him were memberships in both the Belgian and French Academies.

Jongen was at first an imitator of Franck and was later influenced by the German postromantics and the French Impressionists. In his final years he was toying with atonality. He gave up on the only opera he tried. In a final reckoning he excised 104 compositions from his catalog. What was left was almost entirely orchestral (concerti, a symphony, abstract pieces) and chamber music.

RECORDINGS: Recordings are scarce. They include a *Symphonie concertante* for organ and orchestra (at least three recordings), the mature piano concerto of 1943 (Eduardo del Pueyo), the *Legend Dances* Op. 89 (New York Philharmonic Cello Quartet), the *Sonate en duo* for violin and cello (Pierre and Iwan d'Archambeau), Concerto Op. 124 (Berkshire Woodwind Ensemble), several organ works, and piano music played by Marcelle Mercenier and Cécile Muller. Jongen himself recorded his *Petite Suite* for piano.

[1650] GOLLER, Vinzenz (Gol'-ler, Vint'-zentz)
SCHOOLTEACHER, CHOIR DIRECTOR, TEACHER
BORN: 1873
DIED: 1953

After working for a time as a public school teacher, Goller won a government scholarship permitting him to study at the Regensburg Church Music School. He then distinguished himself as choir director in Deggendorf (about forty miles down the Danube) and was hired by the Vienna Academy on the ground floor of its church-music department, which he went on to head. He taught there until he died at eighty. He wrote much religious music, including several Masses, and a cycle of *Offertories* for the church year. RECORDINGS: Franz Haselböck has recorded his organ variations on Praetorius' [360] "Lo, How a Rose."

[1651] SUK, Josef (Sook, Yō'-sef)
VIOLINIST, TEACHER
BORN: Křečovice, January 4, 1874
DIED: Prague, May 29, 1935

Josef Suk, star pupil and son-in-law of Dvořák, was one of the outstanding Czech composers of the second generation. Son, namesake, and pupil of a village school-master-organist, he proceeded, at the age of eleven, to the Prague Conservatory to study violin with the director, Antonín Bennewitz. Among his other teachers were the elder Foerster (see 1520) and the cellist Hanus Wihan, with whom he studied chamber music. He graduated in 1891 but stayed on for a year, chiefly to work with Dvořák, with whose daughter Otilie he fell in love. In 1892 Suk and three other Wihan protégés, Karel Hoffmann, Oscar Nedbal (1874–1930), and Otto Berger joined together to form the Czech String Quartet. Over its long career, it underwent changes of membership—Wihan himself became the cellist from 1894 to 1914 —but Suk remained its second violinist.

By the time he left the Prague Conservatory, Suk was already a practiced composer. He had produced a piano sonata at the age of nine, and a Mass and orchestral works before he graduated. His Op. 1, submitted for the latter event, was a piano quartet, and the *Serenade* Op. 6 for strings, probably his most popular work, followed it a year later. By the time he married Otilie Dvořák in 1898, he was working on his first symphony, Op. 14 in E major. He seemed to be proceeding to a happy and serene career when his world was shattered: in 1904 Dvořák died, and Otilie followed him a little over a year later. The composer sank into a profound depression, which he eventually exorcised with his masterpiece, the second symphony *Asrael,* named after the death-angel and dedicated to the memory of his wife and father-in-law. He followed it with two related orchestral works, *A Summer's Tale* (he had earlier written an overture on Shakespeare's *A Winter's Tale)* and *The Ripening*—all three works are highly subjective and powerful commentaries on life and death. The First World War inspired him to another orchestral trilogy—*Meditation on an Old Czech Chorale, Legend of the Dead Victors,* and *Toward a New Life.* In 1922 he took over the master classes at the conservatory, where in the course of time he was rector for

four years. His best-known pupil was Bohuslav Martinů [1846]. *Toward a New Life,* in a revised version, won him an award at the 1932 Olympic Games in Los Angeles, and he received an honorary doctorate from Brno University in 1933. In the latter year he left the Czech String Quartet, which did not survive his departure. Suk's grandson is the splendid violinist Josef Suk, born in 1924. Besides the works mentioned, Suk wrote music for two plays by Julius Zeyer, *Radúz and Mahulena* and *Under the Apple Tree,* overtures and symphonic poems, some chamber music (mostly small-scale), and a few choral pieces.

RECORDINGS: His recordings with the Czech Quartet include his own Op. 11 quartet. Records of most of the big mature works have come from Czechoslovakia in recent decades (including a complete survey of the piano music), and the Czechs are currently re-recording the major orchestral pieces in digital stereo.

[1652] EYSLER, Edmund (Īz'-ler, Ed'-moont)
PIANIST, TEACHER, CONDUCTOR
BORN: Vienna, March 12, 1874
DIED: Vienna, October 4, 1949

A pupil of the Fuchs brothers at the Vienna Conservatory, Eysler worked for a time as a piano teacher and theater conductor in Vienna. After trying his luck at opera and ballet, he gravitated to operetta and had his greatest hit with his first effort, *Bruder Straubinger,* in 1903. He followed it with nearly sixty others, a handful of which (usually greatly altered) made their way to Broadway between 1909 and 1917 without much success. Though in the 1920s Eysler experimented with "jazz" (as he conceived it), he was happiest in the old-fashioned operetta format. RECORDINGS: There are recordings of excerpts.

[1653] STREICHER, Theodor (Shtrī'-kher, Tā'-ō-dôr)
BORN: Vienna, June 7, 1874
DIED: Wetzelsdorf, Styria, May 28, 1940

Streicher was a direct descendent of Nannette Stein and her husband Johann Andreas Streicher, who founded one of the most important piano firms in Vienna. Theodor originally aspired to be a singer and studied to that end but also had piano lessons from Ferdinand Löwe (who mangled several Bruckner [1293] symphonies) and composition with Leipzig-trained Heinrich

Schulz-Beuthen (1838–1915). Streicher lived most of his life in Vienna. After the death of his first wife, *née* Maria Potpeschnigg, in 1915, he married an English poetess, Edith Thorndike. He wrote some choral and chamber music and orchestrated several ballades by Loewe [1152] but was most successful with his nearly 200 *Lieder*, some of which created a great but very temporary stir around the turn of the century. RECORDINGS: A few of the *Lieder* have been recorded.

[1654] NEUMANN, František *(alias* Franz) (Noi'-mán, Frán'-tyi-shek)
CONDUCTOR
BORN: Přerov, June 16, 1874
DIED: Brno, February 24, 1929

Born in the vicinity of Olomouc in Moravia, Neumann grew up in nearby Prostějov, where his father developed a successful trade in smoked meats. František was apprenticed to a Prague transportation firm, served his requisite year in the army, and joined the family business in 1895. But during his time in Prague, he had taken lessons with Karl Šebor, a conductor and composer. After spending a year in the smoked-meat business, he decided to give music a try and became a pupil of Reinecke [1292] in Leipzig. In 1897 he began a career as an operatic conductor in Karlsruhe, moving on to Hamburg, Regensburg, Linz, Liberec, and Teplice. In 1904 he settled in for fifteen years as chief conductor at Frankfurt-am-Main. At the end of that time he returned to what was now Czechoslovakia and became first *Kapellmeister* and, in 1925, intendant of the opera at Brno, where he conducted the premieres of several of Janáček's [1478] works. Neumann himself wrote 5 operas, 2 ballets, and other music, none of it of any great originality. RECORDINGS: Some of his songs have been recorded.

[1655] KOUSSEVITZKY, Sergei Alexandrovich (Kōō-se-vits'-ki, Sâr'-gā Ál-yek-sàn-drō'-vich)
CONTRABASSIST, PUBLISHER, CONDUCTOR
BORN: Tver, July 26, 1874
DIED: Boston, June 4, 1951

Koussevitzky (his own transliteration) was too unimportant as a composer and too well-known as a conductor to warrant detailing his career here. But it is probably not generally remembered that he began his musical life as a trumpeter in a *stetl* band in Russia

or that he converted from Judaism in order to get into the Moscow Philharmonic Institute. He took up the contrabass because a scholarship was available, became first-desk player at the Bolshoi but won increasing fame as a soloist—the first player of his instrument since Bottesini [1278] to meet with such large-scale acclaim. He gave up the orchestra when in 1905 he married Natalya Ushkova, who was, not incidentally, wealthy. Three years later he began his conducting career by hiring the Berlin Philharmonic for a concert. In 1909 he opened his own publishing house, Editions Russes de Musique, dedicated to promoting new music, which project he furthered by forming his own orchestra to play such works. Until 1914 he plied the Volga by boat every summer, carrying the gospel to the provinces. He survived the 1917 Revolution to become director of the Petrograd State Orchestra but gave it up in 1920 and moved to Paris, where he formed another orchestra and pursued his ideals. In 1924 he was called to Boston to succeed Pierre Monteux at the helm of the Boston Symphony, where he held forth for twenty-five years, bringing the orchestra unprecedented glory and encouraging American composers with commissions. Building on the foundations made by Henry Hadley [1623], he made the Boston Symphony the focus of the Berkshire Music Festival at Tanglewood, where he founded the Berkshire Music Center, a summer school where young musicians might study with more famous ones. (Late in his career, he wrote a *Passacaglia on a Russian Theme* for orchestra.) Koussevitzky composed a few short pieces for his instrument, including a concerto (orchestrated mostly by Glière [1662]). RECORDINGS: The concerto and shorter pieces have been recorded by various subsequent contrabass virtuosi, and Koussevitzky himself made records of two of the small pieces.

[1656] BAIRSTOW, (Sir) Edward Cuthbert
ORGANIST, EDUCATOR, CONDUCTOR
BORN: Huddersfield, August 22, 1874
DIED: York, May 1, 1946

Bairstow was an important figure in modern English church music, as one might expect from a man born in a citadel of choir singing. An 1894 graduate of the University of Durham, he served for a time as organist and choirmaster of various London churches, and as assistant to Sir Frederick Bridge at Westminster Abbey. He received his doctorate in 1901, returned to the north in 1906 to officiate at the Leeds Parish Church, and, from 1913, served as organist and master of the boys at York Minster until his death. He became professor of music at Durham in 1929 and was knighted by George V in 1932. He conducted choral societies all over England, wrote two successful textbooks, *Counterpoint and Harmony* and *The Evolution of Musical Form,* and was coeditor of *The English Psalter.* His anthems are much used in Anglican churches. RECORDINGS: One anthem, *Let All Mortal Flesh Keep Silence,* has been repeatedly recorded.

[1657] SCHOENBERG, Arnold Franz Walter (Shön'-bârg, Âr'-nōlt Frántz Vâl'-ter)
CONDUCTOR, TEACHER
BORN: Vienna, September 13, 1874
DIED: Los Angeles, July 13, 1951

No composer of the twentieth century—perhaps none in the history of Western music—has had so direct and powerful (however temporary) an impact on the subsequent direction of the art as Arnold Schoenberg. Into a world in which former approaches appeared to be bankrupt, he came preaching a radical and apparently fool-proof system, and (though not immediately) was hailed by other musicians as a messiah. By much of the general public, however, he was not accepted at all, and today, more than thirty years after his death, the programming and performance of some of his more advanced works still keep some people away or drive a few out of the hall. It is easy to decry Schoenberg as a self-deluding egotist or a charlatan, but the fact is that he developed his musical concepts out of a deep-seated personal need, and even the most obdurate can recognize in his earlier and more conventional works, such as the *Gurrelieder,* the hand and mind of a great musician. With a little patience too, all but the most intolerant can perhaps come to hear how, even in his most rigidly twelve-tone period, the system worked for him, doubtless because of his unfailing musical instinct. But because that system involves the application of intellectual and rational solutions to what appears to be an emotional and irrational art, its adoption by others—especially as further mechanized by some of the more fanatic or deluded of his disciples—produced much that seems sterile, and there are many who now argue that the whole movement led music not to pastures new but to a cul-de-sac.

The background of both of Schoenberg's parents was Jewish. His father, Samuel,

Hungarian born, was, however, a freethinker who ran a little shoe store. His mother came from Prague. Arnold, the eldest of three children, though of a religious bent, was ironically impatient with dogma. The family had no known musical heritage, but the younger son, Heinrich, eventually became a professional singer. Arnold began violin lessons when he was eight. Shortly afterward he devised a waltz and a polka for two violins. Duos expanded to trios when he encountered a young violist and to quartets when Schoenberg acquired a battered old cello and taught himself to play it by rather unorthodox means. When he was sixteen, his father died and he went to work in a bank. Oscar Adler, one of his friends, helped him with harmony, but for the most part he taught himself by reading scores and composing by rule of thumb. Increasingly attracted to music, he was perversely pleased when his bank failed and his job ended in 1895. Meanwhile he had become cellist in a scratch orchestra, the Polyhymnia, led by Alexander von Zemlinsky **[1621]**, who helped him master counterpoint. Zemlinsky, who had some influence in musical circles, managed to get Schoenberg's D major string quartet (unnumbered in the official canon of his works) performed in 1898 at a concert for members of the Vienna Musicians' Association. It was well received, but the sextet *Verklärte Nacht (Transfigured Night)* was vetoed by the same group a year later, though it and some songs were accepted for publication. Performance of the songs in 1900, however, created an uproar in the concert hall—the first of many the composer was to experience.

No longer regularly employed, Schoenberg was leading a precarious existence. He conducted a workers' chorus and orchestrated operettas (for which there was an insatiable demand in Vienna) by other hopefuls. In 1901 he married Zemlinsky's sister Mathilde and moved to Berlin, where he became music director of an avant-garde cabaret, the Überbrettl, for which he wrote a number of pop songs. (They were not as popular as he hoped.) In 1902, the year in which a daughter, Gertrud, was born, an encounter with Richard Strauss **[1563]** resulted in a grant and a teaching post at the Stern Akademie. This, however, lasted only a year, and in 1903 the Schoenbergs moved back to Vienna. By then Arnold had completed his symphonic poem *Pelleas und Melisande* and the vocal score of the vast cantata *Gurrelieder (Songs of Gurre).* For a few months in Vienna he taught classes in harmony and counterpoint but gave them up for individual private pupils. Among these were Alban Berg [**1789**], Anton Webern [**1773**], and Egon Wellesz [**1799**], who signed aboard in 1904. That year Schoenberg and Zemlinsky organized the Society of Creative Musicians, whose nominal president was Gustav Mahler [**1525**]. Its purpose was the presentation of new music, and it was under the society's auspices that Schoenberg, in 1905, conducted the first performance of his *Pelleas*—shortly before the society's untimely demise.

For the next few years, Schoenberg and his family—to which a son Georg was added in 1906—just managed to get by and sometimes had to borrow. During this time he wrote the first two (numbered) string quartets, and the first chamber symphony, Op. 9. Though he had the aid and (not always comprehending) support of some important musicians in Vienna, notably Mahler, these works tended to send their hearers into paroxysms of rage, for they (the works) were now moving steadily away from tonality—that is, they no longer pretended to be in some particular key to which they would return every so often, however arbitrarily, to demonstrate that they really were. In 1909 he adopted atonality in the Op. 15 song cycle *Das Buch der hängenden Gärten (The Book of the Hanging Gardens)*, the Op. 11 piano pieces, the landmark *5 Orchestral Pieces*, Op. 16, and the "monodrama" *Erwartung (Expectation)*, Op. 17. (Op. 16 had to wait until 1912 to be performed—in London under Sir Henry Wood—and the monodrama was not heard until 1924 in Prague.)

Meanwhile, during this same period, Schoenberg had found another outlet in painting, spurred by his friendship with Wassily Kandinsky, and had his first one-man show in 1910. That same year, with the help of friends in high places, he became what would today be called an adjunct professor at the Akademie. But the job did not fulfill his financial needs, nor lead to anything permanent, so in 1911, after completing his influential treatise on harmony, he returned to the Stern Academy in Berlin. Things did not go much better there; his music raised critical hackles, and attacks on it and its composer in the press apparently kept students away from Schoenberg's classes. The scoring of *Gurrelieder* finally completed, he took on a commission from Albertine Zehme, a Viennese actress. This resulted in *Pierrot Lunaire*, Op. 21, to a set of poems by Albert Guiraud (in German translation) for voice and chamber ensemble. In these he developed *Sprechstimme*, a kind of notated musical speech halfway between declamation and singing, which he had first experimented with in the final movement of

Gurrelieder. After forty rehearsals the work was presented in October 1912, the performers including cellist Hans Kindler (later known as a conductor) and pianist Eduard Steuermann, a Schoenberg disciple. Though several numbers were encored, the critics deplored the work. Nevertheless, the ensemble, with the composer and young Hermann Scherchen alternating as conductors, went on the road with it. Four months later Franz Schreker [**1705**] unveiled *Gurrelieder* in Vienna to what one observer called an ovation—which Schoenberg pointedly ignored. In the meantime Schoenberg was giving a conducting career a try and appeared as far afield as St. Petersburg and London, directing his own compositions.

The outbreak of hostilities in 1914 cost Schoenberg further opportunities as a conductor and most of his students. His friends and a patron kept him afloat. Rejected for service in Germany on medical grounds, he moved back to Vienna in 1915. There he was drafted, and, after a bit of string-pulling, got a one-year hitch in the Deutschmeister Infantry Regiment in December. Influential friends got him out two months early, though considering his desperate economic situation it was a dubious favor. He had completed another monodrama, *Die glückliche Hand (The Lucky Hand)*, in 1913, which waited eleven years for a production. Free to work once again, he occupied his time with a vast oratorio, *Die Jakobsleiter*, intended to symbolize his beliefs about his art and the artist. In 1917 he was again called up for service, but this time he was stationed in Vienna and given minimal duties. Hence he was able to continue with his work. In April he moved to the suburb of Mödling, where he again taught classes. But as the oratorio proceeded, he suddenly found himself committed to a whole new approach, which he called "composing with twelve tones" (he refused to recognize it as a system); since it was inconsistent with the first part of the work at hand, he laid that aside until he could make a reconciliation.

The twelve-tone approach suggested itself as a remedy for increasing difficulties that had appeared in the so-called diatonic system. As long ago as Bach's [**684**] day, equal temperament, essential in keyboard instruments if they were not to be limited to a few tonalities, had rendered diatonicism a convenient fiction rather than a physical fact—i.e., its tuning no longer accurately reflects the aural-acoustical phenomena of the overtone series. Moreover recent tendencies toward free modulation, chromaticism, and atonality had in effect given the composer a palette of twelve tones instead of the eight implied by a given "key." Schoenberg's particular concern was with form and logic, especially as they applied to the musical line ("melody") and the interrelations between musical lines ("counterpoint.") His solution was to forget about the diatonic scale as the alleged basis for composition, and substitute a twelve-tone row *(Reihe)*, as he termed it. A row must include all twelve notes within the octave, in whatever sequence the composer wishes. Any note may immediately succeed itself, but once it is abandoned it may not be repeated until the other eleven notes have been sounded. The row is subject to inversion, retrogression, and retrograde inversion, as well as transposition, and may be stated vertically as well as horizontally. Schoenberg insisted that freedom was not only possible but essential within these strictures—that the row was liberating rather than confining.

As soon as the war ended, Schoenberg founded the Society for Private Musical Performance, dedicated to getting new music played. It was "private" mostly in that reviewers were not admitted. Despite a good deal of sniggering in the newspapers, Schoenberg did not use the organization as a mere showcase for his own works. But the runaway inflation of the era doomed the project, and after a little less than three years and 117 concerts, it was disbanded. Shortly before that happened, there was a benefit that featured chamber arrangements of Johann Strauss [1295] waltzes by Schoenberg, Berg, and Webern.

In 1920 Schoenberg applied the twelve-tone principle for the first time to a set of five piano pieces (Op. 23), which he completed three years later. The next year was an important one in his life. He began it with a series of lectures and an all-Schoenberg festival in Amsterdam and first announced the twelve-tone approach. Though he had not been a practitioner of his faith for many years, and in fact had converted to Protestantism in 1921, he was stunned, when he tried to make reservations at a summer resort, to be told that Jews were not welcomed there. The ugly handwriting was on the wall.

Schoenberg completed his first three twelve-tone pieces—the piano pieces just noted, the Op. 24 *Serenade,* and the Op. 25 piano *Suite*—in 1923. In that year Mathilde Schoenberg died. Less than a year later the composer married Gertrud Kolisch, sister of Rudolf Kolisch, one of his pupils and founder of the Kolisch String Quartet (1922–39). In 1924 Schoenberg was invited to Berlin again to take over the directorship of the master classes at the Berlin Academy left vacant by the death of Busoni [1577] earlier

that year. He completed his Op. 26 wind quintet the same year. In January 1926 he settled in Berlin for one of the most comfortable and productive periods in his life. During it, he completed the Op. 29 *Suite* for chamber septet, the Op. 30 third string quartet, the Op. 31 orchestral *Variations,* the *Begleitungsmusik zu einer Lichtspielszene (Accompaniment for a Cinematic Scene)* Op. 34, and a number of smaller or less important works. In 1928 Gertrud Schoenberg provided him with a comic libretto of her own devising, *Von heute auf morgen (From Today to Tomorrow).* His setting of it, Op. 32, was premiered at Frankfurt-am-Main in 1930 by William (then Wilhelm) Steinberg; the reviews were unenthusiastic. Schoenberg also began work on a big opera, *Moses und Aron,* another attempt at expressing his credo about divine inspiration.

In his army days he began to be bothered by asthmatic attacks. In 1930 these started to give him real trouble, and late the next year he and his wife went to Barcelona for six months, in the hope that he would improve in its climate. In Barcelona their first child, a daughter named Nuria, was born. They returned to Berlin, but on March 1, 1933, Max von Schillings [1597] announced to the faculty of the Berlin Academy that the government meant to tolerate no Jews there. Schoenberg handed in his resignation, packed his bags, and took his family to Paris, where he officially returned to the faith of his fathers. Within a few weeks he had signed a contract to teach in a music school operated by the emigré Russian brothers Jacques, Joseph, and Manfred Malkin in Boston and New York City. The Schoenbergs reached the latter city on October 31. But the job turned out to be generally unsatisfactory, and the combination of overwork, strain, and a northeastern winter laid the composer low. In the early autumn of 1934, despite a tempting offer from the Juilliard School, he fled to California, settled in Hollywood, and taught for a time at USC. This arrangement also turned out to be unsatisfactory, and in 1936 he accepted an appointment as a professor at UCLA, settled in the Brentwood Park section of Los Angeles (for good), and completed his Op. 36 violin concerto and his fourth and final quartet, Op. 37.

It was about this time that he and George Gershwin [1955] developed a friendship, which was, however, abruptly terminated by Gershwin's death in 1937. That same year Gertrud bore Schoenberg (now sixty-three) a son whom they named Rudolf. (He was followed by a brother, Lawrence, in 1941.) The composer enjoyed his family life and the company of his few friends, but he found most of his students a disappointment and took out on them their lack of preparation. Nor was his music even as successful in America as it had been in Europe. One commission came from a Hollywood conductor-composer, Nat Shilkret (1895–), who dreamed up a vast suite on the book of Genesis, whose movements would be contributed by the greatest composers of the day (including Shilkret). Of the few numbers realized, Schoenberg provided the *Prelude*, his Op. 44. MGM movie mogul Irving Thalberg also tried to get him to do the score for the film version of Pearl Buck's *The Good Earth* but gave it up when the composer demanded $50,000 and final say in how his music was to be used. In fact, apart from the liturgical Op. 39 *Kol nidre*, the Op. 42 piano concerto, the Op. 38 second chamber symphony (actually the completion of a project begun thirty-five years earlier), the Op. 43 *Theme and Variations* for band or transcribed for orchestra (in which he reverted to tonality), the Op. 45 String Trio, and perhaps the curious *A Survivor from Warsaw*, Op. 46, Schoenberg wrote little more important music. (The *Jakobsleiter* remains a fragment; *Moses und Aron* lacks its brief final act.)

At seventy Schoenberg was forced to retire on a pension of about $40 a month, which even then did not suffice to pay his bills. Therefore he continued to take private pupils. In 1946 he lectured at the University of Chicago and in the summer of 1948 at the newly opened Music Academy of the West in Santa Barbara. But he was increasingly suffering from the debilities of old age, which included severe asthmatic attacks, a bad heart, diabetes, kidney disease, dropsy, and a hernia, and was unable to do any significant work in his final years. Superstitious about dates and the like, he is said to have insisted that he would die on Friday 13. He did, quite unexpectedly. According to his wife, his final word was "harmony."

RECORDINGS: As a result of Schoenberg's elevation to musical sainthood in the LP era, his music—even such things as the *Brettl-Lieder*, the waltz arrangements, the "realization" of Monn's [809] Concerto for Cello, and the unfinished *Moses und Aron* (three recorded versions already and a fourth to come soon)—have been given almost total attention by record makers. One must cite particularly CBS's multivolume "complete Schoenberg" effort. The final major discographic gap was filled with the recent release of the *Jakobsleiter* fragment under the baton of Pierre Boulez.

[1658] HOLST, Gustav(us) Theodore (von)
(Hōlst, Goos'-tav Thē'-o-dôr)
TROMBONIST, TEACHER, CONDUCTOR
BORN: Cheltenham, September 21, 1874
DIED: London, May 25, 1934

Gustav Holst was a native of the Cotswolds and as a patriotic gesture cleansed his name of Germanisms in 1914. Though his ancestors were ultimately German, his great-grandfather, the first Holst to live in England, was Swedish. Holst's father and mother were both pianists. When the mother, *née* Clara Lediard, died in 1882, Adolphus Holst remarried. He gave his son piano lessons from his earliest years. The boy taught himself the basics of composition, played the organ in a village church, and conducted choirs (and once an orchestra) before his father sent him off to the Royal College of Music in 1893. (A neuritic condition in his arm precluded him from becoming a professional pianist.) After Holst had been turned down twice for scholarships, the RCM awarded him one at the eleventh hour in 1895. His chief teacher was Stanford [1467]; his greatest friend at school was Vaughan Williams [1633], and the relationship lasted all his life. He gave up the piano for the trombone, which he played in summer-resort and theater orchestras and as a member of something called Wurm's White Viennese Band. At the home of the visionary poet William Morris, whither he was called to lead a socialist choir, he met and fell in love with Beatrice Harrison. He graduated in 1898 without any special distinction and joined the orchestra of the Carl Rosa Opera Company, where he sometimes conducted rehearsals. Then he became a member of the Scottish orchestra.

Up to the turn of the century, Holst had written a good deal of music, including a *Cotswolds Symphony*, but little had seen publication. He at first considered an opera-writing career. In 1893 his operetta *Lansdowne Castle*, deeply indebted to Sullivan [1397], was actually performed by amateurs. Another, *The Idea*, intended for children, was in a similar vein. At the RCM he suffered for a time from rampant Wagnerism [1230]. *Ianthe* has been called an amalgam of *Die Walküre* and *Ruddigore*, and Holst burned the score of *The Magic Mirror* as far too imitative. However, when he finally married Beatrice in 1901, he decided to try to live on the proceeds from his music. It didn't work, so in 1903 he embarked on a remarkable but much too demanding teaching career as music master at the Edward Alleyn School in suburban Dulwich. The following year he also took on classes at the Passmore

Edwards Settlement, and in 1905 he began a lifelong intendency at the St. Paul's Girls' School in Hammersmith. In 1907, the year of his daughter Imogen's birth, he shed the settlement job when he was put in charge of music at Morley College. (Imogen later became a fine musician and, until her death on March 9, 1984, her father's most devout apostle.) Given such pressures, composition was impossible save on weekends.

Nevertheless Holst composed. Early on he had developed an interest in Sanskrit literature and, with the intensity he brought to bear on whatever interested him, he set about to learn to read it in the original. This immersion was reflected in his music of the period—the neo-Wagnerian opera *Sita* of 1899–1906, the symphonic poem *Indra* of 1903, the five sets of *Hymns from the Rig Veda* (four for chorus and orchestra, one for voice and piano), and especially the exquisite chamber opera *Sāvitri*. By mid-decade, partially at the urging of Vaughan Williams, Holst had also discovered English folksong. This, building on his love for the vocal music of the Elizabethans and Henry Purcell [581], determined him to learn once and for all how to set English poetry. In 1910 Holst allowed himself a rare vacation in Algeria, which inspired the suite *Beni Mora* for orchestra. But much of his composition in this era was of a practical nature, such as the 1913 *St. Paul's Suite* for strings, designed for his schoolgirl orchestra, and the two suites for military band.

When war broke out in 1914, Holst, whose health was never sound, was rejected for service. For the next two years, inspired by a chat on astrology with a friend, he worked at a set of seven symphonic poems based on the alleged characteristics of the then-known planets. (The savage "Mars, the Bringer of War," was incidentally conceived before the outbreak of hostilities.) When finished, *The Planets* was given a private runthrough in 1918 by Adrian Boult and the New Queen's Hall Orchestra; it was premiered publicly in 1919. *The Planets* was an instantaneous success (though some sneered at it as merely a matter of slick orchestration). The whole matter embarrassed the retiring composer, who never again delivered a work of like popularity. The public was disappointed, but Holst had no interest in fame.

The Holsts had acquired a country refuge at Thaxted in Essex. There, one Whitsunday weekend, a gathering of friends and pupils had produced such happy music making, that the composer set the time aside annually for a sort of private music festival that featured the "Whitsuntide Singers." As the war wound down in 1918, the YMCA sent

Holst to the Balkans and Turkey to organize musical groups, which he did with great success. In 1919 he gave up the Alleyn School when he was appointed to the faculties of the Royal College and of University College at Reading, Berkshire. Despite these increased pressures, Holst continued to compose. He saw his opera *The Perfect Fool* (an indirect satire of Wagner's *Parsifal*) premiered at Covent Garden in 1921; the reviews were mixed, but the ballet music has survived. Somewhat more successful was *At the Boar's Head*—Shakespeare's *Henry IV* lines set to an artful web of folk themes—premiered at Manchester in 1925 and included afterward in the repertoire of the British National Opera Company. The same year brought the initial performance of the *First Choral Symphony* by the local choir under Albert Coates at the Leeds Festival. (A projected second such work was never forthcoming.) It was a triumph, if only because the choir managed to get through it. But it was poorly received later by a London audience, who resented Holst's coldly analytical treatment of Keats's poems.

Early in 1923, while conducting at University College, Holst had lost his footing, toppled backward off the podium, and suffered a concussion. He was forced to give up his post to recuperate. In the spring he sailed for America to fulfill commitments at the University of Michigan. Later that year the *Fugal Overture* and *Fugal Concerto* marked Holst's initial use of a neo-classicism of sorts. On his return to England, he went into such a precipitous decline that his doctors ordered him to retire to Thaxted and take a year off from all duties. (During this time he was made, without consultation, a Fellow of the Royal College.) The success of *The Planets* had gotten much of his music published, and he was able to work without worry—though he always led a Spartan existence. When his sabbatical was over, he returned to London but gave up all duties save for his teaching at St. Paul's and was able to devote himself to composition, with periods of relaxation, which he often devoted to hiking. In 1927, midway through his Thomas Hardy–inspired symphonic poem *Egdon Heath* (regarded by the composer as his greatest work), he decided he needed to see the actual landscape and trudged cross-country to Dorchester, where he had a splendid meeting with the aged novelist. Hardy, however, died before he could hear the completed work, which, considering his distaste for concert music, may have been just as well. That same year Holst was flattered and touched by a festival of his music organized in his birthplace, and he completed the choral ballet *The Morning of the Year* and music for John Masefield's *The Coming of Christ*. The year 1928 produced the *Moorside Suite* for band, and 1929 brought the lovely song settings of Humbert Wolfe, his choral ballet *The Golden Goose*, and the polytonal Concerto for 2 Violins, which brought the composer the London Philharmonic's Gold Medal in 1930. In that year he completed his last opera, *The Wandering Scholar*, the *Choral Fantasia*, and the *Hammersmith Prelude and Scherzo* for band. After that, as his health declined, his productivity fell off. But in 1932 he returned to America to teach at Yale, which awarded him the Howland Prize. (Holst usually managed to dodge proffered honors, but this one delighted him.) One of Holst's students at Yale was Elliott Carter [2130]. Before the semester was out, however, Holst was felled by a bleeding stomach ulcer. He suffered from it for a year and a half and finally submitted to an operation in May 1934. He died two days later, not yet sixty. Though Holst's ascetic later music displeased his contemporaries, who were awaiting another *Planets*, he has now become firmly established as one of the most important figures in the modern English musical renaissance.

RECORDINGS: Holst has been treated well but not exhaustively on records. He himself twice recorded *The Planets* (once acoustically, once electrically) and also made recordings of the *St. Paul's Suite, Beni Mora,* and the two orchestral *Songs Without Words*. All of these have enjoyed modern recordings—*The Planets* more than a score, including three by Boult and a transcription for piano performed by composer Richard Rodney Bennett [2417]. The stage works are represented by *Sāvitri* (two recordings), *The Wandering Scholar, At the Boar's Head*, the choral ballet *The Golden Goose*, dances from *The Perfect Fool* and *The Lure*, and two songs from *The Coming of Christ*. Save for about a dozen early works, all the orchestral and band music has been recorded at least once. A number of choral-orchestral works and song cycles with orchestra remain unrecorded, but there have been recordings of the 1904 *scena* for soprano and orchestra entitled *The Mystic Trumpeter* as well as such choral-orchestral pieces as *Psalm 86*, the *Choral Symphony*, the *Choral Fantasia*, the *Short Festival Te Deum* of 1919, the *Ode to Death*, two of the sets of *Choral Hymns from the Rig-Veda*, and the 1917 *Hymn of Jesus*. A number of additional choral works, including the *Dirge for Two Veterans* and *Mediaeval Scenes*, have also been recorded. Aside from the *Terzetto* for flute, oboe, and viola, the small body of chamber and piano music

is virtually ignored. Of the songs one notes the Wolfe settings and the four pieces for voice and violin. There is even a recording of Colin Matthews's orchestration of ten of the twelve songs in Holst's song cycle *The Dream City*.

[1659] IVES, Charles Edward
ORGANIST, BUSINESSMAN
BORN: Danbury, Conn., October 20, 1874
DIED: New York, May 19, 1954

Almost wholly ignored as a musician in his lifetime, Charles E. Ives has, since his death, been elevated to a position among American composers whose loftiness one suspects is at least partly the result of overreaction. That his gifts and accomplishments were remarkable goes without saying. He was a maverick in the grand American tradition, and none of that kind has been more daring or inventive than he—but one wonders whether every scrawl and doodle he committed to paper should be treasured as a holy relic. Much has been made of his pioneering use of microtones, chord clusters, polyrhythms, atonality, and other advanced techniques; but, however much sweeter unheard music may be than the audible kind, it is likely to have had little impact on the history of music, and so there is no School of Ives.

Ives's musical inquisitiveness and some of the then-unusual devices he used were owing to George Ives, his father. The Iveses had emigrated to New England fifteen years after the Pilgrims landed. George's father was the town banker in Danbury. When George showed an inclination toward music (he was blessed with perfect pitch), he was sent to one Carl Foeppl in the Bronx to study it. Having mastered keyboard instruments and the violin, he became during the Civil War the youngest bandmaster in the Union Army. Mustered out, he came home to teach and lead the Danbury Band—questionable vocations in the eyes of his fellow citizens. On New Year's Day 1874 he married Mary Elizabeth Parmelee, who ten months later gave birth to a son christened Charles Edward. (A second child, Moss, later a successful jurist, followed in 1876.)

George Ives was an Emersonian and spent most of his life quite literally listening for the harmony of the universe. He played with fractional tones, arranged the band in segments throughout the town to produce "quadraphonic" effects, and tried out a "humanophone"—a choir in which each singer was assigned his own note which he produced when called upon. Charles inherited his father's ear. When he was eight, he was turned over to the village barber, formerly one of George's percussionists, to learn to play drums—which he was soon doing under his father's baton. George moreover taught him everything he knew (which was considerable) about how music worked but forbade all experimentation until he had the rules down cold. At eleven Charles became organist of the West Street Congregational Church and three years later moved on to the more prestigious First Baptist Church. By then he was already composing; indeed, a year earlier, the band, somewhat to his embarrassment, had brought that fact to public attention by programming his *Holiday Quick Step.* Meanwhile he was acquiring, not very spectacularly, a general education. After studying at the local grammar school and the Danbury Academy, he was sent for finishing to the Hopkins School in New Haven, where he served as organist at St. Thomas' Episcopal Church. (In all of his church jobs, he had strongly to resist the temptation to spice up the hymntune harmonies, which bored him.) During his secondary-school years, Ives was an outstanding athlete—he played football and pitched for the Hopkins baseball team.

In 1894 he was admitted to Yale University, of which some of his relatives were alumni. He took the general academic course, studying with William Lyon Phelps among others. In his first year he was made chapel organist and took organ lessons from Dudley Buck [1367] and Harry Rowe Shelley, a Dvořák [1386] pupil. At that time Horatio Parker [1556] had just been appointed professor of music. Though his courses were restricted to upperclassmen, he took Ives on from the outset. Parker could make nothing of Ives's experiments and kept a tight rein on him—though the young man indulged his fancy in music written for student use. During his freshman year, however, George Ives, who had at last capitulated to working in the bank to make ends meet, died at forty-nine. It took Charles a long time to recover from the shock.

At Yale Ives continued to be a disappointing student. As a result he was barred from athletics, but he managed to lead a vigorous social life and was a member of several important clubs. He composed steadily—mostly football marches, drinking songs, choruses, and organ pieces, but in 1896 he finished his first string quartet ("From the Salvation Army") and in 1898 his first symphony (much of which Parker made him rewrite in "acceptable" style). By the time he graduated, however, he had decided to make his career in life insurance, on the curiously

idealistic grounds that it was an uplifting and humanitarian calling. With several other recently fledged Yalies, Ives took an apartment (soon dubbed "Poverty Flat") on West Fifty-eighth Street in New York and found employment as a statistician in the actuarial department of the Mutual Insurance Company. He also became organist of the First Presbyterian Church in Bloomfield, New Jersey. After a year he was transferred to the Charles H. Raymond agency, to fill in for the vacationing Julian Myrick. Myrick later said that his replacement was meant to be a permanent one but that Ives's handwriting was so illegible that he (Myrick) was allowed to return and Ives was set to training agents. Meanwhile Ives was studying business law at night and working on a second symphony. In 1900 he became organist of the Central Presbyterian Church in New York, which two years later presented his cantata *The Celestial Country* to generally good reviews. In 1901 he and some of his fellow lodgers seceded to an apartment on Central Park West, and in June 1902 he gave up church-organ playing permanently—leaving a number of manuscripts at Central Presbyterian which were eventually destroyed.

In 1905 he fell in love with a noted Hartford beauty, Harmony Twichell, the sister of a Yale chum. The three-year courtship was not an easy one, since during it she was working as a nurse in Chicago. During this period Ives produced some of his most radical and original works—*The Unanswered Question, Central Park in the Dark* (the two were originally intended to be played in sequence), the *Set for Theater Orchestra,* and *Hallowe'en,* to name only a few. Late in 1906 he suffered what was probably a mild heart attack and, on his doctor's orders, vacationed over Christmas at Old Point Comfort. Myrick went with him to keep an eye on him. They had little in common—Ives was becoming increasingly shy and introverted, whereas Myrick was outgoing and gregarious (a demon tennis player); but they respected each other and worked well together, and by the time they had gotten back to New York, they had decided to strike out for themselves as partners. Under the auspices of Washington Life, they set up as "Ives and Co." But in 1908, shortly after Charles and Harmony were married, Washington Life underwent a merger and the agency was abolished. However, by the new year, the partners were back in business, under Mutual again, as "Ives and Myrick."

Ives was in a very real sense the invisible partner: he reached his private office by an unseen entrance, was ensconced there for most of the time, and discouraged visitors. His employees found him usually gentle and even timid, but he occasionally went into towering rages, and he had very strong opinions, which he expressed in a sort of Whitmanesque rhetoric. For all that, he was a brilliant and innovative businessman. He invented and formulated estate planning. His approach to training his salesmen was revolutionary, for he taught them that their chief function was to educate their clients. His manuals read like Emerson or Thoreau, and one of them, *The Amount to Carry,* came to be regarded as a classic. (If the agent did his job properly, he argued, the customer would know how to decide how much insurance he needed.) The agency grew to be the envy of the insurance world.

After the wedding, the Iveses lived on Eleventh Street, then moved uptown to Twenty-second Street. Charles had continued to compose prodigally, without much hope of—or interest in—performance. At this time he was working on such things as the *New England Holidays, Three Places in New England,* the *"Concord" Sonata* for piano, the *Robert Browning Overture,* and the fourth symphony. (Many of these reused older material, and the chronology of most of Ives's output is dreadfully complex.) In 1911 the couple returned to Connecticut, and the following year they bought land near West Redding, on which a house and barn were built to their specifications. After 1914, however, they wintered in Manhattan and summered at the farm. In 1915, Harmony, who was childless, took over the care of the ailing infant daughter of a poor family, to whom the Iveses had temporarily turned over the gatehouse; later they adopted the child, who was called Edith Osborne Ives.

When America entered the First World War in 1917, the composer had written most of his important music—but had still heard very little of it. Walter Damrosch [1540] had once agreed to conduct a reading of the first symphony but had given it up after the first movement as impossible. Occasionally soloists were invited to try this piece or that, but they were usually baffled or thought their legs were being pulled. Once or twice Ives tried to get amateur orchestras together to test out something, but they invariably proved inadequate to the task.

The outbreak of war in 1914 had outraged the composer, and when his country became involved, it really got to him. When he was not accepted as a volunteer ambulance driver, he devoted his energies to war bonds. In September 1918 he attended a meeting at which he argued so passionately for small-denomination bonds within the reach of the average worker that the idea was accepted and realized in the so-called "baby-bonds." But it was too much for him: that night he suffered a major coronary which laid him up for months. During his convalescence, he had printed up, without copyright and free for the asking, the *"Concord" Sonata,* together with the essays it had inspired from him, and a collection of 114 of his songs. Disappointed by the 1920 election, he sharpened his political thinking and sent to the Congress a constitutional amendment ensuring real democratic participation in government, including the requirement for a public referendum on declarations of war. It was ignored.

Ives was never a well man again, and gradually he gave up almost all of his musical activity. In 1924 he was able to go to England with his wife (they returned in 1934 and 1938 and spent some months on the Continent in 1932–33), but he showed up increasingly rarely at his office and retired for good in 1930. In 1937 he underwent a successful cataract operation, but his health continued to decline, and he often suffered frightening attacks of breathlessness, especially under emotional stress. Meanwhile a small but dedicated group of musicians—it included Aaron Copland [1986], Elliott Carter [2130], Henry Cowell [1934], E. Robert Schmitz, and Nicolas Slonimsky [1893] —had begun to perform and promote his music, though on no very grand scale. In 1947 he was awarded a much-belated Pulitzer Prize for his third symphony (it had been completed in 1904!). Myrick brought over the photographer W. Eugene Smith, who, in celebration of the occasion and despite Ives's belligerent antipathy to cameras, managed the photograph by which he is best known to posterity. Invited to hear Leonard Bernstein [2282] conduct the symphony at the New York Philharmonic, Ives declined, but he sneaked a listen to the broadcast on his cook's little table radio. In 1954, recovering from an operation, he suffered a stroke and died. In 1965 Leopold Stokowski, assisted by David Katz and José Serebrier, conducted the first complete performance of his fourth symphony, regarded by some as Ives's greatest achievement.

RECORDINGS: Ives appealed to the rebellious 1960s, and since then all his major works have been recorded—most of them several times. Large numbers of the minor ones have also been made available, including "reconstructions" from sketches or suggestions (e.g., the fragment for *Orchestral Set No. 3).* CBS issued a commemorative album that includes some home recordings of Ives playing the piano and in conversation.

[1660] WOLFF, Erich (Volf, Ă'-rĕkh)
PIANIST
BORN: Vienna, December 3, 1874
DIED: New York, March 20, 1913

Erich Wolff studied composition at the Vienna Conservatory with Johann Nepomuk Fuchs (1842–99) and piano with Ludwig Door. He became a much sought-after *Lieder* accompanist and was something of an authority on the *Lied*. (He published a study of the songs of Robert Schumann [1211].) Wolff wrote songs himself. Some became favorites of concert singers, and for a time he was hailed as a savior of the German art song. (He was often called "the other Wolf.") His work, however, did not bear out such prognostications, and he died at thirty-nine while on a concert tour of the United States. RECORDINGS: There are a number of song recordings, including an album of c. 1940 by the self-accompanying baritone Ernst Wolff (no relation).

[1661] SCHMIDT, Franz (Shmit, Frănts)
PIANIST, CELLIST, TEACHER, ADMINISTRATOR
BORN: Pozsony (Pressberg, Bratislava),
    December 22, 1874
DIED: Perchtoldsdorf, February 11, 1939

A composer with ideas of his own, Schmidt was long cast in the shadows by the spotlight played on Schoenberg's [1657] Second Vienna School. His father, of German descent, was a china painter by profession but an amateur performer on several instruments. His mother, a Hungarian, played the piano and, according to her son, was his first and best teacher. He spent his childhood in a city where German, Hungarian, and Czech cultures met and was taken in tow by Felizian Moczik, a Franciscan friar who taught him to play the organ in the abbey church. In 1887 he was asked to perform by Helene von Bednarics, a wealthy spinster. She was so delighted with him that she sent him to Vienna to study piano with Theodor Leschetizky. Leschetizky for some reason less than enthusiastic; he told the boy that he was musically unhousebroken, and that anyone named Franz Schmidt had no hope of a musical career. The next year the senior Schmidts moved to Vienna, and for a time Franz had to play for dance schools to help the exchequer. In 1890 he was accepted at the Vienna Conservatory, where he studied counterpoint with Bruckner [1293], theory with Robert Fuchs, and having perhaps understandably abandoned the piano, he studied cello with Ferdinand Hellmesberger. On

graduating in 1896, he was selected from among forty applicants to fill a vacancy in the Imperial Opera Orchestra.

In due time he was promoted to the first desk of his section, a move that won him some enemies. In 1899 he was awarded the Beethoven Prize for his first symphony, and in 1902 the orchestra played it under his direction, winning him an ovation. His success is said to have aroused the jealousy of Gustav Mahler [1525], the general music director. At any rate, not long afterward, while waiting for a performance of *Lohengrin* to begin, Schmidt was summarily ordered to move back to the last seat among the cellos. In 1901 he had also become professor of cello at the conservatory operated by the Friends of Music, and he taught there until the school was taken over by the government in 1908. He eventually resigned from the orchestra (most sources say 1911, but some say 1913). The second symphony was completed in 1913, and a year later the Imperial Opera premiered his *Notre Dame* (after Victor Hugo). It was quite successful and is still played occasionally in German countries. Also in 1914 he returned to the conservatory (now called the Vienna State Academy) to teach piano. Eight years later he was named professor of theory and counterpoint, and director in 1925.

In his private life Schmidt also encountered hardships. He married in 1898. After his wife gave birth to their only child, a daughter, she slipped gradually into a profound depression and spent the rest of her days in a mental hospital. In 1931 Schmidt gave up administration and returned to teaching. The following year his daughter Emma died in childbirth. The father's grief brought on a severe breakdown; he later recorded his emotions in his fourth and last symphony of 1933. In 1937 his doctors told him that he was suffering from inoperable cancer. Sensing that his world was also headed for catastrophe, he threw his energies into writing a great oratorio, *Das Buch mit sieben Siegeln (The Book with Seven Seals,* the text drawn from Revelations). He lived long enough to hear it performed in 1938 but not to witness the debacle it prophesied.

Most of Schmidt's works date from the second decade of the twentieth century or later, for he destroyed most of his earlier efforts. These include another opera, *Fredegundis,* a set of orchestral variations on a hussar's song, 2 string quartets, three quintets for various combinations, and a number of organ works. A concerto and other works for piano, left-hand, were written for the one-armed pianist Paul Wittgenstein, and were later arranged, with Schmidt's concurrence, for two hands by his pupil Franz Wührer.

RECORDINGS: There are recordings of the last three symphonies, the oratorio, the Quintet for Piano and Strings, the Quintet for Clarinet, Piano, and Strings, both of the string quartets, and the orchestral variations. Kurt Rapf has recorded all the organ music. There are at least two pirated versions of *Notre Dame*, one of *Fredegundis,* and several recordings of brief orchestral excerpts.

[1662] GLIÈRE, Reinhold Moritzovich
(Glē-âr', Rīn'-hōld Mō-rēt-zō'-vĕch)
CONDUCTOR, TEACHER, ADMINISTRATOR
BORN: Kiev, January 11, 1875
DIED: Moscow, June 23, 1956

One is tempted to say that Glière's greatest talent was for survival. His name reflects his parentage: his father was a Belgian-born maker of wind instruments. As a child Glière studied the violin and was shortly turning out pieces for domestic musicales. After three years at the Kiev Conservatory, he went in 1894 to that of Moscow. There he continued his violin studies with Jan Hřímalý, one of the many members of a notable Czech musical family. Among his other teachers there were Arensky [1536], Ippolitov-Ivanov [1517], and Taneyev [1492]. He graduated with a gold medal in 1900 and was immediately hired to teach at the Gnessin School in Moscow. In 1905 he was one of the signatories of the manifesto protesting government brutality during that year's uprising. Shortly afterward, no doubt wisely, he left Russia to study conducting with Oscar Fried in Berlin. He returned to Moscow in 1907 and began his conducting career a year later. During the first decade of this century, he wrote a Byron-inspired opera, three piano concerti, quartets, sextets, and an octet for strings, and his 3 symphonies. Of these last, the lengthy programmatic third, *Ilya Murometz,* is generally reckoned his masterpiece, though it might have been by Glazunov [1573] in one of his more fertile moments.

In 1913 Glière returned to Kiev to teach composition at the conservatory, of which he became director a year later. There he weathered the upheaval of 1917, from which he emerged as director of musical education under the new government. In 1920 he returned to the Moscow Conservatory, where he taught until the end of his life (except during World War II). In 1923 he was sent to

Baku to help the Azerbaijanis get their musical culture together. His opera *Shakh-Senem,* premiered at Baku in 1934, was a product of his researches there. Later he was to study and use Ukrainian and Uzbek music. During the 1920s he happily lent his talents to Soviet propaganda. His best-known effort in that direction was the 1927 ballet, *The Red Poppy.* During the 1930s, when musical and other heads were rolling at Stalin's whim, Glière was climbing the bureaucratic ladder, to emerge in 1939 as chairman of the organizing committee of the Composers' Union. Removed to sanctuary during the war, he ground out paeans to the Motherland and the Red Army. He was not only immune to the postwar attacks by Zhdanov on leading artists; he was even praised as a Russian composer of the very first rank (which probably meant that he wrote tunes that officials could whistle). His 1949 ballet *The Bronze Horseman* (after Pushkin) had some currency outside Russia. In his later years he was awarded the Order of the Red Banner, the Order of Merit, an honorary doctorate, the title of Honored People's Artist, and eventually the Stalin Medal. Among the many significant musicians he taught were Khachaturian [2038], Knipper [1958], Miaskovsky [1735], Mossolov [1983], Prokofiev [1851], and Nicolai Rakov (1908–). Glière's success occasionally transcended the fact that most of his 500-odd compositions are in the language and mold of the late nineteenth century.

RECORDINGS: There are recordings of *The Red Poppy, The Bronze Horseman,* the harp concerto, the concerto for soprano voice, and *Ilya Murometz.* Melodiya has also recorded a number of rarer works—among them, the second symphony, the tone poems *The Sirens* and *The Cossacks of Zaporozh,* the orchestral *Fergana Festival,* several other ballet suites, several string quartets, and a *Ballad* for cello and piano—but these recordings have only had limited distribution in the West.

[1663] CARRILLO-TRUJILLO, Julián
Antonio (Cär-rē'-yō Trōō-hē'-yō, Hōōl-yàn' Àn-tōn'-yō)
VIOLINIST, CONDUCTOR, TEACHER, THEORIST
BORN: Ahualulco, January 28, 1875
DIED: Mexico City, September 9, 1965

Visionary and idealist though he was, Julián Carrillo was undoubtedly a more important musical thinker and creator than his current oblivion would suggest. His lineage was Indian, and he was born in the province of San

Luis Potosí in central Mexico. His musical education was perfectly respectable. He began as a violin student in Mexico City and studied composition at the National Conservatory with Melesio Morales, a writer of Italian-style operas. Investigation of the science of acoustics led to his dissatisfaction with the tempered scale and other arbitrary methods of tuning and a search for solutions. In 1895 he found one in a mathematically determined sixteenth tone, which he named *el sonido trece* (the thirteenth sound). However, his traditional training continued in Europe; he studied at the Leipzig Conservatory with Salomon Jadassohn (1831–1902) and learned conducting from Nikisch and Sitt [1452]. For many years he composed more or less according to the rules and never abandoned so doing entirely, though later he moved into atonality. After making something of a name for himself as a violinist in Europe and further study at the Ghent Conservatory, he came home in 1905. For the next few years he played and conducted and pondered what was wrong with the notions of musical form. He alternately suffered and throve in the uneasy political climate of those times. In 1913 he was made director of the National Conservatory but a year later was forced to leave the country. He settled in New York and (as he had in Mexico City) founded his own orchestra. During these years he published texts on harmony, counterpoint, and orchestration, as well as some more general papers reflecting his views on education and the place of the artist in society. He went home again once more in 1918 to head the National Orchestra of Mexico and returned to his post at the conservatory two years later. In 1924, however, he returned to his interest in microtones and became so involved that he resigned his job to devote full time to working out his theories. The result, basically, was the division of the octave into ninety-six parts, notated by a system of numbers in relation to a single line that replaced the traditional staff. Carrillo began composing with these "new" materials and soon won encouragement from adventurous groups and musicians, notably Leopold Stokowski, conductor of the Philadelphia Orchestra, who commissioned several works and later toured Mexico with the microtonal orchestra that Carrillo had organized. The composer also designed a series of microtonal pianos which were eventually built. He continued to write music up to the time of his death at age ninety. RECORDINGS: In 1962 he wrote a microtonal *Mass for Pope John XXIII,* which was recorded by a male choir under Robert Blot. His *Preludio a Cristobal Colón,* played by the

Sonido Trece Ensemble of Havana, was one of the first microtonal works to be recorded. Violinist Robert Gendre and conductor Yves Prin perform the Concerto No. 1 for Violin of 1963 on a Mexican Sonido 13 label recording.

[1664] KREISLER, Fritz (Krīs'-ler, Frits)
VIOLINIST
BORN: Vienna, February 2, 1875
DIED: New York, January 29, 1962

At the height of his career as a performer, Kreisler's name was known to the man on the street, and the home that did not boast at least one Kreisler record (usually of one of his own musical bonbons) was rare. Few were aware, however, that his composition teacher, at the Vienna Conservatory, had been Anton Bruckner [1293]. A true prodigy from the start, he was the son of a successful physician who played the violin and was delighted at his son's talent. (A brother, Hugo, was a cellist and made some records with Fritz.) Fritz began violin lessons at six with old Jacob Dont, sometime teacher of Leopold Auer, and progressed so rapidly that a year later, after he had debuted as assisting artist to Carlotta Patti, he was admitted to the conservatory through a special waiver of the rule that stipulated "no students under fourteen." His violin teachers were the senior Joseph Hellmesberger and Jacques Auber. Kreisler carried off a gold medal in 1885 and moved on to the Paris Conservatoire, where he studied violin with Lambert-Joseph Massart and composition with Delibes [1344], again taking a first prize for his playing in 1887. After a tour of the United States with the pianist Moritz Rosenthal, Kreisler returned to Vienna to complete his academic education and enter medical school. In 1896 he was called up for military service. By then he had decided to abandon medicine for music and was shocked when the Imperial Opera Orchestra rejected him. Two years later, however, he appeared as soloist with the same group in its avatar as the Vienna Philharmonic and the next year began his triumphal progress playing a concerto with the Berlin Philharmonic. He returned to the United States the following year and appeared there both as soloist and *en trio* with Josef Hofmann [1680] and the Belgian cellist Jean Gérardy. Eventually he married an American.

While vacationing in Switzerland in the summer of 1914, he was called up to rejoin his regiment as the war clouds thickened. Two months later he was wounded in an engagement with the Russians in Poland and was discharged for medical reasons. Having recovered, he returned to America that fall and spent the war years there. Because of anti-German sentiment after the spring of 1917, he did not dare appear there from then until after the Armistice. He returned to Europe, but with the Nazi annexation of Austria he settled in France and returned to America for good in 1939. He retired a decade later.

As a composer, Kreisler pretended neither to scope nor profundity. His most ambitious pieces are a string quartet and 2 operettas, *Apple Blossoms* (with Victor Jacoby) and *Sissy.* He specialized in elegant salon pieces for his instruments, most of which he recorded (as have innumerable violinists since.) For years Kreisler also kept introducing "forgotten works" by earlier composers. At last, asked to produce a source, he admitted that he had written them all—shocking the musicologists and amusing almost everyone else.

RECORDINGS: The string quartet and most of the salon pieces have been recorded by Kreisler and others. Oscar Shumsky is, at this writing, recording all the extant solo violin music.

[1665] MELARTIN, Erkki Gustav (Me-lär'-tin, Är'-kē Gōōs'-tàv)
TEACHER, CONDUCTOR, PAINTER, WRITER
BORN: Käkisälmi, February 7, 1875
DIED: Pukinmäki, February 14, 1937

Erkki Melartin was born on Lake Ladoga in a city once called Kexholm, and, now, taken over by the Russians in World War II, as Priozersk. He studied at the Helsingfors Musical Institute with Leipzig-trained Martin Wegelius (1846–1906) and the pianist Ingeborg Hymander. In 1899 he began two years of study abroad—music in Vienna with Robert Fuchs (1847–1927), art in Basle, and other work in Rome and Berlin. In 1901 he came back to Helsingfors to teach at the institute. In 1908 he went to Viipuri (now Russian Viborg) to conduct the orchestra, returning to the institute in 1911 as director, a post he held for a quarter of a century. He was also a painter of talent, the author of a popular book of aphorisms called *Credo,* and a religious mystic. He wrote many serious large-scale compositions—an opera, a ballet, 8 symphonies (including two unfinished works), symphonic poems, string quartets, and so on but was most successful as a writer of piano pieces and songs. RECORDINGS: Some of the songs have been recorded.

[1666] RAVEL, Joseph Maurice (Rà-vel', Zhō-zef' Mō-rēs')
PIANIST, CONDUCTOR
BORN: Ciboure, March 7, 1875
DIED: Paris, December 28, 1937

It is customary to speak of Debussy [1547] and Ravel as the founders of musical Impressionism. The fact is, however, that apart from nationality and contemporaneity, the two did not have much in common—though the younger man once successfully sued the older for stealing the idea of his *Habanera.* Ravel, as individual and "modern" as his idiom was, was a classicist to whom form was essential, even if it came dangerously close to the mechanistic, and who tolerated no inessential fooling around. His favorite composer was Mozart [992], and he disliked the romantic Romantics—though the world of his music is an almost wholly imaginary one. His insistence on bringing his works to a high polish accounts in considerable part for the relative skimpiness of his output. For all his popularity, not everyone agrees on his worth. As a composer for piano who developed the Lisztian [1218] approach and combined it with the ethos of the French clavecinists, he remains unarguably among the greatest (and last). The larger works, however, are praised more for color and technique than for content, and one admired critic, a few years after the composer died, dismissed the whole *oeuvre* as "slick trash."

Ravel's father's people came from the French Alps near Geneva; since the name also appears as "Ravex" and "Ravez," it is thought that they may have been Swiss. Pierre-Joseph Ravel, a baker's son, won first prize for piano at the Geneva Conservatory but elected to make his living as a mechanical engineer of considerable ingenuity. In 1868, for example, he invented a two-cycle petroleum-powered engine that could propel a vehicle but typically did nothing to promote it. After the Franco-Prussian War, he helped build rail lines in Spain, where in 1873 he met and married Marie Delouart, a French Basque fifteen years his junior. The job ran out just before his first son was born, so he left his wife with her family in Ciboure, near Biarritz, and went to Paris to find work. He was successful, and three months after Maurice was born he settled his family in the capital. There a second son, Joseph, who would all his life be Maurice's closest intimate, was born in 1878.

In a reversal of the usual composer's story, Maurice delighted his father by demonstrating musical proclivities at an early age. Accordingly the senior Ravel turned him over to Henri Ghys, a well-known piano teacher, when he was seven. Ghys found the boy "intelligent," and certainly his rapid progress was not impeded by the franc his father awarded him for every thirty minutes of practice. Five years later Maurice began harmony lessons with one Charles-René, a Delibes [1344] pupil who had been once a runner-up for the Prix de Rome. In 1889—the year he discovered oriental music at the Paris Exposition and Russian music in the concert hall—Ravel was admitted to the Paris Conservatoire as a preparatory student in piano (under Eugène Anthiôme). Two years later he was elevated to regular status. His piano teacher was Charles de Bériot (1802–70), who thought him gifted but lazy and in whose class he made friends with the Spaniard Ricardo Viñes, afterward one of his staunchest proponents. Other equally conservative teachers, such as Émile Pessard [1408] and Théodore Dubois [1356], did not know what to make of this apparent rebel, whose written exercises were always more adherent to the rules than their own would have been. Meanwhile, Ravel was refining his tastes. If he preferred the Symbolists in literature, in music he liked lucidity and compactness. Besides Mozart, his tastes inclined to Weber [1124], Chopin [1208], Schumann [1211], Mendelssohn [1200], and Gounod [1258] among the Romantics and Grieg [1410], Liszt [1218], Saint-Saëns [1343] and especially Chabrier [1382] and Satie [1578] among the "moderns." He allegedly played for Chabrier in 1893, and Joseph Ravel arranged for his son to meet Satie in 1895.

In 1895 Ravel left the Conservatoire, where he had not exactly covered himself with glory. He had written a few pieces—e.g., a song or two and a Sérénade grotesque for piano, and in this year he completed a Habanera for two pianos, a Menuet antique (published in 1898) for one piano, and another song, "Un grand sommeil noir" ("A Great Black Sleep") to a Verlaine text. He had apparently given up all hope of becoming a concert pianist. Now twenty, he had attained his full height—barely five feet. Moreover he was underweight, and his large head made him look like a fledgling bird. Perhaps to compensate, he at first affected a curled mustache and a full beard, a three-piece suit, a high collar and cravat, and a swagger stick. (He was always impeccably à la mode all his life.) Friends found him ironic, demanding, and contemptuous of people who did not measure up.

After two years, in which he produced only a couple more songs and another two-piano piece, Entre cloches (Among Bells), he returned to the Conservatoire, where he

found a more understanding teacher in Gabriel Fauré [1424]. Over the next three years Ravel ground out another song, the piano version of the Pavane pour une infante défunte (Pavane for a Long-Dead Infanta), and Shéhérazade, an orchestral overture to an opera that never got written. In 1898 Viñes played the Menuet in a recital and was one of the two pianists who played Sites auriculaires (Auricular Locales—the two two-piano pieces performed in tandem) was premiered at a concert of the Société National de Musique. Neither created much interest. When Ravel made his podium debut a year later, conducting his overture at another concert by the Société, there were some boos. Afterward the critics attacked the piece, and the composer attacked the critics, not entirely to the benefit of his career. Nor was he doing well in school. In 1900 he failed to qualify for the Prix de Rome competition and was scratched from the Conservatoire rolls for never having won a prize there. He continued, however, to audit Fauré's course. Like Berlioz [1175] and Debussy before him, he repeatedly tried for the Prix de Rome. In 1901 he took second place but had no luck the next two years. In 1903 the Conservatoire closed its doors to him even as an auditor. The next year he bypassed the competition, and in 1905 the competition excluded him on the grounds that he had not written his qualifying chorale-and-fugue by the book.

Considering his previous scrupulosity in such matters, it seems likely that Ravel's infractions were deliberate. He was becoming known as a composer—he had already out-Liszted Liszt with his 1901 piano piece Jeux d'eau (Fountains), and produced the song cycle Shéhérazade (based in part on the earlier overture) and the admirable string quartet of 1903. He was a leader of a boisterous group of avant-gardists known as the "Apaches"—a name coined by a timorous news vendor. He frequented the salon of Mme. de St. Marceaux, where he hobnobbed with d'Indy [1462], Debussy, Fauré, Messager [1474], and the painters James McNeill Whistler and Jacques-Émile Blanc, and found sponsors in Cyprien and Ida Godebski. (The Apaches often met chez Godebski, and later the couple would lend Ravel their country home, where he could work undisturbed.) Not surprisingly—and perhaps he had intended to force the issue—Ravel's rejection for the Rome Prize blew up into l'affair Ravel, which toppled Théodore Dubois [1356] and left the reform-minded Fauré at the helm of the Conservatoire. While the storm raged, the composer joined a party that included the painter Pierre Bonnard, on a yacht owned by the publisher Alfred Edwards, husband of Godebski's sister, and for six weeks cruised the Rhine and other rivers and the North Sea.

Despite its upheavals, 1905 was a rather productive year for Ravel. He composed the *Introduction and Allegro*, for harp, flute, clarinet, and strings, and some songs, and completed the *Sonatine* and the five-movement *Miroirs (Mirrors)* for piano. The year 1906 brought the *Mélodies populaires grecques (Greek Folksongs)* and the *Histoires naturelles*—witty settings of animal pieces by Jules Rénard (who did not approve) that dispensed with the antiquated requirement that final *e*'s in French poetry be pronounced. When Jane Bathori introduced them at another SNM concert in 1908, the opposition raised one more ruckus in the hall, and the critics later charged Ravel with theft from Debussy. The year 1907 also brought forth the orchestral *Rapsodie espagnole* (incorporating the *Habanera)*, which its composer conducted at the Concerts Colonne the next spring, creating yet another controversy. Meanwhile he had been hankering to write an opera, but considerations of works by Gerhard Hauptmann and Maurice Maeterlinck had led to even less than the Arabian Nights scheme. Now, however, his Spanish vein turned him to a naughty little comedy, *L'Heure espagnole (The Spanish Hour*—set in a clockshop) by a journalist and sometime-playwright named Franc-Nohain. He completed the music in a few weeks; when he played it for his librettist, the latter complained that it came in four minutes short of the title. They submitted it to Albert Carré, director of the Opéra-Comique, who pronounced the work obscene. Eventually he accepted it but then sat on it until 1911.

In 1908, the senior Ravel, who had been ailing for some years, died. The loss was a profound shock to Maurice, who had continued to live under the family roof, which was by then located in the suburb of Lavallois. He shaved off the beard and mustache, became more sober and reserved, and softpedaled what has been called his arrogance. Despite the psychic upheaval, he managed to write the three-movement *Gaspard de la nuit (Gaspar of the Night)* for piano and the piano-duet suite *Ma mère l'oye (Mother Goose)*, designed for the small hands of the Godebski children, Jean and Mimi. Ravel not only loved children; he was essentially childlike, delighted by toys—especially mechanical toys—and small animals. He liked to refer to Mimi Godebski as his fiancée. She was probably as close as anyone to filling that role, for if Ravel had any sex life at all, he kept it totally hidden.

In 1909 Serge Diaghilev arrived in Paris with his Ballets Russes and took the city by storm. Pleased by Ravel's music, he commissioned a ballet. The result was ultimately *Daphnis et Chloë*, but it was long a-borning, and postpartum vicissitudes delayed its unveiling until 1912. Meanwhile, the musical avant-garde, fed up with the growing conservatism of the SNM, seceded to form the Société Musicale Indépendante (SMI), with Fauré as president and Ravel as a director. At its first concert, in 1910, the Godebski children premiered *Ma mère l'oye*. That summer Igor Stravinsky [1748] came to Paris to oversee the performances of his new ballet *The Firebird* and established a home in Clarens, Switzerland. He and Ravel struck up a friendship—at least for a while. In 1912 Ravel wrote the *Valses nobles et sentimentales*, premiered anonymously at an SMI concert (to let the auditors guess); later that year he orchestrated them and they were used for a ballet, *Adélaide*. He also orchestrated and expanded the *Mother Goose Suite* for similar use. The same year found the composer writing the first of a number of reviews of new music. In 1913, at Diaghilev's request, he and Stravinsky spent the summer in Switzerland attempting an orchestration of Mussorgsky's [1369] *Khovanschina*. It never materialized, but it probably inspired the later Ravelian orchestration of *Pictures at an Exhibition* in 1922, and acquaintance with Stravinsky's *Three Japanese Songs*—themselves triggered by a hearing of Schoenberg's [1657] *Pierrot Lunaire*—bore fruit in the *Trois poèmes de Stéphane Mallarme*, one of Ravel's most uncharacteristic works.

In the summer of 1914, Ravel vacationed, as was his wont, at St.-Jean-de-Luz, near his birthplace. He went earlier than usual and stayed longer, completed his piano trio, and began work on a waltz fantasy tentatively designated as *Vienna!!!* In the midst of his labors, the Germans, to his shock and outrage, invaded Belgium. He went to Bayonne to volunteer but was turned down as too skinny. For a time he worked as a hospital orderly. In 1915 he argued his way into the air force but wound up as a truck driver in motor transport, somewhat to his disgust. (For all his patriotic ardor, however, he refused to join the musical jingoes who demanded a ban on all German music.) However, as one might have guessed, Ravel was not designed for the rugged life; his health began to suffer, and in September 1916 he was hospitalized at Chalons-sur-Marne with amoebic dysentery. Two weeks later he had to undergo an operation. But by December he was able to join his brother on a leave at home. They arrived in time for their mother's death and had only time to bury her before they were called back. After his return to Chalons, Maurice added frostbitten feet to his other miseries and was finally mustered out in March 1917. However, he found the empty house in Lavallois unbearably lonely, and so various friends sheltered him until 1920, when he bought a villa of his own, called Le Belvédère, overlooking the village of Monfort l'Amaury fifteen miles west of Versailles.

Understandably the previous five years had not been fertile ones. The chief product was *Le Tombeau de Couperin (Memorial to Couperin)* for piano in 1917, whose six movements, in the manner of an old suite, were each dedicated to a friend who had died in the war. He orchestrated part of it later, and this too was used as a ballet. In 1920 he completed *Vienna!!!,* now designated as *La Valse, poème choréographique.* (It had been commissioned by Diaghilev, but the ballet version was not forthcoming until 1928.) Ravel was further hampered by persistent insomnia which had developed during the war; it brought on debilitating fits of depression and caused him to spend some time at an Alpine resthome. It was also in 1920 that he began work on an opera to a libretto by the novelist Colette, former wife of his old enemy, the critic "Willy" (Henri-Gauthier-Villars); she had originally conceived of it as a ballet and had sent him a scenario as early as 1916. As *L'Enfant et les sortilèges (The Child and the Spells),* it was not completed until 1925; in its evocation of a magical world, it particularly typifies its composer. Finally, Ravel incurred another scandal in 1920 by rejecting the *Légion d'honneur.*

In 1921 he heard his first American (black) jazz band in Paris, and remembered this when he wrote his second violin sonata (completed in 1927) and his first piano concerto, for the left hand, in 1931. But composition came more slowly now. He had trouble concentrating; he traveled restlessly—Amsterdam, London, Venice—and spent much time in Paris, where he often walked the streets all night. In 1922 he wrote the sonata for violin and cello, one of his least-played works. In 1923 he was still working on the opera and giving lessons to Manuel Rosenthal (1904-), who would conduct its Metropolitan Opera premiere fifty-eight years later. (Ravel eschewed teaching but took on a few pupils in whom he believed. Among them were Vaughan Williams [1633], Roland-Manuel (1891-), and Maurice Delage [1723]; George Gershwin [1955] he turned down as having already mastered his art.) The year 1924 brought the *Tzigane* for violin and piano (or orchestra) and a couple of songs. In 1925, as noted, Raoul Gunsbourg produced the new opera with great success at Monte Carlo, and it was brought to Paris the following year. In 1926 Ravel wrote the *Chansons madécasses (Madagascan Songs,* which he recorded with Madeleine Grey), and the violin sonata followed in 1927. For some time the pianist E. Robert Schmitz had been urging him to come to America, and in the latter year, despite worsening health that defied specific diagnosis, he yielded. He left France in late November and returned five months later, totally exhausted. In between he crisscrossed the American continent horizontally and vertically, conducted his music in several cities, accompanied violinist Joseph Szigeti in New York, saw Hollywood, met Gershwin, suffered from the climate, and worried constantly about how to replenish his supply of French cigarettes.

In 1928 he tackled a commission from the dancer Ida Rubinstein to orchestrate Albéniz' [1523] *Iberia.* When he discovered that this had essentially already been done by the Spanish composer-conductor Enrique Fernández Arbós (1863–1939), he offered to do an original piece, which turned out to be that *tour de force* of eternally various monotony, the *Boléro.* It brought him enormous popularity in every sense of the word (thereby damaging his reputation in some stuffier quarters). That same autumn, 1928, the home folks gave a Ravel Festival in Biarritz, and Oxford conferred an honorary degree on the composer. In response to a commission from the one-armed pianist Paul Wittgenstein, Ravel began a piano concerto for the left hand and was simultaneously inspired to write another for the more common manual complement. Wittgenstein didn't like his work but condescended to play it in Vienna three years later. Ravel finished the other concerto in 1931 and the next year led its first performance in Paris with Marguerite Long as soloist; afterward they toured Europe with it and recorded it. (Ravel also recorded the *Boléro* in one of the slowest performances on disc.) Later in 1932 he wrote and submitted three songs to be considered for Feodor Chaliapin's use in his film of *Don Quixote,* but the producers turned them down for three by Jacques Ibert [1838]. They were Ravel's last works. That fall he suffered a slight concussion in a taxi accident in Paris. Though his doctors denied any connection, by spring he found himself wholly unable to compose. On vacation in the summer, he found while swimming that he could no longer coordinate his movements. Though there were periods of remission, his condition steadily worsened. He tried all sorts of cures. In 1935 Ida Rubinstein paid his way to Morocco via Spain in the company of the sculptor Léon Leyritz, whose bust of Ravel is now in the Paris Opéra. When he returned, the composer felt almost back to normal. But the gain was temporary. Toward the end of 1937 a brain tumor was suspected, and he was hospitalized for an exploratory operation. Shortly after he came out of the anesthetic, he lapsed into a coma and died nine days later at sixty-two. He was buried in Lavallois beside his parents. His illness was finally diagnosed as Pick's Disease.

RECORDINGS: Virtually all of Ravel's music has been many times recorded (the operas somewhat less often). One notes comprehensive surveys of the orchestral material (e.g., by Jean Martinon, Stanisław Skrowaczewski, Seiji Ozawa, André Cluytens) and the piano music (Casadesus, Walter Gieseking, Abbey Simon, Samson François, Vlado Perlemuter [who was coached by the composer], etc.). The songs, stage works, and chamber music have all been well taken care of and, except for the 3 Prix de Rome cantatas and the *Shéhérazade* overture, there are even recordings of most of the variants, orchestrations, and juvenilia. Besides the works previously noted, Ravel conducted the *Introduction and Allegro* for records and made some piano rolls.

[1667] SHAW, Martin Fallas
ORGANIST, EDITOR
BORN: London, March 9, 1875
DIED: Southwold, October 24, 1958

The brothers Shaw—the younger was Geoffrey [1724]—were minor but respectable figures in the recent history of English music. Martin was a pupil of Stanford's [1467] at the Royal College and afterward worked in the theater. In 1900 he provided music for Gordon Craig's staging of Ibsen's *The Vikings* and the same year his own short-lived Purcell Operatic Society put on one of the first modern productions of Purcell's [581] *Dido and Aeneas*. For sixteen years he was a London organist (1908–24) and, as such, helped cleanse English church music of its accumulated dross. He was an indefatigable editor of songbooks and collaborated with Vaughan Williams [1633] on *Songs of Praise* and *The Oxford Book of Carols*. In the 1920s and '30s he turned out several ballad-operas, operettas, pageants, and masques—most notably, perhaps, the music for T. S. Eliot's *The Rock*. Besides these and his church music, he also wrote a string quartet, but was most successful as a songwriter. RE-

CORDINGS: A few songs and choruses have been recorded.

[1668] SZULC, Józef Zygmunt (Shŏŏlts, Yō'-zef Zēg'-mōōnt)
PIANIST
BORN: Warsaw, April 4, 1875
DIED: Paris, April 10, 1956

The son of Henryk Szulc, concertmaster of the Warsaw Opera, Józef Szulc was one of seven musician-brothers. Initially a pianist, he studied with Moszkowski [1479] and Sigismund Noskowski (1846–1909)—there's a limerick there somewhere—at the Warsaw Conservatory. Later he gave up performance for composition and emigrated to Brussels, where he had a success with his ballet, *Une nuit d'Ispahan (One Night in Ispahan)* in 1909 and a triumph with his operetta *Flup* in 1913. After the war, in 1920, *Flup* became the rage of Paris. Szulc followed it with nearly a score of trivial but popular musicals with titles like *Vivette, Flossie,* and *Mannequins,* all full of "shimmies" and "Charlestons." He also wrote some more seriously intended music. A few songs have been recorded, notably a setting of Verlaine's *"Clair de lune"* ("Moonlight"). Szulc's son Józef (b. 1893), a pianist and composer, studied with Busoni [1577] and founded a music school in Cairo.

[1669] NOUGUÈS, Jean (Nŏŏ-gwes', Zhàn)
BORN: Bordeaux, April 25, 1875
DIED: Paris, August 28, 1932

Nouguès wrote his first opera, *Le Roi de Papagey (The King of Papagey)* when he was sixteen, and his *Yannha* was premiered in Bordeaux six years later. Neither it nor *Thamyris* of 1904 created ripples that extended beyond the suburbs. In 1905 *La Mort de Tintagiles (The Death of Tintagiles)* opened and swiftly closed in Paris. But the production in Nice in 1909 of *Quo Vadis?,* based on Henryk Sienkiewicz' best-selling historical novel, created a great stir. There was a successful repetition in Paris, and then the piece was taken up all over the world. (The Chicago Opera produced it both at home and in New York in 1911, with Maggie Teyte in the female lead.) The dozen or so operas and ballets that followed, however, had little success, though Nouguès' music for Rostand's play *Cyrano de Bergerac* enjoyed some currency. RECORDINGS: There are early recordings from *Quo Vadis?* and *L'Aigle (The Eagle)* of 1912.

[1670] GOLESTAN, Stan (Gō'-les-stàn, Stàn)

CRITIC, DIPLOMAT
BORN: Vaslui, May 26, 1875
DIED: Paris, April 22, 1956

Like his younger and greater contemporary Georges Enesco **[1738]**, Stan Golestan played the role of a sort of musical ambassador from Rumania to the West—and was, in fact his country's cultural attaché in Paris for many years. He was also music critic for *Le Figaro*. Again like Enesco, he got his advanced training in Paris—at the Schola Cantorum under d'Indy **[1462]**, Roussel **[1605]**, and later Dukas **[1574]**. In 1905 he founded a journal called *L'Album musical*. He won many honors, including the *Légion d'honneur* (as who did not?). In his use of folk themes in his compositions he seems to have aspired to do for Rumanian music what Bartók **[1734]** did for Hungarian music. Unfortunately he got his folk themes at second hand or invented them. He produced a symphony, other less formal orchestral pieces, 2 string quartets, a violin sonata, a violin concerto, a piano concerto, songs, and other small pieces. RECORDINGS: In his lifetime he was fairly well represented on records—a Rumanian rhapsody, a piece for harp and orchestra, chamber works, etc.

[1671] MONTEMEZZI, Italo (Mōn-tā-med'-zē, Ē'-tà-lō)

CONDUCTOR
BORN: Vigasio, August 4, 1875
DIED: Vigasio, May 15, 1952

Whatever his real achievements as a composer, Montemezzi seems doomed to be remembered (if at all) as a "one-opera" man. He was born in a village near Verona *(Grove* says on May 31), studied piano as a matter of course, and went off to Milan to study engineering. Exposed to music there, he decided to make it his career. After being twice rejected by the Milan Conservatory for lack of grounding, he managed to wangle his way in. His chief teachers there were Carmine Ferroni (1858–1934), a now-forgotten operatic composer, and Saladini, who had replaced the deceased Ponchielli **[1334]**. Though his student-written cantata on the Song of Songs, *Cantico dei cantici,* won a performance by Toscanini, Montemezzi felt he still had much to learn when he graduated in 1900. He taught harmony for a year but found that teaching was not for him. His first opera, *Bianca,* went unperformed, but in 1905 he won deserved applause in Turin

with *Giovanni Gallurese. Hellera* failed four years later, however.

Then the playwright Sem Benelli trimmed down his own very successful play *L'Amore di tre re (The Love of Three Kings),* and Montemezzi set it to music. Its La Scala premiere in 1913 was a huge success, and the work entered the international repertoire for a time. With its seamless symphonic sweep it seemed an advance over the standard Italian "number" opera, though it is not a work whose music one readily remembers. Because it provides two fine dramatic roles (for soprano and basso) it became a vehicle for such singers as Mary Garden, Claudia Muzio, Grace Moore, and Ezio Pinza and is occasionally revived for one or another aspiring musical thespian. In 1918 there followed *La Nave (The Ship),* libretto by Gabriele d'Annunzio. A Cecil B. De Mille epic of a work, it enjoyed some currency for a time and still has passionate proponents. Montemezzi's next opera, *La Notte di Zoraima (Zoraima's Night)* did not appear for thirteen years—and it is only a one-act affair. At the outset of World War II Montemezzi settled in California, where he lived for a decade, frequently appearing as conductor of *L'Amore.* His last opera was the one-act *L'Incantesimo (The Spell),* commissioned by NBC Radio in 1943. Montemezzi also wrote a few orchestral pieces and some chamber music.

RECORDINGS: There are three recordings of *L'Amore di tre re.*

[1672] HAHN, Reynaldo (Hàn, Rā-nàl'-dō)

CONDUCTOR, SINGER, ADMINISTRATOR, WRITER
BORN: Caracas, August 9, 1875
DIED: Paris, January 28, 1947

Hahn's mother was a native of Venezuela; his father, a Jewish merchant, had emigrated there from Hamburg. When the boy was three, the family settled in Paris, where in effect he spent the rest of his life. Musically precocious, he was admitted to the Paris Conservatoire when he was eleven and studied with Massenet **[1396]**, whose influence is particularly clear in Hahn's early songs. One of the earliest—and most famous—songs was *"Si mes vers avaient des ailes"* ("If My Poems Had Wings," text by Victor Hugo), which he produced when he was thirteen. Two years later he wrote a score for a play by Daudet, *L'Obstacle (The Obstacle).* He followed this with a ballet, *Fin d'amour (End of Love)* in 1892, and with Massenet's influence published an album of Verlaine settings, *Chansons grises (Gray Songs),* which contained some of his most popular songs. In 1898 the Opéra-Comique produced his first opera, *L'Île du rêve (The Dream Isle).* Hahn became a member of the salon *précieux* of the Gay Nineties. Possessed with an attractive if wispy baritone voice, he was much in demand as a self-accompanying singer at parties. He was an admirer of Marcel Proust, who based on him a character in his early novel *Jean Santeuil.* Hahn was a friend of Sarah Bernhardt, of whom he published a memoir in 1930. His music was unpretentious, but as both a composer and performer he hid an iron hand in the velvet glove. When, in 1906, Lilli Lehmann revived the then-sporadic Salzburg Festival, she invited him to conduct, and he responded with one of the most authentic performances of *Don Giovanni* heard since Mozart's **[992]** death. In 1919 he was appointed music director at the Cannes Casino, where he produced his opera *Nausicaa,* which was sufficiently successful to be repeated at the Opéra-Comique four years later. (In the interim he had written and seen produced two other operas and four ballets.)

In 1923 Hahn found his proper level with *Ciboulette,* an enormously successful operetta. In 1925 he followed it with the fanciful *Mozart,* a starring vehicle for Sascha Guitry and Yvonne Printemps and then a whole series of musical comedies. In 1935 he returned to the operatic stage with *Le Marchand de Venise (The Merchant of Venice)* which won considerable popularity but did not survive World War II. Despite his Jewish origins, Hahn did survive, remaining in Paris for the duration. The end of the war saw a successful revival of his musical comedy *Malvina* with decor by the tenor Guy Ferrand, Hahn's current intimate. Soon afterward Hahn was elected to the Académie and appointed director of the Opéra but died after little more than a year in office. Ferrand committed suicide from grief.

RECORDINGS: As a singer, Hahn made many recordings, mostly self-accompanied, including renditions of his own songs. He also recorded as an accompanist to Ferrand, Ninon Vallin, and the American baritone Arthur Krackmann, who sang as Arthur Endrèze, and he conducted a performance of his ballet, *Le Bal de Béatrice d'Este (Beatrice d'Este's Ball),* and original-cast excerpts from *Le Marchand de Venise.* There are modern recordings of the ballet score directed by Jean-Pierre Jacquillat, the *Chansons grises* and other songs by tenor Martyn Hill, and a selection of songs by baritone Bruno Laplante. Other discs, mostly pre-LP, include the *Concerto provençal,* the violin so-

nata, a piano sonatina, additional songs, and excerpts from stage and film scores.

[1673] KETÈLBEY, Albert William
CONDUCTOR, CELLIST, PIANIST, ORGANIST, EDITOR, RECORDING EXECUTIVE
BORN: Birmingham (England), August 9, 1875
DIED: Cowes, November 26, 1959

There is a persistent legend that Ketèlbey's real name was William Aston, though it is also said that "Ketèlbey" was inherited from Danish ancestors. He began like a latterday Mozart **[992]**, producing at the age of eleven a piano sonata that won Elgar's **[1499]** praise. Two years later he was named winner of the Queen Victoria Scholarship to London's Trinity College, where he studied composition with Gordon Saunders and mastered several instruments, of which the cello was his favorite. By the time he graduated, at sixteen, he had composed several orchestral and chamber works of which one, a quintet for piano and winds, took the Costa Prize. For the next four years, he served as organist at St. John's Church, Wimbledon. In 1895 he quit to become a freelance conductor and in 1897 became music director of the Vaudeville Theatre in London. His operetta *The Wonder Worker* was produced in 1900. In 1912 a cello piece, *The Phantom Melody,* won two cash awards. Ketèlbey found himself in demand as an editor for various publishers (e.g., Chappell) and eventually became music director of the Columbia Gramophone Company. In 1915 he struck compositional gold with a rather soupy quasi-religious genre piece called *In a Monastery Garden.* Others of an exotic or inspirational nature followed, notably *In a Persian Market, In a Chinese Temple Garden,* and *The Sanctuary of the Heart.* RECORDINGS: These works were played and recorded by bands, organists, xylophonists, and ocarina ensembles, and Ketèlbey was able to give up working before he turned fifty. He continued to compose and arrange (sometimes as "Anton Vodorinski"), and made a number of recordings of his own pieces.

[1674] COLERIDGE-TAYLOR, Samuel
CONDUCTOR, TEACHER
BORN: London, August 15, 1875
DIED: Croyden, September 1, 1912

Samuel Coleridge Taylor (or Coleridge-Taylor as he preferred) enjoyed musical popularity and fame previously denied in English-speaking countries to people of black ancestry. His mother was a white English-woman; his father, a medical doctor from Sierra Leone, returned there for good when Samuel was a small child. The latter grew up in suburban Croyden, where, according to legend, a local theater conductor, Joseph Beckwith, became interested in him when he saw him playing marbles on the street, a violin case beside him. At any rate Beckwith became his teacher, and a Colonel Walters found him a place in a local church choir. At fifteen he was accepted at the Royal College of Music, where he became a pupil of Stanford [1467] and of Charles Wood [1579]. By 1893 he had written choral and chamber pieces, some of which were performed, and was given a scholarship. Before he graduated in 1897, he had turned out several large chamber works and a symphony among other things, had won two prizes, and had gained the advocacy of Elgar [1499]. His orchestral *Ballade in A minor* was commissioned by the Three Choirs Festival and premiered at Gloucester in 1898. This success was eclipsed, however, by that of his cantata *Hiawatha's Wedding Feast,* to Longfellow's verses, conducted by Stanford in November of that same year. Coleridge-Taylor tried to capitalize on its popularity with *The Death of Minnehaha,* a *Hiawatha Overture,* and *Hiawatha's Departure,* all turned out within eighteen months, but none of them attracted as much attention—nor in fact did anything he wrote afterward, though the 1911 cantata, *A Tale of Old Japan,* was more popular than most.

At the end of 1899 Coleridge-Taylor married Jessie Walmisley, who had been his fellow student and came from an English musical family. Racism being widespread in England, her family had opposed the match. They had two children—a son, christened Hiawatha, who was born the following autumn, and Gwendolen in 1903. (She later changed her name to Avril.) The composer supported himself and his family by teaching and conducting. He was made conductor of the Westmorland festival in 1901 and professor of composition at Trinity College in London in 1903. In 1904, the year in which he made his first trip (of three) to the United States, he became conductor of the Handel Society. American blacks saw in his success a symbol of hope, and he became a close friend of the poet Paul Lawrence Dunbar and a supporter of black causes. In 1910 he also became professor of composition at the Guildhall School. Despite his attainments he was never permitted to forget his heritage and, rather ironically, he was actually considering emigrating to the United States

when pneumonia carried him off at the age of thirty-seven.

Besides the works noted, Coleridge-Taylor wrote many others, including an opera, an operetta, scores for half a dozen plays, an Anglican service, various other orchestral and instrumental pieces on the Hiawatha theme, piano and choral pieces, and songs.

RECORDINGS: Though *Hiawatha's Wedding-Feast* is now passé, there are recordings of it as well as the *Petite Suite de Concert* for orchestra, the piano arrangements *(24 Negro Melodies),* the clarinet quintet, and some brief odds and ends.

[1675] KARATIGHIN, Viacheslav Gavrilovich (Kå-rå-tē′-gēn′, Vē-yå′-che-slåv Gå-vrē-lō′-vich)
CHEMIST, CRITIC, EDITOR, TEACHER
BORN: Pavlovsk, September 17, 1875
DIED: Leningrad, December 23, 1925

Though he studied piano with his mother and later took lessons in his spare time from Nicolai Sokolov, a Rimsky-Korsakov [1416] pupil, Karatighin did not turn to music until he was thirty-two. Up to that time he was employed as a chemist by the Imperial Navy. He became an important critic and writer on music, as well as a musicologist and editor. He did important work on Mussorgsky's [1369] two unfinished operas, *Sorochintsk Fair* and *Salammbô,* and published books on Mussorgsky, Scriabin [1625], Schubert [1153], Richard Strauss [1563], Wagner's [1230] *Parsifal,* and the singer Féodor Chaliapin, as well as literally hundreds of articles. He was a passionate advocate of musical progress and helped found a modern music series in St. Petersburg in 1910. In 1916 he became a member of the faculty of that city's conservatory and taught there for the rest of his life. His compositions were mostly in small forms. RE-CORDINGS: An organ prelude and fugue has been recorded by Miroslav Kampelsheimer.

[1676] FÉVRIER, Henry (Fāv-rē-ā′, On-rē′)
CRITIC
BORN: Paris, October 2, 1875
DIED: Paris, July 8, 1957

Once well regarded as a stage composer but now forgotten, Henry Février studied at the Paris Conservatoire with a panoply of prestigious professors, including Fauré [1424], Leroux [1557], Massenet [1396], and the pianist Raoul Pugno. He also took lessons with Messager [1474], of whom he later wrote an admiring memoir. His first opera, *Le Roi aveugle (The Blind King)*, was produced at the Opéra-Comique in 1906; over the next twenty-five years it was followed by nine more operas and operettas. His greatest success was *Monna Vanna*, after a play by Maurice Maeterlinck, which opened in Paris in 1909. A few seasons later it was taken up by the Chicago Opera for Mary Garden, and it remained in the repertoire there for several years. In 1919, Miss Garden appeared in the world premiere of Février's *Gismonda* at the same house. Février also wrote piano pieces and songs and musical criticism. His son is the pianist Jacques Février. RECORDINGS: There are a few old recorded excerpts from the operas.

[1677] LLOBET, Miguel (Lyō-bet', Mēg-wel')
GUITARIST
BORN: Barcelona, October 18, 1875
(Grove gives 1878.)
DIED: Barcelona, February 22, 1938

Miguel Llobet was probably the most important guitarist between Francisco Tárrega **[1469]**, his teacher, and Andrés Segovia, his pupil. Before taking up serious study, he tried painting. Up to the outbreak of World War I, he made Paris his headquarters but spent much time touring, especially in South America. From 1915 to 1917 he was in the United States. After the war he returned to South America and toured with his Argentine pupil Maria Luisa Anido *en duo*. Manuel de Falla **[1688]** wrote his *Homenaje* in memory of Debussy **[1547]**, for Llobet. RECORDINGS: Llobet composed and arranged much music for his instrument, some of which has appeared in recorded guitar recitals.

[1678] CHRISTOV, Dobri (Krēs'-tôf, Dō'-brē)
SCHOOLTEACHER, MUSIC TEACHER, FOLKLORIST, CHOIRMASTER
BORN: Varna, December 14, 1875
DIED: Sofia, January 23, 1941

Christov, one of the first important modern Bulgarian musicians, began his career as a schoolteacher. In 1900 he managed to get to Prague, where he studied with Dvořák **[1386]** at the Prague Conservatory for three years, though his previous musical education was acquired on his own. Afterward he taught and conducted in Sofia. He served as professor of composition and director of the National Conservatory and from 1935 as

choirmaster at the Alexander Nevsky Cathedral. He was a dedicated collector and arranger of Bulgarian folk music, and it was particularly his effort in this area that won him election to the Bulgarian Academy. Much of his output was directed to educational ends, but he also wrote orchestral works and much choral music. RECORDINGS: Several of his liturgical pieces have been recorded by the Svetoslav Obretenov Choir.

[1679] WOLF-FERRARI (*né* Wolf), Ermanno (Volf Fer-rä'-rē, Ãr-mán'-nō)
EDUCATOR
BORN: Venice, January 12, 1876
DIED: Venice, January 21, 1948

Like Busoni **[1577]**, Wolf-Ferrari was torn, in several ways, between Italy and Germany. His mother was a Venetian, whose family name he later added to his own. His father, August Wolf, came from Bavaria; he is usually called a painter, but he was in fact a professional copyist. Though his son showed musical proclivities early, August sent him at sixteen to Rome to learn the paternal trade. He lasted there barely a year. Supposedly he got into amatory troubles and was packed off to Munich where the climate was cooler. At some point—perhaps then, perhaps earlier—he attended the Bayreuth Festival and suffered a violent emotional upset upon exposure to Wagner's **[1230]** music. At any rate, by 1893 he was at the Munich Academy studying with everyone's favorite music teacher, Joseph Rheinberger **[1368]**. He quit in 1895, however, and went home to write an opera, *Irene*, which found no takers and has since disappeared. After vainly seeking his fortune in Milan, he got a production of his oratorio *La Sulamite* in Venice in 1899. This was followed, early in 1900, by the premiere of his opera *Cenerentola (Cinderella)* at La Fenice. It was such a catastrophe that its composer fled to Munich. There he reworked the piece, which was successfully staged in Bremen two years after its initial failure.

In the meantime Wolf-Ferrari had produced two other large and successful choral works, *Talitha Kumi* and *La vita nuova (The New Life*, after Dante), the *Serenade* for strings, and a good deal of chamber music. Up to now his music had showed an eclecticism that ranged from Bach **[684]** to Puccini **[1511]**. Around 1902 he struck on a successful formula: in setting an adaptation of Goldoni's comedy *Le Donne curiose (The Inquisitive Ladies)*, he used a sort of mock-classicism, preponderantly lyrical. The

opening was slated for La Fenice, but musical politics intervened, and the composer
transferred it to Munich, where (in German
translation) it enjoyed a great success in 1903
and was soon taken up everywhere. After
that Wolf-Ferrari regularly first presented
his operas in Germany. A second Goldoni
effort in 1906, *I quattro rusteghi (The Four
Bumpkins,* often called *The School for Fathers),* seemed to confirm the rise of a new
operatic star, and Wolf-Ferrari was hailed as
the "new Mozart." Three years later he had
an enormous success with a two-singer, one-
act trifle, *Il Segreto di Susanna (Suzanne's
Secret* [She smokes! You've come a long way,
baby!]). It is still played for reasons that
transcend its economic attractions.

Wolf-Ferrari's success had brought him
back to Venice in 1903 to run the Liceo Benedetto Marcello. He resigned, however, in
1909 and returned to Bavaria. His next work
came as a shock. *I Gioielli della Madonna
(The Jewels of the Madonna),* which opened
in Berlin on December 23) was a lurid excursion into the lower depths of *verismo* that
out-Heroded Herod. It enjoyed, for a brief
time, a worldwide *succès de scandale.* In fact
the composer's stock was never higher than
during this period, and in 1911–12 he made a
triumphant trip to America, where *Susanna*
and *Gioielli* were produced by the Chicago
Opera and *Donne* by the Metropolitan. In
1913 he returned to his neo-classic style with
L'Amore medico (Doctor Love, after Molière).

Always too sensitive, Wolf-Ferrari was
shocked and horrified by the 1914 war. He
fled to neutral ground in Zürich, where he
worked on a new Goldoni opera, *Gli Amanti
sposi (The Affianced Friends).* But it did not
reach the stage until 1925, in Venice, and indeed for more than a decade he was virtually
unheard from. When he finally returned to
activity, the party was over and it was a different world. Even though his style had matured to a degree, he did not recover his popularity. *Gli Amanti sposi* was followed in
1927 by the fairytale *Das Himmelskleid (The
Heavenly Garment)* in Munich and *Sly* (after
the prologue to Shakespeare's *The Taming
of the Shrew)* at La Scala. Once again the
composer reverted to Goldoni, with some
success, with *La vedova scaltra (The Crafty
Widow),* premiered at Rome in 1931, and *Il
Campiello (The Neighborhood),* at La Scala
in 1936. Perhaps sensing that his operatic
sun had set, Wolf-Ferrari took up writing
orchestral and chamber music again, including a violin concerto, a cello concerto, and a
short symphony. His final operas were *La
Dama boba (The Silly Lady,* after Lope de
Vega), produced at La Scala in 1939, and *Gli*

Dei a Tebe (The Gods at Thebes), at Hannover in 1943. During World War II he taught
at the Salzburg Mozarteum. Afterward he
returned to Zürich but came back to Venice
to die. Some of the operas get occasional revivals.

RECORDINGS: There are several recordings of *Il Segreto di Susanna,* a very early
LP of *L'Amore medico,* and later ones of *I
quattro rusteghi* and *Sly.* Records also offer
the *Serenade,* the 1932 *Idillio-concertino,* the
1933 *Suite-concertino,* the Concerto for English Horn, orchestral excerpts from *I
Gioielli della Madonna,* songs, the 1931 recension of Mozart's *Idomeneo,* and many
operatic excerpts. There are recorded piracies of the operas *Le Donne curiose, I Gioielli
della Madonna, Il Campiello,* of the cantata
La Vita nuova, and of some of the operas
also available commercially.

[1680] HOFMANN, Josef Casimir *(né
Józef Kazimierz)* (Hof'-màn, Yō'-sef
Kä'-zi-mēr)
PIANIST, EDUCATOR, INVENTOR
BORN: Cracow, January 20, 1876
DIED: Los Angeles, February 16, 1957

Josef Hofmann was not only a prodigy, he
was an authentic genius: a musician whose
ear, memory, and technique were the wonder of his colleagues, and a mathematician-
technologist who held many patents. His
mother was a singer, his father Kazimierz a
conductor, pianist, teacher, and composer of
stature. He began teaching Josef when the
latter was three years old. The boy debuted
at six, played with the Berlin Philharmonic
at nine, and began a grueling concert tour of
America with his father at ten. After he had
played several wildly successful concerts, the
Society for the Prevention of Cruelty to
Children stepped in, charging exploitation.
When a Maecenas from New York named
Alfred Corning Clark offered a check for
$50,000 for the boy's further education,
Kazimierz saw the society's point and canceled the rest of the tour. Before they sailed,
however, Josef stopped by Thomas A. Edison's studio to make the first records ever
waxed by an important musician (now long
since vanished).

After a few lessons with Moszkowski
[1479] in Berlin, Hofmann was taken on in
Dresden by Anton Rubinstein **[1309]** as the
only pupil he ever taught privately. Hofmann found his approach odd but useful. In
the spring of 1894 Rubinstein gave him a second Berlin debut, in his (Rubinstein's) D minor piano concerto, with the composer on
the podium (one of his last public appear-

ances). After that Hofmann became a great star on both sides of the Atlantic. Short and increasingly pudgy, his hair close-cropped, he was no matinee idol, but his singing tone and unbelievable technique stood audiences on their heads. (Though he played with more interpretive freedom than might be countenanced today, Hofmann was one of the first virtuosi to insist that the performer's business was playing what a composer had written, not rewriting it.) His hands were quite small, and so he had Steinway build him instruments with narrower keys than normal.

Hofmann became director of the Curtis Institute in Philadelphia and an American citizen in 1926. He helped build the school, founded only two years before, into a first-class conservatory. In 1937 he celebrated his fiftieth American anniversary with a concert at the Metropolitan Opera, which was recorded and eventually made commercially available. He left Curtis in 1938 and gave his final concert in 1946. His last active years showed a decided decline, owing in part to a drinking problem. He spent his final decade in California. Among Hofmann's numerous compositions were a symphony and 5 piano concerti. Some of his pieces were attributed to a mythical invalid composer named Michel Dworsky. ("Dworsky" is Polish for Hofmann or Court Man.)

RECORDINGS: The *Chromaticon* for piano and orchestra is included in the Metropolitan concert, and there are some piano pieces on records. Hofmann, incidentally, left surprisingly few records.

[1681] BRIAN, Havergal (Brī-ȧn, Há-ver-gul)
SALESMAN, CLERK, ETC.; WRITER
BORN: Dresden (Staffordshire), January 29, 1876
DIED: Shoreham-by-Sea, November 28, 1972

Havergal Brian's life story is so incredible that one might almost think it a parody, and the man's courage and fortitude in the face of total neglect are straight out of an inspirational novel. He had little or no formal training in his youth, though he somehow learned to play violin, cello, and organ. At twelve his schooling ended and he became a carpenter's apprentice; at fifteen he was the organist of a local church. Later he became a clerk with a lumber company and then was promoted to traveling salesman. He continued to educate himself, abetted by a certain Halford in Birmingham, who lent him orchestral scores to study. He also taught

himself to read French and German. His first performed compositions were part-songs, which won him some attention. Henry Wood premiered his orchestral *English Suite No. 1* which won him a job reviewing the Hallé Orchestra concerts for *The Musical Times* and an unknown patron who got him a contract with Breitkopf and Härtel. Up until 1910 Brian seemed to be on his way. He had encouragement from Elgar [1499] and performances by Beecham, Bantock [1600], Dan Godfrey, and other well-known or rising conductors. Then abruptly he was dropped. He moved to London in 1912 but was unable to find a means of supporting himself, let alone a congenial one. With the onset of war in 1914, he enlisted, though he was already thirty-eight. After a few months he was mustered out on medical grounds.

For the next several years he lived a precarious existence. In 1922 he became assistant editor for *Musical Opinion*, for which he wrote many articles and editorials. All the while he continued to compose, turning out big works like the 1918 comic opera *The Tigers*, the huge choral *Gothic Symphony* (and four other symphonies), and 2 violin concerti. All were ignored, the composer being tolerantly regarded as an eccentric with delusions of grandeur, and his impetus to write gradually fell off. The editorship dried up with the new world war and, having finished the enormous setting of Shelley's *Prometheus Unbound* in 1944, he laid down his pen. Then, when he was seventy-two, as he himself put it, "the muse returned with a rush." Since no one else was interested, he felt that he might as well end his days writing to please himself. In 1959 he moved to a coastal town in Sussex and there wrote for nine years more. In twenty-one years, 1947–68, he had produced twenty-seven additional symphonies (the last seven in his nineties), the Concerto for Cello, a *Concerto for Orchestra*, and operatic treatments of *Turandot, The Cenci, Faust,* and *Agamemnon,* to cite only his more imposing efforts. Toward the end of his long life (nearly ninety-seven years) there was a small groundswell of demand that his music be played, which resulted in the growth of interest, several books on Brian, and an increasing number of performances.

RECORDINGS: There have been commercial recordings of seven symphonies—nos. 6, 8, 9, 10, 16, 21, and 22—as well as of three of the 5 orchestral *English Suites,* a suite from *The Tigers,* a choral-orchestral setting of *Psalm 23, 2 Herrick Songs, Fantastic Variations,* and a number of smaller orchestral pieces—*Doctor Merryheart, In Memoriam,*

For Valour, Festal Dance, Burlesque Variations on an Original Theme. Some songs for voice and piano have also been recently recorded. In addition there have been pirate records of twenty-one symphonies—nos. 1–5, 8, 9, 13–15, 17–20, 22–26, and 28—and of one violin concerto. (The *Gothic Symphony* [No. 1] recording might be termed a "semipirate," since it was released with the permission of its conductor, the late Sir Adrian Boult.)

[1682] CARPENTER, John Alden
INDUSTRIALIST
BORN: Park Ridge, Ill., February 28, 1876
DIED: Chicago, April 26, 1951

John Alden Carpenter took his Christian names from his Pilgrim ancestor whom Priscilla Mullen chided for not speaking for himself. His father was president of George B. Carpenter and Co., a firm that specialized in supplies for the transportation industry. As a youth Carpenter studied with his mother, a singer, and later with Liszt [1218] pupil Amy Fay (best known for her charming memoirs) and Brahms [1329] pupil William Charles Ernest Seeboeck. In the course of his schooling at Harvard, Carpenter studied with Paine [1366]. On graduating in 1897 he entered the family business, much to Paine's distress. Carpenter did not, however, give up his music. He even managed some lessons in 1906 with his idol, Edward Elgar [1499], and later studied in Chicago with the German-born Bernhard Ziehn, an important theorist, from 1909 until the latter died in 1912. Although he was elevated to the vice presidency of his company in the former year, Carpenter soon began composing, turning out a violin sonata in 1911 and following it with songs, including the cycle *Gitanjali,* and piano pieces. His first orchestral effort, the amusing *Adventures in a Perambulator,* was successfully premiered by the Chicago Symphony under Frederick Stock in 1914. It was succeeded by the first version of the *Concertino for Piano and Orchestra* in 1915, the first version of the first symphony in 1917, and the 1918 ballet *Birthday of the Infanta.* The last-named work was produced by the Chicago Opera, both in Chicago and in New York a year later.

Up to 1920 most of Carpenter's works had been of the international-genteel-eclectic school. Now he felt impelled to make them more "American"—in theme, in inspiration, and even in music. After the orchestral *A Pilgrim Vision* and a piano piece entitled *Tango américain,* he wrote a dance score

based on George Herriman's popular comic strip *Krazy Kat,* which he designated as a "jazz-pantomime"—which meant that there was a saxophone, a "wa-wa" mute, and some syncopation. Nevertheless it was sufficiently different to win Carpenter a comission from Diaghilev for an "American" ballet. Carpenter answered with *Skyscrapers,* which featured overalled workers and flappers. In the end, Diaghilev did not use it, but it got a production by the Metropolitan Opera Company in 1926. Carpenter also did some orchestral pieces dedicated to Paul Whiteman and some songs to texts by the black poet Langston Hughes. After that his production slowed down, later highlights being a 1928 string quartet, the *Song of Faith* for the George Washington Bicentennial in 1932, the orchestral *Sea Drift* (after Whitman) in 1933, the piano quintet in 1934, and the violin concerto, written in 1936, the year he retired from business. Later he revised the *Concertino,* the first symphony, and *Sea Drift,* and wrote a second symphony in 1942, which in a review Virgil Thomson [1928] labeled "rich man's music." Carpenter continued to produce until a few years before his death, but his day was by then over. Before it was, he was awarded several honorary doctorates and other evidences of esteem. If his music is not very original or great (it speaks German with a French accent), it is not stuffy or self-conscious, and Carpenter must be regarded at the very least as a fine art-song composer.

RECORDINGS: There have been several recordings of *Adventures* and of the Tagore song cycle *Gitanjali,* and there is at least one apiece of *Skyscrapers, Krazy Kat, Sea Drift,* the *Concertino,* the Sonata for Violin and Piano, and the String Quartet, as well as a number of songs, including the 1918 cycle *Water Colors.* Carpenter himself conducted a recording of *Song of Faith* and accompanied the alto Mina Hager in *Water Colors.* A two-record set containing the complete solo piano music was just released by New World Records.

[1683] ALFANO, Franco (Ál-fä´-nō, Frän´-kō)
TEACHER, ADMINISTRATOR, PIANIST
BORN: Posillipo, March 8, 1876 *(Grove gives 1875, Hughes's Music Lovers' Encyclopedia 1877.)*
DIED: San Remo, October 27, 1954

A composer of considerable and diverse talent, Alfano appears doomed to be remembered only as the man whose completion of Puccini's [1511] unfinished *Turandot* Toscanini, in a fine fit of theatrics, refused to play at the premiere. Born near Naples, he studied in that city with Longo [1569] and at its conservatory with Paolo Serrao (1830–1907). Then, atypically for an Italian, he spent a year (1895–96) at the Leipzig Conservatory with Salomon Jadassohn (1831–1902) and Sitt [1452], an experience that left its mark on his music. He remained in Germany for several years, appearing as a pianist, and writing operas. There seems to be a difference of opinion as to whether his first opera *Miranda,* completed in 1896, was ever produced, but Breslau put on *La Fonte d'Enschir (The Fountain of Enschir)* in 1898. After that Alfano left Germany for Paris, which staged two ballets for him, and where he drank deeply of Debussy's [1547] music. Alfano's first operatic success, however, was the veristic *Risurrezione (Resurrection)* after Tolstoy, premiered in Turin in 1904. It remained popular in Italy for many years and was for a time in the repertoire of the Chicago Opera as another starring vehicle for Mary Garden (in French!).

After *Risurrezione,* Alfano returned to Italy, living first in Milan and then in San Remo on the Riviera. His next success was *L'Ombra di Don Giovanni (The Shade of Don Juan),* first performed at La Scala in 1914. In 1916 he became professor of composition at the Liceo in Bologna, whose directorship he took over two years later. It was at Bologna in 1921 that he produced his most individual and mature work, *La Leggenda di Sakuntala (The Legend of Sakuntala).* (When the orchestral score was destroyed in World War II, Alfano rewrote it.) In 1923 he became director of the Turin Conservatory, in which city the one-act *Madonna Imperia* was staged in 1927. (It was taken up—and dropped quickly—by the Metropolitan Opera in 1928.)

During the 1920s and 1930s Alfano returned to instrumental music and songs, which he had largely neglected since his early years, producing 3 symphonies (one of them a rewrite), 3 string quartets and other chamber works, and sets of songs to poems by Tagore, among other things. Of his last operas, *L'Ultimo Lord (The Last Lord)* made little impact, *Cyrano de Bergerac* was a surprising success at Rome in 1936 (with its French libretto translated), and *Il Dottor Antonio (Dr. Antonio)* a failure in 1949. During part of the World War II years Alfano was director of the Teatro Massimo in Palermo and taught at the Santa Cecilia Academy in Rome. After the war he was director of the Pesaro Liceo until he retired at seventy-five.

RECORDINGS: There are pre-LP recordings of the second symphony, piano pieces, and operatic excerpts and an LP piracy of *Cyrano.*

[1684] RUGGLES, Carl
VIOLINIST, CONDUCTOR, PAINTER, TEACHER
BORN: East Marion, Mass., March 11, 1876
DIED: Bennington, Vt., October 24, 1971

Ruggles and his friend Charles Ives [1659] are regarded as the patriarchs of modern American music. Both were sterling examples of American individualism, though Ruggles was a more active force and far less productive than Ives. Virgil Thomson [1928] described him in old age as "wiry, salty, disrespectful, and splendidly profane," likening him to Popeye the Sailor Man, whom he resembled facially.

Ruggles was baptized "Charles Sprague," but took to calling himself "Carl" out of an early admiration for German music—notably the songs of Robert Franz [1242]. Though he was born beside the ocean (Buzzard's Bay, at least), there seems no truth to the story that he came from a line of sea captains. As a child he made and played a cigar-box fiddle, graduated to a real one, and eventually had lessons. The family moved to Boston, and there he met a German musician named Josef Claus, who fanned his enthusiasms and taught him some theory. Later he had lessons (though he was not enrolled at Harvard) with John Knowles Paine [1366]. He worked as an engraver, played in theater orchestras, and contemplated a career as a shipbuilder. In 1906 he met and fell in love with a singer, Charlotte Snell. Together, in 1907, they went to Winona, Minnesota (on the Wisconsin border) to teach music. A year later they were married, and Carl became director of the Winona Orchestra, its personnel mostly German and mostly his pupils. One reads that the orchestra was dissolved when its members were interned in 1917 as enemy aliens, but in fact it broke up in 1912, when Ruggles became involved in writing an opera on Gerhardt Hauptmann's *Die versunkene Glocke* (like so much of his work, never finished and eventually destroyed). A son, Micah, was born in 1915. By 1917 Ruggles was back in New York teaching and composing. His first acknowledged composition, however, was a song, "Toys," written for Micah's fourth birthday and published a year later. He then began work on a symphony, whose three movements were to be called "Men," "Angels," and "Sun-Treader." It (as usually happened to

Ruggles's work) went through innumerable revisions, the first movement eventually being discarded and the third cannibalized. Meanwhile he wrote (and rewrote) three songs, of a projected seven, for voice and small orchestra. By then he had become a member of Edgard Varèse's [1774], International Composers' Guild, which premiered them in 1924 as *Vox clamans in deserto (Voice Crying in the Wilderness)*. The group had performed a version of *Angels*, for muted trumpets and bass trumpet, two years earlier. Meanwhile "Sun-Treader" had become "Men," the first movement of another symphony, where it was followed by "Lilacs," and "Marching Mountains," under the overall head of *Men and Mountains*. It was premiered at a ICG concert in December 1924 under the baton of Eugene Goossens [1878]—though Ruggles revised it later for a larger orchestra. He then embarked on still another symphony, to be titled *Portals*, wrote the first movement, revised it for string orchestra (Goossens performed it in 1926), and gave up on the rest. Henry Cowell [1934] published *Portals* and *Men and Mountains* in his New Music Editions, bringing the composer to the attention of Ives, who became his close friend around 1929. In the meantime Ruggles had promised Varèse a new piece, for which he reused the title *Sun-Treader*, but when he could not get it ready for the November 1926 concert, he left the ICG in chagrin.

In 1929, vacationing with Charlotte in Jamaica, Ruggles began painting, and, like his contemporary Schoenberg [1657], soon was having one-man shows. *Sun-Treader* had by 1932 reached a state at which Nicolas Slonimsky [1893] was able to conduct it in Paris. It was published in 1934, but Ruggles kept working at it for most of the rest of his life. (It was not performed in America for more than thirty years.) In 1935 he started composing piano pieces that he called *Evocations*, which by 1943 had reached the number of four. These were also subjected to many revisions and orchestrated. From 1937 to 1943 he taught at the University of Miami. The year after he left, he began another orchestral piece which (as *Organum)* he completed in 1947 (it was premiered in 1949) and also arranged it for two pianos. There followed a long silence, though he continued to paint, more and more abstractly. In 1957 Charlotte Ruggles died unexpectedly. Carl's last completed composition was a simple hymn tune, *Exaltation*, in her memory.

In his later years Ruggles lived in an old converted schoolhouse in Arlington, Vermont, the walls covered with musical sketches in many-colored crayon on big sheets of butcher's paper. Eventually in 1966 he, feeble and almost stone deaf, moved into a retirement home in Bennington. There, with earphones and electronic amplification, the conductor Michael Tilson Thomas let him at last hear *Sun-Treader* from a recording. Ruggles died at ninety-five. His music—what there is of it—is all his own. It is linear (melodically conceived), extremely chromatic, and, though often tonally based, unrelievedly dissonant. Though not a twelve-tonist or a serialist in the formal sense, his ideal was not to repeat a note until more than half of the others (nine was the norm, according to him) had intervened.

RECORDINGS: Apart from various individual recordings, Thomas has produced an album of "The Complete Music of Carl Ruggles," though it does not in fact include the few surviving (disowned) early works (it does include most variant versions of the mature works).

[1685] **LAPARRA, Raoul** (Là-pär'-rà, Rà-ōōl')
CIVIL SERVANT, CRITIC
BORN: Bordeaux, May 13, 1876
DIED: Suresnes, April 4, 1943

Laparra matriculated at the Paris Conservatoire at fourteen and studied with Fauré [1424] and Massenet [1396] among others. In 1903 he was awarded the Grand Prix de Rome. His first opera, *Peau d'âne (Ass's Skin)* was written while he was still a student. In 1908 he wrote his greatest success, *La Habanera*, which won critical praise and three performances at the Metropolitan Opera in 1924. Its Iberian coloration became Laparra's hallmark. His other operas and his incidental music had mostly Spanish themes, and he even wrote a *zarzuela* entitled *Las toreras (The Lady Bullfighters)* in 1929. He also had a measure of success with his last opera, *L'Illustre Fregona (The Famous Fregona)* of 1931. As inspector of musical education and critic for *Le Matin,* he was necessarily a part-time composer until his retirement in 1937. He also wrote orchestral music, piano pieces, and songs. He died in an air raid on a little town near Paris. RECORDINGS: There are old recordings of excerpts from *La Habanera* and *L'Illustre Fregona.*

[1686] **BØRRESEN, Aksel Ejnar Hakon** (Bör'-e-sen, Àk'-sel Ī'-när Hà'-kon)
ADMINISTRATOR
BORN: Copenhagen, June 2, 1876
DIED: Copenhagen, October 6, 1954

A pupil of Svendsen [1379], Hakon Børresen won the Ancker Scholarship in 1901 and used it for a year's study in Germany and France. He was an ardent promoter of modern music, the Danish variety in particular, and was president of the Danish Composers' League for twenty-five years. He was also made an honorary member of the Swedish Academy and of the Norwegian Composers' League. Among his compositions are 3 symphonies, a violin concerto, and 2 string quartets, all of which are well made, conservative, and heavily influenced by Svendsen. Børresen's first opera (of 2), *Den Kongelige Gaest (The Royal Guest)* of 1919, has remained in the Danish repertoire; the second, *Kaddara*, on a Greenland Eskimo theme, has not. However, the 1921 premiere of the work starred Lauritz Melchior, then recently turned tenor. RECORDINGS: Melchior left a recording of an excerpt from *Kaddara*.

[1687] ALPAERTS, Flor (Ål'-pärts, Flôr)
TEACHER, ADMINISTRATOR, CONDUCTOR, EDITOR
BORN: Antwerp, September 12, 1876
DIED: Antwerp, October 5, 1954

Flor Alpaerts graduated from the Royal Conservatory in Antwerp, where he was taught by its founder Peter Benoit (1834–1901), and Benoit's pupil Jan Blockx (1851–1912), considered the Grand Old Men of modern Flemish music. On the practical side Alpaerts learned to play the violin and to conduct, later winning an international reputation in the latter art. Beginning in 1903, he taught at the conservatory for thirty-one years, then directed it for seven more. He conducted the orchestra of Antwerp's Flemish Opera House from 1906 to 1912 and taught for several years at the state teachers' college. In 1919 he was named conductor of the Zoo Concerts. He retired from the conservatory in 1941 and from conducting ten years later. He brought out a complete edition of Benoit's music, and wrote the theory text that became the standard in Belgian schools. His son Jef (1904–73) was a successful conductor and keyboard player, specializing in early music. Among Flor Alpaerts' compositions are a single opera, *Shylock* from 1931, some incidental music, the Concerto for Violin, and symphonic poems. RECORDINGS: Louis Weemaels recorded Alpaerts's orchestral *James Ensor Suite*, based on paintings by that Belgian master.

[1688] FALLA Y MATHEU, Manuel Maria de (Fà'-yà ē Mà-tā'-ōō, Màn'-wel Mà-rē'-à dā)
CONDUCTOR, PIANIST, TEACHER
BORN: Cádiz, November 23, 1876
DIED: Alta Gracia (Argentina), November 14, 1946

It is generally agreed that with Manuel de Falla Spain's modern musical renascence reached its culmination. This is especially remarkable because he did not write a great deal of music, and much of what he wrote he disowned. His paternal ancestry was Valencian. His mother, a Catalan, was a good pianist and his first teacher; he first appeared with her in public when he was eleven, playing a piano-duet version of Haydn's [871] *Seven Last Words*—a Lenten tradition in Cádiz. He also had some lessons in theory from local teachers and became a habitué of the musical salons of a wealthy amateur named Viniegra. Eventually it occurred to him that he wanted to be a composer (he is said to have written an opera in 1887, though it has long since vanished). He entered the Madrid Conservatory in 1898, and before he left two years later, he had written and heard performed several instrumental pieces, including a piano quartet.

Hard-pressed economically (his father had gone bankrupt), Falla embarked on the obvious road that a Spanish composer looking for success would take then: he wrote *zarzuelas*. One, *Los amores de la Inés (The Loves of Inés)*, was staged in the spring of 1902 at the Teatro Comico. It showed no staying power, and the others were ignored —even though Falla had Vives [1622] as his collaborator on two of them. After that he went to Felipe Pedrell [1384], erstwhile teacher of Albéniz [1523] and Granados [1588], for further training. Pedrell's dream was to bring Spanish music to its former glory, and Falla took to heart his insistence on a composer's knowing Spain's musical past and folk music. In 1904, when the Academy of Fine Arts announced a competition for a "Spanish lyrical drama," Falla and his poet-friend Carlos Fernández Shaw worked up and submitted a one-act opera, *La Vida breve (The Brief Life)*, in a sort of Spanish *verismo* vein. It won in 1905, but the judges intimated that its form might stand in the way of its production. Falla promptly extended it to two acts, but he fell victim to theatrical politics and it remained unproduced. Meanwhile at the insistence of José Tragó, his piano teacher at the conservatory, he also competed as a pianist for the Ortiz y Cussó Prize and won it. This success enabled him—somewhat reluctantly—to open a piano studio. After several months of teaching, he went in the summer of 1907 to Paris for a week's vacation. He stayed seven years, Paris having always been his long-term goal.

Not having saved enough money for such a sojourn, he had to continue to take in pupils there. He found that he also had to rethink what being a composer meant, especially in the light of the new ideas and impulses he encountered. He came to know Albéniz, Debussy [1547], Dukas [1574], and Ravel [1666], rewrote much of his opera and at last got it produced at Nice in 1913. The premiere was sufficiently successful to win the work a showing at the Opéra-Comique eight months later. But the only other works from the Paris years were some of the four Albéniz-like *Pièces espagnoles (Spanish Pieces)* for piano, and three songs to texts by Théophile Gautier.

With the onset of the war in the summer of 1914, Falla returned to Spain, where *La Vida breve* enjoyed a great triumph in Madrid that November. There followed the most productive period in the composer's life. We must discount some incidental music for Shakespeare's *Othello* and for two plays by G. Martínez Sierra, since it no longer exists. The seven *Canciónes populares españolas*—making brilliant use of folk material—were completed in 1915. In April of that same year, Falla unveiled his pantomime-ballet *El Amor brujo (Love the Sorcerer)* at the Teatro Lara in Madrid. It had been inspired by the Gypsy dancer Pastora Imperio, the Gypsy stories her mother told him, and *cante jondo* ("flamenco")—which last, though not actually quoted, underlay the music. Much of the audience found the piece vulgar; but, tightened up and danced by La Argentina and Vicente Escudero, it was an overwhelming success in Paris a year later. Finally, 1915 also saw the completion of three "scenes" for piano and orchestra, begun in 1909, which became *Noches en los jardines de España (Nights in the Gardens of Spain)*. This became Falla's most popular work—though it is not his most typical, owing as it does something to French Impressionism. It was first performed in Madrid in April 1916 by the pianist José Cubiles under the baton of Enrique Fernández Arbós. (Falla himself was the pianist at the London premiere five years later.)

Meanwhile Falla had discovered and become fascinated with *El Sombrero de tres picos (The Three-Cornered Hat)*, Pedro de Alarçon's version of an old Spanish tale (which had also inspired Hugo Wolf's [1521] opera *Der Corregidor)*. In 1917 his treatment of it emerged as a pantomime-farce, *El Cor-*

regidor y la molinera (The Corregidor and the Miller's Wife) at the Teatro Eslava in Madrid. Serge Diaghilev saw it and urged Falla to turn it into a full-fledged ballet for his company. The composer complied, and *El Sombrero de tres picos* opened at the Alhambra Theatre at London in July 1919; the decor was by Pablo Picasso, the choreography by Leonid Massine, and the principal dancers were Tamara Karsavina and Massine himself. At about the same time Falla completed a comic opera *Fuego fatuo (Will-o'-the-wisp)*, the libretto by Martínez Sierra, the music derived from Chopin [1208], but it was never produced and part of it has since vanished.

Up to this point, Falla's "Spanish" music had to a considerable degree built on what Albéniz, Granados, and Pedrell had done. But with the 1919 *Fantasia bética* (Andalucia was "Baetica" to the Romans) for piano, the composer moved on to a new and highly individual approach, sometimes described as "ascetic" or "neo-classical," depending on the describer's attitude, in which, looking back to the era of the vihuelists, he strips "Spanishness" to its bare essentials. This style is also to be found in the puppet opera *El Retablo de Maese Pedro (Master Peter's Puppet Show)*, the libretto adapted by the composer from an episode in *Don Quixote*. It was first staged in June 1923 in Paris at the home of the Princesse de Polignac, the Singer sewing-machine heiress, who had commissioned it, though it had had a concert reading in Seville the previous March. (The first public stage performance was in Bristol, England, October 1924). The new phase probably culminated in the Spartan concerto for harpsichord and five instruments, commissioned by Wanda Landowska and first played by her in Barcelona in 1926, and in the 1927 setting of Góngora's *Soneto a Córdoba (Sonnet to Cordova)* for voice and harp.

In 1922 Falla settled in Granada, where he organized a *cante jondo* festival and founded the Orquesta Bética de Cámara, of which he made his pupil Ernesto Halffter [2060] conductor. (Other Falla pupils of note were Halffter's brother Rodolfo [1985] and Joaquín Nin-Culmell [2124].) His composition, however, fell off sharply after the early 1920s. There was some more incidental music for the theater, a couple of part-songs, and a piano arrangement of *The Song of the Volga Boatmen*, none of which he bothered to publish. In 1920 he had written a memorial piece to Debussy for solo guitar; there was also a similarly intended piano piece for Dukas in 1935, and a fanfare on the name of Arbós, but for the most part after 1928 the composer was occupied with a vast project for a sort of oratorio based on the poem *L'Atlántida* by the Catalan Jacint Verdaguer, which was to be, for want of a better term, a musical epic summing up the Spanish spirit as Falla understood it. But the Spanish Civil War and illness prevented him from doing much with it in the 1930s. In 1933–34 he sequestered himself in Majorca. In 1938 Generalissimo Franco named Falla president of the Spanish Institute, but the composer attended no meetings. During part of this period he occupied himself with realizations of old music, mostly Spanish, but again did not publish them. In 1939 he accepted an invitation to Argentina and spent the rest of his life there. That same year he orchestrated the Arbós, Debussy, and Dukas pieces, added one for Pedrell (Pedrelliana), and conducted them in Buenos Aires as *Homenajes (Homages).* This was his last completed work, though he continued to chip away at *Atlántida.* But in 1946 the death of his collaborator José Maria Sert seems to have dealt him a mortal blow, and he died shortly afterward. By Falla's own admission, only about forty percent of the intended composition existed in complete form. Ernesto Halffter, working from sometimes enigmatic sketches, completed it, and conducted it in 1962. A decade later he thoroughly revised it.

RECORDINGS: The second version of *Atlántida* was premiered in 1977 and recorded by Rafael Frühbeck de Burgos. All of Falla's published music has been many times recorded. Of special interest are the *Canciones populares,* the *Soneto,* and the *Amor brujo* solos sung by the soprano Maria Barrientos with Falla at the piano, *El Amor brujo* and *Noches* played by the Orquesta Bética under Ernesto Halffter, and the dances from *El Sombrero* conducted by Arbós.

[1689] KARLOWICZ, Mieczysław
(Kärlw-yō'-vich, Mye-chi'-slwäf)
CONDUCTOR, WRITER
BORN: Wiszniewe, December 11, 1876
DIED: near Zakopane, February 8, 1909

Mieczysław Karłowicz was the son of Jan Karłowicz, a vastly learned Polish nobleman, who wrote musical theory, played the cello, composed, and was a student of Polish folksong. The child was born in the family estate in northeastern Poland—then, as now, Russian territory. He began violin lessons when he was seven. The family moved to Warsaw four years later, where one of his teachers was Stanisław Barcewicz, a some-

time Tchaikovsky [1377] pupil and professor of violin at the conservatory. His composition teacher was Gustaw Roguski [1370]. Karłowicz left the conservatory in 1895 and went to the University of Berlin for a liberal arts degree but continued his musical studies on the side with Heinrich Urban. He returned to Warsaw in 1902 and was active for the next several years as an officer (ultimately director) of the Warsaw Musical Society, helping to foster the "Young Poland" movement represented by Szymanowski [1755] and his friends. For a time Karłowicz conducted the society's string orchestra and in 1906 studied conducting with Nikisch in Leipzig. The next year he settled in the Tatra Mountains, where he could indulge his enthusiasm for winter sports. There he was buried in an avalanche less than two years later. He was thirty-two. His music has been likened to Richard Strauss's [1563], but perhaps Mahler's [1525] comes somewhat closer. Karłowicz edited some previously unpublished Chopin [1208] letters, and wrote a number of articles about his beloved mountains. He composed some songs, but his major output—what there was of it—was orchestral. Besides a symphony, a violin concerto, a *Serenade* for strings, and a *Lithuanian Rhapsody,* there is a handful of symphonic poems: *Returning Waves, Eternal Songs, The Sorrowful Tale,* and *Stanislas and Ann of Auschwitz.* His unfinished *Episode at a Masquerade* was completed by Grzegorz Fitelberg (1879–1953), a member of "Young Poland." RECORDINGS: Most of Karłowicz's music has been recorded by the Polish state recording organization, Muza.

[1690] CASALS, Pau (or Pablo) (Ka-zàls', Pä'-ōō)
CELLIST, PIANIST, CONDUCTOR
BORN: Vendrell, December 29, 1876
DIED: San Juan, P.R., October 22, 1973

Composing was a minor aspect of Casals' many musical talents. Regarded by many as the greatest cellist within memory, he came to the instrument rather late. He learned the keyboards from his father, a sometime organist, studied the violin "seriously," and is said to have successfully tackled several other instruments. He fell in love with the cello when he was eleven and became a pupil of José Garcia. At fourteen he embarked (in Barcelona) on a concert career that would last nearly eighty years. In 1893 he was taken under the wing of the Count de Morphy, a high court official, and was granted a royal scholarship enabling him to study with Tomás Bretón (1850–1923) at the Madrid Conservatory and in 1895 to go to the Brussels Conservatory. That arrangement, however, fell through, and after a short time in Paris Casals returned to Barcelona, where he was first cellist in the opera orchestra.

He announced his musical coming of age in 1899 with performances of Lalo's [1286] concerto in Paris and London, and he quickly established himself as an international drawing card. In 1905 he began a long artistic association with pianist Alfred Cortot and violinist Jacques Thibaud, with whom he later made some much-admired recordings. (Earlier he had appeared *en trio* with Granados [1588] and the violinist Crickboom.) In 1914 he married an American singer, Susan Metcalfe, and performed in concerts as her (piano) accompanist. (An earlier liaison with Guilhermina Suggia, one of his pupils and an important cellist in her own right, was unofficial, though she was billed as "Mme. Casals.") Casals became famous for his performances of the Bach [684] solo cello suites; he first played one in concert in 1909. In 1919 he helped found the École Normale de Musique in Paris, with Cortot as director; until World War II it was a serious rival of the Paris Conservatoire. He also founded at about the same time the Casals Orchestra in Barcelona, which he directed.

Fiercely democratic, Casals made it clear that he had no use for Generalissimo Franco and left Spain in 1936 with a price on his head. He settled in Prades across the border in France—largely Catalan in population— and refused offers of asylum, which came from nations that recognized the Franco government. When World War II did not topple the dictator, Casals announced that he would play no more until Spain should be freed. However, in 1950 his musical colleagues persuaded him to celebrate the two hundredth anniversary of Bach's death with a festival in Prades. This then became an annual affair, moving later to Perpignan, and then to Puerto Rico when Casals settled there in 1956. There, when he was eighty, he married Marta Montañez, another of his pupils. During his later years—he died at ninety-six—he was connected with Rudolf Serkin's summer music school at Marlboro, Vermont, where he gave master classes and conducted the orchestra. Casals' music was unashamedly old-fashioned and lyrical. Early on he wrote a cello concerto, a symphonic poem, and a string quartet, but most of his compositions date from after 1930.

RECORDINGS: Many of his compositions are *sardanas* (the Catalan national dance) and other small instrumental pieces (some of which he recorded), but there is a good deal of liturgical music (recordings by the choir of Montserrat Monastery) and a Christmas oratorio *El Pesebre (The Manger)*, recorded under the composer's direction. The soprano Olga Iglesias has recorded a number of songs.

[1691] DUNHILL, Thomas Frederick
TEACHER, CONDUCTOR, WRITER
BORN: London, February 1, 1877
DIED: Scunthorpe, Lincolnshire, March 13, 1946

Dunhill showed enormous promise as a student at the Royal College of Music, which he entered at sixteen. He studied piano with Franklin Taylor and composition with Stanford [1467] and after his graduation taught there and (concurrently) at Eton. In 1907 he founded a London series of chamber music concerts dedicated to presenting unknown and forgotten British works, including some of his own. He also wrote a symphony and other orchestral works, 2 ballets, and a one-act opera, *The Enchanted Garden*, in 1928. His most successful effort was a 1931 operetta, *Tantivy Towers* to an A. P. Herbert libretto. It had a long run and Dunhill was hailed as a new Sullivan [1397], though detractors said the best thing in the work was the old hunting song "John Peel." He followed this with a second operetta in 1933, *Happy Families*, for which Rose Fyleman wrote the libretto, but no more were forthcoming. Dunhill published studies of chamber music, Sullivan, Mozart [992], and Elgar [1499]. RECORDINGS: About all of his music that has lived on are two songs, "The Cloths of Heaven" and "To the Queen of Heaven," of which there are recordings.

[1692] NOWOWIEJSKI, Feliks (Nō-vō-vyē'-y'skē, Fe'-lēks)
ORGANIST, TEACHER, CONDUCTOR
BORN: Wartenburg, February 7, 1877
DIED: Poznán, January 23, 1946

Nowowiejski's Prussian birthplace is now the Polish town of Barczewo. He attended Stern's Conservatory, the Royal Academy, and the University, all in Berlin, and the School of Church Music in Regensburg. His most important teachers were Max Bruch [1358] in Berlin and Antonín Dvořák [1386] in Prague. In 1902 he was awarded the Meyerbeer Scholarship for his oratorio *The Prodigal Son's Return*, and the next year he won the Paderewski Prize. He lived in Berlin (when not traveling) until 1909, then returned to Poland to conduct in Cracow and

Warsaw. That same year another oratorio, *Quo vadis?*—based on Henryk Sienkiewicz's then-popular historical novel (see also Nouguès **[1669]**)—was successfully premiered in Amsterdam and enjoyed a brief vogue worldwide. After World War I he was appointed professor of organ and church music at the Poznań Conservatory. He gave the post up in 1926 but was active in church music in Poznań for the rest of his life. His Polish contemporaries thought of him as a Wagnerian **[1230]**, but he was really a late Romantic with a nationalistic flavor. He wrote 5 symphonies, a piano concerto, a violin concerto, a string quartet, 2 ballets, keyboard pieces, and songs, but was noted for his choral music and his second opera, *Baltic Legend*. RECORDINGS: There are some recorded excerpts from *Baltic Legend* and a few organ pieces.

[1693] AUBERT, Louis François Marie (Ō-bâr', Lōō-ē' Frȧn-swȧ' Mȧ-rē')
KEYBOARDIST, TEACHER
BORN: Paramé, February 19, 1877
DIED: Paris, January 9, 1968

Louis Aubert seems to have been unrelated to the eighteenth-century family of musicians that included a namesake known as "Aubert *le jeune.*" He began his musical life as a soprano soloist in Paris churches (La Madeleine, Ste. Trinité). Admitted to the Paris Conservatoire at the age of ten, he studied composition with Gabriel Fauré and took most of the prizes the school had to offer—but not the Prix de Rome. He originally planned to be a concert pianist (he studied with Louis Diémer), but when his compositions (especially his songs) began to win critical praise, he abandoned the idea. In 1904 he began writing an opera, *La Forêt bleue (The Blue Forest,* based on fairytales by Charles Perrault). It occupied him almost totally until 1910. It was premiered in Geneva in January 1913 and was produced by the Boston Opera Company (three performances) with a rather second-string cast under André Caplet **[1708]** a few weeks later. The Paris performance was delayed for a decade by the outbreak of war in 1914. Rejected for service, Aubert did his bit, *gratis,* as organist and choirmaster at St. Hippolyte. After completing his opera, the composer went through a period of infatuation with musical Iberianisms, which in 1919 culminated with his orchestral *Habanera,* his most popular and enduring larger work. Never very prolific, he seems to have written little or nothing in the last fifteen of his more than ninety years. RECORDINGS: For records, he con-

ducted his orchestral *Dryade* and selections, after Chopin **[1208]**, from his ballet *La Nuit ensorcelée (The Enchanted Night).* Charles Munch recorded the whole ballet. There is also a recording of the orchestral suite *Feuille d'images (Picture Page),* several of *Habanera,* and a number of various songs.

[1694] BORTKIEVICH, Sergei Eduardovich (Bôrt-kē-yä'-vich, Sâr'-gā Yed-wär-dō'-vich)
PIANIST, TEACHER
BORN: Kharkov, February 28, 1877
DIED: Vienna, October 25, 1952

Bortkievich went to St. Petersburg at nineteen to study law but continued his piano training at the St. Petersburg Conservatory, where he also studied with Liadov **[1485]**. Deciding to become a concert performer, he went to the Leipzig Conservatory for two years (1900–2), then settled in Berlin, where he taught briefly at the Klindworth-Scharwenka Conservatory and from which he made frequent concert tours, increasingly as an apostle for his own music. When war erupted in 1914 he went home to join the Imperial Army. Finding himself *non grata* after the October Revolution, he fled to Constantinople in 1919, then settled permanently in Vienna three years later, becoming (as "Bortkiewicz") an Austrian citizen. In 1938 he published an account of the relationship between Tchaikovsky **[1377]** and Nadezhda von Meck—almost concurrently with Katherine Drinker Bowen's popular treatment "Beloved Friend." Bortkievich extends the Russian Romantic tradition in his music, which includes an opera *Acrobats,* 2 symphonies, 4 piano concerti, a concerto apiece for violin and cello, and other works. RECORDINGS: Marjorie Mitchell has recorded his first piano concerto; Ulla Graf has recorded a two-record set of piano pieces, including the first sonata, *Lamentations et Consolations,* and others.

[1695] BLANCHET, Émile-Robert (Blȧn-shä', Ā-mēl' Rō-bâr')
PIANIST, TEACHER, ALPINIST
BORN: Lausanne, July 17, 1877
DIED: Pully, March 27, 1943

Blanchet was the son and pupil of Charles Blanchet, cathedral organist in Lausanne. Later he studied with Busoni **[1577]** and at the Cologne Conservatory, and eventually made a reputation both as a concert pianist and a mountain climber. In 1904 he became professor of piano at the Lausanne Conser-

vatory and a year later, director of the institution. He gave that post up after three years
but remained on the faculty until 1917, then
retired to concertize and scale peaks. The
bulk of his music consists of piano pieces
and songs. He also published two books on
his hobby. RECORDINGS: A few of his piano
pieces and songs have been recorded.

[1696] DOHNÁNYI, Ernö (Dōkh-nàn'-yē,
Är-nö)
PIANIST, TEACHER, CONDUCTOR, AD-
MINISTRATOR
BORN: Pozsony, July 27, 1877
DIED: New York, February 9, 1960

From having been denigrated politically by
the Communists and artistically by the
Western avant-garde, Dohnányi seems at
last to be recovering his reputation—though
even in the worst times a handful of his
works insisted on remaining popular. He
was born in that polyglot city that has also
been known as Pressburg and Bratislava.
His father, an amateur cellist, taught mathematics in the local *Gymnasium* and introduced the fundamentals of music to his son.
At eight Ernö (who later called himself
Ernst von Dohnányi) took up keyboard
studies with the cathedral organist, Karl
Forstner, and a year later made his first public appearance as pianist in the Mozart [992]
G-minor quartet. By the time he was twelve,
he had written a good deal of music, including two cello sonatas and two string quartets. Having completed his *Gymnasium*
studies, he set out for Budapest to take a
liberal arts degree at Budapest University,
but in 1894 he enrolled at the Royal Hungarian Academy. There he pursued his piano studies with István Thomán (who also
taught Bartók [1734]) and took a course in
composition with Hans Koessler, a pupil of
Rheinberger [1368] and a fervent admirer of
Brahms [1329]. It was Brahms himself who,
struck by Dohnányi's Op. 1 piano quintet
(written when its composer was eighteen),
opened doors for him in Vienna. Dohnányi
spent part of the summer of 1897, immediately following his graduation and his receipt of a royal award for his Symphony in
D Minor, being polished by Eugen d'Albert
[1562] for his concert debut, which took
place that fall. He was immediately acclaimed as a master pianist in Germany and
Austria. A year later his performance of the
Beethoven [1063] fourth concerto in London
(with Hans Richter) created such a furor
that he wound up giving thirty-two concerts
in Great Britain before he could proceed. In
1900 he made his first American tour, travel-

ing for part of it with the Boston Symphony
and featuring his new first concerto, which
he dedicated to d'Albert and which won him
the Bösendorfer Prize.

In 1905 Dohnányi settled in Berlin to
teach at the Hochschule für Musik, gaining
his professorship in 1908. Throughout this
period he continued to concertize and to
compose. He produced such admired works
as the orchestral *Suite in F-sharp Minor*, the
marvelous concerted *Variations on a Nursery
Tune* ("Baa-Baa, Black Sheep" or "Twinkle,
Twinkle Little Star"), the second string
quartet, the piano quintet, etc. After the outbreak of World War I, he returned to Budapest, where he resumed his teaching at the
Budapest Academy and kept music alive in
the darkest days of the conflict with innumerable recitals (all carefully planned to acquaint the public with good music). Early in
1919 the Soviet-backed Béla Kun government elevated him to the directorship of the
academy, but by the end of the year he had
been dismissed when Kun was overthrown
by Admiral Horthy. Nevertheless, Dohnányi remained chief conductor of the Budapest Philharmonic Orchestra. However, he
continued to tour as soloist and increasingly
as guest conductor. (In 1923 he did demonstration performances in America for the
Ampico recording piano, in which he and a
piano roll alternated during performances of
his first concerto.)

In 1928 Dohnányi was invited back to the
Budapest Academy to teach, becoming its
head again six years later. One of his students from this period, who admired him
both as musician and teacher, noted that
probably the most valuable thing Dohnányi
taught his pupils was how to pack a dress
suit. Along with his other posts, the composer was also musical director of the Hungarian Radio Network from 1931. Overwork
and poor health prevented him from doing
much composing during this period of his
life—its major products were a Mass and a
string sextet. The years of World War II are
somewhat puzzling. The left regards him as
a fascist because he stayed on after the Nazi
takeover; the right regards him as a pinko
because he resigned his academy posts
rather than yield to anti-Jewish rules and
protected the Jewish members of his orchestra until he was forced to disband it. The
fact seems to be that, like so many artists, he
was apolitical and put his art before his allegiances. At any rate it was a chastening experience. In the end, after having lost his
two sons to the fighting, he fled to Vienna
ahead of the Russians, in 1944. In England
for a time after the war, he emigrated to Argentina in 1948, and settled in 1949 in Talla-

hassee as a member of the faculty of Florida State University. He also did some teaching at Ohio University, which awarded him an honorary doctorate. He remained vigorous and active to the end of his nearly eighty-three years; his Florida pupils report that to the last he could quote at will from the Beethoven sonatas. In his final years he resumed his long-interrupted recording career. During a session in New York in the midwinter of 1960, he suffered a coronary. Hospitalized, he succumbed to influenza a few days later. His grandson Christoph (b. 1929) has become an internationally celebrated conductor.

An unashamed Romantic composer, Dohnányi was not an epigone of Brahms as is sometimes claimed, for he had more wit, spontaneity, and melodic inspiration. His stage works (3 operas and a mime play) and vocal music have so far withstood revival), but the orchestral and chamber music seems hardy. RECORDINGS: The composer recorded two versions of the *Variations* (there are also numerous recordings by others), his second concerto, and a number of his piano pieces (as well as Beethoven sonatas and other works). The first concerto has been recorded by his pupil Balint Vázsonyi. There are also various recordings of the orchestral *Suite*, the *Symphonic Minutes,* the *Ruralia Hungarica* (in its several forms), and most of the chamber music.

[1697] MARSICK, Armand (Mär-sik', Är-mán')

VIOLINIST, CONDUCTOR, TEACHER
BORN: Liège, September 20, 1877
DIED: Haine-St.-Paul, April 30, 1959

Armand Marsick was born of a prominent musical family. After studies in Liège with Sylvain Dupuis (1856–1941) and Théodore Radoux (1835–1911), and in Nancy with Guy Ropartz [1564], he became concertmaster of the Paris Concerts Colonne. Later appointments as conductor and teacher took him to Athens and Bilbao. In 1927 he returned to Belgium, where he taught and established the Société des Concerts Populaires. Representative works, cast in a conservative post-romantic idiom, include the 1912 orchestral *Tableaux grecs;* the 1920 opera *L'Anneau nuptial;* the 1937 radio drama *Le Visage de la Wallonie;* and the 1950 Quartet in F for Horns, drawing on Greek modal and American folk sources. RECORDINGS: The Caraël Quartet performs the horn quartet.

[1698] TCHESNOKOV, Pavel Grigorievich (Ches'-nō-kof, Pà-vel' Grē-gō-rē-ā'-vich)

CHOIRMASTER, TEACHER
BORN: near Voskresensk, October 24, 1877
DIED: Moscow, March 14, 1944

Born in the countryside fifty miles southeast of Moscow, Tchesnokov was sent to the Synodal School in that city when he was eight. On his graduation ten years later, he was retained to teach the choir. He went on to study with Ippolitov-Ivanov [1517] and Taneyev [1492]. In 1913 he began studies with Vassilenko [1628] at the Moscow Conservatory. Two years later he added to his duties the leadership of the Russian Choral Society. The 1917 Revolution brought an end to his studies and the Choral Society but not immediately to the Synodal School, where he remained until it was closed in 1920. He then became professor of choral singing at the Moscow Conservatory, a post he retained until his death. Later he also became chorus master at the Bolshoi Theater. RECORDINGS: Tchesnokov wrote (expectably) a great deal of practical choral and church music, some of which has been recorded.

[1699] QUILTER, Roger

BORN: Brighton, November 1, 1877
DIED: London, September 21, 1953

The son of Sir Cuthbert Quilter and heir to a handsome income, Roger Quilter was educated at Eton and then became a pupil of Iwan Knorr (1853–1916) at the Frankfurt am Main Conservatory. He was there concurrently with Cyril Scott [1720], Percy Grainger [1749], Balfour Gardiner, and Norman O'Neill—an aggregation that became known as the "Frankfurt Group." A lifelong bachelor, shy and often in poor health, Quilter then lived quietly in the St. John's Wood section of London. For all his reserve and preciosity, his friends knew him as a wit and even a practical joker. From the turn of the century he was famous as the composer of tasteful songs several cuts above the run of the usual drawing-room stuff. He also wrote some delicate orchestral, chamber, and piano pieces, the comic opera *Julia* (produced at Covent Garden in 1935), a couple of ballet scores, and a popular musical for children, *Where the Rainbow Ends* (in whose 1911 premiere, Noël Coward, age eleven, made his stage debut). In the 1930s he accompanied the baritone Mark Raphael in a number of his songs for Columbia Records, and they have been accorded generous phonographic treatment by other singers right down to the present. Quilter, as conductor, also waxed a selection from *Rainbow*. RECORDINGS: There have been several recordings of his popular *Children's Overture* and *Old English Dances*. In his last years, Quilter lapsed into premature senility.

[1700] KARG-ELERT, Sigfrid (Kärg El'-ert, Zēg'-frēt)
PIANIST, ORGANIST, TEACHER
BORN: Obendorf am Neckar, November 21, 1877
DIED: Leipzig, April 9, 1933

If ever anyone backed into musical acclaim, it was Sigfrid Karg, as he was born. His father, a publisher, died when Sigfrid was five, after establishing his family in Leipzig. The boy got enough musical education as a chorister in the Johanneskirche to enable him to begin composing works for his fellows to sing but was then packed off to a teacher-training school to learn a useful profession. He kept up with his music, however, and at nineteen, won a scholarship to the Leipzig Conservatory. On graduating, he embarked on a career as a concert pianist, but an encounter with Grieg [1410] reawakened his compositional itch, and he returned to the conservatory to satisfy it. Having completed his course, he went in 1902 to teach at Magdeburg. But he found that the job did not agree with him and came back to Leipzig to compose in earnest. His Berlin publisher was, around this time, plugging an improved reed organ called the *Kunstharmonium*, the creation of one Johannes Titz. Titz talked Karg into providing music for it. The experience led him from the harmonium to the organ, and eventually to renown as one of the great organists and organ writers of the time. (It was allegedly on the advice of his agent that he became "Karg-Elert," adding his mother's maiden name to his patronymic —which, interpreted, means "stingy.") During World War I he was connected with a military band, which led to an interest in and composition for such musical organizations. In 1919 he succeeded the deceased Max Reger [1637] at the Leipzig Conservatory. He continued to tour, despite declining health, making an extensive journey around the United States the year before he died. He composed voluminously, writing in virtually all forms but the operatic. As a keyboard composer, he trod, like Reger, in the footsteps of Bach [684]. RECORDINGS: There are quite a few organ and harmonium recordings of his music.

[1701] GOLDMAN, Edwin Franko
CORNETIST, BANDMASTER, TEACHER
BORN: Louisville, Ky., January 1, 1878
DIED: New York, February 21, 1956

There is an old saw that military music is to music what military justice is to justice. One of those who alleviated the musical situation was Edwin Franko Goldman. He came to New York at the age of eight and studied with Dvořák. In 1899 he became solo cornet at the Metropolitan Opera, where his uncle, Nahan Franko, was concertmaster and, from 1905, a conductor (the first American native to hold such a post there). Goldman left the orchestra in 1909 and, after teaching for a short time, put together his first band in 1911. In 1918 the Goldman Band Concerts became a New York institution that lasted for more than sixty years. (The band survives today as the Goldman Memorial Band, having been known for a couple of years as the Guggenheim Band.) Among American composers of marches, Goldman's success and popularity was second only to Sousa's [1482]. But he insisted on viewing the band as a serious musical organization, unearthing older music written for wind orchestras and commissioning new pieces from important composers. Goldman founded the American Bandmasters' Association, of which he was first president, and wrote two books on the organization and training of bands, plus a cornet manual. He held two honorary doctorates and other honors. He was succeeded by his son Richard Franko Goldman (1910–80), an important musician in his own right. RECORDINGS: Both Goldmans recorded with the band, and there are many other records of Goldman marches.

[1702] BOUGHTON, Rutland (Bou'-ton, Root'-lånd)
CRITIC, TEACHER, CONDUCTOR
BORN: Aylesbury, January 23, 1878
DIED: London, January 25, 1960

Along with composers who became established and famous, the English musical renaissance of the twentieth century inevitably produced a fringe of interesting and independent composers who remain, for most of us, shadowy. Havergal Brian [1681] is a case in point. Rutland Boughton is another, and it comes as something of a shock to find him described in a recent article as "the most important and significant native-born composer since Henry Purcell" [581].

Boughton began life inauspiciously as the son of a small-time Buckinghamshire grocer. His love of music came from his hymn-singing mother, and he himself was a treble in the village choir. His education at the local grammar school ended when he was fourteen and he became a London apprentice to a firm that promoted brass-band concerts. Discovering that the boy had musical talent and aspirations, his employer found him a teacher and even paid to have one of his songs published. By 1898 he had written a good deal of music, and some of his admirers got up a purse to send him to the Royal College of Music. He spent three years there under the tutelage of Stanford [1467] and Walford Davies [1609]. In 1901 he struck out on his own to make a living as a musician in London. At first he literally starved; then he got a job as a reviewer for the *Daily Mail,* and later he became a conductor at the Haymarket Theatre and an accompanist. In 1903 he was doing sufficiently well to marry, and two years later Granville Bantock [1600] took him into the faculty of his Midlands Institute School of Music.

While at the RCM Boughton had read some socialist literature and had gradually become a dedicated socialist. He also fancied himself a Wagnerian [1230]. Now the two currents ran together with a vision of a "people's opera" that would bring musical and spiritual enlightenment to the masses. (He had already composed two operas that went unperformed.) Since Wagner had focused on a national epic, so would he: the Arthurian legend. He found a collaborator in another young socialist, Reginald Buckley, and set to work on *The Birth of Arthur,* which he completed in 1909. Meanwhile his marriage had gone sour, and in 1910 he took up with Christina Walshe, an artist who saw eye to eye with his views. The liaison and his subsequent divorce forced him to give up his teaching job. (He married Miss Walshe in 1911.)

Nothing daunted, the Boughtons went ahead with plans to establish their Bayreuth at Glastonbury, the reputed site of Arthur's grave. They sent out a call for subscriptions, but few or none were forthcoming; nevertheless they got a lot of help and enthusiasm from up-and-coming performers and from the townspeople. But things took a time to develop, and in the interim Boughton wrote, to a libretto by "Fiona MacLeod" (William Sharp), a non-Arthurian Irish fairytale opera, *The Immortal Hour.* When, on August 5, 1914, the first Glastonbury Festival opened in the town hall, with a piano in lieu of an orchestra, this was the work presented. By now Wagnerian inflation had given way to a reliance on folklike melody, and the work, which was several times repeated, won critical and audience approval.

Boughton was briefly in uniform at the outset of the 1914 war but was back in Glastonbury for the 1915 festival and managed to keep the venture afloat through the summer of 1926. He produced other works besides his own, chiefly by early English composers. In 1915 he did a setting of the nativity play from the Coventry Mystery Cycle, which he called *Bethlehem.* In 1916 the second Arthurian opera, *The Round Table,* was produced (the first was shelved until 1920). Two non-Arthurian works followed—*Alkestis* in 1922 and *The Queen of Cornwall* (based on the Tristan legend) in 1926. Meanwhile a London producer had overcome Boughton's reservations about selling out to capitalistic interests and staged *The Immortal Hour* at the Regent Theatre in October 1922. To everyone's amazement it sustained a run of 376 performances, was taken up elsewhere, and is said during this period to have been played more than 1,000 times throughout England. Covent Garden produced *Alkestis* in 1924.

However, despite so auspicious a success, Boughton was busy digging his own grave. An affair with a pupil, Kathleen Davies, and another divorce (he married Miss Davies in 1923) added fuel to the fire ignited by his communist stance in the public press. As noted, Glastonbury could no longer be maintained, and the Boughtons bought a farm in Gloucestershire. Here Rutland tilled the soil, composed, wrote critical articles, and turned out a book on Bach [684] and another called *The Reality of Music.* He attempted to revive the festival with the third Arthurian opera, *The Lily Maid,* in Stroud in 1934, and the following year with *The Ever Young* (a non-Arthurian work) in Bath, but that was the end of it. The last two works in the Arthurian cycle—*Galahad* of 1944 and *Avalon* of 1945—went unperformed. Boughton's incessant political preachments continued to win him enemies, and he was soon penniless. Bernard Shaw and others went to bat for him and got him a small pension in 1937. He lived another twenty-three years, a militant communist to the last, and died in his sleep two nights after his eighty-second birthday. Besides operas he wrote much other music—symphonies, concerti, choral works, chamber music, and songs, and music for a film version of *Lorna Doone.*

RECORDINGS: For records he conducted a piece from *The Immortal Hour,* of which work commercial records offer a complete version and excerpts, as well as carols from *Bethlehem.* A pirated album also presents the opera complete, plus scenes from *Bethle-*

hem, *Alkestis, The Queen of Cornwall,* and *The Lily Maid.*

[1703] PALMGREN, Selim (Pålm'-gren, Sel'-im)
PIANIST, CONDUCTOR, TEACHER
BORN: Björneborg, February 16, 1878
DIED: Helsinki, December 13, 1951

Palmgren's Finnish birthplace was not named for a future tennis star; a west coast port city, it is now called Pori. Like his older contemporary Armas Järnefelt **[1608]**, Palmgren studied at the Helsingfors Conservatory with Martin Wegelius, and later with Ferruccio Busoni **[1577]**, in Italy. He also studied piano in Germany with Liszt **[1218]** pupil Konrad Ansorge. After three years of such study abroad, he returned to Finland to conduct choruses in the capital and later (1909–12) in Åbo (now Turkku). In 1910 he produced his first opera, *Daniel Hjort,* in Åbo (his second and last was *Peter Schlemihl)* and married the singer Maikki Järnefelt, the divorced wife of the composer. They often toured as a team, Palmgren furnishing the accompaniments. In 1920–21 he made an extensive tour of North America as piano soloist and in 1923 was invited back to the new Eastman School of Music to teach composition. After three years he left to resume his career. Maikki Palmgren died in 1929, and a year later he married Minna Talwik, another singer. In 1936 he accepted the position of professor of harmony and composition at the Helsinki Conservatory, which he retained until his death. A year prior to that melancholy event, he was given an honorary doctorate by Helsinki University. Palmgren wrote a good deal in large forms—the operas, ballets, cantatas, 5 piano concertos—but he was happiest as a miniaturist, especially in his piano writing. In an earlier day many piano pieces, songs, part-songs, and violin works were committed to records. RECORDINGS: Palmgren himself left a couple of records (including one of "May Night," his most popular composition), and his first wife recorded a few songs and folksong arrangements. Pianist Izumi Tateno has recorded the Concerto No. 2 for Piano with Jorma Panula conducting.

[1704] DUPONT, Gabriel Édouard Xavier (Dü-pon', Gä-brē-el' Ä-dwär' G'sà-vyä)
BORN: Caen, March 1, 1878
DIED: Vésinet, August 2, 1914

Dupont's first teacher was his father, organist at the late-Gothic church of St. Pierre in Caen. He then studied privately with André Gedalge (1856–1926) before entering the Paris Conservatoire, where he was a pupil of Massenet **[1396]** and Widor **[1414]**. He was defeated by André Caplet **[1708]** in the 1901 Prix de Rome competition, but three years later his first opera, *La Cabréra,* won the Sonzogno Prize, which included a premiere at the Teatro Lirico in Milan. He continued to attract most attention with his operas— *La Glu (The Birdlime)* in Nice in 1910 and *La Farce du cuvier (The Washtub Farce)* at Brussels in 1912. His best and most ambitious work, the four-act *Antar,* was completed in 1913, but the outbreak of war postponed its Paris premiere until 1921. By the time Dupont had succumbed to lung cancer at the age of thirty-six. During his illness he composed for the piano a sort of diary of his sufferings, *Les Heures dolentes (The Painful Hours),* part of which he managed to orchestrate. He also wrote a string quartet and some orchestral pieces. RECORDINGS: Only a few songs seem to have been recorded.

[1705] SCHREKER, Franz (Shrek'-er, Frânts)
CONDUCTOR, TEACHER
BORN: Monaco, March 23, 1878
DIED: Berlin, March 21, 1934

In the first two decades of this century, Franz Schreker was regarded as an operatic composer slated to take his place among the immortals. But political events and musical "progress" left him at the post, and he has never really been rehabilitated since. Perhaps the only reason he is not celebrated as Monaco's greatest composer is that his father, a Jew, had Austrian citizenship and was working in Monaco as court photographer at the time his son was born. He died ten years later, and Frau Schreker, who came from a noble family fallen on hard times, took her four children back to Vienna to rear them as best she could, which, under the circumstances, was not very well. In 1892, however, a scholarship took Franz to the Vienna Conservatory, where he studied with Robert Fuchs and the violinist Arnold Rosé. By the time he left in 1900, several of his compositions had been performed publicly. In 1902 he gave a concert reading, piano accompanied, of his first opera, *Flammen.* Six years later he had a considerable success with his ballet, *Der Geburtstag der Infantin (The Birthday of the Infanta,* after Oscar Wilde). In the same year he founded the Philharmonic Choir, which he con-

ducted until 1920. (It gave the premiere of
Schoenberg's [1657] *Gurrelieder.*) Soon he
was in love with one of his singers, a young
soprano named Maria Binder, and he married her in November 1909 on her seventeenth birthday.

In 1910 Schreker completed his second opera, *Der ferne Klang (The Distant Peal),* on
which he had been working sporadically for
almost a decade. (He wrote the libretto, as
he did for all his mature operas.) When it
was performed in August 1912, with Maria in
the leading female role, at Frankfurt am
Main, it won an ovation. Schreker was
forthwith appointed professor of composition at the Vienna Academy and was commissioned to write an opera for the Hofoper.
When *Das Spielwerk und die Prinzessin (The
Peal and the Princess)* was unveiled there in
March of the following year, it was a disaster, and the composer remained without
honor in his own city, at least as an operatic
composer. He was, however, very successful
as a teacher and numbered among his Vienna students Alois Hába [1879], Paul Pisk
(1893–), Felix Salmhofer [1974], and the
conductor Josef Rosenstock. He also had the
approval of the Schoenberg circle and a
champion in the critic Paul Bekker.

During the war years Schreker produced
a *Kammersymphonie* but little else. However, in 1918 and 1920 he had two more enormous successes (both in Frankfurt) with *Die
Gezeichneten (The Branded)* and *Der Schatzgräber (The Treasure Digger).* In the latter
year he was invited to Berlin as director of
the Hochschule. His next effort *Irrelohe
(Wandering Flame)* was staged at Cologne in
1924. Both it and *Der singende Teufel (The
Singing Devil),* premiered at Berlin in 1928,
caused controversy, especially in right-wing
quarters. Schreker's Jewishness and his use
of sexual pathology in his libretti made him
a prime target for the rising Nazis. Under
threat, he withdrew *Christophorus,* completed in 1927 but not accepted for performance until 1931 (it was not performed until
very recently). A year later the bully-boys
played havoc with the Berlin premiere of
Der Schmied von Gent (The Smith of Ghent).
He was asked to resign from the Hochschule
für Musik. The Prussian Academy hired
him to teach a master class, but with the
Hitler triumph of 1933, he was kicked out.
That Christmas he suffered a stroke and
died later that winter, two days short of his
fifty-sixth birthday. Maria had retired from
the stage in 1929.

RECORDINGS: In the late 1920s she recorded under her husband's direction scenes
from *Der ferne Klang, Die Gezeichneten,* and
Der Schatzgräber, in all of which she had

created leading roles. There are several LP
recordings of the *Kammersimfonie* and one
apiece of a suite from *Der Geburtstag der
Infantin* and the 1913 *Vorspiel zu einem
Drama (Prelude to a Drama).* There are
also pirate versions of the operas *Die
Gezeichneten* and *Der ferne Klang,* and there
are plans to release *Das Spielwerk, Der
Schatzgräber,* and even *Christophorus.*

[1706] HOLBROOKE, Joseph
PIANIST, CONDUCTOR
BORN: Croyden, July 5, 1878
DIED: London, August 5, 1958

Earlier in this century almost any sizable account of contemporary English music could
be expected to discuss Holbrooke; now he
seems almost wholly forgotten. He learned
the rudiments of music from his father and
appeared as a pianist in a London music hall
when he was only twelve. Later he attended
the Royal Academy, where his composition
teacher was Frederick Corder, a doctrinaire
Wagnerian, and where he won a prestigious
scholarship. He was already composing
(e.g., a string quartet) before he graduated in
1898. He then took occasional conducting
jobs, and concertized as a pianist, devoting a
series to the music of his English contemporaries, though, like his hero Wagner [1230],
he seems to have preferred to live on patronage. Sir August Manns took an interest in
him and in 1900 played the first performance
of his symphonic poem *The Raven.* (Poe was
another of his heroes: he also wrote a choral
symphony entitled *Homage to E. A. Poe,* the
choral-orchestral work *The Bells,* the symphonic poems *Ulalume* and *The Masque of
the Red Death,* the clarinet quintet *Ligeia,*
etc.) Like Boughton [1702], Holbrooke had
socialist leanings and talked of writing "people's music," but his only work that attained
real popularity was a set of orchestral variations on *Three Blind Mice,* also from 1900.
He occasionally attempted to produce another such winner, as with his variations on
"Auld Lang Syne" and "The Girl I Left Behind Me." In 1907 the Irish poet Herbert
Trench (who became manager of the
Haymarket Theatre the next year) commissioned Holbrooke to do a musical treatment
of his poem "Apollo and the Seaman." The
result was a huge symphonic piece whose
first performance also failed to come off for
want of a contrabass sarrusophone. (Like
Brian [1681], Holbrooke was a passionate
advocate of the big Straussian orchestra.)
Beecham conducted, and the poem was projected, via lantern slides, on a screen so that

the audience could follow the work's progress.

Shortly afterward Holbrooke (who had taken to Germanizing his first name as "Josef") was approached by another poet, the future Lord Howard de Walden, who was willing to pay him well to turn into an operatic trilogy the three libretti he had derived from the Welsh *Mabinogian*. Their success marked the apex of Holbrooke's fame. Beecham conducted the premiere of *The Children of Don* in 1912, Nikisch that of *Dylan* (at the Drury Lane Theatre) two years later, and some European performances followed. The third work, *Bronwen*, was not completed until 1922 and had to wait until 1929 to be sung in Huddersfield, Yorkshire. By that time he was passé and gradually lapsed into silence, hampered in part by growing deafness and disillusionment. He died a month after his eightieth birthday.

During his first fifty years Holbrooke wrote prodigiously and uncritically and perhaps won too much exposure and notoriety. Long before he passed on, the reaction had set in, and he was contemptuously dismissed or simply ignored by younger writers. Whether he is salvageable remains to be seen.

RECORDINGS: There were early recordings of the Concerto No. 1 for Piano (subtitled "The Song of Gwynn ap Nudd"), the "Ligeia" quintet, and the "Blind Mice" variations, as well as many small pieces and snippets of larger ones, including some from the *Mabinogian* operas. Holbrooke himself recorded a few piano pieces and a movement of the "Byron" piano quartet. Recently there have been new recordings of the Quartet in G Minor for Piano and Strings, the Quintet in G Major for Clarinet and Strings, the orchestral *Birds of Rhiannon*, the Concerto No. 1 for Piano, the Opp. 71 and 72 *Suites for String Quartet*, and *Songs of the Bottle* for baritone and piano.

[1707] PEDRELL, Carlos (Pä*th*-rel', Kär'-lōs)
EDUCATOR
BORN: Minas, Uruguay, October 16, 1878
DIED: Montrouge, March 9, 1941

Carlos Pedrell was the son of Felipe Pedrell's **[1384]** brother who had emigrated to Uruguay. Carlos went to Spain to study with his uncle and finished up at the Schola Cantorum in Paris with d'Indy **[1462]**. In 1906 he settled in Argentina and worked variously as a professor at the University of

Tucumán and as a public school inspector in Buenos Aires. In 1921, however, he returned to Paris for good. He wrote a handful of operas, ballets, and other works in various categories. RECORDINGS: Some of his guitar pieces have been recorded.

[1708] CAPLET, André (Kå-plä', Àn-drä')
VIOLINIST, TIMPANIST, CONDUCTOR
BORN: Le Havre, November 23, 1878
DIED: Neuilly-sur-Seine, April 22, 1925

Caplet began studying music in Le Havre in childhood and by adolescence was playing violin in local theater orchestras. He was admitted to the Paris Conservatoire at eighteen, studied there with Paul Vidal **[1554]** and Xavier Leroux **[1557]**, among others, and was soon winning notice with such compositions as a quintet for piano and winds, and the *Suite persane* (also for winds). He played timpani at the Concerts Colonne, took on conducting jobs, and was appointed chief conductor at the Odéon in 1899. Two years later he won the Prix de Rome, which eventually took him to Germany, where his career was furthered by Artur Nikisch and Felix Mottl. Shortly after his return to France he became a protégé and friend of Debussy **[1547]**, who in his last illness turned over to him the orchestration of the music for *Le Martyre de Saint Sébastien (The Martyrdom of St. Sebastian)*, which was premiered under Caplet's baton. Caplet also orchestrated *La Boîte à joujoux (The Toy Box)* and some of Debussy's songs and piano pieces. From 1910 to 1914 he conducted the French performances of the short-lived Boston Opera Company. When the war broke out in 1914, he volunteered and served as an infantry sergeant. Wounded and gassed, he was mustered out and spent the rest of his life in frail health, which necessitated his giving up conducting. However, he continued to write music. He died at forty-six of pneumonia. At first strongly influenced by Debussy, Caplet at last managed to develop a style of his own, characterized by references for plainchant and interesting instrumental effects. The bulk of his music is vocal—many fine songs and some notable pieces for women's choir, especially the *Mass* with oboe, cello, and harp. RECORDINGS: The *Mass* has been recorded at least twice. There are also recordings of the *Conte fantastique (Fantastic Tale*, based on Poe's story "The Masque of the Red Death") for harp and strings, the choral *Trois prières (Three Prayers)* the 1923 *Epiphanie* for cello and orchestra, and shorter works.

[1709] DANIELS, Mabel Wheeler

CONDUCTOR, TEACHER
BORN: Swampscott, Mass., November 27, 1878
DIED: Boston, March 10, 1971

Nearly as long-lived as her Boston contemporary Margaret Ruthven Lang [1593], Miss Daniels was also born into a musical family, her father having served a term as president of the Handel and Haydn Society. A 1900 Radcliffe graduate, she studied with Chadwick [1483], then made the requisite trip to Germany to be blessed by Ludwig Thuille [1537] in Munich. She returned to Radcliffe in 1911 to direct the Choral Society for two years, then became head of the music department at Simmons College until 1918. She continued to compose until late in her life and was given honorary degrees by Boston University and Tufts College. She wrote a few operettas, but the bulk of her work was choral. RECORDINGS: There are recordings of an orchestral piece, *Deep Forest,* and of *Observations* for woodwind trio.

[1710] PEDROLLO, Arrigo (Pā-drol'-lō, Är-rē'-gō)

CONDUCTOR, EDUCATOR
BORN: Montebello Vicentino, December 5, 1878
DIED: Vicenza, December 23, 1964

Pedrollo was born near Vicenza, a city on which much of his life was focused. He first studied with his father, the village organist and bandmaster; then, at thirteen, he went to the Milan Conservatory, where his teachers included Gaetano Coronaro, a minor operatic composer from Vicenza. He graduated in 1900 with a performance of his only symphony by Toscanini. Pedrollo, who was of the Wagnerian [1230] persuasion, preferred to write operas. His first one, *Terra promessa (Promised Land),* was produced at Cremona in 1908, and his second, *Juana,* won the Sonzogno Prize in 1914. (Amintore Galli, another of his teachers, was an editor for Sonzogno.) Between 1920 and 1936 Pedrollo had six other operas performed. In 1922 he was appointed head of the Vicenza Conservatory. He interrupted his stay there to teach composition at the Milan Conservatory from 1930 to 1941. He retired at eighty-one and died five years later. Pedrollo also composed some other orchestral works, chamber music, choruses, and songs. RECORDINGS: Pierre Pierlot has recorded his Concertino for Oboe and Strings.

[1711] TRUNK, Richard (Troonk, Rē'-khärt)

PIANIST, CONDUCTOR, CRITIC
BORN: Tauberbischofsheim, February 10, 1879
DIED: Herrsching am Ammersee, June 2, 1968

Richard Trunk, Baden-born, studied in Frankfurt am Main with Iwan Knorr (1853–1916) and then in Munich with Josef Rheinberger [1368]. He was accompanist for a number of performers, including the great *Lieder* singer Eugen Gura, taught singing at the Theresien Gymnasium, and in 1907 became critic for the *Münchner Post.* In 1912 he was chosen to conduct the Arion Society in New York and Newark, but when war broke out two years later, he went home. He became critic for the *Bayrische Staatszeitung* and in 1919 director of a Munich choral society. From 1925 to 1934 he taught and conducted in schools in Cologne, then returned to Munich as president of the Akademie der Tonkunst. At the end of World War II he retired to the Ammersee, a lake west of Munich, where he lived to be nearly ninety. Though he wrote a few instrumental works and in 1916 an operetta *(Herzdame),* Trunk concentrated chiefly on choruses and *Lieder.* RECORDINGS: A number of his songs were recorded.

[1712] DONAUDY, Stefano (Dō-nou'-dē, Stef'-à-nō)

BORN: Palermo, February 21, 1879
DIED: Naples, May 30, 1925

The product of an international marriage—his father was French, his mother Sicilian—Donaudy studied with the director of the Palermo Conservatory, Guglielmo Zuelli, a pupil of Luigi Mancinelli (1848–1921). His first opera, *Folchetto,* was produced in Palermo when he was only thirteen. Five others followed. He also wrote orchestral and piano music, but is chiefly remembered for a series of "arias in the ancient style." RECORDINGS: These arias have long been popular with recording singers.

[1713] BRIDGE, Frank

VIOLIST, CONDUCTOR
BORN: Brighton, February 26, 1879
DIED: Eastbourne, January 10, 1941

In my nonage I saw Frank Bridge presented with the Elizabeth Sprague Coolidge Medal at a Library of Congress concert. I recognized his name from a recording, by Vladimir Rosing, of a song, "Isobel," not far removed from the drawing-room ballad style. His thorny fourth string quartet was played that evening. A quarter of a century passed before I heard a note of his music again. The discrepancy between the two pieces had more than a little to do with the subsequent neglect he suffered. If the present tendency of repentant English critics to elevate him to the stature of a Berg [1789] or a Bartók [1734] is perhaps excessive, there is no question that over his forty creative years the man underwent an amazing development.

Frank Bridge seems to have been unrelated to the earlier composer Sir John Frederick Bridge (1844–1924). He went to the Royal College of Music as a violin student and won a scholarship in 1899 permitting him (inevitably!) to study composition with Stanford [1467]. On graduating he joined the Grimson String Quartet, but after being called on to substitute for the ailing violist of the Joachim Quartet in 1906, he took up the viola and played it in the English String Quartet until 1915. He also soon gained note as a conductor, and when Thomas Beecham organized his New Symphony Orchestra in 1906, he chose Bridge as his assistant. In 1910 Bridge became conductor of Marie Brema's opera company at the Savoy and later worked in the same capacity for Raymond Roze and Beecham at Covent Garden. A friendship with Sir Henry Wood saw Bridge occasionally substituting for him at Queen's Hall and saw Wood promoting Bridge's orchestral music. In 1923 Bridge made a guest-conducting tour of major American cities, during which he presented some of his own pieces. But, a shy and retiring man, he did not really care for the limelight and never accepted a regular conducting post.

As noted, Bridge's early music (some of which he afterward disowned) was nothing special—and therefore was popular. (A song, "Love Went A-Riding," was a longtime favorite as a rip-roaring recital closer.) He also wrote orchestral and choral music from the outset, but his first important development came in his chamber music around 1905, with a string quartet, a piano quartet, and a piano trio, all designated as "Phantasies," indicating an attempt to deal in modern terms with that seventeenth-century English form. In his orchestral music he was initially influenced by the Impressionists and probably by Delius [1539]. The real change came after World War I. Bridge was not in service, but the conflict left on him, as a devout pacifist, profound psychic scars. Beginning with the piano sonata, completed in 1924, his music grew more abstract, darker, and more daringly experimental. He

virtually abandoned vocal music after that time, though his only opera, *The Christmas Rose*, was completed in 1929 after ten years of work. In some of his late music he is dealing with a chromaticism that is almost twelve-tonal, though he was not a practitioner of the Schoenberg [1657] dogma.

It was in 1924 that Bridge met eleven-year-old Benjamin Britten [2215] and took him on as a private pupil. He treated the boy like a son but trained him uncompromisingly, and Britten retained a lifelong affection and admiration for him—evidenced in the orchestral *Variations on a Theme of Frank Bridge* as well as in a recording of Bridge's cello sonata with Mstislav Rostropovich. But those who had loved the early work dismissed the latter efforts (as one critic put it) as deliberate uglification for the sake of keeping up, whereas the "avant-snobs" were unable to get past Bridge's initial conservatism.

RECORDINGS: No doubt thanks in part to Britten's advocacy, Bridge is now being rediscovered, a fact reflected in a small but steady flood of records. These include such ambitious orchestral works as *The Sea, Enter Spring, Oration* (with cello), *Phantasm* (with piano); the slighter *Lament, Summer, 2 Poems, Rebus,* and *There Is a Willow Grows Aslant a Brook;* more popularly directed works such as *Sir Roger de Coverly, Sally in Our Alley,* and *Cherry Ripe;* the early symphonic works *Isabella, Dance Poem,* and *Dance Rhapsody;* the choral-orchestral *A Prayer;* at least two LPs of piano music (including the sonata); the 4 string quartets as well as the *Noveletten,* the *Idylls,* and other short pieces for the medium; the 1925 *Tagore Songs;* the early *Phantasie Trio* and the *Phantasie Quartet;* the Piano Quintet; the String Sextet; miscellaneous chamber pieces; solo piano music; and songs. With the recent release of the opera *The Christmas Rose,* most of Bridge's major works have been recorded. Bridge himself conducted *The Sea* in an acoustical recording and a couple of smaller pieces, and recorded the *Phantasie Quartet* as a member of the English String Quartet.

[1714] WETZEL, Justus Hermann (Vet'-zel, Yōōs'-toos Här'-màn)
MUSICOLOGIST, TEACHER
BORN: Kyritz, March 11, 1879
DIED: Überlingen, December 6, 1973

Wetzel's birthplace was a village between Berlin and Wittenberg. He acquired degrees in art history, philosophy, and science before turning to music as a profession. For two years, 1905–7, he taught at the Riemann Conservatory in Stettin (now Szczecin, Poland). In 1910 he opened a studio in Berlin. In 1926 he accepted a teaching post at the Berlin Academy for Church and School Music, and was promoted to the rank of professor in 1935. From the end of World War II to 1948, he also taught at the Hochschule. He published a theory text and a study of song form, edited many collections of *Lieder,* and wrote several hundred songs of his own. RECORDINGS: A few of his songs may be found on records.

[1715] CLARKE, Robert Coningsby
ORGANIST
BORN: Old Charlton, Kent, March 17, 1879
DIED: Walmer, Kent, January 2, 1934

Clarke was a pupil of Sir John Frederick Bridge and later served as organist at Oxford. He was known as a composer of salon piano pieces and drawing-room songs, the most popular of which was the inspirational "The Blind Ploughman" (text by Margaret Radclyffe-Hall), recorded by the likes of John Charles Thomas and Feodor Chaliapin.

[1716] WIKLUND, Adolf (Vĕk'-lund, Å'-dôlf)
PIANIST, CONDUCTOR
BORN: Långserud, June 5, 1879
DIED: Stockholm, April 3, 1950

Wiklund attended the Stockholm Conservatory, where he studied piano with Richard Andersson, a Clara Schumann [1267] pupil, and composition with Johan Lindegren (1842–1908), who also taught Alfvén [1630]. Wiklund won two successive scholarships that provided him with study in Paris and Berlin (1903–7). After conducting at Karlsruhe for a season and serving as rehearsal pianist at the Court Opera in Berlin for another, he returned to Stockholm. He conducted at the Royal Swedish Opera beginning in 1911 and later led the orchestra of the Stockholm Concert Society. (Sources are hopelessly confused as to the dates; he seems to have left the Royal Swedish Opera in the mid-1920s and to have been succeeded at the other orchestra by Vaclav Talich around 1933). He also made appearances elsewhere in Europe as a conductor and was often soloist in his 2 piano concerti, which are his best works. Wiklund was a thoroughgoing late Romantic who made few concessions to modernism. RECORDINGS: There are record-

ings of both concerti, *Summer Night and Sunrise* for orchestra, the *Three Pieces for Harp and Strings,* piano pieces, songs, and other small-form works.

[1717] GAUBERT, Philippe (Gō-bâr', Fē-lēp')
FLUTIST, CONDUCTOR, TEACHER
BORN: Cahors, July 4, 1879
DIED: Paris, July 10, 1971

One of the finest flutists of his day, Gaubert was a pupil of Taffanel [1421] at the Paris Conservatoire and a first-prize winner for flute in 1894. His composition teacher was Xavier Leroux [1557]. After graduating he filled solo engagements, and played in various Paris orchestras. In 1919 he returned to the Conservatoire as professor of flute and conductor of the orchestra. He also conducted at the Paris Opéra from 1920. He gave up his conductorship at the school in 1938, the year in which he was added to the *Légion d'honneur.* His compositions include 2 operas, 3 ballets, an oratorio, the Concerto for Violin, and other ambitious works, but he is remembered chiefly for his flute music. RECORDINGS: Some of his flute music appears in recorded flute recitals. Gaubert himself appeared on early records, chiefly as obbligatist to Nelly Melba and on electrics as a conductor.

[1718] RESPIGHI, Ottorino (Res-pē'-gē, Ot-tō-rē'-nō)
VIOLIST, TEACHER, ADMINISTRATOR
BORN: Bologna, July 9, 1879
DIED: Rome, April 18, 1936

It is a fact that Respighi was the last Italian composer to win a firm place in the international orchestral repertoire. But there lingers a lot of argument as to whether the works in question have any redeeming musical content or are merely flashy examples of cinematic scoring.

The child of Giuseppe and Erminie Respighi, Ottorino entered the Bologna Liceo at the age of twelve. There he studied viola with Federico Sarti and composition with Giuseppe Martucci (1845–1909). It was at the Liceo too that the musicologist Luigi Torchi developed in him a fascination with early music that colored much of his later work. However, Respighi originally contemplated a performing career and, after graduating in 1899, found a place as first viola at the Russian Imperial Opera in St. Petersburg. During his two seasons there, he studied with Rimsky-Korsakov [1416], whose approach to orchestration also made a lasting impression on him. He then returned to Bologna and for the next few years played wherever the engagements turned up. For a time he was a member of the piano quintet founded by Bruno Mugellini. In 1905 his opera *Il Re Enzo (King Enzo)* was given a student production at the Liceo. (His piano concerto had been heard there three years previously, and he had attained publication —some violin pieces—in 1904.) Respighi's name first resounded internationally, however, when his orchestral *Notturno* was premiered by Rodolfo Ferrari during a 1905 Metropolitan Opera concert in New York. In 1908 the composer went to Berlin for a season; he was bored by Max Bruch's [1358] lectures but bowled over at hearing Strauss's [1563] *Salome*. His immediate reaction was to write a Straussian opera himself. *Semirama* duly stunned the Bolognese in 1910, mostly with its pretentiousness, and dropped out of sight. Respighi's next operatic effort, *Marie Victoire,* completed in 1914, never got a nibble.

Up to then, most of his large-scale music, including a very Straussian *Sinfonia drammatica* of 1915, was highly derivative, though he had already established himself well enough to be called to the Liceo di Santa Cecilia in Rome as professor of composition in 1913. Three years later he found his own voice (eclectic though it was) in the first and best of the three "Roman" suites, *I Fontane di Roma (The Fountains of Rome)*—picture painting to be sure, but undeniably effective picture painting. In 1917 his antiquarianism bore fruit with the first of the orchestrations of *Antiche arie e danze (Ancient Airs and Dances)* whose charm is anything but dependent on accurate scholarship. At forty he married a singer, Elsa Olivieri-Sangiacomo, fifteen years his junior. (A practicing composer, she completed his last opera and wrote a biography of him.) In 1921 Respighi finished his *Concerto gregoriano* for violin and orchestra. The next year saw the premiere of *La Bella dormente nel bosco,* a work with an odd history. Completed in 1909, it was conceived and first presented as a puppet opera, with the singers in the pit. A dozen years later it appeared in Turin as a mime play for children. Finally, in 1966, Respighi's pupil Gianluca Tocchi (1901–   ) revised it as a regular opera. The puppet version was particularly successful and had performances outside of Italy. The fantastic and comic *Belfagor,* produced at La Scala in 1923, was, however, the work that raised the world's expectations of Respighi as the new hope of Italian opera. For a time they

seemed to be realized in *La Campana sommersa (The Sunken Bell,* based on a fairy tale by Gerhart Hauptmann), triumphantly premiered in Hamburg in November 1927 and staged at the Metropolitan Opera a year later with a cast that included Elisabeth Rethberg, Giovanni Martinelli, and Giuseppe de Luca. But it did not survive, and the operas that followed—the one-act "mystery" *Maria Egiziaca (Mary in Egypt)* in 1932 and *La Fiamma (The Flame)* in 1934— were, as one says, no big deal.

In the meantime Respighi had enjoyed further orchestral success with the splashy *I Pini di Roma (The Pines of Rome)* of 1924, with its concluding Mussolinian vision of (noisy) regained imperial glories; the rumbustious *Feste romane (Roman Festivals),* 1928; and to a lesser degree with the more delicate *Trittico botticelliano (Botticellian Triptych)* of 1927 and *Impressioni brasiliane (Brazilian Impressions)* from 1928, the latter written for a tour of Brazil. *Vetrate di chiesa (Church Windows)* of 1925 was mostly orchestrated from some 1919 piano pieces. Much of Respighi's success in fact derived from his transcriptions of other men's work—the ballet *La Boutique fantasque (The Fantastic Toyshop)* and the *Rossiniana* after little pieces by Rossini [1143], *Gli uccelli (The Birds)* after old harpsichord music, and the two later sets of *Antiche arie.* His "free transcription" of Monteverdi's *Orfeo,* 1935, is guaranteed to raise the hackles of every modern scholar.

In 1924 Respighi had been made director of the conservatory, but he preferred merely to teach and resumed his old post two years later. By the time La Scala staged the *Orfeo,* he was already suffering from cancer, to which he succumbed a year later, leaving the opera *Lucrezia* unfinished.

RECORDINGS: With the exception of some of the operas, the *Notturno,* and the symphony, most of the works mentioned previously are plentifully represented on record. Other recordings include the cantata *Didone* and *Lauda per la natività del Signore; Concerto in modo misolidio* for piano and orchestra; *Adagio con variazioni* for cello and orchestra; the *Suite in G Major* for organ and strings; the orchestral *Poema autumnale;* the Sonata for Violin and Piano; the "Doric" String Quartet; the String Quartet in D Major; *Il Tramonto (The Sunset,* after Shelley) for soprano and strings; songs; organ preludes; and piano pieces. Of the operas there are pirated versions of *Belfagor* and *La Campana sommersa,* and commercial recordings of *Lucrezia* and *Maria Egiziaca.*

[1719] IRELAND, John Nicholson
ORGANIST, CHOIRMASTER, TEACHER
BORN: Bowdon, August 13, 1879
DIED: Washington (West Sussex), June 12, 1962

In reply to a presumptuous question, John Ireland is reported to have replied that he did not consider himself a great composer but thought he might be a significant one. Current opinion (especially in England) agrees that he was probably right, though the precise nature of his significance remains elusive. He left little music conceived on a large scale—a piano concerto, a cantata, incidental scores for a film and a radio play, overtures and suites for orchestra and band. The rest of his output consists of practical church music, some fine chamber compositions, some beautifully crafted songs, and the largest body of piano music by any English composer of stature. Nothing he wrote is "English," in the sense that much of Vaughan Williams' [1633] music is—nor is it Irish! None of it is especially "modern," though Ireland admired the Impressionists and, later, Stravinsky [1748]. Rather it is the work of a man who speaks—usually quietly —as he sees fit and evades pigeonholing.

John Ireland was born on the family estate in Cheshire. Both of his parents were writers, his father, Alexander, being editor of the Manchester *Examiner*, Scottish by birth, and a friend of many important literary figures of the day. (There is a lovely story that the visiting Ralph Waldo Emerson found his topper filled with daisies by young John, but since Emerson was last in England seven years before John was born, there appears to be some inaccuracy.) Ireland's childhood is said to have been an unhappy one. In any case he was orphaned shortly after he entered the Royal College of Music in 1893 to study piano with Frederic Cliffe, perhaps best known in his day as an organist. Ireland was thus a contemporary of Holst [1658] and Vaughan Williams at the RCM, though he did not come under Stanford's [1467] tutelage until 1897. Economic necessity forced him to support himself as an organist, and for a time he served as assistant to Walter Alcock (later Sir Walter) at Holy Trinity Church, Sloane Street. When Alcock moved on, Ireland was refused the succession on the grounds that he was too young. However, in 1904 he found a post as organist and choirmaster at St. Luke's Church, Chelsea, in which district he lived until 1939. In 1905 he received his B.Mus. from Durham University, which, twenty-seven years later, conferred an honorary doctorate on him.

Early in the Chelsea years, Ireland picked up a book by the fantasist Arthur Machen in Charing Cross Station and found in that author's mysticism and reference to nameless and forgotten rituals precisely the keynote for his music. Many of his later works allude to Machen stories or are dedicated to Machen. Until 1923 Ireland lived quietly, pretty much out of the public eye. In that year he was summoned back to the RCM to teach composition, which duty made him give up St. Luke's in 1926. During holidays he found refuge in the West Sussex village where he eventually died two months short of his eighty-third birthday, or in the Channel Islands, especially at Le Fauvic in Jersey. At the college he numbered among his pupils Richard Arnell [2270], Benjamin Britten [2215], Alan Bush [1987], E. J. Moeran [1903], and Humphrey Searle [2239]. He retired in 1939 and settled on the island of Guernsey but was forced out by the 1940 German invasion.

Like Frank Bridge [1713], John Ireland underwent a slow musical maturing. Initially he worshipped Brahms [1329]. After Stanford had dismissed his early efforts as "Brahms-and-water," he destroyed most of them, though late in life he resurrected the 1898 Sextet for Clarinet, Horn, and Strings. In 1906 his *Phantasy Trio* (see Bridge, 1713) won second prize in one of the competitions sponsored by the philanthropist and chamber-music addict W. W. Cobbett, and his first violin sonata (of 2) won the top award three years later. Both sonatas attained popular status in England, and his piano music sold well, fulfilling his hope that he would be able to write good music that would reach the average music lover. (St. Luke's installed a memorial window to its former organist.)

RECORDINGS: Ireland himself recorded the first violin sonata with Frederick Grinke, the cello sonata with Antonio Sala, and some piano pieces. Lyrita Records in England recorded, monaurally, all the solo piano music with Ireland's pupil Alan Rowlands, and has embarked on a stereo version with Eric Parkin. The company has also recorded (in stereo) much of the orchestral and incidental music, the cantata *These Things Shall Be,* and a three-disc survey of the songs performed by Benjamin Luxon. Other recordings duplicate some of this material, add several additional orchestral works, and cover most of the chamber works.

[1720] SCOTT, Cyril Meir
PIANIST

BORN: Oxton, September 27, 1879
DIED: Eastbourne, December 31, 1970

It was once conventional to mention Cyril Scott in the same breath with Debussy [1547] and Scriabin [1625] as a leader of the moderns in music. But his insistence on mingling salon potboilers with his more serious efforts—and perhaps the fact that he appeared a rather silly person—relegated him to a not wholly deserved obscurity long before he had lived out his ninety-one years.

Scott was the sickly youngest of the three children born to a pair of middle-aged residents of a Cheshire village. The father, a cultured businessman, was a fine Greek scholar, and the mother, an amateur pianist, had once published a waltz of her own composition. Cyril showed musical proclivities from an early age, and his governess, in the course of taking him to Liverpool to hear Paderewski [1527], discovered that Cyril had perfect pitch. After he had had some piano lessons, his father, still dubious, sent him (his mother in tow) to the Hoch Conservatory in Frankfurt at the age of twelve. There his chief teachers were a Neapolitan pianist named Uzielli and the composer Engelbert Humperdinck [1480]. Scott was brought home after eighteen months and put to study with a Herr Welsing, who turned up drunk for lessons or not at all. In 1895 Scott returned to Frankfurt, where he studied with Ivan Knorr (1853–1916) and became friends with a coterie of young compatriots —Percy Grainger [1749], Balfour Gardiner (1877–1950), and Roger Quilter [1699]. Together they came to be known as "the Frankfurt Group." He also initiated a lifelong friendship with the German poet Stefan George, many of whose verses he later translated.

After three years Scott, now a rather precious young snob sporting unfashionably long hair, came home for good. After effecting his official concert debut in Liverpool, he settled down there to make his living as a pianist and teacher. The pickings were slim: he had two pupils and played Bach [684] once a week for a patron. In 1900 he completed a symphony; it got a mixed reception at its German premiere, and he later disowned it, as he did an orchestral *Heroic Suite*. A piano quartet won him the tag of "Lost Soul" from Stanford [1467] but created something of a stir when Fritz Kreisler [1664] agreed to be the violinist in its first London performance. A second symphony —which Scott later turned into *Three Orchestral Dances*—got an airing by Sir Henry Wood. Along with such ambitious works, however, there were already the aforementioned potboilers—songs to Ernest Dowson (and Cyril Scott) texts and a series of piano pieces blatantly labeled *Frivolous Pieces*. Grainger, as pianist, popularized some of the early music, though it was probably Kreisler's violin transcription of *Lotus Land* that made its composer best known in the worst way.

Scott, a self-proclaimed agnostic and freethinker, began dabbling at around this time in fashionable mysticisms—Eastern philosophies, Christian Science, spiritualism, Vedanta, and especially Theosophy. According to him, freethinking also entered his composition, as evidenced by his rejection of such conventions as key signatures and meter, though his emancipation is perhaps more apparent to the eye than to the ear. Nevertheless, up to World War I at least, his star continued to ascend. He knew everyone in the artistic world who was anyone. He turned out several big choral works and a one-act opera, *The Alchemist*. The premiere of his first piano concerto, which he played under Beecham's direction, won favorable notices. Exempted from military service on medical grounds, he was eventually called up for desk duty, from which he was excused by the personal intervention of Lloyd George, who declared him something like a national treasure.

In the early 1920s Scott made a successful concert tour of the United States and returned to find his housekeeper dead (a suicide) in his apartment. This shock perhaps increased his obsession with spiritualism. He came to depend on the advice of an otherworldly contact identified as Mahatma Koot Hoomi, or "Master K.H." for short. In 1921 K.H. told him that he should marry Rose Allatini, a novelist who wrote as "Eunice Buckley." He did, and she bore him a daughter and a son. Though he continued to compose virtually to the end of his life— later years brought three more operas, several ballets, a third symphony, concerti for violin, cello, piano, harpsichord, and oboe, much chamber music, choral works, piano pieces, and songs—his music attracted less and less notice. He also wrote books—on the mystical properties of his art, on faith healing, and on other aspects of the occult, as well as two autobiographies. In 1939 the outbreak of war dispersed his family. After some years of a lonely existence, he met, through a chance acquaintance, another woman, with whom he came to live (with the blessings of his wife). As he grew very old, anniversaries produced some small and brief kindlings of interest in his music. He died happy, however, assured by the spirits

978

and his horoscope that his time would yet come.

RECORDINGS: Recent recordings by John Ogden with Bernard Herrmann [2175] of both piano concerti and the orchestral *Early One Morning* may signal the beginning of the horoscope prophecy's fulfillment. (Some of the small popular pieces and piano works have also been recorded in the past.)

[1721] NIN Y CASTELLANOS, Joaquín
(Nēn ē Kȧs-tä-yȧ'-nōs, Hwȧ-kēn')
PIANIST, TEACHER, EDITOR, WRITER
BORN: Havana, September 29, 1879
DIED: Havana, October 24, 1949

Though Cuban by birth, Nin grew up and studied in Spain. His piano teacher in Barcelona was one Carlos Vidiella. Nin went on his first concert tour at the age of fifteen. Six years later, in 1902, he went to Paris for further study with Moritz Moszkowski [1479] and became a composition pupil of d'Indy's [1462] at the Schola Cantorum, where he was hired in 1905 to teach piano. From 1908 to 1910 he taught in Berlin; then he returned to Havana to establish a musical magazine, a concert society, and a school. But Havana was apparently not ready for him and, after moving briefly to Brussels, he settled in Paris. There he established himself as a performer, a composer (almost exclusively in small forms), and a musical researcher. He published two books on music and edited and arranged much old Spanish music and Spanish folksong—if not to the tastes of the purists, at least to his own and those of performers and the public. The French government eventually awarded him the *Légion d'honneur*. However, with the outbreak of war in 1939 he returned to Havana for good. Nin was the father of the composer Joaquín Nin-Culmell [2124] and the writer Anaïs Nin. RECORDINGS: Nin recorded a few of his piano pieces and some of his songs and arrangements as accompanist to Ninon Vallin and the violinists Miguel Candela and J. Gautier. There are numerous other song recordings and several of the *Chants d'espagne* for cello (or violin) and piano.

[1722] CANTELOUBE DE MALARET,
Marie-Joseph (Cȧn'-te-loōb dǝ Mȧ-lȧ-
rä', Mȧ-rē' Zhō-zef')
ETHNOMUSICOLOGIST
BORN: Annonay, October 21, 1879
DIED: Grigny, November 4, 1957

Joseph Canteloube was born in the Ardèche in the manufacturing town (fifty miles south of Lyons) that earlier gave birth to the ballooning Montgolfiers. His noble ancestors had lived in the region for centuries. He went to Paris in his youth and studied piano with Amélie Doetzer, who, for what it was worth, had been a pupil of Chopin [1208]. In 1901 he enrolled at the Schola Cantorum, where a fellow Ardèchois, Vincent d'Indy [1462], instilled in him a passion for French folksong. Though the pursuit of same increasingly occupied his time, he was not inactive in composition. His first opera, *Le Mas (The Farmhouse)* won him the 100,000-franc Heugel Prize in 1926, though he had completed it in 1913 and it had to wait until 1929 for the Paris Opéra to produce it. The Opéra also premiered his only other opera, *Vercingétorix*, in 1933. Canteloube (he added the "de Malaret" in honor of the ancestral acres) wrote a symphonic poem, other orchestral and concerted pieces, chamber music, and songs. But his fame rests almost wholly with his folksong arrangements (the concert variety), especially the *Chants d'Auvergne*, collected in the Massif Centrale and magically set for soprano and orchestra. These were first recorded by Madeleine Grey, and have been re-recorded, wholly or in part, many times since. Some of his other arrangements have also been recorded, and there are records of the *Chants de France* and the *Chants d'Augoumois* on which Canteloube himself accompanies a singer named Lucie Daullène. He left a book on French folksong and studies of d'Indy and Sévérac [1644]. (There appears to be some confusion as to where he died. *Grove's V* says Paris, *the New Grove* "Gridny"—but it also lists the man as "Canteloube de Calaret." *Baker's* specifies "Grigny [Dept. of Seine-et-Oise]."

[1723] DELAGE, Maurice Charles (Dǝ-
läzh', Mō-rēs' Shärlz)
BORN: Paris, November 13, 1879
DIED: Paris, September 21, 1961

Maurice Delage came to music late. After working in various occupations, he served a hitch in the army from 1900. Shortly after that date he taught himself to play by ear (cello and piano). In 1904 he met Maurice Ravel [1666], was inspired to try composition, and became his friend for life. It was the cottage that Delage and his wife Nelly had built in Auteuil in 1906 that became the meeting place for the "Apaches." In 1908 Delage wrote a symphonic poem, *Conté par la mer (Told by the Sea)*. The *Quatre poèmes hindous* for soprano and instruments of 1913 reflect his fascination with the East (he made several voyages there). In 1914 he was called up, along with his car, to protect his country, which—much to his disgust—he was assigned to do in Bordeaux, far from the fighting. Most of his small and carefully crafted output was written later—a few orchestral pieces, a string quartet, but mostly songs. RECORDINGS: Janet Baker recorded the *Poèmes hindous.*

[1724] SHAW, Geoffrey Turton
EDUCATOR, ORGANIST
BORN: London, November 14, 1879
DIED: London, April 14, 1943

Like his elder brother Martin **[1667]**, Geoffrey Shaw devoted much of his life to improving English Church music—for which service the brethren were given honorary doctorates by the Archbishop of Canterbury at a joint ceremony in 1932. Geoffrey sang as a choirboy at St. Paul's Cathedral, went to Cambridge at nineteen, won a couple of important scholarships, studied with Stanford **[1467]** and Charles Wood **[1579]**, and graduated in 1902. For the next eight years he taught music at the Gresham School in Holt, Cheshire. In 1920 he succeeded Martin as organist at St. Mary's, Primrose Hill, and in 1928 he succeeded Arthur Somervell **[1553]** as royal staff inspector of music. He retired the year before he died. He wrote an opera, *All at Sea* (produced posthumously at the Royal College of Music), but most of his output consisted of choral pieces and songs. RECORDINGS: A few of his choral pieces and songs may be found in recorded anthologies.

[1725] HARTY, (Sir) Herbert Hamilton
ORGANIST, PIANIST, CONDUCTOR
BORN: Hillsborough, December 4, 1879
DIED: Brighton, February 19, 1941

Hamilton Harty was one of the first conductors from the British Isles to win international fame, though he preferred to think of himself as a composer. He was born in Ireland, in County Down, and was trained by his father, an organist. At the age of twelve, young Harty was himself organist at a church in County Antrim, moving up to posts in Belfast and Dublin. In the latter city he had informal keyboard training from Michele Esposito, professor of piano at the local music academy. He moved to London in 1900 and four years later married the soprano Agnes Nicholls. By then he was well established as a successful concert accompanist, had won a prize in Dublin for a piano trio, and in the year of his marriage was awarded the Hill Prize for a piano quartet. In 1907 his *Comedy Overture* was a hit at the Proms, and Agnes sang his setting of Keats's "Ode to a Nightingale" at the Cardiff Festival. Joseph Szigeti premiered his violin concerto in 1909, and the Cardiff Festival unveiled his orchestral *With the Wild Geese* a year later. The year 1912 brought the orchestral *Variations on a Dublin Air* and the next year his Walt Whitman cantata, *The Mystic Trumpeter.*

It was at about this time that Harty began to make a name for himself as a conductor. In 1920 he was called to Manchester to take over the Hallé Orchestra, which had been floundering for some years. In a short time he turned it into a first-class ensemble—and was knighted for his services to music in 1925. He won particular fame as a Berlioz **[1175]** specialist and introduced a great many works by twentieth-century composers—mostly those who were relatively conservative—both British and foreign. His fame spread through the series of recordings he made with his orchestra, and he was increasingly in demand as a guest conductor. (He first appeared in the United States in 1931.) His frequent absences did not sit well with the members of the board, who took him to task, and he resigned. He spent the rest of his career guest-conducting. After 1920 he produced little, the most original works being a rewrite of his *Irish Symphony* and the 1939 tone poem *Children of Lir.* However, the works with which the large public connected him with were his quite unscholarly symphonic arrangements of suites from Handel's **[683]** *Water Music* and *Royal Fireworks Music*—the only way most people got to hear these compositions prior to 1950—and *A John Field Suite* orchestrated from Field's **[1104]** piano pieces. RECORDINGS: Recordings of the Handel arrangements (including Harty's own) are legion, and there are several of the *John Field Suite.* His own music is late Romantic in style. Until recently it was neglected, save for songs and folksong arrangements, but a new awakening of interest has produced records of the *Irish Symphony,* the *Comedy Overture, With the Wild Geese, In Ireland, Ode to a Nightingale, Londonderry Air, Variations on a Dublin Air, The Children of Lir,* and concerti for violin and piano.

[1726] FRIML, Charles Rudolf (Frē'-mǝl, Chärlz Rōō'-dolf)
PIANIST
BORN: Prague, December 7, 1879
DIED: Hollywood, November 12, 1972

With Victor Herbert [1513] and Sigmund Romberg [1821], Rudolf Friml was one of the holy trinity of American operetta, and like his two fellows he was foreign-born and began as a "serious" musician. His family name is said to have been originally Frimel. His composition teacher at the Prague Conservatory seems to have been Dvořák [1386], though some sources give the elder Foerster [1520]. In the early part of this century, he toured as accompanist to the violinist Jan Kubelik and also as a piano soloist. He settled in New York in 1906 and that same year played the first of his 2 piano concerti with Walter Damrosch [1540] and the New York Symphony. But he was soon better known for his salon pieces and for his skill as an *improvisateur*. Later, as "Roderick Freeman," he tried his hand at songwriting. In 1912 Victor Herbert had a run-in with Emma Trentini, then starring in his *Naughty Marietta*, and refused to honor his contract to provide her with a second starring vehicle. Friml's publisher suggested that he give it a try. The result was *The Firefly*, which opened to rave reviews that December. A year later Friml produced *High Jinks* with almost equal success. Eighteen other operettas and musicals followed in due course, the most popular being *Rose-Marie* in 1924, *The Vagabond King* in 1925, and *The Three Musketeers*, 1927. He became an American citizen and, seeing the handwriting on the wall, moved to Hollywood, where he worked in the studios and got more mileage out of *Rose-Marie* and *The Firefly*, reworked as films for Jeanette MacDonald (with Nelson Eddy in the first, and Alan Jones in the second). In the last years of his long life, he was a frequent guest and performer on televised talk shows. RECORDINGS: As a pianist he recorded some of his little pieces for RCA and for Schirmer. There are innumerable recorded excerpts from the popular operettas.

[1727] MEDTNER, Nikolai Karlovich
(Myet'-ner, Nē'-kō-lī Kär-lō'-vich)
PIANIST, TEACHER
BORN: Moscow, January 5, 1880
DIED: London, November 13, 1951

Among the last considerable composers to come out of czarist Russia, Medtner had his musical roots deep in Romantic soil. Perhaps it had something to do with his German genes, though both his parents were Russian-born. His maternal uncle Fedor Gedike (or Theodore Goedicke), one of his early piano teachers, was a professional pianist and a composer. In 1892 the boy entered the Moscow Conservatory to complete his keyboard studies, which he did in 1900, winning a gold medal. He studied theory with Arensky [1536] at the conservatory, and later with Taneyev [1492]. Medtner immediately went on tour and later that year was awarded the Rubinstein Medal in Vienna. He had been composing for several years, and some pieces had already been published, and he began to devote more time to composition than to performing. In 1909 he was asked back to the conservatory to teach piano. But Medtner was a very shy and inward person who cared neither for the limelight nor public life, and he resigned after a year and moved to Germany. With the outbreak of war in 1914, he returned to Moscow and his post, which he held until the disruptions of the October Revolution in 1917.

In 1919 he married Anna Medtner (née Bratenshi), previously wed to his brother Emil. They stuck it out two more years; then Medtner applied for a permit to tour and, with it in hand, left to settle again in Germany. But the Germany of that era posed too many difficulties, and after a tour of the United States in the winter of 1924-25, he and his wife settled in a Paris suburb. A year or so later he made what turned out to be a farewell tour of Russia. Medtner was not happy in Paris, finding musicians there more interested in the future than in the Romantic past. He toured North America again in 1929-30 and in 1936 left France for London. There he found a small but enthusiastic band of admirers, who helped promote his music. When the bombs began to fall in 1940, one of the group's members, Edna Iles, gave the Medtners shelter at her home in Warwickshire. After the war, the pianist planned another American tour, but the first of the series of heart attacks that eventually carried him off made it impossible.

RECORDINGS: In 1948, there appeared unbidden a Maecenas in the person of Sir Jaya Chamraja Wadiyar, Maharajah of Mysore, who was a fanatic for Medtner's music. He financed a Nikolai Medtner Society, whose mission was to record Medtner's music as performed by its composer. Before death overtook the latter in 1951, he had completed three albums that included the 3 piano concerti, two of the piano sonatas, the Sonata for Soprano Voice and Piano, a score of short piano pieces, and a few songs. He also made an album of songs with Elisabeth Schwarzkopf. Apart from the exceptions noted, 3 violin sonatas, a piano quintet, and a small handful of lesser chamber works, Medtner wrote only piano music and songs. Though basically a throwback to Schumann [1211], his Russian coloration and sharp

sense of form makes him an interesting composer.
RECORDINGS: The LP era has seen a recording of the Concerto No. 3 for Piano, some collections of piano pieces, the 1950 Quintet in C Major for Piano and Strings, and a disc of songs sung by Peter Del Grande.

[1728] SHEPHERD, Arthur
TEACHER, CONDUCTOR, PIANIST
BORN: Paris, Id., February 19, 1880
DIED: Cleveland, January 12, 1958

Arthur Shepherd's parents came from England, and he was born in a Mormon settlement in southeasternmost Idaho. Encouraged by the family, three of the sons became professional musicians. Arthur progressed so rapidly under local tutelage that at the age of twelve he was shipped off to the New England Conservatory. Here, trained by the likes of Chadwick **[1483]** and Percy Goetschius, he was steeped in German conservatism. Graduating with honors in 1897, he returned to the West and settled in Salt Lake City. There he taught piano and conducted a theater orchestra and whatever passed for a symphony in those days. In 1902 his *Ouverture Joyeuse* won the Paderewski Prize, and six years later he was summoned back to his alma mater to teach and conduct the student orchestra. In Boston he struck up friendships with Henry F. Gilbert **[1601]**, and Arthur Farwell **[1629]**. Both got him excited about the idea of an American music, and Farwell published some of his compositions. In 1909 the National Federation of Music Clubs awarded a prize for his first piano sonata and another for one of his songs. In 1917, when the United States became involved in the European war, he joined the army and served as a bandmaster in France. In 1918 the city of Cleveland inaugurated its orchestra and two years later Shepherd was invited to become its associate conductor, in which capacity he initiated a series of concerts for children. In 1926 he was appointed to the faculty of Western Reserve University, where he chaired the music department from 1933 to 1948. He retired in 1950.

Shepherd's music, for all its German roots, was influenced by the Impressionists and by Vaughan Williams **[1633]**. His first symphony, *Horizons* of 1927, perhaps his best-known work, typically used cowboy songs. Shepherd's other orchestral compositions include another symphony, a violin concerto, a *Fantasy Overture on Down East Spirituals*, and another overture with the titillating name of *The Nuptials of Attila*.

There are also cantatas, 4 string quartets and other chamber works, piano pieces, and songs.
RECORDINGS: There are some piano recordings by Grant Johannesen and Vivian Harvey Slater, the Tagore *Triptych for High Voice and String Quartet* sung by Betsy Norden, and a memorial album of songs from Western Reserve sung by Jean Kraft. Louis Lane, who later held Shepherd's associate conductor post with the Cleveland Orchestra, recorded a movement from *Horizons*.

[1729] BLOCH, Ernest
VIOLINIST, CONDUCTOR, TEACHER
BORN: Geneva, July 24, 1880
DIED: Portland, Ore., July 15, 1959

Was Bloch a Franco-Swiss composer as his origins and training suggest? Was he a Jewish composer, as he sometimes claimed to be? Or was he an American composer, as his adopted nationality (and a good many books) indicate? Perhaps it might be best to describe him as a modern international eclectic who sometimes affected quasi-oriental garb. His father was a thriving manufacturer of clocks, specializing, it is said, in the cuckoo variety. Ernest (not to be confused with his contemporary *Ernst* Bloch, a philosopher who wrote on music) studied in his teens with Émile Jaques-Dalcroze (1865–1950), the inventor of "eurhythmics," which taught concentration and coordination through musical rhythms, and the composer of folk-based compositions. At fifteen Bloch wrote a string quartet and an "oriental" symphony. He also studied violin with Louis Rey and by 1897 was deemed good enough to be turned over to Eugène Ysaÿe **[1507]** at the Brussels Conservatory, where he continued his composition studies under Ysaÿe pupil François Rasse **[1635]**. In 1900 he moved on to Frankfurt am Main for a year's work with Iwan Knorr (1853–1916) and then studied briefly with Thuille **[1537]** in Munich, before coming temporarily to rest in Paris in 1903. During all this time he had continued to compose, producing, among other things, another symphony and a violin concerto. None of this work saw print, however; Bloch's first publication was, in fact, a set of songs called *Historiettes au crépuscule (Little Tales at Twilight)*, in 1904.

In 1904 he returned to Geneva, married (the bride was Margarethe Schneider), and did time as a salesman for the family business. (The marriage produced three children, of whom Suzanne [b. 1907] became well known as a lutenist.) Bloch spent most of his spare time over the next half dozen years writing *Macbeth,* his only opera, which was premiered at the Opéra-Comique in Paris in 1910, pronounced "indecipherable," "capricious," and "incoherent," and closed down. It was during this Geneva period that the composer began thinking of himself as a musical spokesman for Judaism. The first products of this stance were the 1913–14 *Trois poèmes juifs (Three Jewish Poems)* for orchestra, *Prelude and 2 Psalms* for soprano and orchestra, and *Psalm 22* for alto or baritone and orchestra. In 1911 he also began teaching a course in aesthetics at the Geneva Conservatory. Four years later he met the cellist Alexander Barjansky, who inspired Bloch's most popular work, the rhapsody *Schelomo (Solomon)* for cello and orchestra. This was completed in 1916, as was the *Israel Symphony* for voices and orchestra. (Suggestive of Jewish music though such works are, Bloch rarely quotes from the real thing.)

By this time Bloch had become a victim of academic politics and was depressed by the war raging in France. He had been doing some conducting for several years and welcomed an invitation to go to the United States in that capacity with Maud Allan's dance troupe. For all his euphoria on arriving in New York, the venture went bankrupt in the wilds of Ohio, and he was left to get back to Manhattan as best he could. But in 1917 things suddenly broke in his favor: the Flonzaly String Quartet included his first quartet in B minor, 1916, in its repertoire; David Mannes gave him a teaching appointment at his school; Karl Muck asked him to conduct the Boston Symphony in the *Trois pièces;* and the Friends of Music put on an all-Bloch concert in New York. From then on—with the signal exception noted below —he identified with America and took out citizenship papers in 1924.

In 1919 Bloch's *Suite for Viola and Piano,* premiered by Louis Bailly of the Flonzaly Quartet and Harold Bauer, won the Coolidge Prize. (There are also versions for viola and orchestra and for cello and piano.) The next year the composer was named director of the new Cleveland Institute of Music. Between then and 1930 he wrote and published the *Episodes* for orchestra, the *Concerto Grosso No. 1,* Piano Quintet No. 1, and some other shorter chamber works, all of his violin-and-piano music (2 sonatas, *Baal Shem, From Jewish Life,* etc.), and several sets of piano pieces. A second opera, *Jézabel,* was aborted, but two other large works completed during this era should be noted, though their importance is questionable. One, an orchestral tribute to his native land, *Helvetia,* had been in the works since 1900.

The other, *America: An Epic Rhapsody,* quotes American music from Indian melodies to Stephen Foster [1299], and culminates in a community-sing chorale that Bloch fervently hoped would be adopted as a new national anthem.

Bloch left Cleveland in 1925 to head the San Francisco Conservatory. In 1929 honorary membership in the St. Cecilia Academy of Rome was conferred on him. When in 1930 a wealthy patron set up a trust to support him for a decade, on condition that he use the time to compose, it was to Italy that he went. Curiously, until the Fascists turned the climate ugly, Bloch was very popular there. The first fruit of his new freedom was the most Jewish of his creations, the *Sacred Service,* commissioned by Gerald Warburg in 1930 and completed three years later. There followed the piano sonata in 1935, *Visions and Prophecies* for piano and *Voice in the Wilderness* for cello and orchestra, both in 1936, and the orchestral *Evocations* in 1937. In the last year an Ernest Bloch Society was founded in England, but in 1938 a revival of *Macbeth* in Naples was hooted down by Mussolini's bully-boys, and Bloch returned to Geneva. There he finished the mature violin concerto and shortly afterward came back to the United States for good. Having finished out his "composing decade," he accepted a professorship at the University of California in Berkeley, where he taught until his retirement in 1952. He continued to be productive; his last two decades brought forth a symphony, a *Sinfonia Breve,* a second *Concerto Grosso* (like the first for string orchestra), several concerted works, four more string quartets, and a second piano quintet. Over his American teaching career Bloch's list of students reads like a who's who of American music: Antheil [1981], Bacon [1949], Chanler [2013], Elwell [1948], Jacobi [1850], Kirchner [2284], Leginska [1805], Moore [1884], Quincy Porter [1932], Rogers [1875], and Sessions [1931], to name only some of the more outstanding. After his retirement he lived on the Oregon coast. He died, after a long battle with cancer, shortly before his seventy-ninth birthday. Among his last works were *Suite Modale* for flute and strings, several suites for unaccompanied violin, viola, and cello, and two meditations entitled *2 Last Poems* ("Funeral Music" and "Life Again?") for flute and orchestra. He left his manuscripts to the Library of Congress.

RECORDINGS: Bloch has been well represented on records, though except for *Schelomo* and a few other popular things, there is no great choice of recordings. Important omissions are *Helvetia, Macbeth* (there are pirated excerpts), *Evocations,* and (apparently) the E-flat symphony of 1956. Bloch himself conducted a recorded performance of the *Sacred Service* and appended a spoken postscript to Stokowski's record of *America.* Recently recordings of the complete string quartets and the Piano Quintet No. 2 have finally appeared.

[1730] STOLZ, Robert Elisabeth (Shtōlts, Rō'-bârt Ā-lēs'-à-bet)
CONDUCTOR
BORN: Graz, August 25, 1880
DIED: West Berlin, June 27, 1975

Together with the likes of Ralph Benatzky [1780], with whom he collaborated on the very successful *Im weissen Rössl (White Horse Inn)* of 1930, Stolz represents the last wheeze of the operetta, already contaminated by the Broadway musical and Hollywood film. As with so many successful pop musicians, Stolz's credentials were excellent. His father was a conductor, his mother a singer; both contributed to his early training, and he made his debut as a pianist in Vienna at the age of seven. He had advanced training from Robert Fuchs (1847–1927) in Vienna and Engelbert Humperdinck [1480] in Berlin. At seventeen he was rehearsal pianist at the Graz Opera. Over the next ten years he worked his way up as a provincial conductor. In 1899 his first operetta *Studentenulke (Student Pranks)* was produced in Marburg (now Maribor, Yugoslavia), where he was number two conductor. In 1907 he was hired by the Theater an der Wien to take over Lehár's [1614] *Die lustige Witwe (The Merry Widow)* in the second year of its run. Stolz kept trying for a real operetta hit—he turned out nearly 70 stage musicals in his more than sixty-five productive years—but had more luck with Viennese popular songs, of which the most famous is perhaps *"Im Prater blühn wieder die Bäume"* ("In the Prater the Trees Are Blooming Again"). The 1920 operetta *Der Tanz ins Glück (Dancing into Happiness)* reached Broadway in 1925 as *Sky High* in a much diluted version. Meanwhile Stolz had moved to Berlin, where he got in on the ground floor of musical films. Here in 1930 he had an enormous success with *Zwei Herzen im Dreivierteltakt (Two Hearts in Three-Quarter Time),* which in 1933 he adapted for the stage as *Der verlorene Walzer (The Lost Waltz).* (Stolz, who had met Johann Strauss, Jr. [1295], in his youth, assumed proprietary rights over his memory and the Viennese waltz tradition.) Stolz returned to Vienna after Hitler rose

to power, fled to Paris at the *Anschluss* of Austria in 1938, and came to America two years later. His 1941 *Night of Love* was a flop on Broadway, but he found plentiful work in the Hollywood studios. In 1943 he was called to New York to direct the New Opera Company's revival of *The Merry Widow* for Jan Kiepura and Marta Eggerth, for whom he had done film scores in Europe; it had a long run. A last Broadway effort was *Mr. Strauss Goes to Boston* in 1945; here, instead of retreading real Strauss tunes, Stolz insisted on providing his own. The show folded ten days after it opened.
RECORDINGS: Stolz went back to Vienna in 1946 and for three decades continued to conduct and record Viennese music. He is said to have written at least 100 film scores and many hundreds of songs. He accompanied Anneliese Rothenberger for a recording of his song cycle *Blumenlieder, (Flower Songs),* Op. 500, and conducted one of his one-act operas, *Die Rosen der Madonna (The Madonna's Roses).*

[1731] INGHELBRECHT, Désiré-Émile (Ing'-el-brekt, Dā-zē-rā' Ā-mēl')
CONDUCTOR, WRITER
BORN: Paris, September 17, 1880
DIED: Paris, February 14, 1965

Inghelbrecht's parents were both musicians, but it did him little good at the Paris Conservatoire, from which he was ejected for lack of application or promise. This did not prevent his composing, which he was doing rather handily shortly after the turn of the century, although in an all too Debussyan [1547] manner. An orchestral violinist, he gradually established himself as a conductor. He held posts in various Parisian theaters, became conductor of the Ballets Suédois in 1920, conducted at the Opéra-Comique for a season, 1924–25, was director of the Concerts Pasdeloup for several years, during which period he also conducted at the Algiers Opera for a season, returned to the Opéra-Comique for another, and in 1934 founded the French National Radio Orchestra. From the end of World War II, he conducted at the Paris Opéra for five years. He was particularly noted as an interpreter of Debussy (with whom he worked for a time) and late in his life made a number of LP recordings of Debussy with the French Radio Orchestra and with the orchestra of the Théâtre des Champs-Elysées. A man with a mordant wit, he wrote several books in his later years, including one on conducting technique, a volume of reminiscences, a study of Debussy, and a guide on how *not* to conduct the operas *Carmen, Faust,* and *Pelléas et Mélisande.*

Once out of his Debussyan phase, which did not last long, Inghelbrecht discovered his own style, which was terse, melodic, clear, and, for the orchestral works, ingeniously instrumented. He often made use of popular or folk songs. Most of his orchestral works have descriptive titles. (A late one, *Vézelay,* evokes the picturesque cathedral village in Burgundy where he had a summer home.) His most popular works were the piano suites in five volumes called *La Nursery,* based on children's songs, which he orchestrated. He also wrote an opera, several ballets, other orchestral works, chamber music, and songs.

RECORDINGS: Inghelbrecht conducted at least two of the pieces from *La Nursery* on records, plus a set of fanfares and the *La Légende du grand St. Nicholas* for orchestra.

[1732] PIZZETTI, Ildebrando (Pid-zet'-tē, Ēl-dä-bràn'-dō)
TEACHER, CONDUCTOR
BORN: Parma, September 20, 1880
DIED: Rome, February 13, 1968

For a while it looked as though Pizzetti would carry the proud banner of Italian music into the twentieth century, but at some point he got out of step and wound up in limbo. His father, Odoardo, was a Parmese piano teacher who moved to nearby Reggio shortly after Ildebrando was born. The latter, throughout his school years, showed no special interest in or aptitude for music, and spent his leisure time writing plays. However, having finished at the *ginnasio* in 1895, he was enrolled in the Parma Conservatory without protest. There the director, Giovanni Tebaldini, a mover and shaker in the movement to reinstate purified Gregorian chant in the Church, got him interested in early music. Meanwhile Pizzetti had lifted (or lowered) his creative sights from spoken drama to music drama. He wrote his first opera, *Sabina,* in 1897 and followed it with *Romeo e Giulietta* in 1899; neither found a producer. He gave some time to several other subjects—e.g., Byron's *Sardanapalus,* Pushkin's *Mazeppa,* Virgil's *Aeneid*—none of which came to fruition. He graduated in 1901 and in 1902 submitted his treatment of Corneille's *Le Cid* to the Sonzogno Competition; it won nothing. However, he was hired as an assistant conductor at the Parma Opera House.

In 1905 Pizzetti was so excited by Gabriele d'Annunzio's still unfinished play *Le Nave (The Ship,* later set by Montemezzi [1671])

that he made a point of meeting the poet. A close friendship followed. D'Annunzio asked him to write the incidental music for the 1908 Rome production. Meanwhile Pizzetti was rethinking his view of opera, concluding that what he wanted to write was not opera but music drama. Song, he said in effect, was song and was fine in its place, but the music dramatist's task was to heighten word meanings, which must be done by converting the rhythms and inflections of speech to musical equivalents. Here he was influenced not by Wagner [1230] but by the aims of the early Florentine opera composers. (He had moved to Florence in 1908 to teach at the Instituto Musicale and was soon expounding his theories in various musical journals. In 1909 d'Annunzio reworked his tragedy *Fedra (Phaedra)* into a libretto for Pizzetti, who set it according to his new principles and got it produced at La Scala in 1915, after getting the runaround at the Rome Opera; it was hailed as a powerful work and a welcome relief from all those dirty *verismo* peasants. In the meantime his music for d'Annunzio's play *La Pisanella (The Girl of Pisa)* had been heard at the Paris production in 1913. But their next collaboration, the opera *Gigliola,* remained on the drawingboard and brought an end to the partnership. It was some time before Pizzetti returned to opera, though in 1917 he wrote music for a play by Belcare, *La sacra rappresentazione di Abram e d'Isaac (The Holy Play of Abraham and Isaac).*

It was also in 1917 that Pizzetti moved up to the directorship of the conservatory. Two years later he succeeded his friend Giannotto Bastianelli, with whom he had founded the journal *Dissonanza* in 1914, as critic of *La Nazione (The Nation).* It was a significant change. Both had originally espoused modernism, but whereas Bastianelli had gone on accepting the extremists, Pizzetti found he was unable to see what they were up to. In December 1922, La Scala brought forth *Debora e Jaele,* which was generally accepted as his most effective opera. Two years later he went to Milan to head the conservatory there. Over the next decade he produced incidental music for a series of Greek tragedies presented among ruins in southern Italy and Sicily and four more operas. One opera was a one-act version of the Abraham play. The most successful of the others was *Fra Gherardo,* premiered at La Scala in 1928, which won a showing at the Metropolitan Opera in 1929, where it was admired but not liked. In 1932 Pizzetti publicly attacked the avant-garde, urging a return to established values—though his music was increasingly showing him to be trapped in his own theories. Four years later he went to Rome to teach at the Accademia di Santa Cecilia, remaining there until 1958. During World War II and after, he returned to opera, turning out eight more, including two for radio. For the fourth, *La Figlia di Jorio (Jorio's Daughter)*, he adapted a play by d'Annunzio and enjoyed something of a success at the Naples premiere in 1954. Though overrated at the time, the next opera, *Assassinio nella cattedrale (Murder in the Cathedral*, based on the play by T. S. Eliot, then riding high), was a huge success at La Scala in 1958 and had showings all over the world. In 1958 he retired from St. Cecilia, where he had served as president from 1947 to 1952, but continued to compose, write, and occasionally conduct. Pizzetti's last opera was *Clitennestra (Clytemnestra*, written in his eighty-fifth year and premiered at La Scala in 1965.

Pizzetti set most store by his stage music but wrote a good deal else. His choral music (including a *Requiem* and some cantatas) and songs have been admired. He also produced a good deal of chamber music (2 string quartets, a piano trio, sonatas for violin and cello). For orchestra he wrote a symphony, a violin concerto, a harp concerto, a *Concerto dell'estate (Summer Concerto)*, a piano concerto entitled *Canti della Stagione alta (Song of the High Season)*, a cello concerto, and some works derived from his experience with Greek drama. He published many articles and several books, and edited the madrigals of Gesualdo [310].

RECORDINGS: On records he is represented by the symphony, the *Concerto dell'estate*, the *Canti della Stagione alta*, a suite from *La Pisanella*, the first violin sonata, songs, and other small pieces. There is a pirated recording of the premiere of *Assassinio*.

[1733] WEIGL, Karl (Vi'-gəl, Kärl)
CONDUCTOR, TEACHER
BORN: Vienna, February 6, 1881
DIED: New York, August 11, 1949

Karl Weigl studied at the Vienna Academy and the University of Vienna. Among his teachers were the pianist Anton Door (a Czerny [1137] pupil!), Robert Fuchs (1847–1927), Alexander von Zemlinsky [1621], and the musicologist Guido Adler. After taking his doctorate, he worked at the Imperial Opera as an assistant to Gustav Mahler [1525] from 1904 until Mahler's departure in 1906. In 1918 he began teaching at the New Conservatory, moving over to the university twelve years later. When the Nazis arrived

in 1938, Weigl and his wife Vally [1970], a former pupil and a composer in her own right, left for America. At first employed by a wing of the New York Philharmonic Society, he later taught at the Hart School, Brooklyn College, and lastly at the New England Conservatory. Though he was highly regarded as a composer in Vienna, he won little recognition here in his lifetime. Since his death, a memorial trust and the apostleship of his widow have managed to get some of his works before the public. (In 1968 Leopold Stokowski conducted the American Symphony in the fifth ["Apocalyptic"] of Weigl's 6 symphonies, twenty-three years after its completion.) Weigl also left 8 string quartets, concertos, sonatas, etc., and many piano pieces, choral music, and *Lieder*. His music is basically late Romantic. RECORDINGS: There are recordings of three of the string quartets, the cello and viola sonatas, *2 Pieces for Cello and Piano*, the *Night Fantasies* for piano, and a good many songs.

[1734] BARTÓK, Béla (Bär'-tok, Bā'-lä)
PIANIST, TEACHER, ETHNOMUSICOLOGIST
BORN: Nagyszentmiklós, March 25, 1881
DIED: New York City, September 26, 1945

Béla Bartók unquestionably ranks as Hungary's greatest and best-known modern composer and as one of the musical giants of the twentieth century on an international scale. Having tried the paths indicated by Wagner [1230] and Debussy [1547], he found in the careful first-hand study of peasant music—in his own country and elsewhere—more basic practices that operated free of supposed "rules," traditional or artificial. These discoveries encouraged him to explore such matters as dissonance, free rhythm, and modality for the sake of their own expressiveness and from them to develop a powerful and energetic language that was peculiarly his own. The music reflected the man: though he was small, frail, and shy, he had enormous drive and an iron will and did whatever he did with passion. Profoundly patriotic, he loathed tyranny in all forms: he willfully hobbled his own career by refusing to play ball with the local dictators Béla Kún and Admiral Horthy, and in his last will he asked that his countrymen name no street for him so long as any in Hungary bore the names of Hitler and Mussolini. Though he taught piano for many years he avoided teaching composition; he left no school of Bartók and produced no major followers, though his influence was and remains widespread.

Bartók's birthplace, 100 miles southeast of Budapest, was in 1920 absorbed by Rumania and is now called Sînnicolau Mare. The elder of two children (his sister was called Erzsebet), he had parents who were musical and who seemed to be in comfortable circumstances. His father, Béla, was in charge of the district agricultural school, played piano and cello, and wrote dance pieces. His mother, the former Paula Voit, was a pianist of ability and training. Young Béla was a sickly child and became as a result bookish and introverted. He exhibited symptoms of musicality quite early, and when he was five, his mother started him on piano lessons. Two years later her husband died unexpectedly, leaving the family with a highly uncertain future. At first they moved to smaller quarters, and Paula Bartók eked out an existence by giving piano lessons. In 1889 she found work as a schoolteacher (ill paid) in Nagyszöllös, 180 miles to the northeast and now Soviet Vinogradov. There she continued to give piano lessons, make her own and her children's clothes, and run the household.

Young Bartók developed rapidly as a pianist. One day in 1890 he played his mother a waltz he had suddenly heard in his mind's ear; she noted down his first composition. It was followed by more little dances and then by some rather ambitious pieces. Discovering that her son had perfect pitch and encouraged by a visiting musician of some authority, she took him to Budapest, where she found the National Conservatory eager to take him on. Deciding he was not ready, she sent him south to Nagyvárad (now Oradea, Rumania) to live with her sister Emma and attend the *Gymnasium*. But neither his academic schooling nor his piano lessons with one Kersch boded well, and in April 1892 she fetched him home. Shortly afterward he made his public debut there as a pianist in a charity concert, playing part of a Beethoven [1063] sonata and his own work, *The River Danube*, inspired by a geography lesson. Around this time, his other maternal aunt, Irma, came to live with the Bartóks and help her hard-pressed sister.

In 1893 the latter took leave from her job, and, hoping to further Béla's musical education thereby, sought a better one in Pozsony (alias Pressburg, now Bratislava), a city with some musical opportunities. But there were no openings, and she spent the year again teaching school, this time in the village of Beszterce (now Rumanian Bristriţa). There were no facilities for musical education there, but the boy kept his hand in by ac-

companying a young local violinist of some talent. But in April 1894 Paula was called back to Pozsony to take a post in the local teachers' college; besides giving her a better salary, it provided her son with free *Gymnasium* tuition. In fact Pozsony proved to be just what he needed. He was able to attend, inexpensively, operas and concerts. He found a good piano teacher in Ferenc Erkel's [1214] son László, who unfortunately died in 1896, and studied harmony and did some advanced composing (e.g., a piano quartet) under one Anton Hyrtl. At the *Gymnasium* the chapel organist was seventeen-year-old Ernö Dohnányi [1696], who became Bartók's idol for a time and whom he succeeded when Dohnányi went off to the conservatory in Budapest. During his years there, Bartók played in several concerts at the *Gymnasium*. In the summer of 1897 he studied briefly with Eugen d'Albert [1562].

Prior to his graduation in 1899, Mrs. Bartók, understanding that the Vienna Conservatory was the best place he could go, took him there for an audition. He was not only admitted but offered an imperial scholarship. However, on Dohnányi's urging, he decided on Budapest. There his future piano professor, István Thomán, told him that the Academy of Music would take him on his (Thomán's) say-so without an audition. A subsequent extended illness kept Bartók away from the piano for most of the time before he returned in September to begin his studies. To his horror the director explained to him that no matter who had promised what, candidates were not accepted sound unheard. In trepidation because of his rustiness, Bartók played for an impromptu examining committee and was admitted with hosannas and advanced standing.

His first two years at the Budapest Academy were interrupted by severe respiratory illnesses, causing the authorities to suggest that he would be well-advised to turn to law or some other less demanding profession. After the first year, he took up quarters in his Aunt Emma's home in Budapest. He had been awarded a small fellowship but had to give lessons to survive, often having to skip meals when his students failed to pay up. Though he made steady progress at the piano, his watery neo-Brahmsian [1329] music did not impress his composition teacher, Hans Koessler (1853–1926), who had taught Dohnányi (and shortly would teach Kodály [1760]), and who was a cousin of Max Reger [1637]. Discouraged, Bartók gave up composing for a time and concentrated on becoming a concert pianist. Among the friends he made in his conservatory years were Adila and Jelly d'Arányi, the violin-playing great-nieces of Joseph Joachim [1321], and he became a central figure in the salon of Emma Gruber, the talented wife of a local businessman who later in her life married Kodály. Thomán had acquainted Bartók with Wagner's scores, which fascinated the neophyte without showing him any particular direction. The revelation came when in 1902 he heard Richard Strauss's [1563] *Also sprach Zarathustra*. He became an ardent Straussian to the degree that he transcribed *Ein Heldenleben* for solo piano, with a performance of which he introduced his professors to his new hero's music. Almost immediately he returned to composition. The most obvious product of this reawakening was the symphonic poem *Kossuth* (after the hero of the Hungarian revolt of 1848), completed in 1903 and played by the Budapest Philharmonic the next year. Meanwhile his concert career was also beginning to bear fruit. Late in 1901 he had been paid 100 florins to play at the Lipótváros Casino (which sum he gave his mother as a Christmas present). After good reviews of performances at the academy, he made a successful debut in Vienna and then treated his birthplace to a concert. He was received there in a veritable triumph. He graduated from the academy in June and spent part of the summer polishing his concert repertoire in Austria with Dohnányi. Then he went off to Berlin to seek his fortune and (unsuccessfully) Richard Strauss.

Bartók had been writing music rather steadily for some time now—mostly piano pieces and songs, but there was also the Symphony in E-flat written in 1902, whose *scherzo* movement had its premiere in 1904, shortly after *Kossuth*. A month before, Jenö Hubay [1509] had played a Bartók violin sonata (not the "official" first), accompanied by its composer. Later that winter Bartók went to Manchester, England, where he stayed at the home of the conductor Hans Richter and was soloist with the Hallé Orchestra in a concert featuring *Kossuth*. After that he took some time off in the Hungarian countryside to compose and practice. From this period came his Opp. 1 and 2—the *Rhapsody* for piano (later with orchestra) and the *Scherzo* for piano and orchestra. In November he went to Vienna to premiere his piano quintet (with the Prill String Quartet) and stayed there to write the Suite No. 1 for orchestra (conducted in Vienna by Ferdinand Löwe the next fall) and to begin the Suite No. 2. Bartók that year spent some weeks in Paris, primarily as an entrant, both as composer and pianist, in the Anton Rubinstein Competition, but also to soak up some culture. As performer he was bested by Wilhelm Backhaus. As creator, he offered the newly orchestrated *Rhapsody* and the quintet. After protests from the performers, the former was played, but they balked completely at the latter, and Bartók had to substitute the sonata (with Lev Zeitlin) instead. His competitors were four nonentities, but (partly because of lack of funds) no prizes were awarded and Bartók took a second honorable mention to one Attilio Brugnoli (1880–1937), much to his disgust.

During his period of quasi-retirement in 1904 Bartók had noted down a folksong from the singing of a peasant girl. What passed for Hungarian folk music at the time (as purveyed by the likes of Liszt and Brahms) was really Gypsy-derived (the *csárdás* of numerous operettas) or composed popular music of the cafés (see Brahms's *Hungarian Dances*). But what Bartók found was the real stuff, and it was becoming rarer by the day. Bartók was fascinated and devoted the summer of 1905 tramping the Hungarian boondocks cajoling such tunes out of the natives. In 1906 he collaborated with Kodály, a sometime acquaintance who had been similarly occupied, to publish twenty such melodies with piano accompaniments. Bartók went on to systematize this music, to study the harmonic implications of the tunes, to use the results as a basis for his own music, and to write often and authoritatively on folk music. From 1907 he used a recording cylinder phonograph in the field; and until war limited him in 1914, he ranged more widely into neighboring countries and even into North Africa to study the interactions of musics. (His conclusion: music, like living organisms, profits from cross-breeding.) Always a lover of the outdoors, he came increasingly to feel at home in, and to identify with, the peasant world in which he spent so much time.

Such research and concertizing took up most of 1906. That spring he served as accompanist to the pubescent violinist Ferenc (or Franz von) Vécsey [1876] on a tour of Spain and Portugal. The next year he succeeded Thomán at the Budapest Academy as professor of piano. In the course of 1907 he completed the *Suite No. 2* for orchestra (premiered by the Budapest Philharmonic in 1909). He also fell deeply in love with Stefi Geyer, a nineteen-year-old violinist and wrote for her a concerto for violin and strings which was not "discovered" until after her death in 1956. (Bartók reused part of it in the two orchestral *Portraits*, Op. 5, he completed in 1908.) Between his appointment to the Academy and 1910, he wrote prodigiously, turning out many piano works (the *Bagatelles, 10 Easy Pieces, For Children, 2 Elegies, 2 Rumanian Dances, 7 Sketches, 4 Dirges,* and *3 Burlesques)* in which his folksong researches played a major role, as well as the *2 Pictures,* Op. 10, for orchestra (also known as *2 Images),* and perhaps most importantly the first string quartet. In these compositions one finds, besides the folksong influence, the impact of Debussy, and occasional vestigial Wagnerian influence.

Shortly after he began teaching at the academy, Bartók encountered among his pupils fourteen-year-old Márta Ziegler and her sister Herma, the daughters of a Budapest police official from Pozsony. He was drawn to Márta, despite the fact that she was half his age, and was taken into the bosom of her family. About two years later, 1909, they were quietly married. After lunch at Paula Bartók's they went out together for a while; when Paula asked if Márta was staying for dinner, she was told they had become man and wife that afternoon. (A son, Béla, was born in 1910.) At the end of the year they visited Paris, where Bartók had an unsatisfactory encounter with d'Indy [1462] and failed to meet Debussy at all. Concurrently four of his friends in Budapest had banded together as the Waldbauer-Kerpely String Quartet with the purpose of performing his chamber music, since no one else seemed so inclined. They premiered the first quartet in an all-Bartók evening on March 19, 1910 (which included the quintet and some of the piano pieces). Later they performed it throughout Europe.

Bartók had no such luck with his first and only opera, *Duke Bluebeard's Castle.* To a Symbolist libretto by Béla Balázs derived from the Perrault fairy tale, it was dedicated to Márta and completed in 1911. The composer submitted it to a national opera competition, but it was rejected. Moreover his publishers were not interested in anything so unsalable, though they tried to ease the blow by commissioning him to produce teaching editions of Classical piano composers. Around the same time Bartók and Kodály, impressed by the French model, tried to organize a Hungarian Musical Society to perform new Hungarian music, but it fizzled for lack of money and interest. The only other composition of 1911 was the *Allegro barbaro* for piano, a piece of polymodal primitivism regarded by some as Bartók's declaration of independence from the trammels of Germanic tradition. For the next several years he composed little and wrote much about folk music. He did not even bother to orchestrate the *4 Pieces* of 1912 until 1921. In 1913 he made his visit to Algeria, where he found the native music, as he had expected,

"purer" and less sophisticated than that of his own country. His next major work—again in collaboration with Balázs—was the ballet *The Wooden Prince,* finished in 1916. It was dedicated to the Italian conductor Egisto Tango, who had come to the Budapest Opera in 1913 after stints at La Scala, Berlin, and the Metropolitan and who was a champion of the new music. Following intensive rehearsals, Tango conducted the first performance on May 12, 1917. It marked a turning point in Bartók's career, for it was a huge success. A year later Tango premiered the opera with equally salutary results, all of which led to the publication of these and other previously ignored Bartók scores.

As previously noted, World War I circumscribed Bartók's folksong researches, though he used the opportunity to continue sorting out what he had collected. Most of the fifteen or so compositions of the period were folksong-based choral and piano pieces, but they also included a suite for piano, the second string quartet, and two sets of original songs. The quartet was first played by the Waldbauer-Kerpely Quartet in 1918. By the end of the war, the composer had been taken into the fold of the prestigious publisher Universal Editions.

That was perhaps the sole benefit Bartók enjoyed at that period in Hungarian history. As part of the Austrian Empire, Hungary began to see that she was on the losing side, and agitation for independence grew. At the end of October 1918, Count Károlyi, the leader of the Radical Party, became head of the government and withdrew Hungarian forces from the conflict. Troops from Rumania and what would soon be Czechoslovakia and Yugoslavia occupied large parts of the country. In mid-November, emulating Lenin, Béla Kún, a one-time insurance agent, came from Russia on a forged passport to effect a Communist takeover. Chaos ensued. Kún was imprisoned, but when it looked as if Hungary would be partitioned among its neighbors, he was freed by the Socialists who agreed to join him. On March 21, Hungary was declared a Soviet state. Kún surrounded himself with a largely Jewish government (accounting to a great degree for subsequent Hungarian anti-Semitism) and set about violently eradicating the opposition. His brutalities, however, alienated more people than they won over, and on August 1 Kún and most of his henchmen fled to Austria. The Rumanians marched into Budapest and looted the city before withdrawing. On January 25, 1920, Hungary was declared a kingless monarchy, and on March 1 Admiral Miklós Horthy was named regent. By the Treaty of Trianon, June 4, much of Hungary's territory and population was awarded to her neighbors.

Two months after Kún took over, the Bartóks were so frightened that they fled their suburban home for Pest, taking only the phonograph cylinders and some books. It was not long before they were able to return, but food was difficult to come by and by summer's end Bartók was ill. He applied for a leave of absence (he was seriously considering emigrating). In October, however, Dohnányi, appointed director of the academy during the Karólyian republic, was dismissed and replaced with Hubay. The faculty resigned in protest without any effect except to place themselves in danger. Hubay announced cryptically that Bartók was essential to his plans—the only response the latter ever got to his request.

The economic and political situation made further field study all but impossible. Despite the upheaval Bartók had managed in 1919 to complete a major work, the ballet *A csodálatos mandarin,* usually translated as *The Miraculous Mandarin* but in one set of notes on a record jacket *The Wonderful Tangerine.* Its setting (a brothel) and its bloody plot prevented its being staged in Hungary until a year after the composer was dead. The year 1920 produced only the *8 Improvisations on Hungarian Folksongs* for piano, written for the Debussy memorial volume published in Paris.

Folksong studies, teaching, life crises, and above all concert tours took up much time in the next few years. For a London visit in the spring of 1922, Bartók wrote his official first violin sonata, dedicated to Jelly d'Arányi, who now lived there and who premiered it with Bartók as pianist. He followed it with a second sonata a year later. Both works represent Bartók's most serious consideration of atonality. In 1922 also Bartók's first two stage works were performed in Frankfurt am Main, and his first violin sonata was featured in the opening concert of the festival of contemporary music given at Salzburg in August. This latter event marked the birth of the International Society for Contemporary Music (ISCM), at whose concerts the composer was represented at least every two years until 1938.

Shortly after World War I, Bartók had fallen in love with another young and talented pupil, Ditta Pásztory. In 1923 he divorced Márta and married her, not without a great deal of guilt and soul searching. In this same period, Paula Bartók, born in what was now Rumania and living in what was now Czechoslovakia, had become a woman without a country and in danger of deprivation of her teacher's pension—a situ-

ation that caused her son no little trouble getting it set to rights. Again, despite the pressures, he managed to compose the orchestral *Dance Suite,* commissioned for the fiftieth anniversary celebration of the union of Buda and Pest. In 1924 he dedicated to Ditta, who had borne him a son, Peter, the *Village Scenes* for voice and piano, three of which he also arranged for chorus and orchestra. There followed two years in which, when Bartók was not concertizing, he was rethinking his approach to music, especially with regard to counterpoint, consequent upon his study of music before Bach [684]. During this time the *Mandarin* was premiered in Cologne (November 1926), and created such protests that further performances were banned. At almost the same time, Bartók completed the first of his 3 piano concerti and premiered it the next summer in Frankfurt with Wilhelm Furtwängler. Other works from late 1926 were the piano sonata and the *Out of Doors Suite* for the same instrument.

In December 1927, Bartók undertook his first American tour. In his debut with the New York Philharmonic (under Willem Mengelberg), he had to substitute the *Rhapsody,* Op. 1, for the first piano concerto, which the orchestra had not mastered, and got better marks for his playing than for his music. He concertized from coast to coast, creating more puzzlement than delight. The trip concluded with the New York premiere of the concerto, this time under Fritz Reiner, who had studied with Bartók in Budapest. The composer had submitted his one-movement third string quartet in a Philadelphia competition sponsored by the Musical Fund Society and back home learned that he and Alfredo Casella [1767] had split the $6,000 first prize.

The year 1928 brought forth *Rhapsodies Nos. 1* and *2,* for violin and piano, the first of which Bartók performed with József Szigeti in Budapest, and the fourth string quartet, premiered there by Waldbauer. Disapproving of the increasingly fascistic trend of the Horthy government, Bartók increasingly tended to avoid Budapest, save at the behest of such friends. Early in 1929, a year that produced only some folksong arrangements, he made a concert tour of Russia and began a valuable friendship with the young conductor Paul Sacher in Basle. The following year he completed the big *Cantata profana (Secular Cantata)* for soloists, chorus, and orchestra, based on Rumanian folk music. It was eventually performed for the first time by the BBC forces in 1934. The year 1930 also produced the second piano concerto, which Bartók played under Hans Rosbaud at Frankfurt in January 1933. His fiftieth birthday was honored by the conferring of the *Légion d'honneur* by France, but it was officially all but ignored at home.

In 1934 Bartók resigned from the academy to join the Academy of Sciences, which offered to finance his preparation of his folksong collection for publication. Apart from arrangements and orchestrations of some early works, the only major composition forthcoming for some time was the fifth string quartet, commissioned by the American patroness, Elisabeth Sprague Coolidge in 1934. In 1936, during which year he did some folksong collecting in Turkey, he wrote on commission from Sacher the *Music for Strings, Percussion, and Celesta,* which was to become one of his most popular compositions.

By 1937 Bartók's world was becoming more circumscribed and more threatening. He had refused to appear in Germany after the Nazis took power. He broke off with Universal Editions and affiliated himself with Boosey and Hawkes in London. The Hungarian papers decried him as a turncoat. Yet he hung on, partly out of patriotism, partly because he could not uproot his aged mother. And he continued to work. He and Ditta first performed the *Sonata for Two Pianos and Percussion* at Basle in January 1938, the year in which he completed the great second violin concerto, dedicated to Zoltán Székely, who played it the following March with Mengelberg and the Amsterdam Concertgebouw Orchestra. In the meantime Szigeti, who settled in the United States two years later, had discovered American jazz and thought Bartók might write something in that line that he (Szigeti) and Benny Goodman might play together. He sent Bartók some records by the Goodman Trio, and Bartók obliged with *Contrasts* for violin, clarinet, and piano (more beholden, however, to Transylvania than to Pennsylvania).

In 1939 the composer completed the set of graded piano pieces *Mikrokosmos,* which he had begun in 1926 for Peter's introduction to the piano, and which had become a sort of epitome of all Bartók himself had discovered about music. Feeling that one year was apt to be pretty much like another, he went to Switzerland for the summer, dashed off the *Divertimento for Strings* for Sacher, and began the sixth string quartet, commissioned by Székely. Midway of his work on it, Hitler and Stalin marched into Poland, and he had to hurry home. He finished the quartet just before his mother died in December. There remaining only technicalities now between him and a life elsewhere, he ordered his papers sent to his publishers in London, and in April 1940 he sailed for America to check out the prospects. He and Szigeti gave a concert under Mrs. Coolidge's sponsorship at the Library of Congress and, with Goodman, recorded *Contrasts* for Columbia Records. Declining an offer to teach at the Curtis Institute, he accepted a post as a visiting assistant at Columbia University at an annual stipend of $3,000, paid by the Alice M. Ditson Fund. He returned to Budapest in May, took care of what could be taken care of, gave a farewell concert on October 8, and set forth with Ditta by way of Italy, unoccupied France, and Spain, to board a freighter in Lisbon. (Peter was to follow.) At the Spanish border customs agents confiscated their baggage, which took more than two months to catch up with them. They reached New York on the penultimate day of October. After a Town Hall duo-recital, the conferring of a doctorate by Columbia University, and a visit to the Hungarian community in Cleveland, the Bartóks settled temporarily in Forest Hills, New York. Following another transcontinental concert tour, they returned to Riverdale, New York. Columbia University offered Bartók the cataloguing of the Yugoslav folk music collected by the late Milman Parry five years earlier. Most of the collection was devoted to "epics," but he found a corollary group of lyric pieces that appealed to him and appeared manageable. The appointment was not guaranteed, however, beyond the end of 1942, and he began investigating other possibilities, including concerts on the West Coast and a job at the University of Washington. Pearl Harbor made such things less likely, however. In the meantime Peter had left Budapest and then dropped out of sight. In April his father ran into him in a Bronx subway station. (In 1944 Peter joined the U.S. Navy and was sent to Panama.)

The Columbia job ran out of funds as scheduled, and things looked grim. The family had, by then, moved to a little apartment on West Fifty-seventh Street in Manhattan. There was small opportunity for concerts, and Bartók adamantly refused anything that looked like charity. The ISCM in Basle had commissioned a version of the two-piano sonata with orchestral accompaniment, which the composer and his wife unveiled on January 21, 1943 with Reiner and the New York Philharmonic. Around this time Bartók became very ill, suffering from terrible weakness and fluctuations of temperature. His weight dropped to eighty-seven. The doctors scratched their heads and sent him to Saranac Lake for the summer. (The bills were met by the American Society of Composers and Publishers, alias ASCAP). At Reiner's instigation, Koussevitzky [1655] commissioned an orchestral work in memory of his wife Natalie. Apparently on the mend, Bartók began work on what would be the *Concerto for Orchestra* in August, finishing it by mid-October. It was the work that would make him accepted by the general public. ASCAP sent him south for the winter, to Asheville, North Carolina. There he felt completely recovered and wrote the solo-violin sonata on commission from Yehudi Menuhin, whose playing had delighted him in New York the previous fall. In the interim, friends and admirers had raised enough money for the Columbia project to continue beginning in April. But by then Bartók had suffered a relapse. This time the doctors could give him a diagnosis: leukemia. In late November and early December he was still strong enough to attend the respective premieres of the sonata and the *Concerto for Orchestra*.

Royalties received from England eased the financial strain. Bartók's publisher Ralph Hawkes commissioned a seventh string quartet, and, with Hawkes's backing, violist William Primrose asked for a concerto. Then the duo-piano team of Rae Bartlett and Ethel Robertson wanted another two-piano concerto. But pneumonia in the spring dealt Bartók a severe setback. He returned to Saranac Lake for the summer of 1945. Peter, discharged, returned from Panama, and word came that the relatives in Hungary were still alive. With what strength he had left, Bartók worked at the viola concerto, which he interrupted with a third piano concerto, intended as a legacy to help Ditta make a living. He died leaving seventeen bars unwritten. These his pupil Tibor Serly [2007] filled in. Serly also took on the inchoate viola concerto, which in its present form is ascribed to Bartók but seems to be mostly Serly's.

RECORDINGS: After Bartók died there was a great upsurge of interest in his music, with the result that very soon most of his major works were available on records. A particular factor in this phenomenon was his son Peter who, as a superb recording engineer, founded Bartók Records to preserve his father's music; unfortunately, after a fine start, he ran into legal blocks set up by copyright holders. Béla Bartók himself made a number of piano recordings, both as soloist and accompanist; Ditta recorded the two-piano sonata with him and, much later, the third piano concerto with Serly. In the past decade or so the Hungarian state recording agency, Hungaroton, has been bringing out a comprehensive recording of all of Bartók's mu-

sic, together with his own recordings, and a survey of his folksong cylinders from his fieldwork. The Canadian Sefel label has recently been issuing a series of digital recordings of Batók's music conducted by Arpád Joó.

[1735] **MIASKOVSKY, Nikolai Yakovlevich** (Mē-yás-kōf′-skē, Nē′-kō-lī Yā-kōf-lyā′-vĕch)
SOLDIER, TEACHER
BORN: Novogeorgievsk, April 20, 1881
DIED: Moscow, August 8, 1950

Perhaps only Havergal Brian [1681] and Alan Hovhaness [2170] in the twentieth century have been more devoted to the symphony than Nikolai Miaskovsky—though Miaskovsky's 27 are considerably less original than Brian's 32 and less prone to exoticism than Hovhaness's 52-plus. At first, though for quite different reasons, the Russian had to struggle almost as hard as the Englishman to get his musical career established. He was born in what is now the Polish town of Plock, where E. T. A. Hoffmann [1086] once spent some dreary years. His father was a military engineer on his way up to a generalship who, seven years later, was transferred to Orenburg in southeast Russia. In 1890, shortly after the family had been retransferred to Kazan, Miaskovsky's mother died, leaving her five children to be reared by their aunt. The lady was a singer and in due course Miaskovsky learned the piano and the violin. Meanwhile the general, insisting that he follow in his footsteps, sent him through a series of military schools. In 1895 General Miaskovsky was moved to St. Petersburg, where, at twenty-one, his son graduated from the Academy of Military Engineering. During his time there, he had some lessons from Nikolai Kazanli, a Rimsky-Korsakov [1416] pupil, and began tentatively to compose. Detailed to Moscow on graduation, he found another teacher in the newly fledged Glière [1662]. After a year he was brought back to St. Petersburg, where he continued his studies with Ivan Kryzhanovsky (1867–1924), another Rimsky pupil—and later an associate of Dr. Pavlov, the reflex man. However, the army would not permit him to enter the conservatory, and when his term was up in 1907, he lacked the money to do so. He made up for the lack by taking on students and winning a scholarship with his first symphony of 1908. At the conservatory he studied for three years with Liadov [1485] and entered into a lifelong friendship with young Serge Prokofiev [1851]. After graduating in 1911, he subsisted as a teacher and musical journalist until 1914, when the war summoned him back to his engineering duties.

The October Revolution found Miaskovsky building a fortress at Revel (later Talinn, Estonia). Though he was apolitical, he had an instinct for survival and, as a member of the Red navy, he held an office job in Moscow until he was mustered out in 1920. The following year he was appointed to a professorship at the Moscow Conservatory, where he taught, much admired for his skill and his probity, for the rest of his life. He helped found the Composers' Union and was active in other musical organizations. Among his notable pupils were Aram Khachaturian [2038], Dmitri Kabalevsky [2058], and Karen Khachaturian [2306]. During World War II he was taken, for his own safety, to Tbilisi (Tiflis) in Georgia, and then to Frunze in Khirgizstan. In 1948 he was one of those blacklisted by Zhdanov for "revisionism," but he held his peace and was soon reinstated. A thoroughgoing eclectic with fine musical instincts and polished skills, he played it safe in his composition. As a result, he enjoyed tremendous success and many honors in the Soviet Union. Of his considerable output, which avoided only stage music, one might note, besides the symphonies, 13 string quartets and 9 piano sonatas. RECORDINGS: Recordings include a concerto apiece for violin and cello, the 2 cello sonatas, about half of the symphonies (No. 21 has enjoyed some popularity here, having been commissioned for the Chicago Symphony Orchestra), the orchestral *Divertimento*, the *Overture in G Major*, numerous string quartets, several piano sonatas, the 2 *Sinfoniettas*, the E-flat major *Serenade*, the *Lyric Concertino*, the orchestrated suite *Links* (originally for piano), and there may be others. All of these recordings—except for some of the chamber music, piano works, and the Symphony No. 21—are (ultimately) of Soviet origin.

[1736] KAZURO, Stanisław (Kä-zōō'-rō, Stä-nē'-släf)
CHOIRMASTER, TEACHER, WRITER
BORN: Teklinapol, August 2, 1881
DIED: Warsaw, November 30, 1961

Born in Russian Poland near what is now Wilnius, Kazuro studied at the Setaccioli Warsaw Conservatory, then with Giacomo Setaccioli (1868–1925), a minor operatic composer, at the St. Cecilia Liceo in Rome, and finally at the Sorbonne in Paris. He spent the rest of his life in Warsaw as a successful teacher and choral conductor. He wrote sol-

feggio manuals and books on musical education. After the Second World War, he was head of the conservatory for six years. He wrote widely in most fields (2 folk operas, 3 oratorios), though the bulk of his compositional output was directed to students. RECORDINGS: The organist Feliks Raczkowski has recorded one of his 12 prelude-and-fugues.

[1737] ZILCHER, Hermann Karl Josef (Tsēl'-kher, Hâr'-mån Kärl Yō'-zef)
PIANIST, CONDUCTOR, EDUCATOR
BORN: Frankfurt am Main, August 18, 1881
DIED: Würzburg, January 1, 1948

Hermann Zilcher got his musical basics from his father, Paul Zilcher, a Frankfurt music teacher, then (so to speak) went down the street to the Hoch Conservatory. There he studied with its successive directors Bernhard Scholz (1835–1916) and Iwan Knorr (1853–1916), while preparing for a career as a concert pianist with James Kwast. He pursued that career in Berlin from 1901 to 1905, during which time his first opera, *Fitzebutze*, was produced. In 1905 he toured the United States with the violinist Franz von Vécsey [1876], then returned to Hoch to teach. He moved on to the Munich Academy in 1908, from which he went in 1920 to serve for twenty-four years as head of the Würzburg Conservatory, where he conducted the faculty orchestra. RECORDINGS: Though Zilcher wrote a number of ambitious works —another opera, oratorios, 5 symphonies— he is to be found on records mostly as a composer of songs and of pieces for the accordion. (He was one of the few serious composers of his time to condescend to that popular instrument, for which he wrote a concerto.)

[1738] ENESCO, Georges (En-es'-kō, Zhôrzh)
VIOLINIST, PIANIST, CONDUCTOR, TEACHER
BORN: Liveni-Virnav, Rumania, August 19, 1881
DIED: Paris, May 3/4, 1955

George Enescu (as he was born and as the Rumanians continue to spell his name) is regarded as the greatest of Rumanian composers so far—which is no big thing, Rumania having been a (rather flexible) entity for less than a century and a half. Various sources give his birthplace as Cordaremi, Dorohoiu, Liveni-Virnaz, and Liveni-Virnav, the most recent source noting that it has been re-named George Enescu; none of these towns, however identical, are discoverable in standard world atlases. As a child, Enesco is said to have learned the violin from a local Gypsy and to have been playing and composing at the age of four. At any rate, three years later he was shipped off to the Vienna Conservatory, where he studied with both Joseph Hellmesbergers and with Robert Fuchs (1847–1927), among others. He gave his first concert (in Rumania) when he was eight. Having graduated in 1894, he decided he needed more seasoning and enrolled at the Paris Conservatory for four years. There he studied with Martin Marsick (a Joachim [1321] pupil) and the black violinist José White [1375], as well as with Théodore Dubois [1356], Fauré [1424], Massenet [1396], and Ambroise Thomas [1217]. By the time he left (with a first prize for violin), he was already known around Paris as a composer and in Rumania as a conductor. (He was also a fine pianist, organist, and cellist.)

To all intents and purposes, Enesco was a Parisian in more than name for the rest of his life. A friend and concert partner of Alfred Cortot, he taught at the École Normale; later he taught at the American Conservatory at Fontainebleau. He toured en trio with pianist Alfredo Casella [1767] and cellist Louis Fournier, and in 1904 organized his own string quartet. However, he maintained an estate in Rumania near Bucharest, kept in touch with music in his country, and returned there as often as his busy schedule permitted. It was in Bucharest in 1903 that he introduced (as conductor) the two very Lisztian [1218] Rumanian Rhapsodies by which he is chiefly known to the broad public. Queen Marie named him her official court violinist, and he founded the symphony orchestra at Iaşi and the Composers' Society. He first appeared in the United States in 1923 with the Philadelphia Orchestra, conducting and playing his own music, and was a guest conductor with the New York Philharmonic in the late 1930s. World War II caught him in Rumania, where he remained quietly on his farm until 1946, when he came to New York to teach. Increasingly incapacitated by arthritis, he gave a farewell concert there in 1950 with his most famous pupil, Yehudi Menuhin (Dinu Lipatti was also a protégé), and returned to Paris. He spent his last ten months totally paralyzed by a stroke.

As a composer, it took Enesco—by nature an eclectic romantic—a long time to find his own voice. He disowned virtually all of the prolix works before 1900. His official Op. 1 is the folkish Poème roumain for orchestra of

1897, but even the 3 completed symphonies come from a period, 1905–21, when he was still flirting with Wagnerism [1230], Impressionism, old-fashioned musical nationalism, and neo-classicism. Eventually he arrived at a sort of Bartókian [1734] use of his native music and a kind of free parlando melodic style. His mature masterpiece is his only opera, Oedipe, which it took him a decade to write; it was produced at the Paris Opéra in 1936 but has been neglected since, save in Rumania. (It makes use of quarter-tones.) Even so his name looms small or is omitted in most histories of modern music.

RECORDINGS: Recordings include the opera, the string octet, the wind dixtuor, all the symphonies, the 3 orchestral suites, the Poème roumain, Concert Overture on Popular Rumanian Themes, the 1954 Chamber Symphony, the 1955 symphonic poem Vox maris, the 3 violin sonatas, the so-called third piano sonata (by Dinu Lipatti [2263]; the second was never set down), songs, and a few small pieces. Enesco himself recorded as conductor (chiefly with Yehudi Menuhin, but he twice led the Rumanian Rhapsodies for records), violinist (including the third sonata, partner of Lipatti, and versions of the second and third with Lipatti, retrieved from wartime radio broadcasts), and pianist.

[1739] EGGEN, Arne (Eg'-gen, Är'-ne)
ORGANIST
BORN: Trondheim, August 28, 1881
DIED: Baerum, October 26, 1955

Norway's political and linguistic history did not favor native opera when it was flourishing elsewhere, and in fact there was no national opera company until 1959. It is not therefore surprising that Norway produced few operatic composers before that date, Arne Eggen being one of the rare exceptions. The younger brother of ethnomusicologist Erik Eggen (1877–1957), who was also a composer, Arne trained to be a schoolteacher. However, when he was twenty-two, he enrolled at the Christiania (Oslo) Conservatory for two years and then spent another at the Leipzig Conservatory. He specialized in organ and in 1908 got a post in a church at Drammen, on the west branch of the Oslo Fjord. During his sixteen years there, he wrote his only symphony and incidental music for Arne Garborg's Liti Kjersti (Little Kirsten). In 1926 he moved to a church in the suburbs of Oslo. The next year he began an eighteen-year term as president of the Norwegian Composers' Association, in which office he was, somewhat confusingly, succeeded by Klaus Egge [2092]. Eggen's operas were late works, the more successful *Olav Liljekrans* dating from 1940 and *Cymbelin* (after Shakespeare) from 1948. Like his brother, he collected folk music, some of which he incorporated in his compositions. He was awarded a lifelong annuity by the government in 1934. RECORDINGS: There are recordings of excerpts from *Olav Liljekrans* and *Liti Kjersti*, and a symphonic poem, *Bøgulv the Fiddler*. Recent extensive recording projects sponsored by the Norwegian government seem to have passed Eggen by, however.

[1740] LÓPEZ BUCHARDO, Carlos
(Lō'-pez Boo-chär'-dō, Kär'-lōs)
TEACHER, ADMINISTRATOR
BORN: Buenos Aires, October 12, 1881
DIED: Buenos Aires, April 21, 1948

López Buchardo began his musical studies in his native city, but his most important teacher was Albert Roussel [1605] in Paris. After he returned to Buenos Aires, he taught. At various times he was director of the Graduate School of Fine Arts at La Plata University, and from 1924 until he died he was director of the Conservatorio Nacionál (of which he was also the founder) in the capital. He twice served as intendant of the Teatro Colón, which produced, under the baton of Tullio Serafin, his only opera *El Sueño de Alma (Alma's Dream)* in 1914. He was married to the singer Brigida Frías. The list of his compositions is not large. Besides the opera, he wrote 3 operettas, a *Mass*, a symphonic suite *Escenas Argentinas (Argentine Scenes;* based on folk themes, it enjoyed considerable popularity, choruses, piano pieces, and songs, including arrangements of folksongs. RECORDINGS: A few songs appear on records.

[1741] CADMAN, Charles Wakefield
ORGANIST, CONDUCTOR,
ETHNOMUSICOLOGIST, CRITIC
BORN: Johnstown, Pa., December 24, 1881
DIED: Los Angeles, December 30, 1946

Like Ethelbert Nevin [1550], Cadman appears doomed to be remembered for his potboilers rather than for his seriously intended music. Though his mother's father was a hymn writer and organ builder, his own father was a steelworker. However, his musical leanings were fostered despite the family's rather straitened circumstances, and he was taught fairly broadly by several Pittsburghers, including Emil Paur, who

had succeeded Victor Herbert [1513] as conductor of the local symphony. Cadman began composing songs and, after a struggle to get them noticed at all, had an enormous hit in 1906 with the sentimental "At Dawning," whose sales eventually reached seven figures. Two years later he became organist of a suburban church, director of the Pittsburgh Male Choir, and reviewer for the Pittsburgh *Dispatch*.

In the meantime Cadman had been caught up in the eleventh-hour tide of interest in American Indian culture. In the summer of 1909 he acquired a recording phonograph and went west to study the music of the Omahas and Winnebagos on location. Shortly afterward he adapted four of the melodies he had collected to verses by his regular lyricist, Nelle Richmond Eberhart, and published them as *Four American Indian Songs*. Their ethnic qualities were largely hidden by the whipped-cream topping, and they (particularly "From the Land of the Sky-Blue Water") further helped make the composer financially independent. Established as an authority on Indian music, Cadman found an Indian singer called Princess Redfeather and in 1910 went off on a successful lecture tour of Europe. For the next several years he capitalized on his reputation as an "Indianist," producing such works as the *Thunderbird Suite* for orchestra and the opera *The Land of the Misty Water* (which found no takers), though he also wrote some purely abstract pieces, including a string quartet, a piano trio, and a piano sonata. Around 1911 he moved to Denver, where he served as a church organist. A second "Indian" opera, to an Eberhart libretto, *Shanewis or The Robin Woman*—the story of an Indian maiden who comes to New York seeking an operatic career—was picked up by the Metropolitan Opera in 1918, the year in which Cadman settled permanently in Los Angeles. It was produced the following season, on a double bill with Henry Gilbert's [1601] ballet *Dance in the Place Congo*, with Sophie Braslau in the title role, and was sufficiently successful to be carried over for another season—the first American opera to be so honored. A third opera, *The Garden of Mystery*, got a New York concert performance in 1925. After 1920 (having dabbled briefly in oriental ethnicities), Cadman seems to have decided to become more broadly "American." Another opera, *A Witch of Salem*, was produced at the Chicago Opera in 1926. Strongly cast (Eide Norena, José Mojica, Charles Hackett), it won considerable praise but only two performances. Later "American" works included a *Suite on American*

Folktunes in 1937, the *Pennsylvania Symphony* of 1940, and the 1945 overture *Huckleberry Finn Goes Fishing.* The *Hollywood Suite* of 1932 reminds us that a decade earlier Cadman had been one of the chief founders of the Hollywood Bowl. Cadman's *Dark Dancers of the Mardi Gras,* 1933 (shades of Henry Gilbert!), for piano and orchestra often featured its composer as soloist.

RECORDINGS: Cadman's more successful songs have been plentifully recorded, especially by singers of an earlier day, and there were one or two contemporaneous excerpts from *Shanewis.* There is also a piano reduction of the 1944 *A Mad Empress Remembers,* originally for cello and orchestra. (The empress was Eugénie of France.)

[1742] HUGHES, Herbert
ETHNOMUSICOLOGIST, CRITIC
BORN: Belfast, March 16, 1882
DIED: Brighton, May 1, 1937

Ulster-born, Herbert Hughes was a graduate of the Royal College of Music in London, class of 1901. His initial interest was in Irish folksong, and he was a founding member of, and editor for, the Irish Folksong Society. He collected and arranged many such songs. He also wrote some incidental music and a few chamber pieces, but the chief focus of his original composition was on songs, many of them parodistic. In 1931 he was appointed critic of the London *Daily Telegraph.* He was the father of Patrick Cairns ("Spike") Hughes (b. 1908), playwright, composer, writer, lecturer, and sometime jazzman. RECORDINGS: His four volumes of *Irish Country Songs* in particular have been the source of innumerable recordings.

[1743] MALIPIERO, Gian Francesco
(Mà-lē-pē-ā'-rō, Jàn Fràn-chã-skō)
TEACHER, ADMINISTRATOR, EDITOR,
WRITER
BORN: Venice, March 18, 1882
DIED: Treviso, August 1, 1973

Regarded in the first half of this century as one of the leading Italian composers (with Casella [1767] and Pizzetti [1732]), Gian Francesco Malipiero suffered eclipse well before he died at the age of ninety-one. It was not so much that he was rejected by the self-proclaimed avant-gardists; it was rather that his music defied classification and often analysis (at least according to the approved methods). Possessed of dynamic energy, he poured forth for seventy years a stream of compositions, editions, articles, and books.

His music often appears to be an overflow of the emotions (though the man was a thinker), and there was unquestionably too much of it, even if one forgets the immature stuff, most of which he destroyed. But the best of it—notably the more individualistic operas—probably should be given another chance.

Malipiero came from an old Venetian family that had included doges. It was musical as well as noble: his grandfather, Francesco (1824–87), had had operas produced in the mid-nineteenth century; his father, Luigi, was a conductor; his brother, Riccardo, was a cellist; and Riccardo's son and namesake (1914–), whom Gian Francesco himself taught, became a notable composer. Gian Francesco's parents' marriage fell apart when he was eleven. As a musician he was a problem from the outset. He was kicked out of the Vienna Conservatory after a year as unpromising. From 1899 he studied at the Liceo in Venice with its director, Marco Enrico Bossi [1534]. Bossi did not think much of him and left him on his own when he moved on to the Bologna Liceo in 1902. Shortly afterward Malipiero became entranced with the old Italian music he found buried in the Marciano Library and began copying it out for his own use. The work provided him with educational underpinning that the classroom had not. Two years later Bossi welcomed him in Bologna.

After he graduated in 1905, Malipiero worked for a time, transcribing music from the playing of the Dalmatian composer Antonio Smareglia (1854–1929). (Smareglia, a passionate Wagnerian [1230] whose compositions were once much admired, had recently gone blind.) Malipiero visited Berlin in 1908 and sat in on some of Bruch's [1358] lectures, like his compatriot Respighi [1718], found them boring. In 1913 he spent some time in Paris—long enough to be shaken by what Debussy [1547] was doing (Debussy found him "ignorant"), to be knocked out of his seat by the premiere of Stravinsky's [1748] *Le Sacre du printemps,* and to be confirmed in a lifelong friendship with Casella. It was at this point that he decided he had been barking up the wrong tree and junked much of his early work, which by that time included four operas and three symphonies. Not much followed for some time. Malipiero was distressed by the outbreak of the 1914 war and spent most of his time in the village of Asolo, northwest of Treviso. In 1917 the Austro-German advance in the Veneto shattered that peace, and he spent the next several years in Rome.

By the end of the war, Malipiero had discovered his own voice. It owed something—

its conviction as to the importance of melody and counterpoint, mostly—to the Renaissance and Baroque music that he loved but virtually nothing to his immediate predecessors or contemporaries. It was unflinchingly diatonic, athematic, and nondevelopmental. The composer attracted most attention with his operas, which were not only musically radical but dramatically experimental. *L'Orfeide* of 1925 is actually three (or nine!) related works. In the first, Orpheus interrupts a traditional *commedia* and condemns the characters as irrelevant; in the second—subtitled "Seven Songs"—we see enacted (and sung) seven tiny unrelated real-life episodes; in the last Orpheus puts a querulous audience to sleep with his singing.

In 1921 Malipiero was appointed to a professorship at the Parma Conservatory. A year later he settled for good in Asolo and, finding teaching at Parma not to his liking, he resigned his post in 1923. The years from 1926 to 1942 were in part devoted to bringing out the first modern edition of the complete works of Claudio Monteverdi [333], but they saw little abatement in his original composition. In 1932 he was persuaded to take up teaching again at the Liceo Marcello in Venice, and seven years later he became its director. He worked hard to bring the school up to his high standards—it became the Conservatorio B. Marcello in 1940—and drew students from all over the world. Shortly after the Second World War was over, he joined the editorial board for the complete edition of Vivaldi's [650] instrumental music, consequent to the discovery of a great hoard of Vivaldi manuscripts two decades earlier. Malipiero himself edited over one hundred of the works; the edition was completed the year before he died. He retired from the conservatory in 1952, when he was seventy, but continued to teach, edit, and compose for nearly twenty more years.

Malipiero's output was too vast to detail here. After he began *L'Orfeide,* he produced 28 more operas, three of them triptychs. Among the more successful or controversial were: *Tre commedie goldoniane (Three Goldoni Comedies),* 1926; *Torneo notturno (Nocturnal Tournament),* 1931; *Il Mistero di Venezia (Venetian Mystery),* 1932; and *I Capricci di Callot (Callot's Caprices),* 1942. Malipiero, a gifted writer, produced most of his own libretti. In the late 1930s and early '40s, he produced a series of operas based on classic authors—Shakespeare, Virgil, Euripides, etc. His last two (one-act operas) were written in 1970. He also wrote 11 numbered symphonies and several unnumbered, 6 ballets, numerous concerti (including 6 for piano) a series of concerted works called "dia-

logues," miscellaneous concerted and/or orchestral works, 8 string quartets, other chamber music, much vocal music (major and minor), and piano pieces. He edited and arranged numerous works by early composers other than those mentioned and published nearly twenty books.

RECORDINGS: Very little evidence of Malipiero's existence has shown up on phonograph records. One notes a concerto apiece for violin and piano, the orchestral *Notturno di canti e balli (Song-and-Dance Nocturne),* the *Fantasie di ogni giorno (Everyday Fantasies),* a selection from *Impressioni dal vero (Impressions of Truth),* *Magister Josephus* for voices and orchestra, *Cimarosiana* (orchestral pieces after Cimarosa), the *Dialoghi* Nos. 3, 4, and 7, the string quartets 1–4 and 7, the *Sonata a tre,* and a few vocal and piano pieces. The operas appear to be represented by a single song arranged from *Filomela e l'infatuato (Philomela and the Infatuated Fellow).*

[1744] WOOD, Haydn
VIOLINIST
BORN: Slaithwaite, March 25, 1882
DIED: London, March 11, 1959

The composer of drawing-room songs of epidemic popularity, Haydn Wood was a Yorkshireman who grew up on the Isle of Man. He was soon stunning the Manx with his fiddling, which got him into the Royal College of Music where, of course, he studied with Stanford [1467]. His violin teacher there was Enrique Fernández Arbós, now remembered as a conductor and the orchestrator of Albéniz' [1523] *Iberia* and *Navarra.* Further training with César Thomson, a star pupil of Vieuxtemps [1270] and Wieniawski [1340], preceded a world tour with the Canadian soprano Emma Albani. In 1909 Wood married Dorothy Court, a popular singer. Though he had written some seriously intended works (and won a prize with a string quartet), he devoted the rest of his career to potboilers. His greatest hits were "Roses of Picardy," written during World War I, and the later "A Brown Bird Singing." RECORDINGS: There are many.

[1745] HOWE, Mary (née Carlisle)
PIANIST
BORN: Richmond, Va., April 4, 1882
DIED: Washington, D.C., September 4, 1964

A society woman and patron of music, Mrs. Howe atypically also made and wrote music as a professional. She is said to have studied, early on, with Richard Burmeister, a Liszt [1218] pupil, in Europe. After the turn of the century she studied at the Peabody Institute in Baltimore, with the director Harold Randolph (a fellow Richmonder), and with the pianist Ernest Hutcheson. After some concertizing—often as a duo with her friend Anne Hull—she married a Washingtonian, Walter Bruce Howe. She came to composition late, studying with Nadia Boulanger and with Reger's [1637] pupil Gustav Strube (1867–1953) at Peabody, from which she graduated finally in 1922. Neither her output nor its contents are large. Her idiom is generally conservative, but the pieces are imaginative and well crafted. She wrote a number of short orchestral pieces, some chamber music, choruses, and a considerable body of interesting songs (published in a collected edition a few years before she died). There are recordings of the tone poems *Stars*, *Sand*, and *Spring Pastoral*, the *Castellana* for two pianos and orchestra (the orchestral pieces are all conducted by William Strickland), songs (sung by Harold Ronk and Katherine Hansel), choruses (Howard University Choir), and some chamber pieces.

[1746] SCHNABEL, Artur (Shnä'-bel Är'-toor)
PIANIST, WRITER, EDITOR, TEACHER
BORN: Lipnik, April 17, 1882
DIED: Axenstein, August 15, 1951

Treated in his day as though he were the voice of Beethoven [1063], and sometimes of God, Schnabel will certainly be remembered as the first pianist to record all thirty-two of the sonatas, and perhaps for his edition of them, which often appears to contain more footnotes than musical ones. A chunky little man with close-cropped hair and mustache, he looked more like a prosperous German small-tradesman than a virtuoso (which he was not). Born in Bohemia, he studied in Vienna with Hans Schmitt, Annette Esipoff (Anna Esipova), and eventually with her husband, Theodor Leschetizky (1830–1915). He also had theory lessons from Eusebius Mandyczewski. Although his teachers warned him that he was too intelligent ever to become a pianist, he was playing in public at the age of eight.

Schnabel settled in Berlin. There he met the six-foot contralto, Therese Behr, a noted *Lieder* singer six years his senior, and married her in 1905. They often appeared in concert together, and their son Karl Ulrich (1909–) became a notable pianist and less notable composer who also accompanied his

mother. In 1912 Artur Schnabel founded the Schnabel Trio, whose other most permanent member was the violinist Carl Flesch. Artur's solo career evolved unspectacularly—he later remarked that he did not begin to understand Beethoven until he was forty—and his first American tour, in 1921, attracted neither attention nor audiences. He had been composing all his mature life, but in this period he discovered twelve-tone music, by which formula he produced most of his works. In 1925 he took up teaching piano at the Berlin Hochschule, where his most famous pupil was Clifford Curzon. He first played the complete Beethoven sonatas in a Berlin concert series in 1927. In 1930 he returned to America, this time with success. A year later he embarked on the great recording project, which took him four years. When the Nazis came to power, he moved to Switzerland, where he gave master classes at Tremezzo on Lake Como. In 1939 he emigrated to the United States, where he joined the faculty of the University of Michigan. He became an American citizen in 1944. However, after the war, he returned to Europe and died in Canton Schwyz, Switzerland. Therese Behr-Schnabel survived her husband by eight years.

RECORDINGS: Late in her career they made an album of *Lieder* recordings. Schnabel's daughter-in-law, Helen (née Fogel), recorded his 1901 piano concerto and some solo pieces, and accompanied Erika Francoulon in some of his songs. There are also recordings of the string trio and the *Duodecimet.*

[1747] MARX, Joseph (Märks, Yō'-zef)
TEACHER, CRITIC, THEORIST
BORN: Graz, May 11, 1882
DIED: Graz, September 3, 1964

Broadly educated and intended for the legal profession, Marx, against family expectations, took a Ph.D. in musical theory at the local university when he was twenty-seven. He had already begun composing *Lieder* as though they were going out of style (which they were) and soon made a name for himself as a songsmith to be watched. In 1914 he became professor of theory at the Vienna Academy of Music. Eight years later he was elevated to the directorship, and when the school became the Hochschule für Musik in 1924, he remained as rector until 1927. From 1931 he was a newspaper reviewer and critic. In the early 1930s he spent some time in Turkey as musical adviser to the government. In 1947 his alma mater conferred an honorary professorship on him. A self-styled "romantic realist," he had no truck with musical progressivism. Though he continued to compose throughout his career, he did not live up to his initial promise. He produced a "Romantic" piano concerto, a program symphony, and chamber music, but his best efforts remain the songs (most of which are also forgotten). He published harmony and counterpoint manuals, a consideration of musical aesthetics, and a collected essays. RECORDINGS: A few songs have attracted a fair number of recordings.

[1748] STRAVINSKY, Igor Fedorovich
PIANIST, CONDUCTOR
BORN: Oranienbaum, June 17, 1882
DIED: New York City, April 6, 1971

When Igor Stravinsky died, there were many who thought of him as the last of the great composers. In part this attitude was owing to the puffery of his sycophants and promoters and in part to the fact that unlike that of many of his contemporaries, his music appealed to a large public; but mostly, one suspects, it was because he was undeniably a great composer. Like so many of that sort, he was not a pathbreaker. Rather one must say that he, more than anyone else, summed up his times. He moved from the late-Romantic onward to Impressionism, primitivism, and neo-classicism to serialism, and, one scholar believes, reconciled himself in his very last works (orchestrations of songs by Hugo Wolf [1521]) with the musical world from which he came. Yet on each of these musical manifestations he placed his own highly personal cachet, and he was protean, doing the new and unexpected from one composition to the next. Finally he was, in the face of a rejection of such things, a lifelong proponent of recognizable melody and sharply defined rhythm.

The Strawinskis came to Russia from Poland in the late eighteenth century. The composer's father, Feodor Ignatievich, was a noted operatic basso at the Maryinsky Theater in St. Petersburg, a singing actor for whom Tchaikovsky [1377] and Rimsky-Korsakov [1416] created parts. As a member of the Kiev Opera in 1873, he married Anna Kholodovsky. The following year, in which Roman, the eldest of their four sons, was born, the father accepted an appointment with the Imperial Opera and moved his family to St. Petersburg, where they remained. Igor was the third child, preceded by Yuri in 1879 and followed by Guri in 1884. His birthplace was a summer resort on the Gulf of Finland. His childhood seems to have been not entirely a happy one: he found his mother cold, feared his father's temper, did not get along with his elder brothers; his best friends were Guri and the servants.

Music was a matter of course in the Stravinsky household. Igor heard his father's daily practice from infancy and was taken to the opera, where he once saw Tchaikovsky plain. At nine he began piano lessons and later had private training in theory and harmony. Accounts differ as to whether his parents encouraged or discouraged a musical career for him, but the fact is that, after Gymnasium, where he was an indifferent student, he was sent to pursue the law at the university, where he was even worse. He enjoyed improvising at the piano, a pastime which led to attempts at composing. After the turn of the century, Feodor Stravinsky developed cancer of the spine. In the summer of 1902 the family went to Bad Wildungen, a German health resort. One of Igor's closest friends at school was Vladimir Rimsky-Korsakov, son of the composer. The Rimsky-Korsakovs were spending the summer with another son, then studying in Germany, and Stravinsky used an invitation to visit them as a chance to show some of his work to the father. Rimsky exhibited no enthusiasm for the music but advised Stravinsky to avoid conservatories and study privately, indicating that he himself would be available for consultation.

In December Feodor died. His son, now twenty, began to assert his independence. He left home for a time but was forced to come back by his mother's "illness." He attended the musicales at the Rimsky-Korsakovs and became part of a group of young proponents of contemporary music, for one of whose concerts he wrote a piano sonata. The following summer he took Rimsky up on his offer and asked for a critique of the sonata. This action led to more or less regular lessons on an informal basis, chiefly devoted to problems of orchestration, of which Stravinsky was to become a master. In 1905 he finished at the university concurrently with the revolution of that year, as a consequence of which upheaval he was once arrested and detained when he innocently wandered into a student protest. In October he became engaged to his cousin Katerina. Cousin marriage being officially frowned on in Russia, they were privately wed in January, the sole participants in the ceremony, other than the priest, being the Rimsky-Korsakov boys. After a year of living with the groom's mother, the pair found an apartment of their own and summered with the in-laws. Their first two children, Feodor and Ludmila, were born in 1907 and 1908 respectively.

In the latter year Rimsky-Korsakov died.

Stravinsky had grown more independent of him but had continued to submit compositions to him. In 1907 Rimsky had arranged a run-through of the first symphony (in E-flat) and a cycle for alto and orchestra, *Faun and Shepherdess*. In 1908 Stravinsky sent the score of his *Fireworks* as a wedding present for Rimsky's daughter Nadeshda and Maximilian Steinberg (a pupil). In reply he received news of the old composer's death. He attended the funeral and afterward wrote a *Chant funèbre*, which was played at a memorial concert in St. Petersburg that fall. (The score later disappeared.) Later on, apparently disapproving of the fact that Stravinsky's music was veering away from his teacher's, the Rimsky-Korsakov family dropped him.

In February 1909 *Fireworks* and the orchestral *Scherzo fantastique* were performed at another St. Petersburg concert. Among the auditors was the impresario Sergei Diaghilev, who was planning a season of Russian ballet and opera for Paris in the spring. Needing a musical expert, he approached Stravinsky for some orchestrations (notably of two Chopin [1208] pieces for *Les Sylphides*). Stravinsky obliged, the season was a success, and when Liadov [1485]—typically—turned down a commission for a new ballet on a folktale about a "firebird" and the rescue of some enchanted princesses, Diaghilev decided to entrust the job to Stravinsky. Flattered, the young composer set to work and finished the full score by April 1910. After a short holiday at Ustilug, he joined the Diaghilev company in Paris. *The Firebird*—orchestra conducted by Gabriel Pierné [1555]—was produced on June 25 and established Stravinsky as a composer to be reckoned with, and he soon knew most of the progressive musicians and artists centered in Paris.

Katerina and the children joined him for a seaside vacation and then decided to stay in the West for a while. In September the Stravinskys produced a second son, christened Sviatoslav Soulima and subsequently called by the second name. (He became a concert pianist.) At first the family lived in Switzerland, then on the French Riviera. Shortly after he had finished *The Firebird*, the composer had imagined a new ballet involving pagan fertility rituals and a human sacrifice. Diaghilev had encouraged him to write it, but when he checked in on him shortly after the child was born, he found his protégé involved with a sort of piano concerto having something to do with a puppet. Needing a new score for 1911 and sensing that this one might do, properly managed, he encouraged Stravinsky to work out a di-

rection with the scenic artist Alexandre Benois. The result was *Petrouchka*, a ballet about the love of a puppet for a ballerina in the setting of a Russian fair. The music, a rhythmic and harmonic advance on *The Firebird*, was a fabric of folk and popular themes. Work on it was interrupted by the composer's illness during the winter, but after his wife and children had returned to Ustilug, he completed the score in Rome in May while Diaghilev was presenting a season there. With Vaclav Nijinsky dancing the title role and Pierre Monteux conducting, *Petrouchka* was first played in Paris on June 13. The score was accepted by Serge Koussevitzky [1655] for publication. Later Stravinsky arranged three movements for piano solo (a "sonata" for Artur Rubinstein).

Its reception encouraged Stravinsky to further experimentation. Returning to Russia, he first wrote a curious and highly dissonant cantata for male choir and orchestra, *Zvezdoliki (Starface*, better known as *The King of the Stars)*, which he dedicated to Debussy [1547]. Though published, this brief work was not performed until 1939, when Franz André conducted it for Belgian Radio. Mostly, however, Stravinsky worked on his "primitive" ballet, which would emerge as *Le Sacre du printemps (The Rite of Spring)*. On account of production difficulties of Nijinsky's ballet to Debussy's *L'Après-midi d'un faune (The Afternoon of a Faun)*, Stravinsky's work had to be put off until the 1913 season. The composer and his family again spent the winter of 1912–13 in Switzerland. During the late fall he was in Berlin for a time, hobnobbed with Arnold Schoenberg [1657], and attended the first performance of his *Pierrot Lunaire*, which Stravinsky liked. But the association did not last, and for a time Stravinsky sneered at Schoenberg's twelve-tone ideas. The new ballet went into rehearsal in the spring while the company toured Hungary, Austria, and England, Nijinsky's avant-garde choreography posing all sorts of problems. While that was going on, the composer was turning out several sets of songs, and working, at Diaghilev's request, with Ravel [1666] on an orchestration of Mussorgsky's [1369] opera *Khovantschina*.

The new ballet was scheduled to be conducted by Pierre Monteux in the new Théâtre des Champs-Elysées. The dress rehearsal went well and Diaghilev decided to finish out the premiere with some turns by star performers. The program never got that far. Legend has it that with the opening high bassoon notes old Saint-Saëns [1343] asked rhetorically "What instrument is *that?*" and stalked out. As the hubbub grew, others loudly proclaimed personal affronts, blows and curses were exchanged, at least one duel was agreed upon, and the evening took on all the look of a riot. Backstage Nijinsky, standing on a chair, was shouting numbers at his dancers, who could hear little or nothing. It may have been the most scandalous premiere in the history of music. The scandal was not repeated at the first London performance six weeks later, which was by contrast something of a triumph. The Nijinsky choreography was, however, jettisoned after that season.

Le Sacre was as far as Stravinsky ever went toward the rejection of musical "rules." Though the work is regarded as a landmark and perhaps the true beginning of "modern" music, the composer did not—could not?—proceed farther in that direction; nor did anyone else of moment. Shortly after the premiere Stravinsky came down with typhoid fever and was ill for six weeks. During the next winter Katerina, pregnant again, was found to have tuberculosis and was placed in a Swiss sanitarium, where she gave birth to a second daughter, named Maria Milena.

During these trying times Stravinsky turned to a commission from the Moscow Free Theater to complete his opera *The Nightingale.* He had begun this work, based on Hans Christian Andersen's fairytale "The Emperor's Nightingale," in his last year with Rimsky, at that time completing only the first of three acts, in a rather impressionistic style. Though the music of the two new acts is not in the *Sacre* vein, it is in a quite different and more individual style. By the time Stravinsky had completed the work, the Free Theater was no more. In April he visited Ernest Ansermet, the young conductor who was to become one of his chief promoters. Ansermet had just been appointed director of the orchestra at Montreux and was programming the early Stravinsky symphony. He initiated the composer's conducting career by persuading him to lead a rehearsal. Meanwhile Diaghilev had gotten funds from the pill magnate Sir Joseph Beecham (father of Sir Thomas, the conductor) for a Paris production of *The Nightingale.* It took place on May 26 and created no great stir. Later, in 1917, Stravinsky extracted from the music a symphonic poem, *Le Chant du rossignol (The Song of the Nightingale).*

His next project was *Les Noces (The Wedding),* a sort of choral ballet based on a Russian peasant wedding and using folk poetry for its text. Finding too little in the West for his purposes, he returned to Russia in July to fetch the requisite books and got back to

Switzerland just before war closed the frontiers. He was not to see his homeland again for nearly forty years. Katerina was still frail, and the family's shifting from one Swiss home to another was not conducive to steady composition, though over the next few years Stravinsky's Russian researches bore fruit in several highly original sets of songs; he also wrote piano pieces for his children and the *Three Pieces* for string quartet. Because of the war Diaghilev's troupe had temporarily disbanded and Stravinsky was cut off from his publishers. Among the many people to whom Ansermet introduced him during this period was the Swiss poet Charles-Ferdinand Ramuz and the Hungarian cimbalom player Aladar Racz. By 1916 Diaghilev had organized a new company (with Ansermet as conductor) and had left for New York on New Year's Day, leaving Stravinsky behind, to his disappointment —though he was able to join them in Spain in the spring. In the interim the Singer sewing-machine heiress, the Princesse de Polignac, asked the composer for a work for chamber orchestra. It was clear that *Les Noces,* then conceived for full symphonic ensemble, would not do, so he suggested a sort of opera-ballet-burlesque, *Renard,* based on a Russian analogue of Chaucer's "The Nuns' Priest's Tale." Ramuz would write the libretto, and the main feature of the orchestra would be the cimbalom (played by Racz), on which instrument Stravinsky worked out the music. Neither it nor *Les Noces* were produced, however, until long after the end of the war.

Since 1915 Stravinsky had been conducting his own works sporadically for the Diaghilev ballet. On what seemed the joyful news of the overthrow of the czar in 1917, he orchestrated *The Song of the Volga Boatmen* to replace the imperial anthem as an opener for the ballet performances. But the times were grim. News came that year of the deaths of his beloved old nurse and his brother Guri. Stravinsky soon realized that he would be unable to live under the Soviet regime. Moreover ballet engagements were becoming scarcer, and early in 1918 the company found itself in Lisbon with nowhere to go. At that juncture Stravinsky and Ramuz back in Switzerland decided that what was in order was a stage work that could be performed with minimal forces. The result (again from Russian folk sources) was *L'Histoire du soldat (The Soldier's Tale)* for seven instrumentalists, readers, and two dancers. Among the dance numbers was a "ragtime," inspired by music Ansermet had brought the composer from America. (This impulse led also to the *Ragtime* for chamber orchestra that same year and the *Piano Rag-Music* of 1919.) The first production of *L'Histoire* (Lausanne, September 28, 1918) was a great success, but Stravinsky's hopes of a series of performances were doomed by the great flu epidemic that followed the war (by which he himself was stricken).

By 1919 the Ballets Russes had revived. Diaghilev was having success with work based on old music arranged by modern composers—e.g., Domenico Scarlatti [687] by Vincenzo Tommasini (1685–1750). When Stravinsky exhibited no interest in having the *Chant du rossignol* choreographed, Diaghilev tempted him with some music by, or attributed to, Pergolesi [782]. Finding that he liked it (to his own surprise) and drawn by Diaghilev's proposal to have Stravinsky's now close friend Pablo Picasso design the ballet, Stravinsky yielded. Diaghilev was disappointed at first with both the designs and the music (the latter was in the *sec* style that came to be Stravinsky's hallmark), but when *Pulcinella* was performed at the Paris Opéra on May 15, 1920, it was an immediate hit. It also marked the composer's entry into neo-classicism.

Faced with the necessity of exile from Russia, Stravinsky decided that Switzerland was too far from the action he was interested in, and after the *Pulcinella* premiere, he moved his household to France—first to Brittany, then to "Coco" Chanel's house outside of Paris, and, by spring 1921, to Biarritz. There, in memory of his off-and-on friendship with Debussy, Stravinsky wrote a piano chorale as his contribution to the commemorative *Tombeau de Debussy;* from it and his recent experiments with instrumental chamber groups came immediately afterward the *Symphonies of Wind Instruments.* In June 1921 he went to London and heard Eugene Goossens [1878] lead a concert performance of *Le Sacre* that once and for all established it as a masterpiece. Goossens had hoped also to premiere the *Symphonies,* but that was done (abominably) by Serge Koussevitzky three days thereafter. Then, with Diaghilev's backing, Stravinsky began work on an opera, *Mavra,* the libretto after Pushkin by Diaghilev's secretary Boris Kochno. Doubtless growing out of the Pergolesi experience, this work was a classical *opera buffa*—set pieces connected by recitatives—with Russian overtones. It was not completed until 1922, having been interrupted by a request from the impresario that he help revise Tchaikovsky's *Sleeping Beauty* for a projected London run. Its 105 performances ended in bankruptcy, but the work served to renew the composer's childhood love of Tchaikovsky. *Renard* (meant to

be pantomimed by acrobats or clowns, the singing roles emanating from the orchestra) at last had, thanks to Diaghilev, its first performance on May 18, 1922, at the Paris Opéra. Two weeks later, on the same stage, Diaghilev repeated it on a bill with the debutante *Mavra,* plus *Petrouchka* and *Le Sacre,* allegedly to impress his guest, the American magnate Otto Kahn, who was backing the company's upcoming tour of the United States. The miniature works were overwhelmed by the big stage and the blockbuster ballets, and *Mavra* had, for the moment, to be reckoned a failure.

In 1922 two significant events occurred in Stravinsky's personal life. Early in the year he met Vera Sudeikine *(née* de Bosset), wife of the painter and scenic artist Sergei Sudeikine, who in 1939 was to become his own wife. And, after much diplomatic maneuvering, Stravinsky went to Germany to meet his mother, who had finally been allowed to leave Russia and who turned out to be as haughty as ever. Having in this same year finally solved the problem of how to orchestrate *Les Noces* (for percussion ensemble and four pianos), he completed that work in April 1923. Diaghilev produced it on June 13—the last "new" Stravinsky ballet to be mounted by his company. Stravinsky's next composition, which he conducted at a Koussevitzky concert the following October, was the abstract *Octet* for winds. Koussevitzky asked for another work and, having rediscovered the piano, the composer decided it would be a piano concerto. When Koussevitzky suggested, on hearing it, that Stravinsky should play the piano part himself, Stravinsky made a couple of short concert tours to test the water and then performed the premiere at Paris in May 1924. (It was scored for piano, woodwinds, brass, string basses, and percussion.) Forgetting momentarily how the second movement began, he covered by an elaborate ritual of sweat mopping before it came back to him. Heartened by his reception on two fronts, he devoted much of the next two years touring Europe and America as a pianist and conductor. He signed a contract with Columbia Records and in 1925 wrote the *Serenade* for piano, the four movements designed to fit on four 12″ record sides.

Stravinsky, who had let his religion slide, had been undergoing in the previous few years a sort of mystical rebirth, at one point even taking a priest into his home to counsel him. In 1926 he was reconfirmed in the Russian Orthodox faith, marking the event with an *a cappella* setting of the Lord's Prayer. The year before, he had decided that he wanted to celebrate Diaghilev's twentieth anniversary as a successful impresario with something special. Stumbling on a life of St. Francis of Assisi and discovering that, unreformed, Francis had chosen to write his secular lyrics in Provençal instead of Italian, he decided by a curious inverse logic to do an "opera-oratorio" in Latin after Sophocles' *Oedipus Tyrannos*. The libretto was written in French by Jean Cocteau and translated by a cleric, the Abbé Jean Danieliou. The music was completed by spring 1924. Stravinsky had hoped to be able somehow to put the work on himself as a surprise for its dedicatee, but the latter had to be called upon in the end. Plans for a full staging quickly dwindled to the more practical solution of a concert performance, and even that had to be salvaged by the generosity of the Princesse de Polignac. In the event, at the premiere *Oedipus*, one of the most marmoreal works of its kind, was preceded by *Petrouchka* (again!). It suffered by the contrast and was badly received—even by Diaghilev.

Diaghilev was typically not happy when Stravinsky's next ballet, *Apollon musagète* (later renamed *Apollo*), was written not for him but on a commission from the American patroness Elizabeth Sprague Coolidge and accused the composer of having no interest in anything but money. Stravinsky salved the hurt by procuring the European rights for him. (The piece was premiered in Washington, D.C., in April 1928). But when the next commission—for a ballet, *Le Baiser de la fée (The Fairy's Kiss)*, after Tchaikovsky themes—came from Paris-based Ida Rubinstein, Diaghilev was furious and broke off further communication. The work got a lukewarm reception at its opening, November 27, 1928, at which Diaghilev took some comfort; nine months later he was dead at fifty-seven, and his company had ceased to exist.

Stravinsky's concert career continued to thrive, and late in 1929, with Ansermet's new Paris Symphony Orchestra, he offered, as soloist, a new work for piano and orchestra, the light-hearted and witty *Capriccio*. About the same time, Koussevitzky again approached him, this time for a symphony to celebrate the fiftieth anniversary of his orchestra, the Boston Symphony. Wishing to place his individual imprint on the concept "symphony" and impelled by his faith, he wrote a choral-orchestral work, the *Symphony of Psalms*, which he did not finish for almost a year. The first performance was actually given by Ansermet in Brussels on December 13, that in Boston following six days later.

Pursuant to a conversation with the Pol-

ish-American violinist Samuel Dushkin in 1931, Willy Strecker of the publishing house of Schott in Mainz suggested that Stravinsky should write some music for violin. When the composer protested that he knew the instrument only superficially (odd for a man who had written a virtuoso part in *L'Histoire d'un soldat!*), Strecker indicated that Dushkin would be glad to serve as his adviser. The partnership proved a happy one: it produced not only the violin concerto in 1931 and the *Duo concertant* in 1932 but also resulted in a series of joint tours of Europe and America through 1935. After the violin pieces were completed, Ida Rubinstein proposed another stage piece, in which she would declaim and mime André Gide's poem *Persephoné*. Gide was an old acquaintance and the two men took on the task. In the end there were balletic sections and parts of the text were sung. Badly produced at the Paris Opéra on April 30, 1934, *Persephoné* ran for only three performances. Gide complained that Stravinsky's music had ruined his prosody; Stravinsky afterward attributed the failure to the bad verse and suggested that the text should be rewritten by, say, W. H. Auden (then high in his favor). Shortly afterward the composer underwent an appendectomy and was so pleased with it that he persuaded his family and many of his friends to have appendectomies.

As of the mid-1930s, Stravinsky was musically a man without a country. Russia was closed to him, though he was still regarded as "Russian." He foreswore Germany when the Nazis came to power in 1933. In 1934, having lived in France for nearly fifteen years, he became a citizen. However, when a year later he was proposed for the seat in the Institut left vacant by the death of Dukas [1574], he was passed over in favor of Florent Schmitt [1615], a musician of far less stature. That same year, 1935, returning to the United States for a tour, he found himself almost popular there. In the meantime his younger son, Soulima, had launched his own career, concentrating on his father's music. For their joint performance Stravinsky wrote the *Concerto for Two Solo Pianos*, which they played in Paris on November 21 and took on tour the next year. That winter (1935–36) he and Nadia Boulanger team-taught a composition course at the École Normale.

In 1936, on a commission from Lincoln Kirstein for his American Ballet, Stravinsky wrote *Jeu de cartes* (later known as *The Card Party)*, derived from three poker hands. The choreography was entrusted to George Balanchine *(né* Georgi Balanchivadze), who, after completing the ballet version of *Le Chant du rossignol* for Diaghilev, had been asked to choreograph *Apollo*. At the Metropolitan Opera House premiere (April 27, 1937), Stravinsky conducted the latter and Balanchine's version of *Le Baiser de la fée* with the new work. That same spring he met, in Washington, D.C., Mr. and Mrs. Robert Woods Bliss, who asked him for a composition to celebrate their thirty years of marriage. Taking his cue from the formal gardens of their estate Dumbarton Oaks near Georgetown University, he wrote a concerto in the style of Bach's [684] *Brandenburgs*. But ill health prevented him from returning to conduct the premiere of the *Dumbarton Oaks Concerto*, which task he delegated to Nadia Boulanger on May 8, 1938.

Political events aside, this was a tragic time for the Stravinskys. Katerina's tuberculosis had spread to her elder daughter, and now her husband was discovered to have it. Ludmila died in the autumn of 1938, Katerina the following March. At that point Stravinsky allowed himself to be hospitalized for five months, during which time his mother also died. At this time he was working on another Bliss commission—the *Symphony in C* for the Chicago Symphony's fiftieth anniversary. He had also accepted the Charles Eliot Norton chair of poetry at Harvard for the academic year 1939–40, for which he was writing (in French, as agreed upon) the requisite lectures. When war began in September, he sailed for New York. He went immediately to Cambridge, where he delivered his lectures (later published) to full houses and held discussion groups with selected students. In January Vera (de Bosset-Sudeikine) followed him, and they were married in March. Soon afterward they went to Mexico and reentered the United States to be eligible for citizenship. Then they settled in Hollywood, where they found a compatible circle of expatriates and became American citizens in 1945.

Stravinsky had completed his symphony in Hollywood in August 1940. He conducted it in Chicago in November. As a great composer resident in the movie capital of the world, he expectably attracted the attention of the studios. Walt Disney, of course, had adapted *Le Sacre* (not protected by copyright) in 1938 for his film *Fantasia*, an action, however high-handed, that had made the composer's name a household word. Stravinsky himself embarked on three or four film projects, all of which failed to jell. There were other odd commissions: through Balanchine he was asked to write the *Circus Polka* for an elephant ballet in the Barnum and Bailey/Ringling Brothers Circus, 1942;

the conductor-arranger Nat Shilkret (1895–) conceived an all-star symposium on the Book of Genesis, for which Stravinsky contributed the choral *Babel*, 1944. For a Billy Rose revue of the same year, *The Seven Lively Arts*, he wrote *Scènes de Ballet* (Rose was appalled at the sparse orchestration, and when the composer refused to let Robert Russell Bennett [1895] "retouch" it, he scrapped much of the music.) Much taken with Woody Herman's swing band, Stravinsky wrote the *Ebony Concerto* for it. There were also more usual commissions—the *Danses concertantes* of 1942 for Werner Janssen's Los Angeles Orchestra, the orchestral *Ode* in memory of Natalie Koussevitzky in 1943, and the *Concerto in D* for strings in 1946, for the Swiss Paul Sacher's Basel Chamber Orchestra. Several works derived from aborted film projects: *Four Norwegian Moods* of 1942, the *Scherzo a la Russe* for Paul Whiteman in 1944, and the *Symphony in Three Movements* in 1945. The second movement of the latter came from a scene for *The Song of Bernadette*, the first and third movements from sketches for a second piano concerto. Finally there were a few independent pieces, notably the *Sonata for 2 Pianos* of 1944 and the *Mass*, begun the same year but not completed until 1948. In 1947 Kerstein, Balanchine, and Stravinsky again joined forces for the ballet *Orpheus*, first produced by the Ballet Society at the City Center in New York on April 28, 1948. It should be noted also that from 1945, when Boosey and Hawkes became his publishers, Stravinsky devoted considerable time to revising his early works in the interest of acquiring for them copyright protection previously denied them by their Russian publication.

Stravinsky had been thinking for some time of writing a full-length opera. In 1947 he was struck by an inspiration for one on seeing William Hogarth's series of eighteenth-century paintings, *The Rake's Progress*, exhibited in Chicago. His friend Aldous Huxley introduced him to the expatriate English poet W. H. Auden. Auden was agreeable and, with *his* friend Chester Kallman, completed the libretto of *The Rake's Progress* in April 1948. The plan was for basically Mozartean [992]—recitatives, arias, ensembles, concerted finales; this was no accident, since Auden and Stravinsky had both agreed that a performance of *Così fan tutte* they had attended together showed them the way—though the work has more of *Don Giovanni*'s darkness. Bidding for the opera, which was not finished until 1951, was high; because of its chamber proportions, Stravinsky gave it to a relatively small house, the Teatro La Fenice, for the 1951 Venice Biennial Festival (though the initial rehearsals were at La Scala, Milan, which lent its chorus and orchestra for the production). The gala premiere—the leads were sung by Elisabeth Schwarzkopf, Robert Rounseville, Otakar Kraus, and Jennie Tourel—took place on September II. Afterward the work made the rounds of the world's leading opera houses, though lately it seems to have fallen into relative desuetude. *The Rake's Progress* marks the end of Stravinsky's neoclassical period.

While he was working on it, the composer met, in 1948, an aspiring conductor named Robert Craft. They had previously corresponded over the possibility of Craft's use of some Stravinsky material for performance in a Stravinsky evening by the New York-based Concert Arts Society, which finally Stravinsky impulsively offered to coconduct free of charge. It was the beginning of a close association that was to last for the rest of his life and that dramatically affected his composing. After Craft's New York ensemble disbanded, he moved to Hollywood, where he soon became part of the Stravinsky household, serving at first as a general musical aide and later as Stravinsky's chief apostle. A devotee of the twelve-tone school, Craft dreamed of bringing Stravinsky and Schoenberg—who lived only a few miles away—together again (though the latter's death in 1951 forestalled that wish). However, having caught Stravinsky's interest with the music of Webern [1773], he saw to it that he became well acquainted with it. Craft helped with the opera, but his influence first appears perhaps in the next composition to be completed, the *Cantata* on medieval English lyrics, written for the Los Angeles Chamber Symphony in 1952, in which Stravinsky explored canonic techniques, as he also did in the 1953 *Septet*, where he also played with a tone row. For the Evenings on the Roof Concerts in Los Angeles, with which the two men were much involved, he made song settings of three Shakespeare lyrics—his first songs in nearly thirty-five years.

Asked in 1953 by Boston University to write a new opera, Stravinsky was directed to Dylan Thomas as a possible librettist. The two met soon afterward, hit it off, and agreed to collaborate when Thomas was to return the following year. Stravinsky went so far as to enlarge his home so that Thomas could live there for the duration, but the next November the poet died after a marathon drinking bout in a New York bar, and all that came of the association was *In Memoriam Dylan Thomas,* a setting of "Do Not Go Gentle into That Good Night" for tenor, strings, and trombones. Stravinsky's

next commission was for the 1956 Venice Festival, for which he produced the *Canticum Sacrum ad honorem Sancti Marci nominis (Hymn in Honor of the Name of St. Mark*—the city's patron saint). The outer movements of this work carry on the studies in canonic polyphony, but the middle section comes at last to grips with serialism. It was performed on September 13, together with an orchestration of J. S. Bach's canonic variations on *Vom Himmel hoch (From Heaven High),* also written for the occasion. The *Canticum* aroused polar responses, and one of the people appalled by Stravinsky's defection to the enemy camp was his old friend Ansermet (originally a mathematician, but no lover of mathematical formulae in music).

Stravinsky was now approaching his seventy-fifth birthday but continued to pursue a demanding schedule as a conductor. His labors were, it is true, mitigated by Craft, who often led rehearsals and sometimes spelled him in concerts. During a Berlin engagement later in 1956, Stravinsky suffered a stroke while conducting but managed to get to the end of the piece and recovered quickly and completely. As part of the birthday celebrations the next year, Craft premiered the score of the new ballet, *Agon,* commissioned by Kerstein and choreographed for twelve dancers of the New York City Ballet by Balanchine. Here, as in the *Canticum,* Stravinsky deliberately moves from the diatonic to the serial and back again. At about the same time, Stravinsky began work on a second commission from Venice, a setting of the Lamentations of Jeremiah entitled *Threni,* this time wholly serial in technique. It was performed on September 23, 1958, as a memorial to Alessandro Piovesan, the festival's director, who died while it was being written.

The next three years were taken up with tours that ultimately included every continent but Antarctica. They also produced Craft's volumes of *Conversations with Stravinsky,* which were spurred by the success of an interview he had conducted with him in 1957. Partly because of time, partly because of the condensation demanded by the new technique, the compositions between 1958 and 1962 contain less than an hour of music. The largest was the twenty-two-minute television piece *The Flood,* commissioned by Breck Shampoo and CBS for national viewing. Based on the biblical story, with a collage libretto drawn by Craft from (chiefly) English late-medieval mystery plays, it involved actors, dancers, and a square-dance caller. On the telecast (June 14, 1962) it was smothered in hyperbole, commercials, and

an inept production. Other works of the period are: the ten-minute *Movements* for piano and orchestra, 1959; the tiny *Epitaphium*
and *Double Canon* of the same year (in
memory of Prince Max von Fürstenberg, patron of the Donaueschingen Festivals, and
the painter Raoul Dufy, respectively); the
1960 *Monumentum pro Gesualdo* (an orchestral reworking of three madrigals by Gesualdo [310]), the 1961 cantata *A Sermon, a
Narrative, and a Prayer* for Paul Sacher; and
the 1962 *Anthem*, a four-part setting of fourteen lines from T. S. Eliot's "Little Gid-
ding."

The year 1962 brought an international
celebration of the composer's eightieth
birthday. He had of course been the recipient of many honors in his lifetime. In January he was given a dinner party at the White
House by President and Mrs. Kennedy—the
first time a composer had been so honored,
according to Craft. Afterward he embarked
on another tour that reached from Canada
to France to South Africa, Germany, Israel,
and back to France. Then, having accepted,
despite the advice of his well-wishers, an invitation personally extended to him a year
before by the secretary-general of the Union
of Soviet Composers, Tikhon Khrennikov
[2208], Stravinsky, Vera, and Craft proceeded to Moscow for a 2½-week stay in
Russia. There Stravinsky heard his music
played (it had long been banned there), conducted some of it himself, renewed old acquaintances and made new ones, and had an
audience with Nikita Khrushchev shortly
before they left. On his return he received a
papal decoration from Pope John XXIII.

The next year, in response to an Israeli
commission, he set *Abraham and Isaac* in
Hebrew for baritone and chamber orchestra.
After that came a handful of small works,
mostly occasional—the little *Elegy for
J.F.K.*, written after the President's assassination; a fanfare for the opening of the New
York State Theater in Lincoln Center; the
Variations for harp, piano, and strings in
memory of Aldous Huxley, 1964; and the *In-
troitus* for male voices and orchestra in
memory of T. S. Eliot, 1965. One last larger
work, the thirteen-minute *Requiem Canticles* (probably for himself) followed in 1966.
Late in 1966 he wrote a song setting of Edward Lear's verse "The Owl and the Pussy-
Cat." In August of the following year, a sudden hemorrhage from a stomach ulcer
marked the beginning of a general physical
decline—though he was still conducting as
recently as May 1967. But the next year he
was sufficiently improved to return to Europe. In May 1968 he orchestrated the two
Wolf songs noted previously. In April 1969

the Stravinskys moved to New York City.
The spells of serious illness grew longer, but
in June 1970 they went to the Évian spa on
the French side of Lake Geneva. Early in
March of 1971 the old man actually returned
to composition, but soon his health gave
way completely and he died on April 6. At
Vera's request his body was taken to Venice
and, after funeral services in St. Mark's, he
was carried in a cortege of gondolas to the
island of San Michele for burial.

RECORDINGS: Stravinsky's major works
have of course been subject to innumerable
recordings at least since the advent of the
microphone. In earlier times he committed
most of his piano works to records himself
(Soulima also did some of them). Thanks to
the farsightedness of the late Goddard
Lieberson [2171] of Columbia Records,
Stravinsky was enabled to leave stereophonic recordings of the entire canon, barring a few unpublished trifles and lost works.

**[1749] GRAINGER, George Percy Al-
dridge**
PIANIST, ETHNOMUSICOLOGIST,
TEACHER, LECTURER, EDITOR,
WRITER
BORN: Brighton, Melbourne, July 8, 1882
DIED: White Plains, N.Y., February 20,
1961

I recall seeing Percy Grainger in a New
York City music store, tweedy in knickers,
freshly arrived on foot from his home in
White Plains. He was then in his mid-sixties.
He was the son of a Melbourne architect but
was his mother's darling. She, a fine pianist
herself, gave him his lessons and sat with
him while he practiced. At ten he began concertizing. He also studied with Louis Pabst,
who had recently opened a conservatory in
Melbourne, Australia. The proceeds from
the concerts were sufficient by the time
Grainger was thirteen to take him and his
mother to Frankfurt am Main. There Mrs.
Grainger found work to support them and
Percy's studies at the Hoch Conservatory,
where his chief teachers were James Kwast
(1852–1927) and Ivan Knorr (1853–1916), and
where he became identified with other English students as a member of the "Frankfurt
Group"—(see Quilter, 1699). He was more
interested in composing than in playing, but
his mother got sick and he had to return to
the concert platform in 1900. The next year
they settled in London, where Mrs. Grainger managed his tours. He appeared as assisting artist with Adelina Patti and soon became a favorite with London society—a position not hampered by his Paderewskian

mop of golden hair and his alabaster good looks. In 1903 he returned to Germany briefly to study with Busoni [1577].

Proud of his Anglo-Saxon heritage—a pride that led to certain notorious mannerisms, such as the substitution in his prose of English-derived terms for their more usual Romance-derived equivalents—Grainger became caught up in the growing enthusiasm for hunting down folk music. He was the first member of the Folk Song Society to tramp about the countryside with a portable recording machine for rural types to sing into. This activity provided him with the bases of many of his best-known pieces and arrangements. Concert tours, folk music, and a love of the outdoors also led him to Scandinavia and a friendship with Edvard Grieg [1410]—and a bit later, Delius [1539]. He was Grieg's preferred interpreter of the piano concerto, and the two were scheduled to perform it together at the 1907 Leeds Festival, but Grieg died in the interim, and the concert became his memorial.

After a decade and a half of energetic composing, arranging, and playing (increasingly his own music), Grainger arrived in New York in 1914. When war broke out in Europe later that year, he decided to stay on and became a citizen in 1918. He did not avoid the war, however, enlisting in the army of the United States in 1917; he was assigned to a coast artillery band and mustered out in 1919. That summer he taught at the Chicago Musical College, to which he returned often over the next decade. In 1921 he bought a home in White Plains. A year later Mrs. Grainger killed herself—a devastating blow to her son, who published a memorial to her (pictures and reproductions of her three manuscript attempts at autobiography). In the years that followed, he composed little but returned to folksong collecting (this time in Denmark) and visited Australia. In 1928 he gave a concert to an audience of 20,000 in the Hollywood Bowl, climaxed by the premiere of his new orchestral piece, *To a Nordic Princess,* and his marriage to the dedicatee, a Swedish poetess and painter named Ella Viola Ström. In the academic year 1932–33 Grainger was chairman of the music department at New York University. In 1934 he returned to Australia to lecture and perform for a year. In 1938 he was back again to open the Grainger Museum at the University of Melbourne, whose support became his delight and his burden for the rest of his life. During World War II he lived in Springfield, Missouri. He died of cancer in White Plains at the age of seventy-nine.

Grainger was in lifelong revolt against meaningless convention—an attitude which unfortunately made most people think of him as a harmless loony. During his early years he was a serious, not to say wholly independent and even revolutionary composer—though one must admit the difficulty of viewing soberly pieces called *Arrival-Platform Humlet* (for solo viola) and *Pritteling Pratteling Pretty Poll Parrot* (two pianos). He tirelessly experimented with new harmonies and new sound sources, and was even a pioneer in electronic music. He was also constantly rearranging and rescoring what he had written, so that chronology is difficult. What got played, however, were little folk-derived and quasi-folksy pieces like *Molly on the Shore, Country Gardens,* and *Handel in the Strand,* which he never intended to be any more than *jeux d'esprit.* (*Country Gardens,* he once said, had more to do with turnips than flowers.)

RECORDINGS: His special genius has only lately begun to be recognized, and almost a dozen LPs have appeared that endeavor to go a little way beyond the obvious, though the surface has barely been scratched. The Grainger centenary in 1982 saw the release and/or reissue of several recordings by Australian EMI. Grainger was a brilliant pianist, but most of his commercial records were made before the day of the microphone, for by the time he died his performing career had long since slid into the doldrums. It is shocking to see on an LP by the Goldman Band "Percy Grainger, pianist)" after the title of his *Children's March.* A version of the Grieg concerto which he arranged for solo piano and recorded on three Duo-Art rolls has been cleverly restored to the original solo part and recorded with the Sydney Symphony under John Hopkins. Perhaps the most unusual pieces committed to disc are *Free Music I* and *Free Music II,* computer-assisted realizations by Australian composer Barry Conyngham (1944–   ) of some of Grainger's most revolutionary sketches, in which even microtonal intervals are abandoned in favor of a continuum of sound. Another notable Australian release is Grainger's *The Warriors,* one of his (relatively) longer works. There is much overlapping between various collections of Grainger's snippets. It is not possible to obtain his complete recorded works without considerable duplication of works.

[1750] HAGEMAN, Richard (Hä'-gə-man)
ACCOMPANIST, CONDUCTOR, TEACHER
BORN: Leeuwarden, July 9, 1882
DIED: Beverly Hills, Calif., March 6, 1966

Richard Hageman was the son and pupil of a Dutch violinist and composer, Maurits Leonard Hageman (1829–1906). Later he studied at the Brussels Conservatory with Gevaert [1303] and pianist-composer Arthur de Greef (1862–1940), a Liszt [1218] pupil. At sixteen he became a rehearsal pianist at the Amsterdam opera house, and he later conducted there. In 1904 he went to Paris and served as accompanist at the Marchesi vocal studio. Two years later he came to the United States as accompanist to the great *diseuse* Yvette Guilbert, who was touring in tandem with music-hall comedian Albert Chevalier. When the tour was over, Hageman remained in New York. He eventually joined the staff of the Metropolitan Opera—most references say in 1908—but he did not conduct a performance there, apparently, before the St. Valentine's Day *Faust* of 1913 and seems to have been used chiefly as a coach and rehearsal conductor. In 1922–23 he conducted *Martha, Manon,* and *The Snow Maiden* at the Chicago Opera and the next year is said to have conducted the "Los Angeles Opera" (since there was no such organization, he undoubtedly conducted tour performances with the Chicago Opera). He also conducted summer performances in Ravinia Park and taught at the Chicago Musical College. Later he was at the Curtis Institute in Philadelphia and is said to have conducted the "Fairmount Symphony Orchestra" there—which presumably means that he conducted the Philadelphia Orchestra at the Robin Hood Dell Concerts in Fairmount Park.

In 1932 Hageman's first opera, *Caponsacchi,* based on Robert Browning's *The Ring and the Book,* was produced in Germany at Freiburg im Breisgau as *Tragödie in Arezzo.* The Edward Johnson management, installed at the Metropolitan Opera in 1934, saw it as a possibility for its native opera program and called Hageman back for a production in the spring of 1936. Staging difficulties delayed it until the next fall. It got front-page publicity when, during rehearsals, Lawrence Tibbett stabbed a chorister with a stage dagger that failed to retract and the poor fellow died of a heart attack. The work itself did not please and was quickly dropped. Hageman settled in the Los Angeles area and worked for Paramount Studios. A second opera, *The Crucible*—unrelated to Arthur Miller's later play—was produced in Los Angeles in 1943.

RECORDINGS: Helen Jepson, who created the soprano lead in Caponsacchi, recorded two scenes from it, but Hageman's memory rests chiefly on a handful of songs, some of which have also been recorded.

[1751] KOWALSKI, Max (Kō-vàl'-skē, Màks)
LAWYER, SINGER, TEACHER
BORN: Kowal, August 10, 1882
DIED: London, June 4, 1956

Born in a *shtetl* between Poznan and Warsaw, Kowalski was reared and educated from the age of one year in Frankfurt am Main. He took a law degree at the nearby University of Marburg, studied voice with the *Lieder* singer Alexander Heinemann in Berlin, and established a legal practice in Frankfurt. After further musical study with Bernhard Sekles (1872–1934), later director of the Hoch Conservatory and teacher of Paul Hindemith [1914], in 1913 Kowalski began publishing *Lieder* of his own. A fellow townsman of his once told me that in Frankfurt the lawyers considered him a fine musician, the musicians an excellent jurist. He was imprisoned in the Buchenwald Concentration Camp by the Nazis but was released just before the attack on Poland in 1939 and took refuge in London. There for a time he lived at a subsistence level, tuning pianos and singing in a synagogue. Later he ran a vocal studio. Apart from a couple of piano pieces, his entire output consisted of songs in the nineteenth-century tradition. Ernst Wolff recorded his *Pierrot Lunaire,* a setting of the same Guiraud poems Schoenberg [1657] had set at almost precisely the same time and that Kowalski's exact contemporary Joseph Marx [1747] would set independently not long after.

[1752] KŘIČKA, Jaroslav (Kr'zēch'-kà, Yà'-rō-slàf)
CONDUCTOR, TEACHER
BORN: Kelč, August 27, 1882
DIED: Prague, January 23, 1969

Like so many Czech composers, Křička was the son of a village schoolmaster. He spent, according to him, a happy childhood in the Moravian hills northwest of Brno and went to high school in nearby Nemecky Brod (now called Havlíčkův Brod). At eighteen he went off to the University in Prague to study law but drifted into music. He entered the Prague Conservatory in 1902, studied composition with the organist-composer Karel Stecker, and proceeded to Berlin for further study in 1905. The following year he found an opening at the Imperial Conservatory at Ekaterinoslav (now Dniepropetrovsk) in the Russian Ukraine. In his three years there he was much influenced by the Russian nationalist school. In 1909 Křička returned to Prague and, after conducting a suburban chorus from some months, was given the directorship of the Prague Hlahol Choral Union, once under Smetana's [1291] charge. In 1917 he produced his first opera *Hypolita* (libretto by his poet-brother Petr, after a novel by Maurice Hewlett). This was followed by several other operas (one after Wilde's *The Canterville Ghost,* another to a libretto by Karel Čapek). Křička also wrote operas for children, a television opera, and a good deal of incidental music for stage, screen, and radio. In 1919 he became professor of composition at the Prague Conservatory and in 1936 moved up to the Master School, but he was ousted after World War II. As a composer he was both prolific and successful. The chief native influence on his music came from his admiration of Vítězslav Novák [1617]. Besides his dramatic works he wrote a symphony, several tone poems and overtures, a great deal of choral music, both sacred and secular, a violin concerto, a violin sonata, chamber music (including 3 string quartets), piano pieces, and many songs—especially children's songs, for which he had an unusual gift. Křička also wrote books and articles about music, including a 1943 study, *Music and Film.* RECORDINGS: Prior to the Second World War he was well represented on Czech records by small pieces and selections from the operas.

[1753] POWELL, John
PIANIST, ETHNOMUSICOLOGIST, ASTRONOMER
BORN: Richmond, Va., September 6, 1882
DIED: Charlottesville, Va., August 15, 1963

John Powell was an FFV and said to be descended from ancient Welsh kings. His father was headmaster of a girls' school in Richmond. His mother, a musical amateur, claimed as an ancestor the poet-composer Nicholas Lanier (1588–1666) and thus distant cousinship with Sidney Lanier [1391]. As a youth Powell studied piano with his sister and with a Liszt [1218] pupil named Hahr. At nineteen he graduated Phi Beta Kappa from the University of Virginia and in 1902 went off to Vienna for five years of piano study with Theodor Leschetizky (1830–1915). During his final year there he also studied composition with Karel Navrátil (1867–1936). He made his concert debut in Berlin in 1907, beginning a successful European career. He made his home in London, where he ran with a rather heady artistic and social set. It was during this time that he tried to talk Joseph Conrad into turning his *Heart of Darkness* into a libretto for him, but nothing

came of it except later inspiration for the *Rhapsodie nègre* for piano and orchestra of 1918, his most popular work.

When war came in 1914, Powell returned to Virginia and concertized in his own country for more than twenty years. As a composer he developed a growing interest in the recovery and use of Anglo-American folk music from the Virginia backwoods. Most of his ensuing works were folk-based—the *Sonata Virginianesque* for violin and piano, the overture *In Old Virginia,* and many concert arrangements. He was a prime mover in the White Top Mountain Folk Music Festivals and organized the State Choral Festivals. He settled in Charlottesville, where in 1916 he founded the Society for the Preservation of Racial Integrity. He was quick to note that he loved his black neighbors but was convinced that only harm could come of interbreeding people and cultures at what he felt were such obviously different evolutionary stages. His friend Daniel Gregory Mason [1648] approved. Powell was also a dedicated amateur astronomer and discovered the comet that bears his name. He retired from the concert platform in 1936 but continued to play privately. In 1951 the state declared a John Powell Day. Besides the works noted, he wrote a symphony, a piano concerto, another for violin, a string quartet, piano sonatas subtitled "Psychologique," "Noble," and "Teutonica," and many smaller pieces—all in a late nineteenth-century idiom.

RECORDINGS: Powell recorded his violin sonata with Eddy Brown and made some private records. There have been commercial recordings of the *Rhapsodie nègre* (Dean Dixon, Calvin Simmons), *In Old Virginia* (Hans-Jürgen Walther), and a slightly abridged version of the *Sonata teutonica* (Roy Hamlin Johnson). Johnson has also recorded the *Sonata psychologique* and *Variations and Double-Fugue on a Theme of J. S. Bach.*

[1754] FRYKLÖF, Harald Leonard (Frü'-kluv, Här-ȧld Lä'-ō-närd)
ORGANIST, TEACHER, EDITOR
BORN: Uppsala, September 14, 1882
DIED: Stockholm, March 11, 1919

Fryklöf was a pupil of Johan Lindegren and Richard Andersson in Stockholm, and also of Philipp Scharwenka [1437] in Berlin. In 1908 he became organist at the Storkyrka in Stockholm and three years later professor of harmony at the Stockholm Conservatory. He was one of the editors of a choral anthology, *Musica sacra,* and wrote a manual on harmonizing hymn tunes. He wrote an overture and a violin sonata, but the bulk of his output consists of organ and piano pieces and songs. RECORDINGS: A few of the songs have been recorded.

[1755] SZYMANOWSKI, Karol Maciej
(Shi-màn-ov´-skē, Kär´-ōl Màts´-yä)
PIANIST
BORN: Tymoszówka, October 6, 1882
DIED: Lausanne, March 29, 1937

Among the thirty-three men treated in *Great Modern Composers,* edited in 1938 by Oscar Thompson, is Karol Szymanowski. He is one of only two or three therein included whose names today might draw a blank stare from the mythical average music lover. Szymanowski's parents were cultured and wealthy Polish landowners. He was born on the family estate near the Ukrainian city of Elisavetgrad, which, in the vicissitudes of Soviet history, has since become Zinovievsk and then Kirovograd. The Szymanowskis considered musical training an essential part of education, and a younger daughter, Stanisława, had a career as a singer and was the dedicatee of some of her brother's songs. As a small child, Karol suffered a fall that left him invalid for some years and permanently lame—and with much time to devote to intellectual and artistic matters. His first music teacher was his father. Later, when he was up and about, he studied in town with a relative, Gustav Neuhaus, the father of Heinrich ("Harry") Neuhaus, who became the teacher of Emil Gilels and Sviatoslav Richter. His academic training came mostly from tutors.

In 1900 Szymanowski completed his Op. 1, a set of Chopinesque [1208] piano preludes, and soon afterward went off to Warsaw for serious study with Sigismund Noskowski (1846–1909), a composer of sorts who had studied with Moniuszko [1263]. Ambitious to produce something more stimulating than the Teutonic-style salon stuff that passed for music in Warsaw, he found backing in three other Noskowski pupils, Ludomir Różycki [1784], Grzegorz (or Gregor) Fitelberg (1879–1953), and Apolinary Szeluta, and support from a wealthy musical amateur, Prince Władysław Lubomirski. Considering themselves the Polish equivalent of the Russian *kuchka,* they became the Association of Young Polish Composers (familiarly known as "Young Poland") and set up their own publishing company in 1905. A year later Fitelberg conducted the Warsaw Philharmonic (of which Noskowski was then director) in a Young Poland concert, which in-

cluded Szymanowski's *Concert Overture in E major* and some of his piano pieces, played by Harry Neuhaus. But Warsaw refused to change, and later that year the group migrated to Berlin and gave a similar concert, which failed to produce headlines.

Szymanowski had been infected with the Wagnerian [1230] virus when at thirteen he was taken to a performance of *Lohengrin,* and he remained in Germany for two years, drinking the heady wine of post-Wagnerian German music. It inspired a symphony (Wagner pudding with Strauss [1563] sauce), that was received so badly at its Warsaw premiere in 1909 that he withdrew it. He had returned to the family estate and the maternal bosom in 1908 and lived there for the next decade, though he traveled a good deal and spent 1911–12 in Vienna. In 1911 Fitelberg premiered the second symphony, which soon had international currency. In 1912, however, the friendship came to an end when Szymanowski (a homosexual) discovered that Fitelberg had been using his bed for clandestine sessions with girlfriends under the very eyes of Mme. Szymanowska's portrait. However, he had found two other eager apostles in the pianist Artur Rubinstein and the violinist Paul Kochanski.

In the summer of 1914 Szymanowski vacationed in North Africa, coming home in August. As he crossed the Russian border, they closed it behind him. World War I had begun. He spent the next three years at Tymoszówka, reading voraciously and composing slowly. He was beginning to develop his own style out of a mix of late Romanticism, Impressionism, Scriabin [1625], and Eastern influences, which last he had come to in his travels and through his reading. He completed a third symphony (with voices, subtitled "Song of the Night"), his first violin concerto, the cantata *Demeter,* and some important violin and piano music. In the fall of 1917 his calm was suddenly shattered when a revolutionary mob descended on the house and burned it. He and his mother had to share quarters with relatives in Elisavetgrad, which was now called Zinovievsk. There, over the next two years, he produced a string quartet, a third piano sonata, and some songs but was chiefly occupied with writing a long erotic novel called *Efebos.* Never published, it perished with its successor, *Tomek,* in the flames of World War II.

Inspired by Poland's independence in a fervent patriotism, Szymanowski found his way back to Warsaw in 1920 and made a home there for his family. Their straitened circumstances now necessitated his putting his career on a paying basis, which he did through a series of concerts, even going to the United States with Rubinstein and Kochanski in 1921. At a postconcert dinner in Warsaw the previous year, however, one of the guests had gotten him interested in Polish folk music. He resolved to do for Polish art music what Stravinsky [1748] had done for Russian music and began to spend time in the Tatra Mountains collecting material. This new phase saw not only the use of folklike themes and rhythms, but also references to old Polish liturgical music and an attempt to evoke a rude primitivism. Meanwhile his first opera, the one-act *Hagith* (completed in 1913 and thus still representative of his German-Romantic period) was produced at Warsaw in 1922 and shortly afterward in Germany. The new folk-oriented stance appeared in *Slopiewnie* (a song cycle for voice and orchestra), the mazurkas and Polish dances for piano, and the second string quartet, and was most fully developed in the *Stabat Mater* and the ballet *Harnasie*.

At this time Szymanowski was as successful and happy as he was ever to be. He was winning worldwide fame as one of the most important composers of the day. He was writing music that satisfied him. He had come to terms with his sexual problems and admitted them to his friends. In 1926 his masterpiece, the opera *Król Roger (King Roger)*, was staged for the first time, and a year later he was offered the directorships of the Warsaw and Cairo conservatories. Good Pole that he was, he chose the former, determined that a new generation of Polish musicians would have the best possible training. The effort proved too much. Always cursed with weak lungs, he was found to be suffering from advanced tuberculosis and resigned in 1929. He spent a year at Zakopane in the Tatras and was pronounced cured. In 1932 he completed the *Symphonie concertante* for piano and orchestra, also known as his fourth symphony, and went on tour with it as soloist. He became terribly fatigued and then suffered an emotional setback when he heard that Kochanski had died (at the age of forty-seven) in New York, shortly after playing the American premiere of Szymanowski's second violin concerto, completed in 1933. His disease flared up again, and he spent another year in bed at a sanitarium in Davos, Switzerland. In 1936 his doctors advised a warm climate, since his illness was not responding to treatment. By now his money was used up, but the government and private well-wishers saw to it that he got to Grasse in Provence. It was too late; he died on Easter Sunday of 1937 at the Dufour Sanitarium in Lausanne. He was fifty-four.

RECORDINGS: Before the LP era, Szymanowski was represented on records only by a single version of the first violin concerto, a few small instrumental pieces, and a handful of songs. Thanks in large part to the efforts of Muza, the state recording trust in Poland and more recently to commercial interests, we have had two recordings of *King Roger*, and one or more apiece of the last three symphonies, the *Concert Overture*, the violin concerti, the ballet-pantomine *Mandragora*, the *Stabat Mater*, *Harnasie*, and most of the music for piano solo, violin and piano, and solo voice. A number of surviving works, including *Hagith* and a few compositions for voice(s) and orchestra, remain unrecorded. As we go to press, a recording of the brief cantata *Demeter* and the vocal-orchestral *Litany to the Virgin Mary* has just appeared.

[1756] DETT, Robert Nathaniel
PIANIST, CHOIRMASTER, TEACHER
BORN: Drummondsville, Quebec, October 11, 1882
DIED: Battle Creek, Mich., October 2, 1943

R. Nathaniel Dett was an important pioneer among black American composers, and one of the first to be honored by the white musical and academic establishment. He was born in a Quebec town that had served as a terminal in slave times for the Underground Railway. His education was thorough, though extended. After studying for a time at the Halstead Conservatory in Lockport, New York, he graduated from Oberlin in 1908. Later he attended Columbia, the University of Pennsylvania, the American Conservatory in Chicago, and Harvard. At the last, in 1920, he won the Bowdoin Prize for literature (for an essay on the music of his people) and the Boott Award for music. Between then and his graduation he had taught for three years at Lane College and two at the Lincoln Institute, also appearing as a concert pianist. In 1913 he was put in charge of the musical program at the Hampton Institute, a Negro school in Tuskegee, Alabama. It was he who honed the choir to a fine edge and won it international fame. The school gave him several leaves of absence to further his own education, as previously indicated. In 1929 he went to Paris for lessons with Nadia Boulanger. Anticipating his fiftieth birthday, Dett retired two years later and opened his own studio in Rochester, New York. He returned twice to academia, however, teaching at Sam Houston College in 1935 and at Bennett College, North Carolina, in 1937. When America entered World War II, he joined the USO and died in harness at Battle Creek, Michigan, where he had been assigned to develop a choir for the Women's Army Corps. He held an honorary M.A. from the Eastman School and honorary Mus.D.'s from Howard University and Oberlin. Dett's compositions were chiefly for chorus and for piano solo. His largest works were the oratorios *The Chariot Jubilee* of 1921 and *The Ordering of Moses* of 1937; his most popular work was the piano suite *In the Bottoms*, which includes "Juba Dance." He also published two important collections of black spirituals, *Religious Folksongs of the Negro* and the four-volume *Dett Collection of Negro Spirituals*. Early in his career he tried his hand at some piano rags. RECORDINGS: The piano suite *In the Bottoms* has been recorded by Natalie Hinderas; there are numerous recordings of the "Juba Dance" movement.

[1757] KÁLMÁN, Imre (Kål′-mån, Ēm′-rå)
CRITIC
BORN: Siófok, October 24, 1882
DIED: Paris, October 30, 1953

Of the post–Johann Strauss **[1295]** generation of "Viennese" operetta composers, only Emmerich Kálmán (as he came to be known) is mentioned in the same breath with Franz Lehár **[1614]**. Born on the shores of Lake Baloton, southwest of Budapest, he entertained hopes of becoming a concert pianist but was thwarted by neuritis. Later he entertained hopes of becoming a lawyer but was thwarted by music. Like so many of his stripe, his musical intents were at first aimed at a higher level. He studied under Hans Koessler at the Budapest Conservatory, where he shared the classroom with Bartók **[1734]** and Kodály **[1760]**. After graduating he produced a symphonic poem, other orchestral pieces, and some *Lieder*, and worked as critic for a Budapest paper for four years, 1904–8. Having successfully tried his hand at popular songs, he wrote an operetta, *Tatárjárás*, in the latter year which became an international success. (As *The Gay Hussars*, it managed nearly six weeks on Broadway in 1909, despite an inadequate production.) After that, Kálmán moved to Vienna, where he averaged about an operetta a year until the 1920s, after which he slowed down a bit. Though he wrote fewer works than Lehár, his own works were more consistently successful. His recipe was to sprinkle the results of a sound technique and melodic fertility liberally with paprika. His greatest subsequent hits were: *Der Zigeunerprimas (The Gypsy Archbishop)*, 1912—a success in New York as *Sari; Die Csárdásfürstin*

(The Csárdás Princess), 1915, or, much altered for Broadway, *Riviera Girl; Die Bajadere (The Bayadere)* 1921, alias *The Yankee Princess; Gräfin Mariza (Countess Mariza)*, 1924; and *Die Zirkusprinzessin (The Circus Princess)*, 1926. In 1927 he collaborated with Robert Stolz **[1730]**, Herbert Stothart, and Oscar Hammerstein II on a Broadway musical with an African locale called *Golden Dawn*, which, despite an incredible plot, ran for six months. With the *Anschluss* of Austria, Kálmán moved to Paris, and in 1940 to America, where he became a citizen. He was working on a musical called *Arizona Lady* when he died. His son, Charles Emmerich, has also written for the musical stage. RECORDINGS: *Countess Mariza* has been recorded complete. Excerpts from *The Bayadere, The Yankee Princess, The Circus Princess, The Czárdás Princess,* and others have been recorded.

[1758] PONCE, Manuel María (Pons, Mån-wel′ Må-rē′-å)
PIANIST, CONDUCTOR, TEACHER
BORN: Fresnillo, December 8, 1882
DIED: Mexico City, April 24, 1948

Though he is generally known for a few salon pieces and drawing-room songs written relatively early in his career, Ponce was an important figure in the history of Mexican music and is generally regarded there as the founder of the nationalistic school. Born in central Mexico four years earlier than he thought he had been, he grew up in Aguascalientes, some miles to the south, where his family settled in his early infancy. His studies were furthered by a sister, Josefina, who taught him to play the piano, and a brother, Antonio, who provided financial backing. At fifteen he became cathedral organist in his hometown and wrote a gavotte for piano which was popularized by the dancer La Argentina. After a year of study in Mexico City from 1900, Ponce concertized, taught, and reviewed. In 1904 he went to the Bologna Liceo, where he studied with Bossi **[1534]** and Luigi Torchi, and a year later to the Stern Conservatory in Berlin for lessons with Liszt **[1218]** disciple Martin Krause. He returned to Mexico in 1908 and a year later joined the faculty of the Mexico City Conservatory, where Carlos Chávez **[1968]** became his pupil in 1910. In 1911 Ponce wrote his first large-scale work, a piano trio; and the following year he introduced his piano concerto (Chopinesque **[1208]** but with Mexican overtones) at a concert devoted to his music. In 1914 he published an album of songs, including "Estrellita." For some rea-

son the collection was not covered by international copyright, and the song became epidemic in performance all over the world.
During the revolutionary upheavals in
mid-decade, Ponce moved to Havana, where
he worked as a newspaper critic for two
years, during which period he made his New
York debut. In 1917 he returned to Mexico
City and his job. In the same year he became
conductor of the National Orchestra and
married Clema Maurel, a singer. Still dissatisfied with the progress of his composing, he
moved to Paris in 1925. Lessons with Paul
Dukas [1574] at the École Normale, and a
friendship struck up with Heitor Villa-Lobos
[1817] gave him renewed confidence and a
sense of direction. He tested out his ideas in
an orchestral triptych, *Chapultepec,* whose
premiere Chávez conducted in 1929. It did
not satisfy the composer, and he revised it
on his return home in 1934, when he briefly
became director of the conservatory. He also
taught folk music at the university during
this period. From the middle to the late
1930s, he was particularly productive, creating Mexican-based works as well as dabbling
in neo-classicism. A friendship with Andrés
Segovia led him in his later years to the guitar. Segovia premiered the *Concierto del sur
(Southern Concerto)* in 1942.

RECORDINGS: Segovia recorded the *Concierto del Sur* and several of Ponce's 7 guitar
sonatas. Besides the works noted previously,
Ponce is represented on domestic records
chiefly by small pieces for piano, guitar
pieces, and songs. Mexican record labels
have dealt far more extensively with his output, including such works as the orchestral
Ferial, concerti for piano and violin, *Es-
tampas nocturnas* and *Romanzetta* for orchestra, and a large number of chamber
works.

[1759] TURINA, Joaquín (Too͞-rē'-na,
  Hwä-kēēn')
PIANIST, TEACHER, WRITER
BORN: Seville, December 9, 1882
DIED: Madrid, January 14, 1949

In terms of the modern rebirth of Spanish
music, Turina is, next to Falla [1688], probably the best-known composer of his generation. He was the son of a painter who
dreamed of his son's becoming a doctor, but
it was not long before he agreed to foster the
boy's inclination toward music. He provided
him with piano training and with theory lessons from the choirmaster of the cathedral.
Young Turina was soon writing music and
made a successful debut as a pianist at fourteen. Around the turn of the century, he
went to Madrid, undertook further piano
studies at the Madrid Conservatory with
José Tragó, Falla's sometime teacher, tried
vainly to get a performance of his first opera,
La Sulamita (The Shulamite Woman), and
did get one performance in 1904 for a
zarzuela which was unsuccessful. In 1905 he
preceded his friend Falla to Paris, where he
studied piano with Moszkowski [1479] and
composition with d'Indy [1462]. Two years
later, subsequent to the first performance
(with the composer as pianist) of his first
opus, a piano quintet in the d'Indy-approved
style, he and Falla were taken to a café by
Albéniz [1523], who preached the doctrine
of Spanish music to Turina. Turina did not
subscribe to it wholly and, along with his
"Spanish" works, continued to produce abstract Impressionist compositions, especially
in the realm of chamber music.

In 1913, the year Turina completed his
studies in Paris, E. F. Arbós conducted the
Procésion del Rocío, an evocation of a Sevil-
lan religious festival, which established
Turina as an important composer. He returned to Spain with the outbreak of the 1914
war, and settled in Madrid, where he was
chorusmaster at the Teatro Real (the opera
house). He attempted a sort of sequel to the
Procésion with the *Evangelio de Navidád
(Christmas Story)* in 1915. In 1920 he produced his two most popular orchestral
works, the *Danzas fantásticas (Fantastic
Dances)* and the *Sinfonía sevillana.* His opera *Jardín de oriente (Eastern Garden)* was
performed at the Teatro Real in 1923. (The
theater closed down in 1925, not to reopen
for forty years.) Turina wrote only three
other orchestral works: the *Canto a Sevilla
(Song to Seville)* with sections for voice and
for recitation, 1927; the "choreographic fantasia" *Ritmos (Rhythms),* 1928; and the *Rap-
sódia sinfonica* for piano and strings, 1931.
The *Oración del torero (Bullfighter's Prayer),*
often played by string orchestras, was originally written for a quartet of lutes(!), as was
the *Recuerdos de la antigua España (Memories of Old Spain).*

In 1930 Turina became professor of composition at the Madrid Conservatory. With
the overthrow of the monarchy in 1931 and
the ensuing civil war, he was out of favor
with the Republicans for his conservative
leanings, but he served the Franco government as a member of the ministry of education and was decorated. In his later years he
limited his piano playing largely to chamber-
music performances with friends and students, though he occasionally conducted in
public. He died of cancer at sixty-six.

Turina seems to have been happiest and
most typical as a composer of piano music,

of which he left a large output, and most
uncomfortable and atypical in chamber music, of which he wrote, among other things,
2 piano trios, a piano quartet, the aforementioned quintet, and 2 violin sonatas. He also
composed some songs, some incidental music, a few organ pieces, and numerous guitar
pieces.

RECORDINGS: There is a performance of
the vocal numbers from *Canto a Sevilla* by
his preferred interpreter, Lola Rodriguez de
Aragón, and a complete recording (minus
the recitations) by Victoria de Los Angeles.
Most of the orchestral works and a good
deal of the piano and guitar music also appear on records, as do some of the songs.
Except for the *Oración,* most of the chamber
music and all of the stage works seem to
have been ignored.

[1760] KODÁLY, Zoltán (Kō-dä'-ē, Zōl'-
tän)
TEACHER, CONDUCTOR, ETHNOMUSI-
COLOGIST, CRITIC
BORN: Kecskemét, December 16, 1882
DIED: Budapest, March 6, 1967

It is customary to speak of Kodály and
Bartók [1734] as though they were the Siamese twins of modern Hungarian music.
They were to be sure close friends and colleagues, and each had immense admiration
and respect for the other. But chiefly influenced by Hungarian folk music and by Debussy [1547], Kodály formed his style early
and was never the radical and restless experimenter that Bartók was. His approach was
vocal and melodic, whereas Bartók's was instrumental and rhythmic. He contributed
far less music to the international concert
repertoire. His chief impact was more on
musical education than on music itself.

Kodály's father, Frigyes, was employed
by the Hungarian railway system, but both
he and his wife were passionate musical amateurs who involved their three children in
domestic music making. Shortly after
Zoltán's birth, his father was transferred to
Szob, north of Budapest, and a year later to
Galánta (now in south-central Czechoslovakia), where he was stationed until 1892.
There the boy had his first schooling and his
introduction to folk music, which he recalled forty years later in his *Dances from
Galánta.* The Kodálys were then moved to
Trnava (then called Nagyszombat), a few
miles to the northwest, and lived there for
eighteen years. Zoltán went to the cathedral
school, sang in the choir, and learned to play
the piano and the violin. When his father
noted jokingly that if someone were to take

up cello, they could have a string quartet,
the boy obliged, teaching himself. By the
time he graduated from school in 1900, he
had been writing music—mostly church
pieces, including a *Mass,* but also some
chamber music for home use—for several
years.

With a scholarship in hand betokening his
fine academic record, he went off to the capital to major in literature at the Eötvös College of the university. Two years later, however, he also enrolled in the Academy of
Music, where he studied with Hans
Koessler, teacher of Dohnányi [1696],
Bartók, and Kálmán [1757]. He seems to
have written little in his college years, apart
from some contributions to student-pro-
duced stage nonsense but took a degree in
composition in 1904 and another in education in 1905. Meanwhile Kodály had developed a growing interest in Hungarian folk
music, and, dissatisfied with what he found
in the collections, he took to the field in the
late summer of the latter year and soon
joined forces with Bartók in an ambitious
plan to publish their findings. To crown the
year, his orchestral piece *Summer Evening*
was chosen to be played at the Academy of
Music graduation that October. The honor
brought with it a traveling fellowship, and
after a short stopover in Berlin in December,
Kodály went to Paris. There he sat in on
Widor's [1414] classes but was chiefly impressed by his discovery of Debussy's music.
In June he was back in Budapest to oversee
the publication of *20 Hungarian Folk Songs*
—purportedly the first volume of the vast
project that was never to come to fruition in
Bartók's or Kodály's lifetime. That fall he
received his Ph.D. for a dissertation on the
poetics of Hungarian folk lyrics. Shortly afterward he returned from the field to accept
a post at the Academy of Music, where
(with unavoidable interruptions) he was to
remain for more than thirty years. He continued his research during vacations and
composed slowly. In 1910 an all-Kodály concert (with Bartók as pianist) unveiled to Budapest the first string quartet, the Op. 10 piano pieces, and the sonata for cello and piano. The audience and the critics seem to
have been not very favorably impressed, but
the event marked the beginning of his worldwide fame. However, the next decade
brought forth very little more—the violin
and cello duo in 1914, the solo cello sonata in
1915, the second string quartet and another
set of piano pieces in 1918, plus a few songs
and other small works.

With Hungarian independence at the end
of World War I, Kodály was appointed second-in-command to Dohnányi at the Acad-

emy of Music in 1919. But later that year the government was overthrown by the Communist regime of Belá Kun, and both directors were ousted. After another governmental change, Kodály was returned to his teaching post in 1922 and commissioned to write a piece for the semicentennial of the united city of Budapest. The result was the *Psalmus Hungaricus* for tenor, choruses, and orchestra, premiered under Dohnányi's baton in November 1923, and, by the end of the decade, famous all over the western world. (Toscanini's production of the work at La Scala in 1928 inaugurated a lifelong friendship between him and the composer.) The *Psalmus* signaled the beginning of a period of vastly increased productivity, particularly in the choral medium, for Kodály had come to regard group-vocal experience as the keystone to musical understanding. The year 1926 saw the first performance of *Háry János,* a work usually classified as an opera but in actuality a sort of folk play with music. The orchestral suite derived from it brought the composer real popularity. This was further ensured by the *Dances from Marosszék* of 1930 and the 1933 *Dances from Galánta* already mentioned. Kodály himself began to appear as a conductor on the international scene in 1927.

During the 1930s Kodály pressed his reform of musical education, taught a course in folk music at the university, edited songs he had collected, and wrote essays, collected in 1937 as *On Hungarian Folk Music.* Besides many smaller vocal compositions and arrangements, he wrote a second opera, *Székelyfonó (The Spinning Room),* in 1932; a big occasional *Te Deum* in 1936; the *Peacock Variations* for orchestra (based on a Hungarian folk song, "The Peacock") in 1939; a *Concerto for Orchestra* (commissioned and premiered by the Chicago Symphony Orchestra) in 1941. Unlike Bartók, he remained in Budapest throughout World War II and wrote a *Missa Brevis* for chorus and orchestra that was premiered in 1945. For a time he and his wife had to hide in a convent as a result of his efforts to save Jewish friends. During the Russian siege of the city, their home was hit, but his papers escaped damage.

The postwar Communist government treated Kodály far differently from the earlier one. It in effect declared him a national hero and showered him with honors, appointed him to several prestigious posts, and adopted his radical teaching methods in the school system. There ensued a whole sequence of decorations, honorary degrees, and other tokens of esteem, both at home

and abroad. Kodály made his first visit to the United States in 1946 as a guest conductor of his own works. In 1959, widowed, he married one of his students, Sarolta Péczely, age nineteen. In 1965, a vigorous eighty-three, he returned to America on an extended lecture tour. (Photographs taken in these years show a saintly-looking man suffused with a sort of inner radiance; but he was always a beautiful human being: according to Antal Dorati [2086], his pupil, in earlier Budapest winters children hailed him as "Christ on skates.") His later works, though very few in number, include a third opera, *Czinka Panna,* of 1948; the Symphony in C Major, premiered in 1961 after a long gestation; and the *Organoedia ad missam lectam* for organ solo, 1966.

RECORDINGS: The Hungarian government has honored Kodály's memory by recording most of his mature output, including the many choral works and songs and the first two "operas." Antal Dorati has done a collection of all the orchestral works, and István Kertesz a version of *Háry János* in which the dialogue is supplanted by an English narration by Peter Ustinov. Vox has issued a set of the chamber works. The Canadian-based Sefel label has issued high-tech recordings of the orchestral works with various Hungarian artists under the baton of Arpad Joó.

[1761] TOSELLI, Enrico (Tō-sel'-lē, En-rē'-kō)
PIANIST, TEACHER
BORN: Florence, March 13, 1883
DIED: Florence, January 15, 1926

Enrico Toselli was in his day famous for two things: a torrid romance and a brief, disastrous marriage, in 1907, with Luise of Tuscany, the former wife of King Frederick August III of Saxony. (After eleven years of marriage to the king and five children, Luisa had run off with her tutor in 1902 and been divorced two years later.) (2) A 1900 song, "Serenata," that achieved epidemic popularity. Apart from these matters, Toselli was a gifted concert pianist, a successful teacher, and a composer of some ambition. He was a pupil of Sgambati [1385] and Martucci [1487]. Luise provided him with a libretto and a scenario for two operettas before the marriage went on the rocks in 1911, and with material for a bestselling book of reminiscences specifically addressed to his unhappy love story; the book was published in 1918.
RECORDINGS: "Serenata" has been recorded in every conceivable form.

[1762] MANÉN, Joan (Mà'-nān, Hwàn)
VIOLINIST, CONDUCTOR, EDITOR,
WRITER
BORN: Barcelona, March 14, 1883
DIED: Barcelona, June 26, 1971

A genuine prodigy, Manén studied with his father from the age of three, took up the violin at five, made his concert debut at seven (after some appearances as a pianist), concertized throughout the Americas at nine, began conducting at ten, and (self-taught) wrote his first composition at thirteen. By the time he reached his majority, he had written three operas and was famous as a performer all over Europe. He settled in Germany in 1909 and was particularly successful there. His 1903 opera *Acté* was produced in revised form (as *Nero und Akté)* at Karlsruhe in 1928. Later he returned to Barcelona. Manén edited the works of Paganini **[1106]** and wrote a book on the violin, two volumes of memoirs, and a dictionary of musical celebrities. RECORDINGS: Manén made acoustical recordings as a violinist. Some of his guitar pieces and songs have been more recently recorded. He also composed ballet scores, some orchestral works, string quartets, and piano pieces.

[1763] HAUER, Josef Matthias (Hou'-er,
Yō'-zef Màt-tē'-às)
TEACHER, ORGANIST
BORN: Wiener Neustadt, March 19, 1883
DIED: Vienna, September 22, 1959

Hauer was the father of twelve-tone music—or so he rather loudly insisted for most of his life. And indeed in a sense he was, but he was never a grandfather. Born in a city south of Vienna, he was certified there in 1902 as a public school teacher and began his career in a nearby village called Krumbach. He was self-taught in music, but his self-training was sufficiently thorough for him to be allowed officially to teach it to others. His official debut as a composer came in 1912 with a work called *Nomos* for piano accompanied by piano or harmonium (four hands). It and the compositions that immediately followed—more keyboard pieces, songs, choruses, and an *Apokalyptische Phantasie* for orchestra—were in effect atonal and rather formless. At the outset of World War I there was some sort of flap over Hauer's patriotism (or lack of it—he was a decidedly eccentric fellow), and he was jailed for a time. In 1915 he moved to Vienna permanently and, stimulated by the company he kept, he began to formulate his philosophy, musical and otherwise. Though he intro-

duced himself to Schoenberg **[1657]**, the two did not by any means see eye to eye. In 1919 the school system retired him (at thirty-six), some of his music was performed at Schoenberg's concert series, and Hauer arrived at his twelve-tone theory, which he explained in a series of books over the next half-dozen years.

Humanity, Hauer reasoned, had been shaped into what it is by the pull of opposite polarities which (to oversimplify vastly) might be summed up as those of spirit and flesh. Music was the result of the tension between *melos* (melody, yes, but implying free flow, best exemplified in the freedom of atonality, unhampered by any external considerations) and *rhythmus* (rhythm, yes, but ultimately regularity implying stasis). By denying its tendency toward *melos,* music had taken a wrong turn, posing grave dangers to mankind. To effect the breakaway, Hauer insisted that the twelve tones of the chromatic scale should be used in nonrepetitive patterns, of which, he calculated, there were 479,001,600 possible. But here Hauer differs sharply from Schoenberg, for Hauer considers his twelve tones as implying two opposed hexachords or six-note scales (though in only two permutations of each can the notes be in the expectable linear sequence—up or down) which would underlay a given composition. The resultant music would be purely intellectual, "depicting" neither external reality nor inner emotions. (Hauer also avoided the contrapuntal complexities essential to Schoenberg's approach).

The discovery of a system within which to work unleashed the creative demon in Hauer, and by the end of the next decade he had 89 opus numbers in his catalog. He produced a series of 8 orchestral suites and other abstract instrumental pieces, but much of his output was devoted to settings of his favorite poet, Friedrich Hölderlin. The music got some exposure, notably at ISCM festivals, and Otto Klemperer **[1794]** did a partial concert performance of Hauer's opera *Salambo,* in 1930. In that same year, the government awarded him an annuity. But Hauer resented the fact that the upstart Schoenberg, who had not unveiled *his* system until 1924, had been deified, whereas his own had not been taken seriously, and he proclaimed *ad nauseam* that he was the *real* founder of twelve-tone music, even so indicating on his stationery—a stance that did not go well with Schoenberg.

Declared unacceptable as a composer by the Nazis in 1938, Hauer became a sort of recluse, happily grinding out hundreds of pieces of all kinds by his formulae—most of them now lost or destroyed. In his last years

the musical world and the Austrian government made belated amends with a series of awards and titles.
RECORDINGS: Very little of Hauer's has been recorded—prior to 1983 I trace three early piano pieces and an LP side of Hölderlin *Lieder* sung by Polly Batic (and credited to *Johann Matthias Hauer!*). Recently the 1750 Arch label has issued a record entitled *Atonale Musik,* consisting of piano pieces from the early 1920s performed by pianist Joseph Kubera.

[1764] NUFFEL, Jules van (Nuf'-fel, Zhülz vån)
ORGANIST, CHOIRMASTER, ADMINISTRATOR, TEACHER, PRIEST, EDITOR
BORN: Hemiksem, March 21, 1883
DIED: Wilrijk, June 29, 1953

Born in a village near Antwerp, Jules van Nuffel learned to love music from his father, a physician. He got his formal training, however, mostly at the seminary at Mechelen (Malines), where he studied for the priesthood. He was ordained in 1907 and remained to teach languages and music there. After the Cathedral of St. Rombaut in Mechelen had sustained severe war damage, he was asked to reorganize the choir in 1916. He made it one of the best in Belgium and stayed on as choirmaster and organist until he died thirty-seven years later. In 1918 he was also named director of the Lemmens Institute of Church Music. During the next decade or so, he helped edit the first modern edition of Philippe de Monte's **[197]** music. In 1946 Pope Pius XII made him a papal chamberlain, with the title of monsignor. As a composer Nuffel remained within the limits of his calling, producing massive and complex organ pieces and much-admired choral works. RECORDINGS: There are a few recordings of organ and choral works.

[1765] GOETZE, Walter (Göt'-zə, Väl'-tår)
BORN: Berlin, April 17, 1883
DIED: Berlin, March 24, 1961

Goetze (not to be confused with Hermann Goetz **[1380]**), started as a writer of sentimental songs. Shortly before World War I he began turning out rather successful operettas and continued to do so for nearly forty years. His greatest hit was the 1919 *Ihre Hoheit die Tänzerin (Her Highness the Ballerina).* RECORDINGS: He is represented on records chiefly by a duet setting of *"Still wie die Nacht"* ("Calm as the Night"—not to be

confused with the solo setting by the pianist Karl Bohm), but there are also excerpts from operettas (e.g., *Der Page des Königs [The King's Page], Liebe im Dreiklang [Love in the Triad]*).

[1766] ZANDONAI, Riccardo (Tsän-dö-nä'-ē, Rik-kär'-dō)
ADMINISTRATOR
BORN: Sacco di Rovereto, May 29, 1883
(Some sources give May 28 or 30)
DIED: Pesaro, June 5, 1944

Representing the last gasp of old-style Italian opera, Zandonai was touted as the new Puccini **[1511]**, though he turned out not to be. Nevertheless he enjoyed considerable success, and his best works have proved resurrectable, at least in Italy. He was born in the Tridentine Alps (which are not made of chewing gum) and in 1893–98 studied in Rovereto with one Gianferrari. At fifteen he became Mascagni's **[1559]** pupil at the Liceo Rossini in Pesaro, graduating in 1902. His first opera, a one-act piece called *La Coppa del re (The King's Cup),* went unperformed. His second, *L'Ucellino d'oro (The Golden Bird),* a fairy tale for children, was produced in his hometown in 1907. The third, *Il Grillo del focolare (The Cricket on the Hearth,* after Charles Dickens) was premiered with considerable success a year later in Turin and won him a contract with the publishing house of Ricordi. Three years later, *Conchita,* a *verismo* effort set in the land of *Carmen* and painted in the colors of *Salome,* made a tremendous but temporary effect at La Scala. *Melenis*—its successor by a year— was a failure. Meanwhile, attracted both by Gabriele d'Annunzio's dramas and by his political views, Zandonai got his permission to make an opera of *Francesca da Rimini.* Adapted by Tito Ricordi for the composer's use, it had a fine success at Turin early in 1914, reached London a few months later, opened at the Metropolitan Opera in December 1916 (with Frances Alda, Giovanni Martinelli, and Pasquale Amato), and remained in the repertoire the following season. Orchestrally rich and dramatically effective, it continues to enjoy revivals (even at the Metropolitan).
In 1915 Zandonai joined d'Annunzio's campaign to restore Trieste to Italy and revive the grandeur that was Rome's, winning himself a place on the Austrian government's hit list. In 1917 he married Tarquinia Tarquini, who had created the title role in *Conchita.* No new opera was forthcoming, however, until 1919, when *La Via della finestra (The Path from the Window)* failed at

Pesaro. Nor did its revised version succeed four years later in liberated Trieste. Meanwhile Zandonai returned to another mediaeval Italian tale of ill-starred love, *Giulietta e Romeo* (closer to Shakespeare's sources than to Shakespeare) and enjoyed another success at Rome in 1922. His last relatively unqualified hit was *I Cavalieri di Ekebu (The Knights of Ekebu)* at La Scala in 1925, based on Selma Lagerlöf's first novel, *Gösta Berlings Saga.* To honor that lady's seventieth birthday, Stockholm gave it a splendid production three years later. In 1928 the San Carlo in Naples premiered a sort of third remake of *Francesca,* called *Giuliano.* It was followed in 1933 by the one-act *Una partita (A Match)* and *La Farsa amorosa (The Love Farce),* an attempt at operatic *commedia dell'arte.* However, in his later years, Zandonai turned more to orchestral music. In 1940 he was appointed director of the (now) Conservatorio Rossini in Pesaro. He was working on another opera, *Il Bacio (The Kiss),* when he died at sixty-one.

RECORDINGS: There have been commercial recordings of *L'Ucellino d'oro, Conchita, Francesca da Rimini,* and *Giulietta e Romeo,* and piracies of *Francesca, Conchita,* and *I Cavalieri d'Ekebu.* (The Swedes recorded the participants of their premiere of the latter in a number of excerpts; other excerpts from the major works are also available.) Apart from a song or two, little else of Zandonai's output—which includes a *Requiem,* symphonic poems, concerted works, cantatas, film scores, piano pieces, and band music—seems to have been recorded.

[1767] CASELLA, Alfredo (Kä-sel´-lä, Äl-frä´-dō)
PIANIST, CONDUCTOR, TEACHER
BORN: Turin, July 25, 1883
DIED: Rome, May 5, 1947

Having called the tune in the musical world since the Renaissance, the Italians refused to recognize in the nineteenth century that they were losing out to other nations, whose music they were generally loath to accept. By the twentieth even opera was failing to progress and the public was mired in the tastes of the past. If a composer wanted to move forward, he had, like Malipiero [1743] and Pizzetti [1732], to find his own way or to take cognizance of the chief developments elsewhere—which was Casella's initial approach and which in many ways colored all his mature output.

Alfredo Casella's father was Carlo Casella, a cellist who taught that instrument at the Liceo in Turin. His mother was a good pianist who began to teach him to play from the age of four. He made his concert debut at eleven and two years later was sent off to the Paris Conservatoire to study with Louis Diémer, Leroux [1557], and eventually with Gabriel Fauré [1424]. In 1899 Casella won a first prize in piano. He left the school in 1902 but at least nominally lived in Paris until the outbreak of war in 1914. In between travels—which took him to, among other places, Germany and Russia—he worked variously as harpsichordist in the Société des Instruments Anciens (organized by members of the Casadesus clan), assistant to Alfred Cortot at the Paris Conservatoire, and conductor. Musicians whom he came to know well included Enesco [1738], Koechlin [1592], Malipiero, and Ravel [1666]. Casella was open to all sorts of musical influences—the German post-Romantics, notably Mahler [1525], the French Impressionists, the Russian nationalists—and his music showed it, without taking many risks. Apart from a considerable number of piano pieces, the early period produced two symphonies, a ballet, an orchestral suite, the symphonic poem *Italia* (which, like Richard Strauss's [1563] *Aus Italien,* quotes Denza's [1426] *"Funiculi-funicula"* as a folk song), songs, and a violin sonata.

Back in Italy after nearly two decades, Casella was hired by the Liceo di Santa Cecilia in Rome to teach piano in 1915. Shocked by the condition in which he found his country's music, he appointed himself its messiah. Seeking out other like-minded young Turks (Italian branch), in 1917 he formed an organization, the Società nazionale di musica, to promote modern music; it soon became the Società Italiana di Musica Moderna. It gave concerts devoted to the avant-garde at which Casella frequently appeared in his various capacities, often performing his own music. This music had suddenly veered sharply toward atonality. The Italians disliked the concerts in general and Casella's music in particular, and by 1919 the Società was out of business; shortly afterward Casella went into a period of compositional hibernation. He also resigned from the Accademia di Santa Cecilia (as the Liceo had become known in the interim) in 1922. He did not, however, give up performing, for he appeared as pianist of the Trio Italiano and increasingly took conducting engagements. (He first appeared in the United States as guest conductor of the Philadelphia Orchestra, in 1921.) But he had failed to create an appetite for modern music in Italy, and more importantly he had failed to create an Italian music—something that the political climate under the Mussolini government, which seized power in 1922, seemed to demand.

According to Casella, while he was traveling through Tuscany in 1923, the ordered landscape revealed to him what the concept of the "Italian" meant to him, and he realized that this quality was expressed in the formalism of Italy's Baroque and Classical composers. With a shout of "Eureka!" he leaped on what turned out to be the Italian model of the neo-classicism that was already juggernauting through Europe. There followed in due course not only *ricercari, toccate,* and *divertimenti,* but also evocations of specific older musicians, as in the *Scarlattiana* of 1927 and the *Paganiniana* of 1942. (There were also a number of abstract works —a third symphony, concerted works for piano, violin, organ, and piano trio, sonatas, and so forth.) Generally speaking the Italian public did not take much better to this phase of Casella's music than it did to the previous one, but the government indicated that it approved.

In 1924 Casella's most successful stage work, the ballet *La Giara (The Jar)* after Pirandello, was first produced in Paris. During the 1920s he returned several times to America and in 1927 was appointed conductor of the Boston Promenade ("Pops") Orchestra. But Bostonians on the Esplanade admired his taste in music no more than the Italians, and after a couple of seasons they replaced him with one of their own named Arthur Fiedler. In 1930 Casella inaugurated, as codirector, the Venice Festival of Contemporary Music (which survived for forty-three years), and two years later he returned to the Accademia di Santa Cecilia and had his only full-length opera, *La Donna serpente (The Serpent Woman),* produced in Rome. (There were also two one-act works, *La Favola d'Orfeo [The Tale of Orpheus],* performed in Venice that same year, and *Il Deserto tentato [The Desert Probed],* inspired by Mussolini's invasion of Ethiopia.)

Casella spent the war years in Italy—uneasily because of his French-Jewish wife and in increasingly bad health. His last composition was a *Missa "Pro pace"* in 1944, celebrating the end of the war for Italy, but he continued occasionally to perform and to write. (His literary efforts include an autobiography, books on Stravinsky [1748], Bach [684], Beethoven [1063], Bartók [1734], and the piano.

RECORDINGS: Recordings are sparse. One notes *Italia, Scarlattiana, Paganiniana,* the *Serenata* (chamber orchestra), suites from *Le Couvent sur l'eau (The Convent by the Water,* an early ballet), the violin concerto, and *La Giara,* the *Cinque pezzi (5 Pieces)* for

string quartet, the 2 cello sonatas, the harp sonata, and piano pieces (including a boxed set of the complete solo piano music on the Italia label).

[1768] INFANTE, Manuel (Ēn-fàn'-tā, Màn-wel')
PIANIST
BORN: Osuna, July 29, 1883
DIED: Paris, April 21, 1958

Infante, a Catalan, studied with Enrique Morera (1865–1942), a pupil of Isaac Albéniz [1523] and Felipe Pedrell [1384] and a successful composer of operas and zarzuelas. Infante lived for most of his mature life in Paris, where he was known as a concert pianist. He wrote an opera, *Almanza,* but most of his output was for his own instrument.
RECORDINGS: There are a few recordings.

[1769] BERNERS, Lord (Sir Gerald Hugh Tyrwhitt-Wilson, Bart.)
POLYMATH
BORN: Apley Park, Bridgnorth, September 18, 1883
DIED: Faringdon House, Berks., April 19, 1950

Gerald Tyrwhitt was the only child of a younger son of an ancient Shropshire family. His by then senile grandfather, a direct descendent of Edward III through John Bourchier, 2nd Baron Berners, the Tudor translator of Froissart, was the thirteenth holder of the title. The boy was sent to Eton, where he was called "the Newt" by his peers; understandably he liked little about the place except its setting and the chance to expand his mind. After graduating, he studied art and languages in Europe and took a course in harmony in Dresden. Later he had a few sessions with Vaughan Williams [1633] and criticism from Casella [1767] and Stravinsky [1748] but otherwise learned music by himself. In 1909 he was appointed honorary cultural attaché to the British Embassy in Constantinople, moving to an analogous position in Rome two years later. His first compositions of note (or notoriety) were written there—three songs to Heine texts, whose flavor may be suggested by his setting *"Du bist wie eine Blume"* ("Thou Art Like a Flower") on the basis of a legend that it was really addressed to a white pig. There followed piano pieces, including the funeral marches for a canary, a statesman, and a rich aunt, and most of his orchestral output: *Three Pieces* and *Fantaisie espagnole.*

In 1919, his uncle having no heir, Tyrwhitt

became 15th Baron (and 5th Baronet) and legally added "Wilson" to his surname. Along with his titles, he inherited a great deal of money and several estates. He chose to live at Faringdon, about fifteen miles southwest of Oxford, where he behaved in a way that would have brought tears to the eyes of Monty Python. He had the doves dyed in assorted colors, put jewelled collars on the dogs, and kept birds-of-paradise on his lawns. The house was usually swarming with what would have been the jet-setters of the day, had there been jets. Eccentricities were not only tolerated; they were actively encouraged. One visitor, for example, brought a live boa constrictor, and another —or so a photo suggests—had her horse in for lunch. The baron, a slight, bald man with a tidy mustache, traveled the roads either in a minuscule car of uncertain make, or a huge Rolls-Royce equipped with a spinet. Sometimes on such jaunts he wore a horrible mask on the back of his head, to the confusion of drivers behind him.

After writing some more songs and piano pieces, Berners was ready for larger matters. In 1924, his only opera, La Carosse du Saint Sacrament (The Carriage of the Holy Sacrament, after Merimée), was produced at the Théâtre des Champs-Elysées in Paris. In spite of extensive later revisions, it never caught on. But the parodistic ballet The Triumph of Neptune (book by Sacheverell Sitwell, choreography by George Balanchine) did when it was produced by Diaghilev in 1926. It was followed in 1930 by the short Luna Park (choreography by Balanchine) as part of a revue. The following year, Berners had, in London, the first of two one-man shows of his paintings. (He was also a superb cook and published, between 1936 and 1945, six novels and two books of memoirs.)

In 1935, over the loud protests of the community, he erected a 140-foot tower on his hilltop at Faringdon, dedicated to the proposition that it could have no conceivable purpose. It became known as the Faringdon Folly. A notice at the foot warned would-be suicides that they jumped at their own risk. The year 1936 brought a new ballet for the burgeoning Sadler's Wells Company, A Wedding Bouquet. The book and chorally-sung text were by Gertrude Stein, the choreography by Frederick Ashton, and the sets and costumes by the composer himself. Berners' last two ballets, both for the same company, were Cupid and Psyche in 1936 and the one-act Les Sirènes, 1946. In the 1940s he turned to film scores, turning out Halfway House in 1944 and Nicholas Nickleby in 1947, plus a couple of songs for Champagne Charlie, also in 1944. During his last few years he was in poor health and saddened by the fact that his way of life had no place in the modern world. He wrote his own epitaph, a clerihew that ends with the lines "But praise to the Lord / He seldom was bored"—which seems to have been true. Though the general musical public tended to dismiss Berners's music as the work of a nut or at best of a minor Satie [1578], real musicians admired and respected his knowledge and craftsmanship.

RECORDINGS: Thomas Beecham twice recorded The Triumph of Neptune. Recently others have come around to the view that he was a talented and witty composer whose works, however much they reflect another time, remain sophisticatedly individual. Meriel and Peter Dickinson have made an LP that includes most of the songs and solo piano pieces, and Menahem Pressler did an earlier recording of the latter. Pianists Peter Lawson and Christopher Scott have recorded the Fantaisie espagnole and Trois morceaux in versions for four-hand piano. There are also recordings of a suite from Les Sirènes, the Fugue for orchestra, and excerpts from Nicholas Nickleby.

[1770] BATH, Hubert
CONDUCTOR
BORN: Barnstaple, November 6, 1883
DIED: Harefield, Middlesex, April 24, 1945

A Devon man, Bath studied at the Royal Academy with the pianist Oscar Beringer and the composer Frederick Corder (1852–1932), a pupil of Hiller's [1219]. He became a popular conductor and—though he occasionally aspired higher—wrote successfully what used to be called "light-classical" music (operettas, one-act operas, cantatas, orchestral pieces, songs). RECORDINGS: His Cornish Rhapsody for orchestra has enjoyed several recordings.

[1771] BAX, (Sir) Arnold Edward Trevor
BORN: Streatham, Surrey, November 8, 1883
DIED: Cork, October 3, 1953

If wishing could have made it so, Arnold Bax would have been born an Irishman. And he tried so hard to be one that critics regularly spoke of the "Celtic" qualities of his music, and some people were sure he was the genuine article. But fate decreed that he be born in a London suburb to cultured and wealthy English Quaker parents. (The poet-playwright Clifford Bax was a younger

brother.) He claimed to have known music
from his cradle and soon reached a point
where even its most labyrinthine complexities held no terrors for him. When he was
fifteen, he entered the Hampstead Conservatory, then under the direction of the future
ethnomusicologist Cecil Sharp. Two years
later he transferred to the Royal Academy,
where he studied composition with Frederick Corder and piano with Tobias Matthay.
(Bax was a brilliant pianist, but, not having
to work for a living and with no taste for the
limelight, he steadfastly refused to play or
conduct in public.) Particularly impressed
with the music of Elgar [1499], Wagner
[1230], and Richard Strauss [1563], he declared in his full maturity that he was still an
unregenerate Romantic. At nineteen he
added a different dimension to his Romanticism when he stumbled on W. B. Yeats's
The Wanderings of Usheen, which took him
into the Celtic twilight. He visited Ireland
repeatedly, hung out with the Dublin *littera-
teurs,* and, as "Dermot O'Byrne," published
three books of Irish tales. Among his earliest
orchestral pieces one finds such titles as
A Connemara Revel, 1905; *Cathaleen-ni-
Hoolihan,* 1905; *An Irish Overture,* 1906; and
Eire (a triptych), 1908-10. (Later he rejected
most of these—except *In the Faery Hills*
from *Eire*—as he did his fearsomely complex chamber works of the period.)

In 1909 Bax fell in love with a Russian
girl, Lyuba Nikolayevna Korolenko, and
vainly pursued her back to Russia, where he
stayed for some months. A few piano pieces
commemorate the visit. After his return to
England, perhaps on the rebound from his
punctured romance, he married a young pianist called Elsita Luisa, the daughter of a
Spanish pianist named Carlos Sobrino.
Though it produced a son and a daughter,
the marriage seems to have been doomed
from the start and ended after a few years.
Its failure, plus the onslaught of World War
I and the Easter Rising in Dublin, shattered
what Bax termed the ivory tower of his
youth and finished the Irish idyll. Yet it
seems all to have had a salutary effect, for it
was about this time that the composer found
his own voice and, beginning with the symphonic poems *The Garden of Fand, November Woods,* and *Tintagel,* and such chamber
works as the *Elegiac Trio,* the first (acknowledged) string quartet, and the second violin
sonata, he entered on his best and most productive period. For most of the rest of his
life he maintained a close liaison with pianist
Harriet Cohen.

In 1922 Bax finished the first of his 7 symphonies, which are probably his most admired works. But there were a score of other

orchestral works, including concerti, and
many chamber compositions, piano pieces,
songs, and choral compositions. Though he
wrote ballet music, dramatic and film scores
(notably one for the 1948 *Oliver Twist),* he
never attempted opera. Except for a restlessness that made it hard for him to stay in one
place very long, his last thirty-five years
were rather uneventful and private. If a minority thought him too modern—his scores
are basically diatonic but tend to be thick-
textured and highly colored—he was generally admired, and his efforts did not go unnoticed. At his coronation in 1937, King
George VI knighted him, and four years
later, on the death of Walford Davies [1609],
appointed him Master of the King's Musick
—somewhat to the discomfort of Bax, who
disliked ceremony. By this time, however,
his musical vein had about run dry. (He
said, defensively, that he supposed he had as
much right to retire as a grocer.) After
World War II Bax spent most of his time at
Storrington, a Sussex village near John Ireland's [1719] retreat. His last works were the
1953 *Coronation March* and a madrigal for
Elizabeth II. Bax hated growing old and had
an irrational fear of his seventieth birthday.
He was spared attaining it by a month, dying suddenly while vacationing in Ireland.

RECORDINGS: All of Bax's symphonies
have been recorded, and Iris Loveridge has
done as much for the whole body of piano
music, including the 4 sonatas. Other
orchestral recordings include *The Garden of
Fand, November Woods, Tintagel, The
Happy Forest, Summer Music, Mediterranean, Northern Ballad No. 1, Overture to a
Picaresque Comedy, The Tale the Pine Trees
Knew,* the *Coronation March,* and selections
from *Oliver Twist.* Of the chamber works
one notes the first string quartet (of 3), the
oboe quintet, the nonet, the *Elegiac Trio,* the
3 violin sonatas, and sonatas for clarinet, viola, and cello, as well as small pieces. Except
for *Mater ora filium* and the madrigal for
Elizabeth, the choral works, like (inexplicably) the songs, have been mostly ignored.

[1772] WIEDERMANN, Bedřich Antonín
(Vē′-der-màn, Be′-der-zhikh Ȧn′-tō-
nyēn)
ORGANIST, VIOLIST, TEACHER
BORN: Ivanovice na Hané, November 10,
1883
DIED: Prague, November 5, 1951

In the familiar pattern of so many Czech
composers, Wiedermann was the son of a
village schoolmaster-organist. After graduating, at the age of twenty, from the Prague

Gymnasium, he decided to enter the priesthood and enrolled at the seminary at Olmütz (Olomouc). After four years there, however, he succumbed to the lure of music and, after a year of organ lessons with Josef Klička at the Prague Conservatory, he devoted another to studying composition with Vitězslav Novák [1617]. In 1910 he went to Brno as cathedral organist, but a year later he returned to Prague to take the analogous post at the Benedictine Monastery and to play viola in the Prague Philharmonic. In 1917 he took over a choir in suburban Karlin and became professor of organ at the Prague Conservatory but continued to give recitals at the monastery. After 1920 the concerts were moved to Smetana Hall, and in the next two decades Wiedermann made several tours, including one to America in 1924. After World War II he taught at the Master School of the conservatory, remaining there when the Communist government rechristened it the Academy of Arts in 1948. Wiedermann wrote choral and organ music in a late-Romantic idiom. RECORDINGS: Some organ pieces have been recorded.

[1773] WEBERN, Anton Friedrich Wilhelm von (Vä'-bern, Än'-tōn Frē'-drikh Vil'-helm fun)
CONDUCTOR, TEACHER
BORN: Vienna, December 3, 1883
DIED: Mittersill, September 15, 1945

After his untimely death, Anton Webern (as he preferred to be known) became one of the most influential composers of his time and the patron saint of the hard-line serialists. A dedicated follower of Schoenberg [1657], he learned to strip twelve-tone music to its lowest common denominator, thus leaving only the concentrated essence of what he had in mind. Some of his worshippers might, however, not have found the man to their refined tastes, for—music aside—he was rather middle-class: a patriot, a family man, a nature lover, and a Bible reader. There have even been some latterday efforts to prove him a Nazi, but though he yearned between the wars for someone to clean up the political and economic mess, and sometimes (as was the fashion in those days) railed privately against the Jews, he was among the first to suffer when Hitler came to power.

Webern's father, Carl Weber von Webern, was a civil engineer in the ministry of agriculture and had inherited a baronetcy, though it was voided when the empire ended in 1918. Frau Webern, *née* Amalie Gehr, was the daughter of a master butcher. Anton was the middle child, between two sisters. His mother gave him piano lessons, but he showed no indication of any real musical talent. When he was seven, the family was transferred to Graz and after four years to Klagenfurt. There he attended the *Gymnasium* and took cello and piano lessons from a Dr. Edwin Komauer, who kindled some musical interest in him—enough to make him experiment with songwriting around the turn of the century. But he was generally a mediocre student, and it is said that he was graduated from the *Gymnasium* in 1902 largely because his teachers liked him. His father wanted him to follow in his own footsteps, but the young man demurred and talked vaguely about a musical career, perhaps as a cellist in some orchestra. At that point the Weberns were restationed in Vienna, where Anton entered the university to take a degree in philosophy. But his chief guide became the musicologist Guido Adler, who saw to it that he acquired the proper basic training. Webern also got some choral and conducting experience in the student Wagner [1230] association and abandoned any further notion of making his living as an instrumental performer. (He never really mastered the piano.) Dissatisfied, however, with the progress (or lack of it) of his composing, he went to Berlin and introduced himself to Pfitzner [1606], with the notion of becoming his pupil, but he found the man so unpleasant that he gave it up. That fall he was steered to Schoenberg, who was then teaching privately in Vienna, made friends with his fellow student Alban Berg [1789], and (though he did not know it) laid the basis for the "Second Vienna School" right there. In 1906 he was the recipient of his Ph.D. from the university for a dissertation on Heinrich Isaac [78] but continued to study with Schoenberg for two more years, his graduation piece there being, so to speak, the *Passacaglia,* Op. 1, for orchestra.

Webern's next several years were not terribly happy ones. Faced with the need to support himself, he became, willy-nilly, a conductor of operettas (a form he came to detest) in such cultural backwaters as Bad Ischl, Teplitz, Danzig (Gdansk), and Stettin (Szczecin), where his associates seemed to view music quite differently from what he did. There were frequent hiatuses between jobs, during some of which he and Berg attempted to raise money to enable Schoenberg to live in the manner to which they felt he should become accustomed (i.e., somewhere above the starvation level). Meanwhile Webern had fallen in love with his cousin, Wilhelmine Mörtl, and married her in February 1911, while he was conducting in Danzig. Two months later she bore him a daughter christened Amalie, who was eventually followed by a brother and two sisters. Early in 1913 Webern walked out of his Stettin job on a pretext of illness and failed to return. He was in fact by then in bad shape, both physically and emotionally, and did not work for some time. In 1915, however, he volunteered for military service. He became an officer and, by the usual military logic, was given a clerical job because he had bad vision. Mustered out in 1917, he went to Prague to take a long-promised post in the German Theater. But this too proved unsatisfactory, and he returned to Vienna, settling in Mödling near his mentor. He was soon a member of the inner circle in the Society for Private Musical Performance and got himself known.

For the next decade, Webern fared rather well. A publishing contract with Universal Edition provided him with a regular income. After directing a *Männerchor* in Mödling, he was put at the helm of the Vienna Workers' Symphony Concerts and the Vienna Workers' Chorus, organizations intended to acculturate the proletariat. He began to make a name for himself as a conductor, not only of the new but also of the classics. He won prizes and commissions. In 1926 he took up teaching at the Jewish Cultural Institute for the Blind for a short time, and a year later began conducting regularly for the Austrian Radio. After that he conducted, as a guest, as far afield as London. And all the while he was steadily, methodically, and painstakingly refining his jeweler's approach to composition. But the chaos in Austria in 1934 that followed Hitler's triumph in Germany overthrew the Social Democrats and robbed Webern of his workers' organizations. For a time he took on private pupils, the most notable of whom was Humphrey Searle [2239]. The *Anschluss* finished the radio work and left Webern branded as a "cultural Bolshevist." He was largely shunned, though Karl Amadeus Hartmann [2072] was his pupil in the early war years. In 1943 he was called into home service as an air-raid warden. Toward the end of the war, his son Peter was killed in Yugoslavia. In the face of the Russian advance, Webern and Wilhelmine closed the house and set out on foot for the Tirol, where their daughters were living. (The Mödling home was later pillaged and vandalized.) By chance a train came along and they rode instead. They were taken in by their second daughter, Maria, although her house was already crowded. On September 15 Webern went to visit his youngest daughter Christine. Her husband was involved in the black market and the American occupation forces had staked out the

house for a raid that evening. After dinner, the composer stepped out on the porch and lit a cigar his son-in-law had given him. A G.I., thinking the match a signal, shot him three times. Webern dragged himself back inside and died. His body was confiscated and the family arrested. Later he was buried in the village cemetery. The soldier was released after pleading self-defense.

RECORDINGS: Webern was a miniaturist: the entire body of his mature work—31 opus numbers—can be performed in about 150 minutes. Much of it has been repeatedly recorded, and Columbia Records has twice issued complete accounts of the canon supervised, respectively, by Robert Craft and Pierre Boulez [2346]), the second of which includes a tape from the Cologne Radio of Webern conducting some Schubert [1153] dances. Some of the early songs have also appeared, and Columbia (CBS) has announced an album of the juvenilia.

[1774] VARÈSE, Edgard Victor Achille
    Charles (Vá-rez′, Ed-gár′ Vĕk-tôr′
    Á-kē′ Shärlz)
    CONDUCTOR
    BORN: Paris, December 22, 1883
    DIED: New York, November 6, 1965

Edgar Varèse, as he called himself after he settled in New York, was perhaps the most radical musical thinker of his time and probably had a more comprehensive impact on the subsequent history of music than even his exact contemporary Anton Webern [1773]. It was he who originated the notion that music was not limited to tones but was organized sound. His gradations of such things as rhythms, timbres, and intensities were taken up by the serialists. John Cage [2192] started where Varèse left off with the exploration of new sound sources. And Varèse was a pioneer in electronic music who was already onto its possibilities by the late 1920s. The remarkable fact about the man as a composer is that he left only a double handful of compositions.

Varèse's mother was Burgundian, and he spent his childhood summers with her people in Burgundy. His father, when the boy was ten, settled with his family in Turin. He planned a practical career for Edgard and saw to it that he was trained in mathematics, science, and technology. This preparation formed his later musical thinking. Meanwhile he had taught himself enough music by the time he was fifteen or so to write a Jules Verne musical, *Martin Pas* (with mandolin accompaniment). Later he managed to take lessons with Giovanni Bolzoni (1841–

1919), a respected composer and conductor who directed the Turin Conservatory and is remembered today only for an innocuous and ubiquitous minuet. By 1903 Varèse's mind was made up and he headed for Paris and the Schola Cantorum. There his education, however much more sophisticated, scarcely foreshadowed his ultimate development, for his teachers were d'Indy [1462], Roussel [1605], Charles Bordes (1863–1909), and later Widor [1414] at the Paris Conservatoire. From 1903 to 1907, however, he composed a number of orchestral pieces. He also founded a chorus and conducted orchestral concerts.

Late in 1907, Varèse pulled up stakes and went to Berlin, where he founded another chorus to sing old polyphonic music and sought out Ferruccio Busoni [1577], whose manifesto on a new musical aesthetics he had read. He was excited by Busoni's demand for the "liberation" of music and found suggestions for how that might be effected in the writings of the physicists Wronsky and Helmholtz. In 1910, thanks to the good offices of Richard Strauss [1563], Josef Stransky conducted a performance of Varèse's symphonic poem *Bourgogne (Burgundy)*. Varèse was at work on an operatic treatment of Hugo von Hoffmannsthal's *Oedipus und die Sphinx* in 1914 when the worsening international situation sent him back to Paris, leaving his belongings and most of his manuscripts in storage. They were destroyed in a fire before he could recover them, and fifty years later he himself destroyed *Bourgogne*. The only work left from the early period is a song for voice and piano. In Paris he joined the French army but became ill and was mustered out the next year, at the end of which, seeing more hope for new music in the New World, he emigrated to New York.

Despite his bucolic experiences in childhood, Varèse was at heart a twentieth-century urbanite, and his new home delighted him, for he loved its roar and dynamism. Though he returned to Europe repeatedly, he remained a New Yorker, conducting most of his professional activity there, marrying an American woman, and acquiring citizenship in 1926. After some initial guest-conducting shots, he founded his own (short-lived) New Symphony Orchestra in 1919, dedicated to the presentation of contemporary music. This aim was better effected by the International Composers' Guild, which he and composer-harpist Carlos Salzedo [1791] founded in 1921 and which presented concerts until 1927. Varèse's next composition, completed in 1921, was entitled *Amériques (Americas)*—a salute to the New World

but also to a new world of music which he intended to create. Though eclectic and influenced by his friend Debussy [1547], it contains, especially in its use of multiple percussion, strong hints of what was to come. It was followed immediately by *Offrandes*, two settings of surrealist poems for soprano and chamber orchestra which Salzedo conducted in April 1922. (*Amériques* was not heard until 1926, in Philadelphia, directed by Leopold Stokowski.)

These two works were, in effect, the composer's farewell to the past. There followed in rapid succession several shockers. The first, *Hyperprism*, caused a minor riot when Varèse introduced it in 1923. Written for woodwinds, brasses, and percussion, it concerns itself not with harmony, counterpoint, and thematic development (at least in any traditional sense) but with juxtapositions of various masses of sound. It was succeeded the next year by *Octandre* for seven winds and double bass, and in 1925 by *Intégrales*, again for winds and percussion. In 1927 Stokowski premiered *Arcana*, in which Varèse transfers a similar approach to an enormous orchestra. Perhaps farthest-out of all was *Ionisation*, for thirteen players of percussion instruments (which included two sirens, but also chimes and a piano), completed in 1931, but first heard in 1933 when Nicholas Slonimsky [1893] conducted it. (He later recorded it.)

In the meantime Varèse had returned to Paris in 1928 for what turned out to be five years, during which time he taught André Jolivet [2073] and discovered the Ondes Martinot and the Theremin, electronic instruments which had been recently discovered. He wrote parts for two of the latter in his next work, *Écuatorial*, in which he combines them with human voices, brasses, piano, organ, and percussion. Slonimsky premiered it in 1934, and in 1936 Varèse wrote for flutist Georges Barrère a solo piece, *Density 21.5* (the title refers to a physical property of the metal—platinum—of which LeRoy's flute was made). An opera projected during this period never saw the light; nor did a truly cosmic project called *Espace* which would link globally scattered performers via radio.

Except for a study for the last-named work, Varèse, for whatever reason, produced nothing more for eighteen years. Over that time he conducted and taught here and there. For some years in the forties he led his Greater New York Chorus, which specialized in polyphonic music (like his earlier ones). Around 1950 he began a big orchestral work, *Déserts*—more about urban deserts and those of the mind and soul than the sandy ones. Three years later the acquisition of a tape recorder fired him up again. With it he first gathered a collage of "concrete" sounds for *Déserts,* which was premiered in Paris in December 1954 by Hermann Scherchen and broadcast in stereophonic sound—the first time a concert had been so relayed there. The next year Varèse provided a soundtrack for a film on Joan Miró. His last completed composition was the *Poème electronique,* designed as "surround sound" for the Philips Pavilion at the Brussels World's Fair in 1958 (and now unrecapturable as conceived). *Nocturnal,* for soprano and bass voices and small orchestra utilizing a text by Anaïs Nin, was completed after Varèse's death by his pupil Chou Wen-Chung **[2331].**

RECORDINGS: Columbia issued Slonimsky's reading of *Ionisation* in the 1930s. In 1950 the Elaine Music Shop in New York produced volume one of a proposed complete works *(Density 21.5, Intégrales, Ionisation, Octandre)* under Frederic Waldman, but the death of the entrepreneur ended the project. However, since then many more Varèse records have appeared, thanks to Maurice Abravanel, Friedrich Cerha, Robert Craft, Pierre Boulez **[2346],** and others, until the entire canon (exclusive of the early song, the study for *Espace,* and the film score) has been made available.

[1775] LHOTKA, Fran (L'hōt'-kà, Fràn)
CONDUCTOR, TEACHER, ADMINISTRATOR, HORNIST
BORN: Mladá Vožice, December 25, 1883
DIED: Zagreb, January 26, 1962

Though the Yugoslavs consider Fran Lhotka one of their more important composers, he was actually born in the outskirts of Budweis (Budejovice) in Bohemia and studied in Prague with Dvořák **[1386],** among others. Like his fellow Czech Křička **[1752],** he taught at the conservatory at Ekaterinoslav (Dniepropetrovsk) in 1908–9. He then settled in Zagreb as a horn player in the opera orchestra. In 1912 he became director of the Lisinski Chorus, and in 1920 he began teaching in the conservatory, which, with time out for a world war, he directed from 1923 to 1952. He wrote 2 operas, concerti, and other smaller things but was most successful as a composer of ballets, which enjoyed a measure of fame outside of Yugoslavia. RECORDINGS: He conducted a recording of the most successful ballet, *The Devil in the Village,* premiered in Zürich in 1935.

[1776] JONGEN, Léon Marie Victor Justin (Zhôn'-gen, Lā-on' Mà-rē' Vēk-tôr' Zhüs-tan')
PIANIST, ORGANIST, CONDUCTOR, TEACHER, ADMINISTRATOR
BORN: Liège, March 2, 1884
DIED: Brussels, November 18, 1969

Léon Jongen, the younger brother of Joseph **[1649]** by nearly a dozen years, entered the Liège Conservatory at the age of twelve and became organist at the church of St. Jacques at fourteen. His first important work was a cantata *Geneviève de Brabant* in 1907, and he followed it in 1909 with another cantata, *La Légende de St. Hubert,* and his first opera, *L'Ardennaise (The Woman of the Ardennes).* He won the Grand Prix de Rome (Belgian variety) in 1913. After a brief turn as a concert pianist, he served in the Belgian army, following the German invasion of August 1914. He returned to the concert trail in 1918, eventually traveling to North Africa and the Far East, where he found employment as a conductor at the opera house in Hanoi in 1927. In 1934 he became professor of fugue at the Brussels Conservatory, then under the direction of his elder brother, whom he succeeded in 1939. He retired in 1949 but continued his activities, writing a violin concerto as a test piece for the Queen Elisabeth Competition when he was seventy-nine. Jongen wrote another opera, *Thomas l'Agnelet* in 1923, an operetta, a ballet, incidental music, film scores, and works in most other classes. RECORDINGS: Léon Jongen conducted for a recording his orchestral suite *Malaisie* (which means "Malaysia," not "discomfort").

[1777] WATTS, Wintter
BORN: Cincinnati, Ohio, March 14, 1884
DIED: Brooklyn, N.Y., November 1, 1962

A product of the Institute of Musical Art (later incorporated into the Juilliard School) in New York, Watts won a Loeb Prize in 1919. Four years later an American Prix de Rome took him to that city for two years further study at the American Academy. Thereafter he lived in Europe until 1931. Though he wrote some more ambitious works, he was quite successful in his lifetime as a composer of effectively tasteful concert songs. RECORDINGS: There are some recordings of the songs.

[1778] VITTADINI, Franco (Vēt-tà-dē'-nē, Frànk'-ō)
ORGANIST, CHOIRMASTER, EDUCATOR

BORN: Pavia, April 9, 1884
DIED: Pavia, November 30, 1948

Vittadini remained a hometown fellow for most of his life. In 1903 he went twenty miles northward to study at the Milan Conservatory. When that did not work out, he moved thirty-five miles farther north to serve as organist-choirmaster in Varese. After a few years he was back in Pavia. Following (an unsuccessful first try at opera, Vittadini created a brief ripple around the globe with *Anima allegra (Happy Soul)*, premiered in Rome in 1921. (It reached the Metropolitan Opera two years later, starred Lucrezia Bori and Giacomo Lauri-Volpi, and had nine performances.) In reward the Pavians put Vittadini in charge of their conservatory, which he ran for twenty-four years. He wrote several other operas and had an Italian success with *La Sagredo,* described by at least one writer as "a sort of nonviolent *Tosca.*" Vittadini's chief problem seems to have been that operatically he was a sort of poor-man's Puccini [1511], just as in his Masses and oratorios he was a sort of poor-man's Perosi [1634]. He also wrote film scores, some orchestral pieces, and much organ music. RECORDINGS: There is a recorded excerpt or two from *Anima allegra.*

[1779] BOERO, Felipe (Bō-ā'-rō, Fā-lē'-pā)

PIANIST, CHOIRMASTER, TEACHER
BORN: Buenos Aires, May 1, 1884
DIED: Buenos Aires, August 9, 1958

Boero studied in Buenos Aires with Leipzig-trained Pablo Berutti and embarked on a career as a concert pianist. In 1912, however, a government prize enabled him to spend some time at the Paris Conservatoire, where he studied with Gabriel Fauré [1424] and Paul Vidal [1554]. With the onset of war in Europe in 1914, he returned to Argentina. His first opera, *Tucumán,* on an Argentine theme, had a great success at the Teatro Colón in 1918. Nine others followed, of which *El Matrero* in 1929 was the most popular and the best known. Boero was also active in music education and from 1935 served as professor and choirmaster in two local teacher-training schools. Besides operas, he wrote orchestral, choral, and piano music. RECORDINGS: There are original-cast and other excerpts from *El Matrero* on records, and some of his orchestral genre pieces.

[1780] BENATZKY, Ralph Rudolf Josef František (Be-nát'-skē, Rålf Rōō'-dolf Yō'-zef Fràn'-tyi-shek)

CONDUCTOR
BORN: Mährisch-Budweis, June 5, 1884
DIED: Zürich, October 17, 1957

Though he became a veritable gusher of light music, Ralph Benatzky did not foresee a musical career for himself. Born in southern Moravia—the town is now Moravské-Budejovice—he grew up in Vienna and took up soldiering. But he was discharged on medical grounds when he was twenty-three. He then went to college and acquired a doctorate in philology in 1911. In the process of his education, he had studied in Munich with Felix Mottl and afterward conducted in that city. He soon, however, returned to Vienna and opened a cabaret. His star singer was a girl called Josma Selim, for whom he began churning out songs and whom he married in 1914. The year before his operetta *Der lachende Dreibund (The Laughing Triple Alliance)* attracted favorable notice in Berlin. After establishing himself as a songsmith and stage composer, he moved to Berlin in the middle 1920s, worked in the film industry, and became one of the most successful composers of the decadent "Berlin operetta," a splashy vaudeville revue held together by a thread of plot. In 1928 *Casanova,* starring Michael Bohnen and Anni Frind was an enormous hit, though his most lasting work, written with Robert Stolz [1730] and others, was *Im weissen Rössl (White Horse Inn)* of 1931. Josma had died in 1930, and the Nazi triumph in 1933 sent Benatzky back to Vienna, then to Paris in 1938, and finally to America and Hollywood in 1940. He settled in Zürich in 1948, where he wrote *Ein Liebestraum (A Dream of Love),* an operetta about Liszt [1218] with music by that composer, and *Don Juans Wiederkehr (Don Juan's Return),* 1953. Of his operettas, only *White Horse Inn* seems to have made it to Broadway; it opened the 1936 season, starred Kitty Carlisle and William Gaxton, and ran for 223 performances. RECORDINGS: There is a complete recording of the German version, an abridged "original-cast" *Casanova,* and many other excerpts and songs.

[1781] LARCHET, John Francis

CONDUCTOR, TEACHER
BORN: Dublin, July 13, 1884
DIED: Dublin, August 10, 1967

An Irish patriot, Larchet was an important force in Irish musical life from his early manhood until his death at eighty-three. He first studied at the Royal Irish Academy. In 1907 he became conductor at the Abbey Theater, then in its great days of Yeats, Synge, and Lady Gregory, and remained there until 1934. He also served as organist in the Jesuit church in Dublin. During the revolutionary years he took baccalaureate and doctoral degrees in music from the University of Dublin. With the passage of the Home Rule Act in 1920, he was named professor of composition at the academy and appointed to the chair of music at University College, where he created a department of music. He retired in 1955. Most of his music —orchestral, choral, solo vocal—was inspired by, or based on, the folk music of his people. RECORDINGS: Milan Horvat recorded two orchestral folk songs *(Dirge of Ossian* and *MacAnanty's Reel)* in a survey of contemporary Irish music.

[1782] GRUENBERG, Louis
PIANIST, TEACHER
BORN: near Brest-Litovsk, August 3, 1884
DIED: Los Angeles, June 9/10, 1964

For a time in the 1920s Europe hailed Louis Gruenberg as the first real American composer of significance. Not long afterward, America hailed him as the Great White Hope of native opera. Time—alas!—has proved both judgments more than immoderate. Gruenberg's chief talent seems to have been for the impermanent gimmick.

Born in a *shtetl* in Russian Poland, Gruenberg was brought to New York in 1886, and studied piano with Adele Margulies there. On hearing Busoni [1577] play in 1901, he was so impressed that he scraped together enough money to follow him to Berlin. There he dogged the great man's footsteps until Busoni agreed to take him on as pupil. Busoni was evidently pleased with him, for he conducted the Berlin Philharmonic for Gruenberg's official pianistic debut in 1912. Shortly thereafter Gruenberg went to Vienna as a student-teacher at the conservatory, and wrote his Op. 1, a children's opera entitled *The Witch of the Brocken.* The next year he set a libretto by Busoni himself, an (Asian) Indian story called *Die Götterbraut (The Bride of the Gods).* He also wrote some chamber music and an orchestral suite, and his first piano concerto was premiered in 1914. Meanwhile his concert career prospered. (At one point we find him joining Louis Closson, Eduard Steuermann, and Anton Webern [1773] in an eight-hand reduction of Schoenberg's [1657]

5 *Pieces for Orchestra* under the composer's direction.) After war broke out in 1914, Gruenberg returned to America—by chance on the same ship as the Busonis.

Having won a prize for his tone poem *The Hill of Dreams* in 1919—the year in which he also wrote the first of his 5 symphonies— Gruenberg opted for a career as a composer. He produced some more eclectic works but became convinced that an American composer should write American music, which he felt should be founded on the most characteristic national musical products—black spirituals and jazz. His 1924 setting of Vachel Lindsay's *The Daniel Jazz* for tenor, clarinet, trumpet, and strings, created a furor at the ISCM Festival in Vienna the next year and won him a contract with International Editions, a leader in the publication of important contemporary music. Gruenberg tried to fulfill expectations with such works as *Jazz Suite, Jazzettes, Jazzberries,* etc., but the charm soon wore off and the relationship was terminated.

In 1930 Gruenberg dusted off his symphony and submitted it to an RCA competition; it won first prize and $5,000 but no recording. The next year the Juilliard School (president: John Erskine) put on Gruenberg's third children's opera, *Jack and the Beanstalk* (librettist: John Erskine), which attracted a short-lived professional production. ("It wasn't much," says a biographer.) In January 1933, however, the composer reached the pinnacle of his fame when the Metropolitan Opera produced his treatment of Eugene O'Neill's *The Emperor Jones,* with Lawrence Tibbett in the title role. Tibbett made the drama compelling, but reviewers were largely unanimous in their opinion that Gruenberg's sketchy music added little to the play. Of his five subsequent operas, only *Green Mansions,* a treatment of W. H. Hudson's novel for radio performance, got any notice—though some listeners were reminded of *Tarzan* soundtracks.

In 1936, after three years of teaching composition at the Chicago Musical College, Gruenberg made his way to the West Coast and the Hollywood studios, where—though he railed against such self-prostitution—he perhaps found his true calling. He scored many pictures and won three Academy Awards for his efforts *(The Fight for Life, So Ends Our Night,* and *Commandos Strike at Dawn).* He died a few weeks before his eightieth birthday, bitter at the neglect that had been accorded his serious efforts for the last thirty years—though Jascha Heifetz had some success with the Concerto for Violin he commissioned in 1944. In spite of considerable publicity, several latter-day attempts to establish Gruenberg's music have failed.

RECORDINGS: Tibbett recorded the arrangement of "Standin' in de Need o' Prayer" from *The Emperor Jones,* and piracies of at least part of the Metropolitan broadcast have circulated. Heifeitz recorded the violin concerto, and pianist Elaine Shaulis has recorded the 1924 *Polychromatics* for piano.

[1783] GRIFFES, Charles Tomlinson
PIANIST, TEACHER
BORN: Elmira, N.Y., September 17, 1884
DIED: New York, April 8, 1920

Though his reputation went for a time into eclipse, owing to the fashions and fatuities of the musical world, it seems now, as it seemed at the time of his too early death, that Charles T. Griffes possessed perhaps the greatest genius among his generation of American composers. His older sister Katharine elected to give him piano lessons when he was a child and then turned him over to her own teacher, one Mary Selena Broughton, who taught piano at Elmira College. While Griffes was acquiring the usual book learning at the Elmira Free Academy, she set about making a gentleman of culture and taste out of him. It was Miss Broughton too who persuaded his doubting parents that he should be a musician, and when he went off to Berlin in midsummer 1903, she helped him survive abroad. At the Stern Conservatory in Berlin, Griffes studied piano with Ernst Jedliczka for the better part of a year. When the latter died in 1904, he was taken on by the brilliant Gottfried Galston, a Leschetizky pupil who was eventually to settle in St. Louis. His chief composition teacher was a minor operatic composer, Philippe-Barthélemy Rüfer (1844–1919). While in Berlin Griffes soaked up the musical and cultural opportunities, increasingly under the guidance of one Emil Joël, a few years his senior, with whom he entered into a close and longtime liaison. It was Joël who led him to Engelbert Humperdinck [1480] in 1905. Humperdinck is usually cited as Griffes's chief teacher, but the fact is that they worked together only about a dozen times, after which Humperdinck begged off because he was too busy with *Königskinder.*

Save for a brief visit home in 1906, Griffes remained in Germany until 1907. The works that he turned out during this period were mostly songs to German texts, skilled but largely derivative, but there were some choral pieces, an overture, and a *Symphonische Phantasie.* Back home he almost immedi-

ately became employed—permanently it eventuated—at the Hackley School for Boys in Tarrytown, New York, where he played the chapel organ and gave piano lessons. Too much has perhaps been made of the oppressiveness of Hackley on Griffes. It is true that most of his charges were not *simpatico* and that the work was time-consuming, but he had summers off, he found friends there, and New York was easily accessible. In what free time he had, Griffes wrote industriously, gradually drifting toward Impressionism and later to experiments with oriental impulses and even more daring ventures. Nor is it true that he wasted his sweetness on the desert air. He found a publisher in Gustav Schirmer, and he was taken up by a number of influential artists, including the pianist Winifred Christie, the singer Eva Gauthier, and the dancer Adolf Bolm. He also enjoyed the friendship and influence of Arthur Farwell [1629] and by early 1919 had been represented by two all-Griffes concerts in New York. The Neighborhood Playhouse presented his ballet *The Kairn of Koridwen* in 1917 and Bolm's company danced his Japanese ballet *Sho-Jo* on tour. Walter Damrosch premiered the *Poem for Flute and Orchestra,* Pierre Monteux and the Boston Symphony *The Pleasure Dome of Kubla Khan,* and Stokowski four of the shorter orchestral pieces.

Legend has it that Griffes died of penury and overwork, but the fact is that he contracted a stubborn lung infection (an empyema) which gradually dragged down his resistance. He succumbed to pneumonia at thirty-five. Among his other major works was a formidable piano sonata and an unfinished "festival drama" after Whitman, *Salut au monde.* There was also a wealth of piano pieces (some later orchestrated), and some of the greatest songs ever written by an American.

RECORDINGS: Recordings include *The Pleasure Dome of Kubla Khan,* the *Poem,* most of the mature short orchestral pieces and transcriptions *(The White Peacock, Clouds, Bacchanale,* and *3 Tone-Pictures*—but none of the stage works), various collections of the piano music, *2 Sketches on Indian Themes* for string quartet, and some songs. Of the last the largest representations are on a New World Records disc, a two-LP Musical Heritage Society album, and on a side by Norman Myrvik.

[1784] RÓŻYCKI, Ludomir (Roo-zhich'-kě, Loo'-dō-myēr)
CONDUCTOR, TEACHER

BORN: Warsaw, November 6, 1884
DIED: Katowice, January 1, 1953

Różycki never quite lived up to the great promise of his early career. His father Aleksander was a composer of sorts and professor of piano at the Warsaw Institute of Music; he taught not only his son but also Arthur Rubinstein, whom he dropped as "not very promising." Ludomir proceeded to the Warsaw Conservatory, where he studied composition with Zygmunt Noskowski (1846–1909), teacher of Szymanowski [1755], Grzegorz Fitelberg (1879–1953), and Apolinary Szeluto, with whom he joined to found the so-called "Young Poland" movement. He graduated in 1903 with a gold medal for composition, and the Warsaw Philharmonic, shortly afterward, performed his symphonic poem *Stańczyk* and his *Ballade* for piano and orchestra. In 1905 he went to Berlin, where he studied with Humperdinck [1480] and won encouragement from Richard Strauss [1563] and the hand of Stefania Mławska. In 1908 he returned to Poland to conduct at the opera house and teach at the conservatory in Lwów. There a year later he successfully premiered his first opera *Bolesław the Bold,* based on his symphonic poem of the same name. He followed it with *Meduza* in 1911, produced in Warsaw, and then set out on his travels. Having visited France, Italy, and Switzerland, he went to Berlin again to try to get a production of his newest opera, *Eros and Psyche.* However, it was the summer of 1914, and before he knew it he was stuck in Berlin for the duration of the war. When he was on the verge of beggary, friends—including soprano Claire Dux, violinist Carl Flesch, and pianist Ignaz Friedman—gave an all-Różycki concert which not only eased the crisis but got his opera premiered in Breslau. It was played repeatedly in central Europe. A second benefit by the Blüthner Orchestra enabled him to survive until he could return to Poland. There he had further successes with *Casanova* in 1923 (conducted by Artur Rodzinski), with *Beatrix Cenci* in 1927, but especially with the 1920 ballet *Pan Twardowski,* which has had over 800 performances in Poland. In 1930 Różycki was awarded a prize by the government and became a professor at the Warsaw Conservatory. By then he had quit writing choral, chamber, and piano music, and the rest of his output fell off badly both in quantity and quality. After World War II he lived and taught in Katowice. RECORDINGS: Barbara Hesse-Bukowska has recorded the *Ballade,* and there are a few other recordings on Polish lists, including a suite from *Pan Twardowski.*

[1785] RANGSTRÖM, Anders Johan Ture (Ràng'-ström, Àn'-ders Yō'-hàn Too'-re)
CRITIC, CONDUCTOR, TEACHER
BORN: Stockholm, November 30, 1884
DIED: Stockholm, May 11, 1947

Originally hoping to be a singer, Rangström studied in Berlin and Munich, which training no doubt explains his success as a vocal writer. His compositional training came chiefly from Johan Lindegren (1842–1908), the church-music man, in Stockholm and from Hans Pfitzner [1606] in Munich. In 1907 he returned to Stockholm and reviewed for various newspapers until 1914. He was much taken with Strindberg's writings, and his 1909 settings of four of his poems led to a friendship between the two. After Strindberg died in 1912, Rangström memorialized him in his first Symphony (of 4), completed in 1914. Meanwhile in 1910 Rangström had opened a successful vocal studio. In 1919, the year in which he made his conducting debut, the Stuttgart Opera premiered *The Crown Bride.* It was based on a Strindberg play for which the playwright specified folk songs; such music, he pointed out to Rangström, must form the basis for any Swedish national music. A second opera, *In the Middle Ages,* was produced in 1921 in Stockholm. The following year Rangström took over the Göteborg Symphony Orchestra from Stenhammar [1619] and was its conductor for three seasons, after which he returned to reviewing for a time. After serving as press officer for the Royal Swedish Opera from 1930 to 1937, he again reviewed until 1942. He left a third opera, *Gilgamesh,* unfinished. His other symphonies—respectively subtitled "My Land," "Song Under the Stars," and "Invocation"—date from 1919, 1931, and 1936. He also wrote music for Strindberg's *To Damascus* and Ibsen's *Brand,* several other orchestral works, a string quartet, choruses, and piano music, but he is chiefly remembered for his art songs, which owe something to folk music but are conceived chiefly in terms of the intonation of the language. RECORDINGS: Many songs have been recorded. There are also records of Symphonies No. 1 (Tor Mann, Leif Segerstam), No. 2 (Segerstam), No. 3 (Janos Fürst), No. 4 (Yuri Ahronovich); *Partita* for violin and orchestra (conducted by Leonard Slatkin), *2 Songs in Old Style* (John Frandsen), the *Divertimento elegiaco* (Carl von Garaguly, Stig Westerberg), the orchestral song cycle *King Erik's Songs* (Frandsen), the piano suite *Legends from Lake Mälaren* after Strindberg (Staffan Scheja), and miscellaneous chamber pieces.

[1786] DIEREN, Bernard van (Dēr'-en, Ber-närd' van)
WRITER
BORN: Rotterdam, December 27, 1884 (Grove's gives 1887, but no one else agrees.)
DIED: London, April 24, 1936

The name and works of Bernard van Dieren were readily invoked by the forward-looking young English artists of the 1920s, but one has the feeling that they admired him more as a thinker and a man than as a composer. His work is oddly uneven, ranging from complex and cerebral polyphony to almost sentimental simplicity. There is little enough of it, and today one hears even less. Though his father was Dutch, three of his grandparents were French. He trained to be a scientist, though his hobbies were playing the violin, drawing, and reading. After trying to compose, he embarked on an intensive course of self-administered musical studies, while he supported himself working in a laboratory. At twenty-five he moved to London and eked out a marginal existence as musical correspondent, which his wife Frieda, sister of the cellist-conductor Hans Kindler, shared with him. Van Dieren was taken up as a sort of guru by the likes of Peter Warlock [1900], Cecil Gray, and Constant Lambert [2074], who did what they could to promote his cause. His largest works were a comic opera, *The Tailor,* and a *Chinese Symphony* for voices and orchestra (on Chinese lyrics); his greatest and perhaps most interesting output was in the field of song, where he often showed ingenuity and exquisite taste in his selection of texts, though it has been said that here he was more concerned with musical problems than with verbal meanings. He also wrote 4 string quartets, a violin sonata, and a few other orchestral works. Besides his many articles he published a study of his friend the sculptor Jacob Epstein in 1920. In 1935 he issued a collection of essays entitled *Down Among the Dead Men.* Always in delicate health, he joined them a year later, aged fifty-one. RECORDINGS: There are a few songs on records, and the string quartets have just been released.

[1787] KERN, Jerome David
PIANIST
BORN: New York, January 27, 1885
DIED: New York, November 11, 1945

Jerome Kern was the first of the great modern writers of American popular songs of the "show-tune" variety and one of those who helped turn the operetta into the more coherently dramatic "musical." However admirable Herbert [1513], Siegmund Romberg [1821], and Friml [1726] were on their own grounds, they were Europeans and wrote in the European tradition.

Kern was the son of a well-to-do businessman who ran water-sprinkling concessions in and around New York. The boy first studied piano with his mother and then with Paolo Gallico, a well-known pianist-composer of the day and the father of the writer Paul Gallico. In 1895 Mr. Kern moved his family to Newark, where he went into merchandising. When Jerome was seventeen, his father sent him to the New York College of Music, where he studied theory and harmony with Austin Pierce and piano with Alexander Lambert, a Liszt [1218] pupil. At the end of the academic year, the elder Kern took his son into the family firm, but he showed such ineptitude for business that his father happily provided him with funds to continue his studies in Heidelberg in 1903–4. Back in New York the next summer, Kern got into the music business on the ground floor, playing for theatrical rehearsals, plugging songs, and trying his hand at some of his own. He was rewarded by having five of them inserted that September in a show called *Mr. Wix of Wickham,* otherwise memorable for introducing the great female impersonator Julian Eltinge to Broadway and for closing as quickly as it opened. His first hit came a year later with "How'd You Like to Spoon with Me?"—added to an operetta called *The Earl and the Girl.* Shortly after that Kern spent some time in London, which he had visited briefly on his earlier trip abroad, where he also wrote some songs for other people's musical plays.

Kern's first complete score was heard in 1912 but not by many. It was for *The Red Petticoat,* a reworking of an earlier disaster, and it managed to survive for sixty-one performances. But he really arrived when seven of his songs, including "They Didn't Believe Me," were added to an English import, *The Girl from Utah*—whose original score was by Paul Rubens (1875–1917) and Sidney Jones [1535]. Audiences immediately recognized that these were something new—easy, subtle, and sophisticated. The next year *Ninety in the Shade,* which closed for lack of funds to pay the cast, marked the beginning of a fruitful partnership with playwright Guy Bolton and producer Ray Comstock. To avoid similar disasters, Comstock took over the tiny Princess Theater (299 seats). The first production there, *Nobody Home,* was advertised as a new kind of musical theater with a "real" plot. It was only moderately successful, and Kern in fact was one of several hands responsible for the score. But it is generally agreed that *Very Good Eddie,* which opened in December 1915 and for which music Kern alone was responsible, lived up to the promises for the early work and marked a turning point in the American musical theater. *Have a Heart* (January 1917) got good reviews (the lyrics were by P. G. Wodehouse) but failed to draw. However, *Oh, Boy!* a month later caused critics and the public to dance in the streets; and *Sally* (produced by Ziegfeld, with a book by Bolton, lyrics by Wodehouse, and ballet music by Herbert), which opened just before Christmas in 1920, stands as one of the great American musicals. The star was Marilyn Miller, who also appeared in *Sunny* of 1925, Kern's first collaboration with Oscar Hammerstein II. Kern and Hammerstein had their greatest and longest-lasting triumph in 1927 with their treatment of Edna Ferber's *Show Boat,* which remains a classic. Among their other successes were *Sweet Adeline* in 1929 and *Music in the Air* (a retrogression toward old-fashioned operetta) in 1932. In 1933 *Roberta,* another summer-theater perennial, initiated the successful careers of two notable comedians, Bob Hope and the tragically short-lived Lyda Roberti, and took Kern to Hollywood for the film version. He stayed to write a dozen film scores. The final Kern-Hammerstein work, *Very Warm for May* of 1939 was a dismal failure, even though it included one of Kern's loveliest songs, "All the Things You Are."

In 1941 the composer obliged Artur Rodzinski with a *Scenario for Orchestra* on *Show Boat* tunes and followed it the next year with an original orchestral work, *Portrait of Mark Twain,* for André Kostelanetz. Both were duly recorded, though sales did not cut into those of Brahms [1329] and Tchaikovsky [1377]. Jerome Kern succumbed to a heart attack at the age of sixty while preparing a New York revival of *Show Boat*—later the first musical to be produced by a major American opera company, the New York City Opera in 1954.

RECORDINGS: There are innumerable recordings of Kern's songs and some abridged versions of his major stage pieces, in addition to several recordings of the previously mentioned *Scenario.*

[1788] KÜNNEKE, Eduard (Kün′-ek-ə, Ed′-wärd)
CONDUCTOR, HORNIST
BORN: Emmerich, January 27, 1885
DIED: Berlin, October 27, 1953

Like Jerome Kern [1787], with whom he shared a birthday, Eduard Künneke made his name as a composer of operetta and musical comedy, though he originally had higher aspirations. He was born on the Rhine near the Dutch border and studied in Berlin with Max Bruch [1358] among others. He remained in Berlin, conducting in various theaters including Max Reinhardt's. His first opera went unperformed, but *Robins Ende (Robin's End)* was produced at Mannheim in 1909 and *Coeur As (Ace of Hearts)* at Dresden in 1913; neither made any impact. After spending the war years in an army band, Künneke returned to Berlin, where one of his first engagements was to conduct Heinrich Berté's (1857–1924) hit operetta *Das Dreimädlerhaus (House of the Three Maidens),* based on the music and purported life of Schubert [1153]. Künneke saw where success lay and turned out *Das Dorf ohne Glocke (The Village Without a Bell),* which succeeded very nicely when he led the premiere in April 1919. After grinding out a couple more operettas, he hit again, more solidly, with *Der Vetter aus Dingsda (The Cousin from You-Know-Where).* It won a Broadway production in 1923, as *Caroline* (set in the Civil War South) but not much acclaim. These facts were duplicated by another work presented as *The Love Song* in 1925, based on the life and music of Offenbach [1264]—and on Berté. Later that year Künneke was invited by the brothers Shubert to supply a score for *Mayflowers,* which survived six weeks. Künneke had more success on home soil, especially after 1933 when, *faute de mieux,* empty, pretentious, formulaic works like *Die lockende Flamme (The Alluring Flame), Die grosse Sünderin (The Great Sinner),* and *Zauberin Lola (Enchantress Lola)* were ballyhooed out of all proportion to their worth. Künneke also wrote for films. Among his "serious" works are 2 piano concerti and a string quartet. RECORDINGS: He recorded some of his own music for records (three orchestral suites), and there are excerpts from several of the operettas.

[1789] BERG, Alban Maria Johannes (Bârg, Ăl′-băn Mă-rē′-ă Yō-hăn′-nes)
CRITIC
BORN: Vienna, February 9, 1885
DIED: Vienna, December 24, 1935

In the Trinity of the so-called "Second Viennese School," which was to have such enormous influence on post–World War II composers, the compassionate Berg would appear to be Son to Schoenberg's [1657] Mo-

saic Father and Webern's [1773] abstract
Spirit. Though devoted to his teacher and a
practitioner of his methods and theories,
Berg never let them stand in the way of saying what he meant. Considering the care
with which he developed his complex structures and the relative brevity of his life, it is
not surprising that he wrote little—though
how little can still astonish: only twenty-two
mature works, several of these being reworkings or arrangements of others. But even for
listeners not yet attuned (after half a century) to his idiom, the mastery shines
through, and the 2 operas are unquestionably among the towering masterpieces of the
twentieth century.

Berg was born in comfortable circumstances, the third of the four children of
Conrad Berg, who was a salesman for an
export firm, and the former Johanna Braun,
daughter of the imperial jeweler, who ran a
shop that sold religious objects. The boy led
a happy life in the bosom of his family,
where matters musical and theatrical were
common pastimes and music lessons a matter of course. His brother Charley (sic!) sang
well, and his younger sister Smaragda, to
whom he was very close, was a fine pianist;
both fanned his own interest. In 1900, however, a heart attack felled Herr Berg at the
age of fifty-four, and this event necessitated
stricter economy for his widow and three
young children. But an aunt came to Berg's
rescue by footing the bill for his lessons. The
following year, without any compositional
training, he began trying his hand at Lieder
writing for home consumption. But a series
of events over the next few months plunged
him into a profound depression that climaxed in a suicide attempt—the death of an
idol, Hugo Wolf [1521]; failure to pass his
high-school graduation examinations; and
the collapse of a passionate love affair. In
1904, having repeated his senior year, he
graduated and that fall went to work as an
apprentice (i.e., unpaid) accountant in a government office that specialized in pigs and
distilleries.

At some point around this time, Charley
Berg read Schoenberg's newspaper ad for
composition students and took some of Alban's manuscripts to him. Schoenberg was
sufficiently impressed to take the latter on—
at first without charge. In 1905 the Bergs
moved to Hietzing, a suburb of Vienna, and
soon afterward came into an inheritance
that solved their most crucial financial problems. Alban worked assiduously at his lessons and in that same year produced the first
of the Sieben frühe Lieder (Seven Early
Songs), the first works he was later to include in his official catalog. During this

same period he was much influenced by
Gustav Mahler [1525] and tremendously impressed by Richard Strauss's [1563] Salome.
By 1906 he had made up his mind to devote
his life to music, and shortly after being ac-
credited as a full-fledged civil servant, he
gave up his job. The following spring he met
and fell in love with a young singer, Helene
Nahowski; her parents, however, opposed
her marrying anyone with such hazy prospects; nor did the severe asthmatic attacks
Berg suffered while on vacation in 1908 help
matters. (He first consulted Siegmund
Freud, the nearest available medical man,
and was deeply impressed by him. Other
contemporary nonmusical influences were
the playwright Frank Wedekind, the painter
Gustav Klimt, the satirist Karl Kraus, and
the architect Adolf Loos.)

Having composed a piano sonata, some
songs, and a string quartet under
Schoenberg's tutelage, Berg became (as
much as he ever did) his own man in 1910.
The next year the quartet and the sonata
were performed in public, though little notice seems to have been taken of them. Be
that as it may, Berg finally married Helene
ten days later and settled on the Traut-
mannsdorfgasse, where they spent the rest of
their lives. In the autumn Schoenberg
moved to Berlin and initially had such a
hard time of it that his devoted pupil set
about to take up a collection for him, which,
however, proved unnecessary. Meanwhile
Berg did what he could to help by working
on the manuscript of Schoenberg's treatise
on harmony and devising an analysis of his
Gurrelieder—the latter task one of several he
undertook for Universal Edition. Berg's next
two compositions were settings of five texts
from postcards from his friend Peter Altenberg the Altenberg Lieder for soprano and
orchestra, and four pieces for clarinet and
piano. In their compactness and brevity,
though not in their style, these works remind one of Webern. Schoenberg, who had
returned temporarily to Vienna for the January 1913 premiere of his Gurrelieder, included two of the Altenberg Lieder in a concert of contemporary Viennese works he
conducted on March 31. The event got out of
hand with his own first Kammersymphonie
(Chamber Symphony), and turned riotous
with the Berg pieces, necessitating the sum-
moning of the police. When Berg visited his
old teacher in Berlin that summer, Schoenberg, typically, castigated him for taking off
in a musical direction that led nowhere.
Berg, also typically, knuckled under and
apologized, and went home to begin what
was to be the almost-Mahlerian [1525] 3
Pieces for Orchestra, hoping that their larger

dimensions and fuller development would mollify the master.

Berg completed the orchestral pieces three days before Archduke Franz Ferdinand was murdered at Sarajevo. Though opposed to the war that followed, he was called up a year later and assigned to a training camp in Hungary. He was not up to the strenuous life this entailed and eleven months later was hospitalized and then transferred to guard duty back home. He found this life almost unbearable, and finally in May 1916 he succeeded in obtaining a desk job in the war ministry. Though it was less demanding physically, he found the endless paperwork virtually precluded his composition. Shortly before war broke out, he had been captivated by a production of *Woyzeck*, a drama about a cloddish soldier driven to desperation, written a century before by the short-lived Georg Büchner, a spiritual ancestor of the Expressionists with whom Berg identified. Berg's wartime experiences increased his sympathy for the protagonist, and he determined to make an opera of the piece. He was mustered out in 1918 and began serious work on it, having already seen where he was going.

Berg managed to make ends meet by teaching (he had three students) and managing some family properties. Shortly after the war Schoenberg, now permanently resident in Vienna again, founded the Society for Private Musical Performances—the music being limited to the contemporary and the privacy requiring subscriptions which were not extended to critics. Berg was asked to take over the running of the society, which task also helped augment his income, but he soon found it more demanding than he had anticipated. In 1920 an article on (or against) Hans Pfitzner [1606], which he wrote for Universal Edition's journal *Musikblätter des Anbruch*, was so well received that it got him a contract as its editor. But an attack of his recurrent illness that summer, and a second article (refused by the journal) supporting Schoenberg against the other Viennese critics—not to mention his own urgency about the opera—brought that potential career to a stop before it began. In 1921 galloping inflation also scuttled the Society, and Berg had the time he wanted in which to compose. He completed *Wozzeck* (as he called it) in midsummer 1922. Alma Mahler, the composer's widow, helped him finance the publication of the vocal score, which he issued the following January, sending out cards to possible buyers. (He had already published the quartet and the clarinet pieces out of his own pocket.)

The year 1923 saw Alban Berg at last be-ginning to be recognized. Two excerpts from the opera were applauded in June at Berlin, when Webern conducted them as part of an "Austrian Music Week," and the string quartet also won praise later that summer when it was played during the second ISCM chamber music festival in Salzburg. Hermann Scherchen encouraged Berg to make a sort of *Wozzeck* suite, which resulted in the *Three Fragments*, which Scherchen conducted with enormous success at the All-German Music Festival in Frankfurt am Main the summer following. In January of that same year, Erich Kleiber, newly appointed music director of the Berlin State Opera, had heard the *Wozzeck* score played by pianist Eduard Steuermann and had immediately contracted to produce the work. Kleiber's appointment had been unpopular with right-wing elements, and his decision precipitated a crisis. The house manager, Max von Schillings [1597], ultimately resigned, and a number of nasty tricks were used to keep *Wozzeck* off the stage. It was, however, put on as scheduled on December 14, 1925, in a predictably hectic atmosphere. There were reviews that damned the opera as utter madness and a few that hailed it as a triumph. It was well received at its Prague premiere in November a year later, though subsequent performances suffered from interruptions that had more to do with politics than with theater or music. Oddly, from today's viewpoint, *Wozzeck* had its first triumph in Leningrad in May 1927. (Leopold Stokowski introduced it to the United States four years later, with Nelson Eddy in the role of the Drum Major, but it was not to reach the Metropolitan Opera for thirty years and the Paris Opera for forty!)

Meanwhile in spite of increasing physical ailments—the asthma was made less bearable by digestive troubles—Berg continued to compose, slowly. When he had finished *Wozzeck* in 1923, he embarked on a *Chamber Concerto*, initially conceived for piano, violin, and ten winds. But when Berg decided to make it a fiftieth-birthday present for his mentor, he added three more winds, thus making the full complement fifteen, the number of instruments Schoenberg called for in his first *Chamber Symphony*, Op. 9, of 1906. In fact Berg's work bristles with numerical and other arcane allusions, reminiscent of mediaeval complexity, and is Berg's first work to toy with dodecaphony. He finished it in 1925, only a few months late, and that same year recomposed an early song, *"Schliesse mir die Augen beide"* ("Close Both My Eyes") in strict twelve-tone style. About the same time he began the *Lyric Suite* for string quartet, which is partly twelve-tonal but demonstrates Berg's refusal to adhere to systems, even Schoenberg's. It was premiered by the Kolisch Quartet early in 1927, and two years later Jascha Horenstein conducted the string-orchestra version of the three middle movements.

Ever since *Wozzeck,* Berg had been looking for material for another opera. After toying with one idea and another, he recalled the impact Wedekind's plays had had on him twenty years before and resolved to use the "Lulu" plays, *Erdgeist (Earth Spirit)* and *Pandoras Büchse (Pandora's Box),* as the basis for his new opera. These works deal with woman as enslaver and victim in a male-dominated world; such problems and their ramifications were not unfamiliar to him since his sister, a lesbian, had found no place in bourgeois society. The first problem was to condense the material into workable form without doing injury to the original—and this task Berg himself took on. In 1929 he interrupted his work to write for a Czech singer, Ružena Herlinger, the concert aria *Der Wein,* to a Baudelaire text translated by Stefan George. Early the next year he was nominated to the Prussian Academy in Berlin but turned down the proposal that he teach a master class there on the ground that such activity would interfere with his work. By now he was doing sufficiently well to buy a car, a small Ford, which he delighted in pushing to sixty-five m.p.h. on the roads. Despite the demands of *Lulu,* he took on, in 1931, editorial work for the journal *23* (a magic number for Berg), founded and published by his student Willi Reich. And a year later he realized a longtime dream, when he purchased a dilapidated summer cabin in Carinthia, which he and his wife made habitable.

The following year the Nazis came to power in Germany, making life there impossible for Schoenberg and many other artists whom Berg knew and admired. Though he was not himself Jewish, his music came under the Nazi ban on "degenerate" art, and he lost his largest market, with serious economic results. He and Helene stayed through an uncomfortable winter at the cabin. Some financial relief was forthcoming when Schoenberg, now in America, negotiated the sale of the *Wozzeck* manuscript to the Library of Congress. In May 1934 Berg finished the short score of *Lulu.* He had been named an honorary director of the Venice Biennial for that summer, and two of his works had been included in the program, but he found that both his name and his music had been dropped, through Nazi-Fascist maneuvering. He protested and was partially reinstated; his trip there was to be his

last one outside Austria. As he had done with *Wozzeck,* Berg arranged a symphonic construct of five pieces from *Lulu.* These Kleiber dared to perform in Berlin in November. They were enthusiastically received by the audience, but the attacks in the press afterward were so brutal that Kleiber resigned within the week and left Germany.

The following January Berg interrupted the scoring of his opera to write a concerto for the American violinist Louis Krasner. Midway through it, Manon Gropius, the beautiful nineteen-year-old daughter of his old friend Alma Mahler, by the architect Walter Gropius, died following an attack of polio. Berg, terribly distressed, decided to dedicate it to her ("to the memory of an angel"), and concluded it with the stunning introduction of a Bach [684] chorale *"Es ist genug."* The work was finished in August. About the same time he incurred what he took to be an insect bite on or near his coccyx. Whatever it was, an abscess developed. After weeks of debilitating pain and fever, blood poisoning set in in mid-December and he was hospitalized. He died early in the morning of Christmas Eve and was buried in the Hietzing Cemetery.

At his death Berg had scored two acts of *Lulu* and part of the third. Just what happened afterward is not entirely clear. Helene Berg maintained that Webern, Schoenberg, and other authorities told her that completion of the final act would be impossible, though there is some thought that she was acting in revenge for the affair she discovered Berg had been carrying on with another woman. At any rate, she steadfastly refused to turn over to anyone the Act III material that remained unpublished, and the opera was premiered as a torso with an artificial ending drawn from the orchestral suite on June 2, 1937, in Zürich, and it continued to be performed in that way until after Helene Berg's death in 1976. Immediately, on the basis of Erwin Stein's complete vocal score and Berg's plentiful fragments, Austrian composer Friedrich Cerha (1926–) finished the scoring, and the complete opera was premiered at Paris in 1979, with Pierre Boulez [2346] conducting.

RECORDINGS: Save perhaps for one or two very minor pieces, all of Berg's work, including the early songs and the finished *Lulu,* is available on records.

[1790] REFICE, (Monsignor) Licinio (Rā-fē'-chā, Lē-chēn'-yō)
PRIEST, CHOIRMASTER, TEACHER
BORN: Patrica, February 12, 1885
DIED: Rio de Janeiro, September 11, 1954

Born in a Roman suburb, Refice had his musical education at the Liceo di Santa Cecilia and studied for the priesthood. After his ordination, his career was furthered by the Vatican, which apparently rather fancied his sentimental style of religious music. In 1910 he began a forty-year career teaching music at the Pontifical School, during thirty-six of which he served as director of the Cappella Liberiana at Santa Maria Maggiore. He also appeared internationally as choirmaster and orchestral conductor (of his own music). For the general public, Refice's tenuous reputation hangs on a single work, the "sacred" opera *Cecilia*, completed in 1923 but not produced until 1934 (in Rome). Various *prime donne*, beginning with Claudia Muzio and including the Renatas Tebaldi and Scotto, have continued to use it as a showcase for their talents. Refice followed *Cecilia* with another opera, *Margherita di Cortona* in 1938 and was working on a third when he was felled by a heart attack while conducting a performance of the first at the Teatro Colón. RECORDINGS: Excerpts from *Cecilia* and a few songs are on records.

[1791]   SALZEDO, Carlos Léon (Sàl-zā'-dō, Kär'-lōs Lä-ôn')
HARPIST, TEACHER, CONDUCTOR
BORN: Arcachon, April 6, 1885
DIED: Waterville, Me., August 17, 1961

The Salzedo family at some point migrated from Spain to the French coast near Bordeaux, where they acquired an *accent aigu* which later disappeared. Carlos Salzedo was the son of Gaston Salzédo, who became professor of voice at the Paris Conservatoire. Carlos studied from the ages of six to nine at the Bordeaux Conservatoire as a piano prodigy, then went to the Paris institution to continue with Charles de Bériot (1802–70) and to take harp from Louis Hasselmans. He graduated at sixteen with first prizes in both areas and toured for four years, before taking a job with an orchestra in Monte Carlo. Toscanini was impressed by him and brought him to New York in 1909 as first harpist of the Metropolitan Opera. Four years later, however, he left to concertize with flutist Georges Barère and cellist Paul Kéfer as part of the Trio de Lutèce. At about this time he began composing, mostly in a modern idiom and almost entirely for the harp, with or without other sound sources. Perhaps the greatest harp virtuoso since Parish-Alvars [1194], he revolutionized harp technique and the instrument itself. In 1921 he joined his immigrant fellow countryman Edgard Varèse [1774] in founding the Inter-

national Composers' Guild, under whose auspices he appeared as a conductor. In 1921 he also founded *The Eolian Review* (later *Eolus*), said to be the first American journal devoted to contemporary music, which he edited until 1933. In 1923 he became an American citizen. He taught at the Juilliard School in New York and founded the harp department of the Curtis Institute in Philadelphia, and in 1931 he inaugurated the Salzedo Harp Colony at Camden, Maine. (The contemporary English composer Leonard Salzedo [1921–   ] is unrelated to him.) RECORDINGS: Carlos Salzedo made a couple of LP recordings for Mercury of some of his shorter pieces and transcriptions and conducted for Columbia his *Concerto for Harp and Seven Winds*, with Lucile Lawrence as soloist. Harpist Heidi Lehwalder recently recorded an album of Salzedo's works for the Nonesuch label.

[1792]   WEINER, Léo (Vī'-ner, Lā'-ō)
TEACHER, MUSIC DIRECTOR
BORN: Budapest, April 16, 1885
DIED: Budapest, September 13, 1960

Weiner was one of the more important Hungarian composers of the Bartók [1734]-Kodály [1760] generation, though he had little in common with those masters other than training by Hans Koessler (1853–1926) at the Royal Academy of Music. Up to his entrance therein in 1901, he was largely self-taught. On graduating in 1905 he was briefly a coach at the Comic Opera, but soon his capture of the Franz Joseph Jubilee Prize enabled him to spend some useful months in the major musical capitals of Europe. On his return in 1908 he obtained successively the professorships of theory, composition, and chamber music at the National Academy. There he became known as a formidable teacher. Among his achievements was the institution of a student orchestra, so well disciplined as not to require a conductor. From his student days on, his meticulous compositions won prize after prize (e.g., the 1922 Coolidge Prize). He retired on a state pension in 1949 and was named "Eminent Artist of the Hungarian People's Republic" four years later. Weiner's music, which is flavored with a dash of paprika but is not folksy in the way of his great contemporaries, is an outgrowth of the central European tradition, which he perfectly understood. Ruthlessly self-critical, he published only about fifty opuses, some of them expansions or arrangements of others (e.g., the 2 violin concerti from the earlier violin sonatas). Weiner's most ambitious effort was the music for the fantasy-play *Csongor es Tünde* by Mihály Vörösmarty, premiered in 1903. His dozen or so orchestral works include a *piano concertino*, 5 *Divertimenti*, a *Serenade*, and a *Hungarian Folkdance Suite*. There are 3 string quartets and other chamber pieces (including a duo for tárogató and cimbalom) and quite a few piano pieces. Weiner made a number of orchestral transcriptions of other composers' music and wrote several musical textbooks. RECORDINGS: There is a representative selection on records (mostly of Hungarian origin)—the piano concertino, the *Divertimenti*, the *Hungarian Folkdance Suite*, the *Serenade*, the second string quartet, *Lakodalmas* for cello and piano, piano pieces, and miscellaneous chamber works.

[1793] RIEGGER, Wallingford
CELLIST, CONDUCTOR, TEACHER, EDITOR
BORN: Albany, Ga., April 29, 1885
DIED: New York, April 2, 1961

A late bloomer but a composer of great skill and seriousness, Riegger proceeded rather swiftly from a sort of flabby post-Romanticism to an uncompromising modernism, ultimately becoming a kind of patriarchal saint in the eyes of the twelve-toners. The child of an affluent lumber dealer, he was born into a household that found literature and music as essential as its daily bread. His mother was a pianist, his father a violinist. While he was still a child, the Rieggers moved to Indianapolis, where the father, Constantin, directed a choir. In 1900 they settled in New York City, where he was sent to the newly opened Institute of Musical Art (later the Juilliard School) to learn cello. There he studied composition with Percy Goetschius (1853–1943), graduating in 1907. In 1908 he went on the still mandatory trek to Germany, where he did further work in composition with Max Bruch [1358] and Edgar Stillman Kelley (1857–1944). He returned two years later to play with the St. Paul Symphony Orchestra in Minnesota and to marry Rose Schramm in 1911. Before leaving Germany, he had done some conducting, and in 1914 he was hired by the municipal theater in Würzburg as assistant to the conductor. He also appeared in Königsberg and in 1916 went back to Berlin to conduct the Blüthner Orchestra, one of the many such independent bodies then operating there. But as the German-American situation grew tenser, he came home the following spring, and for the next four years was on the faculty of Drake University in Des Moines, Iowa.

Whatever Riegger had composed up to then, he kept to himself. He was pretty well convinced that Brahms [1329] represented the ultimate end of musical progress and was horrified by the subsequent radicals. The piano trio that won the Paderewski Prize in 1922 and the setting of Keats's *La Belle dame sans merci* (for four soloists and chamber ensemble) that took the Coolidge Prize two years later would have prepared no one for the mature Riegger. (He was already nearly forty.) But his resettling in New York in 1922 threw him in with some of the farthest-out of the modernists, notably Ruggles [1684] and Varèse [1774], and so badly shook up his thinking that he lapsed into compositional silence for some time. While he was regrouping his musical thinking, he taught at the Institute of Music for a year and at Ithaca College for two. In 1927 the new Riegger emerged in the *Study in Sonority*, an essay for ten violins (or multiples thereof) in unrelieved dissonance. (It is said that his publisher, used to the composer's musical sanity, printed it without studying it, much to his later horror.)

In 1928 Riegger abandoned academia to return once more to New York and work for the cause of contemporary music. He served as an officer of the Pan-American Association of Composers (a Varèse-inspired organization), the American Composers' Alliance, New Music Recordings, and from 1933 the dance division of the WPA's Federal Theater Project. During this period, working for and with such dancers as Martha Graham, Doris Humphrey, and Charles Weidman strongly affected Riegger's style, especially in terms of rhythmic experiments.

But Riegger was interested in composing more than dance accompaniments. In the 1940s he went to work as an editor for the music firm of Harold Flammer. There he not only edited the music of others but also, under various pseudonyms (e.g., the anagrammatic "Gerald Wilfring Gore"), he wrote innumerable choral arrangements and teaching pieces for piano. But in his spare time, he turned to (mostly) abstract and formal chamber and orchestral music, which, over the next twenty years amounted to two thirds of his (signed) published output. Most of it he wrote for his own satisfaction. He wrote 4 symphonies but withdrew the first two. Most of his music is intellectual, contrapuntal, and dissonant. He did in fact use tone rows, but he used them in his own way and began using them before he encountered Schoenberg [1657]. In the course of his later years he numbered among his pupils—who were few and private—Elie Siegmeister [2131], Michael Colgrass [2401], and Morton Feldman [2355]. Shortly before his seventy-sixth birthday, Riegger was walking on a Manhattan street in a spring snowstorm, became entangled in a dog's leash and fell, was kept endlessly waiting in the emergency room of a hospital, and died as a result of his injuries.

RECORDINGS: For a composer who remained in obscurity until his old age, Riegger is well represented on records: the *Piano Trio*, Op. 1; the *Study in Sonority* (string orchestra version), Op. 7; the *Fantasy and Fugue for Organ and Orchestra*, Op. 10; *Dichotomy*, Op. 12; the *New Dance*, Op. 18b; the *Canon and Fugue*, Op. 33, for strings; the *Violin Sonatina*, Op. 39; the *Symphony No. 3*, Op. 42; the *String Quartet No. 2*, Op. 43; the choral *Who Can Revoke*, Op. 44; *Music for Brass Choir*, Op. 45; the *Brass Nonet*, Op. 49; *Music for Orchestra*, Op. 50; the *Woodwind Quintet*, Op. 51; the *Concerto for Piano and Wind Quintet*, Op. 53; the *Variations for Piano and Orchestra*, Op. 54; *Romanza*, Op. 56a, for orchestra; *Dance Rhythms*, Op. 58; the *Symphony No. 4*, Op. 63; *Movement*, Op. 66 (three brasses and piano); the *Variations for Violin and Orchestra*, Op. 71; *Introduction and Fugue for Cello and Winds*, Op. 74; and a few small pieces.

[1794] KLEMPERER, Otto (Klem'-perer, Ot'-tō)
CONDUCTOR, IMPRESARIO
BORN: Breslau (Wrocław), May 14, 1885
DIED: Zürich, July 6, 1973

Relatively few people are aware that Otto Klemperer, one of the great conductors of his day, was also a fairly productive composer. He grew up in Hamburg, where he had piano lessons from his mother. On completing *Gymnasium* in 1901, he went to the Hoch Conservatory in Frankfurt am Main to study with Ivan Knorr (1853–1916) and pianist James Kwast. When two years later Kwast went to the Klindworth-Scharwenka Institute in Berlin, he took Klemperer with him. There Klemperer also studied with Philipp Scharwenka [1437], had composition lessons with Pfitzner [1606], and attracted the attention of Gustav Mahler [1525]. It was Mahler who in 1907 got him his first conducting post at the German Opera in Prague. Over the next twenty-five years, Klemperer worked his way up through various German opera houses— Hamburg, 1910–12; Barmen 1912–14; Strasbourg, 1914–17; Cologne, 1917–24; and Wiesbaden, 1924–27. In 1923, already displaying the famous Klemperer temperament, he refused to become chief conductor of the Berlin State Opera because it did not promise him enough freedom. When, however, that institution opened a satellite at the Kroll Theater, designed to offer new and unusual works, it gave Klemperer *carte blanche* as its general director there. In hindsight, his choice of repertoire is impressive, but normal apathy toward the unknown and growing reaction in Germany to radicalism closed the house by 1931. Klemperer stayed on until 1933. In that year he was awarded the Goethe Medal by the valetudinarian government, in an accident fell off the podium onto his head in Leipzig, and was summarily, as a Jew, discharged by the Berlin State Opera. He moved to Zürich and in 1935 became conductor of the Los Angeles Philharmonic.

After he had for some years suffered blinding headaches—a consequence, Klemperer believed, of his accident—the doctors diagnosed the cause to be a brain tumor. They removed it in 1939 but left him partly paralyzed and unable to go on with his work. He grimly fought back, and forgotten and virtually penniless, returned to Europe, where he was welcomed in a dearth of acceptable conductors. In 1947 he became chief conductor at the Budapest State Opera but gave up when colleagues were denied travel privileges. He lived a precarious existence as guest conductor here and there and made some recordings for Vox Records. Walter Legge decided that he wanted him as permanent conductor for his Philharmonia Orchestra in London, but in 1951 Klemperer slipped on ice in a Canadian airport and was laid up for months with a broken leg. He took his new post in 1955. Now he put his reputation as a prophet of the new behind him and concentrated on the *Mitteleuropäische* classical repertoire. When Legge abandoned the orchestra in 1964, Klemperer stuck with it and remained its conductor until the end of his career. In 1959, while smoking in bed, he set the bedclothes on fire. Trying to douse the flames, he grabbed a bottle of oil of camphor (for his bronchitis) and was terribly burned in the resultant flareup. Again he came back, as he did from a broken hip in 1966. He died at eighty-eight.

RECORDINGS: Klemperer's only opera, *Das Ziel (The Goal)* of 1915, contains a "merry waltz" (in a mental hospital), which he recorded late in his career. But he was not given to blowing his own horn, and I find no trace of records of his *Mass*, his 8 surviving string quartets, his many songs (including 17 for voice and orchestra), or his 6 Mahlerian symphonies (all written after he turned seventy-five!).

[1795] BARRIOS, Pio Agustín (Bär'-yōs,
Pē'-ō A-hōōs-tēn')
GUITARIST, TEACHER
BORN: San Bautista de las Misiones,
May 23, 1885
DIED: San Salvador, August 7, 1944

The Paraguayan Agustín Barrios is not to be
confused with his contemporary, the Spanish guitarist-composer Angel Barrios (1882–
1964). Agustín seems to have been something of an oddball—a sort of proto-hippy—
and so the facts of his life get tangled with
legend. He was, however, emphatically not
the gifted bum he is sometimes made out to
be. He was a trained guitarist who mastered
several languages, read philosophy, and
wrote poetry. At twenty-five he set out on
his travels, becoming widely known and admired throughout South America. Of Indian
ancestry, he is said sometimes to have appeared in Guarany attire as "Barrios
Mangoré," the latter name borrowed from a
legendary Guarany chieftain. He was a pioneer in the modern guitar revival, and was
reportedly the first "classical" guitarist to
make recordings. In 1934 a patron took him
to Europe, where he toured and was compared favorably with Andrés Segovia. In
1939 he was invited to El Salvador to become
professor of guitar at the National Conservatory, and he lived there for the rest of his
days. Legend has it that his funeral virtually
brought business in San Salvador to a halt.
He composed much for the guitar but typically failed to write some pieces down and
lost others or gave them away. (Some pieces
have had to be transcribed from his records.)
RECORDINGS: In recent years, modern-day
guitarists have frequently recorded his music
(e.g., a whole LP by John Williams).

[1796] JOSTEN, Werner Erich (Yōs'-ten,
Vâr'-ner A'-rēkh)
ACCOMPANIST, CONDUCTOR, TEACHER
BORN: Elberfeld, June 12, 1885
DIED: New York, February 6, 1963

The son of a banker, Werner Josten, obedient to paternal wishes, went into banking
himself. But he soon rebelled and went first
to Munich to study music with Rudolf
Siegel, a pupil of Thuille [1537] and Humperdinck [1480], then to Geneva and Jaques-
Dalcroze, finally settling in Paris in 1912. But
the outbreak of the 1914 war drove him back
to Germany. At the end of the hostilities he
became an assistant conductor at the Bavarian State Opera. But the political situation in
Munich was very unstable at the time, and
Josten decided to emigrate to the United

States. He had been writing Lieder for some
time and, shortly after his arrival, an American publisher bought a batch of them and
sent him on the road with various singers, as
accompanist, to publicize them. In 1923
Smith College hired him as professor of
composition; he remained there, a popular
and effective teacher, until his retirement in
1949, becoming an American citizen in 1933.
Perhaps his most impressive accomplishment at Smith was producing the American
premieres of operas by Monteverdi, [333],
Handel [683], and Fux [585]. Basically a Romantic, showing both German and French
influences, Josten was influenced as a composer in the 1920s by African "primitive"
art, which lies behind his 1931 ballet Batoula
and his controversial Jungle for orchestra of
1929. His cause was espoused by both Leopold Stokowski and Serge Koussevitzky
[1655]. RECORDINGS: Stokowski recorded
the 1925 Concerto Sacro I–II (after Mathias
Grünewald's Isenheim Altarpiece, which
also inspired Hindemith [1914]), the premiere of whose first part he had conducted
in 1927. Josten may be heard accompanying
Saramae Endich and William McGrath in
an LP of his songs. Other recordings include
Stokowski's of Jungle and Canzona Seria,
Mischa Elman's of the violin sonatina, Herbert Haefner's of the ballet Endymion, and
William Strickland's of the 1936 Symphony
in F Major.

[1797] BUTTERWORTH, George Sainton
Kaye
CRITIC, ETHNOMUSICOLOGIST, TEACHER
BORN: London, July 12, 1885
DIED: Pozières, August 5, 1916

World War I destroyed no brighter musical
promise than that of George Butterworth.
His father was a lawyer and railway executive and planned for his son to go into law.
It was from his mother, a singer née Julia
Wigan, that he got his love of music. As a
teenager he became quite adept at the keyboards and studied with Thomas Dunhill
[1691] at Eton, where his first compositions
were played by the student orchestra and
where he held the imposing title of "Keeper
of the College Harmonium." He entered Oxford in 1904, but found friends in musicians
like Adrian Boult and was elected president
of the University Musical Club. While at
Oxford he met Cecil Sharp, the folk-song ed-
itor-collector, who got him interested in his
specialty and introduced him to Vaughan
Williams [1633]. On graduating in 1908, he
at first supported himself as a reviewer for
The Times of London and then as a music

teacher at a public school, Radley College. But self-confidence was not Butterworth's long suit, and, feeling it preposterous to attempt to teach others without proper grounding, he enrolled in the Royal College of Music in 1910, where his chief mentor was Charles Wood [1579]. But he gave it up after a few months and went into the field to collect folk music, especially dances. He became something of an expert in the dances themselves and participated in dance festivals both at home and on the Continent. He published his arrangements of some Sussex folk songs he had collected in 1912. Around the same time there appeared his two cycles of Housman songs *(6 Songs from "A Shropshire Lad"* and *Bredon Hill)*—among the most effective settings of that poet ever written. From his version of "Loveliest of Trees," he extracted thematic material for an exquisite orchestral rhapsody, *A Shropshire Lad*. Most of his other extant work— *The Banks of Green Willow* and *Two English Idylls,* both for orchestra; a cycle for voice and strings entitled *Love Blows as the Wind Blows;* and a few smaller pieces—date from this period. Much of his earlier material he destroyed. When England entered the war in 1914, Butterworth at last found a reason for his existence and was one of the first to volunteer. He was killed in action defending a trench in the Battle of the Somme. He was thirty-one. He was awarded a posthumous medal. RECORDINGS: There are several recordings of the song cycles and orchestral pieces.

[1798] HARTMANN, Thomas Alexandrovich de (Härt'-màn, Tō'-mas Áleks-àn-drō'-vich dä)
PIANIST, CONDUCTOR
BORN: Khoruzhevka, Ukraine, September 21, 1885
DIED: Princeton, N.J., March 26, 1956

Thomas de Hartmann numbered among his teachers Anton Arensky [1536], Sergei Taneyev [1492], the pianist Anna Esipova, and Bolesław Jaworski. When he was twenty-two, his ballet *The Blood-Red Flower* was presented by the Imperial Ballet in St. Petersburg with an all-star cast that included Pavlova and Nijinsky. He wrote the first of his 3 completed symphonies in 1915. The 1917 Revolution drove him southward as far as Tbilisi in Georgia. There he met and became a follower of the Armenian-born mystic Georgi Ivanovich Gurdjiev. Gurdjiev, who had founded in Tbilisi the Institute for the Harmonious Development of Man, dedicated to the synthesis of all human

knowledge, included music from various folk sources in his researches and rituals, and it became Hartmann's job to notate the melodies that the master conveyed aurally to him, and to harmonize them. From 1919 to 1921 he made his living teaching in the local conservatory. Events made further flight seem advisable, and after brief stays in Istanbul and Berlin, Hartmann made his way to Paris, whither Gurdjiev and the Institute had preceded him. There he worked, for a time, as a composer of film scores, and gradually became identified with the musical avant-garde. (It was Hartmann who wrote the music for Wassily Kandinsky's expressionist dance drama *Die gelbe Klang [The Yellow Sound],* recently revived in New York City.) In 1928 Hartmann began a systematic collection of Gurdjiev's musical findings, but soon afterward Gurdjiev broke off with all his disciples. Hartmann's most productive period was in the ensuing two decades, in which he produced several concerti, chamber music, songs, and a third ballet, *Babette.* When in 1949 he heard his guru was dying, he visited him and returned to work on his honorific opus, which eventually ran to eight volumes. In 1951 Hartmann moved to New York. He died shortly before a scheduled concert there. RECORDINGS: A song cycle, *Commentaries from Ulysses* (after James Joyce), is sung by Patricia Neway. There are also two discs of Gurdjiev transcriptions played by pianist Herbert Henck and percussionist Trilok Gurtu. The sound track for the movie *Meetings with Remarkable Men* also contains Gurdjiev material as adapted by composer Leonard Rosenman (1924–).

[1799] WELLESZ, Egon Joseph (Vel'-les, Á'-gon Yō'-zef)
MUSICOLOGIST
BORN: Vienna, October 21, 1885
DIED: Oxford, November 9, 1974

Wellesz's scholarly attainments, including important studies in Byzantine music, early polyphony, and Baroque opera, appear to have obscured his not inconsiderable ones in composition. The scion of a wealthy Jewish family, he converted early to Catholicism. He was lured to music by his love for opera and was one of Schoenberg's [1657] early pupils, joining Berg [1789] and Webern [1773] in 1904. His musicological studies were at the University of Vienna with Guido Adler, to whose great series *Denkmäler der Tonkunst in Oesterreich (Monuments of Music in Austria)* he later (1911) contributed an edition of Fux's [585] *Costanza e fortezza (Patience and Fortitude).* He acquired his doctorate in 1909. In 1913 he became professor of music history at the university. Prior to this he had written seventeen opuses, most of them consisting of songs and piano pieces. For the next decade he concentrated chiefly on his research, his teaching, and his promotion (as a founder-officer of the ISCM) of contemporary music. In the 1920s, however, he returned to his first love, the stage, beginning with the opera *Die Prinzessin Girnara (Princess Girnara)*, produced in Hannover in 1921. Within ten years he had seen five more operas staged successfully, as well as four ballets. In 1932 he inaugurated the series of publications *Monumenta Musicae Byzantinae* (sponsored by the Danish Academy) and received an honorary doctorate from Cambridge. In the decade of the 1930s Wellesz wrote mostly vocal music, including two Masses and a number of cantatas.

When Hitler annexed Austria in 1938, Wellesz's origins made him no longer acceptable. He was at the time in Holland to hear Bruno Walter conduct his recently completed *Prosperos Beschwörungen*, Op. 53 *(Prospero's Enchantments)*, and proceeded to England. There he was elected a fellow of Lincoln College, and taught there until he retired. He was given the chair of music history in 1943, held several other prestigious posts, and was on the editorial board of the *Oxford History of Music*, whose first volume he himself wrote. After the war he composed a great deal, completing his last opera, *Incognita*, the last four of his 9 string quartets, and all 9 of his symphonies—the last in 1971. He suffered a stroke a year later and died at eighty-nine in 1974.

Though Wellesz occasionally used a tone row, he was a Viennese rather than a Schoenbergian. His music was more influenced by that of Richard Strauss [1563], Mahler [1525], and Bruckner [1293] but was also reflective of his historical and ethnic interests, and remains unclassifiable.

RECORDINGS: Very little of his work has apparently been recorded. The thoroughly tonal *Octet*, Op. 67, commissioned and recorded by the Vienna Octet, and several minor chamber pieces have been available readily in the United States over the years. There have also been a handful of Austrian recordings, including the 1961 Concerto for Violin, Op. 84, and two movements from String Quartet No. 8, Op. 79.

[1800] POUND, Ezra Loomis
POET, CRITIC, SCHOLAR
BORN: Hailey, Idaho, October 30, 1885
DIED: Venice, November 1, 1972

An intellectually precocious small-town boy from the Smoky Mountains of southern Idaho, Pound enrolled at the University of Pennsylvania at the age of fifteen. His education, however, was wayward, sporadic, and largely self-administered; he studiously avoided requirements that did not appeal to him. He transferred to Hamilton College, left without a degree, taught for two years at Pennsylvania, and then took a job at Wabash College in Indiana, from which he was quickly discharged for failure to conform. In 1908 he left the United States, stayed for a time in Venice, and settled in London, where he became an influential and controversial figure in avant-garde literary circles. He served as music critic for the *New Age* (under the pen name of "Walter Atheling") from 1917 to 1920. In 1924 he moved to Paris and four years later to Rapallo on the Italian Riviera, where he promoted concerts. Over the years his concern with certain evils became obsessive—notably "usury," which he deemed the basic problem of our troubled times, and the Jews as its perpetrator. He remained in Italy during World War II and made a number of anti-American broadcasts on the state radio. He was captured by American troops and imprisoned in a stockade in Pisa as a traitor. Brought back to the United States for trial, he proved such a hot potato that he was declared criminally insane and sent to St. Elizabeth's Hospital, a mental institution in Washington, D.C. There he became the center of a storm, whose fury was increased when he was given the 1949 Bollingen Award for poetry. Finally, in 1958 his friends and admirers got him released on condition that he leave the country. He returned to Venice and lived there with his mistress, the violinist Olga Rudge, until his death at eighty-seven.

Pound was one of the important English-language poets of his time—perhaps more important as an influence than as a creator. Though untaught, he was also a musician of sorts. Apart from his reviews and concerts, he played the bassoon, theorized, and composed. His theories had mostly to do with the relations of poetic rhythms to musical ones (he saw them as all-important and quite complex, and wrote a strange harmony manual based on his notions). As a composer, his reputation, such as it is, rests on his "opera" (or antiopera), *Le Testament de Villon*, completed in 1922. It consists of monophonic settings of Villon poems embedded in a sketchy libretto in "hobo language." George Antheil [1981] provided it with a minimal orchestration based on Pound's indications. The opera was not staged until November 1971 at Berkeley, California. A second such work,

Cavalcanti, had not been performed as of this writing. (Pound also collaborated with pianist Walter Rummel in 1913 on an edition of six troubadour songs, though Pound's part in it is obscure.)

RECORDINGS: Pound's *Le Testament* has been recorded by the Western Opera Theater, a branch of the San Francisco Opera Company. A new 1750 Arch release includes excerpts from *Le Testament* and *Cavalcanti,* and a piece for solo violin.

[1801] TAYLOR, Joseph Deems
LECTURER, CRITIC, ADMINISTRATOR,
STAR OF STAGE, SCREEN, AND RADIO
BORN: New York, December 22, 1885
DIED: New York, July 3, 1966

Deems Taylor committed two unforgivable sins: (1) He was successful as a composer; (2) he was a popularizer as a critic. Nevertheless a generation of American music lovers owes its introduction to the art to his genial, informal, laid-back radio commentaries.

Taylor was not a great composer nor a radical one, but his music too had its effect in its day, and it is interesting to see modern critics finding, to their evident surprise, that it still does. He studied piano from the age of ten and had his secondary education at the Ethical Culture School. At New York University, from which he took a B.A. in 1906, he composed the music for the student shows, one of which, *The Echo* (much reworked and with additional songs by Jerome Kern [1787] and others), had a brief run on Broadway in 1910. On the advice of Victor Herbert [1513], Taylor took up serious musical study, with one Oscar Coon in 1908–11. Meanwhile he was earning a living as a writer. He did editorial work for the Encyclopaedia Britannica, Nelson's Encyclopedia, the *Western Electric News,* and the New York *Sunday Tribune.* In 1912 his Op. 2, a symphonic poem called *The Siren Song* was performed and was followed in 1914 by two cantatas—settings of Holmes's *The Chambered Nautilus* and Alfred Noyes's *The Highwayman.* During much of 1916–17 he was a foreign correspondent for the *Tribune* in France. Then he came home to serve as associate editor for the popular weekly *Collier's* and to compose his Lewis Carroll suite *Through the Looking Glass.* It brought him instant fame and the job of music critic for the New York *World.* He gave that up when the Metropolitan Opera commissioned a work from him. His librettist of choice was Edna St. Vincent Millay, at the peak of her popularity as a poet. The resultant *The King's Henchman* received a gala premiere

on February 17, 1927, with Tullio Serafin conducting and the leads played by Florence Easton, Edward Johnson, and Lawrence Tibbett. It became the first really successful American opera at that house and remained in the repertoire for three seasons. Its success gained Taylor another operatic commission, an honorary doctorate from his university, and the editorship of the magazine *Musical America.* He gave up the last in 1929 to compose *Peter Ibbetson.* It was unveiled in February 1931—the cast included Lucrezia Bori and again Johnson and Tibbett—and it survived for four seasons, or long enough to be heard on a Saturday afternoon broadcast from the Metropolitan.

It was Taylor who, on Christmas Day in 1931, inaugurated those broadcasts and his radio career as commentator. In 1936 he began a seven-year engagement in a similar capacity for the broadcasts of the New York Philharmonic. He also became an officer of ASCAP in 1933 and served as its president from 1942 to 1948. In 1940 he shared the movie screen with Leopold Stokowski, Mickey Mouse, and assorted dinosaurs and hippos in Walt Disney's musical film *Fantasia.* Taylor continued to compose operas *(Ramuntcho, The Dragon)* and orchestral music well into his seventies, but for whatever reason it attracted little notice. He published revised versions of his radio commentaries in three books, the first of which, *Of Men and Music,* was a bestseller. He also wrote a book on Richard Rodgers [2018] and Oscar Hammerstein II. Most of the recordings of his music were made in his heyday. They include *Through the Looking Glass, Portrait of a Lady* (for chamber orchestra), suites from *Peter Ibbetson* and the incidental music for *Casanova,* two scenes from *The King's Henchman* (sung by Lawrence Tibbett), and some songs.

[1802] BECKER, John Joseph
TEACHER, CONDUCTOR, WRITER
BORN: Henderson, Ky., January 22, 1886
DIED: Wilmette, Ill., January 21, 1961

John J. Becker is perhaps the least known of the important American musical mavericks of the early twentieth-century, of whom he became a dedicated promoter. His obscurity is perhaps owing in part to his living in the Middle West rather than in the eastern mainstream and in part to the production problems inherent in his large works. His training was conservative. He graduated from the Cincinnati Conservatory in 1905 and studied variously with the Germans Alexander von Fielitz and Wilhelm Middelschulte and the Dane Carl Busch, all firmly rooted in the Mendelsohn [1200]-Schumann [1211] tradition. He seems to have written nothing worth noting during the decade or so that he taught at North Texas State College. In 1917 he joined the faculty of Notre Dame University, where he directed the Glee Club. His first two symphonies (of 6; Symphony No. 7 was left unfinished) date from around this time. In 1923 he obtained a doctorate from the Wisconsin Conservatory in Milwaukee, and over the next several years he seems to have devoted his creative energies mostly to song writing.

It was Henry Cowell [1934] who in 1928 converted Becker to modernism and inspired him to serious compositional efforts and lifelong experimentation, notably with counterpoint, rhythm, orchestration, and theatrical media. He announced his declaration of independence with his third symphony, *Symphonia brevis,* a year later. That same year he became chairman of the department of fine arts at St. Thomas College in St. Paul, Minnesota. He remained in the Twin Cities for nearly a decade and a half, later teaching at St. Scholastica, conducting choruses and orchestras and, from 1935 to 1941, serving as state director of the Federal Music Project. It was during this period that he wrote most of his "soundpieces" for various instruments or combinations, and his balletic-mimetic-dramatic "stageworks." His last teaching post was at Barat College of the Sacred Heart in Lake Forest, Illinois, where he was on the faculty from 1943 until his retirement at the age of seventy-one. He died on the eve of his seventy-fifth birthday, aware that he was largely forgotten. Among his numerous other compositions there are two operas, an orchestral piece based on Paul Gallico's popular story "The Snow Goose," and a score for a 1949 film of Shakespeare's *Julius Caesar.*

RECORDINGS: Recordings appear to be limited to *The Abongo* (a brief stagework for percussion and dancers), the third symphony, the *Concerto Arabesque* (for piano and orchestra), and his choral-orchestral arrangement of the song *General William Booth Enters Heaven,* by his friend Charles Ives [1659].

[1803] FURTWÄNGLER, Gustav
   Heinrich Ernst Martin Wilhelm
   (Fōōrt'-väng-ler, Gōōs'-táf, Hĭn'-rĭkh
   Árnst Mär-tĭn' Vĭl'-helm)
   CONDUCTOR
   BORN: Berlin, January 25, 1886
   DIED: Baden-Baden, November 30, 1954

Wilhelm Furtwängler's chief fame is of course as a conductor. Execrated by both sides for his supposed political views during the last twenty years of his life, he has since come to be almost venerated in some quarters as one of the supreme interpreters of all time. The son of a professor of archaeology, he had piano lessons as a child and started composing before his family moved to Munich in 1894, where he studied with Rheinberger [1368] and two of Rheinberger's pupils, Anton Beer-Waldbrunn and Max von Schillings [1597]. His dream of being a great composer evaporated when his first symphony was hissed at its Breslau premiere. He began his more practical career in that same city in 1905 as a rehearsal director at the municipal theater and went to Zürich in a similar capacity a year later. There followed two years as assistant to Felix Mottl in Munich and one to Hans Pfitzner [1606] in Strasbourg. In 1911 he was put in charge of orchestral concerts in Lübeck, and later moved on to Mannheim, Vienna, Frankfurt, and Berlin. In 1922 he was named successor to Artur Nikisch (who had died) as chief conductor of both the Leipzig Gewandhaus and the Berlin Philharmonic orchestras. He first conducted in London in 1924 and in New York in 1925, making an enormous impression in both places—though not a favorable one in all quarters (some critics regarded him as too self-indulgent and not respectful of the composer's wishes). A single composition of any consequence, the *Te Deum,* completed in 1910 and revised in 1915, marks the years between 1906 and 1936.

When the Nazis took control in 1933, Furtwängler stayed. He was staunchly German but quite apolitical and viewed the Nazis as one more German government. They were delighted to have so eminent a man cast his lot with theirs, made much of him, and even left the Jewish members of his orchestra alone. But when he suggested certain eminent Jewish performers as soloists for his concerts, he was told no. In 1934 the production of Hindemith's [1914] new opera *Mathis der Maler* was banned at the Berlin State Opera, where Furtwängler was chief conductor. Accounts differ widely on what happened next. He protested in print and either resigned his posts or else was stripped of them. But, contrary to some statements, he did not remain on the shelf until after the war. He was, in fact, back at the helm of the Berlin Philharmonic and conducted it until it disbanded in 1944.

In 1936, following Toscanini's resignation, the New York Philharmonic (on his recommendation) offered the conductorship to Furtwängler. But the latter had made powerful enemies during his guest turns in New York, and when a great public foofaraw was made over his alleged Nazism, the board withdrew the offer. During the years of the Third Reich, Furtwängler returned to composition, producing 2 violin sonatas and the first two of his 3 numbered symphonies, as well as completing a piano concerto begun in 1924. No doubt he needed to take his mind off his troubles. Apart from those troubles already noted, he lost his first wife (the former Zitla Lund) and suffered a severe illness in 1942–43. (He was married in the latter year to Elisabeth Ackermann.) In 1945 he escaped to Switzerland, a step ahead of the Gestapo. On his return to Germany after the war, he was regarded with utmost suspicion by the Americans, who did not let him resume conducting until the spring of 1947. When, two years later, the Chicago Symphony fired Artur Rodzinski, it offered Furtwängler his post, assuming that the smoke had cleared. But another howl against importing Nazis went up, and again the invitation was rescinded. Furtwängler completed his third symphony in 1954 and later that year succumbed to pneumonia.

RECORDINGS: Furtwängler's music is expectably conservative and ponderous in a neo-Brucknerian [1293] way, coming from a man who specialized in the German Romantics. He himself led a recording of his second symphony, and there is one of the second violin sonata. He can be heard as conductor of others' music on innumerable records and as a pianist, accompanying Elisabeth Schwarzkopf in a recital of Hugo Wolf [1521] songs.

[1804] NORDQVIST, Gustaf Lazarus
(Nôrd'-kvist, G̅o̅o̅s'-tåf Lå'-zå-roos)
ORGANIST, TEACHER
BORN: Stockholm, February 12, 1886
DIED: Stockholm, January 28, 1949

Gustaf Nordqvist is not to be confused with his older contemporary Conrad Nordqvist (1840–1920), who coincidentally played the organ and taught harmony at the Stockholm Conservatory. Gustaf studied there from 1901 to 1910. (Conrad left in 1900 and returned in 1910 to teach ensemble playing.) Gustav's chief teachers were the pianist Lennart Lundberg, a Paderewski [1527] pupil, and Ernst Ellberg (1868–1948), teacher of Rosenberg [1866] and Wirén [2075], among others. After further piano study at the Stern Conservatory in Berlin with Arthur Willner, Nordqvist returned to Stockholm to become organist at the Adolf Frederik Church, where he played until his death. He

also taught organ in Stockholm and joined the faculty of the Conservatory in 1924. He specialized, as a composer, in song writing. RECORDINGS: Some of his songs have been recorded.

[1805] LEGINSKA, Ethel (Le-gin'-skà, Eth'-əl)
PIANIST, CONDUCTOR
BORN: Hull, England, April 13, 1886
DIED: Los Angeles, February 26, 1970

Ethel Leginska was clearly a woman ahead of her time. She was born plain Ethel Liggins, the Polish-sounding *nom de combat* having been urged on her by a patroness. Musically precocious, she went to Frankfurt to study at the Hoch Conservatory, but was chiefly known as a Theodor Leschetizky (1830–1915) pupil. She made her concert debut in London and soon became known as a powerful if somewhat erratic performer. In 1907 she married the American composer Emerson Whithorne (1884–1958), *né* Whittern—another Leschetizky pupil, who became her manager for a time. They separated in 1912 and were divorced in 1916. Leginska made her New York debut in 1913 and thereafter spent most of her time in the United States. She studied composition with Rubin Goldmark (1872–1936) and Bloch [1729], and in the 1920s had a good deal of music performed, including the symphonic poem *Beyond the Fields We Know* (after Lord Dunsany) and *Quatre Sujets Barbares* (after paintings by Gauguin). Increasingly she moved into conducting (she premiered the latter work in Munich in 1924), and in the 1930s conducted the Boston Philharmonic (she founded it in 1933), the Chicago Women's Orchestra, and the Boston Women's Orchestra. In 1935 friends raised $5,000 to have her opera *Gale* put on by the foundering Chicago Civic Opera. Four nights before its only performance, conducted by the composer, nothing had been done about staging it, and in the final event the principal, John Charles Thomas, had not bothered to learn his part. Leginska spent her last thirty years teaching piano in Los Angeles. RECORDINGS: The composer made acoustical recordings, and a few of her piano pieces appear on modern records.

[1806] DUPRÉ, Marcel (Dü-prä', Màr-sel')
ORGANIST, TEACHER
BORN: Rouen, May 3, 1886
DIED: Meudon, May 30, 1971

Marcel Dupré, perhaps the most gifted and famous French organist of his generation, came from a family of musicians. His first teacher was his father, Albert Dupré, organist at the church of St. Ouen, and he made his solo debut in Rouen at the age of ten. Two years later he was appointed organist at St. Vivien, and began lessons with Alexandre Guilmant [1351]. In 1901 he heard his oratorio *Le Songe de Jacob (Jacob's Dream)* performed, and in 1902 he entered the Paris Conservatoire. There he continued working with Guilmant and studied as well with Louis Diémer, Vierne [1616], and Widor [1414], and won a string of prizes, including in 1914 the Grand Prix de Rome. He served as Widor's assistant at St. Sulpice from 1906 and was his successor in 1934. In 1916—Dupré was exempted from military service on medical grounds—he took over the ailing Vierne's place at Notre Dame for six years. In 1920 he stunned the musical world by playing, in a series of concerts at the Paris Conservatoire, all of Bach's [684] organ music from memory—a feat that started him on his brilliant international career. In emulation of Guilmant, he had become an even more remarkable *improvisateur,* producing virtually on demand the most complex contrapuntal forms. He often ended his concerts with a symphony on themes (or a sequence of notes) submitted by the audience, and many of his written compositions originated in improvisations. In 1926 Dupré succeeded Gigout [1417] as professor of organ at the Paris Conservatoire. In 1947 he became director of the Fontainebleau Conservatoire, and in 1954 succeeded Claude Delvincourt [1826] as head of the Paris Conservatoire. He resigned two years later and gave up teaching and concertizing about the same time, though he retained his place at St. Sulpice. Dupré was primarily a composer for the organ, both solo and in combination with other bodies of instruments (both large and small), though he wrote some vocal pieces, and a few nonorganic instrumental ones. His pieces are often expectably complex in structure and rather surprisingly dissonant in sound. RECORDINGS: There are a number of recordings of the organ music, including several by Dupré himself, notably his big cycle *Le Chemin de la croix (The Stations of the Cross)* and the *Symphonie-Passion,* Op. 23.

[1807] PIETRI, Giuseppe (Pyā'-trē, Jōo-zep'-pā)
BORN: Sant'Ilario, May 6, 1886
DIED: Milan, August 11, 1946

Giuseppe Pietri may well be the most important composer to come from Elba—which is not saying much. A product of the Milan Conservatory, he produced a string of successful light operas from 1915 into the 1930s. RECORDINGS: An aria from one of them, *Maristella,* has been recorded by several prominent tenors.

[1808] PARAY, Paul Charles (Pà-rā', Pōl Shärlz)
CONDUCTOR
BORN: Le Tréport, May 24, 1886
DIED: Monte Carlo, October 10, 1979

Paul Paray was the son of Auguste Paray, ivory carver and organist of the church of St. Jacques in a fishing village and beach resort near Dieppe on the English Channel. The elder Paray often performed large choral works with forces literally sharked up from the streets; in them his son served as percussionist from the age of five. Paul studied with his father until 1895, when he was sent off to study in Rouen. In 1904 he had his own church there and a year later went to Paris to study at the Paris Conservatoire with, among others, Xavier Leroux [1557]. He capped his student career with the Grand Prix de Rome in 1911. Early in World War I he was captured by the Germans and sat out the duration writing music in a prison camp in Darmstadt. Released at the end of 1918, he found a job conducting a casino orchestra in Cauterets on the Spanish border. His men, mostly Parisian professionals on the take, told him he was wasting his talents there. He returned to Paris and entered his name for consideration as Camille Chevillard's lieutenant at the Concerts Lamoureux. While the slate was being mulled over, he suddenly had to fill in for the indisposed André Caplet [1708] and won the job on the strength of his performance. Three years later, in 1923, he succeeded Chevillard as chief conductor. In 1928 he took over the Monte Carlo Orchestra, and in 1933 he followed Gabriel Pierné [1555] as conductor of the Concerts Colonne. During World War II he returned to Monte Carlo and also aided the *Résistance.* On the liberation of Paris, he returned to the Concerts Colonne.

In 1952 the Detroit Symphony, which had collapsed in a labor dispute a few years earlier, was reorganized and Paray became its conductor. When it moved into the new Ford Auditorium four years later, Paray marked the event with a performance of his 1931 *Mass in Honor of St. Joan of Arc.* He resigned in 1962 (at seventy-six) but kept up a busy conducting schedule in France literally to the day of his death. In 1977 he conducted a concert in Nice celebrating the ninetieth birthday of the painter Marc Chagall, his junior by a year. Among Paray's other (rather conservative) compositions are 2 symphonies, an oratorio, a ballet, and a string quartet.

RECORDINGS: Paray recorded his *Mass in Honor of St. Joan of Arc.*

[1809] ESPLÁ Y TRIAY, Oscar (Es-plá' ē Trē-ā', Os'-cär)
TEACHER, ADMINISTRATOR
BORN: Alicante, August 5, 1886
DIED: Madrid, January 6, 1976

Among recent Spanish composers, Oscar Esplá is probably more important than his rather restricted reputation suggests. His birthplace on the southeastern coast of Spain still exhibits much Moorish influence. As a child he studied there, but his later education bypassed music for a degree in civil engineering and a doctorate in philosophy at the University of Barcelona in 1911. By then, however, his opera *La Bella durmiente (The Sleeping Beauty)* had been performed in Vienna, and in the year of his graduation his orchestral *Suite levantina* won a first prize there in an international competition. He went to Germany, studied briefly there with Reger [1637], and then had a few lessons with Saint-Saëns [1343] in France in 1913. During this period he published books on musicality and aesthetics and a study of Grieg [1410]; his composing between 1912 and 1920 was mostly in smaller forms. At first he eschewed the nationalism which was then the fashion in Spanish music and so was tagged a "German" by his compatriots. Later, however, he developed his own approach to Iberianism, basing some of his compositions on a Moorish-influenced scale of his own devising. His interest in early Spanish music led to his performing edition of the thirteenth-century *El Misterio de Elche (The Elche Mystery)*, which is performed annually at that shrine, which is near Alicante. His most famous composition is probably the orchestral *Don Quijote velando las armas (Don Quixote Guarding His Arms)*, commissioned by Manuel de Falla in 1924. Esplá was given a professorship at the Madrid Conservatory in 1930. After the collapse of the monarchy, he served the republican government as head of the National Music Council and in 1936 was appointed director of the conservatory. But the Fascist victory caused him to go into self-exile in Belgium; he did not return until 1951. In 1958 he opened his own conservatory in Alicante.

He was elected by the Académie française to succeed the Swiss Honegger [1861] in 1955. Esplá composed in almost all standard categories. RECORDINGS: Recordings include *Don Quijote* (Rafael Frübeck de Burgos), the *Canciónes playeras españolas* for soprano and orchestra (Victoria de Los Angeles), the *Sonata española* (Alicia de Larrocha), *Sinfonia gitana, Sonata del sur* for piano and orchestra, the realization of the Elche play, and a number of small pieces.

[1810] YON, Pietro Alessandro (Yon, Pyā'-trō Á-les-sán'-drō)
ORGANIST
BORN: Settimo Vittone, August 8, 1886
DIED: Huntington, N.Y., November 22, 1943

Born on the River Dorea Baltea in the Italian Piedmont, Pietro Yon studied piano with Luca Fumagalli in Milan, then at the Turin Conservatory, before enrolling in the Liceo di Santa Cecilia in Rome, where he continued his keyboard training with Sgambati [1385] and with the organist Remigio Renzi. He completed his studies a year later but remained in Rome for two years, during which time he served as a substitute organist at St. Peter's. In 1907 he emigrated to New York, where for the better part of twenty years he was organist of the Church of St. Francis Xavier, taking time out to return to Rome in the early 1920s to be named honorary organist of St. Peter's. He acquired American citizenship in 1921 and in 1926 became organist of St. Patrick's Cathedral. He wrote a good deal of organ and church music. RECORDINGS: Yon is remembered for a little Christmas piece *Gesù Bambino*, written in 1917, performed and recorded in all sorts of versions.

[1811] CLARKE, Rebecca
VIOLIST
BORN: Harrow, August 27, 1886
DIED: New York City, October 18, 1979

Born into a family where music making was part of daily life, Rebecca Clarke studied the violin in childhood. After she enrolled at the Royal College of Music, she switched to viola, on which she became a notable player. Her composition teacher was Stanford [1467]. After her graduation she appeared with several chamber music ensembles. She played quartets with Jelly d'Aranyi, her sister Adila Fachiri, and Guilhermina Suggia, Casals' [1690] common-law wife. Later she was a founder-member of a piano quartet, the English Ensemble, and violist of the Pro Musica String Quartet. In 1916 she undertook a concert tour of the United States and remained there for some years. Most of her compositions date from this period. She limited herself to chamber works and some exquisite songs, mostly in a rather adventurous harmonic idiom. In 1919 her viola sonata tied Ernest Bloch's [1729] viola suite for first prize in the Elizabeth Sprague Coolidge competition; in the event, Bloch was given the first prize and Clarke the second. Her piano trio, however, was declared a clear winner in 1921. She made a world tour in 1923, then returned to England. In 1944 she married an old classmate, the pianist James Friskin, and made her home with him in New York. RECORDINGS: There are recordings of the trio, the sonata, and a few songs.

[1812] COATES, Eric
VIOLIST, CONDUCTOR
BORN: Hucknall, August 27, 1886
DIED: Chichester, December 23, 1957

Eric Coates, one of the most successful writers of "light-classical" music in his day, seems to have been unrelated to the various musical contemporaries—Albert, Edith, Henry, and John—who bore his surname. He was born and grew up in and around Nottingham, where he learned to play the viola. In 1906 he enrolled at the Royal College, where he continued his viola studies with the great Lionel Tertis and had training in composition from Frederick Corder (1852–1932). After playing in theater orchestras and chamber-music groups, he joined the Queen's Hall Orchestra in 1910. He was promoted to the first desk of the violas in 1912. His chief, Sir Henry Wood, introduced many of his works at the Proms, and by the end of the decade Coates had become so popular that he left to devote the rest of his life composing and appearing as guest conductor of his own music. In the latter capacity he toured the Americas after World War II. His best-known works are the *London Suite* (whose movement "Knightsbridge March" became the BBC signature piece) and *By the Sleepy Lagoon,* and the ballad *Bird Songs at Eventide.* Coates seems to have known a good title when he encountered one —witness *London Again Suite, The Three Bears, The Three Elizabeths, Four Ways, Four Centuries,* etc. RECORDINGS: Coates is well represented on records and expectably recorded many of his own works.

[1813] SCHOECK, Othmar (Shök, Ōt'-mär)
CONDUCTOR, PIANIST
BORN: Brunnen, September 1, 1886
DIED: Zürich, March 8, 1957

Though he is rightly regarded as one of the outstanding Swiss composers of this century, Schoeck has yet to become well known outside the German-speaking world. Born in a village in Schwyz, near Lake Lucerne, he was the son of a prominent painter, Alfred Schoeck, who tried to steer him in his own direction. But the boy seems to have spent more time fooling with music than in the studio, and in 1905 his father gave in and sent him to the Zürich Conservatory, where he studied with several stalwart products of Leipzig and Munich training. The experience, however, seems to have done him no irreparable harm; nor did some months of work with Max Reger [1637] in 1907–8. By that time he had more than a dozen opuses of *Lieder* in print. He then settled in Zürich, where he conducted several *Männerchöre* and married the singer Hilde Bartscher. In 1917 he became conductor of the orchestra in St. Gall. He also appeared in concert as accompanist to his wife and other singers, and the violinist Stefi Geyer, sometime *inamorata* of Belá Bartók [1734]. He was awarded all sorts of honors in his native country as well as the Order of Merit from West Germany. Heart disease necessitated his retirement from conducting in 1944.

Initially a practitioner of middle-European late-Romanticism, as one might expect from his background, Schoeck later developed, on the basis of that impulse, a style all his own and of considerable depth, if not especially "modern." His largest works are his 8 mature operas.

RECORDINGS: Two of his operas have been recorded—*Penthesilea,* his masterpiece of 1925; and *Vom Fischer un syne Fru (Of a Fisherman and His Wife),* 1930. But Schoeck's forte was the *Lied*—whether with piano, orchestral, or chamber-music accompaniment—and his efforts therein have been generously represented on records—notably by Dietrich Fischer-Dieskau, Ernst Haefliger, Thomas Pfeiffer, and Arthur Loosli. There are also recordings of the Concerto for Violin, the Concerto for Horn, the 2 string quartets, and the *Sommernacht* (for strings).

[1814] GURIDI BIDAOLA, Jesús (Goo-rē'-dē Bē-dá-ō'-lā, Hā-zoōs')
ORGANIST, CHOIRMASTER, TEACHER

BORN: Vitoria, September 25, 1886
DIED: Madrid, April 7, 1961

Guridi was the foremost Basque composer of the twentieth-century Spanish musical reawakening. His relatives for several generations back were musicians, and he was already composing at the age of ten. He had his early musical training in nearby Bilbao; then at eighteen he went to Paris, where he studied composition with d'Indy [1462] at the Schola Cantorum. Two years later he went to Joseph Jongen [1649] in Liège. After a few months of further study in Germany, he returned to Bilbao in 1909, where he held forth as a church organist for thirty years and conducted the local choral society for fifteen of them. He also taught at the local music school, was active in furthering the musical life of the town, and collected Basque folk music. Beginning in 1915 he wrote a number of stage works—mostly *zarzuelas*—the majority of which were produced in Madrid. He moved to that city in 1939 and became a professor in its conservatory five years later. He was awarded many official honors. Besides the stage works, his compositions include a symphony, symphonic poems, a *Homenaje a Walt Disney* for piano and orchestra, Masses and other choral works, string quartets, and many songs and folksong arrangements. RECORDINGS: Ataulfo Argenta recorded his orchestral arrangement of *10 Melodias vascas (10 Basque Tunes)*, and there are also recordings of songs and zarzuela selections.

[1815] MADETOJA, Leevi Antti (Mä'-de-tō-yà, Lä'-vē Änt'-tē)
CONDUCTOR, TEACHER, CRITIC
BORN: Oulu, February 17, 1887
DIED: Helsinki, October 6, 1947

Leevi Madetoja was born in the seaport on the Gulf of Bothnia once known as Uleåborg, where he had his early education. In 1906 he went to Helsinki and took a liberal arts degree at the Helsinki University while studying with Sibelius [1575] and Järnefelt [1608]. In 1910–11 he was a pupil of Vincent d'Indy [1462] in Paris, then stopped by Vienna for some work with Robert Fuchs. When he came home in 1912, he conducted the Helsinki Philharmonic Orchestra for two years and the symphony orchestra in Viipuri for two more. He then settled in Helsinki as teacher at the conservatory and critic for the newspaper *Helsingen Sanomat*. He married the poetess L. Onerva who wrote the lyrics for many of his songs. In 1924 his first opera, *Pohjalaisia (The East*

Bothnians), was produced in the capital. It has since become a cornerstone of the Finnish repertoire and has also been performed elsewhere in Europe. Two years later the composer joined the faculty of the university, where he was named professor of music in 1937. A second opera, *Juha*—a story also treated by Aare Merikanto [1882]—appeared in 1934. Madetoja also wrote a ballet, much incidental theater music, a film score, 3 symphonies, and many smaller works. RECORDINGS: The Finnish National Opera has recorded *Pohjalaisia*, and there is a recording of the *Overture to a Comedy* and Symphony No. 3—all conducted by Jorma Panula.

[1816] LINDBERG, Oskar Fredrik (Lind'-bârg, Os'-kár Frā'-drik)
ORGANIST, TEACHER, CONDUCTOR
BORN: Gagnef, February 23, 1887
DIED: Stockholm, April 10, 1955

Lindberg was a Dalesman from the west midlands of Sweden, where many of his relatives were fiddlers. He was the village organist from the age of fourteen. Later he went to Stockholm, studied church music and musical education at the Stockholm Conservatory, and graduated in 1908. For eight years he was organist at the Church of the Trinity there; then in 1914 he took over the analogous post at St. Engelbert's, which he held for forty more years. He taught at the conservatory from 1919 and conducted the orchestra there. He was almost singlehandedly responsible for the 1939 revision of the Swedish hymnbook. Lindberg, a Romantic, wrote a single opera *Fredlös* in 1934, a symphony, symphonic poems, a *Requiem*, and many songs. RECORDINGS: Some few of his songs have been recorded. Orchestral works on record include the *3 Travel Memories* (Stig Rybrant) and *Leksand's Suite* (Nils Grevilius). Organist Hans Fagius has recorded a couple of organ works.

[1817] VILLA-LOBOS, Heitor (Vēl'-là Lō'-bōs, Ā'-tôr)
CELLIST, GUITARIST, CONDUCTOR, TEACHER
BORN: Rio de Janeiro, March 5, 1887
DIED: Rio de Janeiro, December 17, 1959

On the international scene, Villa-Lobos is probably the most famous of Latin-American composers. Largely self-taught, inspired by the popular music of his country (in its manifold manifestations), and a composer who wrote from the gut rather than from the intellect, he burst like a bombshell on a postwar Europe fascinated by primitivism. Later a number of his works became popular favorites, which, together with his creative fecundity and the unclassifiability of his music, helped devalue his stock among the tastemakers. But in Brazil he holds a place of supreme honor, not the least for his innovative and sweeping contributions to musical education, and he will undoubtedly be favorably re-evaluated in the larger world.

Villa-Lobos came to music through both heredity and environment. His maternal grandfather had composed, and his father Raul, a writer and an official of the National Library, was conservatory-trained and famous in Rio for his musical salons. When Heitor, at an early age, began to pick out tunes on the piano, Raul set about to teach him his own instrument, the cello. Some accounts say that the child first used a viola held cello-fashion; others insist that it was a *violão,* a small gut-strung guitar. (Villa-Lobos later became a master of the guitar.) Raul also taught him the clarinet. When Heitor was twelve, his father died. His mother, envisioning a medical career for her son, forbade him the further pursuit of music. He rebelled and took to the streets, inaugurating a long period of bohemian drifting. He survived by playing in *chôros* (itinerant instrumental bands) and working as cellist in theaters and cafés. He also, when things got tight, sold books from his father's fine library. Fascination with Brazil's native music enlarged his sphere of activity. He toured for a while with a roving opera company, worked in a match factory, and, when he could, took field trips that carried him to the Carribean and into the jungles of the Amazon, where he maintained he once played his way out of being a meal for some hungry Indians. (Hyperbole, particularly with regard to himself, was characteristic of Villa-Lobos. A man of enormous energy and appetites, addicted to black cigars and blacker coffee, he had no doubt of his genius and never hesitated to say so.)

Around 1912 he returned to Rio and began to do some serious, if rather academic, composing. A concert of some of the products in 1915 was sufficiently successful to persuade him that he should quit fooling around. He married and undertook studies at the National Institute of Music (cello with Benno Niederberger, composition with Francisco Braga [1868–1945], a Massenet [1396] pupil), while holding down a job in a cinema. But he found the formality stultifying and abandoned his classes to read and to study scores. In 1918 he met and caught the fancy of Darius Milhaud [1868], recently come to Brazil in the entourage of Ambassador Paul Claudel. One morning he invaded the hotel bedroom of Arthur Rubinstein with a group of musicians to demonstrate his talents. Rubinstein forthwith incorporated some of his piano pieces into his programs—though the Brazilians vociferously hissed the sample he offered in Rio. By 1922 he had made sufficient impression locally, however, to receive a commission for a work (about World War I) to welcome the visiting Albert and Elisabeth of Belgium. The result was the third symphony ("War"), which was shortly followed by the fourth ("Victory") and the fifth ("Peace"). The following year, a government grant in hand and the way smoothed by his European admirers, Villa-Lobos sailed for France and seven years residence in Paris (from which he traveled all over Europe and even to Africa). A concert of his music at the Salle Gaveau a year after his arrival was a tremendous success. The composer sent cards to every musician of consequence in the city, saying that he was "at home" on the second Sunday of each month; in a moment of economic misgiving, added a note to each that guests must bring their own refreshments. He profited by exposure to the currents of music then flowing on the Continent but remained very much his own man. In Paris he completed the series of *Chôros,* a quasi-popular form of his own invention for various instruments and combinations (from solo guitar to large orchestra with chorus), and began the *Bachianas Brasileiras,* which purport to do for Brazilian song-and-dance forms what Bach [684] did for the European ones of his day.

By 1930, when he went home for what would be a long period of stability, he was not only famous internationally but a hero in Brazil. Determined to shape, singlehandedly if need be, a true Brazilian musical culture, he plunged into education. His activities in that realm recommended him to President Getulio Vargas, a man sympathetic to the arts, who in 1932 made him national director and supervisor of musical education. Villa-Lobos was particularly effective with children—the more, the better. He taught them what he called "orpheonic effects"—self-produced percussive sound, such as hissing, foot stamping, and hand clapping, and developed a manual sign language (such cheironomy was known to several ancient cultures) to signal notes to massed singers. Each Independence Day he directed choral sings that involved thousands of participants on every occasion. Between 1930 and 1944 he rarely left Brazil, save to visit neighboring countries on educational missions and to attend a music-education convention in Prague in 1936. For all the demands on his time, his productivity continued unabated. (However, many works went unfinished, and in the opinion of many he finished some that he should have junked.)

In 1944 Villa-Lobos made the first of several visits to the United States, where he frequently guest-conducted programs of his own music. After World War II he pursued his conducting career on a worldwide scale and made a number of authoritative recordings in France and Germany, including all of the *Bachianas*. In 1945, with the blessings of the Brazilian government, he initiated an honorary Academy of Music, whose first fifty members he himself hand-picked. He lived to see his concept of the ideal conservatory duplicated in many Brazilian centers and was the recipient of many honors, including membership in the Académie Française and an honorary doctorate from New York University. On his death at the age of seventy-two, he was given a state funeral, and two years later a Villa-Lobos Museum was opened in Rio under the direction of his widow (his second wife) Arminda. In 1971 the Sante Fe Opera presented the posthumous premiere of his third opera, *Yerma*, after Lorca.

Villa-Lobos' output was enormous, and the full extent of it appears still to be uncertain. It includes at least 3 completed operas, ballets, film scores, the 9 *Bachianas*, 13 *Chôros*, 12 symphonies, 5 piano concerti, many other concerti and concerted works, 17 string quartets, and much other chamber music, choral works, songs, and piano pieces.

RECORDINGS: Besides the *Bachianas* recordings (several frequently duplicated by other musicians), there are versions of the second cello concerto, the concerti for harp, harmonica, and guitar, suites from the films *Descobrimento do Brasil (Discovery of Brazil)* and *Green Mansions* (the extensive recorded suite of the latter is entitled *Forest of the Amazon)*, the ballet *Uirapurú*, many of the *Chôros*, the tone poems *Erosão (Erosion, also known as The Origin of the Amazon River)* and *Alvorada na Floresta Tropicale (Dawn in the Tropical Forest)*, at least two symphonies, several piano concerti, *Mômoprecóce* for piano and orchestra, a suite from the opera *Magdalena* (recorded by André Kostelanetz for Columbia but unaccountably never listed in *Schwann* while in print), *Dansas Africanas, Invocation pour la Defense de la Patrie (Invocation for the Defense of the Fatherland), Próle do Bébé (The Baby's Family)* and *Rudepoema (Savage Poem)* for piano, several string quartets, the quartet for wom-

en's voices and instruments, the nonet for men's voices and instruments, the *Fantasia concertante* for cello ensemble, and a fairly good representation of songs, guitar pieces, many miscellaneous chamber pieces, and other piano works. (In addition the Villa-Lobos Museum has issued, semiprivately in Brazil, about a dozen discs, including many works not otherwise available (e.g., the first cello concerto and *The Emperor Jones Suite* for orchestra).

[1818] BRETAN, Nicolae (Brä'-ton, Nē'-kō-lī)
SINGER, OPERATIC EXECUTIVE
BORN: Năsăud, April 6, 1887
DIED: Cluj, December 1, 1968

Bretan first studied at the Cluj Conservatory in Transylvania, won a scholarship to the Vienna Academy in 1908, and wound up graduating from the Budapest Conservatory in 1912, when he embarked on a long career as a singer. The onset of war in 1914 prevented his accepting an offer from the Vienna Volksoper, so instead he settled down as leading baritone of the opera company at Cluj—the second most important troupe in Rumania. Gradually he worked his way into management, retiring in 1944 as general manager. He was also known for his several operas, beginning with *The Evening Star* in 1921. Thanks at least in part to the tireless efforts of his daughter, Bretan has become internationally known since his death for his nearly 250 songs to texts in German, Hungarian, and Rumanian. These, though preponderently introspective and inclined to the melancholic, are of great sensitivity. RECORDINGS: At least three LPs of the songs have appeared, one containing a home recording by the composer of his own rendition of one of his songs.

[1819] TIESSEN, Heinz (Tē'-sen, Hīntz)
CONDUCTOR, TEACHER, WRITER
BORN: Königsberg (Kaliningrad), April 10, 1887
DIED: Berlin, November 29, 1971

Tiessen went to the University of Berlin in 1905 to study law but transferred to the Stern Conservatory, where he studied with the pianist-composer Philipp Rüfer and with Wilhelm Klatte, a pupil of Richard Strauss **[1563]**. Between 1911 and 1917 he reviewed for the *Allgemeine Musikzeitung*. A great admirer of Strauss, Tiessen became his assistant at the Court Opera in 1917 for a brief time. In 1918 he was appointed chief conductor at the Volksbühne Theater, for whose productions he wrote music. From 1920 to 1922 he was choral conductor at the university and then took over a proletarian chorus for which he wrote work songs. From 1925 he taught at the Hochschule, gaining his professorship five years later. When the Nazis came in, they disbanded his chorus, labeled him unacceptable as a composer (although a conservative himself, he was a tireless defender of "degenerate" modernism), but let him keep his teaching post. In 1946 he became director of the Berlin Conservatory but returned to the Hochschule in 1949. Six years later he was put in charge of the musical program at the West Berlin Academy of Fine Arts. Tiessen disowned a good deal of his early music, and much of the rest went up in the flames of the Third Reich. He anticipated Messiaen [2129] by using birdsongs (a subject on which he published a book) in some of his music. Besides orchestral, chamber, instrumental, and choral works, he left several volumes of *Lieder*. RECORDINGS: A few of the *Lieder* have been recorded.

[1820] REESEN, Emil (Rā'-zen, Ā'-mil)
PIANIST, CONDUCTOR
BORN: Copenhagen, May 30, 1887
DIED: 1964

Reesen was the son of Julius Reesen, a Danish army bandmaster. He studied piano with Siegfried Langgaard, pupil of Liszt [1218] and father of the composer Rued Langgaard [1883] and began a concert career as a pianist in 1911. Later he took up conducting and worked as a conductor at the Tivoli Gardens, in various Copenhagen theaters, and for the Danish Radio. His compositions include an opera *The Story of a Mother*, ballets, much incidental music for the theater, orchestral and choral works, and songs. He conducted a recording of his own lovely folk rhapsody *Himmerland*—a work that inexplicably has not become a pop classic.

[1821] ROMBERG, Sigmund
ENGINEER, PIANIST, CONDUCTOR
BORN: Nagy Kaniza, July 29, 1887
DIED: New York, November 9, 1951

The youngest of the Holy Trinity of American operetta, like his elders Herbert [1513] and Friml [1726], was weaned on the Central European tradition of light opera. Unrelated to the several musical Rombergs (see 1051) of the nineteenth century, Sigmund was born in a small town in southwestern

Hungary. He had violin lessons in childhood, but later, after studying in Bucharest and Vienna, he graduated as a civil engineer. While in the latter city, he studied music with Heuberger [1451], and when he became assistant manager of the Theater an der Wien, the chief Viennese operetta house, he burned his bridges. In 1909 he came to New York by way of London, played piano in salon and theater orchestras, and soon became conductor at Bustanoby's Restaurant. His first published compositions caught the attention of the Shubert brothers, who hired him as their house composer. His first show, which opened at the Winter Garden in January 1914, was a revue called *The Whirl of the World;* it lasted five months and left no particular impression. He went on for some time grinding out two and three shows a year, often with collaborators; his name, during this period, was chiefly remembered in connection with several of the annual editions of *The Passing Show*—1914, 1916–19, 1923–24.

Romberg's first unqualified success was the 1917 *Maytime*. (The Jeanette MacDonald–Nelson Eddy film two decades later had little to do with it, aside from preserving some of the music.) The autumn of 1921 brought another hit in *Blossom Time*. It was based on Heinrich Berté's ostensible dramatization of episodes in the life of Franz Schubert [1153], with tunes to match; though Romberg's score, like the book, was Schubert-based, it was an entirely new one. In 1924 Romberg produced his most durable operetta, *The Student Prince*. The Shuberts thought it pretentiously highbrow (!) and Romberg had to sue to get them to stage it. It ran for 608 performances on Broadway and twenty-five years on the road, requiring nine touring companies at the height of its popularity. *The Desert Song* of 1926, also prime Romberg, was not that much of a hit, but it managed 471 performances. *My Maryland*, a 1927 romanticization of the Barbara Frietchie legend, was better received in tryouts (forty weeks) than in New York. The 1928 *Rosalie*, which teamed Romberg with Ira and George Gershwin [1955], P. G. Wodehouse, and Ziegfeld, managed ten weeks; and *New Moon* (in the fall of the same year, completely rewritten after the tryouts) ran more than 500 performances and brought to a close Romberg's heyday and that of the American operetta. He kept trying with little success and finally went to Hollywood. In 1945 he enjoyed an autumnal flareup with *Up in Central Park*—largely redeemed by its skating ballet. Three years after the composer had died, his final score, to *The Girl in Pink Tights*, was heard for ten weeks, surviving that long chiefly because of the presence of the ballerina Zizi Jeanmaire in the title role.

RECORDINGS: Record catalogs are (or were) full of Romberg songs and a few abridged versions of the big hit works. Romberg himself conducted for RCA some samples of his work.

[1822] VALEN, Olav Fartein (Vä′-len, Ō′-låv Fär′-tän)
LIBRARIAN, TEACHER
BORN: Stavanger, August 25, 1887
DIED: Haugesund, December 14, 1952

In the years when atonality and serialism were accepted as the ultimate answers to whatever the question was, Fartein Valen's name was heard more than it is now. In the brief history of Norwegian art music, he represented an abrupt break with the folksy nationalism of the past and an influence on a generation of younger composers. But for most of his life he remained a curiously isolated and lonely figure.

Valen was born on the great fjord in southwest Norway, the son of missionaries, with whom he spent his first six years from infancy in Madagascar. However, he spent the remainder of his youth back in Stavanger, where he took piano lessons. At nineteen he enrolled at Christiania (Oslo) University to study philology but became completely involved with music, taking lessons from the folklorist-composer Catherinus Elling (1858–1942). In 1909 he moved on to the Berlin Hochschule, where Max Bruch [1358] was one of his teachers. But Valen seems to have been blessed or cursed with extremely acute musical hearing, and he found the diatonic system, as preached and practiced, complete nonsense. After two years, he quit but remained in Berlin for five years, reading theory and trying to arrive at a method of composition satisfactory to him. He then returned to Norway and lived at Valevåg in virtual seclusion, studying the music of the Renaissance and Baroque contrapuntalists, which seemed to offer a partial solution to his problem.

Eventually he arrived at a sort of atonal-chromatic-contrapuntal music that used the twelve tones. He did so quite independently of Schoenberg [1657], though in the mid-1920s he not only became familiar with the Schoenbergian system but tried it on for size and adopted certain of its features from time to time. In 1924 he settled in Oslo. He was now thirty-seven and had written exactly five works that pleased him—a *Legende* and a sonata for piano, a violin sonata, a piano

trio, and an *Ave Maria* for voice and orchestra. He attracted some pupils and in 1927 was put in charge of the national music collection at the university. By 1930 he was composing (for him) rather freely and occasionally getting hearings. His recognition was sufficient to win him a government annuity in 1935. But on the whole musicians and public regarded him as an oddity, and three years later he returned to the farm for good. His entire output runs to only forty-four opus numbers, the bulk of it produced in the 1930s. The largest works are 4 symphonies (a fifth was left unfinished), a violin concerto, a piano concerto, and 2 string quartets.

RECORDINGS: All of the finished orchestral and vocal-orchestral works except for the symphonies have been recorded once or twice by the likes of Øivin Fjeldstad, Miltiades Caridis, and Karsten Andersen. Pianist Robert Riefling has offered a two-record set of the complete solo piano music and a performance of the Concerto for Piano under the baton of Fjeldstad. Violinist Arve Tellefsen and conductor Andersen have done the Berg [1789]-like Concerto for Violin. Other recordings include the Piano Trio, the fragmentary *Serenade* for wind quintet, both string quartets, the Sonata for Violin and Piano, and the *Pastorale* for organ.

[1823] SHAPORIN, Yuri Alexandrovich (Shå′-pō-rēn, Yōō′-rē Ål-yek-sån-drō′-vich)
LAWYER, CONDUCTOR, IMPRESARIO, TEACHER
BORN: Glukhov, November 8, 1887
DIED: Moscow, December 9, 1966

An important figure in Russia in the early days of Soviet music, Shaporin is now little more than a name in the West. Born about two hundred miles northeast of Kiev into an artistic family, Shaporin learned cello and piano, but when time came for deciding on a career, he set out toward a liberal arts degree at Kiev University, where he had some training in theory. After two years he transferred to the University of St. Petersburg, where he graduated with a law degree in 1912. Then, at twenty-five, he embarked on a musical curriculum at the St. Petersburg Conservatory, where he studied with, among others, Nikolai Tcherepnin [1642] and Nikolai Alexandrovich Sokolov (1859–1922), who had studied with Rimsky-Korsakov [1416] and later taught Shostakovich [2094]. Caught up in the heady currents of the day, Shaporin became part of a circle of radical young artists. After the October Revolution, he helped found the Grand Drama Theater, where he was associated with Alexander Blok, Maxim Gorky, Vladimir Mayakovsky, and other important playwrights of the day. In his fifteen years with this theater and with the Academic Theater, Shaporin turned out innumerable scores for plays, both classical and modern. He also wrote a choral symphony, 2 piano sonatas, songs, and other works, and worked sporadically on an opera about the Decembrist revolt of 1825, which Shaporin had begun in 1920. The symphony was performed in London in 1935 and was found dull and platitudinous.

At about the same time Shaporin gave up the theater and moved to Klin, near Moscow, ostensibly to complete his opera, but he produced little. He moved to the capital in 1939 and entered a new phase, one of grinding out film scores and oratorios proclaiming Soviet greatness. During World War II he was among the national treasures evacuated to the hinterlands. During this time and briefly after the war, he was a member of the (largely ineffectual) steering committee of the Composers' Union, which fell victim to the infamous 1948 attack on the arts by Zhdanov. For the rest of his life, Shaporin taught composition at the Moscow Conservatory. His opera, *The Decembrists*, was eventually staged in 1953, amid vast hoopla. If it proved static dramatically, the music has been praised as (variously) worthy of Borodin [**1331**], Tchaikovsky [**1377**], and Mussorgsky [**1369**].

RECORDINGS: There is a Soviet recording of *The Decembrists* but little else.

[1824] TOCH, Ernst (Tōkh, Ârnst)
PIANIST, TEACHER
BORN: Vienna, December 7, 1887
DIED: Santa Monica, Calif., October 1, 1964

The son of a Viennese wholesaler of leathers, Ernst Toch taught himself to play the piano and to compose, mostly by copying out scores of masterpieces. By the time he entered the University of Vienna in 1906 as a medical student, he had written a piano concerto and at least six string quartets. In 1909 he won the Mozart Prize, awarded by the city of Frankfurt am Main, and went to the conservatory there to study composition with Iwan Knorr [**1918**] and piano with Willy Rehberg, whose son Walter he himself would teach years later in Berlin. In 1910 Toch won the Mendelssohn Prize. In 1913 he began teaching at the Mannheim Hochschule but was called up for service in the Austrian forces when war broke out a year

later; he soldiered until 1918, with time out to get married in 1916. He returned to his teaching post in 1919 and in 1921 completed a dissertation on melody, later published as *Melodielehre (Melodic Patterns)* for the University of Heidelberg.

Toch remained in the Rhineland for some years and was increasingly admired as a composer. In 1929 he moved to Berlin, where he taught privately and appeared as a pianist. He made a concert tour of the United States in 1932. The rise to power of the Nazis a year later forced him, as a Jew, to leave Germany. He settled in London, where he wrote scores for the films *Catherine the Great* and *The Private Life of Don Juan*. In 1934 he came again to the United States, and after a couple of seasons of teaching at the New School in New York, he gravitated to Hollywood and the film studios. He taught at UCLA and for a decade scored such disparate films as the anti-Nazi *Address Unknown,* the horror fantasy *Dr. Cyclops,* and various Bob Hope comedies. He became an American citizen in 1940. (During the 1940s one of his students was a much younger fellow emigré from Berlin, André Previn.) Toch served as visiting professor at several American Universities, notably Harvard. After the war he returned to Europe for a time but remained California-based. Toch's last twenty years were especially productive, accounting for, among other things, all of his 7 symphonies, of which the third won a Pulitzer Prize in 1956. Toch died of cancer at seventy-six.

Though often lumped with Hindemith [**1914**] and Krenek [**1984**], Toch is a more accessible composer than either, often working within traditional forms (though imaginatively) and eschewing doctrinaire use of atonality. He wrote in most genres, though his 3 operas, all relatively early works, do not loom large in his output (a good deal of which has been lost).

RECORDINGS: Toch himself made recordings of his first (mature) piano concerto of 1926 and his piano quintet. His pupil Previn also recorded the latter work, and his pupil Rehberg once recorded some of his solo piano music. Other recordings include the first, third, and fifth ("Jephta") symphonies; the Concerto for Cello; the *Circus, Pinocchio,* and *Miniature* overtures; the orchestral *Peter Pan, Big Ben,* and *Notturno;* String Quartets Nos. 8, 10, 12, and 13; the String Trio; the *Spitzweg Serenade* for two violins and viola; Sonata No. 1 for Violin and Piano; several chamber pieces for winds; the *Valse* and *Geographical Fugue* for speaking chorus; the song cycles *The Chinese Flute* and *Poems to Martha;* and piano pieces.

[1825] SOJO, Vicente Emilio (Sō'-hō, Vē-sen'-tā Ā-mēl'-yō)
CONDUCTOR, EDUCATOR
BORN: Guatire, December 8, 1887

Born near Caracas, Sojo had some lessons from a local organist and a course in harmony at the Academy in Caracas, but he was largely an autodidact. He was best known as conductor of the Venezuelan Symphony Orchestra and the Orfeon Lamas Choir in Caracas, and he was made director of the National Music School there in 1936. He wrote a string quartet, some Masses and other choral works, and pieces in small forms. RECORDINGS: Alberto Ponce has recorded some of his guitar music.

[1826] DELVINCOURT, Claude (Del-van-coōr', Klôd)
CONDUCTOR, ADMINISTRATOR
BORN: Paris, January 12, 1888
DIED: Orbetello, April 5, 1954

Claude Delvincourt's considerable talent was circumscribed by his equally considerable bad luck. He performed admirably at the Paris Conservatoire, where his teachers included Boëllmann [1549], Widor [1414], and Henri Büsser [1627], and was joint winner of the Prix de Rome in 1913 with the even less fortunate Lili Boulanger [1886]. But fate decreed the trenches for him rather than Rome, and on the last day of 1915 he was so severely wounded that it took him nearly a decade to get his career back on track. His first major work to be performed in fact was his "choreographic poem" *Offrande à Siva* in 1927. Most of his large compositions were intended for some aspect of theater—a comic opera, *La Femme à barbe (The Bearded Lady)* in 1938; the 1948 "mystery" *Lucifer;* incidental music for Sophocles' *Oedipus* in 1939 and for Molière's *Le Bourgeois gentilhomme* in 1948; the 1935 film score *La Croisière jaune (The Yellow Cruise),* and music for the 1937 Paris Exposition. In 1932 Delvincourt was appointed director of the Versailles Conservatoire. Nine years later he succeeded Henri Rabaud [1647] in the analogous capacity at the Paris Conservatoire, just in time for the German occupation. Against considerable odds he managed to keep the school functioning and the student body relatively intact for the duration. True to form he died in a road accident while traveling through Tuscany. RECORDINGS: His work is universally praised for its combination of adventurousness and control, but little of it—a string quartet, a violin sonata, some songs—appears to have been recorded.

[1827] BESLY, Maurice
CONDUCTOR, LAWYER
BORN: Normanby, January 28, 1888
DIED: Horsham, March 20, 1945

A Yorkshireman and Cambridge graduate, Besly had a fling at acting, then took up music at the Leipzig Conservatory (from which the Grand Old Names were now all gone). On graduating he returned to Tonbridge School (where he had prepped) as music master and remained there until the 1914 war broke out two years later. He served brilliantly as a soldier and spent the latter part of 1918 in a German prison camp. After his release, he was appointed director of music at Queen's College, Oxford. Soon he began conducting and in 1924 became conductor of the Scottish Orchestra. Music evidently did not satisfy him as a profession, however, and he finished out his life as a lawyer. As a composer he was not prolific, and is best known for his songs. RECORDINGS: Some of his songs have been recorded.

[1828] DUREY, Louis Edmond (Dü-rā', Loō-ē' Ed-mon')
BORN: Paris, May 27, 1888
DIED: St. Tropez, July 3, 1979

Louis Durey is usually remembered (if at all) as the oldest and most obscure member of that largely mythical group of irreverent postwar French composers known as "Les Six." The son of a printer, Durey took a degree in liberal arts with the intention of becoming a businessman. But an encounter with Debussy's [1547] *Pelléas et Mélisande* awoke his musical interests and sent him for lessons to Léon Saint-Requier, a choirmaster. In 1914 Durey was put in uniform but was released two years later. It was at that point that he began composing, beginning with *Carillons* for piano, four hands. (He had also written a song in 1914.) Though the music of Schoenberg [1657] had triggered this reawakening of interest, Durey was most influenced by Stravinsky [1748] and Satie [1578]. He was soon drawn into the orbit of Jean Cocteau, whence his connection with the rest of Les Six (Auric [1962], Honegger [1861], Milhaud [1868], Poulenc [1960], and Tailleferre [1863]). Though he joined them in a couple of rather ill-assorted musical collaborations, he broke off all links to them in 1921 and moved to St. Tropez, where his parents had settled. He continued to compose throughout the decade. In 1929 he married and soon had to return to Paris to find work that would support his growing family. After that there was little time for music. In 1937 he joined the Communist Party and became secretary general of its musical wing. For some years thereafter he seems not to have composed at all, which is why many reference books write him off at this point in his career. After World War II, however, he took up his pen again. Much of what he wrote in this period—a cantata on Mao Tse-tung's "Long March," music for a film on the Korean War, settings of poems by Ho Chi Minh—was unashamedly propagandistic, but he also wrote a number of nonpolitical and abstract works. He died at ninety-one. RECORDINGS: Recordings include the 1920 Cocteau cantata *Le Printemps au fond de la mer (Spring at the Bottom of the Sea)*, a flute sonatine, a wind quartet, an LP of piano pieces played by Françoise Petit, songs (notably sung by Irène Joachim, Carole Bogard, and Maria Lagios), and a few other short pieces. Durey also wrote a book on instrumentation with Desiré Dondeyne, conductor of the Paris Police Band.

[1829] TALTABULL, Cristofer (Tàl'-tà-bul, Krès'-tō-fer)
PIANIST, TEACHER, CONDUCTOR, CRITIC
BORN: Barcelona, July 28, 1888
DIED: Barcelona, May 1, 1964

The rather picaresque Taltabull is said to have been christened "Cristofer" because he was born on the day the Columbus Monument was dedicated in Barcelona. He had music lessons in school and at the cathedral, and took piano with one Martínez-Imbert. There were later studies with Granados [1588] and Felipe Pedrell [1384], and musical curiosity also drove him to begin putting together what ultimately became a very fine library. In 1908 Taltabull took himself off to Munich and Max Reger [1637]. At some subsequent point he fell in love with a French girl, Lea Masson, only to learn in 1911 that his family had arranged for him to marry a Catalan. He came home to plead his case, lost it, and exiled himself to France, where he worked for a time as an accompanist before settling in Paris in 1913. A year later his parents relented; he married his Lea and returned to Barcelona, where his daughter was born. But soon, leaving his wife and daughter behind until he could get established, he returned to Paris, where he worked for the publisher Durand, taught, and conducted theater and cabaret orches-

tras. With the German invasion of 1940, the Taltabulls fled to Spain, leaving the composer's manuscripts with his sister-in-law in Amiens. In the course of the war, her house was bombed and the music went up in flames. Taltabull returned once more to Paris in 1949 but was denied a work permit and went back to Barcelona for good, serving there for the rest of his life as a reviewer, teacher, and choral conductor. His music has been described as exhibiting a Spanish ethos filtered through French Impressionism. Most of what is extant consists of choral pieces and songs from the postwar period. RECORDINGS: Montserrat Martorell has recorded some of the songs, including a set of *Canciones Xineses* orchestrated by composer Josep Soler (1935–).

[1830] JOHANSEN, David Monrad (Yō-hàn'-sen, Dä'-vēd Mōn'-ràd)
PIANIST, CONDUCTOR, CRITIC
BORN: Vefsn, November 8, 1888
DIED: Sandvika, February 20, 1974

Born in a Norwegian village not far south of the Arctic Circle, Johansen (or Monrad-Johansen, as the name often appears) early fell under the spell of Grieg [1410], of whom he later, in 1934, wrote a standard study. At fifteen he embarked on five years of piano study at the Christiania (Oslo) Conservatory. After six more years of theoretical training by the folklorist Catharinus Elling (1858–1942) and Svendsen's [1379] pupil Iver Holter (1850–1941), he went to Berlin to study with Engelbert Humperdinck [1480] and Robert Kahn (1865–1951) for a year. Johansen's first large-scale composition, the Op. 4 suite for orchestra dates from 1916. In that same year he began his three decades as music critic for various Norwegian newspapers. He also appeared as a concert pianist, and, after 1938, as a conductor, and was active in the promotion of Norwegian music. His own compositions—orchestral, choral, instrumental, and solo-vocal—are rooted in a historical understanding of Norwegian folk music, but also reflect a knowledge of modern techniques. His son, the composer Johan Kvandal (1919–), writes music in a somewhat more advanced idiom. RECORDINGS: The Norwegian government has provided very extensive recorded documentation of Johansen's work on the Philips label. Works recorded include the orchestral works *Pan, Symphonic Fantasy,* and *Symphonic Variations and Fugue;* the song *Sigvat Skald* for tenor and orchestra; the Edda-based oratorio *Voluspaa;* the violin sonata, the flute quintet; several piano suites; and several song cycles.

[1831] TUTHILL, Burnet Corwin
CLARINETIST, CONDUCTOR, EDUCATOR
BORN: New York, November 16, 1888

Tuthill was the son of William Burnet (Tuthill), who designed New York's Carnegie Hall. He was an ardent amateur and schoolband clarinetist, but took nonmusical degrees from Columbia University in 1909 and 1910, and entered on a commercial career. However, he kept up his musical activities, writing an occasional clarinet piece and conducting. In 1919 he and his father founded, to further the cause of native chamber music, the Society for the Publication of American Music, which functioned until 1969. Three years later Tuthill took a job as general manager of the Cincinnati College of Music, which he held until 1930. In 1924 he and Charles N. Boyd, director of the Pittsburgh Musical Institute, founded the National Association of Schools of Music (NASM). Tuthill remained at the college to take a master's degree in music in 1935. Later that year he was appointed chairman of the music department at Southwestern University in Memphis. He also served as conductor of the Memphis Symphony Orchestra from 1938 until its collapse in 1946. He retired in 1959 but continued to compose and compiled important bibliographies of music for the clarinet. He also wrote a history of the NASM and personal memoirs. At this writing he was still living, in Knoxville. Tuthill did not begin composing seriously until he was past forty. He devoted much of his creativity to music for wind instruments, including concerti for clarinet, trombone, and tuba, as well as one for bass viol and band. RECORDINGS: There is a recording of his orchestral *Come Seven*.

[1832] WAYDITCH, Gabriel von (Vī'-dich, Gáb'-rē-el fun)
PIANIST, CONDUCTOR
BORN: Budapest, December 28, 1888
DIED: New York, July 28, 1969

Wayditch's life was unfortunately the stuff of old Hollywood musical melodramas. His father was Baron Aloysius Wajditsch von Verbovac, a physician, physicist, and indefatigable inventor. (He is credited with the 3-D movie, glasses and all, but too early for it to make any impact.) Gabriel studied piano with the great Liszt [1218] pupil Emil von Sauer and composition with Hans

Koessler (1853–1926), quondam mentor of Dohnányi [1696], Bartók [1734], and Kodály [1760]. Infatuated with the music of Wagner [1230] and Richard Strauss [1563], he set out to be an opera composer. But the family fortunes were in decline, his parents' marriage dissolved, and the baron, after a spell as ship's doctor for the Cunard Lines, decided in 1911 that he and his son would seek opportunity in the United States. It never materialized. Gabriel sustained himself as a pianist (sometimes on cruise ships) and as a theatrical conductor. In 1940 he was a member of a trio that had a sustaining program on New York's radio station WNYC. Meanwhile he kept on cranking out operas to the total of fourteen, most of them of a rather lush complexity and some of them of extraordinary length. In 1938 he managed to scrape together enough money to put on a scratch performance of his *Horus,* Fritz Mahler conducting, but about all that came of it was a collection of rather staggering bills. Wayditch, however, maintained unwavering faith that his day would come and kept on working until a heart attack felled him at his desk in his eighty-first year. RECORDINGS: Thanks to his son Ivan, there have been posthumous recordings of *The Caliph's Magician* and *Jesus Before Herod,* both of which might be said to out-Salome *Salome.*

[1833] ZIMBALIST, Efrem Alexandrovich
VIOLINIST, TEACHER
BORN: Rostov on Don, April 9, 1889
    (Other sources say April 7 or 21 or
    May 7, 1889, or April 9, 1890.)
DIED: Denver, Colorado, early 1985.

For forty years Efrem Zimbalist was regarded as one of the great violinists of his time, though today he is probably best known as the shadowy father of an actor who bears his name. (Perhaps he was not so well known in his day; there is an apocryphal story of a radio announcer who introduced him as "Mr. Efrem, the famous zimbalist.") Trained at first by his father, he was placed in the hands of Leopold Auer in 1901. He began his international career in 1907, immediately after his graduation from the St. Petersburg Conservatory. He was first heard in America in 1911 and was so taken with the country that he has remained here ever since. In 1914 he married the soprano Alma Gluck, whose enormous popularity is reflected in the fact that her recording of "Listen to the Mockingbird" was the first by a "classical" singer to sell a million copies. They concertized and made recordings together. (Gluck was the mother, by an earlier marriage, of the writer Marcia Davenport, as well of Efrem Zimbalist, Jr.) She died in 1938. In 1941 Zimbalist was appointed director of the Curtis Institute of Music in Philadelphia, and two years later he married its founder, the heiress Mary Louise Curtis Bok. He officially ended his concert career in 1949 but continued to appear occasionally for several more years. He retired from the conservatory in 1968 and, again a widower, moved to Reno, Nevada, two years later. In recent years he lived in Denver, Colorado. Besides many violin pieces and transcriptions, he wrote an opera, a concerto apiece for violin and cello, other orchestral works, and chamber music. RECORDINGS: There are recordings of a string quartet and a violin sonata as well as of smaller pieces. (There is also a record of a violin sonata by Efrem, Jr.)

[1834] JORDAN, Sverre (Yôr'-dån, Svâr'-re)
PIANIST, CONDUCTOR
BORN: Bergen, May 25, 1889
DIED: Bergen, January 10, 1972

There appears to be some question whether Jordan was born in Christiania or Bergen, but he was closely identified with the latter town for most of his life. Like his close contemporary David Monrad Johansen [1830], he was a pianist, a conductor, and a Grieg [1410] enthusiast who wrote a book about that composer and his music. After studying piano in Norway, he went, in 1907, to Berlin, where he had further lessons with two great Liszt [1218] pupils, José Vianna da Motta and Konrad Ansorge, and studied composition with Wilhelm Klatte, a disciple of Richard Strauss [1563]. After concertizing and guest-conducting for a time, he settled in Bergen, where he reviewed for the local paper and conducted the municipal choir. In 1931 he was appointed conductor at the National Theater there. He retired in 1957. He was a self-proclaimed national Romantic. His music includes concerti, orchestral suites, overtures, incidental music, a quartet, 2 piano trios, violin sonatas, choral and piano music, and songs. RECORDINGS: The songs are his best-known works. They have been represented on records, as has the Sonatina for Flute and Piano of 1955.

[1835] PADILLA, José (Pȧ-dē'-yȧ, Hō-zä')
CONDUCTOR

BORN: Almeria, May 28, 1889
DIED: Madrid, October 25, 1960

Padilla was an international success as both a theatrical composer and songwriter. Born in southeasternmost Spain, he studied at the Madrid Conservatory and then embarked on a career as a theater conductor in both his homeland and South America. He began writing songs for zarzuelas and complete scores. Of the former, El Relicario and Princesita found currency with singers on the international concert circuit, and Valencia, with an English lyric ("Valencia, in my arms I held your charms beneath the southern stars and moon") became something of a popular hit in the United States. In the twenties Padilla moved to Paris and wrote chansons for the big music-hall singers there. In the 1930s he went to Italy for a few years to try his hand at Italian songs. After World War II he returned to Paris for a time. His songs number in the hundreds. RECORDINGS: There are recordings of El Relicario and Princesita.

[1836] GIBBS, Cecil Armstrong
TEACHER
BORN: Great Baddow, August 10, 1889
DIED: Chelmsford, May 12, 1960

An Essex man, Armstrong Gibbs read history at Cambridge, where he became a protégé of one of his music teachers, Edward Dent, later professor of music at that University. On graduating in 1913 with a B.Mus. (he had received his B.A. two years earlier) Gibbs took up public school teaching. Rejected for war service, he settled in at the Wick School at Hove, near Brighton, in 1915. During this period he wrote a fair number of songs, including some settings of Walter de la Mare's poems. In 1919 he persuaded the poet to write a play for the school, music to be supplied by himself. Crossings was duly produced, with Dent in charge and Adrian Boult conducting. Boult was so impressed that he talked Gibbs into chucking it all for a career in music. Gibbs enrolled at the Royal College, where he studied with his old acquaintance Vaughan Williams [1633] and with Boult himself. In 1921 he joined the faculty of the school. He also spent much time judging festival competitions. He retired from the college in 1939. Gibbs composed an enormous amount of music. Much of it is workaday stuff for amateur choirs and orchestras and children's theaters, but it also includes many large-scale serious efforts —an opera on Shakespeare's Twelfth Night, 3 symphonies, several string quartets, etc.

However, he is chiefly admired for the best of his innumerable songs, some of which, like his popular waltz "Dusk," have been recorded.

[1837] GÁL, Hans (Gàl, Hàns)
TEACHER, WRITER, CONDUCTOR, PIANIST
BORN: Brunn, August 5, 1890

Born in a Viennese suburb, Hans Gál studied at the University of Vienna with the musicologists Eusebius Mandyczewski and Guido Adler. He took his doctorate in 1913 and won a prize for composition; later, 1919–29, he taught there. His earliest compositions were chiefly in the areas of choral and chamber music, but in 1919 his first opera, *Der Arzt der Sobeide (The Physician of Sobeida),* was produced in Breslau (Wroclaw). Of the three that followed, *Die heilige Ente (The Sacred Duck)* of 1923 and *Das Lied der Nacht (The Song of the Night)* of 1926 were especially successful. In 1929 Gál was called to Mainz to direct the conservatory, but the Nazi political victory in 1933 drove him back to Vienna and forestalled the production of his fifth (and last) opera. During the next five years he conducted the Madrigal Society and the Concert Orchestra but was forced to flee again in 1938. He settled in Edinburgh, where he was befriended by the great musical scholar Sir Donald Tovey, professor of music at the university, who got him a teaching appointment there. (One of Gál's students was Thea Musgrave [2374].) Gál retired in 1965 but continued to compose and to write. His large list of compositions, in a rather late-Romantic idiom, includes a piano concerto and 4 symphonies but continues to be dominated by chamber and choral works. (He has written few songs and piano pieces.) His writings, witty and often controversial, include studies of Schubert [1153], Brahms [1329], and Wagner [1230]. RECORDINGS: On records there is a *Divertimento* for mandolin and piano.

[1838] IBERT, Jacques François Antoine (Ē-bâr', Zhák Frȧn-swä' Än-twän')
ACTOR, TEACHER, ADMINISTRATOR
BORN: Paris, August 15, 1890
DIED: Paris, February 5, 1962

A dapper Parisian, Jacques Ibert wrote dapper music—clean, crisp, insouciant, witty, unashamedly *derrière-garde,* and sometimes concealing considerable depths—which won him limited popularity and the scorn of the progressive establishment. He learned piano at his mother's knee or somewhere near it. His father envisioned him as a businessman and enrolled him in the Collège Rollin to become one. Ibert, however, saw himself as a thespian, and by the time he was twenty he was coaching declamation at the Paris Conservatoire. He soon succumbed to his environment, took a harmony course with Pessard [1408], and then enrolled as a full-time student. He studied further with André Gédalge (1856–1926), Fauré [1424], and Vidal [1554] and copped several prizes. His education came to a halt with World War I, in which he served as a naval officer but used his leisure time to compose. On his return to the Paris Conservatoire, he won the 1919 Grand Prix de Rome. He thereupon married his fiancée, an artist's daughter named Rose-Marie Veber, and took her off for a three-year honeymoon in Rome. His most important composition during this period was his orchestral *Ballade de la geôle de Reading (Ballad of Reading Gaol,* after Oscar Wilde), which Gabriel Pierné [1555] premiered in 1922. The Iberts' holiday climaxed in a Mediterranean cruise which the composer commemorated in his orchestral suite *Escales (Ports of Call),* which became, somewhat to his regret, his most popular work.

Ibert was a very busy composer over the next fifteen years. Though he wrote all sorts of music, he was chiefly occupied with his first love, the stage. By himself he wrote four operas in a light vein—*Persée et Andromède (Perseus and Andromeda),* 1921; *Angélique,* 1926; *Le Roi d'Yvetot (The King of Yvetot),* 1928; and *Gonzague (Gonzago),* 1930. With his friend Honegger [1861] he also wrote *L'Aiglon (The Eaglet)* in 1937 and *Les Petites Cardinal (The Cardinal Kids)* in 1938. There were several ballet scores, much incidental music (not only for plays, but also for radio), films, and stage spectacles. Some of his most popular pieces derive from such dramatic music—the *Divertissement* of 1930 from the music for Labiche's great farce *The Italian Straw Hat;* the 1932 *Paris* from that for Jules Romain's *Donogoo;* the *Suite élisabéthaine* of 1944 from that for Shakespeare's *A Midsummer Night's Dream.* In 1932 Ibert was asked to write music for a film of *Don Quixote,* to star Feodor Chaliapin. Unknown to each other, so were composers Marcel Delannoy (1898–1962), Falla [1688], Milhaud [1868], and Ravel [1666], in a sort of uncompetitive competition. When it was announced that Ibert's score had been chosen, Ravel sued, but the decision stood.

In 1937 Ibert was appointed director of the Académie de France in Rome. In 1955–56 he served as director of the Paris Opéra and

Opéra-Comique, and in the latter year he was elected to the Académie Française. At the time of his death he was working on an orchestral suite from the 1957 ballet *Tropismes pour des amours imaginaires (Tropisms for Imaginary Love Affairs).*

RECORDINGS: Orchestral recordings include *Divertissement, Paris* (including an older recording conducted by the composer), *Suite elisabethaine, Ballade de la geôle de Reading, Escales, Capriccio, Louisville Concerto, Bostoniana, Ouverture du fête, Symphonie marine, Bacchanale, Symphonie concertante* for oboe and orchestra, ballet music for *Diane de Poitiers, La Licorne, Tropismes pour des amours imaginaires, Les Amours de Jupiter,* and *Le Chevalier errant* (the latter with chorus). There are also recordings of concerti for flute, saxophone, and cello. Chamber music recordings include the very popular *Trois pièces brèves* for winds, an *Entr'acte* for flute or violin and harp or guitar, a Trio for Violin, Cello, and Harp, the string quartet, *Histoires* for piano, and numerous short pieces. Vocal music, apart from the Chaliapin recordings for the film, has only recently begun to appear: the operas *L'Aiglon, Persée et Andromède, Angélique,* and *L'Roi d'Yvetot* in French Radio–derived recordings, as well as a new version of the *Don Quichotte* songs.

[1839] GURNEY, Ivor Bertie
POET, ORGANIST
BORN: Gloucester, August 28, 1890
DIED: Dartford, Kent, December 26, 1937

Ivor Gurney's musical career was, like George Butterworth's [1797], foreshortened by World War I but perhaps even more tragically. One of the four children of a tailor, he experienced a good deal of hardship in his early years. At twelve he joined the choir of Gloucester Cathedral and studied with Herbert Brewer, its director, who appointed him assistant organist in 1906. He got his academic education at King's School, though he perhaps profited even more from access to the fine library of Canon Alfred Cheeseman, his godfather. He also enjoyed the friendship of Herbert Howells [1870], another rising Gloucester musician two years his junior. In 1911 he won a scholarship to the Royal College of Music, where Stanford [1467] found him a brilliant, if difficult, student. At the outbreak of the war, Gurney was rejected for service as too myopic. But he kept trying and was finally given a uniform in 1915 and sent to France a year later. By then he had been composing for some

time. Now, however, he turned to poetry and published his first collection, *Severn and Somme,* in 1917. In that same year he was wounded in the arm and hospitalized in Rouen. But he recovered in time to be involved in the fighting that fall at Passchendale, where he was caught in a mustard-gas attack. After a year in military hospitals, he was shipped home as past rehabilitation. In 1922 he returned to the family home in Gloucester but soon began to suffer delusions and had to be committed to a mental institution. Pronounced incurable, he was transferred to the City of London Hospital at Dartford in Kent. There, though he experienced periods of lucidity, he spent the rest of his life. He wrote many of his finest poems then but gave up composition around 1928. He died of tuberculosis at forty-seven.

In 1918 Gurney published his second and last book of poems, *War's Embers,* but he left around 800 poems all told, which move from pastoralism to a complex metaphysicality. It is said that much of his work, however, exists in too rough or incoherent a state to be salvaged. This also applies to most of his instrumental music and to many of the songs. As a songwriter his chief concern was to fit the right music to the words, and so he was unmoved by the schools and systems of his time.

RECORDINGS: In recent years, after long neglect, a good representation of his songs has been recorded.

[1840] BULLOCK, (Sir) Ernest
ORGANIST, EDUCATOR
BORN: Wigan, September 15, 1890
DIED: Aylesbury, May 24, 1979

A Lancashire lad, Bullock studied organ in Leeds with Edward Bairstow [1656] and took his musical degrees from the University of Durham. He was assistant organist at Manchester Cathedral from 1912 to 1915, when he was taken into the armed forces. For nearly a decade after the war, he was organist and choirmaster at Exeter Cathedral. In 1928 he was appointed organist and master of the choristers at Westminster Abbey, where in 1937 he conducted the music for the coronation of George VI, for which Bullock wrote the fanfares. In 1941 he succeeded to the professorship of music at Glasgow University and the directorship of the Academy of Music and Drama there. King George knighted him in 1951, and in 1952 he became director of the Royal College of Music. In 1953 he wrote most of the *Coronation Fanfares* for Elizabeth II. Bullock retired in 1960. Apart from the ceremonial works

noted, he composed mostly church music.
RECORDINGS: Some of the church music and
the fanfares have been recorded.

[1841] MARTIN, Frank (Mär-ta*n'*, Fránk)
TEACHER, KEYBOARDIST, CONDUCTOR
BORN: Geneva, September 15, 1890
DIED: Naarden, November 21, 1974

Little more than a local celebrity for the first
fifty years of his long life, Frank Martin
emerged in his last few decades as a composer of international stature. Though he
bore some Dutch genes, he was primarily a
descendant of French Huguenots long settled in Switzerland and was in fact the youngest child (of ten) of a Calvinist minister.
His musical development is a classical example of ontogeny duplicating phylogeny. The
melodies of the Huguenot Psalter were in his
blood. In 1900 he was shattered by Bach
[684] when he was taken to a performance of
the *St. Matthew Passion*. His only music
teacher was a local composer, Joseph
Lauber (1864–1952), a product of the Rheinberger **[1368]** mill in Munich and the Massenet **[1396]** factory in Paris. Obedient to his
father's wish, Martin embarked on a mathe-
matical-scientific curriculum, but music got
the upper hand and he did not stay around
for a degree. His earliest compositions were
primarily German Romantic, with Franckian **[1284]** overtones. Some songs for voice
and orchestra, *3 Poèmes païens,* were performed in Vevey as early as 1911. In 1915 he
encountered the conductor Ernest Ansermet, who converted him to Debussy
[1547] and Ravel **[1666]** and officiated at the
premiere of Martin's first major work, the
choral-orchestral *Les Dithyrambes* in 1918.
For the next several years, Martin moved
about quite a bit, both physically and musically, living in Italy and France and trying
to incorporate into his compositions exotic,
ancient, and folk impulses. In 1926 he came
back to Geneva, studied Eurhythmics with
its inventor Jaques-Dalcroze, and taught for
a time in his school. In 1933 he became director of a private music school called the
Technicum Moderne de Musique. It was
during this period that Martin discovered
Schoenberg **[1657]** and began to wrestle with
the twelve-tone concept.

In 1938 Robert Blum commissioned Martin to write a work for the twelve-voice madrigal choir he directed. Martin used as his
foundation Joseph Bédier's recension of the
Tristan story and, over a three-year period
of trial and error, evolved his own twelve-
tone system of what might be called tonal or
harmonic dodecaphony. The result, *Le Vin*

herbé (The Doctored Wine), a "secular oratorio" in which the soloists function both as
characters and chorus members and in
which word meanings and speech rhythms
dictate the melodic lines, was first performed
in Zürich in 1942. Despite the adverse conditions of the time, Martin's fifty-two-year-old
name reverberated around the world. The
composer followed the oratorio almost immediately in 1943 with two other successful
vocal works, *Die Weise von Liebe und Tod
des Cornets Christoph Rilke (The Melody of
Love and Death of Cornet Christoph Rilke),*
also known as *Der Cornet,* and a setting of
six monologues from Hoffmannsthal's version of *Jedermann (Everyman).* As it became obvious that World War II was coming
to an end, Radio Geneva commissioned him
to write an appropriate work to celebrate the
armistice. The result was the oratorio *In
terra pax (Peace on Earth),* duly broadcast
on May 7, 1945. That same year saw the
completion of the *Petite symphonie concertante* for the intriguing combination of
harp, piano, harpsichord, and double string
orchestra, which became a truly popular
concert work.

In 1946 Martin concluded his four-year
term as president of the Swiss Musicians'
Union, pulled up stakes, and moved to Amsterdam, later settling in Naarden, a few
miles to the east of the city. In 1948 he completed his Passion oratorio *Golgotha,* inspired by memories of Bach's works and an
etching of Rembrandt's. Two years later he
began a seven-year series of composition
classes at the Cologne Conservatory. In 1956
his first opera, *Der Sturm (The Tempest,* after Shakespeare), had a successful premiere
in Vienna and shortly afterward a decidedly
unsuccessful repetition at the New York
City Opera in Erich Leinsdorf's only season
as manager there. Martin continued to compose, if not to develop, to within a few
months of his death at eighty-four, completing all but the orchestration of his cantata *Et
la vie l'emporta (And Life Bore Him Away)*
in his final year.

RECORDINGS: Most of the recordings to
date—some under the composer's direction
or supervision—are of music from the peak
years: *Le Vin herbá; Der Cornet; In terra
pax; Golgotha;* the *6 Monologe aus
"Jedermann";* most of the series of *Ballades*
for various solo instruments and orchestra
(or piano) composed between 1938 and 1950;
Sonata da chiesa for viola d'amore and orchestra (or for flute and organ), 1938; *Passacaglia* for organ, 1944; and *8 Préludes* for piano, 1948. Late and early works recorded include: the Piano Quintet No. 1, 1933; concerti for violin, harpsichord, and cello (dat-

ing from 1951, 1952, and 1966, respectively); *Études* for strings, 1956; excerpts from *Der Sturm;* Concerto No. 2 for Piano, 1969; the *Ballade* for viola and chamber orchestra, 1972; the religiously inspired *Polyptique* for violin and two string orchestras, 1973; some guitar pieces; and a few miscellaneous songs and chamber pieces.

[1842] MEDIŅŠ, Jānis (Mā-dēnch', Yä'-nis)
TEACHER, VIOLIST, CONDUCTOR
BORN: Riga, October 9, 1890
DIED: Stockholm, March 4, 1966

One of three composing-and-conducting brothers (the others were Jāzeps and Jēkabs), Mediņš was a pioneer in the brief history of Latvian nationalistic music. Educated in the Riga conservatory, he played viola in the national opera orchestra there from 1913 to 1915. During World War I he composed two operas, *Uguns (Fire)* and *Nakts (Nights),* probably the first Latvian operas, though they were not produced until 1924 (as a single work). After Latvia gained her freedom, he was chief conductor at the National Opera House, and, from 1928, of the National Radio Symphony Orchestra. In 1944 he fled to Germany (his brothers remained behind and won awards from the Soviets) and in 1948 moved permanently to Stockholm. He wrote three more operas, a ballet, concerti, orchestral works, chamber music, and many songs. RECORDINGS: There are recordings of the Concerto No. 2 for Cello, a suite for cello and piano, and a set of piano preludes.

[1843] NYSTROEM, Gösta (Nü'-ström, Yös'-tä)
PAINTER, CRITIC
BORN: Silvberg, October 13, 1890
DIED: Särö, August 9, 1966

Despite a decidedly checkered education, Nystroem became both a painter of reputation and an important and quite individual composer. He was born in west central Sweden but grew up in a suburb of Stockholm, where his father, a trained organist and weekend painter, ran a school. His first music lessons came from his father. Later he studied privately in Stockholm but was rejected as a conservatory student and took a degree in primary education. Around 1915, however, he moved to Copenhagen, where he studied both music and art, and began both composing and painting. In 1920 he went to Paris, losing his manuscripts en

route. There he studied with d'Indy **[1462]**, the conductor Camille Chevillard, and a pupil of Taneyev **[1492]**, Leonid Sabaneyev (1881–1968). In 1932 he finally made his way home and became reviewer for a Göteborg newspaper. He developed a style characterized by polyphony, jagged rhythms, and often extreme dissonance but later tempered it with greater lyricism. His catalog includes a radio opera, a ballet, much incidental music, 6 symphonies, concerti, other orchestral works, 2 string quartets, choral music, and many songs. RECORDINGS: Recordings include: a 1934 suite from the music for *The Merchant of Venice;* the 1939 *Sinfonia Concertante* for cello and orchestra; the first symphony *(Sinfonia breve),* 1931; the second symphony *(Sinfonia espressiva),* 1935; the third symphony *(Sinfonia del mare),* 1948; the 1942 orchestral song cycle *Songs by the Sea* (also a version for soprano and piano); and the *Concerto ricercante* for piano and orchestra, 1959. Pending release is a recording of one of the string quartets (Berwald Quartet).

[1844] DUBENSKY, Arcady (Dōō-ben'-skē, Är-kä'-dē)
VIOLINIST, CONDUCTOR
BORN: Viatka, October 15, 1890
DIED: Tenafly, N.J., October 14, 1966

Born in central Russia, Dubensky graduated in 1909 from the Moscow Conservatory, where he had studied violin with Jan Hřimaly and composition with the German-trained Alexander Ilyinsky (1859–1920). He then played in the orchestra at the Bolshoi Theater until after the October Revolution. In 1919 he escaped to Constantinople, where he played in cabarets. Two years later he emigrated to New York, where he found employment in Walter Damrosch's **[1540]** New York Symphony Orchestra. When it merged in 1928 with Toscanini's Philharmonic, Dubensky was one of those who made the transition. He retired to suburban New Jersey in 1964 and died on the eve of his seventy-sixth birthday. Dubensky did most of his composing in the United States, where his music won frequent performances. Not that he changed the course of the art—his attraction was mostly that of clever novelty. He liked to focus on popular and topical subjects, as witness his *Tom Sawyer Overture,* his *Political Suite* (with Nazi and Communist movements), and his *Stephen Foster: Theme, Variations, and Finale* (based on "Old Folks at Home"). He liked also to write for odd combinations—a quartet for contrabasses, an overture for toy trumpets

and bass drums, a suite for nine flutes. RE-
CORDINGS: There were, in his day, recordings of the *Fugue for 18 Violins, Gossips* for
string orchestra, *Stephen Foster,* and *The
Raven* for reciter and orchestra.

[1845] PINTO, Octavio (Pēn'-tō, Ok-tà'-
vē-ō)
ARCHITECT, PIANIST
BORN: São Paulo, November 3, 1890
DIED: São Paulo, October 31, 1950

Pinto studied music in Paris, notably with
pianist Isidore Philipp, but made his career
as a successful architect in Brazil. In 1922 he
married a fellow Philipp pupil, Guiomar
Novaes, who often played pieces of his composition in recital. RECORDINGS: Novaes recorded his *Scenas infantas.*

[1846] MARTINŮ, Bohuslav (Mär'-tē-nōō,
Bō'-hoo-slàf)
VIOLINIST, TEACHER
BORN: Polička, December 8, 1890
DIED: Liestal, August 28, 1959

Since his death, Martinů's stock as a composer has soared greatly, nowhere more than
in his native Czechoslovakia, where he has
been enshrined among the greatest composers produced by his people. The irony here is
that he enjoyed little success there and, save
for one later brief and ill-advised episode, he
abandoned it for good in his thirty-fourth
year. Nevertheless he remained a Czech at
heart and was much influenced by Czech
music and Czech history. He was born in
eastern Bohemia in a village roughly equidistant from Prague and Brno. His father
was a cobbler who held the post of tower
warden in the church, in the family quarters
of which his son was born. The boy showed
musical proclivities early, learned to play the
violin from the local tailor, and began composing at a fairly sophisticated level at the
age of ten. In 1906 he was sent to the Prague
Conservatory in the hope that he would become a violin virtuoso, but he disliked the
regimentation and found extracurricular interests that ultimately caused him to flunk
out. He was then sent to the Organ School
but could get up no interest in being a
church musician and was dismissed in 1910.
In 1913 he was accepted by the Czech Philharmonic as a second violinist. But to avoid
being drafted into the Austrian army, he left
Prague and sat out the war at home, where
he composed prolifically and gave music lessons. He rejoined the orchestra in 1918. Dissatisfied with his inability to catch on as a

composer, he returned in 1922 to the Prague
Conservatory to study with Suk [1651], but
he found the experience just as depressing as
he had earlier.

In 1923 Martinů packed his bags and went
to Paris, attracted by the music of Roussel
[1605], whose pupil he became. He absorbed
other musical currents as well—Impressionism, jazz, and neo-classicism as promulgated
by Stravinsky [1748] and the Cocteau circle
(see Satie [1578]). Martinů wrote furiously
—operas, ballets, film and radio music,
orchestral and chamber pieces by the yard.
His music gradually began to be taken up,
though it produced little to mitigate his
hand-to-mouth existence. In 1931 he married
Charlotte Quennehen, who undertook to
support him by working as a seamstress—
and soon became seriously ill. At that point
Martinů was awarded the Elizabeth Sprague
Coolidge Prize for his string sextet, the monetary part of which saved the day for the
couple. Just as he was coming into his own
and beginning to win serious attention on an
international scale, however, the Germans
broke through the Maginot Line and headed
for Paris. They had already tagged the composer a "musical degenerate," and he and
his wife fled with what they could carry in a
suitcase. Unable to procure exit visas, they
spent a wretched homeless six months before
winding up in Lisbon. From there, by way of
Bermuda, they made their way to New York
the following March.

In the fall of the same year, Serge Koussevitzky [1655], who knew the composer's earlier work, led the Boston Symphony in the
Concerto grosso, and commissioned a symphony. Other commissions followed, and
soon Martinů's music was being widely
played and, despite a very unsettled existence, he was soon writing with enormous
facility. He made a particular impact with
his *Memorial to Lidiče,* composed in outrage
against the Nazis' vengeful destruction of
that Czech village and its inhabitants, but he
wrote far more important music, including
the first five of his symphonies. At the end of
the war, the Czechs offered him a chair in
the graduate school of the Prague Conservatory. He returned to Paris in 1946 and then
went to Prague, but the subsequent Communist coup drove him away again. In 1947 he
suffered a serious fall that incapacitated him
for a time and from whose effects he never
entirely recovered. By the autumn of 1948,
however, he was well enough to take up his
duties as professor of composition at Princeton University. But he increasingly found
himself unable to come to terms with the
direction American life was taking, and in
1953 he settled in Nice for a time. Two years

later he was back to teach at the Curtis Institute. In that year Charles Munch conducted the Boston Symphony in the premiere of his sixth and last symphony, *Fantaisies symphoniques.* Martinů left the United States for good in 1956 to teach in Rome. Later he moved to Switzerland, where he died of cancer at sixty-nine.

Martinů was musically fluent to the point of glibness, leaving around 400 compositions of all kinds. Among them are 16 operas (two for radio, two for television), 12 ballets, more than a score of concerti and concerted works, 6 symphonies, oratorios, cantatas, a military *Field Mass,* 7 string quartets, etc.— plus many works that defy the usual classifications.

RECORDINGS: Two operas have been recorded complete—*Julietta,* 1937; and *The Greek Passion,* 1959. Choral-orchestral works on records include the 1937 cantata *Bouquet of Flowers,* the 1939 *Field Mass,* the 1955 *Gilgameš,* and the 1959 *Prophecy of Isaiah.* All of the symphonies and two of the ballets—*Istar,* 1922; and *Špaliček,* 1932— have also been recorded. A substantial number of Martinů's many concerted works have been done, including concerti for oboe, violin, cello, piano, harpsichord, violin-and-piano, string quartet, and double string orchestra—among others. Miscellaneous orchestral works recorded include *Memorial to Lidiče,* 1943; *Les Fresques de Piero della Francesca,* 1955; *Parables,* 1959; and many others. The 7 string quartets have been recorded, along with a huge selection of other chamber and keyboard works. However, the list is nowhere near exhaustive of the composer's output. Many, but by no means all, of these recordings are of Czech origin.

[1847] HOYER, Karl (Hoi′-er, Kärl)
ORGANIST, TEACHER
BORN: Weissenfels, January 9, 1891
DIED: Leipzig, June 12, 1936

Saxon-born Karl Hoyer studied at the Leipzig Conservatory with Max Reger [1637], by whom he was much influenced. At twenty he was organist at Reval (now Talinn) in Estonia and was already composing fluently. In 1912 he moved to Chemnitz (now Karl Marx Stadt), where he played for twelve years. Then he was appointed organist of the Nikolaikirche in Leipzig, where he also joined the conservatory faculty. He died at forty-five. His major output is in the realm of organ music. RECORDINGS: Some of his organ music has been recorded.

[1848] SPELMAN, Timothy Mather
ADMINISTRATOR, BAND DIRECTOR
BORN: Brooklyn, January 21, 1891
DIED: Florence, August 21, 1970

In his teens Spelman studied with Harry Rowe Shelley (1858–1947), a pupil of Dvořák [1386]. In 1909 he entered Harvard, where his composition teacher was Edward Burlingame Hill [1632]. On his graduation four years later Spelman won an Elkan Naumberg Fellowship that took him to Munich, where he undertook further studies with the Swiss Walter Courvoisier, protégé and son-in-law of Ludwig Thuille [1537]. Worsening international conditions sent him home in 1915. When America entered the war, Spelman was turned down for military service but did his bit anyway as assistant director of the program to train band musicians for the army. As soon as the fighting was over, he took his bride, poetess Leolyn Louise Everett (frequently his lyricist and librettist), to Florence, where they lived until 1935. After World War II they returned there for good. Fairly conservative and in no way "American," Spelman's music got more attention in Europe than in his fatherland. He wrote several stage works—operas, mime plays, ballets—most of which seem to have gone unperformed. Besides his symphony, oboe concerto, and string quartet, he wrote orchestral and chamber works with descriptive titles (e.g., *The Outcasts of Poker Flat, Dawn in the Woods, Homesick Yankee in North Africa, Le Pavillon sur l'eau),* cantatas, and songs. RECORDINGS: There is a record of his setting of the early mediaeval *Pervigilium Veneris (The All-Night Vigil of Venus).*

[1849] MORENO TORROBA, Federico
(Mō-rā′-nō Tôr-rōb′-vä, Fā-der-ē′-kō)
CONDUCTOR
BORN: Madrid, March 3, 1891
DIED: Spain, 1982

Moreno Torroba was the son and pupil of the organist José Moreno Ballesteros, a professor at the Madrid Conservatory. His chief mentor in composition, however, was Conrado del Campo (1879–1953), a Spanish Wagnerian [1230]. He became known chiefly as a composer of guitar music and of zarzuelas, notably *Luisa Fernanda,* though he has had three goes at writing operas—the last, completed in his ninetieth year, for the tenor Placido Domingo. RECORDINGS: The composer has appeared on records as a conductor of his own works. There are recordings of the zarzuelas *La Caramba, Luisa Fer-*

nanda, and *Maravilla;* the *Concierto de Cas-*
tilla for guitar and orchestra; guitar pieces;
zarzuela excerpts; fantasias; and potpourris.
Recent recordings of late works for guitar(s)
and orchestra include *Homenaje a la segui-*
dilla, Concerto Iberico, and *Dialogos.*

[1850] JACOBI, Frederick

CONDUCTOR, ETHNOMUSICOLOGIST,
TEACHER
BORN: San Francisco, May 4, 1891
DIED: New York, October 24, 1952

Though he has from time to time been pigeonholed as an "Indianist" or a "Hebra-
icist," Frederick Jacobi was really an eclectic. Though he was California born, he was
chiefly educated in New York, where he
studied piano with Rafael Joseffy and Paolo
Gallico and composition with Rubin Goldmark (1872–1936) and graduated from the
Ethical Culture School. Afterward he was a
pupil of the Russian Paul Juon (1872–1940)
at the Berlin Hochschule. From 1913 to 1917
Jacobi was a rehearsal conductor at the Metropolitan Opera House. When the United
States became involved in World War I he
served as a saxophone player in an army
band. Demobilized, he studied in New York
with Ernest Bloch [1729] and spent a good
deal of time studying the music of the
Pueblo Indians in the Southwest. This is reflected in a few compositions written around
the time of his return to New York in 1924
(e.g., the first of his 3 string quartets). His
"Jewish" period, clearly inspired by Bloch,
dates from c. 1930. (Though Bloch is often
said to have written the first complete Jewish musical service by a composer of stature,
Jacobi seems to have beaten him by two
years, completing his first one in 1931.) In
1936 he was appointed professor of composition at the Juilliard Graduate School, a post
he held until his retirement in 1950. At various times he also taught at the University of
California at Berkeley and Mills College in
Oakland, as well as at the Hartt College in
Hartford, Conn. His wife Irene was a pianist. RECORDINGS: Irene Jacobi twice recorded his *Hagiographia,* 1938, for piano and
string quartet. Jacobi himself may be heard
as soloist in a recording of his *Concertino for*
Piano and Strings. Other recordings include
the concerti (one each) for violin and cello,
the *Music Hall Overture,* the *Scherzo* for
wind quintet, the *Ballade* for violin and piano, and a few small works.

[1851] PROKOFIEV, Sergei Sergeivich

(Pru-kôf'-yef, Syir'-gä Syir-gä'-ye-vich)
PIANIST
BORN: Sontsovka, Ukraine, April 23,
1891
DIED: Moscow, March 5, 1953.

Though he was widely regarded as a giant in
his time, Sergei Prokofiev even then was far
from pleasing everyone, and his place in musical history is still up for grabs. By his own
admission he was strongly motivated by a
search for novelty, for a personal and "different" musical idiom, and he had a fondness for the driving "motoric" rhythms so
typical of avant-garde music in the early
twentieth century. At the same time—also
by his own admission—he was, through
early experience, drawn to Classical form,
and his natural utterance was lyrical. In his
clarity, his irony, his vitality, he broke with
the hothouse atmosphere typical of Scriabin
[1625] and Rachmaninoff [1638], but he felt
himself not at home with the fashionable abstraction of Stravinsky [1748] and his followers. Some of his works won immediate
and lasting popularity; others gained small
acceptance over a long period of time. If his
early dissonant works set audiences' teeth on
edge, some of the simplistic ones of his later
period have been viewed askance—in the
West at least. Soviet critics have seen him as
corrupted by his years in capitalist Europe
and America; the West has seen him as crippled by Soviet demands for music for the
masses. Nevertheless it seems likely that for
the foreseeable future the general musical
public will go on listening with pleasure to
the *Classical Symphony, Peter and the Wolf,*
Romeo and Juliet, and a dozen other works
that are now repertoire staples.
    Prokofiev's native village, Sontsovka, in
the Donets basin, took its name from the
Sontsov family, which had a vast estate in
the area. It was managed by Prokofiev's father, a Muscovite who had graduated from
the agricultural college in Moscow. The
composer's mother, the former Maria
Grigorievna Zhitkova, was among other
things a good amateur pianist. Young Sergei
was an only child, the last of three progeny,
his two sisters having died in infancy before
his arrival. He quickly turned out to be a
very bright kid, and his mother encouraged
his experiments at the piano and carefully
taught him what she knew. Inspired by a
domestic conversation (which he did not
quite comprehend) about a famine in India,
he wrote at the age of 5½ an *Indian Galop.*
This was followed by other compositions,
culminating in an opera, *The Giant,* which
got a performance by family members in his

uncle's music room in 1901. On the advice of said uncle and with *entree* provided by a musical friend, Maria took her son early in 1902 to talk with, and play for Sergei Taneyev [1492]. Taneyev (with whom Prokofiev kept up a correspondence) was sufficiently impressed to urge that the boy stick around and get some basics from Yuri Pomerantsiev, a Taneyev pupil. Prokofiev was disappointed and found he hated the lessons, which struck him as useless and boring. (All of his teachers found him rebellious to some degree.)

That summer, 1902, Taneyev sent another pupil, Reinhold Glière [1662], to Sontsovka to get down to compositional training in earnest. Prokofiev liked Glière, whom he bulldozed into letting him write a symphony—of whose hymnbook harmonies Taneyev did not think much. With guidance by mail from his mentors, Prokofiev went on composing furiously but not to the exclusion of other passionate interests—botany, chess, photography, and stamp collecting, for example. He also seems to have been something of a hellraiser among his playmates.

In 1904 his mother took him to St. Petersburg (where she would live with him) to enter the conservatory there. Rimsky-Korsakov [1416] was on the entrance examining board and pronounced him just the sort of pupil he wanted to work with. However, he assigned him to Liadov [1485], who soon did not share his view, for Prokofiev, restive at having to apply rules to his composing, gave him little other than trouble. Nor were the other students, generally of maturer years, much taken with this little whippersnapper. Before the academic year was out, however, revolution had swept the nation, there had been a student protest, Rimsky had been fired, most of the rest of the staff had walked out, and the school was closed.

The conservatory was restored to normal in the spring. The following year Prokofiev studied counterpoint with Liadov (who had promoted him without examination from his harmony course) and piano with Alexander Winkler (a fine technician). He also entered on lifelong friendships with two older pupils, the future composer-critic Boris Asafiev (1884–1949), and the future composer Nikolai Miaskovsky [1735]. On the side Prokofiev wrote steadily and ambitiously, producing, among other things the opera *Undine*, six piano sonatas, a violin sonata, and a string quartet—most of them stillborn or later disavowed.

In his third year the embryo composer began studying orchestration with Rimsky himself. Despite his admiration for Rimsky's music, Prokofiev seems to have regarded his studies as one more onerous necessity, and his teacher wrote him off as slovenly and immature. He fared, however, much better with Nikolai Tcherepnin [1642], under whom he studied score reading and conducting. On New Year's Eve 1908, he made his first appearance as pianist and composer in one of a series of concerts devoted to modern music; the audience responded enthusiastically to his playing, but some found the music puzzling. Nor was the examining board in the spring exactly thrilled with his submissions—the juvenile sixth sonata and a scene from the aborted opera *A Feast in Plague-Time* after Pushkin—but allowed him to graduate as a composer anyhow. Prokofiev, however, decided he also wanted certification as a pianist and returned in the fall to study with Anna Essipova, who found him so disorganized and intractible that she threatened to kick him out.

In 1910 Prokofiev's father died, but his mother saw to it that he continued his studies. Increasingly he came to conduct the student orchestra and operatic performances at the conservatory, and at one concert he led his orchestral pieces *Dreams*, Op. 6, and *Autumnal Sketch*, Op. 8—reportedly rather sticky pieces, now largely forgotten. It was also in 1910 that he played for the first time in Moscow. From that period on, he found himself rapidly becoming famous—or notorious. Attempts to get his music published were, however, at first unsuccessful; but in 1911 Jurgenson gave him a pittance for the (official) first piano sonata (a rewrite of the second juvenile effort) and some other piano pieces. Jurgenson remained his publisher for five years, after which Prokofiev signed an exclusive—and later inconvenient—contract with Serge Koussevitzky [1655]. Still one more opera, *Magdalena*, begun about this time, was aborted, but in 1912 the first piano concerto was hailed in both Moscow and St. Petersburg. In September he completed the second of his mature piano sonatas and probably began the second piano concerto. This, performed a year later in St. Petersburg, after its composer had visited Paris and London, created an uproar, and Alexander Siloti adamantly refused to conduct it in his concert series, saying in so many words that it stank. However, Prokofiev persuaded the conservatory against all precedent to allow him to offer the earlier concerto as his graduation exercise in May 1914 (Nikolas Tcherepnin conducted) and was awarded the Rubinstein Prize with his diploma.

Prokofiev had planned to start immediately on a new opera based on Dostoievsky's *The Gambler* but instead decided to return to London with an acquaintance, Walter

Nuvel, to take in the season of Diaghilev ballets. He had been following the successes of Igor Stravinsky—whom he had met and offended—and perhaps thought that he could do as well. Through Nuvel he met the impresario, played his second concerto for him, and won a commission for a "prehistoric" Russian ballet (Stravinsky's *Sacre du printemps* had épatered large numbers of the bourgeois the year before). The scenario was to be developed by a fashionable avant-garde poet named Sergei Gorodetsky, who came up with a story involving the rescue of a Scythian maiden from an evil god. The work was called *Ala and Lolli.* (Ala was the maiden; Lolli was not her pop but her rescuer.)

Soon after Prokofiev returned home, a war that was to involve most of Europe broke out. As the nominal supporter of his widowed mother, the composer was at first exempt from service; later he won a student deferment by taking classes at the conservatory. While the ballet dragged on, he also wrote a surprisingly direct and lyrical setting of Hans Christian Andersen's *The Ugly Duckling,* and revised his Op. 5 *Sinfonietta* for a performance by Siloti, who had belatedly gotten aboard the Prokofiev bandwagon. In February 1915 Prokofiev, taking his ballet with him, went by way of the Balkans to Italy to unveil it to Diaghilev. The latter arranged to have Bernardino Molinari conduct an all-Prokofiev concert in Rome but flatly rejected the ballet. (Prokofiev had tried to out-*Sacre* Stravinsky, but Diaghilev found the music boring.) Instead he commissioned another, *The Buffoon* (or *Chout)* on a plot found in a collection of Russian folktales lent them by Stravinsky, whom it had supplied with the idea for *The Wedding.* The ballet was finished before the year was out, but the composer sent word (however true) to Diaghilev that the war made his return to Italy impossible, and it had to wait until 1921 when, thanks to inferior choreography and poor timing, it flopped. In the meantime Prokofiev extracted an orchestral suite *(Scythian Suite)* from the earlier ballet and in January 1916 conducted it at a concert of the now wholly converted Siloti, who chortled at the audience's discomfiture.

Having put aside a violin concerto that refused to jell, Prokofiev was now ready to give his full attention to *The Gambler* and made such progress that the Maryinsky Theater scheduled it for the 1916–17 season, thanks to the interest of music director Albert Coates. An encounter with Koussevitzky later that year produced not only the publishing contract previously noted but

also a promise from Koussevitzky to conduct the *Scythian Suite* at Moscow in December. But in December the military called up several key men from the orchestra, and at the last minute the concert was scrubbed. Ironically Leonid Sabaniev, an influential critic and an implacable enemy of Prokofiev, published, unaware of the cancellation, a blistering review of the piece and its performance, and lost his job.

Immersed in preparations for the premiere of *The Gambler,* Prokofiev seems not to have been deeply concerned with the revolution in the winter of 1917. He appears to have been a political *naïf* all his life; and besides, the changeover put the wholly sympathetic Siloti in charge of the Maryinsky Theater. But revolt was in the air, and shortly afterward the singers and musicians announced that the work was impossible to sing or play and that they were not going to try. They were good as their word, and *The Gambler* in fact was not put on until 1929, at Brussels in a considerably revised form.

The year 1917 saw the completion of the first violin concerto and the official first ("Classical") symphony, which was to become its composer's first international success of moment. If the concerto showed his lyric side, the symphony showed his ability to deal with Haydnesque **[871]** form in a modern idiom. He also completed the third and fourth piano sonatas, based on material from (respectively) the third and fifth of the juvenile sonatas and, in the second instance, also from the immature symphony of 1908. (The official second sonata dates from 1912.) He was also working on the third piano concerto and the cantata *Seven, They Are Seven.*

After a Petrograd concert, Prokofiev was introduced to the American magnate Cyrus McCormack, there on a diplomatic mission. Prokofiev had admired McCormack reapers in his childhood, and McCormack was a patron of music back home, so the two hit it off very well. In passing, the industrialist told the composer to look him up if he should ever visit the United States. The remark planted an idea in Prokofiev's mind. But at the importunings of his mother, fretting at a spa in the Caucasus Mountains over the gloomy new reports, he went south to join her and found himself trapped there by the chaos that had broken loose. He finished the cantata and in March 1918, after months of enforced idleness, he decided, come hell or high water, to go home, raise some cash, and head for what he regarded as the Promised Land. In Moscow, after a harrowing journey, he found Koussevitzky, on the eve of his own departure, and managed to extract several thousand rubles in advance (which later proved nigh valueless) from him. Proceeding to Petrograd, he raised more money by giving concerts—premiering the new sonatas and the *Classical Symphony.* He was introduced to a commissar and wangled an open-end passport from him. On May 7 he took what proved to be the last trans-Siberian train for some months.

It was three weeks before he reached Tokyo. He had intended to go first to South America to capitalize on the concert season there, but the delay had rendered that idea impracticable. So, after four concerts in Japan, he sailed instead for San Francisco in August. He would have arrived penniless had not some fellow passengers lent him a few hundred dollars. On disembarking he was detained and grilled for several days on suspicion of being a Bolshevist agent. Then, having heard that New York was where the action was, he took a train thither. He was not met with a red carpet, however appropriate, but other Russian emigrés found him a place to sleep and included him in a Brooklyn Museum concert. On November 20 he gave a solo recital at Aeolian Hall, which drew curiosity seekers and produced reviews depicting him as a Russian wild man. It also produced a contract for him to record some Duo-Art piano rolls and small commissions from a couple of publishers, which latter he rejected as not worth his while. Disappointed in New York, he swallowed his pride and sought out McCormack in Chicago. Here things seemed more promising: Frederick Stock led the Chicago Symphony in the *Scythian Suite* and Cleofonte Campanini agreed to produce a new opera, *The Love for Three Oranges,* based on a fantasy by Carlo Gozzi, at the Civic Opera, giving him a sizable advance. Despite a string of illnesses—scarlet fever, diphtheria, an ulcerated throat—he managed to finish it by autumn 1919 as stipulated. But shortly afterward Campanini succumbed to pneumonia and the plans were shelved. After a few more discouraging months in New York, Prokofiev sailed for Paris in April 1920. There he found Diaghilev reviving plans for *The Buffoon* and spent the summer revising the score.

Returning to Chicago in the fall, he was at loggerheads with the Civic Opera over *The Love for Three Oranges,* and when it became obvious that the new season would not see it staged, he opted for a concert tour that took him to California. There he met Lina Llubera, a Cuban soprano of Russian ancestry, and, apparently for the first time in his life, he fell in love.

In January 1921, after an upheaval at the Chicago Opera, its star soprano Mary Garden was appointed "directa" (her term) and promptly let Prokofiev know that his opera was in the works for the coming season. Returning to Europe, he observed the *Buffoon* disaster, and retired to Brittany, where he quickly wrote his third—and most successful—piano concerto and some songs to texts by the Russian poet Constantin Balmont, whom he found living nearby. Back in America in the fall, he presented the concerto in Chicago (with moderate success) and New York (unsuccessfully), then settled in to see that the opera got staged. After more delays it did, on December 30 with the composer conducting. A flattered public applauded, but the press generally did not. It had one more outing in Chicago and then was offered once in New York, where it was roundly damned. Giving up all hope of a career in America, Prokofiev returned to Europe, settling in Ettal, a Bavarian village near Oberammergau. More normal conditions between Russia and the rest of the world allowed him to have his mother, now ill with a heart condition, brought there. For the next several months he made ends meet by concertizing throughout Western Europe, where the concerto was favorably received. But it was not a productive time: there was a suite from *The Buffoon,* some revisions, and work on *The Fiery Angel,* an opera that gave him endless trouble. In the fall of 1923 he married his Lina and moved to Bellevue, a suburb of Paris.

In Paris Marcel Darrieux gave the long-delayed premiere of the first violin concerto under Koussevitzky's direction. The reviewers execrated it as "sentimental," one of the dirtiest of words in that "neo-classical" era, though they approved the revised second piano concerto and the savage *Seven, They Are Seven.* No one, including the composer, liked the fifth piano sonata, which he revised and re-revised right up to his last days. While all this was going on in 1924, the composer's mother died and his wife bore him a son, who was named Sviatoslav.

Sensing that "modern" music was what was wanted and refusing to fall into the trap of neo-classicism on the Stravinskyan model, Prokofiev now went to work on a complex and dissonant second symphony (which was formally modeled on the last piano sonata of Beethoven [1063]!). Obviously what was wanted was not *this* sort of modern music, for when it was presented in the summer of 1925, it was a disaster. Meanwhile, however, Diaghilev had somewhat wearied of Stravinsky and unexpectedly suggested that Prokofiev write him a "Soviet" ballet. (In fashionable circles the Russian system was beginning to be viewed through pink-tinted glasses.) Prokofiev enthusiastically began a piece that would show the interaction between men and machines in a factory. Diaghilev, for reasons of his own, christened it *Le Pas d'acier (The Steel Step).* Work was interrupted in the fall when the Prokofievs had to return to the United States for a concert tour. Prokofiev himself appeared seven times in five cities with the Boston Symphony, thanks to Koussevitzky, its new conductor and found that his audiences had grown up to the third piano concerto. He also appeared in solo recitals and in joint concerts with Lina. In the spring of 1926 the pair toured Italy and the composer finished the new ballet. That summer he wound up *The Fiery Angel,* which Bruno Walter intended to put on at the Berlin Municipal Opera. He also, on commission from the Steinway Company, wrote an overture (known as the "American") for seventeen musicians.

That fall, despite his misgiving about the censorious activities of the Russian Association of Proletarian Musicians (RAPM), he accepted the latest of several invitations to visit his homeland. The trip, which he undertook in January 1927, was at least on the surface a love feast. But the Russian premiere of *The Love for Three Oranges* was not a success—as the German premiere had not been the previous autumn, and as the French premiere was not to be. In May Prokofiev joined Diaghilev in Monte Carlo to tie up the loose ends of the new ballet. Its premiere in June was sufficiently heartening to elicit a new commission from the impresario: a treatment of the story of the Prodigal Son. When the director Vsevolod Meyerhold proposed that he produce *The Gambler* in Leningrad, Prokofiev turned to the revision of that work, though as it happened the work was rejected by the RAPM, as was *Le Pas d'acier,* as being out of line with Marxist-Leninist thinking. In the meantime the production of *The Flaming Angel* had also fallen through. Prokofiev, who had discovered he could salvage something from his failures by extracting orchestral suites from them, started to act accordingly here but found the material turning into a third symphony, which he completed in 1928, the year his second son (and last child) Oleg was born. That summer Koussevitzky conducted the second act of the opera in a Paris concert, but the whole was not staged (successfully!) until the year after its composer's death.

The new ballet was completed by February 1929 and was accepted by Diaghilev for immediate production. There intervened the Brussels premiere of *The Gambler* in April

(reasonably successful) and that of the third symphony under Pierre Monteux in Paris (generally seen askance by the critics). Despite attempts by some of those involved to scuttle *The Prodigal Son,* it was well received in May, four days after the symphony's debut. It was, however, to be the last Diaghilev commission, for the impresario died suddenly that August. It was successful everywhere the company performed it, and when Prokofiev was asked by Koussevitzky that summer for a new symphony (his fourth) to celebrate the Boston Symphony's golden anniversary, he turned to the new ballet (though chiefly to rejected material originally meant for it).

Having attained to some affluence, Prokofiev treated himself to an automobile, which he proceeded to wreck in October, hurting his hands so that he had to give up his Russian concerts that winter—though he made the trip anyhow. The following spring he and Lina undertook a second North American tour (which included Canada and Cuba)—it was very successful (there was a commission for a string quartet from the Library of Congress) and quite tiring. Nevertheless on his return to Europe, Prokofiev went on concertizing until summer, when he settled down to work on the quartet and on a ballet for the Paris Opera—something about Soviet peasants called *On the Dnieper.* It was danced unsuccessfully in 1932, and both it and the orchestral suite derived from it are among the least-known of the composer's larger works. In 1931 Prokofiev was pleased to receive a commission for a fourth piano concerto from the one-armed Austrian pianist Paul Wittgenstein. Typically Wittgenstein was less than delighted with what he got, refused to play it, and shelved it. (It was not heard until three years after Prokofiev died.) Disappointed, the composer set to work on a fifth (two-handed) piano concerto, which was applauded when he played it in Berlin under Wilhelm Furtwängler [1803] in 1932, on his way back to Russia. That tour was followed by another tour of the United States, where he was now highly regarded and where he heard Bruno Walter give the first performance of *Portraits,* the inevitable suite from *The Gambler.*

By 1933 Prokofiev was so seriously considering a permanent return to Russia that he acquired an apartment in Moscow, though he continued to live a peripatetic existence. Various explanations have been offered for the decision (which became firm in 1936)—the disbanding of the RAPM, the opportunities provided by the Soviet film industry, disenchantment with the bourgeois West—but most commentators think the motive boils down to homesickness. In 1933 his arm was twisted with two commissions—to write a score for a satirical film, *Lieutenant Kijé,* and another for a theatrical extravaganza on Antony and Cleopatra, using material from Shakespeare, Shaw, and Pushkin. The suite drawn from the first was an instant world-wide success; the play was a disaster, and *Egyptian Nights,* based on its music, is virtually forgotten. There were also Western commissions—for a two-violin sonata, a cello concerto, an orchestral piece, and a second violin concerto—the last for Robert Soetans. The orchestral piece, entitled *Symphonic Song* was, in fact, first performed in Moscow in 1934, where it was, according to reports, met with silence. Prokofiev and Soetans successfully and enjoyably toured the concerto in Iberia and North Africa in 1935. But the cello concerto, also unveiled in Russia in 1938, was another failure.

In 1934 Prokofiev was excited by a commission from the Kirov Ballet in Leningrad to write a full-length ballet on Shakespeare's *Romeo and Juliet.* He went to work and had completed the whole thing in piano score by September 1935. He had hardly begun when the Kirov decided against the work, for whatever reason, but he managed to peddle it to the Bolshoi Ballet in Moscow. But when the company heard the music, it rejected it out of hand as "undanceable." True to form, Prokofiev extracted two orchestral suites from the score (later a third and a set of piano arrangements) that served to familiarize the world with the music. Eventually the work was premiered in Brno, Czechoslovakia, in 1938 (Prokofiev did not attend), but Russia had to wait until 1940, when the Kirov finally put it on. It was immediately thereafter proclaimed a masterpiece. The year 1935 saw also the piano suite *Music for Children,* which a dozen years later became the basis of the orchestral *Summer Day Suite.* It was followed in May 1936 by the most successful of all his works for children, *Peter and the Wolf,* for narrator and orchestra.

That same year Prokofiev took the final step: he moved his family to Moscow and they all became Soviet citizens. Shortly before, triggered by Stalin's displeasure with the "immorality" of Shostakovich's **[2094]** opera *Lady Macbeth of the Mtsensk District,* Commissar Georgi Zhdanov had unleashed an attack on that composer's music as being unsuitable to the Soviet state and carrying an implied warning to other composers. Prokofiev was not worried. He had turned out some "mass songs" for the proles; he was writing a big cantata to celebrate the twentieth anniversary of the October Revolution.

He produced a work for recitation and orchestra designed to interest children in the latter; never mind that some grumbled about its "lack of social significance"—it was a palpable hit everywhere. To celebrate the centenary of the death of Pushkin (one of his favorite writers), he was asked to supply music for a film version of the *Queen of Spades* and stagings of *Boris Godunov* and a dramatized *Eugene Onegin.* He had no trouble getting passports for European-American tours at the end of the year and again in 1938; he planned another for 1940. Somewhat ominously, however, the three Pushkin projects went up in smoke. Prokofiev put the music aside for later use and turned his attention to writing a score for the quasi-historical film *Alexander Nevsky,* produced and directed by his friend Sergei Eisenstein. He had stopped off in Hollywood on one of his recent American trips and investigated film music as thoroughly as time would allow. By the autumn of 1940 he had written some remarkable music for a remarkable film, and the "cantata" he drew from it the next year became another Prokofiev classic.

Meanwhile he had decided to write a patriotic opera. For a subject he chose the story of Semyon Kotko (the name became the opera's title), a heroic Ukrainian partisan in the upheavals of 1918, set forth in the novel *I Am a Son of the Working People* by Valentin Kataiev. It was to be produced by the Stanislavsky Theater under the direction of Meyerhold. But in 1939, as he finished the score, he was directed to deal with Serafima Birman, who, he was told, was assuming the burden of the production: Meyerhold had dropped out, owing to overwork. In fact Meyerhold had damned the government's artistic policy, been arrested, and was never heard from again; his wife was later found murdered. *Semyon Kotko* finally saw the light of day in the spring of 1940, during which time Prokofiev completed his sixth piano sonata. Though the opera is now looked upon favorably in Russia, it was disapproved of then and soon vanished from the stage.

It was that same spring that Prokofiev met and was swept off his feet by a young woman writer, Mira Mendelson. He was forty-nine, she twenty-five. Exactly what happened is not clear, but to all intents and purposes he left Lina (probably divorced her) to take up housekeeping with Mira, whom he never officially married. (In 1948 Lina was imprisoned as an enemy agent until after Stalin's death in 1953. In 1959 she sued Mira for a share of Prokofiev's estate. She lost the suit, but afterward the government awarded her a pension.)

At the very outset of their relationship,

Mira urged Prokofiev to try another comic opera and suggested Richard Brinsley Sheridan's *The Duenna*. He liked the idea, she wrote a libretto, and the opera, which was called *Betrothal in a Monastery*, was completed within the year. At the same time the composer was working on another big ballet, *Cinderella*, which the Kirov, delighted with the success of its predecessor, had commissioned. Neither work was, however, to be staged for a long time, owing to Hitler's invasion of Russia in June of 1941. As an artist Prokofiev found himself regarded as a national treasure, and in August he and Mira were removed out of immediate danger far south to Nalchik in the Kabardino-Balkar S.S.R. There he wrote a second string quartet, on folk themes from the region; but more importantly he and Mira worked hard on a new opera, *War and Peace*, based on Tolstoy's epic novel and a product of the uprush of patriotism inspired in the Soviets by the war. Rather oddly, the two had planned a short, intimate opera focusing on the main characters, but the nature of the work and official urging caused it eventually to expand beyond practical bounds.

Toward the end of 1941, the couple was moved farther south to Tbilisi, where an active cultural life perhaps helped make up for cramped quarters, and where the opera was completed in piano score. About the same time the seventh piano sonata was also finished. Then, on the invitation of Eisenstein, whose operations had been moved to Alma Ata in Kazakhstan, near the northwest Chinese border, Prokofiev made the long journey thither to collaborate on a two-part film, *Ivan the Terrible*. Work, however, went at a snail's pace, and the composer, to keep busy and stave off boredom, wrote four other film scores (which appear not to have survived in concert form), reworked the fifth piano sonata, began the choral-orchestral *Ballad of an Unknown Boy*, and made a start on a new opera, *Khan Buzay*, which never got far beyond the planning stage.

At this point the Kirov people contacted him from Perm (later Molotov) in the European Urals to say that they were ready, willing, and able to stage *Cinderella*. Since Eisenstein had not yet got to Part II of his film, Prokofiev took a train for Perm, arriving in mid-1943. In actuality the ballet was not realized for nearly two years (in Moscow), so he devoted part of his Permian period to writing a flute sonata (which, at the request of David Oistrakh, he converted in 1944 into a violin sonata, calling it his second, although he had never completed one begun in 1938). In the autumn he and Mira returned at last to Moscow. There was talk

of a production there of *War and Peace*, but it came to nothing. Prokofiev spent the next several months working on various projects, including Eisenstein's film score and the orchestration of the ballet. During the summer of 1944 he was with a stellar group of Soviet composers at Ivanovno, an estate maintained some fifty miles west of Moscow by their union. The stay produced an eighth piano sonata (first played that December by Emil Gilels), and the fifth symphony, which the composer himself conducted at Moscow in mid-January, 1944. It was hailed as a masterpiece and remains one of his most admired works.

Despite his vigor and energy, Prokofiev had been getting signals that he had inherited his mother's defective circulatory system. Not long after the premiere of the symphony, he suffered a heart spasm at a reception, lost his balance, and toppled down a stairway, incurring a severe brain concussion. He spent the next four months restively in bed. By June, however, he had convinced the physicians that he was well enough to go to Leningrad for a performance of the first half of *War and Peace*. It was all of the work he was to see performed in his lifetime. Returning to Ivanovno in the summer he worked determinedly, doubtless sensing that his time was limited. He wrote a curious instrumental *Ode to the War's End* (scored for eight harps, four pianos, military band, percussion ensemble, and double basses), finished *Ivan the Terrible*, completed the piano score of the sixth symphony, and made real headway on the ninth piano sonata. In November the Bolshoi Ballet managed to beat the Kirov in giving the first performance of *Cinderella*, but attacks of vertigo and migraines sent Prokofiev back to the hospital about that time. When the doctors released him in the spring, he followed their suggestion that he go to some quiet place, moving to a house in Nikolina Gora, a village outside the capital. It was not a productive year. Much of the time he rested while Mira read to him. He did manage finally to complete the first violin sonata, which Oistrakh gave its first public hearing in October. In November the Kirov company presented the first performances of *Betrothal in a Monastery*, and in December the Bolshoi Ballet brought forth its version of *Romeo and Juliet*.

By the end of summer 1947 the new symphony was ready, and shortly afterward he dedicated the completed ninth piano sonata to Sviatoslav Richter, who first played it in public. Prokofiev made the trip to Leningrad in October to hear Yevgeni Mravinsky lead the Leningrad Philharmonic in the premiere of the sixth symphony. Listeners and reviewers alike hailed it as a triumphant thanksgiving for the end of the war. Dogged determination to create in spite of illness and pain drove the composer that fall to completely rework the fourth symphony, to write an orchestral poem, *30 Years*, as an anniversary remembrance of the Revolution, and follow it up with a cantata *Flourish, Mighty Homeland!* to the same end. There was also a sonata for solo violin.

It was at this point that Stalin decided it was time to get the Soviet artists to toe the line, whatever it was. Zhdanov, now a certified hero for his defense of Leningrad during the Nazi siege, was put back on the trail he had begun pursuing a dozen years before. He began by suggesting to the reviewers that they had misjudged the new symphony. They reconsidered, saw that it was no Soviet hymn of victory but a piece of decadent bourgeois cynicism, and said so in print. Zhdanov then summoned to a meeting in Moscow Prokofiev, Shostakovich, Miaskovsky, Aram Khachaturian [2038], Vissarion Shebalin [2017], and Gavril Popov [2054]. Miaskovsky, now sixty-seven and with only two more years to live, ignored the summons. The rest were subjected to a three-day tirade and told to recant their sins in public. These sins were set forth in the press in detail. Those of the culprits who held professorships or other posts were dismissed. The rubberstamp Composers' Union blacklisted much of Prokofiev's output—the ballets of the European years; *The Flaming Angel;* the fifth piano concerto; symphonies nos. 3, 4, and 6; and the sixth through the ninth piano sonatas.

Such actions seem to have had little negative effect on the Russian public and a positive one on Prokofiev: he went back to composing. The Kirov wanted an opera. *The Story of a Real Man,* based on Boris Polevoi's "true novel" about Alexei Meresiev, a heroic Soviet fighter pilot in World War II, was ready by December 1948. Forthwith it was given a concert performance before some bigwigs, pronounced unacceptable, and shelved until 1960, when the Bolshoi staged it. No matter. The Bolshoi wanted a new ballet. He found a plot in a folk tale from the Urals and set to work on *The Stone Flower,* which by 1951 had spun off two orchestral suites, a rhapsody, and a fantasy, though the work as a whole was not staged until 1954. For a brilliant young cellist named Mstislav Rostropovich, who had caught his attention, he devised a sonata.

At the end of August 1949 Prokofiev was incapacitated by a stroke but typically fought his way back and by October was working on a choral-orchestral suite for the children's program of the State Radio, which he completed in January 1950. Later that year, after another setback, he wrote an oratorio, *On Guard for Peace.* Ironically, though he was still under official censure, it won him the 1951 Stalin Prize. Forbidden by his doctors to work more than twenty minutes a day, he began, for Rostropovich, a "symphony-concerto" for cello and orchestra, based on the unsuccessful earlier concerto but initially designated as Concerto No. 2. This was followed by another propagandistic symphonic poem, *The Volga Meets the Don,* commemorating the completion of the canal that joins the two rivers. His head was now teeming with projects—a two-piano concerto, a rewrite of the second symphony, a *Concertino* for cello, another sonata for cello and two more for piano—but he turned his chief attention to a seventh symphony. He completed the piano score in the summer of 1952, but left the writing out of the orchestration to a disciple. Yet he was at the Moscow premiere in October and saw himself vindicated in the reaction of the audience and the press reviews. It was his last completed work (the cello *Concertino* was well enough along to be completed by other hands). In February 1953 he fell ill with influenza, but, though it weakened him still more, he was able by March to work with Lavrovsky, the Bolshoi choreographer, on plans to stage *The Stone Flower.* On the fifth he had another stroke and died that evening. That same day Joseph Stalin also died.

RECORDINGS: It would perhaps be best to detail what has *not* been forthcoming. There are recordings of all the operas from *The Gambler* on; all the ballets in whole or in part; all the mature symphonies, sonatas, concerti, quartets. Even such rarities as the incidental music to *Eugene Onegin* and *Egyptian Nights* have been recorded by Melodiya. Of the film music, only the two works that Prokofiev arranged for concert performance, plus the "oratorio" arranged by Abram Stasevich from *Ivan the Terrible* have appeared. Of the choral and orchestral works there are perhaps some patriotic pieces missing. All of the piano music has been recorded, but the songs have received scant attention. Apart from the early piano rolls, Prokofiev, in the 1930s, recorded the third piano concerto and some piano pieces.

[1852] CHAMPAGNE, Claude (Shàm-pàn-yə, Klōd)
VIOLINIST, EDUCATOR
BORN: Montreal, May 27, 1891
DIED: Montreal, December 21, 1965

At birth Champagne was registered as "Adonaï Desparois." His grandfather was a fiddler, and the future composer cut his teeth on French-Canadian popular music. He learned to play several instruments and to compose after a fashion, but his formal education was truncated. He played saxophone in the Canadian Grenadier Guards Band and taught violin at the Collège du Varenne in Montreal. In 1921 he went to Paris to study seriously—at the Paris Conservatoire with André Gédalge (1856–1926), Koechlin [1592], and Laparra [1685], and at the Schola Cantorum with the Russian violinist-composer Julius Conus (1869–1942). During his eight years there he married and heard his *Suite Canadienne* and his symphonic poem *Hercule et Omphale* premiered by Paris orchestras. He returned to Montreal in 1929 and from 1930 taught at McGill University and the École Vincent d'Indy, as well as serving as coordinator of music education in Catholic elementary schools in the city. In 1942 he founded the Montreal Conservatory of Music and Dramatic Arts, of which he was associate director. In 1945 he was visiting professor at the Conservatory of Rio de Janeiro. In 1964 he was the subject of a documentary film, *Bonsoir, Claude Champagne,* and was the dedicatee of Montreal's new concert hall. He died suddenly the next year while addressing Christmas cards. A good deal of his rather small *oeuvre* is influenced by or based on French-Canadian folk music. (The largest single category is that of choral arrangements.) However, he also—especially in his later works—exhibits a knowledge of modern French music from Debussy [1547] to Messiaen [2129]. RECORDINGS: There is a recording of the 1945 *Symphonie gaspésienne* (said to be his most important work). From Radio Canada we have the orchestral *Paysanna,* 1953; *Danse villageoise,* 1929; the piano concerto, 1948; the orchestral-choral *Suite Canadienne,* 1928; *Images du Canada français;* and *Altitude,* 1960 (the latter also including a prominent part for the electronic Ondes Martenot); and the string quartet, 1951.

[1853] PORTER, Cole Albert

BORN: Peru, Ind., June 9, 1891
DIED: Santa Monica, Calif., October 15, 1964

It is perhaps a surprise to find that Cole Porter, that quintessential American socialite-sophisticate, originated in the Middle West. However, his parents had a great deal of money and meant for him to do the right things with it. His beloved mother taught him the piano, sent him to a local music school, and saw to it that his first composition, *The Bobolink Waltz,* written when he was eleven, was published. Shipped off to the Ivy League, he allegedly prepared for legal studies as a Yale undergraduate, though he spent most of his time writing music for student shows. (To this day his football songs "Bingo Eli Yale" and "Bull Dog" are a part of student culture there.) On graduating in 1913, he enrolled at Harvard Law School, but in 1915, when the song "Esmeralda" was inserted in the Broadway musical *Hands Up*—nominally a Sigmund Romberg [1821] show—Porter apologized to his parents and spent the next year studying music instead.

His first all-original score was heard in New York in 1916 when *See America First* opened (and rapidly closed) at the Maxine Elliott Theater. The story that he fled to France, joined the Foreign Legion, and fought gallantly was one that he himself later perpetrated. In 1919 he studied with d'Indy [1462] at the Schola Cantorum, married, and became a legendary party giver. Most of his songs in the 1920s were heard in social rather than in theatrical circumstances, though his ballet *Within the Quota* was premiered in Paris in 1923. His next Broadway show, *Paris*—he had contributed a song apiece to two others in the interim—opened in 1928 and ran for six months. Its big hit was "Let's Do It," chiefly on account of its lyrics rather than its music—a phenomenon that plagued Porter all of his life. However, for the next three decades, every Porter show was regarded as an occasion, and many of them were brilliant successes—*50 Million Frenchmen,* 1929; *Gay Divorce,* 1932; *Anything Goes,* 1934; *Dubarry Was a Lady,* 1939; *Panama Hattie,* 1940; *Something for the Boys,* 1943; *Mexican Hayride,* 1944; and *Kiss Me, Kate,* 1948. During this same period, 1936–57, Porter did a number of film scores, some based on the stage works, others original. His productivity and success were all the more remarkable because in 1937 his horse had fallen with him, crushing one leg so badly that he lived (despite many operations) in constant agonizing pain and finally had to have it amputated in 1958. His wife died in 1954. His last Broadway show was *Silk Stockings,* which opened in February 1955 and ran for over a year. His last score was *Aladdin* for television in 1958. He lived out his last six years in seclusion in New York.

RECORDINGS: There are innumerable recordings of Porter songs, plus some "original-cast" abridgments of the later shows. Porter made a few recordings accompanying himself at the piano. There is a two-piano recording of the ballet.

[1854] BLISS, (Sir) Arthur Edward Drummond

CONDUCTOR, ADMINISTRATOR, TEACHER
BORN: London, August 2, 1891
DIED: London, March 27, 1975

Arthur Bliss was a composer who began by being dismissed by the musical establishment as hopelessly avant-garde and wound up being dismissed by the avant-garde as hopelessly conservative. Both views were extreme. His father, Francis Edward Bliss, an American of means and taste, had moved to England from Springfield, Massachusetts. His mother, born Agnes Kennard, was an excellent pianist, but her art probably had little impact on her son, since she died when he was four, leaving him with two younger brothers, Kennard and Howard. As a youngster, Bliss showed no special promise in musical terms. He took piano lessons for some years in the growing recognition that he would not have a concert career, and he had a go at the viola. During his five years at Rugby, he wrote a quartet for piano, clarinet, cello, and timpani, whose premiere performance was the occasion for considerable laughter. At Pembroke College, Cambridge, he studied with Charles Wood [1579], graduating in 1913. The next year he entered the Royal College of Music, where he studied for a few months with Stanford [1467]—an experience not to his satisfaction. If, as is often stated, he studied with Vaughan Williams [1633] and Holst [1658], it can only have been after World War I, for neither was there in 1914; but Bliss's memoirs do not bear the allegation out. He volunteered in August 1914, as soon as England entered the struggle, and was in France for most of its duration as an officer on active duty. He was wounded in 1916 in the Battle of the Somme and was gassed at Cambrai shortly before the Armistice.

During the war years Bliss wrote a string quartet, a piano quartet, and other chamber pieces; though they were well received and were published, he later disowned them. Mustered out in 1919, he went into composing on a full-time basis. He received a commission for incidental music for a production of Shakespeare's *As You Like It* at the Lyric Theatre; having thus gotten a foot in the door, he arranged to use the theater for a series of concerts of old and contemporary music, at which he conducted for the first time. A performance of his piano quintet in Paris the next spring, 1920, was a disaster, but it brought him the acquaintance of several of the upcoming French composers of his generation. But it was the London premieres of three experimental compositions for soprano and chamber ensembles that year—*Madam Noy, Rhapsody,* and *Rout*—that got him labeled as a wild man. His storm music for a 1921 production of *The Tempest,* with percussionists all over the theater, seemed to foreshadow some of the "spatial" music of progressives forty years later. During this time Bliss continued to conduct and at one point inherited the Portsmouth Philharmonic from Adrian Boult. The upshot of a love affair (the discovery that another had been preferred to him all along) caused him to destroy several of his manuscripts in a burst of rage. In 1921 he was given a teaching post at the Royal College but soon abandoned it, being sufficiently well off not to have to hold a job. In 1922, under the eye of Vaughan Williams, Bliss composed his *Colour Symphony* (inspired by a manual of heraldry), a much more romantic composition than its immediate predecessors. The premiere in Gloucester Cathedral, at that fall's Gloucester Festival under the composer's baton, was disappointing since the platform was so small that several essential instruments had to be omitted.

In 1923 Francis Bliss, now remarried, decided to return to his homeland, and Arthur went along. They settled in Santa Barbara, California, and Arthur was soon involved in music at Los Angeles and San Francisco. He also tried his hand at acting in Santa Barbara, played opposite twenty-year-old Trudy Hoffmann, fell in love, and married her in the late spring of 1925. The couple returned to London shortly afterward, where their daughters were born in 1926 and 1930. The next several years involved a good deal of traveling, both in Europe and America, but also the composition of several important works, including the oboe and clarinet quintets, the viola sonata, *Music for Strings,* the choral *Pastoral,* and the 1930 oratorio-symphony *Morning Heroes* (in memory of his brother Kennard, who had been killed in the war). In 1933 the Blisses built a home in Somerset overlooking Salisbury Plain. A year later the film magnate Alexander Korda commissioned a score for the H. G. Wells science fiction movie *Things to Come,* thereby setting a precedent in England for having the best composers write film scores. In 1937 Bliss wrote his first ballet, *Checkmate,* for Ninon de Valois and the Sadler's Wells Ballet Company. After serving as a judge on the Brussels Competition

Jury that awarded the Ysaÿe Prize to the young Soviet pianist Emil Gilels, the composer found himself pregnant with a piano concerto and was forthwith commissioned to deliver himself of one for "British Week" at the upcoming New York World's Fair, 1939. The Blisses went for the June 10 premiere (the protagonists were the English pianist Solomon and Sir Adrian Boult), and were caught in America by the outbreak of World War II. Thanks to old friends there, Arthur found employment teaching at the University of California in Berkeley. But the burden of work and the stress of divided loyalties created a long compositional gap, further exacerbated by separation from his family when he went home in 1941 (with a military convoy in which several ships were sunk). In London he was appointed music director of the BBC. (It was Bliss who proposed the Third Programme, devoted to cultural broadcasts.) Finally in the fall of 1943 Trudy and the girls got passage on a Portuguese vessel and joined him at last.

The next year Bliss returned to musical creation with the ballet *Miracle in the Gorbals* for Robert Helpmann, following it with another, *Adam Zero*, in 1946. Satisfied that his musical vein was flowing again, he resigned from the BBC in 1944. In 1949 his first opera, *The Olympians* (libretto by J. B. Priestley), was successfully premiered at Covent Garden. In 1950 he was made Sir Arthur Bliss by King George VI. (In a letter he fantasized a gradual rise in station from "Baron Joy" through the "Marquis of Felicity" and "King Glee" to "Pope Happiness.") In 1951 he wrote the vocal scena *The Enchantress* for Kathleen Ferrier, who died two years later, and in 1952 a piano sonata for the equally tragic Noel Mewton-Wood (a suicide at thirty-one). In 1953 Bliss was named to succeed Sir Arnold Bax [1771] as Master of the (newly enthroned) Queen's Musick. The same year found him arranging the Gay-Pepusch [611] *Beggar's Opera* for the Lawrence Olivier film. Later important works include *Discourse* for orchestra, a violin concerto for Alfredo Campoli, a cello concerto for Mstislav Rostropovich, the orchestral *Meditations on a Theme by John Blow*, *A Knot of Riddles* for baritone and chamber orchestra, a final ballet *The Lady of Shalott*, and an opera for television, *Tobias and the Angel*. He continued to travel widely and to conduct. His last compositions—choral works and *A Wedding Suite* for piano—were written the year before he died.

RECORDINGS: For records Bliss conducted suites from *Checkmate*, *Things to Come*, and *Miracle in the Gorbals*, the *Music for Strings*, the march *Welcome the Queen*, and *Conver-*

sations for chamber ensemble. Other recordings include other versions of most of these, suites from *Adam Zero* and *Christopher Columbus*, *Mélée fantasque*, the revised *Colour Symphony*, *Introduction and Allegro*, the piano concerto, the violin concerto, the cello concerto, the *Edinburgh Overture*, the *Meditations*, *March of Homage*, *Discourse* (all orchestral); the choral-orchestral works *Pastoral* and *Morning Heroes;* the vocal *Madam Noy*, *Rout*, *Serenade*, and *A Knot of Riddles;* a few songs; the oboe and clarinet quintets; and sonatas for viola and for piano.

[1855] GRANDJANY, Marcel Georges Lucien (Gràn-zhà-nē′, Màr-sel′ Zhôrzh Lüs-yon′)
HARPIST, ORGANIST, TEACHER
BORN: Paris, September 3, 1891
DIED: New York, February 24, 1975

After Carlos Salzedo [1791], Grandjany was the best-known virtuoso harpist-composer on the international scene. A prodigy, he was thirteen when he took first prize for harp at the Paris Conservatoire, where he studied the instrument with Henriette Renié and composition with Paul Vidal [1554]. He made his public debut in 1909 at Paris. During the years of World War I he served as organist at the basilica of Sacré Coeur in Montmartre. In 1921 he became professor of harp at the American Conservatory in Fontainebleau, though he continued to concertize. He made his first American appearance three years later. He gave up his teaching post in 1935, emigrated to New York the following year, and was appointed to the faculty of the Juilliard School in 1938. From 1943 he also taught for a score of years at the Montreal Conservatory. Grandjany became an American citizen in 1945. Though he wrote some songs and keyboard pieces, he is best known for his harp compositions, which include a concerto. RECORDINGS: Grandjany recorded his own *Rhapsodie* and *The Children's Hour*. The Louisville Orchestra has recorded his *Aria in Classic Style* for harp and strings.

[1856] GALLON, Noël (Gà-lon′, Nō-el′)
PIANIST, TEACHER
BORN: Paris, September 11, 1891
DIED: Paris, December 26, 1966

Noël Gallon was the younger brother and pupil of the composer Jean Gallon (1878–1959), later professor of harmony at the Paris Conservatoire. Noël himself became a Conservatoire student, taking piano from

Isidor Philipp and composition from Henri Rabaud [1647], among others. Noël was the winner of the 1910 Grand Prix de Rome. In 1920, a year after his brother's appointment, he joined the Paris Conservatoire faculty to teach solfège, later becoming professor of counterpoint. The two Gallons collaborated on the ballet *Hansli le bossu (Hansli the Hunchback)*. Noël also wrote an opera, *Paysans et soldats (Peasants and Soldiers)*, 1911; orchestral and chamber music; and songs—all exquisitely crafted. RECORDINGS: Works on records include a *Cantabile* for clarinet and piano, and some songs.

[1857] PANNAIN, Guido (Pàn-nà'-in, Gwē'-dō)
MUSICOLOGIST, CRITIC, TEACHER
BORN: Naples, November 17, 1891
DIED: Naples, September 6, 1977

Scion of a musical family who provided his early grounding, Pannain studied at the Naples Conservatory and was a 1914 graduate of the Naples University. He returned to the conservatory in 1915 to teach there for forty-six years. By then he was already deeply immersed in research on the music of his native city, on which he became a leading authority. He had also by that time composed a *Requiem,* orchestral pieces, and other works. In 1920 he began a long career as critic for various Neapolitan and Roman publications. Around 1928 he began to take an interest in the directions in which contemporary music was going and wrote a book on modern composers. Perhaps in reaction to what he found, he returned to composition, notably with the late operas *Beatrice Cenci* of 1942 and *Madame Bovary* of 1955, stylistically ripe with nineteenth-century Romanticism. RECORDINGS: There is a scene from *Beatrice Cenci* recorded by Margherita Carosio, who created the title role.

[1858] DONOVAN, Richard Frank
ORGANIST, TEACHER, CONDUCTOR
BORN: New Haven, November 29, 1891
DIED: Middletown, Conn., August 22, 1970

Richard Donovan's career was almost entirely circumscribed by the town of his birth. He took a B.A. from Yale, then acquired a B.Mus. from the Institute of Musical Art (later the Juilliard School) in New York, and studied with Widor [1414] in Paris. He joined the faculty of Smith College in Northampton, Massachusetts, in 1923 but returned to Yale five years later and taught there until 1960, holding the Battell Chair of Theory from 1947. He was also choirmaster-organist at Christ Church in New Haven, conductor of the Bach Cantata Club, and assistant conductor of the New Haven Symphony, as well as an enthusiastic promoter of the Yaddo Festival. His music, always contrapuntal, moved toward the atonal. He wrote orchestral works, including 2 symphonies, but was more productive of choral and chamber music. RECORDINGS: Orchestral or chamber-orchestral works on records include: *New England Chronicle*, 1947; *Suite for Oboe and Strings*, 1945; *Soundings*, 1953; *Epos*, 1963; and *Passacaglia on Vermont Folk Tunes*, 1949. Choral works recorded are the *Mass* and the *Magnificat*. Two chamber works, *Music for Six* and *Elizabethan Lyrics*, have also been released.

[1859] HAUBIEL, Charles Trowbridge *(né Pratt)*
PIANIST, TEACHER, PUBLISHER
BORN: Delta, Ohio, January 30, 1892
DIED: Los Angeles, August 26, 1978

Born in the northwest corner of Ohio, Charles Pratt moved with his parents to New York when he was ten years old. Shortly thereafter he began piano lessons with his sister Florence and began appearing professionally five years later. Following further study with Rudolf Ganz in Berlin (some sources also mention Alexander von Fielitz), he returned in 1913 as accompanist to the Czech violinist Jaroslav Kocián. At some time during this period he took his mother's maiden name, Haubiel, as his own. From 1913 until 1917 he taught piano in Oklahoma, during which period he began to compose. After serving as an officer in World War I, he had his only formal composition training with Rosario Scalero (1870–1954) in New York, where he also undertook advanced piano studies with Josef and Rosina Lhévinne. While still thus engaged, he began teaching at the Juilliard School and at New York University. In 1928 his *Karma Variations* won a first prize in the Columbia Records Schubert-centenary competition (but no recording!). Haubiel left the Juilliard in 1931 and four years later founded the Composer's Press to publish American music (including much of his own). He gave up teaching at NYU in 1947, and in 1954 he married Mary Storke. Twelve years later he sold the press and moved to California, where he died at eighty-six. As a composer, Haubiel began as a Baroque-inspired polyphonist, but later turned to a neo-romantic idiom, in which he wrote a number of American-oriented compositions, including orchestral variations on Foster's [1299] *Swanee River, Pioneers,* and *Ohioana* (violin and piano). RECORDINGS: Some of Haubiel's music was recorded on his own Dorian label and was later transferred to the Orion label. It includes the orchestral *Pioneers, Portraits, Solari, Miniatures,* the *Gothic Variations* for violin and orchestra, sonatas for violin and cello, the chamber piece *In the French Manner, Metamorphoses* for piano, and a few others. (Many of his larger works began as piano pieces.) He himself recorded an LP of teaching pieces published by his press.

[1860] KILPINEN, Yrjö Henrik (Kil'-pē-nen, Ür'-yo Hen'-rik)

TEACHER

BORN: Helsingfors (Helsinki), February 4, 1892

DIED: Helsinki, March 2, 1959

Hailed internationally in the 1930s as the Great Hope of the *Lied,* Kilpinen has fallen into eclipse, though his songs remain popular in his own country. He studied sporadically over a decade at the Helsinki Music Institute, in Vienna, and in Berlin, but was mostly self-taught (which fact perhaps explains the limitations of his music to which some object. Though he wrote some choral pieces and chamber music, his chief output consisted of songs, of which he is said to have produced around 800, many of them still unpublished. He proselytized for *Lieder* throughout Europe, aided by his wife Margaret, a pianist who accompanied many famous singers in them. Musicians in the Third Reich took them up, seeing them as an extension of the nineteenth-century German tradition. Walter Legge of the Gramophone Company wrote a book about them and published an album of recordings sung by the baritone Gerhard Hüsch accompanied by Margaret Kilpinen. In 1942 the composer was given a professorship at the Helsinki Conservatory and six years later was named to the Finnish Academy. The official view today appears to be that most of his work is rather sentimental and simple-minded—one which is perhaps extreme, though one must admit that the songs are often highly romantic. RECORDINGS: There have been more recent recordings by Finnish singers such as TiiNiemela and Martti Talvela and several LPs on the German Da Camera Magna label.

[1861] HONEGGER, Arthur (Ô-ne-gâr', Ar-tür')

VIOLINIST, CONDUCTOR, TEACHER

BORN: Le Havre, March 10, 1892

DIED: Paris, November 27, 1955

One of the more notable members of that ephemeral association of composers tagged "*Les Six français*" by a witty (or desperate) reviewer—and later known simply as "Les Six"—Honegger was probably less in sympathy with the supposed creed of the group or with its mentors (Jean Cocteau and Satie [1578]) than any of his fellows. Despite Honegger's French birth, he was legally Swiss, his parents having come to Le Havre from Switzerland to set up a business in café fixtures. As a child he studied piano with his mother, violin with one Sautreuil, and harmony with an organist named R. C. Martin. When he was seventeen, his father indulged him by sending him to the Zürich Conservatory. His rapid progress there convinced the administration and his family that he should pursue a musical career. In 1911 he returned to Le Havre and for the next several months commuted to Paris for violin lessons with Lucien Capet, founder of the Capet Quartet and professor of violin at the Paris Conservatoire. When his parents moved back to Switzerland the next year, Honegger settled in Paris as a full-time student at the Conservatoire, where his chief teachers were André Gédalge (1856–1926), Widor [1414], and d'Indy [1462]. Though he studied only conducting with the last-named, d'Indy's hard-boiled notions left their mark on the incipient composer, whose other gods were Wagner [1230], Richard Strauss [1563], and, above all, Bach [684]. During his stay at the Conservatoire, Honegger made friends with Darius Milhaud [1868].

In 1914 Honegger was called back to Switzerland for a year's military service. After being discharged, he returned to Paris, where his music was increasingly heard in the concert halls. The nucleus of Les Six was formed in 1916 when he, Georges Auric [1962], Germaine Tailleferre [1863], Francis Poulenc [1960] and Alexis Roland-Manuel (1891–1966) banded together as "Les Nouveaux Jeunes" (The New Young People). The group's inaugural concert at the Théâtre du Vieux-Colombier early in 1918 drew a commission from Jane Bathori, a singer, for music for a sort of masque called *Le Dit des jeux du monde (The Tale of the World's Games)*. By the early 1920s, however, Honegger had virtually divorced himself from the association, abjuring the influences of the music hall and the street fair for sterner stuff.

The opportunity to act on that impulse came early in 1921 with a commission from Swiss playwright René Morax for music for a tragedy about King David. The premiere took place in Mézières in June, Honegger's contribution being singled out for special praise. Thus encouraged, he reworked it as a self-sufficient "dramatic oratorio," *Le Roi David,* which took the musical world by storm from its first presentation in Paris in 1923. Both primitive and polyphonic, it particularly appealed to the general public, much as Georges Rouault's religious paintings did. But just as everyone was deciding that one more supposed modernist had gone conservative, audiences were shocked in 1923 by *Pacific 231,* a study characterized by discord and motoric rhythm, of a big locomotive at full speed—or so Honegger allowed them to believe, admitting privately that the piece was intended as an abstract study in acceleration and deceleration, the title having been a whimsical afterthought.

Honegger never had another success of the enormous magnitude of these. However, one more Biblically inspired work, the opera *Judith,* made an impact when it was introduced at Monte Carlo in 1926, and *Rugby,* a more brutal counterpart of *Pacific 231,* achieved at least notoriety for having been premiered during the halftime of the French-English rugby game at Paris in 1928. These works apart, the late 1920s were a generally fallow period for the composer. Earlier in the decade he had lived for a time with the Irish-Italian singer Claire Croiza *(née* Conelly), who had a son by him. Meanwhile a young pianist, Andrée Vaurabourg, was promoting his piano music in her recitals, and in 1926, after he and Croiza had split up, he married her. She often appeared with him afterward in lecture-recitals. In 1929 Honegger visited America as a guest conductor, and two years later wrote the first of his 5 numbered symphonies on commission from Serge Koussevitzky [1655] in celebration of the Boston Symphony's golden jubilee. (An unnumbered "mimed symphony," *Horace Victorieux,* had appeared in 1921.)

In 1927 Honegger composed a symphonic score for Abel Gance's silent film *Napoléon* (recently revived but with a new musical accompaniment). Over the next two decades he produced an enormous amount of incidental music for stage, radio, and screen; among the film scores one notes music for the 1934 *Crime and Punishment, Mayerling* a year later, and *Pygmalion* in 1938. The 1930s were also marked by a number of more substantial stage works—notably the oratorios *Cris du monde (Cries of the World), Nicolas de Flue,* and most notably *Jeanne d'Arc au bûcher (Joan of Arc at the Stake),* 1938, whose (mostly) nonsinging central role has provided an "operatic" vehicle for actresses otherwise denied access to the stages of important opera houses. One should also mention the 1940 nondramatic oratorio *La Danse des morts (The Dance of Death),* for which Paul Claudel wrote the text, as he had done for *Jeanne.*

Though he might have taken refuge in Switzerland when war erupted in 1939, Honegger elected to stay in Paris, where he aided the French resistance. Otherwise the 1940s are especially notable in his career for having produced his next three symphonies (nos. 3, 4, and 5). In 1947 he returned to America to teach at Tanglewood but was felled by a severe heart attack, which left him semiinvalid for his last eight years. By 1951, however, he was well enough to return to composition and finished his fifth symphony—again for the Boston orchestra. Another heart attack killed him four years later.

RECORDINGS: Honegger conducted several of his own works for the phonograph, including *Le Roi David, Pacific 231, Rugby, Pastorale d'été (Summer Pastoral),* the *Prélude pour la Tempête* and the Concerto for Cello (with Maurice Maréchal). He also accompanied several singers, notably Croiza, in performances of his songs, and appeared as commentator on a disc that offered a sampling of his music. Other musicians have also recorded the aforementioned works a number of times. There are two or more recordings of *Le Roi David, Jeanne d'Arc, La Danse des Morts,* and the *Cantate de Noël.* The opera *Judith,* the 1940 *Nicolas de Flue, Cris du Monde,* and *L'Aiglon* (a 1937 collaboration with Jacques Ibert [1838]) have also been recorded. There is a Soviet recording of *Le Dit des jeux du monde.* The remaining vast body of dramatic music is represented by only a few snippets. None of the ballets have been recorded. Most of the major orchestral works, including the numbered symphonies and *Horace Victorieux* among numerous others, have been recorded. There are representative examples of the chamber, piano, and vocal music.

[1862] **GROFÉ, Ferde** *(né* Ferdinand Rudolph von)
INSTRUMENTALIST, ARRANGER, CONDUCTOR, TEACHER
BORN: New York, March 27, 1892
DIED: Santa Monica, April 3, 1972

Even if Grofé had not written the *Grand Canyon Suite* or orchestrated George

Gershwin's **[1955]** *Rhapsody in Blue,* he would probably have earned a place in musical history as the progenitor of "the big-band sound" in American popular music. He was born into a musical family. His father was a singing actor, his mother a cellist. Her father, Bernard Bierlich, shared the first cello desk at the Metropolitan Opera with Victor Herbert **[1513]**, and later was first cellist of the Los Angeles Philharmonic, where her brother Julius was concertmaster. (She was the teacher of the orchestra's later longtime conductor, Alfred Wallenstein.) The Grofés moved to Los Angeles shortly after their son was born. He learned to read music at a very early age and was soon accompanying his mother. When her husband died in 1899, Mrs. Grofé decided that she was insufficiently equipped to survive as a musician and took her son to Leipzig, where she studied at the conservatory for three years. On returning to Los Angeles, she opened a studio and soon afterward remarried, this time taking a nonmusical spouse.

Grofé's subsequent education—musical and otherwise—was sporadic, and much of it was acquired by osmosis and experiment. For a time he went to the local public schools, where he became acquainted with various band instruments, but at fifteen, his wish to become a professional musician frustrated by his practical stepfather, he ran away from home and supported himself at a number of unskilled jobs, gradually picking up musical engagements as a dance and band musician. He had been writing for a number of years songs that he hoped would be popular, and in 1909 he was commissioned to write a march for the 1909 Elks' reunion, which was subsequently published. Seeing him successful, his family welcomed him home, and he was soon playing viola alongside his uncle in the Philharmonic. In his spare time and in the off-season he played in dance halls up and down the coast (sometimes as "Professor Grofé") and eventually formed his own jazz band in San Francisco, for which he wrote the arrangements. In 1920 Paul Whiteman, who had organized an orchestra of his own in Santa Barbara, took him on as pianist and arranger. His first arrangement to be recorded —"Whispering," on Victor 18690—sold more than a million copies. He moved with the Whiteman Orchestra to New York, where he gave up his role as pianist in 1924 but continued as an arranger until 1931. It was chiefly Grofé who conceived the notion of counterposing solo improvised "breaks" to written-out orchestral *tuttis,* thereby establishing the pattern for such later oleagi-

nous bands as Guy Lombardo's and Lawrence Welk's.

Grofé's success in 1924 with the Gershwin piece made him decide that he wanted to write more ambitious music than he had been producing. His first successful effort was the *Mississippi Suite,* premiered by Whiteman a year later. In 1929 he married Ruth MacGloan and two years later unveiled the *Grand Canyon Suite,* the most wildly successful of all his works. Most of his later efforts were similar—but less happy —attempts to evoke the American landscape. In 1932 he became conductor at the Capitol Theater in New York and was soon much in demand as a guest conductor. He had his own radio series, conducted an all-Grofé concert at Carnegie Hall in 1937, and was appointed to teach orchestration at the Juilliard School in 1939. When America entered World War II, Grofé turned to conducting service bands and USO shows. In 1952 he married for the second time. The bride was a pianist, *née* Anna May Lempton, with whom he later frequently appeared as a duo-pianist. He died a week after his eightieth birthday.

RECORDINGS: Grofé left recordings of his *Aviation Suite,* 1944; *Death Valley Suite,* 1950; *Grand Canyon Suite;* a melodrama, *Atlantic Crossing;* and his D-minor Concerto for Piano (with Jesús María Sanromá as pianist). Other Grofé works on records (mostly led by Whiteman or André Kostelanetz) are the *Hudson River Suite, March for Americans, Metropolis, Mississippi Suite* (several versions), *Three Shades of Blue, Trick or Treat,* and *World's Fair Suite* (composed for the 1964 New York World's Fair). Many first-rank conductors, including Arturo Toscanini, have recorded the *Grand Canyon Suite.* (Just released by CBS as we go to press is a new recording of *Aviation Suite* and *Hudson River Suite.)*

[1863] TAILLEFERRE, Germaine (Tī-yə-fâr', Zher-men')

BORN: Parc-Saint-Maur, April 19, 1892
DIED: Paris, November 7, 1983

Tailleferre was the sole female member of "Les Six," and its predecessor "Les Nouveaux Jeunes"—see Honegger **[1861]**. She embarked on a musical career against parental wishes, was a classmate of Honegger, Auric **[1962]**, and Darius Milhaud **[1868]** at the Paris Conservatoire, and carried off several first prizes there. Later she was one of Ravel's **[1666]** few pupils. Her compositional output was small and carefully crafted. She wrote most of her music after "Les Six" had ceased to be an entity, if it ever was, developing according to her own lights but taking note of what was going on around her. At the outset of World War II, Mlle. Tailleferre moved to New York City, where she lived for some years. She continued to compose well into her eighties. Her *oeuvre* includes operas, ballets, a concerto for piano, another for two pianos (with chorus), a string quartet, sonatas for various instruments, and songs. RECORDINGS: A number of works have been recorded—the *Ballade* for piano and orchestra, 1922; the *Concertino* for harp and orchestra, 1927; the harp sonata; *Overture* to the opera *Il Était un petit navire (There Was a Little Ship); Pastorale* for flute and piano; Trio for Winds; piano pieces; songs. Her contribution to the collectively composed *Les Mariés de la tour Eiffel* has also been recorded.

[1864] NILES, John Jacob
ETHNOMUSICOLOGIST, "FOLKSINGER"
BORN: Louisville, Ky., April 28, 1892
DIED: near Lexington, Ky., May 1, 1980

Niles was the son of a Louisville factotum who carpentered, called square dances, and was active in local politics. The boy's grandfather had manufactured pianos; his mother played them and was a church organist. She taught him to play on a sound classical grounding. His interest in and singing of folksongs dated from his childhood. During the First World War he served in the Army Air Corps and was severely injured in a plane crash. Afterward he studied at the Lyons Conservatory, at the Schola Cantorum in Paris, and with Edgar Stillman Kelley (1857–1944) at the Cincinnati Conservatory. In the late 1920s he published two collections of American soldier songs, the second in collaboration with Douglas Moore [**1884**]. Meanwhile he was spending much of his time tramping the American backwoods collecting folksongs, of which he published several collections. He also learned to make his own dulcimers and lutes to accompany his singing. Around 1940, heralding the first upsurge of popular interest in folk music, RCA Victor recorded (on the prestigious Red Seal series) Niles singing some of his findings. Publicity indicated that he produced his "whisky tenor" (it would now be called countertenor) by standing on his head prior to singing. Much was made of this rude minstrel from the hills, and several of his songs—notably "I wonder as I wander," "Black Is the Color of My True Love's Hair," and "Venezuela"—were taken up by more supposedly sophisticated singers. The first-

named song was an object of wonder to folklorists, who could trace it to no known source or tradition. Later Niles began publishing songs of his own composition, a category to which he eventually admitted the three pieces noted above belonged. He concertized worldwide and occasionally gave courses at prestigious schools such as Juilliard, Curtis, and Eastman. His compositions include an oratorio *Lamentations,* a cantata, and other choral works, as well as many songs, most of which make no pretense of hayseedry. In his mid-eighties he was almost as active as ever on the concert and lecture circuits. RECORDINGS: Apart from his own recordings (which include some of his original songs), there are a few by other singers, notably Mack Harrell and William Parker.

[1865] TAUBER, Richard (Tou'-ber, Rē'-khärt)
SINGER, CONDUCTOR
BORN: Linz, May 16, 1892
DIED: London, January 8, 1948

Tauber was born to fifteen-year-old Elisabeth Denemy, a tyro actress in the Municipal Theater at Linz. His father Richard Anton Tauber, an actor who had appeared with the company the previous season, was unaware that the child was in the offing, and was in fact in the United States when his son was born. Reared by his mother, who became Frau Seiffert, Richard grew up almost literally in a trunk. When the elder Tauber eventually learned of his existence, he assumed full responsibility for his upbringing and gave him his name. He also gave him vocal lessons and a powerful ambition to become an opera singer. But various artists and teachers of stature told him to forget it because he had no voice. His piano teacher Artur Rother (later a noted conductor) persuaded him that he should have a general musical education, and so Tauber enrolled at the Hoch Conservatory at Frankfurt am Main to study conducting and composition —both of which activities he occasionally practiced in the course of his career. Later he met a vocal teacher, Carl Beines of Freiburg im Breisgau, who guaranteed that he could make a singer of him. In 1912 Tauber made his debut as tenor soloist with a Freiburg choir and caused such a stir that he was forthwith offered a contract by the Mannheim opera company. But the elder Tauber had meanwhile become intendant at Chemnitz (now Karl Marx Stadt) and claimed priority for his son's debut. Accordingly young Tauber's first operatic appearance was as Tamino in Mozart's [992] *Die Zauberflöte* at Chemnitz in 1913. (Initially, to avoid confusion with his parent, he billed himself as "Carl Tauber" or "C. Richard Tauber," undoubtedly in tribute to Beines.) Shortly afterward he joined the great Dresden State Opera and by 1915 was singing under Richard Strauss's [1563] direction in Berlin. By 1920 he was the toast of Europe, especially admired as a Mozart singer, and eventually held the title of *Kammersänger* (court singer) in both Germany and Austria. A stocky, florid man who affected a monocle, he was adored by women, undoubtedly for the sensuousness and seductiveness of his singing, which set the model for German lyric tenors. (He was twice married, first to the soprano Carlotta Vanconti, and later to the English actress Diana Napier.) Beginning in the 1920s Tauber's friendship with Franz Lehár [1614] took him increasingly into operetta, and he made several Lehár works—notably *Das Land des Lächelns (The Land of Smiles*—peculiarly his own. The Nazi upheaval sent him to England, where he continued to appear in operas, operettas, films, and concerts up to the very eve of an operation for a cancerous lung, which he did not survive. RECORDINGS: Tauber wrote songs and operettas, notably *Old Chelsea,* 1943, from which he made recordings both as singer and conductor.

[1866] ROSENBERG, Hilding Constantin
(Rō'-sen-ber'y, Hil'-ding Kôn'-stàn-tēn)

ORGANIST, CONDUCTOR, TEACHER
BORN: Bosjökloster, June 21, 1892

At this writing Hilding Rosenberg is ninety-two—the Grand Old Man of Swedish music. A prolific composer who thinks big, he is regarded by many as the most important Swedish composer of this century. A gardener's son, he grew up on a rural estate, where he taught himself to play the violin and the keyboard—the latter well enough to qualify for an organ-playing job in nearby Kalmar (on the southeast coast) when he was seventeen. When the Rosenbergs moved to Trelleborg, at the country's southernmost tip, he found a place there as an orchestral violinist and began writing music. Discovering, however, that he really did not know what he was doing, he (now twenty-two) took a violin sonata which he had written to the Stockholm Conservatory and was admitted as a student on the strength of it. There he studied composition with Ernst Ellberg (1868–1948), but the chief influence on him came from his piano teacher Richard An-

dersson, a Clara Schumann [1267] pupil who taught privately and who saw to it that Rosenberg got a broad education, both musical and academic. Later Rosenberg became friends with Wilhelm Stenhammar [1619], who also exerted a powerful impact on him.

Wanting to be identified as a "Scandinavian" composer, Rosenberg at first took his cue from Sibelius [1575] but was quite unhappy with the symphony that resulted in 1915 and junked all of it but the adagio. In 1920 he went to Dresden for further study, proceeding from there to Paris, always with an ear toward new currents in European music. For a time he experimented with the approaches of Bartók [1734], Stravinsky [1748], and Schoenberg [1657]. After a period spent as a music reviewer in Göteborg, in 1926 he began working with the theater director Per Lindberg in Stockholm, for whom he wrote many of his more than fifty incidental scores for both stage and cinema. In 1927, still dissatisfied with his technique, Rosenberg studied counterpoint with Stenhammar. A few years later he took a course in conducting with Hermann Scherchen, became a coach at the Royal Swedish Opera in 1932, and advanced to first conductor two years later. His first opera, *Resan till Amerika (Voyage to America),* was produced there in 1932. Over the next thirty-eight years he followed it with eight others, including the huge four-part opera-oratorio *Joseph och hans bröder (Joseph and His Brethren,* 1945–48—total running time nearly nine hours). In 1948 he visited the United States as conductor and directed his large-scale fourth symphony, a 1940 choral-orchestral work of seventy-five minutes duration called *Johannes uppenbarelse (The Revelation of St. John).* Rosenberg has also taught, and his pupils include Karl-Birger Blomdahl [2253] and Ingvar Lidholm [2312]. Besides the works noted, Rosenberg has produced 6 ballets, 8 acknowledged symphonies (the last completed at eighty-two), concertos for orchestra (4), violin (2), cello (2), viola, and trumpet; oratorios, cantatas, 12 string quartets, and much other orchestral, choral, and chamber music. By the 1930s he had arrived at his own style—lean, contrapuntal, and diatonic, though in later years he wrote some twelve-tone works.

RECORDINGS: Chiefly of Swedish origin, these include a suite from *Resan till Amerika;* a suite from the 1938 ballet *Orfeus i stan (Orpheus in Town);* Concerto No. 2 for Cello; Concerto No. 2 for Violin; *Lento* for strings; Symphonies Nos. 2, 3, 4, and 6; the *Louisville Concerto* of 1954; the overture to the 1938 opera *The Marionettes;* the 1936

Christmas oratorio *Den heliga natten (The Holy Night)*, which is quite popular in Sweden; the orchestral song cycle *Dagdrivaren (The Herdsman of Days); 14 Chinese Poems* for soprano and piano; a disc of organ works; *Divertimento* for string trio; several string quartets; a set of piano studies; and a few miscellaneous short pieces.

[1867] SORABJI, Kaikhosru Shapurji
(Sō-ráb'-jē, Kĭk-hos'-rōō Shá-poor'-jē)
PIANIST, CRITIC
BORN: Chingford (Essex), August 14, 1892

Sorabji—at the age of ninety-two still active and cantankerous—typically maintains that the facts of his life are no one's business but his own. As given (and he is ignored by many standard references), they are as follows: His father was a successful Indian (Parsi) businessman, his mother a singer of Sicilian and Spanish descent. He was born in a village now at the northeast edge of the London urban sprawl and began composing in his early twenties. Shortly after 1920 he gave a few concerts in Europe and India, then abandoned public performance entirely. Afterward he attracted considerable attention as an astute, acerbic, and highly opinionated reviewer. He published two books of musical criticism: *Around Music* in 1932 and *Mi contra fa* in 1947 (subtitled "The Immoralizings of a Machiavellian Musician"). In 1940 he forbade the performance of any of his works, published or unpublished, and to all intents and purposes vanished from sight as far as the general public was concerned. He wants it known that most of these purported facts are inaccurate and appears especially outraged that some sources claim that he was baptized "Leon Dudley."

The reemergence of Sorabji dates from the early 1970s, when some tapes he had made of his playing found their way to radio and created at least a teapotful of interest among knowledgeable musicians. Around mid-decade, Sorabji gave permission to pianists Michael Habermann and Yonty Solomon to play his music in public, and further relaxations have obviously followed.

For seventy years Sorabji has composed steadily, if not furiously. He has written large- and small-scale orchestral, vocal, and chamber works, but the piano looms largest in his output. On the whole, he thinks big: many of his works (e.g., the *Jami Symphony* for baritone, chorus, and orchestra, which runs to nearly 850 pages of score) are gargantuan, and some of the piano composi-

tions are said to be of a complexity that defies the present state of player technique. His *Opus Clavicembalisticum* (for piano) has, rightly or wrongly, been listed in *The Guinness Book of World Records* as the longest nonrepetitive solo piano composition ever written. Its length is just under four hours. Sorabji has reportedly composed works lasting as long as seven hours. Sorabji has published nothing since the early 1930s. Consequently any evaluation of his music must be based on the very early period plus the few later works recently unveiled in performance. There is talk of likenesses to Busoni [1577], one of the composers execrated by the many, whose cause Sorabji espoused, to Scriabin [1625], to oriental musics, but all that emerges clearly is an image of a highly individual, powerful intellect at work.

RECORDINGS: The complete *Opus Clavicembalisticum* has been recorded (from a concert performance in Utrecht) by Geoffrey Douglas Madge); there are also two LPs of piano pieces by Michael Habermann.

[1868] MILHAUD, Darius (Mē-yō', Där-yüs')
TEACHER, CONDUCTOR, VIOLINIST
BORN: Aix-en-Provence, September 4, 1892
DIED: Geneva, June 22, 1974

Darius Milhaud was perhaps the most famous composer of the mythical "Six"; he was certainly the most prolific, his published works running to nearly 450. He was a compulsive globetrotter, and had, especially as a teacher, a considerable impact on musicians of the next generation in Europe and America. He was a master of his craft, understood (but did not always approve of) the currents of his time, and was intelligent and inventive, doing highly original work in such areas as polytonality and percussion music. Yet he was probably too facile and too unself-critical, for, a handful of works aside, there is little Milhaud that sticks in the repertoire or the memory.

Milhaud's father, a successful exporter, belonged to a Jewish family for centuries settled in Provence. His mother's people were Sephardic Jews from Modena. Milhaud, Sr., was an amateur pianist, his wife an amateur singer, and when their son at four began picking out tunes on the piano, they indulged him in his musical interests. The father taught him piano, and at seven he began violin lessons with Léo Bruquier, a former Paris Conservatoire prizewinner. At ten Milhaud entered the local *lycée*, where he distinguished himself as a brilliant student academically. By the age of twelve he was playing second violin in a string quartet with his teacher. He took harmony lessons from the local bandmaster and had soon written a violin sonata. He had in fact a harmonic sense of his own and was never able to see the link between what he was taught and what he wanted to compose. His closest friends were Léo Latil and Armand Lunel, both budding writers, and later he was strongly influenced by his friendship with other writers—Francis Jammes, Paul Claudel, and Jean Cocteau, among many others.

At sixteen Milhaud passed his baccalaureate examinations and set out with Lunel for Paris and the Conservatoire. He saturated himself in music in the concert halls, delighted in performances by Diaghilev's Ballet Russe, and was bored to distraction by a performance of the Wagner [1230] *Ring*. He continued studying violin with the blind Henri Berthelier, passed the examination, and shortly afterward decided he was tired of the instrument and gave up further study. He took the orchestral class of Paul Dukas [1574], whom he found a poor teacher but an admirable man. After some harmony lessons with Xavier Leroux [1557], he showed him some of his compositions and was told he needed no further study in that field and that he should go to André Gédalge (1856–1926) for composition, which he did. Among the students he came to know Honegger [1861], Ibert [1838], Auric [1962], and Jean Wiéner (1896–); in the summer of 1915 he was introduced to and played tennis with a fifteen-year-old named Francis Poulenc [1960], though he had to be reminded of it when he was reintroduced to him after the war. Beginning in 1910 he composed works that he included in his catalogue of mature compositions: Opp. 1 and 2 were sets of songs by Jammes and Latil respectively. His violin sonata (Op. 3), was performed at a concert of the Société Musicale Indépendente; so was his first string quartet of 1912, which was taken up on the spot for publication by Durand. During the Paris Conservatoire period Milhaud began work on an opera, *La Brebis égarée (The Lost Sheep)*, a setting of a play by Jammes, and had the opportunity to play and sing the first act for the poet. Jammes introduced him to Claudel, St. John Perse (i.e., Saint-Léger Léger), Mme. Chausson, Mme. Daudet, and other important people in the literary and artistic world. Milhaud began his travels in a small way with visits to Spain in 1911 and Germany in 1913. In 1913 he completed *Agamemnon*, the first of an operatic trilogy utilizing Paul Claudel's version of Aeschylus' *Oresteia*.

When war broke out in August 1914, Milhaud was rejected as unfit for service and returned to the Conservatoire, where he won a prize for his two-violin sonata—the only prize, he claimed in his 1949 autobiography, that he was ever awarded. Unable to join the fighting, he engaged in refugee aid. He was presently working on music for Claudel's play *Protée (Proteus)*, trying to suit it to changing plans for production and continued work on the music for the *Oresteia* trilogy. The second part, *Les Choéphores (The Libation Bearers)*, was completed in 1915. In the autumn of 1916 he went into the propaganda wing of the government and was assigned with military standing to the photographic service. Shortly afterward Claudel, newly appointed ambassador to Brazil, decided that Milhaud would make an ideal secretary and had him assigned to his staff. The sights and sounds of Brazil, where he was to remain for two years, had an enormous and productive impact on Milhaud. He encountered the still-struggling Villa-Lobos [1817] and the visiting pianist Arthur Rubinstein and traveled the country with his employer. An encounter with the dancer Nijinsky eventuated in the Claudel-Milhaud ballet *L'Homme et son désir (Man and His Desire)*, though Nijinsky was no longer able to dance by the time it was completed. After the Armistice, Claudel was ordered to Washington for a conference and then home. To get to New York, he commandeered an impounded German liner. It suffered engine trouble that necessitated layovers at Bahia and Pernambuco and then went adrift in the Caribbean without power of communication until the Gulf Stream picked it up and carried it to Barbados. In all, the voyage took nearly two months.

When he returned to Paris, Milhaud found the cultural and intellectual postwar excitement at a rolling boil, some of the movers and shakers being Satie [1578], Cocteau, the singer Jane Bathori, and the conductor Vladimir Golschmann. Reviewing a concert that included songs by Louis Durey [1828] and Milhaud's fourth string quartet, Henri Collet named these two and Auric, Honegger, Poulenc, and Germaine Tailleferre [1863] "The Six," an arbitrarily chosen French counterpart to the Russian "Five." The rather ill-assorted group decided to capitalize on the accident, gave a couple of *Concerts des Six*, and later (without Durey) collaborated on a Cocteau ballet, *Les Mariées de la Tour Eiffel (The Wedding on the Eiffel Tower)*, though the chief product of the linkup was a two-year series of intimate Saturday *soirées*. During this heady period Milhaud dished up another Cocteau ballet, *Le Boeuf sur le toit (The Ox on the Roof)*, named after a Brazilian popular song and originally conceived as a score for a hypothetical film comedy. It was produced in 1919 in a program that included Satie's *Pièces montées*, Auric's *Fox-Trot*, and Poulenc's *Cocardes*. The press thought it all very funny, and the next year it was put on as part of a music-hall show at London's Coliseum, where Milhaud had his first encounter with jazz.

In 1920 Gabriel Pierné [1555] elected to present the *Protée* suite in a Concerts Colonne program. Though today it would raise no eyebrows, the music occasioned an uproar, in the course of which Durey took a poke at another musician. Pierné, nothing daunted, scheduled it again, an action which delayed his election to the Académie by some five years. A year later the concerted piece *Cinq Études* and the long-postponed *L'Homme et son désir*, danced by the Ballets Suédois, occasioned similar uproars, as did the Jammes opera, produced by the Opéra-Comique in 1923, and the collaborative Cocteau ballet. Milhaud's success as a Bad Boy was now assured, and though it was not a role to which he aspired—being, as he himself admitted, immune to comedy—he furthered it with such things as song settings of agricultural and florists' catalogues.

In 1922 Milhaud completed the third *Oresteia* opera, *Les Euménides*, and made his first appearances in the United States, discovering to his chagrin that Leopold Stokowski had arranged for him to make his podium debut as conductor of the Philadelphia Orchestra in a program he was to choose. His musicianship, however, stood him in good stead, and he often conducted thereafter. He also appeared as a pianist in concerted pieces written for his own limited performing talents, lectured at various colleges and was taken to Harlem to hear jazz on the hoof. His announcement to reporters that this was the American music which most stimulated him became front-page news all over the world. The most immediate fruit of this experience, and certainly one of Milhaud's masterpieces, was the 1923 ballet *La Création du monde (The Creation of the World)*, parts of which are straight out of Ellington [1967]. It was followed in 1924 by two more ballets: *Salade* for Leonid Massine and *Le Train bleu (The Blue Train)* for Diaghilev. These were followed by the first two of several short operas, *Les Malheurs d'Orphée (The Misfortunes of Orpheus)*, in a modern Provençal setting, and *Esther de Carpentras*, the first of them commissioned

by the Princesse de Polignac, heiress to the Singer Sewing Machine fortune.

During much of this period Milhaud was restlessly traveling—to Italy, Sardinia, Palestine, Turkey, Russia, and the United States. Part of this activity involved his honeymoon, he having married his cousin Madeleine, an actress. Though he was writing concerti, string quartets, and other abstract works, he was at this point mainly concerned with operas. The year 1927 saw *Le pauvre matelot (The Poor Sailor)*, with a libretto by Cocteau, and in the same year he wrote for Hindemith's [1914] Baden-Baden Festival the first of 3 *opéras-minutes* on mythological themes—the nine-minute *L'enlèvement d'Europe (The Kidnaping of Europa)*; the other two followed in 1929. In the other direction he collaborated again with Claudel on the vast *Christophe Colomb (Christopher Columbus)*, whose Berlin premiere in 1930 involved "mixed media" (movie projections). This was followed in Paris in 1932 by the almost equally ambitious *Maximilien*. In 1929 Milhaud had also embarked on a career as a writer of scores for films; he was to do more than twenty-five in Paris and Hollywood—none of them for major successes, however. In 1932 he also returned to writing incidental music for the theater, providing scores for thirty-odd dramas, ancient and modern. Over the years he wrote a good deal of music for radio.

Milhaud had come down with attacks of illness several times on his travels (he was always notably overweight) and now began to suffer increasingly from the rheumatoid arthritis that was eventually to cripple him. While he was thus ailing in 1930, his son Daniel was born, and Madeleine suffered a slow and painful recovery. Milhaud even tried such things as acupuncture and faith healing for relief, but he was doomed to suffer, often severely, for the rest of his life. By now he had attained international prominence and respect and was regularly called upon to appear at big music festivals, world's fairs, and other occasional events. During the first year of World War II he was mostly bedridden at his home in Provence. After the fall of Paris, however, he and his wife realized they had to get out of France. They managed to make their way to Lisbon, where they found that because of the devalued franc they did not have enough money for passage to New York. But the Portuguese government paid their hotel bills, and eventually the Baroness de Goldschmidt-Rothschild, herself a refugee, arranged their tickets. They reached New York in July 1940 and, after recuperating at the homes of friends, bought a second-hand Ford and drove to Oakland, California, where Milhaud was to teach at Mills College for the next thirty-one years, until his health would no longer permit his traveling. In 1940 Milhaud wrote the first of his 14 symphonies. In 1942 his father died, followed a few months later by his mother; they had been in hiding from the Nazis. In 1946 Milhaud himself was severely ill, but by the end of the following summer he was well enough to take a freighter to France, but there he suffered a relapse and was forced to spend most of his time indoors. From then on, despite indifferent health, he divided his time between teaching at Mills and at the Paris Conservatoire. Among his many successful pupils were William Bolcom [2425], Howard Brubeck [2250], David Brubeck [2310], Ben Johnston [2359], Betsy Jolas [2364], Steve Reich [2419], Seymour Shifrin [2358], and Morton Subotnick [2405]. Later he also became a prime mover (together with Madeleine) in the school connected with the summer festival at Aspen, Colorado.

During this period Milhaud received many commissions and composed as prolifically as before. Most of this work was performed and a good deal of it was recorded, but he seems to have been at his best in the pre-American years and presently seems most likely to be remembered as a leading representative of the spirit of the 1920s.

RECORDINGS: Though the Milhaud discography is quite large, its limitations are consistent with the view expressed above. Of the earlier operas *Les Choéphores, Les Malheurs d'Orphee,* the *opéras-minutes,* and *Christoph Colomb* have been recorded complete. Of the later operas we have only a brief excerpt from the 1943 *Bolivar* and an orchestral suite from *Maximilien.* Most of the pre-1930 ballets are on records, but only the 1936 *Les Songes (The Dreams)* and the 1937 *Carnaval des Londres* among the later works. Similarly, of the stage and film music only that for the early Claudel plays has found its way to records. There is better overall representation of Milhaud's many orchestral and concerted works, but it is spotty throughout (e.g., less than half of the symphonies). The same applied until recently to the chamber music and music for solo instruments. Much of the piano music, the *Suite* for Ondes Martenot, and the complete organ music have been recorded. The French Cybelia label is in the process of recording the complete 18 string quartets and some of the other chamber pieces. The vocal music, both choral and solo, is still rather poorly explored, though a number of significant works have been recorded.

[1869] PONIRIDY, Georges (Pō-nē-rī-dē', Zhôrzh)
VIOLINIST, CIVIL SERVANT
BORN: Constantinople, October 8, 1892

Poniridy's parents were Greek, his name originally being Giorgios Poniridis, but he was educated and established his career in Western Europe. In 1912 he graduated with highest honors and a first prize in violin from the Brussels Conservatory, where he had studied with Paul Gilson [1572] and Eugène Ysaÿe [1507]. Subsequently he moved to Paris, where he undertook further studies at the Schola Cantorum with d'Indy [1462] and Roussel [1605]. His first compositions date from this time, though his important work came much later. He remained in Paris until shortly before World War II, when he moved to Greece, where after the fighting he was an official in the ministry of education. He was solidly grounded in liturgical chant, both Gregorian and Byzantine, and in Greek folk music—materials that underlie his own compositions. He has written much incidental theater music, the ballet *Decameron,* symphonies and other orchestral works, choral pieces, and many smaller-scale items.
RECORDINGS: There is a recording of his *Rhythmes grecs (Greek Rhythms)* for piano.

[1870] HOWELLS, Herbert Norman
ORGANIST, TEACHER, CONDUCTOR
BORN: Lydney, October 17, 1892
DIED: London, February 23, 1983

Howells is highly regarded in England but known here mostly to church musicians. He was born just down the Severn from Gloucester, in which city he studied organ with Herbert Brewer, the cathedral organist, whose assistant he became. It was in Gloucester too that he began his friendship with the ill-starred Ivor Gurney [1839]. Howells began composing on his own and in 1912 won a scholarship to the Royal College of Music, where he studied with Charles Wood [1579], and (inevitably!) with Stanford [1467], whose favorite pupil he is said to have been. His *Mass in the Dorian Mode* was performed in London's (Catholic) Westminster Cathedral later that year, and the following summer Stanford conducted his first piano concerto at Queen's Hall with Arthur Benjamin [1887] as soloist. A life-threatening illness kept Howells out of wartime service. In 1916 his piano quartet became the first work chosen for publication by the Carnegie Trust. A year later he became organist at Salisbury Cathedral but took a turn for the worse and had to resign. By 1920, however, he was sufficiently improved to marry and to accept a teaching appointment at the Royal College, which he held for more than fifty years. He toured South Africa in 1921 and North America two years later. In 1935 he lost his young son, whom he later memorialized in his *Hymnus Paradisi* of 1950, a quasi-Requiem which is his most ambitious and some think greatest work. In 1936 he succeeded Gustav Holst [1658] as music director of St. Paul Girls' School, and a year later he received a D.Mus. from Oxford. Queen Elizabeth made him a Commander of the British Empire in 1953, and in 1954 he was appointed King Edward VII Professor of Music at the University of London. He left St. Paul's in 1962 and the University of London two years later. His output has been small, as have most of his compositions. At the outset of his career he wrote a number of chamber works (quartets, sonatas), music for keyboard, and a few orchestral pieces. In later years he has concentrated on vocal music, especially music for the Anglican service. RECORDINGS: Recordings include the *Hymnus Paradisi*; a good deal of liturgical music; the *Elegy* for viola, string quartet, and strings; the orchestral suite *Music for a Prince* (the dedicatee was Prince Charles); *Merry Eye* (also orchestral); keyboard pieces; and songs.

[1871] ABRAHAM, Paul (Å'-brå-hàm, Poul)
CONDUCTOR, PIANIST
BORN: Apatin, November 2, 1892
DIED: Hamburg, May 6, 1960

Born in a Danube town now located in Yugoslavia, but then in Hungary, Paul Abraham studied at the Academy of Music in Budapest. Like so many creators of operetta, he started out as a serious composer, in his case with some success. The turning point came when he became chief conductor at the Budapest Operetta Theater in 1927. In 1930 he wrote his first operetta, *Viktoria und ihr Husar (Victoria and Her Hussar)*, which was an enormous success in Vienna and later elsewhere. In the manner of the period he combined the Hungarian-Viennese style with what passed for jazz. He had further successes in Germany with *Die Blume von Hawaii (The Flower of Hawaii)* in 1931 and *Ball im Savoy (Dance at the Savoy)* in 1933. Soon after the Nazi triumph in 1933, however, he returned to Vienna, from which he fled to Havana after the *Anschluss.* After a wretched time there he made his way to New York, where in 1946 his mind gave way. In 1956 he was removed to a mental hospital

in Hamburg, where he died. RECORDINGS: There are recordings from the operettas.

[1872] LABUNSKI, Feliks Roderyk (or Felix Roderick)
PIANIST, CRITIC, TEACHER, ADMINISTRATOR
BORN: Ksawerynów, December 27, 1892
DIED: Cincinnati, Ohio, April 8, 1979
(Some sources give April 28)

The son of an engineer, Labunski was born in what is now Ksaverinava in Soviet Latvia. His parents were talented amateur musicians, and his younger brother Wiktor (1895–1974) became a pianist, composer, and director of several American conservatories. Feliks also began as a pianist, graduated from the Warsaw Conservatory, and, with Paderewski's [1527] help, won a scholarship to study with Paul Dukas [1574], Nadia Boulanger, and others at the École Normale in Paris. In 1934 he returned to Poland as director of classical music for the national radio but after two years emigrated to the United States, where Wiktor had preceded him in 1928. Feliks settled in New York, worked as a free-lance critic, and taught composition briefly at Marymount College in Tarrytown. He became an American citizen in 1941. Four years later he joined the faculty of the Cincinnati Conservatory (as it became) and taught there until he retired in 1964. He wrote a ballet, a symphony, 2 string quartets, and other instrumental and vocal works in a pleasant neo-romantic vein. RECORDINGS: Jorge Mester recorded his 1963 *Canto di aspirazione* for orchestra.

[1873] PALAU-BOIX, Manuel (Pà-là'-oo Bō'-iks, Màn-wel')
CONDUCTOR, TEACHER, ETHNOMUSICOLOGIST
BORN: Alfara del Patriarca, January 4, 1893
DIED: Valencia, February 18, 1967

Palau grew up in the countryside in eastern Spain and, after doing a hitch in the army, studied at the Valencia Conservatory from 1914 to 1919. During that period he conducted local popular orchestras and produced a stage piece, *Amor torna,* as early as 1917. Later he went to Paris and took lessons with Charles Koechlin [1592] and Maurice Ravel [1666]. He then returned to Valencia where he spent the rest of his career, first as a teacher at the conservatory and from 1952 as its director. His early compositions were in a popular vein, though the *Tres impre-*

siones orquestrales and the *Poemas de juventud (Poems of Youth)* show something more serious and craftsmanly. A turning point came with the orchestral suite *Gongoriana*, which won the 1927 National Music Prize. Twenty years later his cantata *Atardecer* received another. In the 1930s, perhaps reflecting those troubled times in Spain, his music became less lyrical and more dramatic. In his ripest work there is a synthesis of both characteristics and evidence of great skill. Palau was also a tireless collector of folksongs and under his direction large numbers from the Valencia region were taken down and preserved. RECORDINGS: Narciso Yepes has recorded the 1948 *Concierto levantino* for guitar and orchestra.

[1874] NOVELLO, Ivor
    PIANIST, ACTOR, PLAYWRIGHT
    BORN: Cardiff, January 15, 1893
    DIED: London, March 6, 1951

Ivor Novello was unrelated to the music-publishing Novellos of London. His real name was David Ivor Davies. He was the son of the choral conductor, singer, and music teacher Clara Novello-Davies, whose father had originally nicknamed her "Clara Novello," after a well-known singer of the time (who *was* related to the publishing family). Ivor studied piano and organ and served as a choirboy in the Magdalen College Choir at Oxford. He began his career as a songwriter in his teens, and at twenty-one wrote one of the great hit songs of the World War I, "Keep the Home Fires Burning" (or more properly "Till the Boys Come Home"). Shortly afterward he contributed to some London musicals but then worked for many years on the nonmusical stage, writing, producing, and acting in a series of well-made, if ephemeral, plays. He also appeared in films. In 1935 he starred, in a nonsinging role, in his first operetta, *Glamorous Night* (dialogue and music were all his own). A whole series ensued, cut from the same cloth, all highly successful, especially *The Dancing Years* of 1939, which, despite the conditions, ran all through World War II. Novello (who was no composer in any serious sense) had a gift for effective treacle, though it seems not to have exported well. He died after performing in his *King's Rhapsody*. His last musical, however, was *Gay's the Word* in 1950. RECORDINGS: There are recordings of songs.

[1875] ROGERS, Bernard
    PAINTER, TEACHER
    BORN: New York, February 4, 1893
    DIED: Rochester, N.Y., May 24, 1968

Bernard Rogers was a respected figure among the American composers of his generation and an enormously influential teacher. Though he took piano lessons from the age of twelve, he had no special interest in music until he was taken to one of Walter Damrosch's **[1540]** concerts in 1909. Shortly before that event, he had quit school and gone to work, taking night courses in architecture. However, he was more serious about painting, in which art he aspired to fame and which he kept up all of his life. After his epiphany, he took private music lessons with various people, notably Arthur Farwell **[1629]** and Ernest Bloch **[1729]**. In 1919 his orchestral elegy *To the Fallen* was performed by the New York Philharmonic and won him a Pulitzer Scholarship. In 1921 he took a composition course with Percy Goetschius (1853–1943) at the Institute of Musical Art (Juilliard School). Thereafter he taught, at various times, at the Cleveland Institute of Music and the Julius Hartt School and wrote for *Musical America*. In 1927 a Guggenheim Fellowship enabled him to study in England with Frank Bridge **[1713]** and in France with Nadia Boulanger. Two years later he settled down to teach for the rest of his life at the Eastman School, eventually becoming chairman of the composition department. Among his pupils one notes Jacob Avshalomov **[2287]**, William Bergsma **[2313]**, David Diamond **[2238]**, William Flanagan **[2332]**, Ulysses Kay **[2257]**, Gail Kubik **[2224]**, Burrill Phillips **[2116]**, Peter Mennin **[2328]**, and Vladimir Ussachevsky **[2180]**. In 1947 his one-act opera *The Warrior* (on the Samson story) became the last of the American operas unsuccessfully premiered by the Johnson regime at the Metropolitan Opera. Rogers wrote three other operas, an oratorio, cantatas, 5 symphonies, 2 string quartets, a violin sonata, and much other choral, orchestral, and chamber music, plus a handful of songs. RECORDINGS: A number of orchestral works have been recorded— *Leaves from the Tale of Pinocchio,* 1950; *Japanese Dances* (for wind band), 1933; *Once Upon a Time,* 1934; *Apparitions,* 1967; *Dance Scenes,* 1953; *Variations on a Song by Mussorgsky,* 1960; *Soliloquy* for flute and strings, 1933 (led by Howard Hanson and others).

[1876] VÉCSEY, Franz von (or Ferenc)
    (Vet'-che-ĕ, Frȧnts fun)
    VIOLINIST
    BORN: Budapest, March 23, 1893
    DIED: Rome, April 6, 1935

The son of violinist Lajos Vécsey, Ferenc (later Franz von) studied with him and then, at the age of eight, with Jenö Hubay [1509]. At ten he became Joseph Joachim's [1321] pupil and began his international career as a performer. It was sadly foreshortened by his death a few days after his forty-second birthday. He wrote some pieces for the violin. RECORDINGS: A few of his violin pieces have been recorded.

[1877] MOMPOU, Federico (Mom-pōō', Fā-de-rē'-kō)
PIANIST
BORN: Barcelona, April 16, 1893

Although he is a miniaturist and, in reaction to the increasing complexity of contemporary music, a deliberate "primitive," the Catalan Federico Mompou is by many reckoned the most important piano composer produced by Spain since Falla [1688] and Turina [1759]. Mompou's other compositions are limited to songs plus a few choral pieces and a suite for guitar.) He studied piano with Pedro Serra at the Barcelona Conservatory, making his concert debut in 1908. Three years later he moved to Paris. Though he is often called a compositional autodidact, the records show that he studied composition with Marcel Samuel-Rousseau (1882–1955), and he was much taken with the music of Satie [1578]. The outbreak of war in 1914 drove him home, but he returned when it was over and lived in Paris until the next German invasion sent him back to Barcelona for good. He visited the United States in 1970 but not as a pianist. A very shy and retiring man, he as a matter of fact gave up performing publicly shortly after his debut but continued to play for his friends—and for recordings. RECORDINGS: Late in his life Mompou committed his entire keyboard output to records. Others have also recorded selections and a few songs.

[1878] GOOSSENS, Sir Aynsley Eugene
VIOLINIST, CONDUCTOR
BORN: London, May 26, 1893
DIED: Hillingdon, Middlesex, June 13, 1962

The third Eugene Goossens came from a family overflowing with musical talent. The first, his grandfather, a native of Bruges, was for a time conductor of the Carl Rosa Opera Company in England, and later of the Goossens Male Voice Choir in Liverpool. The second Eugene (our man's father) followed his parent in 1899 to the podium of the Carl

Rosa and was later conductor of the British National Opera in the 1920s. His two daughters, Marie and Sidonie, were noted harpists, and his younger son Leon was one of the great oboists of the century. Their brother Eugene spent much of his childhood in Liverpool and then at the age of ten was sent across the English Channel to the Bruges Conservatory. After a year, however, he returned to Liverpool, where he studied at the Liverpool College of Music for three years until a scholarship led him to the Royal College of Music. There he was a pupil of Stanford [1467] and Charles Wood [1579]. In 1912 Goossens made his first public appearances as a composer-conductor. For a time he played the violin in the orchestra at the Haymarket Theatre and from 1912 to 1915 in the Queen's Hall Orchestra. He was also a member of the Philharmonic String Quartet. In 1916 he became a protégé of Thomas Beecham and conducted the premiere of The Critic, Stanford's penultimate opera. Five years later Goossens was sufficiently well known to form his own orchestra, which gave the English premiere of Stravinsky's Le Sacre du printemps but survived for only a season. Afterward he followed family tradition by conducting some performances with both the Carl Rosa Opera and the British National Opera companies.

In 1923 George Eastman, the Kodak magnate, having decreed that Rochester needed a symphony orchestra, hired Goossens to direct it. He did so for eight years. His first opera, the one-act Judith, was premiered in 1929. In 1931, subsequent to Fritz Reiner's being released from the conductorship of the Cincinnati Symphony when it was discovered that his wife had no official sanction as such, Goossens was asked to take over that body. He remained in Cincinnati for fifteen years and made its orchestra one of the most admired in the country. In 1937 his second and last opera, Don Juan de Mañara with a libretto by Arnold Bennett, was chosen by the Royal Opera House for its Coronation season. When Goossens left Cincinnati in 1946 to head up the New South Wales Conservatory and the Sydney Symphony in Australia, he was honored with a set of ten orchestral variations on a theme of his by as many notable American composers. He was again eminently successful with his Sydney assignment and was rewarded with a knighthood from Queen Elizabeth II in 1955. However, a year later he returned to England in disgrace, having been apprehended by a customs officer with what was then illicit pornographic matter in his baggage. In his last years he continued to conduct for the phonograph, as he had done for many years.

Goossens disowned a good deal of his early music, which was vaguely impressionistic. Later he took a sort of Stravinskian [1748] neo-classical position, producing much that was more interesting to the intellect than to the ear, though for a time he was regarded as a leader of the second generation of English renaissance composers. Besides the operas he produced the oratorio *Apocalypse*, the ballet *L'École en crinoline*, some incidental dramatic scores, 2 symphonies, a concerto each for piano, violin, and oboe (the last for brother Leon), besides other orchestral and chamber pieces and a number of works for piano and solo songs.

RECORDINGS: Goossens did not, as a recording conductor, blow his own horn and left only a few pieces, recorded early, on discs: the *Four Conceits*, the scherzo *Tam O'Shanter*, and the ballet music from *Judith*. Leon recorded the oboe concerto, Sidonie the Op. 37 *Ballade*, and Marie the Op. 6 *Suite* for flute, violin, and harp. Afterward there was a long period in which he was represented only by a few piano pieces. However, a recent upsurge of interest and reevaluation has produced recordings of the first symphony, the complete *Judith*, a *Sinfonietta*, the 1960 *Divertissement*, the James Joyce settings *Chamber Music*, and *4 Conceits* for piano.

[1879] HÁBA, Alois (Hä′-bä, Á′-lois)
TEACHER
BORN: Vizovice, June 21, 1893
DIED: Prague, November 18, 1973

Though Julián Carrillo [1663] and Charles Ives [1659] had experimented with microtonal music, Alois Hába, for what it is worth, should get the credit for promoting it. He came from Moravian peasant stock. His father had a dance band in Vizovice (now in central Czechoslovakia) in which Alois fiddled. (Alois's younger brother Karel [1898–1972] was also a violinist and later studied composition with him.) From the age of fifteen Alois trained as a music teacher at Kroměříž. He graduated in 1912, worked at composition on his own for two years, and then took a job teaching at Bílovice. After a few months, however, he went to Prague to study with Vítězslav Novák [1617] who recognized his talent and encouraged him. After a year, however, he was drafted for war service and wound up in Vienna. There, having read an article on the use of quarter-tones, he recognized what he had heard in the songs his mother taught

him and put theory into practice in his choral *Suite*, Op. 13. In 1918 he became a pupil of Franz Schreker [1705] and at the end of the war took an editorial job with Universal Edition, where he encountered the work of Schoenberg [1657] and other far-out composers of the time, which experience encouraged him to proceed along the radical paths at which Schreker looked askance. Nevertheless he followed the latter to Berlin when he went to teach there at the Hochschule in 1920. However, in that same year he produced a string quartet (his second) in quarter-tones, and the association rapidly fell apart.

Unable to get any action on the implementation of his theories, which he set forth in a monograph in 1922, Hába returned to Prague in 1923 (a good year to leave Germany!) and was soon teaching at the Prague Conservatory. In 1924 he had built the first of three quarter-tone pianos of his own design; later came a clarinet, a trumpet, a guitar, and harmoniums in quarter- and sixth-tones. Having taught his findings for a decade, he was rewarded in 1934 with his own department of microtonal music. His students included the eminent conductors Karel Ančerl and Walter Susskind and a number of young composers. In the war years 1939–45 Hába was, as a modernist, *non grata* with the Germans, but he resumed his place in the latter year and was also appointed director of the National Opera at the Smetana Theater. The Czech government, however, abolished Hába's department in 1951 but continued to hand out honors to him. Contrary to statements that he relapsed into writing very ordinary diatonic music in his last years—though he had never limited himself to microtones in all of his music—he continued his explorations, one of his last works being his Quartet No. 16, in fifth-tones. The bulk of Hába's output consists of choral, chamber, and piano music, though he produced a few orchestral works, including concerti for violin and viola and a *Symphonic Fantasy* for piano and orchestra. His most famous work is his first opera (of 3), *Matka (The Mother)*, written in quarter-tones and premiered in 1929. (The other operas, one in the tempered scale and the other in sixth-tones, have not been performed.)

RECORDINGS: There is a recording of *The Mother*. Other recordings include several of the string quartets, a suite for bass clarinet solo, *Fantasy in Quarter-Tones* for violin solo, several nonets, *Cymbalom Suite*, and *The Path of Life* for orchestra.

[1880] BJÖRKANDER, Nils Frank Fredrik (Byör'-kån-der, Nēls Frånk Fred'-rik)
TEACHER
BORN: Stockholm, June 28, 1893
DIED: Soedertälje, March 5, 1972

Nils Björkander graduated from the Stockholm Conservatory, where he specialized in piano, in 1915. He went into teaching and two years later founded his own music school in Stockholm. He was a highly successful piano teacher. Though he composed a *Concert Fantasy* for piano and orchestra and some chamber pieces and songs, he was best known for his atmospheric piano compositions, which were extremely popular in Sweden; some of these were orchestrated by other composers. RECORDINGS: A few of the piano pieces have been recorded.

[1881] GALLET, Luciano (Gål-låt', Loo-sya'-noo)
ETHNOMUSICOLOGIST, PIANIST, CONDUCTOR
BORN: Rio de Janeiro, June 28, 1893
DIED: Rio de Janeiro, October 29, 1931

Gallet was a graduate of Rio's Instituto Nacional, where he won a gold medal in piano in 1916. He was a friend of Darius Milhaud [1868] during the latter's Brazilian stay and through him became aware of the chief contemporary currents of European music. However, his own chief interest was Brazilian folk music, which he both collected and adapted, and on whose non-Caucasian aspects he became especially authoritative. He taught piano and conducted at the Instituto for more than a decade, winding up as its director in the last year of his brief life. With a few exceptions, his compositions were in chamber-scale forms. RECORDINGS: There are song recordings.

[1882] MERIKANTO, Aarre (Mer'-ē-kån-tō, Är'-re)
TEACHER, PIANIST, CONDUCTOR
BORN: Helsingfors (Helsinki), June 29, 1893
DIED: Helsinki, September 29, 1958

Aarre Merikanto was the son of Oskar Merikanto [1599] and came to music naturally from his home environment. At first he did not intend a career in it, but a course in composition with Erkki Melartin [1665] gave birth to the one-act opera *Helena* (later disowned), a successful concert presentation of which in 1912 caused him to abandon his more "practical" plans. Forthwith his father took him to Leipzig and arranged for him to study for two years with Max Reger [1637]. After returning to Helsinki and giving a concert of his music there, Merikanto took himself to Moscow in late 1915 and studied there with Sergei Vassilenko [1628] for six months. Following two more successful all-Merikanto concerts in Helsinki, in 1917 and 1919 respectively, he settled down to composing an opera, *Juha,* to a libretto by the great Finnish soprano Aino Ackte based on a novel by Juhani Aho. The piece was finished in 1920, but the composer decided that he did not like what he had done and did it all over again. He submitted it in 1922 to the directors of the Helsinki Opera, who rejected it partly because it was too "modern" and partly because of infighting among them. For a decade and more Merikanto continued to write (with little acceptance) music of a highly individual and particularly toughminded kind, influenced to some degree by the later Scriabin [1625]. In 1936 he joined the faculty of the Helsinki Conservatory, where for his last seven years, 1951–58, he was chairman of the composition department. He wrote little music of importance during that whole period but was increasingly admired as a teacher. Among his pupils were Joonas Kokkonen [2318] and Aulis Sallinen (1935–). Merikanto was also known in Finland as an accompanist and conductor. He never got to see *Juha,* though he heard it performed on the radio in 1957. The stage premiere did not take place until five years after his death. The work almost immediately assumed the keystone role in Finland's native operatic repertoire, which, under its inspiration, has steadily expanded ever since (see the Kokkonen article). Merikanto also wrote 3 symphonies, 3 piano concerti, 4 violin concerti, 2 cello concerti, symphonic poems, choral works, and many small pieces. RECORDINGS: There is a recording of the opera *Juha* by Ulf Söderblom and the Finnish National Opera. Other recordings include the second piano concerto, the *Concert Piece* for cello and orchestra, *Partita* for harp and woodwinds, the second violin concerto, and a concerto for violin, clarinet, horn, and string sextet—all by Finnish orchestras or ensembles.

[1883] LANGGAARD, Rued Immanuel (Lång'-gôrd, Rūd Im-mån'-wel)
ORGANIST
BORN: Copenhagen, July 28, 1893
DIED: Ribe, July 10, 1952

Rued Langgaard's father, a Liszt [1218] pupil, was a concert pianist and conservatory teacher, and his mother also played the piano. The boy was making music virtually from the time he could walk and attracted much attention in childhood as a composer and keyboard performer, especially on the organ. He completed a cantata, *Musae triumphantes (The Muses in Triumph),* when he was thirteen; it had a very successful premiere two years later. He wrote the first of his 16 symphonies at eighteen. By then he had moved from an overripe late-Romanticism into an increasingly exploratory and daring approach, which was looked on in Denmark as the work of a madman. In the 1920s, however, he did an abrupt about-face, infuriated by the march toward neo-classicism and returned to the rhetoric and grand gestures of Romanticism. An irascible type, he seems soon to have alienated the entire musical world, and, despite his remarkable qualifications, was unable to find a post as organist until 1940 when he was installed in the cathedral at Ribe, a little city in southwestern Denmark. RECORDINGS: Until very recently the recorded representation was very sparse: a late 1960s abridged recording of *Sfaerenes musik (Music of the Spheres),* one of his more adventurous compositions (for soprano, chorus, and orchestra); the Symphony No. 4 ("The Fall of the Leaf"); and a few chamber pieces. A large number of new releases have just appeared: an unabridged version of *Music of the Spheres;* Symphony No. 6 ("The Heaven Storming"); piano compositions (the second sonata, *Ex est, In the Autumn, Flickering Rays, Insektarium, Le Béguinage);* the second violin sonata; a two-disc set of organ works; and some songs. Imminent for release are the controversial oratorio *Antichrist,* Symphonies Nos. 10 and 14, and the huge *Messis: Part Two* for organ.

[1884] MOORE, Douglas Stuart

TEACHER, ORGANIST
BORN: Cutchogue, N.Y., August 10, 1893
DIED: Greenport, N.Y., July 25, 1969

A native of Long Island, whose ancestors had arrived there 250 years before, Douglas Moore was born and retained a lifelong home about as far from New York City as that body of land allows. He was reared in a cultivated atmosphere but was a rather feckless piano student in childhood. A 1911 graduate of the Hotchkiss School, he wrote his first compositions there—settings of poems by another student named Archibald MacLeish. Proceeding to Yale he pursued an ex-

tracurricular career as a would-be songsmith, with some success, one of his efforts entering the Ivy League football-song repertoire ("Good Night, Harvard"). However, in 1913 he took up serious study of music with David Stanley Smith (1877–1949). Subsequently he caught the attention and won the encouragement of Horatio Parker [1556] and stayed on for two years of postgraduate study with him. On leaving Yale in the war year of 1917, he became a naval officer and amused himself by writing naughty songs for the men, some of which he later included in the collection *Songs My Mother Never Taught Me,* which he edited with John Jacob Niles [1864]. Mustered out early in 1919, Moore spent a year studying in Paris with Vincent d'Indy [1462] and Charles Tournemire [1611] at the Schola Cantorum. He came home long enough to marry Emily Bailey, then returned to Paris for a year under the tutelage of Nadia Boulanger.

In 1921 Moore found a job as general musical factotum at the Cleveland Museum of Art, moonlighting as organist at Western Reserve University. His stay enabled him to study with Ernest Bloch [1729] at the Cleveland Institute. His museum experience inspired him to write *4 Museum Pieces* for an organ recital there. This seems to have been his first essay outside the song genre; he orchestrated the work and conducted the Cleveland Orchestra in it two years later. It was followed in 1926 by the orchestral *Pageant of P. T. Barnum,* signaling the beginning of a lifelong concern with American subjects—the product of a friendship with the poet Vachel Lindsay. This brought Moore a Pulitzer scholarship which took him back to Europe for a year. On his return to New York in 1926 he joined the faculty of Columbia University, and rose to be department head and MacDowell Professor. A Guggenheim fellowship in 1934 permitted him to interrupt his pedagogical duties and write his first opera, the one-act *White Wings* (about street cleaners). It was succeeded a year later by *The Headless Horseman,* a treatment of Washington Irving's *Legend of Sleepy Hollow* to a libretto by Stephen Vincent Benét, intended for high-school use. Moore's first real operatic success came with *The Devil and Daniel Webster,* premiered in 1939, for which Benét again provided a libretto based on his own popular tale. This work continues to be produced by small American opera companies and college music departments. The composer won a Pulitzer Prize for his next operatic effort (exclusive of *The Emperor's New Clothes,* a 1949 opera for children); this was his 1950 treatment of Ole Rölvaag's novel

Giants in the Earth, which, in spite of later revisions, has not shown any staying power. But the "folk opera" *The Ballad of Baby Doe,* commissioned for the centennial of Columbia University and premiered in Central City, Colorado, in 1956, must be reckoned one of the most successful of all American operas. It provided Beverly Sills with her first starring role when it entered the repertoire of the New York City Opera and was later nationally televised. In 1957 Moore wrote *Gallantry,* a piece of satirical dramatic fluff, specifically for television (it was broadcast March 15, 1958). *The Wings of the Dove* (after Henry James) got a respectful reception at the New York City Opera in 1961. Moore retired from Columbia the following year, but continued to teach music appreciation there—a subject on which he had earlier published two popular books. Another opera, *The Greenfield Christmas Tree,* was premiered at Baltimore in 1962. His last opera was *Carry Nation* in 1966. All of his musical life Moore remained an unashamed old-school conservative. Impeccably trained and a scrupulous craftsman, he spiced his music moderately with American idioms. While not especially memorable, it must be admired for its skill and honesty.

RECORDINGS: Recordings include the opera *The Devil and Daniel Webster, The Ballad of Baby Doe* (the original production conducted by Emerson Buckley), and *Carry Nation* (another New York City Opera production); the orchestral *Pageant of P. T. Barnum, Farm Journal, In Memoriam, Cotillion Suite,* and Symphony No. 2 in A Major; the clarinet quintet; and a few songs. Moore's rather small *oeuvre* includes some incidental stage music and several film scores for documentaries.

[1885] MACMILLAN, (Sir) Ernest Alexander Campbell

CONDUCTOR, ORGANIST, EDUCATOR
BORN: Mimico, August 18, 1893
DIED: Toronto, May 6, 1973

Ernest MacMillan was born, in the purlieus of Toronto, into the family of a Scottish Presbyterian minister who was an authority on hymnology. He established himself locally as an organ prodigy, studied both at home and in Great Britain, wrote an operatic treatment of *Snow White* at fourteen, and was holding down a regular job as church organist at fifteen. Two years later he received his B.Mus. from Oxford and then entered the University of Toronto to major in history. In the summer of 1914 he went to Germany to take in the Bayreuth Festival

and spent the next four years in a prison camp as an enemy alien. Fortunately he was able to put them to productive use, writing and conducting musicals for performance by and for the inmates and doing some serious composing, which produced his string quartet and his ode *England,* which served as the thesis that won him his D.Mus. from Oxford. (He also received his B.A. from Toronto *in absentia.*) On returning to Toronto, he took up his church work again, also making tours as an organist. At the same time he taught at the Toronto Academy of Music. In 1926, when it became part of the Toronto Conservatory, MacMillan was named director of the school. A year later he also assumed the position of dean of the music faculty at the University of Toronto. MacMillan was perhaps most important as an educator, making enormous improvements in both institutions and writing several manuals and numerous articles. In 1931 he took over direction of the semiamateur Toronto Symphony and through the years molded it into a professional orchestra of stature. He left the conservatory in 1942, the university a decade later, and the orchestra in 1956. He conducted the Mendelssohn Club Choir in Toronto from 1942 to 1957. In the latter part of his career, he appeared internationally as a guest conductor, went back to giving organ recitals, and was heard frequently as a chamber-music pianist and accompanist. He did much work in various official capacities for Canadian music and delighted in unearthing new talent (tenor Jon Vickers and soprano Lois Marshall were among his discoveries). MacMillan collected Canadian folk music, some of which provided a basis for some of his small body of conservative compositions. RECORDINGS: Seiji Ozawa has recorded his *Two Sketches on French-Canadian Folksongs* for string orchestra.

[1886] BOULANGER, Marie-Juliette Olga ("Lili") (Boo-làn-zhä', Mà-rē' Zhü-lyet' Ol'-gà [Lē-lē'])

BORN: Paris, August 21, 1893
DIED: Mèzy, March 15, 1918

Lili Boulanger had an impressive musical heritage. Her paternal grandfather, a cellist, taught at the Paris Conservatoire; his wife was the famous soprano Marie-Julie Boulanger *(née* Hallinger). Their son Ernest, Lili's father, was a successful opera composer who had won the Prix de Rome in 1835 and who also taught at the Paris Conservatoire; his wife was a former singing pupil, the Russian noblewoman Raissa

Mychetsky. They had four daughters, of whom two survived infancy. The elder was Nadia (1887–1979), one of the great composition teachers of her day. When Lili was born six years later, her father was seventy-seven, her mother thirty-four. That the attendant physician was the father of the great harpist Lily Laskine was symptomatic, for Lili Boulanger was surrounded all of her brief life by everyone who was anyone in French music. By the time she was two, she was already able to carry a tune. Shortly afterward she suffered a near-fatal attack of pneumonia, and from then on was laid low by every passing virus and bacillus. Her father, to whom she was deeply attached, died suddenly when she was six. During her childhood, her interest in music was fostered as much as was possible. She learned to play the harp (from Marcel Tournier and Alphonse Hasselmans), the piano, the cello, and the violin. (She even performed in a couple of student concerts.) She also sat in on some of her sister's conservatory classes, and about 1906 began composing. At sixteen, spurred by her mother's worries about how she would take care of herself (marriage being apparently out of the question) and by Nadia's failure the previous year to win the Grand Prix de Rome, she began serious study with Georges Caussade and Paul Vidal [1554]. Despite repeated statements to the contrary, she did not study with Nadia, though Nadia gave her some help at their country home near Gargenville in the summer of 1911.

In 1912 she was admitted to the Conservatoire and that May went to Compiègne for the preliminaries for the Prix de Rome competition. However, she became too ill to proceed and by November was in such a bad way that she was sent to a sanitarium at Berck on the English Channel. The following spring she was well enough to try again and this time became the first woman ever to win the Grand Prix. (The prize awarded concurrently to Claude Delvincourt [1826] was left over from the previous year.) Her prize-winning piece was the cantata *Faust et Hélène*. That same year she also won the Prix Lepaulle and the Prix Yvonne de Gouy d'Arsy. The appearances and other activities connected with these triumphs further weakened her, and an attack of measles at the end of the year caused more serious complications. However, preceded by all manner of negative and scurrilous rumors, she managed to get to Rome by mid-March of 1914. She was not welcomed by the director, Albert Besnard, who was sure her presence would vitiate his precious discipline. Though she won the backing of the Rome

Academy, she had to go to bed for three weeks. By July, however, she was able to go to France (by special permission) for a vacation. War broke out the next month, and Lili stayed to do what she could by way of war work, particularly helping her fellow students in uniform. She returned to Rome exhausted in early 1916 but set to work on a Maeterlinck opera, *La Princesse Maleine*, with whose lonely *protagoniste* she had long identified. Despite remissions, however, her health continued to deteriorate, and in February 1917 she went to Arcachon to try to recover. But she did not and was moved to Paris, where she underwent an appendectomy—a desperate measure to try to counter intestinal and hepatic troubles that had now grown agonizing. In August she was moved again to the family's summer home, where she died at age twenty-four. Besides the cantata, she left published choral works, songs, piano pieces, and chamber music, and a number of unpublished compositions.

RECORDINGS: There are recordings of the cantata *Faust et Hélène*, the choral-orchestral works *Du fond de l'abîme (From the Bottom of the Abyss), Pie Jesu, Pour les funerailles d'un soldat (For the Funeral of a Soldier), Vieille prière bouddhique (Ancient Buddhist Prayer;* a.k.a. *Daily Prayer for the Whole Universe),* and *Psalms 24* and *129,* the song cycle *Clairières dans le ciel (Clearings of the Sky,* to texts of Francis Jammes), three pieces for violin and piano, and piano pieces.

[1887] BENJAMIN, Arthur
PIANIST, CONDUCTOR, TEACHER
BORN: Sydney, September 18, 1893
DIED: London, April 10, 1960

One of the first Australian-born composers to win international fame, Benjamin got his early schooling in Brisbane. In 1911 he won a scholarship to the Royal College of Music in London, where he studied with Stanford [1467] and specialized in piano (under Frederick Cliffe). In 1914 he joined the British army and was sent to France. Later he flew in the air force and was shot down and captured by the Germans. After the war he went back to Australia, where he taught piano at the Sydney Conservatory. Around the same time, however, he began to compose (mostly in smaller forms), and, deciding that Australia was no place for a burgeoning talent, he returned to London in 1921. Three years later his first string quartet (subtitled "Pastorale Fantasia") won a Carnegie Award and was published. In 1926 Benjamin joined the faculty of the Royal College of Music as professor of piano;

among his students were Benjamin Britten [2215] and the American Lamar Crowson. Though Benjamin could be serious (as in the violin concerto of 1932 or his symphony of 1945), the title of an early orchestral work, *Light Music Suite,* indicates his more usual direction—though it should be noted that he never aims at the trivial or meretricious. His first opera, *The Devil Take Her* of 1931, was enthusiastically promoted by Sir Thomas Beecham. Benjamin followed it almost immediately with *Prima Donna,* which, however, got the cold shoulder for more than fifteen years, finally being premiered in 1949.

As an examiner for the Royal College and Royal Academy, Benjamin traveled to various far-flung parts of the British Empire, which helps explain his several Caribbean-based works, of which the 1938 *Jamaican Rumba* became an instant pops-concert favorite. In 1941 Benjamin, perhaps having undergone one war too many, came to North America, where he taught at Reed College and conducted the Vancouver Symphony. In 1946 he returned to his Royal College post. After the war he wrote a more ambitious opera, *A Tale of Two Cities,* which was premiered by the BBC in 1953. Three years later they did his television opera *Mañana.* At the time of his death, Benjamin was working on an adaptation of Moliere's *Tartuffe,* which was eventually scored and produced in 1964. He also wrote film music, including *The Conquest of Everest, The Ideal Husband,* and Hitchcock's *The Man Who Knew Too Much.*

RECORDINGS: These include the *Jamaican Rumba, Matty Rag,* and other Jamaican pieces; *Overture to an Italian Comedy* (several versions); the oboe concerto, after Cimarosa [962]; *Cotillon* (Frederick Fennell); the harmonica concerto (Larry Adler); the *Concertino* and *Concerto quasi una Fantasia* for piano (Lamar Crowson and the composer); *Heritage March* (Frederick Curzon); *Elegy, Waltz, and Toccata* for viola (William Primrose); *Romantic Fantasy* for violin, viola, and orchestra (Jascha Heifetz and William Primrose); piano pieces (notably an LP by Crowson); and songs.

[1888] PERGAMENT, Moses (Pâr'-gà-ment, Mō'-zes)
VIOLINIST, CONDUCTOR, CRITIC
BORN: Helsingfors (Helsinki), September 21, 1893
DIED: Stockholm, March 5, 1977

Moses Pergament was the son of Orthodox Jewish parents. He studied violin for four years at the St. Petersburg Conservatory (Finland was then still part of Russia), and

spent four more playing in the Helsingfors orchestra and studying at the local university. In 1915 he settled in Stockholm, where he attended the Music High School and acquired Swedish citizenship in 1918. He studied conducting in Berlin at the Stern Conservatory and in fact spent a number of years in Berlin and Paris. Though he wrote some music in his earlier years, he did not settle down to serious composition until he had entered his forties. He returned permanently to Stockholm with the onset of the Second World War and was long an influential critic there, publishing several books on music, including a biography of Jenny Lind. His mature musical style shows influences from all of the places where he lived. The events of the years 1933–45 made him acutely conscious of his Jewish heritage, a fact reflected in such works as: *Dibbuk* for violin and orchestra, 1935; *Rapsodia ebraica* for orchestra, 1935; *Kol nidré* for cello and orchestra, 1949; the 1958 opera *Eli* (libretto by Nelly Sachs), and above all the choral symphony *Den judiska sången (The Jewish Song),* 1944. RECORDINGS: Recordings include the last-named work (conducted by James De Priest), the *4 Chinese Songs* (sung by Berit Lindholm), and the 1928 ballet suite *Krelantems and Eldeling* (Stig Westerberg conducting).

[1889] ABSIL, Jean (Áp-sēl', Zhàn)
TEACHER
BORN: Peruwélz (Bonsecours), October 23, 1893
DIED: Brussels, February 2, 1974

Absil is reckoned one of the more important Belgian composers of the twentieth century, and certainly one of the most prolific. In his days at the Brussels Conservatory he took several first prizes. Later he studied with Paul Gilson [1572]. He won the Prix Agniez in 1921 and second place in the Prix de Rome competition a year later. In 1923 he was appointed director of the Etterbeek Academy in the outskirts of Brussels. During the early 1920s he immersed himself in the music of his important contemporaries and developed his own style of atonalism and a characteristic use of irregular rhythms; he afterward disowned most of the music he wrote before that time. In 1931 he was given a professorship at the Brussels Conservatory, though he continued with his directorial duties. Five years later he founded the association of contemporary Belgian composers known as "La Sirène," and in 1938 he was a cofounder of the *Revue Internationale de Musique.* In the latter year he wrote his first piano concerto as a test piece for aspirants to the Ysaÿe Prize (which was won by Emil Gilels). Absil retired from his professorship in 1959 and from Etterbeek five years later. His large output includes operas, ballets, musicodramatic works for radio, 5 symphonies, a number of concerti for piano, violin, viola, and guitar, cantatas, 4 string quartets, violin sonatas, guitar music, piano music, and songs. RECORDINGS: Absil's most readily obtainable recording has been his saxophone quartet. Other works on record include a setting of Apollinaire's *Le Bestiare* for chorus; ballet music from the opera *Peau d'âne (Ass's Skin)*. Also, under the auspices of the Belgian government, there have been recordings of the *Rapsodie roumaine* for violin and orchestra, the *Threnody for Good Friday* for chorus, and *Asymmetries* for two pianos.

[1890] PISTON, Walter Hamor
TEACHER, VIOLINIST
BORN: Rockland, Me., January 20, 1894
DIED: Belmont, Mass., November 12, 1976

Promoted by Serge Koussevitzky [1655], Walter Piston was toward the end of his life apparently firmly established as one of the Grand Old Men of American orchestral music. But in the last few years his reputation seems to have suffered something of an eclipse—perhaps the inevitable posthumous reaction visited on the famous of a previous generation. His family name was originally Pistone, his grandfather having been an Italian seaman. In 1904 the family settled in Boston, where Walter undertook a craftsmanly curriculum at Mechanic Arts High School (it included blacksmithing), graduating in 1912. His training got him a job as draftsman with the Boston Elevated Railway, and that work led him to the Massachusetts Normal School of Art, where he met his future wife, Kathryn Mason. Meanwhile he had studied enough piano and (particularly) violin to qualify for pickup engagements around Boston. He graduated from art school in 1916 and the following year enlisted in the U.S. Navy, where he was assigned duty as a saxophonist in a band stationed in Boston. (This experience did not prevent him from writing in his textbook *Orchestration* that the saxophone is too sentimental and out of tune to be used in combination with other instruments.) Released in 1919, he studied for a year with Archibald T. Davison, married Kathryn, and entered Harvard as a full-time music student. At

thirty he graduated with highest honors and a Paine Fellowship that took him to Paris for further study—for a time with Dukas [1574] but chiefly with Nadia Boulanger. On his return home in 1926 he fulfilled the final requirement for the modern American musical fairytale: he was appointed to the Harvard faculty and lived happily ever after. He and his wife bought a home in Belmont, Massachusetts where he resided for the rest of his life. His first considerable composition, the *Symphonic Piece* of 1927, was unveiled by the Boston Symphony the following spring; that body gave the premieres of most of his orchestral works, save for those commissioned by other orchestras, including the first of his 8 symphonies in 1938.

A conservative who believed uncompromisingly in the importance of form and technique, Piston was a brilliant teacher, numbering among his students such as Samuel Adler [2372], Leonard Bernstein [2282], Gordon Binkerd [2248], Elliott Carter [2130], Gail Kubik [2224], Robert Moevs [2309], Daniel Pinkham [2330], Harold Shapero [2301], and others. He attained his full professorship in 1944 and was named to the Walter W. Naumburg Chair in 1951. He retired in 1960. He won innumerable honors, awards, and commissions, including Pulitzer Prizes in 1948 (for the third symphony) and in 1960 (for the seventh). With the exception of a couple of choral works, Piston's entire output was instrumental and mostly abstract. Besides the symphonies, it includes a concerto apiece for orchestra, viola, piano, two pianos, clarinet, and flute; 2 concerti for violin; other concerted pieces; miscellaneous orchestral works; chamber music (including 5 string quartets); and a few keyboard pieces. Serious to the point of severity, Piston's music never courted popularity, though his one stage work, the 1938 ballet *The Incredible Flutist*, has attained something like it.

RECORDINGS: The ballet has been recorded both *in toto* and in the form of a suite, together with all of the symphonies, concerti for orchestra and for viola, Concerto No. 1 for Violin, the 1976 Concerto for String Quartet, Winds, and Percussion (one of his last works), the piano concertino, the orchestral *Serenata, Tunbridge Fair* for band, the *Divertimento* for nine instruments, the piano quintet, the piano trio, all of the string quartets, sonatas for flute and for violin, the wind quintet, other wind pieces, the piano *Passacaglia*, the *Chromatic Study on BACH* for organ, and the *Carnival Song* for male voices and brasses.

[1891] KANITZ, Ernest (né Ernst)
TEACHER
BORN: Vienna, April 9, 1894
DIED: Menlo Park, Calif., April 7, 1978

Thanks to the Nazis, Kanitz was another central European composer who made most of his career in the United States. Originally a student of law at the University of Vienna, he spent eight years working at music with Richard Heuberger **[1451]** and Franz Schreker **[1705]**. In 1922 he joined the staff of the Vienna Conservatory. The 1938 *Anschluss* forced him to emigrate to America. He immediately found a position at Winthrop College in Rock Hill, South Carolina. After three years he became head of the music department at Erskine College at Due West in the same state. In 1945 he became a professor at the University of Southern California, remaining there until he reached the mandatory retirement age fourteen years later. However, he continued to teach for another five years at tiny Marymount College, Palos Verdes Estates, California. He died two days before his eighty-fourth birthday. Kanitz, incidentally, did not change his first name to facilitate American pronunciation but to avoid confusion with another Viennese named Ernst Kanitz. He wrote the bulk of his output after he left Austria, including 6 one-act operas, 3 symphonies, and most of his chamber music. RECORDINGS: Recordings include the *Sinfonietta da camera* and the second violin sonata.

[1892] JENSEN, Ludvig Paul Irgens
(Yen'-sen, Lōōd'-vēg Poul Ēr'-genz)
BORN: Oslo, April 13, 1894
DIED: Enna, Sicily, April 11, 1969

There appears to be a difference of opinion as to whether this composer should be listed as here, or as "Irgens Jensen." Though he studied piano, his formal education was in philology and he was almost wholly self-taught in other aspects of music. He began his compositional career exclusively as a songwriter but in the 1920s began branching out into choral and instrumental music. His output was small but his music sufficiently impressive to the Norwegian government to win him a lifetime pension in 1946. His largest work was the 1930 dramatic symphony *Heimferd (Homecoming)*, which he later reworked and presented as an opera. In 1937 he also reworked his music for H. E. Kinck's play *Driftekaren (The Drover)* into a *Partita sinfonica*. Sources also differ on the place of Jensen's death—*Grove* gives Oslo. RECORDINGS: The *Partita sinfonica* has been

recorded, as have the Symphony in D Minor of 1943 (his sole work in that genre), the 1926 *Passacaglia* for orchestra, and the early song cycle *Japanischer Frühling (Japanese Spring)* in its 1957 orchestral dress.

[1893] SLONIMSKY, Nicolas (Slō-nim'-skē, Ni'-kō-làs)
PIANIST, CONDUCTOR, WRITER, LEXICOGRAPHER
BORN: St. Petersburg, April 27, 1894

Television watchers of a generation ago may recall Nicolas Slonimsky's brief moment of popular fame, when as one of the few honest contestants on one of the big-money quiz shows, he smilingly and deferentially demonstrated an encyclopedic knowledge of music—which has long been his stock in trade. His learning in fact extends far beyond the bounds of music. He came from an artistic-intellectual Russian family and was taught piano by his aunt Isabelle Vengerova, who was later to teach Samuel Barber **[2149]**, Leonard Bernstein **[2282]**, and Lukas Foss **[2324]**, among others. His teachers in theory and composition at the St. Petersburg Conservatory were Vassili Kalafati (1869–1942) and Maximilian Steinberg (1883–1946), both Rimsky-Korsakov **[1416]** pupils. Following the October Revolution, Slonimsky fled Petrograd (as it had become). Moving steadily southward, he paused in Kiev long enough for some lessons with Glière **[1662]**, then proceeded by way of Yalta, Constantinople, and Sofia to Paris, where he became Koussevitzky's **[1655]** Man Friday. In 1923 he came to the United States, where he found a job at the newly opened Eastman School of Music in Rochester, New York, seizing the opportunity to study there with Selim Palmgren **[1703]** and the Anglo-Russian conductor Albert Coates. In 1925 Slonimsky rejoined Koussevitzky in Boston but was fired two years later subsequent to a row. He remained in Boston, however, teaching, reviewing, and conducting. To further the cause of contemporary music, he organized the Chamber Orchestra of Boston, which existed from 1927 to 1934. He became increasingly known on the international scene, especially as an apostle of modern music. He was the first to record a work by Varèse **[1774]**—the *Ionization*. In 1937 he published his first book, *Music Since 1900*, a pioneering survey. Slonimsky, who became a United States citizen in 1931, concerned himself more and more with the music of the Americas. In the early 1940s the Pan-American Union sent him on a conducting tour to Latin America, the experience of which he used for the first comprehensive English-language study of music south of the border, *Music in Latin America,* published in 1945. In that year the unexpected death of a faculty member at Harvard catapulted Slonimsky into a post there as lecturer in Slavic languages and literature. A year later the equally sudden death of Oscar Thompson, editor of the *International Cyclopedia of Music and Musicians,* brought him the editorship of that work, which he nursed through five editions. Later he became editor of *Baker's Biographical Dictionary of Musicians,* whose completely revised sixth edition appeared when he was eighty-five. In 1962 the State Department sent him on a lecture tour of Eastern Europe and the Near East. He has taught extensively (and long after the usual retirement age) and has written many books and articles, most of them characterized by his irrepressible sense of humor—e.g., the *Lexicon of Musical Invective,* "Sex and the Music Librarian." Humor also characterizes his music—mostly clever and sometimes searching *jeux d'esprit* in miniature form. (His nephew Sergei [1932–] is a Soviet composer.)

RECORDINGS: Slonimsky has two LPs of musical miniatures, which include song settings of New England epitaphs and popular ads, and a selection of "minitudes" for piano, based on his monumental *Thesaurus of Scales and Musical Patterns* of 1947. There is also a recording of the 1942 orchestral snippet *My Toy Balloon.*

[1894] BOŘKOVEC, Pavel (Bôrzh-kō'-vets, Pà-vel')
TEACHER
BORN: Prague, June 10, 1894
DIED: Prague, July 22, 1972

Bořkovec was a comparatively late bloomer as a composer. He underwent an academic education, despite an early interest in music, and acquired a degree in philosophy. In 1919 he took lessons from Křička [1752] and Foerster [1520]. His early compositions were out of the post-Romantic grab bag. In 1925 he undertook two years of study with Suk [1651] at the Master School of the Prague Conservatory. After that he devoted himself entirely to composition for nearly twenty years. He was influenced by the neo-classic and "motoric" styles of the day, gradually incorporating these with his own lyrical tendencies and an expert handling of counterpoint. With the foundation of the Prague Academy after World War II, he became professor of composition there, retiring in 1964. Among his compositions are two op-

eras, *Satyr* and *Paleček,* a ballet *The Pied Piper,* 3 symphonies, 2 piano concerti, and one each for violin and cello, 5 string quartets, and sonatas for violin and for viola. He was a Czech State Prize winner and held the title of Merited Artist. RECORDINGS: The Concerto No. 2 for Piano has been recorded by pianist Vikterie Svihlikova and Czech orchestral forces.

[1895] BENNETT, Robert Russell
ARRANGER, ORCHESTRATOR, CONDUCTOR
BORN: Kansas City, Mo., June 15, 1894
DIED: New York, August 18, 1981

A prolific composer in his own right, Robert Russell Bennett reigned for half a century as the unparalleled arranger and orchestrator of Broadway musicals. (In his peak season, he had twenty-two shows running concurrently in New York.) His family settled in the United States in colonial times. His father was an orchestral musician and band director, his mother a piano teacher. Stricken with polio at the age of four, he began to take an interest in music during his convalescence and had his first piano lessons from his mother a year later. Over the years he learned to play various other instruments and at fifteen began formal theoretical studies with Carl Busch, founder and director of the Kansas City Symphony and a pupil of J. P. E. Hartmann [1182] and Gade [1248]. Increasingly Bennett worked jobs as a popular musician and in 1916 moved to New York, where he supported himself thus until, completely recovered from his illness, he was taken into the army when the United States declared war on Germany in 1917 and was made a band director. Released in 1919, he found a job orchestrating for the publisher, T. B. Harms, and at the end of the year he married Louise Merrill. In 1922 he struck out on his own as a free-lance orchestrator. The first great hit with which he was connected was Rudolf Friml's [1726] *Rose-Marie* two years later. He brought to his task a skill and sophistication to which Broadway was unused. But he was dissatisfied with so secondary a role, wanting to be known as a composer. After producing a *Charleston Rhapsody,* he was awarded a Guggenheim Fellowship (later renewed), which took him to Europe to study with Nadia Boulanger from 1927 to 1929, during which period he turned out two symphonies and a one-act opera. In 1929 the second symphony (subtitled "Abraham Lincoln") and the orchestral *Sights and Sounds* won him $10,000—two-thirds of the first prize in a competition run by RCA Victor, which he shared with Bloch [1729], Copland [1986], and Gruenberg [1782]. Around 1930 he expanded his activities to Hollywood and spent the years 1936–40 there, turning out an average of eight film scores a year, including one for Hitchcock's *Rebecca* in 1940. He then returned to New York, where he became musical director of the Mutual Broadcasting Company, conducting his own program over station WOR. He also conducted the "Ford Hour" on the air. In March 1943 he emerged as the invisible member of the new reigning musical-comedy Trinity on Broadway with the opening of Richard Rodgers [2018] and Oscar Hammerstein's *Oklahoma!* He enjoyed, of course, further triumphs with both, and a special one with Rodgers for the score for the documentary TV series "Victory at Sea" in 1952. Bennett prospered mightily and should stand as a symbol to parents who think there is no money to be made in the musical profession. He continued to compose throughout most of his long life. RECORDINGS: Original compositions on disc include the Concerto for Violin (Louis Kaufman); *Symphonic Portrait of Gershwin's "Porgy and Bess"; A Symphonic Picture of Jerome Kern; Suite of Old American Dances; Symphonic Songs* (both for band); the *Armed Forces Suite; Commemoration Symphony "Stephen Foster"; The Fun and Faith of William Billings; Symphonic Picture of "My Fair Lady"; Symphonic Picture of "The Sound of Music";* organ sonata; *Song Sonata* for violin and piano (Kaufman); *Hexapoda* for violin and piano (Kaufman, Heifetz); *Rose Variations* for trumpet and piano. (The "Victory at Sea" music has been issued on records in three volumes.)

[1896] MICHELET, Michel (Mē-shel-ā', Mē-shel')
CELLIST
BORN: Kiev, June 26, 1894

Michel Michelet was born Mikhail Levin. He began studying cello in Kiev and continued with Julius Klengel, solo cellist of the Leipzig Gewandhaus Orchestra. He also studied composition with Reger [1637] in Leipzig and, after war broke out in 1914, with Glière [1662] in his hometown. He escaped from Russia after the 1917 Revolution and settled in Paris, where he made a name for himself as a film composer. Fleeing the Nazis, he managed to make his way to the United States in 1941 and took up his career in Hollywood, where he has written scores for innumerable pictures. He has also com-

posed a violin concerto, an opera *Hannele* in 1973, and much music in small forms, including his Sonata for Balalaika and Piano. RECORDINGS: A song cycle entitled *Songs and Arias* has been recorded.

[1897] BARANOVIĆ, Krešimir (Bȧ-rȧn'-ō-vich, Kresh'-ē-mēr)
CONDUCTOR
BORN: Šibenik, July 25, 1894
DIED: Belgrade, September 17, 1975

Born on the Adriatic coast of what was then the Austrian province of Dalmatia, Baranović was trained in Zagreb and later in Vienna. By the time he was twenty-one, he had established himself as a theatrical and operatic conductor. He conducted in Zagreb from 1915 to 1927, in which latter year he became conductor for Anna Pavlova's touring dance troupe. He returned to his Zagreb post in 1928. In 1945 he accepted a professorship at the Belgrade Conservatory, where he also conducted the state radio orchestra. In 1951 he became director of the Belgrade State Philharmonic, and that same year his folk ballet *The Gingerbread Heart* was successful at the Edinburgh Festival. Among his other works are several other ballets and two operas. RECORDINGS: The composer and his orchestra have recorded *The Gingerbread Heart*. There are also Yugoslav recordings of his *Sinfonietta* for string orchestra and *Clouds* for mezzo-soprano and orchestra.

[1898] OVALLE, Jayme (Ō-vȧl'-le, Jā'-me)
CIVIL SERVANT
BORN: Belem, August 5, 1894
DIED: 1955

Ovalle majored in finance at school but picked up sufficient music to play in street bands in Rio de Janeiro. From 1933 to 1937 he was an attaché at the Brazilian Embassy in London. Later he worked in Brazil as a customs agent. An amateur folklorist, he made many arrangements of Brazilian folksongs, whose spirit infected his own music (chiefly in the area of piano pieces and songs). RECORDINGS: A number of his songs have been recorded.

[1899] PIJPER, Willem (Pī'-per, Wil'-em)
CRITIC, EDUCATOR
BORN: Zeist, September 8, 1894
DIED: Leidschendam, March 18, 1947

Willem Pijper stands as one of the key figures in the twentieth-century Dutch musical renaissance, such as it is. Born to working-class parents in a town near Utrecht, he learned his letters and his notes from his father, who played the violin as a hobby. Frail and sickly, he was housebound for years, which he spent educating himself, musically and otherwise. At fourteen he was sufficiently improved to enter high school, but he soon found it rather a waste of his time and dropped out after three years. Since he had decided that he wanted to be a musician, his father, a pious man, sent him to the Utrecht Music School to become a church organist. The director Johan Wagenaar (1862–1941), Pijper's organ teacher and a composer himself, felt that such a career might circumscribe Pijper's talents and urged him to concentrate on composing (which he had been doing since he was five). During his five years at the school the young man wrote feverishly, and by the time he left in 1916, he had completed many small pieces, as well as a piano trio, a string quartet, and some orchestral and choral pieces. The next year he finished his first symphony, a big Mahlerian piece called *Pan*—though other works of this period were not surprisingly Impressionist, since he was an ardent Francophile.

He put such influences behind him around 1918, the year that he began teaching in the High School in Amsterdam and reviewing for the Utrecht *Dagblad,* embracing such compositional devices as polytonality, free rhythms, and the development of compositions from brief motifs or single chords (which he called germ cells). He left the school in 1921 and the newspaper in 1923. In 1925 he became professor of composition at the Amsterdam Conservatory and founder-editor of a journal, *De Muziek,* which survived for four years. He completed his second symphony in 1921 and finished his third and last—his best-known work—in 1926. In 1930 he became director of the Amsterdam Conservatory. Three years later his only completed opera *Halewijn*—he called it a symphonic drama—was premiered in Amsterdam. (A second opera, *Merlijn,* was unfinished.) In 1940 his home in Rotterdam was destroyed along with the rest of the city in a German saturation bombing; with it went most of his manuscripts, including many that had not been published. In his later music, he aimed at compression and simplification. Among his significant compositions are concerti for piano, violin, and cello, 4 completed string quartets (a fifth was unfinished at his death) and other chamber works, choral and keyboard music (including some for carillon), and songs.

RECORDINGS: Recordings which have been available in the United States include the third symphony, the piano concerto, the *Symphonic Epigrams* (written in 1928 for the anniversary of the Concertgebouw Orchestra), the *Adagios for Orchestra,* all but the first of his string quartets, Sonata for Flute and Piano, and a piano sonatina. The Dutch Donemus Foundation has a number of additional recordings of orchestral, vocal, and chamber works in its archives and tentatively plans to release and/or reissue Pijper's complete orchestral works.

[1900] WARLOCK, Peter
CRITIC
BORN: London, October 30, 1894
DIED: London, December 17, 1930

"Peter Warlock" was the creative side of Philip Heseltine, a fine critic and scholar, to whom we owe, at least in part, the resurrection of such early composers as Gesualdo **[310]** and Whythorne **[210].** The Warlock persona was, in the opinion of many, the finest English song writer since Henry Purcell **[581].** The duality of name reflects an apparently irreconcilably split personality.

Heseltine was left fatherless at two. At fourteen he went to Eton for three years and got a little basic musical training there. Vacationing at his uncle's on the French coast in 1910, he met Frederick Delius **[1539],** who lived nearby and became his devoted acolyte, though he took no formal lessons from him. On leaving Eton in 1911, he spent a couple of years in Germany, then entered Oxford to major in classics. At the outbreak of war the following summer, he declared himself a conscientious objector and withdrew from the university. In 1915 he met D. H. Lawrence, was bowled over by his work and his ideas, and strove mightily for the publication of *The Rainbow,* which was then proscribed. Lawrence's typical response was (figuratively) to kick him in the teeth. Heseltine's next enthusiasm was that curious composer Bernard van Dieren **[1786],** who probably had more impact on his music than any other living musician. A marriage at about this time brought no increase in stability and ended in 1924 with a divorce. In 1917 he went to Ireland for a year and there began seriously composing. His writing, like Hugo Wolf's **[1521],** whom he in other ways resembles, came in sudden bursts of frantic creativity, followed by long sterile periods. In 1920 he founded a musical journal, *The Sackbut,* but it lasted only a year. For the next decade he was highly productive of scholarship, editing much early English music, writing articles and books (studies of Delius and, with his friend Cecil Gray,

Gesualdo), and promoting the music of his favorites, notably Delius.

A well-known portrait photo shows hair slicked straight back, and lean, sensitive features marked by a neatly trimmed beard and mustache. Behind the mournful eyes there is a diabolic twinkle. In his other incarnation the quiet scholar was a heroic toper, a master coiner of dirty limericks, a sort of madman whom one glimpses riding his motorcyle stark naked through the English countryside at night. Chaos got the upper hand: shortly before Christmas in his thirty-seventh year, he turned on the gas in his apartment and died. He left no major works. His largest compositions are three small orchestral pieces (the *Capriol Suite* for strings is really arranged from Thoinet Arbeau [189]), three carols for chorus and orchestra, and the song cycle *The Curlew* with chamber ensemble. The rest consists of choral pieces and songs (with a good deal of overlap between the genres). There are about a hundred published songs, ranging (expectably) from bawdy table-thumping drinking songs to some of the most delicate and poignant English *Lieder* ever written. Thirty years ago Hubert Foss lamented that no one had attempted a critical edition of Warlock's music; the gap has not yet been closed.

RECORDINGS: Works like *Capriol Suite, Serenade for Frederick Delius, The Curlew,* and a miscellany of songs and choral pieces have from time to time appeared on major labels. In the past decade several smaller British companies have made a serious and important effort to repair the neglect by recording numerous songs.

[1901] AVSHALOMOV, Aaron (Áv-shäl'-ō-mof, A'-ron)
BORN: Nikolayevsk na Amure, November 11, 1894
DIED: New York, April 26, 1965

The list of significant composers born in Siberia is very small. Aaron Avshalomov, native of a seaport at the mouth of the Amur, would seem to lead all the rest. After studying at the Zürich Conservatory, he made his way at twenty to Peking. There he married an American, fathered the future American composer Jacob Avshalomov [2287], and studied how to synthesize Chinese and Western musics. The first major result was the opera *Kuan Yin,* premiered in Peking in 1925. The 1930s saw a number of major works—the ballets *Soul of the Ch'in, Incense Shadows,* and *Buddha and the Five Planetary Deities,* the orchestral *Peiping Hutungs*

(taken up by Leopold Stokowski), a piano concerto, a violin concerto, and a symphony. Shortly after the premiere of his second opera, *The Great Wall,* Avshalomov brought his family to the United States and settled in New York. Among his later works were three more symphonies. RECORDINGS: Two orchestral works, *Peiping Hutungs* and the piano concerto, have been recorded—both conducted by his son.

[1902] DESSAU, Paul (Des'-sou, Poul)
VIOLINIST, CONDUCTOR
BORN: Hamburg, December 10, 1894
DIED: East Berlin, June 28, 1979

Paul Dessau is perhaps best known in the West (along with Hanns Eisler [1952]) as a successor to Kurt Weill [1978] as Bertolt Brecht's musical interpreter. Dessau was the grandson of a Jewish cantor and first appeared on the concert platform as a child violinist. But after two years of advanced study on the instrument at the Klindworth-Scharwenka Conservatory in Berlin, he gave it up. Subsequent to some study of score reading in Hamburg with Eduard Behm, a onetime protégé of Brahms [1329], he became at eighteen a rehearsal coach at the Hamburg Opera, where he learned the niceties of conducting by watching the big boys. He found a place with an operetta theater at Bremen in 1914, but his engagement was ended when he was called up for military service. In 1918 he became music director of the little Kammerspiele Theater in Hamburg, where his *Lanzelot und Sanderein* was produced the same year. In 1919 he became Klemperer's [1794] assistant at Cologne, spent the 1924–25 season at Mainz, and then found a permanent post at the Municipal Opera in Berlin. It was in Berlin that he got down to composing concert works and also to writing film scores. It all came to an end in 1933 when he fled to Paris, where he became a convert to communism. After a period in Palestine, he emigrated to New York in 1939. In 1942 he met Brecht and joined him in southern California, where he was employed in the film studios. In 1946 he wrote the incidental music for the playwright's *Mutter Courage und ihr Kinder (Mother Courage and Her Children),* following it in 1947 with *Der gute Mensch von Szechuan (The Good Woman of Szechuan).* The pair returned to Germany in 1948, settling by choice in the East Zone of Berlin. The collaboration reached something of a peak for Dessau with the opera *Das Verhör des Lukullus (The Trial of Lucullus),* a condemnation of militarists—with which the

East German government soon found fault (they said it was not forceful enough) and which it closed down. (Eventually, after being repeatedly revised, it found favor as *Die Verurteilung des Lukullus*—"trial" changed to "condemnation"—and was permitted a recording.) In 1960 Dessau settled in Zeuthen outside Berlin, where he taught in the Hochschule. His best-known major work on the international scene is the opera *Puntila*—derived from Brecht's play *Herr Puntila und sein Knecht Matti (Mr. Puntila and His Man Matti)*, for which he had written music in 1949. During his thirty years back in Germany, Dessau often groveled before his masters and wrote much propaganda music. Works of his last years seem to involve a mixture of experimentation and propaganda. These include the 1967 "minimal opera" *Geschäftsbericht*, which lasts exactly 600 seconds, the 1970 choral-orchestral *Lenin*, and the large-scale 1973 opera *Einstein*, described as a Marxist interpretation of Einstein's life and times.

RECORDINGS: Besides *Lukullus* (conducted by Herbert Kegel), recordings under the composer's direction include the opera *Puntila* and two orchestral works—*In Memoriam Bertolt Brecht*, 1957; and *Bach Variations*, 1963. Other East German recordings include *Lenin*, *Einstein*, and several song cycles for soprano and chamber ensemble; there are undoubtedly others behind the Iron Curtain. In addition there is a recording of *A Jewish Chronicle*, a collectively composed work with movements by Blacher [2030], Hartmann [2072], Henze [2361], Dessau himself, and his East German comrade Rudolf Wagner-Régeny (1903–69).

[1903] MOERAN, Ernest John (Mō'-ràn, Er'-nest Jon)
BORN: Heston, Middlesex, December 31, 1894
DIED: Kenmare, County Kerry, December 1, 1950

Little known outside of England in his lifetime, E. J. Moeran's music is, thanks to recordings, making some headway here. Moeran was the son of an Irish-born Anglican parson and an East Anglian mother. While he was still a child, his father was transferred to Bacton on the Norfolk coast, and there Moeran heard mostly hymn tunes and folksongs. He taught himself to read music from the hymnal and studied violin as part of his grammar schooling at nearby Cromer. He was then packed off to Uppingham School in Leicestershire, where he heard his first "serious" music and where

his talents were fostered by the music master, Robert Sterndale Bennett (grandson of Sir William [1246]). On leaving in 1913 he entered the Royal College of Music but left to join the army with the outbreak of war in 1914. He was promoted to an officership a year later. In 1917 he was badly wounded and saw no further service. Mustered out in 1919, he returned to Uppingham to teach. In 1920, when he found his duties were getting in the way of his composing, he quit and went to study privately in London with John Ireland [1719], with whom he worked until 1923. Before that period was over, he had already had songs and other pieces published and had begun collecting and arranging the folksongs on which he had been nurtured. By mid-decade he was known and respected around London as a significant musical figure. Save for a couple of orchestral pieces, however, Moeran concentrated up to 1930 mostly on songs and piano music. Dissatisfied with his limitations, he retired to the Cotswolds to develop his contrapuntal and harmonic language. During this decade he produced a good deal of choral music, some chamber works, and several orchestral pieces, culminating in his only symphony (in G minor) of 1937. The early 1940s saw the violin concerto, the *Rhapsody* for piano and orchestra, the *Sinfonietta*, and the *Overture for a Masque* (written for Walter Legge's concerts for servicemen). In 1945 Moeran married the cellist Peers Coetmore, for whom as a wedding present he wrote a cello concerto (and in 1947 a sonata). On a trip to Ireland late in 1950, he fell into the River Kenmare, apparently the victim of a heart attack and was found dead. Moeran had a gift for melody. In his earlier years he was strongly influenced by Ireland and Delius [1539], but toward the end of his career he developed a more personal style. RECORDINGS: There are recordings of the Symphony, the *Sinfonietta*, the Concerto for Violin, the Concerto for Cello, the Sonata for Cello and Piano (both cello works by Coetmore), the String Trio, *Rhapsody No. 2*, *Two Pieces* for small orchestra, the choral *Songs of Springtime*, the *Overture*, piano pieces, and songs.

[1904] BINDER, Abraham Wolfe
CONDUCTOR, TEACHER
BORN: New York, January 13, 1895
DIED: New York, October 10, 1966

Following the path blazed by Ernest Bloch [1729], Binder identified himself primarily as a Jewish composer. He graduated in 1926 from Columbia University. He was choir director at the YMHA and, under Rabbi Stephen Wise, at the Free Synagogue. In 1931 he was invited to Palestine to conduct the resident symphony orchestra there and in 1937 became professor of liturgical music at the Jewish Institute of Religion in New York. He wrote and arranged much music for worship but also composed secular music, mostly inspired by Jewish history, literature, and folklore—e.g., the opera *A Goat in Chelm;* 2 oratorios, *Judas Maccabaeus* and *Israel Reborn;* and such orchestral works as the *Dybbuk Suite, The Valley of Dry Bones, Holy Land Impressions, The Pioneers, Palestinian Song Suite,* and *In Memory of the Defenders of the Warsaw Ghetto.* RECORDINGS: Amiram Rigai has recorded a piano work, *To a Rose of Sharon.*

[1905] RUDHYAR, Dane (Rud'-yer, Dān)
POLYMATH, ASTROLOGER
BORN: Paris, March 23, 1895

The man who became Dane Rudhyar around 1917 was born Daniel Chennevière, the son of a small-time Parisian manufacturer. He was taught piano and basic theory as a child without exhibiting any great passion for music. When he was twelve, a severe illness and operation permanently undermined his health. He was an omnivorous reader and precocious writer and, despite his setback, graduated a year early from secondary school. Awakened at last to music by Debussy's [1547] *Pelléas et Mélisande,* he sat in on courses at the Paris Conservatoire in 1912–13 and followed orchestral rehearsals with scores. During this period he wrote (and published) some piano pieces and a Nietzsche-inspired book on Debussy, as well as reviews for a local magazine. Exempted from service in 1914 because of his health, he became for a time (like the poet Rainer Marie Rilke) secretary to the sculptor Auguste Rodin.

When in 1916 Chennevière inherited some money, he emigrated to the United States. He had become deeply absorbed in a concept of mixed-media performance or "total theater" called metachory (invented by one Valentine de Saint-Point) and had composed several musical scores to that end. He persuaded the conductor Pierre Monteux to help him mount an evening of metachory (two works entitled *Poèmes ironiques* and *Vision végétale)* at the Metropolitan Opera. The date, April 4, 1917, was not optimum—America declared war on Germany two days later—and the performance was a flop. The next year Rudhyar, as he had become, moved to Canada, where he published a

book of poems and discovered the music of Scriabin [1625], which for a time seems to have had a profound impact on him and his music. A commission from a wealthy Philadelphia matron for music for a Passion Play of her own devising took him in 1920 to California, which, save for a time in Europe in the early 1960s, became his home. There he acted in small movie and stage roles, wrote articles on many subjects, immersed himself in studies of the occult (Eastern and Western), and opened an oriental shop. Having temporarily abandoned composition in 1922, he returned to it in 1925 with a series of piano pieces in a new, individual, and atonal idiom, which generated considerable interest among musicians. By the end of the decade he had quit composing again.

In 1930 Rudhyar married Malya Contento, whose name has a forbidding ring. (The marriage ended in divorce in 1945 and was followed by three more.) He continued to write poetry and philosophy but during this period was chiefly concerned with astrology, of which he formulated a whole new theory and about which he was regarded as an important authority. There was another spurt of composing in the 1950s which produced several orchestral and chamber works, and still another (and riper) period in the mid-1970s. For a decade, 1942–52, Rudhyar made a name for himself as an abstract painter. In 1976 *The Warrior,* his 1921 tone poem for piano and orchestra, finally received its premiere. He married Leyla Rael in 1977 and settled in Palo Alto, California. In 1982 his book *The Magic of Tone and the Art of Music* appeared. He has been the recipient of many prizes, grants, and other honors.

RECORDINGS: The orchestral *Sinfonietta* has been recorded by Jonel Perlea. Two string quartets from 1979, *Advent* and *Crisis and Overcoming,* have been recorded by the Kronos Quartet. Various performers have offered renditions of the following piano works: *3 Paeans, Granites, Stars, Pentagram No. 3, Syntony, Transmutation,* and *Tetragrams Nos. 1, 4, and 5.*

[1906] CASTELNUOVO-TEDESCO, Mario (Kás-tel-nwō'-vō Tä-däs'-kō, Mär'-yō)
TEACHER
BORN: Florence, April 3, 1895
DIED: Hollywood, March 16 (?), 1968

Despite upheavals in his life, Castelnuovo-Tedesco (whose name means "Newcastle-German") was a very prolific composer and at the worst a clever one, though his reputation as a leading modernist has faded. His father was a banker from an old Tuscan Jewish family. The boy learned piano from his mother in secret and so impressed his father when the cat was out of the bag that he gave him his blessing for a musical career. Mario studied piano thereafter with his cousin Edgardo del Valle de Paz at the Luigi Cherubini Institute, and then composition with Ildebrando Pizzetti [1732], graduating in 1918. He had begun composing eight years earlier, addressing himself at first exclusively to piano works (mostly inspired by the Tuscan landscape) and songs. In 1923 he completed an operatic treatment of Machiavelli's black comedy *La Mandragola (The Mandrake)*, which was successfully premiered in Venice three years later, at about the time he finished his second, *Bacco in Toscana (Bacchus in Tuscany)*, premiered at La Scala, in 1931.

Castelnuovo-Tedesco married Clara Porti in 1924. (Their two sons were successful in America as an architect and a physician, respectively.) Soon afterward his discovery of the notebook in which his grandfather had written out Jewish liturgical melodies reminded him of his ethnic background (of which he was to be less pleasantly reminded a decade later), and he produced *Le Danze del Re David (King David's Dances)* for piano, the first of a long series of Jewish-inspired works. A passion for Shakespeare produced a whole series of settings of the lyrics in the 1920s and 11 Shakespearean overtures, beginning in 1930. The 1930s also produced a series of concerti which were taken up by such performers as Jascha Heifetz, Gregor Piatigorsky, and Arturo Toscanini and which gave their composer international fame.

When in 1939 Mussolini, emulating his German partner, cracked down on Italian Jews, Castelnuovo-Tedesco fled with his family to America, settling briefly in Larchmont, New York, and a year later in Beverly Hills, California, where he spent the rest of his life, save for postwar vacations in his beloved Tuscany. He wrote film scores, sometimes pseudonymously, sometimes as a ghost composer. (His best-known effort there—one he admitted—was the score for the Agatha Christie mystery *And Then There Were None (Ten Little Indians)*, directed by René Clair. He also taught, his pupils including André Previn and Henry Mancini. In 1956 the first of his 2 Shakespearean operas, *The Merchant of Venice*, won the Campari competition at La Scala and was premiered five years later in Florence. (The second was *All's Well That Ends Well*, completed in 1958.) Castelnuovo-Te-

desco was a visiting professor at Michigan State University in 1959 and taught regularly at the Los Angeles Conservatory to the end of his life. He died unexpectedly of a heart attack in 1968.

RECORDINGS: Castelnuovo-Tedesco, who occasionally appeared as a pianist, recorded his own *Alt-Wien (Old Vienna), Cipressi (Cypresses)*, and *Études d'ondes (Wave Studies)*. There are many recordings of his guitar works—the 2 concerti for guitar and the concerto for two guitars, the quintet for guitar and strings, the guitar sonata, the suites *Platero y yo (Platero and I, by Andres Segovia)*, the *Romancero gitano (Gypsy romance)* for guitar and voices, and smaller pieces. Heifetz recorded the second violin concerto, subtitled "The Prophets." Other works on record include the Op. 93 *Concertino* for harp and strings, the overture *Much Ado About Nothing*, the orchestral song *Coplas*, a number of sonatas and sonatinas for various instruments, *The Lark* for violin and piano, and other short pieces.

[1907] TOLDRÁ, Eduardo (Tōl-drȧ´, Ed-wär´-dō)
VIOLINIST, CONDUCTOR, TEACHER
BORN: Villanueva y Geltrú, April 7, 1895
DIED: Barcelona, May 31, 1962

A Catalan, Toldrá got the rudiments of music from his father, an amateur, and then studied at the Municipal Music School in Barcelona. At sixteen he began ten years of appearances all over Europe as first violinist of his Renaixement Quartet. In 1921 he returned to Barcelona to teach at his old school, and three years later he also took on the conductorship of the Orquesta Estudios Sinfónicos there. In 1943 he exchanged the latter post for its counterpart at the helm of the newly founded Municipal Orchestra, which he brought to a high state of excellence. He also continued to travel, both as a violinist and conductor. Toldrá did some composing on the side, mostly in smaller forms. RECORDINGS: Some of his songs have been recorded by important Spanish singers such as Conchita Supervia and Victoria de Los Angeles.

[1908] SOWERBY, Leo
ORGANIST, TEACHER, ADMINISTRATOR
BORN: Grand Rapids, Mich., May 1, 1895
DIED: Port Clinton, Ohio, July 7, 1968

Sowerby, the son of an English father and a Canadian mother, was left motherless at

four. The father remarried and the stepmother got him interested in music and saw
to it that he had piano lessons. He began
writing music on his own in childhood.
When he was fourteen, the Sowerbys settled
in Chicago, where he continued his piano
lessons—for a time with Percy Grainger
[1749]—and got some training in theory. In
1913 his first violin concerto was premiered
in an American music concert by the Chicago Symphony. Four years later the same
orchestra gave an all-Sowerby concert, featuring the first concerti for piano and for
cello, the overture *Comes Autumn Time,* and
a soon-to-be-popular Irish folksong arrangement for orchestra, The Irish Washer-
woman. At the end of the year the composer
joined the army, where he rose from bandsman (clarinet) to commissioned band director. He returned to private life and Chicago
in 1919.

Two years later, to his surprise since he
had not entered the competition, he was
named the first recipient of the American
Prix de Rome, which sent him to live and
work at the American Academy in that city
for the next three years. In 1927 he began
thirty-five years as organist at the Episcopal
Cathedral in Chicago (he was almost wholly
self-taught on the instrument). Five years
later he also became professor of composition at the American Conservatory there.
He won the 1945 Pulitzer Prize (awarded in
1946) for his choral-orchestral setting of *The
Canticle of the Sun* (after St. Francis of Assisi). He also received several other prizes
and honors, as well as commissions from
major orchestras. He retired from both his
Chicago posts in 1962 when he was sixty-
seven and then moved to Washington, D.C.,
where he opened the College of Church Musicians, which he headed until he died.
Sowerby wrote 5 orchestral symphonies,
concerti for organ and for violin, 2 concerti
apiece for piano and cello, several cantatas,
2 string quartets, and much else for orchestra, chamber ensembles, organ, piano, and
voices (both massed and solo).

RECORDINGS: Recordings include (orchestral) *Comes Autumn Time, All on a Summer's Day, Prairie* (after Carl Sandburg),
*From the Northland, The Irish Washer-
woman,* and the Concerto for Organ and
Strings; the Symphony in G Major for organ
solo; *Pop Goes the Weasel* for wind quintet;
and keyboard pieces. A classicist at heart,
Sowerby injected American idioms into his
music.

[1909] STILL, William Grant
INSTRUMENTALIST, ARRANGER, ADMIN-
ISTRATOR
BORN: Woodville, Miss., May 11, 1895
DIED: Los Angeles, December 3, 1978

It is probably correct to say that William
Grant Still was the first black American
composer to be accepted as an equal by the
white musical establishment—and one of the
first composers of stature to come from
south of the Mason-Dixon line. His parents
both had college educations; his father in
fact was a professional musician who taught
at Alabama A & M. Unhappily he died
when his son was still a baby. Mrs. Still
moved to Little Rock, where she found a
permanent job as a high school teacher.
There she married a man who happened to
be an opera buff and who introduced his
stepson to the voices of great singers on
records. William also had violin lessons. At
sixteen he matriculated at Wilberforce University, a small Negro college in Ohio, with
an eye to becoming a physician. However,
he spent his time mostly pursuing musical
activities. He taught himself to play reed instruments and soon left school to play in
dance bands. He worked briefly as an arranger for W. C. Handy, the great blues
writer. After a time he returned to Wilberforce, graduating in 1915. After marrying
Grace Bundy, he returned to band work until 1917, when he went to Oberlin on a trust
fund left him by his father. When the country involved itself in the European war, Still
was called into service—as a mess attendant
until news of his performing talents got
around and he was promoted to membership
in the ensemble that played for an officers'
club.

After he had been discharged, he returned
to Oberlin, where the faculty chipped in to
cover his expenses, his money being exhausted. In 1921 he left to play oboe in the
orchestra of the Noble Sissle-Eubie Blake revue *Shuffle Along,* an engagement that lasted
two years. During the show's Boston stand
Still took the opportunity of studying with
George Chadwick [1483], who was so
pleased with his work that he insisted on
teaching him gratis. So afterward did Edgard Varèse [1774] in New York, where for a
time in the middle 1920s Still ran the Black
Swan Phonograph Company. For a time he
tried composing according to Varèse's notions—and won praise and encouragement
for his efforts; but he found that his heart
was not in it and turned to writing a more
conservative sort of music that he hoped
would reflect the ethos of his people. These
efforts reached some sort of culmination in

his *Afro-American Symphony,* premiered in 1931 by Howard Hanson **[1927]** and soon played all over the world. It was the first symphony by a black composer to be played by a major American orchestra (the New York Philharmonic).

But Still's success in this area was insufficient to put bread on the table, and so he led a double life as an increasingly popular orchestrator and arranger. Beginning with Donald Voorhees's radio orchestra, he worked for such employers as the Earl Carroll Vanities, Paul Whiteman, Artie Shaw, and both the radio and television networks. A Guggenheim fellowship in 1934 gave him time to try his hand at an opera, *Blue Steel;* though he had had some ballets produced, he found no takers for it. It was followed by *Troubled Island,* whose libretto was by Verna Arver, whom, his first marriage having gone on the rocks after giving him three children, he married in 1939. In 1940 the pair collaborated on a third opera, *Bayou Legend.* Eventually in 1949 the New York City Opera staged *Troubled Island*—in whiteface and unsuccessfully, but marking the first time a black composer's work had been produced by a major American opera company. *Bayou Legend* had to wait thirty-four years before it was performed, by the Negro Opera/South company, whose production, however, became the first such work ever seen on national American television.

Still had moved to Los Angeles in 1934, where he worked on films (the Bing Crosby version of *Pennies from Heaven,* the original *Lost Horizon)* and later on important TV shows *(Perry Mason, Gunsmoke).* By the end of his long life, his music had been played by most of the great American orchestras, and he had received half a dozen honorary doctorates, several prestige fellowships, and many other honors. His list of works is long and includes 8 operas, 4 ballets, and 5 symphonies (plus 2 that he disowned).

RECORDINGS: Recordings exist of the ballet *Sahdji* (Howard Hanson, Paul Freeman), the *Afro-American Symphony* (Karl Krueger, Freeman), the symphonic poem *Darker America* (Siegfried Landau), excerpts from *Highway No. 1, USA* (Freeman), the orchestral suite *From the Black Belt* (Landau), the *Festive Overture* (Arthur Bennett Lipkin), the band piece *To You America, Ennanga* for harp, piano, and strings, and a number of chamber, piano, and vocal pieces.

[1910] TCHISHKO, Oles Semyonovich
(Chĕsh'-kō, Ōl'-yes Syem-yon-ō'-vich)
SINGER, TEACHER, CONDUCTOR
BORN: Dvurechny Kut, July 3, 1895

Tchishko was born near Kharkov, the son of a Ukrainian peasant. His musical leanings evidenced themselves early, and he became soprano soloist of his grammar school choir. From 1914 he studied law at the University of Kharkov, but he aspired to sing opera and studied voice and composition in his off-hours. After the 1917 Revolution he became a power in Ukrainian musical politics. He seems professionally to have led a catch-as-catch-can existence as a local musical factotum for the next decade or so, during which time he essayed a couple of operas without success. At the age of thirty-six he temporarily abandoned his career, such as it was, for several years of study at the Leningrad Conservatory. In 1937 he completed his opera *The Battleship Potemkin* which, in subject and style, seems to have satisfied both the public and officialdom. He continued to sing, conduct, teach, and organize proletarian and military musical groups. As a singer, he created the leading role of Pierre Bezukhov in Prokofiev's **[1851]** *War and Peace.* Tchishko's work, mostly vocal, leans heavily on folksongs, of which he has made many arrangements. He has also composed for "folk orchestras." The subjects of his choral works are for the most part propagandistic. RECORDINGS: There is a recording of his *Ukrainian Rhapsody* for organ.

[1911] JACOB, Gordon Percival Septimus
TEACHER, CONDUCTOR, ARRANGER, EDITOR
BORN: London, July 5, 1895
DIED: London, June 8, 1984

"A champion of orthodoxy," as one writer terms him, Gordon Jacob is apt to be remembered more for his clever orchestrations of such things as the Chopin **[1208]** *Les Sylphides* and the Schumann **[1211]** *Carnaval* than for his own highly competent compositions. He studied (rather late) at the Royal College of Music (inevitably with Stanford **[1467]** and Parry **[1443]**), taught at Birkbeck and Morley Colleges, and returned in 1926 to the Royal College as a member of its faculty, remaining until 1966. He has served as a musical examiner, conductor, and editor (of the Penguin series of scores). He has also written a good deal on music, notably textbooks on orchestration and score reading. Jacob took a D.Mus. at the University of London in 1935 and has been the recipient of many honors, culminating in the C.B.E. in 1968. He retired from teaching two years earlier. His music, impeccably crafted and often witty, includes 2 ballets, 2 symphonies, several orchestral suites, concerti and concerted works for various instruments (e.g., piano, violin, viola, cello, oboe, horn, bassoon, trombone, and harmonica), some choral works, and a good deal of chamber music. RECORDINGS: Chiefly on British labels, these include a three-hand piano concerto entitled *Concerto for Phyllis and Cyril, Original Suite* for band, *Music for a Festival, William Byrd Suite, Five Pieces for Harmonica and Orchestra, Variations on "Annie Laurie"* (for an ensemble of odd instruments, written for the first Hoffnung Festival), *Mini-Concerto* for clarinet and strings, Concertino for Bassoon and Strings, an overture entitled *The Barber of Seville Goes to the Devil, Divertimento* for Harmonica and Strings Quartet, Quartet for Saxophones, *Rhapsody* for English horn and strings, an oboe sonatina, and other small works.

[1912] ORFF, Carl (Ôrf, Kärl)
TEACHER, CONDUCTOR, MUSICOLOGIST
BORN: Munich, July 11, 1895
DIED: Munich, March 29, 1982

As the composer of the *Carmina Burana,* perhaps the only piece of "serious" new music to have won truly popular acclaim since World War II, Carl Orff has remained a figure of savage controversy since that work burst on the larger world via Eugen Jochum's recording. For all of his mature life, Orff himself jealously guarded his privacy and refused to talk at all about himself. Orff was the scion of an old and cultured Bavarian family, his father being a high officer in the palace guard. He demonstrated musical ability early, both as performer and composer. At nineteen he graduated from the Munich Academy where Hermann Zilcher [1737] had been one of his teachers. Having worked as coach and *répétiteur* at theaters in Munich, Mannheim, and Darmstadt, he did a year of military service near the end of World War I. After experimenting with Impressionism, Straussian postromanticism, and atonality, he went to the reclusive Heinrich Kaminski (1886–1946) in 1920 for further study. (Kaminski, a largely self-taught musical mystic, lived in the home of the painter Franz Marc near the ancient monastery of Benediktbeuren.) Collaboration with the dancer Mary Wigman got Orff interested in Dalcrozian eurhythmics, and in 1924 he joined with Dorothee Günther to open a new sort of music school—the Güntherschule.

Orff became a revolutionary figure in musical education. Students at the school were people seeking careers in teaching eurhyth-

mics. He insisted that they should make their own music to generate movement (and vice versa) and taught them how to improvise skillfully on simple percussion instruments. From this developed his notion of making music an integral part of every child's education from the outset, beginning with simple rhythms (especially as applied to natural vocal utterance) and leading, by way of folk music adapted from all over the world, to a development of the other musical senses and to the ability to "compose" improvisationally. He taught at the Güntherschule until 1936, in the early 1930s formulating his principles in a five-volume graded course *(Schulwerk).* Just as these methods began making real headway in German schools, however, the Nazis came to power, and they became *verboten.*

Meanwhile Orff had turned to old music and in 1925 brought out the first of his three realizations of Monteverdi's **[333]** *Orfeo.* The next year he produced a realization of the same composer's *Il Ballo delle ingrate.* In 1930 Orff became, for three years, conductor of the Munich Bach Society, for which he made similar arrangements. All this time he had been writing music of his own—ballets, operas, choral and orchestral works—virtually all of which he later disowned. The year 1937 saw the premiere of *Carmina Burana (Songs of Beuren),* a "scenic cantata" based on mediaeval poems discovered in the Benediktbeuren library in the previous century. It clearly bore the imprint of Orff's educational notions—a strong emphasis on rhythms, simple melodies, the most basic of harmonies, no modulations. Some felt that it was an abnegation of everything Western music had attained; others felt that it was as refreshing as a glass of cold water. It was followed in 1939 by a similarly conceived "folk-opera," *Der Mond (The Moon).* The war years produced a second such work, *Die Kluge (The Wise Woman),* and a successor to the *Carmina Burana* set to poems of Catullus and called *Catulli Carmina (Catullus' Songs).* This was followed in 1953 by *Il Trionfo di Afrodite (The Triumph of Aphrodite)* to various Latin and Greek erotic poems, the three works being conceived as a trilogy under the blanket title of *Trionfi (Triumphs).*

However, after World War II Orff concerned himself increasingly with the stage, though he refused to call his susequent productions "operas." His first such effort was a 1947 comedy in Bavarian dialect, *Die Bernauerin (The Bernauer Woman),* which is really a play with music, the music being limited to a minimal orchestra and a chorus that hums, chants, and recites as much as it sings. There was another Bavarian work, *Astutuli*, in 1953 and a similarly treated version of Shakespeare's *A Midsummer Night's Dream* a year earlier. Meanwhile in 1949 Orff had produced *Antigonae*, a setting of Sophocles' tragedy in Friedrich Hölderlin's translation. It became the first in a trilogy of Greek tragedies; the others were *Oedipus der Tyrann* (based on Sophocles) in 1959 and *Prometheus* (based on Aeschylus) in 1968. In these works Orff offers his own notion of how Greek drama may have been presented. The orchestra consists of percussion instruments only (though several are tuned), the singing (constant throughout) is primarily chanting. There is little melody and no harmony, the musical impact depending almost entirely on rhythmic effects, most of them hypnotically insistent. A further trilogy of religious "miracle" dramas appeared in the interim: *Comoedia de Christi Resurrectione (Comedy of Christ's Resurrection)*, 1957; *Ludus de Nato Infante Mirificus (Play of the Wondrous Childbirth)*, 1960; and *De Temporum Fine Comoedia (Comedy of the End of Time)*, 1973. In 1962 Orff unwontedly attended a conference on musical education in Toronto, where he both spoke and read from his works. In 1972 he composed *Rota*, a brief ceremonial piece for the Munich Olympics. He died at eighty-six. He was married to the novelist Luise Rinser.

RECORDINGS: Orff left several records on which he reads his two Bavarian plays and the three miracles, as well as *Die Weihnachtsgeschichte (The Christmas Story*, with music by his pupil Gunhild Keetman). There are also recordings of the *Trionfi* and all of the "operas" previously mentioned except the Shakespeare piece. There are various selections from *Schulwerk* (as well as a complete recording entitled *Musica Poetica)* and the few independent choral and orchestral pieces that he continued to claim as his own have also been recorded.

[1913] LONGAS, Federico (Long'-às, Fä-
der-ē'-kō)
PIANIST, EDUCATOR
BORN: Barcelona, August 18, 1895
DIED: Santiago de Chile, June 17, 1968

A fine pianist, Longas was a pupil of Enrique Granados [1588]. He was particularly well known as an accompanist of singers—notably the great tenor Tito Schipa and the soprano Margherita Salvi, who became his wife. The singers, in turn, often sang his lightweight songs. Longas also appeared as a soloist. Until the Fascist victory in Spain, he ran the Academia Longas in Barcelona.

Then he moved to Paris and later settled in New York. RECORDINGS: There are many song recordings.

[1914] HINDEMITH, Paul (Hin'-de-mit,
Poul)
VIOLINIST, VIOLIST, CONDUCTOR,
TEACHER
BORN: Hanau, November 16, 1895
DIED: Frankfurt am Main, December 28,
1963

In the middle years of the twentieth century there was never any doubt that Paul Hindemith was one of the most important composers the era had produced. Progressing from an overripe postromanticism that was linked with Expressionism and often espoused atonality, he moved to a position that reverted to the old Baroque forms newly conceived and that ultimately accepted tonality as the immovable basis of music as we know it. At the present time his stature seems to have been diminished. Perhaps the phenomenon is merely the normal temporary rejection of a titan in reaction to what seems his previous overvaluation—abetted in this instance by the fact that form and tonality have not been admired in certain influential quarters. Or perhaps it is because of the determined earnestness of Hindemith's music, which seems to take itself too seriously even when it is trying to be light or parodistic.

Hindemith was the eldest of the three children of a housepainter; his mother was a shepherd's daughter. Not a great deal is known of his childhood. Hindemith senior seems to have been no more affluent than his calling suggests, and the family moved about a lot before settling in 1902 at Frankfurt. Himself a frustrated musician, he insisted that his children have music lessons. Paul is thought to have studied the violin first with a certain Eugen Reinhardt. Lessons with Anna Hegner when he was twelve led to an all-expenses scholarship at the Hoch Conservatory, where he was a pupil of Adolf Rebner from 1909. The Hindemith children —Paul and Toni on violin, Rudolf on cello —appeared in public with their zither-playing father as the Frankfurter Kindertrio. In the meantime Paul had become a closet composer who went to rather extreme lengths to conceal his shameful activity. When it was discovered, he was put to composition studies in 1912 with Arnold Mendelssohn, a distant relative of the great Felix [1200]. Mendelssohn left in 1913 and Hindemith continued his studies, not altogether happily, with Bernhard Sekles, a Humperdinck [1480] pupil. In these years he participated (with brother Rudolf, who had joined him at the conservatory) in first performances of works by his fellow pupils Ernst Toch [1824] and Hans Rosbaud, the future conductor. The brothers also found occasional jobs playing in salon and theater orchestras. In the summers of 1913 and 1914 Paul found regular employment in Swiss resorts until the outbreak of war sent him scurrying home.

Whether moved by patriotism or his usual restlessness, Hindemith's father Robert, now forty-five, volunteered, was sent to the front in Flanders, and was killed there the next summer, leaving Paul to support his mother and siblings. The young man had already found a place among the first violins at the Frankfurt Opera and was soon promoted to *Konzertmeister*. The chief conductor was Ludwig Rottenberg, who was incidentally Jewish—a fact important in Hindemith's later history. The orchestra also played concerts under Willem Mengelberg, whom Hindemith considered an ass. By now his music —mostly of chamber scale (he was also second violinist in Rebner's string quartet)— was beginning to attract attention, and in 1917, the year he graduated, Breitkopf and Härtel published his Op. 8 cello pieces. At that time Hindemith was a rather unadventurous eclectic to whom Richard Strauss [1563] represented the *ne plus ultra* in music. Soon afterward he was inducted into the army, where he spent the remainder of the war in the field playing bass drum in a band —and violin in a quartet organized by a music-loving commanding officer, who got him promoted to corporal.

Released in 1919, Hindemith returned to his orchestral desk, where he played under a succession of conductors that included Furtwängler [1803], Fritz Busch, Bruno Walter, and Hermann Scherchen. In 1921 Busch conducted the premieres of Hindemith's two little Expressionist operas, *Mörder, Hoffnung der Frauen (Murder, the Hope of Women)* and *Das Nusch-Nuschi* (a Burmese marionette play), scandalizing some of the audience. Rottenberg, however, chose to repeat them the following spring, adding a third, *Sancta Susanna (Saint Susanna)*. Also in 1921, Hindemith's second string quartet was chosen for performance at the second annual festival of contemporary music at Donaueschingen. When the scheduled players balked, the composer (who had taken up the viola) rounded up his brother and the violinists Licco Amar and Walter Casper, who played it. As the Amar Quartet, they continued the association afterward. A year later Hindemith was the talk of the festival for his *Kammermusik No. 1*

(Chamber Music No. 1, for small orchestra) and was soon appointed to its board of directors. Having negotiated a highly favorable publishing contract in 1923 with Schott's of Mainz, he left his orchestral job to allow himself more time for composition. A year later, without announcement and in a private ceremony, he married Gertrud Rottenberg, his former chief's daughter. Shortly afterward he began his first full-length opera *Cardillac,* after E. T. A. Hoffmann [1086]. Carelessly he offered the premiere to both Busch and Otto Klemperer [1794], while Schott was talking terms with Erich Kleiber. After some unpleasantness Busch won out. The premiere, at Dresden in 1926, got mixed reviews, but they were sufficiently favorable to prevent *Cardillac* arrest, though the composer saw fit to virtually rewrite it in 1952.

In 1927, totally inexperienced and with considerable misgivings about his fitness for the role, Hindemith acceded to a request that he teach composition at the Berlin Hochschule. He found not only that the shoe fit but also that the post offered him an opportunity for further education, especially in old music. A year later he, Gertrud, and the model railroad that had become his passion moved to Berlin. Before they did so, however, Hindemith unveiled two new satirical operas at the festival (moved that year, 1927, to Baden-Baden): *Neues vom Tag (News of the Day)* and *Hin und Zurück (There and Back*—a work that reverses itself musically and in terms of action at its midway point). By 1929 the festival had sputtered out, and Hindemith found himself too busy to keep up the string quartet. That same year in Paris he inaugurated a brilliant career as a solo violist (and viola d'amore player), performing under Koussevitzky's baton at Paris in July. Three months later he premiered Walton's [2011] viola concerto in London and shortly afterward began appearing *en trio* with violinist Josef Wolfstahl (later replaced by Szymon Goldberg) and cellist Emanuel Feuermann.

In Berlin Hindemith not only became a brilliant and revolutionary teacher and began to develop his theories about music; he also took a new tack in composing, in considerable degree moved by the thinking of such liberal acquaintances as Bertolt Brecht, with whom he wrote *Lehrstück (Teaching Piece)* in 1929, a propagandistic musical play or revue. He rejected "art for art's sake" and concluded that music should be utilitarian. Accordingly he turned out what he called *Gebrauchsmusik* (roughly "practical music") for the needs of his time. This included music for mechanical keyboards (a score for a Felix the Cat cartoon for mechanical organ) and the electronic trautonium, as well as increasing amounts of material directed to the needs of amateurs, which climaxed in 1932 with the *Plöner Musiktag (Music Day at Plön)*—a complete all-day program for music students in a little town near Kiel. This last work, however, for all practical purposes, saw the end of this phase of Hindemith's career.

In 1933 Hindemith's social views and his changing views of the importance of melody and harmony in music coalesced when he began work on a serious full-length opera about the Renaissance painter Mathias Grünewald and his involvement (unrewarding) with the Peasants' revolt. It was called *Mathis der Maler (Mathias the Painter);* its beginning coincided with the success of a new German leader, Adolf Hilter. Despite his marriage to a Jewish woman, Hindemith took little notice of that event. Goldberg and Feuermann were dismissed from the Hochschule, but he still went on performing with them and teaching at the conservatory. The Nazis were soon, however, proclaiming him a *Kulturbolschewist* preoccupied with sexual perversion, and in 1934, after Furtwängler had conducted the premiere of the symphony that Hindemith had based on the *Mathis* music, they let it be known that the party would not permit further performances of the composer's music. In November a Berlin newspaper published Furtwängler's letter of furious reaction, for which the audience at the Berlin State Opera gave him a standing ovation. The conductor was temporarily removed from his posts, and Hindemith was placed on leave of absence at the Hochschule. However, by spring the fuss seemed to have blown over: the ban on his music was not stringently enforced, though the opera was not allowed to be staged. Hindemith and his wife were permitted to go on an official visit to Turkey for consultation on plans for a conservatory in Ankara, and in 1936 they went back for its opening and for the composer to teach there, though he still nominally held the Hochschule post. In the summer, however, the Nazis exerted new pressures because of his Jewish associations, and by 1937 he found himself virtually a nonperson in Germany. He visited the United States in the spring, concertizing, and in September he resigned his professorship and took his wife back to America, where the Ballet Russe de Monte Carlo gave the premiere of his ballet *Saint Francis,* from which he later extracted the orchestral suite *Nobilissima visione.* On their return to Europe the Hindemiths settled in the little town of Blusch in Switzerland.

They were not worried about their position when Hitler invaded Poland in 1939, but their friends were, and they lured Hindemith back to the United States to a teaching post at the University of Buffalo. (Unknown to him, his salary was paid by an outside benefactor.) Neither the university nor the town pleased him, but he relished teaching at Tanglewood the next summer, 1940, and in the fall was invited to Yale as a visiting professor. There, after many vicissitudes, Gertrud was able to join him. The next year he joined the regular faculty as professor of theory, at an annual salary of $6,500. He became an American citizen in 1945 and remained at Yale, honored by the musical world and placing his cachet on too many future composers to name here. In 1947, in response to many importunings, Hindemith visited Europe, renewing old ties except for that with his brother Rudolf, whom he refused (for whatever reason) ever to see or communicate with again. (Rudolf in fact changed his name to "Hans Lofer," under which sobriquet he wrote some piano sonatas that were later recorded.) Hindemith was adulated everywhere he went and, true to his nature, was rather brusque about receiving the homage. But he was back the following summer, during which he revised *Cardillac* and toured Germany at the request of the Allied military government. The results of the tour were great enthusiasm on the part of the Germans and some remarks to the press by Hindemith quite uncomplimentary to the current state of their music. In 1949 he spent a term at Harvard as Norton Professor. In 1951 he took on, concurrently with his Yale post, a teaching assignment at the University of Zürich. Two years later he settled for good in the village of Blonay in Switzerland and gave up teaching as a profession in 1955. Increasingly he began to appear as a guest conductor, going as far afield as Japan. His last major opera, *Die Harmonie der Welt (The Harmony of the Universe),* on the astronomer Johannes Kepler, was premiered at Munich in 1957. (One other opera, *The Long Christmas Dinner,* to a text by Thornton Wilder, appeared in 1961.) In 1959 Hindemith was persuaded to return to the United States to conduct the premiere of his *Pittsburgh Symphony* (in Pittsburgh); the cold shoulder he received from Yale convinced him that he was regarded there as a defector. Nevertheless he returned to the United States twice more, the last time in 1963. His last works were an organ concerto for the New York Philharmonic and the *Mass* for *a cappella* chorus, premiered (respectively) in April and November of 1963. Back in Switzerland, he fell ill in the late fall and died a little over a month later of an inflammation of the pancreas.

The last twenty-five years of Hindemith's life saw the continued creation of music, though not as productively and with no remarkable changes in his approach after *Mathis der Maler*, which had its first production at Zürich in 1938. Among the more notable later works were: the ballets *Hérodiade, The Four Temperaments,* and *Cupid and Psyche*, a series of concerti for various instruments, five more symphonies (one for band, one based on *Die Harmonie der Welt,* sonatas for virtually all the orchestral instruments, and a contrapuntal *tour de force,* the *Ludus Tonalis (Tonal Games)* for piano.

RECORDINGS: Hindemith recorded many of his own works—as viola soloist, with the Amar Quartet, and as a conductor (in which last capacity he also made an LP of early choral works with his Yale Collegium Musicum). Other recordings include the operas *Cardillac, Hin und Zurück, Mathis der Maler, Wir bauen eine Stadt (We Build a City,* an opera for children), a suite of dances from *Das Nusch-Nuschi,* and the symphonies extracted from *Mathis der Maler* and *Die Harmonie der Welt;* the ballets *Der Dämon (The Demon)* and *Nobilissima Visione; The Four Temperaments* for piano and orchestra; *Symphonic Metamorphosis on Themes of Carl Maria von Weber;* all the other symphonies; the early *Lustige Sinfonietta* and the *Sinfonietta* of 1950; *Concert Music for Strings and Brass* and two other similarly titled works; the 7 *Kammermusik* and the *Kleine Kammermusik;* the 2 cello concerti; concerti for violin, horn, clarinet, trumpet-and-bassoon, organ, harp-and-four-woodwinds, and various concerted works for viola; *Symphonic Dances;* the *Philharmonic Concerto; Requiem for Those We Love* (to Whitman texts), *Apparebit repentina dies,* the 1963 *Mass,* and other choral pieces; the music for trautonium; vocal pieces such as the little cantata *Die Serenaden, Des Todes Tod, Martinslied, Herodiade,* and the huge song cycle *Das Marienleben* in its original and revised versions for voice and piano (but not the orchestrated version), and numerous other songs; all of the piano and solo organ music; and most of the chamber music. A fair number of works remain to be recorded, most notably several operas. That many works are seldom performed is perhaps evidence of Hindemith's uncertain status at the moment.

[1915] DOSTAL, Nico (Dōs'-tȧl, Nē'-kō)

BORN: Korneuberg, November 27, 1895

Nico Dostal's birth in an outer suburb of Vienna is perhaps symbolic of the relation of his operettas to the Viennese tradition. His uncle, Hermann Dostal, was a popular composer of marches. He (Nico) was educated in Linz and rather oddly at the school of church music in Klosterneuburg, though as a matter of fact he wrote some religious music later on. He was employed chiefly as an arranger in various Austrian cities, eventually finding his way to Berlin, where he worked in the film studios and had his first operetta success with *Clivia* in 1933. Over the next decade he produced around an operetta a year (premiered in almost as many German cities). During the 1940s, perhaps understandably, he seems to have written little. He returned to Vienna in 1946 and took up his career again around 1950. RECORDINGS: There are recorded excerpts from such of his musicals as *Monika* and *Die ungarische Hochzeit (The Hungarian Wedding).*

[1916] ROCCA, Lodovico (Rôk'-kȧ, Lō-dō-vē'-kō)

ADMINISTRATOR

BORN: Turin, November 29, 1895

Rocca was educated in Turin and later became a pupil of Giacomo Orefice (1916) at the Milan Conservatory. At the outset of his career, around 1920, he published some rather individual songs and some orchestral pieces, but his heart was chiefly in opera. He finished his first effort around this time, but it *(La Morte di Frine [The Death of Phryne])* had to wait seventeen years for a production at Milan in 1937. The second, *In terra di leggenda (In the Land of Legend),* completed in 1923, did not reach the stage until 1936. Rocca attained his peak with *Il Dibuk (The Dybbuk,* after the Yiddish play by S. Ansky), which was produced at La Scala in 1934, having won a competition there the previous year and created something of a sensation. It was soon being produced internationally; the American premiere was in Detroit in 1936. However, its Italian success was nipped in the bud by Mussolini's anti-Jewish laws, though Rocca himself was not Jewish. He went on to write two more operas, *Monte Ivnor* in 1939 and *L'Uragano (The Storm)* in 1952 but with no special success. In 1940 he was appointed to the directorship of the Turin Conservatory, which he held until he retired twenty-six years later. *Il Dibuk* had occasional revivals after the war—most recently in Turin in 1982, the composer taking a curtain call—but so far has failed to regain its impetus. RECORDINGS:

There are a couple of original-cast excerpts from *Il Dibuk* on records.

[1917] DAVID, Johann Nepomuk (Dä-fēd, Yō'-hän Nā'-pō-mook)

ORGANIST, CHOIRMASTER, TEACHER
BORN: Eferding, November 30, 1895
DIED: Stuttgart, December 22, 1977

David's early career shows a remarkable likeness to Anton Bruckner's **[1293]** in that he was born in a village near Linz, was educated at the monastery of St. Florian, became an organist, and qualified as a schoolteacher. David in fact briefly taught elementary school before and after World War I and resumed his time as a soldier. In 1920 he went to Vienna and studied for three years at the Academy of Music, most importantly with Joseph Marx **[1747]**. Three years later he returned to the Linz area as schoolmaster-organist-choirmaster in the little town of Wels, where he worked for ten years, turning out reams of music in his spare time and acquainting himself with contemporary musical currents. He was eventually particularly influenced on the one hand by Schoenberg **[1657]**, Hindemith **[1914]**, Reger **[1637]**, and Stravinsky **[1748]**, and on the other hand by medieval, Renaissance, and Baroque music. By 1934 he had written his way out of Wels into an appointment as professor of composition at the Leipzig Conservatory, of which he eventually became director. To all intents and purposes he regarded his career as a composer as having started then, for he destroyed the bulk of his previous output. In 1945 his Leipzig home was burned in the aftermath of an air raid, taking most of the rest of his manuscripts with it. For the next three years, he directed the Mozarteum in Salzburg and then taught at the Stuttgart Hochschule until his retirement in 1963. He was the recipient of many prizes, awards, and honorary degrees, and was regarded in German countries as a truly significant composer, though his music does not seem to travel well. He was especially known as a writer of organ and church music, but also produced many instrumental works, including 8 (mature) symphonies, several concerti, and a number of sonatas. He also published studies of music by Bach **[684]** and Mozart **[992]**, and a survey of modern musical history. RECORDINGS: Recordings include the *German Mass*, Symphony No. 5, the oratorio *Ezzolied*, the Concerto for Organ, smaller choral pieces, and works for organ.

[1918] KNORR, Ernst-Lothar von (K'nôr', Ärnst Lō'-tär fun)

VIOLINIST, EDUCATOR
BORN: Eitorf, January 2, 1896
DIED: Heidelberg, October 30, 1973

Born near Cologne, Ernst Knorr studied at that city's conservatory, where he won the Joachim Prize for violin when he was fifteen. (He began writing music at least two years earlier.) After a time as an orchestral violinist, he taught his instrument, from 1925, at the Berlin Hochschule. Later he moved to Frankfurt am Main, where his home and all his manuscripts were destroyed in a 1944 air raid. In 1952 he was appointed director of the Music Academy in Hannover. From 1961 he held a similar post in Heidelberg, where he organized the Heidelberg Kammerorchester. He was also *Konzertmeister* of the Kurpfälzisches Kammerorchester in Mannheim, founded in 1951. In 1932 he produced a theme and variations for five electronic instruments (trautonium, hellertion, theremin, neo-Bechstein piano, and vibraphone). He also wrote string quartets, some orchestral music, and songs but was best known for his choral music and his educational pieces. RECORDINGS: There are recordings of instrumental pieces, including some for accordion, cello, violin, clarinet, and piano.

[1919] WEINBERGER, Jaromír (Vīn'-bâr-ger, Yä'-rō-mēr)

TEACHER
BORN: Prague, January 8, 1896
DIED: St. Petersburg, Fla., August 8, 1967

Briefly hailed in the late 1920s as the Great White Hope (or one of them) of opera, Jaromír Weinberger was one of the more tragic figures in twentieth-century music. He studied with Křička **[1752]** and in 1916 was one of Max Reger's **[1637]** last pupils. Shortly afterward he had a pantomime produced in Prague and in the succeeding years wrote a few instrumental and orchestral pieces. His early career is fairly obscure. In 1922 he came to the United States and taught for a term in Ithaca College, an experience which inspired pieces like *Cowboy's Christmas* and *Banjos*, both for violin and piano. In 1927 the Prague National Theater produced his second opera, *Švanda Dudák (Schwanda the Bagpiper)*, a fantastic comedy inspired by Czech folklore and folk music. (His first opera, *Kocourkov*, never reached the stage.) *Švanda* was brought to the attention of Hans W. Heinsheimer of Universal Editions in Vienna, who, captivated by it, arranged for a production by Joseph Turnau and Herbert Graf in Breslau. As *Schwanda der Dudelsackpfeifer* (a title that inspired the American humorist Frank Sullivan to one of his funniest pieces), it took the operatic world by storm. It reached the Metropolitan Opera in 1931, conducted by Artur Bodansky, with a first-string cast that included Friedrich Schorr, Maria Müller, Karin Branzel, and Gustav Schützendorf. Weinberger almost literally awoke to find himself rich and famous.

But his triumph was the beginning of his tragedy. He was never able to repeat it. There was some small success with his *Frühlingsstürme (Spring Storms)* of 1933, the first of 4 operettas, but the rest of his three other operas—*Die geliebte Stimme (The Beloved Voice)* of 1931, *Lidé z Pokerflatu (The Outcasts of Poker Flat)* in 1932, and *Valdštein (Wallenstein)* in 1937—were failures. When Hitler took over Austria, Weinberger, a Jew, fled to London and shortly afterward to New York. There he dedicated to John Barbirolli and the New York Philharmonic a set of orchestral variations and fugue on "Under the Spreading Chestnut Tree," an English pop tune which he mistook for a folk song. The work had a brief popularity and then was consigned to outer darkness as claptrap. Weinberger continued for a while to write pieces on American (e.g., *Prelude and Fugue on "Dixie"*) and Czech themes, but performances generated little interest, and by 1950 he was virtually forgotten except for the polka and fugue from *Švanda*, a favorite at pops concerts. The opera itself dropped out of the repertory and became a favorite football for critics who had not heard it. Weinberger moved to Florida, where he turned to photography and to writing religious music. One night in his seventy-second year he took a bottle of sleeping pills and was found dead. Fourteen years later, when a recording of *Švanda* (sung in German) was issued, the reviewers all wondered why we had been so long deprived of such a splendid work.

RECORDINGS: In addition to *Švanda*, other Weinberger recordings include *Under the Spreading Chestnut Tree*, the *Czech Rhapsody*, *Prelude to the Festival* for band, *Concerto for Timpani and Brass*, and a few excerpts from the stage works.

[1920] **HERRMANN, Hugo** (Hâr'-màn, Hōō'-gō)
ORGANIST, CONDUCTOR, EDUCATOR
BORN: Ravensburg, April 19, 1896
DIED: Stuttgart, September 7, 1967

Herrmann was the son of a schoolmaster in an old medieval town just north of Lake Constance in Württemberg. He was called up for service in World War I and was severely wounded in action. After he recovered, he took up music—first in Stuttgart, then at the Berlin Hochschule. The sources say that Schreker [**1705**] was one of his teachers there, although Schreker did not come to Berlin until 1920, at which time Herrmann had already spent a year as a church organist in Ludwigsburg (near Stuttgart), where he remained until 1923. In that year he came to the United States, held a church job in Detroit until 1925, and then returned to Germany to conduct a chorus in Reutlingen. Save for a short period at the Wiesbaden Opera at the turn of the decade, he remained there until 1935, when he became director of the conservatory at Trossingen (about fifty miles northwest of his birthplace), from which post he retired in 1962. Herrmann wrote a number of operas, 5 symphonies, 4 string quartets, and much other music. Like his exact contemporary Ernst Knorr [**1918**], Herrmann was much taken with the Hindemithian [**1914**] notion of *Gebrauchsmusik* (practical or utilitarian music) and composed a great deal for students and amateurs. One notes particularly Herrmann's espousal of such lowly instruments as the accordion (for which, among other pieces, he composed 2 concerti) and the harmonica (for which he wrote a manual). RECORDINGS: There are recordings of accordion pieces.

[1921] **SLAVENSKI, Josip** (Slà-ven'-ski, Yō-zip)
TEACHER
BORN: Čakovec, May 11, 1896
DIED: Belgrade, November 30, 1955

Until more evidence is forthcoming, we may have to take on faith Slavenski's Yugoslav compatriots' insistence that he was a true prophet who found little honor among his own people. Though he became a Yugoslav patriot, there is some doubt as to just who his people were. His father was a baker named Stolzer or Štolcer, of German descent, whose home and place of business was then in Hungary, though most of the inhabitants of the town were Croats. From 1913 to 1916 young Stolzer studied at the Budapest Conservatory, with Zoltán Kodály [**1760**] among others. He was then called up for military service and after the war worked in the family bakery for a time. In 1921 he went to Prague for two years to study at its conservatory with Vítezslav Novák [**1617**]. Afterward he settled in Belgrade where he taught first at a private music school and then, from 1937 until his death, at the Academy of Music.

It appears that Slavenski may have been the Yugoslav Charles Ives [1659]. Despite his indoctrination in musical rules, his sense of adventure and an obviously unusual musical ear led him into experiments that appear to have anticipated such things as electronic sound sources, aleatoric techniques, microtonal scales, and other advanced concepts. On the other hand, he was greatly influenced by folk music. His 1929 *Balkanophonia*, which the conductor Erich Kleiber introduced to Western Europe, was a grandiose attempt to synthesize Balkan ethnic musics. Dimitri Mitropoulos also conducted some of his pieces. On his home grounds, however, he won little sympathy from audiences, and he wrote little in his last decade. At the time of his death he was working on a vast piece called *Heliophonia* described as "a cosmic vision." Besides such all-embracing compositions, Slavenski (a pen name at first, but later adopted as his own) wrote more commonplace ones—a violin concerto, 4 string quartets, a piano sonata, stage and film scores.

RECORDINGS: There have been two recordings of his *Religiophonia* under its alternate title *Sinfonia orienta*, a symphonic cantata that is supposed to cover the history of world religions and philosophies. Unfortunately for Slavenski's reputation, it sounds like a bad Hollywood movie score. Other recordings on the Jugoton label include the complete string quartets and the *Slavenska Sonata* for violin and piano.

[1922] CONFALONIERI, Giulio (Cōn-fà-lōn-yâr'-ē, Jōōl'-yō)
CRITIC, BROADCASTER, ADMINISTRATOR
BORN: Milan, May 23, 1896
DIED: Milan, June 29, 1972

Though he was a composer of some success, Confalonieri's monuments will probably be his many books and articles, and the (pirated) recordings of a number of Cherubini [1019] operas which were produced as a result of his enthusiasm in Italy and elsewhere. (He also edited some of these operas and wrote a standard biography of the composer.) Confalonieri took an academic degree from the University of Milan in 1920. He later studied music in Bologna with Franco Alfano [1683] and in Paris with Paul Dukas [1574]. For three years, 1923–26, he lived in London and taught piano, during which time Thomas Beecham engaged him

to write incidental music for a production of Fletcher's *The Faithful Shepherdess*. He then returned to Milan, where he worked for various papers as a reviewer and for the Italian Radio. His reviews sometimes took more direct form: at La Scala in 1951 he hissed loudly throughout the premiere of Menotti's [2177] *The Consul*. In 1954 he became a member of that institution as director of its school for singers and of the Piccola Scala. He was also president of the conservatory at Vercelli in the Piedmont. Among Confalonieri's compositions are several ballets and 2 operas: *L'Habit neuf du régent (The Regent's New Clothes)*, produced at Cannes in 1931; and *Rosaspina (Thornrose)*, at Bergamo in 1939. RECORDINGS: One of the ballets, *Gala*, commissioned by Salvador Dali and named for his wife, has been recorded.

[1923] RIVIER, Jean (Rēv-yā', Zhȧn)
TEACHER
BORN: Villemomble, July 21, 1896

Jean Rivier was born in a Paris suburb to musical parents who moved into the city a few years later. There the boy taught himself to play the cello, though he had no real music lessons as such. He finished school in 1914 in time to enlist for war service, during which he composed in his off-duty hours. In 1918 he was severely gassed and spent the next several years in the hospital. From 1922 to 1926 he studied at the Paris Conservatoire, where he won prizes in counterpoint and fugue but failed to win the Prix de Rome. During this period his first string quartet (of 2) was favorably reviewed. On graduating, he married Marie Peyrissac, herself a musician; they later had a son. By the end of the decade Rivier was well-established as a composer—one who understood how to deal with old forms in modern terms.

In the mid-1930s he became associated with the Groupe du Triton, an association of composers that was seeking a middle ground between the extremes of the radicals Messiaen [2129] and Jolivet [2073] on the one hand and what was left of Les Six on the other; among his associates were Henry Barraud [1976], Emmanuel Bondeville (1898–), and Pierre-Octave Ferroud (1900–36). Toward the end of the decade he became a staff composer for the French National Radio. In 1947 he was appointed to teach composition at the Paris Conservatoire when Milhaud [1868] was absent to fill his American teaching commitments. Rivier was elevated to the professorship in 1962. In private life Rivier is an art collector and a sports buff. The bulk of his compositional

output has been orchestral and includes 7 symphonies and a number of concertos, but he has also written a good deal of chamber and choral music, songs, and a one-act opera, *Vénitienne.*
RECORDINGS: There have been two recordings of Symphony No. 3 for strings and one of No. 5 for orchestra. Also on disc are concerti for flute, trumpet and saxophone, piano *(Concerto breve);* chamber compositions for saxophone quartet, flute and piano, trumpet and organ; and a few piano pieces.

[1924] LECUONA, Ernesto (Lek'-wō'-nà, Âr-nes'-tō)
PIANIST, BANDLEADER
BORN: Guanabacoa, Cuba, August 7, 1896
DIED: Santa Cruz de Tenerife, November 29, 1963

Known for such popular light pieces as *Malagueña* and the song "Siboney," Lecuona was born in a suburb of Havana. His parents were musical, and he had piano lessons from early childhood. He was composing at eleven and teaching music in the city schools at sixteen. A year later he graduated from the Conservatorio Nacional. Subsequently he studied with Joaquín Nin [1721] and, after touring as a concert pianist, formed a Cuban dance band, Lecuona's Cuban Boys, which enjoyed great popularity and made many recordings. For a time Lecuona made his home in New York City. He was known chiefly for his songs and dances but wrote more ambitious things such as a *Rapsodia negra* for piano and orchestra, as well as zarzuelas and scores for radio and movies. After the triumph of Fidel Castro, Lecuona cut his ties with Cuba. He died in the Canary Islands. RECORDINGS: Lecuona recorded a number of his piano pieces—as have other pianists.

[1925] SZELIGOWSKI, Tadeusz (Shel-ē-gov'-skē, Tàd-yōōsh')
LAWYER, TEACHER
BORN: Lwów (Lvov), September 15 (?), 1896
DIED: Poznań, January 10, 1963

Szeligowski's birthdate appears variously as September 12, 13, and 15. He studied piano in his hometown from the age of fourteen, and then composition privately in Cracow while he acquired a law degree at the university there, graduating in 1922. In 1929 he decided to make a career of music and was in Paris for two years under the tutelage of Nadia

Boulanger. On his return, he taught—at first in Vilnius, later in Poznán and Warsaw—until a few months before his death. He began writing piano pieces in the mid-1920s, produced an orchestral suite in 1928, a string quartet the following year, and a concerto for orchestra in 1931. He turned to the stage after World War II, composing 2 ballets and 4 operas. An eclectic, he seems to have followed a recipe of something old, something new, something Polish, and a good deal borrowed. RECORDINGS: His most successful work was the 1951 opera, *The Students' Revolt,* from which excerpts have been recorded. Also on record is the 1937 *Epitaph on the Death of Karol Szymanowski.*

[1926] GERHARD, Roberto (Gâr'-härd, Rō-bâr'-tō)
LIBRARIAN, TEACHER, EDITOR
BORN: Valls, September 25, 1896
DIED: Cambridge (England), January 5, 1970

Of French and Swiss descent, Roberto Gerhard, born in the Spanish province of Tarragona, became through Austrian training an English composer of international modern flavor. He encountered a certain amount of parental opposition before submitting himself to Enrique Granados [1588] for training as a pianist. Unfortunately he chose 1915 to do so. When his teacher went down with the *Sussex* the following spring, Gerhard turned to Granados' own teacher, the septuagenarian Felipe Pedrell [1384], who for some reason saw Gerhard as his logical successor. However, Pedrell died in 1922, so Gerhard made his way to Schoenberg [1657] in Vienna and later followed him to Berlin, remaining with him until 1928. He then returned to Spain, marrying an Austrian girl, Poldi Feichtegger and settling in Barcelona, where he taught for a year at the Escola Normal. Afterward he served as librarian to the Catalan Library in the same institution. He also edited early Spanish music—notably Soler [854]—wrote for musical journals, and made translations of works on music from other languages. In 1938 he went to Warsaw as a judge for the ISCM competition, and on his way home learned that Barcelona had capitulated to Franco. He stopped over in Paris until the summer of the next year, when his friend Edward J. Dent, then president of the ISCM, found a place for him at King's College, Cambridge, as a research scholar. Gerhard contentedly spent his last thirty years there; he took out English citizenship, wrote his critical utterances in the language, and was delighted to be thought of as a British composer. In 1960 he taught for a year at the University of Michigan and spent the summer of 1961 at Tanglewood, but he did not take kindly to teaching. Cambridge gave him an honorary doctorate in 1967.

As a composer Gerhard was a slow starter and a methodical developer. Until he was thirty-five he wrote very little—some chamber music, a few songs and piano pieces, all very eclectic. In the 1930s he went through a Spanish period, producing the ballets *Ariel, Soirées de Barcelona,* the cantata *L'Alta naixença del Rei en jaume,* the orchestral *Albade, interludi i dança,* and a set of Catalan folksongs for voice and orchestra. Immediately after arriving in England, he made up for lost time: he wrote three more ballets, *Don Quixote, Alegrías,* and *Pandora,* and followed them with a neo-classical setting of Sheridan's comedy *The Duenna,* his only opera, which has yet to be staged, though it was performed in concert form in 1951. Here he experimented with Schoenbergian tonal serialism, with which he came to his own terms in the 1950 violin concerto (actually his second, he having given up on an earlier one). Meanwhile he had done homage to his old teacher in a *Cancionero de Pedrell* for soprano and chamber orchestra and the short symphony *Pedrelliana,* the (unnumbered) first of his works in that form, using themes from Pedrell's opera *La Celestina*—both on the centenary of that composer's birth in 1941. In his later works Gerhard arrived at his own notion of overall serialism, quite different from that of Webern [1773] and his followers. (As a dodecaphonicist, Gerhard had insisted that he was not breaking with tonality but reaffirming it.) He also dispensed with the idea of thematic music and used electronics in the third symphony and elsewhere. Nevertheless Gerhard insisted that music was to be heard, not analyzed, and always wrote with that end in mind. Among the important productions of his last years were the concerti for orchestra, for piano, and for harpsichord, the melodrama-cantata *The Plague* (after Camus), and a good deal of chamber music, including a nonet for winds and accordion, a *Concert for 8* (with guitar, mandolin, and accordion), and 2 very tough string quartets as well as a good deal of incidental stage and film music.

RECORDINGS: A portion of Gerhard's sizable output has been recorded. Orchestral works on disc include ballet suites from *Alegrías* (Robert Whitney), and *Don Quixote* (Antal Dorati); *Pedrelliana* (Antonio Ros-Marbá); Symphony No. 1 (Dorati), No. 3 (Frederick Prausnitz), and No. 4 (Colin Davis); *Concerto for Orchestra* (Norman Del

Mar); the Concerto for Violin (Yfrah Neaman with Davis); and the chamber-orchestral works *Libra* and *Leo* (performed by members of the London Sinfonietta under David Atherton). *The Plague* has been recorded by Dorati. Chamber pieces recorded include the Wind Quintet of 1928 (London Wind Quintet) and *Gemini* for violin and piano (Nona Liddell and John Constable).

[1927] HANSON, Howard
CONDUCTOR, TEACHER, ADMINISTRATOR
BORN: Wahoo, Neb., October 28, 1896
DIED: Rochester, N.Y., February 26, 1981

Perhaps no American composer of stature has been so effective in setting the direction of so many in subsequent generations. One is sorely tempted to add "despite the fact that he was born in Wahoo, Nebraska," but there is no doubt that his origins had much to do with what he became—a preserver of the European musical tradition translated into modern American terms. Both his parents emigrated from Sweden. As a child he learned piano (from his mother) and later became a skillful cello player. While in high school he studied music at a local junior college called Luther College. He spent 1912–13 at the University of Nebraska, then freelanced as a cellist until he could afford to go to New York City in the autumn of 1914. There he studied for another year (until the money ran out) with Percy Goetschius and pianist James Friskin at the Institute of Musical Art (the Juilliard School). The following fall he was able to enroll at Northwestern University, where his teachers included the dean of the music school, hymnologist Peter Christian Lutkin, and Rheinberger [1368] pupil Arne Oldberg. (Be it noted that there was no study with Nadia of Paris or Arnold of Vienna: Hanson was homegrown.) In his senior year, 1915–16, he taught music classes there and had his *Symphonic Prelude* performed by the Chicago Symphony under Frederick Stock. (Hanson had been composing ambitiously since he was six.) On graduating he was invited to California to dispense theory and harmony at the College of the Pacific, then located in San Jose. Three years later he was promoted to the deanship of the school's conservatory and produced his Op. 16, music for *California Forest Play of 1920,* a 1920 ballet.

In 1921 Hanson's orchestral piece *Before the Dawn* made him a cowinner with Sowerby [1908] of the first American Prix de

Rome. Accordingly, as stipulated, he moved to Rome, and not long afterward the College of the Pacific moved to Stockton. Among the products of Hanson's stay at the American Academy was his first symphony, subtitled "Nordic." (His music, which often exhibits a sternness that perhaps reflects his Swedish Protestant upbringing, was initially influenced by Grieg [1410], and has often been likened to Sibelius [1575]. When Hanson came home in 1923, he was invited to conduct the Rochester (New York) Philharmonic in the work. On that occasion he met Kodak magnate George Eastman, founder of the orchestra and the music school that bears his name. Eastman was looking for a director for the latter institution, which, under the aegis of the University of Rochester, had become a reality only two years before, and decided that Hanson was his man. Hanson held the directorship with uncommon distinction for forty years.

At the end of his first year in office, 1924–25, Hanson held the first of the annual American music festivals that gave so many American composers (especially those of his enlightened conservative stripe) a chance to be heard. In this sphere his influence was increased by his pioneer series of phonograph records—first for RCA, then for Mercury—in which he conducted the synthetic Eastman-Rochester Symphony in compositions by American composers (including himself). In 1930 his Symphony No. 2, subtitled "Romantic," was premiered by the Boston Symphony under Serge Koussevitsky [1655]. In 1934 his only opera, the Hawthorne-inspired *Merry Mount*, had its world premiere on a Saturday matinee broadcast from the Metropolitan Opera. (The last American work to be presented by the valedictorian Gatti-Casazza regime, it had a *succès d'estime* but was not carried over into the Edward Johnson regime, although Johnson, as singer, had starred in it.) In 1935 Hanson was elected to the National Institute of Arts and Letters, and in 1938 he became a member of the Royal Swedish Academy. His third symphony was premiered nationwide over the radio by the Columbia Broadcasting System in 1937, although Hanson had not written the final movement; not to be outdone, NBC broadcast the work a year later, after it was finished. The fourth symphony, a memorial to his father, brought its composer a Pulitzer Prize in 1944. A list of his other prizes, awards, commissions, and honors would take up another page in this book. So would a list of his notable students, the most important of whom include Dominick Argento [2368], William Bergsma [2313], Ulysses Kay [2257], John La

Montaine [2299], Peter Mennin [2328], Burrill Phillips [2116], and Vladimir Ussachevsky [2180].

A longtime bachelor, Hanson married Margaret Nelson in 1946. In 1961–62 the U.S. State Department sent him abroad with the Eastman Orchestra to spread the American musical gospel to Europe, both Eastern and Western, and to the Middle East. On his retirement in 1964, he was named director of the Institute of American Music at the university, and a dozen years later the Eastman School's new concert hall was named in his honor. Hanson's music is unashamedly but two-fistedly romantic—the kind of big utterance once thought appropriate to a great nation. Besides the works already noted, it includes 7 symphonies (the last, subtitled "The Sea," is a Whitman-choral work dating from his eighty-first year), concerti, many other orchestral and choral works, and a handful of smaller compositions.

RECORDINGS: Despite Hanson's advantageous position vis-à-vis the phonograph, much of his output remains unrecorded. Among the works committed to disc are all of the symphonies; the Concerto for Piano; the Concerto for Organ No. 1; *Serenade* for flute, strings, harp, and orchestra; *Pastorale* for oboe, strings, and harp; *Elegy in Memory of Serge Koussevitsky, Pan and the Priests, Rhythmic Variations on Two Ancient Hymns, Fantasy Variations on a Theme of Youth, "For the First Time",* and *Mosaics* (all orchestral); *Chorale and Alleluia, March Carillon,* and *Young Composer's Guide to the Six-Tone Scale* for wind ensemble or band; the choral-orchestral *Cherubic Hymn, 4 Psalms, Lament for Beowulf, Song of Democracy,* and *Songs from "Drum Taps";* a suite and other excerpts from the opera *Merry Mount;* and the String Quartet.

[1928] THOMSON, Virgil Garnett
ORGANIST, CONDUCTOR, CRITIC
BORN: Kansas City, Mo., November 25, 1896

Though he has long been hailed as a particularly astute and lucid writer on music, and by many leading musicians as one of the foremost American composers of his generation, Thomson has never quite won the respect he would seem to deserve as a musician. His music, strongly influenced by both popular song and dance and by the clean line of Erik Satie [1578], sends the devotees of musical complexity and obscurity into contemptuous guffaws and makes the general public vaguely suspicious of its easiness.

Thomson's ancestors were Scotch-Irish-

Welsh-Virginian Baptists who settled in Missouri. His college-educated father George went from farming to running a hardware store which failed two years before Virgil's birth. He then moved to Kansas City and took a job as a postman. He had married Clara May Gaines in 1883. Their only other child was a daughter, Ruby, born two years later. Despite the hardshell Baptist background, visiting relatives brought music and dancing to the household. A cousin who arrived with a piano gave the boy his first lessons, and after her departure he studied with several local teachers. By the age of ten he was playing dance music for Ruby and her friends. Three years later he made his professional debut as a silent-film pianist and continued to play when needed in theaters and tent shows. A local singer took him on as accompanist and steered him to more professional teachers. One of them taught him organ, and he was soon playing in churches. Thomson graduated from high school in 1913 and worked for a time in the public library, where he read intensively about music. Two years later he enrolled in the recently opened local junior college, but when war with Germany seemed imminent, he enlisted in a National Guard artillery regiment because he liked horses.

After war was declared, Thomson strove in vain to be sent overseas. He resigned his National Guard affiliation, having left the state, was turned down by the Ambulance Corps in Allentown, Pennsylvania, investigated the possibility of a navy band, and rejoined the medical wing of his old regiment. After some months of being shunted about the country, he decided to become an airplane pilot. After he had trained for two months, the military discovered it had a surplus of pilots and shipped him off to Columbia University to learn radio telephony. In due course he was sent to Fort Sill, Oklahoma, for commissioning. His exit was delayed by an attack of the Spanish influenza. He then spent seven weeks in New York waiting for shipping orders. When they came, they were followed immediately by the Armistice. Thomson resigned his commission and went back to college. However, with a loan from the Mormon Church obtained through the father of a girlfriend, he proceeded to Harvard.

At Harvard Thomson studied under and drew the respect of Archibald T. Davidson and Edward Burlingame Hill [1632]. Thomson served as assistant to both, taking over their classes when they were absent and relieving Davidson as chapel organist and conductor of the Glee Club and Choir. Besides the funds provided by his Harvard scholarship and assistantship, he drew $800 a year as regular organist in a North Hampton church. It was the Imagist poet Amy Lowell's friend and biographer, S. Foster Damon, who first introduced him to the music of Satie and the writings of Gertrude Stein. In 1921 Thomson went on a tour of France with the Glee Club as an assistant conductor and, having been awarded a John Knowles Paine Traveling Fellowship, remained behind to study with Nadia Boulanger, whom a Harvard classmate had discovered. He found lodgings in a somewhat disreputable area, met Aaron Copland [1986] at Boulanger's, made friends with Les Six and their guiding spirit Jean Cocteau, was introduced to Satie and Picasso, and wrote reviews for the Boston *Transcript*, one of which eventuated in the Boston Symphony's hiring of Koussevitzky [1655] two years later. At the end of the year he returned to Cambridge with every intention of going back to Paris in 1923. He resumed his assistantship at Harvard, took organ lessons again, served as organist at King's Chapel in Boston, and in the spring gave a concert at the university in which he presented the American premieres of Satie's *Socrate* and Lili Boulanger's [1886] *Pour les funerailles d'un soldat (For a Soldier's Funeral)*. That June he graduated, disappointingly, without distinction and without a renewal of his traveling fellowship. Though he received a grant from the Juilliard Trust, he decided to remain in New York, where he studied conducting (and percussion!) under the auspices of the American Orchestral Association and took further composition lessons with Rosario Scalero (1870–1954). He also picked up extra money writing criticism for such then-prestigious magazines as H. L. Mencken's *American Mercury* and *Vanity Fair*. The next year he returned to Boston, where he continued to write and found yet another church post in Whitinsville southwest of the city. But he and the minister clashed, and in the spring he went back to Kansas City. In September he sailed at last for France, with $500 in capital.

Thomson was headquartered in Paris for fifteen years until the German invasion dislodged him. For more than the first half of that time, he lived a rather precarious economic existence, often getting by on the generosity of friends and family. Up to then he had composed little of consequence—mostly some songs and choral pieces, though his first Paris year produced the nose-thumbing *Sonata da chiesa* for instrumental quintet. But he plunged into the midst of a rich intellectual and social life and came to know virtually everyone who was anyone internationally in the arts. At one time or another, he was closely associated with the composers George Antheil [1981] and Theodore Chanler [2013], the painters Maurice Grosser and Christian Bérard, and the poet Sherry Mangan, but his closest friends were a French *grand-dame,* Louise Langlois, a wild English writer named Mary Butts, and Gertrude Stein.

Antheil took Thomson along one day in 1925 when he was summoned for Miss Stein's inspection. Antheil did not pass muster, but Thomson soon was in the good graces of Miss Stein and her companion Miss Toklas. Gertrude approved of his setting of a short poem of hers, and he proceeded to make others, notably the large-scale *Capitals, Capitals* for four male voices and piano. Thomson demonstrated a unique feeling for words, and soon the two of them were talking about an opera. In November 1927 he found what turned out to be permanent quarters on the Quai Voltaire and began the first act of what Stein had already named *Four Saints in Three Acts,* whose theme, Thomson tells us helpfully, is the religious life as exemplified by Spanish saints in Miss Stein's notion of Spain. He completed the piano score the next summer and went on to finish his orchestral *Symphony on a Hymn Tune.* In that same year he wrote the first of a large series of musical portraits of friends and acquaintances—mostly for piano or violin and piano, but a few for other combinations and many of them later orchestrated.

In the fall of 1928 Thomson took a trip home, visited friends, tried to arouse interest in the opera, had his symphony turned down as too frivolous by Koussevitzky [1655], participated in public performances of *Capitals, Capitals* and the *Sonata da chiesa,* and returned to Paris in March without having made a major impact on his native land. Shortly afterward Darmstadt wanted a look at the opera, but it was ultimately rejected, probably by the then-intendant, Karl Böhm, who preferred the classics. In the next few years, Thomson hobnobbed and worked with the poet Max Jacob, Roy Harris [1947], Marcel Duchamp, and Henri Sauguet [1994], and attempted to teach young Paul Bowles [2165]. In the fall of 1931 Copland included *Capitals, Capitals* in a London concert of modern Americans and persuaded Thomson to return to musical journalism for his journal *Modern Music.* Shortly afterward he saw his first musical publication when the Cos Cob Press (persuaded by Copland) brought out the *Stabat Mater* (to a Jacob text). In 1932 he borrowed passage money from the architect Philip Johnson and went

back to America to arrange a production of *Saints.*

Painting and sculpture had become big business in America, despite the Depression, and Thomson found patrons there, notably in his former Harvard friends Kirk Askew, a dealer, and Everett "Chick" Austin, director of the Hartford Museum, where the premiere was scheduled. Thomson himself planned the production and rounded up the chief engineers, meanwhile living on an occasional lecture and generosity. For many months he was back and forth between France and America, doing the necessary spade work and orchestrating the opera. (Maurice Grosser inked-in the final copy.) In 1933 he and new friends, the exiled Arnold Schoenbergs [1657], sailed for New York, where Thomson would draw the final threads together. His friend Florine Stettheimer had designed sets and costumes. Staging was to be by John Houseman, choreography by young Frederick Ashton, and Alexander Smallens to conduct. Thomson had decided, (rather daringly for 1933) to use an all-black cast. But this was no more startling than the work itself—a verbal construct purposely devoid of plot, character, or coherent action set to a wickedly childlike amalgam of plainchant, ragtime, Sunday-school tunes, and waltzes from the back porches of Kansas City. The sets were mostly of a new and inexpensive plastic material called cellophane. After the Hartford opening the work ran an unexpected six weeks in New York and went on to further success in Chicago. Yet it established Thomson, if at all, rather as an oddity than as a serious composer. Still some commissions were forthcoming and he stayed in America to fill them. There was incidental music for several plays. There were several suggestions for ballets (rejected) including a proposal from James Joyce for one on a scene from *Finnegans Wake.* There were conducting and lecture dates and New Deal–sponsored concerts. In 1936 he was hired by the filmmaker Pare Lorentz and over the next two years produced two remarkable scores for the documentaries *The Plow That Broke the Plains* and *The River,* for which his amanuensis was a young composer named Henry Brant [2213]. He shared an apartment with Houseman and collaborated with him under WPA auspices on a production of *Macbeth* for the American Negro Theater, as well as one with Orson Welles of *The Italian Straw Hat* (Welles's title was "Horse Eats Hat") and another with Joseph Losey on a union propaganda piece. The long-contemplated ballet was finally forthcoming in *Filling Station,* choreographed by Lew Christensen and produced at Hartford in 1938. There was also a House-man-Thomson *Hamlet* for Leslie Howard and an *Antony and Cleopatra* for Tallulah Bankhead. In the midst of all this success, unauthorized junkets to Paris cost Thomson his federal funding.

Late in 1938 he returned to Paris. He gave up on an operatic version of *The Duchess of Malfi* but completed his first book of criticism, *The State of Music.* In 1939 Thomson spent the summer in Italy, where the outbreak of war found him.

The so-called "phony war" seems to have caused Thomson no problems, but the next spring, when the bombs began falling, he decided enough was enough. He exited fairly precariously by way of Spain and Portugal and sailed on a ship overladen with fleeing Americans. No sooner had he arrived in New York than largely on the strength of his book—splendid reviews, poor sales—he was hired to replace Lawrence Gilman, who had died the year before, as music editor of the New York *Herald-Tribune.* Until Thomson left in 1954, he, aided by a fine staff and occasional passing luminaries such as Bowles, John Cage [2192], and Peggy Glanville-Hicks [2197], made the *Trib*'s music pages the most stimulating in the country. Thomson usually said what he felt, which delighted many and won him not a few enemies of considerable stature. During this period he composed many of his orchestral pieces (some of them retreads of portraits and such), largely to provide his burgeoning conducting career with fuel. He renewed his association with Houseman, with whom he again worked on stage, radio, and film projects, found a friend and champion in Sir Thomas Beecham, did another major film score for Robert Flaherty *(Louisiana Story),* which won the 1949 Pulitzer Prize for Music, and at various times incurred the wrath of Toscanini, the New York Philharmonic, and the Metropolitan Opera Company. Just when his music was beginning to be noticed by the big recording companies, he and other composers joined against them in a long antitrust suit which largely nipped such representation in the bud.

As soon as the war was over, Thomson's friends at the French Embassy had him flown to Paris, ostensibly to survey the state of music in France. He reestablished contact with Gertrude Stein, who immediately set to work on the libretto to her "feminist" opera, *The Mother of Us All,* and was allowed to return to his apartment on the grounds that he was Jewish—a longtime assumption of his landlords. He returned to New York in stormy weather on a troopship but was back again in 1946. This time he traveled to Italy,

Belgium, Luxembourg, Germany (East and West), and Austria, making new contacts and renewing old ones. While he was doing so, Gertrude Stein died of cancer, having finished the libretto a few weeks before. As with *Saints,* Maurice Grosser was called on to devise a workable scenario. It was first produced at Columbia University the following spring, prepared by Jack Beeson [2316] and conducted by Otto Luening [1980]. If one discounts the Santa Fe production of the 1970s, it, like its predecessor, has yet to be produced in a major American opera house.

In the early 1950s Thomson did a number of theatrical scores, including those for Capote's *The Grass Harp,* Giraudoux's *Ondine,* and several Shakespeare plays produced by Houseman at the Stratford, Connecticut, festival, as well as the score for the film *The Goddess.* Increasingly he was in demand all over the world as conductor and lecturer, and in 1954 he gave up the *Tribune* post, much to everyone's surprise. He continued to compose, though some of the "new" works were really reworkings of older ones (e.g., the Symphony No. 3 is an orchestral reworking of Quartet No. 2). Most of the 1960s were occupied with the writing of a third opera, *Lord Byron* (libretto by Jack Larson), which was produced at the Juilliard School in 1972. Some were disappointed, but others see it as perhaps his greatest work.

RECORDINGS: Whatever the reason there is no doubt that Thomson has been seriously neglected by the record producers. More than thirty-five years ago he conducted the original cast in an abridged version of *Four Saints,* and it was only recently that a complete recording (conducted by Joel Thome) was released. *The Mother of Us All* has been recorded *in toto* by a trust-backed project, but *Lord Byron* has yet to appear. *Filling Station,* the suites from the Lorentz films and two suites from *Louisiana Story, Symphony on a Hymn Tune,* Symphony No. 3, the Concerto for Cello, Concerto for Flute, *Autumn* (a harp concertino), the orchestral *3 Pictures* and *3 Portraits,* the orchestral *Blake Songs,* the *Stabat Mater, The Feast of Love,* and the String Quartet No. 2 are other larger works on record. But many of the "portraits," the choral pieces, the smaller chamber and piano works, and the songs remain overlooked.

[1929] SZABELSKI, Bolesław (Shà-bel'-skē, Bō-le'-slwáf)
ORGANIST, TEACHER

BORN: Radorya, December 3, 1896
DIED: Katowice, August 27, 1979

Born in a village in what is now east-central Poland, Szabelski studied in Kiev, and, after World War I, at the Warsaw Conservatory with organist Mieczysław Surzyński [1585] and with Roman Statkowski [1519] and Karol Szymanowski [1755]. Having established himself as an organist, Szabelski taught at the Katowice Conservatory from 1929 until the German invasion a decade later, and from after the war until he retired in 1967. Having proved himself a modern master of contrapuntal forms, he proceeded in his later years to explore serialism and other advanced techniques. His output, chiefly orchestral, was small (he was a slow and painstaking composer, and many of his works disappeared during World War II). RECORDINGS: The fourth and fifth of his 5 symphonies (the fifth with chorus) and an orchestral *Toccata* have been recorded by the Polish state recording company Muza.

[1930] ROBERTSON, Leroy
TEACHER
BORN: Fountain Green, Utah, December 21, 1896
DIED: Salt Lake City, July 25, 1971

Utah's composer-laureate began his musical studies in Provo and then went to the New England Conservatory in Boston, where he counted both Chadwick [1483] and Converse [1618] among his teachers. At various other times he had instruction from Ernest Bloch [1729], Ernst Toch [1824], and Hugo Leichtentritt. In 1925 he joined the faculty of Brigham Young University. He took a master's degree at the University of Utah in 1932 and became chairman of his department. In 1947 his *Trilogy* for orchestra won the $25,000 Henry W. Reichold award for American music, and the following year he became professor of composition at the University of Utah. He received his Ph.D. in 1954 from the University of Southern California and retired in 1962 as chairman of the university's music department. Among his orchestral works are several concerti. RECORDINGS: His oratorio *The Book of Mormon* holds high status in Salt Lake City and has been recorded, as have his violin concerto and the concert overture *Punch and Judy.*

[1931] SESSIONS, Roger Huntington
TEACHER

BORN: Brooklyn, December 28, 1896
DIED: Princeton, N.J., March 16, 1985

Roger Sessions's mature work has always been admired by musical intellectuals, but it took the post–World War II victory of musical Teutonism over musical Gallicism to raise him to his latter-day position as Grand Old Man of American music. (Even so, Sessions can scarcely yet be called popular, nor does one often encounter him on concert programs.)

Despite his birthplace, Sessions came of old New England stock and grew up in Hadley, Massachusetts, near Amherst and the Connecticut River. Precocious in every way, he was studying piano at five, wrote his first opera at twelve, and entered Harvard at fourteen. There he engaged in liberal arts studies and edited the *Harvard Review,* fitting music into his schedule where there was time for it. (He had a course with Edward Burlingame Hill [1632].) On acquiring his B.A. in 1915, however, he forthwith enrolled at the Yale School of Music, where he studied with Horatio Parker [1556] and took his B.Mus. two years later. He then returned to his home territory to teach at Smith College, but when he could he pursued further studies in New York with Ernest Bloch [1729]. He married Barbara Foster in 1920, but the union did not last. When Bloch was appointed director of the Cleveland Institute in 1921, he took Sessions along as his assistant. In 1923 Sessions wrote music for a Smith College production of Leonid Andreyev's play *The Black Maskers,* from which he later extracted an orchestral suite that is the first considerable composition to which he owns.

When Bloch and the Cleveland Institute came to a parting of the ways in 1925, Sessions took off for Europe, where he remained for eight years, largely through the adroit exercise of grantsmanship, an art in which he pioneered: he garnered two successive Guggenheims, a three-year Damrosch (in Rome), and a Carnegie. In the course of his stay there he abandoned post-Romanticism for Stravinskian neo-classicism, most prominently exhibited in his first symphony, which Koussevitzky [1655] introduced in Boston in 1927. Shortly afterward he joined Aaron Copland [1986] in presenting a series of concerts of modern American music in New York. The political triumph of Adolf Hitler in 1933 brought him home for good. He taught for two years at Boston University (simultaneously at other Boston and New York schools and privately) and then began the first of two extended stays at

Princeton. The next year he married Elizabeth Franck.

Composition for Sessions took much thought and care, and up to this time his output, apart from the juvenilia which he did not count, consisted of the two large-scale works noted, *3 Chorale-preludes* for organ, a piano sonata, a string quartet, and a single song. In 1935 he completed his Concerto for Violin, on which he had worked for four years. It showed the composer moving in the direction of dodecaphony. A formidable work, it was not performed for another five years, and then by an obscure orchestra and soloist. In 1944 Sessions moved to the University of California at Berkeley, where he taught for the next six years. (He had taught courses during several earlier summers there.) Two years after he arrived, he completed his second symphony, which established him as a highly individual composer and one to be reckoned with. Having found his voice, he stepped up his productivity. The next year saw the premiere of his one-act opera *The Trial of Lucullus* to a libretto by Bertolt Brecht (see also Paul Dessau [1902] for a later setting). In 1952 a Fulbright Fellowship took him back to Europe for a year, after which he returned to Princeton to occupy the Conant Chair until he retired in 1965. But advancing age seemed only to generate more energy in him. Between 1957 and 1968, he completed six more symphonies (Nos. 3–8), Concerto for Piano, the orchestral *Divertimento*, and the big opera *Montezuma* that had occupied him for more than twenty years. (It was premiered with respect but without real success at the Deutsche Oper in Berlin in 1964, and twelve years later Sara Caldwell gave it its first American outing in Boston. The public did not take to it, though Sessions's admirers insist that it is a masterpiece—perhaps more of music than of theater, however.)

Having formally left Princeton, Sessions joined the faculty of the Juilliard School, where he continued to teach with interruptions: in 1966–67 he returned to Berkeley as the (appropriately) Ernest Bloch Professor, and two years later he was Norton Professor at Harvard. Among his innumerable other honors, he held at least eight honorary doctorates. Notable among his innumerable pupils are his Princeton associate Milton Babbitt [2247], Miriam Gideon [2096], Paul Bowles [2165], Mario Davidovsky [2408], David Diamond [2238], Jacob Druckman [2375], Vivian Fine [2214], Ross Lee Finney [2099], Robert Helps [2379], Andrew Imbrie [2314], Leon Kirchner [2284], and Hugo Weisgall [2194]. After his retirement he wrote another symphony (No. 9), a Con-

certo for Violin and Cello, the orchestral *Rhapsody,* the *Concertino* for chamber orchestra, *Concerto for Orchestra,* and the Whitman-based *Requiem: When Lilacs Last in the Dooryard Bloom'd,* the same text used by Hindemith [1914] to a similar end.

RECORDINGS: There are recordings of Symphonies Nos. 1, 2, 3, 7, and 8; the *Concertino;* Concerto for Orchestra; the Concerto for Violin; the *Rhapsody;* the *Divertimento;* the *Black Maskers Suite;* the *Requiem;* String Quartet No. 2; the *Idyll of Theocritus* (soprano and orchestra); the 3 piano sonatas and *From My Diary* for piano; the Sonata for Solo Violin; the Duo for Violin and Piano; and pieces for organ, cello, and piano.

[1932] PORTER, William Quincy
VIOLINIST, EDUCATOR, CONDUCTOR
BORN: New Haven, Conn., February 7, 1897
DIED: Bethany, Conn., November 12, 1966

Quincy Porter ultimately represented the third generation of Porters on the Yale faculty (his father taught theology there). He took up the violin as a child and entered Yale when he was seventeen. He studied with Horatio Parker [1556] and David Stanley Smith (1877–1949), gave violin recitals, conducted the student orchestra, and graduated in 1919. He then trekked off to Paris for some polishing at the Schola Cantorum with d'Indy [1462] and with Lucien Capet, founder of the Capet Quartet. He returned to Yale for his B.Mus. and in 1921 found work in the Capitol Theater orchestra in New York, where he was a colleague of Eugene Ormandy. There he became a pupil of Ernest Bloch [1729], who took him with him the next year when he became director of the Cleveland Institute, to whose faculty he appointed him in 1923. There, as violist, he was a member of the Ribaupierre Quartet, for which he wrote the first two of his 9 string quartets. In 1926 he married violinist Lois Brown, with whom, thanks to a Guggenheim Fellowship, he went off to make beautiful music in Paris two years later. There he continued his production of chamber music. In 1931 he returned to Cleveland for a final year and then went to Vassar to teach and conduct. He began to write more orchestral music, producing his first symphony (of 2) in 1934. He conducted its premiere at a New York Philharmonic concert in 1938, the year he succeeded Frederick Converse [1618] as dean of the faculty of the New England Conservatory in Boston. He became the school's director in 1942, leaving four years later to take a professorship at his alma mater, where he occupied the Battel Chair from 1960 until his retirement in 1965. His *Concerto Concertante* (for two pianos and orchestra) was awarded the Pulitzer Prize in 1953, perhaps the most prestigious of Porter's many awards and honors. Albeit a musical conservative, Porter was a skillful and painstaking artist. Though he wrote some incidental music and songs, he was known best for his instrumental music. RECORDINGS: Porter conducted his own first symphony and *Concerto Concertante* for records. Other recordings included the orchestral *Poem and Dance, New England Episodes, Music for Strings,* the Concerto for Viola, the Symphony No. 2, and the Concerto for Harpsichord, as well as several of the string quartets, the oboe quintet, the flute quintet, the clarinet quintet, the piano sonata, and a few other chamber pieces.

[1933] RIISAGER, Knudåge (Rē'-sà-er, K'nōō'-do-ā)
CIVIL SERVANT, EDUCATOR
BORN: Port Kunda, March 6, 1897
DIED: Copenhagen, December 26, 1974

Although he spent twenty-four years of his mature life in nonmusical work, Riisager was a prolific and interesting composer. He was born in Estonia, the son of a Danish engineer, who brought his family back to Copenhagen three years later. There the boy studied violin and later took theory and composition lessons, but he graduated from the local university with a degree in economics. Some early compositions having been well received, he then spent a year in Paris, where he studied with Roussel [1605] and acquainted himself with contemporary musical trends. In 1925 he wrote the first of his 5 symphonies. A year later he entered the ministry of finance, where he eventually worked his way up to a post of importance. In the early 1930s a government fellowship took him to Leipzig for further study with Hermann Grabner, a pupil of Reger [1637] and a notable pedagogue. During that decade he began to win international notice with his Concertino for Trumpet and especially his ballet *Qaartsiluni* on Eskimo themes (!). In 1937 he became chairman of the Danish Composers' Union, an office he held for twenty-five years. In 1950, his musical career having become too demanding, he resigned from the ministry but six years later acceded to the government's request that he take over the running of the Royal Danish Conservatory. He retired in 1967. Among his

honors was a doctorate from the University of Washington in 1972 and honorary citizenship of that state.

In the 1920s Riisager was regarded as a wild man by his more conservative compatriots. Though he did make use of such advanced concepts as polyrhythms and polytonality, his music—at least what one hears on record—strikes one as typical of the wit and verve of the French neo-classicism of the time. Riisager wrote a single opera, *Susanna,* but was especially successful with ballets, his *Étude* based on studies by Carl Czerny [1137] becoming a worldwide hit for a time.

RECORDINGS: *Étude* has been recorded, as have the trumpet concertino, *Qaartsiluni,* the ballet *Slaraffenland (The Land of Slobs),* the *Little Overture,* sonatas, piano pieces, choral works, and songs.

[1934] COWELL, Henry Dixon
PIANIST, EDITOR, TEACHER
BORN: Menlo Park, Calif., March 11, 1897
DIED: Shady, N.Y., December 10, 1965

In his day Henry Cowell was regarded as one of the most important American progressive composers. Though he was a tireless (and often undisciplined) experimenter and worked hard for the avant-garde, he was, in fact a not very profound musical creator, and his true inclination, despite the outward trappings of his music, was romantic (if not naive). (One is somehow reminded of his poetic contemporary e. e. cummings.)

His father was the immigrant son of an Irish Anglican minister; his mother, an aspiring poet, came from Iowa. The couple soon moved to San Francisco (they would surely have been right at home there in the 1960s). They believed—perhaps not entirely unreasonably—that the education purveyed in the schools was dangerous to one's thinking, and so young Henry, who learned to read and write from his mother, got his from the streets, and in the summers from the farms of the various relatives with whom he stayed. Cowell Senior vanished in 1901, and his wife divorced him in 1902, the year her son took up the violin. Two years later an illness forced him to lay it down permanently, though by then he had absorbed enough music to enable him to compose in his head. When in 1906 the famous earthquake laid the city flat, Mrs. Cowell took her son back to Des Moines, where a brief brush with formal education was quickly ended by his continued poor health. The pair then moved on to New York, where they literally nearly starved to death. By 1909 they were back where they started in Menlo Park, where Henry kept the wolf away by working at odd jobs and peddling wild herbs he had collected.

Eventually when he was thirteen he was sufficiently flush to buy an old piano, which he installed in an outbuilding (there being no room in the little house). He had some lessons from a neighbor but soon found the prescribed approach too limited and began experimenting with the strings and the case as sound sources. He also discovered what he termed tone clusters, produced by depressing several adjacent keys with the fist or elbow or forearm—though surely Ives [1659] was ahead of him here. He proceeded to write a number of compositions embodying his discoveries, which he presented at a concert in San Francisco when he was fifteen, the evening after his birthday. He attracted the attention of Charles Seeger, brother of poet Alan and chairman of the University of California Music Department at Berkeley (later the father of folksinger Pete and husband of composer Ruth Crawford [2000]). Seeger took over Cowell's compositional training and got him admitted to the university as a special student for other musical studies. He fostered the young man's experimental bent, which soon turned to various applications of mathematical-acoustical formulae. In 1916 Cowell went to New York to attend the Institute of Musical Art (the Juilliard School) but soon found it too stodgy and came back to Berkeley, where he began teaching at the university until he was called up to serve in the wartime army. After three months as a cook, he was assigned to a band in Allentown, Pennsylvania, as a conductor and arranger. He spent his spare time writing a book on experimental music, *New Musical Resources,* which, however, had to wait eleven years to be published. Whatever he may have been as a composer, the work revealed a brilliant and farsighted theoretical mind.

After the war Cowell settled in New York, where he studied for a time at the Institute of Applied Music. He played his first New York recital in Carnegie Hall in February 1924 and was greeted with objurgations and chortles from the reviewers. The next year he received a similar reception in Berlin. For some time thereafter he followed the concert trail across both continents, every appearance guaranteed to create a sensation. He was, however, increasingly admired by the progressives, and, on the strength of his reputation as a revolutionary, was the first American invited to play in the Soviet Union, in 1929, where predictably the official

reaction was that he was *too* revolutionary. In 1927 he founded the publication *New Music Quarterly,* which gave first printings to pieces by Ruggles [1684], Ives [1659], Varèse [1774], Riegger [1793], Schoenberg [1657], Cage [2192], and a host of other important moderns. The journal afterward spawned New Records, which allowed a broader public to hear such pieces. A year later Cowell joined the faculty of the New School for Social Research in New York, where he was music director until he retired in 1963. He later also held full-time appointments at Columbia University and the Peabody Conservatory in Baltimore.

Long a student of non-European musics, Cowell obtained a Guggenheim Fellowship in 1930 which enabled him to spend a year investigating them in Berlin under the guidance of important experts. (His interest had been kindled during childhood in San Francisco's Chinatown.) Around 1931, he brought into being, with the aid of Léon Theremin, inventor of the electronic instrument that bears his surname, a device called the rhythmicon, capable of playing polyrhythms at superhuman speeds and complexities in tones derived from the overtone series. In 1931 Cowell wrote a concerto called *Rhythmicana* for rhythmicon and orchestra. In 1936 his success came to an abrupt end when he was picked up in California on a sexual charge. Assuming he would have no trouble proving his innocence, he did not bother to retain a lawyer. Instead he was sentenced to a term in San Quentin. But Cowell had grown up in the school of hard knocks and, despite the hostility of the authorities, he spent his time teaching music to the other inmates. Powerful well-wishers on the outside got him paroled in 1940, and a year later the prosecutor, now convinced that the whole affair had been a railroad job, obtained a full pardon for him. Later that year Cowell married Sidney Robertson, a writer and collector of folk music, with whom he afterward collaborated on an important study of Ives, *Charles Ives and His Music,* published in 1955. During World War II Cowell was in charge of the musical side of the overseas division of the Office of War Information. In his later years Cowell's own music was variously influenced by Irish folk music, early American hymnology (which produced a whole series of "fuguing tunes") and Asian musics, and largely eschewed the "eccentricities" which were his hallmark earlier in his career. Perhaps his most significant compositions are such late works as the Symphony No. 11, which incorporates elements of his early and late styles into a satisfying synthesis. His significant honors, awards, and prestige grants are too many to list. Among his pupils were Cage, Lou Harrison [2266], and (very briefly) George Gershwin [1955].

Cowell's compositions are said to number somewhere between 700 and 1,000, including 21 symphonies; 2 concerti for koto; a concerto apiece for piano, harmonica, accordion, percussion instruments, and harp; and a single opera, *O'Higgins of Chile* (unproduced and unpublished).

RECORDINGS: As a pianist Cowell made a number of recordings of his notorious piano pieces and one of the concerted *Tales of Our Countryside* with Leopold Stokowski. Other recordings include Symphonies Nos. 4, 5, 7, 10, 11, 15, and 16; the orchestral works *Sinfonietta, Synchrony, Persian Set, Saturday Night at the Firehouse, Ancient Desert Drone, Variations, Ballad, Fiddler's Jig, Music 1957,* and *Ongaku;* numerous *Hymns and Fuguing Tunes* for various chamber or orchestral combinations; the vocal-instrumental *Toccanta; ". . . if he please . . ."* for chorus and orchestra; several string quartets; the piano trio; the first violin sonata; several pieces for percussion, including *Homage to Iran* and *Ostinato Pianissimo;* and other chamber and piano works.

[1935] EIMERT, Herbert (Ī'-mert, Her'-bert)
THEORIST, CRITIC, EDITOR, BROAD-CASTER, TEACHER
BORN: Bad Kreuznach, April 8, 1897
DIED: Cologne, December 15, 1972

Eimert offers one more proof that an idea whose time has come is subject to multiple "discovery." After graduating from the Cologne Conservatory in 1924, he took a Ph.D. in musicology at the conservatory in 1931. Before his initial graduation he wrote a guide to twelve-tone theory without having encountered the efforts of either Schoenberg [1657] or Matthias Hauer [1763], and in 1925 he completed a string quartet built on the principles enunciated. That same year he became program annotator for the concerts of the Gürzenich Orchestra in Cologne and shortly afterward joined the staff of the West German Radio. During the Nazi era he was branded a cultural outcast and worked in an editorial capacity on a local newspaper. He returned to his posts after the war, became a pioneer in electronic music, and founded the electronic music studio at the radio station. From 1965 until the year of his death he taught electronic music at the conservatory. RECORDINGS: His electronic compositions

Sélection I, 6 Studies, and *Epitaph für Aikichi Kuboyama* have been recorded, as well as a lecture on electronic music by Eimert himself.

[1936] SAEVERUD, Harald Sigurd Johan (Sā'-ver-ōōd, Här'-åld Sē'-gōōrd Yō'-hån)
PIANIST, TEACHER
BORN: Bergen, April 17, 1897

Harald Saeverud had musical forebears on both sides, one of them being a noted maker of the Hardanger fiddle, a sympathetic-stringed instrument enormously popular in Norway. He was born in Edvard Grieg's [1410] native town, came to music early, taught himself to compose, and conducted the Bergen Orchestra in a concert of his works when he was fifteen. Afterward he undertook more structured studies at the local conservatory and then for a year, 1920–21, at the Musikhochschule in Berlin. He thereupon returned to Bergen, appeared as a pianist and taught privately, and spent his free time composing. Having experimented with post-Brahmsian [1329] Romanticism and atonality, he turned to a lucid and witty neoclassicism, characterized by considerable use of polyphony, and his music began to attract attention outside of Norway. In 1933 a handsome government pension enabled him to compose full-time. He celebrated the next year by visiting the United States and marrying Marie Hvoslef, whose parents had moved there from Norway. During the war years his music became more nationalistic and serious. In 1947 he was asked to write music for a new production of Henrik Ibsen's play *Peer Gynt,* to supplant the hallowed score by Grieg, which the director felt was not in keeping with his concept. Saeverud was more than a little reticent at the notion of overturning a national monument but succeeded in writing a brilliant score, from which, like his predecessor, he extracted two orchestral suites that enjoyed great popularity. The bulk of his work is either orchestral or pianistic and includes a ballet, 9 symphonies, and concerti for various instruments. His son Ketil (1939–), who has recently changed his professional last name to Hvoslef to avoid confusion with his father, has also made a name for himself as a composer. RECORDINGS: Recordings include the *Peer Gynt Suites,* the sixth and seventh symphonies, Concerto for Piano, Concerto for Oboe, *Rondo amoroso, Ballad of Revolt,* and the *Galdreslåtten (Sorcerer's Dance)—* all orchestral—and some piano pieces.

[1937] KORNGOLD, Erich Wolfgang
(Kôrn'-gōlt, Ā'-rikh Volf'-gång)
CONDUCTOR
BORN: Brünn (Brno), May 29, 1897
DIED: Hollywood, Calif., November 29, 1957

Hailed (not without reason) in childhood as a new Mozart **[992]**, Korngold wound up as a man who seemed to have outlived his time. His father Julius was a lawyer who had studied music and who moved to Vienna soon after Erich's birth to serve as assistant to Eduard Hanslick, the all-powerful critic of the *Neue Freie Presse*, whom he succeeded in 1902. At the age of five the boy was playing duets with his father, who had taught him the keyboard. Two years later he was composing. When, at nine, he produced a cantata, *Gold*, Julius decided that music was going to be more than a pastime with him and sent him to study with Robert Fuchs at the Vienna Conservatory. Shortly afterward Gustav Mahler **[1525]** listened to him play the cantata, supposedly muttered "A genius! A genius!" and recommended that he go to Zemlinsky **[1621]** for lessons. Under the latter's eye young Korngold turned out a piano sonata in 1908, and a 1910 ballet, *Der Schneemann (The Snowman)*. His teacher orchestrated it, Emperor Franz Joseph demanded a performance in 1910, and it was subsequently seen all over central Europe. Korngold followed this with a piano trio and another sonata, which Artur Schnabel **[1746]**, with cries of wonder, took unto his bosom for performance. The initial orchestral pieces came in 1911 and 1912—an overture and the *Sinfonietta*. Artur Nikisch commissioned and premiered the first *(Schauspiel-Ouvertüre)* in Munich. There were also some piano pieces and other small chamber works. At sixteen the youth completed two one-act operas—a comedy, *Der Ring des Polykrates (Polykrates' Ring)*, and a piece of Renaissance *verismo* entitled *Violanta*. Bruno Walter, who had played piano in the premiere of the trio, conducted the first performances of both at Munich in 1916. Among others who bestowed kudos on the young phenomenon were Richard Strauss **[1563]** and Giacomo Puccini **[1511]**.

After completing a violin sonata and a piano quintet, Korngold set out on another opera, *Die tote Stadt (The Dead City)*. It at first proved intractable and was interrupted by his country's demand that he take up arms. Actually he spent two years playing for the officer corps. Having discharged his duty, he wrote incidental music for a production of Shakespeare's *Much Ado About Nothing (Viel Lärm um nichts)* and took a

job as conductor at the Hamburg State Opera. There the new opera was first heard in 1920 (with a concurrent production in Cologne). It was an instant (if short-lived) sensation. In Vienna it established Maria Jeritza as an international star, and in New York it was the first German-language opera to play the Metropolitan Opera House after the wartime ban. Latter-day revivals have failed, however, to establish it in the repertoire.

In 1922 Korngold returned to Vienna, where two years later he married Luise von Sonnenthal. (Their son George is now an important record producer.) Korngold busied himself with resuscitating the lesser-known operettas of Johann Strauss, Jr. **[1295]**. When his own next operatic contribution, *Das Wunder der Heliane*, was produced in 1927 (again in Hamburg), there was some muttering that he had not kept up with the times. Nevertheless in 1932 the Viennese still voted him in a poll as one of the two greatest living composers; the other was Schoenberg **[1657]**. In 1929 he began an association with the great theatrical director Max Reinhardt and in 1930 took on a professorship at the Vienna Academy. Another product of this period was a pastiche Strauss operetta that after several vicissitudes reached Broadway in 1934 as *The Great Waltz*, became one of the great musical hits of the decade, and was eventually made into a Hollywood film—almost unrecognizably. That very year Reinhardt, ousted from Germany, went to California to direct a film of Shakespeare's *A Midsummer Night's Dream* (starring Olivia de Haviland, Dick Powell, James Cagney, Joe E. Brown, Mickey Rooney, and the proverbial multitudinous cast), and took Korngold along to arrange the score (mostly based on Mendelssohn **[1200]**). Paramount invited him back the following year to do a film operetta, *Give Us This Night*, for the Polish tenor Jan Kiepura. After that Korngold began a long association with Warner Brothers, initiating it with a score for an Errol Flynn romance, *Captain Blood*. For a short time the composer traveled back and forth between Hollywood and Vienna. But the Nazi incursion in 1938 ended his hopes for a production of his new opera, *Die Kathrin*, and he packed up three generations of Korngolds and settled then in California. (The opera received an unsuccessful premiere in Stockholm the next year.)

In constant demand Korngold wrote at least seventeen new film scores in a few years, grew reasonably wealthy and enormously overweight, and collected three Academy Awards for his efforts (for *Anthony Adverse, The Adventures of Robin*

Hood, and *The Sea Wolf).* In 1942 and again in 1944 he conducted for the New Opera Company in New York. When Julius Korngold died in 1945, his son began to feel that he had betrayed both his father and his own promise. After *Deception* in 1946 he gave up films. He produced a violin concerto and a cello concerto, both based on movie-score material; both got scathing reviews. His only symphony, completed in 1950, was not performed in his lifetime. The Vienna production of *Die Kathrin* in 1950 was a flop. From that time on, the composer suffered a series of heart attacks and strokes that killed him at sixty. His last major work was an orchestral *Theme and Variations* in 1953. Thanks in part to the efforts of his son, there has been some revival of interest in his work.

RECORDINGS: The operas *Violanta* and *Die tote Stadt* have both been recorded, as has a good deal of the film music. Other recordings include the *Sinfonietta,* the Symphony, the *Schauspiel-Ouvertüre,* the Concerto for Violin, the *Much Ado* music, the *Theme and Variations,* the piano trio and quintet, the violin sonata, the second and third piano sonatas, the second string quartet and miscellaneous piano pieces and songs.

[1938] TANSMAN, Alexandre *(né* Aleksander) (Tåns'-mån, Ål-ek-sån'dr')
PIANIST, CONDUCTOR
BORN: Łódź, June 12, 1897

Tansman took up piano in his birthplace under the guidance of Wojciech Gawroński, a disciple of Leschetizky, and began composing at an early age. In 1914 he entered the University of Warsaw to become a lawyer but continued his musical studies on the side, taking composition lessons from Piotr Rytel (1884–1970) and piano from Waldemar Lütschg. He soon abandoned his academic studies, and after the Polish declaration of independence in 1918 he joined the army. By submitting compositions (a piece for violin and piano and a piano sonata) pseudonymously, he managed to win both first and second prize in the 1919 Warsaw Competition. The publicity enabled him to give two highly successful concerts of his music, the proceeds from which took him to Paris, where, save for the years of the German occupation, he spent the rest of his days. After some months of struggle, he was taken up by the dynamic young conductor Vladimir Golschmann, who became a champion of his music. Tansman soon became a very effective apostle for it himself, making annual tours as both pianist and conductor. He was

accepted by the Parisian musical establishment, and struck up a close and lifelong friendship with Igor Stravinsky [1748] by whose neo-classicism and general eclecticism he was affected. The Nazi invasion in 1941 necessitated his fleeing for his life. He wound up in the United States, where he had performed and where his friendships with Golschmann and Stravinsky stood him in good stead. (He had toured with Koussevitzky [1655] and the Boston Symphony in 1927.) For a time he wrote film scores (e.g., *Flesh and Fantasy)* in Hollywood. He returned to Paris in 1946. His wife of sixteen years, *née* Colette Cras, died there in 1953. They had two daughters. Tansman's music is essentially French, but he has experimented with such things as atonality, serialism, and even jazz, and the strongly melodic and rhythmic impulses are often Polish but usually his own. He has been extremely prolific, and his output includes at least 6 operas, 7 ballets, 7 symphonies, 8 string quartets, and works in many other forms. RECORDINGS: Among recordings are the oratorio *Isaiah the Prophet,* the *Triptych* for strings, the orchestral *Capriccio, Musique de Cour* for guitar and orchestra, music from *Flesh and Fantasy,* and a number of smaller pieces for chamber combinations, piano, and guitar.

[1939] BEN-HAIM, Paul (Ben Khả'-ēm, Poul)
TEACHER, ETHNOMUSICOLOGIST, CONDUCTOR
BORN: Munich, July 5, 1897
DIED: Tel Aviv, January 16, 1984

Born Paul Frankenburger, this composer studied music from 1915 to 1920 at the academy in his native city. After a four-year stint as assistant conductor at the Bavarian State Opera there, he moved on to a conductorship at the municipal theater of Augsburg. The rise of the Nazis, however, nipped this phase of his career in the bud, and in 1933 he emigrated to Palestine, where he Hebraicized his name. Up to then Ben-Haim's compositions had been out of the *Mitteleuropäische* bag, but in his new surroundings he turned his attention to the folk music of the area and in attempting to speak for his people, he became one of the patriarchal figures in the music of the new state of Israel. He was aided in his researches by the well-known Palestinian folksinger Bracha Zefira. He did not, however, assume a parochial stance, but left himself open to Arabic and other impulses of the eastern Mediterranean, using not only typical melodic profiles but also rhythms, colorations, and even harmonies. He wrote 2 symphonies, a violin concerto, a cello concerto, and much other music in both large and small forms. RECORDINGS: The suite *From Israel* (Leopold Stokowski); *The Sweet Psalmist of Israel* (Leonard Bernstein); *Concerto for Strings* (Kenneth Alwyn, Izler Solomon); *"To the Chief Musician"* and *Pastorale variée* (Robert Whitney); the violin sonata (Yehudi Menuhin, Sidney Harth); the piano sonata (Menahem Pressler); and many smaller pieces. (Ben-Haim accompanies Ursula Mayer-Reinach in a cycle of songs.) There are also anonymous pirate recordings of the symphonies with a couple of short orchestra pieces and a new commercial recording of Symphony No. 2 conducted by Alwyn.

[1940] AMBROSIUS, Hermann (Ámbröz′-yoos, Här′-màn)
TEACHER
BORN: Hamburg, July 25, 1897

A graduate of the Leipzig Conservatory, Ambrosius studied with Hans Pfitzner **[1606]** in the early 1920s. In 1925 he returned to the conservatory as a professor and taught there until World War II. After the partition of Germany, he settled at Engen in southern Bavaria, where he devoted himself to composition and study. His basically conservative output is said to be very large. RECORDINGS: Ambrosius is represented on records by a suite for guitar and the Concerto for Guitar and Plectrum Orchestra.

[1941] MIGNONE, Francisco Paulo (Mēn-yō′-nä, Fràn-sēs′-kō Pou′-lōo)
FLUTIST, PIANIST, CONDUCTOR,
TEACHER
BORN: São Paulo, September 3, 1897

Mignone's father, a flutist and conductor, gave him his first music lessons, then sent him to the local conservatory. In his student days he doubled as pianist in a cinema orchestra, of which he was soon put in charge. Having established himself as a composer of promise, he went to Italy on a government grant in 1920 and studied at the Milan Conservatory with Vincenzo Ferroni (1858–1934). Save for visits home, he remained there for nine years. In 1924 he wrote his most successful opera, *O contractador dos diamantes (The Diamond Merchant)*, which had an enormously successful premiere in Rio de Janeiro. He followed it in 1928 with *L'innocente (The Innocent)*. The next year he returned to São Paulo to teach at the conservatory. In 1933 he helped found the National School of Music in Rio, where he taught and conducted until his retirement thirty-four years later. He made tours of Europe and the Americas as conductor and pianist, and served as a director of Brazilian radio. Mignone's music at first owed much to his Italian training, then went through a period of intense folk-derived nationalism and emerged as widely eclectic. He has written prolifically in all areas and also moonlighted successfully as a composer of Brazilian pop songs under the pseudonym of "Chico Bororó." RECORDINGS: His available representation on records outside of South America consists mostly of songs, though Mignone himself made a number of recordings as both conductor and pianist in Brazil. (There are also Brazilian recordings of the ballet *The Emerald Hunter* and *12 Études* for guitar.)

[1942] FERNANDEZ, Oscar Lorenzo (Fär-nàn′-des, Ōs′-kär Lō-ren′-zō)
PIANIST, CONDUCTOR, EDUCATOR
BORN: Rio de Janeiro, November 4, 1897
DIED: Rio de Janeiro, August 26, 1948

An even more determined Brazilian musical nationalist than his exact contemporary Francisco Mignone **[1941]**, Fernandez based most of his music on folk themes, borrowed or invented. He studied piano and composition at the National Musical Institute in Rio and gave his first concert of his own works in 1923. The following year he won a prize for his *Trio brasileiro* and was appointed to a professorship at his former school. In 1931 he completed his only opera, the wholly folkbased *Malazarte,* which had much success in Brazil, though its premiere was delayed until 1941. From 1936 until his death he directed the Conservatorio Brasileiro, which he founded. His "Inca" ballet, *Amayá,* was performed in 1939 by the Ballets Russes. RECORDINGS: Recordings include a popular orchestral *Batuque* (accounts disagree as to whether it comes from *Malazarte* or from the suite *Reisado do pastoreio*—or whether there are two), a movement from the prizewinning trio, and a number of songs. (There is also a Brazilian boxed set of the complete piano music performed by Miguel Proença.)

[1943] MARX, Karl
TEACHER, CONDUCTOR
BORN: Munich, November 12, 1897

Not to be in any way confused with his earlier and more famous namesake or with Joseph Marx [**1747**], this Karl Marx set out to become a scientist. Drafted during World War I, he met his fellow Municher Carl Orff [**1912**] in the army and was swayed toward music. Later he was captured and interned in England. After his release he studied with Orff, then became a student at the Munich Academy, where he studied with Anton Beer-Wallbrunn (a pupil of Rheinberger [**1368**]), and the conductor Siegmund von Hausegger, its director. He joined the faculty there in 1924 and four years later was named conductor of the Bach Gesellschaft. During World War II Marx taught in Graz, and afterward, until his retirement in 1966, at the Stuttgart Hochschule. He produced several concerti and a good deal of chamber music but is best known for his choral music. RECORDINGS: Some of his choral music may be found in recorded anthologies.

[**1944**] KOUGUELL, Arkadie (Kōō'-gwoo-el, Ur-kà'-dyi)
PIANIST, TEACHER, ADMINISTRATOR
BORN: Simferopol, December 25, 1897

Born in the Crimea, Kouguell studied at the St. Petersburg Conservatory and was for a time director of a music school in the Crimea. From 1928 until 1948 he ran the Institute of Music at the American University in Beirut, Lebanon. After some time spent teaching in Tel Aviv and Paris, he emigrated to New York in 1952. Much of his music is based on Jewish themes; it includes a ballet, *Jacob and Rachel,* a *Hebrew Rhapsody,* several concerti, choral works, and a good deal of chamber music. RECORDINGS: The *Berceuse* for violin and piano has been recorded.

[**1945**] BAQUIERO FÓSTER, Gerónimo (Bàk-yā'-rō Fōs'-ter, Khā-rō'-nē-mō)
ETHNOMUSICOLOGIST, CRITIC, TEACHER
BORN: Hopelchén, January 7, 1898
DIED: Mexico City, May 20, 1967

Born in the Yucatan Peninsula of Mexico, Baquiero Fóster received enough musical training in Mérida, the provincial capital, to qualify as an army bandsman. By 1922 he had found his way to Mexico City, where he became a disciple of Julián Carrillo [**1663**] and an enthusiastic apostle for his acoustical theories. He was a newspaper reviewer for a time, and from 1929 until 1965 he held a professorship at the National Conservatory. He was best known as a worldwide collector of folk music, the author of many books and articles, and the founder of the *Rivista musical mexicana.* His compositions are largely

folk-based. RECORDINGS: Carlos Chávez [**1968**] recorded his *Huapangos,* not to be confused with a similarly titled work by Pablo Moncayo [**2190**].

[**1946**] RIETI, Vittorio (Rē-ā'-tē, Vit-tō'-rē-ō)
TEACHER
BORN: Alexandria, Egypt, January 28, 1898

Though born in Egypt, Rieti is Italian by parentage and training, and American by citizenship. He studied with pianist Giuseppe Frugatta, a Bazzini [**1256**] pupil, while taking a degree in economics at the University of Milan in 1917, then served in the Italian army. After the war he became a pupil of Respighi [**1718**] in Rome for a couple of years and nominally made his home there until 1940, though he spent much of his time in Paris. His music was taken up by Alfredo Casella [**1767**], who put him on the map. In Paris he came to be well known for his ballets and his dramatic music, much of the latter written for Louis Jouvet's company. When the Germans invaded France, he settled in the United States, where he became a citizen four years later and where he taught in several schools—Peabody, the Chicago Musical College, Queens College, and the Hunter College of Music in New York. He retired from the last in 1964 but continued to be active as a composer. Very much his own man as a stylist, he breaks no trails but writes with irresistible charm and polish. His 6 operas are all small-scale. He wrote more than 12 ballets, 7 symphonies, several concerti, much music for chamber groups and solo instruments, and a few choral pieces and songs. His American publisher has issued several LPs of his music on the Serenus label. There is a Soviet record of the ballet *Barabau.* Other more widely circulated recordings include the harpsichord concerto; the ballet *Capers; Dance Variations, Madrigale,* and *Introduzione e Gioco delle Ore* (all orchestral); the chamber *Partita, Incisioni* for brass quintet, and *Sonata all'Antica* for harpsichord.

[**1947**] HARRIS, Roy Ellsworth
TEACHER
BORN: Chandler, Okla., February 12, 1898
DIED: Santa Monica, Calif., October 1, 1979

Current histories of American music give the impression that somewhere the likeness of Roy Harris is carved on a Mt. Rushmore reserved to American composers. Gangling and at least as hayseedy as Robert Frost, he seemed in the national crisis of the 1930s and 1940s the archetype of his kind—the hymner of the great open spaces and the values of the common man. But the fact remains that by the time he died at eighty-one his sophisticated brand of folksiness was out of fashion and he had been in eclipse for at least two decades.

His origins were appropriate. He was born (in Lincoln County on Lincoln's birthday) to Scotch-Irish parents who had come to Oklahoma in the great land rush, carved out a farm, and built a cabin on it. (He was baptized "Leroy.") After Mrs. Harris's health had been undermined by malaria, the family moved in 1903 to a farm near Covina, California. There Roy learned piano at home and clarinet in the public schools. A passionate reader, he developed artistic and intellectual tastes and in high school developed a coterie of similarly inclined friends with whom he became acquainted with good music through phonograph records, concerts, and opera performances in Los Angeles. On graduating he acquired a farm of his own in 1916 but could not make a go of it and rented it out, later supporting himself as a truckdriver and attending theory classes at the Los Angeles Normal School. After World War I, during which he never got farther than a training program, he went to the University of California at Berkeley to take academic courses, during which time he also had organ and piano lessons. Inspired to try his hand at composing, he wrote a choral work which he showed to Alfred Hertz, conductor of the San Francisco Symphony. Hertz suggested that he get as far away from colleges as possible and find himself a good teacher. This latter Harris did in the person of Arthur Farwell [1629] back in Los Angeles, where he supported himself as a butter-and-egg man for a dairy. He also had help and encouragement from Arthur Bliss [1854]. He advanced rapidly and in March 1926 a piece he wrote for string quartet was played in Los Angeles. Meanwhile Howard Hanson [1927] had accepted his *Andante for Strings,* which he conducted in Rochester the following month and which shortly afterward won first prize and a performance at the Lewisohn Stadium in a contest run by the New York Philharmonic.

Not wanting to miss the New York performance, Harris scraped up enough money to go to New York. There he met Aaron Copland [1986], who sang the praises of Nadia Boulanger to him so seductively that he proceeded to Paris with the backing of a patron,

and remained, thanks to two successive Guggenheim Fellowships. He soon found Nadia's lessons too constraining for his taste, and by mutual agreement he used the opportunity to assiduously explore the music of the great tradition and to compose, checking in with her for advice. The *Concerto for Piano, Clarinet, and String Quartet,* Op. 2, was premiered in Paris in 1927 and won considerable favorable notice.

In 1929 Harris fell down a flight of steps and broke his back. He was returned to the United States for an operation. It was successful, but he had to remain several months in the hospital, where he discovered he could compose without a piano. In 1930 a grant from the Pasadena Music and Arts Association (renewed in 1931) made it possible for Harris to devote his time to composition. The most important product of this period (there were also two string quartets and a sextet) was the first symphony *(Symphony 1933),* on which he worked with the encouragement of Serge Koussevitzky [1655], who first performed it and then recorded it for Columbia Records—the first American symphony ever to be marketed on records. The next year Harris became head of the department of composition at the Westminster Choir School in Princeton, New Jersey. In 1936 he married a pianist named Beula Duffey, who afterward, as Johana Harris, made recordings of several of his works. Harris was now composing at top speed—a piano trio and the *Song for Occupations* for eight-part choir in 1934; the second symphony, choral and orchestral versions of *When Johnny Comes Marching Home,* and the Whitman-based *Symphony for Voices* in 1935; the orchestral *Time Suite* and the piano quintet in 1936; and, perhaps his peak achievement insofar as public acceptance was concerned, the third symphony in 1937. During the summers from 1932 to 1940, he also taught at the Juilliard School in New York. In the latter year he went to Cornell University as composer in residence, and in 1942 he undertook six years of teaching at Colorado College (interrupted for a time in 1945 when he directed the music section of the Overseas Division of the Office of War Information). After that he taught (generally for one-year stints) at, successively, Utah State Agricultural College, Peabody Teachers College in Nashville (two years), Pennsylvania College for Women (five years), the University of Southern Illinois, Indiana University (three years), and the Inter-American University at San Germán, Puerto Rico, before settling down at UCLA in 1961. After his retirement there in 1973, he spent three more years as composer in residence at California State University, Los Angeles, leaving when he was awarded (at seventy-eight) a third Guggenheim Fellowship. The last-named school is the site of the Roy Harris Archive. The composer was the recipient of many honors.

Harris composed 15 symphonies in all; the fourteenth was premiered in 1976 to celebrate the American bicentennial, and he completed the fifteenth in 1978. The fourth, a choral work based on folksongs, was the result of his acquaintance with leading figures in the "folksong revival" of the 1930s and 1940s (e.g., Carl Sandburg, Burl Ives, Pete Seeger, John and Alan Lomax)—an interest further reflected in many later works. In the seventh, for which he was awarded a Naumburg Prize, he experimented with serialism. The tenth is scored for chorus, brass, amplified pianos, and percussion. The bulk of his production was for instruments (orchestra, band, chamber groups, solo instruments) and for chorus. He wrote a couple of ballet scores, music for a documentary film, and a few solo vocal works, but no operas. His music is essentially diatonic and linear, with not infrequent modal references, often seeming simple and rough-hewn and evocative of vast open spaces.

RECORDINGS: Recordings include Symphonies 1, 3, 4, 5, 6, and 7, and the *West Point Symphony* (for band); *When Johnny Comes Marching Home* (both versions); *Kentucky Spring, Elegy and Dance, Epilogue to Profiles in Courage,* and *Fantasy for Piano and Orchestra* (all orchestral); *Cimarron* (band); *Concerto for Amplified Piano, Brasses, Basses, and Percussion; Toccata, Chorale,* and *Fantasy* (all three for organ and brasses); *Concerto for Piano, Clarinet, and String Quartet;* the second and third string quartets; the Quintet for Piano and Strings and the orchestral version thereof; the quintet and sextet for piano and winds; the piano trio; the violin sonata; the piano sonata; *Abraham Lincoln Walks at Midnight* (chamber cantata); *Song for Occupations; Symphony for Voices;* and piano pieces. A modern stereo version of the first symphony is to be released in the near future by the Louisville Orchestra. (Note: Three of the five Harris children made records as members of a rock group, the West Coast Pop Art Experimental Band.)

[1948] ELWELL, Herbert

CRITIC, TEACHER, CONDUCTOR
BORN: Minneapolis, May 10, 1898
DIED: Cleveland, April 17, 1974

After three years, 1916–19, of academic work at the University of Minnesota, during which he studied piano and took some music courses, Elwell became a pupil of Ernest Bloch [1729] in New York. When Bloch left for Cleveland, Elwell left for the American Conservatory in Fontainebleau, where for three years he studied with Nadia Boulanger. In 1923 Elwell won an American Prix de Rome. He was based at the American Academy in that city until 1927, during which time he wrote perhaps his most famous score, the ballet *The Happy Hypocrite,* and married an Italian girl, Maria Cecchini. In 1928 he was appointed head of the composition department at the Cleveland Institute of Music (which Bloch had headed from 1920 to 1925), and he became conductor of its orchestra. Later he became assistant director of the school. From 1930 to 1936 he was program annotator for the Cleveland Orchestra, and in 1932 he became music critic for the Cleveland *Plain Dealer.* He also taught in summer sessions at the Eastman School in Rochester from 1940. He retired from the Cleveland Institute in 1945 but continued to teach summers at Oberlin, and to work for the newspaper until 1962. Elwell wrote a few other orchestral pieces, some choral pieces, and chamber music but was at his best as a songwriter. RECORDINGS: There is a suite from *The Happy Hypocrite,* the *Concert Suite* for violin and orchestra, the *Pastorale* for soprano and orchestra, and some songs.

[1949] BACON, Ernst

PIANIST, CONDUCTOR, TEACHER
BORN: Chicago, May 26, 1898

Ernst Bacon, a particularly distinguished composer of art songs, was the son of a prominent Chicago physician. His mother taught him piano and later entrusted his training to Glenn Dillard Gunn. On his father's insistence, he took an academic degree from Northwestern and did graduate work at the University of Chicago, though he continued with private music lessons. In 1924–25 he studied in Vienna with Karl Weigl [1733] and Franz Schmidt [1661]; then he taught piano and coached opera at the Eastman School, where he studied conducting with Eugene Goossens [1878], the conductor of the Rochester Philharmonic. In 1927 Bacon married Mary Lillie (the union ended in divorce a decade later, and he was subsequently married three more times). Their son Joseph has recorded as a guitarist and lutenist. For two years, 1928–30, Bacon taught at the San Francisco Conservatory.

In 1934–37 he directed the WPA Music Project there and helped found the Bach Festival at Carmel. After a year at Hamilton College in Clinton, New York, he went in 1938 to Converse College in Spartanburg, South Carolina where he was dean and then director of the conservatory until 1947, after which he was at Syracuse University until his retirement in 1963, when he returned to California to live in the Bay Area. Bacon has frequently toured as a pianist and was still giving concerts as recently as 1981. He has written 2 operas (one of them, *A Tree on the Plains,* winning considerable notice in 1942), 2 ballets, 4 symphonies, oratorios, and cantatas, but he has attracted most praise for his large number of songs, which are notable for their sensitivity to the text; many of them are settings of poems by Emily Dickinson. Besides many articles, Bacon has written several books on music—*Our Musical Idiom, Words on Music,* and *Notes on the Piano.* RECORDINGS: There have been recordings of these, as well as the orchestral *The Enchanted Island* and *Ford's Theater,* some piano pieces, and a cello sonata.

[1950] BERTOUILLE, Gérard (Bâr-tōō-wē', Zhā-ràr')
CRITIC
BORN: Tournai, May 26, 1898

Bertouille took a law degree in Brussels and then drifted into music. His chief composition teacher was Jean Absil [1889], but he also studied with the pianist-composer Francis de Bourguignon (1890–1961) and the violinist Martin Marsick. Bertouille's first significant compositions date from the late 1930s; they include a ballet, *Requiem des hommes d'aujourd'hui (Requiem for Men of Today),* 2 symphonies, concerti, quartets, and sonatas. The formal genres are significant: Bertouille is a militant conservative who believes that contemporary music has wandered off down the primrose path, an argument he has set forth in several books. RECORDINGS: There is a recording of a *Prélude* for harps.

[1951] MÜLLER, Paul (Mül'-er, Poul)
CONDUCTOR, TEACHER
BORN: Zürich, June 19, 1898

Switzerland is so full of musical Müllers and Paul Müller's career was so closely identified with Zürich that he took to signing himself "Müller-Zürich." He studied at the Zürich Conservatory—with Busoni [1577] pupil Philipp Jarnach, among others—and later in

Berlin and Paris. In 1927 he returned to teach at the conservatory until his retirement in 1962. He was conductor of the orchestra and of several choirs in Zürich and Lucerne. Beginning as basically a latter-day romantic, he shaped his mature style from a profound knowledge of Renaissance and Baroque polyphony. He wrote some dramatic works (but no opera as such), much choral music, symphonies, concerti, and other orchestral works, chamber music, organ pieces, and songs. RECORDINGS: Works on record include the Symphony No. 2, *Sinfonietta No. 2,* concerti for cello and viola, and the *Capriccio* for flute and piano.

[1952] EISLER, Hanns (Īz'-ler, Hàns)
TEACHER
BORN: Leipzig, July 6, 1898
DIED: Berlin, September 6, 1962

Though Hanns Eisler lived and worked in the United States for several years, he was virtually unknown to the public until his politics gave him a brief moment of notoriety after World War II. His father was a philosopher, and his elder brother Gerhart was a writer of left-wing apologetics. Eisler grew up in Vienna, where he taught himself what he knew about music in his youth. After army service in the last two years of World War I, he took a proofreading job with Universal Editions and studied under Karl Weigl [1733] at the Vienna Conservatory. After a few months he became Schoenberg's [1657] pupil and composed (successfully) for a time under his influence. In 1925 he took a teaching job at the Klindworth-Scharwenka Conservatory in Berlin and a year later joined the Communist Party there. Soon convinced that Schoenbergian music would never reach the common man, he abandoned it for a simpler and more direct approach. With the singing actor Ernst Busch as his chief interpreter and working with left-wing authors (notably Bertolt Brecht), Eisler poured out songs, choruses, cantatas, incidental music for plays, and film scores. Most of this material was designed to help spread the word, though some of it was obviously to satisfy a creative urge. His work was banned by the Nazis in 1933, and he spent several peripatetic years, settling finally in the United States in 1937. He taught at the New School in New York City, wrote music for Clifford Odets's play *Night Music* and a score for a government documentary film, *Soil,* and did research on the problems of writing film music. In 1942 he joined the faculty of the University of Southern California, and during his five-year stay in Los

Angeles he wrote several Hollywood film scores (e.g., *None But the Lonely Heart, So Well Remembered,* and *Woman on the Beach).* Called up in 1947 before the House Un-American Activities Committee for his political affiliations and his blood linkage to Gerhart Eisler, who was labeled a Communist spy, Eisler was found wanting and was ordered deported. So many important people protested (risking their own necks) that the order was rescinded—then Eisler agreed to leave of his own volition. He eventually settled in East Berlin, where he taught and composed (at a furious rate) for the rest of his life. One of his songs was adopted as the national anthem of the DDR, and others became very popular in Iron Curtain countries. His only opera, *Johannes Faustus,* was produced in Berlin in 1953. Most of his output combined words with music, though he produced some chamber music (most of it early) and arranged orchestral suites from some of his dramatic music.

RECORDINGS: In the West Eisler is represented on records by songs (notably an LP sung by drama-scholar and Brechtian Eric Bentley), the first and third piano sonatas, and the Op. 3 *Klavierstücke.* East German recordings include the massive vocal-orchestral *Deutsche Sinfonie* of 1937, several orchestral suites, numerous cantatas and orchestral song cycles, piano music, and songs.

[1953] HAMERIK, Ebbe (Hå´-mer-ik, Eb´-e)
CONDUCTOR
BORN: Copenhagen, September 5, 1898
DIED: at sea, August 11, 1951

Hamerik's family name was originally Hammerich and was retained as such by his uncle Angul, an important historian of Scandinavian music. His own father, Asger Hamerik, was a composer who had just come home when his son was born, after serving twenty-six years as first director of the Peabody Institute in Baltimore. He and the American emigré Frank Van der Stucken (1858–1929) were Ebbe's principal teachers. In 1919 Ebbe began a career as conductor at the Royal Theater in Copenhagen. Five years later he produced his first opera, *Stepan* (set in Soviet Russia), which was premiered in Mainz and later performed in Copenhagen and elsewhere. In the early 1930s Hamerik lived in Austria. His other operas were: *Leonardo da Vinci,* 1939; *Marie Grubbe,* 1940; and *The Traveling Companion,* 1946. He also wrote 5 symphonies, as well as a number of less ambitious works. He was drowned in the Katte-

gat a few weeks before his fifty-third birthday, a result of his passion for sailing. RECORDINGS: There is a recording of his 1942 Wind Quintet.

[1954] BACARISSE, Salvador (Bvà-kà-rès´-se, Sàl-va-*thôr´*)
RADIO EXECUTIVE
BORN: Madrid, September 12, 1898
DIED: Paris, August 5, 1963

Bacarisse studied at the University of Madrid and between 1923 and 1934 was a three-time winner of the National Music Award. He was also music director of the national radio until 1936. He then served on the music council of the republican (loyalist) government until the Fascist victory in 1939, when he fled to Paris. There he worked on musical broadcasts to Spain and won two awards for his radio operas. His stylistic spectrum was large, ranging from dissonant modernism through neo-classicism and neo-romanticism to Spanish nationalism. RECORDINGS: There is a recording (by Narciso Yepes) of his Concerto for Guitar, one of his most popular pieces.

[1955] GERSHWIN, George *(né* Jacob)
PIANIST, CONDUCTOR
BORN: Brooklyn, September 26, 1898
DIED: Hollywood, July 11, 1937

In his brief life George Gershwin produced only a small body of "serious" music. Most of it is flawed in terms of the prescribed rules. Yet no other American composer has won the kind of wide popular acceptance that he has.

Registered incorrectly at birth as Jacob Gershwine, George was the second of the four children of Rose and Morris Gershvin *(né* Gershovitz), immigrants from St. Petersburg. When George was born, his father was working as a shoe designer, but he soon struck out for himself and over the years owned and operated at various times and with reasonable success a stationery store, a cigar store, a bookmaking agency, a hotel, restaurants, and Turkish baths. During George's first twenty years, the family lived at more than twenty-five different addresses, mostly on the Lower East Side. The oldest son, Ira *(né* Israel), became one of the great popular-song lyricists; the younger, Arthur, also wrote songs and even had a Broadway musical produced; the daughter Frankie (Frances) was a talented singer who recorded some of George's songs.

George grew up on the New York streets.

He was a poor student in school and had no use for intellectual pursuits. He discovered music when at nine he heard a friend Max Rosenzweig (later Rosen) practicing the violin. When three years later his mother bought a piano for Ira, George was so much interested that he was given lessons too. After two years with a succession of neighborhood teachers, he discovered Charles Hambitzer, who was a talented (but like his pupil short-lived) pianist and composer. Hambitzer introduced him to the classics and by 1913 had him holding a summer job as pianist in a Catskills hotel and trying his hand at composition. At fifteen Gershwin was working full-time for the publisher Jerome K. Remick as the youngest song plugger in the business. In 1916 Harry von Tilzer published a song of his, "When You Want 'Em You Can't Get 'Em"; it did not catch on, but later that year Sigmund Romberg [1821] used another Gershwin song, "The Making of a Girl" in *The Passing Show of 1916*. It was also in 1916 that Gershwin began cutting piano rolls (many of them pseudonymously).

In 1915, at Hambitzer's urging, Gershwin had begun harmony and theory lessons with Edward Kilenyi, Sr., a Hungarian pupil of Mascagni [1559], afterward known around New York as a theater conductor and as the father of the pianist Edward Kilenyi, Jr. Later George would study sporadically with Rubin Goldmark (1872–1936) and Joseph Schillinger (1895–1943). Despite claims by both that they were his only significant teachers, he seems to have gained little from his association with Goldmark, though he found some of Schillinger's formulas for composing useful in a pinch. Early in 1917 he left Remick. For one night he succeeded Chico Marx as pianist in a Fourteenth Street vaudeville house but flubbed the job so badly that he left without even asking for his pay. Next he was hired as rehearsal pianist for a show called *Miss 1917*, an experience that brought him into contact with important figures on the Broadway scene. Irving Berlin (1888–) offered him a job as an arranger, but Gershwin chose to tour the vaudeville circuit as pianist to the singer Louise Dresser. When he got back, he was hired at thirty-five dollars a week to write songs for the consideration of Max Dreyfus, head of the publishing house of T. B. Harms. Gershwin also served as accompanist for Nora Bayes during the tour of *Ladies First*.

In 1919 Gershwin wrote his first Broadway show, *La La Lucille*, which opened in May and ran for a hundred performances. For the opening of the Capitol Theater later that year, he wrote "Swanee." Al Jolson heard it and added it to the score of *Sinbad*, with which he was touring the country. It was a hit of such enormous proportions (over two million records in its first year!) that it set its composer well on the road to fame and fortune. He was taken on by George White to write the music for his *Scandals*, designed to run competition to Ziegfeld's *Follies*, and did so for five years—until White balked at raising his salary above $125 a week. For the 1922 *Scandals*, he wrote his first opera, a brief one-acter called *Blue Monday* (later known as *135th Street*), but it was cut out after a single performance. Gershwin first drew the attention of serious musicians when the great soprano Eva Gauthier scheduled three of his songs in a recital of modern works at Aeolian Hall in November 1923. He accompanied her in them, and some of the reviewers predicted a great future for him. He was also taken up by New York society and began his career as a young man about town.

Paul Whiteman, who had conducted the only performance of *Blue Monday*, asked Gershwin to write a piece for a concert he was planning, which intended to prove that jazz was serious stuff. Gershwin shrugged off the request until he read in the paper that he was writing a "symphony" to be premiered by Whiteman in a few weeks. The result was the quasi-Lisztian *Rhapsody in Blue*, which Gershwin completed in a two-piano version, and which Ferde Grofé [1862] orchestrated for the Whiteman band (and later for full symphony). The concert took place on February 12, 1924, with Gershwin's piece as the penultimate work in what proved to be a tedious and pretentious series. But when the *Rhapsody* was concluded, the audience came unglued. Some of the critics also liked it, though others found it trite, sentimental, empty, and repetitious—a polarity that Gershwin's serious music occasioned for the rest of his life. In December of the same year, Gershwin had his first hit musical in *Lady, Be Good!* which fulfilled an early dream of writing a show for Fred and Adele Astaire (though perhaps its best song, "The Man I Love," was cut out during the tryouts).

The next year the Gershwins bought a big house on West 103rd Street, in which Ira inhabited the fourth floor and George the fifth, and where a sort of open house seemed to go on all day every day. By now George had been to Europe twice and was on first-name terms with the Prince of Wales, the Duke of Kent, and the Mountbattens, among other luminaries. After two Broadway flops, he hit again with *Tip-Toes* late in 1925 and *Oh Kay!* eleven months later. A month after the second work opened, Walter Damrosch [1540] conducted Gershwin and the New York Symphony in the *Concerto in F,* for piano and orchestra, which he had commissioned after hearing the *Rhapsody.* In 1927 the Gershwins and the Astaires had yet another smash in *Funny Face,* which opened the Alvin Theater, built with the profits from Gershwin's three previous successes. Another European trip the following year saw George lionized by the European musical establishment and inspired *An American in Paris,* premiered by Damrosch and the New York Philharmonic toward the end of that year. (George was called on to play the celesta part in the first recording, filling in for an absent musician.)

By now Gershwin was living a playboy bachelor existence in a penthouse on Riverside Drive. He attracted and was attracted to women but could never bring himself to marry, despite an increasing sense of loneliness and a course of psychoanalysis. Though he had an ego as big as all outdoors (and could not be kept away from the piano at parties, where he improvised brilliantly all evening), he was gregarious and did much to promote the careers of such as Oscar Levant, Vladimir Dukelsky (whom he named "Vernon Duke" [2041]), the emigré Arnold Schoenberg [1657], and many others. He collected art (Picassos, Utrillos, Rouaults, and the like), and at the time of his death had gone a long way toward becoming a fine painter himself.

January 14, 1930, saw the opening of the successful satire *Strike Up the Band* (a new direction for Gershwin) and the composer's debut in Lewisohn Stadium as a conductor of his own music. In 1930 he went to Hollywood to write his first film score (for Twentieth-Century-Fox, a Janet Gaynor-Charles Farrell confection called *Delicious,* at a fee of $70,000.) Themes from the music spawned the work now known as the *Second Rhapsody* but originally called *Rhapsody in Rivets,* which was premiered by none other than Serge Koussevitzky [1655] and the Boston Symphony on January 29, 1932, with the composer as piano soloist. The year 1930 also saw the successful *Girl Crazy,* for which Gershwin discovered Ethel Merman, who introduced "I Got Rhythm." The cast included Ginger Rogers; the orchestra included Benny Goodman, Gene Krupa, Glenn Miller, and Red Nichols. A little over a year later, the brilliant political satire *Of Thee I Sing*—by George S. Kaufman, Morrie Ryskind, and the Gershwins—opened to howls of joy and went on to become the first musical to win a Pulitzer Prize for drama. It was, however, Gershwin's last success; its

sequel *Let 'Em Eat Cake* and *Pardon My English* were both premiered in 1933 and ran less than a hundred performances each. A trip to Cuba in 1932 produced the *Cuban Overture* (at first known as *Rhumba),* premiered by Albert Coates that August in a Lewisohn Stadium concert.

By 1933, despite the Great Depression, Gershwin was a very wealthy man. He moved that year from Riverside Drive to a fourteen-room duplex on Seventy-second Street. The next winter he went on a brief but extensive tour with the Leo Reisman Orchestra, for which he wrote the piano-and-orchestra *Variations on "I Got Rhythm"* and then took on a twice-weekly radio program for station WJZ. Back in 1926 on a sleepless night Gershwin had read *Porgy,* DuBose Heyward's novel of South Carolina Negro life, and had earmarked it for musical treatment. Four years later the Metropolitan Opera had signed a contract with him for an opera, for which he had considered S. Ansky's *The Dybbuk,* though nothing came of it but some sketches. Meanwhile Jerome Kern and Al Jolson had become interested in *Porgy,* and Heyward called Gershwin's hand. The score of what had become a fullfledged opera was completed in the summer of 1935. Gershwin had decided that he preferred a Broadway run to the few showings the Met would be able to offer, and when the work opened in October, the word "opera" was carefully avoided. Moreover, extensive cutting had been done (and in fact it was not until the 1970s that an uncut performance was given publicly.) Nevertheless the work was a triumph with audiences and theatrical critics alike, though the music reviewers were gingerly in their praise. But the work was expensive to produce, and its run of 124 performances and a subsequent tour lost money for the investors. Nevertheless it has become the most successful American opera to date. The Met finally produced it fifty years after its premiere.

Gershwin now turned his attention to films. He moved to Beverly Hills and wrote *Shall We Dance* for Fred Astaire and Ginger Rogers and *A Damsel in Distress* for Astaire, Joan Fontaine, and Gracie Allen. He was then hired by Sam Goldwyn for *The Goldwyn Follies.* But he found himself increasingly dissatisfied, lonely, and depressive. He fell hopelessly in love with Paulette Goddard (then Mrs. Charles Chaplin). Early in 1937 he began to experience blackouts, headaches, and dizzy spells. On July 9 he collapsed and was rushed to the Cedars of Lebanon Hospital. A brain tumor was diagnosed and a specialist-surgeon summoned. But Gershwin had reached such a desperate state by then that a local man had to operate immediately. He found the situation hopeless. Gershwin died twelve hours later, not yet thirty-nine.

RECORDINGS: Though none of Gershwin's shows have been recorded as such (and perhaps not all of the songs), all of his serious music, down to the least important scrap (even including *Blue Monday)* seems to have been committed to disc. It should be noted that Gershwin himself recorded, besides the piano rolls noted, two readings of the *Rhapsody in Blue,* three of the five piano preludes, and a number of piano improvisations on songs.

[1956] RAMIN, Günther (Rá'-mēn, Gün'-ter)
ORGANIST, PIANIST, CONDUCTOR, TEACHER
BORN: Karlsruhe, October 15, 1898
DIED: Leipzig, February 27, 1956

Ramin was trained at the Thomasschule in Leipzig and then at the Leipzig Conservatory, where he studied organ with Karl Straube, who was organist and later cantor at the Thomaskirche. When Straube ascended to the latter post in 1918, Ramin succeeded him at the organ. Three years later he assumed Straube's duties as professor of organ at the conservatory. He also pursued an active career in concert and was one of the most admired organists of his time. In 1935 he was appointed director of the Berlin Philharmonic Chorus, in which post he remained until 1943. He wrote some chamber music, choruses, and songs but as a composer is best known for his editions and compositions for the organ. RECORDINGS: Some of his organ works have been recorded. He himself also made records as an organist.

[1957] MIHALOVICI, Marcel (Mē-há-lō-vē'-chē, Mär-sel')
VIOLINIST
BORN: Bucharest, October 22, 1898

Mihalovici studied violin in his native city with Dimitri Cuclin (1885–), a d'Indy [1462] pupil who was later to teach at Brooklyn College for some years. Placing in a postwar Enesco Competition, he took its sponsor's advice and moved to Paris in 1919. There he too studied with d'Indy and continued at violin with Nestor Lejeune. However, he devoted himself to composition rather than to a concert career. He was one of a group of expatriate composers—Mar-

tinů [1846], Tibor Harsányi (1898–1954), Beck [1997], Tansman [1938], Alexander Tcherepnin [1961], and others—known as *L'École de Paris* (or *Les Constructeurs,* as Roussel [1605] dubbed them), which was if anything more mythical than *Les Six.* Mihalovici married the pianist Monique Haas, who has been instrumental in promoting his music. During the German occupation he was forced to go into hiding but survived. He espoused French citizenship in 1955 and was elected to the Académie in 1964 as a corresponding member. His music (surprisingly influenced by Reger [1637]) includes several operas (one is a treatment of Beckett's *Krapp's Last Tape)* and ballets, much orchestral music (5 symphonies, a violin concerto, other concerted works), string quartets, sonatas, and other chamber works, a sonata and other pieces for piano, choral music, songs, and incidental music for several plays. RECORDINGS: Of French origin, these include the *Esercizio* for strings, *Étude en deux parties* for piano and chamber orchestra (Haas), *Ricercari* for piano (Haas), and the Sonata for Violin and Cello of 1944.

[1958] KNIPPER, Lev Constantinovich (K'nip'-per, Lyof Kon-stàn-tēn-ō'-vich)
MILITARY MAN, TEACHER, ETHNOMUSICOLOGIST
BORN: Tbilisi (Tiflis), December 3, 1898
DIED: Moscow, July 30, 1974

Though he was a prolific composer, Knipper is known to Westerners chiefly for a catchy song, "Meadowlands," which is actually the choral finale of his fourth symphony, subtitled *Poem of the Fighting Komsomol.* He taught himself to play piano. In 1917 he joined the Red Army, to which afterward he was attached in various musical capacities for much of his life, and did a five-year hitch which took him to Siberia. In 1922 he became a student of Glière [1662] at the Gnessin School in Moscow, then went to Berlin to study with Philipp Jarnach, Busoni's [1577] pupil, and finally to Freiburg im Breisgau to study with Julius Weismann from the old Rheinberger [1368] stable. Like many young Soviet composers of the time, he adopted an irreverent modernist style and created something of a stir with his first opera, *The North Wind,* in 1930. And like so many young Soviet composers of the time, he incurred the wrath of Joseph Stalin and was sent off to various remote areas to study folklore, which he reflects in his more dutiful subsequent works. These include 14 (some accounts say 20) fustian symphonies, operas, ballets, dramatic and film scores, lots of orchestral works with inspiring titles, suites based on exotica, suites for children, and songs for soldiers. RECORDINGS: His *Youth Overture* and many versions of "Meadowlands" have been recorded. There may be other recordings from Soviet sources, but his output is obviously regarded as not very exportable.

[1959] LOUCHEUR, Raymond (Lōō-shür′, Rā-môn′)
CIVIL SERVANT, ADMINISTRATOR
BORN: Tourcoing, January 1, 1899
DIED: Nogent-sur-Marne, September 14, 1979

An impeccable composer with impeccable credentials—his chief instructors were Vincent d'Indy **[1462]** and Nadia Boulanger—Loucheur was born in a northern border town near Lille. He was the recipient of the 1928 Prix de Rome. After 1940 he held high positions in the ministry of education, and in 1956 he became director of the Paris Conservatoire for six years. He wrote a ballet, 3 symphonies, several concerti, and a few other orchestral works but seems to have been happiest in small forms. RECORDINGS: Works on record include the ballet suite *Hop Frog*, the orchestral *Rapsodie Malgache (Madagascar Rhapsody)*, the *Dialogue* for flute and harp, and the *Quatre pièces* for flute, harp, and string trio.

[1960] POULENC, Francis Jean Marcel (Pōō-laŋk′, Frän-sēs′ Zhäŋ Mär-sel′)
PIANIST
BORN: Paris, January 7, 1899
DIED: Paris, January 30, 1963

Big, bony, jovial, crewcut, in appearance reminiscent of the comedian Fernandel, Francis Poulenc came gradually to be recognized as one of the most musical and sensitive songwriters of his time, and toward the end of his career as the composer of deeply felt religious music. The son of Émile Poulenc, a manufacturer of pharmaceuticals, he was given a strict religious and classical education. His mother, the former Jenny Royer, was a good pianist, awakened his musical interests when he was a small child, and gave him his first lessons. At the age of eight he was sent to study with Mlle. Boutet de Monvel, a niece of César Franck **[1284]**. Seven years later his pianistic education was taken over by the Spanish virtuoso Ricardo Viñes. (Though Poulenc made a number of piano recordings of pieces by himself and

others, he never developed an outstanding technique.) During this formative period, he tells us, the works that had the greatest impact on him were Debussy's **[1547]** *Danses sacrées et profanes* and Schubert's **[1153]** song cycle *Die Winterreise*—he was perhaps too young to grasp Stravinsky's **[1748]** *Le Sacre du printemps*, whose cataclysmic premiere he attended. Thanks to Viñes, he developed a friendship with Georges Auric **[1962]**, and became a sort of protégé and spiritual godchild of Satie **[1578]**. Thereby he gradually drifted into the group of artistic young Turks who were already thumbing their noses at the establishment.

In 1917—the year his father died, leaving him financially independent—Poulenc, after some attempts at piano music, turned out a spoofing *Rapsodie nègre (Black Rhapsody)* for chamber ensemble with incidental baritone solo, to a gibberish text allegedly written by a Liberian poet named Kangourou. It was performed later that year at one of Jane Bathori's concerts, with the composer singing, the scheduled performer having gotten cold feet at the last moment. A month later Poulenc was drafted for war service. He spent six months at Vincennes, three in an antiaircraft battery in the Vosges, and saw the war end near Chalons-sur-Marne. However, instead of being demobilized, he was returned to Paris to serve as a typist in the ministry of aviation until the autumn of 1921. This assignment brought him back into the thick of the postwar musical upheaval, which in fact he anticipated with a little song cycle, *Le Bestiaire (The Bestiary)* to verses by the avant-garde poet Guillaume Apollinaire. It was soon afterward, in a review of a new music concert promoted by the cellist Félix Delgrange, that the critic Henri Collet half-jokingly called Poulenc and his associates *"Les Six"*—a label that stuck long after they had drifted apart. However, they (minus Louis Durey **[1828]**) hung together long enough to create a scandal with their collective contribution to Jean Cocteau's loony "happening" *Les Mariés sur la Tour Eiffel (The Wedding on the Eiffel Tower)* in June 1921.

It was in 1921 that Poulenc, who so far had produced nothing of substance, faced the facts and sought a real teacher. He found one in Charles Koechlin **[1592]**, and the two worked together for four years, during which time he produced his first major work, the ballet *Les Biches* (literally "The Does" but with the modern slang sense of "The Chicks"), commissioned by Diaghilev for the Ballets Russes in 1923. It was also at this time that Poulenc and Milhaud **[1868]** traveled together to Rome and Vienna to meet the leading avant-garde musical oracles in those cities. For most of the decade Poulenc concentrated on piano pieces and songs. Even there his output was not large, and he later came to regret having published some of these things. In 1926 the *Chansons gaillardes (Wanton Songs,* set to naughty seventeenth-century texts) were introduced by a wispy-voiced fledgling baritone named Pierre Bertin. In 1928 harpsichordist Wanda Landowska unveiled the *Concert champêtre (Rustic Concerto),* and a year later Poulenc was the piano soloist in the ballet score *Aubade* for piano and eighteen winds. Around this time he bought an estate at Noizay, on the Loire near Amboise—more for the sake of privacy than rurality, he being an arch-boulevardier at heart. (From 1935 he maintained a Paris apartment on the Left Bank near the Luxembourg Gardens.)

In 1934 Poulenc again encountered Bertin, who was now calling himself "Bernac" to avoid being confused with the actor Pierre Bertin. The two appeared as a team (Poulenc as accompanist) for the first time at the 1935 Salzburg Festival and were afterward inseparable, both as musicians and friends. It was Bernac's interpretive genius that inspired the composer to the outpouring of songs which characterized most of his ensuing career. The death of a close friend at about this same time reawakened his sense of his Catholic heritage, first evidenced in 1936 in the *Litanies à la vierge noire de Rocamadour (Litanies to the Black Virgin of Rocamadour),* followed by a whole series of devotional compositions, including a *Mass* in 1937, a *Stabat Mater* in 1951, and a *Gloria* in 1961, of major stature. The 1930s also produced the two-piano concerto and the organ concerto, both commissioned by the sewing-machine heiress, the Princesse de Polignac.

In 1939 the outbreak of war summoned the forty-year-old composer back to the antiaircraft guns. He was in Bordeaux when French resistance collapsed the following summer, but instead of heading for the border, he returned to Paris. After he had exorcised his grief and bitterness in several poignant songs, he devoted the war years mostly to music for the stage—drama and film scores, the ballet *Animaux modèles,* and the melodrama *Babar* (on Jean de Brunhof's stories). He also completed his first opera, the one-act surrealist fantasy *Les Mamelles de Tirésias (Tirésias' Breasts)* to a play by Apollinaire, first performed at the Opéra-Comique in 1947. It was from a Bernac-Poulenc recital in Paris just after the war that the general recognition of his songs as the finest since Fauré's [1424] arose. (Some, however, agreeing that they have a fragile

charm, have seen in them one of the more attractive evidences of a general musical decadence.)

In 1948 Poulenc and Bernac made an American tour, in the course of which the composer played the premiere performance of his piano concerto with the Boston Symphony under Koussevitzky [1655]. After that his production tapered off, and he spent much of his time concertizing. His popularity encouraged a move in Noizay to elect him mayor, but he laughingly turned the proposal down. He spent the first half of the 1950s working on his only large opera, *Dialogues des carmélites,* dealing with the self-sacrifice of a group of Carmelite nuns during the French Revolution. It was premiered at La Scala in Milan early in 1957 and made a powerful impression. The United States saw it that autumn in San Francisco, NBC telecast its own production a year later, and in the 1970s it seems to have installed itself in the repertoire at the Metropolitan Opera. It was followed in 1958 by a third opera, *La Voix humaine (The Human Voice),* a treatment of a monodrama by Cocteau dealing with a woman's attempt to handle a crisis in her life on the telephone. Three weeks after his sixty-fourth birthday, Poulenc succumbed in his Paris apartment to an unexpected heart attack. His last major work was the vocal-orchestral *Sept répons des ténèbres (7 Tenebrae Responds)* posthumously premiered by the New York Philharmonic on April 11, 1963. Bernac survived him by sixteen years and published a useful guide to the songs, most of which he recorded with the composer. A more recent recording, calling on several artists, includes the entire canon. The operas and most of the other compositions save the incidental music and film scores have also been committed to records. The *Sept répons* has been available only in an obscure Belgian recording, but a new French version was recently released.

[1961] TCHEREPNIN, Alexander Nikolayevitch (Che-rep′-nēn, Ål-yek-sàn′-der Nē-kō-là-yā′-vich)
PIANIST, CONDUCTOR, TEACHER
BORN: St. Petersburg, January 21, 1899
DIED: Paris, September 29, 1977

The son of Nikolai Tcherepnin [1642], father of Ivan and Serge, Alexander Tcherepnin is perhaps the best-known and (so far) most prolific of the dynasty. He learned to notate music before he learned his letters (at five) and had piano lessons first from his mother, a talented musician, and then from Anna Essipova—though he certainly learned by absorption from the many prominent musicians who frequented the Tcherepnin home. He composed prodigally and uncritically in his youth, and then at eighteen entered the St. Petersburg Conservatory. A few months later, in the face of the upheavals of 1917–18, the Tcherepnin's migrated to Tbilisi, where Alexander studied for a short time with Thomas de Hartmann [1798] before the family moved on to settle in Paris. He studied at the Paris Conservatoire with Gédalge, Vidal [1554], and Isidor Philipp. In 1922 he made his debut as a pianist in an all-Tcherepnin recital and was commissioned by Anna Pavlova to write a ballet *(Ajanta Frescoes)* for her.

Increasingly tours took him afield—to central Europe, England, America—and in the mid-1930s he consummated a love affair with the orient, spending much time concertizing and teaching in both China and Japan, and bringing home a Chinese bride, the pianist Lee Hsien-Ming. World War II bottled him up in Paris. In 1949 he accepted a professorship at DePaul University in Chicago and taught there until his retirement in 1964, taking out American citizenship in 1958 (though he continued to spend much time in Paris). In 1967 he returned to Russia, for the first time in nearly fifty years, on a concert tour. Though his music has Russian roots, it is universally eclectic. Tcherepnin also developed a nine-note scale and some rhythmic inventions that were all his own, though he did not use them systematically. His large catalogue of compositions resists detailing here.

RECORDINGS: His output is fairly well represented by such works as the Op. 87 *Suite for Orchestra;* piano concerti nos. 2 and 5 (the composer as soloist); the harmonica concerto; *10 Bagatelles* for piano and orchestra; Symphonies nos. 2 and 4; *Georgiana Suite;* the brief *Symphonic Prayer;* the ballet suite *Le Gouffre;* the *Triple Concertino* for violin, cello, piano, and orchestra; String Quartet No. 2; the brass quintet; the piano trio; numerous piano pieces (including an LP of the composer playing a program of such); songs. (His son Ivan is represented by a CRI album entitled *Electric Flowers.)*

[1962] AURIC, Georges (Ô-rēk', Zhôrzh)
ADMINISTRATOR, CRITIC
BORN: Lodève, February 15, 1899
DIED: Paris, July 29, 1983

The youngest of the nebulous Les Six—Poulenc [1960] was five weeks older—Georges Auric was born in Languedoc near Montpellier, in which city he first attended both school and conservatory. He began writing music at a disgustingly early age and had turned out reams of it by the time his family moved with him to Paris in 1913. There he was permitted by the Conservatoire to sit in on a counterpoint class. The next year some of his songs were presented in public concerts and he began study with Vincent d'Indy [1462] at the Schola Cantorum. But he found he was allergic to schools and systems and left in 1916. He became infatuated with the music of Satie [1578], fell in with Honegger [1861], Milhaud [1868], and Jean Cocteau, and in 1920 found himself identified as one of Les Six. He also came to know Stravinsky [1748] and played one of the pianos in the premiere of his *Les Noces (The Wedding)* in 1923. A score that he wrote for a production of Molière's *Les Fâcheux (The Bores)* caught the attention of producer Sergei Diaghilev, who had him turn it into a work for his Ballets Russes that same year. A series of successful ballets—*Les Matelots (The Sailors)* 1924; *Pastorale, 1925; Les Enchantements de la fée Alcine (The Enchantments of the Fairy Alcina),* 1929; *Les Concurrences (Rivalries),* 1932 (this writer's introduction to ballet); *Les Imaginaires (Imaginary Beings),* 1934—followed. Auric, a man who admits to thinking in visual images, was particularly attracted to drama (though apart from a disowned juvenile effort he wrote only one opera, *Sous la masque [Beneath the Mask],* 1927). He wrote several later ballets and stage music for plays by Aristophanes, Beaumarchais, Ben Jonson, and others. In 1930, with Cocteau's surrealist classic *Le Sang d'un poète (The Blood of a Poet),* he discovered the film medium and won great praise in 1931 for his score to René Clair's *À nous la liberté (Give Us Liberty).* He married Nora Vilter, a painter, in 1930.

In the cinema Auric found his true calling, and for the last fifty years he produced scores for many important films, including most of Cocteau's most famous efforts, such as *Orphée (Orpheus)* and *La Belle et la bête (Beauty and the Beast).* Here his activity was not confined to France. For English producers he wrote music for, among others, *Dead of Night, Ceasar and Cleopatra,* and *The Lavender Hill Mob.* His score for Hollywood's *Moulin Rouge* included a song—known as "The Song from 'Moulin Rouge' "—which became a bestseller. In 1962 he took on, for four years, the thankless task of running the Paris opera companies. That same year he was elected to the French Académie. Auric's music has been superficially likened to Poulenc's, but in its mature phase it eschews any suspicion of sentimentality for clarity, intelligibility, and detachment. Auric is a firm believer in the primacy of melody, but his seeming simplicity conceals the hand of a master craftsman.

RECORDINGS: The relatively few recordings include the ballets *Les Matelots* and *Les Fâcheux,* and suites from three more, *La Fontaine de jouvence (The Fountain of Youth), Malbrouck s'en va-t-en guerre (Marlborough's Going to War),* and *Phèdre (Phaedra).* Also recorded are the orchestral *Ouverture;* a wind trio; *Partita* and *Double-jeux I–III* for two pianos; *Aria* for flute and piano; *Imaginées,* a set of six suites for various chamber combinations (not to be confused with the ballet *Imaginaires);* music from *À nous la liberté* and *Moulin Rouge;* piano pieces; and songs.

[1963] VLADIGEROV, Panchu (Vlä-dē-jä′-rov, Pản′-choō)

PIANIST, CONDUCTOR, TEACHER
BORN: Zürich, March 13, 1899
DIED: Sofia, September 8, 1978

Vladigerov is one of the more important names in the brief history of Bulgarian art music. His mother, warned that she was facing a difficult delivery, betook herself to a Zürich hospital, where she gave birth to twin boys, sixteen hours and two dates apart —hence his Swiss birthplace. The elder brother, Luben, became a professional violinist. Panchu studied piano in Shumen in northeast Bulgaria where he spent his boyhood, then was a pupil of Dobri Christov [1678] in Sofia. A government scholarship took him to the Berlin Hochschule. He remained in Berlin until 1932 as a conductor for Max Reinhardt at the Deutsches Theater. Returning to his homeland, he taught at the Sofia Academy until he retired in 1972. He has composed prolifically in all forms (especially concerti) in a generally conservative European style, often with folkloristic or exotic touches. Outside Bulgaria his best-known work is his orchestral version of Grigoraş Dinicu's (1889–1949) popular violin piece *Hora staccato.* RECORDINGS: David Oistrakh recorded his *Fantasy on the Bulgarian Dance Theme "Khere."* There have also been scattered recordings of various concerted works from Melodiya, Balkanton, and elsewhere. The Bulgarian state label Balkanton is currently in the process of recording Vladigerov's complete works. The first three boxed sets, consisting of concerted and other orchestral works, comprise twenty-one records. Four additional boxed sets are contemplated!

[1964] BAINES, William

PIANIST
BORN: Horbury, March 26, 1899
DIED: York, November 6, 1922

Born into a poor family in a Yorkshire village, Baines somehow managed a few piano lessons with one Albert Jowett in nearby Leeds but was otherwise wholly self-taught in music. He was particularly influenced by Scriabin [1625] and the Impressionists. By the time he reached seventeen, he had a job accompanying silent films in a local movie house and was already composing for the piano. In 1917 he wrote a symphony and a violin sonata. The year following he was called up for military service. Shortly afterward, already tubercular, he became a victim of the Spanish influenza epidemic. He was ill in bed for nearly four months. Sent home, he resumed his career, composing and playing local concerts, save for a single appearance with the Bournemouth Orchestra sponsored by its conductor, Sir Dan Godfrey. But Baines's health had suffered irreparable damage and, after another extended spell of illness, he died at twenty-three. He left 216 compositions, mostly in manuscript, which, forty years later, his mother gave to the British Museum. RECORDINGS: Eric Parkin recorded an LP of his piano music.

[1965] CASADESUS, Robert Marcel (Cà-sà-dä-süs′, Rō-bâr′ Mär-sel′)

PIANIST, TEACHER
BORN: Paris, April 7, 1899
DIED: Paris, September 19, 1972

Robert Casadesus was at the center of a remarkable three-generation musical dynasty of Catalan descent. Four of his paternal uncles—François, Henri, Marcel, and Marius —were notable as performers, conductors, and teachers, and his Aunt Rose was a concert pianist. (Marius, who toured for a time with his nephew, was also the composer of some fraudulent antiques, including the "Adelaide" concerto ascribed to Mozart [992]). Robert was admitted to the Paris Conservatoire at the age of thirteen, where his most important teachers were Xavier Leroux [1557] and the pianist Louis Diémer, and where he took first prizes in 1913, 1919, and 1920. In the last year he fell in love with a fellow student, a young Marseillaise named Gaby L'Hôte, herself a brilliant pianist. They were married in 1921, and their son Jean (1927–72) also became a pianist of stature, later often appearing with his parents in multipiano pieces, including the three-piano concerto Robert wrote for them in 1965.

Robert Casadesus began his concert career in 1922 but also increasingly turned to teaching. In 1934 he succeeded the redoubtable Isidor Philipp as professor of piano at the American Conservatory (founded in 1918 by Uncle François) at Fontainebleau. The next year he made his American debut with the New York Philharmonic. With the onset of war, he brought his family to the United States, where he remained for the better part of the decade, concertizing, and in the summers teaching first at Newport, Rhode Island, and then at Great Barrington, Massachusetts. Nine months before he died, his son Jean was killed in a Canadian auto crash. Casadesus was an indefatigable composer who wrote 7 symphonies, a ballet, concerti for one or more pianos, orchestral and chamber music, and much for piano solo. RECORDINGS: Those involving the composer and/or his family include the Concerto for Piano; Concerto for 3 Pianos; the Quintet for Piano and Strings; the *Sextuor;* the Nonet; the *Danses méditerranéenes;* the Sonata for Flute and Piano; Sonata No. 2 for Violin and Piano; *Hommage a Chausson;* Sonata No. 4 for Piano; and *8 Études* for piano. Those by other performers include the Sonata for Cello and Piano; Sonata No. 2 for Piano; *3 Berceuses* for piano; and *6 Pièces* for two pianos.

[1966] THOMPSON, Randall

PIANIST, CONDUCTOR, TEACHER
BORN: New York, April 21, 1899
DIED: Boston, July 9, 1984

Not to be confused with his exact contemporary Virgil Thomson (without the *p*), Randall Thompson, though born in Manhattan, came from an old New England family. In the tradition of old New England families, he matriculated at Harvard, where his music teachers were Edward Burlingame Hill [1632], Walter Spalding, and Archibald Davison. Thompson took his B.A. in 1920, studied for a time with Ernest Bloch [1729], and then returned to acquire an M.A. in 1922. At that juncture he won an American Prix de Rome, and lived in Rome at the American Academy for the prescribed three years, producing the orchestral works *Pierrot and Cothurnus* (after Millay), *The Piper at the Gates of Dawn* (after Kenneth Graeme), the string quartet *The Wind in the Willows* (also after Graeme), as well as piano and choral pieces. After his return to America, he took up a teaching career—first at Wellesley, 1927–37 (with interruptions for a couple of Guggenheim Fellowships and the like); then at the University of California at

Berkeley, 1937–39; the Curtis Institute (director), 1939–41; the University of Virginia (chairman of the music department), 1941–46; Princeton, 1946–48; and finally back to Harvard, where he remained until his retirement in 1965. Not a particularly prolific composer and the adherent of no school or system, Thompson has been particularly admired for the second of his 3 symphonies, and for his choral compositions. RECORDINGS: These include Symphonies Nos. 1 and 2; *Mass of the Holy Spirit, The Testament of Freedom, Americana, the Peaceable Kingdom,* and other smaller choral works.

[1967] ELLINGTON, Edward Kennedy ("Duke")

CONDUCTOR, PIANIST
BORN: Washington, D.C., April 29, 1899
DIED: New York, May 24, 1974

Jazz musicians have reluctantly been omitted from this work because their creations are largely improvisational. So was much of Duke Ellington's work, but in his later career he also wrote works that, though they contained improvisatory elements, stand as serious and important musical documents. Ellington's father, a government employee, had a taste for the so-called finer things—which, passed on to his son, accounts for the latter's early-acquired nickname. Duke took piano lessons (from a woman incredibly called Clinkscales) in childhood, became fascinated by ragtime and jazz, and began writing songs at fourteen and playing dance dates shortly afterward. He learned some basic harmony in high school and had some training in deciphering scores from a jazzman called "Doc" Perry. An ability to draw won him a scholarship to the Pratt Institute in New York, but he passed it up to organize his own band and run a sign-painting business in Washington and to marry Edna Thompson. (The marriage, which soon went on the rocks, produced a son, Mercer ([1919–]), who became a talented jazz musician and bandleader.)

In 1922 Ellington tried to go it alone in New York but with no special success. A year later he and five of his men were hired by Barron's, a Harlem nightclub and shortly afterward moved to the Hollywood (later Kentucky) Club on Broadway for four years. There he signed a contract with publisher Irving Mills. In 1927 the band, now expanded to twelve players (most of whom spent their lives in it) returned to Harlem to the Cotton Club, which they turned into one of the great New York nightspots in their five years there. Ellington encouraged the individual styles of each of his performers, at the same time learning his métier from them and making the band the voice of a kind of jazz whose sophistication was something new. Recordings and radio contracts followed. In 1931 he ventured beyond the usual short song form with the eight-minute *Creole Rhapsody* and in 1935 with the twelve-minute *Reminiscing in Tempo*. By then the band had established its independence, had toured Europe in 1933 (a command performance before King George V eventuated in London) and the United States in 1934. (These were the first of many tours.) In 1941 Ellington wrote his first "musical," *Jump for Joy*, which opened and closed in Los Angeles. Two years later the orchestra, now twenty strong, played the first of several Carnegie Hall concerts, this one featuring *Black, Brown, and Beige*, the first of Ellington's several long "symphonic" works. He reached the Broadway stage with *Beggar's Holiday*, the umpteenth adaptation of John Gay's *The Beggar's Opera*, but it ran only three months. He had no better luck twenty years later with *Pousse-Café*, but wrote a number of film scores, beginning with *Anatomy of a Murder* in 1959, and some incidental music for plays (e.g., *Timon of Athens* for the Stratford, Ontario, Shakespeare Festival in 1963). In 1965 Ellington and the band performed the first of his sacred services in San Francisco's Grace Cathedral. Alvin Ailey's dance company performed the ballet *The River* in 1970. An opera, *Boola*, was left unfinished when Ellington died (of cancer) at seventy-five. The band survived under Mercer's direction, though the original members are all gone. (It should be noted that many of the later Ellington works were deeply indebted to his talented arranger Billy Strayhorn, who died —at fifty-two—in 1967.)

RECORDINGS: There are innumerable records (it is said that Ellington produced nearly 6,000 works). Akira Endo and the Louisville Orchestra recently recorded *The River*, and Gunther Schuller [2354] has conducted a selection of Ellington pieces.

[1968] CHÁVEZ Y RAMIREZ, Carlos Antonio de Padua (Chä'-väz ē Rá-mē'-räz, Kär'-lōs Àn-tōn'-yō dā Pád'-wá)
CONDUCTOR, EDUCATOR
BORN: Calzada de Tacuba, June 13, 1899
DIED: Mexico City, August 2, 1978

If one excepts the fluke popularity of Manuel Ponce's [1758] song "Estrellita," Carlos Chávez was the first "serious" Mexican composer to win international success. He was born in a suburb of the capital. His father was of Spanish descent; his mother, part Indian, was left a widow with six children in 1902. Carlos got his first music lessons from an older brother, Manuel, then studied piano with Ponce from 1909 to 1914. Later he continued his lessons with a certain Pedro Luis Ogazón. Otherwise, apart from some grounding in basic theory, he was self-taught as a composer. He began writing piano pieces and making arrangements of popular songs when he was sixteen and completed a symphony three years later. When, after a decade of upheaval, Mexico settled down in 1921, he presented a concert of his own works and won a government commission for a ballet. The result was *El fuego nuevo (The New Fire)*, a work on an Aztec story, but various contretemps prevented its production for seven years. In 1922 Chávez took a bride, Otilia Ortiz, and left on a European honeymoon that lasted until the summer of 1923. He took note of the current musical trends but was otherwise not impressed. A trip to the United States that autumn, however, had a more positive effect: he stayed for four months and returned in 1926 to live for two years in New York City, where he worked closely with Edgard Varèse [1774]. During this time he wrote a good deal of abstract music (some with geometrical titles)—linear, lean, and angular. He went home in 1928 to direct the newly founded Orquesta Sinfónica de México, which was to introduce many new Mexican works including his own. At the same time he became head of the Conservatorio Nacional de Música, where he introduced radical (and successful) methods of teaching. In 1931 he introduced his ballet *H.P.* (i.e., *Horsepower*, originally *Caballos de vapor*, written in the New York years), regarded as the watershed between his first and second periods. A year later he wrote a chamber score for a production of Jean Cocteau's version of *Antigone*, which in 1933 he revised as the one-movement *Sinfonía de Antígona*, his official first symphony.

During the 1930s his leftward political leanings caused Chávez to become concerned with "people's music" and to inaugurate a series of concerts for workers. Now he concentrated on national themes, producing such works as the *Sinfonía India* (his official second symphony, also in one movement), the *Obertura republicana*, the *Cantos de Méjico* for folk instruments, and such choral-orchestral pieces as *El Sol (The Sun)*, *La Paloma Azul (The Blue Bird)*, and *Llamadas*, a "proletarian symphony" on revolutionary songs. In *Xochipilli-Macuilxochitl* he even attempted to re-create ancient Aztec music. In 1940 he led a historic concert of Mexican music at the Museum of Modern Art in New York (in part recorded by Columbia Records). He also did some pioneering investigation into the potential for electronic music.

Chávez resigned from the conservatory in 1933 to head up the fine arts section of the ministry of education but was not happy with the post and returned to his old job. However, he resigned it for good at the end of 1934. The next decade and a half was his most productive period, in which he turned out the ballet *La Hija de Cólquide (the Daughter of Colchis)* for Martha Graham (who produced it as *Dark Meadow),* a good deal of choral music (some to English texts), a concerto for four horns, another for piano, and pieces for chamber ensembles (including the popular *Toccata for Percussion)* and for solo instruments. In 1947 he became director of the new Institute of Fine Arts, which he had helped plan, and a year later he gave up his orchestra. He left the institute in 1952 and spent his remaining years composing (five more symphonies, a violin concerto, the 1945 ballet *Pirámide [Pyramid],* and his only opera *The Visitors,* premiered at Columbia University in 1957). In 1958 he was Charles Elliott Norton Professor at Harvard—one of the innumerable honors bestowed on him. (His final work was the Concerto for Trombone, premiered in 1978; a seventh symphony was left unfinished.) All in all he was probably the most important unifying force in the history of Mexican music.

RECORDINGS: Many of the existing recordings of Chávez's major works were made under his baton. They include all the symphonies, the ballet *H.P., Xochipilli-Macuilxochitl, Paloma azul, Piramide, Corrido de El Sol, Obertura republicana, Le Hija de Colquide (Daughter of Colchis),* the piano and violin concerti, *El Sol,* the 1926 ballet *Los cuatro soles (The Four Suns),* the 1969 *Discovery* for orchestra, *4 Nocturnes* for vocalists and orchestra, and three of the 4 late chamber pieces called *Soli.* Other recordings include the *Toccata for Percussion,* a violin sonatina, small choral pieces, some guitar music, and many piano pieces.

[1969] SANTA CRUZ WILSON, Domingo (Sȧn'-tȧ Krōōz Vil'-sȯn, Dō-mīng'-ō)
DIPLOMAT, TEACHER, ADMINISTRATOR, CONDUCTOR
BORN: La Cruz (Chile), July 5, 1899

While studying law at the University of Chile, Santa Cruz also pursued his musical interests, taking lessons with the composer Enrique Soro (1884–1954) and founding the Sociedad Bach in 1918. On graduating in 1921, he received an appointment as Second Secretary of the Chilean Embassy in Madrid. While there, he indulged himself in further musical study with Conrado del Campo, sometime director of the Madrid Conservatory. Finding that music was more to his liking than diplomacy, he resigned his post and returned to Chile to carry on his work with the Sociedad. Here he made such an impact that the program at the Santiago Conservatory got a good shaking up, and in 1928 he was appointed professor of music history there. A year later he was asked by the university to set up a school of fine arts for it; he became its dean in 1932. Meanwhile in 1931 he had founded the National Association of Symphony Concerts, which he directed for seven years. Among the other organizations that he originated or helped found were the secondary and extension branches of the university's School of Fine Arts, the Chilean Symphony Orchestra, the School of Dance, a chamber music society, the National Association of Composers, at least two musical journals, and many other organizations, awards, etc. Santa Cruz has also lectured on behalf of Chilean music in both Europe and North America. He is perhaps the most important composer to have been produced by his country and certainly the most influential musician. His music, which includes 4 symphonies, an oratorio, and many other examples of orchestral, choral, and chamber music, is in no way nationalistic but derives from the central European tradition of the 1920s and has often been likened to Hindemith's. RECORDINGS: Several early orchestral works have been recorded— Symphony No. 2 for string orchestra of 1948, *5 Short Pieces* for string orchestra of 1943, and *Preludios Dramático* of 1946.

[1970] WEIGL, Vally (Vī'-gȧl, Vȧ'-lē)
THERAPIST, PIANIST, TEACHER
BORN: Vienna, September 11, 1899 (E. Ruth Anderson, *Contemporary American Composers,* gives 1889.)
DIED: New York, N.Y., 1983

A piano pupil of Richard Robert, Mrs. Weigl studied at the University of Vienna with Guido Adler and Karl Weigl [1733], the latter of whom she later married. She worked as a piano teacher in Vienna and Salzburg until the 1938 Nazi *Anschluss* drove her and her husband out of Austria. In New York, where they settled, Vally continued to teach and took graduate courses at Columbia University. In 1955 she became chief music therapist to the New York Medical College. She published a number of articles in this field and became widely known for her work in New York medical circles. On the side she composed, mostly in small forms and, like her husband (who died in 1949), particularly in that of the art song. RECORDINGS: Several song cycles, a clarinet trio, and *Brief Encounters* for wind quartet have been recorded in the last five years.

[1971] DAWSON, William Levi
TROMBONIST, CONDUCTOR
BORN: Anniston, Ala., September 26, 1899 *(Grove* has September 23)

William Dawson was the eldest of the seven children of a man variously described as a "poor black laborer" and a barroom pianist. At an early age he was taken out of school and apprenticed to a cobbler to help support the family. He learned to play trombone and joined a local band led by a man who had once worked at the Tuskegee Institute, which thereafter became Dawson's lodestar. He acquired an education of sorts in odd hours while working at odd jobs and at thirteen ran away to Tuskegee. He spent nine years there, working in the fields to pay for his education and graduating in 1921, at which time he got a job teaching and leading the band at the Kansas Vocational College in Topeka. After a year there, he moved to Kansas City, Missouri, where he played in a concert band, taught at Lincoln High School, and studied with Carl Busch at the Horner Institute. He took a B.Mus. degree there three years later. (His piano trio was performed at the graduation ceremony; he had to take his bows from the black section in the balcony.) He moved on to Chicago, played first trombone in the Civic Symphony, and, under the direction of Adolf Weidig, an old Hamburger who had studied with Rheinberger [1368], took an M.A. in 1927. He celebrated by marrying Cornelia Lampton, who tragically died the next year. He went back to Tuskegee in 1930 and over the next twenty-four years became internationally famous as the director of its choir. As such he wrote many choral pieces and song arrangements, for which he won three Wanamaker prizes. In 1932 he completed his most important composition, the *Negro Folk Symphony*, which the Philadelphia Orchestra under Leopold Stokowski premiered two years later. In 1935 Dawson was married to Cecile Nicholson. In 1952 he revised the symphony. He retired from Tuskegee in 1955 with an honorary doctorate and was sent to

Spain by the State Department the next year to train choruses. He continued to appear as guest choirmaster. RECORDINGS: Stokowski recorded the revised version of the symphony in the early 1960s.

[1972] BÁRDOS, Lajos (Bär'-dōsh, Là'-yōsh)
CONDUCTOR, MUSICOLOGIST, PUBLISHER
BORN: Budapest, October 1, 1899

A specialist in choral music, Lajos Bárdos was a pupil of Zoltán Kodály [1760]. Later he taught at the Academy of Music in Budapest, where he was also choir director at the Church of St. Matthew and conductor of several other choruses at one time or another. He was a cofounder of the publishing firm Hungarian Chorus, which first published many of the choral works of Bártok [1734] and Kodály. As a scholar Bárdos has specialized in medieval and Renaissance choral music and in Hungarian folk music. RECORDINGS: Hungaroton has recorded a representative sampling of his compositions, including sacred and secular pieces and folksong arrangements.

[1973] REVUELTAS, Silvestre (Rāv-wel'-tås, Sĕl-vā'-strā)
VIOLINIST, CONDUCTOR
BORN: Santiago Papasquiaro, December 31, 1899
DIED: Mexico City, October 5, 1940

Revueltas was something of a wild man, both musically and otherwise. He was born in the Mexican state of Durango, the son of a peripatetic and unsuccessful merchant. His talent evidenced itself early, and in 1907 at Colima he began studying the violin. In 1913 he entered the National Conservatory in Mexico City, where he studied for three years with its director, Rafael Tello. During the upheavals of 1916 he went north to Austin, Texas, and then to Chicago, where he studied with Felix Borowski (1872–1956) at the Chicago Musical College. He returned to Mexico and embarked on a concert career there in 1920, but in 1922 he went to New York for further violin study with Otakar Ševcik. A few years later he was working as a theater conductor in Texas and the Deep South. In 1929 he became assistant to Carlos Chávez [1968] at the helm of the Orquesta Sinfónica de México. Shortly afterward, at Chávez's urging, he began composing. Revueltas once said that he liked to listen to all kinds of music—even some of the classics and his own—but preferred the music of the people. Many of his compositions reflect that preference, but they are marked also by wit, irreverence, and true lyricism. Though he wrote a good deal of orchestral music, he produced nothing in large forms except some scores for films and 2 ballets (the second unfinished). In 1933 Revueltas was appointed to the faculty of the conservatory. Three years later he organized his own orchestra, the Orquesta Sinfónica Nacional. It did not survive long, and in 1937 Revueltas went to Spain to work for the ministry of cultural affairs in the Loyalist government. With the Fascist victory, he returned to Mexico and the marginal existence that claimed the lives of his two daughters. Overworked, underfed, and alcoholic (he is said to have composed best when drunk), he died of pneumonia the night of the première of the first of his ballets, *El Renacuajo paseador.* He was not quite forty-one. RECORDINGS: Perhaps his most oft-recorded piece is the orchestral *Sensemayá.* Other recordings include the ballet *El Renacuajo paseador;* the orchestral pieces *Caminos, Alcancias, Itinerarios, Colorines, Janitzio, Cuauhnáhuac,* and *Ventanas;* music derived from his film scores, *Redes* and *La Noche de los Mayas;* the chamber or chamber-orchestral works *Ocho por radio, Homenaje a Garcia Lorca, Planos, Toccata sin fuga, 3 Sonetos,* and *2 Little Serious Pieces;* and several songs for children. Conductor Eduardo Mata has been recording much of the Revueltas canon for Mexican RCA and others.

[1974] SALMHOFER, Felix (Zàlm'-hō-fer, Fā'-liks)
CONDUCTOR, TEACHER
BORN: Vienna, January 22, 1900
DIED: Vienna, September 2, 1975

A distant relative of Franz Schubert [1153], whom he idolized, Salmhofer was the son of a piano mover. He sang as a choirboy in a monastery in Styria and at fourteen entered the Vienna Academy for six years of study with Schreker [1705] and Schmidt [1661]. He taught for a time in a local conservatory and in 1923 married the pianist Margit Gál. He was appointed chief conductor of the Burgtheater, Vienna's most important playhouse, in 1929. In his ten years there he supplied incidental music for dozens of plays. During this period he also wrote several ballets and the operas *Dame in Traum (The Lady in the Dream)* and *Iwan Sergejewitsch Tarassenko,* all produced at the Vienna State Opera. He resigned his post in 1939 after the *Anschluss.* For the ten years immediately following World War II, he conducted at the State Opera and for eight more at the Volksoper. Salmhofer also wrote symphonies, concerti, chamber music, etc. RECORDINGS: A few selections from the operas have been recorded. The song cycle *Heiteres Herbarium* and other songs have also been recorded by Oskar Czerwenka.

[1975] HEAD, Michael Dewar
SINGER, TEACHER
BORN: Eastbourne, January 28, 1900
DIED: Cape Town, August 24, 1976

After toying with the idea of becoming a mechanical engineer, Michael Head enrolled as a student at the Royal Academy, where his composition teacher was Frederick Corder (1852–1932). He went on to teach piano there, rising to a professorship and functioning also as an examiner. He was known to the public as a fine concert baritone, and in 1947 he made a world tour in that capacity. Though he wrote a couple of children's operas and some chamber music, his reputation as a composer rests on a considerable number of attractive songs in the Quilterian [1699] tradition, a number of which appear in recorded recitals. RECORDINGS: At sixty-five Head made a commercial LP of himself singing and playing his own songs.

[1976] BURKHARD, Willy (Bōōrk'-härt, Vi'-lē)
TEACHER
BORN: Évillard-sur-Bienne, April 17, 1900
DIED: Zürich, June 18, 1955

Once spoken of in the same breath as his compatriots Honegger [1861], Martin [1841], and Schoeck [1813], the reputation of the Bernese-born Willy Burkhard—not to be confused with Swiss operetta composer Paul Burkhard (1911–)—seems to have faded. It was not until 1920 that he began serious study of music at the Berne Conservatory. By 1924, however, he had also studied in Leipzig, Munich, and Paris. (The best-known of his teachers was the organist-composer Sigfrid Karg-Elert [1699].) He returned to Berne to teach privately and was appointed to the conservatory there in 1928. In 1933 tuberculosis forced him to resign to recuperate in Davos and later in Montana (Switzerland). In 1942 he settled in Zürich as a member of the faculty of the conservatory. Born in an unlucky year—see Antheil [1981], Berezowsky [1979], Weill [1978]—he found his career abridged by death at the age of fifty-five. His works are neo-Hinde-mithian [1914], contrapuntal, and uncom-promisingly unromantic. He wrote a single opera, *Die Schwarze Spinne (The Black Spi-der)*, 2 oratorios, a *Mass*, and a large body of other sizable choral and vocal works, a rela-tively small amount of orchestral music (in-cluding several concerti), and many works in smaller forms. RECORDINGS: Mostly of Swiss origin, these include the cantata *Herbst; Magnificat* for soprano and strings; *Das ewige Brausen* (song cycle); *Canzona* for flute, oboe, and strings; *Toccata* for orches-tra; Concerto for Violin; String Trio; Sonata for Viola Solo; String Quartet No. 2; pieces for French horn; and some organ works. *Die Schwarze Spinne* has also been recorded.

[1977] BARRAUD, Henry (Bà-rō', On-rē')
VINTNER, RADIO OFFICIAL
BORN: Bordeaux, April 23, 1900

Barraud's parents were in the claret busi-ness. Though French, he spells his first name "Henry." He is variously described as self-taught and as the musical pupil of a local named Vaubourguin. At any rate, though he was composing at an early age, he entered the family business, and it was not until he was twenty-six that he decided to make mu-sic his career. He studied with Dukas [1574] at the Paris Conservatoire and then with Louis Aubert [1693]. Some of his composi-tions were performed by Pierre Monteux in the early 1930s, and he was chosen to oversee the musical aspects of the Paris Exposition in 1937. He then embarked on a career with the national radio. When war broke out in 1939, he became an officer in the infantry, and after the fall of France he worked in the resistance (in which service his brother Jean was murdered by the Gestapo). Just before the liberation of Paris, he helped take over the radio and was appointed music director of the entire system in the late summer of 1944. Four years later he was elevated to the directorship of the Programme National. Barraud is an eclectic who is as apt to draw from the medieval as from the contemporary and is identifiable with no school. He has written (among other things) 2 operas, bal-lets, music for films and plays, large choral works, and 3 symphonies, as well as several books on music and musicians. RECORD-INGS: His 1941 *Offrande à une ombre* (in memory of his brother and the composer Maurice Jaubert [1900–40]) has been re-corded by Paul Paray. Other recordings in-clude the *4 Préludes* for strings (Jean-Fran-çois Paillard), the 1969 symphonic suite *Une Saison en enfer (A Season in Hell)* after

Rimbaud (Andre Girard); the 1965 *Sympho-nie concertante* for trumpet and orchestra (Roger Delmotte trumpet, Manuel Rosen-thal conducting); and the 1972 oratorio *La divine comedie* after Dante (Lorin Maazel).

[1978] WEILL, Kurt Julian (Vīl, Kōōrt Yōōl'-yàn)
BORN: Dessau, March 2, 1900
DIED: New York, April 3, 1950

At this writing Kurt Weill's popularity in America, thirty years after his too early death, has never been higher. The New York City Opera, which has two other Weill works in its repertoire, recently mounted his almost forgotten *Silbersee (Silverlake)* of 1933, and the Metropolitan Opera has just concluded a run of *Mahagonny*, which it broadcast both via radio and television to the nation. As a composer who astutely blended popular music with the most ad-vanced techniques of his time, he bids fair to last.

Weill was the son of a Jewish cantor, who encouraged his musical education. At fifteen the youth began three years of study with a local teacher, Albert Bing, and then in the spring of 1918 went to Berlin, where he at-tended lectures at the university, including those of the philosopher Ernst Cassirer. The following fall he enrolled at the Hochschule, where he studied briefly with Engelbert Humperdinck [1480]. After a semester he left to work as Hans Knappertsbusch's assis-tant at the Dessau Opera and later went to be *Kapellmeister* of the municipal theater of the little Westphalian city of Lüdenscheid. He was already composing and the next year, 1920, he returned to Berlin and pre-sented his work to Busoni [1577], who ac-cepted him in his six-student master class at the Prussian Academy. (A fellow pupil was Dmitri Mitropoulos.) During his three years with Busoni, Weill wrote his first symphony (long thought lost), a divertimento, a *Sinfo-nia Sacra*, a string quartet, and a pantomime ballet, *Zaubernacht (Enchanted Night)*. It was while casting this two years later that he met the young Viennese dancer Lotte Lenja, whom he married in 1926 and who, as sing-ing actress Lotte Lenya, became his chief protagoniste and apostle. In 1925 Weill's Concerto for Violin was premiered in Paris, and in 1926, shortly after Weill's marriage, Fritz Busch conducted his first opera, *Der Protagonist*, a one-acter set to a libretto by expressionist playwright Georg Kaiser, with whom Weill shortly afterward collaborated on another brief opera, *Der Zar lasst sich photographieren (The Czar Has His Picture*

Taken). About this time Weill met the radical (in several senses) poet and playwright Bertolt Brecht, with whom he formed a fruitful partnership. Its first products were the *Mahagonny Songspiel*—later expanded to full length as *Aufstieg und Fall der Stadt Mahagonny (Rise and Fall of the City of Mahagonny),* a picture of total capitalist corruption—and a cantata, *Vom Tod in Wald (Of Death in the Woods).* The year 1928 saw their reworking, in contemporary terms, of John Gay's *Beggar's Opera* as *Der Dreigroschenoper (The Three Penny Opera),* arguably still Weill's best-known work, and the cantata *Lindberghflug* (also known as *Das Ozeanflug),* celebrating the first aerial transatlantic solo crossing. As economic conditions declined and right-wing reaction grew in Germany, the next several works—*Das Berliner Requiem, Happy End,* and the children's opera *Der Jasager (The Affirmer),* which surely influenced such composers as Orff [1912] and Britten [2215]—caused upheavals in the theaters. *Der Silbersee (Silverlake),* premiered early in the fateful year 1933, provoked a riot and was closed down. On the day that Hitler and Hindenburg shook hands in Potsdam, March 21, Weill and Lenya abandoned their possessions and drove to Paris. There Weill wrote (for Lenya and Tilly Losch) the dance piece *Die sieben Todsünden (The Seven Deadly Sins),* and other works produced in Paris and London. In September 1935 the Weills sailed for New York together with playwright Franz Werfel and producer Max Reinhardt, to stage the premiere of *Der Weg der Verheissung* (finally produced as *The Eternal Road* in 1937). When its production was delayed, Weill joined forces with the left-wing Group Theater, an association that eventuated, in November 1936, in the musical pacifist play *Johnny Johnson* (text by Paul Green), which ran for two months (a 1971 revival survived only one night). The following summer Weill went to Canada and re-entered the country to facilitate his acquiring citizenship. In 1938 he established himself as an important figure in the American musical theater with *Knickerbocker Holiday* (with playwright Maxwell Anderson, starring Walter Huston in a singing role!). Even more successful was the Moss Hart collaboration *Lady in the Dark* (with Gertrude Lawrence and introducing Danny Kaye) in January 1941. Another triumph was *One Touch of Venus* in 1943 (book by S. J. Perelman and Ogden Nash, starring Mary Martin). Its successors—*The Firebrand of Florence, Street Scene, Love Life,* and *Lost in the Stars*—were too operatic for the New York theatrical public and had to wait their

time. *Down in the Valley,* a one-act piece based on American folk tunes was, however, unabashedly operatic and became a favorite with small companies and college workshops. During the run of *Lost in the Stars,* Weill suffered a heart attack, was hospitalized, and died two weeks later, a month after his fiftieth birthday. Four years afterward, Lenya opened at the off-Broadway Theater de Lys in Marc Blitzstein's [2065] recension of *Dreigroschenoper* (whose original New York production had flopped); it ran for 2,611 performances.

RECORDINGS: Representation of Weill's nontheatrical music includes the 2 symphonies, the Concerto for Violin, *Vom Tod in Wald, Das Berliner Requiem, Kleine Dreigroschenmusik, Quodlibet, Der Lindberghflug,* the song cycle *Frauentanz,* the 1920 Sonata for Cello and Piano and *Recordare* for chorus. Theatrical music on records includes: complete musical scores of *Der Protagonist, Mahagonny* (both versions), *Silbersee, Dreigroschenoper, Der Jasager, Happy End, Die sieben Todsünden, Down in the Valley,* and *Johnny Johnson;* "original cast" selections from *Knickerbocker Holiday, Lady in the Dark, Street Scene, One Touch of Venus,* and *Lost in the Stars,* as well as *Dreigroschenoper* and *Mahagonny.* Also recorded are a number of selected songs by Lotte Lenya and Teresa Stratas. There is a record of Weill and Ira Gershwin in rehearsal.

[1979] **BEREZOWSKY, Nicolai Tikhonovich** (Bā-rā-zōf'-skē, Nē'-kō-lī Tēkh-ō-nō'-vich)
VIOLINIST, CONDUCTOR, ADMINISTRATOR
BORN: St. Petersburg, May 17, 1900
DIED: New York, August 27, 1953

Musically precocious, Berezowsky studied violin and piano at the Imperial Chapel in St. Petersburg and by the age of seventeen was playing first violin at the opera in Saratov on the southern Volga. After the 1917 Revolution he found a place in the orchestra of the Bolshoi Theater in Moscow. But in 1920 he defected to the West and wound up in New York City two years later. He worked briefly in a theater orchestra, then joined the New York Philharmonic in 1923 and remained there until 1929. Meanwhile he undertook further violin studies under Paul Kochanski at the Juilliard School and studied composition there with Rubin Goldmark (1872–1936). Though he had written an opera as early as 1920, he did not begin composing seriously until after he left the Philharmonic. In the time left him, he wrote 4 symphonies, several concerti (including one for theremin), a good deal of chamber music, and a children's opera on Jean de Brunhof's classic *Babar the Elephant.* In 1931 he joined the staff of the Columbia Broadcasting System, where he established a reputation as a conductor, and in the late 1930s he was second violinist of the renowned Coolidge String Quartet. In his final years he devoted himself particularly to conducting and was becoming widely known as a guest with major orchestras when his career was abruptly cut off by premature death. RECORDINGS: Works on records include *Christmas Festival Overture* (Arthur Bennett Lipkin), *Suite for Brasses* (Roger Voisin); and *Fantasy* for two pianos (Yarbrough and Cowan). Berezowsky made many recordings (of other people's music) with the Coolidge Quartet and recorded as an accompanist-conductor for RCA (e.g., Russian arias with Alexander Kipnis).

[1980] LUENING, Otto Clarence
FLUTIST, CONDUCTOR, TEACHER
BORN: Milwaukee, June 15, 1900

Though he has composed in many forms and styles, Otto Luening is perhaps known today to the public at large as a pioneer in electronic music. His father Eugene, trained at the Leipzig Conservatory, was a pianist, composer, and choral conductor in Milwaukee. In a moment of Rousseauan euphoria, he moved his family to a farm at Wauwatosa. When he was three, Otto began getting the basics of music and language from his mother. When it was clear that he was musically inclined, Eugene took over his training —which meant largely that he let the child teach himself, checking in with him every so often for a progress report. Otto wrote his first composition, a waltz for piano, at five. Two years later his father lost his shirt in the Depression, sold the farm, and joined the faculty of the University of Wisconsin at Madison. An intellectual and a visionary, he clashed with his colleagues and the administration and in 1912 moved his family to Munich, where he set up as a teacher. There Otto was plunged into a world of art and music, continued his self-education, and took up study of the flute. At fifteen he was admitted (with some grumbling about his youth) to the Royal Academy, and he completed the prescribed three-year theory course in six months.

When the United States declared war on Germany in 1917, the senior Luening sent his son and daughter Helene to Zürich. There Otto met or rubbed elbows with the likes of the dadaist writer Tristan Tzara, Lenin, Hermann Hesse, and Busoni [1577]. Luening studied at the local conservatory with Busoni's pupil Philipp Jarnach and the conductor-composer Volkmar Andreae (1879–1962). To support himself, Luening played flute and percussion in the Tonhalle Orchestra and that of the opera, and began his conducting career. He was factotum and sometime actor with the theatrical company run by James Joyce. Busoni went over some of his chamber music and gave him strong encouragement.

In 1920 Luening came home and spent the next five years in Chicago free-lancing, playing in bands and theater orchestras, and teaching. An effort to get an American-oriented opera company off the ground cost him the patronage of Edith Rockefeller McCormick, to whom Andreae had introduced him, and who had been responsible for performances of his music in Chicago. In 1925 the French pianist E. Robert Schmitz showed Luening's sextet to an all-star New York jury, who recommended it for the Venice Festival, and as an indirect result Luening was hired by Howard Hanson [1927] to conduct in the opera department at the Eastman School of Music. The opera department, in which he worked under Eugene Goossens [1878] and Vladimir Rosing, spawned the American Opera Company, which he conducted on tour. He fell uncomfortably in love with one of the sopranos, Ethel Codd, and married her in 1927. In 1928 they broke with Eastman and went to Cologne. Ethel bid fair to catch on with a German opera company, but Otto's expected Guggenheim Fellowship fizzled and they returned to New York, where both worked in radio. A year later the fellowship came through, and Luening wrote his only opera, *Evangeline,* which found no takers. He accepted a teaching job for $3,500 a year at the University of Arizona in 1932, was tempted by Hollywood to write film scores, and two years later went to Vermont to head the music department at the newly fledged Bennington College. He brought famous musicians to the school to perform, conducted, and worked with the drama department but came to feel hemmed in. He and his wife found a studio in New York and spent much time off campus. In 1944 his marriage ended in separation and later divorce. That same year Douglas Moore [1884] persuaded him to become chairman at Barnard College, Columbia University. Subsequently he became director of opera productions at Columbia and presided over the premieres of such works as Menotti's [2177] *The Medium,*

Thomson's *The Mother of Us All,* and in 1948 his own *Evangeline.* In 1949 he became a director of the American Recording Society (ARS), dedicated to making records of American compositions. In 1954 its success encouraged Luening and Moore to join with Oliver Daniel, manager of the American Composers Alliance, to form a new such company, Composers Recordings Incorporated (CRI), which is still going strong. One of its first releases was a disc of electronic music by Luening and Vladimir Ussachevsky [2180], with whom he had teamed up at Columbia two years earlier to set up what became the Columbia-Princeton Electronic Music Center. In 1959 he married Catherine Brunson, a musicologist and teacher. He retired in 1968 but continued to teach classes at both Columbia and the Juilliard School. He has received many honors. His catalog of compositions runs to more than 300 works.

RECORDINGS: Recorded orchestral works include the *Symphonic Fantasia, Kentucky Rondo, Legend* for oboe and strings, *Lyric Scene* for flute and strings, *Prelude to a Hymn Tune,* and *2 Symphonic Interludes.* Instrumental works on disc include the Trio for Flute, Cello, and Piano; *Legend* for oboe, double-bass, and string quartet; String Quartets Nos. 2 and 3; *Short Suite* and *Prelude and Fugue* (both for flute, clarinet, and bassoon); Sonata for Trombone and Piano; *Fantasia* for organ; Sonata No. 1 for Violin and Piano; Sonata for Violin Solo No. 3; Sonata for Piano; *6 Short Sonatas* for piano; and *Suites Nos. 3–5* for flute solo. Recorded electronic-music collaborations with Ussachevsky include *Poem in Cycles and Bells* (with orchestra); *Concerted Piece* (with orchestra); suite from *King Lear; Incantation;* and *Rhapsodic Variations* (with orchestra). Recorded electronic works by Luening alone include *Gargoyles* (with violin); *Synthesis* (with orchestra); *In the Beginning; Fugue and Chorale Fantasy* (with organ); *Fantasy in Space; Invention, Low Speed,* and *Moonflight* (the last three all with flute).

[1981] ANTHEIL, George Johann Carl
(An'-tīl, Jôrj Yō'-hän Kärl)
PIANIST, CONDUCTOR, WRITER
BORN: Trenton, N.J., July 8, 1900
DIED: New York, February 12, 1959

George Antheil first outraged musical conservatives with his avant-gardisms, and later the avant-garde with his defection to conservatism. He was of German-Polish descent, and his first name was originally "Georg." He started piano study at an early age, and from 1914 he journeyed weekly to Philadel-phia for lessons at the school operated by Constantin Sternberg, a Russian-born pupil of Moscheles [1146]. In 1919 he studied with Ernest Bloch [1729] for a few months in New York and then at the Philadelphia Settlement School until 1922, when he left to tour Europe as a pianist. However, he found Berlin to his liking and settled there. He conducted at the State Opera, and his first symphony, subtitled *Zingareska,* was premiered by the Berlin Philharmonic. It was not approved (he later withdrew it), but note was taken of its jazz elements. In 1923 Antheil, who had buckled down to writing deliberately cacophonous and often machine-inspired music, moved to Paris, where he became part of the artistic ferment of the day and was taken up by two of its high priests, James Joyce and Ezra Pound [1800]. He wrote two violin sonatas for Pound's lifelong roommate, Olga Rudge, and helped Pound with his "opera" *Le Testament de Villon.* Pound reciprocated with a document entitled *Antheil and the Treatise on Harmony,* which perhaps tells one more about Pound than about its ostensible subject. *Mr. Bloom and the Cyclops,* an opera based on Joyce's *Ulysses,* however, never got beyond the planning stage.

In 1925 Antheil married Elizabeth Markus, of Austrian descent, and began collaboration with painter Fernand Léger on a score for an abstract film originally called (one assumes, in French) *Message to Mars.* This became the notorious *Ballet mécanique,* scored for, among other things, a player piano, eight grand pianos, anvils, and an airplane motor. It was premiered in 1926 at a private concert given by a wealthy American patroness who, at its conclusion, was tossed in a blanket by two princesses, three baronesses, and a duke. The next year a somewhat modified version performed at New York's Carnegie Hall left all the bourgeois in attendance *épatés.* The work was further revised, for only four pianos, percussion, and a recording of an airplane motor, in 1954. In 1930 Antheil's tabloidlike opera *Transatlantic,* involving American politics and gangsters, was a success at the Frankfurt Opera —supposedly the first American opera to be first presented by a major theater in Germany. But events in 1933 made Antheil's kind of music unwelcome in Germany, and he came home to settle in New York. A second opera, *Helen Retires,* was presented at the Juilliard School in 1934. Helen was from Troy, the libretto was by Juilliard's president John Erskine, and the work was a flop.

For the next several years Antheil largely gave up writing music for writing words. As "Stacey Bishop," he had published a whodunit, *Death in the Dark*, in London in 1930. Now he turned to frankly popular journalism. He had a syndicated column of advice to the lovelorn in newspapers across the country. He wrote regularly for fashionable slick magazines like *Coronet* and *Esquire*. In the latter he produced a stimulating series on the accessibility of women as determined by the effect of glandular dominances on their physical appearances. In 1935 he moved to Hollywood and became a much-sought-after film composer for the next twenty-two years. Shortly afterward he returned to writing other music, now in a frankly romantic style, with jazz and other American references, the marked influence of Prokofiev [1851] and Shostakovich [2094], and a good deal of nose-thumbing. Ultimately this embraced 6 numbered symphonies (the second had come in 1926), an unnumbered one-movement *Jazz Symphony*, the Concerto for Violin, the ballet *Capital of the World*, and 4 operas, of which the most ambitious was *Volpone*. In 1945 he published a breezy autobiography, *Bad Boy of Music*. He died suddenly in his fifty-ninth year.

RECORDINGS: There are several versions of the *Ballet mécanique* in its revised form of 1954. Also recorded are *Capital of the World; Jazz Symphony* (revised version); Symphonies Nos. 4 and 5; *Serenade No. 1* for strings; *McKonkey's Ferry Overture;* three violin sonatas; the trumpet sonata; the *Airplane Sonata* for piano; *La Femme 100 Têtes*, a 1933 piano composition inspired by the art of Max Ernst; *Fragments from Shelley* for chorus, the melodrama *2 Odes of Keats*, and *Blake Songs* (the last three works with the composer at the piano); the opera *The Wish;* and the film score *The Pride and the Passion*.

[1982] ROLDÁN, Amadeo (Rōl-dản', Á-mȧ-dā'-ō)

VIOLINIST, CONDUCTOR TEACHER
BORN: Paris, July 12, 1900
DIED: Havana, March 7, 1939

Roldán's parents were Cuban; theirs was a racially mixed marriage, a fact that clearly has some bearing on their son's later career. When he evidenced musical talent at an early age, he was sent to the Madrid Conservatory, from which he graduated at sixteen, winner of the Sarasate Prize. After embarking on a concert career, he took up the study of composition. In 1921 he settled in Havana. In 1924 the conductor-composer Pedro Sanjuan (1886–1976) appointed him concertmaster of his newly founded Havana Philharmonic Orchestra and, a year later, assistant conductor. In 1927 Roldán founded the Ha-

vana String Quartet, in which he was the first violinist. In 1932 he succeeded Sanjuan and in 1935 was appointed professor of composition at the Havana Conservatory.

Thus sitting as it were in the catbird seat, Roldán was delighted to be able to promote and encourage his musical contemporaries and countrymen. (He was also influential in fostering other artistic and intellectual currents in Cuba.) A serious avant-gardist, he was deeply interested in Afro-Cuban music, whose characteristic sounds he incorporated in many of his compositions. Like his friend Alejandro Garcia Caturla, he was cut off before he reached his full creative maturity. His small catalog of compositions includes two ballets, an overture on Cuban themes, and a number of smaller-scale works. The Castro government renamed the Havana Conservatory as a memorial to him.

RECORDINGS: A few works have been recorded—*Ritmicas* for percussion ensemble, *3 Small Poems* for chamber orchestra, and piano pieces. There may be a few other works recorded in Cuba and released by various Soviet-bloc labels.

[1983] MOSSOLOV, Alexander Vassilievich (Mō'-sō-lof, Ȧl-yek-sản'-der Vȧ-sēl-yā'-vich)

PIANIST
BORN: Kiev, July 29, 1900
DIED: Moscow, July 11, 1973

Mossolov's career is typical of the medieval tragedies acted out by artists in Stalinist Russia. His mother was a singer. (Some sources give his birthdate as August 10 or 11.) When the Revolution had triumphed, he was certified a hero, having been wounded in behalf of the new regime. After studying with Glière [1662] and Miaskovsky [1735], he graduated from the Moscow Conservatory in 1925. He then became a successful concert pianist (the assertion that he was a pupil of Prokofiev [1851] seems suspect, however) and soon was winning praises as an avant-garde composer. As the Soviets' fair-haired boy, he was sent off to international conclaves, and his 1928 orchestral piece *Factory* (or *The Iron-Foundry)* sent shudders through bourgeois concert-goers all over the world. Then a malign fate stepped in. First a briefcase-full of his manuscripts vanished; then Stalin (or a reasonable facsimile thereof) found himself unamused by Mossolov's kind of music. The composer was found guilty of drunkenness and uncouth behavior in public and was delegated to collect folklore in the steppes of central Asia. In the Great Patriotic War he was brought back from official nonexistence and set to writing music to inspire the Gallant Russian People, but he never again assumed any real musical eminence. RECORDINGS: There are some records of his quasi-popular songs and a few old ones of *The Iron Foundry.* Geoffrey Douglas Madge recently recorded the Sonata No. 2 for Piano of 1924 for a small Dutch label. There is also a Soviet recording of the Concerto No. 1 for Piano of 1927.

[1984] KRENEK *(né* Křenek), **Ernst**
(Kren'-ek, Árnst)
PIANIST, CONDUCTOR, CRITIC, TEACHER
BORN: Vienna, August 23, 1900

Cerebral, inventive, prolific, eclectic, sometimes named among the most notable (or notorious) of modern composers, Ernst Krenek's ultimate place in musical history still remains uncertain. Despite his Czech name, his immediate forebears were Austrian, his father being an officer in the Imperial Army. At sixteen he began studying with Franz Schreker [1705] at the Vienna Academy. After a brief hiatus in 1918 for military duty, he continued his studies, both at the academy and the university. During this period a brief marriage to Anna Mahler, daughter of the composer [1525], ended in divorce in 1920. A year later Krenek followed Schreker to Berlin, where he turned out a good deal of music, including three symphonies, three quartets, and two concerti, mostly in a lush romantic idiom, as well as a comic opera, *Der Sprung über den Schatten (The Leap over the Shadow),* which was first staged in Frankfurt am Main in 1924. At the end of 1923, Krenek moved to Zürich, where he turned to atonalism, inspired by his Berlin friendships with Artur Schnabel [1746] and conductor Hermann Scherchen. A trip to Paris, however, directed him toward neoclassicism. In 1925 he became assistant to Paul Bekker, then intendant of the Staatstheater in Cassel, which produced Krenek's atonal *Orpheus und Eurydike* (libretto by the painter Oskar Kokoschka) the following year.

It was in 1926 that Krenek completed his most successful work, the "jazz" opera *Jonny spielt auf (Johnny Strikes Up).* Depicting the global triumph of jazz, the work is a broad satire; the hero, Jonny, is a womanizing black jazzman, who reflects the composer's credo that the artist should be free to live as he pleases. (The "jazz," like most European imitations of the period, is pure cornpone.) Premiered in Leipzig in 1927, *Jonny,* like its protagonist, conquered the world in a

matter of months. (The Metropolitan Opera produced the piece in 1929, with Michael Bohnen and Lawrence Tibbett alternating in the lead role.) Krenek had gone to Wiesbaden with Bekker, who had been appointed manager of the opera there, but, now financially independent, he resigned in 1928, returned to Vienna, married the actress Berta Hermann, and settled down as a newspaper critic, accompanist, and busy composer. Bekker produced three one-act operas by Krenek in Wiesbaden in May 1928, and Leipzig premiered the jazzy *Leben der Orest (Life of Orestes,* to the composer's own libretto) early in 1930.

For a short time Vienna inspired Krenek to a sort of neo-romanticism, most typically perhaps in the song cycle *Reisebuch aus den Österreichischen Alpen (Travel Book from the Austrian Alps),* deliberately modeled on Schubert's [1153] *Winterreise.* But he soon came under the spell of the Second Viennese School and, after considerable agonizing, went twelve-tone in 1933. The system's triumph was announced in a Meyerbeerian [1142] grand opera, *Karl V.* But the German Nazis had already declared Krenek's music offensive to their ears and now exerted sufficient pressure on the Vienna State Opera to cancel the premiere. (The work was first produced in Prague in June 1938.) When Hitler swept into Austria, Krenek emigrated —permanently, as it turned out—to the United States, which he had visited the previous year. After teaching at Vassar for three years, he resigned to become chairman of the music department, and later dean of the School of Fine Arts, at Hamline University in St. Paul, Minnesota, while also lecturing and performing in other schools all over the country. In his early years in America he conceived of an application of mathematics to composition based on changing or "rotating" series. Later he turned to strict serialism, which he then adapted to his own uses, and also wrote a few electronic and chance compositions.

Krenek became a citizen in 1945 and settled in suburban Los Angeles in 1947. Three years later he married Gladys Nordenstrom (1924–), herself a composer. He has continued to compose into his eighties. After the Second World War, he returned to opera, completing eight additional such works (two for television) between 1946 and 1970, the most ambitious being the three-act *Pallas Athene weint (Pallas Athene Weeps)* and the four-act *Der goldene Bock (The Golden Goat,* a treatment of the Golden Fleece myth). In 1966 Krenek and his wife bought a home in Palm Springs, which celebrated his seventy-fifth birthday with a week-long Krenek Festival. He has written, besides libretti and reviews, poetry, plays, and several books on music, both in German and English. His manuscript autobiography rests in the Library of Congress for unveiling fifteen years after its author has gone.

RECORDINGS: Thanks to an ongoing project of Orion Records in California, a fair amount of Krenek's vast output has been produced, though to date, save for an abridged version of *Jonny spielt auf* and a new Austrian recording of *Karl V* (plus some earlier excerpts of the same), the operas, ballets, and most of the larger orchestral works seem to have been ignored. Included on records are these orchestral works —*Symphonic Elegy* (a memorial to Webern [1773]); *3 Merry Marches; Kleine Blasmusik;* Concerto for Violin, Piano, and Small Orchestra; *11 Transparencies; Capriccio* for cello and small orchestra; *From 3 Make 7; Horizon Circled; Kitharaulos* for oboe, harp, and small orchestra; *Static and Ecstatic; Von vorn herein;* and *Music for Strings.* For chorus there is *Lamentatio Jeremiae Prophetiae; The Santa Fe Timetable; Mass for the Birthday of the Mother of God;* and some small pieces. Chamber and instrumental works on disc include the Trio for Violin, Clarinet, and Piano; *Pentagram* for five winds; *Aulokithara* for oboe, harp, and tape; Sonata for Violin and Piano; Sonata for Viola and Piano; *4 Pieces for Oboe and Piano; 5 Pieces for Trombone and Piano;* Sonata for Solo Violin; Sonata for Harp; *Monologue* for clarinet; *Flute Piece in 9 Phases* for flute and piano; *Toccata* for accordion; Sonata for Organ; Sonatas for Piano Nos. 3–5; *Echoes from Austria* for piano; and *4 Bagatelles* for two pianos. Recorded solo vocal works include *The Dissembler* for baritone and orchestra; *Sestina* for voice and ensemble; *Quintina* for soprano, ensemble, and electronic sound; *3 Songs of Verhaeren* for soprano, clarinet, and string quartet; *2 Time Songs of Pandula* for soprano and string quartet; and half a dozen works for voice and piano—*Reisebuch aus den Österreichischen Alpen (Journey Through the Austrian Alps); Fiedellieder (Fiddle Songs); Gesänge des späten Jahres (Songs of the Late Year); 4 Hopkins Songs; Wechselrahmen (Changing Frame);* and *Spätlese (Late Harvest)*—plus a few individual songs. (A recording of the complete string quartets was announced by Orion several years ago but has never appeared.)

[1985] HALFFTER ESCRICHE, Rodolfo
(Hålf'-ter Ā-skrē'-chā, Rō-dol'-fō)
CONDUCTOR, TEACHER, EDITOR, PUBLISHER, CRITIC
BORN: Madrid, October 20, 1900

The son of a German father and a Spanish mother, Rodolfo Halffter is the elder brother of Ernesto Halffter [2060] and the uncle of Cristóbal Halffter (1930–). Though, like Ernesto, Rodolfo was close to Manuel de Falla [1688], he did not study with him in any formal sense, being largely an autodidact. He was a music critic for *La Voz* in the early 1930s and during the Civil War worked for the cultural wing of the Loyalist government. While he was living in Figueras (Catalonia) near the French border, his manuscripts were destroyed in an air raid. He fled on foot and wound up in Paris, where he conducted a concert of his music over the French National Radio in 1938. In the face of general war, the next year he emigrated to Mexico and took out citizenship. In 1940 he joined the faculty of the National Conservatory in Mexico City and also organized a modern dance company. Six years later he became director of the publishing house Ediciones Mexicanas de Música and editor of the journal *Nuestra Música (Our Music),* which he founded. For five years, 1959–64, he was chief of the music department of the Institutio Nacional de Bellas Artes. Most of his earlier music combines Fallan nationalism and French neo-classicism, though in the 1950s he became a pioneer in twelve-tone music. RECORDINGS: Outside of Mexico, suites from the ballets *La Madrugada del panadero (The Baker's Morning)* of 1940 and *Don Lindo de Almeria* of 1935 and the 1944 *Homenaje a Antonio Machado* for piano have been released. Additional works, on Mexican labels, include several orchestral works—*Obertura festiva,* 1953; *3 Pieces for Strings,* 1955; *3 Sonatas de Soler,* 1951; the choral-instrumental *Pregon para una Pascua pobre,* 1969; and the 1937 *Obertura concertante* for piano and orchestra—as well as numerous solo piano pieces.

[1986] COPLAND, Aaron
PIANIST, CONDUCTOR, WRITER, TEACHER
BORN: Brooklyn, N.Y., November 14, 1900

Aaron Copland is perhaps the best known, most admired, and in many ways the most influential American composer of his generation. He has shaped for himself a musical language that seems as American as he meant it to be, and its impact on other composers is inescapable. His father, Harris Copland, emigrated from Russia to England when he was fifteen, where he would have been Kaplan had not the customs registrar had an independent notion of phonics. Three years later he pressed on to New York, where he married Sarah Mittenthal, who had been brought to America from Russia as a small child. He founded a successful department store in Brooklyn, became a man of importance in the Jewish community, and sired five children, of whom Aaron was the youngest. Neither parent was musical, but following the mores of the time, they saw to it that their children had piano lessons. After his sister had taught him what she knew (apparently not much), Aaron at thirteen arranged for lessons with a professional named Leopold Wolfsohn. A couple of years later he determined that he would be a composer and in 1917 began private study with Rubin Goldmark (1872–1936). Like Gershwin [1955], Copland found the conservative Goldmark depressingly limited, but he stuck it out and acquired a solid formal grounding. Meanwhile he was undertaking further piano studies with Clarence Adler and Victor Wittgenstein, working occasionally in the store, and spending his summers as a runner on Wall Street. From these jobs and from his allowance he managed to save up enough money to take him to Europe after he graduated from Boys High School in 1918.

He went in 1920 to study with Paul Vidal [1554] at the newly founded American Conservatory at Fontainebleau. He found Vidal a disappointment—another Goldmark, so to speak. A fellow student, however, dragged him to a class taught by Nadia Boulanger, and he suffered a sort of epiphany. Despite grave reservations about studying composition with a woman, he became her pupil. He worked with her until 1924, sharing quarters with his friend Harold Clurman during the academic year and soaking up contemporary musical currents all over Europe in the summers. As far as Mlle. Boulanger was concerned, Copland could have truthfully said, *"Après moi de déluge,"* for three generations of aspiring American composers came to sit at her feet.

Copland's first published work was a pianistic *jeu d'esprit* entitled *The Cat and the Mouse,* brought out as early as 1921 by Durand et Cie. His first major effort, however, was a "vampire ballet" called *Grogh,* inspired by the film *Nosferatu* and the contemporaneous European balletomania, but it remained unproduced, and Copland later cannibalized it, mostly for the *Dance Symphony,* completed in 1925 but not performed

until 1931. He returned to New York in 1924 and advertised his availability for teaching. There were no takers. However he had a commission from Boulanger to compose an organ concerto for her upcoming American tour. Unfamiliar with the organ and unpracticed in large forms, he went ahead anyway, supporting himself by playing piano in a hotel trio in Milford, Pennsylvania. Providentially Copland had arrived at a lucky moment in history and never had to do that sort of thing again. Boulanger premiered the *Organ Symphony,* as it became known, with the New York Symphony under Walter Damrosch [1540] in January and repeated it in February with the Boston Symphony under its new conductor, Serge Koussevitzky [1655]. It is now regarded by Copland as his official first symphony, the *Dance Symphony* remaining unnumbered. Koussevitzky, whom Copland had known in Paris, asked for a work to play at a November concert for the recently founded League of Composers, which group Copland had already impressed with some of his piano music. The result was *Music for the Theater,* not to be confused with the later *Music for the Movies* and *Music for Radio.* It did not please all the reviewers by any means, but the whole affair had far-reaching consequence. First, Koussevitzky became a champion of Copland's music (and of the music of Copland's friends). Second, Copland assumed in effect the leadership of the League of Composers. Third, he mightily impressed Paul Rosenfeld, the critic and reviewer for *The Dial,* who forthwith found him a patroness in the person of Alma Morgenthau (later backer of the Cos Cob Press, which did valuable work in publishing contemporary American and emigré composers). Copland spent the summer of 1925 at the MacDowell Colony and later became the recipient of the first fellowship given a musician by the newly founded Guggenheim Foundation. It was renewed a year later, allowing Copland to return to Europe in 1926 and 1927. (From his twentieth year he suffered from an unquenchable thirst for travel.) In 1927 Rosenfeld gave up his contemporary music course at the New School in favor of his protégé, who continued to teach it until 1937. Copland also taught sporadically at the Henry Street Settlement and wrote for the League's journal *Modern Music.* The lectures and articles later provided grist for his first two books: *What to Listen for in Music,* 1939; and *Our New Music,* 1941—both of them extremely popular and influential. In 1928 he joined forces with Roger Sessions [1931] in presenting an important series of concerts of contemporary music, the Copland-Sessions

Concerts, which ran in New York City until 1931. In the summer of 1932 Copland inaugurated the music festivals at Yaddo, the artists' retreat at Saratoga Springs, New York; the same year he visited Mexico at the invitation of Carlos Chávez [1968], whom he had promoted when Chávez was living in New York in the late 1920s and who on this occasion premiered Copland's official second symphony, the *Short Symphony*, with the Orquesta Sinfónica de México.

Having moved from determinedly "American" compositions with touches of jazz and other local-color references, such as the Concerto for Piano 1926, to a starkly abstract period that included the *Symphonic Ode* and the *Variations* for piano, Copland now began striving to reach large audiences without sacrificing his stylistic integrity. The Mexican jaunt produced one of the most successful such works, *El Salon Mexico*, completed in 1936 and based on Mexican popular songs. This period saw Copland at his most fertile, and in its twenty or so years included the great ballet scores *Billy the Kid*, *Rodeo*, and *Appalachian Spring*, the operas *The Second Hurricane* (for children) and *The Tender Land*, the third symphony, and such fine dramatic and film scores as *Our Town*, *Of Mice and Men*, and *The Red Pony*. But even though he was composing steadily now, his other activities did not lag. In 1933 he stood as godfather to the Young Composers' Group, consisting of Paul Bowles [2165], Henry Brant [2213], Israel Citkowitz [2134], Lehman Engel (1910–), Vivian Fine [2214], Irwin Heilner (1908–), Bernard Herrmann [2175], Jerome Moross [2211], and Elie Siegmeister [2131], which bowed in a New School concert in mid-January. Two years later the New School devoted a concert apiece to Copland and his friends Roy Harris [1947], Piston [1890], Sessions, and Virgil Thomson [1928], soon to be accepted as the kingpins of the American musical establishment. That same year Copland took over at Harvard for Piston while the latter was on sabbatical, as he did again in 1944. In 1937, together with a number of others, he organized the American Composers' Alliance, an association devoted to publication and allied services, of which he was president until he shifted to ASCAP in 1945. In 1941 and again in 1947 he served as a cultural ambassador to Latin America under government auspices. During the war years he was helpful to young Benjamin Britten [2215], who as a pacifist had sought refuge here. When Koussevitzky inaugurated his summer courses at Tanglewood in 1940, Copland was on the faculty and afterward served as its chief until 1965. Of his

many pupils there the two he perhaps influenced most were Lukas Foss [2324] and Leonard Bernstein [2282]. In 1945 he won the Pulitzer Prize for *Appalachian Spring* (as well as the New York Critics' Circle Award). His score for the film *The Heiress*, after Henry James's novel, won him an Oscar for 1948. (But his writing music for *North Star*, a film about Russian resistance fighters, to a Lillian Hellman script, in 1943, later won him the disapproval of the House Un-American Activities Committee.) In 1951 Copland became the first American-born composer to hold Harvard's Norton Chair of Poetics. Space does not allow citation of his other innumerable honors.

In the *Quartet for Piano and Strings* of 1950 Copland made limited use of twelve-tone technique. In the 1960s he began to gravitate toward serialism and devoted himself increasingly to conducting and lecturing. Although he has kept busy in the latter occupations, he has been regarded as passé by many of the young Turks and, by his own admission, since 1973 he has found himself musically tongue-tied. (Two brief piano works of 1982—*Proclamation* and *Midday Thoughts*—were derived from sketches dating from, respectively 1973 and 1944.) But his place is firmly established.

RECORDINGS: Columbia Records has been sponsoring a long-term recording project that has seen all but minor Copland recorded under his direction or supervision. (*The Tender Land*, however, has appeared only in abridged form, though it has been nationally telecast. A version of the *Organ Symphony* which eliminates the organ part, some of the film music, a few brief miscellani, and the late *Threnodies* for flute and strings remain unrecorded.)

[1987] BUSH, Alan Dudley
PIANIST, CONDUCTOR, TEACHER
BORN: Dulwich, December 22, 1900

Though generally recognized as one of the more important English composers of his generation, Bush has not won easy acceptance, partly perhaps because of his earlier "modernism" and his later political stance. He initially studied at the Royal Academy with Frederick Corder and Tobias Matthay, then had piano lessons with Mabel Lander (who also taught William Busch [1999]), Benno Moiseivitch, and Artur Schnabel [1746]. Busch also put in six years of private study with John Ireland [1719] and then spent two years, 1929–31, at the University of Berlin, studying musicology. From 1925, with the interruption noted, he was a professor at the Royal Academy, where he was the first to lecture on music history (!), and where he was made a fellow in 1938. In 1935 he joined the Communist Party and a year later organized the Workers' Music Association, of which he remained president for much of the rest of his life. After that event he began to modify his hard-boiled style toward something more acceptable to the masses. His several operas have all been consistent with his politics and have been more honored in the Eden to the eastward than at home. Of them *Wat Tyler, The Men of Blackmoor, Guayana Johnny,* and *Joe Hill* have all had their premieres in the German Democratic Republic. Bush has also had success as a conductor in the Socialist bloc, though he has played and conducted on a guest basis in England and for a while directed his own string orchestra. Not all of his pieces have inflammatory titles. RECORDINGS: Bush has had distressingly small representation on records in the West—*Dialectic* for strings; *Variations, Nocturne, and Finale on an Old English Sea Song* for piano and orchestra; Concerto for Violin; and the song cycle *Voices of the Prophets.* (There doesn't seem to be much of his music on records from the Soviet bloc either.)

[1988] TRIGGS, Harold
PIANIST, TEACHER
BORN: Denver, December 25, 1900

Harold Triggs taught at the Juilliard School and at Columbia University. He also appeared as a concert pianist and in duo recitals with Vera Brodsky. His compositions are mostly for his own instrument save for the orchestral *The Bright Land,* taken up by a number of prominent conductors, including Leopold Stokowski. RECORDINGS: *The Bright Land* has been recorded by Howard Hanson [1927].

[1989] McPHEE, Colin Carhart
ETHNOMUSICOLOGIST, CRITIC, PIANIST
BORN: Montreal, March 15, 1901
DIED: Los Angeles, January 7, 1964

Although he was Canadian by birth and American by adoption, Colin McPhee operated musically in a much vaster arena. He studied with Gustav Strube (1867–1953) at the Peabody Institute in Baltimore and in 1921 returned to Canada for further training in piano with Arthur Friedheim in Toronto. In 1924 he premiered his first piano concerto with the Toronto Symphony, then left for Paris, where he was a piano pupil of Isidore

Philipp and brushed up on composition with Paul Le Flem (1881–). The next year he completed the Sonatina for Winds and Piano. He settled in New York, where he and his music profited from his friendship with Edgard Varése [1774]. McPhee's next few years were his most productive period: from them came a first symphony, a second piano concerto (with the accompaniment of a wind octet), a *Sea Chanty Suite* (for voices, pianos, and timpani), and two scores for experimental films.

In 1931 McPhee heard some recordings of East Indian gamelans (orchestras of tuned percussion instruments) and was so fascinated that two years later he took a trip to Bali. There, somewhat to his surprise, he met and married an anthropologist, Jane Belo, built a home, adopted a Balinese boy, and settled down to steep himself in the native music and culture. (The couple later split up; the child, Samphi, became a leading dancer in the Balinese dance troupe that toured the United States in the early 1950s.) McPhee spent the summer of 1936 in Mexico at the invitation of Carlos Chávez [1968], who conducted the premiere of McPhee's most famous work, the gamelan-inspired *Tabuh-Tabuhan.* From this period also came an arrangement of *Balinese Ceremonial Music* for flute and two pianos, *Bali* for orchestra, and a choral work, *From the Revelation of St. John the Divine.* In the face of growing international tensions, he returned to the United States in 1939. During the ensuing war years, he worked with the Office of War Information and wrote two much-admired books that drew on his Balinese experiences —*A House in Bali,* 1946; and *A Club of Small Men,* 1947,—as well as a couple of orchestral pieces inspired by Iroquois Indian music. Later he wrote film music for several U.N. documentaries and a handful of other orchestral works, including two more symphonies. Several prestige awards permitted him no work on a large-scale study of Balinese music and in 1958 he was appointed professor of ethnomusicology at UCLA. He did not live to see the publication of *Music in Bali,* which appeared in 1966. He was regarded as a brilliant jazz critic. His musical output was limited largely to the works cited here.

RECORDINGS: Works recorded include the *Tabuh-Tabuhan,* the 1958 *Nocturne for Orchestra,* the second symphony ("Pastoral"), and the Concerto for Piano and Wind Octet.

[1990] KOUTZEN, Boris
VIOLINIST, TEACHER, CONDUCTOR
BORN: Uman, Ukraine, April 1, 1901

DIED: Mt. Kisco, N.Y., December 10, 1966

Koutzen was the son and pupil of Lev Koutzen, a violinist, who had his own school in Uman. In 1910 the elder Koutzen became a professor at the Kherson Conservatory, and two years later Boris inaugurated his concert career. After the 1917 Revolution, the family settled in Moscow, where as a boy of seventeen Boris became concertmaster at the Bolshoi, a member of the Koussevitzky [1655] orchestra, and a composition pupil of Glière at the Moscow Conservatory. In 1922 he was given permission to study in Germany, whence he proceeded to the United States a year later, was taken into Stokowski's Philadelphia Orchestra, and married pianist Inez Merck in 1924. (Their children, George and Nadia, became well known as a cellist and violinist, respectively.) A year later he began teaching at the Philadelphia Conservatory, whose violin department he headed for more than thirty years. He conducted the Philadelphia Orchestra in his *Poème-Nocturne: Solitude* in 1927 and resigned his post the year following to devote himself to composition and his concert career. In 1937 he returned to orchestral work as a charter member of Toscanini's NBC Symphony, in which he played for eight years. After that he taught until his death at Vassar. In 1958 he organized a chamber orchestra in nearby Chappaqua. On December 9, 1966, following a rehearsal, he suffered a heart attack from which he died. His compositions—mostly instrumental (including several concerti) but also 2 short operas—stem from Russian Romanticism. RECORDINGS: Koutzen's publisher has issued recordings of some of his works on the Serenus label—Concertino for Piano and Orchestra; Sonatina and *Eidolon* for solo piano; Sonatina for 2 Pianos; Sonata for Solo Violin.

[1991] ROGALSKI, Theodor (Rō-gál'-ski, Tä'-ō-dôr)
CONDUCTOR, RADIO EXECUTIVE
BORN: Bucharest, April 11, 1901
DIED: Zürich, February 2, 1954

Theodor Rogalski studied composition at the Bucharest Conservatory with Alfonso Castaldi (1874–1942), a Neapolitan pupil of Giordano [1589] and Cilèa [1580], then in Leipzig with Sigfrid Karg-Elert [1700], and finally in Paris with Vincent d'Indy [1462]. He also had lessons in orchestration with Ravel [1666]. For more than twenty years, 1930–51, he was conductor of the Rumanian Radio Symphony and director of the na-

tional network's musical program. Afterward he was professor of orchestration at the Bucharest Conservatory and chief conductor of the Bucharest Philharmonic. His small and polished compositional output owes a good deal to his country's folk music. RECORDINGS: There are recordings of his most popular work, *3 Rumanian Dances* for orchestra, premiered in 1951.

[1992] POOT, Marcel (Pōt, Mär-sel')
CRITIC, TEACHER, ADMINISTRATOR
BORN: Vilvorde, May 7, 1901

Marcel Poot's witty music has given his name more international currency than that of most of his Belgian contemporaries. The son of Jan Poot, director of the Royal Flemish Theater in Brussels, he was born in the suburbs of that city. After a brief and unsuccessful childhood attempt at being a clarinetist in a band, he grudgingly underwent basic keyboard training and was eventually admitted to the Brussels Conservatory. In 1916, after a short time at the Royal Flemish Conservatory in Antwerp, he found his ideal teacher in Paul Gilson [1572]. Finding it difficult to get performances of their music, Poot and seven other Gilson pupils celebrated the latter's sixtieth birthday in 1925 by organizing as the "Groupe des Synthétistes"; the name did not mean much, the purpose of the union being to bring pressure to bear on concert managers. It attracted the attention of the conductor Arthur Prévost, who conducted a concert of works by its members, which helped establish Poot's name. What also helped was his founding with Gilson, also in 1925, of the *Revue Musicale Belge*, which he edited in its early years.

In 1930, the year the Synthétistes disbanded, Poot was awarded the Rubens Prize and went to Paris for further study with Paul Dukas [1574]. Back in Brussels, he worked his way up to a professorship in the Brussels Conservatory by way of public-school teaching and the Academy of Music in his hometown. He also reviewed for Belgian newspapers and in 1943 received (because of wartime conditions) a largely honorary appointment as inspector of conservatories. In 1949 he became director of the Brussels Conservatory, from which post he retired in 1966. Poot's music comes out of the satiric neo-classical impulse of the 1920s. Though he has written in most genres (including 3 small operas and 2 ballets), he is at his best in instrumental music (5 symphonies, concerti, orchestral suites, much chamber music). He also produced many film and radio scores.

RECORDINGS: There are recordings of the second and fourth symphonies, *Allegro symphonique, 3 Dances,* and *Ouverture joyeuse* (all orchestral); *6 petites pièces* for piano and orchestra; *Octet;* Concertino for Wind Quartet; *Ballade* for saxophone and piano, and *Suite for Piano.*

[1993] EGK *(né Mayer)*, **Werner** (Ek, Vâr′-ner)
CONDUCTOR, TEACHER
BORN: Auchsesheim, May 17, 1901
DIED: Inning, July 10, 1983

Egk was, between the middle 1930s and the early 1960s, one of the most successful opera composers of his time, though he seems now to have gone into eclipse. His *nom de plume* has been speculated upon in terms of various acronyms too silly to bother with here. Born in a village near Augsburg, he had his academic education and private piano lessons in that city, then, at eighteen, moved to Munich, where he studied briefly with Carl Orff **[1912]**. The next year he became a theater director in the raffish suburb of Schwabing across the river from the city proper. Illness sent him in 1924 to Italy, where he remained until 1927, developing a taste for opera. A subsequent sojourn in Berlin, 1928–29, turned him on to the possibilities of radio, and on his return to Munich he joined the staff of Bavarian Radio, which produced his opera *Weihnacht (Christmas)* in 1929. It was followed by *Columbus* in 1933 (later revised for the stage). Egk decided to cast his lot with the new regime and had an enormous success two years later with his folksy *Der Zaubergeige (The Magic Fiddle),* premiered in Frankfurt am Main. (His music shows such disparate influences as Richard Strauss **[1563]** and French neo-classicism, though his insistence on the primacy of singable melody has often been traced to his work with Orff.) His success was rewarded with a government commission for music for the 1936 Olympic Games, another from the Berlin State Opera (which resulted in *Peer Gynt* in 1938), a conductorship at that institution, and, in the war years, the presidency of the German Composers' Union.

With the collapse of the Third Reich, Egk had to undergo "denazification," but he soon reassumed his place in postwar musical activities. In 1948 the sexual explicitness of his ballet *Abraxas* (after Heine's treatment of the Faust legend) created a scandal in Munich and got the work shut down by the Ministry of Education. Equally outraged, Egk moved to Berlin, where he served as director of the Hochschule until 1953, when he stepped down in favor of his friend Boris Blacher **[2030]** and returned to Munich. (He wrote the "libretto"—nonsense syllables— for Blacher's *Abstrakt Oper Nr. 1* of 1953. Egk's 1948 opera *Circe* was a failure, though it fared better in 1966 rewritten as *17 Tage und 4 Minuten (17 Days and 4 Minutes).* *Irische Legende* (after Yeats) was admired at the 1955 Salzburg Festival. *Der Revisor (The Inspector General,* after Gogol) had something of an international success following its Schwetzingen premiere two years later. (Egk himself conducted the New York City Opera company in its American premiere in 1960, but it enjoyed—if that is the word— only three performances.) His last opera was *Die Verlobung in San Domingo (The Betrothal in San Domingo),* the only new work chosen for the opening season of the rebuilt Bavarian State Opera in 1963. He has also written a good deal of orchestral music and other vocal works.

RECORDINGS: On records he may be heard conducting excerpts from *Der Zaubergeige,* from the ballets *Die chinesische Nachtigall (The Chinese Nightingale)* and *Joan von Zarissa,* some of the Olympics music, and the song cycles *Quattro Canzoni (4 Songs)* and *La Tentation de St. Antoine (The Temptation of St. Anthony).* There are other recordings of the last-named, and of the *Französische Suite (French Suite)* and *Kleine Abraxas Suite.* Recently the complete opera *Peer Gynt* has been recorded by Heinz Wallberg. A pirate record contains several orchestral works—*Georgica,* the 1960 *Variations on a Caribbean Theme,* and the 1973 *Moria.*

[1994] SAUGUET, Henri Pierre (Sō-gā′, On-rē′ Pē-âr′)
CRITIC, CONDUCTOR
BORN: Bordeaux, May 18, 1901

Though Sauguet's music has enjoyed considerable success in France, it has not won real popularity outside, perhaps because the composer appears to prefer the calm light of reason to emotionalism. Henri Sauguet was the son of a man named Auguste-Frédéric Poupard, but he has preferred to use his mother's maiden name. The most important of his early teachers was Canteloube **[1722]**. An epistolary friendship with Darius Milhaud **[1868]** brought him to Paris to settle in 1922. There he studied with Charles Koechlin **[1592]**, but he was more profoundly affected by Eric Satie **[1578]**, to whom Milhaud introduced him. In homage to that master, Sauguet banded together with Roger Desormière (later a distin-

guished conductor), the obscure Henri Cli-
quet-Pleyel, and Maxime Jacob to form the
École d'Arceuil, named after Satie's home.
Satie sponsored them in a successful concert
in 1923, but they went their separate ways
after he died in 1925. (Note: Maxime Jacob
[1906–77] is often confused with the poet
Max Jacob [1876–1944]. Oddly both were
converts to Roman Catholicism. Max tried
unsuccessfully to join the Benedictines and
died in a concentration camp. Maxime was
more successful, entering the order in 1930
and becoming Père Clément.)

The concert brought Sauguet commissions for the one-act farce *Le Plumet du colonel (The Colonel's Plume)* and the ballet
Les Roses, both performed in 1924. A giant
success came three years later with a second
ballet, *La Chatte (The Cat),* ordered up for
the Ballets Russe by Diaghilev and choreographed by Georges Balanchine. It provided
Sauguet with a sufficient nest egg to permit
him to forego the clerical jobs by which he
had previously made his living and devote
himself to his métier, though he has since
served as critic for various French newspapers and magazines. Like his music, his life
has been quiet and civilized. His friend
Virgil Thomson [1928] describes him slyly
as "a lean and liverish *bordelais* with damp
hands." Sauguet is a passionate art collector
and has occasionally appeared as an actor.
His largest output has been dramatically directed—more than a score of other ballets,
of which the most popular was *Les Forains
(The Strolling Players,* 1945), half a dozen
operas, of which the most ambitious was *La
Chartreuse de Parme (The Charterhouse of
Parma)* of 1936, on which he worked for ten
years, and a large amount of incidental music for stage, screen, radio, and television.
Sauguet's orchestral works include 4 numbered symphonies; his chamber music includes compositions for saxophone, harmonica, and musical saw. He is a particularly
effective songwriter.

RECORDINGS: On records Sauguet may be
heard as conductor in *Deux mouvements a
la memoire de Paul Gilson* for string orchestra, the ballet suite *Oedipus and the Sphinx*
(a Soviet recording), *The Garden's Concerto*
(for Claude Garden, harmonica player), and
Mélodie concertante for cello and orchestra
(with cellist Mstislav Rostropovich). There
are also recordings of Concerto No. 1 for Piano; *La Chatte;* a suite from *Les Forains;*
Tableaux de Paris and *Les trois lys* (orchestral works); the cantatas *La Voyante* and
L'Oiseau a vu tout cela; Suite royale for solo
harpsichord; String Quartet No. 2; Trio for
Oboe, Clarinet, and Bassoon; and a number
of songs.

[1995] RUBBRA, Charles Edmund (Rub'-
brə, Chärlz Ed'-mund)
PIANIST, TEACHER
BORN: Northampton, May 23, 1901

The son of a factory worker, Edmund Rubbra was encouraged in his musical inclinations by his parents, both of whom loved
music. He somehow managed piano lessons
and hung out in his uncle's music shop,
where he ostensibly demonstrated pianos
and where he saturated himself in music.
Circumstances necessitated his going to
work at fourteen, and he progressed from
office boy to railway clerk. In his musical
explorations he had become addicted to the
music of Cyril Scott [1720], and at fifteen he
promoted an all-Scott concert in Northampton. Scott, getting wind of this quixotic gesture, offered him free lessons, and for several
months Rubbra journeyed to London every
two weeks to work with him. Scott introduced him to the pianist Evlyn Howard-
Jones (male), who helped him get a scholarship at the University of Reading in 1919,
where he and Gustav Holst [1658] were
Rubbra's principal teachers. In 1920 Rubbra
won another scholarship to the Royal College of Music, where he continued with the
same teachers and with R. O. Morris (1886–
1948), who introduced him to counterpoint.
Though Rubbra had played around with
composition from an early age, he composed
slowly in the years after his formal training
—mostly vocal works which already are
marked by the religious mysticism and lyricism that characterize him. In 1933 Rubbra
married Antoinette Chaplin, a violinist, and
wrote his only opera, a one-acter called *Bee-
Bee-Bei.* It was followed over the next six
years by the first three of his 11 symphonies.
With the onset of World War II, he joined
the armed forces as an antiaircraft gunner.
Over the years, however, he had kept up his
piano playing, especially on BBC broadcasts, and in 1942 he and two fellow soldiers,
cellist William Pleeth and violinist Joshua
Glazier, formed a trio. Assigned to a music
unit, they toured camps, playing for the
troops. The trio became so well known that
it survived (with various violinists) until
1956.

After the war Oxford University got serious about music and established its first real
music department. J. A. Westrup (later Sir
Jack) was named professor and invited Rubbra to join the faculty, which he did in 1947.
The following year he converted to Roman
Catholicism (he had already written his
Anglican *Canterbury Mass* in 1945). In 1961
he also joined the Guildhall School. He retired from Oxford in 1968. Though he is ba-

sically a tonal composer, Rubbra often hints at polytonality; obviously sprung from the English tradition, his work is highly individual.

RECORDINGS: Rubbra's Symphonies Nos. 2, 5, 6, 7, 8, and 10 have been recorded, along with several other orchestral pieces—the *Festive Overture, Improvisations on Virginal Pieces by Giles Farnaby, Sinfonia Concertante* for piano and orchestra, *Improvisations* for violin and orchestra, and the *Soliloquy* for cello and orchestra. Choral works on records include the *Missa Cantuariensis, Missa in Honorem Sancti Dominici,* three motets, and the *Inscape: Choral Suite.* The complete solo piano music has been done by Edward Moore; and chamber works recorded include the String Quartet No. 2, Piano Trio, Sonata No. 2 for Violin and Piano, and a couple of pieces for oboe or English horn and piano.

[1996] STAROKADOMSKY, Mikhail Leonidovich (Stá-rō-kà-dōm′-skē, Mēkh-á′-ēl Lā-ō-nē-dō′-vich)
TEACHER, ORGANIST
BORN: Brest-Litovsk, June 13, 1901
DIED: Moscow, April 24, 1954

Starokadomsky graduated in 1928 from the Moscow Conservatory, where he had studied with Miaskovsky [1735] and Sergei Vassilenko [1628]. He, however, remained there for the rest of his life as professor of orchestration. A practitioner of Soviet musical conservatism, he wrote an opera, several musical comedies, some concerti, and other orchestral works, but he was most successful with his songs and keyboard pieces. RECORDINGS: Some of his organ music has been recorded.

[1997] BECK, Conrad
RADIO OFFICIAL
BORN: Lohn, June 16, 1901

Beck, one of the most admired Swiss composers of his generation, at first set out to be a mechanical engineer. Finding the calling too mechanical, he transferred to the Zürich Conservatory, where he studied with its director, Volkmar Andreae (1879–1962). In 1923 he moved to Paris, where he became friends with such composers as Roussel [1605] and Honegger [1861], and where, during his nine-year stay, he was highly productive (the cantata *Der Tod des Oedipus [The Death of Oedipus],* the first five of his 7 symphonies, the first three of his 4 string quartets, and many other pieces). A brilliant

contrapuntalist, he moved from atonalism back toward a sort of compromise with the diatonic. He quickly acquired world fame, and several Beck premieres were played by major American orchestras. In 1932 he returned to Switzerland and settled in Basel, where he soon thereafter completed his most ambitious work, an oratorio on sayings of Angelus Silesius. From 1939 to his retirement in 1966, Beck served as music director for Radio Basel, in which capacity he turned out a good deal of occasional music. RECORDINGS: Works recorded include the Concerto for Viola of 1949; the Symphony No. 7 of 1958 (subtitled "Aeneas-Silvius"); a *Serenade* for flute, clarinet, and strings; *Nocturne* for saxophone and piano; songs; and other small pieces.

[1998] PARTCH, Harry
HOBO
BORN: Oakland, June 24, 1901
DIED: San Diego, September 3 (?), 1974

Even more than Ives [1659] and Ruggles [1684], Harry Partch was the archetypal American maverick—so utterly independent that it is still difficult to see where, if at all, he belongs in the continuity of Western music. He was the third child of disenchanted former missionaries to China. When he was still very young, the family moved to a ranch near Tombstone, Arizona. Both parents were musical, and by the time his mother decided she should give him some lessons, he had already begun playing the harmonium, clarinet, guitar, and mouth organ. About the time he reached his teens, there was another move, to Albuquerque, New Mexico. (Partch was never able to put down roots for the rest of his life.) There he went to high school and began private music lessons. The latter so irritated him by their circumscription of the medium that he soon discontinued them and learned by reading and listening. Having finished his academic education—he saw no reason to go to college—he supported himself however he could, playing in movie theaters, picking grapes, proofreading for a newspaper, and carrying bags in a hotel. Meanwhile he continued to write music, which he had been doing since he was fourteen. His creations included a piano concerto, a symphonic poem, and other works in a romantic-conservative idiom. Having written a string quartet to be played in just intonation (a requirement that presaged his later concern with natural tonal relationships), he found himself so restricted by the rules that he quit to rethink his whole approach. (The ultimate result was his book *The Genesis of a New Music*, which he published in 1949.) One day around 1930, as he later recalled, he threw everything he had ever composed in a pot-bellied stove in Louisiana and set it ablaze.

The basis of his new beginning was a microtonal scale of his own conceiving, which divided the octave into forty-three notes. Since no instrument that he knew had the flexibility to play it, he adapted an ordinary viola to his needs. His first works to follow the indicated direction were a series of settings of poems translated from Li Po, written for chanting voice and adapted viola in the early 1930s. In 1934 he managed to get a grant from the Carnegie Foundation which took him to London and the British Museum, where he explored the history of musical intonation. He also visited the poet W. B. Yeats and got his permission to set his translation of Sophocles' *Oedipos tyrannos* (later rescinded by Yeats's heirs). Back in the United States in 1935, he found his existence more precarious than ever and became a hobo, hopping freights back and forth across the country and working where he could—an experience reflected in such pieces as *U.S. Highball* and his setting of wayside graffiti *(Barstow)*. In 1938 he graduated from adapting instruments to inventing his own, beginning with a sort of lyre which he called a *kithara*. There followed a whole array of plucked or struck instruments, often constructed of found objects and given such names as boo, cloud-chamber bowls, and spoils of war.

In the early years of World War II, Partch found work as a lumberjack. He was so employed in 1943 when he won the first of two successive Guggenheim Fellowships. He introduced *U.S. Highball* to New York in 1944 and that autumn joined the faculty of the University of Wisconsin at Madison in a research capacity. In 1947 he returned to California, where in 1950 he was awarded a third Guggenheim. Over a decade he lived variously in Gualala, Oakland, Sausalito, San Diego, Oaxaca (Mexico), and Santa Fe (New Mexico). In Sausalito he and a handful of disciples lived and worked near an entrance to an abandoned shipyard and produced some of the first records of his music on their own Gate 5 label. In 1951 he was at last permitted to work on *Oedipos*. In it, out of consideration for the actors, he returned to diatonic music but indicated the pitch, rhythmic value, and stress of each word. It was produced at Mills College in Oakland in 1952. After a brief stay in 1957 at Antioch College in Ohio, Partch cast his lot with the University of Illinois at Urbana, which that

spring produced his purely Partchian music drama (or whatever it is), *The Bewitched*, featuring a chorus of Lost Musicians. He followed it in 1960 with *Revelation in the Courthouse Park* (the libretto an updating of Euripides' *The Bacchae)* and in 1963 with *Water, Water*—a sort of early consideration of ecology in eleven prologues, an intermission, and nine epilogues. That year Partch returned again to California, where he lived in Petaluma, Del Mar, Van Nuys, Venice, Los Angeles, and Encinitas, and continued to compose. In 1968 the Whitney Museum in New York gave a retrospective concert of his music in connection with an exhibit of his instruments, and in 1972 a television documentary film, *The Dreamer That Remains*, was made about the man and his work. That year he settled in San Diego. Early in September his body was found in his home, where he had died of a heart attack, probably on the date indicated above.

Apart from its microtonal aspects, there is nothing either complex or forbidding about Harry Partch's music, which some sophisticates have dismissed as simple-minded. Others find it in the attraction of Indian or Javanese music. Its inherent problem is that its performance depends on the availability of the Partchian instruments.

RECORDINGS: Recordings include the Li Po lyrics; *Barstow; The Letter; Castor and Pollux; The Bewitched; Windsong* (or *Daphne of the Dunes*, a film score); *And on the Seventh Day Petals Fell on Petaluma; The Delusion of the Fury* (his last stage work —the boxed set originally contained a bonus record of a lecture by the composer on his instruments but the bonus record has been eliminated from later pressings), and the score of *The Dreamer That Remains*. Partch chants some of the vocal pieces in a gravelly baritone.

[1999] BUSCH, William
PIANIST
BORN: London, June 25, 1901
DIED: Woolacombe, January 30, 1945

The son of naturalized German immigrants, Busch began his musical studies in America at the age of sixteen with one France Woodmansea (where or why remains obscure). At twenty Busch went to Berlin and studied with Hugo Leichtentritt and the pianist Leonid Kreutzer. He then came back to London and continued his studies with John Ireland **[1719]**, Bernard van Dieren **[1786]**, his homonymous contemporary Alan Bush **[1987]**, and a pianist named Mabel Lander. He made a successful London debut as a con-

cert pianist in 1927, but absorption with
composition began to take more and more of
his time. With the onset of the 1939 war,
which depressed him dreadfully, his health
began to fail, and he moved to Devon, where
nevertheless he joined the auxiliary
firefighters. Visiting his wife at the nearby
maternity hospital, where she had gone to
give birth to their daughter, he caught a chill
which progressed to pneumonia and killed
him at forty-three. He left a prelude for orchestra, concerti for piano and cello, a piano
quartet, and a number of smaller works. RE-
CORDINGS: There are recordings of songs by
such as Peter Pears and Janet Baker.

[2000] CRAWFORD (SEEGER), Ruth Porter

TEACHER, ETHNOMUSICOLOGIST
BORN: East Liverpool, Ohio, July 3, 1901
DIED: Chevy Chase, Md., November 18,
1953

Ruth Crawford was the daughter of a Methodist minister serving in an Ohio town near
the Pennsylvania border. She studied piano
there with her mother as a child. When
Ruth was ten, her father was transferred to
Jacksonville, Florida, where she continued
to study privately. Mr. Crawford died two
years later, and she began earning money by
teaching piano in local schools when she was
still in her middle teens. In 1920 she went to
Chicago to study at the American Conservatory, supporting herself as an usherette and
hatcheck girl in local movie theaters and
later, having attained a teaching certificate
and a B.Mus., as a teacher at the conservatory and at the Elmhurst College of Music
nearby. Among her students were the
daughters of poet-folksinger Carl Sandburg,
whom she helped with his folksong anthology *The American Songbag*. During this period some of her piano pieces were performed in New York concerts and published
in *New Music Editions*. She took a master's
degree in 1929, came east for a summer at
the MacDowell Colony in New Hampshire,
and then took up study with Charles Seeger
(1886–1979) in New York. The following year
she won the first Guggenheim Fellowship
ever awarded to a woman and spent a year
in Europe.

On her return to the United States, she
married Seeger and thus became the stepmother of Pete Seeger, and later the mother
of Michael and Peggy Seeger, all known afterward as singers of folksongs. Having already explored increasingly dissonant idioms on her own, she encountered
Schoenberg's [1657] music through her hus-

band and became one of the first Americans
to use the twelve-tone system (in her 1931
string quartet). In 1935 the Seegers settled in
Silver Spring, Maryland, a suburb of Washington, D.C., where Seeger served as assistant director of music for the WPA and music director to the Pan American Union.
Ruth worked with John and Alan Lomax on
the folksong collection at the Library of
Congress, collaborating with them on *Our
Singing Country* and publishing four folksong collections of her own for children. She
was also busy raising four children and
teaching music in local nursery schools and
so wrote very little between her marriage
and her too early death. She had resumed
composition a year or so before she died.
Her few mature compositions were ahead of
their time and have only recently been "discovered."

RECORDINGS: There are recordings of the
Two Movements for Chamber Orchestra,
1926; the *9 Preludes* and *Study in Mixed Accents* for piano, 1928–29; the String Quartet;
the *3 Sandburg Songs*, 1932; the late *Suite for
Wind Quintet*, 1952; the two *Diaphonic
Suites* for solo oboe and for bassoon and
cello, from 1930 and 1931 respectively; the
1929 *Suite No. 2 for 4 Strings and Piano*; and
the Sonata for Violin and Piano.

[2001] FINZI, Gerald Raphael

TEACHER, CONDUCTOR
BORN: London, July 14, 1901
DIED: Oxford, September 27, 1956

Until recently Finzi's music was hardly
known outside of England, but a series of
recordings have created a groundswell of enthusiasm here. The man's relatively brief life
was in many ways a triumph over adversity.
His ancestors were Italian Jews. His father,
a shipbroker, died when Gerald was eight,
and shortly afterward the child lost his three
elder brothers. The repeated shocks left him
withdrawn and shy. Sent off to boarding
school, he stayed for four miserable years
without advancing scholastically and was finally taken out in 1913, when he developed a
talent for faking fainting spells—he was sent
to Switzerland for a year's cure. On his return he fulfilled a longtime wish to study
music by beginning lessons with the organist-composer Ernest Farrar (1885–1918). But
war broke out. Farrar joined the army and
died in the battle of the Somme. From 1917
to 1922 Finzi studied sporadically with Sir
Edward Bairstow [1656], then immured
himself in the Gloucestershire countryside
to compose. He wrote some orchestral pieces
and the first of his settings of Thomas

Hardy. In 1924 his *Severn Rhapsody* attracted some attention, and Adrian Boult urged him to study counterpoint with R. O. Morris (1886–1948). Finzi returned to London in 1925 to do so, got himself known in musical circles, and joined the Royal Academy of Music in 1930 to teach composition. But he found himself unsuited for the pressures and withdrew three years later. He said that his marriage to Joyce Black at about that time saved him from complete collapse. In 1937 they built themselves a retreat in Hampshire, which they made into their own world. Finzi immersed himself in literature and composed slowly and carefully, coming to be recognized among connoisseurs as a musician with an extraordinary sensitivity to words.

A devout pacifist, he was horrified when the Second World War broke out in 1939. But, convincing himself that here duty came before belief, he took a job with the ministry of transport for the duration of the war and conducted concerts of the Newbury String Players, whom he had organized, introducing much old and new English music. In 1951 his doctors told him he had leukemia and could expect to live only a few more years. He told only his family. He died at fifty-five as a result of being exposed to chicken pox at the Gloucestershire Festival. His son Christopher is also a musician.

RECORDINGS: Orchestral works on disc include *A Severn Rhapsody, Introit, Nocturne, Prelude, New Year's Music, Romance, The Fall of a Leaf, 3 Soliloquies* (from a score for *Love's Labour's Lost*), Concerto for Clarinet, *Grand Fantasia and Toccata* for piano and orchestra, Concerto for Cello, and *Eclogue* for piano and strings. Also recorded is the *Interlude* for oboe and strings. Choral works (with or without orchestra) on records include *Intimations of Immortality, Dies Natalis, For St. Cecilia, In Terra Pax, Let Us Garlands Bring, 2 Sonnets by Milton, Farewell to Arms,* anthems, partsongs, psalms. Most of the songs have also been done—in all about ninety percent of his output.

than on any modern "system." He was, unexceptionally, a product of the Paris Conservatoire, where he studied composition with d'Indy [1462] and Vidal [1554], and conducting with Philippe Gaubert [1717]. Several published statements to the contrary, in 1927 he yielded the Grand Prix de Rome to a certain E. Gaujac, having to be content with a second-place finish. He became musical director of a branch of the National Radio and in 1930 of the colonial radio system, which no doubt accounts for his interest in Indochina and other oriental settings. In the latter 1930s the first three of his 9 ballets were produced in Paris. In 1939 he went on active duty with the Alpine *chasseurs,* until the French defeat in 1940. From 1946 to 1950 he was director of the Monte Carlo Opera and later conducted in Marseilles. The government awarded him the Grand Prix de France in 1952. In the 1950s and 1960s he turned out several operas, of which the most ambitious—*Miguel de Mañara, Atlantide,* and the Corsican-set *Sampiero Corso*—enjoyed considerable success. (Corsica was the focus of several orchestral works.) Tomasi also wrote a symphony in 1943; concerti for most members of the wind and string families, between 1947 and 1970; the *Concert asiatique* for percussion and orchestra, 1939; and a large number of smaller works. Among his last compositions were a *Chant pour le Vietnam* and a *Third-World Symphony,* expressive of his outrage at world events of the day. RECORDINGS: Tomasi's larger works are poorly represented on records. Works recorded include the Concerto for Trumpet; *Tam-Tam* for chorus and orchestra; *Semaine Sainte à Cuzco* for piccolo, trumpet, and organ; *Variations sur un thème Corse* for wind quintet; *Printemps* for saxophone and wind quintet; various small instrumental pieces; and songs. The *Divertissement pastoral* for children's chorus and instrumental ensemble and Tomasi's arrangements of *Noëls provençaux* by Nicolas Saboly (1614–75) comprise an album entitled "Christmas Festival in Provence."

[2002] TOMASI, Henri (Tō-mả-sē', On-rē')

CONDUCTOR, RADIO OFFICIAL
BORN: Marseilles, August 17, 1901
DIED: Paris, January 13, 1971

One of the more successful French composers of his time, at least in the short run and *chez lui,* Corsican-descended Henri Tomasi depended for success more on immediate melodic appeal and on exotic coloration

[2003] PEPPING, Ernst (Pep'-ing, Ârnst)

TEACHER
BORN: Duisburg, September 12, 1901
DIED: Berlin, February 1, 1981

Ernst Pepping grew up in Essen and Mülheim in the Ruhr Valley. At twenty-one he matriculated at the Berlin Hochschule, where his composition teacher was Walter Gmeindl. Having made something of a reputation for himself as a composer of instrumental music in the neo-polyphonic style, he gravitated naturally to choral music and specialized in Protestant church music. He became a professor at the School of Church Music in Spandau and established himself as a sort of logical successor to Hugo Distler [2120] as the leading composer in the field. In 1953 he also took on the duties of professor of composition at the Berlin Hochschule. His church music includes a *Mass,* a Christmas oratorio, a cycle of motets for the church year, and many chorales, psalms, and organ pieces. He has also written 3 symphonies, concerti, chamber works, and folksong arrangements. RECORDINGS: A few works have been recorded, including the Christmas oratorio *(The Christmas Story According to Luke), O Haupt voll Blut und Wunden* for baritone and orchestra, the *Te Deum,* and chorale preludes for organ.

[2004] KAUFFMANN, Leo Justinus
(Kouf'-màn, Lā'-ō Yōōs-tē'-noos)
TEACHER, CHOIRMASTER, RADIO EXECUTIVE
BORN: Dammerkirch, September 20, 1901
DIED: Strasbourg, September 25, 1944

Kauffmann's Alsatian birthplace is now called Dannemarie. He had early lessons with his father, then in Strassburg (Strasbourg) with organist-composer Marie-Joseph Erb (1858–1944), a pupil of Saint-Saëns [1343] and Gigout [1417]. Later he studied in Cologne with Busoni's [1577] star pupil Philipp Jarnach and conductor Hermann Abendroth. From 1929 he taught at the Cologne Conservatory, and in 1932 he was put in charge of dramatic music at Radio Cologne. Though he was a rather conservatively romantic composer, the Nazis found him dangerously modernistic and deposed him. For a time he directed a choir in Düren but was later reinstated and permitted to teach at the Strassburg Conservatory after the Germans retook Alsace in 1940. There, five days after his forty-third birthday, he was killed in an air raid. He left 2 operas, several operettas, a symphony, and many songs and choral works. RECORDINGS: There is a recording of a woodwind quintet.

[2005] GROVEN, Eivind (Grō'-ven, E'i'-vin)
ETHNOMUSICOLOGIST, THEORIST, FIDDLER
BORN: Lårdal, October 8, 1901
DIED: 1977

Groven was born and grew up in the Telemark district of Norway, where he became a self-taught virtuoso on the Hardanger fiddle and the Selje flute, the two chief folk instruments of the area. He trained as a schoolteacher, studied briefly—accounts vary between one term and two years—at the Oslo Conservatory, and later in Berlin. (The statement found in some sources that he was a pupil of Gustav Lange [1317] seems suspect, since Lange died a dozen years before Groven was born.) As a folk-music specialist he is regarded in Norway as comparable to Bartók [1734] or Kodály [1760] in Hungary. He has collected hundreds of folktunes, written about the untempered scale common in them, designed an electronic organ adaptable to it, and served as folk-music consultant to the Norwegian state radio. Not surprisingly his own compositions—which include 2 numbered symphonies, a piano concerto, some large choral works, chamber music, and songs—are colored by Norwegian folk music and frequently include roles for the Hardanger fiddle. RECORDINGS: There are recordings of his choral-orchestral *Ballade* and *Solstemning* for flute and piano. Other works, recorded by Philips under the auspices of the Norwegian government, include two large-scale (some say overextended) vocal-orchestral works *Brudgomen (The Bridegroom)* and *Draumkaede,* the brief *Margit Hjuske* (which includes a prominent part for Hardanger fiddle), the overture *Hjarlarljod,* and several discs of songs and piano music.

[2006] GORDON, Gavin Muspratt
SINGER, FILM ACTOR
BORN: Ayr, November 24, 1901
DIED: London, November 18, 1970

Scottish-born Gavin Gordon was a sometime pupil of Vaughan Williams [1633] at the Royal College of Music in London but made his living as an operatic singer and character actor in films. In the early 1930s he turned out three ephemeral ballets, then scored a hit with the Sadler's Wells production in 1935 of his witty and pseudo-classical *The Rake's Progress* (after Hogarth and before Stravinsky [1748]), produced in choreography by Dame Ninette de Valois and later revived. RECORDINGS: A suite from *The Rake's Progress* has been recorded.

[2007] SERLY, Tibor (Ser'-lē, Tē'-bôr)
VIOLIST, CONDUCTOR, TEACHER
BORN: Losonc, November 25, 1901
DIED: London, October 8, 1978

At his funeral Serly was hailed by his *confrère* Géza Frid [2048] as America's greatest composer. Yet he had no entry in the fifth edition of *Grove's,* and most histories of contemporary music mention him only in relationship to Bartók. Tibor Serly was the son of Lajos Serly, a popular composer in Hungary and director of the national operetta theater in Budapest, who brought him to New York in 1905 and made him a citizen in due time. Lajos—who also gave some lessons to George Gershwin [1955]—was his teacher, and Tibor was already writing music by the time he reached his teens. At twenty-one, offered the wherewithal to study in Paris or Budapest, he chose the latter. His teachers were the violinist Jenö Hubay [1509] and the composers Kodály [1760] and Bartók [1734]—marking the beginning of a lifelong friendship with the latter. Serly graduated with highest honors in 1925 from the Budapest Academy of Music and returned to America, where he worked for more than a decade as an orchestral musician—first as a violinist with the Cincinnati Symphony, then from 1927 through 1935 as a violist in the Philadelphia Orchestra.

In 1935 he returned to Budapest to conduct a concert of his own music with the Budapest Philharmonic. He then joined the newly formed NBC Symphony but left in 1938 to devote himself to teaching and composition. It was Serly who was in great measure responsible for Bartók's coming to America and for keeping him from starving after he got here. After the master's death Serly completed the last few bars of the third piano concerto, intended by Bartók as a legacy to his wife Ditta Pasztory (with whom Serly later recorded it). He also "completed" Bartók's viola concerto—though it is now generally agreed that considering the paucity and disarray of Bartók's sketches, the work is more Serly than Bartók. Despite a general tendency of the musical public to dismiss Serly as a rubber stamp of his teacher, he was, in fact, pursuing an independent path, which eventuated in what he termed the *modus lascivus* (a medieval term for the key of C major, a "secular mode"), based on sequences in thirds, and producing eighty-two chromatic scales. Age seemed to have little impact on the pint-size composer's boundless energy, and he attracted innumerable pupils, who reverenced him. One was the pianist Miriam Molin, whom he married, and who became one of his chief apostles. He was killed in a London traffic accident a few weeks before his seventy-seventh birthday, unhappily ending a project to record the bulk of his music.

RECORDINGS: Recordings completed prior to his death include the Concerto for Trombone; *Miniature Suite* (for twelve wind instruments); *Concertino 3 x 3* (piano and orchestra); Concerto for Violin; Concerto for Viola; Concerto for 2 Pianos; Symphony No. 2 (band); *American Elegy; American Fantasy of Quodlibets; Rhapsody for Viola and Piano; Sonata in Modus Lascivus* (violin solo); *4 Songs by James Joyce;* various arrangements including the two Bartók works noted and a completion of the scherzo of Schubert's *Unfinished Symphony.*

[2008] HELY-HUTCHINSON, Christian Victor
TEACHER, RADIO EXECUTIVE
BORN: Cape Town, December 26, 1901
DIED: London, March 11, 1947

Born in South Africa the year his father was appointed governor of Cape Colony there, Victor Hely-Hutchinson returned to England at ten and, after prepping at Eton, took an M.A. and a D.Mus. at Balliol College, Oxford. In 1922 he returned to his birthplace to teach at the university but came back to London in 1924 to join the burgeoning BBC. He was later appointed its regional director in Birmingham, where he succeeded Sir Granville Bantock [1600] in 1934 as professor at the university. In 1944 he followed Arthur Bliss [1854] as music director of the entire BBC, but his intendency was cut short by his death at forty-five. He wrote for orchestra and for chamber ensembles but is best known for his vocal music, notably a series of lighthearted songs—some set to texts of Hilaire Belloc, some parodies of such composers as Handel [683]. RECORDINGS: A number of these songs have been recorded, as has his choral-orchestral *Carol Symphony* on familiar Christmas songs.

[2009] BRUNSWICK, Mark
TEACHER
BORN: New York, January 6, 1902
DIED: London, May 26, 1971

A graduate of Phillips Academy and essentially without musical training, Mark Brunswick took a track much traveled by composers of his generation: between 1922 and 1929 he studied with Rubin Goldmark (1872–1936) in New York, Ernest Bloch [1729] in Cleveland, and Nadia Boulanger in Paris. He then lived and worked in Vienna until 1937, when he returned to New York. There he taught at the Greenwich House Music School until 1946, when he was appointed professor of composition at City College, rising to the chairmanship of his department before retiring in 1967. He succumbed to a heart attack while on vacation, leaving his only opera, a treatment of Ibsen's *The Master Builder,* unfinished. Essentially a neoclassicist influenced by Renaissance contrapuntalism, he wrote a symphony and a couple of large choral-orchestral works *(Lysistrata* and *Eros and Death),* but his main output was a chamber-scale. RECORDINGS: Recordings include the *Septet in Seven Movements* for wind quintet, viola, and cello; the Quartet for Violin, Viola, Cello, and Contrabass; the *7 Trios* for string quartet; and piano pieces.

[2010] DURUFLÉ, Maurice (Dü-rü-flä´, Mô-rēs´)
ORGANIST, TEACHER
BORN: Louviers, January 11, 1902

Born just south of Rouen, Duruflé was a member of the choir of that city's cathedral from the time he was ten until he was sixteen. Then he went to Paris, where he studied first with Tournemire **[1611],** with whom he worked as an assistant at Ste. Clothilde until 1930; then he studied with Vierne **[1616],** for whom he substituted at Notre Dame in 1929–31, and finally with Gigout **[1417]** at the Paris Conservatoire (where he studied composition with Paul Dukas **[1574]** and carried off first prizes in organ, accompaniment, fugue, harmony, and composition). He was named chief organist of the church of St. Étienne-du-Mont in 1930 (a somewhat dubious honor since the main organ was past redemption and remained so). He returned to the conservatory in 1942 to substitute for Marcel Dupré **[1806]** and a year later was appointed professor of harmony. Duruflé has appeared widely as a performer, as has his wife Marie-Madeleine *(née* Chevalier). A meticulous musical craftsman, extremely doubtful of his own abilities, Duruflé has composed a mere handful of works, chiefly for organ or orchestra. His *Requiem,* commissioned during World War II and premiered in 1947, is the most popular work in that form since Fauré's **[1424].** Since that time he was written a *Mass* and four motets. RECORDINGS: There have been several recordings of the *Requiem.* Save for a piece for piano and one for a chamber trio, the entire canon has been recorded with the composer as conductor or with himself or his wife at the console. There are also a number of recordings of his organ works by various performers.

[2011] WALTON, Sir William (Turner)
CONDUCTOR
BORN: Oldham, March 29, 1902
DIED: Ischia, March 8, 1983

With the arrival of young Billy Walton on the musical scene in the 1920s it became obvious that the revival of music in England was no passing phenomenon limited to a single generation. A Lancashire boy, he was the son of a choirmaster and music teacher who encouraged him to follow the path he took. When he was ten, though they had missed their train and thus the required competition, his mother talked Christ Church Cathedral, Oxford, into taking him in as a chorister. He made such a favorable impression there that Sir Hugh Allen, an Oxford professor of music, took it upon himself to instruct the lad. When he left the choir school in 1918, the dean of the college was moved to admit him as an undergraduate despite his tender years. This proved to be a mistake, for though Walton acquitted himself well in music, producing several compositions, he utterly neglected his academic studies and flunked out two years later. Young Sacheverell Sitwell, a classmate, offered him shelter, and for some years he was an unofficial member of the Sitwell family. He and Edith, fifteen years his senior and already known as a poet, set about on a collaboration designed to shock the bourgeois artistic tastes of the day. The result was *Façade,* first privately performed at the Sitwells' and then in a revised version publicly unveiled in 1923. Edith recited her experimental poems to Walton's parodistic music (for a small ensemble). The audience was aghast, someone called the fire department, Edith (for her own safety) was not allowed to take a curtain call, and Billy's name for better or worse was made. (He had in fact previously won a Carnegie Trust Award with his piano quartet in 1921.)

However much the general public was affronted, Walton acquired enough wealthy sponsors to permit him to compose at his own quite deliberate pace until he had established himself. Later that summer the ISCM presented his first string quartet (since withdrawn) at Salzburg. It was not very well received, largely owing to its placement on the program, but it showed that its composer could be serious. In 1926 the ISCM presented, more successfully, his *Portsmouth Point Overture,* and London experienced an expanded version of *Façade* in which Miss Sitwell and Constant Lambert **[2074],** by means of megaphones, shouted the verses through the mouth of a huge mask painted on the curtain. Encouraged by Lambert's success with music for Diaghilev's Ballets Russes, Walton attempted a ballet score; when there were no takers, he converted it into the *Sinfonia Concertante* for piano and orchestra, premiered in 1928. (In 1943 Walton completed an original ballet, *The Quest*, after Spenser's *Faerie Queene*, but his real successes in the medium came in 1940 with *The Wise Virgins*, orchestrated from pieces by Bach [684] and *Façade*, orchestrations of the chamber score in the form of two suites, without the recitations, premiered in 1928 and 1938. [Note: The second *Façade* suite of 1938 is not to be confused with *Façade 2*, about which more later.]) He is also supposed to have had a fairly serious affair with jazz in these interim years, but the only obvious evidences are the mock-jazz pieces in *Façade*.

In 1928 Walton tackled his first large traditional form in the Concerto for Viola, written for Lionel Tertis (the English violist who showed the world the solo possibilities of the instrument) but it was actually first played by Paul Hindemith [1914] at London in 1929. With it Walton exchanged the role of *Wunderkind* for that of a mature composer firmly rooted in tradition. Two years later he created a sensation at the Leeds Festival with his oratorio *Belshazzar's Feast*, the most successful English oratorio since Elgar's (and arguably since Handel's). So popular did Walton become that Sir Hamilton Harty [1725] premiered the first three movements of the first symphony in 1934 before the whole was completed. At about this time Walton found a lucrative outlet for his talents in the British film studios. His first score was for *Escape Me Never* (starring Elisabeth Bergner), followed by *As You Like It* (Bergner and Laurence Olivier); there was also *Major Barbara* (Wendy Hiller and Robert Morley) and the wartime *The First of the Few*, which yielded the popular *Spitfire: Prelude and Fugue*, though his most famous efforts here were the three postwar Olivier-Shakespeare films *Henry V, Hamlet,* and *Richard III.* Just before World War II Walton completed a violin concerto for Jascha Heifetz. Among the major postwar works were the Concerto for Cello, the Symphony No. 2, the *Variations on a Theme by Hindemith* (the theme is from Hindemith's mature cello concerto of 1940), a second string quartet (later adapted for string orchestra as *Sonata for Strings*), and the 1970 *Improvisations on an Impromptu of Britten.* It should be noted too that he was called upon for marches for two royal coronations—*Crown Imperial* for George VI's and *Orb and Sceptre* for Elizabeth II's.

Between the end of the war and 1954, Wal-

ton suffered prolonged labor pains with his first opera, *Troilus and Cressida,* exacerbated by a personal crisis. In 1948 the titled lady usually referred to as his longtime companion died. Walton, then forty-six, went off to Argentina to seek solace and found it in the person of young Susana Gil. Her parents opposed the match because of the discrepancy in their ages, but they were married in December and settled in an old monastery in Ischia, an island in the Bay of Naples. The composer was knighted by King George in 1951. *Troilus* was premiered at Covent Garden three years later. Audiences (and most critics) huzzahed, and major theaters worldwide hurried to produce it—and then shelved it. It was followed in 1967 by a one-act comedy, *The Bear,* after Chekhov. In 1979, for the remarkable American singer-diseuse Cathy Berberian, Walton reworked some pieces not used in the 1926 *Façade* and tacked them onto that as *Façade 2.*

RECORDINGS: Considering Walton's position as a sort of musical monument, it is not surprising that virtually all of his not very large output (save for some early pieces, some of the film and incidental dramatic music, and a few late works) has been committed to records, much of it repeatedly.

[2012] ARÁMBARRI Y GÁRATE, Jesús
(Á-ràm'-bär-rē ē Gá'-rà-tā, Hä-zōōs')
CONDUCTOR
BORN: Bilbao, April 13, 1902
DIED: Madrid, July 11, 1960

Arámbarri first had lessons from his father, who, however, originally saw him as an engineer. When it became obvious that his musical talent would not be denied, he was enrolled at the Conservatorio Vizcaino, where he studied with Jesús Guridi [1814], among others. When he was twenty-seven, a patron sent him to Paris to study with Paul Le Flem. Later he studied with Dukas [1574] and on the advice of conductor Vladimir Golschmann went to Switzerland to learn conducting from Felix Weingartner [1552]. On his return to Bilbao in 1933, he became leader of the Banda Municipal—not, however, with the approval of the local musical establishment. Nevertheless he was entirely successful and by 1939 had created from his organization the first municipal symphony orchestra in Spain. As a result of his taking the orchestra on tour, he was invited to guest-conduct all over the country. In 1953 he was appointed conductor of the Banda Municipal de Madrid. He was regarded as a particularly effective choral conductor. RECORDINGS: Among his compositions is a set of *8 Basque Songs* for soprano and orchestra which has been recorded by Teresa Berganza and by Angeles Chamarro.

[2013] CHANLER, Theodore Ward
TEACHER, REVIEWER
BORN: Newport, R.I., April 29, 1902
DIED: Boston, July 27, 1961

Chanler was the youngest of eight children of well-to-do parents. His artistic tastes were largely founded on his mother's expert piano playing, and on writing and putting on plays with his siblings at their summer home in Geneseo, New York. His interest in formal education was insignificant, so when he was fourteen, his parents sent him off to the Institute of Musical Art (which later became the Juilliard School) in New York. That did not take either, and in 1915 he was placed in the Middlesex School at Concord, Massachusetts, which he left after two refractory years. Now determined to compose, he took some lessons with Arthur Shepherd [1728] and studied piano with a local teacher, Hans Ebell. In 1919 he passed entrance examinations for Harvard, but before the fall term rolled around, he had met Ernest Bloch [1729] and followed him to Cleveland instead. Still determined to make a normal citizen of his son, the elder Chanler got him into Oxford in January of 1923, but while spending the ensuing Christmas holidays with his mother in Paris, Teddy (as he was called) was introduced to Nadia Boulanger and promptly cast his lot with her. She kept him producing for the two years he enjoyed her tutelage, and in his second year he heard Samuel Dushkin premiere his violin sonata. He remained in Europe, producing nothing of consequence until 1930, when he wrote a *Mass* for female voices and organ. After his marriage to Maria de Acosta Sargent, he returned to America, settling in Boston in 1934. When the revered Philip Hale, critic for the *Herald,* died that November, Chanler got his job, but his readers deemed him unfit to fill shoes so large, and he was summarily fired after a few weeks. Shortly afterward he began composing again and turned out a number of exquisitely crafted songs (mostly to texts by Walter De La Mare and Chanler's friend Leonard Feeney). These brought him a prize from the League of Composers and a Guggenheim Fellowship. In 1945 he joined the faculty of the Peabody Conservatory but left after two years. At the time of his death (at fifty-nine), he was teaching at the Longy School in Boston. With the exception of his 1955 chamber opera *The Pot of Fat,* Chanler wrote exclusively in small forms. (One source mentions concerti for violin and for two pianos, but it is corroborated nowhere else.) RECORDINGS: There are recordings of *The Pot of Fat,* the song cycles *8 Epitaphs* and *The Children,* and of various individual songs.

[2014] LOTHAR, Mark (Lō'-tär, Märk)
ACCOMPANIST, CONDUCTOR
BORN: Berlin, May 23, 1902

Lothar began his serious musical studies at the Berlin Hochschule, where he numbered among his teachers Franz Schreker [1705] and the Russian Paul Juon (1872–1940), an Arensky [1536] pupil. In 1921 he became accompanist to the Dutch concert singer Corry Nera, who became, as the accounts coyly put it, "his lifelong companion." (He married her thirteen years later.) For a long time he worked as a theater conductor-composer in Berlin, first for Max Reinhardt at the Deutsche Theater, then for Gustav Gründgens at the Preussische Staatstheater. After World War II he held a similar post at the Bavarian State Theater in Munich. He continued to study when he found the opportunity, working with such men as the *Lieder* composer Justus Wetzel (1879–1973) and Ermanno Wolf-Ferrari [1679]. He was especially successful in Germany as an opera composer *(Schneider Wibbel* won attention in the larger world) and has composed incidental music tirelessly for plays, films, television, and radio. He retired to private life near Munich in 1955. RECORDINGS: Several works have been recorded—*Musik des Einsamen* (song cycle); *The Tale of the Lazy Bear* (narrator, tuba, and orchestra); *8 Haiku* (soprano, flute, viola, percussion, and piano); and other songs.

[2015] DOUGHERTY, Celius
PIANIST
BORN: Glenwood, Minn., May 27, 1902

A graduate of the University of Minnesota, Dougherty came to New York and undertook further study at Juilliard with Josef Lhevinne and Rubin Goldmark (1872–1936). He was for a time part of a duo-piano team and then made a career as a much-admired accompanist (e.g., for Povla Frijsh, Alexander Kipnis, and Maria Kurenko). He wrote an opera, *Many Moons* (after James Thurber) but is best known for his songs. RECORDINGS: Some of his songs have been recorded.

[2016] DAUS, Avraham (Dá'-oos, Áv'-rà-hàm)
CONDUCTOR
BORN: Berlin, June 6, 1902
DIED: Tel Aviv, 1974

Between 1919 and 1922 Daus studied at the Berlin Hochschule and the Munich Academy; then he became an opera conductor in Breslau (Wroclaw). As a Jew he found himself no longer employable in 1933 and fled to Palestine three years later. There he spent twenty-three years fostering music in the *kibbutzim*. In the later part of his composing career he was influenced by Schoenberg's [1657] music. RECORDINGS: There is a recording of his 1968 *Twelfth Sonnet to Orpheus*, for cello and piano.

[2017] SHEBALIN, Vissarion Yakovlevitch (Shà-bà-lēm, Vis-är'-yōn Yà-kōv-lyā'-vich)
TEACHER
BORN: Omsk, June 11, 1902
DIED: Moscow, May 29, 1963

Shebalin was one of the few significant composers to come from Omsk and one of the very few to have seriously weighed the advantages of becoming a farmer against those of a musical career. He was a favorite pupil of Miaskovsky [1735] at the Moscow Conservatory, where he graduated in 1928 but remained to teach. He was a master at fence straddling while preserving a measure of his own integrity, whether his opponents were the young hotheads of the 1920s or the Stalinist toadies of the 1940s. He had particular success with his *Lenin Symphony* in 1933, a big choral-orchestral work based on Vladimir Mayakovsky's poem, which apparently transcended mere propaganda. He also wrote a number of film scores and music for plays and was much in demand during the Great Patriotic War, during which he presided over the rump session of the Moscow Conservatory which remained in that city. Though he was not initially among those attacked by Zhdanov in 1948, he stood up for his associates and was rewarded by being dismissed from the conservatory. He was reinstated after the Khrushchev thaw but in 1953 lost the use of his right hand to a stroke. Nevertheless he learned to compensate and in 1957 was widely praised for his operatic treatment of Shakespeare's *The Taming of the Shrew*. He succumbed to cancer at sixty. RECORDINGS: Excerpts from *The Taming of the Shrew* have been recorded. Additional recordings have circulated primarily in the Soviet Union—among

them, the 1940 Concerto for Violin, the 1930 Concertino for Horn, the Piano Trio, and several of his 9 string quartets.

[2018] RODGERS, Richard Charles
CONDUCTOR
BORN: Hammels Station, N.Y., June 28, 1902
DIED: New York, December 30, 1979

With Richard Rodgers the American musical came of age, turning from a flimsy framework supporting songs and gags toward something very close to opera. It is not surprising, for he adored the theater (and later opera) from childhood. He was the second son of William and Mamie Levy Rodgers. His father *(né* Abrams) was a customs official turned physician; both parents were musical. Young Richard began picking out tunes on the piano at four and soon could play by ear, albeit simply. He was forthwith given piano lessons which lasted only two years against strong resistance. Educated in various city schools, he was also a mediocre student in academic subjects but in at least one served as official pianist. At nine he was writing tunes (which he taught himself to do) and at fourteen began producing full-fledged songs. A year later he contributed seven songs to a benefit musical put on by the Akron Club, a local athletic organization. It was successful enough to get another philanthropic group to ask him to write a benefit musical for them, which the composer conducted at the Waldorf in 1919.

Shortly before, a friend had introduced Rodgers to Lorenz Hart, at twenty-three already a professional lyricist, and a great partnership was born. In the summer of 1919, during which Rodgers began studying at Columbia University, Lew Fields took one of their songs, "Any Old Place with You," for one of his shows, and it later became their first publication. In Rodgers' freshman (and only) year at Columbia, they were selected to do the varsity show (Oscar Hammerstein II was a member of the selection committee), and Fields bought some of the songs for "Poor Little Ritz Girl" which ran for 119 performances. The two took Fields's son Herbert into partnership as librettist; their first effort did not interest even Fields, Sr. Meanwhile Rodgers left Columbia for the Institute of Musical Art, where for two years he got a solid if conservative grounding with the likes of Percy Goetschius and H. E. Krehbiel and wrote three student shows. He left in 1923. For some time he and Hart had no luck cracking Broadway. In 1924, together with the younger Fields, they made it with a satire, *The Melody Man*, but it folded after not quite two months. Pressed by his father, who was supporting him, Rodgers was about to go into the underwear business when the Theatre Guild bit on the notion of a sophisticated revue for a two-performance showing. The result was *The Garrick Gaities*, which proved so successful that eventually the Lunts themselves were dispossessed from the Garrick Theater to permit it a regular run. It lasted six months; Rodgers conducted for the vast wage of eighty-three dollars a week.

After that there were few failures and the successes went from triumph to triumph, culminating with such works as *A Connecticut Yankee, On Your Toes, Babes in Arms, I'd Rather Be Right, The Boys from Syracuse, Pal Joey*, and *By Jupiter*. In 1930 Rodgers married Dorothy Feiner, the sister of a boyhood playmate; their daughters Mary (herself a composer) and Linda were born within the next five years. Despite the successes, however, the partnership with Hart became increasingly difficult because Hart, a diminutive man, lonely, self-conscious, and frustrated, took to drinking and began falling apart. In 1941 Rodgers suggested to his old friend Oscar Hammerstein that he take Hart's place. Their first collaboration, which opened on the last day of March 1943, was *Oklahoma!*—a landmark in the history of American musicals. It welded story, song, and dance into a unity, and ran for more than five years on Broadway—a record at the time. That November Hart came to a revival of *A Connecticut Yankee*, went out on a twenty-four-hour celebration, collapsed, and died five days later. Hollywood afterward celebrated the partnership with the film *Words and Music*, a "biography" with Tom Drake as Rodgers and Mickey Rooney as Hart.

Not all of the Rodgers-Hammerstein collaborations were successes, but the big ones —*Carousel, South Pacific, The King and I*, and *The Sound of Music*—outstripped even the best of the Hart collaborations. One should also mention the film *State Fair* and the television version of *Cinderella* among their notable musicals. After Hammerstein's death in 1960 Rodgers' star declined, and none of his later efforts in the theater met with any real approval. However, his score to the TV documentary series *Victory at Sea* (orchestrated by Robert Russell Bennett [1895], who worked closely with Rodgers for the latter half of his career) was immensely popular, and the recorded suites from it became best sellers. Music for the 1960 documentary series *Winston Churchill: The Valiant Years* was also written by Rod-gers. Rodgers wrote little outside the theater, contributing the ballet *Ghost Town* to the Ballets Russes de Monte Carlo, and a *Nursery Ballet* to Paul Whiteman, and meeting with some success with an odd recorded melodrama *All Points West*.

RECORDINGS: There are copious recordings of the songs, and original-cast versions of the musicals from *Oklahoma!* on. A brief orchestral snippet, *Lagoon*, has been recorded by Andre Kostelanetz. The *Victory at Sea* music makes up three records, and there was also a one-record album of excerpts.

[2019] KRIUKOV, Vladimir Nikolaievich
(Krē-ōō'-kof, Vlåd-yē'-mēr Nē-kō-lī-yā'-vich)
CONDUCTOR, TEACHER, RADIO MAN
BORN: Moscow, July 22, 1902
DIED: Staraya Rusa, June 14, 1960

The elder brother of Nikolai Nikolaievich Kriukov (1908–61), Stalin Prize winner for his film scores, Vladimir studied at the Moscow Conservatory with Georgy Catoire (1861–1926), Grechaninov [1567], and Miaskovsky [1735], graduating in 1925. He later worked for the state radio, conducted in theaters, and taught at the Gnesin School in Moscow. He wrote several operas, beginning with his setting of Pushkin's *The Miserly Knight* when he was fifteen, orchestral and chamber works, and songs. He died at fifty-seven just outside of Moscow; Nikolai committed suicide a year later. RECORDINGS: There is a recording of Vladimir's Concerto for Trumpet.

[2020] WOLPE, Stefan (Vōl'-pe, Stef'-ån)
TEACHER
BORN: Berlin, August 25, 1902
DIED: New York, April 4, 1972

A great teacher and the adored guru of many postwar American composers, including Morton Feldman [2355], Ralph Shapey (1921–), and Ezra Laderman [2342], Wolpe was a man whose will not only enabled him to adapt the musical currents of his time to his own ends but also to overcome enormous personal adversity. He came of a Jewish family; his father was Russian, his mother a Vienna-born Hungarian. Both parents discouraged his musical leanings, and he had no formal training until he was fifteen. Then he made up for lost time by composing furiously. A year later he left home to lead a Bohemian, catch-as-catch-can existence, hanging out with dadaists, other far-out artist types, and revolutionaries. In 1919 he entered the Berlin Hochschule, where he was a rather dissatisfied student (of Franz Schreker's [1705], among others), though he was happier with Busoni [1577], under whose wing he was taken in 1920. He left the school in 1924 and at about the same time destroyed all his early work save for the few pieces that had gotten into print. For the next several years he devoted himself to the musical advancement of the Revolution, writing, so to speak, inspirational music for that purpose by day but pursuing his own atonal ways by night. During this period he discovered jazz, with which he had a romance of some magnitude. In 1927 he married Ola Okuniewska, a painter; the marriage did not last, but it produced a daughter Katharina, who became a concert pianist. In 1931 he began an association with a socialistic theater company, Die Truppe, with an enormously successful musical play, *Die Mausfalle (The Mousetrap)*. Two years later, however, he found himself dangerously *non grata* in his homeland, and fled, taking with him a Rumanian pianist named Irma Schoenberg (no relation to the composer).

After a stay in Vienna, where Wolpe studied with Webern [1773] briefly and a legalization of the union with Irma, they went to Palestine in 1934. There Wolpe taught at the conservatory in Jerusalem for four years and discovered his own solution to the mousetrap of Schoenberg's [1657] twelve-tone system. He also became fascinated by the music of his people, which he explored thoroughly. In 1938 he emigrated to the United States, where he received a number of commissions, and where he taught at various schools (including the experimental Black Mountain College) from 1946. In 1948 he married the poet Hilda Morley. He became chairman of the music department at C. W. Post College on Long Island in 1957. Seven years later he was found to be suffering from incipient Parkinsonism. He continued to teach as long as he could and to compose up to the end, by which time he was virtually helpless. Wolpe's music is very much his own—uncompromising and highly cerebral. RECORDINGS: Wolpe's Symphony has just been released under the direction of Arthur Weisberg. Other recordings include *Chamber Piece No. 1* for fourteen players; *Chamber Piece No. 2; Piece for Trumpet and 7 Instruments; Piece for 2 Instrumental Units;* Quartet for Trumpet, Saxophone, Piano, and Percussion; *Piece for Flute and Piano;* Trio for Flute, Piano, and Cello; Sonata for Violin and Piano; String Quartet; *From Here on Farther* for clarinet, bass clarinet, and piano;

Suite im Hexachord for oboe and clarinet; *Solo Pieces for Trumpet; Piece in 2 Parts for Solo Violin; Piece in 2 Parts for Flute; Second Piece for Violin Alone; Enactments* for two pianos; *Songs from the Hebrew* for voice and piano; and several works for solo piano— *Passacaglia; Pastorale; Presto agitato; Form I;* and *Form IV: Broken Sequences.*

[2021] BALASANYAN, Sergei Artemievich (Bá-là-sàn'-yàn, Sâr'-gā Àrt'-yem-yā'-vēch)
ETHNOMUSICOLOGIST
BORN: Poltoratsk (now Ashkhabad), August 26, 1902

Balasanyan was born, of Armenian lineage, in the present capital of the Turkmen S.S.R., just across the mountains from the Iranian border. On his graduation at age thirty-three from the Moscow Conservatory, where he studied composition with Kabalevsky [2058], two years his junior, he was sent off to Dushanbe (alias Stalinobad), just north of the Afghan border, to help the Tadzhiks create an approvable national art music. He succeeded so well that he was named (among other state honors) "People's Artist of the Tadzhik S.S.R." RECORDINGS: There are recordings of two works that apparently became very popular in Russia, the *7 Armenian Songs* for orchestra and a dance suite from the 1947 ballet *Leili and Medjnun* (which work was also filmed). Also recorded is the Symphony for Strings.

[2022] JERGER, Wilhelm Franz (Yâr'-ger, Vil'-helm Frànts)
MUSICOLOGIST, CONTRABASSIST, TEACHER, ADMINISTRATOR
BORN: Vienna, September 27, 1902
DIED: Linz, April 24, 1978

Jerger began his musical career as a Vienna choirboy, studied at the Vienna Academy with Franz Schalk, Eusebius Mandyczewski, and Guido Adler, and took a baccalaureate degree from the university there. He played bass viol for many years in the Vienna Philharmonic and taught the instrument privately. He gave up that career in 1948 and took a Ph.D. in musicology from the University of Fribourg in Switzerland in 1952, taught there for five years, and then directed the Linz Conservatory until his retirement in 1974. He also composed. RECORDINGS: There is a recording of his *Salzburger Hof- und Barockmusik.*

[2023] NUSSIO, Otmar (Nōōs'-yō, Ōt'-mär)
FLUTIST, CONDUCTOR
BORN: Grosseto, October 23, 1902

Part Hungarian by descent and Tuscan born, Nussio studied at the Milan Conservatory and then with Respighi [1718] in Rome, and made his career in Switzerland, where he settled in 1936 as professor of flute at the Zürich Conservatory. Two years later he was put in charge of the Swiss-Italian Radio Orchestra. His light music concerts in Lugano have made him in effect the Arthur Fiedler of Switzerland. Though he has written some serious if conservative music, most of his compositions are in the category of his concerts. RECORDINGS: There is a recording of his orchestral suite on Swiss folktunes, *Folklore d'Engadine.*

[2024] KAUFMANN, Armin (Kouf'-màn, Àr'-mēn)
VIOLINIST, VIOLIST, TEACHER
BORN: Leberecht (now Itzkany), October 30, 1902
DIED: Vienna, June 30, 1980

Kaufmann was born in a Rumanian town in easternmost Austria-Hungary, of German stock. His father, a composer of sorts, was his first teacher. At the outbreak of war in 1914, the family moved west and settled in Carinthia. Kaufmann continued his musical studies in Brünn (Brno) and then went to Vienna to study with Joseph Marx [1747] at the academy there. He became a professional violist, toured with the Rothschild String Quartet, and in 1938 became first violist of the Vienna Symphony, from which he retired in 1966. He also taught for a time before World War II at the People's Conservatory. He wrote most of his orchestral music (which includes 4 symphonies and a piano concerto) for Franz Litschauer's Vienna Chamber Orchestra. Among his many other compositions are chamber pieces that include variously parts for mandolin, zither, and tarogato (a sort of Hungarian folk clarinet) and many fine songs. RECORDINGS: His *Music for Trumpet and Strings* was recorded.

[2025] RODRIGO, Joaquín (Rōth-rē'-gō, Hwà-kēn')
TEACHER
BORN: Sagunto, November 22, 1902

Thanks largely to the popularity of two works, the Valencia-born Rodrigo is perhaps the best-known Spanish composer of his generation worldwide. He lost his eyesight at the age of three as the result of an accident. His musical gift was noted early, and after taking lessons with local teachers, he went to Paris in 1927 for five years of study with Paul Dukas [1574], getting further help and advice from his countrymen Manuel de Falla [1688] and the pianist Ricardo Viñes. In 1933 he married a Turkish pianist, Victoria Kamhi (who later provided the scenario for his 1955 ballet *Pavana real [Royal Pavane].)* On going home he was awarded a fellowship that enabled him to return to Paris to study musicology with Maurice Emmanuel [1544] and André Pirro. The Spanish Civil War prevented him from going back there until 1939. It was in that year that he completed his first major composition—the one that would make his name—the *Concierto de Aranjuez* for guitar and orchestra. It was premiered in Barcelona in 1940, but world conditions prevented its general triumph for nearly a decade. In 1947 he became the first intendant of the Manuel de Falla Chair at the University of Madrid and shortly afterward was receiving invitations and commissions from both hemispheres. He had another considerable success in 1954 with his *Fantasía para un gentilhombre (Fantasy for a Courtier),* also for guitar and orchestra, based on guitar pieces by Gaspar Sanz [533]. Rodrigo has written a number of other concerted pieces, music for piano and for guitar, a number of fine songs, a zarzuela, and an opera. RECORDINGS: Apart from innumerable recordings of the two most popular concerti, one finds others of the *Concert-Serenade* for harp and orchestra; *Concierto madrigal* for two guitars; *Concierto andaluz* for four guitars; *Concierto de estio* for violin; *Concierto en modo galante* and *Concierto como un divertimento* for cello; *Concierto Pastoral* for flute; and the *Sones en la giralda* for harps. (The *Aranjuez* has also been transcribed for harp.) Other orchestral recordings include *Per la flor del Iliri blau; Musica para un jardin; A la busca del mas allá; Zarabanda lejana y villancico;* the song cycles *Triptic de Mosen Cinto* and *Cuatro madrigales amatorios;* and the cantata *Musica para un Códice Salmantino.* A number of small pieces for guitar and piano have also been recorded.

[2026] SAVAGNONE, Giuseppe (Sà-vàn-yō'-nä, Jōō-sep'-pä)
TEACHER, CONDUCTOR
BORN: Palermo, November 27, 1902

Sicilian-born Giuseppe Savagnone was educated in his native city and has taught at the conservatory there and in Rome. He is described as a philosopher, has conducted choirs, is the inventor of a harmonic system that he designates as "prismatism" (which he explains in a 1966 book on the subject), has composed twelve-tone music, and had an opera, *Millesima seconda,* produced in Palermo in 1949. RECORDINGS: There is a recording of his Concerto for Horn.

[2027] SZABÓ, Ferenc (Sȧ'-bō, Fe-rents')
VIOLINIST, PIANIST, CONDUCTOR,
TEACHER
BORN: Budapest, December 27, 1902
DIED: Budapest, November 4, 1969

Szabó took up study of the violin at fourteen and at nineteen was admitted to the Academy in Budapest, where his most important teachers were Leo Weiner **[1792]** and Zoltan Kodály **[1760]**. In the mid-1920s he was caught up in the proletarian (i.e., Communist) ferment. He conducted something called the Anti-Alcoholic Workers' Choir and later conducted an orchestra in Kispest, just outside the capital. After traveling in central Europe for a couple of years, he gravitated to Russia and settled there. There he turned out works with such titles as *Lenin Is Dead!* and *Class Struggle.* In 1942 he fought for his hosts in the Great Patriotic War and in 1945 came marching home again with the Victorious and Liberating Red Army. He was almost immediately given a professorship at the Budapest Academy and following the upheaval of the mid-1950s was made its director for nearly a decade, 1958–67. Beginning much in step with the middle European modernism of the 1920s, he moved through the populism of the Stalin era to a sound conservatism with decidedly national overtones. RECORDINGS: A number of works have been recorded by Hungaroton—*In Fury Rose the Ocean* (oratorio); *Wolf-Song, Confession,* and *3 Small Choruses* (choral); the ballet suite *Lúdas Matyi; Lyric Suite* for string orchestra; and the Concerto for Orchestra ("Homecoming").

[2028] HIVELY, Wells
PIANIST, TEACHER
BORN: San Joaquin Valley, Calif., 1902
DIED: Palm Beach, Fla., 1969

A product of the Paris Conservatory, the Brussels Conservatory, and the Juilliard School, Hively seems to have been a local celebrity in Palm Beach, Florida, where he taught and played. He composed a one-act opera, *The Sleeping Beauty,* orchestral works, chamber music, and songs. RECORDINGS: Two orchestral works, *Tres Himnos* and *Icarus,* have been recorded by (respectively) Howard Hanson and William Strickland.

[2029] VLASOV, Vladimir Alexandrovich
(Vlȧ'-sof, Vlȧd-yē'-mēr Ȧl-yek-sȧn-drō'-vich)
VIOLINIST, ETHNOMUSICOLOGIST
BORN: Moscow, January 7, 1903

Vlasov was educated in the early Soviet era at the Moscow Conservatory, where he specialized in the violin. Together with his contemporary and fellow student Vladimir Feré, he was shipped off in 1936 to Frunze in the Kirghiz S.S.R. to study the native music and organize a national theater with operas and ballets and other forms of entertainment dear to the heart of all Russian workers. Though the Kirghisi had no tradition for this sort of thing and no notion of Western harmony and such, the intrepid composers, aided by a native musician, Abdylas Moldybaev, managed to put together a music drama called *The Golden Girl* before the year was out. They followed it a year later, still with grave drawbacks, with *Not Death But Life,* a story about the 1916 Kirghiz uprising, which worked well enough to be taken to Moscow for an ethnic hootenanny in 1939. In the latter year a third collaboration, *The Moonlight Beauty,* drawn from the national epic (said to be the longest such work known), featured a ballet whose choreography was based on the movements of native wrestlers, hunters, and cattle breeders (!). This was also taken to Moscow, where it is said to have laid 'em in the aisles. During and after the Great Patriotic War the team continued to turn out operas until Feré's death in 1971. Vlasov, when he was not steeping himself in the local product, wrote concerti, quartets, and other works in the standard Soviet mode of the times. RECORDINGS: His Concerto No. 1 for Cello has been recorded by Mstislav Rostropovich, Gennady Rozhdestvensky conducting.

[2030] BLACHER, Boris (Blȧkh'-er, Bō'-res)
TEACHER
BORN: Newchwang (China), January 19, 1903
DIED: Berlin, January 30, 1975

One of the better known post–World War II German composers, Blacher was nearly fifty before he had any real measure of success or security. Born in a Manchurian port city (variously spelled, and now designated as Yingk'ou) to a German father and a Russian mother, he moved with his family to Irkutsk, Siberia, when he was eleven. He began his musical studies there, then continued them in Harbin (Haerhpin), the Manchurian capital from 1920. He contributed to the city's musical life by orchestrating operas from piano scores for production. In 1922 Herr Blacher took his dependents back to Berlin, just in time for the great postwar financial collapse. On his insistence, Boris set out to become an architect but soon found his way to the Berlin Hochschule, where he studied with Humperdinck's [1480] successor, Friedrich Ernst Koch (1862–1927), until the latter died. Afterward Blacher studied musicology at the university. He wrote a score to accompany a silent film, Bismarck, in 1926, worked as an arranger, and wrote music adventurous enough (coupled with the fact that he had a Jewish grandparent) to make him decidedly unpalatable to the Third Reich. However, he managed to get his music performed (including his 1941 opera Fürstin Tarakanowa [Princess Tarakanova], premiered at Wuppertal in 1941, and two ballets). Thanks to the advocacy of conductor Karl Böhm, he was appointed to the faculty of the Dresden Conservatory in 1938 but was shortly dismissed.

In 1946 he returned to teaching at the music school in Zehlendorf, a Berlin suburb and was brought back to the Hochschule as professor two years later. In his last thirty years he composed successfully, prolifically, and eclectically. He availed himself of such extremes as jazz and twelve-tone music, invented a system of mathematically progressive metrical changes (variable meters), and became an authority on electronic composition. In 1948 he created something of a scandal with his stage piece Die Nachtschwalbe (The Night Swallow) about the sexual underworld, and another with his brief Abstrakte Oper Nr. 1 (1953), which American critic Henry Pleasants (perhaps taking the work too seriously) termed "the worst opera ever written." The libretto to this work, which consists solely of a series of nonsense syllables, was by Werner Egk [1993], whom Blacher succeeded as director of the Hochschule from 1953 until he retired in 1970. Blacher was composer-in-residence at Tanglewood in 1955 and president of the Berlin Academy from 1968 to 1971. He wrote several of his own libretti and contributed substantially to four libretti for his pupil Gottfried von Einem [2276].

RECORDINGS: Blacher has been fairly well represented on records—Abstrakte Oper Nr. 1; (orchestral works) Concertante Musik, Paganini Variations, Concerto No. 2 for Piano, Orchester-Fantasie, Ornamente, and Studie im Pianissimo; (chamber works) Divertimento for trumpet, trombone, and piano; Blues/Espagnola/Rumba philharmonica for twelve cellos; (vocal) Aprèslude, 13 Ways of Looking at a Blackbird, Francesca da Rimini, and 3 Psalms; (piano) Ornamente, 24 Preludes, a sonata, 2 sonatinas, Studie, and 3 Pièces; and (electronic music) Elektronische Impulse.

[2031] RAINIER, Priaulx (Rā-nēr', Prē'-ō)
VIOLINIST, TEACHER
BORN: Howick, South Africa, February 3, 1903

Unusually, in an age when composers have increasingly come from urban musical centers, Priaulx Rainier was born and spent her childhood in a backwoods village in Natal. After some study at the South African College of Music in Cape Town, she entered, at seventeen, the Royal College of Music in London as a violin student of E. Rowsby Woof. Her composition teacher there was Sir John McEwen (1868–1948), though in the late 1930s she took the opportunity of working under Nadia Boulanger in Paris. In 1942 she became professor of harmony and counterpoint at the Royal Academy of Music, of which she was made a fellow a decade later. She retired in 1961. Her compositions date mostly from the post-Boulanger period and are characterized by a sort of pointillistic use of small motifs. RECORDINGS: Although she has composed fairly prolifically for orchestra, she is represented on records only by a number of chamber pieces—Trio for Oboes; the 1939 String Quartet; Quanta for oboe quartet; and the vocal Cycle for Declamation for unaccompanied tenor.

[2032] TREXLER, Georg (Treks'-ler, Gā'-ôrg)
ORGANIST
BORN: Pirna, Saxony, February 3, 1903

Trexler studied with the organist Karl Straube, a latter-day successor of J. S. Bach [684] at the Thomaskirche, and with musicologist-composer Karl Reuter. He was himself organist of Leipzig's Provost's Church until 1971 and a professor at the Leipzig

Conservatory until 1970. He wrote orchestral and chamber music, but mostly religious pieces and works for organ. He was consciously influenced by Bruckner [1293]. RECORDINGS: There are recordings of organ pieces such as the *Introduction and Passacaglia* and the *Meditations* (both on Bruckner themes).

[2033] BLANTER, Matvey Isakovich
(Blån'-ter, Måt-vā'-ē Ē-zå-kō'-vich)
BORN: Potchep, February 10, 1903

Born in a Russian city between Moscow and Kiev, Blanter studied music just before the Revolution in Kursk and just after in Moscow, first at the Moscow Conservatory and then with Georgi Conus (1862–1933). In the heady 1920s he was an enthusiastic proponent of jazz, thus making himself a sitting duck for Stalin's later disapproval. However, he made an adroit recovery and at the height of the Stalinist repressions became extremely successful as a writer of lighthearted theater music and popular songs. In his 1938 song "Katyusha," he achieved a hit of enormous proportions that was sung by Russian troops during World War II and by international adherents of Sovietism afterward. After the Khrushchev "thaw," Blanter again made a pitch for jazz. RECORDINGS: Some of his songs (including "Katyusha") have been recorded.

[2034] LOPATNIKOFF, Nikolai Lvovich
(Lō-påt'-nē-kof, Nē'-kō-lī L'vō'-vich)
PIANIST, TEACHER, ENGINEER
BORN: Reval (Talinn), March 16, 1903
DIED: Pittsburgh, October 7, 1976

The first half of Nikolai Lopatnikoff's (his spelling) life was especially troubled by political events. As a youngster he studied at the St. Petersburg Conservatory but moved with his family to Finland when the October Revolution struck. After further study in Helsinki, he went to Germany, where he studied with the pianist Willi Rehberg and with Ernst Toch [1824]. He married Nora Laschinsky in 1926, took an engineering degree at the University of Karlsruhe in 1928, and settled in Berlin. He was making a solid name for himself (he premiered his 2 piano concerti as soloist in Germany) when the Nazis arrived in 1933 and he decamped for Helsinki again. A year later he moved to London, but the events of 1939 again uprooted him and he settled in the United States. He became a citizen and taught at Carnegie-Mellon Institute from 1945 until

his retirement at sixty-five. In 1951, his wife having died, he married Sara Henderson Hay. An effective practitioner of the neoclassic doctrine (though he claimed to have been influenced by some of the Russian Romantics), he wrote almost exclusively for orchestra or other instrumental combinations. (An opera, *Danton,* remains unstaged, though orchestral excerpts have been performed in concert.) RECORDINGS: Three orchestral works have been recorded—the 1945 Concertino for Orchestra; the 1959 *Music for Orchestra;* and *Variazioni Concertanti,* 1958. The 1946 *Variations and Epilogue* for cello and piano and the Sonata No. 2 for Violin and Piano have also been recorded.

[2035] OLSEN, Carl Gustav Sparre (Ōl'-sen, Kärl Gōōs'-tåf Spär'-re)
VIOLINIST, CONDUCTOR, CRITIC
BORN: Stavanger, April 25, 1903

Sparre Olsen may be considered chiefly a pupil of Fartein Valen [1822], though he later studied with the German Max Butting (1888–1976) and with Percy Grainger [1749]. In 1933, after a decade as violinist with the Oslo Philharmonic, he settled in Bergen, where he played in the local orchestra, conducted a choral society, and wrote music criticism. He was awarded a lifetime pension in 1936. Olsen's music, which includes a number of large choral pieces as well as orchestral and chamber works and songs (the last popular in Norway) is of a strongly nationalistic bent, not at all like the music of Valen. Like Valen, however, Olsen may be described as primarily a miniaturist. RECORDINGS: A number of short orchestral pieces have been recorded—*Canticum; Adagio* for strings; *Serenade* for flute and strings; Concertino for Horn and Strings; and a suite from his incidental music to *Anne of Torp.* Vocal recordings include the 2 *Edda Songs* for soprano and orchestra; 7 *Krokann Songs;* and some songs for chorus. Miscellaneous instrumental snippets on disc include *Metamorphose* for cello solo; the Wind Quintet; *Suite for 3 Woodwinds* for flute, oboe, and clarinet; *Lamento* for clarinet and bassoon; *Variations on a Norwegian Folk Tune* for piano; *Intermezzo* for flute and piano; and 6 *Old Village Songs from Lom* for solo violin.

[2036] BERKELEY, (Sir) Lennox Randall Francis
TEACHER, RADIO OFFICIAL
BORN: Boar's Hill, Oxfordshire, May 12, 1903

Sir Lennox Berkeley's title is honorary—it was bestowed upon him in 1974—but he would have inherited an earldom had not his father fallen out with his parents, joined the Royal Navy (where he rose to a captaincy), and married a Frenchwoman. Though Lennox liked music, he did not study it until he was grown. He was educated at Gresham's and St. George's Schools, then matriculated at Merton College, Oxford, where he read philosophy and French literature, took some organ lessons, and began trying to compose. He showed some of his efforts to the visiting Maurice Ravel [1666], who recommended that he study with Nadia Boulanger. The next year, 1927, Berkeley went to Paris and sat at her feet for five years, inaugurating a lifelong friendship. (Other long-term friendships were with Poulenc [1960] and Benjamin Britten [2215], with the latter of whom Berkeley wrote the *Mont Juic Suite* in 1937.) Not unexpectably he was influenced by Stravinskian [1748] neo-classicism and Parisian musical irreverence—and by Roman Catholicism, to which he converted in 1928. He was a music director under Arthur Bliss [1854] at the BBC during the war years and married a colleague, Elizabeth Bernstein, in 1946. Their son Michael (1947–) has made a name for himself as a composer. In the year of his marriage, Berkeley also began twenty-two years of teaching composition at the Royal Academy of Music, retiring in 1968.

Around 1940 Berkeley struck out in a less laconic, more lyrical vein and a more personal direction, influenced oddly by both Beethoven [1063] and Webern [1773], but not adhering to the serialist gospel. In the 1940s and 1950s he turned out several stage, film, and radio scores. The first of his four operas, *Nelson*, was produced by the Sadler's Wells company in 1954. Britten produced two of the others, the one-act *A Dinner Engagement* of 1954 and *Castaway* of 1967, at his Aldeburgh Festival. In later years Berkeley moved more and more toward atonal writing but usually preserved a tonal point of reference. His output runs to around 100 opus numbers and also includes a ballet, an oratorio, 4 symphonies, several concerti, 3 string quartets, sonatas and other chamber works, and many choral works and songs. RECORDINGS: The first three symphonies have been recorded, together with concerti for piano, two pianos, violin, flute, and guitar. Other orchestral recordings include *Mont Juic; Serenade; Divertimento; Antiphon; Sinfonietta;* and the *4 Ronsard Sonnets* for tenor and orchestra. (There is also a recording of an orchestral transcription of Poulenc's [1960] Sonata for Flute and Pi-

ano.) Among the many chamber recordings are the String Trio; Horn Trio; Duo for Cello and Piano; Sonata for Flute and Piano; Sonatina for Flute and Piano; Sextet for Clarinet, Horn, and Strings; Trio for Oboe and Strings; *Diversions* for eight players; Sonatina and *Palm Court Waltzes* for piano duet; some solo piano pieces; and songs.

[2037] WHITLOCK, Percy William
ORGANIST
BORN: Chatham, June 1, 1903
DIED: Bournemouth, May 1, 1946

A Kentishman, Whitlock was educated at the nearby Rochester Choir School, and at King's School, then won a scholarship to the Guildhall School of Music in London, followed by another to the Royal College of Music. At eighteen he became assistant organist of Rochester Cathedral, a job which he afterward combined with that of organist-choirmaster at the Parish Church in his hometown, and other such posts. In 1930 he went to Bournemouth, where he was in charge of music at St. Stephen's and also organist at the Municipal Pavilion. He died there a month short of his forty-third birthday. He was well-known in England as a recitalist and composed a good deal of music for his instrument. RECORDINGS: Some of his organ music appears in recorded recitals.

[2038] KHACHATURIAN, Aram Ilyich
(Khȧ-chȧ-tōōr'-yȧn, Ȧ'-rȧm Ēl'-yich)
CONDUCTOR
BORN: Tbilisi (Tiflis), June 6, 1903
DIED: Moscow, May 1, 1978

On the strength of a couple of short pieces, Aram Khachaturian enjoyed in America, in his heyday, a popularity probably unshared by any of his Soviet colleagues. He was the son of an impecunious Armenian bookbinder and is said to have taught himself to play piano and to have been a high school bandsman, but he had no music lessons until he had almost reached his majority. The family having moved to Moscow, he began taking cello lessons at the Gnessin School in 1922. Three years later its head and founder Mikhail Gnessin (1883–1957), a pupil of Rimsky-Korsakov [1416] and Liadov [1485], took him into his composition class. In 1929 Khachaturian proceeded to the Moscow Conservatory, where his chief teachers were Miaskovsky [1735] and Vassilenko [1628] and where he met his future wife, the composer Nina Makarova (1908–76). During his years there he continued the composing he had begun with Gnessin, turning out an orchestral suite, most of his chamber music, piano pieces, and hymns of various kinds to the state. He marked his graduation in 1934 with his Symphony No. 1 (of 3), but stayed on for another three years. In 1937 he premiered his Concerto for Piano (with perhaps the only solo for a flexatone written by a major composer) in Moscow, and it was soon being performed around the world. A choral *Song about Stalin* put him in solidly with the authorities, and his Concerto for Violin of 1940 repeated the success of its piano counterpart.

After the German invasion of 1941, Khachaturian was, with other national treasures, removed to the hinterlands. In 1942 his ballet *Gayne*, about fertility and patriotism on a collective farm, was triumphantly performed in Molotov (a town just west of the Urals, known before and since as Perm). A reworking of an earlier unsatisfactory ballet called *Happiness*, it occasioned official disapproval after its initial triumphs, but re-emerged in 1957 with a whole new scenario. Meanwhile its flashy "Sabre Dance" had conquered the U.S.S.R.'s new American allies and at one time was a standard on jukeboxes. The waltz from the incidental music to Lermontov's *Masquerade*, also from 1942, became almost as insistently popular. For all that and notwithstanding his having won both the Lenin and Stalin Prizes, Khachaturian was one of those keelhauled by Comrade Zhdanov in 1948 for bourgeois and formalist proclivities; his third symphony was singled out for especial criticism. Khachaturian groveled abjectly, promised to be good, and wrote film scores about Lenin and the Battle of Stalingrad. (But after Stalin died, he published an article demanding that the government give artists latitude.) He had another big success in Russia with his full-length ballet *Spartacus* of 1954, though enthusiasm was decidedly tempered elsewhere. Like much of the composer's later work—the Symphony No. 3 of 1947, the *Concerto-Rhapsodies*—it seems mostly sugar, dough, and air. In his later years Khachaturian taught at both his former schools and appeared increasingly as guest conductor of his own works. He visited the United States in this capacity in early 1968.

At its best Khachaturian's music is fluently melodic, brilliantly colored in the Rimskian tradition, often reflective of Armenian folk materials, and rarely profound. Apart from the workaday stuff—theater and film music and propaganda—it does not bulk very large; to the works noted, one can add only the Concerto for Cello (the "flute concerto" is merely an adaptation of the violin

piece), the 1943 Symphony No. 2, a couple of overtures, and a few minor pieces.

RECORDINGS: Works on records include the ballets *Gayne* and *Spartacus,* a suite from *Masquerade,* the 1934 *Dance Suite,* Symphonies Nos. 1–3, Concerto for Piano, Concerto for Cello, Concerto for Violin (plus the flute transcription), *Concerto-Rhapsody for Piano and Orchestra, Concerto-Rhapsody for Cello and Orchestra,* a suite from the film *The Battle of Stalingrad,* the *Armenian Dances* for band, the 1956 *Ode to Joy* (for forty violins, ten harps, mezzo-soprano, mixed chorus, and orchestra), some marches for military band, the 1932 Trio for Clarinet, Violin, and Piano, the 1961 Sonata for Piano, and some other piano pieces.

[2039] PERCEVAL, Julio *(né* Jules?)
   (Pâr-se-vàl', Hōōl'-yō)
ORGANIST, TEACHER
BORN: Brussels, July 17, 1903
DIED: Santiago de Chile, September 3, 1963 (Baker's says September 7.)

Perceval studied at the Brussels Conservatory with Paul Gilson **[1572]** and was later a pupil of Marcel Dupré **[1806]** in Paris. He emigrated to Argentina in 1926, Hispanicized his name, and became organist of the Teatro Colón, the Central National College of the university, and the cathedral in Buenos Aires. He was naturalized in 1930, joined the faculty of the University of Cuyo at Mendoza in 1939, and became director of its music school. In 1959 he accepted a professorship with the National Conservatory at Santiago; he died there in an automobile accident four years later. A noted performer and improviser on the organ, he wrote a good deal for that instrument as well as some chamber music and songs. RECORDINGS: A few of the songs have been recorded.

[2040] KADOSA, Pál (Ka-dō'-shà, Pàl)
PIANIST, TEACHER
BORN: Léva, September 6, 1903
DIED: Budapest, March 30, 1983

Hardly known outside his own country, Pál Kadosa is justly admired there as a leading composer of the post-Bartók **[1734]** generation (he studied with Kodály **[1760]**), a splendid performer, and a powerful force for contemporary music. Born and reared in what is now Czechoslovakia (his birthplace is called Levice), he began his concert career in 1923 and graduated from the Budapest Academy in 1927. He immediately took a teaching post at the Fodor School and in 1928 founded a performing group dedicated to the presentation of contemporary music. Through this he became a force in the International Society for Contemporary Music at whose annual festivals he and his music were often featured. Owing to politics he was ousted from his teaching post in 1943 and spent the remaining war years teaching at the Goldmark School. After peace came he received a professorship at the Budapest Academy. He has also served on the Hungarian Arts Council, and is an honorary member of the British Royal Academy of Music. Quite prolific, he wrote an opera, 5 cantatas, 8 symphonies, 4 concerti for piano, 2 for violin, 3 string quartets, and much else. Both his music and his playing were strongly influenced by Bartók. RECORDINGS: The Hungarian state recording agency has issued a number of recordings of Kadosa's works, among them the Symphonies Nos. 4, 5, and 7; Concerti for Piano Nos. 3 and 4; Concerti for Violin Nos. 1 and 2; *Pian e forte* and *Serenade* (both orchestral); several of the string quartets; miscellaneous keyboard pieces; and songs.

[2041] DUKELSKY, Vladimir Alexandrovich *(alias* Vernon Duke)
BORN: Parfianovka, October 10, 1903
DIED: Santa Monica, Calif., January 16, 1969

Immensely successful as a composer of musicals in America, Duke-Dukelsky had previously attained a measure of fame for more "serious" compositions. He came into the world somewhat unexpectedly in a village railway station while his mother was on her way to Pskov. He started composing about the time he learned to speak. Still quite young, he entered the Kiev Conservatory, where he studied with Reinhold Glière [1662] and Boleslav Yavorsky (another Taneyev [1492] pupil). In the aftermath of the 1917 Revolution he drifted southward, reaching Constantinople in 1920. He stayed there the better part of two years, then moved on to New York in 1922, and back to Paris in 1924. Having heard his piano concerto, Diaghilev commissioned him to write a ballet which turned out to be *Zéphyr et Flore,* premiered by the Ballets Russes the following January with choreography by Roland Petit. He remained in Europe for some time, producing an opera *(Demoiselle paysanne (Country Miss),* and meeting Serge Koussevitzky [1655], who was sufficiently impressed to perform the first two of Dukelsky's 3 symphonies.

Dukelsky's friendship with the Gershwins [1955] had gotten him interested in the popular musical stage. His name first appeared in a New York theater program as the writer of a song interpolated in a 1926 operetta, *Katja,* and in 1928 he provided the incidental score for Edgar Wallace's play *The Yellow Mask* in London. The following year he returned to New York and, after contributing several songs to the 1930 revues *Garrick Gaieties* and *Three's a Crowd,* wrote *Walk a Little Faster* in 1932 for Beatrice Lillie and Bobby Clark; it contained his first great hit, "April in Paris." At the suggestion of George Gershwin, Dukelsky became "Vernon Duke" in his pop incarnation; later he adopted the name entirely. There followed the *Ziegfeld Follies* in 1934 and 1936, *The Show Is On, Cabin in the Sky* (his own favorite), Eddie Cantor's *Banjo Eyes,* and several less successful pieces, terminating with *The Littlest Revue* in 1956. Meanwhile Dukelsky had been writing "serious" music too—producing most notably an oratorio, *The End of St. Petersburg* in 1938, 2 ballets— *Le Bal des blanchisseuses (The Laundresses' Ball)* in 1956 and *Souvenir de Monte Carlo*— a third symphony, concerti for violin and for cello, and many smaller works. Later he wrote two more ballets, *Emperor Norton* and *Lady Blue.* With the advent of LP records, he started his own company, the Society for Forgotten Music, which brought out a few oddities. He completed the score for the film *Goldwyn Follies* after Gershwin died and in 1955 published his memoirs, *Passport to Paris.* An article chiding Stravinsky [1748] for defecting to the serialists received a scathing reply, entitled "A Cure for V.D.," almost certainly the brainchild of Stravinsky's Craft-altered ego.

RECORDINGS: Apart from Dukelsky's pop songs, there are recordings of *Souvenir de Monte Carlo,* four song cycles (sung by his widow, mezzosoprano Kay McCracken), Sonata No. 2 for Piano, *Parisian Suite, Surrealist Suite* (all with Duke at the piano), a violin sonata, a string quartet, and other chamber pieces.

[2042] GIANNINI, Vittorio (Gē-à-nē'-nē, Vē-tôr'-yō)
TEACHER
BORN: Philadelphia, October 19, 1903
DIED: New York, November 28, 1966

Vittorio Giannini came from a musical family emigrant from Tuscany. His father, Ferruccio Giannini (1868–1948), was a tenor and is said to have made the first commercial operatic recording (for Emil Berliner in

1896); he later became a manufacturer of plaster statues. Vittorio's elder sister (by ten months to the day), named Dusolina, was one of the great operatic sopranos of her generation. Their mother, née Antoniette Briglia, was a violinist and her children's first teacher. Vittorio did so well that he was posted, at the age of ten, to Milan, where he pursued his violinistic studies under Teresina Tua (alias Maria Felicità Tua, Contessa Franchi-Verney della Valletta, and Sister Maria di Gesù). Returning to America at the outbreak of the 1917 war, he continued private studies in New York until in 1925 he won a double scholarship to Juilliard, enabling him to study there with Rubin Goldmark (1872–1936) and violinist Hans Letz. A year after his 1930 graduation, he married Lucia Avella and a year after that won the American Prix de Rome and a three-year stay at the American Academy in that city. This period saw the composition of chamber and vocal music and culminated in the completion of a first opera, *Lucedia*, which was produced at Munich in 1934. It was as a composer of old-fashioned but stageworthy operas that he became best known, although in due course he produced 4 symphonies, several concerti, and much else. His next operatic effort was a treatment of Hawthorne's *The Scarlet Letter*, premiered in Hamburg in the summer of 1938 with his sister Dusolina as the erring Hester Prynne. His growing success won him several commissions. CBS Radio asked for two short operas and broadcast them as they were finished—*Beauty and the Beast* in 1938 (it was first staged in 1946) and *Blennerhasset* in 1939. In the latter year Giannini also served up an *IBM Symphony* to inaugurate that corporation's new office building in New York and was appointed to the faculty of the Juilliard School, where he taught for the rest of his life. The 1940s saw him writing mostly instrumental music and working on an opera for NBC.

Giannini's first marriage ended in divorce in 1951, and two years later he married Joan Adler. That same year the new opera, a version of Shakespeare's *The Taming of the Shrew*, was premiered in Cincinnati. A year later NBC honored its commitment and telecast it. Probably Giannini's masterpiece and certainly one of the most successful American operas to date, it continues to be performed. Its successors—*The Harvest*, Chicago Lyric Opera, 1961; *The Rehearsal Call*, Juilliard, 1962; and *The Servant of Two Masters*, New York City Opera, 1967—have found no such favor. Giannini's second marriage ended in 1963. A year later he became president of the North Carolina School of the Arts, and two years after that he died in his sleep at sixty-three.

RECORDINGS: The Kansas City Lyric Opera has recorded *The Taming of the Shrew*. Other recordings include the Symphony No. 3 for band, *Divertimento No. 2* for orchestra, and songs.

[2043] KAMINSKI, Joseph (Kȧ-mēn'-skē, Yō'-zef)
VIOLINIST
BORN: Odessa, November 17, 1903
DIED: Gedera, Israel, October 14, 1972

One of the many violinists produced by Odessa (though he was trained mostly in Warsaw), Kaminski was the son of an actress prominent in the Yiddish theater. He studied composition with Friedrich Koch (1862–1927), Humperdinck's **[1480]** successor, at the Berlin Hochschule, and with Hans Gál **[1837]** in Vienna. He became concertmaster of the Warsaw Radio Orchestra and first violin of the Warsaw String Quartet. In 1937 he emigrated to Palestine, where he served as concertmaster in the Palestine (Israel) Philharmonic until 1969. Among his compositions are the String Quartet and concerted pieces for trumpet, harp, and violin. RECORDINGS: There are recordings of violin pieces and the String Quartet.

[2044] SANDOVAL, Miguel (Sȧn'-dō-vȧl, Mēg-wel')
PIANIST, CONDUCTOR, RADIO EXECUTIVE
BORN: Guatemala City, November 22, 1903
DIED: New York, August 24, 1953

When Miguel Sandoval was five years old, Luis Felipe Arias, Guatemala's most notable native-born composer up to that time, was shot down in the street. Such events perhaps explain Sandoval's early emigration to New York, where he became an American citizen in 1925. He made a career as accompanist to many well-known singers. For most of the 1940s he was on the staff of CBS Radio and afterward served as director of Radio Guatemala. RECORDINGS: There are recordings of some of his songs—notably on an LP where he accompanies mezzo-soprano Lydia Ibarrondo in several of them.

[2045] ARRIEU, Claude (Ȧr-yö', Klôd)
TEACHER
BORN: Paris, November 30, 1903

Her first name not withstanding, Claude Arrieu is a woman. She graduated from the Paris Conservatoire, where she had studied with pianist Marguerite Long, Paul Dukas [1574], and Jean Roger-Ducasse [1639], in 1932 carrying off a first prize for composition. In 1946 she joined the staff of the French National Radio. She has written chamber music and orchestral works—notably a series of concerti—in a neat neo-classical vein, but her largest output is in dramatic music—operas (several for television), ballets, film, stage, and radio scores. RE-CORDINGS: There is a recording of her Wind Quintet.

[2046] LAVRY, Marc (Làv'-rē, Märk)
CONDUCTOR, RADIO OFFICIAL
BORN: Riga, December 22, 1903
DIED: Haifa, March 24, 1967

A product of the Leipzig Conservatory, Lavry made a name for himself as a theatrical conductor at Saarbrücken and elsewhere in Germany, and composed in a deliberately popular style. As the Nazis began to consolidate their power, he returned to Riga; and three years later, in 1935, he emigrated to Palestine, where he rapidly became recognized as a composer—no doubt because of his espousal of Jewish music and themes. His 1945 opera Dan Ha'shomer is said to have been the first to a Hebrew libretto ever produced, and rather more incredibly he is said to have been the first Jewish inhabitant of Palestine to write symphonic music. In 1951 he was placed in charge of the musical wing of the international radio station in Jerusalem. Lavry wrote a second opera, an oratorio on the Song of Songs, 2 piano concerti, symphonic poems, etc. RECORDINGS: There are recordings of a Suite concertante for flute, viola, and harp, 3 Jewish Dances for violin and piano, and 5 Country Dances for piano.

[2047] ADDINSELL, Richard
PIANIST
BORN: London, January 13, 1904
DIED: London, November 14/15, 1977

Richard Addinsell was distracted from the study of law at Oxford by the musical ramifications of the theater, and, after a crash introductory course at the Royal College of Music, produced a score for Clemence Dane's play Come of Age (which anniversary Addinsell himself had celebrated just three years earlier). Encouraged, he went off to Germany for further enlighten-

ment. In 1933 he came to the United States to provide music for Eva Le Gallienne's production of Alice in Wonderland and stayed to work in the Hollywood studios. During World War II he was back in England, where he teamed up with comedienne Joyce Grenfell for her one-woman revues and wrote film and radio scores. Among the films whose music he composed, one notes Good-Bye, Mr. Chips, 1939; Blithe Spirit, 1945; The Prince and the Showgirl (with Laurence Olivier and Marilyn Monroe), 1957; and Jean Anouilh's The Waltz of the Toreadors, 1962. But the piece that seems to have guaranteed Addinsell immortality was a Rachmaninoffian [1638] one-movement concerto known as the Warsaw Concerto, from a 1941 film about the Nazi rape of Poland (with Anton Walbrook), called Dangerous Moonlight in Great Britain and Suicide Squadron in the United States. RECORDINGS: There are innumerable recordings of the Warsaw Concerto.

[2048] FRID, Géza (Frēd, Gā'-zà)
PIANIST, TEACHER
BORN: Mármarossziget, January 25, 1904

Frid began studying piano in early childhood with his mother. At eight he went to the Budapest Conservatory, where he was a composition pupil of Kodály [1760] and continued his piano instruction with Bartók [1734]. He graduated in 1924, embarked on a career as a concert pianist, made a tour of Italy in 1926, and traveled over Europe as accompanist to the violinist Zoltán Székely. At the end of this activity in 1929 he remained in Amsterdam, became a part of Dutch musical life, and acquired citizenship in 1948. He continued to appear all over the world as pianist and accompanist and in 1964 became professor of ensemble playing at the Utrecht Conservatory. Besides his opera De zwarte bruid (The Black Bride) and 2 ballets, his large catalogue of rather eclectically modern compositions covers the whole spectrum of musical genres. RECORDINGS: Symphonietta, Concertino for 2 Trumpets and Orchestra, and Fugue for four harps.

[2049] DALLAPICCOLA, Luigi (Dàl'-làpēk'-kō-là, Loo-ē'-jē)
PIANIST, WRITER
BORN: Pisino d'Istria, February 3, 1904
DIED: Florence, February 19, 1975

In the Schoenbergian [1657] atmosphere of the post–World War II period, Dallapiccola was probably the most respected Italian composer of his generation. He was born on Austrian soil in what is now coastal Yugoslavia, the son of a teacher of Latin and Greek. He studied piano in childhood. Suspected, like other Istrian Italians, of treasonable sentiments, the Dallapiccolas were arrested in 1914 and placed in a prison camp. Later they were deported to Austria proper and settled in Graz, where Luigi became addicted to opera. When Istria was turned over to Italy at the end of the war, the Dallapiccolas took up their life there. Luigi commuted to Trieste for music lessons with a certain Antonio Illersberg. At eighteen he settled in Florence, where he continued piano lessons with Ernesto Consolo, a pupil of Sgambati [1385]. A year later he entered the conservatory, from which he graduated in 1931. In his final year he took the place of Consolo, who was dying, and also toured with the violinist Sadro Materassi, performing contemporary compositions. (Dallapiccola's thinking about music had been traumatically shaken up by an early encounter with Debussy's [1547] and a later one with Schoenberg's.

Dallapiccola had been composing seriously from his early years in Florence, and now, in part thanks to the advocacy of Alfredo Casella [1767], began winning notice in more advanced circles, mostly with vocal works. In 1934 he became professor of piano ("as a secondary subject") at the conservatory. Four years later he married Laura Luzzato, an employee of the Biblioteca Nazionale. She was Jewish and lost her job soon thereafter, when Mussolini promulgated his anti-Semitic policies to please his northern ally. At the time Dallapiccola was working on his first opera, Volo di notte (Night Flight, after Antoine de Saint-Exupèry), premiered in Florence in 1940. Already embittered by the Fascist rape of Ethiopia, he decided to voice his opposition in his music. The more immediate result was the 1941 Canti di prigionia (Songs from Captivity), scored for chorus, piano, harps, and percussion, and using some twelve-tone experiments. But the major effort was a second opera, Il Prigioniero (The Prisoner), wholly dodecaphonic (according to the composer's own lights), which occupied him for a decade. Doubly endangered by both his marriage and his politics, he took his family in 1943 to Borgunto, one of the Florentine hill towns, and the following year went into hiding in the homes of friends. It was in 1944 that Laura gave birth to a daughter whom they named Annalibera to celebrate the liberation of Florence and the reattainment of their own freedom. In 1955 he added a third "political" composition with the Canti di liberazione (Songs of Liberation).

In the postwar years, especially after the 1950 production of his "sacred opera" Job in Rome, Dallapiccola turned for a time to mostly small forms (especially songs), which reflected his interest in the methods of Webern [1773]. It was at this time that he became an international figure. He came repeatedly to the United States. He taught at Tanglewood in the summers of 1951 and 1952, was visiting professor of music at Queens College, Long Island, in 1956–57 and 1959–60, and was the intendant of the Chair of Italian Culture at the University of California, Berkeley, in 1962–63. His composing fell off sharply after 1960. His only full-length opera, Ulisse (Ulysses), which it took him eight years to complete, was produced in Berlin in 1968 to mixed reviews. His last finished work, Commiato (Envoi) for soprano and chamber orchestra, is dated 1972.

RECORDINGS: Dallapiccola has been fairly well represented on records. The opera Il Prigioniero, Cori de Michelangelo Buonarotti for chorus with and without orchestra; Canti di prigionia for chorus and chamber orchestra; the choral-orchestral Canti di liberazione; Tempus destruendi/Tempus edificandi for chorus; and a number of orchestral works—2 Pezzi; Tartiniana prima for violin and orchestra; Piccola musica notturna (Little Night Music); Three Questions with Two Answers; and Variations. Instrumental recordings include Ciaccona, intermezzo, e adagio for solo cello; 2 Studi for violin and piano; Tartiniana seconda for violin and piano; Sonatina canonica and Quaderno musicale di Annalibera for piano. Works for voice and ensembles of varying sizes make up a considerable portion of the composer's output. Recordings of these include the early, tonal Divertimento in 4 esercizi; 13 Liriche greche (13 Greek Lyrics); Rencevals (Roncevaux); 4 Liriche di Antonio Machado; Goethe-Lieder; Concerto per la notte di Natale 1956 (Concerto for Christmas Night 1956); Parole di San Paolo (Words of St. Paul); 5 Canti; Preghiere (Prayer); and Sicut umbra.

[2050] SKALKOTTAS, Nikolaos (Skàl-kôt'-tàs, Nē-kō-là'-ōs)
VIOLINIST
BORN: Khalkis, March 21, 1904
DIED: Athena, September 20, 1949

Nikolaos, or Nikos, Skalkottas was the son of a flutist who moved from the island of Euboea (once known as Negroponte, now known as Évvoia or Evia) to Athens when his offspring was still an infant. He and his brother gave the boy his initial music lessons. He showed such promise as a violinist that when he was ten they got him into the Athens Conservatory, from which he graduated six years later with a gold medal for his performance of the Beethoven [1063] concerto. In 1921 he won a scholarship to the Berlin Hochschule, where he studied with the violinist Willy Hess and the composers Robert Kahn (1865–1951) and Paul Juon (1872–1940). In 1925 he began studying privately with Philipp Jarnach, Busoni's [1577] pupil, and decided to concentrate on composition, though he used his violin in pickup jobs to keep afloat. He also had some help from another Busoni pupil, Kurt Weill [1978]. When Jarnach left Berlin for the Cologne Conservatory, Skalkottas, now supported by a Maecenas, gravitated to Arnold Schoenberg [1657], with whom he worked for four years, becoming a devout, if highly individual, twelve-tonist. After that he was on his own. Nothing worked out as he had hoped, and when the Nazis took over in 1933, he fled to Athens with only the clothes on his back. For two years he was unable to write at all and eked out a living as a fiddler in an environment he found wholly hostile to everything he believed in. Then in 1935 the dam burst: he suddenly decided that he must compose and circumstances be damned. Four fifths of his surviving output was written in the next decade (the Berlin works have all been lost), ranging from concerti and orchestral suites through a whole array of chamber works to a few songs. Though he occasionally produced a tonal nationalistic piece in an effort to win recognition from the homefolks, the majority of his compositions are in an idiom that is uncompromisingly personal, but perhaps even freer with the Schoenbergian strictures than Alban Berg [1789] had been. In 1946, despite his continued marginal existence, he married. In due time a child was born. In late summer 1949, when a second was imminent, a hernia that had gone untreated for lack of money became strangulated. Not wanting to alarm his wife, he said nothing. Gangrene set in and he died at the age of forty-five. RECORDINGS: Recordings include a third of the orchestral *36 Greek Dances; 10 Sketches* for strings; the *Little Suite* for strings; the Octet for Winds and Strings; the *Variations on a Greek Folktune* for piano trio; Sonatina, *Little Serenade,* and other pieces for cello and piano; Sonatinas Nos. 3 and 4 for Piano and Violin; Duo for Violin and Viola; String Quartet No. 3; *Suites Nos. 3 and 4 for Piano;* and other piano pieces.

[2051] ANTILL, John Henry
CONDUCTOR, RADIO OFFICIAL, SINGER
BORN: Ashfield, N.S.W., April 8, 1904

Born in a suburb of Sydney, John Antill was a choirboy in that city's Episcopal cathedral, then worked for a time as a draftsman for the railways. At the age of twenty-one he entered the Sydney Conservatory, where he majored in voice and studied composition with Alfred Hill (1870–1960), a product of the Leipzig Conservatory who shared his interest in Australian aboriginal music. Antill sang for a while with a local opera company, then joined the Australian Radio, where he was music director and from 1951 federal music editor. In 1946 Eugene Goossens [1878] premiered an orchestral suite extracted from his then-unperformed ballet *Corroboree,* a remarkable evocation of native ceremonies which was first danced as a ballet in 1950. Antill retired in 1971. He wrote, among other things, 3 operas, and five other ballets, but *Corroboree* remains his best-known work. RECORDINGS: Goossens recorded the suite from *Corroboree,* as did the composer. In addition John Lanchberry recently recorded the complete ballet score for Australian EMI.

[2052] PETRASSI, Goffredo (Pä-träs′-sē, Gof-frä′-dō)
ORGANIST, CONDUCTOR, TEACHER, IMPRESARIO
BORN: Zagarolo, July 16, 1904

No Italian composer of his generation challenges Dallapiccola [2049] more strongly for primacy than his exact contemporary Goffredo Petrassi, who has shown himself more productive, more protean—and more uneven—than he. Petrassi was born in a village near Rome. His family moved into the city when he was seven and he sang there as a choirboy. His education ended when at fourteen he went to work as a clerk in a music store. There he seized the opportunity to learn about music at first hand, and his achievement caught the interest of a customer, Alessandro Bustini, who gave him piano lessons. In 1925 Petrassi was able to study composition with one Vincenzo di Donato and was a pupil from 1928 to 1933 at the St. Cecilia Conservatory, where Bustini was his composition teacher and where he studied organ with Fernando Germani. By the turn of the decade Petrassi was composing and his senior project, *3 Cori (3 Choruses),* won him the admiration and advocacy of Alfredo Casella [1767]. In 1934 he was signed on to teach at the school. His career there was interrupted when he was called to manage the Teatro la Fenice at Venice in 1937, but he returned in 1940 to hold the professorship of composition until he retired in 1974. After an early flirtation with Hindemithian [1914] dissonance, Petrassi moved toward a neo-classic approach based on his understanding of early Italian music. Early in the war years, in 1941, he made his most powerful statement up to that time in his setting of Giacomo Leopardi's *Coro di morti (Chorus of the Dead)* for male chorus, brass, string basses, three pianos, and percussion.

Petrassi's movement through atonality to a sort of Webernian [1773] dodecaphony and eventually to a personal radicalism is clearly shown in his series of 8 orchestral concerti that span a forty-year period from 1931 to 1972. The year 1947 saw the unveiling of his 2 ballets, *La Follia di Orlando (Roland's Madness)* and *Ritratto di Don Chisciotte (Portrait of Don Quixote)*. Petrassi's only 2 operas (each in one act), *Il Cordovano (The Cordovan)* and *La Morte dell'aria (The Death of the Air)*, had their premieres in 1949 and 1950 respectively. Among the several incidental scores of the period is one for the film *Bitter Rice*. The year 1951 brought another powerful choral-orchestral piece, *Noche oscura (Dark Night)*, after St. John of the Cross. In the 1950s and early 1960s the composer traveled a good deal to conduct his music and to fill teaching engagements. He was at Tanglewood in the summer of 1956.

RECORDINGS: Concerti for Orchestra Nos. 1–8 have been recorded complete by Zoltán Peskó (some of them have also been done by others). The ballet *Ritratto di Don Chisciotte*, the chamber symphony *Estri*, *Coro di Morti*, and *Noche oscura* are also on record, along with a considerable selection of smaller-scale works—*Nonsense* for unaccompanied chorus; *Elogio per un'Ombra* for solo violin; *Souffle* for solo flutist; *Ala* for flute and harpsichord; *Introduzione e allegro* for violin and piano; *Nunc* for solo guitar; *Serenata I* for flute, viola, bass, harpsichord, and percussion; *Serenata II* for harp, guitar, and mandolin; *Suoni notturni; 3 per 7;* String Quartet; String Trio; *4 Inni sacri* for tenor, baritone, and organ; *2 Liriche di Saffo;* and *Beatitudines* for baritone and five instrumentalists (a memorial to Martin Luther King, Jr.).

[2053] PIPKOV, Lyubomir (Pēp′-kôf, Lyōō′-bō-měr)
ADMINISTRATOR
BORN: Lovech, September 6, 1904
DIED: Sofia, May 9, 1974

Regarded as one of the most important of Bulgarian composers, Pipkov was born in the north central part of the country, the son of a musician who would have preferred him to follow another calling but at last gave him sufficient training to qualify him for the Sofia Conservatory, from which he graduated in 1926. He then proceeded to Paris and studied at the École Normale de Musique with Paul Dukas [1574] and pianist Yvonne Lefébure, remaining in France until 1932, writing several compositions, including what is said to be the first string quartet by a Bulgarian composer in 1928. On his return to Sofia, he became a member of the staff of the opera house there and served as its general manager in the years immediately following World War II. His mature music leans heavily on Bulgarian folksong. He wrote 3 operas (the second, *Momchil,* is firmly set in the Bulgarian repertoire), a secular oratorio, 4 symphonies, concerti, 3 string quartets, 2 cantatas, and many other works (more than seventy opus numbers). RECORDINGS: Quartet No. 3; selections from the operas; and Symphonies Nos. 1 and 4.

[2054] POPOV, Gavriil Nikolayevitch (Pō′-pôf, Gä′-vrē-il Nē-kō-là-yä′-vich)
BORN: Novocherkask, September 12, 1904
DIED: Repino, February 17, 1972

Though born in a spot remote from cultural centers (near the mouth of the Don), Popov was the scion of a cultured family and, prior to the 1917 Revolution, received a thorough humanistic education. He got his musical training first at the Rostov Conservatory, then at that of Leningrad, where he studied with Maximilian Steinberg (1883–1946), and from which he eventually graduated in 1930. He had already won considerable notice as a composer by that time. Though he was in agreement with Soviet thinking on social matters, he insisted that the composer must be individual and *au courant* with modernism. He even made a speech espousing "Soviet symphonism," indicating that new wine could definitely be poured into old bottles. He managed to skate this thin line for a fairly long time and was one of those in the prewar years most called upon for film scores, and the earlier of his 6 symphonies were admired. This, however, did not save him from condemnation by Comrade Zhdanov in 1948, and his career never recovered. RECORDINGS: His socialist-realist Symphony No. 2 "Fatherland" of 1944 and the Chamber Symphony in C Major have been recorded in the U.S.S.R.

[2055] MOHAUPT, Richard (Mō'-houpt, Rēkh-ärt)
PIANIST, CONDUCTOR
BORN: Breslau (Wroclaw), September 14, 1904
DIED: Reichenau (Austria), July 3, 1957

A graduate of the University of Breslau, Mohaupt studied composition with one Rudolf Bilke and conducting with Julius Prüwer. He began his public career as a pianist and conductor, and was attached to several German opera houses at one time or another. For a time he got along with the Nazis and saw productions of an opera and a ballet in the 1930s, but his refusal to forswear his Jewish spouse made his future in Germany look dismal, and in 1939 he emigrated to the United States. There he became well known, a number of his compositions receiving nationwide broadcasts. He returned to writing for the stage after the war and had productions of three more operas and several ballets. He moved back to Europe in 1955 and died two years later at fifty-two. RECORDINGS: The 1954 opera *Double Trouble* and the 1946 *Stadtpfeifermusik (Town Piper Music)* for orchestra have been recorded by Robert Whitney and the Louisville Orchestra (which commissioned the former work).

[2056] KALNIŅŠ, Jānis (or John) (Kȧl'-nēnch, Yȧ'-nēsh)
ORGANIST, CONDUCTOR, TEACHER
BORN: Pernu, November 3, 1904 (Baker's says Riga, November 2)

Claimed, with propriety, by both Latvians and Canadians, Estonian-born Jānis Kalniņš was the son of Alfreds Kalniņš, composer in 1920 of the first Latvian national opera *(Banuta)*, who lived for a time in New York City. Jānis learned organ from his father, studied at the Riga Conservatory with Joseph Wihtol (or Vitols), and then went to Germany to study conducting with Hermann Abendroth, Leo Blech, and Erich Kleiber. From 1923 to 1933 he was conductor of the National Theater in Riga and then for eleven more years of the National Opera. Wartime conditions and the takeover of Latvia drove him to Stockholm in 1944, where he conducted at the Royal Opera and was awarded the Order of Gustav Vasa. In 1948 he emigrated to Canada and settled in New Brunswick. Now John Kalnins, he became organist in Fredericton, then teacher at the local teachers' college, and in 1962–68 became conductor of the New Brunswick Symphony. His compositions include 4 op-

eras *(Hamlet* and three others), 3 symphonies, a violin concerto, other orchestral music, choral works, chamber music, and songs. RECORDINGS: His cantata *The Long Night* has been recorded by Longins Apkalņš.

[2057] SANTÓRSOLA, Guido (Sȧn-tôr'-sō-la, Gwē'-dō)
VIOLIST, CONDUCTOR, WRITER, ADMINISTRATOR
BORN: Canosa di Puglia, November 18, 1904

Santórsola's parents emigrated from the Italian *mezzogiorno* to São Paulo, Brazil, in 1910. The child showed prodigal abilities and was appearing as a violinist at the age of nine. A graduate of the local conservatory, he obtained a government grant to study at the Naples Conservatory and then at Trinity College in London. He returned to Brazil in 1925, played viola in the Paulist Quartet and in the São Paulo Symphony, taught at the conservatory, and founded the Instituto Musical Brasileiro in São Paulo. He became a Brazilian citizen in 1936, but by then he had already joined the Montevideo Radio Orchestra as a violist. He has since been active chiefly in Uruguay, where he has been director of the Normal School of Music and the opera in Montevideo. He has also written music criticism. He has composed choral, orchestral, and chamber music, but his international reputation depends largely on several works for guitar. RECORDINGS: The Concerto for 2 Guitars and Orchestra and the Concertino for Guitar and Orchestra have been recorded, as have several solo guitar pieces.

[2058] KABALEVSKY, Dmitri Borisovitch (Kȧ-bȧ-lef-skē, D'mē'-trē Bō-rē-sō'-vich)
PIANIST, CONDUCTOR, TEACHER
BORN: St. Petersburg, December 30, 1904

Kabalevsky, with Khatchaturian **[2038]** and Khrennikov **[2208]**, is one of the "three K's" fostered by the early Bolshevist years of the USSR. The son of a government worker, he taught himself to play the piano by ear in childhood. When he was fourteen, the Kabalevskys moved to Moscow, where he began a seven-year apprenticeship at the Scriabin School. His chief teacher was the German-trained Liadov **[1485]** protégé Grigori Catoire (1861–1926). In 1925 he moved on to the Moscow Conservatory, where he studied piano with the great old teacher Alexander Goldenweiser and composition with Miaskovsky [1735]. He completed his studies in 1930 and two years later was appointed to the faculty, where he was soon named professor of piano. During his student years, he experimented with musical collectivism as a member of a group called PROKOLL (an acronym for "Production Collective"); its crowning achievement (if that is the expression) was an oratorio, *The Path of October,* composed by eight persons. But this was a short-term affair, and by the mid-1930s Kabalevsky was being noticed abroad, especially for his early piano concerti and symphonies.

The year 1938 saw the premiere of his first (and best-known) opera *Colas Breugnon* (which he largely rewrote, in greater consistency with Rolland's novel, thirty years later). During the Great Patriotic War, Kabalevsky ground out a quantity of not-so-great propagandistic *Gebrauchsmusik.* As a dependable apologist for socialist realism, he became one of the leading figures in the Organizational Committee. During the Zhdanov attacks on Russian music, he was one of those who groveled and cried *"Mea culpa,"* which action did not endear him to some of his less yielding confreres. In 1956 he was sent to the United States as part of a cultural delegation, and he went on to hold other important governmental posts and to be given government awards. He toured fairly widely both as a pianist and conductor (mostly in his own music). His work is generally conservative, clearly influenced by the old nationalist school, and making some use of folk materials.

RECORDINGS: The opera *Colas Breugnon* (revised version) has been recorded—as have excerpts from the opera *The Taras Family;* the complete 1963 *Requiem;* incidental music for *The Comedians* and for Shakespeare's *Romeo and Juliet;* the Concerto for Violin; Concerti for Cello Nos. 1 and 2; Concerti for Piano Nos. 2–4; Symphonies Nos. 2 and 4; the Op. 57 *Cantata; School Years Rhapsody* for piano and orchestra; *Good Night* for vocal soloists, chorus, and orchestra; the symphonic poem *Spring;* the *Overture Pathetique;* Sonatas for Piano Nos. 2 and 3; a good deal of other piano music; and songs.

[2059] TIPPETT, (Sir) Michael Kemp
TEACHER, CONDUCTOR, WRITER
BORN: London, January 2, 1905

Tippett has apparently inherited Britten's [2215] place as England's best-known living composer (on an international scale). That

he was born nearly eight years earlier may make that statement seem odd, but Tippett was, one might say, tortoise to Britten's hare. (None of his operas, on which much of his fame rests, were produced until after his fiftieth birthday.)

Ultimately of Cornish descent, Tippett grew up in Suffolk, in Provence, and in Italy. After attending a public school in Lincolnshire, he entered the Royal College of Music, where he was a pupil of the sound if stodgy Charles Wood [1579] and R. O. Morris (1886–1948), and (for conducting) the musical knights Adrian Boult and Malcolm Sargent. Apart from these influences, he found himself drawn to a heterogeny of others that included Beethoven [1063], Stravinsky [1748], jazz, and the English Tudor composers. His first job after graduation was as a teacher of French in another public school. He found this constraining, however, and resigned in favor of a private life in a Surrey village. There he made ends meet by writing *Gebrauchsmusik* for local groups. His ballad opera *Robin Hood* was created for unemployed Yorkshire coal miners to produce. He also wrote a symphony and some other works, but in the mid-1930s he disowned all his early compositions and started over. He began to come into his own with the 1937 *Fantasy-Sonata* for piano (the first of his 3 piano sonatas) and the 1939 Concerto for Double String Orchestra, both of which won him considerable attention by way of small-label recordings, but his first major success was his oratorio *A Child of Our Time.* Based on the true story of a tormented young Jew who had assassinated a Nazi diplomat in Paris, and embodying, in lieu of chorales, settings of black spirituals, it was begun two days after the outbreak of the 1939 war, though not produced until 1944. It is not incidental that he sought the advice of T. S. Eliot here. Highly literate, a reader of the Greek classics and modern psychology, Tippett was steeped in the output of his literary contemporaries such as Auden and Spender, and shared their humanitarian and socialistic views. Hence with the outbreak of war he declared himself a conscientious objector and underwent a period of imprisonment.

After Morley College, the night school connected with the Old Vic, had been hit in one of the air raids following the French collapse in 1940, Tippett was asked to become its director and, so to speak, pick up the pieces. He served laudably in this capacity for eleven years, during which time he produced the *Fantasia on a Theme of Handel* (for piano and orchestra), the orchestral *Suite in D Major* (marking the birth of

Prince Charles), the first three string quartets, and the first (numbered) symphony. He resigned his post in 1951 to return to full-time composition. The first and perhaps most successful of his 4 mature operas, *The Midsummer Marriage* (to his own libretto, heavily influenced by Eliot, Yeats, and Jung, *inter alias),* was produced at Covent Garden four years later. The year 1955 also saw the premiere of the Concerto for Piano, and it was followed by several choral works and the second symphony, and, at Coventry in 1962, by a second opera, *King Priam.* In 1959 Tippett was named Commander of the British Empire by Queen Elizabeth. The Concerto for Orchestra appeared in 1963, based in part on material from *King Priam.* The decade of the 1960s also produced the Sonata No. 2 for Piano and the choral *Vision of St. Augustine. The Shires' Suite* of 1970 reflects Tippett's work with the remarkable Leicestershire Schools Symphony Orchestra, whose annual festival he oversees and which he took on a European tour in 1966 (and with which he and several of his important contemporaries have recorded.) That same year he was knighted. Covent Garden produced his third opera, *The Knot Garden,* in 1970. The song cycle *Songs for Dov* was presented in 1971, and Symphony No. 3 followed in 1972. The year 1977 saw the premieres of the fourth opera, *The Ice Break,* and Symphony No. 4. Tippett now lives in rural Wiltshire. Apart from the honors noted, he has received several honorary degrees and membership in the American Academy of Arts and Letters. He has produced most of his own texts and libretti (not to everyone's liking) and has published a book, *Moving into Aquarius.* More recent premieres include the 1978 String Quartet No. 4; the 1979 Concerto for Violin, Viola, and Cello; and the 1984 oratorio *The Mask of Time*—the last two works premiered by Sir Colin Davis in (respectively) London and Boston. *The Mask of Time* was conceived as a companion piece to *A Child of Our Time,* but whereas the earlier work focused on the human condition in the present, *The Mask of Time* has a broader scope, extending from prehistory up to the present time; a third oratorio (or possibly an opera) is contemplated which will focus on the future.

RECORDINGS: There are complete versions of three of the four operas—*The Midsummer Marriage, King Priam,* and *The Knot Garden.* Also recorded are the choral-orchestral *A Child of Our Time, The Shires' Suite,* and *The Vision of St. Augustine;* and the orchestral song cycle *Songs for Dov,* a spin-off of *The Knot Garden;* there are broadcast tapes of *The Mask of Time,* but no announcement of a recording as of this writing. Orchestral recordings include the 4 symphonies; the *Ritual Dances* extracted from *The Midsummer Marriage;* Concerto for Double String Orchestra; *Fantasia on a Theme of Handel* for piano and orchestra; *Little Music* for strings; *Suite in D* (for the birthday of Prince Charles); *Fantasia Concertante on a Theme of Corelli* for strings; *Divertimento on Sellinger's Round* for chamber orchestra; Concerto for Piano; Concerto for Orchestra; and the Concerto for Violin, Viola, Cello, and Orchestra. Other recordings include String Quartets Nos. 1–3; all the piano sonatas; Sonata for 4 Horns; *Fanfare* for brass; the song cycles *Boyhood's End, The Heart's Assurance, Songs for Ariel,* and *Songs for Achilles;* the choral works *The Weeping Babe, Magnificat and Nunc Dimittis, 4 Songs from the British Isles,* and miscellaneous choral pieces. The composer can be heard as conductor of the *Suite in D,* excerpts from *The Shires' Suite,* and in Purcell's 1692 *St. Cecilia Ode.*

[2060] HALFFTER (ESCRICHE), Ernesto (Hálf'-ter Ä-skrē-chä, Är-näs'-tō)
CONDUCTOR
BORN: Madrid, January 16, 1905

Halffter is one of a musical family: his elder brother Rodolfo **[1985]** and his nephew Cristóbal (1930–) are both well-known composers. The proclivity did not extend to his parents, however; it was his grandmother who got him, at the age of four, interested in the piano, she being an Italian-opera buff. Four years later he was given a real teacher. Afterward Manuel de Falla **[1688]** took him on, and he is today perhaps that master's most famous pupil. At eighteen he had his two *Symphonic Sketches* performed in public and a year later was given the conductorship of the Orquesta Bética de Sevilla, which Falla himself had founded and with which Halffter presented premieres of many contemporary works. At twenty-six he attracted international attention with his *Sinfonietta,* whose success was outstripped by the 1928 *Sonatina,* used by the great dancer La Argentina as a ballet score. In 1936, because of the Spanish Civil War, Halffter took his family to Lisbon and remained there until 1960. Halffter's music shows some influence from Ravel **[1666]**, with whom he had a close friendship. Early in his career he developed a film score for a treatment of Mérimée's *Carmen* into a big opera *La Muerte de Carmen (Carmen's Death),* but his most important venture in this field is perhaps his com-

pletion of Falla's fragmentary *Atlántida*. RE-
CORDINGS: Halffter is represented on records by a number of orchestral works—*Sinfonietta, Rapsodia portuguesa* for piano and
orchestra, Concerto for Guitar, *Chanson du
laternier,* and suites from the ballets *Sonatina* and *Cojo enamorado.*

[2061] SANDI, Luis (Sàn'-dē, Lo͞o-ēs')
CONDUCTOR, CRITIC, EDUCATIONIST
BORN: Mexico City, February 22, 1905

A product of Mexico's National Conservatory, Sandi studied violin, voice, and composition there and conducted a student choir.
In 1937 he founded the soon-famous Coro de
Madrigalistas, which he conducted for
twenty-eight years. He taught in Mexican
schools from the mid-1920s and rose to the
directorship of the music section of the ministry of education. Later he held a similar
post in the Fine Arts Institute. He served as
a newspaper reviewer and critic and wrote a
standard musical textbook. His compositions are frequently based on Mexican folk
music. RECORDINGS: There are recordings of
his *Yaqui Music* and a suite from his
"Maya" ballet, *Bonampak.*

[2062] FROMM, Herbert
CONDUCTOR, ORGANIST
BORN: Kitzingen, February 23, 1905

After studying in Munich and conducting
for four years in Bielefeld and Würzburg,
Fromm had his career terminated by the Nazis, and in 1937 he emigrated to the United
States. He soon found employment as a synagogue organist in Buffalo and in 1941 became music director of Temple Israel in Boston, where he officiated for many years. He
has written a good deal of liturgical music
and some more abstract works. RECORD-
INGS: Works recorded include *Transience*
(cantata), *Fantasy* (for piano), String Quartet, *Partita* (for organ), *6 Shakespeare Songs,*
and some cantorials.

[2063] WARREN, Elinor Remick
PIANIST
BORN: Los Angeles, February 23, 1905

Ms. Warren studied privately in Los Angeles
and was already publishing songs by the
time she graduated from the Westlake
School for Girls. She attended Mills College
in Oakland, studied in New York with organist Clarence Dickinson and pianists
Frank LaForge and Paolo Gallico, and in

Paris with Nadia Boulanger. She has appeared as a concert pianist and an accompanist. Among her awards is an honorary doctorate from Occidental College. As a composer she is best known for her songs and
choral music. RECORDINGS: Her 1954 *Suite
for Orchestra* and her 1961 cantata *Abram in
Egypt* have been recorded by William Strickland and Roger Wagner (respectively). A
few songs have also been recorded.

**[2064] LANDRÉ, Guillaume Louis Frédé-
ric, Jr.** (Làn-drā', Gē-yōm' Lo͞o-ē'
Frā-dâr-ēk')
LAWYER, TEACHER
BORN: The Hague, February 24, 1905
DIED: Amsterdam, November 6, 1968

Guillaume Landré was son, namesake, and
pupil of a respected composer, critic,
teacher, and music historian, who was
known as Willem Landré. He did not, however, at first pursue a musical career but
studied law at Utrecht, taking a master's degree in that discipline in 1929. En route, nevertheless, he had composition lessons from
Willem Pijper **[1899]**. Even then he did not
pursue music as a full-time occupation until
he was in his forty-third year, working as a
political science teacher at Amsterdam in
the interim. Afterward he held a number of
important musical and cultural posts in Holland, such as the secretaryship of the Arts
Council, the presidency of the Composers'
Society, and membership on the boards of
the Concertgebouw Orchestra and the Opera Foundation. He was awarded a State
Prize in 1964. He wrote, among other things,
3 operas, 4 symphonies, concerti (including
a *Concertante* for contrabass clarinet), choral works, and chamber music. He was
much influenced by the old Netherlandish
polyphonists. RECORDINGS: The *Anagram-
men* for orchestra has been recorded, but no
new recordings of Landré's work seem to
have appeared in this decade, not even on
Dutch labels.

[2065] BLITZSTEIN, Marc
PIANIST, LECTURER
BORN: Philadelphia, March 2, 1905
DIED: Fort-de-France, Martinique, Janu-
ary 22, 1964

Best known for the deliberately popular music of his Depression-era Brechtian phase,
Blitzstein has proved a difficult composer to
pigeonhole and, perhaps for that reason, one
who has gone into at least a partial eclipse.
He came from a wealthy banking family.

Like so many American rich kids, he seems to have been born with a chip of guilt on his shoulder. Musically he started off as a small-time *Wunderkind*, playing in public at the age of five and soloing with the Philadelphia Orchestra at fifteen. He won a scholarship to the University of Pennsylvania, which ejected him after two years for his refusal to take his athletic requirements seriously. In 1924 he began composition lessons with Rosario Scalero (1870–1954) at the Curtis Institute and piano with Alexander Siloti in New York. In 1926 he made the by then requisite pilgrimage to Nadia Boulanger in Paris and then, somewhat unusually for that period, proceeded to Berlin to be blessed by Schoenberg **[1657]**. While in the latter city he wrote a score for an experimental film, *Hände (Hands)*, the first of the several cinema accompaniments (documentaries for the most part) that would occupy him over the next decade and a half. He returned to the United States late in 1928, concertized, lectured, and wrote musical criticism, chiefly for *Modern Music*. Most of his music during this early period was abstract and fashionably noisy. His first stage piece, a farce called *Triple Sec*, was incorporated into the 1930 (and final) edition of the *Garrick Gaities* (which introduced Imogene Coca to Broadway) but did not last out the revue's relatively brief run. Nevertheless it awakened Blitzstein's interest in the theater. It was followed by the ballet *Cain* and two operas, *The Harpies* and *The Condemned*.

The Condemned, a treatment of the trial and execution of alleged anarchist terrorists Sacco and Vanzetti, reflected Blitzstein's growing concern with left-wing causes. So did his marriage to Eva Goldbeck in 1933. The daughter of a famous opera and operetta singer, Lina Abarbanell, Goldbeck was a socialist writer; tragically, the marriage ended in her death four years later. In 1935 the composer began sitting in on Hanns Eisler's **[1952]** classes at the New School, came to know Bertolt Brecht, and became convinced that he was barking up the wrong tree. From now on his music would be dedicated to delighting the common man and instructing him in social truths. That same year he contributed a skit, *Send in the Militia*, to a rather astonishingly leftish Broadway revue, *Parade*, which lasted five weeks. Then, under Brecht's inspiration and the auspices of the WPA, he wrote a strongly militant musical, *The Cradle Will Rock*. The WPA withdrew under pressure, taking scenery and costumes with it. An injunction was issued forbidding the actors to appear onstage. The musicians' union called its men out. Producer John Houseman and director

Orson Welles found quarters at the Venice Theater; Blitzstein played the score at the piano on a bare stage. The performers bought tickets and performed from their seats among the audience. The piece, twice removed to other theaters, ran for more than 100 showings and was the talk of the season. (Blitzstein also wrote scores for Welles's Mercury Theater productions, including the famous modern-dress *Julius Caesar.*) In 1940 and again in 1941 the composer held Guggenheim fellowships. In January of the latter year he attempted to return to Broadway with another agitprop musical, *No for an Answer*, produced in the minimal way of its predecessor. The license commissioner refused, however, to allow it, on the ground that the theater was not designed for opera.

Following the bombing of Pearl Harbor, Blitzstein enlisted and was attached to the Eighth Air Force in England. Reconciled at last with his country in what he saw as a just cause, he wrote enthusiastically for the Establishment—music for a radio series "Labor for Victory," the film "opera" *Night Shift*, two choral-orchestral extravaganzas—*Freedom Morning* (dedicated to black soldiers) and *The Airborne* (a Hollywoodish hymn to the development of airpower, sometimes referred to as a symphony)—and a score for the Garson Kanin documentary *The True Glory*. After the war Blitzstein composed several scores for Broadway plays, including Lillian Hellman's *Another Part of the Forest*, which led him to its predecessor, *The Little Foxes*. Adapting the book himself, he came up with *Regina*, which he considered a musical and produced as such on Broadway (Forty-sixth St. Theater) in 1949. It ran for two months but later had more success in opera houses. Two later efforts—*Reuben, Reuben* and *Juno*—did not do as well, but a rewriting of Weill's **[1978]** *Dreigroschenoper* as *The Threepenny Opera*, withdrawn after ninety-six performances (with Lotte Lenya) in 1954, was reopened by popular demand a year later and established a record with 2,611 more. In 1962 Blitzstein spent a year as playwright (!)-in-residence at Bennington College in Vermont. At the time he was working on *Sacco and Vanzetti*, commissioned for the opening of the new Metropolitan Opera House. It and several other ambitious projects never came to fruition: on vacation in Martinique in the early winter of 1964, Blitzstein was beaten to death by three French sailors in a barroom argument.

RECORDINGS: Works recorded include *Regina*, abridgments of *The Cradle Will Rock* and *No for an Answer*, *The Airborne*, *Freedom Morning*, and songs. Blitzstein accompanied alto Muriel Smith in an album of songs.

[2066] BOZZA, Eugène (Bō-zà', Ü-zhân)
CONDUCTOR, ADMINISTRATOR
BORN: Nice, April 4, 1905

Bozza, of Italian descent, studied composition with Henri Büsser **[1627]**, Gounod's **[1258]** protégé, at the Paris Conservatoire, and took the Grand Prix de Rome in 1934. He conducted at the Opéra-Comique during the war years and in 1948 became director of the Valenciennes Conservatoire. He wrote a couple of operas, ballets, a symphony, concerti, and a number of chamber works for odd instrumental combinations. RECORDINGS: There are recordings of the Concerto for Saxophone, *Rapsodie niçoise* for violin and orchestra, *Chansons niçoises* for soprano and orchestra (all conducted by the composer); *Variations* for wind quintet; *Scherzo* for saxophone quartet and other saxophone chamber pieces; as well as a considerable number of miscellaneous chamber works for various combinations of woodwinds and brass.

[2067] RAWSTHORNE, Alan
TEACHER
BORN: Haslingden, May 2, 1905
DIED: Cambridge, July 24, 1971

Though his career began late and his fame spread slowly, Alan Rawsthorne became one of the most successful and respected English composers of his generation. Born in the same Lancashire village as his friend actor Robert Donat, he went to dental school and decided to make a career in music only at about the time he reached his majority. He studied piano with Frank Merrick at the Royal Manchester College of Music and continued with Egon Petri in Berlin. From 1932 to 1934 he taught at Darlington Hall School in Devon, then moved to London to seek his musical fortunes. In 1935 he married Jessie Hinchliffe, a violinist, for whom he wrote several works. In 1938 he at last began to win some notice when his *Theme and Variations* for two violins was played at the 1938 ISCM Festival. In 1941 he was called into military service and officially spent the war writing scores for government documentaries, though he found time to pursue his own career, notably with a rewrite of his first piano concerto. (He lost his first violin concerto in an air raid and had to start over, completing it in 1948.) A commission from Sir Thomas Beecham's Royal Philharmonic Orchestra produced the first of 3 symphonies in 1950. (The others followed in 1959 and 1964.) In 1951 his second piano concerto appeared. In 1954 Rawsthorne set T. S. Eliot's *Practical Cats* as a melodrama for Donat, who recorded the work. The same year he married Constant Lambert's **[2074]** widow Isabel and settled in a village in Essex. A second violin concerto followed in 1956. In 1961 he paid tribute to Lambert in the orchestral *Improvisations* on a theme of his. Rawsthorne appeared occasionally as conductor of his own music. That music, harmonically conceived but largely atonal, concerned with form, and initially owing a good deal to Hindemith **[1914]**, remained solidly in the middle of the twentieth-century road. RECORDINGS: Along with *Practical Cats*, the recordings include Rawsthorne's only independent stage work, the ballet *Mme. Chrysanthème;* Concerti for Piano Nos. 1 and 2; Symphonies Nos. 1 and 3; the overture *Street Corner; Symphonic Studies* for orchestra; Concerto for Strings; *Light Music* for strings; Concerto for Clarinet; *Divertimento* for chamber orchestra; String Quartets Nos. 1–3; Quintet for Piano and Strings; Quintet for Piano and Winds; Clarinet Quartet; Sonata for Violin and Piano; *Concertante* for violin and piano; Sonata for Cello and Piano; *Bagatelles* for solo piano; and *Elegy* for solo guitar (his last work, completed by Julian Bream).

[2068] SEIBER, Mátyás György (Sī'-ber, Màch'-yàsh Jörd-ji)
CELLIST, CONDUCTOR, WRITER
BORN: Budapest, May 4, 1905
DIED: Kruger National Park, South Africa, September 24, 1960

Seiber was born into a home where music making was as much part of daily life as sleeping and eating. He took up the cello at ten and at fourteen entered the Budapest Academy, where he was a favorite pupil of Kodály's **[1760]**. Graduating in 1924, Seiber, curious to see the world, led a footloose existence for the next few years, at one point joining the orchestra of a cruise ship plying the Atlantic between Europe and the Americas. In 1928 he settled down in Frankfurt am Main to teach jazz at the Hoch Conservatory. The next year he wrote *Jazzolettes* for a six-piece combo and published a manual for jazz drummers. During the Frankfurt years, Seiber was cellist of the Lenzewsky String Quartet and conducted choirs and theater orchestras. With the Nazi victory in 1933 he returned to Budapest, visited Russia, and then emigrated to England in 1935. For the next several years the problems of making ends meet severely limited his personal efforts at composition, though he wrote for radio and for film cartoons. He also worked for a publisher, brought out an accordion method, lectured, and taught. In 1942 he joined the faculty of Morley College, the Old Vic Theater's educational wing, under the leadership of Michael Tippett [2059] and soon became a much sought-after teacher of composition. He was a cofounder in 1943 of the Society for New Music and founder in 1945 of the Dorian Singers. He married Lilla Bauer in 1947 and settled in the village of Caterham in Surrey. Much of his music was in smaller forms. He exhibits the influences of Kodály, Bartók [1734], and Schoenberg [1657], often with references to jazz and frequently with a leavening of wit. He had a feel for words (in whatever language) and was much admired for his large-scale cantata based on James Joyce's *Ulysses*. In 1959 he collaborated on a jazz-based work, *Improvisations for Jazz Band and Orchestra,* with John Dankworth (who is perhaps best known in America as husband, arranger, and accompanist to the brilliant pop singer Cleo Laine). Among Seiber's full-length film scores was one for an animated version of Orwell's *Animal Farm.* Seiber was killed at fifty-five in an automobile accident while vacationing in South Africa. RECORDINGS: Works recorded include the *Improvisations; Elegy* for viola and small orchestra; *Fantasia concertante* for violin and strings; Concertino for Clarinet and Strings; *Permutazioni a Cinque* for wind quintet; *Introduction and Allegro* for accordion and cello; *3 Fragments from "Portrait of the Artist as a Young Man" for Sprechstimme* narrator, wordless chorus, and ensemble; *4 French Folksongs;* and *3 Morgenstern Lieder.*

[2069] BERGER, Theodor (Bâr'-ger, Tā'-ō-dör)
BORN: Traismauer, May 18, 1905

Born a little to the northwest of Vienna, Berger studied in the latter city, notably with Franz Schmidt [1661], who strongly influenced him. Despite an expectable conservatism, his music is quite vital. He has become highly regarded in his native country and in Germany, to some degree, though he has not really achieved an international name. He likes to experiment with sonorities, both vocal and instrumental. In his mature life he has worked in both Vienna and Hamburg. RECORDINGS: He has (as conductor recorded his 1938 tone poem *Malinconia* for twenty-five separate string parts (reminis-

cent of Richard Strauss's [1563] *Metamorphosen,* but actually its predecessor by several years!). Other recordings include the *Rondino giocoso* for strings, and a *Concerto manuale* for two pianos, percussion, and strings.

[2070] SOWANDE, Fela (Sō-wàn'-dā, Fā'-lā)
ORGANIST, TEACHER
BORN: Oyo, May 29, 1905

The son of a Nigerian tribal chief, Sowande studied music in Lagos, and came to London to seek his fortune. He supported himself as the member of a dance band, as a theater organist and pianist, as accompanist, and as music director for the Colonial Film Unit of the British Ministry of Information; at one time he played second-desk piano with "Fats" Waller during the latter's London appearances. Meanwhile he continued his studies at Trinity College of Music and the Royal College of Organists. During World War II he was a member of the RAF. In 1944 he wrote what became his most popular meld of African and Western music, the *African Suite.* In 1953 he went home to take a post with the national radio system. He made his first visit to the United States in 1957 and a second in 1961, during which he conducted the premiere of his *Nigerian Folk Symphony* in New York. He then accepted a professorial post at Ibadan University but left to teach at Howard University in Washington, D.C. in 1968 and in 1972 moved to the University of Pittsburgh. RECORDINGS: Part of the *African Suite* has been recorded by Paul Freeman and the London Symphony.

[2071] LEIGH, Walter
BORN: London, June 22, 1905
DIED: Tobruk, June 12, 1942

Leigh studied at Christ's College, Cambridge, with E. J. Dent, the noted musicologist and critic and, after graduating in 1926, proceeded to Berlin, where he studied with Hindemith [1914] until 1929. As a composer Leigh was primarily occupied with dramatic media and was particularly admired for his 2 operettas, *Jolly Roger* and *The Pride of the Regiment,* which suggested the revivification of a form moribund since Sullivan [1397]. However, he enlisted early in World War II and was killed in action in North Africa ten days before his thirty-seventh birthday. RECORDINGS: His Concerto for Harpsichord and Strings has been recorded.

[2072] HARTMANN, Karl Amadeus
(Härt'-màn, Kärl Á-mà-dä'-oos)
BORN: Munich, August 2, 1905
DIED: Munich, December 5, 1963

Hartmann studied composition with Joseph Haas, a disciple of Reger [1637], at the Munich Academy and then, in 1927, more satisfactorily with Hermann Scherchen. Though he composed during the 1930s and even won a prize for a string quartet, he was dissatisfied with his achievement and later disowned most of it but kept his official first symphony of 1940 for alto and orchestra on poems by Walt Whitman (which he originally termed "an attempt at a Requiem"). In 1941 he went to Vienna and studied with Webern [1773] for a time. After World War II ended, Hartmann, who had refused to participate in German musical life under the Nazis, founded the Musica Viva Society in Munich, under the sponsorship of the State Opera, dedicated to the performance of new music. Despite this stance, he was himself basically a romantic whose intensely personal music derives from Mahler [1525] and Reger [1637], seasoned with Berg [1789], Stravinsky [1748], and Bartók [1734]. A convinced formalist, he was called by an admiring compatriot "the Last of the Symphonists." His chief monument is his 8 symphonies, of which the last was completed in 1962. RECORDINGS: The symphonies have all been recorded by the German Wergo label (using various conductors and orchestras), which has also recorded the 1963 cantata *Gesangsszene* for baritone and orchestra (his last work) and his contribution (the third movement "Ghetto") to the collaboratively written cantata *A Jewish Song*. Other recordings include the *Concerto funebre* for violin and string orchestra; the cantata *Lamento* for soprano and piano; and the Concerto for Piano, Winds, and Percussion.

[2073] JOLIVET, André (Zhō-lē-vä' Àndrä')
POET, PAINTER, ACTOR, SCENE DESIGNER, CELLIST, TEACHER, CONDUCTOR, ADMINISTRATOR
BORN: Paris, August 8, 1905
DIED: Paris, December 20, 1974

Reared in a family where the good things were taken for granted, Jolivet's problem was not whether he would become an artist, but what art he would specialize in. He was mightily drawn to the theater, and built and operated his own puppet stage as a child. He wrote and improvised at the piano and sketched. At fourteen he began studying painting with Georges Valmier, at fifteen the cello with Louis Feuillard. He also dabbled in theater, both onstage and behind it, with music and without. He took a degree in teaching but at the same time studied musical basics with Abbé Aimé Théodas, choirmaster at the church of Notre Dame de Clignancourt. However, at twenty two, frustrated with an attempt to set one of his poems to music, he buckled down to five years of serious study with Breton composer Paul Le Flem, former student of d'Indy [1462] and Roussel [1605]. In 1930 he encountered Edgard Varèse [1774], who was then sojourning in Paris and was strongly influenced by him. Jolivet began publishing—piano pieces and chamber works—at about this time and caused some stir with his String Quartet of 1934 and a piano work called *Mana,* the latter of which looks toward his notion of music as magic and incantatory ritual. In 1935 he and two contemporaries, Oliver Messiaen **[2129]** and Daniel-Lesur **[2127]**, founded La Spirale, dedicated to the promotion of contemporary chamber music on an international scale. A year later, joined by Yves Baudrier (1906–   ) —the least-known of the group ultimately— they became Jeune France, dedicated to creating a modern French music. Like Les Six, they were never really a school, but, attracting important patronage, they operated effectively to turn around the trivialization that had infected French music for a generation. In 1943 Jolivet fulfilled a long-standing ambition by becoming music director and conductor of the Comédie Française, a post he maintained for sixteen years. He became well known all over the world as a guest conductor of his own music and served as president of the Lamoureux Orchestra concerts in Paris from 1963 to 1968. In an overlapping half decade, 1965–70, he was also professor of composition at the Paris Conservatoire. Though he is said to have been influenced by the Second Viennese School, his music is wholly eclectic and extremely his own and has been highly successful. Many of his titles reflect his concern with primitivism and ritualism. His *oeuvre* is large, embracing an opera, 3 ballets, an oratorio, 2 large cantatas, a great deal of dramatic music for stage and radio, orchestral music that includes 3 numbered symphonies, the Symphony for Strings, a Symphonie de danses, and many concerti, and a considerable amount of vocal and chamber music. RECORDINGS: Both of the cello concerti and the trumpet concerti have been recorded, as well as a concerto apiece for harp, Ondes Martenot, bassoon, piano, and flute. Other orchestral or chamber-orchestral recordings include *5 Danses rituelles;* Symphonies No. 1–3; *Les Amants magnifiques; Suite trans-océane; Andante* for strings; *Suite en concert* for flute and percussion; *Suite delphique* for chamber ensemble (including a part for Ondes Martenot and utilizing various ancient Greek modes); *Heptade* for trumpet and percussion; *Suite liturgique* for chorus and orchestra; *Songe à nouveau rêvé* and *Poèmes intimes* for soprano and orchestra. Other recordings include *Epithalame* for unaccompanied chorus; *Radiophonic Suite No. 2* for winds; *Incantations* for flute; *Chant de linos* for flute, string trio, and harp (also for flute and piano); *Pastorales de noël* for flute, bassoon, and harp; *3 Poèmes* for Ondes Martenot and piano; *Fantaisie-impromptu for saxophone and piano; Suite en concert* for cello; two sonatinas (one for flute and clarinet, the other for oboe and bassoon); Sonatas Nos. 1 and 2 for Piano; *Mana* for piano; *Hymne a l'univers* and *Mandala* for organ; *Suite rhapsodique* for unaccompanied violin; pieces for guitar; and various brief miscellani.

[2074] LAMBERT, Leonard Constant
CONDUCTOR, ARRANGER, WRITER
BORN: London, August 23, 1905
DIED: London, August 21, 1951

Greatly gifted in many ways, Lambert was perhaps his own worst enemy. The son of one respected sculptor, George Washington Lambert, and the brother of another, Maurice Lambert, Constant was a part of the artistic world from his cradle. After being schooled at Christ's Hospital, he matriculated at the Royal College of Music, where he was a student of Vaughan Williams **[1633]**, among others. A member of the Sitwell circle, he was, at twenty one, one of the two reciters in the 1926 scandalous performance of Walton's *Façade.* (The other was Edith Sitwell herself; the two later recorded excerpts from the work.) In the same year the illustrator Edmund Dulac introduced him to Serge Diaghilev, who thereupon ordered a ballet from him. The result was *Romeo and Juliet,* the only commissioned English ballet to be played by the Ballets Russes in Diaghilev's lifetime. It was followed by another ballet, *Pomona,* premiered by Buenos Aires in 1927. Some experimentation with jazz idioms resulted in his very successful *The Rio Grande* of 1929—a sort of anomalous piano concerto with chorus to a text by Sacheverell Sitwell—and in the Sonata for Piano and the Concerto for Piano and 9 Instruments. Lambert's largest purely orchestral effort was the *Music for Orchestra*

of 1927; his largest effort of any kind was the choral "masque" *Summer's Last Will and Testament* of 1936. In 1930 he became one of the founders of the Camargo Society, devoted to continuing ballet in the spirit of Diaghilev, who had meanwhile died. Lambert was its conductor and remained in that post until 1947, by which time the company had become the Sadler's Wells Ballet (later the Royal Ballet). This job, which included not only conducting but arranging music for ballets, cut heavily into Lambert's composing time, and the only large-scale work during this period, besides the masque, was the ballet *Horoscope.* Lambert also wrote and reviewed for various journals and in 1934 produced a book, *Music Ho!,* which was astutely prophetic of the decline of the art in the West. He was on tour with the Sadler's Wells Ballet in Holland when the Germans invaded in 1940 and the troupe managed to escape by a hair, eliciting an *Aubade heroïque* from the composer. The 1940s saw little more than a couple of film scores, and a last ballet, *Tiresias,* appeared in 1950. Meanwhile conducting consumed more of his attention. He appeared at Covent Garden in opera, worked for the BBC, and was associate conductor of the Proms for the 1945 and 1946 seasons. He made many recordings as well. Increasingly known as a specialist in light music, his reputation as a serious musician was the more obscured. He seems to have had few other interests, though he played billiards and was an indefatigable composer of limericks. He gradually lapsed into severe alcoholism, aggravated by diabetes, resigned his conductorship, and died two days shy of his forty-sixth birthday. RECORDINGS: These include *The Rio Grande,* the ballet suites *Pomona* and *Romeo and Juliet,* excerpts from *Horoscope,* the Concerto for Piano and 9 Instruments, music for the film *Anna Karenina,* the *8 Chinese Songs,* and *3 pièces nègres* for piano four hands.

[2075] WIRÉN, Dag Ivar (Vē'-rin, Dåg E'-vär)
CRITIC
BORN: Striberg, October 15, 1905

Wirén was born in the lake country of south central Sweden. At twenty one he began five years of study at the Stockholm Conservatory with Ernst Ellberg (1868–1948) and Oskar Lindberg (1887–1955). He then spent two more years in Paris with the Russian emigré Leonid Sabaneyev, coming home in 1934. Beginning in 1938 he was music critic of the *Svenska Morgonbladet* for eight years. He has held various offices with the Society of

Swedish Composers and is a member of the Royal Academy. In his pre-Paris years his music was Scandinavian-Romantic, but afterward he leaned toward a witty neo-classicism. He once remarked that his credo embraced Bach [684], Mozart [992], and absolute music. Though he has written incidental music for the stage and dramatic pieces for radio and television, his most important works bear out his dictum. They include 5 symphonies, orchestral suites, concerti, chamber music, and piano pieces. RECORDINGS: There are recordings of his *Serenade for Strings* (his best-known work); Symphony No. 4; *Sinfonietta; Triptych* for small orchestra; String Quartets Nos. 2–5; Sonatina for Violin and Piano; *Little Serenade* for guitar; 5 *Ironical Miniatures* for piano; and *Titania* for chorus.

[2076] ALWYN, William

FLUTIST, TEACHER, PAINTER, POET,
CONDUCTOR
BORN: Northampton, November 7, 1905

Alwyn's not inconsiderable reputation has been slow in developing—with reason. The son of a small-time Midlands grocer, he developed a taste for music on his own and was attempting to compose at the age of nine. At fourteen he left school to help out in the store but a year later won admission to the Royal Academy of Music as an inspiring flutist. He spent a year in the reactionary atmosphere there until he encountered John (later Sir John) McEwen (1868–1948), who unveiled for him the wonders of modern music and supervised his general education. In 1923, however, Alwyn's father died, and he had to drop out and make his living, which he did as a flutist—in the London Symphony but also in theater orchestras and at summer resorts. In 1927 he was appointed professor of composition at the Royal Academy of Music. His output in the early years was prodigious—he had already nearly equaled the Beethoven [1063] canon of string quartets by the time he was thirty and had done an oratorio setting of Blake's *The Marriage of Heaven and Hell* in its entirety by 1936. The Concerto for Piano (premiered by his classmate Clifford Curzon) brought him a measure of fame and popularity. But by 1939 Alwyn came to the conclusion that his music was formless and that he needed to acquire real technique. Disowning most of what he had done until then, he set about studying the scores of the composers he most admired, including Debussy [1547], Elgar [1499], Liszt [1218], Puccini [1511],

Scriabin [1625], Stravinsky [1748], and Wagner [1230]. In the war years he turned his hand to film scores, winning much praise for several of them, including *Odd Man Out* in 1947. Among his most admired works are the 5 symphonies. (In the first four he aspired to take up where Beethoven left off and to create a tetralogy that paralleled symphonically what Wagner had done operatically!) Alwyn is also an accomplished painter, poet, and writer, and has supplied some of his own lyrics. His first opera, *The Libertine* of 1969, is a treatment of the Don Juan legend. His second opera, *Miss Julie* after Strindberg, was premiered in a BBC broadcast on February 17, 1977. Although it has not yet been performed on stage, highly favorable reviews of the new recording suggest that it may have a viable future. It has been described as showing the influence of Puccini, Janáček [1478], Szymanowski [1755], and Walton [2011]. RECORDINGS: Lyrita and other British labels have produced a substantial sampling of Alwyn's output. All the symphonies, the *Sinfonietta, The Magic Island, Elizabethan Dances, Concerto Grosso No. 2, Autumn Legend* for English horn and strings, and *Lyra Angelica* for harp and strings are all performed under the composer's direction. Vernon Handley conducts the brief orchestral *Derby Days. Miss Julie* is conducted by Vilem Tausky and features Jill Gomez in the title role. Other recordings include *Naiades* for flute and harp, *Mirages* (song cycle for baritone and piano), *Invocations* for soprano and piano, *A Leave-Taking* for tenor and piano, *Divertimento* for solo flute, the 2 mature string quartets of 1955 and 1975, and a couple of piano works —*Sonata alla Toccata* and *Fantasy Waltzes.*

[2077] CUSHING, Charles

VIOLINIST, CONDUCTOR, CRITIC,
TEACHER
BORN: Oakland, Calif., December 8,
1905

Cushing has been connected with the University of California at Berkeley for most of his life. He took baccalaureate and magisterial degrees there; then, after the prescribed turn with Nedia Boulanger in Paris, he returned to Berkeley to teach and conduct the concert band. He retired in 1970. He composes primarily in the sphere of chamber music. RECORDINGS: Enrique Jorda has recorded the symphonic poem *Cereus,* and there is a performance of the Sonata for Clarinet and Piano by Jerome Rosen.

[2078] MOURAVIEFF, Léon (ex-Lev Muraviev) (Moo-ràv'-yef, Lā'-on)
BORN: Kiev, 1905

Ignored by the standard reference works, Mouravieff has in his seventies attracted several recordings. The son of a Russian father and a German mother, he studied at the Kiev Conservatory with Glière [1662] and at the Moscow Conservatory with Georgy Catoire (1861–1926). After the 1917 Revolution he defected, lived in Italy, then in Germany, and finally settled in Paris. His music exhibits experiments in what might be described as serialized metrics. RECORDINGS: Several works have been recorded—*Dance Metamorphoses* (for strings); one movement of *Nativité* for string trio and orchestra, and *Strophe, Antistrophe, Epode* (for piano).

[2079] GNATTALI, Radamés (Nyàt'-tà-lē, Rà-dà-māz')
PIANIST, VIOLIST, CONDUCTOR
BORN: Pôrto Alegre, January 27, 1906

Towns called Pôrto Alegre are legion in Brazil; Gnattali comes from the one that is the capital of the country's southernmost province, Rio Grande do Sul. His parents came there from Italy to teach music, and he had his first lessons from his mother. Intending to become a concert pianist, he studied at the provincial conservatory and then at the Escola Nacional in Rio de Janiero. After making the concert circuit for a time, he was violist with the Oswald String Quartet. Around 1930 he joined Radio Brazil in Rio as arranger, composer, and conductor, working chiefly in the areas of popular and incidental music. Self-taught as a composer, he gradually moved from light music through a more serious nationalistic phase to a sort of neo-romanticism. But he remains deeply rooted in the popular and folk music of Brazil. RECORDINGS: Guitarist Laurindo Almeida has recorded his *Concêrto de Copacabana* (Gnattali conducting), Concertino for Guitar and Piano, Sonata for Guitar and Cello, and Sonatina for Guitar and Flute. Other recordings include the Concerto for Violin and Concerto for Harp (both with the composer conducting) and the *Suite for Wind Quintet*.

[2080] PITTALUGA, Gustavo (Pit-tà-lōō'-gà, Gōō-stà'-vō)
LAWYER, DIPLOMAT, LIBRARIAN
BORN: Madrid, February 8, 1906

While acquiring a law degree at the University of Madrid, Pittaluga studied with Oscar Esplá [1809]. In the early 1930s he spent some time in Paris, where he was identified with a modernist group called "Triton" (an augmented fourth). (Other members included Henry Barraud [1976] and Jean Rivier [1923]). In 1936 he went to Washington, D.C., as an attaché to the Spanish embassy. When the Loyalists were defeated, he remained in the United States and was for a time librarian of the Museum of Modern Art's film collection in New York. His music dates from the 1930s, during which period he wrote a ballet, a zarzuela, a violin concerto, and a number of other works. RECORDINGS: Songs and piano pieces have been committed to disc.

[2081] GESENSWAY, Louis
VIOLINIST
BORN: Dvinsk, February 19, 1906
DIED: Philadelphia, March 11, 1976

Louis Gesensway was born in Latvia but grew up in Canada, whither his parents emigrated. He took up the violin at four and made something of a stir in his new country as a performing prodigy. He was later a pupil of Luigi von Kunits in Toronto and in 1923 helped him found the New Symphony (later the Toronto Symphony), in which he played until 1926. He then joined the Philadelphia Orchestra, of which he was a member for thirty-five years. In his early years in Philadelphia he continued his studies at the Curtis Institute, notably with Tibor Serly [2007], who sang the praise of Kodály [1760] to him. Leopold Stokowski took an interest in Gesensway and procured him a sabbatical in 1930 so that he could study with Kodály in Budapest. The orchestra later commissioned compositions from him. Though generally a conservative, he did some experimenting with microtones. Gesensway was quite productive: he wrote a children's opera, several concerti, and much orchestral and chamber music. RECORDINGS: Ormandy and the Philadelphia Orchestra recorded his *Four Squares of Philadelphia* for orchestra with narrator of which a critic remarked ambiguously that it did for Philadelphia what Respighi's [1718] "Roman" pieces had done for Rome.

[2082] WILLIAMS, Grace Mary
TEACHER
BORN: Barry, Wales, February 19, 1906
DIED: Barry, Wales, February 10, 1977

Little known outside of Great Britain, Grace Williams is the only female Welsh composer to grace these pages so far. The daughter of a Glamorganshire musician, she learned her basics from her father, took a baccalaureate degree at the University of Wales in 1926, and then went up to London, where she began teaching at the Camden School for Girls and, concurrently, studying with Vaughan Williams [1633] and Jacob [1911] at the Royal College. In 1930 a scholarship enabled her to go to Vienna to put in a year working with Egon Wellesz [1799]. In 1946 she went back to her estate in Barry. Her opera *The Parlour* was produced by the Welsh National Opera, her *Missa Cambrensis* by the 1971 Llandaff Festival, and her *Castell Caernarfon* at the investiture of the present Prince of Wales. RECORDINGS: Encouraged by the sponsorship of the Welsh Arts Council, a substantial number of her works have been released by various British labels—*Fantasia on Welsh Nursery Tunes* and *Penillion* (both orchestral); *Carillons* (for oboe and orchestra); Concerto for Trumpet; *Fairest of Stars* (for soprano and orchestra); Symphony No. 2; and *Ballads* (for orchestra).

[2083] CATURLA, Alejandro García (Kà-tōōr'-là, À-là-hán'-drō Gär-sē'-à)
JURIST
BORN: Remedios, March 7, 1906
DIED: Remedios, November 12, 1940

Though music was an avocation to Caturla, he was regarded as one of the most promising Cuban composers of his day. Born in the north central part of the island, he took composition lessons from Pedro Sanjuán (1886–1976) while studying law at the University of Havana. In 1928 he spent some months with Nadia Boulanger in Paris. His *Danzas cubanas,* which reflect his deep interest in the music of the Cuban blacks (one of whom he married), created a sensation that same year when they were played by the Havana Philharmonic. With his friend Amadeo Roldán [1982], he was the chief proponent of the primitivistic approach known as *Afrocubanismo.* Caturla became a judge in Remedios and founded a chamber orchestra in the neighboring town of Caibarién. He wrote an opera, but perhaps his most successful large-scale work was *Yamba-O,* an effective attempt to evoke the religious rituals of the Cuban Negroes. He was shot dead at the age of thirty four by a man he had tried. RECORDINGS: His 1930 *Primera Suite Cubana* for piano and winds has been recorded, as have some of his songs.

[2084] LOCKWOOD, Normand
TEACHER
BORN: New York, March 19, 1906

Like so many composers whose music is rooted in tradition, Lockwood suffered relative eclipse in the years when the avantgarde was riding high. He came from a musical family and was trained early by his paternal uncle Albert, his father (a professor at the University of Michigan), and his mother (a violinist). At the end of his sophomore year in high school, Uncle Albert took him to Europe. Normand stayed on to study for a year in Rome with Ottorino Respighi [1718]. In 1926 he was home long enough to marry Dorothy Sanders, then took off again for the Boulangerie in Paris, studying with Nadia, when circumstances permitted, for the next six years. In 1928 Frederick Stock conducted the Chicago Symphony in Lockwood's *Odysseus,* which won its composer another stay in the Eternal City via a Prix de Rome. In 1932 he was taken into the faculty of Oberlin College, where he eventually attained an associate professorship and wrote a good deal of not particularly adventurous music, which was nevertheless effective enough to take several prizes. In 1943 he went to New York to write background scores for CBS. For his first two years there he had the additional cushion of two Guggenheim fellowships back to back. In 1945 he began teaching at both the Union Theological Seminary and Columbia University (where he was unbelievably tolerant of the present writer's attempts to understand harmony). That same year Columbia mounted his first opera, *The Scarecrow* (libretto by Dorothy Lockwood).

In the latter part of the New York years, Lockwood often turned to vocal and especially choral music, and he perhaps reached the highest peak of his fame with *Prairie* (text by Carl Sandburg), commissioned by Thor Johnson for the University of Michigan, which he premiered in 1953 with the Philadelphia Orchestra. Meanwhile, when Lockwood was not teaching at the two schools noted above, he was doing so at the Westminster Choir School, Queens College, and Yale. In 1953 he became chairman of the music department at Trinity University in San Antonio and served for two years. In 1961, following appointments at Oregon and Hawaii, he became professor and composer-in-residence at the University of Denver (which in due course produced his other three operas). Lockwood has continued to compose steadily since his retirement in 1974. RECORDINGS: Works on records include the 1950 Concerto No. 1 for Organ and

Brasses, *Inscriptions from the Catacombs* for chorus, *Sonata-Fantasia* for accordion, *Quiet Design* for organ, *Valley Suite* for violin and piano, and *To Margarita de Bayle* for soprano and piano.

[2085] ADASKIN, Murray
TEACHER, VIOLINIST
BORN: Toronto, March 28, 1906

One of three musical brothers, Adaskin began violin studies with the oldest, Harry, and continued over a period of several years with Luigi von Kunits, Kathleen Parlow (in New York), and Marcel Chailley (in Paris). From the age of twenty, he was a violinist in the Toronto Symphony and also played with the Royal York Trio. After writing a few small pieces on his own, he decided that he wanted to compose and in 1944 began studying with John Weinzweig (1913–), Canada's first twelve-tonist, and then went to the United States for further work with Milhaud [1868] and Charles Jones [2155]. His first major work, a suite for orchestra, was played by the Toronto Symphony in 1949, and in 1952 he became chairman of the music department at the University of Saskatchewan. He received many commissions from the CBC and other Canadian organizations, one of which was for the opera *Grant, Warden of the Plains* in 1967. In 1966 his university named him composer-in-residence. He retired in 1973. His output is mostly instrumental (orchestral and chamber music); some of it is based on Canadian material, including Eskimo themes. RECORDINGS: His 1956 *Serenade Concertante* (for orchestra) *Canzona and Rondo* (for violin and piano), and *Rondino* (for nine instruments) are among the works recorded by various performers, mostly issued under the aegis of the Canadian Broadcasting Corporation.

[2086] DORATI, Antal (Dō-rá'-tē, Án'-tál)
CONDUCTOR
BORN: Budapest, April 9, 1906

Though Dorati is known worldwide as one of the important conductors of his time, he is also a composer of talent. The child of musicians, he took up the piano at four, the cello a few years later, and composed precociously (three operas!) before beginning serious study at twelve. His mature training was at the Budapest Academy, at first under Leo Weiner [1792], then for four years with Kodály [1760], whom he came to idolize. In 1924 he was hired as a répétiteur at the Budapest Opera and was soon conducting performances there. In 1928 he went to the Dresden State Opera to assist Fritz Busch, and after a year found a post at Münster, which he held until 1932. Then, finding Germany unhealthy, he became associate conductor (with Efrem Kurtz) of the Ballets Russes de Monte Carlo, with which he toured as far afield as the United States and Australia. He first conducted a symphonic concert in Washington, D.C., in 1937. Early in the war years he made the United States his home, and directed the New Opera Company in New York during its brief but spectacular career. In 1945 he was made director of the Dallas Symphony and did so well that in 1949 he was summoned to Minneapolis to succeed Mitropoulos (who was tapped for the New York Philharmonic). He took out citizenship in 1947. After a brilliant decade in Minneapolis, he asked to be released. In 1962 he began four years as director of the BBC Symphony; then, after a similar stay with the Stockholm Philharmonic, he came full circle to conduct the National Symphony in Washington. As usual he succeeded in healing a sick orchestra but was dumped in 1977 after Rostropovitch had caught the public's fancy. He immediately went to fill concurrent jobs with the moribund Detroit Symphony (from which he resigned in 1982) and the London Philharmonic. He is married to pianist Ilse von Alpenheim, with whom he presently maintains a home in Switzerland. Dorati's best-known compositions (aside from *Graduation Ball*, a ballet-pastiche of Johann Strauss [1295] music) date from his later years and include a symphony, a piano concerto, *Variations on a Theme by Bartók* for piano solo, a *Nocturne and Capriccio* for oboe and string quartet, a cantata *The Way of the Cross*, a cello concerto, and a string quartet. RECORDINGS: The Louisville Orchestra premiered the Concerto for Cello in 1976 and recorded it with cellist Janos Starker (Jorge Mester conducting). All the other works mentioned have been recorded under Dorati's direction or supervision, except the cantata and the string quartet.

[2087] VAN VACTOR, David
FLUTIST, CONDUCTOR, TEACHER
BORN: Plymouth, Ind., May 8, 1906

The product of a small town a few miles south of South Bend, Van Vactor learned to play flute from a barber in nearby Argos sufficiently well to get into a local band. At the proper time, he enrolled at Northwestern University in a pre-med program but became involved in music and after three years

switched to a major in that subject. On graduating, he spent a year in Vienna studying
flute with Josef Niedermayr. He was later in
Paris for a summer under the tutelage of
Paul Dukas [1574] and the great flutist Marcel Moyse. From 1931 until 1943 he played
flute in the Chicago Symphony in the days
of Frederick Stock; the last seven years of
that period he also taught and conducted at
Northwestern. As a member of the North
American Quintet, he toured South America
in 1941 under State Department auspices. In
1943 he moved to Kansas City as first flute
and assistant conductor of the Kansas City
Philharmonic, teaching at the local conservatory. In 1945 and 1946 the U.S. State Department sent him to Brazil and Chile as a
guest conductor, and in 1947 he settled in
Knoxville, Tennessee, as first head of the
School of Fine Arts at the University of Tennessee, and conductor of the Knoxville Symphony. He has made further conducting
tours, both in South America and Europe
and, in 1958, spent a year in Frankfurt am
Main under Fulbright auspices with the
Youth Symphony, studying the impact of
"educational" concerts on children. Van
Vactor has composed copiously, almost entirely in instrumental media, though he has
written a few choral works. RECORDINGS:
Van Vactor has also managed to preserve a
great deal of his effort on records—Symphony No. 1 in D; Symphony No. 2; *Fantasia, Chaconne, and Allegro; Variazione
Solenne; Overture to a Comedy No. 2; Suite
on Chilean Folk Tunes; Sinfonia Breve; Pastoral and Dance* for flute and orchestra; *Recitative and Saltarello; Introduction and
Presto* for strings; *Economy Band; Concerto
à 4* for 3 flutes, harp, and orchestra; Concerto for Viola; *Ode; Sarabanda con variazioni; Passacaglia; Chorale and Allegro; Prelude and March; Etudes* for winds and percussion; *Bagatelles* for strings; Octet for
Brass; Quintet for Flute and Strings; and
two records' worth of miscellaneous works
for various combinations of from one to ten
wind instruments.

[2088] SCHAEUBLE, Hans Joachim
(Shoi'-b'le, Hànts Yō-à'-khēm)
BORN: Arosa, May 29, 1906

A native of the Swiss canton of Grisons,
Schaeuble set out to acquire a liberal arts
degree at the University of Lausanne. But
concerts by Ernest Ansermet and his Suisse
Romande Orchestra quickly caused him to
drop out and take up music. He graduated
from the Leipzig Conservatory in 1931, then
lived and studied in Berlin (where his music

began getting a hearing) until the outbreak
of the 1939 war. He then returned to Switzerland and eventually settled in Zürich. His
music is in a rather conservative, modified
serial style. He has written 2 operas, 3 ballets, a Requiem, 2 symphonies, several concerti, and 3 string quartets. RECORDINGS:
His Concerto for Piano and Strings and *Music for Clarinet and Strings* have been readily
available on records in the United States.
Other records, for Swiss labels, include the
String Quartet, *Music for String Quartet,* Sonata for Piano, and *Monopartita* for two pianos.

**[2089] BALANCHIVADZE, Andrei Me-
litonovitch** (Bà-làn-chē-vàd'-ze, Àn'-
drā Mà-lē-tō-nō'-vich)
TEACHER
BORN: St. Petersburg, June 1, 1906

Balanchivadze's father Meliton, his first
teacher, was a Rimsky-Korsakov [1416] pupil and the promoter of concerts of Georgian
music in St. Petersburg for the twenty years
preceding the 1917 Revolution. (One source
has Andrei born in Kutaisi, Georgia, but
this appears to be wrong.) Andrei's older
brother, Georgi, left Russia in 1924 and
made a reputation as a choreographer; he
westernized his name to "George Balanchine." Andrei's formal musical studies
were obtained at the Tbilisi (Tiflis) Conservatory under Ippolitov-Ivanov [1517] and at
the Leningrad Conservatory under Alexander Zhitomirsky (1881–1937), a pupil of Rimsky-Korsakov, Liadov [1485], and Glazunov
[1573]. He returned to Tbilisi to teach in the
conservatory in 1935 and became professor
of composition in 1962. The composer of ballets, symphonies, concerti, etc., he may be
pigeonholed as a Georgian nationalist. RE-
CORDINGS: The six-movement Concerto No.
4 for Piano and Orchestra, of 1968, and a
brief organ fugue have been recorded.
(There may be additional Soviet recordings.)

[2090] SANDERS, Robert Levine
ORGANIST, CONDUCTOR, TEACHER
BORN: Chicago, July 2, 1906
DIED: Delray Beach, Fla., December 26,
1974

A product of the Chicago (then "Bush")
Conservatory, Robert Sanders was at nineteen the recipient of a master's degree and
an American Prix de Rome, which enabled
him to study with Ottorino Respighi [1718].
After some further study in Paris with Guy
de Lioncourt (1885–1961), a d'Indy [1462]

pupil, he returned to Chicago to teach at the conservatory in 1929. During the next eighteen years in his hometown, he was also on the staffs of the University of Chicago and the Meadville Theological Seminary, organist at the First Unitarian Church, and assistant conductor of the Civic Orchestra. In 1938 he won the New York Philharmonic Prize for his *Little Symphony No. 1* and moved to Indiana University as dean of the music school. After nine years in that post, he served seven more as chairman of the music department at Brooklyn College and then taught there until he retired. Sanders was well-known as a hymnologist (he co-edited a book of hymns). His 1944 ballet *L'Ag'ya* became part of the repertoire of Katherine Dunham's pioneering black dance company. He was particularly effective as a writer for voices (settings of Whitman and T. S. Eliot) and for band. RECORDINGS: There is a recording of his orchestral *Saturday Night*, his most popular work. Other recordings include the Symphony in A, *Little Symphonies No. 1 in G* and *No. 2 in B-flat*, and the Quintet in B-flat for Brass.

[2091] LUTYENS, Agnes Elizabeth (Lut'-yenz, Ag'-nes E-liz'-à-beth)
BORN: London, July 9, 1906
DIED: London, April 15, 1983

Elizabeth Lutyens has been both a pioneer in twelve-tone music in England and a proponent for the recognition of women composers as something more than dogs walking on their hind legs (in Dr. Johnson's image). Her father was Sir Edwin Landseer Lutyens, a notable architect who laid out the plans for New Delhi and whose most familiar work to Westerners is perhaps the Cenotaph in London. After some preliminary study in Paris, she enrolled in the Royal College of Music in London, where her chief composition teacher was the organist-composer Harold Darke (1888–1976) and where her instrument of choice was the viola. In 1931, with fellow students Anne Macnaghten and Iris Lemare, she inaugurated the Macnaghten Concerts, devoted to giving hearings to young composers. (Some early profiters were Britten [2215], Maconchy [2106], and Rawsthorne [2067], as well as Miss Lutyens herself.) The following year the Camargo Society (ancestor of the Royal Ballet) performed her *Birthday of the Infanta* under Constant Lambert's [2074] direction. Up to about 1940, Lutyens was trying to find her own voice. It emerged in her special approach to dodecaphony, at which she arrived without

reference to Schoenberg's [1657] system and which she has further refined. Apart from her "serious" music, she has been kept extremely busy writing film scores and other incidental music. She was married to the conductor Edward Clark, founder of the North Eastern Regional Orchestra in his native Newcastle, who died in 1962. Her friendship with the critic William Glock paid off when he became music director for the BBC, for he was extremely sympathetic to Schoenbergians. Miss Lutyens was honored with the title of C.B.E. in 1969. She has rejected virtually all of her earlier music. The large body that remains includes some dramatic pieces and orchestral works, but is mostly crafted for small ensembles or solo instruments. RECORDINGS: *And Suddenly It's Evening* (chamber cantata to texts of Salvatore Quasimodo); *Quincunx* (for voices and orchestra); *ô saisons, ô châteaux!* (cantata); *Motet* (choral); Wind Quintet; String Quartet No. 6; *5 Bagatelles* (for piano solo).

[2092] EGGE, Klaus (Eg'-gà, Klouz)
EDITOR, CRITIC
BORN: Granserad, July 19, 1906
DIED: Oslo, March 7, 1979

Not to be confused with the Eggen brothers (he succeeded Arne Eggen [1739] as president of the Norges Kunstnerrad), Klaus Egge was a native of Telemark and a product of the Oslo Conservatory, where he studied piano with Nils Larsen (a pupil of Rudolf Ganz), and composition with Fartein Valen [1822]. After further work at the Berlin Hochschule with Walter Gmeindl, he returned to Norway to compose and to edit the journal *Tonekunst* (1935–38). At first much influenced by his country's folk music, he later moved in the direction of the dodecaphonic (e.g., the fourth symphony of 1968). He was granted a life pension by his government in 1949. He wrote 5 symphonies, 3 piano concerti, one concerto each for violin and cello, a ballet, some large choral works, and much chamber music. RECORDINGS: Egge's output has been extensively documented on records, largely thanks to the ongoing series of Philips recordings issued under the auspices of the Norwegian government. Works recorded include Symphonies 1–4; Concerto No. 2 for Piano; Concerto for Violin; Concerto for Cello; String Quartet No. 1; Sonata for Violin and Piano; Sonatas Nos. 1 and 2 for Piano; *Fantasy in Halling-Rhythm* and *Fantasy in Springar-Rhythm* for solo piano; and the Wind Quintet.

[2093] HOMS OLLER, Joaquím (Ōmz Ō'-yer, Hwȧ-kēm')
ENGINEER
BORN: Barcelona, August 21, 1906

In his youth Homs studied cello, but in 1929 he obtained a degree in industrial engineering at the University of Barcelona and took up that profession. In the 1930s, however, he took lessons for several years with Roberto Gerhard [1926] and came to be known as a composer with advanced tendencies. Later he became a pioneer in twelve-tone music in Spain. He has been a rather productive composer but mostly in small-scale works. RECORDINGS: His Wind Octet of 1967 has been recorded by Konstantin Simonovich.

[2094] SHOSTAKOVITCH, Dmitri Dmitrievitch (Shus-tȧ-kō'-vich, D'mē'-trē D'mē-trē-ȧ'-vich)
PIANIST, TEACHER
BORN: St. Petersburg, September 25, 1906
DIED: Moscow, August 9, 1975

If one excepts the sometime-renegade Prokofiev [1851], Shostakovitch is the best known and almost certainly the greatest of Soviet composers. In terms of his general appeal, it is tempting to see him as the last of the great figures in Western music; it is difficult at any rate to think of another who has established himself so firmly in the international repertoire. But one must remember that he drew the sneers of the latter-day avant-garde in the West (for not being sufficiently modern) and from the Russian political establishment (for being too modern). Outside Russia, however, enthusiasm for him has been tempered by his apparently toadying and knuckling under to the Soviets, for whom in general he has been viewed as a sort of official musical spokesman. Recently, though, a purported autobiography, "as told to" a former associate who emigrated to the United States, seems to show him as a man who was increasingly frustrated, embittered, and fearful for his life. Until the truth is sorted out, depictions of him will remain problematic. More recently, the defection to the West of his son Maxim and grandson has made the picture even more puzzling.

Shostakovitch's parents came to St. Petersburg from Siberia. His father, Dmitri Boleslavovitch Shostakovitch, was a government official (variously described as a chemist and an engineer) who liked to sing. His mother, Sofia Vasilievna, had studied piano at the conservatory and was a professional teacher. Her oldest child (of three), Maria,

followed in her path. (The youngest, Zoya, became a veterinarian.) Sofia began teaching her son when he was nine and a year later placed him in Glyaser's Music School. His training lasted through the 1917 Revolution, with which his parents were in sympathy (and on whose rightness he was nurtured), and in 1918 he was admitted to the Petrograd Conservatory as a piano student under Leonid Nikolayev. Five years later he graduated, a highly accomplished performer. Frail and near-sighted, he suffered from hunger during these years and, after his father's death in 1922, seemed on the verge of tuberculosis. Although he had in a moment of despair destroyed the compositions he had written earlier, he decided, encouraged and abetted by Glazunov [1573], to become a composer and spent another two years at the conservatory studying with Maximilian Steinberg (1883–1946). Early on, he had been profoundly taken with Tchaikovsky's [1377] music; later he was fascinated by such Russian moderns as Stravinsky [1748] and Prokofiev. His first major composition, performed in 1926, was the first of his 15 symphonies, which already exhibits the typical admixture of lyricism and acidulousness and which made his name known all over the world. Even today it is one of his most frequently performed orchestral works.

Filled with confidence and patriotic fervor, he followed this first essay with two more symphonies, out and out propaganda pieces dedicated respectively to the October Revolution and Mayday; neither had much impact, even at home. (The second symphony was written in a highly dissonant idiom and sounds rather "advanced" even today.) These were followed by an operatic setting of Gogol's satirical tale, The Nose, first produced in 1930 with an appropriately witty and savage score. Depending on whether one consults Western or Soviet sources, it was either greeted with delight or with alarm; in any case it soon disappeared from the boards for more than forty years. It was followed by several other satirical (but more temperate) works, such as the ballets The Age of Gold and The Bolt. Shostakovitch then embarked on what was to be his only other completed opera, Lady Macbeth of the Mtsensk District, a lurid tale of bourgeois corruption in the old days. Premiered in Leningrad early in 1934, it was rapturously received by public and critics alike, and bid fair to become the greatest Russian operatic success since the days of Rimsky-Korsakov [1416]. Two years later, after it had enjoyed dozens of performances, Stalin decided to take it in. It proved too much for his delicate moral sensibilities, and he stomped out of the opera house in a fury. Soon the critics were attacking it with equal fury as decadent and chaotic. It was summarily withdrawn, and Shostakovitch, wondering what had hit him, also withdrew his then-unperformed fourth symphony as being too negative. (It was not premiered until 1962.) It was only with the fifth symphony, first played in November of 1937, that the composer was officially acceptable again, the work being deemed a proper statement of the upbeat Soviet spirit (assuming that was what Shostakovitch had in mind). There followed, besides the sixth symphony and the first of the 15 string quartets, a good deal of *Gebrauchswerk* such as several film scores, and the reorchestration of Mussorgsky's [1369] *Boris Godunov.*

When the Nazis suddenly turned on their sometime allies in 1941, Shostakovitch, despite his thick glasses, tried to volunteer but was told, "Don't call us—we'll call you." (By then he had been nine years married—to physicist Nina Vasilyevna Vasar—and had two children; Galya, born in 1936, and the future conductor Maxim, born in 1938.) During the first months of the war in Leningrad, he helped organize a theatrical company for the troops, served as a fire warden at the Leningrad Conservatory, where he taught, and worked on his seventh symphony. In late September the authorities ordered him to leave the besieged city, and flew him and his family to Moscow and then to safer ground in the temporary capital of Kyubyshev, where the symphony was premiered the following spring. The American premiere followed in July—a nationwide broadcast by Toscanini and the NBC Symphony with a great publicity buildup and much propaganda for our Heroic Allies. Much was made of the supposed first-movement depiction of the Germans as goose-stepping robots, though the posthumous "autobiography" claims the composer had the Stalinists in mind. Meanwhile the composer had returned to Moscow to teach at the conservatory and to work on an opera, *The Gamblers,* which was unhappily aborted. The eighth symphony, completed in 1943, was heralded with almost as much hoopla as its predecessor, though it did not have immediate popular success, perhaps owing to its graphic depiction of the horrors of war.

Shostakovitch's position as cultural hero seemed assured with his first Order of Lenin award in 1946, but events were already in motion that would topple him again. Evidence of "bourgeois formalism" was detected in the eighth symphony. In 1948—with Prokofiev, Khachaturian [2038], and

several lesser composers—Shostakovitch was a victim of Commissar Zhdanov's attack and was forced virtually to grovel. There followed a period of such propagandistic stuff as a hymn to the Stalin reforestation program. Moreover Shostakovitch was apparently forced into a round of appearances at left-wing "peace conferences," beginning with one in New York in 1949, where he seemed a marmoreal apologist for Russian Communism. (But the "autobiography" says he was convinced that if he did not dance to Stalin's tune, he would be executed.)

Later, though he continued to write such Soviet-oriented works as the eleventh and twelfth symphonies, he also turned out such abstract masterpieces as the tenth symphony and the first violin concerto (not to mention the remarkable later string quartets), and gradually came to be accepted worldwide as a true master, whatever his politics. But his troubles were not over. The thirteenth symphony, a vocal work set to texts by Yevgeni Yevtushenko, including "Babi-Yar" lamenting the Jewish massacre at that infamous site, came under attack and was withdrawn for a time. Shostakovitch's last years were marked by innumerable honors, conferred both at home and abroad, and declining health and spirit. Nina Shostakovitch died in 1954 and her mother-in-law a year later. In 1956 Shostakovich married a schoolteacher, Margarita Andreyevna Kaynova. He traveled to Vienna in 1955 for the opening of the State Opera, to Rome and Oxford in 1958 for honors, and returned to the United States in 1959 and 1973—the latter visit to receive an honorary doctorate at Northwestern University. (He had taught himself English during World War II.) In the 1960s and 1970s he suffered a series of severe heart attacks, one of which at least necessitated heroic measures to resuscitate him. He grew increasingly morbid and pessimistic—as evidenced by such works as the fourteenth symphony, wholly concerned with death, and the tragic mask that one sees in late photographs. His last work, the Sonata for Viola and Piano, Op. 147, was completed in the year of his death.

RECORDINGS: Nearly all of Shostakovitch's important work has been committed to records. This includes all the operas (the original *Lady Macbeth,* its revision as *Katerina Ismailova, The Nose,* and what exists of *The Gambler);* the ballets *The Bolt* and *The Golden Age,* and selections from *The Limpid Brook;* excerpts from the operetta *Moskva Cheryomushki;* scores for such films as *The New Babylon, All Alone, Zoya, Michurin, A Year Is Worth a Lifetime, Pirogov, The Mem-*

orable Year 1919, The Fall of Berlin, The Gadfly, and *Hamlet* (the latter film score of 1964 is not to be confused with the 1932 incidental music for *Hamlet,* which has also been recorded); Symphonies Nos. 1–15 (complete); the Op. 1 *Scherzo* of 1919, the *Festive Overture, Columbus Overture,* and the *Overture on Russian and Kirghiz Folk Themes;* Concerti for Piano Nos. 1 and 2; Concerti for Violin Nos. 1 and 2; Concerti for Cello Nos. 1 and 2; the cantatas *Song of the Forests, The Death of Stepan Razin,* and *The Sun Shines Over the Fatherland;* the complete String Quartets Nos. 1–15, plus Chamber Symphonies Nos. 1 and 2, which are actually orchestral transcriptions by Rudolph Barshai of two of the quartets; Piano Trios Nos. 1 and 2; Sonatas for Piano Nos. 1 and 2; Sonata for Violin and Piano; Sonata for Viola and Piano; Sonata for Cello and Piano; Quintet for Piano and Strings; Concertino for 2 Pianos; 7 *Romances* for soprano, violin, cello, and piano to poems of Alexander Blok; virtually all of the song cycles for voice(s) and piano or orchestra. Many additional minor works (too numerous to list here) have also been recorded. (Possibly the most important unrecorded work at this point is the incidental music to Vladimir Mayakovsky's play *The Bedbug,* 1929.) Shostakovich himself, as pianist, recorded both concerti, the Concertino for 2 Pianos (with Maxim), and some of the Op. 87 set of *24 Preludes and Fugues.*

[2095] CRESTON, Paul *(né* Giuseppe Guttoveggio)
ORGANIST, TEACHER
BORN: New York, October 10, 1906

Self-taught as a composer, Creston is basically a conservative who has, however, explored his art as he understands it with considerable imagination. The son of an immigrant Sicilian laborer, young Creston visited the paternal homeland as a child. He was permitted piano lessons from a neighborhood teacher, and taught himself to play the violin. Economic necessity forced him to give up his schooling in 1921, after which he held a number of office jobs, keeping up his music (both playing and composing) in what spare time he had. Six years later he married Louise Gotto, his sometime coworker and afterward a pioneer Martha Graham dancer. It was then that he changed his name legally, basing his last name on a nickname, "Cris," acquired from a role in a school play. For a short time he was a movie-house organist until the "talkies" came along. At twenty-six he decided that he must become a musician and, rejecting most of what he had

written up to then, began composing seriously. He also resumed keyboard study—one of his teachers was Pietro Yon **[1810]**—and in 1934 became organist at St. Malachy's ("the actors' church") on West Forty-ninth Street, where he played regularly until 1967.

By the mid-1930s Creston's music was beginning to draw serious attention—Henry Cowell **[1934]** published his 7 *Theses* for piano in the *New Music Quarterly* in 1933—and in 1938 Fritz Reiner premiered his *Threnody* (written in memory of his son, the first of three children) with the Pittsburgh Symphony. In 1940 the first of Creston's 6 symphonies attracted the attention of Eugene Ormandy, whose performance of it with the Philadelphia Orchestra in 1943 helped win it that year's New York Critics' Circle Award. The second symphony of 1944, which Creston termed an apotheosis of song and dance, and the Gregorian-based third of 1950 established him as a leading American composer who was showered with commissions. Between the completion of these two works, he led an ABC radio program, "The Hour of Faith." Later he taught briefly at Swarthmore and for a longer stint at the New York College of Music (absorbed by New York University). His fourth and fifth symphonies followed in 1952 and 1956. From 1968 until his retirement in 1975 he was on the faculty of Central Washington State College. In his later work he has explored rhythmic possibilities systematically and has published *Rhythmicon,* a ten-volume treatment of that subject. He has been the recipient of numerous awards and honors, and has held national office in such musical organizations as ASCAP. He has continued to compose orchestral, vocal, and chamber music. His Symphony No. 6 for organ and orchestra was premiered in 1981 by the National Symphony Orchestra in Washington, D.C.

RECORDINGS: Orchestral works on disc include Symphonies Nos. 2 and 3; 2 *Choric Dances; Invocation and Dance; A Rumor; Dance Overture; Walt Whitman; Lydian Ode; Corinthians XIII;* Concertino for Marimba (excerpt); *Partita* for flute, violin, and string orchestra; *Chant of 1942;* and *Suite for Strings.* Works for band on records include *Anatolia; Celebration Overture;* Concerto for Alto Saxophone and Band; *Jubilee; Prelude and Dance; Royce Hall Suite;* and *Zanoni.* Also recorded are *Dedication* for chorus, Sonata for Saxophone and Piano, *Suite for Saxophone and Piano, Fantasy* for trombone and piano, String Quartet, *Suite for Violin and Piano,* and the Trio for Violin, Cello, and Piano.

[2096] GIDEON, Miriam
TEACHER, MUSICOLOGIST
BORN: Greeley, Colo., October 23, 1906

Miriam Gideon's parents were amusical. At the time of her birth, her father Abram was a professor of languages at Colorado State Teachers' College. When she was nine, the Gideons moved to Chicago, where she began piano lessons. A year later they progressed to New York City, where her teacher was Hans Barth (1897–1956), a pupil of Reinecke [1292] and later an experimenter in microtonal composition. She progressed so rapidly that her uncle Henry Gideon, music director of Temple Israel in Boston, took her in charge, seeing her through Girls' High School and a B.A. at Boston University in 1926. She then returned to Manhattan, where over the next several years she tried various teachers, including Marion Bauer (1887–1955), Charles Haubiel [1859], and Lazare Saminsky (1882–1959). The last-named turned her over to Roger Sessions [1931], who exerted a powerful influence on her composition. In 1939 she decided to live in Europe, but political circumstances quickly redecided her to come home. In 1944 she joined the faculty of Brooklyn College, where in 1949 she married a colleague, Frederic Ewen. After study with Paul Henry Láng at Columbia, she took a master's degree in musicology in 1946. During this period she began to win a name for herself as a composer, notably with chamber works and especially those involving word settings (in several languages). In 1954, the year she left Brooklyn College for the Jewish Theological Seminary, she made her first experiment with Jewish liturgical music in *Adon Olom* for soloists, choir, and orchestra. Her only opera to date, *Fortunato,* was finished not long afterward. In 1970 she composed the first Sabbath Morning Service ever commissioned from a woman and followed it with a Friday Evening Service three years later. In 1971 she became professor of composition at the City University of New York. She continued to receive commissions and honors; among the latter was a doctorate from the seminary in 1980. RECORDINGS: Works recorded include the orchestral *Symphonia Brevis* and *Lyric Piece* for strings; a melodrama, *The Adorable Mouse;* and the solo-piano *Suite No. 3.* Also recorded are a number of song cycles for solo voice and various instrumental ensembles—*The Condemned Playground, The Hound of Heaven, Nocturnes, Questions on Nature, Rhymes from the Hill, Seasons of Time, Spirit Over the Dust, The Resounding Lyre, Voices from Elysium,* and *Songs of Youth and Madness*

(the last-named work only with full orchestral accompaniment).

[2097] TALMA, Louise
TEACHER
BORN: Arcachon, October 31, 1906

Some sources to the contrary notwithstanding, Louise Talma was born in France near Bordeaux. However, her parents (both musicians) were Americans. Her father died when she was still a baby. Her mother, a singer, took her back to New York and started her on piano at an early age. Accounts of her later education are conflicting. All agree that in the 1920s she hoped to become a concert pianist and that she took courses at the Institute of Musical Art for most of the decade, winning prizes for both performance and composition. All accounts also have her, rather oddly, taking a B.Mus. at New York University in 1931 and an M.A. at Columbia in 1933; the most recent one, however, says that she initially majored in chemistry at Columbia, graduating in 1930. Whatever else she may have been doing at the time, in 1926 she began teaching piano at the Manhattan School of Music and taking lessons with Isidor Philipp in Paris in the summers. Two years later she joined the faculty of Hunter College, Columbia University, and began studying with Nadia Boulanger during her vacations, an association that lasted until the outbreak of World War II. Nadia exerted a powerful influence on her, causing her to decide that she would prefer composing to performing and to abandon Protestantism for Roman Catholicism. For the last four summers before the war, Miss Talma joined her on the teaching staff at Fontainebleau.

Most of Louise Talma's best work (much of it religiously inspired) came after 1938. At first, expectably, her approach was neo-classical, but in the 1950s she successfully adapted the twelve-tone idiom to her own needs. In 1946 and 1947 she held successive Guggenheim fellowships (the first woman to do so). In 1955 Thornton Wilder wrote her a libretto for a full-length opera, *The Alcestiad.* With its successful premiere at Frankfurt in 1962, she became the first American woman to have an opera produced by a major German company. In 1974 she became the first woman member of the National Institute of Arts and Letters. In 1976, the year she retired from Hunter College, she was named Sanford Fellow at Yale and Clark Lecturer at Scripps College in California. She has published two harmony texts.

RECORDINGS: The 1944 *Toccata* for orchestra has been recorded, along with *3 Duologues* for clarinet and piano, the choral *Corona* (to John Donne texts), and several piano works—Sonata No. 2, *Toccata,* and *6 Etudes.* Just released is a 1979 song cycle, *Diadem* for tenor and ensemble.

[2098] COOKE, Arnold Atkinson
TEACHER, CONDUCTOR
BORN: Gomersal, November 4, 1906

A Yorkshireman, Cooke took a B.A. from Cambridge in 1929 (and a Mus.D. nineteen years later) and went to Berlin to spend four years as a pupil of Hindemith **[1914].** He returned to Cambridge in 1932 to direct the orchestra of the Festival Theater and in 1933 went to the Royal Manchester College of Music as professor of composition. He left in 1938 and in 1941 entered the British Royal Navy to serve for the duration of the war. In 1947 he became professor of composition at the Trinity College of Music in London. His music shows traces of Hindemith's influence, but like so many English composers, Cooke is really an untrammeled eclectic. His compositions include an opera, *Mary Barton;* a ballet, *Jabez and the Devil,* 3 symphonies, concerti for violin and clarinet, and a great deal of chamber music. RECORDINGS: The Symphony No. 3, *Jabez and the Devil,* and the Concerto for Clarinet have been recorded, along with several chamber works— *The Seamew,* a recent work for baritone, oboe, string quartet, and flute; Quartet for Oboe and String Trio; Quartet for Violin, Cello, Recorder, and Harpsichord; Sonata for Clarinet and Piano; and the *Suite for Piano.*

[2099] FINNEY, Ross Lee
TEACHER
BORN: Wells, Minn., December 23, 1906

Born in a village in south central Minnesota, Finney grew up in North Dakota. His mother and two brothers all played instruments. He was introduced early to the piano, and as soon as he was big enough, he took up the cello. When he was twelve, the Finneys settled in Minneapolis, where he was exposed to more structured study. He entered the University of Minnesota in 1923, found it not satisfactory, and graduated in 1927 from Carleton College, where he served as part-time teacher and played in a dance band. The latter job provided him with fare to Paris, where a fellowship paid for lessons with Nadia Boulanger. He spent a postgraduate year at Harvard under the tutelage of

Edward Burlingame Hill **[1632].** In 1929 he began teaching at Smith College in Northampton, Massachusetts, and the following year married Gretchen Ludke, who as Gretchen L. Finney is known for her writings on literature and music. (Finney's brother Theodore is also a successful writer on music and a prominent musical educator.) In 1931 he took a leave to study with Alban Berg **[1789]** in Germany and during these early years had a good deal of informal instruction from Roger Sessions **[1931],** though neither man persuaded him that musical nationalism built on folk music impulses was out. Most of his compositions before 1950 reflect a commitment to such an approach. In 1937 a Guggenheim fellowship allowed him to return to Europe to study with Malipiero **[1743].**

During the early years of World War II, Finney taught at Mt. Holyoke and Hartt College as well as at Smith. In 1944 he was sent to France as a member of the Office of Strategic Services and won a Purple Heart as the result of an unforeseen encounter with a land mine. Afterward, in 1947, he went to the University of Michigan as composer-in-residence. There he ran the department of composition, established a graduate program, and ultimately, after some work with Mario Davidovsky **[2408]** in the Columbia-Princeton Electronic Music Center, set up a similar facility at the University of Michigan, Ann Arbor. In the 1950s he at last became converted to the twelve-tone principle, though in the end he would have to be described as an enlightened eclectic. Virgil Thomson **[1928]** noted, rather snidely, that his music "often glows like the celestial firmament, with a dispersed brilliance untouched by human feeling." For all that, his list of honors, like that of his compositions, is too long to detail here. He retired in 1973. In recent years several of his works have been choreographed by Erick Hawkins.

RECORDINGS: Symphonies Nos. 1–3 have been recorded, along with the Concerto for Saxophone and Winds, Piano Quintet, Piano Trio No. 2, String Quartet No. 6 (of 8), Sonata No. 2 for Cello and Piano, and the *Chromatic Fantasy in E* (also for cello and piano).

[2100] WAXMAN, Franz
PIANIST, CONDUCTOR
BORN: Königshütte, December 24, 1906
DIED: Los Angeles, February 24, 1967

One of the most admired of cinema composers in the golden age of the Hollywood sound film, Waxman was born Franz

Wachsmann to Jewish parents in a town near Crakow now called Krolewska Huta. A protégé of Bruno Walter, he was trained at the Berlin Hochschule, during which time he played piano in a dance orchestra. He caught the attention of film composer Friedrich Holländer (who later also worked in Hollywood, as Frederick Hollander). Holländer gave him a job in 1930 orchestrating and conducting his score for the Marlene Dietrich film *Der blaue Engel (The Blue Angel)*, which established him in the medium. In 1933 Waxman fled the Nazis and wound up in Hollywood, where he eventually won two Academy Awards and scored a large number of prestigious films that included *Captains Courageous, Rebecca, The Philadelphia Story, Sunset Boulevard, Rear Window, The Spirit of St. Louis, Hemingway's Adventures of a Young Man*, and *Peyton Place*. He also worked in television, founded and directed the Los Angeles Music Festival, conducted for Capitol Records, and, being comfortably established, left the screen in 1962 to attend to his own composition. His death, at sixty, interrupted an opera on Stevenson's *Dr. Jekyll and Mr. Hyde.* RECORDINGS: There are recordings of his *Sinfonietta* for strings and timpani and music from most of the films previously mentioned.

[2101] **BADINGS, Henk** (Bàd'-ingz, Henk)
ENGINEER, GEOLOGIST, ACOUSTICIAN, TEACHER
BORN: Bandung, January 17, 1907

Born of Dutch parents in Java, Badings was brought back to Holland at the age of eight to live with a guardian after both parents had died. He had violin lessons and worked at composing but ultimately was sent to the University at Utrecht to become a mining engineer. However, he proceeded with his composing and in his last years there took some lessons with Willem Pijper [1899] and produced several large-scale works, including the first of his 14 symphonies, premiered by Willem Mengelberg and the Concertgebouw Orchestra in 1930. Badings graduated in 1931 and, there being a shortage of mines in Holland, took a job as geologist with the university. But his music soon made such an impression that in 1934 he was appointed to the faculty of the Rotterdam Conservatory and became a director of the Amsterdam Lyceum three years later. Following the German occupation of the Netherlands in 1940, he was appointed head of the Royal Conservatory at The Hague.

After the liberation he was dismissed and for a time was ostracized as a collaborator but was cleared in 1947.

Up to that time he had composed prolifically, experimenting with Classical forms and with scales and tonality. In the early 1950s, however, helped by his technological training, he began to experiment with electronic music and soon came to be revered as one of the pioneers in that field. His first major effort in this area was a 1954 opera for radio, *Orestes*. In 1956 he produced what is said to be the first all-electronic ballet score, *Kain*, and, in 1959, the first all-electronic television opera, *Salto mortale (Death Leap)*. He also wrote microtonal music using a thirty-one tone scale devised by Dutch physicist Adriaan Fokker. (He continued to write music for more traditional media and in fact won several prizes for chamber works in this same decade.) In 1961 he returned to Utrecht as professor of acoustics and a year later became professor of composition at the state conservatory in Stuttgart, where he taught for a decade. His catalog of compositions, which includes most types and genres, is very large.

RECORDINGS: Outside of Holland a small but representative sampling of his instrumental, orchestral, vocal, and electronic output has been issued on records. This includes the Symphony No. 7 "Louisville"; *Armageddon* for soprano, electronics, and wind band; Concerto for Flute and Winds; Octet for Winds and Strings; Sonata for 2 Violins; Sonata No. 3 for Solo Violin; *Passacaglia* for organ and timpani; Sonata for Recorder and Harpsichord; *Ballade* for flute and harp; *Cavatina for Flute and Piano; Cavatina for Alto Flute and Harp; Dialogues* for flute and organ; *Malinconia* for solo saxophone; the song cycle *Chansons orientales;* and several electronic pieces—*Capriccio* for violin and tape; *Evolutions;* and *Genese*. (There are probably other small chamber or instrumental pieces buried in scattered imported anthologies as well.) In addition Badings has over the years been one of the most oft-recorded composers in the Dutch Philips/Donemus/Composers' Voice series of contemporary Dutch music—works recorded in those series include the Symphonies Nos. 3, 8, and 9; Concerto for Piano; Concerto No. 1 for 2 Violins; Concerto for Harp; Sonata No. 2 for Cello and Piano; and the electronic score *Cain and Abel*.

[2102] **PREGER, Leo** (Prâ-zhā', Lā-ō')
BORN: Ajaccio, January 27, 1907
DIED: Ajaccio, December 25, 1965

Corsican by birth, Preger came to Paris and studied with Nadia Boulanger. He became known chiefly as a composer of vocal—and particularly religious—music. RECORDINGS: Four of his motets and some songs are on records.

[2103] GUARNIERI, Camargo Mozart*
(Gwärn-yä'-rē, Kå-mär'-gō Mōt'-zärt)
CONDUCTOR, TEACHER, PIANIST
BORN: Tietê, February 1, 1907

Camargo Guarnieri's father, said to be descended from the violin-making Guarneris of Cremona, was brought to Brazil from Sicily in infancy. He became a small-time flutist, settled in São Paulo (the state), and married, over her parents' objections, a Brazilian aristocrat who bore him nine children. He gave the boy his first music lessons and later, when he moved his family into São Paulo (the city), got him into the conservatory, where he was especially influenced by Mârio de Andrade, an ethnomusicologist. Guarnieri also worked for a publisher and played piano in cinemas and night spots. At twenty he began teaching piano at the conservatory. Three years later he was also conducting a prominent choir and was winning attention for his music. In 1935 he became the city's cultural director. A three-year scholarship in 1938 took him to Paris for further study with Charles Koechlin [1592] and for a course in conducting with Frans Ruhlmann, but the outbreak of World War II a year later sent him home. He then became conductor of the São Paulo Symphony. In 1942 a prize for his Concerto for Violin brought him to the United States under the auspices of the Pan-American Union, where he began an association with the Boston Symphony that brought him many happy returns. In 1960 he returned to the São Paulo Conservatory as chaired professor and director, though he stepped down from the latter office after a year. In 1964 he also became professor of composition at the conservatory in Santos, the port city of São Paulo. Guarnieri, in his use of native elements (rhythms, instruments) and Bachian [684] counterpoint, has been seen as a sort of successor to Villa-Lobos [1817]—who helped further his career. Despite the success of his large-scale works (4 symphonies, 5 piano concerti, 2 violin concerti, several *Chôros* for various instruments and orchestra, etc.), he is probably happier in small forms, and his songs have been particularly admired. RECORDINGS: Domestic releases have included *3*

Dansas for orchestra: *Chôro for Cello and Orchestra; Suite Vila Rica* for orchestra; *Suite IV Centenario* for orchestra; and a few chamber and instrumental pieces—Sonatina for Flute and Piano, 20 of the 50 *Ponteios* for piano, Sonata No. 2 for Violin and Piano, *Estudio No. 1* for guitar, and some songs. A partial listing of records on Brazilian labels includes the Concerti for Piano Nos. 3 and 4; Concerto for Strings and Percussion; Sonata No. 4 for Violin and Piano; Sonata for Piano; and all 50 of the *Ponteios* for piano.

[2104] LANGLAIS, Jean (Làng-lä', Zhàn)
ORGANIST, TEACHER
BORN: La Fontenelle, February 15, 1907

Jean Langlais was born in a Breton village to a stonecutter and a seamstress. After a few months his parents discovered that he was blind. But his handicap proved, in a sense, a blessing, for it gained him an education that he would otherwise not have had: at ten he was admitted to the Institution for Blind Children in Paris. At first a violin student, he later switched to the keyboard and became an organ student of André Marchal in 1923. Four years later he entered the Paris Conservatoire to continue his studies with Marcel Dupré [1806]; in 1930 he took first prizes for organ and for counterpoint, which he had studied with Noël Gallon [1856]. He was then recalled to teach at the Institution for Blind Children and began private organ lessons with Charles Tournemire [1611], with whom he developed a very close relationship. In 1931 Langlais married Jeannette Sartre, a painter, who bore him a son and a daughter, and who faithfully transcribed his music from his Braille notation until her health broke down forty years later. In 1934 he entered Paul Dukas's [1574] composition class as an auditor, but on seeing his work Dukas insisted on his enrolling as a regular student. Dukas died a year later, but Langlais took a first prize in composition at the Conservatoire in 1938. The next year, Tournemire, perhaps with premonitions of his own approaching death, asked Langlais to be prepared to succeed him at Ste. Clothilde. Tournemire died in November, but the war prevented Langlais's succession until 1945. Shortly afterward concert tours worldwide won him a reputation as a first-rank organist. He first appeared in the United States in 1952. In 1960 he became professor of organ at the Schola Cantorum. He suffered a severe heart attack in 1973 and retired three years later. Jeannette Langlais

---

* Most sources give his name thus, but *Grove* has "Mozart Camargo."

died of a heart ailment in 1979. Later Langlais married Marie-Louise Jacquet, a former pupil. His catalog of compositions contains some orchestral and chamber pieces but is largely devoted to liturgical music and organ pieces. RECORDINGS: There are recordings of the *Missa "Salve regina"*, the *Messe solenelle*, the *Missa in simplicitate*, the *Messe en vieux style*, the *Trois Prières* (alto and organ), and many organ works (including a few recorded by the composer). A project by Langlais's student Ann Labounsky to record the entire organ *oeuvre* is in progress.

[2105] ROOS, Robert de (Rōz, Rō'-bârt de)
DIPLOMAT
BORN: The Hague, March 10, 1907
DIED: The Hague, March 18, 1976

De Roos graduated from the Royal Conservatory in The Hague, where he learned violin, viola, and piano, and studied composition with Johan Wagenaar (1862–1941). In 1926 he went to Paris for further piano lessons from Isidor Philipp and also studied privately with Alexis Roland-Manuel (1899–1966) and Charles Koechlin [1592]. During this time he had conducting lessons from Pierre Monteux and later with Hermann Scherchen. Back in Holland, finally, he did some further theoretical work with the composer Sem Dresden (1881–1957). After World War II he spent nearly a decade as cultural attaché to the Dutch embassy in Paris and then served in various higher capacities at the Dutch embassies in Venezuela (with accreditation to Colombia, Peru, Ecuador, and Bolivia), London, and Buenos Aires. His duties appear to have put no crimp in his composing, for his catalogue of publications extends from his twenty-first year to that of his death. RECORDINGS: His *Suggestioni* for orchestra has been recorded.

[2106] MACONCHY, Elizabeth
BORN: Broxbourne, March 19, 1907

Though her parents were Irish, Elizabeth Maconchy was born in England, in Hertfordshire, no matter what one may read elsewhere. Her musical talent evinced itself early, and she entered the Royal College of Music at sixteen to study with Charles Wood [1579] and Ralph Vaughan Williams [1633]. In 1929 a fellowship took her to Prague for a year, where her Concertino for Piano and Orchestra was premiered. Back in London in 1930 Sir Henry Wood played her suite *The Land* at a Promenade Concert. That same

year she married William LeFanu. Subsequent illness, motherhood, and the exigencies of the war years severely curtailed her composing, though she managed four of the 11 string quartets by which she is best known and a handful of other chamber and orchestral pieces. After the war she blossomed, turning out a great deal of music, including 7 operas, a symphony, and much interesting vocal music. The passionate intensity and concentration of her utterance have caused her to be labeled as an "Expressionist," though her music is perhaps closer to middle-period Bartók [1734] than to the Second Viennese School. Her younger daughter, Nicola LeFanu (1947–), is also well known as a composer. RECORDINGS: Works recorded include the *Proud Thames Overture* and the String Quartet No. 5 (both prizewinners), as well as *Ariadne* for soprano and chamber orchestra, *Serenata Concertante* for violin and orchestra, and the Symphony for Double String Orchestra.

[2107] KAUFMANN, Walter
CONDUCTOR, TEACHER, RADIO EXECUTIVE
BORN: Karlsbad, April 1, 1907

A native of what is now Karlovy Vary, Czechoslovakia, Walter Kaufmann was a pupil of Schreker [1705]. At twenty-eight he went to India and served for some years as musical director of Bombay Radio. In 1947 he emigrated to Canada and, after a year of teaching at the Halifax Conservatory, was conductor of the Winnipeg Symphony for nearly a decade. In 1957 he joined the faculty of Indiana University and taught there until his retirement, taking out American citizenship in 1964. He has written 7 operas (several of them premiered in Bloomington), 6 symphonies, and much other music. He has been strongly influenced by oriental music, a subject on which he has published numerous articles and a book. RECORDINGS: His *Partita* for wind quintet has been recorded.

[2108] RÓZSA, Miklós (Rō'-zà, Mēk'-lōsh)
CONDUCTOR, TEACHER
BORN: Budapest, April 18, 1907

Though perhaps best known for his film scores, which have garnered him three Oscars and other awards, Rózsa is also highly respected as a "serious" composer. He spent much of his childhood on the country estate of his father, a rich Hungarian industrialist who envisioned his son as a scientist. Miklós was sawing away at a fiddle, however, when he was five and at eight was giving costume concerts (dressed as the *Wunderkind* Mozart), functioning as violinist and conductor. At the *Gymnasium* in Budapest he promoted concerts. In 1925 he was sent off to the University of Leipzig to study chemistry but found an ally in Hermann Grabner, a pupil of Reger [1637] who talked the elder Rózsa into letting his son transfer to the Leipzig Conservatory, from which he graduated *cum laude* and with a publishing contract with Breitkopf and Härtel in 1929. He remained in Leipzig for some months, teaching at the conservatory, but when an all-Rózsa concert took him to Paris in 1932, he decided to stay. His music was soon being conducted by such big names as Dohnányi [1696], Charles Munch, Bruno Walter, and Karl Böhm. In 1935 a ballet commission took him to London, where he met film magnate Alexander Korda. Korda hired him to do a film score and ended up by making him staff composer. When World War II made further work on a fantasy, *The Thief of Bagdad,* impossible, Korda transferred his entire operation to Hollywood, taking Rózsa with him. The two remained together until 1942—their last joint effort was *The Jungle Book.* Then Rózsa free-lanced, working most frequently for MGM. In 1943 he married Margaret Finlason, joined the faculty of UCLA in 1945, became a citizen in 1946, and in 1955 was elected president of the Screen Composers Association, which office he held for a decade. He retired from the university at the same time he resigned his presidency but has continued to write both for films and for himself. His catalog of noncinematic music runs to more than forty opus numbers, mostly orchestral, instrumental, and choral, his film scores to more than eighty. The former is deeply and intentionally rooted in the peasant music he heard as a child. The same impulse often colors his film music, which is, however, generally more flamboyant. RECORDINGS: Orchestral works recorded include the *Variations on a Hungarian Peasant Song,* Op. 4; *North Hungarian Peasant Songs and Dances,* Op. 5; *Serenade* Op. 10; *Theme, Variations, and Finale,* Op. 13; *3 Hungarian Sketches,* Op. 14; Concerto for Strings, Op. 17; *Variations "The Vintner's Daughter",* Op. 23; Concerto for Violin, Op. 24; *Hungarian Serenade,* Op. 25; *Concert Overture,* Op. 26; *Sinfonia concertante,* Op. 29; Concerto for Piano, Op. 31; and Concerto for Cello, Op. 32. Chamber works on records include *String Trio-Serenade,* Op. 1; Piano Quintet, Op. 2; Duo for Violin and Piano, Op. 7; Duo for Cello and Piano, Op. 8; Sonata for 2 Violins, Op. 15;

String Quartet, Op. 22; and the Sonatina for Clarinet and Guitar, Op. 27. Piano works recorded include the *Variations,* Op. 9; *Bagatelles,* Op. 10; *Kaleidoscope,* Op. 19 (also recorded in an orchestral version); and the Sonata, Op. 20. Choral works include *To Everything There Is a Season,* Op. 20; *Varieties of Life,* Op. 30; and *Psalm 23,* Op. 34. The film discography includes excerpts, arrangements, and complete musical soundtracks from such films as *The Jungle Book, The Thief of Bagdad, Spellbound, The Lost Weekend, Knights of the Round Table, Crisis, Julius Caesar, Lust for Life, The Killers, Ben Hur, El Cid, The King of Kings, Quo Vadis, Lydia, Brute Force,* and *The Naked City,* as well as such late film scores as *Providence, Time After Time, Fedora,* and *Eye of the Needle.*

[2109] MATSUDAIRA, Yoritsune (Mätsoo-dī-rä, Yô-rit-soo-ne)
BORN: Tokyo, May 5, 1907

Matsudaira was one of the first Japanese composers using Western techniques to make an impression outside of Japan. A student of French culture, as well as of music, he began composing in the prescribed neoclassic style of the early 1930s and attracted the sponsorship of Alexander Tcherepnin [1961]. Later he developed an interest in gagaku, the highly formalized (and ultimately Chinese-derived) court music of Japan. This became the basis of his further composition, which gradually accommodated itself to other Western approaches, including twelve-tone writing, strict serialism, and aleatory. His son Yori-Aki (1931–) has explored even farther reaches of avant-gardism. RECORDINGS: Flutist Severino Gazzelloni has recorded the spare solo piece *Somaksah,* which the elder Matsudaira wrote for him. There is also a recording of a *Somaksah* for solo oboe (which may possibly be another version of the same piece).

[2110] HÖLLER, Karl (Höl'-er, Kärl)
ORGANIST, TEACHER
BORN: Bamberg, July 25, 1907

Son and pupil of the Bamberg Cathedral organist Valentin Höller, Karl Höller also was a choirboy there. In 1926 he entered the Würzburg Conservatory, where he studied with Zilcher [1737]. A year later he moved on to Munich, where he studied both at the Hochschule and the university. He remained there to teach from 1933 to 1937, then spent five years on the faculty of the Hochschule in Frankfurt am Main. After the war he returned to Munich, where he became president of the Hochschule from 1954 to 1972. His music—orchestral, chamber, keyboard, and vocal—is of the Hindemithian romantic-polyphonic persuasion, with some influence of French Impressionism. RECORDINGS: The *Variations on "Jesu meine Freude"* for trumpet and orchestra and the Concerto No. 2 for Cello have been recorded. There are also various small chamber pieces in various anthologies.

[2111] MORTENSEN, Otto Jacob
 Hübertz (Môr'-ten-sen, Ot'-tō Yá'-kōb Hü'-bârts)
 TEACHER, CONDUCTOR, PIANIST
 BORN: Copenhagen, August 18, 1907

A 1929 graduate of the Copenhagen Conservatory, Otto Mortensen—not to be confused with the Norwegian composer Finn Mortensen (1922–83)—began his career as a concert pianist; then, in 1937, he began a nineteen-year stint as rehearsal pianist and conductor at the Royal Opera. He taught at the conservatory from 1942 to 1966, and then at the University of Aarhus until he retired in 1974. He has written a symphony, a piano concerto, and 2 string quartets, but has been most successful with his songs. RECORDINGS: Some of his songs are on records.

[2112] SWANSON, Howard
 POSTMAN, IRS AGENT
 BORN: Atlanta, August 18, 1907
 DIED: New York, November 12, 1978

The Swanson family moved to Cleveland when Howard was ten. His mother was musical and two years later somehow managed piano lessons for him. For a time he made ends meet by working on the railroad all the livelong day. Then he got a job as a mail carrier and later became a postal clerk. In 1927 he was admitted to the Cleveland Institute as an evening student and studied with Herbert Elwell **[1948]**. Ten years later he was granted a Rosenwald Fellowship and spent two years studying with Nadia Boulanger in Paris. In 1945, after several years of working full time for the Internal Revenue Service, he decided to give himself over to music. For a long time, very little that was favorable happened and, though he was a quiet man, he became bitter at the lot of the black artist in America. Some of his songs were introduced at a Town Hall debut by his friend Edward Lee Tyler, a remarkable bass-baritone whose career was also stunted by

his color. Swanson won his first real notice when Marian Anderson sang one of his songs in a New York recital. Almost immediately a group of Swanson songs was featured during the 1950 American Composers Festival in New York, and that fall his second symphony (better known as the *Short Symphony*) was introduced by the New York Philharmonic under Dmitri Mitropoulos and won the New York Critics' Circle Award. It would be pleasant to report that Swanson went on to fame and fortune, but the facts are that apart from a third symphony and in 1970 the Trio for Flute, Oboe, and Piano in 1976, he composed little afterward. RECORDINGS: A couple of orchestral works have been recorded—the Concerto for Orchestra and the *Short Symphony*. Other works on disc are the 1976 Trio, the 1949 Suite for Cello and Piano, the 1950 *Night Music* for chamber ensemble, and some songs.

[2113] FELDERHOF, Jan Reindert Adriaan (Fel'-der-hôf, Yàn Rīn-dert Á'-drē-àn)
 TEACHER
 BORN: Bussum, September 25, 1907

After preliminary training at the lyceum in his hometown, just east of Amsterdam, he studied with Sem Dresden (1881–1957) in the Amsterdam Conservatory, where he taught from 1934 to 1954. During the final ten years of that period, he also ran the music school in Bussum. After directing the Rotterdam Conservatory for a year, he became professor of composition at the Utrecht Conservatory, where he worked until 1967. Concurrently, in 1958, he returned to Amsterdam as professor of theory and later served as director. Of a conservative bent, he has written a radio opera, a symphony, and 4 string quartets, among his larger works. RECORDINGS: His Concerto for Flute has been recorded.

[2114] PARTOS, Ödön (Pär'-tōsh, Ö-dön)
 VIOLIST, VIOLINIST, TEACHER
 BORN: Budapest, October 1, 1907
 DIED: Tel Aviv, July 6, 1977

Ödön (or Oedoen, but not Odeon) Partos studied in Budapest, where he was a violin pupil of Hubay **[1509]** and a composition pupil of Kodály **[1760]**. In central Europe he served as concertmaster of various orchestras and also made tours as a soloist. When the outlook for Jews became dismal in 1938, he migrated to Palestine, where he was almost immediately appointed first-desk violist with the national orchestra (which became the present Israel Philharmonic and with which he remained for eighteen years). In 1956 he was given the directorship of the Israel Rubin Academy in Tel Aviv, and in 1961 he became concurrently a member of the faculty of Tel Aviv University. His early compositions were in the modern Hungarian vein, but in Israel he was increasingly influenced by the music of the Near East. Toward the end of his career he experimented with a microtonal scale of thirty-one steps conceived 300 years earlier by the great Dutch scientist Christiaan Huygens and further developed by the Dutch physicist Adriaan Fokker and composer Henk Badings [2101]. Most of his important work dates from the Israeli years and includes 3 viola concerti, a violin concerto, 2 string quartets, and a considerable amount of chamber music. RECORDINGS: Among works recorded are *Yizkor (In Memoriam)* for viola and orchestra; *Agada (Legend)* for viola, piano, and percussion; *Shiluvim (Fusions)* for viola and chamber orchestra; *Visions* for flute, piano, and chamber orchestra; *Nebulae* for wind quintet; String Quartet No. 2 ("Psalms"); and *Prelude* for piano.

[2115] LOUIS FERDINAND von Hohenzollern, Prince of Prussia
BORN: Berlin (?), November 9, 1907

Prince Louis Ferdinand, as the eldest son of Prince Wilhelm, eldest son of the infamous Kaiser Bill, is putative heir to the German throne. Educated at the *Gymnasium* in Potsdam and at the University of Berlin, he holds a Ph.D. He is an amateur composer and has written an autobiography published in the United States as *The Rebel Prince*. RECORDINGS: There is an LP of orchestral pieces and songs.

[2116] PHILLIPS, Burrill
TEACHER, PIANIST
BORN: Omaha, November 9, 1907

Born in Nebraska, Phillips grew up from the age of three in Denver, where he studied piano and played in the high school orchestra. In 1924 he began working his way through the Denver College of Music, where his composition teacher was Edwin Stringham, a Respighi [1718] pupil. From 1925 he was employed as an announcer and musician by a local radio station. Three years later he married Alberta Mayfield, a violinist, giving up school to teach piano. (Alberta later became his lyricist and librettist.) By 1931 he

was able to go to the Eastman School, where he studied with Howard Hanson [1927] and Bernard Rogers [1875], acquired two degrees in two years, and was rewarded for his assiduity by being taken to Eastman's almaternal bosom as a member of her faculty. During his sixteen years there many of his compositions were determinedly illustrative of homey American themes—Miles Standish, Paul Revere, Tom Paine, baseball, village squares, and hoedowns. But he also wrote abstractly for both orchestra and chamber ensembles in a neo-classic vein. In 1949 he moved to the University of Illinois at Urbana, but increasing commissions caused him to resign in 1964 to give more time to composition. Since then he has served as composer-in-residence or visiting professor at Eastman, Juilliard, Colorado College, and the universities of Colorado, Hawaii, Kansas, Southern California, and Texas. RECORDINGS: These include *Selections from McGuffey's Reader* for orchestra; Sonata for Cello and Piano; Sonata for Violin and Harpsichord; Sonata for Organ; and *Canzona III*. (This last is for reciter and chamber orchestra; the original text was by Mrs. Phillips, but the composer invites other poets to supply their own.)

[2117] MANEVICH, Alexander Mendelevich (Mån-yā'-vich, Ål-yek-sån'-der Men-del-yā'-vich)
TEACHER
BORN: Starodube Chernigovsky, January 7, 1908

Born near Bryansk, Russia, Manevich began his musical studies as a cellist. He then studied for a year at the Moscow Conservatory with Anatoly Alexandrov (1888–), a conservative student of Vassilenko's [1628], and for two more with Maximilian Steinberg (1883–1946) in Leningrad. Eventually he returned to the Moscow school, from which he graduated only in 1945! Afterward he taught at the Leningrad Conservatory. He has written an operetta, symphonies, concerti, quartets, etc. RECORDINGS: His Concerto for Clarinet has been recorded by Soviet clarinetist Isaac Roginsky.

[2118] PLANEL, Robert (Plå-nel', Rō-bâr')
CIVIL SERVANT
BORN: Montélimar, January 22, 1908

Born in a city on the lower Rhone, Planel is the brother of the tenor Jean Planel. A graduate of the Paris Conservatoire, he was the

1933 winner of the Grand Prix de Rome, and like so many such victors, he found a cozy niche in the government checking out music teaching in the Paris schools. He managed to find time to compose a ballet and other works in various genres. RECORDINGS: A Concerto for Trumpet has been recorded by French musicians.

[2119] VERRALL, John Weedon
TEACHER, EDITOR
BORN: Britt, Iowa, June 17, 1908

The son of an English-born American IRS agent, Verrall spent his boyhood in a small town in north central Iowa, where he began piano study at age eleven and composition at twelve. When he was fourteen, he was encouraged to study by the touring Sergei Rachmaninoff [1638]. The next year the Verralls moved to Minneapolis, where John became conductor of his high school orchestra. He spent three years from 1928 nominally a student at the Minneapolis College of Music, though during part of that time he was studying with R. O. Morris (1886–1948) and Frank Merrick in London and with Zoltán Kodály [1760] in Budapest. They gave him a B.Mus. anyhow. In 1934 he also acquired a B.A. from the University of Minnesota. Later he studied with Aaron Copland [1986] in 1938, Roy Harris [1947] in 1940, and Frederick Jacobi [1850] in 1945. From 1935 to 1942 he ascended the academic ranks at Hamline College across the river, and in 1935 he married Margaret Larawa. His music attracted the attention of Dimitri Mitropoulos, then conductor of the Minneapolis Symphony, who premiered several of his works, including his first symphony (of 5) with that orchestra and with the New York Philharmonic. In 1942 Verrall joined the faculty of Mt. Holyoke College but was taken into the army the next year as a cryptographer. After he returned to civilian life, he succeeded William Schuman [2158] as director of publications for the firm of G. Schirmer in New York, after a year as a Guggenheim Fellow, but he left soon thereafter, in 1948, to spend his last twenty-five academic years at the University of Washington. His other compositions include 3 operas, 7 string quartets, and several concerti, and he has published a harmony text and other writings on music. For a time he experimented with a nine-tone scale of his own devising. RECORDINGS: Prelude and Allegro for strings, at least two string quartets (nos. 4 and 7), and the 1941 Sonata for Horn and Piano have appeared.

[2120] DISTLER, Hugo (Dist'-ler, Hoo'-gō)
ORGANIST, CONDUCTOR, TEACHER
BORN: Nuremberg, June 24, 1908
DIED: Strausberg bei Berlin, November 1, 1942

One of the masters of Protestant religious music in this century, Hugo Distler (whose surname was his mother's) is said to have been the illegitimate son of a Nuremberg industrialist. When Hugo was still a child, his mother married and emigrated to the United States, leaving him with his grandparents, who seem to have been not wholly grateful for the responsibility. He studied piano at the Dupont School (from which he was twice expelled for fractiousness) and graduated from the Melanchthon Gymnasium in 1927. That autumn he entered the Leipzig Conservatory, where he studied composition with Hermann Grabner, a Reger [1637] pupil, and organ with the great Günther Ramin [1956]. The onset of the Great Depression, however, made it impossible for him to continue, and late in 1930 he was named (not without considerable opposition) successor to the aged Emanuel Kemper at the historic Jakobikirche in Lübeck. Starting virtually from scratch, Distler revitalized the musical life there, notably with a series of musical vesper services, and with the several musical groups he organized or oversaw —and increasingly with his own compositions. In 1933 he married Waltraut Thienhaus, the sister of a pupil, and took on the additional duties of teaching twice a week in Spandau, a Berlin suburb. In 1934 he presented a cantata, at the behest of the Nazis, hymning Ewiges Deutschland—which has since vanished. Guest appearances helped him get known elsewhere in Germany. By 1936 he was teaching at the Lübeck Conservatory as well as in Spandau (he now had two children to support). Meanwhile, the Nazis were making life unbearable for the church people in Lübeck, and in the spring of 1937, ignoring his other commitments, Distler accepted a teaching post at the Württemberg Conservatory in Stuttgart. The family acquired a home in the suburbs (necessitating the composer's having to learn to drive, which he is said to have done wretchedly). Distler immediately founded an oratorio choir, the Esslinger Singkreis, which first appeared in a performance of Monteverdi's [333] Orfeo as edited by Carl Orff [1912], a composer who fascinated the conductor. Though Distler was still in sufficiently good standing with the Nazis to be placed on the local screening board to certify the racial purity of music and musicians, he was increasingly criticized for his adherence to religious music. A guest appearance with his choir at a festival in Graz, in June 1939, however, won him an appointment as professor at the Berlin-Charlottenberg Hochschule for the next year. In the interim Germany invaded Poland, and early in 1940 Distler was called up for a physical but was pronounced too frail to fight. Thus he was able to keep his Berlin commitment in the fall, settling in Strausberg, several miles outside the city. The next year saw the birth of a second daughter, another abortive call-up, and Distler's appointment as director of the Berlin Cathedral Choir. But this proved to be a rather hollow honor, for military needs stripped the organization of qualified male singers, and the Hitler Youth (with official sanction) kept the choirboys away from rehearsals and performances. The situation became increasingly unbearable. In October 1942, while his family was away, Distler was ordered to report for service with a Panzer outfit. After brooding for two weeks, on November 1 he turned on the gas and went to bed. He was thirty-four.

An oratorio and a contemplated opera never got off the drawing board, but Distler lived long enough to publish twenty-one opus numbers of remarkable quality. Apart from a concerto for piano, one for harpsichord, a string quartet, a sonata for two pianos, and another for two violins, Distler's entire output is limited to organ and choral music. RECORDINGS: Much of the organ and choral music has been recorded—notably the *Weihnachtsgeschichte,* the *Totentanz,* the *Choralpassion,* the settings of Eduard Mörike, and many of the important motets.

[2121] FRANCO, Johan Henri Gustav
(Frȧnk'-ō, Yō'-hȧn On-rē Gōōs'-tȧv)
ARCHITECT
BORN: Zaandam, July 12, 1908

The son of a Dutch architect and a painter, Franco studied piano from childhood. After two years as a law student at the University of Amsterdam, he decided to follow in the paternal footsteps and turned to architecture, which profession he practiced briefly. Meanwhile he had been studying composition with Willem Pijper [1899] and had heard several of his own works, including a symphony, performed. In 1934 he packed his bags and sailed for New York, where he lived until called into military service in 1942. During that period he became fascinated with Sir Francis Bacon and particu-

larly with the "Baconian cipher," which is supposed not only to prove that Bacon wrote Shakespeare's plays but also to reveal messages he hid in them. Two results were the orchestral *Baconiana* and *The Virgin Queen's Dream Monologue* (part of an unrealized opera, text derived from the plays via the cipher). In 1948 he married a writer, Eloise Lavrischeff, and settled in Virginia Beach. About the same time he became fascinated with carillon music, once an important aspect of the old Netherlandish art, and has since written half a hundred works for or incorporating the medium. In more recent years he has also written a good deal for guitar and some electronic music. His large output also includes more usual kinds of works, including 5 symphonies, 6 string quartets, orchestral suites, a series of recent works entitled *Concerti lirici* for various instruments and orchestra, other concerted works, and sonatas. RECORDINGS: *The Virgin Queen's Dream Monologue* for soprano and orchestra; Symphony No. 5 ("Cosmos"); *Fantasy* for cello and orchestra; *As the Prophets Foretold* (voices, brass choir, and carillon).

[2122] FRUMERIE, Per Gunnar Fredrik de (Frōō'-mer-ē, Pâr Goon'-är Frā'-drik de)
PIANIST, TEACHER
BORN: Nacka, July 20, 1908

After basic training from his mother, Gunnar de Frumerie, at age twelve, began lessons in nearby Stockholm with Lennart Lundberg, a Paderewski [1527] pupil. Three years later he entered the Stockholm Conservatory, where he studied with composer Ernst Ellberg (1868–1948), graduating in 1928. Afterward he spent three years in further study in Vienna with Liszt [1218] pupil Emil von Sauer and Schoenberg [1657] disciple Erwin Stein (1885–1958), and in Paris with pianist Alfred Cortot and musicologist Leonid Sabaneyev. After 1945 he taught piano at the Stockholm Conservatory. An eclectic of a nationalist-romantic tinge, he has written a successful opera *(Singoalla),* a ballet, several concerti for various instruments, cantatas, and chamber music, but is especially admired as a songwriter. RECORDINGS: There are some recordings of songs and piano pieces. The Louisville Orchestra and Varujan Kojian have recorded the 1941 *Symphonic Variations.* Other recordings include *Music for Nonet;* Piano Trio No. 2; *Pastoral Suite* for flute, harp, and strings; and *Aria* for flute and organ.

[2123] TARP, Svend Erik (Tärp, Svend
Ȧr'-ēk)
TEACHER, EDITOR
BORN: Thisted, August 6, 1908

A native of northwestern Denmark, Tarp
studied composition with Knud Jeppesen
(1892–1974) at the Royal Conservatory in
Copenhagen and had already attracted attention with several chamber and orchestral
works by the time he left in 1931. He spent a
year studying, on scholarship, in Bavaria
and Austria. From 1932 to 1934 he taught
privately and played in a dance band. He
then returned to the conservatory to teach
and from the next year also taught classes at
the university and the Royal Opera School.
After 1942 he was occupied with various official positions in the composers' union and
the national musical publication association,
and as editor for Edition Dania, music publishers. His works include 2 operas (one for
television), as many ballets, 7 symphonies,
suites, overtures, and other orchestral music,
as well as choral, chamber, and piano music,
songs, and a large number of film and radio-
television scores. RECORDINGS: Mostly pre-
LP, these include the *Comedy Overture, Mo-
saic Suite,* piano concerto, *Serenade* for flute
and strings, Duo for flute and viola, and
songs.

[2124] NIN-CULMELL, Joaquín María
(Nēn Kool-mel', Hwȧ-kēn' Mȧ-rē'-ȧ)
PIANIST, CONDUCTOR, TEACHER
BORN: Berlin, September 5, 1908

Nin-Culmell is the son of Spanish composer
Joaquín Nin [1721] and Cuban singer Rosa
Culmell and brother to American writer
Anaïs Nin. His parents moved to Berlin
from Paris shortly before he was born, and
his father decamped while his offspring were
still children. He was Paris-trained (at the
Schola Cantorum and the Paris Conservatoire), his most important teachers being
Paul Dukas [1574] and the pianists Alfred
Cortot and Ricardo Viñes. In the early 1930s
he went to Granada to study with Manuel
de Falla [1688], who left a strong imprint on
his music. During that same decade he
toured as a concert pianist, but at the outset
of World War II he moved to the United
States. He taught for a decade at Williams
College, rising to the chairmanship of the
music department and serving as conductor
of the Berkshire Community Orchestra. He
was on active duty in the Cuban army for a
brief time during the war. In 1950 he went to
Berkeley as chairman of the music department at the University of California and

conductor of the orchestra, and taught there
until he retired in 1974. His rather small list
of compositions includes a ballet, a *Mass,* a
piano concerto, a cello concerto, a piano
quintet, piano pieces, and songs. RECORD-
INGS: There is a recording of his 1962 *Diferencias: Variations pour orchestre* conducted
by Jorge Mester.

[2125] SUCHOŇ, Eugen (Zook-ōn'yȧ',
Oi'-gen)
TEACHER
BORN: Pezinok, September 25, 1908

Perhaps the most prominent Slovak composer of his generation, Suchoň was born in
a little town near Bratislava, the son of the
village organist-schoolteacher (a familiar
pattern in Czechoslovak music). He had his
first piano lessons from his mother and continued with teachers in Bratislava while he
went to high school (where he conducted the
student orchestra). After his 1927 graduation
he studied at the Academy of Music in Bratislava, where his composition teacher Frico
Kafenda, from the Leipzig Conservatory,
had a powerful effect on his musical thinking. In 1931 he went to Prague for two years
with Vítězslav Novák [1617] at the conservatory's master school, where he began to
break away from conservatism. In 1933 he
returned to the Academy of Music and
taught there until 1947 when he took a professorship in the School of Education at the
University of Bratislava. The year 1949 saw
the premiere of his opera *Krútňava (The
Whirlpool),* a strongly nationalistic work to
a Slovak libretto, on which he had worked
for a decade. It was hailed as a masterpiece
and remains a cornerstone of the Slovak repertoire. A second opera, *Svätopluk,* which
originated in incidental music he had written for a play in 1934, was successfully unveiled in 1960; it shows the composer using
twelve-tone elements. A period of poor
health brought Suchoň's teaching to a halt
around this time, but he later returned to the
university as professor of theory, retiring in
1974. RECORDINGS: Both operas have been
recorded, as have a number of orchestral
compositions—*Balladic Suite; Fantasy and
Burlesque* for violin and orchestra; Concerto
for Clarinet; *The Psalm of the Carpathian
Land,* cantata for tenor, mixed choir, and
orchestra; *Metamorphosis on an Original
Theme; Sinfonietta rustica;* and *Symphonic
Fantasy on B-A-C-H* for organ, strings, and
percussion. Additional recordings include
Poème macabre for violin and piano, a piano
version of *Metamorphosis* and one of *Kaleidoscope,* other piano pieces, and two song

cycles for voice and piano, *Ad astra* and *Contemplations.*

[2126] FERGUSON, Howard
PIANIST, TEACHER, MUSICOLOGIST
BORN: Belfast, October 21, 1908

In 1921 the great English pianist Harold Samuel heard Ferguson play and took his training in hand. While studying with Samuel, Ferguson graduated from the Westminster School in London and then attended the Royal College of Music. After giving a concert career a try, however, he abandoned it to compose, though he continued to perform his own works. (He toured the United States doing so in 1953.) In 1948 he began fifteen years of teaching at the Royal Academy. His compositions included a ballet (later disowned), a couple of cantatas, and a piano concerto but were mostly chamber-scale. Having reached Op. 19 in 1959, he gave up composition and turned to editing old keyboard music. RECORDINGS: Recordings include the Octet Op. 4 and the Sonata for Violin and Piano Op. 2 (in which he accompanies Jascha Heifetz).

[2127] DANIEL-LESUR (Dàn-yel' Lə-sür')
PIANIST, ORGANIST, TEACHER, RADIO
OFFICIAL
BORN: Paris, November 19, 1908

Daniel-Lesur was christened Daniel Jean Yves Lesur. Like his mother, *née* Alice Thiboust, he was a pupil of organist-composer Charles Tournemire [1611], though later he studied at the Paris Conservatoire, graduating in 1929. Beginning in 1927, he assisted Tournemire at Ste. Clothilde for a decade and then became organist of the Benedictine Abbey in Paris. He was appointed professor of counterpoint at the Schola Cantorum in 1935. A year later he joined with Olivier Messiaen [2129], André Jolivet [2073], and his own pupil Yves Baudrier (1906–) in an association called La Jeune France (Young France), committed to slaying the neo-classical dragon that to them seemed to be devouring French music. He joined the French National Radio in the spring of 1939, but with the outbreak of war in the fall he joined the army as a demolition expert. When France capitulated in 1940, he moved to the unoccupied area and resumed his duties with the radio network, which he continued after the war was over. He was especially successful in promoting contemporary music. In 1957 he was made director

of the Schola Cantorum. He left in 1964. Since 1969 he has held several musicotheatrical administrative posts in the government. Unsympathetic to musical "systems," Daniel-Lesur (not unlike his friend Jolivet) works on the premise that music is meant to enchant the listener. He writes mostly in smaller forms, but his 1969 opera *Andrea del Sarto* generates much power. RECORDINGS: There is an abridged recording of the opera, as well as the *Symphonie de danses;* the *Sérénade* for strings; the *Pastorale* for chamber orchestra; *Variations* for piano and strings; the 1949 symphonic poem *Andrea del Sarto* (a completely separate work from the opera); *Suite médióvale* for flute, string trio, and harp; and the *Suite française* for four clarinets.

[2128] STEVENS, Halsey
TEACHER, WRITER
BORN: Scott, N.Y., December 3, 1908

A farmer's son from the Finger Lake country, Stevens had music lessons from his tenth year and took a degree in music from nearby Syracuse University in 1931. After four years of musical odd-jobbing, he returned to the university as a graduate student and teacher. In 1937 he was hired as associate professor of music by Dakota Wesleyan University in Mitchell, South Dakota. There he married Harriett Meritt, a ceramic artist, in 1939. In 1941 he became head of the College of Music at Bradley University in Peoria, Illinois. He joined the Naval Reserve in 1943 and, while stationed in California's Bay Area, took the opportunity to study with Ernest Bloch [1729] at the University of California at Berkeley. In the spring of 1946 Stevens joined the faculty of the University of Redlands in California and that fall found a permanent post at the University of Southern California. Two years later he was made chairman of the composition department, an office which he held until his retirement in 1976. In 1953 he published his authoritative critical biography of Béla Bartók [1734]; for some years he also wrote the program notes for the Los Angeles Philharmonic, and he has published many scholarly articles. He has written a considerable body of determinedly tonal but much-praised music. RECORDINGS: Orchestral works recorded include the Symphony No. 1, *Symphonic Dances, Triskelion,* and the Concerto for Clarinet and Strings. Also recorded are sonatas for trombone, trumpet, and horn (each with piano accompaniment), *Suite for Sob Violin,* Sonata for Solo Cello, *Dittico* for saxophone and piano; *Psalm*

CXVIII for chorus; and smaller choral works.

[2129] MESSIAEN, Olivier Eugène Prosper Charles (Mes-sē-àn', Ō-lēv-yā', Ō-zhân' Prōs-pâr' Shärl)
ORGANIST, TEACHER
BORN: Avignon, December 10, 1908

It brooks little argument to say that Olivier Messiaen is the most important name in French music since Ravel [1666], the greatest French musical innovator since Debussy [1547], and—if we exorcise Webern's [1773] restless spirit—the most powerful influence on the post–World War II serial avant-garde. His father, Pierre Messiaen, was a Flemish-descended professor of literature at the University of Grenoble; his mother, Cécile Sauvage, was a poet and a devout Catholic, and her son absorbed both currents—especially the latter, for his faith dominates his life and his music. ("I was born believing," he maintains.) Initially he was largely self-taught in music and had composed a piano impression of Tennyson's poem "The Lady of Shalott" by the time he was nine. About this time the Messiaens moved to Nantes, where some knowledgeable acquaintances persuaded them to enroll the boy in the Paris Conservatoire, which they did in 1919. He doubled his years on earth while there, studying with (notably) Dukas [1574] and Marcel Dupré [1806], as well as Jean and Noël Gallon [1856] and Maurice Emmanuel [1544], and winning first prizes in five fields. In 1931, the youngest chief organist in France (it is said), he ascended for the first time the organ loft of the Ste. Trinité. This has been the chief focus of his life for over forty years; under normal conditions he has played four services every Sunday plus those for feast days and for innumerable weddings, funerals, and other sacraments. (One of the greatest organists of the day, Messiaen has concertized all over the world.) His orchestral work *Les Offrandes oubliées (Forgotten Offerings)* was conducted by Walter Straram that same year, and, over the next few years, was followed by other orchestral, choral, and keyboard works. In 1935 he and his sometime fellow-students André Jolivet [2073] and Daniel-Lesur [2127] banded together to form a group known as "La Spirale," which, with the addition of Yves Baudrier (1906–) the next year, became "Jeune France," dedicated to giving substance to a national music that in the opinion of the group's members had become cynical and trivialized. Also in 1936 Messiaen was appointed to professor-

ships at the Schola Cantorum and the École-Normale.

This meteoric ascent was interrupted by the outbreak of war in 1939. Messiaen was called up almost immediately, was captured in the German breakthrough the next summer, and was interned in a Stalag at Görlitz in Silesia, where he was held for two years. While there he wrote, for the instruments available, a *Quartet pour le fin du temps (Quartet for the End of Time)*, which was performed for the prisoners in 1941. Returning to Paris the next year, he assumed his organ post again and was made professor of harmony at the Conservatoire. (Three years later he became professor of analysis, esthetics, and rhythm, a previously nonexistent position.) Among his innumerable pupils have been such vigorous apostles of the New Music as Pierre Boulez [2346], Karlheinz Stockhausen [2377], Jacques-Louis Monod, and Iannis Xenakis [2321], as well as such less zealous musicians as William Albright [2433], Easley Blackwood [2406], Betsy Jolas [2364], and many others from countries as diverse as Japan and Bulgaria. Another pupil was the pianist Yvonne Loriod, who became his companion of choice and eventually his wife and who has largely devoted her career to playing his music. (Her sister Jeanne officiates over his music for Ondes Martenots.) Since World War II, Messiaen's life has been steadily productive and reasonably uneventful, save for much traveling to concertize, oversee productions, and to guest-teach.

Messiaen does not differentiate between his music and his religion, seeing the one as a natural expression of the other. The sources from which he draws are universal —Gregorian chant, oriental musics (especially Indian), the work of his immediate predecessors (notably Debussy [1547] and the twelve-toners), and natural sounds (especially birdsongs, which he has noted down all over the world). If he hymns Christ and nature, he also sings of human love (in its physical aspect) as consistent with his devotion to praising his Maker. Messiaen has been called a mystic (an appellation he dislikes), though it is his attempts to explain his mystical views of music—the color evocations of sounds, the insistence that voluptuousness transcends sensuality—that fail to communicate much to many people. Over and above this sort of subjectivity, there is a hard-boiled and complex intellectuality that has evinced itself in such devices as "nonretrogradable rhythms" (rhythmic patterns that are palindromic), modes of limited transposition (e.g., a whole-tone scale, such as C-D-E-F sharp-G sharp-A sharp, can be transposed *only* to B-C sharp-D sharp-F-G-A), and modality (or "scale-patterns") applied to such matters as rhythm, intensity, and attack. Indeed, Messiaen may be credited with (or blamed for) much of the emphasis on "total serialization" and other such inaudible systems over the past two or three decades.

Messaien's most recent major work, which he is said to regard as the culmination of his career, is a gigantic opera, *Saint-François d'Assise*. This piece, premiered in Paris on November 28, 1983, has a playing time of nearly five hours, and calls for an orchestra of such size that ample sections of it must be placed outside the pit of even the largest opera house. Messiaen terms *Saint-François* "Franciscan scenes" rather than an "opera" —apparently correctly, since it involves a minimum of dramatic action. Reports suggest that first-nighters found it more interesting to watch the instrumentalists than the stage, and though reviewers paid homage to the orchestral score, one summed up the vocal parts as sounding like "tuckered-out Debussy."

RECORDINGS: Consistent with his stature in the present artistic world, most of Messiaen's music has become available on records, except for a few early works (some of them now disowned) and the new opera, which seems likely to be recorded eventually. Orchestral works on records include *Les Offrandes oubliées,* 1931; *L'Ascension,* 1934; *Hymne,* 1945 (revision of a 1933 work); *Turangalîla-Symphonie,* 1949; *Le Réveil des oiseaux* for piano and orchestra 1953; *Oiseaux exotiques* for piano and small orchestra, 1955; *Chronochromie,* 1960; *7 Haïkaï* for piano, percussion, and small orchestra, 1963; *Couleurs de la Cité Celeste* for piano and small orchestra, 1964; *Et exspecto resurrectionem mortuorum,* 1964; and *Des canyons aux étoiles,* 1974. Choral-orchestral recordings include *3 petites liturgies de la présence divine* for women's voices, piano, Ondes Martenot, percussion, and strings, 1944; and *La Transfiguration de Notre Seigneur Jésus Christ,* 1969. Other vocal recordings include the song cycle *Poèmes pour Mi* (in the 1936 version for soprano and piano and in the 1937 version for soprano and orchestra); *O Sacrum Convivium!* of 1937 (for unaccompanied choir); the song cycle *Chants de terre et de ciel* for soprano and piano, 1938; *Harawi* for soprano and piano, 1945; and *5 Rechants* for twelve solo voices, 1949. Chamber and instrumental recordings include the *8 Préludes* for piano, 1929; *Thème et Variations* for violin and piano, 1932; *Fête des belles eaux* for six Ondes Martenots; *Quatuor pour la fin du temps* for clarinet, violin, cello, and

piano, 1941; *Visions de L'Amen* for two pianos, 1943; *20 Regards sur l'Enfant Jésus,* 1944; *Cantéyodjayâ, Neumes rythmiques,* and *Mode de valeurs et d'intensités,* works for piano from 1949; *Île de Feu I and II* for piano, 1950; *Le Merle noir* for flute and piano, 1951; *Catalogue d'Oiseaux* for piano, 1958; and *La Fauvette des jardins* for piano, 1970. In addition the complete works for organ have been recorded by the composer and others. (Messiaen has also written several didactic books, many articles, and a detailed treatise on his method.)

[2130] CARTER, Elliott Cook, Jr.
TEACHER, CONDUCTOR, CRITIC
BORN: New York, December 11, 1908

In an age when approved music was largely mathematical (or freed of all trammels whatever), Elliott Carter more than held his own as one who successfully combined the highly cerebral with the impulse to free expression. But he did not come easily or rapidly to his present place, and his development is a classic case of ontogeny emulating phylogeny. After graduating from Horace Mann High School in New York, he betook himself at eighteen to Harvard, where he settled in to major in literature. At the same time he was studying piano, and gradually his interest in music took the upper hand so that after graduating in 1930 he stayed on for two years to acquire an M.A. under Piston [1890], Hill [1632], and Holst [1658]. Then, following what had almost become *de rigueur* for American composers, he went to Paris to study with Nadia Boulanger. He wrote incidental music for a performance of Sophocles' *Philoctetes* by the Harvard Classical Club in 1934—apparently his first music to be publicly performed. He also wrote a one-act opera, *Tom and Lily,* that year. He returned to the United States in 1935 and settled in New York City, where he wrote musical criticism and from 1937 to 1939 was music director of the Ballet Caravan (for whom he wrote *The Ball Room Guide* and *Pocahontas).* He married Helen Frost-Jones in 1939 and, doubtless to get on a more solid economic footing, took a job on the faculty of St. John's College (with a curriculum based on the Great Books) at Annapolis. There he was required to teach physics, mathematics, philosophy, and Greek, as well as music. However well the job may have paid, it understandably hampered Carter's productivity, and in 1942 he decamped to Santa Fe, where in short order he completed a symphony. For the next three years he contributed to the war effort as a consultant to the Office of War Information. After the war he returned to teaching—first at the Peabody Conservatory, 1946–48, then at Columbia, to 1950. After that his teaching stints were sporadic, though he put in four years at Yale from 1958. (Other schools where he taught or lectured or served as composer-in-residence were Johns Hopkins, Juilliard, MIT, Cornell, and the American Academy in Rome.)

It was not until he was well into his forties that Carter began to win real respect as a composer. (The 1954 edition of John Tasker Howard's *Our American Music* gives him only a note.) Having begun as a fairly conservative diatonicist, he progressed through chromaticism and modern contrapuntalism to serialism before finding his own voice. En route, he was strongly influenced by such things as jazz, the polyrhythms of Ives [1659], and the motorism of Stravinsky [1748]. Finally he emerged as the eclectic's eclectic—a synthesizer of many of the most important currents of his time. Among his many honors and awards have been two Pulitzer Prizes (for the second and third string quartets, in 1960 and 1973 respectively). In 1970 Virgil Thomson [1928] pronounced him the composer of the most interesting chamber music of his time. Carter's music is extraordinarily complex. Not surprisingly the canon is small, and some of the earlier pieces (e.g., *Tom and Lily*) seem to have dropped out. Besides those mentioned, the major works include a ballet *The Minotaur, Variations for Orchestra,* Double Concerto for Harpsichord, Piano, and Orchestra, Concerto for Piano, Concerto for Orchestra, and *A Symphony of Three Orchestras.* More recent works include *Triple Duo* for six players, three song cycles—*A Mirror on Which to Dwell; Syringa;* and *In Sleep, In Thunder* —and two solo works, *Night Fantasies* for piano and *Changes* for guitar.

RECORDINGS: Most of Carter's mature output has been recorded. Among the orchestral or chamber-orchestral works on records are the ballet suite *Pocahontas;* Symphony No. 1; *Holiday Overture; Elegy* for string orchestra (the version for string quartet is also recorded); ballet music for *The Minotaur; Variations;* Double Concerto for Harpsichord, Piano, and 2 Chamber Orchestras; Concerto for Piano; Concerto for Orchestra; and *A Symphony of Three Orchestras.* Vocal music recorded includes *To Music, Heart Not So Heavy As Mine,* and *Musicians Wrestle Everywhere* for chorus; *Tarantella* for men's chorus and orchestra; *The Harmony of Morning* for women's chorus and strings; *A Mirror on Which to Dwell* for soprano and chamber ensemble; and *Syringa*

for mezzo-soprano, bass, and ensemble. Chamber and instrumental recordings include *Pastoral* for clarinet and piano; Sonata for Piano; Sonata for Cello and Piano; *8 Etudes and a Fantasy* for woodwind quartet; Woodwind Quintet; String Quartets Nos. 1–3; Sonata for Flute, Oboe, Cello, and Harpsichord; *8 Pieces for 4 Timpani;* Duo for Violin and Piano; Brass Quintet; *Night Fantasies* for piano; and *Changes* for guitar.

[2131] SIEGMEISTER, Elie
CONDUCTOR, PIANIST, TEACHER
BORN: New York, January 15, 1909

In his concern for the common man, American roots, and liberal causes, Elie Siegmeister seems the archetypal American composer of the 1930s and 1940s; this side of him, however, tends to obscure the fact that his productivity and the scope and variety of his work extend far beyond such boundaries. The son of a surgeon, he was born in Harlem and grew up in Brooklyn. He was unusually bright and entered Columbia University at fifteen. There he decided after a short time to major in music. His composition teacher was Seth Bingham, a pupil of Horatio Parker [1556], but he also took lessons from Wallingford Riegger [1793] outside. After three years Siegmeister graduated *cum laude* and took the next boat for Paris, the École Normale, and Nadia Boulanger. In Paris he wrote some rather "modern" music, married Hannah Mersel, a young educationist, acquired a *diplome,* and returned to New York in 1932. Two years later he discovered American folk music, thanks to an old lady from the Kentucky hills called Aunt Mollie Jackson. Abandoning (for the nonce) what he considered elitism for "peoples' music," a stance that produced such works as the choral *John Henry* of 1935 and the orchestral works *Ozark Set* and *Prairie Legend,* in 1943 and 1944, respectively. He studied conducting with Albert Stoessel at the Juilliard School and organized a proletarian choir, the American Ballad Singers, with whom he toured and made records until 1945. In 1940 he collaborated with New York *Times* critic Olin Downes, who was sympathetic to his views, on a highly successful folksong collection, *A Treasury of American Song.* Four years later Siegmeister collaborated with another *Times* man, Walter Kerr, on a revue, *Sing Out, Sweet Land,* based on American tunes; sponsored by the Theater Guild and starring Burl Ives and Alfred Drake, it ran for three months on Broadway and got an "original cast" recording from Decca Records. In 1945 Siegmeister attained an even wider fame when Toscanini elected to conduct his *Western Suite* in an NBC Symphony broadcast.

After many years of barnstorming as teacher, lecturer, and conductor, Siegmeister settled in at Hofstra University on Long Island in 1949. There he taught, conducted the orchestra for a dozen years, 1953–65, and retired in 1976 after a decade as composer-in-residence. In his later years he turned away from such obvious folksiness, writing a good deal of abstract music—5 symphonies, concerti, string quartets, sonatas, not to mention 5 operas, a ballet, a film score, and music for plays. He is perhaps at his best as a writer of vocal music, of which he has produced much in all categories. He has also written several books on music.

RECORDINGS: Numerous orchestral works have been recorded—the 1956 Concerto for Clarinet, the 1957 Symphony No. 3, and the 1960 Concerto for Flute (all conducted by Siegmeister), as well as the earlier *Sunday in Brooklyn, Ozark Set, Western Suite,* and *Wilderness Road.* Chamber works recorded include String Quartets Nos. 2 and 3, Sextet for Brass and Percussion, and Sonatas Nos. 1–5 for Violin and Piano (nos. 1, 4, and 5 are played by his daughter and son-in-law, Nancy and Alan Mandel). Other works on records include the *Fantasy and Soliloquy* for solo cello; (for piano) Sonata No. 1 (also known as the *American Sonata,* performed by the composer), Sonata No. 2 (performed by Mandel), *Theme and Variations No. 2, On This Ground,* and *3 Studies;* (for chorus) *American Legends,* performed by the American Ballad Singers; (song cycles and sets for voice and piano) *Elegies for Garcia Lorca, 5 cummings Songs, Madam to You, The Face of War, Songs of Experience, The Strange Funeral in Braddock,* and others; (theater pieces) *Sing Out, Sweet Land* and *Funnybone Alley.*

[2132] FOLPRECHT, Zdeněk (Fôl'-prekht, Zden'-yek)
CONDUCTOR
BORN: Turnov, January 26, 1909
DIED: Prague, October 29, 1961

Folprecht came from a city about fifty miles northeast of Prague. He was schooled in the capital, studying with Foerster at the Prague Conservatory and with Vítězslav Novák **[1617]** and the great conductor Vaclav Talich at the Master School. In 1923 he was hired by the National Theater in Bratislava as a conductor and later also conducted the concerts of the Slovak Philharmonic there. In 1939 he returned to Prague as conductor

of the National Opera. While in Bratislava, he produced an opera, *The Fatal Game of Love.* He also wrote a good deal of incidental music for stage and radio, 4 symphonies, a violin concerto, a piano concerto, 3 string quartets, and many songs and folksong arrangements. RECORDINGS: The *Concertino for Wind-String Nonet* has been recorded.

[2133] BACEWICZ, Grażyna (Bȧt-sā'-vĕch Grȧ-zhĕ'-nȧ)
VIOLINIST, PIANIST, TEACHER
BORN: Lodź, February 5, 1909
DIED: Warsaw, January 17, 1969

Poland's leading twentieth-century woman composer, Grażyna Bacewicz graduated in 1932 from the Warsaw Conservatory, then spent two years studying in Paris with Nadia Boulanger and violinist Carl Flesch. She returned to Lodź in 1934 to teach violin at its conservatory for a year, but much of her time during the next twenty years was spent concertizing. (She frequently performed her own works, both those for violin and piano.) After the war she wrote a good deal of music for radio, including an opera, *The Adventures of King Arthur.* She gave up playing to compose in the 1950s. During her last three years she was professor of composition at the Warsaw Conservatory. She died three weeks short of her sixieth birthday. Bacewicz was primarily a neo-classicist, though in the 1960s she experimented with some of the fashionable techniques of the day. Her output includes another opera, 2 ballets, 5 symphonies, 7 violin concerti, 7 string quartets, and much else. RECORDINGS: The Polish Muza label has been the ultimate source for most such works as the *Music for Strings, 5 Trumpets, and Percussion; Divertimento* for strings; Concerto for Viola; Concerto for 2 Pianos; Piano Quintets Nos. 1 and 2; String Quartets Nos. 4 and 7; Sonata No. 2 for Piano; the *10 Etudes* for piano; and other piano works.

[2134] CITKOWITZ, Israel
TEACHER, CRITIC
BORN: Skierniewice, February 6, 1909
DIED: London, May 4, 1974

Citkowitz is often said to have been born in Russia, which, technically speaking, he was, but his birthplace is actually Poland, between Lodź and Warsaw. His parents emigrated soon after to the United States. His most important music teachers here were Roger Sessions **[1931]** and Aaron Copland **[1986]**. In 1927 he went to Paris for four years of by then seemingly inevitable study with Nadia Boulanger. By the time he got back, he had written two piano pieces and five short songs to texts by James Joyce. Soon afterward Copland liked his String Quartet enough to have it performed at the initial festival at Yaddo in upstate New York. He also had the songs published in New Music Editions. That same year Citkowitz wrote a single movement for string quartet; two years later came a song cycle to poems by William Blake. His peak year was 1936, which produced a Robert Frost cycle and some choral pieces. He seems to have written nothing more except some critical articles. He gave free piano lessons to people who really wanted piano lessons and from 1939 taught for a while at the Dalcroze School in New York City. In 1969 he settled in London. RECORDINGS: Some of the songs have been recorded.

[2135] GENZMER, Harald (Gents'-mer, Hä'-rält)
TEACHER
BORN: Blumenthal, February 9, 1909

Genzmer came from a village in the vicinity of Bremen and began his musical studies as a pianist. From 1928 to 1934 he was at the Berlin Hochschule, where his direction as a composer was profoundly affected by Paul Hindemith **[1914]**. After three years in Breslau (Wrocław) rehearsing opera performances at the municipal theater, he came back to Berlin to teach in a suburban music school. He came to know Friedrich Trautwein, inventor of an early electronic instrument called the trautonium, for which Genzmer wrote a concerto in 1939—but not the first: Hindemith had done that eight years earlier. (Unlike Hindemith, however, Genzmer wrote a second trautonium concerto, in 1952.) After the war Genzmer became professor of composition at the conservatory in Freiburg im Breisgau. In 1957 he transferred to the analogous institution in Munich, from which he retired in 1974. His compositional output is large, solid, and comprehensive (except for dramatic music). RECORDINGS: Works recorded include the Concerto for Trumpet and Strings; *Introduction and Adagio* for strings; *Sinfonietta-Sonatina* for strings; *Sonatina for Strings;* Concerto for Organ; Concerto for Flute; Concertino No. 2 for Piano and Strings; Sonata for Trumpet and Piano; Sonata for Trombone and Piano; Sonata No. 1 for Cello and Piano; Concerto for Organ and Percussion; *Theme and Variations* for glass harp, flute, viola, and cello; Piano Trio; *Symphonic Concerto*

for solo organ; the *Jiménez Cantata* for soprano chorus, and orchestra; and other choral works—*Irische Harfe, Oktober-Narr, Schweigen der Liebe,* and *Vom goldenen Herbst.*

[2136] DZERZHINSKY, Ivan Ivanovich (Tsyer-zhēn'-skē, Ē-vàn Ē-vá-nō'-vich)
PIANIST
BORN: Tambov, April 9, 1909
DIED: Leningrad, January 18, 1978

Save for piano training, Dzerzhinsky had no musical education until he enrolled in Mikhail Gnessin's school at Moscow in 1928. In 1930 he proceeded to the State School of Music in Leningrad and finally to the Leningrad Conservatory. His first opera was a treatment of the novel *And Quiet Flows the Don* (allegedly by Mikhail Sholokhov, though it has been called fraudulent.) He set it in a simple-minded style (no ensembles, among other improvements) which he said was meant for the tastes of the workers, though his detractors insisted that he was unable to do much more. Fortunately or unfortunately Stalin decided that this was his kind of opera, just as he had decided about the same time that Shostakovitch's **[2094]** *Lady Macbeth of Mzensk* was not. This espousal gave Dzerzhinsky not only a great sendoff but considerable power. However, his next effort, a treatment of *Virgin Soil Upturned* (probably genuine Sholokhov) was not so successful, and his several efforts thereafter were quickly buried. With the "thaw" after Stalin's death, Dzerzhinsky published an article warning that without strict control, artists would stray from the true path (i.e., his own). His next, and presumably final, opera, *A Man's Fate* (Sholokhov again) drew such epithets from his fellows as "half-baked," "careless," and "incompetent." RECORDINGS: For all that criticism, some excerpts of *A Man's Fate* were recorded, as well as a few from others of his operas.

[2137] NAGINSKI, Charles
BORN: Cairo, May 29, 1909
DIED: Lenox, Mass., August 4, 1940

A piano pupil of his father, Naginski came to the United States from Egypt when he was eighteen, won a scholarship to the Juilliard School, and studied composition there with Rubin Goldmark (1872–1936), graduating in 1933. He quickly produced 2 symphonies, several other orchestral and chamber works, and a ballet, *The Minotaur.* In 1938 he won an American Prix de Rome. His career ended abruptly when he was drowned in a nearby lake at the age of thirty-one while attending the Berkshire Festival. RECORDINGS: Naginski was particularly admired for his songs, a few of which have been recorded.

[2138] ORR, Robin Kemsley
ORGANIST, TEACHER
BORN: Brechin, June 2, 1909

Though he was born and grew up in a small town in the boondocks of Scotland (near Montrose), Robin Orr had the advantage of access to an organ, built by his father in his home. After basic schooling in Edinburgh he went, at seventeen, to the Royal College of Music in London, where Arthur Benjamin [1887] was his piano teacher. Three years later he became Organ Scholar at Pembroke College, Cambridge, where he studied with E. J. Dent, graduating in 1932. Later in the 1930s he went to Siena to study with Alfredo Casella [1767] and to Paris to study with Nadia Boulanger. In 1933 he took a job at the Sidcot School in Somerset and three years later joined the faculty at the University of Leeds. In 1938 he returned to Cambridge as organist of St. John's College and received his M.A. that same year. After serving in British Intelligence during World War II, he returned to Cambridge to teach, being made a Fellow of St. John's in 1948 and achieving a D.Mus. in 1950. In that year he returned to the Royal College and in 1956 was elected to the Musical Chair at the University of Glasgow. In 1965 he came to Cambridge once more, this time as professor of music. He retired from Cambridge in 1976. Orr has written 2 operas (Full Circle in 1967 and Hermiston in 1975), a good deal of music for the stage, some orchestral material (including 3 symphonies dating from 1963, 1971, and 1978), and a larger number of works for smaller forces. RECORDINGS: The 1963 Symphony in One Movement has been recorded by Alexander Gibson.

[2139] GERSCHEFSKI, Edwin
PIANIST, TEACHER
BORN: Meriden, Conn., June 10, 1909

Gerschefski (or Gershefsky—there seems to be some disagreement about the spelling) went to Yale, where he studied piano with Bruce Simonds. Afterward he had further pianistic training in London and then in Italy with Artur Schnabel [1746]. Returning to New York in 1935, he spent two years studying with the legendary Joseph Schillinger (1895–1943), inventor of a sure-fire mathematical method of composition (which, in book form, once seemed to promise instant fame and fortune to those who felt they had a hit song up their sleeves). After various academic jobs, Gerschefski became chairman of the music department at the University of Georgia in 1960. His list of creations includes film scores, music for orchestra, for band, and for chorus, and a good deal of chamber music. RECORDINGS: Two orchestral works have been recorded—Saugatuck Suite and Fanfare, Fugato, and Finale.

[2140] TEMPLETON, Alec
PIANIST
BORN: Cardiff, Wales, July 4, 1909
DIED: Greenwich, Conn., March 28, 1963

Though Templeton made his fame and fortune largely as a musical entertainer, he was a thoroughly trained musician and a respectable composer. Blind from infancy, he early demonstrated remarkable sensitivity to sounds. He is said to have picked out tunes on the piano at two and to have attempted his first composition at four, the age at which he began formal piano study. He was admitted to the Royal College of Music when still quite young and then spent several years at the Royal Academy, from which he graduated with highest honors in 1931. Four years later he came to the United States, where with a great gift for musical satire and improvisation he soon became a beloved radio personality. His recordings of such takeoffs as Bach Goes to Town and Walter Damrosch [1540] explaining the nonsense song "Three Little Fishes" ("Free Itty Fishy in a Itty Bitty Poo") sold phenomenally. He became an American citizen in 1941. By the time of his early death (at fifty-three), he had largely disappeared from the public eye. He wrote, among other things, 2 piano concerti and some chamber music. Recordings include (besides the jeux d'esprit and an LP of improvisations on Offenbach [1264] and Johann Strauss, Jr. [1295]) a Trio for Flute, Oboe, and Piano, the String Quartet No. 1; and the Pocket-Size Sonata for clarinet and piano.

[2141] MUSHEL, Georgi Alexandrovich
(Mōō'-shel, Gä-ôr'-gē Àl-yek-sàn-drō'-vich)
TEACHER, ETHNOMUSICOLOGIST
BORN: Tambov, July 29, 1909

Originally a pianist, Mushel graduated from the Tambov Conservatory in 1930 and in 1936 from the Moscow Conservatory, where his teachers included Miaskovsky [1735] and pianist Lev Oborin. He then joined the faculty of the Tashkent Conservatory, where his mission was to create a proper music for the Uzbeks on a folk base. Having thoroughly acquainted himself with the latter, he completed the first Uzbek opera, *Farkhad i Shirin* in 1937, which must have established a record for that sort of thing. He followed it the next year with the first Uzbek symphony. He had written two more symphonies, several ballets, concerti, and songs. RE-CORDINGS: Outside of Uzbekistan he is known for his organ music, some of which appears on records. Other works may have appeared on Soviet Melodiya.

[2142] EASDALE, Brian
BORN: Manchester, August 10, 1909

A one-time chorister at Westminster Abbey, Easdale studied at the Royal College of Music under Armstrong Gibbs [1836] and Gordon Jacob [1911], and had already made a reputation as a composer by the time he graduated in 1933. His interest in film music began in the mid-1930s when he supplied music for some documentaries. For a time he and Benjamin Britten [2215] were in charge of music at the Group Theater. At the outset of the 1939 war, Easdale was an artilleryman, but in 1942 he was transferred to India with a film unit and worked almost exclusively in films for the remainder of the decade. His most successful effort—and indeed the only work by which he is known to the world at large—was the score to *The Red Shoes,* a ballet fantasy film that in its day seemed magical but now looks rather tawdry. Easdale also wrote incidental music for the stage, another ballet *The Phoenix,* and 3 operas: *Rapunzel,* 1927; *The Corn King,* 1935; and *The Sleeping Children,* 1951. Little has been heard from him in recent years. RECORDINGS: Some of the ballet music from *The Red Shoes* has been recorded by Vladimir Golschmann, and there was also a soundtrack recording by Muir Matheson. The Modern Brass Ensemble has recorded his *Cantilena.*

[2143] LITAIZE, Gaston Gilbert (Lē-tez', Gàs-tôn' Zhēl-bâr')
ORGANIST, TEACHER
BORN: Ménil-sur-Belvitte, August 11, 1909

Gaston Litaize was born blind in a hamlet in Alsace-Lorraine. Like his contemporary Jean Langlais [2104], he was educated at the Institution for Blind Children in Paris. In 1931 he entered the Paris Conservatoire, where he studied with Marcel Dupré [1806], Henri Büsser [1627], and Maurice Emmanuel [1544]. In his seven years there he took three first prizes in as many subjects and became the first blind person ever to make a showing in the Prix de Rome competition, with a second place in 1938. He played at the Church of St. François Xavier in Paris from 1946 and taught other young blind musicians at his old school. RECORDINGS: He has made a number of recordings and, as composer, is represented on records by organ pieces.

[2144] BERGER, Jean (Bâr'-ger, Jēn)
CONDUCTOR, TEACHER
BORN: Hamm, September 27, 1909

A native of Westphalia, Berger studied with Egon Wellesz [1799] in Vienna and took a doctorate at Heidelberg in 1931. He then went to Paris, where he undertook further study with Louis Aubert [1693], conducted a choral group, and, conditions in Germany having taken a turn for the worse, became a French citizen in 1935. (One guesses that he also became "Jean" then.) When the Germans invaded Poland in 1939, however, he emigrated to South America and worked as a coach in the Rio de Janeiro Opera until 1941, when he came to the United States just in time to be taken into the armed forces. He acquired citizenship in 1943. Since the war he has served on the faculties of Middlebury College, the University of Illinois, and, from 1961, the University of Colorado at Boulder. He has written some instrumental music—notably the *Caribbean Concerto* commissioned by harmonica player Larry Adler in 1942—but is best known for his folksy songs and choral pieces. RECORDINGS: A number of his vocal pieces have been recorded.

[2145] HOLMBOE, Vagn (Holm'-boo'i, Vàn)
CRITIC, TEACHER
BORN: Horsens, December 20, 1909

Vagn Holmboe was born in a port city in Jutland, where his father manufactured paints. Though there was music in the home and though he studied the violin in adolescence, he planned to become a painter. However, the musical impulse was insistent, and at eighteen, having tried his hand at composing, he entered the Royal Conservatory in Copenhagen, where he studied with Nielsen [1571] pupil Knud Jeppesen (1892–1974), and Jeppesen's pupil Finn Høffding (1899–), who had worked in Vienna with Josef Marx [1747]. After two years there he went to Berlin in 1930 for some work with Ernst Toch [1824]. While there he met a Rumanian music student, Meta Graf, whom he married and accompanied to her native country, where they spent some time studying Rumanian folk music from the horse's mouth, so to speak. In 1934 they settled in Denmark, where they continued their folklore studies. Holmboe had begun composing in earnest shortly after the Berlin period but did not make his first real impression until 1939 when the second of his 11 symphonies won first place in an all-Scandinavia competition. After that he composed prodigally and won increasing admiration until he was eclipsed by the avant-garde avalanche of the postwar era. Beginning in 1947, he worked for eight years as critic of the newspaper *Politiken*. In 1955 he was named professor at the Copenhagen Conservatory, where he had been teaching for five years.

Holmboe has no truck with arbitrary "systems," but writes music that is at least as consonant as it is dissonant. Regarded at home as the logical successor to Nielsen, he also admits the influence of Josquin [71], Monteverdi [333], Haydn [871], Beethoven [1063], Brahms [1329], Sibelius [1575], Bartók [1734], and Britten [2215], as well as music of the orient and folk music from such disparate places as Rumania, the Faroë Islands, and points farther north. With Niels Viggo Bentzon [2290] and Hallvard Johnsen (1916–) of Norway, Holmboe has been a leading proponent of "metamorphosis" technique, an approach whereby thematic or chordal germs are subject to constant, seemingly inexorable alterations through the course of a movement or work. His catalog consists of about 150 works (many in large forms) and includes—besides the symphonies—3 operas, a ballet, several *sinfonias,* numerous concerti and other orchestral works, a *Requiem for Nietzsche* and smaller vocal works, 13 chamber concerti, at least 18 string quartets (with more on the way), many sonatas, some piano and organ music, and miscellaneous chamber pieces. A large number of significant works remain unrecorded.

RECORDINGS: Orchestral works committed to disc include Symphonies Nos. 7, 8, and 10, and the Concerto for Cello. Other recordings include the Chamber Concerto No. 11; String Quartets Nos. 1, 3, 7, 8, 11, 15, and 16; Sonata for Cello Solo; *Primavera* for flute, violin, cello, and piano; *Quartetto*

Medico for flute, oboe, clarinet, and piano; Sonata for Solo Flute; *Notturno* for wind quintet; Brass Quintet; Concerto for Brass; *Triade* for trumpet and organ; *Fabula II* for organ; *Suono da bardo* for piano; *Inuit: 3 Igloo Songs* for chorus and percussion; *Moya: 7 Japanese Songs;* Sonatas Nos. 1 and 2 and 5 *Intermezzi* for guitar; and several works for unaccompanied chorus.

[2146] MARTINON, Jean (Mär-tē-nôn', Zhàn)
VIOLINIST, CONDUCTOR
BORN: Lyons, January 10, 1910
DIED: Paris, March 1, 1976

Best known as an international-rank conductor, Martinon began his career as a concert violinist. After preliminary studies at his hometown conservatory, he attended that of Paris, graduating in 1928 with a first prize in violin. He went on, however, to study composition with Albert Roussel [1605] and conducting with Charles Munch and Roger Desormière. A symphony, a symphonette, and his first violin concerto had already won him some notice when his country called him to arms in 1939. He was taken prisoner in the German breakthrough the next spring and was interned for the duration. During that time he wrote *Stalag IX: Musique d'exil* for jazz band, his second symphony *(Hymne)* and two choral-orchestral works. Right after he came home, he was made conductor of the Paris Conservatoire Orchestra and the Bordeaux Symphony. Successively he was director of the Lamoureux, Düsseldorf, and Israel Philharmonic orchestras. In 1963 he answered a call to succeed Rafael Kubelik with the Chicago Symphony. That was his first mistake. Inured to a *Mitteleuropäische* style that had extended from Theodore Thomas and Frederick Stock, Chicagoans did not take kindly to him. After five years of struggle, he gave up and returned to France, where he became conductor of the French National Radio orchestra (ORTF). In 1974 he took over the Residentie Orchestra in The Hague. He died of cancer two years later. He took composing seriously; other works than those noted were an opera *(Hécube),* a third and fourth symphony, an oratorio, four more concerti, 2 string quartets, piano pieces, and songs.

RECORDINGS: Appearing on records are Symphonies No. 2 *(Hymne à la Vie)* and No. 4 *(Altitudes),* Concerto No. 2 for Violin, and *Trois chansons* for chorus. Martinon made, with various orchestras, a long and brilliant series of recordings from the first days of LP (including the fourth symphony cited, with the Chicago Symphony).

[2147] PORRINO, Ennio (Pôr-rē'-nō, En'-nyō)
TEACHER
BORN: Cagliari, January 20, 1910
DIED: Rome, September 25, 1959

A Sardinian, Porrino was a pupil of Respighi **[1718]**, who strongly influenced his music, and was a 1932 graduate of the St. Cecilia Academy in Rome, where he remained to teach for some years. When in 1944 the city capitulated to the Allies, Porrino, a Fascist, went north and became in effect a composer-laureate for Mussolini's "Salò" Republic, named for the town on Lake Garda where the Duce was kept by the Germans. Porrino then taught at the Venice Conservatory, where he wrote a national anthem for the shadowy government of his choice. After the war ended, he taught at the San Pietro Conservatory in Naples, and in 1956 he was made director of the conservatory of his native city. Among his compositions are operas, ballets, an oratorio, orchestral works, and songs. RECORDINGS: Helmut Hunger has recorded his Concerto for Trumpet.

[2148] GALINDO DIMAS, Blas (Gȧ-lēn'-dō Dē'-màs, Blȧs)
CONDUCTOR, TEACHER, ADMINISTRATOR
BORN: San Gabriel, Jalisco, February 3, 1910

Blas Galindo was born into an Indian family in a small town (now called Venustiano Carranza) southwest of Guadalajara. He taught himself organ and clarinet, and in 1931 went to Mexico City to study with Chávez at the conservatory there. In 1936 he and three other Chávez pupils—Daniel Ayala (1906-75), Salvador Contreras (1912–   ), and Pablo Moncayo **[2190]**—formed a sort of avant-garde musical association which came (not unexpectedly) to be known as El Grupo de los Cuatro (The Gang of Four), as which they gave concerts of their own music. At the time Galindo was strongly influenced by native folk music—so much so that it was sometimes hard to tell his compositions from the real folk music. Later he tried his hand at most of the prescribed approaches to progressive music, including electronic and mixed-media works. He studied with Aaron Copland **[1986]** at Tanglewood in the summers of 1941 and 1942. He finally gradu-

ated from the conservatory in 1944. Three years later he became its director, as well as director of the music division of the new Institute of Fine Arts. He left the conservatory in 1961. Later he conducted the orchestras of the Institute of Social Security and the Ballet Popular Mexicano. He was granted a lifetime government pension in 1965. He has written 7 ballets, 3 symphonies, and several concerti (including a short one for electric guitar) among his more orthodox compositions. RECORDINGS: Domestic releases of his works include the Symphony No. 2 of 1957 (Jorge Mester) and *Sones de mariachi* of 1940 (several recordings). Among works only released on Mexican labels are *La Manda, Homenaje a Cervantes,* and *Sinfonia breve* for orchestra, and *Pieces for Piano.*

[2149] BARBER, Samuel Osborne
PIANIST, SINGER
BORN: West Chester, Pa., March 9, 1910
DIED: New York, January 23, 1981

Given a spectacular sendoff at the very outset of his career, Samuel Barber continued all his life to be that rare thing among contemporary American composers—a popular success. And he was that despite—or perhaps because of—an unwavering devotion to musical romanticism. The son and grandson of physicians, he was originally expected to follow in their path. His mother was the former Daisy Beatty, the youngest sister of the great contralto Louise Homer. Samuel was precociously (and even obsessively) musical from earliest childhood. He was playing piano and cello at seven, was composing at eight, and was a church organist at twelve. He profited by the interest and advice of his uncle Sidney Homer **[1568]**—to which he testified years later by editing an album of his songs. It was Homer who persuaded Barber's parents in 1924 to send him to the just-opened Curtis Institute in nearby Philadelphia, to which he commuted every Friday after school. The experiment worked, and he was accepted as a full-time pupil there. His teachers included pianist Isabelle Vengerova (Nicolas Slonimsky's **[1893]** aunt), composition specialist Rosario Scalero (1870–1954), and baritone Emilio de Gogorza. He also entered into a lifelong friendship with fellow pupil Gian-Carlo Menotti **[2177]**, with whom for many years he shared a house in Mt. Kisco, New York. When he was eighteen, his violin sonata won the first of two Bearns Prizes. He also produced the first of his greatly admired songs about this time. Barber, who was a good *baryton-martin,* took his singing seriously; and in 1932, the year of his graduation, RCA Victor recorded his performance of his setting of Matthew Arnold's *Dover Beach*, backed by the Curtis String Quartet. The next year his senior project, the *Overture to The School for Scandal*, was played by the Philadelphia Orchestra, and the year after that the New York Philharmonic performed his *Music for a Scene from Shelley*. The year 1935 also brought him an American Prix de Rome and the first of two successive Pulitzer fellowships. The chief fruits of the Rome stay were the first symphony (the first American work ever played at the Salzburg Festival—by Artur Rodzinski and the Cleveland Orchestra in 1937), his only string quartet, and the *Essay No. 1 for Orchestra*. In 1938 Arturo Toscanini introduced this last work and the *Adagio for Strings* (transcribed from the quartet) to nationwide radio audiences.

When he got back to home soil in 1939, Barber joined the faculty of the Curtis Institute. Though he was profoundly opposed to war, he left after Pearl Harbor to join the Army Air Corps and served as a noncombatant noncom for the duration. His chief official assignment was to write a symphony honoring the Corps, which was premiered by Serge Koussevitzky and the Boston Symphony in 1944 and broadcast worldwide. Barber extensively revised the work three years later and conducted a performance of it for Decca (London) Records. In 1964, however, he rejected it, destroying the manuscript and the rental score and parts, save for a version of the second movement, which he titled *Night Flight*. In 1944 he also wrote the *Capricorn Concerto* for flute, oboe, trumpet, and strings, celebrating the purchase of the Mt. Kisco house, which was called "Capricorn."

After the war prestige commissions produced a stream of works—the Concerto for Cello for Raya Garbousova, a ballet on the Medea story for Martha Graham (originally called *The Serpent Heart*, but better known in its revised form, *The Cave of the Heart*, or as an orchestral suite, *Medea*), a *scena* for soprano Eleanor Steber, *Knoxville: Summer of 1915* (text from James Agee's novel *A Death in the Family*), and a piano sonata for Vladimir Horowitz. In 1957 Barber completed his first opera, the four-act *Vanessa* to a libretto by Menotti. It was premiered at the Metropolitan Opera (with Steber, Regina Reznik, Rosalind Elias, Nicolai Gedda, and Giorgio Tozzi) early in 1958, held over through the next season, recorded by RCA Victor, and revived in 1964—the first American work so treated there since Deems Taylor's **[1801]** *Peter Ibbetson*. Shortly before Barber's death a revival from Menotti's Spo-

leto Festival was telecast nationwide. Barber's second opera, the tiny *A Hand of Bridge* (playing time twenty minutes), was premiered at Spoleto in 1959. A third opera, *Antony and Cleopatra*, was commissioned by the Metropolitan to open the new house at Lincoln Center in 1966. The libretto was extracted from Shakespeare by Franco Zeffirelli, who also served as designer-director-producer. The principals were Leontyne Price, Justino Diaz, and Jess Thomas, with Thomas Schippers conducting and Alvin Ailey as choreographer. The opening was broadcast to the nation. The music was smothered by the production, at various performances the stage machinery malfunctioned, and the work was unmercifully buried, despite persistent cries that it needed a decent chance. (The Juilliard School put on a more successful performance in 1975.) Unfortunately after the fiasco both Barber's productivity and his popularity fell off. He was the recipient of two Pulitzer Prizes, for *Vanessa* in 1958 and for his Concerto for Piano in 1963. He was also a member of the National Institute of Arts and Letters and held an honorary doctorate from Harvard, among many other honors. He died after a long battle with cancer. His last major work completed was the *Essay No. 3* for orchestra; only one movement *(Canzonetta)* of a projected oboe concerto was completed at his death.

RECORDINGS: The operas *A Hand of Bridge, Vanessa,* and (recently) *Antony and Cleopatra* have all been recorded complete, and there is a recording of several scenes from *Antony and Cleopatra* with Leontyne Price. The ballet suites *Medea* and *Souvenirs* have also been recorded, along with most of of the orchestral works—*School for Scandal Overture, Music for a Scene from Shelley,* Symphonies Nos. 1 and 2 (the *Night Flight* movement has also been recorded separately); *Adagio for Strings; Essays Nos. 1–3;* Concerto for Violin; Concerto for Cello; Concerto for Piano; the *Capricorn Concerto; Toccata Festiva* for organ and orchestra; *Die Natali; Serenade for Strings* (a version for string quartet is also recorded); and *Commando March* for band. Vocal-orchestral recordings include *Knoxville: Summer of 1915* for soprano and orchestra; *Prayers of Kierkegaard* for chorus and orchestra; and *Andromache's Farewell,* a dramatic *scena* for soprano and orchestra. Other vocal works recorded include *A Stop-Watch and an Ordnance Map* and *Reincarnation* for chorus; *Dover Beach* for baritone and string quartet; *Nuvoletta, Mélodies passagères,* and *Hermit Songs* for voice and piano; and most of the shorter individual songs except for some of the very late ones. Chamber and instrumental recordings include the String Quartet; *Summer Music* for wind quintet; Sonata for Cello and Piano; *Souvenirs* (version for piano); Sonata for Piano; plus *Excursions, Nocturne (Homage to John Field),* and the 1977 *Ballade*—the last three all for piano. (Perhaps the most important remaining unrecorded orchestral work is *The Lovers* for baritone, mixed chorus, and orchestra, a 1971 setting of love poems by Pablo Neruda.)

[2150] REIF, Paul
ARRANGER
BORN: Prague, March 23, 1910
DIED: New York, July 7, 1978

Originally a violinist, Reif later studied at the Vienna Academy, where his composition teachers were Franz Schmidt **[1661]** and Richard Stöhr. He also studied conducting with Franz Schalk, and, after the latter's death, with Bruno Walter. Richard Strauss **[1563]** deigned to oversee his composition for a time. In 1941 he emigrated to the United States just in time for World War II. While serving with U.S. Intelligence in North Africa, he wrote a popular song, "Dirty Gerty from Bizerte"; another song, "The Sun Never Sets on the AEF," became the theme song of NBC's "Army Hour" radio program. Wounded and decorated, he was mustered out in 1945 and thereafter made his living in the Hollywood studios. He wrote 2 operas and was working on a third when he died. The rest of his output ranges from the serious to the frivolous, none of it designed to shock the bourgeoisie. RECORDINGS: A chamber-orchestral work, *Philidor's Defense,* based on a classic chess opening; *Reverence for Life* and *Monsieur le Pélican* (chamber pieces in honor of Albert Schweitzer); *Banter* for flute and piano; *The Curse of Mauvais-Air* and *8 Vignettes for 4 Singers* (choral); *5 Divertimenti for 4 Strings; Songs on Words of Kenneth Koch; Five-Finger Exercises* (songs to T. S. Eliot texts); and *Duo for 3* (soprano, clarinet, and cello).

[2151] PERAGALLO, Mario (Pä-rä-gàl'-lō, Mär'-yō)
ADMINISTRATOR
BORN: Rome, March 25, 1910

Peragallo's chief teacher was Alfredo Casella **[1767]**, though he first established himself as an operatic composer in the Puccini **[1511]** tradition. During World War II he suffered a sort of Pauline conversion to a modified dodecaphony—so suddenly that he left an opera in his former style unfinished. In the new vein he had considerable national success in 1947 with a sort of madrigal-opera, *La Collina,* based on Edgar Lee Masters' *Spoon River Anthology.* Peragallo was director of the Accademia Filarmonica in Rome in the early 1950s, and more recently has served as president of the Società per Musica Nuova. RECORDINGS: His motet *De profundis* for chorus has been recorded.

[2152] ALEXANDER, Josef
TEACHER
BORN: Boston, May 15, 1910

Alexander served a long apprenticeship. After graduating from the New England Conservatory, he took two degrees at Harvard, where he was a pupil of Piston **[1890]** and Hill **[1632]**. En route he also studied with Copland **[1986]** and Nadia Boulanger. After teaching privately for a time, he accepted an appointment at Brooklyn College in 1943 and taught there until he retired. His compositions include 4 symphonies, written between 1951 and 1968. RECORDINGS: Issued by his publisher, these include *Songs for Eve* for soprano, harp, violin, cello, English horn, and piano; *Pieces for Eight,* and *Burlesque and Fugue* for trumpet and piano.

[2153] STILL, Robert
BORN: London, June 10, 1910
DIED: Bucklebury, Berkshire, January 13, 1971

Still's composing career was lamentably brief for it began late and was ended by death a decade before he reached his allotted threescore-and-ten. He took up music seriously only after he had got his B.A. from Oxford in 1932. He then attended the Royal College of Music. When England declared war on Germany in 1939, he joined the artillery and served for the duration. It was 1954 before he completed the first of his 4 symphonies. Two years later he finished a three-act opera, *Oedipus.* As that might suggest, he was a dedicated amateur of psychology, in which field he published. Other compositions were concerti for violin and piano, 5 string quartets, 3 piano sonatas, several other orchestral and chamber works, and some songs. RECORDINGS: The third and fourth symphonies were recorded by Eugene Goossens **[1878]**.

[2154] REED, Herbert Owen
TEACHER
BORN: Odessa, Mo., June 17, 1910

Not to take anything away from Professor Reed's achievement, his career might, in its outlines, stand for musical success as it is judged in twentieth-century America. Born in Middle America (Harry Truman country), he took degrees in music and French from Louisiana State University, did graduate work with Howard Hanson [1927], and Bernard Rogers [1875], took a Ph.D. in 1939 (he also had lessons with Roy Harris [1947] and Bohuslav Martinů [1846]), joined the faculty of Michigan State University, climbed the academic ladder to a professorship, received a Guggenheim Fellowship (study in Mexico) in 1948 and other awards and grants afterwards, became chairman of his department, wrote and published several musical textbooks, and retired at sixty-five. His catalog of compositions runs from operas to chamber works. RECORDINGS: The Concerto for Cello and two band works—*For the Unfortunate,* and *La Fiesta Mexicana*—have been recorded.

[2155] JONES, Charles
TEACHER
BORN: Tamworth, Ont., June 21, 1910

Canadian-born American composer Charles Jones is to be confused neither with American-born American composer Charles "Big" Jones (1931–   ) nor with American-born Canadian composer Kelsey Jones (1922–   ). The father of our Charles Jones was in fact a United States citizen. The son came to New York at eighteen to study violin at the Juilliard School, where he later studied composition with Bernard Wagenaar (1894–1971). He then became a pupil of, and assistant to, Darius Milhaud [1868] at Mills College in Oakland, worked with him at the Aspen Music School in the summer, and became its director in 1970. He has taught at other schools here and abroad. His music was significantly influenced by Mihaud's basically neo-classical approach. It includes an oratorio on *Piers Plowman,* 4 symphonies, 6 string quartets, and much else. RECORDINGS: Quartet No. 6 and the Sonatina for Violin and Piano have been recorded.

[2156] TARDOS, Béla (Tär'-dōsh, Bā'-là)
INSURANCE MAN, CONDUCTOR, EDITOR, ADMINISTRATOR
BORN: Budapest, June 21, 1910
DIED: Budapest, November 18, 1966

Tardos's father worked in a printery. The boy studied piano from the age of nine, graduating from the Budapest Conservatory ten years later. After trying a concert career, he took a job with an insurance company. While he was working, he studied with Zoltán Kodály [1760] at the Academy of Music and conducted proletarian choruses. In 1941 he helped form the Vándor Ensemble, for which he wrote many choral pieces. Much of his early work was destroyed in the siege of Budapest near the end of World War II. After the war he worked as editor for a publishing house, directed the National Philharmonic Concert Bureau, and from 1955 to his death (at fifty-six) was head of Editio Musica. Most of his surviving music is for voices (cantatas, choruses, songs), but he produced a number of orchestral works, chamber compositions, and an opera, *Laura,* in his last two decades. RECORDINGS: Works recorded by the Hungarian state label include *Evocatio* and *Symphony: In Memoriam Martyrum* for orchestra; the cantatas *The Bitter Years, Upon the Outskirts of the City,* and *The New God;* and several chamber and instrumental works—*Divertimento* for winds, String Quartet No. 3, Sonata for Violin and Piano, and *5 Bagatelles* for piano.

[2157] ROBINSON, Earl
CONDUCTOR, GUITARIST
BORN: Seattle, July 2, 1910

Robinson took a B.A. in 1933 at the University of Washington and was for a brief time a pupil of Aaron Copland [1986]. He then joined the theater wing of the WPA and contributed music for, among other works, a 1935 revue called *Sing for Your Supper.* This was later deemed good enough to close the 1938–39 Broadway season and was cited by a congressional watchdog as evidence of taxes spent on Communist propaganda. One of its numbers, "The Ballad of Uncle Sam," was reworked by radio impresario Norman Corwin in the fall of 1939 and produced on his program "The Pursuit of Happiness" (Paul Robeson, soloist) as "Ballad for Americans." It struck a national patriotic nerve, and Robeson's recording of it sold prodigally. Robinson was duly commissioned to write other works in the same vein—"The Lonesome Train" (on Lincoln's funeral), "The People Yes" (Carl Sandburg), an opera *Sandhog,* but his only other real successes were the songs "Joe Hill" (a left-wing labor song), and "The House I Live In" (another essay on American democracy). RECORDINGS: Among works by Robinson on records are "The Lonesome Train" and "The People Yes."

Those children whose parents insist that a career in music is likely to lead to penury in a cold-water flat should point out to them the case of William Schuman, who has not only attained to Grand Old Manhood among American composers but also to the very top of the corporate ladder. His forebears came from Germany, where they were called Schumann. His father was vice president of a printing firm. If young Shuman had had his druthers, he would have played baseball, a sport for which he has had a life-long passion and which is the focus of his only opera, *The Mighty Casey*, in 1953. (In 1976 it was revised as a cantata and retitled *Casey at the Bat.*) He was educated in New York public schools, playing violin in junior high school, and bass fiddle (self-taught) in high school, where he organized his own dance band and began writing and publishing popular songs—one of which, "Orpheus with His Lute," later formed the thematic basis of his 1963 *Song of Orpheus* for cello and orchestra and the 1978 *In Sweet Music* for soprano, flute, viola, and harp. On graduation, however, he became a copywriter with an advertising firm and started taking courses in the business college of New York University. Two years later, in 1930, his sister dragged him to a New York Philharmonic concert. He promptly quit both his job and his schooling and settled down to study harmony with Max Persin at a music school run by Manfred Malkin. When that closed down, he studied with Charles Haubiel [1859]. Deciding that he needed a way to make a living and support a family eventually, he entered Columbia University's Teachers' College in 1933. Obtaining his B.A. two years later, he spent the summer studying at the Mozarteum in Salzburg, then returned as a junior member of the faculty at Sarah Lawrence College. The following spring he married Frances Prince, to whom he had been engaged for some time (they have a son and a daughter). In the summer he began lessons with Roy Harris [1947], whose rather slavish admirer he became for a time. The discipleship lasted for two years, which saw the performance of Schuman's first symphony and first string quartet and the completion of his second symphony. In 1937 he received his M.A. from Columbia Teachers' College. The next year he was made conductor of the Sarah Lawrence Chorus. In 1939, at the behest of Aaron Copland [1986], Koussevitzky [1655] presented the second symphony in a Boston Symphony concert. It was a disaster, and soon thereafter Schuman disowned the majority of his maiden efforts.

The first fruit of Schuman's endeavor to find his own musical style was the *American Festival Overture*, which Koussevitzky premiered that fall and which became a highly popular work. Its composer was rewarded with two years' worth of Guggenheim fellowships and a commission from the League of Composers and New York's Town Hall for a string quartet. The third symphony (seven more would follow, for a total of 10, including the two withdrawn early efforts) was hailed as a masterpiece in 1941. In 1943 his Walt Whitman cantata *A Free Song* won the first Pulitzer Prize awarded for music. The cantata and the fifth symphony (for strings) were both premiered by Koussevitzky. (Artur Rodzinski and the Cleveland Orchestra had first presented the fourth symphony in 1942.)

So far Schuman's career was following the prescribed outlines for musical success in America. In 1945 he was lured away from the grind of teaching to become editor-in-chief and director of publications for G. Schirmer, a musical publishing house on Forty-third Street (where the present writer had just been promoted from stockboy to salesclerk). Schuman had scarcely gotten his overcoat off when he was offered the presidency of the Juilliard School, which he accepted—though he remained a "special consultant" to Schirmer's until 1952. In his seventeen years at Juilliard he proved a dynamic, innovative, and even revolutionary administrator; yet he managed to keep writing music steadily and, in fact, to produce some of his best work, including three ballet scores for Martha Graham *(Night Journey, Judith, Voyage for a Theater)*, two more symphonies, the violin concerto, and the fourth and last string quartet. In 1962 he resigned to become president of Lincoln Center, where in due course he oversaw the openings of Philharmonic (now Avery Fisher) Hall, the New Metropolitan Opera, the New York State Theater, and the new Juilliard School. The eighth symphony was written for the inauguration of the first-named. He retired in 1969 but not to pasture: he became, in 1970, chairman of the board of the Videorecord Corporation of America and has subsequently served as director of various musical foundations and in 1980 as composer-in-residence at the Aspen Festival.

Recent works by Schuman have included

Symphony No. 9 ("Ardeatine Caves") in 1969; the *Concerto on Old English Rounds* for viola, women's chorus, and orchestra, 1973; *Colloquies* for horn and orchestra, 1980; and *An American Hymn* for orchestra, 1982. Through the years Schuman has gone his own way, largely ignoring the fashionable musical gimmicks of his time and writing music that has immediate appeal but that is in no sense of the terms simpleminded or reactionary.

RECORDINGS: Much of Schuman's output has been recorded, including these works for orchestra—the ballets *Undertow, Night Journey,* and *Judith; American Festival Overture;* Symphonies Nos. 3–9; Concerto for Piano; *Prayer in Time of War; Circus Overture;* Concerto for Violin; *Credendum; New England Triptych; Newsreel; A Song of Orpheus* for cello and orchestra; *Variations on "America"* (transcription of an organ piece by Ives [1659]); *To Thee Old Cause; In Praise of Shahn;* Concerto on Old English Rounds for viola, women's chorus, and orchestra; *An American Hymn;* and *Colloquies* for French horn and orchestra. Works for band on records include *George Washington Bridge, When Jesus Wept* and the *Chester Overture.* Choral recordings include the *Canonic Choruses; Prelude; Te Deum; Carols of Death;* and *Mail Order Madrigals.* Works for solo voice on disc include *The Young Dead Soldiers* for soprano, French horn, and chamber orchestra; *In Sweet Music* for soprano, flute, viola, and harp; and *Time to the Old* for soprano and piano. There are also recordings of the String Quartets Nos. 3 and 4, and *Voyage* for piano. (A recording by Gregg Smith of *Casey at the Bat* was announced by Vox several years ago but has yet to appear.)

[2159] SCHAEFFER, Pierre (Shā-fär′, Pē-âr′)
    ENGINEER, TEACHER, WRITER, THEORIST
    BORN: Nancy, August 14, 1910

There is probably no one who has more claim to the paternity of electronic music directly composed on magnetic tape than Pierre Schaeffer. Though he came from a musical household, he had no real musical training as such. He took a degree in electrical engineering and during the 1930s was a radio technician who wrote novels on the side. Interested in the idea of community, both of human beings and their arts, he was a founder of Jeune France (Young France) and the Studio d'Essai (Experimental Studio), dedicated to exploring various means of interdisciplinary and group expression. During World War II he was active in the Resistance. Afterward he conceived what he called *musique concrète.* On the principle— long before enunciated by Varèse [1774]— that music in a larger sense was patterned sound, he argued that one could compose by juxtaposing and manipulating pre-existent sounds. At first he used whatever sources disc recordings might provide but soon found much greater latitude in tape, particularly in prepared continuous tape loops that, played slow, fast, or backward, could be fed into a "composition." He began to produce short compositions thus. He soon joined with another engineer named Jacques Poullin and composer Pierre Henry (1927–), a pupil of Messiaen [2129], to form the Groupe de Recherche de Musique Concrète or GRMC (Group for Research into Concrete Music). By 1953 the collaboration had produced works as large as a film score, *Masquerage,* and an "opera," *Orphée 53.* For the next five years, however, Schaeffer was too occupied with setting up the overseas service for the RTF to have much time for composing. Free again in 1958, he teamed up with François-Bernard Mâche (1935–) and Luc Ferrari (1929–), both not incidentally Messiaen pupils, to form the Groupe de Recherches Musicales (Group for Musical Research), which succeeded in getting the RTF to support an electronic studio. Shortly afterward Schaeffer turned his attention wholly to theory, publishing a number of articles and books. His chief argument is that "sound objects" can be categorized in various classes and that the normal human ear can be trained clearly to distinguish between them, thus enabling its possessor to learn to combine and manipulate them. On such principles he successfully taught electronic composition at the Paris Conservatoire from 1968. RECORDINGS: It would be accurate to say that Schaeffer's entire *oeuvre* has been recorded, but its chief commercial representation appeared in the mid-1950s on two LPs issued by Ducretet-Thomson.

[2160] BERLINSKI, Herman
    ORGANIST
    BORN: Leipzig, August 18, 1910

The son of Polish Jewish parents, Berlinski began his studies at the Leipzig Conservatory but fled to France with the Nazi political victory in 1933. There he attended the École Normale in Paris, studying piano with Alfred Cortot and composition with Nadia Boulanger. When hostilities broke out in 1939, he joined the Foreign Legion, but the collapse of France necessitated his fleeing once again. In 1941 he reached New York City. There he became a student at Seminary College of the Jewish Theological Seminary, where he earned magisterial and doctoral degrees in the field of sacred music. He served for some time as organist of Temple Emanu-El, and in 1963 was appointed director of music for the Hebrew Congregation in Washington, D.C. He has been heard as a performer all over the United States and Europe. Though he has written instrumental and choral music, he has specialized in organ compositions, strongly colored by Jewish liturgical traditions, including at least 10 organ symphonies. RECORDINGS: Berlinski has recorded his organ symphonies Nos. 2, 3, and 8, and other organ works (e.g., *The Burning Bush, From the World of My Fathers, Kol nidrei*). There is also a recording of his first orchestral symphony, also known as *Symphonic Visions.*

[2161] HEIDEN, Bernhard (Hī'-den, Bärn'-härt)
ORGANIST, CONDUCTOR, ARRANGER,
TEACHER
BORN: Frankfurt am Main, August 24, 1910

Heiden was strongly influenced by Paul Hindemith [1914], his teacher at the Berlin Hochshule, from which he graduated in the fateful year 1933. In 1935 he made his way to Detroit, where he worked as organist, conductor of the Detroit Chamber Orchestra, and staff arranger for Radio Station WWJ. In the war years he was an assistant bandmaster in the U.S. Army. In 1946 he took an M.A. in musicology at Cornell University and joined the faculty of Indiana University, where he spent the rest of his academic career, retiring as chairman of his department. His only opera, *The Darkened City,* was produced there in 1953. He has also written 2 symphonies, several concerti, and much chamber music. RECORDINGS: A number of chamber pieces have been recorded—the Sonata for Saxophone and Piano; Sonata for Horn and Piano; Woodwind Quintet; *Sinfonia* for wind quintet; Quintet for Horn and Strings; *Intrada* for saxophone and wind quintet; *Variations* for tuba and nine horns; *5 Short Pieces* for solo flute; and the Sonata for Violin and Piano. Two orchestral works, *Partita* and *Euphorion,* are on record.

[2162] LIEBERMANN, Rolf (Lē'-ber-màn, Rolf)
RADIO OFFICIAL, IMPRESARIO
BORN: Zürich, September 14, 1910

One of the more controversial figures on the modern scene just after World War II, Liebermann as a composer quickly fizzled out and now is not even a name in several recent histories of twentieth-century music. Though he had some musical training (notably from the conductor Hermann Scherchen), he took a degree in law at the University of Zürich before studying with Vladimir Vogel (1896–), a Busoni [1577]-trained Russian expatriate, in the serious study of composition. He then joined the staff of Radio Zürich. No doubt influenced by his teachers, he espoused dodecaphony as well as other fashionable paths. He briefly created a furor with his 1954 Concerto for Jazzband and Symphony Orchestra—one more doomed attempt to heal the rift between longhair and pop. During the same period several operas claimed some attention —*Leonore 40/45,* after Beethoven's [1063] *Fidelio; Penelope;* and *The School for Wives* (the latter commissioned by the Louisville Orchestra). Liebermann's initiation into the theatrical world led to his appointment as general manager of the Hamburg Opera in 1959. Here he was a great success, restoring the company to international status, and making it a sounding board for contemporary operatic experiment. He also ran the musical programs of the Hamburg and West Berlin radio stations. Arguably the outstanding operatic impresario of his time *(pace* Sir Rudolf Bing), he was put in charge of the long-moribund Paris Opéra in 1973, changing it from a national theater to another big house on the international star circuit. He retired in 1980 but afterward returned to Hamburg. In 1984 he returned to composition after a long silence. RECORDINGS: A pirate record contains the 1949 Symphony No. 1 (a rather conservative blend of Honegger [1861] and Berg [1789]), and the *Girardoux Cantata.* Commercial recordings have been infrequent but have included his opera *The School for Wives,* the *Furioso* for orchestra, and another rendition of the Concerto for Jazzband.

[2163] COHN, Arthur
VIOLINIST, CONDUCTOR, LIBRARIAN,
PUBLISHER, ADMINISTRATOR
BORN: Philadelphia, November 6, 1910

A product of the Combs Conservatory and later of the Juilliard School, where he studied composition with Rubin Goldmark (1872–1936), Cohn has been a central figure in Philadelphia musical life. A fine violinist, he organized and performed in the Dorian String Quartet and later the Stringart Quartet. Sometime conductor of children's concerts with the Philadelphia Orchestra, he has also had several musical organizations of his own—the Symphony Club, the Germantown Symphony, the Philadelphia Little Symphony, and the Haddonfield Symphony (some of these concurrently). He went to work for the Free Library of Philadelphia in 1934 and became director of the Fleisher Collection there from 1940 to 1952. He has also headed the department of music at the Philadelphia School for Social Science and Art and was director of the Settlement Music School there from 1952 to 1956. In 1956 he took an executive post with Mills Music in New York, moved to MCA ten years later, and was most recently director of the Serious Music Division of Carl Fischer. In his spare time he published several books on music and composed steadily. Among his compositions are 6 string quartets; a concerto for flute; another for treble viol, viola d'amore, viola da gamba, bass viol, harpsichord, and orchestra; *Quotations in Percussion* for 103 percussion instruments, 6 players; and something called *Bet It's a Boy* for magic lantern and piano quintet. RECORDINGS: His *Kaddish* for orchestra of 1964 has been recorded by Arthur Bennett Lipkin.

[2164] CHAJES, Julius (Chä′-yes, Yōōl′-yoos)
PIANIST, CONDUCTOR, ADMINISTRATOR, TEACHER
BORN: Lwów (Lvov), December 21, 1910

Polish-born and Vienna-trained, Chajes was, in his European career, known chiefly as a pianist (a pupil of Moritz Rosenthal), though he studied composition with the violinist-composer Hugo Kauder (1888–1972). He went to Palestine in 1934 and taught piano at the conservatory in Tel Aviv for two years, then emigrated to the United States. In 1940 he became music director of Detroit's Jewish Community Center where in 1953 he premiered his piano concerto with the Detroit Symphony. After 1950 he also taught at Wayne State University. He has written an opera, a cello concerto, cantatas and liturgical music, and many chamber works, much of his output being inspired by Judaic music and culture. RECORDINGS: His *Hechassid* for violin and piano has been committed to disc.

[2165] BOWLES, Paul Frederic
NOVELIST, CRITIC
BORN: New York, December 30, 1910

In the 1940s Paul Bowles caused a good deal of twittering among musical sophisticates as the bright-young-man-elect of American music. A decade later he was doing the same in literary circles. Several recent histories of contemporary music bypass him completely. Nor does one hear him much spoken of now around college English departments. He had a brief brush with higher education at the University of Virginia, where he aspired to be a poet. Shortly afterward he encountered Aaron Copland [1986] in New York and traveled with him to Morocco. Copland introduced him to Virgil Thomson [1928] in Paris, where Bowles remained briefly. He is said to have studied with both and with Nadia Boulanger, but Thomson insists that the role of pupil was uncongenial to him and that in actuality he was almost entirely self-taught. Moreover an insatiable taste for the exotic and the novel kept him restlessly on the move—to Latin America, to Spain, and recurrently to North Africa. Thomson introduced him into theatrical circles in New York, where he worked with producers like Orson Welles, George Abbott, and Eddie Dowling, and playwrights like William Saroyan, Tennessee Williams, and Lillian Hellman, producing incidental music for a score of plays (including *The Glass Menagerie*), as well as for a number of movies, mostly documentary. In 1938 he married Jane Sydney Auer, who as Jane Bowles wrote a small body of highly polished fiction. He won a Guggenheim Fellowship in 1941 and joined Thomson as a critic for the *Herald Tribune* in 1942. Toward the end of the decade, he returned to North Africa and took up residence in the native quarter of Tangiers. His novel *The Sheltering Sky* won almost universal acclaim and was succeeded by a volume of short stories, *The Delicate Prey*, whose concern with sadism delighted those eager for stronger music and wilder wine. That about marked the end of the musical phase. A few later books were less noticed. (In recent years his books have been published by such small-press publishers as Black Sparrow. He has continued to live in North Africa and has taught annual writing workshops there.) Apart from the incidental music noted, Bowles wrote 3 operas *(Denmark Vesey, The Wind Remains,* and *Yerma*—the last two to Garcia Lorca plays), several ballets, orchestral and chamber pieces, and songs (which were once especially admired). RECORDINGS: The 1943 opera *The Wind Remains,* the 1954 *Picnic Cantata,* the

1932 *Scènes d'Anabase, Music for a Farce* of 1938, *Sonata for Two Pianos,* piano pieces (a few played by the composer), and some songs have been recorded.

[2166] DEGEN, Helmut (Dā'-gen, Hel'-moot)
ORGANIST, TEACHER
BORN: Aglasterhausen, Baden, January 14, 1911

After studying composition at the Cologne Conservatory with Busoni [1577] pupil Philipp Jarnach and with Wilhelm Maler, Degen, a native of the Heidelberg area, undertook musicology in Bonn with Ludwig Schiedermair and the late Leo Schrade. He served as organist in the little town of Altenkirchen nearby and then taught at the Duisberg Conservatory from 1938 until World War II rendered such things impossible. In more recent times he has taught at the Trossingen Conservatory in Württemberg. Influenced by the schools of Reger [1637] and Hindemith [1914], he took to heart the latter's notion of *Gebrauchsmusik* and wrote many pieces for amateur ensembles. RECORDINGS: A *Fantaisie* for harpsichord and piano has been recorded.

[2167] GRÜNENWALD, Jean-Jacques (Grün-en-vàlt', Zhàn Zhàk)
ORGANIST, TEACHER
BORN: Cran-Gevrier, February 2, 1911
DIED: Paris, December 19, 1982

Admired as one of the great organists of his generation, Grünenwald was born to Swiss parents in a hamlet in the French Alps near Annecy (not in Annexe, as *Grove* has it). His musical training was at the Paris Conservatoire with Marcel Dupré [1806], Henri Büsser [1627], and Noël Gallon [1856], while he was also acquiring a degree in architecture. He won several first prizes at the Conservatoire and was Dupré's assistant at St. Sulpice until 1945. Over the years he toured indefatigably as a recitalist. In 1955 he began a fifteen-year intendancy at the organ of St. Pierre-de-Montrouge in Paris. He taught for three years at the Schola Cantorum in Paris, and five more at the Geneva Conservatory, (1958–66). He wrote an opera, *Sardanapale,* and orchestral and choral works but is most admired for his organ music. RECORDINGS: There are recordings of some of his organ music.

[2168] ALAIN, Jehan-Ariste (À-lan', Zhàn A-rèst')
ORGANIST
BORN: St. Germain-en-Laye, February 3, 1911
DIED: Petit-Puy, June 20, 1940

Jehan Alain was born in a northern suburb of Paris, the oldest of the four children of organist-composer Albert Alain, a pupil of Vierne [1616] and Guilmant [1351]. His younger brother Olivier (1918–) became a critic, pianist, and composer of some stature, his youngest sister Marie-Claire a world-famous organist. Jehan learned to play on the organ his father had built in their home and at thirteen served as Albert's deputy in the local parish church. Later he studied piano with the organist of Versailles Cathedral, Augustin Pierson. In 1927 he entered the Paris Conservatoire, where he studied organ with Marcel Dupré [1806] and composition with Dukas [1574] and Roger-Ducasse [1639]. His slow progress resulted from (1.) a debilitating illness in 1932, (2.) having to support himself, and (3.) an inability to satisfy the pedantic examiners, though he won a prize in 1936 for his organ suite from Les Amis de l'Orgue. The year 1936 was a pivotal one for him: his sister Odile was killed rescuing him in a mountaineering mishap, and he married his longtime sweetheart— and shortly had three mouths to feed instead of one. He made ends meet by giving private lessons and serving as organist at the Paris Church of St. Nicholas-de-Maisons-Lafitte. Meanwhile he was composing slowly but steadily—mostly keyboard pieces but also 3 Masses and a few other choral and instrumental pieces and some songs. He eventually graduated in 1939 with a first prize for organ, but in the growing international tension was almost immediately called into military service. He served for a time on the northern border and saw his third child, born three months later, only once. Caught up in the 1940 retreat, he lost a portfolio full of manuscripts at Dunkirk, from which he was briefly evacuated to England but returned almost immediately. On a mission near Saumur he was killed by gunfire. RECORDINGS: His sister Marie-Claire has recorded all of his surviving organ music.

[2169] McBRIDE, Robert Guyn
WIND-PLAYER, PIANIST, TEACHER
BORN: Tucson, Ariz., February 20, 1911

As an adolescent McBride taught himself piano and reed instruments to the degree that he played in dance bands, theater orchestras, and the Tucson Symphony. He studied at the University of Arizona campus in Tucson, where his chief composition teacher was Otto Luening [1980]. McBride acquired a B.Mus. there in 1933 and an M.Mus. two years later. Luening then brought him to Bennington College in Vermont, where McBride received a Guggenheim Fellowship in 1937, followed by several other awards. He left Bennington in 1946 for eleven years of free-lancing, touring as oboist in a woodwind quintet and writing film scores among his other activities. In 1957 he went back to the University of Arizona to teach, retiring in 1978. In spite of a few gloomy titles like *Depression Sonata* and *Lament for the Parking Problem,* his music is light-hearted, witty, and often jazzy. RECORDINGS: A number of (mostly short) orchestral works have been recorded—*Mexican Rhapsody, Pumpkin Eater's Little Fugue,* Concerto for Violin, *Workout for Small Orchestra, Punch and the Judy, Lonely Landscape, Panorama of Mexico,* and *March of the Be-Bops.* Chamber works on disc include the Oboe Quintet, *Aria and Toccata in Swing* for violin, and *Way Out But Not Too Far* for euphonium and piano.

[2170] HOVHANESS, Alan *(né* Alan Vaness Chakmakjian) (Hōv-hàn'-es, Al'-an)
TEACHER, CONDUCTOR, ORGANIST
BORN: Somerville, Mass., March 8, 1911

Though he is an American by birth, rearing, and residence, Alan Hovhaness probably deserves to be called the most prominent Armenian composer of his generation. His father was an Armenian-born chemistry professor, proud of his heritage—a sentiment to which he found his son at first resistent; his mother was Scottish, and played the harmonium. Alan grew up mostly in Arlington, Massachusetts, whither his family moved not long after he was born. He tried to write music from a very early age. At nine he was turned over to Adelaide Proctor—*not* the lyricist of Sir Arthur Sullivan's [1397] "The Lost Chord"—for piano lessons. Hovhaness was already composing when he began advanced study with Leschetizky pupil Heinrich Gebhard (1878–1963) and entered Tufts University (where his father taught) in 1929. He transferred to the New England Conservatory in 1932 and studied composition with Frederick Converse [1618], graduating in 1934. By then his music had won him a reputation around Boston as an American Sibelius [1575], which he took so much to heart that he made a pilgrimage to

Finland to absorb the landscape. The immediate result was an official first symphony, completed in 1937 and performed by Leslie Heward and the BBC Symphony three years later. (An unofficial one had won him a prize in 1933, but he shortly afterward destroyed it.)

During much of the decade of the 1940s Hovhaness lived a rather precarious existence in Boston on the forty dollars a month he made as organist at the Armenian Church of St. James in nearby Watertown. He had already become interested in his ethnic heritage, a concern that was intensified by his acquaintance with the liturgy and by encounters with other Eastern musics. In 1942 a scholarship enabled him to study with Bohuslav Martinů at Tanglewood. Intensive study of oriental music, philosophies, and religions left him intensely dissatisfied with his compositions up to then—estimated at up to a thousand—and he destroyed most of them. He then began again on a basis of Armenian folktunes, Eastern modes, scales, and rhythms, and other exotic musical devices.

In 1948 Hovhaness joined the faculty of the Boston Conservatory but left in 1951, the year he received a stipend from the National Institute of Arts and Letters and the New York Philharmonic premiered his ninth symphony, called "St. Vartan" after a figure from Armenian legend—an area that inspired most of his work in that period. He settled in New York where, among other compositions, he produced documentary film scores and music for plays (Clifford Odets' *Flowering Peach*) and ballet *(Ardent Song* for Martha Graham). During the 1950s he held three Guggenheim fellowships. In 1959 he married Elizabeth Whittington, was awarded two honorary doctorates, and set out for Asia on a Fulbright fellowship. He was given a hero's welcome in India and especially Japan, to which latter country (and Korea) he returned on a Rockefeller fellowship in 1962, a year in which he also served as composer-in-residence at the University of Hawaii. In recent decades the music of the Far East has become influentially dominant in his creation. The bulk of his music since 1940 adopts the East's avoidance of the trap of diatonic harmony: primarily melodic, melismatic, and incantatory, it does not develop as Western music is expected to but, as one critic put it, it "just goes on and on." This sort of thing provoked snickers from the ruling serialists and aleatorists and puzzlement from many ordinary concertgoers, but such reactions have not fazed the composer, who, like his music, just goes on and on. He continues to win awards and premieres by important orchestras, conductors, and soloists, though no work of his has established itself as a repertoire favorite. His thirty-sixth symphony was first performed in 1979 by Mstislav Rostropovich and the National Symphony Orchestra. At last report he had reached No. 52. A number of his recent works have featured vocal parts composed for his second wife, soprano Hinako Fujihara (whom he married in 1977), as soloist.

RECORDINGS: The list of recorded works by Hovhaness is enormous, though it barely scratches the surface of his vast output. Among works included are at least 20 of the symphonies (Nos. 2, 6, 9, 11, 15, 19, 21, 25, and 40 for orchestra; Nos. 4, 7, 14, 17, 20, and 23 for band; No. 16 for Korean instruments and strings; No. 31 for strings; No. 24 for tenor, chorus, trumpet, violin, and orchestra; No. 38 for trumpet, flute, violin, soprano, and orchestra; and No. 47 for soprano and orchestra). Other orchestral or chamber-orchestral works on record include *And God Created Great Whales* (with taped calls of humpback whales); *Alleluia and Fugue* for strings; *Anahid; Arevakal* (Concerto No. 1 for Orchestra); *Armenian Rhapsodies Nos. 1–3; Artik* (Concerto for Horn and Strings); *Avak the Healer* (cantata for soprano, trumpet, and strings); *Bacchanale; Celestial Fantasy* for strings; Concerto No. 2 for Violin; Concerto No. 7 for Orchestra; *Fantasy on Japanese Woodprints* for xylophone and orchestra; *The Flowering Peach* for chamber ensemble; *Fra Angelico; The Holy City; Hymn to Yerevan* for winds; *In the Beginning Was the Word* for chorus and orchestra (oratorio); *Khaldis* (Concerto for Piano, Trumpets, and Percussion); *King Vahaken (Is There Survival?),* ballet for ensemble; *Lady of Light* for soloists, chorus, and orchestra; *Lousadzak (The Coming of Light)* for piano and strings; *Magnificat* for chorus, soloists, and orchestra; *Meditation on Orpheus; Mountains and Rivers Without End* for ten instruments; *Orbit No. 1* for ensemble; *Prayer of St. Gregory* for trumpet and strings (alternate version for trumpet and organ also recorded); *Prelude and Quadruple Fugue; Requiem and Resurrection* for brass ensemble and percussion; *Return and Rebuild the Desolate Places* (Concerto for Trumpet and Winds); *The Rubáiyát of Omar Khayyám* for narrator, accordion, and orchestra; *Sunrise; Talin* (Concerto for Clarinet and Strings); *Triptych* for chorus and orchestra; and *Ukiyo—the Floating World.* Other vocal recordings include the song cycle *Celestial Canticle* for soprano and piano; *Flute Player of the Armenian Mountains* for voice and piano (not for flute); the cantata *Glory Sings the Setting Sun* for soprano, clarinet, and piano; *Saturn,* twelve pieces for clarinet, soprano, and piano; and numerous individual songs. Chamber and instrumental recordings include the Duet for Violin and Harpsichord; *Fantasy* for piano; *Firdausi* for clarinet, harp, and percussion; *The Garden of Adonis* for flute and harp; *Kirghiz Suite* for violin and piano; *Koke no niwa (Moss Garden)* for English horn, two percussion players, and harp; *Macedonian Mountain Dances* for piano quartet; several quartets for various combinations of winds, strings, and keyboards; *Sharagan and Fugue* for brass; *6 Dances* for brass quintet; Sonata for Solo Flute; Sonata for Solo Harp; *Spirit of Ink* for solo flute; String Quartet No. 2; *Suite for Violin, Piano, and Percussion; Tower Music* for winds and brass; *Tumburu* and *Varuna* (two trios for violin, cello, and piano); *Tzaikerk* for flute, violin, and drums; *Upon Enchanted Ground* for flute, cello, harp, and tamtam; and a number of miscellaneous solo piano pieces.

[2171] LIEBERSON, Goddard
RECORD-COMPANY EXECUTIVE, CRITIC
BORN: Hanley, Staffordshire, April 5, 1911
DIED: New York, May 29, 1977

Goddard Lieberson was a rare example of the record executive who is conversant with music. Though born in England, he came with his family to America in 1915. After study at the University of Washington he won a scholarship to the Eastman School of Music, where he was trained by Bernard Rogers [1875]. On the side he reviewed, wrote articles, and occasionally did cartoons for a local newspaper. After graduating, he settled in New York where he served for a time as an editor of the *International Cyclopedia of Music and Musicians* until he joined Columbia Records in 1939. There he worked his way up to the presidency of the firm and was responsible not only for a catalogue that was remarkable in its taste and variety and eventually included most of the works of such great contemporaries as Copland [1986], Schoenberg [1657], and Stravinsky [1748], but also for backing and helping shape many of the greatest American musicals of the first postwar decades. It was also under Lieberson's direction that the LP record successfully became a reality. He was married to the ballerina-actress Vera Zorina, and their son Peter (1946–) has already made a name for himself as a composer. In 1964 Lieberson was elected head of the Record Industry Association of America. He retired from the presidency of Columbia in 1966. Thereafter the company went whoring after strange gods and plunged into chaos, and in 1973 he returned to take over the reins again. He died of cancer four years later. Lieberson's elegant and witty music was understandably largely a product of his earlier years, 1929–39, and includes incidental music, a ballet, a symphony, choral and chamber works, piano pieces, and songs. Lieberson also published a novel, *Three for Bedroom C*. RECORDINGS: His 1938 String Quartet and the 1963 *Piano Pieces for Advanced Children or Retarded Adults* (written for Peter) have been recorded.

[2172] TATE, Phyllis Margaret Duncan
BORN: Gerrards Cross, April 6, 1911

A Buckinghamshire lass, Phyllis Tate enrolled at seventeen in the Royal Academy of Music, where she majored in piano and timpani and studied composition under Harry Farjeon (1878–1948). By the time she graduated in 1932, she had already written several successful pieces, including an operetta. Three years later she married Alan Frank, later to become head of the music department of the Oxford University Press. After World War II Miss Tate rejected all her early work as immature. Among the strong influences on her official canon are the French neo-classicists, Stravinsky **[1748]**, and Britten **[2215]**. She likes to write for voice and for chamber combinations and solo instruments, including the harmonica. RECORDINGS: The song cycles *Apparitions* and *3 Gaelic Ballads* and the 1947 Sonata for Clarinet and Piano have been recorded.

[2173] REIZENSTEIN, Franz Theodor
(Rīt'-zen-shtīn, Frànts Tā'-ō-dôr)
PIANIST, TEACHER
BORN: Nuremberg, June 7, 1911
DIED: London, October 15, 1968

Something of a prodigy, Franz Reizenstein was reading and writing music at five and not much more than that many years later was an accomplished pianist (holding his own in the family musicales) and had written his first string quartet. In 1930 he entered the Berlin Hochschule, where he studied piano with the Russian expatriate Leonid Kreutzer and composition with Hindemith **[1914]**. In 1934, the Nazis having arrived, he left for England, of which country he eventually became a citizen. He studied at the Royal College of Music with Vaughan Williams **[1633]** and, after receiving his diploma

in 1936, spent two more years working at his pianism under the tutelage of Solomon. Physically disqualified for war duty, he spent World War II as a railroad employee, giving charity concerts in his spare time. After the war he continued to concertize and was particularly successful in chamber-music performances. In 1958 he took up teaching at the Royal Academy and in 1964 became professor of piano at the Royal Manchester College of Music. He died at fifty-seven. His music, solidly grounded, is conservative, accessible, and often witty. He produced an oratorio, a cantata, several concerti, and a good deal of smaller-scale music, as well as music for stage, screen, and radio. RECORDINGS: These include the 1948 Piano Quintet in D Major; Sonatina for Oboe and Piano; *Arabesques* for piano, and *Partita* for recorder and piano (also two spoofs, *Concerto Popolare* and *Let's Fake an Opera* for the Hoffnung Festivals devised by, and later held in memory of, musical cartoonist Gerard Hoffnung).

[2174] BARTOLOZZI, Bruno (Bär-tō-lōd'-zē, Broo'-nō)
VIOLINIST, TEACHER, THEORIST
BORN: Florence, June 8, 1911

A product of the conservatory in his native city, Bartolozzi played in the May Festival Orchestra for twenty-four years, 1941–65, and then taught at his former school. Since the early 1950s he has composed primarily in a twelve-tone style under the influence of his friend and colleague Luigi Dallapiccola **[2049]**. In 1967 he published (apparently in English) a manual entitled *New Sounds for Woodwind*, involving, among other matters, the production of microtones, which he has used sparingly in his own music. He has written a mixed-media stage work and some concerted pieces but composes mostly in small forms. RECORDINGS: There is a recording of his *Variazioni* for violin solo.

[2175] HERRMANN, Bernard
CONDUCTOR
BORN: New York, June 29, 1911
DIED: Los Angeles, December 24, 1975

In recent years Bernard Herrmann has come to be regarded as the most important native-born composer of film scores in Hollywood's Golden Age. A precocious creator, he won a hundred dollars for an orchestral composition he wrote while still a student at DeWitt Clinton High School. That event decided his future for him. He studied with Philip James

(1890–1975) and Percy Grainger [1749] at NYU, and, after taking his degree, studied composition with Bernard Wagenaar (1894–1971) and conducting with Albert Stoessel at the Juilliard. He composed prodigiously during this fledgling period, though later he junked much of what he had produced. He made his Broadway debut at twenty, conducting a ballet of his own composition in the 1932 edition of *Americana,* the last of a sporadic series of revues of that name. Forthwith he founded and conducted the New Chamber Orchestra in an adventurous series of concerts. In 1934 he joined the musical staff of CBS as composer and conductor. Shortly he fell in with Orson Welles, and, after supplying background music for several of his Mercury Theater broadcasts (a regular series), Herrmann followed him to Hollywood to do the score for *Citizen Kane* in 1940, which included a now famous scene from a mythical opera, *Salammbo.* Over the next thirty-five years Herrmann turned out sixty-one film scores, all of high quality (though not always for high-quality films— e.g., *Beneath the Twelve-Mile Reef* or *Jason and the Argonauts).*

In 1940 Herrmann was elevated to the conductorship of the CBS Symphony. That group was hardly intended to challenge its NBC counterpart of those days; but, performing in odd corners of the programming day, Herrmann managed to let Americans hear music most of them had never heard before, including a good deal by their own countrymen. The orchestra was abolished in 1955 by one of those triumphs of executive brainlessness, but by this time Herrmann had discovered Alfred Hitchcock, with whom he made beautiful music through a whole series of films beginning with *The Trouble With Harry* and perhaps peaking in *Vertigo* and *Psycho.* The relationship halted when Hitchcock, urged on by his corporate superiors, rejected the score he had written for the 1966 film *Torn Curtain.* In the 1960s Herrmann moved to England but continued to write film scores, his final one being for the 1975 *Taxi Driver,* the soundtrack of which he completed just before his sudden death of heart failure. Throughout his career Herrmann had continued to write music of his own; and in England, costs being low and he being well provided for, he began recording some of it. Later, when it was recognized that his film music was salable, he also conducted copious selections from that, and finally an attempt was made to get much of his best work on records. Herrmann was not an innovator, save perhaps in orchestration, but his music is skillful and attractive.

RECORDINGS: *Wuthering Heights* (opera); *Moby Dick* (cantata); Symphony; Clarinet Quintet; *Echoes* for string quartet; *The Fantasticks* for vocal quartet; music from *Citizen Kane; All That Money Can Buy; North by Northwest; Psycho; Vertigo; The Seventh Voyage of Sinbad; Journey to the Center of the Earth; Julius Caesar; Torn Curtain; Fahrenheit 451; Obsession; Taxi Driver;* and other films.

[2176] MAURY, Lowndes
TEACHER, ARRANGER, PIANIST
BORN: Butte, Montana, July 7, 1911

A 1931 graduate of the University of Montana, Maury studied at the Chicago Musical College later on and then with Arnold Schoenberg [1657] in 1934, and with Wesley La Violette in California, where he has made his career in the film and television studios. He has returned to Montana on occasion to teach at the State University at Bozeman. He has invented a simplified form of piano notation on three staves. He won a prize for a setting of the Jewish Sabbath Eve service and has written other choral works and a few orchestral ones, but his main output is chamber-size. RECORDINGS: His *Violin Sonata in Memory of the Korean War Dead* has been recorded.

[2177] MENOTTI, Gian Carlo (Me-nôt′-tē, Jän Kär′-lō)
LIBRETTIST, STAGE DIRECTOR, IMPRESARIO
BORN: Cadegliano, July 7, 1911

With the possible exception of Benjamin Britten [2215], Menotti has been the most successful composer of operas since Puccini [1511]—and that despite a lifelong cacophony of hoots and catcalls from the progressives and from much of the critical establishment. Born sixth among the ten musical offspring of a successful Italian importer in the lake country near the Swiss border, he was studying piano (with his mother) at four and writing songs at six. Around 1921 the Menottis moved to Milan, where he haunted the gallery of La Scala and was impelled to write two operas of his own and to arrange productions in a puppet theater that he had at home. At the age of twelve he was admitted to the Milan Conservatory, where he remained for four years, doing minimum work for maximum praise and becoming altogether insufferable. When the elder Menotti died in 1927, his wife took their prodigy to South America with her, where she had to tie up loose ends of the family business, then brought him to Philadelphia, enrolled him in the Curtis Institute and went home. Left to survive—he began with no English—he quickly shaped up. He studied with Rosario Scalero (1870–1954) until 1933, when he graduated with honors. Shortly afterward he began working on a comic opera, *Amelia al ballo (Amelia Goes to the Ball)* in neo-Rossinian style to his own libretto. It was premiered at Curtis (in English), Fritz Reiner conducting, in 1937 and was so successful that the Metropolitan Opera snapped it up the next season and kept it in the repertoire the following year. After that Menotti wrote all of his libretti in English, but he has never renounced his Italian citizenship.

Buoyed up by the signal success of his farce, he wrote another for NBC Radio, *The Old Maid and the Thief*, broadcast in the spring of 1939. Meanwhile the Metropolitan had commissioned from him a full-length opera—one of the four world premieres in the sixteen years of Edward Johnson's regime. A pretentiously allegorical work with little or no dramatic impact, *The Island God* of 1942 turned out to be a disaster. Within the same season Menotti had returned to Curtis to teach and had joined forces with former classmate Samuel Barber [2149] and poet Robert Horan in purchasing a house, dubbed "Capricorn," in Mt. Kisko, New York. Shocked by his failure, he gave up opera for the nonce, though he wrote a piano concerto for Rudolf Firkusny in 1943 and a ballet-score, *Sebastian*, in 1944. However, he returned to the stage in response to a commission from Columbia University's Alice M. Ditson Fund with a Grand Guignol melodrama, *The Medium*, for five singers, a mime, and an orchestra of fourteen, produced at the university in May 1946. It was followed there in 1947 by a two-character piece of fluff called *The Telephone*. That May the two works, backed by the Ballet Society, opened for a limited run on Broadway. Much to everyone's surprise, audience demand held them over for 212 performances—an extraordinary phenomenon for opera in America. This success was largely owing to *The Medium*, which boasted effective if "easy" music (a mix of Puccini and Stravinsky [1748]), a brilliant sense of theatricality, and a remarkable performance in the title role by an aging alto named Marie Powers. Columbia made an original-cast recording, and three years later Menotti directed a film of *The Medium*, with most of the Broadway cast.

Menotti's next opera, *The Consul*, went after out-of-town tryouts directly to Broadway, opening at the Ethel Barrymore Theater on March 15, 1950, with a cast featuring Patricia Neway, Miss Powers again, and the debutant Cornell McNeill. It won general critical hosannas, a run of eight months, a Pulitzer Prize, and the New York Drama Critics' Circle Award. A melodramatic indictment of totalitarian bureaucracy, it was also successful in most nontotalitarian countries, with the important exception of Italy, where it created a flap among Communists and among patriots who considered its composer a traitor. Hard on its heels came the fruits of an NBC television commission, *Amahl and the Night Visitors*, a quasi-Biblical piece about a crippled child and the Magi, aimed at the Christmas trade and telecast on December 24, 1951. Labeled hoky and sentimental in some quarters, it nevertheless exerts an undeniable dewy freshness and has been repeated every year since, with two remakes. After another operatic vacation, which produced a symphonic poem *Apocalypse* and a violin concerto, Menotti came roaring back in 1954 with a third Broadway production, *The Saint of Bleecker Street*. It managed only 92 performances but won awards from both the drama and music critics, and a second Pulitzer Prize. It was followed with a "madrigal comedy," *The Unicorn, the Gorgon, and the Manticore*, a rather transparent fable which has in recent years caught on with college music departments and which was premiered at the Library of Congress in 1956.

At least in terms of immediate acceptance, Menotti can be said to have peaked as a composer in the 1950s. During that period he also wrote the libretto for Barber's opera *Vanessa* and in 1958 inaugurated his Festival of Two Worlds at Spoleto, Italy, which has survived for twenty-five years. In the meantime NBC had commissioned yet another opera, *Maria Golovin*, which was premiered at the Brussels World's Fair on August 20, 1958. It opened—and rapidly closed—on Broadway that fall. A nationwide telecast won it no further plaudits, and the RCA recording was quickly withdrawn from the market. Menotti wrote little or nothing more until 1963 when yet another commission, *Labyrinth*, telecast by NBC, won more praise for its innovatory camera work than for its musicodramatic content. A cantata, *The Death of the Bishop of Brindisi*, which Menotti subsequently tried staging, was heard that same year in Cincinnati, and in October the Paris Opéra-Comique premiered *Le dernier sauvage (The Last Savage)*, originally intended for L'Opéra itself. The Metropolitan took it up three months thereafter (again in English), but it won few friends. Neither did the brief *Martin's Lie* in Bristol a year later. There was another hiatus, punctuated only by a song cycle for Elisabeth Schwarzkopf, until 1968, when the Hamburg Opera staged a short "opera for children," *Help! Help! the Globolinks!* Predicated on a battle between "real" music and that of the avant-garde (represented by electronic sound), it had a brief success with smaller opera groups. *The Leper,* a straight play of 1970, and the operas *The Most Important Man* of 1971 and *Tamu-Tamu* of 1973 fared considerably less well. Convinced that he was the object of a critical conspiracy, Menotti moved his dwelling to a castle near Lothian, Scotland, though since 1977 he has expanded the Spoleto Festival to an annual session in Charleston, South Carolina. Subsequent efforts have left scarcely any wrack behind—*The Hero* and *The Egg,* both from 1976; *The Trial of the Gypsy,* 1978; *La Loca* for Beverly Sills, 1978; and *Chip and His Dog,* 1980. It must be admitted that viewed from a perspective of thirty years even the successful pieces now seem awfully thin stuff.

RECORDINGS: There are one or more complete recordings of a number of the operas— *Amelia al Ballo* (in Italian); *The Old Maid and the Thief; The Medium; The Telephone; The Saint of Bleecker Street; Maria Golovin; Amahl and the Night Visitors;* a Canadian recording of the children's opera *Chip and His Dog;* and a slightly abridged version of *The Consul.* (There are versions of *The Telephone* and *The Medium* in French.) There are also a few instrumental and vocal excerpts from several of the operas. Other works on records include the ballet *Sebastian; The Unicorn, the Gorgon, and the Manticore;* Concerto for Violin; Concerto for Piano; the *Missa O Pulchritudo;* and the cantata *The Death of the Bishop of Brindisi.*

[2178] PETTERSON, Gustaf Allan (Pet'-er-sŏn, Gōō'-stàf Àl'-làn)
VIOLIST
BORN: Västra Ryd, September 19, 1911
DIED: Stockholm, June 20, 1980

It was only in the last dozen years of his stoically tragic life that Allan Petterson's music came into prominence in his homeland and on an international scale. He was born to poverty in a Stockholm slum under conditions that scarred him for life both physically and spiritually. He was largely self-educated. At nineteen he began nine years of work at the Stockholm Conservatory, intending to become a string player but greatly hampered because he could not afford a piano. He composed some songs and chamber works during these years and in

1939 won a Jenny Lind Scholarship that took him to Paris. But the outbreak of World War II sent him quickly home, where he found a place among the violas of the Stockholm Philharmonic. He had further lessons with Karl-Birger Blomdahl [2253], and in 1949 his Concerto for Violin and String Quartet was received with general disapproval. He returned to Paris to work with Honegger [1861] and Schoenberg [1657] disciple René Leibowitz, and in 1953 Heinrich Scherchen conducted his Concerto No. 1 for Strings at the ISCM Festival. Two years before, Petterson had left the orchestra to devote himself entirely to composition, and the first of his 16 symphonies also dates from 1953. In 1963 the progessive rheumatoid arthritis that eventually made him an invalid forced him to give up the viola. In 1968 he won the advocacy of Antal Dorati [2086], then director of the Stockholm Philharmonic, by whose efforts he quickly came to world attention. Petterson's strong concern for the downtrodden is often reflected in his music, notably in the *24 Barefoot Songs* of 1945 and the twelfth symphony to poems by Pablo Neruda, completed in 1974 and subtitled "The Dead in the Marketplace." Against the contemporary grain, he has made the symphony his special province, though in using a vast one-movement form in most of his symphonic works (e.g., the ninth symphony of 1970 is a single movement lasting eighty-five minutes), he has put his own stamp on it. RECORDINGS: There are performances of Symphonies Nos. 2, 6–10, 12, and 14; the cantata *Vox humana;* Concerto No. 1 for Violin and String Quartet; Concerto No. 2 for Violin and Orchestra; Concerto No. 1 for String Orchestra; *Mesto* for strings (actually, one movement of the Concerto No. 3 for String Orchestra); the 7 Sonatas for 2 Violins; the *24 Barefoot Songs* for voice and piano (there are also recordings of eight of the songs arranged for orchestra by Antal Dorati and of a selection of the songs arranged for mixed choir); and a few individual songs.

[2179] NOWAK, Lionel (Nō'-vak, Lī'-ō-nel)
PIANIST, TEACHER, CONDUCTOR
BORN: Cleveland, September 25, 1911

Lionel Nowak began his career in Cleveland as a four-year-old pianist. As an adolescent he was a church organist and choir director and wrote music for his charges. He studied at the Cleveland Institute with pianist Beryl Rubinstein, and with Herbert Elwell [1948] and Quincy Porter [1932], and also had piano lessons from Edwin Fischer and compositional aid from Roger Sessions [1931] and Carl Ruggles [1684]. In the 1930s he accompanied and wrote for the Wiedmann-Humphrey dance troupe. In 1942 he took a teaching post at Converse College in South Carolina, transferred to Syracuse University in 1946, and settled down as professor of piano at Bennington College in 1948. A daughter, Allison (1948–), is also a composer. His rather small output of nonutilitarian works focuses in the area of chamber music. RECORDINGS: His 1961 Concert Piece for kettledrums and strings has been recorded, as have three Soundscapes (one for three woodwinds, one for string quartet, and one for solo piano).

[2180] USSACHEVSKY, Vladimir Alexis
TEACHER
BORN: Hailar, November 3, 1911 (Grove has October 21)

Vladimir Ussachevsky was the son of a Russian colonel resident in Manchuria. The entire family was musical but played and sang only Russian music. The boy began piano lessons with his mother at the age of six and later was an acolyte in a Russian Orthodox church. He was in his middle teens when he first heard Western music. Later he played in dance bands and movie theaters. When he was eighteen he emigrated to California with his mother and his brother. After two years at Pasadena Junior College, he won a scholarship for an orchestral composition, which took him to Pomona College, from which he graduated in 1935. He then spent four years at the Eastman School of Music, studying with Howard Hanson [1927], Burrill Philips [2116], and Bernard Rogers [1875], acquiring his Ph.D. at the end of the line. In 1940 he returned to California to obtain a teacher's certificate from Claremont College. After doing some teaching and choral conducting, he was drafted, taken into military intelligence (because of his oriental background), and sent to the University of Washington for a crash course. There he met and married Elisabeth Kray. He spent the remaining war years at offices in Washington, D.C. After a year of teaching at the Putney School in Vermont, he found a permanent home at Columbia University in 1947.

A few years later he was asked to procure one of those new-fangled tape recorders for his department. He became interested in the gadget, was especially fascinated by how he could manipulate sound with it, and began putting together brief compositions. Curiously he was wholly unaware of what Pierre Schaeffer [2159] was doing in Paris in much

the same way at the same time. He gave his first public demonstration of music created in the new medium in 1952 with Sonic Contours, a work based on piano sounds. Shortly afterward Otto Luening [1980] joined him and in 1954, commissioned by the Louisville Orchestra, they turned out their Rhapsodic Variations for tape and orchestra. Other collaborations were premiered by the Los Angeles Philharmonic and New York Philharmonic or accompanied plays produced by Margaret Webster and Orson Wells. Ussachevsky also continued to create tape works of his own. In 1959 he and Luening, together with Roger Sessions [1931] and Milton Babbitt [2247], founded the Columbia-Princeton Electronic Music Center. Ussachevsky has also created soundtracks for films and television. In recent years he has worked with computerized music and mixed media. Over the years, he has also written a small amount of music for conventional media, including orchestral pieces, a piano sonata, and various chamber pieces. He has received numerous fellowships and other honors.

RECORDINGS: Compositions recorded include Creation: Prologue, Piece for Tape Recorder, Wireless Fantasy, Of Wood and Brass, Computer Piece, Two Sketches, Metamorphosis, Linear Contrasts, Conflict, Pentagram (solo oboe and tape), Missa Brevis (chorus), and 3 Scenes from Creation (with chorus and orchestra). See the article on Luening for a list of recordings of collaborative works.

[2181] BERGMAN, Erik Valdemar (Bârg'-mán, Ä'-rēk Vàl'-de-mär)
CRITIC, CHOIRMASTER, TEACHER
BORN: Nykarleby, November 24, 1911

A significant early Finnish avant-gardist, Bergman was born on the shores of the Gulf of Bothnia in what is now Uusikaarlepyy. He majored in literature and musicology at the University of Helsinki, simultaneously studying at the Helsinki Conservatory, from which he graduated in 1939. In the latter part of the decade, he also had lessons with Joseph Marx [1747] in Vienna and Heinz Tiessen (1887–1971), former lieutenant to Richard Strauss [1563] in Berlin. His career did not really get off the ground until after World War II. He became music critic for Helsinki newspapers in 1945, conducted several choruses and church choirs, and as a composer moved to twelve-tone music, then to serialism, and eventually to some aleatory practice. He was appointed professor of composition at the conservatory (by then the

Sibelius Academy) in 1963. The bulk of his music is choral. RECORDINGS: The Sonatina for Piano, *Energien* (harpsichord), *Aubade* (orchestra), *Concertino da Camera, Colori ed Improvvisazioni* (orchestra), and *Noa* (baritone, chorus, and orchestra) have been recorded by various Scandinavian ensembles and performers.

[2182] PONGRÁCZ, Zoltán (Pōn'-gráts, Zōl'-tàn)
RADIO OFFICIAL, CONDUCTOR, TEACHER
BORN: Diószeg, February 5, 1912

Pongrácz was born in what is now Diosig in northwest Rumania. After five years at the Budapest Academy, where he was Kodály's [1760] composition pupil, he went to Vienna to study with conductor Rudolf Nilius in 1935. Several ambitious compositions—a ballet *The Devil's Gift* and some cantatas— in the years immediately subsequent won him a Franz Josef Prize in 1939. In 1940 he went to the University of Berlin to study exotic musics and stopped by Salzburg in the summer of 1941 on his way home for further conducting lessons with Clemens Krauss. In 1943–44 he was a music director for the Hungarian Radio. After the dust of the war had settled, he became conductor of the Philharmonic Orchestra at Debrecen in eastern Hungary, where he also served as professor at the local conservatory until 1964. About this time he turned to electronic music (he had been a twelve-toner for most of the postwar period). From 1968 he served as an inspector of vocal music in the Budapest schools and in 1975 returned to the Budapest Academy to teach electronic composition. RECORDINGS: Several of his electronic works have been recorded—*Phonothèse, 144 Sounds, Madrigal, In Praise of Folly,* and *Sesquialtera.*

[2183] BROWN, Raynor
ORGANIST, TEACHER
BORN: Des Moines, February 23, 1912

Raynor Brown was trained at the University of Southern California, where he took a master's degree in 1946. He was organist at Los Angeles' Wilshire Presbyterian Church from 1942 and taught at little Biola University in the suburb of La Mirada from 1952. He has written 3 symphonies, but most of his compositions are for band, organ, and wind instruments. RECORDINGS: The fact that his recordings were financed through foundation grants demonstrates an increasingly common phenomenon in the years af-

ter World War II. Works recorded include the Concertino for Harp and Brass; Concertino for Piano and Band; Concertino for 2 Pianos, Brass, and Percussion; *Fantasy and Fugue* for brass; *5 Pieces for Organ, Harp, Brass, and Percussion; Symphony for Clarinet Choir;* and Sonata for Flute and Organ.

[2184] MONTSALVATGE, Bassols Xavier (Mōnt-sàl-vàj', Bà-sōlz' Háv-yâr')
CRITIC, TEACHER
BORN: Gerona, March 11, 1912

Among the better-known of contemporary Spanish composers, Xavier Montsalvatge is an eclectic who avoids identification with musical schools and systems. A Catalan born in the historically much fought-over capital of Spain's northeasternmost province, he entered the Barcelona Conservatory at eleven and remained in its passionately Catalonian atmosphere until 1936, winning several prizes en route. Subsequently he was first heard from as a composer of ballets on the French-Stravinskian [1748] model. He was in part influenced by Catalan folk music but more particularly for a time by that of the West Indies, which he studied and used as a model. He had a local success in 1948 with his children's opera *El Gato in botas (Puss in Boots).* In more recent years he has grown even more consciously eclectic, suiting whatever he deems the proper style to the composition at hand. RECORDINGS: Several brief works for string orchestra— *Danzas concertantes, Americana,* and *Española*—and the *Concierto breve* for piano and orchestra have been recorded, along with the song cycle *Invocaciones al Crucificado (Invocations to the Crucified), Canciones negras (Black Songs),* and several piano pieces *(Sonatine pour Yvette, 3 Divertimenti,* and *Sketch).*

[2185] BERGER, Arthur Victor
CRITIC, TEACHER
BORN: New York, May 15, 1912

As a youngster, Berger taught himself to play piano in emulation of his sister and later to write music. After two years at CCNY, he transferred to NYU in 1930 to get a teaching credential in music. There he became friends with his classmates Jerome Moross [2211] and Bernard Herrmann [2175], came for a time under the spell of Aaron Copland [1986], and tried composing in what he felt was the manner of Schoenberg [1657]. He got his degree in 1933, by which time he was already reviewing for the

New York *Daily Mirror.* A year later, on fellowship, he went to Cambridge, Massachusetts, to study at the Longy School, during which time he took courses with Walter Piston [1890] and others at Harvard, wrote for the Boston *Evening Transcript,* and founded and edited *The Musical Mercury.* Harvard gave him an M.A. in 1936, and a year later he married a young music teacher, Esther Turitz, and sailed for France and Nadia Boulanger. He returned on the eve of World War II to teach for two years at Mills College, where he was colleague and protégé of Darius Milhaud [1868], under whose urging he buckled down to serious composing, now in a French neo-classical style. In 1942 he returned to home territory to teach for a year at Brooklyn College. After that he abandoned academia for posts as critic, first with the New York *Sun* and then with the *Herald Tribune.* In 1953, however, he was named to the Naumburg Chair at Brandeis University, where he remained and where from 1962 he was the first to occupy the Irving Gifford Fine Chair. Esther Berger having died in 1960, he married psychologist Ellen Tessman in 1967. In the 1950s Berger moved into serialism, from which he later retreated to more personal territory. He wrote a handful of orchestral and choral pieces early in his career, but his chief output has been in the realm of chamber music. He also founded the journal *Perspectives in Modern Music* in 1962 and wrote a book-length study of Aaron Copland in 1953. RE-CORDINGS: Works on records include the 1956 *Polyphony* (a Louisville Orchestra commission); *Serenade Concertante* for violin and eleven instruments; *Chamber Music for 13 Players;* String Quartet; Woodwind Quartet in C Major; Duo for Cello and Piano; *3 Pieces for 2 Pianos;* and other keyboard pieces.

[2186] FRANÇAIX, Jean (Fràn-sā' Zhàn)
PIANIST
BORN: Le Mans, May 23, 1912

Already commuting weekly to the Paris Conservatoire, Jean Françaix, on hearing in 1921 of the death of that self-styled old *musicien français* Camille Saint-Saëns [1343], is said to have remarked wearily that it was doubtless his lot to inherit the mantle —one for which his surname seemed to destine him. He could scarcely have missed anyhow: his father was director of the conservatory in Le Mans, where his mother taught voice and directed a choir. After domestic lessons from the age of four, he was entrusted to Nadia Boulanger and pianist Isidor Philipp. Shortly afterward, in 1922, he published a piano suite, *Pour Jacqueline,* dedicated to his infant cousin. In 1930 he took first prize for piano at the Paris Conservatoire, inaugurating a notable performing career. Two years later his compositions began to get public hearings—Pierre Monteux, for example, premiered his only symphony in 1932—and in 1934 he created considerable excitement when he played his Concertino for Piano and Orchestra in Paris. The Ballets Russes de Monte Carlo produced his ballet *Scuola di ballo (Dance School)* with choreography by Léonide Massine, on Boccherini themes, in 1933; and in 1935 the Paris Opéra staged an original dance score, *Le Roi nu (The Naked King* or *The Emperor's New Clothes,* with choreography by Serge Lifar). The Concerto for Piano was first heard in 1936, and the composer played it on his first American visit in 1938 with the New York Philharmonic, Nadia Boulanger conducting. Françaix's first opera, the chamber work *Le Diable boiteux (The Gimpy Devil),* appeared in 1937.

In a world in which music has come more and more to be taken as a deadly serious (place the emphasis on whichever modifier you will) affair, Françaix has gone on producing a stream of beautifully crafted, crystal clear, carefree (a more recent epithet is "frivolous") works of all kinds that take no heed of what is supposed to be musical progress. Occasionally, as in his 1942 oratorio *L'Apocalypse de St. Jean,* he strives for (and achieves) something more profound. He has on occasion concertized with cellist Maurice Gendron and with his own pianist-daughter Claude Paillard-Françaix. His output includes 4 operas, 12 ballets, film scores, much music for orchestra, chamber and choral music, and some songs.

RECORDINGS: A fair portion of his output has been recorded. For the stage we have the chamber opera (or dialogue) for men's voices *Le Diable boiteaux,* the ballets *Scuola di ballo* and *Le Roi nu,* and the "lyric fantasy" *Paris à nous deux* for chamber chorus and saxophone quartet. Orchestral recordings include the Concertino for Piano and Concerto for Piano (versions with Françaix and Boulanger, and with Paillard-Françaix and Françaix); Symphony for Strings; *Serenade* for small orchestra; *Rhapsody* for viola and small orchestra; *Suite for Violin and Orchestra;* Concerto for Bassoon; Concerto for Clarinet; Concerto for Contrabass; Concerto for 2 Pianos; *L'Horloge de Flore (Flora's Clock)* for oboe and chamber orchestra. Chamber works recorded include the String Trio, *Divertissement for String Trio; Divertissement for Bassoon and String Quartet; Di-*

vertissement for Oboe, Clarinet, and Bassoon; *Variations on a Peasant Theme* for piano and winds; Woodwind Quartet; Wind Quintet; Quintet for Flute, Violin, Viola, Cello, and Harp; *Sérénade B-E-A* for string sextet; *Serenade for 12 Instruments; Sérénade comique* and *Petite Quartette* for saxophone quartet; Sonatine for Violin and Piano; Quintet for Clarinet and Strings; *5 Danses exotiques* for saxophone and piano; *Les Vacances* for piano quartet; *Les Petits Paganini* for five violins; and *15 Portraits d'enfants d'Auguste Renoir* for piano, four hands. Solo instrumental recordings include *Suite for Flute Solo; 5 Portraits de jeunes filles* and *8 Anecdotes de Chamfort* for piano; and a few other piano pieces. Vocal recordings include the *Cantate de Méphisto* for bass voice and strings; *5 Chansons pour les enfants* for two sopranos and piano; and *3 Duos* for soprano and string quartet.

[2187] SCOTT, Thomas Jefferson
SINGER, VIOLINIST
BORN: Campbellsburg, Ky., May 28, 1912
DIED: New York, August 12, 1961

Born in the Kentucky hill country near the Indiana border, Tom Scott, as he was generally known, learned the fiddle at home, then became a songwriter and dance-band player. He found his way to Hollywood, where he took lessons from George Antheil **[1981]**. He also studied with Wallingford Riegger **[1793]** in New York. In the first fine flush of concert "folk singing"—the days of Burl Ives, Richard Dyer-Bennett, and Josh White—Scott, who had a fine bass voice, became a popular performer on the circuit and made a number of records. He wrote an opera, symphonies, string quartets, and a number of works with a strongly American or folk bias. He died prematurely at forty-nine. RECORDINGS: Two of Scott's orchestral works have been recorded—*Hornpipe and Chantey* and *Variations on "Binorie"*—along with some folksong arrangements.

[2188] DAHL, Ingolf, (Dȧl, In′-golf)
PIANIST, CONDUCTOR, ARRANGER
BORN: Hamburg, June 9, 1912
DIED: Frutigen, Switzerland, August 7, 1970

A German-born Swede, Dahl was a pupil of Busoni **[1577]**-trained Philipp Jarnach at the Cologne Conservatory. Afterward he studied musicology at the University of Zürich and conducted at that city's opera house. In 1935 he visited America and settled in Los Angeles three years later, where he made a career for himself in radio and film music, mostly as an arranger. He became pianist and conductor of the famous Monday Evening Concerts ("Evenings on the Roof") of contemporary music, during the course of which he became friends with Igor Stravinsky **[1748]**. In 1945 he became a member of the music department of USC, where he taught until his death. He also taught in the summer of the early 1950s at Tanglewood and was director of California's Ojai Festival for two seasons, 1964–66. His music began with thick Central European contrapuntality but moved to a purer sort of neo-classicism. His output was relatively small and is almost all instrumental, inclining toward works of small proportions. RECORDINGS: One orchestral work has been recorded—the 1955 symphonic legend *The Tower of St. Barbara.* Other recordings include the 1949 Concerto for Saxophone and Winds; *Sinfonietta* for band; *Music for Brass Instruments; Allegro and Arioso* for woodwind quintet; *Duettino Concertante* for flute and percussion; *Concertino a tre* for clarinet, violin, and cello; *Sonata da camera* for clarinet and piano; *Divertimento* for viola and piano; *Sonata Seria, Sonata pastorale,* and *Hymne* (all for piano).

[2189] GILLIS, Don
ARRANGER, PRODUCER, SCRIPTWRITER, ADMINISTRATOR
BORN: Cameron, Mo., June 17, 1912
DIED: Columbia, S.C., January 20, 1978

Don Gillis, as composer, was a sort of musical Norman Rockwell. He led a normal smalltown boyhood life, in the course of which he played brasses in a local band and his school orchestra. He also had his own dance band. After the Gillises moved to Fort Worth in 1931, he played in the orchestra at a local radio station and attended Texas Christian University, from which he took a B.A. in 1935 and where he taught for an additional year while acquiring a B.Mus. Then he conducted the orchestra at a local Baptist institution until 1942, when he returned to Station WBAP as producer and began graduate studies at North Texas State University in Denton, where he received an M.Mus. a year later. By then, in part thanks to his radio connections, his work was being heard not only in Texas but around the nation. In 1943 he joined NBC in Chicago and in 1944 was moved to New York, where among other assignments he was producer, scriptwriter, and commentator for Arturo Toscanini's NBC Symphony broadcasts. The conductor was amused by his *Symphony No. 5 1/2*—one of a number of comically aimed compositions by Gillis—and played it on a broadcast. The series ended with Toscanini's retirement in 1954. When NBC tried to disband the orchestra, Gillis headed the effort to save it, and under his presidency it survived for a while as the Symphony of the Air. He later served as vice president of the noted music camp founded by Joe Maddy at Interlochen, Michigan, as chairman of the music department at Southern Methodist University, and from 1968 to 1972 as chairman of the arts program at the small Dallas Baptist College. In 1973 he became composer-in-residence at the University of South Carolina, where he succumbed to a heart attack five years later. His music was determinedly American with folk and jazz elements, but otherwise in an old-fashioned idiom calculated to appeal to the common man. He was extremely productive, his output including 8 operas, a western ballet, 12 symphonies, 6 string quartets, and much other music for orchestra, band, chorus, and instrument combinations, not to mention film scores and a multimedia extravaganza, *Let Us Pray*. Besides radio scripts and his own libretti, he wrote many articles and two books, *The Unfinished Symphony Conductor* and *The Art of Media Instruction*. RECORDINGS: All orchestral, these include *Symphony No. 5 1/2, Tulsa: A Portrait in Oil, The Man Who Invented Music*, and *Frontier Town*.

[2190] MONCAYO GARCÍA, José Pablo
(Mōn-ká'-yō Gär-sē'-à, Hō-zä' Páb'-lō)
PIANIST, PERCUSSIONIST, CONDUCTOR
BORN: Guadalajara, June 29, 1912
DIED: Mexico City, June 16, 1958

Moncayo took up the piano at seventeen and later became a pupil and protégé of Carlos Chávez [1968] at the Mexico City Conservatory. He supported himself by playing in dance bands and cabarets and joined three fellow students, Daniel Ayala (1906–75), Salvador Contreras (1912–), and Blas Galindo [2148] in the Grupo de los Cuatro to produce nationalistic music. In 1932 Chávez appointed him pianist to the Orquesta Sinfónica de Mexico and later its chief percussionist and assistant director. In 1948 Moncayo's opera *La Mulata de Córdoba* had a successful production at the Palace of Fine Arts. He succeeded Chávez as conductor from 1949 to 1952. He died shortly before his forty-sixth birthday. His small output includes 2 symphonies. RECORDINGS: Recordings of his

music, emanating from Mexico and elsewhere, have been fairly numerous and have included several orchestral works—*Homenaje a Cervantes* for two oboes and strings, *Huapango, Cumbres, Bosques, Feria y Danza, Sinfonietta*, and *Tierra de Temporal* (the latter a.k.a. the ballet *Zapata*).

[2191] STEHMAN, Jacques (Stä'-màn, Zhàk)
PIANIST, CRITIC
BORN: Brussels, July 8, 1912
DIED: Heist-aan-Zee, May 20, 1975

Stehman was a pupil of the Belgian Royal Conservatory, where he studied with Jean Absil [1889], Paul Gilson [1572], and the pianist Eduardo Del Pueyo. He later taught there and also appeared as a pianist and gave music reviews in the press and on radio. Among the influences on his undemanding music—which includes a piano concerto and scores for plays and films—were Maurice Ravel [1666] and the jazz of the 1930s. RECORDINGS: The orchestral works *Symphonie de poche* and *Chant funèbre* have been recorded, as have a number of piano pieces—*Matins, Le Tombeau de Ravel, Préludes, Bouquet romantique, Prétexte à danser*, and others.

[2192] CAGE, John
PIANIST, TEACHER, MYCOLOGIST
BORN: Los Angeles, September 5, 1912

For better or worse, John Cage is probably the most influential and by many the most cordially detested of all American composers to date. There is little doubt that in sheer intellectual terms he is a genius, but there is also reason to conclude that he is also a sort of holy fool. His innovations—the "prepared" piano, electronic music, aleatory concepts, indeterminacy, "happenings," etc. —are many and sweeping; but whether in most instances the results qualify as music, save by a kind of Alice-in-Wonderland logic, is questionable, and it remains to be seen whether Cage has liberated the art or, in the desperate way of the twentieth century, painted it into yet one more corner.

Like Ravel's [1666] father Joseph, John Milton Cage, the composer's father, was an ingenious engineer with a turn for invention, most of the products of which failed to make him rich. The younger John was an only child who seems not to have suffered at all from the family's frequent relocations, maintaining a brilliant record throughout his early education save in the matter of learning to play the piano. He was valedictorian and a straight-A student at Los Angeles High School, graduating at sixteen. He entered Pomona College with vague plans to become a preacher and then decided that he wanted to write. But he soon found that he did not see eye to eye with the methods of higher education, dropped out at the end of the academic year in 1930, and went to France with a hazy notion of becoming an architect. He secured a job with a practitioner of that profession named Goldfinger, but when he discovered that such professionals were supposed to specialize in their métier to the exclusion of all other fields of endeavor, he quit. He dabbled in painting, poetry, and piano for a year and a half and then went home. Back in California he worked as a gardener and gave lectures to housewives on modern art, peddling them, so to speak, door to door. Having thus discovered who Schoenberg [1657] was, he took lessons with the pianist Richard Bühlig, who, he had heard, understood Schoenberg's music. Cage worked out his own version of serial technique, which involved twenty-five consecutive tones instead of the canonic twelve. Bühlig sent him to Henry Cowell [1934] with his compositions, and Cowell urged him to seek out Schoenberg himself as a teacher, as soon as he had gotten some proper grounding. Cowell suggested this might be provided best by Adolf Weiss (1891–1971), a Schoenberg pupil who taught in New York.

Cage duly hopped a freight for the East, where he studied with Weiss and Cowell until late 1934, living a marginal existence and working as a handyman in the Brooklyn YMCA. He then returned to Los Angeles and told Schoenberg he wanted to study with him, though he had no money. In a quixotic fit, Schoenberg decided to teach him for free. The lessons under way, Cage took a bride in the person of a sometime art student named Xenia Andreevna Kashevaroff, whom he had met before the New York interlude. They survived on what Cage got as his father's research assistant, plus money from odd jobs. Cage remained an adoring pupil of Schoenberg for nearly three years, though, as was common for Schoenberg's pupils, he got little encouragement and a good deal of browbeating, the chief problem being Cage's inability to comprehend harmony in any meaningful way. Commissioned to do a score for an avantgarde filmmaker who had the quaint notion that every object has its own innate sound, Cage hit on the idea of percussion music, which would not be subject to melodic or harmonic laws, but only to temporal rela-

tionships involving sounds and silences. For some time he concentrated on such music, finding a market for it in modern dance groups, for some of which he worked as a rehearsal pianist.

In 1937 the Cages moved to Seattle, where John worked in the dance classes taught by Bonnie Bird at the Cornish School until 1939 and gave percussion concerts that attracted considerable attention. He met the composer Lou Harrison [2266], who took him to Mills College in the summer to see the avantgarde things happening there. In 1938 he was asked by a dancer at Cornish named Sybilla Fort to write a bacchanale for a solo number she was planning. There was room only for a piano where she was to dance, but Cage, now used to thinking in percussion terms, found he could come up with nothing convincing. Suddenly it occurred to him that by modifying the sounds of the strings he could turn the piano into a percussion instrument. He achieved this with thumbtacks, erasers, and other homely devices, and the "prepared piano" was born. It was also in this period that he worked out a mathematical approach to composition based on time relationships.

After two years with the WPA as a recreational director in San Francisco, during which he vainly tried to corral sponsors for an experimental music center, Cage moved to Chicago in 1941 to teach modern music at the Chicago School of Design. During his stay there, he got a hearing on national radio when CBS, after several contretemps, broadcast a program written by the poet Kenneth Patchen that used a Cage percussion score. Deciding he had arrived, the composer and his wife spent their last dollar on bus tickets to New York and moved in with Max Ernst and his wife Peggy Guggenheim, who had ill-advisedly said, "You must stay with us when you are in New York." Ms. Guggenheim was about to treat Cage to a one-man concert in her gallery until she discovered that he had already arranged one for some months later at the opposition, the Museum of Modern Art and forthwith kicked the couple out of her apartment. Between that time and the MOMA concert in February 1943, the Cages lived on handouts he unblinkingly solicited from whomever he could think of. It was in this period that Cage began his long association with the dancer Merce Cunningham, who had studied at Cornish and danced with Martha Graham. Another research project for his father, being classified "secret," kept Cage out of the draft though it did not pay the bills.

The MOMA concert made Cage's name

and won for him the advocacy of Virgil Thomson [1928], then the most influential critic in America. But Cage was with the general musical public (as he has been ever since) more notorious than famous, and he was distressed that his music was not understood in the way he intended it to be. Meanwhile the marriage had dissolved and Cage had moved into the top floor of an old tenement building on the Lower East Side, which, painted and decorated by his friend the sculptor Richard Lippold, came to be known after its landlord as the Bozza Mansion. Shortly afterward he learned from Gita Sarabhai, an Indian student of his, about the temporal underpinning of Indian music and, more importantly, that the concept of music in Indian philosophy was that it was intended not to communicate anything in and of itself but to prepare the mind for receptivity. Embarking on an intensive study of both oriental and occidental thought, Cage discovered Zen Buddhism in the classes of Daisetz Suzuki at Columbia University and came to the conclusion that his function as a composer was to wake people up to the lives they were unconsciously coasting through.

Shortly afterward he formed a sort of partnership with Merce Cunningham, later becoming musical director of his dance company, and, after they had given a recital at avant-garde Black Mountain College in North Carolina in 1947, they were invited back to teach there the next summer. Instead of giving a course, however, he presented a festival of the music of Erik Satie [1578], in which he had discovered a sympathetic afflatus, at the end of which he suggested that Beethoven [1063] had taken music down the wrong road. In 1949 Maro Ajemian's performance of the Sonatas and Interludes for prepared piano in a New York concert won Cage grants from the Guggenheim Foundation and the National Academy of the Arts. He and Cunningham took off for France, where they concertized and where Cage met the Pierres Schaeffer [2159] and Boulez [2346] and did research on Satie. Shortly after his return, working at his Concerto for Prepared Piano, Cage hit on the idea of scoring it on charts that introduced the element of chance into the interpretation. The results pleased hardly anyone but Cage, except for a budding composer named Morton Feldman [2355]. Feldman introduced him to the pianist-composer David Tudor (1926–) and to a teenage composer named Christian Wolff (1934–), who was a son of the publisher of Pantheon Books), and the four, as a sort of committee, set about to develop Cage's ideas. Together they came up with the concept of indeterminacy

in which only the abstract conditions of the performance are indicated. From one of the elder Wolff's publications Cage learned about the *I Ching*, an ancient Chinese method of fortune telling from the random patterns made by sticks of a special design tossed on a table. He saw in it the possibility of further divorcing himself from his music and composed (if that is the word) *Music of Changes*, in which every note and its ramifications was determined by a complex system of coin tossing, completed in 1951.

Over the years Cage had written three pieces designated as *Imaginary Landscapes* —the second and third for percussion ensembles; the first, in 1939, a pioneering effort in electronic music, using frequency recordings played on variable-speed turntables. The fourth *Imaginary Landscape* made newspaper headlines in 1952. It involved both chance and electronics. Operating on the premise that music, to arouse, should irritate, he scored it for twelve radios, devices whose sounds he found particularly annoying. Each radio had two "players"—one to turn the dial, the other to manipulate volume, and tone controls as specified in the score. It was performed at the end of a long program at Columbia University, after many stations had gone off the air. The patches of static and white noise barely fazed the composer, but the audience was angry and even Virgil Thomson failed to approve. A fifth *Imaginary Landscape*, written in that same year, was Cage's first composition on tape; it consisted of patches from forty-two phonograph records, taped, chopped up, recombined by chance methods and retaped. With Earle Brown [2365], who had joined the inner circle, he expanded this approach in his 1952 *Williams Mix*, which involved both musical sounds and noises similarly broken down and recombined by both mathematical and aleatory processes on a tape carrying eight separate soundtracks. At Black Mountain College in North Carolina that summer, Cage began a productive friendship with the painter Robert Rauschenberg, who was a participant in a "concerted action" conceived by Cage, in which, guided by an aleatory "score," the participants (musicians, poets, dancers, etc.) all (to use a later popular phrase) did their own things simultaneously but independently of each other. This piece is generally regarded as the first "happening," a theatrical movement that enjoyed a brief vogue in the 1960s and regarded Cage as a hero. The year 1952 also produced *Water Music*, in which the performer—ostensibly a pianist—is required to produce, with an array of props, extramusical sounds mostly involving water. In August, at a concert in Woodstock, New York, David Tudor premiered the famous *4′ 33″* (for any instrument) in which, for precisely that long, he sat unmoving at the piano except to open and close the keyboard cover twice to indicate breaks between the movements.

Cage's point in *4′ 33″* is that it forces the listener to hear the *real* music of life that fills the silence—coughs, rustling programs, the wind on the panes. He had arrived at the view that the point of music is not, through the composer's will, to express an ordered view of the cosmos, but, by effacing the composer as far as is possible, to let the cosmos speak for itself. By now he had, except for his intimates, lost the support even of most of the avant-garde musicians. Still he was not satisfied, for in his compositions there were still controlling elements that got in the way of that process.

In 1954 Cage's New York domicile was condemned, and he moved into a sort of commune with David Tudor and several other artists on a farm in New York's Rockland County. There he discovered the joys of mushroom hunting, became an expert, supplied the Four Seasons Restaurant with wild mushrooms for a time and founded the New York Mycological Society. It was also in 1954 that he and Tudor went on a concert tour of Europe, where they elicited mostly laughter and hisses, but at least one auditor, Karlheinz Stockhausen [2377], liked what he heard and proceeded to develop Cagean methods in his own way. Back in America in October 1955, a filmmaker and Cage admirer named Emile de Antonio staged a Cunningham-Cage recital in a high school auditorium in Rockland County that drove away the locals and wowed the avant-garders up from Manhattan.

In 1957–58 Cage composed his *Concert for Piano and Orchestra*. Each instrumental part (composed by chance methods) consists of loose, unnumbered pages. Each performer arranges them as he sees fit, discarding any or all of them at his own discretion the whole controlled only by a specified time limit. A performance with no participants is perfectly possible, but more important in Cage's view is that the likelihood of ever having two identical readings is remote. By now Cage had discovered how to score his music on sets of transparent sheets; the performer got his directions (if so positive a word may be used) by overlaying them as he saw fit. Since the composer could in no wise foresee the results, Cage called this "indeterminacy." In the meantime he had continued to work with the dance company and occasionally taught at the New School, not only on new music but also on Virgil Thomson and mushroom identification. A Town Hall retrospective given him in May 1958 by de Antonio, Rauschenberg, and artist Jasper Johns packed the house, drew both cheers and execrations, and was committed to commercial recordings by George Avakian. That summer Cage taught at Darmstadt and then worked for some months in the Milan Electronic Studio at Luciano Berio's [2352] invitation, producing an indeterminately derived tape piece called *Fontana Mix* after his landlady. While in Milan he participated in a TV quiz show based roughly on the American "$64,000 Question." He espoused mushrooms as his field of expertise and inaugurated each program with a new piece, one of which was *Water Walk,* involving fish, a bathtub, a pressure cooker, and other aqueous devices. He easily made his way to the "top" and won in an unintentionally theatrical cliffhanger, pocketing $6,000 and establishing himself as a star in Italy.

By now Cage was beginning to be taken seriously, and in 1960–61 he held a fellowship at the Center for Advanced Studies at Connecticut's Wesleyan University, where he compiled his first collection of essays *Silence.* In 1962 he and Tudor made a successful tour of Japan. In 1964 the New York Philharmonic under Leonard Bernstein [2282] did a Feldman-Cage-Brown program which included Cage's *Atlas Eclipticalis with Winter Music* (involving contact microphones to distort the instrumental sounds). It not only emptied the hall but drew hisses from the performers. But in succeeding years Cage enjoyed the status of composer-in-residence with the universities of Cincinnati, Illinois and California (at Davis), election to the National Institute of Arts and Letters, and sixtieth-birthday celebrations at the New School and Avery Fisher Hall, as well as an exhibit of his scores. Through all his ups and downs, Cage has remained unbothered, cheerful, and eager for the next step forward.

RECORDINGS: Since a recording freezes forever a given performance, one misses an important dimension of the later Cage works on records. Missing too from perhaps all of them is the visual and theatrical aspect, which cannot really be left out. However, a fair cross section of his work has been thus ineffectually preserved. (The instrumentation of some of the works may vary greatly; what is listed here is descriptive of the recorded performances.) Among the works recorded at the 1958 Town Hall concert are at least one of the percussion works entitled *Construction in Metal, Imaginary Landscape No. 1,* some of the *Sonatas and Interludes* for prepared piano, *6 Short Inventions* for seven instruments, *The Wonderful Widow of 18 Springs, She Is Asleep, Music for Carillon, Williams' Mix* for tape, and the *Concert* for piano and orchestra. Other recordings include the complete *Sonatas and Interludes* for prepared piano; *Music of Changes* for prepared piano; *Études australes* for piano; *Amores* for prepared piano and percussion; *3 Dances* for two amplified prepared pianos; *Winter Music* for four pianos; *A Book of Music* for two prepared pianos; numerous short pieces for solo piano or prepared piano (among them, *A Valentine out of Season, Music for Marcel Duchamp, The Perilous Night, A Room, 7 Haiku, Totem Ancestor, 2 Pastorales,* and *And the Earth Shall Bear Again); HPSCHD,* a collaboration with Lejaren Hiller [2337] for three harpsichords and electronics; *Nocturne* for violin and piano; *6 Melodies* for violin and piano; *27′ 10.554″* for one percussionist; Sonata for Clarinet; *Dream* for viola; *Constructions in Metal I–III* for percussion; *Double Music* for percussion (in collaboration with Lou Harrison [2266]); String Quartet; *26′ 1.1499″* for solo string player; Quartet for 12 Tom-toms (four players); *In a Landscape* for harp; *Chorals, Cheap Imitation,* and *Freeman Etudes,* all for solo violin; a performance-lecture called *Indeterminancy,* with Cage as narrator and David Tudor on electronics; *The Seasons,* a 1947 ballet score for conventional orchestra; *Aria with Fontana Mix* for vocalist and tape; *Fontana Mix* for tape; Concerto for Prepared Piano and Chamber Orchestra (a 1951 work not to be confused with the later *Concert); Cartridge Music* for tape; *Solo for Voice 2* (including a version for chorus); *Solo for Voice 45; Variations II–IV* (tape-collage performance environments); and *Song Books I, II with Empty Words III* for vocal ensemble, speaker, and electronics.

[2193] BARLOW, Wayne Brewster
ORGANIST, TEACHER
BORN: Elyria, Ohio, September 6, 1912

Barlow offers a sterling example of American musico-academic inbreeding. Following youthful lessons in piano and violin, he took to composing, his efforts culminating in a concerted piece performed at his high school graduation. He then took three degrees at the Eastman School of Music in 1934, 1935, and 1937, where his most important teachers were Howard Hanson [1927] and Bernard Rogers [1875]. Concurrently he was organist at the Eastman Baptist Church in Rochester. After receiving his M.A., he studied briefly at USC in the summer of 1935, with

Schoenberg [1657]. On getting his doctorate, he married Helen Hurzen and joined the Eastman faculty, where he lived happily ever after. In 1945 he became organist and choir director at St. Thomas Episcopal Church, moving to Christ Episcopal Church in 1976. In 1955 he spent a year in Denmark as Fulbright lecturer at the universities of Copenhagen and Aarhus. After years of producing (usually to commissions) much music in the conservative mould approved by Eastman, he took up the study of electronic music making at the University of Toronto in 1963 and later in Europe. From 1968 he served as director of his school's electronic music studio and chairman of the department of composition and retired in 1978 from the deanship of the graduate school. He has written a book, *Foundations of Music,* and compositions for orchestra, chorus, and instruments. RECORDINGS: His *Night Song* for orchestra and the rhapsody *The Winter's Passed* for oboe and strings have been recorded.

[2194] WEISGALL, Hugo David
CONDUCTOR, TEACHER, DIPLOMAT
BORN: Eibenschütz (now Ivančice), October 13, 1912

Hugo Weisgall's father, Adolph Joseph Weisgal, was an operetta singer who reverted to family tradition and became the cantor of a synagogue in a town near Brünn (Brno). In 1920 he brought his family to the United States and settled in Baltimore. Hugo came early to music and a love for the stage. He finished high school in 1929 and graduated from the Peabody Institute of Music in 1932. From 1933 he studied off and on with Roger Sessions [1931] until 1941. From 1936 to 1939 he was a pupil of Rosario Scalero's (1870–1954) and Fritz Reiner's at the Curtis Institute in Philadelphia, and in 1941 he obtained —after twelve years of sporadic study their —a Ph.D. in German literature from Johns Hopkins University (no B.A. or M.A.). During most of the years of his higher education he served as choir director at Har Sinai Temple in Baltimore. After some false starts at composition (which he suppressed), his music—notably two ballet scores for the Baltimore Ballet—began to meet with some success in the late 1930s.

In 1942 he joined the U.S. Army and married Nathalie Schulman, a physiologist and amateur musician. For two years he was attached to the Allied Governments in Exile in London, where he conducted the BBC Orchestra in his *American Comedy Overture.* After the war he served as cultural attaché to the American Embassy in Prague, where he wrote a third ballet for the National Theater (which did not use it). He also did a good deal of guest-conducting and was offered orchestral posts but came home in 1948. Over the next several years he taught successively at the Cummington School of the Arts, the Baltimore Institute of Musical Arts, Johns Hopkins University, the Jewish Theological Seminary in New York, the Juilliard School, and Queens College of the City University of New York, where he was named Distinguished University Professor in 1980, serving in that capacity until his retirement several years later.

In the early 1950s Weisgall cast his compositional lot with vocal music and notably with opera. His first mature operatic work, *The Tenor* (on a play by Frank Wedekind), was produced in Baltimore in 1952. It was followed that same year by a setting of a Strindberg monodrama, *The Stronger*, premiered by Weisgall's own Hilltop Opera Company in the same city. A commission from Columbia University's Alice M. Ditson fund produced a more ambitious effort, a treatment of Pirandello's *6 Characters in Search of an Author*. It had three performances at the New York City Opera over two seasons, 1958–60, with a cast that featured Beverly Sills typecast as "The Coloratura," but the review that labeled it "Six Characters in Need of a Composer" seems to have reflected popular reaction. It was in turn succeeded by a treatment of W. B. Yeats's *Purgatory*, presented at the Library of Congress in 1961—Weisgall's first twelvetone work. In *Athaliah*, given a concert performance in 1964, the composer backed off from that approach. His next effort—one by which he set great store—was a World War II allegory, *Nine Rivers from Jordan*. Premiered by the New York City Opera and supported by the Ford Foundation, it was rejected so forcibly in 1968 that Weisgall abandoned the form until 1976, when his *Jenny, or The Hundred Nights* (Juilliard Opera Theater) was more gently received. Weisgall has attracted much attention as an opera composer—largely, one suspects, for his sound dramatic instincts—but the public has not yet accepted his acerbic musical idiom, if it ever will.

RECORDINGS: There are recordings of two operas, *The Tenor* and *The Stronger*, and several song cycles—*4 Poems by Adelaide Crapsey; The Golden Peacock; Fancies and Inventions; Translations; The End of Summer;* and *7 Popular Songs from the Yiddish.*

[2195] NANCARROW, Conlon
TRUMPETER
BORN: Texarkana, Ark., October 27, 1912

A composer who has made unique use of technology, Nancarrow was enrolled in his late teens at the Cincinnati Conservatory. Afterward he worked as a jazz musician and studied privately in Boston with Nicolas Slonimsky [1893], Walter Piston [1890], and Roger Sessions [1931]. He migrated to Europe in 1936 and the following year fought in the Spanish Civil War in the American Abraham Lincoln Brigade on the Loyalist side. When he came home, his passport was confiscated. He moved to Mexico City in 1940 and, except for a 1947 trip to New York in connection with the construction of a device to facilitate his composition, has lived there ever since, taking Mexican nationality in 1956. Though initially he wrote a few pieces of "regular" music, he has composed for many years by cutting mathematically calculated apertures in blank rolls for his Ampico player-pianos. This process allows for prodigies of technique impossible for human fingers. Some of these studies have since been notated by normal means for study, and Merce Cunningham has choreographed several. Composer György Ligeti [2329] has recently become an enthusiastic supporter of Nancarrow and has helped him gain belated recognition in several European music centers. RECORDINGS: A project to record the entire *oeuvre* to date on Nancarrow's instruments has approached completion at this writing.

[2196] JONES, Daniel Jenkyn
EDITOR
BORN: Pembroke, December 7, 1912

Born in southwesternmost Wales, the son of musicians, Jones grew up in the seaport of Swansea. He was composing and writing poetry when scarcely out of rompers, and he learned piano and other instruments. His closest friend was the future poet Dylan Thomas, who used him as a character in a short story, "The Fight." They collaborated on poems, writing alternate lines, as "Walter Bram"—the last name having a scatological application in Welsh—and on such exercises as peering at the Jones maid's bath through the bathroom keyhole. Jones also set a large number of Thomas's early poems to music. He went on to major in English at the University of Wales and wrote a master's thesis on the relation of music to poetry in the Elizabethan age. In between his B.A. and M.A., he studied at the Royal Academy of

Music in London, taking lessons in composition from Harry Farjeon (1878–1948), brother of the poet Eleanor Farjeon, and in conducting from Sir Henry Wood. Jones won the Mendelssohn Scholarship in 1936 and, Leipzig no longer being an essential for such winners, spent a year in Rome, Vienna, and other musical centers in Europe. He was already making a name for himself as a composer when war intervened. From 1940 to 1946 he served in Intelligence for the British army as an officer. After his release he settled in Swansea. In 1951 he received his doctorate from the University of Wales. He has devoted himself mostly to composing, though he occasionally appears as a conductor of his own works. After some deliberate experimentation with Classical forms and oriental influences and a fling at a rather rhetorical neo-romanticism, he developed a style of his own which involves complex meters and sometimes a succession of modes on a systematic basis. Since the war he has written 2 operas, several large choral works, 9 symphonies (the fourth of which he dedicated to Thomas's memory in 1954), a violin concerto, at least 8 string quartets, 5 string trios, and much else. Jones numbers his symphonies in the usual manner, but his string quartets (the genre on which he has concentrated recently) are identified by the year of composition. He was awarded an honorary doctorate in literature by the University of Wales in 1970 and the following year published his important edition of Thomas's poems. RECORDINGS: The cantata The Country Beyond the Stars; Symphonies Nos. 4, 6, 7, 8, and 9; the brief orchestral Dance Fantasy; and String Quartets 1975, 1978, and 1980.

[2197] GLANVILLE-HICKS, Peggy
CRITIC, CONDUCTOR
BORN: Melbourne, December 29, 1912

After a time in Australia at the Melbourne Conservatory studying composition with the director, English conductor-composer Fritz Hart (1874–1949), Peggy Glanville-Hicks came, at nineteen, to London, to enroll at the Royal College of Music. Her teachers there included Ralph Vaughan Williams [1633], Arthur Benjamin [1887], Constant Lambert [2074], Gordon Jacob [1911], and conductor Sir Malcolm Sargent. In 1935 a monetary award enabled her to study in Vienna with Egon Wellesz [1799] and in Paris with Nadia Boulanger. In 1938 she married another product of the Boulangerie, English composer Stanley Bate (1911–59); in the early war years they had a London ballet com-

pany, for which she served as assistant conductor. Shortly, however, they went to Australia and then settled in New York City in 1942. By then the marriage was in trouble and in 1945 Bate went to Brazil, where he remarried after the divorce was effected. Left on her own, Peggy involved herself in matters musical and survived by copying music, lecturing, and writing on music. Virgil Thomson [1928], whose colleague she became at the New York Herald-Tribune in 1948, says she ate little and made her own clothes. She worked tirelessly to get the music of her contemporaries heard, she wrote scores for UNESCO films, she went to India on a musical mission for the Rockefeller Foundation. She composed, mostly chamber music and vocal works; in 1949 she set some of Thomson's reviews as Thomsoniana. (She became an American citizen in 1948.)

Gradually her interest in the oriental and the antique brought a coolly exotic note into her music. Her several operas come from this period. The Transposed Heads (after Thomas Mann) was the first such work commissioned by the Louisville Orchestra. A 1956 Guggenheim Fellowship took her to Greece, with which she fell in love. She settled in Athens in 1959 and the Athens Opera premiered her Nausicaa (after Robert Graves) in 1960, with the young Teresa Stratas in the title role. Sappho, completed in 1963 after Laurence Durrell, was commissioned for the San Francisco Opera but was not produced. Two ballets followed. In 1969 Glanville-Hicks returned to New York for a brain-tumor operation, which left her blind for a time and unable to undertake further composition. She returned to Australia in 1976 to work at the Music Center in Sydney.

RECORDINGS: Works on records include two operas, The Transposed Heads and Nausicaa (the latter abridged); (orchestral works) 3 Gymnopédies, Sinfonia Pacifica, Etruscan Concerto for piano and orchestra, Concerto Romantico for viola and orchestra; (chamber pieces) Sonata for Piano and Percussion, Concertino da Camera (for piano, flute, clarinet, and bassoon), Sonata for Harp; and Letters from Morocco for tenor and chamber orchestra, to texts by Paul Bowles [2165].

[2198] DELLO JOIO, Norman (Del'-lō Joi'-o, Nôr'-man)
ORGANIST, PIANIST, TEACHER
BORN: New York, January 24, 1913

In the years immediately following World War II, Norman Dello Joio often looked like the coming American composer—a new

Samuel Barber [2149], perhaps—but a falling off in productivity and the attacks of the avant-garde on his middle-of-the-road approach (Stravinsky [1748] liked to refer to him as "Norman Jello Doio") have somewhat obscured his reputation. He was the son of Casimir dello Ioio, an Italian-born New York organist, and the godson of Pietro Yon (1886–1943), who was his teacher. From the age of fourteen Dello Joio played in various New York churches and from sixteen in jazz bands. After a year or so at City College, he won a scholarship to the Juilliard School, where he studied with Belgian organist Gaston Déthier and with composer Bernhard Wagenaar (1894–1971). In 1941, the year he finished his studies, his *Sinfonietta* was broadcast by the NBC Symphony, he became music director for a ballet company called the Dance Players (out of New Hope, Pennsylvania), and he began his studies with Paul Hindemith [1914], first at Tanglewood and then at Yale. The association showed in his orchestral *Magnificat*, which won the New York Town Hall Prize the following year—in the course of which he married a ballerina, Grace Baumgold. Following two successive Guggenheim Fellowships, Dello Joio succeeded William Schuman [2158] in 1945 at Sarah Lawrence College.

For the next several years, every Dello Joio premiere was an occasion. His *Variations, Chaconne, and Finale* took the New York Music Critics' Circle Award in 1947. He produced his first opera, *The Triumph of St. Joan*, at Sarah Lawrence in 1950; dissatisfied with it, he turned much of the music into an orchestral symphony similarly named, which was also choreographed and danced by Martha Graham. St. Joan turned up again in another opera, *The Trial at Rouen*, written for television and produced by NBC in 1956. A revised version, confusingly called *The Triumph of St. Joan*, was presented by the New York City Opera in 1959 to a house less than one-third full, but it won its composer another Critics' Circle award. Meanwhile in 1957 *Meditations on Ecclesiastes* for string orchestra (originally a dance score for José Limón) had won that year's Pulitzer Prize.

Dello Joio left Sarah Lawrence in 1950 and in 1956 joined the faculty of the Mannes College of Music, where he taught for sixteen years. A couple of years later he also took on the running of the Ford Foundation's Contemporary Music Project for Creativity in Musical Education which placed composers-in-residence in high schools—his own idea. He won an Emmy Award in 1965 for an NBC television score, *The Louvre*. In 1972 he became dean of the Fine Arts School

at Boston University. Divorced in 1973 from his first wife, he married Barbara Bolton a year later. His major works since 1960 have included the opera *Blood Moon*, the ballet *Heloise and Abelard*, three large Masses, and a number of orchestral works. His son Justin (1954–) is also a composer.

RECORDINGS: Orchestral works recorded include the Concerto for Harp; *Serenade; Variations, Chaconne, and Finale; New York Profiles; The Triumph of St. Joan Symphony; Epigraph; Meditations on Ecclesiastes* and *Air*, both for string orchestra; *Fantasy and Variations* for piano and orchestra; *Homage to Haydn;* and *Air Power*, an orchestral suite derived from music for a television documentary series. Choral recordings include *To St. Cecilia* (set to Dryden's ode); *Mass in Honor of the Eucharist; The Poet's Song; Of Crows and Cluster; Come to Me, My Love;* and the choral-orchestral *Psalm of David*. Recorded chamber pieces include the *Variations and Capriccio* for violin and piano; *Duo concertante* for cello and piano; Sonata for Trumpet and Piano; *The Developing Flutist* for flute and piano; and a few songs. Sonata No. 3, 2 *Nocturnes*, and a *Suite* (all for solo piano); and *Aria and Toccata* for two pianos are also on records. Finally there is an extensive selection of Dello Joio's works for band —*Colonial Ballads, Satiric Dances, Fantasies on a Theme by Haydn, From Every Horizon,* and *Concertante*.

[2199] LUTOSŁAWSKI, Witold (Lōō-tō-slwáf'-skē, Vē'-tōld)
PIANIST, CONDUCTOR, TEACHER
BORN: Warsaw, January 25, 1913

An innovative eclectic who has drawn from most of the important musical impulses of his century, Lutosławski, like his friend Panufnik [2226], is one of the most widely admired Polish composers of his generation. He came from a family of means and education (his mother was a physician). He began piano lessons at eleven, and violin lessons at thirteen. At fifteen he entered the Warsaw Conservatory, graduating nine years later, having also studied some mathematics at the university in passing. The Nazi invasion in 1939 canceled his plans for further study abroad. He survived by working with Panufnik in a two-piano team in cabarets, playing their own arrangements of the classics. (It was this association that also produced the *Paganini Variations* for two pianos in 1941.) Lutosławski managed to flee the 1944 destruction of the city. After the war, he returned, married, and settled down to compose. During this period he, influenced by Bartók [1734], used Polish folk music as the takeoff point for his own. His first symphony was broadcast from Warsaw in 1948. With *Funeral Music* (dedicated to Bartók) ten years later, he first experimented with the twelve-tone approach and also with patterns of dramatic intensities or "sonic form." Attending the Darmstadt Festival in 1961, he was tremendously impressed with John Cage's [2192] aleatory music and thereafter included such techniques in his own music. A year later, with some misgivings, he came to Tanglewood to try his hand at teaching. He has since taught in England, Germany, Scandinavia, and the United States (at Dartmouth and Texas State University). In later works he has included microtones. His output—orchestral (including 3 symphonies), choral, chamber, instrumental, and solo vocal—is small, running to not much more than fifty works. Recent works include the Symphony No. 3 and the Concerto for Oboe, Harp, and Chamber Orchestra, written for oboist Heinz Holliger and harpist Ursula Holliger. In these pieces Lutosławski has remained true to his earlier style and has avoided the neo-tonal approach recently adopted by such Polish colleagues as Penderecki [2407] and Henryk Gorecki (1933–   ). RECORDINGS: Early, neoclassical works on records include the orchestral *Symphonic Variations;* Symphony No. 1; 2 *Children's Songs* for voice and piano; *Overture* for strings; *Little Suite* for orchestra; *Chain of Straw* for soprano, mezzo-soprano, flute, oboe, two clarinets, and bassoon; the Concerto for Orchestra (his most popular work), the *Dance Preludes* for clarinet and chamber orchestra, and the *Paganini Variations* for two pianos. Transitional works recorded include *Funeral Music* (also known as *Trauermusik)* for strings and *5 Songs to Poems of Kazimiera Iłłakowicz* for soprano and orchestra (also recorded in a version for piano), which looks ahead to the objectivity of serialism and back to the ecstatic mysticism of Szymanowski [1755]. Later works recorded include the brief *Postludium* for orchestra; *Epitaph* for oboe and piano; *Venetian Games;* String Quartet; Concerto for Cello; *Mi-parti* for orchestra; Symphony No. 2; *Preludes and Fugues* for strings; *Livre* for orchestra; *3 Poems of Henri Michaux* for chorus and chamber orchestra (two conductors); *Paroles tissées* for tenor and chamber orchestra; and the Concerto for Oboe, Harp, and Chamber Orchestra.

[2200] ADOLPHUS, Milton
CIVIL SERVANT, ADMINISTRATOR
BORN: New York, January 27, 1913

Though he grew up in New York, Adolphus got his compositional training from Rosario Scalero (1870–1954) at the Curtis Institute after he had moved to Philadelphia in 1935. After a short time as director of the Philadelphia Musical Center, he became an official in the state labor department in Harrisburg in 1938 and has remained essentially a weekend composer of accessible and often amusing pieces. His double life has not apparently hampered his productivity: at last count his catalogue showed 13 symphonies and almost twice as many string quartets as Beethoven [1063] wrote. RECORDINGS: Only his *Elegy* for orchestra seems to have been recorded.

[2201] ETLER, Alvin Derald
OBOIST, TEACHER
BORN: Battle Creek, Iowa, February 13, 1913
DIED: Northampton, Mass., June 13, 1973

Born near Sioux City (one source incorrectly gives Battle Creek, Michigan), Alvin Etler devoted his salad years to learning most of the orchestral instruments before adopting the oboe as his own. He was writing, by the time he got out of high school, music of such precocity that a suite for winds was performed in New York by the Georges Barrère Wind Quartet in 1930. That year he entered the University of Illinois but moved to Cleveland in 1932 to study at the Institute of Music and with Arthur Shepherd [1728] at Western Reserve University. From 1938 to 1940 he played oboe under Fabian Sevitzky in the Indianapolis Symphony. In the latter year he received the first of two Guggenheim fellowships and wrote two sinfoniettas premiered in 1941 by Fritz Reiner and the Pittsburgh Symphony. After a tour of Latin America with the North American Woodwind Quartet, he spent four years at Yale studying with Paul Hindemith [1914], teaching winds, and conducting the band. Between 1946 and 1949 he taught at Cornell University and the University of Illinois, then found a permanent post at Smith College, where he eventually held (in succession) two endowed chairs. (He succeeded Werner Josten [1796] at Smith.) His second Guggenheim came in 1963. He was also in charge of the electronic studio at nearby Hampshire College. One source gives the place of his death—thirteen was not his lucky number—as Florence, Massachusetts, which, a suburb of Northampton, appears to be correct. Etler disowned most of his pre-Hindemith work. What remains is chiefly instrumental, moving from a dissonant "American" idiom toward atonality with considerable use of contrapuntal devices. RECORDINGS: A portion of his output has been recorded. Orchestral works include the Concerto for Woodwind Quintet and Orchestra; *Triptych;* Concerto for Clarinet with Chamber Ensemble; Concerto for Brass Quintet. Strings. and Percussion. Instrumental works recorded include the Brass Quintet, *Sonic Sequence* for brass quintet, the Clarinet Sonata, and the Bassoon Sonata.

[2202] RUDZIŃSKI, Witold (Rōōd-zěnch'-skē, Vē'-tōld)
TEACHER, WRITER
BORN: Siebież, March 14, 1913

Born in what was then Lithuania, Rudziński studied at the conservatory of what was then Vilna with the pianist Stanisław Szpinalski and the composer Tadeusz Szeligowski [1925]. He graduated in 1936 and two years later went to Paris to study with Nadia Boulanger and later Charles Koechlin [1592]. He returned to Vilna at the beginning of World War II and taught there until 1942. After the war he taught for two years in Łódź and then settled in Warsaw. His most ambitious works, including his 5 operas, were written after that time, as were his studies of Moniuszko [1263] and Bartók [1734]. In 1957 he took on a professorship in the Graduate School of Music in Warsaw. He has written prolifically in all fields. RECORDINGS: His opera *The Dismissal of the Greek Envoys* and selections from other operas have been recorded.

[2203] BARATI, George
CELLIST, CONDUCTOR
BORN: Györ, April 3, 1913

A graduate of the Budapest Conservatory, Barati became first cellist in the local opera orchestra at twenty-three. Three years later, however, he emigrated to the United States and studied with Sessions [1931] at Princeton until he had to join the war effort as a military band leader. On leaving the service he became a member of the San Francisco Symphony. From 1950 to 1968 he was conductor of the Honolulu Symphony and then returned to the mainland as director of the Santa Cruz Symphony in California. He has written 2 operas, a symphony, string quartets, etc. Some of his pieces—e.g., *Festival Hula, South Seas Suite*—reflect the Hawaiian ethos. RECORDINGS: Several compositions are on discs—the *Chamber Concerto;*

String Quartet No. 1; Quartet for Harpsichord and Strings and *Triple Exposure* for solo cello. As a conductor Barati has recorded with several orchestras, directing his Concerto for Cello and works by both standard and contemporary composers.

[2204] KENNAN, Kent Wheeler
TEACHER
BORN: Milwaukee, Wisc., April 18, 1913

Subsequent to piano lessons in Milwaukee, Kent Kennan matriculated at the University of Michigan, where, after toying with becoming an architect and a writer, he took a course, in his sophomore year, in composition under Hunter Johnson (1906–   ), which turned him toward a career in music. He then transferred to the Eastman School of Music and studied with the almost inevitable Bernard Rogers [1875] and Howard Hanson [1927], taking a bachelor's degree in 1934 and a master's in 1936. In the latter year he won the American Prix de Rome, spending the prescribed three years in that city, where he studied for a time with Ildebrando Pizzetti [1732]. The air must have agreed with him for during that period he produced almost all of his attractive orchestral works and many of his smaller-scale pieces. On his return in 1939 he taught for a year at Kent State, another at the University of Texas, then enlisted in the army and served until 1945 as a bandsman and bandmaster. His *The Unknown Warrior Speaks* for male choir was premiered for Eleanor Roosevelt at the White House in 1944. On being released from service, Kennan returned to Texas for a year, taught for two at Ohio State, and then went back to Texas for good. (Under circumstances too complex to detail here, he graded one of the present writer's counterpoint exercises in 1949.) Kennan has written only a few instrumental pieces since. He has also published several manuals on orchestration and counterpoint. RECORDINGS: Several orchestral works have been recorded—*Night Soliloquy* for flute and strings; *3 Pieces* for orchestra; and *Andante.* Also recorded are the Concertino for Piano and Winds (a 1963 revision of a 1946 work) and the Sonata for Trumpet and Piano.

[2205] DÁVID, Gyula (Dá'-vēd, Dyoo'-lo)
VIOLIST, CONDUCTOR, TEACHER
BORN: Budapest, May 6, 1913
DIED: Budapest, March 14, 1977

Graduating from the Budapest Academy, where he was a pupil of Kodály [1760] in

1938, Dávid became a violist in the Budapest Municipal Symphony until the war shut it down. After hostilities ended, he conducted at the opera until 1950 and has spent most of the time since teaching at the Budapest Academy. His music was at first folk-oriented (he was a folksong collector) but later took the twelve-tone road. He wrote in most categories except religious music and opera. RECORDINGS: The Hungarian state recording agency has issued recordings of the *Dramatic Overture*, Symphony No. 4, Concerto for Violin, Concerto for Viola, Concerto for Horn, *Sinfonietta*, String Quartet No. 1, Sonata for Violin and Piano, and the Sonata for Flute and Piano.

[2206] DUMITRESCU, Ion (Doo-me-tres'-koo, E'-on)
TEACHER, CONDUCTOR
BORN: Oteşani, May 20, 1913 *(Baker's says June 2)*

Ion Dumitrescu is eighteen months older than his composer-brother Gheorghe. Both attended the Bucharest Conservatory from 1934 to 1941. Both studied composition with Dimitri Cuclin, a pupil of d'Indy [1462], both studied conducting with Jonel Perlea. Both conducted at the Bucharest Opera in the war years. More recently both have been professors at the conservatory. Gheorghe wrote several operas and a good deal of choral music; Ion wrote orchestral works and film scores; both wrote symphonies. RECORDINGS: The Rumanian Electrecord firm has recorded Ion's Dumitrescu's Concerto in C Major for string orchestra, Symphony No. 1 and a suite from *The Retezat Mountains* (film score).

[2207] EDMUNDS, John
LIBRARIAN, TEACHER, EDITOR
BORN: San Francisco, June 10, 1913

John Edmunds had his academic education at the University of California in Berkeley, then studied composition with Rosario Scalero (1870–1954) at the Curtis Institute in Philadelphia. In 1941 he took a master's degree with Walter Piston [1890] at Harvard. Others of his teachers have been Roy Harris [1947] at Cornell, Otto Luening [1980] at Columbia, and old-music specialists Arnold Goldsbrough and Thurston Dart in London. Edmunds has taught at Syracuse University and the University of California. After a time in the San Francisco Public Library, he was placed in charge of the American Collection at the music wing of the New York Public Library and was director of the American Music Center, both from 1957 to 1961. He has been the recipient of many grants and fellowships, has edited several collections of folksongs and early songs, and has written or coauthored books and articles. In recent years he has written some stage music (chiefly balletic) and a good deal of choral music, but his reputation rests chiefly on his many superb songs. RECORDINGS: There are all too few recordings of Edmund's songs.

[2208] KHRENNIKOV, Tikhon Nikolaievich (Kren'-ē-kôf, Tē-khōn Nē-kō-lä-yä'-vich)
APARACHNIK
BORN: Yelets, June 10, 1913

Though he gave early evidence of unusual musical ability, Khrennikov's greatest talent has proved to be for survival. Born some 225 miles south of Moscow, he studied at the Gnesin School in that city for 1929 to 1932. He then moved to the Moscow Conservatory, where he was Vissarion Shebalin's [2017] composition pupil. Before his graduation, *magna cum laude* (or the Russian equivalent) in 1936, he attracted much attention with his first piano concerto (of 2) and his first symphony (of 3). He was then house composer for the Vakhtangov Theater and wrote a number of incidental scores for it. (He has also composed for films.) After Stalin had hurled his thunderbolts at Shostakovich's [2094] *Lady Macbeth of Mtzensk*, Khrennikov tried his hand at opera. The result appeared in 1939. Originally called *The Brothers* but officially known as *Into the Storm*, it was not only full of the Stalin-prescribed hummable tunes but was also the first Soviet opera to include Lenin in the *dramatis personae*. It was a great success and was pronounced the model for Soviet opera. During World War II Khrennikov was official musical advisor to the Red Army and completed his second symphony. In 1948 when Comrade Zhdanov administered his critical browbeating to the leading Russian composers, Khrennikov went him one better: he issued a manifesto condemning not only his fellows, but most of the important composers in the West, including the expatriate Stravinsky [1748] and such innocuous figures as Benjamin Britten [2215] and Gian Carlo Menotti [2177]. As a result of his stance, Khrennikov was named head of the Composers Union, which, with an iron hand, he forged into a powerful political entity. (He has been repeatedly reelected, and the members are said to feel him indispensable.) In 1950 Khrennikov unveiled his second opera, a comedy called *Frol Skobeyev.* After the death of Stalin and the onset of the Khrushchev "cultural thaw," Khrennikov became, relatively speaking, a liberal. In 1957 he had another operatic success with *Mother.* Two years later he—with Shostakovich, Kabalevsky [2058], and others—made an official visit to the United States, in the course of which he personally tendered to Stravinsky an invitation to visit his homeland and be his guest. (Stravinsky accepted and went in 1962.) Since visiting the United States Khrennikov has written 2 violin concerti, 2 cello concerti, Symphony No. 3, Concerto No. 2 for Piano, ballets, an operetta, and a children's opera, among other works. He won the Lenin Prize in 1967 and again in 1974. RECORDINGS: Soviet Melodiya has recorded Symphonies Nos. 1–3; Concerti for Violin Nos. 1 and 2; Concerti for Cello Nos. 1 and 2; a suite from *Much Ado About Nothing;* the three-act ballet of 1979, *Hussar Ballad;* songs; choruses; and excerpts from stage and film scores.

[2209] GELBRUN, Artur (Gel'-broͦn,
      Är'-toͦor)
VIOLINIST, TEACHER
BORN: Warsaw, July 11, 1913

A product of the Warsaw Conservatory, Gelbrun proceeded to Rome where he studied at the Santa Cecilia Academy with Alfredo Casella [1767] and then to Zürich for further work with Willy Burkhard [1976]. He also studied conducting *en passant* with Bernardino Molinari and Hermann Scherchen. The European unpleasantness of the late 1930s and 1940s found him in Switzerland, where he made a living playing violin in orchestras. In 1949 he settled in Tel Aviv, where he became professor of composition and conducting at the Academy of Music. He has written an oratorio, several ballets, 3 symphonies, concerti, choral works, and a good deal of chamber music. RECORDINGS: His vocal-orchestral *Lament for the Victims of the Warsaw Ghetto* and *Songs of the Jordan River* and *Esquisses* for flute and harp have been recorded.

[2210] COOLIDGE, Peggy Stuart
PIANIST, CONDUCTOR, THERAPIST
BORN: Swampscott, Mass., July 19, 1913
DIED: New York, May 31, 1981

Born Peggy Stuart, Mrs. Coolidge began piano lessons at five, composing at nine. There was advanced piano study with Leschetizky

pupil Heinrich Gebhard. She also took lessons from Raymond Robinson and Quincy Porter [1932] in Boston but had her sights on performing rather than composing. At twenty-four she wrote an ice ballet, *Cracked Ice,* which was scored by Ferde Grofé [1862] and performed at an ice extravaganza in Madison Square Garden. After studying orchestration, she turned out several other orchestral scores on her own. In the World War II years, Miss Stuart was assistant conductor of the Women's Symphony Orchestra in Boston and busied herself with housing and playing for American servicemen. Afterward she moved to New York and worked as a musical therapist in a mental hospital. In 1952 she married her agent, Joseph R. Coolidge, an old friend from Boston. Later in the decade she broke into writing music for both Hollywood and Broadway. In 1963 the Coolidges visited Austria and Hungary and established ties that led to her especial success in the Eastern bloc, a friendship with the Khachaturians [2038], and the only one-composer concert so far presented in Moscow by an American. Her undemanding music seems to have won more acclaim abroad than at home. RECORDINGS: Works on records include *Rhapsody* for harp and orchestra, 1965; *New England Autumn,* 1971; *Pioneer Dances,* 1970; and *Spirituals in Sunshine and in Shadow,* 1969.

[2211] MOROSS, Jerome
ARRANGER, PIANIST
BORN: Brooklyn, N.Y., August 1, 1913
DIED: Miami, July 25, 1983

Jerome Moross has successfully skated the thin ice between the popular and the "classical," the commercial and the artistic, though historians of music seem unsure of what to do with him and so often omit him. Musically precocious, he was performing and composing ultramodern music before he was out of high school. He then entered New York University in 1929, formed a close friendship there with fellow students Bernard Herrmann [2175] and Arthur Berger [2185] and graduated in 1932 with a B.A. in music education. Meanwhile in 1931 he had received a scholarship to the Juilliard School, where concurrently he studied with Bernard Wagenaar (1894–1971). During this period he attracted considerable attention with his orchestral works *Paeans* (published by Henry Cowell [1934] in his New Music Editions) and *These Everlasting Blues,* his first mature work to cross the pop boundary. Supporting himself as a pianist, he wrote the first of his ballets, *Paul Bunyan,* for Charles Weidman in 1934. The next year he was the chief collaborator on a leftish musical *Parade*—Blitzstein [2065] contributed some numbers—that flopped. In 1938 he wrote *Frankie and Johnny,* the first of a series of ballets-with-song which became a great favorite. The next year he married an actress, Hazel Abrams, and moved to California, where for a decade he arranged and orchestrated film music. His symphony was premiered in Seattle by Sir Thomas Beecham in 1943. An association with lyricist John Latouche covering most of the decade resulted in *Ballet Ballads,* an evening of four song-ballets produced by the Experimental Theater in New York, in 1948. It was so successful that it was moved to Broadway, where it expired after a month. Two Guggenheim Fellowships enabled Moross to write his first opera (not advertised as such), *The Golden Apple,* a treatment of the ancient Troy saga in American rural terms. Produced Off-Broadway in 1952, it won critical hosannas, was moved to Broadway, and suffered much the same fate as its predecessor. Meanwhile Moross had begun writing his own film scores, which included Danny Kaye's *Hans Christian Anderson* and the western *The Big Country.* A second opera *Gentlemen Be Seated* (the Civil War as a minstrel show), was produced by the New York City Opera in its 1963 American season. A third—*Sorry, Wrong Number,* based on a popular radio monodrama—was completed in 1977. In recent years Moross wrote a number of orchestral and chamber works. RECORDINGS: In addition to the soundtrack for *The Big Country,* other works recorded include the stage works *The Golden Apple* and *Frankie and Johnny;* and chamber pieces Concerto for Flute with String Quartet, Sonata for Piano Duet and String Quartet, Sonatina for Clarinet Choir, Sonatina for Bass and Piano, and Sonatina for Brass Quintet.

[2212] BOGATIREV, Anatoli Vasilievich
(Bō-gȧ-tēr′-yof, Ȧ-nȧ-tō′-lē Vȧ-zēl-yā′-vich)
ETHNOMUSICOLOGIST, TEACHER
BORN: Vitebsk, August 13, 1913

The son of a language teacher in a White Russian city, Bogatirev had his meaningful musical education in Minsk, where his composition teacher at the Minsk Conservatory was Vasily Zolotarev (1872–1964), who had studied with Balakirev [1348] and Rimsky-Korsakov [1416]. In the next several years he became an authority on White Russian

folksongs and wrote music—mainly patriotic choral works—based on them. After the war he taught at the White Russian Conservatory in Minsk. His most successful work has been the 1939 folk opera *In the Forest of Polyesye.* He is not to be confused with theorist-musicologist Semyon Semyonovich Bogatirev (1890–1960), known for his completion of Tchaikovsky's [1377] seventh symphony. RECORDINGS: Excerpts of *In the Forest of Polyesye* have been recorded.

[2213] BRANT, Henry Dreyfus
TEACHER
BORN: Montreal, September 15, 1913

Little old ladies tend to cringe at Henry Brant's music as representative of some far-out school devised to torture them; actually it belongs to no school—Brant being a Great American Maverick—and much of it is intended to make them laugh. Though Canadian-born, Brant belongs to the United States by parentage, his father being an American violinist employed in Canada (and later a teacher at McGill University). Young Brant showed his inventive spirit even in childhood and once produced a concert in his back yard consisting of a composition for instruments he had made himself. When he was seventeen, the family moved back to New York, and he spent some time at the Juilliard School studying with Rubin Goldmark (1872–1936), Leopold Mannes (the coinventor of Kodachrome film), and pianist James Friskin. He also studied with Antheil [1981], Copland [1986], and Riegger [1793]. By the time he had left the Juilliard School in the middle 1930s, he had written a symphony, a contrabass concerto, and (more characteristically) a concerto called *Angels and Devils* for flute and an "orchestra" of flutes. Whether his 1938 orchestral *Whoopee in D* celebrated his independence or his marriage to Maxine Picard is not clear.

In the thirties and early forties, Brant made a name for himself as a fine *Gebrauchsmusikant,* arranging, scoring, and composing for radio shows, "big bands" (e.g., Benny Goodman's), and documentary films. Eventually he was hired in 1945 by Columbia University to disseminate these practical skills and was soon teaching concurrently at the Juilliard. His marriage having come unstuck, he was wed to Patricia Gorman in 1948; they have three children. Brant did yeoman service for the music of his time and was instrumental in presenting such radicals as Partch [1998] and Ruggles [1684]. He left his posts in 1955 to enjoy the fruits of grants from the Guggenheim Foundation and the

National Institute of Arts and Letters, and then settled in to teach at Bennington College in Vermont, which has been his headquarters ever since.

On the whole it is useless to try to describe Brant's music without sounding silly. It is endlessly inventive, especially as regards sound sources. One notes a symphony for multiple percussion ensembles, pieces involving kitchen utensils, toys from Woolworth's, massed music boxes, lights played from a pushbutton keyboard, fireworks, and choral works in invented pseudolanguages. One of Brant's fortes is "spatial" or "dimensional" music, in which the placement of various instruments and ensembles is essential to the effect (and thus virtually immune to recording). Such pieces often have a quasi-aleatory element in that each unit goes its own way with only general reference to the others.

RECORDINGS: Works recorded include *Kingdom Come* (for two orchestras and organ); *Machinations* (for percussion, organ, harp, flute, ceramic flute, ocarina, and flageolet); *Hieroglyphics III* (for viola, alto voice, organ, piano, vibraphone, harpsichord, and percussion); *Signs and Alarms* (percussion); *Solar Moth* for fourteen instruments and voice; *Galaxy II* (winds and percussion); *On the Nature of Things* (orchestra); *Angels and Devils* (with three versions, his most recorded work); *Orbits* for sopranino voice, organ, and eighty trombones (!); *Fire Under Water* (chamber ensemble); *Crossing the Bridge Before You Come to It* (chamber ensemble); *An American Requiem* (soprano and wind orchestra); *Millenium II* (brass and percussion); *Millenium IV* (voice and five instruments); *Hieroglyphics I* for violin; Concerto for Trumpet and 9 Instruments; *Crossroads* (four violins); *Verticals Ascending* (winds); and Symphony No. 1 (an early and uncharacteristically conservative work).

[2214] FINE, Vivian
PIANIST, TEACHER
BORN: Chicago, September 28, 1913

Unrelated to her almost exact contemporary Irving Fine [2228], though she appears as pianist in a recent recording of his violin sonata, Vivian Fine became, at normal kindergarten age, a piano pupil at the Chicago Musical College. After three years she studied privately with Djane Lavoie-Herz, who rubbed her nose in the piano works of her own teacher, Alexander Scriabin [1625]. In 1925 she also undertook theoretical and composition studies with Ruth Crawford

[2000]. After a year in high school she gave it up to devote herself to music and had already gotten her compositions noticed in high places by the time she moved to New York at the age of seventeen. In 1933 she began ten years of study with Roger Sessions [1931]. She made her living as an accompanist for various dance companies, and spent a year at the Dalcroze School. In 1935 she married sculptor Benjamin Karp, by whom she had had two daughters. In the latter part of the decade she worked with and wrote ballets for such choreographers as Charles Weidman, Doris Humphrey, and Hanya Holm. After various teaching stints (NYU, SUNY, Juilliard, Connecticut College), she joined the music faculty at Bennington College, Vermont, in 1964. A founder of the American Composers' Alliance, she was its secretary from 1961 to 1965. An avoider of circumscribed systems, Ms. Fine at first leaned toward atonality, then toward the diatonic, and finally compromised between the extremes. Her choice of subjects in her stage and vocal music shows imagination and wit—a ballet, *The Race of Life,* inspired by James Thurber drawings; the choral work *Teisho* on ancient Zen Buddhist documents; an opera, *The Women in the Garden,* whose characters are Gertrude Stein, Virginia Woolf, Emily Dickinson, and Isadora Duncan. RECORDINGS: A sampling of works in various genres has been recorded—(stage) *Alcestis,* the ballet for Martha Graham; (orchestral) *Concertante* for piano and orchestra; (vocal) *Paean* for choir and brasses and *Missa Brevis* for alto and celli; (chamber) Quartet for Brass; and (piano) *Sinfonia and Fugato* and *Momenti.*

[2215] BRITTEN, Edward Benjamin, Lord
PIANIST, CONDUCTOR
BORN: Lowestoft, November 22, 1913
DIED: Aldeburgh, December 4, 1976

In terms of popular acceptance, Benjamin Britten was certainly the most successful opera composer and perhaps the most successful composer of so-called serious music to emerge after World War II (though he began composing considerably before it). Although in the latter part of his career he experimented with twelve-tone technique, his work is always lucid, usually memorable, and often powerfully moving. Yet he rejected the Romantic impulse as self-glorifying. He believed that somehow music had started to go soft with Beethoven [1063], and he once said that he annually played a composition by Brahms [1329] to make sure that that composer was really as bad as he had felt he was.

Born propitiously on the Feast of St. Cecilia, patroness of music, Britten was the son of a prosperous oral surgeon in a busy port city on the North Sea. His mother was a soprano of some local repute and, as secretary of the local choral society, frequently entertained more notable British singers come for concerts. Young Benjamin started playing the piano and composing at the age of five. Later he accompanied his mother on her singing dates, and he salvaged some of his childhood pieces in his now-popular *Simple Symphony* for strings, written when he was twenty. At the age of twelve he encountered Frank Bridge [1713], who offered to take him on as his student, and for the next four years Britten worked with him during his school holidays and retained a reverence for him and his no-nonsense approach for the rest of his own life. On Bridge's insistence he competed for a scholarship at the Royal College of Music and won in 1930. There he studied piano with Harold Samuel and Arthur Benjamin [1887] and went through the motions of studying composition with John Ireland [1719], though his musical mind was by then mature. While still nominally a student, he wrote his oboe quartet, another for strings, a set of choral variations entitled *A Boy Is Born*, and an orchestral *Sinfonietta*, which was performed at London in 1933. In 1934, having won a traveling scholarship, he decided that he wanted to study with Alban Berg [1789] in Vienna, but apparently someone at the college got to his parents with warnings, and they refused to countenance the expedition.

Shortly afterward Dr. Britten died, and his son, who had earlier become one of W. H. Auden's satellites, joined the poet in the documentary film unit of the post office. They collaborated not only on films; Britten wrote incidental music for Auden's plays, and Auden wrote lyrics for Britten to set— notably the early song cycles *Our Hunting Fathers* and *On This Island*, in which the composer was already showing the remarkable ability that brought him to acclaim as one of the greatest word setters in the whole history of English music. In 1937 he paid tribute to his old teacher with *Variations on a Theme of Frank Bridge*. The same year produced his only score for a commercial film, *Love from a Stranger*. In the course of the next he played his piano concerto with Sir Henry Wood.

Britten shared Auden's liberal and pacifist views, which the pair of them emphasized in the cantata *Ballad of Heroes*, premiered by Constant Lambert [2074] in April 1939. Seeing the handwriting on the political wall, Auden emigrated to the United States about this time. In the summer Britten and his lifelong friend and companion, tenor Peter Pears, followed suit. (Mrs. Britten had died in 1938.) They went first to Canada, then to the home of friends in Amityville, Long Island, which they made their headquarters. In 1940 they were briefly with Auden in Brooklyn, and in 1941 they spent some time in Escondido, California. In the former year John Barbirolli introduced Britten's Concerto for Violin at a New York Philharmonic concert; in the latter year the Coolidge Quartet premiered his official first string quartet in Los Angeles. It was also in 1941 that Barbirolli conducted the orchestral *Sinfonia da Requiem*, the result of a commission from the Japanese government, which refused to accept it. Hearing this work, Serge Koussevitzky [1655] urged Britten to write an opera. Britten had in fact already written one—*Paul Bunyan*, to a libretto by Auden—which was produced the following month at Columbia University and was so badly received that Britten withdrew it. (At the end of his life, he restored it to its proper place in the canon, as he did the earliest of the quartets.) Another important product of the American stay was the settings of seven of Michelangelo's sonnets for Pears, for whom he would write all the chief tenor roles in the operas and the majority of the songs.

Britten's pacifism—a lifetime dedication —made him no less concerned for his fellow Britons in their finest and most agonizing hour. He was already mulling over his possible return when he encountered an article by E. M. Forster on the poet George Crabbe, who was from the composer's own East Anglia; this strengthened his resolve. While waiting for a ship, he was told that the Koussevitzky Foundation would support him if he would write another opera. On reaching home, Britten and Pears, rather than accept noncombatant service in the military, took the decidedly unpopular route of declaring themselves conscientious objectors. So certified, they were assigned to keep up home-front morale by concertizing wherever music might help. In what spare time he had, the composer worked on his opera— based on Crabbe's poem "The Borough"— in an old mill he had bought at Snape in East Anglia. Meanwhile the public was introduced to the American works and to such new ones as the choral *Ceremony of Carols*, *Rejoice in the Lamb*, the *Hymn to St. Cecilia*, and the *Festival Te Deum*.

The opera, *Peter Grimes*, was first performed by the Sadler's Wells Opera Company on June 7, 1945, with Pears in the title role. It was a triumph, the like of which had not been seen in England since *The Beggar's Opera*—nor anywhere else for several decades. It quickly made its way around the world, has become established in the international repertoire, has been twice recorded for the phonograph, and was one of the first operas committed to videodisk. Over the ensuing eighteen years, Britten wrote nearly an opera a year—16 operas in all. The immediate follower to *Grimes* was a work for small forces, *The Rape of Lucretia*, premiered at Glyndebourne in 1946. So potent was the Britten magic at that stage that a production was even staged on Broadway in the Ziegfeld Theater. (It closed after a few performances.) *Albert Herring*, a comedy, followed at the same place the following summer. By then there was a coterie of regular Britten performers who consolidated as the English Opera Group, dedicated to performing not only his works, but other English operas, new and old, as well. It was also in 1947 that Britten established his home, for the rest of his life, in the seaside village of Aldeburgh, near Snape, which had been Crabbe's model. The next year he, Pears, and librettist Eric Crozier inaugurated a music festival there which was to be Britten's chief concern thereafter. In 1949 it featured his audience-participation work for children, *Let's Make an Opera*—the opera in question being *The Little Sweep*, which uses mostly children's voices. (Children play a significant role in many of the Britten operas and in some of the songs and choral works.)

Meanwhile Britten had not been idle in other musical forms. The year 1943 had produced the magical *Serenade* for tenor (Pears), horn (Dennis Brain), and strings; 1945 the second quartet and the cycle of Donne sonnets. In 1946 Sir Malcolm Sargent led the Liverpool Philharmonic in the now enormously popular *Young Person's Guide to the Orchestra*, originally for an educational film. The year 1947 brought the cantata *St. Nicholas;* 1948 saw the production of a hybrid work, Britten's arrangement of *The Beggar's Opera* and 1949, the choral-orchestral *Spring Symphony*. (Curiously, save for the 1963 Symphony for Cello and Orchestra, there would be no more really significant orchestral music.) After skipping a year, Britten returned to the stage in 1951 with *Billy Budd*, an all-male setting of a libretto by E. M. Forster and Eric Crozier from Herman Melville's tale, commissioned for the Festival of Britain and introduced at Covent Garden. After another year's hiatus, Covent Garden produced, for the coronation of Elizabeth II, *Gloriana*, a work about Elizabeth I that remains the one neglected work in the canon. Next came one more chamber opera, *The Turn of the Screw*, after Henry James, cast as a set of variations on a twelvetone theme and conducted by the composer at the 1954 Venice Biennale. A trip to the Far East helped inspire the music of Britten's only ballet, *The Prince of the Pagodas*, choreographed by the late John Cranko and produced under the composer's baton at Covent Garden on New Year's Day 1957. The year following, *Noyes Fludde*, an enchanting setting of the medieval Chester "mystery" for church performance by children, pointed ahead to the three short "church parables"—*Curlew River*, 1964; *The Burning Fiery Furnace*, 1966; and *The Prodigal Son*, 1968—produced in the village church at the Aldeburgh Festivals in the years noted. In 1960 came one of Britten's most successful operas, a treatment of Shakespeare's *A Midsummer Night's Dream*, with Oberon sung by a countertenor, and the "rude mechanicals" rudely making fun of some avant-garde affectations.

Around this time, Britten struck up a friendship with Soviet cellist Mstislav Rostropovich and his wife, soprano Galina Vishnevskaya. For Rostropovich he wrote the Symphony for Cello and Orchestra, the Sonata for Cello and Piano, and 3 *Suites for Solo Cello*. Commissioned to do a work to celebrate the rebuilding of Coventry Cathedral, destroyed in a Nazi air raid in the war, he conceived the notion of making as passionate a plea for peace as he knew how. The result was the *War Requiem* of 1962, which combines the Latin Mass with Wilfred Owens' bitter war poems. The soloists were to be Vishnevskaya, Pears, and the great German baritone Dietrich Fischer-Dieskau, but Vishnevskaya was detained in Russia, though she was allowed later to participate in the recording. (Britten afterward wrote a Pushkin cycle for Vishnevskaya, and Blake and Hölderlin cycles for Fischer-Dieskau.) The years 1967 and 1969 respectively produced two cantatas for children's voices, *The Golden Vanity* and *The Children's Crusade*.

In 1971 Britten composed another opera after Henry James, *Owen Wingrave*, for the BBC and the NET Opera Theater in New York. Britten's last opera was *Death in Venice*, after Thomas Mann's novella. He completed it in the spring of 1973, for production at the Festival in the Maltings, the new hall which he had inaugurated at Snape to celebrate the twentieth anniversary. Before the festival opened, Britten was felled by a massive heart attack and had to undergo surgery; he was left a virtual invalid. In 1975, however, he was able to compose again, and in his last years completed his String Quartet No. 3 (actually his fourth), some songs, the cantata *Phaedra,* the orchestral *Suite on English Folktunes,* the *Suite No. 3 for Solo Cello,* and some small choral works. He succumbed to a second attack a year later.

RECORDINGS: Save for *Paul Bunyan, Gloriana,* and the incidental stage and film music, virtually all of Britten's output has been recorded, most of it with the participation of the composer on the podium or at the piano and/or of the dedicatees and original casts. (Sir Colin Davis has expressed a desire to record *Gloriana,* which was recently revived by the English National Opera Company, with considerable success.)

[2216] GOULD, Morton
PIANIST, CONDUCTOR, ARRANGER
BORN: Richmond Hill, N.Y., December 10, 1913

Morton Gould probably qualifies as a genuine prodigy. He could play the piano by ear at four, published a piano piece at six, got a one-year scholarship to the Institute of Musical Art (later known as the Juilliard School) at seven, began study at New York University at thirteen, and had a piano suite published by G. Schirmer at fifteen. His chief piano teachers were Joseph Kardos and Abby Whiteside; he took composition lessons from Vincent Jones at NYU. At seventeen he dropped out of school to contribute to the family finances, at first by working at musical odd jobs in cabarets, theaters, dance bands, and vaudeville. After a year as staff pianist at the Radio City Music Hall, he became a pianist for NBC. In 1934 he moved to the Mutual Network, where he had his own orchestral program, on which he introduced many of his own compositions, including 4 *Symphonettes* (the most famous is the first, the *Latin American,* but the last includes the jazzy *Pavane,* often performed separately and perhaps his best-known piece). The 1943 *American Concertette* for piano and orchestra became best known as *Interplay* after Jerome Robbins used it for a ballet of that name. Other works from this period were premiered by such conductors as Leopold Stokowski, Fritz Reiner, and Vladimir Golschmann.

In 1943 Gould transferred to CBS, where he was orchestra leader for the "Chrysler" and "Cresta Blanca Wine" programs. The next year he married Shirley Bank, and in 1945 his Broadway musical *Billion Dollar Baby* (written with Betty Comden and

Adolph Green) survived for more than half a year. From about this time he began to appear more and more frequently as guest conductor with various orchestras, beginning with the Boston Symphony. From the mid-forties also dates his activity as a composer for films (and later television). He won especial acclaim for his music for the series *World War I.* A second musical, *Arms and the Girl,* ran for four months in 1950. Among Gould's "serious works" are 4 symphonies, the twelve-tone *Jekyll and Hyde Variations* for orchestra, and the ballet *Fall River Legend* (based on the Lizzie Borden story), choreographed by Agnes De Mille for the Ballet Theater.

RECORDINGS: A substantial number of Gould's works have been recorded—(ballets) *Interplay* and *Fall River Legend;* (orchestra) *Latin-American Symphonette, Symphonette No. 2, Pavane* (from the *Symphonette No. 3), Dance Variations* for two pianos and orchestra, *Soundings, Columbia, American Salute, When Johnny Comes Marching Home, Declaration Suite, Venice: Audiograph* for double orchestra and brass choirs, *Vivaldi Gallery* for string quartet and divided orchestras, *Foster Gallery, Burchfield Gallery, Apple Waltzes* (based on materials for an unfinished large-scale collaboration with George Balanchine), *Spirituals, Manhattan Serenade, Cotillion, Festive Music, Philharmonic Waltzes, Quickstep, Legend,* Concerto for Tap-Dancer and Orchestra, *Family Album Suite, Rhapsodies on Familiar Themes* for piano and orchestra, and *Jekyll and Hyde Variations;* (band) *Fanfare for Freedom, American Ballads, Cheers,* Symphony No. 4 "West Point," *Derivations* for clarinet and jazz band, *Ballad, St. Lawrence Suite, Jericho, Formations,* and *Santa Fe Saga;* (television and film scores) *Windjammer, Cinerama Holiday, World War I,* and *Holocaust;* (chamber) *Suite for Tuba and 3 Horns* and Sonata No. 3 for Piano.

[2217] KOMMA, Karl Michael (Kom'-ä, Kärl Mëkh'-ä-el)
MUSICOLOGIST, TEACHER, PIANIST
BORN: Asch, December 24, 1913

Komma's birthplace, now Aš, is the westernmost town in Czechoslovakia. He had his training in Prague, studying composition with Fidelio Friedrich Finke (1891–1968), himself a pupil of Vítězslav Novák **[1617]**. In 1936 he acquired a doctorate in musicology at Heidelberg and taught there until the war broke out. Returning to Czechoslovakia, he headed the conservatory at Liberec during the German occupation. He (perhaps understandably) moved to Bavaria in 1945 and worked in Germany as an accompanist until 1954, when he joined the faculty of the Stuttgart Conservatory. He has published a book on Bohemian music and many articles and has composed in most standard forms. RECORDINGS: Works recorded include the *St. Matthew Passion;* Concerto for Piano; *Signale* for orchestra; *In Praise of Wine* for tenor and piano; *3 Brentano Songs* for soprano, flute, and piano; and *6 Fables of Leonardo Da Vinci* for soprano, baritone, and piano.

[2218] KAPR, Jan (Kåp'r, Yån)
RADIO OFFICIAL, CRITIC, EDITOR, TEACHER
BORN: Prague, March 12, 1914

The son of a professional composer, Kapr studied with his father initially. His career was interrupted by a serious accident, but later he studied at the Prague Conservatory with Jaroslav Řidký (1897–1956), and then with Řidký's teacher Jaroslav Křička [1752]. During the years of World War II he worked as a producer with Radio Prague, then served as a reviewer and later as a senior editor for the state music publishing apparatus. In 1961 he took a professorial post at the Janáček Academy, from which he retired in 1970. He began in the line of succession from the Czech nationalists but gradually moved into serialism and electronics. Among his larger works are an opera, at least 8 symphonies, 2 cantatas, and 2 piano concerti. He has also written film scores, one of which, *New Czechoslovakia*, won him a Stalin Prize in 1951. RECORDINGS: Works issued by his American publisher include *Dialogues* for flute and harp; String Quartet No. 6 (with baritone voice); *Rotazione 9* for piano and string quartet; *Woodcuts* for brasses; Concertino for Clarinet, Cello, Percussion, and Piano; *Intermezzo* for flute and piano; and *Exercises for "Gydli"*. Czech records include the String Quartet No. 3 and Symphony No. 7 ("Childhood Country") for children's chorus and orchestra.

[2219] GROSS, Robert Arthur
VIOLINIST, TEACHER
BORN: Colorado Springs, Colo., March 23, 1914

Robert Gross studied violin at the Juilliard school from the age of twelve, his teachers being the venerable Leopold Auer and Édouard Déthier. He also studied composition with Bernard Wagenaar (1894–1971) and

launched an important concert career. Many compositions were dedicated to him, and he was the first to play publicly the Concerto for Violin of Roger Sessions [1931], with whom he had taken private lessons. (He also put in some time with Schoenberg [1657].) From 1949 Gross taught at Occidental College in Los Angeles, serving two terms as chairman of the music department. He has written 2 operas (one on Ionesco's absurdist play *The Bald Soprano)* but has dealt mostly in chamber music. RECORDINGS: Several chamber works appear on discs—*Epode* (solo cello), *3-4-2* (violin and cello), *Passacaglia* (violin and organ), and *Chacounne* (soprano and violin).

[2220] MELLERS, Wilfrid Howard
MUSICOLOGIST, TEACHER
BORN: Leamington, April 26, 1914

Wilfrid Mellers is (at least outside his own country) better known as a writer *on* than *of* music. After prepping at Leamington College, he entered Cambridge to major in English; later he also took up music. His chief composition teacher was Egon Wellesz [1799], though he was also aided by Edmund Rubbra [1995]. On graduating in 1938 he taught for two years at Dartington Hall. In 1940 he became music editor of *Scrutiny*, and in the war years lectured at Cambridge and the University of Birmingham. In 1946 he brought out his first book, *Music and Society*, followed at two-year intervals by *Studies in Contemporary Music* and the apparently definitive *François Couperin and the French Classical Tradition*. From 1948 to 1959 he taught at Birmingham, during which period he contributed the important segments on sonata form and Romanticism to *Man and His Music*, 1957. From 1960 to 1963 he held the Andrew Mellon Chair at the University of Pittsburgh; the experience resulted in a brilliant study of the conflicting currents in American music, *Music in a New Found Land*. In 1964 he was asked to head up the new department of music at the University of York, which he has made one of the most advanced in England. The preponderance of vocal works among Mellers's output demonstrates the impact thereon of his twin allegiances to words and notes. His fascination with pop music and jazz also makes itself felt. Mellers has been concerned to develop a personal (albeit eclectic) style and as a result has disowned much of what he has written. The official list appears still to include 2 operas, many works for voices (solo and choral), incidental music, and some few instrumental works. RECORDINGS: His cantata *Life Cycle* and the melodrama *Voices and Creatures* have been recorded.

[2221] OHANA, Maurice (Ō-hà'-nà, Mō-rēs')

TEACHER

BORN: Casablanca, June 12, 1914

Ohana's music is almost as international as his life has been. He was born in Morocco. His parents' families were both Andalusian, but his father was a British citizen from Gibraltar and his mother was a Sephardic Jew. He grew up in Bayonne in southern France and studied piano with Frank Marshall in Barcelona. He originally intended to become an architect but by the mid-1930s was pursuing a concert career. In 1937, having decided to devote his life to music, he entered the Schola Cantorum in Paris (where he later taught) and studied composition with Daniel-Lesur [2127]. When war erupted in 1939, Ohana joined the British army. In 1945 he studied with Alfredo Casella [1767] in Rome, then settled in Paris, where his music soon began to win notice. Though he worked for a time with Pierre Schaeffer [2159] in his electronic music research, Ohana has been categorically opposed to systems and movements. His eclecticism has drawn from French Impressionism, Spanish nationalism, *cante jondo*, Sephardic song and dance, and the music of the Berbers and of black Africa. He has also made use of microtonal intervals. A good deal of his output has been for the stage (opera, ballet, incidental music), screen, and radio. RECORDINGS: Two chamber operas—*Syllabaire pour Phèdre (Speller for Phaedra)* and *3 Contes de l'Honorable Fleur (3 Tales of the Honorable Flower)*, the latter an oriental monodrama for soprano and ensemble—have been recorded, as well as the powerful Lorca setting *Llanto por Ignacio Sánchez Mejías* for narrator, baritone, chorus, and small orchestra; *Sarabande* for piano and orchestra; *3 Gráficos* for guitar and orchestra; the choral-orchestral *Cantigas (Songs)*; *Messe* and *Lys de Madrigaux*, both for female voices and ensemble; *Synaxis* for two pianos, percussion, and orchestra; *Signes* for flute, guitar, piano, and percussion; *Cris (Cries)* for *a capella* chorus; *24 Préludes* for piano; *Carillons* for solo harpsichord; *Si le jour parait (If the Day Should Break)* and *Tientos*, both for guitar. (The Concerto for Guitar erroneously listed for a number of years in *Schwann* is actually the *3 Gráficos*, not a separate work.)

[2222] EFFINGER, Cecil

MATHEMATICIAN, INVENTOR, CONDUCTOR, OBOIST, TEACHER

BORN: Colorado Springs, Colo., July 22, 1914

It is an odd coincidence that a small city like Colorado Springs should produce two significant composers (see Robert Gross [2219]) within four months. Effinger, however, so cast his lot with his native state that he might be regarded as its unofficial Composer Laureate. His parents were both in the local school system—his mother a Latin teacher, his father a supervisor of music and a voice teacher. As a schoolboy he played both violin and oboe. In 1931 he entered Colorado College in his hometown to major in mathematics. During his four years there he took some music courses with Frederick Boothroyd, conductor of the local orchestra, and made arrangements for dance bands. On graduation he taught mathematics for a year at the high school, then returned to his alma mater to teach music. In 1937 he also became first oboist in the recently reborn Denver Symphony Orchestra. During that summer he studied with Bernard Wagenaar (1894–1971) and in that of 1939 with Nadia Boulanger. Called up for war service in 1942, he conducted the 506th Army Band (for which he wrote many arrangements) at Fort Logan until 1945; then he was dispatched to teach for a year at the American Conservatory at Biarritz. He married Margaret Wilkins in 1944, a union that ended in divorce.

While in France Effinger began thinking seriously about a problem that had exercised many musical minds: a machine that would print music from type. His "Musicwriter" received a patent ten years later and has been successfully marketed since. He returned to the college for two years in 1946, then settled in at the University of Colorado at Boulder. In 1968 he married a music teacher, Corinne Ann Lindberg, and the next year produced a device called the Tempowatch, which, in contrast to the metronome, which indicates the rate of speed at which something is to be played, indicates the one at which it is *being* played. He has also designed a typewriter for the particular needs of engineers. His considerable musical output so far includes 5 full-scale symphonies and 2 condensed ("little") ones, concerti, string quartets, operas, oratorios, and cantatas. He likes to work in Baroque structures and modern harmonic idioms. A good deal of his music is on American themes. Effinger is one of the few composers one can think of who has played himself (as "Cece" Effinger) in a nationally distributed television commercial. RECORDINGS: His chamber-orchestral *Little Symphony No. 1*, Sonata No. 3 for Piano, String Quartet No. 5, and the oratorio *Paul of Tarsus* have been recorded.

[2223] HAIEFF, Alexei (Hī′-ef, À-lek′-sā)
TEACHER
BORN: Blagoveshchensk, Siberia, August 25, 1914

The seventh child of well-to-do Russian parents, Haieff was born near the Manchurian border, across which the family escaped in 1920. He grew up in Harbin (Haerhpin), where he learned to play the piano and began to compose. Following the Japanese takeover of Manchuria in 1931, Haieff fled to the United States, where he was befriended by Rachmaninoff [1638] and became a fellowship student at the Juilliard School in 1934. His chief teachers there were Rubin Goldmark (1872–1936), Frederick Jacobi [1850], Bernard Wagenaar (1894–1971), and pianist Alexander Siloti. He left in 1938 to study with Nadia Boulanger in Cambridge, Massachusetts, and then in Rome. By the end of the decade his music was being performed by major orchestras and soloists, and he had garnered signal honors—the Lili Boulanger Memorial Award, the American Prix de Rome, two Guggenheim fellowships. He has been visiting professor or composer-in-residence at the American Academy in Rome, SUNY at Buffalo, the Carnegie-Mellon Institute, Brandeis, and the University of Utah. A neo-classicist who owed a good deal to his friendship with Stravinsky [1748], he has composed a small but well-crafted body of works, which includes 2 ballets, 3 symphonies, concerti for piano and violin, and chamber music. At this writing he was living in Rome. He has composed very little since 1970. RECORDINGS: Several orchestral works have been recorded—Concerto No. 1 for Piano, Symphony No. 2, *Ballet in E Major*, and *Divertimento*. Other recordings include the String Quartet No. 1; *Bagatelles* for oboe and bassoon; Sonata for Cello and Piano; and numerous piano works—*4 Juke Box Pieces, 5 Piano Pieces, Bagatelles*, Sonata for Piano, *Gifts and Semblances*, *Notes of Thanks*, and the Sonata for 2 Pianos.

[2224] KUBIK, Gail Thompson
VIOLINIST, CONDUCTOR, TEACHER
BORN: South Coffeyville, Okla., September 5, 1914
DIED: Claremont, Calif., July 20, 1984

Kubik is certainly the only composer from South Coffeyville to have won both an Academy Award—for the 1950 cartoon *Gerald McBoing-Boing*—and a Pulitzer Prize, in 1952. He was the youngest composer to have received that award up to that time. He came from a musical family: his mother sang, his brothers played cello and piano to his violin, and they concertized in Middle America during the 1930s as a group. At fifteen Gail Kubik won a scholarship to the Eastman School of Music (as a violinist) and concurrently completed his high-school education in Rochester. He studied composition with Bernard Rogers [1875] and graduated at nineteen. He then went to Illinois, where he taught violin at Monmouth College and studied with Leo Sowerby [1908] at the American Conservatory in Chicago, from which he took a master's degree in 1936. After a year of teaching at Dakota Wesleyan in South Dakota, he went to Harvard to study for another year with Walter Piston [1890] and made friends with Nadia Boulanger. During this time he played the first performance of the first of his 2 violin concerti with the Chicago Symphony. In 1938 he also entered into his first marriage (of four). After two years of teaching at Teachers' College of Columbia University, he joined the staff of NBC, where he wrote much music for radio shows. In 1942 he was hired by the Office of War Information as its film unit's musical director and a year later transferred to a similar (uniformed) post with the Air Force, for which he wrote a film score, *The Memphis Belle*, which won him an award from the New York Film Critics. Released from the military in 1946, he taught briefly at the University of Southern California; then, thanks to a Guggenheim Fellowship, he returned to composing, writing the opera *A Mirror for the Sky*, the ballet *Frankie and Johnny*, and his first symphony (of 3). Further film work brought him the Oscar noted above in the same year that he won the American Prix de Rome. The *Symphony concertante*, written in Rome, brought him the Pulitzer Prize in 1952.

The three years of residence in Rome stretched to thirteen as an expatriate, during which Kubik wrote, conducted, lectured, and taught (e.g., at Oxford). In 1970 he was appointed composer-in-residence at Scripps College in Claremont, California. Though his later music perhaps increased in complexity, it remained basically neo-classical and was intended for general audiences rather than specialists. In the last decade of his life, his production fell off and was limited chiefly to choral works, which, however, included the large oratorio *A Record of Our Time,* premiered in 1970.

RECORDINGS: Orchestral recordings include the *Symphonie concertante* (composer conducting); *Divertimenti Nos. 1, 2* (the composer again conducting); Symphony No. 2; and the *Prayer and Toccata* for organ and orchestra. Other recorded works include *Scholastica* for chorus; *Theatrical Sketches* for piano trio; the Sonata for Piano; Sonatina for Piano; *Celebrations and Epilogue* for piano; Symphony for 2 Pianos; and Sonatina for Clarinet and Piano.

[2225] CAZDEN, Norman
PIANIST, TEACHER, ETHNOMUSICOLO-GIST
BORN: New York, September 23, 1914
DIED: Bangor, Me., August 18, 1980

A debutant pianist in New York's Town Hall at twelve, young Cazden entered the Institute of Musical Art at thirteen, set up as a teacher at fourteen, and graduated from high school at sixteen and from music school a year later. Thereafter he studied with pianist Ernest Hutcheson and composer Bernard Wagenaar (1894–1971) at the Juilliard School until 1939, serving as a teacher there for his last four years. In the early 1940s he was on the staffs of two local radio stations, and worked as music director of the dance company headed by Doris Humphrey and Charles Weidman. Meanwhile, he had been attending classes at CCNY, majoring in social sciences, and graduated in 1943. That summer—the first of several—as music director of a camp in the Catskills he became fascinated with the folk music of the region, spent much time collecting and arranging it, and later published several collections. Catskill folksongs supplied the basis for some of his own compositions as well, and he wrote a number of articles on the subject. In the autumn of 1943 he began four years in graduate school at Harvard, where, supported by several fellowships and prizes, he studied with Aaron Copland [1986] and Walter Piston [1890] and received a Ph.D. in musicology in 1948. During this time he married Courtney Borden, in 1946, from whom he was divorced twenty-five years and two children later. After more than twenty years in which he taught variously at Vassar, Peabody, and the universities of Michigan and Illinois, as well as privately, he found a permanent home at the University of Maine, where he became a full professor in 1973. Apart from his folklore articles, he wrote a number on musical theory. His music includes a 1944 ballet *The*

Lonely Ones (based on cartoons by William Steig), some incidental music, the "dramatic cantata" *Dingle Hill,* orchestral, choral, and chamber works. RECORDINGS: The orchestral *3 Ballads from the Catskills* and the Sonata No. 4 for Piano are performed on records.

[2226] PANUFNIK, Andrzej (På-nōōf'-nĕk, Än-drä')
PIANIST, CONDUCTOR
BORN: Warsaw, September 24, 1914

The son of Tomasz Panufnik, a famous maker of stringed instruments, and the former Matilda Tonnes, an Englishwoman who had come to Warsaw as a violin student, Andrzej Panufnik began composing at nine. He spent four years, 1932–36, at the Warsaw Conservatory and two more studying conducting with Felix Weingartner [1552] in Vienna. In 1938 he went to Paris to study with Philippe Gaubert [1717], but the worsening international situation sent him home the next summer. During the war years he played in a two-piano team in Warsaw night clubs and theaters with his friend Witold Lutosławski, and lost all of his compositions in the burning of the city in 1944, though he managed to rewrite a few, notably the *Tragic Overture,* inspired by the wartime sufferings of the Poles. After the war he progressed rapidly from the conductorship of the Cracow Philharmonic to that of the Warsaw Philharmonic, and thence to being the state's chief musical emissary abroad, both as composer and conductor. Identified with the international avant-garde, he suddenly found his music being called "bourgeois" and "formalist." In 1952, for the Olympic Games in Helsinki, he wrote the *Heroic Overture.* He was permitted to conduct it there, and it won a gold medal, but it was banned in Poland, and some of the more zealous of the musical adherents of the party demanded that it be burned.

A year later, with his English wife Scarlett (who published an account of the affair, *Out of the City of Fear,* in 1956), he fled to England and settled there. He was conductor of the City of Birmingham Orchestra for two years, 1957–59, and has guest-conducted occasionally since. He became a citizen in 1961 and made his home in Twickenham with his second wife, Camilla. Not surprisingly that setting inspired a big choral composition, *Universal Prayer,* to a text by Alexander Pope, Twickenham's most famous resident. A full-length ballet after Strindberg, *Miss Julie,* appeared in 1970. In his music written after leaving Poland, Panufnik has largely abandoned radical practices for an effective espousal of romantic diatonicism, although in his later years (beginning roughly with the *Universal Prayer* of 1970), he has made increasing use of elaborate formal layouts and mathematical schemata, superimposing a new formal austerity onto his earlier lyricism. In November 1984 his *Arbor cosmica (The Cosmic Tree)* for twelve strings was premiered in New York City, to considerable critical acclaim.

RECORDINGS: Seven of Panufnik's 8 symphonies have been recorded—*Sinfonia rustica, Sinfonia elegiaca, Sinfonia sacra, Sinfonia concertante* (for flute, harp, and strings), *Sinfonia di sfere, Sinfonia mistica,* and the eighth symphony *Sinfonia votiva,* which was commissioned by the Boston Symphony for its one-hundredth-anniversary celebrations in 1980. (Only the seventh symphony, *Metasinfonia,* remains unrecorded.) Other orchestral recordings include the *Tragic Overture; Nocturne; Heroic Overture; Rhapsody; Autumn Music* (for chamber orchestra); *Landscape; Katyń Epitaph; Concerto festivo;* Concertino for Timpani, Percussion, and Strings; Concerto for Violin; and the arrangement *Suite of Ancient Polish Airs and Dances* for strings. Choral-instrumental recordings include the *Universal Prayer* for vocal soloists, choir, three harps, and organ; *Thames Pageant* for narrator, children's chorus, and orchestra; and the brief *Invocation to Peace* for children's chorus and orchestra. Also recorded is *Dreamscape* for soprano and piano. A recent Melodiya release quite unexpectedly contains Panufnik's *Hommage à Chopin* for flute and strings, directed by Gennady Rozhdestvensky.

[2227] GOEB, Roger
TEACHER
BORN: Cherokee, Iowa, October 9, 1914

One of the more promising American composers of the post–World War II era, Roger Goeb came to music late and left it early. As a boy he learned to play piano and trumpet decently but took a degree in agricultural chemistry at the University of Wisconsin in 1936. Having been converted to music by exposure to it, he played dance dates for two years and then went to Paris for a year at the École Normale, where his work was overseen by Nadia Boulanger. He then studied privately with Otto Luening [1980] and at New York University before taking a master's degree at the Cleveland Institute in 1942. The year before he married a dancer, Janey Hoy, who subsequently bore him a son and a daughter. From 1942 to 1944 he

was musical director at a radio station in Norman, Oklahoma; then he taught and studied for a year at the University of Iowa, where he completed his first symphony of 4, for which they gave him a Ph.D. He subsequently taught at Bard College in New York State, at the Juilliard School, and at Stanford University. For some years, until 1962, he directed the American Composers' Alliance and the American Composers' Conference at Bennington College in Vermont every summer. In 1955 Janey Goeb was found to have multiple sclerosis, and later their son became ill with the same disease (she died in 1967, he in 1974). In 1964 Roger Goeb withdrew from music altogether. In his brief career he won much praise and several awards.

RECORDINGS: Works recorded include Symphonies Nos. 3 and 4, the *5 American Dances* for strings, Concertino No. 1 for Trombone and Strings, Concertino No. 2 for Orchestra, Wind Quintet No. 2, and *Prairie Song* for wind quintet.

[2228] FINE, Irving Gifford
TEACHER, CONDUCTOR
BORN: Boston, December 3, 1914
DIED: Boston, August 23, 1962

Except for a couple of visits abroad, Irving Fine—unrelated to composer Vivian Fine [2214]—spent his whole too-brief life in and around Boston. After some youthful piano study, he went to Harvard, was trained there in composition by Edward Burlingame Hill [1632] and Walter Piston [1890], and took a master's degree in 1939. During this period he also studied with Nadia Boulanger in Cambridge (Massachusetts) and with Serge Koussevitzky [1655] at Tanglewood, to learn conducting. In 1939 he went to Paris in the summer for further work with Boulanger, then joined the Harvard staff, where he deputized for G. Wallace Woodworth as conductor of the Glee Club. Two years later he married Verna Rudnick, by whom he had three daughters. He also taught at Tanglewood in the summer of 1946 and 1947 and at Salzburg in that of 1950. In 1950 he left Harvard for Brandeis, where he was successively composer-in-residence, Naumburg Professor of Music, and chairman of the School of Creative Arts. Initially Fine was under the spells of Stravinsky [1748] and Hindemith [1914], then explored twelvetone technique, and finally arrived at a synthesis of his own. His output includes a handful of orchestral works, six chamber compositions, some witty songs and partsongs, and a few piano pieces. He completed his only symphony in 1962 (hence the title

Symphony 1962), recorded it (live in concert) with the Boston Symphony, and conducted it at Tanglewood that summer. A few days later he succumbed to an unexpected heart attack at the age of forty-seven. RECORDINGS: Most of Fine's works have been recorded—*Symphony 1962; Serious Song: A Lament* for strings; *Toccata concertante* and *Diversions*, both for orchestra; *Partita* and *Romanza*, both for wind quintet; *String Quartet; Notturno* for harp and strings; *Fantasia* for string trio; *Music for Piano* (the composer performing); the choral works *Alice in Wonderland, The Hour Glass*, and *McCord's Menagerie;* and the song cycles *Mutability* and *Childhood Fables for Grownups*. Just released is a recording of the Sonata for Violin and Piano (with composer Vivian Fine at the piano).

[2229] LANDOWSKI, Marcel (Làn-dōv'-skē, Màr-sel')
CONDUCTOR, ADMINISTRATOR
BORN: Pont L'Abbé, February 18, 1915

Landowski was born in the southwestern-most coast of Brittany, whither his parents had fled after the German invasion of France. His father Paul Landowski was a sculptor of note. His paternal grandfather, a Pole, had broken out of a Siberian prison, fled to France, and married the daughter of the violinist-composer Henri Vieuxtemps **[1270]**. Marcel studied piano and began composing on his own. When at nineteen he entered the Paris Conservatoire, he resisted the rules until Henri Büsser **[1627]** and Noël Gallon **[1856]** took him firmly in hand. He studied conducting with Philippe Gaubert and became a protégé of Pierre Monteux, who in 1937 introduced two of his choral-orchestral works at a concert of the Paris Orchestre Symphonique. Landowski was in military service from 1939 until the French capitulation in 1940. From 1959 to 1962 he directed the conservatory at his town of residence, Boulogne-sur-Seine, was chief conductor at the Paris Opéra-Comique for the next three years, and then worked for the state department of education and the Ministry of Culture. His music, by his own statement, aims for lucidity and feeling and is particularly effective in dramatic works—4 operas, several ballets, film scores, and *Le Rire de Nils Halerius (The Laughter of Nils Halerius)* in which each of the three acts in turn is an opera, a ballet, and an oratorio. He has also written 3 symphonies, numerous concerti, and a good deal of choral music. RECORDINGS: Stage works on records include the 1956 opera *Le Fou (The Madman)*

and two recent ballets for Roland Petit—the complete *Les Hauts de Hurlevant (Wuthering Heights)* for orchestra and electronic sound and substantial excerpts from *Le Fantôme de l'Opéra (The Phantom of the Opera)* for orchestra. Other orchestral recordings include the Concerto for Ondes Martenot, Strings, and Percussion; Symphonies Nos. 1 and 3; and the Concerto for Trumpet, Orchestra, and Electroacoustic Elements (subtitled "At the End of Grief an Open Window"). Other recordings include *Cantata No. 1: "Jesus Are You There Too?"* for soprano, alto, chorus, organ, and percussion; and the *Notebook for Four Days* for trumpet and organ.

[2230] SURINACH, Carlos (Sōō'-rē-nâch, Kàr'-lōs)
CONDUCTOR
BORN: Barcelona, March 4, 1915

Surinach was the son of a stockbroker and a prizewinning pianist. The latter—his mother —taught him to play, and then in 1928 sent him to José Caminals, who had his own music school in Barcelona, for polishing. While serving in a desk job in the army from 1936 to 1939, he studied with Enrique Morera (1865–1942), a pupil of Isaac Albéniz **[1523]** and of Felipe Pedrell **[1384]**. In 1940 a scholarship took him to Germany, where he studied in Düsseldorf and Berlin. Returning to Barcelona two years later, he conducted the symphony and opera orchestras and produced *Monte Carlo*, the first of his ballet scores. In 1947 he moved to Paris and worked as a guest conductor until 1950 when he emigrated to New York City, where he found work writing music for television commercials. A performance of his *Ritmo jondo* the next year won him a commission for an expanded version for José Limón's dance troupe. This opened the door to a whole series of commissions—from orchestras and television networks, but most especially from dancers and choreographers. Surinach's music was particularly promoted by Martha Graham, Robert Joffrey, and John Butler, who had enormous success with it. He also continued to conduct and made many recordings of his own and other people's music, especially for the phonographic wing of Metro-Goldwyn-Mayer. Much of what he has written is permeated by his understanding of Spanish music and especially of *cante jondo*. He has written for films and has taught briefly at the Carnegie-Mellon Institute in 1966–67 and Queens College in 1974–76. Besides more than a dozen ballets, he has written a one-act opera, 2 numbered symphonies, much other orchestral and instrumental music, and a few choral pieces and songs. RECORDINGS: Both versions of the ballet *Ritmo jondo* have been recorded, as have numerous orchestral compositions—*Sinfonietta flamenca, Hollywood Carnival, Symphonic Variations, Melorhythmic Dramas,* the overture *Feria mágica,* the ballet *Spells and Rhymes, Concierto for Orchestra, Doppio concertino* (for violin, piano, and chamber orchestra), *Concertino* (for piano, strings, and cymbals), Concerto for Piano, *Madrid 1890, Danza Andaluza,* and *Paeans and Dances of Heathen Iberia* (the latter for symphonic band). Chamber pieces recorded include the String Quartet, the *3 Cantos berberes* for sextet, *Tientos* for harpsichord and ensemble, and a few piano pieces.

[2231] BROTT, Alexander
VIOLINIST, CONDUCTOR
BORN: Montreal, March 14, 1915

At the age of thirteen Brott was awarded a five-year scholarship to the conservatory of McGill University, where he specialized in violin. A second scholarship provided another five years at the Juilliard School, where he worked with Sascha Jacobsen, and with Bernard Wagenaar (1894–1971) in composition. A third scholarship was to take him to the Royal College of Music in London in 1939. Unfortunately there was a war, so he returned to Montreal and joined the faculty of McGill University, where he founded the McGill String Quartet and the McGill Chamber Orchestra. He became concertmaster of the Montreal Symphony in 1945 and remained with it for thirteen years; he then conducted the summer concerts from 1960 to 1966. He has been principal conductor of the Kingston (Ontario) Symphony since 1963 and has guest-conducted all over. His music is variously described as of the modern-contrapuntal school and as modern-veneered romanticism. He likes witty titles *(Critic's Corner, 3 on a Spree,* or *Pristine Prisms in Polychrome)* and sometimes writes music to match them. The bulk of his output is for orchestra or instrumental groups, though he has written several choral pieces, a number for vocal soloists, and a ballet score. His son is the conductor Boris Brott. RECORDINGS: There is a composer-directed Soviet performance of his 1960 orchestral work *Spheres in Orbit,* as well as Canadian performances of other orchestral works—*Paraphrase in Polyphony; Triangle, Circle, 4 Squares;* and *The Young Prometheus* (the latter consisting of orchestrations

of early contrapuntal exercises by Beethoven [1063]).

[2232] LE GALLIENNE, Dorian Leon Marlois
RADIO OFFICIAL
BORN: Melbourne, April 19, 1915
DIED: Melbourne, July 29, 1963

A 1938 graduate of Melbourne University, Le Gallienne afterward studied at the Royal College of Music in London with Herbert Howells [1870] and Arthur Benjamin [1887], and somewhat later with Gordon Jacob [1911]. He was in the employ of the Australian Broadcasting System during World War II. His rather small output, which includes 2 ballets, film scores, incidental music, a symphony, and a number of small-form compositions, was sharply curtailed by a terminal illness that eventually carried him off at forty-eight. He had been working on a second symphony at the time of his death; a work entitled *Symphonic Study* was assembled by other hands from his sketches. RECORDINGS: His tuneful *Sinfonietta* for orchestra has been recorded by Anthony Hopkins.

[2233] HANUŠ, Jan (Hà-nōōsh, Yàn)
EDITOR
BORN: Prague, May 2, 1915

Hanuš got his musical education in Prague, mostly from Otakar Jeremiáš (1892–1962), pupil of Vítězslav Novák [1617] and conductor of the local radio symphony. In 1940 he went to work for the music publishing house of F. A. Urbánek and became editor-in-chief after it was nationalized in 1949. From 1963 to 1970 he was managing director of Panton, the state publishing unit for musical books, scores, and records. A rather prolific composer in a rather old-fashioned vein, he has written 4 operas, 2 ballets, at least 6 symphonies, 4 Masses, and much else. RECORDINGS: His American publisher has issued recordings of some of his compositions on the Serenus label, and there are also some on Czech labels. Works recorded include the orchestral Symphony No. 2; *Musica concertante* for cello, piano, winds, and percussion; *Notturni di Praga;* the choral-orchestral *The Czech Year; Little Suite* for nine instruments; *Sonata seria* for violin and percussion; *Sonata variata* for clarinet and piano; and two movements of Concertino for Timpani and Tape. The 1979 Symphony No. 6, recently recorded by Panton, shows the composer utilizing rather unusual sonorities (using the flexatone and electric bass guitar, among other instruments) within a conservative framework.

[2234] PERLE, George
TEACHER
BORN: Bayonne, N.J., May 6, 1915

George Perle began his compositional training with Wesley La Violette (1894–1983) at DePaul University in Chicago, from which he graduated in 1938. During the next two years he studied with Ernst Krenek [1984] and became interested in the twelve-tone system. After taking a master's degree at the American Conservatory in 1942, he did graduate work at NYU with (among others) Kurt Sachs and Gustave Reese. Perle served in both Europe and the Pacific and was stationed in occupied Japan during 1945 and 1946. In 1947 he began teaching at Brooklyn College, then held positions at CCNY, Louisville, and the University of California at Davis. He obtained his Ph.D. at NYU in 1956, with a dissertation on atonality and serialism that was afterward published as a much and justly admired book, *Serial Composition and Atonality,* which has been through several editions. In 1961 he returned to New York as a professor at Queens College. He has held two Guggenheim Fellowships, has had many commissions, and has guest-taught at such schools as Columbia, Yale, Juilliard, and the University of Pennsylvania. Perle has taken his own view of dodecaphony, attempting to reconcile it with the tensions and releases of tonality and harmony-discord, and has set forth his theories in a second book, *Twelve-Tone Tonality.* He has written 2 symphonies, a Concerto for Cello, and other music for both orchestra and band but works chiefly in carefully crafted small forms. RECORDINGS: Two orchestral works, *Rhapsody* and *3 Movements,* have been recorded. Chamber and instrumental recordings include the Quintet for Strings; String Quartets Nos. 5 and 7; Woodwind Quintet No. 3; *Scherzo* for flute, clarinet, violin, and cello; *3 Inventions* for bassoon; *Monody No. 1* for flute; *Monody No. 2* for contrabass; *6 Etudes* and *Toccata* for solo piano; and two song cycles, *2 Rilke Songs* and *13 Dickinson Songs* for voice and piano.

[2235] PALMER, Robert Moffat
TEACHER
BORN: Syracuse, N.Y., June 2, 1915

Palmer, a solid middle-of-the-road composer trained by the approved masters of his time, began writing music in adolescence and won a scholarship to the Eastman School of Music, where inevitably he studied with Howard Hanson [1927] and Bernard Rogers [1875]. He later took some lessons with Roy Harris [1947] and at Tanglewood with Aaron Copland [1986]. He has also been influenced by Bartók [1734] and his longtime friend Quincy Porter [1932], and has made frequent use of the so-called Rimsky-Korsakov [1416] scale. After three years teaching at the University of Kansas, 1940–43, he settled in at Cornell for the rest of his career. He married Alice Westcott in 1940 and has two daughters. He has written a symphony and other orchestral works but has been most effective in chamber forms. RECORDINGS: Two pieces for chamber orchestra have been recorded, *Chamber Music No. 1* and *Memorial Music,* along with a number of works for smaller forces—the Piano Quartet; Quintet for Clarinet, Piano, and Strings; *Nabuchodonosor* for choir and brasses; *Choric Song and Toccata* for wind ensemble; Sonata for Trumpet; *Carmina amoris* for soprano, clarinet, viola, and piano; *Slow, Slow, Fresh Fount* for chorus; and *3 Preludes* and Sonata No. 2 (both for solo piano).

[2236] PERSICHETTI, Vincent
PIANIST, CONDUCTOR, CRITIC
BORN: Philadelphia, June 6, 1915

The son of an Italian-born father and a German-born mother, Persichetti made up his mind to become a musician as soon as he knew what one was. Having mastered the family's player-piano, he began with a manual one at the age of five and was shortly entered at the Combs College of Music, where he got thorough training not only in keyboards and composition but also in the bass viol and the tuba. By the time he turned eleven, he was staff pianist for a local radio station. At sixteen he began twenty years as organist (and later music director) at the Arch Street Presbyterian Church. He wrote conventional music for his courses and modern music in secret. Granted his B.Mus. at Combs in 1936, he returned a year later as head of the department of theory and composition. Meanwhile, in 1937–38, he was studying conducting with Fritz Reiner at the Curtis Institute and, in 1936–39, piano with Olga Samaroff (ex-Mrs. Leopold Stokowski, *née* Lucie Hickenlooper) at the Philadelphia Conservatory. (A transcription of a Bach [684] organ piece that he played by ear at one of his lessons became his first published work.)

After studying composition with Paul Nordoff (1909–) at the conservatory, Persichetti acquired his master's degree in 1941. That same year he married pianist Dorothea Flanagan, who has been his chief pianistic apostle, his concert partner, and the mother of his two children. Persichetti then joined the faculty of the conservatory as head of the composition department. In 1943 he spent part of the summer studying with Roy Harris [1947] and heard the Philadelphia Orchestra under Eugene Ormandy play his *Fables* for narrator and orchestra. He received a doctorate from the conservatory in 1945. In 1947 the first of his 9 symphonies was premiered in Rochester by Howard Hanson [1927], and Persichetti became a member of the faculty of the Juilliard School, where he later became head of the composition department. He also served as director of publications for the Philadelphia music house of Elkan-Vogel. The list of his prestigious fellowships, honors, and commissions is much too long to detail here. Suffice it to note that his *A Lincoln Address,* commissioned for President Nixon's second inauguration, went unperformed because the President disapproved of the antiwar sentiments in the text by his Republican predecessor. Though Persichetti knows and uses up-to-date techniques, he has remained unabashedly on the side of older musical values. He has been extremely prolific in all fields but stage music.

RECORDINGS: Five symphonies have been recorded, including four for orchestra (nos. 4, 5, 8, and 9) and one for symphonic band (no. 6). Other orchestral compositions committed to disc include *The Hollow Men* for trumpet and strings (also recorded in three alternate versions for trumpet with organ or piano or band); the early *Psalm; Serenade No. 5; Introit* for strings; and the recent Concerto for English Horn and Strings (commissioned for Thomas Stacey and the New York Philharmonic). Most of his other works for band have been recorded—*Divertimento, Masquerade, 2 Chorale Preludes, Bagatelles, Pageant, Parable No. 9, So Pure the Star, O Cool Is the Valley,* and *Serenades Nos. 1, 11.* (Additional chamber and solo works recorded include *Serenades Nos. 3, 6, 10, 12; Parables Nos. 2, 3, 4, 8, 11, 14* (also for various solo instruments and combinations); *Pastoral* for wind quintet; Sonata for Solo Cello; Sonata for Organ; Concerto for Piano 4-Hands; Sonata for 2 Pianos; Sonatas Nos. 10–12 for Piano; *Serenade No. 7* for solo piano; and a couple of excerpts from *Poems* for piano. A few choral works have been re-

corded—the *Winter Cantata* for women's chorus, flute, and marimba; and two pieces for *a cappella* chorus, the *Mass* and *A Love.*

[2237] LEGLEY, Victor (Leg-lä′, Vĕk-tôr′)
VIOLIST, RADIO OFFICIAL, TEACHER
BORN: Hazebrouck, June 18, 1915

Termed (properly) a Belgian composer, Legley was, however, born just across the border in northwest France, but he grew up in war-ravaged Ypres (now Ieper), where he began his musical studies. From 1933 to 1935 he majored in viola at the Brussels Conservatory, and in 1936 he became a member of the Belgian Radio Orchestra. Having dabbled in composition for a while, he signed up with Jean Absil [1889] in 1941 and a year later turned out the first of his (at least) 6 symphonies. In 1943 he came in second in the Belgian Prix de Rome competition. After the war he became a director of the Flemish branch of the radio system and a teacher at the Brussels Conservatory. Initially a subscriber to the Central European school of dissonant polyphony, he was later won over to the *Progressiste* movement, which advocated music for the masses. His vast catalogue includes compositions in almost all standard genres. RECORDINGS: His 1944 *Suite for Orchestra,* Symphony No. 6, Concerto No. 2 for Violin, and a few chamber pieces have been recorded.

[2238] DIAMOND, David Leo
VIOLINIST, TEACHER, CONDUCTOR
BORN: Rochester, N.Y., July 9, 1915

The year 1915 produced not only a Perle [2234] but also a Diamond. He was the son of *Mitteleuropäische* Jewish immigrants—his father was a woodworker, his mother a seamstress—and knew hard poverty for much of his early life. He began "composing" in a notation of his own invention in early childhood and took up the violin in elementary school. When he was twelve, his family had to move in with relatives in Cleveland; there his training was taken in hand by a kindly violin teacher named André de Ribaupierre. The Diamonds went back to Rochester in 1929, and David was taken on as a special student at the Eastman School of Music, where he had some advice from Bernard Rogers [1875]. In 1934, the year after he finished high school, he left Eastman and went to New York where he supported himself as best he could, attended classes at the Dalcroze School and the New School, and studied with Roger Sessions

[1931]. In 1935 his *Sinfonietta* won a $2,500 prize in a contest sponsored by Paul Whiteman. At the same time a sponsor paid his expenses to go to Paris and write a ballet in collaboration with choreographer Leonid Massine. (Called *Tom,* it was completed but never produced.) He returned the next year, on her urging, to study with Nadia Boulanger and wrote the orchestral *Psalm* that won him a Juilliard Publication Award. He came back to New York and composed, surviving as a soda jerk and a radio violinist with the "Lucky Strike Hit Parade" program. Such stringencies were relieved in 1938 by the Guggenheim Foundation, which gave him a fellowship (it would do so again in 1941 and 1958) that sent him back to Paris, where he stayed until World War II erupted.

There followed such a spate of awards and commissions as prohibits specification: Diamond was clearly for the nonce the fairhaired boy of American music—a classicist who expressed feeling and whose music had a wide appeal. In 1951 a Fulbright grant took him to Italy, where he settled in Florence for the next fourteen years, save for occasional visits to the United States. Invited to attend his own fiftieth birthday celebration at the Aspen Festival in Colorado in 1965, he stayed to teach at the Manhattan School of Music. After two years he resigned and returned to Rochester, where he devoted himself to composition, occasionally appearing as lecturer and conductor. In 1973 he joined the Juilliard faculty. Extraordinarily productive all his life (he disowned reams of juvenilia) and cautiously "progressive," he suffered some eclipse during the Great Avant Garde Conspiracy.

RECORDINGS: There are a number of orchestral recordings—*Elegy in Memory of Maurice Ravel, Rounds* for string orchestra, Symphony No. 4, *Romeo and Juliet Suite, Timon of Athens: Portrait After Shakespeare,* and *The World of Paul Klee.* Chamber recordings include String Quartets Nos. 4 and 9; Quintet for Flute, Piano, and Strings; Quintet for Clarinet and Strings; Nonet for Strings; *Night Music* for accordion and strings; Sonata for Cello; piano pieces; and songs.

[2239] SEARLE, Humphrey
WRITER, TEACHER, RADIO PRODUCER
BORN: Oxford, August 26, 1915
DIED: London, May 12, 1982

Humphrey Searle was perhaps England's first important native-born adept of the twelve-tone school. Not always a musician, he graduated from Oxford in 1937 as a classi-

cist. He then spent a term at the Royal College in London with John Ireland **[1719]**, Gordon Jacob **[1911]**, and R. O. Morris (1886–1948), and a year at the New Vienna Conservatory. In Vienna he encountered Anton Webern **[1773]**, with whom he took private lessons. He returned to England a year before the outbreak of World War II and took a job with the BBC as a program producer but went into the service in 1940 and did not emerge until 1946. The end of the war found him in Germany, helping Hugh Trevor-Roper round up information on the fate of Adolf Hitler while it was still hot. After two more years with the BBC, during which he became wholly addicted to a Schoenbergian **[1657]** form of dodecaphony, he quit to concentrate on composing and writing on music. The most important products of this interim period were three big choral-orchestral works, two based on poems by Edith Sitwell *(Gold Coast Customs* and *The Shadow of Cain)* and one on material from James Joyce's *Finnegans Wake (Riverrun).* In 1952 Searle became musical adviser to the Sadler's Wells (later Royal) Ballet. In 1954 he published an authoritative study of the music of Liszt **[1218]**, with a new catalogue of the works, and the manual *Twentieth-Century Counterpoint*—both are much admired. Searle gave up his Sadler's Wells post in 1957 (the year his first wife died) but in 1964 served a year at Stanford University as composer-in-residence and then joined the teaching staff of the Royal College of Music. He left in 1976 to fulfill another residency at USC. For all his modernism, Searle is basically influenced by the Romantic, which he often leaves out in plain view; nor is he a doctrinaire twelve-toner. Besides the works noted, he wrote 5 symphonies—between 1953 and 1964—and much else in most genres. The last of his 3 operas, *Hamlet* of 1968, was perhaps the most successful, if that is the word. He also wrote an introductory book on ballet music, published in 1958. RECORDINGS: Searle is sparsely represented on records. Sir Adrian Boult performs his 1953 Symphony No. 1, hornist Barry Tuckwell his *Aubade* for horn and orchestra (with Norman Del Mar conducting), and Josef Krips conducts the Symphony No. 2 of 1958.

[2240] LEE, Dai-Keong (Lē, Dī kē'-ong)
PIANIST, CONDUCTOR, BRASS PLAYER
BORN: Honolulu, September 2, 1915

Of Chinese parentage, Lee has leaned in his compositions heavily on the music of the Pacific islands. He took up piano as a child and in adolescence played it and the trumpet in dance bands; he was also a hornist with the local symphony orchestra. He went to the University of Hawaii in 1933 under the impression that he was going to be a doctor, but after three years music got the upper hand. He came to New York in 1937 for a year of sessions with Roger Sessions [1931], then for three more studied with Frederick Jacobi [1850] at the Juilliard School and with Aaron Copland [1986] at Tanglewood. His first significant compositions—*Prelude and Hula*, 1939; and *Hawaiian Festival Overture*, 1940—attracted considerable attention and were performed by several major American orchestras. Lee's career was interrupted by wartime duty with the air force in New Guinea, 1942–45. In 1950–51 he studied with Otto Luening [1980] at Columbia University. His output has been small but includes 2 symphonies and 4 short operas. Lee is perhaps best known for the incidental music he wrote for the Broadway success *Teahouse of the August Moon* in 1953. RECORDINGS: His 1947 Symphony No. 1 and the 1959 *Polynesian Suite No. 1* have been recorded by George Barati [2203] with the Nuremburg Symphony—not with his own Honolulu Symphony as one would expect.

[2241] LILBURN, Douglas Gordon
TEACHER
BORN: Wanganui, New Zealand, November 2, 1915

The music of Douglas Lilburn, one of New Zealand's most important composers, seems to exemplify ontogeny's duplicating phylogeny. Born on the nation's North Island, he majored in literature and music at Canterbury University in Christchurch, taking the Grainger Prize for an orchestral composition in 1936. He thereupon went to England and studied for three years with Ralph Vaughan Williams [1633], (whom he rather assiduously imitated for a while) at the Royal College of Music. After the Second World War he began teaching at Victoria University in Wellington. From around 1950 to 1961 he traversed the various musical movements of the twentieth century, from neo-classicism to serialism. He then turned to electronic music and founded the first New Zealand electronic studio, at his university, around 1965. RECORDINGS: Among works recorded by the Kiwi label, the 1940 *Aotearoa Overture* and the 1962 Symphony No. 3 have been reissued domestically. Also recorded by Kiwi are the Symphony No. 2, *Concert Overture* for strings, *Canzona 1–4*, *Introduction and Allegro* for strings, *Elegy*

for two violins and strings, *3 Poems of the Sea*, a two-record set of miscellaneous chamber pieces, at least one album of electronic music, *Sings Harry* for tenor and guitar, Quartet for Brass, and scattered miscellanea.

[2242] SVIRIDOV, Georgi Vasilievich
(Svē'-rē-dôf, Gä-ôr'-gē Vä-zēl-yä'-vich)
PIANIST
BORN: Fatezh, December 16, 1915

Sviridov was born in a village in the Kursk region southwest of Moscow and from the age of fourteen attended the conservatory in the provincial capital (also Kursk). Afterward he was a pupil of Shostakovich [2094] at the Leningrad Conservatory, from which he graduated in 1941. After the war he quickly became known as both a concert pianist and as a composer. (He was one of those certified as kosher following the 1948 Zhdanov blast at Soviet musicians.) He has written chamber works and film scores (e.g., *Blizzard* and *Time Forge Ahead!*) but is best known for his vocal music. His greatest successes in Russia, which have won him honors and officerships in the national composers' union, have been mostly propagandistic —e.g., *Poem on Lenin*, *Poem to the Memory of Sergei Yesenin* (a suicide whose poems were suppressed by Stalin), and the *Pathetic Oratorio* (to inflammatory words by Mayakovsky). RECORDINGS: Soviet Melodiya is the ultimate source of most if not all recordings of Sviridov's work. We can attempt only a partial list of recordings here—(orchestral) *Small Triptych* and *Music for Chamber Orchestra;* (choral) *Kursk Songs, Wooden Russia,* and *5 Choruses;* the film score *Blizzard;* and others.

[2243] VALLERAND, Jean (Vàl-ler-rà*n*', Zhà*n*)
VIOLINIST, CONDUCTOR, CRITIC, DIPLO-MAT, TEACHER, RADIO OFFICIAL
BORN: Montreal, December 24, 1915

Vallerand began studying the violin as a child of five and undertook several years of compositional work with Claude Champagne [1852] in 1935. He served as music critic and reviewer for several French-Canadian newspapers and magazines, and taught for a time at the University of Montreal. In 1942 he became secretary of the conservatory there, relinquishing the post twenty-one years later to become director of music for the French section of Radio Canada. In 1966 he went to Paris as cultural attaché at Quebec House, returning in 1971 to become director of the Quebec Conservatory of Music. The bulk of his output was written for radio programs, but he also has a small catalogue of other pieces, including an opera and a violin concerto. He has been influenced by the French post-Romantics and the serialists. RECORDINGS: Of Canadian origin, these include orchestral works (Le Diable dans le beffroi, Prélude, and Cordes en mouvement) and chamber music (Sonata for Violin and Piano, String Quartet, and 4 Poèmes de St. Denys Garneau).

[2244] DUTILLEUX, Henri (Dü-tē-yö', On-rē')
RADIO EXECUTIVE, CONDUCTOR, TEACHER
BORN: Angers, January 22, 1916

Born in the Loire country, Dutilleux was a descendant of artists and musicians. He grew up in Douai and had his first music lessons there. In 1933 he entered the Paris Conservatoire, where his teachers included the Gallon brothers **[1856]** and the conductor-composers Henri Büsser **[1627]** and Philippe Gaubert **[1717].** He won the Grand Prix de Rome in 1938, but the outbreak of general war the next summer foreshortened his stay at the Villa Medici. In 1942–43 he was a chorus master at the Paris Opéra, then joined the French National Radio, where, from 1945 he was a chief conductor in the musical wing. A year later he married Geneviève Joy, who became well known as a concert pianist and duo-pianist; she introduced his piano sonata in 1947. In 1953 Roland Petit's production of Dutilleux's ballet Le Loup (The Wolf) won it high praise and the Prix du Portique. The second symphony was commissioned and first performed by the Boston Symphony in 1959. In 1961 Dutilleux became professor of composition at the École Normale and two years later resigned his radio job. Since 1970 he has taught at the Paris Conservatoire. As a composer Dutilleux has resisted the currents of his time and has found his roots in the music of two generations earlier. A slow and careful creator, his very small output has won disproportionate respect and admiration. RECORDINGS: Aside from numerous disowned early compositions and the 1985 Concerto for Violin, virtually all of Dutilleux's works to date have been recorded. These include the ballet Le Loup; Symphonies Nos. 1 and 2; 5 Métaboles, a cello concerto entitled Tout un monde lointain (A Whole Distant World); Timbre espace mouvement for orchestra; Ainsi la nuit (And So the Night) for string quartet; Sonata

for Oboe and Piano; Sonatine for Flute and Piano; and the Sonata for Piano.

[2245] PARROTT, Horace Ian
TEACHER, WRITER
BORN: London, March 5, 1916

English-born, Ian Parrott has become, by residence, work, and interests, a self-made Welsh composer. While prepping at Harrow he had some composition lessons. On graduating in 1932 he went to the Royal College of Music for two years before transferring to Oxford, where he received concurrent baccalaureate degrees in arts and music in 1937 and a D.Mus. in 1940. He spent the war as an officer in the signal corps in the Middle East and North Africa, then became an examiner at Trinity College, London, and a lecturer at the University of Birmingham. In 1950 he was appointed to the Gregynog Chair of Music at University College, Aberystwyth, Wales, where he remained. Something of an experimenter at first, his more recent music has been colored by his interest in Welsh music, though occasional pieces have an exotic oriental tinge. He has written operas, a ballet, 3 symphonies, concerti, and 4 string quartets, as well as other orchestral, instrumental, and choral works. RECORDINGS: His String Quartet No. 4 and Ceredigian for solo harp are recorded.

[2246] GINASTERA, Alberto Evaristo (Hē-nà-stā'-rà, Ál-bâr'-tō Ā-và-rēs'-tō)
TEACHER, ADMINISTRATOR
BORN: Buenos Aires, April 11, 1916
DIED: Geneva, June 25, 1983

Ginastera was, in the twenty-five years following World War II, the most acclaimed Latin-American composer on the international scene. He began studying piano at seven and entered Alberto Williams's conservatory in Buenos Aires at twelve. In 1936 he moved on to the National Conservatory, from which he graduated two years later summa cum laude. In the intervening year an orchestral performance of his ballet score Panambí put him on the map; the work was danced at the Teatro Colón in 1940 and drew a commission from Lincoln Kirstein for his Ballet Caravan. But by the time Ginastera completed the work—the ballet Estancia—in 1941, the company had folded, and no performance took place for eleven years. Also in 1941 the composer married pianist Mercedes de Toro, and began teaching at the National Conservatory and the Military Academy. The next year he won a Guggenheim fellowship to come to the United States, but wartime conditions prevented his traveling until 1945. Although he fell afoul of the Perón government that year, he was permitted to go anyhow, together with his wife and two children. They stayed for a year, during which the composer studied with Aaron Copland [1986] at Tanglewood and was treated to two all-Ginastera concerts. In 1948, back home and apparently forgiven, he took over direction of the National Conservatory at La Plata and organized the Argentine section of the ISCM, in whose interests he traveled repeatedly to Europe. In 1952 Perón ordered him out of his post, but he returned in 1956 after the dictator was ousted. In 1958 he left to become dean of the music school at the Catholic University and to teach at the University of La Plata. Meanwhile his music was turning away from the rather narrow nationalism of his early efforts, and he had great success in 1961 with his *Cantata para América mágica* for soprano and percussion orchestra and with his Concerto No. 1 for Piano, premiered by Hilde Somer. The next year he was made director of the Center for Advanced Musical Studies in Buenos Aires upon its inauguration and was commissioned by the city to write an opera. Called *Don Rodrigo*, it was premiered two years later and was a great success; in 1966 the New York City Opera chose it as its first production in Lincoln Center, with the young Placido Domingo in the title role. Meanwhile Ginastera was working on a second opera commissioned by the Opera Society of Washington, D.C. Called *Bomarzo* after the strange Renaissance sculpture garden near Viterbo, Italy, it won at least as much fame for its sensational libretto as it did for its musical effectiveness. Premiered in 1967, it is not to be confused with the 1964 cantata *Bomarzo,* a completely separate work. (The opera was initially banned in Buenos Aires.)

In 1969 Ginastera left his wife and, shortly afterward, Argentina; in 1971 he married Aurora Nátola, a cellist, and settled in Geneva, Switzerland. In the same year the Kennedy Center in Washington opened with his third opera, *Beatrix Cenci.* Since then he became less productive and perhaps less prominent. A fourth opera, *Barabbas,* remained unfinished at his death. Works from his final years include String Quartet No. 3 (with soprano), Concerto No. 2 for Piano, his 2 cello concerti, Symphony No. 2, and *Iubilum* for orchestra. Since the early 1960s he has espoused his own very effective form of serialism and has made use of other experimental devices, mostly in the interest of producing new sonorities.

RECORDINGS: He is well represented on records—(stage) *Panambí, Estancia,* the opera *Bomarzo;* (orchestra) *Obertura para el "Fausto" criollo (Overture to the Creole "Faust"), Ollantay, Variaciones concertantes, Pampeana No. 3* (a.k.a. *Pastoral Symphony),* Concerto for Harp; Concerti for Piano Nos. 1 and 2, Concerto for Strings (an arrangement of String Quartet No. 2), and the 1980 *Iubilum;* (chamber) String Quartets Nos. 1 and 2, Piano Quintet, *Impressiones de la Puña* for flute and string quartet, Duo for Flute and Oboe, *Pampeana No. 2* for cello and piano; (piano) Sonata No. 1 for Piano, *12 American Preludes, Danzas argentinas, 3 Pieces, Suite de danzas criollas;* (choral) *Hieremiae Prophetae lamentationes; Cantata para América mágica* for soprano and percussion; and *Milena* for soprano and orchestra.

[2247] BABBITT, Milton Byron
MATHEMATICIAN, TEACHER, THEORIST
BORN: Philadelphia, May 10, 1916

Milton Babbitt is an important pioneer in the serial movement that took hold of a large segment of the avant garde after World War II. Born, like W. C. Fields, in Philadelphia, he is no comedian, perhaps because he moved in childhood to Jackson, Mississippi. There he got his preliminary training in music and shone in mathematics. After a while he came north again, studied, innocuously enough, with Philip James (1890–1975) and Marion Bauer (1887–1955) at New York University and acquired a B.A. at the age of nineteen. He then moved on to Princeton, where he studied privately with Roger Sessions [1931]. Through the latter's recommendation he was hired to teach at the university in 1938. He married Sylvia Miller a year later. He took an M.A. there in 1942, and during the wartime crunch he was called on to teach classes in mathematics. A Webernian [1773] to begin with, he was the first to espouse "total" serial techniques, wherein each element of a composition (e.g., rhythm, dynamics, timbre, as well as tones) is set up in a sequence of twelve differing values, which may be used as is or inverted, and either way in retrograde, horizontally (melodically) or vertically (harmonically), but not until every component has been used in the sequence indicated. He was given a full professorship in 1960, in which year he spelled out his system in an article in *The Musical Quarterly.*

About this time he became interested in electronic music, largely as a more dependable means for handling his system; and in

1959, armed with a Rockefeller grant, he set up the Columbia-Princeton Electronic Music Studio, featuring the RCA Electronic Music Synthesizer. (His fellow board members were Sessions [1931], Luening [1980], and Ussachevsky [2180].) Since then he has composed chiefly electronic music or music for tape and "live" performers; he has not, however, been involved in computer music to any real extent. Babbitt has won many honors and citations. Obviously determined to live down any Lewisian connotations that might attach to his name, Babbitt declares himself firmly in favor of intellectual composition and has written much in its defense. Perhaps because rational music is easier to analyze than emotional music, and certainly because he is a splendid teacher, he has indoctrinated a sort of who's who of the young Turks of the next generation, including Lejaren Hiller [2337], Donald Martino [2393], John Heiss [2428], Thomas Putsché (1929–), Robert Ceely (1930–), David Epstein (1930–), Henry Weinberg (1931–), Peter Westergaard (1931–), Eric Salzman (1933–), John Eaton (1935–), David Ward-Steinman (1936–), and Fred Lerdahl (1943–). Besides Princeton, Babbitt has taught at Salzburg, Darmstadt, and Tanglewood. Music historians are admiring of his intentions, but most seem to agree that his music lacks any human content of the kind that makes the skin horripilate and the eyes moisten.

RECORDINGS: Works recorded include *Composition for 4 Instruments; Composition for 12 Instruments; Composition for Viola and Piano;* String Quartets Nos. 2 and 3; *All Set* for jazz combo; *Duet* for *Arie da Capo* (chamber ensemble); *Paraphrases* (winds, brass, and piano); *3 Compositions for Piano; Semisimple Variations, Partitions,* and *Post-Partitions,* all for solo piano; *Paraphrases* (winds, brass, and piano); *Reflections* (piano and tape); *Composition for Synthesizer; Ensembles for Synthesizer; Du* (soprano and piano); *Phonemena I, II* (soprano and piano, tape); *A Solo Requiem* (soprano and two pianos); *Philomel* and *Vision and Prayer* (soprano and tape).

[2248] BINKERD, Gordon
TEACHER
BORN: Lynch, Neb., May 22, 1916

After studying piano and attending South Dakota Wesleyan University, Binkerd attained a double cachet of establishment respectability by discipleship to Bernard Rogers [1875] at Eastman and Walter Piston [1890] at Harvard. In 1949 he joined the faculty of the University of Illinois at Urbana, where he was a member of the Center of Advanced Studies and chairman of his department. He retired in 1971. He enjoyed the fruits of a suitable number of fellowships, grants, and commissions. He has been identified as a "radical centrist," proving that it is possible to play the ends against the middle. He has written 3 + symphonies (he later disowned and cannibalized the fourth), a lot of choral music, and many less ambitious pieces. RECORDINGS: Symphonies Nos. 1 and 2, the choral *Ad te levavi,* Sonata for Piano, Sonata for Cello and Piano, and Sonata for Violin and Piano have been recorded.

[2249] HARDIN, Louis T. ("Moondog")
INSTRUMENTALIST
BORN: Marysville, Mass., May 26, 1916

Louis Hardin was the son of a sometime Episcopal minister who during the boy's early years tried various means of earning a living in North Carolina, Wisconsin, and Wyoming, finally settling in Hurley, Missouri, in 1929. Louis had gotten the rudiments of music from his mother and was a percussionist in the Hurley High School Band. In his mid-teens he was blinded by the explosion of a dynamite cap, and in 1933 he entered the Iowa School for the Blind, where for the next three years he learned stringed and keyboard instruments and, having mastered Braille, read voraciously in musical theory. After living in Arkansas from 1936 to 1942, he won a scholarship enabling him to continue his studies in Memphis. In 1943 he moved to New York, where he supported himself as a street musician, playing instruments of his own invention. He dubbed himself "Moondog" after a favorite canine and as such he was known by sight to millions— a tall, bearded figure swathed and hooded in coarse cloth, like some leftover Hebrew prophet. He was befriended and aided by many famous musicians, from conductor Artur Rodzinski to jazzmen like Charlie "Bird" Parker. He made a number of recordings which the catalogs classified as jazz, though Hardin did not think of himself as at home in that field. He might in fact be described as a naive contrapuntalist, his "serious" music being simplistically diatonic and rigidly adherent to "Palestrinian" counterpoint. He composes in Braille and then dictates the results to an amanuensis. In 1974 he went on a European tour, discovered (as he had suspected) that Europe was his spiritual home, and settled near Recklinghausen in West Germany. RECORDINGS: At least two classical LP discs of his more ambitious works have appeared, which include the *Mini-Sym No. 1,* three of the *Symphoniques,* the Martha Graham ballet *Witch of Endor,* the *Heimdall Fanfare* (for nine horns), *Logründr* (organ), pieces for string quartet and for piano, etc.

[2250] BRUBECK, Howard
TEACHER
BORN: Concord, Calif., July 11, 1916

One of three musical brothers, Howard Brubeck grew up on the family ranch. His most important teacher was Darius Milhaud **[1868]**. In 1950 he joined the faculty of San Diego State College, where he tried to teach counterpoint to the present writer (with more success than most). A few years later he became involved in an internal hassle in his department and left. He then went to Palomar College in La Mesa, California, where he eventually became dean of humanities. He has written a number of orchestral, choral, and chamber scores. RECORDINGS: His *Dialogues* for jazz combo and symphony orchestra has been recorded.

[2251] WEBER, Ben Brian
RECORDING EXECUTIVE
BORN: St. Louis, July 23, 1916
DIED: New York, May 9, 1979

Ben Weber was one of the first American twelve-tone composers to receive a modicum of attention a few decades back, perhaps because he made his music sound like what people had learned music sounded like. In 1934 his family packed him off to the University of Illinois at Urbana to become a doctor. He lasted a year, then transferred to De Paul University in Chicago, where he specialized in voice and piano, graduating in 1937. He seems to have had no real training in composition, having come to it by instinct. An encounter with Arnold Schoenberg **[1657]** convinced him of the dodecaphonic system's rightness—though he was not doctrinaire about it and forsook it when he wanted to. He settled in New York, worked with various recording companies, taught at the New York College of Music, and took private pupils. He held two Guggenheim fellowships, a commisson from the Ford Foundation, and other honors and awards. Though he wrote concerti for violin and piano and other orchestral works, he composed mostly in small forms. RECORDINGS: Orchestral works recorded include *Symphony on Poems of William Blake* for baritone and chamber

orchestra; *Concert-Aria After Solomon* for soprano and chamber ensemble; *Rapsodie Concertante* for viola and orchestra; *Prelude and Passacaglia; Dolmen: An Elegy;* and the Concerto for Piano. Chamber and instrumental works on records include *Serenade* for flute, oboe, cello, and harpsichord; *Consort of Winds* for wind quintet; String Quartet No. 2; *Sonata da camera* for violin and piano; and a number of works for solo piano —*Episodes; Humoreske; 3 Pieces; 5 Bagatelles; Fantasia;* and the 1978 *Variazioni quasi una fantasia.*

[2252] HUSTON, Thomas Scott, Jr.
TEACHER
BORN: Tacoma, Wash., October 10, 1916

Scott Huston came from a music-making family, learned to play the piano from his mother and other relatives, later had formal lessons, and played for school functions. After a directionless year in college (at Puget Sound), he dropped out, then committed himself in 1938 to the Eastman School of Music, where he studied with Bernard Rogers **[1875]**, Howard Hanson **[1927]**, and Burrill Phillips **[2116]**, acquiring a master's degree in 1942, the year Sir Thomas Beecham conducted the Seattle Symphony in his tone poem *Columbia.* Huston spent the next four years in the navy, then came home to teach for one year at the University of Redlands in California and for three more at the State Teachers' College in Kearney, Nebraska. He then married Natalie Maser, one of his students, and returned to Eastman for his doctorate. In 1951 he joined the faculty of the Cincinnati Conservatory where he remained, save for guest residencies at other colleges. His mature music is basically twelve-tone. He has to his credit 3 symphonies (numbered 3, 4, and 5—two earlier works in the genre having been withdrawn), several large choral works, and much chamber music, often for unusual ensembles. RECORDINGS: His *Lifestyles* for clarinet, cello, and piano; *Phenomena* for baroque quartet; *Sounds at Night* for brass choir; *Suite for Our Times* for brass sextet; and *Penta-Tholoi* for piano.

[2253] BLOMDAHL, Karl-Birger
(Blōōm'-dȧl, Kärl Bēr'-ger)
CONDUCTOR, TEACHER, RADIO OFFICIAL
BORN: Växjö, October 19, 1916
DIED: Kungsängen, June 14, 1968

Karl-Birger Blomdahl was the best-known and most influential Swedish composer of his generation. Born in the south-central part of the country, he studied violin but at eighteen went to Stockholm to become a bio-chemist. Within a year, however, he was studying composition with Hilding Rosenberg [1866] and was already composing by the time he was called up for military service in 1939. Having discharged that duty, he studied with conductor Tor Mann and embarked on a conducting career himself, which, however, he soon gave up. He also, as a composer, quickly escaped the influence of such Scandinavian monoliths as Sibelius [1575] and Nielsen [1571] and adopted Hindemith [1914] as his model. His apartment became a focus for his radical young musical compatriots—Ingvar Lidholm [2312] and Sven-Erik Bäck [2292]—who took to scheduling regular confabs there on Mondays and so became the Monday Club. Traveling in Europe in the middle of the decade, Blomdahl discovered Bartók [1734], Stravinsky [1748], and eventually twelve-tone music. In 1947 he became secretary of the Swedish section of the ISCM, which his group quickly came to control. In 1950 he finished the work generally considered to mark his musical coming of age, his third and last symphony, subtitled "Facets," which shows a judicious mixture of classical formalism, twelve-tone techniques, and Bartókian rhythms—but the composer remained an eclectic who adapted whatever he needed, old or new, to his own ends. From 1956 until his death, he worked with the Swedish Radio, winding up as its music director. He began a successful private career as a teacher in the late 1940s—one of his pupils was Allan Petterson [2178]—and taught at the Royal Academy from 1960 to 1964. By all odds his most successful (or notorious) work was his first opera Aniara, 1959, with a libretto by Erik Lindegren after the popular book-length poem by Harry Martinson. Widely hailed as "the first space opera," it deals with the last doomed remnant of humanity adrift in a spaceship operated by a dying computer that "sings arias" composed on electonic tape. It had considerable currency for a time and is revived periodically in Sweden. Rudolf Bing even considered producing it at the Metropolitan Opera but evidently thought better of it. Later Blomdahl helped set up Sweden's first electronic music studio, in which he composed Altisonans, his last completed work. At the time of his death (at fifty-one) he was working on another quasi-electronic opera, The Saga of the Great Computer. His output included the chamber opera Herr von Hancken, several ballets, music for stage, screen, and radio, orchestral, instrumental, and vocal works. RECORDINGS: There are two recordings of the opera Aniara, one by Werner Janssen and one by Stig Westerberg. Other recordings include ballet suites from Sisyphos and Spel för åtta (Game for Eight); Symphonies Nos. 2 and 3; Chamber Concerto for Piano, Winds, and Percussion; Prelude and Allegro for strings; Forma Ferritonans for orchestra; Dance Suite No. 2 for clarinet, cello, and percussion; Suite for Cello and Piano; Little Suite for bassoon and piano; Trio for Clarinet, Cello, and Piano; I spleglarnas sal (In the Hall of Mirrors), cantata to poems of Erik Lindegren; 5 Italian Songs for voice and piano; Altisonans (electronic); and Resan i denna natt (Voyage of This Night) for soprano and orchestra.

[2254] PAPINEAU-COUTURE, Jean (Pà-pē-nō′ Koō-tür′, Zhàn)
TEACHER, ADMINISTRATOR
BORN: Montreal, November 12, 1916

Papineau-Couture studied piano with his mother, with Claire Laurendeau, and then for some time with Françoise d'Amour (whom he insisted on calling "ma maîtresse d'amour"); she also provided him with the basics of theory and music history. He got a general education at the Collège St. Ignace and the Collège Brébeuf (where he began composing) and had further training in piano and theory with Léo-Pol Morin and Gabriel Cusson. In 1940 he went to Boston and studied at first with Quincy Porter [1932] at the New England Conservatory, and then with Nadia Boulanger, at the Longy School in Cambridge, Massachusetts, and later in California. In 1945 he came home to teach piano at the Collège Brébeuf. He was active in many musical organizations and in 1966 founded the Society for Contemporary Music in Quebec, over which he presided for seven years. During the last five years of this period, he was dean of the music faculty at the University of Montreal. An eclectic, he has experimented with many techniques, both ancient and modern. He has written a number of puppet operas, orchestral and concerted works, vocal music, and a considerable amount for chamber ensembles. RECORDINGS: Canadian performers have done the Pièce concertante No. 1 for piano and orchestra, Concerto Grosso, Concerto for Piano, Psalm 150, String Quartets Nos. 1 and 2, piano pieces, and songs (including notably the song cycle Quatrains).

[2255] BUCCHI, Valentino (Bōōk'-kē, Và-len-tē'-nō)
CRITIC, TEACHER, ADMINISTRATOR
BORN: Florence, November 29, 1916
DIED: Rome, May 9, 1976

A student of Dallapiccola **[2049]**, Bucchi took a degree in philosophy from the University of Florence in 1944 and then for a time wrote reviews for local newspapers. In 1945 he joined the staff of the Florence Conservatory, where he remained until 1957, save for a two-year break in which he taught at the Venice Conservatory. He then taught for a year in Perugia, headed the Philharmonic Academy in Rome for two more, directed the Teatro Comunale in Bologna, and spent his last seven years as an official of Rome Radio. He wrote several operas (and also did performing editions of early musicodramatic pieces), ballets, orchestral, and chamber works. RECORDINGS: His *Concerto lirico* for violin and strings has been recorded.

[2256] EDER, Helmut (Ā'-der, Hel'-moot)
TEACHER
BORN: Linz, December 26, 1916

After studying in Linz's Bruckner Conservatory, Eder soldiered in the Nazi armies in World War II. After that was over, he studied in Munich with Carl Orff **[1912]** and in Stuttgart with Johann Nepomuk David **[1917]**. He returned to the Bruckner Academy in 1950 where he went through a far-out phase, even going so far as to provide Linz with an electronic music studio. In 1967 he was appointed to the faculty at the Mozarteum in Salzburg. He has written 4 operas (one for television), 3 ballets, 3 symphonies, other orchestral works, chamber music, choruses, and songs. RECORDINGS: Several works—Symphony No. 3 for Strings; Double Concerto for Cello, Double Bass, and Orchestra; and Sonatina for Flute and Piano—have been committed to disc.

[2257] KAY, Ulysses Simpson
TEACHER
BORN: Tucson, Ariz., January 7, 1917

Ulysses Kay is almost certainly the first considerable black composer to come out of Tucson. His father, a sometime jockey and cowboy, had settled there as a barber. His mother sang in a choir, a sister played the piano, and a brother the violin. The most notable musical member of the family however, was Kay's maternal uncle, the great

jazzman King Oliver, who insisted the boy get a thorough grounding in piano. Later he learned the violin and the saxophone and participated in music groups in his high school. In 1938 he took a B.Mus. at the University of Arizona, then acquired a master's degree at the Eastman School of Music under Bernard Rogers **[1875]** and Howard Hanson **[1927]**. There ensued a course of study with Paul Hindemith **[1914]** at Tanglewood and Yale. In 1942 he went into service as a bandsman in the U.S. Navy, where he became expert in flute. In 1944 the New York Philharmonic performed his *Of New Horizons,* and in annual succession he won an Alice M. Ditson fellowship, an ABC prize, the Gershwin Memorial Competition, a Rosenwald fellowship, the American Prix de Rome, and a Fulbright fellowship. Returning from Rome in 1952 he became a consultant to BMI. In the mid-1960s he took up teaching—at Boston University, UCLA, and in 1968 at the Herbert Lehman College of New York's City University. In 1965 the American government sent him to Russia on the first cultural exchange of composers between the two nations. Kay has enjoyed many commissions and holds five honorary doctorates. His easily accessible music includes 4 operas and many orchestral and chamber works. RECORDINGS: Works recorded include numerous orchestral pieces —*6 Dances* for strings, Concerto for Orchestra, *Fantasy Variations, Short Overture, Markings, Round Dance and Polka, Umbrian Scenes, Sinfonia in E,* and *Serenade* for orchestra—as well as the Brass Quartet, *Choral Triptych,* and part-songs.

[2258] MORAWETZ, Oscar
TEACHER
BORN: Svetla, January 17, 1917

Morawetz' parents moved downriver to Prague when he was nine. There he learned piano and studied with Křička **[1752]** at the university for a time. After the Nazi invasion he fled to Paris, then to Italy, then to the Dominican Republic, and finally to Toronto, where he was reunited with his parents. He completed his education (through a D.Mus.) at the University of Toronto, while teaching at the Royal Conservatory of Music and has been on the university faculty since 1951. Basically a romantic, he is extremely prolific, especially in orchestral and chamber forms and vocal works and is one of Canada's best-known and most-admired composers. RECORDINGS: His works have been primarily recorded on Canadian labels. These include the *Sinfonietta* for winds and percussion; Concerto No. 1 for Piano; Duo for Violin and Piano; Sonata for Violin and Piano; Trio for Flute, Oboe, and Harpsichord; *Fantasy in D Minor* and other piano pieces; and songs.

[2259] MCCAULEY, William
TEACHER, CONDUCTOR
BORN: Tofield, February 14, 1917

Born in a lakeside village near Edmonton, Alberta, McCauley studied piano, then migrated to Toronto at nineteen, where he found work playing in various hotel and concert orchestras. After studying trombone, he joined the RCAF and served as an assistant bandmaster for the duration of World War II. Then for two years he was a pupil of Healey Willan (1880–1968) at the Toronto Conservatory. On obtaining his B.Mus. he served for two more years as music director at the Ottawa Technical High School and played in the Ottawa Philharmonic. In 1949 he was employed by Crawley Films, for whom he composed and conducted around 100 film scores. In 1954 he founded the choir that bears his name and in 1960 took a doctorate at the Eastman School of Music, where he had studied with Hanson **[1927]**, Rogers **[1875]**, and (surprise!) Hovhaness **[2170]**. Since then he has been successively musical director at the O'Keefe Center in Toronto, York University, and Seneca College. His music (for orchestra, band, chorus, chamber groups, etc.) is light, unpretentious, and amusing. RECORDINGS: His 1958 composition *5 Miniatures for Flute and Strings* has been recorded twice, by Howard Hanson and by the composer.

[2260] GARDNER, John Linton
PIANIST, TEACHER, CONDUCTOR
BORN: Manchester, March 2, 1917

John Linton Gardner is not to be confused with the English conductor John Eliot Gardiner, who is of a later generation. Gardner had a public school education, during which note was taken of his musical talent, and entered Exeter College, Oxford, on a musical scholarship. He distinguished himself in the musical life there and on graduating four years later went on to teach music at Repton School. The war intervened, and a year later he—like Peter Racine Fricker **[2305]**, with whose life Gardner's has certain parallels—joined the RAF. He was a military bandmaster for a time but spent the last two years of combat as a navigator on a bomber. In 1946 he joined the Royal Opera as re-

hearsal director and assistant conductor. His first symphony caused a stir at the Cheltenham Festival (England's annual contemporary music bash) in 1951. In 1952 he left the Royal Opera to teach (as did Fricker) at Morley College. Unlike Fricker, Gardner seemed to thrive on a heavy workload and that same year produced another piece *(Variations on a Waltz of Nielsen)* for Cheltenham, the *Cantiones Sacrae* for the Three Choirs Festival, and a ballet, *Reflection,* for Sadlers Wells. In 1956 he added to his obligations those of teaching at the Royal College of Music and the following year turned out his first and most successful opera, *The Moon and Sixpence.* In 1962, in addition, he became a successor of Gustav Holst **[1658]** at St. Paul's Girls School. When Fricker left for America in 1965, Gardner succeeded him as director at Morley College. In recent years he has turned increasingly to vocal music, adding four more operas to his list and a number of important choral pieces. Gardner is an enthusiastic jazz pianist and is quite unashamed to add jazz and pop elements to his music, which he aims at a general audience. RECORDINGS: The choral works *A Latter Day Athenian Speaks, A Shout,* and *Nearer My God to Thee,* and the *Theme and Variations* for brass have been recorded.

[2261] ERICKSON, Robert
TEACHER
BORN: Marquette, Mich., March 7, 1917

Various accounts of Erickson's career insist that he has or has not followed the serial path, though the opinion that he was one of the earlier native-born composers to do so seems the more accurate. In any case, he seems to have moved out of the strictly serial orbit in recent years. He grew up in a musical household, and attended the Chicago Conservatory. When he was nineteen, he met Ernst Krenek **[1984]** in that city and later became his disciple at Hamline University; for a considerable time he espoused Krenek's brand of contrapuntalism. He took an M.A. in 1947 and taught for a time in St. Paul at St. Catherine College. Then he was chief of theory and composition at the San Francisco Conservatory. During the latter period he studied for a term with Roger Sessions **[1931]** in Berkeley, California. In 1967 he accepted an appointment as professor of music at the University of California at San Diego. He has used electronic techniques, and some of his more recent pieces, in the nature of "happenings," have a decidedly comic flair. RECORDINGS: The serial *Cham-*

ber Concerto; The End of the Mime of Mick, Nick, and the Maggies (choral); Oceans (trumpet and tape); Ricercar a 3 (contrabass and two recorded contrabasses); Ricercar a 5 (trombone and four recorded trombones); General Speech (solo trombonist, proclaiming a speech by Douglas MacArthur through his instrument); The Idea of Order at Key West (soprano and chamber ensemble); Night Music (trumpet and chamber ensemble); Pacific Sirens (chamber ensemble and tape); and End of the Mime (chamber ensemble).

[2262] BOYDELL, Brian
TEACHER, CONDUCTOR, LECTURER
BORN: Dublin, March 17, 1917

Brian Boydell, although born on St. Patrick's Day, has proved something of an anomaly in Irish music in that he has eschewed the Thomas Moore [1093] approach of arranging national melodies so that their identity cannot be mistaken. He seems to have crowded an inordinate amount of education into a brief span: before taking a B.Mus. at the University of Dublin when he was twenty-five, he attended Rugby, the Institute of Evangelical Church Music in Heidelberg, Cambridge University, the Royal College of Music, and the Royal Irish Academy. Around the time of his graduation he took over the conductorship of the Dublin Orchestral Players. Beginning in 1944 he taught voice at the Royal Irish Academy, and he has been a regular and popular lecturer on radio and in other educational institutions, especially in the presentation of music to young people. He has also conducted radio concerts, both in Ireland and in Canada. His music often tends to modality and an artfully antique flavor. RECORDINGS: His orchestral Megalithic Ritual Dances have been recorded by Milan Horvat.

[2263] LIPATTI, Dinu (né Constantin)
(Lē-pàt'-tē, Dē'-noͦo)
PIANIST, TEACHER
BORN: Bucharest, March 19, 1917
DIED: Geneva, December 2, 1950

Dinu Lipatti's progress toward one of the most brilliant pianistic careers in musical history was cut short by his early death. The son of musical parents (his father had studied violin with Pablo de Sarasate [1415]), he was already playing and making up little pieces by the time he was five. In due course he was enrolled in the Bucharest Conservatory where he studied piano with the aptly

named Florica Musicescu and composition with Mihail Jora (1891–1971), a pupil of Max Reger [1637] and Florent Schmitt [1615]. He graduated at fifteen, entered the international competition at Vienna in 1934, where he took second prize for performance and an honorable mention for composition, and then went on to Paris to study with Alfred Cortot, Charles Munch, Nadia Boulanger, and Paul Dukas [1574], who said he had nothing to teach Lipatti. Lipatti made his first recording about this time as Boulanger's piano partner in the Brahms Liebeslieder Walzer; he was identified on the label as "Dina" Lipatti. In 1939 he returned to Rumania, where he married the pianist Madeleine Cantacuzene. Trapped there by the war, they managed to escape in 1943—first to Sweden and then to Switzerland, where Lipatti was given a professorship at the Geneva Conservatory. After the war he resumed his concert career but shortly was found to be suffering from leukemia. His life was prolonged for a time by cortisone treatments (then hideously expensive, but paid for by innumerable musicians and other well-wishers). He was able to make some appearances and to record. He was too weak to complete his last recording session (the Chopin waltzes, of which one had to be omitted) and was thirty-three when he died. He wrote a handful of attractive neo-classical compositions. RECORDINGS: Other performers have recorded three of his works—Concertino in Classic Style for piano and orchestra, Rumanian Dances, and Sonatina for the Left Hand. In addition Lipatti left radio tapes of his performances of the first and third that have been issued on disc.

[2264] YARDUMIAN, Richard
CHOIRMASTER
BORN: Philadelphia, Pa., April 5, 1917

Richard Yardumian was the tenth and last child of an Armenian-born clergyman who had fled the persecutions in 1906. Mrs. Yardumian played the organ and an older son, Elijah, studied piano at the Curtis Institute. In adolescence Richard taught himself piano and composing; by the time he was twenty, he had completed most of his Armenian Suite for orchestra. At that time he joined the Swedenborgian church in suburban Bryn Athyn, married Ruth Seckleman (an assistant of Leopold Stokowski, who had encouraged his musical efforts), and settled down there to rear thirteen children, teach piano, and direct the music at the church. Between 1939 and 1942 he had some lessons, both practical and theoretical, with local musicians. He spent the war years in the army, part of the time in the Philippines. In 1945 Eugene Ormandy conducted his *Desolate City* at a Philadelphia Orchestra concert, inaugurating a close partnership that would account for the premieres of most of Yardumian's major works for the next twenty years. Though the composer has been to some degree inspired by Armenian music, he has worked out a twelve-tone system of his own based on alternating "white-key" and "black-key" intervals of a third. A theme from his *Armenian Suite* has been used as a signature for Voice of America news broadcasts. RECORDINGS: Mostly conducted by Ormandy, these include the orchestral *Armenian Suite;* Symphonies Nos. 1 and 2; *Cantus Animae et Cordis;* Concerto for Violin; *Passacaglia, Recitatives, and Fugue* for piano and orchestra; and *Chorale-Prelude.* The vocal-orchestral *Mass "Come, Creator Spirit"* and *Psalm CXXX* have also been recorded.

[2265] BAINES, Francis Athelstan
CONTRABASSIST, OLD INSTRUMENT
   PLAYER, TEACHER
BORN: Oxford, April 11, 1917

Francis Baines is unrelated to composer William Baines [1964] but is the brother of bassoonist-conductor-scholar Anthony Baines. He graduated from the Royal College of Music and was in military service from 1939 to 1945. In 1947 he joined the London Philharmonic Orchestra as a contrabass player, and was first bassist in the Boyd Neel Orchestra from 1949 to 1951. Afterward he turned to early instruments and became a first-rate viol player as well as an adept of the hurdy-gurdy and the bagpipe; he turns up regularly on records of medieval and Renaissance music. He has lectured and taught at various schools and is on the staff of the Royal College of Music. He has composed film scores, a trumpet concerto, and a good deal of chamber music but in this capacity is best known for his spoofs for the Hoffnung Festivals (inaugurated by the late cartoonist Gerard Hoffnung). RECORDINGS: Some of his Hoffnung Festival pieces have been recorded.

[2266] HARRISON, Lou Silver
TEACHER, DANCER, PIANIST, FLORIST,
   PLAYWRIGHT, CRITIC, POET, SCULP-
   TOR, ETC.
BORN: Portland, Ore., May 14, 1917

It is difficult to sort out the innumerable manifestations of Harrison's fragmented career—or to pigeonhole him as a composer. His two most important teachers were Henry Cowell [1934] in San Francisco and Arnold Schoenberg [1657] in Los Angeles, though he apparently gained much of his knowledge in the San Francisco Public Library. Himself a dancer, he worked as an accompanist for dance classes at Mills College in his early twenties, and it was in the California years that he came to know John Cage [2192], with whom he collaborated on a few pieces. In 1943 Harrison went to New York and became from 1945 to 1948 one of Virgil Thomson's [1928] stable of composer-critics at the New York *Herald Tribune.* At various interims he worked in a flower shop, copied music, and free-lanced as a reviewer. He was among the first to call attention to such Grand Old Mavericks of American music as Ives [1659] and Ruggles [1684]. He edited several of the former's pieces and in 1946 conducted what is said to have been the first performance of Ives's third symphony; he published a monograph on Ruggles. Harrison has also taught from time to time at the iconoclastic Black Mountain College in North Carolina and the Greenwich House School in New York, and most recently at San José State College. A tireless dabbler in the arts, he has written poetry and plays, constructed musical instruments of his own devising, and sculpted (if that is the word) mobiles. He has also set forth some advanced musical theory and invented a direct-to-disc method of musical composition. He is an ardent proponent of Esperanto, which he speaks and writes fluently. Though (expectably for a Schoenberg pupil) he went through a serial phase, his more characteristic pieces reflect medieval and oriental influences. He has written a good deal for percussion, often using odd and homely sound sources and sometimes influenced by Harry Partch [1998]. Harrison is generally admired by his contemporaries, though one seems to detect a common what-have-we-here attitude when he is rather apologetically termed "a marginal figure." RECORDINGS: *Symphony on G; Elegiac Symphony; Pacifika Rondo; Suite for Symphonic Strings; Suite for Violin, Piano, and Small Orchestra;* Concerto for Organ and Percussion; Concerto for Violin and Percussion; Concerto for Flute and Percussion *Canticles No. 1* and *No. 3* for percussion; *Song of Quetzelcoatl* for percussion; *Concerto in slendro* for celeste, two prepared pianos, and percussion; *Fugue for Percussion; Suite for Percussion; Double Music* for percussion (a collaboration with Cage); *Gending Pak Chokro* for gamelan ensemble; incidental music to Yeats's *The Only Jealousy of Emer* for flute, cello, celesta, prepared piano, and string bass; *4 Strict Songs* for eight baritones and orchestra, to Navaho texts; *4 Pieces for Harp; 2 Pieces for Psaltery; Suite for Cello and Harp; Mass* for chorus, trumpet, harp, and strings; *Main Bersama-Sama* for gamelan and French horn; *Threnody for Carlos Chávez* for gamelan and viola; *Serenade* for gamelan and suling; *String Quartet Set;* guitar pieces; *At the Tomb of Charles Ives,* a brief work for chamber ensemble based on ancient Tibetan music; Double Concerto for Violin and Cello with Javanese Gamelan; and the Trio for Violin, Viola, and Cello. (There are also rumors of an impending recording of the recent Symphony No. 3.)

[2267] LAURO, Antonio
GUITARIST
BORN: Cuidad Bolívar, August 3, 1917

Lauro is a product of the Caracas Conservatory, where he studied guitar with Raul Borges. Though he has written orchestral and choral works (and a guitar concerto), his best-known product is his guitar pieces. RECORDINGS: Some of his guitar works have been recorded.

[2268] CORDERO, Roque (Côr-dâ'-rō, Rō'-kā)
CONDUCTOR, TEACHER
BORN: Panama City, August 16, 1917

In his pioneering 1945 survey, *Music in Latin America,* Nicolas Slonimsky **[1893]** was able to find a scratch assortment of seven composers in Panama, of whom only Cordero had written anything beyond the popular level. There is little question now that his name leads all the rest. He studied several instruments in his youth and devoted his creative energies to the usual dance pieces. At seventeen he turned serious and at twenty-one found himself director of the Symphony of the Union Musical, with a *Capriccio interiorano* for band to his credit. Later he played viola in the country's national orchestra. In 1943 he won a scholarship that took him to Hamline University in St. Paul, Minnesota, to study with Ernest Krenek **[1984]**, where he was later supported by Dimitri Mitropoulos. During the latter part of his stay, he served as director of the Institute of Latin-American Studies at the University of Minnesota. He also studied conducting with Stanley Chapple at Tanglewood. In 1950 he returned to Panama to teach composition at the National Institute of Music, where he was director from 1953 to 1964, as well as chief conductor of the Orquesta Sinfónica Nacional. In 1966 he came back to the United States as assistant director of the Latin-American Music Center at Indiana University and adviser to two major publishers (Peer International and Southern Music). Most recently he has taught at Illinois State University. He has been the recipient of a number of fellowships, awards, commissions, and honorary degrees. He was one of the first to be included in the Columbia series of recordings of black composers. His music inclines toward the twelve-tonal. RECORDINGS: *8 Miniatures* for orchestra, 1948; Quintet for Flute, Clarinet, and Strings, 1949; Symphony No. 2, 1956; and *Duo 1954* (two pianos); and Concerto for Violin, 1962.

[2269] WARD, Robert Eugene
CONDUCTOR, TEACHER, EDITOR
BORN: Cleveland, September 13, 1917

Robert Ward is a solid Eastman-trained, nationalistically oriented composer whose earlier acclaim has been somewhat muted by a decrease in production and the temporary triumph of a wilder sort of musical establishment. The son of the owner of a moving-and-storage firm, he had an unexceptional childhood, taking up piano in his mid-teens. Attending the Eastman School of Music from 1935 to 1939, he studied with Rogers **[1875]** and Hanson **[1927]**, the latter of whom premiered several of his student works with the orchestra. He spent the next two years at the Juilliard School acquiring an M.A.; his teachers included Frederick Jacobi **[1850]** and Bernard Wagenaar (1894–1971)—and Aaron Copland **[1986]** at Tanglewood in the summer of 1941. Shortly before leaving Juilliard, he conducted the premiere of his first symphony, which won a Juilliard Publication Award. He also taught at Queens College in 1940–41. During four years in the army, the later ones spent in the Pacific, he wrote, produced, and acted in a revue, *The Life of Riley,* and became a divisional bandmaster. He married Mary Benedict in 1944. Mustered out early in 1946, he completed his degree that spring and remained on the Juilliard faculty for a decade. During that period he also taught for two years at Columbia University, directed the East Third Street Music Settlement School for three, and conducted the Doctors' Orchestra for six. During this period he held fellowships from the National Institute of Arts and Letters and the Guggenheim Foundation, and completed three more of his 5 symphonies.

May 1956 saw the premiere of his first opera, *Pantaloon,* at Columbia University; in the same year he left Juilliard to become vice president and managing editor of the Galaxy Music Company and the Highgate Press. In 1959 the New York City Opera produced *Pantaloon* under the name of its source play, Leonid Andreyev's *He Who Gets Slapped;* the reviews were favorable, the audiences minimal. His next opera, *The Crucible* (after Arthur Miller's play), fared better. Written on a Ford Foundation grant, it was premiered in 1962 by the City Opera to great applause, took both the Pulitzer and New York Critics' Circle Prizes, and has enjoyed occasional performances since, both here and abroad. *The Lady from Colorado,* written for the 1964 Central City Festival, was at least a local success. In 1967 Ward left New York to become chancellor of the North Carolina School of the Arts in Winston-Salem for eight years—a post that seems to have interfered with his productivity. He continued to teach there for two more years and is now on the faculty of Duke University. His fourth opera, *Claudia Legare,* commissioned by the New York City Opera and completed in 1977, has so far not been produced by that company. A fifth opera, *Abelard and Heloise,* appeared in 1980. In June 1982 a sixth opera, *Minutes to Midnight,* concerning the imminence of nuclear war, was premiered by the Greater Miami Opera Company to generally unfavorable reviews.

RECORDINGS: His opera *The Crucible* has been recorded, as have numerous orchestral pieces—Symphonies Nos. 1–3, *Jubilation Overture, Festive Ode, Adagio and Allegro, Divertimento, Euphony, Prairie Overture,* and the Concerto for Piano. Other works on disc include String Quartet No. 1, Sonata No. 1 for Violin and Piano, *Arioso and Tarantelle* for cello and piano, *Fantasia* for brass choir and timpani, and two vocal-orchestral works—*Hush'd Be the Camps Today* and *Sacred Songs for Pantheists.*

[2270] ARNELL, Richard Anthony Sayer
CONDUCTOR, TEACHER
BORN: London, September 15, 1917

Following a public school education, Richard Arnell studied at the Royal College of Music for three years with John Ireland [1719]. In 1939, the year after he had finished there, he came to New York, where he found a publisher for his compositions. In 1943 he was appointed music consultant to the American offices of the BBC and in 1945–46 was conductor of the ILGWU Chorus. He supplied a brass *Prelude and Flourish* for a Winston Churchill visit to Columbia University in 1946. His music caught the fancy of a fellow expatriate, Sir Thomas Beecham, who included some of it in his programs. In 1947 the Ballet Society commissioned from him a work called *Punch and the Child.* He returned to England at the end of that year and was appointed professor of composition at Trinity College, London, in 1948. He later wrote a one-act opera and two more ballets, as well as works for television and "multi-media." Despite such excursions, Arnell is a conservative who has come down flatly against "organized noise." He left Trinity in 1964. Since then he has been a visiting professor at Bowdoin in 1969 and Hofstra in 1970. RECORDINGS: Ballet suites from *Punch and the Child* and *The Great Detective* and the *Serenade* for ten winds and contrabass are on records.

[2271] YUN, Isang (Yoon, Ē'-sàng)
TEACHER
BORN: Tongyong, September 17, 1917

The usual twentieth-century composer biography follows an almost invariable pattern: he acquired one to three degrees, joined a faculty, won several fellowships, and retired at sixty five. Isang Yun's is decidedly atypical, if not especially enviable. The eldest son of Korean poet Ki-hyon Yun, he trained for a commercial career in his native country, then at the Osaka Conservatory as a cello student, and ultimately in Tokyo with the Paris-trained composer Tomojirō Ikenouchi (1906–). In 1943 he was jailed for his work with the Korean anti-Japanese forces, escaped, and spent the rest of the war dodging his pursuers. Afterward he taught high school music in his hometown and in Pusan. In 1950 he married a colleague, Sooja Lee. At the conclusion of the Korean War three years later, Yun was made professor of composition in the University of Seoul, where he wrote a kind of conservative westernized Korean music that he later disowned. In 1956 he went to Paris to study on a government fellowship, taking his wife with him. He remained to imbibe the heady liquor of the avant-garde in Germany—notably at the Darmstadt Festivals in Berlin, where he studied with Blacher [2030] among others, and soon became known as an adept. His failure to return to Korea, which had invested money in him, did not sit well with President Park. The Yuns were declared Communist traitors, kidnaped by Korean Intelligence agents in 1967, dragged back to

Seoul, tried, found guilty, and imprisoned—he for life. International cries of outrage, however, forced the Korean government to reverse itself. In 1969 it released the Yuns and returned them to Germany, where he has since taught at the Hannover and Berlin Conservatories. RECORDINGS: Works recorded are *Loyang, Reák,* and *Fluctuations for orchestra, as well as Music for 7 Instruments, Gasa* for violin and piano, and *Toyaux sonores* for organ. The first two volumes in a series of Japanese recordings of Yun's music have recently appeared, including the Concerto for Clarinet, several short pieces, and Concerto for Violin.

[2272] ADAM, Claus
CELLIST, TEACHER
BORN: Sumatra, November 5, 1917
DIED: New York City, July 5, 1983

The son of an Austrian photographer and social scientist, Adam was born on a Sumatran plantation, but his family returned to Austria when he was six. He sang in a Salzburg choir and studied at the Mozarteum until 1931, when the Adamses moved to the United States. There he specialized in cello (studying at one time with Emanuel Feuermann), became first cellist of Leon Barzin's National Orchestral Association and then in 1940 first cellist of the Minneapolis Symphony under Dimitri Mitropoulos. Pearl Harbor put an abrupt end to that, and during the war he served in the U.S. Army Air Corps. When he was released, he settled in New York, where he studied composition with Stefan Wolpe **[2020]**. Adam was cellist of the New Music Quartet for seven years but is best known as cellist of the Juilliard Quartet, in which he played for nearly twenty years, 1955–74. He taught for many years at the Juilliard School. Despite his training, his music is eclectic. RECORDINGS: The 1973 Concerto for Cello has been recorded by Stephen Kates. Other works on disc are the Sonata for Piano (Jacob Maxin) and the String Quartet (Atlantic Quartet).

[2273] MIHÁLY, András (Mē-hàl'y', Àn'-dràsh)
CELLIST, CONDUCTOR, TEACHER
BORN: Budapest, November 7, 1917

András Mihály majored in cello at the Budapest Academy, where he took a course with Leo Weiner **[1792]**. Later he studied with a Kodály **[1760]** pupil, Pál Kadosa **[2040]**. During the war he formed his own string quartet and came increasingly under

the influence of such moderns as Hindemith **[1914]** and Bartók **[1734]**. In 1944 he was arrested and imprisoned as a Communist and freedom fighter. In the aftermath of the war, he was made first cellist and general secretary at the Budapest Opera. Shortly afterward he became a professor at the Budapest Academy. In 1968 he founded the Budapest Chamber Ensemble, dedicated to contemporary music. For a long time Bartók was the chief influence on his compositions (which range from opera to piano pieces), though recently he has experimented with some of the more advanced devices of his era. RECORDINGS: The state Hungarian recording firm has issued a fair sampling of his output, including the 1962 Symphony No. 3; Concerto for Cello; *3 Movements* for chamber ensemble; *Attila József Songs; 3 Apocrypha* for female voices, clarinet, and percussion; and the cantata *Fly, Poem!* He has also recorded (as conductor) many works of his contemporaries.

[2274] ZBINDEN, Julien-François (Z'bin'-den, Zhül-yàn Fràn-swà')
PIANIST, RADIO OFFICIAL
BORN: Rolle, November 11, 1917

Born in Canton Vaud, Switzerland, Zbinden started piano lessons at eight, attended the Lausanne Conservatory, studied piano and composition in Geneva and graduated in 1938 from the École Normale in Vaud, where he had studied voice and violin. After a career as a jazz pianist, he broke into radio as a studio manager at Radio Lausanne. There he rose in 1959 to be head of musical programming and in 1965 became joint director of Radio Suisse Romande in Geneva. His music has been influenced by the jazz idiom and often (expectably) oriented toward radio performance. RECORDINGS: His Concertino for Trumpet, Strings, and Timpani, and *Concerto da Camera* for piano and strings have been recorded.

[2275] HERVIG, Richard
TEACHER, ADMINISTRATOR
BORN: Story City, Iowa, November 24, 1917

Richard Hervig initially majored in English at Augustana College and spent his first adult years teaching that subject in high school in South Dakota. In 1941 he returned to study music at the University of Iowa with Philip Greeley Clapp (1888–1954), an old Harvard man who had also studied in Germany with Max von Schillings **[1597]**.

After teaching music for a time at Luther College and then at Long Beach State, Hervig became professor of composition and theory at the University of Iowa in 1955. He is also director of the Center for New Music there. Among his compositions are two symphonies. RECORDINGS: Several works are on disc—*Chamber Music for 6 Players,* String Quartet, Sonata No. 1 for Clarinet and Piano, and *Suite for Vibraphone/Marimba.*

[2276] EINEM, Gottfried von (Ī'-nem, Gôt'-frēt fun)
CONDUCTOR
BORN: Bern, January 24, 1918

A musician who has disavowed identification with the fashionable musical -isms (and several other aspects such as the automobile) of his time, Gottfried von Einem has been the most successful Austrian opera composer since World War II. His Swiss origins were owing to his father's having been posted to Bern as military attaché. In 1919 the family settled in Holstein in Germany. His family was highly cultured, his musical leanings were encouraged, and he was educated under the eye of Hindemith **[1914]** at the local Plön Music School. In 1938 he went to Berlin hoping to study with Hindemith who, *non grata* to the Nazis, had, however, moved to Switzerland. Einem found places as a rehearsal coach at the Berlin State Opera and the Bayreuth Festival, and a teacher in another *non grata* composer, Boris Blacher **[2030]**. His ballet *Prinzessin Turandot* was produced at the Dresden State Opera. However, he made no secret of his distaste for the Hitler government. His Concerto for Orchestra was roundly damned in the press (and in effect proscribed), and he and his mother were picked up and jailed by the Gestapo without explanation—an event reflected in his second opera, *Der Prozess (The Trial,* after Franz Kafka). Early in 1945 he managed to flee to Austria and settled in an ancient castle near Salzburg. He married Lianne von Bismarck the next year and soon after became one of the directors of the revived Salzburg Festival. There his first opera *Dantons Tod (Danton's Death)*—libretto by Blacher and the composer after Georg Büchner's nineteenth-century play—was produced to great acclaim in 1947. *Der Prozess,* with the same librettists, followed in 1953. (*Der Prozess* was successfully played by the New York City Opera that same year; the same company gave two performances of *Dantons Tod* in 1966, its first Lincoln Center season.) Of his later operas—*Der Zerrissene (The Tattered),* 1964; *Der Besuch der alten*

Dame (The Visit), 1971; and *Kabale und Liebe (Intrigue and Love),* 1976—the most successful has been the second, to a libretto by Friedrich Dürrenmatt, after his own popular play. (Blacher wrote the other two libretti.) Einem has visited the United States many times and has fulfilled commissions from the New York Philharmonic, Philadelphia, and Louisville orchestras. His wife died in 1962; he has since lived with her mother and his son in Vienna. Besides the operas he has composed a handful of ballets, orchestral, chamber, and vocal works. Some have complained that he borrows indiscriminately from other composers. *("Das ist nicht von Einem; das ist von mehreren"* ["That's not by one man—von Einem—but by several"], wrote one wit.) RECORDINGS: These include the orchestral *Philadelphia Symphony,* Concerto for Piano, *Ballade, Bruckner Dialogue, Capriccio,* and *Meditations.* Chamber works recorded include the String Quartet No. 1, Wind Quintet, and some songs. The opera *Dantons Tod* has recently been issued by German Orfeo.

[2277] WIGGLESWORTH, Frank
TEACHER, EDITOR
BORN: Boston, March 3, 1918

A great-nephew of Elizabeth Sprague Coolidge, American patroness of chamber music, Frank Wigglesworth took degrees from Bard College (in 1940 a part of Columbia University) and Converse College in South Carolina, where he also taught in 1941–42. Among his teachers were Otto Luening **[1980]** and Henry Cowell **[1934]**. After spending World War II in the U.S. Army Air Corps, he returned to New York, where he taught at Greenwich House, Columbia University, and Queens College before settling in at the New School, becoming chairman of the music department in 1965. For a time he was an assistant to Edgard Varèse **[1774]**. In the late 1940s he was a member of the board of editors of New Music Editions and New Music Recordings. Basically a neoclassicist (and a man who admits he likes a good tune), Wigglesworth has written an opera and other stage pieces, 2 symphonies, and a fair amount of other music, including a Trio for Flute, Harp, and Banjo. RECORDINGS: His Symphony No. 1 and *Lake Music* for solo flute have been recorded.

[2278] ZIMMERMANN, Bernd Alois
(Tsim'-mer-màn, Bârnt Á-lō'-ēs)
TEACHER

BORN: Bliesheim, March 20, 1918
DIED: Königsdorf, August 10, 1970

Zimmermann was born near Cologne and went to a monastery school at nearby Steinfeld. Unable to afford full-time advanced training, he did manual labor and played in dance bands while he took courses at the universities of Bonn and Cologne and at the Cologne Conservatory. He was drafted into the *Wehrmacht* and participated in the invasion of France, though he maintained he never fired a shot in the process. Hospitalized shortly thereafter, he was mustered out in 1942 and returned to school. He gave up pursuit of the doctorate, though he took further courses at Darmstadt at the end of the decade. His teachers at various times included Philipp Jarnach, the Schoenbergian René Leibowitz, and Wolfgang Fortner (1907–). He taught at Cologne University from 1950 to 1952. After a stay in Rome in 1957, he joined the staff of the Cologne Conservatory as professor of composition and of media music. (He wrote and arranged many radio scores.) Zimmermann resented having to teach because it took time away from his composition. His output was, in any case, very large. His masterpiece was his only completed opera, *Die Soldaten (The Soldiers)*, a work which often presents several actions simultaneously; after many vicissitudes, it got a Cologne premiere in 1965. Zimmermann was a musical loner, belonging to no school; his music was basically atonal and he developed a technique of quotation that he called *collage*. He was apparently of a manic-depressive tendency, periods of gloomy silence giving way to hearty exuberance—both reflected in his music. Finding himself in his latter years going irreversibly blind, he committed suicide at fifty-two. His last major work was the deeply pessimistic *I Come Again to Contemplate All the Oppression That Is Committed Under the Sun* for two narrators, bass singer, and orchestra. RECORDINGS: His opera *Die Soldaten* has been recorded, along with the Concerto for Violin; Concerto for Cello; Concerto for Oboe; the ballet *Musique pour les soupers du Roi Ubu* (after Alfred Jarry); the orchestral prelude *Photoptosis; Stille und Umkehr (Stillness and Return)* for orchestra; *Die Befristeten (The Limited)* for jazz quintet, derived from music for a radio play; *Intercommunicazione* for cello and piano; Sonata for Solo Cello; *4 Short Studies* for solo cello; *Presence* for piano trio; *Monologe* and *Perspektiven* for piano duet; and *Tratto I and II* (electronic).

[2279] ROCHBERG, George
EDITOR, TEACHER
BORN: Paterson, N.J., July 5, 1918

George Rochberg's *volta face* at the height of his career may be only one of several isolated instances of that sort of thing or may perhaps presage a general disenchantment with doctrinaire musical systems. He grew up in Passaic, N.J., where he studied piano, attempted to compose, became adept at jazz, and tried his hand at songwriting. He took a B.A. at the Montclair State Teachers' College in 1939, won a scholarship to the Mannes School in New York, and studied there with George Szell, Leopold Mannes, and Hans Weisse (1892–1940), a proponent of the Schenker system which argues that every composition is based on its own particular triad. In 1941 he married Gene Rosenfeld. The next year he went into military service, saw action in Europe, and was wounded. After being separated from the army in 1945, Rochberg enrolled at the Curtis Institute, studied there with Rosario Scalero (1870–1954) and Gian Carlo Menotti [2177]—composers who hardly pointed to the direction he was later to take—got his degree in 1947 and joined the faculty the next year. His early music during this period was eclectically modern. A Fulbright grant took him to Italy in 1950, where Luigi Dallapiccola [2049] persuaded him that the twelve-tone row was the one to hoe. On his return he was appointed editor to the Philadelphia publishing firm of Theodore Presser. His first essay in dodecaphony was a set of *Bagatelles* for piano in 1953, and he soon became one of the most enthusiastic proponents of the system. He left Curtis in 1954 and gave up his editorial post in 1960 to chair the department of music at the University of Pennsylvania.

In 1964 Rochberg's twenty-year-old son, a budding literary talent, died of a brain tumor. The father was shattered and abandoned composition for a year. In that time he decided that he could not say what he felt within the confines of serialism. The system led to a *cul-de-sac*, he found, and he told himself that it was the duty of art to affirm life, not the mechanical. Since then he has returned in considerable part to tonality, using, however, a wide variety of devices (often within a given work) ranging from the aleatory and serial to quotations from the whole range of Western music, with some forays into Eastern music. His opera after Herman Melville, *The Confidence Man*, with a libretto by his wife, was completed in 1981.

RECORDINGS: Rochberg is fairly well represented on records, especially in the area of chamber music. Orchestral recordings include *Night Music* for cello and orchestra; Symphonies Nos. 1 and 2 (of 4 to date); Concerto for Violin; and *Music for the Magic Theater* (chamber-orchestra version). Other recordings include the *Chamber Symphony* for nine instruments; *Electrikaleidoscope* for amplified ensemble; *Black Sounds* for wind ensemble; String Quartets Nos. 1–7 (No. 2 with soprano and No. 7 with baritone); *Duo concertante* for violin and cello; *Serenata d'Estate* for chamber ensemble; *Dialogues* for clarinet and piano; *La Bocca della verità* for oboe and piano; *Piano Trio*; *Contra mortem et tempus* for violin, flute, clarinet, and piano; *Caprice-Variations* for solo violin; Quintet for Piano and Strings; *Ukiyo-e: Pictures of the Floating World* for solo harp; *Ukiyo-e II: Slow Fires of Autumn* for flute and harp; *Ricordanza* for cello and piano; *Nach Bach* for harpsichord; *Bagatelles* and *Carnival Music* for piano; *Blake Songs* for soprano and ensemble; *Tableaux* for soprano and ensemble to a text by Rochberg's son; *11 Songs* for voice and piano; and *Songs in Praise of Krishna* for soprano and piano.

[2280] BRÜN, Herbert
TEACHER
BORN: Berlin, July 9, 1918

A Jew, Brün was forced to leave Germany for Palestine in 1936. He studied there with Stefan Wolpe [2020]. Later he also studied at Columbia University but returned to the new state of Israel in 1950, where he taught and lectured. After becoming interested in electronic music, he worked in various European electronic studios and in 1963 joined the faculty of the University of Illinois as an electronicist and particularly as a pioneer in the use of computers in composition. He has also taught at Ohio State. One of his chief interests is in the social significance of music. RECORDINGS: A couple of works have been recorded—*Gestures for 11* for chamber ensemble and *Futility 1964* for reader and electronics.

[2281] GALLOIS-MONTBRUN, Raymond (Gȧl-wȧ' Mon-brön', Rā-mon')
ADMINISTRATOR, VIOLINIST
BORN: Saigon, August 15, 1918

Born in Indochina, Gallois-Montbrun studied at the Paris Conservatoire with Henri Büsser [1627], Noël Gallon [1856], and Jean Gallon (1878–1959). He won the Grand Prix de Rome in 1944, and much good it did him.

For the next dozen years he pursued a concert career as a violinist on the international scene. He began composing seriously during this period, though his most significant work dates from the late 1950s. In 1957 he was appointed director of the conservatory in Versailles and in 1962 of the Paris Conservatoire. RECORDINGS: His *2 Études* for saxophone and piano have been recorded.

[2282] BERNSTEIN, Leonard
CONDUCTOR, PIANIST, LECTURER
BORN: Lawrence, Mass., August 25, 1918

A man of multifarious talents, one of those rare "serious" musicians whose name has become an American household word in his time, Leonard Bernstein is the first native-born conductor to have achieved international status. His parents settled in Massachusetts after immigrating from Russia. Their son's story was the American Dream come true. He went to the prestigious Boston Latin School, and thence to Harvard, where he was a pupil of Edward Burlingame Hill [1632] and Walter Piston [1890], the while he developed a formidable piano technique under Leschetizky pupil Heinrich Gebhard. On graduating in 1939 he entered the Curtis School in Philadelphia, where his teachers included pianist Isabelle Vengerova (another Leschetizky pupil), Fritz Reiner, and Randall Thompson [1966]. He spent his summers at Tanglewood, where he became a student and protégé of Serge Koussevitzky [1655], and eventually his assistant. When Artur Rodzinski took over the New York Philharmonic in 1943, he chose Bernstein as his second-in-command. On the fourteenth of that November, guest conductor Bruno Walter became ill, and Bernstein conducted his program to a nationwide radio audience and made history. He was immediately in demand as guest and recording conductor, and the following January he led the premiere of the first of his 3 symphonies *(Jeremiah)* with the Pittsburgh Symphony. Three months later Jerome Robbins choreographed his ballet *Fancy Free* for the Ballet Theater, and in December Bernstein had his first Broadway hit with *On the Town,* a musical developed from the ballet to a libretto by Betty Comden and Adolph Green. In 1945 he became coconductor (with Leopold Stokowski) of the recently formed and poorly supported New York City Symphony, and a year later its regular conductor until its collapse in the 1947 season. (The year 1946 brought a second Robbins-choreographed ballet, *Facsimile.)* In 1948 he returned to Tanglewood to teach for several seasons and became adviser to the Israel Philharmonic. In April 1949 Koussevitzky premiered his second symphony, *The Age of Anxiety,* inspired by poetry of W. H. Auden, with the composer handling the important piano part.

Bernstein married the beautiful Chilean actress Felicia Montealegre in 1951; she appeared in and recorded his third symphony, *Kaddish,* with him, bore him two children, and died of cancer in 1978. In 1951 too Bernstein joined the faculty of Brandeis University, where he taught until 1956. There he premiered his one-act "soap-opera," *Trouble in Tahiti* in 1952, a year that also saw the opening of the tremendously successful *Wonderful Town* on Broadway. At La Scala in Milan in 1953 he became the first American to conduct a regularly scheduled opera —Cherubini's [1019] *Medea* with Maria Callas (a performance preserved on pirated records). The next year he premiered his *Serenade* for violin, strings, and percussion, after Plato's *Symposium,* at the Venice Festival, with Isaac Stern as soloist, and provided a score for the prizewinning film *On the Waterfront.* His next musical (really an opera), *Candide,* high praise, flopped in 1956 (but, given a new book and brilliant staging, it was revived for a long run eighteen years later). *West Side Story,* a retelling of the Romeo and Juliet story in New York streetgang terms, with a book by Stephen Sondheim [2388], which opened in September of 1957, was something else—one of the most brilliant, successful, and innovative musicals in the history of the American theater and Bernstein's greatest popular success. Having served a term as coconductor with Dimitri Mitropoulos of the New York Philharmonic, Bernstein became in 1958 the second native-born American—the first was Alfred Wallenstein with the Los Angeles Philharmonic—to head a major American orchestra. Almost immediately he inaugurated a series of brilliant television lecture demonstrations with the orchestra and later that year took it on a tour of South America. During the ten years he held the post, he became arguably the best-known and certainly the most-visible conductor in America, whipped a primadonna organization into acquiescing, and even enthusiastic, coherence, and took it on several tours, both eastward and westward. During that period he also conducted at the Metropolitan Opera and with opera companies and symphonies all over the world. Understandably his activities cut into his composing, and the decade saw only the third symphony, *Kaddish,* in 1963 and the *Chichester Psalms,* a commission from Chichester Cathedral in 1965.

As a matinee idol and a figure with one foot in the pop world, "Lenny" came in for a good deal of sniping—nor did his identification with the Kennedys and others of "the beautiful people" or his "radical chic" espousal of such causes as that of the Black Panthers help his image.

In 1969 Bernstein resigned from the New York Philharmonic, ostensibly to return to composition, though he has preserved the title of conductor laureate, has frequently returned as a guest conductor, and took the organization on a bicentennial tour of Europe in 1976. Save for that odd and controversial theater piece *Mass,* written to inaugurate the Kennedy Center in Washington, D.C., in 1971 and later produced on Broadway, the return to composition has so far been neither very productive nor very propitious, having otherwise offered only the 1974 ballet *Dybbuk* (reviews disappointing), the 1976 musical *1600 Pennsylvania Avenue* (an abject failure), the brief 1977 *Slava: A Political Overture* for Rostropovich, the orchestral song cycle *Songfest* of 1978, the 1980 orchestral *Divertimento* (composed for the hundredth anniversary of the Boston Symphony), the 1981 *Halil: Nocturne* for flute and strings, and the 1983 opera *A Quiet Place* (a sequel to *Trouble in Tahiti* which was revised and grafted onto the earlier work in 1984). Response to the last several works has been only slightly more favorable. Though his music, apart from its popular manifestations, has not been highly regarded, some of it bids fair to last longer than a good many contemporaneous works by more profoundly admired composers.

RECORDINGS: With the exception of *1600 Pennsylvania Avenue, A Quiet Place,* and a few songs, virtually all of it has been preserved, mostly in composer-led performances. (Recently Bernstein has recorded *West Side Story* for Deutsche Grammophon.)

[2283] ORREGO-SALAS, Juan Antonio
(Ôr-rā'-gō Sá'-lás, Hwán Án-tōn'-yō)
ARCHITECT, TEACHER, CONDUCTOR, EDITOR, CRITIC
BORN: Santiago de Chile, January 18, 1919

Orrego-Salas is Chile's best-known composer internationally. At sixteen he obtained a baccalaureate degree in liberal arts from the Liceo Alemán. He then embarked on architectural studies at the local Catholic University and on musical training at the National Conservatory under such teachers as Domingo Santa Cruz [1969] and Pedro

Humberto Allende Sarón. In 1938 he founded the choir of the university and served as its conductor for six years, and in 1942, the year he received his architectural degree, he became professor of music history at the conservatory. A Rockefeller fellowship brought him to New York in 1944 to study musicology at Columbia with Paul Henry Láng and ethnomusicology with George Herzog. He then won a Guggenheim fellowship and studied composition with Randall Thompson [1966] at Princeton and Aaron Copland [1986] at Tanglewood. In 1946 he returned to his teaching duties in Santiago, where he also assumed various executive posts in leading musical organizations. He came back to New York in 1948 for the performance of his *Canciones castellanas* at the ISCM Festival and the following year went to Europe at the invitations of the British, French, and Italian governments. On his return to Chile he became music reviewer for the paper *El Mercurio* and editor of the *Revista musical chilena*. In 1954 he returned to the United States on a second Guggenheim fellowship. The next year he became director of the Instituto de Extensión Musical but resigned in 1957 to chair the music department at the university. In 1961 he returned to the United States once again, this time as professor of music at Indiana University and director of its Latin-American Music Center. Two years later the University of Chile awarded him the degree of profesor extraordinario de música. He also holds an honorary doctorate from the Catholic University and has enjoyed many commissions from various American foundations and performers. His compositions include an opera, a Mass, an oratorio, 3 ballets, 2 cantatas, 4 symphonies, concerti, and many other works, as well as some film scores. RECORDINGS: Works recorded include the *Canciones castellanas* (soprano and chamber orchestra); Sextet for Clarinet, Strings, and Piano; *Serenata concertante;* Symphony No. 2 (subtitled "To the Memory of a Wanderer"); and *Missa in tempore discordiae* for tenor, chorus, and orchestra (the latter an Indiana University production).

[2284] KIRCHNER, Leon
PIANIST, TEACHER
BORN: Brooklyn, January 24, 1919

Kirchner's parents, Jewish emigrés from Russia, pulled up stakes again when he was nine and settled in Los Angeles. There he had piano lessons, embarked on a medical career, and studied with Ernst Toch [1824] and Arnold Schoenberg [1657]. Persuaded

that medicine was not for him, he transferred to the University of California at Berkeley, where his teachers included Albert Elkus (1884–1962), Edward Strickland, and (privately) Ernest Bloch [1729], graduating in 1940. He made his way back to New York and took up study with Roger Sessions [1931] there, but it was broken off by the government's insistence that he become a member of the Army Signal Corps. Released after the war, he returned to California and taught variously at the San Francisco Conservatory, Berkeley, USC, and Mills College. He won a Guggenheim in 1948 and in 1949 married Gertrude Schoenberg (not to be confused with the composer's similarly named widow and daughter). After a number of other prestigious awards, Kirchner was named to the Walter Bigelow Rosen Chair of Music at Harvard (in succession to Walter Piston [1890]) in 1961. In 1967 his String Quartet No. 3 (with electronic tape) took the Pulitzer Prize. Despite his serial and twelve-tone training, Kirchner has been a strong antagonist of cerebral music, and has been praised for his own music's passion and expressiveness. He would thus seem a likely candidate for operatic success, but his one venture *Lily* (although—or perhaps because—it was based on Saul Bellow's *Henderson the Rain King)* came a cropper when it was produced by the New York City Opera in 1977. Kirchner has abjured most of his early music, and his more recent output is relatively small. RECORDINGS: Works on records include the Concerto for Piano No. 1 (with the composer as soloist); Concerto for Violin, Cello, Winds, and Percussion; *Lily* for voice and chamber orchestra, derived from sketches for the opera; *Toccata* for strings, winds, and percussion; String Quartets Nos. 1–3; Piano Trio; *Sonata concertante* for violin and piano; Duo for Violin and Piano; and the Sonata for Piano.

[2285] HAUBENSTOCK-RAMATI, Roman (Hou'-ben-shtok Rà-mä'-tē, Rō'-màn)
RADIO OFFICIAL, TEACHER, LIBRARIAN, EDITOR
BORN: Cracow, February 27, 1919

While taking a degree in philosophy at the Jagiełłonian University in Cracow, Haubenstock-Ramati studied music with composers Artur Malawski (1904–57) and Jósef Koffler (1896–1943), a Schoenberg [1657] pupil later massacred by the Nazis. He went on for graduate work in musicology, but this was broken off by the double invasion of Poland in 1939. After the war he served as music director of Radio Cracow until 1950, when he emigrated to Israel. There he taught at the Tel Aviv Academy, in which city he founded the State Music Library, whose head he was until 1956. By that time he had gotten fascinated by the doings of the avant-gardists back in Europe; and, after a brief spell working in the Musique Concrète Studio, he took a job with Universal Editions in Vienna. Since then he has been active in Europe and South America promoting more far-out manifestations of the art. His particular forte in his mature period has been "spatial" music and/or pieces susceptible of performance by indeterminate numbers of participants. He has done an operatic treatment of Kafka's *Amerika,* an antiopera *La Comédie* (for speaking voices and percussion), and some mixed-media pieces. RECORDINGS: His *Interpolation,* a "mobile" for one to three flutes, has been recorded by Severino Gazzelloni. Other recordings include *Catch I* for piano, synthesizer, and tape; *Credentials, or Think, Think Lucky* for speaker and ensemble; *Tableau I* for orchestra; and *Vermutungen über ein Dunkles Haus (Conjectures About a Dark House)* for orchestra.

[2286] FONGAARD, Björn (Foon'-gôrd, Byurn)
GUITARIST, TEACHER
BORN: Oslo, March 2, 1919

Best known outside of Norway as a representative of the extreme avant-garde, Fongaard is a product of (and producer at) the Oslo Conservatory, and of such teachers as (in alphabetical order) Karl Andersen (1903–70), Bjarne Brustad (1895–1978), Sigurd Islandsmoen, and Per Stenberg. He is also the highly prolific author of works in a much more conservative vein (e.g., 23 piano concerti, 21 string quartets, more than 200 sonatas for various instruments), but these are little known outside of Norway. A brilliant guitarist, he has used that instrument as an entree to his innumerable experiments in microtonal relationships. He may also be described as a pioneer in musical science fiction with such works as *Galaxies, Kosmos,* and *Uran 235.* RECORDINGS: Some of his more advanced works on records include *Galaxies* for three microtonally tuned guitars; *Homo sapiens* for tape; *The Space Concerto* for piano and tape; and *Sinfonia* for organ. Also recorded is the 1968 orchestral *Legende,* written in a more conservative, freely tonal idiom, and at least one of his

piano sonatas, Op. III, which falls somewhere in between: a strong work indebted somewhat to Bartók [1734].

[2287] AVSHALOMOV, Jacob
TEACHER, CONDUCTOR
BORN: Tsingtao, China, March 28, 1919

The son of composer Aaron Avshalomov [1901], Jacob Avshalomov was initially indoctrinated in music by his father, then underwent a more or less normal schooling in English and American schools. In 1934 he completed his secondary education and worked for the next few years in Tientsin and Peiping. He also won a regional diving championship. In 1937 he worked in a slaughterhouse in Shanghai and helped his father copy scores and parts in off-hours. With the Japanese invasion that year, he and his mother (a San Franciscan) came to America. Jacob studied for a year with Ernst Toch [1824] in Los Angeles, then at Reed College in Portland, and finally at the Eastman School of Music with Bernard Rogers [1875]. In 1943 he was taken into the U.S. Army and assigned first to London, then to the China desk of the OSS in Washington, where Vladimir Ussachevsky [2180] was a fellow interpreter. On being mustered out, he won an Alice M. Ditson fellowship and taught for a time at Columbia University. (Classes being then swollen by the enormous influx of GIs, Avshalomov is absolved for giving the present writer a passing grade in theory.) He also conducted the university chorus and with it gave the American premieres of several works, including Tippett's [2059] *A Child of Our Time.* His own *Tom o'Bedlam* for chorus took the New York Critics' Circle award for 1953, and in 1954 Avshalomov returned to Portland as permanent conductor of the Portland Junior Symphony (now the Portland Youth Orchestra). Since then he has also taught at Reed, the University of Washington, Northwestern, and Tanglewood. He has written eclectically in various forms, with works for chorus and/or orchestra perhaps predominating. RECORDINGS: Orchestral works on records include the *Sinfonietta,* 1946; *The Taking of T'ung Kuan,* 1948; and *Phases of the Great Land,* 1958 (the latter a tone poem celebrating the achievement of Alaskan statehood). Also recorded are the cantata *How Long, Oh Lord . . . ,* 1949; the 1948 *Prophecy* for tenor, chorus, and organ; and *Lullaby* for solo flute.

[2288] ANHALT, István (Ån'-hàlt, Isht'-vän)
CONDUCTOR, TEACHER
BORN: Budapest, April 12, 1919

Anhalt graduated in 1941 from the Royal Hungarian Academy, where he had been a Kodály [1760] pupil. Since he was Jewish, it seems miraculous that he survived the war and even more so that he was an assistant conductor at the opera house as late as 1945. In 1946 he moved to Paris, where he studied for a time with Nadia Boulanger before emigrating to Montreal on a fellowship in 1949. There he was appointed to the faculty of McGill University, and it is from this time that the bulk of his compositions date. Far more influenced by Schoenberg [1657] than by either of his teachers, he wrote for a period in the dense cerebral style then in fashion among the enlightened, but as time went on he was increasingly (as they say) into electronic music, and in 1963 he set up an electronic studio at McGill. His most recent music coordinates live sound sources with tape. He spent 1969–70 commuting to SUNY in Buffalo as Slee Visiting Professor and two years later accepted the headship of the music department at Queen's University in Kingston, Ontario. Besides electronic music, he has written a ballet, a symphony, and vocal and chamber pieces. RECORDINGS: Among recordings made by various Canadian performers may be included *Cento* (cantata for narrators, voices, and tape); *Foci* (for voices, instruments, and tape); Piano Trio; Sonata for Violin and Piano; *Fantasia* (for piano, performed by Glenn Gould); and *Electronic Compositions No. 3* and *No. 4*.

[2289] AREL, Bülent (A'-rəl, Bü'-lent)
ENGINEER, TEACHER
BORN: Istanbul, April 23, 1919

A graduate of the Ankara Conservatory, Arel served as an engineer at the Ankara radio station from 1951 to 1959 and taught music on the side. He came to America in 1961 and worked in electronic music—first at Yale and then at the Columbia-Princeton Studio, where he was a research assistant. Ten years later he became a member of the music department of SUNY at Stony Brook, New York. The history of Arel's music proceeds from the folkloric to the electronic. Though he has written 2 orchestral symphonies and the Concerto for Piano of 1946, his most recent music has been for tape and/or mixed media. RECORDINGS: Several electronic pieces have been recorded—*Stereo Electronic Music No. 1* and *No. 2, Mimiana*

I–III, and the prelude and postlude from *Sacred Service.* Instrumental or partly instrumental works recorded include *For Violin and Piano, Capriccio for T.V.* for chamber ensemble, and *Music for String Quartet and Tape.*

[2290] BENTZON, Niels Viggo (Bent'-zōn, Nēlz Vig'-gō)
PIANIST, TEACHER
BORN: Copenhagen, August 24, 1919

Related to the composing Hartmanns [1182] on his mother's side and to the more recent composer Jørgen Bentzon (1897–1951) on his father's, Niels Viggo Bentzon could hardly escape being a musician. His mother taught him piano, but then he strove to sidestep his destiny by becoming a jazzman. In 1938, however, he gave in and entered the Copenhagen Conservatory to study the instrument with Christian Christiansen. He also studied theory with Knud Jeppesen (1892–1974), performed brilliantly on all counts, and graduated in 1941. He began composing prolifically almost immediately, and by the end of the decade had completed four of his 13 symphonies, two of his 10 string quartets, three of his 7 violin sonatas, four of his 15 piano sonatas, etc. He has taught at the Copenhagen Conservatory since 1950, and performs as a pianist. The term used to describe much of his earlier music is "neo-classic" and the names of Stravinsky [1748], Hindemith [1914], Sibelius [1575], and even Shostakovitch [2094] and Britten [2215] are evoked as possible influences. Later Bentzon drifted into what he called "metamorphism," involving a constant evolution of thematic material, an approach also used by his countryman Vagn Holmboe [2145]. More recently Bentzon has been partly linked to serialism, though in all fairness, his highly imaginative approach is really *sui generis.* He has produced enormously in all forms. Among his more intriguing titles are *Die Automaten,* an opera on themes from Offenbach's *Les Contes d'Hoffmann; Monkton Blues; Meet the Danes; Suite for Foreigners;* a *Sinfonia Concertante* for six accordions and orchestra; *Suite As Far As Jazz Music Is Concerned; Feature Article on René Descartes; An Arab in Cologne; Bop Serenade; Portrait of Jean-Paul Sartre* (accordion); and *Utilized Termination of a Concert.* RECORDINGS: Orchestral works on record include the *Symphonic Variations; Pezzi sinfonici; Feature Article on René Descartes;* Symphonies Nos. 3, 4, 5, and 7; *Mobiles,* after Alexander Calder; *Sagn* (with chorus); Concerto No. 4 for Piano; and the brief Concerto No. 2 for Flute.

Other recordings include the Quartet No. 3 for Flutes; Sonatas for Piano Nos. 3–5; *The Tempered Piano,* a lengthy opus for piano solo; *Toccata, Paganini Variations,* and *Woodcuts,* all for solo piano; Sonata for 2 Pianos; Concerto for 2 Pianos (unaccompanied); Concerto for 10 Percussionists; *Mosaïque Musicale* for chamber ensemble; String Quartet No. 6; and *Chamber Concerto for 11 Instruments* (with the composer at one of the three pianos).

[2291] DELA, Maurice (Də-lá´, Mō-rēs´)
ORGANIST, ARRANGER
BORN: Montreal, September 10, 1919

Dela came to music quite late, having taken a liberal arts degree at the University of Montreal and then having studied Latin and English there and at Notre Dame University. He began studying the organ in 1940, and in 1944 he undertook a more extensive study of music, including a composition course with Claude Champagne [1852] and, later, orchestration with Leo Sowerby [1908] in Chicago. Since 1947 his pieces, which pursue a safely modern path, have won many Canadian prizes. He makes his living as organist in the Quebec town of Verdun and by writing and arranging for radio and television. He has written 2 symphonies as well as other orchestral and chamber work, plus a few choral pieces and songs. RECORDINGS: Works recorded include the *Scherzo* (orchestra); *Dans tous les cantons!* (strings); *Adagio* (strings); and songs.

[2292] BÄCK, Sven-Erik (Bâk, Sven Ā´-rik)
VIOLINIST, ADMINISTRATOR, CONDUCTOR
BORN: Stockholm, September 16, 1919

Bäck entered the Royal Academy in Stockholm as an embryo violinist in 1938 and then studied composition with Hilding Rosenberg [1866] from 1940 to 1945. He was a member of Blomdahl's [2253] Monday Group along with Ingvar Lidholm [2312]. For the next few years he was violist in the string quartet formed by his teacher Charles Barkel. In 1948 Bäck went to Switzerland to study medieval music at the Schola Cantorum in Basel. After an excursion to Italy in 1951 to do more compositional work with Goffredo Petrassi [2052], he returned to his quartet playing in Stockholm, where he also conducted a chamber orchestra. In 1959 he became director of the music school operated by the Swedish Radio. His music follows a progression typical of his times: beginning in a conservative vein, he moved through serialism to electronic music. He has written several dramatic works, including some for radio or television, plus two electronic ballet scores, and much religious music. Some of the earlier works are in standard forms—a violin concerto, quartets, sonatas. Many of the later ones have the sorts of quirky, nongeneric names fashionable with the avant-garde. RECORDINGS: Bäck conducts two of his 3 chamber operas—*Tranfjädrarna (The Crane Feathers),* based on a Japanese Noh drama; and *Fågeln (The Bird),* after a radio play by the Yugoslav writer Aleksander Obrenovič. Other works recorded include the Symphony for Strings; *Sinfonia da Camera; A Game Around a Game* for orchestra; *Kattresan (Cat Journey),* a cantata for young children; *Favola* for clarinet and percussion ensemble; String Quartets Nos. 2 and 3; *Sonata alla ricercare* for piano; and a number of choral motets. Newly released is the stark, powerful *At the Outermost Edge of the Sea* for chorus, soloists, and orchestra, coupled with the correspondingly "cool" *Signos* for percussion.

[2293] NELHÝBEL, Václav (Nel´-hē-bel, Vä´-tsläf)
RADIO OFFICIAL, CONDUCTOR, TEACHER
BORN: Polanka, Czechoslovakia, September 24, 1919

Nelhýbel studied composition with Jaroslav Řídký (1897–1956) at the Prague Conservatory and musicology at Prague University in the late 1930s and early 1940s, while working as a fledgling conductor for the national radio. In 1942 he went to Switzerland and continued his musicological studies at the University of Fribourg. After working for Swiss Radio for two or three years, he was named musical director of Radio Free Europe in Munich. In 1957 he emigrated to the United States, where he has worked at various schools. He has written operas, ballets, symphonies, and other standard forms but has won most attention for his music for band and for various unusual small instrumental combinations, particularly winds. RECORDINGS: *Étude symphonique* for orchestra; *Chorale* for brass and percussion; *Numismata* for brass septet; Concertino for Chamber Orchestra and Piano; Quartet for Horns; *2 Movements for Chamber Orchestra; 3 Movements for Strings; 3 Modes for Orchestra;* Quartet for Piano and Brass; *3 Intradas* for brass; *Quintetto concertante* for violin, trumpet, trombone, xylophone, and piano; *Slavic March* for brass; Brass Trio; *Suite for*

Trombone and Piano; Arco and Pizzicato and *3 Miniatures* for string trio; *Concertino da Camera* for cello, winds, piano, and percussion; *Auriel Variation* and *Grand Intrada and Tower Music,* both for wind ensemble; *Counterpoint No. 5* for winds; *Concerto Spirituoso No. 1* for twelve flutes, electric harpsichord, and voice; *Concerto Spirituoso No. 3* for electric violin, English horn, French horn, tuba, vibraphone, winds, voice, and percussion; *Outer Space Music* (electronic); *4 Readings from Marlowe's "Doctor Faustus";* and *The House That Jack Built* for voice and quintet. Most of these records were produced by his publisher.

[2294] KAY, Hershy
ARRANGER
BORN: Philadelphia, November 17, 1919
DIED: Danbury, Conn., December 2, 1981

Hershy Kay (no relation to his contemporary Ulysses Kay [2257]) is less well known for his original works than for his clever syntheses of other composers' works. A product of the Curtis Institute, where his composition teacher was Randall Thompson [1966], he went to work early as a New York arranger—for Leonard Bernstein [2282], among others, whose *On the Town* he scored at age twenty-five. Kay's most popular pieces are his ballet scores *Western Symphony* (on western "pop" tunes), *Stars and Stripes* (on Sousa [1482] marches), *Cakewalk* (on Gottschalk [1306] piano pieces), and *Concert* (on Chopin [1208] piano pieces). RECORDINGS: The first three works named are on records, as is his scoring of Gottschalk's *Grande Tarantelle.*

[2295] VAINBERG, Moisei Samuelovich
(Vīn'-bârg, Moy'-sā Sà-mōō-el-ō'-vich)
PIANIST
BORN: Warsaw, December 8, 1919

Born a Polish Jew, Vainberg has miraculously succeeded in winning acceptance as a leading Soviet composer, possibly because his music is neither aggressively "Jewish" nor notably "modern." His family was musical and he studied piano at the Warsaw Conservatory under Józef Turczyński, a Busoni [1577] pupil. With the Nazi invasion of Poland, he sought refuge in Russia, studied at the Minsk Conservatory under aged Balakirev [1348] pupil Vassily Zolotarev (1872–1964), and eventually settled in Moscow. After the Zhdanov purge in 1948, Vainberg was singled out as representative of what the government wanted by its mouthpiece Tikhon Khrennikov [2208] but managed to survive that apparent damnation. Quite prolific, he has produced, among many other works, at least 12 symphonies, at least 12 string quartets, operas (one on Dumas' *Three Musketeers),* ballets, and concerti. RECORDINGS: Mostly of Russian origin, these include the Concerto for Violin; Concerto for Trumpet; Symphonies Nos. 4–7; *Sinfonietta No. 1; Serenade* for orchestra; *Moldavian Rhapsody* for violin and piano; and the Sonatina for Violin and Piano. (The most recent Russian catalogue shows a sudden bareness of Vainberg recordings, whatever that may portend, though a new recording of the 1976 Symphony No. 12 ["In Memoriam Dmitri Shostakovich"] has just been made available in the West.)

[2296] KIM, Earl
TEACHER
BORN: Dinuba, Calif., January 6, 1920

Earl Kim, born to Korean parents in farm country near Fresno, studied with Schoenberg [1657] and with Roger Sessions [1931] at Berkeley, where he took an M.A. in 1952. He then joined Sessions on the Princeton faculty, remaining there until 1967, when he moved on to Harvard. He has turned out several likely young composers, including George Edwards (1943–), John Harbison (1938–), David Del Tredici [2421], and Paul Salerni. Kim's own compositions, mostly for small ensembles (and some for multimedia), generally have odd titles like *Gooseberries, She Said.* Kim is a passionate poker player. RECORDINGS: His *Earthlight* (for soprano, violin, piano, and spotlights, to a pastiche text by Samuel Beckett) has been recorded by soprano Merja Sargon and the Concerto for Violin by Itzhak Perlman.

[2297] FETLER, Paul
TEACHER
BORN: Philadelphia, February 17, 1920

Born in America but reared in Europe (Holland, Latvia, Sweden, Switzerland), Paul Fetler (not to be confused with Alvin Etler [2201]) came home at the outbreak of World War II. Thereafter he studied with David Van Vactor [2087] at Northwestern, with Paul Hindemith [1914] and Quincy Porter [1932] at Yale, and with Boris Blacher [2030] in Berlin. He has now taught for some years at the University of Minnesota, Minneapolis. Neither far out nor in deep, he has composed 4 symphonies among other works and has won a number of prizes and grants. RECORDINGS: Antal Dorati recorded his *Contrasts* for orchestra. The *Pastoral Suite* for piano trio and the cantata *Nothing But Nature* have also been recorded.

[2298] ADDISON, John
TEACHER
BORN: Cobham, March 16, 1920

Surrey-born John Addison went through a public school education with the wish to become a soldier, but at eighteen he entered the Royal College of Music. Fate, however, in the guise of World War II, granted him his original wish a year later, and he soldiered in a tank unit and was wounded at Caën in 1944. Having gotten that out of his system, he returned to the Royal College of Music in 1947 to study with Gordon Jacob [1911], winning the Sullivan Prize after a year. In 1949 he became musical director for a London film company (Boulting Brothers) and in 1950–51 scored several pictures, including the highly successful *Seven Days to Noon*. He returned to the Royal College in 1951 but gave up his post in 1958 to go back to the studios, where he found things more rewarding. He has since scored dozens of films, eventually basing himself in Hollywood, and won an Academy Award for his music to *Tom Jones* in 1963. He is also an ardent mountaineer and maintains a vacation home in the French Alps. Most of his abstract music, which is light, attractive, and witty, dates from his early period and is mostly chamber-size. RECORDINGS: Concert works on records include *Carte Blanche* (ballet suite), Concerto for Trumpet, and *Divertimento No. 9* for brass quintet. More than half a dozen film soundtracks have also been released.

[2299] LA MONTAINE, John
PIANIST, TEACHER
BORN: Oak Park, Ill., March 17, 1920

John La Montaine's mother was a parlor pianist. He himself took up the instrument in early childhood and studied it intensively for twenty years, making his solo debut at the age of eleven. (But he never seriously attempted a concert career, though he may be heard on records playing some of his own music.) At fifteen he entered the American Conservatory in Chicago, at eighteen the Eastman School of Music, where his composition teachers were those Heavenly Twins Bernard Rogers [1875] and Howard Hanson [1927]. After five years of wartime service in

the navy, he returned to the well-worn ascent to Parnassus, studying at Juilliard with Bernard Wagenaar (1894–1971) and at Fontainebleau with Nadia Boulanger. From 1950 to 1954 he was keyboard player with the NBC Symphony under Toscanini's direction. Most of his compositions up to then had been small-scale, and he first came to notice when Leontyne Price premiered his *Songs of the Rose of Sharon* (completed in 1948) with the National Symphony of Washington, D.C., conducted by Howard Mitchell. Mitchell also conducted the same orchestra in the premiere of the Concerto for Piano in November 1958 (with Jorge Bolet as soloist) and the overture *From Sea to Shining Sea* some two years later at the inaugural concert for President Kennedy. The concerto won the Pulitzer Prize for 1959. The year 1961 saw the first performance (in Washington) of *Novellis, Novellis*, written with the aid of two consecutive Guggenheim fellowships. It is the first of a cycle of three settings of medieval mystery plays, the others being his 1967 *The Shephardes Playe* (nationally televised in 1968), and *Erode the Great,* 1969.

Perhaps unwittingly taking a leaf from Olivier Messiaen's [2129] book, La Montaine in the 1960s began traveling to note down birdcalls and other natural sounds, which he used thematically in such works as *Birds of Paradise* (for piano and orchestra) in 1964, the *Te Deum* in 1965, and *Mass of Nature* in 1966. Perhaps the culmination of his efforts in that area is *Wilderness Journal,* a 1972 symphony for bass-baritone, organ, and orchestra to texts of Thoreau. It was premiered by the late singer Donald Gramm, who judged it a masterpiece. On commission from the Pennsylvania State University for the Bicentennial in 1976, La Montaine wrote an "operatic extravagance," *Be Glad Then, America,* using texts and some tunes from the colonial period. From time to time La Montaine has served as visiting professor or composer-in-residence at the Eastman School of Music, the American Academy in Rome, and the University of Utah. In 1977 he was named to the Richard M. Nixon Chair at Whittier College. His ability to compose was severely hampered by cataracts at that time, so he returned to his roots and took up hymn writing, notably in the *Whittier Service* of 1979. In collaboration with a fellow composer, Paul Sifler (1921–), La Montaine has in recent years begun to publish and record many of his works under the Fredonia Press imprint.

RECORDINGS: The Fredonia Press has issued recordings of *Wilderness Journal;* the cantata *The Nine Lessons of Christmas; Incantation* for jazz band; *Conversations* for violin and piano; *6 Sonnets of Shakespeare* for soprano and piano; *12 Relationships* and *Fuguing Set* (both for solo piano); and some miscellaneous piano pieces. Other recordings include the Concerto for Piano; *Birds of Paradise; Songs of the Rose of Sharon;* Sonata for Piano; and some additional keyboard pieces.

[2300] MADERNA, Bruno (Mà-dâr'-nà, Broo'-nō)
CONDUCTOR, TEACHER
BORN: Venice, April 21, 1920
DIED: Darmstadt, November 13, 1973

The eldest member of the leading trinity of the postwar Italian avant-garde—the others being Luciano Berio [2352] and Luigi Nono [2336]—Maderna began his career as a seven-year-old prodigy (violinist and conductor). He graduated from the Santa Cecilia Conservatory in Rome in 1940, then studied with Gian Francesco Malipiero [1743] in Venice and conductor Antonio Guarnieri in Siena. During the war, he served in the Italian army, and after its capitulation fought as a partisan. His compositions in this period were rather inoffensively neo-classical. He was given a teaching post at the Venice Conservatory in 1947. In 1948 he studied conducting with Hermann Scherchen, who converted him to doctrinaire Schoenbergian [1657] twelve-tonism. A few years later he became interested in the possibilities of electronic music, and in 1954 he helped Berio found the Studio di Phonologia of Radio Milan. Meanwhile he had in 1950 inaugurated his conducting career in Germany; he found the musical atmosphere so bracing there that he settled in Darmstadt and became a citizen of West Germany in 1963. He taught variously in Darmstadt, Milan, Salzburg, Rotterdam, and Tanglewood. From 1971 he was chief orchestral conductor at Radio Milan. His later works include aleatory techniques and the use of free "dramatic gesture," but he demanded more form and control than some of his contemporaries, insisting that he preferred his compositions to delight rather than to outrage. He died at fifty-three after a long fight with cancer. In 1975 Pierre Boulez [2346] completed *Rituel* for orchestra, written in Maderna's memory. RECORDINGS: There are a fairly substantial number of his works on disc— (orchestral or chamber-orchestral) Concerti for Oboe Nos. 1 and 3, Concerto for Violin, *Serenata No. 2, Il Giardino religioso (The*

Religious Garden), Quadrivium, Aura, Biogramma, Juilliard Serenade, Hyperion III for flute and orchestra, and the *Grande Aulodia* for flute, oboe, and orchestra; (chamber or solo pieces) *Honeyrêves* for flute and piano, *Viola* for viola, *Dedication* for violin; and (electronic works) *Dimensioni II* and *Continuo.*

[2301] SHAPERO, Harold Samuel
PIANIST, TEACHER
BORN: Lynn, Mass., April 29, 1920

A fledgling pianist at seven, Harold Shapero organized his own dance orchestra seven years later and got it local bookings. As an arranger, he came to the conclusion that he needed training and at sixteen went to Nicholas Slonimsky [1893] in Boston. In 1938 he spent six months at the Malkin Conservatory, where the newly expatriate Ernst Krenek [1984] introduced him to the mysteries of dodecaphony even before he had mastered the mysteries of diatonic harmony. He then entered Harvard, where he studied with Walter Piston [1890] and encountered Stravinsky [1748], who was there as Norton Lecturer. In the summers Shapero worked with Hindemith [1914] at Tanglewood. He graduated in 1941 and won the American Prix de Rome, which, owing to circumstances beyond his control, did not take him to Rome, at least not then. He also won Naumburg and Paine fellowships and spent two more years studying in Cambridge with Nadia Boulanger. In 1945 he married the painter Esther Geller. The next year he won a Guggenheim fellowship (the first of two) and the Gershwin Prize and in 1948 received plaudits for his *Symphony for Classical Orchestra.* After finally spending a year in Rome, he settled into teaching at Brandeis University in 1952—and, one is tempted to say sadly, was never heard from again. And indeed his output since that time has been small. Of all the young neo-classicists in this country, Shapero was one of the most attractive. Aaron Copland [1986] predicted great things of him if he would give up imitating others. There has been little evidence to date that the prophecy will be fulfilled. RECORDINGS: Leonard Bernstein [2282] recorded the celebrated *Symphony for Classical Orchestra.* Other recordings include the *Serenade in D Major* for strings; *3 Sonatas for Piano;* Trumpet Sonata; String Quartet No. 1; and *Partita* for piano and small orchestra. (In recent years, Shapero has experimented with synthesized music, but none of his works in that vein have yet been recorded.)

[2302] KROL, Bernhard (Krōl, Bärn'-härt)
HORNIST
BORN: Berlin, June 24, 1920

Krol was trained in Berlin just before and during World War II at the Mohr Conservatory and the International Institute. He studied composition with Josef Rufer, a pupil of Zemlinsky [1621] and Schoenberg [1657]. For sixteen years Krol was a horn player with the Berlin State Opera Orchestra in East Berlin. In 1961 he came to West Germany and has played since then in the Radio Symphony Orchestra in Stuttgart. He is better known at home than abroad. He has had 2 operas produced and has written in most other genres. He has also published two horn manuals. RECORDINGS: Works in a variety of genres have appeared, primarily on imported labels—*Magnificat Variations* for trumpet and strings; *Linzer Harmoniemusik* for wind quintet; Quartet for Piano and Strings; *Serenata amorosa* for English horn, guitar, piano, and bass; *Antifona* for English horn and organ; *Litania pastorale* for oboe and organ; *Missa muta* for horn and organ; *Laudatio* for horn solo; *Jesu, meine Freude* for trombone and organ; and *Wort-Gottes-Kantate* for chorus.

[2303] LESSARD, John Ayres
TEACHER
BORN: San Francisco, July 3, 1920

A pupil of Nadia Boulanger both abroad and at home (Boston), Lessard held the Cabot Fellowship at Harvard in 1940–41. Having spent the war years in service, he won an Alice M. Ditson fellowship in 1945 and a Guggenheim in 1946. In recent years he has been a member of the faculty of SUNY at Stony Brook, New York. Most of his music is predictably neo-classical. RECORDINGS: Many of them produced by Lessard's publisher, recorded works include the Concerto for Winds and Strings; *Sinfonietta Concertante* for orchestra; Wind Octet; Wind Quintet; *Partita* for wind quintet; *Quodlibets* for two trumpets and trombone; Sonata for Cello; *Fragments from the Cantos of Ezra Pound; Toccata* for harpsichord; and *Threads of Sound Recalled* for piano.

[2304] MIRON, Issachar (Mi-rōn', Is'-à-kär)
BUREAUCRAT, TEACHER, CONDUCTOR
BORN: Kutno, July 5, 1920

Reared in a Polish Jewish community, Miron was the grandson of a noted cantor and composer of cantorials. After learning to play piano and horn, he studied composition and conducting in Warsaw. In 1939 he emigrated to Palestine, then enlisted in the British army for the duration. He wrote many songs during this period, one of which, *"Tzena tzena,"* became an international hit. In the new state of Israel he held a number of posts in the cultural wing of the government. In the early 1960s he emigrated to the United States and settled in New York, where he became chairman of the music department of the Jewish Teachers' Seminary. He has also worked in the recording industry as an arranger, conductor, and producer. He specializes in songs and religious works. RECORDINGS: Two oratorios, *Proverb Canticles* and *Psalms of Israel,* have been recorded, as well as *I Remember* for cello and piano and some songs.

[2305] FRICKER, Peter Racine
TEACHER, ADMINISTRATOR, ORGANIST
BORN: London, September 5, 1920

In the years after World War II, Peter Racine Fricker was regarded as one of the more promising young British composers. But perhaps because he failed to hop aboard one of the many bandwagons that soon got rolling, his reputation has gradually diminished, at least insofar as widespread performance of his music is concerned. A direct descendant of the great French dramatist Jean Racine, he grew up in London, prepped at St. Paul's School, and then went to the Royal College of Music, where he studied with R. O. Morris (1886–1948) and the organist-composer Ernest Bullock. In 1941 Fricker joined the RAF and served in it for five years, three of them in India. On returning to London he worked for a time with Mátyás Seiber [2068] as a private student and assistant. In 1947 horn virtuoso Dennis Brain and his chamber group played Fricker's wind quintet in a BBC broadcast, and from then on, for a time, his ascent was rapid. He joined the faculty of Morley College, worked closely there with Michael Tippett [2059], its director, whom he succeeded in 1953. His first symphony won the Koussevitzky Prize in 1949, and a number of subsequent works received performances at various prestigious festivals. He was also taken notice of by a number of important European conductors. In 1955 he took on, in addition to his Morley College duties, teaching at the Royal College of Music. He also wrote radio and film music, lectured, and did a hundred other odd jobs to make ends meet. In 1964 he went to the University of California at Santa Barbara for a one-year visiting professorship. When he was offered a permanent appointment there, he snapped it up as offering him the money and leisure to compose. Since going there, he has turned out some large works (notably his fourth and fifth symphonies) and a good many chamber works for local performance but nothing that has had the impact of his earlier efforts. Fricker in his earlier years was a sort of neo-Hindemithian [1914] but later developed a style of his own, involving a sort of serialism based on intervals rather than on tones. RECORDINGS: Several orchestral works have been recorded commercially—Symphony No. 1; Concerto for Violin; and *Prelude, Elegy, and Finale.* (There is also a pirate recording of the Symphony No. 5, which is actually a kind of *sinfonia concertante* for organ and orchestra.) Also on commercial records are the Sonata for Cello and Piano, Sonata for Horn and Piano, *3 Arguments* for bassoon and cello, Wind Quintet, String Quintet No. 2, *12 Studies* for piano; and choral pieces. In general Fricker's later works have been severely underexposed, both on records and in concert.

[2306] KHACHATURIAN, Karen Surenovich (Kȧ-chȧ-tōōr'-yȧn, Kä'-ren Sōō-rȧ-nō'-vich)
TEACHER
BORN: Moscow, September 19, 1920

Nephew to the more famous Aram Khachaturian [2038], Karen Khachaturian was studying with Glière's [1662] pupil Genrik Litinsky (later officially doomed to become the "first Yakutsk composer") at the Moscow Conservatory when the 1941 German invasion necessitated Khachaturian's joining an entertainment division of the Red Army. (The accounts do not say how he entertained.) In 1945 he returned to complete his studies under Miaskovsky [1735], Shebalin [2017], and Shostakovich [2094]. At a fairly early age, he became a director of the Composers' Union, where during the Khrushchev "thaw" he cautiously cheered for musical progress. He is on the faculty of the Moscow Conservatory. His compositions include a light opera, a ballet, music for film cartoons, and 2 symphonies. RECORDINGS: His Sonata for Violin and Piano has been recorded by Jascha Heifetz. Other recordings, of Russian origin, include the symphonies (both conducted by Gennady Rozhdestvensky), the ballet *Cippolino* (based on an Italian fairy tale in which the characters

are vegetables), and the Sonata for Cello and Piano.

[2307] ARUTYUNIAN, Alexander Grigori (Ȧ-rōō-tyōōn'-yȧn, Ȧl-yek-sȧn'-der Grē-gō'-rē)
TEACHER, ADMINISTRATOR
BORN: Yerevan, Armenia, September 23, 1920

Arutyunian (sometimes spelled with an initial *H*) graduated from the Yerevan Conservatory on the eve of World War II. After the hostilities he came to Moscow, where, like Karen Khachaturian [2306], he studied composition with Genrik Litinsky. In 1948 his cantata *On the Homeland* was upheld as the kind of music true Russians should write, following the Zhdanov blast at the leading older composers. Arutyunian returned to Yerevan to teach at the conservatory and to be artistic director of the Armenian Philharmonic Orchestra. His music is characterized by folk (and folklike) themes. RECORDINGS: Works recorded include the Concerto for Trumpet, *Concerto-Poem* for violin and orchestra, and the choral *Ballad of the Armenian People.*

[2308] LUNDQUIST, Torbjörn (Loond'-kwist, Tôr'-byörn)
ACCORDIONIST
BORN: Stockholm, September 30, 1920

Lundquist studied composition with Dag Wirén [2075]. He began as a composer in the nationalist tradition and at one point collected Lapp folksongs which he used thematically. In recent years he has written for odd combinations of instruments and other sound sources and has experimented with aleatory techniques. He has composed an opera, 3 symphonies, choral, and chamber works but has made a particular impact with his music for accordion, both solo and in combination with other instruments (e.g., a concerto, a *Duel* for accordion and percussion, and *Stereogram III* for accordion, electric guitar, and xylorimba). RECORDINGS: His *Partita piccola* for accordion solo has been recorded. Other recordings include the Symphony No. 3 *(Sinfonia dolorosa)*, Concerto for Violin, *Landscape* for tuba and strings, and *Engravings* for brass ensemble.

[2309] MOEVS, Robert Walter
PIANIST, TEACHER
BORN: La Crosse, Wisc., December 2, 1920

Grandson of the mayor of La Crosse, Moevs studied piano from early childhood and had some local celebrity as a performer from the age of nine. In 1942 he graduated from Harvard, where he had studied with, *inter alias,* Walter Piston **[1890]** and Edward Burlingame Hill **[1632]**. He immediately joined the U.S. Army Air Corps and became a pilot in the European theater. From the end of the war until 1947 he was stationed in Rumania, but during leave in 1946 he managed lessons with Nadia Boulanger in Paris. After his discharge he continued to study with her at the Paris Conservatoire until 1951, during which time she conducted his choral work *The Bacchantes* in concert. By the time he came home, he was becoming widely known, but he returned to Harvard for a year to get his M.A. While there he won the American Prix de Rome and spent the next three years in Rome, where he married Maria Teresa Marabini, now a professor of archeology and Italian at Rutgers University. At the conclusion of his residency, Moevs returned to Harvard to teach. It was there that he evolved his own approach to serialism, which, he maintains, offers more flexibility than the usual variety. His first major work to use it, the choral-orchestral *Attis I,* premiered by the Boston Symphony in 1960, shook the staid audience even more than most progressive pieces did. Later Moevs was considerably influenced by the music of Pierre Boulez **[2346]**, who performed his *Musica da camera I* at a 1971 New York Philharmonic concert. RECORDINGS: Works on disc include the *Musica da camera I* for chamber orchestra; *Concerto Grosso* for piano, percussion, and orchestra; *Brief Mass* for chorus, organ, vibraphone, guitar, and double bass; *Variazioni* for viola and cello; Sonata for Piano; and other piano pieces.

[2310] BRUBECK, David Warren
PIANIST
BORN: Concord, Calif., December 6, 1920

One of the most important figures in the progressive jazz movement after World War II, Dave Brubeck grew up, like his brothers Henry and Howard **[2250]**, on a ranch near Oakland. He learned piano in childhood but matriculated at the College of the Pacific at Stockton as a prospective veterinary student. He soon, however, switched to music and after graduating in 1942 sought out Darius Milhaud **[1868]**, his brother Howard's teacher, and studied with him—and briefly with Schoenberg **[1657]**. In the latter part of World War II he was an army bandsman,

but in 1946 he returned to Mills College for further work with Milhaud. He organized a jazz trio and for some time played in Bay Area bistros until he was eventually "discovered" by a local disc jockey. The trio, now a quartet, became one of the most innovative, influential, and popular jazz groups of its time. The Brubecks—Dave, his wife, and their six children—made their home in Connecticut, where he more or less settled down after disbanding the quartet in 1967. In recent years his sons Darius, Chris, and Danny have made names for themselves both as rock musicians and in jazz performances with their father. In his "retirement" Brubeck has written several large religious works in collaboration with his wife Iola *(née* Whitlock). RECORDINGS: Three of his religious works have been recorded— *The Light in the Wilderness, Truth Is Fallen,* and *The Gates of Justice.* (There are also innumerable jazz recordings.)

[2311] CARLID, Göte (Kär'-lēd, Y ö'-tə)
LIBRARIAN
BORN: Sandviken, December 26, 1920
DIED: Sundbyberg, June 30, 1953

Born in a city on Lake Storsjön in east-central Sweden, Carlid majored in liberal arts at the University of Uppsala, graduating in 1945. Music he learned for himself; he was particularly influenced by Schoenberg **[1657]** and Varèse **[1774]**. For the next five years he supported himself as a librarian, meanwhile composing, publishing articles, and directing a Stockholm chamber music society. He died at thirty-two, leaving fewer than twenty works. RECORDINGS: His *Monologs* for piano and the *Mass* for string orchestra (nonvocal) have been recorded.

[2312] LIDHOLM, Ingvar Natanael
(Lēd'-hōlm, Ēng'-vär Nå-tå'-nä-el)
VIOLIST, TEACHER, CONDUCTOR, RADIO OFFICIAL
BORN: Jönköping, February 24, 1921

A native of south-central Sweden, Ingvar Lidholm studied with Hilding Rosenberg **[1866]**, Tor Mann, and others at the Royal College of Music in Stockholm, and later in France, Italy, Switzerland, and England. His instrument was the violin, but he switched to viola as an orchestral musician. In 1947 he was appointed conductor of the orchestra at Örebro, a city about a hundred miles west of Stockholm. Nine years later he was put in charge of chamber music broadcasts for Swedish Radio. After another nine years, he came back to his college to teach but in 1975 returned to the radio network as chief musical program planner. Lidholm has been increasingly involved with the avant-garde, for which he has acted as a spokesman, and has progressed from serialism to more "advanced" techniques. He was a charter member of Blomdahl's [2253] Monday Club, along with Sven-Erik Bäck [2292]. RECORDINGS: Orchestral works recorded include the Concerto for Strings; *Poesis; Ritornell; Toccata e canto; Music for Strings* (also recorded in an alternate version for string quartet); *Greetings from an Old World; Kontakion;* and the ballet *Rites.* Vocal works recorded include *Nausicaa Alone* for soprano and orchestra; *The Poet's Night,* a cantata for soprano, chorus, and orchestra; and a number of miscellaneous choral pieces and songs. Chamber and instrumental recordings include *4 Pieces* for cello and piano; Sonata for Flute Solo; *Stamp Music* (an aleatory piece, the score or plan of which appeared on a Swedish postage stamp) in one version for soprano and another for organ; and several piano pieces.

[2313] BERGSMA, William Laurence
TEACHER, ADMINISTRATOR
BORN: Oakland, Calif., April 1, 1921

William Bergsma, of Frisian descent, was unsuccessfully introduced to music by his mother, a former professional singer. He grew up in Redwood City, California, and went to school in Burlingame, where his teachers had more luck. Having learned to compose, Bergsma got into a summer course in 1936 at USC with Howard Hanson [1927] and wrote a ballet called *Paul Bunyan,* music from which was performed back in Burlingame the following year, and by both Hanson in Rochester and Pierre Monteux at San Francisco in 1939. Bergsma attended Stanford University for two years, then in 1940 went to the Eastman School of Music for four, continuing his work with Hanson and taking orchestration from Bernard Rogers [1875]. He also taught there during his last two years and turned out several prizewinning pieces, including the first two of his 4 string quartets. After a year of teaching at Drake University in Des Moines, he came to New York, where in 1946 he married Nancy Nickerson and joined the Juilliard faculty in that order. He worked closely with William Schuman [2158] in rebuilding the curriculum and was appointed associate dean in 1961. During his New York years he continued to compose steadily, producing among other things the first of his 2 symphonies, his

first opera *The Wife of Martin Guerre* (premiered at Juilliard in 1955), and the orchestral *In Celebration,* played at the opening of Lincoln Center. In 1963 Bergsma went to the University of Washington in Seattle, where he taught and ran the music school. Recent large works have included the Concerto for Violin in 1966, his opera *The Murder of Comrade Sharik* in 1973, and the Symphony No. 2 of 1976. Over the years, however, he has tended to work more in small forms. Although he has done some experimenting, his attractive music tends toward the middle of the road. RECORDINGS: There is an abridged version of the opera *The Wife of Martin Guerre* and a recording of the ballet *Gold and the Señor Commandante.* Orchestral works on disc include *Music on a Quiet Theme; The Fortunate Islands* for strings; *Carol on Twelfth Night; March with Trumpets; Chameleon Variations;* and the Concerto for Violin. Chamber and instrumental recordings include String Quartets Nos. 2–4; *Suite for Brass Quartet;* Concerto for Wind Quintet; *Fantastic Variations on a Theme from "Tristan and Isolde"* for viola and piano, *Illegible Canons* for clarinet and percussion, and *Tangents* for piano.

[2314] IMBRIE, Andrew Welsh
TEACHER
BORN: New York, April 6, 1921

Andrew Imbrie grew up and was educated in Princeton, New Jersey (at Lawrenceville School and Princeton University), whither his parents moved when he was six. He studied piano, beginning more than a year earlier, and from 1930 with Leo Ornstein (1892–   ) in nearby Philadelphia, appearing with the Philadelphia Orchestra when he was twelve. In the summer prior to his senior year at Lawrenceville, he studied with Nadia Boulanger in France and then came home to take private lessons with Roger Sessions [1931], continuing under his eye at Princeton from 1938 to 1942. In the last year he completed the first of his 4 string quartets, which won the New York Critics' Circle Award in 1944. Imbrie spent the war years in Washington, D.C., as a Japanese translator for the Army Signal Corps. Separated at last in 1946, he followed Sessions to Berkeley, where he acquired an M.A. and the American Prix de Rome a year later. After two years of residency in Rome, he returned to Berkeley to teach at the university for the remainder of his career, though in 1970 he began doubling as chairman of the department of composition at the San Francisco Conservatory. In 1953 he married Barbara Cushing, daughter of his colleague Charles Cushing [2077]. His compositions have won many prestigious awards. They include 2 operas; 3 symphonies; 2 concerti for piano and a concerto apiece for violin, cello, and flute; and much choral and chamber music. His music is generally contrapuntal, his lines often surprisingly melodic, his harmony dissonant. One recurrent feature of Imbrie's music is the sudden intrusion of bell tones to signal moments of epiphany or transformation. This is especially in evidence in the 1984 *Pilgrimage* for chamber ensemble, as well as in the orchestral *Legend,* Symphony No. 3, and elsewhere. RECORDINGS: Orchestral works on records include the Concerto for Violin, *Legend,* and Symphony No. 3. (A recording by Julius Baker of the Concerto for Flute has been announced several times as forthcoming but has yet to appear.) The Gregg Smith Singers have recorded the early *On the Beach at Night* for chorus and string orchestra. Chamber and instrumental pieces on disc include String Quartets Nos. 1–4; Sonata for Piano; *Serenade* for flute, violin, and piano; *Impromptu* for violin and piano; Sonata for Cello and Piano; *3 Sketches* for trombone and piano; and the brief *Dandelion Wine* for oboe, clarinet, piano, and string quartet (inspired by a collection of stories by Ray Bradbury).

[2315] GOLD, Ernest
LECTURER, WRITER
BORN: Vienna, July 13, 1921

Ernest Gold had his first music lessons from his father and then studied piano at the Vienna Academy. In 1938 he fled the Nazis with his family and settled in New York. There he studied theory with Otto Cesana (1899–), a Brescia-born music educator, and conducting with Brussels-born Léon Barzin. Gold began writing songs for Broadcast Music, Inc. and came up with solid hits in "Practice Makes Perfect" and "Accidentally on Purpose." In 1946 he became an American citizen and decided to try his luck in Hollywood. He was taken on as an arranger in the film studios and later graduated to writing scores for first-line films. He undertook further study with George Antheil [1981] and in 1950 married the soprano Marni Nixon (the film voice for innumerable nonsinging actresses), who has recorded a number of his concert songs. Gold had another runaway hit with the theme from the film *Exodus.* Other film scores include *The Defiant Ones; The Young Philadelphians; On the Beach; Inherit the Wind;*

Judgment at Nuremberg; It's a Mad, Mad, Mad, Mad World; and *Ship of Fools.* Gold's "serious" music includes a symphony, a string quartet, a piano concerto, and many songs. RECORDINGS: Concert works on records include the *Boston Pops March;* Symphony for 5 Instruments; *Songs of Love and Parting* for soprano and orchestra; and miscellaneous songs. A fair number of his film scores have also been recorded.

[2316] BEESON, Jack Hamilton
TEACHER
BORN: Muncie, Ind., July 15, 1921

Though none of his works have as yet attained repertoire status, Jack Beeson is about as successful an opera composer as twentieth-century America has produced. He was born in the city that has been nicknamed "Middletown, U.S.A.," a term that has some application to his music. Sickly as an infant, he survived against all expectations, studied piano, clarinet, and xylophone in Muncie, became addicted to opera through the Metropolitan Opera broadcasts, and tried vainly to write several of his own. In 1939, however, a fellowship took him to the Eastman School of Music where, trained by Howard Hanson [1927], Bernard Rogers [1875], and Burrill Phillips [2116], he acquired a B.A. and an M.A. in 1942–43. His father's death in 1944 allowed him to live and study in New York, where he had lessons from Bartók [1734] in that composer's last months. He joined the faculty of Columbia University (where he had previously done some teaching and studying) in 1945 and has remained there since, serving variously as director of the opera workshop, chairman of the department, and director of music publications for the university press. He married Nora Sigerist in 1947; the next year they went to Rome for two years on Beeson's Prix de Rome. His first opera *Jonah,* completed in 1950, went unperformed. The second, a chamber-size setting of William Saroyan's one-act *Hello, Out There* has remained a favorite with colleges and small companies since its 1954 premiere. *The Sweet Bye and Bye,* based on the life of evangelist Aimee Semple McPherson, was first produced at Juilliard in 1957. *Lizzie Borden* was commissioned by the New York City Opera and produced at Lincoln Center in 1965. A second Saroyan opera, *My Heart's in the Highlands,* written for television, was seen on NET stations in 1970. *Captain Jinks of the Horse Marines,* based on a turn-of-the-century comedy by Clyde Fitch, was commissioned for the National Bicentennial by the National Endowment for the Arts and premiered at Kansas City in 1975. Beeson's most recent opera is another small-scale one-acter, *Dr. Heidegger's Fountain of Youth,* after a story by Nathanial Hawthorne. Appropriately Beeson succeeded Douglas Moore [1884] as MacDowell Professor at Columbia. Beeson has composed other vocal works and admits to a few orchestral, band, and chamber pieces, though he has rejected all of his early efforts in those areas. RECORDINGS: All of the operas but *Jonah* and the TV work, the orchestral Symphony in A, some songs and part-songs, and the Sonata No. 5 for Piano have been recorded.

[2317] ARNOLD, Malcolm Henry
TRUMPETER, CONDUCTOR
BORN: Northampton, England, October 21, 1921

One is tempted to say that Malcolm Arnold writes music by the yard, but that would be to deny its attractiveness. Jovial and extrovert, he simply lets it flow in an outpouring of tunefulness and wit, untroubled by systems or notions of musical progress. At seventeen he won a scholarship to the Royal College of Music, where he specialized in trumpet and studied composition with Gordon Jacob [1911] and conducting with Constant Lambert [2074]. Graduating at twenty, he joined the London Philharmonic as third-desk man, and before the year was out he had been promoted to principal. Already established as a composer of chamber music (he won the Cobbett Prize the year of his graduation), he regularly got up at four a.m. to compose. In 1944 he was drafted, served a few months in the army, and was released on medical grounds in 1945. He then became second trumpet with the BBC Symphony, but was able to get his old job back a few months later. His compositions were now beginning to be noticed and performed by important conductors, and Eduard van Beinum in particular espoused Arnold's cause and also gave him further conductorial training.

In 1948 Arnold figured he could live on his earnings from composition and guest conducting, and gave up orchestral playing permanently. He has since composed voluminously—with particular success in films, his scores including *Hobson's Choice,* the original *1984,* and *The Bridge on the River Kwai* (Academy Award). His less utilitarian music (to date) includes 8 symphonies, 14 concerti, 10 overtures, sets of English, Scottish, and Cornish dances, 3 sinfoniettas, 2 operas, 4

ballets (among them one called *Sweeney Todd)* and innumerable other works—including such *jeux d'esprit* as a Symphony for Toy Instruments and a *Fantasy for Audience and Orchestra.*

RECORDINGS: The ballet *Homage to the Queen* and Symphonies Nos. 1–3 and 5 have been recorded commercially, along with a number of concerted pieces—Concerto for 2 Violins and String Orchestra; *Concerto for Phyllis and Cyril* (for piano, three hands); Concerto for Guitar; *Serenade* for guitar and strings; Concerti for Flute Nos. 1 and 2; and Concerto for Harmonica. Other orchestral compositions on record include Sinfoniettas Nos. 1–3; *Serenade* for small orchestra; *Sound Barrier Rhapsody;* the sets of *English, Scottish,* and *Cornish Dances* for orchestra; *Sarabande and Polka;* and several overtures —*Beckus the Dandipratt; Tam o'Shanter; Peterloo; Leonore No. 4;* and *A Grand Grand Overture* (the last two for the spoofing Hoffnung Festivals). There is also a pirate record of Symphony No. 4 and the *Hong Kong Overture.* Chamber and instrumental recordings include the Quintet for Brass; *Symphony for Brass Instruments;* Sonatina for Clarinet and Piano; *3 Shanties* for wind quintet; *Divertimento* for flute, oboe, and clarinet; and the Piano Trio. There have also been at least ten film soundtracks, mostly from early in Arnold's career.

[2318] KOKKONEN, Joonas (Kok-kō'-nen, Yō'-nås)
PIANIST, CRITIC, TEACHER
BORN: Iisalmi, November 13, 1921

Influenced by Sibelius [1575] and Bartók [1734] and particularly by Bach [684], Kokkonen is perhaps the best-known living Finnish composer on the international scene. Born in the central part of the country, he took a master's degree in musicology from Helsinki University in 1948. A year later he got a diploma from the Sibelius Academy, where he had majored in piano and taken a harmony course with Selim Palmgren [1703]. For the next decade he concertized, wrote reviews, lectured at the Academy, and sharpened his own self-taught compositional skills. He gained a professorship at the Academy in 1959, the year he completed the first of his 3 string quartets. In 1960 he finished the first of his 4 symphonies. His most successful and impressive work to date has been his opera *The Last Temptations.* His student Aulis Sallinen (1935–) has also attained renown as an opera composer recently. RECORDINGS: *The Last Temptations* has been recorded by the

Finnish National Opera. Other recordings include the last three symphonies; Concerto for Cello; *Music for Strings; Sinfonia da Camera,* and . . . *durch einen Spiegel* . . . for chamber orchestra; String Quartets Nos. 1 and 3; Sonata for Cello and Piano; Piano Trio (his Op. 1); *Lux aeterna* for organ; Wind Quintet; piano pieces; and songs.

[2319] KURKA, Robert Frank
VIOLINIST
BORN: Cicero, Ill., December 22, 1921
DIED: New York, December 12, 1957

Robert Kurka studied violin with Kathleen Parlow, *inter alias,* and then composition with Darius Milhaud [1868] and Otto Luening [1980]. In 1951 he won a Guggenheim fellowship which was renewed in 1952. Among his compositions were 5 string quartets, 4 violin sonatas, 3 concerti for various instruments, 2 symphonies, and a suite for winds after Jaroslav Hašek's satirical novel, *The Good Soldier Schweik.* While developing this last piece into a full-length opera, Kurka was stricken with leukemia, to which he succumbed ten days before his thirty-sixth birthday. The opera was successfully produced the following spring by the New York City Opera. RECORDINGS: Several orchestral works are on disc—*The Good Soldier Schweik Suite, Serenade* for small orchestra, and Symphony No. 2.

[2320] KORN, Peter Jona
CONDUCTOR, CRITIC, TEACHER
BORN: Berlin, March 30, 1922

Korn began composing at the age of six and at nine was admitted to the Berlin Hochschule. Two years later he went to England, where he studied with Rubbra [1995] and launched his conducting career (in a school performance) at the age of thirteen. In 1936 he proceeded to Jerusalem, where he studied at the New Conservatory with Stefan Wolpe [2020] and his wife Irma. A third move in 1941 brought him to the United States where, he served in the armed forces and took out citizenship. He settled down in Los Angeles, where at various times he studied with Ingolf Dahl [2188], Hanns Eisler [1952], Miklós Rózsa [2108], Arnold Schoenberg [1657], and Ernst Toch [1824]. He himself taught, wrote reviews and articles, and in 1948 founded the New Orchestra, which was dedicated to modern music and which he conducted. Not surprisingly he experimented for a time with twelve-tone music, but later he became one of the first to de-

clare the system bankrupt and to return to the use of tonality. In 1965 Korn moved back to Germany, where he became director of the Richard Strauss Conservatory in Munich two years later. He has written an opera, 3 symphonies, several concerti, and much else in various forms. RECORDINGS: Several orchestral works are on records— the *Overture "In medias res"; Variations on a Theme from "The Beggar's Opera"* (slightly abridged); and the Concertino for Horn and Double String Orchestra.

[2321] XENAKIS, Iannis (Ze-ná'-kis, Yàn'-nis)
ENGINEER, ARCHITECT, MATHEMATICIAN, TEACHER
BORN: Braïla, May 29, 1922

One of the most cerebral of the important contemporary avant-gardists, Xenakis appears presently to enjoy less prominence than he did a decade ago. Though he was born in a Rumanian city (on the lower Danube), both his parents were Greek—his father was a successful businessman. Ten years later the family went home, and installed Iannis in an English-run prep school on the island of Spetsai. At the age of twelve he began studying music with Aristotle Koundourov, a sometime pupil of Glazunov [1573] and Ippolitov-Ivanov [1517]. However, in 1940 he matriculated at the Polytechnic School in Athens, headed for an engineering career. The Nazi invasion prolonged his studies, for he spent much of his time as a resistance fighter. On New Year's Day 1945 he received a severe facial wound in a skirmish and lost an eye. He was captured, imprisoned, and sentenced to die but managed to escape. After the war he completed his degree, but in 1947 he decamped for France, of which country he eventually became a citizen. He became an assistant to the great architect Le Corbusier and for the next twelve years worked with him on city planning in Marseilles and Nantes, and on such buildings as the convent of LaTourette, the Baghdad stadium, and in 1958 the Philips Pavilion at the Brussels World's Fair (musical decor by Edgard Varèse [1774]). Meanwhile, after some courses with Milhaud [1868] and Honegger [1861], Xenakis embarked in 1950 on two years of concentrated study with Messiaen [2129] at the Paris Conservatoire. He also worked with Hermann Scherchen at Gravesano in Switzerland. In the autumn of 1955 Hans Rosbaud introduced at the Donaueschingen Festival his *Metastasis* for sixty-one players, based on calculus and probability theory and involving constantly evolving *glissandi* (perhaps the most imitable aspect of Xenakis' work. He likened the effect to the singing of an infestation of seventeen-year locusts.) The performance caused a scandal of major proportions. Two years later Xenakis explained his theories (which may simplistically be said to counter Cagean [2192] indeterminacy with mathematical determinacy) in an article, "Elements of Stochastic Music." About the same time he began using a computer to facilitate his calculations and also working in the electronic medium.

Having not seen eye to eye with Le Corbusier for some time, Xenakis decided in 1960 to strike out on his own. By now he had considerable support among the more radical of contemporary musicians and found himself a focal center at modern music festivals and the recipient of a number of commissions. In the middle 1960s he was lecturing and teaching worldwide, and in 1966 he founded the Equipe de Mathématique et d'Automatique Musicale at the École Pratique des Hautes Études in Paris. The following year he set up another such institute at Indiana University, where he held forth until 1972. He has also taught at the Aix, Berkshire, and other festivals. His credo is that music is neither intellectual nor intuitive but a sort of game in which both elements must be brought into balance.

RECORDINGS: Because much of his work involves spatial relationships (often with the audience, which is, for example, surrounded by the orchestra or mixed in with the performers), it is often not done justice by records, though Xenakis has been strongly represented thereon. Orchestral or chamber-orchestral works recorded include *Métastasis; Stratégie* for two conductors and two orchestras; *Jonachaies; Pithoprakta* for strings; *Atrées* for ten instruments; *Achorripsis* for twenty-one instruments; *Aroura* for twelve strings; *Eonta* for piano and brass ensemble; *Synaphai-Connexities* for two pianos and orchestra; *Syrmos* for eighteen strings; the ballet *Antikhthon* for orchestra; *Akrata* for sixteen winds; *ST/10—1,080262* for ten players; and several works for various orchestral groupings "scattered throughout the audience"—*Nomos gamma; Terretektorh;* and *Polytopes.* Works involving choral or choral-orchestral forces on record include *Cendrées;* incidental music for the *Oresteia* and *Medea; Nuits (Nights)* for chorus; and *Polla ta dhina (+),* the latter for children's choir and small orchestra. Instrumental works on disc include *Analogique A* for nine strings; *Nomos alpha* for solo cello; *ST/4-2* for string quartet; *Charisma* for clarinet and cello; *Psappha* for percussion;

Amorsima-Morsima for piano trio and double bass; and two works for solo piano, *Herma* and *Evryali.* Electronic music on disc includes *Analogique B; Diamorphosis I, II; Hibiki Hana Ma; Concret P-H II; Bohor I; Orient-Occident I, III:* and *Persepolis* (music for a light-and-sound show). Relatively few of Xenakis' later compositions have been recorded. A recent release by the Arditi String Quartet contains pieces for various members of the quartet—*Ikhoor* for two violins and cello; *Dikhthas* for violin and piano; *Kottos* for cello; and *Mikka* and *Mikka "S"* for solo violin.

[2322] BANFIELD, Rafaello de
BORN: Newcastle-on-Tyne, June 2, 1922

Of Italian and English parentage, Banfield studied chiefly in Italy—at first with Vito Levi in Trieste, then with Gian Francesco Malipiero [1743] at the Venice Conservatory. Later he worked with Nadia Boulanger in Paris. In the 1950s he attracted some attention with a pair of one-act operas and three ballet scores; but, save for an occasional revival of one of these works, little has been heard of him since. RECORDINGS: His opera *Lord Byron's Love-Letter* and ballet *The Combat* have been recorded.

[2323] HAMILTON, Iain Ellis
TEACHER, ENGINEER
BORN: Glasgow, June 6, 1922

Together with Thea Musgrave [2374], Iain Hamilton represents the first generation of Scots composers to win international notice though he grew up in London. At first music was an avocation with him, he having worked as an engineer until he was twenty-five. At that juncture he switched horses and became a student at both the Royal College of Music and the University of London. His chief composition teacher was William Alwyn [2076]. He was awarded his bachelor's degree in 1950 and for some years thereafter taught both at the university and at Morley College, composing steadily and winning many prizes and awards. Like so many British composers, he evolved a style of his own that is, though dissonant and largely nontonal in some works, unconnected with any of the fashionable "schools." In 1961 he moved to America. He was composer-in-residence in 1962 at Tanglewood and then occupied the Mary Biddle Duke Chair of Music at Duke University until 1971. Lured away by Lehman College of the City University of New York that year, he found conditions there not to his taste and resigned without ever embarking upon his duties. He has written in most conventional forms (and in some not so conventional). From the late 1960s he has occupied himself chiefly with the composition of several large-scale operas —*The Royal Hunt of the Sun; Raleigh's Dream;* and several operas on classical themes. RECORDINGS: Orchestral works on records include the *Scottish Dances; Sinfonia* for two orchestras; Concerto for Violin; and *Voyage* for horn and small orchestra. Other recordings include *Epitaph for This World and Time* for choruses and organs, Sextet, Sonata No. 1 for Piano, *Nocturnes with Cadenzas* for piano, *3 Pieces for Piano,* Sonata for Cello and Piano, *Sonata notturna* for horn and piano, and *Threnos: In Time of War* for organ.

[2324] FOSS *(né Fuchs)*, Lukas
PIANIST, CONDUCTOR, TEACHER, AD-MINISTRATOR
BORN: Berlin, August 15, 1922

Lukas Foss seems to be the most recent in a long succession of composers hailed as the new infant Mozart [992]. He was the son of a professor of philosophy, and his early musical proclivities were encouraged. He was playing and improvising on an accordion at six, began piano lessons at seven (with heavy doses of the classics), and took up theory at nine. In 1933, owing to the political climate in Germany, the Fuchses moved to Paris. There Lukas continued his piano studies with Lazare Lévy (1882–1964), took up the flute with Marcel Moyse, and had lessons in composing from Noël Gallon [1856]. After four years the Fuchses moved finally to the United States. Lukas spent three years at the Curtis Institute in Philadelphia, where his teachers included Rosario Scalero (1870–1954), Randall Thompson [1966], pianist Isabelle Vengerova, and conductor Fritz Reiner. In 1940 he began a close association with Serge Koussevitzky [1655] at Tanglewood, and studied with Hindemith [1914] there, as well as at Yale during the next academic year. In 1942 he became an American citizen and, under the spell of Aaron Copland [1986], wrote a big cantata, *The Prairie,* to texts by Carl Sandburg. That same year he also won a Pulitzer Traveling Fellowship. Koussevitzky conducted the Boston Symphony in a suite from the cantata in 1943, and Robert Shaw premiered the whole work with his recently founded Collegiate Choral in New York in 1944, winning for it the New York Critics' Circle Award. Foss, as he had come to be, had embarked on a successful concert career, and now Koussevitzky named him the symphony's official pianist (and, in effect, his chief assistant). In the same year he completed three ballet scores and his Symphony in G Major. Commissions and awards began to shower on him. In 1945 he was, at twenty-three, the youngest recipient of a Guggenheim fellowship. It was followed in 1950 by a Fulbright and a grant from the American Academy in Rome—to fulfill the requirements of which he left his orchestral post. In 1950 too his first attempt at opera, a treatment of Mark Twain's short story "The Jumping Frog of Calaveras County," was premiered by the opera theater at Indiana University. Foss himself was soloist at the first performance of his Concerto No. 2 for Piano at the Venice Festival in 1951, and shortly afterward he married Cornelia Brendel, an artist. (The concerto won him a second Critics' Circle Award in 1954.) After his return to America in 1952 Foss was named to take Schoenberg's [1657] place on the UCLA faculty, at which school he also conducted the student orchestra. In 1955 a more ambitious opera, *Griffelken,* became the first work to be premiered by the NBC Opera Company on national television. (A third, *Introductions and Goodbyes,* to a libretto by Gian Carlo Menotti [2177], requires only one soloist and takes less than ten minutes to play.)

Up to the mid-1950s Foss had remained a fairly traditional, if ingenious, composer. About that time, however, he became fascinated by the possibilities, as he saw them, of group improvisation, and in 1957 he joined with three other musicians to form the Improvisation Chamber Ensemble, which, working under certain agreed-upon ground rules, concertized and recorded. In 1960 he was sent to Russia by the State Department on a "cultural exchange." After his return he became increasingly identified with the musical avant-garde. That same year Leonard Bernstein [2282] conducted the New York Philharmonic, soprano Adele Addison, and the Improvisation Chamber Ensemble in a song cycle, *Time Cycle,* with improvised interludes for the ensemble. (A year later Foss dropped the interludes and rewrote the orchestral part for the instruments of the ensemble.) It won the composer a third Critics' Circle Award. Afterward Foss tried his hand at all of the gimmicks of the era—indeterminacy, percussion music, unorthodox use of instruments, the-concert-as-theater, game theory, etc.—with results that seem to have endeared him neither to the radicals nor to the conservatives, though he has done yeoman work on behalf of contemporary composers. In 1963 he took over the conductorship of the Buffalo Philharmonic and became director of the Center of Creative and Performing Arts which he founded at SUNY, Buffalo. There and in New York City he directed festivals of so-called progressive music during the 1960s. (He created minor headlines during a Buffalo Festival when one performance featured a nude couple waltzing on the stage.) He left Buffalo in 1970, took over the Brooklyn Philharmonic Orchestra in 1971, served simultaneously as director of the Jerusalem Symphony from 1972 to 1975, and succeeded Kenneth Schermerhorn as conductor of the Milwaukee Symphony in 1981. Since 1969 he has taught on a guest basis at Harvard, the Manhattan School of Music, and the University of Cincinnati.

RECORDINGS: The opera *The Jumping Frog of Calaveras County* has been recorded, along with several other vocal-orchestral works—the cantatas *The Prairie, Song of Songs,* and *A Parable of Death; Psalms* for chorus and orchestra; *Measure for Measure* for tenor and orchestra; the song cycle *Time Cycle* (the chamber version of the latter has also been recorded). Other orchestral works on disc include Concerto No. 2 for Piano; Concerto for Oboe; *Baroque Variations* (one of its movements was earlier recorded as a separate work, *Phorion [Stolen Goods]); Geod;* and *Night Music (for John Lennon)* for brass quintet and orchestra. Other vocal works recorded include *Behold I Build an House* and *3 Airs on O'Hara's Angels* for chorus; *Fragments of Archilochus* for singing and speaking soloists, chorus, and chamber ensemble; *Round a Common Center* for narrator, piano quartet, violin, and voice; and *13 Ways of Looking at a Blackbird* for voice, distant flute, piano, and percussion. Instrumental and chamber works recorded include String Quartets Nos. 1 and 3; *Capriccio* for cello and piano; *Echoi* for clarinet, cello, percussion, and piano; *Elytres* for flute, two violins, and ensemble; *Paradigm* for five instruments and percussion; *Ni bruit, ni vitesse* for two pianos (played by two pianists and two percussionists); *The Cave of the Winds* for wind quintet; *Music for 6* for percussion; *Curriculum vitae* for accordion; and *Solo Observed* for piano, cello, vibraphone, and electric organ. (A recording of *Introductions and Goodbyes* by the Gregg Smith Singers was announced by Vox several years ago but has never appeared.)

[2325] AMIROV, Fikret Meshadi Jamil
(A-mē'rof, Fē'-kret Mā-shá'-dē Jā-mēl')
ADMINISTRATOR

BORN: Ganja (now Kirovabad), Azerbaijan, November 22, 1922

Amirov's father was a virtuoso on the *tar,* the Azerbaijani lute. His son at first followed in his footsteps but in 1939 entered the regional conservatory in Baku. The German invasion of 1941 called him to arms, and he was wounded in action. He finally graduated in 1948, by which time he had already won recognition as a composer for his Concerto for Piano and Violin and two orchestral memorial pieces, and as managing director of the orchestras of Kirovabad and Baku. From 1956 to 1959 he ran the Baku opera house and in the latter year visited the United States with a delegation that included Shostakovich [2094], Kabalevsky [2058], and Khrennikov [2208]. Amirov has written 2 operas, musicals, film scores, and much else but is known in the West chiefly for his *Symphonic Mugam No. 2* (performed by Leopold Stokowski among others), a suite of six brief movements using themes derived from the ancient Azerbaijani counterpart to Indian *ragas.* RECORDINGS: Amirov has composed 3 symphonic *mugamlar,* and all of them have been recorded. Also on Soviet records are the opera *Sevil,* the full-length ballet *1001 Nights,* and the *Nizami Symphony* for strings.

[2326] EVETT, Robert
CRITIC, EDITOR
BORN: Loveland, Colo., November 30, 1922
DIED: Tacoma Park, Md., February 3, 1975

Born in north central Colorado, Evett studied with Roy Harris [1947] in the latter's years at Colorado College in Colorado Springs. Moving to the northeast, he became music critic for *The New Republic* and then took a degree from the Juilliard School. He moved up to the editorship of the magazine's literature-and-arts pages and in 1970 went to Washington, D.C., as literary editor of the Washington *Star.* A traditionalist, he wrote 3 symphonies, concerti, chamber, and choral music. RECORDINGS: His Sonata for Harpsichord, Piano Quintet, Sonata No. 2 for Piano, and the song "Billy in the Darbies" (to a text by Herman Melville) have been recorded.

[2327] POWELL, Mel
PIANIST, TEACHER, ADMINISTRATOR
BORN: New York, February 12, 1923

A piano student of Nadia Reisenberg, Powell began his public career rather precociously as a jazz pianist, notably with the Benny Goodman Orchestra, for which he also wrote arrangements. During this time he had lessons with Joseph Schillinger (1895–1943), Bernard Wagenaar (1894–1971), and Ernst Toch [1824]. In 1948 he began studies with Paul Hindemith [1914] at Yale, graduating in 1952. After teaching at the Mannes College of Music and Queens College, he returned to Yale as a member of the faculty in 1957, leaving twelve years later to become dean of music at the California Institute of the Arts. Surprisingly his music is less influenced by jazz than by the schools of Webern [1773], Cage [2192], and by the electronicists, and some of his later compositions have been regarded as attempts to recreate prehuman emotive noises. RECORDINGS: Classical compositions recorded include *Divertimento* for wind quintet; Piano Trio; *Divertimento for Violin and Harp; Improvisation* for piano, clarinet, and viola; *2 Prayer Settings* for tenor and instrumental quartet; *Haiku Settings* for soprano and string quartet; *Filigree Setting* for string quartet; *Piece for Tape Recorder; Electronic Settings I, II; Events* for tape; and *Étude* for piano. (There are also a number of jazz recordings dating from early in his career.)

[2328] MENNIN (né MENNINI), Peter
TEACHER, ADMINISTRATOR
BORN: Erie, Pa., May 17, 1923
DIED: New York, June 17, 1983

Peter and Louis Mennini (1920–) were the sons of a commercially successful Italian immigrant who loved music. Both studied with the same piano teacher in childhood, both wrote music before their tenth birthdays, both attended the same high school, and both studied with Normand Lockwood [2084] at Oberlin. They had to leave school for wartime military service in the U.S. Army Air Corps (Peter as an officer candidate, discharged in 1943; Louis as a sergeant in England for the duration). Both afterward studied at the Eastman School of Music under Bernard Rogers [1875] and Howard Hanson [1927]. Peter took his B.A. and M.A. in 1945, having already completed his first two symphonies (of 9) and other compositions, and stayed on to complete a Ph.D. in 1947 and to marry a graduate of that year's class, Georganne Bairnson. That same year Louis received his B.A., the master's degree following a year later. (Louis returned in 1949 to teach there, acquiring *his* doctorate in 1961. Later he taught at the

North Carolina School of the Arts and at Mercyhurst College in Erie.) Peter Mennin, who changed his name to avoid confusion with his brother, taught at the Juilliard School from 1947 to 1958, left to head the Peabody Conservatory in Baltimore, was sent to Russia that same year by the State Department, and was named president of Juilliard in 1961. A composer in the solid Eastman tradition, he wrote mostly orchestral and choral music and received numerous awards, grants, and honorary degrees. (Louis has written 2 symphonies and a chamber opera, but his output has been comparatively small.) RECORDINGS: Orchestral works on records include Symphonies Nos. 3–7 (No. 4 is for chorus and orchestra); Concerto for Piano; Concerto for Cello; *Concertato; Canto;* and (for band) *Canzona.* Also recorded are String Quartet No. 2 and *Canto and Toccata* for piano. (Howard Hanson recorded Louis's *Arioso* for string orchestra.)

[2329] LIGETI, György Sándor (Lē-get'-ē, Jörd'ji Shän'-dôr)
TEACHER
BORN: Dicsöszentmárton, Hungary, May 28, 1923

Thanks to Stanley Kubrick's use of György Ligeti's *Atmosphères, Lux aeterna,* and part of the *Requiem* on the soundtrack of his science fiction film *2001: A Space Odyssey,* the composer has enjoyed a sort of popularity denied to most of the avant-garde. He was born in Transylvania in what is now Tirnăveni, Rumania, but grew up in Kolozsvár (now Cluj), in whose conservatory he studied during the early years of World War II. Then he moved to Budapest and studied with Pál Kadosa [2040], among others. (Considering the fate of most Hungarian Jews, one wonders how Ligeti went unscathed.) Immediately after the fighting ended, he entered the Budapest Academy, whose faculty he joined in 1950, a year after his graduation. The repressive conditions of the time stunted his inclination to experiment, and he was kept writing "people's music." During the 1956 uprising, he fled to Vienna and is now an Austrian citizen. His music developed rapidly after that. He began by experimenting with electronic music in the Cologne studio, whither he had been invited by Herbert Eimert [1935], but he seems to have been dissatisfied with the possibilities of the medium. He also found that the limitations of serialism did not attract him. Consequently he developed what he called *Mikropolyphonie,* wherein dense blocks of sound undergo color changes through minute shifts in the warp and woof of their sound fabric. This was first exhibited in the early 1960s in *Apparition, Atmosphères*, and the organ piece *Volumina*, and a bit later was used for contrast (to simple and moving vocal and instrumental statements) in the *Requiem*. He did not, however, cling doggedly to such means of expression but later experimented with unorthodox sounds sources (e.g., nonverbal human sounds in *Aventures*), polyrhythms, and even classical forms. In the fashion of his time, Ligeti has also indulged himself in the parody or "put-on"—a mock "happening" in an audience-participation "lecture" on the future of art, takeoffs of John Cage [2192] and even of himself, and perhaps most notoriously in the *Poème symphonique* for a hundred metronomes.

Ligeti has taught at Darmstadt, the Royal Conservatory in Stockholm, and Stanford University. He is presently professor of composition at the Hamburg Conservatory. He has written many articles, mostly theoretical. According to a recent book by Paul Griffiths, a chronic illness has severely hampered Ligeti's compositional activities since he completed his first opera, *Le Grande Macabre*, in 1977; but he has now resumed work on two long-standing projects, the Concerto for Piano and an opera after Shakespeare's *The Tempest*.

RECORDINGS: A fair portion of Ligeti's output is represented on records. Orchestral works on disc include *Atmosphères;* Concerto for Cello; *Lontano;* Chamber Concerto for 13 Players; Double Concerto for Flute, Oboe, and Orchestra; *Melodien; Ramifications* for strings; and *San Francisco Polyphony*. Vocal recordings include *Aventures* and *Nouvelles aventures*, both for three singers and seven instruments; *Requiem* for soloists, chorus, and orchestra; *Lux aeterna* for sixteen voices; *Night* and *Morning*, two early pieces for unaccompanied chorus to texts of Hungarian poet Sándor Weöres; and *Scenes and Interludes from Le Grande Macabre*, a vocal-orchestral suite. Chamber recordings include String Quartets Nos. 1 and 2; *10 Pieces* and *6 Bagatelles* for woodwind quintet; and the recent Trio for Violin, French Horn, and Piano. Keyboard recordings include *Organ Studies Nos. 1 and 2; Volumina* for organ; *Monument-Selbstportrait-Bewegung* for two pianos; and several pieces for harpsichord—*Continuum; Hungarian Rock (Chaconne);* and *Passacaglia ungherese*. Although Ligeti has largely abandoned the electronic medium, there are two such works on disc—*Articulation* and *Glissandi*.

[2330] PINKHAM, Daniel Rogers
KEYBOARDIST, CONDUCTOR, TEACHER
BORN: Lynn, Mass., June 5, 1923

As the inventor of a best-selling remedy for female complaints, Lydia E. Pinkham has a place in the annals of American medicine. Daniel Pinkham is her great-grandson. He studied with hymnologist Karl Pfatteicher at the Phillips Academy, with Walter Piston [1890] and Aaron Copland [1986] at Harvard (B.A. 1943, M.A. 1944), with Honegger [1861] and Barber [2149] at Tanglewood, and privately with Nadia Boulanger. His chief keyboard teachers were organist E. Power Biggs and harpsichordists Claude-Jean Chiasson, Putnam Aldrich, and Wanda Landowska. In 1946 he took a teaching job at the Boston Conservatory. Besides concertizing as a harpsichordist, he teamed up in 1948 with violinist Robert Brink to present early music recitals. From 1950 he was harpsichordist with the Boston Symphony. After teaching at Simmons College, Boston University, Harvard, and Dartington Hall in England, he cast his lot in 1959 with the New England Conservatory, where he later headed the early music section. Though perhaps best known to the general musical public as a choral arranger, Pinkham has written a chamber opera, 2 symphonies, several concerti and "concertantes," and many choral works. Initially influenced by the neoclassical approaches of Nadia Boulanger and Stravinsky [1748], he has since made judicious use of the twelve-tone row (usually in a harmonic context) and since 1970 has used electronic sound as part of his palette. RECORDINGS: Orchestral recordings include *Concertante No. 1* for violin and harpsichord soli, strings, and celesta; Symphony No. 2; *Signs of the Zodiac* for narrator and orchestra. Chamber and instrumental recordings include *Cantilena and Capriccio* for violin and harpsichord (with Brink and Pinkham); *Partita* for harpsichord (Pinkham); *Proverbs* for organ; *Miracles* for flute and organ; *Diversions* for harp and organ; and Concerto for Harpsichord and Celeste Soli (with Pinkham as soloist). Vocal recordings include the *Christmas Cantata*, smaller choral works, and songs (including several cycles).

[2331] CHOU Wen-Chung (Jou Wen Joong)
ENGINEER, TEACHER, ADMINISTRATOR
BORN: Chefoo (Yent'ai), June 29, 1923

A student of traditional Chinese music, Chou has amalgamated aspects of it with fairly progressive Western techniques in his compositions. Born into a rather large and very musical family in a port city on the Shantung peninsula, he grew up with the sounds of both native and Western music in his ears. In 1937, in the face of the Japanese invasion, the family moved to Shanghai. Later Chou was driven to Kweilin and then to Chungking, from whose university he graduated in 1945 as a civil engineer. The next year a scholarship in architecture took him to Yale, where he quickly saw the error of his ways and transferred (on another scholarship!) to the New England Conservatory in Boston, where Nicolas Slonimsky [1893] urged him to pursue the bicultural path. In 1949 he moved to New York, where he studied briefly with Bohuslav Martinů [1846] and for five years with Edgard Varèse (whose *Nocturnal* he completed after that composer's death and whose official musical executor he is). That same year he wrote his first important composition, the orchestral *Landscapes*. In 1954 he received his M.A. at Columbia, where he had studied for two years under Otto Luening's [1980] direction. Until 1957 he worked with Luening and Vladimir Ussachevsky [2180] on their electronic researches and directed studies in Chinese music and theater. Subsequently he taught at the University of Illinois, Brooklyn College, and Hunter College, before becoming a permanent member of the Columbia music faculty in 1962. Two years previously he had married a compatriot, Yi-An Chang, head of the music department at Abbott Academy in Andover, Massachusetts, and the first native-born Chinese to graduate from the Juilliard School. Into his later music Chou introduced principles based on the I Ching and microtonal variations from pitch, derived from his theory that in Chinese music each tone is an independent entity subject to variation, which accounts for what Western ears hear as "wavering." Since 1969 involvement with Columbia's superstructure in increasingly demanding administrative roles has virtually taken him away from composition. RECORDINGS: Much of his very small output is on records—*Landscapes, All in the Spring Wind,* and *"And the Fallen Petals"* for orchestra; *Suite for Harp and Wind Quintet; The Willows Are New* for piano; *Soliloquy of a Bhiksuni* for trumpet, brass, and percussion; *Cursive* for flute and piano; *Yü ko* for nine players; and *Pien* for piano, winds, and percussion.

[2332] FLANAGAN, William
REVIEWER
BORN: Detroit, August 14, 1923
DIED: New York, August 31 (?), 1969

Educated at first in public schools and then in a Jesuit academy, Flanagan became interested in music through movie background scores, which he tried to recreate on the piano. An ushering job at the Detroit Symphony concerts introduced him to the classical repertoire. He entered college to major in journalism but gave it up when, wholly without prior training, he managed in 1943 to wangle his way into the Eastman School, where he studied under Bernard Rogers [1875] and Burrill Phillips [2116]. He left in 1946, and for two summers was at Tanglewood as a pupil of Aaron Copland [1986]; he also studied with Honegger [1861] and Samuel Barber [2149] there. For two years after that he was a student of David Diamond [2238] in New York. In the late 1950s he was a reviewer for the New York *Herald Tribune* and for most of the 1960s was a regular record critic for *Stereo Review.* An intimate friend of the playwright Edward Albee, Flanagan provided scores for several of his dramas and set some of his poetry to music. In 1963 the New York City Opera commissioned the two of them to write an opera *(The Ice Age),* but it was never completed. William Flanagan's body was discovered in his apartment on the last day of August 1969, where he had died of an overdose of sleeping pills. He wrote a one-act opera, *Bartleby the Scrivener,* as well as orchestral and chamber works, but his chief gift was a true lyric one, best exhibited in his vocal music. RECORDINGS: These include his solo cantata *The Lady of Tearful Regret* to a text of Edward Albee, *Concert Ode* for orchestra, *Chapters from Ecclesiastes* for chorus and wind quintet, *Another August* for soprano and orchestra, and songs.

[2333] HEILLER, Anton (Hīl'-er, Ȧn'-ton)
KEYBOARD PLAYER, CONDUCTOR, TEACHER
BORN: Vienna, September 15, 1923
DIED: Vienna, March 25, 1979

As a student at the Vienna Academy, Anton Heiller specialized in keyboard instruments, and, at 22, became professor of organ in that institution's department of church music. In 1971 he accepted a professorship at the Hochschule für Musik. From shortly after his graduation he was established as one of the great organists of his time and as such won many prizes and honors. He recorded not only as organist, but also as pianist, harpsichordist, conductor, and (at least once, as Neptune in the first recording of Mozart's [992] *Idomeneo)* as a bass singer.

His thoroughly eclectic music is largely made up of works for choir and organ. RE-CORDINGS: His complete organ music and assorted choral pieces have been recorded.

[2334] ROREM, Ned
PIANIST, TEACHER, WRITER
BORN: Richmond, Ind., October 23, 1923

Regarded by many as the General Custer of the art song, Rorem has also composed successfully in other forms and, as an indefatigable autobiographer, has told us more than most of us need to know about his life and loves and other musically borderline tittle-tattle. He was the son of a physician and member of the faculty at Earlham College but grew up in Chicago, where he studied piano and began his lifelong diaries. From 1938 he studied with Leo Sowerby [1908] at the American Conservatory. After two years at Northwestern, 1940–42, and one at Curtis with Rosario Scalero (1870–1954) and Gian Carlo Menotti [2177], he graduated from the Juilliard School, where his chief mentor was Bernard Wagenaar (1894–1971), in 1946, the year his song "The Lordly Hudson" won the Music Library Award as "the best published song of the year." In the next two years he studied in New York with Virgil Thomson [1928], a great influence, and at Tanglewood with Aaron Copland [1986]. In 1948 he received his M.A. from Juilliard and the Gershwin Prize for his *Overture in C*. The next year he followed Paul Bowles's [2165] example and settled in Morocco, where he performed prodigies of composition, turning out an opera, a ballet, a symphony, a piano concerto (his second), and numerous songs, and winning the 1950 Boulanger Prize. The next year a Fulbright fellowship took him to Paris, where he studied with Honegger [1861]. He remained for the next six years as guest of the Vicomtesse de Noailles, hobnobbing with the remaining active members of Les Six and being particularly influenced by Poulenc [1960]. He returned to the United States in 1957, where he has since thrived on commissions, grants, royalties from his music and books, appearances as accompanist to various singers, stands at various schools as composer-in-residence, and most recently, in 1980, as codirector of the undergraduate composition program at Curtis. Handsome and articulate, he has also turned up from time to time on TV talk shows. Gifted with literary taste and style, he is an admirable critic and reviewer. His larger efforts include 6 operas of sorts, 3 symphonies, 3 piano concerti, and incidental music, including that for two Tennessee Williams plays. His songs

are exquisitely chosen as to texts, written with extraordinary skill, grateful to perform, but not, in the way of great songs, usually very musically memorable. His orchestral *Air Music*, commissioned by the Cincinnati Symphony for the American Bicentennial, won the 1976 Pulitzer Prize. RECORDINGS: Orchestral works on disc include *Design; Symphony No. 3; Ideas for Easy Orchestra; Lions; Water Music* for violin, clarinet, and orchestra; and the Concerto No. 3 for Piano (in six movements). Vocal recordings are quite numerous and include excerpts from his opera *Miss Julie;* (song cycles and solo cantatas) *Mourning Scene, King Midas, 4 Dialogues, Poems of Love and the Rain, Some Trees, War Scenes, Gloria, Ariel, Serenade on 5 English Poems, 7 Madrigals, Last Poems of Wallace Stevens, Nantucket Songs,* and *Women's Voices;* and (for chorus) *4 Madrigals, 2 Psalms and a Proverb,* and *Missa Brevis*. Chamber and instrumental recordings include *11 Studies for 11 Players; Trio* for Flute, Cello, and Piano; *The Lovers* for harpsichord, oboe, cello, and percussion; *Day Music* and *Night Music,* both for violin and piano; *The Book of Hours* for flute and harp; *Romeo and Juliet* for flute and guitar; *Suite for Guitar;* Sonata No. 1 for Piano; and *A Quaker Reader* for organ.

[2335] LEES *(né* **Lisniatsky), Benjamin**
TEACHER, PIANIST
BORN: Harbin (Haerhpin), Manchuria, January 8, 1924

Benjamin Lees (as he later abbreviated his name) was, like his exact contemporary Noël Lee [2344], born in China—specifically Manchuria. A year and a half later his Russian parents emigrated to San Francisco and finally settled in Los Angeles in 1940. Young Lees studied piano in both cities. Called up for military service after he finished high school in 1941, he saw stateside duty throughout the war. He came home in 1945 determined to become a musician, a notion with which his parents would not go along. He worked to finance sufficient training to get him into UCLA the following year. There he studied with Ingolf Dahl [2188], Richard Donovan [1858], and Halsey Stevens [2128]. Dissatisfied with his progress, he left the university in 1948, married Leatrice Banks, and settled down to four years of serious study with George Antheil [1981], making ends meet by playing for a ballet school and writing scores for movie cartoons. His compositions were soon attracting notice, his *Profile for Orchestra* winning an airing on NBC Radio in 1952. To have a better base of operations, he moved to New York in 1953, where he was supported by grants (Fromm, Guggenheim, Fulbright). The Fulbright took him to Finland in 1956. Finding Europe congenial, he stayed on, mostly in Vienna, Genoa, and Paris, occasionally teaching and composing, and getting to know many of his counterparts of both his own and the previous generation. In 1963 he came back to America. Since then he has taught or served as composer-in-residence at various schools, including Peabody, Queens College, the University of Wisconsin, and Juilliard. Influenced by Antheil, he has avoided identification with the fashionable movements of his time. His chief musical heroes appear to be Bartók [1734] and Prokofiev [1851]. He has written 2 operas, 3 symphonies, a number of concerti, 2 string quartets, 4 piano sonatas, and about two score other orchestral, instrumental, and vocal works. RECORDINGS: Orchestral works on disc include Symphonies Nos. 2 and 3; Concerto for Violin; Concerto for Orchestra; Concerto for String Quartet and Orchestra; and *Prologue, Capriccio, and Epilogue.* Also recorded are String Quartets Nos. 1 and 2; Sonata No. 2 for Violin and Piano; Sonata for Cello and Piano; and Sonata No. 4 for Piano.

[2336] NONO, Luigi (Nō'-nō, Lōō-ē'-jē)
POLITICIAN, LAWYER, TEACHER, LECTURER
BORN: Venice, January 29, 1924

In an era in which avant-garde music is not only resisted by most audiences but also condemned by the international Communist apparatus, one can only admire the quixoticism of an aging composer who has spent his life purveying it to the proletariat. Thus it is with Luigi Nono, who early became a passionate believer in Marxism and is presently a member of the Central Committee of the Italian Communist Party. He began his musical studies in 1941 at the Benedetto Marcello Conservatory in his native city and audited classes directed by Gian Francesco Malipiero [1743], whom he later rejected as a Fascist. Toward the end of World War II he was a resistance fighter with the Partisans. Afterward he turned to law, graduating from the University of Padua at twenty-two. By that time he had fallen in with Bruno Maderna [2300], with whom he then began serious study. In 1948 he undertook further study with Hermann Scherchen, and between 1950 and 1959 was involved in the contemporary music festivals at Darmstadt. Expectably he followed the path from do-

decaphony to total serialism. As if to seal his allegiance, in 1955 he married Nuria Schoenberg, the composer's [1657] daughter. But in 1960 he went to work in the Milan Studio di Fonologia Musicale, founded by Berio [2352] and Maderna, to develop a mastery of electronic music. (It has been fashionable to speak of the three composers as a sort of Holy Trinity of contemporary Italian music.) Nono has taught, lectured, and propagandized all over the world, including the Soviet Union, where his politics are admired, but where most of his output is regarded as a Nono. His music has become increasingly single-minded and is often wedded to inflammatory texts from what one thinks of as rather unlikely sources—the Communist Manifesto, letters from socialist martyrs, utterances by members of the Viet Cong. (In the early, more adventurous days of National Educational Television, Nono's left-wing opera *Intolleranza 1960* was broadcast nationwide in the United States.) However one feels about Nono's sentiments, it is hard not to regard some of his output as bordering on the hysterical and limited to a given historical era in effectiveness. RECORDINGS: Works recorded include *Y su sangre ya viene cantando* for flute, strings, and percussion; *Polifonica-Monodia-Ritmica* (chamber ensemble); *Como una ola de fuerza y luz* (soprano, piano, orchestra, and tape); *Y entonces comprendio* (voices and tape); *La Fabbrica illuminata* (soprano and tape); *Ricorda costa ti hanno fatto in Auschwitz* (voices and tape); *Ha venido* (soprano voices); *Canciones a Guiomar* (soprano and chamber ensemble); one movement of *Espressione* (orchestra); *A Floresta é jovem e cheja de vida* (oratorio); *". . . Sofferte onde serene . . ."* (two pianos and ensemble); *Contrappunto dialettico alla mente* (chorus and tape); *Sara dolce tacere* (voices); *Per Bastiana* (for three orchestras and tape); *Incontri* (twenty-four instruments); *Omaggio a Emilio Vedora* (tape), and *Canti di vita e d'amore* (soprano, tenor, and orchestra).

[2337] HILLER, Lejaren Arthur, Jr.
CHEMIST, TEACHER
BORN: New York, February 23, 1924

Not surprisingly, the new cerebral music has attracted scientists and technologists to it, Lejaren Hiller providing a sterling example. He went to Princeton University to study chemistry in 1941 and proceeded there to a Ph.D. in that field six years later. However, during this period he took the opportunity of studying with Milton Babbit [2247] and Roger Sessions [1931]. On graduation he took a job as a research chemist with the Du Pont Company, working there for five years. For another five, he was an assistant professor of chemistry at the University of Illinois, but in his spare time pursued his music studies. In 1957 Hiller and Leonard Isaacson successfully programmed the university's ILLIAC computer to "write" a work for string quartet, which they christened the *ILLIAC Suite;* it seems to have been the first (but not the last) computer composition. A year later, with an M.M. degree in hand, Hiller joined the university's music department and founded its Experimental Music Studio. In 1968 he accepted the Slee Visiting Professorship of Music at SUNY, Buffalo, where he also served as Lukas Foss's **[2324]** codirector of the Center for the Creative and Performing Arts and is now full professor. Not all of Hiller's music is technological: he has produced, for example, 2 symphonies, a piano concerto, quartets, and sonatas; he has additionally done a number of mixed-media (and straight) theater pieces. He has also written scholarship in both his fields. RECORDINGS: *An Avalanche for Pitchmen, Prima Donna, Player Piano, Percussionist, and Pre-recorded Playback; Nightmare Music* (film score); *Computer Music* (percussion and tape); *Suite for 2 Pianos and Tape; Algorithms; ILLIAC Suite; Computer Cantata* (with Robert Baker); *HPSCHD* (with John Cage: the first recording in which the listener has some control over the aleatory aspects of the music); String Quartets Nos. 5 and 6; Sonatas Nos. 4 and 5 for Piano; *Jesse James* (4 voices and piano); *5 Appalachian Ballads* (voice and guitar); *Malta* (tuba and tape); Sonata No. 3 for Violin and Piano; *12-Tone Variations* (piano); and *Machine Music* (piano, percussion, and tape).

[2338] DODGSON, Stephen Cuthbert Vivian

BORN: London, March 17, 1924

At eighteen Stephen Dodgson entered the British navy for war service. He emerged in 1946, matriculated at the Royal College of Music, and graduated in 1949. He then spent some time in Italy on a fellowship. He has written, among other things, operas and orchestral works but is perhaps best known for his guitar music, inspired by his friends Julian Bream and John Williams. (Dodgson does not play the instrument himself.) RECORDINGS: His Concerti for Guitar Nos. 1 and 2 have both been recorded, as have the *Duo concertante* for guitar and harpsichord, *Partita* for guitar, Sonata for Brass, *Suite for Brass Septet,* and songs.

[2339] KELEMEN, Milko (Ke-le'-men, Mĕl'-kō)

TEACHER, ADMINISTRATOR

BORN: Podravska Slatina, March 30, 1924

Born in Croatia near the Hungarian border, Kelemen studied piano at home, then attended the Zagreb Conservatory, where, after some work with Messiaen **[2129]** and Tony Aubin (1907–) at the Paris Conservatoire, he joined the teaching staff in 1955. In 1958 he took two years off to study with Wolfgang Fortner (1907–) in Freiburg-in-Breisgau. During his Zagreb years he helped found and later directed the biennial festival devoted to new music, with which latter concern he became increasingly involved. In 1966 he went to Munich and worked for two years in the Siemens electronic studio. From 1969 to 1973 he taught at the Düsseldorf Conservatory, then was appointed professor of music at the Stuttgart Hochschule. Initially folk-inspired, he has explored most of the avant-garde channels and has written prolifically in most forms as well as in nonforms. RECORDINGS: Mostly of Western European origin, these include *Études contrapuntiques* for wind quintet; *Changéant* for cello and orchestra; *Hommage à Heinrich Schütz* for chorus; *Surprise* for strings; *Composé* for two pianos and orchestra; *Floréal* for orchestra; String Quartet No. 2 (also known as *Varia melodia); Fabliau* for organ and microphones; *Passionato* for flute and three choruses; and one word from his pre–avant-garde phrase, the 1955 *Improvisations concertantes* for strings.

[2340] BALLIF, Claude André François (Bȧl-lēf', Klōd Ȧn-drā' Frȧn-swȧ')

TEACHER, MUSICOLOGIST, THEORIST

BORN: Paris, May 22, 1924

Ballif began serious musical study at the Bordeaux Conservatory, then was a pupil of Tony Aubin (1907–), Noël Gallon **[1856]**, and Olivier Messiaen **[2129]** at its Paris analog, and finally in 1951 studied in Berlin with Boris Blacher **[2030]** and musicologist-theorist Josef Rufer. He has taught and lectured sporadically at various schools and institutes in Berlin, Hamburg, and Paris and is on the faculty of the conservatory at Rheims. In 1956 he published a monograph on "metatonality," an extension of tonality based on a scale of eleven notes (the tonality, so-called, being that of the unstated twelfth tone), on which much of his music is based. He has used other adaptations of modern techniques, notably indeterminacy, the use of natural sounds, and electronics. RECORD-INGS: His 4 Sonatas for Organ have been re-corded, as have *Phrases sur le souffle (Phrases on the Breath)* for alto voice, chorus, and instruments; *Imaginaires IV* for organ and brasses; *Un coup de dès* for chorus, percussionists, two contrabasses, and tape (after Mallarmé); and *Airs com-primés* for piano.

[2341] NIGG, Serge (Něg, Sârzh)
EDUCATOR
BORN: Paris, June 6, 1924

As a youngster Nigg studied piano with Ginette Martenot, sister of the inventor of the electronic instrument called the Ondes Martenot. Nigg attended the Paris Conser-vatoire from 1941 to 1946, his composition teacher there being Olivier Messiaen **[2129]**. He then studied with Schoenberg **[1657]** apostle René Leibowitz, and became the first and most militant of the French serialists. Not long afterward his leftist political lean-ings caused him to reject elitist methods for music with a wide popular appeal, chiefly influenced by that of Ravel **[1666]**. As a founder, with Louis Durey **[1828]** and con-ductor Roger Desormière of the Association Française des Musiciens Progressistes, he has been a frequent delegate to the Eastern Bloc, where he has lectured. He visited the United States in 1967 and was appointed in the same year chief inspector of singing in French schools. RECORDINGS: Works re-corded by various French labels include Concerto No. 1 for Violin, Concerto No. 1 for Piano, *Hieronymous Bosch Symphony*, *Visages d'Axel* for orchestra, and *Le Chant de dépossédé*. (These are all works written between 1955 and 1964.)

[2342] LADERMAN, Ezra
TEACHER, ADMINISTRATOR
BORN: New York, June 29, 1924

While a student at New York's High School of Music and Art, Ezra Laderman wrote his first piano concerto (of 2). Serving in the U.S. Army in Germany in 1945, he heard his *Leipzig Symphony* premiered in Wiesbaden. On his return to the United States, he spent four years getting a B.A. at Brooklyn Col-lege in 1950, while he took composition les-sons with Stefan Wolpe **[2020]** on the out-side. He received an M.A. at Columbia two years later, having studied there with Otto Luening **[1980]**, Douglas Moore **[1884]**, and musicologist Paul Henry Láng. He devoted most of the rest of the decade to composi-tion, aided by two Guggenheim fellowships in 1955 and 1958. An opera, *Jacob and the Indians*, was produced at Woodstock, N.Y., in 1957; and another, the one-act *Sarah*, on television in 1959. He taught at Sarah Law-rence (no apparent connection with the op-era) in 1960–61, spent two years abroad in the Eternal City on a Prix de Rome, 1963–65, won a third Guggenheim fellowship in 1964, and returned to Sarah Lawrence for another one-year term in 1965. In the last-named year he wrote a score for the docu-mentary film *The Eleanor Roosevelt Story* that won him an Academy Award the next March. In 1971 CBS televised his opera *And David Wept* (one of several Laderman works on Hebraic themes), and that fall he went to SUNY at Binghamton as professor and composer-in-residence. He remained there until 1979 when he was called to Washington to head the music section of the National Endowment for the Arts. Laderman is mar-ried to the former Aimee Davis, a biologist, and has three children. A fairly conservative composer, he has written 5 operas (the big-gest is *Galileo Galilei*, 1979), 5 symphonies, 2 oratorios, 5 concerti, 6 string quartets, and much vocal and chamber music. RECORD-INGS: Works committed to disc include (orchestral) *Stanzas, The Magic Prison* (with narration, to a text of Archibald MacLeish), and Concerto for Orchestra; (chamber) String Quartets Nos. 1 and 2, *Theme, Varia-tions, and Finale* for wind quintet, Sonata for Flute and Piano, and Duo for Violin and Piano; (song cycles) *Songs for Eve* and *From the Psalms.*

[2343] AITKEN, Hugh
TEACHER
BORN: New York, September 7, 1924

Scion of musical parents, Hugh Aitken had paternal instruction in violin and maternal piano training. Of eminently draftable age, he entered the armed forces in 1942 and served as an air corps navigator. Bolstered by the G.I. Bill, he entered Juilliard, studied with Persichetti **[2236]**, Ward **[2269]**, and Bernard Wagenaar (1894–1971), graduated in 1950, and joined the faculty. In 1971 he went to William Paterson College in New Jersey, where he has chaired the music department and served as associate dean of the College of Arts and Sciences. He has written a piano concerto, cantatas, a ballet, and a good deal of chamber music. RECORDINGS: Works on records include *Cantatas Nos. 1, 3, 4; Suite for Solo Bass; Montages* for solo bassoon; and the *Piano Fantasy.*

[2344] LEE, Noël
PIANIST, TEACHER
BORN: Nanking, December 25, 1924

Despite his oriental place of birth, Noël Lee is unrelated to his older contemporary Dai-Keong Lee **[2240]** and is not Chinese. (There seems, however, to be a relationship between his first name and his birthday.) His parents moved to Lafayette, Indiana, when he was an infant. He began studying the piano at five and composing at six. He went to Harvard on a scholarship, studied composition there with Irving Fine **[2228]** and Walter Piston **[1890]** and continued his pianistic studies at the New England Conservatory. Graduating from both schools in 1948, he went the following year to Paris, where he studied with Nadia Boulanger. Though he has occasionally taught in the United States, he has made Paris his home. His compositions, which include orchestral, vocal, and chamber music, are of a neo-classical cast and unabashedly melodic. He is best known, however, as a pianist and has made dozens of recordings, both as a soloist and with violinist Paul Makanowitzky and in a duo with pianist Christian Ivaldi. RECORDINGS: Works on records include *5 Songs on Poems by Lorca; Caprices on "Schoenberg"* for piano and orchestra; *Convergences* for flute and harpsichord; and *Dialogues* for violin and piano.

[2345] CONSTANT, Marius (Kōn´-stȧnt, Mär´-yoos)
CONDUCTOR, TEACHER
BORN: Bucharest, February 7, 1925

Constant graduated in 1944 from the Bucharest Conservatory and, as winner of the Enesco Prize, went on to study in Paris. A conducting protégé of Jean Fournet at the École Normale, he was also a pupil of Honegger **[1861]** there. Later he attended the Paris Conservatoire, where he worked with Boulanger and perhaps more importantly with Olivier Messiaen **[2129]** and from which he bore away the composition prize on his graduation in 1949. For several years he was chief conductor for the Ballets de Paris, directed by Roland Petit, in which capacity he toured the United States; he wrote a number of ballets for this company. In 1963 he founded the Ars Nova Ensemble, devoted to the performance of new music and to group improvisation. In recent years he has explored a number of avant-garde techniques and has produced mixed-media pieces and stage works that are close to "happenings" (e.g., an "improvised" opera).

He has taught at, among other places, Stanford University. RECORDINGS: Works on records include the ballet *Éloge de la folie (Praise of Folly); 24 Préludes* for orchestra; *Les Chants de Maldoror* (for recitation, twenty-three improvisers, and ten celli); *Winds* (for fourteen winds and double bass); *Traits* (for six to twenty-five players); and *14 Stations* (for one percussionist, playing ninety-two instruments, and six instrumentalists). Also recorded is the snippet by which Constant is perhaps best known to the public at large, the title theme for the television series "The Twilight Zone" (contained on the record album *The Twilight Zone: Volume I*). Constant's musical adaptation of Bizet's **[1363]** *Carmen* for the Peter Brook production *La Tragédie de Carmen* has also been documented on records.

[2346] BOULEZ, Pierre (Bōō-lez´, Pē-âr´)
CONDUCTOR
BORN: Montbrison, March 26, 1925

Pierre Boulez is a child of his time and may be viewed in some respects as a herald of the 1960s. At the outset of his career, his potential dazzled every musician who encountered him. His charisma might be said to have led a whole generation down a primrose path that deltaed into so many *cul-de-sacs.* No one denies his phenomenal musicianship. No one gainsays the power of his intellect. But it now seems possible that in musical history he is as likely to wind up as a curiosity treated in a footnote as he is as a Moses who led music out of the wilderness —or the doldrums.

Boulez was born in a small town in the Lyonnais, not far from St. Étienne. His straitlaced father Léon, an engineer, was an official in a steel plant. Pierre was the third of four children. Like Beethoven **[1063]**, he was named for a deceased elder brother. As a matter of course he was started on piano lessons at the age of six. Later he was soprano soloist in the choir of the local Catholic elementary school, where he distinguished himself academically, especially in mathematics. In 1939 he began going to St. Étienne for weekly music lessons, and he attended school there the next year. In 1941 he entered, at his father's insistence, a pre-engineering curriculum at the University of Lyons. There he met and impressed the soprano Ninon Vallin, who argued his reluctant father into letting him study at the Lyons Conservatory. Attempting to qualify as a pianist, he failed to win acceptance. Nevertheless, on Mme. Vallin's urging, the senior

Boulez let his son concentrate on music courses in his second year.

At eighteen young Boulez was in full rebellion, rejecting (loudly and publicly) his origins, his country, and his religion. He moved to Paris and entered the conservatory there. During his first year he studied counterpoint privately with Mme. Arthur Honegger (Andrée Vaurabourg). The next year he took Olivier Messiaen's [2129] advanced harmony course. He was at first entranced by Messiaen's originality, though later he decided it went nowhere near far enough. (But in 1949 he was to take to heart Messiaen's notions about the serialization of rhythms and intensities.) Meanwhile he supported himself by playing the Ondes Martenot (an electronic instrument for which he wrote some student pieces) in the orchestra of the Folies Bergère.

In 1945 Boulez chanced to hear René Leibowitz conduct Schoenberg's [1657] Woodwind Quintet, Op. 26, and his life was changed once and for all. Leibowitz had studied with Anton Webern [1773] and with Schoenberg himself, and became the latter's self-appointed apostle. It was Leibowitz who in effect introduced Schoenberg's music to France, and it was Leibowitz (rather than Schoenberg) who insisted that the twelve-tone system was a mandatory article of musical faith. Boulez began studying the works of the Second Viennese School under Leibowitz's direction, and the pieces he wrote around that time showed the Schoenbergian influence, though he described their language as that of "controlled hysteria." But typically Boulez found both Schoenberg and Leibowitz too limited and began elevating Webern above Schoenberg as the master for our times. What Boulez wanted was nothing short of total control of his material and its performances, and this gradually led to his theory of serialism, in which not only pitch but all elements of a composition move in rigidly dictated sequences.

Never mind that Milton Babbitt [2247] had hit on the same idea a couple of years before. It was Boulez who preached it like a zealot to rapidly growing numbers of disciples. *This* was the music of the immediate future, and all that had gone before must be ruthlessly destroyed. (Boulez was a great one for solving problems by annihilation: in the 1960s he was urging the torching of opera houses, and he stepped on a good many toes with his 1952 article "Schoenberg Is Dead.") One who was fascinated by Boulez's attitude toward modernism was John Cage [2192], who did much to promote his music

and open doors for him in the earlier stages of his career.

On leaving the Paris Conservatoire in 1946, Boulez became music director for the theater company of Jean-Louis Barrault and Madeleine Renaud, with which he remained for over a decade. Meanwhile he was increasingly attracting attention with such works as the first two piano sonatas and the *Livre pour quatuor (Quartet-Book)* for string quartet. Among those drawn into his orbit for a time were Henri Pousseur [2383], Luciano Berio [2352], and Karlheinz Stockhausen [2377]. His was a name to be conjured with at such avant-garde festivals as those at Donaueschingen and Darmstadt, and his tastes in painting (Klee, Kandinsky, Mondrian) and literature (Joyce, Kafka) became those of his admirers. By the early 1950s he had in such works as *Polyphonie X* (since, like so many of his works, withdrawn) and especially *Structures I* (for two pianos) achieved his goal of total rigidity. (When it was complained that these works failed to communicate, he explained that form is the source of meaning.)

In 1953 Boulez decided it was time to go public with his preachment of the new and persuaded the Barraults to let him use their theater on Sundays for a series of concerts, which came to be called the Domaine Musical and which presented not only the music of Boulez and his group, but also that of selected old masters such as Webern and Stravinsky [1748]. But even as his influence reached its height, some of Boulez's followers were beginning to feel that total serialism was too confining and that there had to be relaxations permitted. One such was Stockhausen: when he discovered Cage, who contrary to Boulez was striving, through the actions of chance, to free his music from all authorial control, there was an irreparable break between him and Boulez. After that Stockhausen became grand guru of the avant-garde as high priest of the aleatory. Boulez was soon apparently seeking a way out: he found it in the poetry of Stephane Mallarmé, who forthwith became his guiding light—for his density of thought, hermetic language, and espousal of "open form," wherein various parts of a work were interchangeable. On the last basis, most of Boulez's relatively few subsequent compositions remain in suspension, having come by their creator to be regarded as parts of greater wholes. On such grounds the third piano sonata has remained unfinished since 1957, and several individual works based on Mallarmé have been conjoined under the title *Pli selon pli (Fold upon Fold)*. Only five new works appeared between 1969 and 1981.

Boulez seems to have slipped into conducting. In the middle 1950s he occasionally presided over some complex piece of chamber music at the Domaine Musical. Two or three times he bailed out other conductors of his own compositions. Late in the decade he moved to Baden-Baden, where he signed a contract with the Southwest German Radio Symphony, which required both composition and conducting. (German radio stations were the chief market for the new music, which they broadcast in late-night programs.) In 1963 he was invited to conduct the French National Radio Orchestra in Stravinsky's *Rite of Spring*. His reading was commercially recorded and at the time was said to mark his first appearance on records as conductor, though in fact he had earlier recorded two concerti by C. P. E. Bach [**801**] (!) and the opera *Christoph Colombe* by Milhaud [**1868**]. The brilliance of Boulez's finely analytical readings made him also the obvious choice to lead the French premiere (after thirty-eight years!) of Alban Berg's [**1789**] *Wozzeck*. In 1964, however, when Minister of Culture André Malraux appointed Marcel Landowski [**2229**] as his musical deputy, Boulez canceled future performances in Paris, forbade that his music be played by government-supported orchestras, and left the Domaine Musical. Nevertheless his reputation as a conductor burgeoned. He was increasingly invited to lead major orchestras, and in 1966 even invaded the sacred German precincts of Bayreuth to conduct *Parsifal*. Ironically in 1968 he was called on to draw up a program of reforms for the Paris Opéra and subsequently was named its director, though the political upheavals of that year rendered the appointment invalid. In 1969 he had become "principal guest conductor" of the Cleveland Orchestra—i.e., he led the modern programs which did not interest Georg Szell. About the same time he was chosen as chief conductor of the BBC Symphony in London and shortly afterward was named to succeed Leonard Bernstein [**2282**] at the helm of the New York Philharmonic. He resolved the conflict by agreeing to conduct four months in each city, leaving him another four for composition.

In the meantime the French government was creating for him the Institut de Recherche et de Coordination Acoustique/Musique (IRCAM). To facilitate its development he left the BBC in 1974 and planned to resign from the New York Philharmonic in 1977 when his second contract would be up. The latter decision was probably just as well: his campaign to bring American audiences into the twentieth century had not worked; irate subscribers had left in droves; many members of the orchestra were fed up with his perfectionism; and the reviewers reported too many performances in which his heart seemed uninvolved. He was replaced by Zubin Mehta, a proponent of the Romantic. However, this did not spell an end to his conducting career by any means: in 1976 he was chosen to conduct the remarkable and controversial Patrice Chereau production of Wagner's Ring at Bayreuth (which was subsequently taped for television and broadcast worldwide). And in 1979 he returned to the Paris Opéra for the first complete performance anywhere of Alban Berg's *Lulu*. As usual with Boulez, earthshaking changes in music have been predicted from his researches. The world is still waiting.

RECORDINGS: Boulez's most successful work with the public has been *Le Marteau sans maître (The Masterless Hammer,* 1954), a treatment for alto and chamber ensemble of a poem by René Char. It has enjoyed several recordings, at least two directed by the composer. Boulez has also recorded the 1948 cantata *Le Soleil des eaux (The Sun on the Waters); Pli selon pli* (twice); *Éclat* for chamber orchestra, 1965; *Éclat-Multiples* (the expanded version of a work that is still in progress); two movements of *Livre* for string quartet; *Livre* for string orchestra (the 1969 revision of the string quartet piece); *Domaines* for solo clarinet and chamber orchestra; and the 1965 *Rituel* for orchestra, written in memory of Bruno Maderna [**2300**]; *Polyphonie X* for eighteen solo instruments; *Cummings ist der Dichter;* the 3 piano sonatas; *Structures* for two pianos; *Messagesquisse* for solo cello and cello ensemble; and the *Étude sur sept sons* for tape. (The *Improvisation sur Mallarmé II* is an excerpt from *Pli selon pli* that has been recorded separately.) Recently Boulez has been recording works written by composers at IRCAM, including pieces by young French composers like Hugues Dufourt (1943–) and Gérard Grisey (1946–), Britishers Harrison Birtwistle [**2410**], and Jonathan Harvey (1939–), the Hungarian György Kurtág (1926–), and (most unpredictably) "serious" works by American rock star Frank Zappa (1940–). These works are anything but doctrinaire; it remains to be seen what impact (if any) such diversity will have on Boulez's own future compositions.

[**2347**] **CHAYNES, Charles** (Shen, Shärl)
VIOLINIST, RADIO OFFICIAL
BORN: Toulouse, July 11, 1925

After initial studies at his hometown conservatory, where he majored in violin, Charles Chaynes transferred to the Paris Conservatoire, where his teachers included Milhaud **[1868]**, Rivier **[1923]**, and the Gallon brothers **[1856]**. He graduated in 1951 and spent the next three years in Rome as a Grand Prix winner. In 1964 he became program director for the Radiodiffusion Française. His music is based on a kind of free atonality. RECORDINGS: Concerto for Organ, Strings, and Percussion; Concerto for Piano; Concerto for Trumpet; *4 Illustrations pour "La Flûte de jade"* for flute and orchestra; *Pour un monde noir* for soprano and orchestra, inspired by music of Africa and Martinique; *Visions concertantes* for guitar and strings; *Erzsevet,* opera monologue for soprano and orchestra; *Poèmes d'Sappho* for soprano and string trio; *Tarquinia* for Ondes Martenot, piano, and percussion; and *M'zab,* a suite for piano based on Arabic music.

[2348] AKUTAGAWA, Yasushi (Ä-kōō-tä-gä-wä, Yä-sōō-shē)
CONDUCTOR
BORN: Tokyo, July 12, 1925

Yasushi Akutagawa is the third son of the novelist Ryunosuke Akutagawa, whose *Rashomon* provided the basis for the classic film. Yasushi was a pupil at the Tokyo Academy of Akira Ifukube (1914–), who was himself a pupil of Alexander Tcherepnin **[1961]**. He also studied conducting at the academy and graduated in 1949. He then spent two further years in graduate study there, during which time his *Trinità Sinfonica* was premiered and given several subsequent performances. In 1950 he won the Japanese Radio Prize for his *Music for Symphony Orchestra.* Three years later he joined forces with Ikuma Dan (1924–) and Toshiro Mayuzumi **[2380]** to promote their own and other contemporary Japanese music. Political interests drew Akutagawa to Russia as a visitor, where he was influenced by the music of Prokofiev **[1851]** and Shostakovich **[2094]**. He has been active as a conductor in Japan. He is perhaps best known in the West for his prize-winning score for the film *Gate of Hell.* He has written 2 operas, 4 ballets, and a good deal of orchestral music. RECORDINGS: Several orchestral works have been recorded—*Music for Symphony Orchestra; Triptyque for Strings; Prima Sinfonia;* and *Trinità Sinfonica.* There is also a recording of music for the film *Village of 8 Gravestones.*

[2349] BOUCOURECHLIEV, André
(Bōō-kōō-rek'-lyev, Än-drä)
PIANIST, CRITIC
BORN: Sofia, July 28, 1925

A prize-winning piano student at the Sofia Conservatory in 1948, Boucourechliev left Bulgaria for Paris a year later to continue his studies with Reine Gianoli at the École Normale, graduating in 1951. He remained there as a teacher of piano to the end of the decade, meanwhile pursuing a concert career and writing on music. He undertook further piano study with Walter Gieseking in 1955 and 1956. About this time he became fascinated by avant-garde music (he had written some unremarkable things previously), spending his summers in Darmstadt, where the action was. In 1957–58 he worked at the Milan electronic music studio and produced *Texte I.* With *Texte II* of 1960, composed in the like facilities of the ORTF in Paris, he combined electronic music with indeterminacy by preparing two tapes to be played together, the second to be started at random relative to the first. In 1963–64 he taught and studied in the United States. Shortly afterward he began the series of aleatory works he termed *Archipels (Archipelagos);* the realization of each depends on how one interprets a score that looks like a navigational map. The composer reviews and writes articles for several French musical journals and has written biographies of Schumann **[1211]**, Chopin **[1208]**, and Beethoven **[1063]** for general readers. RECORDINGS: Works on record include the electronic *Texte I* and *Texte II* as well as *Archipel I* for two pianos and percussion, *Archipel II* for string quartet, *Archipel IV* for piano, and *Ombres* for string orchestra.

[2350] SOMERS, Harry Stuart
PIANIST, MEDIA COMMENTATOR
BORN: Toronto, September 11, 1925

Perhaps Canada's best-known contemporary composer on the international scene, Somers began studying piano with Dorothy Hornfelt when he was fourteen and continued with Reginald Godden at the Royal Conservatory in Toronto from 1941 to 1943. After war service he returned in 1946 to continue piano studies with Weldon Kilburn and, in the summers, with E. Robert Schmitz. His composition teacher at the conservatory was John Weinzweig (1913–). On graduating in 1949 he received a scholarship that gave him a year's study with Milhaud **[1868]** in Paris. Since that time he has devoted his time to composition, sometimes making ends meet by copying music for others and appearing as a performer and radio-television commentator on modern music. His long catalog of works embraces all genres. His style is highly eclectic, making use of both traditional and very advanced techniques. His opera *Louis Riel* was premiered at the Kennedy Center in Washington, D.C., in 1975. RECORDINGS: Works on records include *The Fool* (chamber opera in two scenes); *Sketches* for orchestra; *Passacaglia and Fugue* for orchestra; *Fantasia* for orchestra; *Symphony for Woodwinds, Brass, and Percussion; Scherzo* for strings; *Suite for Harp and Chamber Orchestra; Kuyas* for soprano, flute, and percussion; *5 Songs for Dark Voice and Orchestra; Gloria* (and other choral pieces); String Quartets Nos. 1 and 3; Sonatas Nos. 1 and 2 for Violin and Piano; *Rhapsody* for violin and piano; Sonatas Nos. 3 and 5 for Piano; and some songs. (Other works may have been made briefly available by the CBC.)

[2351] HADZIDAKIS, Manos (Hăd-zē-dă'-kis, Mă'-nōs)
BORN: Xanthi, October 23, 1925

Born in Macedonia, not far from the Bulgarian border, Hadzidakis early became fascinated with the Greek popular idiom, which he incorporated in his music. At nineteen he won attention with his incidental music for Eugene O'Neill's play *Mourning Becomes Electra*. His first published work was a set of piano pieces combining the native touch with Prokofiev **[1851]**. Later he won worldwide fame with his score for the Jules Dassin picture *Never on Sunday*. RECORDINGS: His *Lilacs Out of the Dead Land* has been recorded, as well as *For a Little White Seashell* (for piano) and some songs.

[2352] BERIO, Luciano (Bâr'-yō, Looch-yă'-nō)
PIANIST, CONDUCTOR, TEACHER
BORN: Oneglia, October 24, 1925

The youngest of the Trinity of the Italian avant-garde—the others are Maderna **[2300]** and Nono **[2336]**—Berio is probably more widely known, performed, and admired than either of his fellows nowadays. One indeed finds oneself thinking of him as the grand synthesist, the composer who has pointed up what was most worthwhile in the movement as a whole. Berio was born on the Italian Riviera north of Genoa into a family that had produced several generations of musical Berios. His grandfather was an organist, his father an organist and composer, and both took a hand in his early training. He planned to be a concert pianist, but when a hand was damaged in a 1944 accident, he gave it up. Having a sound academic education, he went to Milan to study law but wound up at the conservatory learning composition from Giorgio Ghedini (1892–1965) and conducting from Carlo Maria Giulini. While a student he supported himself as an accompanist for the vocal classes of Aureliano Pertile and Carmen Melis and as musical factotum (percussionist and conductor) for a small opera company. Shortly after he completed his studies in 1950, he married the extraordinary Armenian-American soprano Cathy Berberian, who had been studying in Milan on a Fulbright fellowship. It can truly be said that they made beautiful music together, for her unusual range, technique, and intelligence inspired him to a number of his most effective (and experimental) vocal compositions. (They also produced a daughter.)

The couple visited the bride's parents in Long Island shortly after the wedding, and Berio found himself seduced by the American scene. He returned a year later—rather extravagantly, one would think—to study with Luigi Dallapiccola **[2049]** at Tanglewood (actually he was financed by a Koussevitzky Scholarship) and was indoctrinated in dodecaphonic mysteries (which typically he turned to his own very individual uses). Back in the United States for a third time in October 1952, he attended Vladimir Ussachevsky's **[2180]** unveiling of his first electronic compositions at the Museum of Modern Art in New York and suffered an epiphany. (Berio is a dedicated Joycean and one of his first twelve-tone compositions was *Chamber Music,* a setting of Joyce poems.) Joining the staff of Radiotelevisione Italiana, he put the new medium to work in scores for some television productions. Meanwhile he continued to compose on paper, producing the orchestral *Nones* and *Allelujah I* (later revised as *Allelujah II)* where, using half a dozen "orchestras" he experiments with "spatial" musical relationships.

Encounters with other avant-garde leaders, chiefly at Darmstadt, led in 1955 to the foundation of the RAI Studio di Fonologia in Milan by Berio and Maderna. Most of the faithful and their followers passed through its doors in the years that Berio directed it. One of his more notable tape compositions is another Joyce-inspired work, *Omaggio a Joyce,* the sound source being Cathy Berberian's reading of a passage from *Ulysses.* But perhaps the most famous—even popular—is the theater piece *Visage* (the soundtrack to an unfilmed movie, Berio has called it) in which a life cycle is traced in twenty minutes by Berberian's voice making nonmusical nonverbal sounds against an electronic background. (The "action" consists of the protagoniste, surrounded by a half dozen other unmoving figures, slowly opening and closing her eyes.) During these years Berio and Maderna staged a series of contemporary music concerts called *Incontri musicali* (Musical Encounters), which spawned a like-named journal that Berio founded and edited.

Snarls of red tape caused Berio to resign from the radio in 1960. He also gave up the magazine and returned to America that summer to teach at Tanglewood, where he and Cathy gave the premiere of *Circles*, imaginative settings of e. e. cummings poems, which use a modicum of indeterminacy. In 1963 Berio began two years of teaching at Mills College in Oakland, California. Then he divided his time between Harvard, Juilliard, and Cologne. About this time the marriage ended (though the musical partnership continued). Remarried, Berio settled in Weehawken, New Jersey, and concentrated his teaching efforts on Juilliard, where he founded and directed the Juilliard Ensemble, a crack contemporary music group. Meanwhile he continued to absorb new impeti, develop, and compose. Notable compositions of the 1960s were the theater piece *Laborintus*, a series of interrelated chamber-ensemble and orchestral *Chemins*, another series of *Sequenze* for various kinds of soloists, and most successfully *Sinfonia*, a big symphony for orchestra and small chorus that uses both musical and verbal quotation in a sort of collage. For Cathy he wrote *Epifanie* (with orchestra), and in a very different vein a set of orchestrally accompanied folksongs, arrangements of songs by the Beatles, and Monteverdi [333] realizations. In 1970 Berio's *Opera* was produced at Santa Fe to cheers from the believers and confusion among the rest.

In 1972 Berio returned to Italy to stay and to the radio to produce an educational TV program, called (in translation) "There's Music and Music." That same year he wrote *Concert for Cathy*, a theater piece that is also an artful synopsis of her career. He has continued to compose prodigiously. He joined Pierre Boulez [2346] in 1974 in the Institut de Recherche et de Coordination Acoustique/Musique (IRCAM) at the newly opened Pompidou Center in Paris, and in 1976 he was named director of the Philharmonic Academy in Rome.

RECORDINGS: Berio has been well-represented on records. Theater pieces such as *Allez-Hop!, Laborintus II,* and *Recital for*

Cathy have been recorded. Orchestral or chamber-orchestral recordings include the Concertino for Clarinet, Violin, Harp, Celeste, and Strings; *Nones; Allelujah II* for five instrumental groups (with two conductors); *Chemins I* for harp and orchestra; *Chemins II* for viola and nine instruments; *Chemins III* for viola and orchestra; *Chemins IV* for oboe and ten strings; Concerto for 2 Pianos; *Points on the Curve to Find* for piano and twenty-two instruments; *Tempi concertati* for flute, violin, two pianos, and percussion; and the *Serenade* for flute and eighteen instruments. Vocal works on record include *Sequenza III* and *5 Variazioni* for solo soprano; *O King* for soprano, flute, clarinet, violin, cello, and piano; *Circles* for soprano, harp, and percussion; *Chamber Music* for soprano, clarinet, cello, and harp; *Epifanie* for soprano and orchestra; *Folk Songs* for mezzo-soprano, cello, and harp; *A-Ronne* and *Cries of London* for chamber chorus (composed for the Swingle Singers II); *Sinfonia* for small chorus, reciters, keyboards, and orchestra (the long-standing Bernstein [2282] recording contains the first four movements, but a new performance by Boulez on Erato is complete with five movements); *Coro* for forty singers and forty instrumentalists; *El Mar la Mar; Agnus; E vó;* and two pieces for voice on tape, *Visage* and *Omaggio à Joyce.* Other recordings include *Perspectives* and *Momenti* for tape; *2 Pezzi* for violin and piano; *Linea* for two pianos, marimba, and vibraphone; *Différences* for flute, clarinet, harp, viola, cello, and tape; *Sincronie* for string quartet; *Gesti; Rounds* for harpsichord; and *Sequenzas I, IV, V, VI,* and *VII* for (respectively) solo flute, piano, trombone, viola, and oboe.

[2353] MAYER, William
WRITER, ADMINISTRATOR
BORN: New York, November 18, 1925

The son of a broker and of a writer of juvenile fiction, Mayer was brought up in a musical household and studied piano as a matter of course. He entered Yale in 1943, was drafted the next year, and returned in 1946. He took a theory course there with Richard Donovan [1858], tried his hand at songwriting, and graduated in 1949. After a summer with Roger Sessions [1931] at Juilliard, he spent three years at the Manhattan School of Music, studying with Felix Salzer, a Shenkerian. He has taught occasionally but has chiefly worked as a writer for the USIA, a reviewer, and since 1966 a director of Composers Recordings Inc. (CRI), where he was named chairman of the board in 1978. His music is fairly conservative, exhibiting lyrical and humorous impulses. He has written operas (notably *A Death in the Family)*, orchestral, choral, and chamber works, and some fine songs. RECORDINGS: For the stage we have *The Greatest Sound Around* and *Hello World!* (both for children) and *Brief Candle* (a six-minute opera). Orchestral recordings include *Essay* for brass and winds; *Concert Piece* for trumpet, strings, and percussion; *Overture for an American; 2 Pastels; Andante for Strings; Octagon* for piano and orchestra; *Dream's End* for chamber orchestra; and the choral-orchestral *Eve of St. Agnes*. Chamber works recorded include *Country Fair* for brass trio; *Brass Quintet; News Items* and *6 Miniatures* for soprano and seven instruments; *Khartoum* for soprano and four instruments; Sonata for Piano; and a few other songs.

[2354] SCHULLER, Gunther
HORNIST, CONDUCTOR, TEACHER, ADMINISTRATOR
BORN: New York, November 22, 1925

Gunther Schuller was the son of Arthur Schuller, longtime violinist in the Metropolitan Opera Orchestra. Of German descent, he was sent to Germany for his primary education, returning in 1936. For the next three years he was a chorister at St. Thomas Church in New York, and a pupil of T. Tertius Noble in the choir school. He took up French horn and, while still in high school, studied it at the Manhattan School of Music. He graduated from the former in the spring of 1942, thereby terminating his education, both musical and academic. That fall he was an extra horn in the New York Philharmonic's premiere of Shostakovich's [2094] Symphony No. 7, toured in the spring with the Ballet Theater, and the next fall was appointed first horn of the Cincinnati Symphony under Eugene Goossens [1878]. Virtually self-taught as a composer, Schuller premiered his own horn concerto with the orchestra two years later. Meanwhile an encounter with Duke Ellington [1967] had turned him on to jazz. He was later to record with Miles Davis, perform with other jazz groups, and make arrangements for the Modern Jazz Quartet. (It was Schuller who coined the term "third stream music" to indicate a union of composed and improvisatory techniques.) He also taught at the Cincinnati Conservatory and married Marjorie Black, one of his students. Before that event, however, he had returned to New York to join the Metropolitan Opera Orchestra, where he was first horn from 1950. In 1951 he

also returned to the Manhattan School of Music to teach his instrument. By 1959, however, he was in so much demand as a composer that he resigned from the orchestra. In 1962, the year he won the first of two consecutive Guggenheim fellowships, he directed the first International Jazz Festival in Washington, D.C. The next year he gave up teaching for conducting, leading a series of contemporary music programs for the Carnegie Hall Foundation and another for radio station WBAI that was afterward syndicated. That summer he was named head of the composition department at Tanglewood, becoming codirector of the program in 1969, and succeeding Copland [1986] as director in 1972. From 1964 to 1967 he taught at Yale, with a year out for residency in Berlin on a Ford Foundation Fellowship. There he began his opera *The Visitation,* premiered with enormous success at Hamburg in 1966. The Hamburg Company later played it at the Metropolitan Opera, where it was less well received (its European success being based in part on its racial theme). In 1967 Schuller became president of the New England Conservatory of Music. The next year he published an authoritative study, *Early Jazz.* At the conservatory he turned special attention to jazz and ragtime, forming and directing a very successful ragtime band. He also orchestrated, and conducted the premiere of, Scott Joplin's [1602] opera *Treemonisha.* Despite Schuller's jazz orientation, most of his serious music is Schoenbergian [1657]. RECORDINGS: Orchestral and chamber-orchestral recordings include the Symphony for Brass and Percussion; *Dramatic Overture; Contours* for chamber orchestra; *7 Studies on Themes of Paul Klee;* Concertino for Jazz Quartet and Orchestra; Symphony (for orchestra); *5 Bagatelles; Triplum No. 1; Transformations* for jazz orchestra; and *3 Invenzione* for chamber orchestra. Chamber and instrumental works (including jazz pieces) on records include the Quartet for Contrabasses; *Suite for Wind Quintet; Abstraction* for jazz ensemble; String Quartets Nos. 1 and 2; Wind Quintet; *Conversations* for jazz and string quartets; *Densities No. 1* for jazz combo; *Night Music* for jazz combo; *Moods* for four tubas; Sonata for Oboe and Piano; *Fantasy* for solo cello; Duo Sonata for Clarinet and Bass Clarinet; Trio for Oboe, Viola, and Horn; *Music for Brass Quintet; Fantasy-Quartet* for four cellos; *Lines and Contrasts* for horns. Schuller has also conducted for records Joplin's opera and his ragtime works, as well as compositions by Ives [1659] and various contemporary composers, from Roger Sessions [1931] to Bruno Maderna [2300].

[2355] FELDMAN, Morton
TEACHER
BORN: New York, January 12, 1926

Initially a piano student, Feldman undertook composition lessons with Wallingford Riegger [1793] and then with Stefan Wolpe [2020]. Predictably his early compositions were of the serialist bent. Shortly, however, he was drawn into the circle of Cage [2192] accolytes, including David Tudor (1926–), Earle Brown [2365], and Christian Wolff (1934–), and became a pioneer of indeterminacy. His compositions, often using graphic notation, provide only the minimal limits in which the performer is to work; within this framework everything else is up to the artist, for whom the composer acts, as it were, as a muse. Like Cage, Feldman believes in the primacy of silence, in which musical sounds hang in uninterrelated isolation. Most of his music might be described as quiet and motionless, the orchestral works slightly less so. Feldman has held a Guggenheim fellowship in 1966, has been a Visiting Composer in Berlin under the auspices of the German Academic Exchange in 1971–72, and has recently occupied the Frederick B. Slee Chair of Composition at SUNY Buffalo. RECORDINGS: Works recorded include *Chorus and Instruments II* for chorus, chimes, and tuba; *For Franz Kline* for soprano, violin, cello, horn, and chimes; *Christian Wolff in Cambridge* for chorus; *For Frank O'Hara* for flute, clarinet, violin, cello, piano, and percussion; *King of Denmark* for solo percussionist; *Rothko Chapel* for chorus, viola, and percussion; *Structures* for string quartet; *Spring of Chosroes* for violin and piano; *The Viola in My Life* for viola; *False Relationships and Extended Ending* for viola; *Out of "Last Pieces"* for orchestra; *Piece for 4 Pianos; Intersection III* for organ, percussion, and winds; *Extensions I, IV* for various instruments; *4 Instruments; 2 Pieces for 2 Pianos; Projection IV; 3 Pieces for String Quartet; Durations* for six instruments; *Vertical Thoughts IV* for piano; and *Piano Piece: To Philip Guston.*

[2356] CHILDS, Barney Sanford
TEACHER
BORN: Spokane, Wash., February 13, 1926

Childs majored in English at the University of Nevada, from which he graduated in 1949. A Rhodes Scholarship took him to Oxford, where he acquired a second B.A. two years later (M.A., 1955). It was only after this that he began anything like formal music study,

working between 1952 and 1955 (in sequence) with Leonard Ratner, Chávez [1968], Copland [1986], and Carter [2130]. He then went to Stanford and in 1959 received a Ph.D. in both his fields of interest. While completing his doctorate, he taught English at the University of Arizona, where he remained until 1965. He then spent a few years deaning, and teaching both music and English, at little Deep Springs College in southeastern California. In 1969 he joined the faculty of the Wisconsin College-Conservatory in Milwaukee and two years later accepted a professorship at the University of Redlands (in California), where he has also served as composer-in-residence. Though he has been to a degree influenced by John Cage [2192], Childs has largely pursued his own way. He wrote 2 symphonies early on, but since then seems to have preferred to write music of chamber proportions except for the Concerto for Clarinet of 1970, a memorable feature of which is a rare solo for bass oboe. RECORDINGS: Works recorded include *Variations sur un chanson de canotier* for brass quintet; *Sonata for Solo Trombone; Music for 2 Flute Players;* Duo for Flute and Bassoon; Trio for Clarinet, Cello, and Piano (in memory of the poet Paul Blackburn); *37 Songs; Mr. T. His Fancy* (contrabass); and choral pieces.

[2357] HOIBY, Lee
PIANIST
BORN: Madison, Wisc., February 17, 1926

Lee Hoiby received much of his education in his hometown, majoring in music at the University of Wisconsin and studying piano with Gunnar Johansen (a pianist who on his own label has recorded the complete works of just about everybody). Intending to pursue a concert career, Hoiby studied further with Egon Petri at Mills College, where he also worked at composition with Milhaud [1868] and took a master's degree in 1952. About to make his New York debut that same year, he defected to Philadelphia when he got a chance to study with Menotti [2177] at the Curtis Institute. This activity was interrupted when a Fulbright grant took him to Rome. (He has since received other grants and awards.) For the next twenty years he made a name for himself as a composer, chiefly of operas and other stage works. At the end of this period he decided to take up his piano career again and made his long-delayed New York debut in Alice Tully Hall in 1977. Since then he has divided his time equally between playing and composing. The opera *Summer and Smoke* has been taped for television and broadcast by PBS. RECORDINGS: His ballet *After Eden,* the Concerto for Piano, *Night Songs* (song cycle), brief excerpts from *Summer and Smoke,* and *Beatrice* have been recorded.

[2358] SHIFRIN, Seymour J.
TEACHER
BORN: New York, February 28, 1926
DIED: Boston, September 26, 1979

Not to be confused with the Hollywood composer Lalo Schifrin (1932–   ), Seymour Shifrin began composition studies with William Schuman [2158] when he was sixteen, then attended Columbia University where he worked with Otto Luening [1980]. He took an M.A. there in 1949, taught there for a year and at CCNY for another. A Fulbright fellowship in 1951 took him to Paris where he studied with Darius Milhaud [1868]. Shifrin became a professor at the University of California at Berkeley in 1952 and remained there for sixteen years before moving on to Brandeis University. He garnered numerous important awards, fellowships, and commissions. Shifrin wrote mostly in smaller forms. RECORDINGS: Works recorded include *3 Pieces for Orchestra; Cantata to the Text of Sophoclean Choruses* for chorus and string quartet; *In eius memoriam* for chamber ensemble; *Serenade for 5 Instruments;* String Quartet No. 4; *Chronicles* for chorus and orchestra; *The Odes of Shang* for chorus; *Satires of Circumstance* (song cycle); *Responses* for piano; *The Nick of Time* for chamber orchestra; *5 Songs* for soprano and piano (his last work), and several earlier songs.

[2359] JOHNSTON, Ben (*né* Benjamin) Burwell, Jr.
TEACHER, PIANIST
BORN: Macon, Ga., March 15, 1926

Ben Johnston began studying piano in Macon, where his father edited a newspaper. He continued after a move to Richmond, Virginia, in 1938, with various teachers including John Powell [1753]. He entered Catholic University in Washington, D.C., in 1944 and then transferred the next year to William and Mary, from which he graduated in 1949. En route he took a few music courses and played piano in dance bands. He buckled down to serious music study at the Cincinnati College-Conservatory (M.Mus., 1950). In 1950 he studied in Gualala, California, with Harry Partch [1998], which training

had an enormous impact on his later development. The next year he was hired to teach at the University of Illinois but delayed fulfilling his contract until he had taken an M.A. (composition studies with Milhaud [1868]) at Mills College. He finally reached Illinois in 1952, where he took the opportunity for further study with Burrill Phillips [2116]. He has taught there ever since. In 1959, on a Guggenheim fellowship, he went to New York, where he studied with John Cage [2192] and at the Columbia-Princeton Electronic Music Center with Otto Luening [1980] and Vladimir Ussachevsky [2180]. It was there that he began experimenting with ideas about microtonal music that had been germinating since his days with Partch. (His earlier music was fairly conservative and included 2 ballets and other theatrical pieces as well as piano music.) Since 1960 his compositions have been largely experimental, using serialism, indeterminacy, and microtones (he has worked with a 142-tone scale). More recently he has also worked to bridge the gap between popular and "serious" music, as with his "rock-opera" *Carmilla* of 1970. RECORDINGS: Duo for Flute and Double-Bass; *Ci-Gît Satie* for voices, double-bass, and percussion; String Quartets Nos. 2, 4, and 6; Sonata for Microtonal Piano; and *Casta Bertram* for double-bass.

[2360] FLOYD, Carlisle Sessions
TEACHER
BORN: Latta, S.C., June 11, 1926

Disproving H. L. Mencken's contention that the American South is the Desert of Bozart, Carlisle Floyd was born in rural South Carolina and grew up wherever the Methodist Church shifted his parson-father. Carlisle had piano lessons from his mother but was perhaps more interested at first in writing and drawing. In 1943 he won a scholarship in music, however, to Converse College, studied there with Ernst Bacon [1949], then followed him to Syracuse University, from which he graduated in 1946. He joined the staff of Florida State University (Tallahassee), where he originated a course in opera writing addressed both to musicians and playwrights (he has written all his own libretti). After a couple of unsatisfactory attempts of his own at the form, he had a great success with *Susannah* (a modern-day account of the biblical tale) at the New York City Opera in 1956. It made the names of the principals, soprano Phyllis Curtin and the late basso Norman Treigle; won its composer a New York Critics' Circle Award, a Guggenheim fellowship, and other honors;

and was selected as the token American opera at the 1958 Brussels World's Fair. Floyd, who writes good old-fashioned opera, has written seven more since then—notably *Wuthering Heights,* 1958; *The Passion of Jonathan Wade,* 1962; *Of Mice and Men,* 1970; *Bilby's Doll,* 1976; and *Willie Stark,* 1981—without duplicating that triumph. (The last-named, drawn from Robert Penn Warren's *All the King's Men,* was telecast nationally.) Floyd's other compositions are limited to a few orchestral pieces, song cycles, and piano works. RECORDINGS: None at the operas have been recorded commercially, though there is a pirate of *Susannah.* The overture *In Celebration* and two orchestral song cycles, *Mystery* and *Pilgrimage* (abridged), have been committed to disc.

[2361] HENZE, Hans Werner (Hent'-se, Hǎns Vâr'-ner)
CONDUCTOR, TEACHER
BORN: Gütersloh, July 1, 1926

Despite his strident left-wing (not to say anarchistic) political stance in recent years, Henze is an eclectic composer who, while rejecting all schools, makes such astute use of what they have to offer that he has enjoyed more success than most of his contemporaries. Many of his attitudes are apparently part of a rejection of the domestic atmosphere of his childhood, where he fretted under the weight of bourgeois values and his schoolmaster father's Nazi tendencies. Despite family opposition, he persisted in trying to teach himself music and at sixteen was accepted by the state conservatory in Brunswick. Two years later he was drafted, but his military career was abruptly ended when he was captured by the British. Freed he found a job as operatic rehearsal coach at Bielefeld, where he had had his academic education. In 1946 he enrolled in the school of church music in Heidelberg, in which town he encountered Wolfgang Fortner (1907–   ), who became his most important composition teacher. Fortner introduced him to the Darmstadt crowd of avant-gardists, from whom he developed a fascination with serialism and studied Schoenbergian [1657] approaches with René Leibowitz and Josef Rufer. In 1948 he became assistant to the conductor of the city theater in Constance and two years later took on the duties of artistic director and conductor at Wiesbaden. He found them too constraining, however, and resigned after a year to compose. In 1952 he created a stir with his opera *Boulevard Solitude,* an updating of the Manon story.

Still unable to come to terms with German life, in part because of his homosexuality, Henze betook himself to Italy, where for three years he lived on the island of Ischia with the poet Ingeborg Bachmann and made friends with the choreographer Sir Frederick Ashton and the composer William Walton [2011]. A second opera, *König Hirsch (King Stag),* based on a play by Carlo Gozzi, was even more successful than the first when it was premiered in Berlin in 1956 under the baton of Hermann Scherchen (with whom Henze had studied conducting in Darmstadt). Several other successful if controversial operas followed—*Der Prinz von Homburg, Elegie für junge Liebenden, Der junge Lord,* and *Die Bassariden* (libretti for the second and fourth translated from the English texts of W. H. Auden and Chester Kallmann). Meanwhile Henze had moved from Ischia to the city of Naples and then, in 1961, built a villa in the Roman hills near Castel Gandolfo. Teaching (e.g., in Salzburg) brought him in contact with the young, and his already radical inclination was intensified by the upheaval among them in the 1960s. Much of his music since has been on provocative social themes. He ostentatiously resigned from the Berlin Academy of Arts and created an uproar at the premiere of *"Medusa"* when his insistence that a red flag be displayed on the stage caused the orchestra to walk out and the police to come in. There followed several expressly political (not to say inflammatory) works—*Versuch über Schweine (Essay on Pigs,* for a reciter who squeals as much as he recites, and orchestra), *El Cimarrón* (a true account of an escape from slavery for reciter and three musicians), *Die langwierige Weg in die Wohnung der Natascha Ungeheuer (The Long, Boring Way to the House of Natasha Monstrous,* an attack on the flabby intellectual left-wingers), and *La Cubana* (a televised "vaudeville" broadcast here on NET). The 1979 ballet *Orpheus* (Stuttgart Ballet) updates the ancient legend from a Marxist perspective but is less harshly polemical than some of its predecessors. At the same time Henze has continued to write abstract music, some of it in traditional forms (6 symphonies, at least 5 string quartets). Some of his recent operas have been *We Come to the River* (Royal Opera House, London, 1976); *Don Chisciotte,* premiered the same year at the festival Henze inaugurated at Montepulciano, Italy; the children's opera *Pollicino* (Cabrillo Festival, California); and *The English Cat* (Paris Opéra) of 1984.
RECORDINGS: Orchestral recordings include Symphonies Nos. 1–6; Concerto No. 1 for Violin; *Ode to the West Wind* for cello

and orchestra; Double Concerto for Oboe, Harp, and Strings; Concerto for Contrabass; Concerto No. 2 for Violin (with tape, voices, and thirty-three instruments); *Compases para Preguntas ensimismadas* for viola and twenty-two players; *Tristan,* preludes for piano, orchestra, and tape; Concerto No. 2 for Piano; ballet music for *Labyrinth, Undine,* and *L'Usignolo dell'imperatore (The Emperor's Nightingale);* concert suite for orchestra from the film *Katharina Blum; Sonata per Archi (Sonata for Strings); Fantasia for Strings,* based on music composed for the film *Young Törless;* and *Telemanniana,* based on themes of Telemann [665]. Dramatic and vocal recordings include *Wiegenlied des Mutter Gottes (Lullaby of the Mother of God)* for children's chorus and small orchestra; *Apollo et Hyacinthus,* cantata for contralto, harpsichord, and chamber orchestra; *Whispers from Heavenly Death,* cantata after Whitman for high voice and eight solo instruments; *Kammermusik I–XII* for tenor, guitar, and chamber ensemble (three of the movements, for solo guitar, are also recorded separately); an hour of excerpts from the full-length opera *Elegie für junge Liebende; Nachstücke und Arien (Nocturnes and Arias)* for soprano and orchestra; *5 Neapolitanische Lieder* for soprano and orchestra; *Being Beauteous,* cantata after Rimbaud for soprano, harp, and four cellos; *Cantata della Fiaba estrema* for soprano, small chorus, and thirteen instruments; *Der junge Lord,* a comic opera; *In Memoriam: Die weisse Rose (In Memory of the White Rose)* for tenor, guitar, and chamber orchestra; *Musen sicilien (Muses of Sicily)* for chorus and orchestra; *Moralitäten (Moralities),* scenic cantatas after Aesop and W. H. Auden for chorus and orchestra; the oratorio *Das Floss der Medusa (The Raft of the Frigate Medusa),* for soloists, chorus, and orchestra; *Versuche über Schweine (Essay on Pigs)* for baritone and chamber orchestra; *El Cimmarón* for baritone, flute, guitar, and percussion; the chamber opera *Die langwierige Weg; Voices,* a collection of twenty-two independent songs for tenor, mezzo-soprano, tape, live electronics, and fifteen instrumentalists playing seventy instruments; and a reorchestration of Carissimi's [471] *Jepthe,* using the instruments of ancient biblical times but mostly preserving the original notes. Chamber and instrumental works on records include the early Sonata for Violin Solo; *Variations* for piano; Sonatina for Flute and Piano; *Chamber Sonata* for violin, piano, and cello; *Concerto per il Marigny* for piano and septet; *Serenade* for cello solo; Wind Quintet; Sonata for Piano; Sonatina for Solo Trumpet; *Royal Winter Music* for

solo guitar; and *12 Variations* for string sextet and harp, as adapted for use in the film *Swann in Love.*

[2362] KUPFERMAN, Meyer
CLARINETIST, TEACHER
BORN: New York, July 3, 1926

Kupferman's father was a devout Jew from Rumania; his mother came from Russia. He began studying clarinet and piano at around ten and graduated from the High School of Music and Art in 1943. He spent two years at Queens College, then made his living for a time as a clarinetist both on pop and classical engagements. Mostly self-taught, he had been composing since his early teens and now wrote arrangements and film scores. He also wrote in 1948 (the year of his marriage to Sylvia Kasten) the one-act opera *In a Garden* to a Gertrude Stein text; it has enjoyed considerable success with small companies. Shortly afterward he committed himself to twelve-tone music for a time but later became freely eclectic. In 1951 he began teaching at Sarah Lawrence College, where he has remained and where he founded an improvisation ensemble. Divorced in 1969, he married the dancer Pai-Fen Chin in 1973. A prolific composer, he has written operas, a ballet, 7 symphonies, and at least 29 *Infinities* (works for various instruments and combinations, all based on the same twelve-tone row). Some of his works are jazz-influenced, some reflect his Jewish heritage. RECORDINGS: His publisher has made available more than twenty of his compositions on Serenus Records. Other recordings include the *Little Symphony; Symphony No. 4; Hallelujah the Hills!;* Concerto for Cello, Tape, and Orchestra; *Superflute* for flute and tape; *Fantasy Sonata* for violin and piano; *Evocation* for cello and piano; *Abracadabra* for piano quartet; *The Celestial City* for piano and tape; *Angel Footprints* for violin and tape; *Infinities 15* for piano, four hands; *Saturnalis* for tuba and amplified cello, and *Line Fantasy* for solo flute.

[2363] GABURO, Kenneth Louis
TEACHER, PUBLISHER
BORN: Somerville, N.J., July 5, 1926

The son of a laundry owner, Kenneth Gaburo got an early start playing the piano and, after a fashion, composing. He put in a year at the Eastman School of Music, then spent most of the war years flying bombing missions as a gunner in the Pacific and playing in an air force jazz group. Returning to

Eastman in 1946, he studied composition with Bernard Rogers [1875], married Yvonne Stevens, and took two degrees—a B.A. in 1948 and an M.A. in 1949. Even the Rochester critics were stunned by the noisiness of his student compositions. After teaching for a year at Kent State in Ohio, he took a job at McNeese State College in Lake Charles, Louisiana, where he wrote his opera *The Snow Queen* (produced there) and his orchestral piece *On a Quiet Theme* that won the 1955 Gershwin Prize. In 1954 he received a Fulbright fellowship and, having declared himself a twelve-toner for the nonce, he spent a year studying with Goffredo Petrassi [2052] in Rome. He then became a teacher and doctoral candidate at the University of Illinois, working in electronic composition. He got his Ph.D. and a divorce in 1962. Two years later he married pianist Virginia Hommel who, as a poet, has collaborated with him on various compositions. An interest in linguistics and the study thereof led Gaburo to the notion of "compositional linguistics," wherein (as nearly as this writer can grasp it) he attempts to synthesize the meaning of music with the abstract sounds of language. He organized his own choir (?), the New Music Choral Ensemble, to deal with his and other advanced choral music, if that is the term. His magnum opus in this period was a vast four-part mixed-media "event" called *Lingua* that runs for about six hours. (Gaburo and his group recorded the audible aspects of *Lingua II: Maledetto*, the focus of which is a fifty-minute oral disquisition on the word "screw"—typical of the wit and humor of those yeasty times.) In mid-*Lingua*, 1968, Gaburo was "translated" to the University of California at San Diego, where he moved increasingly into theatrical "happenings." He left in 1975 to help advance the arts through his own publishing company, the Lingua Press. RECORDINGS: Besides the work noted above, recordings include *Line Studies* (for flute, clarinet, viola, and trombone); *Two* (for mezzo-soprano, alto flute, and contrabass); and *Antiphony II: Poised, Antiphony III: Pearl White Moments, Lemon Drops, For Harry* (an homage to his mentor Harry Partch [1998]), *Fat Millie's Lament*, and *The Wasting of Lucrecetzia* (all for tape, with or without other sound sources).

[2364] JOLAS, Betsy (née Elizabeth)
(Zhō'-làs, Bet'-sē)
TEACHER, WRITER
BORN: Paris, August 5, 1926

Betsy Jolas is the daughter of Eugène Jolas, founder of the literary magazine *Transition* (which first published portions of James Joyce's *Finnegans Wake)*, and his Scottish wife Maria, a well-known translator. World War II drove the family to New York in 1940. Betsy studied music at Bennington College in Vermont, working with Paul Boepple, with whose Dessoff Choirs she served as singer and accompanist. Having gotten her degree in 1946, she returned to France and studied with Messiaen [2129], Milhaud [1868], and others at the Paris Conservatoire until 1955. She then worked for the ORTF for fifteen years as editor of its publication *Écouter aujourdhui (Today's Listening)*. Between 1954 and the present her compositions have won a number of awards, both American and French. In 1971 she became Messiaen's aide at the Paris Conservatoire. Though she has been influenced by serialism and by medieval and Renaissance polyphony, her chief interest has been the human voice as both an instrument and communicator. RECORDINGS: *Stances* for piano and orchestra; *Points d'aube* for viola and thirteen wind instruments; *J.D.E.* for fourteen instruments; *Quatuor II* for soprano and string trio; and *Quatuor III* for strings

[2365] BROWN, Earle
TRUMPETER, RECORDING ENGINEER, ADMINISTRATOR, TEACHER, CONDUCTOR
BORN: Lunenberg, Mass., December 26, 1926

Together with his friends John Cage [2192], Morton Feldman [2355], Christian Wolff (1934–), and their prophet David Tudor (1926–), Earle Brown was one of the pioneers of aleatory music. A failed piano student, he played in dance bands as a youngster, and in the Army Air Force Band in the waning days of World War II. Before and after his military service, he studied mathematics and engineering at Northeastern University in Boston. However, in 1946 he gave that up to study at the Schillinger School of Music, which taught Joseph Schillinger's (1895–1943) foolproof approach to composition, also taking private lessons in arranging. In 1950 he married modern dancer Carolyn Rice and settled in Denver, where he taught privately and began composing twelve-tone pieces. A meeting with John Cage brought him back to New York in 1952, where he was soon set to thinking by contemporary abstract art, notably the paintings of Jackson Pollack and the mobiles of Alexander Calder. Deciding he wanted his music to be free-form and a matter of spatial relationships, he abandoned traditional notation for graphs which defined the parameters of the work in question, within which the performer could operate as he saw fit. Meanwhile he worked as a recording engineer for Capitol Records and later as director of an avant-garde project, Time Records. In the 1960s, separated from his wife, he spent a good deal of time in Europe, where he found a warmer welcome than he had found here. In 1968 he became composer-in-residence at the Peabody Conservatory and while there married Susan Sollins, an official of the fine arts wing of the Smithsonian Institution. Since leaving Peabody in 1973, he has done guest shots with the Rotterdam Philharmonic, the Basel Conservatory, SUNY at Buffalo, the University of California (at Berkeley and Los Angeles), and the California Institute of the Arts. RECORDINGS: Works recorded include *December 1952; Music for Violin, Cello, and Piano; Octet I* for eight tapes; *4 Systems; Music for Cello and Piano; Hodograph I* for flute, piano, and percussion, *Available Forms I* for chamber orchestra; *Novara* for eight instruments; *Times Five* for five instruments and four-channel tape; *Corroboree* for three pianos; *9 Rarebits* for two harpsichords; the String Quartet; and *Small Pieces for Large Chorus*. (In most instances here, the recording represents only one of an infinite number of possible realizations. In the recording, *4 Systems* is performed on amplified cymbals. Of his work *December 1952*, Brown claimed that it could, in December 1953, generate any possible sounds from any combination of players, but demurred when one performer offered "Old Macdonald Had a Farm.")

[2366] MARTIRANO, Salvatore John
(Mȧr-ti-rä'-no, Sal-vȧ-tô'-rä Jon)
TEACHER, PIANIST, CLARINETIST
BORN: Yonkers, N.Y., January 12, 1927

One of the wilder (and more humorous) avant-gardists, Martirano served in the Marine Corps as a band clarinetist, played some jazz piano, and graduated from Oberlin Conservatory (where he studied with Herbert Elwell [1948]) in 1951—the year in which he wrote his first and only opera, *The Magic Stones*. He next spent a year at the Eastman School of Music acquiring an M.M. degree under Bernard Rogers [1875]. From 1952 to 1954 he studied with Dallapiccola [2049] at the Cherubini Conservatory in Florence, and then, on a fellowship, at the American Academy in Rome until 1959. In 1960 he held a Guggenheim fellowship. In 1963 he joined the faculty of the University of Illinois, where he is presently professor of composition. Though his earlier works leaned toward traditional forms, he has moved latterly in the direction of "theater pieces," including *L's G.A.*, which calls for a participating politician who must recite Lincoln's Gettysburg Address while inhaling helium. According to his own words, he has invented a device called the "Sal-Mar Construction . . . a machine designed to produce in real time, composition as fact and process." Martirano's output has so far been small. RECORDINGS: Works recorded include *Mass* (chorus); *O, O, O, O, That Shakespeherean Rag* (chorus and instruments); *Underworld* (theater piece for actors, percussion, two double basses, tenor saxophone, and tape); *Ballad* (amplified singer and instruments); *Octet; L's G.A.; Cocktail Music* (piano); and *Chansons Innocentes* (soprano and piano).

[2367] BÉCAUD, Gilbert (Bā-kō', Zhēl-bâr')
POP SINGER, ACTOR
BORN: Toulon, October 24, 1927

Born François Silly (Sē-yē') in a Mediterranean seaport, Bécaud was educated in the local conservatory and in that of Nice, majoring in piano. However, he turned to writing and singing *chansons* and toured the United States with Edith Piaf. By the mid-1950s his appearances in France caused epidemic female hysteria, and he was being billed as "Monsieur 100,000 Volts." Later he worked in films, both as the star and composer of soundtracks. He has occasionally turned to more serious composition, and the premiere of his *Opéra d'Aran* (after J. M. Synge) at the Paris Opéra in 1962 was the occasion for great excitement. (It is a musically and theatrically effective piece.) RECORDINGS: The *Opéra d'Aran* was recorded by EMI.

[2368] ARGENTO, Dominick
TEACHER
BORN: York, Pa., October 27, 1927

Since the sudden eclipse of the doctrinaire avant-garde in the 1970s, Dominick Argento has increasingly been recognized as an eclectic with something to say. In his mid-teens, inspired by reading musical biographies, he began taking piano lessons and studying theory texts. After a postwar two-year hitch in the army, he studied at the Peabody Insti-

tute with Nicolas Nabokov (1903–78) and
Hugo Weisgall [2194]. Getting his baccalaureate degree in 1951, he was a Fulbright fellow in Florence with Luigi Dallapiccola
[2049] for the next year; in 1954 he returned
to Peabody to take an M.A. under the direction of Henry Cowell [1934]. That autumn
he married soprano Carolyn Bailey, for
whom he has written a number of vocal
works. Proceeding to the Eastman School of
Music on a teaching fellowship, he did doctoral work with Howard Hanson [1927],
Bernard Rogers [1875], and Alan Hovhaness [2170], receiving his Ph.D. in 1957,
which he celebrated with a Rochester production of his one-act comedy *The Boor* (after Chekhov), since seen on German television. After spending another year in Florence on a Guggenheim fellowship, Argento
found happiness and security at the University of Minnesota at Minneapolis. There in
1964 he founded what is now the Minnesota
Opera Company, which has produced several of his works, most successfully *Postcard
from Morocco* in 1971 (much produced since)
and *The Voyage of Edgar Allan Poe* in 1976.
Miss Havisham's Fire (after Dickens) was
commissioned by the New York City Opera
—the last work conducted there by Julius
Rudel at the end of his long term as general
manager in 1979. It pleased the audiences
but not the critics. Argento won the 1975
Pulitzer Prize for his song cycle *From Virginia Woolf's Diary*, and his orchestral *In
Praise of Music* shared a national telecast
with the Beethoven ninth symphony in celebration of the Minnesota Orchestra's
seventy-fifth anniversary. RECORDINGS:
Argento's opera *Postcard from Morocco* was
recorded by the Minnesota Opera. Other recordings include the orchestra *Royal Invitation;* the cantata *Trio Carmina Paschalia* for
women's chorus; the song cycles *6 Elizabethan Songs, Letters from Composers,* and *To
Be Sung Upon the Water* for soprano (accompanied respectively by chamber ensemble, guitar, and clarinet-piano duo); and *Jonah and the Whale* for narrator, soloists,
chorus, and ensemble.

**[2369] BONDON, Jacques Laurent Jules
Désiré** (Bon-don', Zhàk Lō-ràn' Zhül
Dā-zē-rā')
CONDUCTOR, PAINTER, BROADCAST OF-
FICIAL
BORN: Boulbon, December 6, 1927

Born in the Rhone delta, Bondon was initially as attracted to painting as to music
and studied both in nearby Marseilles. At
the end of World War II he migrated to

Paris, was a student for a time at the École
César Franck, and then transferred to the
Conservatoire. His most important teachers
were Koechlin [1592], Rivier [1923], and
Milhaud [1868]. In the period following his
graduation, he was primarily involved in
writing film scores, producing more than
forty in a six-year period. However, in 1962
he gave up this career and a year later
formed a chamber orchestra which, as the
Ensemble Moderne de Paris, became well
known throughout France. Bondon was
commissioned to write the music for the
opening ceremonies for the 1968 Winter
Olympic Games in Grenoble, and since that
time has served as a director of the national
radio and television. Basically a conservative, Bondon has received considerable official support in the form of commissions. A
devotee of fantasy and science fiction, he has
allowed such interests to color such of his
compositions as the 1975 ballet *i.330* and the
orchestral *Musique pour un autre monde
(Music for Another World)* of 1962. RECORD-
INGS: Works on disc include the *Music for
the Olympic Games; Concerto de Mars* for
guitar and orchestra; *Concerto con fuoco* for
guitar and string orchestra; *Kaleidoscope* for
Ondes Martenot and orchestra; *Sonata pour
un ballet; Le Tombeau de Schubert* for piano
quintet; *Les Monts de l'Étoile (The Mountains of the Stars)* for soprano and piano
quintet; *3 Movimenti* for clarinet quartet;
and *Le Soleil multicolore (The Multicolored
Sun)* for flute, viola, and harp.

[2370] DAMASE, Jean-Michel (Dà-mas',
Zhàn Mē-shel')
PIANIST
BORN: Bordeaux, January 27, 1928

Damase's mother was a concert harpist. A
Wunderkind, he was studying with the composer Marcel Samuel-Rousseau (1882–1955)
at five, composing at nine, and a student of
the great pianist Alfred Cortot at the École
Normale in Paris at twelve. Admitted to the
Paris Conservatoire the next year, he won
first prize for piano in 1943, studied with
Henri Büsser [1627], Claude Delvincourt
[1826], and Marcel Dupré [1806], and won
first prize in composition in 1947—as well as
the Grand Prix de Rome. He quickly became known both as a composer (in a neo-
classical vein) and as a concert pianist (he
has toured the United States). Much of his
best-known instrumental music involves the
harp. He has been particularly successful
with his ballets—7 to date—but has also
produced as many operas (two of them to
libretti by Jean Anouilh), a symphony, sev-

eral concerti, chamber music, and songs. RE-
CORDINGS: There is a Russian recording of
his Concertino for Harp with String Orchestra. Other works recorded include *Sonate en
concert* for flute, cello, and piano; *17 Variations* for wind quintet; Sonatina for Flute
and Harp; and some solo piano pieces.

[2371] ALLENDE-BLIN, Juan (Ȧl-yen'-de Blēn, Hwȧn)
TEACHER
BORN: Santiago de Chile, February 24,
1928

Allende-Blin was the son of composer
Adolfo Allende and pianist Rebeca Blin, and
the nephew and pupil of the important nationalist composer Humberto Allende (1885–
1959). He also had lessons with a Dutch emigré named Free Focke. He studied mathematics and architecture at the local university and oboe at the National Conservatory.
Seduced by postwar modernism, he went to
Germany in 1951, studied for a time at the
Detmold Academy, and attended the summer courses at Darmstadt, where he was a
pupil of Messiaen [2129]. He came home to
a professorship at the Santiago Conservatory
in 1954 but abandoned it three years later to
settle in West Germany, where he has been
on the musical staffs of the radio in Hamburg and Frankfurt. He is coinventor of a
sort of outdoor water organ dubbed the
Orgelwiese, for which he has composed. His
music is very advanced in technique. RE-
CORDINGS: Several organ works have been
recorded—*Sons brisés, Sonorités,* and *Mein
blaues Klavier.*

[2372] ADLER, Samuel Hans
TEACHER, CONDUCTOR, VIOLINIST
BORN: Mannheim, March 4, 1928

Unlike most of the innumerable musical Ad-
lers, Samuel is better known for writing music than for performing, conducting, or re-
searching it. The son of a cantor, he spent
much of his childhood in the Mannheim
ghetto and was brought by his parents to
Worcester, Massachusetts, when he was
eleven. Two years later he was playing violin
in the local symphony and studying composition with Herbert Fromm [2062], also a
refugee. Adler majored in music at Boston
University, taking a bachelor's degree there
in 1948, then spent two more years acquiring
an M.A. at Harvard under the tutelage of
Piston [1890], Irving Fine [2228], Hindemith [1914], and Randall Thompson [1966],
studying summers at Tanglewood with Cop-

land [1986] and Koussevitzky [1655]. Called
up for military service in 1950 and stationed
in Germany, he founded and conducted the
Seventh Army Symphony (which he returned to conduct, at the government's request, at the Brussels World's Fair seven
years later). On returning to the United
States, he became director of music at Temple Emanu-El of Dallas in 1953, subsequently held additional conducting jobs in
Dallas, and in 1957 became professor of
composition at North Texas State University. In 1966 Adler left Texas for the Eastman School of Music, where since 1973 he
has headed the department of composition.
He has made three tours of Europe under
U.S. State Department auspices as a conductor and lecturer. He is married to the former
Carol Ellen Stalker and has two daughters.
Adler has won many awards (including the
first Charles Ives Prize), honors, and grants.
His music is thoroughly eclectic. RECORD-
INGS: His opera *The Disappointment* (a "reconstruction" of the first American ballad
opera, whose music had been lost) has been
recorded, along with the Concerto for Flute
and the Symphony No. 4 (the latter a pirate
record). Recorded chamber and instrumental works include the Sonata for Horn and
Piano, *Southwestern Sketches* for winds,
String Quartets Nos. 4 and 6, *Canto 2* for
trombone (one of 9 similarly titled works for
various instruments), *4 Dialogues* for euphonium and marimba, *Xenia: A Dialogue for
Organ and Percussion,* and some keyboard
pieces. Some cantorials and part-songs have
also been done.

[2373] FLAGELLO, Nicolas
VIOLINIST, PIANIST, CONDUCTOR,
TEACHER
BORN: New York, March 15, 1928

The elder son of Italian-born parents in the
garment industry (the younger is the operatic basso Ezio Flagello), Nicolas Flagello
took up piano before he was out of rompers
and violin three years later. In high school
he played both, as well as oboe in the band.
His advanced piano teachers included Adele
Marcus and Harold Bauer, and he was pianist for Friedrich Schorr's vocal classes at the
Manhattan School of Music, from which he
(Flagello) took a bachelor's degree in 1949
and a master's in 1950. At that point he was
admitted to the faculty. He also studied violin with Hugo Kortschak, cello with Gabor
Rejto, oboe with Bruno Labate, and conducting with Dimitri Mitropoulos. His chief
composition teacher, friend, and mentor was
Vittorio Giannini [2042]. For about ten

years Flagello pursued a successful career as a pianist and accompanist. In 1955 a Fulbright fellowship took him to the Santa Cecilia Academy in Rome, where he studied with Ildebrando Pizzetti [1732] and acquired a doctorate in 1956. Though he has continued to teach at the Manhattan School of Music, he helped Giannini with the organization of the North Carolina School of the Arts and taught composition for a year, 1964–65, as head of the department at the Curtis Institute. Since 1960 he has also conducted, at La Scala in Milan, the Chicago Lyric Opera, and the New York City Opera, and has been chief conductor of the Radio Symphony Orchestra in Rome (with which he has recorded). An extraordinarily prolific composer, he belongs to no particular school. He has written 6 operas, and much choral, orchestral, concerted, instrumental, and solo vocal music. Among his many awards and honors is the 1961 New York Critics' Award for a choral piece, *Tristis est anima mea.* He has been twice married and has two sons. RECORDINGS: His perspicacious publisher has issued a number of his works on Serenus Records—the ballet suite *Lautrec;* the orchestral works *Concerto Antoniano* for flute and orchestra, Concerto for Strings, *Burlesca,* and the *Prelude, Ostinato, and Fugue; Lyra* for brass sextet; Sonata for Piano; and the song cycles *Contemplazioni di Michelangelo, Island in the Moon,* and *The Land.* Non-Serenus recordings include *Adoration* for strings and harp, and some band compositions.

[2374] MUSGRAVE, Thea
CONDUCTOR, TEACHER
BORN: Barnton, Midlothian, May 27, 1928

One of the rarest of birds, a successful woman composer of operas (and a Scot at that!), Thea Musgrave became a sort of rallying point in the Women's Movement of the 1970s. She studied at the University of Edinburgh with Hans Gál [1837] and from 1950 to 1954 with Nadia Boulanger in Paris. During the summer of 1953 she was at Dartington Hall as a pupil of Sir William Glock, the school's director, who introduced her to Viennese dodecaphony and to the music of Charles Ives [1659], which had a particular impact on her own. In 1958 she was at Tanglewood, where she came under the influence of Copland [1986] and Milton Babbitt [2247]. Her *Cantata for a Summer's Day* of 1955 and her String Quartet of 1958 were premiered at the Edinburgh Festivals, and her music was soon being played with consider-

able regularity over the BBC. Her first opera, *The Abbot of Drimock,* created no particular stir in 1958, but *The Decision,* premiered at the Sadler's Wells Theater by the New Opera Company in 1967, was more successful and won her a spate of commissions. (Previously she had done some teaching at the University of London and worked as a choral conductor and accompanist.) In 1974 she conducted the premiere of *The Voice of Ariadne* at the Aldeburgh Festival, for which it had been commissioned. (It was played by the New York City Opera in 1977.) Musgrave married the violist Peter Mark, for whom she wrote her Concerto for Viola and *One to Another* for viola and tape. She joined him in 1970 on the faculty of the University of California at Santa Barbara. In 1975 Mark became artistic director of the fledgling Virginia Opera Company in Norfolk, which in 1977 had an outstanding success with Musgrave's *Mary, Queen of Scots* (which was taken up later by the New York City Opera). It was followed in 1979 by her treatment of Dickens's *A Christmas Carol.* With a firm grounding in traditional techniques, and having explored serialism, various forms of indeterminacy, and electronic composition, she has settled into an eclectic style of her own. RECORDINGS: Works recorded include the operas *Mary, Queen of Scots* and *A Christmas Carol;* (orchestral) Concerto for Orchestra, *Chamber Concerto No. 2,* Concerto for Clarinet, *Night Music* for two horns and orchestra, Concerto for Horn; (vocal) *Triptych* for tenor and chamber orchestra; (chamber and instrumental) *Colloquy* for violin and piano, *Monologue* for piano, and *Excursions* for piano.

[2375] DRUCKMAN, Jacob Raphael
TRUMPETER, TEACHER, VIOLINIST
BORN: Philadelphia, June 26, 1928

From the age of ten, Druckman studied violin and composition with Louis Gesensway [2081] and later played trumpet in school and dance bands. In the summer of 1949 he was at Tanglewood as a pupil of Aaron Copland [1986], and subsequently took two degrees at the Juilliard School, with Bernard Wagenaar (1894–1971), Vincent Persichetti [2236], and Peter Mennin [2328]. In June 1954 he married Muriel Topaz, a dancer, and went to Paris on a Fulbright fellowship to study with Tony Aubin (1907–   ) at the École Normale. Afterward both Druckman and his wife taught at Juilliard, and from 1961 to 1967 he divided his teaching duties between that institution and Bard College, up the Hudson. During that period he also studied for a year (1965–66) at the Columbia-Princeton Electronic Music Center, of which he became associate director in 1967. A year later he did further investigation of the medium at the studio of the ORTF in Paris on a Guggenheim Fellowship (his second). The chief compositional products of Druckman's electronic research were four works called *Animus* which pit a live performer against a seemingly antipathetic prerecorded tape. In 1971–72 the composer was in charge of the electronic music studio at Yale. In the latter year he won the Pulitzer Prize for *Windows,* an orchestral work in which snatches of simpler and sometimes familiar music are heard through rifts in a thick sonic fabric. In 1972, too, Druckman left the Juilliard School to direct the electronic studio and teach at Brooklyn College for four years. He then returned to Yale in his former capacity and as chairman of the department of composition. Druckman likes to experiment with sonorities, often using out-of-the-way instruments, and he frequently quotes from other music. Recently Druckman has served as the New York Philharmonic's composer-in-residence and has overseen the 1983 and 1984 Horizons contemporary music festivals in New York City. He has also been working on an opera commissioned by the Metropolitan. RECORDINGS: Works recorded include *Dark Upon the Harp* for soprano, brass quintet, and percussion (no harp); *Lamia* for soprano and orchestra; *Antiphonies* for two choruses; *Incenters* for thirteen instruments; String Quartet No. 2; *Synapse* for tape; *Valentine* for double bass; *Animus I* for trombone and tape; *Animus II* for soprano, percussion, and tape; and *Animus III* for clarinet and tape; *Delizie contente che l'alme beate* for wind quintet and tape; and two orchestral works, *Windows* and *Aureole.*

[2376] BAIRD, Tadeusz (Bârt, Tä-de'-ōōsh)

BORN: Grodzisk Mazowiecki, July 26, 1928
DIED: Warsaw, September 4, 1981

Born near Warsaw, Baird owes his surname to his Scottish ancestry. In the midst of World War II he began studying music in Lodz with Swiss-born Kazimierz Sikorski and Boulanger-trained Bolesław Woytowicz but in 1944 was sent by the Nazis to a labor camp. From 1947 he studied music at the Warsaw Conservatory, and musicology and art history at the university. His early compositions were in a neo-classical idiom, and often on ostensible subjects, that won him

state prizes and a place on the board of the composers' union. Later, when things became more relaxed in Poland, he moved toward a sort of atonal neo-romanticism, influenced by the Viennese tradition from Schubert **[1153]** to Berg **[1789]**. He wrote the opera *Jutro (Tomorrow)* after Joseph Conrad, 3 numbered symphonies, a great deal of incidental music for stage and screen, orchestral works, and chamber music. He was particularly effective as a vocal composer. RECORDINGS: Vocal recordings include the opera *Jutro;* the cantata *Goethe Letters;* the song cycle *Erotica* for soprano and orchestra; *4 Love Sonnets of Shakespeare* for baritone and chamber ensemble; *Chansons des trouvères* for mezzo-soprano, two flutes, and cello; and *4 Songs to Poems of Vesna Parun* for mezzo-soprano and chamber orchestra. Orchestral recordings include Symphony No. 3; *Concerto lugubre* for viola and orchestra; *Psychodrama; Elegeia (Elegy); Scenes* for cello, harp, and orchestra; *Epiphany Music;* the *4 Dialogues* for oboe and chamber orchestra; and *4 Novelettes* for chamber orchestra.

[2377] STOCKHAUSEN, Karlheinz (Shtôk'-hou-zen, Kärl'-hïnts)

CONDUCTOR, TEACHER, PIANIST
BORN: Burg Mödrath, August 22, 1928

Among the acknowledged leaders of the postwar avant-garde, none has been more "avant" than Stockhausen, who, some think, has pushed the concept of what music is about as far as it can be pushed. The son of a schoolmaster in a village near Cologne, he began piano studies at six. His mother died when he was thirteen; a year later his father marched off to war and disappeared forever. Young Stockhausen was placed in a boys' school where he received violin and oboe lessons. By then he was a good enough pianist to pick up money by performing, which he did both in and outside the school. (He is said to have developed an excellent jazz technique.) In 1944 he was drafted and served out the war as an orderly. Set free, he worked for a brief time on a farm and then returned to high school, graduating in 1947. For the next three years he worked for a music teaching degree at the Musikhochschule in Cologne, also taking classes at the university. He graduated in 1950 but stayed around for an additional year to work with Frank Martin **[1841]**. During this period he again moonlighted as a pianist, at one time touring with a magician for whose act he provided atmospheric background.

On leaving school Stockhausen found employment in the Studio for New Music of

Radio Cologne, where he was able to compose and experiment without fear of starving. That summer he began his long connection with the Darmstadt Summer Courses, where he became fascinated with the music of Olivier Messiaen [2129]. A year later, in 1952, he went to the Paris Conservatory to sit at Messiaen's feet. He also studied there with Milhaud [1868], observed the *musique concrète* experiments of Pierre Schaeffer [2159] and his disciples, and made friends with Pierre Boulez [2346]. The following summer his *Kreuzspiel* for orchestra precipitated a near riot at Darmstadt, and he received several commissions from the Baden-Baden radio station. (At the time, perhaps as a reaction to the oppression of the Nazi years, government-subsidized German radio stations were actually in fierce competition for the presentation of contemporary music.) In 1953 Herbert Eimert [1935], in charge of the newly founded electronic studio at Cologne Radio, selected Stockhausen, who was already deeply involved with the medium, as his right-hand man. By this time, influenced by Webern [1773], Messiaen, and Boulez, Stockhausen was committed to "total serialism," on which subject he was writing and lecturing passionately. Dissatisfied with the knowledge he brought to bear on his electronic studio work, he spent three years, 1954–57, taking courses in physics, acoustics, and phonetics. In 1955 he and Eimert brought out the journal *Die Reihe (The Row)*, dedicated to serialism, with the backing of the important publisher Universal Editions of Vienna. Two years later he began teaching at Dortmund and has since taught and lectured worldwide. (In 1958 he toured America and Canada.)

By now Stockhausen had adopted, formulated, and improved upon virtually all of the accepted avant-garde techniques, including John Cage's [2192] aleatory concepts. Taking a leaf from the theorist Joseph Schillinger and from his own teacher Messiaen, Stockhausen saw musical sound as involving four "parameters"—duration, pitch, intensity, and color—all of which, note by note, the electronic composer could actually "create" by manipulation of a basic sine tone. To other such considerations as rhythm and density (of combined sounds) he added that of spatial placement. He argued that since traditional music could be heard perfectly satisfactorily through mechanical reproduction, the new music needed to take an approach that could not be so reproduced—e.g., by the use of multiple performing groups or orchestras, or the placement of loudspeakers. Beginning with a post-Webernian pointillism that argued for the primacy

of the individual note (e.g., *Kontra-Punkte*), Stockhausen moved on to the use of motivic cells which, guided by a few basic rules, the performer could play or sing in whatever order he chose. Increasingly Stockhausen became fascinated with reconciling the polarities of composer control and performer freedom. For example, the composer might work out the game plan with mathematical precision; within its confines the performer or performers would have free rein—one performer might, let us say, "react" as he sees fit to whatever musical cell that might be chosen by another. Or the composer might have the last word by controlling electronically the sounds produced by the performers. Increasingly Stockhausen's vision has become more mystical (not to say indescribable), and he now talks in terms of some kind of total union after the inevitable destruction of the world as we know it. All this of course demands a whole new concept of notation that leaves the old Guidonian scale far behind. It should be added that Stockhausen often intends to bore his audiences as much as to shock them.

In 1963 Stockhausen took over direction of the Cologne Electronic Studio from Eimert, who retired, and about the same time divorced himself from Darmstadt to set up his own courses in Cologne. Three years later he went to the University of California at Davis for a year as a visiting professor, and in 1971 he was appointed professor of composition at the Cologne Musikhochschule. In 1970 the Japanese built him a spherical arena at the Osaka World's Fair wherein he was able to test out his ultimate spatial multimedia concepts. And in 1976 his multimedia piece *Sirius* was premiered at the Aerospace Museum in Washington, D.C. As one sympathetic critic said a decade ago, "Where it will all lead to is anybody's guess." Stockhausen has recently begun a mammoth project which he calls *Licht*—a cycle of seven full-length operas, each named after one of the days of the week. The first such opera, *Donnerstag (Thursday)*, was premiered in 1979. The second, *Samstag (Saturday)*, followed in 1984 at La Scala. The last opera in the series is tentatively to appear by the turn of a new century.

RECORDINGS: Close to ninety percent of Stockhausen's pre-1980 works have been recorded. The list of recordings is as follows—*3 Choruses After Verlaine* and *Choral*, both for unaccompanied chorus; *3 Lieder* for alto and chamber orchestra; Sonatine for Violin and Piano; *Kreuzspiel (Cross Play)* for oboe, bass clarinet, piano, and percussion; *Formel* and *Spiel* for orchestra; *Schlagtrio* for piano and two timpanists; *Punkte* for orchestra;

Kontra-Punkte for ten instruments; *Studie I, II* for tape; *Zeitmässe* for five woodwinds; *Gruppen* for three orchestras; *Gesang der Jünglinge (Song of the Youths)* for tape; *Zyklus* for percussionist; *Klavierstücke I–XI* for piano (Stockhausen recently completed several more piano pieces, but they have not yet been recorded); *Carré* for four orchestras and four choruses; *Refrain* for three instrumentalists; *Kontakte* (two versions: one purely electronic, the other for tape and percussion); *Momente* (two versions: the 1965 version with Martina Arroyo and the longer 1972 version) for soprano, chorus, two organs, and orchestra; *Mikrophonie I* for live electronics (six performers) *Mikrophonie II* for twelve singers, organ, and electronics; *Mixtur* for orchestra and electronics; *Solo* for trombone; *Stop* for orchestra; *Telemusik* for instruments and electronics; *Adieu* for wind quintet; *Hymnen (Anthems)* for electronic and concrete sounds; *Prozession* for tam-tam, viola, piano, tape, and live electronics; *Stimmung* for six vocalists (two versions); *Kurzwellen (Shortwaves)* for piano, tam-tam, viola, and live electronics; about twelve of the fifteen works collectively entitled *Aus den Sieben Tagen (From the Seven Days)* and including *Set Sail for the Sun, Communion, Intensity, It, Upwards, Unlimited,* and others (for various ensembles of generally chamber size); *Spiral* for solo oboe; *Stockhoven-Beethausen Opus 1970,* a multimedia work for four live performers; *Pole* for two performers; *Mantra* for two pianists; *Sternklang (Star Sound)* for five groups of musicians (also known as *Park Music); Trans* for orchestra; *Ylem* for orchestra; *Am Himmel wandre ich . . . (Indianerlieder)* for mezzo-soprano and tenor; *Inori* for orchestra; *Atmen gibt das Leben* (the 1974 version for chorus and the longer 1977 version for chorus and orchestra); *Musik im Bauch (Music in the Belly)* for percussion and musical clocks; *Tierkreis (Zodiac)* for solo violin; four works collectively titled *Für kommende Zeiten (For Times to Come),* including *Japan, Wach, Ceylon* for live electronics, and *Bird of Passage* for five instrumentalists; *Harlekin* and *Der kleine Harlekin* for clarinet; *Sirius* for trumpet, soprano, bass clarinet, bass voice, and electronics; *Donnerstag (Thursday),* the first opera from the cycle *Licht;* and *Der Jahreslauf (The Course of the Year)* for ensemble, an excerpt from the *Licht* sequence.

[2378] KORTE, Karl Richard
TEACHER
BORN: Ossining, N.Y., August 25, 1928

The son of a German-born sculptor and musical amateur, Karl Korte grew up in Englewood, New Jersey, where he played in dance bands. He studied under such teachers as Bergsma **[2313]**, Mennin **[2328]**, and Persichetti **[2236]** at the Juilliard School and privately with Otto Luening **[1980]** and Aaron Copland **[1986]**. He also studied in Italy as a Fulbright fellow, and has received two Guggenheim awards, a Ford Foundation grant, and a number of other prestigious prizes. In 1969 he was winner of the Belgian Queen Elizabeth competition. From 1964 to 1971 he taught at SUNY, Binghamton, and has since served as professor of composition at the University of Texas in Austin. Among his compositions (which involve both twelve-tone and jazz elements) are 3 symphonies, 2 string quartets, and a good deal of music for band and other wind ensembles. RECORDINGS: Works recorded include the Concerto for Piano and Winds; *Pale Is This Good Prince* (oratorio); *Matrix* (winds, piano, and percussion); *"I Think You Would Have Understood"* (jazz ensemble and tape); *Aspects of Love* (song cycle); *4 Blake Songs; Libera me* (choral); and *Remembrances* (flute and tape).

[2379] HELPS, Robert Eugene
PIANIST, TEACHER
BORN: Passaic, N.J., September 23, 1928

Well known as a concert pianist specializing in the modern idiom, Robert Helps studied with Abby Whiteside at Juilliard, where his chief mentor in composition was Roger Sessions **[1931]**. At various other times he attended Columbia University and the University of California at Berkeley (where he taught for a time). He has also taught at Stanford, the San Francisco Conservatory, and the New England Conservatory. More recently he has been on the faculties of Princeton and the Manhattan School of Music. Helps has made a number of recordings as a pianist. Most of his compositions are instrumental, and many of them involve his chosen instrument. RECORDINGS: Symphony No. 1, *Gossamer Noons* for soprano and orchestra, piano pieces, and some songs have been recorded.

[2380] MAYUZUMI, Toshiro (Mä-yōō-zōō-mē, Tōsh-ē-rō)
BROADCAST EXECUTIVE
BORN: Yokohama, February 20, 1929

A composer who has made a highly original amalgam of Eastern and Western techniques (both the traditional and contemporary), Mayuzumi's music is particularly well known outside of Japan. A 1951 graduate and first-prize winner at the Tokyo National Musical Academy, he wrote a piece for voice and chamber orchestra, *Sphenogramme,* which won praise that summer at the ISCM Festival in Frankfurt. A French government scholarship forthwith took him to the Paris Conservatoire and study with Tony Aubin (1907–   ) for a year. He then returned to Japan to spread the gospel of the avant-garde and to pursue experiments in electronic music. He was back in Western Europe in 1956 to attend, and have compositions played at, the summer festivals in Stockholm and Darmstadt. The following year he instituted the Karuisawa Summer Festival in Japan and helped found the Tokyo Institute for Twentieth-Century Music. At around this time he turned to an investigation of oriental music, notably Buddhist chant, *gagaku,* and the "mixed tones" produced by temple bells. Such materials were used in the *Nirvana Symphony* of 1958, whose three movements are designated as "campanologies." He came to the United States in 1960 for a year's study on a Ford Foundation Fellowship, and has made other visits since. In 1976 his opera *Kinkakuji (The Temple of the Golden Pavilion)* was produced in Berlin, marking Mayuzumi's return to composition after a hiatus of several years; based on a novel by Yukio Mishima, the opera is slated to receive its American premiere in 1986. Mayuzumi has also written film scores and musicals. RECORDINGS: Orchestral recordings include the *Mandala Symphony;* the *Phonologie symphonique; Bacchanale; Samsara; Essay* for strings; *Tateyama; Bugaku* (ballet); and *Pieces for Prepared Piano and Strings* (an alternate version for prepared piano and string quartet has also been recorded). Other recordings include the choral-orchestral *Nirvana Symphony; Music with Sculpture* for band; the Concerto for Percussion and Band; the early neo-classical *Divertimento* for ten instruments; *Prelude* for string quartet; and the film score to *The Bible.*

[2381] DENISOV, Edison Vasilievich
(Dā'-nē-sof, Ē'-dē-son Vȧl-zēl-yä'-vēch)
ENGINEER
BORN: Tomsk, April 6, 1929

Denisov, one of the few Soviet composers to experiment with Western avant-garde techniques, is the son of an electrical engineer, who named him after the American inventor of the incandescent bulb. Initially he fol-

lowed in the paternal path, graduating from the University of Tomsk at twenty-two with an engineering degree. At that point he turned to music and spent five years at the Moscow Conservatory. He has been fairly prolific as a composer. At least during the very early part of his career he wrote in traditional forms, from opera to sonata, but in recent years he has used serialism, electronics, and aleatory approaches. Though in this respect he might be regarded as timid by certain circles in the West, it is perhaps significant that he appears to be sparsely represented in the official Soviet record catalog. RECORDINGS: There are American or Western European recordings of his *Cresecendo e diminuendo* for harpsichord and strings, Sonata for Saxophone and Piano, Sonata for Solo Clarinet, Sonata for Cello and Piano, Piano Trio, *Signes en blanc* for piano, Concerto for Piano, and *Peinture (Painting)* for orchestra. There is a Czech recording of *Canon in Memory of Stravinsky* for flute, clarinet, and harp, and at least two Soviet recordings—*The Sun of the Incas* for soprano and eleven instruments and another recording of *Peinture.*

[2382] SCULTHORPE, Peter Joshua
TEACHER
BORN: Launceston, Tasmania, April 29, 1929

One of Australia's more venturesome contemporary composers, Peter Sculthorpe graduated from the Melbourne University Conservatorium in 1950; later he spent two years, 1958–60, at Oxford (Wadham College), studying with Edmund Rubbra [1995] and Egon Wellesz [1799]. In 1963 he was appointed as a lecturer in music at the University of Sydney. He was a Harkness Fellow at Yale in 1965–67 and has taught as a visitor at the University of Sussex in England, 1971–72. Sculthorpe at one time made much use of Asiatic and Australian native music and in recent years has also partaken of most of the paths broken by the Western avant-garde. Very little of his music is known in the Western hemisphere at present, but a pioneering critical study of 1982 by Michael Hannan (University of Queensland Press) suggests that he may be undertaking a grand cross-cultural synthesis of East and West. Sculthorpe has written an opera, *Rites of Passage,* produced by the Sidney Opera in 1974. Other works include at least 10 string quartets; *Sun Music I–IV* for orchestra; *Sun Music for Voices and Percussion;* four works for varying instrumental groupings entitled *Irkanda,* after an aboriginal word meaning "faraway place" *(Irkanda II* is String Quartet No. 5); other orchestral works; much piano music; choral music; and incidental music for the stage and films. RECORDINGS: Among recordings which have been available to some extent in the United States there are *Sun Music I–IV; Irkanda IV* for viola and string orchestra; String Quartets Nos. 8 and 10; *Small Town* for orchestra; and an album of piano and electronic pieces— Sonatina, *2 Easy Pieces, Night Pieces, Landscape,* and *Koto Music I–II.* The Australian Broadcasting Corporation has numerous other works in its tape archives, and a few other scattered works have appeared on obscure Australian labels.

[2383] POUSSEUR, Henri Léon Marie Thérèse (Pōō-ser', On-rē' Lā-ôn' Mà-rē' Tā-res')
TEACHER, ORGANIST, CHOIRMASTER
BORN: Malmédy, Belgium, June 23, 1929

Belgium's most prominent contribution to the far-out wing of the later twentieth century, Henri Pousseur was born in the often war-ravaged area near the German border and studied at first, in 1947–52, at the conservatory of nearby Liège with Jean Absil [1889]. He then spent a year at the Brussels Conservatory and undertook private study with Pierre Boulez [2346]. During these years he appeared innocently enough as a public-school music teacher and as a church choirmaster. In 1954 he became connected with the Cologne electronic studio, where he encountered Karlheinz Stockhausen [2377]. Three years later he worked with Luciano Berio [2352] in the Milan electronic studio. The following year he helped found the APELAC electronic music studio in Brussels. He has taught at the Liège Conservatory, SUNY (Buffalo), Darmstadt, Cologne, and Basel. His music, of which he has produced a great deal, leaves no tone unstirred in its search for auditory novelty, and has passed through and beyond all of the fashionable tics of the avant-garde. Perhaps his most talked-about work has been his 1969 "opera" *Votre Faust,* a collaborative effort with writer Michel Butor, the ending of which the audience is permitted to decide. RECORDINGS: Works on records include *Second Electronic Setting, 2 Prayer Settings, Scambi,* and *3 Visages de Liège* for electronic tape; *Mobile* for two pianos; *Rimes pour différentes sources sonores* for orchestra and electronics; *Jeu de Miroirs de Votre Faust* for piano, voices, and electronic tape; *7 Versets des psaumes de la penitence* for chorus; *Tales and Songs from the Bible of Hell* for voices,

tape, and live electronics; *3 Chants sacrées* for soprano and string trio; *Mnemosyne 2* for voices and chamber ensemble; *Madrigal 2* for ensemble; and *Madrigal 3* for clarinet, piano, violin, cello, and percussion.

[2384] HODDINOTT, Alun
TEACHER, ADMINISTRATOR
BORN: Bargoed, Glamorganshire, August 11, 1929

The most prominent (and prolific) Welsh composer of his generation, Alun Hoddinott took a baccalaureate degree in music from University College in Cardiff in 1949 and studied piano with Arthur Benjamin [1887] in London. He was a member of the faculty of the Cardiff College of Music and Drama from 1951 to 1959, when he returned to his former school as a lecturer. A year later he was given a doctorate and in 1967 became a professor of music there. He is also director of the Cardiff Festival, specializing in contemporary music. His music has been affected by his admiration for such composers as Bartók [1734] and Alan Rawsthorne [2067], and he has experimented with serial techniques but must in the end be regarded as an eclectic. Since 1970 he has written 4 operas (two of them for television), but most of his output—which includes at least 5 symphonies, concerti for various instruments, string quartets, and sonatas—is instrumental. RECORDINGS: Orchestral works on disc include Symphonies Nos. 2, 3, and 5; *Sinfoniettas No. 1* and *No. 2;* Concerti for Piano Nos. 2 and 3; Concerto for Clarinet; Concerto for Horn; Concerto for Harp; *Concerto Grosso No. 1* and *No. 2; Divertimento; Nocturnes and Cadenzas* for cello and orchestra; *Overture Jack Straw; ... the Sun, the Great Luminary of the Universe ... ; Landscapes; Variants; Investiture Dances;* and *Welsh Dances.* Chamber and instrumental recordings include the Septet; String Quartet No. 1; Piano Trio; Sonatas Nos. 1 and 3 for Violin and Piano; Sonata for Cello and Piano; Sonata for Clarinet and Piano; Sonatas for Piano Nos. 1, 2, 5, and 6; and miscellaneous piano pieces. Vocal recordings include *Roman Dream* for soprano, piano, and harp; the choral-orchestral cantata *Sinfonia fidei;* and other choral pieces.

[2385] GARANT, Albert Antonio Serge (Gà-ran', Àl-bâr' Àn-tōn'-yō Sârzh)
CLARINETIST, CONDUCTOR, TEACHER, ADMINISTRATOR
BORN: Quebec, September 22, 1929

Born into a family of passionate musical amateurs, Serge Garant found school not to his taste and, by request of the authorities, discontinued his formal education in his early teens. Shortly afterward the Garants moved to Sherbrooke (near the Vermont-New Hampshire borders) and Serge began teaching himself various instruments. He was soon playing saxophone and clarinet in dance combos and in the local symphony. He discovered music of the Schoenbergian [1657] school and learned the idiom from scores. After some desultory composition studies in Montreal with Claude Champagne [1852], he went in 1951 to Paris, where he took a course under Messiaen [2129] and studied counterpoint with Andrée Vaurabourg, the wife of Arthur Honegger [1861]. Excited by the music of Boulez [2346], he committed himself to serialism, though of a rather personal variety. After a year he came home and worked variously as an arranger, accompanist, and cocktail pianist. In 1954 in conjunction with several other Canadian modernists, he began promoting the new music in concerts that eventually became a regular feature of the annual Montreal Festival. In recent years he has conducted throughout Canada, taught composition at the University of Montreal, and directed the Société de Musique Contemporaine in Quebec. Though he has written orchestral pieces and scores for documentary films, most of his output is of chamber dimensions. RECORDINGS: Among works on records are *Anerca* for voice and instruments, using Eskimo poems as texts; *Offrande I* for orchestra; *Phrases I* for voice and instruments; *Jeu à quatre, Offrande III,* and *Circuits II* for various chamber groups; songs; and piano pieces.

[2386] CRUMB, George Henry
TEACHER
BORN: Charleston, W.Va., October 24, 1929

The son of trained instrumentalists, George Crumb was steeped in music and taught himself to play piano and compose (almost obsessively) by the time he reached adolescence. Graduating at seventeen, he spent three years in a local music school, Mason College, during which he married a fellow student, Elizabeth May Brown. He then took a master's degree at the University of Illinois under the direction of Eugene Weigel (1910–   ), a pupil of Hindemith [1914], and proceeded to the University of Michigan for further graduate study with Ross Lee Finney [2099]. His 1954 String Quartet and the

1955 Sonata for Solo Cello both in a generally atonal idiom won prizes, and in the latter year Crumb went to Berlin on a Fulbright fellowship to study with Boris Blacher [2030].

In 1958 he taught for a year at Hollins College, near Roanoke, Virginia, and received his doctorate of musical arts from Michigan in 1959. Until 1964, Crumb taught piano at the University of Colorado. After a brief flirtation with serialism, he produced his first truly characteristic work, *Night Music I,* in 1964. Inspired, like much of his music of the 1964–70 period, by the poetry of Federico Garcia Lorca, it is characterized by extraordinary delicacy and unusual and haunting sounds. After a year as a visitor at the Center for Creative and Performing Arts in Buffalo, he came to rest at the University of Pennsylvania in Philadelphia. A Guggenheim Fellowship in 1967 was followed by the 1968 Pulitzer Prize for his orchestral *Echoes of Time and the River,* in which some members of the orchestra are not only asked to produce unusual sounds with their instruments, but to shout, whistle, whisper, and (optionally) march in procession across the stage. Later works include stunningly placed quotations from familiar music and wisps of melody that catch at the throat. At least four honorary doctorates, as well as other awards, have been conferred on the composer.

RECORDINGS: Almost all of his works have been recorded, except for the 1954 String Quartet, some recent piano music, and the 1977 *Star Child* for soloists, choruses, and large orchestra. Recordings include the Sonata for Solo Cello; *Variazioni* for orchestra; *Night Music I* for soprano, piano, and percussion; *4 Nocturnes (Night Music II)* for violin and piano; *Madrigals, Book I* for soprano, vibraphone, and double bass; *Madrigals, Book II* for soprano, alto flute, and percussion; *11 Echoes of Autumn 1965* for violin, alto flute, clarinet, and piano; *Echoes of Time and the River* for orchestra; *Songs, Drones, and Refrains of Death* for amplified instruments (double bass, piano, and guitar) and percussion; *Madrigals, Book III* for soprano, harp, and percussion; *Madrigals, Book IV* for soprano, flute, harp, double bass, and percussion; *Night of the 4 Moons* for alto flute, banjo, electric cello, and percussion; *Black Angels* for amplified string quartet; *Ancient Voices of Children* for soprano, boy soprano, and chamber orchestra; *Lux Aeterna* for soprano, bass flute, sitar, and two percussionists; *Voice of the Whale* for flute, cello, and piano; *Makrokosmos I, II* for piano; *Makrokosmos III (Music for a Summer Evening)* for two amplified pianos and two percussionists; *Makrokosmos IV (Celestial Mechanics)* for amplified piano, four hands; *Dream Sequence* for chamber ensemble; *Apparition* (after Whitman) for soprano and piano; the early *5 Piano Pieces* and the recent *Gnomic Variations* for piano; and *A Haunted Landscape* for orchestra (first performed by Arthur Weisberg and the New York Philharmonic in June 1984).

[2387] PETROVICS, Emil (Pet'-rō-vēch, E'-mil)
CONDUCTOR, PIANIST, TEACHER
BORN: Zrenjanin, Yugoslavia, February 9, 1930

The Hungarians insist that Petrovics' birthplace was called Nagybecskerek, but that was its name before he put in his appearance. He spent most of his childhood in Belgrade, then moved to Budapest, where he first began studying composition with Reszö Sugár (1919–), a Kodály [1760] pupil. In 1951 he entered the Budapest Academy where his teachers included Ferenc Szabó [2027], János Viski (1906–61), and Ferenc Farkas (1905–). Graduating in 1957, he held a four-year engagement as conductor at the Petöfi Theater, then taught at the Academy of Dramatic Art until 1969, when he became professor of composition at the Academy of Music. He moved from a sort of neo-classicism, much beholden to Ravel [1666] of whom he published a study, to a Bergian [1789] dodecaphony. He has been especially successful with his three operas, premiered between 1961 and 1969. RECORDINGS: Two one-act operas, *C'est la guerre* and *Lysistrate,* and the full-length opera *Crime and Punishment* have been recorded, along with his oratorio *The Book of Jonah, Cantatas Nos. 1–4,* and the String Quartet.

[2388] SONDHEIM, Stephen Joshua
LYRICIST
BORN: New York, March 22, 1930

Stephen Sondheim, though famed as a writer of musicals, has come perhaps closer than anyone else to creating an American opera grown out of the popular musical stage. At Williams College, from which he graduated in 1950, he wrote a number of student shows. He then studied for a time with Milton Babbitt [2247]. In 1956 he wrote music for *The Girls of Summer* and the following year was asked by Leonard Bernstein [2282] to supply lyrics for *West Side Story.* He has also served as lyricist for other musicals not his own, the most notable of which was *Gypsy.* He pro-

vided music and lyrics for *A Funny Thing Happened on the Way to the Forum,* and his own libretti to a series of increasingly successful works, including *Anyone Can Whistle* in 1964, *Company* in 1970, and *Follies* in 1971. *A Little Night Music,* based on an Ingmar Bergman film, was an overwhelming success in 1973. (The last three named won Tony Awards for best musical score in New York productions.) His next work, the 1976 *Pacific Overtures,* in which he experimented with Japanese themes, was a critical success but proved too rich for its audiences. *Sweeney Todd,* 1979, designed as a real opera but remodeled for Broadway, succeeded, however, in spite of an extraordinarily gruesome and cynical story and has been televised by PBS. Sondheim has also written television and movie scores, and his songs have been the focus of a revue, *Side by Side by Sondheim.* His most recent musical, *Sunday in the Park with George,* again garnered critical raves, a considerable amount of audience appreciation, and a Pulitzer Prize. RECORDINGS: There are many individual songs, the musical portions of all the shows from 1964 onward, and a virtually complete recording of *Sweeney Todd.*

[2389] ASHLEY, Robert
ADMINISTRATOR
BORN: Ann Arbor, Mich., March 28, 1930

Robert Ashley, who has taken music into remote climes, was graduated in 1952 from the University of Michigan, virtually in his own backyard. He then spent some time in New York at the Manhattan School of Music studying composition with Wallingford Riegger [1793], and having his mind enlarged by John Cage [2192]. Returning to Michigan in 1957, he studied psychoacoustics with Roberto Gerhard [1926]. That same year he joined forces with fellow student Gordon Mumma (1935–) and painter-sculptor Milton Cohen to produce mixed-media events which they termed "space theater." They formalized their effort a year later in the Cooperative Studio for Electronic Music, where artists of all sorts put their heads together to produce, in the term of the day, total theater. In 1961 all this came to fruition in the first ONCE Festival (of eight), to which Ashley's initial contribution was a piece called *Public Opinion Descends Upon the Demonstrators.* Between 1965 and 1969 he took the ONCE Ensemble on tour, and a year later joined with Mumma, David Behrman, and Alvin Lucier (1931–) in the Sonic Arts Union. This last was an electronic-music performing group that used such media as tape recorders, synthesizers, microphones, telephones, and computers in their presentations. In 1969 Ashley moved to Oakland, California, to direct the Contemporary Music Center at Mills College. He has done scores for experimental films and once, in 1959, wrote a piano sonata. RECORDINGS: The early Sonata for Piano has been recorded, along with a number of more typical pieces—*Symphony "In Memoriam Crazy Horse"* for twenty (or more) instruments; *The Wolfman* for voice and tape; *She Was a Visitor* for voices; *Automatic Writing* for tape; *Purposeful Lady Slow Afternoon* for live electronic instruments; *Automatic Writing* for tape; and several LPs of episodes and segments from his huge "performance opera" *Perfect Lives (Private Parts)*. Newly released on cassettes only is a boxed set of what purports to be the complete *Perfect Lives*.

[2390] AUSTIN, Larry Don
TEACHER, ADMINISTRATOR, EDITOR,
TRUMPETER
BORN: Duncan, Okla., September 12,
1930

From the receipt of a childhood birthday trumpet, Larry Austin (born in southern Oklahoma, schooled in Vernon, Texas) quickly developed into a jazzman, a fact that left its mark on his work, even though he eventually progressed to electronics and mixed-media. Between 1947 and 1952 he acquired two degrees in music at North Texas State University. Drafted into the military in the latter year, he was assigned as a staff arranger-composer to an army radio station in San Antonio, where he studied languages on his own time and married Edna Navarro, a nurse. After a summer studying with Darius Milhaud [1868] at Mills College in 1955, he spent three years at the University of California, Berkeley, studying composition with Andrew Imbrie [2314] and teaching as a graduate assistant. In 1958 he became a member of the faculty of the University of California at Davis. There he began experimenting with jazz composition and, abetted by Gunther Schuller [2354], wrote *Improvisations for Orchestra and Jazz Soloists*. Premiered by Schuller with the National Symphony in 1962 and telecast in 1964 by Leonard Bernstein [2282] and the New York Philharmonic, it created something of a stir. With his New Music Ensemble, organized in 1963, Austin soon moved to controlled group improvisation, which he termed "open style." After a year in Rome, 1964–65, on a

fellowship from the university, Austin returned to hobnob with such visiting celebrities as Cage [2192] and Stockhausen [2377], whose notions encouraged him to move into musical theater and mixed-media, involving variously lights, sculptures, films, projections, mobiles, mimes, mirrors, trapdoors, and pajamas. After a summer course at Stanford in 1969 involving computer music, Austin occupied himself with tape music. In 1972 he went to Tampa to head the music department at the University of South Florida, and in 1978 he returned to North Texas State to teach. RECORDINGS: Works on records include *Piano Variations* and *Piano Set in Open Style* for solo piano; *Current* for clarinet and piano; *Canadian Coastlines* for computer; *Improvisations for Orchestra and Jazz Soloists;* and several "hybrid" works for electronically altered instruments or voices —*Quadrants: Event Complex No. 1* (wind ensemble); *Catalogo Voce* (bass-baritone voice); *Maroon Bells* (tenor voice and piano); and *Second Fantasy on Ives's Universe Symphony—The Heavens* (clarinet, viola, keyboards, percussion, and soprano).

[2391] TAKEMITSU, Toru (Tá-ke-mit-
soo, Tō-rōō)
BORN: Tokyo, October 8, 1930

Takemitsu, one of the most widely performed of contemporary Japanese composers, seems to have demonstrated no startling proclivity for music in his youth. In the aftermath of World War II, he worked as a mess boy in an American officers' club in Yokohama and studied briefly with a composer named Yasuji Kiyose (1900–   ), a pupil of Alexander Tcherepnin [1961]. He contracted tuberculosis and while convalescing in 1948 he decided that he must himself write music. Most of his subsequent knowledge of his art he acquired himself, in great part through intelligent listening. He has been influenced chiefly by twentieth-century composers from Debussy [1547] on, as well as by Japanese music and natural sounds. By 1950 he was already being performed, and a year later he joined with several of his compatriots to form the experimental group Jitsuken Kohbo. At first he worked largely in limited forms and with tape, but in 1957 the death of a friend elicited his first orchestral work, a *Requiem* for strings.
In 1966, together with Toshi Ichiyanagi (1933–   ) and conductor Seiji Ozawa, Takemitsu founded the biennial contemporary music festival Orchestral Space. It was Takemitsu who was chiefly responsible for the 1970 Osaka Exposition's spherical mul-

timedia concert hall that enabled Karlheinz Stockhausen [2377] to realize some of his more extreme dreams. Takemitsu has eschewed teaching and other such public activities, and spends much of his time composing in a hideaway in the mountains north of Tokyo. He has successfully amalgamated Japanese music with advanced Western techniques and sometimes calls for native instruments as soloists. A good deal of his music depends on the placement of the performers, who often interract as groups of soloists rather than as orchestral masses. Besides a large catalog of more abstract pieces, Takemitsu has produced several film scores, notably that for *A Woman of the Dunes.*

RECORDINGS: Takemitsu has been quite well-represented on records, domestic and imported. Orchestral works recorded include *Textures; Requiem* for strings; *The Dorian Horizon* for seventeen strings; *November Steps I,* with biwa and shakuhachi soloists; *Green (November Steps II); Asterism* for piano and orchestra; *Arc* for piano and orchestra; *Coral Island* for soprano and orchestra; *Tree Music; Quatrain I* for piano, clarinet, violin, cello, and orchestra; *A Flock Descends into the Pentagonal Garden; Cassiopeia* for percussion group and orchestra; *Gitimalya* for marimba and orchestra; *Winter; Marginalia;* the film score *Legacy for the Future;* and *In an Autumn Garden* for gagaku orchestra. Other recordings include *Stanza I* for piano, guitar, harp, vibraphone, and female voice; *Ring* for flute, terz-guitar, and lute; *Valeria* for violin, cello, guitar, two piccolos, and organ; *Sacrifice* for alto flute, lute, and vibraphone; *Quatrain II* for piano, clarinet, violin, and cello; *Water Ways* for two harps, two vibraphones, piano, clarinet, violin, and cello; *Waves* for solo clarinet with French horn, two trombones, and bass drum; *Hika* for violin and piano; *A Way a Lone* for string quartet; *Bryce* for flute, two harps, two marimbas, and percussion; *Toward the Sea* for alto flute and guitar; *Rain Tree* and *Munari by Munari* for percussion; *Water Music* and *Vocalism Ai* for tape; and works for keyboards—*Corona; Far Away; Piano Distance;* and *Undisturbed Rest.* (One unfortunate reality for the American collector of Japanese music is that most direct-import Japanese recordings contain liner notes *entirely* in Japanese.)

[2392] AMRAM, David Werner

BRASS PLAYER, PIANIST, CONDUCTOR
BORN: Philadelphia, Pa., November 17, 1930

One of the more successful of those composers who have attempted to bridge the widening gulf to pop music, Amram led a peripatetic childhood in Philadelphia, small towns in Florida and Pennsylvania, and Washington, D.C. By the time he reached puberty, he had graduated from the bugle to the trumpet, tuba, and horn, which he played variously in school and dance bands. After an abortive year as a music major at Oberlin Conservatory, he transferred in 1948 to George Washington University in Washington, D.C., where he kept up his jazz interests and from which he graduated in 1952 with a major in European history. Drafted, he spent two years in the Seventh Army Symphony, founded two years before by Samuel Adler [2372], in Germany. After spending an extra year in Paris as a night club musician, he came back to New York in 1955, where he studied composition with Vittorio Giannini [2042] and conducting with Jonel Perlea. Having made a name for himself as a jazzman, he formed his own combo, with which he made recordings. He also composed for films, for the Off-Broadway theaters, and eventually for Broadway productions. Toward the end of the decade he began producing concert works, resulting in an all-Amram concert at Town Hall in 1960 and another in 1962. In 1961 he also wrote a *Sacred Service* for the Park Avenue Synagogue, a performance of which in 1967 marked his New York conducting debut. In 1965 his first opera *The Final Ingredient,* also on a Jewish theme, was nationally telecast by ABC. A second, *Twelfth Night,* was successfully premiered at the Lake George Opera Festival three years later, in a production by Amram's longtime colleague Joseph Papp. During the 1970s Amram traveled all over the world under the sponsorship of the U.S. State Department and, leading a jazz group thither in 1977, was the first American musician to visit Cuba in sixteen years. In 1979 he married Lora Lee Ecobelli and received an honorary doctorate from Moravian College in Bethlehem, Pennsylvania. Amram has been composer-in-residence at the Marboro Festival in Vermont and (the first such) with the New York Philharmonic Orchestra. His music makes no attempt to join the fashionable modes of the day. RECORDINGS: Several orchestral works have been recorded—the *Shakespearean Concerto; Ode to Lord Buckley; Elegy* for violin and orchestra; and the Triple Concerto for Winds, Brass, Jazz Quintets, and Orchestra. Chamber recordings include the Piano Sonata; Violin Sonata; *Dirge and Variations* for piano trio; Quintet for Winds; and *Portraits* for piano quartet. There was also a two-record album entitled *No More Walls,* which contains a selection of short pop, jazz, ethnic, and classical pieces, reflecting Amram's cross-cultural outlook.

[2393] MARTINO, Donald James
CLARINETIST, ARRANGER, TEACHER
BORN: Plainfield, N.J., May 16, 1931

Taking up the clarinet in elementary school and playing in high school instrumental groups, Donald Martino went to Syracuse University in 1948 to become a professional clarinetist. There his composition teacher, Ernst Bacon [1949], suggested he was cut out for higher things. Still undecided, he moved on to Princeton in 1952 to do graduate work in history, but gave in to his inclinations and took an M.F.A. under the direction of Roger Sessions [1931] and Milton Babbitt [2247] in 1954. While still a student there in 1953 he married Mari Rice and won several awards for composition, including a Koussevitzky Fellowship. A Fulbright fellowship in 1954 (renewed in 1955) took him to Florence to study with Luigi Dallapiccola [2049]. On his return, he taught for a year at the East Third Street Music Settlement School in New York, and two more at Princeton, padding the family budget with jazz gigs and arranging. From 1959 to 1969 he held a professorship at Yale and taught several summers at Tanglewood. By then a rather doctrinaire dodecaphony in his music had been considerably tempered by an admiration for nineteenth-century German Romanticism. In 1969, after having received a number of prestigious grants, Martino became chairman of the department of composition at the New England Conservatory of Music in Boston, and, his first marriage having ended in divorce, married Lora Harvey. In 1974 he won the Pulitzer Prize for his *Notturno* for flutes, clarinets, violin, viola, cello, and piano. Martino became full professor of music at Brandeis University in 1980. He has made one essay into mixed-media theater, but otherwise the bulk of his output has been instrumental or choral. RECORDINGS: There is a recording of the Triple Concerto for Clarinet, Bass Clarinet, Contrabass Clarinet, and Chamber Orchestra. Chamber works on disc include *Quodlibets* for flute; *A Set for Clarinet;* Trio for Clarinet, Violin, and Piano; *Frammenti* for oboe and double bass; *Fantasy-Variations* for solo violin; Concerto for Wind Quintet; *B-a-b-b-i-t-t* for Clarinet; *Notturno;* and *Strata.* His choral works, *7 Pious Pieces* and *Paradiso Choruses,* have also been recorded.

[2394] DLUGOSZEWSKI, Lucia (Dloo-gō-chef'-skē, Loo-chē'-à)
TEACHER, PERCUSSIONIST, POET, PIANIST
BORN: Detroit, June 16, 1931

Though Lucia Dlugoszewski has been writing music for thirty years, she was known and admired until recently only by a small group of advanced artists in (mostly) other fields. Though she studied music at the Detroit Conservatory, she attended Wayne State University as a physics major and premed student. However, increasingly fascinated with the mathematical ramifications of contemporary music, she traipsed off to New York to study with Edgard Varèse [1774] and others. In 1947 she won the Tomkins Prize for poetry; she published a book of poetry in 1969. She found a place composing for theater and dance companies. For the needs of her musical concepts she invented a vast array of percussion instruments and a "timbre" piano whose strings are bowed as well as struck. She has taught at the New School and at NYU, and has served for some years as music director for the Erick Hawkins Dance Company. (She has written on modern dance and on aesthetics.) Her first concert (at the Five Spot Café in 1958) was arranged by sculptor David Smith. In 1966 she won an award from the National Institute of Arts and Letters, which institution joined with the New York Philharmonic in 1975 to commission *Abyss and Caress.* Though Ms. Dlugoszewski's music is nothing if not "advanced," it possesses a stunning delicacy and imagination. RECORDINGS: *Fire Fragile Flight* for chamber orchestra; *Space Is a Diamond* for solo trumpet; *Angels of the Inmost Heaven* for brasses; *Tender Theatre Flight Nageire* for brasses and percussion—a tiny sampling of a vast output.

[2395] ELKUS, Jonathan
TEACHER, CONDUCTOR, BASSOONIST
BORN: San Francisco, August 8, 1931

The son of composer Albert Elkus (1884–1962), Jonathan Elkus grew up in the focal center of West Coast music and musicians. He did his undergraduate work at the University of California in Berkeley, where his father taught from 1935 to 1951 and where he studied with Charles Cushing [2077]. He then took a master's degree under Ernst Bacon [1949] and Leonard Ratner (1916–   ) at Stanford and undertook study in composition with Darius Milhaud [1868] at Mills. In 1957 he joined the faculty of Lehigh University in Bethlehem, Pennsylvania, where he taught and directed the bands. Over the next decade and a half he turned out several operas, of which the most successful has been *Tom Sawyer,* a work for children that has been internationally performed. In 1973, inspired by what was then called the counterculture, Elkus moved with his wife and son to Provincetown, Rhode Island, to live on his creativity. He is the author of a 1974 monograph on Charles Ives [1659] and American band music. RECORDINGS: The song cycle *After Their Kind* and some band pieces have been recorded.

[2396] BUSSOTTI, Sylvano (Boos-sôt'-tē, Sil-và'-nō)

POLYMATH

BORN: Florence, October 1, 1931

Among avant-garde composers, Bussotti appears to be the radical's radical. A member of an intellectual and artistic family, he began as something of a violin prodigy. At the age of nine he was sent to the Florence Conservatory, where he studied with Luigi Dallapiccola [2049]. Having been indoctrinated in the mysteries of twelve-tone music, he quit at the age of thirteen. Later in Paris and elsewhere he studied composition privately. He cast aside serialism for indeterminacy and other more revolutionary approaches and then did an about-face and increasingly relied on quotation from and imitation of the musical past—both his own and his country's. He also experimented in total theater, the culmination of his efforts being the 1972 opera *Lorenzaccio* for which he designed sets and costumes and served as stage director. He has also made a name for himself as a painter and writer. Recently Bussotti's orchestral music has been championed by conductor Giuseppe Sinopoli. RECORDINGS: *Coeur pour batteur—Positively Yes* for percussion and electronics; *Pièces de Chair III: Voix de femme* for female voice and tape; *Marbre* for string orchestra and piano; *Couple* for flute and piano; *Phrase à Trois* for string trio; *Ancora odono i colli* for mixed vocal sextet; *Il Nudo (The Naked One)* for soprano, piano, and string quartet; *O* for female voice; *Siciliano* and *5 frammenti all'Italia* for chorus; *Ultima Rara* for guitar and vocal ensemble; *Rara* for solo cello; *Rara Requiem* for vocal soloists, two choruses, instrumental soloists, and orchestra; *Bergkristal,* ballet after Adalbert Stifter for orchestra; *Lorenzaccio-Symphonie* for orchestra; and *Il Catalogo è Questo* for orchestra (with flutes obbligati).

[2397] WILLIAMSON, Malcolm Benjamin Graham Christopher

PIANIST, ORGANIST

BORN: Sydney, November 21, 1931

As an adolescent Malcolm Williamson studied violin, horn, and piano in Sydney and was a composition pupil of Sir Eugene Goossens [1878]. In 1950 he spent a few months in London studying with Elizabeth Lutyens [2091] and came back three years later for more lessons and to settle permanently. Fascinated by the music of Olivier Messiaen [2129], he became a virtuoso organist and also converted to Roman Catholicism. For a time he worked as a nightclub pianist. His earliest surviving works were written for his own keyboard performance or for a broad public, as with his rather ordinary hymns and carols. Then for a time he wrote big orchestral pieces—symphonies and concerti—influenced to a degree by Messiaen and serialism but generally eclectic. His first two operas, *Our Man in Havana* (produced by Sadler's Wells in 1963) and *English Eccentrics* (produced at Aldeburgh in 1964), were fairly successful and generally admired. Increasingly, however, from the mid-1960s Williamson seems to have rejected "modernism" for an attempt to be popular by using simple (some say simple-minded) tunes and such devices as audience participation—one more evidence of the musical malaise of the times. In 1975 he was named to succeed Sir Arthur Bliss [1854] as Master of the Queen's Musick. RECORDINGS: Two children's operas have been recorded, *The Happy Prince* and *Julius Caesar Jones.* Other vocal recordings include *The Brilliant and the Dark* for chorus and orchestra, to a text by Ursula Vaughan Williams; *Symphony for Voices* and *The Musicians of Bremen* for unaccompanied chorus; anthems; songs; and hymns. Orchestral recordings include the Concerto for Organ and the Concerto No. 3 for Piano (both played by the composer); Concerto for Violin; *Sinfonietta;* Symphony No. 1 "Elevamini"; *Sinfonia concertante* for piano and orchestra; *The Display,* a "ballet symphony"; *Santiago de Espada Overture;* and a number of short pieces for string orchestra—*Azure; The Bridge That Van Gogh Painted and the French Camargue; Lento;* and *Epitaphs for Edith Sitwell.* Chamber and instrumental recordings include *Pas de quatre* for wind quartet and piano; Piano Quintet; Piano Trio; Sonata No. 2 for Piano and other piano pieces; Sonata for 2 Pianos; *Symphony for Organ Solo;* and *Vision of Christ-Phoenix* for organ.

[2398] AHROLD, Frank
PIANIST, CONDUCTOR
BORN: Long Beach, Calif., December 12, 1931

Ahrold studied composition with John Vincent (1902–) and Lukas Foss **[2324]** at UCLA. Later he returned to Long Beach, where in the 1960s he conducted the Civic Chorus, the local chamber orchestra, and the Civic Light Opera. He then moved to San Francisco and became pianist of the Oakland Symphony in 1973. He has written nearly 200 compositions of all kinds, many on commission. RECORDINGS: *Song Without Words* (for strings); *Second Coming* (for tenor and orchestra); and *3 Poems of Sylvia Plath* (for voice and piano).

[2399] KAGEL, Mauricio Raúl (Kä'-gel, Mou-rēs'-yō Rä-ōōl')
CONDUCTOR, TEACHER, DIRECTOR, PRODUCER
BORN: Buenos Aires, December 24, 1931

If Kagel does not quite rank with the superstars of avant-garde music, few of them have managed to incorporate so many of the trends of their times in their work, and few have had more exposure on phonograph records. A liberal arts major at the University of Buenos Aires, he studied theory with Juan Carlos Paz (1901–72), a pioneer South American twelve-tone composer, and keyboards, strings, voice, and conducting with others. He gives chief credit for his intellectual development to thinkers and writers of his acquaintance, notably Jorge Luis Borges. From 1949 he worked as a pianist and conductor at the Teatro Colón, adviser to the progressive Agrupación Nueva Música and to the bureau of cultural activities at the university, and director of the Argentine Film Society. As a composer he was self-taught and an iconoclast and experimenter from the outset. A fellowship took him to Germany. In 1957 he settled in Cologne and he worked in the electronic studio there (pursuing further investigations in the studios of Munich and Utrecht later on). He conducted the Rhineland Chamber Orchestra for a time, lectured at the Darmstadt Festivals, and was Slee Professor at SUNY, Buffalo, New York, in 1964–65. In 1969 he became director of the New Music Institute at the Cologne Conservatory, where he founded the Ensemble for New Music and where he was given the rank of professor in 1974. Kagel is also known as a playwright and filmmaker.

To put it much too simply, Kagel has extended the notion of music beyond those of tonality, atonality, and patterned noise to embrace all aspects of art—and, one is inclined to say, of life. He has explored the electronic, the aleatory, the percussive, language as sound, action music, unorthodox ways of playing instruments, unorthodox instruments, mixed media, and drug-induced composition. He has been influenced by surrealism, absurdism, dadaism, slapstick comedy, and classical movies. In most instances recordings deprive one, for better or worse, of several dimensions of his work.

RECORDINGS: *Transición I* for electronic sound; *Transición II* for piano, percussion, and tape; String Sextet; *Pandorasbox* for magnetic tape (also recorded in a revised version for accordion solo); *Heterophonie* for orchestra; *Improvisation ajoutée* for organ; *Prima Vista; Match* for two cellos and percussion; *Musik für Renaissance Instrumente* for twenty-three instruments; *Exotica* for six players; *Phantasie für Orgel mit Obbligati* (for organ); *Hallelujah* for unaccompanied chorus; *Der Schall* for chamber ensemble; *Ludwig Van*, film score with fragments of Beethoven's **[1063]** works; *Atem* for wind soloist and tape; *Unter Strom* for three players; *Tactil* for three pianos and a stringed instrument; *Unguis incarnatus est; Acustica* for sound generators, speakers, and ensemble; *Anagramma* for four soloists, speaking choir, and ensemble; *Sur Scène*, a theater piece for six participants (some actors and some musicians); *Staatstheater*, another theater piece for "operatic forces."

[2400] LAZAROF, Henri
TEACHER, CONDUCTOR
BORN: Sofia, April 12, 1932

After studying at the Sofia Academy, Lazarof moved from Bulgaria to Israel in 1949 and studied for three years with Paul Ben-Haim **[1939]** at the New Academy in Jerusalem. From 1955 to 1957 he was in Rome working under the guidance of Goffredo Petrassi **[2052]** at the St. Cecilia Academy. Then a fellowship brought him to Brandeis University, where Harold Shapero **[2301]** conducted him to an M.F.A. in 1959. That same year he found employment at UCLA teaching French, but in 1962 he was given a professorship in the music department, where he has remained. His music, largely instrumental, steers a middle course between neo-classicism and serialism, with occasional use of electronics. RECORDINGS: Orchestral recordings include *Tempi concertati* for violin, viola, and chamber orchestra; *Structures Sonores;* Concerto for Cello; *Textures* for piano and five ensembles; *Spec-*

trum for trumpet, orchestra, and tape; Concerto for Flute (with James Galway); and *Volo (3 Canti da Requiem)* for viola and two string ensembles. Chamber, instrumental, and choral recordings include *Concertino da Camera* for wind quintet; *Inventions* for viola and piano; *Rhapsody* for viola and piano; *Espaces* for ten instruments; Octet for Winds; *Cadences II–VI* for various solo instruments and tape; *Continuum* for string trio; *Concertazioni* for trumpet, six instruments, and tape; *Duo 1973* for cello and piano; *Chamber Concerto No. 3* for twelve instruments; *Adieu* for clarinet and piano; and *8 Canti* for chorus.

[2401] COLGRASS, Michael
PERCUSSIONIST, TEACHER
BORN: Chicago, April 22, 1932

Michael Colgrass knew from childhood that he wanted to be a drummer and acted on the impulse by buying a set of drums at the age of ten with money he had earned himself. He taught himself to play and had his own jazz band by the time he reached high school. At eighteen he went to the University of Illinois, where he studied percussion with Paul Price and composition with Eugene Weigel, who was trained by Hindemith [1914]. Colgrass studied in the summer of 1952 with Lukas Foss [2324] at Tanglewood, and in that of 1953 with Darius Milhaud [1868] at Aspen, Colorado. His schooling was interrupted by the nation's insistence that he help protect her shores for two years, which he did as a percussionist in the Seventh Army Symphony (founded by Samuel Adler [2372]) in Germany. He returned to the university in 1956, to complete his B.A., then settled in New York City as a free-lance percussionist. He has played for opera, ballet, and in many musicals, one of the first being Bernstein's [2282] *West Side Story.* Most of his music up to then had been for percussion. At the turn of the decade he had lessons from Wallingford Riegger [1793] and Ben Weber [2251] and had a go at twelve-tone music. A sudden brief (but temporary) attack of amnesia following a concert caused Colgrass not only to put a limit on his playing engagements but also to rethink what he was doing. He decided that he wanted to please audiences rather than peers and from then on wrote highly imaginative music of a decidedly melodic and harmonic cast. In 1968 he married Ulla Rasmussen, with whom he now edits the journal *Music Magazine.* A Rockefeller Fellowship took him to Europe that year, where he studied theater with the Polish Theater Laboratory and Milan's Piccolo Teatro, specializing in pantomime and *commedia dell'arte,* which he has used in some of his theatrical works and which he teaches. His *Déjà vu* for percussion quartet and orchestra won the 1978 Pulitzer Prize. RECORDINGS: *Three Brothers* for percussion; *Variations* for four drums and viola; *As Quiet As . . .* for orchestra; *The Earth's a Baked Apple* for chorus and orchestra, with lyrics by Colgrass; *Concertmasters* for three violins and orchestra; *Fantasy-Variations* for percussion; *Percussion Music; New People,* song cycle for mezzo-soprano, viola, and piano; *Déjà vu* for percussion quartet and orchestra; and *Light Spirit* for flute, viola, percussion, and guitar.

[2402] OLIVEROS, Pauline
TEACHER
BORN: Houston, Tex., May 30, 1932

A black-belt karate expert, Pauline Oliveros has carried the idea of music to what some may consider the brink. She was not always so inclined. She grew up in a rather musically typical American environment, studied piano with her mother (a piano teacher), violin and accordion with other locals, and French horn in high school. She was also student director of her junior high school band. In 1949 she entered the University of Houston, where she took a composition course and wrote some (it would seem) rather ordinary pieces. She left the university in 1952 and moved to San Francisco, where she acquired a B.A. at San Francisco State College, with a major in composition. At the same time she studied privately with Robert Erickson [2261], a pupil of Ernst Krenek [1984] and Roger Sessions [1931]. She began working with an improvisation group and writing music that was, for want of a better term, Webernian [1773]. Meanwhile it was beginning to dawn on her that what she wanted to deal with (and make others hear) was not music but the sound of existence on earth. In 1961 she, Morton Subotnick [2405], and Ramon Sender founded the San Francisco Tape Music Center, and for the next several years she occupied herself with the possible ways of using electronic tape, at times in connection with live improvisation-and-action. When the center was absorbed into Mills College in 1966, she became its director, but a year later she went to San Diego to teach at the University of California and has remained there. About that time she began moving toward music-as-spectacle, which came to involve everything from card tricks to piano moving. This phase in turn led to the most recent one of music-as-ritual, evidenced in what Ms. Oliveros terms "sonic meditations" which, from third-party descriptions, appear to have as a constant something like prolonged and shifting drones, and in which the audience is asked to participate. (One such work appears to have involved a meal shared by performers and "listeners.") According to the composer's own statement, she sees the purpose of her music as being to raise the total consciousness of the participants. Like most such works, hers suffer in being limited to a phonograph record. RECORDINGS: *I of IV* for two-channel tape; *Outline* for flute, contrabass, and percussion; and *Sound Patterns* for voices.

[2403] GOEHR, Peter Alexander
TEACHER
BORN: Berlin, August 10, 1932

Walter Goehr (1903–60), a Schoenberg [1657] pupil and later well known to record collectors as a conductor, fled with his family to England when his son Alexander was a year old. Alexander had lessons from his father and was a friend and contemporary of Birtwistle [2410], Maxwell Davies [2411], and John Ogdon at the Royal Manchester College. After graduation, he spent some time studying with Messiaen [2129] in Paris. He has traveled widely and has taught at Morley College, Yale University, and Cambridge University, where he is presently professor of music. His interest in musical theater and multimedia concepts led to his foundation of the Music Theater Ensemble in 1967. The chief influences on his music have been Schoenberg and Messiaen. RECORDINGS: *Little Symphony;* Concerto for Violin; *Romanza* for cello and orchestra; *Metamorphosis/Dance,* a ballet based on the Circe legend; *2 Choruses; 3 Pieces, Capriccio,* and *Nonomiya* for solo piano; *4 Songs from the Japanese; Piano Trio;* and *String Quartet No. 2.*

[2404] SHCHEDRIN, Rodion Constantinovitch (Sh'chā'-drēn, Rōd'-yôn Kŏnstán-tē-nŏ'-vich)
PIANIST
BORN: Moscow, December 16, 1932

Shchedrin is one of the few Soviet composers born since the Revolution who has made any kind of impact on the Western world. He also, in his flirtation with atonalism and aleatory, might be described as Russia's token modernist. (He has, however, taken care to deplore those, such as Edison Denisov

[2381], who dare more.) His father was a writer on music and encouraged his precocious son, whose musical education, however, was disrupted by the German invasion in 1941. Afterward he studied at the Moscow Choral Academy and then at the Moscow Conservatory, where his most important teachers were Yuri Shaporin [1823] and the pianist Yakov Flier. By the time he had graduated in 1955 he had already won considerable notice with a string quartet, a piano quintet, and the first of his 3 piano concerti. These included a good deal of material based on Russian folk music and, more typically, on street songs. In 1960 he produced his highly successful ballet *The Humpbacked Horse* and followed it a year later with an opera much praised by the Soviet establishment, *Not Love Alone.* A street-song piece of 1963, *Ozorni'ye chashtushki*—variously translated as "Merry Melodies," "Racy Rhymes," or "Lewd Limericks" and also known as Concerto for Orchestra No. 1. —attained something like pops-concert immortality. Shchedrin's marriage to the great ballerina Maya Plisetskaya produced *The Carmen Ballet* (Bizet [1363] arranged for percussion and strings) and the full-length *Anna Karenina.* RECORDINGS: The full-length opera after Gogol, *Dead Souls,* has recently been recorded by Soviet Melodiya, which is likewise the source of the full-length ballets *Anna Karenina* and *The Seagull,* along with the *Carmen Ballet* and suites from *The Humpbacked Horse* and *Not Love Alone.* There is also an orchestral work, *Anna Karenina: Romantic Music,* which is not part of the ballet score. Other recordings include Symphonies Nos. 1 and 2; Concerti for Piano Nos. 1–3; Concerti for Orchestra No. 1 ("Merry Melodies") and No. 2 ("The Bells"), *Symphonic Fanfares* for orchestra; *Poetoria* for voices and ensemble; and *Polyphonic Book* for piano.

[2405] SUBOTNICK, Morton
CLARINETIST, TEACHER, CONDUCTOR
BORN: Los Angeles, April 14, 1933

As a mature composer, Subotnick has worked almost entirely with electronic music and music-as-theater. After piano lessons with his mother, he took up the clarinet. In his teens he taught himself to compose after a fashion and put in a year with Leon Kirchner [2284]. In 1952 he transferred to the University of Denver, where he majored in English and played in the local symphony. These activities were temporarily halted in 1953, when he was called up for army service and stationed for three years in San

Francisco, during which time he kept up lessons with Kirchner, who moved to Mills College in Oakland in 1954. Subotnick completed work for his degree in Denver in 1958 and took an M.Mus. at Mills a year later. He taught there until 1962. During the Mills years he founded, with Pauline Oliveros [2402] and Ramon Sender, the San Francisco Tape Music Center. He was also music director for the Halperin Dance Company, as well as for the Mills College Performing Group (for new music), which he founded.

After a couple of serial compositions, Subotnick turned to the tape medium. But almost from the first his tape works involved live performers, audience participation, and sometimes film. A series of works called *Play!* involved aspect of games and rituals (the fourth is specified for four game players, four musicians, two conductors, two films, and tape.) In 1966 Subotnick moved to New York, where briefly he served as music director of the Repertory Theater in Lincoln Center, music director at the discothèque The Electric Circus, and artist-in-residence at the School of the Arts at New York University. In 1967 Nonesuch Records commissioned from him an all-electronic work called *Silver Apples of the Moon*—the first electronic work composed specifically for a commercial record. This was successful and was followed by several other such works. After teaching as a visitor at the universities of Maryland and Pittsburgh, Subotnick returned to California in the capacity of associate dean at the California Institute of the Arts in Valencia, where at this writing he is chairman of the composition department and director of the electronic studio. For the U.S. Bicentennial he produced, on commission from the National Endowment for the Arts, a large orchestral work, *Before the Butterfly*, premiered by Zubin Mehta and the Los Angeles Philharmonic. It involved electronic modifications of the instrumental sounds, a technique he has used since in his so-called "ghost-pieces" in which the prerecorded tape is not heard but serves to effect changes in the sounds produced by a live source. Subotnick is married to Joan La Barbara (1947–   ), an avant-garde vocalist and composer, and has two children from one of his two earlier marriages.

RECORDINGS: *Silver Apples of the Moon, The Wild Bull, Touch, Sidewinder, Four Butterflies, Until Spring,* and *A Sky of Cloudless Sulphur* (all electronic); *Liquid Strata* for piano and tape; *Prelude No. 4* for piano and tape; *Laminations* for orchestra and tape; *After the Butterfly* for trumpet and chamber orchestra; *Axolotl* for cello and tape; *The Wild Beasts* for trombone, piano, and tape;

The First Dream of Light for tuba and piano; *Ascent into Air* for ten instruments and computer-generated sound; *A Fluttering of Wings* for string quartet and electronic sounds; and *Parallel Lines* for orchestra and electronic sounds. Just released is *The Last Dream of the Beast* for soprano, instruments, and "ghost" electronics.

[2406] BLACKWOOD, Easley
PIANIST, TEACHER
BORN: Indianapolis, April 21, 1933

The son of an authority on the game of bridge, Blackwood was something of a piano prodigy, playing a Mozart [992] concerto in public at nine, and appearing with the local symphony orchestra at fourteen. (He went on to establish a name for himself in the twentieth-century repertoire.) At fifteen he studied at Tanglewood with Olivier Messiaen [2129] and then had lessons with Bernhard Heiden [2161] at Indiana University. On Heiden's recommendation, he transferred to Yale to study with Paul Hindemith [1914], acquiring his baccalaureate degree in 1953 and his master's in 1954. A Fulbright fellowship took him to France in the latter year to study with Nadia Boulanger. He remained there until 1956, completing the first of his 5 symphonies and winning the Lili Boulanger Prize en route. In 1958 Blackwood was hired as an assistant professor by the University of Chicago and has remained there ever since. The following spring Charles Munch premiered the symphony, a big romantic work, with the Boston Symphony. It was several times repeated, taken up by other major orchestras, accorded the Koussevitzky Prize, published, and recorded by RCA. Since then Blackwood has moved toward complexity, dissonance, and, in some degree, toward serialism. His output has been slim—four more symphonies (the last in 1978), five concerti for clarinet, oboe, flute, violin, and piano, respectively, a *Symphonic Fantasy*, and a dozen chamber works, none of them received with the éclat enjoyed by the first symphony. He has also written a multimedia opera, *Four Letters from Gulliver*, in collaboration with Frank Lewin and Elliot Kaplan, produced in 1975 by the Minnesota Opera. RECORDINGS: Works recorded include the Chamber Symphony for 14 Winds, Symphony No. 1, Concerto for Violin, Sonata for Flute and Harpsichord; and Sonata No. 2 for Violin and Piano. There is also an album, privately produced by the composer, of his *12 Microtonal Etudes* for electronic keyboards.

[2407] PENDERECKI, Krzysztof (Pen-de-ret'-skē, K'zhēsh'-tôf)
TEACHER, CONDUCTOR, ADMINISTRA-TOR, VIOLINIST
BORN: Dębica, November 23, 1933

Whatever it may mean, Penderecki has been more successful in appealing to a wide audience than almost any avant-garde composer of his generation. Born in a Polish town to the east of Cracow, he grew up in a nonmusical atmosphere and with only a general interest in the art. At seventeen he went to Cracow to study humanities at the university. For his own amusement he taught himself to play the violin and began to compose traditionally oriented pieces for himself. Dissatisfied with his efforts, he took some lessons with one Skołyszewski, then became a private pupil of the important but obscure modernist composer Artur Malawski (1904–57). Meanwhile he had decided that music was the career for him and entered the Cracow Conservatory. In his final year there, Malawski having died, Penderecki's composition teacher was Stanisław Wiechowicz (1893–1963). He graduated in 1958. The following year Penderecki entered three compositions *(Emanations; The Psalms of David; and Strophes)* in the "youth" category of the annual competition held by the Union of Polish Composers and won all three top awards. Coming as they did at the time of Poland's cultural "thaw," these pieces were already in an advanced and highly personal idiom.

From the time of his graduation until 1966, Penderecki taught at the Cracow Conservatory. He was particularly active during this period, producing a major percentage of the works by which he is best known. Perhaps his most generally successful work to date has been the 1960 *Threnody for the Victims of Hiroshima,* a harrowing piece for fifty-two strings, in which the *glissandi* conjure up such horrors as air-raid sirens, the scream of planes, and howls of agony. (The programmatic title is an afterthought, since the work was originally written as an abstract study in sonority.) For all his modernism—he uses the full range of accepted avant-garde devices and experiments with unorthodox sounds and sound sources—Penderecki is, however, firmly grounded in tradition. With the *St. Luke Passion,* completed in 1965, he expanded his palette to include standard forms and tonal devices. In 1966 the composer went to West Germany, where the work was premiered with overwhelming success in Münster and where he taught at the Essen Conservatory until 1972. In 1968 Hamburg State Opera premiered his

first operatic effort, *The Devils of Loudun,* which generated much excitement, not alone for the "topless" nuns in a scene of diabolic possession. This was followed by another religious work, *Utrenja,* derived from the Slavic liturgy. In 1972 Penderecki was named rector of the Cracow Conservatory, but a year later he was in the United States, where he taught for a time at Yale (and later at Aspen). About this time he began to appear as conductor of his own music and has made a number of recordings in that capacity. He has been showered with awards, prizes, and honorary doctorates, and is an honorary member of the British Royal Academy and of its counterparts in Sweden and both Germanies. With the dark-hued Concerto for Violin of 1976 Penderecki's style moved in a somewhat neo-tonal direction. Among his more recent important commissions was one for an opera from the Chicago Lyric Opera Company. After several delays and cumulative anticipation, *Paradise Lost* (libretto by Christopher Fry after John Milton) was produced on the penultimate evening of November 1978. The most favorable reaction was that it was a brave try. In 1980 Penderecki completed his Symphony No. 2 ("Christmas"), a work which has aroused considerable controversy and consternation because it is written in a shockingly conservative, nineteenth-century style.

For all his ingenuity, Penderecki seems chiefly to rely on shock or surface effect, a direct assault on the emotions through the ear. Whether this represents a new and viable direction or only another desperate way to produce one last quiver in moribund audiences is not yet possible to say.

RECORDINGS: The opera *The Devils of Loudun* has been recorded, along with a large number of choral and/or vocal-orchestral pieces—*The Psalms of David* for chorus and chamber ensemble; *Strophes* for soprano, narrator, and ten instruments; *Dimensions of Time and Silence* for wordless chorus, strings, and percussion; *Stabat Mater* for unaccompanied chorus (later incorporated into the *St. Luke Passion; St. Luke Passion* for narrator, soloists, choruses, and orchestra; *Dies Irae (Auschwitz Oratorio)* for soloists and orchestra; *Miserere; Utrenja (Morning Prayer),* oratorio in two parts for soloists, choruses, and orchestra (the first part, *The Entombment of Christ,* was also recorded separately); *Kosmogonia* for soloists, chorus, and orchestra; *Ecloga VIII* for six male voices unaccompanied; *Canticum Canticorum Salomonis (Song of Songs)* for chorus and chamber orchestra; *Magnificat* for soloists, choruses, and orchestra; *The*

Awakening of Jacob for voices, orchestra, and twelve ocarinas; *Te Deum* for soloists, orchestra, and chorus; and *Lacrimosa,* an excerpt from a newly completed *Polish Requiem* for Solidarity. Orchestral and instrumental recordings include *Emanations* for two string orchestras; *3 Miniatures* for violin and piano; *Anaklasis* for string orchestra and percussion; *Threnody to the Victims of Hiroshima* for fifty-two strings; String Quartet No. 1 (of 2); *Fonogrammi* for three flutes, strings, and percussion; *Polymorphia* for forty-eight strings; *Kanon* for fifty-two strings and tape; *Fluorescences* for orchestra; Sonata for Cello and Orchestra; *De Natura Sonoris Nos. 1 and 2* for orchestra; *Capriccio No. 2* for violin and orchestra; *Pittsburgh Overture* for wind band; *Capriccio per Siegfried Palm* for solo cello; *Actions* for jazz ensemble; Symphonies Nos. 1 and 2; *Partita* for harpsichord, amplified instruments, and orchestra; Concerto for Cello; and the Concerto for Violin—not to be confused with an earlier (unrecorded) Concerto for Violino Grande (a five-string violin).

[2408] DAVIDOVSKY, Mario
TEACHER
BORN: Buenos Aires, March 4, 1934

The son of a devout Jewish family, Davidovsky began studying violin at the age of seven, had training in composition, and worked toward a law degree. However, he soon decided to be a musician. He wrote a number of abstract instrumental and orchestral works, some of which won prizes, and founded the Argentine Society of Young Composers. He came to Tanglewood in 1958 to hear his *Noneto* played. In 1960 he received the first of his two Guggenheim and two Rockefeller fellowships and returned to study at the Columbia-Princeton Electronic Music Center—and, it turned out, to stay. He married Ellen Blaustein the following year and began turning out the series of electronic compositions for which he is best known. These include the 3 *Electronic Studies,* 1961–65, and the series of *Synchronisms* (8 so far) for various instruments or instrumental groups and tape. After various guest shots at teaching, he became professor of music at CUNY in 1969. He is also associate director of the Columbia-Princeton Center. *Synchronism No. 6* won the 1971 Pulitzer Prize. Since then he has returned to writing for instruments and has also composed what he terms a cantata-opera, *Scenes from Shir Ha-Shirim,* 1976. His *Divertimento* for cello and orchestra, premiered by the American Composers' Orchestra in November 1984, although by no means tonal, is a distinctly virtuosic showpiece, with a darker atmosphere than its title would lead one to expect. RECORDINGS: *Electronic Studies Nos. 1–3; Synchronisms Nos. 1–3, 5, 6, 8; Inflexions* for fourteen instruments; *Chacona* for piano trio; *Junctures* for flute, clarinet, and violin; and *Pennplay* for sixteen instruments.

[2409] REYNOLDS, Roger
ENGINEER, TEACHER
BORN: Detroit, July 13, 1934

Reynolds began as an engineer, taking a baccalaureate at Michigan in 1957. He then returned to study music for three years with Ross Lee Finney [2099] and Roberto Gerhard [1926], with the latter of whom he also worked at Tanglewood. In succession he won a Fulbright, which took him to the Cologne Electronic Music Studio; a Guggenheim, which took him to France and Italy; and an Institute of Current World Affairs fellowship, which took him to Japan for three years, 1966–69. On his return he accepted a professorship in music and cultural studies at the University of California at San Diego. He helped to found and run contemporary music festivals at Ann Arbor (The ONCE Festival) and in Japan. He has known and been influenced by Varèse [1774] and Cage [2192] and has also been influenced by Charles Ives [1659] and Buckminster Fuller. Reynolds has written a number of works involving electronics and mixed media and has recently been involved in the development of advanced computer-music systems, as exemplified in his recent *Fiery Winds II* for orchestra and computer-realized sounds. RECORDINGS: *The Emperor of Ice Cream* for eight voices, piano, percussion, and contrabass; *Fantasy for Pianist; Ambages* for Flute; *Quick Are the Mouths of Earth* for chamber orchestra; *Blind Men* for twenty-four voices, brasses, and percussion; *Ping* for flute, piano, harmonium, cymbal, tamtam, slides, and tape; *Traces* for piano, flute, cello, and six tapes; *From Behind the Unreasoning Mask* for trombone, percussion, and tape; *Voicespace I–IV,* performed by the Extended Vocal Techniques Ensemble; and . . . *the Serpent-Snapping Eye* for trumpet, percussion, and piano, with computer-synthesized sound.

[2410] BIRTWISTLE, Harrison
CLARINETIST, TEACHER
BORN: Accrington, Lancashire, July 15, 1934

Birtwistle studied at the Royal Manchester College of Music, and was a contemporary there of Alexander Goehr [2403], Peter Maxwell Davies [2411], and pianist John Ogdon, with whom he performed contemporary music. Later he studied with the great clarinetist Reginald Kell at the Royal Academy of Music in London. For a time he worked as a performer and taught at a Dorsetshire school from 1962 to 1965. In 1967 he and Maxwell Davies founded the Pierrot Players in London. When Davies took them over three years later as the Fires of London, Birtwistle and fellow clarinetist Alan Hacker founded their own group, called Matrix. Birtwistle has also taught at Princeton, Swarthmore, and SUNY Buffalo, and in 1975 became music director of the National Theater in London. His surname should not evoke pastoral reveries: the terms generally used to describe his music are "harsh," "violent," "strident," and "astringent." His chief influences have been Varèse [1774], Webern [1773], Stravinsky [1748], and medieval polyphony. His chamber opera *Punch and Judy* created a sensation, not wholly favorable, at Aldeburgh in 1968. (He has since written another, *Orpheus.)* Several of his works are interrelated. RECORDINGS: Works on records include the opera *Punch and Judy; Chronometer* and *The Triumph of Time* for orchestra; *Refrains and Choruses* for wind quintet; *Tragoedia* for winds, strings, and harp; *Verses for Ensembles* for winds, brass, and percussion; *Précis* for piano; (vocal) *Ring a Dumb Carillon, Nenia— The Death of Orpheus, The Fields of Sorrow,* and . . . *agm* . . . for sixteen voices and three instrumental groups (with fragmentary texts from Sappho).

[2411] DAVIES, Peter Maxwell
TEACHER, CONDUCTOR
BORN: Manchester, September 8, 1934

Davies, one of the more successful and influential British moderns, is a graduate of the University of Manchester and the Royal Manchester School of Music. Here he developed an interest in early polyphony, though his instincts were basically Schoenbergian [1657]. In 1957 he won an Italian government fellowship that permitted him to study in Rome with Goffredo Petrassi [2052], where his Webernian [1773] *Prolation* for orchestra won the Olivetti Prize in 1959. From that year until 1962 he taught, with great success, at the Cirencester Grammar School. Then, on a Harkness fellowship (granted on Aaron Copland's [1986] enthusiastic recommendation), he studied at Princeton with

Roger Sessions [1931] until 1964. In 1966–67 he spent a year as composer-in-residence at the University of Adelaide in Australia, and, on his return, he, together with his Manchester schoolmate Harrison Birtwistle [2410], founded a virtuoso chamber group called the Pierrot Players to perform contemporary music. (The name and makeup are taken from Schoenberg's *Pierrot Lunaire.)* In 1970 Birtwistle dropped out and Davies renamed the group The Fires of London (for which he has written numerous works). That same year he established his home in the Orkney Islands—not a bad place to be these days if you can stand the weather. He has not, however, turned hermit and has been featured at recent music festivals at Aspen, New York City, Dartington, and Montepulciano. Davies has not adhered to strict serialism, but has developed his own style, which often involves parody and deliberate uglification. He is rumored to be at work on a piece for violin and orchestra, being written for Isaac Stern, who plans to record it. RECORDINGS: Works on disc include the Sonata for Trumpet and Piano; *St. Michael Sonata* for seventeen winds; *O Magnum Mysterium* for choir, instrumental ensemble, and organ; *Second Fantasia on an In Nomine of John Taverner* for orchestra; *Revelation and Fall* for soprano and chamber ensemble; *Antechrist* for chamber ensemble; *Hymnos* for clarinet and piano; *L'Homme arme* for chamber ensemble and speaker; *Points and Dances from "Taverner"* for orchestra; *St. Thomas Wake* for orchestra; *8 Songs for a Mad King* for male voice and ensemble (perhaps his most macabre piece on records) *Vesalii Icones* for cello, winds, and piano; *From Stone to Thorn* for soprano and chamber ensemble; *Tenebrae super Gesualdo* for soprano, guitar, and chamber ensemble; *Ave Maris Stella* for chamber ensemble; *Image, Reflections, Shadow* for ensemble; *Dark Angels* for soprano and guitar; *The Bairns of Brugh; Runes from a Holy Island;* Symphony No. 1 (of 3 so far); the ballet *Salome; Hill Runes* for guitar; Sonata for Piano; and an album of *Renaissance and Baroque Realizations* for ensemble.

[2412] MATHIAS, William James
TEACHER
BORN: Whitland, Wales, November 1, 1934

Like his compatriot and contemporary Alun Hoddinott [2384], William Mathias has won an international reputation accorded to few Welsh composers. A pupil of Ian Parrott

[2245] at University College of Music in Aberystwyth, he graduated in 1956 and spent the ensuing year in London studying on scholarship with Lennox Berkeley [2036] at the Royal Academy of Music, of which institution he was elected a fellow a decade later. Since 1959 he has taught at the University College of North Wales in Bangor, save for a year at the University of Edinburgh, 1968–69, and is now a professor of music there. His considerable output—rapidly approaching one hundred opus numbers—carefully pursues a middle-of-the-road path, influenced by Welsh music, Hindemith [1914], Stravinsky [1748], Bartók [1734], and more recently Tippett [2059]. RECORDINGS: Orchestral works on records include the *Dance Overture; Invocation and Dance;* Symphony No. 1; *Sinfonietta;* Concerto No. 3 for Piano; Concerto for Harp; *Celtic Dances; Laudi; Vistas;* and *Vivat Regina* (the latter for band). Vocal recordings include *Lux Aeterna* for chorus, soloists, and orchestra; *Ave Rex* and *Elegy for a Prince* for chorus; and other choral works. There are also recordings of organ and piano pieces.

[2413] RILEY, Terry
PIANIST, SAXOPHONIST, TEACHER
BORN: Colfax, Calif., June 24, 1935

Riley has been categorized as a "minimalist" composer, a term applied to those who rejected the complexities of the serialists and the chaos of the aleatorists for sometimes stultifyingly simple music. He was born in the Sierra foothills near Sacramento, studied at the University of California in Berkeley with Robert Erickson [2261], Seymour Shifrin [2358], and William Denny, played piano in San Francisco's Tenderloin, and received his M.A. in 1961. Under the spell of his fellow student La Monte Young (1935–), later the leading proponent of "conceptualism" (which might be summed up as "music is whatever you think it is"), Riley then moved to New York. In 1962 he proceeded to Europe to work at the electronic studios of the ORTF where, like Steve Reich [2419], he became fascinated by the accoustical phenomena (and psychic states) produced by very gradually overlapping sonic repetitions. In the way of the burgeoning "counterculture," he led the life of a wandering minstrel, playing in a Place Pigalle bar, touring France with a nightclub act, and doing street theater in Stockholm. Having devised several tapes, in 1964 he composed his *In C,* in which any number of musicians, picking and choosing among short musical phrases in the key of C, produce effects similar to those described above. The cumulative tedium produced by such music, and Riley's preference for improvisation to written music, inevitably led him to the music of India. In 1970 he and Young went off to India to study with Pandit Pran Nath, an Indian singer they had met. In 1972 Riley joined the Mills College faculty. He reputedly occupied much of his time in the 1970s studying Indian music. Up to 1971 Riley had composed about ten works. Then there was a long hiatus of about ten years' duration. He has resurfaced recently with several new record albums, has begun to concertize again, and has written music for the Kronos String Quartet. RECORDINGS: His early recordings include *In C; A Rainbow in Curved Air; Dorian Reeds* for soprano saxophone and electronics; *Persian Surgery Dervishes* for electric organ and electronics; and *Poppy Nogood and the Phantom Band.* Recent recordings include *Shri Camel* for electric organ and *The Descending Moonshine Dervishes,* also for solo organ.

[2414] SCHICKELE, Peter
BASSOONIST, TEACHER, WRITER, MUSIKER
BORN: Ames, Iowa, July 17, 1935

Best known for his outrageous alter ego, P. D. Q. Bach (1807–1742?), Sebastian's ne'er-do-well mythical cadet son, Schickele is actually a serious musician and has the credentials to prove it. In his youth he was bassoonist in the Fargo-Moorhead Symphony, which helps civilize the North Dakota-Minnesota border (a locale almost certainly responsible for the "University of Southern North Dakota at Hoople," site of the P. D. Q. Bach researches of one "Professor Schickele.") He then acquired a B.A. in music at Swarthmore and worked toward his M.S. in 1960 with Bergsma [2313], and Persichetti [2236] at the Juilliard School. He also had some lessons with Roy Harris [1947]. He has taught at Juilliard, Swarthmore, and Aspen, and has received his share of grants and commissions. In his Juilliard years he founded the Composers' Circle. P. D. Q. Bach was invented in 1965— a thoroughly inept, not to say drunken, Baroque composer who allegedly wrote for bargain-counter tenors and off-coloraturas, and for such instruments as the left-handed sewer flute and the windbreaker. The humor is hardly subtle but usually irresistible, and as a result P.D.Q. has monopolized much of Schickele's time. He appears in P.D.Q. concerts and on records in both instrumental and vocal capacities (he has a dreadful bass voice), and has written *The Definitive Biography of P. D. Q. Bach,* 1976. In 1967 he helped form the collaborative compositional group The Open Window with Robert Dennis (1933–) and Stanley Walden (1923–). Schickele has written a small amount of abstract music under his own name, some of which explores the realm of the far-out, and some of which reflects the apparently unconquerable comedic impulse. He has also produced a good deal of *Gebrauchsmusik* for the stage and the electronic media, including songs for the nude revue *Oh Calcutta.* RECORDINGS: *Fantastic Garden* for orchestra; *The Lowest Trees Have Tops* (cantata); *Diversions* for oboe, clarinet, and bassoon; *Elegies* for clarinet and piano; *Summer Trio* for flute, cello, and piano; *Pentangle* for French horn and orchestra; *Songs from "The Knight of the Burning Pestle"* for soloists and ensemble; *Windows* for clarinet and guitar; and numerous P. D. Q. Bach LPs, the most recent containing *Blaues Gras* and the *No-No Nonette.*

[2415] FIŠER, Luboš (Fēsh'-er, Lōō'-bōsh)
BORN: Prague, September 20, 1935

Fišer was a student at the Prague Conservatory and Academy of Pavel Bořkovec [1894] and of Emil Hlobil (1901–), who had himself been taught by Suk [1651] and Krička [1752]. He completed his work there in 1960. By then he had already written 2 symphonies, a string quartet, and sonatas for piano and violin. He has since been a very successful composer of film scores and stage works (notably the comic opera *The Good Soldier Schweik,* not to be confused with similar works by Robert Kurka [2319] and others.) In 1971–72 he was composer-in-residence with the American Wind Symphony in Pittsburgh. RECORDINGS: Works recorded include *15 Prints from Dürer's Apocalypse* for orchestra, winner of a UNESCO prize in 1966; Requiem for chorus and orchestra, 1968; and Concerto for Piano.

[2416] MAW, John Nicholas
BORN: Grantham, November 5, 1935

Described as a neo-Bergian [1789], and determinedly aloof from the music-as-antics fad of his times, Maw remains little known outside of England. He was born and grew up in a Lincolnshire market town, came to London at twenty, and studied composition with Lennox Berkeley [2036] at the Royal Academy of Music. He spent a year in Paris, 1958–59, studying on scholarship with Nadia

Boulanger and made his first real impact with *Scenes and Arias,* introduced at the London Proms in 1962. His second opera, *The Rising of the Moon,* was at least a *succès d'estime* at Glyndebourne in 1970. Since then he has produced mostly chamber-scale works for voices and/or instruments, some of which show the influence of Britten [2215]. He has taught on occasion at Cambridge and at the University of Exeter. RECORDINGS: Works on records include *Scenes and Arias* for voices and orchestra, *Sinfonia,* Sonata for Strings and 2 Horns, *Life Studies* for fifteen strings, *La Vita nuova* for soprano and chamber ensemble, and the song cycle *The Voice of Love* for voice and piano.

[2417] BENNETT, Richard Rodney
PIANIST, TEACHER
BORN: Broadstairs, Kent, March 29, 1936

Despite the similarity of names, Richard Rodney Bennett is unrelated to the American Robert Russell Bennett [1895]. Born in a beach resort near Canterbury, he had his first music lessons from his mother, a sometime pupil of Gustav Holst [1658]. After advanced training from Howard Ferguson [2126] and Lennox Berkeley [2036] at the Royal Academy of Music, from which he graduated in 1956, he studied in Paris on scholarship with Pierre Boulez [2346] until 1959. Rather than pursuing the path suggested by that redoubtable composer, Bennett turned for a time to writing quasi-popular music. He wrote effective scores for the films *Far from the Madding Crowd, Nicholas and Alexandra,* and *Murder on the Orient Express,* and jazz-based pieces like *Jazz Calendar* for twelve instruments and *Soliloquy* for voices and ensemble. He also wrote several operas, including *The Mines of Sulphur,* produced with some success at Sadler's Wells in 1965, and a treatment of Conrad's *Victory,* produced with little success in 1970 at Covent Garden. At the same time he produced a number of works (among them 2 symphonies in 1966 and 1968) in a fairly conservative dodecaphonic idiom. More recently he has experimented with instrumental works that imply some sort of unstated drama, but he remains an eclectic more admired by the general public than by the tastemakers. RECORDINGS: Orchestral works on disc include the *Aubade,* Symphony No. 1, and Concerto for Guitar. Vocal recordings include *Spells* for soprano, chorus, and orchestra; *The House of Sleep* for six male voices; the children's opera *All the King's Men;* and some songs. Chamber and instrumental recordings include *Calendar* for ensemble; *Jazz Calendar* for ensemble; Trio for Flute, Oboe, and Piano; *Commedia IV* for brass quintet, and some piano pieces. Film scores on records include *Far From the Madding Crowd; Murder on the Orient Express; Equus; Yanks; Billion Dollar Brain;* and *Lady Caroline Lamb.* (Bennett can also be heard as pianist in a transcription of Holst's [1658] *The Planets.)*

[2418] AMY, Gilbert (À-mē', Zhēl-bâr')
CONDUCTOR
BORN: Paris, August 29, 1936

A piano student from an early age and trained in the arts and humanities, Amy graduated from the Paris Conservatoire in 1960, having studied there with Milhaud [1868] and Messiaen [2129]. During the same period he came under the influence of Pierre Boulez [2346], particularly at Darmstadt. His earliest compositions already showed an affinity with Webern [1773], and Boulez had a powerful impact on his development. In 1962 Amy was appointed to an assistant conductorship at the Odéon. Quickly becoming known in that capacity, he succeeded Boulez at the Domaine Musical concerts in 1967, remaining their chief conductor until they were terminated six years later. His knowledge of the orchestra is also reflected in his music, in which he has increasingly experimented with new and modified sound colors. He has composed, besides concert material, music for several plays and films. In recent years Amy has moved away, slightly, from the severities of Boulez toward the sonorous mysticism of Messiaen. RECORDINGS: *Inventions* for flute, piano, harp, and percussion; *Diaphonies* for two identical chamber orchestras; *Strophe* for soprano and orchestra; *Sonata pian' e forte* for soprano, mezzo-soprano, and twelve instruments; *Trajectoires* for violin and orchestra; *Relais* for two trumpets, two trombones, and horn.

[2419] REICH, Steve (*né* Stephen Michael)
PERCUSSIONIST, TEACHER
BORN: New York, October 3, 1936

Steve Reich is generally regarded as one of the leading "minimalist" composers—a term of not very specific application. His mother was the former June Carroll, a lyricist who collaborated on some of the songs for the revue *New Faces of 1952.* Reich began as a piano student but quit because of stage fright. In high school he took up drums and played in jazz groups and dance bands. He attended Cornell University, where he took some music courses, graduating *cum laude* with a major in philosophy and a scholarship to the Harvard graduate school in 1957. However, he gave it up to study composition with Hall Overton (1920–72) in New York, where he subsequently attended Juilliard. His chief teachers there were Vincent Persichetti [2236] and William Bergsma [2313]. He also continued to play and listen to progressive jazz. In 1961 he moved on to Mills College in California, where he served as a teaching assistant and studied with Darius Milhaud [1868] and Luciano Berio [2352], though Berio and he did not see eye to eye. Receiving his M.A. in 1963, he remained in the Bay Area, writing for a mime company, driving a cab, and working with his own improvisation group. This last he soon gave up for tape music, working at the San Francisco Tape Music Center. Here he created his first two notable works, *It's Gonna Rain* and *Come Out.* The first is based on a tape of a three-word phrase from a hellfire sermon, the second on "come out to show them," part of a black youth's testimony in a police-brutality trial. By using tape loops and doubling the voices from two to eight times, and by letting the doublings move from a unison gradually out of synchronization with each other and back to unison, he produced a curiously hypnotic and percussive pair of compositions.

Returning to New York in 1966, he organized a performance group, Steve Reich and Musicians—at least until recently, a Reich composition required Reich among the performers—and transferred this concept to "live" music. Here he became increasingly concerned with the manipulation of rhythms by "phrase shifting"; in *Four Organs,* for example, the musical material is a single chord, the widening or decreasing durations of the individual tones creating such musical movement as there is. Such experiments came to involve more performers and to become more complex. He gave this up in the mid-1970s to write for symphony orchestra such works as *Music for a Large Ensemble,* where, using a sequence of eleven chords, he explores melody, harmony, rhythm, and color "in depth." (One has the sense that in Reich's history one is seeing the birth of music recapitulated.) He owes something to his acquaintance with medieval music and Bach and to his studies of Balinese, African, and Jewish liturgical music. His music has become quite popular, especially with younger listeners. Recent works include the Jewish-inspired *Tehillim* for vocalists and ensemble (it was also arranged for orchestra and performed, less successfully, by the New York Philharmonic) and the large-scale theatrical piece *The Desert Music,* after a poem by William Carlos Williams.

RECORDINGS: The two early tape pieces, *It's Gonna Rain* and *Come Out,* are on records, along with *Violin Phase* for violin and tape; *4 Organs* for four organs and maracas; *Drumming* for tuned percussion, piccolo, voices; *6 Pianos; Music for Mallet Instruments, Voices, and Organ; Music for Pieces of Wood* (performed by Hungarian musicians, evidence that Reich's music is making an impact in Eastern Europe); *Music for 18 Musicians; Music for a Large Ensemble* (for twenty-nine musicians or so); *Octet* for winds and strings; *Eight Lines,* an orchestral version of *Octet; Tehillim* for chorus and ensemble; and *Vermont Counterpoint* for flutes (overdubbed).

[2420] GLASS, Philip
FLUTIST, ORGANIST
BORN: Baltimore, January 31, 1937

With Steve Reich [2419], Glass is one of the leading (and eminently successful) proponents of musical "minimalism." His path to that position was, however, more tortuous than Reich's. He began as a juvenile violin student but switched to flute, which he studied at the Peabody Conservatory from 1945 to 1952. He took a B.A. from the University of Chicago at nineteen, then spent four more years at the Juilliard School under the eyes of Vincent Persichetti [2236] and William Bergsma [2313]—and with Milhaud [1868] at Aspen in the summer of 1960. He was in Pittsburgh from 1962 to 1964 as composer-in-residence for the public school system. During these and the Juilliard years, he wrote prolifically, winning citations and publication. The year 1964, which brought him a $10,000 award from the Ford Foundation and a Fulbright fellowship, marked the apex and the turning point of this stage of his career. Although he dutifully went to Paris for study with Nadia Boulanger, his heart was not in it. Travels in Asia and Africa made him conscious of other kinds of music than what he had been trained in. Working for sitarist Ravi Shankar in Paris in 1965 turned the trick. He returned to New York and studied Indian music with Alla Rakha in 1967 and thenceforth based his compositions on quasi-Indian rhythmic and melodic principles. Later he added the simplest of harmonies and modulations. He founded his own performance group—three wind players (saxophones doubling flutes),

three performers on electronic organs, and a sound engineer. He soon began to win a following, particularly among devotees of rock music and "New Age" fusion.

In 1976, with his "opera" *Einstein on the Beach,* a gigantic multimedia work written with avant-garde theater man Robert Wilson, Glass moved from being a cult figure to worldwide celebrity (or notoriety, at least). Although Einstein (or several of him) appears in the work, it is without a story or vocal soloists and presents a series of disjunct and often surrealistic pictures. The piece was premiered at the Avignon Festival, played in several European cities, and was scheduled for a one-shot performance at the Metropolitan Opera (not *by* the company, however) in November. Demand was so great that a second performance had to be arranged. Glass recorded the work on the Tomato record label. He gave a wildly successful concert of his own music at Carnegie Hall in 1978 and two more at a Greenwich, Village night spot called the Bottom Line a year later. In 1980 his second opera (a real one but in Sanskrit), called *Satyagraha* and ostensibly about Gandhi, was premiered in Amsterdam. In 1984 his third opera, *Akhnaten,* was premiered in Stuttgart.

RECORDINGS: Early in his career Glass issued his works on his own Chatham Square label. Among works recorded thereby were *Music in Similar Motion* for three electric organs, two soprano saxophones, and flute; *Music in Fifths* for organ and two soprano saxophones, and *Music with Changing Parts.* Later recordings include *Glassworks; North Star, Facades* for flutes and strings; *Modern Love Waltz* for ensemble; *The Photographer* for violin, chorus, and ensemble; the film soundtrack to *Koyaanisquatsi; Strung Out* for solo violin; *Dressed Like an Egg* (preliminary sketches for his first opera) for two vocalists and organ; and the opera *Einstein on the Beach.* The second opera, *Satyagraha,* and *Danceworks* are his most recent recordings.

[2421] DEL TREDICI, David (Del Tred'-i-chē, Dā'-vid)
PIANIST, TEACHER
BORN: Cloverdale, Calif., March 16, 1937

David Del Tredici came from California wine country in Sonoma County, where he taught himself to play the piano. Later he studied with Bernard Abramowitsch in San Francisco and became a formidable technician and local celebrity. In 1955 he entered the University of California at Berkeley, where he studied with Andrew Imbrie

[2314], Arnold Elson, and Seymour Shifrin [2358], and caught up on his sleep in a freshman English class taught by this writer (with whom he shares a birthday). Under the urging of Darius Milhaud [1868] during a summer at Aspen, he began composing in a fashionably complex and dissonant style. In 1959 he won a Woodrow Wilson Fellowship, on which he spent two years at Princeton studying with Sessions [1931] and Earl Kim [2296]. After a time studying piano in New York with Robert Helps [2379], he returned to take an M.F.A. in 1964. He spent the next two summers at Tanglewood, and the two that followed as composer-in-residence at the Marboro Festival, winning a Guggenheim Fellowship in 1966. In 1967 he joined the Harvard faculty but left in 1971. At about the same time he began to have second thoughts about where his creative direction was taking him and began to draw elements of popular, folk, and old-fashioned diatonic music into his own. This coincided with the beginning of a musical love affair with the *Alice* books of Lewis Carroll that resulted in a whole series of compositions based on those works. The culmination came in 1976 with the imprecisely named *Final Alice*, premiered by Sir Georg Solti with the Chicago Symphony and soprano Barbara Hendricks; it was quickly taken up by other major orchestras and greeted with standing ovations by audiences and with a mixture of hosannas and withering contempt by the critics. One of its sequels, *In Memory of a Summer Day*, was awarded the 1980 Pulitzer Prize, and *its* successor was nationally televised that same year from the inaugural of the Louise M. Davies Symphony Hall in San Francisco. Del Tredici has taught part-time at Boston University since 1973. RECORDINGS: *Fantasy Pieces* for piano, *Scherzo* for piano duet, *I Hear an Army, Night Conjure Verse, Syzygy* (the last three for soprano and instruments), *Final Alice, In Memory of a Summer Day*, and *Acrostic Song* for guitar.

[2422] CROSSE, Gordon
TEACHER
BORN: Bury, Lancashire, December 1, 1937

Apparently more interested in establishing contact with audiences than demonstrating his mastery of the required mysteries, Gordon Crosse studied with Egon Wellesz [1799] at Oxford and later with Goffredo Petrassi [2052] at the Santa Cecilia Academy in Rome. He has since taught at the universities of Birmingham and Essex. Though he often uses serial techniques, he has been strongly influenced by the likes of Britten [2215] and Maxwell Davies [2411] and has been admired chiefly for his operas (including several for children) and other stage pieces. RECORDINGS: His opera monologue after Yeats, *Purgatory*, has been recorded, as have *Changes* for voices and orchestra, *Concerto da Camera* for violin and ensemble, and *Some Marches on a Ground* for orchestra.

[2423] CORIGLIANO, John, Jr.
PIANIST, TEACHER, RADIO AND TELEVISION DIRECTOR AND PRODUCER
BORN: New York, February 16, 1938

Composer John Corigliano's father (1901–75) was concertmaster of the New York Philharmonic under Artur Rodzinski, Dmitri Mitropoulos, and Leonard Bernstein [2282]; his mother was a talented pianist. He studied piano as a child and began composing early. In 1959 he took a B.A. from Columbia University, where his most influential teacher was Otto Luening [1980]. He also studied with Vittorio Giannini [2042] at the Manhattan School of Music and with Paul Creston [2095]. In the chamber music competition at the Spoleto Festival in Italy in 1964, his Sonata for Violin and Piano was the unanimous selection for the top award. In the interim he had worked as programme annotator for New York "good music station" WXQR and as station WBAI's music director. From 1961 to 1972 he was associate producer with CBS for the New York Philharmonic's televised Young People's Concerts. Since that time he has taught at the Manhattan School and at Lehman College of CUNY. Though his music is unquestionably "modern," Corigliano would seem to be one of those of the younger generation who are turning away from the systems (or nonsystems) so eagerly advocated by their elders. (One should perhaps note in this context his much-praised 1980 film score for *Altered States*, nominated for an Academy Award, and his pop arrangement of Bizet's [1363] operatic masterpiece in 1970 as *The Naked Carmen*.) Corigliano was recently commissioned to write an opera for New York's Metropolitan Opera. RECORDINGS: Concerto for Piano; *Poem in October* for tenor and orchestra; Sonata for Violin and Piano (with Corigliano, Sr., as soloist); *Tournaments Overture; Elegy* for orchestra; Concerto for Clarinet; and Concerto for Oboe.

[2424] SOLLBERGER, Harvey Dene
FLUTIST, TEACHER
BORN: Cedar Rapids, Iowa, May 11, 1938

Sollberger graduated in 1960 from the University of Iowa, where he studied with Yale-trained Philip Bezanson (1916–75) and Iowa-trained Eldon Obrecht. He then did graduate work at Columbia with Jack Beeson [2316] and Otto Luening [1980], attaining his M.A. in 1964. He also studied flute with Samuel Baron and Betty Mather, is regarded as a superb performer, especially of contemporary music, of which he has made a number of recordings. While still graduate students, he and Charles Wuorinen [2426] organized the Group for Contemporary Music, of which Sollberger has been codirector. His wife Sophie is also a distinguished flutist. He taught at Columbia University from 1964 to 1971 and has since been on the faculty of the Manhattan School of Music. He has also served as visiting professor at CUNY Stony Brook, and holds summer workshops for flutists at the Flute Farm. He has won many awards and grants. He has been influenced by Milton Babbitt [2247] and Stefan Wolpe [2020] among others. Save for his incidental music to Sophocles' *Antigone* for narrator, chorus, and tape, Sollberger has so far stuck to chamber-size compositions. RECORDINGS: *Chamber Variations* for twelve players; *Divertimento* for flute, cello, and piano; *Riding the Wind I* for flute and five instruments; *Solos for Violin and 5 Instruments; Grand Quartet* for flutes; *Impromptu* for piano; *Sunflowers* for flute and vibraphone; and *Angel and Stone* for flute and piano.

[2425] BOLCOM, William Elden
PIANIST, TEACHER
BORN: Seattle, May 26, 1938

William Bolcom is perhaps still better known as a ragtime pianist and an authority on American popular music than as a composer. His mother, a schoolteacher, is said to have played classical records incessantly while she was carrying him to persuade him to become a great musician. It seems to have worked: prodigiously gifted, he was playing and composing at a disgustingly early age, and at eleven was admitted as a special student to the University of Washington, where he studied piano with Berthe Ponsonby Jacobson, theory and composition with George McKay (1899–1970) and John Verrall [2119]. Later, as a regular student, he took a poetry course with Theodore Roethke and graduated in 1958. He studied with Milhaud

[1868] at Aspen and at Mills College and in 1959 followed him to the Paris Conservatoire, where he also was a pupil of Rivier [1923] and Messiaen [2129]. He spent a summer at Darmstadt but was not fatally contaminated. He came back to the United States in 1961, having thrived on several fellowships in his years abroad, to pick up his master's degree from Mills (already granted), and to take Stanford University's first doctorate in composition (under the supervision of Leland Smith [1925–   ], a Milhaud pupil) in 1964. He then spent another year in Paris on a Guggenheim fellowship, and returned to teach successively at the University of Washington, Queens College, Yale, and New York University. From around 1967 he became interested in ragtime, wrote piano rags of his own, and increasingly composed as he saw fit (which has often involved popular elements). In 1973 he settled down to teach at the University of Michigan. Two years later, after two unsuccessful marriages, he wedded the remarkable singer Joan Morris, with whom he has frequently appeared on the stage and on television in recitals of old American popular music. He has made many recordings with her and several of ragtime solos. RECORDINGS: *12 Etudes* for piano; *Black Host* for organ and percussion; *Frescoes* for two keyboard players; *Commedia for (Almost) Eighteenth-Century Orchestra; Open House* for tenor and orchestra; Piano Quartet; *Whisper Moon* for chamber ensemble; Concerto for Piano; Sonata No. 2 for Violin and Piano; *Duo Fantasy* and *Graceful Ghost,* both for violin and piano; and a number of piano rags (some of them collaborations with William Albright [2433].)

[2426] WUORINEN, Charles (Wô'-ri-nen, Chärlz)
TEACHER, PIANIST, SINGER
BORN: New York, June 9, 1938

For a while it appeared that Charles Wuorinen's whole meteoric career would unfold in the bosom of Columbia University. The son of a professor of history there, he studied piano, began composing at the age of five, had private lessons with his father's colleagues Jack Beeson [2316] and Vladimir Ussachevsky [2180], and won the New York Philharmonic Young Composers' Prize before he was out of high school. Still composing furiously, he went through a liberal arts curriculum at Columbia, studying composition with Otto Luening [1980], and working as a piano accompanist, choral singer, and recording engineer in his spare time. In 1960 he won an Alice M. Ditson fellowship and an Arthur Rose fellowship in 1961, in which year he graduated with a Phi Beta Kappa key. He proceeded with graduate work on a teaching fellowship. In 1962 he and Harvey Sollberger [2424] organized (with Wuorinen as pianist) the Group for Contemporary Music, designed to play new music and financed by the university. Wuorinen got his master's degree in 1963 and became a member of the music department. His music, already atonal, began to exhibit Babbitry [2247] and to pursue more or less strict serialism. He also began to experiment with electronics. In the midst of a continued shower of awards, fellowships, and commissions, he used a synthesizer to compose *Time's Encomium* for Nonesuch Records. It won the 1970 Pulitzer Prize. A year later, for whatever reason, Wuorinen was denied tenure by the university, which also discontinued support of his performing group. Since then he has been on the staff of the Manhattan School of Music. His music in recent years has mellowed and has even shown flashes of humor. It includes his only opera, *The W. of Babylon*, a quasi-pornographic parody with, the composer stoutly maintains, redeeming social values. There is also *A Reliquary for Igor Stravinsky*, built on themes from unfinished works turned over to him by Stravinsky's widow, and a sacred oratorio, *The Celestial Sphere*. RECORDINGS: Many of Wuorinen's recordings involve members of the Group for Contemporary Music. Orchestral works on disc include the early Symphony No. 3, Concerto No. 1 for Piano, Concerto for Amplified Violin, *Grand Bamboula* for strings, and the *Two-Part Symphony*. The electronic *Time's Encomium* was recorded by the label (Nonesuch) that commissioned it. Recorded chamber or chamber-orchestra pieces include the Chamber Concerto for Flute and 10 Players; Chamber Concerto for Cello and 10 Instruments; Chamber Concerto for Tuba, Winds, and Percussion; *Speculum Speculi* for ensemble; *Arabia Felix* for flute, bassoon, guitar, violin, vibraphone, and piano; *Bearbeitung über das Glogauer Liederbuch* for flute, clarinet, violin, and contrabass; *New York Notes* for chamber ensemble; *Percussion Symphony* for large percussion ensemble; *Joan's* for flute, violin, clarinet, cello, and piano; Percussion Duo for percussion and piano; *Prelude and Fugue, Janissary Music*, and *Ringing Changes* for percussion; *Composition for Oboe and Piano;* String Trio; *Variations* for bassoon, harp, and timpani; *6 Pieces for Violin and Piano; Making Ends Meet* for piano duet; *The Winds* for eight winds; String Quartet; *Psalm 39* for

baritone and guitar; *Piano Variations;* and Sonata No. 1 for Piano.

[2427] CHIHARA, Paul Seiko (Chi-hä'-rå, Päl Sī'-kō)
TEACHER
BORN: Seattle, Wash., July 9, 1938

The son of Japanese parents, Paul Chihara spent four childhood years with them in a "relocation camp" for potential traitors in Idaho, 1941–45. They then returned to Seattle, where he took a B.A. in English literature at the University of Washington in 1960. A master's in the same subject followed at Cornell University a year later. Chihara had up to then studied piano and taken some music courses as a sideline, but now he decided to make it his career. After a year with Nadia Boulanger in Paris, he returned to Cornell and, under the direction of Robert Palmer [2235], attained a D.M.A. in 1965. Next a Fulbright fellowship took him to Berlin to study a year with Ernst Pepping [2003]. Since then he has studied at Tanglewood with Gunther Schuller [2354] and gone to Japan to study oriental music. In 1966 he began teaching at UCLA, where he founded and directed the Twice Ensemble. He was also adviser to the Los Angeles Monday Evening Concerts. He has since resigned from his university post in order to compose. Though he began as a serialist and uses most of the modern techniques, his music is an amalgam of impulses, including medieval and oriental. He has written a film score, *Prince of the City*, several ballets, concerti, two heterogeneous series of compositions, one inspired by trees (and other plant life), another subsumed under the head of *Ceremonies*, and some choral works. RECORDINGS: Works on records include the complete ballet *The Tempest* (not to be confused with a contemporaneous score by the Norwegian Arne Nordheim [1931–]); *Branches* for two bassoons and percussion; *Willow, Willow* for bass flute, tuba, and percussion; *Driftwood* for violin, 2 violas, and cello; *Logs VI* for amplified string bass and tape; *Grass* for double-bass and orchestra; *Ceremony I* for oboe, 2 cellos, double-bass, and percussion; *Ceremony II (Incantations)* for flute, 2 cellos, and percussion; *Ceremony III* for small orchestra; *Ceremony IV (Symphony in Celebration)* for orchestra; *Wind Song* for cello and orchestra; Concerto for Saxophone; *Redwood* for viola and percussion; *The Beauty of the Rose Is in Its Passing* for bassoon, 2 horns, harp, and percussion; Piano Trio; *Elegy* for piano trio; *Missa Carminum Brevis: Folk Song Mass, Magnifi-*

cat, and *Ave Maria-Scarborough Fair*, all for chorus; and the film music for *Prince of the City*.

[2428] HEISS, John
FLUTIST, TEACHER
BORN: New York, October 23, 1938

John Heiss majored in English at Lehigh University, where he played first flute in the band and took music courses with Jonathan Elkus [2395]. On graduating, he went to Princeton to major in music and later did graduate work at Columbia, eventually acquiring a doctorate. Among his teachers he numbers Milton Babbitt [2247], Edward Cone (1917–), Earl Kim [2296], Otto Luening [1980], Peter Westergaard (1931–), and (at Aspen) Darius Milhaud [1868]. He has received a number of important prizes and commissions. He has taught at MIT and Columbia and has been on the faculty of the New England Conservatory since 1967. From its foundation in 1969 he was for five years first flutist of Musica Viva, a Boston chamber group devoted to twentieth-century music. RECORDINGS: *Inventions, Contours, and Colors* for chamber orchestra; *Songs of Nature* for soprano and chamber ensemble; *Quartet* for flute, clarinet, cello, and piano; *4 Movements* for three flutes; and *Capriccio* for flute, clarinet, and percussion.

[2429] KOLB, Barbara
CLARINETIST, TEACHER
BORN: Hartford, Conn., February 10, 1939

Barbara Kolb's father was a musician and director of a Hartford radio station. She took up clarinet at the age of eleven and played in school bands but was proceeding toward a commercial art career until she realized that her heart and talents did not agree with that plan. Against parental misgivings, she enrolled at the Hartt College of Music, where she took a B.A. in 1961 and an M.A. in 1965. She also studied with Gunther Schuller [2354] and Lukas Foss [2324] at Tanglewood during several summers. She kept up her clarinet studies and played in the Hartford Symphony. In 1966 a Fulbright fellowship took her to Vienna for a year, and three years later she became the first woman to win the American Prix de Rome. (From 1972 to 1975 she was a trustee of the American Academy in Rome.) She has since had commissions from foundations (Fromm and Koussevitzky), fellowships (two Gug-

genheims and a Ford Foundation award), and other tokens of recognition. Her music to date has been mostly small-scale and makes judicious use of the serial, the aleatory, and the electronic, as well as of established techniques. RECORDINGS: *3 Place Settings; Rebuttal* for two clarinets; *Trobar Clus* for thirteen instruments; *Chansons Bas* for voice, harp, and percussion; *Spring-River-Flowers-Moon-Night* for two pianos and tape; *Looking for Claudio* for guitar and tape; *Figments* for flute; *Solitaire* for piano, vibraphone, and tape; *3 Lullabies* for guitar; *Homage to Keith Jarrett and Gary Burton* for flute and vibraphone; and *Songs Before an Adieu* for soprano, flute (plus alto flute), and guitar.

[2430] BROUWER, Leo (Brou'-wer, Lä'-ō)
GUITARIST, TEACHER
BORN: Havana, March 1, 1939

Brouwer took up the guitar at an early age, had some basic music lessons from an aunt, and was publishing compositions for his instrument by the time he was seventeen. Shortly after the success of Fidel Castro in 1959, Brouwer came to the United States for serious study at the Juilliard School, where his teachers included Vincent Persichetti [2236] and Stefan Wolpe [2020], and at the Hartt College of Music, where he studied with Isadore Freed (1900–60) and lutenist Joseph Iadone. On his return to Cuba he became an official of Radio Havana, was put in charge of the music wing of the Cuban film industry, and joined the faculty of the Havana Conservatory, where he was shortly named professor of composition. He was also voted a government annuity for his services as musical spokesman for the brave new Cuban world. Originally concerned with native folk influences, he quickly hopped on the bandwagon of the international avant-garde and at last reports was exploring the worlds of the electronic and the aleatory. He continues to concertize and to record as a guitarist. (The blurb on one of his records notes that he has been at pains to learn "Cuban works" by Rodrigo [2025], Stravinsky [1748], and Torelli [578].) RECORDINGS: There are recordings of solo guitar pieces played by the composer and such other guitarists as John Williams and Turibio Santos. Williams has also recorded the 1972 Concerto for Guitar. Additional works on records include the *6 Estudios Sencilios* for mandolin and guitar and the Sonata for Piano ("Pian e forte").

[2431] TISHCHENKO, Boris Ivanovich
(Tish-chen'-kō, Bô'-ris Ē-vȧ-nō'-vich)
PIANIST, TEACHER
BORN: Leningrad, March 23, 1939

World War II and its aftermath dictated that Tishchenko postpone his musical education until 1953. After a year in an elementary school, he moved on to the Rimsky-Korsakov College and then to the Leningrad Conservatory. Among his composition teachers were Shostakovich [2904] pupils Galina Ustvolskaya (1919–) and Orest Yevlakhov. He graduated as a composer in 1962 and received his piano certification in 1963. In the latter year his Concerto for Cello, Winds, Harmonium, and Percussion, dedicated to Mstislav Rostropovich, won first prize in a competition at the Prague Spring Festival. For two years after he graduated, Tishchenko studied with Shostakovich himself. Shostakovich reportedly put much stock in his pupil's talent and once reorchestrated Tishchenko's Concerto for Cello as a birthday present for him. Tishchenko's strongly individualistic musical style is clearly indebted to the late works of Shostakovich but also shows the impact of such diverse influences as Mussorgsky [1369] and (perhaps) Webern [1773]. A member of the faculty of his alma mater, Tishchenko had, at last reports, written an opera for chorus, ballets, 5 numbered symphonies, concerti, cantatas, film scores, and many smaller works. RECORDINGS: Orchestral works represented on disc include the Concerto for Cello, Winds, Harmonium, and Percussion; Concerto for Violin; Concerto for Piano; Concerto for Flute, Piano, and Chamber Ensemble; Concerto for Harp; Symphony No. 3 for two vocalists and chamber orchestra; the brief Sinfonia robusta for an orchestra which includes ten French horns; Yaroslavna, a full-length "ballet meditation" for chorus and orchestra; and Suzdal for soprano, tenor, and chamber ensemble (consisting of sparsely but effectively orchestrated songs and dances from a film score). Other recordings include String Quartets Nos. 1 and 3; Invention No. 3 for organ; 3 Romances to Poems by Marina Tsvetaeva for mezzo-soprano and piano; 3 Choruses to Words by Yuĕfu for choir; a few solo piano pieces; and the Sonata for Solo Cello.

[2432] TAVENER, John Kenneth
ORGANIST
BORN: London, January 28, 1944

John Tavener, who thinks he may be related to the sixteenth-century John Taverner [128] (note the orthography) is a product of the Highgate School and the Royal Academy of Music, where he studied with Lennox Berkeley [2036] and David Lumsdaine (1931–), a Sydney-born pupil of Mátyás Seiber [2068]. After a few early compositions, Tavener won some attention in 1965, the year of his graduation, with two dramatic cantatas, The Cappemakers and Cain and Abel, the latter of which owed something to late-period Stravinsky [1748]. The next year his quite individual dramatic cantata The Whale, for narrator, vocal soloists, chorus, and orchestra (with considerable use of unorthodox sounds) won critical huzzas. It was followed four years later by the Celtic Requiem, which incorporates children's singing games and hymn tunes with advanced techniques. Tavener's cause was for a time espoused by the Beatles, who recorded on their own Apple label these two works, among others. Though he is the regular organist of a Presbyterian chapel, he has identified himself musically with Roman Catholicism and increasingly with mysticism, and has converted to Ba'Hai. His opera Thérèse was premiered at Covent Garden in 1979. RECORDINGS: These include The Whale; the Celtic Requiem; Nomine Jesu for five male speakers, mezzo-soprano, chorus, two alto flutes, organ, and harpsichord; and Coplas for chorus, soloists, and tape—the last two works on texts by St. John of the Cross.

[2433] ALBRIGHT, William Hugh
PIANIST, ORGANIST, CHOIR DIRECTOR, TEACHER
BORN: Gary, Ind., October 20, 1944

William Albright was admitted to the Juilliard School at the age of fifteen. After three years he went briefly to the Eastman School of Music, then to the University of Michigan, where he studied with Hugh Aitken [2343], Leslie Bassett (1923–), and Ross Lee Finney [2099]. At twenty he won the first of two Koussevitzky awards for composition (the second at twenty-two). In 1968 a Fulbright fellowship took him to Paris to study with Olivier Messiaen [2129] and Max Deutsch. He was also a pupil of George Rochberg [2279] at Tanglewood and of the organist Marilyn Mason. On the completion of his training in 1970, having acquired several other notable prizes, he was retained on the Michigan faculty and became associate director of the university's electronic music studio. His friend and associate William

Bolcom [2425] reawakened an early interest in ragtime, and he writes and performs music in the ragtime and jazz idioms. His "straight" compositions, though couched in the approved musical language of his time, often reflect his pop interests. RECORDINGS: *Organbooks I* and *II, Juba,* and *Neuma* (all with the composer performing on organ); *The King of Instruments* for organ and narrator; *Take That* for percussion; *Grand Sonata in Rag* for piano; *Pianoagogo* and *5 Chromatic Dances* for piano; and an LP disc of Albright playing his own rags.